THE PARALLEL APOCRYPHA

THE PARALLEL APOCRYPHA

Greek Text

King James Version

Douay Old Testament

The Holy Bible by Ronald Knox

Today's English Version

New Revised Standard Version

New American Bible

New Jerusalem Bible

John R. Kohlenberger III

General Editor

New York Oxford

OXFORD UNIVERSITY PRESS

OXFORD UNIVERSITY PRESS

Oxford New York
Athens Auckland Bangkok Bogota Bombay Buenos Aires
Calcutta Cape Town Dar es Salaam Delhi Florence Hong Kong
Istanbul Karachi Kuala Lumpur Madras Madrid Melbourne
Mexico City Nairobi Paris Singapore Taipei Tokyo Toronto

and associated companies in
Berlin Ibadan

Published by Oxford University Press, Inc.
198 Madison Avenue, New York, New York 10016

Design and Typesetting by
John R. Kohlenberger III and Multnomah Graphics
Portland, Oregon

COPYRIGHT NOTICES

IMPRIMATUR:
BERNARDUS CARD. GRIFFIN
ARCHIEPISCOPUS WESTMONASTERIENSIS

WESTMONASTERII, DIE 8 DECEMBRIS 1954

Imprimatur:
Most Reverend William H. Keeler, D.D.
President, National Conference of Catholic Bishops
March 10, 1993

1 3 5 7 9 8 6 4 2
Printed in the United States of America

Contents

The Books of the Apocrypha

The Apocryphal/Deuterocanonical Books are listed here in four groupings, as follows:

(a) *Books and Additions to Esther and Daniel that are in the Roman Catholic, Greek, and Slavonic Bibles*

The Books of the Apocrypha in Alphabetical Order

Acknowledgments

The Publisher wishes to thank all those who have contributed to this volume:

The translation owners, particularly those of the New American Bible, New Jerusalem Bible, and The Holy Bible by Ronald Knox, who allowed modification of the apparatus and text of their Bible to better fit the parallel format.

Peachtree Editorial and Proofreading Service, who proofread the entire volume.

Leslie Phillips, for helpful consultation on the overall design.

Deborah Darcy, for quietly accomplishing the innumerable tasks, major and minor, that were an integral part of bringing this project to completion.

Preface to Today's English Version

In September 1966 the American Bible Society published *The New Testament in Today's English Version*, a translation intended for people everywhere for whom English is either their mother tongue or an acquired language. Shortly thereafter the United Bible Societies requested the American Bible Society to undertake on its behalf a translation of the Old Testament following the same principles. Accordingly the American Bible Society appointed a group of translators to prepare the translation. In 1971 this group added a British consultant recommended by the British and Foreign Bible Society. The translation of the Old Testament now appears together with the fourth edition of the New Testament.

In a section between the Old Testament and the New Testament this Bible contains two series of books: (1) Tobit, Judith, Esther (Greek text), Wisdom of Solomon, Sirach, Baruch, Letter of Jeremiah, Song of the Three Young Men, Susanna, Bel and the Dragon, 1 Maccabees, and 2 Maccabees, and (2) 1 Esdras, 2 Esdras, and the Prayer of Manasseh. With the exception of 2 Esdras, these books formed part of the Septuagint Greek text of the Old Testament which was in circulation at the time of Christ. The first series of books are accepted by Roman Catholics as part of the canon of the Old Testament; and both series are regarded by many Protestants (including especially Anglicans, Episcopalians, and Lutherans) as worthy of at least private reading, though they are not regarded as a basis for doctrine. For further information about these books, see the Introductions to the respective series.

With the exception of 2 Esdras, the basic text for the two sections of books occurring before the New Testament is the Greek text printed in the Septuagint (3rd edition, 1949), edited by Alfred Rahlfs. For 2 Esdras the text is the Latin text printed in *Biblia Sacra* (1st edition, 1969), edited by Robert Weber.

Preface to the Apocryphal/Deuterocanonical Books of the New Revised Standard Version

When the King James or Authorized Version of the Bible was published in 1611, it contained, between the Old and the New Testaments, the books of the Apocrypha. These are books and portions of books that appear in the Latin Vulgate, either as part of the Old Testament or as an appendix, but are not in the Hebrew Bible. With the exception of 2 Esdras, these books appear also in the Greek version of the Old Testament that is known as the Septuagint.

In the course of time printers began to issue editions of the King James Bible without the books of the Apocrypha, and when the American Standard Version of the Bible was published in 1901, it did not include the Apocrypha. After the Revised Standard Version of the Bible was issued in 1952, a request came from the General Convention of the Protestant Episcopal Church that the Standard Bible Committee undertake also the revision of the English translation of the Apocrypha. This work was accomplished in 1957. It was on the basis of this version that the text of a 'Common Bible,' approved by both Roman Catholics and Protestants, was issued in 1973. Subsequently, in order to include all the texts accepted as Deuterocanonical by Eastern Orthodox Churches, the Standard Bible Committee prepared a version of 3 and 4 Maccabees and Psalm 151. These were issued in 1977, and the expanded edition of the Apocryphal/Deuterocanonical Books was endorsed by representatives of Orthodox communions. Since the contents of the collection known as Deuterocanonical Books vary among the churches that recognize them as authoritative, in the interest of clear identification they have been arranged in the New Revised Standard Version in four sections (see the Table of Contents).

For the translation of the Apocryphal/Deuterocanonical Books the Committee made use of a number of texts. In the case of most of the books the basic text was the standard edition of the Greek Septuagint prepared by Alfred Rahlfs and published by the Württemberg Bible Society (Stuttgart, 1935). For several of the books the more recently published individual volumes of Göttingen Septuagint project were utilized. For the book of Tobit it was decided to follow the form of the Greek text found in codex Sinaiticus (supported as it is by evidence from Qumran); where this text is defective, it was supplemented and corrected by other Greek manuscripts. For the three Additions to Daniel (namely, Susanna, the Prayer of Azariah and the Song of the Three Jews, and Bel and the Dragon) the Committee continued to use the Greek version attributed to Theodotion (the so-called "Theodotion-Daniel"). In translating Ecclesiasticus (Sirach), while constant reference was made to the Hebrew fragments of a large portion of this book (those discovered at Qumran and Masada as well as those recovered from the Cairo Geniza), the Committee generally followed the Greek text (including verse numbers) published by Joseph Ziegler in the Göttingen Septuagint (1965). But in many places the Committee has translated the Hebrew text when this provides a reading that is clearly superior to the Greek; the Syriac and Latin versions were also consulted throughout and occasionally adopted. The basic text adopted in rendering 2 Esdras is the Latin version given in the Biblia Sacra, edited by Robert Weber (Stuttgart, 1971). This was supplemented by consulting the Latin text as edited by R.L. Bensly (1895) and by Bruno Violet (1910), as well as the several Oriental versions of 2 Esdras, namely, the Syriac, Ethiopic, Arabic (two forms, referred to as Arabic 1 and Arabic 2), Armenian, and Georgian versions. Finally, since the Additions to the Book of Esther are disjointed and unintelligible as they stand in most editions of the Apocrypha, we have provided them with their original context by translating the whole of the Greek version of Esther from Robert Hanhart's Göttingen edition (1983).

For the Committee,
Bruce M. Metzger

Contributors

Mary Chilton Callaway
Associate Professor of Old Testament
Fordham University

D.A. Carson
Research Professor of New Testament
Trinity Evangelical Divinity School

John J. Collins
Professor of the Hebrew Bible and Post-Biblical Judaic Studies
University of Chicago

Demetrios J. Constantelos
Charles Cooper Townsend, Sr. Distinguished Professor of History and Religious Studies
The Richard Stockton College of New Jersey

Walter J. Harrelson
Distinguished Professor of Hebrew Bible, Emeritus
Vanderbilt University

Judith L. Kovacs
Lecturer in Religious Studies
University of Virginia

Sarah J. Tanzer
Associate Professor of Judaism and Christian Origins
McCormick Theological Seminary

The Contents and Character of the Apocryphal/Deuterocanonical Books

Judith L. Kovacs

These 18 books (or additions to books) are all Jewish works not included in the Hebrew Bible but accepted as canonical (i.e. authoritative Scripture) by some Christian groups. (The only exception is 4 Maccabees, which does not have authoritative status but is printed in Greek Bibles as an appendix; see table of contents for a classification of these books according to their status in the Roman Catholic, Greek, and Slavonic Bibles.) The term "Apocrypha" derives from a Greek word meaning "hidden things"; whether the term was originally a positive designation (esoteric teaching) or a negative one (books that should be hidden because they are false) remains a matter of dispute. The adjective "deuterocanonical" indicates that these books became recognized as Scripture at a later time than the books of the Old Testament (OT). These works are written in several different literary genres: they include historical narratives, fictional narratives, poetic and wisdom books, sermons and treatises, and an apocalypse. All were probably composed in the first three centuries B.C.E. (=B.C.) or the first century C.E. (=A.D.). In addition to the apocryphal books discussed here, many other Jewish writings of this period survive, including the Dead Sea Scrolls and some works from a group of writings called the Pseudepigrapha (literally "works written under a pseudonym"), which includes apocalypses, testaments, interpretive paraphrases of OT narratives, and poetry. Also from this period are the extensive writings of Philo of Alexandria, who interpreted Jewish Scripture in light of Greek philosophy, and the works of the Jewish historian Josephus.

The books of the Apocrypha were composed in three different languages: Greek, Hebrew, and Aramaic. Several survive only in translations into other languages, and in some cases we are not certain about the original language of composition. For most books the place and approximate date of writing can be assigned only tentatively. A number of books probably come from Israel (e.g. 1 Maccabees, Sirach), and several others from the large Jewish community at Alexandria in Egypt (e.g. Wisdom of Solomon, 3 Maccabees, 4 Maccabees).

We know the name of only one author, Jesus son of Sirach (Hebrew: Joshua ben Sira), a scribe who taught in Jerusalem, sometime around 180. (All dates are B.C.E. unless otherwise noted.) The anonymous author of 2 Maccabees tells us that his work is an abridgement of a work in five books by a certain "Jason of Cyrene" (2.23). The other books are all anonymous or pseudonymous; several are attributed to OT figures such as David, Solomon, and Jeremiah.

The apocryphal books need to be read in light of the history and culture of the times in which they were written. They draw on the history narrated in the OT and presuppose subsequent historical developments, the most important of which are here summarized. Two events of OT history that figure prominently in the Apocrypha are the destruction of the city of Jerusalem, with its temple, by the Babylonians in 587 and the Exile of leading Jews in Babylon from 587-538 (hereafter referred to as the Exile). The Exile ended in 538 when Cyrus, the new king of Persia and recent victor over Babylon, issued an edict allowing the exiles to return to Judea (the area around Jerusalem, all that survived of the original kingdoms of Judah and Israel).

The historical narratives of the OT end around the year 420, after describing the rebuilding of the temple and the restoration of the people in the land. We know almost nothing of Jewish history during the rest of the period of Persian domination, which ends with the rise of Alexander the Great. Alexander, the son of Philip of Macedon, astonished the world by a swift series of victories (336-30) that made him the new lord of Greece, the Persian Empire, and Egypt.

After Alexander's premature death in 323, his vast empire was divided among his generals, who fought for decades over the right to succeed him. Two rival successors, Seleucus, king of northern Syria and Babylon, and Ptolemy, king of Egypt and Coele-Syria (southern Syria and Israel), laid claim to Israel. Under their heirs, Israel was the site of frequent battles and changed hands many times. Israel came under the rule of the Ptolemies in 301 and was taken by the Seleucids in 200.

The period Alexander initiated is called the "Hellenistic" (i.e. Greek-speaking) period because Alexander and his successors encouraged their subject populations to take over Greek language, culture, and religion. As vehicles for their dissemination, they established new cities modeled after the Greek *polis* (city-state), including Alexandria in Egypt and many cities in Israel. These cities had an enrolled body of Greek citizens and temples, theatres, schools, and gymnasia on the Greek model.

After Israel passed into Seleucid control, the pressure on Jews to adopt Greek culture increased, especially under Antiochus IV, who assumed the throne in 175. He established a body of citizens in Jerusalem, led by the Hellenized Jew Jason (who paid Antiochus to establish him as high priest) and by his successor Menelaus. When pious Jews opposed these corrupt high priests and their Hellenizing policies, Antiochus' response was severe. In 169 he attacked Jerusalem, plundered the temple, murdered many Jews, and sold others into slavery. Two years later he took even sterner measures, outlawing the religion which had provoked the resistance. Observance of the Law of Moses (the central teachings of the Jewish religion, contained in the books of Genesis through Deuteronomy) became a crime, and the temple in Jerusalem was desecrated by the establishment of a polytheistic cult.

These measures caused many Jews to give up their religion, but they also increased the determination of the Jews who opposed Antiochus. In 167 a priest of the Hasmonean family, Mattathias, together with his five sons, started an armed revolt. This revolt is named the Maccabean revolt after Judas, called Maccabeus (the "Hammer"), who assumed leadership upon his father Mattathias' death. In 164 Judas recaptured the temple mountain, purified the temple, and reestablished traditional worship, an event still celebrated every year in the Jewish festival of Hanukkah.

Conflict continued between the Hasmoneans—led after Judas' death by his brothers Jonathan and Simon—and a rapid succession of Seleucid rulers. The Hasmoneans gradually gained power, largely as the result of shrewd alliances with rival Seleucid factions. In 141 the Hasmonean Simon gained political independence for Judea by siding with Demetrius II. The people acclaimed Simon as governor and "high priest for ever" (1 Macc. 14.41), thus establishing the priestly Hasmonean dynasty, which was to rule Judea until the Roman conquest in 63.

Subsequent Hasmonean rulers took advantage of the decline in Seleucid power to increase the territory of Judea and have themselves declared "king." Their reigns were marked by violence and increased factionalism among the Jews. It is in this period that we first hear of the Jewish groups Pharisees, Sadducees, and Essenes. Dispute among rival claimants to the Hasmonean throne in 67-63 led the Romans to step in. Much of the newly reconquered territory was given to the Roman governor of Syria, and Judea and Jerusalem became directly subject to Rome.

Roman rule did not bring an end to the strife, as the descendants of the Hasmoneans, the various factions in the Roman civil wars, and the Idumean family of Antipater (the father of Herod the Great) vied for power over the region. After over a century of Roman rule, the Jews revolted in 66 C.E. The results of the ensuing Jewish War were catastrophic; in 70 C.E. the Romans destroyed the city of Jerusalem. The second temple was burned down, never to be rebuilt.

This brief survey of Jewish history between 587 B.C.E. and 70 C.E. has focused on the land of Israel. The books of the Apocrypha also give us glimpses of a wider Jewish community, called the *diaspora* or the dispersion, spread throughout the Mediterranean world. The dispersion resulted partly from forced exile (the deportation of the 10 tribes of the Northern kingdom of Israel to Assyria in 722 and the Exile of many Judeans to Babylon in 587) and partly from voluntary migration. During the period of the Apocrypha, there were sizable Jewish communities outside of Israel, particularly in Babylon and in Egypt, where Alexandria had become an important center for Jewish learning.

The apocryphal books, written from this historical background, have several common themes. One is the question of how Jews are to respond to the challenge of Hellenism, an issue which was particularly acute in the dispersion, where Jews lived as a minority. The heroes and heroines of several books serve as examples of how diaspora Jews can live a law-observant life, and the divine favors granted to them (e.g. miraculous rescues) underscore the benefits of faithfulness to the law and reverence for the temple. Many works contain polemic against the worship of gentile gods (idolatry). On the other hand, there is considerable evidence of the influence of Greek culture on the apocryphal literature. Several books were composed in Greek, many show the influence of Greek rhetoric and literary conventions, and some take over ideas from Greek philosophy (including the immortality of the soul).

A second issue running though these books is the question of how to interpret the sufferings and misfortunes of individual Jews and of the people as a whole. A common theme in the short stories is the vindication of the Jew who is persecuted for his or her piety. Writings in various genres wrestle with the question of the theological meaning of the sufferings of the people of Israel, especially the events of 722 (destruction of the Northern tribes), 587 (first destruction of Jerusalem), 167 (persecution of Antiochus IV), and 70 C.E. (second destruction of Jerusalem). The theme of exile pervades these works, sometimes in the form of the narrative setting and sometimes as the subject of explicit theological reflection. The image of exile is suggestive not only of the major disasters in the history of the people but also of the problems of ordinary existence of Jews in the dispersion.

The authors of apocryphal works made use of many of the works that later came to be known as the OT (Hebrew Bible), and they reiterate central themes of the OT such as law, covenant, and divine wisdom. For example, many books address the theological problem of the people's suffering by reiterating the view of the prophets and the authors of 1-2 Kings: the destruction of Jerusalem and the Exile are interpreted as divine punishment for the people's sins. Israel's sufferings are thus given meaning, belief in divine justice is supported, and the hope is held out that Israel's repentance will be the prelude to a glorious restoration.

The rest of this essay will consider the individual books, grouped according to their literary genres: (1) historical narratives; (2) fictional narratives; (3) poetic and wisdom books; (4) sermons and treatises; (5) apocalypse. All quotations are from the New Revised Standard Version (NRSV).

Historical Narratives

Four apocryphal works (1 Esdras and 1, 2, and 3 Maccabees) illustrate the continued importance of this genre in post-Biblical Judaism. Like the ten OT books in this genre (Joshua, Judges, 1-2 Samuel, 1-2 Kings, 1-2 Chronicles, Ezra and Nehemiah), all are theological histories, whose authors are more interested in conveying the religious meaning of history than in strict historical accuracy in the modern sense. We consider them in the order of the events they describe. First Esdras reproduces, with minor changes, much of what is reported in 2 Chr. 35-36, Ezra, and Neh. 1-8, from king Josiah of Jerusalem (621) through the reforms of Ezra (around 445). The most significant difference is the addition of the story of the three young bodyguards of Darius, king of Persia (521-486) in 1 Esd. 3.1–5.6. Adapting an old tale, the author tells of a rhetorical contest in which three men give speeches on "what one thing is strongest." The winner, here identified with Zerubbabel, a descendant of king David, gains as his reward Darius' promise to rebuild the temple in Jerusalem (a detail improbable in itself and contradicted by other evidence).

The name of 3 Maccabees is misleading; it does not concern the events of the Maccabean revolt but describes the trials of Egyptian Jews some 50 years earlier, during the reign of Ptolemy IV (222-204). The book has two parts, both of which encourage Jews facing persecution from gentiles to be faithful to the law and the temple. The first part tells of Ptolemy IV's attack on Jerusalem in 217 and his desecration of the "holy of holies" (the inner sanctuary of the temple), an act punished when God strikes him with paralysis. Ptolemy recovers and returns to Egypt with the intention of enslaving the Alexandrian Jews, unless they agree to become initiated into the mysteries of Dionysus (2.27-30). In the second part the author attributes to this Ptolemy an action which other sources assign to a later king, Ptolemy VIII (145-116): the king seeks to exterminate the Jews of Egypt by shutting them up in the hippodrome and prepares to set upon them drunken and enraged elephants, an action averted only by divine intervention. Impressed, the king repents and becomes a supporter of the Jews.

First and Second Maccabees are our main sources for historical events in Israel in the second century B.C.E. First Maccabees treats the period from about 169 to 139, while 2 Maccabees describes the period between about 180 and 161, giving more details about Antiochus and the early days of the revolt (cf. 1 Macc. 1–7). After a paragraph about Alexander the Great and his successors, 1 Macc. 1 describes the "sinful root" Antiochus IV, who writes to all his subjects "that all should be one people, and that each should give up his customs" (1.41), a command that all the gentiles, and some of the Jews, obey. He also writes letters to Jerusalem and the cities of Judah directing them:

> . . . to forbid burnt offerings and sacrifices and drink offerings in the sanctuary, to profane sabbaths and festivals, to defile the sanctuary and the priests, to build altars and sacred precincts and shrines for idols, to sacrifice swine [regarded as unclean in Jewish law] and unclean animals, and to leave their sons uncircumcised. (1.45-48)

The king proceeds to have copies of the law burned and to erect "a desolating sacrilege" (1.54; cf. Dan. 11.31)—an altar to the Greek god Zeus—within the sacred precincts of the temple.

All Jews are forced to take a stand. Many choose the easy course of apostasy, giving up their ancestral religion to save their lives or to assure their standing in society. Mattathias and his five sons serve as paradigms for the response of pious Jews. Lamenting the profanation of the temple (2.7-13), and burning with "zeal for the law" (2.26), Mattathias defies the king's order to sacrifice to Greek gods:

> Even if all the nations that live under the rule of the king obey him, and have chosen to obey his commandments, every one of them abandoning the religion of their ancestors, I and my sons and my brothers will continue to live by the covenant of our ancestors. Far be it from us to desert the law and the ordinances. (2.19-21)

Mattathias then flees to the hills and begins an armed revolt, carried on after his death under the leadership of his sons Judas, Jonathan, and Simon. A key event in the narrative is Judas' purification and rededication of the temple (4.36-59; cf. 2 Macc. 10.1-8). Many passages in 1 Maccabees praise the exploits of the Hasmoneans; the book as a whole gives an account of the origins of the new Hasmonean dynasty and serves to legitimate it.

The early events of Maccabean times (including Antiochus' forced Hellenization) are told in a more explicitly theological way in 2 Maccabees, with several accounts of direct divine interventions. Special emphasis is put on the sanctity of the temple and on the deeds of pious martyrs (e.g. the story of the seven brothers and their mother in 7.1-42). The author shares the view of history expressed in

Deuteronomy and 1-2 Kings: the people's sins bring divine retribution in history, while their repentance (here aided by the special devotion of the martyrs) restores God's favor and thus their fortunes.

Fictional Narratives

This genre is represented in the OT by Ruth and Esther, and by a series of tales in the first half of the book of Daniel (chs. 1-6). The Apocrypha contains narrative additions to Esther and Daniel, as well as the short stories Judith and Tobit. The fictional setting of all these stories relates them to key events in Jewish history.

As it appears in the Hebrew Bible, Esther lacks an explicit religious element and does not even mention the name of God. Six additions found in the Greek, Latin, and Slavonic versions supply this missing element, for instance, by introducing a prayer of Esther.

Of the three additions to the Greek version of the book of Daniel, two (Susanna and Bel and the Dragon) are short stories set in the Babylonian Exile. (The third will be discussed below.) Susanna is a beautiful and pious Jew, educated "according to the law of Moses" (v. 3), who is falsely accused of adultery. Her story differs from other narratives of this period in that the villains are not idolatrous gentiles but Jews. Susanna's accusers are two elders—prominent members of the Jewish community—who become hostile when she rejects their advances. In her distress, Susanna cries out to God, who hears her prayer and sends Daniel to rescue her through clever refutation of the elders' false testimony.

In Bel and the Dragon, the wise and pious Daniel is pitted against the gods of the Babylonians and their priests. First he unmasks the god Bel (Marduk)—the chief deity of Babylon—as a fraud, and then he kills a large dragon worshiped by the Babylonians by feeding it a mixture of "pitch, fat, and hair," which causes the dragon to burst. After Daniel's victories over the pagan gods, the Babylonian priests have him thrown into a den of hungry lions (compare Dan. 6.16-24), a danger from which God miraculously rescues him. This tale is typical of several apocryphal works that polemicize against gentile religion by ridiculing its idols.

One indication of the fictional nature of Judith is the confusion in its historical setting: it takes place (1.1) "during the reign of Nebuchadnezzar" (the Babylonian king who ruled from 605-562, here mistakenly called king of the Assyrians) but presents the people of Israel as recently returned from Exile (4.3). (The Exile ended in 538, twenty-five years or more after the events narrated in Judith.) The chief protagonists are Holofernes, the Assyrian general sent to subdue the people of Israel and force them to worship only Nebuchadnezzar, and Judith (whose name means "the Jewess"), a pious widow who uses her wisdom and her female charms to defeat him. Gaining entrance to Holofernes' tent, Judith beheads him, leads her people in a rout of the enemy, and thus averts the threat to people and temple and demonstrates that the God of Israel, not Nebuchadnezzar, is the only God. This book encourages strict observance of the law (dietary laws, fasting, etc.) and portrays God as the deliverer of his people. The prayer of Judith stresses the graciousness and power of God and the surprising way this power shows itself:

> Here now are the Assyrians, a greatly increased force, priding themselves in their horses and riders, boasting in the strength of their foot soldiers, and trusting in shield and spear, in bow and sling . . . crush their arrogance by the hand of a woman. For your strength does not depend upon numbers, nor your might upon the powerful. But you are the God of the lowly, helper of the oppressed, upholder of the weak, protector of the forsaken, savior of those without hope. (9.7, 10-11)

The story of Tobit is set in Assyria after the fall of the Northern Kingdom in 722 (see 2 Kgs. 17). Tobit is a model of piety, who reveres the temple in Jerusalem and scrupulously observes the Law of Moses even in exile. The book uses a complicated plot to illustrate the miraculous power of God. The author sets the stage by telling two stories of suffering: the righteous Tobit is struck blind, and, in a far country, his kinswoman Sarah is loved by a demon, who has kept her a childless widow by killing her seven successive husbands on their wedding nights. The sufferings of both are resolved through the action of God's angelic representative Raphael. Disguised as a human, Raphael leads Tobit's son Tobias to Sarah and teaches him the magical cures that relieve Sarah of her demon and Tobit of his blindness. Tobias falls in love with Sarah and thus fulfills the admonition of his father to avoid foreign women and marry one of his own kin (4.12).

Tobit deals with the problem of suffering, both of the individual and of the Jewish nation; several passages lament the dispersion. The book ends with the prediction of the return of the tribes to Israel and the conversion of the gentiles: "Then the nations in the whole world will all be converted and worship God in truth. They will all abandon their idols . . . ." (14.6).

Poetic and Wisdom Books

Included here are three brief poetic works ascribed to OT figures (Psalm 151, The Prayer of Manasseh, and the Prayer of Azariah and the Song of the Three Jews), two books carrying on the wisdom traditions of late OT books (Sirach and the Wisdom of Solomon) and Baruch, a work that includes wisdom poems.

Psalm 151, ascribed to David "after he had fought in single combat with Goliath," celebrates his victory over the Philistine giant. The Prayer of Manasseh is a psalm of repentance, attributed to Manasseh king of Judah. He was the arch-villain of 2 Kings (see ch. 21), whose idolatrous practices are said to have caused the terrible punishment of Judah in 587. (See also 2 Chr. 33, which says that Manasseh, in exile in Babylon, prayed for forgiveness.) This prayer typifies the penitential mood of many apocryphal works.

Between Daniel 3.23 and 3.24 the Greek and Latin Bibles insert the Prayer of Azariah and the Song of the Three Jews. In Babylon, the righteous Jews, Azariah (Abednego), Shadrach, and Meshach are being tested in the fiery furnace. Azariah's prayer expresses repentance, and interprets the events of 587 as the righteous judgment of God: "For we, O Lord, have become fewer than any nation, and are brought low this day in all the world because of our sins" (v. 14). The prayer ends in a plea to God to have mercy, remembering his promises to Abraham and accepting his people's repentance. There follows a description of the divine rescue of Azariah and his companions from the fire, which prepares for the Song of the Three Jews, a general praise of God.

The Wisdom of Jesus, Son of Sirach (in Hebrew, Joshua ben Sira), the only book of the Apocrypha published in the author's own name (see 50.27), was written early in the second century B.C.E., probably in Jerusalem, by a Jewish scribe—a professional student and teacher of the "Law and the Prophets" and of the wisdom traditions (see the Prologue to Sirach). It survives in a Greek translation by the author's grandson, who wanted to make his grandfather's wisdom available "for those living abroad who wished to gain learning, and are disposed to live according to the law" (Prologue). Sirach was named "Ecclesiasticus" ("the church's book") in the early Latin church, an indication of the high regard in which it was held. The fifty-one chapters of Sirach contain words of practical wisdom similar to Proverbs, poems on Wisdom (personified as a woman), hymns praising the creative powers of God, and a recital of Israel's history in the form of praise of her heroes. It has much in common with OT wisdom books, especially Proverbs, but differs in combining wisdom teaching with central OT themes such as law, covenant, and sacred history. "Lady Wisdom" is identified with "the book of the covenant . . . the law that Moses commanded us" (24.23). The author shares the covenantal theology of Deuteronomy, with its blessings and curses, and he expects rewards and punishments in this life. Many passages speak of sin, repentance, and atonement. The survey of the heroes of Israel's history (chs. 44-50) puts particular emphasis on Aaron; it ends with praise of the high priest Simon II (219-196), who repaired the temple and the walls of Jerusalem (50.1-21).

The Wisdom of Solomon claims to be by king Solomon (see chs. 7-9) but internal evidence suggests that it was written in Greek by an Alexandrian Jew. It is an example of how an educated Jew of the dispersion combined the traditional themes of Jewish wisdom with ideas drawn from Greek rhetoric and philosophy (e.g. the four cardinal virtues of Platonic and Stoic philosophy and the Platonic ideas of the pre-existence of the soul and of the dualism of soul and body). The book is an exhortation to follow the life of wisdom, identified with the righteous and holy life demanded by the law. One difference from Sirach is the belief that the wise are rewarded with immortality. Chapters 10-19 describe God's action in history, especially during the time of the exodus from Egypt; the events are interpreted in a series of contrasts of God's treatment of the Israelites with his punishment of the Egyptians (e.g. how God gave the Israelites water from the rock but turned the Egyptians' water supply into blood). This section contains a long polemic against idolatry and pagan religion, with special emphasis on Egyptian religion (chs. 13-15).

The book of Baruch is probably a work of the first or second century B.C.E., written in the name of Jeremiah's friend and secretary (see Jer. 36.4). It is set in the Exile, from which Baruch writes a letter (in prose) to the people left behind in Judah, counseling them to repent, publicly confess their sins, and beg God to bring back the exiles (1.1–3.8). Baruch is a good example of the impact of the tragic events of 587 on later generations. Making use of ideas from Deuteronomy and Jeremiah, the author views the destruction of Jerusalem as God's calling into effect of the covenant curses (see Deut. 27-28):

> So to this day there have clung to us the calamities and the curses which the Lord declared through Moses his servant. . . . He made them subject to all the kingdoms around us, to be an object of scorn and desolation among all the surrounding peoples, where the Lord has scattered them. They were brought down and not raised up, because our nation sinned against the Lord our God, in not heeding his voice. (1.20; 2.4-5)

According to Baruch, the prophets, unheeded in their own day, are now proved correct.

Baruch is included here among the poetic and wisdom books because of the last two chapters, which were probably originally independent. The wisdom poem in 3.9–4.3 equates wisdom with the law and attributes the Exile to Israel's forsaking "the fountain of wisdom" (3.12). The book ends with a poem (4.5–5.9) in which Jerusalem, personified as a woman who has lost her children (the exiles), counsels them to beg for God's mercy and predicts their restoration to the land and the punishment of their enemies.

Sermons and Treatises

The Letter of Jeremiah and 4 Maccabees are prose works of exhortation and instruction. The Letter of Jeremiah claims to be a letter the prophet Jeremiah sent to the first group of exiles in Babylon (Jer. 29.1). Actually it is a sermon composed during the Hellenistic period, which seeks to combat gentile religion by arguing that its cult-images (idols) are impotent and thus cannot be gods.

Although not given canonical status by any religious group, 4 Maccabees is included as an appendix in some manuscripts of the ancient Greek Bible and is revered in the Eastern Orthodox Churches. Like the Wisdom of Solomon, 4 Maccabees makes use of Greek philosophy; here the debt is great (especially to the Stoics) and explicitly acknowledged ("the subject that I am about to discuss is most philosophical," 1.1). In style and tone, this work is much closer to the writings of the first-century Jewish philosopher Philo than to any books of the OT or Apocrypha.

The author defines his thesis by adapting a topic commonly discussed in Hellenistic philosophy— that "devout reason is sovereign over the emotions" (1.1; the term "devout" is added by the author), but his real concern is to demonstrate that the Jewish religion is a training in philosophy and virtue. He identifies wisdom (defined in Stoic terms, 1.16) with "education in the [Jewish] law" (1.17). Examples from the OT (chs. 2-3) prove that the law leads to control of the emotions and thus to virtue (especially the four cardinal virtues). The heart of the work (chs. 4-12) is devoted to a philosophical exposition of the stories of pious Jews martyred under Antiochus IV—the aged Eleazar and seven unnamed brothers with their mother (an elaboration of 2 Macc. 6.12–7.42). The tortures of the cruel Antiochus are described in excruciating detail and combined with dialogues between the martyrs and their torturers. The martyrs appear as true philosophers, their reason strengthened by training in the Law of Moses. The text glorifies at once the martyrs of Maccabean times and the religion they represent. Martyrdom is presented as a means of expiation; it turns away God's anger from his guilty people, so that God restores their fortunes by allowing Antiochus to be defeated (17.20-22). Like several other apocryphal books, 4 Maccabees envisions an afterlife (at least for some people): the martyrs are promised immortality, while Antiochus will suffer eternal punishment.

Apocalypse

We conclude our discussion of the Apocrypha with one book written in the literary genre apocalypse. Like the apocalypse of Daniel in the OT and the NT book of Revelation, 2 Esdras is a work that claims to reveal the secrets of heaven and of history (especially the end of history). Like other apocalypses, it makes use of visions and elaborate imagery (e.g. symbolic animals). Second Esdras (called 4 Ezra in Latin manuscripts) is written in the name of Ezra, the post-exilic scribe. (We discuss here the core of the book, chs. 3-14; chs. 1-2 and 15-16 are later Christian additions.) Probably the last book of the Apocrypha to be written (c. 100 C.E.), 2 Esdras is an anguished reflection on the second fall of Jerusalem in 70 C.E. The fictional setting in the Babylonian Exile draws attention to the obvious parallel between the Roman destruction of the temple and that by the Babylonians six centuries before.

A series of visions and dialogues between Ezra and an angelic revealer explore the question of God's justice. Although he accepts the view that Jerusalem was destroyed as divine punishment, Ezra raises this question: since the Jews are no worse than the Babylonians (Romans), why has God allowed the gentiles to destroy their nation and rule over them (3.28-35)? Ezra's question is not given a direct answer, but he is told that the end of this present evil age is near, and that in the age to come there will be a general resurrection of the dead, followed by rewards for the righteous and punishment for the wicked. (Note that this is a different view of afterlife from the immortality of the soul taught in Wisdom of Solomon and 4 Maccabees.) One vision (9.27–10.59) portrays Zion (Jerusalem) as a woman lamenting her children; before Ezra's eyes she is transformed into a glorious city, a promise of restoration. In another vision (11.1–12.39) Ezra sees Rome, symbolized as a great eagle, being defeated by the "lion of Judah" (the Messiah). The end of the book portrays Ezra in his role as scribe: he renews the law (see the report in Nehemiah 8) and exhorts the people to be obedient. The book concludes with a promise that those who follow the "law of life" will obtain mercy after death: "and then the names of the righteous shall become manifest" (14.30).

A View From History: The Place of the Apocrypha in the Jewish Community

SARAH J. TANZER

All of the texts included in the Apocrypha are Jewish, having their origins within various Jewish communities in antiquity, and as such reflecting (to varying degrees) issues within the lives of those communities. Yet, to the best of our knowledge, they were never formed into one collection by Jews [1], and therefore one cannot write about the place of the Apocrypha in the Jewish community. With the exception of those texts preserved among the Dead Sea Scrolls and part of Ben Sira, most of these texts have come down to us through the hands of Christian copyists. In spite of this, each of the individual Jewish texts included in this volume of the Christian Apocrypha contributes to our picture of the development of Judaism in the Graeco-Roman period in communities inside Israel, as well as those in the Diaspora. It is much more difficult to conjure up a historical picture of the role that these different texts have played in the Jewish community from the Graeco-Roman period until now. We are provided with little glimpses where issues of canon surface and also through a survey of the texts of the Apocrypha in Jewish literature, festival celebrations, and the arts. For most of these texts the evidence provides us with only the barest of hints, and for some we have virtually no evidence—apart from sheer speculation. We are left with the faintest of glimmers when we try to assess how the Jewish community has historically viewed these Jewish texts.

Although they have been included in the Septuagint [2], there are several books of the Apocrypha for which we have virtually no evidence to indicate how they were historically viewed by the Jewish community. These include: Bel and the Dragon (among the additions to the Book of Daniel), 3 Maccabees [3], the Prayer of Manasseh, Greek Ezra (1 Esdras) and Greek Esther (Additions to the Book of Esther).

Issues of Canon

While for many of these texts a relatively late date of composition may have precluded their inclusion among either the second or third sections of the Jewish Bible (the Prophets or the Writings) [4], for most we can only speculate as to why they were not included. The speculation is often along lines of Halakhah (legal commentary), looking for ways in which a particular book may have violated a point of

1. One might argue that the Septuagint, the translation of the Hebrew Bible into Greek by Jews, includes the Apocrypha. But the Septuagint was inherited by early Christianity, the codices which attest a collection of Apocrypha are late (4th and 5th centuries C.E.), they do not include all the Apocrypha, and they are Christian, following the Christian rather than the Jewish arrangement of books. All this suggests that the Apocrypha as a collection within the Septuagint may be a Christian innovation. At least, there is no evidence to suggest that the books of the Apocrypha were a part of any Jewish translation of the Hebrew Bible into Greek. More about this below.

2. See note 1 above. Some of these books do show up among the 4th and 5th century C.E. Christian codices (Vaticanus, Sinaiticus, and Alexandrinus).

3. 3 Maccabees is intriguing. Though we know nothing about its continuing impact on Judaism, chapters six and seven of the book may be related to the origination of an annual celebration by Egyptian Jews similar to the feast of Purim.

4. Roger Beckwith (*The Old Testament Canon of the New Testament Church*, Grand Rapids, MI: 1985) has argued exhaustively that by the 2nd century B.C.E. the "canon" of the Jewish Bible was fixed. The evidence, however, for the third section of the Jewish Bible (the Writings) does not seem so clear cut. At the very least, well into the 1st century C.E. there is a haziness about the books which were included in the Writings and the shape of some of those books (e.g., Psalms), though the number of books included in the Jewish Bible is already accurately reported by Josephus and 4th Ezra (2 Esdras).

Halakhah. For example, it has been suggested that Judith was rejected because, contrary to the prohibition concerning Ammonites in Deuteronomy 23.3, it records the conversion to Judaism of Achior, an Ammonite. Or perhaps, as Harry Orlinsky suggested, the problem was that Achior's conversion included only circumcision and not the prescribed ritual purification by water in the mikveh [5]. Speculation based on contradiction of Halakhah has also been offered for Susanna (about punishment of discredited witnesses) and for Tobit (about acceptable marriage practices). In the case of those texts which are additions to canonical texts (for instance, the various additions to Esther and Daniel), the fact that they were recognizable as additions—and in some cases clumsy additions at that—may have hampered their chances for inclusion. In the case of Greek Esther—despite its own numerous merits—the continuing debate about the sacredness of the book of Esther into the first centuries C.E. in rabbinic circles would have been enough to keep Greek Esther out of the Jewish Bible. Of course all of this is speculation, and we simply do not know why certain books were not included in the Jewish Bible [6].

In the past it has been argued that the Septuagint, a translation of the Bible for Greek-speaking Jews, gives us evidence of a wider canon in use among Alexandrian Jews, because it includes the books of the Apocrypha (with the exception of 4 Ezra). The studies of Albert Sundberg, Jr. [7] and Roger Beckwith [8] have effectively demolished this thesis on several grounds, only a few of which are noted here. The original grounds for a wider Alexandrian canon were the larger codices of the Septuagint from the fourth and fifth centuries C.E. (Codices is the plural of codex, which means a manuscript in bound book form rather than a scroll.) These codices (Vaticanus, Sinaiticus, and Alexandrinus) include most of the books of the Apocrypha, though Sinaiticus excludes 2 and 3 Maccabees, Vaticanus totally excludes the Books of Maccabees, and Alexandrinus "adds" the Psalms of Solomon! Two major obstacles to any theory advocating a wider canon among Alexandrian Jews are: (1) These codices are Christian: they do not follow the three-fold division of the Jewish Bible. They do not agree about which of the texts of the Apocrypha to include and where to incorporate them. (2) Since there is evidence that in the 2nd century C.E. Jews seem largely to have discarded the Septuagint in favor of translations which better suited their controversy with the Church (for example, Aquila's translation), these comprehensive codices from the fourth and fifth centuries should not be used as evidence of Jewish practice. In fact, since the Septuagint was appropriated by Christianity, these codices may provide early evidence that the Apocrypha was a Christian innovation. The evidence does not support a "wider" Alexandrian Jewish canon which would have included the books of the Apocrypha, and we simply do not know what sort of biblical canon Alexandrian Jews may have had.

There is very little discussion in rabbinic literature about these Jewish texts of the Apocrypha. What concerns us here is the issue of canon. [9] Only two of these books are discussed by rabbinic sources in a way that demonstrates that their "authority" or "sacredness" was an issue: Baruch and Ben Sira (Sirach). The evidence for Baruch is very limited and far from conclusive. However, among some of the rabbis the figure of Baruch was viewed as Jeremiah's attendant and therefore one who shared in his prophetic gifts, [10] and the book itself gives directions that it shall be read publicly "in the house of the Lord on the days of the festivals and at appointed seasons" (1.14). If it was read in the synagogue in

5. H.M. Orlinsky, *Essays in Biblical Culture and Bible Translation*. New York: 1974, p. 218.
6. Shaye Cohen (*From the Maccabees to the Mishnah*. Philadelphia: 1987, p. 190) has noted that "there are no objective and absolute criteria that will distinguish works that were included from those which were not."
7. *The Old Testament of Early Church*. Cambridge, MA: 1964.
8. *The Old Testament Canon*.
9. Some of the books of the Apocrypha may have been excluded from any discussion of "sacredness" at the outset by virtue of having been written in Greek (2-4 Maccabees and Wisdom of Solomon) or totally in Aramaic (Tobit). This is because Mishnah Yadayim 4.5 proclaims that a biblical scroll only makes the hands unclean (see below) if it has been written in Hebrew or Hebrew with Aramaic.
10. Sifre on Number 78; Seder Olam Rabbah 20; Bab. Megillah 14b; and Jer. Sotah 9.12.

whatever narrow circles, this would indicate that it had some sort of authoritative status even though it was not considered sacred in the same way as the books which made it into the Jewish canon.

The evidence for Ben Sira is much more wide-ranging and intriguing, and points to a book which was highly authoritative in rabbinic circles and well-esteemed in Palestine though it never achieved full canonical status. The rabbinic evidence is inconsistent, though the inconsistencies themselves are clues that this book was very highly valued, generating the divergent and strongly stated views which are found in the Talmud and midrashim (varieties of comment on scripture) and eliciting numerous scholarly attempts to reconcile the rabbinic evidence from the 11th century right up to the present. Briefly, in the rabbinic evidence are the following points about Ben Sira [11]: (1) It is discussed among the "outside books" where it is stated that it is forbidden to read the book of Ben Sira (by Rabbi Akiba). [12] (2) It is said to have been withdrawn by the rabbis, and yet they expound all the good passages contained in it. [13] (3) It is said not to "make the hands unclean" [14]—though this is a mysterious expression, it means that the book is not recognized as sacred scripture; Mishnah Yadayim 3.5 gives us the general principle: "All the Sacred Scriptures make the hands unclean" and Mishnah Yadayim 4.6 adds: "As to their preciousness, so is their uncleanness." [15] (4) It is not to be brought into the house for intensive study. [16] (5) It is quoted numerous times, and the introductory formulae for these citations give indications about how the book was regarded. Of special interest is the formula, "it is written in the Book of Ben Sira," which is parallel to formulae used for books for the Jewish Bible and so could imply canonical status. However, it has been pointed out that there may be a difference between "it is written" (the book not being named—a formula used with authoritative Scriptures) and "it is written in the Book of Ben Sira" (the book is named—an authoritative text is being quoted, but not necessarily a sacred one.) [17] One other factor which is often noted are the numerous recensions of Ben Sira in Hebrew and Greek from the 1st century B.C.E. onward, indicating that the text of Ben Sira was not stabilized. Sid Leiman has interpreted this as one more signal that Ben Sira never attained canonical biblical status as all the books in the Jewish Bible have stabilized texts. In sum, while there is never a challenge to the declaration that Ben Sira does not make the hands unclean, yet long after Akiba had banned the book, rabbis continue to cite Ben Sira as if it was authoritative. The rabbinic sources suggest that Ben Sira was a dangerous book (it had to be banned!), widely used and respected, and therefore it may have been too tempting to treat it as a sacred canonical book.

The presence of certain texts of the Apocrypha among the Dead Sea Scrolls both raises an issue of canon and demonstrates the value of these texts for one Jewish community in antiquity. Four texts of the Apocrypha have been identified among the Dead Sea Scrolls. Four copies of Tobit in Aramaic and one in Hebrew (4Q196-200) have been found, perhaps indicating that the book circulated early in two languages. Among the five copies of Tobit, parts of all of its fourteen chapters are represented. [18] All of the Aramaic copies agree with the longer Greek text of Tobit found in the Codex Sinaiticus, suggesting that the Aramaic represents the more original form. Two small pieces of the Hebrew text of Ben Sira

11. For the rabbinic evidence I am especially indebted to Sid Z. Leiman (*The Canonization of Hebrew Scripture: The Talmudic and Midrashic Evidence*. Hamden, Conn.: 1976.), who has collected the sources together.
12. Sanhedrin 100b and Jer. Sanhedrin 28a—though this latter passage may indicate that casual reading is permissible.
13. Ibid.
14. Tosefta Yadayim 2.13.
15. The debates about which books make the hands unclean begin at Yavneh toward the end of the 1st century C.E. Yavneh should not be regarded as a meeting at which decisions were made about the Jewish biblical canon, but rather as debates which responded to a process which had been going on for a long time.
16. Koheleth Rabbah 12.12.
17. Beckwith, *The Old Testament Canon*, pp. 378-379.
18. So James C. Vanderkam, *The Dead Sea Scrolls Today*. Grand Rapids, MI: 1994, pp. 34-35. The copies of Tobit among the Dead Sea Scrolls have been translated and recently published by Joseph Fitzmyer in *Discoveries in the Judean Desert*. Oxford: 1995 (Volume XIX).

have been found in caves 2 and 11 at Qumran. Though Ben Sira was originally composed in Hebrew and must have circulated in Hebrew for several centuries (note the extensive discussion of it in rabbinic literature), the Hebrew text eventually passed out of use in most Jewish communities and was no longer copied. These two smaller pieces from Qumran join with other twentieth-century discoveries (a substantial amount of the text found in the Cairo Geniza and a copy of several chapters found at Masada) to shed light on the lost Hebrew original. Also found among the Dead Sea Scrolls at Qumran is one copy of the Letter of Jeremiah (from cave 7—written in Greek, apparently the original language) and Psalm 151 which is the conclusion to the Psalms Scroll from cave 11. The presence of these four texts at Qumran tells us that they were valued as a part of the library of the community of Jews (most likely Essenes) who lived at Qumran between the mid 2nd century B.C.E. and 68 C.E.

Psalm 151 is a part of the large Psalms Scroll from cave 11 which has raised an issue about canon at the time of the Qumran community.[19] The book of Psalms divides into five sections ("books"): (1) Psalms 1-41; (2) Psalms 42-72; (3) Psalms 73-89; (4) Psalms 90-106; and (5) Psalms 107-150 [or 151]. The cave 11 Psalms Scroll incorporates nine texts (including Psalm 151) not found in the Masoretic book of Psalms—all of them found in the last two sections of the book. In addition there now appear to be two other copies of this variant form of the book of Psalms (from caves 11 and 4), suggesting that the cave 11 Psalms Scroll "allows us to be privy to a time in the development of the Psalter when books four and five fluctuated considerably"[20], and when Psalm 151 was a part of an official Jewish collection of Psalms.

The Apocrypha in Jewish Literature, Festival Celebrations and the Arts

What we know about the use of the Apocrypha in Jewish literature, festival celebrations and in the arts varies from the sketchiest of details to the more than a dozen medieval midrashim and liturgical pieces which build upon the story of Judith. What follows is a brief survey.

4 Ezra. The impact of 4 Ezra can be discerned through the extraordinary wealth of translations of this text and the number of later writings that depend on it.

Prayer of Azariah. Though there is no clear evidence of how the Prayer of Azariah may have been used in Jewish communities prior to the early Middle Ages, it does appear in the 10th century Hebrew historical narrative "Josippon,"[21] and in the 12th century "Chronicles of Jerahmeel."[22] Selections from many of the texts of the Apocrypha are found in these two works.

Susanna. Several variants and allusions to the Susanna story show up in later Jewish literature including the Babylonian Talmud (b. Sanhedrin 93a), Josippon and the Chronicles of Jerahmeel.

Tobit. Because it is often so difficult to date texts of the Apocrypha and Pseudepigrapha with precision, it can be hard to decide which text has influenced another or if one is dealing with a common source. Nevertheless, it has been asserted that one can find the influence of Tobit in the books of Jubilees, the Testament of Job and the Testimony of Solomon.[23] Its popularity even beyond the Qumran community is attested to by several medieval Jewish versions of the Tobit story.

1, 2, and 4 Maccabees. These three books of Maccabees have played a significant role in the Jewish

19. I am dependent here on the excellent and more detailed discussion of James Vanderkam in *The Dead Sea Scrolls Today* (pp. 135-139).
20. Vanderkam, *The Dead Sea Scrolls Today*, p. 138. The first three sections of the book of Psalms seem much more firmly fixed.
21. Josippon (composed in southern Italy) describes Jewish history in the Graeco-Roman period focusing especially on the Jewish wars against Rome and ending with the fall of Masada. It served as a major source of information for this period, and was therefore frequently quoted by Bible and Talmud commentators in the Middle Ages. The author was unknown, but the work came to be ascribed to the Jewish historian, Josephus.
22. Jerahmeel Ben Solomon was a chronicler in southern Italy in the 12th century. He compiled numerous writings from Jewish and non-Jewish sources in his Chronicles, including some of the texts of the Apocrypha.
23. Carey A. Moore, "Tobit, Book of" *Anchor Bible Dictionary*. Vol. VI, p. 592.

community, though it is not always possible to separate them when assessing their impact. The first century Jewish historian Josephus relied on at least 1 Maccabees in relating Jewish history in the Hasmonean period. First and Second Maccabees served as sources for Josippon in the 10th century. One of the more popular medieval Hebrew stories was the Scroll of Antiochus which included some of the better known parts of the books of Maccabees. The story of the martyrdom of the woman and her seven sons, recounted in both 2 and 4 Maccabees,[24] has remained popular in Judaism ever since. It is the only story from the books of Maccabees that is known and related in rabbinic literature—though it may have come into rabbinic circles through oral traditions rather than by way of the books of Maccabees.[25] The Jewish concepts of resurrection and prayers for the dead originate primarily in 2 Maccabees. The stories and details relating to the celebrations of the minor festival of Hanukkah are drawn more from 1 and 2 Maccabees than from rabbinic literature including: the story of the victory of the Hasmoneans against the Seleucids, the different martyrdom stories, celebration of the dedication of the altar (1 Maccabees), celebration of the cleansing and rededication of the Temple (2 Maccabees), and the celebration lasting for eight days.

Ben Sira. The impact of Ben Sira has been especially evident in rabbinic literature where the sayings of Ben Sira have been cited by rabbis of all eras and even sayings which were not Ben Sira's have been erroneously ascribed to him. Further, many ideas found for the first time in Ben Sira are picked up by the rabbis and advocated by them in Aggadic literature (stories or preaching) as are customs taken from Ben Sira and promoted in the Halakhah. One also finds Ben Sira's influence on ancient Hebrew prayers and in *Piyyutim* (Jewish liturgical poems of the early medieval period). A hint of the continued reverence for Ben Sira is found in the Middle Ages, during which a new pseudepigraphic work, the "Alfabet de-Ben Sira," is attributed to the sage.[26]

Judith. Without a doubt, the heroic and gory details of the Judith story captured the imagination of the Jewish people. We have more than a dozen midrashim and liturgical pieces based on Judith which date from the tenth to the 19th centuries and several more allusions to Judith and critical discussions of the midrashim by rabbis from the Middle Ages. While there is an overlap between many of the midrashim, the accounts are too long and detailed to be summarized here. However, typical of many of the accounts is the conflation of three elements: (1) the story of an endangered fiancée during Hasmonean times; (2) the traditional Judith story; (3) changing the city which she saves from Bethulia to Jerusalem. Often there are many changed elements from the original account: sometimes the characters are not named, sometimes they are named but their position has changed (e.g. Holofernes becomes king of the Greeks or Judith becomes a young, beautiful woman or even the endangered fiancée, or—in one account—the reincarnation of Jael, etc.), Judith goes before the enemy king and he proposes marriage (an old motif!) and so on.[27] One of the most intriguing aspects of many of these medieval texts is the association of Judith with the festival of Hanukkah.[28] Rabbi Samuel Ben Meir (12th century) writes, "At Purim give thanks to Esther, at Hanukkah give thanks to Judith."[29] Not only is she associated with the eight days of the festival and lauded as the one by whose hand the miracle happened, there is

24. 4 Maccabees greatly expands the account in 2 Maccabees to serve the purpose of that book.
25. There are significant discrepancies between the principal rabbinic accounts (Lam. R 1.50; Gittin 57b; Seder Eliyahu R 29) and the stories in 2 and 4 Maccabees. In rabbinic literature, probably to increase the impact of the story, the sons are portrayed as young children. It is intriguing that rabbinic literature does not recount the martyrdom of Eleazar found in both 2 and 4 Maccabees.
26. However, other than the name and a few sayings it has nothing in common with the original Ben Sira.
27. The various texts and explication of the texts are presented in A.M. Dubarle, O.P., *Judith Formes Et Sens Des Diverses Traditions*. Rome: 1966.
28. This association of Judith with Hanukkah is heavily criticized for its artificiality by two revered rabbis of the 16th and 17th centuries.
29. Dubarle, *Judith*. p. 105.

evidence that Judith was actually incorporated into the Hanukkah celebration: there are liturgical hymns for the first and second Sabbaths of Hanukkah celebrating Judith's role, it became customary to eat a platter of cheese (based on midrashim in which Judith brings a platter of cheese to Holofernes or the enemy king before beheading him), and there is even a 16th century Hanukkah menorah which depicts Judith holding the head of Holofernes! The association of the story of Judith with Hanukkah did not continue into the present era, but fascination with the book of Judith has continued inspiring (between the Middle Ages and now) numerous plays, liturgical music and operas in the Jewish community.

The Apocryphal/Deuterocanonical Books: An Orthodox View

Demetrios J. Constantelos

The official canon of the Old Testament section of the Holy Scriptures in the Orthodox Christian Church today includes forty-nine books. As some of the Bible's books have been designated by a name indicating a specific category such as historical (Pentateuch, Judges, etc.), poetic and didactic (Psalms, Job, Proverbs, etc.), prophetic (Isaiah, Jeremiah, etc.) likewise there are in the Old Testament ten books known as deuterocanonical (second canon). That is, in addition to the 39 books of the Palestinian Judaism's canon, the Orthodox Church's canon includes 10 books of Hellenistic Judaism. In a slightly different arrangement all 49 books, known as the Septuagint, made up the Holy Scriptures of the early Christian Church.

The term Apocrypha is used by the Orthodox for several books which have been omitted from the Old Testament canon, such as Enoch, The Apocalypse of Abraham, the Testament of the 12 Patriarchs, The Book of Jubilees, Job's Testament, Psalms of Solomon, The Apocryphon of Ezekiel, Martyrdom of Isaiah, The Life of Adam and Eve, Lives of the Prophets, The Ascension of Moses, Revelation of Baruch, Revelation of Esdras, The Epistle of Aristeas and several more written in Hebrew, Aramaic, Greek, and Syriac between 200 B.C.E. and 150 C.E. Several of these books are also called Pseudepigrapha, meaning books with false attributions.

The Deuterocanonical Books in the Early Christian Church

The canonical status of the ten deuterocanonical books of the Old Testament was greatly influenced by their place in the early Christian community's life and worship. While the Orthodox Church subscribes to the historical method and is not averse to change and reconsideration, it strongly believes in maintaining a fidelity to and continuity with the principles, doctrines, ethos, and liturgical life of the early and medieval church.

The question remains: Why does the contemporary Orthodox Church continue to use the larger or Alexandrian canon of 49 Old Testament books? First of all because this collection of Old Testament books was the official Scripture used by the Apostolic Church. The early Church as a Greek speaking church, both in the eastern and the western parts of the Roman Empire, used the Greek translation of the Alexandrian Jewish canon, the Septuagint.

The importance of the Greek Old Testament for early Christianity is indicated by the presence of many quotations in the writings of the New Testament. Out of 350 Old Testament passages in the New Testament, more than 300 of them are taken from the Septuagint, including the deuterocanonical books. In addition to quotations and allusions in the four gospels and the book of the Acts of the Apostles, the Apostles and other writers of the New Testament books copied either directly or paraphrased from the Septuagint's deuterocanonical books. For instance:

Romans 1.18-20 and Wisdom of Solomon 13.1ff

Romans 9.3; 10.1 and Prayer of Manasseh, esp. 8-9

1 Corinthians 2.10-16 and Judith 8.14
Hebrews 1.3 and Wisdom of Solomon 7.26
Hebrews 11.32-39 and 2 Maccabees 6.18-27
James 3.5-9 and Sirach 5.13
Revelation 8.2 and Tobit 12.15

In addition to New Testament writers, the apostolic fathers (Polycarp, Epistle of Barnabas), apologists (Justin, Irenaeus), and leading Church fathers and ecclesiastical writers (Clement of Alexandria, Origen) cited these books, thereby giving them authority and providing a basis for their canonicity. To be sure there were disagreements among the Church Fathers of the first five centuries over the canonical status of the deuterocanonical books, but the opinion of major Church Fathers such as Athanasios of Alexandria, Basil of Caesarea, Gregory of Nyssa, John Chrysostom, Cyril of Alexandria, Theodoretos of Cyrrhus, Ephraim the Syrian, Lactantius, Ambrose of Milan, and Augustine of Hippo settled the issue on the side of their canonicity. Nevertheless, the deuterocanonical books were not considered as sources for official doctrine. From as early as the fourth century they were also designated as Anaginoskomena: books that can be read for spiritual edification and instruction.

The Deuterocanonical Books in the Liturgy

Liturgy and liturgical services such as the Eucharistic liturgy, Baptism, Marriage ceremony, Unction, and others contain biblical passages and allusions not only from the canonical books but also from the deuterocanonical ones. For example the Liturgy of the Presanctified Gifts (in use from around 200 C.E. and celebrated today on each Wednesday and Friday during the Great Lent before Easter and on a few other days), the Liturgies under the names of Basil of Caesarea and John Chrysostom, and the services of Baptism, Chrism, Marriage, and Holy Unction include 511 passages from canonical Old Testament books and 56 from the deuterocanonical ones, including 1 Esdras, Tobit, Judith, Wisdom of Solomon, Wisdom of Sirach, the three books of Maccabees, and even the 4th book of the Maccabees, which appears as an appendix to the deuterocanonical books.

For the Orthodox in general, the Old Testament is propaideutic to (a preparation for) the New. As there are two periods in the history of Divine Economy and in the Christian Church, one preparatory and the other fulfillment, likewise there are two divisions in the Holy Scriptures: the Old and the New Testaments. It is for this reason that no Old Testament lectionaries are found in the Divine Liturgy. With the exception of psalmic verses in hymns of the Divine Liturgy, the Liturgy's lections are from the New Testament. Old Testament excerpts and lections are read during Vesper services which are preparatory to the Eucharistic service—the celebration of the death and the resurrection of Christ and communion with Him.

Most of the deuterocanonical readings in Vesper services are selected from the wisdom literature, the Wisdom of Solomon in particular. For example, in the Vespers of St. Basil, January 1, a lengthy lection is a compilation of passages from the Wisdom of Solomon; the Vespers of St. Theodosios the Koinobiarches, Jan. 11, includes three lections from the same book (3.1-9; 5.15-23; 6.1-3; 4.7-15). The Vespers of St. Anthony (Jan.17) includes three lections from the Wisdom of Solomon. A lection from the same book is read in the Vespers of SS Athanasios and Kyrillos of Alexandria (Jan. 18) as well as in the Vespers of St. Gregory the Theologian (Jan. 25), the Vespers of the Three Hierarchs (Jan. 30), the Vespers of St. Charalampes (Feb. 10), the Vespers of St. George (April 23), etc.; the Vespers of St. Anna, the mother of Theotokos (the "God-bearer," that is, Mary, the Mother of Christ) (July 25), the Vespers of St. Panteleemon (July 27), the beheading of John the Baptist (Aug. 29). Indeed, a survey of all Vesper Services commemorating major saints reveals that the book of Wisdom of Solomon is widely used and the most popular of all Old Testament lections.

Unlike Vespers in honor of Saints, in Vespers commemorating the Theotokos (Mother of Christ) and Christ, the Lections are taken from various Old Testament books: Genesis, Exodus, Deuteronomy, Joshua, Kings I and II (Septuagint III and IV), Judges, Proverbs, Isaiah, Jeremiah, Ezekiel, Daniel, and Malachi. Vespers commemorating apostles (June 29, for Peter and Paul, September 26 for John the Evangelist, November 30 for St. Andrew) and so on, include lections from the New Testament's Catholic Epistles.

With the exception of the book of Psalms, the Wisdom of Solomon is used in church services more frequently than any other Old Testament book. It is perhaps this liturgical usage of the deuterocanonical books that has contributed to their canonical status in the Orthodox Church. The conscience and practice of the Church in history counts more than theological opinion. But from as early as the fourth century the deuterocanonical books stand on a lower level than the rest of the Old Testament books.

Other Indications of the Authority of the Deuterocanonical Books

That the deuterocanonical books were considered authentic by the Greek Church during the Byzantine millennia (330-1453 C.E.) and beyond is indicated by the wide use of them by authors of Lives of Saints, and also Church Fathers in sermons, homilies, and epistles (examples: Lives of St. Nikon and Petros of Argos; homilies of Cappadocian Fathers, St. Photios, St. Gregory Palamas).

Even though there is no official decree of the Church by an Ecumenical Synod concerning the canonicity of these books, there are acts by several local councils which reveal that the early Church used the larger or Alexandrian canon of the Bible. Decisions of councils such as Laodicea (343, 381), Hippo (393), Carthage (397-419), and the Council in Trullo (619) confirm the validity of the deuterocanonical books. Later councils of the Orthodox Church such as those of Constantinople (1638), Jassy (1642), and especially the very influential Council of Jerusalem (1672) made no distinction between shorter and longer lists of canonical Old Testament books.

The attitude of the Church in history toward the deuterocanonical books (apostles, apostolic fathers, apologists, major Church fathers, and Church councils) indicate that the Christian Church did not see the Palestinian canon (the Hebrew Scriptures) as a definitively closed book. God's presence, renewing and guiding the faithful, provides the ground for an understanding of the Orthodox Church's attitude not only toward the Scriptures as a larger collection but of the importance of Holy Tradition, including the decisions of councils whose deliberations have been adopted by ecumenical councils. God did not reveal Himself "once and no more" (Martin Buber) because God is active whether through elect persons or through the beauty, the order, the mystery, the personal experience of devout persons in the world.

Thus God's involvement in the life and history of ancient Israel did not stop with the events of the fourth century B.C.E. God did not leave himself *amartyron*, "without witness," between the period of 250 B.C.E. to 200 C.E. when the deuterocanonical and the New Testament books were written. Furthermore both the deuterocanonical books and the apocryphal/pseudepigraphal writings are of great historical significance for an understanding of later Judaism and early Christianity.

It seems that serious questions regarding the canonicity of the deuterocanonical books were not raised until after the Sixth Ecumenical Council in Trullo, either in the Greek Byzantine or the Slavic and Armenian Churches. Theologians such as John of Damascus and Patriarch Nicephoros following the opinion of Athanasios accepted the deuterocanonical books, but on a lower level than the rest of the Old Testament. On the other hand, Patriarch Photios (d. 891) included the longer canon in his *Nomocanon* and his *Syntagma of Canons* without differentiating between canonical and deuterocanonical.

The issue was reopened at the beginning of the seventeenth century by the *Confession of Faith* attributed to Patriarch Kyrillos Loukaris. Under the influence of Protestantism, he had adopted the shorter canon. But his Homologia Pisteos was condemned by Church Synods of Constantinople (1638), Jassy (1642), and especially of Jerusalem (1672). Kyrillos' position on the canon of the Scriptures was, however, defended by several Greek theologians of the nineteenth and twentieth centuries. Today the Greek-speaking church subscribes to the longer canon, making no distinction between protocanonical and deuterocanonical.

The Russian Orthodox position has not been as clear. For several centuries, its position was greatly determined by the opinion of Philaret of Moscow, who had accepted the shorter canon. But he was accused (1619-1633) of Protestant inclinations and influences. Nevertheless Philaret's views influenced the Russian Church for many years. It seems that ambiguities exist among Orthodox theologians in Russia even today. It is not rare, nevertheless, to find in all Orthodox churches theologians, both lay and clergy, who consider the deuterocanonical books divinely inspired and of equal value to other Old Testament books.

The Apocryphal/Deuterocanonical Books: A Catholic View

John J. Collins

The books known as "Apocrypha" in Protestant tradition are evaluated differently in the Catholic Church. Tobit, Judith, the additions to Esther and Daniel, Sirach, Wisdom of Solomon, Baruch (including the Letter of Jeremiah), and 1 and 2 Maccabees are all accepted as canonical scriptures. (The additions to Esther and Daniel are regarded simply as parts of those books.) First and Second Esdras, the Prayer of Manasseh, and 3 and 4 Maccabees are not canonical and have no special status. The term "Apocrypha" in Catholic parlance refers to the entire corpus of non-canonical Jewish or Christian writings from the biblical period, including the Pseudepigrapha. In 1566, however, a distinction was introduced by Sixtus of Sienna between "protocanonical" books, that were acknowledged by the entire Church from the beginning, and "deuterocanonical" books that were added later. The Protestant "Apocrypha" are commonly referred to as "deuterocanonical" in Catholic publications. The deuterocanonical books are recognized as fully canonical, but it is acknowledged that they are absent from the Hebrew scriptures and were added secondarily to the canon.

The Debate About Canonicity

Catholic tradition in the Middle Ages took its cue from St. Augustine, who included the deuterocanonical books in his list of the scriptures. Nonetheless some variation persisted. On the one hand, additional books were included in biblical manuscripts: for instance, the Psalms and Odes of Solomon in the Septuagint or Greek Bible, and 1 and 2 Esdras in the Latin Vulgate. On the other hand, several authoritative Church figures continued to express preference for the shorter Hebrew canon, or to express doubts about the canonicity of the deuterocanonical writings. The list of such figures includes Gregory the Great, John Damascene, Hugh of St. Victor, and Nicholas of Lyra. Nicholas, in the 14th century, wrote a commentary on the protocanonical Bible in which he followed the Hebrew and drew on Jewish exegetes. He added a commentary on the "uncanonical" books of Wisdom, Sirach, Judith, Tobit, and 1 and 2 Maccabees. He also wrote a pamphlet on the differences between the Vulgate translation and the Hebrew original. His role as a precursor for the Reformation view of the canon was acknowledged in the Latin ditty: *Si Lyra no lyrasset, Luther non saltasset*—"If Lyra had not played the lyre, Luther would not have danced."

Even at the time of the Reformation, several Catholic scholars expressed views that were close to those of the Reformers on the subject of the canon. Cardinal Ximenes, who published the *Complutensian Polyglot* in 1514-17, stated in the Preface that the books printed in Greek, but not available in Hebrew, were received by the Church for edification rather than for the establishment of doctrine. Erasmus accepted the authority of the Church in approving the additional books, but added that "it is of great importance to know in what spirit the Church approves a thing. It surely does not wish Judith, Tobit, and Wisdom to have the same weight as the Pentateuch." Later, in an exposition of the Creed in 1533, he distinguished between those books that it would be impious to doubt and those that have been received into ecclesiastical use. In the latter category he included not only Wisdom, Sirach, Tobit, Judith, and the Additions to Daniel, but also Esther. He again questioned whether these books had the same authority as the others. The most famous Catholic proponent of the shorter canon in this era, however, was Cardinal Cajetan, the papal legate before whose tribunal Luther was summoned to appear at Augsburg in 1518, and a staunch foe of the reformers. Cajetan wrote a commentary on "the authentic historical books" of the Old Testament, which are found in the Hebrew canon. He acknowledged that Judith, Tobit, and the books of Maccabees can be called "canonical" but insisted that they stood outside the ancient canon. In an extraordinarily bold statement he argued that "the words of councils and of doctors must alike be revised by the judgment of Jerome."

Cajetan died in 1534. The Council of Trent was convened in 1545. In April 1546 a decree was promulgated concerning the inspired scriptures of the Old Testament. The deuterocanonical books were interspersed with the books of the Hebrew canon, and all were declared to be of equal validity. The decree pronounced an anathema upon "anyone who does not receive these entire books, with all their parts, as they are accustomed to be read in the Catholic Church and are found in the ancient edition of the Latin Vulgate, as sacred and canonical." (The anathema only concerned the reception of the books, not the primacy of the Vulgate text.) The books of 1 and 2 Esdras and the Prayer of Manasseh were omitted. In basing its decision on Jerome's Vulgate, the Council confirmed the majority Church tradition of more than a thousand years. It was ironic, however, that Jerome had been the champion of the *Hebraica veritas* and of the shorter Hebrew canon.

Liturgical Use

Whatever the controversies about their canonical status, the deuterocanonical books have figured quite prominently in Catholic liturgy and theology. Two deuterocanonical passages figure prominently in liturgies of the Virgin Mary. The first scripture reading (traditionally, the Epistle) for the common Mass of the Blessed Virgin is taken from Sirach (Ecclesiasticus) 24.9-11: "From the beginning and before all ages I was created, and for all ages I will not cease to be. . . ." The speaker in Sirach is personified Wisdom, but the passage is here applied to Mary, presumably because Wisdom is also feminine. Catholic theology does not teach that Mary was pre-existent, but passages describing pre-existent wisdom are regularly applied to her in the liturgy nonetheless. Another passage from Sirach 24 is chosen as the first reading for the feast of the Queenship of the Blessed Virgin (May 31): "I came out of the mouth of the Most High, the first-born before all creatures. I dwelt in the highest places, and my throne is in a pillar of cloud." On the feasts of the Nativity of the Virgin (September 8) and the Immaculate Conception (December 8) the readings are taken from Proverbs 8, which also deals with personified Wisdom. These passages (Proverbs 8 and Sirach 24) associate the female figure of wisdom very closely with God. The liturgical veneration of the Virgin Mary, in the Catholic Church before the Second Vatican Council (1962-65), also tended in this direction, and went further than formal theological doctrines on the subject. There has been a sharp decline in Marian devotion since Vatican II. The most recent Catholic theological work on the figure of wisdom has used these biblical passages to argue from a feminist perspective for a feminine side of God. (See Elizabeth Johnson, *She Who Is: The Mystery of God in Feminist Theological Discourse* [1992].)

The second deuterocanonical text that figures prominently in traditional liturgies of the Virgin Mary is Judith 13.18-20, supplemented by 15.9. This is the first reading for the feast of the Assumption of the Virgin into Heaven (August 15): "You are blessed by the Most High God above all women on the earth . . . You are the glory of Jerusalem, the joy of Israel, the honor of our people." This passage also provides the text for the Gradual (a short hymnic prayer following the first reading) for the feast of the Immaculate Conception. It is obviously chosen because of the verses cited above. Other verses may seem less appropriate: ". . .blessed be the Lord God, who created the heavens and the earth, who has guided you to strike the head of the leader of our enemies" (Judith 13.18). As applied to Mary, however, this verse recalls the familiar Catholic iconography of the Virgin crushing the head of the snake, Satan, which in turn arises from applying to Mary Genesis 3.15 ("I will put enmity between you and the woman").

The liturgical use of these texts with reference to the Virgin Mary involves a transfer of imagery that is in accordance with traditional typological interpretation, but ignores the literal sense and context of the passages in question. A more straightforward use of deuterocanonical texts can be found in the liturgy for the dead. The first reading for the anniversary Mass is taken from 2 Maccabees 12.43-44, which tells how Judas Maccabee collected money from his soldiers to provide a sin offering for their fallen comrades, who were found to be wearing idolatrous amulets. The author comments: "In doing this he acted well and honorably, taking account of the resurrection. For if he were not expecting that those who had fallen would rise again, it would have been superfluous and foolish to pray for the dead. But if he was looking to the splendid reward that is laid up for those who fall asleep in godliness, it was a holy and pious thought. Therefore he made atonement for the dead that they might be delivered from their sin." This passage is cited in support of the idea of making atonement for the dead, which is also a purpose of the anniversary Mass. It is quite doubtful whether this is what Judas Maccabee had in mind. He was probably making atonement on behalf of the army, lest it be punished for the transgression of those who had worn amulets. The author of 2 Maccabees interprets his action in the light of his own belief in resurrection. A more vivid expression of that belief is found in the story of the martyrs in 2 Maccabees 7, but that passage does not authorize the custom of praying and making atonement for the dead.

Two other apocryphal passages provide familiar and beautiful prayers for the dead. One is the chant "Justorum animae in manu Dei sunt" ("The souls of the just are in the hand of God"), which is taken from Wisdom of Solomon 3.1. The other is the most familiar prayer for the dead, which is used in the Introit of the Burial Mass and intermittently in the burial service (and has also been immortalized many times in music): "Requiem aeternam dona eis Domine, et lux perpetua luceat eis" ("eternal rest grant unto them, O Lord, and may perpetual light shine upon them"). This famous prayer is adapted from 2 Esdras 2.34-35, one of the apocryphal books that was rejected as non-canonical by the Council of Trent: "Therefore I say to you, O nations that hear and understand, 'Await your shepherd; he will give you everlasting rest, because he who will come at the end of the age is close at hand. Be ready for the rewards of the kingdom, because the eternal light will shine upon you for evermore.'" The liturgy for the dead also appeals to a source that has even less canonical authority than 2 Esdras. The chant "Dies irae" begins by announcing that on "the day of wrath" the world will dissolve into ashes, as David and *the sibyl* attest. While the sibylline oracles were never accorded scriptural authority, the sibyl was widely respected in the Catholic Church in the Middle Ages.

Theological Influence

The main point at issue in the debates about the canon in the Reformation period was not appropriateness for liturgical use, but for the establishment of doctrine. While the deuterocanonical books do not serve as sole authorities for any Catholic doctrine, they have a bearing on some doctrinal discussions.

The Hebrew Bible is notoriously lacking in attestations of immortality and resurrection. The only undisputed reference to resurrection in the Hebrew scriptures is in Daniel 12. In the Apocrypha, belief in resurrection is clearly attested in 2 Maccabees. More important, however, is the support of the Wisdom of Solomon for the immortality of the soul, an idea that presupposes Greek anthropology and is alien to Hebrew thought. In addition to the statement about the souls of the righteous cited above, Wisdom declares that "God created man for incorruption, and made him in the image of his own eternity" (2.23) and also that "a perishable body weighs down the soul, and this earthy tent burdens the thoughtful mind" (9.14-15). On this point, the deuterocanonical book provides an important foundation for the Catholic tradition, which affirms both the resurrection of the body and the immortality of the soul.

The insistence of the Reformers that salvation is by grace and not by works led to acrimonious debates on the value of good works. The Book of Tobit begins by reciting the various good works of Tobit. It does not however claim that these works atoned for sin, and so their salvific value could still be disputed.

The most important theological issue raised in the Apocrypha is undoubtedly that of natural theology. The Wisdom of Solomon 13.5 blames those who admired creation but failed to acknowledge the creator: "For from the greatness and beauty of created things comes a corresponding perception of their Creator." This passage anticipates the statement of St. Paul in Romans 1: "For what can be known about God is plain to them, because God has shown it to them. Ever since the creation of the world his eternal power and divine nature, invisible though they are, have been understood and seen through the things he has made." The possibility of knowing God from nature has been one of the most fundamental points of dispute between Catholic and Protestant theologians. The classic position of Thomas Aquinas in the *Summa Theologica*, First Part, Article 12, cites Romans, but not Wisdom. Yet the discussion seems closer to the formulation of Wisdom: "Our natural knowledge takes its beginning from sense. Hence our natural knowledge can go as far it can be led by sensible things. But our mind cannot be led by sense so far as to see the essence of God, because the sensible effects of God do not equal the power of God as their cause. Hence from the knowledge of sensible things the whole power of God cannot be known; nor therefore can His essence be seen. But because they are His effects and depend on their cause, we can be led from them so far as to know of God whether He exists, and to know of Him what must necessarily belong to Him as the first cause of all things, exceeding all things caused by Him."

The First Vatican Council defined the possibility of a sure knowledge of God "by the natural light of human reason from created realities." Even though it also affirmed the need for faith beyond reason for salvation, and acknowledged that humanity needs revelation in order to grasp even natural truths with certainty and without error, the role accorded to human reason has been the subject of much Protestant polemic, especially in the theology of Karl Barth. While the Wisdom of Solomon is not a necessary foundation for the Catholic position, it is highly congenial to it. The biblical wisdom literature is the part of the biblical corpus that lends itself most readily to some form of natural theology. Since the Apocrypha contain two major wisdom books, Wisdom and Sirach, this aspect of the tradition is greatly strengthened by their inclusion. Both of the these books, but especially the Wisdom of Solomon, attempt to combine the biblical tradition with the categories of Hellenistic philosophy. This fusion of Greek and Hebrew thought is constitutive for Christian theology in the Catholic tradition.

Happily, doctrinal debates about good works and natural theology are now mainly of historical interest. Contemporary Catholic scholars scarcely differ from their Protestant colleagues in their appreciation of the historical importance of the apocryphal literature, whether it is classified as canonical or not. Nonetheless, the tendency to inclusiveness, and to blurring the line between canon and tradition, remain typical of a Catholic as distinct from a Protestant sensibility.

Further Reading

C. C. Torrey, *The Apocryphal Literature* (1945) has a lively account of the debates about the canon.

R. E. Brown, et al. *The New Jerome Biblical Commentary* (1990) contains a helpful discussion of canonicity (by R. E. Brown and R. F. Collins, 1034-54) and contemporary Catholic commentaries on the individual deuterocanonical books.

The Apocryphal/Deuterocanonical Books: An Anglican/Episcopal View

Mary Chilton Callaway

The story of the Apocrypha in Anglican tradition illuminates some of the most distinctive historical and theological aspects of Anglicanism. Although its historical roots are in England, and the Archbishop of Canterbury is its spiritual leader, the Anglican Communion includes seventy-five million Christians worldwide. Anglicans do not have an official and binding statement of doctrine; questions of policy are best addressed through their history and liturgy. The documents defining the content of the faith for Anglicans are the Holy Scriptures, the Nicene Creed, and the Book of Common Prayer. The Anglican understanding of the Apocrypha is embedded in the history of the English Bible and the liturgy of the Church.

The Apocrypha and the Origins of the English Bible

For nearly twelve centuries, from the appearance of the Vulgate (Jerome's Latin translation of the Scriptures) in 382 to the Council of Trent in 1546, the Apocrypha was defined in the western Church by the subtle understanding of Jerome. Recognizing that Christianity had inherited from Judaism a double legacy in the 24 books of the Hebrew Old Testament and the 36 or so books of its Greek translation (known as the Septuagint), Jerome included the extra books in his version, but noted in his preface that "men may read them to the edifying of the people, but not to confirm and strengthen the doctrine of the Church."

For centuries Jerome's translation served as the official Scriptures of the western Church. Most Christians, however, were not aware of the distinction Jerome had made between two classes of biblical books. They knew the Bible from allusions in sermons, stained glass windows, songs, and popular dramatizations. Stories from the Apocrypha were well represented, together with a host of local legends and details of popular piety that were interwoven with biblical stories.

Three developments in Europe between the fourteenth and sixteenth centuries led to a permanent change in the way Christians thought about the Bible, and ultimately shaped the Anglican understanding of the Apocrypha. The first was the evolution of the English language. For the first seven centuries of Christianity in England, the Bible was available only in Latin. In the seventh century Caedmon wrote a poetic version of portions of the Old Testament, and in the next two centuries paraphrases of Psalms and Bible stories into Anglo-Saxon circulated freely. The challenge of turning biblical idioms into Anglo-Saxon and Anglo-Norman pressed the development of the English language forward. The earliest translation of the entire Bible into English, made by the Oxford scholars John Wycliffe and Nicholas of Hereford in 1382, appeared when English had finally eclipsed French as the language of England, and interest in an English Bible was widespread. Wycliffe's edition, though it contained the Apocrypha, included a Preface citing Jerome's judgment that the books of the Apocrypha were "without authority of belief." Wycliffe's translation implicitly challenged two long-accepted Church traditions: the Vulgate as the authoritative Bible, and inclusion of the books of the

Apocrypha among the books of the Old Testament canon. The first Bible in English therefore linked the Apocrypha to the question of Church authority. In spite of Wycliffe's reputation as a heretic and the Archbishop's prohibition against reading the Bible in English, the Wycliffe Bible was widely read and dominated English Christianity for a century. Over two hundred manuscripts are still in existence.

The second significant development affecting the role of the Apocrypha in English Christianity was widespread scholarly interest in the original languages of the Bible. In 1333 Nicolas of Lyra, a Christian scholar of Jewish parents, published an exegetical study of the Old Testament, in which he distinguished between the canonical Hebrew scriptures and the additional books included in the Vulgate. Early in the sixteenth century the publication of Hebrew grammars and dictionaries made study of the Old Testament in its original language possible for Christian scholars. It was the study of Hebrew with a rabbi in Bethlehem that had originally led Jerome to describe the extra books of the Christian Old Testament as useful for edification but not for doctrine; twelve centuries later the same kind of study led English and German scholars to question the status of these books.

The third historical factor influencing the role of the Apocrypha was the invention of the printing press, leading to the widespread availability of printed Bibles in homes. In the sixteenth century the technology of printing converged with the widespread renaissance of interest in Greek and Hebrew among the learned clergy and the desire for English translations of the Bible among the laity. An important result was the publication of Myles Coverdale's "Great Bible" of 1535, including the Apocrypha grouped together in a unit between the Old and New Testaments and called Hagiographa (the Greek for "holy writings"). A lengthy essay introduced the books and cited Jerome in the argument for printing them as an appendix to the Old Testament, concluding that "we have separated them, and let them be addended, that they may be better known: to the intent that men may know of which books witness ought to be received, and of which not." The books of Judith, Maccabees (especially 2 Maccabees) and 3 and 4 Esdras (1 and 2 Esdras in this volume) were singled out as "the more suspect and the less received." The reader was cautioned not to confuse "the laws of the living God" with "men's inventions, uncertain imagination and phantasy."

Coverdale's placement of the Apocrypha between the Testaments was indebted to Martin Luther's German version of 1534. This printing convention would prove crucial in the controversies over the Apocrypha that developed during the next century. Binding a Bible without the Apocrypha became a simple matter of omitting a fascicle (a group of pages); printers in England and Europe could produce marketable versions to suit a variety of theological positions. For the English church, the printed Bible with the Apocrypha between the Testaments functioned as a physical reminder of the Apocrypha's special place in the canon of Scripture. It was a graphic statement of Jerome's conclusion that the books of the Apocrypha were to be included with the Hebrew canon but interpreted according to a different set of rules.

The Apocrypha and the Book of Common Prayer

When Thomas Cranmer wrote the first Prayer Book in 1549 he shaped the monastic offices into services that could be used by laity in their homes as well as in a public service. The morning offices of Matins, Lauds, and Prime he combined into Morning Prayer; the evening offices of Vespers and Compline became Evensong. In his preface, Cranmer said that the ancient fathers had ordered the common prayers of the Church to insure the reading of Scripture in course, to the end that "the people, by daily hearing of Holy Scripture read in the church, should continually profit more and more in the knowledge of God, and be more inflamed with the love of his true religion." A significant part of his prayer book therefore was the Lectionary, which provided three lessons, from the Old Testament, Gospels, and Epistles for every service, morning and evening. Cranmer followed the Breviary that Cardinal Francesco de Quinones, General of the Franciscans, had revised for Pope Clement VII in 1529. This lectionary provided for reading the entire Old Testament through every year once, and the New Testament three times. Cranmer excepted "certain books and chapters, which be least edifying, and might best be spared, and therefore be left unread," but most of the Apocrypha was included, as it was in the Roman Breviary. The Prayer Book revision of 1559, under Queen Elizabeth I, added a table of Scripture readings appointed for Sundays and fixed holy days, and the books of Wisdom and Ecclesiasticus were well represented.

Cranmer wove words from the Apocrypha into liturgies and some of these remain in Anglican liturgies today. The *Benedicite omnia opera Domini Domino* ("O all the works of the Lord, bless ye the Lord"), also called the Song of the Three Young Men in the Fiery Furnace from the Additions to Daniel, served as a canticle to follow the second lesson in Morning Prayer. The Eucharist included two offertory sentences from the Book of Tobit:

> Give almose [alms, charitable donations] of thy goods, and turn never thy face from any poor man, and then the face of the Lord shall not be turned away from thee.
> Be merciful after thy power: if thou hast much, give plenteously, if thou has little, do thy diligence gladly to give of that little: for so gatherest thou thyself a good reward in the day of necessity.

The service of Holy Matrimony included an allusion to the wedding night of Tobias and Sarah in Tobit 7-8 in prayer for the bride and groom asking that God "look mercifully upon them from heaven, and bless them: And as thou didst send thy Angel Raphael to Thobie and Sara, the daughter of Raguel, to their great comfort; so vouchsafe to send thy blessing upon these thy servants."

Besides using the Apocrypha in daily and Sunday liturgies, the English Church clarified their status in the Articles of Religion, drawn up in 1553 in response to the celebrations of the Council of Trent. The Articles spelled out what would come to be known as the *via media*, the middle road between Rome and Geneva, on a number of theological issues, as an important Anglican characteristic. Article VI addresses the Scriptures:

> Holy Scripture containeth all things necessary to Salvation: So that whatsoever is neither read therein, nor may be proved thereby, although it be sometime received of the faithful, as godly, and profitable for an order and comeliness: Yet no man ought to be constrained to believe it, as an article of faith, or repute it requisite to the necessity of Salvation.

In this statement the English Church began with the Reformers' principle of *sola scriptura*, but it went on to define the canon of Scripture using Jerome's distinction between the Apocrypha and the books of the Jewish canon:

> And the other Books (as Hierome saith) the Church doth read for example of life and instructions of manners; but yet doth it not apply them to establish any doctrine.

The list names fourteen books of the Apocrypha, including the Prayer of Manesses and Third and Fourth Esdras, all three of which had been dropped by the Council of Trent. The English Church took a position on Scripture that was partly indebted to the emerging Reformation theologies of Europe but was also faithful to the most ancient tradition of the Catholic Church. It is the forging of a middle way between these two that defines the Anglican understanding of the Apocrypha.

Controversies in the English Church

In the following century the delicate theological balance that characterized the Anglican Church was often threatened. In 1603 the Puritans presented a petition to James I pressing their requirements for an English Church purified of all Roman elements, one of which was that only "the canonical Scriptures. . . be read in the Church." The conference of clergy and scholars appointed by James I responded by ordering that "a translation be made of the whole Bible, as consonant as can be to the original Hebrew and Greek and that this be set out and printed without any marginal notes, and only used in all churches of England in Time of divine service." The result of this compromise with the Puritans was the Authorized Version of 1611, which combined Reformation zeal for the original languages of the Bible (and the insistence on printed Bibles free of ecclesiastical interpretations) with the ancient tradition of including the books of the Apocrypha. King James himself was ambivalent about the Apocrypha, and wrote about the books that "some of them are as like the ditement [words, statements] of the spirit of God as an egge is to an oyster." In further compromise with the Puritans, therefore, the conference declared that "such Apocrypha as have any repugnance to canonical Scripture shall be removed and not read" in the services of the church. Four lessons from the Apocrypha were removed from Cranmer's lectionary and replaced by Old Testament passages. The offending texts included parts of Bel and the Dragon and the Book of Tobit, deemed "putrid" and "frivolous" by the Puritans. Also eliminated were the 25th chapter of Sirach and a good part of chapter 26; the misogyny of these writings, read regularly in Sunday service, was corrosive, and to the Puritans was evidence that these were human writings, not inspired by God. Sirach 46.19-20, because of its approving mention of the "witch" of Endor, was cut out; the fear of witchcraft persisted in England (and in the American colonies) after it had vanished in Europe.

Puritans continued to press the English Church to have no readings at all from the Apocrypha, which they deemed to be merely human writings. Publishers who wanted to broaden their markets began publishing Bibles for Puritans by removing the Apocrypha. When the new translation authorized by James I began to appear in large numbers without the Apocrypha, the Archbishop of Canterbury ruled that anyone who printed an English Bible without the Apocrypha would be fined and imprisoned for one year.

During the next two centuries the Apocrypha was part of a continuing debate in the English Church. For many heirs of the Reformers in the eighteenth and nineteenth centuries the distinction between tradition, understood as human judgment, and Scripture, the inspired word of God, was crucial. The Scottish bishops had succeeded in limiting Apocrypha readings in the Scottish Prayer Book. In 1870, when Evangelical fervor was at its height in England, the readings from the Apocrypha in the lectionary of the Book of Common Prayer were reduced from 132 to 44. The role of the Apocrypha in the English Church of the nineteenth century therefore reflected the debates about the nature of Anglicanism.

The Apocrypha in the Episcopal Church

The Anglican Church in America followed English custom until 1789, when the new Constitution of the United States required a decision of the American Anglicans. Anglican clergy in the former colonies could not give allegiance to the English king as the head of the church and defender of the faith. They began to hold regional conventions to adapt the polity and liturgy of their churches to the new political realities. In 1789 delegates from all the colonies held a convention in Philadelphia to approve a proposed American version of Cranmer's Book of Common Prayer, a work that had been in progress for six years. The question of whether Anglicanism could be defined apart from English politics was answered in 1789 by the establishment of the Protestant Episcopal Church in America. The Episcopal Church strove to maintain the delicate balance between Catholic and Reformation principles that characterized Anglicanism in England, and it adopted a revision of Cranmer's Prayer Book that was still quite close to the Elizabethan book of 1662.

The cultural ethos of the young republic naturally influenced American Anglicans. The use of the Apocrypha in liturgy and lectionary was an issue in the American revision of the Prayer Book, and the debates it generated nicely characterize the way the culture influenced theological thinking. The dominant ethos in the colonies was Protestant, with the Puritan influence still strong in New England. One of the Prayer book revisers wrote in 1785 about the Apocrypha in the liturgy: ". . . the reading of the Apocrypha has been so old an objection to our Church, that I believe it would be taken well if we were to substitute others." The use of the *Benedicite* (the Song of the Three Young Men in the Fiery Furnace) as a canticle at the principal Sunday service was a particular irritant; it remained, but with the Te Deum as an alternative canticle. Further, the clergy and scholars who revised the Prayer Book for American use were as affected by the climate of the Age of Reason as the statesmen who had written the Constitution. The historically ambiguous position of the Apocrypha in the canon from the beginning, together with the numerous narrative elements that many found an offense to reason, were particularly problematic. The drafters of the first American Book of Common Prayer dropped all readings from the Apocrypha from the weekday lectionary, but many readings from Sirach and Wisdom for fixed holy days remained.

The attitude toward the Apocrypha in the Episcopal Church was affected by the broader ecclesiastical movements of the eighteenth and nineteenth centuries. In 1827 the British and Foreign Bible Society had ceased using money given to them for the purpose of publishing the Apocrypha, and editions of the King James Version without the Apocrypha became the norm in America. The revision of the Prayer Book lectionary in 1892 reflected the strength of the Evangelical movement in America, for all readings from the Apocrypha save three, from Sirach and Wisdom, were eliminated from the lessons appointed for fixed holy days. The Prayer Book revision of 1928, however, partly influenced by the Oxford Movement, with its appreciation of the Catholic heritage of the Anglican Church, restored more than thirty of the Apocrypha readings to the daily lectionary. Although the Prayer Book was not revised again until 1979, the General Convention of the Episcopal Church approved several changes in the lectionary, all of which moved toward broader use of the Apocrypha. In 1943 Apocrypha lessons for fixed holy days were restored. All of these readings were from Sirach and Wisdom. By 1954 the lectionary included 111 readings from the Apocrypha, ranging through 2 Esdras, Tobit, Baruch, 1 Maccabees, the Additions to Daniel, as well as Wisdom and Sirach. The revision of 1979 was influenced by Vatican II and the liturgical movements of the 1960s, and its lectionary is very close to that of the Roman Catholic Church. Today Episcopalians in church on Sunday regularly hear readings from Wisdom and Ecclesiasticus as the First Lesson; at Morning Prayer they may chant the Song of the Three Young Men and at the service of the Burial of the Dead they often hear a reading from Wisdom 3. An Episcopalian who reads the Bible daily following the Prayer Book Lectionary will read parts of most the books of the Apocrypha.

The Apocryphal/Deuterocanonical Books: A Protestant View

WALTER J. HARRELSON

The literature of the Apocrypha provided one of the contested points at the beginning of the Protestant Reformation. For Martin Luther, the apocryphal literature had its appropriate place in the Christian Bible, even though it lacked the authority of the Old Testament. Accordingly, in his 1534 translation of the entire Bible, he collected the apocryphal writings from their location in the Latin Vulgate and placed them together at the end of the Old Testament collection as an appendix, preceded by an introduction that explained his reasons for doing so. Luther would surely not have spent the time and energy required for rendering these writings into German if he had not been convinced of their value for the Christian community.

Luther's motivation for placing the Apocrypha in an appendix is plain. He knew that these writings were not to be found in the Hebrew Bible used by the Jewish community. St. Jerome long ago had made note of this fact and had retained only a portion of the apocryphal writings then available to him. Luther also recognized that certain texts of the Apocrypha supported, or were used to support, Christian doctrines and practices that he rejected, such as the doctrine of purgatory and prayer services for the dead (1 Maccabees 12.43-46) and the great emphasis upon almsgiving (Tobit). In Luther's case, however, the critical import of the Hebrew Scriptures was their testimony to Christ; what counts in the Scriptures of the Jews is "what pertains to Christ." Theoretically, Luther and the other Reformers could have used the apocryphal literature to discover "types," or symbolic foreshadowing, of Christ and Christian teachings, but they did not do so. Nevertheless, Luther preserved the writings, despite their not having the authoritative standing that the Jewish Bible did.

With John Calvin the situation was different. Calvin took a more rigorous line than that of St. Jerome: God's revelation was tied in a distinctive way to the books of the Old and New Testaments, and Calvin firmly identified these books as the thirty-nine in the Old Testament canon and the twenty-seven in the New Testament canon. He did not write expository commentaries on the apocryphal books, as he did on almost all the books of the Hebrew Scriptures, though he made frequent allusions to them. Like Luther, Calvin noted that only in a few apocryphal texts could support be found for certain Roman Catholic doctrines and practices that these Reformers rejected: prayers for the dead and the notion of purgatory; the efficacy of almsgiving and martyrdom, etc. But it was Calvin who laid the greater stress upon a fixed and limited canon as the revealed Word of God.

While the literature of the Apocrypha supplied subjects and themes for literary artists, composers, and painters, both Protestant and Catholic, within Protestant church life and scholarship the Apocrypha clearly occupied a position inferior to that of the Hebrew Scriptures. Article VI of the Anglican Thirty-Nine Articles affirms the value of the Apocrypha "for example of life and instruction of manners," but speaks against the use of the apocryphal texts in support of Christian doctrine. The British and Foreign Bible Societies and the American Bible Society have until recently regularly excluded the Apocrypha from their editions of the Bible.

During the last half century a remarkable change has occurred. Even conservative Protestant groups that stress the literal and infallible truth of the canonical sixty-six books are quite well aware of the value of the apocryphal literature for a thorough understanding of Jewish and Christian life and faith. These groups rarely raise objections to the inclusion of the Apocrypha with the rest of the biblical books.

Fifty years ago, the translators of the Revised Standard Version of the Bible, a work sponsored largely by Protestant churches, faced a quite different situation. The first RSV edition of the Apocrypha (1957) did not appear until five years after the publication of the Old and New Testaments (1952). The translation recognized that the publication of the Apocrypha was not nearly as urgent as that of the canonical Protestant Bible. Many purchasers of the RSV, they knew, would not accept a Bible that included the Apocrypha.

By contrast, the earliest editions of the New Revised Standard Version of the Bible in 1990 already contained the Apocrypha. Purchasers would have to ask for an edition without the Apocrypha in 1990 and following; in 1965 and following, purchasers would have to ask for an edition that *did* include the Apocrypha.

Today, Protestants tend not to focus on the makeup of the Bible but on its interpretation. The inclusion of the Apocrypha is widely acceptable, even though the books fail to receive the regular treatment in pulpit and in church school. Protestant scholarship, however, is heavily involved in the interpretation of the apocryphal works. In such series as the Anchor Bible commentaries and the Hermeneia commentaries, volumes are devoted to the books of the Apocrypha as well as to many of the pseudepigraphical works.

Among the best-known works of the Apocrypha are the Wisdom of Solomon, Sirach (Ben Sira or Ecclesiasticus), Judith, and Tobit. Susanna is fairly well known, and so are 1 Maccabees (for Jewish history between the Testaments) and 2 Maccabees (important especially for its stories of the Jewish martyrs). None of the books of the Apocrypha is entirely ignored in Protestant circles today, not even those that had been published only as an appendix to the Roman Catholic Vulgate (1 and 2 Esdras and the Prayer of Manasseh) or had been included only in some Greek and other Orthodox Christian Bibles (Psalm 151, and 3 and 4 Maccabees). All of these are included in the New Revised Standard Version, a practice that has made the NRSV an acceptable Bible for most Christian bodies.

The NRSV has continued the Protestant practice of placing all of the apocryphal works together, between the Old and New Testaments. The contents and order of the books of the Apocrypha in the NRSV differ from the arrangement and contents of most collections. The translators placed 1 and 2 Esdras and the Prayer of Manasseh toward the end of the collection, since those works are found only as an appendix to the Vulgate Bible, and they added Psalm 151, 3 Maccabees and 4 Maccabees to close the collection, thereby including all of the books that the Greek and Russian churches accept as deuterocanonical.

Particularly valuable among Protestant communities have been the following themes found within the literature of the Apocrypha:

- The immortality of the soul (Wisdom of Solomon 3), which is related to and often contrasted with the theme of bodily resurrection
- A readiness to risk life and honor in faithfulness to God's demands (Judith 9 and the martyr stories of 2 Maccabees)
- The identification of Wisdom with God's Law (Sirach 24 and Baruch 3-5)
- The many and often eloquent prayers of the Apocrypha (Greek Esther, the prayer of Azariah, and prayers of Judith, Tobias, Sarah, and Tobit)
- The place of Jerusalem in the Last Days (Baruch 5, 2 Esdras 9-10)

Women occupy an important place in the apocryphal literature. Contemporary scholars have turned to the Apocrypha to fill out the evidence for the place of women in the world of ancient Israel, Judaism, and Christianity. Among the most striking and memorable of these female figures are Judith; Sarah and

Anna in the Book of Tobit; Esther in the Greek form of the Book of Esther; the figure of Wisdom in Sirach, Wisdom of Solomon, and Baruch; the mother of the seven martyred sons in 2 Maccabees; and Susanna in the Additions to Daniel. Another is the grieving woman of 2 Esdras who is suddenly transformed into the city of Zion being restored and enlarged.

The fact that recent editions of the Apocrypha include the entire deuterocanonical collection as found in Roman Catholic and Orthodox Bibles is a great boon to the study and use of the Apocrypha. Scholars and students of the Bible now have easy access to the whole of the apocryphal writings claimed by the churches. And happily, this large collection can now be supplemented with an English translation of the major literature of the Dead Sea Scrolls and of the Old Testament Pseudepigrapha.

Protestant Christians clearly give first place to the Hebrew Scriptures and to the New Testament. Even so, there are signs that the Apocrypha may soon gain a much larger place in the life of the Christian community. Literary study of the whole of Scripture naturally enough focuses upon some of the literary gems of the Apocrypha (Susanna, Judith, Tobit, some of the prayers). Fresh studies of the period from Ezra/Nehemiah to the beginning of the Rabbinical movement, supported by archaeological investigations and by new literary discoveries like the Dead Sea Scrolls, bring the Apocrypha into greater prominence. And the general change within Protestantism toward claiming for the life of faith the entire literary and theological heritage of Jewish and early Christian literature brings the Apocrypha into greater prominence among theologians, clergy, educators and publishers. The current *Parallel Apocrypha* is a clear example of this change.

The life and faith of the Protestant community are much enriched by the literature and thought of the Apocrypha. Nowhere in the Hebrew Scriptures is there as clear an articulation of the view that the human self has eternal life in and with God as we find in the Wisdom of Solomon (Wisdom 3). The understanding of the Prologue to the Gospel of John is greatly illuminated by texts such as Sirach 24 and Baruch 3-5. In those apocryphal texts, it is God's gift of the Law (Torah) that is identified with the Wisdom that was present with God at the creation (Proverbs 8.22-31). And the theme of martyrdom in fidelity to the will of God, which for the early Christian community will become a theme of massive importance, appears nowhere in the Hebrew Scriptures, but is firmly fixed in the Maccabean literature (see especially 2 Maccabees 7).

The Apocrypha also contains a version of the Book of Esther that, unlike the Hebrew Esther, reveals a deep piety, a readiness to resort to God in praise and petition. Greek Esther is a thoroughly religious work; it is valuable indeed to see that the Jewish community offered two such distinct pictures of the heroine of the festival of Purim and her associates.

Often it has been observed that even Christopher Columbus was influenced by one of the books of the Apocrypha as he sought to gain support for his plan to sail west in order to discover another route to the Indies. He read the reference in 2 Esdras 6.42 as support for his view that the western route to the Indies was not nearly as distant as had been supposed. According to 2 Esdras, he pointed out, the surface of the earth was six-sevenths land, which must mean that the western sea could not be as vast as had been claimed!

Today, Protestants approach the Apocrypha very much as do other readers. The change in perspective can be noted by reference to a quotation from one of the important reference works of the early 1960s, *The Interpreter's Dictionary of the Bible*:[1]

> The long-standing controversy regarding the canonicity of the Apoc[rypha] has thus ended in a stalemate [between Protestant and Catholic interpretations].

Today, there is no stalemate at all. The literature and thought of the Apocrypha are regularly addressed within the Protestant community, even though it remains the case that no Protestant church

1. *The Interpreter's Dictionary of the Bible*, I (Nashville: Abingdon, 1962), p. 165.

body assigns the Apocrypha equal canonical authority with the Old Testament. "Canonical" is not the question today in most circles. Protestants are, on the whole, content with the question of the value and illumination that the Apocrypha provide for the community of faith. Such value and illumination are unmistakable and weighty.

Selected Bibliography

Anderson, G.W., "Canonical and Non-Canonical," *Cambridge History of the Bible*, Vol. I, pp. 113-19. Cambridge: Cambridge University Press, 1970.

Goodspeed, Edgar J. *The Story of the Apocrypha*. Chicago: University of Chicago Press, 1939.

Gowan, Donald E. ed. *Bridge Between the Testaments*: Reappraisal of Judaism from the Exile to the Birth of Christianity, Pittsburgh Theological Monographs: No.6. Pittsburgh: Pickwick Publisher, Ltd., 1976.

Metzger, Bruce M. *An Introduction to the Apocrypha*. New York: Oxford University Press, 1957.

Metzger, Bruce M., ed. *The Oxford Annotated Apocrypha*. New York: Oxford University Press, 1994.

Nickelsburg, George W. E. *Jewish Literature Between the Bible and Mishnah*. Philadelphia: Augsburg Fortress Publishers, 1981.

Stone, Michael E., ed. *Jewish Writings of the Second Temple Period*. Compendia rerum iudaicarum ad novum testamentum. Minneapolis, MN: Augsburg Fortress Publishers, 1984.

The Apocryphal/Deuterocanonical Books: An Evangelical View

D. A. Carson

Evangelicalism is on many points so diverse a movement that it would be presumptuous to speak of the evangelical view of the Apocrypha. Two axes of evangelical diversity are particularly important for the subject at hand. First, while many evangelicals belong to independent and/or congregational churches, many others belong to movements within national or mainline churches. (If we include charismatics among evangelicals—an alignment with which most charismatics would concur—then in the world-wide movement independent or congregational evangelicals make up the overwhelming majority of evangelicals.) These independent evangelical groups often reflect, as we shall see, rather different perspectives on the Apocrypha from those of evangelicals in mainline or national churches. Second, more than many religious movements, evangelicalism embraces an extraordinary range of intellectual training and awareness. Thus not a few evangelical leaders at the lower end of the educational spectrum will scarcely have heard of the Apocrypha, much less read it; if they have heard of it, it will only be as something bad connected somehow with Catholics and their view of revelation and tradition. But at the upper end of the educational spectrum, though the Apocrypha will not be accepted as Scripture, it is known, sometimes studied, and universally recognized to form part of the matrix of the world in which the New Testament came to birth.

Evangelicals of all stripes adopt the classic Protestant view that the Apocrypha should not be considered part of the canon of Scripture. What Mallau says of Baptists could be said of all evangelicals: they "took over the essential theological decisions of the Reformation . . . [and] said no more than other Protestants about deuterocanonical writings."[1] This means, of course, that they think of these books as "apocryphal" and not as "deuterocanonical." The latter term was coined by Sixtus of Sienna in 1566 to distinguish two groups of books. On this view, the "protocanonical" books are the books of Scripture received as inspired by the entire Church from the beginning, while "deuterocanonical" refers to those books and parts of books whose authority and inspiration came to be recognized a little later, after the matter had been debated by certain Fathers. Thus for Roman Catholics, "deuterocanonical" does not carry overtones of "less than canonical" or "second tier of canonicity," still less "apocryphal"; for Protestants, "Apocrypha" seems still to be the best designation. The list of canonical Old Testament books accepted by the Council of Trent in 1546 includes all those fourteen or fifteen books normally referred to collectively as the Apocrypha, minus the Prayer of Manasseh and 1 and 2 Esdras. Traditionally, Protestants have restricted themselves, so far as the Old Testament is concerned, to the books of the Hebrew canon. (The nomenclature is problematic, because some of the Apocrypha almost certainly sprang from Semitic originals. But it is clear enough what is meant.)

Objections to Canonicity

Because most of the fifteen books of the Apocrypha are found in the Greek translation of the Old Testament known as the Septuagint (LXX), and it was the Greek form of the Old Testament that circu-

1. Hans-Harold Mallau, "The Attitude of the Baptists to the Deuterocanonical Writings," *The Apocrypha in Ecumenical Perspective*, UBS Monograph Series 6, ed. Siegried Meurer, tr. Paul Ellingworth (Reading: UBS, 1992) 129.

lated widely in the Hellenistic church, many have argued that (a) the Septuagint represents an Alexandrian (as opposed to a Palestinian) canon, and that (b) the early church, using a Greek Bible, therefore clearly bought into this alternative canon. In any case, (c) the Hebrew canon was not "closed" until Jamnia (around 85 C.E.), so the earliest Christians could not have thought in terms of a closed Hebrew canon. "It seems therefore that the Protestant position must be judged a failure on historical grounds."[2]

But serious objections are raised by traditional Protestants, including evangelicals, against these points. (a) Although the LXX translations were undertaken before Christ, the LXX evidence that has come down to us is both late and mixed. An important early manuscript like Codex Vaticanus (4th cent.) includes all the Apocrypha except 1 and 2 Maccabees; Codex Sinaiticus (4th cent.) has Tobit, Judith, 1 and 2 Maccabees, Wisdom, and Ecclesiasticus; another, Codex Alexandrinus (5th cent.) boasts all the apocryphal books plus 3 and 4 Maccabees and the Psalms of Solomon. In other words, there is no evidence here for a well-delineated set of additional canonical books. (b) More importantly, as the LXX has come down to us, it is a Christian collection that has undergone the move from scrolls to codices (i.e. books bound like ours, with many "books" within the one volume). This meant that for the first time things were being bound together that had never been bound together before. As Metzger puts it:

> Books which heretofore had never been regarded by the Jews as having any more than a certain edifying significance were now placed by Christian scribes in one codex side by side with the acknowledged books of the Hebrew canon. Thus it would happen that what was first a matter of convenience in making such books of secondary status available among Christians became a factor in giving the impression that all of the books within such a codex were to be regarded as authoritative.[3]

(c) Ancient sources yield very little evidence supporting the view that Alexandria produced its own canon, and the notion that diaspora Judaism went its own way in this respect faces some extraordinarily difficult historical criticism.[4] (d) Two Alexandrian church Fathers, Origen and Athanasius, give lists of Old Testament books that differ but little from the traditional Jewish reckoning.[5] (e) The Council of Jamnia may have discussed the status of one or two books (as Luther did a millennium and a half later); there is no convincing evidence that Jamnia actually "closed" the Hebrew canon.[6] (f) Despite arguments to the contrary,[7] the New Testament writers rarely allude to books of the Apocrypha, and do not cite them as Scripture, the way they do with Old Testament books.

2. Marvin E. Tate, "Old Testament Apocalyptic and the Old Testament Canon," *Review and Expositor* 65 (1968) 353. Cf. also A. C. Sundberg, Jr., "The Protestant Old Testament Canon: Should It Be Re-Examined?" *Catholic Biblical Quarterly* 28 (1966) 199.
3. Bruce M. Metzger, An Introduction to the Apocrypha (New York: Oxford University Press, 1957) 178.
4. Albert C. Sundberg, Jr., *The Old Testament of the Early Church* (Cambridge: Harvard University Press, 1964) 52, passim.
5. For Origen, see Euseb. H.E. 4.26; Athanasius, Ep. List. 39.
6. See, for example, Sid Z. Leiman, *The Canonization of the Hebrew Scriptures* (Hamden: Archon, 1976) 121-124; Jack P. Lewis, "What Do We Mean by Jabneh?" *Journal of Bible and Religion* 32 (1964) 132; Robert C. Newman, "The Council of Jamnia and the Old Testament Canon," *Westminster Theological Journal* 38 (1976) 319-349; Gÿuunter Stemberger, "Die sogenannte 'Synode von Jabne' und das frÿuuhe Christentum," *Journal of Biblical Literature* 29 (1977) 14-21; D. E. Aune, "On the Origins of the 'Council of Javneh' Myth," *Journal of Biblical Literature* 110 (1991) 491-493; Roger T. Beckwith, *The Old Testament Canon and the New Testament Church* (Grand Rapids: Eerdmans, 1985) 275; cf. David Kraemer, "The Formation of Rabbinic Canon: Authority and Boundaries," *Journal of Biblical Literature* 110 (1991) 613-630.
7. A not uncommon example is found in Peter Stuhlmacher, "The Significance of the Old Testament Apocrypha and Pseudepigrapha for the Understanding of Jesus and Christology," in *The Apocrypha in Ecumenical Perspective*, op. cit. 2. He says that the "most important evidence" that the NT cites the Apocrypha as Scripture is: Mk. 10.19, quoting Ex. 20.12-16 and Deut. 5.16-20, and then Sir. 4.1; 2 Tim. 2.19, quoting Num. 16.5, but also Sir. 17.26 (Stuhlmacher offers two more cases of "quoting" pseudepigraphical sources, which need not concern us here). These two instances, the "most important evidence," are not convincing. Even if the words "do not defraud" (Mk. 10.19) are drawn from Sir. 4.1 (and I am uncertain that this is the case, for certainly the entire phrase in Sirach is not cited), the primary reference to the decalogue (Ex. 20 and Deut. 5) is unambiguous; the additional words may be part of common halakhic expansion. The second quotation in 2 Tim. 2.19 is not at all close to Sir. 17.26. Many commentators think it is a generalized summary of the exhortation in Num. 16.26, using language found elsewhere in the OT; the first part of it is reminiscent of the LXX of Joel 3.5.

During the first two centuries or so, most Greek and Latin church fathers, including Irenaeus, Tertullian, Clement of Alexandria, and Cyprian (none of whom knew Hebrew) quote passages from the Apocrypha as "Scripture": undoubtedly these books were circulating, and in some cases were revered. Only a few fathers at this stage were interested in the limits of the Palestinian Jewish canon (e.g. Melito of Sardis) or the differences between, say, the Hebrew text of Daniel and the additional story of Susanna in the Greek version (e.g. Africanus). The turning point came with Jerome, who in his Latin translation followed the order of the Hebrew canon and by means of prefaces drew attention to the separate category of the apocryphal books. Later copyists of the Latin Vulgate did not always preserve these prefaces, with the result that during the medieval period the Western church customarily regarded these additional books as part of Scripture.

For evangelicals, these disputes cannot be dismissed as arcane bits of obscure history. Because of their high view as to the nature of Scripture, the delineation of the boundaries of Scripture is of fundamental importance. It is not simply that the prophetic "Thus says the LORD," ubiquitous in many strands of the Old Testament, is conspicuous by its absence from the Apocrypha; it is something more. Since evangelicals strongly insist that their beliefs and doctrine be grounded in Scripture, to exclude the Apocrypha is to unseat, say, the doctrine of purgatory, which finds precious little support outside the Apocrypha.

The Value of the Apocrypha

Yet despite these negative judgments about the Apocrypha, informed evangelicals have important reasons for knowing these books well. These may be grouped into three categories, though the latter two overlap.

First, those who belong to Protestant national or mainline traditions are aware that within their traditions the books of the Apocrypha are designated with some such encomium as "useful to be read in the churches" or the like. The Anglican Book of Common Prayer, for example, from 1549 onwards, included prescribed lessons from the Apocrypha. Those who wished to forbid the practice, on the grounds that the sufficiency of Scripture might be jeopardized, were told by the Bishops of the Savoy Conference (1661) that the same objection could be raised against sermons. The comment was both astute and disingenuous: astute, because the sufficiency of Scripture was never designed to shut down the reading of all other material, and disingenuous, because the real issue was not the mere reading of other material, but the reading of it in a context in which confusion between canonical and extra-canonical authority might prevail. In any case, these branches of Evangelicalism have certain historical and denominational reasons for knowing the Apocrypha, indeed for knowing it well enough to distinguish it from Scripture. All of this must be contrasted with Trent, which pronounced its anathema on anyone who "does not accept as sacred and canonical the aforesaid books in their entirety and with all their parts, as they have been accustomed to be read in the Catholic Church and as they are contained in the old Latin Vulgate Edition." For accuracy's sake, one should note that "the aforesaid books" excluded 1 and 2 Esdras and the Prayer of Manasseh even though they had been included in some manuscripts of the Vulgate. In the official Vulgate edition of 1592, these are printed as an appendix after the New Testament, "lest they should perish altogether." The phrase "in their entirety and with all their parts" refers to the Letter of Jeremiah, read as ch. 6 of Baruch, the Additions of Esther with Esther, and the various additions to Daniel—Song of the Three Young Men, Susanna, Bel and the Dragon—with Daniel.

Second, precisely because of their high view of Scripture, evangelicals are perennially interested in the dimensions of texts that purport to provide historical information and perspectives relating to the times and places embraced by Scripture. Although, like all good readers, evangelicals are interested in different literary genres, not for them an approach to, say, narrative, that treats a purportedly historical narrative text as if it can be properly interpreted by studying only its narrative properties while ignoring its extra-textual referents. While acknowledging the cultural "locatedness" of any interpreter, not for them the unqualified open-endedness of some postmodern readers. This means that sources, not least the Apocrypha, that help fill in the large holes in our knowledge of Second Temple Judaism—the history, culture, social structures, and beliefs of what used to be more commonly called the intertestamental period—will be treasured.

The issue is not simply the sequence of events that bring us from the Persian period to first-century Palestine under the Roman superpower, but how outlooks, values, and structures of thought and of society changed. Thus devotional literature like the Prayer of Manasseh is as important as historical literature like 1 Maccabees and 1 Esdras; the liturgical cast of the Prayer of Azariah and the Song of the Three Young Men is of as great interest as the legendary material in Bel and the Dragon; the view of women in Judith and Susanna is as compelling as the fiery rhetoric and exaggerated numbers in 2 Maccabees; a didactic narrative like Tobit, with its indebtedness not only to the Old Testament but to sources like the Story of Ahikar, the fable of the Grateful Dead and a tractate of the god Khons, is as informative as the quite different didactic books of wisdom literature, Ecclesiasticus and the Wisdom of Solomon. It has even been suggested that the Letter of Jeremiah provided later writers with a model of how letters—that most common form of communication in the ancient world—might be used for religious purposes, a point of no small interest to readers of the letters of the New Testament.

Third, allied with the interest of evangelicals in the historical dimensions of the biblical texts (and therefore of extrabiblical texts that clarify that dimension) is their interest in the theological dimension. Evangelicals are invariably interested in how things hold together, not merely in atomistic exegesis. Moreover, they hold to the notion that revelation is normally mediated through the language and experience of particular people in particular times and places. That means that if from the perspective of canonical authority they exclude the Apocrypha, from the perspective of understanding the language and categories of the New Testament writers they cannot afford to do so. The Apocrypha constitutes an important part of the historical and theological matrix in which the New Testament came to birth, along with, of course, material such as the Dead Sea Scrolls, Philo and Josephus, the pseudepigrapha, the earlier strands of the rabbinic corpus, the vast Graeco-Roman corpus, and more.

This reality prompts many important questions that have a critical bearing on biblical interpretation, and thus on theological structures. To what extent do the accounts of the Maccabean martyrs provide a model for vicarious suffering? How do linguistic usage and common beliefs help shape Christological titles in the New Testament? To what extent does the propensity of this literature (not least the Apocrypha) to elevate God and emphasize his transcendence, sometimes at the expense of his personal engagement, open up more space for angels and other mediators? To what extent do the three so-called traditional acts of piety—almsgiving, fasting, and prayer—come to fruition in this literature, and what is their relation to, say, the Sermon on the Mount?

However strongly evangelicals, as part of the larger Protestant tradition, reject the Apocrypha as Scripture, they can no more dismiss this corpus from all consideration than they can write off the world and culture into which the Christ was born, and in which the New Testament was written.

The Texts and Translations of The Parallel Apocrypha

JOHN R. KOHLENBERGER III

With this volume, Oxford University Press publishes the first parallel edition of the eighteen books recognized as apocryphal or deuterocanonical by the Protestant, Anglican, Roman Catholic, and Orthodox communities. The other articles contained in this volume represent these communities as well as the Jewish community, which produced these books, and discuss more thoroughly the concepts and definitions of "apocryphal" and "deuterocanonical." Here, however, it is helpful to include a chart that summarizes the categories and locations of these books in the Bibles of these Christian communities:

Protestant/Anglican	Catholic	Orthodox
Apocrypha	*Deuterocanonical O.T.*	*Deuterocanonical O.T.*
Tobit	Tobit	Tobit
Judith	Judith	Judith
Additions to Esther	Esther (with Additions)	Esther (with Additions)
Wisdom of Solomon	Wisdom of Solomon	Wisdom of Solomon
Ecclesiasticus (Sirach)	Ecclesiasticus (Sirach)	Ecclesiasticus (Sirach)
Baruch	Baruch 1–5	Baruch 1–5
Letter of Jeremiah	Baruch 6	Baruch 6
[Additions to Daniel:]		
Prayer of Azariah	Daniel 3.24-90	Daniel 3.24-90
Susanna	Daniel 13	Susanna (before Daniel in Greek)
Bel and the Dragon	Daniel 14	Daniel 13
1 Maccabees	1 Maccabees	1 Maccabees
2 Maccabees	2 Maccabees	2 Maccabees
	Apocrypha [1]	
1 Esdras	1 (or 3) Esdras	1 (or 3) Esdras
Prayer of Manasseh	Prayer of Manasseh	Prayer of Manasseh (Ode 12)
Psalm 151 [2]	Psalm 151	Psalm 151
3 Maccabees [2,3]	*not in the Vulgate*	3 Maccabees
2 Esdras	2 (or 4) Esdras	2 (or 4) Esdras
4 Maccabees [2]	*not in the Vulgate*	4 Maccabees

In this article, the oldest (and shortest) terms "Apocrypha" and "apocryphal" are used to refer to these eighteen books.

1. The six books listed as apocryphal are not included in any major English translation by Roman Catholics. 1 and 2 (3 and 4) Esdras, the Prayer of Manasseh, and Psalm 151 are in an appendix to the Latin Vulgate.
2. Psalm 151 and 3 and 4 Maccabees are not part of the traditional Apocrypha found in Protestant and ecumenical translations. Third Maccabees was included in some editions of the Great Bible. All three are found only in the Expanded Apocryphas of the Revised Standard Version and the New Revised Standard Version.
3. Third Maccabees is included in some editions of Taverner's Bible.

The books of the Apocrypha originated within the Jewish communities of Judea and Alexandria between 200 B.C.E. and 100 C.E. Most were originally written in Hebrew or Aramaic; the Wisdom of Solomon, 2, 3, and 4 Maccabees, and portions of 2 Esdras were written in Greek. By the end of the first century C.E. all of the books of the Apocrypha were translated and perpetuated in Greek. Only portions of Tobit, Sirach, and Psalm 151 survive in Hebrew or Aramaic. The Greek-speaking Orthodox Church has adopted the Greek Old Testament, including the Apocrypha, as its official Bible, while the rest of Christendom has needed its Bible in translation.

From the second century to the present, the Roman Catholic Church has had its Scriptures in Latin, declaring the Vulgate its "authentical" translation in 1546. Regardless of the official position of the Roman Church, Christians have always desired their Scriptures in their native language. The invention of the printing press in the mid-fifteenth century and the Protestant Reformation of the sixteenth century sparked an explosion of translation activity. By the end of the sixteenth century, Bibles had been printed in sixteen European languages. In England, from Tyndale's New Testament to the King James Version, the English Bible went through a succession of no less than a dozen revisions and three hundred printings, and every whole Bible contained the Apocrypha.

The rich history of the English Bible continues to this day, with more than sixty versions of the New Testament or whole Bibles in print at the close of the twentieth century. *The Parallel Apocrypha* brings together the Greek (or Latin for 2 Esdras) text and seven significant English translations of the Apocrypha, three Protestant and four Catholic. The Greek (or Latin) and Protestant translations run across the top of the page, the Catholic translations across the bottom of the page, both rows in the order in which the versions were published. The Greek Old Testament represents this collection in its oldest existing language. Second Esdras is presented in Latin, as only a fragment of the Greek edition survives. The Douay Old Testament and the King James Version are the classic English versions of Roman Catholicism and Protestantism, respectively, representing as well the Latin and Greek sources of the Apocrypha. The Knox translation is the last Roman Catholic version based on the Latin Vulgate. Like its more modern Protestant counterpart, Today's English Version (The Good News Bible), it is a free-form "dynamic equivalent" rendering. The New American Bible and the New Jerusalem Bible are the latest descendants of the Douay translation, but are based on the Greek rather than the Latin text, the former more of a word-for-word translation, the latter freer and more literary. The New Revised Standard Version is the latest ecumenical translation and follows the maxim, "As literal as possible, as free as necessary."

Used in concert, these versions illustrate Augustine's famous statement, "variety of translations is profitable for finding out the sense of the Scriptures."

Hebrew, Greek, and Latin Sources of the English Bible

The Church was born with a Bible in hand: the Greek translation of the Hebrew Scriptures, the Septuagint (LXX). Within a century, Christians had created their own Scriptures in Greek, later called the New Testament (NT) as the Hebrew Scriptures were called the Old Testament (OT). The oldest copies of the Greek Bible, codices (books rather than scrolls) from the fourth and fifth centuries C.E., contain books from both testaments as well as books of the Apocrypha. No two codices have the same collection of apocryphal books, possibly because these books were never considered canonical within Judaism. Nonetheless books of the Apocrypha were in the earliest Christian Bibles.

The earliest translations of the NT were into Latin. The Latin translations of the OT were also from the Greek. Citations in early Christian writings witness to the existence of Latin versions in Africa and Europe in the mid and late second century. Desiring to standardize the diverse Old Latin text, Pope Damasus assigned the work to the learned scholar Jerome in 382. Jerome revised the Latin Gospels in

Rome (382-385) and completed the books of the OT by 406. Acts through Revelation were also revised from the Old Latin, probably in Rome, but not by Jerome. Jerome made a distinction between the 39 books of the Hebrew canon, which he translated from the Hebrew and Aramaic, and the books outside of that canon, which he translated from Greek or Aramaic. These latter he termed "Apocrypha," and produced them only under papal insistence. Jerome translated (or paraphrased) 1 Esdras, Tobit, and Judith from Aramaic, and the additions to Daniel and Esther from Greek. Later translators added Wisdom, Sirach, 1 and 2 Maccabees, and Baruch, which already existed in the Old Latin. The *versio vulgata*, or "common translation," dominated western Christianity for more than a millennium (more than 8,000 manuscripts survive) and remains the official Bible of Roman Catholicism.

The first printed book was the Latin Vulgate. The Gutenberg Bible, also called the Mazarin or forty-two-line Bible, was completed in 1455 or 1456. By the end of the fifteenth century, over 100 editions of the Latin Bible had been printed in Germany, Switzerland, Venice and France. Official editions were produced under the authority of Popes Sixtus V (1590) and Clement VIII (1592, corrected in 1593 and 1598).

The Bible was also published in multi-language or polyglot editions. Foremost was the Complutensian Polyglot, begun at the university of Alcalá (Complutum) in 1502 at the expense of Cardinal Ximénes. Issued in six expertly printed folio volumes (1522, printed 1514-17), the OT had the Hebrew, Latin and Greek (interlinear with Latin) in parallel columns. The Pentateuch in addition had the Aramaic Targum (an expansive Jewish paraphrase) with Latin translation. The NT had the Greek and Latin in parallel columns, keyed phrase by phrase with a system of superscript letters. The eight-volume Royal Polyglot (Antwerp, 1569-72) updated the texts of the Complutensian and added Syriac to both testaments. Both publications contained dictionaries to their biblical texts; the Royal Polyglot also included grammars. Each provided substantial resources to biblical scholars and translators.

Although the NT volume of the Complutensian Polyglot was the first printed Greek text (1514), the first published was Johann Froben's printing of Desiderius Erasmus' Greek and Latin NT (Basel, 1516). The Aldine press issued a complete Greek Bible in Venice in 1518/19, combining the LXX with Erasmus' NT. Another edition of the Greek OT was produced under the auspices of Pope Sixtus V in 1587, the Sixtina Romana.

Rahlfs' Septuagint and Weber's Vulgate

The first critical edition of the LXX was published between 1788 and 1827 under the direction of Robert Holmes of Oxford and his successor James Parsons. Tischendorf published his *Vetus Testamentum Graece iuxta LXX Interpretes* in 1850. The next major edition began at Cambridge in 1883 with the goal of presenting the text of codex Vaticanus (B) with all major variants noted. A four-volume "handy" edition of *The Old Testament in Greek* was published between 1887 and 1894, edited by Henry Barclay Swete. The larger Cambridge LXX, edited by Brooke, McLean, and Thackeray, was interrupted by the war in 1940 and was never completed. Nine portions were published, including Genesis through Esther and the apocryphal 1 Esdras, Judith, and Tobit.

The standard editions of the LXX in use today are the popular *Septuaginta* of Alfred Rahlfs and the *Septuaginta, Vetus Testamentum Graecum*, the latter of which began appearing in volumes in 1931, with Rahlfs' *Psalmi cum Odis*. The Göttingen Septuagint currently has more than twenty volumes in print. Because Rahlfs' LXX serves as the base text for most modern versions, and because it is complete, it was chosen for inclusion in *The Parallel Apocrypha*.

While the Clementine Vulgate (1592, rev. 1593, 1598) remains the official text of the Roman Catholic church, newer editions of the Latin text have been produced. Wordsworth and White assembled a critical edition of the NT (Oxford, 1889-1954). Pope Pius X commissioned a revision of the Vulgate which began in 1907. Most of the OT has been completed.

The standard edition of the Vulgate in use today is the *Biblia Sacra Iuxta Vulgatam Versionem*, originally edited by Robert Weber (Stuttgart, 1969) and now in its fourth edition by Roger Gryson (1994). The text of 2 Esdras (4 Ezrae in the Vulgate) is taken from the appendix to the Vulgate, as no complete Greek text exists.

Format and Features. The text of Rahlfs and Weber are printed in paragraph style. Poetry in Rahlfs is indicated by up to two levels of indentation. Because of their diverse textual histories, Rahlfs presents Tobit in two forms, BA (Vaticanus-Alexandrinus) and S (Sinaiticus), and Daniel in 𝔊 (Greek-LXX) and Θ′ (Theodotion, as found in B and A). *The Parallel Apocrypha* reproduces the text of S in Tobit, filling in 4.7b-19a and 13.8-11a from BA, and the text of Θ′ in the additions to Daniel, as is done in most modern translations.

Words and phrases that are textually uncertain are set off in square brackets ([ ]) in Rahlfs. No documentation or critical apparatus accompanies the texts as reproduced here; students of LXX should consult the latest editions of Rahlfs or Göttingen and of Weber.

English Bible Translations through the Sixteenth Century

The earliest known examples of English translation are the Anglo-Saxon poetic paraphrases of Caedmon in the seventh century, but the first complete Bible did not appear until the fourteenth century. John Wycliffe, "the Morning Star of the Reformation," and his colleagues at Oxford prepared two complete English Bibles from the Vulgate. The first (c. 1384) was very literal. Translated by Nicholas of Hereford as far as Baruch 3.20, and continued by other scholars, it possibly contains Wycliffe's own NT as well as bearing his name. The second, following Wycliffe's death in 1384, was rendered in more idiomatic English, probably by John Purvey. Its use was severely restricted by the Council of Oxford (1407-08) and was prohibited in 1414. The Wycliffe Bible paved the way for the English Bibles of the sixteenth century, but because it was based on the Latin Vulgate, it did not directly influence the idiom of the translations that followed. The Wycliffite translations, based as they were on the Vulgate, did contain the books of the Apocrypha within the OT.

The condemnation of Wycliffe's version suppressed English Bible translation for a time. Although printing reached England in 1476, the Bible was published only in Latin. But many desired, with William Tyndale, to "cause a boy that driveth the plough to know more of the Scripture" than the papal clerics. To this end Tyndale unsuccessfully sought approval to produce an English translation in 1523. With the assistance of William Roye, he translated the NT while in Hamburg in 1524-25. Printing began in Cologne, but persecution moved them to flee to Worms, where the testament was completed. Smuggled testaments were being sold—and burned—in England in early 1526. In exile in Antwerp, Tyndale translated and published the Pentateuch and the Psalms in 1530, Jonah in 1531 and revised NTs in 1534 and 1535. He left Joshua through Chronicles in manuscript when he was martyred for heresy in 1536. That year saw the first printing in England of Tyndale's NT. More than forty editions of his NT, published between 1525 and 1566, are known.

In 1535 Myles Coverdale issued the first complete English Bible, translated from Latin with heavy dependence on Tyndale and on Luther's German Bible. Following Jerome and Luther, the books of the Apocrypha were in their own section, with the exception of Baruch "whom we have set amonge the prophetes next unto Jeremy, because he was his reader." Although not an authorized version, the Coverdale Bible was licensed. In 1537 an edition of Coverdale became the first complete English Bible printed in England, this time with Baruch relocated to the Apocrypha section. Also in 1537, John Rogers published a Bible under the pseudonym Thomas Matthew. Rogers drew upon Tyndale's NT and supplemented extant portions of Tyndale's OT with his own revision of Coverdale. Matthew's was the first

English Bible to include the Prayer of Manasseh. Despite containing the condemned work of Tyndale, Matthew's Bible was licensed.

Richard Taverner's revision of Matthew's Bible was published in 1539, again with an Apocrypha section between the Testaments. It was overshadowed that same year by Coverdale's revision of Matthew's Bible, called the Great Bible for its size. The Apocrypha section was titled "The volume of bokes called Hagiographa." This was the first authorized version "appointed to the use of the Churches." A small octavo volume printed in 1540 contained a selection of wisdom books from the Great Bible that were "very good and profytable for every Chrysten man for to knowe." It included the canonical Proverbs, Ecclesiastes, and Song of Songs, with the apocryphal Wisdom and Ecclesiasticus. A five-volume edition of Taverner's Old Testament and Apocrypha appeared in 1549-51. The Apocrypha volume of 1549 was the first stand-alone English Apocrypha, the first to contain 3 Maccabees, and had new translations of 3 (1) Esdras, Tobit, and Judith by Edmund Becke.

In 1557, William Whittingham published a NT from exile in Geneva; John Calvin wrote its preface. In 1560, collaborating with Anthony Gilby and Thomas Sampson, Whittingham published the Geneva Bible. Though never formally licensed or authorized, the Geneva or "Breeches Bible" (for its rendering of Gen. 3.7) became the most popular English version of its day and went through at least 140 printings through 1644. A notable printing error occurred in the early editions (to 1576) when the negative was left out of the last clause of Ecclesiasticus 15.13: "The Lord hateth all abominacion [of errour:] and they that feare God, wil loue it." In keeping with its evaluation of the Apocrypha as "bokes, which were not received by a comune consent to be red and expounded publikely in the Church," the otherwise annotated Geneva Bible had only cross references, alternate renderings, and chapter summaries in the Apocrypha. "The Prayer of Manasseh King of the Iewes," noted as "apocryphe" in the contents, was nonetheless printed at the end of 2 Chronicles, with three annotations. An edition of 1599 lists the Apocrypha in its contents, but the section was omitted from most copies. This is perhaps the first English Bible intentionally bound without an Apocrypha. The Bishops' Bible of 1568 was a revision, mostly by bishops of the Church of England, intended to provide an alternative to the anti-Catholic and pro-Calvinistic notes of the Geneva Bible.

The Douay-Rheims Translation

Roman Catholics became the persecuted party in England in the days of Elizabeth, as Protestants had been earlier in the century. In 1546 the Council of Trent had declared the Latin Vulgate the "authentic" text of the Roman Church. But the growing number and influence of Protestant Bible translations required a vernacular translation for English-speaking Catholic priests and laypeople. William Allen, president of the English college at Rheims (or Rhemes), in 1578 instigated an English translation "with the object of healthfully counteracting the corruptions whereby the heretics have so long lamentably deluded almost the whole of our countrymen." English exile Gregory Martin translated two chapters a day, which were then reviewed by Allen and Richard Bristow.

The New Testament was published at Rheims in 1582. Martin translated the whole of the OT before his death in 1584, but it was not published until 1609-10 in Douay (or Doway or Douai), thus the composite title for the version. The text herein is referred to as the Douay Old Testament, as its counterpart was labeled the Rheims New Testament in *The Precise Parallel New Testament* (Oxford, 1995). Before publication the OT was "conformed to the most perfect Latin Edition," the authorized edition of Vulgate published under the authority of Pope Clement VIII in 1592, for which Richard Allen served as a reviser. The Clementine Vulgate was also the basis of the last translation from Latin, that of Ronald Knox (see below).

The Douay Old Testament was chosen for inclusion in *The Parallel Apocrypha* as the first and most influential Catholic translation of the Bible into English, for its Latin textual base, and as the oldest continuously-printed English Bible translation.

Textual base. "We translate the old Vulgar Latin text, not the common Greek text," states the Preface. Among the reasons listed for this choice are the antiquity of the Vulgate, its correction by Jerome, its continuous use in the Church since that time, its use by the Fathers, because the Council of Trent declared it authentical, because the Latin was to be preferred to the Greek where the languages disagreed, and because most of the ancient heretics were Greek and had corrupted their Greek Scriptures. The differences between the Latin and Greek textual bases are most noticeable in the books of Tobit and Judith, which Jerome paraphrased and abridged freely. The book of Esther is a composite translation in the Vulgate: chapters 1.1–10.3 are translated from the Hebrew and 10.4–16.24 from the Greek. This is apparent in the rendering of proper names, such as Assuerus/Artaxerxes. The book has been rearranged in *The Parallel Apocrypha* to match the Greek order followed by the modern versions.

Style. Because of its precise translation of the Vulgate, the most noted (and criticized) feature of the Douay-Rheims is its unnatural reflection of Latin vocabulary and syntax. However, the most extreme latinisms were edited out by Richard Challoner in his eighteenth century revisions. Remnants of the Latin original are clearly seen in proper names, such as Tobias (Tobit), Assuerus (Ahasuerus), and Elias (Elijah).

Subsequent editions. The Douay-Rheims versions was revised by Richard Challoner in 1750 and 1763-64. Its American printing of 1899 is still reprinted by TAN Books (Rockford, IL) and is the text reproduced in this volume.

The King James or Authorized Version

The Geneva Bible was the Bible of Shakespeare and Bunyan. It was brought to the Americas on the Mayflower. But its Calvinistic notes were not universally appreciated. James I of England, to whom the first Scottish printing of the Geneva Bible had been dedicated (1579), called a conference of theologians and churchmen at Hampton Court in 1604 and heard a proposal from Puritan John Reynolds for "a newe translation of the Bible, because those which were allowed in the raignes of Henrie the eight, and Edward the sixt, were corrupt and not aunswerable to the truth of the Originall." James was intrigued by the proposal that no annotations would be included with the translation, for he was not fond of the notes of the Geneva Bible. So the king accepted the proposal and became its patron.

Six panels of forty-seven (perhaps as many as fifty-seven) "learned men" from Westminster, Cambridge and Oxford set about the task of revising the previous century's English Bible tradition. A panel of seven scholars at Cambridge was entrusted with the Apocrypha. The translators were to follow the Bishops' Bible as closely as possible, using the translations of Tyndale, Matthew, Coverdale, Great and Geneva when they agreed more closely with the original languages. When each group finished its portion, twelve men (two from each group) reviewed the whole. Thomas Bilson and Miles Smith were the final editors, Smith providing the excellent Preface "The Translators to the Reader," which unfortunately is no longer reprinted in modern editions.

The version of 1611 was published by Robert Barker, owner of the Royal Printer's patent. Though there exist no documents for its authorization, the version has popularly been called *the* Authorized Version (AV) or the King James Version (KJV). After countless editions, thousands of revisions (authorized and unauthorized), and untold millions of copies, the KJV remains the most circulated and influential English Bible ever. As such, it is a necessary inclusion in *The Parallel Apocrypha*.

Textual base. The KJV was based on the Greek and Hebrew texts of the sixteenth century, but also drew on the Latin. Second Esdras and the Prayer of Manasseh were both translated from Latin, as the Greek text of the latter was not published until Walton's Polyglot of 1657. Unique to the Apocrypha is the use of brackets ([ ]) to mark words, phrases, and verses found in Latin but not in Greek (e.g., Baruch 4.6; Sirach 1.7). The LXX texts of sixteenth century were based primarily on manuscripts from the Vatican library, notably codex Vaticanus (B) from the fourth century. Although B is the text preferred for most subsequent printings of the LXX, most modern scholars prefer the text of Sinaiticus (S or א) for Tobit and the revision attributed to Theodotion for the additions to Daniel. The KJV does follow the text of B for Tobit and of Theodotion for the additions to Daniel. The book of Esther is a composite translation in the KJV: chapters 1.1–10.3 are translated from the Hebrew and 10.4–16.24 from the Greek. This is apparent in the rendering of proper names, such as Mordecai/Mardocheus and Ahasuerus/Artexerxes. The book has been rearranged in *The Parallel Apocrypha* to match the Greek order followed by the modern versions. The book of Sirach has an additional preface not found in the LXX, attributed to Athanasius in the marginal note, which is reproduced in a footnote at the beginning of the book. The Prayer of Manasseh has no verse numbers in the KJV, but for the purpose of *The Parallel Apocrypha*, verse numbers have been introduced into the running text.

Style. The KJV is often characterized as a word-for-word or "formal-equivalence" translation, highly regarded for its literary quality. The Apocrypha, however, is considered its least impressive section, owing most likely to the low regard in which these books were held by their Protestant translators. As a revision of the English versions of the sixteenth century, it compares well to the contemporary Douay translation.

Subsequent editions. No version of the English Bible has been more regularly reprinted than the KJV, nor has any suffered more abuse at the hands of publishers and printers. There have been the "Wicked Bible" (1631), so called for leaving "not" out of Exodus 20.14, the "Unrighteous Bible" (1653), which allows the unrighteous to inherit the kingdom in 1 Corinthians 6.9, and the "Vinegar Bible" (1717), which misspells the parable of the vineyard in Luke 20.9. Ironically, an edition of 1612 misprints "princes" in Psalm 119.161 to read "Printers have persecuted me without cause."

In an attempt to correct the thousands of careless errors that had crept into the text, as well as to make the spelling and punctuation of the KJV more consistent throughout, noted revisions were prepared by Paris and Therold in 1762, Blayney in 1769 and Scrivener in 1873. The KJV reproduced in this volume follows the Oxford standard edition, which derives from Blayney.

The New American Bible

The Douay-Rheims-Challoner translation remained the standard English translation for Roman Catholics well into the twentieth century. There were many private translations of the Vulgate, such as that by Francis Patrick Kenrick, Bishop of Philadelphia (1849-60), designed to update the idiom of the standard version. But only that of Ronald Knox received significant attention (see below).

After five years of labor by twenty-seven Catholic scholars, a new American translation of the Latin NT was released in 1941. Titled the Confraternity Version, for its development under the auspices of the Confraternity of Christian Doctrine, it was a conscious revision of the Rheims-Challoner NT in light of the best Latin texts, once again with reference to the Greek. For the next two years, work proceeded on the OT.

On September 30, 1943, Pope Pius XII issued an encyclical on scripture studies, *Divino afflante Spiritu*, which profoundly influenced the nature of Catholic scholarship and Bible translation. In part, he wrote:

> We ought to explain the original text which was written by the inspired author himself and has more authority and greater weight than any, even the very best, translation whether ancient or modern. This can be done all the more easily and fruitfully if to the knowledge of languages be joined a real skill in literary criticism of the same text.

In the spirit of the encyclical, in 1944 the Bishops' Committee of the Confraternity of Christian Doctrine requested members of The Catholic Biblical Association of America to produce a translation based on the original languages. The OT was issued in segments from 1952 to 1969, the NT in 1970. Of the fifty translators that worked on the project, forty-six were Catholic and four were Protestant. The resultant New American Bible (NAB) was the first translation in American English produced from the original languages by Catholic scholars and was the first produced by Catholics with the cooperation of Protestant scholars. In 1978 a thorough revision of the NT was commissioned to reflect advances in scholarship and to satisfy needs identified through pastoral experience.

Textual base. Sirach is based on the original Hebrew as far as it is preserved and is supplemented and corrected from Greek and the other ancient versions. The Hebrew portions of Esther (1.1–10.3) are translated from Hebrew; the Greek additions to Esther and Daniel are translated from Greek, the latter specifically from Theodotion. Tobit is translated from S. The other deuterocanonical books are based on the standard Greek text.

The standard edition of the NAB is accompanied by voluminous interpretive notes. For the purposes of *The Parallel Apocrypha*, the Confraternity graciously allowed these to be limited to eleven notes dealing with text critical issues.

Style. The editorial board aimed to produce a version as accurate and faithful to the original languages as is possible in English, and thus strove to develop a readable, dignified, formal-equivalent translation. Traditional language is regularly used, as in the "holocausts, sacrifices, and libations" of 1 Maccabees 1.45 (compare Douay), as opposed to the "burnt offerings and sacrifices and drink offerings" of the KJV and NRSV or "burnt offerings, grain offerings, or wine offerings" of the TEV. Archaic pronouns and verb forms are avoided, however, as in "You are righteous, O Lord" (Tobit 3.2), as opposed to "Thou art just, O Lord" (Douay and KJV).

In addition to being a direct descendant of the Douay-Rheims-Challoner tradition, the NAB is currently the best-selling Catholic translation. Its scholarship and style commend it to both Catholics and Protestants for devotional reading and for careful study.

The Holy Bible by Ronald Knox

Ronald Knox was the son of an Anglican priest, an outstanding student of the classics, and a writer of vigorous prose and detective novels. He converted to Catholicism at age twenty-nine and in 1939 began a translation of the Bible into contemporary English. In his *Trials of a Translator*, he explained his working principle as not "How shall I make this foreigner talk English?" but "What would an Englishman have said to express the same?" The NT was published in 1945 and the OT in 1949; the first complete Bible in 1955, and its second edition in 1956.

Textual base. Knox based his translation on the Clementine Vulgate of 1592, the official text of the Roman Catholic church. His numerous footnotes regularly point out difficulties in interpreting the Latin and differences between the Latin and the Greek, as at Tobit 1.25 and 2.22. The book of Esther is a composite translation in the Vulgate: chapters 1.1–10.3 are translated from the Hebrew and 10.4–16.24 from the Greek. This is apparent in the rendering of proper names, such as Assuerus/Artaxerxes. The book has been rearranged in *The Parallel Apocrypha* to match the Greek order followed by the modern versions. In the original edition, Knox had alerted the readers of the contextual location of the Greek additions in subheads and footnotes. These have been retained, although the wording has been slightly modified so that "above" and "below" relate accurately to the rearrangement.

Style. Knox has been criticized for his slavish adherence to the Clementine Vulgate, in light of better available resources, but he has rarely been criticized for the quality of his translation. Powerful, elegant, and literary, his language is characterized by the inversion of predicates and modifiers to the beginning of the clause, as in Daniel's confession of faith in Bel 24, "my own God I worship still; living God is none but he." Though translating in the mid-twentieth century, Knox still used archaic second person pronouns and verb forms, as in Bel 5, "wilt thou have it Bel is not a living god?" Hundreds of annotations point out difficulties in interpretation and differences between the Latin and Greek texts, as illustrated in the previous paragraph.

Standard editions of the Knox translation have verse numbers in the margin rather than in the text, so that the prose reads more like normal English literature and less like a Bible. For the purpose of *The Parallel Apocrypha*, and with the kind permission of the copyright holder, the verse numbers were incorporated into the running text. The editor assumes all responsibility for any errors in versification that may have been unintentionally introduced in this process.

The Knox Translation of the Bible was chosen for inclusion in *The Parallel Apocrypha* as the last official Catholic translation of the Latin Bible into English and for its outstanding, literary, "dynamic equivalent" translation. It is interesting to compare the relationship of the free-form Knox and the literalistic Douay translation with the free-form TEV and the literalistic KJV.

The New Jerusalem Bible

The Jerusalem Bible (JB) of 1966 was the first official Roman Catholic Bible translated into English from the original Hebrew, Aramaic, and Greek. Though a direct translation, it was influenced by the French *La Bible de Jérusalem*, produced by the Ecole Biblique in Jerusalem and published in Paris in 1956. The notes of the JB were translated from the French edition of 1961. Of the twenty-seven principal translators that worked under general editor Alexander Jones, the best known is J. R. R. Tolkien. The JB is regarded for its literary quality, including the unique styles the various translators brought to their books, the extensive annotations, and the use of the proper name "Yahweh" throughout the OT, where most English versions use "LORD."

The New Jerusalem Bible (NJB) was undertaken in response to a new edition of *La Bible de Jérusalem,* published in 1973. Henry Wansbrough served as the general editor and Alan Neame as the principal OT translator. The NJB appeared in 1985.

Textual base. The NJB was translated "directly from the Hebrew, Greek or Aramaic." In standard editions of the NJB, portions of books that are known only in Greek (e.g., Esther and Daniel) are printed in italics. In *The Parallel Apocrypha*, italics are used for the Greek additions to Esther, but because the Greek additions to Daniel are printed as separate books, they are not italicized. Tobit is based on the Greek text of S, the additions to Daniel on Theodotion, and Sirach is based primarily on the Greek and supplemented by the Hebrew.

Style. The NJB has a more consistent translation style than the JB, yet it remains literary and readable. It is especially strong in poetry. The general editor's foreword states, "Paraphrase has been avoided more rigorously than in the first edition; . . . Key terms in the originals . . . have been rendered throughout (with very few exceptions) by the same English word." "Considerable efforts have also been made, though not at all costs," to use gender-inclusive language. Thus, "my child" is used through Sirach in place of "my son" (e.g., 2.1; 3.12, 17), "blessed is the man" becomes "happy is anyone" (Sirach 14.1, 2), and so on. Of the copious notes to the Reader's Edition of the NJB, *The Parallel Apocrypha* presents 62 notes primarily relating key cross-references and parallel passages and explanations of word plays.

The New Jerusalem Bible was chosen for inclusion in *The Parallel Apocrypha* as a companion to the NAB, the other modern Catholic version, and for its excellent literary translation. These scholarly Catholic translations compare well to the NRSV, the latest scholarly ecumenical translation.

Today's English Version (The Good News Bible)

The American Bible Society (ABS) first published the NT, titled Good News for Modern Man, in 1966. The version was primarily the work of one man, Robert G. Bratcher, Research Associate of the Translations Department of the ABS, and was reviewed by consultants to both the American and the British and Foreign Bible Societies. Bratcher, an experienced missionary translator, had undertaken the project in 1964.

The tremendous success of the NT prompted the formation of a committee to translate the OT. Bratcher chaired the committee of seven, whose work was reviewed by eight Bible specialists representing seven religious groups, by English stylists, and by the Translations Committee of the ABS. The Good News Bible or The Bible in Today's English Version (TEV) is simple to read, but it was not translated simply. The TEV was published with the sixty-six books of the Protestant canon in 1976. Three members of the OT committee then translated the Apocrypha, which was completed in 1978 and first published in 1979. The second edition of the TEV appeared in 1992.

Textual base. The Apocrypha of the TEV was based on Rahlfs' LXX and the available volumes of Göttingen. Tobit was based on S, supplemented and corrected by other Greek manuscripts, and the three additions to Daniel were based on Theodotion. Sirach has many footnotes relating to Hebrew variants. Second Esdras was based on the first edition (1969) of Weber's Latin version, supplemented by other editions and ancient versions. Esther was completely translated from the Greek, as it was in the NRSV. Textual choices and variant readings are regularly documented in the footnotes of the TEV.

Style. The TEV was the first translation that was associated with the term "dynamic equivalence." Most traditional translations, such as Douay and the KJV, are "formal equivalent," meaning that they try as much as is possible to translate word-for-word and even form-for-form. The result is usually understandable English, but is often not idiomatic English. "Dynamic equivalent" translations render the original languages into idiomatic English, taking into account all of the words and forms of the originals, but with "no attempt to reproduce in English the parts of speech, sentence structure, word order and grammatical devices of the original languages." Because of the translators' desire to reflect the original languages accurately in idiomatic English, many clauses and sentences are reversed in order, thus creating many composite verses, such as Tobit 4.3-4 and 10-11. The TEV also has the smallest vocabulary and simplest sentence structure of the versions in *The Parallel Apocrypha*. For further information, please consult the Preface to Today's English Version on page x.

Today's English Version of the Bible was chosen for inclusion in *The Parallel Apocrypha* as a unique Protestant translation, "dynamic equivalent" and easy reading. It is interesting to compare the relationship of the free-form Knox and the literalistic Douay translation with the free-form TEV and the literalistic KJV.

The New Revised Standard Version

Protestant Bible translation did not begin with the KJV, nor did it end there. Among the early alternatives to the KJV were Daniel Mace's Greek and English diglot (1729), William Whiston's NT (1745), and John Wesley's NT (1755), which departed from the KJV in 12,000 places. But no English version seriously challenged the near monopoly of the KJV as *the* English Bible until 1870, when an interdenominational group of 55 translators was commissioned to create a revision of the KJV in Britain. In 1872 an American committee was invited to participate. The NT of the Revised Version (RV) was published in 1881, its OT in 1885, and Apocrypha in 1895. The American committee issued the American Standard Version (ASV) 1901.

As rigorous formal-equivalent translations, the RV and ASV were praised for their accuracy, but not for their readability. They were used by scholars, but did not even come close to replacing the KJV in popular use. So in 1937 the International Council of Religious Education authorized a revision of the ASV (the rights to which it had acquired in 1928). Thirty scholars headed by Luther A. Weigle generated the Revised Standard Version (RSV) NT in 1946, the OT in 1952, and the Apocrypha in 1957 (expanded in 1977).

The RSV combined traditional ecclesiastical language with modern critical scholarship and won an instant audience. Eventually it was officially authorized for use by Protestant, Anglican, Roman Catholic and Eastern Orthodox bodies. It remained the standard version of English biblical scholarship into the 1990s when its own revision appeared.

The revision of the RSV began in 1974, overseen by the RSV Bible Committee. This continuing body of scholars is comprised of about thirty members, both male and female, representing various Protestant denominations, Roman Catholicism and Eastern Orthodoxy, as well as one Jewish member. The main goals of the revision were to accommodate the language of the RSV to more contemporary English, to update its scholarship, and to eliminate gender-biased language. The New Revised Standard Version (NRSV) was published in 1990 to strong praise and wide acceptance.

Text. Most of the Apocrypha was translated from Rahlfs' LXX and the individual volumes of Göttingen, the latter of which sometimes has different verse numbers (e.g., in Sirach). Tobit was based on S, supplemented and corrected by other Greek manuscripts, and the three additions to Daniel were based on Theodotion. Sirach was translated from the Göttingen text, with constant reference to the Hebrew fragments discovered at Qumran, Masada, and the Cairo Geniza. Second Esdras was based on Weber's Latin version, supplemented by other editions and ancient versions. Esther was completely translated from the Greek, as it was in the TEV. Textual choices and variant readings are well documented in the nearly 1,400 footnotes of the NRSV Apocrypha.

Style. The NRSV revisers followed the maxim, "As literal as possible, as free as necessary." As a result, the NRSV is primarily a formal-equivalent translation. When the translators chose a freer rendering, footnotes call attention to a more formal or technical translation of the Greek or Hebrew text.

Significant in this category are notes that document the rendering of gender-inclusive Greek terms with gender-inclusive English. For example, when the Greek word *adelphos* does not specifically refer to a male relative, it is rendered "brothers and sisters" in Judith 7.30 (cf. the footnote). Because English does not have a common gender third person pronoun, the NRSV uses the second person singular or third person plural to avoid using "he" and "him" to refer to "anyone" or "everyone." Such renderings are not documented in the notes, but compare "the man . . . him" (KJV, Douay) to "those . . . them" in Sirach 9.18-19.

The best documented of the versions in *The Parallel Apocrypha*, the NRSV provides an excellent guide to the precise translation of the Rahlfs Greek text into readable English, as well as a model for communicating that translation in gender-inclusive language. For further information, please consult the Preface to the Apocryphal/Deuterocanonical Books of the NRSV on page xi.

For Further Study

The Parallel Apocrypha provides the Greek text and seven English versions that can be used to explore issues of text, word meanings, interpretation and communication. For those who wish to go deeper in their studies, the following are some leading resources.

More thorough definitions of Greek words may be found in Greek lexicons and word study books. The latest and most useful Greek lexicons to the NT, which cover most of the vocabulary of the Apocrypha, are *A Greek-English Lexicon of the New Testament*, Bauer, Arndt, Gingrich and Danker (Chicago: U. of Chicago and Grand Rapids: Zondervan, 1979) and *Greek-English Lexicon of the New*

Testament Based on Semantic Domains, Louw and Nida (New York: United Bible Societies, 1988). The only lexicon to cover the whole vocabulary of the Greek books of the Apocrypha is the unabridged *Greek-English Lexicon* by Liddell, Scott, and Jones (Oxford, 1843, 9th ed. 1940). *The Analytical Lexicon to the Septuagint* by Bernard A. Taylor (Grand Rapids: Zondervan, 1994) gives a parsing and a lexical form for each word in the LXX.

Concordances index the vocabulary of a Bible translation. The original editions of Alexander Cruden's *Concordance* to the KJV included a section on the books of the Apocrypha. Last reprinted as *Cruden's Unabridged Concordance* (Grand Rapids: Baker, 1980), it is not currently available. *The NRSV Concordance Unabridged* (Grand Rapids: Zondervan, 1991), by John R. Kohlenberger III, indexes all occurrences of every word in the NRSV, including the Apocryphal/Deuterocanonical books. The classic Greek *Concordance to the Septuagint* by Edwin Hatch and Henry A. Redpath (Oxford, 1897) is currently in reprint from Baker Book House.

Commentaries are the most handy, and often the most thorough, source for analyzing any passage of the Apocrypha and for explaining differences in its textual base and interpretation. Among the best series of critical commentaries for detailed study are the Anchor Bible (New York: Doubleday) and Hermeneia (Philadelphia: Fortress), both as yet incomplete on the books of the Apocrypha. The one-volume *New Jerome Biblical Commentary* (Englewood Cliffs: Prentice Hall, 1990) and four volumes of *The Cambridge Bible Commentary* (Cambridge, 1972-4) comment on all books of the Catholic canon; the former includes excellent articles on canon, texts, and translations.

THE PARALLEL APOCRYPHA

GREEK OLD TESTAMENT

ΤΩΒΙΤ

1 Βίβλος λόγων Τωβιθ τοῦ Τωβιηλ τοῦ Ανανιηλ τοῦ Αδουηλ
τοῦ Γαβαηλ τοῦ Ραφαηλ τοῦ Ραγουηλ ἐκ τοῦ σπέρματος
Ασιηλ ἐκ φυλῆς Νεφθαλιμ, 2 ὃς ᾐχμαλωτεύθη ἐν ταῖς
ἡμέραις Ενεμεσσαρου τοῦ βασιλέως τῶν Ἀσσυρίων ἐκ
Θισβης, ἥ ἐστιν ἐκ δεξιῶν Κυδιως τῆς Νεφθαλιμ ἐν τῇ ἄνω
Γαλιλαίᾳ ὑπεράνω Ασσηρ ὀπίσω [ὁδοῦ] δυσμῶν ἡλίου ἐξ
ἀριστερῶν Φογωρ.

3 Ἐγὼ Τωβιθ ὁδοῖς ἀληθείας ἐπορευόμην καὶ ἐν δικαιοσύ-
ναις πάσας τὰς ἡμέρας τῆς ζωῆς μου καὶ ἐλεημοσύνας
πολλὰς ἐποίησα τοῖς ἀδελφοῖς μου καὶ τῷ ἔθνει μου τοῖς
πορευθεῖσιν μετ' ἐμοῦ ἐν τῇ αἰχμαλωσίᾳ εἰς τὴν χώραν τῶν
Ἀσσυρίων εἰς Νινευη. 4 καὶ ὅτε ἤμην ἐν τῇ χώρᾳ μου ἐν γῇ
Ισραηλ καὶ ὅτε ἤμην νέος, πᾶσα ἡ φυλὴ Νεφθαλιμ τοῦ
πατρός μου ἀπέστησαν ἀπὸ τοῦ οἴκου Δαυιδ τοῦ πατρός μου
καὶ ἀπὸ Ιερουσαλημ πόλεως τῆς [ἐκλεγείσης] ἐκ πασῶν φυλῶν Ισραηλ εἰς τὸ θυσιάζειν πάσαις φυλαῖς Ισραηλ· καὶ
ἡγιάσθη ὁ ναὸς τῆς κατασκηνώσεως τοῦ θεοῦ καὶ ᾠκοδομήθη
ἐν αὐτῇ εἰς πάσας τὰς γενεὰς τοῦ αἰῶνος. 5 πάντες οἱ
ἀδελφοί μου καὶ ὁ οἶκος Νεφθαλιμ τοῦ πατρός μου, ἐθυσίαζον ἐκεῖνοι τῷ μόσχῳ, ὃν ἐποίησεν Ιεροβεαμ ὁ βασιλεὺς
Ισραηλ ἐν Δαν, ἐπὶ πάντων ὀρέων τῆς Γαλιλαίας. 6 κἀγὼ
μονώτατος ἐπορευόμην πολλάκις εἰς Ιεροσόλυμα ἐν ταῖς
ἑορταῖς, καθὼς γέγραπται ἐν παντὶ Ισραηλ ἐν προστάγματι

KING JAMES VERSION

TOBIT

1 The book of the words of Tobit, son of Tobiel, the son of Ananiel, the son of Aduel, the son of Gabael, of the seed of Asael, of the tribe of Nephthali;

2 Who in the time of Enemessar king of the Assyrians was led captive out of Thisbe, which is at the right hand of that city, which is called properly Nephthali in Galilee above Aser.

3 I Tobit have walked all the days of my life in the way of truth and justice, and I did many almsdeeds to my brethren, and my nation, who came with me to Nineve, into the land of the Assyrians.

4 And when I was in mine own country, in the land of Israel, being but young, all the tribe of Nephthali my father fell from the house of Jerusalem, which was chosen out of all the tribes of Israel, that all the tribes should sacrifice *there,* where the temple of the habitation of the most High was consecrated and built for all ages.

5 Now all the tribes which together revolted, and the house of my father Nephthali, sacrificed unto the heifer Baal.

6 But I alone went often to Jerusalem at the feasts, as it was ordained unto all the people of Israel by an everlasting

DOUAY OLD TESTAMENT

THE BOOK OF TOBIAS

1 TOBIAS of the tribe and city of Nephtali, (which is in the upper parts of Galilee above Naasson, beyond the way that leadeth to the west, having on the right hand the city of Sephet,)

2 When he was made captive in the days of Salmanasar king of the Assyrians, even in his captivity, forsook not the way of truth,

3 But every day gave all he could get to his brethren his fellow captives, that were of his kindred.

4 And when he was younger than any of the tribe of Nephtali, yet did he no childish thing in his work.

5 Moreover when all went to the golden calves which Jeroboam king of Israel had made, he alone fled the company of all,

6 And went to Jerusalem to the temple of the Lord, and

KNOX TRANSLATION

THE BOOK OF TOBIAS

1 THERE was a man of Nephthali dwelling in the city of
that name, which lies in the hill-country of Galilee,
beyond Naasson, by the road leading westwards with Sephet
on the left of it. His name was Tobias; 2 and when he was
carried off as a prisoner by the Assyrians under king
Salmanasar, he would not make his exile an excuse for
deserting true religion. 3 Every day he would share whatever
means he had with his fellow-captives, that were men of his
own clan.

4 Even when he was a boy, and was of least regard among
the men of Nephthali, no boyish levity did his acts display.
5 While the rest had recourse to the golden calves Jeroboam
had set up when he reigned in Israel, Tobias shunned their
company and went his own way; 6 went up to Jerusalem to
the Lord's temple, and worshipped the Lord that was God of

TODAY'S ENGLISH VERSION

THE BOOK OF TOBIT

1 I am Tobit and this is the story of my life. My father was
Tobiel, my grandfather was Ananiel, and my great-
grandfather was Aduel. Aduel's father was Gabael; his
grandfather was Raphael; and his great-grandfather was
Raguel, who belonged to the clan of Asiel, a part of the tribe
of Naphtali. 2 During the time that Shalmaneser was emper-
or of Assyria, I was taken captive in my hometown of Thisbe,
located in northern Galilee, south of Kadesh in Naphtali,
northwest of Hazor, and north of Phogor.
3 All my life I have been honest and have tried to do what
was right. I often gave money to help needy relatives and
other Jews who had been deported with me to Nineveh, the
capital of Assyria.
4 When I was young, I lived in northern Israel. All the
tribes in Israel were supposed to offer sacrifices in Jerusalem.
It was the one city that God had chosen from among all the
Israelite cities as the place where his Temple was to be built
for his holy and eternal home. But my entire tribe of
Naphtali rejected the city of Jerusalem and the kings
descended from David. 5 Like everyone else in this tribe, my
own family used to go to the city of Dan in the mountains of
northern Galilee to offer sacrifices to the gold bull-calf which
King Jeroboam of Israel had set up there.
6 I was the only one in my family who regularly went to
Jerusalem to celebrate the religious festivals, as the Law of

NEW REVISED STANDARD VERSION

a) The books and parts of books from Tobit through 2 Maccabees are recognized as Deuterocanonical Scripture by the Roman Catholic, Greek, and Russian Orthodox Churches.

TOBIT

1 This book tells the story of Tobit son of Tobiel son of
Hananiel son of Aduel son of Gabael son of Raphael son
of Raguel of the descendants[a] of Asiel, of the tribe of
Naphtali, 2 who in the days of King Shalmaneser[b] of the
Assyrians was taken into captivity from Thisbe, which is to
the south of Kedesh Naphtali in Upper Galilee, above Asher
toward the west, and north of Phogor.
3 I, Tobit, walked in the ways of truth and righteousness
all the days of my life. I performed many acts of charity for
my kindred and my people who had gone with me in exile to
Nineveh in the land of the Assyrians. 4 When I was in my
own country, in the land of Israel, while I was still a young
man, the whole tribe of my ancestor Naphtali deserted the
house of David and Jerusalem. This city had been chosen
from among all the tribes of Israel, where all the tribes of
Israel should offer sacrifice and where the temple, the
dwelling of God, had been consecrated and established for all
generations forever.
5 All my kindred and our ancestral house of Naphtali sacrificed to the calf[c] that King Jeroboam of Israel had erected in
Dan and on all the mountains of Galilee. 6 But I alone went
often to Jerusalem for the festivals, as it is prescribed for all
Israel by an everlasting decree. I would hurry off to

a Other ancient authorities lack *of Raphael son of Raguel of the descendants*
b Gk *Enemessaros* *c* Other ancient authorities read *heifer*

NEW AMERICAN BIBLE

THE BOOK OF TOBIT

1 This book tells the story of Tobit, son of Tobiel, son of
Hananiel, son of Aduel, son of Gabael of the family of
Asiel, of the tribe of Naphtali, 2 who during the reign of
Shalmaneser, king of Assyria, was taken captive from
Thisbe, which is south of Kedesh Naphtali in upper Galilee,
above and to the west of Asser, north of Phogor.
3 I, Tobit, have walked all the days of my life on the paths
of truth and righteousness. I performed many charitable
works for my kinsmen and my people who had been deported with me to Nineveh, in Assyria. 4 When I lived as a young
man in my own country, Israel, the entire tribe of my forefather Naphtali had broken away from the house of David and
from Jerusalem. This city had been singled out of all Israel's
tribes, so that they all might offer sacrifice in the place where
the temple, God's dwelling, had been built and consecrated
for all generations to come. 5 All my kinsmen, like the rest of
the tribe of my forefather Naphtali, used to offer sacrifice on
all the mountains of Galilee as well as to the young bull
which Jeroboam, king of Israel, had made in Dan.
6 I, for my part, would often make the pilgrimage alone to
Jerusalem for the festivals, as is prescribed for all Israel by

NEW JERUSALEM BIBLE

TOBIT

1 The tale of Tobit son of Tobiel, son of Ananiel, son of
Aduel, son of Gabael, of the lineage of Asiel and tribe of
Naphtali. 2 In the days of Shalmaneser king of Assyria, he
was exiled from Thisbe, which is south of Kedesh-Naphtali in
Upper Galilee, above Hazor, some distance to the west, north
of Shephat.
3 I, Tobit, have walked in paths of truth and in good works
all the days of my life. I have given much in alms to my
brothers and fellow country-folk, exiled like me to Nineveh in
the country of Assyria. 4 In my young days, when I was still
at home in the land of Israel, the whole tribe of Naphtali my
ancestor broke away from the House of David and from
Jerusalem, though this was the city chosen out of all the
tribes of Israel for their sacrifices; here, the Temple—God's
dwelling-place—had been built and hallowed for all generations to come. 5 All my brothers and the House of Naphtali
sacrificed on every hill-top in Galilee to the calf that
Jeroboam king of Israel had made at Dan.
6 Often I was quite alone in making the pilgrimage to
Jerusalem, fulfilling the Law that binds all Israel perpetually.

GREEK OLD TESTAMENT

αἰωνίῳ· τὰς ἀπαρχὰς καὶ τὰ πρωτογενήματα καὶ τὰς δεκάτας τῶν κτηνῶν καὶ τὰς πρωτοκουρίας τῶν προβάτων ἔχων
ἀπέτρεχον εἰς Ιεροσόλυμα 7 καὶ ἐδίδουν αὐτὰ τοῖς ἱερεῦσιν
τοῖς υἱοῖς Ααρων πρὸς τὸ θυσιαστήριον καὶ τὴν δεκάτην τοῦ
σίτου καὶ τοῦ οἴνου καὶ ἐλαίου καὶ ῥοῶν καὶ τῶν σύκων καὶ
τῶν λοιπῶν ἀκροδρύων τοῖς υἱοῖς Λευι τοῖς θεραπεύουσιν ἐν
Ιερουσαλημ. καὶ τὴν δεκάτην τὴν δευτέραν ἀπεδεκάτιζον
ἀργυρίῳ τῶν ἓξ ἐτῶν καὶ ἐπορευόμην καὶ ἐδαπάνων αὐτὰ ἐν
Ιερουσαλημ καθ' ἕκαστον ἐνιαυτόν. 8 καὶ ἐδίδουν αὐτὰ τοῖς
ὀρφανοῖς καὶ ταῖς χήραις καὶ προσηλύτοις τοῖς προσκει-
μένοις τοῖς υἱοῖς Ισραηλ εἰσέφερον καὶ ἐδίδουν αὐτοῖς ἐν τῷ
τρίτῳ ἔτει καὶ ἠσθίομεν αὐτὰ κατὰ τὸ πρόσταγμα τὸ προσ-
τεταγμένον περὶ αὐτῶν ἐν τῷ νόμῳ Μωσῆ καὶ κατὰ τὰς ἐντολάς, ἃς ἐνετείλατο Δεββωρα ἡ μήτηρ Ανανιηλ τοῦ πατρὸς
ἡμῶν, ὅτι ὀρφανὸν κατέλιπέν με ὁ πατὴρ καὶ ἀπέθανεν.
9 καὶ ὅτε ἐγενήθην ἀνήρ, ἔλαβον γυναῖκα ἐκ τοῦ σπέρματος
τῆς πατριᾶς ἡμῶν καὶ ἐγέννησα ἐξ αὐτῆς υἱὸν καὶ ἐκάλεσα
τὸ ὄνομα αὐτοῦ Τωβιαν. 10 μετὰ τὸ αἰχμαλωτισθῆναί με εἰς
'Ασσυρίους καὶ ὅτε ᾐχμαλωτίσθην, εἰς Νινευη ἐπορευόμην·
καὶ πάντες οἱ ἀδελφοί μου καὶ οἱ ἐκ τοῦ γένους μου ἤσθιον
ἐκ τῶν ἄρτων τῶν ἐθνῶν, 11 ἐγὼ δὲ συνετήρησα τὴν ψυχήν
μου μὴ φαγεῖν ἐκ τῶν ἄρτων τῶν ἐθνῶν. 12 καὶ ὅτε ἐμεμνή-
μην τοῦ θεοῦ μου ἐν ὅλῃ ψυχῇ μου, 13 καὶ ἔδωκέν μοι ὁ
ὕψιστος χάριν καὶ μορφὴν ἐνώπιον Ενεμεσσαρου, καὶ ἠγόραζον αὐτῷ πάντα τὰ πρὸς τὴν χρῆσιν· 14 καὶ ἐπορευόμην εἰς
Μηδίαν καὶ ἠγόραζον αὐτῷ ἐκεῖθεν ἕως αὐτὸν ἀποθανεῖν.

KING JAMES VERSION

decree, having the firstfruits and tenths of increase, with that which was first shorn; and them gave I at the altar to the priests the children of Aaron.

7 The first tenth part of all increase I gave to the sons of Aaron, who ministered at Jerusalem: another tenth part I sold away, and went, and spent it every year at Jerusalem:

8 And the third I gave unto them to whom it was meet, as Debora my father's mother had commanded me, because I was left an orphan by my father.

9 Furthermore, when I was come to the age of a man, I married Anna of mine own kindred, and of her I begat Tobias.

10 And when we were carried away captives to Nineve, all my brethren and those that were of my kindred did eat of the bread of the Gentiles.

11 But I kept myself from eating;

12 Because I remembered God with all my heart.

13 And the most High gave me grace and favour before Enemessar, so that I was his purveyor.

14 And I went into Media, and left in trust with Gabael,

DOUAY OLD TESTAMENT

there adored the Lord God of Israel, offering faithfully all his firstfruits, and his tithes,

7 So that in the third year he gave all his tithes to the proselytes, and strangers.

8 These and such like things did he observe when but a boy according to the law of God.

9 But when he was a man, he took to wife Anna of his own tribe, and had a son by her, whom he called after his own name,

10 And from his infancy he taught him to fear God, and to abstain from all sin.

11 And when by the captivity he with his wife and his son and all his tribe was come to the city of Ninive,

12 (When all ate of the meats of the Gentiles) he kept his soul and never was defiled with their meats.

13 And because he was mindful of the Lord with all his heart, God gave him favour in the sight of Salmanasar the king.

14 And he gave him leave to go whithersoever he would, with liberty to do whatever he had a mind.

15 He therefore went to all that were in captivity, and gave them wholesome admonitions.

16 And when he was come to Rages a city of the Medes, and had ten talents of silver of that with which he had been honoured by the king:

17 And when amongst a great multitude of his kindred,

KNOX TRANSLATION

Israel. First-fruit and tithe he duly offered, 7 and every third
year he tithed his goods afresh, for the needs of wanderers
and homeless folk. 8 By such acts as these he shewed, even
in boyhood, what loyalty he had for the law of God; 9 when
he grew up it was a maiden of his own tribe, called Anna,
that he wedded, and their son, called by his father's name,
10 was brought up to fear God and keep clear of every fault.
11 Such was he, when, like all his tribe, he was carried
away, with his wife and his son, to Nineve. 12 All the rest
might share the food of the Gentiles, he would not lose his
innocence, he would not defile himself by eating what the
law forbade. 13 And God, finding his heart so loyal to the
divine commands, won him favour with king Salmanasar.
14 From this king he had leave to go where he would, and
spend his time as he would; 15 so he made a round of all his
fellow-exiles, giving them such good counsel as might avail
them. 16 Once he was at a Median city called Rages, and had
with him ten talents of silver, a gift from the king's bounty.
17 To what use should he put it? He found there a fellow-

TODAY'S ENGLISH VERSION

Moses commands everyone to do. I would hurry off to
Jerusalem with the first part of my harvest, the first-born of
my animals, a tenth of my cattle, and the freshly clipped
wool from my sheep. Then I would stand before the altar in
the Temple, and give these offerings to the priests, the
descendants of Aaron. 7 I would give a tenth of my grain,
wine, olive oil, pomegranates, figs, and other fruits to the
Levites who served God in Jerusalem. Every year, except the
seventh year when the land was at rest,[a] I would sell a second tenth of my possessions and spend the money in
Jerusalem on the festival meal.

8 But every third year, I would give a third tithe[b] to widows
and orphans and to foreigners living among my people, and
we would eat the festival meal together. I did this in keeping
with the Law of Moses, which Deborah, the mother of my
grandfather Ananiel, had taught me to obey. (I had been left
an orphan when my father died.)

9 When I grew up, I married Anna, a member of my own
tribe. We had a son and named him Tobias. 10 Later, I was
taken captive and deported to Assyria, and that is how I
came to live in Nineveh.

While we lived in Nineveh, all my relatives and the other
Jews used to eat the same kind of food as the other people
who lived there, 11 but I refused to do so. 12 Since I took seriously the commands of the Most High God, 13 he made
Emperor Shalmaneser respect me, and I was placed in charge
of purchasing all the emperor's supplies.

14 Before the emperor died, I made regular trips to the land

[a] THE LAND WAS AT REST: *See Lv 25.1-7.* [b] a third tithe; *some manuscripts have* the money.

NEW REVISED STANDARD VERSION

Jerusalem with the first fruits of the crops and the firstlings
of the flock, the tithes of the cattle, and the first shearings of
the sheep. 7 I would give these to the priests, the sons of
Aaron, at the altar; likewise the tenth of the grain, wine,
olive oil, pomegranates, figs, and the rest of the fruits to the
sons of Levi who ministered at Jerusalem. Also for six years I
would save up a second tenth in money and go and distribute it in Jerusalem. 8 A third tenth[a] I would give to the
orphans and widows and to the converts who had attached
themselves to Israel. I would bring it and give it to them in
the third year, and we would eat it according to the ordinance decreed concerning it in the law of Moses and according to the instructions of Deborah, the mother of my father
Tobiel,[b] for my father had died and left me an orphan.
9 When I became a man I married a woman,[c] a member of
our own family, and by her I became the father of a son
whom I named Tobias.

10 After I was carried away captive to Assyria and came
as a captive to Nineveh, everyone of my kindred and my people ate the food of the Gentiles, 11 but I kept myself from eating the food of the Gentiles. 12 Because I was mindful of God
with all my heart, 13 the Most High gave me favor and good
standing with Shalmaneser,[d] and I used to buy everything
he needed. 14 Until his death I used to go into Media, and

a A third tenth added from other ancient authorities *b* Lat: Gk *Hananiel*
c Other ancient authorities add *Anna* *d* Gk *Enemessaros*

NEW AMERICAN BIBLE

perpetual decree. Bringing with me the first fruits of the field
and the firstlings of the flock, together with a tenth of my
income and the first shearings of the sheep, I would hasten
to Jerusalem 7 and present them to the priests, Aaron's sons,
at the altar. To the Levites who were doing service in
Jerusalem I would give the tithe of grain, wine, olive oil,
pomegranates, figs, and other fruits. And except for sabbatical years, I used to give a second tithe in money, which each
year I would go and disburse in Jerusalem. 8 The third tithe I
gave to orphans and widows, and to converts who were living with the Israelites. Every third year I would bring them
this offering, and we ate it in keeping with the decree of the
Mosaic law and the commands of Deborah, the mother of my
father Tobiel; for when my father died, he left me an orphan.
9 When I reached manhood, I married Anna, a woman of
our own lineage. By her I had a son whom I named Tobiah.
10 Now after I had been deported to Nineveh, all my brothers
and relatives ate the food of heathens, 11 but I refrained from
eating that kind of food. 12 Because of this wholehearted service of God, 13 the Most High granted me favor and status
with Shalmaneser, so that I became purchasing agent for all
his needs. 14 Every now and then until his death I would go

NEW JERUSALEM BIBLE

I would hurry to Jerusalem with the first yield of fruits and
beasts, the tithe of cattle and the sheep's first shearings. 7 I
would give these to the priests, the sons of Aaron, for the
altar. To the Levites ministering at Jerusalem I would give
my tithe of wine and corn, olives, pomegranates and other
fruits. Six years in succession I took the second tithe in
money and went and paid it annually at Jerusalem. 8 I gave
the third to orphans and widows and to the strangers who
live among the Israelites; I brought it them as a gift every
three years. When we ate, we obeyed both the ordinances of
the law of Moses and the exhortations of Deborah the mother of our ancestor Ananiel; for my father had died and left
me an orphan. 9 When I came to man's estate, I married a
woman from our kinsfolk whose name was Anna; she bore
me a son whom I called Tobias.

10 When the banishment into Assyria came, I was taken
away and went to Nineveh. All my brothers and the people of
my race ate the food of the heathen, 11 but for my part I was
careful not to eat the food of the heathen. 12 And because I
had kept faith with my God with my whole heart, 13 the
Most High granted me the favour of Shalmaneser, and I
became the king's purveyor. 14 Until his death I used to

GREEK OLD TESTAMENT

καὶ παρεθέμην Γαβαήλῳ βαλλάντια τῷ ἀδελφῷ τῷ Γαβρι ἐν
τῇ χώρᾳ τῆς Μηδίας, ἀργυρίου τάλαντα δέκα.
15 Καὶ ὅτε ἀπέθανεν Ενεμασσαρ καὶ ἐβασίλευσεν Σενναχηριμ υἱὸς αὐτοῦ ἀντ᾽ αὐτοῦ, καὶ αἱ ὁδοὶ τῆς Μηδίας ἀπέστησαν, καὶ οὐκέτι ἠδυνάσθην πορευθῆναι εἰς τὴν Μηδίαν. 16 ἐν
ταῖς ἡμέραις Ενεμεσσαρου ἐλεημοσύνας πολλὰς ἐποίησα τοῖς
ἀδελφοῖς μου τοῖς ἐκ τοῦ γένους μου· 17 τοὺς ἄρτους μου ἐδίδουν τοῖς πεινῶσιν καὶ ἱμάτια τοῖς γυμνοῖς, καὶ εἴ τινα τῶν
ἐκ τοῦ ἔθνους μου ἐθεώρουν τεθνηκότα καὶ ἐρριμμένον ὀπίσω
τοῦ τείχους Νινευη, ἔθαπτον αὐτόν. 18 καὶ εἴ τινα ἀπέκτεινεν
Σενναχηριμ, ὅτε ἀπῆλθεν φεύγων ἐκ τῆς Ιουδαίας ἐν ἡμέραις
τῆς κρίσεως, ἧς ἐποίησεν ἐξ αὐτοῦ ὁ βασιλεὺς τοῦ οὐρανοῦ
περὶ τῶν βλασφημιῶν, ὧν ἐβλασφήμησεν, ἔθαψα· πολλοὺς γὰρ
ἀπέκτεινεν ἐν τῷ θυμῷ αὐτοῦ ἐκ τῶν υἱῶν Ισραηλ, καὶ ἔκλε-
πτον τὰ σώματα αὐτῶν καὶ ἔθαπτον· καὶ ἐζήτησεν αὐτὰ
Σενναχηριμ καὶ οὐχ εὗρεν αὐτά. 19 καὶ ἐπορεύθη εἷς τις τῶν
ἐκ τῆς Νινευη καὶ ὑπέδειξεν τῷ βασιλεῖ περὶ ἐμοῦ ὅτι ἐγὼ
θάπτω αὐτούς, καὶ ἐκρύβην· καὶ ὅτε ἐπέγνων ὅτι ἔγνω περὶ
ἐμοῦ ὁ βασιλεὺς καὶ ὅτι ζητοῦμαι τοῦ ἀποθανεῖν, ἐφοβήθην
καὶ ἀπέδρασα. 20 καὶ ἡρπάγη πάντα, ὅσα ὑπῆρχέν μοι, καὶ οὐ
κατελείφθη μοι οὐδέν, ὃ οὐκ ἀνελήμφθη εἰς τὸ βασιλικόν, πλὴν
Αννας τῆς γυναικός μου καὶ Τωβια τοῦ υἱοῦ μου. 21 καὶ οὐ
διῆλθον ἡμέραι τεσσαράκοντα ἕως οὗ ἀπέκτειναν αὐτὸν οἱ δύο
υἱοὶ αὐτοῦ· καὶ ἔφυγον εἰς τὰ ὄρη Αραρατ, καὶ ἐβασίλευσεν
Σαχερδονος υἱὸς αὐτοῦ μετ᾽ αὐτόν. καὶ ἔταξεν Αχιχαρον τὸν
Αναηλ τὸν τοῦ ἀδελφοῦ μου υἱὸν ἐπὶ πᾶσαν τὴν ἐκλογιστίαν
τῆς βασιλείας αὐτοῦ, καὶ αὐτὸς εἶχεν τὴν ἐξουσίαν ἐπὶ πᾶσαν

KING JAMES VERSION

the brother of Gabrias, at Rages a city of Media ten talents of silver.

15 Now when Enemessar was dead, Sennacherib his son reigned in his stead; whose estate was troubled, that I could not go into Media.

16 And in the time of Enemessar I gave many alms to my brethren, and gave my bread to the hungry,

17 And my clothes to the naked: and if I saw any of my nation dead, or cast about the walls of Nineve, I buried him.

18 And if the king Sennacherib had slain any, when he was come, and fled from Judea, I buried them privily; for in his wrath he killed many; but the bodies were not found, when they were sought for of the king.

19 And when one of the Ninevites went and complained of me to the king, that I buried them, and hid myself; understanding that I was sought for to be put to death, I withdrew myself for fear.

20 Then all my goods were forcibly taken away, neither was there any thing left me, beside my wife Anna and my son Tobias.

21 And there passed not five and fifty days, before two of his sons killed him, and they fled into the mountains of Ararath; and Sarchedonus his son reigned in his stead; who

DOUAY OLD TESTAMENT

he saw Gabelus in want, who was one of his tribe, taking a note of his hand he gave him the aforesaid sum of money.

18 But after a long time, Salmanasar the king being dead, when Sennacherib his son, who reigned in his place, had a hatred for the children of Israel:

19 Tobias daily went among all his kindred, and comforted them, and distributed to every one as he was able, out of his goods:

20 He fed the hungry, and gave clothes to the naked, and was careful to bury the dead, and they that were slain.

21 And when king Sennacherib was come back, fleeing from Judea by reason of the slaughter that God had made about him for his blasphemy, and being angry slew many of the children of Israel, Tobias buried their bodies.

22 But when it was told the king, he commanded him to be slain, and took away all his substance.

23 But Tobias fleeing naked away with his son and with his wife, lay concealed, for many loved him.

24 But after forty-five days, the king was killed by his own sons.

KNOX TRANSLATION

tribesman of his own, called Gabelus, who was in great
need; to him, then, he lent the aforesaid silver under a bond.
18 Time passed; Salmanasar died, and the throne passed to
his son Sennacherib, who was no friend to the Jews; 19 and
now it was Tobias' daily task to visit his own clansmen,
comforting them and providing for each of them as best he
could, out of what store he had; 20 it was for him to feed the
hungry, to clothe the naked, to honour with careful burial
men that had died of sickness, and men slain. 21 When
Sennacherib came home from Judaea, escaping while he
might from the divine vengeance his blasphemies had
brought upon him, he killed many an Israelite in his anger;
and these too Tobias would bury. 22 When this came to the
king's ears, he gave orders that Tobias should be put to
death, and seized all his property; 23 but he escaped, with
his wife and son, into safe hiding; destitute as he was, he
had many friends. 24 And then, forty-five days later,
Sennacherib was murdered by his own sons, 25 whereupon

Today's English Version

of Media to buy things for him there. Once, when I was in
the city of Rages in Media, I left some bags of money there
with Gabael, Gabrias' brother, and asked him to keep them
for me. There were more than 600 pounds of silver coins in
those bags. 15 When Shalmaneser died, his son Sennacherib
succeeded him as emperor. It soon became so dangerous to
travel on the roads in Media that I could no longer go there.

16 While Shalmaneser was still emperor, I took good care of
my own people whenever they were in need. 17 If they were
hungry, I shared my food with them; if they needed clothes, I
gave them some of my own. Whenever I saw that the dead
body of one of my people had been thrown outside the city
wall, I gave it a decent burial.

18 One day Sennacherib cursed God, the King of Heaven;
God punished him, and Sennacherib had to retreat from
Judah. On his way back to Media he was so furious that he
killed many Israelites. But I secretly removed the bodies and
buried them; and when Sennacherib later searched for the
bodies, he could not find them.

19 Then someone from Nineveh told the emperor that I was
the one who had been burying his victims. As soon as I realized that the emperor knew all about me and that my life
was in danger, I became frightened. So I ran away and hid.
20 Everything I owned was seized and put in the royal treasury. My wife Anna and my son Tobias were all I had left.

21 About six weeks later, two of Sennacherib's sons assassinated him and then escaped to the mountains of Ararat.
Another son, Esarhaddon, became emperor and put Ahikar,
my brother Anael's son, in charge of all the financial affairs

New Revised Standard Version

buy for him there. While in the country of Media I left bags
of silver worth ten talents in trust with Gabael, the brother of
Gabri. 15 But when Shalmaneser[a] died, and his son Sennacherib reigned in his place, the highways into Media
became unsafe and I could no longer go there.

16 In the days of Shalmaneser[a] I performed many acts of
charity to my kindred, those of my tribe. 17 I would give my
food to the hungry and my clothing to the naked; and if I saw
the dead body of any of my people thrown out behind the wall
of Nineveh, I would bury it. 18 I also buried any whom King
Sennacherib put to death when he came fleeing from Judea in
those days of judgment that the king of heaven executed upon
him because of his blasphemies. For in his anger he put to
death many Israelites; but I would secretly remove the bodies
and bury them. So when Sennacherib looked for them he
could not find them. 19 Then one of the Ninevites went and
informed the king about me, that I was burying them; so I hid
myself. But when I realized that the king knew about me and
that I was being searched for to be put to death, I was afraid
and ran away. 20 Then all my property was confiscated; nothing was left to me that was not taken into the royal treasury
except my wife Anna and my son Tobias.

21 But not forty[b] days passed before two of Sennacherib's[c] sons killed him, and they fled to the mountains of
Ararat, and his son Esar-haddon[d] reigned after him. He
appointed Ahikar, the son of my brother Hanael[e] over all the
accounts of his kingdom, and he had authority over the

a Gk *Enemessaros* *b* Other ancient authorities read either *forty-five* or *fifty* *c* Gk *his* *d* Gk *Sacherdonos* *e* Other authorities read *Hananael*

New American Bible

to Media to buy goods for him. I also deposited several
pouches containing a great sum of money with my kinsman
Gabael, son of Gabri, who lived at Rages, in Media. 15 But
when Shalmaneser died and his son Sennacherib succeeded
him as king, the roads to Media became unsafe, so I could no
longer go there.

16 During Shalmaneser's reign I performed many charitable
works for my kinsmen and my people. 17 I would give my
bread to the hungry and my clothing to the naked. If I saw
one of my people who had died and been thrown outside the
walls of Nineveh, I would bury him. 18 I also buried anyone
whom Sennacherib slew when he returned as a fugitive from
Judea during the days of judgment decreed against him by
the heavenly King because of the blasphemies he had
uttered. In his rage he killed many Israelites, but I used to
take their bodies by stealth and bury them; so when
Sennacherib looked for them, he could not find them. 19 But
a certain citizen of Nineveh informed the king that it was I
who buried the dead. When I found out that the king knew
all about me and wanted to put me to death, I went into hiding; then in my fear I took to flight. 20 Afterward, all my
property was confiscated; I was left with nothing. All that I
had was taken to the king's palace, except for my wife Anna
and my son Tobiah.

21 But less than forty days later the king was assassinated
by two of his sons, who then escaped into the mountains of
Ararat. His son Esarhaddon, who succeeded him as king,
placed Ahiqar, my brother Anael's son, in charge of all the
accounts of his kingdom, so that he took control over the

New Jerusalem Bible

travel to Media, where I transacted business on his behalf,
and I deposited sacks of silver worth ten talents with Gabael
the brother of Gabrias at Rhages in Media.

15 On the death of Shalmaneser his son Sennacherib succeeded; the roads into Media were barred, and I could no
longer go there. 16 In the days of Shalmaneser I had often
given alms to the people of my race; 17 I gave my bread to
the hungry and clothes to those who lacked them; and I
buried, when I saw them, the bodies of my country-folk
thrown over the walls of Nineveh.

18 I also buried those who were killed by Sennacherib.
When Sennacherib was beating a disorderly retreat from
Judaea after the King of heaven had punished his blasphemies, he killed a great number of Israelites in his rage. So I
stole their bodies to bury them; Sennacherib looked for them
and could not find them. 19 A Ninevite went and told the
king it was I who had buried them secretly. When I knew
that the king had been told about me and saw myself being
hunted by men who would put me to death, I was afraid and
fled. 20 All my goods were seized; they were all confiscated
by the treasury; nothing was left me but my wife Anna and
my son Tobias.

21 Less than forty days after this, the king was murdered
by his two sons, who then fled to the mountains of Ararat.
His son Esarhaddon succeeded. Ahikar the son of my brother
Anael, was appointed chancellor of the exchequer for the

GREEK OLD TESTAMENT

τὴν διοίκησιν. 22 τότε ἠξίωσεν Αχιχαρος περὶ ἐμοῦ, καὶ
κατῆλθον εἰς τὴν Νινευη. Αχιχαρος γὰρ ἦν ὁ ἀρχιοινοχόος
καὶ ἐπὶ τοῦ δακτυλίου καὶ διοικητὴς καὶ ἐκλογιστὴς ἐπὶ
Σενναχηριμ βασιλέως Ἀσσυρίων, καὶ κατέστησεν αὐτὸν
Σαχερδονος ἐκ δευτέρας. ἦν δὲ ἐξάδελφός μου καὶ ἐκ τῆς συγ-
γενείας μου.

2 Καὶ ἐπὶ Σαχερδονος βασιλέως κατῆλθον εἰς τὸν οἶκόν
μου, καὶ ἀπεδόθη μοι ἡ γυνή μου Αννα καὶ Τωβιας ὁ υἱός
μου. καὶ ἐν τῇ πεντηκοστῇ τῇ ἑορτῇ ἡμῶν, ἥ ἐστιν ἁγία
[ἑπτὰ] ἑβδομάδων, ἐγενήθη μοι ἄριστον καλόν, καὶ ἀνέπεσα
τοῦ ἀριστῆσαι. 2 καὶ παρετέθη μοι ἡ τράπεζα, καὶ παρετέθη
μοι ὀψάρια πλείονα, καὶ εἶπα τῷ Τωβια τῷ υἱῷ μου Παιδίον,
βάδιζε καὶ ὃν ἂν εὕρῃς πτωχὸν τῶν ἀδελφῶν ἡμῶν ἐκ
Νινευητῶν αἰχμαλώτων, ὃς μέμνηται ἐν ὅλῃ καρδίᾳ αὐτοῦ,
καὶ ἄγαγε αὐτὸν καὶ φάγεται κοινῶς μετ᾽ ἐμοῦ· καὶ ἰδὲ
προσμενῶ σε, παιδίον, μέχρι τοῦ σε ἐλθεῖν. 3 καὶ ἐπορεύθη
Τωβιας ζητῆσαί τινα πτωχὸν τῶν ἀδελφῶν ἡμῶν. καὶ
ἐπιστρέψας λέγει Πάτερ. καὶ εἶπα αὐτῷ Ἰδοὺ ἐγώ, παιδίον.
καὶ ἀποκριθεὶς εἶπεν Πάτερ, ἰδοὺ εἷς ἐκ τοῦ ἔθνους ἡμῶν
πεφόνευται καὶ ἔρριπται ἐν τῇ ἀγορᾷ καὶ αὐτόθι νῦν
ἐστραγγάληται. 4 καὶ ἀναπηδήσας ἀφῆκα τὸ ἄριστον πρὶν ἢ
γεύσασθαί με αὐτοῦ καὶ ἀναιροῦμαι αὐτὸν ἐκ τῆς πλατείας
καὶ εἰς ἓν τῶν οἰκιδίων ἔθηκα μέχρι τοῦ τὸν ἥλιον δύειν καὶ
θάψω αὐτόν. 5 ἐπιστρέψας οὖν ἐλουσάμην καὶ ἤσθιον τὸν
ἄρτον μετὰ πένθους. 6 καὶ ἐμνήσθην τοῦ ῥήματος τοῦ
προφήτου, ὅσα ἐλάλησεν Αμως ἐπὶ Βαιθηλ λέγων

KING JAMES VERSION

appointed over his father's accounts, and over all his affairs,
Achiacharus my brother Anael's son.

22 And Achiacharus intreating for me, I returned to
Nineve. Now Achiacharus was cupbearer, and keeper of the
signet, and steward, and overseer of the accounts: and
Sarchedonus appointed him next unto him: and he was my
brother's son.

2 Now when I was come home again, and my wife Anna
was restored unto me, with my son Tobias, in the feast
of Pentecost, which is the holy feast of the seven weeks,
there was a good dinner prepared me, in the which I sat
down to eat.

2 And when I saw abundance of meat, I said to my son,
Go and bring what poor man soever thou shalt find out of
our brethren, who is mindful of the Lord; and, lo, I tarry for
thee.

3 But he came again, and said, Father, one of our nation
is strangled, and is cast out in the marketplace.

4 Then before I had tasted of any meat, I started up, and
took him up into a room until the going down of the sun.

5 Then I returned, and washed myself, and ate my meat
in heaviness,

6 Remembering that prophecy of Amos, as he said, Your

DOUAY OLD TESTAMENT

25 And Tobias returned to his house, and all his substance was restored to him.

2 BUT after this, when there was a festival of the Lord,
and a good dinner was prepared in Tobias's house,

2 He said to his son: Go, and bring some of our tribe that
fear God, to feast with us.

3 And when he had gone, returning he told him, that one
of the children of Israel lay slain in the street. And he forthwith leaped up from his place at the table, and left his dinner, and came fasting to the body:

4 And taking it up carried it privately to his house, that
after the sun was down, he might bury him cautiously.

5 And when he had hid the body, he ate bread with
mourning and fear,

6 Remembering the word which the Lord spoke by Amos

KNOX TRANSLATION

Tobias came back home, and had all his goods restored to
him.[a]

2 Soon after this, one of the Lord's feast-days came round,
and Tobias, his table richly spread, 2 would have his son
go out and invite fellow-tribesmen and fellow-worshippers of
theirs, to share the banquet. 3 Go out he did, but came back
bearing ill news; he had found an Israelite lying murdered in
the open street. His father, without more ado, sprang up
from where he sat, leaving his dinner untasted; he would not
break his fast till he had found the body, 4 wrapped it about
and carried it home with him, to bury it in secret when night
fell. 5 A sad and anxious meal was his, with such a guest
hidden under his roof; 6 he remembered those words the
Lord had put into the mouth of Amos, Your feast-days shall

a Both in the Hebrew and in the Greek versions which survive to us, Tobias speaks in the first person throughout this chapter, and the whole story is differently told, though its substance is the same.

TODAY'S ENGLISH VERSION

of the empire. 22 This was actually the second time Ahikar was appointed to this position, for when Sennacherib was emperor of Assyria, Ahikar had been wine steward, treasurer, and accountant, and had been in charge of the official seal. Since Ahikar was my nephew, he put in a good word for me with the emperor, and I was allowed to return to Nineveh.

2 When I returned home I was reunited with my wife Anna and my son Tobias. At the Harvest Festival, which is also called the Festival of Weeks, I sat down to a delicious meal. 2 When I saw how much food there was on the table, I said to Tobias, "Son, go out and find one of our people who is living in poverty here in exile, someone who takes God's commands seriously. Bring him back with you, so that he can share this festival meal with us. I won't start eating until you come back."

3 So Tobias went out to look for such a person. But he quickly returned, shouting, "Father! Father!"

"Yes, what is it?" I asked.

"One of our people has just been murdered! Someone strangled him and threw his body into the marketplace."

4 I jumped up and left the table without even touching my food. I removed the body from the street and carried it to a little shed, where I left it until sunset, when I could bury it. 5 Then I returned home and washed, so as to purify myself. In deep sorrow I ate my dinner. 6 I was reminded of what the prophet Amos had said to the people of Bethel,

NEW REVISED STANDARD VERSION

entire administration. 22 Ahikar interceded for me, and I returned to Nineveh. Now Ahikar was chief cupbearer, keeper of the signet, and in charge of administration of the accounts under King Sennacherib of Assyria; so Esar-haddon[a] reappointed him. He was my nephew and so a close relative.

2 Then during the reign of Esar-haddon[a] I returned home, and my wife Anna and my son Tobias were restored to me. At our festival of Pentecost, which is the sacred festival of weeks, a good dinner was prepared for me and I reclined to eat. 2 When the table was set for me and an abundance of food placed before me, I said to my son Tobias, "Go, my child, and bring whatever poor person you may find of our people among the exiles in Nineveh, who is wholeheartedly mindful of God,[b] and he shall eat together with me. I will wait for you, until you come back." 3 So Tobias went to look for some poor person of our people. When he had returned he said, "Father!" And I replied, "Here I am, my child." Then he went on to say, "Look, father, one of our own people has been murdered and thrown into the market place, and now he lies there strangled." 4 Then I sprang up, left the dinner before even tasting it, and removed the body[c] from the square[d] and laid it[c] in one of the rooms until sunset when I might bury it.[c] 5 When I returned, I washed myself and ate my food in sorrow. 6 Then I remembered the prophecy of Amos, how he said against Bethel,[e]

a Gk *Sacherdonos* *b* Lat: Gk *wholeheartedly mindful* *c* Gk *him* *d* Other ancient authorities lack *from the square* *e* Other ancient authorities read *against Bethlehem*

NEW AMERICAN BIBLE

entire administration. 22 Then Ahiqar interceded on my behalf, and I was able to return to Nineveh. For under Sennacherib, king of Assyria, Ahiqar had been chief cupbearer, keeper of the seal, administrator, and treasurer; and Esarhaddon reappointed him. He was a close relative—in fact, my nephew.

2 Thus under King Esarhaddon I returned to my home, and my wife Anna and my son Tobiah were restored to me. Then on our festival of Pentocost, the feast of Weeks, a fine dinner was prepared for me, and I reclined to eat. 2 The table was set for me, and when many different dishes were placed before me, I said to my son Tobiah: "My son, go out and try to find a poor man from among our kinsmen exiled here in Nineveh. If he is a sincere worshiper of God, bring him back with you, so that he can share this meal with me. Indeed, son, I shall wait for you to come back."

3 Tobiah went out to look for some poor kinsman of ours. When he returned he exclaimed, "Father!" I said to him, "What is it, son?" He answered, "Father, one of our people has been murdered! His body lies in the market place where he was just strangled!" 4 I sprang to my feet, leaving the dinner untouched; and I carried the dead man from the street and put him in one of the rooms, so that I might bury him after sunset. 5 Returning to my own quarters, I washed myself and ate my food in sorrow. 6 I was reminded of the oracle pronounced by the prophet Amos against Bethel:

NEW JERUSALEM BIBLE

kingdom and given the main ordering of affairs. 22 Ahikar then interceded for me and I was allowed to return to Nineveh, since Ahikar had been chief cupbearer, keeper of the signet, administrator and treasurer under Sennacherib king of Assyria, and Esarhaddon had kept him in office. He was a relation of mine; he was my nephew.

2 In the reign of Esarhaddon, therefore, I returned home, and my wife Anna was restored to me with my son Tobias. At our feast of Pentecost (the feast of Weeks) there was a good dinner. I took my place for the meal; 2 the table was brought to me and various dishes were brought. I then said to my son Tobias, 'Go, my child, and seek out some poor, loyal-hearted man among our brothers exiled in Nineveh, and bring him to share my meal. I will wait until you come back, my child.' 3 So Tobias went out to look for some poor man among our brothers, but he came back again and said, 'Father!' I replied, 'What is it, my child?' He went on, 'Father, one of our nation has just been murdered; he has been strangled and then thrown down in the market place; he is there still.' 4 I sprang up at once, left my meal untouched, took the man from the market place and laid him in one of my rooms, waiting until sunset to bury him. 5 I came in again and washed myself and ate my bread in sorrow, 6 remembering the words of the prophet Amos concerning Bethel:

GREEK OLD TESTAMENT

Στραφήσονται ὑμῶν αἱ ἑορταὶ εἰς πένθος
καὶ πᾶσαι αἱ ᾠδαὶ ὑμῶν εἰς θρῆνος

καὶ ἔκλαυσα. 7 καὶ ὅτε ἔδυ ὁ ἥλιος, ᾠχόμην καὶ ὀρύξας
ἔθαψα αὐτόν. 8 καὶ οἱ πλησίον μου κατεγέλων λέγοντες Οὐ
φοβεῖται οὐκέτι· ἤδη γὰρ ἐπεζητήθη τοῦ φονευθῆναι περὶ
τοῦ πράγματος τούτου καὶ ἀπέδρα, καὶ πάλιν ἰδοὺ θάπτει
τοὺς νεκρούς. 9 καὶ αὐτῇ τῇ νυκτὶ ἐλουσάμην καὶ εἰσῆλθον
εἰς τὴν αὐλήν μου καὶ ἐκοιμήθην παρὰ τὸν τοῖχον τῆς
αὐλῆς, καὶ τὸ πρόσωπόν μου ἀνακεκαλυμμένον διὰ τὸ καῦμα·
10 καὶ οὐκ ᾔδειν ὅτι στρουθία ἐν τῷ τοίχῳ ἐπάνω μού εἰσιν,
καὶ ἐκάθισεν τὸ ἀφόδευμα αὐτῶν εἰς τοὺς ὀφθαλμούς μου
θερμὸν καὶ ἐπήγαγεν λευκώματα. καὶ ἐπορευόμην πρὸς τοὺς
ἰατροὺς θεραπευθῆναι, καὶ ὅσῳ ἐνεχρίοσάν με τὰ φάρμακα,
τοσούτῳ μᾶλλον ἐξετυφλοῦντο οἱ ὀφθαλμοί μου τοῖς λευκώ-
μασιν μέχρι τοῦ ἀποτυφλωθῆναι· καὶ ἤμην ἀδύνατος τοῖς
ὀφθαλμοῖς ἔτη τέσσαρα. καὶ πάντες οἱ ἀδελφοί μου ἐλυποῦν-
το περὶ ἐμοῦ, καὶ Αχιαχαρος ἔτρεφέν με ἔτη δύο πρὸ τοῦ
αὐτὸν βαδίσαι εἰς τὴν Ἐλυμαΐδα.

KING JAMES VERSION

feasts shall be turned into mourning, and all your mirth into lamentation.

7 Therefore I wept: and after the going down of the sun I went and made a grave, and buried him.

8 But my neighbours mocked me, and said, This man is not yet afraid to be put to death for this matter: who fled away; and yet, lo, he burieth the dead again.

9 The same night also I returned from the burial, and slept by the wall of my courtyard, being polluted, and my face was uncovered:

10 And I knew not that there were sparrows in the wall, and mine eyes being open, the sparrows muted warm dung into mine eyes; and a whiteness came in mine eyes; and I went to the physicians, but they helped me not: moreover Achiacharus did nourish me, until I went into Elymais.

DOUAY OLD TESTAMENT

the prophet: Your festival days shall be turned into lamentation and mourning.

7 So when the sun was down, he went and buried him.

8 Now all his neighbours blamed him, saying: Once already commandment was given for thee to be slain because of this matter, and thou didst scarce escape the sentence of death, and dost thou again bury the dead?

9 But Tobias fearing God more than the king, carried off the bodies of them that were slain, and hid them in his house, and at midnight buried them.

10 Now it happened one day, that being wearied with burying, he came to his house, and cast himself down by the wall and slept,

11 And as he was sleeping, hot dung out of a swallow's nest fell upon his eyes, and he was made blind.

12 Now this trial the Lord therefore permitted to happen to him, that an example might be given to posterity of his patience, as also of holy Job.

13 For whereas he had always feared God from his infancy, and kept his commandments, he repined not against God because the evil of blindness had befallen him,

14 But continued immoveable in the fear of God, giving thanks to God all the days of his life.

15 For as the kings insulted over holy Job: so his relations and kinsmen mocked at his life, saying:

16 Where is thy hope, for which thou gavest alms, and buriedst the dead?

17 But Tobias rebuked them, saying: Speak not so:

18 For we are the children of saints, and look for that life

KNOX TRANSLATION

end in lamentation and sad thoughts. 7 Night fell at last, and
the body was buried in safety; 8 but his neighbours shook
their heads over it, Here was sentence of death passed on
thee for such doings of thine; from that sentence thou wast
barely reprieved, and art thou back at thy grave-digging?
9 But still Tobias feared God much, and the king little; still
the bodies of murdered men were stolen away, hidden in his
house, and at dead of night buried.

10 But toil brought weariness, and one morning, when he
came home, he threw himself down in the shadow of the
wall, and quickly fell asleep. 11 As he slept, warm droppings
from a swallow's nest fell into his eyes, and he became
blind. 12 This was but a trial which the Lord allowed to befall
him, so that he might leave to later ages, as God's servant
Job did, a document of patience. 13 Here was a man that had
feared God and obeyed his commandments from infancy; he
was smitten with blindness; did he thereupon complain, God
was using him ill? 14 No, he remained as stout-hearted a
worshipper of God as before, and never a day passed but he
returned thanks for the gift of life. 15 Kinsman and clansman
might taunt him, as Job was taunted by his fellow chieftains;
might call him a fool for his pains, 16 and ask whether this
was the reward he had hoped for when he gave alms, and
went a-burying; 17 Tobias took them up short. Nay, said he,
never talk thus; 18 we come of holy stock, you and I, and

TODAY'S ENGLISH VERSION

"Your festivals will be turned into funerals,
and your glad songs will become cries of grief."

I began to weep.

7 After sunset I went out, dug a grave, and buried the man. 8 My neighbors thought I was crazy. "Haven't you learned anything?" they asked. "You have already been hunted down once for burying the dead, and you would have been killed if you had not run away. But here you are doing the same thing all over again."

9 That night I washed, so as to purify myself, and went out into my courtyard to sleep by the wall. It was a hot night, and I did not pull the cover up over my head. 10 Sparrows were on the wall right above me, but I did not know it. Their warm droppings fell into my eyes, causing a white film to form on them. I went to one doctor after another, but the more they treated me with their medicines, the worse my eyes became, until finally I was completely blind.

For four years I could see nothing. My relatives were deeply concerned about my condition, and Ahikar supported me for two years before he went to the land of Elam.

NEW REVISED STANDARD VERSION

"Your festivals shall be turned into mourning,
and all your songs into lamentation."

And I wept.

7 When the sun had set, I went and dug a grave and buried him. 8 And my neighbors laughed and said, "Is he still not afraid? He has already been hunted down to be put to death for doing this, and he ran away; yet here he is again burying the dead!" 9 That same night I washed myself and went into my courtyard and slept by the wall of the courtyard; and my face was uncovered because of the heat. 10 I did not know that there were sparrows on the wall; their fresh droppings fell into my eyes and produced white films. I went to physicians to be healed, but the more they treated me with ointments the more my vision was obscured by the white films, until I became completely blind. For four years I remained unable to see. All my kindred were sorry for me, and Ahikar took care of me for two years before he went to Elymais.

NEW AMERICAN BIBLE

"Your festivals shall be returned into mourning,
And all your songs into lamentation."

7 And I wept. Then at sunset I went out, dug a grave, and buried him.

8 The neighbors mocked me, saying to one another: "Will this man never learn! Once before he was hunted down for execution because of this very thing; yet now that he has escaped, here he is again burying the dead!"

9 That same night I bathed, and went to sleep next to the wall of my courtyard. Because of the heat I left my face uncovered. 10 I did not know there were birds perched on the wall above me, till their warm droppings settled in my eyes, causing cataracts. I went to see some doctors for a cure, but the more they anointed my eyes with various salves, the worse the cataracts became, until I could see no more. For four years I was deprived of eyesight, and all my kinsmen were grieved at my condition. Ahiqar, however, took care of me for two years, until he left for Elymais.

NEW JERUSALEM BIBLE

*I shall turn your festivals into mourning
and all your singing into lamentation.*[a]

7 And I wept. When the sun was down, I went and dug a grave and buried him. 8 My neighbours laughed and said, 'See! He is not afraid any more.' (You must remember that a price had been set on my head earlier for this very thing.) 'Once before he had to flee, yet here he is, beginning to bury the dead again.'

9 That night I took a bath; then I went into the courtyard and lay down by the courtyard wall. Since it was hot I left my face uncovered. 10 I did not know that there were sparrows in the wall above my head; their hot droppings fell into my eyes. This caused white spots to form, which I went to have treated by the doctors. But the more ointments they tried me with, the more the spots blinded me, and in the end, I became completely blind. I remained without sight four years; all my brothers were distressed on my behalf; and Ahikar provided for my upkeep for two years, until he left for Elymais.

[a] **2** Am 8:10.

GREEK OLD TESTAMENT

11 Καὶ ἐν τῷ χρόνῳ ἐκείνῳ Αννα ἡ γυνή μου ἠριθεύετο ἐν
τοῖς ἔργοις τοῖς γυναικείοις. 12 καὶ ἀπέστελλε τοῖς κυρίοις
αὐτῶν, καὶ ἀπεδίδουν αὐτῇ τὸν μισθόν. καὶ ἐν τῇ ἑβδόμῃ τοῦ
Δύστρου ἐξέτεμε τὸν ἱστὸν καὶ ἀπέστειλεν αὐτὸν τοῖς
κυρίοις, καὶ ἔδωκαν αὐτῇ τὸν μισθὸν πάντα καὶ ἔδωκαν αὐτῇ
ἐφ᾽ ἑστίᾳ ἔριφον ἐξ αἰγῶν. 13 καὶ ὅτε εἰσῆλθεν πρός με, ὁ
ἔριφος ἤρξατο κράζειν· καὶ ἐκάλεσα αὐτὴν καὶ εἶπα Πόθεν
τὸ ἐρίφιον τοῦτο; μήποτε κλεψιμαῖόν ἐστιν; ἀπόδος αὐτὸ
τοῖς κυρίοις αὐτοῦ· οὐ γὰρ ἐξουσίαν ἔχομεν ἡμεῖς φαγεῖν
οὐδὲν κλεψιμαῖον. 14 καὶ λέγει μοι αὐτή Δόσει δέδοταί μοι
ἐπὶ τῷ μισθῷ. καὶ οὐκ ἐπίστευον αὐτῇ καὶ ἔλεγον ἀποδοῦναι
τοῖς κυρίοις καὶ προσηρυθρίων χάριν τούτου πρὸς αὐτήν·
εἶτα ἀποκριθεῖσα λέγει μοι Καὶ ποῦ εἰσιν αἱ ἐλεημοσύναι
σου; ποῦ εἰσιν αἱ δικαιοσύναι σου; ἰδὲ ταῦτα μετὰ σοῦ
3 γνωστά ἐστιν. — 1 καὶ περίλυπος γενόμενος τῇ ψυχῇ
καὶ στενάξας ἔκλαυσα καὶ ἠρξάμην προσεύχεσθαι μετὰ
στεναγμῶν 2 Δίκαιος εἶ, κύριε, καὶ πάντα τὰ ἔργα σου δίκαια, καὶ πᾶσαι αἱ ὁδοί σου ἐλεημοσύνη καὶ ἀλήθεια· σὺ
κρίνεις τὸν αἰῶνα. 3 καὶ νῦν σύ, κύριε, μνήσθητί μου καὶ
ἐπίβλεψον καὶ μή με ἐκδικήσῃς ταῖς ἁμαρτίαις μου καὶ ἐν
τοῖς ἀγνοήμασίν μου καὶ τῶν πατέρων μου, οἷς ἥμαρτον

KING JAMES VERSION

11 And my wife Anna did take women's works to do.

12 And when she had sent them home to the owners, they paid her wages, and gave her also besides a kid.

13 And when it was in my house, and began to cry, I said unto her, From whence is this kid? is it not stolen? render it to the owners; for it is not lawful to eat any thing that is stolen.

14 But she replied upon me, It was given for a gift more than the wages. Howbeit I did not believe her, but bade her render it to the owners: and I was abashed at her. But she replied upon me, Where are thine alms and thy righteous deeds? behold, thou and all thy works are known.

3 Then I being grieved did weep, and in my sorrow prayed, saying,

2 O Lord, thou art just, and all thy works and all thy ways are mercy and truth, and thou judgest truly and justly for ever.

3 Remember me, and look on me, punish me not for my sins and ignorances, and *the sins of* my fathers, who have sinned before thee:

DOUAY OLD TESTAMENT

which God will give to those that never change their faith from him.

19 Now Anna his wife went daily to weaving work, and she brought home what she could get for their living by the labour of her hands.

20 Whereby it came to pass, that she received a young kid, and brought it home:

21 And when her husband heard it bleating, he said: Take heed, lest perhaps it be stolen: restore ye it to its owners, for it is not lawful for us either to eat or to touch any thing that cometh by theft.

22 At these words his wife being angry answered: It is evident thy hope is come to nothing, and thy alms now appear.

23 And with these, and other such like words she upbraided him.

3 THEN Tobias sighed, and began to pray with tears,

2 Saying: Thou art just, O Lord, and all thy judgments are just, and all thy ways mercy, and truth, and judgment:

3 And now, O Lord, think of me, and take not revenge of my sins, neither remember my offences, nor those of my parents.

KNOX TRANSLATION

God has life waiting for us if we will but keep faith with him.
19 His wife Anna went every day to work at the loom, bringing home what earnings she could; 20 and one day it was a
kid that was given her for her wages. 21 When she brought
this home, and its bleating reached her husband's ears, he
made great ado for fear it had been stolen; Nay, he said, this
must be restored to its owner; never shall it be said that we
ate stolen food, or soiled our hands with theft! 22 Fine talk,[a]
said she, but the like hopes have played thee false already;
what hast thou to shew, now, for all thy almsgiving? With
such taunts as these even his wife assailed him.[b]
3 So at last Tobias fell a-sighing, and he prayed still, but
wept as he prayed. Lord, 2 he said, thou hast right on
thy side; no award of thine but is deserved, no act of thine
but tells of mercy, of faithfulness, and of justice. 3 Yet
bethink thee, Lord, of my case; leave my sins unpunished,
my guilt, and the guilt of my parents, forgotten. 4 If we are

a These words are not in the original; they have been inserted to elucidate the train of thought, which is here much confused. It seems probable that Anna meant, 'Why should you make such a point of being honest, when Providence has given you such a poor reward for being charitable?'

b In this chapter the Hebrew and Greek versions still give the story in the first person. But here they correspond more nearly with the Vulgate Latin (and with the Aramaic text from which it was translated); the chief difference, is the omission of verses 12-18.

TODAY'S ENGLISH VERSION

11 After Ahikar left, my wife Anna had to go to work, so she took up weaving, like many other women. 12 The people she worked for would pay her when she delivered the cloth. One spring day, she cut a finished piece of cloth from the loom and took it to the people who had ordered it. They paid her the full price and also gave her a goat.

13 When Anna came home with the goat, it began to bleat. I called out, "Where did that goat come from? You stole it, didn't you? Take it straight back to its owners. It's not right to eat stolen food!"

14 "No!" she replied. "It was given to me as a gift in addition to what I got for the cloth." But I didn't believe her, and I blushed for shame for what she had done. I ordered her to return the goat to its owners, but she had the last word. "Now I see what you are really like!" she shouted. "Where is all that concern of yours for others? What about all those good deeds you used to do?"

3 I was so embarrassed and ashamed that I sighed and began to cry. Then, as I choked back my tears, I prayed:

2 "You are righteous, O Lord!
You are merciful[a] in all you do,
faithful in all your ways.
You are the judge of this world.[b]
3-4 I beg you, treat me with kindness.
Do not punish me for my sins,
not even for sins of which I am unaware.

[a] merciful; *some manuscripts add* and just. [b] You are the judge of this world; *some manuscripts have* You are always fair and just when you judge.

NEW REVISED STANDARD VERSION

11 At that time, also, my wife Anna earned money at women's work. 12 She used to send what she made to the owners and they would pay wages to her. One day, the seventh of Dystrus, when she cut off a piece she had woven and sent it to the owners, they paid her full wages and also gave her a young goat for a meal. 13 When she returned to me, the goat began to bleat. So I called her and said, "Where did you get this goat? It is surely not stolen, is it? Return it to the owners; for we have no right to eat anything stolen." 14 But she said to me, "It was given to me as a gift in addition to my wages." But I did not believe her, and told her to return it to the owners. I became flushed with anger against her over this. Then she replied to me, "Where are your acts of charity? Where are your righteous deeds? These things are known about you!"[a]

3 Then with much grief and anguish of heart I wept, and with groaning began to pray:

2 "You are righteous, O Lord,
and all your deeds are just;
all your ways are mercy and truth;
you judge the world.[b]
3 And now, O Lord, remember me
and look favorably upon me.
Do not punish me for my sins
and for my unwitting offenses
and those that my ancestors committed before you.

[a] Or *to you*; Gk *with you* [b] Other ancient authorities read *you render true and righteous judgment forever*

NEW AMERICAN BIBLE

11 At that time my wife Anna worked for hire at weaving cloth, the kind of work women do. 12 When she sent back the goods to their owners, they would pay her. Late in winter she finished the cloth and sent it back to the owners. They paid her the full salary, and also gave her a young goat for the table. 13 On entering my house the goat began to bleat. I called to my wife and said: "Where did this goat come from? Perhaps it was stolen! Give it back to its owners; we have no right to eat stolen food! 14 But she said to me, "It was given to me as a bonus over and above my wages." Yet I would not believe her; and told her to give it back to its owners. I became very angry with her over this. So she retorted: "Where are your charitable deeds now? Where are your virtuous acts? See! Your true character is finally showing itself!"

3 Grief-stricken in spirit, I groaned and wept aloud. Then with sobs I began to pray:

2 "You are righteous, O Lord,
and all your deeds are just;
All your ways are mercy and truth;
you are the judge of the world.
3 And now, O Lord, may you be mindful of me,
and look with favor upon me.
Punish me not for my sins,
nor for my inadvertent offenses,
nor for those of my fathers.

NEW JERUSALEM BIBLE

11 My wife Anna then undertook woman's work; she would spin wool and take cloth to weave; 12 she used to deliver whatever had been ordered from her and then receive payment. Now on the seventh day of the month of Dystros, she finished a piece of work and delivered it to her customers. They paid her all that was due, and into the bargain presented her with a kid for a meal. 13 When the kid came into my house, it began to bleat. I called to my wife and said, 'Where does this creature come from? Suppose it has been stolen! Let the owners have it back; we have no right to eat stolen goods'. 14 She said, 'No, it was a present given me over and above my wages.' I did not believe her, and told her to give it back to the owners (I felt deeply ashamed of her). To which, she replied, 'What about your own alms? What about your own good works? Everyone knows what return you have had for them.'

3 Then, sad at heart, I sighed and wept, and began this prayer of lamentation:

2 You are just, O Lord,
and just are all your works.
All your ways are grace and truth,
and you are the Judge of the world.

3 Therefore, Lord,
remember me, look on me.
Do not punish me for my sins
or for my needless faults
or those of my ancestors.

GREEK OLD TESTAMENT

ἐναντίον σου [4] καὶ παρήκουσα τῶν ἐντολῶν σου. καὶ ἔδωκας ἡμᾶς εἰς ἁρπαγὴν καὶ αἰχμαλωσίαν καὶ θάνατον καὶ εἰς παραβολὴν καὶ λάλημα καὶ ὀνειδισμὸν ἐν πᾶσιν τοῖς ἔθνεσιν, ἐν οἷς ἡμᾶς διεσκόρπισας. [5] καὶ νῦν πολλαί σου αἱ κρίσεις ὑπάρχουσιν ἀληθιναὶ ποιῆσαι ἐξ ἐμοῦ περὶ τῶν ἁμαρτιῶν μου, ὅτι οὐκ ἐποιήσαμεν τὰς ἐντολάς σου καὶ οὐκ ἐπορεύθημεν ἀληθινῶς ἐνώπιόν σου. [6] καὶ νῦν κατὰ τὸ ἀρεστόν σου ποίησον μετ᾽ ἐμοῦ καὶ ἐπίταξον ἀναλαβεῖν τὸ πνεῦμά μου ἐξ ἐμοῦ, ὅπως ἀπολυθῶ ἀπὸ προσώπου τῆς γῆς καὶ γένωμαι γῆ· διὸ λυσιτελεῖ μοι ἀποθανεῖν μᾶλλον ἢ ζῆν, ὅτι ὀνειδισμοὺς ψευδεῖς ἤκουσα, καὶ λύπη πολλὴ μετ᾽ ἐμοῦ. κύριε, ἐπίταξον ὅπως ἀπολυθῶ ἀπὸ τῆς ἀνάγκης ταύτης, ἀπόλυσόν με εἰς τὸν τόπον τὸν αἰώνιον καὶ μὴ ἀποστρέψῃς τὸ πρόσωπόν σου, κύριε, ἀπ᾽ ἐμοῦ· διὸ λυσιτελεῖ μοι ἀποθανεῖν μᾶλλον ἢ βλέπειν ἀνάγκην πολλὴν ἐν τῇ ζωῇ μου καὶ μὴ ἀκούειν ὀνειδισμούς.

[7] Ἐν τῇ ἡμέρᾳ ταύτῃ συνέβη Σαρρα τῇ θυγατρὶ Ραγουηλ τοῦ ἐν Ἐκβατάνοις τῆς Μηδίας καὶ αὐτὴν ἀκοῦσαι ὀνειδισμοὺς ὑπὸ μιᾶς τῶν παιδισκῶν τοῦ πατρὸς ἑαυτῆς, [8] διότι ἦν

KING JAMES VERSION

4 For they obeyed not thy commandments: wherefore thou hast delivered us for a spoil, and unto captivity, and unto death, and for a proverb of reproach to all the nations among whom we are dispersed.

5 And now thy judgments are many and true: deal with me according to my sins and my fathers': because we have not kept thy commandments, neither have walked in truth before thee.

6 Now therefore deal with me as seemeth best unto thee, and command my spirit to be taken from me, that I may be dissolved, and become earth: for it is profitable for me to die rather than to live, because I have heard false reproaches, and have much sorrow: command therefore that I may now be delivered out of this distress, and go into the everlasting place: turn not thy face away from me.

7 It came to pass the same day, that in Ecbatane a city of Media Sara the daughter of Raguel was also reproached by her father's maids;

DOUAY OLD TESTAMENT

4 For we have not obeyed thy commandments, therefore are we delivered to spoil and to captivity, and death, and are made a fable, and a reproach to all nations, amongst which thou hast scattered us.

5 And now, O Lord, great are thy judgments, because we have not done according to thy precepts, and have not walked sincerely before thee:

6 And now, O Lord, do with me according to thy will, and command my spirit to be received in peace: for it is better for me to die, than to live.

7 Now it happened on the same day, that Sara daughter of Raguel, in Rages a city of the Medes, received a reproach from one of her father's servant maids,

KNOX TRANSLATION

doomed to loss, to banishment and to death, if thou hast made us a by-word and a laughing-stock in all the countries to which thou hast banished us, it is because we have defied thy commandments; [5] it was fitting punishment, Lord, for the men who neglected thy bidding, and were half-hearted followers of thine. [6] And now, Lord, do with me as thy will is, give the word, and take my spirit to thyself in peace; for me, death is more welcome than life.[a]

[7] Now turn we to Rages[b] a city in Media, and another soul that must undergo taunts on this same day, Sara, the daughter of Raguel. It was one of her father's maid-servants that

a The Hebrew and the Greek versions are still in the first person but the substance of Tobias' prayer is the same. *b* All the other versions here have Ecbatana as the name of the Median city, 'Rages' is probably a copyist's error, cf. 1. 16 and 9. 3.

TODAY'S ENGLISH VERSION

My ancestors rebelled and disobeyed[a] your commands,
but do not punish me for their sins.
You let our people be plundered,
taken captive and killed.
You made an example of our people,
an object of contempt and disgrace
in all the nations where you scattered us.
5 You have often judged my ancestors for their sins
and punished me for mine.
We were disloyal and rejected your commands,
so our punishment has always been just.
6 "Now treat me as you please.
Take my life away and free me from this world;
let my body return to the earth.
I would be better off dead.
I am tormented by insults I don't deserve,
and weighed down with despair.
Lord, give the command—
bring all my troubles to an end,
take me to my eternal rest.
Don't reject my prayer.
I would rather die than live in misery
and face such cruel insults."

7 That same day in the city of Ecbatana in Media, it happened that Sarah, the daughter of a man named Raguel, was
insulted by one of her father's servant women. 8 Sarah had

[a] My ancestors . . . disobeyed; *some manuscripts have* I disobeyed.

NEW REVISED STANDARD VERSION

They sinned against you,
4 and disobeyed your commandments.
So you gave us over to plunder, exile, and death,
to become the talk, the byword, and an object of reproach
among all the nations among whom you have dispersed us.
5 And now your many judgments are true
in exacting penalty from me for my sins.
For we have not kept your commandments
and have not walked in accordance with truth before you.
6 So now deal with me as you will;
command my spirit to be taken from me,
so that I may be released from the face of the earth and become dust.
For it is better for me to die than to live,
because I have had to listen to undeserved insults,
and great is the sorrow within me.
Command, O Lord, that I be released from this distress;
release me to go to the eternal home,
and do not, O Lord, turn your face away from me.
For it is better for me to die
than to see so much distress in my life
and to listen to insults."

7 On the same day, at Ecbatana in Media, it also happened that Sarah, the daughter of Raguel, was reproached by

NEW AMERICAN BIBLE

"They sinned against you,
4 and disobeyed your commandments.
So you handed us over to plundering, exile, and death,
till we were an object lesson, a byword, a reproach
in all the nations among whom you scattered us.

5 "Yes, your judgments are many and true
in dealing with me as my sins
and those of my fathers deserve.
For we have not kept your commandments,
nor have we trodden the paths of truth before you.

6 "So now, deal with me as you please,
and command my life breath to be taken from me,
that I may go from the face of the earth into dust.
It is better for me to die than to live,
because I have heard insulting calumnies,
and I am overwhelmed with grief.

"Lord, command me to be delivered from such anguish;
let me go to the everlasting abode;
Lord, refuse me not.
For it is better for me to die
than to endure so much misery in life,
and to hear these insults!"

7 On the same day, at Ecbatana in Media, it so happened
that Raguel's daughter Sarah also had to listen to abuse,

NEW JERUSALEM BIBLE

4 For we have sinned against you
and broken your commandments;
and you have given us over to be plundered,
to captivity and death,
to be the talk, the laughing-stock and scorn
of all the nations among whom you have dispersed us.

5 And now all your decrees are true
when you deal with me as my faults deserve,
and those of my ancestors.
For we have neither kept your commandments
nor walked in truth before you.

6 So now, do with me as you will;
be pleased to take my life from me;
so that I may be delivered from earth
and become earth again.
Better death than life for me,
for I have endured groundless insult
and am in deepest sorrow.

Lord, be pleased
to deliver me from this affliction.
Let me go away to my everlasting home;
do not turn your face from me, O Lord.
Better death for me than life prolonged
in the face of unrelenting misery:
I can no longer bear to listen to insults.

7 It chanced on the same day that Sarah the daughter of
Raguel, who lived in Media at Ecbatana, also heard insults

GREEK OLD TESTAMENT

ἐκδεδομένη ἀνδράσιν ἑπτά, καὶ Ασμοδαῖος τὸ δαιμόνιον τὸ
πονηρὸν ἀπέκτεννεν αὐτοὺς πρὶν ἢ γενέσθαι αὐτοὺς μετ'
αὐτῆς, καθάπερ ἀποδεδειγμένον ἐστὶν ταῖς γυναιξίν. καὶ
εἶπεν αὐτῇ ἡ παιδίσκη Σὺ εἶ ἡ ἀποκτέννουσα τοὺς ἄνδρας
σου· ἰδοὺ ἤδη ἀπεκδέδοσαι ἑπτὰ ἀνδράσιν καὶ ἑνὸς αὐτῶν οὐκ
ὠνομάσθης. 9 τί ἡμᾶς μαστιγοῖς περὶ τῶν ἀνδρῶν σου, ὅτι
ἀπέθανον; βάδιζε μετ' αὐτῶν, καὶ μὴ ἴδοιμεν υἱόν σου μηδὲ
θυγατέρα εἰς τὸν αἰῶνα. 10 ἐν τῇ ἡμέρᾳ ἐκείνῃ ἐλυπήθη ἐν τῇ
ψυχῇ καὶ ἔκλαυσεν καὶ ἀναβᾶσα εἰς τὸ ὑπερῷον τοῦ πατρὸς
αὐτῆς ἠθέλησεν ἀπάγξασθαι. καὶ πάλιν ἐλογίσατο καὶ λέγει
Μήποτε ὀνειδίσωσιν τὸν πατέρα μου καὶ ἐροῦσιν αὐτῷ Μία
σοι ὑπῆρχεν θυγάτηρ ἀγαπητὴ καὶ αὐτὴ ἀπήγξατο ἀπὸ τῶν
κακῶν· καὶ κατάξω τὸ γῆρας τοῦ πατρός μου μετὰ λύπης εἰς
ᾅδου· χρησιμώτερόν μοί ἐστιν μὴ ἀπάγξασθαι, ἀλλὰ δεηθῆναι
τοῦ κυρίου ὅπως ἀποθάνω καὶ μηκέτι ὀνειδισμοὺς ἀκούσω ἐν
τῇ ζωῇ μου. 11 ἐν αὐτῷ τῷ καιρῷ διαπετάσασα τὰς χεῖρας
πρὸς τὴν θυρίδα ἐδεήθη καὶ εἶπεν Εὐλογητὸς εἶ, θεὲ ἐλεήμων,
καὶ εὐλογητὸν τὸ ὄνομά σου εἰς τοὺς αἰῶνας, καὶ εὐλογησάτωσάν σε πάντα τὰ ἔργα σου εἰς τὸν αἰῶνα. 12 καὶ νῦν ἐπὶ
σὲ τὸ πρόσωπόν μου καὶ τοὺς ὀφθαλμούς μου ἀνέβλεψα·
13 εἰπὸν ἀπολυθῆναί με ἀπὸ τῆς γῆς καὶ μὴ ἀκούειν με

KING JAMES VERSION

8 Because that she had been married to seven husbands, whom Asmodeus the evil spirit had killed, before they had lain with her. Dost thou not know, said they, that thou hast strangled thine husbands? thou hast had already seven husbands, neither wast thou named after any of them.

9 Wherefore dost thou beat us for them? if they be dead, go thy ways after them, let us never see of thee either son or daughter.

10 When she heard these things, she was very sorrowful, so that she thought to have strangled herself; and she said, I am the only daughter of my father, and if I do this, it shall be a reproach unto him, and I shall bring his old age with sorrow unto the grave.

11 Then she prayed toward the window, and said, Blessed art thou, O Lord my God, and thine holy and glorious name is blessed and honourable for ever: let all thy works praise thee for ever.

12 And now, O Lord, I set mine eyes and my face toward thee,

13 And say, Take me out of the earth, that I may hear no more the reproach.

DOUAY OLD TESTAMENT

8 Because she had been given to seven husbands, and a devil named Asmodeus had killed them, at their first going in unto her.

9 So when she reproved the maid for her fault, she answered her, saying: May we never see son, or daughter of thee upon the earth, thou murderer of thy husbands.

10 Wilt thou kill me also, as thou hast already killed seven husbands? At these words she went into an upper chamber of her house: and for three days and three nights did neither eat nor drink:

11 But continuing in prayer with tears besought God, that he would deliver her from this reproach.

12 And it came to pass on the third day, when she was making an end of her prayer, blessing the Lord,

13 She said: Blessed is thy name, O God of our fathers: who when thou hast been angry, wilt shew mercy, and in the time of tribulation forgivest the sins of them that call upon thee.

14 To thee, O Lord, I turn my face, to thee I direct my eyes.

15 I beg, O Lord, that thou loose me from the bond of this reproach, or else take me away from the earth.

KNOX TRANSLATION

taunted her; 8 and the ground of it was that she had been
married seven times, but each of her husbands in turn had
been killed, at the time of his bedding with her, by an evil
spirit that was named Asmodaeus. 9 This maid, then, upon
being reproved for some fault, had answered, God send we
never see son or daughter of thine brought to light!
Murderess, where are those husbands of thine? 10 Wouldst
thou make as short work with me as thou didst with those
seven? At that, Sara withdrew to an upper room of the
house, and for three days and nights would neither eat nor
drink; 11 all this time she spent in prayer, begging with tears
that God would free her of the suspicion.
12 And at last on the third day, her time of prayer ended,
she blessed the name of the Lord after this fashion:
13 Blessed is thy name, O God of our fathers, who, though
thy anger be roused, shewest mercy still, who dost pardon
the sinner that cries out to thee in time of need! 14 To thee,
Lord, I turn; on thee my eyes are fixed; 15 and, Lord, my
prayer is that thou wouldst either rid me of this clogging suspicion, or else take me away from earth. 16 Thou, Lord, canst

TODAY'S ENGLISH VERSION

been married seven times, but the evil demon, Asmodeus,
killed each husband before the marriage could be consummated. The servant woman said to Sarah, "You husband
killer! Look at you! You've already had seven husbands, but
not one of them lived long enough to give you a son.[a] 9 Why
should you take it out on us? Why don't you go and join
your dead husbands? I hope we never see a child of yours!"
10 Sarah was so depressed that she burst into tears and
went upstairs determined to hang herself. But when she
thought it over, she said to herself, "No, I won't do it! People
would insult my father and say, 'You had only one child, a
daughter whom you loved dearly, but she hanged herself
because she felt so miserable.' Such grief would bring my
gray-haired father to his grave, and I would be responsible. I
won't kill myself; I'll just beg the Lord to let me die. Then I
won't have to listen to those insults any longer!"
11 Then Sarah stood by the window, raised her arms in
prayer, and said,

"God of mercy, worthy of our praise,
may your name always be honored,
may all your creation praise you forever.
12 "Lord, I look to you for help.
13 Speak the word and set me free from this life;
then I will no longer have to hear these insults.

[a] but . . . son; *some manuscripts have* but it hasn't done you a bit of good.

NEW REVISED STANDARD VERSION

one of her father's maids. 8 For she had been married to
seven husbands, and the wicked demon Asmodeus had killed
each of them before they had been with her as is customary
for wives. So the maid said to her, "You are the one who
kills[a] your husbands! See, you have already been married to
seven husbands and have not borne the name of[b] a single
one of them. 9 Why do you beat us? Because your husbands
are dead? Go with them! May we never see a son or daughter
of yours!"
10 On that day she was grieved in spirit and wept. When
she had gone up to her father's upper room, she intended to
hang herself. But she thought it over and said, "Never shall
they reproach my father, saying to him, 'You had only one
beloved daughter but she hanged herself because of her distress.' And I shall bring my father in his old age down in sorrow to Hades. It is better for me not to hang myself, but to
pray the Lord that I may die and not listen to these reproaches anymore." 11 At that same time, with hands outstretched
toward the window, she prayed and said,
"Blessed are you, merciful God!
Blessed is your name forever;
let all your works praise you forever.
12 And now, Lord,[c] I turn my face to you,
and raise my eyes toward you.
13 Command that I be released from the earth
and not listen to such reproaches any more.

[a] Other ancient authorities read *strangles* [b] Other ancient authorities read *have had no benefit from* [c] Other ancient authorities lack *Lord*

NEW AMERICAN BIBLE

from one of her father's maids. 8 For she had been married
to seven husbands, but the wicked demon Asmodeus killed
them off before they could have intercourse with her, as it is
prescribed for wives. So the maid said to her: "You are the
one who strangles your husbands! Look at you! You have
already been married seven times, but you have had no joy
with any one of your husbands. 9 Why do you beat us?
Because your husbands are dead? Then why not join them!
May we never see a son or daughter of yours!"
10 That day she was deeply grieved in spirit. She went in
tears to an upstairs room in her father's house with the
intention of hanging herself. But she reconsidered, saying to
herself: "No! People would level this insult against my
father: 'You had only one beloved daughter, but she hanged
herself because of ill fortune!' And thus would I cause my
father in his old age to go down to the nether world laden
with sorrow. It is far better for me not to hang myself, but to
beg the Lord to have me die, so that I need no longer live to
hear such insults."
11 At that time, then, she spread out her hands, and facing
the window, poured out this prayer:

"Blessed are you, O Lord, merciful God!
Forever blessed and honored is your holy name;
may all your works forever bless you.
12 And now, O Lord, to you I turn my face
and raise my eyes.
13 Bid me to depart from the earth,
never again to hear such insults.

NEW JERUSALEM BIBLE

from one of her father's maids. 8 For she had been given in
marriage seven times, and Asmodeus, the worst of demons,
had killed her bridegrooms one after another before ever they
had slept with her as man with wife. The servant-girl said,
'Yes, you kill your bridegrooms yourself. That makes seven
already to whom you have been given, and you have not
once been in luck yet. 9 Just because your bridegrooms have
died, that is no reason for punishing us. Go and join them,
and may we be spared the sight of any child of yours!'
10 That day, she grieved, she sobbed, and she went up to her
father's room intending to hang herself. But then she
thought, 'Suppose they were to blame my father! They would
say, "You had an only daughter whom you loved, and now
she has hanged herself for grief." I cannot cause my father a
sorrow which would bring down his old age to the dwelling
of the dead. I should do better not to hang myself, but to beg
the Lord to let me die and not live to hear any more insults.'
11 And at this, by the window, with outstretched arms she
said this prayer:

You are blessed, O God of mercy!
May your name be blessed for ever,
and may all things you have made
bless you everlastingly.

12 And now I turn my face
and I raise my eyes to you.
13 Let your word deliver me from earth;
I can hear myself insulted no longer.

GREEK OLD TESTAMENT

μηκέτι ὀνειδισμούς. [14] σὺ γινώσκεις, δέσποτα, ὅτι καθαρά εἰμι ἀπὸ πάσης ἀκαθαρσίας ἀνδρὸς [15] καὶ οὐχὶ ἐμόλυνά μου τὸ ὄνομα καὶ οὐδὲ τὸ ὄνομα τοῦ πατρός μου ἐν τῇ γῇ τῆς αἰχμαλωσίας μου. μονογενής εἰμι τῷ πατρί μου, καὶ οὐχ ὑπάρχει αὐτῷ ἕτερον τέκνον, ἵνα κληρονομήσῃ αὐτόν, οὐδὲ ἀδελφὸς αὐτῷ ἐγγὺς οὔτε συγγενὴς αὐτῷ ὑπάρχει, ἵνα συντηρήσω ἐμαυτὴν αὐτῷ γυναῖκα. ἤδη ἀπώλοντό μοι ἑπτά, καὶ ἵνα τί μοί ἐστιν ἔτι ζῆν; καὶ εἰ μή σοι δοκεῖ ἀποκτεῖναί με, κύριε, νῦν εἰσάκουσον ὀνειδισμόν μου.

[16] Ἐν αὐτῷ τῷ καιρῷ εἰσηκούσθη ἡ προσευχὴ ἀμφοτέρων ἐνώπιον τῆς δόξης τοῦ θεοῦ, [17] καὶ ἀπεστάλη Ραφαηλ ἰάσασθαι τοὺς δύο, Τωβιν ἀπολῦσαι τὰ λευκώματα ἀπὸ τῶν ὀφθαλμῶν αὐτοῦ, ἵνα ἴδῃ τοῖς ὀφθαλμοῖς τὸ φῶς τοῦ θεοῦ, καὶ Σαρραν τὴν Ραγουηλ δοῦναι αὐτὴν Τωβια τῷ υἱῷ Τωβιθ γυναῖκα καὶ λῦσαι Ασμοδαιον τὸ δαιμόνιον τὸ πονηρὸν ἀπ᾽ αὐτῆς, διότι Τωβια ἐπιβάλλει κληρονομῆσαι αὐτὴν παρὰ πάντας τοὺς θέλοντας λαβεῖν αὐτήν. ἐν ἐκείνῳ τῷ καιρῷ ἐπέστρεψεν Τωβιθ ἀπὸ τῆς αὐλῆς εἰς τὸν οἶκον αὐτοῦ καὶ Σαρρα ἡ τοῦ Ραγουηλ καὶ αὐτὴ κατέβη ἐκ τοῦ ὑπερῴου.

KING JAMES VERSION

14 Thou knowest, Lord, that I am pure from all sin with man,

15 And that I never polluted my name, nor the name of my father, in the land of my captivity: I am the only daughter of my father, neither hath he any child to be his heir, neither any near kinsman, nor any son of his alive, to whom I may keep myself for a wife: my seven husbands are already dead; and why should I live? but if it please not thee that I should die, command some regard to be had of me, and pity taken of me, that I hear no more reproach.

16 So the prayers of them both were heard before the majesty of the great God.

17 And Raphael was sent to heal them both, that is, to scale away the whiteness of Tobit's eyes, and to give Sara the daughter of Raguel for a wife to Tobias the son of Tobit; and to bind Asmodeus the evil spirit; because she belonged to Tobias by right of inheritance. The selfsame time came Tobit home, and entered into his house, and Sara the daughter of Raguel came down from her upper chamber.

DOUAY OLD TESTAMENT

16 Thou knowest, O Lord, that I never coveted a husband, and have kept my soul clean from all lust.

17 Never have I joined myself with them that play: neither have I made myself partaker with them that walk in lightness.

18 But a husband I consented to take, with thy fear, not with my lust.

19 And either I was unworthy of them, or they perhaps were not worthy of me: because perhaps thou hast kept me for another man.

20 For thy counsel is not in man's power.

21 But this every one is sure of that worshippeth thee, that his life, if it be under trial, shall be crowned: and if it be under tribulation, it shall be delivered: and if it be under correction, it shall be allowed to come to thy mercy.

22 For thou art not delighted in our being lost: because after a storm thou makest a calm, and after tears and weeping thou pourest in joyfulness.

23 Be thy name, O God of Israel, blessed for ever.

24 At that time the prayers of them both were heard in the sight of the glory of the most high God:

25 And the holy angel of the Lord, Raphael was sent to heal them both, whose prayers at one time were rehearsed in the sight of the Lord.

KNOX TRANSLATION

bear me witness that I lusted never after man; still have I guarded my soul from shameful desire, [17] nor kept company with the wanton, nor cast in my lot with the lovers of dalliance. [18] If I consented to take a husband, law of thine was my rule, not lust of mine. [19] It seems I was unworthy of these men's love, or perhaps they of mine; it may be thou wast reserving me for another husband; [20] thy designs are beyond our human reach. [21] But this at least all thy true worshippers know; never was a life of trials but had its crown; never distress from which thou couldst not save; never punishment but left a gateway to thy mercy. [22] Not thine to plot eagerly for our undoing; the storm passes, and thou grantest clear weather again; tears and sighs are over, and thou fillest the cup with rejoicing; blessed be thy name, [23] God of Israel, for ever! [a]

[24] Two prayers that day reached the bright presence of the most high God; [25] and Raphael, one of the Lord's holy angels, was sent out, bearing common deliverance to the suppliants of a single hour.

a The prayer of Sara is given in a quite different form by the other versions, including our present Aramaic text. From this point onwards, all the versions tell the story in the third person.

TODAY'S ENGLISH VERSION

14 You know, O Lord, that I'm still a virgin;
I have never been defiled by a man.
15 Never have I disgraced myself or my father's name,
as long as we have lived in this land of exile.
My father has no other child to be his heir,
and there is no relative[a] whom I can marry.
I have already lost seven husbands,
so why should I live any longer?
But if it is not your will to take my life,
at least show mercy to me.
Don't let me hear those insults again!"[b]

16 As Tobit and Sarah were praying, God in heaven heard
their prayers 17 and sent his angel Raphael to help them. He
was sent to remove the white film from Tobit's eyes, so that
he could see again, and to arrange a marriage between Sarah
and Tobit's son Tobias, who, as her cousin, had the right to
marry her. Raphael was also ordered to expel the demon
Asmodeus from Sarah. At the very moment that Tobit went
back into his house from the courtyard, Sarah, in her house
in Ecbatana, was coming downstairs.

[a] RELATIVE: *In Israel it was customary to marry within one's own tribe.*
[b] at least . . . again; *some manuscripts have* at least listen to my complaint.

NEW REVISED STANDARD VERSION

14 You know, O Master, that I am innocent
of any defilement with a man,
15 and that I have not disgraced my name
or the name of my father in the land of my exile.
I am my father's only child;
he has no other child to be his heir;
and he has no close relative or other kindred
for whom I should keep myself as wife.
Already seven husbands of mine have died.
Why should I still live?
But if it is not pleasing to you, O Lord, to take my life,
hear me in my disgrace."

16 At that very moment, the prayers of both of them were
heard in the glorious presence of God. 17 So Raphael was
sent to heal both of them: Tobit, by removing the white films
from his eyes, so that he might see God's light with his eyes;
and Sarah, daughter of Raguel, by giving her in marriage to
Tobias son of Tobit, and by setting her free from the wicked
demon Asmodeus. For Tobias was entitled to have her before
all others who had desired to marry her. At the same time
that Tobit returned from the courtyard into his house, Sarah
daughter of Raguel came down from her upper room.

NEW AMERICAN BIBLE

14 "You know, O Master, that I am innocent
of any impure act with a man,
15 And that I have never defiled my own name
or my father's name in the land of my exile.

"I am my father's only daughter,
and he has no other child to make his heir,
Nor does he have a close kinsman or other relative
whom I might bide my time to marry.
I have already lost seven husbands;
why then should I live any longer?
But if it please you, Lord, not to slay me,
look favorably upon me and have pity on me;
never again let me hear these insults!"

16 At that very time, the prayer of these two suppliants was
heard in the glorious presence of Almighty God. 17 So
Raphael was sent to heal them both: to remove the cataracts
from Tobit's eyes, so that he might again see God's sunlight;
and to marry Raguel's daughter Sarah to Tobit's son Tobiah,
and then drive the wicked demon Asmodeus from her. For
Tobiah had the right to claim her before any other who might
wish to marry her.

In the very moment that Tobit returned from the courtyard
to his house, Raguel's daughter Sarah came downstairs from
her room.

NEW JERUSALEM BIBLE

14 O Lord, you know
that I have remained pure;
no man has touched me;
15 I have not dishonoured your name
or my father's name
in this land of exile.

I am my father's only daughter,
he has no other child as heir;
he has no brother at his side,
nor has he any kinsman left
for whom I ought to keep myself.

I have lost seven husbands already;
why should I live any longer?
If it does not please you to take my life,
then look on me with pity;
I can no longer bear to hear myself defamed.

16 This time the prayer of each of them found favour before
the glory of God, 17 and Raphael was sent to bring remedy to
them both. He was to take the white spots from the eyes of
Tobit, so that he might see God's light with his own eyes;
and he was to give Sarah the daughter of Raguel as bride to
Tobias son of Tobit, and to rid her of Asmodeus, that worst
of demons. For it was to Tobias before all other suitors that
she belonged by right. Tobit was coming back from the courtyard into the house at the same moment as Sarah the daughter of Raguel was coming down from the upper room.

GREEK OLD TESTAMENT

4 Ἐν τῇ ἡμέρᾳ ἐκείνῃ ἐμνήσθη Τωβιθ τοῦ ἀργυρίου, ὃ
παρέθετο Γαβαήλῳ ἐν Ῥάγοις τῆς Μηδίας, 2 καὶ εἶπεν
ἐν τῇ καρδίᾳ αὐτοῦ Ἰδοὺ ἐγὼ ᾐτησάμην θάνατον· τί οὐχὶ
καλῶ Τωβιαν τὸν υἱόν μου καὶ ὑποδείξω αὐτῷ περὶ τοῦ ἀργυρίου τούτου πρὶν ἀποθανεῖν με; 3 καὶ ἐκάλεσεν Τωβιαν
τὸν υἱὸν αὐτοῦ, καὶ ἦλθεν πρὸς αὐτόν· καὶ εἶπεν αὐτῷ Θάψον
με καλῶς. καὶ τίμα τὴν μητέρα σου καὶ μὴ ἐγκαταλίπῃς
αὐτὴν πάσας τὰς ἡμέρας τῆς ζωῆς αὐτῆς καὶ ποίει τὸ
ἀρεστὸν ἐνώπιον αὐτῆς καὶ μὴ λυπήσῃς τὸ πνεῦμα αὐτῆς ἐν
παντὶ πράγματι. 4 μνήσθητι αὐτῆς, παιδίον, ὅτι κινδύνους
πολλοὺς ἑώρακεν ἐπὶ σοὶ ἐν τῇ κοιλίᾳ αὐτῆς. καὶ ὅταν ἀποθάνῃ, θάψον αὐτὴν παρ᾽ ἐμοὶ ἐν ἑνὶ τάφῳ. 5 καὶ πάσας τὰς
ἡμέρας σου, παιδίον, τοῦ κυρίου μνημόνευε καὶ μὴ θελήσῃς
ἁμαρτεῖν καὶ παραβῆναι τὰς ἐντολὰς αὐτοῦ· δικαιοσύνας
ποίει πάσας τὰς ἡμέρας τῆς ζωῆς σου καὶ μὴ πορευθῇς ταῖς
ὁδοῖς τῆς ἀδικίας. 6 διότι οἱ ποιοῦντες ἀλήθειαν εὐοδωθή-
σονται ἐν τοῖς ἔργοις αὐτῶν. 7 καὶ πᾶσιν τοῖς ποιοῦσιν
δικαιοσύνην ⟦BA:[a] ἐκ τῶν ὑπαρχόντων σοι ποίει ἐλεημοσύνην, καὶ μὴ φθονεσάτω σου ὁ ὀφθαλμὸς ἐν τῷ ποιεῖν σε
ἐλεημοσύνην· μὴ ἀποστρέψῃς τὸ πρόσωπόν σου ἀπὸ παντὸς
πτωχοῦ, καὶ ἀπὸ σοῦ οὐ μὴ ἀποστραφῇ τὸ πρόσωπον τοῦ
θεοῦ. 8 ὡς σοὶ ὑπάρχει, κατὰ τὸ πλῆθος ποίησον ἐξ αὐτῶν
ἐλεημοσύνην· ἐὰν ὀλίγον σοι ὑπάρχῃ, κατὰ τὸ ὀλίγον μὴ
φοβοῦ ποιεῖν ἐλεημοσύνην· 9 θέμα γὰρ ἀγαθὸν θησαυρίζεις
σεαυτῷ εἰς ἡμέραν ἀνάγκης. 10 διότι ἐλεημοσύνη ἐκ θανάτου ῥύεται καὶ οὐκ ἐᾷ εἰσελθεῖν εἰς τὸ σκότος. 11 δῶρον γὰρ
ἀγαθόν ἐστιν ἐλεημοσύνη πᾶσι τοῖς ποιοῦσιν αὐτὴν ἐνώπιον

a Verses 7b–19a, missing in ℵ (S), are supplemented from B and A.

KING JAMES VERSION

4 In that day Tobit remembered the money which he had committed to Gabael in Rages of Media,

2 And said with himself, I have wished for death; wherefore do I not call for my son Tobias, that I may signify to him *of the money* before I die?

3 And when he had called him, he said, My son, when I am dead, bury me; and despise not thy mother, but honour her all the days of thy life, and do that which shall please her, and grieve her not.

4 Remember, my son, that she saw many dangers for thee, *when thou wast* in her womb; and when she is dead, bury her by me in one grave.

5 My son, be mindful of the Lord our God all thy days, and let not thy will be set to sin, or to transgress his commandments: do uprightly all thy life long, and follow not the ways of unrighteousness.

6 For if thou deal truly, thy doings shall prosperously succeed to thee, and to all them that live justly.

7 Give alms of thy substance; and when thou givest alms, let not thine eye be envious, neither turn thy face from any poor, and the face of God shall not be turned away from thee.

8 If thou hast abundance, give alms accordingly: if thou have but a little, be not afraid to give according to that little:

9 For thou layest up a good treasure for thyself against the day of necessity.

10 Because that alms do deliver from death, and suffereth not to come into darkness.

11 For alms is a good gift unto all that give it in the sight of the most High.

DOUAY OLD TESTAMENT

4 THEREFORE when Tobias thought that his prayer was heard that he might die, he called to him Tobias his son,

2 And said to him: Hear, my son, the words of my mouth, and lay them as a foundation in thy heart.

3 When God shall take my soul, thou shalt bury my body: and thou shalt honour thy mother all the days of her life:

4 For thou must be mindful what and how great perils she suffered for thee in her womb.

5 And when she also shall have ended the time of her life, bury her by me.

6 And all the days of thy life have God in thy mind: and take heed thou never consent to sin, nor transgress the commandments of the Lord our God.

7 Give alms out of thy substance, and turn not away thy face from any poor person: for so it shall come to pass that the face of the Lord shall not be turned from thee.

8 According to thy ability be merciful.

9 If thou have much give abundantly: if thou have little, take care even so to bestow willingly a little.

10 For thus thou storest up to thyself a good reward for the day of necessity.

11 For alms deliver from all sin, and from death, and will not suffer the soul to go into darkness.

12 Alms shall be a great confidence before the most high God, to all them that give it.

KNOX TRANSLATION

4 And now, thinking that his prayer for death was to be
granted, the elder Tobias called his son to him 2 and
gave him a charge; Let these rules of mine, said he, be the
frame-work of thy life, my son.
3 When God takes my soul to himself, give this body of
mine burial, and give thy mother her due[a] while her life
lasts; 4 do not forget what hazard she underwent to bear
thee in her womb; 5 and when she, too, has lived out her
allotted span of years, bury her at my side. 6 And do thou,
while thou hast life, think ever upon God, nor lend thyself to
any sinful design, nor leave the commandments of the Lord
our God unfulfilled. 7 Use thy wealth in giving of alms;
never turn thy back on any man who is in need, and the
Lord, in thy own need, will have eyes for thee. 8 Shew to
others what kindness thy means allow, 9 giving much, if
much is thine, if thou hast little, cheerfully sharing that little. 10 To do this is but to lay up a store against the day of
distress; 11 alms-deeds were ever a sovereign way of escape
from guilt and death, a bar against the soul's passage into
darkness; 12 none has less to fear when he stands before the
most high God than he who does them.

a Literally, 'honour', but this was, according to St Jerome, a regular idiom among the Jews.

TODAY'S ENGLISH VERSION

4 That same day, Tobit remembered the money that he
had left with Gabael at Rages in Media. 2He thought to
himself, "Now that I have asked God to let me die, I should
call my son Tobias and tell him about the money."
3-4So Tobit called Tobias and said to him, "Son, when I die,
give me a proper burial. And after I'm gone, show respect to
your mother. Take care of her for the rest of her life, and
when she dies, bury her beside me. Remember, she risked
her life to bring you into this world, so try to make her happy
and never do anything that would worry her.
5"Every day of your life, keep the Lord our God in mind.
Never sin deliberately or disobey any of his commands.
Always do what is right and never get involved in anything
evil. 6Be honest, and you will succeed in whatever you do.
7"Give generously to anyone who faithfully obeys God.[a]
If you are stingy in giving to the poor, God will be stingy in
giving to you. 8Give according to what you have. The more
you have, the more you should give. Even if you have only
a little, be sure to give something. 9This is as good as
money saved. You will have your reward in a time of trouble. 10-11Taking care of the poor is the kind of offering that
pleases God in heaven. Do this, and you will be kept safe
from the dark world of the dead.

[a] *The translation of verses 7b-19b, accidentally omitted in the Greek manuscript that this translation normally follows, is based on other Greek manuscripts.*

NEW REVISED STANDARD VERSION

4 That same day Tobit remembered the money that he had
left in trust with Gabael at Rages in Media, 2and he said
to himself, "Now I have asked for death. Why do I not call
my son Tobias and explain to him about the money before I
die?" 3Then he called his son Tobias, and when he came to
him he said, "My son, when I die,[a] give me a proper burial.
Honor your mother and do not abandon her all the days of
her life. Do whatever pleases her, and do not grieve her in
anything. 4Remember her, my son, because she faced many
dangers for you while you were in her womb. And when she
dies, bury her beside me in the same grave.
5 "Revere the Lord all your days, my son, and refuse to sin
or to transgress his commandments. Live uprightly all the
days of your life, and do not walk in the ways of wrongdoing;
6for those who act in accordance with truth will prosper in all
their activities. To all those who practice righteousness[b] 7give
alms from your possessions, and do not let your eye begrudge
the gift when you make it. Do not turn your face away from
anyone who is poor, and the face of God will not be turned
away from you. 8If you have many possessions, make your
gift from them in proportion; if few, do not be afraid to give
according to the little you have. 9So you will be laying up a
good treasure for yourself against the day of necessity. 10For
almsgiving delivers from death and keeps you from going into
the Darkness. 11Indeed, almsgiving, for all who practice it, is
an excellent offering in the presence of the Most High.

a Lat *b* The text of codex Sinaiticus goes directly from verse 6 to verse 19, reading *To those who practice righteousness 19the Lord will give good counsel.* In order to fill the lacuna verses 7 to 18 are derived from other ancient authorities

NEW AMERICAN BIBLE

4 That same day Tobit remembered the money he had
deposited with Gabael at Rages in Media, and he
thought, 2"Now that I have asked for death, why should I
not call my son Tobiah and let him know about this money
before I die?" 3So he called his son Tobiah; and when he
came, he said to him: "My son, when I die, give me a decent
burial. Honor your mother, and do not abandon her as long
as she lives. Do whatever pleases her, and do not grieve her
spirit in any way. 4Remember, my son, that she went
through many trials for your sake while you were in her
womb. And when she dies, bury her in the same grave with
me.
5"Through all your days, my son, keep the Lord in mind,
and suppress every desire to sin or to break his commandments. Perform good works all the days of your life, and do
not tread the paths of wrongdoing. 6For if you are steadfast
in your service, your good works will bring success, not only
to you, but also to all those who live uprightly.
7"Give alms from your possessions. Do not turn your face
away from any of the poor, and God's face will not be turned
away from you. 8Son, give alms in proportion to what you
own. If you have great wealth, give alms out of your abundance; if you have but little, distribute even some of that.
But do not hesitate to give alms; 9you will be storing up a
goodly treasure for yourself against the day of adversity.
10Almsgiving frees one from death, and keeps one from
going into the dark abode. 11Alms are a worthy offering in
the sight of the Most High for all who give them.

NEW JERUSALEM BIBLE

4 The same day Tobit remembered the silver that he had
left with Gabael at Rhages in Media 2and thought, 'I
have come to the point of praying for death; I should do well
to call my son Tobias and tell him about the money before I
die.' 3He summoned his son Tobias and told him, 'When I
die, give me an honourable burial. Honour your mother, and
never abandon her all the days of your life. Do all that she
wants, and give her no reason for sorrow. 4Remember, my
child, all the risks she ran for your sake when you were in
her womb. And when she dies, bury her at my side in the
same grave.
5'My child, be faithful to the Lord all your days. Never
entertain the will to sin or to transgress his laws. Do good
works all the days of your life, never follow ways that are
not upright; 6for if you act in truthfulness, you will be successful in all your actions, as everyone is who practises what
is upright.
7'Set aside part of your goods for almsgiving. Never turn
your face from the poor and God will never turn his from
you. 8Measure your alms by what you have; if you have
much, give more; if you have little, do not be afraid to give
less in alms. 9So doing, you will lay up for yourself a great
treasure for the day of necessity. 10For almsgiving delivers
from death and saves people from passing down to darkness.
11Almsgiving is a most effective offering for all those who do
it in the presence of the Most High.

GREEK OLD TESTAMENT

τοῦ ὑψίστου. 12 πρόσεχε σεαυτῷ, παιδίον, ἀπὸ πάσης
πορνείας καὶ γυναῖκα πρῶτον λαβὲ ἀπὸ τοῦ σπέρματος τῶν
πατέρων σου· μὴ λάβῃς γυναῖκα ἀλλοτρίαν, ἣ οὐκ ἔστιν ἐκ
τῆς φυλῆς τοῦ πατρός σου, διότι υἱοὶ προφητῶν ἐσμεν. Νωε,
Αβρααμ, Ισαακ, Ιακωβ οἱ πατέρες ἡμῶν ἀπὸ τοῦ αἰῶνος
μνήσθητι, παιδίον, ὅτι οὗτοι πάντες ἔλαβον γυναῖκας ἐκ τῶν
ἀδελφῶν αὐτῶν καὶ εὐλογήθησαν ἐν τοῖς τέκνοις αὐτῶν, καὶ
τὸ σπέρμα αὐτῶν κληρονομήσει γῆν. 13 καὶ νῦν, παιδίον,
ἀγάπα τοὺς ἀδελφούς σου καὶ μὴ ὑπερηφανεύου τῇ καρδίᾳ
σου ἀπὸ τῶν ἀδελφῶν σου καὶ τῶν υἱῶν καὶ θυγατέρων τοῦ
λαοῦ σου λαβεῖν σεαυτῷ ἐξ αὐτῶν γυναῖκα, διότι ἐν τῇ
ὑπερηφανίᾳ ἀπώλεια καὶ ἀκαταστασία πολλή, καὶ ἐν τῇ
ἀχρειότητι ἐλάττωσις καὶ ἔνδεια μεγάλη· ἡ γὰρ ἀχρειότης
μήτηρ ἐστὶν τοῦ λιμοῦ. 14 μισθὸς παντὸς ἀνθρώπου, ὃς ἐὰν
ἐργάσηται, παρὰ σοὶ μὴ αὐλισθήτω, ἀλλὰ ἀπόδος αὐτῷ
παραυτίκα, καὶ ἐὰν δουλεύσῃς τῷ θεῷ, ἀποδοθήσεταί σοι.
πρόσεχε σεαυτῷ, παιδίον, ἐν πᾶσι τοῖς ἔργοις σου καὶ ἴσθι
πεπαιδευμένος ἐν πάσῃ ἀναστροφῇ σου. 15 καὶ ὃ μισεῖς,
μηδενὶ ποιήσῃς. οἶνον εἰς μέθην μὴ πίῃς, καὶ μὴ πορευθήτω
μετὰ σοῦ μέθη ἐν τῇ ὁδῷ σου. 16 ἐκ τοῦ ἄρτου σου δίδου
πεινῶντι καὶ ἐκ τῶν ἱματίων σου τοῖς γυμνοῖς. πᾶν, ὃ ἐὰν
περισσεύσῃ σοι, ποίει ἐλεημοσύνην, καὶ μὴ φθονεσάτω σου ὁ
ὀφθαλμὸς ἐν τῷ ποιεῖν σε ἐλεημοσύνην. 17 ἔκχεον τοὺς
ἄρτους σου ἐπὶ τὸν τάφον τῶν δικαίων καὶ μὴ δῷς τοῖς
ἁμαρτωλοῖς. 18 συμβουλίαν παρὰ παντὸς φρονίμου ζήτησον
καὶ μὴ καταφρονήσῃς ἐπὶ πάσης συμβουλίας χρησίμης.
19 καὶ ἐν παντὶ καιρῷ εὐλόγει κύριον τὸν θεὸν καὶ παρ' αὐτοῦ
αἴτησον ὅπως αἱ ὁδοί σου εὐθεῖαι γένωνται, καὶ πᾶσαι αἱ

KING JAMES VERSION

12 Beware of all whoredom, my son, and chiefly take a wife of the seed of thy fathers, and take not a strange woman to wife, which is not of thy father's tribe: for we are the children of the prophets, Noe, Abraham, Isaac, and Jacob: remember, my son, that our fathers from the beginning, even that they all married wives of their own kindred, and were blessed in their children, and their seed shall inherit the land.

13 Now therefore, my son, love thy brethren, and despise not in thy heart thy brethren, the sons and daughters of thy people, in *not* taking a wife of them: for in pride is destruction and much trouble, and in lewdness is decay and great want: for lewdness is the mother of famine.

14 Let not the wages of any man, which hath wrought for thee, tarry with thee, but give him it out of hand: for if thou serve God, he will also repay thee: be circumspect, my son, in all things thou doest, and be wise in all thy conversation.

15 Do that to no man which thou hatest: drink not wine to make thee drunken: neither let drunkenness go with thee in thy journey.

16 Give of thy bread to the hungry, and of thy garments to them that are naked; and according to thine abundance give alms; and let not thine eye be envious, when thou givest alms.

17 Pour out thy bread on the burial of the just, but give nothing to the wicked.

18 Ask counsel of all that are wise, and despise not any counsel that is profitable.

19 Bless the Lord thy God alway, and desire of him that thy ways may be directed, and that all thy paths and

DOUAY OLD TESTAMENT

13 Take heed to keep thyself, my son, from all fornication, and beside thy wife never endure to know a crime.

14 Never suffer pride to reign in thy mind, or in thy words: for from it all perdition took its beginning.

15 If any man hath done any work for thee, immediately pay him his hire, and let not the wages of thy hired servant stay with thee at all.

16 See thou never do to another what thou wouldst hate to have done to thee by another.

17 Eat thy bread with the hungry and the needy, and with thy garments cover the naked.

18 Lay out thy bread, and thy wine upon the burial of a just man, and do not eat and drink thereof with the wicked.

19 Seek counsel always of a wise man.

20 Bless God at all times: and desire of him to direct thy ways, and that all thy counsels may abide in him.

KNOX TRANSLATION

13 Keep clear, my son, of fornication; save for thy wife,
never let woman's name be linked with thine. 14 In thought
and word of thine, pride must never bear rule; thence it was
all our undoing came. 15 There and then pay thy workman
his wages; do not let the hire he has earned remain in thy
keeping; 16 never use another as thou wert loth thyself to be
used. 17 Share thy bread with the hungry and the poor; in
thy garments let the naked go clad. 18 Bestow thy meat and
thy drink upon a just man's burying, never share them with
sinners.[a] 19 Still take a wise man's counsel over thy doings;
20 but praise God all the while, and ask him to guide thy
paths aright; let all thy designs repose in him.

a The meaning of this verse is very obscure, and some think there is a corruption in the text. The versions have, not 'bestow', but 'pour out'; it was a common heathen practice to pour libations of wine over the tombs of the dead, but the mention of bread would in that case be confusing, and the Septuagint Greek has simply 'Pour out thy loaves' without any mention of wine. It is possible there is some reference to providing entertainment for the mourners at a pauper funeral, but the allusion seems far-fetched. For the custom of providing the mourners at a funeral with food, cf. Jer. 16. 8.

TODAY'S ENGLISH VERSION

12 "Son, be on your guard against prostitutes. Above all, marry a woman of our tribe, because we are descendants of the prophets. Do not marry anyone who is not related to us. Remember that Noah, Abraham, Isaac and Jacob, our earliest ancestors, all married relatives. God blessed them with children, and so their descendants will inherit the land of Israel. 13 Son, be loyal to your own relatives. Don't be too proud to marry one of them. Such pride leads to terrible frustration and ruin, just as laziness brings on severe poverty and causes starvation.

14 "Pay your workers each day; never keep back their wages overnight. Honor God in this way, and he will reward you. Behave properly at all times. 15 Never do to anyone else anything that you would not want someone to do to you.

"Do not drink so much wine that you get drunk, and do not let drinking become a habit.

16 "Give food to the hungry and clothes to people in need. If you are prosperous, give generously, and do it gladly!

17 "When one of God's faithful people has died, prepare food for the family,[a] but never do this when someone evil dies.

18 "Take the advice of sensible people, and never treat any useful advice lightly.

19 "Take advantage of every opportunity to praise the Lord your God. Ask him to make you prosper in whatever you set

[a] prepare . . . family; *or* put food on his grave.

NEW REVISED STANDARD VERSION

12 "Beware, my son, of every kind of fornication. First of all, marry a woman from among the descendants of your ancestors; do not marry a foreign woman, who is not of your father's tribe; for we are the descendants of the prophets. Remember, my son, that Noah, Abraham, Isaac, and Jacob, our ancestors of old, all took wives from among their kindred. They were blessed in their children, and their posterity will inherit the land. 13 So now, my son, love your kindred, and in your heart do not disdain your kindred, the sons and daughters of your people, by refusing to take a wife for yourself from among them. For in pride there is ruin and great confusion. And in idleness there is loss and dire poverty, because idleness is the mother of famine.

14 "Do not keep over until the next day the wages of those who work for you, but pay them at once. If you serve God you will receive payment. Watch yourself, my son, in everything you do, and discipline yourself in all your conduct. 15 And what you hate, do not do to anyone. Do not drink wine to excess or let drunkenness go with you on your way. 16 Give some of your food to the hungry, and some of your clothing to the naked. Give all your surplus as alms, and do not let your eye begrudge your giving of alms. 17 Place your bread on the grave of the righteous, but give none to sinners. 18 Seek advice from every wise person and do not despise any useful counsel. 19 At all times bless the Lord God, and ask him that your ways may be made straight and that all your paths and

NEW AMERICAN BIBLE

12 "Be on your guard, son, against every form of immorality, and above all, marry a woman of the lineage of your forefathers. Do not marry a stranger who is not of your father's tribe, because we are sons of the prophets. My boy, keep in mind Noah, Abraham, Isaac, and Jacob, our fathers from of old; all of them took wives from among their own kinsmen and were blessed in their children. Remember that their posterity shall inherit the land. 13 Therefore, my son, love your kinsmen. Do not be so proudhearted toward your kinsmen, the sons and daughters of your people, as to refuse to take a wife for yourself from among them. For in such arrogance there is ruin and great disorder. Likewise, in worthlessness there is decay and dire poverty, for worthlessness is the mother of famine.

14 "Do not keep with you overnight the wages of any man who works for you, but pay him immediately. If you thus behave as God's servant, you will receive your reward. Keep a close watch on yourself, my son, in everything you do, and discipline yourself in all your conduct. 15 Do to no one what you yourself dislike. Do not drink wine till you become drunk, nor let drunkenness accompany you on your way.

16 "Give to the hungry some of your bread, and to the naked some of your clothing. Whatever you have left over, give away as alms; and do not begrudge the alms you give. 17 Be lavish with your bread and wine at the burial of the virtuous, but do not share them with sinners.

18 "Seek counsel from every wise man, and do not think lightly of any advice that can be useful. 19 At all times bless the Lord God, and ask him to make all your paths straight and

NEW JERUSALEM BIBLE

12 'My child, avoid all loose conduct. Choose a wife of your father's stock. Do not take a foreign wife outside your father's tribe, because we are the children of the prophets. Remember Noah, Abraham, Isaac and Jacob, our ancestors from the beginning. All of them took wives from their own kindred, and they were blessed in their children, and their race will inherit the earth. 13 You, too, my child, must love your own brothers; never presume to despise your brothers, the sons and daughters of your people; choose your wife from among them. For pride brings ruin and much worry; idleness causes need and poverty, for the mother of famine is idleness.

14 'Do not keep back until next day the wages of those who work for you; pay them at once. If you serve God you will be rewarded. Be careful, my child, in all you do, well-disciplined in all your behaviour. 15 Do to no one what you would not want done to you. Do not drink wine to the point of drunkenness; do not let excess be your travelling companion.

16 'Give your bread to those who are hungry, and your clothes to those who lack clothing. Of whatever you own in plenty, devote a proportion to almsgiving; and when you give alms, do it ungrudgingly. 17 Be generous with bread and wine on the graves of upright people, but not for the sinner.

18 'Ask advice of every wise person; never scorn any profitable advice. 19 Bless the Lord God in everything; beg him to guide your ways and bring your paths and purposes to their

GREEK OLD TESTAMENT

τρίβοι καὶ βουλαὶ εὐοδωθῶσιν· διότι πᾶν ἔθνος οὐκ ἔχει
βουλήν,]] δώσει κύριος αὐτοῖς βουλὴν ἀγαθήν· καὶ ὃν ἂν θέλῃ
κύριος, ταπεινοῖ ἕως ᾅδου κατωτάτω. καὶ νῦν, παιδίον,
μνημόνευε τὰς ἐντολὰς ταύτας, καὶ μὴ ἐξαλειφθήτωσαν ἐκ
τῆς καρδίας σου. 20 καὶ νῦν, παιδίον, ὑποδεικνύω σοι ὅτι
δέκα τάλαντα ἀργυρίου παρεθέμην Γαβαήλῳ τῷ τοῦ Γαβρι ἐν
Ῥάγοις τῆς Μηδίας. 21 καὶ μὴ φοβοῦ, παιδίον, ὅτι ἐπτωχεύ-
σαμεν· ὑπάρχει σοι πολλὰ ἀγαθά, ἐὰν φοβηθῇς τὸν θεὸν καὶ
φύγῃς ἀπὸ πάσης ἁμαρτίας καὶ ποιήσῃς τὰ ἀγαθὰ ἐνώπιον
κυρίου τοῦ θεοῦ σου.

5 Τότε ἀποκριθεὶς Τωβιας εἶπεν Τωβιθ τῷ πατρὶ αὐτοῦ
Πάντα, ὅσα ἐντέταλσαί μοι, ποιήσω, πάτερ· 2 πῶς δὲ
δυνήσομαι αὐτὸ λαβεῖν παρ' αὐτοῦ καὶ αὐτὸς οὐ γινώσκει με
καὶ ἐγὼ οὐ γινώσκω αὐτόν; τί σημεῖον δῶ αὐτῷ καὶ ἐπιγνῷ
με καὶ πιστεύσῃ μοι καὶ δῷ μοι τὸ ἀργύριον; καὶ τὰς ὁδοὺς
τὰς εἰς Μηδίαν οὐ γινώσκω τοῦ πορευθῆναι ἐκεῖ. 3 τότε
ἀποκριθεὶς Τωβιθ εἶπεν Τωβια τῷ υἱῷ αὐτοῦ Χειρόγραφον
αὐτοῦ ἔδωκέν μοι, καὶ χειρόγραφον ἔδωκα αὐτῷ· καὶ διεῖλον
εἰς δύο, καὶ ἐλάβομεν ἑκάτερος ἕν, καὶ ἔθηκα μετὰ τοῦ ἀρ-
γυρίου· καὶ νῦν ἰδοὺ ἔτη εἴκοσι ἀφ' οὗ παρεθέμην τὸ ἀργύριον τοῦτο ἐγώ. καὶ νῦν, παιδίον, ζήτησον σεαυτῷ ἄνθρωπον
πιστόν, ὃς πορεύσεται μετὰ σοῦ, καὶ δώσομεν αὐτῷ μισθόν,
ἕως ὅτου ἔλθῃς. καὶ λαβὲ παρ' αὐτοῦ τὸ ἀργύριον τοῦτο.
4 ἐξῆλθεν δὲ Τωβιας ζητῆσαι ἄνθρωπον, ὃς πορεύσεται μετ'
αὐτοῦ εἰς Μηδίαν, ὃς ἐμπειρεῖ τῆς ὁδοῦ, καὶ ἐξῆλθεν καὶ
εὗρεν Ραφαηλ τὸν ἄγγελον ἑστηκότα ἀπέναντι αὐτοῦ καὶ
οὐκ ἔγνω ὅτι ἄγγελος τοῦ θεοῦ ἐστιν· 5 καὶ εἶπεν αὐτῷ

KING JAMES VERSION

counsels may prosper: for every nation hath not counsel; but the Lord himself giveth all good things, and he humbleth whom he will, as he will; now therefore, my son, remember my commandments, neither let them be put out of thy mind.

20 And now I signify this to thee, that I committed ten talents to Gabael the *son* of Gabrias at Rages in Media.

21 And fear not, my son, that we are made poor: for thou hast much wealth, if thou fear God, and depart from all sin, and do that which is pleasing in his sight.

5 Tobias then answered and said, Father, I will do all things which thou hast commanded me:

2 But how can I receive the money, seeing I know him not?

3 Then he gave him the handwriting, and said unto him, Seek thee a man which may go with thee, whiles I yet live, and I will give him wages: and go and receive the money.

4 Therefore when he went to seek a man, he found Raphael that was an angel.

DOUAY OLD TESTAMENT

21 I tell thee also, my son, that I lent ten talents of silver, while thou wast yet a child, to Gabelus, in Rages a city of the Medes, and I have a note of his hand with me:

22 Now therefore inquire how thou mayst go to him, and receive of him the foresaid sum of money, and restore to him the note of his hand.

23 Fear not, my son: we lead indeed a poor life, but we shall have many good things if we fear God, and depart from all sin, and do that which is good.

5 THEN Tobias answered his father, and said: I will do all things, father, which thou hast commanded me.

2 But how I shall get this money, I cannot tell; he knoweth not me, and I know not him: what token shall I give him? nor did I ever know the way which leadeth thither.

3 Then his father answered him, and said: I have a note of his hand with me, which when thou shalt shew him, he will presently pay it.

4 But go now, and seek thee out some faithful man, to go with thee for his hire: that thou mayst receive it, while I yet live.

5 Then Tobias going forth, found a beautiful young man, standing girded, and as it were ready to walk.

6 And not knowing that he was an angel of God, he

KNOX TRANSLATION

21 This too I would have thee know, my son, that long
since, when thou wert but a child, I lent ten talents of silver
to a citizen of Rages in Media, called Gabelus, and I have his
bond still. 22 Do thou find means to reach his home, and so
recover from him the sum I speak of, in return for his bond.
23 Never lose heart, my son, though we lead, thou and I, the
life poor men lead. Fear we but God, shun guilt, and do the
good we can, blessings shall be ours in abundance.[a]

5 Father, answered the young Tobias, I will do all thy bidding; 2 but as for recovering the money, I have little
hope. Here is one who is a stranger to me, and I to him;
what proof can I bring forward? Meanwhile, I must find my
way to Rages, and of that I have no experience. 3 Nay, said
his father, I have the man's bond here; do but shew him
that, and he will restore the money without more ado. 4 Up
then, and find some man of credit, that will go with thee
upon condition of a due reward; must I die before thou bring
the money back to me? 5 With that, his son went out, and at
the door stood a young man of noble mien, all girt about, as
if he were ready for a journey. 6 Little he knew that this was
an angel of God, as he gave him welcome; Fair sir, he asked,

a The other versions differ greatly in the account they give of Tobias' advice to his son, the Aramaic text being nearest to the Vulgate.

TODAY'S ENGLISH VERSION

out to do. He does not give his wisdom to the people of any
other nation. He is the source of all good things, but he can
also destroy you and bring you to certain death, if he wishes.
"Remember all my instructions. Don't forget them for one
minute.
20 "Tobias, I want you to know that I once left a large sum
of money with Gabrias' son, Gabael, at Rages in Media.
21 We're poor now, but don't worry. If you obey God and
avoid sin, he will be pleased with you and make you prosperous."
5 Then Tobias answered his father, "I'll do everything you
told me. 2 But how can I get the money back from
Gabael? We have never even met each other. How can I
prove to him who I am, so that he will trust me and give me
the money? Besides that, I don't know how to get to Media."
3 Tobit replied, "Gabael and I both signed a document. I
then tore it in two, and we each took a half. I put his half
with the money. That was twenty years ago! Now, go and
find a reliable person to travel with you to Media and back,
and we will pay him when you return. But you must get the
money that I left with Gabael."
4 Tobias then went out to look for someone who knew the
way to Media and would travel with him. Almost as soon as
he left the house, he found himself face-to-face with
Raphael. Tobias did not know that Raphael was an angel of
God, 5 so he asked him where he was from.

NEW REVISED STANDARD VERSION

plans may prosper. For none of the nations has understanding, but the Lord himself will give them good counsel; but if
he chooses otherwise, he casts down to deepest Hades. So
now, my child, remember these commandments, and do not
let them be erased from your heart.
20 "And now, my son, let me explain to you that I left ten
talents of silver in trust with Gabael son of Gabrias, at Rages
in Media. 21 Do not be afraid, my son, because we have
become poor. You have great wealth if you fear God and flee
from every sin and do what is good in the sight of the Lord
your God."
5 Then Tobias answered his father Tobit, "I will do everything that you have commanded me, father; 2 but how
can I obtain the money[a] from him, since he does not know
me and I do not know him? What evidence[b] am I to give him
so that he will recognize and trust me, and give me the
money? Also, I do not know the roads to Media, or how to
get there." 3 Then Tobit answered his son Tobias, "He gave
me his bond and I gave him my bond. I[c] divided his in two;
we each took one part, and I put one with the money. And
now twenty years have passed since I left this money in
trust. So now, my son, find yourself a trustworthy man to go
with you, and we will pay him wages until you return. But
get back the money from Gabael."[d]
4 So Tobias went out to look for a man to go with him to
Media, someone who was acquainted with the way. He went
out and found the angel Raphael standing in front of him;
but he did not perceive that he was an angel of God.

a Gk *it* *b* Gk *sign* *c* Other authorities read *He* *d* Gk *from him*

NEW AMERICAN BIBLE

to grant success to all your endeavors and plans. For no pagan
nation possesses good counsel, but the Lord himself gives all
good things. If the Lord chooses, he raises a man up; but if he
should decide otherwise, he casts him down to the deepest
recesses of the nether world. So now, my son, keep in mind my
commandments, and never let him be erased from your heart.
20 "And now, son, I wish to inform you that I have deposited a great sum of money with Gabri's son Gabael at Rages in
Media. 21 Do not be discouraged, my child, because of our
poverty. You will be a rich man if you fear God, avoid all sin,
and do what is right before the Lord your God."
5 Then Tobiah replied to his father Tobit: "Everything that
you have commanded me, father, I will do. 2 But how
shall I be able to obtain the money from him, since he does
not know me nor do I know him? What can I show him to
make him recognize me and trust me, so that he will give me
the money? I do not even know which roads to take for the
journey into Media!" 3 Tobit answered his son Tobiah: "We
exchanged signatures on a document written in duplicate; I
divided it into two parts, and each of us kept one; his copy I
put with the money. Think of it, twenty years have already
passed since I deposited that money! So now, my son, find
yourself a trustworthy man who will make the journey with
you. We will, of course, give him a salary when you return;
but get back that money from Gabael."
4 Tobiah went to look for someone acquainted with the
roads who would travel with him to Media. As soon as he
went out, he found the angel Raphael standing before him,
though he did not know that this was an angel of God.

NEW JERUSALEM BIBLE

end. For wisdom is not the property of every nation; their
desire for what is good is conferred by the Lord. At his will
he lifts up or he casts down to the depths of the dwelling of
the dead. So now, my child, remember these precepts and
never let them fade from your heart.
20 'Now, my child, I must tell you I have left ten talents of
silver with Gabael son of Gabrias, at Rhages in Media. 21 Do
not be afraid, my child, if we have grown poor. You have
great wealth if you fear God, if you shun every kind of sin
and if you do what is pleasing to the Lord your God.'
5 Tobias then replied to his father Tobit, 'Father, I shall do
everything you have told me. 2 But how am I to recover
the silver from him? He does not know me, nor I him. What
token am I to give him for him to believe me and hand the
silver over to me? And besides, I do not know what roads to
take for this journey into Media.' 3 Then Tobit answered his
son Tobias, 'Each of us set his signature to a note which I
cut in two, so that each could keep half of it. I took one
piece, and put the other with the silver. To think it was twenty years ago I left this silver in his keeping! And now, my
child, find a trustworthy travelling companion—we shall pay
him for his time until you arrive back—and then go and collect the silver from Gabael.'
4 Tobias went out to look for a man who knew the way to
go with him to Media. Outside he found Raphael the angel
standing facing him, though he did not guess he was an

GREEK OLD TESTAMENT

Πόθεν εἶ, νεανίσκε; καὶ εἶπεν αὐτῷ Ἐκ τῶν υἱῶν Ισραηλ τῶν
ἀδελφῶν σου καὶ ἐλήλυθα ὧδε ἐργατεύεσθαι. καὶ εἶπεν αὐτῷ
Ἐπίστῃ τὴν ὁδὸν πορευθῆναι εἰς Μηδίαν; 6 καὶ εἶπεν αὐτῷ
Ναί, πολλάκις ἐγὼ ἐγενόμην ἐκεῖ καὶ ἐμπειρῶ καὶ ἐπίσταμαι
τὰς ὁδοὺς πάσας. πλεονάκις ἐπορεύθην εἰς Μηδίαν καὶ ηὐλι-
ζόμην παρὰ Γαβαήλῳ τῷ ἀδελφῷ ἡμῶν τῷ οἰκοῦντι ἐν
Ῥάγοις τῆς Μηδίας, καὶ ἀπέχει ὁδὸν ἡμερῶν δύο τεταγμένων ἀπὸ Ἐκβατάνων εἰς Ῥάγα· κεῖνται γὰρ ἐν τῷ ὄρει.
7 καὶ εἶπεν αὐτῷ Μεῖνόν με, νεανίσκε, μέχρι ὅτου εἰσελθὼν
ὑποδείξω τῷ πατρί μου· χρείαν γὰρ ἔχω ἵνα βαδίσῃς μετ'
ἐμοῦ, καὶ δώσω σοι τὸν μισθόν σου. 8 καὶ εἶπεν αὐτῷ Ἰδοὺ
ἐγὼ προσκαρτερῶ, μόνον μὴ χρονίσῃς. 9 καὶ εἰσελθὼν
Τωβιας ὑπέδειξεν Τωβιθ τῷ πατρὶ αὐτοῦ καὶ εἶπεν αὐτῷ
Ἰδοὺ ἄνθρωπον εὗρον τῶν ἀδελφῶν ἡμῶν τῶν υἱῶν Ισραηλ.
καὶ εἶπεν αὐτῷ Κάλεσόν μοι τὸν ἄνθρωπον, ὅπως ἐπιγνῶ τί
τὸ γένος αὐτοῦ καὶ ἐκ ποίας φυλῆς ἐστιν καὶ εἰ πιστός
ἐστιν ἵνα πορευθῇ μετὰ σοῦ, παιδίον. 10 καὶ ἐξῆλθεν Τωβιας
καὶ ἐκάλεσεν αὐτὸν καὶ εἶπεν αὐτῷ Νεανίσκε, ὁ πατήρ καλεῖ
σε. καὶ εἰσῆλθεν πρὸς αὐτόν, καὶ ἐχαιρέτισεν αὐτὸν Τωβιθ
πρῶτος. καὶ εἶπεν αὐτῷ Χαίρειν σοι πολλὰ γένοιτο. καὶ
ἀποκριθεὶς Τωβιθ εἶπεν αὐτῷ Τί μοι ἔτι ὑπάρχει χαίρειν; καὶ
ἐγὼ ἄνθρωπος ἀδύνατος τοῖς ὀφθαλμοῖς καὶ οὐ βλέπω τὸ
φῶς τοῦ οὐρανοῦ, ἀλλ' ἐν τῷ σκότει κεῖμαι ὥσπερ οἱ νεκροὶ
οἱ μηκέτι θεωροῦντες τὸ φῶς. ζῶν ἐγὼ ἐν νεκροῖς εἰμι,
φωνὴν ἀνθρώπων ἀκούω καὶ αὐτοὺς οὐ βλέπω. καὶ εἶπεν αὐτῷ
Θάρσει, ἐγγὺς παρὰ τῷ θεῷ ἰάσασθαί σε, θάρσει. καὶ εἶπεν

KING JAMES VERSION

5 But he knew not; and he said unto him, Canst thou go with me to Rages? and knowest thou those places well?

6 To whom the angel said, I will go with thee, and I know the way well: for I have lodged with our brother Gabael.

7 Then Tobias said unto him, Tarry for me, till I tell my father.

8 Then he said unto him, Go, and tarry not. So he went in and said to his father, Behold, I have found one which will go with me. Then he said, Call him unto me, that I may know of what tribe he is, and whether he be a trusty man to go with thee.

9 So he called him, and he came in, and they saluted one another.

DOUAY OLD TESTAMENT

saluted him, and said: From whence art thou, good young man?

7 But he answered: Of the children of Israel. And Tobias said to him: Knowest thou the way that leadeth to the country of the Medes?

8 And he answered: I know it: and I have often walked through all the ways thereof, and I have abode with Gabelus our brother, who dwelleth at Rages a city of the Medes, which is situate in the mount of Ecbatana.

9 And Tobias said to him: Stay for me, I beseech thee, till I tell these same things to my father.

10 Then Tobias going in told all these things to his father. Upon which his father being in admiration, desired that he would come in unto him.

11 So going in he saluted him, and said: Joy be to thee always.

12 And Tobias said: What manner of joy shall be to me, who sit in darkness, and see not the light of heaven?

13 And the young man said to him: Be of good courage, thy cure from God is at hand.

KNOX TRANSLATION

whence comest thou? 7 And on hearing that he had been
among the men of Israel, Why then, said he, thou knowest
the road from here to Media? 8 I know it well, he answered;
no step of it but I have marched often enough, when I would
visit a fellow-countryman of ours who lives there; one
Gabelus. The city where he dwells, Rages, is in Media, in the
hill-country about Ecbatana.
9 Wait for me here, Tobias asked of him, while I give my
father news of this. 10 Then he went back, and told the story
to his father, who was all astonishment, and would have
the stranger brought in. 11 So in he came, and wished him
abiding happiness. 12 Happiness! Tobias said; little happiness for me, that sit here in the dark, and see never the light
of day! 13 Take courage, the stranger said, God means thy

TODAY'S ENGLISH VERSION

"I am an Israelite," Raphael answered, "one of your distant relatives, and I have come here to Nineveh to find work."

"Do you know the way to Media?" Tobias asked.

6 "Yes, I do," Raphael replied. "I have been there many times, and I know all the roads well. I used to stay with our relative Gabael, who lives there in the town of Rages.[a] It takes at least two days to travel there from Ecbatana, the capital city, because Rages is up in the mountains."

7 Then Tobias said to Raphael, "Wait here for me, my friend, while I go in and tell my father. I would like for you to travel with me, and I will pay you for the journey."

8 "All right," Raphael said, "I'll wait, but don't take too long."

9 Tobias went in and told his father, "I have found an Israelite to travel with me."

"Call the man in," Tobit replied. "I would like to know what family and tribe he belongs to, and whether he is a reliable traveling companion for you."

So Tobias went out and called to Raphael, "My father would like to meet you." When Raphael came in, Tobit greeted him first.

Then Raphael returned the greeting, "I hope all is well with you."

But Tobit replied, "How can all be well with me? I'm blind and can't see a thing. It's like being dead and no longer able to see the light. I might as well be dead! I can hear people talking, but I can't see them."

"Cheer up!" Raphael said to him. "God is going to cure you soon, so don't worry!"

[a] Rages; *Greek* Ecbatana.

NEW REVISED STANDARD VERSION

5 Tobias[a] said to him, "Where do you come from, young man?" "From your kindred, the Israelites," he replied, "and I have come here to work." Then Tobias[b] said to him, "Do you know the way to go to Media?" 6 "Yes," he replied, "I have been there many times; I am acquainted with it and know all the roads. I have often traveled to Media, and would stay with our kinsman Gabael who lives in Rages of Media. It is a journey of two days from Ecbatana to Rages; for it lies in a mountainous area, while Ecbatana is in the middle of the plain." 7 Then Tobias said to him, "Wait for me, young man, until I go in and tell my father; for I do need you to travel with me, and I will pay you your wages." 8 He replied, "All right, I will wait; but do not take too long."

9 So Tobias[b] went in to tell his father Tobit and said to him, "I have just found a man who is one of our own Israelite kindred!" He replied, "Call the man in, my son, so that I may learn about his family and to what tribe he belongs, and whether he is trustworthy enough to go with you."

10 Then Tobias went out and called him, and said, "Young man, my father is calling for you." So he went in to him, and Tobit greeted him first. He replied, "Joyous greetings to you!" But Tobit retorted, "What joy is left for me any more? I am a man without eyesight; I cannot see the light of heaven, but I lie in darkness like the dead who no longer see the light. Although still alive, I am among the dead. I hear people but I cannot see them." But the young man[b] said, "Take courage; the time is near for God to heal you; take

a Gk *He* *b* Gk *he*

NEW AMERICAN BIBLE

5 Tobiah said to him, "Who are you, young man?" He replied, "I am an Israelite, one of your kinsmen. I have come here to work." Tobiah said, "Do you know the way to Media?" 6 The other replied: "Yes, I have been there many times. I know the place well and I know all the routes. I have often traveled to Media; I used to stay with our kinsman Gabael, who lives at Rages in Media. It is a good two days' travel from Ecbatana to Rages, for Rages is situated at the mountains, Ecbatana out on the plateau." 7 Tobiah said to him, "Wait for me, young man, till I go back and tell my father; for I need you to make the journey with me. I will, of course, pay you." 8 Raphael replied, "Very well, I will wait for you; but do not be long."

9 Tobiah went back to tell his father Tobit what had happened. He said to him, "I have just found a man who is one of our own Israelite kinsmen!" Tobit said, "Call the man, so that I may find out what family and tribe he comes from, and whether he is trustworthy enough to travel with you, son." Tobiah went out to summon the man saying, "Young man, my father would like to see you."

10 When Raphael entered the house, Tobit greeted him first. Raphael said, "Hearty greetings to you!" Tobit replied: "What joy is left for me any more? Here I am, a blind man who cannot see God's sunlight, but must remain in darkness, like the dead who no longer see the light! Though alive, I am among the dead. I can hear a man's voice, but I cannot see him." Raphael said, "Take courage! God has healing in store for

NEW JERUSALEM BIBLE

angel of God. 5 He said, 'Where do you come from, friend?' The angel replied, 'I am one of your brother Israelites; I have come to these parts to look for work.' Tobias asked, 'Do you know the road to Media?' 6 The other replied, 'Certainly I do, I have been there many times; I have knowledge and experience of all the ways. I have often been to Media and stayed with Gabael one of our kinsmen who lives at Rhages in Media. It usually takes two full days to get from Ecbatana to Rhages; Rhages lies in the mountains, and Ecbatana is in the middle of the plain.' 7 Tobias said, 'Wait for me, friend, while I go and tell my father; I need you to come with me; I shall pay you for your time.' 8 The other replied, 'Good, I shall wait; but do not be long.'

9 Tobias went in and told his father that he had found one of their brother Israelites. And the father said, 'Fetch him in; I want to find out about his family and tribe. I must see if he is going to be a reliable companion for you, my child.' So Tobias went out and called him, 'Friend,' he said, 'my father wants you.'

10 The angel came into the house; Tobit greeted him, and the other answered, wishing him happiness in plenty. Tobit replied, 'Can I ever be happy again? I am a blind man; I no longer see the light of heaven; I am sunk in darkness like the dead who see the light no more. I am a man buried alive; I hear people speak but cannot see them.' The angel said, 'Take comfort; before long God will heal you. Take comfort.'

GREEK OLD TESTAMENT

αὐτῷ Τωβιθ Τωβιας ὁ υἱός μου θέλει πορευθῆναι εἰς Μηδίαν·
εἰ δυνήσῃ συνελθεῖν αὐτῷ καὶ ἀγαγεῖν αὐτόν; καὶ δώσω σοι
τὸν μισθόν σου, ἄδελφε. καὶ εἶπεν αὐτῷ Δυνήσομαι πορευθῆναι μετ᾽ αὐτοῦ, καὶ ἐπίσταμαι ἐγὼ τὰς ὁδοὺς πάσας, καὶ
πολλάκις ᾠχόμην εἰς Μηδίαν καὶ διῆλθον πάντα τὰ πεδία
αὐτῆς, καὶ τὰ ὄρη καὶ πάσας τὰς ὁδοὺς αὐτῆς ἐγὼ γινώσκω.
11 καὶ εἶπεν αὐτῷ Ἄδελφε, ποίας πατριᾶς εἶ καὶ ἐκ ποίας
φυλῆς; ὑπόδειξόν μοι, ἄδελφε. 12 καὶ εἶπεν Τί χρείαν ἔχεις
φυλῆς; καὶ εἶπεν αὐτῷ Βούλομαι γνῶναι τὰ κατ᾽ ἀλήθειαν
τίνος εἶ, ἄδελφε, καὶ τί τὸ ὄνομά σου. 13 καὶ εἶπεν αὐτῷ
Ἐγὼ Αζαριας Ανανιου τοῦ μεγάλου, τῶν ἀδελφῶν σου.
14 καὶ εἶπεν αὐτῷ Ὑγιαίνων ἔλθοις καὶ σῳζόμενος, ἄδελφε·
καὶ μή μοι πικρανθῇς, ἄδελφε, ὅτι τὴν ἀλήθειαν ἐβουλόμην
γνῶναι καὶ τὴν πατριάν σου. καὶ σὺ τυγχάνεις ἀδελφὸς ὤν,
καὶ ἐκ γενεᾶς καλῆς καὶ ἀγαθῆς εἶ σύ· ἐγίνωσκον Ανανιαν
καὶ Ναθαν τοὺς δύο υἱοὺς Σεμε[λ]ιου τοῦ μεγάλου, καὶ αὐτοὶ
συνεπορεύοντό μοι εἰς Ιερουσαλημ καὶ προσεκύνουν μετ᾽
ἐμοῦ ἐκεῖ καὶ οὐκ ἐπλανήθησαν. οἱ ἀδελφοί σου ἄνθρωποι
ἀγαθοί· ἐκ ῥίζης ἀγαθῆς εἶ σύ, καὶ χαίρων ἔλθοις. 15 καὶ
εἶπεν αὐτῷ Ἐγώ σοι δίδωμι μισθὸν τὴν ἡμέραν δραχμὴν καὶ
τὰ δέοντά σοι ὁμοίως τῷ υἱῷ μου· 16 καὶ πορεύθητι μετὰ τοῦ
υἱοῦ μου, καὶ ἔτι προσθήσω σοι τῷ μισθῷ. 17 καὶ εἶπεν αὐτῷ
ὅτι Πορεύσομαι μετ᾽ αὐτοῦ· καὶ μὴ φοβηθῇς, ὑγιαίνοντες
ἀπελευσόμεθα καὶ ὑγιαίνοντες ἐπιστρέψομεν πρὸς σέ, διότι

KING JAMES VERSION

10 Then Tobit said unto him, Brother, shew me of what tribe and family thou art.

11 To whom he said, Dost thou seek for a tribe or family, or an hired man to go with thy son? Then Tobit said unto him, I would know, brother, thy kindred and name.

12 Then he said, I am Azarias, the son of Ananias the great, and of thy brethren.

13 Then Tobit said, Thou art welcome, brother; be not now angry with me, because I have enquired to know thy tribe and thy family; for thou art my brother, of an honest and good stock: for I know Ananias and Jonathas, sons of that great Samaias, as we went together to Jerusalem to worship, and offered the firstborn, and the tenths of the fruits; and they were not seduced with the error of our brethren: my brother, thou art of a good stock.

14 But tell me, what wages shall I give thee? *wilt thou* a drachm a day, and things necessary, as to mine own son?

15 Yea, moreover, if ye return safe, I will add something to thy wages.

DOUAY OLD TESTAMENT

14 And Tobias said to him: Canst thou conduct my son to Gabelus at Rages, a city of the Medes? and when thou shalt return, I will pay thee thy hire.

15 And the angel said to him: I will conduct him thither, and bring him back to thee.

16 And Tobias said to him: I pray thee, tell me, of what family, or what tribe art thou?

17 And Raphael the angel answered: Dost thou seek the family of him thou hirest, or the hired servant himself to go with thy son?

18 But lest I should make thee uneasy, I am Azarias the son of the great Ananias.

19 And Tobias answered: Thou art of a great family. But I pray thee be not angry that I desired to know thy family.

20 And the angel said to him: I will lead thy son safe, and bring him to thee again safe.

KNOX TRANSLATION

soon recovery. 14 Then Tobias asked, Wilt thou take my son
with thee, and guide him to Media, to Rages, and so to the
house of Gabelus? There shall be a reward awaiting thee on
thy return. 15 I will take him there, said the angel, and bring
him home again besides. 16 Then Tobias would know of
what household or tribe he came. 17 It was indeed no other
than the angel Raphael that spoke to him; What, he
answered, is it my lineage, not myself, thou wouldst have
for thy son's escort? 18 But set thy mind at rest; my name is
Azarias,[a] and a man of renown, Ananias, was my father.
19 Forgive me, Tobias said, for doubting thy lineage; thou
comest of good stock indeed.
20 Raphael, then, promised to conduct the boy safely and
bring him safely home, 21 and Tobias bade them good speed;

a The name Azarias means 'God has brought aid', and the name Ananias 'God has been merciful', as if the angel had chosen a name to signify the nature of his office. St Athanasius explains that he was actually wearing the appearance of the living Azarias and was appointed by divine Providence to represent him; he was, so to speak, Azarias' second self. The purpose of concealing his angelic nature was evidently so as to make proof of the elder Tobias' faith (cf. verse 27 below).

TODAY'S ENGLISH VERSION

Tobit then said, "My son Tobias wants to go to Media. Can you go with him and show him the way? I will pay you, of course."

Raphael replied, "Certainly I can go with him. I have traveled there many times and I know all the roads in the mountains and on the plains."

10 Tobit questioned him further, "Tell me, my friend, what family and tribe do you belong to?"

11 But Raphael asked, "Why do you need to know that?"

"Tell me the truth," said Tobit. "What is your name, and who are you?"

12 Raphael replied, "My name is Azarias, and I am the son of the older Ananias, one of your relatives."

13 Then Tobit said to him, "Welcome to our home! God bless you, my son. Please don't be offended because I wanted to know the truth about you and your family. As it turns out, you are from a good family and a relative at that! I knew Ananias and Nathan, the two sons of the older Shemaiah. They were always loyal to their religion. We used to travel together to Jerusalem and worship there. Your relatives are fine people, and you come from good stock. Have a safe journey."

14 Tobit continued, "I will pay the normal daily wage plus expenses for both of you. 15 Be a good companion to Tobias, and I will add a bonus to your wages."

16 "I will go with him," Raphael said. "And don't worry; we will get there and back safely. The roads are not dangerous."

NEW REVISED STANDARD VERSION

courage." Then Tobit said to him, "My son Tobias wishes to go to Media. Can you accompany him and guide him? I will pay your wages, brother." He answered, "I can go with him and I know all the roads, for I have often gone to Media and have crossed all its plains, and I am familiar with its mountains and all of its roads."

11 Then Tobit[a] said to him, "Brother, of what family are you and from what tribe? Tell me, brother." 12 He replied, "Why do you need to know my tribe?" But Tobit[a] said, "I want to be sure, brother, whose son you are and what your name is." 13 He replied, "I am Azariah, the son of the great Hananiah, one of your relatives." 14 Then Tobit said to him, "Welcome! God save you, brother. Do not feel bitter toward me, brother, because I wanted to be sure about your ancestry. It turns out that you are a kinsman, and of good and noble lineage. For I knew Hananiah and Nathan,[b] the two sons of Shemeliah,[c] and they used to go with me to Jerusalem and worshiped with me there, and were not led astray. Your kindred are good people; you come of good stock. Hearty welcome!"

15 Then he added, "I will pay you a drachma a day as wages, as well as expenses for yourself and my son. So go with my son, 16 and[d] I will add something to your wages." Raphael[e] answered, "I will go with him; so do not fear. We shall leave in good health and return to you in good health, because the way is safe." 17 So Tobit[a] said to

a Gk *he* *b* Other ancient authorities read *Jathan* or *Nathaniah*
c Other ancient authorities read *Shemaiah* *d* Other ancient authorities add *when you return safely* *e* Gk *He*

NEW AMERICAN BIBLE

you; so take courage!" Tobit then said: "My son Tobiah wants to go to Media. Can you go with him to show him the way? I will of course pay you, brother." Raphael answered: "Yes, I can go with him, for I know all the routes. I have often traveled to Media and crossed all its plains and mountains; so I know every road well." 11 Tobit asked, "Brother, tell me, please, what family and tribe are you from?" 12 Raphael said: "Why? Do you need a tribe and a family? Or are you looking for a hired man to travel with your son?" Tobit replied, "I wish to know truthfully whose son you are, brother, and what your name is."

13 Raphael answered, "I am Azariah, son of Hananiah the elder, one of your own kinsmen." 14 Tobit exclaimed: "Welcome! God save you, brother! Do not be provoked with me, brother, for wanting to learn the truth about your family. So it turns out that you are a kinsman, and from a noble and good line! I knew Hananiah and Nathaniah, the two sons of Shemaiah the elder; with me they used to make the pilgrimage to Jerusalem, where we would worship together. No, they did not stray from the right path; your kinsmen are good men. You are certainly of good lineage, and welcome!"

15 Then he added: "For each day you are away I will give you the normal wages, plus expenses for you and for my son. If you go with my son, 16 I will even add a bonus to your wages!" Raphael replied: "I will go with him; have no fear. In good health we shall leave you, and in good health we shall return to you, for the way is safe." 17 Tobit said,

NEW JERUSALEM BIBLE

Tobit said, 'My son Tobias wishes to go to Media. Will you join him as his guide? Brother, I will pay you.' He replied, 'I am willing to go with him; I know all the ways; I have often been to Media, I have crossed all its plains and mountains, and I know all its roads.' 11 Tobit said, 'Brother, what family and what tribe do you belong to? Will you tell me, brother?' 12 'What does my tribe matter to you?' the angel said. Tobit said, 'I want to be quite sure whose son you are and what your name is.' 13 The angel said, 'I am Azarias, son of the great Ananias, one of your kinsmen.' 14 'Welcome and greetings, brother! Do not be offended at my wanting to know the name of your family; I find you are my kinsman of a good and honourable line. I know Ananias and Nathan, the two sons of the great Shemaiah. They used to go to Jerusalem with me; we have worshipped together there and they have never strayed from the right path. Your brothers are worthy men; you come of good stock; welcome.'

15 He went on, 'I engage you at a drachma a day, with the same expenses as my own son's. Complete the journey with my son 16 and I shall go beyond the agreed wage.' The angel replied, 'I shall complete the journey with him. Do not be afraid. On the journey outward all will be well; on the journey back all will be well; the road is safe.' 17 Tobit said,

GREEK OLD TESTAMENT

ἡ ὁδὸς ἀσφαλής. καὶ εἶπεν αὐτῷ Εὐλογία σοι γένοιτο, ἄδελφε. καὶ ἐκάλεσεν τὸν υἱὸν αὐτοῦ καὶ εἶπεν αὐτῷ Παιδίον, ἑτοίμασον τὰ πρὸς τὴν ὁδὸν καὶ ἔξελθε μετὰ τοῦ ἀδελφοῦ σου, καὶ ὁ θεὸς ὁ ἐν τῷ οὐρανῷ διασώσαι ὑμᾶς ἐκεῖ καὶ ἀποκαταστήσαι ὑμᾶς πρὸς ἐμὲ ὑγιαίνοντας, καὶ ὁ ἄγγελος αὐτοῦ συνοδεύσαι ὑμῖν μετὰ σωτηρίας, παιδίον. καὶ ἐξῆλθεν πορευθῆναι τὴν ὁδὸν αὐτοῦ καὶ ἐφίλησεν τὸν πατέρα αὐτοῦ καὶ τὴν μητέρα, καὶ εἶπεν αὐτῷ Τωβιθ Πορεύου ὑγιαίνων. — [18] καὶ ἔκλαυσεν ἡ μήτηρ αὐτοῦ καὶ εἶπεν πρὸς Τωβιθ Τί ὅτι ἀπέστειλας τὸ παιδίον μου; οὐχὶ αὐτὸς ῥάβδος τῆς χειρὸς ἡμῶν ἐστιν καὶ αὐτὸς εἰσπορεύεται καὶ ἐκπορεύεται ἐνώπιον ἡμῶν; [19] ἀργύριον τῷ ἀργυρίῳ μὴ φθάσαι, ἀλλὰ περίψημα τοῦ παιδίου ἡμῶν γένοιτο. [20] ὡς δέδοται ζῆν ἡμῖν παρὰ τοῦ κυρίου, τοῦτο ἱκανὸν ἡμῖν. [21] καὶ εἶπεν αὐτῇ Μὴ λόγον ἔχε· ὑγιαίνων πορεύσεται τὸ παιδίον ἡμῶν καὶ ὑγιαίνων ἐλεύσεται πρὸς ἡμᾶς, καὶ οἱ ὀφθαλμοί σου ὄψονται ἐν τῇ ἡμέρᾳ, ᾗ ἂν ἔλθῃ πρὸς σὲ ὑγιαίνων· [22] μὴ λόγον ἔχε, μὴ φοβοῦ περὶ αὐτῶν, ἀδελφή· ἄγγελος γὰρ ἀγαθὸς συνελεύσεται αὐτῷ, καὶ εὐοδωθήσεται ἡ ὁδὸς αὐτοῦ, καὶ ὑποστρέψει ὑγιαίνων. [23] καὶ ἐσίγησεν κλαίουσα.

6 Καὶ ἐξῆλθεν τὸ παιδίον καὶ ὁ ἄγγελος μετ᾽ αὐτοῦ, καὶ ὁ κύων ἐξῆλθεν μετ᾽ αὐτοῦ καὶ ἐπορεύθη μετ᾽ αὐτῶν· καὶ ἐπορεύθησαν ἀμφότεροι, καὶ ἔτυχεν αὐτοῖς νὺξ μία, καὶ ηὐλίσθησαν ἐπὶ τοῦ Τίγριδος ποταμοῦ. [2] καὶ κατέβη τὸ παιδίον περινίψασθαι τοὺς πόδας εἰς τὸν Τίγριν ποταμόν, καὶ ἀναπηδήσας ἰχθὺς μέγας ἐκ τοῦ ὕδατος ἐβούλετο κατα-

KING JAMES VERSION

16 So they were well pleased. Then said he to Tobias, Prepare thyself for the journey, and God send you a good journey. And when his son had prepared all things for the journey, his father said, Go thou with this man, and God, which dwelleth in heaven, prosper your journey, and the angel of God keep you company. So they went forth both, and the young man's dog with them.

17 But Anna his mother wept, and said to Tobit, Why hast thou sent away our son? is he not the staff of our hand, in going in and out before us?

18 Be not greedy to add money to money: but let it be as refuse in respect of our child.

19 For that which the Lord hath given us to live with doth suffice us.

20 Then said Tobit to her, Take no care, my sister; he shall return in safety, and thine eyes shall see him.

21 For the good angel will keep him company, and his journey shall be prosperous, and he shall return safe.

22 Then she made an end of weeping.

6 And as they went on their journey, they came in the evening to the river Tigris, and they lodged there.

2 And when the young man went down to wash himself, a fish leaped out of the river, and would have devoured him.

DOUAY OLD TESTAMENT

21 And Tobias answering, said: May you have a good journey, and God be with you in your way, and his angel accompany you.

22 Then all things being ready, that were to be carried in their journey, Tobias bade his father and his mother farewell, and they set out both together.

23 And when they were departed, his mother began to weep, and to say: Thou hast taken the staff of our old age, and sent him away from us.

24 I wish the money for which thou hast sent him, had never been.

25 For our poverty was sufficient for us, that we might account it as riches, that we saw our son.

26 And Tobias said to her: Weep not, our son will arrive thither safe, and will return safe to us, and thy eyes shall see him.

27 For I believe that the good angel of God doth accompany him, and doth order all things well that are done about him, so that he shall return to us with joy.

28 At these words his mother ceased weeping, and held her peace.

6 AND Tobias went forward, and the dog followed him, and he lodged the first night by the river of Tigris.

2 And he went out to wash his feet, and behold a monstrous fish came up to devour him.

3 And Tobias being afraid of him, cried out with a loud voice, saying: Sir, he cometh upon me.

KNOX TRANSLATION

God be with you, said he, on your journey, and may his angel bear you company! [22] Then, when his pack was ready, the young Tobias bade his father and mother farewell, and the travellers set out together. [23] Now that the boy had gone, his mother fell a-weeping; Here was the only support of our old age, said she, why hast thou passed him on into other hands? [24] Would to God the money thou hast sent him to claim had never been thine! [25] We were content in our poverty; the very sight of the lad was riches enough. [26] Dry thy tears, Tobias answered; safe will he fare, this son of ours, and safe return; those eyes shall have sight of him again. [27] I hold it for truth that some good angel of the Lord escorts him, to see that all goes well with him and grant him happy return. [28] Thus comforted, the mother dried her tears and complained no more.[a]

6 Tobias, meanwhile, was on the march, with his dog at his heels; they did not make their first halt until they reached the river Tigris. [2] And when he went down to wash

[a] The outlines of the story are the same here in all the versions, but there is enough difference of detail to make it clear that they do not follow a single manuscript source.

TODAY'S ENGLISH VERSION

"God be with you!" Tobit replied. Then he called Tobias
and said to him, "Son, get everything ready that you need for
the journey, so that the two of you can be on your way. May
God and his angel watch over you both and bring you back
to me safe and sound."
Before leaving for Media, Tobias kissed his father and
mother good-bye. Tobit said again, "Have a safe journey!"
17 Then his mother began to cry. "How could you send my
son away like this?" she complained. "He's our only means
of support. Who will take care of us now? 18 Is that money
so important to you that you are willing to risk your own
son's life to get it back? 19 Why can't we be content to live
on what the Lord has given us?"
20 "Calm down," Tobit said to her. "He will get there and
back safely, and with your own eyes you will see him return
home safe and sound. 21 Now stop worrying about them,
dear. A good angel will go with Tobias. He will have a successful journey and will come back in good health." At that,
Anna calmed down and stopped crying.

6 So Tobias and the angel started out toward Media, taking Tobias' dog along with them. They walked on until
sunset, then camped by the Tigris River. 2 Tobias had gone
down to wash his feet in the river, when suddenly a huge
fish jumped up out of the water and tried to swallow one of

NEW REVISED STANDARD VERSION

him, "Blessings be upon you, brother."
Then he called his son and said to him, "Son, prepare supplies for the journey and set out with your brother. May God
in heaven bring you safely there and return you in good
health to me; and may his angel, my son, accompany you
both for your safety."
Before he went out to start his journey, he kissed his father
and mother. Tobit then said to him, "Have a safe journey."
18 But his mother[a] began to weep, and said to Tobit,
"Why is it that you have sent my child away? Is he not the
staff of our hand as he goes in and out before us? 19 Do not
heap money upon money, but let it be a ransom for our child.
20 For the life that is given to us by the Lord is enough for us."
21 Tobit[b] said to her, "Do not worry; our child will leave in
good health and return to us in good health. Your eyes will
see him on the day when he returns to you in good health.
Say no more! Do not fear for them, my sister. 22 For a good
angel will accompany him; his journey will be successful, and
he will come back in good health." 1 So she stopped
weeping.

6 The young man went out and the angel went with him;
2 and the dog came out with him and went along with them.
So they both journeyed along, and when the first night overtook them they camped by the Tigris river. 3 Then the young
man went down to wash his feet in the Tigris river. Suddenly
a large fish leaped up from the water and tried to swallow the

a Other ancient authorities add *Anna* *b* Gk *He*

NEW AMERICAN BIBLE

"God bless you, brother." Then he called his son and said to
him: "My son, prepare whatever you need for the journey,
and set out with your kinsman. May God in heaven protect
you on the way and bring you back to me safe and sound;
and may his angel accompany you for safety, my son."
Before setting out on his journey, Tobiah kissed his father
and mother. Tobit said to him, "Have a safe journey." 18 But
his mother began to weep. She said to Tobit: "Why have you
decided to send my child away? Is he not the staff to which
we cling, ever there with us in all that we do? 19 I hope more
money is not your chief concern! Rather let it be a ransom
for our son! 20 What the Lord has given us to live on is certainly enough for us." 21 Tobit reassured her. "Have no such
thought. Our son will leave in good health and come back to
us in good health. Your own eyes will see the day when he
returns to you safe and sound. 22 So, no such thought; do
not worry about them, my love. For a good angel will go
with him, his journey will be successful, and he will return
unharmed." 1 Then she stopped weeping.

6
2 When the boy left home, accompanied by the angel, the
dog followed Tobiah out of the house and went with him.
The travelers walked till nightfall, and made camp beside the
Tigris River. 3 Now when the boy went down to wash his
feet in the river, a large fish suddenly leaped out of the water

NEW JERUSALEM BIBLE

'Blessings on you, brother!' Then he turned to his son. 'My
child', he said, 'prepare what you need for the journey, and
set off with your brother. May God in heaven protect you
abroad and bring you both back to me safe and sound! May
his angel go with you and protect you, my child!'
Tobias left the house to set out and kissed his father and
mother. Tobit said, 'A happy journey!' 18 His mother burst
into tears and said to Tobit, 'Why must you send my child
away? Is he not the staff of our hands, as he goes about
before us? 19 Surely money is not the only thing that matters? Surely it is not as precious as our child? 20 The way of
life God had already given us was good enough.' 21 He said,
'Do not think such thoughts. Going away and coming back,
all will be well with our child. You will see for yourself when
he comes back safe and sound! Do not think such thoughts;
do not worry on their account, my sister. 22 A good angel
will go with him; he will have a good journey and come back
to us well and happy.'

6 And she dried her tears.

2 The boy left with the angel, and the dog followed behind.
The two walked on, and when the first evening came they
camped beside the Tigris. 3 The boy had gone down to the
river to wash his feet, when a great fish leapt out of the

GREEK OLD TESTAMENT

πιεῖν τὸν πόδα τοῦ παιδαρίου, καὶ ἔκραξεν. 3 καὶ ὁ ἄγγελος
τῷ παιδαρίῳ εἶπεν Ἐπιλαβοῦ καὶ ἐγκρατὴς τοῦ ἰχθύος
γενοῦ. καὶ ἐκράτησεν τὸ παιδάριον τοῦ ἰχθύος καὶ ἀνήνεγκεν αὐτὸν ἐπὶ τὴν γῆν. 4 καὶ εἶπεν αὐτῷ ὁ ἄγγελος
Ἀνάσχισον τὸν ἰχθὺν καὶ ἔξελε τὴν χολὴν καὶ τὴν καρδίαν
καὶ τὸ ἧπαρ αὐτοῦ καὶ ἀπόθες αὐτὰ μετὰ σαυτοῦ καὶ τὰ
ἔγκατα ἔκβαλε· ἔστιν γὰρ εἰς φάρμακον χρήσιμον ἡ χολὴ
καὶ ἡ καρδία καὶ τὸ ἧπαρ αὐτοῦ. 5 καὶ ἀνασχίσας τὸ παιδάριον τὸν ἰχθὺν συνήγαγεν τὴν χολὴν καὶ τὴν καρδίαν καὶ
τὸ ἧπαρ καὶ ὤπτησεν τοῦ ἰχθύος καὶ ἔφαγεν καὶ ἀφῆκεν ἐξ
αὐτοῦ ἡλισμένον. — 6 καὶ ἐπορεύθησαν ἀμφότεροι κοινῶς,
ἕως ἤγγισαν εἰς Μηδίαν. 7 καὶ τότε ἠρώτησεν τὸ παιδάριον
τὸν ἄγγελον καὶ εἶπεν αὐτῷ Αζαρια ἄδελφε, τί τὸ φάρμακον
ἐν τῇ καρδίᾳ καὶ τῷ ἥπατι τοῦ ἰχθύος καὶ ἐν τῇ χολῇ; 8 καὶ
εἶπεν αὐτῷ Ἡ καρδία καὶ τὸ ἧπαρ τοῦ ἰχθύος, κάπνισον ἐνώπιον ἀνθρώπου ἢ γυναικός, ᾧ ἀπάντημα δαιμονίου ἢ πνεύματος πονηροῦ, καὶ φεύξεται ἀπ᾽ αὐτοῦ πᾶν ἀπάντημα καὶ οὐ
μὴ μείνωσιν μετ᾽ αὐτοῦ εἰς τὸν αἰῶνα· 9 καὶ ἡ χολή, ἐγχρῖ-
σαι ἀνθρώπου ὀφθαλμούς, οὗ λευκώματα ἀνέβησαν ἐπ᾽ αὐτῶν,
ἐμφυσῆσαι ἐπ᾽ αὐτοὺς ἐπὶ τῶν λευκωμάτων, καὶ ὑγιαίνουσιν.
10 Καὶ ὅτε εἰσῆλθεν εἰς Μηδίαν καὶ ἤδη ἤγγιζεν εἰς
Ἐκβάτανα, 11 λέγει Ραφαηλ τῷ παιδαρίῳ Τωβια ἄδελφε. καὶ
εἶπεν αὐτῷ Ἰδοὺ ἐγώ. καὶ εἶπεν αὐτῷ Ἐν τοῖς Ραγουήλου
τὴν νύκτα ταύτην δεῖ ἡμᾶς αὐλισθῆναι, καὶ ὁ ἄνθρωπος συγγενής σού ἐστιν, καὶ ἔστιν αὐτῷ θυγάτηρ, ᾗ ὄνομα Σαρρα·
12 καὶ υἱὸς ἄρσην οὐδὲ θυγάτηρ ὑπάρχει αὐτῷ πλὴν Σαρρας
μόνης, καὶ σὺ ἔγγιστα αὐτῆς εἶ παρὰ πάντας ἀνθρώπους

KING JAMES VERSION

3 Then the angel said unto him, Take the fish. And the young man laid hold of the fish, and drew it to land.

4 To whom the angel said, Open the fish, and take the heart and the liver and the gall, and put them up safely.

5 So the young man did as the angel commanded him; and when they had roasted the fish, they did eat it: then they both went on their way, till they drew near to Ecbatane.

6 Then the young man said to the angel, Brother Azarias, to what use is the heart and the liver and the gall of the fish?

7 And he said unto him, Touching the heart and the liver, if a devil or an evil spirit trouble any, we must make a smoke thereof before the man or the woman, and the party shall be no more vexed.

8 As for the gall, *it is good* to anoint a man that hath whiteness in his eyes, and he shall be healed.

9 And when they were come near to Rages,

10 The angel said to the young man, Brother, to day we shall lodge with Raguel, who is thy cousin; he also hath one only daughter, named Sara; I will speak for her, that she may be given thee for a wife.

11 For to thee doth the right of her appertain, seeing thou only art of her kindred.

DOUAY OLD TESTAMENT

4 And the angel said to him: Take him by the gill, and draw him to thee. And when he had done so, he drew him out upon the land, and he began to pant before his feet.

5 Then the angel said to him: Take out the entrails of this fish, and lay up his heart, and his gall, and his liver for thee: for these are necessary for useful medicines.

6 And when he had done so, he roasted the flesh thereof, and they took it with them in the way: the rest they salted as much as might serve them, till they came to Rages the city of the Medes.

7 Then Tobias asked the angel, and said to him: I beseech thee, brother Azarias, tell me what remedies are these things good for, which thou hast bid me keep of the fish?

8 And the angel, answering, said to him: If thou put a little piece of its heart upon coals, the smoke thereof driveth away all kind of devils, either from man or from woman, so that they come no more to them.

9 And the gall is good for anointing the eyes, in which there is a white speck, and they shall be cured.

10 And Tobias said to him: Where wilt thou that we lodge?

11 And the angel answering, said: Here is one whose name is Raguel, a near kinsman of thy tribe, and he hath a daughter named Sara, but he hath no son nor any other daughter beside her.

KNOX TRANSLATION

the dust from his feet, up came a monstrous fish as if it
would have devoured him. 3 At this, he cried out in an
extreme of fear, Help, sir; he means mischief. 4 But the angel
bade him catch it by the gill and pull it towards him; so catch
it he did, and brought it out on to the dry land, where it lay
struggling at his feet. 5 This fish, the angel told him, is
worth the bowelling; heart and gall and liver of it thou must
keep by thee, sovereign remedies all. 6 This done, he roasted
part of the meat, which they ate on their journey, and salted
the rest, to serve them for provisions till they should reach
Rages in Media.
7 And now Tobias had a question to ask of the angel; Tell
me, good Azarias, said he, what healing virtue lies in those
parts of the fish I must needs keep by me? 8 Its heart,
answered he, has this virtue, that if a morsel of it be laid on
the coals, the smoke will rid man or woman of the fiend's
harassing, and that for ever. 9 As for the gall, it is a sovereign salve for healing eyes that have a white film binding
them.[a] 10 And for our journey, said Tobias, what is the next
stage of that? 11 Our host's name is Raguel, the angel told
him, a tribesman and a kinsman of thy own. He has a
daughter called Sara, and neither chick nor child besides.

a The fish called by the ancients callionymus, or uranoscopus, was supposed to be a specific in cases of leucoma; it was, however, a salt-water fish. In verses 1-9 the other versions vary hardly at all, but from this point onward they shew considerable difference, and have nothing corresponding to verses 16-22 of the Vulgate.

TODAY'S ENGLISH VERSION

his feet. Tobias let out a yell, 3 and the angel called to him,
"Grab that fish! Don't let it get away."
Then Tobias grabbed the fish and dragged it up on the
bank.
4 "Cut the fish open," the angel instructed, "and take out
its gall bladder, heart, and liver. Keep these with you; they
can be used for medicine, but throw away the guts."
5 Tobias did as the angel had told him. Then he cooked the
fish, ate part of it, and salted the rest to take along with him.
The two continued on together until they were near Media.
6 Then Tobias asked, "Azarias, my friend, what diseases can
be cured by this gall bladder, heart, and liver?"
7 The angel answered, "The heart and liver can be burned
and used to chase away a demon or an evil spirit that is tormenting someone. The attacks will stop immediately, and
the person will never be troubled again. 8 You can use the
gall bladder to treat someone whose eyes are covered with a
white film. Just rub it on his eyes and blow on the film, and
he will be able to see again."
9 When they had reached Media and were approaching the
city of Ecbatana, 10 Raphael said, "Tobias, my friend."
"Yes, what is it?" Tobias asked.
Raphael continued, "Tonight we will stay at the home of
your relative Raguel. He has only one child, a daughter
named Sarah, 11 and since you are her closest relative, you

NEW REVISED STANDARD VERSION

young man's foot, and he cried out. 4 But the angel said to
the young man, "Catch hold of the fish and hang on to it!" So
the young man grasped the fish and drew it up on the land.
5 Then the angel said to him, "Cut open the fish and take out
its gall, heart, and liver. Keep them with you, but throw away
the intestines. For its gall, heart, and liver are useful as medicine." 6 So after cutting open the fish the young man gathered together the gall, heart, and liver; then he roasted and
ate some of the fish, and kept some to be salted.
The two continued on their way together until they were
near Media.[a] 7 Then the young man questioned the angel
and said to him, "Brother Azariah, what medicinal value is
there in the fish's heart and liver, and in the gall?" 8 He
replied, "As for the fish's heart and liver, you must burn
them to make a smoke in the presence of a man or woman
afflicted by a demon or evil spirit, and every affliction will
flee away and never remain with that person any longer.
9 And as for the gall, anoint a person's eyes where white
films have appeared on them; blow upon them, upon the
white films, and the eyes[b] will be healed."
10 When he entered Media and already was approaching
Ecbatana,[c] 11 Raphael said to the young man, "Brother
Tobias." "Here I am," he answered. Then Raphael[d] said to
him, "We must stay this night in the home of Raguel. He is
your relative, and he has a daughter named Sarah. 12 He has
no male heir and no daughter except Sarah only, and you, as
next of kin to her, have before all other men a hereditary

a Other ancient authorities read *Ecbatana* *b* Gk *they* *c* Other ancient authorities read *Rages* *d* Gk *he*

NEW AMERICAN BIBLE

and tried to swallow his foot. He shouted in alarm. 4 But the
angel said to him, "Take hold of the fish and don't let it get
away!" The boy seized the fish and hauled it up on the
shore. 5 The angel then told him: "Cut the fish open and take
out its gall, heart, and liver, and keep them with you; but
throw away the entrails. Its gall, heart, and liver make useful
medicines." 6 After the lad had cut the fish open, he put
aside the gall, heart, and liver. Then he broiled and ate part
of the fish; the rest he salted and kept for the journey.
7 Afterward they traveled on together till they were near
Media. The boy asked the angel this question: "Brother
Azariah, what medicinal value is there in the fish's heart,
liver, and gall?" 8 He answered: "As regards the fish's heart
and liver, if you burn them so that the smoke surrounds a
man or a woman who is afflicted by a demon or evil spirit,
the affliction will leave him completely, and no demons will
ever return to him again. 9 And as for the gall, if you rub it
on the eyes of a man who has cataracts, blowing into his
eyes right on the cataracts, his sight will be restored."
10 When they had entered Media and were getting close to
Ecbatana, 11 Raphael said to the boy, "Brother Tobiah!" He
answered, "Yes, what is it?" Raphael continued: "Tonight we
must stay with Raguel, who is a relative of yours. He has a
daughter named Sarah, 12 but no other child. Since you are
Sarah's closest relative, you before all other men have the

NEW JERUSALEM BIBLE

water and tried to swallow his foot. The boy gave a shout
4 and the angel said, 'Catch the fish; do not let it go.' The boy
mastered the fish and pulled it onto the bank. 5 The angel
said, 'Cut it open; take out gall, heart and liver; set these
aside and throw the entrails away, for gall and heart and
liver have curative properties.' 6 The boy cut the fish open
and took out gall and heart and liver. He fried part of the
fish for his meal and kept some for salting. Then they
walked on again together until they were nearly in Media.
7 Then the boy asked the angel this question, 'Brother
Azarias, what can the fish's heart, liver and gall cure?' 8 He
replied, 'You burn the fish's heart and liver, and their smoke
is used in the case of a man or woman plagued by a demon
or evil spirit; any such affliction disappears for good, leaving
no trace. 9 As regards the gall, this is used as an eye ointment for anyone having white spots on his eyes; after using
it, you have only to blow on the spots to cure them.'
10 They entered Media and had nearly reached Ecbatana
11 when Raphael said to the boy, 'Brother Tobias.' 'Yes?' he
replied. The angel went on, 'Tonight we are to stay with
Raguel, who is a kinsman of yours. He has a daughter called
Sarah, 12 but apart from Sarah he has no other son or
daughter. Now you are her next of kin; she belongs to you

GREEK OLD TESTAMENT

κληρονομῆσαι αὐτήν, καὶ τὰ ὄντα τῷ πατρὶ αὐτῆς σοὶ δικαιοῦται κληρονομῆσαι· καὶ τὸ κοράσιον φρόνιμον καὶ ἀνδρεῖον
καὶ καλὸν λίαν, καὶ ὁ πατὴρ αὐτῆς καλός. 13 καὶ εἶπεν
Δεδικαίωταί σοι λαβεῖν αὐτήν· καὶ ἄκουσόν μου, ἄδελφε, καὶ
λαλήσω τῷ πατρὶ περὶ τοῦ κορασίου τὴν νύκτα ταύτην, ἵνα
λημψόμεθά σοι αὐτὴν νύμφην· καὶ ὅταν ἐπιστρέψωμεν ἐκ
Ῥάγων, ποιήσομεν τὸν γάμον αὐτῆς. καὶ ἐπίσταμαι ὅτι οὐ
μὴ δυνηθῇ Ραγουηλ κωλῦσαι αὐτὴν ἀπὸ σοῦ ἢ ἐγγυᾶσθαι
ἑτέρῳ, ὀφειλήσειν θάνατον κατὰ τὴν κρίσιν τῆς βίβλου
Μωυσέως διὰ τὸ γινώσκειν ὅτι σοὶ κληρονομία καθήκει
λαβεῖν τὴν θυγατέρα αὐτοῦ παρὰ πάντα ἄνθρωπον. καὶ νῦν
ἄκουσόν μου, ἄδελφε, καὶ λαλήσομεν περὶ τοῦ κορασίου τὴν
νύκτα ταύτην καὶ μνηστευσόμεθά σοι αὐτήν· καὶ ὅταν
ἐπιστρέψωμεν ἐκ Ῥάγων, λημψόμεθα αὐτὴν καὶ ἀπάξομεν
αὐτὴν μεθ' ἡμῶν εἰς τὸν οἶκόν σου. 14 τότε ἀποκριθεὶς
Τωβιας εἶπεν τῷ Ραφαηλ Αζαρια ἄδελφε, ἤκουσα ὅτι ἑπτὰ
ἤδη ἐδόθη ἀνδράσιν, καὶ ἀπέθανον ἐν τοῖς νυμφῶσιν αὐτῶν
τὴν νύκτα, ὁπότε εἰσεπορεύοντο πρὸς αὐτήν, καὶ ἀπέθνη-
σκον. καὶ ἤκουσα λεγόντων αὐτῶν ὅτι δαιμόνιον ἀποκτέννει
αὐτούς. 15 καὶ νῦν φοβοῦμαι ἐγώ — ὅτι αὐτὴν οὐκ ἀδικεῖ,
ἀλλ' ὃς ἂν θελήσῃ ἐγγίσαι αὐτῆς, ἀποκτέννει αὐτόν· μονογενής εἰμι τῷ πατρί μου — μὴ ἀποθάνω καὶ κατάξω τὴν
ζωὴν τοῦ πατρός μου καὶ τῆς μητρός μου μετ' ὀδύνης ἐπ'
ἐμοὶ εἰς τὸν τάφον αὐτῶν· καὶ υἱὸς ἕτερος οὐχ ὑπάρχει αὐτοῖς, ἵνα θάψῃ αὐτούς. 16 καὶ λέγει αὐτῷ Οὐ μέμνησαι τὰς
ἐντολὰς τοῦ πατρός σου, ὅτι ἐνετείλατό σοι λαβεῖν γυναῖκα

KING JAMES VERSION

12 And the maid is fair and wise: now therefore hear me, and I will speak to her father; and when we return from Rages we will celebrate the marriage: for I know that Raguel cannot marry her to another according to the law of Moses, but he shall be guilty of death, because the right of inheritance doth rather appertain to thee than to any other.

13 Then the young man answered the angel, I have heard, brother Azarias, that this maid hath been given to seven men, who all died in the marriage chamber.

14 And now I am the only son of my father, and I am afraid, lest, if I go in unto her, I die, as the other before: for a wicked spirit loveth her, which hurteth no body, but those which come unto her: wherefore I also fear lest I die, and bring my father's and my mother's life because of me to the grave with sorrow: for they have no other son to bury them.

15 Then the angel said unto him, Dost thou not remember the precepts which thy father gave thee, that thou shouldest marry a wife of thine own kindred? wherefore hear me, O my

DOUAY OLD TESTAMENT

12 All his substance is due to thee, and thou must take her to wife.

13 Ask her therefore of her father, and he will give her thee to wife.

14 Then Tobias answered, and said: I hear that she hath been given to seven husbands, and they all died: moreover I have heard, that a devil killed them.

15 Now I am afraid, lest the same thing should happen to me also: and whereas I am the only child of my parents, I should bring down their old age with sorrow to hell.

KNOX TRANSLATION

12 Of all he possesses thou mayest be heir, if thou wilt claim
his daughter's hand in marriage; 13 thou hast but to ask
him, and she is thine.
14 I hear stories told of this maid, Tobias answered; how
she has been betrothed seven times, and to every bridegroom
it brought death; how it was a fiend, if the tale be true, that
made away with them. 15 If the like befall me too, it would
go hard with those parents of mine; I am all the children
they have, they are old now, and this were to give them a
cheerless passage to the grave. 16 Heed me well, answered

TODAY'S ENGLISH VERSION

have the right to marry her. You also have the right to inherit
all her father's property. 12 She is sensible, brave, and very
beautiful; and her father is a good man. Tonight I'll discuss
the marriage proposal with her father, and he will consent to
give her to you as your bride. Then, when we return home
from the town of Rages, we will celebrate the marriage.
Raguel cannot refuse to let you marry her, and he cannot let
any other man have her. If he did, then according to the Law
of Moses he would deserve the death penalty. He knows that
you are the only man who has the right to marry his daughter and receive the inheritance, so follow my advice. Raguel
and I will discuss the matter tonight and arrange your
engagement to Sarah. When we get back from the city of
Rages, we will take her home with us."
13 Tobias then said to Raphael, "Azarias, my friend, I have
already heard about Sarah's seven former husbands, and
how each one dropped dead on his wedding night, even
before he could get to bed. 14 According to the story I heard,
a demon killed them. He doesn't harm Sarah, but he kills
every man who tries to get near her. I am afraid of this
demon. I am an only child, and if I were to die, the sorrow
would send my parents to their graves. They don't even have
another son to bury them."
15 The angel replied, "Have you already forgotten your
father's instructions? He told you to marry a woman from

NEW REVISED STANDARD VERSION

claim on her. Also it is right for you to inherit her father's
possessions. Moreover, the girl is sensible, brave, and very
beautiful, and her father is a good man." 13 He continued,
"You have every right to take her in marriage. So listen to
me, brother; tonight I will speak to her father about the girl,
so that we may take her to be your bride. When we return
from Rages we will celebrate her marriage. For I know that
Raguel can by no means keep her from you or promise her to
another man without incurring the penalty of death according to the decree of the book of Moses. Indeed he knows that
you, rather than any other man, are entitled to marry his
daughter. So now listen to me, brother, and tonight we shall
speak concerning the girl and arrange her engagement to
you. And when we return from Rages we will take her and
bring her back with us to your house."
14 Then Tobias said in answer to Raphael, "Brother
Azariah, I have heard that she already has been married to
seven husbands and that they died in the bridal chamber. On
the night when they went in to her, they would die. I have
heard people saying that it was a demon that killed them.
15 It does not harm her, but it kills anyone who desires to
approach her. So now, since I am the only son my father
has, I am afraid that I may die and bring my father's and
mother's life down to their grave, grieving for me—and they
have no other son to bury them."
16 But Raphael[a] said to him, "Do you not remember your
father's orders when he commanded you to take a wife from

a Gk *he*

NEW AMERICAN BIBLE

right to marry her. Also, her father's estate is rightfully yours
to inherit. Now the girl is sensible, courageous, and very
beautiful; and her father loves her dearly." 13 He continued:
"Since you have the right to marry her, listen to me, brother.
Tonight I will ask the girl's father to let us have her as your
bride. When we return from Rages, we will hold the wedding
feast for her. I know that Raguel cannot keep her from you
or let her become engaged to another man; that would be a
capital crime according to the decree in the Book of Moses,
and he knows that it is your right, before all other men, to
marry his daughter. So heed my words, brother; tonight we
must speak for the girl, so that we may have her engaged to
you. And when we return from Rages, we will take her and
bring her back with us to your house."
14 Tobiah objected, however: "Brother Azariah, I have
heard that this woman has already been married seven
times, and that her husbands died in their bridal chambers.
On the very night they approached her, they dropped dead.
And I have heard it said that it was a demon who killed
them. 15 So now I too am afraid of this demon. Because he
loves her, he does not harm her; but he does slay any man
who wishes to come close to her. I am my father's only child.
If I should die, I would bring my father and mother down to
their grave in sorrow over me. And they have no other son to
bury them!"
16 Raphael said to him: "Do you not remember your
father's orders? He commanded you to marry a woman from

NEW JERUSALEM BIBLE

before anyone else and you may claim her father's inheritance. She is a thoughtful, courageous and very lovely girl,
and her father loves her dearly. 13 You have the right to
marry her. Listen, brother; this very evening I shall speak
about the girl to her father and arrange for her to be
betrothed to you, and when we come back from Rhages we
can celebrate the marriage. I assure you, Raguel has no right
whatever to refuse you or to betroth her to anyone else. That
would be asking for death, as prescribed in the Book of
Moses, once he is aware that kinship gives you the pre-eminent right to marry his daughter. So listen, brother. This very
evening we shall speak about the girl and ask for her hand
in marriage. When we come back from Rhages we shall fetch
her and take her home with us.'
14 Tobias replied to Raphael, 'Brother Azarias, I have been
told that she has already been given in marriage seven times
and that each time her bridegroom has died in the bridal
room. He died the same night as he entered her room; and I
have heard people say it was a demon that killed them,
15 and this makes me afraid. To her the demon does no harm
because he loves her, but as soon as a man tries to approach
her, he kills him. I am my father's only son, and I have no
wish to die. I do not want my father and mother to grieve
over me for the rest of their lives; they have no other son to
bury them.' 16 The angel said, 'Have you forgotten your
father's advice? After all, he urged you to choose a wife from

GREEK OLD TESTAMENT

ἐκ τοῦ οἴκου τοῦ πατρός σου; καὶ νῦν ἄκουσόν μου, ἄδελφε,
καὶ μὴ λόγον ἔχε τοῦ δαιμονίου τούτου καὶ λαβέ· καὶ γινώσκω ἐγὼ ὅτι τὴν νύκτα ταύτην δοθήσεταί σοι γυνή. 17 καὶ
ὅταν εἰσέλθῃς εἰς τὸν νυμφῶνα, λαβὲ ἐκ τοῦ ἥπατος τοῦ
ἰχθύος καὶ τὴν καρδίαν καὶ ἐπίθες ἐπὶ τὴν τέφραν τῶν θυμιαμάτων, καὶ ἡ ὀσμὴ πορεύσεται, καὶ ὀσφρανθήσεται τὸ
δαιμόνιον καὶ φεύξεται καὶ οὐκέτι μὴ φανῇ περὶ αὐτὴν τὸν
πάντα αἰῶνα. 18 καὶ ὅταν μέλλῃς γίνεσθαι μετ' αὐτῆς, ἐξ-
εγέρθητε πρῶτον ἀμφότεροι καὶ προσεύξασθε καὶ δεήθητε
τοῦ κυρίου τοῦ οὐρανοῦ, ἵνα ἔλεος γένηται καὶ σωτηρία ἐφ'
ὑμᾶς. καὶ μὴ φοβοῦ, σοὶ γάρ ἐστιν μεμερισμένη πρὸ τοῦ
αἰῶνος, καὶ σὺ αὐτὴν σώσεις, καὶ μετὰ σοῦ πορεύσεται, καὶ
ὑπολαμβάνω ὅτι ἔσονταί σοι ἐξ αὐτῆς παιδία καὶ ἔσονταί
σοι ὡς ἀδελφοί, μὴ λόγον ἔχε. 19 καὶ ὅτε ἤκουσεν Τωβιας
τῶν λόγων Ραφαηλ καὶ ὅτι ἔστιν αὐτῷ ἀδελφὴ ἐκ τοῦ σπέρματος τοῦ οἴκου τοῦ πατρὸς αὐτοῦ, λίαν ἠγάπησεν αὐτήν,
καὶ ἡ καρδία αὐτοῦ ἐκολλήθη εἰς αὐτήν.

7 Καὶ ὅτε εἰσῆλθεν εἰς Ἐκβάτανα, λέγει αὐτῷ Αζαρια
ἄδελφε, ἀπάγαγέ με εὐθεῖαν πρὸς Ραγουηλ τὸν ἀδελφὸν
ἡμῶν. καὶ ἀπήγαγεν αὐτὸν εἰς τὸν οἶκον Ραγουήλου, καὶ
εὗρον αὐτὸν καθήμενον παρὰ τὴν θύραν τῆς αὐλῆς καὶ
ἐχαιρέτισαν αὐτὸν πρῶτοι, καὶ εἶπεν αὐτοῖς Χαίρετε πολλά,
ἀδελφοί, καὶ καλῶς ἤλθατε ὑγιαίνοντες. καὶ ἤγαγεν αὐτοὺς
εἰς τὸν οἶκον αὐτοῦ. 2 καὶ εἶπεν Εδνα τῇ γυναικὶ αὐτοῦ Ὡς
ὅμοιος ὁ νεανίσκος οὗτος Τωβει τῷ ἀδελφῷ μου. 3 καὶ ἠρώτησεν αὐτοὺς Εδνα καὶ εἶπεν αὐτοῖς Πόθεν ἐστέ, ἀδελφοί;
καὶ εἶπαν αὐτῇ Ἐκ τῶν υἱῶν Νεφθαλιμ ἡμεῖς τῶν αἰχμα-

KING JAMES VERSION

brother; for she shall be given thee to wife; and make thou
no reckoning of the evil spirit; for this same night shall she
be given thee in marriage.
16 And when thou shalt come into the marriage chamber,
thou shalt take the ashes of perfume, and shalt lay upon
them some of the heart and liver of the fish, and shalt make
a smoke with it:
17 And the devil shall smell it, and flee away, and never
come again any more: but when thou shalt come to her, rise
up both of you, and pray to God which is merciful, who will
have pity on you, and save you: fear not, for she is appointed unto thee from the beginning; and thou shalt preserve
her, and she shall go with thee. Moreover I suppose that she
shall bear thee children. Now when Tobias had heard these
things, he loved her, and his heart was effectually joined to
her.

7 And when they were come to Ecbatane, they came to the
house of Raguel, and Sara met them: and after they had
saluted one another, she brought them into the house.
2 Then said Raguel to Edna his wife, How like is this
young man to Tobit my cousin!
3 And Raguel asked them, From whence are ye, brethren?
To whom they said, We are of the sons of Nephthalim, which
are captives in Nineve.

DOUAY OLD TESTAMENT

16 Then the angel Raphael said to him: Hear me, and I
will shew thee who they are, over whom the devil can prevail.
17 For they who in such manner receive matrimony, as to
shut out God from themselves, and from their mind, and to
give themselves to their lust, as the horse and mule, which
have not understanding, over them the devil hath power.
18 But thou when thou shalt take her, go into the chamber, and for three days keep thyself continent from her, and
give thyself to nothing else but to prayers with her.
19 And on that night lay the liver of the fish on the fire,
and the devil shall be driven away.
20 But the second night thou shalt be admitted into the
society of the holy Patriarchs.
21 And the third night thou shalt obtain a blessing that
sound children may be born of you.
22 And when the third night is past, thou shalt take the
virgin with the fear of the Lord, moved rather for love of children than for lust, that in the seed of Abraham thou mayst
obtain a blessing in children.

7 AND they went in to Raguel, and Raguel received them
with joy.
2 And Raguel looking upon Tobias, said to Anna his wife:
How like is this young man to my cousin?
3 And when he had spoken these words, he said: Whence
are ye young men our brethren?
4 But they said: We are of the tribe of Nephtali, of the captivity of Ninive.

KNOX TRANSLATION

Raphael, and thou shalt hear why the fiend has power to
hurt some and not others. 17 The fiend has power over such
as go about their marrying with all thought of God shut out
of their hearts and minds, wholly intent on their lust, as if
they were horse or mule, brutes without reason. 18 Not such
be thy mating, when thou hast won thy bride. For three days
deny thyself her favours, and the time you spend together,
spend all in prayer. 19 The first night, burn the liver of yonder fish, and therewith the fiend shall be driven away. 20 On
the second night, union thou shalt have, but with the company of the holy patriarchs.[a] 21 The third night, thy prayer
shall win thee a blessing, of children safely born to thee and
to her. 22 Then, when the third night is past, take the maid
to thyself with the fear of the Lord upon thee, moved rather
by the hope of begetting children than by any lust of thine.
So, in the true line of Abraham, thou shalt have joy of thy
fatherhood.

7 To Raguel, then, they went, and right gladly he welcomed them; 2 he no sooner caught sight of Tobias than
he said to his wife Anna,[b] Here is a young man has the very
look of my cousin Tobias! 3 Then he asked them, Whence
come you, fellow-countrymen? 4 And, upon hearing that
they were of Nephthali's tribe, exiles dwelling at Nineve,

[a] The meaning of this mystical allusion is unknown. [b] This seems to be a mistake in the Latin; the other versions call Raguel's wife Edna.

TODAY'S ENGLISH VERSION

your own tribe. So, listen carefully to what I say. Don't worry about the demon. Marry Sarah! I know that tonight Raguel will let Sarah marry you. 16When you go into the bedroom, take the fish's heart and liver with you and place them on the burning incense, 17so that the odor will spread throughout the room. When the demon smells it, he will leave and never come near Sarah again. But before you consummate the marriage, both of you must get up and pray for the Lord in heaven to be merciful to you and to protect you. Don't be afraid. Sarah was meant to be yours from the beginning of creation. You will rescue her from the demon, and she will go with you to your home. You and Sarah will have many children, whom you will love very much. So don't worry!"

Tobias listened very carefully to what Raphael had to say. He knew that Sarah was a relative on his father's side of the family. He began to fall in love with her and looked forward to marrying her.

7 When Tobias and the angel Raphael had entered the city of Ecbatana, Tobias said, "Azarias, my friend, take me to see Raguel as quickly as you can." The angel brought him to Raguel's house, where they found him sitting at the entrance to his courtyard. Raphael and Tobias greeted him first; then he replied, "Come in, my friends. You are welcome in my home."

Raguel brought them into his house 2and said to his wife Edna, "Doesn't this young man look just like my cousin Tobit?"

3Edna asked them, "Where do you come from?"

"We are Israelites of the tribe of Naphtali," Tobias and

NEW REVISED STANDARD VERSION

your father's house? Now listen to me, brother, and say no more about this demon. Take her. I know that this very night she will be given to you in marriage. 17When you enter the bridal chamber, take some of the fish's liver and heart, and put them on the embers of the incense. An odor will be given off; 18the demon will smell it and flee, and will never be seen near her any more. Now when you are about to go to bed with her, both of you must first stand up and pray, imploring the Lord of heaven that mercy and safety may be granted to you. Do not be afraid, for she was set apart for you before the world was made. You will save her, and she will go with you. I presume that you will have children by her, and they will be as brothers to you. Now say no more!" When Tobias heard the words of Raphael and learned that she was his kinswoman,[a] related through his father's lineage, he loved her very much, and his heart was drawn to her.

7 Now when they[b] entered Ecbatana, Tobias[c] said to him, "Brother Azariah, take me straight to our brother Raguel." So he took him to Raguel's house, where they found him sitting beside the courtyard door. They greeted him first, and he replied, "Joyous greetings, brothers; welcome and good health!" Then he brought them into his house. 2He said to his wife Edna, "How much the young man resembles my kinsman Tobit!" 3Then Edna questioned them, saying, "Where are you from, brothers?" They answered, "We belong to the descendants of Naphtali who

a Gk *sister* *b* Other ancient authorities read *he* *c* Gk *he*

NEW AMERICAN BIBLE

your own family. So now listen to me, brother; do not give another thought to this demon, but marry Sarah. I know that tonight you shall have her for your wife! 17When you go into the bridal chamber, take the fish's liver and heart, and place them on the embers for the incense. 18As soon as the demon smells the odor they give off, he will flee and never again show himself near her. Then when you are about to have intercourse with her, both of you first rise up to pray. Beg the Lord of heaven to show you mercy and grant you deliverance. But do not be afraid, for she was set apart for you before the world existed. You will save her, and she will go with you. And I suppose that you will have children by her, who will take the place of brothers for you. So do not worry."

When Tobiah heard Raphael say that she was his kinswoman, of his own family's lineage, he fell deeply in love with her, and his heart became set on her.

7 When they entered Ecbatana, Tobiah said, "Brother Azariah, lead me straight to our kinsman Raguel." So he brought him to the house of Raguel, whom they found seated by his courtyard gate. They greeted him first. He said to them, "Greetings to you too, brothers! Good health to you, and welcome!" When he brought them into his home, 2he said to his wife Edna, "This young man looks just like my kinsman Tobit!" 3So Edna asked them, "Who are you, brothers?" They answered, "We are of the exiles from

NEW JERUSALEM BIBLE

your father's family. Listen then, brother. Do not worry about the demon; take her. This very evening, I promise, she will be given you as your wife. 17Then once you are in the bridal room, take the heart and liver of the fish and lay a little of it on the burning incense. The reek will rise, 18the demon will smell it and flee, and there is no danger that he will ever be found near the girl again. Then, before you sleep together, first stand up, both of you, and pray. Ask the Lord of heaven to grant you his grace and protection. Do not be afraid; she was destined for you from the beginning, and you are the one to save her. She will follow you, and I pledge my word she will give you children who will be like brothers to you. Do not worry.' And when Tobias heard Raphael say this, when he understood that Sarah was his sister, a kinswoman of his father's family, he fell so deeply in love with her that he could no longer call his heart his own.

7 As they entered Ecbatana, Tobias said, 'Brother Azarias, take me at once to our brother Raguel's.' And he showed him the way to the house of Raguel, whom they found sitting beside his courtyard door. They greeted him first, and he replied, 'Welcome and greetings, brothers.' And he took them into his house. 2He said to his wife Edna, 'How like my brother Tobit this young man is!' 3Edna asked them where they came from; they said, 'We are sons of Naphtali exiled in

GREEK OLD TESTAMENT

λωτισθέντων ἐν Νινευη. 4 καὶ εἶπεν αὐτοῖς Γινώσκετε Τωβιν
τὸν ἀδελφὸν ἡμῶν; καὶ εἶπαν αὐτῇ Γινώσκομεν ἡμεῖς αὐτόν.
5 καὶ εἶπεν αὐτοῖς Ὑγιαίνει; καὶ εἶπαν αὐτῇ Ὑγιαίνει καὶ
ζῇ· καὶ εἶπεν Τωβιας Ὁ πατήρ μού ἐστιν. 6 καὶ ἀνεπήδησεν
Ραγουηλ καὶ κατεφίλησεν αὐτὸν καὶ ἔκλαυσεν καὶ ἐλάλησεν
καὶ εἶπεν αὐτῷ Εὐλογία σοι γένοιτο, παιδίον, ὁ τοῦ καλοῦ
καὶ ἀγαθοῦ πατρός. ὢ ταλαιπώρων κακῶν, ὅτι ἐτυφλώθη ἀνὴρ
δίκαιος καὶ ποιῶν ἐλεημοσύνας. καὶ ἐπιπεσὼν ἐπὶ τὸν
τράχηλον Τωβια τοῦ ἀδελφοῦ αὐτοῦ ἔκλαυσεν. 7 καὶ Εδνα ἡ
γυνὴ αὐτοῦ ἔκλαυσεν αὐτόν, καὶ Σαρρα ἡ θυγάτηρ αὐτῶν
ἔκλαυσεν καὶ αὐτή. 8 καὶ ἔθυσεν κριὸν ἐκ προβάτων καὶ
ὑπεδέξατο αὐτοὺς προθύμως.

9 Καὶ ὅτε ἐλούσαντο καὶ ἐνίψαντο καὶ ἀνέπεσαν δειπνῆσαι,
εἶπεν Τωβιας τῷ Ραφαηλ Αζαρια ἄδελφε, εἰπὸν Ραγουηλ
ὅπως δῷ μοι Σαρραν τὴν ἀδελφήν μου. 10 καὶ ἤκουσεν
Ραγουηλ τὸν λόγον καὶ εἶπεν τῷ παιδί Φάγε καὶ πίε καὶ
ἡδέως γενοῦ τὴν νύκτα ταύτην· οὐ γάρ ἐστιν ἄνθρωπος ᾧ
καθήκει λαβεῖν Σαρραν τὴν θυγατέρα μου πλὴν σοῦ, ἄδελφε,
ὡσαύτως δὲ καὶ ἐγὼ οὐκ ἔχω ἐξουσίαν δοῦναι αὐτὴν ἑτέρῳ
ἀνδρὶ πλὴν σοῦ, ὅτι σὺ ἔγγιστά μου· καὶ μάλα τὴν ἀλήθειάν
σοι ὑποδείξω, παιδίον. 11 ἔδωκα αὐτὴν ἑπτὰ ἀνδράσιν τῶν
ἀδελφῶν ἡμῶν, καὶ πάντες ἀπέθανον τὴν νύκτα ὁπότε εἰσεπορεύοντο πρὸς αὐτήν. καὶ νῦν, παιδίον, φάγε καὶ πίε, καὶ
κύριος ποιήσει ἐν ὑμῖν. 12 καὶ εἶπεν Τωβιας Οὐ μὴ φάγω ἐντεῦθεν οὐδὲ μὴ πίω, ἕως ἂν διαστήσῃς τὰ πρὸς ἐμέ. καὶ

KING JAMES VERSION

4 Then he said to them, Do ye know Tobit our kinsman? And they said, We know him. Then said he, Is he in good health?

5 And they said, He is both alive, and in good health: and Tobias said, He is my father.

6 Then Raguel leaped up, and kissed him, and wept,

7 And blessed him, and said unto him, Thou art the son of an honest and good man. But when he had heard that Tobit was blind, he was sorrowful, and wept.

8 And likewise Edna his wife and Sara his daughter wept. Moreover they entertained them cheerfully; and after that they had killed a ram of the flock, they set store of meat on the table. Then said Tobias to Raphael, Brother Azarias, speak of those things of which thou didst talk in the way, and let this business be dispatched.

9 So he communicated the matter with Raguel: and Raguel said to Tobias, Eat and drink, and make merry:

10 For it is meet that thou shouldest marry my daughter: nevertheless I will declare unto thee the truth.

11 I have given my daughter in marriage to seven men, who died that night they came in unto her: nevertheless for the present be merry. But Tobias said, I will eat nothing here, till we agree and swear one to another.

DOUAY OLD TESTAMENT

5 And Raguel said to them: Do you know Tobias my brother? And they said: We know him.

6 And when he was speaking many good things of him, the angel said to Raguel: Tobias concerning whom thou inquirest is this young man's father.

7 And Raguel went to him, and kissed him with tears, and weeping upon his neck, said: A blessing be upon thee, my son, because thou art the son of a good and most virtuous man.

8 And Anna his wife, and Sara their daughter wept.

9 And after they had spoken, Raguel commanded a sheep to be killed, and a feast to be prepared. And when he desired them to sit down to dinner,

10 Tobias said: I will not eat nor drink here this day, unless thou first grant me my petition, and promise to give me Sara thy daughter.

11 Now when Raguel heard this he was afraid, knowing what had happened to those seven husbands, that went in unto her: and he began to fear lest it might happen to him also in like manner: and as he was in suspense, and gave no answer to his petition,

12 The angel said to him: Be not afraid to give her to this man, for to him who feareth God is thy daughter due to be his wife: therefore another could not have her.

KNOX TRANSLATION

5 Do you know my cousin, Tobias? Yes, they said, we know
him well. 6 With that, Raguel fell to singing his cousin's
praises, but the angel cut him short: Thou dost well to ask
about Tobias; this is his son. 7 Thereupon Raguel threw his
arms about him, and wept, and kissed him, and wept again;
A blessing on thee, my son, cried he; 'tis a good man, a good
excellent man, thou hast for thy father! 8 And there stood his
wife Anna, and their daughter Sara, in tears like himself.
9 When they had spent some time in talk, Raguel would
have a ram killed, and a feast made. But it was in vain he
urged them to fall to; 10 Neither eat nor drink will I in this
house, Tobias said, until thou dost grant a request of mine.
And my request is for the hand of thy daughter Sara in marriage. 11 Upon hearing this, Raguel was much taken aback;
he had not forgotten what befell those other seven men that
went near her bed; and the fear assailed him, What if this
one fares no better? But while he hummed and hawed over
his answer, 12 the angel said, Do not be afraid to give him
thy daughter's hand; for his pious care she was destined,
that is why those other wooers could not gain their suit.

TODAY'S ENGLISH VERSION

Raphael answered, "but we are now living in exile in the city
of Nineveh in Assyria."
4 Edna said, "Do you know our cousin Tobit?"
"We certainly do know him," they answered.
"How is he?" she asked.
5 "He is alive and well," they replied.
Then Tobias added, "Tobit is my father." 6 At that Raguel
got up, and with tears of joy in his eyes he kissed Tobias.
7 Then he said, "God bless you, my child. Your father is a good
and noble man. What a terrible tragedy that such an honest
and generous man should have lost his sight!" He threw his
arms around Tobias' neck and wept on his shoulder. 8 His
wife Edna and his daughter Sarah also wept for Tobit.

Raguel gave Tobias and Raphael a warm welcome and had
one of his rams slaughtered. After the guests had bathed and
were about to sit down to eat, Tobias said to Raphael,
"Azarias, my friend, when are you going to ask Raguel to let
me marry Sarah?"
9 But Raguel overheard the question and said to Tobias,
10 "Eat and drink something first and enjoy yourself this
evening. You have the right to marry Sarah, and I cannot let
anyone else marry her, because you are my closest relative.
But I must tell you the truth, my son. 11 I have already given
her to seven men, all of them relatives. Each one died on his
wedding night, as soon as he entered the bedroom. But now,
my son, have something to eat and drink. The Lord will take
care of you both."
Tobias replied, "I won't eat or drink until you give me your
word."

NEW REVISED STANDARD VERSION

are exiles in Nineveh." 4 She said to them, "Do you know our
kinsman Tobit?" And they replied, "Yes, we know him."
Then she asked them, "Is he[a] in good health?" 5 They
replied, "He is alive and in good health." And Tobias added,
"He is my father!" 6 At that Raguel jumped up and kissed
him and wept. 7 He also spoke to him as follows, "Blessings
on you, my child, son of a good and noble father![b] O most
miserable of calamities that such an upright and beneficent
man has become blind!" He then embraced his kinsman
Tobias and wept. 8 His wife Edna also wept for him, and
their daughter Sarah likewise wept. 9 Then Raguel[c] slaughtered a ram from the flock and received them very warmly.

When they had bathed and washed themselves and had
reclined to dine, Tobias said to Raphael, "Brother Azariah,
ask Raguel to give me my kinswoman[d] Sarah." 10 But
Raguel overheard it and said to the lad, "Eat and drink, and
be merry tonight. For no one except you, brother, has the
right to marry my daughter Sarah. Likewise I am not at liberty to give her to any other man than yourself, because you
are my nearest relative. But let me explain to you the true
situation more fully, my child. 11 I have given her to seven
men of our kinsmen, and all died on the night when they
went in to her. But now, my child, eat and drink, and the
Lord will act on behalf of you both." But Tobias said, "I will
neither eat nor drink anything until you settle the things that

a Other ancient authorities add *alive and* *b* Other ancient authorities add *When he heard that Tobit had lost his sight, he was stricken with grief and wept. Then he said,* *c* Gk *he* *d* Gk *sister*

NEW AMERICAN BIBLE

Naphtali at Nineveh." 4 She said, "Do you know our kinsman Tobit?" They answered, "Indeed we do!" She asked, "Is
he well?" 5 They answered, "Yes, he is alive and well." Then
Tobiah exclaimed, "He is my father!" 6 Raguel sprang up
and kissed him, shedding tears of joy. 7 But when he heard
that Tobit had lost his eyesight, he was grieved and wept
aloud. He said to Tobiah: "My child, God bless you! You are
the son of a noble and good father. But what a terrible misfortune that such a righteous and charitable man should be
afflicted with blindness!" He continued to weep in the arms
of his kinsman Tobiah. 8 His wife Edna also wept for Tobit;
and even their daughter Sarah began to weep.
9 Afterward, Raguel slaughtered a ram from the flock and
gave them a cordial reception. When they had bathed and
reclined to eat, Tobiah said to Raphael, "Brother Azariah, ask
Raguel to let me marry my kinswoman Sarah." 10 Raguel
overheard the words; so he said to the boy: "Eat and drink
and be merry tonight, for no man is more entitled to marry
my daughter Sarah than you, brother. Besides, not even I
have the right to give her to anyone but you, because you are
my closest relative. But I will explain the situation to you very
frankly. 11 I have given her in marriage to seven men, all of
whom were kinsmen of ours, and all died on the very night
they approached her. But now, son, eat and drink. I am sure
the Lord will look after you both." Tobiah answered, "I will
eat or drink nothing until you set aside what belongs to me."

NEW JERUSALEM BIBLE

Nineveh.' 4 'Do you know our brother Tobit?' 'Yes.' 'How is
he?' 5 'He is alive and well.' And Tobias added, 'He is my
father.' 6 Raguel leapt to his feet and kissed him and wept.
7 Then, finding words, he said, 'Blessings on you, child! You
are the son of a noble father. How sad it is that someone so
bright and full of good deeds should have gone blind!' He fell
on the neck of his kinsman Tobias and wept. 8 And his wife
Edna wept for him, and so did his daughter Sarah. 9 Raguel
killed a ram from the flock, and they gave them a warm welcome.

They washed and bathed and sat down to table. Then
Tobias said to Raphael, 'Brother Azarias, will you ask Raguel
to give me my sister Sarah?' 10 Raguel overheard the words,
and said to the young man, 'Eat and drink, and make the
most of your evening; no one else has the right to take my
daughter Sarah— no one but you, my brother. In any case
even I am not at liberty to give her to anyone else, since you
are her next of kin. However, my boy, I must be frank with
you: 11 I have tried to find a husband for her seven times
among our kinsmen, and all of them have died the first
evening, on going to her room. But for the present, my boy,
eat and drink; the Lord will grant you his grace and peace.'
Tobias spoke out, 'I will not hear of eating and drinking till
you have come to a decision about me.' Raguel answered,

GREEK OLD TESTAMENT

εἶπεν αὐτῷ Ραγουηλ ὅτι Ποιῶ, καὶ αὐτὴ δίδοταί σοι κατὰ τὴν κρίσιν τῆς βίβλου Μωυσέως, καὶ ἐκ τοῦ οὐρανοῦ κέκριταί σοι δοθῆναι· κομίζου τὴν ἀδελφήν σου. ἀπὸ τοῦ νῦν σὺ ἀδελφὸς εἶ αὐτῆς καὶ αὐτὴ ἀδελφή σου· δέδοταί σοι ἀπὸ τῆς σήμερον καὶ εἰς τὸν αἰῶνα· καὶ ὁ κύριος τοῦ οὐρανοῦ εὐοδώσει ὑμᾶς, παιδίον, τὴν νύκτα ταύτην καὶ ποιήσαι ἐφ' ὑμᾶς ἔλεος καὶ εἰρήνην. 13 καὶ ἐκάλεσεν Ραγουηλ Σαρραν τὴν θυγατέρα αὐτοῦ, καὶ ἦλθεν πρὸς αὐτόν, καὶ λαβόμενος τῆς χειρὸς αὐτῆς παρέδωκεν αὐτὴν αὐτῷ καὶ εἶπεν Κόμισαι κατὰ τὸν νόμον καὶ κατὰ τὴν κρίσιν τὴν γεγραμμένην ἐν τῇ βίβλῳ Μωυσέως δοῦναί σοι τὴν γυναῖκα, ἔχε καὶ ἄπαγε πρὸς τὸν πατέρα σου ὑγιαίνων· καὶ ὁ θεὸς τοῦ οὐρανοῦ εὐοδώσαι ὑμῖν εἰρήνην. 14 καὶ ἐκάλεσεν τὴν μητέρα αὐτῆς. καὶ εἶπεν ἐνεγκεῖν βιβλίον καὶ ἔγραψεν συγγραφὴν βιβλίου συνοικήσεως καὶ ὡς δίδωσιν αὐτὴν αὐτῷ γυναῖκα κατὰ τὴν κρίσιν τοῦ Μωυσέως νόμου. ἀπ' ἐκείνου ἤρξαντο φαγεῖν καὶ πιεῖν. 15 καὶ ἐκάλεσεν Ραγουηλ Εδναν τὴν γυναῖκα αὐτοῦ καὶ εἶπεν αὐτῇ Ἀδελφή, ἑτοίμασον τὸ ταμίειον τὸ ἕτερον καὶ εἰσάγαγε αὐτὴν ἐκεῖ. 16 καὶ βαδίσασα ἔστρωσεν εἰς τὸ ταμίειον, ὡς εἶπεν αὐτῇ, καὶ ἤγαγεν αὐτὴν ἐκεῖ καὶ ἔκλαυσεν περὶ αὐτῆς καὶ ἀπεμάξατο τὰ δάκρυα καὶ εἶπεν αὐτῇ 17 Θάρσει, θύγατερ, ὁ κύριος τοῦ οὐρανοῦ δῴη σοι χαρὰν ἀντὶ τῆς λύπης σου· θάρσει, θύγατερ. καὶ ἐξῆλθεν.

8 Καὶ ὅτε συνετέλεσαν τὸ φαγεῖν καὶ πιεῖν, ἠθέλησαν κοιμηθῆναι. καὶ ἀπήγαγον τὸν νεανίσκον καὶ εἰσήγαγον αὐτὸν εἰς τὸ ταμίειον. 2 καὶ ἐμνήσθη Τωβιας τῶν λόγων

KING JAMES VERSION

12 Raguel said, Then take her from henceforth according to the manner, for thou art her cousin, and she is thine, and the merciful God give you good success in all things.

13 Then he called his daughter Sara, and she came to her father, and he took her by the hand, and gave her to be wife to Tobias, saying, Behold, take her after the law of Moses, and lead her away to thy father. And he blessed them;

14 And called Edna his wife, and took paper, and did write an instrument *of covenants,* and sealed it.

15 Then they began to eat.

16 After Raguel called his wife Edna, and said unto her, Sister, prepare another chamber, and bring her in thither.

17 Which when she had done as he had bidden her, she brought her thither: and she wept, and she received the tears of her daughter, and said unto her,

18 Be of good comfort, my daughter; the Lord of heaven and earth give thee joy for this thy sorrow: be of good comfort, my daughter.

8 And when they had supped, they brought Tobias in unto her.

DOUAY OLD TESTAMENT

13 Then Raguel said: I doubt not but God hath regarded my prayers and tears in his sight.

14 And I believe he hath therefore made you come to me, that this maid might be married to one of her own kindred, according to the law of Moses: and now doubt not but I will give her to thee.

15 And taking the right hand of his daughter, he gave it into the right hand of Tobias, saying: The God of Abraham, and the God of Isaac, and the God of Jacob be with you, and may he join you together, and fulfil his blessing in you.

16 And taking paper they made a writing of the marriage.

17 And afterwards they made merry, blessing God.

18 And Raguel called to him Anna his wife, and bade her prepare another chamber.

19 And she brought Sara her daughter in thither, and she wept.

20 And she said to her: Be of good cheer, my daughter: the Lord of heaven give thee joy for the trouble thou hast undergone.

8 AND after they had supped, they brought in the young man to her.

KNOX TRANSLATION

13 Why then, answered Raguel, all those prayers and sighs of mine were not wasted; God has granted them audience; 14 and I doubt not his design in bringing you here was to have my daughter matched with one of her own kin, as the law of Moses bade. Then he said to Tobias, Have no fear, she is thine. 15 And so, taking his daughter's right hand and putting it into the right hand of Tobias, he gave them his blessing: May the God of Abraham, Isaac and Jacob be with you and himself join you in one, and fulfil his merciful purpose in you.

16 So they took paper, and signed a contract of marriage; 17 then they sat down to their feasting, and gave thanks to God. 18 Meanwhile Raguel called Anna aside, and bade her have a fresh room in readiness. 19 Into this she brought her daughter Sara, weeping as she did so; 20 then she said, Do not lose heart, daughter; thou hast had sadness enough; may the Lord of heaven give thee gladness in exchange. [a]

8 When the feasting was over, bridegroom was led to bride-chamber. 2 And now, remembering what the angel

a The correspondence between the various versions is fairly close in this chapter, but the Vulgate is not a direct translation from any of the others.

TODAY'S ENGLISH VERSION

12 Raguel agreed. "Certainly I will," he said. "I will give her
to you just as the Law of Moses commands. God in heaven
has arranged this marriage, so take her as your wife. From
now on, you belong to each other. Sarah is yours today and
forever. May the Lord of heaven keep both of you safe
tonight. May he be merciful and kind to you."

13 Then Raguel called his daughter. When she came in, he
took her by the hand and gave her to Tobias with his blessing,
"Take her to be your wife according to the teachings in the
Law of Moses. Take her safely with you to your father's house.
May the God of heaven give you a happy life together."

14 Raguel asked his wife to bring him a blank scroll so that
he could write out the marriage contract. Edna brought him
the scroll, and Raguel wrote out the agreement, saying that
Sarah was given to Tobias according to the teachings in the
Law of Moses. 15 After the ceremony they began the meal.

16 Raguel called his wife and said, "Get the spare room
ready, my dear, and take Sarah there."

17 Edna made up the bed as Raguel had told her. Then she
took Sarah into the room with her, and Sarah began to cry.[a]
But Edna wiped away her tears and said, 18 "Don't worry,
Sarah. I'm sure the Lord of heaven will make you happy this
time and not sad. So cheer up, my dear." Then Edna left the
room.

8 When they had finished the meal, and it was time to go
to bed, Sarah's parents led young Tobias to the bedroom. 2 He remembered Raphael's instructions, so he took

[a] and Sarah began to cry; *some manuscripts have* and she began to cry.

NEW REVISED STANDARD VERSION

pertain to me." So Raguel said, "I will do so. She is given to
you in accordance with the decree in the book of Moses, and
it has been decreed from heaven that she be given to you.
Take your kinswoman;[a] from now on you are her brother
and she is your sister. She is given to you from today and
forever. May the Lord of heaven, my child, guide and prosper
you both this night and grant you mercy and peace." 12 Then
Raguel summoned his daughter Sarah. When she came to
him he took her by the hand and gave her to Tobias,[b] saying, "Take her to be your wife in accordance with the law
and decree written in the book of Moses. Take her and bring
her safely to your father. And may the God of heaven prosper
your journey with his peace." 13 Then he called her mother
and told her to bring writing material; and he wrote out a
copy of a marriage contract, to the effect that he gave her to
him as wife according to the decree of the law of Moses.
14 Then they began to eat and drink.

15 Raguel called his wife Edna and said to her, "Sister,
get the other room ready, and take her there." 16 So she went
and made the bed in the room as he had told her, and
brought Sarah[c] there. She wept for her daughter.[c] Then,
wiping away the tears,[d] she said to her, "Take courage, my
daughter; the Lord of heaven grant you joy[e] in place of your
sorrow. Take courage, my daughter." Then she went out.

8 When they had finished eating and drinking they wanted to retire; so they took the young man and brought
him into the bedroom. 2 Then Tobias remembered the words

a Gk *sister* *b* Gk *him* *c* Gk *her* *d* Other ancient authorities read *the tears of her daughter* *e* Other ancient authorities read *favor*

NEW AMERICAN BIBLE

Raguel said to him: "I will do it. She is yours according to
the decree of the Book of Moses. Your marriage to her has
been decided in heaven! Take your kinswoman; from now on
you are her love, and she is your beloved. She is yours today
and ever after. And tonight, son, may the Lord of heaven
prosper you both. May he grant you mercy and peace."
12 Then Raguel called his daughter Sarah, and she came to
him. He took her by the hand and gave her to Tobiah with
the words: "Take her according to the law. According to the
decree written in the Book of Moses she is your wife. Take
her and bring her back safely to your father. And may the
God of heaven grant both of you peace and prosperity."
13 He then called her mother and told her to bring a scroll, so
that he might draw up a marriage contract stating that he
gave Sarah to Tobiah as his wife according to the decree of
the Mosaic law. Her mother brought the scroll, and he drew
up the contract, to which they affixed their seals.

14 Afterward they began to eat and drink. 15 Later Raguel
called his wife Edna and said, "My love, prepare the other
bedroom and bring the girl there." 16 She went and made the
bed in the room, as she was told, and brought the girl there.
After she had cried over her, she wiped away the tears and
said: 17 "Be brave, my daughter. May the Lord of heaven
grant you joy in place of your grief. Courage, my daughter."
Then she left.

8 When they had finished eating and drinking, the girl's
parents wanted to retire. They brought the young man
out of the dining room and led him into the bedroom. 2 At

NEW JERUSALEM BIBLE

'Very well. Since, by the prescription of the Book of Moses
she is given to you, Heaven itself decrees she shall be yours.
I therefore entrust your sister to you. From now on you are
her brother and she is your sister. She is given to you from
today for ever. The Lord of heaven favour you tonight, my
child, and grant you his grace and peace.' 12 Raguel called
for his daughter Sarah, took her by the hand and gave her to
Tobias with these words, 'I entrust her to you; the law and
the ruling recorded in the Book of Moses assign her to you as
your wife. Take her; bring her home safe and sound to your
father's house. The God of heaven grant you a good journey
in peace.' 13 Then he turned to her mother and asked her to
fetch him writing paper. He drew up the marriage contract,
and so he gave his daughter as bride to Tobias according to
the ordinance of the Law of Moses.

14 After this they began to eat and drink. 15 Raguel called
his wife Edna and said, 'My sister, prepare the second room
and take her there.' 16 She went and made the bed in this
room as he had ordered, and took her daughter to it. She
wept over her, then wiped away her tears and said, 'Courage,
daughter! May the Lord of heaven turn your grief to joy!
Courage, daughter!' And she went out.

8 When they had finished eating and drinking and it
seemed time to go to bed, the young man was taken
from the dining room to the bedroom. 2 Tobias remembered

GREEK OLD TESTAMENT

Ραφαηλ καὶ ἔλαβεν τὸ ἧπαρ τοῦ ἰχθύος καὶ τὴν καρδίαν ἐκ τοῦ βαλλαντίου, οὗ εἶχεν, καὶ ἐπέθηκεν ἐπὶ τὴν τέφραν τοῦ θυμιάματος. [3] καὶ ἡ ὀσμὴ τοῦ ἰχθύος ἐκώλυσεν, καὶ ἀπέδραμεν τὸ δαιμόνιον ἄνω εἰς τὰ μέρη Αἰγύπτου, καὶ βαδίσας Ραφαηλ συνεπόδισεν αὐτὸν ἐκεῖ καὶ ἐπέδησεν παραχρῆμα. [4] καὶ ἐξῆλθον καὶ ἀπέκλεισαν τὴν θύραν τοῦ ταμιείου. καὶ ἠγέρθη Τωβιας ἀπὸ τῆς κλίνης καὶ εἶπεν αὐτῇ Ἀδελφή, ἀνάστηθι, προσευξώμεθα καὶ δεηθῶμεν τοῦ κυρίου ἡμῶν, ὅπως ποιήσῃ ἐφ᾽ ἡμᾶς ἔλεος καὶ σωτηρίαν. [5] καὶ ἀνέστη, καὶ ἤρξαντο προσεύχεσθαι καὶ δεηθῆναι ὅπως γένηται αὐτοῖς σωτηρία, καὶ ἤρξατο λέγειν Εὐλογητὸς εἶ, ὁ θεὸς τῶν πατέρων ἡμῶν, καὶ εὐλογητὸν τὸ ὄνομά σου εἰς πάντας τοὺς αἰῶνας τῆς γενεᾶς. εὐλογησάτωσάν σε οἱ οὐρανοὶ καὶ πᾶσα ἡ κτίσις σου εἰς πάντας τοὺς αἰῶνας. [6] σὺ ἐποίησας τὸν Αδαμ καὶ ἐποίησας αὐτῷ βοηθὸν στήριγμα Ευαν τὴν γυναῖκα αὐτοῦ, καὶ ἐξ ἀμφοτέρων ἐγενήθη τὸ σπέρμα τῶν ἀνθρώπων· καὶ σὺ εἶπας ὅτι Οὐ καλὸν εἶναι τὸν ἄνθρωπον μόνον, ποιήσωμεν αὐτῷ βοηθὸν ὅμοιον αὐτῷ. [7] καὶ νῦν οὐχὶ διὰ πορνείαν ἐγὼ λαμβάνω τὴν ἀδελφήν μου ταύτην, ἀλλ᾽ ἐπ᾽

KING JAMES VERSION

2 And as he went, he remembered the words of Raphael, and took the ashes of the perfumes, and put the heart and the liver of the fish thereupon, and made a smoke *therewith*.

3 The which smell when the evil spirit had smelled, he fled into the utmost parts of Egypt, and the angel bound him.

4 And after that they were both shut in together, Tobias rose out of the bed, and said, Sister, arise, and let us pray that God would have pity on us.

5 Then began Tobias to say, Blessed art thou, O God of our fathers, and blessed *is* thy holy and glorious name for ever; let the heavens bless thee, and all thy creatures.

6 Thou madest Adam, and gavest him Eve his wife for an helper and stay: of them came mankind: thou hast said, It is not good that man should be alone; let us make unto him an aid like unto himself.

7 And now, O Lord, I take not this my sister for lust, but

DOUAY OLD TESTAMENT

2 And Tobias remembering the angel's word, took out of his bag part of the liver, and laid it upon burning coals.

3 Then the angel Raphael took the devil, and bound him in the desert of upper Egypt.

4 Then Tobias exhorted the virgin, and said to her: Sara, arise, and let us pray to God to day, and to morrow, and the next day: because for these three nights we are joined to God: and when the third night is over, we will be in our own wedlock.

5 For we are the children of saints, and we must not be joined together like heathens that know not God.

6 So they both arose, and prayed earnestly both together that health might be given them,

7 And Tobias said: Lord God of our fathers, may the heavens and the earth, and the sea, and the fountains, and the rivers, and all thy creatures that are in them, bless thee.

8 Thou madest Adam of the slime of the earth, and gavest him Eve for a helper.

9 And now, Lord, thou knowest, that not for fleshly lust

KNOX TRANSLATION

had said, he took out from his wallet a piece of the fish's
liver, which he burnt on live coals. [3] With that, the evil spirit
fled; it was overtaken by the angel Raphael in the waste
lands of Upper Egypt, and there held prisoner. [4] Next, Tobias
must plead with his bride; Leave thy bed, Sara; to-day, and
to-morrow, and the day after, let us pray God for mercy.
These three nights are set apart for our union with God;
when the third is over, we will be joined in one, thou and I.
[5] We come of holy lineage; not for us to mate blindly, like the
heathen that have no knowledge of God. [6] Side by side they
kept vigil, and prayed together that no plague should mar
their mating. [7] Lord God of our fathers, Tobias said, praise
be to thee from heaven and earth, from seas and fountains
and rivers, and from all creatures of thine that make in these
their homes! [8] When Adam was made of earth's clay, it was
by thy hand; when Eve was sent to cheer him, it was of thy
gift. [9] Thou, Lord, art my witness that I wed this sister of
mine not from love of dalliance; only in the dear hope of

TODAY'S ENGLISH VERSION

the fish's liver and heart out of the bag where he had been
keeping them. Then he placed them on the burning incense.
3 The smell drove the demon away from them, and he fled to
Egypt.[a] Raphael chased after him and caught him there. At
once he bound him hand and foot.

4 When Tobias and Sarah were alone behind closed doors,
Tobias got up from the bed and said to his wife, "Get up,
dear. Let's pray for the Lord to be merciful and to protect us."
5 Sarah got up so that they could pray together and ask God
for his protection. Then Tobias prayed:

"God of our ancestors, you are worthy of praise.
May your name be honored forever and ever
by all your creatures in heaven and on earth.
6 You created Adam and gave him his wife Eve
to be his helper and support.
They became the parents of the whole human race.
You said, 'It is not good for man to live alone.
I will make a suitable helper for him.'
7 Lord, I have chosen Sarah because it is right,
not because I lusted for her.

[a] EGYPT: *Egypt was thought of as the most remote part of the world and the home of demons and evil spirits.*

NEW REVISED STANDARD VERSION

of Raphael, and he took the fish's liver and heart out of the
bag where he had them and put them on the embers of the
incense. 3 The odor of the fish so repelled the demon that he
fled to the remotest parts[a] of Egypt. But Raphael followed
him, and at once bound him there hand and foot.

4 When the parents[b] had gone out and shut the door of
the room, Tobias got out of bed and said to Sarah,[c] "Sister,
get up, and let us pray and implore our Lord that he grant us
mercy and safety." 5 So she got up, and they began to pray
and implore that they might be kept safe. Tobias[d] began by
saying,

"Blessed are you, O God of our ancestors,
and blessed is your name in all generations forever.
Let the heavens and the whole creation bless you
forever.
6 You made Adam, and for him you made his wife Eve
as a helper and support.
From the two of them the human race has sprung.
You said, 'It is not good that the man should be alone;
let us make a helper for him like himself.'
7 I now am taking this kinswoman of mine,
not because of lust,
but with sincerity.

a Or *fled through the air to the parts* b Gk *they* c Gk *her* d Gk *He*

NEW AMERICAN BIBLE

this point Tobiah, mindful of Raphael's instructions, took the
fish's liver and heart from the bag which he had with him,
and placed them on the embers for the incense. 3 The demon,
repelled by the odor of the fish, fled into Upper Egypt;
Raphael pursued him there and bound him hand and foot.
Then Raphael returned immediately.

4 When the girl's parents left the bedroom and closed the
door behind them, Tobiah arose from bed and said to his
wife, "My love, get up. Let us pray and beg our Lord to have
mercy on us and to grant us deliverance." 5 She got up, and
they started to pray and beg that deliverance might be theirs.
He began with these words:

"Blessed are you, O God of our fathers;
praised be your name forever and ever.
Let the heavens and all your creation
praise you forever.
6 You made Adam and you gave him his wife Eve
to be his help and support;
and from these two the human race descended.
You said, 'It is not good for the man to be alone;
let us make him a partner like himself.'
7 Now, Lord, you know that I take this wife of mine
not because of lust,
but for a noble purpose.

NEW JERUSALEM BIBLE

Raphael's advice; he went to his bag, took the fish's heart
and liver out of it and put some on the burning incense.
3 The reek of the fish distressed the demon, who fled through
the air to Egypt. Raphael pursued him there, shackled him
and strangled him forthwith.

4 The parents meanwhile had gone out and shut the door
behind them. Tobias rose from the bed, and said to Sarah,
'Get up, my sister! You and I must pray and petition our Lord
to win his grace and his protection.' 5 She stood up, and
they began praying for protection, and this was how he
began:

You are blessed, O God of our fathers;
blessed too is your name
for ever and ever.
Let the heavens bless you
and all things you have made
for evermore.
6 You it was who created Adam,
you who created Eve his wife
to be his help and support;
and from these two the human race was born.
You it was who said,
'It is not right that the man should be alone;
let us make him a helper like him.'[a]
7 And so I take my sister
not for any lustful motive,
but I do it in singleness of heart.

[a] **8** Gn 2:18.

GREEK OLD TESTAMENT

ἀληθείας. ἐπίταξον ἐλεῆσαί με καὶ αὐτὴν καὶ συγκαταγηρᾶ-
σαι κοινῶς. 8 καὶ εἶπαν μεθ' ἑαυτῶν Αμην αμην. 9 καὶ
ἐκοιμήθησαν τὴν νύκτα.
10 Καὶ ἀναστὰς Ραγουηλ ἐκάλεσεν τοὺς οἰκέτας μεθ'
ἑαυτοῦ, καὶ ᾤχοντο καὶ ὤρυξαν τάφον· εἶπεν γάρ Μήποτε
ἀποθάνῃ καὶ γενώμεθα κατάγελως καὶ ὀνειδισμός. 11 καὶ
ὅτε συνετέλεσαν ὀρύσσοντες τὸν τάφον, ἦλθεν Ραγουηλ εἰς
τὸν οἶκον καὶ ἐκάλεσεν τὴν γυναῖκα αὐτοῦ 12 καὶ εἶπεν
Ἀπόστειλον μίαν τῶν παιδισκῶν καὶ εἰσελθοῦσα ἰδέτω εἰ
ζῇ· καὶ εἰ τέθνηκεν, ὅπως ἂν θάψωμεν αὐτόν, ὅπως μηδεὶς
γνῷ. 13 καὶ ἀπέστειλαν τὴν παιδίσκην καὶ ἧψαν τὸν λύχνον
καὶ ἤνοιξαν τὴν θύραν, καὶ εἰσῆλθεν καὶ εὗρεν αὐτοὺς καθεύ-
δοντας καὶ ὑπνοῦντας κοινῶς. 14 καὶ ἐξελθοῦσα ἡ παιδίσκη
ὑπέδειξεν αὐτοῖς ὅτι ζῇ καὶ οὐδὲν κακόν ἐστιν. 15 καὶ
εὐλόγησαν τὸν θεὸν τοῦ οὐρανοῦ καὶ εἶπαν Εὐλογητὸς εἶ,
θεέ, ἐν πάσῃ εὐλογίᾳ καθαρᾷ· εὐλογείτωσάν σε εἰς πάντας
τοὺς αἰῶνας. 16 καὶ εὐλογητὸς εἶ ὅτι εὔφρανάς με, καὶ οὐκ
ἐγένετο καθὼς ὑπενόουν, ἀλλὰ κατὰ τὸ πολὺ ἔλεός σου
ἐποίησας μεθ' ἡμῶν. 17 καὶ εὐλογητὸς εἶ ὅτι ἠλέησας δύο
μονογενεῖς. ποίησον αὐτοῖς, δέσποτα, ἔλεος καὶ σωτηρίαν

KING JAMES VERSION

uprightly: *therefore* mercifully ordain that we may become aged together.

8 And she said with him, Amen.

9 So they slept both that night. And Raguel arose, and went and made a grave,

10 Saying, *I fear* lest he also be dead.

11 But when Raguel was come into his house,

12 He said unto his wife Edna, Send one of the maids, and let her see whether he be alive: if *he be* not, that we may bury him, and no man know it.

13 So the maid opened the door, and went in, and found them both asleep,

14 And came forth, and told them that he was alive.

15 Then Raguel praised God, and said, O God, thou art worthy to be praised with all pure and holy praise; therefore let thy saints praise thee with all thy creatures; and let all thine angels and thine elect praise thee for ever.

16 Thou art to be praised, for thou hast made me joyful; and that is not come to me which I suspected; but thou hast dealt with us according to thy great mercy.

17 Thou art to be praised, because thou hast had mercy of two that were the only begotten children of their fathers:

DOUAY OLD TESTAMENT

do I take my sister to wife, but only for the love of posterity, in which thy name may be blessed for ever and ever.

10 Sara also said: Have mercy on us, O Lord, have mercy on us, and let us grow old both together in health.

11 And it came to pass about the cockcrowing, Raguel ordered his servants to be called for, and they went with him together to dig a grave.

12 For he said: Lest perhaps it may have happened to him, in like manner as it did to the other seven husbands, that went in unto her.

13 And when they had prepared the pit, Raguel went back to his wife, and said to her:

14 Send one of thy maids, and let her see if he be dead, that I may bury him before it be day.

15 So she sent one of her maidservants, who went into the chamber, and found them safe and sound, sleeping both together.

16 And returning she brought the good news: and Raguel and Anna his wife blessed the Lord,

17 And said: We bless thee, O Lord God of Israel, because it hath not happened as we suspected.

18 For thou hast shewn thy mercy to us, and hast shut out from us the enemy that persecuted us.

19 And thou hast taken pity upon two only children. Make them, O Lord, bless thee more fully: and to offer up to

KNOX TRANSLATION

leaving a race behind me, a race in whose destiny, Lord, may
thy name be ever blessed! 10 And thus Sara prayed, Have
mercy on us, Lord, have mercy on us; safe from all harm
grow we old together, he and I!
11 And now it was cock-crow, and Raguel had all his men
out betimes to help him dig the grave; 12 Like enough,
thought he, this one will have fared no better than the other
seven that took her to wife. 13 Their digging done, he went
back to his wife, 14 and bade her send one of her maids to
find out if Tobias were dead; it were best to have him in his
grave before the sun was up. 15 So the maid went on her
errand, and ventured into the bride-chamber, where both lay
asleep together, safe and sound. 16 When she returned with
that good news, Raguel and Anna fell to praising the Lord;
17 God of Israel, said they, we thank thee that our fears were
vain! 18 Great mercy hast thou shewn us, in ridding us of the
fiend's pursuit; 19 great mercy hast thou shewn on these
two, Tobias' only child and ours. Ever may their hearts, Lord,

TODAY'S ENGLISH VERSION

Please be merciful to us
and grant that we may grow old together."

8 Then they both said "Amen" 9 and went to bed for the
night.

Later that night, Raguel called his servants, and together
they went out to dig a grave, 10 because Raguel thought,
"Tobias will probably die too, and people will laugh and
make fun of us." 11 When they finished digging the grave,
Raguel went back into the house and said to his wife,
12 "Send one of the servant women to find out if Tobias is
still alive. If he isn't, then we will bury him before anyone
finds out." 13 They then sent a servant woman to take a
lamp and see if he was still alive. As she opened the door,
she could see that both of them were sound asleep. 14 So she
went back and told Raguel and Edna that Tobias was alive
and unharmed. 15 Then Raguel[a] praised the God of heaven:

"You are worthy of our praise, O God.
May your people praise you forever,
may they praise you with pure hearts.
16 I praise you because you have made me glad;
you have been merciful to us,
and my worst fears did not come true.
17 You deserve our praise, O Lord;
you were merciful to this young couple,
the only children of their parents.
Now, grant them your mercy and protection.

[a] Raguel; *some manuscripts have* they.

NEW REVISED STANDARD VERSION

Grant that she and I may find mercy
and that we may grow old together."

8 And they both said, "Amen, Amen." 9 Then they went to
sleep for the night.

But Raguel arose and called his servants to him, and they
went and dug a grave, 10 for he said, "It is possible that he
will die and we will become an object of ridicule and derision." 11 When they had finished digging the grave, Raguel
went into his house and called his wife, 12 saying, "Send one
of the maids and have her go in to see if he is alive. But if he
is dead, let us bury him without anyone knowing it." 13 So
they sent the maid, lit a lamp, and opened the door; and she
went in and found them sound asleep together. 14 Then the
maid came out and informed them that he was alive and
that nothing was wrong. 15 So they blessed the God of heav-
en, and Raguel[a] said,

"Blessed are you, O God, with every pure blessing;
let all your chosen ones bless you.[b]
Let them bless you forever.
16 Blessed are you because you have made me glad.
It has not turned out as I expected,
but you have dealt with us according to your great
mercy.
17 Blessed are you because you had compassion
on two only children.
Be merciful to them, O Master, and keep them safe;

a Gk *they* *b* Other ancient authorities lack this line

NEW AMERICAN BIBLE

Call down your mercy on me and on her,
and allow us to live together to a happy old age."

8 They said together, "Amen, amen," 9 and went to bed for
the night.

But Raguel got up and summoned his servants. With him
they went out to dig a grave, 10 for he said, "I must do this,
because if Tobiah should die, we would be subjected to ridicule
and insult." 11 When they had finished digging the grave,
Raguel went back into the house and called his wife, 12 saying, "Send one of the maids in to see whether Tobiah is alive
or dead, so that if necessary we may bury him without anyone's knowing about it." 13 She sent the maid, who lit a lamp,
opened the bedroom door, went in, and found them sound
asleep together. 14 The maid went out and told the girl's parents that Tobiah was alive, and that there was nothing wrong.
15 Then Raguel praised the God of heaven in these words:

"Blessed are you, O God, with every holy and pure
blessing!
Let all your chosen ones praise you;
let them bless you forever!
16 Blessed are you, who have made me glad;
what I feared did not happen.
Rather you have dealt with us
according to your great mercy.
17 Blessed are you, for you were merciful
toward two only children.
Grant them, Master, mercy and deliverance,

NEW JERUSALEM BIBLE

Be kind enough to have pity on her and on me
and bring us to old age together.

8 And together they said, 'Amen, Amen,' 9 and lay down for
the night.

But Raguel rose and called his servants, who came and
helped him dig a grave. 10 He had thought, 'Heaven grant he
does not die! We should be overwhelmed with ridicule and
shame.' 11 When the grave was ready, Raguel went back to
the house, called his wife 12 and said, 'Will you send a maid
to the room to see if Tobias is still alive? For if he is dead, we
may be able to bury him without anyone else knowing.'
13 They sent the maid, lit the lamp, opened the door and the
maid went in. She found the two fast asleep together; 14 she
came out again and whispered, 'He is not dead; all is well.'
15 Then Raguel blessed the God of heaven with these words:

You are blessed, my God,
with every blessing that is pure;
may you be blessed for evermore!

16 You are blessed for having made me glad.
What I feared has not happened,
instead you have shown us
your boundless mercy.

17 You are blessed for taking pity
on this only son, this only daughter.
Grant them, Master, your mercy and your protection;

GREEK OLD TESTAMENT

καὶ συντέλεσον τὴν ζωὴν αὐτῶν μετ᾽ εὐφροσύνης καὶ ἐλέου. 18 τότε εἶπεν τοῖς οἰκέταις αὐτοῦ χῶσαι τὸν τάφον πρὸ τοῦ ὄρθρον γενέσθαι.

19 Καὶ τῇ γυναικὶ εἶπεν ποιῆσαι ἄρτους πολλούς. καὶ εἰς τὸ βουκόλιον βαδίσας ἤγαγεν βόας δύο καὶ κριοὺς τέσσαρας καὶ εἶπεν συντελεῖν αὐτούς, καὶ ἤρξαντο παρασκευάζειν. 20 καὶ ἐκάλεσεν Τωβιαν καὶ εἶπεν αὐτῷ Δέκα τεσσάρων ἡμερῶν οὐ μὴ κινηθῇς ἐντεῦθεν, ἀλλ᾽ αὐτοῦ μενεῖς ἔσθων καὶ πίνων παρ᾽ ἐμοὶ καὶ εὐφρανεῖς τὴν ψυχὴν τῆς θυγατρός μου τὴν κατωδυνωμένην· 21 καὶ ὅσα μοι ὑπάρχει, λάμβανε αὐτόθεν τὸ ἥμισυ καὶ ὕπαγε ὑγιαίνων πρὸς τὸν πατέρα σου· καὶ τὸ ἄλλο ἥμισυ, ὅταν ἀποθάνω ἐγώ τε καὶ ἡ γυνή μου, ὑμέτερόν ἐστιν. θάρσει, παιδίον, ἐγώ σου ὁ πατὴρ καὶ Εδνα ἡ μήτηρ σου, καὶ παρὰ σοῦ ἐσμεν ἡμεῖς καὶ τῆς ἀδελφῆς σου ἀπὸ τοῦ νῦν εἰς τὸν αἰῶνα· θάρσει, παιδίον.

9 Τότε ἐκάλεσεν Τωβιας Ραφαηλ καὶ εἶπεν αὐτῷ 2 Αζαρια ἄδελφε, παράλαβε μετὰ σεαυτοῦ τέσσαρας οἰκέτας καὶ καμήλους δύο καὶ πορεύθητι εἰς Ῥάγας καὶ ἧκε παρὰ Γαβαήλῳ καὶ δὸς αὐτῷ τὸ χειρόγραφον καὶ κόμισαι τὸ ἀργύριον καὶ παράλαβε αὐτὸν μετὰ σοῦ εἰς τοὺς γάμους. 3-4 γὰρ γινώσκεις ὅτι ἔσται ἀριθμῶν ὁ πατὴρ τὰς ἡμέρας, καὶ ἐὰν χρονίσω ἡμέραν μίαν, λυπήσω αὐτὸν λίαν· καὶ θεωρεῖς τί ὤμοσεν Ραγουηλ, καὶ οὐ δύναμαι παραβῆναι τὸν ὅρκον αὐτοῦ. 5 καὶ ἐπορεύθη Ραφαηλ καὶ οἱ τέσσαρες οἰκέται καὶ αἱ δύο

KING JAMES VERSION

grant them mercy, O Lord, and finish their life in health with joy and mercy.

18 Then Raguel bade his servants to fill the grave.

19 And he kept the wedding feast fourteen days.

20 For before the days of the marriage were finished, Raguel had said unto him by an oath, that he should not depart till the fourteen days of the marriage were expired;

21 And then he should take the half of his goods, and go in safety to his father; and should have the rest when I and my wife be dead.

9 Then Tobias called Raphael, and said unto him,

2 Brother Azarias, take with thee a servant, and two camels, and go to Rages of Media to Gabael, and bring me the money, and bring him to the wedding.

3 For Raguel hath sworn that I shall not depart.

4 But my father counteth the days; and if I tarry long, he will be very sorry.

5 So Raphael went out, and lodged with Gabael, and gave

DOUAY OLD TESTAMENT

thee a sacrifice of thy praise, and of their health, that all nations may know, that thou alone art God in all the earth.

20 And immediately Raguel commanded his servants, to fill up the pit they had made, before it was day.

21 And he spoke to his wife to make ready a feast, and prepare all kind of provisions that are necessary for such as go a journey.

22 He caused also two fat kine, and four wethers to be killed, and a banquet to be prepared for all his neighbours, and all his friends.

23 And Raguel adjured Tobias, to abide with him two weeks.

24 And of all things which Raguel possessed, he gave one half to Tobias, and made a writing, that the half that remained should after their decease come also to Tobias.

9 THEN Tobias called the angel to him, whom he took to be a man, and said to him: Brother Azarias, I pray thee hearken to my words:

2 If I should give myself to be thy servant I should not make a worthy return for thy care.

3 However, I beseech thee, to take with thee beasts and servants, and to go to Gabelus to Rages the city of the Medes: and to restore to him his note of hand, and receive of him the money, and desire him to come to my wedding.

4 For thou knowest that my father numbereth the days: and if I stay one day more, his soul will be afflicted.

5 And indeed thou seest how Raguel hath adjured me, whose adjuring I cannot despise.

6 Then Raphael took four of Raguel's servants, and two

KNOX TRANSLATION

swell with thankfulness, ever may these lives thou hast preserved be a sacrifice of praise to thee, till all the Gentiles around them know thee for the only God that rules on earth!

20 With that, Raguel bade his men fill up the newly dug
grave before sunrise; 21 bade his wife spread a feast, and
prepare such food as the travellers needed. 22 Two fat heifers
and four rams must be slaughtered and a banquet made for
all his neighbours and friends. 23 And now he was urgent
with Tobias to be his guest for two whole weeks; 24 half of
all his goods he bestowed upon him there and then, while the rest, as he declared in writing, should follow when he and Anna died.[a]

9 And now Tobias took the angel aside and, though he still did not guess this was more than man, spoke as follows:
Pray bear with this request of mine, friend Azarias. 2 No
return could I make for all thy watchful care of me, though I
should dedicate myself to be thy slave. 3 Instead of that, I am
still asking thee for a favour; that thou wouldst journey on to Rages in Media, with what beasts, what retinue thou wilt, and seek out Gabelus there. Give him back his bond, recover the debt, and bid him to my wedding-feast. 4 Thou canst
guess how my father is counting the days till my return; no fresh day of my absence but brings with it a fresh sorrow;
5 yet thou seest how earnestly Raguel pleads with me to stay on, and that plea I cannot bring myself to refuse.

6 So Raphael took with him four of Raguel's men, and two

a The course of the story is the same in the other versions, except that they represent Tobias' marriage as having been consummated on his wedding night.

TODAY'S ENGLISH VERSION

Let them live out their lives in happiness and love."
18 Then Raguel ordered his servants to fill in the grave before dawn.

19 Raguel told his wife to bake enough bread for a big feast. Then he went out to the herd and brought back two oxen and four rams, which he ordered his servants to slaughter in preparation for the wedding feast. 20 He called for Tobias and vowed[a] that he would not let him leave for two weeks. "Stay, and we will eat and drink together," he said. "It will do my daughter good after her terrible suffering. 21 Then you may take half of what I own and go back to your parents safe and sound. You will inherit the other half when Edna and I die. Have no doubts about our love for you; from now on you are as much our son as Sarah is our daughter. You can be sure of that, my son."

9 Then Tobias called Raphael and said to him, 2 "Azarias, take four of the servants with you, and two camels, and go to Gabael's house in the town of Rages. Give him the signed document, so that he will give you the money. Then bring him back with you for the wedding feast. 3-4 You know that my father is counting the days until I come home, and he will be very upset if I am even one day late. You know, too, how Raguel insists that I must stay, and I cannot disappoint him."

5 So Raphael and the four servants went to Rages in

[a] vowed; *some manuscripts have* said.

NEW REVISED STANDARD VERSION

bring their lives to fulfillment
in happiness and mercy."

18 Then he ordered his servants to fill in the grave before daybreak.

19 After this he asked his wife to bake many loaves of bread; and he went out to the herd and brought two steers and four rams and ordered them to be slaughtered. So they began to make preparations. 20 Then he called for Tobias and swore on oath to him in these words:[a] "You shall not leave here for fourteen days, but shall stay here eating and drinking with me; and you shall cheer up my daughter, who has been depressed. 21 Take at once half of what I own and return in safety to your father; the other half will be yours when my wife and I die. Take courage, my child. I am your father and Edna is your mother, and we belong to you as well as to your wife[b] now and forever. Take courage, my child."

9 Then Tobias called Raphael and said to him, 2 "Brother Azariah, take four servants and two camels with you and travel to Rages. Go to the home of Gabael, give him the bond, get the money, and then bring him with you to the wedding celebration. 4 For you know that my father must be counting the days, and if I delay even one day I will upset him very much. 3 You are witness to the oath Raguel has sworn, and I cannot violate his oath."[c] 5 So Raphael with the four servants and two camels went to Rages in Media

a Other ancient authorities read *Tobias and said to him* *b* Gk *sister*
c In other ancient authorities verse 3 precedes verse 4

NEW AMERICAN BIBLE

and bring their lives to fulfillment
with happiness and mercy."

18 Then he told his servants to fill in the grave before dawn.

19 He asked his wife to bake many loaves of bread; he himself went out to the herd and picked out two steers and four rams which he ordered to be slaughtered. So the servants began to prepare the feast. 20 He summoned Tobiah and made an oath in his presence, saying: "For fourteen days you shall not stir from here, but shall remain here eating and drinking with me; and you shall bring joy to my daughter's sorrowing spirit. 21 Take, to begin with, half of whatever I own when you go back in good health to your father; the other half will be yours when I and my wife die. Be of good cheer, my son! I am your father, and Edna is your mother; and we belong to you and to your beloved now and forever. So be happy, son!"

9 Then Tobiah called Raphael and said to him: 2 "Brother Azariah, take along with you four servants and two camels and travel to Rages. Go to Gabael's house and give him this bond. Get the money and then bring him along with you to the wedding celebration. 4 For you know that my father is counting the days. If I should delay my return by a single day, I would cause him intense grief. 3 You witnessed the oath that Raguel has sworn; I cannot violate his oath."
5 So Raphael, together with the four servants and two

NEW JERUSALEM BIBLE

let them live out their lives
in happiness and in mercy.

18 And he made his servants fill the grave in before dawn broke.

19 He told his wife to make an ovenful of bread; he went to his flock, brought back two oxen and four sheep and gave orders for them to be cooked; and preparations began. 20 He called Tobias and said, 'I will not hear of your leaving here for a fortnight. You are to stay where you are, eating and drinking, with me. You will make my daughter happy again after all her troubles. 21 After that, take away a half of all I have, and take her safe and sound back to your father. When my wife and I are dead you shall have the other half. Courage, my boy! I am your father, and Edna is your mother. We are your parents in future, as we are your sister's. Courage, my son!'

9 Then Tobias turned to Raphael. 2 'Brother Azarias,' he said, 'take four servants and two camels and leave for Rhages. 3 Go to Gabael's house, give him the receipt and see about the money; then invite him to come with you to my wedding feast. 4 You know that my father must be counting the days and that I cannot lose a single one without worrying him. 5 You see what Raguel has pledged himself to do; I am bound by his oath.' So Raphael left for Rhages in Media with the four servants and two camels. They stayed with

GREEK OLD TESTAMENT

κάμηλοι εἰς Ῥάγας τῆς Μηδίας καὶ ηὐλίσθησαν παρὰ Γαβαήλῳ· καὶ ἔδωκεν αὐτῷ τὸ χειρόγραφον αὐτοῦ καὶ ὑπέδειξεν αὐτῷ περὶ Τωβιου τοῦ υἱοῦ Τωβιθ ὅτι ἔλαβεν γυναῖκα καὶ ὅτι καλεῖ αὐτὸν εἰς τὸν γάμον. καὶ ἀναστὰς παρηρίθμησεν αὐτῷ τὰ θυλάκια σὺν ταῖς σφραγῖσιν, καὶ συνέθηκαν αὐτά. 6 καὶ ὤρθρισαν κοινῶς καὶ εἰσῆλθον εἰς τὸν γάμον. καὶ εἰσῆλθον εἰς τὰ Ραγουηλ καὶ εὗρον Τωβιαν ἀνακείμενον, καὶ ἀνεπήδησεν καὶ ἠσπάσατο αὐτόν, καὶ ἔκλαυσεν καὶ εὐλόγησεν αὐτὸν καὶ εἶπεν αὐτῷ Καλὲ καὶ ἀγαθέ, ἀνδρὸς καλοῦ καὶ ἀγαθοῦ, δικαίου καὶ ἐλεημοποιοῦ, δῴη σοι κύριος εὐλογίαν οὐρανοῦ καὶ τῇ γυναικί σου καὶ τῷ πατρί σου καὶ τῇ μητρὶ τῆς γυναικός σου· εὐλογητὸς ὁ θεός, ὅτι εἶδον Τωβιν τὸν ἀνεψιόν μου ὅμοιον αὐτῷ.

10 Ἑκάστην δὲ ἡμέραν ἐξ ἡμέρας ἐλογίζετο Τωβιθ τὰς ἡμέρας ἐν πόσαις πορεύσεται καὶ ἐν πόσαις ἐπιστρέψει· καὶ ὅτε συνετελέσθησαν αἱ ἡμέραι καὶ ὁ υἱὸς αὐτοῦ οὐ παρῆν, 2 εἶπεν Μήποτε κατεσχέθη ἐκεῖ; ἢ μήποτε ἀπέθανεν ὁ Γαβαηλ καὶ οὐδεὶς αὐτῷ δίδωσιν τὸ ἀργύριον; 3 καὶ ἤρξατο λυπεῖσθαι. 4 καὶ Αννα ἡ γυνὴ αὐτοῦ λέγει

KING JAMES VERSION

him the handwriting: who brought forth bags which were sealed up, and gave them to him.

6 And early in the morning they went forth both together, and came to the wedding: and Tobias blessed his wife.

10 Now Tobit his father counted every day: and when the days of the journey were expired, and they came not,

2 Then Tobit said, Are they detained? or is Gabael dead, and there is no man to give him the money?

3 Therefore he was very sorry.

DOUAY OLD TESTAMENT

camels, and went to Rages the city of the Medes: and finding Gabelus, gave him his note of hand, and received of him all the money.

7 And he told him concerning Tobias the son of Tobias, all that had been done: and made him come with him to the wedding.

8 And when he was come into Raguel's house he found Tobias sitting at the table: and he leaped up, and they kissed each other: and Gabelus wept, and blessed God,

9 And said: The God of Israel bless thee, because thou art the son of a very good and just man, and that feareth God, and doth almsdeeds:

10 And may a blessing come upon thy wife and upon your parents.

11 And may you see your children, and your children's children, unto the third and fourth generation: and may your seed be blessed by the God of Israel, who reigneth for ever and ever.

12 And when all had said, Amen, they went to the feast: but the marriage feast they celebrated also with the fear of the Lord.

10 BUT as Tobias made longer stay upon occasion of the marriage, Tobias his father was solicitous, saying: Why thinkest thou doth my son tarry, or why is he detained there?

2 Is Gabelus dead, thinkest thou, and no man will pay him the money?

3 And he began to be exceeding sad, both he and Anna his wife with him: and they began both to weep together:

KNOX TRANSLATION

camels; went to Rages in Media and sought out Gabelus there; gave him the bond, and recovered the debt in full. 7 Then he recounted to him the younger Tobias' history, and brought him back to take part in the wedding-feast. 8 Tobias, who was sitting at table when Gabelus entered the house, sprang up to welcome him; and when they had embraced, Gabelus wept, and praised God for their meeting. 9 The God of Israel bless thee, he cried, for the son of an excellent honest man, his true worshipper, and a great giver of alms! 10 May the name of this thy bride, the names of her parents and thine, be used for an example of blessedness! 11 May you live to see sons of yours, and sons of theirs again, and a fourth generation to succeed the third! May your posterity win a blessing from the God of Israel, that reigns everlastingly! 12 All said Amen to that, and so they fell to and feasted; yet was there no merry-making over this wedding but such as became God's worshippers.

10 While the younger Tobias lingered thus over his marriage, his father fell into an extreme of anxiety. What means this long delay on my son's part? he asked. What has detained him? 2 Can it be that Gabelus is dead, and there is no recovering the debt? 3 Great lament he made, and his wife Anna with him, and fast fell the tears of both, that the

TODAY'S ENGLISH VERSION

Media, where they stayed at Gabael's house. Raphael gave him the signed document and told him that Tobit's son Tobias had recently married, and that Gabael was invited to the wedding feast. At once Gabael counted out the bags of money, which were still sealed, and they loaded them on the
camels.[a] 6Very early the next morning, they set out for the wedding feast. When Raphael and Gabael came to Raguel's house, they found Tobias at dinner. Tobias immediately got up and greeted Gabael. With tears in his eyes Gabael returned the greeting and added, "You are just like your honest and generous father. May the Lord in heaven bless you and your wife, your mother-in-law, and your father. Praise God! He has let me live to see my cousin Tobias, who looks so much like his father."

10 Meanwhile, every day Tobit was keeping count of the time needed to travel to Rages and back. When the time was up and his son had not returned, Tobit said to his
wife, 2"What can be keeping him? Do you suppose Gabael has died? Maybe there is no one to give him the money."
3Tobit was very worried.

[a] loaded them on the camels; *some manuscripts have* stacked them up.

NEW REVISED STANDARD VERSION

and stayed with Gabael. Raphael[a] gave him the bond and informed him that Tobit's son Tobias had married and was inviting him to the wedding celebration. So Gabael[b] got up and counted out to him the money bags, with their seals
intact; then they loaded them on the camels.[c] 6In the morning they both got up early and went to the wedding celebration. When they came into Raguel's house they found Tobias reclining at table. He sprang up and greeted Gabael,[d] who wept and blessed him with the words, "Good and noble son of a father good and noble, upright and generous! May the Lord grant the blessing of heaven to you and your wife, and to your wife's father and mother. Blessed be God, for I see in Tobias the very image of my cousin Tobit."

10 Now, day by day, Tobit kept counting how many days Tobias[b] would need for going and for returning. And when the days had passed and his son did not appear,
2he said, "Is it possible that he has been detained? Or that Gabael has died, and there is no one to give him the
money?" 3And he began to worry. 4His wife Anna said,

a Gk *He* *b* Gk *he* *c* Other ancient authorities lack *on the camels*
d Gk *him*

NEW AMERICAN BIBLE

camels, traveled to Rages in Media, where they stayed at Gabael's house. Raphael gave Gabael his bond and told him about Tobit's son Tobiah, and that he had married and was inviting him to the wedding celebration. Gabael promptly checked over the sealed moneybags, and they placed them on the camels.

6The following morning they got an early start and traveled to the wedding celebration. When they entered Raguel's house, they found Tobiah reclining at table. He sprang up and greeted Gabael, who wept and blessed him, exclaiming: "O noble and good child, son of a noble and good, upright and charitable man, may the Lord grant heavenly blessing to you and to your wife, and to your wife's father and mother. Blessed be God, because I have seen the very image of my cousin Tobit!"

10 Meanwhile, day by day, Tobit was keeping track of the time Tobiah would need to go and to return. When the number of days was reached and his son did not
appear, 2he said, "I wonder what has happened. Perhaps he has been detained there; or perhaps Gabael is dead, and
there is no one to give him the money." 3And he began to

NEW JERUSALEM BIBLE

Gabael, and Raphael showed him the receipt. He told him about the marriage of Tobias son of Tobit and gave him his invitation to the wedding feast. Gabael started counting out the sacks to him—the seals were intact—and they loaded
them on to the camels. 6Early in the morning they set off together for the feast, and reached Raguel's house where they found Tobias dining. He rose to greet Gabael, who burst into tears and blessed him with the words, 'Excellent son of a father beyond reproach, just and generous in his dealings! The Lord give heaven's blessing to you, to your wife, to your wife's father and mother! Blessed be God for granting me the sight of this living image of my cousin Tobit!'

10 Every day, meanwhile, Tobit kept reckoning the days required for the journey there and the journey back. The full number went by, and still his son had not come.
2Then he thought, 'I hope he has not been delayed there! I hope Gabael is not dead, so that no one will give him the sil-
ver.' 3And he began to worry. 4His wife Anna kept saying,

GREEK OLD TESTAMENT

Ἀπώλετο τὸ παιδίον μου καὶ οὐκέτι ὑπάρχει ἐν τοῖς ζῶσιν·
καὶ ἤρξατο κλαίειν καὶ θρηνεῖν περὶ τοῦ υἱοῦ αὐτῆς καὶ
εἶπεν 5 Οὐαί μοι, τέκνον, ὅτι ἀφῆκά σε πορευθῆναι, τὸ φῶς
τῶν ὀφθαλμῶν μου. 6 καὶ Τωβιθ ἔλεγεν αὐτῇ Σίγα, μὴ λόγον
ἔχε, ἀδελφή, ὑγιαίνει· καὶ μάλα περισπασμὸς αὐτοῖς ἐγένετο ἐκεῖ, καὶ ὁ ἄνθρωπος ὁ πορευθεὶς μετ᾽ αὐτοῦ πιστός
ἐστιν καὶ εἷς τῶν ἀδελφῶν ἡμῶν· μὴ λυποῦ περὶ αὐτοῦ,
ἀδελφή, ἤδη παρέσται. 7 καὶ εἶπεν αὐτῷ Σίγα ἀπ᾽ ἐμοῦ καὶ
μή με πλάνα· ἀπώλετο τὸ παιδίον μου. καὶ ἐκπηδήσασα
περιεβλέπετο τὴν ὁδόν, ᾗ ᾤχετο ὁ υἱὸς αὐτῆς, καθ᾽ ἡμέραν
καὶ οὐκ ἐπείθετο οὐδενί, καὶ ὅτε ἔδυ ὁ ἥλιος, εἰσπορευομένη
ἐθρήνει καὶ ἔκλαιεν τὴν νύκτα ὅλην καὶ οὐκ εἶχεν ὕπνον.
8 Καὶ ὅτε συνετελέσθησαν αἱ δέκα τέσσαρες ἡμέραι τοῦ
γάμου, ἃς ὤμοσεν Ραγουηλ ποιῆσαι τῇ θυγατρὶ αὐτοῦ,
εἰσῆλθεν πρὸς αὐτὸν Τωβιας καὶ εἶπεν Ἐξαπόστειλόν με,
γινώσκω γὰρ ἐγὼ ὅτι ὁ πατήρ μου καὶ ἡ μήτηρ μου οὐ
πιστεύουσιν ὅτι ὄψονταί με ἔτι· καὶ νῦν ἀξιῶ σε, πάτερ,
ὅπως ἐξαποστείλῃς με καὶ πορευθῶ πρὸς τὸν πατέρα μου·
ἤδη ὑπέδειξά σοι ὡς ἀφῆκα αὐτόν. 9 καὶ εἶπεν Ραγουηλ τῷ
Τωβια Μεῖνον, παιδίον, μεῖνον μετ᾽ ἐμοῦ, καὶ ἐγὼ ἀπο-
στέλλω ἀγγέλους πρὸς Τωβιν τὸν πατέρα σου καὶ ὑποδείξου-
σιν αὐτῷ περὶ σοῦ. καὶ εἶπεν αὐτῷ Μηδαμῶς, ἀξιῶ σε ὅπως
ἐξαποστείλῃς με ἐντεῦθεν πρὸς τὸν πατέρα μου. 10 καὶ
ἀναστὰς Ραγουηλ παρέδωκεν Τωβια Σαρραν τὴν γυναῖκα

KING JAMES VERSION

4 Then his wife said unto him, My son is dead, seeing he stayeth long; and she began to bewail him, and said,

5 *Now I care for nothing,* my son, *since I have let thee go,* the light of mine eyes.

6 To whom Tobit said, Hold thy peace, take no care, for he is safe.

7 But she said, Hold thy peace, and deceive me not; my son is dead. And she went out every day into the way which they went, and did eat no meat on the daytime, and ceased not whole nights to bewail her son Tobias, until the fourteen days of the wedding were expired, which Raguel had sworn that he should spend there. Then Tobias said to Raguel, Let me go, for my father and my mother look no more to see me.

8 But his father in law said unto him, Tarry with me, and I will send to thy father, and they shall declare unto him how things go with thee.

9 But Tobias said, No; but let me go to my father.

10 Then Raguel arose, and gave him Sara his wife, and

DOUAY OLD TESTAMENT

because their son did not return to them on the day appointed.

4 But his mother wept and was quite disconsolate, and said: Woe, woe is me, my son; why did we send thee to go to a strange country, the light of our eyes, the staff of our old age, the comfort of our life, the hope of our posterity?

5 We having all things together in thee alone, ought not to have let thee go from us.

6 And Tobias said to her: Hold thy peace, and be not troubled, our son is safe: that man with whom we sent him is very trusty.

7 But she could by no means be comforted, but daily running out looked round about, and went into all the ways by which there seemed any hope he might return, that she might if possible see him coming afar off.

8 But Raguel said to his son in law: Stay here, and I will send a messenger to Tobias thy father, that thou art in health.

9 And Tobias said to him: I know that my father and mother now count the days, and their spirit is grievously afflicted within them.

10 And when Raguel had pressed Tobias with many words, and he by no means would hearken to him, he delivered Sara unto him, and half of all his substance in

KNOX TRANSLATION

appointed day was over and their son not yet returned. 4 The
mother's grief there was no consoling; My son, my son, she
cried, why did we ever let thee go on thy travels? The light of
our eyes, the support of our old age, our comfort in life, our
hope of posterity when we are gone; 5 all this thou wert, and
thou alone; how could we let thee leave our sight? 6 All in
vain did Tobias try to comfort her, with, Peace, woman;
never disquiet thyself; there is nought amiss with our son; it
was a trusty companion we sent with him. 7 Comfort she
would have none; no day passed but she would rise from her
place and view the landscape all about, or roam the streets,
hoping she might get some rumour, some distant glimpse of
his return.
8 Meanwhile, Raguel was pressing his son-in-law to stay
on; I will send a message to thy father, said he, to assure
him of thy safety. 9 But Tobias would have none of it; No
question, said he, but my father and mother are counting the
days, and tormenting their hearts over me. 10 Still Raguel
plied him with entreaties, and still could not win his consent. So at last he gave Sara into Tobias' keeping, and with

TODAY'S ENGLISH VERSION

4 Then Anna said, "My son is dead. I'm sure of it." She
began to weep and to mourn for Tobias, 5 "Oh, my son, the
joy of my life, why did I ever let you leave home?"
6 Tobit tried to comfort her. "Calm down, my dear," he said.
"Don't worry. He will be all right. Something unexpected is
probably keeping them there longer than we counted on.
Besides, his companion is a reliable man and a relative at
that. Don't let yourself get so upset over him, dear. I'm sure
he is already on his way home."
7 But she replied, "Be quiet and leave me alone! Don't try
to fool me. My son is dead." Each day she would rush out of
the house to the road which Tobias had taken and would
watch for him until sunset. She would let no one comfort
her,[a] and when she returned home she would weep and
mourn for her son all night long, without sleeping.
The two-week wedding feast which Raguel had promised
to hold for his daughter Sarah came to an end. So Tobias
went to him and asked, "Please let me go home now. I'm certain my parents have given up all hope of ever seeing me
again. Please, Raguel, let me go home to my father. I have
already told you the condition he was in when I left."
8 But Raguel answered, "Stay, my son. Stay here with me. I
will send messengers to your father to tell him that you are
all right."
9 But Tobias insisted, "No, I can't! Please let me go back to
my father."
10 So Raguel gave Tobias his bride Sarah without further

[a] She would let no one comfort her; *some manuscripts have* She would not eat a bite.

NEW REVISED STANDARD VERSION

"My child has perished and is no longer among the living."
And she began to weep and mourn for her son, saying,
5 "Woe to me, my child, the light of my eyes, that I let you
make the journey." 6 But Tobit kept saying to her, "Be quiet
and stop worrying, my dear;[a] he is all right. Probably something unexpected has happened there. The man who went
with him is trustworthy and is one of our own kin. Do not
grieve for him, my dear;[a] he will soon be here." 7 She
answered him, "Be quiet yourself! Stop trying to deceive me!
My child has perished." She would rush out every day and
watch the road her son had taken, and would heed no one.[b]
When the sun had set she would go in and mourn and weep
all night long, getting no sleep at all.
Now when the fourteen days of the wedding celebration
had ended that Raguel had sworn to observe for his daughter, Tobias came to him and said, "Send me back, for I know
that my father and mother do not believe that they will see
me again. So I beg of you, father, to let me go so that I may
return to my own father. I have already explained to you
how I left him." 8 But Raguel said to Tobias, "Stay, my child,
stay with me; I will send messengers to your father Tobit and
they will inform him about you." 9 But he said, "No! I beg
you to send me back to my father." 10 So Raguel promptly
gave Tobias his wife Sarah, as well as half of all his

[a] Gk *sister* [b] Other ancient authorities read *and she would eat nothing*

NEW AMERICAN BIBLE

worry. 4 His wife Anna said, "My son has perished and is no
longer among the living!" And she began to weep aloud and
to wail over her son: 5 "Alas, my child, light of my eyes, that
I let you make this journey!" 6 But Tobit kept telling her:
"Hush, do not think about it, my love; he is safe! Probably
they have to take care of some unexpected business there.
The man who is traveling with him is trustworthy, and is
one of our own kinsmen. So do not worry over him, my love.
He will be here soon." 7 But she retorted, "Stop it, and do not
lie to me! My child has perished!" She would go out and
keep watch all day at the road her son had taken, and she
ate nothing. At sunset she would go back home to wail and
cry the whole night through, getting no sleep at all.
Now at the end of the fourteen-day wedding celebration
which Raguel had sworn to hold for his daughter, Tobiah
went to him and said: "Please let me go, for I know that my
father and mother do not believe they will ever see me again.
So I beg you, father, let me go back to my father. I have
already told you how I left him." 8 Raguel said to Tobiah:
"Stay, my child, stay with me. I am sending messengers to
your father Tobit, and they will give him news of you." 9 But
Tobiah insisted, "No, I beg you to let me go back to my
father."
10 Raguel then promptly handed over to Tobiah Sarah his

NEW JERUSALEM BIBLE

'My son is dead! He is no longer among the living!' And she
began to weep and mourn over her son. She kept saying,
5 'Alas! I should never have let you leave me, my child, you,
the light of my eyes.' 6 And Tobit would reply, 'Hush, my sister! Do not worry. All is well with him. Something has happened there to delay them. His companion is someone we
can trust, one of our kinsmen at that. Do not lose heart, my
sister. 7 He will soon be here.' But all she would say was,
'Leave me alone; do not try to deceive me. My child is dead.'
And every day she would go abruptly out to watch the road
by which her son had left. She trusted no eyes but her own.
Once the sun had set she would come home again, only to
weep and moan all night, unable to sleep.
After the fourteen days of feasting that Raguel had sworn
to keep for his daughter's marriage, Tobias came to him and
said, 'Let me go now; my father and mother must have lost
all hope of seeing me again. So I beg you, father, to let me
return to my father's house; I have told you the plight he
was in when I left him.' 8 Raguel said to Tobias, 'Stay, my
son, stay with me. I shall send messengers to your father
Tobit to give him news of you.' 9 But Tobias pressed him,
'No, I beg you to let me go back to my father's house.'
10 Without more ado, Raguel committed Sarah his bride into

GREEK OLD TESTAMENT

αὐτοῦ καὶ τὸ ἥμισυ πάντων τῶν ὑπαρχόντων αὐτῷ, παῖδας
καὶ παιδίσκας, βόας καὶ πρόβατα, ὄνους καὶ καμήλους,
ἱματισμὸν καὶ ἀργύριον καὶ σκεύη· [11] καὶ ἐξαπέστειλεν αὐτοὺς ὑγιαίνοντας καὶ ἠσπάσατο αὐτὸν καὶ εἶπεν αὐτῷ
Ὑγίαινε, παιδίον, ὑγιαίνων ὕπαγε· ὁ κύριος τοῦ οὐρανοῦ
εὐοδώσαι ὑμᾶς καὶ Σαρραν τὴν γυναῖκά σου, καὶ ἴδοιμι ὑμῶν
παιδία πρὸ τοῦ ἀποθανεῖν με. [12] καὶ εἶπεν Σαρρα τῇ θυγατρὶ
αὐτοῦ Ὕπαγε πρὸς τὸν πενθερόν σου, ὅτι ἀπὸ τοῦ νῦν αὐτοὶ
γονεῖς σου ὡς οἱ γεννήσαντές σε· βάδιζε εἰς εἰρήνην,
θύγατερ, ἀκούσαιμί σου ἀγαθὴν ἀκοήν, ἕως ζῶ. καὶ ἀπα-
σπασάμενος ἀπέλυσεν αὐτούς. [13] καὶ Εδνα λέγει Τωβια
Τέκνον καὶ ἄδελφε ἠγαπημένε, ἀποκαταστήσαι σε κύριος
καὶ ἴδοιμί σου τέκνα, ἕως ζῶ, καὶ Σαρρας τῆς θυγατρός μου
πρὸ τοῦ με ἀποθανεῖν· ἐνώπιον τοῦ κυρίου παρατίθεμαί σοι
τὴν θυγατέρα μου ἐν παραθήκῃ, μὴ λυπήσῃς αὐτὴν πάσας
τὰς ἡμέρας τῆς ζωῆς σου· παιδίον, εἰς εἰρήνην· ἀπὸ τοῦ νῦν
ἐγώ σου μήτηρ καὶ Σαρρα ἀδελφή, εὐοδωθείημεν πάντες ἐν
τῷ αὐτῷ πάσας τὰς ἡμέρας ἐν τῇ ζωῇ ἡμῶν. καὶ κατεφίλησεν ἀμφοτέρους καὶ ἀπέστειλεν ὑγιαίνοντας. [14] καὶ
ἀπῆλθεν Τωβιας ἀπὸ Ραγουηλ ὑγιαίνων καὶ χαίρων καὶ
εὐλογῶν τῷ κυρίῳ τοῦ οὐρανοῦ καὶ τῆς γῆς, τῷ βασιλεῖ τῶν
πάντων, ὅτι εὐόδωκεν τὴν ὁδὸν αὐτοῦ. καὶ εἶπεν αὐτῷ
Εὐοδώθη σοι τιμᾶν αὐτοὺς πάσας τὰς ἡμέρας τῆς ζωῆς
αὐτῶν.

11 Καὶ ὡς ἤγγισαν εἰς Κασεριν, ἥ ἐστιν κατέναντι
Νινευη, εἶπεν Ραφαηλ [2] Σὺ γινώσκεις πῶς ἀφήκαμεν

KING JAMES VERSION

half his goods, servants, and cattle, and money:
11 And he blessed them, and sent them away, saying, The
God of heaven give you a prosperous journey, my children.
12 And he said to his daughter, Honour thy father and thy
mother in law, which are now thy parents, that I may hear
good report of thee. And he kissed her. Edna also said to
Tobias, The Lord of heaven restore thee, my dear brother,
and grant that I may see thy children of my daughter Sara
before I die, that I may rejoice before the Lord: behold, I commit my daughter unto thee of special trust; wherefore do not
entreat her evil.

11 After these things Tobias went his way, praising God
that he had given him a prosperous journey, and
blessed Raguel and Edna his wife, and went on his way till
they drew near unto Nineve.
2 Then Raphael said to Tobias, Thou knowest, brother,
how thou didst leave thy father:

DOUAY OLD TESTAMENT

menservants, and womenservants, in cattle, in camels, and
in kine, and in much money, and sent him away safe and
joyful from him,
11 Saying: The holy angel of the Lord be with you in your
journey, and bring you through safe, and that you may find
all things well about your parents, and my eyes may see
your children before I die.
12 And the parents taking their daughter kissed her, and
let her go:
13 Admonishing her to honour her father and mother in
law, to love her husband, to take care of the family, to govern the house, and to behave herself irreprehensibly.

11 AND as they were returning they came to Charan,
which is in the midway to Ninive, the eleventh day.
2 And the angel said: Brother Tobias, thou knowest how
thou didst leave thy father.

KNOX TRANSLATION

her half his goods, men and maid servants, sheep and
camels and cows, and of money a great sum, and let him go
his way, safe and content. [11] The Lord's holy angel, said he,
go with you on your journey, and bring you home without
scathe, to find that all is well, Tobias and Anna both. And
may my life be spared to see children born of you. [12] So
Raguel and Anna embraced their daughter, and kissed her,
and set her on her way, [13] full of good counsel to the last;
how she was to give father-in-law and mother-in-law their
due, love her husband, be mistress in her own house, order it
well, and prove herself the perfection of a woman.

11 On the eleventh day of their homeward journey, they
halted in the middle of it at a place that looks out
towards Nineve (called Charan). [a] [2] And here the angel said,
Friend Tobias, remember how eagerly thy father awaits thee.

a The name of the place reached by the travellers is variously given in the different versions. If it was really Charan, it must have been quite different from the well-known city of that name, which stood miles away to the west.

TODAY'S ENGLISH VERSION

delay. He also gave Tobias half of everything he owned: slaves, cattle, sheep, donkeys, camels, clothes, money, and furniture. 11 Raguel embraced Tobias and sent them on their way with his blessing, "Good-bye, my son. Have a safe journey. May the Lord of heaven protect you and Sarah. And may I live to see your children." 12 Raguel then said to Sarah, "Go with your husband and live in his parents' house. From now on they are as much your parents as your own mother and I are. Let me hear only good things about you as long as I live." After saying good-bye he sent them on their way.

Then Edna said to Tobias, "Tobias my dear child, may the Lord bring you safely home. And may he let me live to see your children. The Lord is my witness; I am placing my daughter in your care. Never, at any time in your life, do anything that would break her heart. Have a safe journey, Tobias. From now on, Sarah is your wife and I am your mother. May we all prosper as long as we live." Then Edna kissed them both and sent them safely on their way.

11 When Tobias left, he was as happy as could be. He praised the Lord of heaven and earth, the King of all the world, because his journey had been so successful, and he promised to honor Raguel and his wife as long as they lived.[a]

As they came near the city of Kaserin, just outside Nineveh, 2 Raphael said, "Tobias, you know the condition

[a] successful, and . . . lived; *or* successful. And Raguel made Tobias promise to honor him and Edna as long as they lived.

NEW REVISED STANDARD VERSION

property: male and female slaves, oxen and sheep, donkeys and camels, clothing, money, and household goods. 11 Then he saw them safely off; he embraced Tobias[a] and said, "Farewell, my child; have a safe journey. The Lord of heaven prosper you and your wife Sarah, and may I see children of yours before I die." 12 Then he kissed his daughter Sarah and said to her, "My daughter, honor your father-in-law and your mother-in-law,[b] since from now on they are as much your parents as those who gave you birth. Go in peace, daughter, and may I hear a good report about you as long as I live." Then he bade them farewell and let them go. Then Edna said to Tobias, "My child and dear brother, the Lord of heaven bring you back safely, and may I live long enough to see children of you and of my daughter Sarah before I die. In the sight of the Lord I entrust my daughter to you; do nothing to grieve her all the days of your life. Go in peace, my child. From now on I am your mother and Sarah is your beloved wife.[c] May we all prosper together all the days of our lives." Then she kissed them both and saw them safely off. 13 Tobias parted from Raguel with happiness and joy, praising the Lord of heaven and earth, King over all, because he had made his journey a success. Finally, he blessed Raguel and his wife Edna, and said, "I have been commanded by the Lord to honor you all the days of my life."[d]

11 When they came near to Kaserin, which is opposite Nineveh, Raphael said, 2 "You are aware of how we

a Gk *him* *b* Other ancient authorities lack parts of *Then . . . mother-in-law* *c* Gk *sister* *d* Lat: Meaning of Gk uncertain

NEW AMERICAN BIBLE

wife, together with half of all his property: male and female slaves, oxen and sheep, asses and camels, clothing, money, and household goods. 11 Bidding them farewell, he let them go. He embraced Tobiah and said to him: "Good-bye, my son. Have a safe journey. May the Lord of heaven grant prosperity to you and to your wife Sarah. And may I see children of yours before I die!" 12 Then he kissed his daughter Sarah and said to her: "My daughter, honor your father-in-law and your mother-in-law, because from now on they are as much your parents as the ones who brought you into the world. Go in peace, my daughter; let me hear good reports about you as long as I live." Finally he said goodbye to them and sent them away.

13 Then Edna said to Tobiah: "My child and beloved kinsman, may the Lord bring you back safely, and may I live long enough to see children of you and of my daughter Sarah before I die. Before the Lord, I entrust my daughter to your care. Never cause her grief at any time in your life. Go in peace, my child. From now on I am your mother, and Sarah is your beloved. May all of us be prosperous all the days of our lives." She kissed them both and sent them away in peace.

14 When Tobiah left Raguel, he was full of happiness and joy, and he blessed the Lord of heaven and earth, the King of all, for making his journey so successful. Finally he said goodbye to Raguel and his wife Edna, and added, "May I honor you all the days of my life!"

11 Then they left and began their return journey. When they were near Kaserin, just before Nineveh, 2 Raphael said: "You know how we left your father. 3 Let us

NEW JERUSALEM BIBLE

his keeping. He gave Tobias half his wealth, slaves, men and women, oxen and sheep, donkeys and camels, clothes and money and household things. 11 And so he let them leave happily. To Tobias he said these parting words, 'Good health, my son, and a happy journey! May the Lord of heaven be gracious to you and to your wife Sarah! I hope to see your children before I die.' 12 To his daughter Sarah he said, 'Go now to your father-in-law's house, since henceforward they are as much your parents as those who gave you life. Go in peace, my daughter, I hope to hear nothing but good of you, as long as I live.' He said goodbye to them and let them go.

Edna in her turn said to Tobias, 'Dear son and brother, may it please the Lord to bring you back again! I hope to live long enough to see the children of you and my daughter Sarah before I die. In the sight of the Lord I give my daughter into your keeping. Never make her unhappy as long as you live. Go in peace, my son. Henceforward I am your mother and Sarah is your sister. May we all live happily for the rest of our lives!' And she kissed them both and saw them set out happily.

13 Tobias left Raguel's house with his mind at ease. In his gladness he blessed the Lord of heaven and earth, the King of all that is, for the happy issue of his travels. He gave this blessing to Raguel and his wife Edna, 'May it be my happiness to honour you for the rest of my life!'

11 They were nearly at Kaserin, opposite Nineveh, 2 when Raphael said, 'You know the plight in which

GREEK OLD TESTAMENT

τὸν πατέρα σου· 3 προδράμωμεν τῆς γυναικός σου καὶ
ἑτοιμάσωμεν τὴν οἰκίαν, ἐν ᾧ ἔρχονται. 4 καὶ ἐπορεύθησαν
ἀμφότεροι κοινῶς, καὶ εἶπεν αὐτῷ Λαβὲ μετὰ χεῖρας τὴν
χολήν. καὶ συνῆλθεν αὐτοῖς ὁ κύριος ἐκ τῶν ὀπίσω αὐτοῦ καὶ
Τωβια. 5 καὶ Αννα ἐκάθητο περιβλεπομένη τὴν ὁδὸν τοῦ υἱοῦ
αὐτῆς. 6 καὶ προσενόησεν αὐτὸν ἐρχόμενον καὶ εἶπεν τῷ
πατρὶ αὐτοῦ Ἰδοὺ ὁ υἱός σου ἔρχεται καὶ ὁ ἄνθρωπος ὁ
πορευθεὶς μετ᾽ αὐτοῦ. 7 καὶ Ραφαηλ εἶπεν Τωβια πρὸ τοῦ
ἐγγίσαι αὐτὸν πρὸς τὸν πατέρα Ἐπίσταμαι ὅτι οἱ ὀφθαλμοὶ
αὐτοῦ ἀνεῳχθήσονται· 8 ἔμπλασον τὴν χολὴν τοῦ ἰχθύος εἰς
τοὺς ὀφθαλμοὺς αὐτοῦ, καὶ ἀποστύψει τὸ φάρμακον καὶ
ἀπολεπίσει τὰ λευκώματα ἀπὸ τῶν ὀφθαλμῶν αὐτοῦ, καὶ
ἀναβλέψει ὁ πατήρ σου καὶ ὄψεται τὸ φῶς. 9 καὶ ἀνέδραμεν
[Αννα] καὶ ἐπέπεσεν ἐπὶ τὸν τράχηλον τοῦ υἱοῦ αὐτῆς καὶ
εἶπεν αὐτῷ Εἶδόν σε, παιδίον· ἀπὸ τοῦ νῦν ἀποθανοῦμαι. καὶ
ἔκλαυσεν. 10 καὶ ἀνέστη Τωβις καὶ προσέκοπτεν τοῖς ποσὶν
καὶ ἐξῆλθεν τὴν θύραν τῆς αὐλῆς, 11 καὶ ἐβάδισεν Τωβιας

KING JAMES VERSION

3 Let us haste before thy wife, and prepare the house.

4 And take in thine hand the gall of the fish. So they went their way, and the dog went after them.

5 Now Anna sat looking about toward the way for her son.

6 And when she espied him coming, she said to his father, Behold, thy son cometh, and the man that went with him.

7 Then said Raphael, I know, Tobias, that thy father will open his eyes.

8 Therefore anoint thou his eyes with the gall, and being pricked therewith, he shall rub, and the whiteness shall fall away, and he shall see thee.

9 Then Anna ran forth, and fell upon the neck of her son, and said unto him, Seeing I have seen thee, my son, from henceforth I am content to die. And they wept both.

10 Tobit also went forth toward the door, and stumbled: but his son ran unto him,

DOUAY OLD TESTAMENT

3 If it please thee therefore, let us go before, and let the family follow softly after us, together with thy wife, and with the beasts.

4 And as this their going pleased him, Raphael said to Tobias: Take with thee of the gall of the fish, for it will be necessary. So Tobias took some of that gall and departed.

5 But Anna sat beside the way daily, on the top of a hill, from whence she might see afar off.

6 And while she watched his coming from that place, she saw him afar off, and presently perceived it was her son coming: and returning she told her husband, saying: Behold thy son cometh.

7 And Raphael said to Tobias: As soon as thou shalt come into thy house, forthwith adore the Lord thy God: and giving thanks to him, go to thy father, and kiss him.

8 And immediately anoint his eyes with this gall of the fish, which thou carriest with thee. For be assured that his eyes shall be presently opened, and thy father shall see the light of heaven, and shall rejoice in the sight of thee.

9 Then the dog, which had been with them in the way, ran before, and coming as if he had brought the news, shewed his joy by his fawning and wagging his tail.

10 And his father that was blind, rising up, began to run stumbling with his feet: and giving a servant his hand, went to meet his son.

11 And receiving him kissed him, as did also his wife, and they began to weep for joy.

12 And when they had adored God, and given him thanks, they sat down together.

KNOX TRANSLATION

3 How sayest thou? Should not we two hurry on together,
and leave thy wife to follow at leisure with the servants and
the beasts? 4 When this was agreed upon, he bade Tobias
take some of the fish's gall with him, for he would need it;
take it he did, and they set out together.
5 There sat Anna, where she sat every day, on the brow of
the hill, whence she could scan the country far and wide.
6 From that seat of hers she saw them coming, a long distance away, and knew at once it was her son that came.
Back home she ran, and told her husband, Thy son! He is
coming!
7 Thy home once reached, Raphael said to Tobias, pay worship to the Lord thy God first, and return thanks to him.
Then go up to thy father, and embrace him, 8 and rub on his
eyes, without more ado, some of the fish's gall thou hast
with thee. I promise thee it will not be long before his eyes
are opened; once more he will look on the light of day, and
have a father's joy at the sight of thee.
9 Yet he was not to reach the house first. The dog that had
accompanied him on his travels ran on before him, heralding
the good news with the caress of his wagging tail. 10 Up
sprang the father, blind though he were, and made for the
door, running and stumbling as he ran. A servant must take
him by the hand before he could go out to meet his son;
11 but meet him he did, embraced and kissed him, and his
wife too must embrace the boy and kiss him, and then they
both wept over him; but they were tears of joy. 12 So they
paid God worship, and gave him thanks, and sat down
together.

TODAY'S ENGLISH VERSION

your father was in when we left him. 3 We should go on
ahead of your wife and get the house ready before everyone
else arrives. 4 Be sure to bring the fish's gall bladder with
you." So they went on ahead, and Tobias' dog ran along
with[a] them.
5 Meanwhile, Anna sat looking down the road for her son.
6 Suddenly she saw him coming and she shouted out to
Tobit, "Look! Our son is coming, and his friend is with him!"
7 Before they reached Tobit, Raphael said to Tobias, "Your
father will be able to see again. 8 Just put the fish's gall bladder on his eyes like a plaster. The medicine will make the
white film shrivel up so that you can peel it off, and your
father will then regain his eyesight."
9 Anna ran to her son, threw her arms around him, and
exclaimed, "Now that I have seen you alive, my child, I can
die in peace!" And she wept for joy.
10 Tobit got up and stumbled out through the entrance of

[a] Tobias' dog . . . with; *some manuscripts have* the Lord accompanied.

NEW REVISED STANDARD VERSION

left your father. 3 Let us run ahead of your wife and prepare
the house while they are still on the way." 4 As they went on
together Raphael[a] said to him, "Have the gall ready." And
the dog[b] went along behind them.
5 Meanwhile Anna sat looking intently down the road by
which her son would come. 6 When she caught sight of him
coming, she said to his father, "Look, your son is coming,
and the man who went with him!"
7 Raphael said to Tobias, before he had approached his
father, "I know that his eyes will be opened. 8 Smear the gall
of the fish on his eyes; the medicine will make the white
films shrink and peel off from his eyes, and your father will
regain his sight and see the light."
9 Then Anna ran up to her son and threw her arms
around him, saying, "Now that I have seen you, my child, I
am ready to die." And she wept. 10 Then Tobit got up and
came stumbling out through the courtyard door. Tobias went

a Gk *he* *b* Codex Sinaiticus reads *And the Lord*

NEW AMERICAN BIBLE

hurry on ahead of your wife to prepare the house while the
rest of the party are still on the way." 4 So they both went on
ahead and Raphael said to Tobiah, "Have the gall in your
hand!" And the dog ran along behind them.
5 Meanwhile, Anna sat watching the road by which her son
was to come. 6 When she saw him coming, she exclaimed to
his father, "Tobit, your son is coming, and the man who
traveled with him!"
7 Raphael said to Tobiah before he reached his father: "I
am certain that his eyes will be opened. 8 Smear the fish gall
on them. This medicine will make the cataracts shrink and
peel off from his eyes; then your father will again be able to
see the light of day."
9 Then Anna ran up to her son, threw her arms around
him, and said to him, "Now that I have seen you again, son,
I am ready to die!" And she sobbed aloud. 10 Tobit got up
and stumbled out through the courtyard gate. Tobiah went

NEW JERUSALEM BIBLE

we left your father; 3 let us go on ahead of your wife and
prepare the house ourselves while she travels behind with
the others.' 4 They went on together (Raphael warned Tobias
to take the gall with him) and the dog followed them.
5 Anna was sitting, watching the road by which her son
would come. 6 She was sure at once it must be he and said
to the father, 'Here comes your son, with his companion.'
7 Raphael said to Tobias before he reached his father, 'I
give you my word that your father's eyes will open. 8 You
must put the fish's gall to his eyes; the medicine will smart
and will draw a filmy white skin off his eyes. And your
father will no more be blind but will be able to see the light.'
9 The mother ran forward and threw her arms round her
son's neck. 'Now I can die,' she said, 'I have seen you again.'
And she wept. 10 Tobit rose to his feet and stumbled across
the courtyard through the door. Tobias came on towards him

GREEK OLD TESTAMENT

πρὸς αὐτόν, καὶ ἡ χολὴ τοῦ ἰχθύος ἐν τῇ χειρὶ αὐτοῦ, καὶ
ἐνεφύσησεν εἰς τοὺς ὀφθαλμοὺς αὐτοῦ καὶ ἐλάβετο αὐτοῦ
καὶ εἶπεν Θάρσει, πάτερ· καὶ ἐπέβαλεν τὸ φάρμακον ἐπ'
αὐτὸν καὶ ἐπέδωκεν. 12 καὶ ἀπελέπισεν ἑκατέραις ταῖς
χερσὶν αὐτοῦ ἀπὸ τῶν κανθῶν τῶν ὀφθαλμῶν αὐτοῦ. 13 καὶ
ἔπεσεν ἐπὶ τὸν τράχηλον αὐτοῦ καὶ ἔκλαυσεν καὶ εἶπεν αὐτῷ
Εἶδόν σε, τέκνον τὸ φῶς τῶν ὀφθαλμῶν μου. 14 καὶ εἶπεν
Εὐλογητὸς ὁ θεός, καὶ εὐλογητὸν τὸ ὄνομα τὸ μέγα αὐτοῦ,
καὶ εὐλογημένοι πάντες οἱ ἄγγελοι οἱ ἅγιοι αὐτοῦ· γένοιτο
τὸ ὄνομα τὸ μέγα αὐτοῦ ἐφ' ἡμᾶς, καὶ εὐλογητοὶ πάντες οἱ
ἄγγελοι εἰς πάντας τοὺς αἰῶνας. ὅτι αὐτὸς ἐμαστίγωσέν
με, καὶ ἰδοὺ βλέπω Τωβιαν τὸν υἱόν μου. 15 καὶ εἰσῆλθεν
Τωβιας χαίρων καὶ εὐλογῶν τὸν θεὸν ἐν ὅλῳ τῷ στόματι αὐτοῦ, καὶ ἐπέδειξεν Τωβιας τῷ πατρὶ αὐτοῦ ὅτι εὐοδώθη ἡ
ὁδὸς αὐτοῦ, καὶ ὅτι ἐνήνοχεν ἀργύριον, καὶ ὡς ἔλαβεν
Σαρραν τὴν θυγατέρα Ραγουηλ γυναῖκα, καὶ ὅτι ἰδοὺ παρα-
γίνεται καὶ ἔστιν σύνεγγυς τῆς πύλης Νινευη.

16 Καὶ ἐξῆλθεν [Τωβιθ] εἰς ἀπάντησιν τῆς νύμφης αὐτοῦ
χαίρων καὶ εὐλογῶν τὸν θεὸν πρὸς τὴν πύλην Νινευη· καὶ
ἰδόντες αὐτὸν οἱ ἐν Νινευη πορευόμενον καὶ διαβαίνοντα
αὐτὸν πάσῃ τῇ ἰσχύι αὐτοῦ καὶ ὑπὸ μηδενὸς χειραγωγου-
μενον ἐθαύμασαν, καὶ Τωβιθ ἐξωμολογεῖτο ἐναντίον αὐτῶν
ὅτι ἠλέησεν αὐτὸν ὁ θεὸς καὶ ὅτι ἤνοιξεν τοὺς ὀφθαλμοὺς

KING JAMES VERSION

11 And took hold of his father: and he strake of the gall
on his father's eyes, saying, Be of good hope, my father.
12 And when his eyes began to smart, he rubbed them;
13 And the whiteness pilled away from the corners of his
eyes: and when he saw his son, he fell upon his neck.
14 And he wept, and said, Blessed art thou, O God, and
blessed is thy name for ever; and blessed are all thine holy
angels:
15 For thou hast scourged, and hast taken pity *on me:* for,
behold, I see my son Tobias. And his son went in rejoicing,
and told his father the great things that had happened to
him in Media.
16 Then Tobit went out to meet his daughter in law at the
gate of Nineve, rejoicing, and praising God: and they which
saw him go marvelled, because he had received his sight.
17 But Tobit gave thanks before them, because God had

DOUAY OLD TESTAMENT

13 Then Tobias taking of the gall of the fish, anointed his
father's eyes.
14 And he stayed about half an hour: and a white skin
began to come out of his eyes, like the skin of an egg.
15 And Tobias took hold of it, and drew it from his eyes,
and immediately he recovered his sight.
16 And they glorified God, both he and his wife and all
that knew him.
17 And Tobias said: I bless thee, O Lord God of Israel,
because thou hast chastised me, and thou hast saved me:
and behold I see Tobias my son.
18 And after seven days Sara his son's wife, and all the
family arrived safe, and the cattle, and the camels, and an
abundance of money of his wife's: and that money also
which he had received of Gabelus:
19 And he told his parents all the benefits of God, which
he had done to him by the man that conducted him.

KNOX TRANSLATION

13 Then it was that Tobias took out the fish's gall, and
rubbed it on his father's eyes. 14 He waited, maybe, for half
an hour, and then a white film, like the white of an egg,
began to separate itself from the eyes; 15 he took hold of this
and pulled it away, and immediately his father's sight was
restored. 16 How they praised God, he and his wife and all
who knew them! 17 I thank thee, Lord God of Israel, the old
man cried; from thee my chastisement, from thee my deliverance came; I thank thee for eyes that see, and eyes that see
Tobias, my son!
18 It was a week before his daughter-in-law Sara reached
Nineve, with all her retinue safe and sound; the farm stock,
too, she brought with her, and the camels, and all the money
she was dowered with, besides the sum paid over by
Gabelus. 19 Meanwhile, her husband told his parents the
whole story; all the mercies God had shewn him through the

TODAY'S ENGLISH VERSION

the courtyard. 11 Tobias went up to him, holding the fish's
gall bladder in his hand. He blew on his father's eyes and
steadied him. "Don't worry now, father," he said. 12-13 Tobias
then applied the gall, and beginning from the corners of
Tobit's eyes, he peeled away the white film. 14 Tobit threw
his arms around Tobias' neck and wept for joy. Then he
exclaimed, "I can see you! My son, the light of my eyes!

"Praise God. Praise him for his greatness.
Praise all his holy angels.
May he continue to bless us.
Praise all his angels forever.
15 He brought this illness upon me,
but now I can see my son Tobias!"

Then Tobias went happily into the house, praising God at
the top of his voice. He told his father how successful he had
been, that he had not only brought back the money, but had
married Raguel's daughter Sarah, who was on her way and
would soon arrive.

16 Tobit was excited and praised God as he went out to
meet his son's bride at the city gate. When the people of
Nineveh saw him, they were amazed, because he was walking on his own, with no one leading him by the hand.
17 Tobit praised God and told everyone how God in his mercy
had restored his sight.

NEW REVISED STANDARD VERSION

up to him, 11 with the gall of the fish in his hand, and holding him firmly, he blew into his eyes, saying, "Take courage,
father." With this he applied the medicine on his eyes, 12 and
it made them smart.[a] 13 Next, with both his hands he peeled
off the white films from the corners of his eyes. Then Tobit[b]
saw his son and[c] threw his arms around him, 14 and he
wept and said to him, "I see you, my son, the light of my
eyes!" Then he said,

"Blessed be God,
and blessed be his great name,
and blessed be all his holy angels.
May his holy name be blessed[d]
throughout all the ages.
15 Though he afflicted me,
he has had mercy upon me.[e]
Now I see my son Tobias!"

So Tobit went in rejoicing and praising God at the top of his
voice. Tobias reported to his father that his journey had been
successful, that he had brought the money, that he had married Raguel's daughter Sarah, and that she was, indeed, on
her way there, very near to the gate of Nineveh.

16 Then Tobit, rejoicing and praising God, went out to
meet his daughter-in-law at the gate of Nineveh. When the
people of Nineveh saw him coming, walking along in full
vigor and with no one leading him, they were amazed.
17 Before them all, Tobit acknowledged that God had been

a Lat: Meaning of Gk uncertain *b* Gk *he* *c* Other ancient authorities lack *saw his son and* *d* Codex Sinaiticus reads *May his great name be upon us and blessed be all the angels* *e* Lat: Gk lacks this line

NEW AMERICAN BIBLE

up to him 11 with the fish gall in his hand, and holding him
firmly, blew into his eyes. "Courage, father," he said. 12 Next
he smeared the medicine on his eyes, 13 and it made them
smart. Then, beginning at the corners of Tobit's eyes, Tobiah
used both hands to peel off the cataracts. When Tobit saw
his son, he threw his arms around him 14 and wept. He
exclaimed, "I can see you, son, the light of my eyes!" Then
he said:

"Blessed be God,
and praised be his great name,
and blessed be all his holy angels.
May his holy name be praised
throughout all the ages,
15 Because it was he who scourged me,
and it is he who has had mercy on me.
Behold, I now see my son Tobiah!"

Then Tobit went back in, rejoicing and praising God with full
voice. Tobiah told his father that his journey had been a success; that he had brought back the money; and that he had
married Raguel's daughter Sarah, who would arrive shortly,
for she was approaching the gate of Nineveh.

16 Rejoicing and praising God, Tobit went out to the gate of
Nineveh to meet his daughter-in-law. When the people of
Nineveh saw him walking along briskly, with no one leading
him by the hand, they were amazed. 17 Before them all Tobit
proclaimed how God had mercifully restored sight to his

NEW JERUSALEM BIBLE

11 (he had the fish's gall in his hand). He blew into his eyes
and said, steadying him, 'Take courage, father!' With this he
applied the medicine, left it there a while, 12 then with both
hands peeled away a filmy skin from the corners of his eyes.
13 Then his father fell on his neck 14 and wept. He exclaimed,
'I can see you, my son, the light of my eyes!' And he said:

Blessed be God!
Blessed be his great name!
Blessed be all his holy angels!
Blessed be his great name
for evermore!
15 For, having afflicted me,
he has had pity on me
and now I see my son Tobias!

Tobias went indoors, joyfully blessing God at the top of his
voice. Then he told his father everything; how his journey
had been successful and he had brought the silver back; how
he had married Sarah the daughter of Raguel; how she was
following him now, close behind, and could not be far from
the gates of Nineveh.

16 Tobit set off to the gates of Nineveh to meet his daughter-in-law, giving joyful praise to God as he went. When the
people of Nineveh saw him walking without a guide and
stepping forward as briskly as of old, they were astonished.
17 Tobit described to them how God had taken pity on him

GREEK OLD TESTAMENT

αὐτοῦ. 17 καὶ ἤγγισεν Τωβιθ Σαρρα τῇ γυναικὶ Τωβια τοῦ υἱοῦ αὐτοῦ καὶ εὐλόγησεν αὐτὴν καὶ εἶπεν αὐτῇ Εἰσέλθοις ὑγιαίνουσα, θύγατερ, καὶ εὐλογητὸς ὁ θεός σου, ὃς ἤγαγέν σε πρὸς ἡμᾶς, θύγατερ· καὶ εὐλογημένος ὁ πατήρ σου, καὶ εὐλογημένος Τωβιας ὁ υἱός μου, καὶ εὐλογημένη σύ, θύγατερ· εἴσελθε εἰς τὴν οἰκίαν σου ὑγιαίνουσα ἐν εὐλογίᾳ καὶ χαρᾷ, εἴσελθε, θύγατερ. 18 ἐν τῇ ἡμέρᾳ ταύτῃ ἐγένετο χαρὰ πᾶσιν τοῖς Ιουδαίοις τοῖς οὖσιν ἐν Νινευη. 19 καὶ παρεγένοντο Αχικαρ καὶ Ναβαδ οἱ ἐξάδελφοι αὐτοῦ χαίροντες πρὸς Τωβιν.

12 Καὶ ὅτε ἐπετελέσθη ὁ γάμος, ἐκάλεσεν Τωβιθ Τωβιαν τὸν υἱὸν αὐτοῦ καὶ εἶπεν αὐτῷ Παιδίον, ὅρα δοῦναι τὸν μισθὸν τῷ ἀνθρώπῳ τῷ πορευθέντι μετὰ σοῦ [καὶ] προσθεῖναι αὐτῷ εἰς τὸν μισθόν. 2 καὶ εἶπεν αὐτῷ Πάτερ, πόσον αὐτῷ δώσω τὸν μισθόν; οὐ βλάπτομαι διδοὺς αὐτῷ τὸ ἥμισυ τῶν ὑπαρχόντων, ὧν ἐνήνοχεν μετ' ἐμοῦ. 3 ἐμὲ ἀγείοχεν ὑγιαίνοντα καὶ τὴν γυναῖκά μου ἐθεράπευσεν καὶ τὸ ἀργύριον ἤνεγκεν μετ' ἐμοῦ καὶ σὲ ἐθεράπευσεν· πόσον αὐτῷ ἔτι δῶ μισθόν; 4 καὶ εἶπεν αὐτῷ Τωβις Δικαιοῦται αὐτῷ, παιδίον, λαβεῖν τὸ ἥμισυ πάντων, ὧν ἔχων ἦλθεν. 5 καὶ ἐκάλεσεν αὐτὸν καὶ εἶπεν Λαβὲ τὸ ἥμισυ πάντων, ὧν ἔχων ἦλθες, εἰς τὸν μισθόν σου καὶ ὕπαγε ὑγιαίνων.

6 Τότε ἐκάλεσεν τοὺς δύο κρυπτῶς καὶ εἶπεν αὐτοῖς Τὸν θεὸν εὐλογεῖτε καὶ αὐτῷ ἐξομολογεῖσθε ἐνώπιον πάντων τῶν ζώντων ἃ ἐποίησεν μεθ' ὑμῶν ἀγαθά, τοῦ εὐλογεῖν καὶ

KING JAMES VERSION

mercy on him. And when he came near to Sara his daughter in law, he blessed her, saying, Thou art welcome, daughter: God be blessed, which hath brought thee unto us, and *blessed be* thy father and thy mother. And there was joy among all his brethren which were at Nineve.

18 And Achiacharus, and Nasbas his brother's son, came:

19 And Tobias' wedding was kept seven days with great joy.

12 Then Tobit called his son Tobias, and said unto him, My son, see that the man have his wages, which went with thee, and thou must give him more.

2 And Tobias said unto him, O father, it is no harm to me to give him half of those things which I have brought:

3 For he hath brought me again to thee in safety, and made whole my wife, and brought me the money, and likewise healed thee.

4 Then the old man said, It is due unto him.

5 So he called the angel, and he said unto him, Take half of all that ye have brought, and go away in safety.

6 Then he took them both apart, and said unto them, Bless God, praise him, and magnify him, and praise him for the things which he hath done unto you in the sight of all that live. It is good to praise God, and exalt his name, and

DOUAY OLD TESTAMENT

20 And Achior and Nabath the kinsmen of Tobias came, rejoicing for Tobias, and congratulating with him for all the good things that God had done for him.

21 And for seven days they feasted and rejoiced all with great joy.

12 THEN Tobias called to him his son, and said to him: What can we give to this holy man, that is come with thee?

2 Tobias answering, said to his father: Father, what wages shall we give him? or what can be worthy of his benefits?

3 He conducted me and brought me safe again, he received the money of Gabelus, he caused me to have my wife, and he chased from her the evil spirit, he gave joy to her parents, myself he delivered from being devoured by the fish, thee also he hath made to see the light of heaven, and we are filled with all good things through him. What can we give him sufficient for these things?

4 But I beseech thee, my father, to desire him, that he would vouchsafe to accept of one half of all things that have been brought.

5 So the father and the son calling him, took him aside: and began to desire him that he would vouchsafe to accept of half of all things that they had brought.

6 Then he said to them secretly: Bless ye the God of heaven, give glory to him in the sight of all that live, because he hath shewn his mercy to you.

KNOX TRANSLATION

man that was his guide. 20 Tobias' cousins, Achior and Nabath, came with glad hearts to congratulate him over the blessings he had received; 21 and for a whole week they all kept high festival, and rejoiced together.

12 And now Tobias took his son aside and asked him, What payment shall we make to this heaven-sent companion of thine? 2 Payment? answered he; why, what reward can ever suffice for all the services he did me? 3 He it was that escorted me safely, going and coming; recovered the debt from Gabelus; won me my bride; rid her of the fiend's attack; engaged the gratitude of her parents; rescued me from the fish's onslaught; and to thee restored the light of day. Through him, we have been loaded with benefits; is it possible to make any return for all these? 4 Do this, father, at least; ask him to accept half of all the wealth that has come to us.

5 So both of them, father and son, beckoned him aside, and would have prevailed on him to accept half of their new-found wealth. 6 But he, with a finger on his lip,[a] bade them give their thanks to the God of heaven. To him, he said, offer your praises for all men to hear; he it is that has shewn

[a] Literally, 'in secret', but as the three had already gone apart, it seems best to understand the words as referring to some *gesture* of secrecy.

TODAY'S ENGLISH VERSION

When Tobit met Sarah, he greeted her, "Welcome, daughter! Praise God for bringing you to us, my daughter. May God
bless your father, as well as you and my son Tobias.
Welcome to your new home. May you always be blessed with
good health and happiness. Come in, daughter!"

It was a day of great joy for all the Jews of Nineveh.
18 Tobit's nephews Ahikar and Nadab came by to share
Tobit's happiness with him.

12 When the wedding feast was over, Tobit called his
son Tobias and said to him, "Son, be sure to pay
your traveling companion, and don't forget to give him a
bonus."

2 Tobias asked him, "Father, how much do you think I
should pay him? I wouldn't mind giving him half of everything we brought back with us. 3 He brought me back home
safe and sound; he went to get the money for me from
Gabael; he rid my wife of a demon; and he cured your blindness. How much of a bonus should I give him?"

4 Tobit answered, "Give him half of what he helped you
bring back. He well deserves that."

5 Tobias then called Raphael and said to him, "Here is half
of what you helped me bring back. You have earned it; have
a safe journey home.

6 Then Raphael called the two men aside and said to them,
"Praise God and tell everyone about the good things he has

NEW REVISED STANDARD VERSION

merciful to him and had restored his sight. When Tobit met
Sarah the wife of his son Tobias, he blessed her saying,
"Come in, my daughter, and welcome. Blessed be your God
who has brought you to us, my daughter. Blessed be your
father and your mother, blessed be my son Tobias, and
blessed be you, my daughter. Come in now to your home,
and welcome, with blessing and joy. Come in, my daughter."
So on that day there was rejoicing among all the Jews who
were in Nineveh. 18 Ahikar and his nephew Nadab were also
present to share Tobit's joy. With merriment they celebrated
Tobias's wedding feast for seven days, and many gifts were
given to him.[a]

12 When the wedding celebration was ended, Tobit
called his son Tobias and said to him, "My child, see
to paying the wages of the man who went with you, and give
him a bonus as well." 2 He replied, "Father, how much shall
I pay him? It would do no harm to give him half of the possessions brought back with me. 3 For he has led me back to
you safely, he cured my wife, he brought the money back
with me, and he healed you. How much extra shall I give
him as a bonus?" 4 Tobit said, "He deserves, my child, to
receive half of all that he brought back." 5 So Tobias[b] called
him and said, "Take for your wages half of all that you
brought back, and farewell."

6 Then Raphael[b] called the two of them privately and said
to them, "Bless God and acknowledge him in the presence of
all the living for the good things he has done for you. Bless

a Other ancient authorities lack parts of this sentence *b* Gk *he*

NEW AMERICAN BIBLE

eyes. When Tobit reached Sarah, the wife of his son Tobiah,
he greeted her: "Welcome, my daughter! Blessed be your God
for bringing you to us, daughter! Blessed are your father and
your mother. Blessed is my son Tobiah, and blessed are you,
daughter! Welcome to your home with blessing and joy.
Come in, daughter!" That day there was joy for all the Jews
who lived in Nineveh. 18 Ahiqar and his nephew Nadab also
came to rejoice with Tobit. They celebrated Tobiah's wedding
feast for seven happy days, and he received many gifts.

12 When the wedding celebration came to an end, Tobit
called his son Tobiah and said to him, "Son, see to it
that you give what is due to the man who made the journey
with you; give him a bonus too." 2 Tobiah said: "Father, how
much shall I pay him? It would not hurt me at all to give him
half of all the wealth he brought back with me. 3 He led me
back safe and sound; he cured my wife; he brought the
money back with me; and he cured you. How much of a
bonus should I give him?" 4 Tobit answered, "It is only fair,
son, that he should receive half of all that he brought back."
5 So Tobiah called Raphael and said, "Take as your wages
half of all that you have brought back, and go in peace."

6 Raphael called the two men aside privately and said to
them: "Thank God! Give him the praise and the glory. Before
all the living, acknowledge the many good things he has

NEW JERUSALEM BIBLE

and had opened his eyes. Then Tobit met Sarah the bride of
his son Tobias, and blessed her in these words. 'Welcome,
daughter! Blessed be your God for sending you to us, my
daughter. Blessings on your father, blessings on my son
Tobias, blessings on yourself, my daughter. Welcome now to
your own house in joyfulness and in blessedness. Come in,
my daughter.' That day brought joy to the Jews of Nineveh,
18 and his cousins Ahikar and Nadab came to share in Tobit's
happiness.

12 When the wedding feast was over, Tobit called his
son Tobias and said, 'My son, you ought to think
about paying the amount due to your fellow traveller; give
him more than the figure agreed on.' 2 'Father,' he replied,
'how much am I to give him for his help? Even if I give him
half the goods he brought back with me, I shall not be the
loser. 3 He has brought me back safe and sound, he has
cured my wife, he has brought the money back too, and now
he has cured you as well. How much am I to give him for all
this?' 4 Tobit said, 'He has richly earned half what he
brought back'. 5 So Tobias called his companion and said,
'Take half of what you brought back, in payment for all you
have done, and go in peace.'

6 Then Raphael took them both aside and said, 'Bless God,
utter his praise before all the living for the favour he has

GREEK OLD TESTAMENT

ὑμνεῖν τὸ ὄνομα αὐτοῦ· τοὺς λόγους τοῦ θεοῦ ὑποδείκνυτε
πᾶσιν ἀνθρώποις ἐντίμως καὶ μὴ ὀκνεῖτε ἐξομολογεῖσθαι
αὐτῷ. 7 μυστήριον βασιλέως κρύπτειν καλόν, τὰ δὲ ἔργα τοῦ
θεοῦ ἀνακαλύπτειν καὶ ἐξομολογεῖσθαι ἐντίμως. τὸ ἀγαθὸν
ποιεῖτε, καὶ κακὸν οὐχ εὑρήσει ὑμᾶς. 8 ἀγαθὸν προσευχὴ
μετὰ ἀληθείας καὶ ἐλεημοσύνη μετὰ δικαιοσύνης μᾶλλον ἢ
πλοῦτος μετὰ ἀδικίας. καλὸν ποιῆσαι ἐλεημοσύνην μᾶλλον ἢ
θησαυρίσαι χρυσίον. 9 ἐλεημοσύνη ἐκ θανάτου ῥύεται, καὶ
αὐτὴ ἀποκαθαίρει πᾶσαν ἁμαρτίαν· οἱ ποιοῦντες ἐλεημοσύνην χορτασθήσονται ζωῆς. 10 οἱ ποιοῦντες ἁμαρτίαν καὶ
ἀδικίαν πολέμιοί εἰσιν τῆς ἑαυτῶν ψυχῆς. 11 πᾶσαν τὴν
ἀλήθειαν ὑμῖν ὑποδείξω καὶ οὐ μὴ κρύψω ἀφ᾽ ὑμῶν πᾶν ῥῆμα·
ἤδη ὑμῖν ὑπέδειξα καὶ εἶπον Μυστήριον βασιλέως καλὸν κρύ-
ψαι καὶ τὰ ἔργα τοῦ θεοῦ ἀνακαλύπτειν ἐνδόξως. 12 καὶ νῦν
ὅτε προσηύξω καὶ Σαρρα, ἐγὼ προσήγαγον τὸ μνημόσυνον
τῆς προσευχῆς ὑμῶν ἐνώπιον τῆς δόξης κυρίου· καὶ ὅτε
ἔθαπτες τοὺς νεκρούς, ὡσαύτως. 13 καὶ ὅτε οὐκ ὤκνησας
ἀναστῆναι καὶ καταλιπεῖν σου τὸ ἄριστον καὶ ᾤχου καὶ
περιέστειλες τὸν νεκρόν, τότε ἀπέσταλμαι ἐπὶ σὲ πειράσαι
σε. 14 καὶ ἅμα ἀπέσταλκέν με ὁ θεὸς ἰάσασθαί [σε] καὶ
Σαρραν τὴν νύμφην σου. 15 ἐγώ εἰμι Ραφαηλ, εἷς τῶν ἑπτὰ
ἀγγέλων, οἳ παρεστήκασιν καὶ εἰσπορεύονται ἐνώπιον τῆς
δόξης κυρίου.

16 Καὶ ἐταράχθησαν οἱ δύο καὶ ἔπεσαν ἐπὶ πρόσωπον
αὐτῶν καὶ ἐφοβήθησαν. 17 καὶ εἶπεν αὐτοῖς Μὴ φοβεῖσθε,

KING JAMES VERSION

honourably to shew forth the works of God; therefore be not slack to praise him.

7 It is good to keep close the secret of a king, but it is honourable to reveal the works of God. Do that which is good, and no evil shall touch you.

8 Prayer is good with fasting and alms and righteousness. A little with righteousness is better than much with unrighteousness. It is better to give alms than to lay up gold:

9 For alms doth deliver from death, and shall purge away all sin. Those that exercise alms and righteousness shall be filled with life:

10 But they that sin are enemies to their own life.

11 Surely I will keep close nothing from you. For I said, It was good to keep close the secret of a king, but that it was honourable to reveal the works of God.

12 Now therefore, when thou didst pray, and Sara thy daughter in law, I did bring the remembrance of your prayers before the Holy One: and when thou didst bury the dead, I was with thee likewise.

13 And when thou didst not delay to rise up, and leave thy dinner, to go and cover the dead, thy good deed was not hid from me: but I was with thee.

14 And now God hath sent me to heal thee and Sara thy daughter in law.

15 I am Raphael, one of the seven holy angels, which present the prayers of the saints, and which go in and out before the glory of the Holy One.

16 Then they were both troubled, and fell upon their faces: for they feared.

DOUAY OLD TESTAMENT

7 For it is good to hide the secret of a king: but honourable to reveal and confess the works of God.

8 Prayer is good with fasting and alms more than to lay up treasures of gold:

9 For alms delivereth from death, and the same is that which purgeth away sins, and maketh to find mercy and life everlasting.

10 But they that commit sin and iniquity, are enemies to their own soul.

11 I discover then the truth unto you, and I will not hide the secret from you.

12 When thou didst pray with tears, and didst bury the dead, and didst leave thy dinner, and hide the dead by day in thy house, and bury them by night, I offered thy prayer to the Lord.

13 And because thou wast acceptable to God, it was necessary that temptation should prove thee.

14 And now the Lord hath sent me to heal thee, and to deliver Sara thy son's wife from the devil.

15 For I am the angel Raphael, one of the seven, who stand before the Lord.

16 And when they had heard these things, they were troubled, and being seized with fear they fell upon the ground on their face.

17 And the angel said to them: Peace be to you, fear not.

KNOX TRANSLATION

mercy to you. 7 Kings have their counsel that must be kept
secret; God's ways are open, and he honours them best who
proclaims them openly.
8 Prayer, fasting, and alms, said he, here is better treasure
to lay up than any store of gold. 9 Almsgiving is death's
avoiding, is guilt's atoning, is the winning of mercy and of
life eternal; 10 the sinners, the wrong-doers, are enemies to
their own souls. 11 Come, let me tell you the whole truth of
the matter, bring the hidden purpose of it to light. 12 When
thou, Tobias, wert praying, and with tears, when thou wert
burying the dead, leaving thy dinner untasted, so as to hide
them all day in thy house, and at night give them funeral, I,
all the while, was offering that prayer of thine to the Lord.
13 Then, because thou hadst won his favour, needs must that
trials should come, and test thy worth. 14 And now, for thy
healing, for the deliverance of thy son's wife Sara from the
fiend's attack, he has chosen me for his messenger. 15 Who
am I? I am the angel Raphael, and my place is among those
seven who stand in the presence of the Lord.
16 Upon hearing this, they were both mazed with terror,
and fell down trembling, face to earth. 17 Peace be with you,

TODAY'S ENGLISH VERSION

done for you, so that they too will honor him and sing his
praises. Let everyone know what God has done. Never stop
praising him.
7 "It's a good idea to keep a king's secret, but what God
does should be told everywhere, so that he may be praised
and honored.
"If you do good, no harm will come to you.
8 "It is better to pray sincerely and to please God by helping
the poor than to be rich and dishonest. It is better to give to
the poor than to store up gold. 9 Such generosity will save
you from death and will wash away all your sins. Those who
give to the poor will live full lives, 10 but those who live a
life of sin and wickedness are their own worst enemies.
11 "I have already told you that a king's secret ought to be
kept, but the things God does should be told to everyone.
Now I will reveal to you the full truth and keep nothing back.
12 Tobit, when you and Sarah prayed to the Lord, I was the
one who brought your prayers into his glorious presence. I
did the same thing each time you buried the dead. 13 On the
day you got up from the table without eating your meal in
order to bury that corpse, God sent me to test you. 14 But he
also sent me to cure you and to rescue your daughter-in-law,
Sarah, from her troubles. 15 I am Raphael, one of the seven
angels who stand in the glorious presence of the Lord, ready
to serve him."
16 Tobit and Tobias were terrified and fell to the ground,
trembling with fear. 17 But Raphael said to them, "Don't be

NEW REVISED STANDARD VERSION

and sing praise to his name. With fitting honor declare to all
people the deeds[a] of God. Do not be slow to acknowledge
him. 7 It is good to conceal the secret of a king, but to
acknowledge and reveal the works of God, and with fitting
honor to acknowledge him. Do good and evil will not overtake you. 8 Prayer with fasting[b] is good, but better than both
is almsgiving with righteousness. A little with righteousness
is better than wealth with wrongdoing.[c] It is better to give
alms than to lay up gold. 9 For almsgiving saves from death
and purges away every sin. Those who give alms will enjoy a
full life, 10 but those who commit sin and do wrong are their
own worst enemies.
11 "I will now declare the whole truth to you and will
conceal nothing from you. Already I have declared it to you
when I said, 'It is good to conceal the secret of a king, but to
reveal with due honor the works of God.' 12 So now when
you and Sarah prayed, it was I who brought and read[d] the
record of your prayer before the glory of the Lord, and likewise whenever you would bury the dead. 13 And that time
when you did not hesitate to get up and leave your dinner to
go and bury the dead, 14 I was sent to you to test you. And
at the same time God sent me to heal you and Sarah your
daughter-in-law. 15 I am Raphael, one of the seven angels
who stand ready and enter before the glory of the Lord."
16 The two of them were shaken; they fell face down, for
they were afraid. 17 But he said to them, "Do not be afraid;

a Gk *words*; other ancient authorities read *words of the deeds* *b* Codex Sinaiticus *with sincerity* *c* Lat *d* Lat: Gk lacks *and read*

NEW AMERICAN BIBLE

done for you, by blessing and extolling his name in song.
Before all men, honor and proclaim God's deeds, and do not
be slack in praising him. 7 A king's secret it is prudent to
keep, but the works of God are to be declared and made
known. Praise them with due honor. Do good, and evil will
not find its way to you. 8 Prayer and fasting are good, but
better than either is almsgiving accompanied by righteousness. A little with righteousness is better than abundance
with wickedness. It is better to give alms than to store up
gold; 9 for almsgiving saves one from death and expiates
every sin. Those who regularly give alms shall enjoy a full
life; 10 but those habitually guilty of sin are their own worst
enemies.
11 "I will now tell you the whole truth; I will conceal nothing at all from you. I have already said to you, 'A king's
secret it is prudent to keep, but the works of God are to be
made known with due honor.' 12 I can now tell you that
when you, Tobit, and Sarah prayed, it was I who presented
and read the record of your prayer before the Glory of the
Lord; and I did the same thing when you used to bury the
dead. 13 When you did not hesitate to get up and leave your
dinner in order to go and bury the dead, 14 I was sent to put
you to the test. At the same time, however, God commissioned me to heal you and your daughter-in-law Sarah. 15 I
am Raphael, one of the seven angels who enter and serve
before the Glory of the Lord."
16 Stricken with fear, the two men fell to the ground. 17 But
Raphael said to them: "No need to fear; you are safe. Thank

NEW JERUSALEM BIBLE

shown you. Bless and extol his name. Proclaim before all
people the deeds of God as they deserve, and never tire of
giving him thanks. 7 It is right to keep the secret of a king,
yet right to reveal and publish the works of God as they
deserve. Do what is good, and no evil can befall you.
8 'Prayer with fasting and alms with uprightness are better
than riches with iniquity. Better to practise almsgiving than
to hoard up gold. 9 Almsgiving saves from death and purges
every kind of sin. Those who give alms have their fill of
days; 10 those who commit sin and do evil bring harm on
themselves.
11 'I am going to tell you the whole truth, hiding nothing
from you. I have already told you that it is right to keep the
secret of a king, yet right too to reveal in a worthy way the
words of God. 12 So you must know that when you and
Sarah were at prayer, it was I who offered your supplications
before the glory of the Lord and who read them; so too when
you were burying the dead. 13 When you did not hesitate to
get up and leave the table to go and bury a dead man, I was
sent to test your faith, 14 and at the same time God sent me
to heal you and your daughter-in-law Sarah. 15 I am
Raphael, one of the seven angels who stand ever ready to
enter the presence of the glory of the Lord.'
16 They were both overwhelmed with awe; they fell on their
faces in terror. 17 But the angel said, 'Do not be afraid; peace

Greek Old Testament

εἰρήνη ὑμῖν· τὸν θεὸν εὐλογεῖτε εἰς πάντα τὸν αἰῶνα.
18 ἐγὼ ὅτε ἤμην μεθ' ὑμῶν, οὐχὶ τῇ ἐμῇ χάριτι ἤμην μεθ'
ὑμῶν. ἀλλὰ τῇ θελήσει τοῦ θεοῦ· αὐτὸν εὐλογεῖτε κατὰ
πάσας τὰς ἡμέρας, αὐτῷ ὑμνεῖτε. 19 καὶ ἐθεωρεῖτέ με ὅτι
οὐκ ἔφαγον οὐθέν, ἀλλὰ ὅρασις ὑμῖν ἐθεωρεῖτο. 20 καὶ νῦν
εὐλογεῖτε ἐπὶ τῆς γῆς κύριον καὶ ἐξομολογεῖσθε τῷ θεῷ.
ἰδοὺ ἐγὼ ἀναβαίνω πρὸς τὸν ἀποστείλαντά με. γράψατε
πάντα ταῦτα τὰ συμβάντα ὑμῖν. καὶ ἀνέβη. 21 καὶ ἀνέστη-
σαν· καὶ οὐκέτι ἠδύναντο ἰδεῖν αὐτόν. 22 καὶ ηὐλόγουν καὶ
ὕμνουν τὸν θεὸν καὶ ἐξωμολογοῦντο αὐτῷ ἐπὶ τὰ ἔργα αὐτοῦ
τὰ μεγάλα ταῦτα, ὡς ὤφθη αὐτοῖς ἄγγελος θεοῦ.

13 Καὶ εἶπεν
2 Εὐλογητὸς ὁ θεὸς ὁ ζῶν εἰς τὸν αἰῶνα καὶ ἡ
βασιλεία αὐτοῦ,
ὅτι αὐτὸς μαστιγοῖ καὶ ἐλεᾷ,
κατάγει ἕως ᾅδου κατωτάτω τῆς γῆς,
καὶ αὐτὸς ἀνάγει ἐκ τῆς ἀπωλείας τῆς μεγάλης,
καὶ οὐκ ἔστιν οὐδέν, ὃ ἐκφεύξεται τὴν χεῖρα αὐτοῦ.
3 ἐξομολογεῖσθε αὐτῷ, οἱ υἱοὶ Ισραηλ, ἐνώπιον τῶν ἐθνῶν,
ὅτι αὐτὸς διέσπειρεν ὑμᾶς ἐν αὐτοῖς.
4 καὶ ἐκεῖ ὑπέδειξεν ὑμῖν τὴν μεγαλωσύνην αὐτοῦ,

King James Version

17 But he said unto them, Fear not, for it shall go well with you; praise God therefore.

18 For not of any favour of mine, but by the will of our God I came; wherefore praise him for ever.

19 All these days I did appear unto you; but I did neither eat nor drink, but ye did see a vision.

20 Now therefore give God thanks: for I go up to him that sent me; but write all things which are done in a book.

21 And when they arose, they saw him no more.

22 Then they confessed the great and wonderful works of God, and how the angel of the Lord had appeared unto them.

13 Then Tobit wrote a prayer of rejoicing, and said, Blessed be God that liveth for ever, and blessed be his kingdom.

2 For he doth scourge, and hath mercy: he leadeth down to hell, and bringeth up again: neither is there any that can avoid his hand.

3 Confess him before the Gentiles, ye children of Israel: for he hath scattered us among them.

4 There declare his greatness, and extol him before all the

Douay Old Testament

18 For when I was with you, I was there by the will of God: bless ye him, and sing praises to him.

19 I seemed indeed to eat and to drink with you: but I use an invisible meat and drink, which cannot be seen by men.

20 It is time therefore that I return to him that sent me: but bless ye God, and publish all his wonderful works.

21 And when he had said these things, he was taken from their sight, and they could see him no more.

22 Then they lying prostrate for three hours upon their face, blessed God: and rising up, they told all his wonderful works.

13 AND Tobias the elder opening his mouth, blessed the Lord, and said: Thou art great, O Lord, for ever, and thy kingdom is unto all ages:

2 For thou scourgest, and thou savest: thou leadest down to hell, and bringest up again: and there is none that can escape thy hand.

3 Give glory to the Lord, ye children of Israel, and praise him in the sight of the Gentiles:

4 Because he hath therefore scattered you among the Gentiles, who know not him, that you may declare his

Knox Translation

the angel said; do not be afraid. 18 It was God's will, not
mine, brought me to your side; to him pay the thanks and
praise you owe. 19 I was at your side, eating and drinking,
but only in outward show; the food, the drink I live by,
man's eyes cannot see. 20 And now the time has come when
I must go back to him who sent me; give thanks to God, and
tell the story of his great deeds. 21 With that, he was caught
away from their eyes, and no more might they see of him.[a]
22 For three hours together, face to earth, they gave thanks to
God; and when they rose up, it was to tell the story of all
these marvels.

13 It was thus, when he found utterance, that the elder
Tobias sang praise to the Lord: Great is thy name,
Lord, for ever; thy kingdom cannot fail. 2 Thine to scourge,
thine to pity; thou dost bring men to the grave and back
from the grave; from thy power there is no deliverance.
3 Sons of Israel, make his name known, publish it for all the
Gentiles to hear; 4 if he has dispersed you among heathen
folk who know nothing of him, it was so that you might tell
them the story of his great deeds, convince them that he, and

a In the Aramaic text we now have, Raphael goes away without disclosing his identity.

TODAY'S ENGLISH VERSION

afraid; everything is all right. Always remember to praise
God. 18 He wanted me to come and help you; I did not come
on my own. So sing God's praises as long as you live.
19 When you thought you saw me eating, I did not really eat
anything; it only seemed so. 20 While you are on this earth,
you must praise the Lord God and give him thanks. Now I
must go back to him who sent me. Write down everything
that has happened to you."
21 Then Raphael disappeared into the sky. Tobit and Tobias
stood up, but they could no longer see him. 22 They began to
sing hymns of praise, giving thanks for all the mighty deeds
God had done while his angel Raphael had been with them.

13 Then Tobit prayed:

"Praise the eternal God,
praise the one who rules.
2 He punishes us; then he shows us mercy.
He sends us down to the world of the dead,
then he brings us up from the grave.
No one can escape his power.

3 "People of Israel, give thanks among the nations,
where he sent you into exile;
4 even there he showed his great power.

NEW REVISED STANDARD VERSION

peace be with you. Bless God forevermore. 18 As for me,
when I was with you, I was not acting on my own will, but
by the will of God. Bless him each and every day; sing his
praises. 19 Although you were watching me, I really did not
eat or drink anything—but what you saw was a vision. 20 So
now get up from the ground,[a] and acknowledge God. See, I
am ascending to him who sent me. Write down all these
things that have happened to you." And he ascended.
21 Then they stood up, and could see him no more. 22 They
kept blessing God and singing his praises, and they acknowledged God for these marvelous deeds of his, when an angel
of God had appeared to them.

13 Then Tobit[b] said:
"Blessed be God who lives forever,
because his kingdom[c] lasts throughout all ages.
2 For he afflicts, and he shows mercy;
he leads down to Hades in the lowest regions of the
earth,
and he brings up from the great abyss,[d]
and there is nothing that can escape his hand.
3 Acknowledge him before the nations, O children of
Israel;
for he has scattered you among them.
4 He has shown you his greatness even there.

a Other ancient authorities read *now bless the Lord on earth* *b* Gk *he*
c Other ancient authorities read *forever, and his kingdom* *d* Gk *from destruction*

NEW AMERICAN BIBLE

God now and forever. 18 As for me, when I came to you it
was not out of any favor on my part, but because it was
God's will. So continue to thank him every day; praise him
with song. 19 Even though you watched me eat and drink, I
did not really do so; what you were seeing was a vision.
20 So now get up from the ground and praise God. Behold, I
am about to ascend to him who sent me; write down all
these things that have happened to you." 21 When Raphael
ascended, they rose to their feet and could no longer see him.
22 They kept thanking God and singing his praises; and they
continued to acknowledge these marvelous deeds which he
had done when the angel of God appeared to them.

13 Then Tobit composed this joyful prayer:

Blessed be God who lives forever,
because his kingdom lasts for all ages.
2 For he scourges and then has mercy;
he casts down to the depths of the netherworld,
and he brings up from the great abyss.
No one can escape his hand.

3 Praise him, you Israelites, before the Gentiles,
for though he has scattered you among them,
4 he has shown you his greatness even there.

NEW JERUSALEM BIBLE

be with you. Bless God for ever. 18 As far as I was concerned,
when I was with you, my presence was not by any decision
of mine, but by the will of God; he is the one whom you
must bless as long as you live, he the one that you must
praise. 19 You thought you saw me eating, but that was
appearance and no more. 20 Now bless the Lord on earth and
give thanks to God. I am about to return to him who sent me
from above. Write down all that has happened.' And he rose
in the air. 21 When they stood up again, he was no longer
visible. They praised God with hymns; they thanked him for
having performed such wonders; had not an angel of God
appeared to them?

13 And he said:

Blessed be God who lives for ever,
for his reign endures throughout all ages!
2 For he both punishes and pardons;
he sends people down to the depths of the underworld
and draws them up from utter Destruction;
no one can escape his hand.
3 Declare his praise before the nations,
you who are the children of Israel!
For if he has scattered you among them,
4 there too he has shown you his greatness.

GREEK OLD TESTAMENT

καὶ ὑψοῦτε αὐτὸν ἐνώπιον παντὸς ζῶντος,
καθότι αὐτὸς ἡμῶν κύριός ἐστιν, καὶ αὐτὸς θεὸς ἡμῶν
καὶ αὐτὸς πατὴρ ἡμῶν καὶ αὐτὸς θεὸς εἰς πάντας τοὺς
αἰῶνας.
5 μαστιγώσει ὑμᾶς ἐπὶ ταῖς ἀδικίαις ὑμῶν
καὶ πάντας ὑμᾶς ἐλεήσει ἐκ πάντων τῶν ἐθνῶν,
ὅπου ἂν διασκορπισθῆτε ἐν αὐτοῖς.
6 ὅταν ἐπιστρέψητε πρὸς αὐτὸν ἐν ὅλῃ τῇ καρδίᾳ ὑμῶν
καὶ ἐν ὅλῃ τῇ ψυχῇ ὑμῶν ποιῆσαι ἐνώπιον αὐτοῦ
ἀλήθειαν,
τότε ἐπιστρέψει πρὸς ὑμᾶς
καὶ οὐ μὴ κρύψῃ τὸ πρόσωπον αὐτοῦ ἀφ᾽ ὑμῶν οὐκέτι.
7 καὶ νῦν θεάσασθε ἃ ἐποίησεν μεθ᾽ ὑμῶν,
καὶ ἐξομολογήσασθε αὐτῷ ἐν ὅλῳ τῷ στόματι ὑμῶν·
καὶ εὐλογήσατε τὸν κύριον τῆς δικαιοσύνης
καὶ ὑψώσατε τὸν βασιλέα τῶν αἰώνων.—
8 [[BA:[a] ἐγὼ ἐν τῇ γῇ τῆς αἰχμαλωσίας μου ἐξομολογοῦμαι
αὐτῷ
καὶ δεικνύω τὴν ἰσχὺν καὶ τὴν μεγαλωσύνην αὐτοῦ
ἔθνει ἁμαρτωλῶν
Ἐπιστρέψατε, ἁμαρτωλοί, καὶ ποιήσατε δικαιοσύνην
ἐνώπιον αὐτοῦ·
τίς γινώσκει εἰ θελήσει ὑμᾶς καὶ ποιήσει ἐλεημοσύνην
ὑμῖν;
9 τὸν θεόν μου ὑψῶ
καὶ ἡ ψυχή μου τὸν βασιλέα τοῦ οὐρανοῦ

a Verses 8–11a, missing in ℵ (S), are supplemented from B and A.

KING JAMES VERSION

living: for he is our Lord, and he is the God our Father for ever.

5 And he will scourge us for our iniquities, and will have mercy again, and will gather us out of all nations, among whom he hath scattered us.

6 If ye turn to him with your whole heart, and with your whole mind, and deal uprightly before him, then will he turn unto you, and will not hide his face from you. Therefore see what he will do with you, and confess him with your whole mouth, and praise the Lord of might, and extol the everlasting King. In the land of my captivity do I praise him, and declare his might and majesty to a sinful nation. O ye sinners, turn and do justice before him: who can tell if he will accept you, and have mercy on you?

7 I will extol my God, and my soul shall praise the King of heaven, and shall rejoice in his greatness.

DOUAY OLD TESTAMENT

wonderful works, and make them know that there is no other almighty God besides him.

5 He hath chastised us for our iniquities: and he will save us for his own mercy.

6 See then what he hath done with us, and with fear and trembling give ye glory to him: and extol the eternal King of worlds in your works.

7 As for me, I will praise him in the land of my captivity: because he hath shewn his majesty toward a sinful nation.

8 Be converted therefore, ye sinners, and do justice before God, believing that he will shew his mercy to you.

9 And I and my soul will rejoice in him.

KNOX TRANSLATION

no other, is God all-powerful. 5 He it is that has scourged us
for our sins; he it is that will deliver us in his mercy. 6 Look
and see how he has dealt with us, and then give thanks to
him, but with trembling awe in your hearts; let your own
deeds acclaim him, king of all the ages. 7 I, at least, in this
land of exile, will be the spokesman of his praise, tell the
story of his dread dealings with a sinful race. 8 Come back,
sinners, and do his will; doubt not that he will shew you
mercy. 9 Here at least, while I live, is a soul that finds

TODAY'S ENGLISH VERSION

Let all who live hear your praise.
The Lord is our God and father forever.
5 "Though he punished you for your wickedness,
he will be merciful and bring you home
from among the nations where he scattered you.
6 "Turn to him with all your heart and soul,
live in loyal obedience to him.
Then he will turn to you to help you
and will no longer hide himself.
Remember what God has done for you,
and give thanks with all your heart.
Praise the righteous Lord;
honor the eternal King.

"Although I live in exile in a foreign land,
I will give thanks to the Lord
and will speak of his great strength to a nation of sinners.
'Turn away from your sins, and do what pleases God!
Perhaps he will be gracious
and show you his mercy.'

7 "I praise my God and rejoice in his greatness;
my whole being honors the King of heaven.

NEW REVISED STANDARD VERSION

Exalt him in the presence of every living being,
because he is our Lord and he is our God;
he is our Father and he is God forever.
5 He will afflict[a] you for your iniquities,
but he will again show mercy on all of you.
He will gather you from all the nations
among whom you have been scattered.
6 If you turn to him with all your heart and with all your soul,
to do what is true before him,
then he will turn to you
and will no longer hide his face from you.
So now see what he has done for you;
acknowledge him at the top of your voice.
Bless the Lord of righteousness,
and exalt the King of the ages.[b]
In the land of my exile I acknowledge him,
and show his power and majesty to a nation of sinners:
'Turn back, you sinners, and do what is right before him;
perhaps he may look with favor upon you and show you mercy.'
7 As for me, I exalt my God,
and my soul rejoices in the King of heaven.

a Other ancient authorities read *He afflicted* *b* The lacuna in codex Sinaiticus, verses 6b to 10a, is filled in from other ancient authorities

NEW AMERICAN BIBLE

Exalt him before every living being,
because he is the Lord our God,
our Father and God forever.
5 He scourged you for your iniquities,
but will again have mercy on you all.
He will gather you from all the Gentiles
among whom you have been scattered.
6 When you turn back to him with all your heart,
to do what is right before him,
Then he will turn back to you,
and no longer hide his face from you.

So now consider what he has done for you,
and praise him with full voice.
Bless the Lord of righteousness,
and exalt the King of the ages.

In the land of my exile I praise him,
and show his power and majesty to a sinful nation.
"Turn back, you sinners! do the right before him:
perhaps he may look with favor upon you
and show you mercy.

7 "As for me, I exalt my God,
and my spirit rejoices in the King of heaven.

NEW JERUSALEM BIBLE

Extol him before all the living;
he is our Lord
and he is our God;
he is our Father,
and he is God for ever and ever.
5 Though he punishes you for your iniquities,
he will take pity on you all;
he will gather you from every nation
wherever you have been scattered.
6 If you return to him
with all your heart and all your soul,
behaving honestly towards him,
then he will return to you
and hide his face from you no longer.
Consider how well he has treated you;
loudly give him thanks.
Bless the Lord of justice
and extol the King of the ages.

I for my part sing his praise
in the country of my exile;
I make his power and greatness known
to a nation that has sinned.
Sinners, return to him;
let your conduct be upright before him;
perhaps he will be gracious to you
and take pity on you.
7 I for my part extol God
and my soul rejoices

GREEK OLD TESTAMENT

καὶ ἀγαλλιάσεται τὴν μεγαλωσύνην αὐτοῦ.
10 λεγέτωσαν πάντες καὶ ἐξομολογείσθωσαν αὐτῷ ἐν
Ιεροσολύμοις
Ιεροσόλυμα πόλις ἁγία,
μαστιγώσει ἐπὶ τὰ ἔργα τῶν υἱῶν σου
καὶ πάλιν ἐλεήσει τοὺς υἱοὺς τῶν δικαίων.
11 ἐξομολογοῦ τῷ κυρίῳ ἀγαθῶς
καὶ εὐλόγει τὸν βασιλέα τῶν αἰώνων,⟧
καὶ πάλιν ἡ σκηνή σου οἰκοδομηθήσεταί σοι μετὰ χαρᾶς.
12 καὶ εὐφράναι ἐν σοὶ πάντας τοὺς αἰχμαλώτους
καὶ ἀγαπήσαι ἐν σοὶ πάντας τοὺς ταλαιπώρους
εἰς πάσας τὰς γενεὰς τοῦ αἰῶνος.
13 φῶς λαμπρὸν λάμψει εἰς πάντα τὰ πέρατα τῆς γῆς.
ἔθνη πολλὰ μακρόθεν [ἥξει σοι]
καὶ κάτοικοι πάντων τῶν ἐσχάτων τῆς γῆς πρὸς τὸ
ὄνομα τὸ ἅγιόν σου
καὶ τὰ δῶρα αὐτῶν ἐν ταῖς χερσὶν αὐτῶν ἔχοντες τῷ
βασιλεῖ τοῦ οὐρανοῦ·
γενεαὶ γενεῶν δώσουσιν ἐν σοὶ ἀγαλλίαμα,
καὶ ὄνομα τῆς ἐκλεκτῆς εἰς τὰς γενεὰς τοῦ αἰῶνος.
14 ἐπικατάρατοι πάντες, οἳ ἐροῦσιν λόγον σκληρόν,
ἐπικατάρατοι ἔσονται πάντες οἱ καθαιροῦντές σε
καὶ κατασπῶντες τὰ τείχη σου
καὶ πάντες οἱ ἀνατρέποντες τοὺς πύργους σου

KING JAMES VERSION

8 Let all men speak, and let all praise him for *his* righteousness.

9 O Jerusalem, the holy city, he will scourge thee for thy children's works, and will have mercy again on the sons of the righteous.

10 Give praise to the Lord, *for he is* good: and praise the everlasting King, that his tabernacle may be builded in thee again with joy, and let him make joyful there in thee those that are captives, and love in thee for ever those that are miserable.

11 Many nations shall come from far to the name of the Lord God with gifts in their hands, even gifts to the King of heaven; all generations shall praise thee with great joy.

12 Cursed *are* all they which hate thee, and blessed shall all be which love thee for ever.

DOUAY OLD TESTAMENT

10 Bless ye the Lord, all his elect, keep days of joy, and give glory to him.

11 Jerusalem, city of God, the Lord hath chastised thee for the works of thy hands.

12 Give glory to the Lord for thy good things, and bless the God eternal, that he may rebuild his tabernacle in thee, and may call back all the captives to thee, and thou mayst rejoice for ever and ever.

13 Thou shalt shine with a glorious light: and all the ends of the earth shall worship thee.

14 Nations from afar shall come to thee: and shall bring gifts, and shall adore the Lord in thee, and shall esteem thy land as holy.

15 For they shall call upon the great name in thee.

16 They shall be cursed that shall despise thee: and they shall be condemned that shall blaspheme thee: and blessed shall they be that shall build thee up.

KNOX TRANSLATION

content in him. 10 Bless the Lord, souls whom the Lord has
chosen; keep high festival in his honour.
11 Jerusalem, city of God, what divine punishments thy
own ill deeds have brought on thee! 12 Yet thank the Lord for
the blessings that are thine, praise him, the eternal God. So
may he rebuild thy dwelling-place, recall thy exiles, give thee
joy that shall last for ever. 13 Thou shalt yet shine with dazzling brightness, for all the ends of the world to worship
thee. 14 From far away, nations shall come bringing their
gifts, to worship the Lord within those walls of thine; shall
reckon thy soil holy ground, 15 so great the name they shall
invoke within thee. 16 Cursed shall they be that despise thee,
condemned shall they be that blaspheme thee, blessed shall

TODAY'S ENGLISH VERSION

8 "Let everyone tell of his greatness
and sing his praises in Jerusalem.

9 "Jerusalem, Holy City of our God,
he will punish you for the sins of your people,
but he will be merciful to all who do right.
10 So give thanks to the Lord, for he is good.
Praise the eternal King.[a]
Your Temple will be rebuilt,
and your people will be happy again.

"May the Lord make all your exiles glad,
may he take care of your suffering people
for as long as time shall last.

11 "Jerusalem, your light will shine brightly for all the
world,
and from far away many nations will come to you.
Their people will come to honor the Lord your God,
they will bring gifts for the King of heaven.
In your streets many generations will sing joyful praise,
your name will endure forever as God's chosen city.
12 A curse will be on all who make threats against you,
on all who destroy you and tear down your walls,

[a] *Some manuscripts do not have verses 6b-10a* Although I live . . . Praise the eternal King.

NEW REVISED STANDARD VERSION

8 Let all people speak of his majesty,
and acknowledge him in Jerusalem.
9 O Jerusalem, the holy city,
he afflicted[a] you for the deeds of your hands,[b]
but will again have mercy on the children of the
righteous.
10 Acknowledge the Lord, for he is good,[c]
and bless the King of the ages,
so that his tent[d] may be rebuilt in you in joy.
May he cheer all those within you who are captives,
and love all those within you who are distressed,
to all generations forever.
11 A bright light will shine to all the ends of the earth;
many nations will come to you from far away,
the inhabitants of the remotest parts of the earth to
your holy name,
bearing gifts in their hands for the King of heaven.
Generation after generation will give joyful praise in
you;
the name of the chosen city will endure forever.
12 Cursed are all who speak a harsh word against you;
cursed are all who conquer you
and pull down your walls,
all who overthrow your towers

a Other ancient authorities read *will afflict* *b* Other ancient authorities read *your children* *c* Other ancient authorities read *Lord worthily* *d* Or *tabernacle*

NEW AMERICAN BIBLE

8 Let all men speak of his majesty,
and sing his praises in Jerusalem."
9 O Jerusalem, holy city,
he scourged you for the works of your hands,
but will again pity the children of the righteous.
10 Praise the Lord for his goodness,
and bless the King of the ages,
so that his tent may be rebuilt in you with joy.
May he gladden within you all who were captives;
all who were ravaged may he cherish within you
for all generations to come.

11 A bright light will shine to all parts of the earth;
many nations shall come to you from afar,
And the inhabitants of all the limits of the earth,
drawn to you by the name of the Lord God,
Bearing in their hands their gifts for the King of
heaven.
Every generation shall give joyful praise in you,
and shall call you the chosen one,
through all ages forever.

12 Accursed are all who speak a harsh word against you;
accursed are all who destroy you
and pull down your walls,
And all who overthrow your towers

NEW JERUSALEM BIBLE

in the King of heaven.
Let his greatness 8 be on every tongue,
his praises be sung in Jerusalem.

9 Jerusalem, Holy City,
God has scourged you for what you have done
but will still take pity on the children of the upright.
10 Thank the Lord as he deserves
and bless the King of the ages,
that your Temple may be rebuilt with joy within you;
within you he may comfort every exile,
and within you he may love all those who are
distressed,
for all generations to come.
11 A bright light will shine
over all the regions of the earth;
many nations will come from far away,
from all the ends of the earth,
to dwell close to the holy name of the Lord God,
with gifts in their hands for the King of heaven.
Within you, generation after generation
will proclaim their joy,
and the name of her who is Elect will endure
through the generations to come.
12 Cursed be any who affront you,
cursed be any who destroy you,
who throw down your walls,
who rase your towers,

GREEK OLD TESTAMENT

καὶ ἐμπυρίζοντες τὰς οἰκήσεις σου·
καὶ εὐλογητοὶ ἔσονται πάντες εἰς τὸν αἰῶνα οἱ φοβούμενοί σε.
15 τότε πορεύθητι καὶ ἀγαλλίασαι πρὸς τοὺς υἱοὺς τῶν δικαίων,
ὅτι πάντες ἐπισυναχθήσονται
καὶ εὐλογήσουσιν τὸν κύριον τοῦ αἰῶνος.
μακάριοι οἱ ἀγαπῶντές σε,
καὶ μακάριοι οἳ χαρήσονται ἐπὶ τῇ εἰρήνῃ σου·
16 καὶ μακάριοι πάντες οἱ ἄνθρωποι,
οἳ ἐπὶ σοὶ λυπηθήσονται ἐπὶ πάσαις ταῖς μάστιξίν σου,
ὅτι ἐν σοὶ χαρήσονται καὶ ὄψονται πᾶσαν τὴν χαράν σου εἰς τὸν αἰῶνα.
ἡ ψυχή μου, εὐλόγει τὸν κύριον τὸν βασιλέα τὸν μέγαν.
17 ὅτι Ιερουσαλημ οἰκοδομηθήσεται, τῇ πόλει οἶκος αὐτοῦ εἰς πάντας τοὺς αἰῶνας.
μακάριος ἔσομαι, ἂν γένηται τὸ κατάλειμμα τοῦ σπέρματός μου
ἰδεῖν τὴν δόξαν σου καὶ ἐξομολογήσασθαι τῷ βασιλεῖ τοῦ οὐρανοῦ.
καὶ αἱ θύραι Ιερουσαλημ σαπφείρῳ καὶ σμαράγδῳ οἰκοδομηθήσονται
καὶ λίθῳ τιμίῳ πάντα τὰ τείχη σου·
οἱ πύργοι Ιερουσαλημ χρυσίῳ οἰκοδομηθήσονται
καὶ οἱ προμαχῶνες αὐτῶν χρυσίῳ καθαρῷ·
αἱ πλατεῖαι Ιερουσαλημ ἄνθρακι ψηφολογηθήσονται καὶ λίθῳ Σουφιρ.
18 καὶ αἱ θύραι Ιερουσαλημ ᾠδὰς ἀγαλλιάματος ἐροῦσιν,
καὶ πᾶσαι αἱ οἰκίαι αὐτῆς ἐροῦσιν Αλληλουια,

KING JAMES VERSION

13 Rejoice and be glad for the children of the just: for they shall be gathered together, and shall bless the Lord of the just.

14 O blessed *are* they which love thee, *for* they shall rejoice in thy peace: blessed *are* they which have been sorrowful for all thy scourges; for they shall rejoice for thee, when they have seen all thy glory, and shall be glad for ever.

15 Let my soul bless God the great King.

16 For Jerusalem shall be built up with sapphires, and emeralds, and precious stone: thy walls and towers and battlements with pure gold.

17 And the streets of Jerusalem shall be paved with beryl and carbuncle and stones of Ophir.

18 And all her streets shall say, Alleluia; and they shall

DOUAY OLD TESTAMENT

17 But thou shalt rejoice in thy children, because they shall all be blessed, and shall be gathered together to the Lord.

18 Blessed are all they that love thee, and that rejoice in thy peace.

19 My soul, bless thou the Lord, because the Lord our God hath delivered Jerusalem his city from all her troubles.

20 Happy shall I be if there shall remain of my seed, to see the glory of Jerusalem.

21 The gates of Jerusalem shall be built of sapphire, and of emerald, and all the walls thereof round about of precious stones.

22 All its streets shall be paved with white and clean stones: and Alleluia shall be sung in its streets.

KNOX TRANSLATION

they be that build thee again. 17 What joy wilt thou have of
thy children, a blessed race, gathered in the Lord's fold
anew! 18 A blessing on all that love thee, on all that welcome
thy good news! 19 Give thanks, my soul, to the Lord, the
Lord our God who has delivered Jerusalem, his own city,
from all the afflictions she endured; 20 happy I count myself,
if any posterity of mine is left to see Jerusalem in her splendour. 21 Sapphire and emerald Jerusalem's gates shall be, of
precious stones the wall that rings her round; 22 shining
white and clean the pavement of her streets; no quarter of
her but shall echo the Alleluia-chant of praise. 23 Blessed be

TODAY'S ENGLISH VERSION

on all who demolish your towers and burn your homes.
But all who honor you will be blessed forever.

13 "Rejoice, Jerusalem, because of your righteous people;
they will be gathered together from exile
to praise the Lord of the ages.

14 "Happy are all who love you
and are pleased to see you prosper.
Those who mourn over your suffering now
will one day be happy;
your happiness will bring them joy forever.

15 "I praise the Lord, the great King;
16 Jerusalem will be rebuilt
and will be his home forever.

"Jerusalem, how happy I will be
when my descendants can see your splendor
and give thanks to the King of heaven.

"Your gates will be built with sapphires and emeralds,
and all your walls with precious stones.
Your towers will be made of gold,
and their fortifications of pure gold.
17 Your streets will be paved with rubies and precious jewels.
18 Joyful songs will ring out from your gates,
and from all your houses people will shout,
'Praise the Lord! Praise the God of Israel!'

NEW REVISED STANDARD VERSION

and set your homes on fire.
But blessed forever will be all who revere you.[a]
13 Go, then, and rejoice over the children of the righteous,
for they will be gathered together
and will praise the Lord of the ages.
14 Happy are those who love you,
and happy are those who rejoice in your prosperity.
Happy also are all people who grieve with you
because of your afflictions;
for they will rejoice with you
and witness all your glory forever.
15 My soul blesses[b] the Lord, the great King!
16 For Jerusalem will be built[c] as his house for all ages.
How happy I will be if a remnant of my descendants
should survive
to see your glory and acknowledge the King of
heaven.
The gates of Jerusalem will be built with sapphire and
emerald,
and all your walls with precious stones.
The towers of Jerusalem will be built with gold,
and their battlements with pure gold.
The streets of Jerusalem will be paved
with ruby and with stones of Ophir.
17 The gates of Jerusalem will sing hymns of joy,
and all her houses will cry, 'Hallelujah!

a Other ancient authorities read *who build you up* *b* Or *O my soul, bless*
c Other ancient authorities add *for a city*

NEW AMERICAN BIBLE

and set fire to your homes;
but forever blessed are all those who build you up.

13 Go, then, rejoice over the children of the righteous,
who shall all be gathered together
and shall bless the Lord of the ages.
14 Happy are those who love you,
and happy those who rejoice in your prosperity.

Happy are all the men who shall grieve over you,
over all your chastisements,
For they shall rejoice in you
as they behold all your joy forever.

15 My spirit blesses the Lord, the great King;
16 Jerusalem shall be rebuilt as his home forever.
Happy for me if a remnant of my offspring survive
to see your glory and to praise the King of heaven!

The gates of Jerusalem shall be built with sapphire and
emerald,
and all your walls with precious stones.
The towers of Jerusalem shall be built with gold,
and their battlements with pure gold.
17 The streets of Jerusalem shall be paved
with rubies and stones of Ophir;
18 The gates of Jerusalem shall sing hymns of gladness,
and all her houses shall cry out, "Alleluia!"

NEW JERUSALEM BIBLE

who burn your houses!
Eternally blessed be he who rebuilds you!
13 Then you will exult, and rejoice
over the children of the upright,
for they will all have been gathered in
and will bless the Lord of the ages.

14 Blessed are those who love you,
blessed those who rejoice over your peace,
blessed those who have mourned
over all your punishment!
For they will soon rejoice within you,
witness all your blessedness in days to come.
15 My soul blesses the Lord, the great King
16 because Jerusalem will be built anew
and his house for ever and ever.

What bliss, if one of my family be left
to see your glory and praise the King of heaven!
The gates of Jerusalem will be built
of sapphire and of emerald,
and all your walls of precious stone,
the towers of Jerusalem will be built of gold
and their battlements of pure gold.
17 The streets of Jerusalem will be paved
with ruby and with stones from Ophir;
the gates of Jerusalem will resound
with songs of exultation;
and all her houses will say,
'Alleluia! Blessed be the God of Israel.'

GREEK OLD TESTAMENT

εὐλογητὸς ὁ θεὸς τοῦ Ισραηλ·
καὶ εὐλογητοὶ εὐλογήσουσιν τὸ ὄνομα τὸ ἅγιον εἰς τὸν
αἰῶνα καὶ ἔτι.

14 καὶ συνετελέσθησαν οἱ λόγοι τῆς ἐξομολογήσεως Τωβιθ.

2 Καὶ ἀπέθανεν ἐν εἰρήνῃ ἐτῶν ἑκατὸν δώδεκα καὶ ἐτάφη ἐνδόξως ἐν Νινευη. καὶ ἑξήκοντα δύο ἐτῶν ἦν, ὅτε ἐγένετο ἀνάπειρος τοῖς ὀφθαλμοῖς, καὶ μετὰ τὸ ἀναβλέψαι αὐτὸν ἔζησεν ἐν ἀγαθοῖς καὶ ἐλεημοσύνας ἐποίησεν· καὶ ἔτι προσέθετο εὐλογεῖν τὸν θεὸν καὶ ἐξομολογεῖσθαι τὴν μεγαλωσύνην τοῦ θεοῦ. 3 καὶ ὅτε ἀπέθνησκεν, ἐκάλεσεν Τωβιαν τὸν υἱὸν αὐτοῦ καὶ ἐνετείλατο αὐτῷ λέγων Παιδίον, ἀπάγαγε τὰ παιδία σου 4 καὶ ἀπότρεχε εἰς Μηδίαν, ὅτι πιστεύω ἐγὼ τῷ ῥήματι τοῦ θεοῦ ἐπὶ Νινευη, ἃ ἐλάλησεν Ναουμ, ὅτι πάντα ἔσται καὶ ἀπαντήσει ἐπὶ Αθουρ καὶ Νινευη, καὶ ὅσα ἐλάλησαν οἱ προφῆται τοῦ Ισραηλ, οὓς ἀπέστειλεν ὁ θεός, πάντα ἀπαντήσει, καὶ οὐ μηθὲν ἐλαττονωθῇ ἐκ πάντων τῶν ῥημάτων, καὶ πάντα συμβήσεται τοῖς καιροῖς αὐτῶν, καὶ ἐν τῇ Μηδίᾳ ἔσται σωτηρία μᾶλλον ἤπερ ἐν Ἀσσυρίοις καὶ ἐν Βαβυλῶνι· διὸ γινώσκω ἐγὼ καὶ πιστεύω ὅτι πάντα, ἃ εἶπεν ὁ θεός, συντελεσθήσεται καὶ ἔσται, καὶ οὐ μὴ διαπέσῃ ῥῆμα ἐκ τῶν λόγων· καὶ οἱ ἀδελφοὶ ἡμῶν οἱ κατοικοῦντες ἐν τῇ γῇ Ισραηλ πάντες διασκορπισθήσονται καὶ αἰχμαλωτισθήσονται ἐκ τῆς γῆς τῆς ἀγαθῆς, καὶ ἔσται πᾶσα ἡ γῆ τοῦ Ισραηλ ἔρημος, καὶ Σαμάρεια καὶ Ιερουσαλημ ἔσται ἔρημος καὶ ὁ οἶκος τοῦ θεοῦ ἐν λύπῃ καὶ καυθήσεται μέχρι χρόνου. 5 καὶ

KING JAMES VERSION

praise him, saying, Blessed be God, which hath extolled it for ever.

14 So Tobit made an end of praising God.

2 And he was eight and fifty years old when he lost his sight, which was restored to him after eight years: and he gave alms, and he increased in the fear of the Lord God, and praised him.

3 And when he was very aged, he called his son, and the six sons of his son, and said to him, My son, take thy children; for, behold, I am aged, and am ready to depart out of this life.

4 Go into Media, my son, for I surely believe those things which Jonas the prophet spake of Nineve, that it shall be overthrown; and that for a time peace shall rather be in Media; and that our brethren shall lie scattered in the earth from that good land: and Jerusalem shall be desolate, and the house of God in it shall be burned, and shall be desolate for a time;

DOUAY OLD TESTAMENT

23 Blessed be the Lord, who hath exalted it, and may he reign over it for ever and ever, Amen.

14 AND the words of Tobias were ended. And after Tobias was restored to his sight, he lived two and forty years, and saw the children of his grandchildren.

2 And after he had lived a hundred and two years, he was buried honourably in Ninive.

3 For he was six and fifty years old when he lost the sight of his eyes, and sixty when he recovered it again.

4 And the rest of his life was in joy, and with great increase of the fear of God he departed in peace.

5 And at the hour of his death he called unto him his son Tobias and his children, seven young men, his grandsons, and said to them:

6 The destruction of Ninive is at hand: for the word of the

KNOX TRANSLATION

the Lord, that has set her on the heights; may he reign there for ever, reign for ever as her king. Amen.[a]

14 Such was the song of Tobias. He lived forty-two years after recovering his sight, lived to see his great-grand-children; 2 then, dying at the age of a hundred and two, he was buried with due honour in the town of Nineve. 3 He lost his sight at the age of fifty-six, recovered it at the age of sixty, 4 and lived out the rest of his life in great content, his course ever untroubled, his conscience ever more tender towards God.

5 On his death-bed, he called his seven grandsons to him, with their father Tobias, and spoke thus: 6 The Lord's words must needs come true; it will not be long before Nineve is

a The Aramaic text has nothing corresponding to this chapter. Some think that verses 11-23 are a separate psalm, which has been attached accidentally to the canticle of Tobias. If we understand these sentiments as having been expressed by Tobias, it must have been by way of prophecy; the dates given in the next chapter shew that he cannot have been alive at the time when Jerusalem was sacked by the king of Babylon.

TODAY'S ENGLISH VERSION

"Jerusalem, God will bless your people,
and they will praise his holy name forever."

With these words Tobit ended his song of praise.

14 1-2Tobit was 62 years old when he became blind, but after his sight had been restored, he lived a very full life. Once again he gave generously to the poor, and he continued to praise God and tell of his greatness. Tobit died a peaceful death at the age of 112, and was given an honorable burial in Nineveh.
3But just before Tobit died, he sent for his son Tobias and
told him, 4"My son, take your children and go at once to Media. I believe that God's judgment which his prophet Nahum announced against Nineveh is about to take place. Everything that God's prophets told Israel about Nineveh and Assyria will happen. It will all come true, every word of it, when the right time comes. I am absolutely convinced that everything God has said is sure to come true. God does not break his promises. It will be safer for you in Media than in Assyria or Babylon.

"Those Jews who live in Israel will all be scattered and taken from that good land into exile. All Israel will become a wasteland; Samaria and Jerusalem will be abandoned cities. God's Temple will be burned to the ground and will lie in
complete ruin for a while. 5But God will have mercy on his

NEW REVISED STANDARD VERSION

Blessed be the God of Israel!'
and the blessed will bless the holy name forever and ever."

14 So ended Tobit's words of praise.
2 Tobit[a] died in peace when he was one hundred twelve years old, and was buried with great honor in Nineveh. He was sixty-two[b] years old when he lost his eyesight, and after regaining it he lived in prosperity, giving alms and continually blessing God and acknowledging God's majesty.
3 When he was about to die, he called his son Tobias and the seven sons of Tobias[c] and gave this command: "My son,
take your children 4and hurry off to Media, for I believe the word of God that Nahum spoke about Nineveh, that all these things will take place and overtake Assyria and Nineveh. Indeed, everything that was spoken by the prophets of Israel, whom God sent, will occur. None of all their words will fail, but all will come true at their appointed times. So it will be safer in Media than in Assyria and Babylon. For I know and believe that whatever God has said will be fulfilled and will come true; not a single word of the prophecies will fail. All of our kindred, inhabitants of the land of Israel, will be scattered and taken as captives from the good land; and the whole land of Israel will be desolate, even Samaria and Jerusalem will be desolate. And the temple of God in it will be burned to the ground, and it will be desolate for a while.[d]

a Gk *He* *b* Other ancient authorities read *fifty-eight* *c* Lat: Gk lacks *and the seven sons of Tobias* *d* Lat: Other ancient authorities read *of God will be in distress and will be burned for a while*

NEW AMERICAN BIBLE

"Blessed be God who has raised you up!
may he be blessed for all ages!"
For in you they shall praise his holy name forever.

The end of Tobit's hymn of praise.

14 Tobit died peacefully at the age of a hundred and twelve, and received an honorable burial in Nineveh.
2He was sixty-two years old when he lost his eyesight, and after he recovered it he lived in prosperity, giving alms and continually blessing God and praising the divine Majesty.
3Just before he died, he called his son Tobiah and Tobiah's seven sons, and gave him this command: "Son, take your
children 4and flee into Media, for I believe God's word which was spoken by Nahum against Nineveh. It shall all happen, and shall overtake Assyria and Nineveh; indeed, whatever was said by Israel's prophets, whom God commissioned, shall occur. Not one of all the oracles shall remain unfulfilled, but everything shall take place in the time appointed for it. So it will be safer in Media than in Assyria or Babylon. For I know and believe that whatever God has spoken will be accomplished. It shall happen, and not a single word of the prophecies shall prove false.

"As for our kinsmen who dwell in Israel, they shall all be scattered and led away into exile from the Good Land. The entire country of Israel shall become desolate; even Samaria and Jerusalem shall become desolate! God's temple there shall be burnt to the ground and shall be desolate for a

NEW JERUSALEM BIBLE

Within you they will bless the holy name
for ever and ever.

14 The end of the hymns of Tobit.
Tobit died when he was a hundred and twelve years
old and received an honourable burial in Nineveh. 2He had
been sixty-two when he went blind; and after his cure, he lived in comfort, practising almsgiving and continually praising God and extolling his greatness. 3When he was at the
point of death he summoned his son Tobias and gave him
these instructions, 4'My son, take your children and hurry away to Media, since I believe the word of God pronounced over Nineveh by Nahum. Everything will come true, everything happen that the emissaries of God, the prophets of Israel, have predicted against Assyria and Nineveh; not one of their words will prove empty. It will all take place in due time. You will be safer in Media than in Assyria or in Babylonia. Since I for my part know and believe that everything God has said will come true; so it will be, and not a word of the prophecies will fail.

'A census will be taken of our brothers living in the land of Israel and they will be exiled far from their own fair country. The entire territory of Israel will become a desert, and Samaria and Jerusalem will become a desert, and the house
of God, for a time, will be laid waste and burnt. 5Then once

GREEK OLD TESTAMENT

πάλιν ἐλεήσει αὐτοὺς ὁ θεός, καὶ ἐπιστρέψει αὐτοὺς ὁ θεὸς
εἰς τὴν γῆν τοῦ Ισραηλ, καὶ πάλιν οἰκοδομήσουσιν τὸν οἶκον,
καὶ οὐχ ὡς τὸν πρῶτον, ἕως τοῦ χρόνου, οὗ ἂν πληρωθῇ ὁ
χρόνος τῶν καιρῶν. καὶ μετὰ ταῦτα ἐπιστρέψουσιν ἐκ τῆς
αἰχμαλωσίας αὐτῶν πάντες καὶ οἰκοδομήσουσιν Ιερουσαλημ
ἐντίμως, καὶ ὁ οἶκος τοῦ θεοῦ ἐν αὐτῇ οἰκοδομηθήσεται,
καθὼς ἐλάλησαν περὶ αὐτῆς οἱ προφῆται τοῦ Ισραηλ. 6 καὶ
πάντα τὰ ἔθνη τὰ ἐν ὅλῃ τῇ γῇ, πάντες ἐπιστρέψουσιν καὶ
φοβηθήσονται τὸν θεὸν ἀληθινῶς, καὶ ἀφήσουσιν πάντες τὰ
εἴδωλα αὐτῶν, τοὺς πλανῶντας ψευδῆ τὴν πλάνησιν αὐτῶν,
καὶ εὐλογήσουσιν τὸν θεὸν τοῦ αἰῶνος ἐν δικαιοσύνῃ.
7 πάντες οἱ υἱοὶ τοῦ Ισραηλ οἱ σῳζόμενοι ἐν ταῖς ἡμέραις
ἐκείναις μνημονεύοντες τοῦ θεοῦ ἐν ἀληθείᾳ ἐπισυναχθήσονται καὶ ἥξουσιν εἰς Ιερουσαλημ καὶ οἰκήσουσιν τὸν αἰῶνα ἐν τῇ γῇ Αβρααμ μετὰ ἀσφαλείας, καὶ παραδοθήσεται
αὐτοῖς. καὶ χαρήσονται οἱ ἀγαπῶντες τὸν θεὸν ἐπ' ἀληθείας,
καὶ οἱ ποιοῦντες τὴν ἁμαρτίαν καὶ τὴν ἀδικίαν ἐκλείψουσιν
ἀπὸ πάσης τῆς γῆς. 8-9 νῦν, παιδία, ἐγὼ ὑμῖν ἐντέλλομαι·
δουλεύσατε τῷ θεῷ ἐν ἀληθείᾳ καὶ ποιήσατε τὸ ἀρεστὸν ἐνώπιον αὐτοῦ, καὶ τοῖς παιδίοις ὑμῶν ἐνυποταγήσεται ποιεῖν
δικαιοσύνην καὶ ἐλεημοσύνην καὶ ἵνα ὦσιν μεμνημένοι τοῦ
θεοῦ καὶ εὐλογῶσιν τὸ ὄνομα αὐτοῦ ἐν παντὶ καιρῷ ἐν ἀληθείᾳ καὶ ὅλῃ τῇ ἰσχύι αὐτῶν. καὶ νῦν σύ, παιδίον, ἔξελθε ἐκ
Νινευη καὶ μὴ μείνῃς ὧδε· ἐν ᾗ ἂν ἡμέρᾳ θάψῃς τὴν μητέρα
σου μετ' ἐμοῦ, αὐτῇ τῇ ἡμέρᾳ μὴ αὐλισθῇς ἐν τοῖς ὁρίοις
αὐτῆς. ὁρῶ γὰρ ὅτι πολλὴ ἀδικία ἐν αὐτῇ, καὶ δόλος πολὺς
συντελεῖται ἐν αὐτῇ, καὶ οὐκ αἰσχύνονται. 10 ἰδέ, παιδίον,
ὅσα Ναδαβ ἐποίησεν Αχικάρῳ τῷ ἐκθρέψαντι αὐτόν· οὐχὶ

KING JAMES VERSION

5 And that again God will have mercy on them, and bring them again into the land, where they shall build a temple, but not like to the first, until the time of that age be fulfilled; and afterward they shall return from *all* places of their captivity, and build up Jerusalem gloriously, and the house of God shall be built in it for ever with a glorious building, as the prophets have spoken thereof.

6 And all nations shall turn, and fear the Lord God truly, and shall bury their idols.

7 So shall all nations praise the Lord, and his people shall confess God, and the Lord shall exalt his people; and all those which love the Lord God in truth and justice shall rejoice, shewing mercy to our brethren.

8 And now, my son, depart out of Nineve, because that those things which the prophet Jonas spake shall surely come to pass.

9 But keep thou the law and the commandments, and shew thyself merciful and just, that it may go well with thee.

10 And bury me decently, and thy mother with me; but tarry no longer at Nineve. Remember, my son, how Aman handled Achiacharus that brought him up, how out of light

DOUAY OLD TESTAMENT

Lord must be fulfilled: and our brethren, that are scattered abroad from the land of Israel, shall return to it.

7 And all the land thereof that is desert shall be filled with people, and the house of God which is burnt in it, shall again be rebuilt: and all that fear God shall return thither.

8 And the Gentiles shall leave their idols, and shall come into Jerusalem, and shall dwell in it.

9 And all the kings of the earth shall rejoice in it, adoring the King of Israel.

10 Hearken therefore, my children, to your father: serve the Lord in truth, and seek to do the things that please him:

11 And command your children that they do justice and almsdeeds, and that they be mindful of God, and bless him at all times in truth, and with all their power.

12 And now, children, hear me, and do not stay here: but as soon as you shall bury your mother by me in one sepulchre, without delay direct your steps to depart hence:

13 For I see that its iniquity will bring it to destruction.

KNOX TRANSLATION

destroyed. After that, our exiled brethren will be able to
return to the land of Israel; 7 the deserted country-side will
be populous once again, and its temple, long since destroyed
by fire, will be built anew, and all those who fear God will
find their way back to it. 8 Then the Gentiles, too, will forsake their false gods; will betake themselves to Jerusalem,
and find a home there; 9 all the kings of the earth will take
pride in it, as they pay worship to the king who reigns in
Israel. [a]

10 This, then, my sons, is your father's testament: Keep
true to the Lord's service, studying ever to carry out his will;
11 and hand on this charge to your children, that they should
do what the law enjoins and give alms freely, that they
should keep God ever in mind, offering him faithful praise at
all times, and with all their strength. 12 And you, my sons,
heed well this warning of mine; do not linger in this country,
but leave it as soon as you have laid your mother to rest at
my side, to share my grave; 13 there is guilt at Nineve, I see
well, that must needs bring it to ruin.

a Tobias' prophecy in verses 6-9, like many in the Old Testament, foreshortens the perspective of history; relating first to the conquest of Assyria by Babylon in 612, then to the conquest of Babylon by Persia in 539, and the restoration of the Jewish exiles, then to the Messianic kingdom. In the Greek text, the destruction of Jerusalem by Nabuchodonosor is explicitly mentioned.

TODAY'S ENGLISH VERSION

people again, and he will bring them back to the land of Israel. They will rebuild the Temple, but it will not be as splendid as the first Temple, not until the proper time has come. But when that time does come, all the people of Israel will return from exile, and they will rebuild the city of Jerusalem in all its former splendor. They will rebuild God's Temple in Jerusalem, just as Israel's prophets have foretold.

6 "Then all the nations in the world will come back to God. They will worship him as the only true God and give up the idols that led them into false worship. 7 The nations of the world will praise the everlasting God by doing what he demands.

"At that time God will save all the people of Israel who have been faithful to him. He will bring them together to Jerusalem, and let them take possession of the land of Abraham, and there they will live securely forever. All who love God with their heart and soul will rejoice, but all sinners and evil people will be wiped off the face of the earth.

8 "Now, my children, follow my instructions. Worship God sincerely and do what is pleasing to him. 9 Bring up your children to do what is right. Teach them that they must give to the poor and must always remember to praise God with all sincerity.

10 "Tobias, my son, leave Nineveh now. Do not stay here. As soon as you bury your mother beside me, leave; do not stay another night within the city limits. It is a wicked city and full of immorality; the people here have no sense of shame. Remember what Nadab did to Ahikar his own uncle who had brought him up. He tried to kill Ahikar and forced

NEW REVISED STANDARD VERSION

5 "But God will again have mercy on them, and God will bring them back into the land of Israel; and they will rebuild the temple of God, but not like the first one until the period when the times of fulfillment shall come. After this they all will return from their exile and will rebuild Jerusalem in splendor; and in it the temple of God will be rebuilt, just as the prophets of Israel have said concerning it. 6 Then the nations in the whole world will all be converted and worship God in truth. They will all abandon their idols, which deceitfully have led them into their error; 7 and in righteousness they will praise the eternal God. All the Israelites who are saved in those days and are truly mindful of God will be gathered together; they will go to Jerusalem and live in safety forever in the land of Abraham, and it will be given over to them. Those who sincerely love God will rejoice, but those who commit sin and injustice will vanish from all the earth. 8,9 So now, my children, I command you, serve God faithfully and do what is pleasing in his sight. Your children are also to be commanded to do what is right and to give alms, and to be mindful of God and to bless his name at all times with sincerity and with all their strength. So now, my son, leave Nineveh; do not remain here. 10 On whatever day you bury your mother beside me, do not stay overnight within the confines of the city. For I see that there is much wickedness within it, and that much deceit is practiced within it, while the people are without shame. See, my son, what Nadab did to Ahikar who had reared him. Was he not, while still alive,

NEW AMERICAN BIBLE

while. 5 But God will again have mercy on them and bring them back to the land of Israel. They shall rebuild the temple, but it will not be like the first one, until the era when the appointed times shall be completed. Afterward all of them shall return from their exile, and they shall rebuild Jerusalem with splendor. In her the temple of God shall also be rebuilt; yes, it will be rebuilt for all generations to come, just as the prophets of Israel said of her. 6 All the nations of the world shall be converted and shall offer God true worship; all shall abandon their idols which have deceitfully led them into error, 7 and shall bless the God of the ages in righteousness. Because all the Israelites who are to be saved in those days will truly be mindful of God, they shall be gathered together and go to Jerusalem; in security shall they dwell forever in the land of Abraham, which will be given over to them. Those who sincerely love God shall rejoice, but those who become guilty of sin shall completely disappear from the land.

9 "Now, children, I give you this command: serve God faithfully and do what is right before him; you must tell your children to do what is upright and to give alms, to be mindful of God and at all times to bless his name sincerely and with all their strength.

8 "Now, as for you, my son, depart from Nineveh; do not remain here. 10 The day you bury your mother next to me, do not even stay overnight within the confines of the city. For I see that people here shamelessly commit all sorts of wickedness and treachery. Think, my son, of all that Nadab did to Ahiqar, the very one who brought him up: Ahiqar went down

NEW JERUSALEM BIBLE

again God will take pity on them and bring them back to the land of Israel. They will rebuild his house, although it will be less beautiful than the first, until the time is fulfilled. But after this, all will return from captivity and rebuild Jerusalem in all her glory, and the house of God will be rebuilt within her as the prophets of Israel have foretold. 6 And all the people of the whole earth will be converted and will reverence God with all sincerity. All will renounce their false gods who have led them astray into error, 7 and will bless the God of ages in uprightness. All the Israelites spared in those days will remember God in sincerity of heart. They will come and gather in Jerusalem and thereafter dwell securely in the land of Abraham, which will be theirs. And those who sincerely love God will rejoice. And those who commit sin and wickedness will vanish from the earth.

8 'And now, my children, I lay this duty on you; serve God sincerely, and do what is pleasing to him. And lay on your children the obligation to behave uprightly, to give alms, to keep God in mind and to bless his name always, sincerely and with all their might.

9 'So then, my son, leave Nineveh, do not stay here. 10 As soon as you have buried your mother next to me, go the same day, whenever it may be, and do not linger in this country where I see wickedness and perfidy unashamedly triumphant. Consider, my child, all the things done by Nadab to his foster-father Ahikar. Was not Ahikar forced to go

GREEK OLD TESTAMENT

ζῶν κατηνέχθη εἰς τὴν γῆν; καὶ ἀπέδωκεν ὁ θεὸς τὴν ἀτιμίαν κατὰ πρόσωπον αὐτοῦ, καὶ ἐξῆλθεν εἰς τὸ φῶς Αχικαρος,
καὶ Ναδαβ εἰσῆλθεν εἰς τὸ σκότος τοῦ αἰῶνος, ὅτι ἐζήτησεν
ἀποκτεῖναι Αχικαρον· ἐν τῷ ποιῆσαι ἐλεημοσύνην ἐξῆλθεν
ἐκ τῆς παγίδος τοῦ θανάτου, ἣν ἔπηξεν αὐτῷ Ναδαβ, καὶ
Ναδαβ ἔπεσεν εἰς τὴν παγίδα τοῦ θανάτου, καὶ ἀπώλεσεν
αὐτόν. 11 καὶ νῦν, παιδία, ἴδετε τί ποιεῖ ἐλεημοσύνη, καὶ τί
ποιεῖ ἀδικία, ὅτι ἀποκτέννει· καὶ ἰδοὺ ἡ ψυχή μου ἐκλείπει.
— καὶ ἔθηκαν αὐτὸν ἐπὶ τὴν κλίνην, καὶ ἀπέθανεν· καὶ
ἐτάφη ἐνδόξως.
12 Καὶ ὅτε ἀπέθανεν ἡ μήτηρ αὐτοῦ, ἔθαψεν αὐτὴν Τωβιας
μετὰ τοῦ πατρὸς αὐτοῦ. καὶ ἀπῆλθεν αὐτὸς καὶ ἡ γυνὴ αὐτοῦ
εἰς Μηδίαν καὶ ᾤκησεν ἐν Ἐκβατάνοις μετὰ Ραγουήλου τοῦ
πενθεροῦ αὐτοῦ. 13 καὶ ἐγηροβόσκησεν αὐτοὺς ἐντίμως καὶ
ἔθαψεν αὐτοὺς ἐν Ἐκβατάνοις τῆς Μηδίας καὶ ἐκληρονόμησεν τὴν οἰκίαν Ραγουήλου καὶ Τωβιθ τοῦ πατρὸς αὐτοῦ.
14 καὶ ἀπέθανεν ἐτῶν ἑκατὸν δέκα ἑπτὰ ἐνδόξως. 15 καὶ
εἶδεν καὶ ἤκουσεν πρὸ τοῦ ἀποθανεῖν αὐτὸν τὴν ἀπώλειαν
Νινευη καὶ εἶδεν τὴν αἰχμαλωσίαν αὐτῆς ἀγομένην εἰς
Μηδίαν, ἣν ᾐχμαλώτισεν Αχιαχαρος ὁ βασιλεὺς τῆς
Μηδίας, καὶ εὐλόγησεν τὸν θεὸν ἐν πᾶσιν, οἷς ἐποίησεν ἐπὶ
τοὺς υἱοὺς Νινευη καὶ Αθουριας. ἐχάρη πρὶν τοῦ ἀποθανεῖν
ἐπὶ Νινευη καὶ εὐλόγησεν κύριον τὸν θεὸν εἰς τοὺς αἰῶνας
τῶν αἰώνων. ἀμήν.

KING JAMES VERSION

he brought him into darkness, and how he rewarded him again: yet Achiacharus was saved, but the other had his reward: for he went down into darkness. Manasses gave alms, and escaped the snares of death which they had set for him: but Aman fell into the snare, and perished.

11 Wherefore now, my son, consider what alms doeth, and how righteousness doth deliver. When he had said these things, he gave up the ghost in the bed, being an hundred and eight and fifty years old; and he buried him honourably.

12 And when Anna his mother was dead, he buried her with his father. But Tobias departed with his wife and children to Ecbatane to Raguel his father in law,

13 Where he became old with honour, and he buried his father and mother in law honourably, and he inherited their substance, and his father Tobit's.

14 And he died at Ecbatane in Media, being an hundred and seven and twenty years old.

15 But before he died he heard of the destruction of Nineve, which was taken by Nabuchodonosor and Assuerus: and before his death he rejoiced over Nineve.

DOUAY OLD TESTAMENT

14 And it came to pass that after the death of his mother, Tobias departed out of Ninive with his wife, and children, and children's children, and returned to his father and mother in law.

15 And he found them in health in a good old age: and he took care of them, and he closed their eyes: and all the inheritance of Raguel's house came to him: and he saw his children's children to the fifth generation.

16 And after he had lived ninety-nine years in the fear of the Lord, with joy they buried him.

17 And all his kindred, and all his generation continued in good life, and in holy conversation, so that they were acceptable both to God, and to men, and to all that dwelt in the land.

KNOX TRANSLATION

14 So, when his mother died, Tobias, with his wife, sons
and grandsons left Nineve. He betook himself to his wife's
parents instead, 15 and found them thriving still, well content in their old age. Tenderly he cared for them, and when
they died it was he that closed their eyes in death. Then he
became heir to all Raguel possessed, and himself lived to see
a fresh generation yet, descendants of his own. 16 Ninety-
nine years he lived in the fear of God, and with full hearts
they buried him. 17 No kith or kin of his but persevered in
uprightness and holy living; God's favour they had and
man's alike, well loved by all their neighbours.

TODAY'S ENGLISH VERSION

him to go into hiding in a tomb. Ahikar came back into the light of day, but God sent Nadab down into everlasting darkness for what he had done. Ahikar escaped the deadly trap which Nadab had set for him, because Ahikar[a] had given generously to the poor. But Nadab fell into that fatal trap and it destroyed him. 11 So now, my children, you see what happens to those who show their concern for others, and how death awaits those who treat others unjustly. But now I am very weak."

Then they laid Tobit on his bed. He died and was given an honorable burial. 12 Later on, Tobit's wife died and was buried beside her husband. Then Tobias and his wife moved to Ecbatana in Media, where they lived with Raguel, Tobias' father-in-law. 13 Tobias took care of Edna and Raguel in their old age and showed them great respect. When at last they died, he buried them at Ecbatana. Tobias inherited Raguel's estate, as he had inherited the estate of his father Tobit.

14 At the ripe old age of 117 Tobias died, 15 having lived long enough to hear about the destruction of Nineveh and to see King Cyaxares[b] of Media take the people away as captives. Tobias praised God for the way that he had punished the people of Nineveh and Assyria. As long as he lived he gave thanks for what God had done to Nineveh.

[a] Ahikar; *or* I. [b] *Probable text* Cyaxares; *Greek unclear.*

NEW REVISED STANDARD VERSION

brought down into the earth? For God repaid him to his face for this shameful treatment. Ahikar came out into the light, but Nadab went into the eternal darkness, because he tried to kill Ahikar. Because he gave alms, Ahikar[a] escaped the fatal trap that Nadab had set for him, but Nadab fell into it himself, and was destroyed. 11 So now, my children, see what almsgiving accomplishes, and what injustice does—it brings death! But now my breath fails me."

Then they laid him on his bed, and he died; and he received an honorable funeral. 12 When Tobias's mother died, he buried her beside his father. Then he and his wife and children[b] returned to Media and settled in Ecbatana with Raguel his father-in-law. 13 He treated his parents-in-law[c] with great respect in their old age, and buried them in Ecbatana of Media. He inherited both the property of Raguel and that of his father Tobit. 14 He died highly respected at the age of one hundred seventeen[d] years. 15 Before he died he heard[e] of the destruction of Nineveh, and he saw its prisoners being led into Media, those whom King Cyaxares[f] of Media had taken captive. Tobias[g] praised God for all he had done to the people of Nineveh and Assyria; before he died he rejoiced over Nineveh, and he blessed the Lord God forever and ever. Amen.[h]

a Gk *he*; other ancient authorities read *Manasses* *b* Codex Sinaiticus lacks *and children* *c* Gk *them* *d* Other authorities read other numbers *e* Codex Sinaiticus reads *saw and heard* *f* Cn: Codex Sinaiticus *Ahikar*; other ancient authorities read *Nebuchadnezzar and Ahasuerus* *g* Gk *He* *h* Other ancient authorities lack *Amen*

NEW AMERICAN BIBLE

alive into the earth! Yet God made Nadab's disgraceful crime rebound against him. Ahiqar came out again into the light, but Nadab went into the everlasting darkness, for he had tried to kill Ahiqar. Because Ahiqar had given alms to me, he escaped from the deadly trap Nadab had set for him. But Nadab himself fell into the deadly trap, and it destroyed him. 11 So, my children, note well what almsgiving does, and also what wickedness does—it kills! But now my spirit is about to leave me."

12 They placed him on his bed and he died; and he received an honorable burial. When Tobiah's mother died, he buried her next to his father. He then departed with his wife and children for Media, where he settled in Ecbatana with his father-in-law Raguel. 13 He took respectful care of his aging father-in-law and mother-in-law; and he buried them at Ecbatana in Media. Then he inherited Raguel's estate as well as that of his father Tobit. 14 He died at the venerable age of a hundred and seventeen. 15 But before he died, he heard of the destruction of Nineveh and saw its effects. He witnessed the exile of the city's inhabitants when Cyaxares, king of Media, led them captive into Media. Tobiah praised God for all that he had done against the citizens of Nineveh and Assyria. Before dying he rejoiced over Nineveh's destruction, and he blessed the Lord God forever and ever. Amen.

NEW JERUSALEM BIBLE

underground, though still a living man? But God made the criminal pay for his outrage before his victim's eyes, since Ahikar came back to the light of day, while Nadab went down to everlasting darkness in punishment for plotting against Ahikar's life. Because of his good works Ahikar escaped the deadly snare Nadab had laid for him, and Nadab fell into it to his own ruin. 11 So, my children, you see what comes of almsgiving, and what wickedness leads to, I mean to death. But now breath fails me.'

They laid him back on his bed; he died and was buried with honour.

12 When his mother died, Tobias buried her beside his father. Then he left for Media with his wife and children. He lived in Ecbatana with Raguel, his father-in-law. 13 He treated the ageing parents of his wife with every care and respect, and later buried them in Ecbatana in Media. Tobias inherited the patrimony of Raguel besides that of his father Tobit. 14 Much honoured, he lived to the age of a hundred and seventeen years. 15 Before he died he witnessed the ruin of Nineveh. He saw the Ninevites taken prisoner and deported to Media by Cyaxares king of Media. He blessed God for everything he inflicted on the Ninevites and Assyrians. Before his death he had the opportunity of rejoicing over the fate of Nineveh, and he blessed the Lord God for ever and ever. Amen.

GREEK OLD TESTAMENT

ΙΟΥΔΙΘ

1 Ἔτους δωδεκάτου τῆς βασιλείας Ναβουχοδονοσορ, ὃς
ἐβασίλευσεν Ἀσσυρίων ἐν Νινευη τῇ πόλει τῇ μεγάλῃ,
ἐν ταῖς ἡμέραις Αρφαξαδ, ὃς ἐβασίλευσεν Μήδων ἐν
Ἐκβατάνοις, 2 καὶ ᾠκοδόμησεν ἐπ᾽ Ἐκβατάνων κύκλῳ τείχη
ἐκ λίθων λελαξευμένων εἰς πλάτος πηχῶν τριῶν καὶ εἰς
μῆκος πηχῶν ἓξ καὶ ἐποίησεν τὸ ὕψος τοῦ τείχους πηχῶν
ἑβδομήκοντα καὶ τὸ πλάτος αὐτοῦ πηχῶν πεντήκοντα 3 καὶ
τοὺς πύργους αὐτοῦ ἔστησεν ἐπὶ ταῖς πύλαις αὐτῆς πηχῶν
ἑκατὸν καὶ τὸ πλάτος αὐτῆς ἐθεμελίωσεν εἰς πήχεις
ἑξήκοντα 4 καὶ ἐποίησεν τὰς πύλας αὐτῆς πύλας διεγειρο-
μένας εἰς ὕψος πηχῶν ἑβδομήκοντα καὶ τὸ πλάτος αὐτῆς
πήχεις τεσσαράκοντα εἰς ἐξόδους δυνάμεως δυνατῶν αὐτοῦ
καὶ διατάξεις τῶν πεζῶν αὐτοῦ. 5 καὶ ἐποίησεν πόλεμον ἐν
ταῖς ἡμέραις ἐκείναις ὁ βασιλεὺς Ναβουχοδονοσορ πρὸς
βασιλέα Αρφαξαδ ἐν τῷ πεδίῳ τῷ μεγάλῳ, τοῦτό ἐστιν πεδι-
΄ον ἐν τοῖς ὁρίοις Ραγαυ. 6 καὶ συνήντησαν πρὸς αὐτὸν
πάντες οἱ κατοικοῦντες τὴν ὀρεινὴν καὶ πάντες οἱ κατοικοῦντες τὸν Εὐφράτην καὶ τὸν Τίγριν καὶ τὸν Ὑδάσπην καὶ
πεδία Αριωχ βασιλέως Ἐλυμαίων, καὶ συνῆλθον ἔθνη πολλὰ
εἰς παράταξιν υἱῶν Χελεουδ. 7 καὶ ἀπέστειλεν Ναβουχοδονοσορ βασιλεὺς Ἀσσυρίων ἐπὶ πάντας τοὺς κατοικοῦντας
τὴν Περσίδα καὶ ἐπὶ πάντας τοὺς κατοικοῦντας πρὸς δυσμαῖς, τοὺς κατοικοῦντας τὴν Κιλικίαν καὶ Δαμασκὸν καὶ
τὸν Λίβανον καὶ Ἀντιλίβανον, καὶ πάντας τοὺς κατοικοῦντας
κατὰ πρόσωπον τῆς παραλίας 8 καὶ τοὺς ἐν τοῖς ἔθνεσι τοῦ
Καρμήλου καὶ Γαλααδ καὶ τὴν ἄνω Γαλιλαίαν καὶ τὸ μέγα

KING JAMES VERSION

JUDITH

1 In the twelfth year of the reign of Nabuchodonosor, who reigned in Nineve, the great city; in the days of Arphaxad, which reigned over the Medes in Ecbatane,

2 And built in Ecbatane walls round about of stones hewn three cubits broad and six cubits long, and made the height of the wall seventy cubits, and the breadth thereof fifty cubits:

3 And set the towers thereof upon the gates of it, an hundred cubits *high,* and the breadth thereof in the foundation threescore cubits:

4 And he made the gates thereof, even gates that were raised to the height of seventy cubits, and the breadth of them was forty cubits, for the going forth of his mighty armies, and for the setting in array of his footmen:

5 Even in those days king Nabuchodonosor made war with king Arphaxad in the great plain, which is the plain in the borders of Ragau.

6 And there came unto him all they that dwelt in the hill country, and all that dwelt by Euphrates, and Tigris, and Hydaspes, and the plain of Arioch the king of the Elymeans, and very many nations of the sons of Chelod, assembled themselves to the battle.

7 Then Nabuchodonosor king of the Assyrians sent unto all that dwelt in Persia, and to all that dwelt westward, and to those that dwelt in Cilicia, and Damascus, and Libanus, and Antilibanus, and to all that dwelt upon the sea coast,

8 And to those among the nations that were of Carmel, and Galaad, and the higher Galilee, and the great plain of Esdrelon,

DOUAY OLD TESTAMENT

THE BOOK OF JUDITH

1 NOW Arphaxad king of the Medes had brought many nations under his dominions, and he built a very strong city, which he called Ecbatana,

2 Of stones squared and hewed: he made the walls thereof seventy cubits broad, and thirty cubits high, and the towers thereof he made a hundred cubits high. But on the square of them, each side was extended the space of twenty feet.

3 And he made the gates thereof according to the height of the towers:

4 And he gloried as a mighty one in the force of his army and in the glory of his chariots.

5 Now in the twelfth year of his reign, Nabuchodonosor king of the Assyrians, who reigned in Ninive the great city, fought against Arphaxad and overcame him,

6 In the great plain which is called Ragua, about the Euphrates, and the Tigris, and the Jadason, in the plain of Erioch the king of the Elicians.

7 Then was the kingdom of Nabuchodonosor exalted, and his heart was elevated: and he sent to all that dwelt in Cilicia and Damascus, and Libanus,

8 And to the nations that are in Carmelus, and Cedar, and to the inhabitants of Galilee in the great plain of Asdrelon,

KNOX TRANSLATION

THE BOOK OF JUDITH

1 ARPHAXAD, king of Media, the conqueror of many
nations, built a princely city, which he called Ecbatana.
Of stones cut and squared he built it, 2 with walls seventy
cubits thick and thirty cubits high, and towers reaching the
height of a hundred cubits. 3 Each of these towers was twenty feet square, and at the foot of them he set gates to match
their height.[a] 4 And he boasted much of his great army, of
his fine chariots; 5 till at last war was levied upon him by
the Assyrian king Nabuchodonosor,[b] then in the twelfth year
of his reign, with his capital at Nineve. This Nabuchodonosor
defeated him 6 in the great plain called Ragua, where
Euphrates flows, and Tigris, and Jadason, in the lowland
country belonging to Erioch, king of the Elici.
7 Thus to Nabuchodonosor in his turn, came power and
pride. To distant lands he had sent out his demand for aid;
to Cilicia, Damascus, and the Lebanon, 8 to Carmel, and
Cedar, and Galilee about the wide Esdrelon plain, 9 Samaria,

a The measurements here are uncertain, since the Greek gives a different account of them. *b* No Nabuchodonosor king of Assyria is known from other sources. Probably the story relates to some conqueror known to history under another name, but there is no agreement among scholars about his identity. We cannot, therefore, be certain what is the period in which the action of the book takes place.

TODAY'S ENGLISH VERSION

THE BOOK OF JUDITH

1 While King Nebuchadnezzar was ruling over the Assyrians from his capital city of Nineveh, King Arphaxad ruled over the Medes from his capital city of Ecbatana. 2 Around Ecbatana King Arphaxad built a wall 105 feet high and 75 feet thick of cut stones; each stone was 4 1/2 feet thick and 9 feet long. 3 At each gate he built a tower 150 feet high, with a foundation 90 feet thick. 4 Each gateway was 105 feet high and 60 feet wide—wide enough for his whole army to march through, with the infantry in formation.

5 In the twelfth year of his reign King Nebuchadnezzar went to war against King Arphaxad in the large plain around the city of Rages. 6 Many nations joined forces with King Arphaxad—all the people who lived in the mountains, those who lived along the Tigris, Euphrates, and Hydaspes rivers, as well as those who lived in the plain ruled by King Arioch of Elam. Many nations joined this Chelodite alliance.

7 Then King Nebuchadnezzar of Assyria sent a message to the Persians and to the people to the west, in the regions of Cilicia, Damascus, Lebanon, Antilebanon, to those along the coast, 8 and in the regions of Carmel, Gilead, northern Galilee,

NEW REVISED STANDARD VERSION

JUDITH

1 It was the twelfth year of the reign of Nebuchadnezzar, who ruled over the Assyrians in the great city of Nineveh. In those days Arphaxad ruled over the Medes in Ecbatana. 2 He built walls around Ecbatana with hewn stones three cubits thick and six cubits long; he made the walls seventy cubits high and fifty cubits wide. 3 At its gates he raised towers one hundred cubits high and sixty cubits wide at the foundations. 4 He made its gates seventy cubits high and forty cubits wide to allow his armies to march out in force and his infantry to form their ranks. 5 Then King Nebuchadnezzar made war against King Arphaxad in the great plain that is on the borders of Ragau. 6 There rallied to him all the people of the hill country and all those who lived along the Euphrates, the Tigris, and the Hydaspes, and, on the plain, Arioch, king of the Elymeans. Thus, many nations joined the forces of the Chaldeans.[a]

7 Then Nebuchadnezzar, king of the Assyrians, sent messengers to all who lived in Persia and to all who lived in the west, those who lived in Cilicia and Damascus, Lebanon and Antilebanon, and all who lived along the seacoast, 8 and those among the nations of Carmel and Gilead, and Upper Galilee and the great plain of Esdraelon, 9 and all who were

a Syr: Gk *Cheleoudites*

NEW AMERICAN BIBLE

THE BOOK OF JUDITH

1 It was the twelfth year of the reign of Nebuchadnezzar, king of the Assyrians in the great city of Nineveh. At that time Arphaxad ruled over the Medes in Ecbatana. 2 Around this city he built a wall of blocks of stone, each three cubits in height and six in length. He made the wall seventy cubits high and fifty thick. 3 At the gates he raised towers of a hundred cubits, with a thickness of sixty cubits at the base. 4 The gateway he built to a height of seventy cubits, with an opening forty cubits wide for the passage of his chariot forces and the marshaling of his infantry. 5 Then King Nebuchadnezzar waged war against King Arphaxad in the vast plain, in the district of Ragae. 6 To him there rallied all the inhabitants of the mountain region, all who dwelt along the Euphrates, the Tigris, and the Hydaspes, and King Arioch of the Elamites, in the plain. Thus many nations came together to resist the people of Cheleoud.

7 Now Nebuchadnezzar, king of the Assyrians, sent messengers to all the inhabitants of Persia, and to all those who dwelt in the West: to the inhabitants of Cilicia and Damascus, Lebanon and Anti-Lebanon, to all who dwelt along the seacoast, 8 to the peoples of Carmel, Gilead, Upper Galilee, and the vast plain of Esdraelon, 9 to all those in

NEW JERUSALEM BIBLE

JUDITH

1 It was the twelfth year of Nebuchadnezzar who reigned over the Assyrians in the great city of Nineveh. Arphaxad was then reigning over the Medes in Ecbatana. 2 He surrounded this city with walls of dressed stones three cubits thick and six cubits long, making the rampart seventy cubits high and fifty cubits wide. 3 At the gates he placed towers one hundred cubits high and, at the foundations, sixty cubits wide, 4 the gates themselves being seventy cubits high and forty wide to allow his forces to march out in a body and his infantry to parade freely.

5 About this time King Nebuchadnezzar gave battle to King Arphaxad in the great plain lying in the territory of Ragae. 6 Supporting him were all the peoples from the highlands, all from the Euphrates and Tigris and Hydaspes, and those from the plains who were subject to Arioch, king of the Elymaeans. Thus many nations had mustered to take part in the battle of the Cheleoudites.

7 Nebuchadnezzar king of the Assyrians sent a message to all the inhabitants of Persia, to all the inhabitants of the western countries, Cilicia, Damascus, Lebanon, Anti-Lebanon, to all those along the coast, 8 to the peoples of Carmel, Gilead, Upper Galilee, the great plain of Esdraelon,

GREEK OLD TESTAMENT

πεδίον Εσδρηλων 9 καὶ πάντας τοὺς ἐν Σαμαρείᾳ καὶ ταῖς
πόλεσιν αὐτῆς καὶ πέραν τοῦ Ιορδάνου ἕως Ιερουσαλημ καὶ
Βατανη καὶ Χελους καὶ Καδης καὶ τοῦ ποταμοῦ Αἰγύπτου
καὶ Ταφνας καὶ Ραμεσση καὶ πᾶσαν γῆν Γεσεμ 10 ἕως τοῦ
ἐλθεῖν ἐπάνω Τάνεως καὶ Μέμφεως καὶ πάντας τοὺς κατοικοῦντας τὴν Αἴγυπτον ἕως τοῦ ἐλθεῖν ἐπὶ τὰ ὅρια τῆς
Αἰθιοπίας. 11 καὶ ἐφαύλισαν πάντες οἱ κατοικοῦντες πᾶσαν
τὴν γῆν τὸ ῥῆμα Ναβουχοδονοσορ βασιλέως Ἀσσυρίων καὶ
οὐ συνῆλθον αὐτῷ εἰς τὸν πόλεμον, ὅτι οὐκ ἐφοβήθησαν αὐτόν, ἀλλ᾽ ἦν ἐναντίον αὐτῶν ὡς ἀνὴρ εἷς, καὶ ἀνέστρεψαν
τοὺς ἀγγέλους αὐτοῦ κενοὺς ἐν ἀτιμίᾳ προσώπου αὐτῶν.
12 καὶ ἐθυμώθη Ναβουχοδονοσορ ἐπὶ πᾶσαν τὴν γῆν ταύτην
σφόδρα καὶ ὤμοσε κατὰ τοῦ θρόνου καὶ τῆς βασιλείας αὐτοῦ
εἰ μὴν ἐκδικήσειν πάντα τὰ ὅρια τῆς Κιλικίας καὶ Δαμα-
σκηνῆς καὶ Συρίας ἀνελεῖν τῇ ῥομφαίᾳ αὐτοῦ καὶ πάντας
τοὺς κατοικοῦντας ἐν γῇ Μωαβ καὶ τοὺς υἱοὺς Αμμων καὶ
πᾶσαν τὴν Ιουδαίαν καὶ πάντας τοὺς ἐν Αἰγύπτῳ ἕως τοῦ
ἐλθεῖν ἐπὶ τὰ ὅρια τῶν δύο θαλασσῶν. 13 καὶ παρετάξατο ἐν
τῇ δυνάμει αὐτοῦ πρὸς Αρφαξαδ βασιλέα ἐν τῷ ἔτει τῷ
ἑπτακαιδεκάτῳ καὶ ἐκραταιώθη ἐν τῷ πολέμῳ αὐτοῦ καὶ
ἀνέστρεψεν πᾶσαν τὴν δύναμιν Αρφαξαδ καὶ πᾶσαν τὴν
ἵππον αὐτοῦ καὶ πάντα τὰ ἅρματα αὐτοῦ 14 καὶ ἐκυρίευσε
τῶν πόλεων αὐτοῦ καὶ ἀφίκετο ἕως Ἐκβατάνων καὶ ἐκράτησε
τῶν πύργων καὶ ἐπρονόμευσε τὰς πλατείας αὐτῆς καὶ τὸν
κόσμον αὐτῆς ἔθηκεν εἰς ὄνειδος αὐτῆς 15 καὶ ἔλαβε τὸν
Αρφαξαδ ἐν τοῖς ὄρεσι Ραγαυ καὶ κατηκόντισεν αὐτὸν ἐν
ταῖς σιβύναις αὐτοῦ καὶ ἐξωλέθρευσεν αὐτὸν ἕως τῆς

KING JAMES VERSION

9 And to all that were in Samaria and the cities thereof, and beyond Jordan unto Jerusalem, and Betane, and Chellus, and Kades, and the river of Egypt, and Taphnes, and Ramesse, and all the land of Gesem,

10 Until ye come beyond Tanis and Memphis, and to all the inhabitants of Egypt, until ye come to the borders of Ethiopia.

11 But all the inhabitants of the land made light of the commandment of Nabuchodonosor king of the Assyrians, neither went they with him to the battle; for they were not afraid of him: yea, he was before them as one man, and they sent away his ambassadors from them without effect, and with disgrace.

12 Therefore Nabuchodonosor was very angry with all this country, and sware by his throne and kingdom, that he would surely be avenged upon all those coasts of Cilicia, and Damascus, and Syria, and that he would slay with the sword all the inhabitants of the land of Moab, and the children of Ammon, and all Judea, and all that were in Egypt, till ye come to the borders of the two seas.

13 Then he marched in battle array with his power against king Arphaxad in the seventeenth year, and he prevailed in his battle: for he overthrew all the power of Arphaxad, and all his horsemen, and all his chariots,

14 And became lord of his cities, and came unto Ecbatane, and took the towers, and spoiled the streets thereof, and turned the beauty thereof into shame.

15 He took also Arphaxad in the mountains of Ragau, and smote him through with his darts, and destroyed him utterly that day.

DOUAY OLD TESTAMENT

9 And to all that were in Samaria, and beyond the river Jordan even to Jerusalem, and all the land of Jesse till you come to the borders of Ethiopia.

10 To all these Nabuchodonosor king of the Assyrians, sent messengers:

11 But they all with one mind refused, and sent them back empty, and rejected them without honour.

12 Then king Nabuchodonosor being angry against all that land, swore by his throne and kingdom that he would revenge himself of all those countries.

KNOX TRANSLATION

and all the country beyond Jordan as far as Jerusalem, and
the land of Gessen[a] right up to the borders of Ethiopia.
10 And of all the peoples to whom Nabuchodonosor, the
Assyrian king, sent out his messengers, 11 there was not one
but had refused, and sent them away thwarted and despised.
12 So now, in anger, Nabuchodonosor swore by his royal
throne to avenge himself on these countries, one and all.[b]

[a] 'Gessen'; this is given in the Vulgate as 'Jesse', probably through a copyist's error; Gessen is mentioned in the Septuagint Greek. [b] Here and in the following chapters the story is told in different language and at somewhat greater length in the Septuagint Greek.

TODAY'S ENGLISH VERSION

and Jezreel Valley. 9-10 The message also went to the people living in Samaria and the nearby towns, to those in the area west of the Jordan River as far as the cities of Jerusalem, Bethany, Chelous, and Kadesh, and to the district of Goshen. The message was also taken to the Egyptian cities of Tahpanhes, Rameses, Tanis, and Memphis, and the district up the Nile River to the Ethiopian[a] border. 11 But everyone in this whole region ignored King Nebuchadnezzar's appeal and refused to take part in the war. They thought that he had no chance of winning the war, so they were not afraid of him and sent his messengers back disgraced and empty-handed.

12 This made Nebuchadnezzar so furious that he vowed he would risk his entire kingdom to take revenge on all those people. He vowed that he would put to death the entire population of Cilicia, Damascus, Syria, Moab, Ammon, Judah, and Egypt—everyone from the Mediterranean Sea to the Persian Gulf.

13 In the seventeenth year of his reign King Nebuchadnezzar led his army into battle against King Arphaxad. He defeated all of Arphaxad's forces, including his entire cavalry, and all his charioteers. 14 Then Nebuchadnezzar occupied all the towns in the land of Media and advanced against the city of Ecbatana. He captured the city's towers, looted its markets, and made that beautiful city a ruin. 15 He captured King Arphaxad in the mountains around Rages and killed

[a] *Greek* Ethiopian: *Ethiopia is the name given in Graeco-Roman times to the extensive territory south of the First Cataract of the Nile River. Cush was the ancient (Hebrew) name of this region which included within its borders most of modern Sudan and some of present-day Ethiopia (Abyssinia).*

NEW REVISED STANDARD VERSION

in Samaria and its towns, and beyond the Jordan as far as Jerusalem and Bethany and Chelous and Kadesh and the river of Egypt, and Tahpanhes and Raamses and the whole land of Goshen, 10 even beyond Tanis and Memphis, and all who lived in Egypt as far as the borders of Ethiopia. 11 But all who lived in the whole region disregarded the summons of Nebuchadnezzar, king of the Assyrians, and refused to join him in the war; for they were not afraid of him, but regarded him as only one man.[a] So they sent back his messengers empty-handed and in disgrace.

12 Then Nebuchadnezzar became very angry with this whole region, and swore by his throne and kingdom that he would take revenge on the whole territory of Cilicia and Damascus and Syria, that he would kill with his sword also all the inhabitants of the land of Moab, and the people of Ammon, and all Judea, and every one in Egypt, as far as the coasts of the two seas.

13 In the seventeenth year he led his forces against King Arphaxad and defeated him in battle, overthrowing the whole army of Arphaxad and all his cavalry and all his chariots. 14 Thus he took possession of his towns and came to Ecbatana, captured its towers, plundered its markets, and turned its glory into disgrace. 15 He captured Arphaxad in the mountains of Ragau and struck him down with his spears, thus destroying him once and for all. 16 Then he

[a] Or *a man*

NEW AMERICAN BIBLE

Samaria and its cities, and west of the Jordan as far as Jerusalem, Bethany, Chelous, Kadesh, and the River of Egypt; to Tahpanhes, Raamses, all the land of Goshen, 10 Tanis, Memphis and beyond, and to all the inhabitants of Egypt as far as the borders of Ethiopia.

11 But the inhabitants of all that land disregarded the summons of Nebuchadnezzar, king of the Assyrians, and would not go with him to the war. They were not afraid of him but regarded him as a lone individual opposed to them, and turned away his envoys emptyhanded, in disgrace. 12 Then Nebuchadnezzar fell into a violent rage against all that land, and swore by his throne and his kingdom that he would avenge himself on all the territories of Cilicia and Damascus and Syria, and also destroy with his sword all the inhabitants of Moab, Ammon, the whole of Judea, and those living anywhere in Egypt as far as the borders of the two seas.

13 In the seventeenth year he proceeded with his army against King Arphaxad, and was victorious in his campaign. He routed the whole force of Arphaxad, his entire cavalry and all his chariots, 14 and took possession of his cities. He pressed on to Ecbatana and took its towers, sacked its marketplaces, and turned its glory into shame. 15 Arphaxad himself he overtook in the mountains of Ragae, ran him through with spears, and utterly destroyed him. 16 Then he returned

NEW JERUSALEM BIBLE

9 to the people of Samaria and its outlying towns, to those beyond Jordan, as far away as Jerusalem, Bethany, Chelous, Kadesh, the river of Egypt, Tahpanhes, Rameses and the whole territory of Goshen, 10 beyond Tanis too and Memphis, and to all the inhabitants of Egypt as far as the frontiers of Ethiopia. 11 But the inhabitants of these countries ignored the summons of Nebuchadnezzar king of the Assyrians and did not rally to him to make war. They were not afraid of him, since in their view he appeared isolated. Hence they sent his ambassadors back with nothing achieved and in disgrace. 12 Nebuchadnezzar was furious with all these countries. He swore by his throne and kingdom to take revenge on all the territories of Cilicia, Damascus and Syria, of the Moabites and of the Ammonites, of Judaea and Egypt as far as the limits of the two seas, and to ravage them with the sword.

13 In the seventeenth year, he gave battle with his whole army to King Arphaxad and in this battle defeated him. He routed Arphaxad's entire army and all his cavalry and chariots; 14 he occupied his towns and advanced on Ecbatana; he seized its towers and plundered its market places, reducing its former magnificence to a mockery. 15 He later captured Arphaxad in the mountains of Ragae and, thrusting him through with his spears, destroyed him once and for all.

GREEK OLD TESTAMENT

ἡμέρας ἐκείνης. 16 καὶ ἀνέστρεψεν μετ' αὐτῶν αὐτὸς καὶ
πᾶς ὁ σύμμικτος αὐτοῦ, πλῆθος ἀνδρῶν πολεμιστῶν πολὺ
σφόδρα, καὶ ἦν ἐκεῖ ῥαθυμῶν καὶ εὐωχούμενος αὐτὸς καὶ ἡ
δύναμις αὐτοῦ ἐφ' ἡμέρας ἑκατὸν εἴκοσι.

2 Καὶ ἐν τῷ ἔτει τῷ ὀκτωκαιδεκάτῳ δευτέρᾳ καὶ εἰκάδι
τοῦ πρώτου μηνὸς ἐγένετο λόγος ἐν οἴκῳ Ναβουχοδονοσορ βασιλέως Ἀσσυρίων ἐκδικῆσαι πᾶσαν τὴν γῆν
καθὼς ἐλάλησεν. 2 καὶ συνεκάλεσεν πάντας τοὺς θεράποντας αὐτοῦ καὶ πάντας τοὺς μεγιστᾶνας αὐτοῦ καὶ ἔθετο
μετ' αὐτῶν τὸ μυστήριον τῆς βουλῆς αὐτοῦ καὶ συνετέλεσεν
πᾶσαν τὴν κακίαν τῆς γῆς ἐκ τοῦ στόματος αὐτοῦ, 3 καὶ
αὐτοὶ ἔκριναν ὀλεθρεῦσαι πᾶσαν σάρκα οἳ οὐκ ἠκολούθησαν
τῷ λόγῳ τοῦ στόματος αὐτοῦ. 4 καὶ ἐγένετο ὡς συνετέλεσεν
τὴν βουλὴν αὐτοῦ, ἐκάλεσεν Ναβουχοδονοσορ βασιλεὺς
Ἀσσυρίων τὸν Ολοφέρνην ἀρχιστράτηγον τῆς δυνάμεως
αὐτοῦ δεύτερον ὄντα μετ' αὐτὸν καὶ εἶπεν πρὸς αὐτόν
5 Τάδε λέγει ὁ βασιλεὺς ὁ μέγας, ὁ κύριος πάσης τῆς γῆς
Ἰδοὺ σὺ ἐξελεύσῃ ἐκ τοῦ προσώπου μου καὶ λήμψῃ μετὰ
σεαυτοῦ ἄνδρας πεποιθότας ἐν ἰσχύι αὐτῶν, πεζῶν εἰς
χιλιάδας ἑκατὸν εἴκοσι καὶ πλῆθος ἵππων σὺν ἀναβάταις
χιλιάδας δέκα δύο, 6 καὶ ἐξελεύσῃ εἰς συνάντησιν πάσῃ τῇ
γῇ ἐπὶ δυσμάς, ὅτι ἠπείθησαν τῷ ῥήματι τοῦ στόματός μου,
7 καὶ ἀπαγγελεῖς αὐτοῖς ἑτοιμάζειν γῆν καὶ ὕδωρ, ὅτι ἐξελεύσομαι ἐν θυμῷ μου ἐπ' αὐτοὺς καὶ καλύψω πᾶν τὸ πρόσωπον τῆς γῆς ἐν τοῖς ποσὶν τῆς δυνάμεώς μου καὶ δώσω
αὐτοὺς εἰς διαρπαγὴν αὐτοῖς, 8 καὶ οἱ τραυματίαι αὐτῶν
πληρώσουσιν τὰς φάραγγας αὐτῶν, καὶ πᾶς χειμάρρους καὶ
ποταμὸς ἐπικλύζων τοῖς νεκροῖς αὐτῶν πληρωθήσεται· 9 καὶ

KING JAMES VERSION

16 So he returned afterward to Nineve, both he and all his
company of sundry nations, being a very great multitude of
men of war, and there he took his ease, and banqueted, both
he and his army, an hundred and twenty days.

2 And in the eighteenth year, the two and twentieth day of
the first month, there was talk in the house of Nabuchodonosor king of the Assyrians, that he should, as he said,
avenge himself on all the earth.
2 So he called unto him all his officers, and all his nobles,
and communicated with them his secret counsel, and concluded the afflicting of the whole earth out of his own mouth.
3 Then they decreed to destroy all flesh, that did not obey
the commandment of his mouth.
4 And when he had ended his counsel, Nabuchodonosor
king of the Assyrians called Holofernes the chief captain of
his army, which was next unto him, and said unto him,
5 Thus saith the great king, the lord of the whole earth,
Behold, thou shalt go forth from my presence, and take with
thee men that trust in their own strength, of footmen an
hundred and twenty thousand; and the number of horses
with their riders twelve thousand.
6 And thou shalt go against all the west country, because
they disobeyed my commandment.
7 And thou shalt declare unto them, that they prepare for
me earth and water: for I will go forth in my wrath against
them, and will cover the whole face of the earth with the feet
of mine army, and I will give them for a spoil unto them:
8 So that their slain shall fill their valleys and brooks, and
the river shall be filled with their dead, till it overflow:

DOUAY OLD TESTAMENT

2 IN the thirteenth year of the reign of Nabuchodonosor,
the two and twentieth day of the first month, the word
was given out in the house of Nabuchodonosor king of the
Assyrians, that he would revenge himself.
2 And he called all the ancients, and all the governors,
and his officers of war, and communicated to them the secret
of his counsel:
3 And he said that his thoughts were to bring all the earth
under his empire.
4 And when this saying pleased them all, Nabuchodonosor, the king, called Holofernes the general of his armies,
5 And said to him: Go out against all the kingdoms of the
west, and against them especially that despised my commandment.

KNOX TRANSLATION

2 It was on the twenty-second day of the first month, in
the thirteenth year of his reign, that this resolve was
taken at Nabuchodonosor's court. 2 He summoned all his
councillors, chieftains and commanders, and put before them
his secret design; 3 his thought, he told them, was to bring
the whole world under his allegiance. 4 With this, all agreed;
whereupon he summoned Holofernes, that commanded his
forces, and said, 5 March out and make war on the western
kingdoms, those especially that made light of my summons.

TODAY'S ENGLISH VERSION

him. After Arphaxad's death, 16 Nebuchadnezzar and his
entire army returned to Nineveh with all the loot taken in
battle. There they relaxed and feasted for four months.

2 In the eighteenth year of Nebuchadnezzar's reign, on the
twenty-second day of the first month of that year, he
and his advisers decided to carry out his threat to take
revenge on all those countries that had refused to help him.
2-3 The king called his general staff and senior officers together and reported in detail how those countries had betrayed
him. He and his officers agreed that everyone who had
refused to help him in the war should be put to death. Then
he described to them his plan of attack.

4 At the close of the meeting, Nebuchadnezzar gave the following command to Holofernes, who was the general in
command of his armies and second in command to the king:
5 "I, Nebuchadnezzar, the great king and ruler of all the
earth, command you to choose some experienced soldiers:
120,000 infantry and 12,000 cavalry. 6 Then attack the
lands to the west because they refused to respond to my
appeal for help. 7 Warn them that they must prepare their
offerings of earth and water to show that they have surrendered unconditionally. I will make them feel the full force of
my anger and completely destroy them. My armies will
march over every foot of their land and plunder it as they go.
8 I will fill the valleys with their dead bodies and will choke
up every stream and river with so many corpses that they

NEW REVISED STANDARD VERSION

returned to Nineveh, he and all his combined forces, a vast
body of troops; and there he and his forces rested and feasted for one hundred twenty days.

2 In the eighteenth year, on the twenty-second day of the
first month, there was talk in the palace of Nebuchadnezzar, king of the Assyrians, about carrying out his revenge
on the whole region, just as he had said. 2 He summoned all
his ministers and all his nobles and set before them his
secret plan and recounted fully, with his own lips, all the
wickedness of the region.[a] 3 They decided that every one
who had not obeyed his command should be destroyed.

4 When he had completed his plan, Nebuchadnezzar, king
of the Assyrians, called Holofernes, the chief general of his
army, second only to himself, and said to him, 5 "Thus says
the Great King, the lord of the whole earth: Leave my presence and take with you men confident in their strength, one
hundred twenty thousand foot soldiers and twelve thousand
cavalry. 6 March out against all the land to the west, because
they disobeyed my orders. 7 Tell them to prepare earth and
water, for I am coming against them in my anger, and will
cover the whole face of the earth with the feet of my troops,
to whom I will hand them over to be plundered. 8 Their
wounded shall fill their ravines and gullies, and the swelling

a Meaning of Gk uncertain

NEW AMERICAN BIBLE

home with all his numerous, motley horde of warriors; and
there he and his army relaxed and feasted for a hundred and
twenty days.

2 In the eighteenth year, on the twenty-second day of the
first month, there was a discussion in the palace of
Nebuchadnezzar, king of the Assyrians, about taking
revenge on the whole world, as he had threatened. 2 He
summoned all his ministers and nobles, laid before them his
secret plan, and urged the total destruction of those countries. 3 They decided to do away with all those who had
refused to comply with the order he had issued.

4 When he had completed his plan, Nebuchadnezzar, king
of the Assyrians, summoned Holofernes, general in chief of
his forces, second to himself in command, and said to him:
5 "Thus says the great king, the lord of all the earth: Go forth
from my presence, take with you men of proven valor, a
hundred and twenty thousand infantry and twelve thousand
cavalry, 6 and proceed against all the land of the West,
because they did not comply with the order I issued. 7 Tell
them to have earth and water ready, for I will come against
them in my wrath; I will cover all the land with the feet of
my soldiers, to whom I will deliver them as spoils. 8 Their
slain shall fill their ravines and wadies, the swelling torrent

NEW JERUSALEM BIBLE

16 He then retired with his troops and all who had joined
forces with him: a vast horde of armed men. Then he and his
army gave themselves up to carefree feasting for a hundred
and twenty days.

2 In the eighteenth year, on the twenty-second day of the
first month, a rumour ran through the palace that
Nebuchadnezzar king of the Assyrians was to have his
revenge on all the countries, as he had threatened.
2 Summoning his general staff and senior officers, he held a
secret conference with them, and with his own lips pronounced utter destruction on the entire area. 3 It was then
decreed that everyone should be put to death who had not
answered the king's appeal.

4 When the council was over, Nebuchadnezzar king of the
Assyrians sent for Holofernes, general-in-chief of his armies
and subordinate only to himself. He said to him, 5 'Thus
speaks the Great King, lord of the whole world, "Go; take
men of proven valour, about a hundred and twenty thousand
foot soldiers and a strong company of horse with twelve
thousand cavalrymen; 6 then advance against all the western lands, since these people have disregarded my call. 7 Bid
them have earth and water ready, because in my rage I am
about to march on them; the feet of my soldiers will cover
the whole face of the earth, and I shall plunder it. 8 Their
wounded will fill the valleys and the torrents, and rivers,

GREEK OLD TESTAMENT

ἄξω τὴν αἰχμαλωσίαν αὐτῶν ἐπὶ τὰ ἄκρα πάσης τῆς γῆς.
10 σὺ δὲ ἐξελθὼν προκαταλήμψῃ μοι πᾶν ὅριον αὐτῶν, καὶ
ἐκδώσουσίν σοι ἑαυτούς, καὶ διατηρήσεις ἐμοὶ αὐτοὺς εἰς
ἡμέραν ἐλεγμοῦ αὐτῶν· 11 ἐπὶ δὲ τοὺς ἀπειθοῦντας οὐ
φείσεται ὁ ὀφθαλμός σου τοῦ δοῦναι αὐτοὺς εἰς φόνον καὶ
ἁρπαγὴν ἐν πάσῃ τῇ γῇ σου. 12 ὅτι ζῶν ἐγὼ καὶ τὸ κράτος
τῆς βασιλείας μου, λελάληκα καὶ ποιήσω ταῦτα ἐν χειρί μου.
13 καὶ σὺ δὲ οὐ παραβήσῃ ἕν τι τῶν ῥημάτων τοῦ κυρίου σου,
ἀλλὰ ἐπιτελῶν ἐπιτελέσεις καθότι προστέταχά σοι, καὶ οὐ
μακρυνεῖς τοῦ ποιῆσαι αὐτά. 14 καὶ ἐξῆλθεν Ολοφέρνης ἀπὸ
προσώπου τοῦ κυρίου αὐτοῦ καὶ ἐκάλεσεν πάντας τοὺς δυνάστας καὶ τοὺς στρατηγοὺς καὶ ἐπιστάτας τῆς δυνάμεως
Ασσουρ 15 καὶ ἠρίθμησεν ἐκλεκτοὺς ἄνδρας εἰς παράταξιν,
καθότι ἐκέλευσεν αὐτῷ ὁ κύριος αὐτοῦ, εἰς μυριάδας δέκα
δύο καὶ ἱππεῖς τοξότας μυρίους δισχιλίους, 16 καὶ διέταξεν
αὐτοὺς ὃν τρόπον πολέμου πλῆθος συντάσσεται. 17 καὶ
ἔλαβεν καμήλους καὶ ὄνους καὶ ἡμιόνους εἰς τὴν ἀπαρτίαν
αὐτῶν, πλῆθος πολὺ σφόδρα, καὶ πρόβατα καὶ βόας καὶ αἶγας
εἰς τὴν παρασκευὴν αὐτῶν, ὧν οὐκ ἦν ἀριθμός, 18 καὶ ἐπισιτισμὸν παντὶ ἀνδρὶ εἰς πλῆθος καὶ χρυσίον καὶ ἀργύριον
ἐξ οἴκου βασιλέως πολὺ σφόδρα. 19 καὶ ἐξῆλθεν αὐτὸς καὶ
πᾶσα ἡ δύναμις αὐτοῦ εἰς πορείαν τοῦ προελθεῖν βασιλέως
Ναβουχοδονοσορ καὶ καλύψαι πᾶν τὸ πρόσωπον τῆς γῆς

KING JAMES VERSION

9 And I will lead them captives to the utmost parts of all the earth.

10 Thou therefore shalt go forth, and take beforehand for me all their coasts: and if they will yield themselves unto thee, thou shalt reserve them for me till the day of their punishment.

11 But concerning them that rebel, let not thine eye spare them; but put them to the slaughter, and spoil them wheresoever thou goest.

12 For as I live, and by the power of my kingdom, whatsoever I have spoken, that will I do by mine hand.

13 And take thou heed that thou transgress none of the commandments of thy lord, but accomplish them fully, as I have commanded thee, and defer not to do them.

14 Then Holofernes went forth from the presence of his lord, and called all the governors and captains, and the officers of the army of Assur;

15 And he mustered the chosen men for the battle, as his lord had commanded him, unto an hundred and twenty thousand, and twelve thousand archers on horseback;

16 And he ranged them, as a great army is ordered for the war.

17 And he took camels and asses for their carriages, a very great number; and sheep and oxen and goats without number for their provision:

18 And plenty of victual for every man of the army, and very much gold and silver out of the king's house.

19 Then he went forth and all his power to go before king Nabuchodonosor in the voyage, and to cover all the face of

DOUAY OLD TESTAMENT

6 Thy eye shall not spare any kingdom, and all the strong cities thou shalt bring under my yoke.

7 Then Holofernes called the captains, and officers of the power of the Assyrians: and he mustered men for the expedition, as the king commanded him, a hundred and twenty thousand fighting men on foot, and twelve thousand archers, horsemen.

8 And he made all his warlike preparations to go before with a multitude of innumerable camels, with all provisions sufficient for the armies in abundance, and herds of oxen, and flocks of sheep, without number.

9 He appointed corn to be prepared out of all Syria in his passage.

10 But gold and silver he took out of the king's house in great abundance.

11 And he went forth he and all the army, with the chariots, and horsemen, and archers, who covered the face of the earth, like locusts.

KNOX TRANSLATION

6 Nowhere let pity melt thy eye; no fortified town but must be brought under my dominion.

7 Thereupon Holofernes summoned all the chieftains and
commanders of the Assyrian army, and mustered a force to
march out and do the king's bidding, a hundred and twenty
thousand that went on foot, and twelve thousand mounted
archers. 8 And his baggage-train he sent on beforehand, a
long array of camels, well laden with all his army needed,
herds of oxen, too, and flocks of sheep, past all counting. 9 A
supply of corn from the whole of Syria was to meet him as
he passed, 10 and he had great store of gold and silver from
the royal treasury.

11 Then he himself set out at the head of his forces, chariots and horsemen and archers and the rest, that swarmed like locusts on the ground.

TODAY'S ENGLISH VERSION

will all overflow. 9 I will take captive all those who are left
alive and carry them off to the ends of the earth.
10 "But you, Holofernes, are ordered to go ahead of me and
occupy all their territories in advance. If they surrender to
you, hold them for me until I come to punish them. 11 But if
they resist, do not spare them. Kill them and loot the entire
region under your control. 12 I have taken a solemn vow,
and at the risk of my life and my royal power I am determined to do what I have vowed to do. 13 Do not disobey me
in any way. I am your king; remember that, and carry out
without delay every order that I have given you."
14 So Holofernes left the king and called together all the
commanders, generals, and officers of the Assyrian army.
15 Just as the king had ordered, he chose 120,000 of the best
infantrymen and 12,000 of the best mounted archers 16 and
arranged them in battle formation. 17 He also took along a
very large number of camels, donkeys, and mules to carry
the equipment, as well as many sheep, cattle, and goats for
food. 18 Every soldier received plenty of rations and a large
payment of gold and silver from the royal treasury.
19 Then Holofernes and his entire army set out, advancing
ahead of King Nebuchadnezzar. The chariots, the cavalry,

NEW REVISED STANDARD VERSION

river shall be filled with their dead. 9 I will lead them away
captive to the ends of the whole earth. 10 You shall go and
seize all their territory for me in advance. They must yield
themselves to you, and you shall hold them for me until the
day of their punishment. 11 But to those who resist show no
mercy, but hand them over to slaughter and plunder
throughout your whole region. 12 For as I live, and by the
power of my kingdom, what I have spoken I will accomplish
by my own hand. 13 And you—take care not to transgress
any of your lord's commands, but carry them out exactly as I
have ordered you; do it without delay."
14 So Holofernes left the presence of his lord, and summoned all the commanders, generals, and officers of the
Assyrian army. 15 He mustered the picked troops by divisions as his lord had ordered him to do, one hundred twenty
thousand of them, together with twelve thousand archers on
horseback, 16 and he organized them as a great army is mar-
shaled for a campaign. 17 He took along a vast number of
camels and donkeys and mules for transport, and innumerable sheep and oxen and goats for food; 18 also ample
rations for everyone, and a huge amount of gold and silver
from the royal palace.
19 Then he set out with his whole army, to go ahead of
King Nebuchadnezzar and to cover the whole face of the

NEW AMERICAN BIBLE

shall be choked with their dead; 9 and I will deport them as
exiles to the very ends of the earth.
10 "You go before me and take possession of all their territories for me. If they surrender to you, guard them for me till
the day of their punishment. 11 As for those who resist, show
them no quarter, but deliver them up to slaughter and plunder in each country you occupy. 12 For as I live, and by the
strength of my kingdom, what I have spoken I will accomplish by my power. 13 Do not disobey a single one of the
orders of your lord; fulfill them exactly as I have commanded
you, and do it without delay."
14 So Holofernes left the presence of his lord, and summoned all the princes, and the generals and officers of the
Assyrian army. 15 He mustered a hundred and twenty thousand picked troops, as his lord had commanded, and twelve
thousand mounted archers, 16 and grouped them into a complete combat force. 17 He took along a very large number of
camels, asses, and mules for their baggage; innumerable
sheep, cattle, and goats for their food supply; 18 abundant
provisions for each man, and much gold and silver from the
royal palace.
19 Then he and his whole army proceeded on their expedition in advance of King Nebuchadnezzar, to cover all the

NEW JERUSALEM BIBLE

blocked with their dead, will overflow. 9 I shall lead them
captive to the ends of the earth. 10 Now go! Begin by conquering this whole region for me. If they surrender to you,
hold them for me until the time comes to punish them.
11 But if they resist, look on no one with clemency, hand
them over to slaughter and plunder throughout the territory
entrusted to you. 12 For by my life and by the living power of
my kingdom I have spoken. All this I shall do by my power.
13 And you, neglect none of your master's commands, act
strictly according to my orders without further delay." '
14 Leaving the presence of his sovereign, Holofernes immediately summoned all the marshals, generals and officers of
the Assyrian army 15 and detailed the picked troops as his
master had ordered, about a hundred and twenty thousand
men and a further twelve thousand mounted archers. 16 He
organised these in the normal battle formation. 17 He then
secured vast numbers of camels, donkeys and mules to carry
the baggage, and innumerable sheep, oxen and goats for
food supplies. 18 Every man received full rations and a generous sum of gold and silver from the king's purse.
19 He then set out for the campaign with his whole army,
in advance of King Nebuchadnezzar, to overwhelm the whole

GREEK OLD TESTAMENT

πρὸς δυσμαῖς ἐν ἅρμασι καὶ ἱππεῦσι καὶ πεζοῖς ἐπιλέκτοις
αὐτῶν· 20 καὶ πολὺς ὁ ἐπίμικτος ὡς ἀκρὶς συνεξῆλθον αὐτοῖς καὶ ὡς ἡ ἄμμος τῆς γῆς, οὐ γὰρ ἦν ἀριθμὸς ἀπὸ
πλήθους αὐτῶν. 21 καὶ ἀπῆλθον ἐκ Νινευη ὁδὸν τριῶν ἡμερῶν
ἐπὶ πρόσωπον τοῦ πεδίου Βεκτιλεθ καὶ ἐπεστρατοπέδευσαν
ἀπὸ Βεκτιλεθ πλησίον τοῦ ὄρους τοῦ ἐπ' ἀριστερᾷ τῆς ἄνω
Κιλικίας. 22 καὶ ἔλαβεν πᾶσαν τὴν δύναμιν αὐτοῦ, τοὺς
πεζοὺς καὶ τοὺς ἱππεῖς καὶ τὰ ἅρματα αὐτοῦ, καὶ ἀπῆλθεν
ἐκεῖθεν εἰς τὴν ὀρεινήν. 23 καὶ διέκοψεν τὸ Φουδ καὶ Λουδ
καὶ ἐπρονόμευσεν υἱοὺς πάντας Ρασσις καὶ υἱοὺς Ισμαηλ
τοὺς κατὰ πρόσωπον τῆς ἐρήμου πρὸς νότον τῆς Χελεων.
24 καὶ παρῆλθεν τὸν Εὐφράτην καὶ διῆλθεν τὴν Μεσοποταμίαν καὶ κατέσκαψεν πάσας τὰς πόλεις τὰς ὑψηλὰς τὰς ἐπὶ
τοῦ χειμάρρου Αβρωνα ἕως τοῦ ἐλθεῖν ἐπὶ θάλασσαν. 25 καὶ
κατελάβετο τὰ ὅρια τῆς Κιλικίας καὶ κατέκοψε πάντας τοὺς
ἀντιστάντας αὐτῷ καὶ ἦλθεν ἕως ὁρίων Ιαφεθ τὰ πρὸς νότον
κατὰ πρόσωπον τῆς Ἀραβίας. 26 καὶ ἐκύκλωσεν πάντας
τοὺς υἱοὺς Μαδιαμ καὶ ἐνέπρησεν τὰ σκηνώματα αὐτῶν καὶ
ἐπρονόμευσεν τὰς μάνδρας αὐτῶν. 27 καὶ κατέβη εἰς πεδίον
Δαμασκοῦ ἐν ἡμέραις θερισμοῦ πυρῶν καὶ ἐνέπρησεν πάντας
τοὺς ἀγροὺς αὐτῶν καὶ τὰ ποίμνια καὶ τὰ βουκόλια ἔδωκεν
εἰς ἀφανισμὸν καὶ τὰς πόλεις αὐτῶν ἐσκύλευσεν καὶ τὰ
πεδία αὐτῶν ἐξελίκμησεν καὶ ἐπάταξεν πάντας τοὺς νεανίσκους αὐτῶν ἐν στόματι ῥομφαίας. — 28 καὶ ἐπέπεσεν φόβος
καὶ τρόμος αὐτοῦ ἐπὶ τοὺς κατοικοῦντας τὴν παραλίαν τοὺς

KING JAMES VERSION

the earth westward with their chariots, and horsemen, and their chosen footmen.

20 A great number also sundry countries came with them like locusts, and like the sand of the earth: for the multitude was without number.

21 And they went forth of Nineve three days' journey toward the plain of Bectileth, and pitched from Bectileth near the mountain which is at the left hand of the upper Cilicia.

22 Then he took all his army, his footmen, and horsemen, and chariots, and went from thence into the hill country;

23 And destroyed Phud and Lud, and spoiled all the children of Rasses, and the children of Ismael, which were toward the wilderness at the south of the land of the Chellians.

24 Then he went over Euphrates, and went through Mesopotamia, and destroyed all the high cities that were upon the river Arbonai, till ye come to the sea.

25 And he took the borders of Cilicia, and killed all that resisted him, and came to the borders of Japheth, which were toward the south, over against Arabia.

26 He compassed also all the children of Madian, and burned up their tabernacles, and spoiled their sheepcotes.

27 Then he went down into the plain of Damascus in the time of wheat harvest, and burnt up all their fields, and destroyed their flocks and herds, also he spoiled their cities, and utterly wasted their countries, and smote all their young men with the edge of the sword.

28 Therefore the fear and dread of him fell upon all the inhabitants of the sea coasts, which were in Sidon and

DOUAY OLD TESTAMENT

12 And when he had passed through the borders of the Assyrians, he came to the great mountains of Ange, which are on the left of Cilicia: and he went up to all their castles, and took all the strong places.

13 And he took by assault the renowned city of Melothus, and pillaged all the children of Tharsis, and the children of Ismahel, who were over against the face of the desert, and on the south of the land of Cellon.

14 And he passed over the Euphrates, and came into Mesopotamia: and he forced all the stately cities that were there, from the torrent of Mambre, till one comes to the sea:

15 And he took the borders thereof, from Cilicia to the coasts of Japheth, which are towards the south.

16 And he carried away all the children of Madian, and stripped them of all their riches, and all that resisted him he slew with the edge of the sword.

17 And after these things he went down into the plains of Damascus in the days of the harvest, and he set all the corn on fire, and he caused all the trees and vineyards to be cut down.

18 And the fear of them fell upon all the inhabitants of the land.

KNOX TRANSLATION

12 Leaving Assyria, he first reached the high mountains of
Ange, on the left-hand side of Cilicia, scaling all their fast-
nesses and reducing all their garrisons. 13 Then he broke
into the city of Melothi, that resisted him stubbornly, and
ravaged all the country which belonged to the sons of
Tharsis, and to the Ismaelites, facing the desert, to the south
of Cellon. 14 Then he crossed Euphrates into Mesopotamia,
and stormed every stronghold between the river Mambre and
the sea. 15 All the land of Mesopotamia he overran, from
Cilicia on the north to the frontier of Japheth on the south,
16 drove the Madianites from their homes and plundered their
goods, putting all who resisted him to the sword.[a] 17 And at
last he came down on to the plain of Damascus, in harvest
time, burnt all the crops there and had all the trees and vineyards cut down. 18 And a great dread of him fell upon the
whole country-side.

a The place-names given in verses 12-16 cannot be identified with certainty: many of them differ in the different versions.

TODAY'S ENGLISH VERSION

and the infantry marched out to overrun the entire western
region. 20 Other troops went with them. There were so many
that it was impossible to count them—they were like a
swarm of locusts or like grains of sand in the desert.
21 Three days after they had left the city of Nineveh, they
reached the plains around Bectileth near the mountains
north of Cilicia, where they set up camp. 22 From there
Holofernes advanced into the hill country with his entire
army, his infantry, cavalry, and chariots. 23 He totally
destroyed the countries of Libya and Lydia, then plundered
all the people of Rassis and the Ishmaelites who lived on the
edge of the desert, south of the land of the Chelleans.
24 Then Holofernes crossed the Euphrates River and
marched through the land of Mesopotamia, completely
destroying all the walled towns along the Abron River as far
as the sea. 25 He seized the territory of Cilicia, killing everyone who resisted him, and went as far as the southern borders of the land of Japheth, near Arabia. 26 He surrounded
the Midianites, burned down their tents, and slaughtered
their sheep.
27 Holofernes went down into the plains around Damascus
during the wheat harvest, burned all the fields, slaughtered
the flocks and herds, looted the towns, devastated the entire
countryside, and killed all the young men. 28 Panic seized all
the people who lived along the Mediterranean Sea, and they

NEW REVISED STANDARD VERSION

earth to the west with their chariots and cavalry and picked
foot soldiers. 20 Along with them went a mixed crowd like a
swarm of locusts, like the dust[a] of the earth—a multitude
that could not be counted.
21 They marched for three days from Nineveh to the plain
of Bectileth, and camped opposite Bectileth near the mountain that is to the north of Upper Cilicia. 22 From there
Holofernes[b] took his whole army, the infantry, cavalry, and
chariots, and went up into the hill country. 23 He ravaged
Put and Lud, and plundered all the Rassisites and the
Ishmaelites on the border of the desert, south of the country
of the Chelleans. 24 Then he followed[c] the Euphrates and
passed through Mesopotamia and destroyed all the fortified
towns along the brook Abron, as far as the sea. 25 He also
seized the territory of Cilicia, and killed everyone who resisted him. Then he came to the southern borders of Japheth,
facing Arabia. 26 He surrounded all the Midianites, and
burned their tents and plundered their sheepfolds. 27 Then
he went down into the plain of Damascus during the wheat
harvest, and burned all their fields and destroyed their flocks
and herds and sacked their towns and ravaged their lands
and put all their young men to the sword.
28 So fear and dread of him fell upon all the people who
lived along the seacoast, at Sidon and Tyre, and those who

a Gk *sand* *b* Gk *he* *c* Or *crossed*

NEW AMERICAN BIBLE

western region with their chariots and cavalry and regular
infantry. 20 A huge, irregular force, too many to count, like
locusts or the dust of the earth, went along with them.
21 After a three-day march from Nineveh, they reached the
plain of Bectileth, and from Bectileth they next encamped
near the mountains to the north of Upper Cilicia. 22 From
there Holofernes took his whole force, the infantry, calvary,
and chariots, and marched into the mountain region. 23 He
devastated Put and Lud, and plundered all the Rassisites and
the Ishmaelites on the border of the desert toward the south
of Chaldea.
24 Then, following the Euphrates, he went through
Mesopotamia, and battered down every fortified city along
the Wadi Abron, until he reached the sea. 25 He seized the
territory of Cilicia, and cut down everyone who resisted him.
Then he proceeded to the southern borders of Japheth,
toward Arabia. 26 He surrounded all the Midianites, burned
their tents, and plundered their sheepfolds. 27 Descending to
the plain of Damascus at the time of the wheat harvest, he
set fire to all their fields, destroyed their flocks and herds,
despoiled their cities, devastated their plains, and put all
their youths to the sword.
28 The fear and dread of him fell upon all the inhabitants of
the coastland, upon those in Sidon and Tyre, and those who

NEW JERUSALEM BIBLE

western region with his chariots, his horsemen and his
picked body of foot. 20 A motley gathering followed in his
rear, as numerous as locusts or the grains of sand on the
ground; there was no counting their multitude.
21 Thus they set out from Nineveh and marched for three
days towards the Plain of Bectileth. From Bectileth they went
on to pitch camp near the mountains that lie to the north of
Upper Cilicia. 22 From there Holofernes advanced into the
highlands with his whole army, infantry, horsemen, chariots. 23 He cut his way through Put and Lud, carried away
captive all the sons of Rassis and sons of Ishmael living on
the verge of the desert south of Cheleon, 24 marched along
the Euphrates, crossed Mesopotamia, rased all the fortified
towns controlling the Wadi Abron and reached the sea.
25 Next he attacked the territories of Cilicia, butchering all
who offered him resistance, advanced on the southern frontiers of Japheth, facing Arabia, 26 completely encircled the
Midianites, burned their tents and plundered their sheepfolds, 27 made his way down to the Damascus plain at the
time of the wheat harvest, set fire to the fields, destroyed the
flocks and herds, sacked the towns, laid the countryside
waste and put all the young men to the sword. 28 Fear and
trembling seized all the coastal peoples; those of Sidon and

GREEK OLD TESTAMENT

ὄντας ἐν Σιδῶνι καὶ ἐν Τύρῳ καὶ τοὺς κατοικοῦντας Σουρ καὶ Οκινα καὶ πάντας τοὺς κατοικοῦντας Ιεμνααν, καὶ οἱ κατοικοῦντες ἐν Ἀζώτῳ καὶ Ἀσκαλῶνι ἐφοβήθησαν αὐτὸν σφόδρα.

3 [1] καὶ ἀπέστειλαν πρὸς αὐτὸν ἀγγέλους λόγοις εἰρηνικοῖς λέγοντες [2] Ἰδοὺ ἡμεῖς οἱ παῖδες Ναβουχοδονοσορ βασιλέως μεγάλου παρακείμεθα ἐνώπιόν σου, χρῆσαι ἡμῖν καθὼς ἀρεστόν ἐστιν τῷ προσώπῳ σου· [3] ἰδοὺ αἱ ἐπαύλεις ἡμῶν καὶ πᾶς τόπος ἡμῶν καὶ πᾶν πεδίον πυρῶν καὶ τὰ ποίμνια καὶ τὰ βουκόλια καὶ πᾶσαι αἱ μάνδραι τῶν σκηνῶν ἡμῶν παράκειται πρὸ προσώπου σου, χρῆσαι καθὸ ἂν ἀρέσκῃ σοι· [4] ἰδοὺ καὶ αἱ πόλεις ἡμῶν καὶ οἱ κατοικοῦντες ἐν αὐταῖς δοῦλοί σοί εἰσιν, ἐλθὼν ἀπάντησον αὐταῖς ὡς ἔστιν ἀγαθὸν ἐν ὀφθαλμοῖς σου. [5] καὶ παρεγένοντο οἱ ἄνδρες πρὸς Ολοφέρνην καὶ ἀπήγγειλαν αὐτῷ κατὰ τὰ ῥήματα ταῦτα. [6] καὶ κατέβη ἐπὶ τὴν παραλίαν αὐτὸς καὶ ἡ δύναμις αὐτοῦ καὶ ἐφρούρωσε τὰς πόλεις τὰς ὑψηλὰς καὶ ἔλαβεν ἐξ αὐτῶν εἰς συμμαχίαν ἄνδρας ἐπιλέκτους. [7] καὶ ἐδέξαντο αὐτὸν αὐτοὶ καὶ πᾶσα ἡ περίχωρος αὐτῶν μετὰ στεφάνων καὶ χορῶν καὶ τυμπάνων. [8] καὶ κατέσκαψεν πάντα τὰ ὅρια αὐτῶν καὶ τὰ ἄλση αὐτῶν ἐξέκοψεν, καὶ ἦν δεδομένον αὐτῷ

KING JAMES VERSION

Tyrus, and them that dwelt in Sur and Ocina, and all that dwelt in Jemnaan; and they that dwelt in Azotus and Ascalon feared him greatly.

3 So they sent ambassadors unto him to treat of peace, saying,

2 Behold, we the servants of Nabuchodonosor the great king lie before thee; use us as shall be good in thy sight.

3 Behold, our houses, and all our places, and all our fields of wheat, and flocks, and herds, and all the lodges of our tents, lie before thy face; use them as it pleaseth thee.

4 Behold, even our cities and the inhabitants thereof are thy servants; come and deal with them as seemeth good unto thee.

5 So the men came to Holofernes, and declared unto him after this manner.

6 Then came he down toward the sea coast, both he and his army, and set garrisons in the high cities, and took out of them chosen men for aid.

7 So they and all the country round about received them with garlands, with dances, and with timbrels.

8 Yet he did cast down their frontiers, and cut down their

DOUAY OLD TESTAMENT

3 THEN the kings and the princes of all the cities and provinces, of Syria, Mesopotamia, and Syria Sobal, and Libya, and Cilicia sent their ambassadors, who coming to Holofernes, said:

2 Let thy indignation towards us cease: for it is better for us to live and serve Nabuchodonosor the great king, and be subject to thee, than to die and to perish, or suffer the miseries of slavery.

3 All our cities and our possessions, all mountains and hills, and fields, and herds of oxen, and flocks of sheep, and goats, and horses, and camels, and all our goods, and families are in thy sight:

4 Let all we have be subject to thy law.

5 Both we and our children are thy servants.

6 Come to us a peaceable lord, and use our service as it shall please thee.

7 Then he came down from the mountains with horsemen, in great power, and made himself master of every city, and all the inhabitants of the land.

8 And from all the cities he took auxiliaries valiant men, and chosen for war.

9 And so great a fear lay upon all those provinces, that the inhabitants of all the cities, both princes and nobles, as well as the people, went out to meet him at his coming.

10 And received him with garlands, and lights, and dances, and timbrels, and flutes.

11 And though they did these things, they could not for all that mitigate the fierceness of his heart:

12 For he both destroyed their cities, and cut down their groves.

KNOX TRANSLATION

3 And now from every city and province, from the Syrians of Mesopotamia and Sobal and from (Libya[a] and) Cilicia, king and chieftain sent envoys to Holofernes. [2] Spare us thy further vengeance, they said; better we should live as slaves to the great king Nabuchodonosor, under thy commands, than be reduced by slaughter, undergoing massacre and slavery both. [3] Cities and lands, mountain and hill and plain, ox and sheep and goat and horse and camel, all that we have, and our own households too, lie at thy mercy; [4] dispose of them all as thou wilt; [5] we, and our children with us, are thy slaves. [6] Come to us as our master, so thou come to us in peace, and make what use thou wilt of our surrender.

[7] Then, with his horsemen and all his armed strength, he came down from the hill-country and made city and citizen his own, [8] levying from their townships all the bravest men, all the picked warriors, for his own service. [9] Such dread of him lay on these provinces, that chiefs and nobles came out from every town, with the common sort at their heels, [10] to meet him, welcoming him with crowns and processions by torch-light, dancing in his honour to the music of tambour and flute. [11] Yet might they not, even so, win over that relentless heart; [12] cities must be razed to the ground, and forest-shrines cut down; [13] king Nabuchodonosor had bidden

a Perhaps a copyist's mistake for 'Lebanon' or 'Lycia'.

TODAY'S ENGLISH VERSION

shook with fear. Everyone in the towns of Tyre, Sidon, Sur, Ocina, Jamnia, Ashdod, and Ashkelon was terrified.

3 All these nations sent a peace delegation to King Nebuchadnezzar with this message: [2]"We remain loyal to you, great King Nebuchadnezzar; we are ready to serve you and obey any command that you may wish to give us. [3]Our buildings, all our land, our wheat fields, our livestock, and our tents are at your disposal; use them in any way you wish. [4]Our people will be your slaves, and you may use our towns as you please."

[5]After the peace delegation had brought this message, [6]Holofernes led Nebuchadnezzar's army down to the Mediterranean coast. He stationed guards in all the walled towns and selected certain local men in each of the towns as reserve troops. [7]The people in the towns and in the surrounding countryside welcomed Holofernes by wearing wreaths of flowers and dancing to the beat of drums. [8]But Holofernes destroyed all their places of worship[a] and cut down their sacred trees. He had been ordered to destroy all

[a] *One ancient translation* places of worship; *Greek* territory.

NEW REVISED STANDARD VERSION

lived in Sur and Ocina and all who lived in Jamnia. Those who lived in Azotus and Ascalon feared him greatly.

3 They therefore sent messengers to him to sue for peace in these words: [2]"We, the servants of Nebuchadnezzar, the Great King, lie prostrate before you. Do with us whatever you will. [3]See, our buildings and all our land and all our wheat fields and our flocks and herds and all our encampments[a] lie before you; do with them as you please. [4]Our towns and their inhabitants are also your slaves; come and deal with them as you see fit."

5 The men came to Holofernes and told him all this. [6]Then he went down to the seacoast with his army and stationed garrisons in the fortified towns and took picked men from them as auxiliaries. [7]These people and all in the countryside welcomed him with garlands and dances and tambourines. [8]Yet he demolished all their shrines[b] and cut down their sacred groves; for he had been commissioned to

[a] Gk *all the sheepfolds of our tents* [b] Syr: Gk *borders*

NEW AMERICAN BIBLE

dwelt in Sur and Ocina, and the inhabitants of Jamnia. Those in Azotus and Ascalon also feared him greatly.

3 They therefore sent messengers to him to sue for peace in these words: [2]"We, the servants of Nebuchadnezzar the great king, lie prostrate before you; do with us as you will. [3]Our dwellings and all our wheat fields, our flocks and herds, and all our encampments are at your disposal; make use of them as you please. [4]Our cities and their inhabitants are also at your service; come and deal with them as you see fit."

[5]After the spokesmen had reached Holofernes and given him this message, [6]he went down with his army to the seacoast, and stationed garrisons in the fortified cities; from them he impressed picked troops as auxiliaries. [7]The people of these cities and all the inhabitants of the countryside received him with garlands and dancing to the sound of timbrels. [8]Nevertheless, he devastated their whole territory and cut down their sacred groves, for he had been commissioned

NEW JERUSALEM BIBLE

Tyre, those of Sur, Ocina and Jamnia. The populations of Azotos and Ascalon were panic-stricken.

3 They therefore sent envoys to him to sue for peace, to say, [2]'We are servants of the great King Nebuchadnezzar; we lie prostrate before you. Treat us as you think fit. [3]Our cattle-farms, all our land, all our wheat fields, our flocks and herds, all the sheep-folds in our encampments are at your disposal. Do with them as you please. [4]Our towns and their inhabitants too are at your service; go and treat them as you think fit.' [5]These men came to Holofernes and delivered the message as above.

[6]He then made his way down to the coast with his army and stationed garrisons in all the fortified towns, levying outstanding men there as auxiliaries. [7]The people of these cities and of all the other towns in the neighbourhood welcomed him, wearing garlands and dancing to the sound of tambourines. [8]But he demolished their shrines and cut down their sacred trees, carrying out his commission to

GREEK OLD TESTAMENT

ἐξολεθρεῦσαι πάντας τοὺς θεοὺς τῆς γῆς, ὅπως αὐτῷ μόνῳ
τῷ Ναβουχοδονοσορ λατρεύσωσι πάντα τὰ ἔθνη, καὶ πᾶσαι
αἱ γλῶσσαι καὶ αἱ φυλαὶ αὐτῶν ἐπικαλέσωνται αὐτὸν εἰς
θεόν. 9 καὶ ἦλθεν κατὰ πρόσωπον Εσδρηλων πλησίον τῆς
Δωταιας, ἥ ἐστιν ἀπέναντι τοῦ πρίονος τοῦ μεγάλου τῆς
Ιουδαίας, 10 καὶ κατεστρατοπέδευσαν ἀνὰ μέσον Γαιβαι καὶ
Σκυθῶν πόλεως, καὶ ἦν ἐκεῖ μῆνα ἡμερῶν εἰς τὸ συλλέξαι
πᾶσαν τὴν ἀπαρτίαν τῆς δυνάμεως αὐτοῦ.

4 Καὶ ἤκουσαν οἱ υἱοὶ Ισραηλ οἱ κατοικοῦντες ἐν τῇ
Ιουδαίᾳ πάντα, ὅσα ἐποίησεν Ολοφέρνης τοῖς ἔθνεσιν ὁ
ἀρχιστράτηγος Ναβουχοδονοσορ βασιλέως Ἀσσυρίων, καὶ ὃν
τρόπον ἐσκύλευσεν πάντα τὰ ἱερὰ αὐτῶν καὶ ἔδωκεν αὐτὰ
εἰς ἀφανισμόν, 2 καὶ ἐφοβήθησαν σφόδρα σφόδρα ἀπὸ
προσώπου αὐτοῦ καὶ περὶ Ιερουσαλημ καὶ τοῦ ναοῦ κυρίου
θεοῦ αὐτῶν ἐταράχθησαν. 3 ὅτι προσφάτως ἦσαν ἀναβεβη-
κότες ἐκ τῆς αἰχμαλωσίας, καὶ νεωστὶ πᾶς ὁ λαὸς συνελέ-
λεκτο τῆς Ιουδαίας, καὶ τὰ σκεύη καὶ τὸ θυσιαστήριον καὶ ὁ
οἶκος ἐκ τῆς βεβηλώσεως ἡγιασμένα ἦν. 4 καὶ ἀπέστειλαν
εἰς πᾶν ὅριον Σαμαρείας καὶ Κωνα καὶ Βαιθωρων καὶ
Βελμαιν καὶ Ιεριχω καὶ εἰς Χωβα καὶ Αισωρα καὶ τὸν αὐλῶνα
Σαλημ 5 καὶ προκατελάβοντο πάσας τὰς κορυφὰς τῶν ὀρέων
τῶν ὑψηλῶν καὶ ἐτείχισαν τὰς ἐν αὐτοῖς κώμας καὶ παρέθεντο εἰς ἐπισιτισμὸν εἰς παρασκευὴν πολέμου, ὅτι προσφάτως ἦν τὰ πεδία αὐτῶν τεθερισμένα. 6 καὶ ἔγραψεν Ιωακιμ ὁ
ἱερεὺς ὁ μέγας, ὃς ἦν ἐν ταῖς ἡμέραις ἐν Ιερουσαλημ, τοῖς

KING JAMES VERSION

groves: for he had decreed to destroy all the gods of the land, that all nations should worship Nabuchodonosor only, and that all tongues and tribes should call upon him as god.

9 Also he came over against Esdraelon near unto Judea, over against the great strait of Judea.

10 And he pitched between Geba and Scythopolis, and there he tarried a whole month, that he might gather together all the carriages of his army.

4 Now the children of Israel, that dwelt in Judea, heard all that Holofernes the chief captain of Nabuchodonosor king of the Assyrians had done to the nations, and after what manner he had spoiled all their temples, and brought them to nought.

2 Therefore they were exceedingly afraid of him, and were troubled for Jerusalem, and for the temple of the Lord their God:

3 For they were newly returned from the captivity, and all the people of Judea were lately gathered together: and the vessels, and the altar, and the house, were sanctified after the profanation.

4 Therefore they sent into all the coasts of Samaria, and the villages, and to Bethoron, and Belmen, and Jericho, and to Choba, and Esora, and to the valley of Salem:

5 And possessed themselves beforehand of all the tops of the high mountains, and fortified the villages that were in them, and laid up victuals for the provision of war: for their fields were of late reaped.

6 Also Joacim the high priest, which was in those days in Jerusalem, wrote to them that dwelt in Bethulia, and

DOUAY OLD TESTAMENT

13 For Nabuchodonosor the king had commanded him to destroy all the gods of the earth, that he only might be called God by those nations which could be brought under him by the power of Holofernes.

14 And when he had passed through all Syria Sobal, and all Apamea, and all Mesopotamia, he came to the Idumeans into the land of Gabaa,

15 And he took possession of their cities, and stayed there for thirty days, in which days he commanded all the troops of his army to be united.

4 THEN the children of Israel, who dwelt in the land of Juda, hearing these things, were exceedingly afraid of him.

2 Dread and horror seized upon their minds, lest he should do the same to Jerusalem and to the temple of the Lord, that he had done to other cities and their temples.

3 And they sent into all Samaria round about, as far as Jericho, and seized upon all the tops of the mountains:

4 And they compassed their towns with walls, and gathered together corn for provision for war.

5 And Eliachim the priest wrote to all that were over

KNOX TRANSLATION

him destroy all traces of the countryside gods, so that the
nations overpowered by Holofernes might acknowledge no
other god but himself. 14 Then, after traversing the Syrian
country of Sobal, and Apamea, and Mesopotamia, he reached
the Idumaeans that dwelt in the land of Gabaa. 15 Their cities surrendered to him, and he made a halt of thirty days
there, during which he bade all the forces under his command rally to his side.

4 Consternation fell on all the Israelites that dwelt in Juda,
at the news of his coming; 2 fear struck deep at their
anxious hearts, that Jerusalem and its temple might fare as
other cities and temples had fared. 3 So they sent the word
round all the Samaritan country, and back again to Jericho,
that all the mountain-heights were to be occupied; 4 the villages on them were put in a state of defence, and corn stored
up in readiness for the campaign. 5 Nay, the high priest
Eliachim sent letters even further afield; the hill-folk that

TODAY'S ENGLISH VERSION

the gods of the land so that all the nations and tribes would
worship only Nebuchadnezzar and pray to him as a god.
9 Then Holofernes passed through Jezreel Valley near
Dothan, which faces the main ridge of the mountains of
Judah, 10 and set up camp between Geba and Scythopolis. He
stayed there for a month in order to get supplies for his
army.

4 The people of Judah heard what Holofernes, the commander of King Nebuchadnezzar's armies, had done to
the other nations. They heard how he had looted and
destroyed all their temples, 2 and they were terrified of him
and afraid of what he might do to Jerusalem and to the
Temple of the Lord their God. 3 They had only recently
returned home to Judah from exile and had just rededicated
the Temple and its utensils and its altar after they had been
defiled. 4 So they sent a warning to the whole region of
Samaria and to the towns of Kona, Beth Horon, Belmain,
Jericho, Choba, and Aesora, and to Salem Valley. 5 They
immediately occupied the mountaintops, fortified the villages
on the mountains, and stored up food in preparation for war.
It was fortunate that they had recently harvested their fields.
6 The High Priest Joakim, who was in Jerusalem at that
time, wrote to the people in the towns of Bethulia and

NEW REVISED STANDARD VERSION

destroy all the gods of the land, so that all nations should
worship Nebuchadnezzar alone, and that all their dialects
and tribes should call upon him as a god.
9 Then he came toward Esdraelon, near Dothan, facing
the great ridge of Judea; 10 he camped between Geba and
Scythopolis, and remained for a whole month in order to collect all the supplies for his army.

4 When the Israelites living in Judea heard of everything
that Holofernes, the general of Nebuchadnezzar, the
king of the Assyrians, had done to the nations, and how he
had plundered and destroyed all their temples, 2 they were
therefore greatly terrified at his approach; they were alarmed
both for Jerusalem and for the temple of the Lord their God.
3 For they had only recently returned from exile, and all the
people of Judea had just now gathered together, and the
sacred vessels and the altar and the temple had been consecrated after their profanation. 4 So they sent word to every
district of Samaria, and to Kona, Beth-horon, Belmain, and
Jericho, and to Choba and Aesora, and the valley of Salem.
5 They immediately seized all the high hilltops and fortified
the villages on them and stored up food in preparation for
war—since their fields had recently been harvested.
6 The high priest, Joakim, who was in Jerusalem at the
time, wrote to the people of Bethulia and Betomesthaim,

NEW AMERICAN BIBLE

to destroy all the gods of the earth, so that every nation
might worship Nebuchadnezzar alone, and every people and
tribe invoke him as a god. 9 At length Holofernes reached
Esdraelon in the neighborhood of Dothan, the approach to
the main ridge of the Judean mountains; 10 he set up his
camp between Geba and Scythopolis, and stayed there a
whole month to refurbish all the equipment of his army.

4 When the Israelites who dwelt in Judea heard of all that
Holofernes, commander in chief of Nebuchadnezzar,
king of the Assyrians, had done to the nations, and how he
had despoiled all their temples and destroyed them, 2 they
were in extreme dread of him, and greatly alarmed for
Jerusalem and the temple of the LORD, their God. 3 Now, they
had lately returned from exile, and only recently had all the
people of Judea been gathered together, and the vessels, the
altar, and the temple been purified from profanation. 4 So
they sent word to the whole region of Samaria, to Kona,
Beth-horon, Belmain, and Jericho, to Choba and Aesora, and
to the valley of Salem. 5 The people there posted guards on
all the summits of the high mountains, fortified their villages, and since their fields had recently been harvested,
stored up provisions in preparation for war.
6 Joakim, who was high priest in Jerusalem in those days,
wrote to the inhabitants of Bethulia [and Betomesthaim],

NEW JERUSALEM BIBLE

destroy all local gods so that the nations should worship
Nebuchadnezzar alone and people of every language and
nationality should hail him as a god.
9 Thus he reached the edge of Esdraelon, in the neighbourhood of Dothan, a village facing the great ridge of Judaea.
10 He pitched camp between Geba and Scythopolis and stayed
there a full month to re-provision his forces.

4 When the Israelites living in Judaea heard how Holofernes, general-in-chief of Nebuchadnezzar king of the
Assyrians, had treated the various nations, plundering their
temples and destroying them, 2 they were thoroughly
alarmed at his approach and trembled for Jerusalem and the
Temple of the Lord their God. 3 They had returned from captivity only a short time before, and the resettlement of the
people in Judaea and the reconsecration of the sacred furnishings, of the altar, and of the Temple, which had been
profaned, were of recent date.
4 They therefore alerted the whole of Samaria, Kona, Beth-
Horon, Belmain, Jericho, Choba, Aesora and the Salem valley. 5 They occupied the summits of the highest mountains
and fortified the villages on them; they laid in supplies for
the coming war, as the fields had just been harvested.
6 Joakim the high priest, resident in Jerusalem at the time,
wrote to the inhabitants of Bethulia and of Betomesthaim,

GREEK OLD TESTAMENT

κατοικοῦσι Βαιτυλουα καὶ Βαιτομεσθαιμ, ἥ ἐστιν ἀπέναντι
Εσδρηλων κατὰ πρόσωπον τοῦ πεδίου τοῦ πλησίον Δωθαϊμ,
[7] λέγων διακατασχεῖν τὰς ἀναβάσεις τῆς ὀρεινῆς, ὅτι δι᾽
αὐτῶν ἦν ἡ εἴσοδος εἰς τὴν Ιουδαίαν, καὶ ἦν εὐχερῶς διακω-
λῦσαι αὐτοὺς προσβαίνοντας στενῆς τῆς προσβάσεως οὔσης
ἐπ᾽ ἄνδρας τοὺς πάντας δύο. [8] καὶ ἐποίησαν οἱ υἱοὶ Ισραηλ
καθὰ συνέταξεν αὐτοῖς Ιωακιμ ὁ ἱερεὺς ὁ μέγας καὶ ἡ γερουσία παντὸς δήμου Ισραηλ, οἳ ἐκάθηντο ἐν Ιερουσαλημ. —
[9] καὶ ἀνεβόησαν πᾶς ἀνὴρ Ισραηλ πρὸς τὸν θεὸν ἐν ἐκτενείᾳ
μεγάλῃ καὶ ἐταπείνωσαν τὰς ψυχὰς αὐτῶν ἐν ἐκτενείᾳ
μεγάλῃ. [10] αὐτοὶ καὶ αἱ γυναῖκες αὐτῶν καὶ τὰ νήπια αὐτῶν
καὶ τὰ κτήνη αὐτῶν καὶ πᾶς πάροικος καὶ μισθωτὸς καὶ ἀρ-
γυρώνητος αὐτῶν ἐπέθεντο σάκκους ἐπὶ τὰς ὀσφύας αὐτῶν.
[11] καὶ πᾶς ἀνὴρ Ισραηλ καὶ γυνὴ καὶ τὰ παιδία οἱ κατοικοῦντες ἐν Ιερουσαλημ ἔπεσον κατὰ πρόσωπον τοῦ ναοῦ καὶ
ἐσποδώσαντο τὰς κεφαλὰς αὐτῶν καὶ ἐξέτειναν τοὺς σάκκους αὐτῶν κατὰ πρόσωπον κυρίου· [12] καὶ τὸ θυσιαστήριον
σάκκῳ περιέβαλον καὶ ἐβόησαν πρὸς τὸν θεὸν Ισραηλ ὁμοθυμαδὸν ἐκτενῶς τοῦ μὴ δοῦναι εἰς διαρπαγὴν τὰ νήπια αὐτῶν
καὶ τὰς γυναῖκας εἰς προνομὴν καὶ τὰς πόλεις τῆς κληρονομίας αὐτῶν εἰς ἀφανισμὸν καὶ τὰ ἅγια εἰς βεβήλωσιν καὶ
ὀνειδισμὸν ἐπίχαρμα τοῖς ἔθνεσιν. [13] καὶ εἰσήκουσεν κύριος

KING JAMES VERSION

Betomestham, which is over against Esdraelon toward the open country, near to Dothaim,

7 Charging them to keep the passages of the hill country: for by them there was an entrance into Judea, and it was easy to stop them that would come up, because the passage was straight, for two men at the most.

8 And the children of Israel did as Joacim the high priest had commanded them, with the ancients of all the people of Israel, which dwelt at Jerusalem.

9 Then every man of Israel cried to God with great fervency, and with great vehemency did they humble their souls:

10 Both they, and their wives, and their children, and their cattle, and every stranger and hireling, and their servants bought with money, put sackcloth upon their loins.

11 Thus every man and woman, and the little children, and the inhabitants of Jerusalem, fell before the temple, and cast ashes upon their heads, and spread out their sackcloth before the face of the Lord: also they put sackcloth about the altar,

12 And cried to the God of Israel all with one consent earnestly, that he would not give their children for a prey, and their wives for a spoil, and the cities of their inheritance to destruction, and the sanctuary to profanation and reproach, and for the nations to rejoice at.

DOUAY OLD TESTAMENT

against Esdrelon, which faceth the great plain near Dothain, and to all by whom there might be a passage of way, that they should take possession of the ascents of the mountains, by which there might be any way to Jerusalem, and should keep watch where the way was narrow between the mountains.

6 And the children of Israel did as the priest of the Lord Eliachim had appointed them.

7 And all the people cried to the Lord with great earnestness, and they humbled their souls in fastings, and prayers, both they and their wives.

8 And the priests put on haircloths, and they caused the little children to lie prostrate before the temple of the Lord, and the altar of the Lord they covered with haircloth.

9 And they cried to the Lord the God of Israel with one accord, that their children might not be made a prey, and their wives carried off, and their cities destroyed, and their holy things profaned, and that they might not be made a reproach to the Gentiles.

10 Then Eliachim the high priest of the Lord went about all Israel and spoke to them,

11 Saying: Know ye that the Lord will hear your prayers, if you continue with perseverance in fastings and prayers in the sight of the Lord.

12 Remember Moses the servant of the Lord, who overcame Amalec that trusted in his own strength, and in his power, and in his army, and in his shields, and in his chariots, and in his horsemen, not by fighting with the sword, but by holy prayers:

13 So shall all the enemies of Israel be, if you persevere in this work which you have begun.

KNOX TRANSLATION

lived facing Esdrelon across the wide plain around Dothain,
controlling the passes to the south, must occupy all the hill-
paths leading to Jerusalem, standing ever on guard where
the defile was narrowest. [6] Such orders from Eliachim, the
Lord's high priest, the Israelites faithfully carried out.
[7] Meanwhile, in good earnest, the whole nation made
appeal to the Lord, doing penance, men and women alike,
with fast and prayer. [8] Garb of sackcloth the priests wore,
and bade the very infants lie prostrate before the temple
gates; in sackcloth they veiled the Lord's own altar; [9] and so
with one voice they made appeal to the Lord, the God of
Israel. Were they to see their children slaves, their women-
folk allotted as spoil, their cities razed, their sanctuary profaned? Were they to become the scorn of the Gentiles? [10] And
Eliachim, the Lord's high priest, went about everywhere
among the Israelite folk with words of comfort. [11] Be sure,
said he, that the Lord will listen to your plea, if you pray on,
fast on, in his presence. [12] Remember how Amelec, long ago,
boasted of their overwhelming strength, of their great army,
shields and chariots and horsemen; and it was by the holy
prayers he offered, not by the sword, that the Lord's servant
Moses defeated them.[a] [13] So shall it be with all Israel's enemies, will you but persevere in your undertaking. [14] Thus

[a] Ex. 17. 12.

TODAY'S ENGLISH VERSION

Betomesthaim, which face Jezreel Valley near Dothan. [7]He
ordered them to occupy the mountain passes which led into
the land of Judah, where it would be easy to withstand an
attack, since the approach was only wide enough for two
people at a time to pass. [8]The Israelites carried out the
orders given to them by the High Priest Joakim and the
Council which met in Jerusalem.

[9]The leaders of Israel prayed earnestly to God and fasted.
[10]They put on sackcloth—they and their wives, their children, their livestock, and every resident foreigner, every slave
and hired laborer. [11-12]They also covered the altar with sackcloth. Then all the men, women, and children in Jerusalem
lay face down on the ground in front of the Temple; they lay
there in the Lord's presence, all in sackcloth, their heads covered with ashes. They joined together in earnest prayer to the
God of Israel, begging him not to let their children be captured, their wives carried off, or their home towns destroyed.
They pleaded with him not to give the Gentiles the satisfaction of destroying the Temple and dishonoring it. [13]The Lord

NEW REVISED STANDARD VERSION

which faces Esdraelon opposite the plain near Dothan,
[7]ordering them to seize the mountain passes, since by them
Judea could be invaded; and it would be easy to stop any
who tried to enter, for the approach was narrow, wide
enough for only two at a time to pass.

8 So the Israelites did as they had been ordered by the
high priest Joakim and the senate of the whole people of
Israel, in session at Jerusalem. [9]And every man of Israel
cried out to God with great fervor, and they humbled themselves with much fasting. [10]They and their wives and their
children and their cattle and every resident alien and hired
laborer and purchased slave—they all put sackcloth around
their waists. [11]And all the Israelite men, women, and children living at Jerusalem prostrated themselves before the
temple and put ashes on their heads and spread out their
sackcloth before the Lord. [12]They even draped the altar with
sackcloth and cried out in unison, praying fervently to the
God of Israel not to allow their infants to be carried off and
their wives to be taken as booty, and the towns they had
inherited to be destroyed, and the sanctuary to be profaned
and desecrated to the malicious joy of the Gentiles.

NEW AMERICAN BIBLE

which is on the way to Esdraelon, facing the plain near
Dothan, [7]and instructed them to keep firm hold of the
mountain passes, since these offered access to Judea. It
would be easy to ward off the attacking forces, as the defile
was only wide enough for two abreast. [8]The Israelites carried out the orders given them by Joakim, the high priest,
and the senate of the whole people of Israel, which met in
Jerusalem.

[9]All the men of Israel cried to God with great fervor and
did penance— [10]they, along with their wives, and children,
and domestic animals. All their resident aliens, hired laborers, and slaves also girded themselves with sackcloth. [11]And
all the Israelite men, women, and children who lived in
Jerusalem prostrated themselves in front of the temple building, with ashes strewn on their heads, displaying their sackcloth covering before the LORD. [12]The altar, too, they draped
in sackcloth; and with one accord they cried out fervently to
the God of Israel not to allow their children to be seized, their
wives to be taken captive, the cities of their inheritance to be
ruined, or the sanctuary to be profaned and mocked for the
nations to gloat over.

NEW JERUSALEM BIBLE

two towns facing Esdraelon, towards the plain of Dothan.
[7]He ordered them to occupy the mountain passes, the only
means of access to Judaea, for there it would be easy for
them to halt an attacking force, the narrowness of the
approach not allowing men to advance more than two
abreast. [8]The Israelites carried out the orders of Joakim the
high priest and of the people's Council of Elders in session at
Jerusalem.

[9]All the men of Israel cried most fervently to God and
humbled themselves before him. [10]They, their wives, their
children, their cattle, all their resident aliens, hired or slave,
wrapped sackcloth round their loins. [11]All the Israelites in
Jerusalem, including women and children, lay prostrate in
front of the Temple, and with ashes on their heads stretched
out their hands before the Lord. [12]They draped the altar
itself in sackcloth and fervently joined together in begging
the God of Israel not to let their children be carried off, their
wives distributed as booty, the towns of their heritage
destroyed, the Temple profaned and desecrated for the

GREEK OLD TESTAMENT

τῆς φωνῆς αὐτῶν καὶ εἰσεῖδεν τὴν θλῖψιν αὐτῶν· καὶ ἦν ὁ
λαὸς νηστεύων ἡμέρας πλείους ἐν πάσῃ τῇ Ιουδαίᾳ καὶ
Ιερουσαλημ κατὰ πρόσωπον τῶν ἁγίων κυρίου παντοκράτορος. 14 καὶ Ιωακιμ ὁ ἱερεὺς ὁ μέγας καὶ πάντες οἱ παρεστηκότες ἐνώπιον κυρίου ἱερεῖς καὶ οἱ λειτουργοῦντες κυρίῳ
σάκκους περιεζωσμένοι τὰς ὀσφύας αὐτῶν προσέφερον τὴν
ὁλοκαύτωσιν τοῦ ἐνδελεχισμοῦ καὶ τὰς εὐχὰς καὶ τὰ
ἑκούσια δόματα τοῦ λαοῦ, 15 καὶ ἦν σποδὸς ἐπὶ τὰς κιδάρεις
αὐτῶν, καὶ ἐβόων πρὸς κύριον ἐκ πάσης δυνάμεως εἰς
ἀγαθὸν ἐπισκέψασθαι πᾶν οἶκον Ισραηλ.

5 Καὶ ἀνηγγέλη Ολοφέρνῃ ἀρχιστρατήγῳ δυνάμεως
Ασσουρ διότι οἱ υἱοὶ Ισραηλ παρεσκευάσαντο εἰς πόλεμον καὶ τὰς διόδους τῆς ὀρεινῆς συνέκλεισαν καὶ ἐτείχισαν
πᾶσαν κορυφὴν ὄρους ὑψηλοῦ καὶ ἔθηκαν ἐν τοῖς πεδίοις
σκάνδαλα. 2 καὶ ὠργίσθη θυμῷ σφόδρα καὶ ἐκάλεσεν πάντας
τοὺς ἄρχοντας Μωαβ καὶ τοὺς στρατηγοὺς Αμμων καὶ πάντας σατράπας τῆς παραλίας 3 καὶ εἶπεν αὐτοῖς Ἀναγγεί-
λατε δή μοι, υἱοὶ Χανααν, τίς ὁ λαὸς οὗτος ὁ καθήμενος ἐν
τῇ ὀρεινῇ, καὶ τίνες ἃς κατοικοῦσιν πόλεις, καὶ τὸ πλῆθος
τῆς δυνάμεως αὐτῶν, καὶ ἐν τίνι τὸ κράτος αὐτῶν καὶ ἡ
ἰσχὺς αὐτῶν, καὶ τίς ἀνέστηκεν ἐπ' αὐτῶν βασιλεὺς
ἡγούμενος στρατιᾶς αὐτῶν, 4 καὶ διὰ τί κατενωτίσαντο τοῦ
μὴ ἐλθεῖν εἰς ἀπάντησίν μοι παρὰ πάντας τοὺς κατοικοῦντας ἐν δυσμαῖς. — 5 καὶ εἶπεν πρὸς αὐτὸν Αχιωρ ὁ ἡγούμενος πάντων υἱῶν Αμμων Ἀκουσάτω δὴ λόγον ὁ κύριός μου
ἐκ στόματος τοῦ δούλου σου, καὶ ἀναγγελῶ σοι τὴν ἀλήθειαν
περὶ τοῦ λαοῦ τούτου, ὃς κατοικεῖ τὴν ὀρεινὴν ταύτην,

KING JAMES VERSION

13 So God heard their prayers, and looked upon their afflictions: for the people fasted many days in all Judea and Jerusalem before the sanctuary of the Lord Almighty.

14 And Joacim the high priest, and all the priests that stood before the Lord, and they which ministered unto the Lord, had their loins girt with sackcloth, and offered the daily burnt offerings, with the vows and free gifts of the people,

15 And had ashes on their mitres, and cried unto the Lord with all their power, that he would look upon all the house of Israel graciously.

5 Then was it declared to Holofernes, the chief captain of the army of Assur, that the children of Israel had prepared for war, and had shut up the passages of the hill country, and had fortified all the tops of the high hills, and had laid impediments in the champaign countries:

2 Wherewith he was very angry, and called all the princes of Moab, and the captains of Ammon, and all the governors of the sea coast,

3 And he said unto them, Tell me now, ye sons of Chanaan, who this people is, that dwelleth in the hill country, and what are the cities that they inhabit, and what is the multitude of their army, and wherein is their power and strength, and what king is set over them, or captain of their army;

4 And why have they determined not to come and meet me, more than all the inhabitants of the west.

5 Then said Achior, the captain of all the sons of Ammon, Let my lord now hear a word from the mouth of thy servant, and I will declare unto thee the truth concerning this people,

DOUAY OLD TESTAMENT

14 So they being moved by this exhortation of his, prayed to the Lord, and continued in the sight of the Lord.

15 So that even they who offered the holocausts to the Lord, offered the sacrifices to the Lord girded with haircloths, and with ashes upon their head.

16 And they all begged of God with all their heart, that he would visit his people Israel.

5 AND it was told Holofernes the general of the army of the Assyrians, that the children of Israel prepared themselves to resist, and had shut up the ways of the mountains.

2 And he was transported with exceeding great fury and indignation, and he called all the princes of Moab and the leaders of Ammon.

3 And he said to them: Tell me what is this people that besetteth the mountains: or what are their cities, and of what sort, and how great: also what is their power, or what is their multitude: or who is the king over their warfare:

4 And why they above all that dwell in the east, have despised us, and have not come out to meet us, that they might receive us with peace?

5 Then Achior captain of all the children of Ammon answering, said: If thou vouchsafe, my lord, to hear, I will tell the truth in thy sight concerning this people, that

KNOX TRANSLATION

encouraged, they kept their posture of entreaty, there in the
Lord's presence; 15 the very priests who offered him sacrifice,
did so in sackcloth, with ashes on their heads; 16 and with all
their hearts they prayed, every one of them, that God would
bring deliverance to his people of Israel.

5 When news reached Holofernes, the Assyrian commander, that the Israelites were for offering resistance, and
had secured the mountain passes, 2 he broke out into a great
fury of indignation. He summoned all the chiefs of Moab and
Ammon to his presence; 3 What folk are these, he asked, that
would hold the mountain-heights? Are their cities so prosperous or so well defended, are they so brave or so numerous, have they a commander so skilled in war, 4 that they
alone defy us, and will not come out to meet and welcome
us, like the other nations around them?

5 It was Achior, chief paramount of the Ammonites, that
answered him. My lord, said he, if thou wilt hear me out, I
will tell the whole truth to thy face, about these mountain-

TODAY'S ENGLISH VERSION

heard their prayers and saw their distress. For many days the
people of Judah and Jerusalem continued their fast in front of
the Temple of the Lord Almighty. 14 The High Priest Joakim,
the priests, and all the others who served in the Lord's
Temple, wore sackcloth when they offered the daily burnt
offering, the freewill offerings of the people, and the offerings made to fulfill a vow. 15 They put ashes on their turbans and cried out in prayer to the Lord, begging him to
have mercy on the whole nation.

5 When Holofernes, the Assyrian general, heard that the
Israelites had prepared for war, blocked the mountain
passes, fortified the mountaintops, and set up roadblocks in
the plains, 2 he boiled over with anger. He called together all
the Moabite rulers, all the Ammonite generals, and all the
governors of the region along the Mediterranean coast 3 and
said to them, "You live in Canaan, so tell me about the people who live in these mountains. Which cities do they occupy? How large is their army? What is the source of their
power and strength? Who is the king who leads their army?
4 Why have they alone, of all the people in the west, refused
to come out and surrender to me?"

5 Then Achior, the leader of all the Ammonites, answered
Holofernes, "Sir, if you will please be so kind as to listen to
me, I will tell you the truth about these people who live in

NEW REVISED STANDARD VERSION

13 The Lord heard their prayers and had regard for their
distress; for the people fasted many days throughout Judea
and in Jerusalem before the sanctuary of the Lord Almighty.
14 The high priest Joakim and all the priests who stood before
the Lord and ministered to the Lord, with sackcloth around
their loins, offered the daily burnt offerings, the votive offerings, and freewill offerings of the people. 15 With ashes on
their turbans, they cried out to the Lord with all their might
to look with favor on the whole house of Israel.

5 It was reported to Holofernes, the general of the Assyrian army, that the people of Israel had prepared for war
and had closed the mountain passes and fortified all the
high hilltops and set up barricades in the plains. 2 In great
anger he called together all the princes of Moab and the commanders of Ammon and all the governors of the coastland,
3 and said to them, "Tell me, you Canaanites, what people is
this that lives in the hill country? What towns do they inhabit? How large is their army, and in what does their power
and strength consist? Who rules over them as king and leads
their army? 4 And why have they alone, of all who live in the
west, refused to come out and meet me?"

5 Then Achior, the leader of all the Ammonites, said to
him, "May my lord please listen to a report from the mouth
of your servant, and I will tell you the truth about this people
that lives in the mountain district near you. No falsehood

NEW AMERICAN BIBLE

13 The LORD heard their cry and had regard for their distress. For the people observed a fast of many days' duration
throughout Judea, and before the sanctuary of the LORD
Almighty in Jerusalem. 14 The high priest Joakim, and all the
priests in attendance on the LORD who served his altar, were
also girded with sackcloth as they offered the daily holocaust, the votive offerings, and the free-will offerings of the
people. 15 With ashes upon their turbans, they cried to the
LORD with all their strength to look with favor on the whole
house of Israel.

5 It was reported to Holofernes, commander in chief of the
Assyrian army, that the Israelites were ready for battle,
and had blocked the mountain passes, fortified the summits
of all the higher peaks, and placed roadblocks in the plains.
2 In great anger he summoned all the rulers of the Moabites,
the generals of the Ammonites, and all the satraps of the
seacoast 3 and said to them: "Now tell me, you Canaanites,
what sort of people is this that dwells in the mountains?
Which cities do they inhabit? How large is their army? In
what does their power and strength consist? Who has set
himself up as their king and the leader of their army? 4 Why
have they refused to come out to meet me along with all the
other inhabitants of the West?"

5 Then Achior, the leader of all the Ammonites, said to
him: "My lord, hear this account from your servant; I will
tell you the truth about this people that lives near you [that

NEW JERUSALEM BIBLE

heathen to gloat over. 13 The Lord heard them and looked
kindly on their distress.

The people fasted for many days throughout Judaea as
well as in Jerusalem before the sanctuary of the Lord
Almighty. 14 Joakim the high priest and all who stood before
the Lord, the Lord's priests and ministers, wore sackcloth
round their loins as they offered the perpetual burnt offering
and the votive and voluntary offerings of the people. 15 With
ashes on their turbans they earnestly called on the Lord to
look kindly on the House of Israel.

5 Holofernes, general-in-chief of the Assyrian army,
received the intelligence that the Israelites were preparing for war, that they had closed the mountain passes, fortified all the high peaks and laid obstructions in the plains.
2 Holofernes was furious. He summoned all the princes of
Moab, all the generals of Ammon and all the satraps of the
coastal regions. 3 'Men of Canaan,' he said, 'tell me: what
people is this that occupies the hill-country? What towns
does it inhabit? How large is its army? What are the sources
of its power and strength? Who is the king who rules it and
commands its army? 4 Why have they disdained to wait on
me, as all the western peoples have?'

5 Achior, leader of all the Ammonites, replied, 'May my lord
be pleased to listen to what your servant is going to say. I
shall give you the facts about these mountain folk whose

GREEK OLD TESTAMENT

πλησίον σοῦ οἰκοῦντος, καὶ οὐκ ἐξελεύσεται ψεῦδος ἐκ τοῦ
στόματος τοῦ δούλου σου. 6 ὁ λαὸς οὗτός εἰσιν ἀπόγονοι
Χαλδαίων. 7 καὶ παρῴκησαν τὸ πρότερον ἐν τῇ Μεσοποταμίᾳ, ὅτι οὐκ ἐβουλήθησαν ἀκολουθῆσαι τοῖς θεοῖς τῶν
πατέρων αὐτῶν, οἳ ἐγένοντο ἐν γῇ Χαλδαίων· 8 καὶ ἐξέβη-
σαν ἐξ ὁδοῦ τῶν γονέων αὐτῶν καὶ προσεκύνησαν τῷ θεῷ τοῦ
οὐρανοῦ, θεῷ ᾧ ἐπέγνωσαν, καὶ ἐξέβαλον αὐτοὺς ἀπὸ
προσώπου τῶν θεῶν αὐτῶν, καὶ ἔφυγον εἰς Μεσοποταμίαν
καὶ παρῴκησαν ἐκεῖ ἡμέρας πολλάς. 9 καὶ εἶπεν ὁ θεὸς
αὐτῶν ἐξελθεῖν ἐκ τῆς παροικίας αὐτῶν καὶ πορευθῆναι εἰς
γῆν Χανααν, καὶ κατῴκησαν ἐκεῖ καὶ ἐπληθύνθησαν χρυσίῳ
καὶ ἀργυρίῳ καὶ ἐν κτήνεσιν πολλοῖς σφόδρα. 10 καὶ κατέβησαν εἰς Αἴγυπτον, ἐκάλυψεν γὰρ τὸ πρόσωπον τῆς γῆς
Χανααν λιμός, καὶ παρῴκησαν ἐκεῖ μέχρις οὗ διετράφησαν·
καὶ ἐγένοντο ἐκεῖ εἰς πλῆθος πολύ, καὶ οὐκ ἦν ἀριθμὸς τοῦ
γένους αὐτῶν. 11 καὶ ἐπανέστη αὐτοῖς ὁ βασιλεὺς Αἰγύπτου
καὶ κατεσοφίσατο αὐτοὺς ἐν πόνῳ καὶ πλίνθῳ, ἐταπείνωσαν
αὐτοὺς καὶ ἔθεντο αὐτοὺς εἰς δούλους. 12 καὶ ἀνεβόησαν
πρὸς τὸν θεὸν αὐτῶν, καὶ ἐπάταξεν πᾶσαν τὴν γῆν
Αἰγύπτου πληγαῖς, ἐν αἷς οὐκ ἦν ἴασις. καὶ ἐξέβαλον αὐτοὺς
οἱ Αἰγύπτιοι ἀπὸ προσώπου αὐτῶν. 13 καὶ κατεξήρανεν ὁ
θεὸς τὴν ἐρυθρὰν θάλασσαν ἔμπροσθεν αὐτῶν 14 καὶ ἤγαγεν
αὐτοὺς εἰς ὁδὸν τοῦ Σινα καὶ Καδης Βαρνη· καὶ ἐξέβαλον
πάντας τοὺς κατοικοῦντας ἐν τῇ ἐρήμῳ 15 καὶ ᾤκησαν ἐν γῇ

KING JAMES VERSION

which dwelleth near thee, and inhabiteth the hill countries: and there shall no lie come out of the mouth of thy servant.

6 This people are descended of the Chaldeans:

7 And they sojourned heretofore in Mesopotamia, because they would not follow the gods of their fathers, which were in the land of Chaldea.

8 For they left the way of their ancestors, and worshipped the God of heaven, the God whom they knew: so they cast them out from the face of their gods, and they fled into Mesopotamia, and sojourned there many days.

9 Then their God commanded them to depart from the place where they sojourned, and to go into the land of Chanaan: where they dwelt, and were increased with gold and silver, and with very much cattle.

10 But when a famine covered all the land of Chanaan, they went down into Egypt, and sojourned there, while they were nourished, and became there a great multitude, so that one could not number their nation.

11 Therefore the king of Egypt rose up against them, and dealt subtilly with them, and brought them low with labouring in brick, and made them slaves.

12 Then they cried unto their God, and he smote all the land of Egypt with incurable plagues: so the Egyptians cast them out of their sight.

13 And God dried the Red sea before them,

14 And brought them to mount Sina, and Cades-Barne, and cast forth all that dwelt in the wilderness.

DOUAY OLD TESTAMENT

dwelleth in the mountains, and there shall not a false word come out of my mouth.

6 This people is of the offspring of the Chaldeans.

7 They dwelt first in Mesopotamia, because they would not follow the gods of their fathers, who were in the land of the Chaldeans.

8 Wherefore forsaking the ceremonies of their fathers, which consisted in the worship of many gods,

9 They worshipped one God of heaven, who also commanded them to depart from thence, and to dwell in Charan. And when there was a famine over all the land, they went down into Egypt, and there for four hundred years were so multiplied, that the army of them could not be numbered.

10 And when the king of Egypt oppressed them, and made slaves of them to labour in clay and brick, in the building of his cities, they cried to their Lord, and he struck the whole land of Egypt with divers plagues.

11 And when the Egyptians had cast them out from them, and the plague had ceased from them, and they had a mind to take them again, and bring them back to their service,

12 The God of heaven opened the sea to them in their flight, so that the waters were made to stand firm as a wall on either side, and they walked through the bottom of the sea and passed it dry foot.

13 And when an innumerable army of the Egyptians pursued after them in that place, they were so overwhelmed with the waters, that there was not one left, to tell what had happened to posterity.

14 And after they came out of the Red Sea, they abode in

KNOX TRANSLATION

folk; never a false word shalt thou hear from me. 6 They
come of Chaldaean stock, 7 but they made their abode in
Mesopotamia, because they had no mind to worship the old
gods of Chaldaea; 8 gods a many their fathers' worship
owned, but they forsook it, 9 to worship one God only, the
God of heaven. He it was bade them remove thence, and
dwell in Charan. At a time when famine overspread the
world, they took refuge in Egypt; and there, when four hundred years had passed,[a] they had grown so numerous that
there was no counting the muster of them. 10 The king of
Egypt oppressed them, forcing them to make bricks of clay
and build cities for him; so they cried out to this Lord of
theirs, and he smote the whole land of Egypt with plagues of
every sort, 11 till at last the Egyptians were fain to be rid of
them. But not for long; plagued no more, they tried to capture the men of Israel and make slaves of them anew. 12 To
these, as they fled, the God of heaven opened a path through
the sea, whose waves stood firm as a wall to right and left
while they marched across its floor dry-shod; 13 and when a
great army from Egypt sought to follow them, it was overwhelmed in those waters, so that never a man escaped to tell
his children the story.

14 The Red Sea once passed, they took for their own the

a The four hundred years are probably reckoned as elapsing between Abraham and Moses; cf. a similar calculation in Ac. 13. 20.

Today's English Version

the mountains near your camp. I will not lie to you. 6 These people are the descendants of some Babylonians 7-8 who abandoned the ways of their ancestors in order to worship the God of heaven. Finally, they were driven out of their land because they refused to worship their ancestors' gods. Then they fled to Mesopotamia, where they settled and lived for a long time.

9 "Afterward, their god told them to leave Mesopotamia and go to the land of Canaan, where they settled and became very rich in gold, silver, and livestock. 10 Later, when a famine struck all the land of Canaan, these Israelites, as they were later called, went down to Egypt and stayed there as long as there was enough food. While they were there, they became a large nation with so many people that they could not be counted. 11 So the king of Egypt turned against them. He took advantage of them and put them to work making bricks. He oppressed them and made them slaves. 12 But they prayed to their god, and he sent disasters that left the Egyptians helpless. When the Egyptians drove them out of the country, 13 their god dried up the Red Sea in front of them, 14 and then led them along the way to Sinai and Kadesh Barnea.

"The Israelites drove out all the people who lived in the

New Revised Standard Version

shall come from your servant's mouth. 6 These people are descended from the Chaldeans. 7 At one time they lived in Mesopotamia, because they did not wish to follow the gods of their ancestors who were in Chaldea. 8 Since they had abandoned the ways of their ancestors, and worshiped the God of heaven, the God they had come to know, their ancestors[a] drove them out from the presence of their gods. So they fled to Mesopotamia, and lived there for a long time. 9 Then their God commanded them to leave the place where they were living and go to the land of Canaan. There they settled, and grew very prosperous in gold and silver and very much livestock. 10 When a famine spread over the land of Canaan they went down to Egypt and lived there as long as they had food. There they became so great a multitude that their race could not be counted. 11 So the king of Egypt became hostile to them; he exploited them and forced them to make bricks. 12 They cried out to their God, and he afflicted the whole land of Egypt with incurable plagues. So the Egyptians drove them out of their sight. 13 Then God dried up the Red Sea before them, 14 and he led them by the way of Sinai and Kadesh-barnea. They drove out all the people of the desert,

a Gk *they*

New American Bible

inhabits this mountain region]; no lie shall escape your servant's lips.

6 "These people are descendants of the Chaldeans. 7 They formerly dwelt in Mesopotamia, for they did not wish to follow the gods of their forefathers who were born in the land of the Chaldeans. 8 Since they abandoned the way of their ancestors, and acknowledged with divine worship the God of heaven, their forefathers expelled them from the presence of their gods. So they fled to Mesopotamia and dwelt there a long time. 9 Their God bade them leave their abode and proceed to the land of Canaan. Here they settled, and grew very rich in gold, silver, and a great abundance of livestock. 10 Later, when famine had gripped the whole land of Canaan, they went down into Egypt. They stayed there as long as they found sustenance, and grew into such a great multitude that the number of their race could not be counted. 11 The king of Egypt, however, rose up against them, shrewdly forced them to labor at brickmaking, oppressed and enslaved them. 12 But they cried to their God, and he struck the land of Egypt with plagues for which there was no remedy. When the Egyptians expelled them, 13 God dried up the Red Sea before them, 14 and led them along the route to Sinai and Kadesh-barnea. First they drove out all the inhabitants of the

New Jerusalem Bible

home lies close to you. You will hear no lie from the mouth of your servant. 6 These people are descended from the Chaldaeans. 7 They once came to live in Mesopotamia, because they did not want to follow the gods of their ancestors who lived in Chaldaea. 8 They abandoned the way of their ancestors to worship the God of heaven, the God they learnt to acknowledge. Banished from the presence of their own gods, they fled to Mesopotamia where they lived for a long time. 9 When God told them to leave their home and set out for Canaan, they settled there and accumulated gold and silver and great herds of cattle. 10 Next, famine having overwhelmed the land of Canaan, they went down to Egypt where they stayed till they were well nourished. There they became a great multitude, a race beyond counting. 11 But the king of Egypt turned against them and exploited them by forcing them to make bricks; he degraded them, reducing them to slavery. 12 They cried to their God, who struck the entire land of Egypt with incurable plagues, and the Egyptians expelled them. 13 God dried up the Red Sea before them 14 and led them forward by way of Sinai and Kadesh-Barnea. Having driven off all the inhabitants of the desert,

GREEK OLD TESTAMENT

Αμορραίων καὶ πάντας τοὺς Εσεβωνίτας ἐξωλέθρευσαν ἐν τῇ
ἰσχύι αὐτῶν. καὶ διαβάντες τὸν Ιορδάνην ἐκληρονόμησαν
πᾶσαν τὴν ὀρεινήν 16 καὶ ἐξέβαλον ἐκ προσώπου αὐτῶν τὸν
Χαναναῖον καὶ τὸν Φερεζαῖον καὶ τὸν Ιεβουσαῖον καὶ τὸν
Συχεμ καὶ πάντας τοὺς Γεργεσαίους καὶ κατῴκησαν ἐν αὐτῇ
ἡμέρας πολλάς. 17 καὶ ἕως οὐχ ἥμαρτον ἐνώπιον τοῦ θεοῦ
αὐτῶν, ἦν μετ' αὐτῶν τὰ ἀγαθά, ὅτι θεὸς μισῶν ἀδικίαν μετ'
αὐτῶν ἐστιν. 18 ὅτε δὲ ἀπέστησαν ἀπὸ τῆς ὁδοῦ, ἧς διέθετο
αὐτοῖς, ἐξωλεθρεύθησαν ἐν πολλοῖς πολέμοις ἐπὶ πολὺ σφόδρα καὶ ᾐχμαλωτεύθησαν εἰς γῆν οὐκ ἰδίαν, καὶ ὁ ναὸς τοῦ
θεοῦ αὐτῶν ἐγενήθη εἰς ἔδαφος, καὶ αἱ πόλεις αὐτῶν ἐκρα-
τήθησαν ὑπὸ τῶν ὑπεναντίων. 19 καὶ νῦν ἐπιστρέψαντες ἐπὶ
τὸν θεὸν αὐτῶν ἀνέβησαν ἐκ τῆς διασπορᾶς, οὗ διεσπάρησαν
ἐκεῖ, καὶ κατέσχον τὴν Ιερουσαλημ, οὗ τὸ ἁγίασμα αὐτῶν,
καὶ κατῳκίσθησαν ἐν τῇ ὀρεινῇ, ὅτι ἦν ἔρημος. 20 καὶ νῦν,

KING JAMES VERSION

15 So they dwelt in the land of the Amorites, and they destroyed by their strength all them of Esebon, and passing over Jordan they possessed all the hill country.

16 And they cast forth before them the Chanaanite, the Pherezite, the Jebusite, and the Sychemite, and all the Gergesites, and they dwelt in that country many days.

17 And whilst they sinned not before their God, they prospered, because the God that hateth iniquity was with them.

18 But when they departed from the way which he appointed them, they were destroyed in many battles very sore, and were led captives into a land that was not their's, and the temple of their God was cast to the ground, and their cities were taken by the enemies.

19 But now are they returned to their God, and are come up from the places where they were scattered, and have possessed Jerusalem, where their sanctuary is, and are seated in the hill country; for it was desolate.

DOUAY OLD TESTAMENT

the deserts of mount Sina, in which never man could dwell, or son of man rested.

15 There bitter fountains were made sweet for them to drink, and for forty years they received food from heaven.

16 Wheresoever they went in without bow and arrow, and without shield and sword, their God fought for them and overcame.

17 And there was no one that triumphed over this people, but when they departed from the worship of the Lord their God.

18 But as often as beside their own God, they worshipped any other, they were given to spoil, and to the sword, and to reproach.

19 And as often as they were penitent for having revolted from the worship of their God, the God of heaven gave them power to resist.

20 So they overthrew the king of the Chanaanites, and of the Jebusites, and of the Pherezites, and of the Hethites, and of the Hevites, and of the Amorrhites, and all the mighty ones in Hesebon, and they possessed their lands, and their cities:

21 And as long as they sinned not in the sight of their God, it was well with them: for their God hateth iniquity.

22 And even some years ago when they had revolted from the way which God had given them to walk therein, they were destroyed in battles by many nations, and very many of them were led away captive into a strange land.

23 But of late returning to the Lord their God, from the different places wherein they were scattered, they are come together and are gone up into all these mountains, and possess Jerusalem again, where their holies are.

KNOX TRANSLATION

desert country about Sinai, that never yet gave man a home,
gave wanderer a resting-place; 15 there from brackish fountains fresh water sprang, there, for forty years, heaven itself
sent them nourishment. 16 Go where they would, without
bow or arrow, shield or spear, God fought for them, and won
the victory; 17 there was no beating down such a people as
this, save when they forsook the worship of the Lord their
God; 18 only when they worshipped some god other than
himself, their own God, would he let them be plundered, and
slaughtered, and treated with insult. 19 Even then, did they
but repent of their revolt from his allegiance, the God of
heaven would give them strength to resist their assailants.
20 So it was they overthrew kings a many, Chanaanite and
Jebusite, Pherezite and Hethites and Hevite; the Amorrhite
king, too, and all the warrior chiefs of Hesebon; took possession of their lands, and garrisoned their cities.
21 All went well with them, so long as no sin of theirs
offended his eye, the God that is an enemy to all wrong.
22 But there was a time, these many years back, when they
forsook the old paths God had given them to follow; then, in
battle after battle, nation after nation defeated them, and a
multitude of them were borne away as captives into an alien
land; 23 it was but lately that they turned to their God again,
and he reunited the scattered remnants of them. So they
returned to these hills, and took possession anew of
Jerusalem, where their sanctuary is. 24 Of this, then, my lord,

TODAY'S ENGLISH VERSION

southern part of Canaan, 15 occupied the land of the Amorites, wiped out the people of Heshbon, crossed the Jordan River, and took possession of the entire mountain region. 16 They drove out the Canaanites, the Perizzites, the Jebusites, the Shechemites, and all the Girgashites. The Israelites have now lived in these mountains for a long time.

17 "Their god hates wickedness, and as long as they did not sin against him, they prospered. 18 But when they disobeyed him, they suffered heavy losses in many wars and were finally taken away as captives to a foreign country. The temple of their god was leveled and their cities were occupied by their enemies. 19 But now that they have returned to their god, they have come back home from the countries where they had been scattered. They have again taken possession of the city of Jerusalem, where their temple is, and have resettled in the mountains that had remained uninhabited.

NEW REVISED STANDARD VERSION

15 and took up residence in the land of the Amorites, and by their might destroyed all the inhabitants of Heshbon; and crossing over the Jordan they took possession of all the hill country. 16 They drove out before them the Canaanites, the Perizzites, the Jebusites, the Shechemites, and all the Gergesites, and lived there a long time.

17 "As long as they did not sin against their God they prospered, for the God who hates iniquity is with them. 18 But when they departed from the way he had prescribed for them, they were utterly defeated in many battles and were led away captive to a foreign land. The temple of their God was razed to the ground, and their towns were occupied by their enemies. 19 But now they have returned to their God, and have come back from the places where they were scattered, and have occupied Jerusalem, where their sanctuary is, and have settled in the hill country, because it was uninhabited.

NEW AMERICAN BIBLE

desert; 15 then they settled in the land of the Amorites, destroyed all the Heshbonites by main force, crossed the Jordan, and took possession of the whole mountain region. 16 They expelled the Canaanites, the Perizzites, the Jebusites, the Shechemites, and all the Gergesites; and they lived in these mountains a long time.

17 "As long as the Israelites did not sin in the sight of their God, they prospered, for their God, who hates wickedness, was with them. 18 But when they deviated from the way he prescribed for them, they were ground down steadily, more and more, by frequent wars, and finally taken as captives into foreign lands. The temple of their God was razed to the ground, and their cities were occupied by their enemies. 19 But now that they have returned to their God, they have come back from the Dispersion wherein they were scattered, and have repossessed Jerusalem, where their sanctuary is, and have settled again in the mountain region which was unoccupied.

NEW JERUSALEM BIBLE

15 they settled in the land of the Amorites and in their strength exterminated the entire population of Heshbon. Then, having crossed the Jordan, they took possession of all the hill-country, 16 driving out the Canaanites before them and the Perizzites, Jebusites, Shechemites and all the Girgashites, and lived there for many years. 17 All the while they did not sin before their God, prosperity was theirs, for they have a God who hates wickedness. 18 But when they turned from the path he had marked out for them some were exterminated in a series of battles, others were taken captive to a foreign land. The Temple of their God was rased to the ground and their towns were seized by their enemies. 19 Then having turned once again to their God, they came back from the places to which they had been dispersed and scattered, regained possession of Jerusalem, where they have their Temple, and reoccupied the hill-country which had been

GREEK OLD TESTAMENT

δέσποτα κύριε, εἰ μὲν ἔστιν ἀγνόημα ἐν τῷ λαῷ τούτῳ καὶ ἁμαρτάνουσιν εἰς τὸν θεὸν αὐτῶν καὶ ἐπισκεψόμεθα ὅτι ἔστιν ἐν αὐτοῖς σκάνδαλον τοῦτο, καὶ ἀναβησόμεθα καὶ ἐκπολεμήσομεν αὐτούς. 21 εἰ δ' οὐκ ἔστιν ἀνομία ἐν τῷ ἔθνει αὐτῶν, παρελθέτω δὴ ὁ κύριός μου, μήποτε ὑπερασπίσῃ ὁ κύριος αὐτῶν καὶ ὁ θεὸς αὐτῶν ὑπὲρ αὐτῶν, καὶ ἐσόμεθα εἰς ὀνειδισμὸν ἐναντίον πάσης τῆς γῆς. — 22 καὶ ἐγένετο ὡς ἐπαύσατο Αχιωρ λαλῶν τοὺς λόγους τούτους, καὶ ἐγόγγυσεν πᾶς ὁ λαὸς ὁ κυκλῶν τὴν σκηνὴν καὶ περιεστώς, καὶ εἶπαν οἱ μεγιστᾶνες Ολοφέρνου καὶ πάντες οἱ κατοικοῦντες τὴν παραλίαν καὶ τὴν Μωαβ συγκόψαι αὐτόν 23 Οὐ γὰρ φοβηθησόμεθα ἀπὸ υἱῶν Ισραηλ, ἰδοὺ γὰρ λαὸς ἐν ᾧ οὐκ ἔστιν δύναμις οὐδὲ κράτος εἰς παράταξιν ἰσχυράν· 24 διὸ δὴ ἀναβησόμεθα, καὶ ἔσονται εἰς κατάβρωσιν πάσης τῆς στρατιᾶς σου, δέσποτα Ολοφέρνη. —

6 1 καὶ ὡς κατέπαυσεν ὁ θόρυβος τῶν ἀνδρῶν τῶν κύκλῳ τῆς συνεδρίας, καὶ εἶπεν Ολοφέρνης ἀρχιστράτηγος δυνάμεως Ασσουρ πρὸς Αχιωρ ἐναντίον παντὸς τοῦ δήμου ἀλλοφύλων καὶ πρὸς πάντας υἱοὺς Μωαβ 2 Καὶ τίς εἶ σύ, Αχιωρ καὶ οἱ μισθωτοὶ τοῦ Εφραιμ, ὅτι ἐπροφήτευσας ἐν ἡμῖν καθὼς σήμερον καὶ εἶπας τὸ γένος Ισραηλ μὴ πολεμῆσαι, ὅτι ὁ θεὸς αὐτῶν ὑπερασπιεῖ αὐτῶν; καὶ τίς θεὸς εἰ μὴ Ναβουχοδονοσορ; οὗτος ἀποστελεῖ τὸ κράτος αὐτοῦ καὶ ἐξολεθρεύσει αὐτοὺς ἀπὸ προσώπου τῆς γῆς, καὶ οὐ ῥύσεται αὐτοὺς ὁ θεὸς αὐτῶν· 3 ἀλλ' ἡμεῖς οἱ δοῦλοι αὐτοῦ πατάξομεν αὐτοὺς ὡς ἄνθρωπον ἕνα, καὶ οὐχ ὑποστήσονται τὸ κράτος τῶν ἵππων ἡμῶν. 4 κατακαύσομεν

KING JAMES VERSION

20 Now therefore, my lord and governor, if there be any error in this people, and they sin against their God, let us consider that this shall be their ruin, and let us go up, and we shall overcome them.

21 But if there be no iniquity in their nation, let my lord now pass by, lest their Lord defend them, and their God be for them, and we become a reproach before all the world.

22 And when Achior had finished these sayings, all the people standing round about the tent murmured, and the chief men of Holofernes, and all that dwelt by the sea side, and in Moab, spake that he should kill him.

23 For, *say they*, we will not be afraid of the face of the children of Israel: for, lo, it is a people that have no strength nor power for a strong battle.

24 Now therefore, lord Holofernes, we will go up, and they shall be a prey to be devoured of all thine army.

6 And when the tumult of men that were about the council was ceased, Holofernes the chief captain of the army of Assur said unto Achior and all the Moabites before all the company of other nations,

2 And who art thou, Achior, and the hirelings of Ephraim, that thou hast prophesied among us as to day, and hast said, that we should not make war with the people of Israel, because their God will defend them? and who is God but Nabuchodonosor?

3 He will send his power, and will destroy them from the face of the earth, and their God shall not deliver them: but we his servants will destroy them as one man; for they are not able to sustain the power of our horses.

DOUAY OLD TESTAMENT

24 Now therefore, my lord, search if there be any iniquity of theirs in the sight of their God: let us go up to them, because their God will surely deliver them to thee, and they shall be brought under the yoke of thy power:

25 But if there be no offence of this people in the sight of their God, we cannot resist them, because their God will defend them: and we shall be a reproach to the whole earth.

26 And it came to pass, when Achior had ceased to speak these words, all the great men of Holofernes were angry, and they had a mind to kill him, saying to each other:

27 Who is this, that saith the children of Israel can resist king Nabuchodonosor, and his armies, men unarmed, and without force, and without skill in the art of war?

28 That Achior therefore may know that he deceiveth us, let us go up into the mountains: and when the bravest of them shall be taken, then shall he with them be stabbed with the sword:

29 That every nation may know that Nabuchodonosor is god of the earth, and besides him there is no other.

6 AND it came to pass when they had left off speaking, that Holofernes being in a violent passion, said to Achior:

2 Because thou hast prophesied unto us, saying: That the nation of Israel is defended by their God, to shew thee that there is no God, but Nabuchodonosor:

3 When we shall slay them all as one man, then thou also shalt die with them by the sword of the Assyrians, and all Israel shall perish with thee:

KNOX TRANSLATION

assure thyself first; has any guilt of theirs lost them the favour of their God? Then indeed march we against them; none more ready than this God of theirs to hand them over to thee, fit subjects for thy over-mastering yoke. 25 If fault he has none to find with his own people, then meet them in battle we may not; he himself will be their defender, and ours will be a plight for all the world to mock at.

26 At these words of Achior's, Holofernes' lords were full of indignation, and thought to make an end of him. What talk is this? they said to one another. 27 Can the men of Israel, without arms, without valour, without skill in war, hold out against king Nabuchodonosor and his troops? 28 Scale we yonder heights, to prove Achior a liar, and when we have mastered the defenders, let Achior be put to the sword with the rest. 29 Let us prove to the whole world that Nabuchodonosor rules it, and other god there is none.

6 When their talk had died down, Holofernes himself, in a transport of rage, said to Achior, 2 This, then, is thy prophecy, that the race of Israel will find protection in their God? Thou hast a lesson still to learn; that Nabuchodonosor is god, and he only. 3 So be it; when the Israelites fall like one man, thou too shalt feel the sword of Assyria, and share

TODAY'S ENGLISH VERSION

20 "Sir, if these people are now sinning against their god,
even unknowingly, and if we can be sure that they are guilty
of some offense, we can successfully attack them. 21 But if
they have not disobeyed the law of their god, then you
should leave them alone, or he will defend them, and we will
be disgraced before the whole world."
22 When Achior had finished his speech, all the people
standing around the tent began to protest. Holofernes' own
senior officers, as well as the Moabites and those from the
Mediterranean coast, demanded that Achior be put to death.
23 "Why should we be afraid of these Israelites?" they
asked. "They are weak; they can't put up a strong defense.
24 Let's go ahead! General Holofernes, your great army will
slaughter them easily."

6 When the noise of the crowd around the council had
subsided, Holofernes spoke to Achior in front of the
entire group, those from the Mediterranean coast, the Moabites, and the Ammonite mercenaries.[a]
2 "Achior,[b] who do you think you are, acting like a prophet? Who are you to tell us not to go to war against the
Israelites because some god will defend them? Nebuchadnezzar is our god, and that's all that matters. He will send
his army and wipe these Israelites off the face of the earth.
Their god can't help them. 3 But we serve Nebuchadnezzar,
and we will beat them as easily as if their whole army were
one man. They will not be able to hold their ground against

[a] the Ammonite mercenaries; *some manuscripts do not have these words.*
[b] Achior; *some manuscripts add* you and your hired soldiers from Ephraim; *others add* you and your mercenaries from Ammon.

NEW REVISED STANDARD VERSION

20 "So now, my master and lord, if there is any oversight
in this people and they sin against their God and we find out
their offense, then we can go up and defeat them. 21 But if
they are not a guilty nation, then let my lord pass them by;
for their Lord and God will defend them, and we shall
become the laughingstock of the whole world."
22 When Achior had finished saying these things, all the
people standing around the tent began to complain;
Holofernes' officers and all the inhabitants of the seacoast
and Moab insisted that he should be cut to pieces. 23 They
said, "We are not afraid of the Israelites; they are a people
with no strength or power for making war. 24 Therefore let
us go ahead, Lord Holofernes, and your vast army will swallow them up."

6 When the disturbance made by the people outside the
council had died down, Holofernes, the commander of
the Assyrian army, said to Achior[a] in the presence of all the
foreign contingents:
2 "Who are you, Achior and you mercenaries of Ephraim,
to prophesy among us as you have done today and tell us
not to make war against the people of Israel because their
God will defend them? What god is there except Nebuchadnezzar? He will send his forces and destroy them from the
face of the earth. Their God will not save them; 3 we the
king's[b] servants will destroy them as one man. They cannot
resist the might of our cavalry. 4 We will overwhelm them;[c]

[a] Other ancient authorities add *and to all the Moabites* [b] Gk *his*
[c] Other ancient authorities add *with it*

NEW AMERICAN BIBLE

20 "So now, my lord and master, if these people are at
fault, and are sinning against their God, and if we verify this
offense of theirs, then we shall be able to go up and conquer
them. 21 But if they are not a guilty nation, then your lordship should keep his distance; otherwise their LORD and God
will shield them, and we shall become the laughingstock of
the whole world."
22 Now when Achior had concluded his recommendation,
all the people standing round about the tent murmured; and
the officers of Holofernes and all the inhabitants of the seacoast and of Moab alike said he should be cut to pieces.
23 "We are not afraid of the Israelites," they said, "for they
are a powerless people, incapable of a strong defense. 24 Let
us therefore attack them; your great army, Lord Holofernes,
will swallow them up."

6 When the noise of the crowd surrounding the council
had subsided, Holofernes, commander in chief of the
Assyrian army, said to Achior, in the presence of the whole
throng of coast-land peoples, of the Moabites, and of the
Ammonite mercenaries: 2 "Who are you, Achior, to prophesy
among us as you have done today, and to tell us not to fight
against the Israelites because their God protects them? What
god is there beside Nebuchadnezzar? He will send his force
and destroy them from the face of the earth. Their God will
not save them; 3 but we, the servants of Nebuchadnezzar,
will strike them down as one man, for they will be unable to
withstand the force of our cavalry. 4 We will overwhelm

NEW JERUSALEM BIBLE

left deserted. 20 So, now, master and lord, if this people has
committed any fault, if they have sinned against their God,
let us first be sure that they really have this reason to fail,
then advance and attack them. 21 But if their nation is guiltless, my lord would do better to abstain, for fear that their
Lord and God should protect them. We should then become
the laughing-stock of the whole world.'
22 When Achior had ended this speech, all the people
crowding round the tent began protesting. Holofernes' own
senior officers, as well as all the coastal peoples and the
Moabites, threatened to tear him limb from limb. 23 'Why
should we be afraid of the Israelites? They are a weak and
powerless people, quite unable to stand a stiff attack.
24 Forward! Advance! Your army, Holofernes our master, will
swallow them in one mouthful!'

6 When the uproar of those crowding round the council
had subsided, Holofernes, general-in-chief of the Assyrian army, reprimanded Achior in front of the whole crowd of
foreigners and Ammonites. 2 'Achior, who do you think you
are, you and the Ephraimite mercenaries, playing the prophet
like this with us today, and trying to dissuade us from making war on the people of Israel? You claim their God will protect them. And who is God if not Nebuchadnezzar? He himself will display his power and wipe them off the face of the
earth, and their God will certainly not save them. 3 But we,
his servants, shall destroy them as easily as a single individual. They can never resist the strength of our cavalry. 4 We

GREEK OLD TESTAMENT

γὰρ αὐτοὺς ἐν αὐτοῖς, καὶ τὰ ὄρη αὐτῶν μεθυσθήσεται ἐν τῷ
αἵματι αὐτῶν, καὶ τὰ πεδία αὐτῶν πληρωθήσεται τῶν νεκρῶν
αὐτῶν, καὶ οὐκ ἀντιστήσεται τὸ ἴχνος τῶν ποδῶν αὐτῶν
κατὰ πρόσωπον ἡμῶν, ἀλλὰ ἀπωλείᾳ ἀπολοῦνται, λέγει ὁ
βασιλεὺς Ναβουχοδονοσορ ὁ κύριος πάσης τῆς γῆς. εἶπεν
γάρ, οὐ ματαιωθήσεται τὰ ῥήματα τῶν λόγων αὐτοῦ. 5 σὺ δέ,
Αχιωρ μισθωτὲ τοῦ Αμμων, ὃς ἐλάλησας τοὺς λόγους τούτους ἐν ἡμέρᾳ ἀδικίας σου, οὐκ ὄψει ἔτι τὸ πρόσωπόν μου
ἀπὸ τῆς ἡμέρας ταύτης, ἕως οὗ ἐκδικήσω τὸ γένος τῶν ἐξ
Αἰγύπτου· 6 καὶ τότε διελεύσεται ὁ σίδηρος τῆς στρατιᾶς
μου καὶ ὁ λαὸς τῶν θεραπόντων μου τὰς πλευράς σου, καὶ
πεσῇ ἐν τοῖς τραυματίαις αὐτῶν, ὅταν ἐπιστρέψω. 7 καὶ
ἀποκαταστήσουσίν σε οἱ δοῦλοί μου εἰς τὴν ὀρεινὴν καὶ θή-
σουσίν σε ἐν μιᾷ τῶν πόλεων τῶν ἀναβάσεων, 8 καὶ οὐκ
ἀπολῇ ἕως οὗ ἐξολεθρευθῇς μετ᾽ αὐτῶν. 9 καὶ εἴπερ ἐλπίζεις
τῇ καρδίᾳ σου ὅτι οὐ συλλημφθήσονται, μὴ συμπεσέτω σου
τὸ πρόσωπον· ἐλάλησα, καὶ οὐδὲν διαπεσεῖται τῶν ῥημάτων
μου. — 10 καὶ προσέταξεν Ολοφέρνης τοῖς δούλοις αὐτοῦ, οἳ
ἦσαν παρεστηκότες ἐν τῇ σκηνῇ αὐτοῦ, συλλαβεῖν τὸν
Αχιωρ καὶ ἀποκαταστῆσαι αὐτὸν εἰς Βαιτυλουα καὶ
παραδοῦναι εἰς χεῖρας υἱῶν Ισραηλ. 11 καὶ συνέλαβον αὐτὸν
οἱ δοῦλοι αὐτοῦ καὶ ἤγαγον αὐτὸν ἔξω τῆς παρεμβολῆς εἰς
τὸ πεδίον καὶ ἀπῆραν ἐκ μέσου τῆς πεδινῆς εἰς τὴν ὀρεινὴν
καὶ παρεγένοντο ἐπὶ τὰς πηγάς, αἳ ἦσαν ὑποκάτω
Βαιτυλουα. 12 καὶ ὡς εἶδαν αὐτοὺς οἱ ἄνδρες τῆς πόλεως ἐπὶ
τὴν κορυφὴν τοῦ ὄρους, ἀνέλαβον τὰ ὅπλα αὐτῶν καὶ

KING JAMES VERSION

4 For with them we will tread them under foot, and their mountains shall be drunken with their blood, and their fields shall be filled with their dead bodies, and their footsteps shall not be able to stand before us, for they shall utterly perish, saith king Nabuchodonosor, lord of all the earth: for he said, None of my words shall be in vain.

5 And thou, Achior, an hireling of Ammon, which hast spoken these words in the day of thine iniquity, shalt see my face no more from this day, until I take vengeance of this nation that came out of Egypt.

6 And then shall the sword of mine army, and the multitude of them that serve me, pass through thy sides, and thou shalt fall among their slain, when I return.

7 Now therefore my servants shall bring thee back into the hill country, and shall set thee in one of the cities of the passages:

8 And thou shalt not perish, till thou be destroyed with them.

9 And if thou persuade thyself in thy mind that they shall not be taken, let not thy countenance fall: I have spoken it, and none of my words shall be in vain.

10 Then Holofernes commanded his servants, that waited in his tent, to take Achior, and bring him to Bethulia, and deliver him into the hands of the children of Israel.

11 So his servants took him, and brought him out of the camp into the plain, and they went from the midst of the plain into the hill country, and came unto the fountains that were under Bethulia.

12 And when the men of the city saw them, they took up

DOUAY OLD TESTAMENT

4 And thou shalt find that Nabuchodonosor is lord of the whole earth: and then the sword of my soldiers shall pass through thy sides, and thou shalt be stabbed and fall among the wounded of Israel, and thou shalt breathe no more till thou be destroyed with them.

5 But if thou think thy prophecy true, let not thy countenance sink, and let the paleness that is in thy face, depart from thee, if thou imaginest these my words cannot be accomplished.

6 And that thou mayst know that thou shalt experience these things together with them, behold from this hour thou shalt be associated to their people, that when they shall receive the punishment they deserve from my sword, thou mayst fall under the same vengeance.

7 Then Holofernes commanded his servants to take Achior, and to lead him to Bethulia, and to deliver him into the hands of the children of Israel.

8 And the servants of Holofernes taking him, went through the plains: but when they came near the mountains, the slingers came out against them.

KNOX TRANSLATION

their utter ruin. 4 Proof thou shalt have first, that Nabuchodonosor is the world's supreme lord; then, no more
breathing-space given thee, thou shalt perish with the rest,
shalt lie where Israel lies, with Assyrian steel between thy
ribs. 5 What, does thy face fall, sir Oracle? Why those pale
cheeks, if thou knowest all my threats are vain? 6 Nay, be
assured thou shalt learn the truth when the Israelites learn
it, no sooner. Henceforth thy lot shall be thrown in with
theirs; only when my sword falls on them shalt thou feel my
vengeance.
7 With that, Holofernes bade his men lay hold of Achior
and bear him off to Bethulia,[a] and so hand him over to the
men of Israel. 8 Lay hold of him they did, and set out on
their journey across the plain, but when they reached the
mountain spurs, out came slingers to meet them. 9 So they

a No town called Bethulia is elsewhere mentioned. Some think that the names, both of persons and of places, have been deliberately replaced by fictitious ones throughout this book.

TODAY'S ENGLISH VERSION

our cavalry; 4 it will overwhelm them. The mountains will be
soaked with their blood, and the valleys will be filled with
their corpses. After our attack, they will be completely wiped
out; not a trace of them will be left. This is the command of
Nebuchadnezzar, the lord of the whole earth, and he doesn't
speak idle words. 5 Achior, you are nothing but an Ammonite mercenary, and you talk like a traitor. You will not see me
again until I come and punish this race of runaway slaves.
6 And when I do, my soldiers will put you to death. You will
be just another name on the casualty list.

7 "Now my men will take you into the mountains and leave
you in one of the Israelite towns, 8 and you will die with the
people there. 9 Why look so worried, Achior? Don't you think
the town can stand against me? I will carry out all my
threats; you can be sure of that!"

10 Then Holofernes ordered his men, who were waiting in
his tent, to seize Achior, take him to Bethulia, and hand him
over to the Israelites. 11 So the men seized Achior and took
him out of the camp into the valley. From there they led him
into the mountains, as far as the spring which was below
Bethulia.

12 When the men of that town saw them approaching, they
picked up their weapons and ran to the top of the hill. Every

NEW REVISED STANDARD VERSION

their mountains will be drunk with their blood, and their
fields will be full of their dead. Not even their footprints will
survive our attack; they will utterly perish. So says King
Nebuchadnezzar, lord of the whole earth. For he has spoken;
none of his words shall be in vain.

5 "As for you, Achior, you Ammonite mercenary, you have
said these words in a moment of perversity; you shall not see
my face again from this day until I take revenge on this race
that came out of Egypt. 6 Then at my return the sword of my
army and the spear[a] of my servants shall pierce your sides,
and you shall fall among their wounded. 7 Now my slaves
are going to take you back into the hill country and put you
in one of the towns beside the passes. 8 You will not die
until you perish along with them. 9 If you really hope in your
heart that they will not be taken, then do not look downcast!
I have spoken, and none of my words shall fail to come
true."

10 Then Holofernes ordered his slaves, who waited on
him in his tent, to seize Achior and take him away to
Bethulia and hand him over to the Israelites. 11 So the slaves
took him and led him out of the camp into the plain, and
from the plain they went up into the hill country and came to
the springs below Bethulia. 12 When the men of the town
saw them,[b] they seized their weapons and ran out of the

a Lat Syr: Gk *people* *b* Other ancient authorities add *on the top of the hill*

NEW AMERICAN BIBLE

them with it, and the mountains shall be drunk with their
blood, and their plains filled with their corpses. Not a trace
of them shall survive our attack: they shall utterly perish,
says King Nebuchadnezzar, lord of all the earth; for he has
spoken, and his words shall not remain unfulfilled. 5 As for
you, Achior, you Ammonite mercenary, for saying these
things in a moment of perversity you shall not see my face
after today, until I have taken revenge on this race of people
from Egypt. 6 Then at my return, the sword of my army or
the spear of my servants will pierce your sides, and you shall
fall among their slain. 7 My servants will now conduct you
to the mountain region, and leave you at one of the towns
along the ascent. 8 You shall not die till you are destroyed
together with them. 9 If you still cherish the hope that they
will not be taken, then there is no need for you to be downcast. I have spoken, and my words shall not prove false in
any respect."

10 Then Holofernes ordered the servants who were standing
by in his tent to seize Achior, conduct him to Bethulia, and
hand him over to the Israelites. 11 So the servants took him
in custody and brought him out of the camp into the plain.
From there they led him into the mountain region till they
reached the springs below Bethulia. 12 When the men of the
city saw them, they seized their weapons and ran out of the

NEW JERUSALEM BIBLE

shall burn them all. Their mountains will be drunk with their
blood and their plains filled with their corpses. Far from
being able to resist us, every one of them will die; thus says
King Nebuchadnezzar, lord of the whole world. For he has
spoken, and his words will not prove empty. 5 As for you,
Achior, you Ammonite mercenary, who in a rash moment
said these words, you will not see my face again until the
day when I have taken my revenge on this brood from Egypt.
6 And then the swords of my soldiers and the spears of my
officers will pierce your sides. You will fall among their
wounded, the moment I turn on Israel. 7 My servants will
now take you into the hill-country and leave you near one of
the towns in the passes; 8 you will not die, until you share
their ruin. 9 No need to look so sad if you cherish the secret
hope that they will not be captured! I have spoken; none of
my words will prove idle.'

10 Holofernes having commanded his tent-orderlies to seize
Achior, to take him to Bethulia and to hand him over to the
Israelites, 11 the orderlies took him, escorted him out of the
camp and across the plain, and then, making for the hill-
country, reached the springs below Bethulia. 12 As soon as
the men of the town sighted them, they snatched up their

GREEK OLD TESTAMENT

ἀπῆλθον ἔξω τῆς πόλεως ἐπὶ τὴν κορυφὴν τοῦ ὄρους, καὶ πᾶς
ἀνὴρ σφενδονήτης διεκράτησαν τὴν ἀνάβασιν αὐτῶν καὶ
ἔβαλλον ἐν λίθοις ἐπ' αὐτούς. 13 καὶ ὑποδύσαντες ὑποκάτω
τοῦ ὄρους ἔδησαν τὸν Αχιωρ καὶ ἀφῆκαν ἐρριμμένον ὑπὸ τὴν
ῥίζαν τοῦ ὄρους καὶ ἀπῴχοντο πρὸς τὸν κύριον αὐτῶν.
14 καταβάντες δὲ οἱ υἱοὶ Ισραηλ ἐκ τῆς πόλεως αὐτῶν ἐπέστησαν αὐτῷ καὶ λύσαντες αὐτὸν ἀπήγαγον εἰς τὴν Βαιτυλουα καὶ κατέστησαν αὐτὸν ἐπὶ τοὺς ἄρχοντας τῆς πόλεως
αὐτῶν, 15 οἳ ἦσαν ἐν ταῖς ἡμέραις ἐκείναις, Οζιας ὁ τοῦ
Μιχα ἐκ τῆς φυλῆς Συμεων καὶ Χαβρις ὁ τοῦ Γοθονιηλ καὶ
Χαρμις υἱὸς Μελχιηλ. 16 καὶ συνεκάλεσαν πάντας τοὺς
πρεσβυτέρους τῆς πόλεως, καὶ συνέδραμον πᾶς νεανίσκος
αὐτῶν καὶ αἱ γυναῖκες εἰς τὴν ἐκκλησίαν, καὶ ἔστησαν τὸν
Αχιωρ ἐν μέσῳ παντὸς τοῦ λαοῦ αὐτῶν, καὶ ἐπηρώτησεν
αὐτὸν Οζιας τὸ συμβεβηκός. 17 καὶ ἀποκριθεὶς ἀπήγγειλεν
αὐτοῖς τὰ ῥήματα τῆς συνεδρίας Ολοφέρνου καὶ πάντα τὰ
ῥήματα, ὅσα ἐλάλησεν ἐν μέσῳ τῶν ἀρχόντων υἱῶν Ασσουρ,
καὶ ὅσα ἐμεγαλορρημόνησεν Ολοφέρνης εἰς τὸν οἶκον
Ισραηλ. 18 καὶ πεσόντες ὁ λαὸς προσεκύνησαν τῷ θεῷ καὶ
ἐβόησαν λέγοντες 19 Κύριε ὁ θεὸς τοῦ οὐρανοῦ, κάτιδε ἐπὶ
τὰς ὑπερηφανίας αὐτῶν καὶ ἐλέησον τὴν ταπείνωσιν τοῦ
γένους ἡμῶν καὶ ἐπίβλεψον ἐπὶ τὸ πρόσωπον τῶν ἡγιασμένων σοι ἐν τῇ ἡμέρᾳ ταύτῃ. 20 καὶ παρεκάλεσαν τὸν

KING JAMES VERSION

their weapons, and went out of the city to the top of the hill: and every man that used a sling kept them from coming up by casting of stones against them.

13 Nevertheless having gotten privily under the hill, they bound Achior, and cast him down, and left him at the foot of the hill, and returned to their lord.

14 But the Israelites descended from their city, and came unto him, and loosed him, and brought him to Bethulia, and presented him to the governors of the city:

15 Which were in those days Ozias the son of Micha, of the tribe of Simeon, and Chabris the son of Gothoniel, and Charmis the son of Melchiel.

16 And they called together all the ancients of the city, and all their youth ran together, and their women, to the assembly, and they set Achior in the midst of all their people. Then Ozias asked him of that which was done.

17 And he answered and declared unto them the words of the council of Holofernes, and all the words that he had spoken in the midst of the princes of Assur, and whatsoever Holofernes had spoken proudly against the house of Israel.

18 Then the people fell down and worshipped God, and cried unto God, saying,

19 O Lord God of heaven, behold their pride, and pity the low estate of our nation, and look upon the face of those that are sanctified unto thee this day.

DOUAY OLD TESTAMENT

9 Then turning out of the way by the side of the mountain, they tied Achior to a tree hand and foot, and so left him bound with ropes, and returned to their master.

10 And the children of Israel coming down from Bethulia, came to him, and loosing him they brought him to Bethulia, and setting him in the midst of the people, asked him what was the matter, that the Assyrians had left him bound.

11 In those days the rulers there, were Ozias the son of Micha of the tribe of Simeon, and Charmi, called also Gothoniel.

12 And Achior related in the midst of the ancients, and in the presence of all the people, all that he had said being asked by Holofernes: and how the people of Holofernes would have killed him for this word,

13 And how Holofernes himself being angry had commanded him to be delivered for this cause to the Israelites: that when he should overcome the children of Israel, then he might command Achior also himself to be put to death by diverse torments, for having said: The God of heaven is their defender.

14 And when Achior had declared all these things, all the people fell upon their faces, adoring the Lord, and all of them together mourning and weeping poured out their prayers with one accord to the Lord,

15 Saying: O Lord God of heaven and earth, behold their pride, and look on our low condition, and have regard to the face of thy saints, and shew that thou forsakest not them that trust on thee, and that thou humblest them that presume of themselves, and glory in their own strength.

KNOX TRANSLATION

let the mountains alone, tied Achior hand and foot to a tree,
and went back to their master, leaving Achior there with the
ropes round him. 10 But now the men of Israel ventured
down from Bethulia, and came to his side; he was set free
and taken back to the town with them. There he must stand
up before the general assembly of the people and satisfy their
questioning: what moved the Assyrians to leave him thus
bound?

11 The chieftains there at this time were the Simeonite,
Ozias son of Micha, and Charmi, who was also called
Gothoniel. 12 Before these and all the elders, in full view of
the people, Achior told them what answer he had made to
Holofernes' question; how the bystanders had been for
killing him outright; 13 in what angry fashion Holofernes
had given orders for his surrender to Israel, only so that he
too, in the hour of their defeat, might be doomed to execution; and of all the punishments he was threatened with,
only for saying, They have the God of heaven to defend
them. 14 When Achior had finished his story, the people
bowed down with one accord, face to earth, offering the Lord
worship and entreaty; all was weeping and lament. 15 Lord,
they cried, God of heaven and earth, leave not this insolence
unregarded, our distress unrelieved, the prayer of thy chosen
servants unheeded! Give proof, now, that those who trust in
thee are never forsaken, that the presumptuous, who boast
of their own strength, are ever brought low! 16 So they made

TODAY'S ENGLISH VERSION

man who used a sling as a weapon rained stones down on
Holofernes' soldiers, and this stopped them from coming any
farther up the mountain. 13 The Assyrians were forced to
take cover along the mountainside, where they tied Achior
up and left him lying at the foot of the mountain. Then they
returned to Holofernes.
14 Later, when the Israelites came down from Bethulia,
they untied Achior, brought him into the town, and took him
before the town officials, 15 who at that time were Uzziah
son of Micah, of the tribe of Simeon, Chabris son of Gothoniel, and Charmis son of Melchiel. 16 The officials called
together the town elders, and all the women and the young
men also ran to the assembly. Achior was brought before the
people, and Uzziah began questioning him. 17 Achior told
them what had been said at Holofernes' war council, what
he himself had said to the Assyrian officers, and how
Holofernes had boasted about what he would do to the
Israelites. 18 When the people heard this, they fell on their
knees and worshiped God. They prayed: 19 "O Lord God of
heaven, look how our boastful enemies have humiliated your
people! Have pity on us and help us." 20 Then they reassured

NEW REVISED STANDARD VERSION

town to the top of the hill, and all the slingers kept them
from coming up by throwing stones at them. 13 So having
taken shelter below the hill, they bound Achior and left him
lying at the foot of the hill, and returned to their master.
14 Then the Israelites came down from their town and
found him; they untied him and brought him into Bethulia
and placed him before the magistrates of their town, 15 who
in those days were Uzziah son of Micah, of the tribe of
Simeon, and Chabris son of Gothoniel, and Charmis son of
Melchiel. 16 They called together all the elders of the town,
and all their young men and women ran to the assembly.
They set Achior in the midst of all their people, and Uzziah
questioned him about what had happened. 17 He answered
and told them what had taken place at the council of
Holofernes, and all that he had said in the presence of the
Assyrian leaders, and all that Holofernes had boasted he
would do against the house of Israel. 18 Then the people fell
down and worshiped God, and cried out:
19 "O Lord God of heaven, see their arrogance, and have
pity on our people in their humiliation, and look kindly
today on the faces of those who are consecrated to you."

NEW AMERICAN BIBLE

city to the crest of the ridge; and all the slingers blocked the
ascent of Holofernes' servants by hurling stones upon them.
13 So they took cover below the mountain, where they bound
Achior and left him lying at the foot of the mountain; then
they returned to their lord.
14 The Israelites came down to him from their city, loosed
him, and brought him into Bethulia. They haled him before
the rulers of the city, 15 who in those days were Uzziah, son
of Micah of the tribe of Simeon, Chabris, son of Gothoniel,
and Charmis, son of Melchiel. 16 They then convened all the
elders of the city; and all their young men, as well as the
women, gathered in haste at the place of assembly. They
placed Achior in the center of the throng, and Uzziah questioned him about what had happened. 17 He replied by giving them an account of what was said in the council of
Holofernes, and of all his own words among the Assyrian
officers, and of all the boasting threats of Holofernes against
the house of Israel.
18 At this the people fell prostrate and worshiped God; and
they cried out: 19 "LORD, God of heaven, behold their arrogance! Have pity on the lowliness of our people, and look
with favor this day on those who are consecrated to you."

NEW JERUSALEM BIBLE

weapons, left the town and made for the mountain tops,
while all the slingers pelted them with stones to prevent
them from coming up. 13 However, they managed to take
cover at the foot of the slope, where they bound Achior and
left him lying at the bottom of the mountain and returned to
their master.
14 The Israelites then came down from their town, stopped
by him, unbound him and took him to Bethulia, where they
brought him before the chief men of the town, 15 who at that
time were Uzziah son of Micah of the tribe of Simeon,
Chabris son of Gothoniel and Charmis son of Melchiel.
16 These summoned all the elders of the town. The young
men and the women also hurried to the assembly. Achior
was made to stand with all the people surrounding him, and
Uzziah questioned him about what had happened. 17 He
answered by telling them what had been said at Holofernes'
council, and what he himself had said in the presence of the
Assyrian leaders, and how Holofernes had bragged of what
he would do to the House of Israel. 18 At this the people fell
to the ground and worshipped God. 19 'Lord God of heaven,'
they cried, 'take notice of their arrogance and have pity on
the humiliation of our race. Look kindly today on those who
are consecrated to you.' 20 They then spoke reassuringly to

GREEK OLD TESTAMENT

Αχιωρ καὶ ἐπῄνεσαν αὐτὸν σφόδρα, 21 καὶ παρέλαβεν αὐτὸν
Οζιας ἐκ τῆς ἐκκλησίας εἰς οἶκον αὐτοῦ καὶ ἐποίησεν πότον
τοῖς πρεσβυτέροις, καὶ ἐπεκαλέσαντο τὸν θεὸν Ισραηλ εἰς
βοήθειαν ὅλην τὴν νύκτα ἐκείνην.

7 Τῇ δὲ ἐπαύριον παρήγγειλεν Ολοφέρνης πάσῃ τῇ στρατιᾷ αὐτοῦ καὶ παντὶ τῷ λαῷ αὐτοῦ, οἳ παρεγένοντο ἐπὶ
τὴν συμμαχίαν αὐτοῦ, ἀναζευγνύειν ἐπὶ Βαιτυλουα καὶ τὰς
ἀναβάσεις τῆς ὀρεινῆς προκαταλαμβάνεσθαι καὶ ποιεῖν
πόλεμον πρὸς τοὺς υἱοὺς Ισραηλ. 2 καὶ ἀνέζευξεν ἐν τῇ
ἡμέρᾳ ἐκείνῃ πᾶς ἀνὴρ δυνατὸς αὐτῶν· καὶ ἡ δύναμις αὐτῶν
ἀνδρῶν πολεμιστῶν χιλιάδες πεζῶν ἑκατὸν ἑβδομήκοντα καὶ
ἱππέων χιλιάδες δέκα δύο χωρὶς τῆς ἀποσκευῆς καὶ τῶν ἀνδρῶν, οἳ ἦσαν πεζοὶ ἐν αὐτοῖς, πλῆθος πολὺ σφόδρα. 3 καὶ
παρενέβαλον ἐν τῷ αὐλῶνι πλησίον Βαιτυλουα ἐπὶ τῆς
πηγῆς καὶ παρέτειναν εἰς εὖρος ἐπὶ Δωθαϊμ ἕως Βελβαιμ
καὶ εἰς μῆκος ἀπὸ Βαιτυλουα ἕως Κυαμωνος, ἥ ἐστιν ἀπέναντι τοῦ Εσδρηλων. 4 οἱ δὲ υἱοὶ Ισραηλ, ὡς εἶδον αὐτῶν τὸ

KING JAMES VERSION

20 Then they comforted Achior, and praised him greatly.

21 And Ozias took him out of the assembly unto his house, and made a feast to the elders; and they called on the God of Israel all that night for help.

7 The next day Holofernes commanded all his army, and all his people which were come to take his part, that they should remove their camp against Bethulia, to take aforehand the ascents of the hill country, and to make war against the children of Israel.

2 Then their strong men removed their camps in that day, and the army of the men of war was an hundred and seventy thousand footmen, and twelve thousand horsemen, beside the baggage, and other men that were afoot among them, a very great multitude.

3 And they camped in the valley near unto Bethulia, by the fountain, and they spread themselves in breadth over Dothaim even to Belmaim, and in length from Bethulia unto Cyamon, which is over against Esdraelon.

4 Now the children of Israel, when they saw the multitude

DOUAY OLD TESTAMENT

16 So when their weeping was ended, and the people's prayer, in which they continued all the day, was concluded, they comforted Achior,

17 Saying: The God of our fathers, whose power thou hast set forth, will make this return to thee, that thou rather shalt see their destruction.

18 And when the Lord our God shall give this liberty to his servants, let God be with thee also in the midst of us: that as it shall please thee, so thou with all thine mayst converse with us.

19 Then Ozias, after the assembly was broken up, received him into his house, and made him a great supper.

20 And all the ancients were invited, and they refreshed themselves together after their fast was over.

21 And afterwards all the people were called together, and they prayed all the night long within the church, desiring help of the God of Israel.

7 BUT Holofernes on the next day gave orders to his army, to go up against Bethulia.

2 Now there were in his troops a hundred and twenty thousand footmen, and two and twenty thousand horsemen, besides the preparations of those men who had been taken, and who had been brought away out of the provinces and cities of all the youth.

3 All these prepared themselves together to fight against the children of Israel, and they came by the hillside to the top, which looketh toward Dothain, from the place which is called Belma, unto Chelmon, which is over against Esdrelon.

4 But the children of Israel, when they saw the multitude

KNOX TRANSLATION

an end of weeping; and now, their day of public prayer over,
they offered Achior consolation. 17 The God of our fathers,
they told him, will give thee thy reward. Thou hast been the
herald of his great deeds, and thou shalt live to see the
downfall of thy enemies. 18 Then, when the Lord our God
has granted his servants deliverance, may he still be with
thee, thy own God, here in our midst; thou and thine shall be
made free of our company.
19 And now Ozias, dismissing the assembly, bade Achior to
his house and made a great feast for him; 20 all the elders,
too, were bidden, and together they refreshed themselves,
now the fast was over. 21 But afterwards all the people were
summoned from their homes anew; and in solemn assembly,
the whole night long, they prayed to the God of Israel, to win
deliverance.

7 Next day, Holofernes ordered his troops to march on
Bethulia. 2 He had a hundred and twenty thousand foot
and twenty-two thousand horse under his command, besides
forced levies from the manhood of all the regions and cities
he had overrun. 3 This whole army now prepared to attack
the Israelites, advancing up the mountain-slopes to a height
which commands the Dothian plain, all the way from Belma
to Chelmon, near Esdrelon. 4 Face to earth the men of Israel

TODAY'S ENGLISH VERSION

Achior and praised him for what he had done. 21 After the
assembly was over, Uzziah took Achior home with him, and
gave a banquet there for the elders. All that night they
prayed to the God of Israel for help.

7 1-2 The next day Holofernes gathered his whole army
together, as well as his allied forces. It was an immense
army, consisting of 170,000 infantry and 12,000 cavalry,
not counting the support troops who took care of the equipment. He ordered them to march on Bethulia, seize the
mountain passes, and attack the Israelites. So they moved
out 3 and set up camp beside the spring in the valley near
Bethulia. The camp was so wide that it spread out toward
the town of Dothan as far as Balbaim, and so long that it
stretched from Bethulia to Cyamon, which faces Jezreel
Valley.

4 When the Israelites saw the size of the army, they were

NEW REVISED STANDARD VERSION

20 Then they reassured Achior, and praised him highly.
21 Uzziah took him from the assembly to his own house and
gave a banquet for the elders; and all that night they called
on the God of Israel for help.

7 The next day Holofernes ordered his whole army, and all
the allies who had joined him, to break camp and move
against Bethulia, and to seize the passes up into the hill
country and make war on the Israelites. 2 So all their warriors marched off that day; their fighting forces numbered
one hundred seventy thousand infantry and twelve thousand
cavalry, not counting the baggage and the foot soldiers handling it, a very great multitude. 3 They encamped in the valley near Bethulia, beside the spring, and they spread out in
breadth over Dothan as far as Balbaim and in length from
Bethulia to Cyamon, which faces Esdraelon.

4 When the Israelites saw their vast numbers, they were

NEW AMERICAN BIBLE

20 Then they reassured Achior and praised him highly.
21 Uzziah brought him from the assembly to his home, where
he gave a banquet for the elders. That whole night they
called upon the God of Israel for help.

7 The following day Holofernes ordered his whole army,
and all the allied troops that had come to his support, to
move against Bethulia, seize the mountain passes, and
engage the Israelites in battle. 2 That same day all their
fighting men went into action. Their forces numbered a hundred and seventy thousand infantry and twelve thousand
horsemen, not counting the baggage train or the men who
accompanied it on foot—a very great army. 3 They encamped
at the spring in the valley near Bethulia, and spread out in
breadth toward Dothan as far as Balbaim, and in length from
Bethulia to Cyamon, which faces Esdraelon.

4 When the Israelites saw how many there were, they said

NEW JERUSALEM BIBLE

Achior and praised him warmly. 21 After the assembly
Uzziah took him home and gave a banquet for the elders; all
that night they called on the God of Israel for help.

7 The following day Holofernes issued orders to his whole
army and to the whole host of auxiliaries who had
joined him, to break camp and march on Bethulia, to occupy
the mountain passes and so open the campaign against the
Israelites. 2 The troops broke camp that same day. The actual
fighting force numbered one hundred and twenty thousand
infantry and twelve thousand cavalry, not to mention the
baggage train with the vast number of men on foot concerned with that. 3 They penetrated the valley in the neighbourhood of Bethulia, near the spring, and deployed on a
wide front from Dothan to Balbaim and, in depth, from
Bethulia to Cyamon, which faces Esdraelon. 4 When the
Israelites saw this horde, they were all appalled and said to

GREEK OLD TESTAMENT

πλῆθος, ἐταράχθησαν σφόδρα καὶ εἶπαν ἕκαστος πρὸς τὸν
πλησίον αὐτοῦ Νῦν ἐκλείξουσιν οὗτοι τὸ πρόσωπον τῆς γῆς
πάσης, καὶ οὔτε τὰ ὄρη τὰ ὑψηλὰ οὔτε αἱ φάραγγες οὔτε οἱ
βουνοὶ ὑποστήσονται τὸ βάρος αὐτῶν. 5 καὶ ἀναλαβόντες
ἕκαστος τὰ σκεύη τὰ πολεμικὰ αὐτῶν καὶ ἀνακαύσαντες
πυρὰς ἐπὶ τοὺς πύργους αὐτῶν ἔμενον φυλάσσοντες ὅλην
τὴν νύκτα ἐκείνην. 6 τῇ δὲ ἡμέρᾳ τῇ δευτέρᾳ ἐξήγαγεν
Ολοφέρνης πᾶσαν τὴν ἵππον αὐτοῦ κατὰ πρόσωπον τῶν υἱῶν
Ισραηλ, οἳ ἦσαν ἐν Βαιτυλουα, 7 καὶ ἐπεσκέψατο τὰς ἀναβάσεις τῆς πόλεως αὐτῶν καὶ τὰς πηγὰς τῶν ὑδάτων
ἐφώδευσεν καὶ προκατελάβετο αὐτὰς καὶ ἐπέστησεν αὐταῖς
παρεμβολὰς ἀνδρῶν πολεμιστῶν, καὶ αὐτὸς ἀνέζευξεν εἰς
τὸν λαὸν αὐτοῦ. — 8 καὶ προσελθόντες αὐτῷ πάντες ἄρχοντες υἱῶν Ησαυ καὶ πάντες οἱ ἡγούμενοι τοῦ λαοῦ Μωαβ καὶ
οἱ στρατηγοὶ τῆς παραλίας εἶπαν 9 Ἀκουσάτω δὴ λόγον ὁ
δεσπότης ἡμῶν, ἵνα μὴ γένηται θραῦσμα ἐν τῇ δυνάμει σου.
10 ὁ γὰρ λαὸς οὗτος τῶν υἱῶν Ισραηλ οὐ πέποιθαν ἐπὶ τοῖς
δόρασιν αὐτῶν, ἀλλ᾽ ἐπὶ τοῖς ὕψεσι τῶν ὀρέων, ἐν οἷς αὐτοὶ
ἐνοικοῦσιν ἐν αὐτοῖς. οὐ γάρ ἐστιν εὐχερὲς προσβῆναι ταῖς
κορυφαῖς τῶν ὀρέων αὐτῶν. 11 καὶ νῦν, δέσποτα, μὴ πολέμει
πρὸς αὐτοὺς καθὼς γίνεται πόλεμος παρατάξεως, καὶ οὐ
πεσεῖται ἐκ τοῦ λαοῦ σου ἀνὴρ εἷς. 12 ἀνάμεινον ἐπὶ τῆς
παρεμβολῆς σου διαφυλάσσων πάντα ἄνδρα ἐκ τῆς δυνάμεώς
σου, καὶ ἐπικρατησάτωσαν οἱ παῖδές σου τῆς πηγῆς τοῦ
ὕδατος, ἣ ἐκπορεύεται ἐκ τῆς ῥίζης τοῦ ὄρους, 13 διότι

KING JAMES VERSION

of them, were greatly troubled, and said every one to his neighbour, Now will these men lick up the face of the earth; for neither the high mountains, nor the valleys, nor the hills, are able to bear their weight.

5 Then every man took up his weapons of war, and when they had kindled fires upon their towers, they remained and watched all that night.

6 But in the second day Holofernes brought forth all his horsemen in the sight of the children of Israel which were in Bethulia,

7 And viewed the passages up to the city, and came to the fountains of their waters, and took them, and set garrisons of men of war over them, and he himself removed toward his people.

8 Then came unto him all the chief of the children of Esau, and all the governors of the people of Moab, and the captains of the sea coast, and said,

9 Let our lord now hear a word, that there be not an overthrow in thine army.

10 For this people of the children of Israel do not trust in their spears, but in the height of the mountains wherein they dwell, because it is not easy to come up to the tops of their mountains.

11 Now therefore, my lord, fight not against them in battle array, and there shall not so much as one man of thy people perish.

12 Remain in thy camp, and keep all the men of thine army, and let thy servants get into their hands the fountain of water, which issueth forth of the foot of the mountain:

DOUAY OLD TESTAMENT

of them, prostrated themselves upon the ground, putting ashes upon their heads, praying with one accord, that the God of Israel would shew his mercy upon his people.

5 And taking their arms of war, they posted themselves at the places, which by a narrow pathway lead directly between the mountains, and they guarded them all day and night.

6 Now Holofernes, in going round about, found that the fountain which supplied them with water, ran through an aqueduct without the city on the south side: and he commanded their aqueduct to be cut off.

7 Nevertheless there were springs not far from the walls, out of which they were seen secretly to draw water, to refresh themselves a little rather than to drink their fill.

8 But the children of Ammon and Moab came to Holofernes, saying: The children of Israel trust not in their spears, nor in their arrows, but the mountains are their defence, and the steep hills and precipices guard them.

9 Wherefore that thou mayst overcome them without joining battle, set guards at the springs that they may not draw water out of them, and thou shalt destroy them without

KNOX TRANSLATION

bowed down, and threw dust on their heads, as they saw the
enemy's numbers, beseeching God with one accord to grant
his people deliverance; 5 then, taking up their arms, they
mounted guard over the approaches of the narrow defile that
leads between the mountains, where they kept watch day
and night. 6 Holofernes, looking for a devious path to cir-
cumvent them, came upon the springs which fed their aqueduct, south of the city and beyond its enclosure; so he gave
orders that their supply of water should be cut off. 7 A few
springs remained, not far from the wall, from which they still
drew water, enough to revive their spirits but scarce enough
to quench their thirst. This they did by stealth, but not unobserved; 8 and now the men of Ammon and Moab offered
their advice to Holofernes. Not in bow or lance, said they, do
the Israelites put their trust; it is the hill-country that
befriends them; these mountains with their headlong slopes
are all the defence they need. 9 Wouldst thou defeat them
without battle joined? Then set a guard over these springs of
theirs, and let them draw water no longer. Either thou wilt

TODAY'S ENGLISH VERSION

terrified and said to one another, "Those soldiers are going to eat up everything in sight. There's not enough food in the mountains, valleys, and hills put together to feed an army like that." 5But in spite of their fear, all the Israelites took up their weapons, lighted signal fires on the towers, and remained on guard duty all night. 6The next day Holofernes led out his entire cavalry so that the Israelites in Bethulia could see them. 7He inspected the approaches to the town and the springs that supplied its water. He seized the springs and stationed guards there, before returning to camp.

8All the leaders of the Edomite and Moabite forces, along with the commanders of the troops from the Mediterranean coast, came to Holofernes and said, 9"Sir, if you listen to our advice, your troops will not suffer heavy losses. 10These Israelites do not rely on their weapons for defense but rather on the height of the mountains where they live, since the mountains are not easy to climb. 11So then, General Holofernes, if you do not make a direct attack on them, your whole army will suffer no casualties. 12Stay in your camp and keep your soldiers in their quarters. Just command your men to blockade the springs at the foot of the mountains,

NEW REVISED STANDARD VERSION

greatly terrified and said to one another, "They will now strip clean the whole land; neither the high mountains nor the valleys nor the hills will bear their weight." 5Yet they all seized their weapons, and when they had kindled fires on their towers, they remained on guard all that night.

6 On the second day Holofernes led out all his cavalry in full view of the Israelites in Bethulia. 7He reconnoitered the approaches to their town, and visited the springs that supplied their water; he seized them and set guards of soldiers over them, and then returned to his army.

8 Then all the chieftains of the Edomites and all the leaders of the Moabites and the commanders of the coastland came to him and said, 9"Listen to what we have to say, my lord, and your army will suffer no losses. 10This people, the Israelites, do not rely on their spears but on the height of the mountains where they live, for it is not easy to reach the tops of their mountains. 11Therefore, my lord, do not fight against them in regular formation, and not a man of your army will fall. 12Remain in your camp, and keep all the men in your forces with you; let your servants take possession of the spring of water that flows from the foot of the mountain,

NEW AMERICAN BIBLE

to one another in great dismay: "Soon they will devour the whole country. Neither the high mountains nor the valleys and hills can support the mass of them." 5Yet they all seized their weapons, lighted fires on their bastions, and kept watch throughout the night.

6On the second day Holofernes led out all his cavalry in the sight of the Israelites who were in Bethulia. 7He reconnoitered the approaches to their city and located their sources of water; these he seized, stationing armed detachments around them, while he himself returned to his troops.

8All the commanders of the Edomites and all the leaders of the Ammonites, together with the generals of the seacoast, came to Holofernes and said: 9"Sir, listen to what we have to say, that there may be no losses among your troops. 10These Israelites do not rely on their spears, but on the height of the mountains where they dwell; it is not easy to reach the summit of their mountains. 11Therefore, sir, do not attack them in regular formation; thus not a single one of your troops will fall. 12Stay in your camp, and spare all your soldiers. Have some of your servants keep control of the source of water that flows out at the base of the mountain,

NEW JERUSALEM BIBLE

each other, 'Now they will lick the whole country clean. Not even the loftiest peaks, the gorges or the hills will be able to stand the weight of them.' 5Each man snatched up his arms; they lit beacons on their towers and spent the whole night on watch.

6On the second day Holofernes deployed his entire cavalry in sight of the Israelites in Bethulia. 7He reconnoitred the slopes leading up to the town, located the water-points, seized them and posted pickets over them and returned to the main body. 8The chieftains of the sons of Esau, all the leaders of the Moabites and the generals of the coastal district then came to him and said, 9'If our master will be pleased to listen to us, his forces will not sustain a single wound. 10These Israelites do not rely so much on their spears as on the height of the mountains where they live. And admittedly it is not at all easy to scale these heights of theirs.

11'This being the case, master, avoid engaging them in a pitched battle and then you will not lose a single man. 12Stay in camp, keep all your troops there too, while your servants seize the spring which rises at the foot of the mountain,

GREEK OLD TESTAMENT

ἐκεῖθεν ὑδρεύονται πάντες οἱ κατοικοῦντες Βαιτυλουα, καὶ
ἀνελεῖ αὐτοὺς ἡ δίψα, καὶ ἐκδώσουσι τὴν πόλιν αὐτῶν· καὶ
ἡμεῖς καὶ ὁ λαὸς ἡμῶν ἀναβησόμεθα ἐπὶ τὰς πλησίον κορυφὰς τῶν ὀρέων καὶ παρεμβαλοῦμεν ἐπ' αὐταῖς εἰς προφυλακὴν τοῦ μὴ ἐξελθεῖν ἐκ τῆς πόλεως ἄνδρα ἕνα. 14 καὶ τακή-
σονται ἐν τῷ λιμῷ αὐτοὶ καὶ αἱ γυναῖκες αὐτῶν καὶ τὰ τέκνα
αὐτῶν, καὶ πρὶν ἐλθεῖν τὴν ῥομφαίαν ἐπ' αὐτοὺς καταστρω-
θήσονται ἐν ταῖς πλατείαις τῆς οἰκήσεως αὐτῶν. 15 καὶ
ἀνταποδώσεις αὐτοῖς ἀνταπόδομα πονηρὸν ἀνθ' ὧν ἐστασία-
σαν καὶ οὐκ ἀπήντησαν τῷ προσώπῳ σου ἐν εἰρήνῃ. — 16 καὶ
ἤρεσαν οἱ λόγοι αὐτῶν ἐνώπιον Ολοφέρνου καὶ ἐνώπιον πάντων τῶν θεραπόντων αὐτοῦ, καὶ συνέταξε ποιεῖν καθὰ ἐλάλησαν. 17 καὶ ἀπῆρεν παρεμβολὴ υἱῶν Αμμων καὶ μετ' αὐτῶν
χιλιάδες πέντε υἱῶν Ασσουρ καὶ παρενέβαλον ἐν τῷ αὐλῶνι
καὶ προκατελάβοντο τὰ ὕδατα καὶ τὰς πηγὰς τῶν ὑδάτων
τῶν υἱῶν Ισραηλ. 18 καὶ ἀνέβησαν οἱ υἱοὶ Ησαυ καὶ οἱ υἱοὶ
Αμμων καὶ παρενέβαλον ἐν τῇ ὀρεινῇ ἀπέναντι Δωθαϊμ. καὶ
ἀπέστειλαν ἐξ αὐτῶν πρὸς νότον καὶ ἀπηλιώτην ἀπέναντι
Εγρεβηλ, ἥ ἐστιν πλησίον Χους, ἥ ἐστιν ἐπὶ τοῦ χειμάρρου
Μοχμουρ. καὶ ἡ λοιπὴ στρατιὰ τῶν Ἀσσυρίων παρενέβαλον
ἐν τῷ πεδίῳ καὶ ἐκάλυψαν πᾶν τὸ πρόσωπον τῆς γῆς, καὶ αἱ
σκηναὶ καὶ αἱ ἀπαρτίαι αὐτῶν κατεστρατοπέδευσαν ἐν ὄχλῳ
πολλῷ καὶ ἦσαν εἰς πλῆθος πολὺ σφόδρα.
19 Καὶ οἱ υἱοὶ Ισραηλ ἀνεβόησαν πρὸς κύριον θεὸν αὐτῶν,
ὅτι ὠλιγοψύχησεν τὸ πνεῦμα αὐτῶν, ὅτι ἐκύκλωσαν πάντες
οἱ ἐχθροὶ αὐτῶν καὶ οὐκ ἦν διαφυγεῖν ἐκ μέσου αὐτῶν. 20 καὶ

KING JAMES VERSION

13 For all the inhabitants of Bethulia have their water thence; so shall thirst kill them, and they shall give up their city, and we and our people shall go up to the tops of the mountains that are near, and will camp upon them, to watch that none go out of the city.

14 So they and their wives and their children shall be consumed with famine, and before the sword come against them, they shall be overthrown in the streets where they dwell.

15 Thus shalt thou render them an evil reward; because they rebelled, and met not thy person peaceably.

16 And these words pleased Holofernes and all his servants, and he appointed to do as they had spoken.

17 So the camp of the children of Ammon departed, and with them five thousand of the Assyrians, and they pitched in the valley, and took the waters, and the fountains of the waters of the children of Israel.

18 Then the children of Esau went up with the children of Ammon, and camped in the hill country over against Dothaim: and they sent some of them toward the south, and toward the east, over against Ekrebel, which is near unto Chusi, that is upon the brook Mochmur; and the rest of the army of the Assyrians camped in the plain, and covered the face of the whole land; and their tents and carriages were pitched to a very great multitude.

19 Then the children of Israel cried unto the Lord their God, because their heart failed, for all their enemies had compassed them round about, and there was no way to escape out from among them.

DOUAY OLD TESTAMENT

sword, or at least being wearied out they will yield up their city, which they suppose, because it is situate in the mountains, to be impregnable.

10 And these words pleased Holofernes, and his officers, and he placed all round about a hundred men at every spring.

KNOX TRANSLATION

compass their deaths, and no blood shed, or, worn down at last, they will yield into thy hands the city they think impregnable.

10 This advice commended itself to Holofernes and his lords, and he set a hundred men to guard each of the wells

TODAY'S ENGLISH VERSION

13 because that's where the people of Bethulia come to draw
their water. Then, when they are dying of thirst, they will
surrender their town to you. Meanwhile, we and our men
will go up to the tops of the surrounding mountains, where
we will set up camp and keep anyone from leaving the town.
14 Everyone will starve to death—men, women, and children.
Even before we attack, the streets will be littered with their
corpses. 15 In this way you can make them pay for their
rebellion and for refusing to surrender peacefully to you."

16 Holofernes and his entire staff were pleased with this
suggestion, so he gave orders to put the plan into action.
17 The Moabites and 5,000 Assyrians moved their camp into
the valley to control the source of the town's water. 18 The
Edomites and the Ammonites went up into the mountains
and set up their camp opposite the town of Dothan. They
sent some of their men to the southeast in the direction of
Acraba, near Chusi, which is beside the Mochmur River. The
rest of the Assyrian army set up camp in the valley. Their
camp was spread out over the whole countryside, because
the number of tents and the amount of equipment needed for
such a large army were immense.

19 Then the Israelites cried out to the Lord their God for
help. They had lost their courage, for with the enemy all
around them there was no way to escape. 20 The entire

NEW REVISED STANDARD VERSION

13 for this is where all the people of Bethulia get their water.
So thirst will destroy them, and they will surrender their
town. Meanwhile, we and our people will go up to the tops
of the nearby mountains and camp there to keep watch to
see that no one gets out of the town. 14 They and their wives
and children will waste away with famine, and before the
sword reaches them they will be strewn about in the streets
where they live. 15 Thus you will pay them back with evil,
because they rebelled and did not receive you peaceably."

16 These words pleased Holofernes and all his attendants,
and he gave orders to do as they had said. 17 So the army of
the Ammonites moved forward, together with five thousand
Assyrians, and they encamped in the valley and seized the
water supply and the springs of the Israelites. 18 And the
Edomites and Ammonites went up and encamped in the hill
country opposite Dothan; and they sent some of their men
toward the south and the east, toward Egrebeh, which is
near Chusi beside the Wadi Mochmur. The rest of the
Assyrian army encamped in the plain, and covered the whole
face of the land. Their tents and supply trains spread out in
great number, and they formed a vast multitude.

19 The Israelites then cried out to the Lord their God, for
their courage failed, because all their enemies had surrounded

NEW AMERICAN BIBLE

13 for that is where the inhabitants of Bethulia get their
water. Then thirst will begin to carry them off, and they will
surrender their city. Meanwhile, we and our men will go up
to the summits of the nearby mountains, and encamp there
to guard against anyone's leaving the city. 14 They and their
wives and children will languish with hunger, and even
before the sword strikes them they will be laid low in the
streets of their city. 15 Thus you will render them dire punishment for their rebellion and their refusal to meet you
peacefully."

16 Their words pleased Holofernes and all his ministers,
and he ordered their proposal to be carried out. 17 Thereupon
the Moabites moved camp, together with five thousand
Assyrians. They encamped in the valley, and held the water
supply and the springs of the Israelites. 18 The Edomites and
the Ammonites went up and encamped in the mountain
region opposite Dothan; and they sent some of their men to
the south and to the east opposite Egrebel, near Chusi, which
is on Wadi Mochmur. The rest of the Assyrian army was
encamped in the plain, covering the whole countryside. Their
enormous store of tents and equipment was spread out in
profusion everywhere.

19 The Israelites cried to the LORD, their God, for they were
disheartened, since all their enemies had them surrounded,
and there was no way of slipping through their lines. 20 The

NEW JERUSALEM BIBLE

13 since that is what provides the population of Bethulia with
their water supply. Thirst will then force them to surrender
their town. Meanwhile, we and our men will climb the nearest mountain tops and form advance posts there to prevent
anyone from leaving the town. 14 Hunger will waste them,
with their wives and children, and before the sword can reach
them they will already be lying in the streets outside their
houses. 15 And you will make them pay dearly for their defiance and their refusal to meet you peaceably.'

16 Their words pleased Holofernes as well as all his officers, and he decided to do as they suggested. 17 Accordingly,
a troop of Moabites moved forward with a further five thousand Assyrians. They penetrated the valley and seized the
Israelites' waterpoints and springs. 18 Meanwhile the Edomites and Ammonites went and took up positions in the highlands opposite Dothan, sending some of their men to the
south-east opposite Egrebel near Chous on the Wadi
Mochmur. The rest of the Assyrian army took up positions in
the plain, covering every inch of the ground; their tents and
equipment made an immense encampment, so vast were
their numbers.

19 The Israelites called on the Lord their God, dispirited
because the enemy had surrounded them and cut all line of

GREEK OLD TESTAMENT

ἔμεινεν κύκλῳ αὐτῶν πᾶσα παρεμβολὴ Ασσουρ, οἱ πεζοὶ καὶ
ἅρματα καὶ οἱ ἱππεῖς αὐτῶν, ἡμέρας τριάκοντα τέσσαρας.
καὶ ἐξέλιπεν πάντας τοὺς κατοικοῦντας Βαιτυλουα πάντα
τὰ ἀγγεῖα αὐτῶν τῶν ὑδάτων, 21 καὶ οἱ λάκκοι ἐξεκενοῦντο,
καὶ οὐκ εἶχον πιεῖν εἰς πλησμονὴν ὕδωρ ἡμέραν μίαν, ὅτι ἐν
μέτρῳ ἐδίδοσαν αὐτοῖς πιεῖν. 22 καὶ ἠθύμησεν τὰ νήπια
αὐτῶν, καὶ αἱ γυναῖκες καὶ οἱ νεανίσκοι ἐξέλιπον ἀπὸ τῆς
δίψης καὶ ἔπιπτον ἐν ταῖς πλατείαις τῆς πόλεως καὶ ἐν
ταῖς διόδοις τῶν πυλῶν, καὶ οὐκ ἦν κραταίωσις ἔτι ἐν αὐτοῖς. — 23 καὶ ἐπισυνήχθησαν πᾶς ὁ λαὸς ἐπὶ Οζιαν καὶ
τοὺς ἄρχοντας τῆς πόλεως, οἱ νεανίσκοι καὶ αἱ γυναῖκες καὶ
τὰ παιδία, καὶ ἀνεβόησαν φωνῇ μεγάλῃ καὶ εἶπαν ἐναντίον
πάντων τῶν πρεσβυτέρων 24 Κρίναι ὁ θεὸς ἀνὰ μέσον ὑμῶν
καὶ ἡμῶν, ὅτι ἐποιήσατε ἐν ἡμῖν ἀδικίαν μεγάλην οὐ λα-
λήσαντες εἰρηνικὰ μετὰ υἱῶν Ασσουρ. 25 καὶ νῦν οὐκ ἔστιν ὁ
βοηθὸς ἡμῶν, ἀλλὰ πέπρακεν ἡμᾶς ὁ θεὸς εἰς τὰς χεῖρας
αὐτῶν τοῦ καταστρωθῆναι ἐναντίον αὐτῶν ἐν δίψῃ καὶ ἀπωλείᾳ μεγάλῃ. 26 καὶ νῦν ἐπικαλέσασθε αὐτοὺς καὶ ἔκδοσθε
τὴν πόλιν πᾶσαν εἰς προνομὴν τῷ λαῷ Ολοφέρνου καὶ πάσῃ
τῇ δυνάμει αὐτοῦ. 27 κρεῖσσον γὰρ ἡμῖν γενηθῆναι αὐτοῖς
εἰς διαρπαγήν· ἐσόμεθα γὰρ εἰς δούλους, καὶ ζήσεται ἡ
ψυχὴ ἡμῶν, καὶ οὐκ ὀψόμεθα τὸν θάνατον τῶν νηπίων ἡμῶν
ἐν ὀφθαλμοῖς ἡμῶν καὶ τὰς γυναῖκας καὶ τὰ τέκνα ἡμῶν ἐκ-
λειπούσας τὰς ψυχὰς αὐτῶν. 28 μαρτυρόμεθα ὑμῖν τὸν οὐρανὸν καὶ τὴν γῆν καὶ τὸν θεὸν ἡμῶν καὶ κύριον τῶν πατέρων
ἡμῶν, ὃς ἐκδικεῖ ἡμᾶς κατὰ τὰς ἁμαρτίας ἡμῶν καὶ κατὰ τὰ

KING JAMES VERSION

20 Thus all the company of Assur remained about them, both their footmen, chariots, and horsemen, four and thirty days, so that all their vessels of water failed all the inhabitants of Bethulia.

21 And the cisterns were emptied, and they had not water to drink their fill for one day; for they gave them drink by measure.

22 Therefore their young children were out of heart, and their women and young men fainted for thirst, and fell down in the streets of the city, and by the passages of the gates, and there was no longer any strength in them.

23 Then all the people assembled to Ozias, and to the chief of the city, both young men, and women, and children, and cried with a loud voice, and said before all the elders,

24 God be judge between us and you: for ye have done us great injury, in that ye have not required peace of the children of Assur.

25 For now we have no helper: but God hath sold us into their hands, that we should be thrown down before them with thirst and great destruction.

26 Now therefore call them unto you, and deliver the whole city for a spoil to the people of Holofernes, and to all his army.

27 For it is better for us to be made a spoil unto them, than to die for thirst: for we will be his servants, that our souls may live, and not see the death of our infants before our eyes, nor our wives nor our children to die.

28 We take to witness against you the heaven and the earth, and our God and Lord of our fathers, which punisheth

DOUAY OLD TESTAMENT

11 And when they had kept this watch for full twenty days, the cisterns, and the reserve of waters failed among all the inhabitants of Bethulia, so that there was not within the city, enough to satisfy them, no not for one day, for water was daily given out to the people by measure.

12 Then all the men and women, young men, and children, gathering themselves together to Ozias, all together with one voice,

13 Said: God be judge between us and thee, for thou hast done evil against us, in that thou wouldst not speak peaceably with the Assyrians, and for this cause God hath sold us into their hands.

14 And therefore there is no one to help us, while we are cast down before their eyes in thirst, and sad destruction.

15 And now assemble ye all that are in the city, that we may of our own accord yield ourselves all up to the people of Holofernes.

16 For it is better, that being captives we should live and bless the Lord, than that we should die, and be a reproach to all flesh, after we have seen our wives and our infants die before our eyes.

17 We call to witness this day heaven and earth, and the God of our fathers, who taketh vengeance upon us according to

KNOX TRANSLATION

all about. 11 When this watch had been kept for twenty days
together, the people of Bethulia had no water left in tank or
cistern, not a full supply for one day; for now a daily
allowance was made to each. 12 Thereupon all of them, husbands and wives, young men and children, gathered about
Ozias, all uttering a single cry of complaint. 13 God give
judgement, they said, between us and thee; an ill turn thou
hast done us, in refusing to come to terms with the
Assyrians. Now God has given them the mastery over us;
14 none brings aid; we lie at their mercy, cruelly undone by
thirst. 15 Come, muster all the citizens, and let us all surrender at discretion to the army of Holofernes. 16 Better we
should be prisoners, still thanking the Lord for our lives
spared, than ourselves be slaughtered, first winning the
whole world's reproaches by letting our wives and little ones
be slaughtered before our very eyes. 17 We adjure you by
heaven and earth, and by the God of our fathers, who now
takes such vengeance on us for our sins, to surrender the

TODAY'S ENGLISH VERSION

Assyrian army—infantry, chariots, and cavalry—blockaded
Bethulia for thirty-four days until the town ran out of water.
21 All the reservoirs and cisterns went dry, so that the drinking water had to be rationed, and not a day passed when
there was enough water to go around. 22 Children were
becoming weak; everywhere throughout the town women
and young people were collapsing. No one had any strength
left.

23 All the people of the town—men, women, and children
alike—gathered around Uzziah and the town officials and
shouted in protest, 24 "God will punish you for what you
have done to us! You are to blame for what is happening,
because you did not make peace with the Assyrians. 25 There
is no one to help us now! God has put us in their power. We
are exhausted and dying of thirst. 26 Call the Assyrians now
and surrender to them, and let Holofernes and his army take
the town and loot it. 27 We are better off as prisoners of war.
They will make us slaves, but at least we will be alive, and
we won't have to watch our wives and children dying before
our eyes. 28 Heaven and earth are witnesses against you, and
so is our God, the Lord of our ancestors, who is punishing us

NEW REVISED STANDARD VERSION

them, and there was no way of escape from them. 20 The
whole Assyrian army, their infantry, chariots, and cavalry,
surrounded them for thirty-four days, until all the water con-
tainers of every inhabitant of Bethulia were empty; 21 their
cisterns were going dry, and on no day did they have enough
water to drink, for their drinking water was rationed. 22 Their
children were listless, and the women and young men fainted
from thirst and were collapsing in the streets of the town and
in the gateways; they no longer had any strength.

23 Then all the people, the young men, the women, and
the children, gathered around Uzziah and the rulers of the
town and cried out with a loud voice, and said before all the
elders, 24 "Let God judge between you and us! You have
done us a great injury in not making peace with the Assyrians. 25 For now we have no one to help us; God has sold us
into their hands, to be strewn before them in thirst and
exhaustion. 26 Now summon them and surrender the whole
town as booty to the army of Holofernes and to all his forces.
27 For it would be better for us to be captured by them.[a] We
shall indeed become slaves, but our lives will be spared, and
we shall not witness our little ones dying before our eyes,
and our wives and children drawing their last breath. 28 We
call to witness against you heaven and earth and our God,
the Lord of our ancestors, who punishes us for our sins and

a Other ancient authorities add *than to die of thirst*

NEW AMERICAN BIBLE

whole Assyrian camp, infantry, chariots, and cavalry, kept
them thus surrounded for thirty-four days. All the reservoirs
of water failed the inhabitants of Bethulia, 21 and the cisterns ran dry, so that on no day did they have enough to
drink, but their drinking water was rationed. 22 Their children fainted away, and the women and youths were consumed with thirst and were collapsing in the streets and
gateways of the city, with no strength left in them.

23 All the people, therefore, including youths, women, and
children, went in a crowd to Uzziah and the rulers of the
city. They set up a great clamor and said before the elders:
24 "God judge between you and us! You have done us grave
injustice in not making peace with the Assyrians. 25 There is
no help for us now! Instead, God has sold us into their
power by laying us prostrate before them in thirst and utter
exhaustion. 26 Therefore, summon them and deliver the
whole city as booty to the troops of Holofernes and to all his
forces; 27 we would be better off to become their prey. We
should indeed be made slaves, but at least should live, and
not have to behold our little ones dying before our eyes and
our wives and children breathing out their souls. 28 We
adjure you by heaven and earth, and by our God, the LORD of
our forefathers, who is punishing us for our sins and those

NEW JERUSALEM BIBLE

retreat. 20 For thirty-four days the Assyrian army, infantry,
chariots, cavalrymen, had them surrounded. Every water-jar
the inhabitants of Bethulia had was empty, 21 their storage-
wells were drying up; on no day could a man drink his fill,
since their water was rationed. 22 Their little children pined
away, the women and young men grew weak with thirst;
they collapsed in the streets and gateways of the town; they
had no strength left.

23 Young men, women, children, the whole people
thronged clamouring round Uzziah and the chief men of the
town, shouting in the presence of the assembled elders,
24 'May God be judge between you and us! For you have
done us great harm, by not suing for peace with the
Assyrians. 25 And now there is no one to help us. God has
delivered us into their hands to be prostrated before them in
thirst and utter helplessness. 26 Call them in at once; hand
the whole town over to be sacked by Holofernes' men and all
his army. 27 After all, we should be much better off as their
booty than we are now; no doubt we shall be enslaved, but
at least we shall be alive and not see our little ones dying
before our eyes or our wives and children perishing. 28 By
heaven and earth and by our God, the Lord of our fathers,

GREEK OLD TESTAMENT

ἁμαρτήματα τῶν πατέρων ἡμῶν, ἵνα μὴ ποιήσῃ κατὰ τὰ ῥήματα ταῦτα ἐν τῇ ἡμέρᾳ τῇ σήμερον. [29] καὶ ἐγένετο κλαυθμὸς μέγας ἐν μέσῳ τῆς ἐκκλησίας πάντων ὁμοθυμαδόν, καὶ ἐβόησαν πρὸς κύριον τὸν θεὸν φωνῇ μεγάλῃ. — [30] καὶ εἶπεν πρὸς αὐτοὺς Οζιας Θαρσεῖτε, ἀδελφοί, διακαρτερήσωμεν ἔτι πέντε ἡμέρας, ἐν αἷς ἐπιστρέψει κύριος ὁ θεὸς ἡμῶν τὸ ἔλεος αὐτοῦ ἐφ' ἡμᾶς, οὐ γὰρ ἐγκαταλείψει ἡμᾶς εἰς τέλος. [31] ἐὰν δὲ διέλθωσιν αὗται καὶ μὴ ἔλθῃ ἐφ' ἡμᾶς βοήθεια, ποιήσω κατὰ τὰ ῥήματα ὑμῶν. [32] καὶ ἐσκόρπισεν τὸν λαὸν εἰς τὴν ἑαυτοῦ παρεμβολήν, καὶ ἐπὶ τὰ τείχη καὶ τοὺς πύργους τῆς πόλεως αὐτῶν ἀπῆλθον καὶ τὰς γυναῖκας καὶ τὰ τέκνα εἰς τοὺς οἴκους αὐτῶν ἀπέστειλαν· καὶ ἦσαν ἐν ταπεινώσει πολλῇ ἐν τῇ πόλει.

8 Καὶ ἤκουσεν ἐν ἐκείναις ταῖς ἡμέραις Ιουδιθ θυγάτηρ Μεραρι υἱοῦ Ωξ υἱοῦ Ιωσηφ υἱοῦ Οζιηλ υἱοῦ Ελκια υἱοῦ Ανανιου υἱοῦ Γεδεων υἱοῦ Ραφαϊν υἱοῦ Αχιτωβ υἱοῦ Ηλιου υἱοῦ Χελκιου υἱοῦ Ελιαβ υἱοῦ Ναθαναηλ υἱοῦ Σαλαμιηλ υἱοῦ

KING JAMES VERSION

us according to our sins and the sins of our fathers, that he do not according as we have said this day.

29 Then there was great weeping with one consent in the midst of the assembly; and they cried unto the Lord God with a loud voice.

30 Then said Ozias to them, Brethren, be of good courage, let us yet endure five days, in the which space the Lord our God may turn his mercy toward us; for he will not forsake us utterly.

31 And if these days pass, and there come no help unto us, I will do according to your word.

32 And he dispersed the people, every one to their own charge; and they went unto the walls and towers of their city, and sent the women and children into their houses: and they were very low brought in the city.

8 Now at that time Judith heard thereof, which was the daughter of Merari, the son of Ox, the son of Joseph, the son of Oziel, the son of Elcia, the son of Ananias, the son of Gedeon, the son of Raphaim, the son of Acitho, the son of Eliu, the son of Eliab, the son of Nathanael, the son of Samael, the son of Salasadai, the son of Israel.

DOUAY OLD TESTAMENT

our sins, conjuring you to deliver now the city into the hand of the army of Holofernes, that our end may be short by the edge of the sword, which is made longer by the drought of thirst.

18 And when they had said these things, there was great weeping and lamentation of all in the assembly, and for many hours with one voice they cried to God, saying:

19 We have sinned with our fathers, we have done unjustly, we have committed iniquity:

20 Have thou mercy on us, because thou art good, or punish our iniquities by chastising us thyself, and deliver not them that trust in thee to a people that knoweth not thee,

21 That they may not say among the Gentiles: Where is their God?

22 And when being wearied with these cries, and tired with these weepings, they held their peace,

23 Ozias rising up all in tears, said: Be of good courage, my brethren, and let us wait these five days for mercy from the Lord.

24 For perhaps he will put a stop to his indignation, and will give glory to his own name.

25 But if after five days be past there come no aid, we will do the things which you have spoken.

8 NOW it came to pass, when Judith a widow had heard these words, who was the daughter of Merari, the son of Idox, the son of Joseph, the son of Ozias, the son of Elai, the son of Jamnor, the son of Gedeon, the son of Raphaim, the son of Achitob, the son of Melchias, the son of Enan, the son of Nathanias, the son of Salathiel, the son of Simeon, the son of Ruben:

KNOX TRANSLATION

town to Holofernes' army. If we must die, let it be a swift death at the sword's point, not a lingering death from this parching thirst.
[18] All this was said, and with that the whole throng fell to weeping and lamenting bitterly; and for many hours together they cried out to God as with a single voice: [19] We have
taken part in our fathers' sins; we are guilty men, rebels against thee. [20] Do thou, in thy great love, take pity on us; or
if punished we must be, let it be under thy own rod; do not abandon us, that still acknowledge thy name, to the mercy of men who never knew thee! [21] Wouldst thou have the heathen asking, What has become of their God? [22] At last they
grew weary of their clamour; they had wept enough; and when silence was restored, [23] Ozias rose from his place,
bathed in tears, and spoke to them. Brethren, said he, be calm and patient. These five next days, let us still look to the Lord for deliverance; [24] perhaps his anger will relent, perhaps he means to win himself fresh renown. [25] If at the end
of those five days no help has reached us, rest assured we will act on the counsel you have given.

8 Now turn we to one whom all this news concerned; a widow called Judith, that was descended (from Ruben)[a] through Merari, Idox, Joseph, Ozias, Elai, Jamnor, Gedeon, Raphaim, Achitob, Melchias, Enrac, Nathanias, Salathiel and

a 'Son of Ruben' can hardly be taken literally, unless the names are deliberately fictitious. The phrase does not appear in the Septuagint Greek, which differs here in several other features.

TODAY'S ENGLISH VERSION

for their sins as well as ours. We can only hope and pray that
he will not let these terrible things happen to us today."[a]
29 Everyone there began to weep loudly and to pray to the
Lord their God. 30 Then Uzziah said to them, "Don't give up,
my friends! Let's wait five more days to see if the Lord our
God will be merciful to us. Surely he will not abandon us
completely. 31 But if no help comes after five days, then I
will do as you say." 32 So Uzziah dismissed the people. All
the men returned to their guard posts on the walls and towers, while the women and children went back to their homes.
The morale of the entire town was very low.

8 At that time, Judith heard about Uzziah's decision. She
was the daughter of Merari, the granddaughter of Ox
and the great-granddaughter of Joseph. Joseph's ancestors
were Oziel, Elkiah, Ananias, Gideon, Raphaim, Ahitub,
Elijah, Hilkiah, Eliab, Nathanael, Salamiel, Sarasadai, and

[a] We can . . . today; *some Greek manuscripts and ancient translations have* We demand that you surrender, as we have asked you to do today.

NEW REVISED STANDARD VERSION

the sins of our ancestors; do today the things that we have
described!"
29 Then great and general lamentation arose throughout
the assembly, and they cried out to the Lord God with a loud
voice. 30 But Uzziah said to them, "Courage, my brothers and
sisters![a] Let us hold out for five days more; by that time the
Lord our God will turn his mercy to us again, for he will not
forsake us utterly. 31 But if these days pass by, and no help
comes for us, I will do as you say."
32 Then he dismissed the people to their various posts,
and they went up on the walls and towers of their town. The
women and children he sent home. In the town they were in
great misery.

8 Now in those days Judith heard about these things: she
was the daughter of Merari son of Ox son of Joseph son
of Oziel son of Elkiah son of Ananias son of Gideon son of
Raphain son of Ahitub son of Elijah son of Hilkiah son of
Eliab son of Nathanael son of Salamiel son of Sarasadai son

[a] Gk *Courage, brothers*

NEW AMERICAN BIBLE

of our forefathers, to do as we have proposed, this very day."
29 All in the assembly with one accord broke into shrill
wailing and loud cries to the LORD their God. 30 But Uzziah
said to them, "Courage, my brothers! Let us wait five days
more for the LORD our God, to show his mercy toward us; he
will not utterly forsake us. 31 But if those days pass without
help coming to us, I will do as you say." 32 Then he dispersed the men to their posts, and they returned to the walls
and towers of the city; the women and children he sent to
their homes. Throughout the city they were in great misery.

8 Now in those days Judith, daughter of Merari, son of
Joseph, son of Oziel, son of Elkiah, son of Ananias, son
of Gideon, son of Raphain, son of Ahitob, son of Elijah, son
of Hilkiah, son of Eliab, son of Nathanael, son of Salamiel,
son of Sarasadai, son of Simeon, son of Israel, heard of this.
2 Her husband, Manasseh, of her own tribe and clan, had

NEW JERUSALEM BIBLE

who is punishing us for our sins and the sins of our ancestors, we implore you to take this course now, today.'
29 Bitter lamentations rose from the whole assembly, and
they all cried loudly to the Lord God.
30 Then Uzziah spoke to them, 'Take heart, brothers! Let us
hold out five days more. By then the Lord our God will take
pity on us, for he will not desert us altogether. 31 At the end
of this time, if no help is forthcoming, I shall do as you have
said.' 32 With that he dismissed the people to their various
quarters. The men went to man the walls and towers of the
town, sending the women and children home. The town was
full of despondency.

8 Judith was informed at the time of what had happened.
She was the daughter of Merari son of Ox, son of Joseph,
son of Oziel, son of Elkiah, son of Ananias, son of Gideon,
son of Raphaim, son of Ahitub, son of Elijah, son of Hilkiah,
son of Eliab, son of Nathanael, son of Salamiel, son of

GREEK OLD TESTAMENT

Σαρασαδαι υἱοῦ Ισραηλ. 2 καὶ ὁ ἀνὴρ αὐτῆς Μανασσης τῆς
φυλῆς αὐτῆς καὶ τῆς πατριᾶς αὐτῆς. καὶ ἀπέθανεν ἐν
ἡμέραις θερισμοῦ κριθῶν· 3 ἐπέστη γὰρ ἐπὶ τοὺς δεσμεύον-
τας τὰ δράγματα ἐν τῷ πεδίῳ, καὶ ὁ καύσων ἦλθεν ἐπὶ τὴν
κεφαλὴν αὐτοῦ, καὶ ἔπεσεν ἐπὶ τὴν κλίνην αὐτοῦ καὶ ἐτελεύτησεν ἐν Βαιτυλουα τῇ πόλει αὐτοῦ, καὶ ἔθαψαν αὐτὸν μετὰ
τῶν πατέρων αὐτοῦ ἐν τῷ ἀγρῷ τῷ ἀνὰ μέσον Δωθαϊμ καὶ
Βαλαμων. 4 καὶ ἦν Ιουδιθ ἐν τῷ οἴκῳ αὐτῆς χηρεύουσα ἔτη
τρία καὶ μῆνας τέσσαρας. 5 καὶ ἐποίησεν ἑαυτῇ σκηνὴν ἐπὶ
τοῦ δώματος τοῦ οἴκου αὐτῆς καὶ ἐπέθηκεν ἐπὶ τὴν ὀσφὺν
αὐτῆς σάκκον, καὶ ἦν ἐπ' αὐτῆς τὰ ἱμάτια τῆς χηρεύσεως
αὐτῆς. 6 καὶ ἐνήστευε πάσας τὰς ἡμέρας τῆς χηρεύσεως
αὐτῆς χωρὶς προσαββάτων καὶ σαββάτων καὶ προνουμηνιῶν
καὶ νουμηνιῶν καὶ ἑορτῶν καὶ χαρμοσυνῶν οἴκου Ισραηλ.
7 καὶ ἦν καλὴ τῷ εἴδει καὶ ὡραία τῇ ὄψει σφόδρα· καὶ
ὑπελίπετο αὐτῇ Μανασσης ὁ ἀνὴρ αὐτῆς χρυσίον καὶ ἀργύριον καὶ παῖδας καὶ παιδίσκας καὶ κτήνη καὶ ἀγρούς, καὶ
ἔμενεν ἐπ' αὐτῶν. 8 καὶ οὐκ ἦν ὃς ἐπήνεγκεν αὐτῇ ῥῆμα
πονηρόν, ὅτι ἐφοβεῖτο τὸν θεὸν σφόδρα. — 9 καὶ ἤκουσεν τὰ
ῥήματα τοῦ λαοῦ τὰ πονηρὰ ἐπὶ τὸν ἄρχοντα, ὅτι ὠλιγοψύ-
χησαν ἐν τῇ σπάνει τῶν ὑδάτων, καὶ ἤκουσεν πάντας τοὺς
λόγους Ιουδιθ, οὓς ἐλάλησεν πρὸς αὐτοὺς Οζιας, ὡς ὤμοσεν
αὐτοῖς παραδώσειν τὴν πόλιν μετὰ ἡμέρας πέντε τοῖς
Ἀσσυρίοις. 10 καὶ ἀποστείλασα τὴν ἅβραν αὐτῆς τὴν
ἐφεστῶσαν πᾶσιν τοῖς ὑπάρχουσιν αὐτῆς ἐκάλεσεν Χαβριν
καὶ Χαρμιν τοὺς πρεσβυτέρους τῆς πόλεως αὐτῆς, 11 καὶ

KING JAMES VERSION

2 And Manasses was her husband, of her tribe and kindred, who died in the barley harvest.

3 For as he stood overseeing them that bound sheaves in the field, the heat came upon his head, and he fell on his bed, and died in the city of Bethulia: and they buried him with his fathers in the field between Dothaim and Balamo.

4 So Judith was a widow in her house three years and four months.

5 And she made her a tent upon the top of her house, and put on sackcloth upon her loins, and ware her widow's apparel.

6 And she fasted all the days of her widowhood, save the eves of the sabbaths, and the sabbaths, and the eves of the new moons, and the new moons, and the feasts and solemn days of the house of Israel.

7 She was also of a goodly countenance, and very beautiful to behold: and her husband Manasses had left her gold, and silver, and menservants, and maidservants, and cattle, and lands; and she remained upon them.

8 And there was none that gave her an ill word; for she feared God greatly.

9 Now when she heard the evil words of the people against the governor, that they fainted for lack of water; for Judith had heard all the words that Ozias had spoken unto them, and that he had sworn to deliver the city unto the Assyrians after five days;

10 Then she sent her waitingwoman, that had the government of all things that she had, to call Ozias and Chabris and Charmis, the ancients of the city.

DOUAY OLD TESTAMENT

2 And her husband was Manasses, who died in the time of the barley harvest:

3 For he was standing over them that bound sheaves in the field; and the heat came upon his head, and he died in Bethulia his own city, and was buried there with his fathers.

4 And Judith his relict was a widow now three years and six months.

5 And she made herself a private chamber in the upper part of her house, in which she abode shut up with her maids.

6 And she wore haircloth upon her loins, and fasted all the days of her life, except the sabbaths, and new moons, and the feasts of the house of Israel.

7 And she was exceedingly beautiful, and her husband left her great riches, and very many servants, and large possessions of herds of oxen, and flocks of sheep.

8 And she was greatly renowned among all, because she feared the Lord very much, neither was there any one that spoke an ill word of her.

9 When therefore she had heard that Ozias had promised that he would deliver up the city after the fifth day, she sent to the ancients Chabri and Charmi.

KNOX TRANSLATION

Simeon. 2 She had been married to one Manasses, but lost
him when the barley was a-reaping; 3 he must needs be hurrying his men on as they bound the sheaves on his farm,
while the sun beat fierce on his head, and of that stroke he
died, and was laid to rest with his fathers, there in his native
town of Bethulia. 4 Judith had now been left a widow these
three years and six months past; 5 ever she dwelt cloistered
among her maid-servants, in a secret bower she had made
for herself on the roof of her house, 6 wearing sackcloth
about her waist and keeping fast continually, save on the
sabbath and the new moon and what other holidays were
observed in Israel. 7 She was a woman very fair to see, and
her husband had left her great wealth, a full household, and
lands well stocked with cattle and sheep; 8 a woman of high
repute everywhere, and the Lord's devout worshipper; no
man had a word to say in her dispraise.
9 This Judith, then, when she heard how Ozias had promised to surrender the city in five days' time, would have two
of the elders, Chabri and Charmi, pay her a visit.[a] 10 And

[a] The Greek text says she sent for Ozias as well (cf. verses 28 and 34).

TODAY'S ENGLISH VERSION

Israel. 2 Judith's husband Manasseh, who belonged to the same tribe and clan, had died during the barley harvest. 3 He had suffered a sunstroke while in the fields supervising the farm workers and later died in bed at home in Bethulia. He was buried in the family tomb in the field between Dothan and Balamon.

4 For three years and four months, Judith had lived as a widow. 5 In her grief she built a little shelter on the roof of her house and lived there, wearing sackcloth. 6 She fasted during that entire period except when fasting was forbidden: the day before the Sabbath and the Sabbath itself, the eve of the New Moon Festival and the Festival itself, and all the festivals and holidays observed by the people of Israel. 7 Judith was a very beautiful woman. Her husband had left her gold and silver, servants and slaves, livestock and fields. She continued to supervise the estate, 8 and no one ever said anything bad about Judith. She was a very religious woman.

9 Judith heard how the people were complaining bitterly against Uzziah, now that the water shortage had broken their morale. She learned that in answer to their complaints he had promised to surrender the town to the Assyrians after five days. 10 Judith sent a slave, the woman who managed her business affairs, to invite Uzziah,[a] Chabris, and Charmis, the town officials, to her home.

[a] Uzziah; *some Greek manuscripts do not have this word.*

NEW REVISED STANDARD VERSION

of Israel. 2 Her husband Manasseh, who belonged to her tribe and family, had died during the barley harvest. 3 For as he stood overseeing those who were binding sheaves in the field, he was overcome by the burning heat, and took to his bed and died in his town Bethulia. So they buried him with his ancestors in the field between Dothan and Balamon. 4 Judith remained as a widow for three years and four months 5 at home where she set up a tent for herself on the roof of her house. She put sackcloth around her waist and dressed in widow's clothing. 6 She fasted all the days of her widowhood, except the day before the sabbath and the sabbath itself, the day before the new moon and the day of the new moon, and the festivals and days of rejoicing of the house of Israel. 7 She was beautiful in appearance, and was very lovely to behold. Her husband Manasseh had left her gold and silver, men and women slaves, livestock, and fields; and she maintained this estate. 8 No one spoke ill of her, for she feared God with great devotion.

9 When Judith heard the harsh words spoken by the people against the ruler, because they were faint for lack of water, and when she heard all that Uzziah said to them, and how he promised them under oath to surrender the town to the Assyrians after five days, 10 she sent her maid, who was in charge of all she possessed, to summon Uzziah and[a] Chabris and Charmis, the elders of her town. 11 They came to her, and she said to them:

a Other ancient authorities lack *Uzziah and* (see verses 28 and 35)

NEW AMERICAN BIBLE

died at the time of the barley harvest. 3 While he was in the field supervising those who bound the sheaves, he suffered sunstroke; and he died of this illness in Bethulia, his native city. He was buried with his forefathers in the field between Dothan and Balamon. 4 The widowed Judith remained three years and four months at home, 5 where she set up a tent for herself on the roof of her house. She put sackcloth about her loins and wore widow's weeds. 6 She fasted all the days of her widowhood, except sabbath eves and sabbaths, new moon eves and new moons, feastdays and holidays of the house of Israel. 7 She was beautifully formed and lovely to behold. Her husband, Manasseh, had left her gold and silver, servants and maids, livestock and fields, which she was maintaining. 8 No one had a bad word to say about her, for she was a very God-fearing woman. 9 When Judith, therefore, heard of the harsh words which the people, discouraged by their lack of water, had spoken against their ruler, and of all that Uzziah had said to them in reply, swearing that he would hand over the city to the Assyrians at the end of five days, 10 she sent the maid who was in charge of all her things to ask Uzziah, Chabris, and Charmis, the elders of the city, to visit her. 11 When they came, she said to them: "Listen to me, you rulers of the people of Bethulia. What you

NEW JERUSALEM BIBLE

Sarasadai, son of Israel. 2 Her husband Manasseh, of her own tribe and family, had died at the time of the barley harvest. 3 He was supervising the men as they bound up the sheaves in the field when he caught sunstroke and had to take to his bed. He died in Bethulia, his home town, and was buried with his ancestors in the field that lies between Dothan and Balamon. 4 As a widow, Judith stayed inside her home for three years and four months. 5 She had had an upper room built for herself on the roof. She wore sackcloth next to the skin and dressed in widow's weeds. 6 She fasted every day of her widowhood except for the Sabbath eve, the Sabbath itself, the eve of New Moon, the feast of New Moon and the joyful festivals of the House of Israel. 7 Now she was very beautiful, charming to see. Her husband Manasseh had left her gold and silver, menservants and maidservants, herds and land; and she lived among all her possessions 8 without anyone finding a word to say against her, so devoutly did she fear God.

9 Hearing how the water shortage had demoralised the people and how they had complained bitterly to the headman of the town, and being also told what Uzziah had said to them and how he had given them his oath to surrender the town to the Assyrians in five days' time, 10 Judith immediately sent the serving-woman who ran her household to summon Chabris and Charmis, two elders of the town. 11 When these came in she said:

GREEK OLD TESTAMENT

ἦλθον πρὸς αὐτήν, καὶ εἶπεν πρὸς αὐτούς Ἀκούσατε δή μου,
ἄρχοντες τῶν κατοικούντων ἐν Βαιτυλουα· ὅτι οὐκ εὐθὴς ὁ
λόγος ὑμῶν, ὃν ἐλαλήσατε ἐναντίον τοῦ λαοῦ ἐν τῇ ἡμέρᾳ
ταύτῃ καὶ ἐστήσατε τὸν ὅρκον τοῦτον, ὃν ἐλαλήσατε ἀνὰ
μέσον τοῦ θεοῦ καὶ ὑμῶν καὶ εἴπατε ἐκδώσειν τὴν πόλιν τοῖς
ἐχθροῖς ἡμῶν, ἐὰν μὴ ἐν αὐταῖς ἐπιστρέψῃ κύριος βοήθειαν
ὑμῖν. 12 καὶ νῦν τίνες ἐστὲ ὑμεῖς, οἳ ἐπειράσατε τὸν θεὸν ἐν
τῇ ἡμέρᾳ τῇ σήμερον καὶ ἵστατε ὑπὲρ τοῦ θεοῦ ἐν μέσῳ υἱῶν
ἀνθρώπων; 13 καὶ νῦν κύριον παντοκράτορα ἐξετάζετε καὶ
οὐθὲν ἐπιγνώσεσθε ἕως τοῦ αἰῶνος. 14 ὅτι βάθος καρδίας ἀνθρώπου οὐχ εὑρήσετε καὶ λόγους τῆς διανοίας αὐτοῦ οὐ
διαλήμψεσθε· καὶ πῶς τὸν θεόν, ὃς ἐποίησεν πάντα ταῦτα,
ἐρευνήσετε καὶ τὸν νοῦν αὐτοῦ ἐπιγνώσεσθε καὶ τὸν λογισμὸν αὐτοῦ κατανοήσετε; μηδαμῶς, ἀδελφοί, μὴ παροργ-
ίζετε κύριον τὸν θεὸν ἡμῶν. 15 ὅτι ἐὰν μὴ βούληται ἐν ταῖς
πέντε ἡμέραις βοηθῆσαι ἡμῖν, αὐτὸς ἔχει τὴν ἐξουσίαν ἐν
αἷς θέλει σκεπάσαι ἡμέραις ἢ καὶ ὀλεθρεῦσαι ἡμᾶς πρὸ
προσώπου τῶν ἐχθρῶν ἡμῶν. 16 ὑμεῖς δὲ μὴ ἐνεχυράζετε
τὰς βουλὰς κυρίου τοῦ θεοῦ ἡμῶν, ὅτι οὐχ ὡς ἄνθρωπος ὁ
θεὸς ἀπειληθῆναι οὐδ᾽ ὡς υἱὸς ἀνθρώπου διαιτηθῆναι.
17 διόπερ ἀναμένοντες τὴν παρ᾽ αὐτοῦ σωτηρίαν ἐπικαλε-
σώμεθα αὐτὸν εἰς βοήθειαν ἡμῶν, καὶ εἰσακούσεται τῆς
φωνῆς ἡμῶν, ἐὰν ᾖ αὐτῷ ἀρεστόν. 18 ὅτι οὐκ ἀνέστη ἐν ταῖς
γενεαῖς ἡμῶν οὐδέ ἐστιν ἐν τῇ ἡμέρᾳ τῇ σήμερον οὔτε φυλὴ
οὔτε πατριὰ οὔτε δῆμος οὔτε πόλις ἐξ ἡμῶν, οἳ προσκυνοῦσι
θεοῖς χειροποιήτοις, καθάπερ ἐγένετο ἐν ταῖς πρότερον

KING JAMES VERSION

11 And they came unto her, and she said unto them, Hear me now, O ye governors of the inhabitants of Bethulia: for your words that ye have spoken before the people this day are not right, touching this oath which ye made and pronounced between God and you, and have promised to deliver the city to our enemies, unless within these days the Lord turn to help you.

12 And now who are ye that have tempted God this day, and stand instead of God among the children of men?

13 And now try the Lord Almighty, but ye shall never know any thing.

14 For ye cannot find the depth of the heart of man, neither can ye perceive the things that he thinketh: then how can ye search out God, that hath made all these things, and know his mind, or comprehend his purpose? Nay, my brethren, provoke not the Lord our God to anger.

15 For if he will not help us within these five days, he hath power to defend us when he will, even every day, or to destroy us before our enemies.

16 Do not bind the counsels of the Lord our God: for God is not as man, that he may be threatened; neither is he as the son of man, that he should be wavering.

17 Therefore let us wait for salvation of him, and call upon him to help us, and he will hear our voice, if it please him.

18 For there arose none in our age, neither is there any now in these days, neither tribe, nor family, nor people, nor city, among us, which worship gods made with hands, as hath been aforetime.

DOUAY OLD TESTAMENT

10 And they came to her, and she said to them: What is this word, by which Ozias hath consented to give up the city to the Assyrians, if within five days there come no aid to us?

11 And who are you that tempt the Lord?

12 This is not a word that may draw down mercy, but rather that may stir up wrath, and enkindle indignation.

13 You have set a time for the mercy of the Lord, and you have appointed him a day, according to your pleasure.

14 But forasmuch as the Lord is patient, let us be penitent for this same thing, and with many tears let us beg his pardon:

15 For God will not threaten like man, nor be inflamed to anger like the son of man.

16 And therefore let us humble our souls before him, and continuing in an humble spirit, in his service:

17 Let us ask the Lord with tears, that according to his will so he would shew his mercy to us: that as our heart is troubled by their pride, so also we may glorify in our humility.

18 For we have not followed the sins of our fathers, who forsook their God, and worshipped strange gods.

KNOX TRANSLATION

thus she greeted them, Is it true Ozias has promised he will
hand the city over to the Assyrians, if in five days no rescue
comes to you? 11 By what right, sirs, do you put the Lord's
goodness to such a test? 12 This is no way to win it; rather,
we shall earn his displeasure, add fuel to his vengeance.
13 What, would you set a date to the Lord's mercies, bid him
keep tryst with you on a day of your own appointing?
14 Well for us that he, at least, is patient; repent we, and
with flowing tears ask his pardon! 15 He will not overwhelm
us with reproaches, as men do; not his the human anger
that bursts into flame. 16 Abate we our pride, and wait on
him with chastened spirits; 17 entreat him with tears to
grant us relief at a time of his own choosing. Then shall we,
who stand aghast now at the pride of our enemies, triumph
in the reward of our humility. 18 It is something that we
have not followed the evil example of our forefathers, who
forsook their own God and worshipped alien gods instead,

Today's English Version

11 When the officials arrived, Judith said to them, "Please listen to me. You are the leaders of the people of Bethulia, but you were wrong to speak to the people as you did today. You should not have made a solemn promise before God that you would surrender the town to our enemies if the Lord did not come to our aid within a few days. 12 What right do you have to put God to the test as you have done today? Who are you to put yourselves in God's place in dealing with human affairs? 13 It is the Lord Almighty that you are putting to the test! Will you never learn? 14 There is no way that you can understand what is in the depths of a human heart or find out what a person is thinking. Yet you dare to read God's mind and interpret his thoughts! How can you claim to understand God, the Creator? No, my friends, you must stop arousing the anger of the Lord our God! 15 If he decides not to come to our aid within five days, he still may rescue us at any time he chooses. Or he may let our enemies destroy us. 16 But you must not lay down conditions for the Lord our God! Do you think that he is like one of us? Do you think you can bargain with him or force him to make a decision? 17 No! Instead, we should ask God for his help and wait patiently for him to rescue us. If he wants to, he will answer our cry for help. 18 We do not worship gods made with human hands. Not one of our clans, tribes, towns, or cities has ever done that, even though our ancestors used to do so.

New Revised Standard Version

"Listen to me, rulers of the people of Bethulia! What you have said to the people today is not right; you have even sworn and pronounced this oath between God and you, promising to surrender the town to our enemies unless the Lord turns and helps us within so many days. 12 Who are you to put God to the test today, and to set yourselves up in the place of[a] God in human affairs? 13 You are putting the Lord Almighty to the test, but you will never learn anything! 14 You cannot plumb the depths of the human heart or understand the workings of the human mind; how do you expect to search out God, who made all these things, and find out his mind or comprehend his thought? No, my brothers, do not anger the Lord our God. 15 For if he does not choose to help us within these five days, he has power to protect us within any time he pleases, or even to destroy us in the presence of our enemies. 16 Do not try to bind the purposes of the Lord our God; for God is not like a human being, to be threatened, or like a mere mortal, to be won over by pleading. 17 Therefore, while we wait for his deliverance, let us call upon him to help us, and he will hear our voice, if it pleases him.

18 "For never in our generation, nor in these present days, has there been any tribe or family or people or town of ours that worships gods made with hands, as was done in

a Or *above*

New American Bible

said to the people today is not proper. When you promised to hand over the city to our enemies at the end of five days unless within that time the LORD comes to our aid, you interposed between God and yourselves this oath which you took. 12 Who are you, then, that you should have put God to the test this day, setting yourselves in the place of God in human affairs? 13 It is the LORD Almighty for whom you are laying down conditions; will you never understand anything? 14 You cannot plumb the depths of the human heart or grasp the workings of the human mind; how then can you fathom God, who has made all these things, discern his mind, and understand his plan?

"No, my brothers, do not anger the LORD our God. 15 For if he does not wish to come to our aid within the five days, he has it equally within his power to protect us at such time as he pleases, or to destroy us in the face of our enemies. 16 It is not for you to make the LORD our God give surety for his plans.

"God is not man that he should be moved by threats,
nor human, that he may be given an ultimatum.

17 "So while we wait for the salvation that comes from him, let us call upon him to help us, and he will hear our cry if it is his good pleasure. 18 For there has not risen among us in recent generations, nor does there exist today, any tribe, or clan, or town, or city of ours that worships gods made by hands, as happened in former days. 19 It was for such conduct that our forefathers were handed over to the

New Jerusalem Bible

'Listen to me, leaders of the people of Bethulia. You were wrong to speak to the people as you did today and to bind yourself by oath, in defiance of God, to surrender the town to our enemies if the Lord did not come to your help within a set number of days. 12 Who are you, to put God to the test today, you, of all people, to set yourselves above him? 13 You put the Lord Almighty to the test! You do not understand anything, and never will. 14 If you cannot sound the depths of the human heart or unravel the arguments of the human mind, how can you fathom the God who made all things, or sound his mind or unravel his purposes? No, brothers, do not provoke the anger of the Lord our God. 15 Although it may not be his will to help us within the next five days, he has the power to protect us for as many days as he pleases, just as he has the power to destroy us before our enemies. 16 But you have no right to demand guarantees where the designs of the Lord our God are concerned. For God is not to be threatened as a human being is, nor is he, like a mere human, to be cajoled. 17 Rather, as we wait patiently for him to save, let us plead with him to help us. He will hear our voice if such is his good pleasure.

18 'And indeed of recent times and still today there is not one tribe of ours, or family, or village, or town that has worshipped gods made by human hand, as once was done,

GREEK OLD TESTAMENT

ἡμέραις. 19 ὧν χάριν ἐδόθησαν εἰς ῥομφαίαν καὶ εἰς
διαρπαγὴν οἱ πατέρες ἡμῶν καὶ ἔπεσον πτῶμα μέγα ἐνώπιον
τῶν ἐχθρῶν ἡμῶν. 20 ἡμεῖς δὲ ἕτερον θεὸν οὐκ ἔγνωμεν πλὴν
αὐτοῦ· ὅθεν ἐλπίζομεν ὅτι οὐχ ὑπερόψεται ἡμᾶς οὐδ᾽ ἀπὸ
τοῦ γένους ἡμῶν. 21 ὅτι ἐν τῷ λημφθῆναι ἡμᾶς οὕτως καὶ
λημφθήσεται πᾶσα ἡ Ιουδαία, καὶ προνομευθήσεται τὰ ἅγια
ἡμῶν, καὶ ἐκζητήσει τὴν βεβήλωσιν αὐτῶν ἐκ τοῦ αἵματος
ἡμῶν 22 καὶ τὸν φόνον τῶν ἀδελφῶν ἡμῶν καὶ τὴν αἰχμαλωσίαν τῆς γῆς καὶ τὴν ἐρήμωσιν τῆς κληρονομίας ἡμῶν ἐπιστρέψει εἰς κεφαλὴν ἡμῶν ἐν τοῖς ἔθνεσιν, οὗ ἐὰν δουλεύ-
σωμεν ἐκεῖ, καὶ ἐσόμεθα εἰς πρόσκομμα καὶ εἰς ὄνειδος
ἐναντίον τῶν κτωμένων ἡμᾶς. 23 ὅτι οὐ κατευθυνθήσεται ἡ
δουλεία ἡμῶν εἰς χάριν, ἀλλ᾽ εἰς ἀτιμίαν θήσει αὐτὴν κύριος
ὁ θεὸς ἡμῶν. 24 καὶ νῦν, ἀδελφοί, ἐπιδειξώμεθα τοῖς
ἀδελφοῖς ἡμῶν, ὅτι ἐξ ἡμῶν κρέμαται ἡ ψυχὴ αὐτῶν, καὶ τὰ
ἅγια καὶ ὁ οἶκος καὶ τὸ θυσιαστήριον ἐπεστήρισται ἐφ᾽
ἡμῖν. 25 παρὰ ταῦτα πάντα εὐχαριστήσωμεν κυρίῳ τῷ θεῷ
ἡμῶν, ὃς πειράζει ἡμᾶς καθὰ καὶ τοὺς πατέρας ἡμῶν.
26 μνήσθητε ὅσα ἐποίησεν μετὰ Αβρααμ καὶ ὅσα ἐπείρασεν
τὸν Ισαακ καὶ ὅσα ἐγένετο τῷ Ιακωβ ἐν Μεσοποταμίᾳ τῆς
Συρίας ποιμαίνοντι τὰ πρόβατα Λαβαν τοῦ ἀδελφοῦ τῆς
μητρὸς αὐτοῦ. 27 ὅτι οὐ καθὼς ἐκείνους ἐπύρωσεν εἰς ἐτα-
σμὸν τῆς καρδίας αὐτῶν, καὶ ἡμᾶς οὐκ ἐξεδίκησεν, ἀλλ᾽ εἰς
νουθέτησιν μαστιγοῖ κύριος τοὺς ἐγγίζοντας αὐτῷ. — 28 καὶ

KING JAMES VERSION

19 For the which cause our fathers were given to the sword, and for a spoil, and had a great fall before our enemies.

20 But we know none other god, therefore we trust that he will not dispise us, nor any of our nation.

21 For if we be taken so, all Judea shall lie waste, and our sanctuary shall be spoiled; and he will require the profanation thereof at our mouth.

22 And the slaughter of our brethren, and the captivity of the country, and the desolation of our inheritance, will he turn upon our heads among the Gentiles, wheresoever we shall be in bondage; and we shall be an offence and a reproach to all them that possess us.

23 For our servitude shall not be directed to favour: but the Lord our God shall turn it to dishonour.

24 Now therefore, O brethren, let us shew an example to our brethren, because their hearts depend upon us, and the sanctuary, and the house, and the altar, rest upon us.

25 Moreover let us give thanks to the Lord our God, which trieth us, even as he did our fathers.

26 Remember what things he did to Abraham, and how he tried Isaac, and what happened to Jacob in Mesopotamia of Syria, when he kept the sheep of Laban his mother's brother.

27 For he hath not tried us in the fire, as he did them, for the examination of their hearts, neither hath he taken vengeance on us: but the Lord doth scourge them that come near unto him, to admonish them.

DOUAY OLD TESTAMENT

19 For which crime they were given up to their enemies, to the sword, and to pillage, and to confusion: but we know no other God but him.

20 Let us humbly wait for his consolation, and the Lord our God will require our blood of the afflictions of our enemies, and he will humble all the nations that shall rise up against us, and bring them to disgrace.

21 And now, brethren, as you are the ancients among the people of God, and their very soul resteth upon you: comfort their hearts by your speech, that they may be mindful how our fathers were tempted that they might be proved, whether they worshipped their God truly.

22 They must remember how our father Abraham was tempted, and being proved by many tribulations, was made the friend of God.

23 So Isaac, so Jacob, so Moses, and all that have pleased God, passed through many tribulations, remaining faithful.

24 But they that did not receive the trials with the fear of the Lord, but uttered their impatience and the reproach of their murmuring against the Lord,

25 Were destroyed by the destroyer, and perished by serpents.

26 As for us therefore let us not revenge ourselves for these things which we suffer.

27 But esteeming these very punishments to be less than our sins deserve, let us believe that these scourges of the Lord, with which like servants we are chastised, have happened for our amendment, and not for our destruction.

KNOX TRANSLATION

19 dooming themselves thus to massacre, to plunder, and to
insult at the hands of their enemies. At least we acknowledge one God, and him only. 20 Wait we humbly till he
sends us relief; he will avenge our wrongs by bringing misfortune on our enemies; he, the Lord our God, will bring the
invader low, and disappoint him of his prize.
21 You, brethren, are among the elders of the people; their
lives are in your charge. Yours to hearten them, by reminding them what trials our fathers underwent, to shew whether
they were God's worshippers indeed; 22 how Abraham was
put to the proof, tested by long endurance, before he became
God's friend; 23 how Isaac, Jacob, Moses, and all who won
God's favour, must be loyal to him under great affliction
first. 24 And what of those others, who could not hold out,
submitting to the divine will, under these trials; who bore
themselves impatiently, and did the Lord despite by complaining against him? 25 These were the men the destroying
angel slew, the men who fell a prey to serpents. 26 It is our
turn to suffer now, and never a word said in remonstrance;
27 think we the Lord's rod too light a punishment for our
sins, believe we that he is punishing us as his servants, to
chasten, not to destroy.

Today's English Version

19That is why God let their enemies kill them and take everything they had. It was a great defeat! 20But since we worship no other God but the Lord, we can hope that he will not
reject us or any of our people.

21"If our town is taken by the enemy, the entire region of
Judah will then fall, and our Temple in Jerusalem will be
looted. And God will make us pay with our lives for allowing
the Temple to be defiled. 22He will hold us responsible for
the slaughter and captivity of our people and for the destruction of the land we have inherited. We will be despised and
mocked by the people in those nations to which we will be
taken as slaves. 23We are not going to win the favor of our
enemies by surrendering to them now.[a] If we do surrender,
the Lord our God will see that we are put to shame.

24"No, my friends, we should set an example for our own
people. Not only their lives, but the fate of the Temple and
the altar depend on us. 25The Lord our God is putting us to
the test, just as he tested our ancestors, and we should be
thankful for that. 26Remember how he put Abraham and
Isaac to the test, and what happened to Jacob while he was
working as a shepherd for his uncle Laban in Mesopotamia.
27God is not testing our loyalty as severely as he did theirs.
God is not sending this punishment on us as revenge, but as
a warning to us who worship him."

[a] We are not . . . now; *or* No good will ever come out of our slavery.

New Revised Standard Version

days gone by. 19That was why our ancestors were handed
over to the sword and to pillage, and so they suffered a great
catastrophe before our enemies. 20But we know no other
god but him, and so we hope that he will not disdain us or
any of our nation. 21For if we are captured, all Judea will be
captured and our sanctuary will be plundered; and he will
make us pay for its desecration with our blood. 22The
slaughter of our kindred and the captivity of the land and the
desolation of our inheritance—all this he will bring on our
heads among the Gentiles, wherever we serve as slaves; and
we shall be an offense and a disgrace in the eyes of those
who acquire us. 23For our slavery will not bring us into
favor, but the Lord our God will turn it to dishonor.

24 "Therefore, my brothers, let us set an example for our
kindred, for their lives depend upon us, and the sanctuary—
both the temple and the altar—rests upon us. 25In spite of
everything let us give thanks to the Lord our God, who is
putting us to the test as he did our ancestors. 26Remember
what he did with Abraham, and how he tested Isaac, and
what happened to Jacob in Syrian Mesopotamia, while he
was tending the sheep of Laban, his mother's brother. 27For
he has not tried us with fire, as he did them, to search their
hearts, nor has he taken vengeance on us; but the Lord
scourges those who are close to him in order to admonish
them."

New American Bible

sword and to pillage, and fell with great destruction before
our enemies. 20But since we acknowledge no other god but
the LORD, we hope that he will not disdain us or any of our
people. 21If we are taken, all Judea will fall, our sanctuary
will be plundered, and God will make us pay for its profanation with our life's blood. 22For the slaughter of our kinsmen, for the taking of exiles from the land, and for the devastation of our inheritance, he will lay the guilt on our
heads. Wherever we shall be enslaved among the nations,
we shall be a mockery and a reproach in the eyes of our
masters. 23Our enslavement will not be turned to our benefit, but the LORD our God will maintain it to our disgrace.

24"Therefore, my brothers, let us set an example for our
kinsmen. Their lives depend on us, and the defense of the
sanctuary, the temple, and the altar rests with us. 25Besides
all this, we should be grateful to the LORD our God, for
putting us to the test, as he did our forefathers. 26Recall
how he dealt with Abraham, and how he tried Isaac, and all
that happened to Jacob in Syrian Mesopotamia while he was
tending the flocks of Laban, his mother's brother. 27Not for
vengeance did the LORD put them in the crucible to try their
hearts, nor has he done so with us. It is by way of admonition that he chastises those who are close to him."

New Jerusalem Bible

19which was the reason why our ancestors were delivered
over to sword and sack, and perished in misery at the hands
of our enemies. 20We for our part acknowledge no other God
but him; and so we may hope he will not look on us disdainfully or desert our nation.

21'If indeed they capture us, as you expect, then all Judaea
will be captured too, and our holy places plundered, and we
shall answer with our blood for their profanation. 22The
slaughter of our brothers, the captivity of our country, the
unpeopling of our heritage, will recoil on our own heads
among the nations whose slaves we shall become, and our
new masters will look down on us as an outrage and a disgrace; 23for our surrender will not reinstate us in their
favour; no, the Lord our God will make it a thing to be
ashamed of. 24So now, brothers, let us set an example to
our brothers, since their lives depend on us, and the sanctuary—Temple and altar—rests on us.

25'All this being so, let us rather give thanks to the Lord
our God who, as he tested our ancestors, is now testing us.
26Remember how he treated Abraham, all the ordeals of
Isaac, all that happened to Jacob in Syrian Mesopotamia
while he kept the sheep of Laban, his mother's brother.
27For as these ordeals were intended by him to search their
hearts, so now this is not vengeance that God is exacting on
us, but a warning inflicted by the Lord on those who are
near his heart.'

GREEK OLD TESTAMENT

εἶπεν πρὸς αὐτὴν Οζιας Πάντα, ὅσα εἶπας, ἐν ἀγαθῇ καρδίᾳ
ἐλάλησας, καὶ οὐκ ἔστιν ὃς ἀντιστήσεται τοῖς λόγοις σου·
29 ὅτι οὐκ ἐν τῇ σήμερον ἡ σοφία σου πρόδηλός ἐστιν, ἀλλ᾽
ἀπ᾽ ἀρχῆς ἡμερῶν σου ἔγνω πᾶς ὁ λαὸς τὴν σύνεσίν σου,
καθότι ἀγαθόν ἐστιν τὸ πλάσμα τῆς καρδίας σου. 30 ἀλλὰ ὁ
λαὸς δεδίψηκεν σφόδρα καὶ ἠνάγκασαν ἡμᾶς ποιῆσαι καθὰ
ἐλαλήσαμεν αὐτοῖς καὶ ἐπαγαγεῖν ἐφ᾽ ἡμᾶς ὅρκον, ὃν οὐ
παραβησόμεθα. 31 καὶ νῦν δεήθητι περὶ ἡμῶν, ὅτι γυνὴ
εὐσεβὴς εἶ, καὶ ἀποστελεῖ κύριος τὸν ὑετὸν εἰς πλήρωσιν
τῶν λάκκων ἡμῶν, καὶ οὐκ ἐκλείψομεν ἔτι. 32 καὶ εἶπεν πρὸς
αὐτοὺς Ιουδιθ Ἀκούσατέ μου, καὶ ποιήσω πρᾶγμα ὃ ἀφίξεται
εἰς γενεὰς γενεῶν υἱοῖς τοῦ γένους ἡμῶν. 33 ὑμεῖς στή-
σεσθε ἐπὶ τῆς πύλης τὴν νύκτα ταύτην, καὶ ἐξελεύσομαι
ἐγὼ μετὰ τῆς ἅβρας μου, καὶ ἐν ταῖς ἡμέραις, μεθ᾽ ἃς
εἴπατε παραδώσειν τὴν πόλιν τοῖς ἐχθροῖς ἡμῶν, ἐπισκέψε-
ται κύριος τὸν Ισραηλ ἐν χειρί μου· 34 ὑμεῖς δὲ οὐκ ἐξερευ-
νήσετε τὴν πρᾶξίν μου, οὐ γὰρ ἐρῶ ὑμῖν ἕως τοῦ τελεσθῆναι
ἃ ἐγὼ ποιῶ. 35 καὶ εἶπεν Οζιας καὶ οἱ ἄρχοντες πρὸς αὐτήν
Πορεύου εἰς εἰρήνην, καὶ κύριος ὁ θεὸς ἔμπροσθέν σου εἰς
ἐκδίκησιν τῶν ἐχθρῶν ἡμῶν. 36 καὶ ἀποστρέψαντες ἐκ τῆς
σκηνῆς ἐπορεύθησαν ἐπὶ τὰς διατάξεις αὐτῶν.

9 Ιουδιθ δὲ ἔπεσεν ἐπὶ πρόσωπον καὶ ἐπέθετο σποδὸν ἐπὶ
τὴν κεφαλὴν αὐτῆς καὶ ἐγύμνωσεν ὃν ἐνεδεδύκει

KING JAMES VERSION

28 Then said Ozias to her, All that thou hast spoken hast thou spoken with a good heart, and there is none that may gainsay thy words.

29 For this is not the first day wherein thy wisdom is manifested; but from the beginning of thy days all the people have known thy understanding, because the disposition of thine heart is good.

30 But the people were very thirsty, and compelled us to do unto them as we have spoken, and to bring an oath upon ourselves, which we will not break.

31 Therefore now pray thou for us, because thou art a godly woman, and the Lord will send us rain to fill our cisterns, and we shall faint no more.

32 Then said Judith unto them, Hear me, and I will do a thing, which shall go throughout all generations to the children of our nation.

33 Ye shall stand this night in the gate, and I will go forth with my waitingwoman: and within the days that ye have promised to deliver the city to our enemies the Lord will visit Israel by mine hand.

34 But enquire not ye of mine act: for I will not declare it unto you, till the things be finished that I do.

35 Then said Ozias and the princes unto her, Go in peace, and the Lord God be before thee, to take vengeance on our enemies.

36 So they returned from the tent, and went to their wards.

9 Then Judith fell upon her face, and put ashes upon her head, and uncovered the sackcloth wherewith she was

DOUAY OLD TESTAMENT

28 And Ozias and the ancients said to her: All things which thou hast spoken are true, and there is nothing to be reprehended in thy words.

29 Now therefore pray for us, for thou art a holy woman, and one fearing God.

30 And Judith said to them: As you know that what I have been able to say is of God:

31 So that which I intend to do prove ye if it be of God, and pray that God may strengthen my design.

32 You shall stand at the gate this night, and I will go out with my maidservant: and pray ye, that as you have said, in five days the Lord may look down upon his people Israel.

33 But I desire that you search not into what I am doing, and till I bring you word let nothing else be done but to pray for me to the Lord our God.

34 And Ozias the prince of Juda said to her: Go in peace, and the Lord be with thee to take revenge of our enemies. So returning they departed.

9 AND when they were gone, Judith went into her oratory: and putting on haircloth, laid ashes on her head: and

KNOX TRANSLATION

28 All thou sayest is true, Ozias and the elders confessed,
beyond cavil. 29 Pray for us, holy woman as thou art, and
the Lord's true worshipper. 30 Why then, said Judith, if you
recognize the words I say as God's words, 31 judge for yourselves whether the deed I mean to do is of God's ordaining;
and pray him to bring my design to effect. 32 Stand at the
gate this night, while I pass beyond it with my handmaid for
company, and pray that the Lord bring Israel relief within the
five days you spoke of. 33 But what my design is, never ask
me; till I come back and give you news, I would have nothing of you but your prayers to the Lord our God. 34 Go in
peace, Ozias said, and the Lord be with thee, to the confusion of our enemies. And with that they left her, and withdrew.

9 When they had gone, Judith went to her place of prayer, sackcloth her garb, ashes sprinkled over her head, and

TODAY'S ENGLISH VERSION

28 Then Uzziah answered Judith, "Everything you have
said makes good sense, and no one can argue with it. 29 This
is not the first time you have shown wisdom. Ever since you
were a child, all of us have recognized the soundness and
maturity of your judgment. 30 But our people are dying of
thirst. They forced us to say what we did and to make a
solemn promise, which we cannot break. 31 So now, since
you are a deeply religious woman, pray for our people; ask
the Lord to send rain to fill our cisterns, so that we can get
our strength back."

32 "All right," Judith replied, "I am going to do something
which our Jewish people will never forget. 33 Tonight, the
three of you must stand guard at the gate so that my slave
woman and I can leave the town. And before the day comes
on which you have promised to surrender, the Lord will use
me to rescue the people of Israel. 34 But you must not ask me
what I am going to do; I will explain it to you when it is all
over."

35 Uzziah and the other officials said to her, "You have our
blessing. May the Lord our God guide you as you take
revenge on our enemies." Then they left Judith's rooftop
shelter and returned to their posts.

9 Then Judith put ashes on her head, opened her robe to
reveal the sackcloth she was wearing under her clothes,

NEW REVISED STANDARD VERSION

28 Then Uzziah said to her, "All that you have said was
spoken out of a true heart, and there is no one who can deny
your words. 29 Today is not the first time your wisdom has
been shown, but from the beginning of your life all the people have recognized your understanding, for your heart's disposition is right. 30 But the people were so thirsty that they
compelled us to do for them what we have promised, and
made us take an oath that we cannot break. 31 Now since
you are a God-fearing woman, pray for us, so that the Lord
may send us rain to fill our cisterns. Then we will no longer
feel faint from thirst."

32 Then Judith said to them, "Listen to me. I am about to
do something that will go down through all generations of
our descendants. 33 Stand at the town gate tonight so that I
may go out with my maid; and within the days after which
you have promised to surrender the town to our enemies, the
Lord will deliver Israel by my hand. 34 Only, do not try to
find out what I am doing; for I will not tell you until I have
finished what I am about to do."

35 Uzziah and the rulers said to her, "Go in peace, and
may the Lord God go before you, to take vengeance on our
enemies." 36 So they returned from the tent and went to their
posts.

9 Then Judith prostrated herself, put ashes on her head,
and uncovered the sackcloth she was wearing. At the

NEW AMERICAN BIBLE

28 Then Uzziah said to her: "All that you have said was
spoken with good sense, and no one can gainsay your
words. 29 Not today only is your wisdom made evident, but
from your earliest years all the people have recognized your
prudence, which corresponds to the worthy dispositions of
your heart. 30 The people, however, were so tortured with
thirst that they forced us to speak to them as we did, and to
bind ourselves by an oath that we cannot break. 31 But now,
God-fearing woman that you are, pray for us that the LORD
may send rain to fill up our cisterns, lest we be weakened
still further."

32 Then Judith said to them: "Listen to me! I will do something that will go down from generation to generation
among the descendants of our race. 33 Stand at the gate
tonight to let me pass through with my maid; and within the
days you have specified before you will surrender the city to
our enemies, the LORD will rescue Israel by my hand. 34 You
must not inquire into what I am doing, for I will not tell you
until my plan has been accomplished." 35 Uzziah and the
rulers said to her, "Go in peace, and may the LORD God go
before you to take vengeance upon our enemies!" 36 Then
they withdrew from the tent and returned to their posts.

9 Judith threw herself down prostrate, with ashes strewn
upon her head, and wearing nothing over her sackcloth.

NEW JERUSALEM BIBLE

28 Uzziah replied, 'Everything you have just said comes
from an honest heart and no one will contradict a word of it.
29 Not that today is the first time your wisdom has been displayed; from your earliest years all the people have known
how shrewd you are and of how sound a heart. 30 But,
parched with thirst, the people forced us to act as we had
promised them and to bind ourselves by an inviolable oath.
31 You are a devout woman; pray to the Lord, then, to send
us a downpour to fill our storage-wells, so that our faintness
may pass.'

32 Judith replied, 'Listen to me, I intend to do something,
the memory of which will be handed down to the children of
our race from age to age. 33 Tonight you must be at the gate
of the town. I shall make my way out with my attendant.
Before the time fixed by you for surrendering the town to our
enemies, the Lord will make use of me to rescue Israel.
34 You must not ask what I intend to do; I shall not tell you
until I have done it.' 35 Uzziah and the chief men said, 'Go in
peace. May the Lord show you a way to take revenge on our
enemies.' 36 And leaving the upper room they went back to
their posts.

9 Judith threw herself face to the ground, scattered ashes
on her head, undressed as far as the sackcloth she was

GREEK OLD TESTAMENT

σάκκον, καὶ ἦν ἄρτι προσφερόμενον ἐν Ιερουσαλημ εἰς τὸν
οἶκον τοῦ θεοῦ τὸ θυμίαμα τῆς ἑσπέρας ἐκείνης, καὶ ἐβόησεν φωνῇ μεγάλῃ Ιουδιθ πρὸς κύριον καὶ εἶπεν 2 Κύριε ὁ
θεὸς τοῦ πατρός μου Συμεων, ᾧ ἔδωκας ἐν χειρὶ ῥομφαίαν
εἰς ἐκδίκησιν ἀλλογενῶν, οἳ ἔλυσαν μήτραν παρθένου εἰς
μίασμα καὶ ἐγύμνωσαν μηρὸν εἰς αἰσχύνην καὶ ἐβεβήλωσαν
μήτραν εἰς ὄνειδος. εἶπας γάρ Οὐχ οὕτως ἔσται, καὶ ἐποίη-
σαν· 3 ἀνθ' ὧν ἔδωκας ἄρχοντας αὐτῶν εἰς φόνον καὶ τὴν
στρωμνὴν αὐτῶν, ἣ ᾐδέσατο τὴν ἀπάτην αὐτῶν, ἀπατηθεῖ-
σαν εἰς αἷμα καὶ ἐπάταξας δούλους ἐπὶ δυνάσταις καὶ
δυνάστας ἐπὶ θρόνους αὐτῶν 4 καὶ ἔδωκας γυναῖκας αὐτῶν
εἰς προνομὴν καὶ θυγατέρας αὐτῶν εἰς αἰχμαλωσίαν καὶ
πάντα τὰ σκῦλα αὐτῶν εἰς διαίρεσιν υἱῶν ἠγαπημένων ὑπὸ
σοῦ, οἳ καὶ ἐζήλωσαν τὸν ζῆλόν σου καὶ ἐβδελύξαντο μίασμα
αἵματος αὐτῶν καὶ ἐπεκαλέσαντό σε εἰς βοηθόν· ὁ θεὸς ὁ
θεὸς ὁ ἐμός, καὶ εἰσάκουσον ἐμοῦ τῆς χήρας. 5 σὺ γὰρ
ἐποίησας τὰ πρότερα ἐκείνων καὶ ἐκεῖνα καὶ τὰ μετέπειτα
καὶ τὰ νῦν καὶ τὰ ἐπερχόμενα διενοήθης, καὶ ἐγενήθησαν ἃ

KING JAMES VERSION

clothed; and about the time that the incense of that evening was offered in Jerusalem in the house of the Lord Judith cried with a loud voice, and said,

2 O Lord God of my father Simeon, to whom thou gavest a sword to take vengeance of the strangers, who loosened the girdle of a maid to defile her, and discovered the thigh to her shame, and polluted her virginity to her reproach; for thou saidst, It shall not be so; and yet they did so:

3 Wherefore thou gavest their rulers to be slain, so that they dyed their bed in blood, being deceived, and smotest the servants with their lords, and the lords upon their thrones;

4 And hast given their wives for a prey, and their daughters to be captives, and all their spoils to be divided among thy dear children; which were moved with thy zeal, and abhorred the pollution of their blood, and called upon thee for aid: O God, O my God, hear me also a widow.

5 For thou hast wrought not only those things, but also the things which fell out before, and which ensued after; thou hast thought upon the things which are now, and which are to come.

DOUAY OLD TESTAMENT

falling down prostrate before the Lord, she cried to the Lord, saying:

2 O Lord God of my father Simeon, who gavest him a sword to execute vengeance against strangers, who had defiled by their uncleanness, and uncovered the virgin unto confusion:

3 And who gavest their wives to be made a prey, and their daughters into captivity: and all their spoils to be divided to thy servants, who were zealous with thy zeal: assist, I beseech thee, O Lord God, me a widow.

4 For thou hast done the things of old, and hast devised one thing after another: and what thou hast designed hath been done.

KNOX TRANSLATION

thus, falling down before the Lord, she cried for mercy:
2 Lord God of my father Simeon, thou didst put a sword in
his hand to punish the alien for foul wrong done, for a virgin
stripped and shamed;[a] 3 thou didst mark down their wives
for spoil, their daughters for slavery, their goods as forfeit, to
reward the men who had thy honour at heart. Listen now, O
Lord my God, to a widow's prayer. 4 Thine are the deeds of
long ago; that this event should succeed that, was of thy

a The murder of the Sichemites by Simeon and Levi is apparently condemned by Jacob (Gen. 34. 30; 49. 5-6). But evidently the Simeonites only preserved the tradition that their ancestor had shewed a laudable zeal for God's service, in taking vengeance for the contamination of the Israelite stock with alien blood.

TODAY'S ENGLISH VERSION

and bowed down with her face to the floor. It was the time
that the evening incense was being offered in the Temple in
Jerusalem, and Judith prayed in a loud voice: 2“O Lord, the
God of my ancestor Simeon, remember how you armed
Simeon with a sword to take revenge on those foreigners
who seized Dinah, who was a virgin, tore off her clothes,[a]
and defiled her; they stripped her naked and shamed her;
they raped her and disgraced her, even though you had forbidden this. 3That is why you let their leaders be killed—put
to death on the same bed where they had raped the woman.[b]
You destroyed them all, slaves, princes, and rulers on their
thrones. 4You let their wives be carried off, their daughters
taken captive, and their possessions plundered by the
Israelites, your chosen people, who were eager to do your
will. Dinah's brothers were furious because of this disgrace
to their family, so they called on you for help.
“O my God, listen to my prayer, the prayer of a widow.
5Your hand guided all that happened then, and all that happened before and after. You have planned it all—what is
happening now, and what is yet to be. Your plans have

[a] *Probable text* clothes; *Greek unclear.* [b] *Probable text* put to death . . . woman; *Greek unclear.*

NEW REVISED STANDARD VERSION

very time when the evening incense was being offered in the
house of God in Jerusalem, Judith cried out to the Lord with
a loud voice, and said,
2 “O Lord God of my ancestor Simeon, to whom you gave
a sword to take revenge on those strangers who had torn off
a virgin's clothing[a] to defile her, and exposed her thighs to
put her to shame, and polluted her womb to disgrace her; for
you said, ‘It shall not be done’—yet they did it; 3so you
gave up their rulers to be killed, and their bed, which was
ashamed of the deceit they had practiced, was stained with
blood, and you struck down slaves along with princes, and
princes on their thrones. 4You gave up their wives for booty
and their daughters to captivity, and all their booty to be
divided among your beloved children who burned with zeal
for you and abhorred the pollution of their blood and called
on you for help. O God, my God, hear me also, a widow.
5 “For you have done these things and those that went
before and those that followed. You have designed the things
that are now, and those that are to come. What you had in

a Cn: Gk *loosed her womb*

NEW AMERICAN BIBLE

While the incense was being offered in the temple of God in
Jerusalem that evening, Judith prayed to the LORD with a loud
voice: 2“LORD, God of my forefather Simeon! You put a
sword into his hand to take revenge upon the foreigners who
had immodestly loosened the maiden's girdle, shamefully
exposed her thighs, and disgracefully violated her body. This
they did, though you forbade it. 3Therefore you had their
rulers slaughtered; and you covered with their blood the bed
in which they lay deceived, the same bed that had felt the
shame of their own deceiving. You smote the slaves together
with their princes, and the princes together with their servants. 4Their wives you handed over to plunder, and their
daughters to captivity; and all the spoils you divided among
your favored sons, who burned with zeal for you, and in
their abhorrence of the defilement of their kinswoman, called
on you for help.
5“O God, my God, hear me also, a widow. It is you who
were the author of those events and of what preceded and
followed them. The present, also, and the future you have
planned. Whatever you devise comes into being; 6the things

NEW JERUSALEM BIBLE

wearing and cried loudly to the Lord. At the same time in
Jerusalem the evening incense was being offered in the
Temple of God. Judith said:

2 Lord, God of my ancestor Simeon,
you armed him with a sword to take vengeance on the
foreigners
who had undone a virgin's belt to her shame,
laid bare her thigh to her confusion,
violated her womb to her dishonour,
since, though you said, ‘This must not be,’ they did it.
3 For this you handed their leaders over to slaughter,
and their bed, defiled by their treachery,
was itself betrayed in blood.
You struck the slaves with the chieftains
and the chieftains with their retainers.
4 You left their wives to be carried off,
their daughters to be taken captive,
and their spoils to be shared out
among the sons you loved,
who had been so zealous for you,
had loathed the stain put on their blood
and called on you for help.

O God, my God,
now hear this widow too;
5 for you have made the past,
and what is happening now, and what will follow.
What is, what will be, you have planned;
what has been, you designed.

GREEK OLD TESTAMENT

ἐνενοήθης, [6]καὶ παρέστησαν ἃ ἐβουλεύσω καὶ εἶπαν Ἰδοὺ πάρεσμεν· πᾶσαι γὰρ αἱ ὁδοί σου ἕτοιμοι, καὶ ἡ κρίσις σου ἐν προγνώσει. [7]ἰδοὺ γὰρ Ἀσσύριοι ἐπληθύνθησαν ἐν δυνάμει αὐτῶν, ὑψώθησαν ἐφ' ἵππῳ καὶ ἀναβάτῃ, ἐγαυρίασαν ἐν βραχίονι πεζῶν, ἤλπισαν ἐν ἀσπίδι καὶ ἐν γαίσῳ καὶ τόξῳ καὶ σφενδόνῃ καὶ οὐκ ἔγνωσαν ὅτι σὺ εἶ κύριος συντρίβων πολέμους. [8]κύριος ὄνομά σοι· σὺ ῥάξον αὐτῶν τὴν ἰσχὺν ἐν δυνάμει σου καὶ κάταξον τὸ κράτος αὐτῶν ἐν τῷ θυμῷ σου· ἐβουλεύσαντο γὰρ βεβηλῶσαι τὰ ἅγιά σου, μιᾶναι τὸ σκήνωμα τῆς καταπαύσεως τοῦ ὀνόματος τῆς δόξης σου, καταβαλεῖν σιδήρῳ κέρας θυσιαστηρίου σου. [9]βλέψον εἰς ὑπερηφανίαν αὐτῶν, ἀπόστειλον τὴν ὀργήν σου εἰς κεφαλὰς αὐτῶν, δὸς ἐν χειρί μου τῆς χήρας ὃ διενοήθην κράτος. [10]πάταξον δοῦλον ἐκ χειλέων ἀπάτης μου ἐπ' ἄρχοντι καὶ ἄρχοντα ἐπὶ θεράποντι αὐτοῦ, θραῦσον αὐτῶν τὸ ἀνάστεμα

KING JAMES VERSION

6 Yea, what things thou didst determine were ready at hand, and said, Lo, we are here: for all thy ways are prepared, and thy judgments are in thy foreknowledge.

7 For, behold, the Assyrians are multiplied in their power; they are exalted with horse and man; they glory in the strength of their footmen; they trust in shield, and spear, and bow, and sling; and know not that thou art the Lord that breakest the battles: the Lord is thy name.

8 Throw down their strength in thy power, and bring down their force in thy wrath: for they have purposed to defile thy sanctuary, and to pollute the tabernacle where thy glorious name resteth, and to cast down with sword the horn of thy altar.

9 Behold their pride, and send thy wrath upon their heads: give into mine hand, which am a widow, the power that I have conceived.

10 Smite by the deceit of my lips the servant with the prince, and the prince with the servant: break down their stateliness by the hand of a woman.

DOUAY OLD TESTAMENT

5 For all thy ways are prepared, and in thy providence thou hast placed thy judgments.

6 Look upon the camp of the Assyrians now, as thou wast pleased to look upon the camp of the Egyptians, when they pursued armed after thy servants, trusting in their chariots, and in their horsemen, and in a multitude of warriors.

7 But thou lookedst over their camp, and darkness wearied them.

8 The deep held their feet, and the waters overwhelmed them.

9 So may it be with these also, O Lord, who trust in their multitude, and in their chariots, and in their pikes, and in their shields, and in their arrows, and glory in their spears,

10 And know not that thou art our God, who destroyest wars from the beginning, and the Lord is thy name.

11 Lift up thy arm as from the beginning, and crush their power with thy power: let their power fall in their wrath, who promise themselves to violate thy sanctuary, and defile the dwelling place of thy name, and to beat down with their sword the horn of thy altar.

12 Bring to pass, O Lord, that his pride may be cut off with his own sword.

13 Let him be caught in the net of his own eyes in my regard, and do thou strike him by the graces of the words of my lips.

14 Give me constancy in my mind, that I may despise him: and fortitude that I may overthrow him.

15 For this will be a glorious monument for thy name, when he shall fall by the hand of a woman.

KNOX TRANSLATION

contriving; [5]all thy designs are long a-brewing, all thy awards made in full foreknowledge.

[6]Turn thy eyes now to yonder Assyrian camp, as thou didst let them fall long ago on the Egyptians, the armed host that went in pursuit of thy servants, boasting so proudly of its chariots and horsemen, its warrior strength. [7]One glance from thee, and on that camp darkness fell; [8]their feet were sucked down into the depths, and the waters closed above them! [9]So be it, Lord, with these others, that boast of their great array, now of chariots, now of pike and shield, of arrow and lance, [10]and know not the name thou bearest, thou, our God, crushing the invader still. [11]Lift up thy hand, as it was lifted up long ago; break power of theirs with power of thine! Helpless may they lie beneath thy vengeance, who now think to profane thy holy place, dishonour the very shrine of thy name, violate, at the sword's point, the sanctity of thy altar.

[12]The sword of Holofernes! Lord, if it might be his own pride's undoing! [13]Be the eyes he casts on me a lure to catch himself, the professions of love I make, his deathblow! [14]Too bold be my heart to fear, too resolute to spare him! [15]Let him fall by a woman's hand, and all the glory of it will be ascribed to thy name. [16]Not in the mustering of great

TODAY'S ENGLISH VERSION

always been carried out. 6 Whatever you want to be done is
as good as done. You know in advance all that you will do
and what decisions you will make. 7 Now the Assyrians are
stronger than ever; they take pride in their cavalry and their
infantry. They rely on their weapons, but they do not know
that you, O Lord, are a warrior who ends war. The Lord is
your name. 8 In your anger, use your power to shatter their
mighty army. They plan to defile your Temple, where you are
worshiped, and to hack off the corners of your altar with
their swords. 9 Look how proud and boastful they are! Pour
out your fury upon them! I am only a widow, but give me
the strength to carry out my plan. 10 Use my deceitful words
to strike them all dead, master and slave alike. Let a woman's strength break their pride. 11 Your power does not

NEW REVISED STANDARD VERSION

mind has happened; 6 the things you decided on presented
themselves and said, 'Here we are!' For all your ways are
prepared in advance, and your judgment is with foreknowledge.
7 "Here now are the Assyrians, a greatly increased force,
priding themselves in their horses and riders, boasting in the
strength of their foot soldiers, and trusting in shield and
spear, in bow and sling. They do not know that you are the
Lord who crushes wars; the Lord is your name. 8 Break their
strength by your might, and bring down their power in your
anger; for they intend to defile your sanctuary, and to pollute
the tabernacle where your glorious name resides, and to
break off the horns[a] of your altar with the sword. 9 Look at
their pride, and send your wrath upon their heads. Give to
me, a widow, the strong hand to do what I plan. 10 By the
deceit of my lips strike down the slave with the prince and
the prince with his servant; crush their arrogance by the
hand of a woman.

a Syr: Gk *horn*

NEW AMERICAN BIBLE

you decide on come forward and say, 'Here we are!' All your
ways are in readiness, and your judgment is made with foreknowledge.
7 "Here are the Assyrians, a vast force, priding themselves
on horse and rider, boasting of the power of their infantry,
trusting in shield and spear, bow and sling. They do not
know that

8 " 'You, the LORD, crush warfare;
Lord is your name.'

"Shatter their strength in your might, and crush their force
in your wrath; for they have resolved to profane your sanctuary, to defile the tent where your glorious name resides, and
to overthrow with iron the horns of your altar. 9 See their
pride, and send forth your wrath upon their heads. Give me,
a widow, the strong hand to execute my plan. 10 With the
guile of my lips, smite the slave together with the ruler, the
ruler together with his servant; crush their pride by the hand
of a woman.

NEW JERUSALEM BIBLE

6 Your purposes stood forward;
'See, here we are!' they said.
For all your ways are prepared
and your judgements delivered with foreknowledge.
7 See the Assyrians, with their army abounding
glorying in their horses and their riders,
exulting in the strength of their infantry.
Trust as they may in shield and spear,
in bow and sling,
in you they have not recognised the Lord,
the breaker of battle-lines;
8 yours alone is the title of Lord.

Break their violence with your might,
in your anger bring down their strength.
For they plan to profane your holy places,
to defile the tabernacle, the resting place of your
glorious name,
and to hack down the horn of your altar.
9 Observe their arrogance,
send your fury on their heads,
give the strength I have in mind
to this widow's hand.
10 By guile of my lips
strike down slave with master,
and master with retainer.
Break their pride
by a woman's hand.

GREEK OLD TESTAMENT

ἐν χειρὶ θηλείας. 11 οὐ γὰρ ἐν πλήθει τὸ κράτος σου, οὐδὲ ἡ
δυναστεία σου ἐν ἰσχύουσιν, ἀλλὰ ταπεινῶν εἶ θεός, ἐλατ-
τόνων εἶ βοηθός, ἀντιλήμπτωρ ἀσθενούντων, ἀπεγνωσμένων
σκεπαστής, ἀπηλπισμένων σωτήρ. 12 ναὶ ναὶ ὁ θεὸς τοῦ
πατρός μου καὶ θεὸς κληρονομίας Ισραηλ, δέσποτα τῶν
οὐρανῶν καὶ τῆς γῆς, κτίστα τῶν ὑδάτων, βασιλεῦ πάσης
κτίσεώς σου, σὺ εἰσάκουσον τῆς δεήσεώς μου 13 καὶ δὸς λόγον μου καὶ ἀπάτην εἰς τραῦμα καὶ μώλωπα αὐτῶν, οἳ κατὰ
τῆς διαθήκης σου καὶ οἴκου ἡγιασμένου σου καὶ κορυφῆς
Σιων καὶ οἴκου κατασχέσεως υἱῶν σου ἐβουλεύσαντο σκληρά.
14 καὶ ποίησον ἐπὶ παντὸς ἔθνους σου καὶ πάσης φυλῆς
ἐπίγνωσιν τοῦ εἰδῆσαι ὅτι σὺ εἶ ὁ θεὸς θεὸς πάσης δυνάμεως καὶ κράτους καὶ οὐκ ἔστιν ἄλλος ὑπερασπίζων τοῦ γένους Ισραηλ εἰ μὴ σύ.

10 Καὶ ἐγένετο ὡς ἐπαύσατο βοῶσα πρὸς τὸν θεὸν
Ισραηλ καὶ συνετέλεσεν πάντα τὰ ῥήματα ταῦτα,
2 καὶ ἀνέστη ἀπὸ τῆς πτώσεως καὶ ἐκάλεσεν τὴν ἅβραν
αὐτῆς καὶ κατέβη εἰς τὸν οἶκον, ἐν ᾧ διέτριβεν ἐν αὐτῷ ἐν
ταῖς ἡμέραις τῶν σαββάτων καὶ ἐν ταῖς ἑορταῖς αὐτῆς,
3 καὶ περιείλατο τὸν σάκκον, ὃν ἐνεδεδύκει, καὶ ἐξεδύσατο
τὰ ἱμάτια τῆς χηρεύσεως αὐτῆς καὶ περιεκλύσατο τὸ σῶμα

KING JAMES VERSION

11 For thy power standeth not in multitude, nor thy might in strong men: for thou art a God of the afflicted, an helper of the oppressed, an upholder of the weak, a protector of the forlorn, a saviour of them that are without hope.

12 I pray thee, I pray thee, O God of my father, and God of the inheritance of Israel, Lord of the heavens and earth, Creator of the waters, King of every creature, hear thou my prayer:

13 And make my speech and deceit to be their wound and stripe, who have purposed cruel things against thy covenant, and thy hallowed house, and against the top of Sion, and against the house of the possession of thy children.

14 And make every nation and tribe to acknowledge that thou art the God of all power and might, and that there is none other that protecteth the people of Israel but thou.

10 Now after that she had ceased to cry unto the God of Israel, and had made an end of all these words,

2 She rose where she had fallen down, and called her maid, and went down into the house, in the which she abode in the sabbath days, and in her feast days,

3 And pulled off the sackcloth which she had on, and put off the garments of her widowhood, and washed her body all

DOUAY OLD TESTAMENT

16 For thy power, O Lord, is not in a multitude, nor is thy pleasure in the strength of horses, nor from the beginning have the proud been acceptable to thee: but the prayer of the humble and the meek hath always pleased thee.

17 O God of the heavens, creator of the waters, and Lord of the whole creation, hear me a poor wretch, making supplication to thee, and presuming of thy mercy.

18 Remember, O Lord, thy covenant, and put thou words in my mouth, and strengthen the resolution in my heart, that thy house may continue in thy holiness:

19 And all nations may acknowledge that thou art God, and there is no other besides thee.

10 AND it came to pass, when she had ceased to cry to the Lord, that she rose from the place wherein she lay prostrate before the Lord.

2 And she called her maid, and going down into her house she took off her haircloth, and put away the garments of her widowhood,

3 And she washed her body, and anointed herself with the

KNOX TRANSLATION

armies, Lord, thy power is shewn; not on the well-horsed
warrior thy choice falls; never did boasting earn thy favour.
Still from a humble soul, an obedient will, the prayer must
come that wins thee. 17 God of the heavens, maker of the
floods, Lord of this universal frame, listen to the defenceless
plea of one who trusts only in thy mercy. 18 Bethink thee,
Lord, of thy covenant; grant my lips utterance, my heart firm
resolve; so shall thy temple ever remain inviolate, 19 so shall
all the Gentiles learn that thou art God, and hast none to
rival thee.

10 Then, her plea for the divine succour ended, Judith
rose from the ground where she lay prostrate in the
Lord's presence, 2 called her maid-servant to her, and went
downstairs into her house. Flung aside, now, the sackcloth,
folded away her widow's weeds; 3 she bathed herself,

TODAY'S ENGLISH VERSION

depend on the size and strength of an army. You are a God who cares for the humble and helps the oppressed. You give support and protection to people who are weak and helpless; you save those who have lost hope. 12 Now hear my prayer, O God of my ancestor Simeon, the God in whom Israel trusts, ruler of heaven and earth, creator of the rivers and the seas, king of all creation. Hear my prayer and 13 let my deceitful words wound and kill those who have planned such cruelty against your covenant and your holy Temple, against Mount Zion and the land you have given your people. 14 Make your whole nation and every tribe recognize that you are God, almighty and all-powerful, and that you alone protect the people of Israel!"

10 When Judith had finished her prayer to the God of Israel, 2 she stood up, called her slave woman, and went down into the house as she always did on Sabbaths and festival days. 3 She took off the sackcloth and her widow's clothes, took a bath, and put on rich perfumes. She

NEW REVISED STANDARD VERSION

11 "For your strength does not depend on numbers, nor your might on the powerful. But you are the God of the lowly, helper of the oppressed, upholder of the weak, protector of the forsaken, savior of those without hope. 12 Please, please, God of my father, God of the heritage of Israel, Lord of heaven and earth, Creator of the waters, King of all your creation, hear my prayer! 13 Make my deceitful words bring wound and bruise on those who have planned cruel things against your covenant, and against your sacred house, and against Mount Zion, and against the house your children possess. 14 Let your whole nation and every tribe know and understand that you are God, the God of all power and might, and that there is no other who protects the people of Israel but you alone!"

10 When Judith[a] had stopped crying out to the God of Israel, and had ended all these words, 2 she rose from where she lay prostrate. She called her maid and went down into the house where she lived on sabbaths and on her festal days. 3 She removed the sackcloth she had been wearing, took off her widow's garments, bathed her body with

a Gk *she*

NEW AMERICAN BIBLE

11 "Your strength is not in numbers, nor does your power depend upon stalwart men; but you are the God of the lowly, the helper of the oppressed, the supporter of the weak, the protector of the forsaken, the savior of those without hope.

12 "Please, please, God of my forefather, God of the heritage of Israel, LORD of heaven and earth, Creator of the waters, King of all you have created, hear my prayer! 13 Let my guileful speech bring wound and wale on those who have planned dire things against your covenant, your holy temple, Mount Zion, and the homes your children have inherited. 14 Let your whole nation and all the tribes know clearly that you are the God of all power and might, and that there is no other who protects the people of Israel but you alone."

10 As soon as Judith had thus concluded, and ceased her invocation to the God of Israel, 2 she rose from the ground. She called her maid and they went down into the house, which she used only on sabbaths and feast days. 3 She took off the sackcloth she had on, laid aside the garments of her widowhood, washed her body with water, and

NEW JERUSALEM BIBLE

11 Your strength does not lie in numbers,
nor your might in strong men;
since you are the God of the humble,
the help of the oppressed,
the support of the weak,
the refuge of the forsaken,
the Saviour of the despairing.
12 Please, please, God of my father,
God of the heritage of Israel,
Master of heaven and earth,
Creator of the waters,
King of your whole creation,
hear my prayer.
13 Give me a beguiling tongue
to wound and kill
those who have formed such cruel designs
against your covenant,
against your holy dwelling-place,
against Mount Zion,
against the house belonging to your sons.
14 And demonstrate to every nation, every tribe,
that you are the Lord, God of all power, all might,
and that the race of Israel has no protector but you.

10 Thus Judith called on the God of Israel. When she had finished praying, 2 she got up from the floor, summoned her maid and went down into the rooms which she used on Sabbath days and festivals. 3 There she removed the sackcloth she was wearing and taking off her widow's

GREEK OLD TESTAMENT

ὕδατι καὶ ἐχρίσατο μύρῳ παχεῖ καὶ διέξανε τὰς τρίχας τῆς
κεφαλῆς αὐτῆς καὶ ἐπέθετο μίτραν ἐπ᾽ αὐτῆς καὶ ἐνεδύσατο
τὰ ἱμάτια τῆς εὐφροσύνης αὐτῆς, ἐν οἷς ἐστολίζετο ἐν ταῖς
ἡμέραις τῆς ζωῆς τοῦ ἀνδρὸς αὐτῆς Μανασση, [4] καὶ ἔλαβεν
σανδάλια εἰς τοὺς πόδας αὐτῆς καὶ περιέθετο τοὺς χλιδῶ-
νας καὶ τὰ ψέλια καὶ τοὺς δακτυλίους καὶ τὰ ἐνώτια καὶ
πάντα τὸν κόσμον αὐτῆς καὶ ἐκαλλωπίσατο σφόδρα εἰς
ἀπάτησιν ὀφθαλμῶν ἀνδρῶν, ὅσοι ἂν ἴδωσιν αὐτήν. [5] καὶ
ἔδωκεν τῇ ἅβρᾳ αὐτῆς ἀσκοπυτίνην οἴνου καὶ καψάκην
ἐλαίου καὶ πήραν ἐπλήρωσεν ἀλφίτων καὶ παλάθης καὶ ἄρτων
καθαρῶν καὶ περιεδίπλωσε πάντα τὰ ἀγγεῖα αὐτῆς καὶ
ἐπέθηκεν αὐτῇ. [6] καὶ ἐξήλθοσαν ἐπὶ τὴν πύλην τῆς πόλεως
Βαιτυλουα καὶ εὕροσαν ἐφεστῶτα ἐπ᾽ αὐτῇ Οζιαν καὶ τοὺς
πρεσβυτέρους τῆς πόλεως Χαβριν καὶ Χαρμιν· [7] ὡς δὲ εἶδον
αὐτὴν καὶ ἦν ἠλλοιωμένον τὸ πρόσωπον αὐτῆς καὶ τὴν
στολὴν μεταβεβληκυῖαν αὐτῆς, καὶ ἐθαύμασαν ἐπὶ τῷ κάλλει
αὐτῆς ἐπὶ πολὺ σφόδρα καὶ εἶπαν αὐτῇ [8] Ὁ θεὸς τῶν πατέρων ἡμῶν δῴη σε εἰς χάριν καὶ τελειώσαι τὰ ἐπιτηδεύ-
ματά σου εἰς γαυρίαμα υἱῶν Ισραηλ καὶ ὕψωμα Ιερουσαλημ.
[9] καὶ προσεκύνησεν τῷ θεῷ καὶ εἶπεν πρὸς αὐτούς Ἐπι-
τάξατε ἀνοῖξαί μοι τὴν πύλην τῆς πόλεως, καὶ ἐξελεύσομαι
εἰς τελείωσιν τῶν λόγων, ὧν ἐλαλήσατε μετ᾽ ἐμοῦ· καὶ
συνέταξαν τοῖς νεανίσκοις ἀνοῖξαι αὐτῇ καθότι ἐλάλησεν.
[10] καὶ ἐποίησαν οὕτως. καὶ ἐξῆλθεν Ιουδιθ, αὐτὴ καὶ ἡ παιδίσκη αὐτῆς μετ᾽ αὐτῆς. ἀπεσκόπευον δὲ αὐτὴν οἱ ἄνδρες τῆς
πόλεως ἕως οὗ κατέβη τὸ ὄρος, ἕως διῆλθεν τὸν αὐλῶνα καὶ

KING JAMES VERSION

over with water, and anointed herself with precious ointment, and braided the hair of her head, and put on a tire upon it, and put on her garments of gladness, wherewith she was clad during the life of Manasses her husband.

4 And she took sandals upon her feet, and put about her her bracelets, and her chains, and her rings, and her earrings, and all her ornaments, and decked herself bravely, to allure the eyes of all men that should see her.

5 Then she gave her maid a bottle of wine, and a cruse of oil, and filled a bag with parched corn, and lumps of figs, and with fine bread; so she folded all these things together, and laid them upon her.

6 Thus they went forth to the gate of the city of Bethulia, and found standing there Ozias, and the ancients of the city, Chabris and Charmis.

7 And when they saw her, that her countenance was altered, and her apparel was changed, they wondered at her beauty very greatly, and said unto her,

8 The God, the God of our fathers, give thee favour, and accomplish thine enterprizes to the glory of the children of Israel, and to the exaltation of Jerusalem. Then they worshipped God.

9 And she said unto them, Command the gates of the city to be opened unto me, that I may go forth to accomplish the things whereof ye have spoken with me. So they commanded the young men to open unto her, as she had spoken.

10 And when they had done so, Judith went out, she, and her maid with her; and the men of the city looked after her, until she was gone down the mountain, and till she had passed the valley, and could see her no more.

DOUAY OLD TESTAMENT

best ointment, and plaited the hair of her head, and put a bonnet upon her head, and clothed herself with the garments of her gladness, and put sandals on her feet, and took her bracelets, and lilies, and earlets, and rings, and adorned herself with all her ornaments.

4 And the Lord also gave her more beauty: because all this dressing up did not proceed from sensuality, but from virtue: and therefore the Lord increased this her beauty, so that she appeared to all men's eyes incomparably lovely.

5 And she gave to her maid a bottle of wine to carry, and a vessel of oil, and parched corn, and dry figs, and bread and cheese, and went out.

6 And when they came to the gate of the city, they found Ozias, and the ancients of the city waiting.

7 And when they saw her they were astonished, and admired her beauty exceedingly.

8 But they asked her no question, only they let her pass, saying: The God of our fathers give thee grace, and may he strengthen all the counsel of thy heart with his power, that Jerusalem may glory in thee, and thy name may be in the number of the holy and just.

9 And they that were there said, all with one voice: So be it, so be it.

10 But Judith praying to the Lord, passed through the gates, she and her maid.

KNOX TRANSLATION

anointed herself with the finest myrrh, parted and tied her
hair. The garments of happier days she donned anew, put on
her sandals, took bracelet and anklet, ear-ring and finger-
ring; decked herself with every ornament she had. [4] The Lord
himself lent grace to her mien; manly resolve, not woman's
wantonness, was the occasion of her finery, and he would
enhance her beauty till all beholders should vow there was
never woman so fair. [5] A bottle of wine she bade her serving-
maid carry, and a phial of oil, parched corn and dry figs, and
bread, and cheese, and so she went out on her journey.
[6] When they reached the gates, they found Ozias and the
elders of the city awaiting them there; [7] and no sooner did
these catch sight of her, than they fell into a great wonderment of her beauty. [8] Still they did not question her, but let
her pass; May the God of our fathers, they said, grant thee
his favour, and his strength speed whatever design is in thy
heart. Cause may Jerusalem have to be proud of thee; may
thy name live among the holy and the just! [9] And all the
bystanders, as with one voice, said Amen to that.
[10] So, with a prayer to the Lord, Judith passed out at the
gate, and her maid-servant with her. [11] At break of day,

TODAY'S ENGLISH VERSION

brushed her hair, tied a ribbon around it, and dressed herself
in the fine clothes she used to wear on joyful occasions when
her husband Manasseh was still alive. 4 She put on sandals
and all her finest jewelry: rings and earrings, and bracelets
on her wrists and ankles. She made herself so beautiful that
she was sure to attract the attention of any man who saw
her. 5 Judith gave her slave woman a leather bag of wine
and a jar of oil to carry. She filled a bag with roasted barley,
cakes of dried figs, and several loaves of bread baked according to Jewish food laws. She carefully wrapped all the food
and dishes and gave them to her slave. 6 Then the two
women left the house and went to the gates of Bethulia,
where they found Uzziah and the town officials, Chabris and
Charmis, standing guard. 7 When the men saw Judith after
she had changed clothes and put on make-up, they were
struck by her beauty and said to her, 8 "May the God of our
ancestors bless you and make your plan successful, so that
you may bring glory to Jerusalem and victory to Israel."

Judith prayed 9 and then said, "Order the gates to be
opened for me. I am on my way to do what we were talking
about." Then they ordered the young men to open the gates
for her, 10 and Judith and her slave left the city. The men
watched her as she went down the mountain into the valley,
until she was out of sight.

NEW REVISED STANDARD VERSION

water, and anointed herself with precious ointment. She
combed her hair, put on a tiara, and dressed herself in the
festive attire that she used to wear while her husband
Manasseh was living. 4 She put sandals on her feet, and put
on her anklets, bracelets, rings, earrings, and all her other
jewelry. Thus she made herself very beautiful, to entice the
eyes of all the men who might see her. 5 She gave her maid a
skin of wine and a flask of oil, and filled a bag with roasted
grain, dried fig cakes, and fine bread;[a] then she wrapped up
all her dishes and gave them to her to carry.

6 Then they went out to the town gate of Bethulia and
found Uzziah standing there with the elders of the town,
Chabris and Charmis. 7 When they saw her transformed in
appearance and dressed differently, they were very greatly
astounded at her beauty and said to her, 8 "May the God of
our ancestors grant you favor and fulfill your plans, so that
the people of Israel may glory and Jerusalem may be exalted." She bowed down to God.

9 Then she said to them, "Order the gate of the town to be
opened for me so that I may go out and accomplish the
things you have just said to me." So they ordered the young
men to open the gate for her, as she requested. 10 When they
had done this, Judith went out, accompanied by her maid.
The men of the town watched her until she had gone down
the mountain and passed through the valley, where they lost
sight of her.

a Other ancient authorities add *and cheese*

NEW AMERICAN BIBLE

anointed it with rich ointment. She arranged her hair and
bound it with a fillet, and put on the festive attire she had
worn while her husband, Manasseh, was living. 4 She chose
sandals for her feet, and put on her anklets, bracelets, rings,
earrings, and all her other jewelry. Thus she made herself
very beautiful, to captivate the eyes of all the men who
should see her.

5 She gave her maid a leather flask of wine and a cruse of
oil. She filled a bag with roasted grain, fig cakes, bread and
cheese; all these provisions she wrapped up and gave to the
maid to carry.

6 Then they went out to the gate of the city of Bethulia and
found Uzziah and the elders of the city, Chabris and Charmis,
standing there. 7 When these men saw Judith transformed in
looks and differently dressed, they were very much astounded at her beauty and said to her, 8 "May the God of our
fathers bring you to favor, and make your undertaking a success, for the glory of the Israelites and the exaltation of
Jerusalem."

Judith bowed down to God. Then she said to them,
9 "Order the gate of the city opened for me, that I may go to
carry out the business we discussed." So they ordered the
youths to open the gate for her as she requested. 10 When
they did so, Judith and her maid went out. The men of the
city kept her in view as she went down the mountain and
crossed the valley; then they lost sight of her.

NEW JERUSALEM BIBLE

dress, she washed all over, anointed herself plentifully with
perfumes, dressed her hair, wrapped a turban round it and
put on the robe of joy she used to wear when her husband
Manasseh was alive. 4 She put sandals on her feet, put on
her necklaces, bracelets, rings, earrings and all her jewellery,
and made herself beautiful enough to beguile the eye of any
man who saw her. 5 Then she handed her maid a skin of
wine and a flask of oil, filled a bag with barley girdle-cakes,
cakes of dried fruit and pure loaves, and wrapping all these
provisions up gave them to her as well. 6 They then went
out, making for the town gate of Bethulia. There they found
Uzziah waiting with the two elders of the town, Chabris and
Charmis. 7 When they saw Judith, her face so changed and
her clothes so different, they were lost in admiration of her
beauty. They said to her:

> 8 May the God of our ancestors keep you in his favour!
> May he crown your designs with success
> to the glory of the children of Israel,
> to the greater glory of Jerusalem!

9 Judith worshipped God, and then she said, 'Have the
town gate opened for me so that I can go out and fulfil all
the wishes you expressed to me.' They did as she asked and
gave orders to the young men to open the gate for her.
10 This done, Judith went out accompanied by her maid,
while the men of the town watched her all the way down the
mountain and across the valley, until they lost sight of her.

GREEK OLD TESTAMENT

οὐκέτι ἐθεώρουν αὐτήν. — 11 καὶ ἐπορεύοντο ἐν τῷ αὐλῶνι
εἰς εὐθεῖαν, καὶ συνήντησεν αὐτῇ προφυλακὴ τῶν Ἀσσυρίων.
12 καὶ συνέλαβον αὐτὴν καὶ ἐπηρώτησαν Τίνων εἶ καὶ πόθεν
ἔρχῃ καὶ ποῦ πορεύῃ; καὶ εἶπεν Θυγάτηρ εἰμὶ τῶν Εβραίων
καὶ ἀποδιδράσκω ἀπὸ προσώπου αὐτῶν, ὅτι μέλλουσιν δίδοσθαι ὑμῖν εἰς κατάβρωμα· 13 κἀγὼ ἔρχομαι εἰς τὸ πρόσωπον
Ολοφέρνου ἀρχιστρατήγου δυνάμεως ὑμῶν τοῦ ἀπαγγεῖλαι
ῥήματα ἀληθείας καὶ δείξω πρὸ προσώπου αὐτοῦ ὁδὸν καθ'
ἣν πορεύσεται καὶ κυριεύσει πάσης τῆς ὀρεινῆς, καὶ οὐ
διαφωνήσει τῶν ἀνδρῶν αὐτοῦ σὰρξ μία οὐδὲ πνεῦμα ζωῆς.
14 ὡς δὲ ἤκουσαν οἱ ἄνδρες τὰ ῥήματα αὐτῆς καὶ κατενόη-
σαν τὸ πρόσωπον αὐτῆς — καὶ ἦν ἐναντίον αὐτῶν θαυμάσιον
τῷ κάλλει σφόδρα —, καὶ εἶπαν πρὸς αὐτήν 15 Σέσωκας τὴν
ψυχήν σου σπεύσασα καταβῆναι εἰς πρόσωπον τοῦ κυρίου
ἡμῶν· καὶ νῦν πρόσελθε ἐπὶ τὴν σκηνὴν αὐτοῦ, καὶ ἀφ' ἡμῶν
προπέμψουσίν σε, ἕως παραδώσουσίν σε εἰς χεῖρας αὐτοῦ·
16 ἐὰν δὲ στῇς ἐναντίον αὐτοῦ, μὴ φοβηθῇς τῇ καρδίᾳ σου,
ἀλλὰ ἀνάγγειλον κατὰ τὰ ῥήματά σου, καὶ εὖ σε ποιήσει.
17 καὶ ἐπέλεξαν ἐξ αὐτῶν ἄνδρας ἑκατὸν καὶ παρέζευξαν
αὐτῇ καὶ τῇ ἅβρᾳ αὐτῆς, καὶ ἤγαγον αὐτὰς ἐπὶ τὴν σκηνὴν
Ολοφέρνου. 18 καὶ ἐγένετο συνδρομὴ ἐν πάσῃ τῇ παρεμβολῇ,
διεβοήθη γὰρ εἰς τὰ σκηνώματα ἡ παρουσία αὐτῆς. καὶ
ἐλθόντες ἐκύκλουν αὐτήν, ὡς εἱστήκει ἔξω τῆς σκηνῆς
Ολοφέρνου, ἕως προσήγγειλαν αὐτῷ περὶ αὐτῆς. 19 καὶ ἐθαύμαζον ἐπὶ τῷ κάλλει αὐτῆς καὶ ἐθαύμαζον τοὺς υἱοὺς Ισραηλ
ἀπ' αὐτῆς, καὶ εἶπεν ἕκαστος πρὸς τὸν πλησίον αὐτοῦ Τίς

KING JAMES VERSION

11 Thus they went straight forth in the valley: and the first watch of the Assyrians met her,

12 And took her, and asked her, Of what people art thou? and whence comest thou? and whither goest thou? And she said, I am a woman of the Hebrews, and am fled from them: for they shall be given you to be consumed:

13 And I am coming before Holofernes the chief captain of your army, to declare words of truth; and I will shew him a way, whereby he shall go, and win all the hill country, without losing the body or life of any one of his men.

14 Now when the men heard her words, and beheld her countenance, they wondered greatly at her beauty, and said unto her,

15 Thou hast saved thy life, in that thou hast hasted to come down to the presence of our lord: now therefore come to his tent, and some of us shall conduct thee, until they have delivered thee to his hands.

16 And when thou standest before him, be not afraid in thine heart, but shew unto him according to thy word; and he will entreat thee well.

17 Then they chose out of them an hundred men to accompany her and her maid; and they brought her to the tent of Holofernes.

18 Then was there a concourse throughout all the camp: for her coming was noised among the tents, and they came about her, as she stood without the tent of Holofernes, till they told him of her.

19 And they wondered at her beauty, and admired the children of Israel because of her, and every one said to his

DOUAY OLD TESTAMENT

11 And it came to pass, when she went down the hill, about break of day, that the watchmen of the Assyrians met her, and stopped her, saying: Whence comest thou? or whither goest thou?

12 And she answered: I am a daughter of the Hebrews, and I am fled from them, because I knew they would be made a prey to you, because they despised you, and would not of their own accord yield themselves, that they might find mercy in your sight.

13 For this reason I thought with myself, saying: I will go to the presence of the prince Holofernes, that I may tell him their secrets, and shew him by what way he may take them, without the loss of one man of his army.

14 And when the men had heard her words, they beheld her face, and their eyes were amazed, for they wondered exceedingly at her beauty.

15 And they said to her: Thou hast saved thy life by taking this resolution, to come down to our lord.

16 And be assured of this, that when thou shalt stand before him, he will treat thee well, and thou wilt be most acceptable to his heart. And they brought her to the tent of Holofernes, telling him of her.

KNOX TRANSLATION

while she was yet making her way down the mountain-
slope, she fell in with the advance-guard of the Assyrians,
who stopped her, and asked whence she came, whither she
was bound? 12 A Hebrew, she said, but I have given my fel-
low-country-men the slip, well knowing that the city must
fall into your hands. Why did they defy you, and refuse to
surrender, instead of throwing themselves on your mercy?
13 What was I to do? I determined to win audience with your
general, Holofernes, and tell him of their secret plans; shew
him, too, means by which he may reduce the city without
losing a man of his army. 14 Her story told, they must next
scan her face; and now their eyes dazzled with the admiration they had of her beauty. 15 It has been the saving of thy
life, they told her, this plan thou hast formed of betaking
thyself to our master yonder. 16 Of this be well assured, once
thou hast found thy way to his presence he will use thee
well; none so welcome as thou. And so they led her to
Holofernes' tent, and advised him of her coming.

TODAY'S ENGLISH VERSION

11 As the two women were walking through the valley, an Assyrian patrol met them. 12 They arrested Judith and questioned her, "What is your nationality? Where did you come from, and where are you going?"

"I am a Hebrew," she answered, "but I am running away from the Israelites because God is going to let you destroy them. 13 I am on my way to see Holofernes, the general in command of your army, to give him some reliable information. I can show him how to advance into the mountains and take control of the entire region without a single casualty."

14 The men stared at her because she was so beautiful. They listened to her story and said, 15 "You have saved your life by coming down here to see our general. Some of us will take you to his headquarters and present you to him. 16 Do not be afraid of him. Just tell him what you have told us, and he will treat you well." 17 They assigned a hundred men to escort Judith and her slave to the headquarters of Holofernes.

18 There was great commotion in the Assyrian camp as news of Judith's arrival spread from tent to tent. While she stood outside the tent of Holofernes waiting to be presented to him, many Assyrian soldiers came and stood around her. 19 They were greatly impressed by her beauty and wondered what kind of people the Israelites were. "Who can have

NEW REVISED STANDARD VERSION

11 As the women[a] were going straight on through the valley, an Assyrian patrol met her 12 and took her into custody. They asked her, "To what people do you belong, and where are you coming from, and where are you going?" She replied, "I am a daughter of the Hebrews, but I am fleeing from them, for they are about to be handed over to you to be devoured. 13 I am on my way to see Holofernes the commander of your army, to give him a true report; I will show him a way by which he can go and capture all the hill country without losing one of his men, captured or slain."

14 When the men heard her words, and observed her face—she was in their eyes marvelously beautiful—they said to her, 15 "You have saved your life by hurrying down to see our lord. Go at once to his tent; some of us will escort you and hand you over to him. 16 When you stand before him, have no fear in your heart, but tell him what you have just said, and he will treat you well."

17 They chose from their number a hundred men to accompany her and her maid, and they brought them to the tent of Holofernes. 18 There was great excitement in the whole camp, for her arrival was reported from tent to tent. They came and gathered around her as she stood outside the tent of Holofernes, waiting until they told him about her. 19 They marveled at her beauty and admired the Israelites, judging them by her. They said to one another, "Who can

a Gk *they*

NEW AMERICAN BIBLE

11 As Judith and her maid walked directly across the valley, they encountered the Assyrian outpost. 12 The men took her in custody and asked her, "To what people do you belong? Where do you come from, and where are you going?" She replied: "I am a daughter of the Hebrews, and I am fleeing from them, because they are about to be delivered up to you as prey. 13 I have come to see Holofernes, the general in chief of your forces, to give him a trustworthy report; I will show him the route by which he can ascend and take possession of the whole mountain district without a single one of his men suffering injury or loss of life."

14 When the men heard her words and gazed upon her face, which appeared wondrously beautiful to them, they said to her, 15 "By coming down thus promptly to see our master, you have saved your life. Now go to his tent; some of our men will accompany you to present you to him. 16 When you stand before him, have no fear in your heart; give him the report you speak of, and he will treat you well." 17 So they detailed a hundred of their men as an escort for her and her maid, and these conducted them to the tent of Holofernes.

18 When the news of her arrival spread among the tents, a crowd gathered in the camp. They came and stood around her as she waited outside the tent of Holofernes, while he was being informed about her. 19 They marveled at her beauty, regarding the Israelites with wonder because of her, and

NEW JERUSALEM BIBLE

11 As the women were making straight through the valley, an advance unit of Assyr ians intercepted them, 12 and, seizing Judith, began to question her. 'Which side are you on? Where do you come from? Where are you going?' 'I am a daughter of the Hebrews,' she replied, 'and I am fleeing from them since they will soon be your prey. 13 I am on my way to see Holofernes, the general of your army, to give him trustworthy information. I shall show him the road to take if he wants to capture all the hill-country without losing one man or one life.' 14 As the men listened to what she was saying, they stared in astonishment at the sight of such a beautiful woman. 15 'It will prove the saving of you,' they said to her, 'coming down to see our master of your own accord. You had better go to his tent; some of our men will escort you and hand you over to him. 16 Once you are in his presence do not be afraid. Tell him what you have just told us and you will be well treated.' 17 They then detailed a hundred of their men as escort for herself and her attendant, and these led them to the tent of Holofernes.

18 News of her coming had already spread through the tents, and there was a general stir in the camp. She was still outside the tent of Holofernes waiting to be announced, when a crowd began forming round her. 19 They were immediately impressed by her beauty and impressed with the

GREEK OLD TESTAMENT

καταφρονήσει τοῦ λαοῦ τούτου, ὃς ἔχει ἐν ἑαυτῷ γυναῖκας τοιαύτας; ὅτι οὐ καλόν ἐστιν ὑπολείπεσθαι ἐξ αὐτῶν ἄνδρα ἕνα, οἳ ἀφεθέντες δυνήσονται κατασοφίσασθαι πᾶσαν τὴν γῆν. 20 καὶ ἐξῆλθον οἱ παρακαθεύδοντες Ολοφέρνῃ καὶ πάντες οἱ θεράποντες αὐτοῦ καὶ εἰσήγαγον αὐτὴν εἰς τὴν σκηνήν. 21 καὶ ἦν Ολοφέρνης ἀναπαυόμενος ἐπὶ τῆς κλίνης αὐτοῦ ἐν τῷ κωνωπίῳ, ὃ ἦν ἐκ πορφύρας καὶ χρυσίου καὶ σμαράγδου καὶ λίθων πολυτελῶν καθυφασμένων. 22 καὶ ἀνήγγειλαν αὐτῷ περὶ αὐτῆς, καὶ ἐξῆλθεν εἰς τὸ προσκήνιον, καὶ λαμπάδες ἀργυραῖ προάγουσαι αὐτοῦ. 23 ὡς δὲ ἦλθεν κατὰ πρόσωπον αὐτοῦ Ιουδιθ καὶ τῶν θεραπόντων αὐτοῦ, ἐθαύμασαν πάντες ἐπὶ τῷ κάλλει τοῦ προσώπου αὐτῆς. καὶ πεσοῦσα ἐπὶ πρόσωπον προσεκύνησεν αὐτῷ, καὶ ἤγειραν αὐτὴν οἱ δοῦλοι αὐτοῦ.

11 Καὶ εἶπεν πρὸς αὐτὴν Ολοφέρνης Θάρσησον, γύναι, μὴ φοβηθῇς τῇ καρδίᾳ σου, ὅτι ἐγὼ οὐκ ἐκάκωσα ἄνθρωπον ὅστις ᾑρέτικεν δουλεύειν βασιλεῖ Ναβουχοδονοσορ πάσης τῆς γῆς. 2 καὶ νῦν ὁ λαός σου ὁ κατοικῶν τὴν ὀρεινὴν εἰ μὴ ἐφαύλισάν με, οὐκ ἂν ἦρα τὸ δόρυ μου ἐπ' αὐτούς. ἀλλὰ αὐτοὶ ἑαυτοῖς ἐποίησαν ταῦτα. 3 καὶ νῦν λέγε μοι τίνος ἕνεκεν ἀπέδρας ἀπ' αὐτῶν καὶ ἦλθες πρὸς ἡμᾶς. ἥκεις γὰρ εἰς σωτηρίαν· θάρσει, ἐν τῇ νυκτὶ ταύτῃ ζήσῃ καὶ εἰς τὸ λοιπόν· 4 οὐ γὰρ ἔστιν ὃς ἀδικήσει σε, ἀλλ' εὖ σε ποιήσει, καθὰ γίνεται τοῖς δούλοις τοῦ κυρίου μου βασιλέως Ναβουχοδονοσορ. 5 καὶ εἶπεν πρὸς αὐτὸν Ιουδιθ Δέξαι τὰ ῥήματα τῆς δούλης σου, καὶ λαλησάτω ἡ παιδίσκη σου κατὰ πρόσωπόν σου, καὶ οὐκ ἀναγγελῶ ψεῦδος τῷ κυρίῳ μου ἐν τῇ νυκτὶ

KING JAMES VERSION

neighbour, Who would despise this people, that have among them such women? surely it is not good that one man of them be left, who being let go might deceive the whole earth.

20 And they that lay near Holofernes went out, and all his servants, and they brought her into the tent.

21 Now Holofernes rested upon his bed under a canopy, which was woven with purple, and gold, and emeralds, and precious stones.

22 So they shewed him of her; and he came out before his tent with silver lamps going before him.

23 And when Judith was come before him and his servants, they all marvelled at the beauty of her countenance; and she fell down upon her face, and did reverence unto him: and his servants took her up.

11 Then said Holofernes unto her, Woman, be of good comfort, fear not in thine heart: for I never hurt any that was willing to serve Nabuchodonosor, the king of all the earth.

2 Now therefore, if thy people that dwelleth in the mountains had not set light by me, I would not have lifted up my spear against them: but they have done these things to themselves.

3 But now tell me wherefore thou art fled from them, and art come unto us: for thou art come for safeguard; be of good comfort, thou shalt live this night, and hereafter:

4 For none shall hurt thee, but entreat thee well, as they do the servants of king Nabuchodonosor my lord.

5 Then Judith said unto him, Receive the words of thy servant, and suffer thine handmaid to speak in thy presence, and I will declare no lie to my lord this night.

DOUAY OLD TESTAMENT

17 And when she was come into his presence, forthwith Holofernes was caught by his eyes.

18 And his officers said to him: Who can despise the people of the Hebrews, who have such beautiful women, that we should not think it worth our while for their sakes to fight against them?

19 And Judith seeing Holofernes sitting under a canopy, which was woven of purple and gold, with emeralds and precious stones:

20 After she had looked on his face, bowed down to him, prostrating herself to the ground. And the servants of Holofernes lifted her up, by the command of their master.

11 THEN Holofernes said to her: Be of good comfort, and fear not in thy heart: for I have never hurt a man that was willing to serve Nabuchodonosor the king.

2 And if thy people had not despised me, I would never have lifted up my spear against them.

3 But now tell me, for what cause hast thou left them, and why it hath pleased thee to come to us?

4 And Judith said to him: Receive the words of thy

KNOX TRANSLATION

17 No sooner did she stand before him, than Holofernes' eyes made him her prisoner. 18 Meanwhile, his lords were saying to one another, Who shall belittle the Hebrew folk, or doubt they are worth the attacking, when for prize there are such women as this? 19 As for Judith, she saw only Holofernes, as he sat there with a canopy over him, a canopy of purple, with gold and emeralds and other precious stones worked into it. 20 She looked him full in the face, then did reverence, bowing down to earth, until his servants raised her to her feet, at their master's bidding.

11 Compose thyself, Holofernes said; no need thy heart should misgive thee. None ever yet came to harm through me, that would do homage to my lord Nabuchodonosor; 2 never had lance of mine been raised against thy own people, if they had not defied me. 3 Tell me, what moved thee to part from their company and betake thyself to us? 4 My lord, said Judith, I have counsel for thee; do but

TODAY'S ENGLISH VERSION

contempt for people whose women are so beautiful?" they asked one another. "We had better kill all the men, or else these Jews will be able to charm the whole world."

20 Then Holofernes' bodyguard and his personal servants came out and led Judith into the tent. 21 Holofernes was resting on his bed under a mosquito net woven of purple and gold thread and decorated with emeralds and other precious stones. 22 When the men told him that Judith had arrived, he came to the outer part of the tent. Silver lamps were carried ahead of him. 23 When Judith came near him and his servants, they were all astonished at her beauty. She bowed down to the ground before Holofernes, but his servants helped her to her feet.

11 Holofernes said to Judith, "Don't worry; there's no need for you to be afraid. I have never hurt anyone who was willing to serve Nebuchadnezzar, king of the whole world. 2 Even now, if your people up in the mountains had not insulted me, I would not have declared war on them. They have brought all this trouble on themselves. 3 But tell me, why have you left them and come to us? You will be safe here. No need to be afraid! We have spared your life tonight, and you are in no danger for the future. 4 No one here will harm you; everyone will treat you well, like all other servants of my master, Nebuchadnezzar."

5 Then Judith said to Holofernes, "Allow me to speak to you, my lord, and please listen to what I have to say. I will

NEW REVISED STANDARD VERSION

despise these people, who have women like this among them? It is not wise to leave one of their men alive, for if we let them go they will be able to beguile the whole world!"

20 Then the guards of Holofernes and all his servants came out and led her into the tent. 21 Holofernes was resting on his bed under a canopy that was woven with purple and gold, emeralds and other precious stones. 22 When they told him of her, he came to the front of the tent, with silver lamps carried before him. 23 When Judith came into the presence of Holofernes[a] and his servants, they all marveled at the beauty of her face. She prostrated herself and did obeisance to him, but his slaves raised her up.

11 Then Holofernes said to her, "Take courage, woman, and do not be afraid in your heart, for I have never hurt anyone who chose to serve Nebuchadnezzar, king of all the earth. 2 Even now, if your people who live in the hill country had not slighted me, I would never have lifted my spear against them. They have brought this on themselves. 3 But now tell me why you have fled from them and have come over to us. In any event, you have come to safety. Take courage! You will live tonight and ever after. 4 No one will hurt you. Rather, all will treat you well, as they do the servants of my lord King Nebuchadnezzar."

5 Judith answered him, "Accept the words of your slave, and let your servant speak in your presence. I will say nothing false to my lord this night. 6 If you follow out the words

a Gk *him*

NEW AMERICAN BIBLE

they said to one another, "Who can despise this people that has such women among them? It is not wise to leave one man of them alive, for if any were to be spared they could beguile the whole world." 20 The guard of Holofernes and all his servants came out and ushered her into the tent. 21 Now Holofernes was reclining on his bed under a canopy with a netting of crimson and gold, emeralds and other precious stones. 22 When they announced her to him, he came out to the antechamber, preceded by silver lamps; 23 and when Holofernes and his servants beheld Judith, they all marveled at the beauty of her face. She threw herself down prostrate before him, but his servants raised her up.

11 Then Holofernes said to her: "Take courage, lady; have no fear in your heart! Never have I harmed anyone who chose to serve Nebuchadnezzar, king of all the earth. 2 Nor would I have raised my spear against your people who dwell in the mountain region, had they not despised me and brought this upon themselves. 3 But now tell me why you fled from them and came to us. In any case, you have come to safety. Take courage! Your life is spared tonight and for the future. 4 No one at all will harm you. Rather, you will be well treated, as are all the servants of my lord, King Nebuchadnezzar."

5 Judith answered him: "Listen to the words of your servant, and let your handmaid speak in your presence! I will tell no lie to my lord this night, 6 and if you follow out the

NEW JERUSALEM BIBLE

Israelites because of her. 'Who could despise a people who have women like this?' they kept saying. 'Better not leave one of them alive; let any go and they could twist the whole world round their fingers!'

20 The bodyguard and adjutants of Holofernes then came out and led Judith into the tent. 21 Holofernes was resting on his bed under a canopy of purple and gold studded with emeralds and precious stones. 22 The men announced her and he came out to the entrance to the tent, with silver torches carried before him.

23 When Judith confronted the general and his adjutant, the beauty of her face astonished them all. She fell on her face and did homage to him, but his servants raised her from the ground.

11 'Courage, woman,' Holofernes said, 'do not be afraid. I have never hurt anyone who chose to serve Nebuchadnezzar, king of the whole world. 2 Even now, if your nation of mountain dwellers had not insulted me, I would not have raised a spear against them. This was their fault, not mine. 3 But tell me, why have you fled from them and come to us? . . . Anyhow, this will prove the saving of you. Courage! You will live through this night, and many after. 4 No one will hurt you. On the contrary, you will be treated as well as any who serve my lord King Nebuchadnezzar.'

5 Judith said, 'Please listen favourably to what your slave has to say. Permit your servant to speak in your presence, I shall speak no word of a lie to my lord tonight. 6 You have

GREEK OLD TESTAMENT

ταύτῃ. [6] καὶ ἐὰν κατακολουθήσῃς τοῖς λόγοις τῆς παιδίσκης σου, τελείως πρᾶγμα ποιήσει μετὰ σοῦ ὁ θεός, καὶ οὐκ
ἀποπεσεῖται ὁ κύριός μου τῶν ἐπιτηδευμάτων αὐτοῦ. [7] ζῇ
γὰρ βασιλεὺς Ναβουχοδονοσορ πάσης τῆς γῆς καὶ ζῇ τὸ
κράτος αὐτοῦ, ὃς ἀπέστειλέν σε εἰς κατόρθωσιν πάσης
ψυχῆς, ὅτι οὐ μόνον ἄνθρωποι διὰ σὲ δουλεύουσιν αὐτῷ, ἀλλὰ
καὶ τὰ θηρία τοῦ ἀγροῦ καὶ τὰ κτήνη καὶ τὰ πετεινὰ τοῦ
οὐρανοῦ διὰ τῆς ἰσχύος σου ζήσονται ἐπὶ Ναβουχοδονοσορ
καὶ πάντα τὸν οἶκον αὐτοῦ. [8] ἠκούσαμεν γὰρ τὴν σοφίαν
σου καὶ τὰ πανουργεύματα τῆς ψυχῆς σου, καὶ ἀνηγγέλη
πάσῃ τῇ γῇ ὅτι σὺ μόνος ἀγαθὸς ἐν πάσῃ βασιλείᾳ καὶ δυνατὸς ἐν ἐπιστήμῃ καὶ θαυμαστὸς ἐν στρατεύμασιν πολέμου.
[9] καὶ νῦν ὁ λόγος, ὃν ἐλάλησεν Αχιωρ ἐν τῇ συνεδρίᾳ σου,
ἠκούσαμεν τὰ ῥήματα αὐτοῦ, ὅτι περιεποιήσαντο αὐτὸν οἱ
ἄνδρες Βαιτυλουα, καὶ ἀνήγγειλεν αὐτοῖς πάντα, ὅσα ἐξελά-
λησεν παρὰ σοί. [10] διό, δέσποτα κύριε, μὴ παρέλθῃς τὸν λόγον αὐτοῦ, ἀλλὰ κατάθου αὐτὸν ἐν τῇ καρδίᾳ σου, ὅτι ἐστὶν
ἀληθής. οὐ γὰρ ἐκδικᾶται τὸ γένος ἡμῶν, οὐ κατισχύει
ῥομφαία ἐπ᾽ αὐτούς, ἐὰν μὴ ἁμάρτωσιν εἰς τὸν θεὸν αὐτῶν.
[11] καὶ νῦν ἵνα μὴ γένηται ὁ κύριός μου ἔκβολος καὶ ἄπρα-
κτος καὶ ἐπιπεσεῖται θάνατος ἐπὶ πρόσωπον αὐτῶν, καὶ
κατελάβετο αὐτοὺς ἁμάρτημα, ἐν ᾧ παροργιοῦσιν τὸν θεὸν
αὐτῶν, ὁπηνίκα ἂν ποιήσωσιν ἀτοπίαν. [12] ἐπεὶ παρεξέλιπεν
αὐτοὺς τὰ βρώματα καὶ ἐσπανίσθη πᾶν ὕδωρ, ἐβουλεύσαντο
ἐπιβαλεῖν τοῖς κτήνεσιν αὐτῶν καὶ πάντα, ὅσα διεστείλατο
αὐτοῖς ὁ θεὸς τοῖς νόμοις αὐτοῦ μὴ φαγεῖν, διέγνωσαν

KING JAMES VERSION

6 And if thou wilt follow the words of thine handmaid, God will bring the thing perfectly to pass by thee; and my lord shall not fail of his purposes.

7 As Nabuchodonosor king of all the earth liveth, and as his power liveth, who hath sent thee for the upholding of every living thing: for not only men shall serve him by thee, but also the beasts of the field, and the cattle, and the fowls of the air, shall live by thy power under Nabuchodonosor and all his house.

8 For we have heard of thy wisdom and thy policies, and it is reported in all the earth, that thou only art excellent in all the kingdom, and mighty in knowledge, and wonderful in feats of war.

9 Now as concerning the matter, which Achior did speak in thy council, we have heard his words; for the men of Bethulia saved him, and he declared unto them all that he had spoken unto thee.

10 Therefore, O lord and governor, reject not his word; but lay it up in thine heart, for it is true: for our nation shall not be punished, neither can the sword prevail against them, except they sin against their God.

11 And now, that my lord be not defeated and frustrate of his purpose, even death is now fallen upon them, and their sin hath overtaken them, wherewith they will provoke their God to anger, whensoever they shall do that which is not fit to be done:

12 For their victuals fail them, and all their water is scant, and they have determined to lay hands upon their cattle, and purposed to consume all those things, that God hath forbidden them to eat by his laws:

DOUAY OLD TESTAMENT

handmaid, for if thou wilt follow the words of thy handmaid, the Lord will do with thee a perfect thing.

5 For as Nabuchodonosor the king of the earth liveth, and his power liveth which is in thee for chastising of all straying souls: not only men serve him through thee, but also the beasts of the field obey him.

6 For the industry of thy mind is spoken of among all nations, and it is told through the whole world, that thou only art excellent, and mighty in all his kingdom, and thy discipline is cried up in all provinces.

7 It is known also what Achior said, nor are we ignorant of what thou hast commanded to be done to him.

8 For it is certain that our God is so offended with sins, that he hath sent word by his prophets to the people, that he will deliver them up for their sins.

9 And because the children of Israel know they have offended their God, thy dread is upon them.

10 Moreover also a famine hath come upon them, and for drought of water they are already to be counted among the dead.

11 And they have a design even to kill their cattle, and to drink the blood of them.

12 And the consecrated things of the Lord their God which

KNOX TRANSLATION

take the advice this handmaid of thine offers, and the Lord
shall do great things with thee. [5] By the life of Nabuchodonosor I swear it,[a] by the power of Nabuchodonosor, committed to thee here and now for the punishment of rebellious
spirits! All men, nay, the brute beasts themselves, thou
tamest to his will; [6] of thy unwearied labours all nations
know; a world acclaims thee for the best and greatest of his
subjects; no province but speaks of thy wise government.
[7] It is common knowledge among us what Achior said to
thee, and what doom thou hast pronounced in return. [8] His
words have come true; God is indeed angered by our sins, so
angered that he has sent warning through his prophets, he
means to put our guilty race in thy power, [9] and if the
Israelites tremble at thy coming, it is because they know they
have lost their God's favour. [10] And now, with famine
threatening them, doomed to perish from lack of water,
[11] they have taken a worse resolve. They mean to kill their
cattle and drink the blood; [12] they mean to satisfy their own

a This refers, presumably to what has gone just before. Both the Latin and the Septuagint Greek imply, on the contrary, that it refers to what follows; but in the Hebrew original Judith is more Likely to have given emphasis to the promise in verse 4, than to a string of conventional compliments.

TODAY'S ENGLISH VERSION

tell you the truth. 6 If you follow my advice, God will do
something great with you, and my lord will not fail in his
plan. 7 For I swear to you by the life and strength of
Nebuchadnezzar, king of the whole world, who sent you to
bring order to all the subjects of his kingdom, that not only
have you made people serve him, but because of you even
the wild animals, the livestock, and the birds obey him.
Because of you, Nebuchadnezzar and his entire kingdom will
prosper.[a] 8 We have heard how wise and clever you are. The
whole world knows that you are the most competent, skilled,
and accomplished general in the whole Assyrian Empire.
9 Achior was rescued by the men of Bethulia, and has told us
what he said at your war council. 10 Please, sir, do not dismiss lightly what Achior told you, but take it seriously,
because it is true. No one can harm or conquer our people
unless they sin against their God.
11 "But you will not suffer any setbacks, nor will you fail to
achieve your goal. When the Israelites sin and make their
God angry, they will die. 12 Their food supply has already
run out, and the water shortage has become serious, so they
have decided to kill their livestock and eat foods that God's
Law clearly forbids them to eat. 13 They have decided to eat

[a] not only . . . prosper; *Greek unclear.*

NEW REVISED STANDARD VERSION

of your servant, God will accomplish something through you,
and my lord will not fail to achieve his purposes. 7 By the
life of Nebuchadnezzar, king of the whole earth, and by the
power of him who has sent you to direct every living being!
Not only do human beings serve him because of you, but
also the animals of the field and the cattle and the birds of
the air will live, because of your power, under Nebuchadnezzar and all his house. 8 For we have heard of your wisdom and skill, and it is reported throughout the whole world
that you alone are the best in the whole kingdom, the most
informed and the most astounding in military strategy.
9 "Now as for Achior's speech in your council, we have
heard his words, for the people of Bethulia spared him and
he told them all he had said to you. 10 Therefore, lord and
master, do not disregard what he said, but keep it in your
mind, for it is true. Indeed our nation cannot be punished,
nor can the sword prevail against them, unless they sin
against their God.
11 "But now, in order that my lord may not be defeated
and his purpose frustrated, death will fall upon them, for a
sin has overtaken them by which they are about to provoke
their God to anger when they do what is wrong. 12 Since
their food supply is exhausted and their water has almost
given out, they have planned to kill their livestock and have
determined to use all that God by his laws has forbidden
them to eat. 13 They have decided to consume the first fruits

NEW AMERICAN BIBLE

words of your handmaid, God will give you complete success, and my lord will not fail in any of his undertakings.
7 By the life of Nebuchadnezzar, king of all the earth, and by
the power of him who has sent you to set all creatures
aright! not only do men serve him through you; but even the
wild beasts and the cattle and the birds of the air, because of
your strength, will live for Nebuchadnezzar and his whole
house. 8 Indeed, we have heard of your wisdom and sagacity, and all the world is aware that throughout the kingdom
you alone are competent, rich in experience, and distinguished in military strategy.
9 "As for Achior's speech in your council, we have heard of
it. When the men of Bethulia spared him, he told them all he
had said to you. 10 So then, my lord and master, do not disregard his word, but bear it in mind, for it is true. For our
people are not punished, nor does the sword prevail against
them, except when they sin against their God. 11 But now
their guilt has caught up with them by which they bring the
wrath of their God upon them whenever they do wrong; so
that my lord will not be repulsed and fail, but death will
overtake them. 12 Since their food gave out and all their
water ran low, they decided to kill their animals, and determined to consume all the things which God in his laws forbade them to eat. 13 They decreed that they would use up the

NEW JERUSALEM BIBLE

only to follow your servant's advice and God will bring your
work to a successful conclusion; in what my lord undertakes
he will not fail. 7 Long life to Nebuchadnezzar, king of the
whole world, who has sent you to set every living soul to
rights; may his power endure! Since, thanks to you, he is
served not only by human beings, but because of your might
the wild animals themselves, the cattle, and the birds of the
air are to live in the service of Nebuchadnezzar and his
whole House.
8 'We have indeed heard of your genius and adroitness of
mind. It is known everywhere in the world that throughout
the empire you have no rival for ability, wealth of experience
and brilliance in waging war. 9 We have also heard what
Achior said in his speech to your council. The men of
Bethulia having spared him, he has told them everything
that he said to you. 10 Now, master and lord, do not disregard what he said; keep it in your mind, since it is true; our
nation will not be punished, the sword will indeed have no
power over them, unless they sin against their God. 11 But as
it is, my lord need expect no repulse or setback, since death
is about to fall on their heads, for sin has gained a hold over
them, provoking the anger of their God each time that they
commit it. 12 As they are short of food and their water is giving out, they have resolved to fall back on their cattle and
decided to make use of all the things that God has, by his
laws, forbidden them to eat. 13 Not only have they made up

GREEK OLD TESTAMENT

δαπανῆσαι. 13 καὶ τὰς ἀπαρχὰς τοῦ σίτου καὶ τὰς δεκάτας
τοῦ οἴνου καὶ τοῦ ἐλαίου, ἃ διεφύλαξαν ἁγιάσαντες τοῖς
ἱερεῦσιν τοῖς παρεστηκόσιν ἐν Ιερουσαλημ ἀπέναντι τοῦ
προσώπου τοῦ θεοῦ ἡμῶν, κεκρίκασιν ἐξαναλῶσαι, ὧν οὐδὲ
ταῖς χερσὶν καθῆκεν ἅψασθαι οὐδένα τῶν ἐκ τοῦ λαοῦ. 14 καὶ
ἀπεστάλκασιν εἰς Ιερουσαλημ, ὅτι καὶ οἱ ἐκεῖ κατοικοῦντες
ἐποίησαν ταῦτα, τοὺς μετακομίσοντας αὐτοῖς τὴν ἄφεσιν
παρὰ τῆς γερουσίας. 15 καὶ ἔσται ὡς ἂν ἀναγγείλῃ αὐτοῖς
καὶ ποιήσωσιν, δοθήσονταί σοι εἰς ὄλεθρον ἐν τῇ ἡμέρᾳ
ἐκείνῃ. 16 ὅθεν ἐγὼ ἡ δούλη σου ἐπιγνοῦσα ταῦτα πάντα
ἀπέδρων ἀπὸ προσώπου αὐτῶν, καὶ ἀπέστειλέν με ὁ θεὸς
ποιῆσαι μετὰ σοῦ πράγματα, ἐφ᾽ οἷς ἐκστήσεται πᾶσα ἡ γῆ,
ὅσοι ἐὰν ἀκούσωσιν αὐτά. 17 ὅτι ἡ δούλη σου θεοσεβής ἐστιν
καὶ θεραπεύουσα νυκτὸς καὶ ἡμέρας τὸν θεὸν τοῦ οὐρανοῦ·
καὶ νῦν μενῶ παρὰ σοί, κύριέ μου, καὶ ἐξελεύσεται ἡ δούλη
σου κατὰ νύκτα εἰς τὴν φάραγγα καὶ προσεύξομαι πρὸς τὸν
θεόν, καὶ ἐρεῖ μοι πότε ἐποίησαν τὰ ἁμαρτήματα αὐτῶν.
18 καὶ ἐλθοῦσα προσανοίσω σοι, καὶ ἐξελεύσῃ σὺν πάσῃ τῇ
δυνάμει σου, καὶ οὐκ ἔστιν ὃς ἀντιστήσεταί σοι ἐξ αὐτῶν.
19 καὶ ἄξω σε διὰ μέσου τῆς Ιουδαίας ἕως τοῦ ἐλθεῖν ἀπέναντι Ιερουσαλημ καὶ θήσω τὸν δίφρον σου ἐν μέσῳ αὐτῆς,
καὶ ἄξεις αὐτοὺς ὡς πρόβατα, οἷς οὐκ ἔστιν ποιμήν, καὶ οὐ
γρύξει κύων τῇ γλώσσῃ αὐτοῦ ἀπέναντί σου· ὅτι ταῦτα
ἐλαλήθη μοι κατὰ πρόγνωσίν μου καὶ ἀπηγγέλη μοι, καὶ

KING JAMES VERSION

13 And are resolved to spend the firstfruits of the corn, and the tenths of wine and oil, which they had sanctified, and reserved for the priests that serve in Jerusalem before the face of our God; the which things it is not lawful for any of the people so much as to touch with their hands.

14 For they have sent some to Jerusalem, because they also that dwell there have done the like, to bring them a licence from the senate.

15 Now when they shall bring them word, they will forthwith do it, and they shall be given thee to be destroyed the same day.

16 Wherefore I thine handmaid, knowing all this, am fled from their presence; and God hath sent me to work things with thee, whereat all the earth shall be astonished, and whosoever shall hear it.

17 For thy servant is religious, and serveth the God of heaven day and night: now therefore, my lord, I will remain with thee, and thy servant will go out by night into the valley, and I will pray unto God, and he will tell me when they have committed their sins:

18 And I will come and shew it unto thee: then thou shalt go forth with all thine army, and there shall be none of them that shall resist thee.

19 And I will lead thee through the midst of Judea, until thou come before Jerusalem; and I will set thy throne in the midst thereof; and thou shalt drive them as sheep that have no shepherd, and a dog shall not so much as open his mouth at thee: for these things were told me according to my foreknowledge, and they were declared unto me, and I am sent to tell thee.

DOUAY OLD TESTAMENT

God forbade them to touch, in corn, wine, and oil, these have they purposed to make use of, and they design to consume the things which they ought not to touch with their hands: therefore because they do these things, it is certain they will be given up to destruction.

13 And I thy handmaid knowing this, am fled from them, and the Lord hath sent me to tell thee these very things.

14 For I thy handmaid worship God even now that I am with thee, and thy handmaid will go out, and I will pray to God,

15 And he will tell me when he will repay them for their sins, and I will come and tell thee, so that I may bring thee through the midst of Jerusalem, and thou shalt have all the people of Israel, as sheep that have no shepherd, and there shall not so much as one dog bark against thee:

16 Because these things are told me by the providence of God.

17 And because God is angry with them, I am sent to tell these very things to thee.

KNOX TRANSLATION

needs with the hallowed corn, wine, and oil offered to the
Lord their God, tasting what they are forbidden to touch.
This done, it is certain they will involve themselves in ruin.
13 Hearing such news, what marvel if I shun their fellowship? Thy handmaid now; the Lord has sent me to tell thee
of all this. 14 Thy handmaid, but my own God I must still
worship, though I be dwelling in thy camp. Suffer me, my
lord, to go beyond its bounds, and offer prayer to God; 15 so
he will make it known to me, when he means to punish their
guilt, and I will come and tell thee. Then I will take thee into
the heart of Jerusalem, and thou wilt find the whole people
of Israel defenceless as strayed sheep, not a dog to bark at
thee. 16 It is God's providence has advised me of all this;
17 his vengeance that has sent me to warn thee of it.

TODAY'S ENGLISH VERSION

the wheat set aside from the early harvest and the tithes of wine and oil, which are holy and are reserved for the priests who serve God in Jerusalem. The rest of us are forbidden even to touch this sacred food, 14 but since the people in Jerusalem have already broken this law, the people of our town have sent messengers to the Council there requesting permission to do the same. 15 On the day that they receive permission and actually eat the food, you will be able to destroy them. 16 As soon as I learned about this, I ran away from my people. God has sent me to do something with you that will amaze everyone in the entire world who hears about it. 17 Sir, I am a religious woman; I worship the God of heaven day and night. I will stay here in your camp, and each night I will go out into the valley to pray to God, and he will tell me when the Israelites have sinned. 18 As soon as I find out, I will come and tell you, and you can march out with your whole army. The Israelites will not be able to defend themselves against you. 19 I will guide you through the central part of the land of Judah until we come to Jerusalem, where I will crown you king in the center of the city. You will scatter the people of Jerusalem like sheep without a shepherd. Not even a dog will dare to growl at you. God has revealed these things to me in advance and has sent me to report them to you."

NEW REVISED STANDARD VERSION

of the grain and the tithes of the wine and oil, which they had consecrated and set aside for the priests who minister in the presence of our God in Jerusalem—things it is not lawful for any of the people even to touch with their hands. 14 Since even the people in Jerusalem have been doing this, they have sent messengers there in order to bring back permission from the council of the elders. 15 When the response reaches them and they act upon it, on that very day they will be handed over to you to be destroyed.

16 "So when I, your slave, learned all this, I fled from them. God has sent me to accomplish with you things that will astonish the whole world wherever people shall hear about them. 17 Your servant is indeed God-fearing and serves the God of heaven night and day. So, my lord, I will remain with you; but every night your servant will go out into the valley and pray to God. He will tell me when they have committed their sins. 18 Then I will come and tell you, so that you may go out with your whole army, and not one of them will be able to withstand you. 19 Then I will lead you through Judea, until you come to Jerusalem; there I will set your throne.[a] You will drive them like sheep that have no shepherd, and no dog will so much as growl at you. For this was told me to give me foreknowledge; it was announced to me, and I was sent to tell you."

a Or *chariot*

NEW AMERICAN BIBLE

first fruits of grain and the tithes of wine and oil which they had sanctified and reserved for the priests who minister in the presence of our God in Jerusalem: things which no layman should even touch with his hands. 14 They have sent messengers to Jerusalem to bring back to them authorization from the council of the elders; for the inhabitants there have also done these things. 15 On the very day when the response reaches them and they act upon it, they will be handed over to you for destruction.

16 "As soon as I, your handmaid, learned all this, I fled from them. God has sent me to perform with you such deeds that people throughout the world will be astonished on hearing of them. 17 Your handmaid is, indeed, a God-fearing woman, serving the God of heaven night and day. Now I will remain with you, my lord; but each night your handmaid will go out to the ravine and pray to God. He will tell me when the Israelites have committed their crimes. 18 Then I will come and let you know, so that you may go out with your whole force, and not one of them will be able to withstand you. 19 I will lead you through Judea, till you come to Jerusalem, and there I will set up your judgment seat. You will drive them like sheep that have no shepherd, and not even a dog will growl at you. This was told me, and announced to me in advance, and I in turn have been sent to tell you."

NEW JERUSALEM BIBLE

their minds to eat the first-fruits of corn and the tithes of wine and oil, though these have been consecrated by them and set apart for the priests who serve in Jerusalem in the presence of our God, and may not lawfully even be handled by ordinary people, 14 but they have sent men to Jerusalem—where the inhabitants are doing much the same—to bring them back authorisation from the Council of Elders. 15 Now this will be the outcome: when the permission arrives and they act on it, that very day they will be delivered over to you for destruction.

16 'When I, your servant, came to know all this, I fled from them. God has sent me to do things with you at which the world will be astonished when it hears. 17 Your servant is a devout woman; she honours the God of heaven day and night. I therefore propose, my lord, to stay with you. I, your servant, shall go out every night into the valley and pray to God to let me know when they have committed their sin. 18 I shall then come and tell you, so that you can march out with your whole army; and none of them will be able to resist you. 19 I shall be your guide right across Judaea until you reach Jerusalem; there I shall enthrone you in the very middle of the city. And then you can round them up like shepherd-less sheep, with never a dog daring to bark at you. Foreknowledge tells me this; this has been foretold to me and I have been sent to reveal it to you.'

GREEK OLD TESTAMENT

ἀπεστάλην ἀναγγεῖλαί σοι. — 20 καὶ ἤρεσαν οἱ λόγοι αὐτῆς ἐναντίον Ολοφέρνου καὶ ἐναντίον πάντων τῶν θεραπόντων αὐτοῦ, καὶ ἐθαύμασαν ἐπὶ τῇ σοφίᾳ αὐτῆς καὶ εἶπαν 21 Οὐκ ἔστιν τοιαύτη γυνὴ ἀπ᾽ ἄκρου ἕως ἄκρου τῆς γῆς ἐν καλῷ προσώπῳ καὶ συνέσει λόγων. 22 καὶ εἶπεν πρὸς αὐτὴν Ολοφέρνης Εὖ ἐποίησεν ὁ θεὸς ἀποστείλας σε ἔμπροσθεν τοῦ λαοῦ τοῦ γενηθῆναι ἐν χερσὶν ἡμῶν κράτος, ἐν δὲ τοῖς φαυλίσασι τὸν κύριόν μου ἀπώλειαν. 23 καὶ νῦν ἀστεία εἶ σὺ ἐν τῷ εἴδει σου καὶ ἀγαθὴ ἐν τοῖς λόγοις σου· ὅτι ἐὰν ποιήσῃς καθὰ ἐλάλησας, ὁ θεός σου ἔσται μου θεός, καὶ σὺ ἐν οἴκῳ βασιλέως Ναβουχοδονοσορ καθήσῃ καὶ ἔσῃ ὀνομαστὴ παρὰ πᾶσαν τὴν γῆν.

12 Καὶ ἐκέλευσεν εἰσαγαγεῖν αὐτὴν οὗ ἐτίθετο τὰ ἀργυρώματα αὐτοῦ καὶ συνέταξεν καταστρῶσαι αὐτῇ ἀπὸ τῶν ὀψοποιημάτων αὐτοῦ καὶ τοῦ οἴνου αὐτοῦ πίνειν. 2 καὶ εἶπεν Ιουδιθ Οὐ φάγομαι ἐξ αὐτῶν, ἵνα μὴ γένηται σκάνδαλον, ἀλλ᾽ ἐκ τῶν ἠκολουθηκότων μοι χορηγηθήσεται. 3 καὶ εἶπεν πρὸς αὐτὴν Ολοφέρνης Ἐὰν δὲ ἐκλίπῃ τὰ ὄντα μετὰ σοῦ, πόθεν ἐξοίσομέν σοι δοῦναι ὅμοια αὐτοῖς; οὐ γάρ ἐστιν μεθ᾽ ἡμῶν ἐκ τοῦ γένους σου. 4 καὶ εἶπεν Ιουδιθ πρὸς αὐτόν Ζῇ ἡ ψυχή σου, κύριέ μου, ὅτι οὐ δαπανήσει ἡ δούλη σου τὰ ὄντα μετ᾽ ἐμοῦ, ἕως ἂν ποιήσῃ κύριος ἐν χειρί μου ἃ ἐβουλεύσατο. 5 καὶ ἠγάγοσαν αὐτὴν οἱ θεράποντες Ολοφέρνου εἰς τὴν σκηνήν, καὶ ὕπνωσεν μέχρι μεσούσης τῆς νυκτός. καὶ ἀνέστη πρὸς τὴν ἑωθινὴν φυλακήν. 6 καὶ

KING JAMES VERSION

20 Then her words pleased Holofernes and all his servants; and they marvelled at her wisdom, and said,

21 There is not such a woman from one end of the earth to the other, both for beauty of face, and wisdom of words.

22 Likewise Holofernes said unto her, God hath done well to send thee before the people, that strength might be in our hands, and destruction upon them that lightly regard my lord.

23 And now thou art both beautiful in thy countenance, and witty in thy words: surely if thou do as thou hast spoken, thy God shall be my God, and thou shalt dwell in the house of king Nabuchodonosor, and shalt be renowned through the whole earth.

12 Then he commanded to bring her in where his plate was set; and bade that they should prepare for her of his own meats, and that she should drink of his own wine.

2 And Judith said, I will not eat thereof, lest there be an offence: but provision shall be made for me of the things that I have brought.

3 Then Holofernes said unto her, If thy provision should fail, how should we give thee the like? for there be none with us of thy nation.

4 Then said Judith unto him, As thy soul liveth, my lord, thine handmaid shall not spend those things that I have, before the Lord work by mine hand the things that he hath determined.

5 Then the servants of Holofernes brought her into the tent, and she slept till midnight, and she arose when it was toward the morning watch,

DOUAY OLD TESTAMENT

18 And all these words pleased Holofernes, and his servants, and they admired her wisdom, and they said one to another:

19 There is not such another woman upon earth in look, in beauty, and in sense of words.

20 And Holofernes said to her: God hath done well who sent thee before the people, that thou mightest give them into our hands:

21 And because thy promise is good, if thy God shall do this for me, he shall also be my God, and thou shalt be great in the house of Nabuchodonosor, and thy name shall be renowned through all the earth.

12 THEN he ordered that she should go in where his treasures were laid up, and bade her tarry there, and he appointed what should be given her from his own table.

2 And Judith answered him and said: Now I cannot eat of these things which thou commandest to be given me, lest sin come upon me: but I will eat of the things which I have brought.

3 And Holofernes said to her: If these things which thou hast brought with thee fail thee, what shall we do for thee?

4 And Judith said: As thy soul liveth, my lord, thy handmaid shall not spend all these things till God do by my hand that which I have purposed. And his servants brought her into the tent which he had commanded.

KNOX TRANSLATION

18 This was welcome hearing for Holofernes and all that served under him; what prudence was hers! They told one another, 19 Never was a woman such as this, so fair to look upon, so wise to listen to. 20 And Holofernes said to her, God has been good indeed, sending thee here in advance of thy people, so as to give them up into our hands. 21 These are fair promises thou makest; will he but bring them to fulfilment, thy God shall be my God too, and thou thyself, at Nabuchodonosor's court, shalt be held in high honour; wide as the world shall be thy renown.

12 And now Holofernes would have her repair to the tent where he kept his treasures, and lodge there; and he was for sending food to her there from his own table. 2 But Judith told him, Eat I may not of the portion thou wouldst assign me; that were a grave fault; I have brought my own provisions with me. 3 Ay, thou hast brought them, Holofernes said, but how if they should not suffice? How shall we fend for thee? 4 My lord, answered Judith, as thou art a living man, God will prosper thy handmaid's undertaking before ever these are spent. So his servants shewed her to the tent he had designed for her; 5 but as she entered it,

Today's English Version

20 Holofernes and his personal servants were pleased with what Judith had said, and they admired her wisdom. 21 "She must be the wisest and most beautiful woman in the world," they commented one to another.

22 Then Holofernes said to her, "It's a good thing that God has sent you here to bring us victory and to destroy those who have insulted King Nebuchadnezzar. 23 Not only are you beautiful, but you know how to make a speech. If you do as you have promised, your God will be my God. You will live in King Nebuchadnezzar's palace and will be famous throughout the world."

12 Holofernes commanded his men to take Judith to the table which was set with his silverware and to serve her some of his own special food and wine. 2 But Judith refused. "I cannot eat your food," she said, "for I would be breaking the laws of my God. I will eat only what I have brought with me."

3 "But what will you do when your food and wine are gone?" Holofernes asked. "Where will we get more food for you? There are no Israelites here in our camp."

4 "Sir," Judith answered, "as surely as you live, I have more than enough food to last until the Lord has used me to carry out his plan."

5 Then Holofernes' personal servants led Judith to a tent. She slept there until the time of the morning watch just

New Revised Standard Version

20 Her words pleased Holofernes and all his servants. They marveled at her wisdom and said, 21 "No other woman from one end of the earth to the other looks so beautiful or speaks so wisely!" 22 Then Holofernes said to her, "God has done well to send you ahead of the people, to strengthen our hands and bring destruction on those who have despised my lord. 23 You are not only beautiful in appearance, but wise in speech. If you do as you have said, your God shall be my God, and you shall live in the palace of King Nebuchadnezzar and be renowned throughout the whole world."

12 Then he commanded them to bring her in where his silver dinnerware was kept, and ordered them to set a table for her with some of his own delicacies, and with some of his own wine to drink. 2 But Judith said, "I cannot partake of them, or it will be an offense; but I will have enough with the things I brought with me." 3 Holofernes said to her, "If your supply runs out, where can we get you more of the same? For none of your people are here with us." 4 Judith replied, "As surely as you live, my lord, your servant will not use up the supplies I have with me before the Lord carries out by my hand what he has determined."

5 Then the servants of Holofernes brought her into the tent, and she slept until midnight. Toward the morning

New American Bible

20 Her words pleased Holofernes and all his servants; they marveled at her wisdom and exclaimed, 21 "No other woman from one end of the world to the other looks so beautiful and speaks so wisely!" 22 Then Holofernes said to her: "God has done well in sending you ahead of your people, to bring victory to our arms, and destruction to those who have despised my lord. 23 You are fair to behold, and your words are well spoken. If you do as you have said, your God will be my God; you shall dwell in the palace of King Nebuchadnezzar, and shall be renowned throughout the earth."

12 Then he ordered them to lead her into the room where his silverware was kept, and bade them set a table for her with his own delicacies to eat and his own wine to drink. 2 But Judith said, "I will not partake of them, lest it be an occasion of sin; but I shall be amply supplied from the things I brought with me." 3 Holofernes asked her: "But if your provisions give out, where shall we get more of the same to provide for you? None of your people are with us." 4 Judith answered him, "As surely as you, my lord, live, your handmaid will not use up her supplies till the LORD accomplishes by my hand what he has determined."

5 Then the servants of Holofernes led her into the tent, where she slept till midnight. In the night watch just before

New Jerusalem Bible

20 Her words pleased Holofernes, and all his adjutants. Full of admiration at her wisdom they exclaimed, 21 'There is no woman like her from one end of the earth to the other, so lovely of face and so wise of speech!' 22 Holofernes said, 'God has done well to send you ahead of the others. Strength will be ours, and ruin theirs who have insulted my lord. 23 As for you, you are as beautiful as you are eloquent; if you do as you have promised, your God shall be my God, and you yourself shall make your home in the palace of King Nebuchadnezzar and be famous throughout the world.'

12 With that he had her brought in to where his silver dinner service was already laid, and had his own food served to her and his own wine poured out for her. 2 But Judith said, 'I would rather not eat this, in case I incur some fault. What I have brought will be enough for me.' 3 'Suppose your provisions run out,' Holofernes asked, 'how could we get more of the same sort? We have no one belonging to your race here.' 4 'May your soul live, my lord,' Judith answered, 'the Lord will have used me to accomplish his plan, before your servant has finished these provisions.' 5 Holofernes' adjutants then took her to a tent where she slept until midnight. A little before the morning watch, she

GREEK OLD TESTAMENT

ἀπέστειλεν πρὸς Ολοφέρνην λέγουσα Ἐπιταξάτω δὴ ὁ κύριός μου ἐᾶσαι τὴν δούλην σου ἐπὶ προσευχὴν ἐξελθεῖν· [7] καὶ προσέταξεν Ολοφέρνης τοῖς σωματοφύλαξιν μὴ διακωλύειν αὐτήν. καὶ παρέμεινεν ἐν τῇ παρεμβολῇ ἡμέρας τρεῖς. καὶ ἐξεπορεύετο κατὰ νύκτα εἰς τὴν φάραγγα Βαιτυλουα καὶ ἐβαπτίζετο ἐν τῇ παρεμβολῇ ἐπὶ τῆς πηγῆς τοῦ ὕδατος.
[8] καὶ ὡς ἀνέβη, ἐδέετο τοῦ κυρίου θεοῦ Ισραηλ κατευθῦναι τὴν ὁδὸν αὐτῆς εἰς ἀνάστημα τῶν υἱῶν τοῦ λαοῦ αὐτοῦ·
[9] καὶ εἰσπορευομένη καθαρὰ παρέμενεν ἐν τῇ σκηνῇ, μέχρι οὗ προσηνέγκατο τὴν τροφὴν αὐτῆς πρὸς ἑσπέραν.

[10] Καὶ ἐγένετο ἐν τῇ ἡμέρᾳ τῇ τετάρτῃ ἐποίησεν Ολοφέρνης πότον τοῖς δούλοις αὐτοῦ μόνοις καὶ οὐκ ἐκάλεσεν εἰς τὴν κλῆσιν οὐδένα τῶν πρὸς ταῖς χρείαις. [11] καὶ εἶπεν Βαγῴᾳ τῷ εὐνούχῳ, ὃς ἦν ἐφεστηκὼς ἐπὶ πάντων τῶν αὐτοῦ Πεῖσον δὴ πορευθεὶς τὴν γυναῖκα τὴν Εβραίαν, ἥ ἐστιν παρὰ σοί, τοῦ ἐλθεῖν πρὸς ἡμᾶς καὶ φαγεῖν καὶ πιεῖν μεθ' ἡμῶν·
[12] ἰδοὺ γὰρ αἰσχρὸν τῷ προσώπῳ ἡμῶν εἰ γυναῖκα τοιαύτην παρήσομεν οὐχ ὁμιλήσαντες αὐτῇ· ὅτι ἐὰν ταύτην μὴ ἐπισπασώμεθα, καταγελάσεται ἡμῶν. [13] καὶ ἐξῆλθεν Βαγώας ἀπὸ προσώπου Ολοφέρνου καὶ εἰσῆλθεν πρὸς αὐτὴν καὶ εἶπεν Μὴ ὀκνησάτω δὴ ἡ παιδίσκη ἡ καλὴ αὕτη ἐλθοῦσα πρὸς τὸν κύριόν μου δοξασθῆναι κατὰ πρόσωπον αὐτοῦ καὶ πίεσαι μεθ' ἡμῶν εἰς εὐφροσύνην οἶνον καὶ γενηθῆναι ἐν τῇ ἡμέρᾳ ταύτῃ ὡς θυγάτηρ μία τῶν υἱῶν Ασσουρ, αἳ παρεστήκασιν ἐν οἴκῳ Ναβουχοδονοσορ. [14] καὶ εἶπεν πρὸς αὐτὸν Ιουδιθ Καὶ τίς εἰμι ἐγὼ ἀντεροῦσα τῷ κυρίῳ μου; ὅτι πᾶν, ὃ ἔσται ἐν τοῖς ὀφθαλμοῖς αὐτοῦ ἀρεστόν, σπεύσασα ποιήσω, καὶ ἔσται τοῦτό μοι ἀγαλλίαμα ἕως ἡμέρας θανάτου μου. [15] καὶ

KING JAMES VERSION

6 And sent to Holofernes, saying, Let my lord now command that thine handmaid may go forth unto prayer.

7 Then Holofernes commanded his guard that they should not stay her: thus she abode in the camp three days, and went out in the night into the valley of Bethulia, and washed herself in a fountain of water by the camp.

8 And when she came out, she besought the Lord God of Israel to direct her way to the raising up of the children of her people.

9 So she came in clean, and remained in the tent, until she did eat her meat at evening.

10 And in the fourth day Holofernes made a feast to his own servants only, and called none of the officers to the banquet.

11 Then said he to Bagoas the eunuch, who had charge over all that he had, Go now, and persuade this Hebrew woman which is with thee, that she come unto us, and eat and drink with us.

12 For, lo, it will be a shame for our person, if we shall let such a woman go, not having had her company; for if we draw her not unto us, she will laugh us to scorn.

13 Then went Bagoas from the presence of Holofernes, and came to her, and he said, Let not this fair damsel fear to come to my lord, and to be honoured in his presence, and drink wine, and be merry with us, and be made this day as one of the daughters of the Assyrians, which serve in the house of Nabuchodonosor.

14 Then said Judith unto him, Who am I now, that I should gainsay my lord? surely whatsoever pleaseth him I will do speedily, and it shall be my joy unto the day of my death.

DOUAY OLD TESTAMENT

5 And when she was going in, she desired that she might have liberty to go out at night and before day to prayer, and to beseech the Lord.

6 And he commanded his chamberlains, that she might go out and in, to adore her God as she pleased, for three days.

7 And she went out in the nights into the valley of Bethulia, and washed herself in a fountain of water.

8 And as she came up, she prayed to the Lord the God of Israel, that he would direct her way to the deliverance of his people.

9 And going in, she remained pure in the tent, until she took her own meat in the evening.

10 And it came to pass on the fourth day, that Holofernes made a supper for his servants, and said to Vagao his eunuch: Go, and persuade that Hebrew woman, to consent of her own accord to dwell with me.

11 For it is looked upon as shameful among the Assyrians, if a woman mock a man, by doing so as to pass free from him.

12 Then Vagao went in to Judith, and said: Let not my good maid be afraid to go in to my lord, that she may be honoured before his face, that she may eat with him and drink wine and be merry.

13 And Judith answered him: Who am I, that I should gainsay my lord?

14 All that shall be good and best before his eyes, I will do. And whatsoever shall please him, that shall be best to me all the days of my life.

KNOX TRANSLATION

she asked that she might be allowed to leave it each night, before day broke, and, praying, make her peace with the Lord. [6] So he gave orders to his chamberlains, that for the next three days she should be allowed to come and go as she would, for the worship of her God; [7] each night she went out to the vale of Bethulia, and washed herself in a fountain there, [8] and prayed, as she came up out of the water, the God of Israel would speed her errand for his people's deliverance. [9] Then she guarded herself against defilement by keeping her tent all day, till she made her meal at sun-down.
[10] On the fourth day, Holofernes made a banquet for his own attendants, and sent his chamberlain Vagoa with an invitation to her. Prevail if thou canst, said he, on this Hebrew woman to grant me, of her own free will, her favours. [11] (Great shame the Assyrians hold it in a man, if any woman fools him, and contrives to escape from his company unmolested.) [12] So Vagoa waited on Judith, and said, Fair lady, make no scruple to appear as an honoured guest in my master's presence, to eat with him, and make merry over the wine. [13] It is not for me, Judith answered, to gainsay my lord in this. [14] Whim and will of his shall be whim and will of mine; I ask no better, all my life, than to obey his

TODAY'S ENGLISH VERSION

before dawn, when she got up 6 and sent a message to Holofernes requesting permission to go out into the valley to pray. 7 Holofernes ordered his guards to let Judith leave the camp. So for three days Judith lived in the camp, and each night she would go out to the valley near Bethulia and bathe at the spring. 8 After she had bathed, she would pray to the Lord God to guide her in her plan to bring victory to Israel. 9 Then she would return to the camp ritually pure and remain in her tent until after the evening meal.

10 On the fourth day of Judith's stay in the camp, Holofernes gave a banquet for his highest ranking officers, but he did not invite any of the officers who were on duty. 11 He said to Bagoas, the eunuch who was in charge of his personal affairs, "Go and persuade the Hebrew woman, who is in your care, to come to my tent to eat and drink with us. 12 It would be a shame to pass up an opportunity to make love to a woman like that. If I don't try to seduce her, she will laugh at me."

13 So Bagoas left Holofernes and went to Judith. "Lovely lady," he said, "the general invites you to his tent for some drinks. Come and enjoy yourself like the Assyrian women who serve in Nebuchadnezzar's palace. This is a great honor."

14 "I shall be glad to accept," Judith answered. "How could I refuse? I'll remember this happy night as long as I live."

NEW REVISED STANDARD VERSION

watch she got up 6 and sent this message to Holofernes: "Let my lord now give orders to allow your servant to go out and pray." 7 So Holofernes commanded his guards not to hinder her. She remained in the camp three days. She went out each night to the valley of Bethulia, and bathed at the spring in the camp.[a] 8 After bathing, she prayed the Lord God of Israel to direct her way for the triumph of his[b] people. 9 Then she returned purified and stayed in the tent until she ate her food toward evening.

10 On the fourth day Holofernes held a banquet for his personal attendants only, and did not invite any of his officers. 11 He said to Bagoas, the eunuch who had charge of his personal affairs, "Go and persuade the Hebrew woman who is in your care to join us and to eat and drink with us. 12 For it would be a disgrace if we let such a woman go without having intercourse with her. If we do not seduce her, she will laugh at us."

13 So Bagoas left the presence of Holofernes, and approached her and said, "Let this pretty girl not hesitate to come to my lord to be honored in his presence, and to enjoy drinking wine with us, and to become today like one of the Assyrian women who serve in the palace of Nebuchadnezzar." 14 Judith replied, "Who am I to refuse my lord? Whatever pleases him I will do at once, and it will be a joy to me until the day of my death." 15 So she proceeded to dress

a Other ancient authorities lack *in the camp* *b* Other ancient authorities read *her*

NEW AMERICAN BIBLE

dawn, she rose 6 and sent this message to Holofernes, "Give orders, my lord, to let your handmaid go out for prayer." 7 So Holofernes ordered his bodyguard not to hinder her. Thus she stayed in the camp three days. Each night she went out to the ravine of Bethulia, where she washed herself at the spring of the camp. 8 After bathing, she besought the LORD, the God of Israel, to direct her way for the triumph of his people. 9 Then she returned purified to the tent, and remained there until her food was brought to her toward evening.

10 On the fourth day Holofernes gave a banquet for his servants alone, to which he did not invite any of the officers. 11 And he said to Bagoas, the eunuch in charge of his household: "Go and persuade this Hebrew woman in your care to come and to eat and drink with us. 12 It would be a disgrace for us to have such a woman with us without enjoying her company. If we do not entice her, she will laugh us to scorn."

13 So Bagoas left the presence of Holofernes, and came to Judith and said, "So fair a maiden should not be reluctant to come to my lord to be honored by him, to enjoy drinking wine with us, and to be like one of the Assyrian women who live in the palace of Nebuchadnezzar." 14 She replied, "Who am I to refuse my lord? Whatever is pleasing to him I will promptly do. This will be a joy for me till the day of my death."

NEW JERUSALEM BIBLE

got up. 6 She had already sent this request to Holofernes, 'Let my lord kindly give orders for your servant to be allowed to go out and pray,' 7 and Holofernes had ordered his guards not to prevent her. She stayed in the camp for three days; she went out each night to the valley of Bethulia and washed at the spring where the picket had been posted. 8 As she went she prayed to the Lord God of Israel to guide her in her plan to relieve the children of her people. 9 Having purified herself, she would return and stay in her tent until her meal was brought her in the evening.

10 On the fourth day Holofernes gave a banquet, inviting only his own staff and none of the other officers. 11 He said to Bagoas, the officer in charge of his personal affairs, 'Go and persuade that Hebrew woman you are looking after to come and join us and eat and drink in our company. 12 We shall be disgraced if we let a woman like this go without seducing her. If we do not seduce her, everyone will laugh at us!' 13 Bagoas then left Holofernes and went to see Judith. 'Would this young and lovely woman condescend to come to my lord?' he asked. 'She will occupy the seat of honour opposite him, drink the joyful wine with us and be treated today like one of the Assyrian ladies who stand in the palace of Nebuchadnezzar.' 14 'Who am I', Judith replied, 'to resist my lord? I shall not hesitate to do whatever he wishes, and doing this will be my joy to my dying day.'

GREEK OLD TESTAMENT

διαναστᾶσα ἐκοσμήθη τῷ ἱματισμῷ καὶ παντὶ τῷ κόσμῳ τῷ
γυναικείῳ, καὶ προσῆλθεν ἡ δούλη αὐτῆς καὶ ἔστρωσεν αὐτῇ
κατέναντι Ολοφέρνου χαμαὶ τὰ κώδια, ἃ ἔλαβεν παρὰ
Βαγώου εἰς τὴν καθημερινὴν δίαιταν αὐτῆς εἰς τὸ ἐσθίειν
κατακλινομένην ἐπ' αὐτῶν. 16 καὶ εἰσελθοῦσα ἀνέπεσεν
Ιουδιθ, καὶ ἐξέστη ἡ καρδία Ολοφέρνου ἐπ' αὐτήν, καὶ
ἐσαλεύθη ἡ ψυχὴ αὐτοῦ, καὶ ἦν κατεπίθυμος σφόδρα τοῦ
συγγενέσθαι μετ' αὐτῆς. καὶ ἐτήρει καιρὸν τοῦ ἀπατῆσαι
αὐτὴν ἀφ' ἧς ἡμέρας εἶδεν αὐτήν. 17 καὶ εἶπεν πρὸς αὐτὴν
Ολοφέρνης Πίε δὴ καὶ γενήθητι μεθ' ἡμῶν εἰς εὐφροσύνην.
18 καὶ εἶπεν Ιουδιθ Πίομαι δή, κύριε, ὅτι ἐμεγαλύνθη τὸ ζῆν
μου ἐν ἐμοὶ σήμερον παρὰ πάσας τὰς ἡμέρας τῆς γενέσεώς
μου. 19 καὶ λαβοῦσα ἔφαγεν καὶ ἔπιεν κατέναντι αὐτοῦ ἃ
ἡτοίμασεν ἡ δούλη αὐτῆς. 20 καὶ ηὐφράνθη Ολοφέρνης ἀπ'
αὐτῆς καὶ ἔπιεν οἶνον πολὺν σφόδρα, ὅσον οὐκ ἔπιεν πώποτε
ἐν ἡμέρᾳ μιᾷ ἀφ' οὗ ἐγεννήθη.

13 Ὡς δὲ ὀψία ἐγένετο, ἐσπούδασαν οἱ δοῦλοι αὐτοῦ
ἀναλύειν. καὶ Βαγώας συνέκλεισεν τὴν σκηνὴν
ἔξωθεν καὶ ἀπέκλεισεν τοὺς παρεστῶτας ἐκ προσώπου τοῦ
κυρίου αὐτοῦ, καὶ ἀπῴχοντο εἰς τὰς κοίτας αὐτῶν· ἦσαν γὰρ
πάντες κεκοπωμένοι διὰ τὸ ἐπὶ πλεῖον γεγονέναι τὸν πότον.
2 ὑπελείφθη δὲ Ιουδιθ μόνη ἐν τῇ σκηνῇ, καὶ Ολοφέρνης
προπεπτωκὼς ἐπὶ τὴν κλίνην αὐτοῦ· ἦν γὰρ περικεχυμένος
αὐτῷ ὁ οἶνος. 3 καὶ εἶπεν Ιουδιθ τῇ δούλῃ αὐτῆς στῆναι ἔξω
τοῦ κοιτῶνος αὐτῆς καὶ ἐπιτηρεῖν τὴν ἔξοδον αὐτῆς
καθάπερ καθ' ἡμέραν, ἐξελεύσεσθαι γὰρ ἔφη ἐπὶ τὴν
προσευχὴν αὐτῆς. καὶ τῷ Βαγώᾳ ἐλάλησεν κατὰ τὰ ῥήματα

KING JAMES VERSION

15 So she arose, and decked herself with her apparel and all her woman's attire, and her maid went and laid soft skins on the ground for her over against Holofernes, which she had received of Bagoas for her daily use, that she might sit and eat upon them.

16 Now when Judith came in and sat down, Holofernes his heart was ravished with her, and his mind was moved, and he desired greatly her company; for he waited a time to deceive her, from the day that he had seen her.

17 Then said Holofernes unto her, Drink now, and be merry with us.

18 So Judith said, I will drink now, my lord, because my life is magnified in me this day more than all the days since I was born.

19 Then she took and ate and drank before him what her maid had prepared.

20 And Holofernes took great delight in her, and drank more wine than he had drunk at any time in one day since he was born.

13 Now when the evening was come, his servants made haste to depart, and Bagoas shut his tent without, and dismissed the waiters from the presence of his lord; and they went to their beds: for they were all weary, because the feast had been long.

2 And Judith was left alone in the tent, and Holofernes lying along upon his bed: for he was filled with wine.

3 Now Judith had commanded her maid to stand without her bedchamber, and to wait for her coming forth, as she did daily: for she said she would go forth to her prayers, and she spake to Bagoas according to the same purpose.

DOUAY OLD TESTAMENT

15 And she arose and dressed herself out with her garments, and going in she stood before his face.

16 And the heart of Holofernes was smitten, for he was burning with the desire of her.

17 And Holofernes said to her: Drink now, and sit down and be merry; for thou hast found favour before me.

18 And Judith said: I will drink my lord, because my life is magnified this day above all my days.

19 And she took and ate and drank before him what her maid had prepared for her.

20 And Holofernes was made merry on her occasion, and drank exceeding much wine, so much as he had never drunk in his life.

13 AND when it was grown late, his servants made haste to their lodgings, and Vagao shut the chamber doors, and went his way.

2 And they were all overcharged with wine.

3 And Judith was alone in the chamber.

4 But Holofernes lay on his bed, fast asleep, being exceedingly drunk.

5 And Judith spoke to her maid to stand without before the chamber, and to watch:

KNOX TRANSLATION

pleasure. 15 With that, she rose up and threw her robe about
her, and so made her way into Holofernes' presence; 16 fast
beat his heart within him, such was his longing for her
charms. 17 Drink with me, he said; fall to, and make merry;
thou art right welcome. 18 And Judith answered, Drink I will,
my lord; never was a day in my life so proud as this. 19 So
she ate and drank with him, but only what her serving-maid
had prepared for her. 20 And Holofernes, basking in her
smiles, drank ever deeper; never drank Holofernes as on that
night.

13 And now it was late; his attendants were fain to
make for their beds, leaving Vagoa, the last of them,
to shut the doors of the banqueting-room; 2 the wine had
made drowsy men of them. 3 In the banqueting-room, Judith
was now left alone, 4 save for Holofernes, that lay full length
on his couch by the table, in drunken sleep. 5 Her maid she
left at the door, to keep watch; 6 she herself, standing by the

TODAY'S ENGLISH VERSION

15 So Judith got up and put on her prettiest clothes. Her slave woman went ahead of her and placed on the ground in front of Holofernes the lamb skins that Bagoas had given Judith to sit on when she ate. 16 Judith came into the tent and sat down there. Holofernes was aroused when he saw her and had an uncontrollable desire to make love to her. From the first day he had seen her, he had been waiting for a chance to seduce her. 17 "Join us for a drink and enjoy yourself," he said to her.

18 "I'll be glad to, sir," Judith replied; "this is the happiest day of my life." 19 But even then Judith ate and drank only what her slave had prepared. 20 Holofernes was so charmed by her that he drank more wine than he had ever drunk at one time in his whole life.

13 Finally, when it got late, the guests excused themselves and left. Bagoas then closed up the tent from the outside and prevented Holofernes' servants from going in. So they all went to bed; everyone was very tired because the banquet had lasted so long. 2 Judith was left alone in the tent with Holofernes who was lying drunk on his bed. 3 Judith's slave woman was waiting outside the tent for Judith to go and pray, as she had done each night. Judith had also told Bagoas that she would be going out to pray as usual.

NEW REVISED STANDARD VERSION

herself in all her woman's finery. Her maid went ahead and spread for her on the ground before Holofernes the lambskins she had received from Bagoas for her daily use in reclining.

16 Then Judith came in and lay down. Holofernes' heart was ravished with her and his passion was aroused, for he had been waiting for an opportunity to seduce her from the day he first saw her. 17 So Holofernes said to her, "Have a drink and be merry with us!" 18 Judith said, "I will gladly drink, my lord, because today is the greatest day in my whole life." 19 Then she took what her maid had prepared and ate and drank before him. 20 Holofernes was greatly pleased with her, and drank a great quantity of wine, much more than he had ever drunk in any one day since he was born.

13 When evening came, his slaves quickly withdrew. Bagoas closed the tent from outside and shut out the attendants from his master's presence. They went to bed, for they all were weary because the banquet had lasted so long. 2 But Judith was left alone in the tent, with Holofernes stretched out on his bed, for he was dead drunk.

3 Now Judith had told her maid to stand outside the bedchamber and to wait for her to come out, as she did on the other days; for she said she would be going out for her prayers. She had said the same thing to Bagoas. 4 So

NEW AMERICAN BIBLE

15 Thereupon she proceeded to put on her festive garments and all her feminine adornments. Meanwhile her maid went ahead and spread out on the ground for her in front of Holofernes the fleece Bagoas had furnished for her daily use in reclining at her dinner. 16 Then Judith came in and reclined on it. The heart of Holofernes was in rapture over her, and his spirit was shaken. He was burning with the desire to possess her, for he had been biding his time to seduce her from the day he saw her. 17 Holofernes said to her, "Drink and be merry with us!" 18 Judith replied, "I will gladly drink, my lord, for at no time since I was born have I ever enjoyed life as much as I do today." 19 She then took the things her maid had prepared, and ate and drank in his presence. 20 Holofernes, charmed by her, drank a great quantity of wine, more than he had ever drunk on one single day in his life.

13 When it grew late, his servants quickly withdrew. Bagoas closed the tent from the outside and excluded the attendants from their master's presence. They went off to their beds, for they were all tired from the prolonged banquet. 2 Judith was left alone in the tent with Holofernes, who lay prostrate on his bed, for he was sodden with wine. 3 She had ordered her maid to stand outside the bedroom and wait, as on the other days, for her to come out; she said she would be going out for her prayer. To Bagoas she had said this also.

NEW JERUSALEM BIBLE

15 So she got up and put on her dress and all her feminine adornments. Her maid preceded her, and on the floor in front of Holofernes spread the fleece which Bagoas had given Judith for her daily use to lie on as she ate.

16 Judith came in and took her place. The heart of Holofernes was ravished at the sight; his very soul was stirred. He was seized with a violent desire to sleep with her; and indeed since the first day he saw her, he had been waiting for an opportunity to seduce her. 17 'Drink then!' Holofernes said. 'Enjoy yourself with us!' 18 'I am delighted to do so, my lord, for since my birth I have never felt my life more worthwhile than today.' 19 She took what her maid had prepared, and ate and drank facing him. 20 Holofernes was so enchanted with her that he drank far more wine than he had drunk on any other day in his life.

13 It grew late and his staff hurried away. Bagoas closed the tent from the outside, having shown out those who still lingered in his lord's presence. They went to their beds wearied with too much drinking, 2 and Judith was left alone in the tent with Holofernes who had collapsed wine-sodden on his bed. 3 Judith then told her maid to stay just outside the bedroom and wait for her to come out, as she did every morning. She had let it be understood she would be going out to her prayers and had also spoken of her intention to Bagoas.

GREEK OLD TESTAMENT

ταῦτα. 4 καὶ ἀπήλθοσαν πάντες ἐκ προσώπου, καὶ οὐδεὶς κατελείφθη ἐν τῷ κοιτῶνι ἀπὸ μικροῦ ἕως μεγάλου· καὶ στᾶσα Ιουδιθ παρὰ τὴν κλίνην αὐτοῦ εἶπεν ἐν τῇ καρδίᾳ αὐτῆς Κύριε ὁ θεὸς πάσης δυνάμεως, ἐπίβλεψον ἐν τῇ ὥρᾳ ταύτῃ ἐπὶ τὰ ἔργα τῶν χειρῶν μου εἰς ὕψωμα Ιερουσαλημ· 5 ὅτι νῦν καιρὸς ἀντιλαβέσθαι τῆς κληρονομίας σου καὶ ποιῆσαι τὸ ἐπιτήδευμά μου εἰς θραῦσμα ἐχθρῶν, οἳ ἐπανέστησαν ἡμῖν. 6 καὶ προσελθοῦσα τῷ κανόνι τῆς κλίνης, ὃς ἦν πρὸς κεφαλῆς Ολοφέρνου, καθεῖλεν τὸν ἀκινάκην αὐτοῦ ἀπ' αὐτοῦ 7 καὶ ἐγγίσασα τῆς κλίνης ἐδράξατο τῆς κόμης τῆς κεφαλῆς αὐτοῦ καὶ εἶπεν Κραταίωσόν με, κύριε ὁ θεὸς Ισραηλ, ἐν τῇ ἡμέρᾳ ταύτῃ. 8 καὶ ἐπάταξεν εἰς τὸν τράχηλον αὐτοῦ δὶς ἐν τῇ ἰσχύι αὐτῆς καὶ ἀφεῖλεν τὴν κεφαλὴν αὐτοῦ ἀπ' αὐτοῦ. 9 καὶ ἀπεκύλισε τὸ σῶμα αὐτοῦ ἀπὸ τῆς στρωμνῆς καὶ ἀφεῖλε τὸ κωνώπιον ἀπὸ τῶν στύλων· καὶ μετ' ὀλίγον ἐξῆλθεν καὶ παρέδωκεν τῇ ἅβρᾳ αὐτῆς τὴν κεφαλὴν Ολοφέρνου, 10 καὶ ἐνέβαλεν αὐτὴν εἰς τὴν πήραν τῶν βρωμάτων αὐτῆς. καὶ ἐξῆλθον αἱ δύο ἅμα κατὰ τὸν ἐθισμὸν αὐτῶν ἐπὶ τὴν προσευχήν· καὶ διελθοῦσαι τὴν παρεμβολὴν ἐκύκλωσαν τὴν φάραγγα ἐκείνην καὶ προσανέβησαν τὸ ὄρος Βαιτυλουα καὶ ἦλθοσαν πρὸς τὰς πύλας αὐτῆς.

11 Καὶ εἶπεν Ιουδιθ μακρόθεν τοῖς φυλάσσουσιν ἐπὶ τῶν πυλῶν Ἀνοίξατε ἀνοίξατε δὴ τὴν πύλην· μεθ' ἡμῶν ὁ θεὸς ὁ θεὸς ἡμῶν ποιῆσαι ἔτι ἰσχὺν ἐν Ισραηλ καὶ κράτος κατὰ τῶν ἐχθρῶν, καθὰ καὶ σήμερον ἐποίησεν. 12 καὶ ἐγένετο ὡς ἤκουσαν οἱ ἄνδρες τῆς πόλεως αὐτῆς τὴν φωνὴν αὐτῆς, ἐσπούδασαν τοῦ καταβῆναι ἐπὶ τὴν πύλην τῆς πόλεως αὐτῶν καὶ συνεκάλεσαν τοὺς πρεσβυτέρους τῆς πόλεως.

KING JAMES VERSION

4 So all went forth, and none was left in the bedchamber, neither little nor great. Then Judith, standing by his bed, said in her heart, O Lord God of all power, look at this present upon the works of mine hands for the exaltation of Jerusalem.

5 For now is the time to help thine inheritance, and to execute mine enterprizes to the destruction of the enemies which are risen against us.

6 Then she came to the pillar of the bed, which was at Holofernes' head, and took down his fauchion from thence,

7 And approached to his bed, and took hold of the hair of his head, and said, Strengthen me, O Lord God of Israel, this day.

8 And she smote twice upon his neck with all her might, and she took away his head from him,

9 And tumbled his body down from the bed, and pulled down the canopy from the pillars; and anon after she went forth, and gave Holofernes his head to her maid;

10 And she put it in her bag of meat: so they twain went together according to their custom unto prayer: and when they passed the camp, they compassed the valley, and went up the mountain of Bethulia, and came to the gates thereof.

11 Then said Judith afar off to the watchmen at the gate, Open, open now the gate: God, even our God, is with us, to shew his power yet in Jerusalem, and his forces against the enemy, as he hath even done this day.

12 Now when the men of her city heard her voice, they made haste to go down to the gate of their city, and they called the elders of the city.

DOUAY OLD TESTAMENT

6 And Judith stood before the bed praying with tears, and the motion of her lips in silence,

7 Saying: Strengthen me, O Lord God of Israel, and in this hour look on the works of my hands, that as thou hast promised, thou mayst raise up Jerusalem thy city: and that I may bring to pass that which I have purposed, having a belief that it might be done by thee.

8 And when she had said this, she went to the pillar that was at his bed's head, and loosed his sword that hung tied upon it.

9 And when she had drawn it out, she took him by the hair of his head, and said: Strengthen me, O Lord God, at this hour.

10 And she struck twice upon his neck, and cut off his head, and took off his canopy from the pillars, and rolled away his headless body.

11 And after a while she went out, and delivered the head of Holofernes to her maid, and bade her put it into her wallet.

12 And they two went out according to their custom, as it were to prayer, and they passed the camp, and having compassed the valley, they came to the gate of the city.

13 And Judith from afar off cried to the watchmen upon the walls: Open the gates for God is with us, who hath shewn his power in Israel.

14 And it came to pass, when the men had heard her voice, that they called the ancients of the city.

KNOX TRANSLATION

couch, wept silently, and silently moved her lips in prayer. 7 Lord God of Israel, she said, give me strength! Now guide these hands aright, and give Jerusalem the relief thou hast promised; now be the task performed, but for the hope of thy aid, undreamed of! 8 With that, she went to the head of the couch, and unfastened the scimitar that hung there; 9 unsheathed it, and caught the sleeping man by the hair; Lord God, she said, strengthen me now! 10 Twice the scimitar fell on his neck, and cut clean through it; down came the canopy from the pillars, down fell the headless body to the earth, 11 and ere long she was at the doors, giving the severed head to her maid-servant and bidding her thrust it away into the wallet she carried. 12 Then they went out, both of them, right through the camp, as if bound on their customary errand of prayer; but this time they took the winding path along the valley, right up to the city gates.

13 Far away rang the cry of Judith to the watchmen on the city walls, Open the gates! God is on our side. Open the gates! His power yet lives in Israel. 14 These, upon hearing her voice, ran to tell the elders of the city, 15 and all, high

TODAY'S ENGLISH VERSION

4 All the guests and servants were now gone, and Judith
and Holofernes were alone in the tent. Judith stood by
Holofernes' bed and prayed silently, "O Lord, God Almighty,
help me with what I am about to do for the glory of
Jerusalem. 5 Now is the time to rescue your chosen people
and to help me carry out my plan to destroy the enemies who
are threatening us." 6 Judith went to the bedpost by
Holofernes' head and took down his sword. 7 She came closer, seized Holofernes by the hair of his head, and said,
"O Lord, God of Israel, give me strength now." 8 Then Judith
raised the sword and struck him twice in the neck as hard as
she could, chopping off his head. 9 She rolled his body off
the bed and took down the mosquito net from the bedposts.
Then she came out and gave Holofernes' head to her slave,
10 who put it in the food bag.

Then the two women left together, as they always did
when they went to pray. After they had walked through the
Assyrian camp, they crossed the valley and went up the
mountainside until they came to the gates of Bethulia.
11 When they were a short distance away, Judith called out to
the guards at the gate, "Open the gate! Open the gate! Our
God is still with us. Today he has once again shown his
strength in Israel and used his power against our enemies."

12 When the men heard her voice, they hurried down to the
gates and called for the town officials. 13 Everyone, young

NEW REVISED STANDARD VERSION

everyone went out, and no one, either small or great, was
left in the bedchamber. Then Judith, standing beside his bed,
said in her heart, "O Lord God of all might, look in this hour
on the work of my hands for the exaltation of Jerusalem.
5 Now indeed is the time to help your heritage and to carry
out my design to destroy the enemies who have risen up
against us."

6 She went up to the bedpost near Holofernes' head, and
took down his sword that hung there. 7 She came close to
his bed, took hold of the hair of his head, and said, "Give me
strength today, O Lord God of Israel!" 8 Then she struck his
neck twice with all her might, and cut off his head. 9 Next
she rolled his body off the bed and pulled down the canopy
from the posts. Soon afterward she went out and gave
Holofernes' head to her maid, 10 who placed it in her food
bag.

Then the two of them went out together, as they were
accustomed to do for prayer. They passed through the camp,
circled around the valley, and went up the mountain to
Bethulia, and came to its gates. 11 From a distance Judith
called out to the sentries at the gates, "Open, open the gate!
God, our God, is with us, still showing his power in Israel
and his strength against our enemies, as he has done
today!"

12 When the people of her town heard her voice, they hurried down to the town gate and summoned the elders of the

NEW AMERICAN BIBLE

4 When all had departed, and no one, small or great, was
left in the bedroom, Judith stood by Holofernes' bed and said
within herself: "O LORD, God of all might, in this hour look
graciously on my undertaking for the exaltation of
Jerusalem; 5 now is the time for aiding your heritage and for
carrying out my design to shatter the enemies who have
risen against us." 6 She went to the bedpost near the head of
Holofernes, and taking his sword from it, 7 drew close to the
bed, grasped the hair of his head, and said, "Strengthen me
this day, O God of Israel!" 8 Then with all her might she
struck him twice in the neck and cut off his head. 9 She
rolled his body off the bed and took the canopy from its supports. Soon afterward, she came out and handed over the
head of Holofernes to her maid, 10 who put it into her food
pouch; and the two went off together as they were accustomed to do for prayer.

They passed through the camp, and skirting the ravine,
reached Bethulia on the mountain. As they approached its
gates, 11 Judith shouted to the guards from a distance:
"Open! Open the gate! God, our God, is with us. Once more
he has made manifest his strength in Israel and his power
against our enemies; he has done it this very day." 12 When
the citizens heard her voice, they quickly descended to their
city gate and summoned the city elders. 13 All the people,

NEW JERUSALEM BIBLE

4 By now everyone had left Holofernes, and no one, either
important or unimportant, was left in the bedroom. Standing
beside the bed, Judith murmured to herself:

Lord God, to whom all strength belongs,
prosper what my hands are now to do
for the greater glory of Jerusalem;
5 now is the time to recover your heritage
and to further my plans
to crush the enemies arrayed against us.

6 With that she went up to the bedpost by Holofernes' head
and took down his scimitar; 7 coming closer to the bed she
caught him by the hair and said, 'Make me strong today,
Lord God of Israel!' 8 Twice she struck at his neck with all
her might, and cut off his head. 9 She then rolled his body
off the bed and pulled down the canopy from the bedposts.
After which, she went out and gave the head of Holofernes to
her maid 10 who put it in her food bag. The two then left the
camp together, as they always did when they went to pray.
Once they were out of the camp, they skirted the ravine,
climbed the slope to Bethulia and made for the gates.

11 From a distance, Judith shouted to the guards on the
gates, 'Open the gate! Open! For the Lord our God is with us
still, displaying his strength in Israel and his might against
our enemies, as he has done today!' 12 Hearing her voice, the
townsmen hurried down to the town gate and summoned

GREEK OLD TESTAMENT

13 καὶ συνέδραμον πάντες ἀπὸ μικροῦ ἕως μεγάλου αὐτῶν,
ὅτι παράδοξον ἦν αὐτοῖς τὸ ἐλθεῖν αὐτήν, καὶ ἤνοιξαν τὴν
πύλην καὶ ὑπεδέξαντο αὐτὰς καὶ ἅψαντες πῦρ εἰς φαῦσιν
περιεκύκλωσαν αὐτάς. 14 ἡ δὲ εἶπεν πρὸς αὐτοὺς φωνῇ
μεγάλῃ Αἰνεῖτε τὸν θεόν, αἰνεῖτε· αἰνεῖτε τὸν θεόν, ὃς οὐκ
ἀπέστησεν τὸ ἔλεος αὐτοῦ ἀπὸ τοῦ οἴκου Ισραηλ, ἀλλ᾽
ἔθραυσε τοὺς ἐχθροὺς ἡμῶν διὰ χειρός μου ἐν τῇ νυκτὶ ταύτῃ. 15 καὶ προελοῦσα τὴν κεφαλὴν ἐκ τῆς πήρας ἔδειξεν καὶ
εἶπεν αὐτοῖς Ἰδοὺ ἡ κεφαλὴ Ολοφέρνου ἀρχιστρατήγου
δυνάμεως Ασσουρ, καὶ ἰδοὺ τὸ κωνώπιον, ἐν ᾧ κατέκειτο ἐν
ταῖς μέθαις αὐτοῦ· καὶ ἐπάταξεν αὐτὸν ὁ κύριος ἐν χειρὶ
θηλείας. 16 καὶ ζῇ κύριος, ὃς διεφύλαξέν με ἐν τῇ ὁδῷ μου,
ᾗ ἐπορεύθην, ὅτι ἠπάτησεν αὐτὸν τὸ πρόσωπόν μου εἰς
ἀπώλειαν αὐτοῦ, καὶ οὐκ ἐποίησεν ἁμάρτημα μετ᾽ ἐμοῦ εἰς
μίασμα καὶ αἰσχύνην. 17 καὶ ἐξέστη πᾶς ὁ λαὸς σφόδρα καὶ
κύψαντες προσεκύνησαν τῷ θεῷ καὶ εἶπαν ὁμοθυμαδόν
Εὐλογητὸς εἶ, ὁ θεὸς ἡμῶν ὁ ἐξουδενώσας ἐν τῇ ἡμέρᾳ τῇ
σήμερον τοὺς ἐχθροὺς τοῦ λαοῦ σου. 18 καὶ εἶπεν αὐτῇ
Οζιας Εὐλογητὴ σύ, θύγατερ, τῷ θεῷ τῷ ὑψίστῳ παρὰ
πάσας τὰς γυναῖκας τὰς ἐπὶ τῆς γῆς, καὶ εὐλογημένος

KING JAMES VERSION

13 And then they ran all together, both small and great, for it was strange unto them that she was come: so they opened the gate, and received them, and made a fire for a light, and stood round about them.

14 Then she said to them with a loud voice, Praise, praise God, praise God, I say, for he hath not taken away his mercy from the house of Israel, but hath destroyed our enemies by mine hands this night.

15 So she took the head out of the bag, and shewed it, and said unto them, Behold the head of Holofernes, the chief captain of the army of Assur, and behold the canopy, wherein he did lie in his drunkenness; and the Lord hath smitten him by the hand of a woman.

16 As the Lord liveth, who hath kept me in my way that I went, my countenance hath deceived him to his destruction, and yet hath he not committed sin with me, to defile and shame me.

17 Then all the people were wonderfully astonished, and bowed themselves, and worshipped God, and said with one accord, Blessed be thou, O our God, which hast this day brought to nought the enemies of thy people.

18 Then said Ozias unto her, O daughter, blessed art thou of the most high God above all the women upon the earth;

DOUAY OLD TESTAMENT

15 And all ran to meet her from the least to the greatest: for they now had no hopes that she would come.

16 And lighting up lights they all gathered round about her: and she went up to a higher place, and commanded silence to be made. And when all had held their peace,

17 Judith said: Praise ye the Lord our God, who hath not forsaken them that hope in him.

18 And by me his handmaid he hath fulfilled his mercy, which he promised to the house of Israel: and he hath killed the enemy of his people by my hand this night.

19 Then she brought forth the head of Holofernes out of the wallet, and shewed it them, saying: Behold the head of Holofernes the general of the army of the Assyrians, and behold his canopy, wherein he lay in his drunkenness, where the Lord our God slew him by the hand of a woman.

20 But as the same Lord liveth, his angel hath been my keeper both going hence, and abiding there, and returning from thence hither: and the Lord hath not suffered me his handmaid to be defiled, but hath brought me back to you without pollution of sin, rejoicing for his victory, for my escape, and for your deliverance.

21 Give all of you glory to him, because he is good, because his mercy endureth for ever.

22 And they all adored the Lord, and said to her: The Lord hath blessed thee by his power, because by thee he hath brought our enemies to nought.

23 And Ozias the prince of the people of Israel, said to her: Blessed art thou, O daughter, by the Lord the most high God, above all women upon the earth.

KNOX TRANSLATION

and low, went out to meet her; they had thought never to see
her again. 16 There, by torch-light, they gathered round her,
and she, mounting on to higher ground, bade them keep
silence. Silence was made, 17 and thus Judith began, Praise
the Lord our God; he does not forsake those who put their
trust in him. 18 Through me, his handmaid, deliverance has
come to Israel's race, as he promised; through me, this night,
the enemy of his people lies slain. 19 With that, she took
Holofernes' head out of the wallet where it lay hidden. Look
upon this head, she cried, and know that the Assyrian army
has lost its general. Look upon this, the canopy he lay under,
in drunken sleep, when the Lord our God smote him, and by
the hand of a woman. 20 And, as the Lord is a living God,
well did his angel watch over me, thither going, there abiding, and thence returning. The Lord would not have his own
handmaid stained with sin; he has brought me back to you
inviolate, to glory in his triumph, my preservation, and your
deliverance. 21 One and all, then, give thanks to the Lord;
the Lord is gracious, his mercy endures for ever!
22 Thereupon all of them offered the Lord worship; and to
her they said, With his own power the Lord has blessed thee,
and by thy means has brought our enemies to nothing!
23 And Ozias, that was the Israelites' commander, said to her,
Blessing be thine, my daughter, from the Lord God, the most
high, such as no other woman on earth can claim! 24 Blessed

TODAY'S ENGLISH VERSION

and old, ran together to the gate. No one could believe that Judith had come back. They opened the gate for her and her slave and welcomed them. Then, when they had lit a fire to give some light and had gathered around the two women, 14 Judith shouted, "Praise God, give him praise! Praise God, who has not held back his mercy from the people of Israel. Tonight he has used me to destroy our enemies." 15 She then took the head out of the food bag and showed it to the people. "Here," she said, "is the head of Holofernes, the general of the Assyrian army, and here is the mosquito net from his bed, where he lay in a drunken stupor. The Lord used a woman to kill him. 16 As the Lord lives, I swear that Holofernes never touched me, although my beauty deceived him and brought him to his ruin. I was not defiled or disgraced; the Lord took care of me through it all."

17 Everyone in the city was utterly amazed. They bowed down and worshiped God, praying together, "Our God, you are worthy of great praise. Today you have triumphed over the enemies of your people."

18 Then Uzziah said, "Judith, my dear, the Most High God has blessed you more than any other woman on earth. How

NEW REVISED STANDARD VERSION

town. 13 They all ran together, both small and great, for it seemed unbelievable that she had returned. They opened the gate and welcomed them. Then they lit a fire to give light, and gathered around them. 14 Then she said to them with a loud voice, "Praise God, O praise him! Praise God, who has not withdrawn his mercy from the house of Israel, but has destroyed our enemies by my hand this very night!"

15 Then she pulled the head out of the bag and showed it to them, and said, "See here, the head of Holofernes, the commander of the Assyrian army, and here is the canopy beneath which he lay in his drunken stupor. The Lord has struck him down by the hand of a woman. 16 As the Lord lives, who has protected me in the way I went, I swear that it was my face that seduced him to his destruction, and that he committed no sin with me, to defile and shame me."

17 All the people were greatly astonished. They bowed down and worshiped God, and said with one accord, "Blessed are you our God, who have this day humiliated the enemies of your people."

18 Then Uzziah said to her, "O daughter, you are blessed by the Most High God above all other women on earth; and

NEW AMERICAN BIBLE

from the least to the greatest, hurriedly assembled, for her return seemed unbelievable. They opened the gate and welcomed the two women. They made a fire for light; and when they gathered around the two, 14 Judith urged them with a loud voice: "Praise God, praise him! Praise God, who has not withdrawn his mercy from the house of Israel, but has shattered our enemies by my hand this very night." 15 Then she took the head out of the pouch, showed it to them, and said: "Here is the head of Holofernes, general in charge of the Assyrian army, and here is the canopy under which he lay in his drunkenness. The LORD struck him down by the hand of a woman. 16 As the LORD lives, who has protected me in the path I have followed, I swear that it was my face that seduced Holofernes to his ruin, and that he did not sin with me to my defilement or disgrace."

17 All the people were greatly astonished. They bowed down and worshiped God, saying with one accord, "Blessed are you, our God, who today have brought to nought the enemies of your people." 18 Then Uzziah said to her: "Blessed are you, daughter, by the Most High God, above all

NEW JERUSALEM BIBLE

the elders. 13 Everyone, great and small, came running down, since her arrival was unexpected. They threw the gate open, welcomed the women, lit a fire to see by and crowded round them. 14 Then Judith raised her voice and said, 'Praise God! Praise him! Praise the God who has not withdrawn his mercy from the House of Israel, but has shattered our enemies by my hand tonight!' 15 She pulled the head out of the bag and held it for them to see. 'This is the head of Holofernes, general-in-chief of the Assyrian army; here is the canopy under which he lay drunk! The Lord has struck him down by the hand of a woman! 16 Glory to the Lord who has protected me in the course I took! My face seduced him, only to his own undoing; he committed no sin with me to shame me or disgrace me.'

17 Overcome with emotion, the people all prostrated themselves and worshipped God, exclaiming with one voice, 'Blessings on you, our God, for confounding your people's enemies today!' 18 Uzziah then said to Judith:

> May you be blessed, my daughter, by God Most High,
> beyond all women on earth;

GREEK OLD TESTAMENT

κύριος ὁ θεός, ὃς ἔκτισεν τοὺς οὐρανοὺς καὶ τὴν γῆν, ὃς
κατεύθυνέν σε εἰς τραῦμα κεφαλῆς ἄρχοντος ἐχθρῶν ἡμῶν·
19 ὅτι οὐκ ἀποστήσεται ἡ ἐλπίς σου ἀπὸ καρδίας ἀνθρώπων
μνημονευόντων ἰσχὺν θεοῦ ἕως αἰῶνος. 20 καὶ ποιῆσαι σοι
αὐτὰ ὁ θεὸς εἰς ὕψος αἰώνιον τοῦ ἐπισκέψασθαί σε ἐν
ἀγαθοῖς, ἀνθ᾽ ὧν οὐκ ἐφείσω τῆς ψυχῆς σου διὰ τὴν ταπείνωσιν τοῦ γένους ἡμῶν, ἀλλ᾽ ἐπεξῆλθες τῷ πτώματι ἡμῶν ἐπ᾽
εὐθεῖαν πορευθεῖσα ἐνώπιον τοῦ θεοῦ ἡμῶν. καὶ εἶπαν πᾶς ὁ
λαός Γένοιτο γένοιτο.

14 Καὶ εἶπεν πρὸς αὐτοὺς Ιουδιθ Ἀκούσατε δή μου,
ἀδελφοί, καὶ λαβόντες τὴν κεφαλὴν ταύτην κρεμά-
σατε αὐτὴν ἐπὶ τῆς ἐπάλξεως τοῦ τείχους ὑμῶν. 2 καὶ

KING JAMES VERSION

and blessed be the Lord God, which hath created the heavens and the earth, which hath directed thee to the cutting off of the head of the chief of our enemies.

19 For this thy confidence shall not depart from the heart of men, which remember the power of God for ever.

20 And God turn these things to thee for a perpetual praise, to visit thee in good things, because thou hast not spared thy life for the affliction of our nation, but hast revenged our ruin, walking a straight way before our God. And all the people said, So be it, so be it.

14 Then said Judith unto them, Hear me now, my brethren, and take this head, and hang it upon the highest place of your walls.

DOUAY OLD TESTAMENT

24 Blessed be the Lord who made heaven and earth, who hath directed thee to the cutting off the head of the prince of our enemies.

25 Because he hath so magnified thy name this day, that thy praise shall not depart out of the mouth of men who shall be mindful of the power of the Lord for ever, for that thou hast not spared thy life, by reason of the distress and tribulation of thy people, but hast prevented our ruin in the presence of our God.

26 And all the people said: So be it, so be it.

27 And Achior being called for came, and Judith said to him: The God of Israel, to whom thou gavest testimony, that he revengeth himself of his enemies, he hath cut off the head of all the unbelievers this night by my hand.

28 And that thou mayst find that it is so, behold the head of Holofernes, who in the contempt of his pride despised the God of Israel: and threatened thee with death, saying: When the people of Israel shall be taken, I will command thy sides to be pierced with a sword.

29 Then Achior seeing the head of Holofernes, being seized with a great fear he fell on his face upon the earth, and his soul swooned away.

30 But after he had recovered his spirits he fell down at her feet, and reverenced her, and said:

31 Blessed art thou by thy God in every tabernacle of Jacob, for in every nation which shall hear thy name, the God of Israel shall be magnified on occasion of thee.

14 AND Judith said to all the people: Hear me, my brethren, hang ye up this head upon our walls.

KNOX TRANSLATION

be the Lord, maker of heaven and earth, for sending thee out
to wound the head of our arch-enemy. 25 Such high renown
he has given thee this day, that the praise of thee shall never
die on men's lips, so long as they hold the Lord's power in
remembrance. Thy own life thou wouldst not prize, when thy
countrymen were in need and great affliction; thou wouldst
avert our rum, with our God to speed thee. 26 And to that all
the people said Amen.

27 Then Achior was summoned, and thus Judith greeted
him: No credit hast thou lost, by averring that the God of
Israel did not spare his enemies; by my hand, this night, he
has cut down the chief of those who gave thee the lie.
28 Was it not Holofernes that defied the God of Israel, in his
proud insolence, and threatened thyself with death? When
Israel was conquered, thou too, he said, shouldst be put to
the sword. To prove which was the truer prophet, here is his
head. 29 Upon seeing the head of Holofernes, Achior was in
such a great taking of fear that he fell to earth in a swoon.
30 Then, coming back to his senses and taking heart again,
he did reverence, bowing low at her feet; 31 Wherever the
sons of Jacob dwell, said he, God has made thy name a name
of blessing; wherever thy renown reaches through the world,
the God of Israel shall be glorified in the telling of it.

14 Hang we this head from the battlements, Judith said
to the people; and now, brethren, here is my plan.

Today's English Version

worthy of praise is the Lord God who created heaven and
earth! He guided you as you cut off the head of our deadliest
enemy. 19 Your trust in God will never be forgotten by those
who tell of God's power. 20 May God give you everlasting
honor for what you have done. May he reward you with
blessings, because you remained faithful to him and did not
hesitate to risk your own life to relieve the oppression of
your people."

All the people replied, "Amen, amen!"

14 Then Judith said to them, "My friends, please follow
my advice. In the morning, take this head and hang

New Revised Standard Version

blessed be the Lord God, who created the heavens and the
earth, who has guided you to cut off the head of the leader of
our enemies. 19 Your praise[a] will never depart from the
hearts of those who remember the power of God. 20 May God
grant this to be a perpetual honor to you, and may he reward
you with blessings, because you risked your own life when
our nation was brought low, and you averted our ruin, walking in the straight path before our God." And all the people
said, "Amen. Amen."

14 Then Judith said to them, "Listen to me, my friends.
Take this head and hang it upon the parapet of your

[a] Other ancient authorities read *hope*

New American Bible

the women on earth; and blessed be the LORD God, the creator of heaven and earth, who guided your blow at the head
of the chief of our enemies. 19 Your deed of hope will never
be forgotten by those who tell of the might of God. 20 May
God make this redound to your everlasting honor, rewarding
you with blessings, because you risked your life when your
people were being oppressed, and you averted our disaster,
walking uprightly before our God." And all the people
answered, "Amen! Amen!"

14 Then Judith said to them: "Listen to me, my brothers.
Take this head and hang it on the parapet of your

New Jerusalem Bible

and blessed be the Lord God,
Creator of heaven and earth,
who guided you to cut off the head
of the leader of our enemies!
19 The trust which you have shown
will not pass from human hearts,
as they commemorate
the power of God for evermore.
20 God grant you may be always held in honour
and rewarded with blessings,
since you did not consider your own life
when our nation was brought to its knees,
but warded off our ruin,
walking in the right path before our God.

And the people all said, 'Amen! Amen!'

14 Judith said, 'Listen to me, brothers. Take this head
and hang it on your battlements. 2 When morning

GREEK OLD TESTAMENT

ἔσται ἡνίκα ἐὰν διαφαύσῃ ὁ ὄρθρος καὶ ἐξέλθῃ ὁ ἥλιος ἐπὶ
τὴν γῆν, ἀναλήμψεσθε ἕκαστος τὰ σκεύη τὰ πολεμικὰ ὑμῶν
καὶ ἐξελεύσεσθε πᾶς ἀνὴρ ἰσχύων ἔξω τῆς πόλεως καὶ
δώσετε ἀρχηγὸν εἰς αὐτοὺς ὡς καταβαίνοντες ἐπὶ τὸ πεδίον
εἰς τὴν προφυλακὴν υἱῶν Ασσουρ, καὶ οὐ καταβήσεσθε. 3 καὶ
ἀναλαβόντες οὗτοι τὰς πανοπλίας αὐτῶν πορεύσονται εἰς
τὴν παρεμβολὴν αὐτῶν καὶ ἐγεροῦσι τοὺς στρατηγοὺς τῆς
δυνάμεως Ασσουρ· καὶ συνδραμοῦνται ἐπὶ τὴν σκηνὴν
Ολοφέρνου καὶ οὐχ εὑρήσουσιν αὐτόν, καὶ ἐπιπεσεῖται ἐπ'
αὐτοὺς φόβος, καὶ φεύξονται ἀπὸ προσώπου ὑμῶν. 4 καὶ
ἐπακολουθήσαντες ὑμεῖς καὶ πάντες οἱ κατοικοῦντες πᾶν
ὅριον Ισραηλ καταστρώσατε αὐτοὺς ἐν ταῖς ὁδοῖς αὐτῶν.
5 πρὸ δὲ τοῦ ποιῆσαι ταῦτα καλέσατέ μοι Αχιωρ τὸν
Αμμανίτην, ἵνα ἰδὼν ἐπιγνοῖ τὸν ἐκφαυλίσαντα τὸν οἶκον
τοῦ Ισραηλ καὶ αὐτὸν ὡς εἰς θάνατον ἀποστείλαντα εἰς
ἡμᾶς. 6 καὶ ἐκάλεσαν τὸν Αχιωρ ἐκ τοῦ οἴκου Οζια· ὡς δὲ
ἦλθεν καὶ εἶδεν τὴν κεφαλὴν Ολοφέρνου ἐν χειρὶ ἀνδρὸς
ἑνὸς ἐν τῇ ἐκκλησίᾳ τοῦ λαοῦ, ἔπεσεν ἐπὶ πρόσωπον, καὶ
ἐξελύθη τὸ πνεῦμα αὐτοῦ. 7 ὡς δὲ ἀνέλαβον αὐτόν, προσέπεσεν τοῖς ποσὶν Ιουδιθ καὶ προσεκύνησεν τῷ προσώπῳ αὐτῆς
καὶ εἶπεν Εὐλογημένη σὺ ἐν παντὶ σκηνώματι Ιουδα καὶ ἐν
παντὶ ἔθνει, οἵτινες ἀκούσαντες τὸ ὄνομά σου ταραχθήσον-
ται· 8 καὶ νῦν ἀνάγγειλόν μοι ὅσα ἐποίησας ἐν ταῖς
ἡμέραις ταύταις. καὶ ἀπήγγειλεν αὐτῷ Ιουδιθ ἐν μέσῳ τοῦ
λαοῦ πάντα, ὅσα ἦν πεποιηκυῖα ἀφ' ἧς ἡμέρας ἐξῆλθεν ἕως
οὗ ἐλάλει αὐτοῖς. 9 ὡς δὲ ἐπαύσατο λαλοῦσα, ἠλάλαξεν ὁ
λαὸς φωνῇ μεγάλῃ καὶ ἔδωκεν φωνὴν εὐφρόσυνον ἐν τῇ πόλει

KING JAMES VERSION

2 And so soon as the morning shall appear, and the sun shall come forth upon the earth, take ye every one his weapons, and go forth every valiant man out of the city, and set ye a captain over them, as though ye would go down into the field toward the watch of the Assyrians; but go not down.

3 Then they shall take their armour, and shall go into their camp, and raise up the captains of the army of Assur, and they shall run to the tent of Holofernes, but shall not find him: then fear shall fall upon them, and they shall flee before your face.

4 So ye, and all that inhabit the coast of Israel, shall pursue them, and overthrow them as they go.

5 But before ye do these things, call me Achior the Ammonite, that he may see and know him that despised the house of Israel, and that sent him to us, as it were to his death.

6 Then they called Achior out of the house of Ozias; and when he was come, and saw the head of Holofernes in a man's hand in the assembly of the people, he fell down on his face, and his spirit failed.

7 But when they had recovered him, he fell at Judith's feet, and reverenced her, and said, Blessed art thou in all the tabernacles of Juda, and in all nations, which hearing thy name shall be astonished.

8 Now therefore tell me all the things that thou hast done in these days. Then Judith declared unto him in the midst of the people all that she had done, from the day that she went forth until that hour she spake unto them.

9 And when she had left off speaking, the people shouted with a loud voice, and made a joyful noise in their city.

DOUAY OLD TESTAMENT

2 And as soon as the sun shall rise, let every man take his arms, and rush ye out, not as going down beneath, but as making an assault.

3 Then the watchmen must needs run to awake their prince for the battle.

4 And when the captains of them shall run to the tent of Holofernes, and shall find him without his head wallowing in his blood, fear shall fall upon them.

5 And when you shall know that they are fleeing, go after them securely, for the Lord will destroy them under your feet.

KNOX TRANSLATION

2 At sunrise, arm all of you, and go out to the attack; but this
attack of yours will be a feint, you will not go down into the
plain. 3 It will suffice to make the advance guards retreat,
and rouse their general; 4 and when their leaders hasten to
the tent of Holofernes, to find his headless body lying in a
pool of blood, they will be overcome by terror. 5 Then, once
assured that they are ready for flight, go out after them
undismayed, and the Lord will beat them to dust under your
feet.

TODAY'S ENGLISH VERSION

it on the town wall. 2 Appoint a leader for yourselves, and at sunrise have all your able-bodied men take their weapons and march out of the town with him, as if they were going down into the valley to attack the Assyrian outpost. 3 The Assyrian guards will grab their weapons and rush back to camp to wake up their officers. The officers will run to Holofernes' tent but will not find him, and the whole army will be terrified and retreat as you advance against them. 4 Then you and all the other Israelites will be able to follow them and kill them as they retreat. 5 But before you do any of this, send Achior the Ammonite to me. I want to see if he recognizes Holofernes, the man who spoke of Israel with contempt and sent Achior to us, thinking he would be killed along with the rest of us."

6 So they called Achior from Uzziah's house. But when he came and saw the head of Holofernes in the hands of one of the men, Achior fainted and fell to the floor. 7 When they had helped him up, Achior bowed at Judith's feet in respect. "May every family in the land of Judah praise you," he said, "and may every nation tremble with terror when they hear your name. 8 Please tell me how you managed to do this."

While all the people were gathered around, Judith told him everything that she had done from the day she left the town until that moment. 9 When she had finished her story, the people cheered so loudly that the whole town echoed with

NEW REVISED STANDARD VERSION

wall. 2 As soon as day breaks and the sun rises on the earth, each of you take up your weapons, and let every able-bodied man go out of the town; set a captain over them, as if you were going down to the plain against the Assyrian outpost; only do not go down. 3 Then they will seize their arms and go into the camp and rouse the officers of the Assyrian army. They will rush into the tent of Holofernes and will not find him. Then panic will come over them, and they will flee before you. 4 Then you and all who live within the borders of Israel will pursue them and cut them down in their tracks. 5 But before you do all this, bring Achior the Ammonite to me so that he may see and recognize the man who despised the house of Israel and sent him to us as if to his death."

6 So they summoned Achior from the house of Uzziah. When he came and saw the head of Holofernes in the hand of one of the men in the assembly of the people, he fell down on his face in a faint. 7 When they raised him up he threw himself at Judith's feet, and did obeisance to her, and said, "Blessed are you in every tent of Judah! In every nation those who hear your name will be alarmed. 8 Now tell me what you have done during these days."

So Judith told him in the presence of the people all that she had done, from the day she left until the moment she began speaking to them. 9 When she had finished, the people raised a great shout and made a joyful noise in their

NEW AMERICAN BIBLE

wall. 2 At daybreak, when the sun rises on the earth, let each of you seize his weapons, and let all the able-bodied men rush out of the city under command of a captain, as if about to go down into the plain against the advance guard of the Assyrians, but without going down. 3 They will seize their armor and hurry to their camp to awaken the generals of the Assyrian army. When they run to the tent of Holofernes and do not find him, panic will seize them, and they will flee before you. 4 Then you and all the other inhabitants of the whole territory of Israel will pursue them and strike them down in their tracks. 5 But before doing this, summon for me Achior the Ammonite, that he may see and recognize the one who despised the house of Israel and sent him here to meet his death."

6 So they called Achior from the house of Uzziah. When he came and saw the head of Holofernes in the hand of one of the men in the assembly of the people, he fell forward in a faint. 7 Then, after they lifted him up, he threw himself at the feet of Judith in homage, saying: "Blessed are you in every tent of Judah; and in every foreign nation, all who hear of you will be struck with terror. 8 But now, tell me all that you did during these days." So Judith told him, in the presence of the people, all that she had been doing from the day she left till the time she began speaking to them. 9 When she finished her account, the people cheered loudly, and their

NEW JERUSALEM BIBLE

comes and the sun is up, let every man take his arms and every able-bodied man leave the town. Appoint a leader for them, as if you meant to march down to the plain against the Assyrian advanced post. But you must not do this. 3 The Assyrians will gather up their equipment, make for their camp and wake up their commanders; they in turn will rush to the tent of Holofernes and not be able to find him. They will then be seized with panic and flee at your advance. 4 All you and the others who live in the territory of Israel will have to do is to give chase and slaughter them as they retreat.

5 'But before you do this, call me Achior the Ammonite, for him to see and identify the man who held the House of Israel in contempt, the man who sent him to us as someone already doomed to die.' 6 So they had Achior brought from Uzziah's house. No sooner had he arrived and seen the head of Holofernes held by a member of the people's assembly than he fell on his face in a faint. 7 They lifted him up. He then threw himself at Judith's feet and, prostrate before her, exclaimed:

May you be blessed in all the tents of Judah
and in every nation;
those who hear your name
will be seized with dread!

8 'Now tell me everything that you have done in these past few days.' And surrounded by the people, Judith told him everything she had done from the day she left Bethulia to the moment when she was speaking. 9 When she came to the end, the people cheered at the top of their voices until the

GREEK OLD TESTAMENT

αὐτῶν. 10 ἰδὼν δὲ Αχιωρ πάντα, ὅσα ἐποίησεν ὁ θεὸς τοῦ
Ισραηλ, ἐπίστευσεν τῷ θεῷ σφόδρα καὶ περιετέμετο τὴν
σάρκα τῆς ἀκροβυστίας αὐτοῦ καὶ προσετέθη εἰς τὸν οἶκον
Ισραηλ ἕως τῆς ἡμέρας ταύτης.
11 Ἡνίκα δὲ ὁ ὄρθρος ἀνέβη, καὶ ἐκρέμασαν τὴν κεφαλὴν
Ολοφέρνου ἐκ τοῦ τείχους, καὶ ἀνέλαβεν πᾶς ἀνὴρ τὰ ὅπλα
αὐτοῦ καὶ ἐξήλθοσαν κατὰ σπείρας ἐπὶ τὰς ἀναβάσεις τοῦ
ὄρους. 12 οἱ δὲ υἱοὶ Ασσουρ ὡς εἶδον αὐτούς, διέπεμψαν ἐπὶ
τοὺς ἡγουμένους αὐτῶν· οἱ δὲ ἦλθον ἐπὶ τοὺς στρατηγοὺς
καὶ χιλιάρχους καὶ ἐπὶ πάντα ἄρχοντα αὐτῶν. 13 καὶ
παρεγένοντο ἐπὶ τὴν σκηνὴν Ολοφέρνου καὶ εἶπαν τῷ ὄντι
ἐπὶ πάντων τῶν αὐτοῦ Ἔγειρον δὴ τὸν κύριον ἡμῶν, ὅτι
ἐτόλμησαν οἱ δοῦλοι καταβαίνειν ἐφ᾽ ἡμᾶς εἰς πόλεμον, ἵνα
ἐξολεθρευθῶσιν εἰς τέλος. 14 καὶ εἰσῆλθεν Βαγώας καὶ
ἔκρουσε τὴν αὐλαίαν τῆς σκηνῆς· ὑπενόει γὰρ καθεύδειν
αὐτὸν μετὰ Ιουδιθ. 15 ὡς δ᾽ οὐθεὶς ἐπήκουσεν, διαστείλας
εἰσῆλθεν εἰς τὸν κοιτῶνα καὶ εὗρεν αὐτὸν ἐπὶ τῆς χελωνίδος
ἐρριμμένον νεκρόν, καὶ ἡ κεφαλὴ αὐτοῦ ἀφῄρητο ἀπ᾽ αὐτοῦ.
16 καὶ ἐβόησεν φωνῇ μεγάλη μετὰ κλαυθμοῦ καὶ στεναγμοῦ
καὶ βοῆς ἰσχυρᾶς καὶ διέρρηξεν τὰ ἱμάτια αὐτοῦ. 17 καὶ

KING JAMES VERSION

10 And when Achior had seen all that the God of Israel had done, he believed in God greatly, and circumcised the flesh of his foreskin, and was joined unto the house of Israel unto this day.

11 And as soon as the morning arose, they hanged the head of Holofernes upon the wall, and every man took his weapons, and they went forth by bands unto the straits of the mountain.

12 But when the Assyrians saw them, they sent to their leaders, which came to their captains and tribunes, and to every one of their rulers.

13 So they came to Holofernes' tent, and said to him that had the charge of all his things, Waken now our lord: for the slaves have been bold to come down against us to battle, that they may be utterly destroyed.

14 Then went in Bagoas, and knocked at the door of the tent; for he thought that he had slept with Judith.

15 But because none answered, he opened it, and went into the bedchamber, and found him cast upon the floor dead, and his head was taken from him.

16 Therefore he cried with a loud voice, with weeping, and sighing, and a mighty cry, and rent his garments.

DOUAY OLD TESTAMENT

6 Then Achior seeing the power that the God of Israel had wrought, leaving the religion of the Gentiles, he believed God, and circumcised the flesh of his foreskin, and was joined to the people of Israel, with all the succession of his kindred until this present day.

7 And immediately at break of day, they hung up the head of Holofernes upon the walls, and every man took his arms, and they went out with a great noise and shouting.

8 And the watchmen seeing this, ran to the tent of Holofernes.

9 And they that were in the tent came, and made a noise before the door of the chamber to awake him, endeavouring by art to break his rest, that Holofernes might awake, not by their calling him, but by their noise.

10 For no man durst knock, or open and go into the chamber of the general of the Assyrians.

11 But when his captains and tribunes were come, and all the chiefs of the army of the king of the Assyrians, they said to the chamberlains:

12 Go in, and awake him, for the mice, coming out of their holes, have presumed to challenge us to fight.

13 Then Vagao going into his chamber, stood before the curtain, and made a clapping with his hands: for he thought that he was sleeping with Judith.

14 But when with hearkening, he perceived no motion of one lying, he came near to the curtain, and lifting it up, and seeing the body of Holofernes, lying upon the ground, without the head, weltering in his blood, he cried out with a loud voice, with weeping, and rent his garments.

KNOX TRANSLATION

6 (Meanwhile Achior, such visible proof before his eyes of
what Israel's God could do, cast heathenry aside and learned
to believe in God. He would be circumcised, and reckoned
among Israel's folk, and so his posterity remain to this day.)
7 No sooner was day dawned, and Holofernes' head raised
aloft on the battlements, than all took up their arms, and
sallied out with a great stir and noise of shouting, 8 whereupon the enemy's advance guard hastened back to
Holofernes' tent. 9 The guards there went to the door of the
banqueting-room and bustled to and fro; rouse their lord
they must, but they had rather make this show of commotion and disturb him with their din, than wake him outright;
10 never a man in all the Assyrian army durst knock at the
door or go in. 11 But now chief and captain and commander
in the Assyrian king's service were waiting there, and they
said to Holofernes' attendants, 12 Go in and rouse him; these
Israelite rats have left their holes, and are boldly offering battle. 13 Upon this, Vagoa went into the room where he lay,
and stood behind the curtain clapping his hands; no doubt
had he but Holofernes was there with Judith for his bed-fel-
low. 14 Then, when his ears told him that the sleeper had not
moved, he went closer to the curtain and lifted it. And when
he saw the headless body of Holofernes lying there on the
ground, weltering in its own blood, he gave a loud cry of
lament, and tore his garments about him. 15 Making his way

TODAY'S ENGLISH VERSION

sounds of joy. 10 When Achior heard all that the God of
Israel had done, he became a firm believer. He was circumcised and made a member of the Israelite community, as his
descendants are to the present day.
11 The next morning the Israelites hung the head of
Holofernes on the wall of the town. All of them took up their
weapons and went out in companies to the slopes in front of
the town. 12 When the Assyrians saw what was happening,
they sent word to their officers, and these reported the matter
to their superiors. 13 These men then went to Holofernes'
tent and said to Bagoas, "Wake up the general! Those worthless Israelites have dared to come down from the mountain
to attack us; they are just asking to be destroyed."
14 Bagoas went in and clapped his hands in front of the
sleeping quarters of the tent, thinking that Holofernes was in
bed with Judith. 15 When there was no answer, he drew the
curtain aside and went in, and there he found the headless
body sprawled over a footstool. 16 Bagoas let out a yell. He
screamed, tore his clothes, and started groaning and weeping.

NEW REVISED STANDARD VERSION

town. 10 When Achior saw all that the God of Israel had
done, he believed firmly in God. So he was circumcised, and
joined the house of Israel, remaining so to this day.
11 As soon as it was dawn they hung the head of Holofernes on the wall. Then they all took their weapons, and
they went out in companies to the mountain passes.
12 When the Assyrians saw them they sent word to their commanders, who then went to the generals and the captains
and to all their other officers. 13 They came to Holofernes'
tent and said to the steward in charge of all his personal
affairs, "Wake up our lord, for the slaves have been so bold
as to come down against us to give battle, to their utter
destruction."
14 So Bagoas went in and knocked at the entry of the
tent, for he supposed that he was sleeping with Judith.
15 But when no one answered, he opened it and went into the
bedchamber and found him sprawled on the floor dead, with
his head missing. 16 He cried out with a loud voice and wept
and groaned and shouted, and tore his clothes. 17 Then he

NEW AMERICAN BIBLE

city resounded with shouts of joy. 10 Now Achior, seeing all
that the God of Israel had done, believed firmly in him. He
had the flesh of his foreskin circumcised, and he has been
united with the house of Israel to the present day.
11 At daybreak they hung the head of Holofernes on the
wall. Then all the Israelite men took up their arms and went
to the slopes of the mountain. 12 When the Assyrians saw
them, they notified their captains; these, in turn, went to the
generals and division leaders and all their other commanders. 13 They came to the tent of Holofernes and said to the
one in charge of all his things, "Waken our master, for the
slaves have dared come down to give us battle, to their utter
destruction." 14 Bagoas went in, and knocked at the entry of
the tent, presuming that he was sleeping with Judith. 15 As
no one answered, he parted the curtains, entered the bedroom, and found him lying on the floor, a headless corpse.
16 He broke into a loud clamor of weeping, groaning, and
howling, and rent his garments. 17 Then he entered the tent

NEW JERUSALEM BIBLE

town echoed. 10 Achior, recognising all that the God of Israel
had done, believed ardently in him and, accepting circumcision, was permanently incorporated into the House of Israel.
11 At daybreak they hung the head of Holofernes on the
ramparts. Every man took his arms and they all went out in
groups to the slopes of the mountain. 12 Seeing this, the
Assyrians sent word to their leaders, who in turn reported to
the generals, the captains of thousands and all the other officers; 13 and these in their turn reported to the tent of Holofernes. 'Rouse our master,' they said to his major-domo,
'these slaves have dared to march down on us to attack—
and to be wiped out to a man!' 14 Bagoas went inside and
struck the curtain dividing the tent, thinking that Holofernes
was sleeping with Judith. 15 But as no one seemed to hear,
he drew the curtain and went into the bedroom, to find him
thrown down dead on the threshold, with his head cut off.
16 He gave a great shout, wept, sobbed, shrieked and rent his

GREEK OLD TESTAMENT

εἰσῆλθεν εἰς τὴν σκηνήν, οὗ ἦν Ιουδιθ καταλύουσα, καὶ οὐχ
εὗρεν αὐτήν· καὶ ἐξεπήδησεν εἰς τὸν λαὸν καὶ ἐβόησεν
18 Ἠθέτησαν οἱ δοῦλοι, ἐποίησεν αἰσχύνην μία γυνὴ τῶν
Εβραίων εἰς τὸν οἶκον τοῦ βασιλέως Ναβουχοδονοσορ· ὅτι
ἰδοὺ Ολοφέρνης χαμαί, καὶ ἡ κεφαλὴ οὐκ ἔστιν ἐπ' αὐτῷ.
19 ὡς δὲ ἤκουσαν ταῦτα τὰ ῥήματα οἱ ἄρχοντες τῆς δυνάμεως Ασσουρ, τοὺς χιτῶνας αὐτῶν διέρρηξαν, καὶ ἐταράχθη
αὐτῶν ἡ ψυχὴ σφόδρα, καὶ ἐγένετο αὐτῶν κραυγὴ καὶ βοὴ
15 μεγάλη σφόδρα ἐν μέσῳ τῆς παρεμβολῆς. 1 καὶ ὡς
ἤκουσαν οἱ ἐν τοῖς σκηνώμασιν ὄντες, ἐξέστησαν
ἐπὶ τὸ γεγονός, 2 καὶ ἐπέπεσεν ἐπ' αὐτοὺς τρόμος καὶ
φόβος, καὶ οὐκ ἦν ἄνθρωπος μένων κατὰ πρόσωπον τοῦ πλησίον ἔτι, ἀλλ' ἐκχυθέντες ὁμοθυμαδὸν ἔφευγον ἐπὶ πᾶσαν
ὁδὸν τοῦ πεδίου καὶ τῆς ὀρεινῆς. 3 καὶ οἱ παρεμβεβληκότες
ἐν τῇ ὀρεινῇ κύκλῳ Βαιτυλουα καὶ ἐτράπησαν εἰς φυγήν. καὶ
τότε οἱ υἱοὶ Ισραηλ, πᾶς ἀνὴρ πολεμιστὴς ἐξ αὐτῶν, ἐξεχύ-
θησαν ἐπ' αὐτούς. 4 καὶ ἀπέστειλεν Οζιας εἰς Βαιτομα-
σθαιμ καὶ Βηβαι καὶ Χωβαι καὶ Κωλα καὶ εἰς πᾶν ὅριον
Ισραηλ τοὺς ἀπαγγέλλοντας ὑπὲρ τῶν συντετελεσμένων καὶ
ἵνα πάντες ἐπεκχυθῶσιν τοῖς πολεμίοις εἰς τὴν ἀναίρεσιν
αὐτῶν. 5 ὡς δὲ ἤκουσαν οἱ υἱοὶ Ισραηλ, πάντες ὁμοθυμαδὸν
ἐπέπεσον ἐπ' αὐτοὺς καὶ ἔκοπτον αὐτοὺς ἕως Χωβα.
ὡσαύτως δὲ καὶ οἱ ἐξ Ιερουσαλημ παρεγενήθησαν καὶ ἐκ
πάσης τῆς ὀρεινῆς, ἀνήγγειλαν γὰρ αὐτοῖς τὰ γεγονότα τῇ
παρεμβολῇ τῶν ἐχθρῶν αὐτῶν· καὶ οἱ ἐν Γαλααδ καὶ οἱ ἐν
τῇ Γαλιλαίᾳ ὑπερεκέρασαν αὐτοὺς πληγῇ μεγάλῃ, ἕως οὗ

KING JAMES VERSION

17 After he went into the tent where Judith lodged: and when he found her not, he leaped out to the people, and cried,

18 These slaves have dealt treacherously; one woman of the Hebrews hath brought shame upon the house of king Nabuchodonosor: for, behold, Holofernes *lieth* upon the ground without a head.

19 When the captains of the Assyrians' army heard these words, they rent their coats, and their minds were wonderfully troubled, and there was a cry and a very great noise throughout the camp.

15 And when they that were in the tents heard, they were astonished at the thing that was done.

2 And fear and trembling fell upon them, so that there was no man that durst abide in the sight of his neighbour, but rushing out all together, they fled into every way of the plain, and of the hill country.

3 They also that had camped in the mountains round about Bethulia fled away. Then the children of Israel, every one that was a warrior among them, rushed out upon them.

4 Then sent Ozias to Betomasthem, and to Bebai, and Chobai, and Cola, and to all the coasts of Israel, such as should tell the things that were done, and that all should rush forth upon their enemies to destroy them.

5 Now when the children of Israel heard it, they all fell upon them with one consent, and slew them unto Chobai: likewise also they that came from Jerusalem, and from all the hill country, (for men had told them what things were done in the camp of their enemies,) and they that were in Galaad,

DOUAY OLD TESTAMENT

15 And he went into the tent of Judith, and not finding her, he ran out to the people,

16 And said: One Hebrew woman hath made confusion in the house of king Nabuchodonosor: for behold Holofernes lieth upon the ground, and his head is not upon him.

17 Now when the chiefs of the army of the Assyrians had heard this, they all rent their garments, and an intolerable fear and dread fell upon them, and their minds were troubled exceedingly.

18 And there was a very great cry in the midst of their camp.

15 AND when all the army heard that Holofernes was beheaded, courage and counsel fled from them, and being seized with trembling and fear they thought only to save themselves by flight:

2 So that no one spoke to his neighbour, but hanging down the head, leaving all things behind, they made haste to escape from the Hebrews, who, as they heard, were coming armed upon them, and fled by the ways of the fields, and the paths of the hills.

3 So the children of Israel seeing them fleeing, followed after them. And they went down sounding with trumpets and shouting after them.

4 And because the Assyrians were not united together, they went without order in their flight; but the children of Israel pursuing in one body, defeated all that they could find.

5 And Ozias sent messengers through all the cities and countries of Israel.

6 And every country, and every city, sent their chosen

KNOX TRANSLATION

to Judith's tent, and finding her gone, he ran out to where
the others stood; 16 Here is great despite done, he cried, to
the court of king Nabuchodonosor, and one Jewish woman
its author! Holofernes lies there felled to the earth, and no
head on his body!
17 At this news, all the Assyrian leaders tore their garments; a craven fear fell on them they could not master, and
their spirits were cowed utterly; 18 never was such a cry as
went up then from the heart of the Assyrian camp.
15 When word of this outrage upon Holofernes spread
through the army, plan and purpose had they none;
taking counsel only of the fear that shook their limbs, they
sought refuge in flight. 2 None might say a word to his
neighbour, none might lift his head; they left all behind, and
hastened to make good their escape from the rumoured
onslaught of the Hebrews, some taking the roads across the
plain, some the mountain tracks. 3 The Israelites, when they
saw their backs turned, went in pursuit, and swept down the
hill-side with blowing of trumpets and a great shouting at
their heels. 4 The Assyrians, in their headlong flight, could
not hold together, and their enemies, pursuing them in
orderly array, need only catch them to overpower them; 5 so
Ozias sent out messengers to all Israel, city-dwellers and
country-dwellers alike, 6 and none but sent out the flower of
their manhood, ready armed for the pursuit. At the sword's

Today's English Version

17 He went into the tent where Judith had stayed, but of course he did not find her. He rushed out and shouted to the officers, 18 "They have tricked us! One Israelite woman has disgraced Nebuchadnezzar's whole kingdom. Look in there! Holofernes is lying dead on the ground and his head is gone!" 19 When the officers heard this, they tore their clothes in grief; and as the panic spread, wild cries and shouts were heard throughout the camp.

15 When the soldiers heard what had happened, they were horrified 2 and began to tremble with fear. They all scattered in different directions from the camp, making no effort to stay together as they tried to escape along the paths in the mountains and valleys. 3 The soldiers who had camped in the mountains around Bethulia also began to retreat. Then all the Israelite soldiers came charging down on them.

4 Uzziah sent messengers to the towns of Betomesthaim, Bebai, Choba, and Kola, and throughout the land of Israel to tell everyone what had happened and to urge them to join in pursuing and destroying the enemy. 5 When they received the message, they all attacked the Assyrians and chased them as far as Choba, slaughtering them as they went. Even the people of Jerusalem and others living in the mountains joined the attack when the messengers told them what had happened in the Assyrian camp. The people of the regions of Gilead and Galilee blocked the path of the retreating

New Revised Standard Version

went to the tent where Judith had stayed, and when he did not find her, he rushed out to the people and shouted, 18 "The slaves have tricked us! One Hebrew woman has brought disgrace on the house of King Nebuchadnezzar. Look, Holofernes is lying on the ground, and his head is missing!"

19 When the leaders of the Assyrian army heard this, they tore their tunics and were greatly dismayed, and their loud cries and shouts rose up throughout the camp.

15 When the men in the tents heard it, they were amazed at what had happened. 2 Overcome with fear and trembling, they did not wait for one another, but with one impulse all rushed out and fled by every path across the plain and through the hill country. 3 Those who had camped in the hills around Bethulia also took to flight. Then the Israelites, everyone that was a soldier, rushed out upon them. 4 Uzziah sent men to Betomasthaim[a] and Choba and Kola, and to all the frontiers of Israel, to tell what had taken place and to urge all to rush out upon the enemy to destroy them. 5 When the Israelites heard it, with one accord they fell upon the enemy,[b] and cut them down as far as Choba. Those in Jerusalem and all the hill country also came, for they were told what had happened in the camp of the enemy. The men in Gilead and in Galilee outflanked them with great

a Other ancient authorities add *and Bebai* *b* Gk *them*

New American Bible

where Judith had her quarters; and, not finding her, he rushed out to the troops and cried: 18 "The slaves have duped us! A single Hebrew woman has brought disgrace on the house of King Nebuchadnezzar. Here is Holofernes headless on the ground!"

19 When the commanders of the Assyrian army heard these words, they rent their tunics and were seized with consternation. Loud screaming and howling arose in the camp.

15 On hearing what had happened, those still in their tents were amazed, 2 and overcome with fear and trembling. No one kept ranks any longer; they scattered in all directions, and fled along every road, both through the valley and in the mountains. 3 Those also who were stationed in the mountain district around Bethulia took to flight. Then all the Israelite warriors overwhelmed them.

4 Uzziah sent messengers to Betomasthaim, to Choba and Kona, and to the whole country of Israel to report what had happened, that all might fall upon the enemy and destroy them. 5 On hearing this, all the Israelites, with one accord, attacked them and cut them down as far as Choba. Even those from Jerusalem and the rest of the mountain region took part in this, for they too had been notified of the happenings in the camp of their enemies. The Gileadites and the Galileans struck the enemy's flanks with great slaughter,

New Jerusalem Bible

clothes. 17 He then went into the tent which Judith had occupied and could not find her either. Then, rushing out to the men, he shouted, 18 'The slaves have rebelled! A single Hebrew woman has brought shame on the House of Nebuchadnezzar. Holofernes is lying dead on the ground, without his head!'

19 When they heard this, the leaders of the Assyrian army tore their tunics in consternation, and the camp rang with their wild cries and their shouting.

15 When the men who were still in their tents heard the news they were appalled. 2 Panic-stricken and trembling, no two of them could keep together, the rout was complete, with one accord they fled along every track across the plain or through the mountains. 3 The men who had been bivouacking in the mountains round Bethulia were fleeing too. Then all the Israelite warriors charged down on them. 4 Uzziah sent messengers to Betomasthaim, Bebai, Choba, Kola, throughout the whole territory of Israel, to inform them of what had happened and to urge them all to hurl themselves on the enemy and annihilate them. 5 As soon as the Israelites heard the news, they fell on them as one man and massacred them all the way to Choba. The men of Jerusalem and the entire mountain country also rallied to them, once they had been informed of the events in the enemy camp. Then the men of Gilead and Galilee attacked them on the

GREEK OLD TESTAMENT

παρῆλθον Δαμασκὸν καὶ τὰ ὅρια αὐτῆς. 6 οἱ δὲ λοιποὶ οἱ
κατοικοῦντες Βαιτυλουα ἐπέπεσαν τῇ παρεμβολῇ Ασσουρ
καὶ ἐπρονόμευσαν αὐτοὺς καὶ ἐπλούτησαν σφόδρα. 7 οἱ δὲ
υἱοὶ Ισραηλ ἀναστρέψαντες ἀπὸ τῆς κοπῆς ἐκυρίευσαν τῶν
λοιπῶν, καὶ αἱ κῶμαι καὶ ἐπαύλεις ἐν τῇ ὀρεινῇ καὶ πεδινῇ
ἐκράτησαν πολλῶν λαφύρων, ἦν γὰρ πλῆθος πολὺ σφόδρα.
8 Καὶ Ιωακιμ ὁ ἱερεὺς ὁ μέγας καὶ ἡ γερουσία τῶν υἱῶν
Ισραηλ οἱ κατοικοῦντες ἐν Ιερουσαλημ ἦλθον τοῦ θεάσασθαι
τὰ ἀγαθά, ἃ ἐποίησεν κύριος τῷ Ισραηλ, καὶ τοῦ ἰδεῖν τὴν
Ιουδιθ καὶ λαλῆσαι μετ' αὐτῆς εἰρήνην. 9 ὡς δὲ εἰσῆλθον
πρὸς αὐτήν, εὐλόγησαν αὐτὴν πάντες ὁμοθυμαδὸν καὶ εἶπαν
πρὸς αὐτήν Σὺ ὕψωμα Ιερουσαλημ, σὺ γαυρίαμα μέγα τοῦ
Ισραηλ, σὺ καύχημα μέγα τοῦ γένους ἡμῶν· 10 ἐποίησας
ταῦτα πάντα ἐν χειρί σου, ἐποίησας τὰ ἀγαθὰ μετὰ Ισραηλ,
καὶ εὐδόκησεν ἐπ' αὐτοῖς ὁ θεός. εὐλογημένη γίνου παρὰ τῷ
παντοκράτορι κυρίῳ εἰς τὸν αἰῶνα χρόνον. καὶ εἶπεν πᾶς ὁ
λαός Γένοιτο. 11 καὶ ἐλαφύρευσεν πᾶς ὁ λαὸς τὴν παρεμβολὴν ἐφ' ἡμέρας τριάκοντα· καὶ ἔδωκαν τῇ Ιουδιθ τὴν
σκηνὴν Ολοφέρνου καὶ πάντα τὰ ἀργυρώματα καὶ τὰς κλίνας
καὶ τὰ ὁλκεῖα καὶ πάντα τὰ κατασκευάσματα αὐτοῦ, καὶ
λαβοῦσα αὐτὴ ἐπέθηκεν ἐπὶ τὴν ἡμίονον αὐτῆς καὶ ἔζευξεν
τὰς ἁμάξας αὐτῆς καὶ ἐσώρευσεν αὐτὰ ἐπ' αὐτῶν. 12 καὶ

KING JAMES VERSION

and in Galilee, chased them with a great slaughter, until they were past Damascus and the borders thereof.

6 And the residue, that dwelt at Bethulia, fell upon the camp of Assur, and spoiled them, and were greatly enriched.

7 And the children of Israel that returned from the slaughter had that which remained; and the villages and the cities, that were in the mountains and in the plain, gat many spoils: for the multitude was very great.

8 Then Joacim the high priest, and the ancients of the children of Israel that dwelt in Jerusalem, came to behold the good things that God had shewed to Israel, and to see Judith, and to salute her.

9 And when they came unto her, they blessed her with one accord, and said unto her, Thou art the exaltation of Jerusalem, thou art the great glory of Israel, thou art the great rejoicing of our nation:

10 Thou hast done all these things by thine hand: thou hast done much good to Israel, and God is pleased therewith: blessed be thou of the Almighty Lord for evermore. And all the people said, So be it.

11 And the people spoiled the camp the space of thirty days: and they gave unto Judith Holofernes his tent, and all his plate, and beds, and vessels, and all his stuff: and she took it, and laid it on her mule; and made ready her carts, and laid them thereon.

DOUAY OLD TESTAMENT

young men armed after them, and they pursued them with the edge of the sword until they came to the extremities of their confines.

7 And the rest that were in Bethulia went into the camp of the Assyrians, and took away the spoils, which the Assyrians in their flight had left behind them, and they were laden exceedingly.

8 But they that returned conquerors to Bethulia, brought with them all things that were theirs, so that there was no numbering of their cattle, and beasts, and all their moveables, insomuch that from the least to the greatest all were made rich by their spoils.

9 And Joachim the high priest came from Jerusalem to Bethulia with all his ancients to see Judith.

10 And when she was come out to him, they all blessed her with one voice, saying: Thou art the glory of Jerusalem, thou art the joy of Israel, thou art the honour of our people:

11 For thou hast done manfully, and thy heart has been strengthened, because thou hast loved chastity, and after thy husband hast not known any other: therefore also the hand of the Lord hath strengthened thee, and therefore thou shalt be blessed for ever.

12 And all the people said: So be it, so be it.

13 And thirty days were scarce sufficient for the people of Israel to gather up the spoils of the Assyrians.

14 But all those things that were proved to be the peculiar goods of Holofernes, they gave to Judith in gold, and silver, and garments and precious stones, and all household stuff, and they all were delivered to her by the people.

KNOX TRANSLATION

point they followed them, to the very frontiers of their
domain. 7 As for the folk who had been left behind in
Bethulia, they made their way into the Assyrian camp,
whence they carried off all the Assyrians had left behind
when they fled, and it was no light load they brought home
with them. 8 When the victorious army returned, with the
spoils taken from their enemies, there was no counting the
cattle and the pack-beasts and the plunder of all sorts; none,
high or low, but was enriched with the booty.
9 And now the high priest Joacim[a] came to Bethulia, with
all that were his fellow elders at Jerusalem, asking to see
Judith; 10 and when she answered his summons, all with
one voice began to extol her; Thou art the boast of
Jerusalem, the joy of Israel, the pride of our people; 11 thou
hast played a man's part, and kept thy courage high. Not
unrewarded thy love of chastity, that wouldst never take a
second husband in thy widowhood; the Lord gave thee firm-
ness of resolve, and thy name shall be ever blessed. 12 And
to that all the people said Amen.
13 Scarce did thirty days suffice for the men of Israel to
gather the Assyrian spoils. 14 Among these, all that proved to
be Holofernes' own went to Judith herself, gold and silver,
clothes and jewels, and furniture of every sort; all these the
people handed over to her, 15 keeping high festival, while

a The only high priest we know of as bearing this name held office during the early days of the Persian empire, long after the fall of Assyria (Neh. 12. 10). Once more, the suggestion seems possible that the names in the story have been artificially supplied.

Today's English Version

Assyrians and inflicted heavy losses on them. They pursued them as far as the region around Damascus.

6 The rest of the people in Bethulia went down to the Assyrian camp, plundered it and carried away enough loot to make themselves very rich. 7 When the Israelite soldiers returned from the slaughter, they helped themselves to what was left. There was so much of it that the people of the towns and villages in the hill country also shared in the loot.

8 The High Priest Joakim and the Council of Israel came from Jerusalem to see for themselves what great things the Lord had done for his people and to meet Judith and congratulate her. 9 When they arrived, they all praised her, "You are Jerusalem's crowning glory, the heroine of Israel, the pride and joy of our people! 10 You have won this great victory for Israel by yourself. God, the Almighty, is pleased with what you have done. May he bless you as long as you live."

All the people responded, "Amen."

11 It took the people thirty days to finish looting the camp of the Assyrians. Judith was given Holofernes' tent, all his silver, his bowls, his couches, and all his furniture. She took them and loaded as much as she could on her mule; then she brought her wagons and loaded them too. 12 All the Israelite

New Revised Standard Version

slaughter, even beyond Damascus and its borders. 6 The rest of the people of Bethulia fell upon the Assyrian camp and plundered it, acquiring great riches. 7 And the Israelites, when they returned from the slaughter, took possession of what remained. Even the villages and towns in the hill country and in the plain got a great amount of booty, since there was a vast quantity of it.

8 Then the high priest Joakim and the elders of the Israelites who lived in Jerusalem came to witness the good things that the Lord had done for Israel, and to see Judith and to wish her well. 9 When they met her, they all blessed her with one accord and said to her, "You are the glory of Jerusalem, you are the great boast of Israel, you are the great pride of our nation! 10 You have done all this with your own hand; you have done great good to Israel, and God is well pleased with it. May the Almighty Lord bless you forever!" And all the people said, "Amen."

11 All the people plundered the camp for thirty days. They gave Judith the tent of Holofernes and all his silver dinnerware, his beds, his bowls, and all his furniture. She took them and loaded her mules and hitched up her carts and piled the things on them.

New American Bible

even beyond Damascus and its territory. 6 The remaining inhabitants of Bethulia swept down on the camp of the Assyrians, plundered it, and acquired great riches. 7 The Israelites who returned from the slaughter took possession of what was left, till the towns and villages in the mountains and on the plain were crammed with the enormous quantity of booty they had seized.

8 The high priest Joakim and the elders of the Israelites, who dwelt in Jerusalem, came to see for themselves the good things that the LORD had done for Israel, and to meet and congratulate Judith. 9 When they had visited her, all with one accord blessed her, saying:

"You are the glory of Jerusalem,
the surpassing joy of Israel;
You are the splendid boast of our people.
10 With your own hand you have done all this;
You have done good to Israel,
and God is pleased with what you have wrought.
May you be blessed by the LORD Almighty
forever and ever!"

And all the people answered, "Amen!"

11 For thirty days the whole populace plundered the camp, giving Judith the tent of Holofernes, with all his silver, his couches, his dishes, and all his furniture, which she accepted. She harnessed her mules, hitched her wagons to them, and loaded these things on them.

New Jerusalem Bible

flank and struck at them fiercely till they neared Damascus and its territory. 6 All the other inhabitants of Bethulia fell on the Assyrian camp and looted it to their great profit. 7 The Israelites returning from the slaughter seized what was left. The hamlets and villages of the mountain country and the plain also captured a great deal of booty, since there were vast stores of it.

8 Joakim the high priest and the entire Council of Elders of Israel, who were in Jerusalem, came to gaze on the benefits that the Lord had lavished on Israel and to see Judith and congratulate her. 9 On coming to her house, they blessed her with one accord, saying:

You are the glory of Jerusalem!
You are the great pride of Israel!
You are the highest honour of our race!

10 By doing all this with your own hand
you have deserved well of Israel,
and God has approved what you have done.
May you be blessed by the Lord Almighty
in all the days to come!

And the people all said, 'Amen!'

11 The people looted the camp for thirty days. They gave Judith the tent of Holofernes, all his silver plate, his divans, his drinking bowls and all his furniture. She took this, loaded her mule, harnessed her carts and heaped the things

GREEK OLD TESTAMENT

συνέδραμεν πᾶσα γυνὴ Ισραηλ τοῦ ἰδεῖν αὐτὴν καὶ εὐλόγησαν αὐτὴν καὶ ἐποίησαν αὐτῇ χορὸν ἐξ αὐτῶν, καὶ ἔλαβεν
θύρσους ἐν ταῖς χερσὶν αὐτῆς καὶ ἔδωκεν ταῖς γυναιξὶν ταῖς
μετ᾽ αὐτῆς. 13 καὶ ἐστεφανώσαντο τὴν ἐλαίαν, αὐτὴ καὶ αἱ
μετ᾽ αὐτῆς, καὶ προῆλθεν παντὸς τοῦ λαοῦ ἐν χορείᾳ ἡγου-
μένη πασῶν τῶν γυναικῶν, καὶ ἠκολούθει πᾶς ἀνὴρ Ισραηλ
ἐνωπλισμένοι μετὰ στεφάνων καὶ ὕμνουν ἐν τῷ στόματι
αὐτῶν. 14 καὶ ἐξῆρχεν Ιουδιθ τὴν ἐξομολόγησιν ταύτην ἐν
παντὶ Ισραηλ, καὶ ὑπερεφώνει πᾶς ὁ λαὸς τὴν αἴνεσιν ταύτην

16 καὶ εἶπεν Ιουδιθ
Ἐξάρχετε τῷ θεῷ μου ἐν τυμπάνοις,
ᾄσατε τῷ κυρίῳ ἐν κυμβάλοις,
ἐναρμόσασθε αὐτῷ ψαλμὸν καὶ αἶνον,
ὑψοῦτε καὶ ἐπικαλεῖσθε τὸ ὄνομα αὐτοῦ,
2 ὅτι θεὸς συντρίβων πολέμους κύριος,
ὅτι εἰς παρεμβολὰς αὐτοῦ ἐν μέσῳ λαοῦ
ἐξείλατό με ἐκ χειρὸς καταδιωκόντων με.
3 ἦλθεν Ασσουρ ἐξ ὀρέων ἀπὸ βορρᾶ,
ἦλθεν ἐν μυριάσι δυνάμεως αὐτοῦ,
ὧν τὸ πλῆθος αὐτῶν ἐνέφραξεν χειμάρρους,
καὶ ἡ ἵππος αὐτῶν ἐκάλυψεν βουνούς.
4 εἶπεν ἐμπρήσειν τὰ ὅριά μου
καὶ τοὺς νεανίσκους μου ἀνελεῖν ἐν ῥομφαίᾳ
καὶ τὰ θηλάζοντά μου θήσειν εἰς ἔδαφος
καὶ τὰ νήπιά μου δώσειν εἰς προνομὴν
καὶ τὰς παρθένους μου σκυλεῦσαι.

KING JAMES VERSION

12 Then all the women of Israel ran together to see her, and blessed her, and made a dance among them for her: and she took branches in her hand, and gave also to the women that were with her.

13 And they put a garland of olive upon her and her maid that was with her, and she went before all the people in the dance, leading all the women: and all the men of Israel followed in their armour with garlands, and with songs in their mouths.

16 Then Judith began to sing this thanksgiving in all Israel, and all the people sang after her this song of praise.

2 And Judith said, Begin unto my God with timbrels, sing unto my Lord with cymbals: tune unto him a new psalm: exalt him, and call upon his name.

3 For God breaketh the battles: for among the camps in the midst of the people he hath delivered me out of the hands of them that persecuted me.

4 Assur came out of the mountains from the north, he came with ten thousands of his army, the multitude whereof stopped the torrents, and their horsemen have covered the hills.

5 He bragged that he would burn up my borders, and kill my young men with the sword, and dash the sucking children against the ground, and make mine infants as a prey, and my virgins as a spoil.

DOUAY OLD TESTAMENT

15 And all the people rejoiced, with the women, and virgins, and young men, playing on instruments and harps.

16 THEN Judith sung this canticle to the Lord, saying:
2 Begin ye to the Lord with timbrels, sing ye to the Lord with cymbals, tune unto him a new psalm, extol and call upon his name.

3 The Lord putteth an end to wars, the Lord is his name.

4 He hath set his camp in the midst of his people, to deliver us from the hand of all our enemies.

5 The Assyrian came out of the mountains from the north in the multitude of his strength: his multitude stopped up the torrents, and their horses covered the valleys.

6 He bragged that he would set my borders on fire, and kill my young men with the sword, to make my infants a prey, and my virgins captives.

KNOX TRANSLATION

man and maid, wed and unwedded, played flute and harp together.

16 Then Judith herself sang to the Lord, and this was
Judith's song: 2 Strike up, tambour, and cymbals
beat in the Lord's honour, sound a fresh song of praise; high
enthrone him, call aloud upon his name! 3 What power
divine crushes the enemy, but the Lord's great name? 4 Here
in the midst of his people he lies encamped; come what
enemy may, he grants deliverance.

5 Came the Assyrian from the northern hills in his great
strength, the valleys choked with his marching columns, the
mountain glens black with his horses; 6 to send fire through
our country-side, put our warriors to the sword, mark down
our children for slavery, our maidens for spoil. 7 Great

TODAY'S ENGLISH VERSION

women came to see her; they sang her praises and danced in her honor. On this joyful occasion Judith and the other women waved ivy-covered branches [13]and wore wreaths of olive leaves on their heads. Judith took her place at the head of the procession to lead the women as they danced. All the men of Israel followed, wearing wreaths of flowers on their heads, carrying their weapons, and singing songs of praise.

16 Then Judith sang a song of thanksgiving there with all Israel present, and the people joined in this song of praise. [2]She sang,

"Praise my God and sing to him;
praise the Lord with drums and cymbals;
play a new song for him.
Praise him and call on him for help.
[3]The Lord is a warrior who ends war.
He rescued me from my pursuers
and brought me back to his people's camp.
[4]Down from the mountains of the north came the Assyrians,
with their tens of thousands of soldiers.
Their troops blocked the rivers in the valleys;
their cavalry covered the mountains.
[5]They threatened to set fire to our country,
slaughter our young men,
dash our babies to the ground,
take our children away as captives,
and carry off all our young women.

NEW REVISED STANDARD VERSION

12 All the women of Israel gathered to see her, and blessed her, and some of them performed a dance in her honor. She took ivy-wreathed wands in her hands and distributed them to the women who were with her; [13]and she and those who were with her crowned themselves with olive wreaths. She went before all the people in the dance, leading all the women, while all the men of Israel followed, bearing their arms and wearing garlands and singing hymns.

14 Judith began this thanksgiving before all Israel, and all
16 the people loudly sang this song of praise. [1]And
Judith said,

Begin a song to my God with tambourines,
sing to my Lord with cymbals.
Raise to him a new psalm;[a]
exalt him, and call upon his name.
2 For the Lord is a God who crushes wars;
he sets up his camp among his people;
he delivered me from the hands of my pursuers.
3 The Assyrian came down from the mountains of the north;
he came with myriads of his warriors;
their numbers blocked up the wadis,
and their cavalry covered the hills.
4 He boasted that he would burn up my territory,
and kill my young men with the sword,
and dash my infants to the ground,
and seize my children as booty,
and take my virgins as spoil.

a Other ancient authorities read *a psalm and praise*

NEW AMERICAN BIBLE

[12]All the women of Israel gathered to see her; and they blessed her and performed a dance in her honor. She took branches in her hands and distributed them to the women around her. [13]and she and the other women crowned themselves with garlands of olive leaves. At the head of all the people, she led the women in the dance, while the men of Israel followed in their armor, wearing garlands and singing hymns.

[14]Judith led all Israel in this song of thanksgiving, and the people swelled this hymn of praise:

16 "Strike up the instruments,
a song to my God with timbrels,
chant to the LORD with cymbals;
Sing to him a new song,
exalt and acclaim his name.
[2]For the LORD is God; he crushes warfare,
and sets his encampment among his people;
he snatched me from the hands of my persecutors.

[3]"The Assyrian came from the mountains of the north,
with the myriads of his forces he came;
Their numbers blocked the torrents, their horses covered the hills.
[4]He threatened to burn my land,
put my youths to the sword,
Dash my babes to the ground,
make my children a prey,
and seize my virgins as spoil.

NEW JERUSALEM BIBLE

into them. [12]All the women of Israel, hurrying to see her,
formed choirs of dancers in her honour. Judith took wands of
vine-leaves in her hand and distributed them to the women
who accompanied her; [13]she and her companions put on
wreaths of olive. Then she took her place at the head of the
procession and led the women as they danced. All the men of
Israel, armed and garlanded, followed them, singing hymns.
[14]With all Israel round her, Judith broke into this song of
thanksgiving and the whole people sang this hymn:

16 Break into song for my God, to the tambourine,
sing in honour of the Lord, to the cymbal,
let psalm and canticle mingle for him,
extol his name, invoke it!
[2]For the Lord is a God who breaks battle-lines;
he has pitched his camp in the middle of his people
to deliver me from the hands of my oppressors.

[3]Assyria came down from the mountains of the north,
came with tens of thousands of his army.
Their multitude blocked the ravines,
their horses covered the hills.
[4]He threatened to burn up my country,
destroy my young men with the sword,
dash my sucklings to the ground,
make prey of my little ones,
carry off my maidens;
[5]but the Lord Almighty has thwarted them
by a woman's hand.

GREEK OLD TESTAMENT

5 κύριος παντοκράτωρ ἠθέτησεν αὐτοὺς
ἐν χειρὶ θηλείας.
6 οὐ γὰρ ὑπέπεσεν ὁ δυνατὸς αὐτῶν ὑπὸ νεανίσκων,
οὐδὲ υἱοὶ τιτάνων ἐπάταξαν αὐτόν,
οὐδὲ ὑψηλοὶ γίγαντες ἐπέθεντο αὐτῷ,
ἀλλὰ Ιουδιθ θυγάτηρ Μεραρι
ἐν κάλλει προσώπου αὐτῆς παρέλυσεν αὐτόν,
7 ἐξεδύσατο γὰρ στολὴν χηρεύσεως αὐτῆς
εἰς ὕψος τῶν πονούντων ἐν Ισραηλ,
ἠλείψατο τὸ πρόσωπον αὐτῆς ἐν μυρισμῷ
8 καὶ ἐδήσατο τὰς τρίχας αὐτῆς ἐν μίτρᾳ
καὶ ἔλαβεν στολὴν λινῆν εἰς ἀπάτην αὐτοῦ·
9 τὸ σανδάλιον αὐτῆς ἥρπασεν ὀφθαλμὸν αὐτοῦ,
καὶ τὸ κάλλος αὐτῆς ᾐχμαλώτισεν ψυχὴν αὐτοῦ,
διῆλθεν ὁ ἀκινάκης τὸν τράχηλον αὐτοῦ.
10 ἔφριξαν Πέρσαι τὴν τόλμαν αὐτῆς,
καὶ Μῆδοι τὸ θράσος αὐτῆς ἐταράχθησαν·
11 τότε ἠλάλαξαν οἱ ταπεινοί μου,
καὶ ἐφοβήθησαν οἱ ἀσθενοῦντές μου καὶ ἐπτοήθησαν,
ὕψωσαν τὴν φωνὴν αὐτῶν καὶ ἀνετράπησαν·
12 υἱοὶ κορασίων κατεκέντησαν αὐτοὺς
καὶ ὡς παῖδας αὐτομολούντων ἐτίτρωσκον αὐτούς,
ἀπώλοντο ἐκ παρατάξεως κυρίου μου.

KING JAMES VERSION

6 But the Almighty Lord hath disappointed them by the hand of a woman.

7 For the mighty one did not fall by the young men, neither did the sons of the Titans smite him, nor high giants set upon him: but Judith the daughter of Merari weakened him with the beauty of her countenance.

8 For she put off the garment of her widowhood for the exaltation of those that were oppressed in Israel, and anointed her face with ointment, and bound her hair in a tire, and took a linen garment to deceive him.

9 Her sandals ravished his eyes, her beauty took his mind prisoner, and the fauchion passed through his neck.

10 The Persians quaked at her boldness, and the Medes were daunted at her hardiness.

11 Then my afflicted shouted for joy, and my weak ones cried aloud; but they were astonished: these lifted up their voices, but they were overthrown.

12 The sons of the damsels have pierced them through, and wounded them as fugatives' children: they perished by the battle of the Lord.

DOUAY OLD TESTAMENT

7 But the almighty Lord hath struck him, and hath delivered him into the hands of a woman, and hath slain him.

8 For their mighty one did not fall by young men, neither did the sons of Titan strike him, nor tall giants oppose themselves to him, but Judith the daughter of Merari weakened him with the beauty of her face.

9 For she put off her the garments of widowhood, and put on her the garments of joy, to give joy to the children of Israel.

10 She anointed her face with ointment, and bound up her locks with a crown, she took a new robe to deceive him.

11 Her sandals ravished his eyes, her beauty made his soul her captive, with a sword she cut off his head.

12 The Persians quaked at her constancy, and the Medes at her boldness.

13 Then the camp of the Assyrians howled, when my lowly ones appeared, parched with thirst.

14 The sons of the damsels have pierced them through, and they have killed them like children fleeing away: they perished in battle before the face of the Lord my God.

KNOX TRANSLATION

despite the Lord Almighty did him, that he should fall into a
woman's power for his death-blow. 8 Not by warriors' hands
the tyrant fell; not giants smote him, not heroes of the old
time barred his path; it was Judith, Merari's daughter,
Judith's fair face that was his undoing. 9 Laid aside, now,
her widow's weeds; festal her array must be; a feast waits
for the sons of Israel. 10 Ointment, there, for her cheeks, a
band for her straying locks, a robe new-wrought to ensnare
him! 11 Her very sandals thralled his eyes; he lay there, his
heart beauty's prisoner, while the sharp steel pierced his
neck through. 12 Stood Persian, stood Mede aghast at the
boldness of her resolve; 13 loud rang the cry of the Assyrian
camp, when the hard-pressed defenders sallied out against
them, parched with thirst! 14 Slaves, did they call us? But we
gave them cold steel; cut them down where, like slaves, they
ran; one glance from the Lord our God, and the battle was
lost.

TODAY'S ENGLISH VERSION

6 But the Lord Almighty tricked them;
he used a woman to stop them.
7 Their hero was not slain by young soldiers
or attacked and killed by mighty giants.
It was Judith, the daughter of Merari,
who brought him down with her beauty.
8 She gave victory to the oppressed people of Israel,
when she took off her widow's clothes,
and put on a linen dress to entice him.
She put on her rich perfumes
and tied a ribbon around her hair.
9 Her dainty sandal caught his eye;
her beauty captured his heart.
Then the sword slashed through his neck.
10 The Persians trembled at her daring;
the Medes were amazed at her bravery.
11 Then our people shouted in victory.
They had been weak and oppressed,
but they forced the enemy to retreat in panic and
fear.
12 We are the descendants of slaves,
but our enemies turned and ran;
we killed them like runaway slaves.
They were destroyed by the army of the Lord.

NEW REVISED STANDARD VERSION

5 But the Lord Almighty has foiled them
by the hand of a woman.[a]
6 For their mighty one did not fall by the hands of the
young men,
nor did the sons of the Titans strike him down,
nor did tall giants set upon him;
but Judith daughter of Merari
with the beauty of her countenance undid him.

7 For she put away her widow's clothing
to exalt the oppressed in Israel.
She anointed her face with perfume;
8 she fastened her hair with a tiara
and put on a linen gown to beguile him.
9 Her sandal ravished his eyes,
her beauty captivated his mind,
and the sword severed his neck!
10 The Persians trembled at her boldness,
the Medes were daunted at her daring.

11 Then my oppressed people shouted;
my weak people cried out,[b] and the enemy[c] trembled;
they lifted up their voices, and the enemy[c] were
turned back.
12 Sons of slave-girls pierced them through
and wounded them like the children of fugitives;
they perished before the army of my Lord.

a Other ancient authorities add *he has confounded them* *b* Other ancient authorities read *feared* *c* Gk *they*

NEW AMERICAN BIBLE

5 "But the LORD Almighty thwarted them,
by a woman's hand he confounded them.
6 Not by youths was their mighty one struck down,
nor did titans bring him low,
nor huge giants attack him;
But Judith, the daughter of Merari,
by the beauty of her countenance disabled him.
7 She took off her widow's garb
to raise up the afflicted in Israel.
She anointed her face with fragrant oil;
8 with a fillet she fastened her tresses
and put on a linen robe to beguile him.
9 Her sandals caught his eyes,
and her beauty captivated his mind.
The sword cut through his neck.

10 "The Persians were dismayed at her daring,
the Medes appalled at her boldness.
11 When my lowly ones shouted, they were terrified;
when my weaklings cried out, they trembled;
at the sound of their war cry, they took to flight.
12 The sons of slave girls pierced them through;
the supposed sons of rebel mothers cut them down;
they perished before the ranks of my LORD.

NEW JERUSALEM BIBLE

6 For their hero did not fall at the young men's hands,
it was not the sons of Titans struck him down,
no proud giants made that attack,
but Judith, the daughter of Merari,
who disarmed him with the beauty of her face.
7 She laid aside her widow's dress
to raise up those who were oppressed in Israel;
she anointed her face with perfume,
8 bound her hair under a turban,
put on a linen gown to seduce him.
9 Her sandal ravished his eye,
her beauty took his soul prisoner
and the scimitar cut through his neck!
10 The Persians trembled at her boldness,
the Medes were daunted by her daring.
11 These were struck with fear when my lowly ones raised
the war cry,
these were seized with terror when my weak ones
shouted,
and when they raised their voices these gave ground.
12 The children of mere girls ran them through,
pierced them like the offspring of deserters.
They perished in the battle of my Lord!

GREEK OLD TESTAMENT

13 ὑμνήσω τῷ θεῷ μου ὕμνον καινόν
Κύριε, μέγας εἶ καὶ ἔνδοξος,
θαυμαστὸς ἐν ἰσχύι, ἀνυπέρβλητος.
14 σοὶ δουλευσάτω πᾶσα ἡ κτίσις σου·
ὅτι εἶπας, καὶ ἐγενήθησαν·
ἀπέστειλας τὸ πνεῦμά σου, καὶ ᾠκοδόμησεν·
καὶ οὐκ ἔστιν ὃς ἀντιστήσεται τῇ φωνῇ σου.
15 ὄρη γὰρ ἐκ θεμελίων σὺν ὕδασιν σαλευθήσεται,
πέτραι δ᾽ ἀπὸ προσώπου σου ὡς κηρὸς τακήσονται·
ἔτι δὲ τοῖς φοβουμένοις σε,
σὺ εὐιλατεύσεις αὐτοῖς.
16 ὅτι μικρὸν πᾶσα θυσία εἰς ὀσμὴν εὐωδίας,
καὶ ἐλάχιστον πᾶν στέαρ εἰς ὁλοκαύτωμά σοι·
ὁ δὲ φοβούμενος τὸν κύριον μέγας διὰ παντός.
17 οὐαὶ ἔθνεσιν ἐπανιστανομένοις τῷ γένει μου·
κύριος παντοκράτωρ ἐκδικήσει αὐτοὺς ἐν ἡμέρᾳ κρίσεως
δοῦναι πῦρ καὶ σκώληκας εἰς σάρκας αὐτῶν,
καὶ κλαύσονται ἐν αἰσθήσει ἕως αἰῶνος.

18 Ὡς δὲ ἤλθοσαν εἰς Ιερουσαλημ, προσεκύνησαν τῷ θεῷ,
καὶ ἡνίκα ἐκαθαρίσθη ὁ λαός, ἀνήνεγκαν τὰ ὁλοκαυτώματα

KING JAMES VERSION

13 I will sing unto the Lord a new song: O Lord, thou art great and glorious, wonderful in strength, and invincible.

14 Let all creatures serve thee: for thou spakest, and they were made, thou didst send forth thy spirit, and it created them, and there is none that can resist thy voice.

15 For the mountains shall be moved from their foundations with the waters, the rocks shall melt as wax at thy presence: yet thou art merciful to them that fear thee.

16 For all sacrifice is too little for a sweet savour unto thee, and all the fat is not sufficient for thy burnt offering: but he that feareth the Lord is great at all times.

17 Woe to the nations that rise up against my kindred! the Lord Almighty will take vengeance of them in the day of judgment, in putting fire and worms in their flesh; and they shall feel them, and weep for ever.

18 Now as soon as they entered into Jerusalem, they worshipped the Lord; and as soon as the people were purified,

DOUAY OLD TESTAMENT

15 Let us sing a hymn to the Lord, let us sing a new hymn to our God.

16 O Adonai, Lord, great art thou, and glorious in thy power, and no one can overcome thee.

17 Let all thy creatures serve thee: because thou hast spoken, and they were made: thou didst send forth thy spirit, and they were created, and there is no one that can resist thy voice.

18 The mountains shall be moved from the foundations with the waters: the rocks shall melt as wax before thy face.

19 But they that fear thee, shall be great with thee in all things.

20 Woe be to the nation that riseth up against my people: for the Lord almighty will take revenge on them, in the day of judgment he will visit them.

21 For he will give fire, and worms into their flesh, that they may burn, and may feel for ever.

22 And it came to pass after these things, that all the people, after the victory, came to Jerusalem to adore the Lord:

KNOX TRANSLATION

15 A hymn, a new hymn, sing we to the Lord our God.
16 Great and glorious thou art, Lord Adonai; there is no outmatching thy wondrous power. 17 Let all thy creatures do
thee service; were they not made at tiny word, fashioned by
a breath from thee? When thou commandest, none but must
obey. 18 Rain-swept, the mountains quake from their depths,
the rocks melt like wax at thy coming. 19 Yet great, by thy
measure, are those that fear thee, in all their doings great.
20 Woe to the nations that levy war on my people; when the
time comes for judgement, the Lord Almighty will execute
vengeance on them; he will not spare. 21 Their flesh the fire
shall scorch, the worm shall devour; lament they must and
bear their pain for ever.
22 And now, their victory won, all went to Jerusalem to worship the Lord there; once they were cleansed of defilement,

TODAY'S ENGLISH VERSION

13 "I will sing a new song to my God.
O Lord, you are strong and glorious!
You have never been defeated.
14 Let all your creatures serve you.
You gave the command,
and all of them came into being;
you breathed on them,
and all of them were created.
No one can oppose your command.
15 The mountains and the seas tremble,
and rocks melt like wax when you come near.
But there is mercy for all who obey you.
16 The Lord is more pleased with those who obey him
than with all the choice meat on the altar,
or with all the most fragrant sacrifices.
17 The nations who rise up against my people are doomed.
The Lord Almighty will punish them on
Judgment Day.
He will send fire and worms to devour their bodies,
and they will weep in pain forever."

18 When the people arrived in Jerusalem, they purified
themselves and worshiped God. They presented their burnt

NEW REVISED STANDARD VERSION

13 I will sing to my God a new song:
O Lord, you are great and glorious,
wonderful in strength, invincible.
14 Let all your creatures serve you,
for you spoke, and they were made.
You sent forth your spirit,[a] and it formed them;[b]
there is none that can resist your voice.
15 For the mountains shall be shaken to their foundations
with the waters;
before your glance the rocks shall melt like wax.
But to those who fear you
you show mercy.
16 For every sacrifice as a fragrant offering is a small
thing,
and the fat of all whole burnt offerings to you is a
very little thing;
but whoever fears the Lord is great forever.
17 Woe to the nations that rise up against my people!
The Lord Almighty will take vengeance on them in
the day of judgment;
he will send fire and worms into their flesh;
they shall weep in pain forever.

18 When they arrived at Jerusalem, they worshiped God.
As soon as the people were purified, they offered their burnt

a Or *breath* *b* Other ancient authorities read *they were created*

NEW AMERICAN BIBLE

13 "A new hymn I will sing to my God.
O LORD, great are you and glorious,
wonderful in power and unsurpassable.
14 Let your every creature serve you;
for you spoke, and they were made,
You sent forth your spirit, and they were created;
no one can resist your word.
15 The mountains to their bases, and the seas, are shaken;
the rocks, like wax, melt before your glance.

"But to those who fear you,
you are very merciful.
16 Though the sweet odor of every sacrifice is a trifle,
and the fat of all holocausts but little in your sight,
one who fears the LORD is forever great.

17 "Woe to the nations that rise against my people!
the LORD Almighty will requite them;
in the day of judgment he will punish them:
He will send fire and worms into their flesh,
and they shall burn and suffer forever."

18 The people then went to Jerusalem to worship God; when
they were purified, they offered their holocausts, free-will

NEW JERUSALEM BIBLE

13 I shall sing a new song to my God.
Lord, you are great, you are glorious,
wonderfully strong, unconquerable.
14 May your whole creation serve you!
For you spoke and things came into being,
you sent your breath and they were put together,
and no one can resist your voice.

15 Should mountains be tossed from their foundations
to mingle with the waves,
should rocks melt
like wax before your face,
to those who fear you,
you would still be merciful.

16 A little thing indeed
is a sweetly smelling sacrifice,
still less the fat
burned for you in burnt offering;
but whoever fears the Lord
is great for ever.

17 Woe to the nations
who rise against my race!
The Lord Almighty
will punish them on judgement day.
He will send fire and worms in their flesh
and they will weep with pain for evermore.

18 When they reached Jerusalem they fell on their faces
before God and, once the people had been purified, they

GREEK OLD TESTAMENT

αὐτῶν καὶ τὰ ἑκούσια αὐτῶν καὶ τὰ δόματα. 19 καὶ ἀνέθηκεν
Ιουδιθ πάντα τὰ σκεύη Ολοφέρνου, ὅσα ἔδωκεν ὁ λαὸς αὐτῇ,
καὶ τὸ κωνώπιον, ὃ ἔλαβεν ἑαυτῇ ἐκ τοῦ κοιτῶνος αὐτοῦ, εἰς
ἀνάθημα τῷ θεῷ ἔδωκεν. 20 καὶ ἦν ὁ λαὸς εὐφραινόμενος ἐν
Ιερουσαλημ κατὰ πρόσωπον τῶν ἁγίων ἐπὶ μῆνας τρεῖς, καὶ
Ιουδιθ μετ' αὐτῶν κατέμεινεν.

21 Μετὰ δὲ τὰς ἡμέρας ταύτας ἀνέζευξεν ἕκαστος εἰς τὴν
κληρονομίαν αὐτοῦ, καὶ Ιουδιθ ἀπῆλθεν εἰς Βαιτυλουα καὶ
κατέμεινεν ἐπὶ τῆς ὑπάρξεως αὐτῆς. καὶ ἐγένετο κατὰ τὸν
καιρὸν αὐτῆς ἔνδοξος ἐν πάσῃ τῇ γῇ. 22 καὶ πολλοὶ ἐπεθύμησαν αὐτήν, καὶ οὐκ ἔγνω ἀνὴρ αὐτὴν πάσας τὰς ἡμέρας
τῆς ζωῆς αὐτῆς, ἀφ' ἧς ἡμέρας ἀπέθανεν Μανασσης ὁ ἀνὴρ
αὐτῆς καὶ προσετέθη πρὸς τὸν λαὸν αὐτοῦ. 23 καὶ ἦν προ-
βαίνουσα μεγάλη σφόδρα καὶ ἐγήρασεν ἐν τῷ οἴκῳ τοῦ ἀνδρὸς αὐτῆς ἔτη ἑκατὸν πέντε· καὶ ἀφῆκεν τὴν ἅβραν αὐτῆς
ἐλευθέραν. καὶ ἀπέθανεν εἰς Βαιτυλουα, καὶ ἔθαψαν αὐτὴν ἐν
τῷ σπηλαίῳ τοῦ ἀνδρὸς αὐτῆς Μανασση, 24 καὶ ἐπένθησεν
αὐτὴν οἶκος Ισραηλ ἡμέρας ἑπτά. καὶ διεῖλεν τὰ ὑπάρχοντα
αὐτῆς πρὸ τοῦ ἀποθανεῖν αὐτὴν πᾶσι τοῖς ἔγγιστα Μανασση τοῦ ἀνδρὸς αὐτῆς καὶ τοῖς ἔγγιστα τοῦ γένους αὐτῆς.
25 καὶ οὐκ ἦν ἔτι ὁ ἐκφοβῶν τοὺς υἱοὺς Ισραηλ ἐν ταῖς
ἡμέραις Ιουδιθ καὶ μετὰ τὸ ἀποθανεῖν αὐτὴν ἡμέρας πολλάς.

KING JAMES VERSION

they offered their burnt offerings, and their free offerings, and their gifts.

19 Judith also dedicated all the stuff of Holofernes, which the people had given her, and gave the canopy, which she had taken out of his bedchamber, for a gift unto the Lord.

20 So the people continued feasting in Jerusalem before the sanctuary for the space of three months, and Judith remained with them.

21 After this time every one returned to his own inheritance, and Judith went to Bethulia, and remained in her own possession, and was in her time honourable in all the country.

22 And many desired her, but none knew her all the days of her life, after that Manasses her husband was dead, and was gathered to his people.

23 But she increased more and more in honour, and waxed old in her husband's house, being an hundred and five years old, and made her maid free; so she died in Bethulia: and they buried her in the cave of her husband Manasses.

24 And the house of Israel lamented her seven days: and before she died, she did distribute her goods to all them that were nearest of kindred to Manasses her husband, and to them that were nearest of her kindred.

25 And there was none that made the children of Israel any more afraid in the days of Judith, nor a long time after her death.

DOUAY OLD TESTAMENT

and as soon as they were purified, they all offered holocausts, and vows, and their promises.

23 And Judith offered for an anathema of oblivion all the arms of Holofernes, which the people gave her, and the canopy that she had taken away out of his chamber.

24 And the people were joyful in the sight of the sanctuary, and for three months the joy of this victory was celebrated with Judith.

25 And after those days every man returned to his house, and Judith was made great in Bethulia, and she was most renowned in all the land of Israel.

26 And chastity was joined to her virtue, so that she knew no man all the days of her life, after the death of Manasses her husband.

27 And on festival days she came forth with great glory.

28 And she abode in her husband's house a hundred and five years, and made her handmaid free, and she died, and was buried with her husband in Bethulia.

29 And all the people mourned for seven days.

30 And all the time of her life there was none that troubled Israel, nor many years after her death.

31 But the day of the festivity of this victory is received by the Hebrews in the number of holy days, and is religiously observed by the Jews from that time until this day.

KNOX TRANSLATION

burnt-sacrifice was done, vow and promise were paid by all
alike. 23 As for Judith, she kept none of Holofernes' spoil, that
the people had given her, nor the canopy she had carried off
from his banqueting-room, for herself; she offered them up as
a thing forfeit.[a] 24 High festival the people kept, there before
the sanctuary; for three whole months they solemnized their
victory, and Judith among them. 25 Then they dispersed to
their homes, and Judith, back at Bethulia, was held in great
renown; in all Israel, none so honoured as she. 26 So well, in
her, did chastity mate with valour; once her husband was
dead, she never had knowledge of man again. 27 When she
left her house on festival days, great reverence was hers
indeed. 28 And for the serving-maid, Judith let her go free.

There, then, Judith lived on in her husband's dwelling-
place, and a hundred and five years had passed before she
was laid to rest at his side at Bethulia; 29 and the whole people bewailed her for seven days together. 30 All the while she
lived, and long after her death, was never enemy that disturbed the peace of Israel. 31 In the Hebrew calendar, a day
of rejoicing commemorates her victory; in such honour have
the Jews held it from that day to this.

a Literally, 'as an anathema of forgetfulness'; in the Greek, 'as an offering'. If the Vulgate rendering is right, the phrase probably alludes to the proceedings mentioned in Deut. 13. 16, Jos. 7. 24.

TODAY'S ENGLISH VERSION

offerings, freewill offerings, and gifts. 19 Judith dedicated to God all of Holofernes' property, which the people had given to her. And as a special offering in fulfillment of a vow, she presented to the Lord the mosquito net which she had taken from Holofernes' bed. 20 For three months the people continued to celebrate in front of the Temple in Jerusalem, and Judith stayed there with them.

21 When the celebrations had ended, everyone returned home, and Judith went back to Bethulia to live on her own estate. For the rest of her life she was famous throughout the land of Israel. 22 Many men wanted to marry her, but she never remarried after the death of her husband Manasseh. 23-24 Her fame continued to spread, and she lived in the house her husband had left her. Before she died, Judith divided her property among her husband's and her own close relatives and set her slave woman free. When she died in Bethulia at the age of 105, she was buried beside her husband, and the people of Israel mourned her death for seven days. 25 As long as Judith lived, and for many years after her death, no one dared to threaten the people of Israel.

NEW REVISED STANDARD VERSION

offerings, their freewill offerings, and their gifts. 19 Judith also dedicated to God all the possessions of Holofernes, which the people had given her; and the canopy that she had taken for herself from his bedchamber she gave as a votive offering. 20 For three months the people continued feasting in Jerusalem before the sanctuary, and Judith remained with them.

21 After this they all returned home to their own inheritances. Judith went to Bethulia, and remained on her estate. For the rest of her life she was honored throughout the whole country. 22 Many desired to marry her, but she gave herself to no man all the days of her life after her husband Manasseh died and was gathered to his people. 23 She became more and more famous, and grew old in her husband's house, reaching the age of one hundred five. She set her maid free. She died in Bethulia, and they buried her in the cave of her husband Manasseh; 24 and the house of Israel mourned her for seven days. Before she died she distributed her property to all those who were next of kin to her husband Manasseh, and to her own nearest kindred. 25 No one ever again spread terror among the Israelites during the lifetime of Judith, or for a long time after her death.

NEW AMERICAN BIBLE

offerings, and gifts. 19 Judith dedicated, as a votive offering to God, all the things of Holofernes that the people had given her, as well as the canopy that she herself had taken from his bedroom. 20 For three months the people continued their celebration in Jerusalem before the sanctuary, and Judith remained with them.

21 When those days were over, each one returned to his inheritance. Judith went back to Bethulia and remained on her estate. For the rest of her life she was renowned throughout the land. 22 Many wished to marry her, but she gave herself to no man all the days of her life from the time of the death and burial of her husband, Manasseh. 23 She lived to be very old in the house of her husband, reaching the advanced age of a hundred and five. She died in Bethulia, where they buried her in the tomb of her husband, Manasseh; 24 and the house of Israel mourned her for seven days. Before she died, she distributed her goods to the relatives of her husband, Manasseh, and to her own relatives; and to the maid she gave her freedom.

25 During the life of Judith and for a long time after her death, no one again disturbed the Israelites.

NEW JERUSALEM BIBLE

presented their burnt offerings, voluntary offerings and gifts. 19 All Holofernes' property given her by the people, and the canopy she herself had stripped from his bed, Judith vowed to God as a dedicated offering. 20 For three months the people gave themselves up to rejoicings in front of the Temple in Jerusalem, where Judith stayed with them.

21 When this was over, everyone returned home. Judith went back to Bethulia and lived on her property; as long as she lived, she enjoyed a great reputation throughout the country. 22 She had many suitors, but all her days, from the time her husband Manasseh died and was gathered to his people, she never gave herself to another man. 23 Her fame spread more and more, the older she grew in her husband's house; she lived to the age of one hundred and five. She emancipated her maid, then died in Bethulia and was buried in the cave where Manasseh her husband lay. 24 The House of Israel mourned her for seven days. Before her death she had distributed her property among her own relations and those of her husband Manasseh.

25 Never again during the lifetime of Judith, nor indeed for a long time after her death, did anyone trouble the Israelites.

GREEK OLD TESTAMENT

The versification of Rahlfs' *Septuaginta* follows that of the Hebrew when the contents of the Greek and Hebrew texts parallel. The versification of the Greek additions is followed by the New Jerusalem Bible and parallels the other systems as follows:

1:1^{a}-1^{l}	= 11:2-12	= A.1-11
1:1^{m}-1^{r}	= 12:1-6	= A.12-17
[1:1^{s}	= 1:1	= 1:1]
3:13^{a}-13^{g}	= 13:1-7	= B.1-7
4:17^{a}-17^{i}	= 13:8-18	= C.1-11
4:17^{k}-17^{z}	= 14:1-19	= C.12-30
5:1^{a}-1^{f}; 2^{a}-2^{b}	= 15:1-16	= D.1-16
8:12^{a}-12^{x}	= 16:1-24	= E.1-24
10:3^{a}-3^{k}	= 10:4-13	= F.1-9
10:3^{l}	= 11:1	= F.10

ΕΣΘΗΡ

1 1a Ἔτους δευτέρου βασιλεύοντος Ἀρταξέρξου τοῦ
μεγάλου τῇ μιᾷ τοῦ Νισα ἐνύπνιον εἶδεν Μαρδοχαῖος ὁ
τοῦ Ιαΐρου τοῦ Σεμεΐου τοῦ Κισαιου ἐκ φυλῆς Βενιαμιν,
1b Ιουδαῖος οἰκῶν ἐν Σούσοις τῇ πόλει, ἄνθρωπος μέγας θεραπεύων ἐν τῇ αὐλῇ τοῦ βασιλέως. 1c δὲ ἐκ τῆς αἰχμαλωσίας,
ἧς ᾐχμαλώτευσεν Ναβουχοδονοσορ ὁ βασιλεὺς Βαβυλῶνος ἐξ
Ιερουσαλημ μετὰ Ιεχονιου τοῦ βασιλέως τῆς Ιουδαίας.

KING JAMES VERSION

The translators of the King James or Authorized Version followed Jerome and the Latin Vulgate in their translation and arrangement of the Book of Esther. Chapters 1:1—10:3 are translated from the Hebrew text and are placed in the Old Testament section. Chapters 10:4—16:24, "The rest of the Chapters of the Booke of Esther, which are found neither in the Hebrew, nor in the Calde," were translated from the Greek text and placed in the Apocrypha section. The chapter and verse numbers for the Greek additions followed the Latin rather than the Greek.

For this volume, the Hebrew and Greek portions are combined and arranged to match the order of Greek text and the other English versions. As in the case of the Douay, Knox, and New Revised Standard Version, the Latin chapter and verse numbers have been preserved.

ESTHER
(Hebrew and Greek Combined)

11 2 In the second year of the reign of Artexerxes the
great, in the first day of the month Nisan, Mardocheus the son of Jairus, the son of Semei, the son of Cisai, of
the tribe of Benjamin, had a dream;
3 Who was a Jew, and dwelt in the city of Susa, a great
man, being a servitor in the king's court.
4 He was also one of the captives, which Nabuchodonosor
the king of Babylon carried from Jerusalem with Jechonias
king of Judea; and this was his dream:

DOUAY OLD TESTAMENT

The Douay Old Testament is based on the Latin Vulgate of Jerome. Jerome translated the Book of Esther from two sources: he first translated the Hebrew Book of Esther in its entirety and then appended to this his translation of the Greek additions to Esther, out of the context and sequence of the Greek edition of Esther.

For this volume, the Douay translation is rearranged to match the order of Greek text and the other English versions. As in the case of the King James Version, Knox, and New Revised Standard Version, the Latin chapter and verse numbers have been preserved.

THE BOOK OF ESTHER

11 2 In the second year of the reign of Artaxerxes the
great, in the first day of the month Nisan, Mardochai
the son of Jair, the son of Semei, the son of Cis, of the tribe
of Benjamin:
3 A Jew who dwelt in the city of Susan, a great man and
among the first of the king's court, had a dream.
4 Now he was of the number of the captives, whom Nabuchodonosor king of Babylon had carried away from Jerusalem with Jechonias king of Juda:

KNOX TRANSLATION

Monsignor Knox's translation is based on the Latin Vulgate of Jerome. Jerome translated the Book of Esther from two sources: he first translated the Hebrew Book of Esther in its entirety and then appended to this his translation of the Greek additions to Esther, out of the context and sequence of the Greek edition of Esther.

For this volume, the Knox translation is rearranged to match the order of Greek text and the other English versions. As in the case of the Douay, King James Version, and New Revised Standard Version, the Latin chapter and verse numbers have been preserved.

THE BOOK OF ESTHER

(Verses 2-12 of this chapter, and the whole of chapter 12, appear in the Septuagint Greek as the introduction to the whole book. In part, they are a duplicate of 2. 5, 6, 21-23.)

11 2 On the first day of the month Nisan, in the second
year of the great Artaxerxes, a vision came in a dream
to Mardochaeus the Benjamite, who was descended from Cis
through Jairi and Semei. 3 Although a Jew, he dwelt at Susan,
and was a man of consequence in the royal court;[a] 4 he
belonged to that band of exiles who were carried off from
Jerusalem by Nabuchodonosor, king of Babylon, together with

[a] See note on 2. 5 below. Here the reference is clearly to Mardochaeus himself; probably he only 'belonged' to the band of exiles carried off in 588 B.C. in the sense of being descended from them.

TODAY'S ENGLISH VERSION

The Book of Esther *in Greek is a translation, adaptation, and expansion of* The Book of Esther *in Hebrew. The chain of events is much the same, but there are many variations in text, including different proper names and a strong religious tone. The six additions, shown as Chapters A–F in this translation, provide a different introduction and conclusion, introduce documents in an official style, and emphasize the religious elements by the addition of prayers and accounts of how they were answered.*

THE BOOK OF ESTHER

(The Greek Version)

A [a] 1-3Mordecai, a Jew who belonged to the tribe of Benjamin, was taken into exile, along with King Jehoiachin of Judah, when King Nebuchadnezzar of Babylonia captured Jerusalem. Mordecai was the son of Jair, a descendant of Kish and Shimei. He now lived in the Persian city of Susa, where he was an important official in the royal court of Xerxes the great king.

During the second year of Xerxes' reign, on the first day of

[a] *Chapter A 1-17 corresponds to chapters 11.2—12.6 in a number of English translations.*

NEW REVISED STANDARD VERSION

The deuterocanonical portions of the Book of Esther are several additional passages found in the Greek translation of the Hebrew Book of Esther, a translation that differs also in other respects from the Hebrew text (the latter is translated in the NRSV Old Testament). The disordered chapter numbers come from the displacement of the additions to the end of the canonical Book of Esther by Jerome in his Latin translation and from the subsequent division of the Bible into chapters by Stephen Langton, who numbered the additions consecutively as though they formed a direct continuation of the Hebrew text. So that the additions may be read in their proper context, the whole of the Greek version is here translated, though certain familiar names are given according to their Hebrew rather than their Greek form; for example, Mordecai and Vashti instead of Mardocheus and Astin. The order followed is that of the Greek text, but the chapter and verse numbers conform to those of the King James or Authorized Version. The additions, conveniently indicated by the letters A–F, are located as follows: A, before 1.1; B, after 3.13; C and D, after 4.17; E, after 8.12; F, after 10.3.

ESTHER

(The Greek Version Containing the Additional Chapters)

ADDITION A

11 [a] 2In the second year of the reign of Artaxerxes the Great, on the first day of Nisan, Mordecai son of Jair son of Shimei[b] son of Kish, of the tribe of Benjamin, had a dream. 3He was a Jew living in the city of Susa, a great man, serving in the court of the king. 4He was one of the captives whom King Nebuchadnezzar of Babylon had brought from Jerusalem with King Jeconiah of Judea. And

a Chapters 11.2—12.6 correspond to chapter A 1-17 in some translations.
b Gk *Semeios*

NEW AMERICAN BIBLE

The text of Esther, written originally in Hebrew, was transmitted in two forms: a short Hebrew form and a longer Greek version. The latter contains 107 additional verses, inserted at appropriate places within the Hebrew form of the text. A few of these seem to have a Hebrew origin while the rest are Greek in original composition. It is possible that the Hebrew form of the text is original throughout. If it systematically omits reference to God and his Providence over Israel, this is perhaps due to fear of irreverent response. The Greek text with the above-mentioned additions is possibly a later literary paraphrase in which the author seeks to have the reader share his sentiments. This standard Greek text is pre-Christian in origin. The church has accepted the additions as equally inspired with the rest of the book.

In the present translations, the portions preceded by the letters A through F indicate the underlying Greek additions referred to above. The regular chapter numbers apply to the Hebrew text.

Since the New American Bible version of Esther inserts translations of the additional Greek passages into a translation of the Hebrew text, the designation "deuterocanonical" properly applies only to the Greek insertions.

THE BOOK OF ESTHER

A In the second year of the reign of the great King Ahasuerus, on the first day of Nisan, Mordecai, son of Jair, son of Shimei, son of Kish, of the tribe of Benjamin, had a dream. 2He was a Jew residing in the city of Susa, a prominent man who served at the king's court, 3and one of the captives whom Nebuchadnezzar, king of Babylon, had taken from Jerusalem with Jeconiah, king of Judah.

NEW JERUSALEM BIBLE

The book of Esther has two forms: one short, in Hebrew; one long, in Greek. The Greek version contains the following passages not found in the Hebrew: the dream of Mordecai, 1:1a-r and its explanation, 10:3a-k; two edicts of Ahaseuerus, 3:13a-g and 8:12a-v, the prayer of Mordecai, 4:17a-i the prayer of Esther, 4:17k-z a second account of Esther's appeal to Ahasuerus, 5:1a-f and 5:2a-b; an appendix explaining the origin of the Greek version, 10:3l. Jerome placed his translation of these passages after the translated Hebrew text (Vulg. 10:4–16:24); in our own translation they have been left where the Greek text has them, but in italics.

Since the New Jerusalem Bible version of Esther inserts translations of the additional Greek passages into a translation of the Hebrew text, the designation "deuterocanonical" properly applies only to the Greek insertions.

ESTHER

1a [a] *In the second year of the reign of the Great King, Ahasuerus, on the first day of Nisan, a dream came to Mordecai son of Jair, son of Shimei, son of Kish, of the tribe of Benjamin,* 1b*a Jew living at Susa and holding high office at the royal court.* 1c*He was one of the captives whom Nebuchadnezzar king of Babylon had deported from Jerusalem with Jeconiah king of Judah.*

a 1 Throughout the book the passages printed in italics are contained in the Gk text but are not in the Hebr.

GREEK OLD TESTAMENT

1d τοῦτο αὐτοῦ τὸ ἐνύπνιον· καὶ ἰδοὺ φωναὶ καὶ θόρυβος,
βρονταὶ καὶ σεισμός, τάραχος ἐπὶ τῆς γῆς. 1e ἰδοὺ δύο δράκοντες μεγάλοι ἕτοιμοι προῆλθον ἀμφότεροι παλαίειν, καὶ
ἐγένετο αὐτῶν φωνὴ μεγάλη· 1f τῇ φωνῇ αὐτῶν ἡτοιμάσθη
πᾶν ἔθνος εἰς πόλεμον ὥστε πολεμῆσαι δικαίων ἔθνος.
1g ἰδοὺ ἡμέρα σκότους καὶ γνόφου, θλῖψις καὶ στενοχωρία,
κάκωσις καὶ τάραχος μέγας ἐπὶ τῆς γῆς. 1h ἐταράχθη
δίκαιον πᾶν ἔθνος φοβούμενοι τὰ ἑαυτῶν κακὰ καὶ ἡτοιμά-
σθησαν ἀπολέσθαι καὶ ἐβόησαν πρὸς τὸν θεόν. 1i δὲ τῆς
βοῆς αὐτῶν ἐγένετο ὡσανεὶ ἀπὸ μικρᾶς πηγῆς ποταμὸς
μέγας, ὕδωρ πολύ· 1k καὶ ὁ ἥλιος ἀνέτειλεν, καὶ οἱ ταπεινοὶ
ὑψώθησαν καὶ κατέφαγον τοὺς ἐνδόξους. — 1l διεγερθεὶς
Μαρδοχαῖος ὁ ἑωρακὼς τὸ ἐνύπνιον τοῦτο καὶ τί ὁ θεὸς
βεβούλευται ποιῆσαι, εἶχεν αὐτὸ ἐν τῇ καρδίᾳ καὶ ἐν παντὶ
λόγῳ ἤθελεν ἐπιγνῶναι αὐτὸ ἕως τῆς νυκτός. 1m ἡσύχασεν
Μαρδοχαῖος ἐν τῇ αὐλῇ μετὰ Γαβαθα καὶ Θαρρα τῶν δύο
εὐνούχων τοῦ βασιλέως τῶν φυλασσόντων τὴν αὐλὴν 1n τε
αὐτῶν τοὺς λογισμοὺς καὶ τὰς μερίμνας αὐτῶν ἐξηρεύνησεν
καὶ ἔμαθεν ὅτι ἑτοιμάζουσιν τὰς χεῖρας ἐπιβαλεῖν Ἀρταξέρξῃ τῷ βασιλεῖ, καὶ ὑπέδειξεν τῷ βασιλεῖ περὶ αὐτῶν·
1o ἐξήτασεν ὁ βασιλεὺς τοὺς δύο εὐνούχους, καὶ ὁμολογή-
σαντες ἀπήχθησαν. 1p ἔγραψεν ὁ βασιλεὺς τοὺς λόγους

KING JAMES VERSION

5 Behold a noise of a tumult, with thunder, and earthquakes, and uproar in the land:

6 And, behold, two great dragons came forth ready to fight, and their cry was great.

7 And at their cry all nations were prepared to battle, that they might fight against the righteous people.

8 And lo a day of darkness and obscurity, tribulation and anguish, affliction and great uproar, upon earth.

9 And the whole righteous nation was troubled, fearing their own evils, and were ready to perish.

10 Then they cried unto God, and upon their cry, as it were from a little fountain, was made a great flood, even much water.

11 The light and the sun rose up, and the lowly were exalted, and devoured the glorious.

12 Now when Mardocheus, who had seen this dream, and what God had determined to do, was awake, he bare this dream in mind, and until night by all means was desirous to know it.

12 And Mardocheus took his rest in the court with Gabatha and Tharra, the two eunuchs of the king, and keepers of the palace.

2 And he heard their devices, and searched out their purposes, and learned that they were about to lay hands upon Artexerxes the king; and so he certified the king of them.

3 Then the king examined the two eunuchs, and after that they had confessed it, they were strangled.

DOUAY OLD TESTAMENT

5 And this was his dream: Behold there were voices, and tumults, and thunders, and earthquakes, and a disturbance upon the earth.

6 And behold two great dragons came forth ready to fight one against another.

7 And at their cry all nations were stirred up to fight against the nation of the just.

8 And that was a day of darkness and danger, of tribulation and distress, and great fear upon the earth.

9 And the nation of the just was troubled fearing their own evils, and was prepared for death.

10 And they cried to God: and as they were crying, a little fountain grew into a very great river, and abounded into many waters.

11 The light and the sun rose up, and the humble were exalted, and they devoured the glorious.

12 And when Mardochai had seen this, and arose out of his bed, he was thinking what God would do: and he kept it fixed in his mind, desirous to know what the dream should signify.

12 AND he abode at that time in the king's court with Bagatha and Thara the king's eunuchs, who were porters of the palace.

2 And when he understood their designs, and had diligently searched into their projects, he learned that they went about to lay violent hands on king Artaxerxes, and he told the king thereof.

3 Then the king had them both examined, and after they had confessed, commanded them to be put to death.

KNOX TRANSLATION

the king of Juda, Jechonias. 5 His dream was this: Mutterings
and uproar at first, thunder and earthquake, and commotion
all over the world, 6 and from these two dragons disengaged
themselves, ready to join battle. 7 Roused by their clamour,
the whole world rose to levy war against one innocent nation;
8 it was a time of darkness and of peril, of affliction and sore
need, and great fear brooded over all the earth. 9 Then this
innocent nation, terrified by the misfortunes which threatened it, already marked down to die, cried out to the Lord.
10 And at their cry, a great river grew out of a little spring, and
rolled on in full flood; 11 the sun returned, and the sunlight,
the weak triumphed now, and tyranny fell a prey to their
onslaught. 12 All this Mardochaeus saw, and rose from his
bed still wondering what the divine purpose was; still the
vision haunted his mind, and he longed to know what was
the meaning of it.

12 ...At this time his days were passed at the king's
palace, and two of the royal chamberlains, Bagatha
and Thara, were much in his company. 2 When he came to
know their minds better, and read the secret of their ambi-
tions, he became aware that they were plotting against the
king's life, and warned the king of his danger. 3 Both, upon
examination, confessed their guilt, and were sent to execution; 4 and the king had the story recorded in his archives;

TODAY'S ENGLISH VERSION

the month of Nisan, Mordecai had a dream. 4He dreamed
that there was great noise and confusion, loud thunder, and
an earthquake, with terrible turmoil on the earth. 5Then two
huge dragons appeared, ready to fight each other. 6They
made a dreadful noise, and all the nations got ready to make
war against God's nation of righteous people. 7For the
world it was a day of darkness and gloom, trouble and distress, destruction and ruin. 8All of God's righteous people
were troubled, in great fear of what was about to happen to
them. They prepared for death, 9but they cried out to God
for help. In the dream their prayer was answered by a great
river which came flowing out of a small spring. 10The day
dawned, the sun rose, and the humble people were made
strong and destroyed their arrogant enemies.

11Mordecai woke up from this dream in which he saw
what God planned to do. He thought about it all day and
tried to understand what it meant.

12While Mordecai was resting in the courtyard of the
palace, where two of the king's eunuchs, Gabatha and
Tharra, were on guard, 13he overheard them plotting together. He listened carefully to what they were saying and
learned that they were making plans to kill the king. So
Mordecai went to King Xerxes and told him about the plot of
the two eunuchs. 14The king had them questioned, and
when they confessed, they were led away and executed.

NEW REVISED STANDARD VERSION

this was his dream: 5Noises[a] and confusion, thunders and
earthquake, tumult on the earth! 6Then two great dragons
came forward, both ready to fight, and they roared terribly.
7At their roaring every nation prepared for war, to fight
against the righteous nation. 8It was a day of darkness and
gloom, of tribulation and distress, affliction and great tumult
on the earth! 9And the whole righteous nation was troubled;
they feared the evils that threatened them,[b] and were ready
to perish. 10Then they cried out to God; and at their outcry,
as though from a tiny spring, there came a great river, with
abundant water; 11light came, and the sun rose, and the
lowly were exalted and devoured those held in honor.

12 Mordecai saw in this dream what God had determined
to do, and after he awoke he had it on his mind, seeking all
day to understand it in every detail.

12 Now Mordecai took his rest in the courtyard with
Gabatha and Tharra, the two eunuchs of the king
who kept watch in the courtyard. 2He overheard their conversation and inquired into their purposes, and learned that
they were preparing to lay hands on King Artaxerxes; and he
informed the king concerning them. 3Then the king examined the two eunuchs, and after they had confessed it, they
were led away to execution. 4The king made a permanent

a Or *Voices* *b* Gk *their own evils*

NEW AMERICAN BIBLE

4This was his dream. There was noise and tumult, thunder
and earthquake—confusion upon the earth. 5Two great
dragons came on, both poised for combat. They uttered a
mighty cry, 6and at their cry every nation prepared for war,
to fight against the race of the just. 7It was a dark and
gloomy day. Tribulation and distress, evil and great confusion, lay upon the earth. 8The whole race of the just were
dismayed with fear of the evils to come upon them, and were
at the point of destruction. 9Then they cried out to God, and
as they cried, there appeared to come forth a great river, a
flood of water from a little spring. 10The light of the sun
broke forth; the lowly were exalted and they devoured the
nobles.

11Having seen this dream and what God intended to do,
Mordecai awoke. He kept it in mind, and tried in every way,
until night, to understand its meaning.

12Mordecai lodged at the court with Bagathan and Thares,
two eunuchs of the king who were court guards. 13He overheard them plotting, investigated their plans, and discovered
that they were preparing to lay hands on King Ahasuerus. So
he informed the king about them, 14and the king had the
two eunuchs questioned and, upon their confession, put to

NEW JERUSALEM BIBLE

1d*This was his dream. There were cries and noise, thunder*
and earthquakes, and disorder over the whole earth. 1e*Then*
two great dragons came forward, each ready for the fray, and
set up a great roar. 1f*At the sound of them every nation*
made ready to wage war against the nation of the just. 1g*A*
day of darkness and gloom, of affliction and distress, oppres-
sion and great disturbance on earth! 1h*The entire upright*
nation was thrown into consternation at the fear of the evils
awaiting it and prepared for death, crying out to God. 1i*Then*
from its cry, as from a little spring, there grew a great river,
a flood of water. 1k*Light came as the sun rose, and the hum-*
ble were raised up and devoured the mighty.

1l*On awakening from this dream and vision of God's*
designs, Mordecai thought deeply about the matter, trying
his best all day to discover what its meaning might be.

1m*Mordecai was lodging at court with Bigthan and Teresh,*
two of the king's eunuchs who guarded the palace. 1n*Having*
got wind of their plotting and gained knowledge of their
designs, he discovered that they were preparing to assassi-
nate King Ahasuerus, and he warned the king against them.
1o*The king gave orders for the two officers to be tortured; they*
confessed and were executed. 1p*He then had these events*

Greek Old Testament

τούτους εἰς μνημόσυνον, καὶ Μαρδοχαῖος ἔγραψεν περὶ τῶν
λόγων τούτων· 1q ἐπέταξεν ὁ βασιλεὺς Μαρδοχαίῳ θεραπεύ-
ειν ἐν τῇ αὐλῇ καὶ ἔδωκεν αὐτῷ δόματα περὶ τούτων. 1r ἦν
Αμαν Αμαδαθου Βουγαῖος ἔνδοξος ἐνώπιον τοῦ βασιλέως.
καὶ ἐζήτησεν κακοποιῆσαι τὸν Μαρδοχαῖον καὶ τὸν λαὸν αὐτοῦ ὑπὲρ τῶν δύο εὐνούχων τοῦ βασιλέως.

1s Καὶ ἐγένετο μετὰ τοὺς λόγους τούτους ἐν ταῖς ἡμέραις
Ἀρταξέρξου — οὗτος ὁ Ἀρταξέρξης ἀπὸ τῆς Ἰνδικῆς ἑκατὸν
εἴκοσι ἑπτὰ χωρῶν ἐκράτησεν — 2 ἐν αὐταῖς ταῖς ἡμέραις,
ὅτε ἐθρονίσθη ὁ βασιλεὺς Ἀρταξέρξης ἐν Σούσοις τῇ πόλει,
3 ἐν τῷ τρίτῳ ἔτει βασιλεύοντος αὐτοῦ δοχὴν ἐποίησεν τοῖς
φίλοις καὶ τοῖς λοιποῖς ἔθνεσιν καὶ τοῖς Περσῶν καὶ Μήδων
ἐνδόξοις καὶ τοῖς ἄρχουσιν τῶν σατραπῶν. 4 καὶ μετὰ ταῦτα
μετὰ τὸ δεῖξαι αὐτοῖς τὸν πλοῦτον τῆς βασιλείας αὐτοῦ καὶ
τὴν δόξαν τῆς εὐφροσύνης τοῦ πλούτου αὐτοῦ ἐπὶ ἡμέρας
ἑκατὸν ὀγδοήκοντα, 5 ὅτε δὲ ἀνεπληρώθησαν αἱ ἡμέραι τοῦ
γάμου, ἐποίησεν ὁ βασιλεὺς πότον τοῖς ἔθνεσιν τοῖς εὑρε-
θεῖσιν εἰς τὴν πόλιν ἐπὶ ἡμέρας ἓξ ἐν αὐλῇ οἴκου τοῦ βασιλέως 6 κεκοσμημένῃ βυσσίνοις καὶ καρπασίνοις τεταμένοις
ἐπὶ σχοινίοις βυσσίνοις καὶ πορφυροῖς ἐπὶ κύβοις χρυσοῖς
καὶ ἀργυροῖς ἐπὶ στύλοις παρίνοις καὶ λιθίνοις. κλῖναι χρυσαῖ καὶ ἀργυραῖ ἐπὶ λιθοστρώτου σμαραγδίτου λίθου καὶ

King James Version

4 And the king made a record of these things, and Mardocheus also wrote thereof.

5 So the king commanded Mardocheus to serve in the court, and for this he rewarded him.

6 Howbeit Aman the son of Amadathus the Agagite, who was in great honour with the king, sought to molest Mardocheus and his people because of the two eunuchs of the king.

1 Now it came to pass in the days of Ahasuerus, (this *is* Ahasuerus which reigned, from India even unto Ethiopia, *over* an hundred and seven and twenty provinces:)

2 *That* in those days, when the king Ahasuerus sat on the throne of his kingdom, which *was* in Shushan the palace,

3 In the third year of his reign, he made a feast unto all his princes and his servants; the power of Persia and Media, the nobles and princes of the provinces, *being* before him:

4 When he shewed the riches of his glorious kingdom and the honour of his excellent majesty many days, *even* an hundred and fourscore days.

5 And when these days were expired, the king made a feast unto all the people that were present in Shushan the palace, both unto great and small, seven days, in the court of the garden of the king's palace;

6 *Where were* white, green, and blue, *hangings,* fastened with cords of fine linen and purple to silver rings and pillars

Douay Old Testament

4 But the king made a record of what was done: and Mardochai also committed the memory of the thing to writing.

5 And the king commanded him, to abide in the court of the palace, and gave him presents for the information.

6 But Aman the son of Amadathi the Bugite was in great honour with the king, and sought to hurt Mardochai and his people, because of the two eunuchs of the king who were put to death.

1 IN the days of Assuerus, who reigned from India to Ethiopia over a hundred and twenty-seven provinces:

2 When he sat on the throne of his kingdom, the city Susan was the capital of his kingdom.

3 Now in the third year of his reign he made a great feast for all the princes, and for his servants, for the most mighty of the Persians, and the nobles of the Medes, and the governors of the provinces in his sight,

4 That he might shew the riches of the glory of his kingdom, and the greatness, and boasting of his power, for a long time, to wit, for a hundred and fourscore days.

5 And when the days of the feast were expired, he invited all the people that were found in Susan, from the greatest to the least: and commanded a feast to be made seven days in the court of the garden, and of the wood, which was planted by the care and the hand of the king.

6 And there were hung up on every side sky coloured, and green, and violet hangings, fastened with cords of silk, and of purple, which were put into rings of ivory, and were held up with marble pillars. The beds also were of gold and silver,

Knox Translation

Mardochaeus himself has also left an account of it. 5 The
royal orders were, that he should be rewarded for the information given, and lodged at the palace;[a] 6 but already he
had an enemy, Aman son of Amadathi, the Bugaean. This
Aman was in high favour with the king, and owed both
Mardochaeus and his nation a grudge for bringing the two
chamberlains to their death.

1 Now turn we to the days of Assuerus,[b] that was lord of
a hundred and twenty-seven provinces, from India on
this side to Ethiopia on that, 2 and was firmly established on
the throne of his kingdom, with the city of Susan for his capital. 3 It was now the third year of his reign, and he held
high feast for all his lords and vassals; Persian warriors,
Median notables, and the governor of every province, were
his guests. 4 All should have proof of his royal splendour, of
the power and pride that were his; and long they kept holiday, for a hundred and eighty days together. 5 And when the
festivity drew to an end, he would entertain all the folk of
Susan, high and low; for a whole week a banquet was
spread for them at the gates of his garden, amid trees planted by art at the royal bidding. 6 On every side, fastened by
ivory rings to marble columns, hung canopies, some white,
some flaxen, some violet, with cords of fine linen and purple
thread; couches of gold and silver were set here and there on

a This appears to conflict with 6. 3 below. We are perhaps meant to understand that the royal orders were never carried out, because Aman interfered with the execution of them. The word Bugaean in verse 6 is of doubtful significance; some think it was a title accorded to certain royal chamberlains. *b* Assuerus is the name given on inscriptions to that king Xerxes who was defeated by the Greeks at Salamis in 480 B.C.

TODAY'S ENGLISH VERSION

15The king had an account of this written in the official
records, and Mordecai also wrote an account of it. 16Then
the king appointed Mordecai to a position at court and gave
him many gifts as a reward for what he had done.

17But Haman son of Hammedatha, a Bougaean who was
respected by the king, tried to cause trouble for Mordecai and
his people the Jews, because Mordecai had been responsible
for the death of the two eunuchs.

1 1-2These things happened in the time of King Xerxes,
who ruled 127 provinces, all the way from India to
Ethiopia,[a] from his royal throne in Susa, Persia's capital city.
3In the third year of his reign, the king gave a banquet for all
his advisers, the representatives of the other countries, the
noblemen from Persia and Media, and the governors of the
provinces. 4For six whole months he made a show of the
riches of the imperial court with magnificent and expensive
celebrations.

5After the feast[b] the king gave a banquet for the people of
other nations who were in the city. It lasted a week and was
held in the palace courtyard, 6which was decorated with
linen and cotton curtains, held by cords of purple linen
attached to silver and gold blocks on marble and stone
columns. Couches made of gold and silver had been placed in

[a] *Greek* Ethiopia: *Ethiopia is the name given in Graeco-Roman times to the extensive territory south of the First Cataract of the Nile River. Cush was the ancient (Hebrew) name of this region which included within its borders most of modern Sudan and some of present-day Ethiopia (Abyssinia).*
[b] feast; *some manuscripts have* wedding feast.

NEW REVISED STANDARD VERSION

record of these things, and Mordecai wrote an account of
them. 5And the king ordered Mordecai to serve in the court,
and rewarded him for these things. 6But Haman son of
Hammedatha, a Bougean, who was in great honor with the
king, determined to injure Mordecai and his people because
of the two eunuchs of the king.

END OF ADDITION A

1 It was after this that the following things happened in
the days of Artaxerxes, the same Artaxerxes who ruled
over one hundred twenty-seven provinces from India to
Ethiopia.[a] 2In those days, when King Artaxerxes was
enthroned in the city of Susa, 3in the third year of his reign,
he gave a banquet for his Friends and other persons of various nations, the Persians and Median nobles, and the governors of the provinces. 4After this, when he had displayed to
them the riches of his kingdom and the splendor of his bountiful celebration during the course of one hundred eighty
days, 5at the end of the festivity[b] the king gave a drinking
party for the people of various nations who lived in the city.
This was held for six days in the courtyard of the royal
palace, 6which was adorned with curtains of fine linen and
cotton, held by cords of purple linen attached to gold and silver blocks on pillars of marble and other stones. Gold and
silver couches were placed on a mosaic floor of emerald,

a Other ancient authorities lack *to Ethiopia* *b* Gk *marriage feast*

NEW AMERICAN BIBLE

death. 15Then the king had these things recorded; Mordecai,
too, put them into writing. 16The king also appointed
Mordecai to serve at the court, and rewarded him for his
actions.

17Haman, however, son of Hammedatha the Agagite, who
was in high honor with the king, sought to harm Mordecai
and his people because of the two eunuchs of the king.

1 During the reign of Ahasuerus—this was the Ahasuerus
who ruled over a hundred and twenty-seven provinces
from India to Ethiopia — 2while he was occupying the royal
throne in the stronghold of Susa, 3in the third year of his
reign, he presided over a feast for all his officers and ministers: the Persian and Median aristocracy, the nobles, and the
governors of the provinces. 4For as many as a hundred and
eighty days, he displayed the glorious riches of his kingdom
and the resplendent wealth of his royal estate.

5At the end of this time the king gave a feast of seven days
in the garden court of the royal palace for all the people,
great and small, who were in the stronghold of Susa. 6There
were white cotton draperies and violet hangings, held by
cords of crimson byssus from silver rings on marble pillars.
Gold and silver couches were on the pavement, which was of

NEW JERUSALEM BIBLE

*entered in his Record Book, while Mordecai himself also wrote
an account of them.* 1q*The king then appointed Mordecai to
an office at court and rewarded him with presents.* 1r*But
Haman son of Hammedatha, the Agagite, who enjoyed high
favour with the king, determined to injure Mordecai in
revenge for the affair of the king's two officers.*

1 It was in the days of Ahasuerus, the Ahasuerus whose
empire stretched from India to Ethiopia and comprised
one hundred and twenty-seven provinces. 2In those days,
when King Ahasuerus was sitting on his royal throne in the
citadel of Susa, 3in the third year of his reign, he gave a
banquet at his court for all his officers-of-state and ministers, Persian and Median army-commanders, nobles and provincial governors. 4Thus he displayed the riches and splendour of his empire and the pomp and glory of his majesty;
the festivities went on for a long time, a hundred and eighty
days.

5When this period was over, for seven days the king gave
a banquet for all the people living in the citadel of Susa, to
high and low alike, on the esplanade in the gardens of the
royal palace. 6There were white and violet hangings fastened with cords of fine linen and purple thread to silver
rings on marble columns, couches of gold and silver on a

GREEK OLD TESTAMENT

πιννίνου καὶ παρίνου λίθου καὶ στρωμναὶ διαφανεῖς ποικίλως
διηνθισμέναι, κύκλῳ ῥόδα πεπασμένα· 7 ποτήρια χρυσᾶ καὶ
ἀργυρᾶ καὶ ἀνθράκινον κυλίκιον προκείμενον ἀπὸ ταλάντων
τρισμυρίων· οἶνος πολὺς καὶ ἡδύς, ὃν αὐτὸς ὁ βασιλεὺς
ἔπινεν. 8 ὁ δὲ πότος οὗτος οὐ κατὰ προκείμενον νόμον
ἐγένετο, οὕτως δὲ ἠθέλησεν ὁ βασιλεὺς καὶ ἐπέταξεν τοῖς
οἰκονόμοις ποιῆσαι τὸ θέλημα αὐτοῦ καὶ τῶν ἀνθρώπων. 9 καὶ
Αστιν ἡ βασίλισσα ἐποίησε πότον ταῖς γυναιξὶν ἐν τοῖς
βασιλείοις, ὅπου ὁ βασιλεὺς ᾿Αρταξέρξης. 10 ἐν δὲ τῇ ἡμέρᾳ
τῇ ἑβδόμῃ ἡδέως γενόμενος ὁ βασιλεὺς εἶπεν τῷ Αμαν καὶ
Βαζαν καὶ Θαρρα καὶ Βωραζη καὶ Ζαθολθα καὶ Αβαταζα καὶ
Θαραβα, τοῖς ἑπτὰ εὐνούχοις τοῖς διακόνοις τοῦ βασιλέως
᾿Αρταξέρξου, 11 εἰσαγαγεῖν τὴν βασίλισσαν πρὸς αὐτὸν
βασιλεύειν αὐτὴν καὶ περιθεῖναι αὐτῇ τὸ διάδημα καὶ δεῖξαι
αὐτὴν πᾶσιν τοῖς ἄρχουσιν καὶ τοῖς ἔθνεσιν τὸ κάλλος
αὐτῆς, ὅτι καλὴ ἦν. 12 καὶ οὐκ εἰσήκουσεν αὐτοῦ Αστιν ἡ
βασίλισσα ἐλθεῖν μετὰ τῶν εὐνούχων. καὶ ἐλυπήθη ὁ βασιλεὺς
καὶ ὠργίσθη 13 καὶ εἶπεν τοῖς φίλοις αὐτοῦ Κατὰ ταῦτα
ἐλάλησεν Αστιν, ποιήσατε οὖν περὶ τούτου νόμον καὶ κρίσιν.

KING JAMES VERSION

of marble: the beds *were of* gold and silver, upon a pavement of red, and blue, and white, and black, marble.

7 And they gave *them* drink in vessels of gold, (the vessels being diverse one from another,) and royal wine in abundance, according to the state of the king.

8 And the drinking *was* according to the law; none did compel: for so the king had appointed to all the officers of his house, that they should do according to every man's pleasure.

9 Also Vashti the queen made a feast for the women *in* the royal house which *belonged* to king Ahasuerus.

10 On the seventh day, when the heart of the king was merry with wine, he commanded Mehuman, Biztha, Harbona, Bigtha, and Abagtha, Zethar, and Carcas, the seven chamberlains that served in the presence of Ahasuerus the king,

11 To bring Vashti the queen before the king with the crown royal, to shew the people and the princes her beauty: for she *was* fair to look on.

12 But the queen Vashti refused to come at the king's commandment by *his* chamberlains: therefore was the king very wroth, and his anger burned in him.

13 Then the king said to the wise men, which knew the times, (for so *was* the king's manner toward all that knew law and judgment:

DOUAY OLD TESTAMENT

placed in order upon a floor paved with porphyry and white marble: which was embellished with painting of wonderful variety.

7 And they that were invited, drank in golden cups, and the meats were brought in divers vessels one after another. Wine also in abundance and of the best was presented, as was worthy of a king's magnificence.

8 Neither was there any one to compel them to drink that were not willing, but as the king had appointed, who set over every table one of his nobles, that every man might take what he would.

9 Also Vasthi the queen made a feast for the women in the palace, where king Assuerus was used to dwell.

10 Now on the seventh day, when the king was merry, and after very much drinking was well warmed with wine, he commanded Mauman, and Bazatha, and Harbona, and Bagatha, and Abgatha, and Zethar, and Charcas, the seven eunuchs that served in his presence,

11 To bring in queen Vasthi before the king, with the crown set upon her head, to shew her beauty to all the people and the princes: for she was exceeding beautiful.

12 But she refused, and would not come at the king's commandment, which he had signified to her by the eunuchs. Whereupon the king, being angry, and inflamed with a very great fury,

13 Asked the wise men, who according to the custom of the kings, were always near his person, and all he did was by their counsel, who knew the laws, and judgments of their forefathers:

KNOX TRANSLATION

a floor of malachite and marble, wondrously patterned.
7 From golden cups they drank, and the very trenchers on
which the meat was served were ever of new design. Wine
they had in plenty, and of rare vintage, as befitted a king's
state; 8 nor was any man compelled to drink; the king had
set one of his nobles at the head of each table, bidding him
see that each man drank as drink he would. 9 For the
women the queen, Vasthi, held a banquet too, in Assuerus'
own palace.
10 The seventh day had come; the king's heart was merry,
warmed by long draughts of wine; and now he had an
errand for the seven chamberlains that waited on him,
Maumam, Bazatha, Harbona, Bagatha, Abgatha, Zethar and
Charchas. 11 They were to bring queen Vasthi into the king's
presence, wearing the royal crown, so that he might display
her person to the rabble as well as to his lords; hers was no
common beauty. 12 Vain was the royal summons the chamberlains brought her; she would not come. Whereupon the
king broke out into a great passion of rage, 13 and was fain
to take counsel of the wise men that were ever about his person, after the fashion of courts; theirs was still the advice he
followed, theirs the knowledge of ancient law and precedent.

TODAY'S ENGLISH VERSION

the courtyard, which was paved with green and white marble
and mother-of-pearl. The couches were spread with a fine,
thin fabric of many colors, with roses around the edges.
7 There were gold and silver cups, and one of them, decorated
with jewels worth more than a thousand tons of silver, had
been set out for display. There was plenty of good wine from
the king's own supply. 8 There were no limits on the drinks.
The king had given orders to the palace servants that they
should provide him and his guests with as much as they
wanted.
9 Meanwhile, inside the royal palace Queen Vashti was giving a banquet for the women.
10 On the seventh day of his banquet the king was feeling
happy, so he called in the seven eunuchs who were his personal servants, Haman, Bazan, Tharra, Boraze, Zatholta,
Abataza, and Tharaba. 11 He ordered them to bring in the
queen, so that he could place the royal crown on her head
and show her off to the officials and all his guests, for she
was a beautiful woman. 12 But Queen Vashti refused to obey
and would not come with the servants. This embarrassed the
king and made him furious.
13 He told his advisers about Vashti's reply and asked them
to give a legal opinion about what he should do. 14-15 Three

NEW REVISED STANDARD VERSION

mother-of-pearl, and marble. There were coverings of gauze,
embroidered in various colors, with roses arranged around
them. 7 The cups were of gold and silver, and a miniature
cup was displayed, made of ruby, worth thirty thousand talents. There was abundant sweet wine, such as the king himself drank. 8 The drinking was not according to a fixed rule;
but the king wished to have it so, and he commanded his
stewards to comply with his pleasure and with that of the
guests.
9 Meanwhile, Queen Vashti[a] gave a drinking party for the
women in the palace where King Artaxerxes was.
10 On the seventh day, when the king was in good
humor, he told Haman, Bazan, Tharra, Boraze, Zatholtha,
Abataza, and Tharaba, the seven eunuchs who served King
Artaxerxes, 11 to escort the queen to him in order to proclaim
her as queen and to place the diadem on her head, and to
have her display her beauty to all the governors and the people of various nations, for she was indeed a beautiful
woman. 12 But Queen Vashti[a] refused to obey him and
would not come with the eunuchs. This offended the king
and he became furious. 13 He said to his Friends, "This is
how Vashti[a] has answered me.[b] Give therefore your ruling
and judgment on this matter." 14 Arkesaeus, Sarsathaeus,

a Gk *Astin* *b* Gk *Astin has said thus and so*

NEW AMERICAN BIBLE

porphyry, marble, mother-of-pearl, and colored stones.
7 Liquor was served in a variety of golden cups, and the royal
wine flowed freely, as befitted the king's munificence. 8 By
ordinance of the king the drinking was unstinted, for he had
instructed all the stewards of his household to comply with
the good pleasure of everyone.
9 Queen Vashti also gave a feast for the women inside the
royal palace of King Ahasuerus.
10 On the seventh day, when the king was merry with
wine, he instructed Mehuman, Biztha, Harbona, Bigtha,
Abagtha, Zethar, and Carkas, the seven eunuchs who attended King Ahasuerus, 11 to bring Queen Vashti into his presence wearing the royal crown, that he might display her
beauty to the populace and the officials, for she was lovely to
behold. 12 But Queen Vashti refused to come at the royal
order issued through the eunuchs. At this the king's wrath
flared up, and he burned with fury. 13 He conferred with the
wise men versed in the law, because the king's business was
conducted in general consultation with lawyers and jurists.

NEW JERUSALEM BIBLE

pavement of porphyry, marble, mother-of-pearl and precious
stones. 7 For drinking there were golden cups of various
design and plenty of wine provided by the king with royal
liberality. 8 The royal edict did not, however, make drinking
obligatory, the king having instructed the officials of his
household to treat each guest according to the guest's own
wishes.
9 Queen Vashti, for her part, gave a banquet for the women
in the royal palace of King Ahasuerus. 10 On the seventh
day, when the king was merry with wine, he commanded
Mehuman, Biztha, Harbona, Bigtha, Abagtha, Zethar and
Carkas, the seven officers in attendance on the person of
King Ahasuerus, 11 to bring Queen Vashti before the king,
crowned with her royal diadem, in order to display her beauty to the people and the officers-of-state, since she was very
beautiful. 12 But Queen Vashti refused to come at the king's
command delivered by the officers. The king was very angry
at this and his rage grew hot. 13 Addressing himself to the
wise men who were versed in the law—it being the practice
to refer matters affecting the king to expert lawyers and

GREEK OLD TESTAMENT

14 καὶ προσῆλθεν αὐτῷ Αρκεσαιος καὶ Σαρσαθαιος καὶ Μαλη-
σεαρ οἱ ἄρχοντες Περσῶν καὶ Μήδων οἱ ἐγγὺς τοῦ βασιλέως
οἱ πρῶτοι παρακαθήμενοι τῷ βασιλεῖ 15 καὶ ἀπήγγειλαν αὐτῷ
κατὰ τοὺς νόμους ὡς δεῖ ποιῆσαι Αστιν τῇ βασιλίσσῃ, ὅτι
οὐκ ἐποίησεν τὰ ὑπὸ τοῦ βασιλέως προσταχθέντα διὰ τῶν
εὐνούχων. 16 καὶ εἶπεν ὁ Μουχαιος πρὸς τὸν βασιλέα καὶ
τοὺς ἄρχοντας Οὐ τὸν βασιλέα μόνον ἠδίκησεν Αστιν ἡ
βασίλισσα, ἀλλὰ καὶ πάντας τοὺς ἄρχοντας καὶ τοὺς
ἡγουμένους τοῦ βασιλέως 17 [καὶ γὰρ διηγήσατο αὐτοῖς τὰ
ῥήματα τῆς βασιλίσσης καὶ ὡς ἀντεῖπεν τῷ βασιλεῖ]. ὡς οὖν
ἀντεῖπεν τῷ βασιλεῖ Ἀρταξέρξῃ, 18 οὕτως σήμερον αἱ τυραν-
νίδες αἱ λοιπαὶ τῶν ἀρχόντων Περσῶν καὶ Μήδων ἀκούσασαι
τὰ τῷ βασιλεῖ λεχθέντα ὑπ' αὐτῆς τολμήσουσιν ὁμοίως
ἀτιμάσαι τοὺς ἄνδρας αὐτῶν. 19 εἰ οὖν δοκεῖ τῷ βασιλεῖ,
προσταξάτω βασιλικόν, καὶ γραφήτω κατὰ τοὺς νόμους
Μήδων καὶ Περσῶν· καὶ μὴ ἄλλως χρησάσθω, μηδὲ εἰσελθάτω
ἔτι ἡ βασίλισσα πρὸς αὐτόν, καὶ τὴν βασιλείαν αὐτῆς δότω ὁ
βασιλεὺς γυναικὶ κρείττονι αὐτῆς. 20 καὶ ἀκουσθήτω ὁ νόμος
ὁ ὑπὸ τοῦ βασιλέως, ὃν ἐὰν ποιῇ, ἐν τῇ βασιλείᾳ αὐτοῦ, καὶ
οὕτως πᾶσαι αἱ γυναῖκες περιθήσουσιν τιμὴν τοῖς ἀνδράσιν
ἑαυτῶν ἀπὸ πτωχοῦ ἕως πλουσίου. 21 καὶ ἤρεσεν ὁ λόγος τῷ
βασιλεῖ καὶ τοῖς ἄρχουσι, καὶ ἐποίησεν ὁ βασιλεὺς καθὰ

KING JAMES VERSION

14 And the next unto him *was* Carshena, Shethar, Admatha, Tarshish, Meres, Marsena, *and* Memucan, the seven princes of Persia and Media, which saw the king's face, *and* which sat the first in the kingdom;)

15 What shall we do unto the queen Vashti according to law, because she hath not performed the commandment of the king Ahasuerus by the chamberlains?

16 And Memucan answered before the king and the princes, Vashti the queen hath not done wrong to the king only, but also to all the princes, and to all the people that *are* in all the provinces of the king Ahasuerus.

17 For *this* deed of the queen shall come abroad unto all women, so that they shall despise their husbands in their eyes, when it shall be reported, The king Ahasuerus commanded Vashti the queen to be brought in before him, but she came not.

18 *Likewise* shall the ladies of Persia and Media say this day unto all the king's princes, which have heard of the deed of the queen. Thus *shall there arise* too much contempt and wrath.

19 If it please the king, let there go a royal commandment from him, and let it be written among the laws of the Persians and the Medes, that it be not altered, That Vashti come no more before king Ahasuerus; and let the king give her royal estate unto another that is better than she.

20 And when the king's decree which he shall make shall be published throughout all his empire, (for it is great,) all the wives shall give to their husbands honour, both to great and small.

21 And the saying pleased the king and the princes; and the king did according to the word of Memucan:

DOUAY OLD TESTAMENT

14 (Now the chief and nearest him were, Charsena, and Sethar, and Admatha, and Tharsis, and Mares, and Marsana, and Mamuchan, seven princes of the Persians, and of the Medes, who saw the face of the king, and were used to sit first after him:)

15 What sentence ought to pass upon Vasthi the queen, who had refused to obey the commandment of king Assuerus, which he had sent to her by the eunuchs?

16 And Mamuchan answered, in the hearing of the king and the princes: Queen Vasthi hath not only injured the king, but also all the people and princes that are in all the provinces of king Assuerus.

17 For this deed of the queen will go abroad to all women, so that they will despise their husbands, and will say: King Assuerus commanded that queen Vasthi should come in to him, and she would not.

18 And by this example all the wives of the princes of the Persians and the Medes will slight the commandments of their husbands: wherefore the king's indignation is just.

19 If it please thee, let an edict go out from thy presence, and let it be written according to the law of the Persians and of the Medes, which must not be altered, that Vasthi come in no more to the king, but another, that is better than her, be made queen in her place.

20 And let this be published through all the provinces of thy empire, (which is very wide,) and let all wives, as well of the greater as of the lesser, give honour to their husbands.

21 His counsel pleased the king, and the princes: and the king did according to the counsel of Mamuchan.

KNOX TRANSLATION

14 (The chief of them, and the nearest to his person, were
Charsena, Sethar, Admatha, Tharsis, Mares, Marsana and
Mamuchan; these seven princes of Persia and Media attended on him always, and had places next himself.) 15 What
sentence should he pass on queen Vasthi, to whom he, king
Assuerus, had sent a summons through his chamberlains,
and in vain?

16 Thereupon, in the hearing of the king and his nobles,
Mamuchan thus spoke: Queen Vasthi has put a slight, not
upon the king's grace only, but on all men, high and low, in
his dominions. 17 All our women-folk will hear what she has
done, and all will set their husbands at defiance, reminding
them how king Assuerus sent for queen Vasthi, and she
would not come. 18 Not a wife in Persia or Media but will
disobey her husband more lightly for this example; the king
has good reason to be angry. 19 So please thee, let an edict
go out in thy name, by the laws of Persia and Media irrevocable, forbidding Vasthi ever to come into the royal presence
again. Let the crown pass to some head worthier than hers.
20 In all the broad lands under thy domain let this decree be
published; so to all husbands, high and low, their wives
shall pay due honour henceforward.

21 King and nobles liked the plan well, and the king did as

TODAY'S ENGLISH VERSION

of them, who were closest to the king and held the highest
offices, came and told him what the law required and what
should be done to Queen Vashti for disobeying the command
he had given her through his servants. They were Arkesaeus,
Sarsathaeus, and Malesear, officials of Persia and Media.
16Then the king told his officials and the governors of
Media and Persia how the queen had defied him. So
Muchaeus said to the king and everyone present: "Queen
Vashti has insulted not only you but all of us as well. 17-18As
soon as our wives hear what the queen has done, they will
be bold enough to defy their husbands and treat them with
disrespect in the same way that Vashti has treated you. 19If,
then, it please Your Majesty, issue a royal proclamation that
Vashti may never again appear before the king. Have it written into the laws of Media and Persia. Then give her place as
queen to some better woman. There is no other way.
20When your proclamation is made known all over this
empire, then every woman will treat her husband with proper respect, whether he is rich or poor."
21The king and his officials liked this idea, and the king

NEW REVISED STANDARD VERSION

and Malesear, then the governors of the Persians and Medes
who were closest to the king—Arkesaeus, Sarsathaeus, and
Malesear, who sat beside him in the chief seats—came to
him 15and told him what must be done to Queen Vashti[a] for
not obeying the order that the king had sent her by the
eunuchs. 16Then Muchaeus said to the king and the governors, "Queen Vashti[a] has insulted not only the king but also
all the king's governors and officials" 17(for he had reported
to them what the queen had said and how she had defied the
king). "And just as she defied King Artaxerxes, 18so now the
other ladies who are wives of the Persian and Median governors, on hearing what she has said to the king, will likewise
dare to insult their husbands. 19If therefore it pleases the
king, let him issue a royal decree, inscribed in accordance
with the laws of the Medes and Persians so that it may not
be altered, that the queen may no longer come into his presence; but let the king give her royal rank to a woman better
than she. 20Let whatever law the king enacts be proclaimed
in his kingdom, and thus all women will give honor to their
husbands, rich and poor alike." 21This speech pleased the
king and the governors, and the king did as Muchaeus had

a Gk *Astin*

NEW AMERICAN BIBLE

14He summoned Carshena, Shethar, Admatha, Tarshish,
Meres, Marsena and Memucan, the seven Persian and
Median officials who were in the king's personal service and
held first rank in the realm, 15and asked them, "What is to
be done by law with Queen Vashti for disobeying the order of
King Ahasuerus issued through the eunuchs?"
16In the presence of the king and of the officials, Memucan
answered: "Queen Vashti has not wronged the king alone,
but all the officials and the populace throughout the
provinces of King Ahasuerus. 17For the queen's conduct will
become known to all the women, and they will look with disdain upon their husbands when it is reported, 'King
Ahasuerus commanded that Queen Vashti be ushered into
his presence, but she would not come.' 18This very day the
Persian and Median ladies who hear of the queen's conduct
will rebel against all the royal officials, with corresponding
disdain and rancor. 19If it please the king, let an irrevocable
royal decree be issued by him and inscribed among the laws
of the Persians and Medes, forbidding Vashti to come into
the presence of King Ahasuerus and authorizing the king to
give her royal dignity to one more worthy than she. 20Thus,
when the decree which the king will issue is published
throughout his realm, vast as it is, all wives will honor their
husbands, from the greatest to the least."
21This proposal found acceptance with the king and the
officials, and the king acted on the advice of Memucan. 22He

NEW JERUSALEM BIBLE

jurists— 14he summoned Carshena, Shethar, Admatha,
Tarshish, Meres, Marsena and Memucan, seven Persian and
Median officers-of-state who had privileged access to the
royal presence and occupied the leading positions in the
kingdom. 15'According to law,' he said, 'what is to be done
to Queen Vashti for not obeying the command of King
Ahasuerus delivered by the officers?' 16In the presence of
the king and the officers-of-state, Memucan replied, 'Queen
Vashti has wronged not only the king but also all the officers-of-state and all the peoples inhabiting the provinces of
King Ahasuerus. 17The queen's conduct will soon become
known to all the women, who will adopt a contemptuous
attitude towards their own husbands. They will say, "King
Ahasuerus himself commanded Queen Vashti to appear
before him and she did not come." 18Before the day is out,
the wives of the Persian and Median officers-of-state will be
telling every one of the king's officers-of-state what they
have heard about the queen's behaviour; and that will mean
contempt and anger all round. 19If it is the king's pleasure,
let him issue a royal edict, to be irrevocably incorporated into
the laws of the Persians and Medes, to the effect that Vashti
is never to appear again before King Ahasuerus, and let the
king confer her royal dignity on a worthier woman. 20Let
this edict issued by the king be proclaimed throughout his
empire—which is great—and all the women will henceforth
bow to the authority of their husbands, both high and low
alike.'
21This speech pleased the king and the officers-of-state,

GREEK OLD TESTAMENT

ἐλάλησεν ὁ Μουχαιος. 22 καὶ ἀπέστειλεν εἰς πᾶσαν τὴν βασιλείαν κατὰ χώραν κατὰ τὴν λέξιν αὐτῶν ὥστε εἶναι φόβον αὐτοῖς ἐν ταῖς οἰκίαις αὐτῶν.

2 Καὶ μετὰ τοὺς λόγους τούτους ἐκόπασεν ὁ βασιλεὺς τοῦ θυμοῦ καὶ οὐκέτι ἐμνήσθη τῆς Αστιν μνημονεύων οἷα ἐλάλησεν καὶ ὡς κατέκρινεν αὐτήν. 2 καὶ εἶπαν οἱ διάκονοι τοῦ βασιλέως Ζητηθήτω τῷ βασιλεῖ κοράσια ἄφθορα καλὰ τῷ εἴδει· 3 καὶ καταστήσει ὁ βασιλεὺς κωμάρχας ἐν πάσαις ταῖς χώραις τῆς βασιλείας αὐτοῦ, καὶ ἐπιλεξάτωσαν κοράσια παρθενικὰ καλὰ τῷ εἴδει εἰς Σουσαν τὴν πόλιν εἰς τὸν γυναικῶνα, καὶ παραδοθήτωσαν τῷ εὐνούχῳ τοῦ βασιλέως τῷ φύλακι τῶν γυναικῶν, καὶ δοθήτω σμῆγμα καὶ ἡ λοιπὴ ἐπιμέλεια· 4 καὶ ἡ γυνή, ἣ ἂν ἀρέσῃ τῷ βασιλεῖ, βασιλεύσει ἀντὶ Αστιν. καὶ ἤρεσεν τῷ βασιλεῖ τὸ πρᾶγμα, καὶ ἐποίησεν οὕτως.

5 Καὶ ἄνθρωπος ἦν Ιουδαῖος ἐν Σούσοις τῇ πόλει, καὶ ὄνομα αὐτῷ Μαρδοχαῖος ὁ τοῦ Ιαϊρου τοῦ Σεμεϊου τοῦ Κισαιου ἐκ φυλῆς Βενιαμιν, 6 ὃς ἦν αἰχμάλωτος ἐξ Ιερουσαλημ, ἣν ᾐχμαλώτευσεν Ναβουχοδονοσορ βασιλεὺς Βαβυλῶνος. 7 καὶ ἦν τούτῳ παῖς θρεπτή, θυγάτηρ Αμιναδαβ ἀδελφοῦ πατρὸς αὐτοῦ, καὶ ὄνομα αὐτῇ Εσθηρ· ἐν δὲ τῷ μεταλλάξαι αὐτῆς τοὺς γονεῖς ἐπαίδευσεν αὐτὴν ἑαυτῷ εἰς

KING JAMES VERSION

22 For he sent letters into all the king's provinces, into every province according to the writing thereof, and to every people after their language, that every man should bear rule in his own house, and that *it* should be published according to the language of every people.

2 After these things, when the wrath of king Ahasuerus was appeased, he remembered Vashti, and what she had done, and what was decreed against her.

2 Then said the king's servants that ministered unto him, Let there be fair young virgins sought for the king:

3 And let the king appoint officers in all the provinces of his kingdom, that they may gather together all the fair young virgins unto Shushan the palace, to the house of the women, unto the custody of Hege the king's chamberlain, keeper of the women; and let their things for purification be given *them:*

4 And let the maiden which pleaseth the king be queen instead of Vashti. And the thing pleased the king; and he did so.

5 *Now* in Shushan the palace there was a certain Jew, whose name *was* Mordecai, the son of Jair, the son of Shimei, the son of Kish, a Benjamite;

6 Who had been carried away from Jerusalem with the captivity which had been carried away with Jeconiah king of Judah, whom Nebuchadnezzar the king of Babylon had carried away.

7 And he brought up Hadassah, that *is,* Esther, his uncle's daughter: for she had neither father nor mother, and the maid *was* fair and beautiful; whom Mordecai, when her

DOUAY OLD TESTAMENT

22 And he sent letters to all the provinces of his kingdom, as every nation could hear and read, in divers languages and characters, that the husbands should be rulers and masters in their houses: and that this should be published to every people.

2 AFTER this, when the wrath of king Assuerus was appeased, he remembered Vasthi, and what she had done and what she had suffered:

2 And the king's servants and his officers said: Let young women be sought for the king, virgins and beautiful,

3 And let some persons be sent through all the provinces to look for beautiful maidens and virgins: and let them bring them to the city of Susan, and put them into the house of the women under the hand of Egeus the eunuch, who is the overseer and keeper of the king's women: and let them receive women's ornaments, and other things necessary for their use.

4 And whosoever among them all shall please the king's eyes, let her be queen instead of Vasthi. The word pleased the king: and he commanded it should be done as they had suggested.

5 There was a man in the city of Susan, a Jew, named Mardochai, the son of Jair, the son of Semei, the son of Cis, of the race of Jemini,

6 Who had been carried away from Jerusalem at the time that Nabuchodonosor king of Babylon carried away Jechonias king of Juda,

7 And he had brought up his brother's daughter Edissa, who by another name was called Esther: now she had lost both her parents: and was exceeding fair and beautiful. And

KNOX TRANSLATION

Mamuchan had advised, 22 sent a letter to each nation in the tongue it spoke, the characters it used, decreeing that a man should be lord and master in his own house, and the whole world must take note of it.[a]

2 With time, the rage of Assuerus cooled down, but he had not forgotten Vasthi's offence, or her dismissal. 2 And now his courtiers and attendants offered him their counsel, It is time we made search for beauty and maidenhood, to console the king's grace. 3 It would be well if commissioners were sent into all the provinces, to look out fair damsels that are maidens still, and bring them here to Susan. There let them be handed over to the chamberlain Egeus, that has charge of the women's quarters in the palace, and an allowance be made them for adding art to their beauty, and for all else they need. 4 And she, who most of all wins the royal favour, shall be queen instead of Vasthi. The king liked this counsel well, and gave orders that it should be put into effect.

5 There was a Jew called Mardochaeus living at Susan, descended through Jair and Semei from Cis the Benjamite,[b] 6 who was carried off from Jerusalem by the Babylonian king Nabuchodonosor at the same time as king Jechonias of Juda. 7 A ward this man had, a niece of his called Edissa, or Esther, that had lost both her parents. Beauty was hers of form and

a Instead of this last phrase, the Hebrew text has 'and should speak the tongue of his own people,' an expression difficult to account for. *b* If Assuerus is identified with Xerxes, the words 'who was carried off' should perhaps be applied to Cis, not to Mardochaeus; otherwise Mardochaeus must have been more than a hundred years old. But see note *a* on page 166. According to the Hebrew text and the Septuagint Greek, Esther was cousin, not niece, to Mardochaeus. So in 2. 15 below 'his brother' should, according to the Hebrew, be 'his nephew'.

Today's English Version

did as Muchaeus suggested. 22 To each of the royal provinces he sent a message in the language of that province, saying that every husband must be respected in his own home.

2 Later the king's anger cooled down. Although he no longer mentioned Vashti, he kept thinking about how he had condemned her. 2 So some of the king's advisers suggested, "Why don't you make a search to find some beautiful young women of good character? 3 You can appoint officials in every province of the empire and have them bring all these beautiful young virgins to your harem here in Susa. Put them in the care of Hegai, the eunuch who is in charge of your women, and let them be given cosmetics and whatever else they may need. 4 Then take the young woman you like best and make her queen in Vashti's place."

The king thought this was good advice, so he followed it.

5 There in Susa lived a Jew named Mordecai son of Jair; he was from the tribe of Benjamin and was a descendant of Kish and Shimei. 6 He was among the captives whom King Nebuchadnezzar of Babylonia had taken into exile from Jerusalem. 7 Mordecai was the guardian of Esther, the daughter of his uncle Aminadab. She was a beautiful young

New Revised Standard Version

recommended. 22 The king sent the decree into all his kingdom, to every province in its own language, so that in every house respect would be shown to every husband.

2 After these things, the king's anger abated, and he no longer was concerned about Vashti[a] or remembered what he had said and how he had condemned her. 2 Then the king's servants said, "Let beautiful and virtuous girls be sought out for the king. 3 The king shall appoint officers in all the provinces of his kingdom, and they shall select beautiful young virgins to be brought to the harem in Susa, the capital. Let them be entrusted to the king's eunuch who is in charge of the women, and let ointments and whatever else they need be given them. 4 And the woman who pleases the king shall be queen instead of Vashti."[a] This pleased the king, and he did so.

5 Now there was a Jew in Susa the capital whose name was Mordecai son of Jair son of Shimei[b] son of Kish, of the tribe of Benjamin; 6 he had been taken captive from Jerusalem among those whom King Nebuchadnezzar of Babylon had captured. 7 And he had a foster child, the daughter of his father's brother, Aminadab, and her name

a Gk *Astin* *b* Gk *Semeios*

New American Bible

sent letters to all the royal provinces, to each province in its own script and to each people in its own language, to the effect that every man should be lord in his own home.

2 After this, when King Ahasuerus' wrath had cooled, he thought over what Vashti had done and what had been decreed against her. 2 Then the king's personal attendants suggested: "Let beautiful young virgins be sought for the king. 3 Let the king appoint commissaries in all the provinces of his realm to bring together all beautiful young virgins to the harem in the stronghold of Susa. Under the care of the royal eunuch Hegai, custodian of the women, let cosmetics be given them. 4 Then the girl who pleases the king shall reign in place of Vashti." This suggestion pleased the king, and he acted accordingly.

5 There was in the stronghold of Susa a certain Jew named Mordecai, son of Jair, son of Shimei, son of Kish, a Benjaminite, 6 who had been exiled from Jerusalem with the captives taken with Jeconiah, king of Judah, whom Nebuchadnezzar, king of Babylon, had deported. 7 He was foster father to Hadassah, that is, Esther, his cousin; for she had lost both father and mother. The girl was beautifully

New Jerusalem Bible

and the king did as Memucan advised. 22 He sent letters to all the provinces of the kingdom, to each province in its own script and to each nation in its own language, ensuring that every husband should be master in his own house.

2 Some time after this, when the king's wrath had subsided, Ahasuerus remembered Vashti, how she had behaved, and the measures taken against her. 2 The king's gentlemen-in-waiting said, 'A search should be made on the king's behalf for beautiful young virgins, 3 and the king appoint commissioners throughout the provinces of his realm to bring all these beautiful young virgins to the citadel of Susa, to the harem under the authority of Hegai the king's eunuch, custodian of the women. Here he will give them whatever they need for enhancing their beauty, 4 and the girl who pleases the king can take Vashti's place as queen.' This advice pleased the king and he acted on it.

5 Now in the citadel of Susa there lived a Jew called Mordecai son of Jair, son of Shimei, son of Kish, of the tribe of Benjamin, 6 who had been deported from Jerusalem among the captives taken away with Jeconiah king of Judah by Nebuchadnezzar king of Babylon, 7 and was now bringing up a certain Hadassah, otherwise called Esther, his uncle's daughter, who had lost both father and mother; the girl had a good figure and a beautiful face, and on the death

GREEK OLD TESTAMENT

γυναῖκα· καὶ ἦν τὸ κοράσιον καλὸν τῷ εἴδει. 8 καὶ ὅτε ἠκούσθη τὸ τοῦ βασιλέως πρόσταγμα, συνήχθησαν κοράσια πολλὰ
εἰς Σουσαν τὴν πόλιν ὑπὸ χεῖρα Γαι, καὶ ἤχθη Εσθηρ πρὸς
Γαι τὸν φύλακα τῶν γυναικῶν. 9 καὶ ἤρεσεν αὐτῷ τὸ κοράσιον καὶ εὗρεν χάριν ἐνώπιον αὐτοῦ, καὶ ἔσπευσεν αὐτῇ δοῦναι τὸ σμῆγμα καὶ τὴν μερίδα καὶ τὰ ἑπτὰ κοράσια τὰ ἀπο-
δεδειγμένα αὐτῇ ἐκ βασιλικοῦ καὶ ἐχρήσατο αὐτῇ καλῶς καὶ
ταῖς ἅβραις αὐτῆς ἐν τῷ γυναικῶνι· 10 καὶ οὐχ ὑπέδειξεν
Εσθηρ τὸ γένος αὐτῆς οὐδὲ τὴν πατρίδα, ὁ γὰρ Μαρδοχαῖος
ἐνετείλατο αὐτῇ μὴ ἀπαγγεῖλαι. 11 καθ' ἑκάστην δὲ ἡμέραν
ὁ Μαρδοχαῖος περιεπάτει κατὰ τὴν αὐλὴν τὴν γυναικείαν
ἐπισκοπῶν τί Εσθηρ συμβήσεται. 12 οὗτος δὲ ἦν καιρὸς
κορασίου εἰσελθεῖν πρὸς τὸν βασιλέα, ὅταν ἀναπληρώσῃ
μῆνας δέκα δύο· οὕτως γὰρ ἀναπληροῦνται αἱ ἡμέραι τῆς
θεραπείας, μῆνας ἓξ ἀλειφόμεναι ἐν σμυρνίνῳ ἐλαίῳ καὶ
μῆνας ἓξ ἐν τοῖς ἀρώμασιν καὶ ἐν τοῖς σμήγμασιν τῶν
γυναικῶν, 13 καὶ τότε εἰσπορεύεται πρὸς τὸν βασιλέα· καὶ ὃ
ἐὰν εἴπῃ, παραδώσει αὐτῇ συνεισέρχεσθαι αὐτῇ ἀπὸ τοῦ
γυναικῶνος ἕως τῶν βασιλείων. 14 δείλης εἰσπορεύεται καὶ
πρὸς ἡμέραν ἀποτρέχει εἰς τὸν γυναικῶνα τὸν δεύτερον, οὗ
Γαι ὁ εὐνοῦχος τοῦ βασιλέως ὁ φύλαξ τῶν γυναικῶν, καὶ

KING JAMES VERSION

father and mother were dead, took for his own daughter.

8 So it came to pass, when the king's commandment and his decree was heard, and when many maidens were gathered together unto Shushan the palace, to the custody of Hegai, that Esther was brought also unto the king's house, to the custody of Hegai, keeper of the women.

9 And the maiden pleased him, and she obtained kindness of him; and he speedily gave her her things for purification, with such things as belonged to her, and seven maidens, *which were* meet to be given her, out of the king's house: and he preferred her and her maids unto the best *place* of the house of the women.

10 Esther had not shewed her people nor her kindred: for Mordecai had charged her that she should not shew *it.*

11 And Mordecai walked every day before the court of the women's house, to know how Esther did, and what should become of her.

12 Now when every maid's turn was come to go in to king Ahasuerus, after that she had been twelve months, according to the manner of the women, (for so were the days of their purifications accomplished, *to wit,* six months with oil of myrrh, and six months with sweet odours, and with *other* things for the purifying of the women;)

13 Then thus came *every* maiden unto the king; whatsoever she desired was given her to go with her out of the house of the women unto the king's house.

14 In the evening she went, and on the morrow she returned into the second house of the women, to the custody of Shaashgaz, the king's chamberlain, which kept the

DOUAY OLD TESTAMENT

her father and mother being dead, Mardochai adopted her for his daughter.

8 And when the king's ordinance was noised abroad, and according to his commandment many beautiful virgins were brought to Susan, and were delivered to Egeus the eunuch: Esther also among the rest of the maidens was delivered to him to be kept in the number of the women.

9 And she pleased him, and found favour in his sight. And he commanded the eunuch to hasten the women's ornaments, and to deliver to her her part, and seven of the most beautiful maidens of the king's house, and to adorn and deck out both her and her waiting maids.

10 And she would not tell him her people nor her country. For Mardochai had charged her to say nothing at all of that:

11 And he walked every day before the court of the house, in which the chosen virgins were kept, having a care for Esther's welfare, and desiring to know what would befall her.

12 Now when every virgin's turn came to go in to the king, after all had been done for setting them off to advantage, it was the twelfth month: so that for six months they were anointed with oil of myrrh, and for other six months they used certain perfumes and sweet spices.

13 And when they were going in to the king, whatsoever they asked to adorn themselves they received: and being decked out, as it pleased them, they passed from the chamber of the women to the king's chamber.

14 And she that went in at evening, came out in the morning, and from thence she was conducted to the second house, that was under the hand of Susagaz the eunuch, who

KNOX TRANSLATION

face, and when her parents died, Mardochaeus adopted her
as his own daughter. 8 In accordance with the king's bidding, Esther was carried off among many other fair maidens
to Susan, and there handed over to the chamberlain Egeus,
to be kept in waiting with the rest. 9 Her charms won his
favour, and he bade her attendant set about the anointing of
her without more ado; choice foods should be allotted to her,
and seven maids, the fairest in all the palace, to wait on her,
adorning with all his art her person and theirs. 10 Of her race
and country she had told him nothing; concerning that,
Mardochaeus had enjoined silence on her; 11 and he himself
walked to and fro, every day, before the lodging of those fair
pensioners, so great was his care for Esther and of what
would befall her.
12 It was a full twelvemonth before a maiden's turn came,
to be the king's bride; first she must add art to her beauty,
anointing herself for six months with oil, and for six with
paints and powders. 13 Ever the bride was given what
adornment she would, and so, in finery of her own choosing, passed out from the maidens' lodging to the royal bedchamber. 14 Each morning, the bride of yesternight was
escorted to a new home, where the chamberlain Susagazi,
master of the royal concubines, had charge of her, nor might

TODAY'S ENGLISH VERSION

woman, and after the death of her parents, Mordecai brought
her up until she was grown.[a]
8 When the king had issued his new proclamation, many
young women were being brought to Susa, and Esther was
among them. She too was put in the royal palace in the care
of Hegai, who had charge of the harem. 9 Hegai liked Esther,
and she won his favor. He lost no time in beginning her
beauty treatment of massage and special diet. He assigned
seven young women specially chosen from the royal palace
to serve her, and he treated her and her servants well.
10 Now, on the advice of Mordecai, Esther had kept secret
the fact that she was Jewish. 11 Every day Mordecai would
walk back and forth in front of the courtyard of the harem,
watching to see what was going to happen to her.
12 The regular beauty treatment for the young women lasted a year: massages with oil of myrrh for six months and
with beauty creams and cosmetics for six more. 13 After
that, each young woman was handed over to the person
appointed to conduct her from the harem to the palace, and
she was taken to the king. 14 She would go there in the
evening, and the next morning she would be taken to
another harem and put in the care of Hegai, the eunuch in

[a] until she was grown; *or* and planned to marry her.

NEW REVISED STANDARD VERSION

was Esther. When her parents died, he brought her up to
womanhood as his own. The girl was beautiful in appearance. 8 So, when the decree of the king was proclaimed, and
many girls were gathered in Susa the capital in custody of
Gai, Esther also was brought to Gai, who had custody of the
women. 9 The girl pleased him and won his favor, and he
quickly provided her with ointments and her portion of
food,[a] as well as seven maids chosen from the palace; he
treated her and her maids with special favor in the harem.
10 Now Esther had not disclosed her people or country, for
Mordecai had commanded her not to make it known. 11 And
every day Mordecai walked in the courtyard of the harem, to
see what would happen to Esther.
12 Now the period after which a girl was to go to the king
was twelve months. During this time the days of beautifica-
tion are completed—six months while they are anointing
themselves with oil of myrrh, and six months with spices
and ointments for women. 13 Then she goes in to the king;
she is handed to the person appointed, and goes with him
from the harem to the king's palace. 14 In the evening she
enters and in the morning she departs to the second harem,
where Gai the king's eunuch is in charge of the women; and

a Gk lacks *of food*

NEW AMERICAN BIBLE

formed and lovely to behold. On the death of her father and
mother, Mordecai had taken her as his own daughter.
8 When the king's order and decree had been obeyed and
many maidens brought together to the stronghold of Susa
under the care of Hegai, Esther also was brought in to the
royal palace under the care of Hegai, custodian of the
women. 9 The girl pleased him and won his favor. So he
promptly furnished her with cosmetics and provisions. Then
picking out seven maids for her from the royal palace, he
transferred both her and her maids to the best place in the
harem. 10 Esther did not reveal her nationality or family, for
Mordecai had commanded her not to do so.
11 Day by day Mordecai would walk about in front of the
court of the harem, to learn how Esther was faring and what
was to become of her.
12 Each girl went in turn to visit King Ahasuerus after the
twelve months' preparation decreed for the women. Of this
period of beautifying treatment, six months were spent with
oil of myrrh, and the other six months with perfumes and
cosmetics. 13 Then, when the girl was to visit the king, she
was allowed to take with her from the harem to the royal
palace whatever she chose. 14 She would go in the evening
and return in the morning to a second harem under the care
of the royal eunuch Shaashgaz, custodian of the concubines.

NEW JERUSALEM BIBLE

of her parents Mordecai had adopted her as his daughter.
8 On the promulgation of the royal command and edict a
great number of girls were brought to the citadel of Susa
where they were entrusted to Hegai. Esther, too, was taken
to the king's palace and entrusted to Hegai, the custodian of
the women. 9 The girl pleased him and won his favour. Not
only did he quickly provide her with all she needed for her
dressing room and her meals, but he gave her seven special
maids from the king's household and transferred her and her
maids to the best part of the harem. 10 Esther had not
divulged her race or parentage, since Mordecai had forbidden
her to do so. 11 Mordecai walked up and down in front of the
courtyard of the harem all day and every day, to learn how
Esther was and how she was being treated.
12 Each girl had to appear in turn before King Ahasuerus
after a delay of twelve months fixed by the regulations for
the women; this preparatory period was occupied as follows:
six months with oil of myrrh, and six months with spices
and lotions commonly used for feminine beauty treatment.
13 When each girl went to the king, she was given whatever
she wanted to take with her, since she then moved from the
harem into the royal household. 14 She went there in the
evening, and the following morning returned to another
harem entrusted to the care of Shaashgaz, the king's officer,

GREEK OLD TESTAMENT

οὐκέτι εἰσπορεύεται πρὸς τὸν βασιλέα, ἐὰν μὴ κληθῇ ὀνόματι. 15 ἐν δὲ τῷ ἀναπληροῦσθαι τὸν χρόνον Εσθηρ τῆς θυγατρὸς Αμιναδαβ ἀδελφοῦ πατρὸς Μαρδοχαίου εἰσελθεῖν πρὸς
τὸν βασιλέα οὐδὲν ἠθέτησεν ὧν αὐτῇ ἐνετείλατο ὁ εὐνοῦχος
ὁ φύλαξ τῶν γυναικῶν· ἦν γὰρ Εσθηρ εὑρίσκουσα χάριν παρὰ
πάντων τῶν βλεπόντων αὐτήν. 16 καὶ εἰσῆλθεν Εσθηρ πρὸς
Ἀρταξέρξην τὸν βασιλέα τῷ δωδεκάτῳ μηνί, ὅς ἐστιν Αδαρ,
τῷ ἑβδόμῳ ἔτει τῆς βασιλείας αὐτοῦ. 17 καὶ ἠράσθη ὁ
βασιλεὺς Εσθηρ, καὶ εὗρεν χάριν παρὰ πάσας τὰς παρθένους, καὶ ἐπέθηκεν αὐτῇ τὸ διάδημα τὸ γυναικεῖον. 18 καὶ
ἐποίησεν ὁ βασιλεὺς πότον πᾶσι τοῖς φίλοις αὐτοῦ καὶ ταῖς
δυνάμεσιν ἐπὶ ἡμέρας ἑπτὰ καὶ ὕψωσεν τοὺς γάμους Εσθηρ
καὶ ἄφεσιν ἐποίησεν τοῖς ὑπὸ τὴν βασιλείαν αὐτοῦ. 19 ὁ
δὲ Μαρδοχαῖος ἐθεράπευεν ἐν τῇ αὐλῇ. 20 ἡ δὲ Εσθηρ οὐχ
ὑπέδειξεν τὴν πατρίδα αὐτῆς. οὕτως γὰρ ἐνετείλατο αὐτῇ

KING JAMES VERSION

concubines: she came in unto the king no more, except the king delighted in her, and that she were called by name.

15 Now when the turn of Esther, the daughter of Abihail the uncle of Mordecai, who had taken her for his daughter, was come to go in unto the king, she required nothing but what Hegai the king's chamberlain, the keeper of the women, appointed. And Esther obtained favour in the sight of all them that looked upon her.

16 So Esther was taken unto king Ahasuerus into his house royal in the tenth month, which *is* the month Tebeth, in the seventh year of his reign.

17 And the king loved Esther above all the women, and she obtained grace and favour in his sight more than all the virgins; so that he set the royal crown upon her head, and made her queen instead of Vashti.

18 Then the king made a great feast unto all his princes and his servants, *even* Esther's feast; and he made a release to the provinces, and gave gifts, according to the state of the king.

19 And when the virgins were gathered together the second time, then Mordecai sat in the king's gate.

20 Esther had not *yet* shewed her kindred nor her people;

DOUAY OLD TESTAMENT

had the charge over the king's concubines: neither could she return any more to the king, unless the king desired it, and had ordered her by name to come.

15 And as the time came orderly about, the day was at hand, when Esther, the daughter of Abihail the brother of Mardochai, whom he had adopted for his daughter, was to go in to the king. But she sought not women's ornaments, but whatsoever Egeus the eunuch the keeper of the virgins had a mind, he gave her to adorn her. For she was exceeding fair, and her incredible beauty made her appear agreeable and amiable in the eyes of all.

16 So she was brought to the chamber of king Assuerus the tenth month, which is called Tebeth, in the seventh year of his reign.

17 And the king loved her more than all the women, and she had favour and kindness before him above all the women, and he set the royal crown on her head, and made her queen instead of Vasthi.

18 And he commanded a magnificent feast to be prepared for all the princes, and for his servants, for the marriage and wedding of Esther. And he gave rest to all the provinces, and bestowed gifts according to princely magnificence.

19 And when the virgins were sought the second time, and gathered together, Mardochai stayed at the king's gate,

20 Neither had Esther as yet declared her country and people, according to his commandment. For whatsoever he

KNOX TRANSLATION

she ever find her way back to the king, save at his will and
on his express summons.
15 So the day came when it was the turn of 15 Esther,
Abihail's child, daughter now to his brother Mardochaeus, to
be a king's bride. For her adorning, she had no request to
make; let the chamberlain Egeus, since the maidens were
under his charge, deck her as he would. But oh, she was fair;
she had beauty past all belief, to win men's favour and their
love. 16 It was in Tebeth, the tenth month, in the seventh
year of Assuerus' reign, that she was escorted to the royal
bed-chamber.[a] 17 More than all those others she won the
king's heart, more than all she enjoyed his loving favour; on
her head he set the royal crown, and made her his queen in
place of Vasthi. 18 And he had a great feast prepared for all
his lords and vassals, Esther's bridal feast. To all his dominions he granted a public holiday, and made them gifts, with
princely liberality, besides.
19 And now, the brides summoned and housed anew,[b]
Mardochaeus took up his post at the gates of the palace
itself. 20 Still faithful to his bidding, Esther had said no word

a The slow progress of events may be partly explained, if Assuerus is Xerxes, by his absence during the time of his campaign against Greece.

b Literally, in the Hebrew text, 'when the maidens were collected a second time', in the Latin, 'when the maidens were sought out and collected a second time'. Commentators are much exercised to know how a repetition of the procedure mentioned in verse 3 should have been either likely in itself, or relevant to the present context. The rendering given above is based on what seems the most probable interpretation; the brides had now passed out of Egeus' care into the seraglio proper (verse 14); Mardochaeus, therefore, deserted his post at the entrance of Egeus' establishment (verse 11), and mingled with the hangers-on at the gates of the palace itself.

TODAY'S ENGLISH VERSION

charge. She would not go to the king again unless he asked
for her by name.
15 The time came for Esther, the daughter of Aminadab the
uncle of Mordecai, to go to the king. She had done everything that Hegai had advised, and she was admired by everyone who saw her. 16 So in Xerxes' seventh year as king, in
the twelfth month, the month of Adar, she was brought to
the king. 17 He fell in love with Esther, who pleased him
more than any of the others, and he placed the queen's
crown on her head. 18 Then the king gave a week-long banquet for all his advisers and administrators to celebrate his
marriage to Esther. He also granted a reduction of taxes for
the whole empire.
19 Meanwhile Mordecai had been appointed to a high
administrative position. 20 As for Esther, she had still not let
it be known that she was Jewish. Mordecai had told her not

NEW REVISED STANDARD VERSION

she does not go in to the king again unless she is summoned
by name.
15 When the time was fulfilled for Esther daughter of
Aminadab, the brother of Mordecai's father, to go in to the
king, she neglected none of the things that Gai, the eunuch
in charge of the women, had commanded. Now Esther found
favor in the eyes of all who saw her. 16 So Esther went in to
King Artaxerxes in the twelfth month, which is Adar, in the
seventh year of his reign. 17 And the king loved Esther and
she found favor beyond all the other virgins, so he put on
her the queen's diadem. 18 Then the king gave a banquet
lasting seven days for all his Friends and the officers to celebrate his marriage to Esther; and he granted a remission of
taxes to those who were under his rule.
19 Meanwhile Mordecai was serving in the courtyard.
20 Esther had not disclosed her country—such were the

NEW AMERICAN BIBLE

She could not return to the king unless he was pleased with
her and had her summoned by name.
15 As for Esther, daughter of Abihail and adopted daughter
of his nephew Mordecai, when her turn came to visit the
king, she did not ask for anything but what the royal eunuch
Hegai, custodian of the women, suggested. Yet she won the
admiration of all who saw her. 16 Esther was led to King
Ahasuerus in his palace in the tenth month, Tebeth, in the
seventh year of his reign. 17 The king loved Esther more than
all other women, and of all the virgins she won his favor and
benevolence. So he placed the royal diadem on her head and
made her queen in place of Vashti. 18 Then the king gave a
great feast in honor of Esther to all his officials and ministers, granting a holiday to the provinces and bestowing gifts
with royal bounty.
19 [To resume: From the time the virgins had been brought
together, and while Mordecai was passing his time at the

2, 19-23: This is a resumption, in a slightly different form, of the story already told in Est A, 12-15.

NEW JERUSALEM BIBLE

custodian of the concubines. She did not go to the king any
more, unless he was particularly pleased with her and had
her summoned by name.
15 But when it was the turn of Esther the daughter of
Abihail, whose nephew Mordecai had adopted her as his own
daughter, to go into the king's presence, she did not ask for
anything beyond what had been assigned her by Hegai, the
king's officer, custodian of the women. Esther won the
approval of all who saw her. 16 She was brought to King
Ahasuerus in his royal apartments in the tenth month,
which is called Tebeth, in the seventh year of his reign;
17 and the king liked Esther better than any of the other
women; none of the other girls found so much favour and
approval with him. So he set the royal diadem on her head
and proclaimed her queen instead of Vashti.
18 The king then gave a great banquet, Esther's banquet,
for all his officers-of-state and ministers, decreed a holiday
for all the provinces and distributed largesse with royal
prodigality.
19 When Esther, like the other girls, had been transferred
to the second harem, 20 she did not divulge her parentage
or race, in obedience to the orders of Mordecai, whose

GREEK OLD TESTAMENT

Μαρδοχαῖος φοβεῖσθαι τὸν θεὸν καὶ ποιεῖν τὰ προστάγματα αὐτοῦ, καθὼς ἦν μετ' αὐτοῦ, καὶ Εσθηρ οὐ μετήλλαξεν τὴν ἀγωγὴν αὐτῆς.

21 Καὶ ἐλυπήθησαν οἱ δύο εὐνοῦχοι τοῦ βασιλέως οἱ ἀρχι-
σωματοφύλακες ὅτι προήχθη Μαρδοχαῖος, καὶ ἐζήτουν ἀποκτεῖναι Ἀρταξέρξην τὸν βασιλέα. 22 καὶ ἐδηλώθη Μαρδοχαίῳ ὁ λόγος, καὶ ἐσήμανεν Εσθηρ, καὶ αὐτὴ ἐνεφάνισεν τῷ
βασιλεῖ τὰ τῆς ἐπιβουλῆς. 23 ὁ δὲ βασιλεὺς ἤτασεν τοὺς δύο
εὐνούχους καὶ ἐκρέμασεν αὐτούς. καὶ προσέταξεν ὁ βασιλεὺς καταχωρίσαι εἰς μνημόσυνον ἐν τῇ βασιλικῇ βιβλιοθήκῃ
ὑπὲρ τῆς εὐνοίας Μαρδοχαίου ἐν ἐγκωμίῳ.

3 Μετὰ δὲ ταῦτα ἐδόξασεν ὁ βασιλεὺς Ἀρταξέρξης Αμαν
Αμαδαθου Βουγαῖον καὶ ὕψωσεν αὐτόν, καὶ ἐπρωτο-
βάθρει πάντων τῶν φίλων αὐτοῦ. 2 καὶ πάντες οἱ ἐν τῇ αὐλῇ
προσεκύνουν αὐτῷ, οὕτως γὰρ προσέταξεν ὁ βασιλεὺς ποιῆ-
σαι· ὁ δὲ Μαρδοχαῖος οὐ προσεκύνει αὐτῷ. 3 καὶ ἐλάλησαν
οἱ ἐν τῇ αὐλῇ τοῦ βασιλέως τῷ Μαρδοχαίῳ Μαρδοχαῖε, τί
παρακούεις τὰ ὑπὸ τοῦ βασιλέως λεγόμενα; 4 καθ' ἑκάστην
ἡμέραν ἐλάλουν αὐτῷ, καὶ οὐχ ὑπήκουεν αὐτῶν· καὶ ὑπέ-
δειξαν τῷ Αμαν Μαρδοχαῖον τοῖς τοῦ βασιλέως λόγοις ἀντι-
τασσόμενον· καὶ ὑπέδειξεν αὐτοῖς ὁ Μαρδοχαῖος ὅτι

KING JAMES VERSION

as Mordecai had charged her: for Esther did the commandment of Mordecai, like as when she was brought up with him.

21 In those days, while Mordecai sat in the king's gate, two of the king's chamberlains, Bigthan and Teresh, of those which kept the door, were wroth, and sought to lay hand on the king Ahasuerus.

22 And the thing was known to Mordecai, who told *it* unto Esther the queen; and Esther certified the king *thereof* in Mordecai's name.

23 And when inquisition was made of the matter, it was found out; therefore they were both hanged on a tree: and it was written in the book of the chronicles before the king.

3 After these things did king Ahasuerus promote Haman the son of Hammedatha the Agagite, and advanced him, and set his seat above all the princes that *were* with him.

2 And all the king's servants, that *were* in the king's gate, bowed, and reverenced Haman: for the king had so commanded concerning him. But Mordecai bowed not, nor did *him* reverence.

3 Then the king's servants, which *were* in the king's gate, said unto Mordecai, Why transgressest thou the king's commandment?

4 Now it came to pass, when they spake daily unto him, and he hearkened not unto them, that they told Haman, to see whether Mordecai's matters would stand: for he had told them that he *was* a Jew.

DOUAY OLD TESTAMENT

commanded, Esther observed: and she did all things in the same manner as she was wont at that time when he brought her up a little one.

21 At that time, therefore, when Mardochai abode at the king's gate, Bagathan and Thares, two of the king's eunuchs, who were porters, and presided in the first entry of the palace, were angry: and they designed to rise up against the king, and to kill him.

22 And Mardochai had notice of it, and immediately he told it to queen Esther: and she to the king in Mardochai's name, who had reported the thing unto her.

23 It was inquired into, and found out: and they were both hanged on a gibbet. And it was put in the histories, and recorded in the chronicles before the king.

3 AFTER these things, king Assuerus advanced Aman, the son of Amadathi, who was of the race of Agag: and he set his throne above all the princes that were with him.

2 And all the king's servants, that were at the doors of the palace, bent their knees, and worshipped Aman: for so the emperor had commanded them, only Mardochai did not bend his knee, nor worship him.

3 And the king's servants that were chief at the doors of the palace, said to him: Why dost thou alone not observe the king's commandment?

4 And when they were saying this often, and he would not hearken to them, they told Aman, desirous to know whether he would continue in his resolution: for he had told them that he was a Jew.

KNOX TRANSLATION

about her race or her country; still, as in her nursery days,
she remembered and did all he told her. 21 And it was while
Mardochaeus haunted the palace gates that two of the royal
chamberlains, Bagathan and Thares, door-keepers both at
the palace entry, grew disaffected, and would have made a
murderous attack on the king's person. 22 Mardochaeus
came to hear of it, and told queen Esther; she, naming him
as her informant, told her husband. 23 The charge was investigated, and found true; the two conspirators were hanged,
and the circumstance was put on record, being entered in the
king's own archives.

3 It was after this that king Assuerus bestowed high rank
upon an Agagite, Aman the son of Amadathi, bidding
him take precedence of all his other nobles. 2 And all the
royal attendants at the palace gates must bow the knee and
do Aman reverence, such were their orders. But Mardochaeus
went his own way, and would neither bow nor bend. 3 Often
the king's men asked him at the palace doors why he thus
defied the royal bidding, 4 but still he gave them no heed, till
at last they told Aman of it. Would he still be so stiff in his
opinions? They had learned from him by now that he was a

TODAY'S ENGLISH VERSION

to tell anyone, and she obeyed him in this, just as she had
obeyed him when she was a little girl under his care. She
continued to worship God and carry out God's commands,
without abandoning her Jewish ways.
21 When the king promoted Mordecai to a higher position,
the two palace eunuchs who were officers of the king's bodyguard became angry and plotted to assassinate the king.
22 Mordecai learned about it and told Queen Esther, who then
told the king the details of the plot. 23 The king had the two
men questioned, and both men were hanged. To honor
Mordecai, the king ordered an account of this to be written
down in the royal records, so that his valuable service would
be remembered.
3 Some time later King Xerxes honored a man named
Haman son of Hammedatha, a Bougaean, by promoting
him to the position of prime minister. 2 The king ordered all
the officials in his service to show their respect for Haman by
bowing to him. They all did so, except Mordecai, who refused
to bow to Haman. 3 The other officials in the royal service
asked him why he was disobeying the king's command.
4 Day after day they urged him to give in, but he would not
listen to them. "I am a Jew," he explained, "and I cannot bow
to Haman." So they told Haman how Mordecai was defying

NEW REVISED STANDARD VERSION

instructions of Mordecai; but she was to fear God and keep
his laws, just as she had done when she was with him. So
Esther did not change her mode of life.
21 Now the king's eunuchs, who were chief bodyguards,
were angry because of Mordecai's advancement, and they
plotted to kill King Artaxerxes. 22 The matter became known
to Mordecai, and he warned Esther, who in turn revealed the
plot to the king. 23 He investigated the two eunuchs and
hanged them. Then the king ordered a memorandum to be
deposited in the royal library in praise of the goodwill shown
by Mordecai.
3 After these events King Artaxerxes promoted Haman son
of Hammedatha, a Bougean, advancing him and granting him precedence over all the king's[a] Friends. 2 So all who
were at court used to do obeisance to Haman,[b] for so the
king had commanded to be done. Mordecai, however, did not
do obeisance. 3 Then the king's courtiers said to Mordecai,
"Mordecai, why do you disobey the king's command?" 4 Day
after day they spoke to him, but he would not listen to them.
Then they informed Haman that Mordecai was resisting the
king's command. Mordecai had told them that he was a Jew.

a Gk *all his* *b* Gk *him*

NEW AMERICAN BIBLE

king's gate, 20 Esther had not revealed her family or nationality, because Mordecai had told her not to; and Esther continued to follow Mordecai's instructions, just as she had
when she was being brought up by him. 21 And during the
time that Mordecai spent at the king's gate, Bagathan and
Thares, two of the royal eunuchs who guarded the entrance,
had plotted in anger to lay hands on King Ahasuerus.
22 When the plot became known to Mordecai, he told Queen
Esther, who in turn informed the king for Mordecai. 23 The
matter was investigated and verified, and both of them were
hanged on a gibbet. This was written in the annals for the
king's use.]
3 After these events King Ahasuerus raised Haman, son of
Hammedatha the Agagite, to high rank, seating him
above all his fellow officials. 2 All the king's servants who
were at the royal gate would kneel and bow down to Haman,
for that is what the king had ordered in his regard. Mordecai,
however, would not kneel and bow down. 3 The king's servants who were at the royal gate said to Mordecai, "Why do
you disobey the king's order?" 4 When they had reminded
him day after day and he would not listen to them, they
informed Haman, to see whether Mordecai's explanation was
acceptable, since he had told them that he was a Jew.

NEW JERUSALEM BIBLE

instructions she continued to follow as when she had been
under his care. 21 At this time Mordecai was attached to the
Chancellery and two malcontents, Bigthan and Teresh, officers in the king's service as Guards of the Threshold, plotted to assassinate King Ahasuerus. 22 Mordecai came to
hear of this and informed Queen Esther, who in turn, on
Mordecai's authority, told the king. 23 The matter was
investigated and proved to be true. The two conspirators
were sent to the gallows, and the incident was recorded in
the Annals, in the royal presence.
3 Shortly afterwards, King Ahasuerus singled out Haman
son of Hammedatha, a native of Agag, for promotion.
He raised him in rank, granting him precedence over all his
colleagues, the other officers-of-state, 2 and all the royal officials employed at the Chancellery used to bow low and prostrate themselves whenever Haman appeared—such was the
king's command. Mordecai refused either to bow or to prostrate himself. 3 'Why do you flout the royal command?' the
officials of the Chancellery asked Mordecai. 4 Day after day
they asked him this, but he took no notice of them. In the
end they reported the matter to Haman, to see whether
Mordecai would persist in his attitude, since he had told
them that he was a Jew. 5 Haman could see for himself that

GREEK OLD TESTAMENT

Ιουδαῖός ἐστιν. 5 καὶ ἐπιγνοὺς Αμαν ὅτι οὐ προσκυνεῖ αὐτῷ
Μαρδοχαῖος, ἐθυμώθη σφόδρα 6 καὶ ἐβουλεύσατο ἀφανίσαι
πάντας τοὺς ὑπὸ τὴν Ἀρταξέρξου βασιλείαν Ιουδαίους.
7 καὶ ἐποίησεν ψήφισμα ἐν ἔτει δωδεκάτῳ τῆς βασιλείας
Ἀρταξέρξου καὶ ἔβαλεν κλήρους ἡμέραν ἐξ ἡμέρας καὶ μῆνα
ἐκ μηνὸς ὥστε ἀπολέσαι ἐν μιᾷ ἡμέρᾳ τὸ γένος
Μαρδοχαίου, καὶ ἔπεσεν ὁ κλῆρος εἰς τὴν τεσσαρεσκαιδεκάτην τοῦ μηνός, ὅς ἐστιν Αδαρ. 8 καὶ ἐλάλησεν πρὸς τὸν
βασιλέα Ἀρταξέρξην λέγων Ὑπάρχει ἔθνος διεσπαρμένον ἐν
τοῖς ἔθνεσιν ἐν πάσῃ τῇ βασιλείᾳ σου, οἱ δὲ νόμοι αὐτῶν
ἔξαλλοι παρὰ πάντα τὰ ἔθνη, τῶν δὲ νόμων τοῦ βασιλέως
παρακούουσιν, καὶ οὐ συμφέρει τῷ βασιλεῖ ἐάσαι αὐτούς.
9 εἰ δοκεῖ τῷ βασιλεῖ, δογματισάτω ἀπολέσαι αὐτούς, κἀγὼ
διαγράψω εἰς τὸ γαζοφυλάκιον τοῦ βασιλέως ἀργυρίου
τάλαντα μύρια. 10 καὶ περιελόμενος ὁ βασιλεὺς τὸν δακτύλιον ἔδωκεν εἰς χεῖρα τῷ Αμαν σφραγίσαι κατὰ τῶν γεγραμμένων κατὰ τῶν Ιουδαίων. 11 καὶ εἶπεν ὁ βασιλεὺς τῷ Αμαν
Τὸ μὲν ἀργύριον ἔχε, τῷ δὲ ἔθνει χρῶ ὡς βούλει. 12 καὶ
ἐκλήθησαν οἱ γραμματεῖς τοῦ βασιλέως μηνὶ πρώτῳ τῇ
τρισκαιδεκάτῃ καὶ ἔγραψαν, ὡς ἐπέταξεν Αμαν, τοῖς

KING JAMES VERSION

5 And when Haman saw that Mordecai bowed not, nor did him reverence, then was Haman full of wrath.

6 And he thought scorn to lay hands on Mordecai alone; for they had shewed him the people of Mordecai: wherefore Haman sought to destroy all the Jews that *were* throughout the whole kingdom of Ahasuerus, *even* the people of Mordecai.

7 In the first month, that *is,* the month Nisan, in the twelfth year of king Ahasuerus, they cast Pur, that *is,* the lot, before Haman from day to day, and from month to month, *to* the twelfth *month,* that *is,* the month Adar.

8 And Haman said unto king Ahasuerus, There is a certain people scattered abroad and dispersed among the people in all the provinces of thy kingdom; and their laws *are* diverse from all people; neither keep they the king's laws: therefore it *is* not for the king's profit to suffer them.

9 If it please the king, let it be written that they may be destroyed: and I will pay ten thousand talents of silver to the hands of those that have the charge of the business, to bring *it* into the king's treasuries.

10 And the king took his ring from his hand, and gave it unto Haman the son of Hammedatha the Agagite, the Jews' enemy.

11 And the king said unto Haman, The silver *is* given to thee, the people also, to do with them as it seemeth good to thee.

12 Then were the king's scribes called on the thirteenth day of the first month, and there was written according to all that Haman had commanded unto the king's lieutenants,

DOUAY OLD TESTAMENT

5 Now when Aman had heard this, and had proved by experience that Mardochai did not bend his knee to him, nor worship him, he was exceeding angry.

6 And he counted it nothing to lay his hands upon Mardochai alone: for he had heard that he was of the nation of the Jews, and he chose rather to destroy all the nation of the Jews that were in the kingdom of Assuerus.

7 In the first month (which is called Nisan) in the twelfth year of the reign of Assuerus, the lot was cast into an urn, which in Hebrew is called Phur, before Aman, on what day and what month the nation of the Jews should be destroyed: and there came out the twelfth month, which is called Adar.

8 And Aman said to king Assuerus: There is a people scattered through all the provinces of thy kingdom, and separated one from another, that use new laws and ceremonies, and moreover despise the king's ordinances: and thou knowest very well that it is not expedient for thy kingdom that they should grow insolent by impunity.

9 If it please thee, decree that they may be destroyed, and I will pay ten thousand talents to thy treasurers.

10 And the king took the ring that he used, from his own hand, and gave it to Aman, the son of Amadathi of the race of Agag, the enemy of the Jews,

11 And he said to him: As to the money which thou promisest, keep it for thyself: and as to the people, do with them as seemeth good to thee.

12 And the king's scribes were called in the first month Nisan, on the thirteenth day of the same month: and they wrote, as Aman had commanded, to all the king's lieutenants,

KNOX TRANSLATION

Jew. 5 Aman, when he heard their story, and proved the
truth of it for himself, that Mardochaeus would neither bow
nor bend, fell into a great passion of rage; 6 and, hearing
that he was a Jew, he would not be content with laying
hands on Mardochaeus only; the whole race, throughout all
Assuerus' dominions, should be brought to ruin for it. 7 It
was in the twelfth year of the reign, in Nisan, the first month
of it, that the lot (which the Hebrews call Pur) was cast into
the urn in Aman's presence, to determine the day and month
when he would make an end of the Jews; and the month
chosen was the twelfth month, Adar.
8 So now Aman said to king Assuerus, There is a race
spread here and there throughout thy domains that follows
strange law and custom, in defiance of the royal decrees;
judge whether it consorts with thy royal dignity that licence
should embolden them. 9 Be it thy pleasure to decree their
destruction, and I promise thee an increase of ten thousand
talents to thy revenue. 10 There and then Assuerus took off
the ring he wore on his hand, and gave it to the Agagite
Aman, son of Amadathi, the Jews' enemy; 11 Keep it for thy
own use, said he, the money thou offerest, and as for the
people, do what thou wilt with them. 12 So, on the thirteenth
day of that month, Nisan, the royal secretaries were summoned, and a decree was made in Aman's sense. Governor

TODAY'S ENGLISH VERSION

the king's orders. 5 Haman was furious when he realized
that Mordecai was not going to bow to him, 6 and so he
made plans to kill every Jew in the whole Persian Empire.
7 In the twelfth year of King Xerxes' reign, Haman ordered
the lots to be cast to find out the right day and month to
destroy the Jews, all in a single day. The fourteenth day of
the month of Adar was the date chosen.
8 So Haman told the king, "There is a certain race of people
scattered among the nations all over your empire. They
observe customs that are not like those of any other people.
Moreover, they do not obey the laws of the empire, so it is
not in your best interests to tolerate them. 9 If it please Your
Majesty, issue a decree that they are to be put to death. If
you do this, I promise to put 375 tons of silver into the royal
treasury."
10 The king took off his ring, which was used to stamp official proclamations, and gave it to Haman to seal the decree
that was to be written against the Jews. 11 The king told him,
"Keep the money, and do whatever you want with that race
of people."
12 So on the thirteenth day of the first month, Haman
called the king's secretaries and dictated a proclamation to
be translated into every language in the empire and to be
sent to all the rulers and governors. It was issued in the

NEW REVISED STANDARD VERSION

5 So when Haman learned that Mordecai was not doing obeisance to him, he became furiously angry, 6 and plotted to
destroy all the Jews under Artaxerxes' rule.
7 In the twelfth year of King Artaxerxes Haman[a] came to
a decision by casting lots, taking the days and the months
one by one, to fix on one day to destroy the whole race of
Mordecai. The lot fell on the fourteenth[b] day of the month of
Adar.
8 Then Haman[a] said to King Artaxerxes, "There is a certain nation scattered among the other nations in all your
kingdom; their laws are different from those of every other
nation, and they do not keep the laws of the king. It is not
expedient for the king to tolerate them. 9 If it pleases the
king, let it be decreed that they are to be destroyed, and I will
pay ten thousand talents of silver into the king's treasury."
10 So the king took off his signet ring and gave it to Haman
to seal the decree[c] that was to be written against the Jews.
11 The king told Haman, "Keep the money, and do whatever
you want with that nation."
12 So on the thirteenth day of the first month the king's
secretaries were summoned, and in accordance with
Haman's instructions they wrote in the name of King
Artaxerxes to the magistrates and the governors in every

a Gk *he* *b* Other ancient witnesses read *thirteenth*; see 8.12
c Gk lacks *the decree*

NEW AMERICAN BIBLE

5 When Haman observed that Mordecai would not kneel and
bow down to him, he was filled with anger. 6 Moreover, he
thought it was not enough to lay hands on Mordecai alone.
Since they had told Haman of Mordecai's nationality, he
sought to destroy all the Jews, Mordecai's people, throughout
the realm of King Ahasuerus. 7 In the first month, Nisan, in
the twelfth year of King Ahasuerus, the **pur,** or lot, was cast in
Haman's presence, to determine the day and the month for
the destruction of Mordecai's people on a single day, and the
lot fell on the thirteenth day of the twelfth month, Adar.
8 Then Haman said to King Ahasuerus: "Dispersed among
the nations throughout the provinces of your kingdom, there
is a certain people living apart, with laws differing from
those of every other people. They do not obey the laws of the
king, and so it is not proper for the king to tolerate them. 9 If
it please the king, let a decree be issued to destroy them; and
I will deliver to the procurators ten thousand silver talents
for deposit in the royal treasury." 10 The king took the signet
ring from his hand and gave it to Haman, son of Hammedatha the Agagite, the enemy of the Jews. 11 "The silver
you may keep," the king said to Haman, "but as for this people, do with them whatever you please."
12 So the royal scribes were summoned; and on the thirteenth day of the first month they wrote, at the dictation of
Haman, an order to the royal satraps, the governors of every

3, 7: Pur: a Babylonian word which the Hebrew translates as goral, "lot." This word is preserved in the text because its plural, purim, became the name of the feast of Purim commemorating the deliverance of the Jews; cf Est 9, 24. 26.

NEW JERUSALEM BIBLE

Mordecai did not bow or prostrate himself in his presence; he
became furiously angry. 6 And, on being told what race
Mordecai belonged to, he thought it beneath him merely to
get rid of Mordecai, but made up his mind to wipe out all the
members of Mordecai's race, the Jews, living in Ahasuerus'
entire empire.
7 In the first month, that is the month of Nisan, of the
twelfth year of King Ahasuerus, the *pur*[a] (that is, the lot)
was cast in Haman's presence, to determine the day and the
month. The lot falling on the twelfth month, which is Adar,
8 Haman said to King Ahasuerus, 'There is a certain unassim-
ilated nation scattered among the other nations throughout
the provinces of your realm; their laws are different from
those of all the other nations, and the royal laws they ignore;
hence it is not in the king's interests to tolerate them. 9 If
their destruction be signed, so please the king, I am ready to
pay ten thousand talents of silver to the king's receivers, to
be credited to the royal treasury.'
10 The king then took his signet ring off his hand and gave
it to Haman son of Hammedatha, the persecutor of the Jews.
11 'Keep the money,' he said, 'and you can have the people
too; do what you like with them.'
12 The royal scribes were therefore summoned for the thirteenth day of the first month, when they wrote out the orders
addressed by Haman to the king's satraps, to the governors

[a] **3** From this the name of the feast on which the book is read, Purim, is derived. It is a joyful feast, characterised by banquets.

GREEK OLD TESTAMENT

στρατηγοῖς καὶ τοῖς ἄρχουσιν κατὰ πᾶσαν χώραν ἀπὸ Ἰνδικῆς ἕως τῆς Αἰθιοπίας, ταῖς ἑκατὸν εἴκοσι ἑπτὰ χώραις, τοῖς τε ἄρχουσι τῶν ἐθνῶν κατὰ τὴν αὐτῶν λέξιν δι' Ἀρταξέρξου τοῦ βασιλέως. 13 καὶ ἀπεστάλη διὰ βιβλιαφόρων εἰς τὴν Ἀρταξέρξου βασιλείαν ἀφανίσαι τὸ γένος τῶν Ιουδαίων ἐν ἡμέρᾳ μιᾷ μηνὸς δωδεκάτου, ὅς ἐστιν Αδαρ, καὶ διαρπάσαι τὰ ὑπάρχοντα αὐτῶν. — 13a δὲ ἐπιστολῆς ἐστιν τὸ ἀντίγραφον τόδε Βασιλεὺς μέγας Ἀρταξέρξης τοῖς ἀπὸ τῆς Ἰνδικῆς ἕως τῆς Αἰθιοπίας ἑκατὸν εἴκοσι ἑπτὰ χωρῶν ἄρχουσι καὶ τοπάρχαις ὑποτεταγμένοις τάδε γράφει 13b ἐπάρξας ἐθνῶν καὶ πάσης ἐπικρατήσας οἰκουμένης ἐβουλήθην, μὴ τῷ θράσει τῆς ἐξουσίας ἐπαιρόμενος, ἐπιεικέστερον δὲ καὶ μετὰ ἠπιότητος ἀεὶ διεξάγων, τοὺς τῶν ὑποτεταγμένων ἀκυμάτους διὰ παντὸς καταστῆσαι βίους, τήν τε βασιλείαν ἥμερον καὶ πορευτὴν μέχρι περάτων παρεξόμενος ἀνανεώσασθαί τε τὴν ποθουμένην τοῖς πᾶσιν ἀνθρώποις εἰρήνην. 13c δέ μου τῶν συμβούλων πῶς ἂν ἀχθείη τοῦτο ἐπὶ πέρας, σωφροσύνῃ παρ' ἡμῖν διενέγκας καὶ ἐν τῇ εὐνοίᾳ ἀπαραλλάκτως καὶ βεβαίᾳ πίστει ἀποδεδειγμένος καὶ δεύτερον τῶν βασιλειῶν γέρας ἀπενηνεγμένος Αμαν 13d ἡμῖν ἐν πάσαις ταῖς κατὰ τὴν οἰκουμένην φυλαῖς

KING JAMES VERSION

and to the governors that *were* over every province, and to the rulers of every people of every province according to the writing thereof, and *to* every people after their language; in the name of king Ahasuerus was it written, and sealed with the king's ring.

13 And the letters were sent by posts into all the king's provinces, to destroy, to kill, and to cause to perish, all Jews, both young and old, little children and women, in one day, *even* upon the thirteenth *day* of the twelfth month, which is the month Adar, and *to take* the spoil of them for a prey.

13 The copy of the letters was this: The great king Artexerxes writeth these things to the princes and governors that are under him from India unto Ethiopia, in an hundred and seven and twenty provinces.

2 After that I became lord over many nations, and had dominion over the whole world, not lifted up with presumption of my authority, but carrying myself alway with equity and mildness, I purposed to settle my subjects continually in a quiet life, and making my kingdom peaceable, and open for passage to the utmost coasts, to renew peace, which is desired of all men.

3 Now when I asked my counsellors how this might be brought to pass, Aman, that excelled in wisdom among us, and was approved for his constant good will and stedfast fidelity, and had the honour of the second place in the kingdom,

4 Declared unto us, that in all nations throughout the

DOUAY OLD TESTAMENT

and to the judges of the provinces, and of divers nations, as every nation could read, and hear according to their different languages, in the name of king Assuerus: and the letters, sealed with his ring,

13 Were sent by the king's messengers to all provinces, to kill and destroy all the Jews, both young and old, little children, and women, in one day, that is, on the thirteenth of the twelfth month, which is called Adar, and to make a spoil of their goods.

13 AND this was the copy of the letter: Artaxerxes the great king who reigneth from India to Ethiopia, to the princes and governors of the hundred and twenty-seven provinces, that are subject to his empire, greeting.

2 Whereas I reigned over many nations, and had brought all the world under my dominion, I was not willing to abuse the greatness of my power, but to govern my subjects with clemency and lenity, that they might live quietly without any terror, and might enjoy peace, which is desired by all men.

3 But when I asked my counsellors how this might be accomplished, one that excelled the rest in wisdom and fidelity, and was second after the king, Aman by name,

4 Told me that there was a people scattered through the

KNOX TRANSLATION

and chieftain must receive a letter, each in the language and the characters of his own province or tribe, sent in the name of king Assuerus and sealed with his royal seal. 13 All through his dominions the couriers went out on their errand, bearing death and ruin to all the Jews, to young and old, to women and little children with the rest. The day fixed for their massacre and the seizing of their goods was the thirteenth day of the twelfth month, Adar.

(The following seven verses are found in the Septuagint Greek after 3. 13 above, with the rubric, Here is a copy of the letter.)

13 The great king Artaxerxes, to the governors of the hundred and twenty-seven provinces between India and Ethiopia, and to all his vassal chiefs, sends greeting. 2 Wide as I rule, the world's conqueror, I would not abuse this great power of mine; mild and indulgent my sway should be, and my subjects live in undisturbed tranquillity; peace is man's greatest boon. 3 So I asked my counsellors how this end might best be achieved; and among them Aman, who ranks next to my person; no counsellor so wise or so trusty as he. 4 He it was told me of a race scattered

TODAY'S ENGLISH VERSION

name of King Xerxes and sent to all the 127 provinces,
which stretched from India to Ethiopia.[a] 13 Runners took
this proclamation to every province of the empire. It contained the instructions that on a single day in the twelfth
month, the month of Adar, all Jews were to be killed and
their belongings confiscated.[b]

B [c] This is a copy of the decree:
"King Xerxes the Great sends the following decree to the
governors of his 127 provinces, from India to Ethiopia,[a] and
to their subordinate officials:
2 "After I became ruler of many nations and master of the
whole world, I resolved that my subjects should always live
at peace. I wanted this, not because of pride in my power but
because I was always reasonable and governed my subjects
with kindness. I determined to renew the peace that everyone
longs for and to do what was necessary to create a civilized
kingdom, safe for travel from one border to another.
3 "I asked my advisers how to accomplish this goal, and
Haman made a suggestion. He is distinguished among us as
a man of great wisdom, and at all times he has demonstrated his concern for the welfare of the kingdom. Because of his
unfailing loyalty, he has been raised to the second highest
position in the empire. 4 Recently Haman told us about a

[a] *Greek* Ethiopia: *Ethiopia is the name given in Graeco-Roman times to the extensive territory south of the First Cataract of the Nile River. Cush was the ancient (Hebrew) name of this region which included within its borders most of modern Sudan and some of present-day Ethiopia (Abyssinia).*
[b] *Chapter 3 continues after chapter B.* [c] *Chapter B 1-7 corresponds to chapter 13.1-7 in a number of English translations.*

NEW REVISED STANDARD VERSION

province from India to Ethiopia. There were one hundred
twenty-seven provinces in all, and the governors were
addressed each in his own language. 13 Instructions were
sent by couriers throughout all the empire of Artaxerxes to
destroy the Jewish people on a given day of the twelfth
month, which is Adar, and to plunder their goods.

ADDITION B

13 [a] This is a copy of the letter: "The Great King, Artaxerxes, writes the following to the governors of the
hundred twenty-seven provinces from India to Ethiopia and
to the officials under them:
2 "Having become ruler of many nations and master of
the whole world (not elated with presumption of authority
but always acting reasonably and with kindness), I have
determined to settle the lives of my subjects in lasting tranquility and, in order to make my kingdom peaceable and
open to travel throughout all its extent, to restore the peace
desired by all people.
3 "When I asked my counselors how this might be accomplished, Haman—who excels among us in sound judgment,
and is distinguished for his unchanging goodwill and steadfast fidelity, and has attained the second place in the kingdom— 4 pointed out to us that among all the nations in the

a Chapter 13.1-7 corresponds to chapter B 1-7 in some translations.

NEW AMERICAN BIBLE

province, and the officials of every people, to each province
in its own script and to each people in its own language. It
was written in the name of King Ahasuerus and sealed with
the royal signet ring. 13 Letters were sent by couriers to all
the royal provinces, that all the Jews, young and old, including women and children, should be killed, destroyed, wiped
out in one day, the thirteenth day of the twelfth month,
Adar, and that their goods should be seized as spoil.

B This is a copy of the letter:
"The great King Ahasuerus writes to the satraps of the
hundred and twenty-seven provinces from India to Ethiopia,
and the governors subordinate to them, as follows: 2 When I
came to rule many peoples and to hold sway over the whole
world, I determined not to be carried away with the sense of
power, but always to deal fairly and with clemency; to provide for my subjects a life of complete tranquillity; and by
making my government humane and effective as far as the
borders, to restore the peace desired by all men. 3 When I
consulted my counselors as to how this might be accomplished, Haman, who excels among us in wisdom, who is
outstanding for constant devotion and steadfast loyalty, and
who has gained the second rank in the kingdom, 4 brought it
to our attention that, mixed in with all the races throughout

NEW JERUSALEM BIBLE

ruling each province and to the principal officials of each
people, to each province in its own script and to each people
in its own language. The edict was signed in the name of
King Ahasuerus and sealed with his ring, 13 and letters were
sent by runners to every province of the realm, ordering the
destruction, slaughter and annihilation of all Jews, young
and old, including women and children, on the same day—
the thirteenth day of the twelfth month, which is Adar—and
the seizing of their possessions.
13a *The text of the letter was as follows:*

*'The Great King, Ahasuerus, to the governors of the hun-
dred and twenty-seven provinces stretching from India to
Ethiopia, and to their subordinate district commissioners:*
13b *'Being placed in authority over many nations and ruling the whole world, I have resolved never to be carried
away by the insolence of power, but always to rule with
moderation and clemency, so as to assure for my subjects a
life ever free from storms and, offering my kingdom the
benefits of civilisation and free transit from end to end, to
restore that peace which all men desire.* 13c *In consultation
with our advisers as to how this aim is to be effected, we
have been informed by one of them, eminent among us for
prudence and well proved for his unfailing devotion and
unshakeable trustworthiness, and in rank second only to
our majesty, Haman by name,* 13d *that there is, mingled*

GREEK OLD TESTAMENT

ἀναμεμεῖχθαι δυσμενῆ λαόν τινα τοῖς νόμοις ἀντίθετον
πρὸς πᾶν ἔθνος τά τε τῶν βασιλέων παραπέμποντας διηνεκῶς διατάγματα πρὸς τὸ μὴ κατατίθεσθαι τὴν ὑφ᾽ ἡμῶν
κατευθυνομένην ἀμέμπτως συναρχίαν. 13e οὖν τόδε τὸ ἔθνος
μονώτατον ἐν ἀντιπαραγωγῇ παντὶ διὰ παντὸς ἀνθρώπῳ κείμενον διαγωγὴν νόμων ξενίζουσαν παραλλάσσον καὶ δυσνο-
οῦν τοῖς ἡμετέροις πράγμασιν τὰ χείριστα συντελοῦν κακὰ
καὶ πρὸς τὸ μὴ τὴν βασιλείαν εὐσταθείας τυγχάνειν· 13f οὖν
τοὺς σημαινομένους ὑμῖν ἐν τοῖς γεγραμμένοις ὑπὸ Αμαν
τοῦ τεταγμένου ἐπὶ τῶν πραγμάτων καὶ δευτέρου πατρὸς
ἡμῶν πάντας σὺν γυναιξὶ καὶ τέκνοις ἀπολέσαι ὁλορριζεὶ
ταῖς τῶν ἐχθρῶν μαχαίραις ἄνευ παντὸς οἴκτου καὶ φειδοῦς
τῇ τεσσαρεσκαιδεκάτῃ τοῦ δωδεκάτου μηνὸς Αδαρ τοῦ ἐνε-
στῶτος ἔτους, 13g οἱ πάλαι καὶ νῦν δυσμενεῖς ἐν ἡμέρᾳ μιᾷ
βιαίως εἰς τὸν ᾅδην κατελθόντες εἰς τὸν μετέπειτα χρόνον
εὐσταθῆ καὶ ἀτάραχα παρέχωσιν ἡμῖν διὰ τέλους τὰ πράγματα. — 14 τὰ δὲ ἀντίγραφα τῶν ἐπιστολῶν ἐξετίθετο κατὰ
χώραν, καὶ προσετάγη πᾶσι τοῖς ἔθνεσιν ἑτοίμους εἶναι εἰς
τὴν ἡμέραν ταύτην. 15 ἐσπεύδετο δὲ τὸ πρᾶγμα καὶ εἰς
Σουσαν· ὁ δὲ βασιλεὺς καὶ Αμαν ἐκωθωνίζοντο, ἐταράσσετο
δὲ ἡ πόλις.

KING JAMES VERSION

world there was scattered a certain malicious people, that had laws contrary to all nations, and continually despised the commandments of kings, so as the uniting of our kingdoms, honourably intended by us, cannot go forward.

5 Seeing then we understand that this people alone is continually in opposition unto all men, differing in the strange manner of their laws, and evil affected to our state, working all the mischief they can, that our kingdom may not be firmly established:

6 Therefore have we commanded, that all they that are signified in writing unto you by Aman, who is ordained over the affairs, and is next unto us, shall all, with their wives and children, be utterly destroyed by the sword of their enemies, without all mercy and pity, the fourteenth day of the twelfth month Adar of this present year:

7 That they, who of old and now also are malicious, may in one day with violence go into the grave, and so ever hereafter cause our affairs to be well settled, and without trouble.

3 14 The copy of the writing for a commandment to be given in every province was published unto all people, that they should be ready against that day.

15 The posts went out, being hastened by the king's commandment, and the decree was given in Shushan the palace. And the king and Haman sat down to drink; but the city Shushan was perplexed.

DOUAY OLD TESTAMENT

whole world, which used new laws, and acted against the customs of all nations, despised the commandments of kings, and violated by their opposition the concord of all nations.

5 Wherefore having learned this, and seeing one nation in opposition to all mankind using perverse laws, and going against our commandments, and disturbing the peace and concord of the provinces subject to us,

6 We have commanded that all whom Aman shall mark out, who is chief over all the provinces, and second after the king, and whom we honour as a father, shall be utterly destroyed by their enemies, with their wives and children, and that none shall have pity on them, on the fourteenth day of the twelfth month Adar of this present year:

7 That these wicked men going down to hell in one day, may restore to our empire the peace which they had disturbed.

3 14 And the contents of the letters were to this effect, that all provinces might know and be ready against that day.

15 The couriers that were sent made haste to fulfil the king's commandment. And immediately the edict was hung up in Susan, the king and Aman feasting together, and all the Jews that were in the city weeping.

KNOX TRANSLATION

about the world that lives by strange laws, and usages
unknown to the rest of mankind; thinks lightly of the royal
decrees, and by dissenting from them mars the concord of
nations. 5 Strange news, that one people should revolt
against the whole of mankind; should follow misguided customs, slight our edicts, and disturb the peaceful order of our
empire! 6 This Aman, next to the king in dignity, is one we
reverence like a father; in all our provinces, he is supreme.
He will name the malefactors, who must be put to death with
their wives and children, and no mercy shewn, on the fourteenth of Adar in this present year. 7 In one day let them all
be hurried to the grave, so that our realm may recover the
peace they have denied it.

3 14 The tenour of the letter, sent out to warn all the
provinces and have them in readiness for the stated day,
was this... [a] 15 No time the couriers lost in following out the
royal command; at Susan, the decree was posted up forthwith, and before the king and Aman had finished their wine,
all the Jewish citizens were in tears.

a This verse is probably the rubric introducing the copy of a decree, perhaps in the Chaldaean language. See 13. 1. In the Hebrew text there is no trace of any omission. At the end of verse 15, instead of 'all the Jewish citizens were in tears' this text reads 'the city of Susan was perplexed'.

TODAY'S ENGLISH VERSION

certain unruly people scattered among all the other peoples
of the empire. He explained to us that these people have
their own laws, are opposed to every other nation, and constantly ignore royal commands. As a result of their attitude,
we are not able to establish the kind of unified government
which we earnestly intend for the empire.
5 "These people are hostile to our government and commit
terrible crimes which threaten the security of the empire.
They follow strange customs, obey their own laws, and stand
alone in their constant opposition to all people. 6 In the light
of these facts, we recommend the slaughter of the people
referred to by Haman, our prime minister. All of them,
including women and children, must be put to death; no one
is to be spared. They are our enemies; we will show them no
pity. This order is to be carried out this year on the fourteenth day of the twelfth month, the month of Adar. 7 These
people, who have caused so much trouble for so long, will all
die a violent death in a single day. From then on, our government will be secure and stable."

3 14 The contents of the proclamation were made public in
every province, and everyone was ordered to be prepared
for that day.
15 The decree was also rapidly made public in the capital
city of Susa. And while the king and Haman got drunk, the
city of Susa was thrown into confusion.

NEW REVISED STANDARD VERSION

world there is scattered a certain hostile people, who have
laws contrary to those of every nation and continually disregard the ordinances of kings, so that the unifying of the
kingdom that we honorably intend cannot be brought about.
5 We understand that this people, and it alone, stands constantly in opposition to every nation, perversely following a
strange manner of life and laws, and is ill-disposed to our
government, doing all the harm they can so that our kingdom may not attain stability.
6 "Therefore we have decreed that those indicated to you
in the letters written by Haman, who is in charge of affairs
and is our second father, shall all—wives and children
included—be utterly destroyed by the swords of their enemies, without pity or restraint, on the fourteenth day of the
twelfth month, Adar, of this present year, 7 so that those
who have long been hostile and remain so may in a single
day go down in violence to Hades, and leave our government
completely secure and untroubled hereafter."

END OF ADDITION B

3 14 Copies of the document were posted in every province,
and all the nations were ordered to be prepared for that
day. 15 The matter was expedited also in Susa. And while the
king and Haman caroused together, the city of Susa[a] was
thrown into confusion.

a Gk *the city*

NEW AMERICAN BIBLE

the world, there is one people of bad will, which by its laws
is opposed to every other people and continually disregards
the decrees of kings, so that the unity of empire blamelessly
designed by us cannot be established.
5 "Having noted, therefore, that this most singular people
is continually at variance with all men, lives by divergent
and alien laws, is inimical to our interests, and commits the
worst crimes, so that stability of government cannot be
obtained, 6 we hereby decree that all those who are indicated
to you in the letters of Haman, who is in charge of the
administration and is a second father to us, shall, together
with their wives and children, be utterly destroyed by the
swords of their enemies, without any pity or mercy, on the
fourteenth day of the twelfth month, Adar, of the current
year; 7 so that when these people, whose present ill will is of
long standing, have gone down into the nether world by a
violent death on one same day, they may at last leave our
affairs stable and undisturbed for the future."

3 14 A copy of the decree to be promulgated as law in every
province was published to all the peoples, that they
might be prepared for that day. 15 The couriers set out in
haste at the king's command; meanwhile, the decree was
promulgated in the stronghold of Susa. The king and Haman
then sat down to feast, but the city of Susa was thrown into
confusion.

NEW JERUSALEM BIBLE

among all the tribes of the earth, a certain ill-disposed peo-
ple, opposed by its laws to every other nation and continu-
ally defying the royal ordinances, in such a way as to
obstruct that form of government assured by us to the gen-
eral good.
13e *'Considering therefore that this people, unique of its*
kind, is in complete opposition to all humanity from which
it differs by its outlandish laws, that it is hostile to our
interests and that it commits the most heinous crimes, to
the point of endangering the stability of the realm:
13f *'We command that those persons designated to you in*
the letters written by Haman, who was appointed to watch
over our interests and is a second father to us, be all
destroyed, root and branch, including women and children,
by the swords of their enemies, without any pity or mercy,
on the fourteenth day of the twelfth month, Adar, of the
present year, 13g *so that, these past and present malcon-*
tents being in one day forcibly thrown down to Hades, our
government may henceforward enjoy perpetual stability
and peace.'

14 Copies of this decree, to be promulgated as law in each
province, were published to the various peoples, so that each
might be ready for the day aforementioned. 15 At the king's
command, the runners set out with all speed; the decree was
first promulgated in the citadel of Susa.
While the king and Haman gave themselves up to feasting
and drinking, consternation reigned in the city of Susa.

GREEK OLD TESTAMENT

4 Ὁ δὲ Μαρδοχαῖος ἐπιγνοὺς τὸ συντελούμενον διέρρηξεν τὰ ἱμάτια αὐτοῦ καὶ ἐνεδύσατο σάκκον καὶ κατεπάσατο σποδὸν καὶ ἐκπηδήσας διὰ τῆς πλατείας τῆς πόλεως ἐβόα φωνῇ μεγάλῃ Αἴρεται ἔθνος μηδὲν ἠδικηκός. 2 καὶ ἦλθεν ἕως τῆς πύλης τοῦ βασιλέως καὶ ἔστη· οὐ γὰρ ἦν ἐξὸν αὐτῷ εἰσελθεῖν εἰς τὴν αὐλὴν σάκκον ἔχοντι καὶ σποδόν. 3 καὶ ἐν πάσῃ χώρᾳ, οὗ ἐξετίθετο τὰ γράμματα, κραυγὴ καὶ κοπετὸς καὶ πένθος μέγα τοῖς Ιουδαίοις, σάκκον καὶ σποδὸν ἔστρωσαν ἑαυτοῖς. 4 καὶ εἰσῆλθον αἱ ἅβραι καὶ οἱ εὐνοῦχοι τῆς βασιλίσσης καὶ ἀνήγγειλαν αὐτῇ, καὶ ἐταράχθη ἀκούσασα τὸ γεγονὸς καὶ ἀπέστειλεν στολίσαι τὸν Μαρδοχαῖον καὶ ἀφελέσθαι αὐτοῦ τὸν σάκκον, ὁ δὲ οὐκ ἐπείσθη. 5 ἡ δὲ Εσθηρ προσεκαλέσατο Αχραθαῖον τὸν εὐνοῦχον αὐτῆς, ὃς παρειστήκει αὐτῇ, καὶ ἀπέστειλεν μαθεῖν αὐτῇ παρὰ τοῦ Μαρδοχαίου τὸ ἀκριβές. 7 ὁ δὲ Μαρδοχαῖος ὑπέδειξεν αὐτῷ τὸ γεγονὸς καὶ τὴν ἐπαγγελίαν, ἣν ἐπηγγείλατο Αμαν τῷ βασιλεῖ εἰς τὴν γάζαν ταλάντων μυρίων, ἵνα ἀπολέσῃ τοὺς Ιουδαίους. 8 καὶ τὸ ἀντίγραφον τὸ ἐν Σούσοις ἐκτεθὲν ὑπὲρ τοῦ ἀπολέσθαι αὐτοὺς ἔδωκεν αὐτῷ δεῖξαι τῇ Εσθηρ καὶ εἶπεν αὐτῷ ἐντείλασθαι αὐτῇ εἰσελθούσῃ παραιτήσασθαι τὸν βασιλέα καὶ ἀξιῶσαι αὐτὸν περὶ τοῦ λαοῦ μνησθεῖσα ἡμερῶν

KING JAMES VERSION

4 When Mordecai perceived all that was done, Mordecai rent his clothes, and put on sackcloth with ashes, and went out into the midst of the city, and cried with a loud and a bitter cry;

2 And came even before the king's gate: for none *might* enter into the king's gate clothed with sackcloth.

3 And in every province, whithersoever the king's commandment and his decree came, *there was* great mourning among the Jews, and fasting, and weeping, and wailing; and many lay in sackcloth and ashes.

4 So Esther's maids and her chamberlains came and told *it* her. Then was the queen exceedingly grieved; and she sent raiment to clothe Mordecai, and to take away his sackcloth from him: but he received *it* not.

5 Then called Esther for Hatach, *one* of the king's chamberlains, whom he had appointed to attend upon her, and gave him a commandment to Mordecai, to know what it *was*, and why it *was*.

6 So Hatach went forth to Mordecai unto the street of the city, which *was* before the king's gate.

7 And Mordecai told him of all that had happened unto him, and of the sum of the money that Haman had promised to pay to the king's treasuries for the Jews, to destroy them.

8 Also he gave him the copy of the writing of the decree that was given at Shushan to destroy them, to shew *it* unto Esther, and to declare *it* unto her, and to charge her that she should go in unto the king, to make supplication unto him, and to make request before him for her people.

DOUAY OLD TESTAMENT

4 NOW when Mardochai had heard these things, he rent his garments, and put on sackcloth, strewing ashes on his head: and he cried with a loud voice in the street in the midst of the city, shewing the anguish of his mind.

2 And he came lamenting in this manner even to the gate of the palace: for no one clothed with sackcloth might enter the king's court.

3 And in all provinces, towns, and places, to which the king's cruel edict was come, there was great mourning among the Jews, with fasting, wailing, and weeping, many using sackcloth and ashes for their bed.

4 Then Esther's maids and her eunuchs went in, and told her. And when she heard it she was in a consternation: and she sent a garment, to clothe him, and to take away the sackcloth: but he would not receive it.

5 And she called for Athach the eunuch, whom the king had appointed to attend upon her, and she commanded him to go to Mardochai, and learn of him why he did this.

6 And Athach going out went to Mardochai, who was standing in the street of the city, before the palace gate:

7 And Mardochai told him all that had happened, how Aman had promised to pay money into the king's treasures, to have the Jews destroyed.

8 He gave him also a copy of the edict which was hanging up in Susan, that he should shew it to the queen, and admonish her to go in to the king, and to entreat him for her people.

KNOX TRANSLATION

4 When the news reached Mardochaeus, he tore his garments about him; put on sackcloth, and sprinkled ashes on his head; and as he went through the open square in the heart of the city, loud lament betrayed the bitterness of his grief. 2 Lamenting he made his way to the outer gates of the palace; further than that he might not go, into the royal court, with sackcloth for his wear. 3 So it was everywhere; never a province, town or district the cruel edict reached but there was mourning and fasting, wailing and weeping among the Jewish folk, and of sackcloth and ashes many among them made their beds.

4 Esther heard, from her maidservants and from the chamberlains, what Mardochaeus did; she was bewildered at the news, and sent out clothes for him to wear instead of his sackcloth, but he would have none of it. 5 Then she sent for Athach, the chamberlain whom the king had deputed for her needs, bidding him go and ask Mardochaeus what his doings meant. 6 There in the public square, before the gate that led to the palace, Athach found him, and heard from him all the news; 7 of the money Aman had promised to the royal treasury in return for the Jews' destruction. 8 Mardochaeus gave him a copy, too, of the edict which had been posted in Susan, bidding him shew it to the queen; go she must into the king's presence, and plead there the cause of her people. [a]

[a] An amplification of this verse is to be found in 15. 1-3, where see notes.

TODAY'S ENGLISH VERSION

4 When Mordecai learned of all that had been done, he
tore his clothes in anguish. Then he dressed in sackcloth, covered his head with ashes, and ran through the city
crying loudly, "An innocent nation is being destroyed!"
2 When he came to the entrance of the palace, he stopped. He
did not go in because no one in sackcloth and ashes was
allowed inside. 3 Throughout all the provinces, wherever the
king's proclamation was made known, there was loud
mourning among the Jews. They wept, wailed, and put on
sackcloth and ashes.

4 When Esther's servant women and eunuchs told her what
Mordecai was doing, she was deeply disturbed. She sent
Mordecai some clothes to put on instead of the sackcloth, but
he would not accept them. 5 Then she called Hathach, one of
the palace eunuchs appointed as her servant, and told him to
go to Mordecai and get the details of what was happening.[a]
7 Mordecai told him everything that had happened and how
Haman had promised to put 375 tons of silver into the royal
treasury if all the Jews were killed. 8 He gave Hathach a copy
of the proclamation that had been issued in Susa, ordering
the destruction of the Jews. Mordecai asked him to take it to
Esther so that she might go and plead with the king and beg
him to have mercy on her people. "Tell her," he said, "to

[a] *Some manuscipts add verse 6:* Hathach went to Mordecai in the city square at the entrance to the palace.

NEW REVISED STANDARD VERSION

4 When Mordecai learned of all that had been done, he
tore his clothes, put on sackcloth, and sprinkled himself
with ashes; then he rushed through the street of the city,
shouting loudly: "An innocent nation is being destroyed!"
2 He got as far as the king's gate, and there he stopped,
because no one was allowed to enter the courtyard clothed in
sackcloth and ashes. 3 And in every province where the
king's proclamation had been posted there was a loud cry of
mourning and lamentation among the Jews, and they put on
sackcloth and ashes. 4 When the queen's[a] maids and
eunuchs came and told her, she was deeply troubled by what
she heard had happened, and sent some clothes to Mordecai
to put on instead of sackcloth; but he would not consent.
5 Then Esther summoned Hachratheus, the eunuch who
attended her, and ordered him to get accurate information
for her from Mordecai.[b]

7 So Mordecai told him what had happened and how
Haman had promised to pay ten thousand talents into the
royal treasury to bring about the destruction of the Jews.
8 He also gave him a copy of what had been posted in Susa
for their destruction, to show to Esther; and he told him to
charge her to go in to the king and plead for his favor in

a Gk *When her* *b* Other ancient witnesses add [6]*So Hachratheus went out to Mordecai in the street of the city opposite the city gate.*

NEW AMERICAN BIBLE

4 When Mordecai learned all that was happening, he tore
his garments, put on sackcloth and ashes, and walked
through the city, crying out loudly and bitterly, 2 till he came
before the royal gate, which no one clothed in sackcloth
might enter. 3 (Likewise in each of the provinces, wherever
the king's legal enactment reached, the Jews went into deep
mourning, with fasting, weeping, and lament; they all slept
on sackcloth and ashes.)

4 Queen Esther's maids and eunuchs came and told her.
Overwhelmed with anguish, she sent garments for Mordecai
to put on, so that he might take off his sackcloth; but he
refused. 5 Esther then summoned Hathach, one of the king's
eunuchs whom he had placed at her service, and commanded
him to find out what this action of Mordecai meant and the
reason for it. 6 So Hathach went out to Mordecai in the public
square in front of the royal gate, 7 and Mordecai told him all
that had happened, as well as the exact amount of silver
Haman had promised to pay to the royal treasury for the
slaughter of the Jews. 8 He also gave him a copy of the written decree for their destruction which had been promulgated
in Susa, to show and explain to Esther. He was to instruct her
to go to the king; she was to plead and intercede with him in

NEW JERUSALEM BIBLE

4 When Mordecai learned what had happened, he tore his
garments and put on sackcloth and ashes. Then he
walked into the centre of the city, wailing loudly and bitterly,
2 until he arrived in front of the Chancellery, which no one
clothed in sackcloth was allowed to enter. 3 And in every
province, no sooner had the royal command and edict
arrived, than among the Jews there was great mourning,
fasting, weeping and wailing, and many lay on sackcloth
and ashes.

4 When Queen Esther's maids and officers came and told
her, she was overcome with grief. She sent clothes for
Mordecai to put on instead of his sackcloth, but he refused
them. 5 Esther then summoned Hathach, an officer whom
the king had appointed to wait on her, and ordered him to go
to Mordecai and enquire what the matter was and why he
was acting in this way.

6 Hathach went out to Mordecai in the city square in front
of the Chancellery, 7 and Mordecai told him what had happened to him personally, and also about the sum of money
which Haman had offered to pay into the royal treasury to
procure the destruction of the Jews. 8 He also gave him a
copy of the edict of extermination published in Susa for
him to show Esther for her information, with the message
that she was to go to the king and implore his favour and
plead with him for the race to which she belonged.

GREEK OLD TESTAMENT

ταπεινώσεώς σου ὡς ἐτράφης ἐν χειρί μου, διότι Αμαν ὁ
δευτερεύων τῷ βασιλεῖ ἐλάλησεν καθ᾽ ἡμῶν εἰς θάνατον·
ἐπικάλεσαι τὸν κύριον καὶ λάλησον τῷ βασιλεῖ περὶ ἡμῶν
καὶ ῥῦσαι ἡμᾶς ἐκ θανάτου. 9 εἰσελθὼν δὲ ὁ Αχραθαῖος
ἐλάλησεν αὐτῇ πάντας τοὺς λόγους τούτους. 10 εἶπεν δὲ
Εσθηρ πρὸς Αχραθαῖον Πορεύθητι πρὸς Μαρδοχαῖον καὶ
εἰπὸν ὅτι 11 Τὰ ἔθνη πάντα τῆς βασιλείας γινώσκει ὅτι πᾶς
ἄνθρωπος ἢ γυνή, ὃς εἰσελεύσεται πρὸς τὸν βασιλέα εἰς τὴν
αὐλὴν τὴν ἐσωτέραν ἄκλητος, οὐκ ἔστιν αὐτῷ σωτηρία· πλὴν
ᾧ ἐκτείνει ὁ βασιλεὺς τὴν χρυσῆν ῥάβδον, οὗτος σωθήσεται·
κἀγὼ οὐ κέκλημαι εἰσελθεῖν πρὸς τὸν βασιλέα, εἰσὶν αὗται
ἡμέραι τριάκοντα. 12 καὶ ἀπήγγειλεν Αχραθαῖος Μαρδοχαίῳ
πάντας τοὺς λόγους Εσθηρ. 13 καὶ εἶπεν Μαρδοχαῖος πρὸς
Αχραθαῖον Πορεύθητι καὶ εἰπὸν αὐτῇ Εσθηρ, μὴ εἴπῃς
σεαυτῇ ὅτι σωθήσῃ μόνη ἐν τῇ βασιλείᾳ παρὰ πάντας τοὺς

KING JAMES VERSION

9 And Hatach came and told Esther the words of Mordecai.

10 Again Esther spake unto Hatach, and gave him commandment unto Mordecai;

11 All the king's servants, and the people of the king's provinces, do know, that whosoever, whether man or woman, shall come unto the king into the inner court, who is not called, *there is* one law of his to put *him* to death, except such to whom the king shall hold out the golden sceptre, that he may live: but I have not been called to come in unto the king these thirty days.

12 And they told to Mordecai Esther's words.

13 Then Mordecai commanded to answer Esther, Think not with thyself that thou shalt escape in the king's house, more than all the Jews.

DOUAY OLD TESTAMENT

15 AND he commanded her (no doubt but he was Mardochai) to go to the king, and petition for her people, and for her country.

2 Remember, (said he,) the days of thy low estate, how thou wast brought up by my hand, because Aman the second after the king hath spoken against us unto death.

3 And do thou call upon the Lord, and speak to the king for us, and deliver us from death.

4 9 And Athach went back and told Esther all that Mardochai had said.

10 She answered him, and bade him say to Mardochai:

11 All the king's servants, and all the provinces that are under his dominion, know, that whosoever, whether man or woman, cometh into the king's inner court, who is not called for, is immediately to be put to death without any delay: except the king shall hold out the golden sceptre to him, in token of clemency, that so he may live. How then can I go in to the king, who for these thirty days now have not been called unto him?

12 And when Mardochai had heard this,

13 He sent word to Esther again, saying: Think not that thou mayst save thy life only, because thou art in the king's house, more than all the Jews:

KNOX TRANSLATION

(*The three verses which follow represent a section found by St Jerome as a detached fragment in the Latin version current before his time. But they correspond to the Septuagint Greek text of 4. 8, where the Hebrew and Vulgate texts stop short after the words 'Go she must into the king's presence, and plead there the cause of her people'. This phrase, however, is verbally different in the Vulgate of 4. 8 and 15. 1. In our present context St Jerome has added the note,* The speaker is evidently Mardochaeus.)

15 ...So he bade her claim audience with the king, and
intercede for her people and for her country.
2 Remember, said he, the days of thy humbler fortunes, and
how it was my care nurtured thee. Now thou art matched
against Aman, that is next to the king's person; he pleads for
our overthrow, and it is thine to plead for our preservation.
3 Ask aid of the Lord, and seek the king's audience....

4 9 So Athach went back with his message. 10 But she sent
this answer: 11 No subject of the king's grace, no province in his domains, but knows the inner court of the palace to be sacred. Man or woman entering it unbidden dies there and then; unless indeed the king should grant them life, by holding out his gold sceptre in token of pardon. These thirty days past I have not been summoned to the king's presence; how can I venture in?

12 Upon receiving this message, 13 Mardochaeus answered,
Do not flatter thyself that a royal court will shelter thee in
the general massacre of thy countrymen. 14 Keep silence, and

Today's English Version

remember the days when she was just an ordinary person
being brought up under my care. Now, since Haman, the
king's prime minister, has spoken against us and demands
our death, she must pray to the Lord and then speak to the
king about us. She must save us from death."

9 So Hathach did this, 10 and Esther gave him this message
to take back to Mordecai: 11 "If anyone, man or woman, goes
to the inner courtyard and sees the king without being summoned, that person will be sentenced to death. Everyone in
the empire knows that. Only if the king holds out his gold
scepter to him can his life be spared. But it has been a month
now since the king has sent for me."

12 When Mordecai received Esther's message, 13 he sent her
this warning: "Esther, don't imagine that you are safer than
any of the other Jews in the empire. 14 If you keep quiet at a

New Revised Standard Version

behalf of the people. "Remember," he said, "the days when
you were an ordinary person, being brought up under my
care—for Haman, who stands next to the king, has spoken
against us and demands our death. Call upon the Lord; then
speak to the king in our behalf, and save us from death."

9 Hachratheus went in and told Esther all these things.
10 And she said to him, "Go to Mordecai and say, 11 'All
nations of the empire know that if any man or woman goes
to the king inside the inner court without being called, there
is no escape for that person. Only the one to whom the king
stretches out the golden scepter is safe—and it is now thirty
days since I was called to go to the king.' "

12 When Hachratheus delivered her entire message to
Mordecai, 13 Mordecai told him to go back and say to her,
"Esther, do not say to yourself that you alone among all the

New American Bible

behalf of her people. B, 8 "Remember the days of your lowly
estate," Mordecai had him say, "when you were brought up
in my charge; for Haman, who is second to the king, has
asked for our death. B, 9 Invoke the LORD and speak to the
king for us; save us from death."

9 Hathach returned to Esther and told her what Mordecai
had said. 10 Then Esther replied to Hathach and gave him
this message for Mordecai: 11 "All the servants of the king
and the people of his provinces know that any man or
woman who goes to the king in the inner court without
being summoned, suffers the automatic penalty of death,
unless the king extends to him the golden scepter, thus sparing his life. Now as for me, I have not been summoned to the
king for thirty days."

12 When Esther's words were reported to Mordecai, 13 he
had this reply brought to her: "Do not imagine that because
you are in the king's palace, you alone of all the Jews will

B, 8f: These verses belong to ch B.

New Jerusalem Bible

8a *'Remember your humbler circumstances,' he said, 'when
you were fed by my hand. Since Haman, the second person in
the realm, has petitioned the king for our deaths,* 8b *invoke
the Lord, speak to the king for us and save us from death!'*

9 Hathach came back and told Esther what Mordecai had
said; 10 and she replied with the following message for
Mordecai, 11 'Royal officials and people living in the
provinces alike all know that for anyone, man or woman,
who approaches the king in the private apartments without
having been summoned there, there is only one law: he must
die, unless the king, by pointing his golden sceptre towards
him, grants him his life. And I have not been summoned to
the king for the last thirty days.'

12 These words of Esther were reported to Mordecai, 13 who
sent back the following reply, 'Do not suppose that, because
you are in the king's palace, you are going to be the one Jew

GREEK OLD TESTAMENT

Ιουδαίους. 14 ὡς ὅτι ἐὰν παρακούσῃς ἐν τούτῳ τῷ καιρῷ,
ἄλλοθεν βοήθεια καὶ σκέπη ἔσται τοῖς Ιουδαίοις, σὺ δὲ καὶ ὁ
οἶκος τοῦ πατρός σου ἀπολεῖσθε· καὶ τίς οἶδεν εἰ εἰς τὸν
καιρὸν τοῦτον ἐβασίλευσας; 15 καὶ ἐξαπέστειλεν Εσθηρ τὸν
ἥκοντα πρὸς αὐτὴν πρὸς Μαρδοχαῖον λέγουσα 16 Βαδίσας
ἐκκλησίασον τοὺς Ιουδαίους τοὺς ἐν Σούσοις καὶ νηστεύ-
σατε ἐπ᾽ ἐμοὶ καὶ μὴ φάγητε μηδὲ πίητε ἐπὶ ἡμέρας τρεῖς
νύκτα καὶ ἡμέραν, κἀγὼ δὲ καὶ αἱ ἅβραι μου ἀσιτήσομεν, καὶ
τότε εἰσελεύσομαι πρὸς τὸν βασιλέα παρὰ τὸν νόμον, ἐὰν
καὶ ἀπολέσθαι με ᾖ.
17 Καὶ βαδίσας Μαρδοχαῖος ἐποίησεν ὅσα ἐνετείλατο
αὐτῷ Εσθηρ, 17a ἐδεήθη κυρίου μνημονεύων πάντα τὰ ἔργα
κυρίου καὶ εἶπεν 17b κύριε βασιλεῦ πάντων κρατῶν, ὅτι ἐν
ἐξουσίᾳ σου τὸ πᾶν ἐστιν, καὶ οὐκ ἔστιν ὁ ἀντιδοξῶν σοι ἐν
τῷ θέλειν σε σῶσαι τὸν Ισραηλ· 17c σὺ ἐποίησας τὸν οὐρανὸν
καὶ τὴν γῆν καὶ πᾶν θαυμαζόμενον ἐν τῇ ὑπ᾽ οὐρανὸν καὶ
κύριος εἶ πάντων, καὶ οὐκ ἔστιν ὃς ἀντιτάξεταί σοι τῷ
κυρίῳ. 17d πάντα γινώσκεις. σὺ οἶδας, κύριε, ὅτι οὐκ ἐν ὕβρει
οὐδὲ ἐν ὑπερηφανίᾳ οὐδὲ ἐν φιλοδοξίᾳ ἐποίησα τοῦτο, τὸ μὴ

KING JAMES VERSION

14 For if thou altogether holdest thy peace at this time, *then* shall there enlargement and deliverance arise to the Jews from another place; but thou and thy father's house shall be destroyed: and who knoweth whether thou art come to the kingdom for *such* a time as this?

15 Then Esther bade *them* return Mordecai *this answer,*

16 Go, gather together all the Jews that are present in Shushan, and fast ye for me, and neither eat nor drink three days, night or day: I also and my maidens will fast likewise; and so will I go in unto the king, which *is* not according to the law: and if I perish, I perish.

17 So Mordecai went his way, and did according to all that Esther had commanded him.

13 8 Then Mardocheus thought upon all the works of the Lord, and made his prayer unto him,

9 Saying, O Lord, Lord, the King Almighty: for the whole world is in thy power, and if thou hast appointed to save Israel, there is no man that can gainsay thee:

10 For thou hast made heaven and earth, and all the wondrous things under the heaven.

11 Thou art Lord of all things, and there is no man that can resist thee, which art the Lord.

12 Thou knowest all things, and thou knowest, Lord, that it was neither in contempt nor pride, nor for any desire of glory, that I did not bow down to proud Aman.

DOUAY OLD TESTAMENT

14 For if thou wilt now hold thy peace, the Jews shall be delivered by some other occasion: and thou, and thy father's house shall perish. And who knoweth whether thou art not therefore come to the kingdom, that thou mightest be ready in such a time as this?

15 And again Esther sent to Mardochai in these words:

16 Go, and gather together all the Jews whom thou shalt find in Susan, and pray ye for me. Neither eat nor drink for three days and three nights: and I with my handmaids will fast in like manner, and then I will go in to the king, against the law, not being called, and expose myself to death and to danger.

17 So Mardochai went, and did all that Esther had commanded him.

13 8 But Mardochai besought the Lord, remembering all his works,

9 And said: O Lord, Lord, almighty king, for all things are in thy power, and there is none that can resist thy will, if thou determine to save Israel.

10 Thou hast made heaven and earth, and all things that are under the cope of heaven.

11 Thou art Lord of all, and there is none that can resist thy majesty.

12 Thou knowest all things, and thou knowest that it was not out of pride and contempt, or any desire of glory, that I refused to worship the proud Aman,

KNOX TRANSLATION

the Jews will find some other means of deliverance; on thee
and thine destruction shall fall. Who knows, but thou hast
reached the throne only to be ready for such an opportunity
as this? 15 Then Esther sent word, 16 Go and muster all the
Jews thou canst find in Susan, and pray for me. Spend three
days and nights without food or drink, while I and my maidens fast too. Then I will break the law by appearing in the
king's presence unsummoned, though I must die for it.
17 And Mardochaeus went away, to do as Esther had bidden
him.

(*The rest of this chapter* [*13. 8-18*], *the whole of chapter 14 and chapter 15 verses 4-19 follow, in the Septuagint Greek, at the end of chapter 4 above.*)

13 8 So Mardochaeus bethought him of all the Lord's
great deeds in time past, and thus he prayed: 9 O
Lord, thou art the sovereign Lord and King of all things;
nothing but is subject to thy power; who then can withstand
thy will, if thou art minded to deliver Israel? 10 Heaven and
earth and all that heaven's vault contains is thy creation;
11 thy dominion is universal, thy royalty unchallengeable.
12 Thou knowest, who knowest all things, that if I refused
proud Aman yonder my greeting, it was no pride of mine, no
scorn, no ambition of mine that moved me. 13 For Israel's

TODAY'S ENGLISH VERSION

time like this, help will come to the Jews in some other way
and they will be saved, but you will die and your father's
family will come to an end. Yet, who knows? Maybe it was
for a time like this that you were made queen!"
15 Esther sent Mordecai this reply: 16 "Go and gather all the
Jews in Susa together; hold a fast and pray for me. Don't eat
or drink anything for three days and nights. My servant
women and I will be doing the same. After that, I will go to
the king, even though it is against the law. If I must die for
doing it, I will die."
17 Mordecai then left and did everything that Esther had
told him to do.
C[a] Mordecai prayed to the Lord, calling to mind what the
Lord had done in the past: 2 "O Lord, you are the Lord
and King of all creation, and everything obeys your commands. If you wish to save Israel, no one can stop you.
3 You made heaven and earth and all the wonderful things
on earth. 4 You are the Lord of all, and there is no one who
can stand against you. 5 You know all things. You know,
Lord, that when I refused to bow to that arrogant Haman, it
was not because I was arrogant or trying to impress people.
6-7 I simply did not want to honor any human being more
than I honor God. I refuse to bow to anyone but you, my

[a] *Chapter C 1-30 corresponds to chapters 13.8—14.19 in a number of English translations.*

NEW REVISED STANDARD VERSION

Jews will escape alive. 14 For if you keep quiet at such a time
as this, help and protection will come to the Jews from
another quarter, but you and your father's family will perish.
Yet, who knows whether it was not for such a time as this
that you were made queen?" 15 Then Esther gave the messenger this answer to take back to Mordecai: 16 "Go and
gather all the Jews who are in Susa and fast on my behalf;
for three days and nights do not eat or drink, and my maids
and I will also go without food. After that I will go to the
king, contrary to the law, even if I must die." 17 So Mordecai
went away and did what Esther had told him to do.

ADDITION C

13 8[a] Then Mordecai[b] prayed to the Lord, calling to
remembrance all the works of the Lord.
9 He said, "O Lord, Lord, you rule as King over all things,
for the universe is in your power and there is no one who
can oppose you when it is your will to save Israel, 10 for you
have made heaven and earth and every wonderful thing
under heaven. 11 You are Lord of all, and there is no one
who can resist you, the Lord. 12 You know all things; you
know, O Lord, that it was not in insolence or pride or for any
love of glory that I did this, and refused to bow down to this

[a] Chapters 13.8—15.16 correspond to chapters C 1-30 and D 1-16 in some translations. [b] Gk *he*

NEW AMERICAN BIBLE

escape. 14 Even if you now remain silent, relief and deliverance will come to the Jews from another source; but you and
your father's house will perish. Who knows but that it was
for a time like this that you obtained the royal dignity?"
15 Esther sent back to Mordecai the response: 16 "Go and
assemble all the Jews who are in Susa; fast on my behalf, all
of you, not eating or drinking, night or day, for three days. I
and my maids will also fast in the same way. Thus prepared,
I will go to the king, contrary to the law. If I perish, I perish!"
C Mordecai went away and did exactly as Esther had commanded. 1 Recalling all that the LORD had done, he
prayed to him 2 and said: "O Lord God, almighty King, all
things are in your power, and there is no one to oppose you
in your will to save Israel. 3 You made heaven and earth and
every wonderful thing under the heavens. 4 You are LORD of
all, and there is no one who can resist you, LORD. 5 You
know all things. You know, O LORD, that it was not out of
insolence or pride or desire for fame that I acted thus in not
bowing down to the proud Haman. 6 Gladly would I have

NEW JERUSALEM BIBLE

to escape. 14 No; if you persist in remaining silent at such a
time, relief and deliverance will come to the Jews from another quarter, but both you and your father's whole family will
perish. Who knows? Perhaps you have come to the throne
for just such a time as this.'
15 Whereupon Esther sent this reply to Mordecai, 16 'Go and
assemble all the Jews now in Susa and fast for me. Do not eat
or drink day or night for three days. For my part, I and my
waiting-women shall keep the same fast, after which I shall
go to the king in spite of the law; and if I perish, I perish.'
17 Mordecai went away and carried out Esther's instructions.
17a *Then calling to mind all the wonderful works of the*
Lord, he offered this prayer:

17b *Lord, Lord, Almighty King,*
everything is subject to your power,
and there is no one who can withstand you
in your determination to save Israel.
17c *You have made heaven and earth,*
and all the marvels that are under heaven.
You are the Master of the universe
and no one can resist you, Lord.

17d *You know all things,*
you, Lord, know
that neither pride, self-esteem nor vainglory
prompted me to do what I have done:
to refuse to prostrate myself
before proud Haman.

GREEK OLD TESTAMENT

προσκυνεῖν τὸν ὑπερήφανον Αμαν, ὅτι ηὐδόκουν φιλεῖν πέλματα ποδῶν αὐτοῦ πρὸς σωτηρίαν Ισραηλ· [17e] ἐποίησα τοῦτο, ἵνα μὴ θῶ δόξαν ἀνθρώπου ὑπεράνω δόξης θεοῦ, καὶ οὐ προσκυνήσω οὐδένα πλὴν σοῦ τοῦ κυρίου μου καὶ οὐ ποιήσω αὐτὰ ἐν ὑπερηφανίᾳ. [17f] νῦν, κύριε ὁ θεὸς ὁ βασιλεὺς ὁ θεὸς Αβρααμ, φεῖσαι τοῦ λαοῦ σου, ὅτι ἐπιβλέπουσιν ἡμῖν εἰς καταφθορὰν καὶ ἐπεθύμησαν ἀπολέσαι τὴν ἐξ ἀρχῆς κληρονομίαν σου· [17g] ὑπερίδῃς τὴν μερίδα σου, ἣν σεαυτῷ ἐλυτρώσω ἐκ γῆς Αἰγύπτου· [17h] τῆς δεήσεώς μου καὶ ἱλάσθητι τῷ κλήρῳ σου καὶ στρέψον τὸ πένθος ἡμῶν εἰς εὐωχίαν, ἵνα ζῶντες ὑμνῶμέν σου τὸ ὄνομα, κύριε, καὶ μὴ ἀφανίσῃς στόμα αἰνούντων σοι. — [17i] πᾶς Ισραηλ ἐκέκραξαν ἐξ ἰσχύος αὐτῶν, ὅτι θάνατος αὐτῶν ἐν ὀφθαλμοῖς αὐτῶν.

[17k] Καὶ Εσθηρ ἡ βασίλισσα κατέφυγεν ἐπὶ τὸν κύριον ἐν ἀγῶνι θανάτου κατειλημμένη καὶ ἀφελομένη τὰ ἱμάτια τῆς δόξης αὐτῆς ἐνεδύσατο ἱμάτια στενοχωρίας καὶ πένθους καὶ ἀντὶ τῶν ὑπερηφάνων ἡδυσμάτων σποδοῦ καὶ κοπριῶν ἔπλησεν τὴν κεφαλὴν αὐτῆς καὶ τὸ σῶμα αὐτῆς ἐταπείνωσεν

KING JAMES VERSION

13 For I could have been content with good will for the salvation of Israel to kiss the soles of his feet.

14 But I did this, that I might not prefer the glory of man above the glory of God: neither will I worship any but thee, O God, neither will I do it in pride.

15 And now, O Lord God and King, spare thy people: for their eyes are upon us to bring us to nought; yea, they desire to destroy the inheritance, that hath been thine from the beginning.

16 Despise not the portion, which thou hast delivered out of Egypt for thine own self.

17 Hear my prayer, and be merciful unto thine inheritance: turn our sorrow into joy, that we may live, O Lord, and praise thy name: and destroy not the mouths of them that praise thee, O Lord.

18 All Israel in like manner cried most earnestly unto the Lord, because their death was before their eyes.

14 Queen Esther also, being in fear of death, resorted unto the Lord:

2 And laid away her glorious apparel, and put on the garments of anguish and mourning: and instead of precious ointments, she covered her head with ashes and dung, and

DOUAY OLD TESTAMENT

13 (For I would willingly and readily for the salvation of Israel have kissed even the steps of his feet,)

14 But I feared lest I should transfer the honour of my God to a man, and lest I should adore any one except my God.

15 And now, O Lord, O king, O God of Abraham, have mercy on thy people, because our enemies resolve to destroy us, and extinguish thy inheritance.

16 Despise not thy portion, which thou hast redeemed for thyself out of Egypt.

17 Hear my supplication, and be merciful to thy lot and inheritance, and turn our mourning into joy, that we may live and praise thy name, O Lord, and shut not the mouths of them that sing to thee.

18 And all Israel with like mind and supplication cried to the Lord, because they saw certain death hanging over their heads.

14 QUEEN Esther also, fearing the danger that was at hand, had recourse to the Lord.

2 And when she had laid away her royal apparel, she put on garments suitable for weeping and mourning: instead of divers precious ointments, she covered her head with ashes

KNOX TRANSLATION

sake, willingly enough would I kiss the dust his feet have
trodden, [14] did not fear withhold me from giving man that
reverence which is God's due, from worshipping aught else
than thee, my God. [15] God of Abraham, our Lord and King,
now as ever have mercy on thy people, now when our enemies threaten to destroy us, and put an end to thy ancient
right. [16] Wilt thou make so little of the possession thou didst
win for thyself in Egypt? [17] Nay, listen to my prayer, have
mercy on the people thou claimest for thy own; turn our sadness, Lord, into rejoicing, and let us live to bless thy name;
do not silence the lips that sing thy praise. [18] Such was the
mind, such was the prayer of all Israel, as they cried out to
the Lord that day, with doom hanging over their heads.

14 And what of queen Esther? She too had recourse to the Lord, in her fear of the danger that threatened.
[2] Laid aside were those royal robes of hers, her array must
tell only of grief and lament; dust and dung should be all her

TODAY'S ENGLISH VERSION

Lord; and this is not because of pride. If it would help to save
Israel, I would be willing even to kiss the soles of his feet.
8-9"And now, O Lord, God and King, God of Abraham,
spare your people; save us from our enemies. They are determined to destroy us; they are looking for a chance. Long ago
you chose us to be your people and rescued us from the land
of Egypt. Do not abandon us now. 10We are your chosen
people, so listen to my prayer and be gracious to us. Turn
our misfortune into joy so that we may live to sing your
praises. Save us from death so that we can keep on
praising you."
11And all the people of Israel prayed loudly and earnestly
because they were sure that they were going to die.
12Queen Esther, in deep agony, turned to the Lord. 13She
took off her splendid robes and put on garments of mourning
and grief. Instead of her rich perfumes, she put ashes and

NEW REVISED STANDARD VERSION

proud Haman; 13for I would have been willing to kiss the
soles of his feet to save Israel! 14But I did this so that I
might not set human glory above the glory of God, and I will
not bow down to anyone but you, who are my Lord; and I
will not do these things in pride. 15And now, O Lord God
and King, God of Abraham, spare your people; for the eyes of
our foes are upon us[a] to annihilate us, and they desire to
destroy the inheritance that has been yours from the beginning. 16Do not neglect your portion, which you redeemed for
yourself out of the land of Egypt. 17Hear my prayer, and
have mercy upon your inheritance; turn our mourning into
feasting that we may live and sing praise to your name,
O Lord; do not destroy the lips[b] of those who praise you."
18 And all Israel cried out mightily, for their death was
before their eyes.
14 Then Queen Esther, seized with deadly anxiety, fled
to the Lord. 2She took off her splendid apparel and
put on the garments of distress and mourning, and instead
of costly perfumes she covered her head with ashes and

a Gk *for they are eying us* *b* Gk *mouth*

NEW AMERICAN BIBLE

kissed the soles of his feet for the salvation of Israel. 7But I
acted as I did so as not to place the honor of man above that
of God. I will not bow down to anyone but you, my LORD. It is
not out of pride that I am acting thus. 8And now, LORD God,
King, God of Abraham, spare your people, for our enemies
plan our ruin and are bent upon destroying the inheritance
that was yours from the beginning. 9Do not spurn your portion, which you redeemed for yourself out of Egypt. 10Hear
my prayer; have pity on your inheritance and turn our sorrow into joy: thus we shall live to sing praise to your name,
O LORD. Do not silence those who praise you."
11All Israel, too, cried out with all their strength, for death
was staring them in the face.
12Queen Esther, seized with mortal anguish, likewise had
recourse to the LORD. 13Taking off her splendid garments,
she put on garments of distress and mourning. In place of
her precious ointments she covered her head with dirt and

NEW JERUSALEM BIBLE

Gladly would I have kissed the soles of his feet,
had this assured the safety of Israel.

17e*But what I have done, I have done,*
rather than place the glory of a man
above the glory of God;
and I shall not prostrate myself to anyone
except, Lord, to you,
and, in so doing, I shall not be acting in pride.
17f*And now, Lord God,*
King, God of Abraham
spare your people!
For our ruin is being plotted,
there are plans to destroy your ancient heritage.
17g*Do not overlook your inheritance,*
which you redeemed from Egypt to be yours.
17h*Hear my supplication,*
have mercy on your heritage,
and turn our grief into rejoicing,
so that we may live, Lord, to hymn your name.
Do not suffer the mouths
of those who praise you to perish.

17i*And all Israel cried out with all their might, since death*
was staring them in the face.
17k*Queen Esther also took refuge with the Lord in the mor-*
tal peril which had overtaken her. She took off her sumptuous
robes and put on sorrowful mourning. Instead of expensive
perfumes, she covered her head with ashes and dung. She

GREEK OLD TESTAMENT

σφόδρα καὶ πάντα τόπον κόσμου ἀγαλλιάματος αὐτῆς
ἔπλησε στρεπτῶν τριχῶν αὐτῆς καὶ ἐδεῖτο κυρίου θεοῦ
Ισραηλ καὶ εἶπεν 17l μου ὁ βασιλεὺς ἡμῶν, σὺ εἶ μόνος·
βοήθησόν μοι τῇ μόνῃ καὶ μὴ ἐχούσῃ βοηθὸν εἰ μὴ σέ, ὅτι
κίνδυνός μου ἐν χειρί μου. 17m ἤκουον ἐκ γενετῆς μου ἐν
φυλῇ πατριᾶς μου ὅτι σύ, κύριε, ἔλαβες τὸν Ισραηλ ἐκ πάντων τῶν ἐθνῶν καὶ τοὺς πατέρας ἡμῶν ἐκ πάντων τῶν προγόνων αὐτῶν εἰς κληρονομίαν αἰώνιον καὶ ἐποίησας αὐτοῖς
ὅσα ἐλάλησας. 17n νῦν ἡμάρτομεν ἐνώπιόν σου, καὶ παρέδωκας ἡμᾶς εἰς χεῖρας τῶν ἐχθρῶν ἡμῶν, ἀνθ' ὧν ἐδοξάσαμεν
τοὺς θεοὺς αὐτῶν· δίκαιος εἶ, κύριε. 17o νῦν οὐχ ἱκανώθησαν
ἐν πικρασμῷ δουλείας ἡμῶν, ἀλλὰ ἔθηκαν τὰς χεῖρας αὐτῶν
ἐπὶ τὰς χεῖρας τῶν εἰδώλων αὐτῶν ἐξᾶραι ὁρισμὸν στόματός
σου καὶ ἀφανίσαι κληρονομίαν σου καὶ ἐμφράξαι στόμα αἰνούντων σοι καὶ σβέσαι δόξαν οἴκου σου καὶ θυσιαστήριόν σου

KING JAMES VERSION

she humbled her body greatly, and all the places of her joy she filled with her torn hair.

3 And she prayed unto the Lord God of Israel, saying, O my Lord, thou only art our King: help me, desolate woman, which have no helper but thee:

4 For my danger is in mine hand.

5 From my youth up I have heard in the tribe of my family, that thou, O Lord, tookest Israel from among all people, and our fathers from all their predecessors, for a perpetual inheritance, and thou hast performed whatsoever thou didst promise them.

6 And now we have sinned before thee: therefore hast thou given us into the hands of our enemies,

7 Because we worshipped their gods: O Lord, thou art righteous.

8 Nevertheless it satisfieth them not, that we are in bitter captivity: but they have stricken hands with their idols,

9 That they will abolish the thing that thou with thy mouth hast ordained, and destroy thine inheritance, and stop the mouth of them that praise thee, and quench the glory of thy house, and of thine altar,

DOUAY OLD TESTAMENT

and dung, and she humbled her body with fasts: and all the places in which before she was accustomed to rejoice, she filled with her torn hair.

3 And she prayed to the Lord the God of Israel, saying: O my Lord, who alone art our king, help me a desolate woman, and who have no other helper but thee.

4 My danger is in my hands.

5 I have heard of my father that thou, O Lord, didst take Israel from among all nations, and our fathers from all their predecessors, to possess them as an everlasting inheritance, and thou hast done to them as thou hast promised.

6 We have sinned in thy sight, and therefore thou hast delivered us into the hands of our enemies:

7 For we have worshipped their gods. Thou art just, O Lord.

8 And now they are not content to oppress us with most hard bondage, but attributing the strength of their hands to the power of their idols,

9 They design to change thy promises, and destroy thy inheritance, and shut the mouths of them that praise thee, and extinguish the glory of thy temple and altar,

KNOX TRANSLATION

anointing now. Her body she tamed with fasting; only her
torn locks hung where once she had loved to adorn her beauty. 3 In such guise she made her plea to the Lord, the God of
Israel; Lord, our King, thou reignest alone; befriend a lonely
heart that can find help nowhere but in thee. 4 The peril I
must take upon me is plain to view. 5 Lord, my childhood's
lessons are still unforgotten; I know that Israel, for all time,
is the people of thy choice, chosen stock of a chosen race; I
know that thy warnings have come true, and if thou hast
given our enemies the mastery, 6 it is because we sinned
against thee, 7 by worshipping the gods they worshipped; in
all this, Lord, thou art nothing to blame. 8 But now they are
not content with holding us down under a cruel yoke; strong
in the fancied protection of these false gods, 9 they would
fain set all thy promises aside, leave thee no possession on
earth at all. They would silence the voices that praise thee,
dim the glories of thy temple and thy altar;[a] 10 nothing must

a This verse gives a hint that Aman had special designs against the restored Jewish exiles at Jerusalem, whose existence is nowhere else alluded to in the Book of Esther.

TODAY'S ENGLISH VERSION

dung on her head. She did all she could to destroy any dignity in her appearance. She let her tangled and uncombed hair
hang down over her body that she had always taken such
care to beautify. 14 She prayed to the Lord God of Israel, "My
Lord and King, only you are God. I am all alone, and I have
no one to turn to but you. Help me! 15 I am about to risk my
life. 16 O Lord, as long as I can remember, my family has told
me how you chose Israel from all the nations and how in
ancient times you singled out our ancestors to be your people forever. You have kept all your promises to them.

17 "But we sinned against you. You handed us over to our
enemies because we worshiped their gods. 18 We deserved
your punishment, O Lord. 19 But our enemies are no longer
satisfied just to see us in slavery. They have made a solemn
promise to their idols 20 not only to destroy the people who
praise you, but to do away with your Law and to remove forever the glory of your house and altar. 21 They want the

NEW REVISED STANDARD VERSION

dung, and she utterly humbled her body; every part that she
loved to adorn she covered with her tangled hair. 3 She
prayed to the Lord God of Israel, and said: "O my Lord, you
only are our king; help me, who am alone and have no
helper but you, 4 for my danger is in my hand. 5 Ever since I
was born I have heard in the tribe of my family that you,
O Lord, took Israel out of all the nations, and our ancestors
from among all their forebears, for an everlasting inheritance, and that you did for them all that you promised.
6 And now we have sinned before you, and you have handed
us over to our enemies 7 because we glorified their gods. You
are righteous, O Lord! 8 And now they are not satisfied that
we are in bitter slavery, but they have covenanted with their
idols 9 to abolish what your mouth has ordained, and to
destroy your inheritance, to stop the mouths of those who
praise you and to quench your altar and the glory of your

NEW AMERICAN BIBLE

ashes. She afflicted her body severely; all her festive adornments were put aside, and her hair was wholly disheveled.

14 Then she prayed to the LORD, the God of Israel, saying:
"My LORD, our King, you alone are God. Help me, who am
alone and have no help but you, 15 for I am taking my life in
my hand. 16 As a child I was wont to hear from the people of
the land of my fore-fathers that you, O LORD, chose Israel
from among all peoples, and our fathers from among all
their ancestors, as a lasting heritage, and that you fulfilled
all your promises to them. 17 But now we have sinned in
your sight, and you have delivered us into the hands of our
enemies, 18 because we worshiped their gods. You are just, O
LORD. 19 But now they are not satisfied with our bitter servitude, but have undertaken 20 to do away with the decree you
have pronounced, and to destroy your heritage; to close the
mouths of those who praise you, and to extinguish the glory
of your temple and your altar; 21 to open the mouths of the

NEW JERUSALEM BIBLE

*mortified her body severely, and the former scenes of her hap-
piness and elegance were now littered with tresses torn from
her hair. She besought the Lord God of Israel in these words:*

17l *My Lord, our King, the Only One,
come to my help, for I am alone
and have no helper but you
and am about to take my life in my hands.*

17m *I have been taught from infancy
in the bosom of my family
that you, Lord, have chosen
Israel out of all the nations
and our ancestors out of all before them,
to be your heritage for ever;
and that you have treated them as you promised.*

17n *But we have sinned against you
and you have handed us over to our enemies
for paying honour to their gods.
Lord, you are upright.*

17o *But they are not satisfied
with the bitterness of our slavery:
they have pledged themselves to their idols
to abolish the decree that your own lips have uttered,
to blot out your heritage,
to stop the mouths of those who praise you,
to quench your altar and the glory of your House,*

17p *and instead to open the mouths of the heathen,*

GREEK OLD TESTAMENT

17p ἀνοῖξαι στόμα ἐθνῶν εἰς ἀρετὰς ματαίων καὶ θαυμα-
σθῆναι βασιλέα σάρκινον εἰς αἰῶνα. 17q παραδῷς, κύριε, τὸ
σκῆπτρόν σου τοῖς μὴ οὖσιν, καὶ μὴ καταγελασάτωσαν ἐν τῇ
πτώσει ἡμῶν, ἀλλὰ στρέψον τὴν βουλὴν αὐτῶν ἐπ᾽ αὐτούς,
τὸν δὲ ἀρξάμενον ἐφ᾽ ἡμᾶς παραδειγμάτισον. 17r κύριε,
γνώσθητι ἐν καιρῷ θλίψεως ἡμῶν καὶ ἐμὲ θάρσυνον, βασιλεῦ
τῶν θεῶν καὶ πάσης ἀρχῆς ἐπικρατῶν· 17s λόγον εὔρυθμον
εἰς τὸ στόμα μου ἐνώπιον τοῦ λέοντος καὶ μετάθες τὴν καρδίαν αὐτοῦ εἰς μῖσος τοῦ πολεμοῦντος ἡμᾶς εἰς συντέλειαν
αὐτοῦ καὶ τῶν ὁμονοούντων αὐτῷ· 17t δὲ ῥῦσαι ἐν χειρί σου
καὶ βοήθησόν μοι τῇ μόνῃ καὶ μὴ ἐχούσῃ εἰ μὴ σέ, κύριε.
17u γνῶσιν ἔχεις καὶ οἶδας ὅτι ἐμίσησα δόξαν ἀνόμων καὶ
βδελύσσομαι κοίτην ἀπεριτμήτων καὶ παντὸς ἀλλοτρίου.
17w οἶδας τὴν ἀνάγκην μου, ὅτι βδελύσσομαι τὸ σημεῖον τῆς
ὑπερηφανίας μου, ὅ ἐστιν ἐπὶ τῆς κεφαλῆς μου ἐν ἡμέραις

KING JAMES VERSION

10 And open the mouths of the heathen to set forth the praises of the idols, and to magnify a fleshly king for ever.

11 O Lord, give not thy sceptre unto them that be nothing, and let them not laugh at our fall; but turn their device upon themselves, and make him an example, that hath begun this against us.

12 Remember, O Lord, make thyself known in time of our affliction, and give me boldness, O King of the nations, and Lord of all power.

13 Give me eloquent speech in my mouth before the lion: turn his heart to hate him that fighteth against us, that there may be an end of him, and of all that are likeminded to him:

14 But deliver us with thine hand, and help me that am desolate, and which have no other help but thee.

15 Thou knowest all things, O Lord; thou knowest that I hate the glory of the unrighteous, and abhor the bed of the uncircumcised, and of all the heathen.

16 Thou knowest my necessity: for I abhor the sign of my high estate, which is upon mine head in the days wherein I

DOUAY OLD TESTAMENT

10 That they may open the mouths of Gentiles, and praise the strength of idols, and magnify for ever a carnal king.

11 Give not, O Lord, thy sceptre to them that are not, lest they laugh at our ruin: but turn their counsel upon themselves, and destroy him that hath begun to rage against us.

12 Remember, O Lord, and shew thyself to us in the time of our tribulation, and give me boldness, O Lord, king of gods, and of all power:

13 Give me a well ordered speech in my mouth in the presence of the lion, and turn his heart to the hatred of our enemy, that both he himself may perish, and the rest that consent to him.

14 But deliver us by thy hand, and help me, who have no other helper, but thee, O Lord, who hast the knowledge of all things.

15 And thou knowest that I hate the glory of the wicked, and abhor the bed of the uncircumcised, and of every stranger.

16 Thou knowest my necessity, that I abominate the sign of my pride and glory, which is upon my head in the days of

KNOX TRANSLATION

be heard but the chant of the Gentiles boasting of their false
gods, offering their endless praises to a mortal king.
11 Lord, wilt thou yield thy sceptre to gods that are no gods?
Must the heathen laugh over our downfall? Let their own
scheming recoil on them; bring him to a swift end, the man
who has loosed his fury on us! 12 Lord, bethink thee of our
need, give proof of thy power; Lord, that hast no rival in heav-
en or earth, grant me confidence. 13 Frame my utterance, as I
speak with this fierce lord of mine, and embitter him against
our enemy, bringing ruin on Aman and all that take Aman's
part. 14 So let thy power deliver us; grant help where help save
thine is none. Lord, thou knowest all things; 15 thou knowest
how I hate the splendours of a godless court, how unwillingly
I mate with an alien lord, a lord uncircumcised. 16 The sport of
ill-chance, how little I love the proud emblem of royalty I must
wear before the world! Loathsome to me as the rags we

TODAY'S ENGLISH VERSION

whole world to praise worthless idols and stand in awe of
mortal kings forever.
22 "Lord, these gods are nothing; do not surrender your
power to them or give our enemies the chance to laugh at
our downfall. Instead, turn their evil plans against them, and
make an example of that man who first planned our destruction.
23 "Remember us, O Lord. Come to us in this time of trouble. Give me courage, King of all gods and Ruler over all
earthly powers. 24 Give me the right words to say when I go
in to face Xerxes, that savage lion. Change his heart so that
he will turn against Haman, our enemy, and destroy him
and his gang. 25 Come to our rescue, O Lord. Help me; I am
all alone, and I have no one to turn to but you.
26 "You know everything, Lord. You know that I hate the
honor I receive from these Gentiles. I detest the thought of
having sex with any of these uncircumcised heathen. 27 But
you know that I have no choice. I hate the crown I have to
wear as queen on official occasions. I never wear it unless I

NEW REVISED STANDARD VERSION

house, 10 to open the mouths of the nations for the praise of
vain idols, and to magnify forever a mortal king.
11 "O Lord, do not surrender your scepter to what has no
being; and do not let them laugh at our downfall; but turn
their plan against them, and make an example of him who
began this against us. 12 Remember, O Lord; make yourself
known in this time of our affliction, and give me courage,
O King of the gods and Master of all dominion! 13 Put
eloquent speech in my mouth before the lion, and turn his
heart to hate the man who is fighting against us, so that
there may be an end of him and those who agree with him.
14 But save us by your hand, and help me, who am alone and
have no helper but you, O Lord. 15 You have knowledge of all
things, and you know that I hate the splendor of the wicked
and abhor the bed of the uncircumcised and of any alien.
16 You know my necessity—that I abhor the sign of my proud
position, which is upon my head on days when I appear in

NEW AMERICAN BIBLE

heathen to acclaim their false gods, and to extol an earthly
king forever.
22 "O LORD, do not relinquish your scepter to those that are
nought. Let them not gloat over our ruin, but turn their own
counsel against them and make an example of our chief
enemy. 23 Be mindful of us, O LORD. Manifest yourself in the
time of our distress and give me courage, King of gods and
Ruler of every power. 24 Put in my mouth persuasive words
in the presence of the lion and turn his heart to hatred for
our enemy, so that he and those who are in league with him
may perish. 25 Save us by your power, and help me, who am
alone and have no one but you, O LORD.
"You know all things. 26 You know that I hate the glory of
the pagans, and abhor the bed of the uncircumcised or of
any foreigner. 27 You know that I am under constraint, that I
abhor the sign of grandeur which rests on my head when I

NEW JERUSALEM BIBLE

to sing the praise of worthless idols
and for ever to idolise a king of flesh.

17q *Do not yield your sceptre, Lord,*
to what does not exist.
Never let our ruin be matter for laughter.
Turn these plots against their authors,
and make an example
of the man who leads the attack on us.
17r *Remember, Lord; reveal yourself*
in the time of our distress.

As for me, give me courage,
King of gods and Master of all powers!
17s *Put persuasive words into my mouth*
when I face the lion;
change his feeling into hatred for our enemy,
so that he may meet his end,
and all those like him!

17t *As for ourselves, save us by your hand,*
and come to my help, for I am alone
and have no one but you, Lord.
17u *You have knowledge of all things,*
and you know that I hate honours from the godless,
that I loathe the bed of the uncircumcised,
of any foreigner whatever.
17w *You know I am under constraint,*
that I loathe the symbol of my high position
bound round my brow when I appear at court;

GREEK OLD TESTAMENT

ὀπτασίας μου· βδελύσσομαι αὐτὸ ὡς ῥάκος καταμηνίων καὶ
οὐ φορῶ αὐτὸ ἐν ἡμέραις ἡσυχίας μου. 17x οὐκ ἔφαγεν ἡ δούλη σου τράπεζαν Αμαν καὶ οὐκ ἐδόξασα συμπόσιον βασιλέως
οὐδὲ ἔπιον οἶνον σπονδῶν· 17y οὐκ ηὐφράνθη ἡ δούλη σου ἀφ᾽
ἡμέρας μεταβολῆς μου μέχρι νῦν πλὴν ἐπὶ σοί, κύριε ὁ θεὸς
Αβρααμ. 17z θεὸς ὁ ἰσχύων ἐπὶ πάντας, εἰσάκουσον φωνὴν
ἀπηλπισμένων καὶ ῥῦσαι ἡμᾶς ἐκ χειρὸς τῶν πονηρευο-
μένων· καὶ ῥῦσαί με ἐκ τοῦ φόβου μου.
5 Καὶ ἐγενήθη ἐν τῇ ἡμέρᾳ τῇ τρίτῃ, ὡς ἐπαύσατο προσ-
ευχομένη, ἐξεδύσατο τὰ ἱμάτια τῆς θεραπείας καὶ περι-
εβάλετο τὴν δόξαν αὐτῆς 1a γενηθεῖσα ἐπιφανὴς ἐπικαλε-
σαμένη τὸν πάντων ἐπόπτην θεὸν καὶ σωτῆρα παρέλαβεν
τὰς δύο ἅβρας καὶ τῇ μὲν μιᾷ ἐπηρείδετο ὡς τρυφερευο-
μένη, ἡ δὲ ἑτέρα ἐπηκολούθει κουφίζουσα τὴν ἔνδυσιν
αὐτῆς, 1b αὐτὴ ἐρυθριῶσα ἀκμῇ κάλλους αὐτῆς, καὶ τὸ
πρόσωπον αὐτῆς ἱλαρὸν ὡς προσφιλές, ἡ δὲ καρδία αὐτῆς
ἀπεστενωμένη ἀπὸ τοῦ φόβου. 1c εἰσελθοῦσα πάσας τὰς
θύρας κατέστη ἐνώπιον τοῦ βασιλέως, καὶ αὐτὸς ἐκάθητο
ἐπὶ τοῦ θρόνου τῆς βασιλείας αὐτοῦ καὶ πᾶσαν στολὴν τῆς
ἐπιφανείας αὐτοῦ ἐνεδεδύκει, ὅλος διὰ χρυσοῦ καὶ λίθων
πολυτελῶν, καὶ ἦν φοβερὸς σφόδρα. 1d ἄρας τὸ πρόσωπον
αὐτοῦ πεπυρωμένον δόξῃ ἐν ἀκμῇ θυμοῦ ἔβλεψεν, καὶ ἔπεσεν

KING JAMES VERSION

shew myself, and that I abhor it as a menstruous rag, and that I wear it not when I am private by myself,

17 And that thine handmaid hath not eaten at Aman's table, and that I have not greatly esteemed the king's feast, nor drunk the wine of the drink offerings.

18 Neither had thine handmaid any joy since the day that I was brought hither to this present, but in thee, O Lord God of Abraham.

19 O thou mighty God above all, hear the voice of the forlorn, and deliver us out of the hands of the mischievous, and deliver me out of my fear.

15 And upon the third day, when she had ended her prayer, she laid away her mourning garments, and put on her glorious apparel.

2 And being gloriously adorned, after she had called upon God, who is the beholder and saviour of all things, she took two maids with her:

3 And upon the one she leaned, as carrying herself daintily;

4 And the other followed, bearing up her train.

5 And she was ruddy through the perfection of her beauty, and her countenance was cheerful and very amiable: but her heart was in anguish for fear.

6 Then having passed through all the doors, she stood before the king, who sat upon his royal throne, and was clothed with all his robes of majesty, all glittering with gold and precious stones; and he was very dreadful.

7 Then lifting up his countenance that shone with majesty, he looked very fiercely upon her: and the queen fell

DOUAY OLD TESTAMENT

my public appearance, and detest it as a menstruous rag, and wear it not in the days of my silence,

17 And that I have not eaten at Aman's table, nor hath the king's banquet pleased me, and that I have not drunk the wine of the drink offerings:

18 And that thy handmaid hath never rejoiced, since I was brought hither unto this day, but in thee, O Lord, the God of Abraham.

19 O God, who art mighty above all, hear the voice of them, that have no other hope, and deliver us from the hand of the wicked, and deliver me from my fear.

15 4 And on the third day she laid away the garments she wore, and put on her glorious apparel.

5 And glittering in royal robes, after she had called upon God the ruler and Saviour of all, she took two maids with her,

6 And upon one of them she leaned, as if for delicateness and overmuch tenderness she were not able to bear up her own body.

7 And the other maid followed her lady, bearing up her train flowing on the ground.

8 But she with a rosy colour in her face, and with gracious and bright eyes, hid a mind full of anguish, and exceeding great fear.

9 So going in she passed through all the doors in order, and stood before the king, where he sat upon his royal throne, clothed with his royal robes, and glittering with gold, and precious stones, and he was terrible to behold.

10 And when he had lifted up his countenance, and with burning eyes had shewn the wrath of his heart, the queen

KNOX TRANSLATION

women cast aside, how gladly I tear it from my brow, in this
cool hour! 17 At Aman's board I would never sit; even the
king's banquets have no taste for me, nor would I drink the
wine from which he pours libation. 18 Ever since they brought
me here, comfort thy handmaid had none, Lord God of
Abraham, save in thee! 19 Lord, that hast power over all men,
listen to this cry of despair; save us all from the clutches of our
enemies, and rid me of these fears that daunt me!

(*The remaining verses of this chapter* [*15. 4-19*] *represent an alternative version, in the Septuagint Greek, of the opening of chapter 5, and resume the narrative from 14. 19 above, which is the end of chapter 4 in the Greek. The main phrases of 5. 1-2 can be distinguished here in 15. 4, 9, 15.*)

15 4 When the third day came, she laid aside the garb of
prayer,[a] and put on all her fine array, 5 queenly
robes that dazzled the eye. One prayer she offered to the God
who alone rules, alone can save; then bade two of her wait-
ing-maids bear her company. 6 On one she leant, as though
her dainty form must needs be supported; 7 the other followed her mistress as train-bearer. 8 Alluring beauty of
flushed cheek and shining eye hid a heart grief-stricken, a
heart chilled with an overwhelming fear. 9 Door after door
she passed, till she reached the king's presence, where he sat
on his royal throne, royally clad, amid a glitter of gold and
jewels; terrible of mien. 10 No sooner had he looked up, his
fiery glance betraying his angry humour, than the queen

a This is perhaps the sense of the Greek; the Latin, probably through a confusion between *oration* and *ornation*, has 'the garb of her adornment', which gives no good sense.

TODAY'S ENGLISH VERSION

have to; it's as disgusting as last month's rag. 28 I refuse to eat at Haman's table or honor the king by attending his parties, and I have never drunk any of the wine dedicated to his gods. 29 Since I came here, the only thing that has brought me joy is my worship of you, Lord God of Abraham.

30 "Almighty God, listen to the prayer of your people. Rescue us from these evildoers, and take away my fear."

D[a] Queen Esther prayed for three days. Then she took off the clothes she had been wearing and put on her splendid robes again. 2-3 In all her royal splendor, she prayed again to her God and savior, who sees everything. Walking like a queen, she left her room accompanied by two servant women, one of them escorting her by the arm and 4 the other holding up the train of her robe. 5 Queen Esther's face was radiantly beautiful. She looked as cheerful as she was lovely, but in her heart she was terror-stricken. 6 She passed through all the doors and entered the throne room, where she stood before the king. He was seated on his royal throne, dressed in his glorious robes, which were covered with gold and precious jewels. It was an awe-inspiring sight. 7 His face glowed with splendor, but when he saw Esther, he stared at her with fierce anger. She grew weak and turned pale; she

[a] *Chapter D 1-15 corresponds to chapter 15.1-16 in a number of English translations.*

NEW REVISED STANDARD VERSION

public. I abhor it like a filthy rag, and I do not wear it on the days when I am at leisure. 17 And your servant has not eaten at Haman's table, and I have not honored the king's feast or drunk the wine of libations. 18 Your servant has had no joy since the day that I was brought here until now, except in you, O Lord God of Abraham. 19 O God, whose might is over all, hear the voice of the despairing, and save us from the hands of evildoers. And save me from my fear!"

END OF ADDITION C

ADDITION D

15 On the third day, when she ended her prayer, she took off the garments in which she had worshiped, and arrayed herself in splendid attire. 2 Then, majestically adorned, after invoking the aid of the all-seeing God and Savior, she took two maids with her; 3 on one she leaned gently for support, 4 while the other followed, carrying her train. 5 She was radiant with perfect beauty, and she looked happy, as if beloved, but her heart was frozen with fear. 6 When she had gone through all the doors, she stood before the king. He was seated on his royal throne, clothed in the full array of his majesty, all covered with gold and precious stones. He was most terrifying.

7 Lifting his face, flushed with splendor, he looked at her in fierce anger. The queen faltered, and turned pale and

NEW AMERICAN BIBLE

appear in public; abhor it like a polluted rag, and do not wear it in private. 28 I, your handmaid, have never eaten at the table of Haman, nor have I graced the banquet of the king or drunk the wine of libations. 29 From the day I was brought here till now, your handmaid has had no joy except in you, O LORD, God of Abraham. 30 O God, more powerful than all, hear the voice of those in despair. Save us from the power of the wicked, and deliver me from my fear."

D On the third day, putting an end to her prayers, she took off her penitential garments and arrayed herself in her royal attire. 2 In making her state appearance, after invoking the all-seeing God and savior, she took with her two maids; 3 on the one she leaned gently for support, 4 while the other followed her, bearing her train. 5 She glowed with the perfection of her beauty and her countenance was as joyous as it was lovely, though her heart was shrunk with fear. 6 She passed through all the portals till she stood face to face with the king, who was seated on his royal throne, clothed in full robes of state, and covered with gold and precious stones, so that he inspired great awe. 7 As he looked up, his features ablaze with the height of majestic anger, the queen staggered, changed color, and leaned

NEW JERUSALEM BIBLE

I loathe it as if it were a filthy rag
and do not wear it on my days of leisure.
17x *Your servant has not eaten at Haman's table,*
nor taken pleasure in the royal banquets,
nor drunk the wine of libations.
17y *Nor has your servant found pleasure*
from the day of her promotion until now
except in you, Lord, God of Abraham.
17z *O God, whose strength prevails over all,*
listen to the voice of the desperate,
save us from the hand of the wicked,
and free me from my fear!

5 1a *On the third day, when she had finished praying, she took off her suppliant's mourning attire and dressed herself in her full splendour. Radiant as she then appeared, she invoked God who watches over all people and saves them. With her, she took two ladies-in-waiting. With a delicate air she leaned on one, while the other accompanied her carrying her train.* 1b *Rosy with the full flush of her beauty, her face radiated joy and love: but her heart shrank with fear.* 1c *Having passed through door after door, she found herself in the presence of the king. He was sitting on his royal throne, dressed in all his robes of state, glittering with gold and precious stones—a formidable sight.* 1d *He looked up, afire with majesty and, blazing with anger, saw her. The queen sank to*

GREEK OLD TESTAMENT

ἡ βασίλισσα καὶ μετέβαλεν τὸ χρῶμα αὐτῆς ἐν ἐκλύσει καὶ κατεπέκυψεν ἐπὶ τὴν κεφαλὴν τῆς ἅβρας τῆς προπορευομένης. 1e μετέβαλεν ὁ θεὸς τὸ πνεῦμα τοῦ βασιλέως εἰς πραΰτητα, καὶ ἀγωνιάσας ἀνεπήδησεν ἀπὸ τοῦ θρόνου αὐτοῦ καὶ ἀνέλαβεν αὐτὴν ἐπὶ τὰς ἀγκάλας αὐτοῦ, μέχρις οὗ κατέστη, καὶ παρεκάλει αὐτὴν λόγοις εἰρηνικοῖς καὶ εἶπεν αὐτῇ 1f ἔστιν, Εσθηρ; ἐγὼ ὁ ἀδελφός σου, θάρσει, οὐ μὴ ἀποθάνῃς, ὅτι κοινὸν τὸ πρόσταγμα ἡμῶν ἐστιν· πρόσελθε. 2 καὶ ἄρας τὴν χρυσῆν ῥάβδον ἐπέθηκεν ἐπὶ τὸν τράχηλον αὐτῆς καὶ ἠσπάσατο αὐτὴν καὶ εἶπεν Λάλησόν μοι. 2a εἶπεν αὐτῷ Εἶδόν σε, κύριε, ὡς ἄγγελον θεοῦ, καὶ ἐταράχθη ἡ καρδία μου ἀπὸ φόβου τῆς δόξης σου· ὅτι θαυμαστὸς εἶ, κύριε, καὶ τὸ πρόσωπόν σου χαρίτων μεστόν. 2b δὲ τῷ διαλέγεσθαι αὐτὴν ἔπεσεν ἀπὸ ἐκλύσεως αὐτῆς, καὶ ὁ βασιλεὺς ἐταράσσετο, καὶ πᾶσα ἡ θεραπεία αὐτοῦ παρεκάλει αὐτήν. 3 καὶ εἶπεν ὁ

KING JAMES VERSION

down, and was pale, and fainted, and bowed herself upon the head of the maid that went before her.

8 Then God changed the spirit of the king into mildness, who in a fear leaped from his throne, and took her in his arms, till she came to herself again, and comforted her with loving words, and said unto her,

9 Esther, what is the matter? I am thy brother, be of good cheer:

10 Thou shalt not die, though our commandment be general: come near.

11 And so be held up his golden sceptre, and laid it upon her neck,

12 And embraced her, and said, Speak unto me.

13 Then said she unto him, I saw thee, my lord, as an angel of God, and my heart was troubled for fear of thy majesty.

14 For wonderful art thou, lord, and thy countenance is full of grace.

15 And as she was speaking, she fell down for faintness.

16 Then the king was troubled, and all his servants comforted her.

5 [a] Now it came to pass on the third day, that Esther put on *her* royal *apparel,* and stood in the inner court of the king's house, over against the king's house: and the king sat upon his royal throne in the royal house, over against the gate of the house.

2 And it was so, when the king saw Esther the queen standing in the court, *that* she obtained favour in his sight: and the

a 5:1-2 translate the Hebrew text expanded on in the Greek (Addition D).

DOUAY OLD TESTAMENT

sunk down, and her colour turned pale, and she rested her weary head upon her handmaid.

11 And God changed the king's spirit into mildness, and all in haste and in fear he leaped from his throne, and holding her up in his arms, till she came to herself, caressed her with these words:

12 What is the matter, Esther? I am thy brother, fear not.

13 Thou shalt not die: for this law is not made for thee, but for all others.

14 Come near then, and touch the sceptre.

15 And as she held her peace, he took the golden sceptre, and laid it upon her neck, and kissed her, and said: Why dost thou not speak to me?

16 She answered: I saw thee, my lord, as an angel of God, and my heart was troubled for fear of thy majesty.

17 For thou, my lord, art very admirable, and thy face is full of graces.

18 And while she was speaking, she fell down again, and was almost in a swoon.

19 But the king was troubled, and all his servants comforted her.

5 [a] AND on the third day Esther put on her royal apparel, and stood in the inner court of the king's house, over against the king's hall: now he sat upon his throne in the hall of the palace, over against the door of the house.

2 And when he saw Esther the queen standing, she pleased his eyes, and he held out toward her the golden

a 5:1-2 translate the Hebrew text expanded on in the Greek (Addition D).

KNOX TRANSLATION

swooned away; white went her cheeks, as she leaned her head, fainting, on the maid that stood by.

11 And now God changed the king's mood all at once to mildness; he started from his throne in trembling haste, and was fain to hold her in his arms till she came to herself; and still with soothing words he reassured her: 12 Esther, what is amiss with thee? Were I thy own brother, thou hadst not less cause to fear. 13 Thy life is safe; to others the law forbids entry, never to thee; 14 thou hast but to come near, and touch my sceptre. 15 And with that, for she was voiceless still, he raised his golden sceptre and touched her neck with it; then kissed her, and asked, What, hast thou no word for me? 16 My lord, she said, the sight of thee overawed me, as if I had seen one of God's angels; such reverence does thy majesty inspire. 17 For indeed, my lord, there is nothing about thee but must be admired, nothing in thy looks but is gracious. 18 Even as she spoke, once again her strength failed her; and she was near to fainting.; 19 the king was all anxiety, and his courtiers must needs come about him, seeking to allay her fears.

5 [a] The third day came, and Esther put on her royal robes; and, so clad, made her appearance before the king's palace, within the royal (that is, the inner) court. There sat the king on his throne, in the palace council chamber, facing the main door; 2 he saw Esther, his queen, standing there without, and the sight of her won his heart. Out went the

a 5:1-2 translate the Hebrew text expanded on in the Greek (Addition D).

TODAY'S ENGLISH VERSION

almost fainted and had to lean her head on her attendant's
shoulder.
8 But God changed the king's anger into tender concern. He
quickly rose from his throne and took her in his arms until
she was able to stand. He calmed her with comforting words.
9 "What is it, Esther?" he said to her. "I am your husband.
There's no need to be afraid. 10 Our law applies only to ordinary people; you will not die. 11 Come here to me." 12 He lifted his gold scepter and touched her on the neck with it. Then
he kissed her and said, "Tell me what you want."
13 "When I looked at you, my lord, I thought I was seeing
an angel of God," the queen answered, "and I was overcome
by your awesome majesty. 14 You are so marvelous and your
face is so full of kindness."
15 But while she was speaking, she fainted again. 16 The
king was concerned about her, and all his attendants tried to
revive her.

NEW REVISED STANDARD VERSION

faint, and collapsed on the head of the maid who went in
front of her. 8 Then God changed the spirit of the king to
gentleness, and in alarm he sprang from his throne and took
her in his arms until she came to herself. He comforted her
with soothing words, and said to her, 9 "What is it, Esther? I
am your husband.[a] Take courage; 10 You shall not die, for
our law applies only to our subjects.[b] Come near."
11 Then he raised the golden scepter and touched her
neck with it; 12 he embraced her, and said, "Speak to me."
13 She said to him, "I saw you, my lord, like an angel of God,
and my heart was shaken with fear at your glory. 14 For you
are wonderful, my lord, and your countenance is full of
grace." 15 And while she was speaking, she fainted and fell.
16 Then the king was agitated, and all his servants tried to
comfort her.

END OF ADDITION D

a Gk *brother* *b* Meaning of Gk uncertain

NEW AMERICAN BIBLE

weakly against the head of the maid in front of her. 8 But
God changed the king's anger to gentleness. In great anxiety
he sprang from his throne, held her in his arms until she
recovered, and comforted her with reassuring words.
9 "What is it, Esther?" he said to her. "I am your brother.
Take courage! 10 You shall not die because of this general
decree of ours. 11 Come near!" 12 Raising the golden scepter,
he touched her neck with it, embraced her, and said, "Speak
to me."
13 She replied: "I saw you, my lord, as an angel of God, and
my heart was troubled with fear of your majesty. 14 For you
are awesome, my lord, though your glance is full of kindness." 15 As she said this, she fainted. 16 The king became
troubled and all his attendants tried to revive her.

5 [Now on the third day, Esther put on her royal garments
and stood in the inner courtyard, looking toward the
royal palace, while the king was seated on his royal throne
in the audience chamber, facing the palace doorway. 2 He
saw Queen Esther standing in the courtyard, and made her

5, 1f: The Hebrew text here translated is a short form of the account already given in Greek.

NEW JERUSALEM BIBLE

the floor. As she fainted, the colour drained from her face and
her head fell against the lady-in-waiting beside her. 1e *But*
God changed the king's heart, inducing a milder spirit. He
sprang from his throne in alarm and took her in his arms
until she recovered, comforting her with soothing words.
1f *'What is the matter, Esther?' he said. 'I am your brother.*
Take heart, you are not going to die; our order applies only to
ordinary people. Come to me.' 2 *And raising his golden scep-*
tre he laid it on Esther's neck, embraced her and said, 'Speak
to me.' 2a *'Sire,' she said, 'to me you looked like one of God's*
angels, and my heart was moved with fear of your majesty.
For you are a figure of wonder, my lord, and your face is full
of graciousness.' 2b *But as she spoke she fell down in a faint.*
The king grew more agitated, and his courtiers all set about

GREEK OLD TESTAMENT

βασιλεύς Τί θέλεις, Εσθηρ, καὶ τί σού ἐστιν τὸ ἀξίωμα; ἕως τοῦ ἡμίσους τῆς βασιλείας μου καὶ ἔσται σοι. [4]εἶπεν δὲ Εσθηρ Ἡμέρα μου ἐπίσημος σήμερόν ἐστιν· εἰ οὖν δοκεῖ τῷ βασιλεῖ, ἐλθάτω καὶ αὐτὸς καὶ Αμαν εἰς τὴν δοχήν, ἣν ποιήσω σήμερον. [5]καὶ εἶπεν ὁ βασιλεύς Κατασπεύσατε Αμαν, ὅπως ποιήσωμεν τὸν λόγον Εσθηρ· καὶ παραγίνονται ἀμφότεροι εἰς τὴν δοχήν, ἣν εἶπεν Εσθηρ. [6]ἐν δὲ τῷ πότῳ εἶπεν ὁ βασιλεὺς πρὸς Εσθηρ Τί ἐστιν, βασίλισσα Εσθηρ; καὶ ἔσται σοι ὅσα ἀξιοῖς. [7]καὶ εἶπεν Τὸ αἴτημά μου καὶ τὸ ἀξίωμά μου· [8]εἰ εὗρον χάριν ἐνώπιον τοῦ βασιλέως, ἐλθάτω ὁ βασιλεὺς καὶ Αμαν ἐπὶ τὴν αὔριον εἰς τὴν δοχήν, ἣν ποιήσω αὐτοῖς, καὶ αὔριον ποιήσω τὰ αὐτά.

[9]Καὶ ἐξῆλθεν ὁ Αμαν ἀπὸ τοῦ βασιλέως ὑπερχαρὴς εὐφραινόμενος. ἐν δὲ τῷ ἰδεῖν Αμαν Μαρδοχαῖον τὸν Ιουδαῖον ἐν τῇ αὐλῇ ἐθυμώθη σφόδρα. [10]καὶ εἰσελθὼν εἰς τὰ ἴδια ἐκάλεσεν τοὺς φίλους καὶ Ζωσαραν τὴν γυναῖκα αὐτοῦ

KING JAMES VERSION

king held out to Esther the golden sceptre that *was* in his hand. So Esther drew near, and touched the top of the sceptre.

3 Then said the king unto her, What wilt thou, queen Esther? and what *is* thy request? it shall be even given thee to the half of the kingdom.

4 And Esther answered, If *it seem* good unto the king, let the king and Haman come this day unto the banquet that I have prepared for him.

5 Then the king said, Cause Haman to make haste, that he may do as Esther hath said. So the king and Haman came to the banquet that Esther had prepared.

6 And the king said unto Esther at the banquet of wine, What *is* thy petition? and it shall be granted thee: and what *is* thy request? even to the half of the kingdom it shall be performed.

7 Then answered Esther, and said, My petition and my request *is;*

8 If I have found favour in the sight of the king, and if it please the king to grant my petition, and to perform my request, let the king and Haman come to the banquet that I shall prepare for them, and I will do to morrow as the king hath said.

9 Then went Haman forth that day joyful and with a glad heart: but when Haman saw Mordecai in the king's gate, that he stood not up, nor moved for him, he was full of indignation against Mordecai.

10 Nevertheless Haman refrained himself: and when he came home, he sent and called for his friends, and Zeresh his wife.

DOUAY OLD TESTAMENT

sceptre, which he held in his hand: and she drew near, and kissed the top of his sceptre.

3 And the king said to her: What wilt thou, queen Esther? what is thy request? if thou shouldst even ask one half of the kingdom, it shall be given to thee.

4 But she answered: If it please the king, I beseech thee to come to me this day, and Aman with thee to the banquet which I have prepared.

5 And the king said forthwith: Call ye Aman quickly, that he may obey Esther's will. So the king and Aman came to the banquet which the queen had prepared for them.

6 And the king said to her, after he had drunk wine plentifully: What dost thou desire should be given thee? and for what thing askest thou? although thou shouldst ask the half of my kingdom, thou shalt have it.

7 And Esther answered: My petition and request is this:

8 If I have found favour in the king's sight, and if it please the king to give me what I ask, and to fulfil my petition: let the king and Aman come to the banquet which I have prepared them, and to morrow I will open my mind to the king.

9 So Aman went out that day joyful and merry. And when he saw Mardochai sitting before the gate of the palace, and that he not only did not rise up to honour him, but did not so much as move from the place where he sat, he was exceedingly angry:

10 But dissembling his anger, and returning into his house, he called together to him his friends, and Zares his wife:

KNOX TRANSLATION

golden sceptre he bore, and as she drew near to kiss the tip of it, [3]Why, Esther, said he, what is thy errand? Ask me for half my kingdom, and it is thine. [4]My lord king, she answered, do me the honour of dining with me to-day; I have a feast prepared; and bring Aman with thee. [5]The king, without more ado, had Aman summoned to wait, there and then, on Esther's pleasure; and both of them went to the feast she had prepared. [6]Deep drank the king that day, and said to Esther, What wouldst thou? Tell me what thy desire is? Be it half my kingdom, it shall not be denied thee. [7]What would I have? said she. I ask no more than this; [8]since the king's grace is ready to humour my whim, to grant me what I ask, do me the favour to dine with me to-morrow, and Aman with thee; then I will make known to the royal ear what my request is.

[9]A proud man was Aman that day, and he went home treading on air. But Mardochaeus still sat at the palace door; rise up he would not, nor stir from his post. [10]And Aman, seeing it, fell into a rage. He gave no mark of it then, but when he reached home he called all his friends about him, and his wife Zares among them, and opened his mind. [11]He

TODAY'S ENGLISH VERSION

5[a] 3 "What is it, Esther?" the king asked. "Tell me what
you want, and you shall have it—even if it is half of
my empire."
4 Esther replied, "Today is a special day for me. If it please
my lord, I would like you and Haman to be my guests
tonight at a banquet I am preparing for you."
5 The king then ordered Haman to come quickly, so that
they could be Esther's guests. So the king and Haman went
to Esther's banquet. 6 Over the wine the king again said to
her, "Tell me what you want, Queen Esther."
7 Esther replied, 8 "If my lord is kind enough to grant my
request, I would like you and Haman to be my guests tomorrow at another banquet that I will prepare for you. It will be
just like this one."
9 When Haman left the king he was happy and in a good
mood, until he saw Mordecai the Jew in the courtyard of the
palace. That made him furious, 10 but he went on home.
Then he invited his friends to his house and asked his wife

a In Greek, chapter D replaces verses 1 and 2 in Hebrew.

NEW REVISED STANDARD VERSION

5[a] 3 The king said to her, "What do you wish, Esther?
What is your request? It shall be given you, even to half
of my kingdom." 4 And Esther said, "Today is a special day
for me. If it pleases the king, let him and Haman come to the
dinner that I shall prepare today." 5 Then the king said,
"Bring Haman quickly, so that we may do as Esther desires."
So they both came to the dinner that Esther had spoken
about. 6 While they were drinking wine, the king said to
Esther, "What is it, Queen Esther? It shall be granted you."
7 She said, "My petition and request is: 8 if I have found
favor in the sight of the king, let the king and Haman come
to the dinner that I shall prepare them, and tomorrow I will
do as I have done today."
9 So Haman went out from the king joyful and glad of
heart. But when he saw Mordecai the Jew in the courtyard,
he was filled with anger. 10 Nevertheless, he went home and
summoned his friends and his wife Zosara. 11 And he told

a In Greek, Chapter D replaces verses 1 and 2 in Hebrew.

NEW AMERICAN BIBLE

welcome by extending toward her the golden staff which he
held. She came up to him, and touched the top of the staff.]
3 Then the king said to her, "What is it, Queen Esther?
What is your request? Even if it is half of my kingdom, it
shall be granted you." 4 "If it please your majesty," Esther
replied, "come today with Haman to a banquet I have prepared." 5 And the king ordered, "Have Haman make haste to
fulfill the wish of Esther."
So the king went with Haman to the banquet Esther had
prepared. 6 During the drinking of the wine, the king said to
Esther, "Whatever you ask for shall be granted, and whatever request you make shall be honored, even if it is for half
my kingdom." 7 Esther replied: "This is my petition and
request: 8 if I have found favor with the king and if it pleases
your majesty to grant my petition and honor my request,
come with Haman tomorrow to a banquet which I shall prepare for you; and then I will do as you ask."
9 That day Haman left happy and in good spirits. But when
he saw that Mordecai at the royal gate did not rise, and
showed no fear of him, he was filled with anger toward him.
10 Haman restrained himself, however, and went home,
where he summoned his friends and his wife Zeresh. 11 He

NEW JERUSALEM BIBLE

reviving her. 3 'What is the matter, Queen Esther?' the king
said. 'Tell me what you want; even if it is half my kingdom, I
grant it you.' 4 'Would it please the king,' Esther replied, 'to
come with Haman today to the banquet I have prepared for
him?' 5 The king said, 'Tell Haman to come at once, so that
Esther may have her wish.'
6 So the king and Haman came to the banquet that Esther
had prepared and, during the banquet, the king again said to
Esther, 'Tell me your request; I grant it to you. Tell me what
you want; even if it is half my kingdom, it is yours for the
asking.' 7 'What do I want, what is my request?' Esther
replied. 8 'If I have found favour in the king's eyes, and if it
is his pleasure to grant what I ask and to agree to my
request, let the king and Haman come to the banquet I
intend to give them tomorrow, and then I shall do as the
king says.'
9 Haman left full of joy and high spirits that day; but when
he saw Mordecai at the Chancellery, neither standing up nor
stirring at his approach, he felt a gust of anger. 10 He
restrained himself, however. Returning home, he sent for his
friends and Zeresh his wife 11 and held forth to them about

GREEK OLD TESTAMENT

11 καὶ ὑπέδειξεν αὐτοῖς τὸν πλοῦτον αὐτοῦ καὶ τὴν δόξαν, ἣν
ὁ βασιλεὺς αὐτῷ περιέθηκεν, καὶ ὡς ἐποίησεν αὐτὸν πρωτεύ-
ειν καὶ ἡγεῖσθαι τῆς βασιλείας. 12 καὶ εἶπεν Αμαν Οὐ
κέκληκεν ἡ βασίλισσα μετὰ τοῦ βασιλέως οὐδένα εἰς τὴν
δοχὴν ἀλλ᾽ ἢ ἐμέ, καὶ εἰς τὴν αὔριον κέκλημαι· 13 καὶ ταῦτά
μοι οὐκ ἀρέσκει, ὅταν ἴδω Μαρδοχαῖον τὸν Ιουδαῖον ἐν τῇ
αὐλῇ. 14 καὶ εἶπεν πρὸς αὐτὸν Ζωσαρα ἡ γυνὴ αὐτοῦ καὶ οἱ
φίλοι Κοπήτω σοι ξύλον πηχῶν πεντήκοντα, ὄρθρου δὲ εἰπὸν
τῷ βασιλεῖ καὶ κρεμασθήτω Μαρδοχαῖος ἐπὶ τοῦ ξύλου· σὺ
δὲ εἴσελθε εἰς τὴν δοχὴν σὺν τῷ βασιλεῖ καὶ εὐφραίνου. καὶ
ἤρεσεν τὸ ῥῆμα τῷ Αμαν, καὶ ἡτοιμάσθη τὸ ξύλον.

6 Ὁ δὲ κύριος ἀπέστησεν τὸν ὕπνον ἀπὸ τοῦ βασιλέως
τὴν νύκτα ἐκείνην, καὶ εἶπεν τῷ διδασκάλῳ αὐτοῦ εἰσ-
φέρειν γράμματα μνημόσυνα τῶν ἡμερῶν ἀναγινώσκειν
αὐτῷ. 2 εὗρεν δὲ τὰ γράμματα τὰ γραφέντα περὶ Μαρδοχαίου, ὡς ἀπήγγειλεν τῷ βασιλεῖ περὶ τῶν δύο εὐνούχων τοῦ
βασιλέως ἐν τῷ φυλάσσειν αὐτοὺς καὶ ζητῆσαι ἐπιβαλεῖν
τὰς χεῖρας Ἀρταξέρξῃ. 3 εἶπεν δὲ ὁ βασιλεύς Τίνα δόξαν ἢ
χάριν ἐποιήσαμεν τῷ Μαρδοχαίῳ; καὶ εἶπαν οἱ διάκονοι τοῦ
βασιλέως Οὐκ ἐποίησας αὐτῷ οὐδέν. 4 ἐν δὲ τῷ πυνθάνεσθαι
τὸν βασιλέα περὶ τῆς εὐνοίας Μαρδοχαίου ἰδοὺ Αμαν ἐν τῇ
αὐλῇ· εἶπεν δὲ ὁ βασιλεύς Τίς ἐν τῇ αὐλῇ; ὁ δὲ Αμαν
εἰσῆλθεν εἰπεῖν τῷ βασιλεῖ κρεμάσαι τὸν Μαρδοχαῖον ἐπὶ

KING JAMES VERSION

11 And Haman told them of the glory of his riches, and the multitude of his children, and all *the things* wherein the king had promoted him, and how he had advanced him above the princes and servants of the king.

12 Haman said moreover, Yea, Esther the queen did let no man come in with the king unto the banquet that she had prepared but myself; and to morrow am I invited unto her also with the king.

13 Yet all this availeth me nothing, so long as I see Mordecai the Jew sitting at the king's gate.

14 Then said Zeresh his wife and all his friends unto him, Let a gallows be made of fifty cubits high, and to morrow speak thou unto the king that Mordecai may be hanged thereon: then go thou in merrily with the king unto the banquet. And the thing pleased Haman; and he caused the gallows to be made.

6 On that night could not the king sleep, and he commanded to bring the book of records of the chronicles; and they were read before the king.

2 And it was found written, that Mordecai had told of Bigthana and Teresh, two of the king's chamberlains, the keepers of the door, who sought to lay hand on the king Ahasuerus.

3 And the king said, What honour and dignity hath been done to Mordecai for this? Then said the king's servants that ministered unto him, There is nothing done for him.

4 And the king said, Who *is* in the court? Now Haman was come into the outward court of the king's house, to

DOUAY OLD TESTAMENT

11 And he declared to them the greatness of his riches, and the multitude of his children, and with how great glory the king had advanced him above all his princes and servants.

12 And after this he said: Queen Esther also hath invited no other to the banquet with the king, but me: and with her I am also to dine to morrow with the king:

13 And whereas I have all these things, I think I have nothing, so long as I see Mardochai the Jew sitting before the king's gate.

14 Then Zares his wife, and the rest of his friends answered him: Order a great beam to be prepared, fifty cubits high, and in the morning speak to the king, that Mardochai may be hanged upon it, and so thou shalt go full of joy with the king to the banquet. The counsel pleased him, and he commanded a high gibbet to be prepared.

6 THAT night the king passed without sleep, and he commanded the histories and chronicles of former times to be brought him. And when they were reading them before him,

2 They came to that place where it was written, how Mardochai had discovered the treason of Bagathan and Thares the eunuchs, who sought to kill king Assuerus.

3 And when the king heard this, he said: What honour and reward hath Mardochai received for this fidelity? His servants and ministers said to him: He hath received no reward at all.

4 And the king said immediately: Who is in the court? for Aman was coming in to the inner court of the king's house,

KNOX TRANSLATION

recounted to them how great his wealth was, how many children were his, what honour the king had done him by promoting him to be the chief of all his nobles and courtiers.
12 More, he said; it was but this day queen Esther gave the
king a banquet, and would have me and none other for his
fellow-guest; to-morrow I must dine with her again, with the
king present. 13 All this is mine, he said, and all this is nothing to me, while I yet see Mardochaeus sitting there at the
palace gate.
14 But they had a remedy for this, his wife Zares and those
friends of his. Have a gallows made, fifty cubits high, so that
to-morrow thou canst bid the king have Mardochaeus
hanged on it. Then thou mayst go light-hearted enough, to
feast with the king. This counsel Aman liked well, and he
gave his men orders to have a high gallows in readiness.

6 All that night the king could not sleep; so he would have
the annals of his reign brought to him, the record of
times past, and they began to read these out in his presence.
2 In the reading of them, they came upon the story of the plot
made by two chamberlains, Bagathan and Thares, to murder
the king, and how Mardochaeus gave information of it.
3 And for this loyalty, the king asked, what honours or
rewards were given to Mardochaeus? But page and courtier
were agreed, Mardochaeus was never the better for it. 4 Who
is out there in the court? the king asked. It was Aman, come
into the inner court to find audience with the king, and have

TODAY'S ENGLISH VERSION

Zeresh to join them. 11 He boasted to them about how rich
he was and about the honor the king had paid him when he
promoted him to high office and made him prime minister.
12 "What is more," Haman said, "Queen Esther gave a banquet for no one but the king and me, and we are invited back
tomorrow. 13 But none of this means a thing to me as long
as I see that Jew Mordecai sitting in the courtyard of the
palace."

14 Then his wife and all his friends suggested, "Why don't
you have a gallows put up, seventy-five feet high? Tomorrow
morning you can ask the king to have Mordecai hanged on
it, and then you can go with the king to the banquet and
enjoy yourself." Haman thought it was a good idea, so he
had the gallows built.

6 That night the Lord kept the king from sleeping, so the
king ordered his private secretary to bring the official
records of the empire and read them to him. 2 He read the
account of how Mordecai had uncovered a plot to assassinate the king—the plot made by the two eunuchs who
served as palace guards. 3 The king asked, "How have we
honored and rewarded Mordecai for this?"

His servants answered, "You have done nothing for him."

4 Now just as the king was inquiring about Mordecai's
good deed, Haman entered the courtyard. He had come to

NEW REVISED STANDARD VERSION

them about his riches and the honor that the king had
bestowed on him, and how he had advanced him to be the
first in the kingdom. 12 And Haman said, "The queen did not
invite anyone to the dinner with the king except me; and I
am invited again tomorrow. 13 But these things give me no
pleasure as long as I see Mordecai the Jew in the courtyard."
14 His wife Zosara and his friends said to him, "Let a gallows
be made, fifty cubits high, and in the morning tell the king to
have Mordecai hanged on it. Then, go merrily with the king
to the dinner." This advice pleased Haman, and so the gallows was prepared.

6 That night the Lord took sleep from the king, so he gave
orders to his secretary to bring the book of daily records,
and to read to him. 2 He found the words written about
Mordecai, how he had told the king about the two royal
eunuchs who were on guard and sought to lay hands on
King Artaxerxes. 3 The king said, "What honor or dignity did
we bestow on Mordecai?" The king's servants said, "You
have not done anything for him." 4 While the king was
inquiring about the goodwill shown by Mordecai, Haman
was in the courtyard. The king asked, "Who is in the courtyard?" Now Haman had come to speak to the king about

NEW AMERICAN BIBLE

recounted the greatness of his riches, the large number of his
sons, and just how the king had promoted him and placed
him above the officials and royal servants. 12 "Moreover,"
Haman added, "Queen Esther invited no one but me to the
banquet with the king; again tomorrow I am to be her guest,
with the king. 13 Yet none of this satisfies me as long as I
continue to see the Jew Mordecai sitting at the royal gate."
14 His wife Zeresh and all his friends said to him, "Have a
gibbet set up, fifty cubits in height, and in the morning ask
the king to have Mordecai hanged on it. Then go to the banquet with the king in good cheer." This suggestion pleased
Haman, and he had the gibbet erected.

6 That night the king, unable to sleep, asked that the
chronicle of notable events be brought in. While this was
being read to him, 2 the passage occurred in which Mordecai
reported Bagathan and Teresh, two of the royal eunuchs who
guarded the entrance, for seeking to lay hands on King
Ahasuerus. 3 The king asked, "What was done to reward and
honor Mordecai for this?" The king's attendants replied,
"Nothing was done for him."

4 "Who is in the court?" the king asked. Now Haman had
entered the outer court of the king's palace to suggest to the

NEW JERUSALEM BIBLE

his dazzling wealth, his many children, how the king had
raised him to a position of honour and promoted him over
the heads of the king's officers-of-state and ministers.
12 'What is more,' he added, 'Queen Esther has just invited
me and the king—no one else except me—to a banquet she
was giving, and better still she has invited me and the king
again tomorrow. 13 But what do I care about all this when
all the while I see Mordecai the Jew sitting there at the
Chancellery?' 14 'Have a fifty-cubit gallows run up,' said
Zeresh his wife and all his friends, 'and in the morning ask
the king to have Mordecai hanged on it. Then you can go
with the king to the banquet, without a care in the world!'
Delighted with this advice, Haman had the gallows erected.

6 That night the king could not sleep; he called for the
Record Book, or Annals, to be brought and read to him.
2 They contained an account of how Mordecai had denounced
Bigthan and Teresh, two of the king's eunuchs serving as
Guards of the Threshold, who had plotted to assassinate
King Ahasuerus. 3 'And what honour and dignity', the king
asked, 'was conferred on Mordecai for this?' 'Nothing has
been done for him,' the gentlemen-in-waiting replied. 4 The
king then said, 'Who is outside in the antechamber?' Haman
had, that very moment, entered the outer antechamber of the

GREEK OLD TESTAMENT

τῷ ξύλῳ, ᾧ ἡτοίμασεν. 5 καὶ εἶπαν οἱ διάκονοι τοῦ βασιλέως
Ἰδοὺ Αμαν ἕστηκεν ἐν τῇ αὐλῇ· καὶ εἶπεν ὁ βασιλεύς Καλέσατε αὐτόν. 6 εἶπεν δὲ ὁ βασιλεὺς τῷ Αμαν Τί ποιήσω τῷ
ἀνθρώπῳ, ὃν ἐγὼ θέλω δοξάσαι; εἶπεν δὲ ἐν ἑαυτῷ Αμαν Τίνα
θέλει ὁ βασιλεὺς δοξάσαι εἰ μὴ ἐμέ; 7 εἶπεν δὲ πρὸς τὸν
βασιλέα Ἄνθρωπον, ὃν ὁ βασιλεὺς θέλει δοξάσαι, 8 ἐνεγκά-
τωσαν οἱ παῖδες τοῦ βασιλέως στολὴν βυσσίνην, ἣν ὁ
βασιλεὺς περιβάλλεται, καὶ ἵππον, ἐφ' ὃν ὁ βασιλεὺς ἐπι-
βαίνει, 9 καὶ δότω ἑνὶ τῶν φίλων τοῦ βασιλέως τῶν ἐνδόξων
καὶ στολισάτω τὸν ἄνθρωπον, ὃν ὁ βασιλεὺς ἀγαπᾷ, καὶ ἀνα-
βιβασάτω αὐτὸν ἐπὶ τὸν ἵππον καὶ κηρυσσέτω διὰ τῆς
πλατείας τῆς πόλεως λέγων Οὕτως ἔσται παντὶ ἀνθρώπῳ, ὃν
ὁ βασιλεὺς δοξάζει. 10 εἶπεν δὲ ὁ βασιλεὺς τῷ Αμαν Καθὼς
ἐλάλησας, οὕτως ποίησον τῷ Μαρδοχαίῳ τῷ Ιουδαίῳ τῷ
θεραπεύοντι ἐν τῇ αὐλῇ, καὶ μὴ παραπεσάτω σου λόγος ὧν
ἐλάλησας. 11 ἔλαβεν δὲ Αμαν τὴν στολὴν καὶ τὸν ἵππον καὶ
ἐστόλισεν τὸν Μαρδοχαῖον καὶ ἀνεβίβασεν αὐτὸν ἐπὶ τὸν
ἵππον καὶ διῆλθεν διὰ τῆς πλατείας τῆς πόλεως καὶ
ἐκήρυσσεν λέγων Οὕτως ἔσται παντὶ ἀνθρώπῳ, ὃν ὁ
βασιλεὺς θέλει δοξάσαι. 12 ἐπέστρεψεν δὲ ὁ Μαρδοχαῖος εἰς
τὴν αὐλήν, Αμαν δὲ ὑπέστρεψεν εἰς τὰ ἴδια λυπούμενος

KING JAMES VERSION

speak unto the king to hang Mordecai on the gallows that he had prepared for him.

5 And the king's servants said unto him, Behold, Haman standeth in the court. And the king said, Let him come in.

6 So Haman came in. And the king said unto him, What shall be done unto the man whom the king delighteth to honour? Now Haman thought in his heart, To whom would the king delight to do honour more than to myself?

7 And Haman answered the king, For the man whom the king delighteth to honour,

8 Let the royal apparel be brought which the king *useth* to wear, and the horse that the king rideth upon, and the crown royal which is set upon his head:

9 And let this apparel and horse be delivered to the hand of one of the king's most noble princes, that they may array the man *withal* whom the king delighteth to honour, and bring him on horseback through the street of the city, and proclaim before him, Thus shall it be done to the man whom the king delighteth to honour.

10 Then the king said to Haman, Make haste, *and* take the apparel and the horse, as thou hast said, and do even so to Mordecai the Jew, that sitteth at the king's gate: let nothing fail of all that thou hast spoken.

11 Then took Haman the apparel and the horse, and arrayed Mordecai, and brought him on horseback through the street of the city, and proclaimed before him, Thus shall it be done unto the man whom the king delighteth to honour.

12 And Mordecai came again to the king's gate. But Haman hasted to his house mourning, and having his head covered.

DOUAY OLD TESTAMENT

to speak to the king, that he might order Mardochai to be hanged upon the gibbet which was prepared for him.

5 The servants answered: Aman standeth in the court, and the king said: Let him come in.

6 And when he was come in, he said to him: What ought to be done to the man whom the king is desirous to honour? But Aman thinking in his heart, and supposing that the king would honour no other but himself,

7 Answered: The man whom the king desireth to honour,

8 Ought to be clothed with the king's apparel, and to be set upon the horse that the king rideth upon, and to have the royal crown upon his head,

9 And let the first of the king's princes and nobles hold his horse, and going through the street of the city, proclaim before him and say: Thus shall he be honoured, whom the king hath a mind to honour.

10 And the king said to him: Make haste and take the robe and the horse, and do as thou hast spoken to Mardochai the Jew, who sitteth before the gates of the palace. Beware thou pass over any of those things which thou hast spoken.

11 So Aman took the robe and the horse, and arraying Mardochai in the street of the city, and setting him on the horse, went before him, and proclaimed: This honour is he worthy of, whom the king hath a mind to honour.

12 But Mardochai returned to the palace gate: and Aman made haste to go to his house, mourning and having his head covered:

KNOX TRANSLATION

Mardochaeus hanged on his gallows; 5 so when they told
him it was Aman, Let him come in, the king said.
6 Aman, said Assuerus, when he came in, what should a
king do, if his heart is set on raising one of his subjects to
great honour? And Aman, casting about in his mind, could
think of no other man that would be so marked out for the
royal favour, but himself. 7 Why, said he, if such a man is to
be honoured indeed, 8 he should be dressed in royal robes,
mounted on the king's own horse, and crowned with the
royal crown; 9 and let him ride through the city streets, with
the noblest of all the king's vassals crying out at his bridle-
rein, So he rides, whom most the king would honour. 10 Lose
no time, then, the king answered; bring robe and horse, and
do as much thyself for the Jew Mardochaeus, that sits there
at the palace gates. And have a care that none of the ceremonies thou speakest of goes unobserved.
11 So Aman must bring robe and horse, must dress
Mardochaeus and mount him, and then go through the city
streets at his bridle-rein, crying out, So he rides, whom most
the king would honour. 12 That done, Mardochaeus went
back to his post at the palace gates, while Aman made the
best of his way home, weeping loud and hiding away his

Today's English Version

ask the king to have Mordecai hanged on the gallows that
was now ready.
"Who is that in the courtyard?" the king asked.
5 The servants answered, "It is Haman; he is waiting to
see you."
"Show him in," said the king.
6 So Haman came in, and the king said to him, "There is
someone I wish very much to honor. What should I do for
this man?"
Haman thought to himself, "Now who could the king want
to honor so much? Me, of course."
7-8 So he answered the king, "Let the royal servants bring a
fine linen robe for this man—one that you yourself wear.
And let them bring a horse that you yourself ride. 9 Then put
that robe on the man you like so much and then have the
nobleman lead him, mounted on the horse, through the city
square. Have the nobleman announce as they go: 'See how
the king rewards a man whom he wishes to honor!' "
10 Then the king said to Haman, "Fine! Do all that for
Mordecai the Jew, who holds a high position in the palace;
don't leave out a thing."
11 So Haman got the robe and the horse, and he put the
robe on Mordecai. Mordecai got on the horse, and Haman led
him through the city square, announcing to the people as
they went: "See how the king rewards a man whom he
wishes to honor!"
12 Mordecai then went back to the courtyard while Haman
hurried home, covering his face in embarrassment. 13 He told

New Revised Standard Version

hanging Mordecai on the gallows that he had prepared.
5 The servants of the king answered, "Haman is standing in
the courtyard." And the king said, "Summon him." 6 Then
the king said to Haman, "What shall I do for the person
whom I wish to honor?" And Haman said to himself, "Whom
would the king wish to honor more than me?" 7 So he said
to the king, "For a person whom the king wishes to honor,
8 let the king's servants bring out the fine linen robe that the
king has worn, and the horse on which the king rides, 9 and
let both be given to one of the king's honored Friends, and
let him robe the person whom the king loves and mount him
on the horse, and let it be proclaimed through the open
square of the city, saying, 'Thus shall it be done to everyone
whom the king honors.' " 10 Then the king said to Haman,
"You have made an excellent suggestion! Do just as you
have said for Mordecai the Jew, who is on duty in the courtyard. And let nothing be omitted from what you have proposed." 11 So Haman got the robe and the horse; he put the
robe on Mordecai and made him ride through the open
square of the city, proclaiming, "Thus shall it be done to
everyone whom the king wishes to honor." 12 Then Mordecai
returned to the courtyard, and Haman hurried back to his
house, mourning and with his head covered. 13 Haman told

New American Bible

king that Mordecai should be hanged on the gibbet he had
raised for him. 5 The king's servants answered him, "Haman
is waiting in the court." "Let him come in," the king said.
6 When Haman entered, the king said to him, "What should
be done for the man whom the king wishes to reward?" Now
Haman thought to himself, "Whom would the king more
probably wish to reward than me?" 7 So he replied to the
king: "For the man whom the king wishes to reward 8 there
should be brought the royal robe which the king wore and
the horse on which the king rode when the royal crown was
placed on his head. 9 The robe and the horse should be consigned to one of the noblest of the king's officials, who must
clothe the man the king wishes to reward, have him ride on
the horse in the public square of the city, and cry out before
him, 'This is what is done for the man whom the king
wishes to reward.' " 10 Then the king said to Haman:
"Hurry! Take the robe and horse as you have proposed, and
do this for the Jew Mordecai, who is sitting at the royal gate.
Do not omit anything you proposed." 11 So Haman took the
robe and horse, clothed Mordecai, had him ride in the public
square of the city, and cried out before him, "This is what is
done for the man whom the king wishes to reward."
12 Mordecai then returned to the royal gate, while Haman
hurried home, his head covered in grief. 13 When he told his

New Jerusalem Bible

private apartments, to ask the king to have Mordecai hanged
on the gallows which he had just put up for the purpose.
5 So the king's gentlemen-in-waiting replied, 'It is Haman out
in the antechamber.' 'Bring him in,' the king said, 6 and, as
soon as Haman came in, went on to ask, 'What is the right
way to treat a man whom the king wishes to honour?'
'Whom', thought Haman, 'would the king wish to honour, if
not me?' 7 So he replied, 'If the king wishes to honour someone, 8 royal robes should be brought from the king's
wardrobe, and a horse from the king's stable, sporting a
royal diadem on its head. 9 The robes and horse should be
entrusted to one of the noblest of the king's officers-of-state,
who should then array the man whom the king wishes to
honour and lead him on horseback through the city square,
proclaiming before him: "This is the way a man shall be
treated whom the king wishes to honour." ' 10 'Hurry,' the
king said to Haman, 'take the robes and the horse, and do
everything you have just said to Mordecai the Jew, who
works at the Chancellery. On no account leave out anything
that you have mentioned.'
11 So taking the robes and the horse, Haman arrayed
Mordecai and led him on horseback through the city square,
proclaiming before him: 'This is the way a man shall be
treated whom the king wishes to honour.' 12 After this
Mordecai returned to the Chancellery, while Haman went
hurrying home in dejection and covering his face. 13 He told

GREEK OLD TESTAMENT

κατὰ κεφαλῆς. 13 καὶ διηγήσατο Αμαν τὰ συμβεβηκότα
αὐτῷ Ζωσαρα τῇ γυναικὶ αὐτοῦ καὶ τοῖς φίλοις, καὶ εἶπαν
πρὸς αὐτὸν οἱ φίλοι καὶ ἡ γυνή Εἰ ἐκ γένους Ιουδαίων Μαρδοχαῖος, ἦρξαι ταπεινοῦσθαι ἐνώπιον αὐτοῦ, πεσὼν πεσῇ· οὐ
μὴ δύνῃ αὐτὸν ἀμύνασθαι, ὅτι θεὸς ζῶν μετ' αὐτοῦ. — 14 ἔτι
αὐτῶν λαλούντων παραγίνονται οἱ εὐνοῦχοι ἐπισπεύδοντες
τὸν Αμαν ἐπὶ τὸν πότον, ὃν ἡτοίμασεν Εσθηρ.

7 Εἰσῆλθεν δὲ ὁ βασιλεὺς καὶ Αμαν συμπιεῖν τῇ βασιλίσσῃ. 2 εἶπεν δὲ ὁ βασιλεὺς Εσθηρ τῇ δευτέρᾳ ἡμέρᾳ
ἐν τῷ πότῳ Τί ἐστιν, Εσθηρ βασίλισσα, καὶ τί τὸ αἴτημά σου
καὶ τί τὸ ἀξίωμά σου; καὶ ἔστω σοι ἕως τοῦ ἡμίσους τῆς
βασιλείας μου. 3 καὶ ἀποκριθεῖσα εἶπεν Εἰ εὗρον χάριν ἐνώπιον τοῦ βασιλέως, δοθήτω ἡ ψυχή μου τῷ αἰτήματί μου καὶ
ὁ λαός μου τῷ ἀξιώματί μου· 4 ἐπράθημεν γὰρ ἐγώ τε καὶ ὁ
λαός μου εἰς ἀπώλειαν καὶ διαρπαγὴν καὶ δουλείαν, ἡμεῖς
καὶ τὰ τέκνα ἡμῶν εἰς παῖδας καὶ παιδίσκας, καὶ παρή-
κουσα· οὐ γὰρ ἄξιος ὁ διάβολος τῆς αὐλῆς τοῦ βασιλέως.
5 εἶπεν δὲ ὁ βασιλεύς Τίς οὗτος, ὅστις ἐτόλμησεν ποιῆσαι
τὸ πρᾶγμα τοῦτο; 6 εἶπεν δὲ Εσθηρ Ἄνθρωπος ἐχθρὸς Αμαν
ὁ πονηρὸς οὗτος. Αμαν δὲ ἐταράχθη ἀπὸ τοῦ βασιλέως καὶ
τῆς βασιλίσσης. 7 ὁ δὲ βασιλεὺς ἐξανέστη ἐκ τοῦ συμποσίου

KING JAMES VERSION

13 And Haman told Zeresh his wife and all his friends every *thing* that had befallen him. Then said his wise men and Zeresh his wife unto him, If Mordecai *be* of the seed of the Jews, before whom thou hast begun to fall, thou shalt not prevail against him, but shalt surely fall before him.

14 And while they *were* yet talking with him, came the king's chamberlains, and hasted to bring Haman unto the banquet that Esther had prepared.

7 So the king and Haman came to banquet with Esther the queen.

2 And the king said again unto Esther on the second day at the banquet of wine, What *is* thy petition, queen Esther? and it shall be granted thee: and what *is* thy request? and it shall be performed, *even* to the half of the kingdom.

3 Then Esther the queen answered and said, If I have found favour in thy sight, O king, and if it please the king, let my life be given me at my petition, and my people at my request:

4 For we are sold, I and my people, to be destroyed, to be slain, and to perish. But if we had been sold for bondmen and bondwomen, I had held my tongue, although the enemy could not countervail the king's damage.

5 Then the king Ahasuerus answered and said unto Esther the queen, Who is he, and where is he, that durst presume in his heart to do so?

6 And Esther said, The adversary and enemy *is* this wicked Haman. Then Haman was afraid before the king and the queen.

7 And the king arising from the banquet of wine in his

DOUAY OLD TESTAMENT

13 And he told Zares his wife, and his friends, all that had befallen him. And the wise men whom he had in counsel, and his wife answered him: If Mardochai be of the seed of the Jews, before whom thou hast begun to fall, thou canst not resist him, but thou shalt fall in his sight.

14 As they were yet speaking, the king's eunuchs came, and compelled him to go quickly to the banquet which the queen had prepared.

7 SO the king and Aman went in, to drink with the queen.

2 And the king said to her again the second day, after he was warm with wine: What is thy petition, Esther, that it may be granted thee? and what wilt thou have done: although thou ask the half of my kingdom, thou shalt have it.

3 Then she answered: If I have found favour in thy sight, O king, and if it please thee, give me my life for which I ask, and my people for which I request.

4 For we are given up, I and my people, to be destroyed, to be slain, and to perish. And would God we were sold for bondmen and bondwomen: the evil might be borne with, and I would have mourned in silence: but now we have an enemy, whose cruelty redoundeth upon the king.

5 And king Assuerus answered and said: Who is this, and of what power, that he should do these things?

6 And Esther said: It is this Aman that is our adversary and most wicked enemy. Aman hearing this was forthwith astonished, not being able to bear the countenance of the king and of the queen.

7 But the king being angry rose up, and went from the

KNOX TRANSLATION

head. 13 To his wife Zares and to all his friends he told the
story of what befell; but from wife and counsellors he could
get no comfort. If he is of the Jewish race,[a] they said, this
Mardochaeus who has begun to outmatch thee, thou wilt
never get the better of him; yield to him thou must. 14 And
even as they spoke, in came the royal chamberlains, and
hurried him off to the feast the queen had prepared for him.

7 So met they once again, the king and Aman, over the
queen's wine. 2 And once again, his heart warmed by
drinking, Assuerus would know what Esther's mind might
be; what was it she would have? Half of his kingdom should
be hers for the asking. 3 My lord king, she said, if this is
indeed thy gracious pleasure, one gift I would ask, my life;
one boon, the preservation of my people. 4 Must we be
crushed to nothing, I and my people; must we perish by massacre? To that we are doomed. If we were only marked down
for slaves and bondwomen, our lot should be bravely borne;
I would have nursed my grief in silence. But here is an
enemy whose cruel designs concern the king's grace. 5 Who
is this man? Assuerus asked. Where is the insolence to be
found that would make such an attempt as this? 6 One
enemy we have, said Esther, one schemer's malice we fear,
and he is here in thy presence; Aman.

Upon hearing this, Aman was struck dumb, and could look
neither king nor queen in the eyes. 7 The king rose angrily

a This is generally interpreted as an allusion to the divine protection enjoyed by the Jewish people. But we should have expected to find such an argument supported by reference to the events of Jewish history (cf. Judith 5. 6-25); and it is perhaps only a hostile reference to the Jews, implying that if once they rise to power they are careful not to lose it.

TODAY'S ENGLISH VERSION

his wife and all his friends everything that had happened to
him. Then they all said to him, "You are beginning to lose
power to Mordecai. He is a Jew, and you cannot overcome
him. He will certainly defeat you, for the living God is
with him!"
14 While they were still talking, the palace eunuchs arrived
to take Haman to Esther's banquet.

7 And so the king and Haman went to eat with Esther
2 for a second time. Over the wine the king asked her
again, "Now, Queen Esther, what do you want? Tell me and
you shall have it. I'll even give you half the empire."
3 Queen Esther answered, "If it please Your Majesty to
grant my humble request, my wish is that I may live and
that my people may live. 4 My people and I have been sold
into slavery; our possessions have been plundered, and now
we are to be destroyed—all of us, including our children, will
be slaves—and so far I have kept quiet. It isn't right that our
enemy should be a member of the royal court."
5 Then King Xerxes asked Esther, "Who dares to do such a
thing?"
6 Esther answered, "Our enemy is this evil man Haman!"
In terror Haman faced the king and queen. 7 The king got

NEW REVISED STANDARD VERSION

his wife Zosara and his friends what had befallen him. His
friends and his wife said to him, "If Mordecai is of the Jewish
people, and you have begun to be humiliated before him, you
will surely fall. You will not be able to defend yourself,
because the living God is with him."
14 While they were still talking, the eunuchs arrived and
hurriedly brought Haman to the banquet that Esther had

7 prepared. 1 So the king and Haman went in to drink
with the queen. 2 And the second day, as they were
drinking wine, the king said, "What is it, Queen Esther?
What is your petition and what is your request? It shall be
granted to you, even to half of my kingdom." 3 She
answered and said, "If I have found favor with the king, let
my life be granted me at my petition, and my people at my
request. 4 For we have been sold, I and my people, to be
destroyed, plundered, and made slaves—we and our children—male and female slaves. This has come to my knowledge. Our antagonist brings shame on[a] the king's court."
5 Then the king said, "Who is the person that would dare to
do this thing?" 6 Esther said, "Our enemy is this evil man
Haman!" At this, Haman was terrified in the presence of the
king and queen.
7 The king rose from the banquet and went into the

a Gk *is not worthy of*

NEW AMERICAN BIBLE

wife Zeresh and all his friends everything that had happened
to him, his advisers and his wife Zeresh said to him, "If
Mordecai, before whom you are beginning to decline, is of
the Jewish race, you will not prevail against him, but will
surely be defeated by him."
14 While they were speaking with him, the king's eunuchs
arrived and hurried Haman off to the banquet Esther had
prepared.

7 So the king of Haman went to the banquet with Queen
Esther. 2 Again, on this second day, during the drinking
of the wine, the king said to Esther, "Whatever you ask,
Queen Esther, shall be granted you. Whatever request you
make shall be honored, even for half the kingdom." 3 Queen
Esther replied: "If I have found favor with you, O king, and if
it pleases your majesty, I ask that my life be spared, and I
beg that you spare the lives of my people. 4 For my people
and I have been delivered to destruction, slaughter, and
extinction. If we were to be sold into slavery I would remain
silent, but as it is, the enemy will be unable to compensate
for the harm done to the king." 5 "Who and where," said
King Ahasuerus to Queen Esther, "is the man who has dared
to do this?" 6 Esther replied, "The enemy oppressing us is
this wicked Haman." At this, Haman was seized with dread
of the king and queen.
7 The king left the banquet in anger and went into the

NEW JERUSALEM BIBLE

his wife Zeresh and all his friends what had just happened.
His wife Zeresh and his friends said, 'You are beginning to
fall, and Mordecai to rise; if he is Jewish, you will never get
the better of him. With him against you, your fall is certain.'
14 While they were still talking, the king's officers arrived
in a hurry to escort Haman to the banquet that Esther was
giving.

7 The king and Haman went to Queen Esther's banquet,
2 and this second day, during the banquet, the king
again said to Esther, 'Tell me your request, Queen Esther. I
grant it to you. Whatever you want; even if it is half my
kingdom, it is yours for the asking.' 3 'If I have found favour
in your eyes, O king,' Queen Esther replied, 'and if it please
your majesty, grant me my life—that is my request; and the
lives of my people—that is what I want. 4 For we have been
handed over, my people and I, to destruction, slaughter and
annihilation; had we merely been sold as slaves and servant-
girls, I should not have said anything; but in the present
case, it will be beyond the persecutor's means to make good
the loss that the king is about to sustain.' 5 King Ahasuerus
interrupted Queen Esther, 'Who is this man?' he exclaimed.
'Where is the man who has thought of doing such a thing?'
6 Esther replied, 'The persecutor, the enemy? Why, this
wretch Haman!' Haman quaked with terror in the presence
of the king and queen. 7 In a rage the king got up from the

GREEK OLD TESTAMENT

εἰς τὸν κῆπον· ὁ δὲ Αμαν παρῃτεῖτο τὴν βασίλισσαν, ἑώρα γὰρ ἑαυτὸν ἐν κακοῖς ὄντα. 8 ἐπέστρεψεν δὲ ὁ βασιλεὺς ἐκ τοῦ κήπου, Αμαν δὲ ἐπιπεπτώκει ἐπὶ τὴν κλίνην ἀξιῶν τὴν βασίλισσαν· εἶπεν δὲ ὁ βασιλεύς Ὥστε καὶ τὴν γυναῖκα βιάζῃ ἐν τῇ οἰκίᾳ μου; Αμαν δὲ ἀκούσας διετράπη τῷ προσώπῳ. 9 εἶπεν δὲ Βουγαθαν εἷς τῶν εὐνούχων πρὸς τὸν βασιλέα Ἰδοὺ καὶ ξύλον ἡτοίμασεν Αμαν Μαρδοχαίῳ τῷ λαλήσαντι περὶ τοῦ βασιλέως, καὶ ὤρθωται ἐν τοῖς Αμαν ξύλον πηχῶν πεντήκοντα. εἶπεν δὲ ὁ βασιλεὺς Σταυρωθήτω ἐπ' αὐτοῦ. 10 καὶ ἐκρεμάσθη Αμαν ἐπὶ τοῦ ξύλου, ὃ ἡτοίμασεν Μαρδοχαίῳ. καὶ τότε ὁ βασιλεὺς ἐκόπασεν τοῦ θυμοῦ.

8 Καὶ ἐν αὐτῇ τῇ ἡμέρᾳ ὁ βασιλεὺς Ἀρταξέρξης ἐδωρήσατο Εσθηρ ὅσα ὑπῆρχεν Αμαν τῷ διαβόλῳ, καὶ Μαρδοχαῖος προσεκλήθη ὑπὸ τοῦ βασιλέως, ὑπέδειξεν γὰρ Εσθηρ ὅτι ἐνοικείωται αὐτῇ. 2 ἔλαβεν δὲ ὁ βασιλεὺς τὸν δακτύλιον, ὃν ἀφείλατο Αμαν, καὶ ἔδωκεν αὐτὸν Μαρδοχαίῳ, καὶ κατέστησεν Εσθηρ Μαρδοχαῖον ἐπὶ πάντων τῶν Αμαν. 3 καὶ προσθεῖσα ἐλάλησεν πρὸς τὸν βασιλέα καὶ προσέπεσεν πρὸς τοὺς πόδας αὐτοῦ καὶ ἠξίου ἀφελεῖν τὴν Αμαν κακίαν καὶ ὅσα ἐποίησεν τοῖς Ιουδαίοις. 4 ἐξέτεινεν δὲ ὁ βασιλεὺς

KING JAMES VERSION

wrath *went* into the palace garden: and Haman stood up to make request for his life to Esther the queen; for he saw that there was evil determined against him by the king.

8 Then the king returned out of the palace garden into the place of the banquet of wine; and Haman was fallen upon the bed whereon Esther *was*. Then said the king, Will he force the queen also before me in the house? As the word went out of the king's mouth, they covered Haman's face.

9 And Harbonah, one of the chamberlains, said before the king, Behold also, the gallows fifty cubits high, which Haman had made for Mordecai, who had spoken good for the king, standeth in the house of Haman. Then the king said, Hang him thereon.

10 So they hanged Haman on the gallows that he had prepared for Mordecai. Then was the king's wrath pacified.

8 On that day did the king Ahasuerus give the house of Haman the Jews' enemy unto Esther the queen. And Mordecai came before the king; for Esther had told what he *was* unto her.

2 And the king took off his ring, which he had taken from Haman, and gave it unto Mordecai. And Esther set Mordecai over the house of Haman.

3 And Esther spake yet again before the king, and fell down at his feet, and besought him with tears to put away the mischief of Haman the Agagite, and his device that he had devised against the Jews.

DOUAY OLD TESTAMENT

place of the banquet into the garden set with trees. Aman also rose up to entreat Esther the queen for his life, for he understood that evil was prepared for him by the king.

8 And when the king came back out of the garden set with trees, and entered into the place of the banquet, he found Aman was fallen upon the bed on which Esther lay, and he said: He will force the queen also in my presence, in my own house. The word was not yet gone out of the king's mouth, and immediately they covered his face.

9 And Harbona, one of the eunuchs that stood waiting on the king, said: Behold the gibbet which he hath prepared for Mardochai, who spoke for the king, standeth in Aman's house, being fifty cubits high. And the king said to him: Hang him upon it.

10 So Aman was hanged on the gibbet, which he had prepared for Mardochai: and the king's wrath ceased.

8 ON that day king Assuerus gave the house of Aman, the Jews' enemy, to queen Esther, and Mardochai came in before the king. For Esther had confessed to him that he was her uncle.

2 And the king took the ring which he had commanded to be taken again from Aman, and gave it to Mardochai. And Esther set Mardochai over her house.

3 And not content with these things, she fell down at the king's feet and wept, and speaking to him besought him, that he would give orders that the malice of Aman the Agagite, and his most wicked devices which he had invented against the Jews, should be of no effect.

KNOX TRANSLATION

from his place, left the banqueting-room, and went out to walk in the garden, among his trees. With that, Aman rose too, intent on winning his pardon from queen Esther; doubt he might not that the king was bent on his undoing. 8 Thus minded, he fell sprawling across the couch on which Esther lay; and so the king found him, when he returned from garden to banqueting-room. What, cried he, will he ravish the queen before my eyes, and in my own house? And before the words were out of his mouth Aman was gagged and blindfold.

9 And now Harbona, one of the chamberlains in attendance on the king's person, came forward; What of the gallows, said he, fifty cubits high, that stands there by Aman's house, ready for Mardochaeus, that saved the king's life?[a] Let Aman himself hang on it, said the king. 10 So Aman was hanged on the gallows he had raised for Mardochaeus; and with that, the king's angry mood was appeased.

8 That same day, Assuerus made a present to Esther of Aman's house, that was the Jews' enemy, and gave audience to Mardochaeus; for now Esther had told him that this was her uncle. 2 He took back, too, the ring he had bade Aman wear, and gave it to Mardochaeus instead; and Mardochaeus was given charge of Esther's house. 3 Nor would Esther be content, till she had fallen weeping at the king's feet and prayed him to prevent the mischief Aman had thought to do by his false plotting against the Jews. 4 The golden sceptre

a Literally, 'spoke good for the king', that is, gave useful information.

TODAY'S ENGLISH VERSION

up from the table and went outside to the palace gardens.
Haman could see that he was in a dangerous situation, so he
stayed behind to beg Queen Esther for his life. 8He had just
thrown himself down on Esther's couch to beg for mercy,
when the king came back into the room from the gardens.
Seeing this, the king cried out, "Are you going to rape my
wife here in my own palace?"

When Haman heard this, he turned away in despair.
9Then one of the eunuchs, whose name was Bougathan,
said, "Haman has even gone so far as to build a gallows at
his house so that he can hang Mordecai, who warned Your
Majesty about the plot. And it's seventy-five feet high!"

"Hang Haman on it!" the king commanded.

10So Haman was hanged on the gallows that he had built
for Mordecai. Then the king's anger cooled down.

8 That same day King Xerxes gave Queen Esther all the
property of Haman, the enemy of the Jews. Esther told
the king that Mordecai was related to her, and Mordecai was
invited to enter the king's presence. 2The king took off his
ring with his seal on it (which he had taken back from
Haman) and gave it to Mordecai. Esther put Mordecai in
charge of Haman's property.

3Then Esther spoke to the king again, throwing herself at
his feet. She begged him to do something to stop the evil plot
that Haman had made against the Jews. 4The king held out

NEW REVISED STANDARD VERSION

garden, and Haman began to beg for his life from the queen,
for he saw that he was in serious trouble. 8When the king
returned from the garden, Haman had thrown himself on the
couch, pleading with the queen. The king said, "Will he dare
even assault my wife in my own house?" Haman, when he
heard, turned away his face. 9Then Bugathan, one of the
eunuchs, said to the king, "Look, Haman has even prepared
a gallows for Mordecai, who gave information of concern to
the king; it is standing at Haman's house, a gallows fifty
cubits high." So the king said, "Let Haman be hanged on
that." 10So Haman was hanged on the gallows he had prepared for Mordecai. With that the anger of the king abated.

8 On that very day King Artaxerxes granted to Esther all
the property of the persecutor[a] Haman. Mordecai was
summoned by the king, for Esther had told the king[b] that he
was related to her. 2The king took the ring that had been
taken from Haman, and gave it to Mordecai; and Esther set
Mordecai over everything that had been Haman's.

3 Then she spoke once again to the king and, falling at
his feet, she asked him to avert all the evil that Haman had
planned against the Jews. 4The king extended his golden

a Gk *slanderer* *b* Gk *him*

NEW AMERICAN BIBLE

garden of the palace, but Haman stayed to beg Queen Esther
for his life, since he saw that the king had decided on his
doom. 8When the king returned from the garden of the
palace to the banquet hall, Haman had thrown himself on
the couch on which Esther was reclining; and the king
exclaimed, "Will he also violate the queen while she is with
me in my own house!" Scarcely had the king spoken, when
the face of Haman was covered over.

9Harbona, one of the eunuchs who attended the king,
said, "At the house of Haman stands a gibbet fifty cubits
high. Haman prepared it for Mordecai, who gave the report
that benefited the king." The king answered, "Hang him on
it." 10So they hanged Haman on the gibbet which he had
made ready for Mordecai, and the anger of the king abated.

8 That day King Ahasuerus gave the house of Haman,
enemy of the Jews, to Queen Esther; and Mordecai was
admitted to the king's presence, for Esther had revealed his
relationship to her. 2The king removed his signet ring from
Haman, and transferred it into the keeping of Mordecai; and
Esther put Mordecai in charge of the house of Haman.

3In another audience with the king, Esther fell at his feet
and tearfully implored him to revoke the harm done by
Haman the Agagite, and the plan he had devised against the

NEW JERUSALEM BIBLE

banquet and went into the palace garden; while Haman,
realising that the king was determined on his ruin, stayed
behind to beg Queen Esther for his life.

8When the king came back from the palace garden into the
banqueting hall, he found Haman sprawled across the couch
where Esther was reclining. 'What!' the king exclaimed. 'Is
he going to rape the queen in my own palace?' The words
were scarcely out of his mouth than a veil was thrown over
Haman's face. 9In the royal presence, Harbona, one of the
officers, said, 'There is that fifty-cubit gallows, too, which
Haman ran up for Mordecai, who spoke up to the king's
great advantage. It is all ready at his house.' 'Hang him on
it,' said the king. 10So Haman was hanged on the gallows
which he had erected for Mordecai, and the king's wrath subsided.

8 That same day King Ahasuerus gave Queen Esther the
house of Haman, the persecutor of the Jews. Mordecai
was presented to the king, Esther having revealed their
mutual relationship. 2The king, who had recovered his
signet ring from Haman, took it off and gave it to Mordecai,
while Esther gave Mordecai charge of Haman's house.

3Esther again went to speak to the king. She fell at his
feet, weeping and imploring his favour, to frustrate the malice that Haman the Agagite had been plotting against the

Greek Old Testament

Εσθηρ τὴν ῥάβδον τὴν χρυσῆν, ἐξηγέρθη δὲ Εσθηρ παρεστη-
κέναι τῷ βασιλεῖ. 5 καὶ εἶπεν Εσθηρ Εἰ δοκεῖ σοι καὶ εὗρον
χάριν, πεμφθήτω ἀποστραφῆναι τὰ γράμματα τὰ ἀπεσταλμένα ὑπὸ Αμαν τὰ γραφέντα ἀπολέσθαι τοὺς Ιουδαίους, οἵ
εἰσιν ἐν τῇ βασιλείᾳ σου· 6 πῶς γὰρ δυνήσομαι ἰδεῖν τὴν
κάκωσιν τοῦ λαοῦ μου καὶ πῶς δυνήσομαι σωθῆναι ἐν τῇ
ἀπωλείᾳ τῆς πατρίδος μου; 7 καὶ εἶπεν ὁ βασιλεὺς πρὸς
Εσθηρ Εἰ πάντα τὰ ὑπάρχοντα Αμαν ἔδωκα καὶ ἐχαρισάμην
σοι καὶ αὐτὸν ἐκρέμασα ἐπὶ ξύλου, ὅτι τὰς χεῖρας ἐπήνεγκε
τοῖς Ιουδαίοις, τί ἔτι ἐπιζητεῖς; 8 γράψατε καὶ ὑμεῖς ἐκ
τοῦ ὀνόματός μου ὡς δοκεῖ ὑμῖν καὶ σφραγίσατε τῷ δακτυλίῳ μου· ὅσα γὰρ γράφεται τοῦ βασιλέως ἐπιτάξαντος καὶ
σφραγισθῇ τῷ δακτυλίῳ μου, οὐκ ἔστιν αὐτοῖς ἀντειπεῖν.
9 ἐκλήθησαν δὲ οἱ γραμματεῖς ἐν τῷ πρώτῳ μηνί, ὅς ἐστι
Νισα, τρίτῃ καὶ εἰκάδι τοῦ αὐτοῦ ἔτους, καὶ ἐγράφη τοῖς
Ιουδαίοις ὅσα ἐνετείλατο τοῖς οἰκονόμοις καὶ τοῖς ἄρχουσιν

King James Version

4 Then the king held out the golden sceptre toward Esther. So Esther arose, and stood before the king,

5 And said, If it please the king, and if I have found favour in his sight, and the thing *seem* right before the king, and I *be* pleasing in his eyes, let it be written to reverse the letters devised by Haman the son of Hammedatha the Agagite, which he wrote to destroy the Jews which *are* in all the king's provinces:

6 For how can I endure to see the evil that shall come unto my people? or how can I endure to see the destruction of my kindred?

7 Then the king Ahasuerus said unto Esther the queen and to Mordecai the Jew, Behold, I have given Esther the house of Haman, and him they have hanged upon the gallows, because he laid his hand upon the Jews.

8 Write ye also for the Jews, as it liketh you, in the king's name, and seal *it* with the king's ring: for the writing which is written in the king's name, and sealed with the king's ring, may no man reverse.

9 Then were the king's scribes called at that time in the third month, that *is,* the month Sivan, on the three and twentieth *day* thereof; and it was written according to all that Mordecai commanded unto the Jews, and to the lieutenants,

Douay Old Testament

4 But he, as the manner was, held out the golden sceptre with his hand, which was the sign of clemency: and she arose up and stood before him,

5 And said: If it please the king, and if I have found favour in his sight, and my request be not disagreeable to him, I beseech thee, that the former letters of Aman the traitor and enemy of the Jews, by which he commanded that they should be destroyed in all the king's provinces, may be reversed by new letters.

6 For how can I endure the murdering and slaughter of my people?

7 And king Assuerus answered Esther the queen, and Mardochai the Jew: I have given Aman's house to Esther, and I have commanded him to be hanged on a gibbet, because he durst lay hands on the Jews.

8 Write ye therefore to the Jews, as it pleaseth you, in the king's name, and seal the letters with my ring. For this was the custom, that no man durst gainsay the letters which were sent in the king's name, and were sealed with his ring.

9 Then the king's scribes and secretaries were called for (now it was the time of the third month which is called Siban) the three and twentieth day of the month, and letters were written, as Mardochai had a mind, to the Jews, and to

Knox Translation

was held out, in sign of the royal favour, and she rose to her
feet and stood fronting him. 5 Please it the king's grace, she
said, to look favourably on my suit, and find nothing in it to
his disadvantage. I would have new dispatches sent out, to
revoke the order made by Aman, our crafty enemy, for the
slaying of the Jews in all thy domains. 6 How can I bear to see
my own people exterminated by massacre? 7 Nay, said the
king to Esther and Mardochaeus; Aman's house I have granted to Esther, and Aman himself I have sent to the gallows, for
daring to lift his hand against the Jews. 8 But letters sent in
the king's name and signed with his ring, by the custom of the
realm, none must ever revoke.[a] Write rather in my name,
under the royal seal, orders for the Jewish people to obey, in
whatever sense likes you best.
9 So, on the twenty-third day of the third month, Siban,
they summoned notary and scribe of the royal household,
and at Mardochaeus' bidding they issued orders to the Jewish
people. Letters were sent to all the chieftains, governors and

a The Greek and Latin versions have 'withstand' instead of 'revoke' (the same Hebrew word is used here as in verse 5). This obscures what seems to be the point of the whole passage. Although Aman is dead, the royal edict sent out by him cannot, according to the law of the Medes and Persians, be revoked (1. 19 above). Assuerus is in the same difficulty as Darius in Daniel 6. 15. He therefore tells Mardochaeus and Esther, not to rescind the existing decree, but to frame another, *addressed to the Jews,* which will have the effect of thwarting it. Their letter calls on the Jews to arm against the Gentiles, as Aman's decree had, in effect, called on the Gentiles to arm against the Jews (3. 13). While, therefore, the action of the Jews on the thirteenth of Adar can be represented as an act of vengeance (verses 12 and 13), it also was an act of self-defence (verse 11); if they had not armed, their enemies would have instituted a successful pogrom under the (still unrepealed) edict of Aman.

TODAY'S ENGLISH VERSION

the gold scepter to her, so she stood up 5and said, "If it
please Your Majesty and if you care about me, please issue a
proclamation to keep Haman's orders from being carried
out—those orders he gave for the destruction of all the Jews
in the empire. 6How can I endure it if this disaster comes on
my people? How can I go on living if my whole nation is
destroyed?"

7Then the king said to Esther, "I have hanged Haman for
his plot against the Jews, and I have given you his property.
If that is not enough, 8you may write to the Jews whatever
you like; and you may write it in my name and stamp it with
the royal seal, for a proclamation issued in the king's name
and stamped with the royal seal cannot be revoked."

9On the twenty-third day of the first month, the month of
Nisan, the king's secretaries were called and letters were
written to the Jews and to the governors and administrators

NEW REVISED STANDARD VERSION

scepter to Esther, and she rose and stood before the king.
5Esther said, "If it pleases you, and if I have found favor, let
an order be sent rescinding the letters that Haman wrote and
sent to destroy the Jews in your kingdom. 6How can I look
on the ruin of my people? How can I be safe if my ancestral
nation[a] is destroyed?" 7The king said to Esther, "Now that
I[b] have granted all of Haman's property to you and have
hanged him on a tree because he acted against the Jews,
what else do you request? 8Write in my name what you
think best and seal it with my ring; for whatever is written at
the king's command and sealed with my ring cannot be con-
travened."

9 The secretaries were summoned on the twenty-third day
of the first month, that is, Nisan, in the same year; and all
that he commanded with respect to the Jews was given in
writing to the administrators and governors of the provinces

a Gk *country* *b* Gk *If I*

NEW AMERICAN BIBLE

Jews. 4The king stretched forth the golden scepter to Esther.
So she rose and, standing in his presence, 5said: "If it
pleases your majesty and seems proper to you, and if I have
found favor with you and you love me, let a document be
issued to revoke the letters which that schemer Haman, son
of Hammedatha the Agagite, wrote for the destruction of the
Jews in all the royal provinces. 6For how can I witness the
evil that is to befall my people, and how can I behold the
destruction of my race?"

7King Ahasuerus then said to Queen Esther and to the Jew
Mordecai: "Now that I have given Esther the house of
Haman, and they have hanged him on the gibbet because he
attacked the Jews, 8you in turn may write in the king's
name what you see fit concerning the Jews and seal the letter
with the royal signet ring." For whatever is written in the
name of the king and sealed with the royal signet ring cannot be revoked.

9At that time, on the twenty-third day of the third month,
Sivan, the royal scribes were summoned. Exactly as
Mordecai dictated, they wrote to the Jews and to the satraps,

NEW JERUSALEM BIBLE

Jews. 4The king held out the golden sceptre to her, whereupon Esther stood up and faced him. 5'If such is the king's
good pleasure,' she said, 'and if I have found favour before
him, if my petition seems proper to him and if I myself am
pleasing to his eyes, may he be pleased to issue a written
revocation of the letters which Haman son of Hammedatha,
the Agagite, has had written, ordering the destruction of the
Jews throughout the royal provinces. 6For how can I look
on, while my people suffer what is proposed for them? How
can I bear to witness the extermination of my relatives?'

7King Ahasuerus said to Queen Esther and to Mordecai the
Jew, 'I for my part have given Esther Haman's house, and
have had him hanged on the gallows for planning to destroy
the Jews. 8You, for your part, write what you please as
regards the Jews, in the king's name, and seal it with the
king's signet; for any edict written in the king's name and
sealed with his signet is irrevocable.' 9The royal scribes were
summoned at once—it was the third month, the month of
Sivan, on the twenty-third day—and at Mordecai's dictation
an order was written to the Jews, the satraps, governors and

GREEK OLD TESTAMENT

τῶν σατραπῶν ἀπὸ τῆς Ἰνδικῆς ἕως τῆς Αἰθιοπίας, ἑκατὸν εἴκοσι ἑπτὰ σατραπείαις κατὰ χώραν καὶ χώραν, κατὰ τὴν ἑαυτῶν λέξιν. 10 ἐγράφη δὲ διὰ τοῦ βασιλέως καὶ ἐσφραγίσθη τῷ δακτυλίῳ αὐτοῦ, καὶ ἐξαπέστειλαν τὰ γράμματα διὰ βιβλιαφόρων, 11 ὡς ἐπέταξεν αὐτοῖς χρῆσθαι τοῖς νόμοις αὐτῶν ἐν πάσῃ πόλει βοηθῆσαί τε αὐτοῖς καὶ χρῆσθαι τοῖς ἀντιδίκοις αὐτῶν καὶ τοῖς ἀντικειμένοις αὐτῶν ὡς βούλονται, 12 ἐν ἡμέρᾳ μιᾷ ἐν πάσῃ τῇ βασιλείᾳ Ἀρταξέρξου, τῇ τρισκαιδεκάτῃ τοῦ δωδεκάτου μηνός, ὅς ἐστιν Αδαρ.

12a Ὧν ἐστιν ἀντίγραφον τῆς ἐπιστολῆς τὰ ὑπογεγραμμένα 12b μέγας Ἀρταξέρξης τοῖς ἀπὸ τῆς Ἰνδικῆς ἕως τῆς Αἰθιοπίας ἑκατὸν εἴκοσι ἑπτὰ σατραπείαις χωρῶν ἄρχουσι καὶ τοῖς τὰ ἡμέτερα φρονοῦσι χαίρειν. 12c τῇ πλείστῃ τῶν εὐεργετούντων χρηστότητι πυκνότερον τιμώμενοι μεῖζον ἐφρόνησαν καὶ οὐ μόνον τοὺς ὑποτεταγμένους ἡμῖν ζητοῦσι κακοποιεῖν, τόν τε κόρον οὐ δυνάμενοι φέρειν καὶ τοῖς ἑαυτῶν εὐεργέταις ἐπιχειροῦσι μηχανᾶσθαι· 12d τὴν εὐχαριστίαν οὐ μόνον ἐκ τῶν ἀνθρώπων ἀνταναιροῦντες, ἀλλὰ καὶ τοῖς τῶν ἀπειραγάθων κόμποις ἐπαρθέντες τοῦ τὰ πάντα κατοπτεύοντος ἀεὶ θεοῦ μισοπόνηρον ὑπολαμβάνουσιν

KING JAMES VERSION

and the deputies and rulers of the provinces which *are* from India unto Ethiopia, an hundred twenty and seven provinces, unto every province according to the writing thereof, and unto every people after their language, and to the Jews according to their writing, and according to their language.

10 And he wrote in the king Ahasuerus' name, and sealed *it* with the king's ring, and sent letters by posts on horseback, *and* riders on mules, camels, *and* young dromedaries:

11 Wherein the king granted the Jews which *were* in every city to gather themselves together, and to stand for their life, to destroy, to slay, and to cause to perish, all the power of the people and province that would assault them, *both* little ones and women, and *to take* the spoil of them for a prey,

12 Upon one day in all the provinces of king Ahasuerus, *namely,* upon the thirteenth *day* of the twelfth month, which *is* the month Adar.

16 The great king Artexerxes unto the princes and governors of an hundred and seven and twenty provinces from India unto Ethiopia, and unto all our faithful subjects, greeting.

2 Many, the more often they are honoured with the great bounty of their gracious princes, the more proud they are waxen,

3 And endeavour to hurt not our subjects only, but not being able to bear abundance, do take in hand to practise also against those that do them good:

4 And take not only thankfulness away from among men, but also lifted up with the glorious words of lewd persons, that were never good, they think to escape the justice of God, that seeth all things, and hateth evil.

DOUAY OLD TESTAMENT

the governors, and to the deputies, and to the judges, who were rulers over the hundred and twenty-seven provinces, from India even to Ethiopia: to province and province, to people and people, according to their languages and characters, and to the Jews, according as they could read and hear.

10 And these letters which were sent in the king's name, were sealed with his ring, and sent by posts: who were to run through all the provinces, to prevent the former letters with new messages.

11 And the king gave orders to them, to speak to the Jews in every city, and to command them to gather themselves together, and to stand for their lives, and to kill and destroy all their enemies with their wives and children and all their houses, and to take their spoil.

12 And one day of revenge was appointed through all the provinces, to wit, the thirteenth of the twelfth month Adar.

16 THE great king Artaxerxes, from India to Ethiopia, to the governors and princes of a hundred and twenty-seven provinces, which obey our command, sendeth greeting.

2 Many have abused unto pride the goodness of princes, and the honour that hath been bestowed upon them:

3 And not only endeavour to oppress the king's subjects, but not bearing the glory that is given them, take in hand to practise also against them that gave it.

4 Neither are they content not to return thanks for benefits received, and to violate in themselves the laws of humanity, but they think they can also escape the justice of God who seeth all things.

KNOX TRANSLATION

judges who ruled the hundred and twenty-seven provinces between India and Ethiopia, written to each province or tribe in the characters it used and in the language it spoke; to the Jews, in their own characters and their own language. 10 And these letters, written under the royal seal in the king's name, were sent out by post-boys, that must carry them from province to province before the earlier decree could be executed. 11 City by city the Jews must be brought together, so that they could muster their whole number and fight for their lives. They might slay their enemies till they made an end of them, with their wives and children and all their households, and divide their goods as plunder. 12 The day fixed everywhere for this act of retribution was the thirteenth day of the twelfth month, Adar....

(This chapter appears in the Septuagint Greek after 8. 12. The letter here given is addressed throughout to the king's Gentile subjects; which suggests that two separate missives are referred to in 8. 9.)

16 The great king Artaxerxes, to the governors of the hundred and twenty-seven provinces between India and Ethiopia, and to all his vassal chiefs, sends greeting. 2 The favour of princes has often bred insolence in those whom they advanced to high rank; 3 they oppress their fellow-subjects, and are even prompted by their good fortune to plot against the authors of it; 4 deaf to the claims of gratitude and of humanity, they think to escape the all-seeing

TODAY'S ENGLISH VERSION

of all 127 provinces from India to Ethiopia.[a] The letters were
written to each province in its own language. 10 They were
written in the name of the king and stamped with the royal
seal and they were delivered by runners.
11 These letters explained that the king would allow the
Jews in every city of the empire to live by their own laws and
organize for self-defense. They were permitted to treat their
opponents and enemies in any way they liked. 12 This decree
was to take effect throughout the Persian Empire on the thirteenth day of Adar, the twelfth month.[b]

E[c] This is a copy of the decree:
"Greetings from King Xerxes the Great to the governors
of the 127 provinces, which extend from India to Ethiopia,[a]
and to all those who are loyal to us.
2 "Many people become increasingly arrogant when honors
are given to them and favors are done for them. 3 They do
not know what to do with so much good fortune, so they not
only try to harm our subjects, but they even scheme against
those who grant them favors. 4 They are never grateful for
what people do for them, and they even think they can
escape the judgment of God, who hates evil and sees everything. In their arrogance they listen to the flattery of ignorant, sinful people.

[a] *Greek* Ethiopia: *Ethiopia is the name given in Graeco-Roman times to the extensive territory south of the First Cataract of the Nile River. Cush was the ancient (Hebrew) name of this region which included within its borders most of modern Sudan and some of present-day Ethiopia (Abyssinia).*
[b] *Chapter 8 continues after chapter E.* [c] *Chapter E 1-24 corresponds to chapter 16.1-24 in a number of English translations.*

NEW REVISED STANDARD VERSION

from India to Ethiopia, one hundred twenty-seven provinces,
to each province in its own language. 10 The edict was
written[a] with the king's authority and sealed with his ring,
and sent out by couriers. 11 He ordered the Jews in every city
to observe their own laws, to defend themselves, and to act
as they wished against their opponents and enemies 12 on a
certain day, the thirteenth of the twelfth month, which is
Adar, throughout all the kingdom of Artaxerxes.

ADDITION E

16[b] The following is a copy of this letter:
"The Great King, Artaxerxes, to the governors of the
provinces from India to Ethiopia, one hundred twenty-seven
provinces, and to those who are loyal to our government,
greetings.
2 "Many people, the more they are honored with the most
generous kindness of their benefactors, the more proud do
they become, 3 and not only seek to injure our subjects, but
in their inability to stand prosperity, they even undertake to
scheme against their own benefactors. 4 They not only take
away thankfulness from others, but, carried away by the
boasts of those who know nothing of goodness, they even
assume that they will escape the evil-hating justice of God,

a Gk *It was written* *b* Chapter 16.1-24 corresponds to chapter E 1-24 in some translations.

NEW AMERICAN BIBLE

governors, and officials of the hundred and twenty-seven
provinces from India to Ethiopia: to each province in its own
script and to each people in its own language, and to the
Jews in their own script and language. 10 These letters,
which he wrote in the name of King Ahasuerus and sealed
with the royal signet ring, he sent by mounted couriers riding thoroughbred royal steeds. 11 In these letters the king
authorized the Jews in each and every city to group together
and defend their lives, and to kill, destroy, wipe out, along
with their wives and children, every armed group of any
nation or province which should attack them, and to seize
their goods as spoil 12 throughout the provinces of King
Ahasuerus, on a single day, the thirteenth of the twelfth
month, Adar.

E The following is a copy of the letter:
"King Ahasuerus the Great to the governors of the
provinces in the hundred and twenty-seven satrapies from
India to Ethiopia, and to those responsible for our interests:
Greetings!
2 "Many have become the more ambitious the more they
were showered with honors through the bountiful generosity
of their patrons. 3 Not only do they seek to do harm to our
subjects; incapable of bearing such greatness, they even
begin plotting against their own benefactors. 4 Not only do
they drive out gratitude from among men; with the arrogant
boastfulness of those to whom goodness has no meaning,
they suppose they will escape the vindictive judgment of the
all-seeing God.

NEW JERUSALEM BIBLE

principal officials of the provinces stretching from India to
Ethiopia, a hundred and twenty-seven provinces, to each
province in its own script, and to each people in its own language, and to the Jews in their own script and language.
10 These letters, written in the name of King Ahasuerus and
sealed with the king's signet, were carried by couriers mounted on horses from the king's own stud-farms. 11 In them the
king granted the Jews, in whatever city they lived, the right to
assemble in self-defence, with permission to destroy, slaughter and annihilate any armed force of any people or province
that might attack them, together with their women and children, and to plunder their possessions, 12 with effect from the
same day throughout the provinces of King Ahasuerus—the
thirteenth day of the twelfth month, which is Adar.

12a *The text of the letter was as follows:*

12b *'The Great King, Ahasuerus, to the satraps of the hun-*
dred and twenty-seven provinces which stretch from India
to Ethiopia, to the provincial governors and to all our loyal
subjects, greeting:
12c *'Many people, repeatedly honoured by the extreme*
bounty of their benefactors, only grow the more arrogant. It
is not enough for them to seek our subjects' injury, but
unable as they are to support the weight of their own sur-
feit they turn to scheming against their benefactors them-
selves. 12d *Not content with banishing gratitude from the*
human heart, but elated by the plaudits of people unac-
quainted with goodness, notwithstanding that all is for
ever under the eye of God, they expect to escape his justice,

GREEK OLD TESTAMENT

ἐκφεύξεσθαι δίκην. 12e δὲ καὶ πολλοὺς τῶν ἐπ᾽ ἐξουσίαις
τεταγμένων τῶν πιστευθέντων χειρίζειν φίλων τὰ πράγματα
παραμυθία μεταιτίους αἱμάτων ἀθῴων καταστήσασα περιέ-
βαλε συμφοραῖς ἀνηκέστοις 12f τῆς κακοηθείας ψευδεῖ
παραλογισμῷ παραλογισαμένων τὴν τῶν ἐπικρατούντων
ἀκέραιον εὐγνωμοσύνην. 12g δὲ ἔξεστιν, οὐ τοσοῦτον ἐκ τῶν
παλαιοτέρων ὧν παρεδώκαμεν ἱστοριῶν, ὅσα ἐστὶν παρὰ
πόδας ὑμᾶς ἐκζητοῦντας ἀνοσίως συντετελεσμένα τῇ τῶν
ἀνάξια δυναστευόντων λοιμότητι, 12h προσέχειν εἰς τὰ
μετὰ ταῦτα εἰς τὸ τὴν βασιλείαν ἀτάραχον τοῖς πᾶσιν
ἀνθρώποις μετ᾽ εἰρήνης παρεξόμεθα 12i ταῖς μεταβολαῖς, τὰ
δὲ ὑπὸ τὴν ὄψιν ἐρχόμενα διακρίνοντες ἀεὶ μετ᾽ ἐπιεικε-
στέρας ἀπαντήσεως. 12k γὰρ Αμαν Αμαδαθου Μακεδών,
ταῖς ἀληθείαις ἀλλότριος τοῦ τῶν Περσῶν αἵματος καὶ πολὺ
διεστηκὼς τῆς ἡμετέρας χρηστότητος, ἐπιξενωθεὶς ἡμῖν
12l ἧς ἔχομεν πρὸς πᾶν ἔθνος φιλανθρωπίας ἐπὶ τοσοῦτον
ὥστε ἀναγορεύεσθαι ἡμῶν πατέρα καὶ προσκυνούμενον ὑπὸ
πάντων τὸ δεύτερον τοῦ βασιλικοῦ θρόνου πρόσωπον δια-
τελεῖν, 12m ἐνέγκας δὲ τὴν ὑπερηφανίαν ἐπετήδευσεν τῆς
ἀρχῆς στερῆσαι ἡμᾶς καὶ τοῦ πνεύματος 12n τε ἡμέτερον
σωτῆρα καὶ διὰ παντὸς εὐεργέτην Μαρδοχαῖον καὶ τὴν
ἄμεμπτον τῆς βασιλείας κοινωνὸν Εσθηρ σὺν παντὶ τῷ τούτων ἔθνει πολυπλόκοις μεθόδων παραλογισμοῖς αἰτησάμενος

KING JAMES VERSION

5 Oftentimes also fair speech of those, that are put in trust to manage their friends' affairs, hath caused many that are in authority to be partakers of innocent blood, and hath enwrapped them in remediless calamities:

6 Beguiling with the falsehood and deceit of their lewd disposition the innocency and goodness of princes.

7 Now ye may see this, as we have declared, not so much by ancient histories, as ye may, if ye search what hath been wickedly done of late through the pestilent behaviour of them that are unworthily placed in authority.

8 And we must take care for the time to come, that our kingdom may be quiet and peaceable for all men,

9 Both by changing our purposes, and always judging things that are evident with more equal proceeding.

10 For Aman, a Macedonian, the son of Amadatha, being indeed a stranger from the Persian blood, and far distant from our goodness, and as a stranger received of us,

11 Had so far forth obtained the favour that we shew toward every nation, as that he was called our father, and was continually honoured of all men, as the next person unto the king.

12 But he, not bearing his great dignity, went about to deprive us of our kingdom and life:

13 Having by manifold and cunning deceits sought of us the destruction, as well of Mardocheus, who saved our life, and continually procured our good, as also of blameless Esther, partaker of our kingdom, with their whole nation.

DOUAY OLD TESTAMENT

5 And they break out into so great madness, as to endeavour to undermine by lies such as observe diligently the offices committed to them, and do all things in such manner as to be worthy of all men's praise,

6 While with crafty fraud they deceive the ears of princes that are well meaning, and judge of others by their own nature.

7 Now this is proved both from ancient histories, and by the things which are done daily, how the good designs of kings are depraved by the evil suggestions of certain men.

8 Wherefore we must provide for the peace of all provinces.

9 Neither must you think, if we command different things, that it cometh of the levity of our mind, but that we give sentence according to the quality and necessity of times, as the profit of the commonwealth requireth.

10 Now that you may more plainly understand what we say, Aman the son of Amadathi, a Macedonian both in mind and country, and having nothing of the Persian blood, but with his cruelty staining our goodness, was received being a stranger by us:

11 And found our humanity so great towards him, that he was called our father, and was worshipped by all as the next man after the king:

12 But he was so far puffed up with arrogancy, as to go about to deprive us of our kingdom and life.

13 For with certain new and unheard of devices he hath sought the destruction of Mardochai, by whose fidelity and good services our life was saved, and of Esther the partner of our kingdom, with all their nation:

KNOX TRANSLATION

scrutiny of God. 5 A madness comes over them, and they
assail with false charges the very men who win the praise of
all by faithfulness to their duties; 6 what easier, than to
abuse with calumny the confidence of an unsuspecting ruler,
who fancies all men to be as honest as himself? 7 That men
will so practise on the credulity of princes is evident both
from history and from daily experience; 8 no little foresight
is needed, if the welfare of a great empire is to be preserved.
9 The orders given yesterday must be reversed to-day; not
from any caprice of ours, but because we have to consider
the changing needs of the moment, in the best interests of
the commonwealth.

10 But to our matter. We took under our protection, some
time since, one Aman, son of Amadathi, a stranger; a Macedonian by race, with no share of our Persian blood, a Macedonian in his nature, whose cruel temper sorts ill with our
Persian kindliness.[a] 11 He received from us nothing but
friendly usage; we would have him called our father, we
would have reverence paid to him as one that stood next to
the king's person. 12 And he? So was his heart swelled with
pride, that he went about to deprive us of our royalty, and of
life itself. 13 First, with daring unheard-of, he would compass the death of two persons, through the general massacre
of their race; Mardochaeus, to whose loyalty we owe life
itself, and Esther, the queen-consort of our realm. 14 Then,

[a] Aman has been described elsewhere as an Agagite or a Bugaean, neither of which terms can be explained with certainty. Macedonia would be regarded as a natural enemy of Persia at any time from 480 B.C. onwards.

TODAY'S ENGLISH VERSION

5 "It often happens also that friends who have been
entrusted with administrative responsibilities exert pressure
on those in authority. They make their leaders their partners
in killing people and bring about misfortunes that can never
be remedied. 6 These friends, by their lies and deceitful ways,
take advantage of the good will of their rulers.

7 "You can see examples of this misuse of power not only
in the stories that have been handed down to us from the
past, but in the more recent outrageous things which have
happened among you.

8 "I intend to make sure that in the future my kingdom will
remain untroubled and peaceful for all people. 9 This can be
done by changing certain policies and by judging fairly each
situation that comes to my attention.

10 "Consider, for example, the case of Haman son of
Hammedatha, a Macedonian. He is a foreigner with no
Persian blood and with no trace of my generosity; but I welcomed him, 11 and he received the benefit of my concern and
love for all people. He was, in fact, proclaimed 'Father' of the
empire and received more honor than anyone else, except the
king.

12 "But his arrogance knew no limits, and he tried to murder me and take over the empire. 13 In his crafty and deceitful way, he asked that Mordecai be put to death—Mordecai,
who once saved my life and who has always supported me.
He even asked for the death of Esther, our blameless queen,
and in fact, the death of all the Jewish people. 14 His purpose

NEW REVISED STANDARD VERSION

who always sees everything. 5 And often many of those who
are set in places of authority have been made in part responsible for the shedding of innocent blood, and have been
involved in irremediable calamities, by the persuasion of
friends who have been entrusted with the administration of
public affairs, 6 when these persons by the false trickery of
their evil natures beguile the sincere goodwill of their sover-
eigns.

7 "What has been wickedly accomplished through the
pestilent behavior of those who exercise authority unworthily can be seen, not so much from the more ancient records
that we hand on, as from investigation of matters close at
hand.[a] 8 In the future we will take care to render our kingdom quiet and peaceable for all, 9 by changing our methods
and always judging what comes before our eyes with more
equitable consideration. 10 For Haman son of Hammedatha,
a Macedonian (really an alien to the Persian blood, and quite
devoid of our kindliness), having become our guest,
11 enjoyed so fully the goodwill that we have for every nation
that he was called our father and was continually bowed
down to by all as the person second to the royal throne.
12 But, unable to restrain his arrogance, he undertook to
deprive us of our kingdom and our life,[b] 13 and with intricate craft and deceit asked for the destruction of Mordecai,
our savior and perpetual benefactor, and of Esther, the
blameless partner of our kingdom, together with their whole

a Gk *matters beside* (your) *feet* *b* Gk *our spirit*

NEW AMERICAN BIBLE

5 "Often, too, the fair speech of friends entrusted with the
administration of affairs has induced many placed in authority to become accomplices in the shedding of innocent blood,
and has involved them in irreparable calamities 6 by deceiving with malicious slander the sincere good will of rulers.
7 This can be verified in the ancient stories that have been
handed down to us, but more fully when one considers the
wicked deeds perpetrated in your midst by the pestilential
influence of those undeserving of authority. 8 We must provide for the future, so as to render the kingdom undisturbed
and peaceful for all men, 9 taking advantage of changing
conditions and deciding always with equitable treatment
matters coming to our attention.

10 "For instance, Haman, son of Hammedatha, a Macedonian, certainly not of Persian blood, and very different
from us in generosity, was hospitably received by us. 11 He
so far enjoyed the good will which we have toward all peoples that he was proclaimed 'father of the king,' before
whom everyone was to bow down; he attained the rank second to the royal throne. 12 But, unequal to this dignity, he
strove to deprive us of kingdom and of life; 13 and by weaving intricate webs of deceit, he demanded the destruction of
Mordecai, our savior and constant benefactor, and of Esther,
our blameless royal consort, together with their whole race.

NEW JERUSALEM BIBLE

so hostile to the wicked. 12e *Thus it has often happened to*
those placed in authority that, having entrusted friends
with the conduct of affairs and allowed themselves to be
influenced by them, they find themselves sharing with
these the guilt of innocent blood and involved in irremedia-
ble misfortunes, 12f *the upright intentions of rulers having*
been misled by false arguments of the evilly disposed.
12g *This may be seen without recourse to the history of earli-*
er times to which we have referred; you have only to look at
what is before you, at the crimes perpetrated by a plague of
unworthy officials. 12h *For the future, we shall exert our*
efforts to assure the tranquillity and peace of the realm for
all, 12i *by adopting new policies and by always judging*
matters that are brought to our notice in the most equi-
table spirit.

12k *'Thus Haman son of Hammedatha, a Macedonian,*
without a drop of Persian blood and far removed from our
goodness, enjoyed our hospitality 12l *and was treated by us*
with the benevolence which we show to every nation, even
to the extent of being proclaimed our 'father' and being
accorded universally the prostration of respect as second in
dignity to the royal throne. 12m *But he, unable to keep with-*
in his own high rank, schemed to deprive us of our realm
and of our life. 12n *Furthermore, by tortuous wiles and*
arguments, he would have had us destroy Mordecai, our
saviour and constant benefactor, with Esther the blameless
partner of our majesty, and their whole nation besides.

GREEK OLD TESTAMENT

εἰς ἀπώλειαν· [12o] γὰρ τῶν τρόπων τούτων ᾠήθη λαβὼν ἡμᾶς ἐρήμους τὴν τῶν Περσῶν ἐπικράτησιν εἰς τοὺς Μακεδόνας μετάξαι. [12p] δὲ τοὺς ὑπὸ τοῦ τρισαλιτηρίου παραδεδομένους εἰς ἀφανισμὸν Ιουδαίους εὑρίσκομεν οὐ κακούργους ὄντας, δικαιοτάτοις δὲ πολιτευομένους νόμοις, [12q] δὲ υἱοὺς τοῦ ὑψίστου μεγίστου ζῶντος θεοῦ τοῦ κατευθύνοντος ἡμῖν τε καὶ τοῖς προγόνοις ἡμῶν τὴν βασιλείαν ἐν τῇ καλλίστῃ διαθέσει. [12r] οὖν ποιήσετε μὴ προσχρησάμενοι τοῖς ὑπὸ Αμαν Αμαδαθου ἀποσταλεῖσι γράμμασιν διὰ τὸ αὐτὸν τὸν ταῦτα ἐξεργασάμενον πρὸς ταῖς Σούσων πύλαις ἐσταυρῶσθαι σὺν τῇ πανοικίᾳ, τὴν καταξίαν τοῦ τὰ πάντα ἐπικρατοῦντος θεοῦ διὰ τάχους ἀποδόντος αὐτῷ κρίσιν, [12s] δὲ ἀντίγραφον τῆς ἐπιστολῆς ταύτης ἐκθέντες ἐν παντὶ τόπῳ μετὰ παρρησίας ἐᾶν τοὺς Ιουδαίους χρῆσθαι τοῖς ἑαυτῶν νομίμοις καὶ συνεπισχύειν αὐτοῖς ὅπως τοὺς ἐν καιρῷ θλίψεως ἐπιθεμένους αὐτοῖς ἀμύνωνται τῇ τρισκαιδεκάτῃ τοῦ δωδεκάτου μηνὸς Αδαρ τῇ αὐτῇ ἡμέρᾳ· [12t] γὰρ ὁ πάντα δυναστεύων θεὸς ἀντ' ὀλεθρίας τοῦ ἐκλεκτοῦ γένους ἐποίησεν αὐτοῖς εὐφροσύνην. [12u] ὑμεῖς οὖν ἐν ταῖς ἐπωνύμοις ὑμῶν ἑορταῖς ἐπίσημον ἡμέραν μετὰ πάσης εὐωχίας ἄγετε, ὅπως καὶ νῦν καὶ μετὰ ταῦτα σωτηρία ᾖ ἡμῖν καὶ τοῖς εὐνοοῦσιν Πέρσαις, τοῖς δὲ ἡμῖν ἐπιβουλεύουσιν μνημόσυνον τῆς

KING JAMES VERSION

14 For by these means he thought, finding us destitute of friends, to have translated the kingdom of the Persians to the Macedonians.

15 But we find that the Jews, whom this wicked wretch hath delivered to utter destruction, are no evildoers, but live by most just laws:

16 And that they be children of the most high and most mighty living God, who hath ordered the kingdom both unto us and to our progenitors in the most excellent manner.

17 Wherefore ye shall do well not to put in execution the letters sent unto you by Aman the son of Amadatha.

18 For he, that was the worker of these things, is hanged at the gates of Susa with all his family: God, who ruleth all things, speedily rendering vengeance to him according to his deserts.

19 Therefore ye shall publish the copy of this letter in all places, that the Jews may freely live after their own laws.

20 And ye shall aid them, that even the same day, being the thirteenth day of the twelfth month Adar, they may be avenged on them, who in the time of their affliction shall set upon them.

21 For Almighty God hath turned to joy unto them the day, wherein the chosen people should have perished.

22 Ye shall therefore among your solemn feasts keep it an high day with all feasting:

23 That both now and hereafter there may be safety to us, and the well affected Persians; but to those which do conspire against us a memorial of destruction.

DOUAY OLD TESTAMENT

14 Thinking that after they were slain, he might work treason against us left alone without friends, and might transfer the kingdom of the Persians to the Macedonians.

15 But we have found that the Jews, who were by that most wicked man appointed to be slain, are in no fault at all, but contrariwise, use just laws,

16 And are the children of the highest and the greatest, and the ever living God, by whose benefit the kingdom was given both to our fathers and to us, and is kept unto this day.

17 Wherefore know ye that those letters which he sent in our name, are void and of no effect.

18 For which crime both he himself that devised it, and all his kindred hang on gibbets, before the gates of this city Susan: not we, but God repaying him as he deserved.

19 But this edict, which we now send, shall be published in all cities, that the Jews may freely follow their own laws.

20 And you shall aid them that they may kill those who had prepared themselves to kill them, on the thirteenth day of the twelfth month, which is called Adar.

21 For the almighty God hath turned this day of sadness and mourning into joy to them.

22 Wherefore you shall also count this day among other festival days, and celebrate it with all joy, that it may be known also in times to come,

23 That all they who faithfully obey the Persians, receive a worthy reward for their fidelity: but they that are traitors to their kingdom, are destroyed for their wickedness.

KNOX TRANSLATION

when their deaths had left us unbefriended, he would plot
against our own empire and transfer it to the Macedonians. [a]
15 Meanwhile, the race this inhuman wretch had marked
down for slaughter, the Jewish race, proves to have deserved
no blame whatever. The laws they follow are just; 16 they are
the children of that most high, most powerful and ever-living
God by whose favour my fathers won this realm, and I maintain it.

17 Take note, then, that the directions which were sent out
by Aman under our name are to be left unheeded. [b] 18 He, the
author of this plot, hangs now on a gibbet, here at the gates
of Susan, with all his kindred; to God, not to us, thanks are
due that he has received his deserts. 19 The decree we are
now sending you, giving the Jews liberty to follow their own
laws, is to be posted up in every city of the realm; 20 and you
must furnish them with the means to make an end of all
those who would have compassed their murder, on the thirteenth day of Adar, the last month of the year. 21 Here is a
day marked down for mourning and lament, turned by God
Almighty into a day of triumph for them; 22 you too must
keep it as one of the year's holidays, and observe it with due
rejoicing; so making it known to posterity 23 that Persia's
loyal subjects are well rewarded for their loyalty, and that all
who plot against her sovereignty atone for their crime with

a This verse, like the notice in 12. 6 which connects Aman with the disloyal chamberlains, suggests the existence of a fuller version of the story, from which our narrative was abridged. *b* Literally, 'are cancelled', but this seems to have been technically impossible; cf. note on 8. 8. 'Left unheeded' is the sense of the Septuagint Greek.

TODAY'S ENGLISH VERSION

was to leave us helpless and to allow the Macedonians to
take over the Persian Empire. 15 Even though this wicked
criminal plotted to wipe out the Jews, I find that they are not
traitors at all but are governed by very just laws. 16 They
worship the living God, the highest and greatest God, who
has kept our empire in its excellent condition from the time
of our ancestors until our own day.

17 "Therefore I advise you not to carry out the instructions
issued in the letters sent out by Haman. 18 He is the person
responsible for all of this, and he has been hanged, along
with his entire family, at the gates of Susa. God, who governs all things, has given him the speedy punishment that he
deserved.

19 "I order you to post copies of this decree in every public
place. Permit the Jews to live by their own customs, 20 and
give them support when they defend themselves against
those who attack them on the day set for their destruction,
the thirteenth day of Adar, the twelfth month. 21 God, who
governs all things, has turned that day of destruction into a
day of celebration for his chosen people.

22 "Include this day among your national holidays and celebrate it as a festival. 23 Now and in the future it will remind
us and all our allies of the way God watches over our nation,
and those who plot against us will be reminded of God's
threat of destruction.

NEW REVISED STANDARD VERSION

nation. 14 He thought that by these methods he would catch
us undefended and would transfer the kingdom of the
Persians to the Macedonians.

15 "But we find that the Jews, who were consigned to
annihilation by this thrice-accursed man, are not evildoers,
but are governed by most righteous laws 16 and are children
of the living God, most high, most mighty,[a] who has directed
the kingdom both for us and for our ancestors in the most
excellent order.

17 "You will therefore do well not to put in execution the
letters sent by Haman son of Hammedatha, 18 since he, the
one who did these things, has been hanged at the gate of Susa
with all his household—for God, who rules over all things,
has speedily inflicted on him the punishment that he deserved.

19 "Therefore post a copy of this letter publicly in every
place, and permit the Jews to live under their own laws.
20 And give them reinforcements, so that on the thirteenth
day of the twelfth month, Adar, on that very day, they may
defend themselves against those who attack them at the time
of oppression. 21 For God, who rules over all things, has
made this day to be a joy for his chosen people instead of a
day of destruction for them.

22 "Therefore you shall observe this with all good cheer
as a notable day among your commemorative festivals, 23 so
that both now and hereafter it may represent deliverance for
you[b] and the loyal Persians, but that it may be a reminder of
destruction for those who plot against us.

a Gk *greatest* *b* Other ancient authorities read *for us*

NEW AMERICAN BIBLE

14 For by such measures he hoped to catch us defenseless and
to transfer the rule of the Persians to the Macedonians.
15 But we find that the Jews, who were doomed to extinction
by this arch-criminal, are not evildoers, but rather are governed by very just laws 16 and are the children of the Most
High, the living God of majesty, who has maintained the
kingdom in a flourishing condition for us and for our forebears.

17 "You will do well, then, to ignore the letter sent by
Haman, son of Hammedatha, 18 for he who composed it has
been hanged, together with his entire household, before the
gates of Susa. Thus swiftly has God, who governs all,
brought just punishment upon him.

19 "You shall exhibit a copy of this letter publicly in every
place, to certify that the Jews may follow their own laws,
20 and that you may help them on the day set for their ruin,
the thirteenth day of the twelfth month, Adar, to defend
themselves against those who attack them. 21 For God, the
ruler of all, has turned that day for them from one of
destruction of the chosen race into one of joy. 22 Therefore,
you too must celebrate this memorable day among your designated feasts with all rejoicing, 23 so that both now and in
the future it may be, for us and for loyal Persians, a celebration of victory, and for those who plot against us a reminder
of destruction.

NEW JERUSALEM BIBLE

12o *He thought by these means to leave us without support
and so to transfer the Persian empire to the Macedonians.*

12p *'But we find that the Jews, marked out for annihilation by this arch-scoundrel, are not criminals: they are in
fact governed by the most just of laws.* 12q *They are children of the Most High, the great and living God to whom
we and our ancestors owe the continuing prosperity of our
realm.* 12r *You will therefore do well not to act on the letters
sent by Haman son of Hammedatha, since their author has
been hanged at the gates of Susa with his whole household: a fitting punishment, which God, Master of the
Universe, has speedily inflicted on him.* 12s *Put up copies of
this letter everywhere, allow the Jews to observe their own
customs without fear, and come to their help against anyone who attacks them on the day originally chosen for their
maltreatment, that is, the thirteenth day of the twelfth
month, which is Adar.* 12t *For the all-powerful God has
made this day a day of joy and not of ruin for the chosen
people.* 12u *You, for your part, among your solemn festivals
celebrate this as a special day with every kind of feasting,
so that now and in the future, for you and for Persians of
good will, it may commemorate your rescue, and for your
enemies may stand as a reminder of their ruin.*

GREEK OLD TESTAMENT

ἀπωλείας. 12x πᾶσα δὲ πόλις ἢ χώρα τὸ σύνολον, ἥτις κατὰ
ταῦτα μὴ ποιήσῃ, δόρατι καὶ πυρὶ καταναλωθήσεται μετ’
ὀργῆς. οὐ μόνον ἀνθρώποις ἄβατος, ἀλλὰ καὶ θηρίοις καὶ
πετεινοῖς εἰς τὸν ἅπαντα χρόνον ἔχθιστος κατασταθήσεται.
13 τὰ δὲ ἀντίγραφα ἐκτιθέσθωσαν ὀφθαλμοφανῶς ἐν πάσῃ τῇ
βασιλείᾳ, ἑτοίμους τε εἶναι πάντας τοὺς Ιουδαίους εἰς ταύτην τὴν ἡμέραν πολεμῆσαι αὐτῶν τοὺς ὑπεναντίους.
14 Οἱ μὲν οὖν ἱππεῖς ἐξῆλθον σπεύδοντες τὰ ὑπὸ τοῦ
βασιλέως λεγόμενα ἐπιτελεῖν· ἐξετέθη δὲ τὸ πρόσταγμα καὶ
ἐν Σούσοις. 15 ὁ δὲ Μαρδοχαῖος ἐξῆλθεν ἐστολισμένος τὴν
βασιλικὴν στολὴν καὶ στέφανον ἔχων χρυσοῦν καὶ διάδημα
βύσσινον πορφυροῦν· ἰδόντες δὲ οἱ ἐν Σούσοις ἐχάρησαν.
16 τοῖς δὲ Ιουδαίοις ἐγένετο φῶς καὶ εὐφροσύνη· 17 κατὰ
πόλιν καὶ χώραν, οὗ ἂν ἐξετέθη τὸ πρόσταγμα, οὗ ἂν ἐξετέθη τὸ ἔκθεμα, χαρὰ καὶ εὐφροσύνη τοῖς Ιουδαίοις, κώθων
καὶ εὐφροσύνη, καὶ πολλοὶ τῶν ἐθνῶν περιετέμνοντο καὶ
ἰουδάιζον διὰ τὸν φόβον τῶν Ιουδαίων.
9 Ἐν γὰρ τῷ δωδεκάτῳ μηνὶ τρισκαιδεκάτῃ τοῦ μηνός, ὅς
ἐστιν Αδαρ, παρῆν τὰ γράμματα τὰ γραφέντα ὑπὸ τοῦ

KING JAMES VERSION

24 Therefore every city and country whatsoever, which
shall not do according to these things, shall be destroyed
without mercy with fire and sword, and shall be made not
only unpassable for men, but also most hateful to wild
beasts and fowls for ever.
8 13 The copy of the writing for a commandment to be
given in every province *was* published unto all people,
and that the Jews should be ready against that day to avenge
themselves on their enemies.
14 *So* the posts that rode upon mules *and* camels went
out, being hastened and pressed on by the king's commandment. And the decree was given at Shushan the palace.
15 And Mordecai went out from the presence of the king
in royal apparel of blue and white, and with a great crown of
gold, and with a garment of fine linen and purple: and the
city of Shushan rejoiced and was glad.
16 The Jews had light, and gladness, and joy, and honour.
17 And in every province, and in every city, whithersoever
the king's commandment and his decree came, the Jews had
joy and gladness, a feast and a good day. And many of the
people of the land became Jews; for the fear of the Jews fell
upon them.
9 Now in the twelfth month, that *is,* the month Adar, on
the thirteenth day of the same, when the king's commandment and his decree drew near to be put in execution,
in the day that the enemies of the Jews hoped to have power
over them, (though it was turned to the contrary, that the
Jews had rule over them that hated them;)

DOUAY OLD TESTAMENT

24 And let every province and city, that will not be partaker
of this solemnity, perish by the sword and by fire, and be
destroyed in such manner as to be made unpassable, both to
men and beasts, for an example of contempt, and disobedience.
8 13 And this was the content of the letter, that it should
be notified in all lands and peoples that were subject to
the empire of king Assuerus, that the Jews were ready to be
revenged of their enemies.
14 So the swift posts went out carrying the messages, and
the king's edict was hung up in Susan.
15 And Mardochai going forth out of the palace, and from
the king's presence, shone in royal apparel, to wit, of violet
and sky colour, wearing a golden crown on his head, and
clothed with a cloak of silk and purple. And all the city
rejoiced and was glad.
16 But to the Jews a new light seemed to rise, joy, honour,
and dancing.
17 And in all peoples, cities, and provinces, whithersoever
the king's commandments came, there was wonderful rejoicing, feasts and banquets, and keeping holy day: insomuch
that many of other nations and religion, joined themselves to
their worship and ceremonies. For a great dread of the name
of the Jews had fallen upon all.
9 SO on the thirteenth day of the twelfth month, which as
we have said above is called Adar, when all the Jews
were designed to be massacred, and their enemies were
greedy after their blood, the case being altered, the Jews
began to have the upper hand, and to revenge themselves of
their adversaries.

KNOX TRANSLATION

death. 24 Be there province or city that will not take its part
in this observance, let it be laid waste with fire and sword;
man nor beast shall tread its ways hereafter; to warn men
what doom they suffer, that set edict of ours at defiance.
8 13 A copy of the letter warning the Jews everywhere in
Assuerus' empire, to be prepared for vengeance.... [a]
14 Swiftly the post-boys went about their errand, and in
Susan the royal edict was hung up for all to see.
15 When Mardochaeus came out from his audience with the
king, resplendent in royal robes of violet and white, a gold
crown on his head, his cloak of purple and lawn, the whole
city welcomed him with rejoicing and applause; 16 for the
Jews, it was a dawn of new hope, a day of gladness and triumphant glory.
17 As each tribe, city and province received the royal letter,
there was feasting and carousal and holiday; and many there
were, of alien race and alien creed, that submitted themselves to Jewish rite and observance; such terror the name of
Jewry struck into their hearts.
9 So Adar came, the last month of the year, and the thirteenth day of Adar. All preparations had been made, by
bloodthirsty enemies, for a massacre of the Jews on that day,
but instead, the Jews had the better of them, and could set
about avenging themselves. 2 City by city, town by town,

a See note on 3. 14, and also that on 16. 1.

TODAY'S ENGLISH VERSION

24 "Every province, every city, without exception, which does not obey these orders will feel my anger. It will be destroyed in battle and burned to the ground. No human being will ever go there again, and even the birds and wild animals will avoid it forever.

8[a] 13 "Post copies of this decree in plain view in every province, so that all the Jews can be ready to fight their enemies when that day comes."

14 Messengers on horses rode off at top speed to carry out the orders of the king, and the decree was also made public in Susa.

15 Mordecai left the palace, wearing royal robes, a turban of fine purple linen, and a gold crown. When the people of Susa saw him, they cheered, 16 and the Jews were happy and joyful. 17 They held a joyful holiday with feasting and happiness in every city and province, wherever the king's proclamation was posted. In fact, many Gentiles were circumcised and became Jews, because they were now afraid of them.

9 On the thirteenth day of Adar, the day on which the royal proclamation was to take effect, 2 it was the

[a] *Verses 1-12 precede chapter E.*

NEW REVISED STANDARD VERSION

24 "Every city and country, without exception, that does not act accordingly shall be destroyed in wrath with spear and fire. It shall be made not only impassable for human beings, but also most hateful to wild animals and birds for all time.

END OF ADDITION E

8 13 "Let copies of the decree be posted conspicuously in all the kingdom, and let all the Jews be ready on that day to fight against their enemies."

14 So the messengers on horseback set out with all speed to perform what the king had commanded; and the decree was published also in Susa. 15 Mordecai went out dressed in the royal robe and wearing a gold crown and a turban of purple linen. The people in Susa rejoiced on seeing him. 16 And the Jews had light and gladness 17 in every city and province wherever the decree was published; wherever the proclamation was made, the Jews had joy and gladness, a banquet and a holiday. And many of the Gentiles were circumcised and became Jews out of fear of the Jews.

9 Now on the thirteenth day of the twelfth month, which is Adar, the decree written by the king arrived. 2 On that

NEW AMERICAN BIBLE

24 "Every city and province, without exception, that does not observe this decree shall be ruthlessly destroyed with fire and sword, so that it will be left not merely untrodden by men, but even shunned by wild beasts and birds forever."

8 13 A copy of the letter to be promulgated as law in each and every province was published among all the peoples, so that the Jews might be prepared on that day to avenge themselves on their enemies. 14 Couriers mounted on royal steeds sped forth in haste at the king's order, and the decree was promulgated in the stronghold of Susa.

15 Mordecai left the king's presence clothed in a royal robe of violet and of white cotton, with a large crown of gold and a cloak of crimson byssus. The city of Susa shouted with joy, 16 and there was splendor and merriment for the Jews, exultation and triumph. 17 In each and every province and in each and every city, wherever the king's order arrived, there was merriment and exultation, banqueting and feasting for the Jews. And many of the peoples of the land embraced Judaism, for they were seized with a fear of the Jews.

9 When the day arrived on which the order decreed by the king was to be carried out, the thirteenth day of the twelfth month, Adar, on which the enemies of the Jews had expected to become masters of them, the situation was reversed: the Jews became masters of their enemies. 2 The

NEW JERUSALEM BIBLE

12v *'Every city and, more generally, every country, which does not follow these instructions, will be mercilessly devastated with fire and sword, and made not only inaccessible to human beings but hateful to wild animals and even birds for ever.'*

13 Copies of this edict, to be promulgated as law in each province, were published to the various peoples, so that the Jews could be ready on the day stated to avenge themselves on their enemies. 14 The couriers, mounted on the king's horses, set out in great haste and urgency at the king's command. The edict was also published in the citadel of Susa. 15 Mordecai left the royal presence in a princely gown of violet and white, with a great golden crown and a cloak of fine linen and purple. The city of Susa shouted for joy. 16 For the Jews there was light and gladness, joy and honour. 17 In every province and in every city, wherever the king's command and decree arrived, there was joy and gladness among the Jews, with feasting and holiday-making. Of the country's population many became Jews, since now the Jews were feared.

9 The king's command and decree came into force on the thirteenth day of the twelfth month, Adar, and the day on which the enemies of the Jews had hoped to crush them produced the very opposite effect: the Jews it was who crushed their enemies. 2 In their towns throughout the

GREEK OLD TESTAMENT

βασιλέως. 2 ἐν αὐτῇ τῇ ἡμέρᾳ ἀπώλοντο οἱ ἀντικείμενοι
τοῖς Ιουδαίοις. οὐδεὶς γὰρ ἀντέστη φοβούμενος αὐτούς. 3 οἱ
γὰρ ἄρχοντες τῶν σατραπῶν καὶ οἱ τύραννοι καὶ οἱ βασιλι-
κοὶ γραμματεῖς ἐτίμων τοὺς Ιουδαίους. ὁ γὰρ φόβος Μαρδοχαίου ἐνέκειτο αὐτοῖς. 4 προσέπεσεν γὰρ τὸ πρόσταγμα τοῦ
βασιλέως ὀνομασθῆναι ἐν πάσῃ τῇ βασιλείᾳ. 6 καὶ ἐν
Σούσοις τῇ πόλει ἀπέκτειναν οἱ Ιουδαῖοι ἄνδρας πεντακοσίους 7 τόν τε Φαρσαννεσταιν καὶ Δελφων καὶ Φασγα 8 καὶ
Φαρδαθα καὶ Βαρεα καὶ Σαρβαχα 9 καὶ Μαρμασιμα καὶ
Αρουφαιον καὶ Αρσαιον καὶ Ζαβουθαιθαν, 10 τοὺς δέκα υἱοὺς
Αμαν Αμαδαθου Βουγαίου τοῦ ἐχθροῦ τῶν Ιουδαίων, καὶ
διήρπασαν. — 11 ἐν αὐτῇ τῇ ἡμέρᾳ ἐπεδόθη ὁ ἀριθμὸς τῷ
βασιλεῖ τῶν ἀπολωλότων ἐν Σούσοις. 12 εἶπεν δὲ ὁ βασιλεὺς
πρὸς Εσθηρ Ἀπώλεσαν οἱ Ιουδαῖοι ἐν Σούσοις τῇ πόλει
ἄνδρας πεντακοσίους. ἐν δὲ τῇ περιχώρῳ πῶς οἴει ἐχρήσαντο; τί οὖν ἀξιοῖς ἔτι καὶ ἔσται σοι; 13 καὶ εἶπεν Εσθηρ τῷ

KING JAMES VERSION

2 The Jews gathered themselves together in their cities throughout all the provinces of the king Ahasuerus, to lay hand on such as sought their hurt: and no man could withstand them; for the fear of them fell upon all people.

3 And all the rulers of the provinces, and the lieutenants, and the deputies, and officers of the king, helped the Jews; because the fear of Mordecai fell upon them.

4 For Mordecai *was* great in the king's house, and his fame went out throughout all the provinces: for this man Mordecai waxed greater and greater.

5 Thus the Jews smote all their enemies with the stroke of the sword, and slaughter, and destruction, and did what they would unto those that hated them.

6 And in Shushan the palace the Jews slew and destroyed five hundred men.

7 And Parshandatha, and Dalphon, and Aspatha,

8 And Poratha, and Adalia, and Aridatha,

9 And Parmashta, and Arisai, and Aridai, and Vajezatha,

10 The ten sons of Haman the son of Hammedatha, the enemy of the Jews, slew they; but on the spoil laid they not their hand.

11 On that day the number of those that were slain in Shushan the palace was brought before the king.

12 And the king said unto Esther the queen, The Jews have slain and destroyed five hundred men in Shushan the palace, and the ten sons of Haman; what have they done in the rest of the king's provinces? now what *is* thy petition? and it shall be granted thee: or what *is* thy request further? and it shall be done.

DOUAY OLD TESTAMENT

2 And they gathered themselves together in every city, and town, and place, to lay their hands on their enemies, and their persecutors. And no one durst withstand them, for the fear of their power had gone through every people.

3 And the judges of the provinces, and the governors, and lieutenants, and every one in dignity, that presided over every place and work, extolled the Jews for fear of Mardochai:

4 For they knew him to be prince of the palace, and to have great power: and the fame of his name increased daily, and was spread abroad through all men's mouths.

5 So the Jews made a great slaughter of their enemies, and killed them, repaying according to what they had prepared to do to them:

6 Insomuch that even in Susan they killed five hundred men, besides the ten sons of Aman the Agagite, the enemy of the Jews: whose names are these:

7 Pharsandatha, and Delphon, and Esphatha,

8 And Phoratha, and Adalia, and Aridatha,

9 And Phermesta, and Arisai, and Aridai, and Jezatha.

10 And when they had slain them, they would not touch the spoils of their goods.

11 And presently the number of them that were killed in Susan was brought to the king.

12 And he said to the queen: The Jews have killed five hundred men in the city of Susan, besides the ten sons of Aman: how many dost thou think they have slain in all the provinces? What askest thou more, and what wilt thou have me to command to be done?

KNOX TRANSLATION

region by region they banded themselves together, ready to
strike the first blow against the men that hated and persecuted them. None dared withstand them, so wide-spread the
fear their rise to power had engendered; 3 judge and governor and chieftain, ruler and administrator everywhere had
no praise too high for the Jewish people, for dread of
Mardochaeus; 4 did he not hold the first place at court, high
in the royal favour? Every day his fame grew, and he was in
all men's mouths.
5 Great havoc the Jews wrought among their enemies that
day, slaying the very men who had marked them down for
slaughter; 6 in Susan alone they put five hundred men to
death, not counting the ten sons of Aman the Agagite. Ten
sons he had, 7 Pharsandatha, Delphon, Esphatha, 8 Phoratha, Adalia, Aridatha, 9 Phermestha, Arisai, Adirai and
Jezatha; 10 all these they slew, and would take nothing of
theirs for plunder. 11 And now, learning the number of those
who had been killed at Susan, 12 the king said to the queen,
In Susan alone the Jews have slain five hundred men, and
Aman's ten sons besides; here is massacre indeed, if in all
my dominions they have done the like. Tell me, what more
wouldst thou have me do for thee? 13 Please it the king's

TODAY'S ENGLISH VERSION

enemies of the Jews who were wiped out. People everywhere
were afraid of the Jews, and no one could stand against
them. 3In fact, the provincial governors, the administrators,
and the royal scribes showed respect for the Jews, because
they were all afraid of Mordecai. 4-5The royal decree had
made his name known throughout the empire.
6In Susa, the capital city itself, the Jews killed five hundred people 7-10and looted their property. Among them were
the ten sons of Haman son of Hammedatha, a Bougaean, the
enemy of the Jews: Pharsannestain, Delphon, Phasga, Phara-
datha, Barea, Sarbacha, Marmasima, Arouphaeus, Arsaeus,
and Zabouthaeus.
11That same day the number of people killed in Susa was
reported to the king. 12He then said to Esther, "In Susa
alone the Jews have killed five hundred people. What must
they have done out in the provinces! Tell me what else you
want, and you shall have it."

NEW REVISED STANDARD VERSION

same day the enemies of the Jews perished; no one resisted,
because they feared them. 3The chief provincial governors,
the princes, and the royal secretaries were paying honor to
the Jews, because fear of Mordecai weighed upon them.
4The king's decree required that Mordecai's name be held in
honor throughout the kingdom.[a] 6Now in the city of Susa
the Jews killed five hundred people, 7including Pharsannestain, Delphon, Phasga, 8Pharadatha, Barea, Sarbacha,
9Marmasima, Aruphaeus, Arsaeus, Zabutheus, 10the ten
sons of Haman son of Hammedatha, the Bougean, the
enemy of the Jews—and they indulged[b] themselves in plunder.
11 That very day the number of those killed in Susa was
reported to the king. 12The king said to Esther, "In Susa, the
capital, the Jews have destroyed five hundred people. What
do you suppose they have done in the surrounding country-
side? Whatever more you ask will be done for you." 13And

a Meaning of Gk uncertain. Some ancient authorities add verse 5, *So the Jews struck down all their enemies with the sword, killing and destroying them, and they did as they pleased to those who hated them.* *b* Other ancient authorities read *did not indulge*

NEW AMERICAN BIBLE

Jews mustered in their cities throughout the provinces of
King Ahasuerus to attack those who sought to do them
harm, and no one could withstand them, but all peoples
were seized with a fear of them. 3Moreover, all the officials
of the provinces, the satraps, governors, and royal procurators supported the Jews from fear of Mordecai; 4for Mordecai
was powerful in the royal palace, and the report was spreading through all the provinces that he was continually growing in power.
5The Jews struck down all their enemies with the sword,
killing and destroying them; they did to their enemies as
they pleased. 6In the stronghold of Susa, the Jews killed and
destroyed five hundred men. 7They also killed Parshandatha, Dalphon, Aspatha, 8Porathai, Adalia, Aridatha,
9Parmashta, Arisai, Aridai, and Vaizatha, 10the ten sons of
Haman, son of Hammedatha, the foe of the Jews. However,
they did not engage in plundering.
11On the same day, when the number of those killed in the
stronghold of Susa was reported to the king, 12he said to
Queen Esther: "In the stronghold of Susa the Jews have
killed and destroyed five hundred men, as well as the ten
sons of Haman. What must they have done in the other royal
provinces! You shall again be granted whatever you ask, and
whatever you request shall be honored." 13So Esther said,

NEW JERUSALEM BIBLE

provinces of King Ahasuerus, the Jews assembled to strike at
those who had planned to injure them. No one resisted them,
since the various peoples were now all afraid of them.
3Provincial officers-of-state, satraps, governors and royal
officials, all supported the Jews for fear of Mordecai. 4And
indeed Mordecai was a power in the palace and his fame was
spreading through all the provinces; Mordecai was steadily
growing more powerful.
5So the Jews struck down all their enemies with the sword,
with resulting slaughter and destruction, and worked their
will on their opponents. 6In the citadel of Susa alone, the
Jews put to death and slaughtered five hundred men,
7notably Parshandatha, Dalphon, Aspatha, 8Poratha,
Adalia, Aridatha, 9Parmashtha, Arisai, Aridai and Jezatha,
10the ten sons of Haman son of Hammedatha, the persecutor
of the Jews. But they took no plunder.
11The number of those killed in the citadel of Susa was
reported to the king that same day. 12The king said to
Queen Esther, 'In the citadel of Susa the Jews have killed
five hundred men and also the ten sons of Haman. What
must they have done in the other provinces of the realm?
Tell me your request; I grant it to you. Tell me what else you
would like; it is yours for the asking.' 13'If such is the

Greek Old Testament

βασιλεῖ Δοθήτω τοῖς Ιουδαίοις χρῆσθαι ὡσαύτως τὴν αὔριον
ὥστε τοὺς δέκα υἱοὺς κρεμάσαι Αμαν. 14 καὶ ἐπέτρεψεν
οὕτως γενέσθαι καὶ ἐξέθηκε τοῖς Ιουδαίοις τῆς πόλεως τὰ
σώματα τῶν υἱῶν Αμαν κρεμάσαι. 15 καὶ συνήχθησαν οἱ
Ιουδαῖοι ἐν Σούσοις τῇ τεσσαρεσκαιδεκάτῃ τοῦ Αδαρ καὶ
ἀπέκτειναν ἄνδρας τριακοσίους καὶ οὐδὲν διήρπασαν. —
16 οἱ δὲ λοιποὶ τῶν Ιουδαίων οἱ ἐν τῇ βασιλείᾳ συνήχθησαν
καὶ ἑαυτοῖς ἐβοήθουν καὶ ἀνεπαύσαντο ἀπὸ τῶν πολεμίων·
ἀπώλεσαν γὰρ αὐτῶν μυρίους πεντακισχιλίους τῇ τρισκαιδεκάτῃ τοῦ Αδαρ καὶ οὐδὲν διήρπασαν. 17 καὶ ἀνεπαύσαντο
τῇ τεσσαρεσκαιδεκάτῃ τοῦ αὐτοῦ μηνὸς καὶ ἦγον αὐτὴν
ἡμέραν ἀναπαύσεως μετὰ χαρᾶς καὶ εὐφροσύνης. 18 οἱ δὲ
Ιουδαῖοι οἱ ἐν Σούσοις τῇ πόλει συνήχθησαν καὶ τῇ τεσσαρεσκαιδεκάτῃ καὶ οὐκ ἀνεπαύσαντο· ἦγον δὲ καὶ τὴν
πεντεκαιδεκάτην μετὰ χαρᾶς καὶ εὐφροσύνης. 19 διὰ τοῦτο
οὖν οἱ Ιουδαῖοι οἱ διεσπαρμένοι ἐν πάσῃ χώρᾳ τῇ ἔξω
ἄγουσιν τὴν τεσσαρεσκαιδεκάτην τοῦ Αδαρ ἡμέραν ἀγαθὴν
μετ᾿ εὐφροσύνης ἀποστέλλοντες μερίδας ἕκαστος τῷ πλησίον, οἱ δὲ κατοικοῦντες ἐν ταῖς μητροπόλεσιν καὶ τὴν
πεντεκαιδεκάτην τοῦ Αδαρ ἡμέραν εὐφροσύνην ἀγαθὴν
ἄγουσιν ἐξαποστέλλοντες μερίδας τοῖς πλησίον.

King James Version

13 Then said Esther, If it please the king, let it be granted to the Jews which *are* in Shushan to do to morrow also according unto this day's decree, and let Haman's ten sons be hanged upon the gallows.

14 And the king commanded it so to be done: and the decree was given at Shushan; and they hanged Haman's ten sons.

15 For the Jews that *were* in Shushan gathered themselves together on the fourteenth day also of the month Adar, and slew three hundred men at Shushan; but on the prey they laid not their hand.

16 But the other Jews that *were* in the king's provinces gathered themselves together, and stood for their lives, and had rest from their enemies, and slew of their foes seventy and five thousand, but they laid not their hands on the prey,

17 On the thirteenth day of the month Adar; and on the fourteenth day of the same rested they, and made it a day of feasting and gladness.

18 But the Jews that *were* at Shushan assembled together on the thirteenth *day* thereof, and on the fourteenth thereof; and on the fifteenth *day* of the same they rested, and made it a day of feasting and gladness.

19 Therefore the Jews of the villages, that dwelt in the unwalled towns, made the fourteenth day of the month Adar *a day of* gladness and feasting, and a good day, and of sending portions one to another.

Douay Old Testament

13 And she answered: If it please the king, let it be granted to the Jews, to do to morrow in Susan as they have done to day, and that the ten sons of Aman may be hanged upon gibbets.

14 And the king commanded that it should be so done. And forthwith the edict was hung up in Susan, and the ten sons of Aman were hanged.

15 And on the fourteenth day of the month Adar the Jews gathered themselves together, and they killed in Susan three hundred men: but they took not their substance.

16 Moreover through all the provinces which were subject to the king's dominion the Jews stood for their lives, and slew their enemies and persecutors: insomuch that the number of them that were killed amounted to seventy-five thousand, and no man took any of their goods.

17 Now the thirteenth day of the month Adar was the first day with them all of the slaughter, and on the fourteenth day they left off. Which they ordained to be kept holy day, so that all times hereafter they should celebrate it with feasting, joy, and banquets.

18 But they that were killing in the city of Susan, were employed in the slaughter on the thirteenth and fourteenth day of the same month: and on the fifteenth day they rested. And therefore they appointed that day to be a holy day of feasting and gladness.

19 But those Jews that dwelt in towns not walled and in villages, appointed the fourteenth day of the month Adar for banquets and gladness, so as to rejoice on that day, and send one another portions of their banquets and meats.

Knox Translation

grace, she answered, let the Jews be free to continue this
day's work to-morrow; and let the bodies of Aman's sons be
hanged on gibbets. 14 So the king gave orders as she asked.
No sooner was the decree posted up, than gallows were
made for the bodies of Aman's sons; 15 and on the fourteenth day of Adar the Jews mustered afresh, killing three
hundred citizens of Susan, but taking nothing of theirs for
plunder.

16 All over the king's dominions, the Jews fought for their
lives, and put to death the enemies that persecuted them, till
seventy-five thousand of them lay slain, and no plunder
taken. 17 Everywhere it was on the thirteenth of Adar they
began laying about them, and next day they slew no more;
so it was this day, the fourteenth, they made into a holiday,
to be observed thenceforward with feast, and rejoicing, and
carousal. 18 In the city of Susan itself, the killing went on for
two days; it was the fifteenth day, when their work was
over, that they set apart for feasting and merrymaking;
19 but in the unwalled towns and villages round about,
carouse and rejoicing and the sharing out of dainties began

TODAY'S ENGLISH VERSION

13Esther answered, "Let the Jews in Susa do again tomorrow what they were allowed to do today. And have the bodies of Haman's ten sons hung up." 14The king agreed and
permitted the Jews to put the bodies of Haman's ten sons on
public display. 15On the fourteenth day of Adar the Jews of
Susa got together again and killed three hundred more people in the city. But they did no looting.

16The Jews in the provinces also organized and defended
themselves. They rid themselves of their enemies by killing
15,000 people on the thirteenth day of Adar, but they did no
looting. 17On the next day, the fourteenth, there was no
more killing, and the Jews made it a joyful holiday of rest
and feasting. 18The Jews of Susa, however, made the fifteenth a holiday, since they had slaughtered their enemies
on the thirteenth and fourteenth and did not stop until the
fifteenth. 19This is why Jews who live in small towns
observe the fourteenth day of the month of Adar as a holiday, a time of giving gifts of food to one another, while the
Jews in the large cities celebrate the holiday in the same way
on the fifteenth.

NEW REVISED STANDARD VERSION

Esther said to the king, "Let the Jews be allowed to do the
same tomorrow. Also, hang up the bodies of Haman's ten
sons." 14So he permitted this to be done, and handed over to
the Jews of the city the bodies of Haman's sons to hang up.
15The Jews who were in Susa gathered on the fourteenth and
killed three hundred people, but took no plunder.

16 Now the other Jews in the kingdom gathered to defend
themselves, and got relief from their enemies. They destroyed
fifteen thousand of them, but did not engage in plunder.
17On the fourteenth day they rested and made that same day
a day of rest, celebrating it with joy and gladness. 18The
Jews who were in Susa, the capital, came together also on
the fourteenth, but did not rest. They celebrated the fifteenth
with joy and gladness. 19On this account then the Jews who
are scattered around the country outside Susa keep the fourteenth of Adar as a joyful holiday, and send presents of food
to one another, while those who live in the large cities keep
the fifteenth day of Adar as their joyful holiday, also sending
presents to one another.

NEW AMERICAN BIBLE

"If it pleases your majesty, let the Jews in Susa be permitted
again tomorrow to act according to today's decree, and let
the ten sons of Haman be hanged on gibbets." 14The king
then gave an order to this effect, and the decree was published in Susa. So the ten sons of Haman were hanged,
15and the Jews in Susa mustered again on the fourteenth of
the month of Adar and killed three hundred men in Susa.
However, they did not engage in plundering.

16The other Jews, who dwelt in the royal provinces, also
mustered and defended themselves, and obtained rest from
their enemies. They killed seventy-five thousand of their
foes, without engaging in plunder, 17on the thirteenth day
of the month of Adar. On the fourteenth of the month they
rested, and made it a day of feasting and rejoicing.

18(The Jews in Susa, however, mustered on the thirteenth
and fourteenth of the month. But on the fifteenth they rested,
and made it a day of feasting and rejoicing.) 19That is why
the rural Jews, who dwell in villages, celebrate the fourteenth
of the month of Adar as a day of rejoicing and feasting, a holiday on which they send gifts of food to one another.

NEW JERUSALEM BIBLE

king's pleasure,' Esther replied, 'let the Jews of Susa be
allowed to enforce today's decree tomorrow as well. And as
for the ten sons of Haman, let their bodies be hanged on the
gallows.' 14Whereupon, the king having given the order,
the edict was promulgated in Susa and the ten sons of
Haman were hanged. 15Thus the Jews of Susa reassembled
on the fourteenth day of the month of Adar and killed three
hundred men in the city. But they took no plunder.

16The other Jews who lived in the king's provinces also
assembled to defend their lives and rid themselves of their
enemies. They slaughtered seventy-five thousand of their
opponents. But they took no plunder. 17This was on the
thirteenth day of the month of Adar. On the fourteenth day
they rested and made it a day of feasting and gladness.
18But for the Jews of Susa, who had assembled on the thirteenth and fourteenth days, the fifteenth was the day they
rested, making that a day of feasting and gladness. 19This is
why Jewish country people, those who live in undefended
villages, keep the fourteenth day of the month of Adar as a
day of gladness, feasting and holiday-making, and the
exchanging of presents with one another, 19a*whereas for*
those who live in cities the day of rejoicing and exchanging
presents with their neighbours is the fifteenth day of Adar.

GREEK OLD TESTAMENT

20 Ἔγραψεν δὲ Μαρδοχαῖος τοὺς λόγους τούτους εἰς
βιβλίον καὶ ἐξαπέστειλεν τοῖς Ιουδαίοις, ὅσοι ἦσαν ἐν τῇ
Ἀρταξέρξου βασιλείᾳ, τοῖς ἐγγὺς καὶ τοῖς μακράν, 21 στῆσαι τὰς ἡμέρας ταύτας ἀγαθὰς ἄγειν τε τὴν τεσσαρεσκαιδεκάτην καὶ τὴν πεντεκαιδεκάτην τοῦ Αδαρ — 22 ἐν γὰρ
ταύταις ταῖς ἡμέραις ἀνεπαύσαντο οἱ Ιουδαῖοι ἀπὸ τῶν
ἐχθρῶν αὐτῶν — καὶ τὸν μῆνα, ἐν ᾧ ἐστράφη αὐτοῖς [ὅς ἦν
Αδαρ] ἀπὸ πένθους εἰς χαρὰν καὶ ἀπὸ ὀδύνης εἰς ἀγαθὴν
ἡμέραν, ἄγειν ὅλον ἀγαθὰς ἡμέρας γάμων καὶ εὐφροσύνης
ἐξαποστέλλοντας μερίδας τοῖς φίλοις καὶ τοῖς πτωχοῖς.
23 καὶ προσεδέξαντο οἱ Ιουδαῖοι, καθὼς ἔγραψεν αὐτοῖς ὁ
Μαρδοχαῖος, 24 πῶς Αμαν Αμαδαθου ὁ Μακεδὼν ἐπολέμει
αὐτούς, καθὼς ἔθετο ψήφισμα καὶ κλῆρον ἀφανίσαι αὐτούς,
25 καὶ ὡς εἰσῆλθεν πρὸς τὸν βασιλέα λέγων κρεμάσαι τὸν
Μαρδοχαῖον· ὅσα δὲ ἐπεχείρησεν ἐπάξαι ἐπὶ τοὺς Ιουδαίους
κακά, ἐπ᾽ αὐτὸν ἐγένοντο, καὶ ἐκρεμάσθη αὐτὸς καὶ τὰ τέκνα αὐτοῦ. 26 διὰ τοῦτο ἐπεκλήθησαν αἱ ἡμέραι αὗται
Φρουραι διὰ τοὺς κλήρους, ὅτι τῇ διαλέκτῳ αὐτῶν καλοῦνται
Φρουραι, διὰ τοὺς λόγους τῆς ἐπιστολῆς ταύτης καὶ ὅσα
πεπόνθασιν διὰ ταῦτα καὶ ὅσα αὐτοῖς ἐγένετο· 27 καὶ ἔστησεν καὶ προσεδέχοντο οἱ Ιουδαῖοι ἐφ᾽ ἑαυτοῖς καὶ ἐπὶ τῷ

KING JAMES VERSION

20 And Mordecai wrote these things, and sent letters unto all the Jews that *were* in all the provinces of the king Ahasuerus, *both* nigh and far,

21 To stablish *this* among them, that they should keep the fourteenth day of the month Adar, and the fifteenth day of the same, yearly,

22 As the days wherein the Jews rested from their enemies, and the month which was turned unto them from sorrow to joy, and from mourning into a good day: that they should make them days of feasting and joy, and of sending portions one to another, and gifts to the poor.

23 And the Jews undertook to do as they had begun, and as Mordecai had written unto them;

24 Because Haman the son of Hammedatha, the Agagite, the enemy of all the Jews, had devised against the Jews to destroy them, and had cast Pur, that *is,* the lot, to consume them, and to destroy them;

25 But when *Esther* came before the king, he commanded by letters that his wicked device, which he devised against the Jews, should return upon his own head, and that he and his sons should be hanged on the gallows.

26 Wherefore they called these days Purim after the name of Pur. Therefore for all the words of this letter, and *of that* which they had seen concerning this matter, and which had come unto them,

27 The Jews ordained, and took upon them, and upon

DOUAY OLD TESTAMENT

20 And Mardochai wrote all these things, and sent them comprised in letters to the Jews that abode in all the king's provinces, both those that lay near and those afar off,

21 That they should receive the fourteenth and fifteenth day of the month Adar for holy days, and always at the return of the year should celebrate them with solemn honour:

22 Because on those days the Jews revenged themselves of their enemies, and their mourning and sorrow were turned into mirth and joy, and that these should be days of feasting and gladness, in which they should send one to another portions of meats, and should give gifts to the poor.

23 And the Jews undertook to observe with solemnity all they had begun to do at that time, which Mardochai by letters had commanded to be done.

24 For Aman, the son of Amadathi of the race of Agag, the enemy and adversary of the Jews, had devised evil against them, to kill them and destroy them: and had cast Phur, that is, the lot.

25 And afterwards Esther went in to the king, beseeching him that his endeavours might be made void by the king's letters: and the evil that he had intended against the Jews, might return upon his own head. And so both he and his sons were hanged upon gibbets.

26 And since that time these days are called Phurim, that is, of lots: because Phur, that is, the lot, was cast into the urn. And all things that were done, are contained in the volume of this epistle, that is, of this book:

27 And the things that they suffered, and that were afterwards changed, the Jews took upon themselves and their

KNOX TRANSLATION

on the fourteenth. 20 So Mardochaeus wrote to all the king's
Jewish subjects, near and far, 21 setting all this out and bidding them observe both the fourteenth and the fifteenth,
22 year by year, as the days of Jewry's vengeance, when
weeping and lament gave place to mirth and gladness. There
was to be feasting on both days, and on both days rejoicing;
dainties should be exchanged, and gifts made to the poor.
23 So the will they then had and the orders Mardochaeus
sent became a yearly rite; 24 to recall how Amadathi's son,
Aman the Agagite, thought to vent his enmity against the
Jews by murderously destroying them, and how he consulted
Put, the lot; 25 how Esther sought audience with the king,
praying for a royal decree that should thwart his design, and
make his malice fall on his own head; and how Aman and
his sons went to the gallows. 26 This feast has ever been
known as the feast of Purim, because of Aman's lot-taking.
Here in this letter, nay, this book you have been reading, the
whole story has been set out, 27 deeds done, griefs borne,
and strange vicissitudes. And the Jews pledged themselves

TODAY'S ENGLISH VERSION

20 Mordecai had these events written down in a book and
sent it to all the Jews, near and far, throughout the Persian
Empire, 21 telling them to observe the fourteenth and fifteenth days of Adar as holidays. 22 These were the days on
which the Jews had rid themselves of their enemies. The Jews
were to observe the whole month as a holiday, for this was a
month that had been turned from a time of grief and despair
into a time of joy and happiness. They were told to observe
these days with feasts and parties, giving gifts of food to
friends and to the poor. 23 So the Jews accepted all that
Mordecai had written.

24 Mordecai had recorded how Haman son of Hammedatha, a Macedonian, had fought against the Jewish people,
how he had made a decree and cast lots to determine the
day he would destroy them, 25 and how he had gone to the
king to request that Mordecai be hanged. But Haman suffered the same fate he had planned for the Jews—he and his
sons were hanged from the gallows. 26-28 Because of
Mordecai's letter, because of all they had suffered, and
because of all that had happened to them, the Jews accepted
Mordecai's suggestion and made it a rule for themselves,

NEW REVISED STANDARD VERSION

20 Mordecai recorded these things in a book, and sent it
to the Jews in the kingdom of Artaxerxes both near and far,
21 telling them that they should keep the fourteenth and fifteenth days of Adar, 22 for on these days the Jews got relief
from their enemies. The whole month (namely, Adar), in
which their condition had been changed from sorrow into
gladness and from a time of distress to a holiday, was to be
celebrated as a time for feasting[a] and gladness and for sending presents of food to their friends and to the poor.

23 So the Jews accepted what Mordecai had written to
them 24—how Haman son of Hammedatha, the Macedonian,[b] fought against them, how he made a decree and cast
lots[c] to destroy them, 25 and how he went in to the king,
telling him to hang Mordecai; but the wicked plot he had
devised against the Jews came back upon himself, and he
and his sons were hanged. 26 Therefore these days were
called "Purim," because of the lots (for in their language this
is the word that means "lots"). And so, because of what was
written in this letter, and because of what they had experienced in this affair and what had befallen them, Mordecai
established this festival,[d] 27 and the Jews took upon themselves, upon their descendants, and upon all who would join

a Gk *of weddings* *b* Other ancient witnesses read *the Bougean* *c* Gk *a lot* *d* Gk *he established* (it)

NEW AMERICAN BIBLE

20 Mordecai recorded these events and sent letters to all the
Jews, both near and far, in all the provinces of King
Ahasuerus. 21 He ordered them to celebrate every year both
the fourteenth and the fifteenth of the month of Adar 22 as
the day on which the Jews obtained rest from their enemies
and as the month which was turned for them from sorrow
into joy, from mourning into festivity. They were to observe
these days with feasting and gladness, sending food to one
another and gifts to the poor. 23 The Jews took upon themselves for the future this observance which they instituted at
the written direction of Mordecai.

24 Haman, son of Hammedatha the Agagite, the foe of all
the Jews, had planned to destroy them and had cast the **pur,**
or lot, for the time of their defeat and destruction. 25 Yet,
when Esther entered the royal presence, the king ordered in
writing that the wicked plan Haman had devised against the
Jews should instead be turned against Haman and that he
and his sons should be hanged on gibbets. 26 And so these
days have been named Purim after the word **pur.**

Thus, because of all that was contained in this letter, and
because of what they had witnessed and experienced in this
affair, 27 the Jews established and took upon themselves,

NEW JERUSALEM BIBLE

20 Mordecai committed these events to writing. Then he
sent letters to all the Jews living in the provinces of King
Ahasuerus, both near and far, 21 enjoining them to celebrate
the fourteenth and fifteenth days of the month of Adar every
year, 22 as the days on which the Jews had rid themselves of
their enemies, and the month in which their sorrow had been
turned into gladness, and mourning into a holiday. He therefore told them to keep these as days of festivity and gladness
when they were to exchange presents and make gifts to the
poor.

23 Once having begun, the Jews continued observing these
practices, Mordecai having written them an account 24 of
how Haman son of Hammedatha, the Agagite, the persecutor
of all the Jews, had plotted their destruction and had cast the
pur, that is, the lot, for their overthrow and ruin; 25 but how,
when he went back to the king to ask him to order the hanging of Mordecai, the wicked scheme which he had devised
against the Jews recoiled on his own head, and both he and
his sons were hanged on the gallows; 26 and that, hence,
these days were called Purim, from the word *pur*. And so,
because of what was written in this letter, and because of
what they had seen for themselves and of what had happened to them, 27 the Jews willingly bound themselves, their

GREEK OLD TESTAMENT

σπέρματι αὐτῶν καὶ ἐπὶ τοῖς προστεθειμένοις ἐπ' αὐτῶν
οὐδὲ μὴν ἄλλως χρήσονται· αἱ δὲ ἡμέραι αὗται μνημόσυνον
ἐπιτελούμενον κατὰ γενεὰν καὶ γενεὰν καὶ πόλιν καὶ πα-
τριὰν καὶ χώραν· [28] αἱ δὲ ἡμέραι αὗται τῶν Φρουραι ἀχθή-
σονται εἰς τὸν ἅπαντα χρόνον, καὶ τὸ μνημόσυνον αὐτῶν οὐ
μὴ ἐκλίπῃ ἐκ τῶν γενεῶν. [29] καὶ ἔγραψεν Εσθηρ ἡ βασίλισσα
θυγάτηρ Αμιναδαβ καὶ Μαρδοχαῖος ὁ Ιουδαῖος ὅσα ἐποίησαν
τό τε στερέωμα τῆς ἐπιστολῆς τῶν Φρουραι. [31] καὶ Μαρδοχαῖος καὶ Εσθηρ ἡ βασίλισσα ἔστησαν ἑαυτοῖς καθ' ἑαυτῶν
καὶ τότε στήσαντες κατὰ τῆς ὑγιείας αὐτῶν καὶ τὴν βουλὴν
αὐτῶν· [32] καὶ Εσθηρ λόγῳ ἔστησεν εἰς τὸν αἰῶνα, καὶ
ἐγράφη εἰς μνημόσυνον.

10 Ἔγραψεν δὲ ὁ βασιλεὺς τέλη ἐπὶ τὴν βασιλείαν τῆς
τε γῆς καὶ τῆς θαλάσσης. [2] καὶ τὴν ἰσχὺν αὐτοῦ καὶ
ἀνδραγαθίαν πλοῦτόν τε καὶ δόξαν τῆς βασιλείας αὐτοῦ,
ἰδοὺ γέγραπται ἐν βιβλίῳ βασιλέων Περσῶν καὶ Μήδων εἰς

KING JAMES VERSION

their seed, and upon all such as joined themselves unto them, so as it should not fail, that they would keep these two days according to their writing, and according to their *appointed* time every year;

28 And *that* these days *should be* remembered and kept throughout every generation, every family, every province, and every city; and *that* these days of Purim should not fail from among the Jews, nor the memorial of them perish from their seed.

29 Then Esther the queen, the daughter of Abihail, and Mordecai the Jew, wrote with all authority, to confirm this second letter of Purim.

30 And he sent the letters unto all the Jews, to the hundred twenty and seven provinces of the kingdom of Ahasuerus, *with* words of peace and truth,

31 To confirm these days of Purim in their times *appointed,* according as Mordecai the Jew and Esther the queen had enjoined them, and as they had decreed for themselves and for their seed, the matters of the fastings and their cry.

32 And the decree of Esther confirmed these matters of Purim; and it was written in the book.

10 And the king Ahasuerus laid a tribute upon the land, and *upon* the isles of the sea.

2 And all the acts of his power and of his might, and the declaration of the greatness of Mordecai, whereunto the king advanced him, *are* they not written in the book of the chronicles of the kings of Media and Persia?

DOUAY OLD TESTAMENT

seed, and upon all that had a mind to be joined to their religion, so that it should be lawful for none to pass these days without solemnity: which the writing testifieth, and certain times require, as the years continually succeed one another.

28 These are the days which shall never be forgot: and which all provinces in the whole world shall celebrate throughout all generations: neither is there any city wherein the days of Phurim, that is, of lots, must not be observed by the Jews, and by their posterity, which is bound to these ceremonies.

29 And Esther the queen, the daughter of Abihail, and Mardochai the Jew, wrote also a second epistle, that with all diligence this day should be established a festival for the time to come.

30 And they sent to all the Jews that were in the hundred and twenty-seven provinces of king Assuerus, that they should have peace, and receive truth,

31 And observe the days of lots, and celebrate them with joy in their proper time: as Mardochai and Esther had appointed, and they undertook them to be observed by themselves and by their seed, fasts, and cries, and the days of lots,

32 And all things which are contained in the history of this book, which is called Esther.

10 AND king Assuerus made all the land, and all the islands of the sea tributary.

2 And his strength and his empire, and the dignity and greatness wherewith he exalted Mardochai, are written in the books of the Medes, and of the Persians:

KNOX TRANSLATION

and their children, with all who in after times should seek
admission to their way of worship, to observe two days in
each year, at the fixed time by this record determined.[a]
[28] Never must the observance die out with the passing of
years, where there are Jews living in any part of the world; in
every city the feast of Lots must be kept by the Jews, and by
all those on whom their ancestral customs are binding.
[29] There was a second letter written by queen Esther,
Abihail's daughter, and the Jew Mardochaeus, confirming
this ordinance for ever; [30] it went out to all the Jews in the
hundred and twenty-seven provinces of Assuerus' realm,
wishing them health and assuring them that they had her
warrant [31] for keeping Purim feast with yearly rejoicing. And
they, at the bidding of Mardochaeus and Esther, bound
themselves and their children to keep it in mind; the fasting,
and the cries for aid, the casting of the lots, [32] and all else
that is recorded in this book, the book of Esther.

10 This Assuerus received tribute from the whole mainland, and from the islands out at sea; [2] how great
his reign was, you may learn from the Annals of the Medes
and Persians. There, too, you will read of the high honours
to which he raised Mardochaeus; [3] how Mardochaeus, a Jew,

a Verses 20-27, the interpretation of which is in several places uncertain, are taken by some as implying that Mardochaeus' letter set out at length the story of what had been happening at Susan, and that the Book of Esther itself is either a copy of, or an abridgement made from, this document.

TODAY'S ENGLISH VERSION

their descendants, and anyone that might become a Jew,
that these days should be properly observed as a memorial,
generation after generation, in every city, province, and
country. The Jews were to remember and observe these days
of Purim for all time to come and never neglect them. (The
holidays are called Purim because "purim" in their language
is the word for "lots.")
29-30 Then Queen Esther, the daughter of Aminadab, along
with Mordecai the Jew, wrote down what they had done,
putting the queen's full authority behind the letter about
Purim. 31 They both took responsibility for establishing the
festival and made up their minds to observe it at all costs.[a]
32 Esther established the festival forever, and a written record
was made of her official decree.
10 King Xerxes imposed taxes on the people of the
coastal regions of his empire as well as on those of
the interior. 2 His power and virtue, as well as the wealth
and splendor of his empire, are recorded in the official
records of the kings of Persia and Media. 3 Mordecai was

[a] at all costs; *Greek unclear.*

NEW REVISED STANDARD VERSION

them, to observe it without fail.[a] These days of Purim should
be a memorial and kept from generation to generation, in
every city, family, and country. 28 These days of Purim were
to be observed for all time, and the commemoration of them
was never to cease among their descendants.
29 Then Queen Esther daughter of Aminadab along with
Mordecai the Jew wrote down what they had done, and gave
full authority to the letter about Purim.[b] 31 And Mordecai
and Queen Esther established this decision on their own
responsibility, pledging their own well-being to the plan.[c]
32 Esther established it by a decree forever, and it was written
for a memorial.
10 The king levied a tax upon his kingdom both by land
and sea. 2 And as for his power and bravery, and the
wealth and glory of his kingdom, they were recorded in the
annals of the kings of the Persians and the Medes.

a Meaning of Gk uncertain *b* Verse 30 in Heb is lacking in Gk: *Letters were sent to all the Jews, to the one hundred twenty-seven provinces of the kingdom of Ahasuerus, in words of peace and truth.* *c* Meaning of Gk uncertain

NEW AMERICAN BIBLE

their descendants, and all who should join them, the inviolable obligation of celebrating these two days every year in
the manner prescribed by this letter, and at the time appointed. 28 These days were to be commemorated and kept in
every generation, by every clan, in every province, and in
every city. These days of Purim were never to fall into disuse
among the Jews, nor into oblivion among their descendants.
29 Queen Esther, daughter of Abihail and of Mordecai the
Jew, wrote to confirm with full authority this second letter
about Purim, 30 when Mordecai sent documents concerning
peace and security to all the Jews in the hundred and twenty-
seven provinces of Ahasuerus' kingdom. 31 Thus were established, for their appointed time, these days of Purim which
Mordecai the Jew and Queen Esther had designated for the
Jews, just as they had previously enjoined upon themselves
and upon their race the duty of fasting and supplication.
32 The command of Esther confirmed these prescriptions for
Purim and was recorded in the book.
10 King Ahasuerus laid tribute on the land and on the
islands of the sea. 2 All the acts of his power and
valor, as well as a detailed account of the greatness of
Mordecai, whom the king promoted, are recorded in the
chronicles of the kings of Media and Persia. 3 The Jew

NEW JERUSALEM BIBLE

descendants and all who should join them, to celebrate these
two days without fail, in the manner prescribed and at the
time appointed, year after year. 28 Thus commemorated and
celebrated from generation to generation, in every family, in
every province, in every city, these days of Purim will never
be abrogated among the Jews, nor will their memory perish
from their race.
29 Queen Esther, the daughter of Abihail, wrote with full
authority to ratify this second letter, 30 and sent letters to all
the Jews of the hundred and twenty-seven provinces of the
realm of Ahasuerus, in terms of peace and loyalty 31 enjoining them to observe these days of Purim at the appointed
time, as Mordecai the Jew had recommended, and in the
manner prescribed for themselves and their descendants,
with additional ordinances for fasts and lamentations.
32 The ordinance of Esther fixed the law of Purim, which was
then recorded in a book.
10 King Ahasuerus put not only the mainland under
tribute but the Mediterranean islands as well. 2 All
his feats of power and valour, and the account of the high
honour to which he raised Mordecai: all this is recorded in
the Book of the Annals of the Kings of Media and Persia.

GREEK OLD TESTAMENT

μνημόσυνον. 3 ὁ δὲ Μαρδοχαῖος διεδέχετο τὸν βασιλέα
Ἀρταξέρξην καὶ μέγας ἦν ἐν τῇ βασιλείᾳ καὶ δεδοξασμένος
ὑπὸ τῶν Ιουδαίων· καὶ φιλούμενος διηγεῖτο τὴν ἀγωγὴν
παντὶ τῷ ἔθνει αὐτοῦ.

3a Καὶ εἶπεν Μαρδοχαῖος Παρὰ τοῦ θεοῦ ἐγένετο ταῦτα·
3b γὰρ περὶ τοῦ ἐνυπνίου, οὗ εἶδον περὶ τῶν λόγων τούτων·
οὐδὲ γὰρ παρῆλθεν ἀπ' αὐτῶν λόγος. 3c μικρὰ πηγή, ἣ ἐγένετο ποταμὸς καὶ ἦν φῶς καὶ ἥλιος καὶ ὕδωρ πολύ· Εσθηρ
ἐστὶν ὁ ποταμός, ἣν ἐγάμησεν ὁ βασιλεὺς καὶ ἐποίησεν
βασίλισσαν. 3d δὲ δύο δράκοντες ἐγώ εἰμι καὶ Αμαν. 3e δὲ
ἔθνη τὰ ἐπισυναχθέντα ἀπολέσαι τὸ ὄνομα τῶν Ιουδαίων.
3f δὲ ἔθνος τὸ ἐμόν, οὗτός ἐστιν Ισραηλ οἱ βοήσαντες πρὸς
τὸν θεὸν καὶ σωθέντες. καὶ ἔσωσεν κύριος τὸν λαὸν αὐτοῦ,
καὶ ἐρρύσατο κύριος ἡμᾶς ἐκ πάντων τῶν κακῶν τούτων, καὶ
ἐποίησεν ὁ θεὸς τὰ σημεῖα καὶ τὰ τέρατα τὰ μεγάλα, ἃ οὐ
γέγονεν ἐν τοῖς ἔθνεσιν. 3g τοῦτο ἐποίησεν κλήρους δύο,
ἕνα τῷ λαῷ τοῦ θεοῦ καὶ ἕνα πᾶσι τοῖς ἔθνεσιν· 3h ἦλθον οἱ
δύο κλῆροι οὗτοι εἰς ὥραν καὶ καιρὸν καὶ εἰς ἡμέραν κρίσεως
ἐνώπιον τοῦ θεοῦ καὶ ἐν πᾶσι τοῖς ἔθνεσιν, 3i ἐμνήσθη ὁ
θεὸς τοῦ λαοῦ αὐτοῦ καὶ ἐδικαίωσεν τὴν κληρονομίαν αὐτοῦ.

KING JAMES VERSION

3 For Mordecai the Jew *was* next unto king Ahasuerus, and great among the Jews, and accepted of the multitude of his brethren, seeking the wealth of his people, and speaking peace to all his seed.

4 Then Mardocheus said, God hath done these things.

5 For I remember a dream which I saw concerning these matters, and nothing thereof hath failed.

6 A little fountain became a river, and there was light, and the sun, and much water: this river is Esther, whom the king married, and made queen:

7 And the two dragons are I and Aman.

8 And the nations were those that were assembled to destroy the name of the Jews:

9 And my nation is this Israel, which cried to God, and were saved: for the Lord hath saved his people, and the Lord hath delivered us from all those evils, and God hath wrought signs and great wonders, which have not been done among the Gentiles.

10 Therefore hath he made two lots, one for the people of God, and another for all the Gentiles.

11 And these two lots came at the hour, and time, and day of judgment, before God among all nations.

12 So God remembered his people, and justified his inheritance.

DOUAY OLD TESTAMENT

3 And how Mardochai of the race of the Jews, was next after king Assuerus: and great among the Jews, and acceptable to the people of his brethren, seeking the good of his people, and speaking those things which were for the welfare of his seed.

4 Then Mardochai said: God hath done these things.

5 I remember a dream that I saw, which signified these same things: and nothing thereof hath failed.

6 The little fountain which grew into a river, and was turned into a light, and into the sun, and abounded into many waters, is Esther, whom the king married, and made queen.

7 But the two dragons are I and Aman.

8 The nations that were assembled are they that endeavoured to destroy the name of the Jews.

9 And my nation is Israel, who cried to the Lord, and the Lord saved his people: and he delivered us from all evils, and hath wrought great signs and wonders among the nations:

10 And he commanded that there should be two lots, one of the people of God, and the other of all the nations.

11 And both lots came to the day appointed already from that time before God to all nations:

12 And the Lord remembered his people, and had mercy on his inheritance.

KNOX TRANSLATION

became next in rank to the king himself, a great name among Jewish names, a man well loved by his fellows, that sought his people's good and brought blessings on their race.

(The remaining verses of chapter 10, with verse 1 of chapter 11, occur at the end of the Septuagint Greek; they may, however, have been displaced, being an extract from some fuller narrative. The dream referred to is described in chapter 11.)

4 ...All this has been God's doing, Mardochaeus said. 5 I
have not forgotten the dream I had, and all this was foretold
in it; not a word but has come true. 6 I dreamt of a little
spring that grew into a river, spreading out into sun and
sunlight, and so went rolling on in full tide. This was Esther,
the king's bride that became his queen. 7 I dreamt of two
dragons; of these, I was one, and Aman the other. 8 I dreamt
of nations mustering for battle; these were the men that
would have blotted out the Jewish name. 9 And the single
nation in my dream was Israel; did not Israel cry out to the
Lord, and win his protection, win deliverance from its
wrongs? Wondrous proof he gave of his power, for all the
world to see. 10 Two dooms he ordained, one for God's people and one for the Gentiles, 11 and either should take effect,
all the world over, after an interval of time divinely decreed;
12 then it was the Lord shewed he remembered his own people still, pitied his own servants still. 13 With eager and glad

TODAY'S ENGLISH VERSION

second in rank only to King Xerxes himself. He was a great
man in the empire and was honored by his fellow Jews. He
was greatly loved, for he sought the welfare of his people.

F[a] Then Mordecai said, "God has caused all these things to
happen! 2 And I am reminded of the dream I had about
all of this. Every detail of the dream has come true: 3 the
small spring that became a river, the dawn that turned into
sunlight, and the abundance of water. The river is Esther,
whom the king married and made his queen. 4 The two dragons represent Haman and me. 5 The nations are all those
who have gathered together to destroy the Jews. 6 My nation
is Israel, which cried out to God for help and was saved. The
Lord saved his people! He rescued us from all these evils and
performed great miracles and wonders that have never happened among other nations. 7 That is because God prepared
one destiny for his own people and another for all other
nations. 8 Then came the day and the hour when these two
destinies were to be decided; the time had come for God to
make a decision about the nations. 9 God remembered his
chosen people and gave the verdict in their favor. 10 So each

[a] *Chapter F 1-10 corresponds to chapters 10.4—11.1 in a number of English translations.*

NEW REVISED STANDARD VERSION

3 Mordecai acted with authority on behalf of King Artaxerxes
and was great in the kingdom, as well as honored by the
Jews. His way of life was such as to make him beloved to his
whole nation.

ADDITION F

4[a] And Mordecai said, "These things have come from God;
5 for I remember the dream that I had concerning these matters, and none of them has failed to be fulfilled. 6 There was
the little spring that became a river, and there was light and
sun and abundant water—the river is Esther, whom the king
married and made queen. 7 The two dragons are Haman and
myself. 8 The nations are those that gathered to destroy the
name of the Jews. 9 And my nation, this is Israel, who cried
out to God and was saved. The Lord has saved his people;
the Lord has rescued us from all these evils; God has done
great signs and wonders, wonders that have never happened
among the nations. 10 For this purpose he made two lots,
one for the people of God and one for all the nations, 11 and
these two lots came to the hour and moment and day of decision before God and among all the nations. 12 And God
remembered his people and vindicated his inheritance. 13 So

[a] Chapter 10.4-13 and 11.1 correspond to chapter F 1-11 in some translations.

NEW AMERICAN BIBLE

Mordecai was next in rank to King Ahasuerus, in high standing among the Jews, and was regarded with favor by his
many brethren, as the promoter of his people's welfare and
the herald of peace for his whole race.

F Then Mordecai said: "This is the work of God. 2 I recall
the dream I had about these very things, and not a single detail has been left unfulfilled— 3 the tiny spring that
grew into a river, the light of the sun, the many waters. The
river is Esther, whom the king married and made queen.
4 The two dragons are myself and Haman. 5 The nations are
those who assembled to destroy the name of the Jews, 6 but
my people is Israel, who cried to God and was saved.

"The LORD saved his people and delivered us from all these
evils. God worked signs and great wonders, such as have not
occurred among the nations. 7 For this purpose he arranged
two lots: one for the people of God, the second for all the
other nations. 8 These two lots were fulfilled in the hour, the
time, and the day of judgment before God and among all the
nations. 9 God remembered his people and rendered justice
to his inheritance.

NEW JERUSALEM BIBLE

3 And Mordecai the Jew was next in rank to King Ahasuerus. He was a man held in respect among the Jews,
esteemed by thousands of his brothers, a man who sought
the good of his people and cared for the welfare of his entire
race.

3a *And Mordecai said, 'All this is God's doing.* 3b *I remember the dream I had about these matters, nothing of which
has failed to come true:* 3c *the little spring that became a
river, the light that shone, the sun, the flood of water. Esther
is the river—she whom the king married and made queen.*
3d *The two dragons are Haman and myself.* 3e *The nations are
those that banded together to blot out the name of Jew.* 3f *The
single nation, mine, is Israel, those who cried out to God and
were saved. Yes, the Lord has saved his people, the Lord has
delivered us from all these evils, God has worked such signs
and great wonders as have never occurred among the
nations.*

3g *'Two destinies he appointed, one for his own people, one
for the nations at large.* 3h *And these two destinies were
worked out at the hour and time and day laid down by God,
involving all the nations.* 3i *In this way God has remembered
his people and vindicated his heritage;* 3k *and for them these*

GREEK OLD TESTAMENT

3k ἔσονται αὐτοῖς αἱ ἡμέραι αὗται ἐν μηνὶ Αδαρ τῇ τεσσαρεσκαιδεκάτῃ καὶ τῇ πεντεκαιδεκάτῃ τοῦ αὐτοῦ μηνὸς μετὰ συναγωγῆς καὶ χαρᾶς καὶ εὐφροσύνης ἐνώπιον τοῦ θεοῦ κατὰ γενεὰς εἰς τὸν αἰῶνα ἐν τῷ λαῷ αὐτοῦ Ισραηλ.

3l Ἔτους τετάρτου βασιλεύοντος Πτολεμαίου καὶ Κλεοπάτρας εἰσήνεγκεν Δωσίθεος, ὃς ἔφη εἶναι ἱερεὺς καὶ Λευίτης, καὶ Πτολεμαῖος ὁ υἱὸς αὐτοῦ τὴν προκειμένην ἐπιστολὴν τῶν Φρουραι, ἣν ἔφασαν εἶναι καὶ ἑρμηνευκέναι Λυσίμαχον Πτολεμαίου τῶν ἐν Ιερουσαλημ.

KING JAMES VERSION

13 Therefore those days shall be unto them in the month Adar, the fourteenth and fifteenth day of the same month, with an assembly, and joy, and with gladness before God, according to the generations for ever among his people.

11 In the fourth year of the reign of Ptolemeus and Cleopatra, Dositheus, who said he was a priest and Levite, and Ptolemeus his son, brought this epistle of Phurim, which they said was the same, and that Lysimachus the son of Ptolemeus, that was in Jerusalem, had interpreted it.

DOUAY OLD TESTAMENT

13 And these days shall be observed in the month of Adar on the fourteenth, and fifteenth day of the same month, with all diligence, and joy of the people gathered into one assembly, throughout all the generations hereafter of the people of Israel.

11 IN the fourth year of the reign of Ptolemy and Cleopatra, Dositheus, who said he was a priest, and of the Levitical race, and Ptolemy his son brought this epistle of Phurim, which they said Lysimachus the son of Ptolemy had interpreted in Jerusalem.

KNOX TRANSLATION

hearts all must come together and observe that time, the fourteenth and fifteenth days of Adar, as long as Israel's race shall last.

11 This document about the feast of Purim, said to have been translated by Lysimachus son of Ptolemy, a native of Jerusalem, was first made public in the fourth year of king Ptolemy and queen Cleopatra, by Dosithaeus, who claimed to be a priest of true Levite descent, and his son, who was also called Ptolemy.[a]

a The dating here is obscure. Taken in conjunction with 12. 1, this verse seems to imply that the vision was seen *after* the incidents described in chapter 1 and in chapter 2. 1-20. But those incidents began with the third year of the reign, and it is difficult to see how we are still in the second. But probably chapter 12 is a separate fragment of the story, not closely connected with chapter 11 in date. 'Artaxerxes' is the Greek translator's rendering of 'Assuerus' throughout this book; the Latin has hitherto given him his Hebrew name Assuerus.

TODAY'S ENGLISH VERSION

year for all time to come God's people will gather together in his presence on the fourteenth and fifteenth of the month of Adar, and celebrate with joy and happiness."

During the fourth year of the reign of Ptolemy and Cleopatra, a man named Dositheus, who claimed to be a levitical priest, brought the preceding letter about the Purim festival. He was accompanied by his son Ptolemy, and they declared that the letter was genuine and that it had been translated by Lysimachus, son of Ptolemy, a member of a Jerusalem family.

NEW REVISED STANDARD VERSION

they will observe these days in the month of Adar, on the
fourteenth and fifteenth[a] of that month, with an assembly
and joy and gladness before God, from generation to genera-
11 tion forever among his people Israel." 1 In the fourth
year of the reign of Ptolemy and Cleopatra, Dositheus, who said that he was a priest and a Levite,[b] and his son
Ptolemy brought to Egypt[c] the preceding Letter about Purim,
which they said was authentic and had been translated by
Lysimachus son of Ptolemy, one of the residents of
Jerusalem.

END OF ADDITION F

a Other ancient authorities lack *and fifteenth* *b* Or *priest, and Levitas* *c* Cn: Gk *brought in*

NEW AMERICAN BIBLE

10 "Gathering together with joy and happiness before God,
they shall celebrate these days on the fourteenth and fifteenth of the month Adar throughout all future generations
of his people Israel."

F, 10: The Greek text of Esther contains a postscript as follows: In the fourth year of the reign of Ptolemy and Cleopatra, Dositheus, who said he was a priest and Levite, and his son Ptolemy brought the present letter of Purim, saying that it was genuine and that Lysimachus, son of Ptolemy, of the community of Jerusalem, had translated it. The date referred to in this postscript is most probably 78-77 B.C., in the reign of Ptolemy XII and Cleopatra V.

NEW JERUSALEM BIBLE

days, the fourteenth and fifteenth of the month of Adar, are to
be days of assembly, of joy and of gladness before God,
through all generations and for ever among his people Israel.'
31 *In the fourth year of the reign of Ptolemy and Cleopatra,*
Dositheus, who affirmed that he was a priest and Levite, and
Ptolemy his son brought the foregoing letter concerning
Purim. They vouched for its authenticity, the translation hav-
ing been made by Lysimachus son of Ptolemy, a member of
the Jerusalem community.

GREEK OLD TESTAMENT

ΣΟΦΙΑ ΣΑΛΩΜΩΝΟΣ

1 Ἀγαπήσατε δικαιοσύνην, οἱ κρίνοντες τὴν γῆν,
φρονήσατε περὶ τοῦ κυρίου ἐν ἀγαθότητι
καὶ ἐν ἁπλότητι καρδίας ζητήσατε αὐτόν.
2 ὅτι εὑρίσκεται τοῖς μὴ πειράζουσιν αὐτόν,
ἐμφανίζεται δὲ τοῖς μὴ ἀπιστοῦσιν αὐτῷ.
3 σκολιοὶ γὰρ λογισμοὶ χωρίζουσιν ἀπὸ θεοῦ,
δοκιμαζομένη τε ἡ δύναμις ἐλέγχει τοὺς ἄφρονας.
4 ὅτι εἰς κακότεχνον ψυχὴν οὐκ εἰσελεύσεται σοφία
οὐδὲ κατοικήσει ἐν σώματι κατάχρεῳ ἁμαρτίας.
5 ἅγιον γὰρ πνεῦμα παιδείας φεύξεται δόλον
καὶ ἀπαναστήσεται ἀπὸ λογισμῶν ἀσυνέτων
καὶ ἐλεγχθήσεται ἐπελθούσης ἀδικίας.
6 φιλάνθρωπον γὰρ πνεῦμα σοφία
καὶ οὐκ ἀθῳώσει βλάσφημον ἀπὸ χειλέων αὐτοῦ·
ὅτι τῶν νεφρῶν αὐτοῦ μάρτυς ὁ θεὸς
καὶ τῆς καρδίας αὐτοῦ ἐπίσκοπος ἀληθὴς
καὶ τῆς γλώσσης ἀκουστής.
7 ὅτι πνεῦμα κυρίου πεπλήρωκεν τὴν οἰκουμένην,
καὶ τὸ συνέχον τὰ πάντα γνῶσιν ἔχει φωνῆς.
8 διὰ τοῦτο φθεγγόμενος ἄδικα οὐδεὶς μὴ λάθῃ,
οὐδὲ μὴ παροδεύσῃ αὐτὸν ἐλέγχουσα ἡ δίκη.

KING JAMES VERSION

THE WISDOM OF SOLOMON

1 Love righteousness, ye that be judges of the earth: think of the Lord with a good (heart,) and in simplicity of heart seek him.

2 For he will be found of them that tempt him not; and sheweth himself unto such as do not distrust him.

3 For froward thoughts separate from God: and his power, when it is tried, reproveth the unwise.

4 For into a malicious soul wisdom shall not enter; nor dwell in the body that is subject unto sin.

5 For the holy spirit of discipline will flee deceit, and remove from thoughts that are without understanding, and will not abide when unrighteousness cometh in.

6 For wisdom is a loving spirit; and will not acquit a blasphemer of his words: for God is witness of his reins, and a true beholder of his heart, and a hearer of his tongue.

7 For the Spirit of the Lord filleth the world: and that which containeth all things hath knowledge of the voice.

8 Therefore he that speaketh unrighteous things cannot be hid: neither shall vengeance, when it punisheth, pass by him.

DOUAY OLD TESTAMENT

THE BOOK OF WISDOM

1 LOVE justice, you that are the judges of the earth. Think of the Lord in goodness, and seek him in simplicity of heart.

2 For he is found by them that tempt him not: and he sheweth himself to them that have faith in him.

3 For perverse thoughts separate from God: and his power, when it is tried, reproveth the unwise:

4 For wisdom will not enter into a malicious soul, nor dwell in a body subject to sins.

5 For the Holy Spirit of discipline will flee from the deceitful, and will withdraw himself from thoughts that are without understanding, and he shall not abide when iniquity cometh in.

6 For the spirit of wisdom is benevolent, and will not acquit the evil speaker from his lips: for God is witness of his reins, and he is a true searcher of his heart, and a hearer of his tongue.

7 For the spirit of the Lord hath filled the whole world: and that, which containeth all things, hath knowledge of the voice.

8 Therefore he that speaketh unjust things cannot be hid, neither shall the chastising judgment pass him by.

KNOX TRANSLATION

THE BOOK OF WISDOM

1 LISTEN, all you who are judges here on earth. Learn to
love justice; learn to think high thoughts of what God is,
and with sincere hearts aspire to him. 2 Trust him thou
must, if find him thou wouldst; he does not reveal himself to
one that challenges his power. 3 Man's truant thoughts may
keep God at a distance, but when the test of strength comes,
folly is shewn in its true colours; 4 never yet did wisdom find
her way into the schemer's heart, never yet made her home
in a life mortgaged to sin. 5 A holy thing it is, the spirit that
brings instruction; how it shrinks away from the touch of
falsehood, holds aloof from every rash design! It is a touchstone, to betray the neighbourhood of wrong-doing. 6 A good
friend to man is this spirit of wisdom, that convicts the blasphemer of his wild words; God can witness his secret
thoughts, can read his heart unerringly, and shall his utterance go unheard? 7 No, the spirit of the Lord fills the whole
world; bond that holds all things in being, it takes cogni-
sance of every sound we utter; 8 how should ill speech go
unmarked, or the scrutiny of justice pass it by? 9 The hidden

Today's English Version

THE WISDOM OF SOLOMON

1 Love justice, you rulers of the world. Set your minds sincerely on the Lord, and look for him with all honesty.
2 Those who do not try to test him will find him; he will show
himself to those who trust him. 3 Dishonest thoughts separate people from God, and if we are foolish enough to test
him, his power will put us to shame. 4 Wisdom will never be
at home with anyone who is deceitful or a slave of sin.
5 Everyone who is holy has learned to stay away from deceitful people. He will not stay around when foolish thoughts
are being expressed; he will not feel comfortable when injustice is done.
6 Wisdom is a spirit that is friendly to people, but she will
not forgive anyone who speaks against God, for God knows
our feelings and thoughts, and hears our every word. 7 Since
the Lord's spirit fills the entire world, and holds everything
in it together, she knows every word that people say. 8 No
one who speaks wickedly will escape notice; sooner or later
he will receive just punishment. 9 The intentions of ungodly

New Revised Standard Version

THE WISDOM OF SOLOMON

1 Love righteousness, you rulers of the earth,
think of the Lord in goodness
and seek him with sincerity of heart;
2 because he is found by those who do not put him to the
test,
and manifests himself to those who do not distrust him.
3 For perverse thoughts separate people from God,
and when his power is tested, it exposes the foolish;
4 because wisdom will not enter a deceitful soul,
or dwell in a body enslaved to sin.
5 For a holy and disciplined spirit will flee from deceit,
and will leave foolish thoughts behind,
and will be ashamed at the approach of
unrighteousness.

6 For wisdom is a kindly spirit,
but will not free blasphemers from the guilt of their
words;
because God is witness of their inmost feelings,
and a true observer of their hearts, and a hearer of their
tongues.
7 Because the spirit of the Lord has filled the world,
and that which holds all things together knows what is
said,
8 therefore those who utter unrighteous things will not
escape notice,
and justice, when it punishes, will not pass them by.

New American Bible

THE BOOK OF WISDOM

1 Love justice, you who judge the earth;
think of the Lord in goodness,
and seek him in integrity of heart;
2 Because he is found by those who test him not,
and he manifests himself to those who do not
disbelieve him.
3 For perverse counsels separate a man from God,
and his power, put to the proof, rebukes the
foolhardy;
4 Because into a soul that plots evil wisdom enters not,
nor dwells she in a body under debt of sin.
5 For the holy spirit of discipline flees deceit
and withdraws from senseless counsels;
and when injustice occurs it is rebuked.
6 For wisdom is a kindly spirit,
yet she acquits not the blasphemer of his guilty lips;
Because God is the witness of his inmost self
and the sure observer of his heart
and the listener to his tongue.
7 For the spirit of the Lord fills the world,
is all-embracing, and knows what man says.
8 Therefore no one who utters wicked things can go
unnoticed,
nor will chastising condemnation pass him by.

New Jerusalem Bible

THE BOOK OF WISDOM

1 Love uprightness you who are rulers on earth,
be properly disposed towards the Lord
and seek him in simplicity of heart;
2 for he will be found by those who do not put him to the
test,
revealing himself to those who do not mistrust him.
3 Perverse thoughts, however, separate people from God,
and power, when put to the test, confounds the stupid.
4 Wisdom will never enter the soul of a wrong-doer,
nor dwell in a body enslaved to sin;
5 for the holy spirit of instruction flees deceitfulness,
recoils from unintelligent thoughts,
is thwarted by the onset of vice.
6 Wisdom is a spirit friendly to humanity,
though she will not let a blasphemer's words go
unpunished;
since God observes the very soul
and accurately surveys the heart,
listening to every word.
7 For the spirit of the Lord fills the world,
and that which holds everything together knows every
word said.
8 No one who speaks what is wrong will go undetected,
nor will avenging Justice pass by such a one.

GREEK OLD TESTAMENT

9 ἐν γὰρ διαβουλίοις ἀσεβοῦς ἐξέτασις ἔσται,
λόγων δὲ αὐτοῦ ἀκοὴ πρὸς κύριον ἥξει
εἰς ἔλεγχον ἀνομημάτων αὐτοῦ·
10 ὅτι οὖς ζηλώσεως ἀκροᾶται τὰ πάντα,
καὶ θροῦς γογγυσμῶν οὐκ ἀποκρύπτεται.
11 Φυλάξασθε τοίνυν γογγυσμὸν ἀνωφελῆ
καὶ ἀπὸ καταλαλιᾶς φείσασθε γλώσσης·
ὅτι φθέγμα λαθραῖον κενὸν οὐ πορεύσεται,
στόμα δὲ καταψευδόμενον ἀναιρεῖ ψυχήν.
12 μὴ ζηλοῦτε θάνατον ἐν πλάνῃ ζωῆς ὑμῶν
μηδὲ ἐπισπᾶσθε ὄλεθρον ἐν ἔργοις χειρῶν ὑμῶν·
13 ὅτι ὁ θεὸς θάνατον οὐκ ἐποίησεν
οὐδὲ τέρπεται ἐπ᾽ ἀπωλείᾳ ζώντων.
14 ἔκτισεν γὰρ εἰς τὸ εἶναι τὰ πάντα,
καὶ σωτήριοι αἱ γενέσεις τοῦ κόσμου,
καὶ οὐκ ἔστιν ἐν αὐταῖς φάρμακον ὀλέθρου
οὔτε ᾅδου βασίλειον ἐπὶ γῆς.
15 δικαιοσύνη γὰρ ἀθάνατός ἐστιν.
16 Ἀσεβεῖς δὲ ταῖς χερσὶν καὶ τοῖς λόγοις
προσεκαλέσαντο αὐτόν,
φίλον ἡγησάμενοι αὐτὸν ἐτάκησαν
καὶ συνθήκην ἔθεντο πρὸς αὐτόν,
ὅτι ἄξιοί εἰσιν τῆς ἐκείνου μερίδος εἶναι.

2 εἶπον γὰρ ἐν ἑαυτοῖς λογισάμενοι οὐκ ὀρθῶς
Ὀλίγος ἐστὶν καὶ λυπηρὸς ὁ βίος ἡμῶν,

KING JAMES VERSION

9 For inquisition shall be made into the counsels of the ungodly: and the sound of his words shall come unto the Lord for the manifestation of his wicked deeds.

10 For the ear of jealousy heareth all things: and the noise of murmurings is not hid.

11 Therefore beware of murmuring, which is unprofitable; and refrain your tongue from backbiting: for there is no word so secret, that shall go for nought: and the mouth that belieth slayeth the soul.

12 Seek not death in the error of your life: and pull not upon yourselves destruction with the works of your hands.

13 For God made not death: neither hath he pleasure in the destruction of the living.

14 For he created all things, that they might have their being: and the generations of the world were healthful; and there is no poison of destruction in them, nor the kingdom of death upon the earth:

15 (For righteousness is immortal:)

16 But ungodly men with their works and words called *it* to them: for when they thought to have it their friend, they consumed to nought, and made a covenant with it, because they are worthy to take part with it.

2 For the *ungodly* said, reasoning with themselves, but not aright, Our life is short and tedious, and in the death of

DOUAY OLD TESTAMENT

9 For inquisition shall be made into the thoughts of the ungodly: and the hearing of his words shall come to God, to the chastising of his iniquities.

10 For the ear of jealousy heareth all things, and the tumult of murmuring shall not be hid.

11 Keep yourselves therefore from murmuring, which profiteth nothing, and refrain your tongue from detraction, for an obscure speech shall not go for nought: and the mouth that belieth, killeth the soul.

12 Seek not death in the error of your life, neither procure ye destruction by the works of your hands.

13 For God made not death, neither hath he pleasure in the destruction of the living.

14 For he created all things that they might be: and he made the nations of the earth for health: and there is no poison of destruction in them, nor kingdom of hell upon the earth.

15 For justice is perpetual and immortal.

16 But the wicked with works and words have called it to them: and esteeming it a friend have fallen away, and have made a covenant with it: because they are worthy to be of the part thereof.

2 FOR they have said, reasoning with themselves, *but* not right: The time of our life is short and tedious, and in

KNOX TRANSLATION

counsel of the godless will all come to light; no word of it but
reaches the divine hearing, and betrays their wicked design;
10 that jealous ear is still listening, and all their busy murmuring shall stand revealed.
11 Beware, then, of whispering, and to ill purpose; ever let
your tongues refrain from calumny. Think not that the secret
word goes for nought; lying lips were ever the soul's destroying. 12 Death for its goal, is not life's aim missed? Labours
he well, that labours to bring doom about his ears? 13 Death
was never of God's fashioning; not for his pleasure does life
cease to be; 14 what meant his creation, but that all created
things should have being? No breed has he created on earth
but for its thriving; none carries in itself the seeds of its own
destruction. Think not that mortality bears sway on earth;[a]
15 no end nor term is fixed to a life well lived...[b] 16 It is the
wicked that have brought death on themselves, by word and
deed of their own; court death, and melt away in its
embrace, keep tryst with it, and lay claim to its partnership.

2 Reason they offer, yet reason all amiss. Their hearts tell them, So brief our time here, so full of discomfort, and

a What is said here is understood by some as referring only to human life; others take it as implying that mortality in general owes its origin to the fall of Adam. *b* This verse seems to be incomplete; the old Sixtine Vulgate adds, on the authority of certain Latin manuscripts, the phrase 'death is earned only by wrong-doing'.

TODAY'S ENGLISH VERSION

people will be closely examined; their words will be reported
to the Lord, and then they will get the punishment that their
wickedness deserves. 10 God will tolerate no challenge, and
since he hears everything, you cannot hide your complaining
from him. 11 So be sure that you do not go around complaining—it does no good—and don't engage in bitter talk. The
most secret things you say will have their consequences, and
lying will destroy your soul.
12 Do not bring on your own death by sinful actions.
13 God did not invent death, and when living creatures die, it
gives him no pleasure. 14 He created everything so that it
might continue to exist, and everything he created is wholesome and good. There is no deadly poison in them. No, death
does not rule this world, 15 for God's justice does not die.
16 Ungodly people have brought death on themselves by
the things they have said and done. They yearn for death as
if it were a lover. They have gone into partnership with
death, and it is just what they deserve.

2 Wicked people are wrong when they say to themselves,
"Our life is short and full of sorrow, and when its end

NEW REVISED STANDARD VERSION

9 For inquiry will be made into the counsels of the ungodly,
and a report of their words will come to the Lord,
to convict them of their lawless deeds;
10 because a jealous ear hears all things,
and the sound of grumbling does not go unheard.
11 Beware then of useless grumbling,
and keep your tongue from slander;
because no secret word is without result,[a]
and a lying mouth destroys the soul.

12 Do not invite death by the error of your life,
or bring on destruction by the works of your hands;
13 because God did not make death,
and he does not delight in the death of the living.
14 For he created all things so that they might exist;
the generative forces[b] of the world are wholesome,
and there is no destructive poison in them,
and the dominion[c] of Hades is not on earth.
15 For righteousness is immortal.

16 But the ungodly by their words and deeds summoned
death;[d]
considering him a friend, they pined away
and made a covenant with him,
because they are fit to belong to his company.

2 For they reasoned unsoundly, saying to themselves,
"Short and sorrowful is our life,

a Or *will go unpunished* *b* Or *the creatures* *c* Or *palace* *d* Gk *him*

NEW AMERICAN BIBLE

9 For the devices of the wicked man shall be scrutinized,
and the sound of his words shall reach the LORD,
for the chastisement of his transgressions;
10 Because a jealous ear hearkens to everything,
and discordant grumblings are no secret.
11 Therefore guard against profitless grumbling,
and from calumny withhold your tongues;
For a stealthy utterance does not go unpunished,
and a lying mouth slays the soul.
12 Court not death by your erring way of life,
nor draw to yourselves destruction by the works of
your hands.
13 Because God did not make death,
nor does he rejoice in the destruction of the living.
14 For he fashioned all things that they might have being;
and the creatures of the world are wholesome,
And there is not a destructive drug among them
nor any domain of the nether world on earth,
15 For justice is undying.
16 It was the wicked who with hands and words invited
death,
considered it a friend, and pined for it,
and made a covenant with it,
Because they deserve to be in its possession,

2 1 they who said among themselves, thinking not aright:
"Brief and troublous is our lifetime;

NEW JERUSALEM BIBLE

9 For the schemes of the godless will be examined,
and a report of his words will reach the Lord
to convict him of his crimes.
10 There is a jealous ear that overhears everything,
not even a murmur of complaint escapes it.
11 So beware of uttering frivolous complaints,
restrain your tongue from finding fault;
even what is said in secret has repercussions,
and a lying mouth deals death to the soul.

12 Do not court death by the errors of your ways,
nor invite destruction through the work of your hands.
13 For God did not make Death,
he takes no pleasure in destroying the living.
14 To exist—for this he created all things;
the creatures of the world have health in them,
in them is no fatal poison,
and Hades has no power over the world:
15 for uprightness is immortal.
16 But the godless call for Death with deed and word,
counting him friend, they wear themselves out for him;
with him they make a pact,
worthy as they are to belong to him.

2 And this is the false argument they use,
'Our life is short and dreary,

GREEK OLD TESTAMENT

καὶ οὐκ ἔστιν ἴασις ἐν τελευτῇ ἀνθρώπου,
καὶ οὐκ ἐγνώσθη ὁ ἀναλύσας ἐξ ᾅδου.
2 ὅτι αὐτοσχεδίως ἐγενήθημεν
καὶ μετὰ τοῦτο ἐσόμεθα ὡς οὐχ ὑπάρξαντες·
ὅτι καπνὸς ἡ πνοὴ ἐν ῥισὶν ἡμῶν,
καὶ ὁ λόγος σπινθὴρ ἐν κινήσει καρδίας ἡμῶν,
3 οὗ σβεσθέντος τέφρα ἀποβήσεται τὸ σῶμα
καὶ τὸ πνεῦμα διαχυθήσεται ὡς χαῦνος ἀήρ.
4 καὶ τὸ ὄνομα ἡμῶν ἐπιλησθήσεται ἐν χρόνῳ,
καὶ οὐθεὶς μνημονεύσει τῶν ἔργων ἡμῶν·
καὶ παρελεύσεται ὁ βίος ἡμῶν ὡς ἴχνη νεφέλης
καὶ ὡς ὁμίχλη διασκεδασθήσεται
διωχθεῖσα ὑπὸ ἀκτίνων ἡλίου
καὶ ὑπὸ θερμότητος αὐτοῦ βαρυνθεῖσα.
5 σκιᾶς γὰρ πάροδος ὁ καιρὸς ἡμῶν,
καὶ οὐκ ἔστιν ἀναποδισμὸς τῆς τελευτῆς ἡμῶν,
ὅτι κατεσφραγίσθη καὶ οὐδεὶς ἀναστρέφει.
6 δεῦτε οὖν καὶ ἀπολαύσωμεν τῶν ὄντων ἀγαθῶν
καὶ χρησώμεθα τῇ κτίσει ὡς ἐν νεότητι σπουδαίως·
7 οἴνου πολυτελοῦς καὶ μύρων πλησθῶμεν,
καὶ μὴ παροδευσάτω ἡμᾶς ἄνθος ἔαρος·
8 στεψώμεθα ῥόδων κάλυξιν πρὶν ἢ μαρανθῆναι·
9 μηδεὶς ἡμῶν ἄμοιρος ἔστω τῆς ἡμετέρας ἀγερωχίας,
πανταχῇ καταλίπωμεν σύμβολα τῆς εὐφροσύνης,
ὅτι αὕτη ἡ μερὶς ἡμῶν καὶ ὁ κλῆρος οὗτος.

KING JAMES VERSION

a man there is no remedy: neither was there any man known to have returned from the grave.

2 For we are born at all adventure: and we shall be hereafter as though we had never been: for the breath in our nostrils is as smoke, and a little spark in the moving of our heart:

3 Which being extinguished, our body shall be turned into ashes, and our spirit shall vanish as the soft air,

4 And our name shall be forgotten in time, and no man shall have our works in remembrance, and our life shall pass away as the trace of a cloud, and shall be dispersed as a mist, that is driven away with the beams of the sun, and overcome with the heat thereof.

5 For our time is a very shadow that passeth away; and after our end there is no returning: for it is fast sealed, so that no man cometh again.

6 Come on therefore, let us enjoy the good things that are present: and let us speedily use the creatures like as in youth.

7 Let us fill ourselves with costly wine and ointments: and let no flower of the spring pass by us:

8 Let us crown ourselves with rosebuds, before they be withered:

9 Let none of us go without his part of our voluptuousness: let us leave tokens of our joyfulness in every place: for this is our portion, and our lot is this.

DOUAY OLD TESTAMENT

the end of a man there is no remedy, and no man hath been known to have returned from hell:

2 For we are born of nothing, and after this we shall be as if we had not been: for the breath in our nostrils is smoke: and speech a spark to move our heart,

3 Which being put out, our body shall be ashes, and our spirit shall be poured abroad as soft air, and our life shall pass away as the trace of a cloud, and shall be dispersed as a mist, which is driven away by the beams of the sun, and overpowered with the heat thereof:

4 And our name in time shall be forgotten, and no man shall have any remembrance of our works.

5 For our time is *as* the passing of a shadow, and there is no going back of our end: for it is fast sealed, and no man returneth.

6 Come therefore, and let us enjoy the good things that are present, and let us speedily use the creatures as in youth.

7 Let us fill ourselves with costly wine, and ointments: and let not the flower of the time pass by us.

8 Let us crown ourselves with roses, before they be withered: let no meadow escape our riot.

9 Let none of us go without his part in luxury: let us everywhere leave tokens of joy: for this is our portion, and this *our* lot.

KNOX TRANSLATION

death brings no remedy! Never a man yet made good his title
to have come back from the grave! 2 Whence came we, none
can tell; and it will be all one hereafter whether we lived or
no. What is our breath, but a passing vapour; what is our
reason, but a spark that sets the brain whirling? 3 Quench
that spark, and our body is turned to ashes; like a spent
sigh, our breath is wasted on the air; like the cloud-wrack
our life passes away, unsubstantial as the mist yonder sun
disperses with its ray, bears down with its heat. 4 Time will
surely efface our memory, and none will mark the record of
our doings. 5 Only a passing shadow, this life of ours, and
from its end there is no returning; the doom is sealed, and
there is no acquittal.
6 Come then (they say), let us enjoy pleasure, while pleasure is ours; youth does not last, and creation is at our call;
7 of rich wine and well spiced take we our fill. Spring shall
not cheat us of her blossoming; 8 crown we our heads with
roses ere they wither; be every meadow the scene of our
wanton mirth. 9 Share we the revels all alike, leave traces
everywhere of our joyous passing; no part or lot have we but
this.

TODAY'S ENGLISH VERSION

comes, there is no escape. No one has ever been known to
come back from the world of the dead. 2 We were born by
chance, and after life is over, we will be as if we had never
been born at all. Our breath is no more than a puff of smoke;
our mind is nothing more than a spark thrown off by the
beating of our heart. 3 When that spark dies, our body will
crumble into ashes, and our breath will become part of the
empty air. 4 In time, no one will remember anything we ever
did, and even our names will be forgotten. Our lives will
pass away like the traces of clouds and vanish like fog in the
heat of the sun. 5 Our time on earth is like a passing shadow. There is no escape from the day of our death; it is fixed,
and no one can postpone it."

6 The wicked say, "Come on, then, let's enjoy the good
things of life, and live in this world the way we did when we
were young and free of care! 7 Let's drink the most expensive wines and use the finest perfumes. Let's not miss a single flower in the springtime! 8 Before the roses wither, let's
pick them and wear them in our hair! 9 Let's all join in and
leave signs everywhere of our carefree revelry! Life owes us
that much!

NEW REVISED STANDARD VERSION

and there is no remedy when a life comes to its end,
and no one has been known to return from Hades.
2 For we were born by mere chance,
and hereafter we shall be as though we had never been,
for the breath in our nostrils is smoke,
and reason is a spark kindled by the beating of our
hearts;
3 when it is extinguished, the body will turn to ashes,
and the spirit will dissolve like empty air.
4 Our name will be forgotten in time,
and no one will remember our works;
our life will pass away like the traces of a cloud,
and be scattered like mist
that is chased by the rays of the sun
and overcome by its heat.
5 For our allotted time is the passing of a shadow,
and there is no return from our death,
because it is sealed up and no one turns back.

6 "Come, therefore, let us enjoy the good things that
exist,
and make use of the creation to the full as in youth.
7 Let us take our fill of costly wine and perfumes,
and let no flower of spring pass us by.
8 Let us crown ourselves with rosebuds before they
wither.
9 Let none of us fail to share in our revelry;
everywhere let us leave signs of enjoyment,
because this is our portion, and this our lot.

NEW AMERICAN BIBLE

neither is there any remedy for man's dying,
nor is anyone known to have come back from the
nether world.
2 For haphazard were we born,
and hereafter we shall be as though we had not been;
Because the breath in our nostrils is a smoke
and reason is a spark at the beating of our hearts,
3 And when this is quenched, our body will be ashes
and our spirit will be poured abroad like unresisting
air,
4 Even our name will be forgotten in time,
and no one will recall our deeds.
So our life will pass away like the traces of a cloud,
and will be dispersed like a mist
pursued by the sun's rays
and overpowered by its heat.
5 For our lifetime is the passing of a shadow;
and our dying cannot be deferred
because it is fixed with a seal; and no one returns.
6 Come, therefore, let us enjoy the good things that are
real,
and use the freshness of creation avidly.
7 Let us have our fill of costly wine and perfumes,
and let no springtime blossom pass us by;
8 let us crown ourselves with rosebuds ere they wither.
9 Let no meadow be free from our wantonness;
everywhere let us leave tokens of our rejoicing,
for this our portion is, and this our lot.

NEW JERUSALEM BIBLE

there is no remedy when our end comes,
no one is known to have come back from Hades.
2 We came into being by chance
and afterwards shall be as though we had never been.
The breath in our nostrils is a puff of smoke,
reason a spark from the beating of our hearts;
3 extinguish this and the body turns to ashes,
and the spirit melts away like the yielding air.
4 In time, our name will be forgotten,
nobody will remember what we have done;
our life will pass away like wisps of cloud,
dissolving like the mist
that the sun's rays drive away
and that its heat dispels.
5 For our days are the passing of a shadow,
our end is without return,
the seal is affixed and nobody comes back.
6 'Come then, let us enjoy the good things of today,
let us use created things with the zest of youth:
7 take our fill of the dearest wines and perfumes,
on no account forgo the flowers of spring
8 but crown ourselves with rosebuds before they wither,
9 no meadow excluded from our orgy;
let us leave the signs of our revelry everywhere,
since this is our portion, this our lot!

GREEK OLD TESTAMENT

10 καταδυναστεύσωμεν πένητα δίκαιον,
μὴ φεισώμεθα χήρας
μηδὲ πρεσβύτου ἐντραπῶμεν πολιὰς πολυχρονίους·
11 ἔστω δὲ ἡμῶν ἡ ἰσχὺς νόμος τῆς δικαιοσύνης,
τὸ γὰρ ἀσθενὲς ἄχρηστον ἐλέγχεται.
12 ἐνεδρεύσωμεν τὸν δίκαιον, ὅτι δύσχρηστος ἡμῖν ἐστιν
καὶ ἐναντιοῦται τοῖς ἔργοις ἡμῶν
καὶ ὀνειδίζει ἡμῖν ἁμαρτήματα νόμου
καὶ ἐπιφημίζει ἡμῖν ἁμαρτήματα παιδείας ἡμῶν·
13 ἐπαγγέλλεται γνῶσιν ἔχειν θεοῦ
καὶ παῖδα κυρίου ἑαυτὸν ὀνομάζει·
14 ἐγένετο ἡμῖν εἰς ἔλεγχον ἐννοιῶν ἡμῶν,
βαρύς ἐστιν ἡμῖν καὶ βλεπόμενος,
15 ὅτι ἀνόμοιος τοῖς ἄλλοις ὁ βίος αὐτοῦ,
καὶ ἐξηλλαγμέναι αἱ τρίβοι αὐτοῦ·
16 εἰς κίβδηλον ἐλογίσθημεν αὐτῷ,
καὶ ἀπέχεται τῶν ὁδῶν ἡμῶν ὡς ἀπὸ ἀκαθαρσιῶν·
μακαρίζει ἔσχατα δικαίων
καὶ ἀλαζονεύεται πατέρα θεόν.
17 ἴδωμεν εἰ οἱ λόγοι αὐτοῦ ἀληθεῖς,
καὶ πειράσωμεν τὰ ἐν ἐκβάσει αὐτοῦ·
18 εἰ γάρ ἐστιν ὁ δίκαιος υἱὸς θεοῦ, ἀντιλήμψεται αὐτοῦ
καὶ ῥύσεται αὐτὸν ἐκ χειρὸς ἀνθεστηκότων.
19 ὕβρει καὶ βασάνῳ ἐτάσωμεν αὐτόν,
ἵνα γνῶμεν τὴν ἐπιείκειαν αὐτοῦ
καὶ δοκιμάσωμεν τὴν ἀνεξικακίαν αὐτοῦ·

KING JAMES VERSION

10 Let us oppress the poor righteous man, let us not spare the widow, nor reverence the ancient gray hairs of the aged.

11 Let our strength be the law of justice: for that which is feeble is found to be nothing worth.

12 Therefore let us lie in wait for the righteous; because he is not for our turn, and he is clean contrary to our doings: he upbraideth us with our offending the law, and objecteth to our infamy the transgressings of our education.

13 He professeth to have the knowledge of God: and he calleth himself the child of the Lord.

14 He was made to reprove our thoughts.

15 He is grievous unto us even to behold: for his life is not like other men's, his ways are of another fashion.

16 We are esteemed of him as counterfeits: he abstaineth from our ways as from filthiness: he pronounceth the end of the just to be blessed, and maketh his boast that God is his father.

17 Let us see if his words be true: and let us prove what shall happen in the end of him.

18 For if the just man be the son of God, he will help him, and deliver him from the hand of his enemies.

19 Let us examine him with despitefulness and torture, that we may know his meekness, and prove his patience.

DOUAY OLD TESTAMENT

10 Let us oppress the poor just man, and not spare the widow, nor honour the ancient grey hairs of the aged.

11 But let our strength be the law of justice: for that which is feeble, is found to be nothing worth.

12 Let us therefore lie in wait for the just, because he is not for our turn, and he is contrary to our doings, and upbraideth us with transgressions of the law, and divulgeth against us the sins of our way of life.

13 He boasteth that he hath the knowledge of God, and calleth himself the son of God.

14 He is become a censurer of our thoughts.

15 He is grievous unto us, even to behold: for his life is not like other men's, and his ways are very different.

16 We are esteemed by him as triflers, and he abstaineth from our ways as from filthiness, and he preferreth the latter end of the just, and glorieth that he hath God for his father.

17 Let us see then if his words be true, and let us prove what shall happen to him, and we shall know what his end shall be.

18 For if he be the true son of God, he will defend him, and will deliver him from the hands of his enemies.

19 Let us examine him by outrages and tortures, that we may know his meekness and try his patience.

KNOX TRANSLATION

10 Helpless innocence shall lie at our mercy; not for us to
spare the widow, to respect the venerable head, grown white
with years. 11 Might shall be our right, weakness count for
proof of worthlessness. 12 Where is he, the just man? We
must plot to be rid of him; he will not lend himself to our
purposes. Ever he must be thwarting our plans; transgress
we the law, he is all reproof, depart we from the traditions of
our race, he denounces us. 13 What, would he claim knowledge of divine secrets, give himself out as the son of God?
14 The touchstone, he, of our inmost thoughts; 15 we cannot
bear the very sight of him, his life so different from other
men's, the path he takes, so far removed from theirs! 16 No
better than false coin he counts us, holds aloof from our
doings as though they would defile him; envies the just their
future happiness, boasts of a divine parentage. 17 Put we his
claims, then, to the proof; let experience shew what his lot
shall be, what end awaits him. 18 If to be just is to be God's
son indeed, then God will take up his cause, will save him
from the power of his enemies.[a] 19 Outrage and torment, let
these be the tests we use; let us see that gentleness of his in
its true colours, find out what his patience is worth.

[a] Cf. Mt. 27. 43.

TODAY'S ENGLISH VERSION

10 "We'll oppress the poor, even if they are righteous. We'll
show no respect for widows or old people. 11 We'll call ourselves right if we are strong enough to get what we want. No
one ever got anywhere by being weak! 12 Righteous people
are nothing but a nuisance, so let's look for chances to get
rid of them. They are against what we do; they accuse us of
breaking the Law of Moses and violating the traditions of
our ancestors. 13 They claim to know God, and they call
themselves the Lord's children. 14 We can't stand the sight of
people like that; what they are contradicts our whole way of
thinking. 15 They are not like other people; they have strange
ways. 16 They think that our moral standards are so corrupt
that everything we do should be avoided. They boast of having God for their Father, and believe that when all is said
and done, only the righteous will be happy. 17 But we'll see
if that's true! Let's see what will happen when it's time for
them to die! 18 If the righteous really are God's children, God
will save them from their enemies. 19 So let's put them to the
test. We'll be cruel to them, and torment them; then we'll
find out how calm and reasonable they are! We'll find out
just how much they can stand! 20 We'll condemn them to a

NEW REVISED STANDARD VERSION

10 Let us oppress the righteous poor man;
let us not spare the widow
or regard the gray hairs of the aged.
11 But let our might be our law of right,
for what is weak proves itself to be useless.

12 "Let us lie in wait for the righteous man,
because he is inconvenient to us and opposes our
actions;
he reproaches us for sins against the law,
and accuses us of sins against our training.
13 He professes to have knowledge of God,
and calls himself a child[a] of the Lord.
14 He became to us a reproof of our thoughts;
15 the very sight of him is a burden to us,
because his manner of life is unlike that of others,
and his ways are strange.
16 We are considered by him as something base,
and he avoids our ways as unclean;
he calls the last end of the righteous happy,
and boasts that God is his father.
17 Let us see if his words are true,
and let us test what will happen at the end of his life;
18 for if the righteous man is God's child, he will help him,
and will deliver him from the hand of his adversaries.
19 Let us test him with insult and torture,
so that we may find out how gentle he is,
and make trial of his forbearance.

a Or *servant*

NEW AMERICAN BIBLE

10 Let us oppress the needy just man;
let us neither spare the widow
nor revere the old man for his hair grown white with
time.
11 But let our strength be our norm of justice;
for weakness proves itself useless.
12 Let us beset the just one, because he is obnoxious to us;
he sets himself against our doings,
Reproaches us for transgressions of the law
and charges us with violations of our training.
13 He professes to have knowledge of God
and styles himself a child of the LORD.
14 To us he is the censure of our thoughts;
merely to see him is a hardship for us,
15 Because his life is not like other men's,
and different are his ways.
16 He judges us debased;
he holds aloof from our paths as from things impure.
He calls blest the destiny of the just
and boasts that God is his Father.
17 Let us see whether his words be true;
let us find out what will happen to him.
18 For if the just one be the son of God, he will defend him
and deliver him from the hand of his foes.
19 With revilement and torture let us put him to the test
that we may have proof of his gentleness
and try his patience.

NEW JERUSALEM BIBLE

10 'As for the upright man who is poor, let us oppress him;
let us not spare the widow,
nor respect old age, white-haired with many years.
11 Let our might be the yardstick of right,
since weakness argues its own futility.
12 Let us lay traps for the upright man, since he annoys us
and opposes our way of life,
reproaches us for our sins against the Law,
and accuses us of sins against our upbringing.
13 He claims to have knowledge of God,
and calls himself a child of the Lord.
14 We see him as a reproof to our way of thinking,
the very sight of him weighs our spirits down;
15 for his kind of life is not like other people's,
and his ways are quite different.
16 In his opinion we are counterfeit;
he avoids our ways as he would filth;
he proclaims the final end of the upright as blessed
and boasts of having God for his father.
17 Let us see if what he says is true,
and test him to see what sort of end he will have.
18 For if the upright man is God's son, God will help him
and rescue him from the clutches of his enemies.
19 Let us test him with cruelty and with torture,
and thus explore this gentleness of his
and put his patience to the test.

GREEK OLD TESTAMENT

20 θανάτῳ ἀσχήμονι καταδικάσωμεν αὐτόν,
ἔσται γὰρ αὐτοῦ ἐπισκοπὴ ἐκ λόγων αὐτοῦ.
21 Ταῦτα ἐλογίσαντο, καὶ ἐπλανήθησαν·
ἀπετύφλωσεν γὰρ αὐτοὺς ἡ κακία αὐτῶν,
22 καὶ οὐκ ἔγνωσαν μυστήρια θεοῦ
οὐδὲ μισθὸν ἤλπισαν ὁσιότητος
οὐδὲ ἔκριναν γέρας ψυχῶν ἀμώμων.
23 ὅτι ὁ θεὸς ἔκτισεν τὸν ἄνθρωπον ἐπ' ἀφθαρσίᾳ
καὶ εἰκόνα τῆς ἰδίας ἀϊδιότητος ἐποίησεν αὐτόν·
24 φθόνῳ δὲ διαβόλου θάνατος εἰσῆλθεν εἰς τὸν κόσμον,
πειράζουσιν δὲ αὐτὸν οἱ τῆς ἐκείνου μερίδος ὄντες.

3 Δικαίων δὲ ψυχαὶ ἐν χειρὶ θεοῦ,
καὶ οὐ μὴ ἅψηται αὐτῶν βάσανος.
2 ἔδοξαν ἐν ὀφθαλμοῖς ἀφρόνων τεθνάναι,
καὶ ἐλογίσθη κάκωσις ἡ ἔξοδος αὐτῶν
3 καὶ ἡ ἀφ' ἡμῶν πορεία σύντριμμα,
οἱ δέ εἰσιν ἐν εἰρήνῃ.
4 καὶ γὰρ ἐν ὄψει ἀνθρώπων ἐὰν κολασθῶσιν,
ἡ ἐλπὶς αὐτῶν ἀθανασίας πλήρης·
5 καὶ ὀλίγα παιδευθέντες μεγάλα εὐεργετηθήσονται,
ὅτι ὁ θεὸς ἐπείρασεν αὐτοὺς
καὶ εὗρεν αὐτοὺς ἀξίους ἑαυτοῦ·
6 ὡς χρυσὸν ἐν χωνευτηρίῳ ἐδοκίμασεν αὐτοὺς
καὶ ὡς ὁλοκάρπωμα θυσίας προσεδέξατο αὐτούς.

KING JAMES VERSION

20 Let us condemn him with a shameful death: for by his own saying he shall be respected.

21 Such things they did imagine, and were deceived: for their own wickedness hath blinded them.

22 As for the mysteries of God, they knew them not: neither hoped they for the wages of righteousness, nor discerned a reward for blameless souls.

23 For God created man to be immortal, and made him to be an image of his own eternity.

24 Nevertheless through envy of the devil came death into the world: and they that do hold of his side do find it.

3 But the souls of the righteous are in the hand of God, and there shall no torment touch them.

2 In the sight of the unwise they seemed to die: and their departure is taken for misery,

3 And their going from us to be utter destruction: but they are in peace.

4 For though they be punished in the sight of men, yet is their hope full of immortality.

5 And having been a little chastised, they shall be greatly rewarded: for God proved them, and found them worthy for himself.

6 As gold in the furnace hath he tried them, and received them as a burnt offering.

DOUAY OLD TESTAMENT

20 Let us condemn him to a most shameful death: for there shall be respect had unto him by his words.

21 These things they thought, and were deceived: for their own malice blinded them.

22 And they knew not the secrets of God, nor hoped for the wages of justice, nor esteemed the honour of holy souls.

23 For God created man incorruptible, and to the image of his own likeness he made him.

24 But by the envy of the devil, death came into the world:

25 And they follow him that are of his side.

3 BUT the souls of the just are in the hand of God, and the torment of death shall not touch them.

2 In the sight of the unwise they seemed to die: and their departure was taken for misery:

3 And their going away from us, for utter destruction: but they are in peace.

4 And though in the sight of men they suffered torments, their hope is full of immortality.

5 Afflicted in few things, in many they shall be well rewarded: because God hath tried them, and found them worthy of himself.

6 As gold in the furnace he hath proved them, and as a victim of a holocaust he hath received them, and in time there shall be respect had to them.

KNOX TRANSLATION

20 Sentenced let him be to a shameful death; by his own way
of it, he shall find deliverance.[a]
21 So false the calculations that are blinded by human malice! 22 The secret purposes of God they might not fathom;
how should they foresee that holiness is requited, how
should they pass true award on a blameless life? 23 God, to
be sure, framed man for an immortal destiny, the created
image of his own endless being; 24 but, since the devil's envy
brought death into the world, 25 they make him their model
that take him for their master.[b]

3 But the souls of the just are in God's hands, and no torment, in death itself, has power to reach them. 2 Dead?
Fools think so; think their end loss, 3 their leaving us, annihilation; but all is well with them. 4 The world sees nothing
but the pains they endure; they themselves have eyes only
for what is immortal; 5 so light their suffering, so great the
gain they win! God, all the while, did but test them, and testing them found them worthy of him. 6 His gold, tried in the
crucible, his burnt-sacrifice, graciously accepted, they do but
wait for the time of their deliverance; 7 then they will shine

a Some would render, less plausibly, 'he shall be judged by his words'.
b 'They make him their model'; the Greek text has, 'they experience it', i.e. death.

TODAY'S ENGLISH VERSION

shameful death. After all, they say that God will protect
them."
21 That is how evil people think, but they are wrong. They
are blinded by their own wickedness. 22 They have never
known God's secrets, never hoped for the rewards of a holy
and blameless life. 23 When God created us, he did not
intend for us to die; he made us like himself. 24 It was the
Devil's jealousy that brought death into the world, and those
who belong to the Devil are the ones who will die.

3 But righteous people are protected by God and will never
suffer torment. 2 It is a foolish mistake to think that
righteous people die and that their death is a terrible evil.
3 They leave us, but it is not a disaster. In fact, the righteous
are at peace. 4 It might appear that they have suffered punishment, but they have the confident hope of immortality.
5-6 Their sufferings were minor compared with the blessings
they will receive. God has tested them, like gold in a furnace,
and found them worthy to be with him. He has accepted
them, just as he accepts the sacrifices which his worshipers
burn on the altar.

NEW REVISED STANDARD VERSION

20 Let us condemn him to a shameful death,
for, according to what he says, he will be protected."

21 Thus they reasoned, but they were led astray,
for their wickedness blinded them,
22 and they did not know the secret purposes of God,
nor hoped for the wages of holiness,
nor discerned the prize for blameless souls;
23 for God created us for incorruption,
and made us in the image of his own eternity,[a]
24 but through the devil's envy death entered the world,
and those who belong to his company experience it.

3 But the souls of the righteous are in the hand of God,
and no torment will ever touch them.
2 In the eyes of the foolish they seemed to have died,
and their departure was thought to be a disaster,
3 and their going from us to be their destruction;
but they are at peace.
4 For though in the sight of others they were punished,
their hope is full of immortality.
5 Having been disciplined a little, they will receive great
good,
because God tested them and found them worthy of
himself;
6 like gold in the furnace he tried them,
and like a sacrificial burnt offering he accepted them.

a Other ancient authorities read *nature*

NEW AMERICAN BIBLE

20 Let us condemn him to a shameful death;
for according to his own words, God will take care of
him."
21 These were their thoughts, but they erred;
for their wickedness blinded them,
22 And they knew not the hidden counsels of God;
neither did they count on a recompense of holiness
nor discern the innocent souls' reward.
23 For God formed man to be imperishable;
the image of his own nature he made him.
24 But by the envy of the devil, death entered the world,
and they who are in his possession experience it.

3 But the souls of the just are in the hand of God,
and no torment shall touch them.
2 They seemed, in the view of the foolish, to be dead;
and their passing away was thought an affliction
3 and their going forth from us, utter destruction.
But they are in peace.
4 For if before men, indeed, they be punished,
yet is their hope full of immortality;
5 Chastised a little, they shall be greatly blessed,
because God tried them
and found them worthy of himself.
6 As gold in the furnace, he proved them,
and as sacrificial offerings he took them to himself.

NEW JERUSALEM BIBLE

20 Let us condemn him to a shameful death
since God will rescue him—or so he claims.'
21 This is the way they reason, but they are misled,
since their malice makes them blind.
22 They do not know the hidden things of God,
they do not hope for the reward of holiness,
they do not believe in a reward for blameless souls.
23 For God created human beings to be immortal,
he made them as an image of his own nature;
24 Death came into the world only through the Devil's
envy,
as those who belong to him find to their cost.

3 But the souls of the upright are in the hands of God,
and no torment can touch them.
2 To the unenlightened, they appeared to die,
their departure was regarded as disaster,
3 their leaving us like annihilation;
but they are at peace.
4 If, as it seemed to us, they suffered punishment,
their hope was rich with immortality;
5 slight was their correction, great will their blessings be.
God was putting them to the test
and has proved them worthy to be with him;
6 he has tested them like gold in a furnace,
and accepted them as a perfect burnt offering.

GREEK OLD TESTAMENT

7 καὶ ἐν καιρῷ ἐπισκοπῆς αὐτῶν ἀναλάμψουσιν
καὶ ὡς σπινθῆρες ἐν καλάμῃ διαδραμοῦνται·
8 κρινοῦσιν ἔθνη καὶ κρατήσουσιν λαῶν,
καὶ βασιλεύσει αὐτῶν κύριος εἰς τοὺς αἰῶνας.
9 οἱ πεποιθότες ἐπ᾽ αὐτῷ συνήσουσιν ἀλήθειαν,
καὶ οἱ πιστοὶ ἐν ἀγάπῃ προσμενοῦσιν αὐτῷ·
ὅτι χάρις καὶ ἔλεος τοῖς ἐκλεκτοῖς αὐτοῦ.
10 Οἱ δὲ ἀσεβεῖς καθὰ ἐλογίσαντο ἕξουσιν ἐπιτιμίαν
οἱ ἀμελήσαντες τοῦ δικαίου καὶ τοῦ κυρίου ἀποστάντες·
11 σοφίαν γὰρ καὶ παιδείαν ὁ ἐξουθενῶν ταλαίπωρος,
καὶ κενὴ ἡ ἐλπὶς αὐτῶν, καὶ οἱ κόποι ἀνόνητοι,
καὶ ἄχρηστα τὰ ἔργα αὐτῶν·
12 αἱ γυναῖκες αὐτῶν ἄφρονες,
καὶ πονηρὰ τὰ τέκνα αὐτῶν,
ἐπικατάρατος ἡ γένεσις αὐτῶν.
13 ὅτι μακαρία στεῖρα ἡ ἀμίαντος,
ἥτις οὐκ ἔγνω κοίτην ἐν παραπτώματι,
ἕξει καρπὸν ἐν ἐπισκοπῇ ψυχῶν,
14 καὶ εὐνοῦχος ὁ μὴ ἐργασάμενος ἐν χειρὶ ἀνόμημα
μηδὲ ἐνθυμηθεὶς κατὰ τοῦ κυρίου πονηρά,
δοθήσεται γὰρ αὐτῷ τῆς πίστεως χάρις ἐκλεκτὴ
καὶ κλῆρος ἐν ναῷ κυρίου θυμηρέστερος.

KING JAMES VERSION

7 And in the time of their visitation they shall shine, and run to and fro like sparks among the stubble.

8 They shall judge the nations, and have dominion over the people, and their Lord shall reign for ever.

9 They that put their trust in him shall understand the truth: and such as be faithful in love shall abide with him: for grace and mercy is to his saints, and he hath care for his elect.

10 But the ungodly shall be punished according to their own imaginations, which have neglected the righteous, and forsaken the Lord.

11 For whoso despiseth wisdom and nurture, he is miserable, and their hope is vain, their labours unfruitful, and their works unprofitable:

12 Their wives are foolish, and their children wicked:

13 Their offspring is cursed. Wherefore blessed is the barren that is undefiled, which hath not known the sinful bed: she shall have fruit in the visitation of souls.

14 And *blessed is* the eunuch, which with his hands hath wrought no iniquity, nor imagined wicked things against God: for unto him shall be given the special gift of faith, and an inheritance in the temple of the Lord more acceptable to his mind.

DOUAY OLD TESTAMENT

7 The just shall shine, and shall run to and fro like sparks among the reeds.

8 They shall judge nations, and rule over people, and their Lord shall reign for ever.

9 They that trust in him, shall understand the truth: and they that are faithful in love shall rest in him: for grace and peace is to his elect.

10 But the wicked shall be punished according to their own devices: who have neglected the just, and have revolted from the Lord.

11 For he that rejecteth wisdom, and discipline, is unhappy: and their hope is vain, and their labours without fruit, and their works unprofitable.

12 Their wives are foolish, and their children wicked.

13 Their offspring is cursed: for happy is the barren: and the undefiled, that hath not known bed in sin: she shall have fruit in the visitation of holy souls.

14 And the eunuch, that hath not wrought iniquity with his hands, nor thought wicked things against God: for the precious gift of faith shall be given to him, and a most acceptable lot in the temple of God.

KNOX TRANSLATION

out, these just souls, unconquerable as the sparks that break
out, now here, now there, among the stubble.[a] 8 Theirs to sit
in judgement on nations, to subdue whole peoples, under a
Lord whose reign shall last for ever. 9 Trust him if thou wilt,
true thou shalt find him;[b] faith waits for him calmly and lovingly; who claims his gift, who shall attain peace, if not they,
his chosen servants?[c]

10 But dearly shall the wicked pay for their error,[d] for the
claims of right forgotten, for the Lord's will defied. 11 Their
case is pitiable indeed, who make light of true wisdom and
of ordered living; vain their hope, profitless their toil, barren
their achievement. 12 Light women are the wives they wed,
worthless is their brood; 13 a curse lies on their begetting.
Blessed, rather, her lot, that childless is, yet chaste, that
never knew the bed of shame; offspring she will not lack,
when holy souls have their reward. 14 Nay, let there be some
eunuch that has kept his hands clear of wrong, has never
harboured treasonable thought against the Lord; he too with
rare gifts shall be faithfully rewarded, shall have the portion
that most contents him in God's holy place.[e] 15 A noble

a Mt. 13. 43. *b* 'Trust him if thou wilt, true thou shalt find him'; literally, 'those who trust in him shall understand truth'. The word 'truth' in the Old Testament refers, as a rule, either to human loyalty or to divine fidelity. *c* 'His chosen servants'; the Greek text gives, 'His holy ones; who shall find deliverance, if not his chosen servants?' *d* Or perhaps, 'The scheming of the wicked shall recoil on them in punishment'.
e Cf. Deut. 23. I; Is. 56. 3. 'He too with rare gifts shall be faithfully rewarded'; literally, 'He too shall be given a rare gift of fidelity'.

TODAY'S ENGLISH VERSION

7 When God comes to reward the righteous, they will blaze
out against the wicked like fire in dry straw. 8 They will rule
over nations and peoples, and the Lord will be their king forever. 9 Those who have put their trust in God will come to
understand the truth of his ways. Those who have been
faithful will live with him in his love, for he is kind and merciful to the ones whom he has chosen.[a]
10 The ungodly, however, will get the punishment their
wicked thoughts deserve, because they rebelled against the
Lord and ignored what was right.[b] 11 A man who has no use
for wisdom or education has a miserable life in store for him.
He has nothing to hope for. His labors are useless, and he
will never accomplish anything worthwhile. 12 The woman
he marries will turn out to be irresponsible, and his children
will go wrong. 13 All his descendants will be under a curse.
On Judgment Day God will reward the woman who has
never been able to have a child, provided she has not been
guilty of adultery. Then she will be happy. 14 On that day,
even the man who has been castrated will be rewarded with
happiness, if he has kept the Law and has not stored up
resentment against the Lord. Because he has been faithful,
he will receive a special reward more precious than having
children: a place in the Lord's heavenly Temple. 15 Honest

[a] *Some manuscripts add* and he protects his own people *(see 4.15).*
[b] what was right; *or* righteous people.

NEW REVISED STANDARD VERSION

7 In the time of their visitation they will shine forth,
and will run like sparks through the stubble.
8 They will govern nations and rule over peoples,
and the Lord will reign over them forever.
9 Those who trust in him will understand truth,
and the faithful will abide with him in love,
because grace and mercy are upon his holy ones,
and he watches over his elect.[a]

10 But the ungodly will be punished as their reasoning
deserves,
those who disregarded the righteous[b]
and rebelled against the Lord;
11 for those who despise wisdom and instruction are
miserable.
Their hope is vain, their labors are unprofitable,
and their works are useless.
12 Their wives are foolish, and their children evil;
13 their offspring are accursed.
For blessed is the barren woman who is undefiled,
who has not entered into a sinful union;
she will have fruit when God examines souls.
14 Blessed also is the eunuch whose hands have done no
lawless deed,
and who has not devised wicked things against the Lord;
for special favor will be shown him for his faithfulness,
and a place of great delight in the temple of the Lord.

a Text of this line uncertain; omitted by some ancient authorities. Compare 4.15 *b* Or *what is right*

NEW AMERICAN BIBLE

7 In the time of their visitation they shall shine,
and shall dart about as sparks through stubble;
8 They shall judge nations and rule over peoples,
and the LORD shall be their King forever.
9 Those who trust in him shall understand truth,
and the faithful shall abide with him in love:
Because grace and mercy are with his holy ones,
and his care is with his elect.
10 But the wicked shall receive a punishment to match
their thoughts,
since they neglected justice and forsook the LORD.
11 For he who despises wisdom and instruction is doomed.
Vain is their hope, fruitless are their labors,
and worthless are their works.
12 Their wives are foolish and their children wicked;
accursed is their brood.
13 Yes, blessed is she who, childless and undefiled,
knew not transgression of the marriage bed;
she shall bear fruit at the visitation of souls.
14 So also the eunuch whose hand wrought no misdeed,
who held no wicked thoughts against the LORD—
For he shall be given fidelity's choice reward
and a more gratifying heritage in the LORD's temple.

NEW JERUSALEM BIBLE

7 At their time of visitation, they will shine out;
as sparks run through the stubble, so will they.
8 They will judge nations, rule over peoples,
and the Lord will be their king for ever.
9 Those who trust in him will understand the truth,
those who are faithful will live with him in love;
for grace and mercy await his holy ones,
and he intervenes on behalf of his chosen.

10 But the godless will be duly punished for their
reasoning,
for having neglected the upright and deserted the Lord.
11 Yes, wretched are they who scorn wisdom and
discipline:
their hope is void,
their toil unavailing,
their achievements unprofitable;
12 their wives are reckless,
their children depraved,
their descendants accursed.

13 Blessed the sterile woman if she be blameless,
and has not known an unlawful bed,
for she will have fruit at the visitation of souls.
14 Blessed, too, the eunuch whose hand commits no
crime,
and who harbours no resentment against the Lord:
a special favour will be granted to him for his loyalty,
a most desirable portion in the temple of the Lord.

GREEK OLD TESTAMENT

15 ἀγαθῶν γὰρ πόνων καρπὸς εὐκλεής,
καὶ ἀδιάπτωτος ἡ ῥίζα τῆς φρονήσεως.
16 τέκνα δὲ μοιχῶν ἀτέλεστα ἔσται,
καὶ ἐκ παρανόμου κοίτης σπέρμα ἀφανισθήσεται.
17 ἐάν τε γὰρ μακρόβιοι γένωνται, εἰς οὐθὲν
λογισθήσονται,
καὶ ἄτιμον ἐπ' ἐσχάτων τὸ γῆρας αὐτῶν·
18 ἐάν τε ὀξέως τελευτήσωσιν, οὐχ ἕξουσιν ἐλπίδα
οὐδὲ ἐν ἡμέρᾳ διαγνώσεως παραμύθιον·
19 γενεᾶς γὰρ ἀδίκου χαλεπὰ τὰ τέλη.

4 κρείσσων ἀτεκνία μετὰ ἀρετῆς·
ἀθανασία γάρ ἐστιν ἐν μνήμῃ αὐτῆς,
ὅτι καὶ παρὰ θεῷ γινώσκεται καὶ παρὰ ἀνθρώποις.
2 παροῦσάν τε μιμοῦνται αὐτὴν
καὶ ποθοῦσιν ἀπελθοῦσαν·
καὶ ἐν τῷ αἰῶνι στεφανηφοροῦσα πομπεύει
τὸν τῶν ἀμιάντων ἄθλων ἀγῶνα νικήσασα.
3 πολύγονον δὲ ἀσεβῶν πλῆθος οὐ χρησιμεύσει
καὶ ἐκ νόθων μοσχευμάτων οὐ δώσει ῥίζαν εἰς βάθος
οὐδὲ ἀσφαλῆ βάσιν ἑδράσει·
4 κἂν γὰρ ἐν κλάδοις πρὸς καιρὸν ἀναθάλῃ,
ἐπισφαλῶς βεβηκότα ὑπὸ ἀνέμου σαλευθήσεται
καὶ ὑπὸ βίας ἀνέμων ἐκριζωθήσεται.
5 περικλασθήσονται κλῶνες ἀτέλεστοι,
καὶ ὁ καρπὸς αὐτῶν ἄχρηστος, ἄωρος εἰς βρῶσιν

KING JAMES VERSION

15 For glorious is the fruit of good labours: and the root of wisdom shall never fall away.

16 As for the children of adulterers, they shall not come to their perfection, and the seed of an unrighteous bed shall be rooted out.

17 For though they live long, yet shall they be nothing regarded: and their last age shall be without honour.

18 Or, if they die quickly, they have no hope, neither comfort in the day of trial.

19 For horrible is the end of the unrighteous generation.

4 Better it is to have no children, and to have virtue: for the memorial thereof is immortal: because it is known with God, and with men.

2 When it is present, men take example at it; and when it is gone, they desire it: it weareth a crown, and triumpheth for ever, having gotten the victory, striving for undefiled rewards.

3 But the multiplying brood of the ungodly shall not thrive, nor take deep rooting from bastard slips, nor lay any fast foundation.

4 For though they flourish in branches for a time; yet standing not fast, they shall be shaken with the wind, and through the force of winds they shall be rooted out.

5 The imperfect branches shall be broken off, their fruit

DOUAY OLD TESTAMENT

15 For the fruit of good labours is glorious, and the root of wisdom never faileth.

16 But the children of adulterers shall not come to perfection, and the seed of the unlawful bed shall be rooted out.

17 And if they live long, they shall be nothing regarded, and their last old age shall be without honour.

18 And if they die quickly, they shall have no hope, nor speech of comfort in the day of trial.

19 For dreadful are the ends of a wicked race.

4 O HOW beautiful is the chaste generation with glory: for the memory thereof is immortal: because it is known both with God and with men.

2 When it is present, they imitate it: and they desire it when it hath withdrawn itself, and it triumpheth crowned for ever, winning the reward of undefiled conflicts.

3 But the multiplied brood of the wicked shall not thrive, and bastard slips shall not take deep root, nor any fast foundation.

4 And if they flourish in branches for a time, yet standing not fast, they shall be shaken with the wind, and through the force of winds they shall be rooted out.

5 For the branches not being perfect, shall be broken, and

KNOX TRANSLATION

harvest good men reap from their labours; wisdom is a root
which never yet cast its crop. 16 Not so the adulterers; never
look for children of theirs to thrive; the offspring of the
unhallowed wedlock will vanish away.[a] 17 Live they long,
they shall be held in no regard, in their late age unhonoured;
18 die they soon, they shall die without hope, no comfort to
sustain them in the day when all comes to light. 19 Bitterly
they shall rue it hereafter, the race of the evil-doers.

4 How fair a thing is the unwedded life[b] that is nobly
lived! Think not the memory of it can fade; God and
man alike preserve the record; 2 in life how eagerly imitated,
in death how long regretted, in eternity how crowned with
triumph, the conquest gained in fields of honourable striving! 3 Let the wicked gender as they will, it shall nothing
avail them; what, should those bastard slips ever strike their
roots deep, base the tree firm? 4 Burgeon they may for a little, but the wind will shake their frail hold; root and all, the
storm will carry them away. 5 Half-formed, the boughs will

a Some think that adultery, here as often in the Old Testament, is used by a metaphor for the worship of false gods. *b* In the Greek text, 'even a childless life'.

TODAY'S ENGLISH VERSION

deeds are like a tree that bears marvelous fruit. Wisdom is
like a root that is alive and can always send up new shoots.
16 But children born of adultery or of a forbidden union
will die an early death. 17 Yet even if they do live a long
time, they will never amount to anything. They will not be
respected in their old age, 18 and if they die young, they will
have no hope or comfort on Judgment Day. 19 Children born
of a forbidden union suffer a miserable fate.

4 It is better to have virtue, even if it means having no
children. Your virtue will be recognized by other people
and by God, and you will be remembered for it forever.
2 Virtue provides an example for people to follow; when it is
not there, they miss it. It has always been the finest prize a
person can win, and it always will be so. It is the noblest of
all the good qualities a person can have.
3 No matter how many children are born of a forbidden
union, none of them will ever amount to anything. They are
illegitimate; they can never lay a firm foundation for themselves, never take deep root. 4 Like trees with shallow roots,
they put out leaves for a while, but they sway in the wind,
and storms uproot them. 5 Their branches snap off before

NEW REVISED STANDARD VERSION

15 For the fruit of good labors is renowned,
and the root of understanding does not fail.
16 But children of adulterers will not come to maturity,
and the offspring of an unlawful union will perish.
17 Even if they live long they will be held of no account,
and finally their old age will be without honor.
18 If they die young, they will have no hope
and no consolation on the day of judgment.
19 For the end of an unrighteous generation is grievous.

4 Better than this is childlessness with virtue,
for in the memory of virtue[a] is immortality,
because it is known both by God and by mortals.
2 When it is present, people imitate[b] it,
and they long for it when it has gone;
throughout all time it marches, crowned in triumph,
victor in the contest for prizes that are undefiled.
3 But the prolific brood of the ungodly will be of no use,
and none of their illegitimate seedlings will strike a
deep root
or take a firm hold.
4 For even if they put forth boughs for a while,
standing insecurely they will be shaken by the wind,
and by the violence of the winds they will be uprooted.
5 The branches will be broken off before they come to
maturity,
and their fruit will be useless,

a Gk *it* *b* Other ancient authorities read *honor*

NEW AMERICAN BIBLE

15 For the fruit of noble struggles is a glorious one;
and unfailing is the root of understanding.
16 But the children of adulterers will remain without issue,
and the progeny of an unlawful bed will disappear.
17 For should they attain long life, they will be held in no
esteem,
and dishonored will their old age be at last;
18 While should they die abruptly, they have no hope
nor comfort in the day of scrutiny;
19 for dire is the end of the wicked generation.

4 Better is childlessness with virtue;
for immortal is its memory:
because both by God is it acknowledged, and by men.
2 When it is present men imitate it,
and they long for it when it is gone;
And forever it marches crowned in triumph,
victorious in unsullied deeds of valor.
3 But the numerous progeny of the wicked shall be of no
avail;
their spurious offshoots shall not strike deep root
nor take firm hold.
4 For even though their branches flourish for a time,
they are unsteady and shall be rocked by the wind
and, by the violence of the winds, uprooted;
5 Their twigs shall be broken off untimely,
and their fruit be useless, unripe for eating,

NEW JERUSALEM BIBLE

15 For the fruit of honest labours is glorious,
and the root of understanding does not decay.
16 But the children of adulterers will not reach maturity,
the offspring of an unlawful bed will disappear.
17 Even if they live long, they will count for nothing,
their old age will go unhonoured at the last;
18 while if they die early, they have neither hope
nor comfort on the day of judgement,
19 for the end of a race of evil-doers is harsh.

4 Better to have no children yet to have virtue,
since immortality perpetuates its memory;
for God and human beings both recognise it.
2 Present, we imitate it,
absent, we long for it;
crowned, it holds triumph through eternity,
having striven for untainted prizes and emerged the
victor.
3 But the offspring of the godless come to nothing,
however prolific,
sprung from a bastard stock, they will never strike deep
roots,
never put down firm foundations.
4 They may branch out for a time,
but, on unsteady foundations, they will be rocked by
the wind
and uprooted by the force of the storm;
5 their branches, yet unformed, will be snapped off,
their fruit be useless,

GREEK OLD TESTAMENT

καὶ εἰς οὐθὲν ἐπιτήδειος·
6 ἐκ γὰρ ἀνόμων ὕπνων τέκνα γεννώμενα
μάρτυρές εἰσιν πονηρίας κατὰ γονέων ἐν ἐξετασμῷ
αὐτῶν.
7 Δίκαιος δὲ ἐὰν φθάσῃ τελευτῆσαι, ἐν ἀναπαύσει
ἔσται·
8 γῆρας γὰρ τίμιον οὐ τὸ πολυχρόνιον
οὐδὲ ἀριθμῷ ἐτῶν μεμέτρηται,
9 πολιὰ δέ ἐστιν φρόνησις ἀνθρώποις
καὶ ἡλικία γήρως βίος ἀκηλίδωτος.
10 εὐάρεστος θεῷ γενόμενος ἠγαπήθη
καὶ ζῶν μεταξὺ ἁμαρτωλῶν μετετέθη·
11 ἡρπάγη, μὴ κακία ἀλλάξῃ σύνεσιν αὐτοῦ
ἢ δόλος ἀπατήσῃ ψυχὴν αὐτοῦ·
12 βασκανία γὰρ φαυλότητος ἀμαυροῖ τὰ καλά,
καὶ ῥεμβασμὸς ἐπιθυμίας μεταλλεύει νοῦν ἄκακον.
13 τελειωθεὶς ἐν ὀλίγῳ ἐπλήρωσεν χρόνους μακρούς·
14 ἀρεστὴ γὰρ ἦν κυρίῳ ἡ ψυχὴ αὐτοῦ,
διὰ τοῦτο ἔσπευσεν ἐκ μέσου πονηρίας·
οἱ δὲ λαοὶ ἰδόντες καὶ μὴ νοήσαντες
μηδὲ θέντες ἐπὶ διανοίᾳ τὸ τοιοῦτο,
15 ὅτι χάρις καὶ ἔλεος ἐν τοῖς ἐκλεκτοῖς αὐτοῦ
καὶ ἐπισκοπὴ ἐν τοῖς ὁσίοις αὐτοῦ.

KING JAMES VERSION

unprofitable, not ripe to eat, yea, meet for nothing.

6 For children begotten of unlawful beds are witnesses of wickedness against their parents in their trial.

7 But though the righteous be prevented with death, yet shall he be in rest.

8 For honourable age is not that which standeth in length of time, nor that is measured by number of years.

9 But wisdom is the gray hair unto men, and an unspotted life is old age.

10 He pleased God, and was beloved of him: so that living among sinners he was translated.

11 Yea, speedily was he taken away, lest that wickedness should alter his understanding, or deceit beguile his soul.

12 For the bewitching of naughtiness doth obscure things that are honest; and the wandering of concupiscence doth undermine the simple mind.

13 He, being made perfect in a short time, fulfilled a long time:

14 For his soul pleased the Lord: therefore hasted he *to take him away* from among the wicked.

15 This the people saw, and understood it not, neither laid they up this in their minds, That his grace and mercy is with his saints, and that he hath respect unto his chosen.

DOUAY OLD TESTAMENT

their fruits shall be unprofitable, and sour to eat, and fit for nothing.

6 For the children that are born of unlawful beds, are witnesses of wickedness against their parents in their trial.

7 But the just man, if he be prevented with death, shall be in rest.

8 For venerable old age is not that of long time, nor counted by the number of years: but the understanding of a man is grey hairs.

9 And a spotless life is old age.

10 He pleased God and was beloved, and living among sinners he was translated.

11 He was taken away lest wickedness should alter his understanding, or deceit beguile his soul.

12 For the bewitching of vanity obscureth good things, and the wandering of concupiscence overturneth the innocent mind.

13 Being made perfect in a short space, he fulfilled a long time:

14 For his soul pleased God: therefore he hastened to bring him out of the midst of iniquities: but the people see this, and understand not, nor lay up such things in their hearts:

15 That the grace of God, and his mercy is with his saints, and that he hath respect to his chosen.

KNOX TRANSLATION

be snapped off, and their fruit go to waste, unripe, unprofitable. 6 And indeed, when the day of reckoning comes,
needs must they should be cited as witnesses against their
own parents, these, the children of their shame, by unlawful
dalliance begotten.[a]
7 Not so the innocent; though he should die before his
time, rest shall be his. 8 A seniority there is that claims reverence, owing nothing to time, not measured by the lapse of
years; 9 count a man grey-haired when he is wise, ripe of age
when his life is stainless. 10 Divine favour, divine love banished him from a life he shared with sinners; 11 caught him
away, before wickedness could pervert his thoughts, before
wrong-doing could allure his heart; 12 such witchery evil
has, to tarnish honour, such alchemy do the roving passions
exercise even on minds that are true metal. 13 With him,
early achievement counted for long apprenticeship; 14 so
well the Lord loved him, from a corrupt world he would
grant him swift release.
15 The world looks on, uncomprehending; a hard lesson it
is to learn, that God does reward, does pity his chosen
friends, does grant his faithful servants deliverance. 16 Did

a Some think that the author is condemning, not literal adultery, but marriage with the heathen.

TODAY'S ENGLISH VERSION

they mature; their fruit never ripens, and it is good for nothing. 6 On Judgment Day children born of a forbidden union
will testify to the sin of their parents and act as witnesses
against them.

7 Righteous people, however, will find rest, even if they die
young. 8 We honor old age, but not just because a person
has lived a long time. 9 Wisdom and righteousness are signs
of the maturity that should come with old age.

10 Once there was a man named Enoch who pleased God,
and God loved him. While Enoch was still living among sinners, God took him away, 11 so that evil and falsehood could
not corrupt his mind and soul. (12 We all know that people
can be so fascinated by evil that they cannot recognize what
is good even when they are looking right at it. Innocent people can be so corrupted with desire that they can think of
nothing but what they want.) 13 This man Enoch achieved in
a few years' time a perfection that other people could never
attain in a complete lifetime. 14 The Lord was pleased with
Enoch's life and quickly took him out of this wicked world.
People were aware of his departure but didn't understand.
They never seemed to learn the lesson 15 that God is kind
and merciful to his own people; he protects those whom he
has chosen.

NEW REVISED STANDARD VERSION

not ripe enough to eat, and good for nothing.
6 For children born of unlawful unions
are witnesses of evil against their parents when God
examines them.[a]
7 But the righteous, though they die early, will be at rest.
8 For old age is not honored for length of time,
or measured by number of years;
9 but understanding is gray hair for anyone,
and a blameless life is ripe old age.

10 There were some who pleased God and were loved by
him,
and while living among sinners were taken up.
11 They were caught up so that evil might not change their
understanding
or guile deceive their souls.
12 For the fascination of wickedness obscures what is
good,
and roving desire perverts the innocent mind.
13 Being perfected in a short time, they fulfilled long years;
14 for their souls were pleasing to the Lord,
therefore he took them quickly from the midst of
wickedness.
15 Yet the peoples saw and did not understand,
or take such a thing to heart,
that God's grace and mercy are with his elect,
and that he watches over his holy ones.

a Gk *at their examination*

NEW AMERICAN BIBLE

and fit for nothing.
6 For children born of lawless unions
give evidence of the wickedness of their parents,
when they are examined.

7 But the just man, though he die early, shall be at rest.
8 For the age that is honorable comes not with the
passing of time,
nor can it be measured in terms of years.
9 Rather, understanding is the hoary crown for men,
and an unsullied life, the attainment of old age.
10 He who pleased God was loved;
he who lived among sinners was transported—
11 Snatched away, lest wickedness pervert his mind
or deceit beguile his soul;
12 For the witchery of paltry things obscures what is right
and the whirl of desire transforms the innocent mind.
13 Having become perfect in a short while,
he reached the fullness of a long career;
14 for his soul was pleasing to the LORD,
therefore he sped him out of the midst of wickedness.
But the people saw and did not understand,
nor did they take this into account.

4, 15: The verse here omitted repeats the last two lines of Wis 3, 9.

NEW JERUSALEM BIBLE

too unripe to eat,
fit for nothing.
6 For children begotten of unlawful bed
witness, when put on trial, to their parents'
wickedness.
7 The upright, though he die before his time, will find
rest.
8 Length of days is not what makes age honourable,
nor number of years the true measure of life;
9 understanding, this is grey hairs,
untarnished life, this is ripe old age.
10 Having won God's favour, he has been loved
and, as he was living among sinners, has been taken
away.
11 He has been carried off so that evil may not warp his
understanding
or deceitfulness seduce his soul;
12 for the fascination of evil throws good things into the
shade,
and the whirlwind of desire corrupts a simple heart.
13 Having come to perfection so soon, he has lived long;
14 his soul being pleasing to the Lord,
he has hurried away from the wickedness around him.

Yet people look on, uncomprehending;
and it does not enter their heads
15 that grace and mercy await his chosen ones
and that he intervenes on behalf of his holy ones.

GREEK OLD TESTAMENT

16 κατακρινεῖ δὲ δίκαιος καμὼν τοὺς ζῶντας ἀσεβεῖς
καὶ νεότης τελεσθεῖσα ταχέως πολυετὲς γῆρας ἀδίκου·
17 ὄψονται γὰρ τελευτὴν σοφοῦ
καὶ οὐ νοήσουσιν τί ἐβουλεύσατο περὶ αὐτοῦ
καὶ εἰς τί ἠσφαλίσατο αὐτὸν ὁ κύριος.
18 ὄψονται καὶ ἐξουθενήσουσιν·
αὐτοὺς δὲ ὁ κύριος ἐκγελάσεται,
19 καὶ ἔσονται μετὰ τοῦτο εἰς πτῶμα ἄτιμον
καὶ εἰς ὕβριν ἐν νεκροῖς δι' αἰῶνος,
ὅτι ῥήξει αὐτοὺς ἀφώνους πρηνεῖς
καὶ σαλεύσει αὐτοὺς ἐκ θεμελίων,
καὶ ἕως ἐσχάτου χερσωθήσονται
καὶ ἔσονται ἐν ὀδύνῃ,
καὶ ἡ μνήμη αὐτῶν ἀπολεῖται.
20 ἐλεύσονται ἐν συλλογισμῷ ἁμαρτημάτων αὐτῶν δειλοί,
καὶ ἐλέγξει αὐτοὺς ἐξ ἐναντίας τὰ ἀνομήματα αὐτῶν.

5 Τότε στήσεται ἐν παρρησίᾳ πολλῇ ὁ δίκαιος
κατὰ πρόσωπον τῶν θλιψάντων αὐτὸν
καὶ τῶν ἀθετούντων τοὺς πόνους αὐτοῦ.
2 ἰδόντες ταραχθήσονται φόβῳ δεινῷ

KING JAMES VERSION

16 Thus the righteous that is dead shall condemn the ungodly which are living; and youth that is soon perfected the many years and old age of the unrighteous.

17 For they shall see the end of the wise, and shall not understand what God in his counsel hath decreed of him, and to what end the Lord hath set him in safety.

18 They shall see him, and despise him; but God shall laugh them to scorn: and they shall hereafter be a vile carcase, and a reproach among the dead for evermore.

19 For he shall rend them, and cast them down headlong, that they shall be speechless; and he shall shake them from the foundation; and they shall be utterly laid waste, and be in sorrow; and their memorial shall perish.

20 And when they cast up the accounts of their sins, they shall come with fear: and their own iniquities shall convince them to their face.

5 Then shall the righteous man stand in great boldness before the face of such as have afflicted him, and made no account of his labours.

2 When they see it, they shall be troubled with terrible

DOUAY OLD TESTAMENT

16 But the just that is dead, condemneth the wicked that are living, and youth soon ended, the long life of the unjust.

17 For they shall see the end of the wise man, and shall not understand what God hath designed for him, and why the Lord hath set him in safety.

18 They shall see him, and shall despise him: but the Lord shall laugh them to scorn.

19 And they shall fall after this without honour, and be a reproach among the dead for ever: for he shall burst them puffed up and speechless, and shall shake them from the foundations, and they shall be utterly laid waste: they shall be in sorrow, and their memory shall perish.

20 They shall come with fear at the thought of their sins, and their iniquities shall stand against them to convict them.

5 THEN shall the just stand with great constancy against those that have afflicted them, and taken away their labours.

2 These seeing it, shall be troubled with terrible fear, and

KNOX TRANSLATION

they know it, the death of the just man, with its promise
early achieved, is a reproach to the wicked that live yet in
late old age. 17 But what see they? Here is a man dead, and
all his wisdom could not save him. That the Lord planned all
this, and for the saving of him, does not enter their minds.
18 What wonder if the sight fills them with contempt? And
they themselves, all the while, are earning the Lord's contempt; they themselves, doomed to lie there dishonoured
among the dead, eternally a laughing-stock! 19 How they
will stand aghast, when he pricks the bubble of their pride![a]
Ruins they shall be, overthrown from the foundation, land
for ever parched dry; bitter torment shall be theirs, and their
name shall perish irrecoverably. Alas, the long tally of their
sins! 20 Trembling they shall come forward, and the record of
their misdeeds shall rise up to confront them.

5 How boldly, then, will the just man appear, to meet his
old persecutors, that thwarted all his striving! 2 And
they, in what craven fear they will cower at the sight of him,

a Literally, 'when he breaks them asunder, all puffed up as they are'. The sense of the Greek text is probably, 'When he throws them down headlong'.

TODAY'S ENGLISH VERSION

16 Even when righteous people are dead and gone, they put
to shame the wicked people who live on after them. In their
old age the wicked will be disgraced by young people who
have already achieved perfection. 17 The wise may die
young, but the wicked will never understand that this is the
Lord's way of taking them off to safety. 18 They make light
of a wise person's death, but the Lord will soon be laughing
at them. When they die, they will not be given an honorable
burial. Even the dead will hold them in scorn and disgust
forever. 19 God will throw them to the ground and make
them speechless. Like buildings shaken from their foundations, they will be reduced to piles of ruins. They will be in
torment. People will soon forget all about them. 20 They will
come in fear to the Judgment, where their sins will be counted; they will stand condemned by their own lawless actions.
5 On that day someone righteous, full of confidence, will
stand before those who oppressed him and made light of
his labors. 2 They will be amazed to see him safe and will

NEW REVISED STANDARD VERSION

16 The righteous who have died will condemn the ungodly
who are living,
and youth that is quickly perfected[a] will condemn the
prolonged old age of the unrighteous.
17 For they will see the end of the wise,
and will not understand what the Lord purposed for
them,
and for what he kept them safe.
18 The unrighteous[b] will see, and will have contempt for
them,
but the Lord will laugh them to scorn.
After this they will become dishonored corpses,
and an outrage among the dead forever;
19 because he will dash them speechless to the ground,
and shake them from the foundations;
they will be left utterly dry and barren,
and they will suffer anguish,
and the memory of them will perish.

20 They will come with dread when their sins are reckoned
up,
and their lawless deeds will convict them to their face.
5 Then the righteous will stand with great confidence
in the presence of those who have oppressed them
and those who make light of their labors.
2 When the unrighteous[c] see them, they will be shaken
with dreadful fear,

a Or *ended* *b* Gk *They* *c* Gk *they*

NEW AMERICAN BIBLE

16 Yes, the just man dead condemns the sinful who live,
and youth swiftly completed
condemns the many years of the wicked man grown
old.
17 For they see the death of the wise man
and do not understand what the LORD intended for
him,
or why he made him secure.
18 They see, and hold him in contempt;
but the LORD laughs them to scorn.
19 And they shall afterward become dishonored corpses
and an unceasing mockery among the dead.
For he shall strike them down speechless and prostrate
and rock them to their foundations;
They shall be utterly laid waste
and shall be in grief
and their memory shall perish.
20 Fearful shall they come, at the counting up of their
sins,
and their lawless deeds shall convict them to their
face.

5 Then shall the just one with great assurance confront
his oppressors who set at nought his labors.
2 Seeing this, they shall be shaken with dreadful fear,

NEW JERUSALEM BIBLE

16 The upright who dies condemns the godless who
survive,
and youth quickly perfected condemns the lengthy old
age of the wicked.
17 These people see the end of the wise
without understanding what the Lord has in store
or why he has taken such a one to safety;
18 they look on and sneer,
but the Lord will laugh at them.
19 Soon they will be corpses without honour,
objects of horror among the dead for ever.
For he will shatter them and fling them headlong and
dumbfounded.
He will shake them from their foundations;
they will be utterly laid waste,
a prey to grief,
and their memory will perish.
20 When the count of their sins has been drawn up, in
terror they will come,
and their crimes, confronting them, will accuse them.
5 Then the upright will stand up boldly
to face those who had oppressed him
and had thought so little of his sufferings.
2 And, seeing him, they will be seized with terrible fear,

GREEK OLD TESTAMENT

καὶ ἐκστήσονται ἐπὶ τῷ παραδόξῳ τῆς σωτηρίας·
3 ἐροῦσιν ἐν ἑαυτοῖς μετανοοῦντες
καὶ διὰ στενοχωρίαν πνεύματος στενάξονται καὶ
ἐροῦσιν
4 Οὗτος ἦν, ὃν ἔσχομέν ποτε εἰς γέλωτα
καὶ εἰς παραβολὴν ὀνειδισμοῦ οἱ ἄφρονες·
τὸν βίον αὐτοῦ ἐλογισάμεθα μανίαν
καὶ τὴν τελευτὴν αὐτοῦ ἄτιμον.
5 πῶς κατελογίσθη ἐν υἱοῖς θεοῦ
καὶ ἐν ἁγίοις ὁ κλῆρος αὐτοῦ ἐστιν;
6 ἄρα ἐπλανήθημεν ἀπὸ ὁδοῦ ἀληθείας,
καὶ τὸ τῆς δικαιοσύνης φῶς οὐκ ἐπέλαμψεν ἡμῖν,
καὶ ὁ ἥλιος οὐκ ἀνέτειλεν ἡμῖν·
7 ἀνομίας ἐνεπλήσθημεν τρίβοις καὶ ἀπωλείας
καὶ διωδεύσαμεν ἐρήμους ἀβάτους,
τὴν δὲ ὁδὸν κυρίου οὐκ ἐπέγνωμεν.
8 τί ὠφέλησεν ἡμᾶς ἡ ὑπερηφανία;
καὶ τί πλοῦτος μετὰ ἀλαζονείας συμβέβληται ἡμῖν;
9 παρῆλθεν ἐκεῖνα πάντα ὡς σκιὰ
καὶ ὡς ἀγγελία παρατρέχουσα·
10 ὡς ναῦς διερχομένη κυμαινόμενον ὕδωρ,
ἧς διαβάσης οὐκ ἔστιν ἴχνος εὑρεῖν
οὐδὲ ἀτραπὸν τρόπιος αὐτῆς ἐν κύμασιν·
11 ἢ ὡς ὀρνέου διιπτάντος ἀέρα
οὐθὲν εὑρίσκεται τεκμήριον πορείας,
πληγῇ δὲ μαστιζόμενον ταρσῶν πνεῦμα κοῦφον

KING JAMES VERSION

fear, and shall be amazed at the strangeness of his salvation, so far beyond all that they looked for.

3 And they repenting and groaning for anguish of spirit shall say within themselves, This was he, whom we had sometimes in derision, and a proverb of reproach:

4 We fools accounted his life madness, and his end to be without honour:

5 How is he numbered among the children of God, and his lot is among the saints!

6 Therefore have we erred from the way of truth, and the light of righteousness hath not shined unto us, and the sun of righteousness rose not upon us.

7 We wearied ourselves in the way of wickedness and destruction: yea, we have gone through deserts, where there lay no way: but as for the way of the Lord, we have not known it.

8 What hath pride profited us? or what good hath riches with *our* vaunting brought us?

9 All those things are passed away like a shadow, and as a post that hasted by;

10 And as a ship that passeth over the waves of the water, which when it is gone by, the trace thereof cannot be found, neither the pathway of the keel in the waves;

11 Or as when a bird hath flown through the air, there is no token of her way to be found, but the light air being beaten with the stroke of her wings, and parted with the violent

DOUAY OLD TESTAMENT

shall be amazed at the suddenness of their unexpected salvation.

3 Saying within themselves, repenting, and groaning for anguish of spirit: These are they, whom we had some time in derision, and for a parable of reproach.

4 We fools esteemed their life madness, and their end without honour.

5 Behold how they are numbered among the children of God, and their lot is among the saints.

6 Therefore we have erred from the way of truth, and the light of justice hath not shined unto us, and the sun of understanding hath not risen upon us.

7 We wearied ourselves in the way of iniquity and destruction, and have walked through hard ways, but the way of the Lord we have not known.

8 What hath pride profited us? or what advantage hath the boasting of riches brought us?

9 All those things are passed away like a shadow, and like a post that runneth on,

10 And as a ship that passeth through the waves: whereof when it is gone by, the trace cannot be found, nor the path of its keel in the waters:

11 Or as when a bird flieth through the air, of the passage of which no mark can be found, but only the sound of the wings beating the light air, and parting it by the force of her

KNOX TRANSLATION

amazed at the sudden reversal of his fortunes! 3 Inward
remorse will wring a groan from those hearts: Why, these
were the men we made into a laughing-stock and a by-word!
4 We, poor fools, mistook the life they lived for madness,
their death for ignominy; 5 and now they are reckoned as
God's own children, now it is among his holy ones that their
lot is cast.[a]
6 Far, it seems, did our thoughts wander from the true
path; never did the ray of justice enlighten them, never the
true sun shone. 7 Weary it proved, the reckless way of ruin,
lonely were the wastes we travelled, who missed the path the
Lord meant for us. 8 What advantage has it brought us, all
our pomp and pride? How are we the better for all our vaunted wealth? 9 Nothing of that but is gone, unsubstantial as a
shadow, swift as courier upon his errand. 10 The ship that
ploughs angry waves, what trace is left of her passage? How
wilt thou track her keel's pathway through the deep? 11 The
bird's flight through air what print betrays? So fiercely
lashed the still breeze with the beating of her pinions, as she
cleaves her noisy way through heaven, wings flapping, and

a vv. 3-5: 'These were the men...' in the Greek text, 'This is the man...' the singular being used throughout.

TODAY'S ENGLISH VERSION

tremble with terrible fear. 3 Then they will regret what they
did, and groaning in anguish they will say to each other:
4 "This is the one we made fun of. We thought he was a joke.
What fools we were! We thought he was crazy to live the
way he did, and when he died, we didn't honor him. 5 And
now here he is, one of God's own children, with a place of
his own among God's people. 6 We were the ones who wandered off the right road. We never lived in the light of righteousness; we never caught the first glimmer of its light.
7 All our lives we wandered across unmarked deserts, instead
of following the road which the Lord wanted us to travel.
And this lawlessness led us to ruin. 8 We were so proud of
ourselves—we bragged about how rich we were—and now,
what good has it done us? 9 All those things are gone now;
they have disappeared like a shadow, like something you
hear and then forget.

10 "A ship sails across the waves of the ocean, but when it
is gone, it leaves no trace. You cannot tell it was ever there.
11 A bird flies through the air, but leaves no sign that it has
been there. It speeds along, riding through the thin air by the

NEW REVISED STANDARD VERSION

and they will be amazed at the unexpected salvation of
the righteous.
3 They will speak to one another in repentance,
and in anguish of spirit they will groan, and say,
4 "These are persons whom we once held in derision
and made a byword of reproach—fools that we were!
We thought that their lives were madness
and that their end was without honor.
5 Why have they been numbered among the children of
God?
And why is their lot among the saints?
6 So it was we who strayed from the way of truth,
and the light of righteousness did not shine on us,
and the sun did not rise upon us.
7 We took our fill of the paths of lawlessness and
destruction,
and we journeyed through trackless deserts,
but the way of the Lord we have not known.
8 What has our arrogance profited us?
And what good has our boasted wealth brought us?

9 "All those things have vanished like a shadow,
and like a rumor that passes by;
10 like a ship that sails through the billowy water,
and when it has passed no trace can be found,
no track of its keel in the waves;
11 or as, when a bird flies through the air,
no evidence of its passage is found;
the light air, lashed by the beat of its pinions

NEW AMERICAN BIBLE

and amazed at the unlooked-for salvation.
3 They shall say among themselves, rueful
and groaning through anguish of spirit:
"This is he whom once we held as a laughingstock
and as a type for mockery, 4 fools that we were!
His life we accounted madness,
and his death dishonored.
5 See how he is accounted among the sons of God;
how his lot is with the saints!
6 We, then, have strayed from the way of truth,
and the light of justice did not shine for us,
and the sun did not rise for us.
7 We had our fill of the ways of mischief and of ruin;
we journeyed through impassable deserts,
but the way of the LORD we knew not.
8 What did our pride avail us?
What have wealth and its boastfulness afforded us?
9 All of them passed like a shadow
and like a fleeting rumor;
10 Like a ship traversing the heaving water,
of which, when it has passed, no trace can be found,
no path of its keel in the waves.
11 Or like a bird flying through the air;
no evidence of its course is to be found—
But the fluid air, lashed by the beat of pinions,

NEW JERUSALEM BIBLE

amazed that he should have been so unexpectedly
saved.
3 Stricken with remorse, they will say to one another
with groans and labouring breath,
4 'This is the one whom we used to mock,
making him the butt of our insults, fools that we were!
His life we regarded as madness,
his ending as without honour.
5 How has he come to be counted as one of the children
of God
and to have his lot among the holy ones?
6 Clearly we have strayed from the way of truth;
the light of justice has not shone for us,
the sun has not risen for us.
7 We have left no path of lawlessness or ruin unexplored,
we have crossed deserts where there was no track,
but the way of the Lord is one we have never known.
8 What good has arrogance been to us?
What has been the purpose of our riches and
boastfulness?
9 All those things have passed like a shadow,
passed like a fleeting rumour.
10 Like a ship that cuts through heaving waves—
leaving no trace to show where it has passed,
no wake from its keel in the waves.
11 Or like a bird flying through the air—
leaving no proof of its passing;
it whips the light air with the stroke of its pinions,

GREEK OLD TESTAMENT

καὶ σχιζόμενον βίᾳ ῥοίζου
κινουμένων πτερύγων διωδεύθη,
καὶ μετὰ τοῦτο οὐχ εὑρέθη σημεῖον ἐπιβάσεως ἐν αὐτῷ·
12 ἢ ὡς βέλους βληθέντος ἐπὶ σκοπὸν
τμηθεὶς ὁ ἀὴρ εὐθέως εἰς ἑαυτὸν ἀνελύθη
ὡς ἀγνοῆσαι τὴν δίοδον αὐτοῦ·
13 οὕτως καὶ ἡμεῖς γεννηθέντες ἐξελίπομεν
καὶ ἀρετῆς μὲν σημεῖον οὐδὲν ἔσχομεν δεῖξαι,
ἐν δὲ τῇ κακίᾳ ἡμῶν κατεδαπανήθημεν.
14 ὅτι ἐλπὶς ἀσεβοῦς ὡς φερόμενος χνοῦς ὑπὸ ἀνέμου
καὶ ὡς πάχνη ὑπὸ λαίλαπος διωχθεῖσα λεπτὴ
καὶ ὡς καπνὸς ὑπὸ ἀνέμου διεχύθη
καὶ ὡς μνεία καταλύτου μονοημέρου παρώδευσεν.
15 Δίκαιοι δὲ εἰς τὸν αἰῶνα ζῶσιν,
καὶ ἐν κυρίῳ ὁ μισθὸς αὐτῶν,
καὶ ἡ φροντὶς αὐτῶν παρὰ ὑψίστῳ.
16 διὰ τοῦτο λήμψονται τὸ βασίλειον τῆς εὐπρεπείας
καὶ τὸ διάδημα τοῦ κάλλους ἐκ χειρὸς κυρίου,
ὅτι τῇ δεξιᾷ σκεπάσει αὐτοὺς
καὶ τῷ βραχίονι ὑπερασπιεῖ αὐτῶν.
17 λήμψεται πανοπλίαν τὸν ζῆλον αὐτοῦ
καὶ ὁπλοποιήσει τὴν κτίσιν εἰς ἄμυναν ἐχθρῶν·
18 ἐνδύσεται θώρακα δικαιοσύνην
καὶ περιθήσεται κόρυθα κρίσιν ἀνυπόκριτον·

KING JAMES VERSION

noise and motion of them, is passed through, and therein afterwards no sign where she went is to be found;

12 Or like as when an arrow is shot at a mark, it parteth the air, which immediately cometh together again, so that a man cannot know where it went through:

13 Even so we in like manner, as soon as we were born, began to draw to our end, and had no sign of virtue to shew; but were consumed in our own wickedness.

14 For the hope of the ungodly is like dust that is blown away with the wind; like a thin froth that is driven away with the storm; like as the smoke which is dispersed here and there with a tempest, and passeth away as the remembrance of a guest that tarrieth but a day.

15 But the righteous live for evermore; their reward also is with the Lord, and the care of them is with the most High.

16 Therefore shall they receive a glorious kingdom, and a beautiful crown from the Lord's hand: for with his right hand shall he cover them, and with his arm shall he protect them.

17 He shall take to him his jealousy for complete armour, and make the creature his weapon for the revenge of *his* enemies.

18 He shall put on righteousness as a breastplate, and true judgment instead of an helmet.

DOUAY OLD TESTAMENT

flight; she moved her wings, and hath flown through, and there is no mark found afterwards of her way:

12 Or as when an arrow is shot at a mark, the divided air presently cometh together again, so that the passage thereof is not known:

13 So we also being born, forthwith ceased to be: and have been able to shew no mark of virtue: but are consumed in our wickedness.

14 Such things as these the sinners said in hell:

15 For the hope of the wicked is as dust, which is blown away with the wind, and as a thin froth which is dispersed by the storm: and a smoke that is scattered abroad by the wind: and as the remembrance of a guest of one day that passeth by.

16 But the just shall live for evermore: and their reward is with the Lord, and the care of them with the most High.

17 Therefore shall they receive a kingdom of glory, and a crown of beauty at the hand of the Lord: for with his right hand he will cover them, and with his holy arm he will defend them.

18 And his zeal will take armour, and he will arm the creature for the revenge of his enemies.

19 He will put on justice as a breastplate, and will take true judgment instead of a helmet.

KNOX TRANSLATION

is gone; and afterwards, what sign of her going? 12 Or be it
some arrow, shot at a mark, that pierces the air, how quick
the wound closes, the journey is forgotten! 13 So with us it
was all one, our coming to birth and our ceasing to be; no
trace might we leave behind us of a life well lived; we spent
ourselves on ill-doing.
14 (Such is the lament of sinners, there in the world
beneath.[a]) 15 Short-lived are all the hopes of the godless,
thistle-down in the wind, flying spray before the storm,
smoke that whirls away in the breeze; as soon forgotten as
the guest that comes for a day, and comes no more. 16 It is
the just that will live for ever; the Lord has their recompense
waiting for them, the most high God takes care of them.
17 How glorious is that kingdom, how beautiful that crown,
which the Lord will bestow on them! His right hand is there
to protect them, his holy arm to be their shield. 18 Indignantly
he will take up arms, mustering all the forces of creation for
vengeance on his enemies. 19 His own faithfulness is the
breastplate he will put on, unswerving justice the helmet he

a The words enclosed in brackets are not found in the Greek text.

TODAY'S ENGLISH VERSION

force of its wings, leaving behind no trace of its passing.
12 An arrow splits the air when it is shot at a target, but at
once the air closes up behind it, and no one can tell where it
passed. 13 It is the same with us—we were born, and then
we ceased to be. We left no sign of virtue behind us; we were
destroyed by our wickedness."
14 What hope do wicked people have? Only the hope of
straw blown about in the wind, the hope of ocean foam[a]
that disappears in the storm, the hope of smoke in the
breeze. Their hope lasts no longer than our memory of a
guest who stays one day and leaves the next.
15 But the righteous live on forever. The Lord will reward
them; the Most High will protect them. 16 He will give them
royal splendor and a magnificent crown. He will shield them
with his powerful arm. 17 He will go out into battle determined to defeat his enemies, and use the creation itself as a
weapon. 18 Righteousness will be his armor, genuine justice

[a] ocean foam; *some manuscripts have* frost.

NEW REVISED STANDARD VERSION

and pierced by the force of its rushing flight,
is traversed by the movement of its wings,
and afterward no sign of its coming is found there;
12 or as, when an arrow is shot at a target,
the air, thus divided, comes together at once,
so that no one knows its pathway.
13 So we also, as soon as we were born, ceased to be,
and we had no sign of virtue to show,
but were consumed in our wickedness."
14 Because the hope of the ungodly is like thistledown[a]
carried by the wind,
and like a light frost[b] driven away by a storm;
it is dispersed like smoke before the wind,
and it passes like the remembrance of a guest who
stays but a day.

15 But the righteous live forever,
and their reward is with the Lord;
the Most High takes care of them.
16 Therefore they will receive a glorious crown
and a beautiful diadem from the hand of the Lord,
because with his right hand he will cover them,
and with his arm he will shield them.
17 The Lord[c] will take his zeal as his whole armor,
and will arm all creation to repel[d] his enemies;
18 he will put on righteousness as a breastplate,
and wear impartial justice as a helmet;

a Other ancient authorities read *dust* *b* Other ancient authorities read *spider's web* *c* Gk *He* *d* Or *punish*

NEW AMERICAN BIBLE

and cleft by the rushing force
Of speeding wings, is traversed:
and afterward no mark of passage can be found in it.
12 Or as, when an arrow has been shot at a mark,
the parted air straightway flows together again
so that none discerns the way it went through—
13 Even so we, once born, abruptly came to nought
and held no sign of virtue to display,
but were consumed in our wickedness."
14 Yes, the hope of the wicked is like thistledown borne on
the wind,
and like fine, tempest-driven foam;
Like smoke scattered by the wind,
and like the passing memory of the nomad camping
for a single day.
15 But the just live forever,
and in the LORD is their recompense,
and the thought of them is with the Most High.
16 Therefore shall they receive the splendid crown,
the beauteous diadem, from the hand of the LORD—
For he shall shelter them with his right hand,
and protect them with his arm.
17 He shall take his zeal for armor
and he shall arm creation to requite the enemy;
18 He shall don justice for a breastplate
and shall wear sure judgment for a helmet;

NEW JERUSALEM BIBLE

tears it apart in its whirring rush,
drives its way onward with sweeping wing,
and afterwards no sign is seen of its passage.
12 Or like an arrow shot at a mark,
the pierced air closing so quickly on itself,
there is no knowing which way the arrow has passed.
13 So with us: scarcely born, we disappear;
of virtue not a trace have we to show,
we have spent ourselves in our own wickedness!'
14 For the hope of the godless is like chaff carried on the
wind,
like fine spray driven by the storm;
it disperses like smoke before the wind,
goes away like the memory of a one-day guest.
15 But the upright live for ever,
their recompense is with the Lord,
and the Most High takes care of them.
16 So they will receive the glorious crown
and the diadem of beauty from the Lord's hand;
for he will shelter them with his right hand
and with his arm he will shield them.
17 For armour he will take his jealous love,
he will arm creation to punish his enemies;
18 he will put on justice as a breastplate,
and for helmet wear his forthright judgement;

GREEK OLD TESTAMENT

19 λήμψεται ἀσπίδα ἀκαταμάχητον ὁσιότητα,
20 ὀξυνεῖ δὲ ἀπότομον ὀργὴν εἰς ῥομφαίαν,
συνεκπολεμήσει δὲ αὐτῷ ὁ κόσμος ἐπὶ τοὺς
παράφρονας.
21 πορεύσονται εὔστοχοι βολίδες ἀστραπῶν
καὶ ὡς ἀπὸ εὐκύκλου τόξου τῶν νεφῶν ἐπὶ σκοπὸν
ἁλοῦνται,
22 καὶ ἐκ πετροβόλου θυμοῦ πλήρεις ῥιφήσονται χάλαζαι·
ἀγανακτήσει κατ' αὐτῶν ὕδωρ θαλάσσης,
ποταμοὶ δὲ συγκλύσουσιν ἀποτόμως·
23 ἀντιστήσεται αὐτοῖς πνεῦμα δυνάμεως
καὶ ὡς λαῖλαψ ἐκλικμήσει αὐτούς·
καὶ ἐρημώσει πᾶσαν τὴν γῆν ἀνομία,
καὶ ἡ κακοπραγία περιτρέψει θρόνους δυναστῶν.

6 Ἀκούσατε οὖν, βασιλεῖς, καὶ σύνετε·
μάθετε, δικασταὶ περάτων γῆς·
2 ἐνωτίσασθε, οἱ κρατοῦντες πλήθους
καὶ γεγαυρωμένοι ἐπὶ ὄχλοις ἐθνῶν·
3 ὅτι ἐδόθη παρὰ κυρίου ἡ κράτησις ὑμῖν
καὶ ἡ δυναστεία παρὰ ὑψίστου,
ὃς ἐξετάσει ὑμῶν τὰ ἔργα καὶ τὰς βουλὰς διερευνήσει·
4 ὅτι ὑπηρέται ὄντες τῆς αὐτοῦ βασιλείας οὐκ ἐκρίνατε
ὀρθῶς
οὐδὲ ἐφυλάξατε νόμον
οὐδὲ κατὰ τὴν βουλὴν τοῦ θεοῦ ἐπορεύθητε.
5 φρικτῶς καὶ ταχέως ἐπιστήσεται ὑμῖν,

KING JAMES VERSION

19 He shall take holiness for an invincible shield.

20 His severe wrath shall he sharpen for a sword, and the world shall fight with him against the unwise.

21 Then shall the right aiming thunderbolts go abroad; and from the clouds, as from a well drawn bow, shall they fly to the mark.

22 And hailstones full of wrath shall be cast *as* out of a stone bow, and the water of the sea shall rage against them, and the floods shall cruelly drown them.

23 Yea, a mighty wind shall stand up against them, and like a storm shall blow them away: thus iniquity shall lay waste the whole earth, and ill dealing shall overthrow the thrones of the mighty.

6 Hear therefore, O ye kings, and understand; learn, ye that be judges of the ends of the earth.

2 Give ear, ye that rule the people, and glory in the multitude of nations.

3 For power is given you of the Lord, and sovereignty from the Highest, who shall try your works, and search out your counsels.

4 Because, being ministers of his kingdom, ye have not judged aright, nor kept the law, nor walked after the counsel of God;

5 Horribly and speedily shall he come upon you: for a

DOUAY OLD TESTAMENT

20 He will take equity for an invincible shield:

21 And he will sharpen his severe wrath for a spear, and the whole world shall fight with him against the unwise.

22 Then shafts of lightning shall go directly from the clouds, as from a bow well bent, they shall be shot out, and shall fly to the mark.

23 And thick hail shall be cast upon them from the stone casting wrath: the water of the sea shall rage against them, and the rivers shall run together in a terrible manner.

24 A mighty wind shall stand up against them, and as a whirlwind shall divide them: and their iniquity shall bring all the earth to a desert, and wickedness shall overthrow the thrones of the mighty.

6 WISDOM is better than strength, and a wise man is better than a strong man.

2 Hear therefore, ye kings, and understand: learn, ye that are judges of the ends of the earth.

3 Give ear, you that rule the people, and that please yourselves in multitudes of nations:

4 For power is given you by the Lord, and strength by the most High, who will examine your works, and search out your thoughts:

5 Because being ministers of his kingdom, you have not judged rightly, nor kept the law of justice, nor walked according to the will of God.

6 Horribly and speedily will he appear to you: for a most

KNOX TRANSLATION

wears, 20 a right cause his shield unfailing. 21 See, where he
whets the sword of strict retribution, and the whole order of
nature is banded with him against his reckless foes! 22 Well-
aimed fly his thunder-bolts, sped far and wide from yonder
cloud-arch, never missing their mark. 23 Teeming hailstorms
shall whirl about them, the artillery of his vengeance; fiercely
the sea's waves shall roar against them, pitilessly the floods
cut them off; 24 the storm-wind shall rise in their faces, and
scatter them as the gust scatters chaff. The whole earth ransacked, and the thrones of the mighty pulled down, by their
own disobedience, their own malignancy!

6 (Wisdom more avails than strength; for a man of prudence, the warrior is no match.)[a] 2 A word, then, for
kings' ears to hear, kings' hearts to heed; a message for you,
rulers, wherever you be! 3 Listen well, all you that have multitudes at your command, foreign hordes to do your bidding.
4 Power is none but comes to you from the Lord, nor any royalty but from One who is above all. He it is that will call you
to account for your doings, with a scrutiny that reads your
inmost thoughts; 5 you that held his commission and were
false to it, justice neglected, the law set aside, his divine will
transgressed. 6 Swift and terrible shall be his coming; strictly

a Verses 1 and 23 are not found in the Greek text.

TODAY'S ENGLISH VERSION

will be his helmet, 19 holiness will be his invincible shield.
20 He will sharpen his stern anger into a sword, and the
forces of nature will join him in battle against those who are
foolish enough to oppose him. 21 Bolts of lightning will
strike right on target, as if the Lord had made a bow out of
the clouds and was shooting arrows. 22 Hailstones will beat
down on his enemies with terrible force. The oceans and
rivers will come rushing over them in a devastating flood.
23 Great windstorms will blow them away like straw.
Lawlessness will be the ruin of the whole world. Evil actions
will cause governments to fall.

6 So then, you kings, you rulers the world over, listen to
what I say, and learn from it. 2 You govern many lands
and are proud that so many people are under your rule, 3 but
this authority has been given to you by the Lord Most High.
He will examine what you have done and what you plan to
do. 4 You rule on behalf of God and his kingdom, and if you
do not govern justly, if you do not uphold the law, if you do
not live according to God's will, 5 you will suffer sudden and

NEW REVISED STANDARD VERSION

19 he will take holiness as an invincible shield,
20 and sharpen stern wrath for a sword,
and creation will join with him to fight against his
frenzied foes.
21 Shafts of lightning will fly with true aim,
and will leap from the clouds to the target, as from a
well-drawn bow,
22 and hailstones full of wrath will be hurled as from a
catapult;
the water of the sea will rage against them,
and rivers will relentlessly overwhelm them;
23 a mighty wind will rise against them,
and like a tempest it will winnow them away.
Lawlessness will lay waste the whole earth,
and evildoing will overturn the thrones of rulers.

6 Listen therefore, O kings, and understand;
learn, O judges of the ends of the earth.
2 Give ear, you that rule over multitudes,
and boast of many nations.
3 For your dominion was given you from the Lord,
and your sovereignty from the Most High;
he will search out your works and inquire into your
plans.
4 Because as servants of his kingdom you did not rule
rightly,
or keep the law,
or walk according to the purpose of God,
5 he will come upon you terribly and swiftly,

NEW AMERICAN BIBLE

19 He shall take invincible rectitude as a shield
20 and whet his sudden anger for a sword,
And the universe shall war with him against the
foolhardy.
21 Well-aimed shafts of lightnings shall go forth
and from the clouds as from a well-drawn bow shall
leap to the mark;
22 and as from his sling, wrathful hailstones shall be
hurled.
The water of the sea shall be enraged against them
and the streams shall abruptly overflow;
23 A mighty wind shall confront them
and a tempest winnow them out;
Thus lawlessness shall lay the whole earth waste
and evildoing overturn the thrones of potentates.

6 Hear, therefore, kings, and understand;
learn, you magistrates of the earth's expanse!
2 Hearken, you who are in power over the multitude
and lord it over throngs of peoples!
3 Because authority was given you by the LORD
and sovereignty by the Most High,
who shall probe your works and scrutinize your
counsels!
4 Because, though you were ministers of his kingdom,
you judged not rightly,
and did not keep the law,
nor walk according to the will of God,
5 Terribly and swiftly shall he come against you,

NEW JERUSALEM BIBLE

19 he will take up invincible holiness for shield,
20 of his pitiless wrath he will forge a sword,
and the universe will march with him to fight the
reckless.
21 Bolts truly aimed, the shafts of lightning will leap,
and from the clouds, as from a full-drawn bow, fly to
their mark;
22 and the catapult will hurl hailstones charged with fury.
The waters of the sea will rage against them,
the rivers engulf them without pity,
23 a mighty gale will rise against them
and winnow them like a hurricane.
Thus wickedness will lay the whole earth waste
and evil-doing bring down the thrones of the mighty.

6 Listen then, kings, and understand;
rulers of remotest lands, take warning;
2 hear this, you who govern great populations,
taking pride in your hosts of subject nations!
3 For sovereignty is given to you by the Lord
and power by the Most High,
who will himself probe your acts and scrutinise your
intentions.
4 If therefore, as servants of his kingdom, you have not
ruled justly
nor observed the law,
nor followed the will of God,
5 he will fall on you swiftly and terribly.

GREEK OLD TESTAMENT

ὅτι κρίσις ἀπότομος ἐν τοῖς ὑπερέχουσιν γίνεται.
6 ὁ γὰρ ἐλάχιστος συγγνωστός ἐστιν ἐλέους,
δυνατοὶ δὲ δυνατῶς ἐτασθήσονται·
7 οὐ γὰρ ὑποστελεῖται πρόσωπον ὁ πάντων δεσπότης
οὐδὲ ἐντραπήσεται μέγεθος,
ὅτι μικρὸν καὶ μέγαν αὐτὸς ἐποίησεν
ὁμοίως τε προνοεῖ περὶ πάντων,
8 τοῖς δὲ κραταιοῖς ἰσχυρὰ ἐφίσταται ἔρευνα.
9 πρὸς ὑμᾶς οὖν, ὦ τύραννοι, οἱ λόγοι μου,
ἵνα μάθητε σοφίαν καὶ μὴ παραπέσητε·
10 οἱ γὰρ φυλάξαντες ὁσίως τὰ ὅσια ὁσιωθήσονται,
καὶ οἱ διδαχθέντες αὐτὰ εὑρήσουσιν ἀπολογίαν.
11 ἐπιθυμήσατε οὖν τῶν λόγων μου,
ποθήσατε καὶ παιδευθήσεσθε.
12 Λαμπρὰ καὶ ἀμάραντός ἐστιν ἡ σοφία
καὶ εὐχερῶς θεωρεῖται ὑπὸ τῶν ἀγαπώντων αὐτὴν
καὶ εὑρίσκεται ὑπὸ τῶν ζητούντων αὐτήν,
13 φθάνει τοὺς ἐπιθυμοῦντας προγνωσθῆναι.
14 ὁ ὀρθρίσας πρὸς αὐτὴν οὐ κοπιάσει·
πάρεδρον γὰρ εὑρήσει τῶν πυλῶν αὐτοῦ.
15 τὸ γὰρ ἐνθυμηθῆναι περὶ αὐτῆς φρονήσεως τελειότης,
καὶ ὁ ἀγρυπνήσας δι᾽ αὐτὴν ταχέως ἀμέριμνος ἔσται·
16 ὅτι τοὺς ἀξίους αὐτῆς αὐτὴ περιέρχεται ζητοῦσα

KING JAMES VERSION

sharp judgment shall be to them that be in high places.

6 For mercy will soon pardon the meanest: but mighty men shall be mightily tormented.

7 For he which is Lord over all shall fear no man's person, neither shall he stand in awe of any man's greatness: for he hath made the small and great, and careth for all alike.

8 But a sore trial shall come upon the mighty.

9 Unto you therefore, O kings, do I speak, that ye may learn wisdom, and not fall away.

10 For they that keep holiness holily shall be judged holy: and they that have learned such things shall find what to answer.

11 Wherefore set your affection upon my words; desire them, and ye shall be instructed.

12 Wisdom is glorious, and never fadeth away: yea, she is easily seen of them that love her, and found of such as seek her.

13 She preventeth them that desire her, in making herself first known unto them.

14 Whoso seeketh her early shall have no great travail: for he shall find her sitting at his doors.

15 To think therefore upon her is perfection of wisdom: and whoso watcheth for her shall quickly be without care.

16 For she goeth about seeking such as are worthy of her,

DOUAY OLD TESTAMENT

severe judgment shall be for them that bear rule.

7 For to him that is little, mercy is granted: but the mighty shall be mightily tormented.

8 For God will not except any man's person, neither will he stand in awe of any man's greatness: for he made the little and the great, and he hath equally care of all.

9 But a greater punishment is ready for the more mighty.

10 To you, therefore, O kings, are these my words, that you may learn wisdom, and not fall from it.

11 For they that have kept just things justly, shall be justified: and they that have learned these things, shall find what to answer.

12 Covet ye therefore my words, and love them, and you shall have instruction.

13 Wisdom is glorious, and never fadeth away, and is easily seen by them that love her, and is found by them that seek her.

14 She preventeth them that covet her, so that she first sheweth herself unto them.

15 He that awaketh early to seek her, shall not labour: for he shall find her sitting at his door.

16 To think therefore upon her, is perfect understanding: and he that watcheth for her, shall quickly be secure.

17 For she goeth about seeking such as are worthy of her,

KNOX TRANSLATION

his doom falls where heads rise high. 7 For the meanest,
there may be pardon; for greatness, greater torment is
reserved. 8 What, should he cringe before high rank, stand in
awe of a name, he, the Lord of a universe, that made great
and little alike, that cares alike for all? 9 Who most has
power, him the sharpest pains await. 10 Do you, then, royal
sirs (for my warning touches none so nearly), learn wisdom's
lesson, and save yourselves from ruin. 11 He that would find
soul's health, holy must be and hallowed precepts observe;
master these he must, if he would make good his defence.
12 Cherish these warnings of mine, and greedily devour them
for your instruction.

13 The bright beacon of wisdom, that never burns dim, how
readily seen by eyes that long for it, how open to their
search! 14 Nay, she is beforehand with these her suitors,
ready to make herself known to them; 15 no toilsome quest
is his, that is up betimes to greet her; she is there, waiting at
his doors. 16 Why, to entertain the very thought of her is
maturity of the mind; one night's vigil, and all thy cares are
over. 17 She goes her rounds, to find men worthy of her

TODAY'S ENGLISH VERSION

terrible punishment. Judgment is especially severe on those
in power. 6 Common people may be mercifully forgiven for
their wrongs, but those in power will face a severe judgment. 7 The Lord of all is not afraid of anyone, no matter
how great they are. He himself made everyone, great and
common alike, and he provides for all equally, 8 but he will
judge the conduct of rulers more strictly. 9 It is for you,
mighty kings, that I write these words, so that you may
know how to act wisely and avoid mistakes. 10 These are
holy matters, and if you treat them in a holy manner, you
yourselves will be considered holy. If you have learned this
lesson, you will be able to defend yourselves at the
Judgment. 11 So then, make my teaching your treasure and
joy, and you will be well instructed.

12 Wisdom shines bright and never grows dim; those who
love her and look for her can easily find her. 13 She is quick
to make herself known to anyone who desires her. 14 Get up
early in the morning to find her, and you will have no problem; you will find her sitting at your door. 15 To fasten your
attention on Wisdom is to gain perfect understanding. If you
look for her, you will soon find peace of mind, 16 because
she will be looking for those who are worthy of her, and she

NEW REVISED STANDARD VERSION

because severe judgment falls on those in high places.
6 For the lowliest may be pardoned in mercy,
but the mighty will be mightily tested.
7 For the Lord of all will not stand in awe of anyone,
or show deference to greatness;
because he himself made both small and great,
and he takes thought for all alike.
8 But a strict inquiry is in store for the mighty.
9 To you then, O monarchs, my words are directed,
so that you may learn wisdom and not transgress.
10 For they will be made holy who observe holy things in holiness,
and those who have been taught them will find a defense.
11 Therefore set your desire on my words;
long for them, and you will be instructed.

12 Wisdom is radiant and unfading,
and she is easily discerned by those who love her,
and is found by those who seek her.
13 She hastens to make herself known to those who desire her.
14 One who rises early to seek her will have no difficulty,
for she will be found sitting at the gate.
15 To fix one's thought on her is perfect understanding,
and one who is vigilant on her account will soon be free from care,
16 because she goes about seeking those worthy of her,

NEW AMERICAN BIBLE

because judgment is stern for the exalted—
6 For the lowly may be pardoned out of mercy
but the mighty shall be mightily put to the test.
7 For the Lord of all shows no partiality,
nor does he fear greatness,
Because he himself made the great as well as the small,
and he provides for all alike;
8 but for those in power a rigorous scrutiny impends.
9 To you, therefore, O princes, are my words addressed
that you may learn wisdom and that you may not sin.
10 For those who keep the holy precepts hallowed shall be found holy,
and those learned in them will have ready a response.
11 Desire therefore my words;
long for them and you shall be instructed.
12 Resplendent and unfading is Wisdom,
and she is readily perceived by those who love her,
and found by those who seek her.
13 She hastens to make herself known in anticipation of men's desire;
14 he who watches for her at dawn shall not be disappointed,
for he shall find her sitting by his gate.
15 For taking thought of her is the perfection of prudence,
and he who for her sake keeps vigil shall quickly be free from care;
16 Because she makes her own rounds, seeking those worthy of her,

NEW JERUSALEM BIBLE

On the highly placed a ruthless judgement falls;
6 the lowly are pardoned, out of pity,
but the mighty will be mightily tormented.
7 For the Lord of all does not cower before anyone,
he does not stand in awe of greatness,
since he himself has made small and great
and provides for all alike;
8 but a searching trial awaits those who wield power.
9 So, monarchs, my words are meant for you,
so that you may learn wisdom and not fall into error;
10 for those who in holiness observe holy things will be adjudged holy,
and, accepting instruction from them, will find their defence in them.
11 Set your heart, therefore, on what I have to say,
listen with a will, and you will be instructed.
12 Wisdom is brilliant, she never fades.
By those who love her, she is readily seen,
by those who seek her, she is readily found.
13 She anticipates those who desire her by making herself known first.
14 Whoever gets up early to seek her will have no trouble
but will find her sitting at the door.
15 Meditating on her is understanding in its perfect form,
and anyone keeping awake for her will soon be free from care.
16 For she herself searches everywhere for those who are worthy of her,

GREEK OLD TESTAMENT

καὶ ἐν ταῖς τρίβοις φαντάζεται αὐτοῖς εὐμενῶς
καὶ ἐν πάσῃ ἐπινοίᾳ ὑπαντᾷ αὐτοῖς.
17 ἀρχὴ γὰρ αὐτῆς ἡ ἀληθεστάτη παιδείας ἐπιθυμία,
φροντὶς δὲ παιδείας ἀγάπη,
18 ἀγάπη δὲ τήρησις νόμων αὐτῆς,
προσοχὴ δὲ νόμων βεβαίωσις ἀφθαρσίας,
19 ἀφθαρσία δὲ ἐγγὺς εἶναι ποιεῖ θεοῦ·
20 ἐπιθυμία ἄρα σοφίας ἀνάγει ἐπὶ βασιλείαν.
21 εἰ οὖν ἥδεσθε ἐπὶ θρόνοις καὶ σκήπτροις, τύραννοι λαῶν,
τιμήσατε σοφίαν, ἵνα εἰς τὸν αἰῶνα βασιλεύσητε.
22 τί δέ ἐστιν σοφία καὶ πῶς ἐγένετο, ἀπαγγελῶ
καὶ οὐκ ἀποκρύψω ὑμῖν μυστήρια,
ἀλλὰ ἀπ᾽ ἀρχῆς γενέσεως ἐξιχνιάσω
καὶ θήσω εἰς τὸ ἐμφανὲς τὴν γνῶσιν αὐτῆς
καὶ οὐ μὴ παροδεύσω τὴν ἀλήθειαν.
23 οὔτε μὴν φθόνῳ τετηκότι συνοδεύσω,
ὅτι οὗτος οὐ κοινωνήσει σοφίᾳ.
24 πλῆθος δὲ σοφῶν σωτηρία κόσμου,
καὶ βασιλεὺς φρόνιμος εὐστάθεια δήμου.
25 ὥστε παιδεύεσθε τοῖς ῥήμασίν μου, καὶ ὠφεληθήσεσθε.

KING JAMES VERSION

sheweth herself favourably unto them in the ways, and meeteth them in every thought.

17 For the very true beginning of her is the desire of discipline; and the care of discipline is love;

18 And love is the keeping of her laws; and the giving heed unto her laws is the assurance of incorruption;

19 And incorruption maketh us near unto God:

20 Therefore the desire of wisdom bringeth to a kingdom.

21 If your delight be then in thrones and sceptres, O ye kings of the people, honour wisdom, that ye may reign for evermore.

22 As for wisdom, what she is, and how she came up, I will tell you, and will not hide mysteries from you: but will seek her out from the beginning of her nativity, and bring the knowledge of her into light, and will not pass over the truth.

23 Neither will I go with consuming envy; for such a man shall have no fellowship with wisdom.

24 But the multitude of the wise is the welfare of the world: and a wise king is the upholding of the people.

25 Receive therefore instruction through my words, and it shall do you good.

DOUAY OLD TESTAMENT

and she sheweth herself to them cheerfully in the ways, and meeteth them with all providence.

18 For the beginning of her is the most true desire of discipline.

19 And the care of discipline is love: and love is the keeping of her laws: and the keeping of her laws is the firm foundation of incorruption:

20 And incorruption bringeth near to God.

21 Therefore the desire of wisdom bringeth to the everlasting kingdom.

22 If then your delight be in thrones, and sceptres, O ye kings of the people, love wisdom, that you may reign for ever.

23 Love the light of wisdom, all ye that bear rule over peoples.

24 Now what wisdom is, and what was her origin, I will declare: and I will not hide from you the mysteries of God, but will seek her out from the beginning of her birth, and bring the knowledge of her to light, and will not pass over the truth:

25 Neither will I go with consuming envy: for such a man shall not be partaker of wisdom.

26 Now the multitude of the wise is the welfare of the whole world: and a wise king is the upholding of the people.

27 Receive therefore instruction by my words, and it shall be profitable to you.

KNOX TRANSLATION

favours; in the open street unveils that smiling face of hers,
comes deliberately to meet them. 18 The very first step
towards wisdom is the desire for discipline, 19 and how
should a man care for discipline without loving it, or love it
without heeding its laws, or heed its laws without winning
immortality, 20 or win immortality without drawing near to
God? 21 A royal road it is, then, this desire for wisdom,
22 and you, that have nations under your sway, as you value
throne and sceptre, must hold wisdom in honour; how else
shall your reign be eternal? 23 (A welcome light hers should
be to the world's princes.)
24 What wisdom is, whence came its birth, I will now make
known to you. Not for me to withhold the secret; from first to
last I will tell the story of her origin, bring to light all that
may be known of her, no word of the truth passed by.
25 Withhold it? Nay, the pale miser that grudges his store
was never friend of mine; no such character befits the wise.
26 Wide let wisdom be spread, for the more health of
mankind; what better security for a people, than prudence on
the throne? 27 Learn, then, who will, the lesson of discernment; at my charges, and to his profit.

TODAY'S ENGLISH VERSION

will find you wherever you are. She is kind and will be with
you in your every thought.
17 Wisdom begins when you sincerely want to learn. To
desire Wisdom is to love her; 18 to love her is to keep her
laws; to keep her laws is to be certain of immortality;
19 immortality will bring you close to God. 20 This desire for
Wisdom can prepare you to rule a kingdom. 21 So then, you
that rule the nations, if you value your thrones and symbols
of authority, honor Wisdom so that you may rule forever.
22 I will tell you what Wisdom is, and how she came to be.
I will not keep anything secret. I will trace her history from
the beginning and make knowledge of her open to all. I will
not ignore any part of the truth. 23 No jealous desire to
guard my own knowledge will make me hold back anything.
Wisdom has nothing in common with such an attitude.
24 No indeed—the more wise people there are, the safer the
world will be. A sensible king can be depended on to give his
people this kind of security. 25 So then, learn what I am
about to teach you, and you will profit from it.

NEW REVISED STANDARD VERSION

and she graciously appears to them in their paths,
and meets them in every thought.

17 The beginning of wisdom[a] is the most sincere desire for
instruction,
and concern for instruction is love of her,
18 and love of her is the keeping of her laws,
and giving heed to her laws is assurance of
immortality,
19 and immortality brings one near to God;
20 so the desire for wisdom leads to a kingdom.
21 Therefore if you delight in thrones and scepters,
O monarchs over the peoples,
honor wisdom, so that you may reign forever.
22 I will tell you what wisdom is and how she came to be,
and I will hide no secrets from you,
but I will trace her course from the beginning of
creation,
and make knowledge of her clear,
and I will not pass by the truth;
23 nor will I travel in the company of sickly envy,
for envy[b] does not associate with wisdom.
24 The multitude of the wise is the salvation of the world,
and a sensible king is the stability of any people.
25 Therefore be instructed by my words, and you will
profit.

a Gk *Her beginning* *b* Gk *this*

NEW AMERICAN BIBLE

and graciously appears to them in the ways,
and meets them with all solicitude.
17 For the first step toward discipline is a very earnest
desire for her;
then, care for discipline is love of her;
18 love means the keeping of her laws;
To observe her laws is the basis for incorruptibility;
19 and incorruptibility makes one close to God;
20 thus the desire for Wisdom leads up to a kingdom.
21 If, then, you find pleasure in throne and scepter, you
princes of the peoples,
honor Wisdom, that you may reign as kings forever.
22 Now what Wisdom is, and how she came to be, I shall
relate;
and I shall hide no secrets from you,
But from the very beginning I shall search out
and bring to light knowledge of her,
nor shall I diverge from the truth.
23 Neither shall I admit consuming jealousy to my
company,
because that can have no fellowship with Wisdom.
24 A great number of wise men is the safety of the world,
and a prudent king, the stability of his people;
25 so take instruction from my words, to your profit.

NEW JERUSALEM BIBLE

benevolently appearing to them on their ways,
anticipating their every thought.
17 For Wisdom begins with the sincere desire for
instruction,
care for instruction means loving her,
18 loving her means keeping her laws,
attention to her laws guarantees incorruptibility,
19 and incorruptibility brings us near to God;
20 the desire for Wisdom thus leads to sovereignty.
21 If then thrones and sceptres delight you, monarchs of
the nations,
honour Wisdom, so that you may reign for ever.
22 What Wisdom is and how she was born, I shall now
explain;
I shall hide no mysteries from you,
but shall follow her steps from the outset of her origin,
setting out what we know of her in full light,
without departing from the truth.
23 Blighting envy is no companion for me,
for envy has nothing in common with Wisdom.
24 In the greatest number of the wise lies the world's
salvation,
in a sagacious king the stability of a people.
25 Learn, therefore, from my words; the gain will be yours.

GREEK OLD TESTAMENT

7 Εἰμὶ μὲν κἀγὼ θνητὸς ἄνθρωπος ἴσος ἅπασιν
καὶ γηγενοῦς ἀπόγονος πρωτοπλάστου·
καὶ ἐν κοιλίᾳ μητρὸς ἐγλύφην σὰρξ
2 δεκαμηνιαίῳ χρόνῳ παγεὶς ἐν αἵματι
ἐκ σπέρματος ἀνδρὸς καὶ ἡδονῆς ὕπνῳ συνελθούσης.
3 καὶ ἐγὼ δὲ γενόμενος ἔσπασα τὸν κοινὸν ἀέρα
καὶ ἐπὶ τὴν ὁμοιοπαθῆ κατέπεσον γῆν
πρώτην φωνὴν τὴν ὁμοίαν πᾶσιν ἴσα κλαίων·
4 ἐν σπαργάνοις ἀνετράφην καὶ φροντίσιν.
5 οὐδεὶς γὰρ βασιλέων ἑτέραν ἔσχεν γενέσεως ἀρχήν,
6 μία δὲ πάντων εἴσοδος εἰς τὸν βίον ἔξοδός τε ἴση.
7 διὰ τοῦτο εὐξάμην, καὶ φρόνησις ἐδόθη μοι·
ἐπεκαλεσάμην, καὶ ἦλθέν μοι πνεῦμα σοφίας.
8 προέκρινα αὐτὴν σκήπτρων καὶ θρόνων
καὶ πλοῦτον οὐδὲν ἡγησάμην ἐν συγκρίσει αὐτῆς·
9 οὐδὲ ὡμοίωσα αὐτῇ λίθον ἀτίμητον,
ὅτι ὁ πᾶς χρυσὸς ἐν ὄψει αὐτῆς ψάμμος ὀλίγη,
καὶ ὡς πηλὸς λογισθήσεται ἄργυρος ἐναντίον αὐτῆς·
10 ὑπὲρ ὑγίειαν καὶ εὐμορφίαν ἠγάπησα αὐτὴν
καὶ προειλόμην αὐτὴν ἀντὶ φωτὸς ἔχειν,
ὅτι ἀκοίμητον τὸ ἐκ ταύτης φέγγος.
11 ἦλθεν δέ μοι τὰ ἀγαθὰ ὁμοῦ πάντα μετ' αὐτῆς
καὶ ἀναρίθμητος πλοῦτος ἐν χερσὶν αὐτῆς·
12 εὐφράνθην δὲ ἐπὶ πᾶσιν, ὅτι αὐτῶν ἡγεῖται σοφία,
ἠγνόουν δὲ αὐτὴν γενέτιν εἶναι τούτων.

KING JAMES VERSION

7 I myself also am a mortal man, like to all, and the offspring of him that was first made of the earth,

2 And in my mother's womb was fashioned to be flesh in the time of ten months, being compacted in blood, of the seed of man, and the pleasure that came with sleep.

3 And when I was born, I drew in the common air, and fell upon the earth, which is of like nature, and the first voice which I uttered was crying, as all others do.

4 I was nursed in swaddling clothes, and that with cares.

5 For there is no king that had any other beginning of birth.

6 For all men have one entrance into life, and the like going out.

7 Wherefore I prayed, and understanding was given me: I called *upon God,* and the spirit of wisdom came to me.

8 I preferred her before sceptres and thrones, and esteemed riches nothing in comparison of her.

9 Neither compared I unto her any precious stone, because all gold in respect of her is as a little sand, and silver shall be counted as clay before her.

10 I loved her above health and beauty, and chose to have her instead of light: for the light that cometh from her never goeth out.

11 All good things together came to me with her, and innumerable riches in her hands.

12 And I rejoiced in *them* all, because wisdom goeth before them: and I knew not that she was the mother of them.

DOUAY OLD TESTAMENT

7 I MYSELF also am a mortal man, like all *others,* and of the race of him, that was first made of the earth, and in the womb of my mother I was fashioned to be flesh.

2 In the time of ten months I was compacted in blood, of the seed of man, and the pleasure of sleep concurring.

3 And being born I drew in the common air, and fell upon the earth, that is made alike, and the first voice which I uttered was crying, as all *others* do.

4 I was nursed in swaddling clothes, and with great cares.

5 For none of the kings had any other beginning of birth.

6 For all men have one entrance into life, and the like going out.

7 Wherefore I wished, and understanding was given me: and I called upon God, and the spirit of wisdom came upon me:

8 And I preferred her before kingdoms and thrones, and esteemed riches nothing in comparison of her.

9 Neither did I compare unto her any precious stone: for all gold in comparison of her, is as a little sand, and silver in respect to her shall be counted as clay.

10 I loved her above health and beauty, and chose to have her instead of light: for her light cannot be put out.

11 Now all good things came to me together with her, and innumerable riches through her hands,

12 And I rejoiced in all these: for this wisdom went before me, and I knew not that she was the mother of them all.

KNOX TRANSLATION

7 What of myself? Was not Solomon a mortal man like the
rest of you, come down from that first man that was a
thing of clay?[a] I, too, was flesh and blood; 2 ten months I
lay a-fashioning in my mother's womb; of woman's body my
stuff came, and of man's procreation; midnight joys went to
the making of me. 3 Born was I, and born drew in the common air; dust amid the dust I fell, and, baby-fashion, my
first utterance was a cry; 4 swaddled I must be, and cared
for, like the rest. 5 Tell me, was ever king had other manner
of coming to be? 6 By one gate all enter life, by one gate all
leave it.
7 Whence, then, did the prudence spring that endowed me?
Prayer brought it; to God I prayed, and the spirit of wisdom
came upon me.[b] 8 This I valued more than kingdom or
throne; I thought nothing of my riches in comparison.
9 There was no jewel I could match with it; all my treasures
of gold were a handful of dust beside it, my silver seemed
but base clay in presence of it. 10 I treasured wisdom more
than health or beauty, preferred her to the light of day; hers
is a flame which never dies down. 11 Together with her all
blessings came to me; boundless prosperity was her gift.
12 All this I enjoyed, with wisdom to prepare my way for me,
never guessing that it all sprang from her. 13 The lessons she

a Solomon's name is not mentioned in the original; but it is certainly he who is represented as speaking in this and the following chapters.
b Cf. III Kg. 3. 9.

TODAY'S ENGLISH VERSION

7 1-2 Like every human being, I am mortal. I am a descendant of that first man, who was made from the soil. I
was conceived from the sperm of a man, in the pleasure of
intercourse. For nine months my flesh took shape in the
blood of my mother's womb. 3 When I was born, I came into
the world like anyone else. I began to breathe the same air
we all breathe; and like everyone else, the first sound I made
was a cry. 4 I was wrapped in cloths and cared for. 5 No king
ever began life differently. 6 For all of us, there is one way
into life, and there is one way out.
7 Realizing that I was only human, I prayed and was given
understanding. The spirit of Wisdom came to me. 8 I regarded her more highly than any throne or crown. Wealth was
nothing compared to her. 9 Precious jewels could not equal
her worth; beside Wisdom all the gold in the world is a handful of sand, and silver is nothing more than clay. 10 I valued
her more than health and good looks. Hers is a brightness
that never grows dim, and I preferred it to any other light.
11 When Wisdom came to me, all good things came with
her. She brought me untold riches. 12 I was happy with them
all, because Wisdom had brought them to me. I had not realized before that she was the source of all these things.

NEW REVISED STANDARD VERSION

7 I also am mortal, like everyone else,
a descendant of the first-formed child of earth;
and in the womb of a mother I was molded into flesh,
2 within the period of ten months, compacted with blood,
from the seed of a man and the pleasure of marriage.
3 And when I was born, I began to breathe the common
air,
and fell upon the kindred earth;
my first sound was a cry, as is true of all.
4 I was nursed with care in swaddling cloths.
5 For no king has had a different beginning of existence;
6 there is for all one entrance into life, and one way out.
7 Therefore I prayed, and understanding was given me;
I called on God, and the spirit of wisdom came to me.
8 I preferred her to scepters and thrones,
and I accounted wealth as nothing in comparison with
her.
9 Neither did I liken to her any priceless gem,
because all gold is but a little sand in her sight,
and silver will be accounted as clay before her.
10 I loved her more than health and beauty,
and I chose to have her rather than light,
because her radiance never ceases.
11 All good things came to me along with her,
and in her hands uncounted wealth.
12 I rejoiced in them all, because wisdom leads them;
but I did not know that she was their mother.

NEW AMERICAN BIBLE

7 I too am a mortal man, the same as all the rest,
and a descendant of the first man formed of earth.
And in my mother's womb I was molded into flesh
2 in a ten-months' period—body and blood,
from the seed of man, and the pleasure that
accompanies marriage.
3 And I too, when born, inhaled the common air,
and fell upon the kindred earth;
wailing, I uttered that first sound common to all.
4 In swaddling clothes and with constant care I was
nurtured.
5 For no king has any different origin or birth,
6 but one is the entry into life for all; and in one same
way they leave it.
7 Therefore I prayed, and prudence was given me;
I pleaded, and the spirit of Wisdom came to me.
8 I preferred her to scepter and throne,
And deemed riches nothing in comparison with her,
9 nor did I liken any priceless gem to her;
Because all gold, in view of her, is a little sand,
and before her, silver is to be accounted mire.
10 Beyond health and comeliness I loved her,
And I chose to have her rather than the light,
because the splendor of her never yields to sleep.
11 Yet all good things together came to me in her company,
and countless riches at her hands;
12 And I rejoiced in them all, because Wisdom is their
leader,
though I had not known that she is the mother of these.

NEW JERUSALEM BIBLE

7 I too am mortal like everyone else,
a descendant of the first man formed from the earth.
I was modelled in flesh inside a mother's womb,
2 where, for ten months, in blood I acquired substance—
the result of virile seed and pleasure, sleep's
companion.
3 I too, when I was born, drew in the common air,
I fell on the same ground that bears us all,
and crying was the first sound I made, like everyone
else.
4 I was nurtured in swaddling clothes, with every care.
5 No king has known any other beginning of existence;
6 for there is only one way into life, and one way out of it.
7 And so I prayed,[a] and understanding was given me;
I entreated, and the spirit of Wisdom came to me.
8 I esteemed her more than sceptres and thrones;
compared with her, I held riches as nothing.
9 I reckoned no precious stone to be her equal,
for compared with her, all gold is a pinch of sand,
and beside her, silver ranks as mud.
10 I loved her more than health or beauty,
preferred her to the light,
since her radiance never sleeps.
11 In her company all good things came to me,
and at her hands incalculable wealth.
12 All these delighted me, since Wisdom brings them,
though I did not then realise that she was their mother.

[a] **7** Cf. 1 K 3:4–14.

GREEK OLD TESTAMENT

13 ἀδόλως τε ἔμαθον ἀφθόνως τε μεταδίδωμι,
τὸν πλοῦτον αὐτῆς οὐκ ἀποκρύπτομαι·
14 ἀνεκλιπὴς γὰρ θησαυρός ἐστιν ἀνθρώποις,
ὃν οἱ κτησάμενοι πρὸς θεὸν ἐστείλαντο φιλίαν
διὰ τὰς ἐκ παιδείας δωρεὰς συσταθέντες.
15 Ἐμοὶ δὲ δῴη ὁ θεὸς εἰπεῖν κατὰ γνώμην
καὶ ἐνθυμηθῆναι ἀξίως τῶν δεδομένων,
ὅτι αὐτὸς καὶ τῆς σοφίας ὁδηγός ἐστιν
καὶ τῶν σοφῶν διορθωτής.
16 ἐν γὰρ χειρὶ αὐτοῦ καὶ ἡμεῖς καὶ οἱ λόγοι ἡμῶν
πᾶσά τε φρόνησις καὶ ἐργατειῶν ἐπιστήμη.
17 αὐτὸς γάρ μοι ἔδωκεν τῶν ὄντων γνῶσιν ἀψευδῆ
εἰδέναι σύστασιν κόσμου καὶ ἐνέργειαν στοιχείων,
18 ἀρχὴν καὶ τέλος καὶ μεσότητα χρόνων,
τροπῶν ἀλλαγὰς καὶ μεταβολὰς καιρῶν,
19 ἐνιαυτοῦ κύκλους καὶ ἄστρων θέσεις,
20 φύσεις ζῴων καὶ θυμοὺς θηρίων,
πνευμάτων βίας καὶ διαλογισμοὺς ἀνθρώπων,
διαφορὰς φυτῶν καὶ δυνάμεις ῥιζῶν,
21 ὅσα τέ ἐστιν κρυπτὰ καὶ ἐμφανῆ ἔγνων·
ἡ γὰρ πάντων τεχνῖτις ἐδίδαξέν με σοφία.
22 Ἔστιν γὰρ ἐν αὐτῇ πνεῦμα νοερόν, ἅγιον,
μονογενές, πολυμερές, λεπτόν,

KING JAMES VERSION

13 I learned diligently, and do communicate *her* liberally: I do not hide her riches.

14 For she is a treasure unto men that never faileth: which they that use become the friends of God, being commended for the gifts that come from learning.

15 God hath granted me to speak as I would, and to conceive as is meet for the things that are given me: because it is he that leadeth unto wisdom, and directeth the wise.

16 For in his hand are both we and our words; all wisdom also, and knowledge of workmanship.

17 For he hath given me certain knowledge of the things that are, namely, to know how the world was made, and the operation of the elements:

18 The beginning, ending, and midst of the times: the alterations of the turning *of the sun,* and the change of seasons:

19 The circuits of years, and the positions of stars:

20 The natures of living creatures, and the furies of wild beasts: the violence of winds, and the reasonings of men: the diversities of plants, and the virtues of roots:

21 And all such things as are either secret or manifest, them I know.

22 For wisdom, which is the worker of all things, taught me: for in her is an understanding spirit, holy, one only, manifold, subtil, lively, clear, undefiled, plain, not subject to

DOUAY OLD TESTAMENT

13 Which I have learned without guile, and communicate without envy, and her riches I hide not.

14 For she is an infinite treasure to men! which they that use, become the friends of God, being commended for the gift of discipline.

15 And God hath given to me to speak as I would, and to conceive thoughts worthy of those things that are given me: because he is the guide of wisdom, and the director of the wise:

16 For in his hand are both we, and our words, and all wisdom, and the knowledge and skill of works.

17 For he hath given me the true knowledge of the things that are: to know the disposition of the whole world, and the virtues of the elements,

18 The beginning, and ending, and midst of the times, the alterations of their courses, and the changes of seasons,

19 The revolutions of the year, and the dispositions of the stars,

20 The natures of living creatures, and rage of wild beasts, the force of winds, and reasonings of men, the diversities of plants, and the virtues of roots,

21 And all such things as are hid and not foreseen, I have learned: for wisdom, which is the worker of all things, taught me.

22 For in her is the spirit of understanding: holy, one, manifold, subtile, eloquent, active, undefiled, sure, sweet,

KNOX TRANSLATION

taught me are riches honestly won, shared without stint,
openly proclaimed; 14 a treasure men will find incorruptible.
Those who enjoy it are honoured with God's friendship, so
high a value he sets on her instruction.

15 God's gift it is, if speech answers to thought of mine,
and thought of mine to the message I am entrusted with.
Who else can shew wise men the true path, check them
when they stray? 16 We are in his hands, we and every word
of ours; our prudence in act, our skill in craftsmanship.
17 Sure knowledge he has imparted to me of all that is; how
the world is ordered, what influence have the elements,
18 how the months[a] have their beginning, their middle, and
their ending, how the sun's course alters and the seasons
revolve, 19 how the years have their cycles, the stars their
places. 20 To every living thing its own breed, to every beast
its own moods; the winds[b] rage, and men think deep
thoughts; the plants keep their several kinds, and each root
has its own virtue; 21 all the mysteries and all the surprises
of nature were made known to me; wisdom herself taught
me, that is the designer of them all.

22 Mind-enlightening is the influence that dwells in her; set
high. apart; one in its source, yet manifold in its operation;

a Literally, 'The times'. *b* Or perhaps 'the spirits', either human or diabolic.

TODAY'S ENGLISH VERSION

13 I was sincere in learning from her, and now I am glad to
share what I learned. 14 No one can ever exhaust the treasures of Wisdom. Use those treasures and you are God's
friends; he approves of what you learn from her.
15 I pray to God that my thoughts may be worthy of what I
have learned, and that I may speak according to his will. He
is Wisdom's guide; he gives correction to those who are wise.
16 We are under his power and authority—we ourselves, our
words, all our understanding and skills. 17 It is he who gave
me true knowledge of the forces of nature: what the world is
made of; how the elements behave; 18 how the calendar is
determined by the movements of the sun, the changing seasons, 19 the constellations, and the cycles of years. 20 He has
taught me about the nature of living creatures, the behavior
of wild animals, the force of the winds, the reasoning powers
of human beings, the different kinds of plants, and the use
of their roots as medicine. 21 I learned things that were well
known and things that had never been known before,
22 because Wisdom, who gave shape to everything that
exists, was my teacher.
The spirit of Wisdom is intelligent and holy. It is of one
nature but reveals itself in many ways. It is not made of any
material substance, and it moves about freely. It is clear,

NEW REVISED STANDARD VERSION

13 I learned without guile and I impart without grudging;
I do not hide her wealth,
14 for it is an unfailing treasure for mortals;
those who get it obtain friendship with God,
commended for the gifts that come from instruction.

15 May God grant me to speak with judgment,
and to have thoughts worthy of what I have received;
for he is the guide even of wisdom
and the corrector of the wise.
16 For both we and our words are in his hand,
as are all understanding and skill in crafts.
17 For it is he who gave me unerring knowledge of what
exists,
to know the structure of the world and the activity of
the elements;
18 the beginning and end and middle of times,
the alternations of the solstices and the changes of the
seasons,
19 the cycles of the year and the constellations of the stars,
20 the natures of animals and the tempers of wild animals,
the powers of spirits[a] and the thoughts of human beings,
the varieties of plants and the virtues of roots;
21 I learned both what is secret and what is manifest,
22 for wisdom, the fashioner of all things, taught me.

There is in her a spirit that is intelligent, holy,
unique, manifold, subtle,

a Or *winds*

NEW AMERICAN BIBLE

13 Simply I learned about her, and ungrudgingly do I share—
her riches I do not hide away;
14 For to men she is an unfailing treasure;
those who gain this treasure win the friendship of God,
to whom the gifts they have from discipline commend
them.
15 Now God grant I speak suitably
and value these endowments at their worth:
For he is the guide of Wisdom
and the director of the wise.
16 For both we and our words are in his hand,
as well as all prudence and knowledge of crafts.
17 For he gave me sound knowledge of existing things,
that I might know the organization of the universe
and the force of its elements,
18 The beginning and the end and the midpoint of times,
the changes in the sun's course and the variations of
the seasons.
19 Cycles of years, positions of the stars,
20 natures of animals, tempers of beasts,
Powers of the winds and thoughts of men,
uses of plants and virtues of roots—
21 Such things as are hidden I learned, and such as are
plain;
22 for Wisdom, the artificer of all, taught me.

For in her is a spirit
intelligent, holy, unique,
Manifold, subtle, agile,

NEW JERUSALEM BIBLE

13 What I learned diligently, I shall pass on liberally,
I shall not conceal how rich she is.
14 For she is to human beings an inexhaustible treasure,
and those who acquire this win God's friendship,
commended to him by the gifts of instruction.

15 May God grant me to speak as he would wish
and conceive thoughts worthy of the gifts I have received,
since he is both guide to Wisdom and director of sages;
16 for we are in his hand, yes, ourselves and our sayings,
and all intellectual and all practical knowledge.
17 He it was who gave me sure knowledge of what exists,
to understand the structure of the world and the action
of the elements,
18 the beginning, end and middle of the times,
the alternation of the solstices and the succession of the
seasons,
19 the cycles of the year and the position of the stars,
20 the natures of animals and the instincts of wild beasts,
the powers of spirits and human mental processes,
the varieties of plants and the medical properties of roots.
21 And now I understand everything, hidden or visible,
for Wisdom, the designer of all things, has instructed me.
22 For within her is a spirit[a] intelligent, holy,
unique, manifold, subtle,

a **7** The peak of OT writing on Wisdom (cf. Jb 28; Pr 8:22). The twenty-one qualities show Wisdom originating and participating in God, inseparable from him but working in the world.

GREEK OLD TESTAMENT

εὐκίνητον, τρανόν, ἀμόλυντον,
σαφές, ἀπήμαντον, φιλάγαθον, ὀξύ,
23 ἀκώλυτον, εὐεργετικόν, φιλάνθρωπον,
βέβαιον, ἀσφαλές, ἀμέριμνον,
παντοδύναμον, πανεπίσκοπον
καὶ διὰ πάντων χωροῦν πνευμάτων
νοερῶν καθαρῶν λεπτοτάτων.
24 πάσης γὰρ κινήσεως κινητικώτερον σοφία,
διήκει δὲ καὶ χωρεῖ διὰ πάντων διὰ τὴν καθαρότητα·
25 ἀτμὶς γάρ ἐστιν τῆς τοῦ θεοῦ δυνάμεως
καὶ ἀπόρροια τῆς τοῦ παντοκράτορος δόξης εἰλικρινής·
διὰ τοῦτο οὐδὲν μεμιαμμένον εἰς αὐτὴν παρεμπίπτει.
26 ἀπαύγασμα γάρ ἐστιν φωτὸς ἀιδίου
καὶ ἔσοπτρον ἀκηλίδωτον τῆς τοῦ θεοῦ ἐνεργείας
καὶ εἰκὼν τῆς ἀγαθότητος αὐτοῦ.
27 μία δὲ οὖσα πάντα δύναται
καὶ μένουσα ἐν αὑτῇ τὰ πάντα καινίζει
καὶ κατὰ γενεὰς εἰς ψυχὰς ὁσίας μεταβαίνουσα
φίλους θεοῦ καὶ προφήτας κατασκευάζει·
28 οὐθὲν γὰρ ἀγαπᾷ ὁ θεὸς εἰ μὴ τὸν σοφίᾳ συνοικοῦντα.
29 ἔστιν γὰρ αὕτη εὐπρεπεστέρα ἡλίου
καὶ ὑπὲρ πᾶσαν ἄστρων θέσιν.
φωτὶ συγκρινομένη εὑρίσκεται προτέρα·
30 τοῦτο μὲν γὰρ διαδέχεται νύξ,
σοφίας δὲ οὐ κατισχύει κακία.

KING JAMES VERSION

hurt, loving the thing that is good, quick, which cannot be letted, ready to do good,

23 Kind to man, stedfast, sure, free from care, having all power, overseeing all things, and going through all understanding, pure, and most subtil, spirits.

24 For wisdom is more moving than any motion: she passeth and goeth through all things by reason of her pureness.

25 For she is the breath of the power of God, and a pure influence flowing from the glory of the Almighty: therefore can no defiled thing fall into her.

26 For she is the brightness of the everlasting light, the unspotted mirror of the power of God, and the image of his goodness.

27 And being but one, she can do all things: and remaining in herself, she maketh all things new: and in all ages entering into holy souls, she maketh them friends of God, and prophets.

28 For God loveth none but him that dwelleth with wisdom.

29 For she is more beautiful than the sun, and above all the order of stars: being compared with the light, she is found before it.

30 For after this cometh night: but vice shall not prevail against wisdom.

DOUAY OLD TESTAMENT

loving that which is good, quick, which nothing hindereth, beneficent,

23 Gentle, kind, steadfast, assured, secure, having all power, overseeing all things, and containing all spirits, intelligible, pure, subtile.

24 For wisdom is more active than all active things: and reacheth everywhere by reason of her purity.

25 For she is a vapour of the power of God, and a certain pure emanation of the glory of the almighty God: and therefore no defiled thing cometh into her.

26 For she is the brightness of eternal light, and the unspotted mirror of God's majesty, and the image of his goodness.

27 And being but one, she can do all things: and remaining in herself the same, she reneweth all things, and through nations conveyeth herself into holy souls, she maketh the friends of God and prophets.

28 For God loveth none but him that dwelleth with wisdom.

29 For she is more beautiful than the sun, and above all the order of the stars: being compared with the light, she is found before it.

30 For after this cometh night, but no evil can overcome wisdom.

KNOX TRANSLATION

subtle, yet easily understood. An influence quick in movement, inviolable, persuasive, gentle, right-thinking, keen-
edged, irresistible, beneficent, 23 kindly, gracious, steadfast,
proof against all error and all solicitude. Nothing is beyond
its power, nothing hidden from its view, and such capacity
has it that it can pervade the minds of all living men; so pure
and subtle an essence is thought. 24 Nothing so agile that it
can match wisdom for agility; nothing can penetrate this
way and that, etherial as she. 25 Steam that ascends from
the fervour of divine activity, pure effluence of his glory who
is God all-powerful, she feels no passing taint; 26 she, the
glow that radiates from eternal light, she, the untarnished
mirror of God's majesty, she, the faithful image of his goodness. 27 Alone, with none to aid her, she is all-powerful; herself ever unchanged, she makes all things new; age after age
she finds her way into holy men's hearts, turning them into
friends and spokesmen of God. 28 Her familiars it is, and
none other, that God loves. 29 Brightness is hers beyond the
brightness of the sun, and all the starry host; match her with
light itself, and she outvies it; 30 light must still alternate
with darkness, but where is the conspiracy can pull down
wisdom from her throne?

TODAY'S ENGLISH VERSION

clean, and confident; it cannot be harmed.[a] It loves what is
good. It is sharp and unconquerable, 23 kind, and a friend of
humanity. It is dependable and sure, and has no worries. It
has power over everything, and sees everything. It penetrates
every spirit that is intelligent and pure, no matter how delicate its substance may be.
24 Wisdom moves more easily than motion itself; she is so
pure that she penetrates everything. 25 She is a breath of
God's power—a pure and radiant stream of glory from the
Almighty. Nothing that is defiled can ever steal its way into
Wisdom. 26 She is a reflection of eternal light, a perfect mirror of God's activity and goodness. 27 Even though Wisdom
acts alone, she can do anything. She makes everything new,
although she herself never changes. From generation to
generation she enters the souls of holy people, and makes
them God's friends and prophets. 28 There is nothing that
God loves more than people who are at home with Wisdom.
29 Wisdom is more beautiful than the sun and all the constellations. She is better than light itself, 30 because night
always follows day, but evil never overcomes Wisdom.

[a] cannot be harmed; *or* does no harm.

NEW REVISED STANDARD VERSION

mobile, clear, unpolluted,
distinct, invulnerable, loving the good, keen,
irresistible, 23 beneficent, humane,
steadfast, sure, free from anxiety,
all-powerful, overseeing all,
and penetrating through all spirits
that are intelligent, pure, and altogether subtle.
24 For wisdom is more mobile than any motion;
because of her pureness she pervades and penetrates all things.
25 For she is a breath of the power of God,
and a pure emanation of the glory of the Almighty;
therefore nothing defiled gains entrance into her.
26 For she is a reflection of eternal light,
a spotless mirror of the working of God,
and an image of his goodness.
27 Although she is but one, she can do all things,
and while remaining in herself, she renews all things;
in every generation she passes into holy souls
and makes them friends of God, and prophets;
28 for God loves nothing so much as the person who lives with wisdom.
29 She is more beautiful than the sun,
and excels every constellation of the stars.
Compared with the light she is found to be superior,
30 for it is succeeded by the night,
but against wisdom evil does not prevail.

NEW AMERICAN BIBLE

clear, unstained, certain,
Not baneful, loving the good, keen,
unhampered, beneficent, 23 kindly,
Firm, secure, tranquil,
all-powerful, all-seeing,
And pervading all spirits,
though they be intelligent, pure and very subtle.
24 For Wisdom is mobile beyond all motion,
and she penetrates and pervades all things by reason of her purity.
25 For she is an aura of the might of God
and a pure effusion of the glory of the Almighty;
therefore nought that is sullied enters into her.
26 For she is the refulgence of eternal light,
the spotless mirror of the power of God,
the image of his goodness.
27 And she, who is one, can do all things,
and renews everything while herself perduring;
And passing into holy souls from age to age,
she produces friends of God and prophets.
28 For there is nought God loves, be it not one who dwells with Wisdom.
29 For she is fairer than the sun
and surpasses every constellation of the stars.
Compared to light, she takes precedence;
30 for that, indeed, night supplants,
but wickedness prevails not over Wisdom.

NEW JERUSALEM BIBLE

mobile, incisive, unsullied,
lucid, invulnerable, benevolent, shrewd,
23 irresistible, beneficent, friendly to human beings,
steadfast, dependable, unperturbed,
almighty, all-surveying,
penetrating all intelligent, pure and most subtle spirits.
24 For Wisdom is quicker to move than any motion;
she is so pure, she pervades and permeates all things.
25 She is a breath of the power of God,
pure emanation of the glory of the Almighty;
so nothing impure can find its way into her.
26 For she is a reflection of the eternal light,
untarnished mirror of God's active power,
and image of his goodness.
27 Although she is alone, she can do everything;
herself unchanging, she renews the world,
and, generation after generation, passing into holy souls,
she makes them into God's friends and prophets;
28 for God loves only those who dwell with Wisdom.
29 She is indeed more splendid than the sun,
she outshines all the constellations;
compared with light, she takes first place,
30 for light must yield to night,
but against Wisdom evil cannot prevail.

GREEK OLD TESTAMENT

8 διατείνει δὲ ἀπὸ πέρατος ἐπὶ πέρας εὐρώστως
καὶ διοικεῖ τὰ πάντα χρηστῶς.
2 Ταύτην ἐφίλησα καὶ ἐξεζήτησα ἐκ νεότητός μου
καὶ ἐζήτησα νύμφην ἀγαγέσθαι ἐμαυτῷ
καὶ ἐραστὴς ἐγενόμην τοῦ κάλλους αὐτῆς.
3 εὐγένειαν δοξάζει συμβίωσιν θεοῦ ἔχουσα,
καὶ ὁ πάντων δεσπότης ἠγάπησεν αὐτήν·
4 μύστις γάρ ἐστιν τῆς τοῦ θεοῦ ἐπιστήμης
καὶ αἱρετὶς τῶν ἔργων αὐτοῦ.
5 εἰ δὲ πλοῦτός ἐστιν ἐπιθυμητὸν κτῆμα ἐν βίῳ,
τί σοφίας πλουσιώτερον τῆς τὰ πάντα ἐργαζομένης;
6 εἰ δὲ φρόνησις ἐργάζεται,
τίς αὐτῆς τῶν ὄντων μᾶλλόν ἐστιν τεχνῖτις;
7 καὶ εἰ δικαιοσύνην ἀγαπᾷ τις,
οἱ πόνοι ταύτης εἰσὶν ἀρεταί·
σωφροσύνην γὰρ καὶ φρόνησιν ἐκδιδάσκει,
δικαιοσύνην καὶ ἀνδρείαν,
ὧν χρησιμώτερον οὐδέν ἐστιν ἐν βίῳ ἀνθρώποις.
8 εἰ δὲ καὶ πολυπειρίαν ποθεῖ τις,
οἶδεν τὰ ἀρχαῖα καὶ τὰ μέλλοντα εἰκάζει,
ἐπίσταται στροφὰς λόγων καὶ λύσεις αἰνιγμάτων,
σημεῖα καὶ τέρατα προγινώσκει
καὶ ἐκβάσεις καιρῶν καὶ χρόνων.
9 ἔκρινα τοίνυν ταύτην ἀγαγέσθαι πρὸς συμβίωσιν

KING JAMES VERSION

8 *Wisdom* reacheth from one end to another mightily: and sweetly doth she order all things.

2 I loved her, and sought *her* out from my youth, I desired to make *her* my spouse, and I was a lover of her beauty.

3 In that she is conversant with God, she magnifieth her nobility: yea, the Lord of all things himself loved her.

4 For she is privy to the mysteries of the knowledge of God, and a lover of his works.

5 If riches be a possession to be desired in this life; what is richer than wisdom, that worketh all things?

6 And if prudence work; who of all that are is a more cunning workman than she?

7 And if a man love righteousness, her labours are virtues: for she teacheth temperance and prudence, justice and fortitude: which are such things, as men can have nothing more profitable in their life.

8 If a man desire much experience, she knoweth things of old, and conjectureth *aright* what is to come: she knoweth the subtilties of speeches, and can expound dark sentences: she foreseeth signs and wonders, and the events of seasons and times.

9 Therefore I purposed to take her to me to live with me,

DOUAY OLD TESTAMENT

8 SHE reacheth therefore from end to end mightily, and ordereth all things sweetly.

2 Her have I loved, and have sought her out from my youth, and have desired to take her for my spouse, and I became a lover of her beauty.

3 She glorifieth her nobility by being conversant with God: yea and the Lord of all things hath loved her.

4 For it is she that teacheth the knowledge of God, and is the chooser of his works.

5 And if riches be desired in life, what is richer than wisdom, which maketh all things?

6 And if sense do work: who is a more artful worker than she of those things that are?

7 And if a man love justice: her labours have great virtues; for she teacheth temperance, and prudence, and justice, and fortitude, which are such things as men can have nothing more profitable in life.

8 And if a man desire much knowledge: she knoweth things past, and judgeth of things to come: she knoweth the subtilties of speeches, and the solutions of arguments: she knoweth signs and wonders before they be done, and the events of times and ages.

9 I purposed therefore to take her to me to live with me:

KNOX TRANSLATION

8 Bold is her sweep from world's end to world's end, and
everywhere her gracious ordering manifests itself.
2 She, from my youth up has been my heart's true love, my
heart's true quest; she was the bride I longed for, enamoured
of her beauty. 3 Was I moved by noble birth? No better claim
than hers, who dwells in God's palace, marked out by the
4 Ruler of the world as his favourite; the mistress of his
craftsmanship, the arbiter of his plans.[a] 5 Or should life's
dearest aim be wealth? Why then, who has more wealth at
her disposal than wisdom, that turns all to account? 6 Or if
sound judgement is man's business, who else on earth goes
to work so skilfully as she?[b] 7 If thy desire be for honest living, man's excellences are the fruit she labours to produce;
temperance and prudence she teaches, justice and fortitude,
and what in life avails man more? 8 Or if wide knowledge be
thy ambition, she can inform thee of what is past, make conjecture of the future; she is versed in the subtleties of debate,
in the reading of all riddles; marvels and portents she can
foretell, and what events time or season will bring.
9 Her, then, I would take to myself, to share my home; to

a The exact meaning of verses 3 and 4 is uncertain. *b* Or perhaps, 'Who but she is the contriver of all that is?'

TODAY'S ENGLISH VERSION

8 1 Her great power reaches into every part of the world,
and she sets everything in useful order.
2 Wisdom has been my love. I courted her when I was
young and wanted to make her my bride. I fell in love with
her beauty. 3 She glorifies her noble origin by living with
God, the Lord of all, who loves her. 4 She is familiar with
God's mysteries and helps determine his course of action.
5 Is it good to have riches in this life? Nothing can make
you richer than Wisdom, who makes everything function.
6 Is knowledge a useful thing to have? Nothing is better than
Wisdom, who has given shape to everything that exists. 7 Do
you love justice? All the virtues are the result of Wisdom's
work: justice and courage, self-control and understanding.
Life can offer us nothing more valuable than these. 8 Do you
want to have wide experience? Wisdom knows the lessons of
history and can anticipate the future. She knows how to
interpret what people say and how to solve problems. She
knows the miracles that God will perform, and how the
movements of history will develop.
9 So I decided to take Wisdom home to live with me,

NEW REVISED STANDARD VERSION

8 She reaches mightily from one end of the earth to the
other,
and she orders all things well.
2 I loved her and sought her from my youth;
I desired to take her for my bride,
and became enamored of her beauty.
3 She glorifies her noble birth by living with God,
and the Lord of all loves her.
4 For she is an initiate in the knowledge of God,
and an associate in his works.
5 If riches are a desirable possession in life,
what is richer than wisdom, the active cause of all
things?
6 And if understanding is effective,
who more than she is fashioner of what exists?
7 And if anyone loves righteousness,
her labors are virtues;
for she teaches self-control and prudence,
justice and courage;
nothing in life is more profitable for mortals than these.
8 And if anyone longs for wide experience,
she knows the things of old, and infers the things to
come;
she understands turns of speech and the solutions of
riddles;
she has foreknowledge of signs and wonders
and of the outcome of seasons and times.
9 Therefore I determined to take her to live with me,

NEW AMERICAN BIBLE

8 Indeed, she reaches from end to end mightily
and governs all things well.
2 Her I loved and sought after from my youth;
I sought to take her for my bride
and was enamored of her beauty.
3 She adds to nobility the splendor of companionship
with God;
even the LORD of all loved her.
4 For she is instructress in the understanding of God,
the selector of his works.
5 And if riches be a desirable possession in life,
what is more rich than Wisdom, who produces all
things?
6 And if prudence renders service,
who in the world is a better craftsman than she?
7 Or if one loves justice,
the fruits of her works are virtues;
For she teaches moderation and prudence,
justice and fortitude,
and nothing in life is more useful for men than these.
8 Or again, if one yearns for copious learning,
she knows the things of old, and infers those yet to
come.
She understands the turns of phrases and the solutions
of riddles;
signs and wonders she knows in advance
and the outcome of times and ages.
9 So I determined to take her to live with me,

NEW JERUSALEM BIBLE

8 Strongly she reaches from one end of the world to the
other
and she governs the whole world for its good.
2 Wisdom I loved and searched for from my youth;
I resolved to have her as my bride,
I fell in love with her beauty.
3 She enhances her noble birth by sharing God's life,
for the Master of All has always loved her.
4 Indeed, she shares the secrets of God's knowledge,
and she chooses what he will do.
5 If in this life wealth is a desirable possession,
what is more wealthy than Wisdom whose work is
everywhere?
6 Or if it be the intellect that is at work,
who, more than she, designs whatever exists?
7 Or if it be uprightness you love,
why, virtues are the fruit of her labours,
since it is she who teaches temperance and prudence,
justice and fortitude;
nothing in life is more useful for human beings.
8 Or if you are eager for wide experience,
she knows the past, she forecasts the future;
she knows how to turn maxims, and solve riddles;
she has foreknowledge of signs and wonders,
and of the unfolding of the ages and the times.
9 I therefore determined to take her to share my life,

GREEK OLD TESTAMENT

εἰδὼς ὅτι ἔσται μοι σύμβουλος ἀγαθῶν
καὶ παραίνεσις φροντίδων καὶ λύπης.
10 ἕξω δι᾽ αὐτὴν δόξαν ἐν ὄχλοις
καὶ τιμὴν παρὰ πρεσβυτέροις ὁ νέος·
11 ὀξὺς εὑρεθήσομαι ἐν κρίσει
καὶ ἐν ὄψει δυναστῶν θαυμασθήσομαι·
12 σιγῶντά με περιμενοῦσιν καὶ φθεγγομένῳ προσέξουσιν
καὶ λαλοῦντος ἐπὶ πλεῖον
χεῖρα ἐπιθήσουσιν ἐπὶ στόμα αὐτῶν.
13 ἕξω δι᾽ αὐτὴν ἀθανασίαν
καὶ μνήμην αἰώνιον τοῖς μετ᾽ ἐμὲ ἀπολείψω.
14 διοικήσω λαούς, καὶ ἔθνη ὑποταγήσεταί μοι·
15 φοβηθήσονταί με ἀκούσαντες τύραννοι φρικτοί,
ἐν πλήθει φανοῦμαι ἀγαθὸς καὶ ἐν πολέμῳ ἀνδρεῖος.
16 εἰσελθὼν εἰς τὸν οἶκόν μου προσαναπαύσομαι αὐτῇ·
οὐ γὰρ ἔχει πικρίαν ἡ συναναστροφὴ αὐτῆς
οὐδὲ ὀδύνην ἡ συμβίωσις αὐτῆς,
ἀλλὰ εὐφροσύνην καὶ χαράν.
17 ταῦτα λογισάμενος ἐν ἐμαυτῷ
καὶ φροντίσας ἐν καρδίᾳ μου
ὅτι ἀθανασία ἐστὶν ἐν συγγενείᾳ σοφίας
18 καὶ ἐν φιλίᾳ αὐτῆς τέρψις ἀγαθὴ
καὶ ἐν πόνοις χειρῶν αὐτῆς πλοῦτος ἀνεκλιπὴς
καὶ ἐν συγγυμνασίᾳ ὁμιλίας αὐτῆς φρόνησις

KING JAMES VERSION

knowing that she would be a counsellor of good things, and a comfort in cares and grief.

10 For her sake I shall have estimation among the multitude, and honour with the elders, though I be young.

11 I shall be found of a quick conceit in judgment, and shall be admired in the sight of great men.

12 When I hold my tongue, they shall bide my leisure, and when I speak, they shall give good ear unto me: if I talk much, they shall lay their hands upon their mouth.

13 Moreover by the means of her I shall obtain immortality, and leave behind me an everlasting memorial to them that come after me.

14 I shall set the people in order, and the nations shall be subject unto me.

15 Horrible tyrants shall be afraid, when they do but hear of me; I shall be found good among the multitude, and valiant in war.

16 After I am come into mine house, I will repose myself with her: for her conversation hath no bitterness; and to live with her hath no sorrow, but mirth and joy.

17 Now when I considered these things in myself, and pondered them in my heart, how that to be allied unto wisdom is immortality;

18 And great pleasure it is to have her friendship; and in the works of her hands are infinite riches; and in the exercise of conference with her, prudence; and in talking with

DOUAY OLD TESTAMENT

knowing that she will communicate to me of her good things, and will be a comfort in my cares and grief.

10 For her sake I shall have glory among the multitude, and honour with the ancients, though I be young:

11 And I shall be found of a quick conceit in judgment, and shall be admired in the sight of the mighty, and the faces of princes shall wonder at me.

12 They shall wait for me when I hold my peace, and they shall look upon me when I speak, and if I talk much they shall lay their hands on their mouths.

13 Moreover by the means of her I shall have immortality: and shall leave behind me an everlasting memory to them that come after me.

14 I shall set the people in order: and nations shall be subject to me.

15 Terrible kings hearing shall be afraid of me: among the multitude I shall be found good, and valiant in war.

16 When I go into my house, I shall repose myself with her: for her conversation hath no bitterness, nor her company any tediousness, but joy and gladness.

17 Thinking these things with myself, and pondering them in my heart, that to be allied to wisdom is immortality,

18 And that there is great delight in her friendship, and inexhaustible riches in the works of her hands, and in the exercise of conference with her, wisdom, and glory in the

KNOX TRANSLATION

be my counsellor in prosperity, my solace in anxiety and
grief. 10 Through her (said I) I shall win fame in the assembly, find honour, though so young, amidst the elders. 11 If I
sit in judgement, quick wit shall be mine, that shall strike
awe into the princes when I appear before them, the admiration of the great. 12 Am I silent? They wait my leisure; speak
I, they take heed; flows my speech on, they listen, hand on
lip. 13 She, too, will bring me immortality; imperishable the
name I shall leave to after ages. 14 Mine to rule peoples, and
have nations at my call; 15 dread tyrants to daunt by the
very name of me, the name of a king so loved by his people,
so brave in battle. 16 Then home again, to rest upon her
bosom; no shrewish mate, no tedious housewife, joy and
contentment all of her.

17 So ran my thoughts, and well in my heart I pondered
them. Wisdom, that brought such kinship with immortality,
whose friendship was such dear delight, 18 whose exercise
brought me credit unfailing, her daily comradeship a training

TODAY'S ENGLISH VERSION

because I knew that she would give me good advice and
encourage me in times of trouble and grief. 10 I thought to
myself, "Because of her I will be honored wherever people
come together. The old men will respect me, even though I
am young. 11 They will find that my opinions show deep
insight, and those in power will admire me. 12 When I am
silent, they will wait for me to speak, and when I speak, they
will pay attention. Even when I speak at length, they will listen with concentration. 13 Because of Wisdom I will gain
immortality; I will live forever in the memory of those who
come after me. 14 I will hold power over nations and peoples;
15 dreaded tyrants will be seized with fear at the mention of
my name. I will be famous, as a good king and as a brave
soldier. 16 When I come home to Wisdom, I will find contentment because there is no conflict or pain in living with her,
only happiness and joy."

17 And so I thought it over: to be wedded to Wisdom is to
live forever, 18 to love her is to be perfectly happy, to do her
work is to be rich beyond measure, to share her company is to

NEW REVISED STANDARD VERSION

knowing that she would give me good counsel
and encouragement in cares and grief.
10 Because of her I shall have glory among the multitudes
and honor in the presence of the elders, though I am
young.
11 I shall be found keen in judgment,
and in the sight of rulers I shall be admired.
12 When I am silent they will wait for me,
and when I speak they will give heed;
if I speak at greater length,
they will put their hands on their mouths.
13 Because of her I shall have immortality,
and leave an everlasting remembrance to those who
come after me.
14 I shall govern peoples,
and nations will be subject to me;
15 dread monarchs will be afraid of me when they hear of
me;
among the people I shall show myself capable, and
courageous in war.
16 When I enter my house, I shall find rest with her;
for companionship with her has no bitterness,
and life with her has no pain, but gladness and joy.
17 When I considered these things inwardly,
and pondered in my heart
that in kinship with wisdom there is immortality,
18 and in friendship with her, pure delight,
and in the labors of her hands, unfailing wealth,
and in the experience of her company, understanding,

NEW AMERICAN BIBLE

knowing that she would be my counselor while all
was well,
and my comfort in care and grief.
10 For her sake I should have glory among the masses,
and esteem from the elders, though I be but a youth.
11 I should become keen in judgment,
and should be a marvel before rulers.
12 They would abide my silence and attend my utterance;
and as I spoke on further,
they would place their hands upon their mouths.
13 For her sake I should have immortality
and leave to those after me an everlasting memory.
14 I should govern peoples, and nations would be my
subjects—
15 terrible princes, hearing of me, would be afraid;
in the assembly I should appear noble, and in war
courageous.
16 Within my dwelling, I should take my repose beside
her;
For association with her involves no bitterness
and living with her no grief,
but rather joy and gladness.
17 Thinking thus within myself,
and reflecting in my heart
That there is immortality in kinship with Wisdom,
18 and good pleasure in her friendship,
and unfailing riches in the works of her hands,
And that in frequenting her society there is prudence,

NEW JERUSALEM BIBLE

knowing that she would be my counsellor in prosperity
and comfort me in cares and sorrow.
10 'Thanks to her, I shall be admired by the masses
and honoured, though young, by the elders.
11 I shall be reckoned shrewd as a judge,
and the great will be amazed at me.
12 They will wait on my silences,
and pay attention when I speak;
if I speak at some length, they will lay their hand on
their lips.
13 By means of her, immortality will be mine,
I shall leave an everlasting memory to my successors.
14 I shall govern peoples, and nations will be subject to
me;
15 at the sound of my name fearsome despots will be
afraid;
I shall show myself kind to the people and valiant in
battle.
16 'When I go home I shall take my ease with her,
for nothing is bitter in her company,
when life is shared with her there is no pain,
nothing but pleasure and joy.'
17 Having meditated on all this,
and having come to the conclusion
that immortality resides in kinship with Wisdom,
18 noble contentment in her friendship,
inexhaustible riches in her activities,
understanding in cultivating her society,

GREEK OLD TESTAMENT

καὶ εὔκλεια ἐν κοινωνίᾳ λόγων αὐτῆς,
περιῄειν ζητῶν ὅπως λάβω αὐτὴν εἰς ἐμαυτόν.
19 παῖς δὲ ἤμην εὐφυὴς
ψυχῆς τε ἔλαχον ἀγαθῆς,
20 μᾶλλον δὲ ἀγαθὸς ὢν ἦλθον εἰς σῶμα ἀμίαντον.
21 γνοὺς δὲ ὅτι οὐκ ἄλλως ἔσομαι ἐγκρατής, ἐὰν μὴ ὁ θεὸς δῷ
— καὶ τοῦτο δ' ἦν φρονήσεως τὸ εἰδέναι τίνος ἡ χάρις —,
ἐνέτυχον τῷ κυρίῳ καὶ ἐδεήθην αὐτοῦ
καὶ εἶπον ἐξ ὅλης τῆς καρδίας μου

9 Θεὲ πατέρων καὶ κύριε τοῦ ἐλέους
ὁ ποιήσας τὰ πάντα ἐν λόγῳ σου
2 καὶ τῇ σοφίᾳ σου κατασκευάσας ἄνθρωπον,
ἵνα δεσπόζῃ τῶν ὑπὸ σοῦ γενομένων κτισμάτων
3 καὶ διέπῃ τὸν κόσμον ἐν ὁσιότητι καὶ δικαιοσύνῃ
καὶ ἐν εὐθύτητι ψυχῆς κρίσιν κρίνῃ,
4 δός μοι τὴν τῶν σῶν θρόνων πάρεδρον σοφίαν
καὶ μή με ἀποδοκιμάσῃς ἐκ παίδων σου.
5 ὅτι ἐγὼ δοῦλος σὸς καὶ υἱὸς τῆς παιδίσκης σου,
ἄνθρωπος ἀσθενὴς καὶ ὀλιγοχρόνιος
καὶ ἐλάσσων ἐν συνέσει κρίσεως καὶ νόμων·
6 κἂν γάρ τις ᾖ τέλειος ἐν υἱοῖς ἀνθρώπων,
τῆς ἀπὸ σοῦ σοφίας ἀπούσης εἰς οὐδὲν λογισθήσεται.
7 σύ με προείλω βασιλέα λαοῦ σου
καὶ δικαστὴν υἱῶν σου καὶ θυγατέρων·

KING JAMES VERSION

her, a good report; I went about seeking how to take her to me.

19 For I was a witty child, and had a good spirit.

20 Yea rather, being good, I came into a body undefiled.

21 Nevertheless, when I perceived that I could not otherwise obtain her, except God gave her me; and that was a point of wisdom also to know whose gift she was; I prayed unto the Lord, and besought him, and with my whole heart I said,

9 O God of my fathers, and Lord of mercy, who hast made all things with thy word,

2 And ordained man through thy wisdom, that he should have dominion over the creatures which thou hast made,

3 And order the world according to equity and righteousness, and execute judgment with an upright heart:

4 Give me wisdom, that sitteth by thy throne; and reject me not from among thy children:

5 For I thy servant and son of thine handmaid am a feeble person, and of a short time, and too young for the understanding of judgment and laws.

6 For though a man be never so perfect among the children of men, yet if thy wisdom be not with him, he shall be nothing regarded.

7 Thou hast chosen me to be a king of thy people, and a judge of thy sons and daughters:

DOUAY OLD TESTAMENT

communication of her words: I went about seeking, that I might take her to myself.

19 And I was a witty child and had received a good soul.

20 And whereas I was more good, I came to a body undefiled.

21 And as I knew that I could not otherwise be continent, except God gave it, and this also was a point of wisdom, to know whose gift it was: I went to the Lord, and besought him, and said with my whole heart:

9 GOD of my fathers, and Lord of mercy, who hast made all things with thy word,

2 And by they wisdom hast appointed man, that he should have dominion over the creature that was made by thee,

3 That he should order the world according to equity and justice, and execute justice with an upright heart:

4 Give me wisdom, that sitteth by thy throne, and cast me not off from among thy children:

5 For I am thy servant, and the son of thy handmaid, a weak man, and of short time, and falling short of the understanding of judgment and laws.

6 For if one be perfect among the children of men, yet if thy wisdom be not with him, he shall be nothing regarded.

7 Thou hast chosen me to be king of thy people, and a judge of thy sons and daughters.

KNOX TRANSLATION

in sound judgement, the eloquence she inspired an earnest of
renown; win her for myself I must, and went about to attain
my purpose. 19 I was, indeed, a boy of good parts, and nobility of nature had fallen to my lot; 20 gentle birth above the
common had endowed me with a body free from blemish.[a]
21 But to be master of myself was a thing I could not hope to
come by, except of God's bounty; I was wise enough already
to know whence the gift came. So to the Lord I turned, and
made my request of him, praying with all my heart in these
words following:

9 God of our fathers, Lord of all mercy, thou by thy word
hast made all things, 2 and thou in thy wisdom hast
contrived man to rule thy creation, 3 to order the world by a
law of right living and of just dealing, and give true award in
the honest purpose of his heart. 4 Wisdom I ask of thee, the
same wisdom that dwells so near thy throne; do not grudge
me a place among thy retinue. 5 Am I not thy servant, and to
thy service born? Mortal man thou seest me, the puny creature of an hour, a mind unapt for judgement and the making
of laws. 6 Grow man to what perfection he will, if he lacks
the wisdom that comes from thee, he is nothing; 7 and me
thou hast chosen to reign over thy people; from me sons and
daughters of thine must seek for redress! 8 More than this,

a The Greek would naturally be taken to mean, 'Or rather, gentle birth had endowed me...'. But it is difficult to institute the desired contrast between this and the preceding verse, whatever rendering of them is adopted. The translation given above assumes that 'good' means 'nobly born', which is the primary sense of the word in Greek. Literally, 'And being more good I came into an undefiled body'.

TODAY'S ENGLISH VERSION

have sound judgment, to converse with her is to be honored.
Then I was determined to take Wisdom as my bride. 19 I had
a pleasant personality even as a child. I had been fortunate
enough to receive a good soul, or rather, I was given a sound
body to live in because I was already good. 20 Still, I realized
that I would never receive Wisdom unless God gave her to
me—and knowing that only God could give her to me was
itself a sign of understanding. So I prayed, begging the Lord
with all my heart:

9 "God of my ancestors, merciful Lord, by your word you
created everything. 2 By your Wisdom you made us
humans to rule all creation, 3 to govern the world with holiness and righteousness, to administer justice with integrity.
4 Give me the Wisdom that sits beside your throne; give me a
place among your children. 5 I am your slave, as was my
mother before me. I am only human. I am not strong, and
my life will be short. I have little understanding of the Law
or of how to apply it. 6 Even if someone is perfect, he will be
thought of as nothing without the Wisdom that comes from
you. 7 You chose me over everyone else to be the king of
your own people, to judge your sons and daughters. 8 You

NEW REVISED STANDARD VERSION

and renown in sharing her words,
I went about seeking how to get her for myself.
19 As a child I was naturally gifted,
and a good soul fell to my lot;
20 or rather, being good, I entered an undefiled body.
21 But I perceived that I would not possess wisdom unless
God gave her to me—
and it was a mark of insight to know whose gift she
was—
so I appealed to the Lord and implored him,
and with my whole heart I said:

9 "O God of my ancestors and Lord of mercy,
who have made all things by your word,
2 and by your wisdom have formed humankind
to have dominion over the creatures you have made,
3 and rule the world in holiness and righteousness,
and pronounce judgment in uprightness of soul,
4 give me the wisdom that sits by your throne,
and do not reject me from among your servants.
5 For I am your servant[a] the son of your serving girl,
a man who is weak and short-lived,
with little understanding of judgment and laws;
6 for even one who is perfect among human beings
will be regarded as nothing without the wisdom that
comes from you.
7 You have chosen me to be king of your people
and to be judge over your sons and daughters.

a Gk *slave*

NEW AMERICAN BIBLE

and fair renown in sharing her discourses,
I went about seeking to take her for my own.
19 Now, I was a well-favored child,
and I came by a noble nature;
20 or rather, being noble, I attained an unsullied body.
21 And knowing that I could not otherwise possess her
except God gave it—
and this, too, was prudence, to know whose is the
gift—
I went to the LORD and besought him,
and said with all my heart:

9 God of my fathers, LORD of mercy,
you who have made all things by your word
2 And in your wisdom have established man
to rule the creatures produced by you,
3 To govern the world in holiness and justice,
and to render judgment in integrity of heart:
4 Give me Wisdom, the attendant at your throne,
and reject me not from among your children;
5 For I am your servant, the son of your handmaid,
a man weak and short-lived
and lacking in comprehension of judgment and of
laws.
6 Indeed, though one be perfect among the sons of men,
if Wisdom, who comes from you, be not with him,
he shall be held in no esteem.
7 You have chosen me king over your people
and magistrate for your sons and daughters.

NEW JERUSALEM BIBLE

and renown in conversing with her,
I went all ways, seeking how to get her.
19 I was a boy of happy disposition,
I had received a good soul as my lot,
20 or rather, being good, I had entered an undefiled body;
21 but, realising that I could never possess Wisdom unless
God gave her to me,
—a sign of intelligence in itself, to know in whose gift
she lay—
I prayed[a] to the Lord and entreated him,
and with all my heart I said:

9 'God of our ancestors, Lord of mercy,
who by your word have made the universe,
2 and in your wisdom have fitted human beings
to rule the creatures that you have made,
3 to govern the world in holiness and saving justice
and in honesty of soul to dispense fair judgement,
4 grant me Wisdom, consort of your throne,
and do not reject me from the number of your children.
5 For I am your servant, son of your serving maid,
a feeble man, with little time to live,
with small understanding of justice and the laws.
6 Indeed, were anyone perfect among the sons of men,
if he lacked the Wisdom that comes from you, he would
still count for nothing.

7 'You have chosen me to be king over your people,
to be judge of your sons and daughters.

a **8** Cf. 1 K 3:6–9.

GREEK OLD TESTAMENT

8 εἶπας οἰκοδομῆσαι ναὸν ἐν ὄρει ἁγίῳ σου
καὶ ἐν πόλει κατασκηνώσεώς σου θυσιαστήριον,
μίμημα σκηνῆς ἁγίας, ἣν προητοίμασας ἀπ᾽ ἀρχῆς.
9 καὶ μετὰ σοῦ ἡ σοφία ἡ εἰδυῖα τὰ ἔργα σου
καὶ παροῦσα, ὅτε ἐποίεις τὸν κόσμον,
καὶ ἐπισταμένη τί ἀρεστὸν ἐν ὀφθαλμοῖς σου
καὶ τί εὐθὲς ἐν ἐντολαῖς σου.
10 ἐξαπόστειλον αὐτὴν ἐξ ἁγίων οὐρανῶν
καὶ ἀπὸ θρόνου δόξης σου πέμψον αὐτήν,
ἵνα συμπαροῦσά μοι κοπιάσῃ,
καὶ γνῶ τί εὐάρεστόν ἐστιν παρὰ σοί.
11 οἶδε γὰρ ἐκείνη πάντα καὶ συνίει
καὶ ὁδηγήσει με ἐν ταῖς πράξεσί μου σωφρόνως
καὶ φυλάξει με ἐν τῇ δόξῃ αὐτῆς·
12 καὶ ἔσται προσδεκτὰ τὰ ἔργα μου,
καὶ διακρινῶ τὸν λαόν σου δικαίως
καὶ ἔσομαι ἄξιος θρόνων πατρός μου.
13 τίς γὰρ ἄνθρωπος γνώσεται βουλὴν θεοῦ;
ἢ τίς ἐνθυμηθήσεται τί θέλει ὁ κύριος;
14 λογισμοὶ γὰρ θνητῶν δειλοί,
καὶ ἐπισφαλεῖς αἱ ἐπίνοιαι ἡμῶν·
15 φθαρτὸν γὰρ σῶμα βαρύνει ψυχήν,
καὶ βρίθει τὸ γεῶδες σκῆνος νοῦν πολυφρόντιδα.

KING JAMES VERSION

8 Thou hast commanded me to build a temple upon thy holy mount, and an altar in the city wherein thou dwellest, a resemblance of the holy tabernacle, which thou hast prepared from the beginning.

9 And wisdom was with thee: which knoweth thy works, and was present when thou madest the world, and knew what was acceptable in thy sight, and right in thy commandments.

10 O send her out of thy holy heavens, and from the throne of thy glory, that being present she may labour with me, that I may know what is pleasing unto thee.

11 For she knoweth and understandeth all things, and she shall lead me soberly in my doings, and preserve me in her power.

12 So shall my works be acceptable, and then shall I judge thy people righteously, and be worthy to sit in my father's seat.

13 For what man is he that can know the counsel of God? or who can think what the will of the Lord is?

14 For the thoughts of mortal men are miserable, and our devices are but uncertain.

15 For the corruptible body presseth down the soul, and the earthy tabernacle weigheth down the mind that museth upon many things.

DOUAY OLD TESTAMENT

8 And hast commanded me to build a temple on thy holy mount, and an altar in the city of thy dwelling place, a resemblance of thy holy tabernacle, which thou hast prepared from the beginning:

9 And thy wisdom with thee, which knoweth thy works, which then also was present when thou madest the world, and knew what was agreeable to thy eyes, and what was right in thy commandments.

10 Send her out of thy holy heaven, and from the throne of thy majesty, that she may be with me, and may labour with me, that I may know what is acceptable with thee:

11 For she knoweth and understandeth all things, and shall lead me soberly in my works, and shall preserve me by her power.

12 So shall my works be acceptable, and I shall govern thy people justly, and shall be worthy of the throne of my father.

13 For who among men is he that can know the counsel of God? or who can think what the will of God is?

14 For the thoughts of mortal men are fearful, and our counsels uncertain.

15 For the corruptible body is a load upon the soul, and the earthly habitation presseth down the mind that museth upon many things.

KNOX TRANSLATION

thou hast bidden me raise thee temple and altar, upon this
mountain, in the holy city where thou dwellest, model of
that holy tabernacle, made long ago, whose pattern was of
thy own devising.[a] 9 Wisdom was with thee then,[b] privy to
all thy designs, she who stood by thee at the world's creation, and knows thy whole will, the whole tenour of thy
commandments. 10 From that heavenly sanctuary, that high
throne of thine, send her out still on thy errand, to be at my
side too, and share my labours! How else should thy will be
made clear to me? 11 For her, no secret, no riddle is too dark;
her prudent counsel will be my guide, the fame of her my
protection. 12 So shall my task be accomplished as thou
wouldst have it be; so shall I give this people of thine just
awards, no unworthy heir of the throne my father left me.
13 What God's purpose is, how should man discover, how
should his mind master the secret of the divine will? 14 So
hesitating our human thoughts, so hazardous our conjec-
tures! 15 Ever the soul is weighed down by a mortal body,
earth-bound cell that clogs the manifold activity of its

a Literally, 'Which thou didst make ready beforehand from the beginning'. The rendering given assumes a reference to the tabernacle in the desert, and the pattern of it shewn to Moses on Mount Sinai. Others would interpret the verse as alluding to God's dwelling-place in heaven. *b* Or perhaps, 'Wisdom is ever at thy side'.

TODAY'S ENGLISH VERSION

told me to build a temple on your sacred mountain, an altar
in Jerusalem, the city you chose as your home. It is a copy of
that temple in heaven, which you prepared at the beginning.
9 Wisdom is with you and knows your actions; she was
present when you made the world. She knows what pleases
you, what is right and in accordance with your commands.
10 Send her from the holy heavens, down from your glorious
throne, so that she may work at my side, and I may learn
what pleases you. 11 She knows and understands everything, and will guide me intelligently in what I do. Her glory
will protect me. 12 Then I will judge your people fairly, and
be worthy of my father's throne. My actions will be acceptable.
13 "Who can ever learn the will of God? 14 Human reason
is not adequate for the task, and our philosophies tend to
mislead us, 15 because our mortal bodies weigh our souls
down. The body is a temporary structure made of earth, a
burden to the active mind. 16 All we can do is make guesses

NEW REVISED STANDARD VERSION

8 You have given command to build a temple on your
holy mountain,
and an altar in the city of your habitation,
a copy of the holy tent that you prepared from the
beginning.
9 With you is wisdom, she who knows your works
and was present when you made the world;
she understands what is pleasing in your sight
and what is right according to your commandments.
10 Send her forth from the holy heavens,
and from the throne of your glory send her,
that she may labor at my side,
and that I may learn what is pleasing to you.
11 For she knows and understands all things,
and she will guide me wisely in my actions
and guard me with her glory.
12 Then my works will be acceptable,
and I shall judge your people justly,
and shall be worthy of the throne[a] of my father.
13 For who can learn the counsel of God?
Or who can discern what the Lord wills?
14 For the reasoning of mortals is worthless,
and our designs are likely to fail;
15 for a perishable body weighs down the soul,
and this earthy tent burdens the thoughtful[b] mind.

a Gk *thrones* *b* Or *anxious*

NEW AMERICAN BIBLE

8 You have bid me build a temple on your holy mountain
and an altar in the city that is your dwelling place,
a copy of the holy tabernacle which you had
established from of old.
9 Now with you is Wisdom, who knows your works
and was present when you made the world;
Who understands what is pleasing in your eyes
and what is conformable with your commands.
10 Send her forth from your holy heavens
and from your glorious throne dispatch her
That she may be with me and work with me,
that I may know what is your pleasure,
11 For she knows and understands all things,
and will guide me discreetly in my affairs
and safeguard me by her glory;
12 Thus my deeds will be acceptable,
and I shall judge your people justly
and be worthy of my father's throne.
13 For what man knows God's counsel,
or who can conceive what the LORD intends?
14 For the deliberations of mortals are timid,
and unsure are our plans.
15 For the corruptible body burdens the soul
and the earthen shelter weighs down the mind that
has many concerns.

NEW JERUSALEM BIBLE

8 You have bidden me build a temple on your holy
mountain,
and an altar in the city where you have pitched your
tent,
a copy of the holy Tent which you prepared at the
beginning.
9 With you is Wisdom, she who knows your works,
she who was present when you made the world;
she understands what is pleasing in your eyes
and what agrees with your commandments.
10 Despatch her from the holy heavens,
send her forth from your throne of glory
to help me and to toil with me
and teach me what is pleasing to you;
11 since she knows and understands everything
she will guide me prudently in my actions
and will protect me with her glory.
12 Then all I do will be acceptable,
I shall govern your people justly
and be worthy of my father's throne.

13 'What human being indeed can know the intentions of
God?
And who can comprehend the will of the Lord?
14 For the reasoning of mortals is inadequate,
our attitudes of mind unstable;
15 for a perishable body presses down the soul,
and this tent of clay weighs down the mind with its
many cares.

GREEK OLD TESTAMENT

16 καὶ μόλις εἰκάζομεν τὰ ἐπὶ γῆς
καὶ τὰ ἐν χερσὶν εὑρίσκομεν μετὰ πόνου·
τὰ δὲ ἐν οὐρανοῖς τίς ἐξιχνίασεν;
17 βουλὴν δέ σου τίς ἔγνω, εἰ μὴ σὺ ἔδωκας σοφίαν
καὶ ἔπεμψας τὸ ἅγιόν σου πνεῦμα ἀπὸ ὑψίστων;
18 καὶ οὕτως διωρθώθησαν αἱ τρίβοι τῶν ἐπὶ γῆς,
καὶ τὰ ἀρεστά σου ἐδιδάχθησαν ἄνθρωποι,
καὶ τῇ σοφίᾳ ἐσώθησαν.
10 Αὕτη πρωτόπλαστον πατέρα κόσμου
μόνον κτισθέντα διεφύλαξεν
καὶ ἐξείλατο αὐτὸν ἐκ παραπτώματος ἰδίου
2 ἔδωκέν τε αὐτῷ ἰσχὺν κρατῆσαι ἁπάντων.
3 ἀποστὰς δὲ ἀπ' αὐτῆς ἄδικος ἐν ὀργῇ αὐτοῦ
ἀδελφοκτόνοις συναπώλετο θυμοῖς.
4 δι' ὃν κατακλυζομένην γῆν πάλιν ἔσωσεν σοφία
δι' εὐτελοῦς ξύλου τὸν δίκαιον κυβερνήσασα.
5 αὕτη καὶ ἐν ὁμονοίᾳ πονηρίας ἐθνῶν συγχυθέντων

KING JAMES VERSION

16 And hardly do we guess aright at things that are upon earth, and with labour do we find the things that are before us: but the things that are in heaven who hath searched out?

17 And thy counsel who hath known, except thou give wisdom, and send thy Holy Spirit from above?

18 For so the ways of them which lived on the earth were reformed, and men were taught the things that are pleasing unto thee, and were saved through wisdom.

10 She preserved the first formed father of the world, that was created alone, and brought him out of his fall,

2 And gave him power to rule all things.

3 But when the unrighteous went away from her in his anger, he perished also in the fury wherewith he murdered his brother.

4 For whose cause the earth being drowned with the flood, wisdom again preserved it, and directed the course of the righteous in a piece of wood of small value.

5 Moreover, the nations in their wicked conspiracy being

DOUAY OLD TESTAMENT

16 And hardly do we guess aright at things that are upon earth: and with labour do we find the things that are before us. But the things that are in heaven, who shall search out?

17 And who shall know thy thought, except thou give wisdom, and send thy Holy Spirit from above:

18 And so the ways of them that are upon earth may be corrected, and men may learn the things that please thee?

19 For by wisdom they were healed, whosoever have pleased thee, O Lord, from the beginning.

10 SHE preserved him, that was first formed by God the father of the world, when he was created alone,

2 And she brought him out of his sin, and gave him power to govern all things.

3 But when the unjust went away from her in his anger, he perished by the fury wherewith he murdered his brother.

4 For whose cause, when water destroyed the earth, wisdom healed it again, directing the course of the just by contemptible wood.

5 Moreover when the nations had conspired together to consent to wickedness, she knew the just, and preserved him

KNOX TRANSLATION

thought. 16 Hard enough to read the riddle of our life here,
with laborious search ascertaining what lies so close to hand;
and would we trace out heaven's mysteries too? 17 Thy purposes none may know, unless thou dost grant thy gift of wisdom, sending out from high heaven thy own holy spirit.
18 Thus ever were men guided by the right way, here on earth,
and learned to know thy will; 19 ever since the world began
wisdom was the salve they used, that have won thy favour.[a]
10 When man was but newly made, the lonely father of
this created world, she it was that watched over him,
2 and set him free from wrong-doing of his own,[b] and gave
him the mastery over all things else. 3 Against her Cain
rebelled,[c] when he did foul wrong, and by murderous spite
against his brother compassed his own ruin. 4 Who but she,
when the world was a-drowning for Cain's fault;[d] gave it a
second term of life, steering, on a paltry raft, one innocent
man to safety? 5 And when the nations went their several
ways;[e] banded in a single conspiracy of wickedness, of one

a This verse is represented in the Greek text by four words, meaning 'And were saved (or, healed) by wisdom'. *b* It is not clear whether the final words of this verse refer to Adam's original innocence, or to his deliverance from the death-penalty after he had sinned. *c* This chapter, in the original, mentions no proper names; a few of them have here been supplied, in accordance with modern usage. *d* 'For Cain's fault' is an expression difficult to account for, except on the view that the 'sons of God' mentioned in Gen. 6. 2, are the descendants of Seth, the 'children of men' those of Cain. *e* The Latin here obscures the sense of the original, by describing the nations as 'coming together'. According to the Greek text, they 'were confounded', almost certainly a reference to Gen. 11. 7, where the same verb is used. Mankind, for its sin, was split up into a multitude of nations, but Wisdom saw to it that one of these, with Abraham as its founder, should be different from the rest.

TODAY'S ENGLISH VERSION

about things on earth; we must struggle to learn about
things that are close to us. Who, then, can ever hope to
understand heavenly things? 17 No one has ever learned
your will, unless you first gave him Wisdom, and sent your
holy spirit down to him. 18 In this way people on earth have
been set on the right path, have learned what pleases you,
and have been kept safe by Wisdom."

10 Wisdom protected the father of the world, the first
man that was ever formed, when he alone had been
created. She saved him from his own sinful act 2 and gave
him the strength to master everything on earth.

3 But there was an unrighteous man who abandoned
Wisdom; he destroyed himself by killing his brother in a fit
of anger.

4 Because of that sin, the earth was flooded, but Wisdom
saved it again. She guided a righteous man in his flimsy
wooden boat.

5 Once when the nations were frustrated in their wicked

NEW REVISED STANDARD VERSION

16 We can hardly guess at what is on earth,
and what is at hand we find with labor;
but who has traced out what is in the heavens?
17 Who has learned your counsel,
unless you have given wisdom
and sent your holy spirit from on high?
18 And thus the paths of those on earth were set right,
and people were taught what pleases you,
and were saved by wisdom."

10 Wisdom[a] protected the first-formed father of the
world, when he alone had been created;
she delivered him from his transgression,
2 and gave him strength to rule all things.
3 But when an unrighteous man departed from her in his
anger,
he perished because in rage he killed his brother.
4 When the earth was flooded because of him, wisdom
again saved it,
steering the righteous man by a paltry piece of wood.

5 Wisdom[a] also, when the nations in wicked agreement
had been put to confusion,

a Gk *She*

NEW AMERICAN BIBLE

16 And scarce do we guess the things on earth,
and what is within our grasp we find with difficulty;
but when things are in heaven, who can search them
out?
17 Or who ever knew your counsel, except you had given
Wisdom
and sent your holy spirit from on high?
18 And thus were the paths of those on earth made
straight,
and men learned what was your pleasure,
and were saved by Wisdom.

10 She preserved the first-formed father of the world
when he alone had been created;
And she raised him up from his fall,
2 and gave him power to rule all things.
3 But when the unjust man withdrew from her in his
anger,
he perished through his fratricidal wrath.
4 When on his account the earth was flooded, Wisdom
again saved it,
piloting the just man on frailest wood.
5 She, when the nations were sunk in universal
wickedness,

NEW JERUSALEM BIBLE

16 It is hard enough for us to work out what is on earth,
laborious to know what lies within our reach;
who, then, can discover what is in the heavens?
17 And who could ever have known your will, had you not
given Wisdom
and sent your holy Spirit from above?
18 Thus have the paths of those on earth been
straightened
and people have been taught what pleases you,
and have been saved, by Wisdom.'

10 [a] It was Wisdom who protected the first man to be
fashioned,
the father of the world, who had been created all alone,
she it was who rescued him from his fall
2 and gave him the strength to subjugate all things.
3 But when in his wrath a wicked man deserted her,
he perished in his fratricidal fury.
4 When because of him the earth was drowned, it was
Wisdom again who saved it,
piloting the upright man on valueless timber.
5 Again, when, concurring in wickedness, the nations
had been thrown into confusion,

a **10** v. 1 Adam, v. 3 Cain, v. 4 Noah, v. 5 Abraham, v. 6 Lot, v. 10 Jacob,
v. 13 Joseph.

GREEK OLD TESTAMENT

ἔγνω τὸν δίκαιον καὶ ἐτήρησεν αὐτὸν ἄμεμπτον θεῷ
καὶ ἐπὶ τέκνου σπλάγχνοις ἰσχυρὸν ἐφύλαξεν.
6 αὕτη δίκαιον ἐξαπολλυμένων ἀσεβῶν ἐρρύσατο
φυγόντα καταβάσιον πῦρ Πενταπόλεως,
7 ἧς ἔτι μαρτύριον τῆς πονηρίας
καπνιζομένη καθέστηκε χέρσος,
καὶ ἀτελέσιν ὥραις καρποφοροῦντα φυτά,
ἀπιστούσης ψυχῆς μνημεῖον ἑστηκυῖα στήλη ἁλός.
8 σοφίαν γὰρ παροδεύσαντες
οὐ μόνον ἐβλάβησαν τοῦ μὴ γνῶναι τὰ καλά,
ἀλλὰ καὶ τῆς ἀφροσύνης ἀπέλιπον τῷ βίῳ μνημόσυνον,
ἵνα ἐν οἷς ἐσφάλησαν μηδὲ λαθεῖν δυνηθῶσιν.
9 σοφία δὲ τοὺς θεραπεύοντας αὐτὴν ἐκ πόνων ἐρρύσατο.
10 αὕτη φυγάδα ὀργῆς ἀδελφοῦ δίκαιον
ὡδήγησεν ἐν τρίβοις εὐθείαις·
ἔδειξεν αὐτῷ βασιλείαν θεοῦ
καὶ ἔδωκεν αὐτῷ γνῶσιν ἁγίων·
εὐπόρησεν αὐτὸν ἐν μόχθοις
καὶ ἐπλήθυνεν τοὺς πόνους αὐτοῦ·
11 ἐν πλεονεξίᾳ κατισχυόντων αὐτὸν παρέστη
καὶ ἐπλούτισεν αὐτόν·
12 διεφύλαξεν αὐτὸν ἀπὸ ἐχθρῶν
καὶ ἀπὸ ἐνεδρευόντων ἠσφαλίσατο·

KING JAMES VERSION

confounded, she found out the righteous, and preserved him blameless unto God, and kept him strong against his tender compassion toward his son.

6 When the ungodly perished, she delivered the righteous man, who fled from the fire which fell down upon the five cities.

7 Of whose wickedness even to this day the waste land that smoketh is a testimony, and plants bearing fruit that never come to ripeness: and a standing pillar of salt *is* a monument of an unbelieving soul.

8 For regarding not wisdom, they gat not only this hurt, that they knew not the things which were good; but also left behind them to the world a memorial of their foolishness: so that in the things wherein they offended they could not so much as be hid.

9 Rut wisdom delivered from pain those that attended upon her.

10 When the righteous fled from his brother's wrath, she guided him in right paths, shewed him the kingdom of God, and gave him knowledge of holy things, made him rich in his travails, and multiplied *the fruit of* his labours.

11 In the covetousness of such as oppressed him she stood by him, and made him rich.

12 She defended him from his enemies, and kept him safe

DOUAY OLD TESTAMENT

without blame to God, and kept him strong against the compassion for his son.

6 She delivered the just man who fled from the wicked that were perishing, when the fire came down upon Pentapolis:

7 Whose land for a testimony of their wickedness is desolate, and smoketh to this day, and the trees bear fruits that ripen not, and a standing pillar of salt is a monument of an incredulous soul.

8 For regarding not wisdom, they did not only slip in this, that they were ignorant of good things, but they left also unto men a memorial of their folly, so that in the things in which they sinned, they could not so much as lie hid.

9 But wisdom hath delivered from sorrow them that attend upon her.

10 She conducted the just, when he fled from his brother's wrath, through the right ways, and shewed him the kingdom of God, and gave him the knowledge of the holy things, made him honourable in his labours, and accomplished his labours.

11 In the deceit of them that overreached him, she stood by him, and made him honourable.

12 She kept him safe from his enemies, and she defended

KNOX TRANSLATION

man's innocence she still took note; Abraham must be kept
irreproachable in God's service, and steeled against pity for
his own child. 6 Here was another innocent man, Lot, that
owed his preservation to Wisdom, when godless folk were
perishing all around him. Escape he should, when fire came
down upon the Cities of the Plain; 7 those five cities whose
shame is yet unforgotten, while smoke issues from the barren soil, and never tree bears seasonable fruit, and the pillar
of salt stands monument to an unbelieving soul. 8 Fatal
neglect of Wisdom's guidance, that could blind their eyes to
the claims of honour, and leave the world such a memorial
of their folly, as should make the record of their sins unmistakable!

9 But those who cherish her, Wisdom brings safely out of
all their striving. 10 When Jacob, her faithful servant, was in
flight from his brother's anger, she guided him straight to his
goal, and on the way shewed him the heavenly kingdom,
gave him knowledge of holy things. She enriched him by his
toil, and gave all his labours a happy issue. 11 Knavery went
about to get the better of him, but she stood by him and
prospered him; 12 kept him safe from his enemies, protected

TODAY'S ENGLISH VERSION

plans, Wisdom recognized a righteous man and kept him
innocent in God's sight. She gave him strength to obey God's
command in spite of his love for his son.
6 Wisdom rescued a righteous man while ungodly people
were dying. He escaped the flames that destroyed the Five
Cities. 7 You can still see the evidence of their wickedness.
The land there is barren and smoking. The plants bear fruit
that never ripens, and a pillar of salt stands as a monument
to one who did not believe. 8 The people of those cities
ignored Wisdom and could not tell right from wrong. Not
only that, but the remains of their cities still remind us of the
foolish way they lived, so that their failure can never be forgotten. 9 But Wisdom rescued her servants from the danger.
10 A righteous man once had to escape from his brother's
anger, and Wisdom guided him in the right way. She showed
him God's kingdom and allowed him to know about holy
things.[a] She made him prosperous and successful in his
work. 11 When others were greedy for what he had, and
wanted to take it away from him, Wisdom stood by him
and made him rich. 12 She protected him from his enemies
who were waiting for a chance to attack him. She gave him

[a] holy things; *or* angels.

NEW REVISED STANDARD VERSION

recognized the righteous man and preserved him
blameless before God,
and kept him strong in the face of his compassion for
his child.
6 Wisdom[a] rescued a righteous man when the ungodly
were perishing;
he escaped the fire that descended on the Five Cities.[b]
7 Evidence of their wickedness still remains:
a continually smoking wasteland,
plants bearing fruit that does not ripen,
and a pillar of salt standing as a monument to an
unbelieving soul.
8 For because they passed wisdom by,
they not only were hindered from recognizing the good,
but also left for humankind a reminder of their folly,
so that their failures could never go unnoticed.

9 Wisdom rescued from troubles those who served her.
10 When a righteous man fled from his brother's wrath,
she guided him on straight paths;
she showed him the kingdom of God,
and gave him knowledge of holy things;
she prospered him in his labors,
and increased the fruit of his toil.
11 When his oppressors were covetous,
she stood by him and made him rich.
12 She protected him from his enemies,
and kept him safe from those who lay in wait for him;

a Gk *She* *b* Or *on Pentapolis*

NEW AMERICAN BIBLE

knew the just man, kept him blameless before God,
and preserved him resolute against pity for his child.
6 She delivered the just man from among the wicked who
were being destroyed,
when he fled as fire descended upon Pentapolis—
7 Where as a testimony to its wickedness,
there yet remain a smoking desert,
Plants bearing fruit that never ripens,
and the tomb of a disbelieving soul, a standing pillar
of salt.
8 For those who forsook Wisdom
first were bereft of knowledge of the right,
And then they left mankind a memorial of their folly—
so that they could not even be hidden in their fall.
9 But Wisdom delivered from tribulations those who
served her.
10 She, when the just man fled from his brother's anger,
guided him in direct ways,
Showed him the kingdom of God
and gave him knowledge of holy things;
She prospered him in his labors
and made abundant the fruit of his works,
11 Stood by him against the greed of his defrauders,
and enriched him;
12 She preserved him from foes,
and secured him against ambush,

NEW JERUSALEM BIBLE

she singled out the upright man, preserved him
blameless before God
and fortified him against pity for his child.
6 She it was who, while the godless perished, saved the
upright man
as he fled from the fire raining down on the Five Cities,
7 in witness against whose evil ways
a desolate land still smokes,
where plants bear fruit that never ripens
and where, monument to an unbelieving soul, there
stands a pillar of salt.
8 For, by ignoring the path of Wisdom,
not only did they suffer the loss of not knowing the
good,
but they left the world a memorial to their folly,
so that their offences could not pass unnoticed.
9 But Wisdom delivered her servants from their ordeals.
10 The upright man, fleeing from the anger of his brother,
was led by her along straight paths.
She showed him the kingdom of God
and taught him the knowledge of holy things.
She brought him success in his labours
and gave him full return for all his efforts;
11 she stood by him against grasping and oppressive men
and she made him rich.
12 She preserved him from his enemies
and saved him from the traps they set for him.

GREEK OLD TESTAMENT

καὶ ἀγῶνα ἰσχυρὸν ἐβράβευσεν αὐτῷ,
ἵνα γνῷ ὅτι παντὸς δυνατωτέρα ἐστὶν εὐσέβεια.
13 αὕτη πραθέντα δίκαιον οὐκ ἐγκατέλιπεν,
ἀλλὰ ἐξ ἁμαρτίας ἐρρύσατο αὐτόν·
14 συγκατέβη αὐτῷ εἰς λάκκον
καὶ ἐν δεσμοῖς οὐκ ἀφῆκεν αὐτόν,
ἕως ἤνεγκεν αὐτῷ σκῆπτρα βασιλείας
καὶ ἐξουσίαν τυραννούντων αὐτοῦ·
ψευδεῖς τε ἔδειξεν τοὺς μωμησαμένους αὐτὸν
καὶ ἔδωκεν αὐτῷ δόξαν αἰώνιον.
15 Αὕτη λαὸν ὅσιον καὶ σπέρμα ἄμεμπτον
ἐρρύσατο ἐξ ἔθνους θλιβόντων·
16 εἰσῆλθεν εἰς ψυχὴν θεράποντος κυρίου
καὶ ἀντέστη βασιλεῦσιν φοβεροῖς ἐν τέρασι καὶ σημείοις.
17 ἀπέδωκεν ὁσίοις μισθὸν κόπων αὐτῶν,
ὡδήγησεν αὐτοὺς ἐν ὁδῷ θαυμαστῇ
καὶ ἐγένετο αὐτοῖς εἰς σκέπην ἡμέρας
καὶ εἰς φλόγα ἄστρων τὴν νύκτα.
18 διεβίβασεν αὐτοὺς θάλασσαν ἐρυθρὰν
καὶ διήγαγεν αὐτοὺς δι' ὕδατος πολλοῦ·
19 τοὺς δὲ ἐχθροὺς αὐτῶν κατέκλυσεν
καὶ ἐκ βάθους ἀβύσσου ἀνέβρασεν αὐτούς.
20 διὰ τοῦτο δίκαιοι ἐσκύλευσαν ἀσεβεῖς

KING JAMES VERSION

from those that lay in wait, and in a sore conflict she gave him the victory; that he might know that godliness is stronger than all.

13 When the righteous was sold, she forsook him not, but delivered him from sin: she went down with him into the pit,

14 And left him not in bonds, till she brought him the sceptre of the kingdom, and power against those that oppressed him: as for them that had accused him, she shewed them to be liars, and gave him perpetual glory.

15 She delivered the righteous people and blameless seed from the nation that oppressed them.

16 She entered into the soul of the servant of the Lord, and withstood dreadful kings in wonders and signs;

17 Rendered to the righteous a reward of their labours, guided them in a marvellous way, and was unto them for a cover by day, and a light of stars in the night season;

18 Brought them through the Red sea, and led them through much water:

19 But she drowned their enemies, and cast them up out of the bottom of the deep.

20 Therefore the righteous spoiled the ungodly, and

DOUAY OLD TESTAMENT

him from seducers, and gave him a strong conflict, that he might overcome, and know that wisdom is mightier than all.

13 She forsook not the just when he was sold, but delivered him from sinners: she went down with him into the pit.

14 And in bands she left him not, till she brought him the sceptre of the kingdom, and power against those that oppressed him: and shewed them to be liars that had accused him, and gave him everlasting glory.

15 She delivered the just people, and blameless seed from the nations that oppressed them.

16 She entered into the soul of the servant of God, and stood against dreadful kings in wonders and signs.

17 And she rendered to the just the wages of their labours, and conducted them in a wonderful way: and she was to them for a covert by day, and for the light of stars by night:

18 And she brought them through the Red Sea, and carried them over through a great water.

19 But their enemies she drowned in the sea, and from the depth of hell she brought them out. Therefore the just took the spoils of the wicked.

KNOX TRANSLATION

him from their scheming. She would have him wrestle manfully, and prove that there is no strength like the strength of
wisdom. 13 When Joseph, in his innocence, was sold for a
slave, Wisdom did not desert him, did not leave him among
the guilty, but went down with him into his dungeon. 14 Fast
he was bound, but she had not finished with him till she gave him dominion over a whole kingdom, and power to do what he would with his persecutors. So she brought home the lie to those who had traduced him, and won him everlasting fame.

15 So, too, with that innocent people of Israel, that unoffending race; did she not deliver them from the nations that
kept them under? 16 Did she not enter into the heart of God's
servant, confronting dread rulers with portent and with miracle? 17 Did she not restore to men ill-used the just reward of
their labours? She, too, led them out on their miraculous journey, affording them shelter by day and starry radiance at
night. 18 She made a passage for them through the Red Sea,
brought them safely through those leagues of water, 19 and
churned up the bodies of their drowned enemy from those unfathomed depths. So, enriched by the spoils of the godless,

TODAY'S ENGLISH VERSION

victory in a hard fight, so that he might realize that nothing
can make a person stronger than serving God.
13 Once a righteous man was sold into slavery, but Wisdom
did not abandon him. She kept him safe from sin. She went
to prison with him 14 and never left him until she had given
him power over an empire and made him the ruler of people
who had once oppressed him. She let it be known that a
false accusation had been made against him, and she gave
him eternal honor.
15 Wisdom once rescued an innocent and holy people from
a nation of oppressors. 16 She entered the soul of one of
God's servants and[a] stood up to dreaded kings by performing miracles. 17 She rewarded God's people for their hardships. She guided them along a miraculous journey. She
gave them shade during the day and brilliant starlight at
night. 18 She led them through the deep waters of the Red
Sea, 19 but she drowned their enemies and washed their bodies up on the shore. 20 And so the righteous looted the

[a] and; *or* who.

NEW REVISED STANDARD VERSION

in his arduous contest she gave him the victory,
so that he might learn that godliness is more powerful
than anything else.

13 When a righteous man was sold, wisdom[a] did not
desert him,
but delivered him from sin.
She descended with him into the dungeon,
14 and when he was in prison she did not leave him,
until she brought him the scepter of a kingdom
and authority over his masters.
Those who accused him she showed to be false,
and she gave him everlasting honor.

15 A holy people and blameless race
wisdom delivered from a nation of oppressors.
16 She entered the soul of a servant of the Lord,
and withstood dread kings with wonders and signs.
17 She gave to holy people the reward of their labors;
she guided them along a marvelous way,
and became a shelter to them by day,
and a starry flame through the night.
18 She brought them over the Red Sea,
and led them through deep waters;
19 but she drowned their enemies,
and cast them up from the depth of the sea.
20 Therefore the righteous plundered the ungodly;

a Gk *she*

NEW AMERICAN BIBLE

And she gave him the prize for his stern struggle
that he might know that devotion to God
is mightier than all else.
13 She did not abandon the just man when he was sold,
but delivered him from sin.
14 She went down with him into the dungeon,
and did not desert him in his bonds,
Until she brought him the scepter of royalty
and authority over his oppressors,
Showed those who had defamed him false,
and gave him eternal glory.
15 The holy people and blameless race—it was she
who delivered them from the nation that oppressed
them.
16 She entered the soul of the LORD's servant,
and withstood fearsome kings with signs and
portents;
17 she gave the holy ones the recompense of their
labors,
Conducted them by a wondrous road,
and became a shelter for them by day
and a starry flame by night.
18 She took them across the Red Sea
and brought them through the deep waters—
19 But their enemies she overwhelmed,
and cast them up from the bottom of the depths.
20 Therefore the just despoiled the wicked;

NEW JERUSALEM BIBLE

In an arduous struggle she awarded him the prize,
to teach him that piety is stronger than all.
13 She did not forsake the upright man when he was sold,
but snatched him away from sin;
14 she accompanied him down into the pit,
nor did she abandon him in his chains
until she had brought him the sceptre of a kingdom
and authority over his despotic masters,
thus exposing as liars those who had traduced him,
and giving him honour everlasting.
15 It was Wisdom who delivered a holy people,
a blameless race, from a nation of oppressors.
16 She entered the soul of a servant of the Lord,
and withstood fearsome kings with wonders and signs.
17 To the holy people she gave the wages of their labours;
she guided them by a marvellous road,
herself their shelter by day—
and their starlight through the night.
18 She brought them across the Red Sea,
leading them through an immensity of water,
19 whereas she drowned their enemies,
then spat them out from the depths of the abyss.
20 So the upright despoiled the godless;

GREEK OLD TESTAMENT

καὶ ὕμνησαν, κύριε, τὸ ὄνομα τὸ ἅγιόν σου
τήν τε ὑπέρμαχόν σου χεῖρα ᾔνεσαν ὁμοθυμαδόν·
21 ὅτι ἡ σοφία ἤνοιξεν στόμα κωφῶν
καὶ γλώσσας νηπίων ἔθηκεν τρανάς.

11 Εὐόδωσεν τὰ ἔργα αὐτῶν ἐν χειρὶ προφήτου ἁγίου.
2 διώδευσαν ἔρημον ἀοίκητον
καὶ ἐν ἀβάτοις ἔπηξαν σκηνάς·
3 ἀντέστησαν πολεμίοις καὶ ἐχθροὺς ἠμύναντο.
4 ἐδίψησαν καὶ ἐπεκαλέσαντό σε,
καὶ ἐδόθη αὐτοῖς ἐκ πέτρας ἀκροτόμου ὕδωρ
καὶ ἴαμα δίψης ἐκ λίθου σκληροῦ.
5 δι᾽ ὧν γὰρ ἐκολάσθησαν οἱ ἐχθροὶ αὐτῶν,
διὰ τούτων αὐτοὶ ἀποροῦντες εὐεργετήθησαν.
6 ἀντὶ μὲν πηγῆς ἀενάου ποταμοῦ
αἵματι λυθρώδει ταραχθέντος
7 εἰς ἔλεγχον νηπιοκτόνου διατάγματος
ἔδωκας αὐτοῖς δαψιλὲς ὕδωρ ἀνελπίστως
8 δείξας διὰ τοῦ τότε δίψους
πῶς τοὺς ὑπεναντίους ἐκόλασας.
9 ὅτε γὰρ ἐπειράσθησαν, καίπερ ἐν ἐλέει παιδευόμενοι,
ἔγνωσαν πῶς μετ᾽ ὀργῆς κρινόμενοι ἀσεβεῖς
ἐβασανίζοντο·
10 τούτους μὲν γὰρ ὡς πατὴρ νουθετῶν ἐδοκίμασας,

KING JAMES VERSION

praised thy holy name, O Lord, and magnified with one accord thine hand, that fought for them.

21 For wisdom opened the mouth of the dumb, and made the tongues of them that cannot speak eloquent.

11 She prospered their works in the hand of the holy prophet.

2 They went through the wilderness that was not inhabited, and pitched tents in places where there lay no way.

3 They stood against their enemies, and were avenged of their adversaries.

4 When they were thirsty, they called upon thee, and water was given them out of the flinty rock, and their thirst was quenched out of the hard stone.

5 For by what things their enemies were punished, by the same they in their need were benefited.

6 For instead of a fountain of a perpetual running river troubled with foul blood,

7 For a manifest reproof of that commandment, whereby the infants were slain, thou gavest unto them abundance of water by a means which they hoped not for:

8 Declaring by that thirst then how thou hadst punished their adversaries.

9 For when they were tried, albeit but in mercy chastised, they knew how the ungodly were judged in wrath and tormented, thirsting in another manner than the just.

10 For these thou didst admonish and try, as a father:

DOUAY OLD TESTAMENT

20 And they sung to thy holy name, O Lord, and they praised with one accord thy victorious hand.

21 For wisdom opened the mouth of the dumb, and made the tongues of infants eloquent.

11 SHE prospered their works in the hands of the holy prophet.

2 They went through wildernesses that were not inhabited, and in desert places they pitched their tents.

3 They stood against their enemies, and revenged themselves of their adversaries.

4 They were thirsty, and they called upon thee, and water was given them out of the high rock, and a refreshment of their thirst out of the hard stone.

5 For by what things their enemies were punished, when their drink failed them, while the children of Israel abounded therewith and rejoiced:

6 By the same things they in their need were benefited.

7 For instead of a fountain of an ever running river, thou gavest human blood to the unjust.

8 And whilst they were diminished for a manifest reproof of their murdering the infants, thou gavest to thine abundant water unlooked for:

9 Shewing by the thirst that was then, how thou didst exalt thine, and didst kill their adversaries.

10 For when they were tried, and chastised with mercy, they knew how the wicked were judged with wrath and tormented.

11 For thou didst admonish and try them as a father: but

KNOX TRANSLATION

20 they extolled, O Lord, thy holy name, proclaimed with one
voice thy sovereign power; 21 Wisdom opened the dumb
mouths, and made the lips of infants[a] vocal with praise.

11 With Moses set apart for his spokesman,[b] to what
good issue he brought all their enterprises! 2 Through
desert solitudes they journeyed on, pitching their camp far
from the haunts of men; 3 boldly they confronted their
enemy, and overcame his malice. 4 When they were thirsty,
on thy name they called, and out of the rock's sheer face
water was given to heal their thirst, out of the hard flint.
5 Strange likeness between the punishment that befell their
enemies,[c] who went thirsty while Israel had drink to their
heart's content, 6 and the relief of their want Israel now experienced!
7 Thou who once, into defiling blood, hadst troubled
the sources of a living stream, 8 to avenge a murderous edict
against new-born children, didst now give thy people abundant
water to drink, by means unlooked for. 9 How ill it had
gone with their adversaries in Egypt, that thirst of theirs in
the desert plainly shewed them; 10 in mercy schooled, yet
sorely tried, they learned to know what torments the wicked
had undergone, forfeit to thy vengeance. 11 For Israel, only a
test of their faith; only a father's correction; for Egypt, as

a Unless the word 'infants' is to be understood metaphorically (of the Jews, as a people newly born by their ransoming from Egypt), this verse seems to preserve a tradition not found in Ex. 15. 1, that even little children took part in the song of Moses. *b* The word 'Moses', here and in verse 14, like the names of Egyptian and Israelite, has been inserted for the sake of clearness. *c vv.* 5-14: The thought of this whole passage is obscurely expressed in the original, and it is still further obscured by the Latin translation in verses 8 and 13, where the Greek has to be used as a guide, if we are to obtain any tolerable sense.

TODAY'S ENGLISH VERSION

ungodly. They sang hymns to your holy name, O Lord; together they praised you for defending them. [21]Wisdom gave speech to those who could not speak; she even caused babies to speak clearly.

11 Wisdom brought success to the people of Israel through a holy prophet. [2]They traveled across a desert where no one lived and camped in places where no human being had ever been. [3]They stood up to their enemies and fought them off. [4]When your people grew thirsty, they called to you, Lord, and you gave them water flowing out of solid rock. [5]The disasters that punished the Egyptians saved your people when they were in trouble.

[6-8]Because those enemies decreed that the babies of your people should be killed, you stirred up the sources of their everflowing river and made it foul with blood.

In the desert you let your people go thirsty, to give them a taste of how you had punished their enemies. And then, when they least expected it, you gave them plenty of water. [9]When they were being tested, even though it was a merciful discipline, they learned how wicked people were tortured when you judged them in anger. [10]You tested your people, as parents test their children, to warn them. But you judged

NEW REVISED STANDARD VERSION

they sang hymns, O Lord, to your holy name,
and praised with one accord your defending hand;
21 for wisdom opened the mouths of those who were mute,
and made the tongues of infants speak clearly.

11 Wisdom[a] prospered their works by the hand of a holy prophet.
2 They journeyed through an uninhabited wilderness,
and pitched their tents in untrodden places.
3 They withstood their enemies and fought off their foes.
4 When they were thirsty, they called upon you,
and water was given them out of flinty rock,
and from hard stone a remedy for their thirst.
5 For through the very things by which their enemies were punished,
they themselves received benefit in their need.
6 Instead of the fountain of an ever-flowing river,
stirred up and defiled with blood
7 in rebuke for the decree to kill the infants,
you gave them abundant water unexpectedly,
8 showing by their thirst at that time
how you punished their enemies.
9 For when they were tried, though they were being disciplined in mercy,
they learned how the ungodly were tormented when judged in wrath.
10 For you tested them as a parent[b] does in warning,

a Gk *She* b Gk *a father*

NEW AMERICAN BIBLE

and they sang, O LORD, your holy name
and praised in unison your conquering hand—
21 Because Wisdom opened the mouths of the dumb,
and gave ready speech to infants.

11 She made their affairs prosper through the holy prophet.
2 They journeyed through the uninhabited desert,
and in solitudes they pitched their tents;
3 they withstood enemies and took vengeance on their foes.
4 When they thirsted, they called upon you,
and water was given them from the sheer rock,
assuagement for their thirst from the hard stone.
5 For by the things through which their foes were punished
they in their need were benefited.
6 Instead of a spring, when the perennial river
was troubled with impure blood
7 as a rebuke to the decree for the slaying of infants,
You gave them abundant water in an unhoped-for way,
8 once you had shown by the thirst they then had
how you punished their adversaries.
9 For when they had been tried, though only mildly chastised,
they recognized how the wicked, condemned in anger, were being tormented.
11 Both those afar off and those close by were afflicted:
10 the latter you tested, admonishing them as a father;

NEW JERUSALEM BIBLE

Lord, they extolled your holy name,
and with one accord praised your protecting hand;
21 for Wisdom opened the mouths of the dumb
and made eloquent the tongues of babes.

11 She made their actions successful, by means of a holy prophet.
2 They journeyed through an unpeopled desert
and pitched their tents in inaccessible places.
3 They stood firm against their enemies, fought off their foes.
4 On you they called when they were thirsty,
and from the rocky cliff water was given them,
from hard stone a remedy for their thirst.
5 Thus, what had served to punish their enemies
became a benefit for them in their difficulties.
6 Whereas their enemies had only the ever-flowing source
of a river fouled with mingled blood and mud,
7 to punish them for their decree of infanticide,
you gave your people, against all hope, water in abundance,
8 once you had shown by the thirst that they were experiencing
how severely you were punishing their enemies.
9 From their own ordeals, which were only loving correction,
they realised how an angry sentence was tormenting the godless;
10 for you had tested your own as a father admonishes,

GREEK OLD TESTAMENT

ἐκείνους δὲ ὡς ἀπότομος βασιλεὺς καταδικάζων
ἐξήτασας.
11 καὶ ἀπόντες δὲ καὶ παρόντες ὁμοίως ἐτρύχοντο·
12 διπλῆ γὰρ αὐτοὺς ἔλαβεν λύπη
καὶ στεναγμὸς μνημῶν τῶν παρελθόντων·
13 ὅτε γὰρ ἤκουσαν διὰ τῶν ἰδίων κολάσεων
εὐεργετημένους αὐτούς, ᾔσθοντο τοῦ κυρίου.
14 ὃν γὰρ ἐν ἐκθέσει πάλαι ῥιφέντα ἀπεῖπον χλευάζοντες,
ἐπὶ τέλει τῶν ἐκβάσεων ἐθαύμασαν
οὐχ ὅμοια δικαίοις διψήσαντες.
15 ἀντὶ δὲ λογισμῶν ἀσυνέτων ἀδικίας αὐτῶν,
ἐν οἷς πλανηθέντες ἐθρήσκευον ἄλογα ἑρπετὰ καὶ
κνώδαλα εὐτελῆ,
ἐπαπέστειλας αὐτοῖς πλῆθος ἀλόγων ζῴων εἰς
ἐκδίκησιν,
16 ἵνα γνῶσιν ὅτι, δι᾽ ὧν τις ἁμαρτάνει, διὰ τούτων
κολάζεται.
17 οὐ γὰρ ἠπόρει ἡ παντοδύναμός σου χεὶρ
καὶ κτίσασα τὸν κόσμον ἐξ ἀμόρφου ὕλης
ἐπιπέμψαι αὐτοῖς πλῆθος ἄρκων ἢ θρασεῖς λέοντας

KING JAMES VERSION

but the other, as a severe king, thou didst condemn and punish.

11 Whether they were absent or present, they were vexed alike.

12 For a double grief came upon them, and a groaning for the remembrance of things past.

13 For when they heard by their own punishments the other to be benefited, they had some feeling of the Lord.

14 For whom they rejected with scorn, when he was long before thrown out at the casting forth *of the infants,* him in the end, when they saw what came to pass, they admired.

15 But for the foolish devices of their wickedness, wherewith being deceived they worshipped serpents void of reason, and vile beasts, thou didst send a multitude of unreasonable beasts upon them for vengeance;

16 That they might know, that wherewithal a man sinneth, by the same also shall he be punished.

17 For thy Almighty hand, that made the world of matter without form, wanted not means to send among them a multitude of bears, or fierce lions,

DOUAY OLD TESTAMENT

the others, as a severe king, thou didst examine and condemn.

12 For whether absent or present, they were tormented alike.

13 For a double affliction came upon them, and a groaning for the remembrance of things past.

14 For when they heard that by their punishments the others were benefited, they remembered the Lord, wondering at the end of what was come to pass.

15 For whom they scorned before, when he was thrown out at the time of his being wickedly exposed to perish, him they admired in the end, when they saw the event: their thirsting being unlike to that of the just.

16 But for the foolish devices of their iniquity, because some being deceived worshipped dumb serpents and worthless beasts, thou didst send upon them a multitude of dumb beasts for vengeance:

17 That they might know that by what things a man sinneth, by the same also he is tormented.

18 For thy almighty hand, which made the world of matter without form, was not unable to send upon them a multitude of bears, or fierce lions,

KNOX TRANSLATION

from a king, stern scrutiny and stern doom. 12 Tidings from
far away, that racked the Egyptians no less than their own
former sufferings; 13 anguish redoubled, as they groaned over
the memory of things past! 14 That the same plague of thirst
which had tortured themselves should be the source of
Israel's rejoicing! Then indeed they felt the Lord's power, then
indeed they wondered at the revenge time had brought;
15 wondered at Moses, whom their insolence had long ago dis-
inherited, when they exposed him with the other children.
Thirst, that had been Egypt's enemy, had no terrors for the
just.

16 So lost to piety were these Egyptians, such foolish reasonings led them astray, that they worshipped brute[a] reptiles, and despicable vermin. And swarms of brute beasts
thou didst send to execute thy vengeance, 17 for the more
proof that a man's own sins are the instrument of his punishment. 18 Thy power knows no restraint, the power that
created an ordered world out of dark chaos. It had been easy
to send a plague of bears upon them, or noble lions; 19 or to

a It seems likely that the author meant rather, 'inconsiderable', cf. verse 17. The Egyptians, who were credited with worshipping beetles, were punished by plagues of insects.

TODAY'S ENGLISH VERSION

their enemies like a stern king and condemned them. 11 They
suffered, whether they were near your people or far from
them. 12 Their sorrow was doubled; they groaned as they
looked back on what had happened. 13 When they learned
that their punishment had been of benefit to your people,
they realized that it was your work, Lord. 14 The Egyptians
had refused to have anything to do with that man who, long
before as a baby, had been thrown out and exposed; but as
things worked out, they came to be amazed at him. The righteous never suffered a thirst like theirs.

15 Their wickedness misled them into silly ideas, so that
they worshiped snakes and other disgusting animals, creatures without any powers of reason. Because of this, you
punished them with millions of such animals, 16 and taught
them that punishment for sin takes the same form as the sin
itself. 17 Your almighty power, Lord, created the world out of
material that had no form at all. You could easily have punished those people by sending an invasion of bears or savage

NEW REVISED STANDARD VERSION

but you examined the ungodly[a] as a stern king does in
condemnation.
11 Whether absent or present, they were equally
distressed,
12 for a twofold grief possessed them,
and a groaning at the memory of what had occurred.
13 For when they heard that through their own
punishments
the righteous[b] had received benefit, they perceived it
was the Lord's doing.
14 For though they had mockingly rejected him who long
before had been cast out and exposed,
at the end of the events they marveled at him,
when they felt thirst in a different way from the
righteous.

15 In return for their foolish and wicked thoughts,
which led them astray to worship irrational serpents
and worthless animals,
you sent upon them a multitude of irrational creatures
to punish them,
16 so that they might learn that one is punished by the
very things by which one sins.
17 For your all-powerful hand,
which created the world out of formless matter,
did not lack the means to send upon them a multitude
of bears, or bold lions,

a Gk *those* *b* Gk *they*

NEW AMERICAN BIBLE

the former as a stern king you probed and
condemned.
12 For a twofold grief took hold of them
and a groaning at the remembrance of the ones who
had departed.
13 For when they heard that the cause of their own
torments
was a benefit to these others, they recognized the
LORD.
14 Him who of old had been cast out in exposure they
indeed mockingly rejected;
but in the end of events, they marveled at him,
since their thirst proved unlike that of the just.
15 And in return for their senseless, wicked thoughts,
which misled them into worshiping dumb serpents
and worthless insects,
You sent upon them swarms of dumb creatures for
vengeance;
16 that they might recognize that a man is punished by
the very things through which he sins.
17 For not without means was your almighty hand,
that had fashioned the universe from formless
matter,
to send upon them a drove of bears or fierce lions,

NEW JERUSALEM BIBLE

but the others you had punished as a pitiless king
condemns,
11 and, whether far or near, they were equally afflicted.
12 For a double sorrow seized on them,
and a groaning at the memory of the past;
13 when they learned that the punishments they were
receiving
were beneficial to the others, they realised it was the
Lord,
14 while for the man whom long before they had exposed
and later mockingly rebuffed,
they felt only admiration when all was done,
having suffered a thirst so different from that of the
upright.
15 For their foolish and wicked notions which led them
astray
into worshipping mindless reptiles and contemptible
beetles,
you sent a horde of mindless animals to punish them
16 and to teach them that the agent of sin is the agent of
punishment.
17 And indeed your all-powerful hand which created
the world from formless matter, did not lack means
to unleash a horde of bears or savage lions on them

GREEK OLD TESTAMENT

18 ἢ νεοκτίστους θυμοῦ πλήρεις θῆρας ἀγνώστους
ἤτοι πυρπνόον φυσῶντας ἄσθμα
ἢ βρόμον λικμωμένους καπνοῦ
ἢ δεινοὺς ἀπ᾿ ὀμμάτων σπινθῆρας ἀστράπτοντας,
19 ὧν οὐ μόνον ἡ βλάβη ἠδύνατο συνεκτρῖψαι αὐτούς,
ἀλλὰ καὶ ἡ ὄψις ἐκφοβήσασα διολέσαι.
20 καὶ χωρὶς δὲ τούτων ἑνὶ πνεύματι πεσεῖν ἐδύναντο
ὑπὸ τῆς δίκης διωχθέντες
καὶ λικμηθέντες ὑπὸ πνεύματος δυνάμεώς σου·
ἀλλὰ πάντα μέτρῳ καὶ ἀριθμῷ καὶ σταθμῷ διέταξας.
21 τὸ γὰρ μεγάλως ἰσχύειν σοι πάρεστιν πάντοτε,
καὶ κράτει βραχίονός σου τίς ἀντιστήσεται;
22 ὅτι ὡς ῥοπὴ ἐκ πλαστίγγων ὅλος ὁ κόσμος ἐναντίον σου
καὶ ὡς ῥανὶς δρόσου ὀρθρινὴ κατελθοῦσα ἐπὶ γῆν.
23 ἐλεεῖς δὲ πάντας, ὅτι πάντα δύνασαι,
καὶ παρορᾷς ἁμαρτήματα ἀνθρώπων εἰς μετάνοιαν.
24 ἀγαπᾷς γὰρ τὰ ὄντα πάντα
καὶ οὐδὲν βδελύσσῃ ὧν ἐποίησας·
οὐδὲ γὰρ ἂν μισῶν τι κατεσκεύασας.
25 πῶς δὲ διέμεινεν ἄν τι, εἰ μὴ σὺ ἠθέλησας,
ἢ τὸ μὴ κληθὲν ὑπὸ σοῦ διετηρήθη;

KING JAMES VERSION

18 Or unknown wild beasts, full of rage, newly created, breathing out either a fiery vapour, or filthy scents of scattered smoke, or shooting horrible sparkles out of their eyes:

19 Whereof not only the harm might dispatch them at once, but also the terrible sight utterly destroy them.

20 Yea, and without these might they have fallen down with one blast, being persecuted of vengeance, and scattered abroad through the breath of thy power: but thou hast ordered all things in measure and number and weight.

21 For thou canst shew thy great strength at all times when thou wilt; and who may withstand the power of thine arm?

22 For the whole world before thee is as a little grain of the balance, yea, as a drop of the morning dew that falleth down upon the earth.

23 But thou hast mercy upon all; for thou canst do all things, and winkest at the sins of men, because they should amend.

24 For thou lovest all the things that are, and abhorrest nothing which thou hast made: for never wouldest thou have made any thing, if thou hadst hated it.

25 And how could any thing have endured, if it had not been thy will? or been preserved, if not called by thee?

DOUAY OLD TESTAMENT

19 Or unknown beasts of a new kind, full of rage: either breathing out a fiery vapour, or sending forth a stinking smoke, or shooting horrible sparks out of their eyes:

20 Whereof not only the hurt might be able to destroy them, but also the very sight might kill them through fear.

21 Yea and without these, they might have been slain with one blast, persecuted by their own deeds, and scattered by the breath of thy power: but thou hast ordered all things in measure, and number, and weight.

22 For great power always belonged to thee alone: and who shall resist the strength of thy arm?

23 For the whole world before thee is as the least grain of the balance, and as a drop of the morning dew, that falleth down upon the earth:

24 But thou hast mercy upon all, because thou canst do all things, and overlookest the sins of men for the sake of repentance.

25 For thou lovest all things that are, and hatest none of the things which thou hast made: for thou didst not appoint, or make any thing hating it.

26 And how could any thing endure, if thou wouldst not? or be preserved, if not called by thee.

KNOX TRANSLATION

form new creatures, of a ferocity hitherto unknown, breathing fiery breath, churning out foul fumes, terrible sparks
darting from their eyes; 20 so that men would die of fear at
their very aspect, without waiting for proof of their power to
do harm. 21 Nay, without more ado thou mightest have overthrown them with a single blast; all at once their sins should
have found them out, thy fierce breath whirled them away;
but no, all thou doest is done in exact measure, all is nicely
calculated and weighed.

22 No moment passes but thou, if thou wilt, canst shew
thyself supreme; that arm has power there is no withstand-
ing; 23 the whole world, matched against thee, is but a scruple on the balance, is but a drop of dew, falling to earth at
sunrise. 24 Only thou art all-merciful, as befits the Almighty,
and dost overlook our human slips, in hope of our repentance. 25 All things thou lovest, nor holdest any of thy creatures in abhorrence; hate and create thou couldst not, 26 nor
does aught abide save at thy will, whose summoning word

TODAY'S ENGLISH VERSION

lions. 18 You could have created new and terrible animals,
that could breathe fire or roar and send out clouds of smoke,
or shoot out fearful sparks from their eyes. 19 You could
have made animals like these that would not have to attack
those people to kill them, but could scare them to death just
by looking at them. 20 But this was not necessary. You could
have pursued them with your justice or struck them dead at
the slightest hint of your power. But you have chosen to
measure, count, and weigh everything you do.
21 You can show your great power any time you wish, and
no one can stand up against it. 22 In your sight the whole
world is a grain of sand, barely heavy enough to tip a pair of
scales, a drop of dew on the ground in the morning. 23 You
are powerful enough to do anything, but you are merciful to
everyone; you overlook our sins and give us time to repent.
24 You love everything that exists; you do not despise anything that you have made. If you had not liked it, you would
not have made it in the first place. 25 How could anything
last, if you did not want it to? How could it endure, if you

NEW REVISED STANDARD VERSION

18 or newly-created unknown beasts full of rage,
or such as breathe out fiery breath,
or belch forth a thick pall of smoke,
or flash terrible sparks from their eyes;
19 not only could the harm they did destroy people,[a]
but the mere sight of them could kill by fright.
20 Even apart from these, people[b] could fall at a single breath
when pursued by justice
and scattered by the breath of your power.
But you have arranged all things by measure and number and weight.

21 For it is always in your power to show great strength,
and who can withstand the might of your arm?
22 Because the whole world before you is like a speck that tips the scales,
and like a drop of morning dew that falls on the ground.
23 But you are merciful to all, for you can do all things,
and you overlook people's sins, so that they may repent.
24 For you love all things that exist,
and detest none of the things that you have made,
for you would not have made anything if you had hated it.
25 How would anything have endured if you had not willed it?
Or how would anything not called forth by you have been preserved?

a Gk *them* b Gk *they*

NEW AMERICAN BIBLE

18 Or new-created, wrathful, unknown beasts
to breathe forth fiery breath,
Or pour out roaring smoke,
or flash terrible sparks from their eyes.
19 Not only could these attack and completely destroy them;
even their frightful appearance itself could slay.
20 Even without these, they could have been killed at a single blast,
pursued by retribution
and winnowed out by your mighty spirit;
But you have disposed all things by measure and number and weight.
21 For with you great strength abides always;
who can resist the might of your arm?
22 Indeed, before you the whole universe is as a grain from a balance,
or a drop of morning dew come down upon the earth.
23 But you have mercy on all, because you can do all things;
and you overlook the sins of men that they may repent.
24 For you love all things that are
and loathe nothing that you have made;
for what you hated, you would not have fashioned.
25 And how could a thing remain, unless you willed it;
or be preserved, had it not been called forth by you?

NEW JERUSALEM BIBLE

18 or unknown beasts, newly created, full of rage,
breathing out fire,
or puffing out stinking smoke,
or flashing fearful sparks from their eyes,
19 beasts able not only to destroy them, being so savage,
but even to strike them dead by their terrifying appearance.
20 However, without these, one breath could have blown them over,
pursued by Justice,
whirled away by the breath of your power.
You, however, ordered all things by measure, number and weight.
21 For your great power is always at your service,
and who can withstand the might of your arm?
22 The whole world, for you, can no more than tip a balance,
like a drop of morning dew falling on the ground.
23 Yet you are merciful to all, because you are almighty,
you overlook people's sins, so that they can repent.
24 Yes, you love everything that exists,
and nothing that you have made disgusts you,
since, if you had hated something, you would not have made it.
25 And how could a thing subsist, had you not willed it?
Or how be preserved, if not called forth by you?

GREEK OLD TESTAMENT

26 φείδη δὲ πάντων, ὅτι σά ἐστιν, δέσποτα φιλόψυχε·
12 τὸ γὰρ ἄφθαρτόν σου πνεῦμά ἐστιν ἐν πᾶσιν.
2 Διὸ τοὺς παραπίπτοντας κατ' ὀλίγον ἐλέγχεις
καὶ ἐν οἷς ἁμαρτάνουσιν ὑπομιμνῄσκων νουθετεῖς,
ἵνα ἀπαλλαγέντες τῆς κακίας πιστεύσωσιν ἐπὶ σέ,
κύριε.
3 καὶ γὰρ τοὺς πάλαι οἰκήτορας τῆς ἁγίας σου γῆς
4 μισήσας ἐπὶ τῷ ἔχθιστα πράσσειν,
ἔργα φαρμακειῶν καὶ τελετὰς ἀνοσίους
5 τέκνων τε φονὰς ἀνελεήμονας
καὶ σπλαγχνοφάγον ἀνθρωπίνων σαρκῶν θοῖναν καὶ
αἵματος,
ἐκ μέσου μύστας θιάσου
6 καὶ αὐθέντας γονεῖς ψυχῶν ἀβοηθήτων,
ἐβουλήθης ἀπολέσαι διὰ χειρῶν πατέρων ἡμῶν,
7 ἵνα ἀξίαν ἀποικίαν δέξηται θεοῦ παίδων
ἡ παρὰ σοὶ πασῶν τιμιωτάτη γῆ.
8 ἀλλὰ καὶ τούτων ὡς ἀνθρώπων ἐφείσω
ἀπέστειλάς τε προδρόμους τοῦ στρατοπέδου σου
σφῆκας,
ἵνα αὐτοὺς κατὰ βραχὺ ἐξολεθρεύσωσιν.
9 οὐκ ἀδυνατῶν ἐν παρατάξει ἀσεβεῖς δικαίοις
ὑποχειρίους δοῦναι
ἢ θηρίοις δεινοῖς ἢ λόγῳ ἀποτόμῳ ὑφ' ἓν ἐκτρῖψαι,

KING JAMES VERSION

26 But thou sparest all: for they are thine, O Lord, thou lover of souls.

12 For thine incorruptible Spirit is in all things.

2 Therefore chastenest thou them by little and little that offend, and warnest them by putting them in remembrance wherein they have offended, that leaving their wickedness they may believe on thee, O Lord.

3 For it was thy will to destroy by the hands of our fathers both those old inhabitants of thy holy land,

4 Whom thou hatedst for doing most odious works of witchcrafts, and wicked sacrifices;

5 And also those merciless murderers of children, and devourers of man's flesh, and the feasts of blood,

6 With their priests out of the midst of their idolatrous crew, and the parents, that killed with their own hands souls destitute of help:

7 That the land, which thou esteemedst above all other, might receive a worthy colony of God's children.

8 Nevertheless even those thou sparedst as men, and didst send wasps, forerunners of thine host, to destroy them by little and little.

9 Not that thou wast unable to bring the ungodly under the hand of the righteous in battle, or to destroy them at once with cruel beasts, or with one rough word:

DOUAY OLD TESTAMENT

27 But thou sparest all: because they are thine, O Lord, who lovest souls.

12 O HOW good and sweet is thy spirit, O Lord, in all things!

2 And therefore thou chastisest them that err, by little and little: and admonishest them, and speakest to them, concerning the things wherein they offend: that leaving their wickedness, they may believe in thee, O Lord.

3 For those ancient inhabitants of thy holy land, whom thou didst abhor,

4 Because they did works hateful to thee by their sorceries, and wicked sacrifices,

5 And *those* merciless murderers of their own children, and eaters of men's bowels, and devourers of blood from the midst of thy consecration,

6 And *those* parents sacrificing with their own hands helpless souls, it was thy will to destroy by the hands of our parents,

7 That the land which of all is most dear to thee might receive a worthy colony of the children of God.

8 Yet even those thou sparedst as men, and didst send wasps, forerunners of thy host, to destroy them by little and little.

9 Not that thou wast unable to bring the wicked under the just by war, or by cruel beasts, or with one rough word to destroy them at once:

KNOX TRANSLATION

holds them in being. 27 They are thine, and thou sparest
them; all things that live thou lovest, thou, the Master of
them all.
12 Thy kindly influence, Lord, thy gracious influence is
all about us. 2 Tender, at the first false step, is thy
rebuke; thou dost remind and warn us that we have gone
astray, to make us leave our sinning and have faith in thee.
3 So it was with the former inhabitants of this thy holy land.
4 Good reason thou hadst to be their enemy; of what
detestable practices were they not guilty, with those sorceries
and unhallowed rites of theirs! 5 Murderers that would not
spare their own children, that feasted on human flesh,
human entrails and blood, they must have no share in thy
covenant. 6 Thy will was that our fathers should root them
out, these unnatural murderers of their own defenceless children;[a] 7 and this land, dear to thee as no other, should be
more worthily peopled by the sons of God. 8 Yet they, too,
were men, and thou wouldst deal gently with them; thou
wouldst send hornets as the vanguard of thy invading host,
to wear them down gradually.[b] 9 Not that it was beyond thy
power to give piety the mastery over godlessness by victory
in battle, by some plague of ravening monsters, or by one

a vv. 5, 6: The Greek text is here clearly wrong, and cannot be restored with certainty. In the Latin, 'they must have no share in thy covenant' is literally 'away from the midst of thy sacrament', and the word 'murderers', through an error, has been translated 'authors'. *b* See Ex. 23. 28.

TODAY'S ENGLISH VERSION

had not created it? 26 You have allowed it all to exist, O Lord, because it is yours, and you love every living thing.

12 1 Your immortal spirit is in every one of them, 2 and so you gently correct those who sin against you. You remind them of what they are doing, and warn them about it, so that they may abandon their evil ways and put their trust in you, Lord.

3-4 You hated the people who lived in your holy land long ago, because they did horrible things: they practiced magic and conducted unholy worship; 5 they killed children without mercy and ate the flesh and blood of human beings. They were initiated into secret rituals[a] 6 in which parents murdered their own defenseless children. It was your will for our ancestors to destroy these people, 7 so that the land which you consider the most precious of all lands would be a suitable home for your people. 8 But even in this you showed mercy toward their enemies, since they were only human beings. You sent hornets ahead of your army, to destroy the enemy gradually. 9 You could have allowed the righteous to destroy those ungodly people in battle; you could have wiped them out immediately with wild animals or with one harsh

[a] They were . . . rituals; *Greek unclear.*

NEW REVISED STANDARD VERSION

26 You spare all things, for they are yours, O Lord, you
who love the living.

12 For your immortal spirit is in all things.
2 Therefore you correct little by little those who
trespass,
and you remind and warn them of the things through
which they sin,
so that they may be freed from wickedness and put
their trust in you, O Lord.

3 Those who lived long ago in your holy land
4 you hated for their detestable practices,
their works of sorcery and unholy rites,
5 their merciless slaughter[a] of children,
and their sacrificial feasting on human flesh and blood.
These initiates from the midst of a heathen cult,[b]
6 these parents who murder helpless lives,
you willed to destroy by the hands of our ancestors,
7 so that the land most precious of all to you
might receive a worthy colony of the servants[c] of God.
8 But even these you spared, since they were but mortals,
and sent wasps[d] as forerunners of your army
to destroy them little by little,
9 though you were not unable to give the ungodly into
the hands of the righteous in battle,
or to destroy them at one blow by dread wild animals or
your stern word.

a Gk *slaughterers* *b* Meaning of Gk uncertain *c* Or *children*
d Or *hornets*

NEW AMERICAN BIBLE

26 But you spare all things, because they are yours, O LORD
and lover of souls,

12 for your imperishable spirit is in all things!
2 Therefore you rebuke offenders little by little,
warn them, and remind them of the sins they are
committing,
that they may abandon their wickedness and believe
in you, O LORD!
3 For, truly, the ancient inhabitants of your holy land,
4 whom you hated for deeds most odious—
Works of witchcraft and impious sacrifices;
5 a cannibal feast of human flesh
and of blood, from the midst of . . .—
These merciless murderers of children,
6 and parents who took with their own hands
defenseless lives,
You willed to destroy by the hands of our fathers,
7 that the land that is dearest of all to you
might receive a worthy colony of God's children.
8 But even these, as they were men, you spared,
and sent wasps as forerunners of your army
that they might exterminate them by degrees.
9 Not that you were without power to have the wicked
vanquished in battle by the just,
or wiped out at once by terrible beasts or by one
decisive word;

12, 5: And of blood, from the midst of . . . : this line is obscure in the current Greek text and in all extant translations.

NEW JERUSALEM BIBLE

26 No, you spare all, since all is yours, Lord, lover of life!

12 For your imperishable spirit is in everything!
2 And thus, gradually, you correct those who offend;
you admonish and remind them of how they have
sinned,
so that they may abstain from evil and trust in you,
Lord.

3 The ancient inhabitants of your holy land
4 you hated for their loathsome practices,
their acts of sorcery, and unholy rites.
5 Those ruthless murderers of children,
those eaters of entrails at feasts of human flesh and of
blood,
those initiates of secret brotherhoods,
6 those murderous parents of defenceless beings,
you determined to destroy at our ancestors' hands,
7 so that this land, dearer to you than any other,
might receive a worthy colony of God's children.
8 Even so, since these were human, you treated them
leniently,
sending hornets as forerunners of your army,
to exterminate them little by little.
9 Not that you were unable to hand the godless over to
the upright in pitched battle
or destroy them at once by savage beasts or one harsh
word;

GREEK OLD TESTAMENT

10 κρίνων δὲ κατὰ βραχὺ ἐδίδους τόπον μετανοίας
οὐκ ἀγνοῶν ὅτι πονηρὰ ἡ γένεσις αὐτῶν
καὶ ἔμφυτος ἡ κακία αὐτῶν
καὶ ὅτι οὐ μὴ ἀλλαγῇ ὁ λογισμὸς αὐτῶν εἰς τὸν αἰῶνα.
11 σπέρμα γὰρ ἦν κατηραμένον ἀπ᾽ ἀρχῆς,
οὐδὲ εὐλαβούμενός τινα ἐφ᾽ οἷς ἡμάρτανον ἄδειαν ἐδίδους.
12 τίς γὰρ ἐρεῖ Τί ἐποίησας;
ἢ τίς ἀντιστήσεται τῷ κρίματί σου;
τίς δὲ ἐγκαλέσει σοι κατὰ ἐθνῶν ἀπολωλότων ἃ σὺ ἐποίησας;
ἢ τίς εἰς κατάστασίν σοι ἐλεύσεται ἔκδικος κατὰ ἀδίκων ἀνθρώπων;
13 οὔτε γὰρ θεός ἐστιν πλὴν σοῦ, ᾧ μέλει περὶ πάντων,
ἵνα δείξῃς ὅτι οὐκ ἀδίκως ἔκρινας,
14 οὔτε βασιλεὺς ἢ τύραννος ἀντοφθαλμῆσαι δυνήσεταί σοι περὶ ὧν ἐκόλασας.
15 δίκαιος δὲ ὢν δικαίως τὰ πάντα διέπεις
αὐτὸν τὸν μὴ ὀφείλοντα κολασθῆναι καταδικάσαι
ἀλλότριον ἡγούμενος τῆς σῆς δυνάμεως.
16 ἡ γὰρ ἰσχύς σου δικαιοσύνης ἀρχή,
καὶ τὸ πάντων σε δεσπόζειν πάντων φείδεσθαί σε ποιεῖ.

KING JAMES VERSION

10 But executing thy judgments upon them by little and little, thou gavest them place of repentance, not being ignorant that they were a naughty generation, and that their malice was bred in them, and that their cogitation would never be changed.

11 For it was a cursed seed from the beginning; neither didst thou for fear of any man give them pardon for those things wherein they sinned.

12 For who shall say, What hast thou done? or who shall withstand thy judgment? or who shall accuse thee for the nations that perish, whom thou hast made? or who shall come to stand against thee, to be revenged for the unrighteous men?

13 For neither is there any God but thou that careth for all, to whom thou mightest shew that thy judgment is not unright.

14 Neither shall king or tyrant be able to set his face against thee for any whom thou hast punished.

15 Forsomuch then as thou art righteous thyself, thou orderest all things righteously: thinking it not agreeable with thy power to condemn him that hath not deserved to be punished.

16 For thy power is the beginning of righteousness, and because thou art the Lord of all, it maketh thee to be gracious unto all.

DOUAY OLD TESTAMENT

10 But executing thy judgments by degrees thou gavest them place of repentance, not being ignorant that they were a wicked generation, and their malice natural, and that their thought could never be changed.

11 For it was a cursed seed from the beginning: neither didst thou for fear of any one give pardon to their sins.

12 For who shall say to thee: What hast thou done? or who shall withstand thy judgment? or who shall come before thee *to be* a revenger of wicked men? or who shall accuse thee, if the nations perish, which thou hast made?

13 For there is no other God but thou, who hast care of all, that thou shouldst shew that thou dost not give judgment unjustly.

14 Neither shall king, nor tyrant in thy sight inquire about them whom thou hast destroyed.

15 For so much then as thou art just, thou orderest all things justly: thinking it not agreeable to thy power, to condemn him who deserveth not to be punished.

16 For thy power is the beginning of justice: and because thou art Lord of all, thou makest thyself gracious to all.

KNOX TRANSLATION

word of doom. 10 But no, their sentence should be executed
by degrees, giving them opportunity to repent; though indeed
thou knewest well that theirs was a worthless breed, of a
malice so ingrained, that they would turn aside from their ill
devices never; 11 from its beginnings, an accursed race.

Nor, if thou wast patient with the sinner, was it human
respect that persuaded thee to it. 12 Thy acts who shall question, thy doom who shall gainsay? Will some champion arise
to challenge thee on behalf of these rebels, tax thee with
unmaking the peoples thou hast made? 13 God there is none
save thou, that hast a whole world for thy province; and
shall thy justice abide our question? 14 Punish thou mayst as
punish thou wilt; king nor emperor can be bold to outface
thee. 15 So high beyond our censure, and therewithal so just
in thy dealings! To condemn the innocent were unworthy of
such majesty as thine; 16 of all justice, thy power is the true
source, universal lordship the ground of universal love!

TODAY'S ENGLISH VERSION

command. 10 But instead, you carried out your sentence
gradually, to give them a chance to repent, even though you
knew that they came from evil stock, that they had been
wicked since birth, and that they would never change their
way of thinking. 11 Their whole nation was cursed from the
start, and though you had not punished them for their sins,
it was not because you were afraid of anyone.
12 You created those wicked people, and no one can speak
in their defense or condemn you for destroying them. No one
can question what you have done or challenge your judgment. 13 All things are under your care, and there is no other
god to whom you must justify your decisions. 14 No king or
ruler on earth can accuse you of punishing those people
unfairly. 15 You are righteous, and you rule everything righteously. You have never used your power to condemn a person who does not deserve to be punished. 16 Your strength is
the source of justice. You can show mercy to everyone,
because you are the Lord of all. 17 You show your strength

NEW REVISED STANDARD VERSION

10 But judging them little by little you gave them an
opportunity to repent,
though you were not unaware that their origin[a] was evil
and their wickedness inborn,
and that their way of thinking would never change.
11 For they were an accursed race from the beginning,
and it was not through fear of anyone that you left
them unpunished for their sins.

12 For who will say, "What have you done?"
or will resist your judgment?
Who will accuse you for the destruction of nations that
you made?
Or who will come before you to plead as an advocate
for the unrighteous?
13 For neither is there any god besides you, whose care is
for all people,[b]
to whom you should prove that you have not judged
unjustly;
14 nor can any king or monarch confront you about those
whom you have punished.
15 You are righteous and you rule all things righteously,
deeming it alien to your power
to condemn anyone who does not deserve to be
punished.
16 For your strength is the source of righteousness,
and your sovereignty over all causes you to spare all.

a Or *nature* *b* Or *all things*

NEW AMERICAN BIBLE

10 But condemning them bit by bit, you gave them space
for repentance.
You were not unaware that their race was wicked
and their malice ingrained,
And that their dispositions would never change;
11 for they were a race accursed from the beginning.
Neither out of fear for anyone
did you grant amnesty for their sins.
12 For who can say to you, "What have you done?"
or who can oppose your decree?
Or when peoples perish, who can challenge you, their
maker;
or who can come into your presence as vindicator of
unjust men?
13 For neither is there any god besides you who have the
care of all,
that you need show you have not unjustly
condemned;
14 Nor can any king or prince confront you on behalf of
those you have punished.
15 But as you are just, you govern all things justly;
you regard it as unworthy of your power
to punish one who has incurred no blame.
16 For your might is the source of justice;
your mastery over all things makes you lenient to all.

NEW JERUSALEM BIBLE

10 but, by carrying out your sentences gradually, you gave
them a chance to repent,
although you knew that they were inherently evil,
innately wicked,
11 and fixed in their cast of mind;
for they were a race accursed from the beginning.
Nor was it from awe of anyone that you let their sins go
unpunished.
12 For who is there to ask, 'What have you done?'
Or who is there to disagree with your sentence?
Who to arraign you for destroying nations which you
have created?
Who to confront you by championing the wicked?
13 For there is no god, other than you, who cares for every
one,
to whom you have to prove that your sentences have
been just.
14 No more could any king or despot challenge you over
those whom you have punished.
15 For, being upright yourself, you rule the universe
uprightly,
and hold it as incompatible with your power
to condemn anyone who has not deserved to be
punished.
16 For your strength is the basis of your saving justice,
and your sovereignty over all makes you lenient to all.

GREEK OLD TESTAMENT

17 ἰσχὺν γὰρ ἐνδείκνυσαι ἀπιστούμενος ἐπὶ δυνάμεως τελειότητι
καὶ ἐν τοῖς εἰδόσι τὸ θράσος ἐξελέγχεις·
18 σὺ δὲ δεσπόζων ἰσχύος ἐν ἐπιεικείᾳ κρίνεις
καὶ μετὰ πολλῆς φειδοῦς διοικεῖς ἡμᾶς·
πάρεστιν γάρ σοι, ὅταν θέλῃς, τὸ δύνασθαι.
19 Ἐδίδαξας δέ σου τὸν λαὸν διὰ τῶν τοιούτων ἔργων
ὅτι δεῖ τὸν δίκαιον εἶναι φιλάνθρωπον,
καὶ εὐέλπιδας ἐποίησας τοὺς υἱούς σου
ὅτι διδοῖς ἐπὶ ἁμαρτήμασιν μετάνοιαν.
20 εἰ γὰρ ἐχθροὺς παίδων σου καὶ ὀφειλομένους θανάτῳ
μετὰ τοσαύτης ἐτιμωρήσω προσοχῆς καὶ διέσεως
δοὺς χρόνους καὶ τόπον, δι᾽ ὧν ἀπαλλαγῶσι τῆς κακίας,
21 μετὰ πόσης ἀκριβείας ἔκρινας τοὺς υἱούς σου,
ὧν τοῖς πατράσιν ὅρκους καὶ συνθήκας ἔδωκας ἀγαθῶν ὑποσχέσεων;
22 Ἡμᾶς οὖν παιδεύων τοὺς ἐχθροὺς ἡμῶν ἐν μυριότητι μαστιγοῖς,
ἵνα σου τὴν ἀγαθότητα μεριμνῶμεν κρίνοντες,
κρινόμενοι δὲ προσδοκῶμεν ἔλεος.

KING JAMES VERSION

17 For when men will not believe that thou art of a full power, thou shewest thy strength, and among them that know it thou makest their boldness manifest.

18 But thou, mastering thy power, judgest with equity, and orderest us with great favour: for thou mayest use power when thou wilt.

19 But by such works hast thou taught thy people that the just man should be merciful, and hast made thy children to be of a good hope that thou givest repentance for sins.

20 For if thou didst punish the enemies of thy children, and the condemned to death, with such deliberation, giving them time and place, whereby they might be delivered from their malice:

21 With how great circumspection didst thou judge thine own sons, unto whose fathers thou hast sworn, and made covenants of good promises?

22 Therefore, whereas thou dost chasten us, thou scourgest our enemies a thousand times more, to the intent that, when we judge, we should carefully think of thy goodness, and when we ourselves are judged, we should look for mercy.

DOUAY OLD TESTAMENT

17 For thou shewest thy power, when men will not believe thee to be absolute in power, and thou convincest the boldness of them that know thee not.

18 But thou being master of power, judgest with tranquillity; and with great favour disposest of us: for thy power is at hand when thou wilt.

19 But thou hast taught thy people by such works, that they must be just and humane, and hast made thy children to be of a good hope: because in judging thou givest place for repentance for sins.

20 For if thou didst punish the enemies of thy servants, and that deserved to die, with so great deliberation, giving them time and place whereby they might be changed from their wickedness:

21 With what circumspection hast thou judged thy own children, to whose parents thou hast sworn and made covenants of good promises?

22 Therefore whereas thou chastisest us, thou scourgest our enemies very many ways, to the end that when we judge we may think on thy goodness: and when we are judged, we may hope for thy mercy.

KNOX TRANSLATION

17 Only when thy omnipotence is doubted wilt thou assert thy
mastery, their rashness making manifest, who will not
acknowledge thee;[a] 18 elsewhere, with such power at thy
disposal, a lenient judge thou provest thyself, riding us with
a light rein, and keeping thy terrors in reserve.
19 Two lessons thy people were to learn from these dealings
of thine; ever should justice and mercy go hand in hand,
never should thy own children despair of fore-stalling thy
justice by repentance. 20 What, so patient, so unhurrying, in
thy vengeance on the doomed enemies of thy chosen race;
always delay, always the opportunity given them to repent of
their misdeeds; 21 and wouldst thou shew less anxious care
in trying the cause of thy own children, bound to thee from
of old by a sworn covenant so rich in mercies? 22 It is for our
instruction, then, that thou usest such exquisite care in the
punishing of our enemies;[b] judge we, let us imitate thy
clemency, abide we judgement, let us ever hope for pardon.

a The Greek text, probably by an error, gives 'who acknowledge thee'.
b The first half of this verse is ordinarily rendered, 'In chastening us, thou dost scourge our enemies ten thousandfold'; but it will be seen that such considerations are out of harmony with the rest of the sentence.

TODAY'S ENGLISH VERSION

when people doubt that your power is perfect, and you punish anyone who knows your power but dares to ignore it.
18 Even though you have absolute power, you are a merciful
judge. You could take action against us whenever you like,
but instead, you rule us with great patience.
19 By the things you have done you have taught your people that a person who is righteous must also be kind. You
have given your people abundant hope by allowing them to
repent of their sins. 20 You were very careful and patient in
punishing your people's enemies; even when they deserved
to die, you gave them every opportunity to give up their sinful ways. 21 But you judged your own people very strictly,
even though you had made covenants with their ancestors
and had solemnly promised to give them good things.
22 Yes, you punish us, but you punish our enemies ten
thousand times more, so that when we judge others, we may
remember your goodness, and when we are being judged, we
may look for mercy.

NEW REVISED STANDARD VERSION

17 For you show your strength when people doubt the
completeness of your power,
and you rebuke any insolence among those who know
it.[a]
18 Although you are sovereign in strength, you judge with
mildness,
and with great forbearance you govern us;
for you have power to act whenever you choose.

19 Through such works you have taught your people
that the righteous must be kind,
and you have filled your children with good hope,
because you give repentance for sins.
20 For if you punished with such great care and
indulgence[b]
the enemies of your servants[c] and those deserving of
death,
granting them time and opportunity to give up their
wickedness,
21 with what strictness you have judged your children,
to whose ancestors you gave oaths and covenants full
of good promises!
22 So while chastening us you scourge our enemies ten
thousand times more,
so that, when we judge, we may meditate upon your
goodness,
and when we are judged, we may expect mercy.

a Meaning of Gk uncertain *b* Other ancient authorities lack *and indulgence*; others read *and entreaty* *c* Or *children*

NEW AMERICAN BIBLE

17 For you show your might when the perfection of your
power is disbelieved;
and in those who know you, you rebuke temerity.
18 But though you are master of might, you judge with
clemency,
and with much lenience you govern us;
for power, whenever you will, attends you.
19 And you taught your people, by these deeds,
that those who are just must be kind;
And you gave your sons good ground for hope
that you would permit repentance for their sins.
20 For these were enemies of your servants, doomed to
death;
yet, while you punished them with such solicitude
and pleading,
granting time and opportunity to abandon
wickedness,
21 With what exactitude you judged your sons,
to whose fathers you gave the sworn covenants of
goodly promises!
22 Us, therefore, you chastise, and our enemies with a
thousand blows you punish,
that we may think earnestly of your goodness when
we judge,
and, when being judged, may look for mercy.

NEW JERUSALEM BIBLE

17 You show your strength when people will not believe in
your absolute power,
and you confound any insolence in those who do know
it.
18 But you, controlling your strength, are mild in
judgement, and govern us with great lenience,
for you have only to will, and your power is there.
19 By acting thus, you have taught your people
that the upright must be kindly to his fellows,
and you have given your children the good hope
that after sins you will grant repentance.
20 For, if with such care and indulgence you have
punished
your children's enemies, though doomed to death,
and have given them time and place to be rid of their
wickedness,
21 with what exact attention have you not judged your
children,
to whose ancestors, by oaths and covenants, you made
such generous promises?
22 Thus, you instruct us, when you punish our enemies in
moderation,
that we should reflect on your kindness when we judge,
and, when we are judged, we should look for mercy.

GREEK OLD TESTAMENT

23 ὅθεν καὶ τοὺς ἐν ἀφροσύνῃ ζωῆς βιώσαντας ἀδίκως
διὰ τῶν ἰδίων ἐβασάνισας βδελυγμάτων·
24 καὶ γὰρ τῶν πλάνης ὁδῶν μακρότερον ἐπλανήθησαν
θεοὺς ὑπολαμβάνοντες τὰ καὶ ἐν ζῴοις τῶν αἰσχρῶν ἄτιμα
νηπίων δίκην ἀφρόνων ψευσθέντες.
25 διὰ τοῦτο ὡς παισὶν ἀλογίστοις
τὴν κρίσιν εἰς ἐμπαιγμὸν ἔπεμψας.
26 οἱ δὲ παιγνίοις ἐπιτιμήσεως μὴ νουθετηθέντες
ἀξίαν θεοῦ κρίσιν πειράσουσιν.
27 ἐφ᾽ οἷς γὰρ αὐτοὶ πάσχοντες ἠγανάκτουν,
ἐπὶ τούτοις, οὓς ἐδόκουν θεούς, ἐν αὐτοῖς κολαζόμενοι
ἰδόντες, ὃν πάλαι ἠρνοῦντο εἰδέναι, θεὸν ἐπέγνωσαν ἀληθῆ·
διὸ καὶ τὸ τέρμα τῆς καταδίκης ἐπ᾽ αὐτοὺς ἐπῆλθεν.

13 Μάταιοι μὲν γὰρ πάντες ἄνθρωποι φύσει, οἷς παρῆν θεοῦ ἀγνωσία
καὶ ἐκ τῶν ὁρωμένων ἀγαθῶν οὐκ ἴσχυσαν εἰδέναι τὸν ὄντα
οὔτε τοῖς ἔργοις προσέχοντες ἐπέγνωσαν τὸν τεχνίτην,
2 ἀλλ᾽ ἢ πῦρ ἢ πνεῦμα ἢ ταχινὸν ἀέρα
ἢ κύκλον ἄστρων ἢ βίαιον ὕδωρ
ἢ φωστῆρας οὐρανοῦ πρυτάνεις κόσμου θεοὺς ἐνόμισαν.

KING JAMES VERSION

23 Wherefore, whereas men have lived dissolutely and unrighteously, thou hast tormented them with their own abominations.

24 For they went astray very far in the ways of error, and held them for gods, which even among the beasts of their enemies were despised, being deceived, as children of no understanding.

25 Therefore unto them, as to children without the use of reason, thou didst send a judgment to mock them.

26 But they that would not be reformed by that correction, wherein he dallied with them, shall feel a judgment worthy of God.

27 For, look, for what things they grudged, when they were punished, that is, for them whom they thought to be gods; [now] being punished in them, when they saw it, they acknowledged him to be the true God, whom before they denied to know; and therefore came extreme damnation upon them.

13 Surely vain are all men by nature, who are ignorant of God, and could not out of the good things that are seen know him that is: neither by considering the works did they acknowledge the workmaster;

2 But deemed either fire, or wind, or the swift air, or the circle of the stars, or the violent water, or the lights of heaven, to be the gods which govern the world.

DOUAY OLD TESTAMENT

23 Wherefore thou hast also greatly tormented them who in their life have lived foolishly and unjustly, by the same things which they worshipped.

24 For they went astray for a long time in the ways of error, holding those things for gods which are the most worthless among beasts, living after the manner of children without understanding.

25 Therefore thou hast sent a judgment upon them as senseless children to mock them.

26 But they that were not amended by mockeries and reprehensions, experienced the worthy judgment of God.

27 For seeing with indignation that they suffered by those very things which they took for gods, when they were destroyed by the same, they acknowledged him the true God, whom in time past they denied that they knew: for which cause the end also of their condemnation came upon them.

13 BUT all men are vain, in whom there is not the knowledge of God: and who by these good things that are seen, could not understand him that is, neither by attending to the works have acknowledged who was the workman:

2 But have imagined either the fire, or the wind, or the swift air, or the circle of the stars, or the great water, or the sun and moon, to be the gods that rule the world.

KNOX TRANSLATION

23 And so it was that thou didst plague the Egyptians,[a]
that were knaves and fools both; their own false gods should
be the undoing of them. 24 This was the worst error of all
their erring, that they worshipped the meanest of beasts as
gods; silly children had been no more credulous. 25 Why
then, these silly children should have play-time penalties
first; 26 of those play-time penalties if they took no heed,
then at last they should feel how a God can punish.
27 Humiliated they well might be at those sufferings of theirs,
the very gods they worshipped the instruments of their distress; a sight enough to convince them that he was the true God, whom all this while they had rejected! But no, they must needs bring upon themselves the full rigours of justice.

13 What folly it argues in man's nature, this ignorance
of God! So much good seen, and he, who is existent
Good,[b] not known! Should they not learn to recognise the
Artificer by the contemplation of his works? 2 Instead, they
have pointed us to fire, or wind, or to the nimble air, wheeling stars, or tempestuous waves, or sun and moon, and
made gods of them, to rule the world! 3 Perhaps the beauty

a The word 'Egyptians' does not occur in the original, but the reference of this passage is almost certainly to them; cf. 11. 15 above. For 'didst plague' the Latin version has, 'didst inflict the utmost torments upon', but this misses the sense. The plagues of lice, flies, locusts, etc., are here contrasted, as being comparatively light, with the last two plagues, to be mentioned in chs. 17 and 18. *b* Or perhaps simply, 'who is'.

TODAY'S ENGLISH VERSION

23 And so you tormented those who were foolish enough to
live wickedly—you tormented them with the horrible things
they worshiped. 24 They had wandered far away from the
truth and worshiped the most disgusting and horrible animals. They were deceived as easily as little children. 25 And
so you punished them for their stupidity, and your judgment
made them look like fools. 26 It was a light punishment, but
those who pay no attention to such warnings deserve to feel
the full weight of God's judgment. 27 When they were punished with those creatures they considered gods, they became
bitterly disillusioned and recognized that the true God was
the one they had always refused to acknowledge. That is
why they suffered the final punishment.

13 Anyone who does not know God is simply foolish.
Such people look at the good things around them
and still fail to see the living God. They have studied the
things he made, but they have not recognized the one who
made them. 2 Instead, they suppose that the gods who rule
the world are fire or wind or storm or the circling stars or
rushing water or the heavenly bodies. 3 People were so

NEW REVISED STANDARD VERSION

23 Therefore those who lived unrighteously, in a life of folly,
you tormented through their own abominations.
24 For they went far astray on the paths of error,
accepting as gods those animals that even their
enemies[a] despised;
they were deceived like foolish infants.
25 Therefore, as though to children who cannot reason,
you sent your judgment to mock them.
26 But those who have not heeded the warning of mild
rebukes
will experience the deserved judgment of God.
27 For when in their suffering they became incensed
at those creatures that they had thought to be gods,
being punished by means of them,
they saw and recognized as the true God the one whom
they had before refused to know.
Therefore the utmost condemnation came upon them.

13 For all people who were ignorant of God were foolish
by nature;
and they were unable from the good things that are
seen to know the one who exists,
nor did they recognize the artisan while paying heed to
his works;
2 but they supposed that either fire or wind or swift air,
or the circle of the stars, or turbulent water,
or the luminaries of heaven were the gods that rule the
world.

a Gk *they*

NEW AMERICAN BIBLE

23 Hence those unjust also, who lived a life of folly,
you tormented through their own abominations.
24 For they went far astray in the paths of error,
taking for gods the worthless and disgusting among
beasts,
deceived like senseless infants.
25 Therefore as though upon unreasoning children,
you sent your judgment on them as a mockery;
26 But they who took no heed of punishment which was
but child's play
were to experience a condemnation worthy of God.
27 For in the things through which they suffered distress,
since they were tortured by the very things they
deemed gods,
They saw and recognized the true God
whom before they had refused to know;
with this, their final condemnation came upon them.

13 For all men were by nature foolish who were in
ignorance of God,
and who from the good things seen did not succeed
in knowing him who is,
and from studying the works did not discern the
artisan;
2 But either fire, or wind, or the swift air,
or the circuit of the stars, or the mighty water,
or the luminaries of heaven, the governors of the
world, they considered gods.

NEW JERUSALEM BIBLE

23 And this is why people leading foolish and wicked lives
were tortured by you with their own abominations;
24 for they had strayed too far on the paths of error
by taking the vilest and most despicable of animals for
gods,
being deluded like silly little children.
25 So, as to children with no sense,
you gave them a sentence making fools of them.
26 Those, however, who would not take warning from a
mocking reproof
were soon to endure a sentence worthy of God.
27 The creatures that made them suffer and against which
they protested,
those very creatures that they had taken for gods and
by which they were punished they saw in their
true light;
and he whom hitherto they had refused to know, they
realised was true God.
And this is why the final condemnation fell on them.

13 Yes, naturally stupid are all who are unaware of God,
and who, from good things seen, have not been able
to discover Him-who-is,
or, by studying the works, have not recognised the
Artificer.
2 Fire, however, or wind, or the swift air,
the sphere of the stars, impetuous water, heaven's lamps,
are what they have held to be the gods who govern the
world.

GREEK OLD TESTAMENT

3 ὧν εἰ μὲν τῇ καλλονῇ τερπόμενοι ταῦτα θεοὺς
ὑπελάμβανον,
γνώτωσαν πόσῳ τούτων ὁ δεσπότης ἐστὶ βελτίων,
ὁ γὰρ τοῦ κάλλους γενεσιάρχης ἔκτισεν αὐτά·
4 εἰ δὲ δύναμιν καὶ ἐνέργειαν ἐκπλαγέντες,
νοησάτωσαν ἀπ' αὐτῶν πόσῳ ὁ κατασκευάσας αὐτὰ
δυνατώτερός ἐστιν·
5 ἐκ γὰρ μεγέθους καὶ καλλονῆς κτισμάτων
ἀναλόγως ὁ γενεσιουργὸς αὐτῶν θεωρεῖται.
6 ἀλλ' ὅμως ἐπὶ τούτοις μέμψις ἐστὶν ὀλίγη,
καὶ γὰρ αὐτοὶ τάχα πλανῶνται
θεὸν ζητοῦντες καὶ θέλοντες εὑρεῖν·
7 ἐν γὰρ τοῖς ἔργοις αὐτοῦ ἀναστρεφόμενοι διερευνῶσιν
καὶ πείθονται τῇ ὄψει, ὅτι καλὰ τὰ βλεπόμενα.
8 πάλιν δ' οὐδ' αὐτοὶ συγγνωστοί·
9 εἰ γὰρ τοσοῦτον ἴσχυσαν εἰδέναι
ἵνα δύνωνται στοχάσασθαι τὸν αἰῶνα,
τὸν τούτων δεσπότην πῶς τάχιον οὐχ εὗρον;
10 Ταλαίπωροι δὲ καὶ ἐν νεκροῖς αἱ ἐλπίδες αὐτῶν,
οἵτινες ἐκάλεσαν θεοὺς ἔργα χειρῶν ἀνθρώπων,
χρυσὸν καὶ ἄργυρον τέχνης ἐμμελέτημα
καὶ ἀπεικάσματα ζῴων
ἢ λίθον ἄχρηστον χειρὸς ἔργον ἀρχαίας.

KING JAMES VERSION

3 With whose beauty if they being delighted took them to be gods; let them know how much better the Lord of them is: for the first author of beauty hath created them.

4 But if they were astonished at their power and virtue, let them understand by them, how much mightier he is that made them.

5 For by the greatness and beauty of the creatures proportionably the maker of them is seen.

6 But yet for this they are the less to be blamed: for they peradventure err, seeking God, and desirous to find him.

7 For being conversant in his works they search *him* diligently, and believe their sight: because the things are beautiful that are seen.

8 Howbeit neither are they to be pardoned.

9 For if they were able to know so much, that they could aim at the world; how did they not sooner find out the Lord thereof?

10 But miserable are they, and in dead things is their hope, who called them gods, which are the works of men's hands, gold and silver, to shew art in, and resemblances of beasts, or a stone good for nothing, the work of an ancient hand.

DOUAY OLD TESTAMENT

3 With whose beauty, if they, being delighted, took them to be gods: let them know how much the Lord of them is more beautiful than they: for the first author of beauty made all those things.

4 Or if they admired their power and their effects, let them understand by them, that he that made them, is mightier than they:

5 For by the greatness of the beauty, and of the creature, the creator of them may be seen, so as to be known thereby.

6 But yet as to these they are less to be blamed. For they perhaps err, seeking God, and desirous to find him.

7 For being conversant among his works, they search: and they are persuaded that the things are good which are seen.

8 But then again they are not to be pardoned.

9 For if they were able to know so much as to make a judgment of the world: how did they not more easily find out the Lord thereof?

10 But unhappy are they, and their hope is among the dead, who have called gods the works of the hands of men, gold and silver, the inventions of art, and the resemblances of beasts, or an unprofitable stone the work of an ancient hand.

KNOX TRANSLATION

of such things bewitched them into mistaking it for divinity?
Ay, but what of him who is Master of them all; what excellence must be his, the Author of all beauty, that could make
them! 4 Or was it power, and power's exercise, that awoke
their wonderment? Why then, how many times greater must
he be, who contrived it! 5 Such great beauty[a] even creatures
have, reason is well able to contemplate the Source from
which these perfections came.
6 Yet, if we find fault with men like these, their fault is little by comparison; err they may, but their desire is to find
God, and it is in that search they err. 7 They stop short in
their enquiry at the contemplation of his creatures, trusting
only in the senses, that find such beauty there. 8 Excuse
them, then, we may not; 9 if their thoughts could reach far
enough to form a judgement about the world around them,
how is it they found, on the way, no trace of him who is
Master of it? 10 But there are men more wretched yet, men
who repose all their confidence in a world of shadows. They
give the name of god to what is made by human art, gold
and silver that human workmanship has turned into the
likeness of living things, blocks of senseless stone that
human hands have carved, long ago.

a Some manuscripts of the Greek read, 'such greatness and beauty'.

TODAY'S ENGLISH VERSION

delighted with the beauty of these things that they thought
they must be gods, but they should have realized that these
things have a master and that he is much greater than all of
them, for he is the creator of beauty, and he created them.
4 Since people are amazed at the power of these things, and
how they behave, they ought to learn from them that their
maker is far more powerful. 5 When we realize how vast and
beautiful the creation is, we are learning about the Creator at
the same time.

6 But maybe we are too harsh with these people. After all,
they may have really wanted to find God, but couldn't.
7 Surrounded by God's works, they keep on looking at them,
until they are finally convinced that because the things they
see are so beautiful, they must be gods. 8 But still, these people really have no excuse. 9 If they had enough intelligence
to speculate about the nature of the universe, why did they
never find the Lord of all things?

10 But the most miserable people of all are those who rest
their hopes on lifeless things, who worship things that have
been made by human hands—images of animals artistically
made from gold and silver, or some useless stone carved by

NEW REVISED STANDARD VERSION

3 If through delight in the beauty of these things people
assumed them to be gods,
let them know how much better than these is their Lord,
for the author of beauty created them.
4 And if people[a] were amazed at their power and working,
let them perceive from them
how much more powerful is the one who formed them.
5 For from the greatness and beauty of created things
comes a corresponding perception of their Creator.
6 Yet these people are little to be blamed,
for perhaps they go astray
while seeking God and desiring to find him.
7 For while they live among his works, they keep
searching,
and they trust in what they see, because the things that
are seen are beautiful.
8 Yet again, not even they are to be excused;
9 for if they had the power to know so much
that they could investigate the world,
how did they fail to find sooner the Lord of these things?

10 But miserable, with their hopes set on dead things, are
those
who give the name "gods" to the works of human hands,
gold and silver fashioned with skill,
and likenesses of animals,
or a useless stone, the work of an ancient hand.

a Gk *they*

NEW AMERICAN BIBLE

3 Now if out of joy in their beauty they thought them
gods,
let them know how far more excellent is the Lord
than these;
for the original source of beauty fashioned them.
4 Or if they were struck by their might and energy,
let them from these things realize how much more
powerful is he who made them.
5 For from the greatness and the beauty of created things
their original author, by analogy, is seen.
6 But yet, for these the blame is less;
For they indeed have gone astray perhaps,
though they seek God and wish to find him.
7 For they search busily among his works,
but are distracted by what they see, because the
things seen are fair.
8 But again, not even these are pardonable.
9 For if they so far succeeded in knowledge
that they could speculate about the world,
how did they not more quickly find its LORD?

10 But doomed are they, and in dead things are their
hopes,
who termed gods things made by human hands:
Gold and silver, the product of art, and likenesses of
beasts,
or useless stone, the work of an ancient hand.

NEW JERUSALEM BIBLE

3 If, charmed by their beauty, they have taken these for
gods,
let them know how much the Master of these excels
them,
since he was the very source of beauty that created
them.
4 And if they have been impressed by their power and
energy,
let them deduce from these how much mightier is he
that has formed them,
5 since through the grandeur and beauty of the creatures
we may, by analogy, contemplate their Author.

6 Small blame, however, attaches to them,
for perhaps they go astray
only in their search for God and their eagerness to find
him;
7 familiar with his works, they investigate them
and fall victim to appearances, seeing so much beauty.
8 But even so, they have no excuse:
9 if they are capable of acquiring enough knowledge
to be able to investigate the world,
how have they been so slow to find its Master?
10 But wretched are they, with their hopes set on dead
things,
who have given the title of gods to human artefacts,
gold or silver, skilfully worked,
figures of animals,
or useless stone, carved by some hand long ago.

GREEK OLD TESTAMENT

11 εἰ δὲ καί τις ὑλοτόμος τέκτων εὐκίνητον φυτὸν
ἐκπρίσας
περιέξυσεν εὐμαθῶς πάντα τὸν φλοιὸν αὐτοῦ
καὶ τεχνησάμενος εὐπρεπῶς
κατεσκεύασεν χρήσιμον σκεῦος εἰς ὑπηρεσίαν ζωῆς,
12 τὰ δὲ ἀποβλήματα τῆς ἐργασίας
εἰς ἑτοιμασίαν τροφῆς ἀναλώσας ἐνεπλήσθη,
13 τὸ δὲ ἐξ αὐτῶν ἀπόβλημα εἰς οὐθὲν εὔχρηστον,
ξύλον σκολιὸν καὶ ὄζοις συμπεφυκός,
λαβὼν ἔγλυψεν ἐν ἐπιμελείᾳ ἀργίας αὐτοῦ
καὶ ἐμπειρίᾳ συνέσεως ἐτύπωσεν αὐτό,
ἀπείκασεν αὐτὸ εἰκόνι ἀνθρώπου
14 ἢ ζῴῳ τινὶ εὐτελεῖ ὡμοίωσεν αὐτὸ
καταχρίσας μίλτῳ καὶ φύκει ἐρυθήνας χρόαν αὐτοῦ
καὶ πᾶσαν κηλῖδα τὴν ἐν αὐτῷ καταχρίσας
15 καὶ ποιήσας αὐτῷ αὐτοῦ ἄξιον οἴκημα
ἐν τοίχῳ ἔθηκεν αὐτὸ ἀσφαλισάμενος σιδήρῳ.
16 ἵνα μὲν οὖν μὴ καταπέσῃ, προενόησεν αὐτοῦ
εἰδὼς ὅτι ἀδυνατεῖ ἑαυτῷ βοηθῆσαι·
καὶ γάρ ἐστιν εἰκὼν καὶ χρείαν ἔχει βοηθείας.
17 περὶ δὲ κτημάτων καὶ γάμων αὐτοῦ καὶ τέκνων
προσευχόμενος
οὐκ αἰσχύνεται τῷ ἀψύχῳ προσλαλῶν
καὶ περὶ μὲν ὑγιείας τὸ ἀσθενὲς ἐπικαλεῖται,
18 περὶ δὲ ζωῆς τὸ νεκρὸν ἀξιοῖ,
περὶ δὲ ἐπικουρίας τὸ ἀπειρότατον ἱκετεύει,
περὶ δὲ ὁδοιπορίας τὸ μηδὲ βάσει χρῆσθαι δυνάμενον,

DOUAY OLD TESTAMENT

11 Or if an artist, a carpenter, hath cut down a tree proper for his use in the wood, and skilfully taken off all the bark thereof, and with his art, diligently formeth a vessel profitable for the common uses of life,

12 And useth the chips of his work to dress his meat:

13 And taking what was left thereof, which is good for nothing, being a crooked piece of wood, and full of knots, carveth it diligently when he hath nothing else to do, and by the skill of his art fashioneth it and maketh it like the image of a man:

14 Or the resemblance of some beast, laying it over with vermilion, and painting it red, and covering every spot that is in it:

15 And maketh a convenient dwelling place for it, and setting it in a wall, and fastening it with iron,

16 Providing for it, lest it should fall, knowing that it is unable to help itself: for it is an image, and hath need of help.

17 And then maketh prayer to it, inquiring concerning his substance, and his children, or his marriage. And he is not ashamed to speak to that which hath no life:

18 And for health he maketh supplication to the weak, and for life prayeth to that which is dead, and for help calleth upon that which is unprofitable:

19 And for a good journey he petitioneth him that cannot

KING JAMES VERSION

11 Now a carpenter that felleth timber, after he hath sawn down a tree meet for the purpose, and taken off all the bark skilfully round about, and hath wrought it handsomely, and made a vessel thereof fit for the service of man's life;

12 And after spending the refuse of his work to dress his meat, hath filled himself;

13 And taking the very refuse among those which served to no use, being a crooked piece of wood, and full of knots, hath carved it diligently, when he had nothing else to do, and formed it by the skill of his understanding, and fashioned it to the image of a man;

14 Or made it like some vile beast, laying it over with vermilion, and with paint colouring it red, and covering every spot therein;

15 And when he had made a convenient room for it, set it in a wall, and made it fast with iron:

16 For he provided for it that it might not fall, knowing that it was unable to help itself; for it is an image, and hath need of help:

17 Then maketh he prayer for his goods, for his wife and children, and is not ashamed to speak to that which hath no life.

18 For health he calleth upon that which is weak: for life prayeth to that which is dead: for aid humbly beseecheth that which hath least means to help: and for a good journey he asketh of that which cannot set a foot forward:

KNOX TRANSLATION

11 What would you? Here is a craftsman in wood has been
to the forest and sawed off a fine straight branch; deftly he
strips off the bark, and fashions, with patient skill, some
piece of carpentry apt for man's needs. 12 As for the chips in
his workshop, they cook his meal for him, to eat and take his
fill. 13 But one more piece of refuse wood is left, that is fit for
nothing; so crooked is it and so gnarled. See him, in an idle
moment, pick it up and spend his leisure carving it! A master
craftsman this; ere long it has taken shape, made into a
man's likeness; 14 or it may be he gives it the form of a
senseless beast. And now he paints it with ochre; ruddled it
must be till all its native colour is lost, all its faults hidden
away. 15 That done, he must find a suitable room to house
it, and there lets it into the wall, making it fast with iron
clamps. 16 No pains does he spare to keep it from falling; fall
if it does, it shall find no remedy; please you, this is but an
image, and cannot shift for itself!
17 And so, unashamed, for home and children and wife he
utters his prayer, addressing himself all the while to a senseless thing. 18 A weak, foolish thing, and for health he asks
it; dead, and he will have life of it; shiftless, and he will have
aid of it. 19 How should it set forward his journeyings, that

TODAY'S ENGLISH VERSION

someone years ago. 11 A skilled woodworker may saw down
some suitable tree, carefully strip off the bark, and then,
with skillful craftsmanship, make from it an object that will
serve some useful purpose. 12 He will take the leftover pieces
and use them as firewood to cook a meal that he can sit
down to and enjoy. 13 But among that scrap wood he may
take one piece that isn't good for anything—maybe it's
crooked and full of knots—and carefully carve it in his
leisure time, using spare moments to shape it into the crude
image of a person, 14 or maybe of some worthless animal.
He paints it all over with red, covering up every flaw in the
work. 15 Then he prepares a suitable place in the wall for it
and fastens it in place with iron nails. 16 He is careful to
keep it from falling, because he knows it is only an idol and
needs help; it cannot help itself. 17 But he is not ashamed to
pray to this lifeless thing about his marriage, his children,
and his possessions. 18 It is weak, but he prays to it for
health. It is dead, but he prays to it for life. It has no experience, but he prays to it for help. It cannot walk, but he prays

NEW REVISED STANDARD VERSION

11 A skilled woodcutter may saw down a tree easy to handle
and skillfully strip off all its bark,
and then with pleasing workmanship
make a useful vessel that serves life's needs,
12 and burn the cast-off pieces of his work
to prepare his food, and eat his fill.
13 But a cast-off piece from among them, useful for nothing,
a stick crooked and full of knots,
he takes and carves with care in his leisure,
and shapes it with skill gained in idleness;[a]
he forms it in the likeness of a human being,
14 or makes it like some worthless animal,
giving it a coat of red paint and coloring its surface red
and covering every blemish in it with paint;
15 then he makes a suitable niche for it,
and sets it in the wall, and fastens it there with iron.
16 He takes thought for it, so that it may not fall,
because he knows that it cannot help itself,
for it is only an image and has need of help.
17 When he prays about possessions and his marriage and
children,
he is not ashamed to address a lifeless thing.
18 For health he appeals to a thing that is weak;
for life he prays to a thing that is dead;
for aid he entreats a thing that is utterly inexperienced;
for a prosperous journey, a thing that cannot take a
step;

a Other ancient authorities read *with intelligent skill*

NEW AMERICAN BIBLE

11 A carpenter may saw out a suitable tree
and skillfully scrape off all its bark,
And deftly plying his art,
produce something fit for daily use,
12 and use up the refuse from his handiwork in
preparing his food, and have his fill;
13 Then the good-for-nothing refuse from these remnants,
crooked wood grown full of knots,
he takes and carves to occupy his spare time.
This wood he models with listless skill,
and patterns it on the image of a man
14 or makes it resemble some worthless beast.
When he has daubed it with red and crimsoned its
surface with red stain,
and daubed over every blemish in it,
15 He makes a fitting shrine for it
and puts it on the wall, fastening it with a nail.
16 Thus lest it fall down he provides for it,
knowing that it cannot help itself;
for, truly, it is an image and needs help.
17 But when he prays about his goods or marriage or
children,
he is not ashamed to address the thing without a
soul.
And for vigor he invokes the powerless;
18 and for life he entreats the dead;
And for aid he beseeches the wholly incompetent,
and about travel, something that cannot even walk.

NEW JERUSALEM BIBLE

11 Take a woodcutter. He fells a suitable tree,
neatly strips off the bark all over
and then with admirable skill
works the wood into an object useful in daily life.
12 The bits left over from his work
he uses for cooking his food, then eats his fill.
13 There is still a good-for-nothing bit left over,
a gnarled and knotted billet:
he takes it and whittles it with the concentration of his
leisure hours,
he shapes it with the skill of experience,
he gives it a human shape
14 or perhaps he makes it into some vile animal,
smears it with ochre, paints its surface red,
coats over all its blemishes.
15 He next makes a worthy home for it,
lets it into the wall, fixes it with an iron clamp.
16 Thus he makes sure that it will not fall down—
being well aware that it cannot help itself,
since it is only an image, and needs to be helped.
17 And yet, if he wishes to pray for his goods, for his
marriage, for his children,
he does not blush to harangue this lifeless thing—
for health, he invokes what is weak,
18 for life, he pleads with what is dead,
for help, he goes begging to total inexperience,
for a journey, what cannot even use its feet,

GREEK OLD TESTAMENT

19 περὶ δὲ πορισμοῦ καὶ ἐργασίας καὶ χειρῶν ἐπιτυχίας
τὸ ἀδρανέστατον ταῖς χερσὶν εὐδράνειαν αἰτεῖται.

14 Πλοῦν τις πάλιν στελλόμενος καὶ ἄγρια μέλλων
διοδεύειν κύματα
τοῦ φέροντος αὐτὸν πλοίου σαθρότερον ξύλον
ἐπιβοᾶται.
2 ἐκεῖνο μὲν γὰρ ὄρεξις πορισμῶν ἐπενόησεν,
τεχνῖτις δὲ σοφία κατεσκεύασεν·
3 ἡ δὲ σή, πάτερ, διακυβερνᾷ πρόνοια,
ὅτι ἔδωκας καὶ ἐν θαλάσσῃ ὁδὸν
καὶ ἐν κύμασι τρίβον ἀσφαλῆ
4 δεικνὺς ὅτι δύνασαι ἐκ παντὸς σῴζειν,
ἵνα κἂν ἄνευ τέχνης τις ἐπιβῇ.
5 θέλεις δὲ μὴ ἀργὰ εἶναι τὰ τῆς σοφίας σου ἔργα·
διὰ τοῦτο καὶ ἐλαχίστῳ ξύλῳ πιστεύουσιν ἄνθρωποι
ψυχὰς
καὶ διελθόντες κλύδωνα σχεδίᾳ διεσώθησαν.
6 καὶ ἀρχῆς γὰρ ἀπολλυμένων ὑπερηφάνων γιγάντων
ἡ ἐλπὶς τοῦ κόσμου ἐπὶ σχεδίας καταφυγοῦσα
ἀπέλιπεν αἰῶνι σπέρμα γενέσεως τῇ σῇ κυβερνηθεῖσα
χειρί.
7 εὐλόγηται γὰρ ξύλον, δι᾽ οὗ γίνεται δικαιοσύνη·

KING JAMES VERSION

19 And for gaining and getting, and for good success of his hands, asketh ability to do of him, that is most unable to do any thing.

14 Again, one preparing himself to sail, and about to pass through the raging waves, calleth upon a piece of wood more rotten than the vessel that carrieth him.

2 For verily desire of gain devised that, and the workman built it by his skill.

3 But thy providence, O Father, governeth it: for thou hast made a way in the sea, and a safe path in the waves;

4 Shewing that thou canst save from all danger: yea, though a man went to sea without art.

5 Nevertheless thou wouldest not that the works of thy wisdom should be idle, and therefore do men commit their lives to a small piece of wood, and passing the rough sea in a weak vessel are saved.

6 For in the old time also, when the proud giants perished, the hope of the world governed by thy hand escaped in a weak vessel, and left to all ages a seed of generation.

7 For blessed is the wood whereby righteousness cometh.

DOUAY OLD TESTAMENT

walk: and for getting, and for working, and for the event of all things he asketh him that is unable to do any thing.

14 AGAIN, another designing to sail, and beginning to make his voyage through the raging waves, calleth upon a piece of wood more frail than the wood that carrieth him.

2 For this the desire of gain devised, and the workman built it by his skill.

3 But thy providence, O Father, governeth it: for thou hast made a way even in the sea, and a most sure path among the waves,

4 Shewing that thou art able to save out of all things, yea though a man went to sea without art.

5 But that the works of thy wisdom might not be idle: therefore men also trust their lives even to a little wood, and passing over the sea by ship are saved.

6 And from the beginning also when the proud giants perished, the hope of the world fleeing to a vessel, which was governed by thy hand, left to the world seed of generation.

7 For blessed is the wood, by which justice cometh.

KNOX TRANSLATION

cannot walk? What service should it do, if trade he want, or skill, or good fortune, that is every way unserviceable?

14 Nay, here is one that will go a-voyaging, the wild
waves for his pathway, and perishable wood to carry
him, yet he makes his prayer to a piece of wood more perishable yet! 2 As for the ship's timbers, it was man's covetousness that made the need for them, and man's skill that fashioned them; 3 but it is thy fatherly Providence that brings her
safe to port; thou hast made the sea into a high road men
may travel by without harm, 4 as if thou wouldst prove to us
how strong is thy protection, though the sailor have little
skill. 5 So careful art thou that the gifts thy wisdom affords
us should not go unused; man ventures his life on a few
planks, and the frail barque gives him safe conduct across
the waves. 6 And what marvel? At the beginning of all, when
the giants perished in their pride, was not such a barque the
refuge of all the world's hopes? Yet thy hand was at the
helm, and the seed of life was saved for posterity. 7 A blessing on the wood that can so procure salvation! 8 But yonder

TODAY'S ENGLISH VERSION

to it for a successful journey. 19 Its hands have no power,
but he asks it to help him—in business, in making money,
and in his work.

14 In the same way, a man getting ready to sail on the
raging sea will call for help from a piece of wood that
is not as strong as the ship he is about to board. 2 Someone
designed the ship out of a desire for profit, and a craftsman
built it with skill. 3 But it is your care, O Father, that steers
it; you give it a safe path through the waves of the sea.
4 People may go to sea even if they have no skill, because you
can save them from any danger. 5 It is your will that the
things you have made by your wisdom should be put to use.
And so people can cross the sea in a boat and come safely to
land, because they trust their lives to that small piece of
wood.
6 This was how it was in ancient times, when a proud race
of giants was dying away. The hope of the world escaped on
such a boat under your guidance and left the world a new
generation to carry on the human race. 7 A blessing was on
Noah's wooden boat that allowed righteousness to survive,

NEW REVISED STANDARD VERSION

19 for money-making and work and success with his hands
he asks strength of a thing whose hands have no strength.

14 Again, one preparing to sail and about to voyage over raging waves
calls upon a piece of wood more fragile than the ship that carries him.
2 For it was desire for gain that planned that vessel,
and wisdom was the artisan who built it;
3 but it is your providence, O Father, that steers its course,
because you have given it a path in the sea,
and a safe way through the waves,
4 showing that you can save from every danger,
so that even a person who lacks skill may put to sea.
5 It is your will that works of your wisdom should not be without effect;
therefore people trust their lives even to the smallest piece of wood,
and passing through the billows on a raft they come safely to land.
6 For even in the beginning, when arrogant giants were perishing,
the hope of the world took refuge on a raft,
and guided by your hand left to the world the seed of a new generation.
7 For blessed is the wood by which righteousness comes.

NEW AMERICAN BIBLE

19 And for profit in business and success with his hands
he asks facility of a thing with hands completely inert.

14 Again, one preparing for a voyage and about to traverse the wild waves
cries out to wood more unsound than the boat that bears him.
2 For the urge for profits devised this latter,
and Wisdom the artificer produced it.
3 But your providence, O Father! guides it,
for you have furnished even in the sea a road,
and through the waves a steady path,
4 Showing that you can save from any danger,
so that even one without skill may embark.
5 But you will that the products of your Wisdom be not idle;
therefore men trust their lives even to frailest wood,
and have been safe crossing the surge on a raft.
6 For of old, when the proud giants were being destroyed,
the hope of the universe, who took refuge on a raft,
left to the world a future for his race, under the guidance of your hand.
7 For blest is the wood through which justice comes about;

NEW JERUSALEM BIBLE

19 for profit, an undertaking, and success in pursuing his craft,
he asks skill from something whose hands have no skill whatever.

14 Or someone else, taking ship to cross the wild waves,
loudly invokes a piece of wood[a] frailer than the vessel that bears him.
2 Agreed, the ship is the product of a craving for gain,
its building embodies the wisdom of the shipwright;
3 but your providence, Father, is what steers it,
you having opened a pathway even through the sea,
and a safe way over the waves,
4 showing that you can save, whatever happens,
so that, even without experience, someone may put to sea.
5 It is not your will that the works of your Wisdom should be sterile,
so people entrust their lives to the smallest piece of wood,
cross the waves on a raft, yet are kept safe and sound.
6 Why, in the beginning, when the proud giants were perishing,
the hope of the world took refuge on a raft
and, steered by your hand, preserved the seed of a new generation for the ages to come.
7 For blessed is the wood which serves the cause of uprightness

a **14** A ship's figurehead.

GREEK OLD TESTAMENT

8 τὸ χειροποίητον δέ, ἐπικατάρατον αὐτὸ καὶ ὁ ποιήσας
αὐτό,
ὅτι ὁ μὲν ἠργάζετο, τὸ δὲ φθαρτὸν θεὸς ὠνομάσθη.
9 ἐν ἴσῳ γὰρ μισητὰ θεῷ καὶ ὁ ἀσεβῶν καὶ ἡ ἀσέβεια
αὐτοῦ·
10 καὶ γὰρ τὸ πραχθὲν σὺν τῷ δράσαντι κολασθήσεται.
11 διὰ τοῦτο καὶ ἐν εἰδώλοις ἐθνῶν ἐπισκοπὴ ἔσται,
ὅτι ἐν κτίσματι θεοῦ εἰς βδέλυγμα ἐγενήθησαν
καὶ εἰς σκάνδαλα ψυχαῖς ἀνθρώπων
καὶ εἰς παγίδα ποσὶν ἀφρόνων.
12 Ἀρχὴ γὰρ πορνείας ἐπίνοια εἰδώλων,
εὕρεσις δὲ αὐτῶν φθορὰ ζωῆς.
13 οὔτε γὰρ ἦν ἀπ' ἀρχῆς οὔτε εἰς τὸν αἰῶνα ἔσται·
14 κενοδοξίᾳ γὰρ ἀνθρώπων εἰσῆλθεν εἰς τὸν κόσμον,
καὶ διὰ τοῦτο σύντομον αὐτῶν τὸ τέλος ἐπενοήθη.
15 ἀώρῳ γὰρ πένθει τρυχόμενος πατὴρ
τοῦ ταχέως ἀφαιρεθέντος τέκνου εἰκόνα ποιήσας
τόν ποτε νεκρὸν ἄνθρωπον νῦν ὡς θεὸν ἐτίμησεν

KING JAMES VERSION

8 But that which is made with hands is cursed, as well it, as he that made it: he, because he made it; and it, because, being corruptible, it was called god.

9 For the ungodly and his ungodliness are both alike hateful unto God.

10 For that which is made shall be punished together with him that made it.

11 Therefore even upon the idols of the Gentiles shall there be a visitation: because in the creature of God they are become an abomination, and stumblingblocks to the souls of men, and a snare to the feet of the unwise.

12 For the devising of idols was the beginning of *spiritual* fornication, and the invention of them the corruption of life.

13 For neither were they from the beginning, neither shall they be for ever.

14 For by the vain glory of men they entered into the world, and therefore shall they come shortly to an end.

15 For a father afflicted with untimely mourning, when he hath made an image of his child soon taken away, now honoured him as a god, which was then a dead man, and

DOUAY OLD TESTAMENT

8 But the idol that is made by hands, is cursed, as well it, as he that made it: he because he made it; and it because being frail it is called a god.

9 But to God the wicked and his wickedness are hateful alike.

10 For that which is made, together with him that made it, shall suffer torments.

11 Therefore there shall be no respect had even to the idols of the Gentiles: because the creatures of God are turned to an abomination, and a temptation to the souls of men, and a snare to the feet of the unwise.

12 For the beginning of fornication is the devising of idols: and the invention of them is the corruption of life.

13 For neither were they from the beginning, neither shall they be for ever.

14 For by the vanity of men they came into the world: and therefore they shall be found to come shortly to an end.

15 For a father being afflicted with bitter grief, made to himself the image of his son who was quickly taken away: and him who then had died as a man, he began now to worship as

KNOX TRANSLATION

idol is accursed, no less than the man who made it; he for
his wicked design, and the lifeless thing for the legend of
divinity that was attached to it. 9 Sinner and sin, God hates
both; 10 pardon is none for deed or doer. 11 Thus it is that a
time of reckoning will come for these idols the Gentiles
make; part of God's creation though they be, he detests
them, so have they entangled men's souls, and laid a trap for
fools.

12 When idols were first devised, then began unfaithfulness; there was death in the invention of them. 13 For indeed
they were no part of man's life from the first, nor shall be at
the last; 14 it was but man's folly brought them into the
world, and there shall be a short way with them yet. 15 Here
was some father, bowed with sorrow before his time, his
child untimely lost; the likeness of those features once made,
to mortal man (that was dead besides) he would pay divine

TODAY'S ENGLISH VERSION

8 but a curse is on an idol made by human hands. A curse is
also on the one who makes it, because he works on this perishable thing and then calls it a god. 9 Ungodly people and
these ungodly things they make are equally hated by God,
10 who will punish both the things made and the people who
made them. 11 And so God's judgment will fall on pagan
idols, because, even though they are made from something
God created, they became horrible things that trap the souls
of foolish people.

12 Sexual immorality began when idols were invented.
They have corrupted human life ever since they were first
made. 13 Idols have not always existed, nor will they exist
forever. 14 It was human pride that brought them into the
world, and that is why a quick end has been planned for
them.

15 Once there was a father who was overwhelmed with
grief at the untimely death of his child, so he made an image
of that child who had been suddenly taken from him. He
then honored a dead human being as a god, and handed on

NEW REVISED STANDARD VERSION

8 But the idol made with hands is accursed, and so is the
one who made it—
he for having made it, and the perishable thing because
it was named a god.
9 For equally hateful to God are the ungodly and their
ungodliness;
10 for what was done will be punished together with the
one who did it.
11 Therefore there will be a visitation also upon the
heathen idols,
because, though part of what God created, they became
an abomination,
snares for human souls
and a trap for the feet of the foolish.

12 For the idea of making idols was the beginning of
fornication,
and the invention of them was the corruption of life;
13 for they did not exist from the beginning,
nor will they last forever.
14 For through human vanity they entered the world,
and therefore their speedy end has been planned.

15 For a father, consumed with grief at an untimely
bereavement,
made an image of his child, who had been suddenly
taken from him;
he now honored as a god what was once a dead human
being,

NEW AMERICAN BIBLE

8 but the handmade idol is accursed, and its maker as
well:
he for having produced it, and it, because though
corruptible, it was termed a god.
9 Equally odious to God are the evildoer and his evil
deed;
10 and the thing made shall be punished with its
contriver.
11 Therefore upon even the idols of the nations shall a
visitation come,
since they have become abominable amid God's
works,
Snares for the souls of men
and a trap for the feet of the senseless.

12 For the source of wantonness is the devising of idols;
and their invention was a corruption of life.
13 For in the beginning they were not,
nor shall they continue forever;
14 for by the vanity of men they came into the world,
and therefore a sudden end is devised for them.
15 For a father, afflicted with untimely mourning,
made an image of the child so quickly taken from
him,
And now honored as a god what was formerly a dead
man

NEW JERUSALEM BIBLE

8 but accursed the man-made idol, yes, it and its maker,
he for having made it, and it because, though
perishable, it has been called god.
9 For God holds the godless and his godlessness in equal
hatred;
10 both work and workman will alike be punished.
11 Hence even the idols of the nations will have a
visitation
since, in God's creation, they have become an
abomination,
a scandal for human souls,
a snare for the feet of the foolish.

12 The idea of making idols was the origin of fornication,
their discovery corrupted life.
13 They did not exist at the beginning, they will not exist
for ever;
14 human vanity brought them into the world,
and a quick end is therefore reserved for them.
15 A father afflicted by untimely mourning
has an image made of his child so soon carried off,[a]
and now pays divine honours to what yesterday was
only a corpse,

[a] **14** The Gk custom of giving the dead divine rank.

GREEK OLD TESTAMENT

καὶ παρέδωκεν τοῖς ὑποχειρίοις μυστήρια καὶ τελετάς·
16 εἶτα ἐν χρόνῳ κρατυνθὲν τὸ ἀσεβὲς ἔθος ὡς νόμος ἐφυλάχθη.
17 καὶ τυράννων ἐπιταγαῖς ἐθρησκεύετο τὰ γλυπτά,
οὓς ἐν ὄψει μὴ δυνάμενοι τιμᾶν ἄνθρωποι διὰ τὸ μακρὰν οἰκεῖν
τὴν πόρρωθεν ὄψιν ἀνατυπωσάμενοι
ἐμφανῆ εἰκόνα τοῦ τιμωμένου βασιλέως ἐποίησαν,
ἵνα ὡς παρόντα τὸν ἀπόντα κολακεύωσιν διὰ τῆς σπουδῆς.
18 εἰς ἐπίτασιν δὲ θρησκείας καὶ τοὺς ἀγνοοῦντας
ἡ τοῦ τεχνίτου προετρέψατο φιλοτιμία·
19 ὁ μὲν γὰρ τάχα κρατοῦντι βουλόμενος ἀρέσαι
ἐξεβιάσατο τῇ τέχνῃ τὴν ὁμοιότητα ἐπὶ τὸ κάλλιον·
20 τὸ δὲ πλῆθος ἐφελκόμενον διὰ τὸ εὔχαρι τῆς ἐργασίας
τὸν πρὸ ὀλίγου τιμηθέντα ἄνθρωπον νῦν σέβασμα ἐλογίσαντο.
21 καὶ τοῦτο ἐγένετο τῷ βίῳ εἰς ἔνεδρον,
ὅτι ἢ συμφορᾷ ἢ τυραννίδι δουλεύσαντες ἄνθρωποι
τὸ ἀκοινώνητον ὄνομα λίθοις καὶ ξύλοις περιέθεσαν.

KING JAMES VERSION

delivered to those that were under him ceremonies and sacrifices.

16 Thus in process of time an ungodly custom grown strong was kept as a law, and graven images were worshipped by the commandments of kings.

17 Whom men could not honour in presence, because they dwelt far off, they took the counterfeit of his visage from far, and made an express image of a king whom they honoured, to the end that by this their forwardness they might flatter him that was absent, as if he were present.

18 Also the singular diligence of the artificer did help to set forward the ignorant to more superstition.

19 For he, peradventure willing to please one in authority, forced all his skill to make the resemblance of the best fashion.

20 And so the multitude, allured by the grace of the work, took him now for a god, which a little before was but honoured as a man.

21 And this was an occasion to deceive the world: for men, serving either calamity or tyranny, did ascribe unto stones and stocks the incommunicable name.

DOUAY OLD TESTAMENT

a god, and appointed him rites and sacrifices among his servants.

16 Then in process of time, wicked custom prevailing, this error was kept as a law, and statues were worshipped by the commandment of tyrants.

17 And those whom men could not honour in presence, because they dwelt far off, they brought their resemblance from afar, and made an express image of the king whom they had a mind to honour: that by this their diligence, they might honour as present, him that was absent.

18 And to the worshipping of these, the singular diligence also of the artificer helped to set forward the ignorant.

19 For he being willing to please him that employed him, laboured with all his art to make the resemblance in the best manner.

20 And the multitude of men, carried away by the beauty of the work, took him now for a god that a little before was but honoured as a man.

21 And this was the occasion of deceiving human life: for men serving either their affection, or their kings, gave the incommunicable name to stones and wood.

KNOX TRANSLATION

honours, and with that, rites of initiation must become the
tradition of his clan. 16 As time went on, impious habit grew
into impious custom. A king would have his own likeness
adored, 17 and his subjects, living far away, so that they
could not do obeisance to him in person, would have his
present image set up in their view, eager to pay his absent
royalty their adulation. 18 And if any spur were needed yet
for their ignorant superstition, the rivalry of craftsmen
afforded it; 19 each of these sought to please his master by
improving the portrait, with the utmost abuse of his skill,
20 till at last the vulgar, carried away by so much grace of art,
would account him a god whom yesterday they reverenced
as mortal man. 21 So, unawares, the world was caught in the
ambush; under the stress, now of bereavement, now of royal
policy, men imparted to stocks and stones the incommunicable name of God.

TODAY'S ENGLISH VERSION

secret rituals and ceremonies to those who were under his
authority. 16 As time went on, this ungodly custom became
stronger. Finally it became law, and idols were being worshiped at the command of powerful rulers. 17 When people
lived too far away to honor a ruler in his presence but were
eager to pay honor to this absent king, they would imagine
what he must look like, and would then make a likeness of
him. 18 The ambitious artists who made these likenesses
caused this worship to spread, even among people who did
not know the king. 19 An artist might want to please some
ruler, and so he would use his skill to make the likeness better looking than the actual person. 20 Then people would be
so attracted by the work of art, that the one whom they had
earlier honored now became the object of their worship.
21 So all this became a deadly trap, because people who were
grieving, or under royal authority, would take objects of
stone or wood, and give them the honor reserved for the
One God.

NEW REVISED STANDARD VERSION

and handed on to his dependents secret rites and
initiations.
16 Then the ungodly custom, grown strong with time, was
kept as a law,
and at the command of monarchs carved images were
worshiped.
17 When people could not honor monarchs[a] in their
presence, since they lived at a distance,
they imagined their appearance far away,
and made a visible image of the king whom they honored,
so that by their zeal they might flatter the absent one as
though present.

18 Then the ambition of the artisan impelled
even those who did not know the king to intensify their
worship.
19 For he, perhaps wishing to please his ruler,
skillfully forced the likeness to take more beautiful form,
20 and the multitude, attracted by the charm of his work,
now regarded as an object of worship the one whom
shortly before they had honored as a human
being.
21 And this became a hidden trap for humankind,
because people, in bondage to misfortune or to royal
authority,
bestowed on objects of stone or wood the name that
ought not to be shared.

a Gk *them*

NEW AMERICAN BIBLE

and handed down to his subjects mysteries and
sacrifices.
16 Then, in time, the impious practice gained strength and
was observed as law,
and graven things were worshiped by princely
decrees.
17 Men who lived so far away that they could not honor
him in his presence
copied the appearance of the distant king
And made a public image of him they wished to honor,
out of zeal to flatter him when absent, as though
present.
18 And to promote this observance among those to whom
it was strange,
the artisan's ambition provided a stimulus.
19 For he, mayhap in his determination to please the ruler,
labored over the likeness to the best of his skill;
20 And the masses, drawn by the charm of the
workmanship,
soon thought he should be worshiped who shortly
before was honored as a man.
21 And this became a snare for mankind,
that men enslaved to either grief or tyranny
conferred the incommunicable Name on stocks and
stones.

NEW JERUSALEM BIBLE

handing on mysteries and ceremonies to his people;
16 time passes, the custom hardens and is observed as
law.
17 Rulers were the ones who ordered that statues should
be worshipped:
people who could not honour them in person, because
they lived too far away,
would have a portrait made of their distant
countenance,
to have an image that they could see of the king whom
they honoured;
meaning, by such zeal, to flatter the absent as if he
were present.
18 Even people who did not know him
were stimulated into spreading his cult by the artist's
enthusiasm;
19 for the latter, doubtless wishing to please his ruler,
exerted all his skill to surpass the reality,
20 and the crowd, attracted by the beauty of the work,
mistook for a god someone whom recently they had
honoured as a man.
21 And this became a snare for life:
that people, whether enslaved by misfortune or by
tyranny,
should have conferred the ineffable Name on sticks and
stones.

GREEK OLD TESTAMENT

22 Εἶτ᾽ οὐκ ἤρκεσεν τὸ πλανᾶσθαι περὶ τὴν τοῦ θεοῦ γνῶσιν,
ἀλλὰ καὶ ἐν μεγάλῳ ζῶντες ἀγνοίας πολέμῳ
τὰ τοσαῦτα κακὰ εἰρήνην προσαγορεύουσιν.
23 ἢ γὰρ τεκνοφόνους τελετὰς ἢ κρύφια μυστήρια
ἢ ἐμμανεῖς ἐξάλλων θεσμῶν κώμους ἄγοντες
24 οὔτε βίους οὔτε γάμους καθαροὺς ἔτι φυλάσσουσιν,
ἕτερος δ᾽ ἕτερον ἢ λοχῶν ἀναιρεῖ ἢ νοθεύων ὀδυνᾷ.
25 πάντα δ᾽ ἐπιμὶξ ἔχει αἷμα καὶ φόνος, κλοπὴ καὶ δόλος,
φθορά, ἀπιστία, τάραχος, ἐπιορκία,
26 θόρυβος ἀγαθῶν, χάριτος ἀμνηστία,
ψυχῶν μιασμός, γενέσεως ἐναλλαγή,
γάμων ἀταξία, μοιχεία καὶ ἀσέλγεια.
27 ἡ γὰρ τῶν ἀνωνύμων εἰδώλων θρησκεία
παντὸς ἀρχὴ κακοῦ καὶ αἰτία καὶ πέρας ἐστίν·
28 ἢ γὰρ εὐφραινόμενοι μεμήνασιν ἢ προφητεύουσιν ψευδῆ
ἢ ζῶσιν ἀδίκως ἢ ἐπιορκοῦσιν ταχέως·
29 ἀψύχοις γὰρ πεποιθότες εἰδώλοις
κακῶς ὀμόσαντες ἀδικηθῆναι οὐ προσδέχονται.
30 ἀμφότερα δὲ αὐτοὺς μετελεύσεται τὰ δίκαια,
ὅτι κακῶς ἐφρόνησαν περὶ θεοῦ προσέχοντες εἰδώλοις
καὶ ἀδίκως ὤμοσαν ἐν δόλῳ καταφρονήσαντες ὁσιότητος·

KING JAMES VERSION

22 Moreover this was not enough for them, that they erred in the knowledge of God; but whereas they lived in the great war of ignorance, those so great plagues called they peace.

23 For whilst they slew their children in sacrifices, or used secret ceremonies, or made revellings of strange rites;

24 They kept neither lives nor marriages any longer undefiled: but either one slew another traiterously, or grieved him by adultery.

25 So that there reigned in all men without exception blood, manslaughter, theft, and dissimulation, corruption, unfaithfulness, tumults, perjury,

26 Disquieting of good men, forgetfulness of good turns, defiling of souls, changing of kind, disorder in marriages, adultery, and shameless uncleanness.

27 For the worshipping of idols not to be named is the beginning, the cause, and the end, of all evil.

28 For either they are mad when they be merry, or prophesy lies, or live unjustly, or else lightly forswear themselves.

29 For insomuch as their trust is in idols, which have no life; though they swear falsely, yet they look not to be hurt.

30 Howbeit for both causes shall they be justly punished: both because they thought not well of God, giving heed unto idols, and also unjustly swore in deceit, despising holiness.

DOUAY OLD TESTAMENT

22 And it was not enough for them to err about the knowledge of God, but whereas they lived in a great war of ignorance, they call so many and so great evils peace.

23 For either they sacrifice their own children, or use hidden sacrifices, or keep watches full of madness,

24 So that now they neither keep life, nor marriage undefiled, but one killeth another through envy, or grieveth him by adultery:

25 And all things are mingled together, blood, murder, theft and dissimulation, corruption and unfaithfulness, tumults and perjury, disquieting of the good,

26 Forgetfulness of God, defiling of souls, changing of nature, disorder in marriage, and the irregularity of adultery and uncleanness.

27 For the worship of abominable idols is the cause, and the beginning and end of all evil.

28 For either they are mad when they are merry: or they prophesy lies, or they live unjustly, or easily forswear themselves.

29 For whilst they trust in idols, which are without life, though they swear amiss, they look not to be hurt.

30 But for two things they shall be justly punished, because they have thought not well of God, giving heed to idols, and have sworn unjustly, in guile despising justice.

KNOX TRANSLATION

22 Nor were they content with these false notions of God's
nature; living in a world besieged by doubt, they misnamed
its innumerable disorders a state of peace. 23 Peace, amidst
their rites of child-murder, their dark mysteries, their vigils
consecrated to frenzy! 24 Peace, while there is no respect for
life, or for wedlock undefiled; always the murderous
ambush, the jealous pangs of a husband betrayed! 25 All is a
welter of bloodshed and murder, theft and fraud, corruption
and disloyalty, sedition and perjury; 26 honest men are
assailed, kindnesses forgotten, souls defiled, breeds confused, marriages unsettled; adultery reigns and wantonness.
27 Name we all these, name we never the idols whose worship is the cause, the beginning and end, of all these!
28 Their ecstasies are but raving, their prophecies are but lies;
ill live their worshippers, and lightly forswear themselves.
29 And no marvel; what hurt should they take from the oath
falsely sworn, since all their faith is in dead gods? 30 But
indeed they shall pay both scores, idolaters that thought so
ill of God, and perjurers that by their treason slighted all

TODAY'S ENGLISH VERSION

22 One thing led to another. It was not enough to be wrong
about the knowledge of God. They lived in a state of evil
warfare, but they were so ignorant that they called it peace.
23 They murdered children in their initiation rituals, celebrated secret mysteries, and held wild ceremonial orgies with
unnatural practices. 24 They no longer kept their lives or
their marriages pure. A man might kill another by an act of
treachery or cause him grief by committing adultery with his
wife. 25 Everything was a complete riot of bloody murder,
robbery, deceit, corruption, faithlessness, disorder, falsehood, 26 harassment of innocent people, ingratitude, moral
decay, sexual perversion, broken marriages, adultery, and
immorality. 27 The worship of idols, whose names should
never be spoken, is the beginning and the end, the cause
and the result of every evil. 28 People who worship them lose
control of themselves in ecstasy, or pass off lies as prophecies, or live wickedly, or break their word without hesitation.
29 They tell lies under oath and expect no punishment,
because the idols they put their trust in are lifeless. 30 But
punishment will finally catch up with them, for two reasons:
first, they were in error about God when they worshiped
idols, and second, they had so little regard for holiness that
they made false statements to deceive people. 31 When

NEW REVISED STANDARD VERSION

22 Then it was not enough for them to err about the
knowledge of God,
but though living in great strife due to ignorance,
they call such great evils peace.
23 For whether they kill children in their initiations, or
celebrate secret mysteries,
or hold frenzied revels with strange customs,
24 they no longer keep either their lives or their marriages
pure,
but they either treacherously kill one another, or grieve
one another by adultery,
25 and all is a raging riot of blood and murder, theft and
deceit, corruption, faithlessness, tumult, perjury,
26 confusion over what is good, forgetfulness of favors,
defiling of souls, sexual perversion,
disorder in marriages, adultery, and debauchery.
27 For the worship of idols not to be named
is the beginning and cause and end of every evil.
28 For their worshipers[a] either rave in exultation,
or prophesy lies, or live unrighteously, or readily
commit perjury;
29 for because they trust in lifeless idols
they swear wicked oaths and expect to suffer no harm.
30 But just penalties will overtake them on two counts:
because they thought wrongly about God in devoting
themselves to idols,
and because in deceit they swore unrighteously through
contempt for holiness.

a Gk *they*

NEW AMERICAN BIBLE

22 Then it was not enough for them to err in their
knowledge of God;
but even though they live in a great war of
ignorance,
they call such evils peace.
23 For while they celebrate either child-slaying sacrifices or
clandestine mysteries,
or frenzied carousals in unheard-of rites,
24 They no longer safeguard either lives or pure wedlock;
but each either waylays and kills his neighbor, or
aggrieves him by adultery.
25 And all is confusion—blood and murder, theft and
guile,
corruption, faithlessness, turmoil, perjury,
26 Disturbance of good men, neglect of gratitude,
besmirching of souls, unnatural lust,
disorder in marriage, adultery and shamelessness.
27 For the worship of infamous idols
is the reason and source and extremity of all evil.
28 For they either go mad with enjoyment, or prophesy
lies,
or live lawlessly or lightly forswear themselves.
29 For as their trust is in soulless idols,
they expect no harm when they have sworn falsely.
30 But on both counts shall justice overtake them:
because they thought ill of God and devoted
themselves to idols,
and because they deliberately swore false oaths,
despising piety.

NEW JERUSALEM BIBLE

22 It is not enough, however, for them to have such
misconceptions about God;
for, living in the fierce warfare of ignorance,
they call these terrible evils peace.
23 With their child-murdering rites, their occult mysteries,
or their frenzied orgies with outlandish customs,
24 they no longer retain any purity in their lives or their
marriages,
one treacherously murdering another or wronging him
by adultery.
25 Everywhere a welter of blood and murder, theft and fraud,
corruption, treachery, riot, perjury,
26 disturbance of decent people, forgetfulness of favours,
pollution of souls, sins against nature,
disorder in marriage, adultery and debauchery.
27 For the worship of idols with no name
is the beginning, cause, and end of every evil.
28 For these people either carry their merrymaking to the
point of frenzy,
or they prophesy what is not true, or they live wicked
lives,
or they perjure themselves without hesitation;
29 since they put their trust in lifeless idols
they do not reckon their false oaths can harm them.

30 But they will be justly punished for this double crime:
for degrading the concept of God by adhering to idols;
and for wickedly perjuring themselves in contempt for
what is holy.

GREEK OLD TESTAMENT

31 οὐ γὰρ ἡ τῶν ὀμνυμένων δύναμις,
ἀλλ' ἡ τῶν ἁμαρτανόντων δίκη
ἐπεξέρχεται ἀεὶ τὴν τῶν ἀδίκων παράβασιν.

15 Σὺ δέ, ὁ θεὸς ἡμῶν, χρηστὸς καὶ ἀληθής,
μακρόθυμος καὶ ἐλέει διοικῶν τὰ πάντα.
2 καὶ γὰρ ἐὰν ἁμάρτωμεν, σοί ἐσμεν, εἰδότες σου τὸ κράτος·
οὐχ ἁμαρτησόμεθα δέ, εἰδότες ὅτι σοὶ λελογίσμεθα.
3 τὸ γὰρ ἐπίστασθαί σε ὁλόκληρος δικαιοσύνη,
καὶ εἰδέναι σου τὸ κράτος ῥίζα ἀθανασίας.
4 οὔτε γὰρ ἐπλάνησεν ἡμᾶς ἀνθρώπων κακότεχνος ἐπίνοια
οὐδὲ σκιαγράφων πόνος ἄκαρπος,
εἶδος σπιλωθὲν χρώμασιν διηλλαγμένοις,
5 ὧν ὄψις ἄφροσιν εἰς ὄρεξιν ἔρχεται,
ποθεῖ τε νεκρᾶς εἰκόνος εἶδος ἄπνουν.
6 κακῶν ἐρασταὶ ἄξιοί τε τοιούτων ἐλπίδων
καὶ οἱ δρῶντες καὶ οἱ ποθοῦντες καὶ οἱ σεβόμενοι.
7 Καὶ γὰρ κεραμεὺς ἁπαλὴν γῆν θλίβων ἐπίμοχθον
πλάσσει πρὸς ὑπηρεσίαν ἡμῶν ἓν ἕκαστον·
ἀλλ' ἐκ τοῦ αὐτοῦ πηλοῦ ἀνεπλάσατο
τά τε τῶν καθαρῶν ἔργων δοῦλα σκεύη
τά τε ἐναντία, πάντα ὁμοίως·
τούτων δὲ ἑτέρου τίς ἑκάστου ἐστὶν ἡ χρῆσις,
κριτὴς ὁ πηλουργός.

KING JAMES VERSION

31 For it is not the power of them by whom they swear: but it is the just vengeance of sinners, that punisheth always the offence of the ungodly.

15 But thou, O God, art gracious and true, longsuffering, and in mercy ordering all things.

2 For if we sin, we are thine, knowing thy power: but we will not sin, knowing that we are counted thine.

3 For to know thee is perfect righteousness: yea, to know thy power is the root of immortality.

4 For neither did the mischievous invention of men deceive us, nor an image spotted with divers colours, the painter's fruitless labour;

5 The sight whereof enticeth fools to lust after it, and so they desire the form of a dead image, that hath no breath.

6 Both they that make them, they that desire them, and they that worship them, are lovers of evil things, and are worthy to have such things to trust upon.

7 For the potter, tempering soft earth, fashioneth every vessel with much labour for our service: yea, of the same clay he maketh both the vessels that serve for clean uses, and likewise also all such as serve to the contrary: but what is the use of either sort, the potter himself is the judge.

DOUAY OLD TESTAMENT

31 For it is not the power of them, by whom they swear, but the just vengeance of sinners always punisheth the transgression of the unjust.

15 BUT thou, our God, art gracious and true, patient, and ordering all things in mercy.

2 For if we sin, we are thine, knowing thy greatness: and if we sin not, we know that we are counted with thee.

3 For to know thee is perfect justice: and to know thy justice, and thy power, is the root of immortality.

4 For the invention of mischievous men hath not deceived us, nor the shadow of a picture, a fruitless labour, a graven figure with divers colours,

5 The sight whereof enticeth the fool to lust after it, and he loveth the lifeless figure of a dead image.

6 The lovers of evil things deserve to have no better things to trust in, both they that make them, and they that love them, and they that worship them.

7 The potter also tempering soft earth, with labour fashioneth every vessel for our service, and of the same clay he maketh both vessels that are for clean uses, and likewise such as serve to the contrary: but what is the use of these vessels, the potter is the judge.

KNOX TRANSLATION

honour; 31 not the power he swore by, but the justice that
keeps watch over sinners, walks ever close on the heels of ill-
doing.

15 For us, thou art God; thou, beneficent and truthful,
thou, always patient and merciful towards the world
thou governest. 2 Sin we, still we are thy worshippers; have
we not proof of thy power? Sin we not, of this, too, we have
proof, that thou wilt count us for thy own. 3 To know thee as
thou art, is the soul's full health; to have proof of thy power,
is the root whence springs immortality. 4 Not for us to be led
astray by foolish tales of man's imagining, by the sculptor's
barren art, as he picks out some image with motley colours,
5 to set fools gaping at the sight of a lifeless shadow, all
seeming and no breathing. 6 Lovers they are of their own
ruin, worthy of the fond hopes they cherish, that make such
things, or sigh after them, or do them reverence.
7 Despise we not the potter's toil, that works the pliant
earth between his fingers, and makes a cup here, a dish there
for our use. Serve they noble ends or base, all alike come
from the same clay, and what employment each of them
shall find, it is the potter's right to determine. 8 But very ill is

TODAY'S ENGLISH VERSION

unrighteous people commit sin, they will be hunted down,
not by the power of whatever thing they swear by, but by the
punishment that sinners deserve.
15 But you, our God, are kind and true and patient. You
rule the universe with mercy. 2 Even if we sin, we
know your power and are still yours. But because we know
that we belong to you, we will not sin. 3 Knowing you is perfect righteousness. Recognizing your power is where immortality begins. 4 We have not been misled by any evil product
of human skill, by any useless object painted by some artist,
or by any idol smeared with different colors. 5 The sight of
such things arouses the passions of foolish people and
makes them desire a dead, lifeless image. 6 Anyone who
makes such a thing or desires it or worships it is in love with
something evil, and gets what he deserves when he places
his hopes in it.
7 A potter works the soft clay and carefully shapes each
object for our use. Some things he makes are put to good
use, and some are not, but he makes them all from the same
clay, and shapes them in the same manner. The potter himself decides which objects shall be used for what purposes.

NEW REVISED STANDARD VERSION

31 For it is not the power of the things by which people
swear,[a]
but the just penalty for those who sin,
that always pursues the transgression of the
unrighteous.

15 But you, our God, are kind and true,
patient, and ruling all things[b] in mercy.
2 For even if we sin we are yours, knowing your power;
but we will not sin, because we know that you
acknowledge us as yours.
3 For to know you is complete righteousness,
and to know your power is the root of immortality.
4 For neither has the evil intent of human art misled us,
nor the fruitless toil of painters,
a figure stained with varied colors,
5 whose appearance arouses yearning in fools,
so that they desire[c] the lifeless form of a dead image.
6 Lovers of evil things and fit for such objects of hope[d]
are those who either make or desire or worship them.

7 A potter kneads the soft earth
and laboriously molds each vessel for our service,
fashioning out of the same clay
both the vessels that serve clean uses
and those for contrary uses, making all alike;
but which shall be the use of each of them
the worker in clay decides.

a Or *of the oaths people swear* *b* Or *ruling the universe* *c* Gk *and he desires* *d* Gk *such hopes*

NEW AMERICAN BIBLE

31 For not the might of those that are sworn by
but the retribution of sinners
ever follows upon the transgression of the wicked.

15 But you, our God, are good and true,
slow to anger, and governing all with mercy.
2 For even if we sin, we are yours, and know your might;
but we will not sin, knowing that we belong to you.
3 For to know you well is complete justice,
and to know your might is the root of immortality.
4 For neither did the evil creation of men's fancy deceive
us,
nor the fruitless labor of painters,
A form smeared with varied colors,
5 the sight of which arouses yearning in the senseless
man,
till he longs for the inanimate form of a dead image.
6 Lovers of evil things, and worthy of such hopes
are they who make them and long for them and
worship them.

7 For truly the potter, laboriously working the soft earth,
molds for our service each several article:
Both the vessels that serve for clean purposes
and their opposites, all alike;
As to what shall be the use of each vessel of either class
the worker in clay is the judge.

NEW JERUSALEM BIBLE

31 For it is not the power of the things by which they
swear
but the punishment reserved for sinners
that always follows the offences of wicked people.

15 But you, our God, are kind and true,
slow to anger, governing the universe with mercy.
2 Even if we sin, we are yours, since we acknowledge
your power,
but we will not sin, knowing we count as yours.
3 To know you is indeed the perfect virtue,
and to know your power is the root of immortality.
4 We have not been duped by inventions of misapplied
human skill,
or by the sterile work of painters,
by figures daubed with assorted colours,
5 the sight of which sets fools yearning
and hankering for the lifeless form of an unbreathing
image.
6 Lovers of evil and worthy of such hopes
are those who make them, those who want them and
those who worship them.

7 Take a potter, now, laboriously working the soft earth,
shaping each object for us to use.
Out of the self-same clay,
he models vessels intended for a noble use
and those for a contrary purpose, all alike:
but which of these two uses each will have
is for the potter himself to decide.

GREEK OLD TESTAMENT

8 καὶ κακόμοχθος θεὸν μάταιον ἐκ τοῦ αὐτοῦ πλάσσει
πηλοῦ
ὃς πρὸ μικροῦ ἐκ γῆς γενηθεὶς
μετ᾽ ὀλίγον πορεύεται ἐξ ἧς ἐλήμφθη,
τὸ τῆς ψυχῆς ἀπαιτηθεὶς χρέος.
9 ἀλλ᾽ ἔστιν αὐτῷ φροντὶς οὐχ ὅτι μέλλει κάμνειν
οὐδ᾽ ὅτι βραχυτελῆ βίον ἔχει,
ἀλλ᾽ ἀντερείδεται μὲν χρυσουργοῖς καὶ ἀργυροχόοις
χαλκοπλάστας τε μιμεῖται
καὶ δόξαν ἡγεῖται ὅτι κίβδηλα πλάσσει.
10 σποδὸς ἡ καρδία αὐτοῦ, καὶ γῆς εὐτελεστέρα ἡ ἐλπὶς
αὐτοῦ,
πηλοῦ τε ἀτιμότερος ὁ βίος αὐτοῦ,
11 ὅτι ἠγνόησεν τὸν πλάσαντα αὐτὸν
καὶ τὸν ἐμπνεύσαντα αὐτῷ ψυχὴν ἐνεργοῦσαν
καὶ ἐμφυσήσαντα πνεῦμα ζωτικόν,
12 ἀλλ᾽ ἐλογίσαντο παίγνιον εἶναι τὴν ζωὴν ἡμῶν
καὶ τὸν βίον πανηγυρισμὸν ἐπικερδῆ,
δεῖν γάρ φησιν ὅθεν δή, κἂν ἐκ κακοῦ, πορίζειν.
13 οὗτος γὰρ παρὰ πάντας οἶδεν ὅτι ἁμαρτάνει
ὕλης γεώδους εὔθραυστα σκεύη καὶ γλυπτὰ δημιουργῶν.

KING JAMES VERSION

8 And employing his labours lewdly, he maketh a vain god of the same clay, even he which a little before was made of earth himself, and within a little while after returneth to the same, out of the which he was taken, when his life which was lent him shall be demanded.

9 Notwithstanding his care is, not that he shall have much labour, nor that his life is short: but striveth to excel goldsmiths and silversmiths, and endeavoureth to do like the workers in brass, and counteth it his glory to make counterfeit things.

10 His heart is ashes, his hope is more vile than earth, and his life of less value than clay:

11 Forasmuch as he knew not his Maker, and him that inspired into him an active soul, and breathed in a living spirit.

12 But they counted our life a pastime, and our time here a market for gain: for, say they, we must be getting every way, though it be by evil means.

13 For this man, that of earthly matter maketh brittle vessels and graven images, knoweth himself to offend above all others.

DOUAY OLD TESTAMENT

8 And of the same clay by a vain labour he maketh a god: he who a little before was made of earth himself, and a little after returneth to the same out of which he was taken, when his life which was lent him shall be called for again.

9 But his care is, not that he shall labour, nor that his life is short, but he striveth with the goldsmiths and silversmiths: and he endeavoureth to do like the workers in brass, and counteth it a glory to make vain things.

10 For his heart is ashes, and his hope vain earth, and his life more base than clay:

11 Forasmuch as he knew not his maker and him that inspired into him the soul that worketh, and that breathed into him a living spirit.

12 Yea and they have counted our life a pastime, and the business of life to be gain, and that we must be getting every way, even out of evil.

13 For that man knoweth that he offendeth above all others, who of earthly matter maketh brittle vessels, and graven *gods*.

KNOX TRANSLATION

that toil bestowed, when he uses the same clay to fashion
some god that is no god. Bethink thee, potter, that it is but a
little while since thou thyself wast fashioned out of the same
earth, and ere long, when the lease of thy soul falls due, to
that earth thou shalt return. 9 But no, he never looks forward to the day when he will be past work; how short life is,
he recks not; he must vie with goldsmith and silversmith, he
must be even with his neighbour that works in bronze; in
puppet-making[a] all his hope lies of winning fame. 10 O heart
of dust, O ambition worthless as the sand, life than his own
clay more despicable! 11 No thought for the God that was his
own fashioner, quickened him with the pulse of energy,
breathed into him a living spirit! 12 Existence, for him, only
a toy to be played with; our life here, only a market-place,
where a man must needs get his living by fair means or foul!
13 Such a man, as no other, sins with his eyes open; from the
same earthenware he will make you fragile pot or carved effi-
gy as you will.

a Rather, according to the Greek text, 'in passing false coin'. The imputation seems to be that such workmen covered over their clay figures with metal leaf; even as images, they were false; how much more as gods!

TODAY'S ENGLISH VERSION

8 He is a human being who was himself formed from earth
only a short while earlier, and after a little while, when he
must return the soul that was lent to him, he will go back to
the same earth. He is a human being, but he wastes his labor
shaping a useless god out of the same clay that he uses to
make pots. 9 His life will be short, and he will soon have to
die, but he is not concerned about that. He wants to compete
with those who work in gold, silver, and bronze, and make
things like they do. He takes great pride in the things he
makes, but they are counterfeit. 10 His heart is made of
ashes. His hope is cheaper than dirt. His life is not worth as
much as his clay, 11 because he never came to know the God
who shaped him, who breathed into him an active soul and
a living spirit. 12 He thinks of human life as just a game, a
market where he can make a profit. He believes that he must
make money however he can, even by evil ways. 13 This
man, who makes idols and fragile pots from the same clay,
knows better than anyone else that he is sinning.

NEW REVISED STANDARD VERSION

8 With misspent toil, these workers form a futile god from the same clay—
these mortals who were made of earth a short time before
and after a little while go to the earth from which all mortals are taken,
when the time comes to return the souls that were borrowed.

9 But the workers are not concerned that mortals are destined to die
or that their life is brief,
but they compete with workers in gold and silver,
and imitate workers in copper;
and they count it a glorious thing to mold counterfeit gods.

10 Their heart is ashes, their hope is cheaper than dirt,
and their lives are of less worth than clay,

11 because they failed to know the one who formed them
and inspired them with active souls
and breathed a living spirit into them.

12 But they considered our existence an idle game,
and life a festival held for profit,
for they say one must get money however one can, even by base means.

13 For these persons, more than all others, know that they sin
when they make from earthy matter fragile vessels and carved images.

NEW AMERICAN BIBLE

8 And with misspent toil he molds a meaningless god
from the selfsame clay;
though he himself shortly before was made from the earth
And after a little, is to go whence he was taken,
when the life that was lent him is demanded back.

9 But his concern is not that he is to die
nor that his span of life is brief;
Rather, he vies with goldsmiths and silversmiths
and emulates molders of bronze,
and takes pride in modeling counterfeits.

10 Ashes his heart is! more worthless than earth is his hope,
and more ignoble than clay his life;

11 Because he knew not the one who fashioned him,
and breathed into him a quickening soul,
and infused a vital spirit.

12 Instead, he esteemed our life a plaything,
and our span of life a holiday for gain;
"For one must," says he, "make profit every way, be it even out of evil."

13 For this man more than any knows that he is sinning,
when out of earthen stuff he creates fragile vessels and idols alike.

NEW JERUSALEM BIBLE

8 Then—ill-spent effort!—from the same clay he models a futile god,
although so recently made out of earth himself
and shortly to return to what he was taken from,
when asked to give back the soul that has been lent to him.

9 Even so, he does not worry about having to die
or about the shortness of his life,
but strives to outdo the goldsmiths and silversmiths,
imitates the bronzeworkers,
and prides himself on modelling counterfeits.

10 Ashes, his heart;
more vile than earth, his hope;
more wretched than clay, his life!

11 For he has misconceived the One who has modelled him,
who breathed an active soul into him
and inspired a living spirit.

12 What is more, he looks on this life of ours as a kind of game,
and our time here like a fair, full of bargains.
'However foul the means,' he says, 'a man must make a living.'

13 He, more than any other, knows he is sinning,
he who from one earthy stuff makes both brittle pots and idols.

GREEK OLD TESTAMENT

14 πάντες δὲ ἀφρονέστατοι καὶ τάλανες ὑπὲρ ψυχὴν νηπίου
οἱ ἐχθροὶ τοῦ λαοῦ σου καταδυναστεύσαντες αὐτόν,
15 ὅτι καὶ πάντα τὰ εἴδωλα τῶν ἐθνῶν ἐλογίσαντο θεούς,
οἷς οὔτε ὀμμάτων χρῆσις εἰς ὅρασιν
οὔτε ῥῖνες εἰς συνολκὴν ἀέρος
οὔτε ὦτα ἀκούειν
οὔτε δάκτυλοι χειρῶν εἰς ψηλάφησιν
καὶ οἱ πόδες αὐτῶν ἀργοὶ πρὸς ἐπίβασιν.
16 ἄνθρωπος γὰρ ἐποίησεν αὐτούς,
καὶ τὸ πνεῦμα δεδανεισμένος ἔπλασεν αὐτούς·
οὐδεὶς γὰρ αὐτῷ ὅμοιον ἄνθρωπος ἰσχύει πλάσαι θεόν·
17 θνητὸς δὲ ὢν νεκρὸν ἐργάζεται χερσὶν ἀνόμοις·
κρείττων γάρ ἐστιν τῶν σεβασμάτων αὐτοῦ,
ὧν αὐτὸς μὲν ἔζησεν, ἐκεῖνα δὲ οὐδέποτε.—
18 καὶ τὰ ζῷα δὲ τὰ ἔχθιστα σέβονται·
ἀνοίᾳ γὰρ συγκρινόμενα τῶν ἄλλων ἐστὶ χείρονα·
19 οὐδ' ὅσον ἐπιποθῆσαι ὡς ἐν ζῴων ὄψει καλὰ τυγχάνει,
ἐκπέφευγεν δὲ καὶ τὸν τοῦ θεοῦ ἔπαινον καὶ τὴν εὐλογίαν αὐτοῦ.

16 Διὰ τοῦτο δι' ὁμοίων ἐκολάσθησαν ἀξίως
καὶ διὰ πλήθους κνωδάλων ἐβασανίσθησαν.

KING JAMES VERSION

14 And all the enemies of thy people, that hold them in subjection, are most foolish, and are more miserable than very babes.

15 For they counted all the idols of the heathen to be gods: which neither have the use of eyes to see, nor noses to draw breath, nor ears to hear, nor fingers of hands to handle; and as for their feet, they are slow to go.

16 For man made them, and he that borrowed his own spirit fashioned them: but no man can make a god like unto himself.

17 For being mortal, he worketh a dead thing with wicked hands: for he himself is better than the things which he worshippeth: whereas he lived *once,* but they never.

18 Yea, they worshipped those beasts also that are most hateful: for being compared together, some are worse than others.

19 Neither are they beautiful, so much as to be desired in respect of beasts: but they went without the praise of God and his blessing.

16 Therefore by the like were they punished worthily, and by the multitude of beasts tormented.

DOUAY OLD TESTAMENT

14 But all the enemies of thy people that hold them in subjection, are foolish, and unhappy, and proud beyond measure:

15 For they have esteemed all the idols of the heathens for gods, which neither have the use of eyes to see, nor noses to draw breath, nor ears to hear, nor fingers of hands to handle, and as for their feet, they are slow to walk.

16 For man made them: and he that borroweth his own breath, fashioned them. For no man can make a god like to himself.

17 For being mortal himself, he formeth a dead thing with his wicked hands. For he is better than they whom he worshippeth, because he indeed hath lived, though he were mortal, but they never.

18 Moreover they worship also the vilest creatures: but things without sense compared to these, are worse than they.

19 Yea, neither by sight can any man see good of these beasts. But they have fled from the praise of God, and from his blessing.

16 FOR these things, and by the like things to these, they were worthily punished, and were destroyed by a multitude of beasts.

KNOX TRANSLATION

14 Fools all, and doomed to misery beyond the common
doom of tyrants,[a] were the enemies that from time to time
have lorded it over thy people. 15 Gods, for them, were all the
idols of the heathen, with their sightless eyes, their nostrils
that never drew breath, deaf ears, unfeeling hands, and feet
that still would walk, yet still tarry; 16 gods man-made, gods
of his fashioning that is a debtor for the very breath he
draws. For indeed, the gods man fashions are less than himself; 17 vain his impiety, since he is but mortal, they already
dead; better he than they, since he lived once, and they
never. 18 And what beasts are these they worship? Of all
beasts, the most hateful; such models they have foolishly
chosen as cannot vie with the others;[b] 19 as have no beauty,
even beast-fashion, to make them desirable; the least honourable of God's creatures and the least blessed.

16 Fittingly, then, were the Egyptians plagued by such beasts as these, that swarmed to their undoing.[c]

a According to the Greek text (itself probably corrupt), 'of infants'.
b This is probably the sense of the Greek; the Latin version here can hardly be translated. *c* The names 'Egypt' and 'Egyptians' have, as before, been inserted to make the sense of the original plainer. The same is to be said of the following words: 'frogs' in verse 3, 'brazen serpent' in verse 7, and 'manna' in verse 27.

TODAY'S ENGLISH VERSION

[14]But the most foolish of all people, showing less sense
than babies, were the enemies who oppressed your people,
O Lord. [15]They thought that all their pagan idols were gods,
even though idols cannot see with their eyes, cannot breathe
through their nose, cannot hear with their ears, cannot feel
with their fingers, and cannot walk on their legs. [16]Some-
one whose spirit is only borrowed made them. No one can
ever make a god that is equal to a human being. [17]Every
person will sooner or later die, but anything he makes with
his wicked hands is dead from the start. He himself is better
than what he worships. He at least is alive, but what he worships is not, and never has been. [18]Such people worship the
most disgusting animals, including even the least intelligent
ones. [19]Even as animals they are not attractive enough to
make anyone want them. God himself passed them by when
he put his approval and blessing on the rest of creation.

16 [1]And so it was appropriate that these people were
punished by such creatures—tormented by swarms
of them.

NEW REVISED STANDARD VERSION

14 But most foolish, and more miserable than an infant,
are all the enemies who oppressed your people.
15 For they thought that all their heathen idols were gods,
though these have neither the use of their eyes to see
with,
nor nostrils with which to draw breath,
nor ears with which to hear,
nor fingers to feel with,
and their feet are of no use for walking.
16 For a human being made them,
and one whose spirit is borrowed formed them;
for none can form gods that are like themselves.
17 People are mortal, and what they make with lawless
hands is dead;
for they are better than the objects they worship,
since[a] they have life, but the idols[b] never had.

18 Moreover, they worship even the most hateful animals,
which are worse than all others when judged by their
lack of intelligence;
19 and even as animals they are not so beautiful in
appearance that one would desire them,
but they have escaped both the praise of God and his
blessing.

16 Therefore those people[c] were deservedly punished
through such creatures,
and were tormented by a multitude of animals.

a Other ancient authorities read *of which* *b* Gk *but they* *c* Gk *they*

NEW AMERICAN BIBLE

[14]But all quite senseless, and worse than childish in
mind,
are the enemies of your people who enslaved them.
[15]For they esteemed all the idols of the nations, gods,
which have no use of the eyes for vision,
nor nostrils to snuff the air,
Nor ears to hear,
nor fingers on their hands for feeling;
even their feet are useless to walk with.
[16]For a man made them;
one whose spirit has been lent him fashioned them.
For no man succeeds in fashioning a god like himself;
[17] being mortal, he makes a dead thing with his lawless
hands.
For he is better than the things he worships;
he at least lives, but never they.

[18]And besides, they worship the most loathsome beasts—
for compared as to folly, these are worse than the
rest,
[19]Nor for their looks are they good or desirable beasts,
but they have escaped both the approval of God and
his blessing.

16 Therefore they were fittingly punished by similar
creatures,
and were tormented by a swarm of insects.

NEW JERUSALEM BIBLE

[14]But most foolish, more pitiable even than the soul of a
little child,
are the enemies who once played the tyrant with your
people,
[15]and have taken all the idols of the heathen for gods;
these can use neither their eyes for seeing
nor their nostrils for breathing the air
nor their ears for hearing
nor the fingers on their hands for handling
nor their feet for walking.
[16]They have been made, you see, by a human being,
modelled by a being whose own breath is borrowed.
No man can model a god to resemble himself;
[17]subject to death, his impious hands can produce
only something dead.
He himself is worthier than the things he worships;
he will at least have lived, but never they.
[18]And they worship even the most loathsome of animals,
worse than the rest in their degree of stupidity,
[19]without a trace of beauty—if that is what is attractive
in animals—
and excluded from God's praises and blessing.

16 Thus they were appropriately punished by similar
creatures
and tormented by swarms of vermin.

GREEK OLD TESTAMENT

2 ἀνθ᾽ ἧς κολάσεως εὐεργετήσας τὸν λαόν σου
εἰς ἐπιθυμίαν ὀρέξεως ξένην γεῦσιν
τροφὴν ἡτοίμασας ὀρτυγομήτραν,
3 ἵνα ἐκεῖνοι μὲν ἐπιθυμοῦντες τροφὴν
διὰ τὴν εἰδέχθειαν τῶν ἐπαπεσταλμένων
καὶ τὴν ἀναγκαίαν ὄρεξιν ἀποστρέφωνται,
αὐτοὶ δὲ ἐπ᾽ ὀλίγον ἐνδεεῖς γενόμενοι
καὶ ξένης μετάσχωσι γεύσεως.
4 ἔδει γὰρ ἐκείνοις μὲν ἀπαραίτητον ἔνδειαν ἐπελθεῖν
τυραννοῦσιν,
τούτοις δὲ μόνον δειχθῆναι πῶς οἱ ἐχθροὶ αὐτῶν
ἐβασανίζοντο.
5 Καὶ γὰρ ὅτε αὐτοῖς δεινὸς ἐπῆλθεν θηρίων θυμὸς
δήγμασίν τε σκολιῶν διεφθείροντο ὄφεων,
οὐ μέχρι τέλους ἔμεινεν ἡ ὀργή σου·
6 εἰς νουθεσίαν δὲ πρὸς ὀλίγον ἐταράχθησαν
σύμβολον ἔχοντες σωτηρίας εἰς ἀνάμνησιν ἐντολῆς
νόμου σου·
7 ὁ γὰρ ἐπιστραφεὶς οὐ διὰ τὸ θεωρούμενον ἐσῴζετο,
ἀλλὰ διὰ σὲ τὸν πάντων σωτῆρα.
8 καὶ ἐν τούτῳ δὲ ἔπεισας τοὺς ἐχθροὺς ἡμῶν
ὅτι σὺ εἶ ὁ ῥυόμενος ἐκ παντὸς κακοῦ·

KING JAMES VERSION

2 Instead of which punishment, dealing graciously with thine own people, thou preparedst for them meat of a strange taste, even quails to stir up their appetite:

3 To the end that they, desiring food, might for the ugly sight of the beasts sent among them lothe even that, which they must needs desire; but these, suffering penury for a short space, might be made partakers of a strange taste.

4 For it was requisite, that upon them exercising tyranny should come penury, which they could not avoid: but to these it should only be shewed how their enemies were tormented.

5 For when the horrible fierceness of beasts came upon these, and they perished with the stings of crooked serpents, thy wrath endured not for ever:

6 But they were troubled for a small season, that they might be admonished, having a sign of salvation, to put them in remembrance of the commandment of thy law.

7 For he that turned himself toward it was not saved by the thing that he saw, but by thee, that art the Saviour of all.

8 And in this thou madest thine enemies confess, that it is thou who deliverest from all evil:

DOUAY OLD TESTAMENT

2 Instead of which punishment, dealing well with thy people, thou gavest them their desire of delicious food, of a new taste, preparing for them quails for their meat:

3 To the end that they indeed desiring food, by means of those things that were shewn and sent among them, might loathe even that which was necessary to satisfy their desire. But these, after suffering want for a short time, tasted a new meat.

4 For it was requisite that inevitable destruction should come upon them that exercised tyranny: but to these it should only be shewn how their enemies were destroyed.

5 For when the fierce rage of beasts came upon these, they were destroyed with the bitings of crooked serpents.

6 But thy wrath endured not for ever, but they were troubled for a short time for their correction, having a sign of salvation to put them in remembrance of the commandment of thy law.

7 For he that turned to it, was not healed by that which he saw, but by thee the Saviour of all.

8 And in this thou didst shew to our enemies, that thou art he who deliverest from all evil.

KNOX TRANSLATION

2 Thy own people no plague befell; pined their queasy stomach for dainties, thou wouldst feed them on quails. 3 Though
hunger drove them to food, the men of Egypt turned away with loathing from the necessaries they craved, so foul the sight of the frogs that came to punish them. Thy own people should go wanting for a little, only so as to prepare them for the dainties that would follow. 4 Their oppressors must feel
the pinch of poverty; for themselves, the sight of another's chastisement should be lesson enough. 5 When they them-
selves encountered brute malice, and the bites of writhing serpents threatened them with destruction, 6 thy vengeance
did not go to all lengths; enough that they should be warned by a brief experience of distress; they should be put in mind of thy law, yet have the assurance that thou wouldst come to their rescue. 7 For indeed, he who turned to look did not win
safety from the brazen serpent which met his eyes, but from thee, who alone canst save.

8 No better proof could our enemies have, that from all

TODAY'S ENGLISH VERSION

2 But you, O Lord, did not punish your people in this way;
instead, you showed them kindness. You sent them quails to
eat, a rare, delicious food to satisfy their hunger. 3 You did
all this so that the idolaters, when they were hungry, would
be unable to eat because of the disgusting creatures sent to
them. Your people, however, suffered hunger only a short
while, and then they ate the finest food. 4 It was necessary
for the oppressors to suffer relentless need, while your people
saw how their enemies were being tormented.
5 When terrible, fierce snakes attacked your people and
were killing them with their poison, you did not remain
angry long enough to destroy your people. 6 This trouble
lasted for only a little while, as a warning. Then you gave
them a healing symbol, the bronze snake, to remind them of
what your Law requires. 7 If a person looked at that symbol,
he was cured of the snakebite—not by what he saw, but by
you, the savior of all mankind. 8 By doing this, you also convinced our enemies that you are the one who rescues people

NEW REVISED STANDARD VERSION

2 Instead of this punishment you showed kindness to
your people,
and you prepared quails to eat,
a delicacy to satisfy the desire of appetite;
3 in order that those people, when they desired food,
might lose the least remnant of appetite[a]
because of the odious creatures sent to them,
while your people,[b] after suffering want a short time,
might partake of delicacies.
4 For it was necessary that upon those oppressors
inescapable want should come,
while to these others it was merely shown how their
enemies were being tormented.

5 For when the terrible rage of wild animals came upon
your people[c]
and they were being destroyed by the bites of writhing
serpents,
your wrath did not continue to the end;
6 they were troubled for a little while as a warning,
and received a symbol of deliverance to remind them of
your law's command.

7 For the one who turned toward it was saved, not by the
thing that was beheld,
but by you, the Savior of all.
8 And by this also you convinced our enemies
that it is you who deliver from every evil.

a Gk *loathed the necessary appetite* *b* Gk *they* *c* Gk *them*

NEW AMERICAN BIBLE

2 Instead of this punishment, you benefited your people
with a novel dish, the delight they craved,
by providing quail for their food;
3 That those others, when they desired food,
since the creatures sent to plague them were so
loathsome,
should be turned from even the craving of
necessities,
While these, after a brief period of privation,
partook of a novel dish.
4 For upon those oppressors, inexorable want had to
come;
but these needed only be shown how their enemies
were being tormented.
5 For when the dire venom of beasts came upon them
and they were dying from the bite of crooked
serpents,
your anger endured not to the end.
6 But as a warning, for a short time they were terrorized,
though they had a sign of salvation, to remind them
of the precept of your law.
7 For he who turned toward it was saved,
not by what he saw,
but by you, the savior of all.
8 And by this also you convinced our foes
that you are he who delivers from all evil.

NEW JERUSALEM BIBLE

2 In contrast to this punishment, you did your people a
kindness
and, to satisfy their sharp appetite,
provided quails—a luscious rarity—for them to eat.
3 Thus the Egyptians,
at the repulsive sight of the creatures sent against them,
were to find that, though they longed for food,
they had lost their natural appetite;
whereas your own people, after a short privation,
were to have a rare relish for their portion.
4 Inevitable that relentless want should seize on the
former oppressors;
enough for your people to be shown
how their enemies were being tortured.
5 Even when the fearful rage of wild animals overtook
them
and they were perishing from the bites of writhing
snakes,
your retribution did not continue to the end.
6 Affliction struck them briefly, by way of warning,
and they had a saving token[a] to remind them of the
commandment of your Law,
7 for whoever turned to it was saved, not by what he
looked at,
but by you, the Saviour of all.
8 And by such means you proved to our enemies
that you are the one who delivers from every evil;

a **16** The bronze snake, Nb 21:4–9.

GREEK OLD TESTAMENT

9 οὓς μὲν γὰρ ἀκρίδων καὶ μυιῶν ἀπέκτεινεν δήγματα,
καὶ οὐχ εὑρέθη ἴαμα τῇ ψυχῇ αὐτῶν,
ὅτι ἄξιοι ἦσαν ὑπὸ τοιούτων κολασθῆναι·
10 τοὺς δὲ υἱούς σου οὐδὲ ἰοβόλων δρακόντων ἐνίκησαν
ὀδόντες,
τὸ ἔλεος γάρ σου ἀντιπαρῆλθεν καὶ ἰάσατο αὐτούς.
11 εἰς γὰρ ὑπόμνησιν τῶν λογίων σου ἐνεκεντρίζοντο
καὶ ὀξέως διεσῴζοντο,
ἵνα μὴ εἰς βαθεῖαν ἐμπεσόντες λήθην
ἀπερίσπαστοι γένωνται τῆς σῆς εὐεργεσίας.
12 καὶ γὰρ οὔτε βοτάνη οὔτε μάλαγμα ἐθεράπευσεν
αὐτούς,
ἀλλὰ ὁ σός, κύριε, λόγος ὁ πάντας ἰώμενος.
13 σὺ γὰρ ζωῆς καὶ θανάτου ἐξουσίαν ἔχεις
καὶ κατάγεις εἰς πύλας ᾅδου καὶ ἀνάγεις·
14 ἄνθρωπος δὲ ἀποκτέννει μὲν τῇ κακίᾳ αὐτοῦ,
ἐξελθὸν δὲ πνεῦμα οὐκ ἀναστρέφει
οὐδὲ ἀναλύει ψυχὴν παραλημφθεῖσαν.
15 Τὴν δὲ σὴν χεῖρα φυγεῖν ἀδύνατόν ἐστιν·
16 ἀρνούμενοι γάρ σε εἰδέναι ἀσεβεῖς
ἐν ἰσχύι βραχίονός σου ἐμαστιγώθησαν
ξένοις ὑετοῖς καὶ χαλάζαις καὶ ὄμβροις διωκόμενοι
ἀπαραιτήτοις
καὶ πυρὶ καταναλισκόμενοι.
17 τὸ γὰρ παραδοξότατον, ἐν τῷ πάντα σβεννύντι ὕδατι

KING JAMES VERSION

9 For them the bitings of grasshoppers and flies killed, neither was there found any remedy for their life: for they were worthy to be punished by such.

10 But thy sons not the very teeth of venomous dragons overcame: for thy mercy was *ever* by them, and healed them.

11 For they were pricked, that they should remember thy words; and were quickly saved, that not falling into deep forgetfulness, they might be continually mindful of thy goodness.

12 For it was neither herb, nor mollifying plaister, that restored them to health: but thy word, O Lord, which healeth all things.

13 For thou hast power of life and death: thou leadest to the gates of hell, and bringest up again.

14 A man indeed killeth through his malice: and the spirit, when it is gone forth, returneth not; neither the soul received up cometh again.

15 But it is not possible to escape thine hand.

16 For the ungodly, that denied to know thee, were scourged by the strength of thine arm: with strange rains, hails, and showers, were they persecuted, that they could not avoid, and through fire were they consumed.

17 For, which is most to be wondered at, the fire had

DOUAY OLD TESTAMENT

9 For the bitings of locusts, and of flies killed them, and there was found no remedy for their life: because they were worthy to be destroyed by such things.

10 But not even the teeth of venomous serpents overcame thy children: for thy mercy came and healed them.

11 For they were examined for the remembrance of thy words, and were quickly healed, lest falling into deep forgetfulness, they might not be able to use thy help.

12 For it was neither herb, nor mollifying plaster that healed them, but thy word, O Lord, which healeth all things.

13 For it is thou, O Lord, that hast power of life and death, and leadest down to the gates of death, and bringest back again:

14 A man indeed killeth through malice, and when the spirit is gone forth, it shall not return, neither shall he call back the soul that is received:

15 But it is impossible to escape thy hand.

16 For the wicked that denied to know thee, were scourged by the strength of thy arm, being persecuted by strange waters, and hail, and rain, and consumed by fire.

17 And which was wonderful, in water, which extinguisheth

KNOX TRANSLATION

peril thou alone deliverest. 9 Bite of locust or sting of fly was
the undoing of them; no salve could be found against the
mortal punishment they had deserved. 10 And here were
these sons of thine, unvanquished even by the teeth of venomous serpents, because thy mercy came out to meet them
and gave relief. 11 They must feel the prick, to remind them
of the commandments they had from thee, and then quickly
be rescued before they sank into deep lethargy, beyond the
reach of thy succour. 12 Herb nor plaster it was that cured
them, but thy word, Lord, that all healing gives. 13 Lord of
life as of death, thou canst bring us down to the grave and
back from the grave; 14 thine is not the fatal stroke man
deals in spite, that banishes life beyond recall, imprisons the
soul for ever.

15 Truly, thine is a power there is no escaping; 16 the uplifted arm that plagued impious Egypt, where thou wast treated
as a stranger. Strange, indeed, to that country were the rains
that hunted them down, the fierce hail-storms; the fire, too,
that wasted them. 17 Wonder beyond all wont, that in water,

TODAY'S ENGLISH VERSION

from every evil. 9Our enemies died from the bites of locusts
and flies; no way was found to cure them, because they
deserved to be punished by such creatures. 10But even poisonous snakes could not overcome your people, because you
had mercy, helped them, and cured them. 11They were bitten
so that they would remember your commands, but they were
quickly rescued, in order to keep them from forgetting you
completely and depriving themselves of your kindness. 12No
medicine or ointment cured them. They were restored to
health by your word, O Lord, the word which heals all
humanity. 13You have power over life and death; you can
bring a person to the brink of death and back again.
14A wicked person may kill someone, but cannot bring the
dead person back to life or rescue a soul imprisoned in the
world of the dead.

15No one can possibly escape from you. 16Look at those
ungodly people: they refused to recognize you as God, so you
punished them with your great power. They were overtaken
by terrible storms of rain and hail and were completely
destroyed by fire. 17The most amazing thing was that the

NEW REVISED STANDARD VERSION

9 For they were killed by the bites of locusts and flies,
and no healing was found for them,
because they deserved to be punished by such things.
10 But your children were not conquered even by the fangs
of venomous serpents,
for your mercy came to their help and healed them.
11 To remind them of your oracles they were bitten,
and then were quickly delivered,
so that they would not fall into deep forgetfulness
and become unresponsive[a] to your kindness.
12 For neither herb nor poultice cured them,
but it was your word, O Lord, that heals all people.
13 For you have power over life and death;
you lead mortals down to the gates of Hades and back
again.
14 A person in wickedness kills another,
but cannot bring back the departed spirit,
or set free the imprisoned soul.

15 To escape from your hand is impossible;
16 for the ungodly, refusing to know you,
were flogged by the strength of your arm,
pursued by unusual rains and hail and relentless
storms,
and utterly consumed by fire.
17 For—most incredible of all—in water, which quenches
all things,

a Meaning of Gk uncertain

NEW AMERICAN BIBLE

9For the bites of locusts and of flies slew them,
and no remedy was found to save their lives
because they deserved to be punished by such means;
10But not even the fangs of poisonous reptiles overcame
your sons,
for your mercy brought the antidote to heal them.
11For as a reminder of your injunctions, they were stung,
and swiftly they were saved,
Lest they should fall into deep forgetfulness
and become unresponsive to your beneficence.
12For indeed, neither herb nor application cured them,
but your all-healing word, O LORD!
13For you have dominion over life and death;
you lead down to the gates of the nether world, and
lead back.
14Man, however, slays in his malice,
but when the spirit has come away, it does not
return,
nor can he bring back the soul once it is confined.
15But your hand none can escape.
16For the wicked who refused to know you
were punished by the might of your arm,
Pursued by unwonted rains and hailstorms and
unremitting downpours,
and consumed by fire.
17For against all expectation, in water which quenches
anything,

NEW JERUSALEM BIBLE

9for them, the bites of locusts and flies proved fatal
and no remedy could be found to save their lives,
since they deserved to be punished by such creatures.

10But your children,
not even the fangs of poisonous snakes could bring
them down;
for your mercy came to their help and cured them.
11One sting—how quickly healed!—
to remind them of your pronouncements
rather than that, by sinking into deep forgetfulness,
they should be cut off from your kindness.
12No herb, no poultice cured them,
but your all-healing word, Lord.
13Yes, you are the one with power over life and death,
bringing to the gates of Hades and back again.
14A human being out of malice may put to death,
but cannot bring the departed spirit back
or free the soul that Hades has once received.

15It is not possible to escape your hand.
16The godless who refused to acknowledge you
were scourged by the strength of your arm,
pursued by no ordinary rains, hail and unrelenting
downpours,
and consumed by fire.
17Even more wonderful, in the water—which quenches
all—

GREEK OLD TESTAMENT

πλεῖον ἐνήργει τὸ πῦρ,
ὑπέρμαχος γὰρ ὁ κόσμος ἐστὶν δικαίων·
18 ποτὲ μὲν γὰρ ἡμεροῦτο φλόξ,
ἵνα μὴ καταφλέξῃ τὰ ἐπ' ἀσεβεῖς ἀπεσταλμένα ζῷα,
ἀλλ' αὐτοὶ βλέποντες εἰδῶσιν ὅτι θεοῦ κρίσει
ἐλαύνονται·
19 ποτὲ δὲ καὶ μεταξὺ ὕδατος ὑπὲρ τὴν πυρὸς δύναμιν
φλέγει,
ἵνα ἀδίκου γῆς γενήματα διαφθείρῃ.
20 ἀνθ' ὧν ἀγγέλων τροφὴν ἐψώμισας τὸν λαόν σου
καὶ ἕτοιμον ἄρτον ἀπ' οὐρανοῦ παρέσχες αὐτοῖς
ἀκοπιάτως
πᾶσαν ἡδονὴν ἰσχύοντα καὶ πρὸς πᾶσαν ἁρμόνιον
γεῦσιν·
21 ἡ μὲν γὰρ ὑπόστασίς σου τὴν σὴν πρὸς τέκνα
ἐνεφάνιζεν γλυκύτητα,
τῇ δὲ τοῦ προσφερομένου ἐπιθυμίᾳ ὑπηρετῶν
πρὸς ὅ τις ἐβούλετο μετεκιρνᾶτο.
22 χιὼν δὲ καὶ κρύσταλλος ὑπέμεινε πῦρ καὶ οὐκ ἐτήκετο,
ἵνα γνῶσιν ὅτι τοὺς τῶν ἐχθρῶν καρποὺς
κατέφθειρε πῦρ φλεγόμενον ἐν τῇ χαλάζῃ
καὶ ἐν τοῖς ὑετοῖς διαστράπτον·
23 τοῦτο πάλιν δ', ἵνα τραφῶσιν δίκαιοι,
καὶ τῆς ἰδίας ἐπιλέλησται δυνάμεως.

KING JAMES VERSION

more force in the water, that quencheth all things: for the world fighteth for the righteous.

18 For sometime the flame was mitigated, that it might not burn up the beasts that were sent against the ungodly; but themselves might see and perceive that they were persecuted with the judgment of God.

19 And at another time it burneth even in the midst of water above the power of fire, that it might destroy the fruits of an unjust land.

20 Instead whereof thou feddest thine own people with angels' food, and didst send them from heaven bread prepared without their labour, able to content every man's delight, and agreeing to every taste.

21 For thy sustenance declared thy sweetness unto thy children, and serving to the appetite of the eater, tempered itself to every man's liking.

22 But snow and ice endured the fire, and melted not, that they might know that fire burning in the hail, and sparkling in the rain, did destroy the fruits of the enemies.

23 But this again did even forget his own strength, that the righteous might be nourished.

DOUAY OLD TESTAMENT

all things, the fire had more force: for the world fighteth for the just.

18 For at one time, the fire was mitigated, that the beasts which were sent against the wicked might not be burned, but that they might see and perceive that they were persecuted by the judgment of God.

19 And at another time the fire, above its own power, burned in the midst of water, to destroy the fruits of a wicked land.

20 Instead of which things thou didst feed thy people with the food of angels, and gavest them bread from heaven prepared without labour; having in it all that is delicious, and the sweetness of every taste.

21 For thy sustenance shewed thy sweetness to thy children, and serving every man's will, it was turned to what every man liked.

22 But snow and ice endured the force of fire, and melted not: that they might know that fire burning in the hail and flashing in the rain destroyed the fruits of the enemies.

23 But this same again, that the just might be nourished, did even forget its own strength.

KNOX TRANSLATION

the all-quenching, fire should rage its fiercest; no element
but must rally in the cause of right. 18 Here the flame would
burn low, to spare those creatures a scorching, that were thy
emissaries against the godless; doubt there should be none,
for any who saw it, but divine justice was at his heels.
19 Here, in the very midst of the water it would burn as never
fire burned yet, to blast all the fruits of that accursed land.
And thy own people, Lord? 20 Them thou didst foster with
the food of angels; bread from heaven thou didst set before
them, which no labour of theirs had made ready, every taste
uniting that could bring content, of every appetite the welcome choice. 21 So would thy own nature manifest a father's
universal love; this food should humour the eater's whim,
turning itself into that which he craved most. 22 In Egypt,
snow and ice had resisted the fire, never melting; plain it
was that this fire, which shone out amid the hailstones and
the rain, was in alliance with them to burn up and destroy
the enemy's harvest. 23 Now, once again, fire forgot its own
nature, this time, to give faithful souls their nourishment! [a]

[a] *vv.* 22, 23: The meaning here is not very clearly expressed; it is, that fire twice failed to produce its natural effect, once when it did not melt the hailstones which fell in Egypt, and again when it did not melt the manna in the cooking-pots of the Israelites (see verse 27 below, and Ex. 16. 21).

TODAY'S ENGLISH VERSION

fire burned all the more fiercely in the water, which usually
puts fire out. All the forces of nature fight to defend those
who are righteous. 18At one point the flames died down, so
that they wouldn't destroy the creatures sent to punish the
ungodly. Those people had to learn that they were being
overtaken by your judgment. 19But at another point, when
surrounded by water, the flames burned more fiercely than
fire had ever burned before, and so destroyed the crops on
the land where those unrighteous people lived.
20But this disaster did not strike your people. Instead, you
gave them the food of angels. From heaven you sent down
bread that was ready to eat, and they did not have to prepare
it. The food you gave delighted everyone, no matter what his
taste. 21All this showed how lovingly you care for your children. That food satisfied the desire of everyone who ate it; it
was changed to suit each person's taste. 22It was food that
under normal circumstances would vanish away like snow
or ice, but now it did not melt even in the fire. This was
meant to teach your people that the same fire that was
destroying their enemies' crops during the heavy downpour
of rain and hail 23held back its power, so that your own
righteous people might have food.

NEW REVISED STANDARD VERSION

the fire had still greater effect,
for the universe defends the righteous.
18 At one time the flame was restrained,
so that it might not consume the creatures sent against
the ungodly,
but that seeing this they might know
that they were being pursued by the judgment of God;
19 and at another time even in the midst of water it
burned more intensely than fire,
to destroy the crops of the unrighteous land.
20 Instead of these things you gave your people food of
angels,
and without their toil you supplied them from heaven
with bread ready to eat,
providing every pleasure and suited to every taste.
21 For your sustenance manifested your sweetness toward
your children;
and the bread, ministering[a] to the desire of the one
who took it,
was changed to suit everyone's liking.
22 Snow and ice withstood fire without melting,
so that they might know that the crops of their enemies
were being destroyed by the fire that blazed in the hail
and flashed in the showers of rain;
23 whereas the fire,[b] in order that the righteous might be
fed,
even forgot its native power.

a Gk *and it, ministering* *b* Gk *this*

NEW AMERICAN BIBLE

the fire grew more active;
For the universe fights on behalf of the just.
18For now the flame was tempered
so that the beasts might not be burnt up that were
sent upon the wicked,
but that these might see and know they were struck
by the judgment of God;
19And again, even in the water, fire blazed beyond its
strength
so as to consume the produce of the wicked land.
20Instead of this, you nourished your people with food of
angels
and furnished them bread from heaven, ready to
hand, untoiled-for,
endowed with all delights and conforming to every
taste.
21For this substance of yours revealed your sweetness
toward your children,
and serving the desire of him who received it,
was blended to whatever flavor each one wished.
22Yet snow and ice withstood fire and were not melted,
that they might know that their enemies' fruits
Were consumed by a fire that blazed in the hail
and flashed lightning in the rain.
23But this fire, again, that the just might be nourished,
forgot even its proper strength;

NEW JERUSALEM BIBLE

the fire[a] raged fiercer than ever;
for the elements fight for the upright.
18At one moment, the fire would die down,
to avoid consuming the animals sent against the
godless
and to make clear to them by that sight, that the
sentence of God was pursuing them;
19at another, in the very heart of the water, it would burn
more fiercely than fire
to ruin the produce of a wicked land.
20How differently with your people! You gave them the
food of angels,
from heaven untiringly providing them bread already
prepared,
containing every delight, to satisfy every taste.
21And the substance you gave
showed your sweetness towards your children,
for, conforming to the taste of whoever ate it,
it transformed itself into what each eater wished.
22Snow and ice endured the fire, without melting;
this was to show them that, to destroy the harvests of
their enemies,
fire would burn even in hail and flare in falling rain,
23whereas, on the other hand, it would even forget its
own strength
in the service of feeding the upright.

a **16** Cf. the lightning of Ex 9:24.

GREEK OLD TESTAMENT

24 Ἡ γὰρ κτίσις σοὶ τῷ ποιήσαντι ὑπηρετοῦσα
ἐπιτείνεται εἰς κόλασιν κατὰ τῶν ἀδίκων
καὶ ἀνίεται εἰς εὐεργεσίαν ὑπὲρ τῶν ἐπὶ σοὶ
πεποιθότων.
25 διὰ τοῦτο καὶ τότε εἰς πάντα μεταλλευομένη
τῇ παντοτρόφῳ σου δωρεᾷ ὑπηρέτει
πρὸς τὴν τῶν δεομένων θέλησιν,
26 ἵνα μάθωσιν οἱ υἱοί σου, οὓς ἠγάπησας, κύριε,
ὅτι οὐχ αἱ γενέσεις τῶν καρπῶν τρέφουσιν ἄνθρωπον,
ἀλλὰ τὸ ῥῆμά σου τοὺς σοὶ πιστεύοντας διατηρεῖ.
27 τὸ γὰρ ὑπὸ πυρὸς μὴ φθειρόμενον
ἁπλῶς ὑπὸ βραχείας ἀκτῖνος ἡλίου θερμαινόμενον
ἐτήκετο,
28 ὅπως γνωστὸν ᾖ ὅτι δεῖ φθάνειν τὸν ἥλιον ἐπ᾽
εὐχαριστίαν σου
καὶ πρὸς ἀνατολὴν φωτὸς ἐντυγχάνειν σοι·
29 ἀχαρίστου γὰρ ἐλπὶς ὡς χειμέριος πάχνη τακήσεται
καὶ ῥυήσεται ὡς ὕδωρ ἄχρηστον.

17 Μεγάλαι γάρ σου αἱ κρίσεις καὶ δυσδιήγητοι·
διὰ τοῦτο ἀπαίδευτοι ψυχαὶ ἐπλανήθησαν.
2 ὑπειληφότες γὰρ καταδυναστεύειν ἔθνος ἅγιον ἄνομοι
δέσμιοι σκότους καὶ μακρᾶς πεδῆται νυκτὸς

KING JAMES VERSION

24 For the creature that serveth thee, who art the Maker, increaseth his strength against the unrighteous for their punishment, and abateth his strength for the benefit of such as put their trust in thee.

25 Therefore even then was it altered into all fashions, and was obedient to thy grace, that nourisheth all things, according to the desire of them that had need:

26 That thy children, O Lord, whom thou lovest, might know, that it is not the growing of fruits that nourisheth man: but that it is thy word, which preserveth them that put their trust in thee.

27 For that which was not destroyed of the fire, being warmed with a little sunbeam, soon melted away:

28 That it might be known, that we must prevent the sun to give thee thanks, and at the dayspring pray unto thee.

29 For the hope of the unthankful shall melt away as the winter's hoar frost, and shall run away as unprofitable water.

17 For great are thy judgments, and cannot be expressed: therefore unnurtured souls have erred.

2 For when unrighteous men thought to oppress the holy nation; they being shut up in their houses, the prisoners of

DOUAY OLD TESTAMENT

24 For the creature serving thee the Creator, is made fierce against the unjust for their punishment; and abateth its strength for the benefit of them that trust in thee.

25 Therefore even then it was transformed into all things, and was obedient to thy grace that nourisheth all, according to the will of them that desired it of thee:

26 That thy children, O Lord, whom thou lovedst, might know that it is not the growing of fruits that nourisheth men, but thy word preserveth them that believe in thee.

27 For that which could not be destroyed by fire, being warmed with a little sunbeam presently melted away:

28 That it might be known to all, that we ought to prevent the sun to bless thee, and adore thee at the dawning of the light.

29 For the hope of the unthankful shall melt away as the winter's ice, and shall run off as unprofitable water.

17 FOR thy judgments, O Lord, are great, and thy words cannot be expressed: therefore undisciplined souls have erred.

2 For while the wicked thought to be able to have dominion over the holy nation, *they themselves being* fettered with the bonds of darkness, and a long night, shut up in their

KNOX TRANSLATION

24 So well does thy creation obey thee, its author, now exerting all its powers to punish the wicked, now abating its force to do thy loyal followers a service!

25 Why should nature, seconding that universal bounty of
thine, go to all shifts to meet the needs of thy suppliants,
26 but for the instruction of thy own children, Lord, children
so well beloved? They were to learn that man lives, not by
the ripening of crops, but by thy word, ever protecting the
souls that trust in thee. 27 This manna, that never shrank
from the fire while it was a-cooking, would melt before the
heat of the sun's first feeble ray. 28 What meant this, but
that we must be up before the sun to give thee thanks, seeking thy audience with day's earliest light? 29 Thankless if a
man be, like the hoar frost of winter his hopes shall dissolve;
like water that goes to waste they shall vanish.

17 High above us, Lord, are thy judgements, mysterious
thy dealings; no skill had those Egyptian hearts to
understand them. 2 They had thought to exercise barbarous
tyranny over a nation consecrated to thee. And now they lay,
shut close under their own roofs, darkness their dungeon,
their sentence a long-drawn night, exiled from the gifts of

TODAY'S ENGLISH VERSION

24 You created the universe; it is at your command. All creation uses its power to punish unrighteous people, but it
becomes mild and kind to those who put their trust in you.
25 Creation assumed all kinds of forms to show how you provide generously for all who pray to you.[a] 26 This happened
so that the people whom you loved, O Lord, might learn that
they are not fed by what they can grow. It is your word that
maintains those who put their trust in you. 27 The food that
was not destroyed by the fire melted when the first ray of
sunlight warmed it. 28 This was to teach us that we must get
up before daybreak to give you thanks, and pray as the sun
comes up. 29 But an ungrateful person's hope will melt away
like frost, and drain away like water that is not being used.

17 O Lord, your acts of judgment are marvelous and
hard to explain; that is why people who had not been
taught about them went astray. 2 When lawless people imagined that they had your holy nation in their power, they were
themselves imprisoned in a long night of darkness. They lay

[a] pray to you; *or* are in need.

NEW REVISED STANDARD VERSION

24 For creation, serving you who made it,
exerts itself to punish the unrighteous,
and in kindness relaxes on behalf of those who trust in you.
25 Therefore at that time also, changed into all forms,
it served your all-nourishing bounty,
according to the desire of those who had need,[a]
26 so that your children, whom you loved, O Lord, might learn
that it is not the production of crops that feeds humankind
but that your word sustains those who trust in you.
27 For what was not destroyed by fire
was melted when simply warmed by a fleeting ray of the sun,
28 to make it known that one must rise before the sun to give you thanks,
and must pray to you at the dawning of the light;
29 for the hope of an ungrateful person will melt like wintry frost,
and flow away like waste water.

17 Great are your judgments and hard to describe;
therefore uninstructed souls have gone astray.
2 For when lawless people supposed that they held the holy nation in their power,
they themselves lay as captives of darkness and prisoners of long night,

[a] Or *who made supplication*

NEW AMERICAN BIBLE

24 For your creation, serving you, its maker,
grows tense for punishment against the wicked,
but is relaxed in benefit for those who trust in you.
25 Therefore at that very time, transformed in all sorts of ways,
it was serving your all-nourishing bounty
according to what they needed and desired;
26 That your sons whom you loved might learn, O LORD,
that it is not the various kinds of fruits that nourish man,
but it is your word that preserves those who believe you!
27 For what was not destroyed by fire,
when merely warmed by a momentary sunbeam, melted;
28 So that men might know that one must give you thanks before the sunrise,
and turn to you at daybreak.
29 For the hope of the ingrate melts like a wintry frost
and runs off like useless water.

17 For great are your judgments, and hardly to be described;
therefore the unruly souls were wrong.
2 For when the lawless thought to enslave the holy nation,
shackled with darkness, fettered by the long night,

NEW JERUSALEM BIBLE

24 For the creation, being at the service of you, its Creator,
tautens to punish the wicked
and slackens for the benefit of those who trust in you.
25 And this is why, by changing into all things,
it obediently served your all-nourishing bounty,
conforming to the wishes of those who were in need;
26 so that your beloved children, Lord, might learn
that the various crops are not what provide nourishment,
but your word which preserves all who believe in you.
27 For that which fire could not destroy
melted in the heat of a single fleeting sunbeam,
28 to show that, to give you thanks, we must rise before the sun
and meet you at the dawning of the day;
29 whereas the hope of the ungrateful melts like winter frost
and flows away like water running to waste.

17 Yes, your judgements are great and impenetrable,
which is why uninstructed souls have gone astray.
2 While the wicked supposed they had a holy nation in their power,
they themselves lay prisoners of the dark,[a] in the fetters of long night,

[a] **17** Cf. Ex 10:21–23. It is here supposed that darkness came on some while light continued for others.

GREEK OLD TESTAMENT

κατακλεισθέντες ὀρόφοις φυγάδες τῆς αἰωνίου
προνοίας ἔκειντο.
3 λανθάνειν γὰρ νομίζοντες ἐπὶ κρυφαίοις ἁμαρτήμασιν
ἀφεγγεῖ λήθης παρακαλύμματι
ἐσκορπίσθησαν θαμβούμενοι δεινῶς
καὶ ἰνδάλμασιν ἐκταρασσόμενοι.
4 οὐδὲ γὰρ ὁ κατέχων αὐτοὺς μυχὸς ἀφόβους
διεφύλαττεν,
ἦχοι δ' ἐκταράσσοντες αὐτοὺς περιεκόμπουν,
καὶ φάσματα ἀμειδήτοις κατηφῆ προσώποις
ἐνεφανίζετο.
5 καὶ πυρὸς μὲν οὐδεμία βία κατίσχυεν φωτίζειν,
οὔτε ἄστρων ἔκλαμπροι φλόγες
καταυγάζειν ὑπέμενον τὴν στυγνὴν ἐκείνην νύκτα.
6 διεφαίνετο δ' αὐτοῖς μόνον
αὐτομάτη πυρὰ φόβου πλήρης,
ἐκδειματούμενοι δὲ τῆς μὴ θεωρουμένης ἐκείνης ὄψεως
ἡγοῦντο χείρω τὰ βλεπόμενα.
7 μαγικῆς δὲ ἐμπαίγματα κατέκειτο τέχνης,
καὶ τῆς ἐπὶ φρονήσει ἀλαζονείας ἔλεγχος ἐφύβριστος·
8 οἱ γὰρ ὑπισχνούμενοι δείματα καὶ ταραχὰς ἀπελαύνειν
ψυχῆς νοσούσης,
οὗτοι καταγέλαστον εὐλάβειαν ἐνόσουν.
9 καὶ γὰρ εἰ μηδὲν αὐτοὺς ταραχῶδες ἐφόβει,
κνωδάλων παρόδοις καὶ ἑρπετῶν συριγμοῖς
ἐκσεσοβημένοι

KING JAMES VERSION

darkness, and fettered with the bonds of a long night, lay [there] exiled from the eternal providence.

3 For while they supposed to lie hid in their secret sins, they were scattered under a dark veil of forgetfulness, being horribly astonished, and troubled with [strange] apparitions.

4 For neither might the corner that held them keep them from fear: but noises [as of waters] falling down sounded about them, and sad visions appeared unto them with heavy countenances.

5 No power of the fire might give them light: neither could the bright flames of the stars endure to lighten that horrible night.

6 Only there appeared unto them a fire kindled of itself, very dreadful: for being much terrified, they thought the things which they saw to be worse than the sight they saw not.

7 As for the illusions of art magick, they were put down, and their vaunting in wisdom was reproved with disgrace.

8 For they, that promised to drive away terrors and troubles from a sick soul, were sick themselves of fear, worthy to be laughed at.

9 For though no terrible thing did fear them; yet being scared with beasts that passed by, and hissing of serpents,

DOUAY OLD TESTAMENT

houses, lay *there* exiled from the eternal providence.

3 And while they thought to lie hid in their obscure sins, they were scattered under a dark veil of forgetfulness, being horribly afraid and troubled with exceeding great astonishment.

4 For neither did the den that held them, keep them from fear: for noises coming down troubled them, and sad visions appearing to them, affrighted them.

5 And no power of fire could give them light, neither could the bright flames of the stars enlighten that horrible night.

6 But there appeared to them a sudden fire, very dreadful: and being struck with the fear of that face, which was not seen, they thought the things which they saw to be worse:

7 And the delusions of their magic art were put down, and their boasting of wisdom was reproachfully rebuked.

8 For they who promised to drive away fears and troubles from a sick soul, were sick themselves of a fear worthy to be laughed at.

9 For though no terrible thing disturbed them: yet being scared with the passing by of beasts, and hissing of serpents,

KNOX TRANSLATION

thy eternal Providence. 3 Did they hope, under that dark veil
of oblivion, to find a cloak for secret sinning? Nay, they were
scattered far apart, and in grievous dread of the terrors that
came to daunt them. 4 Lie snug in their hidden lairs they
might not; noises swept down, echoing about their affrighted
ears, and boding visions of sad faces cowed their spirits.
5 Fire itself no light could give them, nor star's clear beam
illuminate that hideous night; 6 only now and again a blaze
shone out, not of their kindling, terrible to behold; and fear
of this unseen radiance lent fresh horror to the sights it
shewed.[a]
7 A mockery, now, seemed those magic arts of theirs; ignominious the rebuff to their boasted cunning. 8 The very men
who had professed to rid ailing minds of all discomposure
and disquiet, were now themselves sick with apprehension,
to their great discomfiture. 9 Even when no alarms were
present to disturb them, the memory of prowling beast and
hissing serpent filled them with mortal tremors, till they shut

a The original is here very obscure; it runs, literally, 'Only a self-lighted beacon shone upon them at intervals, full of terror, and being afraid of that vision which escaped their observation, they thought the things seen worse'.

TODAY'S ENGLISH VERSION

in their own houses, shut off from your eternal care. 3They
thought that their sins had been secret and unnoticed,
shielded from view by a dark curtain of forgetfulness, but
now they were horribly afraid, confused, and terrified by
ghostly forms. 4Not even the dark corners where they lay
could protect them from fear. They were surrounded by horrible noises; grim ghosts with gloomy faces appeared before
their eyes. 5No fire had power to give them light, and the
brilliant stars could do nothing to relieve that deathly darkness. 6There was only a dreadful fire, lit by no human hand,
that shone on them, and in their terror they believed that the
real world was even worse than the things they imagined.
7The illusions produced by their magic tricks were put to
shame, and all the wisdom they had boasted of came to
nothing. 8They had claimed they could drive away all the
fears and illnesses of sick minds, but now they themselves
were sick with silly, groundless fears. 9Even though nothing
dangerous had actually happened, they were terrified by
hissing snakes and animals advancing on them. 10And so

NEW REVISED STANDARD VERSION

shut in under their roofs, exiles from eternal
providence.
3 For thinking that in their secret sins they were
unobserved
behind a dark curtain of forgetfulness,
they were scattered, terribly[a] alarmed,
and appalled by specters.
4 For not even the inner chamber that held them
protected them from fear,
but terrifying sounds rang out around them,
and dismal phantoms with gloomy faces appeared.
5 And no power of fire was able to give light,
nor did the brilliant flames of the stars
avail to illumine that hateful night.
6 Nothing was shining through to them
except a dreadful, self-kindled fire,
and in terror they deemed the things that they saw
to be worse than that unseen appearance.
7 The delusions of their magic art lay humbled,
and their boasted wisdom was scornfully rebuked.
8 For those who promised to drive off the fears and
disorders of a sick soul
were sick themselves with ridiculous fear.
9 For even if nothing disturbing frightened them,
yet, scared by the passing of wild animals and the
hissing of snakes

a Other ancient authorities read *unobserved, they were darkened behind a dark curtain of forgetfulness, terribly*

NEW AMERICAN BIBLE

they lay confined beneath their own roofs as exiles
from the eternal providence.
3 For they who supposed their secret sins were hid
under the dark veil of oblivion
Were scattered in fearful trembling,
terrified by apparitions.
4 For not even their inner chambers kept them fearless,
for crashing sounds on all sides terrified them,
and mute phantoms with somber looks appeared.
5 No force, even of fire, was able to give light,
nor did the flaming brilliance of the stars
succeed in lighting up that gloomy night.
6 But only intermittent, fearful fires
flashed through upon them;
And in their terror they thought beholding these was
worse
than the times when that sight was no longer to be
seen.
7 And mockeries of the magic art were in readiness,
and a jeering reproof of their vaunted shrewdness.
8 For they who undertook to banish fears and terrors
from the sick soul
themselves sickened with a ridiculous fear.
9 For even though no monstrous thing frightened them,
they shook at the passing of insects and the hissing
of reptiles,

NEW JERUSALEM BIBLE

confined under their own roofs, banished from eternal
providence.
3 While they thought to remain unnoticed with their
secret sins,
curtained by dark forgetfulness,
they were scattered in fearful dismay,
terrified by apparitions.
4 The hiding place sheltering them could not ward off
their fear;
terrifying noises echoed round them;
and gloomy, grim-faced spectres haunted them.
5 No fire had power enough to give them light,
nor could the brightly blazing stars
illuminate that dreadful night.
6 The only light for them was a great, spontaneous
blaze—
a fearful sight to see!
And in their terror, once that sight had vanished,
they thought what they had seen more terrible than
ever.
7 Their magical illusions were powerless now,
and their claims to intelligence were ignominiously
confounded;
8 for those who promised to drive out fears and disorders
from sick souls
were now themselves sick with ludicrous fright.
9 Even when there was nothing frightful to scare them,
the vermin creeping past and the hissing of reptiles
filled them with panic;

GREEK OLD TESTAMENT

διώλλυντο ἔντρομοι
καὶ τὸν μηδαμόθεν φευκτὸν ἀέρα προσιδεῖν ἀρνούμενοι.
10 δειλὸν γὰρ ἰδίῳ πονηρία μάρτυρι καταδικαζομένη,
ἀεὶ δὲ προσείληφεν τὰ χαλεπὰ συνεχομένη τῇ
συνειδήσει·
11 οὐθὲν γάρ ἐστιν φόβος εἰ μὴ προδοσία τῶν ἀπὸ
λογισμοῦ βοηθημάτων,
12 ἔνδοθεν δὲ οὖσα ἥττων ἡ προσδοκία
πλείονα λογίζεται τὴν ἄγνοιαν τῆς παρεχούσης τὴν
βάσανον αἰτίας.
13 οἱ δὲ τὴν ἀδύνατον ὄντως νύκτα
καὶ ἐξ ἀδυνάτου ᾅδου μυχῶν ἐπελθοῦσαν
τὸν αὐτὸν ὕπνον κοιμώμενοι
14 τὰ μὲν τέρασιν ἠλαύνοντο φαντασμάτων,
τὰ δὲ τῆς ψυχῆς παρελύοντο προδοσίᾳ·
αἰφνίδιος γὰρ αὐτοῖς καὶ ἀπροσδόκητος φόβος ἐπεχύθη.
15 εἶθ᾽ οὕτως, ὃς δή ποτ᾽ οὖν ἦν ἐκεῖ καταπίπτων,
ἐφρουρεῖτο εἰς τὴν ἀσίδηρον εἱρκτὴν κατακλεισθείς·
16 εἴ τε γὰρ γεωργὸς ἦν τις ἢ ποιμὴν
ἢ τῶν κατ᾽ ἐρημίαν ἐργάτης μόχθων,
προλημφθεὶς τὴν δυσάλυκτον ἔμενεν ἀνάγκην,
μιᾷ γὰρ ἁλύσει σκότους πάντες ἐδέθησαν·
17 εἴ τε πνεῦμα συρίζον

KING JAMES VERSION

10 They died for fear, denying that they saw the air, which could of no side be avoided.

11 For wickedness, condemned by her own witness, is very timorous, and being pressed with conscience, always forecasteth grievous things.

12 For fear is nothing else but a betraying of the succours which reason offereth.

13 And the expectation from within, being less, counteth the ignorance more than the cause which bringeth the torment.

14 But they sleeping the same sleep that night, which was indeed intolerable, and which came upon them out of the bottoms of inevitable hell,

15 Were partly vexed with monstrous apparitions, and partly fainted, their heart failing them: for a sudden fear, and not looked for, came upon them.

16 So then whosoever there fell down was straitly kept, shut up in a prison without iron bars.

17 For whether he were husbandman, or shepherd, or a labourer in the field, he was overtaken, and endured that necessity, which could not be avoided: for they were all bound with one chain of darkness.

18 Whether it were a whistling wind, or a melodious

DOUAY OLD TESTAMENT

they died for fear: and denying that they saw the air, which could by no means be avoided.

10 For whereas wickedness is fearful, it beareth witness of its condemnation: for a troubled conscience always forecasteth grievous things.

11 For fear is nothing else but a yielding up of the succours from thought.

12 And while there is less expectation from within, the greater doth it count the ignorance of that cause which bringeth the torment.

13 But they that during that night, in which nothing could be done, and which came upon them from the lowest and deepest hell, slept the same sleep,

14 Were sometimes molested with the fear of monsters, sometimes fainted away, their soul failing them: for a sudden and unlooked for fear was come upon them.

15 Moreover if any of them had fallen down, he was kept shut up in prison without irons.

16 For if any one were a husbandman, or a shepherd, or a labourer in the field, and was suddenly overtaken, he endured a necessity from which he could not fly.

17 For they were all bound together with one chain of darkness. Whether it were a whistling wind, or the melodi-

KNOX TRANSLATION

their eyes against the sight of empty air, we must all
breathe.[a] 10 So cowardly a thing is wickedness, it pro-
nounces its own condemnation; hard pressed by conscience,
it forecasts ever the worst. 11 What else is timorousness, but
a betrayal of the vantage-ground reason gives us?
12 Imagination, already defeated within its own stronghold,
fears the unknown more than it fears the true source of its
misery. 13 Whether the darkness that held them bound were
true night, or that darkness which comes up from the lowest
depths of the grave, their bemused senses could not well distinguish;[b] 14 now monstrous apparitions came indeed to
scare them, now it was but their own faint hearts made cow-
ards of them; in a moment dismay was all about them, and
took them unawares.
15 Into this prison, then, that needed no bars to secure it,
all fell alike, whatever their condition; 16 tiller of the fields,
or shepherd, or workman that plied his task out in the
desert, each was caught at his post, each must abide the
inevitable lot, 17 by darkness, like all his fellows, held in
thrall. Did the wind whistle, or bird utter tuneful notes deep

a 'We must all breathe'; literally, according to the Latin version, 'which cannot possibly be avoided'; but the sense of the Greek is probably 'which there is no reason to dread'. *b* *vv.* 11-14: There is much obscurity here, and perhaps some corruption in the text. Of verse 13, only conjectural interpretation is possible; it runs, literally, 'sleeping the same sleep the really impossible night and (the night) coming upon them from the depths of an impossible lower world'.

TODAY'S ENGLISH VERSION

they died, shaking with fear, afraid even to open their eyes,
yet unable to keep them shut.
11 Wickedness is cowardly in itself and stands self-condemned.[a] Someone with a guilty conscience will always
imagine things to be worse than they really are. 12 Fear is
nothing but the failure to use the help that reason gives.
13 When you lack the confidence to rely on reason, you give
in to the fears caused by ignorance.
14 All night long those people slept the same restless sleep,
even though the night held no power over them, since it
came from the powerless depths of the world of the dead.
15 They were chased by hideous forms and lay paralyzed as
they surrendered themselves to the sudden, unexpected fear
that came over them. 16 People would suddenly collapse and
lie locked in the chains of their own fear. 17 Farmers, shepherds, and laborers out in the countryside were captured by
the same inevitable fate and bound in the darkness by the
same invisible chain. 18-19 They were panic-stricken by the
sighing of the wind or by the singing of birds in the trees or

[a] Wickedness . . . self-condemned; *Greek unclear.*

NEW REVISED STANDARD VERSION

10 they perished in trembling fear,
refusing to look even at the air, though it nowhere
could be avoided.
11 For wickedness is a cowardly thing, condemned by its
own testimony;[a]
distressed by conscience, it has always exaggerated[b]
the difficulties.
12 For fear is nothing but a giving up of the helps that
come from reason;
13 and hope, defeated by this inward weakness,
prefers ignorance of what causes the torment.
14 But throughout the night, which was really powerless
and which came upon them from the recesses of
powerless Hades,
they all slept the same sleep,
15 and now were driven by monstrous specters,
and now were paralyzed by their souls' surrender;
for sudden and unexpected fear overwhelmed them.
16 And whoever was there fell down,
and thus was kept shut up in a prison not made of iron;
17 for whether they were farmers or shepherds
or workers who toiled in the wilderness,
they were seized, and endured the inescapable fate;
for with one chain of darkness they all were bound.
18 Whether there came a whistling wind,

[a] Meaning of Gk uncertain [b] Other ancient authorities read *anticipated*

NEW AMERICAN BIBLE

10 And perished trembling,
reluctant to face even the air that they could nowhere
escape.
11 For wickedness, of its nature cowardly, testifies in its
own condemnation,
and because of a distressed conscience, always
magnifies misfortunes.
12 For fear is nought but the surrender of the helps that
come from reason;
13 and the more one's expectation is of itself uncertain,
the more one makes of not knowing the cause that
brings on torment.
14 So they, during that night, powerless though it was,
that had come upon them from the recesses of a
powerless nether world,
while all sleeping the same sleep,
15 Were partly smitten by fearsome apparitions
and partly stricken by their soul's surrender;
for fear came upon them, sudden and unexpected.
16 Thus, then, whoever was there fell
into that unbarred prison and was kept confined.
17 For whether one was a farmer, or a shepherd,
or a worker at tasks in the wasteland,
Taken unawares, he served out the inescapable
sentence;
18 for all were bound by the one bond of darkness.
And were it only the whistling wind,

NEW JERUSALEM BIBLE

10 they died convulsed with fright,
refusing even to look at empty air, which cannot be
eluded anyhow!
11 Wickedness is confessedly very cowardly, and it
condemns itself;
under pressure from conscience it always assumes the
worst.
12 Fear, indeed, is nothing other
than the failure of the help offered by reason;
13 the less you rely within yourself on this,
the more alarming it is not to know the cause of your
suffering.
14 And they, all locked in the same sleep,
while that darkness lasted—which was in fact quite
powerless
and had issued from the depths of equally powerless
Hades—
15 were now chased by monstrous spectres,
now paralysed by the fainting of their souls;
for a sudden, unexpected terror had attacked them.
16 And thus, whoever it might be that fell there
stayed clamped to the spot in this prison without bars.
17 Whether he was ploughman or shepherd,
or somebody at work in the desert,
he was still overtaken and suffered the inevitable fate,
for all had been bound by the one same chain of
darkness.
18 The soughing of the wind,

GREEK OLD TESTAMENT

ἢ περὶ ἀμφιλαφεῖς κλάδους ὀρνέων ἦχος εὐμελὴς
ἢ ῥυθμὸς ὕδατος πορευομένου βίᾳ
ἢ κτύπος ἀπηνὴς καταρριπτομένων πετρῶν
18 ἢ σκιρτώντων ζῴων δρόμος ἀθεώρητος
ἢ ὠρυομένων ἀπηνεστάτων θηρίων φωνὴ
ἢ ἀντανακλωμένη ἐκ κοιλότητος ὀρέων ἠχώ,
παρέλυεν αὐτοὺς ἐκφοβοῦντα.
19 ὅλος γὰρ ὁ κόσμος λαμπρῷ κατελάμπετο φωτὶ
καὶ ἀνεμποδίστοις συνείχετο ἔργοις·
20 μόνοις δὲ ἐκείνοις ἐπετέτατο βαρεῖα νὺξ
εἰκὼν τοῦ μέλλοντος αὐτοὺς διαδέχεσθαι σκότους,
ἑαυτοῖς δὲ ἦσαν βαρύτεροι σκότους.

18 Τοῖς δὲ ὁσίοις σου μέγιστον ἦν φῶς·
ὧν φωνὴν μὲν ἀκούοντες μορφὴν δὲ οὐχ ὁρῶντες,
ὅτι μὲν οὐ κἀκεῖνοι ἐπεπόνθεισαν, ἐμακάριζον,
2 ὅτι δ' οὐ βλάπτουσιν προηδικημένοι, ηὐχαρίστουν
καὶ τοῦ διενεχθῆναι χάριν ἐδέοντο.
3 ἀνθ' ὧν πυριφλεγῆ στῦλον
ὁδηγὸν μὲν ἀγνώστου ὁδοιπορίας,
ἥλιον δὲ ἀβλαβῆ φιλοτίμου ξενιτείας παρέσχες.
4 ἄξιοι μὲν γὰρ ἐκεῖνοι στερηθῆναι φωτὸς καὶ
φυλακισθῆναι σκότει

KING JAMES VERSION

noise of birds among the spreading branches, or a pleasing fall of water running violently,

19 Or a terrible sound of stones cast down, or a running that could not be seen of skipping beasts, or a roaring voice of most savage wild beasts, or a rebounding echo from the hollow mountains; these things made them to swoon for fear.

20 For the whole world shined with clear light, and none were hindered in their labour:

21 Over them only was spread an heavy night, an image of that darkness which should afterward receive them: but yet were they unto themselves more grievous than the darkness.

18 Nevertheless thy saints had a very great light, whose voice they hearing, and not seeing their shape, because they also had not suffered the same things, they counted them happy.

2 But for that they did not hurt them *now,* of whom they had been wronged before, they thanked them, and besought them pardon for that they had been enemies.

3 Instead whereof thou gavest them a burning pillar of fire, both to be a guide of the unknown journey, and an harmless sun to entertain them honourably.

4 For they were worthy to be deprived of light, and impris-

DOUAY OLD TESTAMENT

ous voice of birds, among the spreading branches of trees, or a fall of water running down with violence,

18 Or the mighty noise of stones tumbling down, or the running that could not be seen of beasts playing together, or the roaring voice of wild beasts, or a rebounding echo from the highest mountains: these things made them to swoon for fear.

19 For the whole world was enlightened with a clear light, and none were hindered in their labours.

20 But over them only was spread a heavy night, an image of that darkness which was to come upon them. But they were to themselves more grievous than the darkness.

18 BUT thy saints had a very great light, and they heard their voice indeed, but did not see their shape. And because they also did not suffer the same things, they glorified thee:

2 And they that before had been wronged, gave thanks, because they were not hurt now: and asked this gift, that there might be a difference.

3 Therefore they received a burning pillar of fire for a guide of the way which they knew not, and thou gavest them a harmless sun of a good entertainment.

4 The others indeed were worthy to be deprived of light,

KNOX TRANSLATION

amid the boughs; were it the dull roar of some waterfall,
18 or the sudden crash of tumbling rocks, or the padding feet
of beasts that gambolled past them unseen, or the howl of
wild things ravening, or a booming echo from the mountain
hollows, it was all one; it would startle them into a great
quaking of fear. 19 All around them the world was bathed in
the clear sunlight, and men went about their tasks unhindered; 20 over them alone this heavy curtain of night was
spread, image of the darkness that should be their next
abode. Yet each man had a burden heavier to bear than darkness itself, the burden of his own companionship.

18 Brightest of all, that light shone on thy chosen people.
These neighbours of theirs, heard but not seen, the
Egyptians must congratulate on their escape from the common
doom, 2 thank them for letting vengeance be, and ask forgiveness for past ill-will.[a] 3 To these thou gavest, not darkness,
but a pillar of burning fire, to be the guide of their unfamiliar
journey, a sun, all gracious welcome, that brought no harm.[b]
4 A fitting punishment it was for the Egyptians, this loss of
light; fitting that they should be imprisoned in darkness,

a vv. 1, 2: The Greek text (which is rendered above) has here been misunderstood by the Latin translator, and the version he gives altogether misrepresents the sense of the passage; it runs: 'Brightest of all the light shone on thy chosen people. They heard the voice of these, but did not see their form. And they glorified thee for their escape from the common doom, thanking thee that they were not now, as they had been formerly, the sufferers; and they made a request of thee, that thou wouldst distinguish' (between themselves and the Egyptians). The words 'Egypt', 'Egyptians', 'Israel', and 'Aaron', though not in the original, have been supplied in this chapter as before. *b* The Greek text probably means, 'which should preserve them from harm during their ambitious travels'.

TODAY'S ENGLISH VERSION

by the roar of rushing water or by the rumble of falling rock
or by the sound of unseen creatures running about or by the
savage roaring of wild animals or by the echoes from the
mountains. 20 In the full light of day, the rest of the world
went about its business undisturbed. 21 Only those people
were covered by this heavy night, a foretaste of the darkness
of death that was waiting for them. They were a burden to
themselves that was even heavier than the darkness.

18 Yet all the while a brilliant light was shining for your
holy people. Their enemies heard their voices, but
couldn't see them. They envied the good fortune of your people, who were not suffering. 2 Those enemies could at least
be thankful that the people they had wronged were not taking vengeance on them now, and so they begged them to
leave.[a]

3 Then you guided your people as they traveled through a
country they did not know. You guided them with a pillar of
fire. It was like a sun that would not harm them on that glorious journey. 4 But their enemies, who were not allowed to
see the light, deserved to be prisoners in darkness, because

[a] begged them to leave; *or* begged their forgiveness for their past hostility.

NEW REVISED STANDARD VERSION

or a melodious sound of birds in wide-spreading
 branches,
or the rhythm of violently rushing water,
19 or the harsh crash of rocks hurled down,
or the unseen running of leaping animals,
or the sound of the most savage roaring beasts,
or an echo thrown back from a hollow of the mountains,
it paralyzed them with terror.
20 For the whole world was illumined with brilliant light,
and went about its work unhindered,
21 while over those people alone heavy night was spread,
an image of the darkness that was destined to receive
 them;
but still heavier than darkness were they to themselves.

18 But for your holy ones there was very great light.
Their enemies[a] heard their voices but did not see
 their forms,
and counted them happy for not having suffered,
2 and were thankful that your holy ones,[b] though
 previously wronged, were doing them no injury;
and they begged their pardon for having been at
 variance with them.[b]
3 Therefore you provided a flaming pillar of fire
as a guide for your people's[c] unknown journey,
and a harmless sun for their glorious wandering.
4 For their enemies[d] deserved to be deprived of light and
 imprisoned in darkness,

a Gk *They* *b* Meaning of Gk uncertain *c* Gk *their* *d* Gk *those persons*

NEW AMERICAN BIBLE

or the melodious song of birds in the spreading
 branches,
Or the steady sound of rushing water,
19 or the rude crash of overthrown rocks,
Or the unseen gallop of bounding animals,
or the roaring cry of the fiercest beasts,
Or an echo resounding from the hollow of the hills,
these sounds, inspiring terror, paralyzed them.
20 For the whole world shone with brilliant light
and continued its works without interruption;
21 Over them alone was spread oppressive night,
an image of the darkness that next should come
 upon them;
yet they were to themselves more burdensome than
 the darkness.

18 But your holy ones had very great light;
And those others, who heard their voices but did not
 see their forms,
since now they themselves had suffered, called them
 blest;
2 And because they who formerly had been wronged did
 not harm them, they thanked them,
and pleaded with them, for the sake of the difference
 between them.
3 Instead of this, you furnished the flaming pillar
which was a guide on the unknown way,
and the mild sun for an honorable migration.
4 For those deserved to be deprived of light and
 imprisoned by darkness,

NEW JERUSALEM BIBLE

the tuneful noise of birds in the spreading branches,
the measured beat of water in its powerful course,
the headlong din of rocks cascading down,
19 the unseen course of bounding animals,
the roaring of the most savage of wild beasts,
the echo rebounding from the clefts in the mountains,
all held them paralysed with fear.
20 For the whole world shone with the light of day
and, unhindered, went about its work;
21 over them alone there spread a heavy darkness,
image of the dark that would receive them.
But heavier than the darkness was the burden they
 were to themselves.

18 For your holy ones, however, there was a very great
 light.
The Egyptians, who could hear them but not see them,
called them fortunate because they had not suffered
 too;
2 they thanked them for doing no injury in return for
 previous wrongs
and asked forgiveness for their past ill-will.
3 In contrast to the darkness, you gave your people a
 pillar of blazing fire
to guide them on their unknown journey,
a mild sun for their ambitious migration.
4 But well those others deserved to be deprived of light
and imprisoned in darkness,

GREEK OLD TESTAMENT

οἱ κατακλείστους φυλάξαντες τοὺς υἱούς σου,
δι' ὧν ἤμελλεν τὸ ἄφθαρτον νόμου φῶς τῷ αἰῶνι
δίδοσθαι.
5 Βουλευσαμένους δ' αὐτοὺς τὰ τῶν ὁσίων ἀποκτεῖναι
νήπια
καὶ ἑνὸς ἐκτεθέντος τέκνου καὶ σωθέντος
εἰς ἔλεγχον τὸ αὐτῶν ἀφείλω πλῆθος τέκνων
καὶ ὁμοθυμαδὸν ἀπώλεσας ἐν ὕδατι σφοδρῷ.
6 ἐκείνη ἡ νὺξ προεγνώσθη πατράσιν ἡμῶν,
ἵνα ἀσφαλῶς εἰδότες οἷς ἐπίστευσαν ὅρκοις
ἐπευθυμήσωσιν.
7 προσεδέχθη ὑπὸ λαοῦ σου
σωτηρία μὲν δικαίων, ἐχθρῶν δὲ ἀπώλεια·
8 ᾧ γὰρ ἐτιμωρήσω τοὺς ὑπεναντίους,
τούτῳ ἡμᾶς προσκαλεσάμενος ἐδόξασας.
9 κρυφῇ γὰρ ἐθυσίαζον ὅσιοι παῖδες ἀγαθῶν
καὶ τὸν τῆς θειότητος νόμον ἐν ὁμονοίᾳ διέθεντο
τῶν αὐτῶν ὁμοίως καὶ ἀγαθῶν
καὶ κινδύνων μεταλήμψεσθαι τοὺς ἁγίους
πατέρων ἤδη προαναμέλποντες αἴνους.

KING JAMES VERSION

oned in darkness, who had kept thy sons shut up, by whom the uncorrupt light of the law was to be given unto the world.

5 And when they had determined to slay the babes of the saints, one child being cast forth, and saved, to reprove them, thou tookest away the multitude of their children, and destroyedst them altogether in a mighty water.

6 Of that night were our fathers certified afore, that assuredly knowing unto what oaths they had given credence, they might afterwards be of good cheer.

7 So of thy people was accepted both the salvation of the righteous, and destruction of the enemies.

8 For wherewith thou didst punish our adversaries, by the same thou didst glorify us, whom thou hadst called.

9 For the righteous children of good men did sacrifice secretly, and with one consent made a holy law, that the saints should be like partakers of the same good and evil, the fathers now singing out the songs of praise.

DOUAY OLD TESTAMENT

and imprisoned in darkness, who kept thy children shut up, by whom the pure light of the law was to be given to the world.

5 And whereas they thought to kill the babes of the just, one child being cast forth, and saved, to reprove them, thou tookest away a multitude of their children, and destroyedst them all together in a mighty water.

6 For that night was known before by our fathers, that assuredly knowing what oaths they had trusted to, they might be of better courage.

7 So thy people received the salvation of the just, and destruction of the unjust.

8 For as thou didst punish the adversaries: so thou didst also encourage and glorify us.

9 For the just children of good men were offering sacrifice secretly, and they unanimously ordered a law of justice: that the just should receive both good and evil alike, singing now the praises of the fathers.

KNOX TRANSLATION

who had kept thy own sons in prison; thy own sons, through
whom that law, which is light unfailing, was to be given to
the world. 5 It was their purpose, besides, to slay all the children born of that holy stock; but one child survived exposure
and lived to rebuke them; through him thou didst destroy
Egypt's own children in their thousands, and drown its
assembled host in the rushing waves. 6 Of what should
befall that night, our fathers had good warning; confidence
in thy sworn protection should keep them unafraid. 7 A welcome gift it was to thy people, rescue for the just, and doom
for their persecutors; 8 at one stroke thou didst punish our
enemies, and make us proud men by singling us out for thyself.

9 In secret they offered their sacrifice, children of a nobler race, all set apart; with one accord they ratified the divine covenant, which bound them to share the same blessings and the same perils; singing for prelude their ancestral

TODAY'S ENGLISH VERSION

they had made prisoners of your people. And it was through
your people that the eternal light of the Law was going to be
given to the world.
5 When your enemies were carrying out their resolve to kill
the babies of your holy people, there was one child who was
abandoned but later rescued. Then you punished your enemies by killing a great number of their own children. You
drowned their whole army at one time in the rushing waters.
6 But our ancestors had been told in advance of what would
happen that night, so that they would be cheered and
encouraged by confident trust in your promises to them.
7 Your people knew that you would rescue the righteous
nation and destroy their enemies. 8 With the same act you
punished our enemies and did us the glorious honor of calling us to yourself.
9 During all this time devout people from this righteous
nation were secretly offering sacrifices, giving their word to
each other that they would keep God's law and share each
other's blessings and dangers. Already they were chanting
those ancient hymns of praise. 10 But their enemies' pitiful

NEW REVISED STANDARD VERSION

those who had kept your children imprisoned,
through whom the imperishable light of the law was to
be given to the world.

5 When they had resolved to kill the infants of your holy
ones,
and one child had been abandoned and rescued,
you in punishment took away a multitude of their
children;
and you destroyed them all together by a mighty flood.
6 That night was made known beforehand to our
ancestors,
so that they might rejoice in sure knowledge of the
oaths in which they trusted.
7 The deliverance of the righteous and the destruction of
their enemies
were expected by your people.
8 For by the same means by which you punished our
enemies
you called us to yourself and glorified us.
9 For in secret the holy children of good people offered
sacrifices,
and with one accord agreed to the divine law,
so that the saints would share alike the same things,
both blessings and dangers;
and already they were singing the praises of the
ancestors.[a]

[a] Other ancient authorities read *dangers, the ancestors already leading the songs of praise*

NEW AMERICAN BIBLE

who had kept your sons confined
through whom the imperishable light of the law was
to be given to the world.
5 When they determined to put to death the infants of the
holy ones,
and when a single boy had been cast forth but saved,
As a reproof you carried off their multitude of sons
and made them perish all at once in the mighty
water.
6 That night was known beforehand to our fathers,
that, with sure knowledge of the oaths in which they
put their faith, they might have courage.
7 Your people awaited
the salvation of the just and the destruction of their
foes.
8 For when you punished our adversaries,
in this you glorified us whom you had summoned.
9 For in secret the holy children of the good were offering
sacrifice
and putting into effect with one accord the divine
institution,
That your holy ones should share alike the same good
things and dangers,
having previously sung the praises of the fathers.

NEW JERUSALEM BIBLE

for they had kept in captivity your children,
by whom the incorruptible light of the Law was to be
given to the world.
5 As they had resolved to kill the infants of the holy ones,
and as of those exposed only one child had been saved,
you punished them by carrying off their horde of
children
and by destroying them all in the wild water.
6 That night had been known in advance to our
ancestors,
so that, well knowing him in whom they had put their
trust, they would be sure of his promises.
7 Your people thus were waiting
both for the rescue of the upright and for the ruin of the
enemy;
8 for by the very vengeance that you exacted on our
adversaries,
you glorified us by calling us to you.
9 So the holy children of the good offered sacrifice in
secret
and with one accord enacted this holy law:
that the holy ones should share good things and
dangers alike;
and forthwith they chanted the hymns of the ancestors.

GREEK OLD TESTAMENT

10 ἀντήχει δ' ἀσύμφωνος ἐχθρῶν ἡ βοή,
καὶ οἰκτρὰ διεφέρετο φωνὴ θρηνουμένων παίδων·
11 ὁμοίᾳ δὲ δίκῃ δοῦλος ἅμα δεσπότῃ κολασθεὶς
καὶ δημότης βασιλεῖ τὰ αὐτὰ πάσχων,
12 ὁμοθυμαδὸν δὲ πάντες ἐν ἑνὶ ὀνόματι θανάτου
νεκροὺς εἶχον ἀναριθμήτους·
οὐδὲ γὰρ πρὸς τὸ θάψαι οἱ ζῶντες ἦσαν ἱκανοί,
ἐπεὶ πρὸς μίαν ῥοπὴν ἡ ἐντιμοτέρα γένεσις αὐτῶν διέφθαρτο.
13 πάντα γὰρ ἀπιστοῦντες διὰ τὰς φαρμακείας
ἐπὶ τῷ τῶν πρωτοτόκων ὀλέθρῳ ὡμολόγησαν θεοῦ υἱὸν λαὸν εἶναι.
14 ἡσύχου γὰρ σιγῆς περιεχούσης τὰ πάντα
καὶ νυκτὸς ἐν ἰδίῳ τάχει μεσαζούσης
15 ὁ παντοδύναμός σου λόγος ἀπ' οὐρανῶν ἐκ θρόνων βασιλείων
ἀπότομος πολεμιστὴς εἰς μέσον τῆς ὀλεθρίας ἥλατο γῆς
ξίφος ὀξὺ τὴν ἀνυπόκριτον ἐπιταγήν σου φέρων
16 καὶ στὰς ἐπλήρωσεν τὰ πάντα θανάτου
καὶ οὐρανοῦ μὲν ἥπτετο, βεβήκει δ' ἐπὶ γῆς.
17 τότε παραχρῆμα φαντασίαι μὲν ὀνείρων δεινῶν ἐξετάραξαν αὐτούς,
φόβοι δὲ ἐπέστησαν ἀδόκητοι,

KING JAMES VERSION

10 But on the other side there sounded an ill according cry of the enemies, and a lamentable noise was carried abroad for children that were bewailed.

11 The master and the servant were punished after one manner; and like as the king, so suffered the common person.

12 So they all together had innumerable dead with one kind of death; neither were the living sufficient to bury them: for in one moment the noblest offspring of them was destroyed.

13 For whereas they would not believe any thing by reason of the enchantments; upon the destruction of the firstborn, they acknowledged this people to be the sons of God.

14 For while all things were in quiet silence, and that night was in the midst of her swift course,

15 Thine Almighty word leaped down from heaven out of thy royal throne, as a fierce man of war into the midst of a land of destruction,

16 And brought thine unfeigned commandment as a sharp sword, and standing up filled all things with death; and it touched the heaven, but it stood upon the earth.

17 Then suddenly visions of horrible dreams troubled them sore, and terrors came upon them unlooked for.

DOUAY OLD TESTAMENT

10 But on the other side there sounded an ill according cry of the enemies, and a lamentable mourning was heard for the children that were bewailed.

11 And the servant suffered the same punishment as the master, and a common man suffered in like manner as the king.

12 So all alike had innumerable dead, with one kind of death. Neither were the living sufficient to bury them; for in one moment the noblest offspring of them was destroyed.

13 For whereas they would not believe any thing before by reason of the enchantments, then first upon the destruction of the firstborn, they acknowledged the people to be of God.

14 For while all things were in quiet silence, and the night was in the midst of her course,

15 Thy almighty word leapt down from heaven from thy royal throne, as a fierce conqueror into the midst of the land of destruction,

16 *With* a sharp sword carrying thy unfeigned commandment, and he stood and filled all things with death, and standing on the earth reached even to heaven.

17 Then suddenly visions of evil dreams troubled them, and fears unlooked for came upon them.

KNOX TRANSLATION

hymns of praise. 10 But music was none in the enemy's cry
that answered them; here all was dirge for children untimely
mourned. 11 Slave and master, prince and peasant, a common doom met them, and a common loss; 12 death levelled
all under one title; unnumbered everywhere the slain, nor
might the living suffice to bury them; all in one moment, the
flower of their race had perished. 13 Against those earlier
plagues, sorcery had hardened their hearts; Israel they recognized for God's children only when the first-born died.

14 There was a hush of silence all around, and night had
but finished half her swift journey, 15 when from thy heavenly throne, Lord, down leaped thy word omnipotent. Never
lighted sterner warrior on a doomed land; 16 never was
sword so sharp, errand so unmistakable; thy word that could
spread death everywhere, that trod earth, yet reached up to
heaven. 17 All at once came terror in their dreams; phantoms
dismayed, and sudden alarms overtook them; 18 and when

TODAY'S ENGLISH VERSION

cries of grief echoed everywhere, as they mourned for their
dead children. 11 Masters suffered the same punishment as
their slaves; the king endured the same loss as the common
people. 12 There were too many dead bodies to count. There
were not enough people left to bury them all. In a single
moment their dearest children died; all of them met death in
the same way. 13 These people had paid no attention to any
warning, but relied instead on their magical powers. But
when their first-born sons were killed, then they recognized
that Israel was God's son.
14 The short night was half over, and all was quiet and
peaceful, 15 when suddenly your threats were carried out! An
invincible word of judgment sped from your royal throne in
heaven, straight down to that doomed land. It came like a
soldier in fierce attack, 16 carrying out your firm command
with a fearful weapon, standing with feet on the ground and
head touching the sky, filling the land with death. 17 At that
moment the people who were about to die had terrible nightmares and were seized by sudden fear. 18 All over the land

NEW REVISED STANDARD VERSION

10 But the discordant cry of their enemies echoed back,
and their piteous lament for their children was spread
abroad.
11 The slave was punished with the same penalty as the
master,
and the commoner suffered the same loss as the king;
12 and they all together, by the one form[a] of death,
had corpses too many to count.
For the living were not sufficient even to bury them,
since in one instant their most valued children had
been destroyed.
13 For though they had disbelieved everything because of
their magic arts,
yet, when their firstborn were destroyed, they
acknowledged your people to be God's child.
14 For while gentle silence enveloped all things,
and night in its swift course was now half gone,
15 your all-powerful word leaped from heaven, from the
royal throne,
into the midst of the land that was doomed,
a stern warrior
16 carrying the sharp sword of your authentic command,
and stood and filled all things with death,
and touched heaven while standing on the earth.
17 Then at once apparitions in dreadful dreams greatly
troubled them,
and unexpected fears assailed them;

a Gk *name*

NEW AMERICAN BIBLE

10 But the discordant cry of their enemies responded,
and the piteous wail of mourning for children was
borne to them.
11 And the slave was smitten with the same retribution as
his master;
even the plebeian suffered the same as the king.
12 And all alike by a single death
had countless dead;
For the living were not even sufficient for the burial,
since at a single instant their nobler offspring were
destroyed.
13 For though they disbelieved at every turn on account of
sorceries,
at the destruction of the first-born they acknowledged
that the people was God's son.
14 For when peaceful stillness compassed everything
and the night in its swift course was half spent,
15 Your all-powerful word from heaven's royal throne
bounded, a fierce warrior, into the doomed land,
16 bearing the sharp sword of your inexorable decree.
And as he alighted, he filled every place with death;
he still reached to heaven, while he stood upon the
earth.
17 Then, forthwith, visions in horrible dreams perturbed
them
and unexpected fears assailed them;

NEW JERUSALEM BIBLE

10 In echo came the discordant cries of their enemies,
and the pitiful wails of people mourning for their
children
could be heard from far away.
11 One and the same punishment had struck slave and
master alike,
and now commoner and king had the same sufferings
to endure.
12 Struck by the same death, all had innumerable dead.
There were not enough living left to bury them,
for, at one stroke, the flower of their offspring had
perished.
13 Those whose spells had made them completely
incredulous,
when faced with the destruction of their first-born,
acknowledged this people to be child of God.

14 When peaceful silence lay over all,
and night had run the half of her swift course,
15 down from the heavens, from the royal throne,
leapt your all-powerful Word
like a pitiless warrior into the heart of a land doomed to
destruction.
Carrying your unambiguous command like a sharp
sword,
16 it stood, and filled the universe with death;
though standing on the earth, it touched the sky.
17 Immediately, dreams and gruesome visions
overwhelmed them with terror,

GREEK OLD TESTAMENT

18 καὶ ἄλλος ἀλλαχῇ ῥιφεὶς ἡμίθνητος
δι᾽ ἣν ἔθνῃσκον αἰτίαν ἐνεφάνιζεν·
19 οἱ γὰρ ὄνειροι θορυβήσαντες αὐτοὺς τοῦτο
προεμήνυσαν,
ἵνα μὴ ἀγνοοῦντες δι᾽ ὃ κακῶς πάσχουσιν ἀπόλωνται.
20 Ἥψατο δὲ καὶ δικαίων πεῖρα θανάτου,
καὶ θραῦσις ἐν ἐρήμῳ ἐγένετο πλήθους.
ἀλλ᾽ οὐκ ἐπὶ πολὺ ἔμεινεν ἡ ὀργή·
21 σπεύσας γὰρ ἀνὴρ ἄμεμπτος προεμάχησεν
τὸ τῆς ἰδίας λειτουργίας ὅπλον
προσευχὴν καὶ θυμιάματος ἐξιλασμὸν κομίσας·
ἀντέστη τῷ θυμῷ καὶ πέρας ἐπέθηκε τῇ συμφορᾷ
δεικνὺς ὅτι σός ἐστιν θεράπων·
22 ἐνίκησεν δὲ τὸν χόλον οὐκ ἰσχύι τοῦ σώματος,
οὐχ ὅπλων ἐνεργείᾳ,
ἀλλὰ λόγῳ τὸν κολάζοντα ὑπέταξεν
ὅρκους πατέρων καὶ διαθήκας ὑπομνήσας.
23 σωρηδὸν γὰρ ἤδη πεπτωκότων ἐπ᾽ ἀλλήλων νεκρῶν
μεταξὺ στὰς ἀνέκοψε τὴν ὀργὴν
καὶ διέσχισεν τὴν πρὸς τοὺς ζῶντας ὁδόν.
24 ἐπὶ γὰρ ποδήρους ἐνδύματος ἦν ὅλος ὁ κόσμος,
καὶ πατέρων δόξαι ἐπὶ τετραστίχου λίθων γλυφῆς,
καὶ μεγαλωσύνη σου ἐπὶ διαδήματος κεφαλῆς αὐτοῦ.

KING JAMES VERSION

18 And one thrown here, and another there, half dead, shewed the cause of his death.

19 For the dreams that troubled them did foreshew this, lest they should perish, and not know why they were afflicted.

20 Yea, the tasting of death touched the righteous also, and there was a destruction of the multitude in the wilderness: but the wrath endured not long.

21 For then the blameless man made haste, and stood forth to defend them; and bringing the shield of his proper ministry, even prayer, and the propitiation of incense, set himself against the wrath, and so brought the calamity to an end, declaring that he was thy servant.

22 So he overcame the destroyer, not with strength of body, nor force of arms, but with a word subdued he him that punished, alleging the oaths and covenants made with the fathers.

23 For when the dead were now fallen down by heaps one upon another, standing between, he stayed the wrath, and parted the way to the living.

24 For in the long garment was the whole world, and in the four rows of the stones was the glory of the fathers graven, and thy Majesty upon the diadem of his head.

DOUAY OLD TESTAMENT

18 And one thrown here, another there, half dead, shewed the cause of his death.

19 For the visions that troubled them foreshewed these things, lest they should perish and not know why they suffered these evils.

20 But the just also were afterwards touched by an assault of death, and there was a disturbance of the multitude in the wilderness: but thy wrath did not long continue.

21 For a blameless man made haste to pray for the people, bringing forth the shield of his ministry, prayer, and by incense making supplication, withstood the wrath, and put an end to the calamity, shewing that he was thy servant.

22 And he overcame the disturbance, not by strength of body nor with force of arms, but with a word he subdued him that punished them, alleging the oaths and covenant made with the fathers.

23 For when they were now fallen down dead by heaps one upon another, he stood between and stayed the assault, and cut off the way to the living.

24 For in the priestly robe which he wore, was the whole world: and in the four rows of the stones the glory of the fathers was graven, and thy majesty was written upon the diadem of his head.

KNOX TRANSLATION

they lay a-dying, each fallen where fall he must, they confessed what fault it was they expiated; 19 all was foretold by
the dreams that so disquieted them; they were not suffered
to perish ignorant of their offence.

20 There was a time, too, when God's own people tasted the
bitterness of death; out there in the desert a plague fell upon
the common folk; but not for long this vengeance lasted. 21 A
peerless champion they found, in Aaron, that quickly took up
the shield of his appointed ministry; the power of intercession that was his, and the atoning incense, held thy wrath in
check, and brought the calamity to an end; none could doubt
now he was the man of thy choice! 22 Not by strength of
body, not by prowess in arms, he won the victory;[a] by persuasion he disarmed resistance, calling to mind the sworn
covenant of our race. 23 Already the corpses were piled thick
one on another; but he kept vengeance at bay, standing in
between to breach the path between dead and living. 24 Such
blazonings he bore; what meant that long robe of his but the
whole world's orbit, the four rows of gems but the great
deeds of our first fathers, the mitre on his head but thy own

a That is, according to the Latin version, 'he overcame the multitude', but some manuscripts of the Greek text give, 'he overcame the (divine) anger'.

TODAY'S ENGLISH VERSION

they lay half-dead and let it be known why they were dying.
19 They knew why they were dying, because their horrible
dreams had told them.
20 Death also came to the righteous nation, for an epidemic
struck many of them while they were in the desert, but your
anger did not last long. 21 There was a certain blameless
man who quickly took action to defend them. Acting as their
priest, Aaron offered prayers and burned the incense used in
asking forgiveness of sins. With prayers and incense as his
weapons, he withstood your anger and ended the disaster.
By doing this he proved that he was your servant. 22 He
overcame the bitter difficulty,[a] but not by his own strength
or by military force. Instead, he used prayer to stop the punishment, appealing to the promises you solemnly gave to our
ancestors. 23 Dead bodies were already lying in piles, but he
stepped in to hold your anger back and to keep it from harm-
ing those who were left alive. 24 He wore a long robe decorated with symbols of the universe. In honor of our ancestors
he wore four rows of engraved stones on his chest, and your
own majesty was represented by the ornament on his turban.

[a] *Probable text* bitter difficulty; *Greek* crowd.

NEW REVISED STANDARD VERSION

18 and one here and another there, hurled down half dead,
made known why they were dying;
19 for the dreams that disturbed them forewarned them of
this,
so that they might not perish without knowing why
they suffered.

20 The experience of death touched also the righteous,
and a plague came upon the multitude in the desert,
but the wrath did not long continue.
21 For a blameless man was quick to act as their champion;
he brought forward the shield of his ministry,
prayer and propitiation by incense;
he withstood the anger and put an end to the disaster,
showing that he was your servant.
22 He conquered the wrath[a] not by strength of body,
not by force of arms,
but by his word he subdued the avenger,
appealing to the oaths and covenants given to our
ancestors.
23 For when the dead had already fallen on one another in
heaps,
he intervened and held back the wrath,
and cut off its way to the living.
24 For on his long robe the whole world was depicted,
and the glories of the ancestors were engraved on the
four rows of stones,
and your majesty was on the diadem upon his head.

[a] Cn: Gk *multitude*

NEW AMERICAN BIBLE

18 And cast half-dead, one here, another there,
each was revealing the reason for his dying.
19 For the dreams that disturbed them had proclaimed this
beforehand,
lest they perish unaware of why they suffered ill.
20 But the trial of death touched at one time even the just,
and in the desert a plague struck the multitude;
Yet not for long did the anger last.
21 For the blameless man hastened to be their champion,
bearing the weapon of his special office,
prayer and the propitiation of incense;
He withstood the wrath and put a stop to the calamity,
showing that he was your servant.
22 And he overcame the bitterness
not by bodily strength, not by force of arms;
But by word he overcame the smiter,
recalling the sworn covenants with their fathers.
23 For when corpses had already fallen one on another in
heaps,
he stood in the midst and checked the anger,
and cut off the way to the living.
24 For on his full-length robe was the whole world,
and the glories of the fathers were carved in four
rows upon the stones,
and your grandeur was on the crown upon his head.

NEW JERUSALEM BIBLE

unexpected fears assailed them.
18 Hurled down, some here, some there, half dead,
they were able to say why they were dying;
19 for the dreams that had troubled them
had warned them why beforehand,
so that they should not perish without knowing why
they were being afflicted.

20 Experience of death, however, touched the upright too,
and a great many were struck down in the desert.
But the Retribution did not last long,
21 for a blameless man hurried to their defence.
Wielding the weapons of his sacred office,
prayer and expiating incense,
he confronted Retribution and put an end to the plague,
thus showing that he was your servant.
22 He overcame Hostility, not by physical strength,
nor by force of arms;
but by word he prevailed over the Punisher,
by recalling the oaths made to the Fathers, and the
covenants.
23 Already the corpses lay piled in heaps,
when he interposed and beat Retribution back
and cut off its approach to the living.
24 For the whole world was on his flowing robe,
the glorious names of the Fathers engraved on the four
rows of stones,
and your Majesty on the diadem on his head.

GREEK OLD TESTAMENT

25 τούτοις εἶξεν ὁ ὀλεθρεύων, ταῦτα δὲ ἐφοβήθη·
ἦν γὰρ μόνη ἡ πεῖρα τῆς ὀργῆς ἱκανή.

19 Τοῖς δὲ ἀσεβέσιν μέχρι τέλους ἀνελεήμων θυμὸς
ἐπέστη·
προῄδει γὰρ αὐτῶν καὶ τὰ μέλλοντα,
2 ὅτι αὐτοὶ ἐπιτρέψαντες τοῦ ἀπιέναι
καὶ μετὰ σπουδῆς προπέμψαντες αὐτοὺς
διώξουσιν μεταμεληθέντες.
3 ἔτι γὰρ ἐν χερσὶν ἔχοντες τὰ πένθη
καὶ προσοδυρόμενοι τάφοις νεκρῶν
ἕτερον ἐπεσπάσαντο λογισμὸν ἀνοίας
καὶ οὓς ἱκετεύοντες ἐξέβαλον, τούτους ὡς φυγάδας
ἐδίωκον.
4 εἷλκεν γὰρ αὐτοὺς ἡ ἀξία ἐπὶ τοῦτο τὸ πέρας ἀνάγκη
καὶ τῶν συμβεβηκότων ἀμνηστίαν ἐνέβαλεν,
ἵνα τὴν λείπουσαν ταῖς βασάνοις προσαναπληρώσωσιν
κόλασιν,
5 καὶ ὁ μὲν λαός σου παράδοξον ὁδοιπορίαν πειράσῃ,
ἐκεῖνοι δὲ ξένον εὕρωσι θάνατον.
6 ὅλη γὰρ ἡ κτίσις ἐν ἰδίῳ γένει πάλιν ἄνωθεν διετυποῦτο
ὑπηρετοῦσα ταῖς σαῖς ἐπιταγαῖς,
ἵνα οἱ σοὶ παῖδες φυλαχθῶσιν ἀβλαβεῖς.
7 ἡ τὴν παρεμβολὴν σκιάζουσα νεφέλη,
ἐκ δὲ προϋφεστῶτος ὕδατος ξηρᾶς ἀνάδυσις γῆς
ἐθεωρήθη,

KING JAMES VERSION

25 Unto these the destroyer gave place, and was afraid of them: for it was enough that they only tasted of the wrath.

19 As for the ungodly, wrath came upon them without mercy unto the end: for he knew before what they would do;

2 How that having given them leave to depart, and sent them hastily away, they would repent and pursue them.

3 For whilst they were yet mourning and making lamentation at the graves of the dead, they added another foolish device, and pursued them as fugitives, whom they had intreated to be gone.

4 For the destiny, whereof they were worthy, drew them unto this end, and made them forget the things that had already happened, that they might fulfil the punishment which was wanting to their torments:

5 And that thy people might pass a wonderful way: but they might find a strange death.

6 For the whole creature in his proper kind was fashioned again anew, serving the peculiar commandments that were given unto them, that thy children might be kept without hurt:

7 *As namely,* a cloud shadowing the camp; and where water stood before, dry land appeared; and out of the Red

DOUAY OLD TESTAMENT

25 And to these the destroyer gave place, and was afraid of them: for the proof only of wrath was enough.

19 BUT as to the wicked, even to the end there came upon them wrath without mercy. For he knew before also what they would do:

2 For when they had given them leave to depart, and had sent them away with great care, they repented, and pursued after them.

3 For whilst they were yet mourning, and lamenting at the graves of the dead, they took up another foolish device: and pursued them as fugitives whom they had pressed to be gone:

4 For a necessity, of which they were worthy, brought them to this end: and they lost the remembrance of those things which had happened, that their punishment might fill up what was wanting to their torments:

5 And that thy people might wonderfully pass through, but they might find a new death.

6 For every creature according to its kind was fashioned again *as* from the beginning, obeying thy commandments, that thy children might be kept without hurt.

7 For a cloud overshadowed their camp, and where water was before, dry land appeared, and in the Red Sea a way

KNOX TRANSLATION

greatness? 25 In awe of these shrank the destroying angel
away; for thy own people, some taste of thy vengeance
should be enough.

19 It was not so with their impious enemies; with them,
God decreed that pitiless justice should run its
course, knowing well what ill-doing of theirs lay yet in store;
2 how the very men who had allowed the Israelites to depart,
nay, set them eagerly on their way, would soon repent of it
and march out in pursuit.[a] 3 The business of mourning still
in hand, the grave-sides of the dead still calling for their
tears, they must needs betake themselves to a fresh desperate shift; they would hunt down as fugitives the unwelcome
guests of yesterday. 4 Fitting destiny, that lured them to a
fitting doom, made them forget the past, and led them on to
complete their tale of suffering and of punishment! 5 For thy
people, a strange sea-faring; for those others, an unexampled manner of death!

6 Each form of nature, in its own proper sphere, was formed
anew as from the beginning, obedient to the new laws thou
hadst given it, for the greater safety of thy children. 7 Such
was the cloud that over-shadowed their camp; such the dry
land that appeared where water stood before; the Red Sea

[a] The word 'Israelites', like the other proper names used in this chapter, has been supplied so as to make the original text less obscure.

TODAY'S ENGLISH VERSION

25 The Angel of Death was afraid of these things, and gave
up. It was only a slight experience of your wrath, but it was
enough.

19 But the godless continued to feel your pitiless anger
until the very end. You knew what they would do
before they did it. 2 You knew that even though they let your
people go and made them leave quickly, they would change
their minds and pursue them. 3-4 While the Egyptians were
still mourning at the graves of their dead, they forgot why all
this had happened, and they foolishly decided that the people they had begged to leave were runaways. So they chased
after them. They were led into this as part of the punishment
they deserved, so that they would suffer the rest of the torments they were due to receive. 5 They were to meet a
strange death, while your people continued on their miraculous journey.
6 The whole nature of the universe was changed at your
command so that your people would not be harmed. 7 They
saw the cloud over their camp and dry land where water had

NEW REVISED STANDARD VERSION

25 To these the destroyer yielded, these he[a] feared;
for merely to test the wrath was enough.

19 But the ungodly were assailed to the end by pitiless anger,
for God[b] knew in advance even their future actions:
2 how, though they themselves had permitted[c] your people to depart
and hastily sent them out,
they would change their minds and pursue them.
3 For while they were still engaged in mourning,
and were lamenting at the graves of their dead,
they reached another foolish decision,
and pursued as fugitives those whom they had begged and compelled to leave.
4 For the fate they deserved drew them on to this end,
and made them forget what had happened,
in order that they might fill up the punishment that their torments still lacked,
5 and that your people might experience[d] an incredible journey,
but they themselves might meet a strange death.
6 For the whole creation in its nature was fashioned anew,
complying with your commands,
so that your children[e] might be kept unharmed.
7 The cloud was seen overshadowing the camp,
and dry land emerging where water had stood before,

a Other ancient authorities read *they* *b* Gk *he* *c* Other ancient authorities read *had changed their minds to permit* *d* Other ancient authorities read *accomplish* *e* Or *servants*

NEW AMERICAN BIBLE

25 To these names the destroyer yielded, and these he feared;
for the mere trial of anger was enough.

19 But the wicked, merciless wrath assailed until the end.
For he knew beforehand what they were yet to do:
2 That though they themselves had agreed to the departure
and had anxiously sent them on their way,
they would regret it and pursue them.
3 For while they were still engaged in funeral rites
and were mourning at the burials of the dead,
They adopted another senseless plan;
and those whom they had sent away with entreaty,
they pursued as fugitives.
4 For a compulsion suited to this ending drew them on,
and made them forgetful of what had befallen them,
That they might fill out the torments of their punishment,
5 and your people might experience a glorious journey
while those others met an extraordinary death.
6 For all creation, in its several kinds, was being made over anew,
serving its natural laws,
that your children might be preserved unharmed.
7 The cloud overshadowed their camp;
and out of what had before been water, dry land was seen emerging:

NEW JERUSALEM BIBLE

25 From these the Destroyer recoiled, he was afraid of these.
This one experience of Retribution was enough.

19 But the godless were assailed by merciless anger to the very end,
for he knew beforehand what they would do,
2 how, after letting his people leave and hastening their departure,
they would change their minds and give chase.
3 They were actually still conducting their mourning rites
and lamenting at the tombs of their dead,
when another mad scheme came into their heads
and they set out to pursue, as though runaways,
the people whom they had expelled and begged to go.
4 A well-deserved fate urged them to this extreme
and made them forget what had already happened,
so that they would add to their torments
the one punishment outstanding
5 and, while your people were experiencing a journey contrary to all expectations,
would themselves meet an extraordinary death.
6 For the whole creation, submissive to your commands,
had its very nature re-created,
so that your children should be preserved from harm.
7 Overshadowing the camp there was the cloud;
where there had been water, dry land was seen to rise;

GREEK OLD TESTAMENT

ἐξ ἐρυθρᾶς θαλάσσης ὁδὸς ἀνεμπόδιστος
καὶ χλοηφόρον πεδίον ἐκ κλύδωνος βιαίου·
8 δι᾽ οὗ πανεθνεὶ διῆλθον οἱ τῇ σῇ σκεπαζόμενοι χειρὶ
θεωρήσαντες θαυμαστὰ τέρατα.
9 ὡς γὰρ ἵπποι ἐνεμήθησαν
καὶ ὡς ἀμνοὶ διεσκίρτησαν
αἰνοῦντές σε, κύριε, τὸν ῥυσάμενον αὐτούς.
10 ἐμέμνηντο γὰρ ἔτι τῶν ἐν τῇ παροικίᾳ αὐτῶν,
πῶς ἀντὶ μὲν γενέσεως ζῴων ἐξήγαγεν ἡ γῆ σκνῖπα,
ἀντὶ δὲ ἐνύδρων ἐξηρεύξατο ὁ ποταμὸς πλῆθος
βατράχων.
11 ἐφ᾽ ὑστέρῳ δὲ εἶδον καὶ γένεσιν νέαν ὀρνέων,
ὅτε ἐπιθυμίᾳ προαχθέντες ᾐτήσαντο ἐδέσματα τρυφῆς·
12 εἰς γὰρ παραμυθίαν ἐκ θαλάσσης ἀνέβη αὐτοῖς
ὀρτυγομήτρα.
13 Καὶ αἱ τιμωρίαι τοῖς ἁμαρτωλοῖς ἐπῆλθον
οὐκ ἄνευ τῶν προγεγονότων τεκμηρίων τῇ βίᾳ τῶν
κεραυνῶν·
δικαίως γὰρ ἔπασχον ταῖς ἰδίαις αὐτῶν πονηρίαις,
καὶ γὰρ χαλεπωτέραν μισοξενίαν ἐπετήδευσαν.
14 οἱ μὲν γὰρ τοὺς ἀγνοοῦντας οὐκ ἐδέχοντο παρόντας·
οὗτοι δὲ εὐεργέτας ξένους ἐδουλοῦντο.
15 καὶ οὐ μόνον, ἀλλ᾽ ἥ τις ἐπισκοπὴ ἔσται αὐτῶν,
ἐπεὶ ἀπεχθῶς προσεδέχοντο τοὺς ἀλλοτρίους·

KING JAMES VERSION

sea a way without impediment; and out of the violent stream a green field:

8 Wherethrough all the people went that were defended with thy hand, seeing thy marvellous strange wonders.

9 For they went at large like horses, and leaped like lambs, praising thee, O Lord, who hadst delivered them.

10 For they were yet mindful of the things that were done while they sojourned in the strange land, how the ground brought forth flies instead of cattle, and how the river cast up a multitude of frogs instead of fishes.

11 But afterwards they saw a new generation of fowls, when, being led with their appetite, they asked delicate meats.

12 For quails came up unto them from the sea for their contentment.

13 And punishments came upon the sinners not without former signs by the force of thunders: for they suffered justly according to their own wickedness, insomuch as they used a more hard and hateful behaviour toward strangers.

14 For the *Sodomites* did not receive those, whom they knew not when they came: but these brought friends into bondage, that had well deserved of them.

15 And not only so, but peradventure some respect shall be had of those, because they used strangers not friendly:

DOUAY OLD TESTAMENT

without hinderance, and out of the great deep a springing field:

8 Through which all the nation passed which was protected with thy hand, seeing thy miracles and wonders.

9 For they fed on their food like horses, and they skipped like lambs, praising thee, O Lord, who hadst delivered them.

10 For they were yet mindful of those things which had been done in the time of their sojourning, how the ground brought forth flies instead of cattle, and how the river cast up a multitude of frogs instead of fishes.

11 And at length they saw a new generation of birds, when being led by their appetite they asked for delicate meats.

12 For to satisfy their desire, the quail came up to them from the sea: and punishments came upon the sinners, not without foregoing signs by the force of thunders: for they suffered justly according to their own wickedness.

13 For they exercised a more detestable inhospitality *than any:* others indeed received not strangers unknown to them, but these brought their guests into bondage that had deserved well of them.

14 And not only so, but in another respect also they were worse: for the others against their will received the strangers.

KNOX TRANSLATION

unlaboriously crossed, a grassy floor spread out amid the
surging billows! 8 So, sheltered by thy hand, they passed on
their way, a whole nation of them, strange marvels seen in
their passage; 9 lighthearted as horse at pasture or frisking
lamb, they chanted praises to thee, Lord, their rescuer.
10 Such, too, were their memories of Egypt itself; memories of
the land that bred lice and could breed no beasts else, the
river that could spawn frogs, yet never a fish lived there.
11 Later on, they were to see how birds could be the subject of
a new creation, when their appetites craved for richer fare,
and quails came up from the sea to content them.
12 Nor were the Egyptians punished without warning; the
thunders that terrified them were but echoes of the past. Did
not their own wickedness deserve the pains they suffered,
13 a race even more inhospitable than the men of Sodom
before them? These did but refuse a welcome when strangers
came to their doors; the Egyptians condemned their own
guests, their own benefactors, to slavery. 14 It is one thing to
be called to account for unfriendly treatment of alien folk;

TODAY'S ENGLISH VERSION

been. There was a grass-covered plain between the stormy
waves of the Red Sea, making it easy for them to cross over.
8 All your people, under your protection, saw this miracle and
went across. 9 They pranced about like horses let out to pasture; they skipped about like lambs and praised you, Lord,
for saving them. 10 They still remembered what life had been
like when they were slaves—how the earth bred gnats
instead of cattle, how the river produced huge numbers of
frogs instead of fish. 11-12 Later, when they desperately wanted better food, quails came up from the sea to satisfy their
hunger. The quail was a bird they had never seen before.
13 But violent thunder gave warning of the punishment
that was coming on those sinners. They suffered a well-
deserved punishment for their great wickedness. No nation
had ever hated strangers so bitterly. 14 Other people had
been known to refuse welcome to strangers who came to
them, but these people made slaves of those who were their
guests and who had shown them kindness. 15 Every nation
will be punished if it does not welcome foreigners, 16 but

NEW REVISED STANDARD VERSION

an unhindered way out of the Red Sea,
and a grassy plain out of the raging waves,
8 where those protected by your hand passed through as one nation,
after gazing on marvelous wonders.
9 For they ranged like horses,
and leaped like lambs,
praising you, O Lord, who delivered them.
10 For they still recalled the events of their sojourn,
how instead of producing animals the earth brought forth gnats,
and instead of fish the river spewed out vast numbers of frogs.
11 Afterward they saw also a new kind[a] of birds,
when desire led them to ask for luxurious food;
12 for, to give them relief, quails came up from the sea.

13 The punishments did not come upon the sinners
without prior signs in the violence of thunder,
for they justly suffered because of their wicked acts;
for they practiced a more bitter hatred of strangers.
14 Others had refused to receive strangers when they came to them,
but these made slaves of guests who were their benefactors.
15 And not only so—but, while punishment of some sort will come upon the former
for having received strangers with hostility,

a Or *production*

NEW AMERICAN BIBLE

Out of the Red Sea an unimpeded road,
and a grassy plain out of the mighty flood.
8 Over this crossed the whole nation sheltered by your hand,
after they beheld stupendous wonders.
9 For they ranged about like horses,
and bounded about like lambs,
praising you, O Lord! their deliverer.
10 For they were still mindful of what had happened in their sojourn:
how instead of the young of animals the land brought forth gnats,
and instead of fishes the river swarmed with countless frogs.
11 And later they saw also a new kind of bird
when, prompted by desire, they asked for pleasant foods;
12 For to appease them quail came to them from the sea.
13 And the punishments came upon the sinners
only after forewarnings from the violence of the thunderbolts.
For they justly suffered for their own misdeeds,
since indeed they treated their guests with the more grievous hatred.
14 For those others did not receive unfamiliar visitors,
but these were enslaving beneficent guests.
15 And not that only; but what punishment was to be theirs
since they received strangers unwillingly!

NEW JERUSALEM BIBLE

the Red Sea became an unimpeded way,
the tempestuous waves, a green plain;
8 sheltered by your hand, the whole nation passed across,
gazing at these amazing prodigies.
9 They were like horses at pasture,
they skipped like lambs,
singing your praises, Lord, their deliverer.
10 For they still remembered the events of their exile,
how the land had bred mosquitoes instead of animals
and the River had disgorged millions of frogs instead of fish.
11 Later they were to see a new way for birds to come into being,
when, goaded by greed, they demanded something tasty,
12 and quails came up out of the sea to satisfy them.
13 On the sinners, however, punishments rained down
not without violent thunder as early warning;
and they suffered what their own crimes had justly deserved
since they had shown such bitter hatred to foreigners.
14 Others, indeed, had failed to welcome strangers who came to them,
but the Egyptians had enslaved their own guests and benefactors.
15 The sinners, moreover, will certainly be punished for it,
since they gave the foreigners a hostile welcome;

GREEK OLD TESTAMENT

16 οἱ δὲ μετὰ ἑορτασμάτων
εἰσδεξάμενοι τοὺς ἤδη τῶν αὐτῶν μετεσχηκότας δικαίων
δεινοῖς ἐκάκωσαν πόνοις.
17 ἐπλήγησαν δὲ καὶ ἀορασίᾳ
ὥσπερ ἐκεῖνοι ἐπὶ ταῖς τοῦ δικαίου θύραις,
ὅτε ἀχανεῖ περιβληθέντες σκότει
ἕκαστος τῶν ἑαυτοῦ θυρῶν τὴν δίοδον ἐζήτει.
18 Δι᾽ ἑαυτῶν γὰρ τὰ στοιχεῖα μεθαρμοζόμενα,
ὥσπερ ἐν ψαλτηρίῳ φθόγγοι τοῦ ῥυθμοῦ τὸ ὄνομα διαλλάσσουσιν,
πάντοτε μένοντα ἤχῳ,
ὅπερ ἐστὶν εἰκάσαι ἐκ τῆς τῶν γεγονότων ὄψεως ἀκριβῶς·
19 χερσαῖα γὰρ εἰς ἔνυδρα μετεβάλλετο,
καὶ νηκτὰ μετέβαινεν ἐπὶ γῆς·
20 πῦρ ἴσχυεν ἐν ὕδατι τῆς ἰδίας δυνάμεως,
καὶ ὕδωρ τῆς σβεστικῆς φύσεως ἐπελανθάνετο·
21 φλόγες ἀνάπαλιν εὐφθάρτων ζῴων
οὐκ ἐμάραναν σάρκας ἐμπεριπατούντων,
οὐδὲ τηκτὸν κρυσταλλοειδὲς εὔτηκτον γένος ἀμβροσίας τροφῆς.
22 Κατὰ πάντα γάρ, κύριε, ἐμεγάλυνας τὸν λαόν σου καὶ ἐδόξασας
καὶ οὐχ ὑπερεῖδες ἐν παντὶ καιρῷ καὶ τόπῳ παριστάμενος.

KING JAMES VERSION

16 But these very grievously afflicted them, whom they had received with feastings, and were already made partakers of the same laws with them.

17 Therefore even with blindness were these stricken, as those were at the doors of the righteous man: when, being compassed about with horrible great darkness, every one sought the passage of his own doors.

18 For the elements were changed in themselves by a kind of harmony, like as in a psaltery notes change the name of the tune, and yet are always sounds; which may well be perceived by the sight of the things that have been done.

19 For earthly things were turned into watery, and the things, that before swam in the water, now went upon the ground.

20 The fire had power in the water, forgetting his own virtue: and the water forgat his own quenching nature.

21 On the other side, the flames wasted not the flesh of the corruptible living things, though they walked therein; neither melted they the icy kind of heavenly meat, that was of nature apt to melt.

22 For in all things, O Lord, thou didst magnify thy people, and glorify them, neither didst thou lightly regard them: but didst assist them in every time and place.

DOUAY OLD TESTAMENT

15 But these grievously afflicted them whom they had received with joy, and who lived under the same laws.

16 But they were struck with blindness: as those others were at the doors of the just man, when they were covered with sudden darkness, and every one sought the passage of his own door.

17 For while the elements are changed in themselves, as in an instrument the sound of the quality is changed, yet all keep their sound: which may clearly be perceived by the very sight.

18 For the things of the land were turned into things of the water: and the things before swam in the water passed upon the land.

19 The fire had power in water above its own virtue, and the water forgot its quenching nature.

20 On the other side, the flames wasted not the flesh of corruptible animals walking therein, neither did they melt that good food, which was apt to melt as ice. For in all things thou didst magnify thy people, O Lord, and didst honour them, and didst not despise them, but didst assist them at all times, and in every place.

KNOX TRANSLATION

15 but these Egyptians had received the Israelites into their
midst with rejoicing, had admitted them to rights of citizenship, and then turned on them with savage ill-treatment.
16 No wonder blindness fell on them, as upon the men of
Sodom at Lot's door! But in Egypt the darkness was so bewildering that a man could not find his way through the doors of his own house.

17 All the elements may be transposed among themselves, keeping up the same answering rhythm, like the notes of a harp altering their mood; so much we may infer with certainty from the sights that have been witnessed in the past.[a]
18 Land-beasts turned to water-beasts, and the firm ground
was trodden by creatures born to swim. 19 Fire surpassed its
own nature, when water forgot to quench it; 20 then fire, in
its turn, could not waste the frail flesh of living creatures that traversed it, nor melt that heavenly food that melted easily as ice. No means wouldst thou neglect, Lord, to magnify thy people and win them renown; never wouldst thou leave them unregarded, but always and everywhere camest to their side.[b]

a The meaning of this passage is highly doubtful, and it is possible that the text has been badly transmitted. But the notion seems to be that the history of miracle shews a kind of reciprocity between the elements, earth yielding to water and then water to land, ice to fire and then fire to ice.

b *vv.* 18-20: It is not certain, from the context, whether these verses refer entirely to the period of the Exodus.

TODAY'S ENGLISH VERSION

these people, who had earlier welcomed the foreigners with
happy celebrations and treated them as equals, later made
them suffer cruelly. 17 These people were also struck with
blindness, like the men of Sodom who came to the door of
that righteous man Lot. They found themselves in total darkness, as each one groped around to find his own door.
18 On a harp each string keeps its own pitch, but each
sound can be combined with others to make different
melodies. That is how it was in those days, when the very
elements entered into new combinations. Look at what happened! 19 Land animals took to the water, and swimming
creatures came up on the land. 20 Fire burned even in water,
which could not put it out. 21 And yet the flames could not
burn the flesh of the perishable creatures walking in them
and did not melt that heavenly food that would ordinarily
have melted like frost.
22 Lord, you have made your people great—glorious in all
respects. You have never neglected them. You have given
them help, always, everywhere.

NEW REVISED STANDARD VERSION

16 the latter, having first received them with festal
celebrations,
afterward afflicted with terrible sufferings
those who had already shared the same rights.
17 They were stricken also with loss of sight—
just as were those at the door of the righteous man—
when, surrounded by yawning darkness,
all of them tried to find the way through their own doors.

18 For the elements changed[a] places with one another,
as on a harp the notes vary the nature of the rhythm,
while each note remains the same.[b]
This may be clearly inferred from the sight of what took
place.
19 For land animals were transformed into water creatures,
and creatures that swim moved over to the land.
20 Fire even in water retained its normal power,
and water forgot its fire-quenching nature.
21 Flames, on the contrary, failed to consume
the flesh of perishable creatures that walked among them,
nor did they melt[c] the crystalline, quick-melting kind of
heavenly food.

22 For in everything, O Lord, you have exalted and
glorified your people,
and you have not neglected to help them at all times
and in all places.

a Gk *changing* *b* Meaning of Gk uncertain *c* Cn: Gk *nor could be melted*

NEW AMERICAN BIBLE

16 Yet these, after welcoming them with festivities,
oppressed with awful toils
those who now shared with them the same rights.
17 And they were struck with blindness,
as those others had been at the portals of the just—
When, surrounded by yawning darkness,
each sought the entrance of his own gate.
18 For the elements, in variable harmony among
themselves,
like strings of the harp, produce new melody,
while the flow of music steadily persists.
And this can be perceived exactly from a review of what
took place.
19 For land creatures were changed into water creatures,
and those that swam went over on to the land.
20 Fire in water maintained its own strength,
and water forgot its quenching nature;
21 Flames, by contrast, neither consumed the flesh
of the perishable animals that went about in them,
nor melted the icelike, quick-melting kind of
ambrosial food.
22 For every way, O LORD! you magnified and glorified
your people;
unfailing, you stood by them in every time and
circumstance.

NEW JERUSALEM BIBLE

16 but the latter, having given a festive reception
to people who already shared the same rights as
themselves,
later overwhelmed them with terrible labours.
17 Hence they were struck with blindness,
like the sinners at the gate of the upright,
when, yawning darkness all around them,
each had to grope his way through his own door.
18 A new attuning of the elements occurred,
as on a harp the notes may change their rhythm,
though all the while preserving the same tone;
and this is just what happened:
19 land animals became aquatic,
swimming ones took to the land,
20 fire reinforced its strength in water,
and water forgot the power of extinguishing it;
21 flames, on the other hand, did not char the flesh
of delicate animals that ventured into them;
nor did they melt the heavenly food
resembling ice and as easily melted.
22 Yes, Lord, in every way you have made your people
great and glorious;
you have never failed to help them at any time or place.

GREEK OLD TESTAMENT

ΣΟΦΙΑ ΣΙΡΑΧ

ΠΡΟΛΟΓΟΣ

Πολλῶν καὶ μεγάλων ἡμῖν διὰ τοῦ νόμου καὶ τῶν
 προφητῶν
καὶ τῶν ἄλλων τῶν κατ' αὐτοὺς ἠκολουθηκότων
 δεδομένων
ὑπὲρ ὧν δέον ἐστὶν ἐπαινεῖν τὸν Ισραηλ παιδείας
 καὶ σοφίας,
καὶ ὡς οὐ μόνον αὐτοὺς τοὺς ἀναγινώσκοντας δέον
 ἐστὶν ἐπιστήμονας γίνεσθαι,
ἀλλὰ καὶ τοῖς ἐκτὸς δύνασθαι τοὺς φιλομαθοῦντας
 χρησίμους εἶναι
καὶ λέγοντας καὶ γράφοντας,
ὁ πάππος μου Ἰησοῦς ἐπὶ πλεῖον ἑαυτὸν δοὺς
εἴς τε τὴν τοῦ νόμου
καὶ τῶν προφητῶν
καὶ τῶν ἄλλων πατρίων βιβλίων ἀνάγνωσιν
καὶ ἐν τούτοις ἱκανὴν ἕξιν περιποιησάμενος
προήχθη καὶ αὐτὸς συγγράψαι τι τῶν εἰς παιδείαν
 καὶ σοφίαν ἀνηκόντων,
ὅπως οἱ φιλομαθεῖς καὶ τούτων ἔνοχοι γενόμενοι
πολλῷ μᾶλλον ἐπιπροσθῶσιν διὰ τῆς ἐννόμου βιώσεως.
Παρακέκλησθε οὖν
μετ' εὐνοίας καὶ προσοχῆς
τὴν ἀνάγνωσιν ποιεῖσθαι

KING JAMES VERSION

THE WISDOM OF JESUS THE SON OF SIRACH, OR, ECCLESIASTICUS

The Prologue of the Wisdom of Jesus *the Son of* Sirach.[a]

Whereas many and great things have been delivered unto us by the law and the prophets, and by others that have followed their steps, for the which things Israel ought to be commended for learning and wisdom; and whereof not only the readers must needs become skilful themselves, but also they that desire to learn be able to profit them which are without, both by speaking and writing: my grandfather Jesus, when he had much given himself to the reading of the law, and the prophets, and other books of our fathers, and had gotten therein good judgment, was drawn on also himself to write something pertaining to learning and wisdom; to the intent that those which are desirous to learn, and are addicted to these things, might profit much more in living according to the law. Wherefore let me intreat you to read it with favour and attention, and to pardon us,

a The KJV also includes the following "Prologue made by an uncertain author," concerning which the marginal note states: "*Some refer this Prologue to Athanasius, because it is found in his Synopsis.*"

THIS Jesus was the son of Sirach, and grandchild to Jesus of the same name with him: this man therefore lived in the latter times, after the people had been led away captive, and called home again, and almost after all the prophets. Now his grandfather Jesus, as he himself witnesseth, was a man of great diligence and wisdom among the Hebrews, who did not only gather the grave and short sentences of wise men, that had been before him, but himself also uttered some of his own, full of much understanding and

DOUAY OLD TESTAMENT

ECCLESIASTICUS

THE PROLOGUE

THE knowledge of many and great things hath been shewn us by the law, and the prophets, and others that have followed them: for which things Israel is to be commended for doctrine and wisdom, because not only they that speak must needs be skilful, but strangers also, both speaking and writing, may *by their means* become most learned. My grandfather Jesus, after he had much given himself to a diligent reading of the law, and the prophets, and other books, that were delivered to us from our fathers, had a mind also to write something himself, pertaining to doctrine and wisdom: that such as are desirous to learn, and are made knowing in these things, may be more and more attentive in mind, and be strengthened to live according to the law. I entreat you therefore to come with benevolence, and to

KNOX TRANSLATION

THE BOOK OF ECCLESIASTICUS

PREFACE

MANY are the important truths conveyed to us by the law, by the prophets and by those other writers who have followed them. Israel must be given credit for its own philosophical tradition, suited not only to instruct those who talk its language, but to reach, in spoken or written form, the outside world too, and bring it great enlightenment. No wonder if my own grandfather, Jesus, who had devoted himself to the careful study of the law, the prophets, and our other ancestral records, had a mind to put something in writing himself that should bear on this philosophical tradition, to claim the attention of eager students who had already mastered it, and to encourage their observance of the law.

I must beg its readers to come well-disposed to their task, and to follow me closely, making allowances for me wherever

TODAY'S ENGLISH VERSION

SIRACH
The Wisdom of Jesus, Son of Sirach (Ecclesiasticus)

FOREWORD

The Law, the Prophets, and the later writers have left us a wealth of valuable teachings, and we should praise Israel for the instruction and wisdom they provide. But it is not enough that those who read them should gain understanding for themselves. Anyone who values learning should be able to help others by what he himself says and writes. That is why my grandfather Jesus devoted himself to reading the Law, the Prophets, and the other books of our ancestors. After he had mastered them, he was led to write a book of his own in order to share his wisdom and learning with others, so that anyone who shared his love for learning should have his book available as well, and be all the more able to live according to the Law.

Let me urge you, then, to read this book carefully and with an open mind. And please be patient in those places

NEW REVISED STANDARD VERSION

ECCLESIASTICUS, OR THE WISDOM OF JESUS SON OF SIRACH

THE PROLOGUE

Many great teachings have been given to us through the Law and the Prophets and the others[a] that followed them, and for these we should praise Israel for instruction and wisdom. Now, those who read the scriptures must not only themselves understand them, but must also as lovers of learning be able through the spoken and written word to help the outsiders. So my grandfather Jesus, who had devoted himself especially to the reading of the Law and the Prophets and the other books of our ancestors, and had acquired considerable proficiency in them, was himself also led to write something pertaining to instruction and wisdom, so that by becoming familiar also with his book[b] those who love learning might make even greater progress in living according to the law.

You are invited therefore to read it with goodwill and attention, and to be indulgent in cases where, despite our

a Or *other books* *b* Gk *with these things*

NEW AMERICAN BIBLE

SIRACH
(Ecclesiasticus)

FOREWORD

Many important truths have been handed down to us through the law, the prophets, and the later authors; and for these the instruction and wisdom of Israel merit praise. Now, those who are familiar with these truths must not only understand them themselves but, as lovers of wisdom, be able, in speech and in writing, to help others less familiar. Such a one was my grandfather, Jesus, who, having devoted himself for a long time to the diligent study of the law, the prophets, and the rest of the books of our ancestors, and having developed a thorough familiarity with them, was moved to write something himself in the nature of instruction and wisdom, in order that those who love wisdom might, by acquainting themselves with what he too had written, make even greater progress in living in conformity with the divine law.

You therefore are now invited to read it in a spirit of attentive good will, with indulgence for any apparent failure on

NEW JERUSALEM BIBLE

NOTE: The numbering of the verses is based on a Latin text which included several additions to the original. In some cases whole verses are missed out in this edition.

ECCLESIASTICUS

TRANSLATOR'S FOREWORD

1 The Law, the Prophets, 2 and the other writers succeeding
them have passed on to us great lessons, 3 in consequence of
which Israel must be commended for learning and wisdom.
4 Furthermore, it is a duty, not only to acquire learning by
reading, 5 but also, once having acquired it, to make oneself
of use to people outside 6 by what one can say or write. 7 My
grandfather Jesus, having long devoted himself to the reading 8 of the Law, 9 the Prophets 10 and other books of the
Fathers 11 and having become very learned in them, 12 himself decided to write something on the subjects of learning
and wisdom, 13 so that people who wanted to learn might,
by themselves accepting these disciplines, 14 learn how better to live according to the Law.

15 You are therefore asked 16 to read this book 17 with good
will and attention 18 and to show indulgence 19 in those

GREEK OLD TESTAMENT

καὶ συγγνώμην ἔχειν
ἐφ᾽ οἷς ἂν δοκῶμεν
τῶν κατὰ τὴν ἑρμηνείαν πεφιλοπονημένων τισὶν τῶν λέξεων ἀδυναμεῖν·
οὐ γὰρ ἰσοδυναμεῖ
αὐτὰ ἐν ἑαυτοῖς Εβραϊστὶ λεγόμενα καὶ ὅταν μεταχθῇ εἰς ἑτέραν γλῶσσαν·
οὐ μόνον δὲ ταῦτα,
ἀλλὰ καὶ αὐτὸς ὁ νόμος καὶ αἱ προφητεῖαι
καὶ τὰ λοιπὰ τῶν βιβλίων
οὐ μικρὰν ἔχει τὴν διαφορὰν ἐν ἑαυτοῖς λεγόμενα.
Ἐν γὰρ τῷ ὀγδόῳ καὶ τριακοστῷ ἔτει ἐπὶ τοῦ Εὐεργέτου βασιλέως
παραγενηθεὶς εἰς Αἴγυπτον καὶ συγχρονίσας
εὑρὼν οὐ μικρᾶς παιδείας ἀφόμοιον
ἀναγκαιότατον ἐθέμην καὶ αὐτός τινα προσενέγκασθαι σπουδήν καὶ φιλοπονίαν τοῦ μεθερμηνεῦσαι τήνδε τὴν βίβλον
πολλὴν ἀγρυπνίαν καὶ ἐπιστήμην προσενεγκάμενος
ἐν τῷ διαστήματι τοῦ χρόνου
πρὸς τὸ ἐπὶ πέρας ἀγαγόντα τὸ βιβλίον ἐκδόσθαι
καὶ τοῖς ἐν τῇ παροικίᾳ βουλομένοις φιλομαθεῖν
προκατασκευαζομένους τὰ ἤθη
ἐννόμως βιοτεύειν.

1 Πᾶσα σοφία παρὰ κυρίου
καὶ μετ᾽ αὐτοῦ ἐστιν εἰς τὸν αἰῶνα.
2 ἄμμον θαλασσῶν καὶ σταγόνας ὑετοῦ
καὶ ἡμέρας αἰῶνος τίς ἐξαριθμήσει;

KING JAMES VERSION

wherein we may seem to come short of some words, which we have laboured to interpret. For the same things uttered in Hebrew, and translated into another tongue, have not the same force in them: and not only these things, but the law itself, and the prophets, and the rest of the books, have no small difference, when they are spoken in their own language. For in the eight and thirtieth year coming into Egypt, when Euergetes was king, and continuing there some time, I found a book of no small learning: therefore I thought it most necessary for me to bestow some diligence and travail to interpret it; using great watchfulness and skill in that space to bring the book to an end, and set it forth for them also, which in a strange country are willing to learn, being prepared before in manners to live after the law.

1 All wisdom *cometh* from the Lord, and is with him for ever.
2 Who can number the sand of the sea, and the drops of
rain, and the days of eternity?

wisdom. When as therefore the first Jesus died, leaving this book almost perfected, Sirach his son receiving it after him left it to his own son Jesus, who, having gotten it into his hands, compiled it all orderly into one volume, and called it Wisdom, intituling it both by his own name, his father's name, and his grandfather's; alluring the hearer by the very name of Wisdom to have a greater love to the study of this book. It containeth therefore wise sayings, dark sentences, and parables, and certain particular ancient godly stories of men that pleased God; also his prayer and song; moreover, what benefits God had vouchsafed his people, and what plagues he had heaped upon their enemies. This Jesus did imitate Solomon, and was no less famous for wisdom and learning, both being indeed a man of great learning, and so reputed also.

DOUAY OLD TESTAMENT

read with attention, and to pardon us for those things wherein we may seem, while we follow the image of wisdom, to come short in the composition of words; for the Hebrew words have not the same force in them when translated into another tongue. And not only these, but the law also itself, and the prophets, and the rest of the books, have no small difference, when they are spoken in their own language. For in the eight and thirtieth year coming into Egypt, when Ptolemy Evergetes was king, and continuing there a long time, I found there books left, of no small nor contemptible learning. Therefore I thought it good, and necessary for me to bestow some diligence and labour to interpret this book; and with much watching and study in some space of time, I brought the book to an end, and set it forth for the service of them that are willing to apply their mind, and to learn how they ought to conduct themselves, who purpose to lead their life according to the law of the Lord.

1 ALL wisdom is from the Lord God, and hath been always with him, and is before all time.
2 Who hath numbered the sand of the sea, and the drops
of rain, and the days of the world? Who hath measured the

KNOX TRANSLATION

I seem to have failed in the right marshalling of words, as I pass on wisdom at second hand. Hebrew words lose their force when they are translated into another language; moreover, when the Hebrews read out the law, the prophets, and the other books among themselves, they read them out in a greatly different form.

It was in my thirty-eighth year,[a] in the reign of Euergetes, that I went to Egypt and spent some time there. When I found writings preserved there which were of high doctrinal value, it seemed to me right and fitting that I, too, should be at some pains; I would set about translating this book. Learning I gave to the task and long labour, and so brought it to an end; and so I offer the book to all who are ready to apply their minds to it, and learn how a man must frame his conduct if he would live by the divine law.

1 All wisdom has one source; it dwelt with the Lord God before ever time began. 2 Sand thou mayst count, or the
rain-drops, or the days of the world's abiding; heaven-height

a In the original, 'the thirty-eighth year'; probably the author refers to 132 B.C., the thirty-eighth regnal year of Ptolemy Euergetes II. If the year meant is that of his own age, he may equally well have lived under Ptolemy Euergetes I (247-222 B.C.).

TODAY'S ENGLISH VERSION

where, in spite of all my diligent efforts, I may not have translated some phrases very well. What was originally written in Hebrew does not always have exactly the same sense when it is translated into another language.[a] That is true not only of this book, but even of the Law itself, the Prophets, and the other books. The translations differ quite a bit from the original.

I came to Egypt in the thirty-eighth year of King Euergetes' reign and stayed for some time. While I was there, I had the opportunity for a good deal of study and felt the necessity of translating the following book. I wanted to use all my diligence and skill to complete it and make it available for all those living in foreign lands who wish to learn and who have the strength of character to live by the Law of Moses.

1 All wisdom comes from the Lord,
and Wisdom is with him forever.
2 Who can count raindrops or the sand along the shore?
Who can count the days of eternity?

[a] *The book of Sirach was written in Hebrew, but the writer of this foreword translated it into Greek.*

NEW REVISED STANDARD VERSION

diligent labor in translating, we may seem to have rendered some phrases imperfectly. For what was originally expressed in Hebrew does not have exactly the same sense when translated into another language. Not only this book, but even the Law itself, the Prophecies, and the rest of the books differ not a little when read in the original.

When I came to Egypt in the thirty-eighth year of the reign of Euergetes and stayed for some time, I found opportunity for no little instruction.[a] It seemed highly necessary that I should myself devote some diligence and labor to the translation of this book. During that time I have applied my skill day and night to complete and publish the book for those living abroad who wished to gain learning and are disposed to live according to the law.

1 All wisdom is from the Lord,
and with him it remains forever.
2 The sand of the sea, the drops of rain,
and the days of eternity—who can count them?

[a] Other ancient authorities read *I found a copy affording no little instruction*

NEW AMERICAN BIBLE

our part, despite earnest efforts, in the interpretation of particular passages. For words spoken originally in Hebrew are not as effective when they are translated into another language. That is true not only of this book but of the law itself, the prophets and the rest of the books, which differ no little when they are read in the original.

I arrived in Egypt in the thirty-eighth year of the reign of King Euergetes, and while there, I found a reproduction of our valuable teaching. I therefore considered myself in duty bound to devote some diligence and industry to the translation of this book. Many sleepless hours of close application have I devoted in the interval to finishing the book for publication, for the benefit of those living abroad who wish to acquire wisdom and are disposed to live their lives according to the standards of the law.

1 All wisdom comes from the LORD
and with him it remains forever.
2 The sand of the seashore, the drops of rain,
the days of eternity: who can number these?

NEW JERUSALEM BIBLE

places where, notwithstanding our efforts at interpretation,
we may seem 20 to have failed to give an adequate rendering
of this or that expression; 21 the fact is that there is no
equivalent 22 for things originally written in Hebrew when it
is a question of translating them into another language;
23 what is more, 24 the Law itself, the Prophets 25 and the
other books 26 differ considerably in translation from what
appears in the original text.

27 It was in the thirty-eighth year of the late King
Euergetes[a] 28 that, coming to Egypt and spending some time
here, 29 and finding life here consistent with a high degree of
wisdom, 30 I became convinced of an immediate duty to
apply myself in my turn with pains and diligence to the
translation of the book that follows; 31 and I spent much
time and learning on it 32 in the course of this period, 33 to
complete the work and to publish the book 34 for the benefit
of those too who, domiciled abroad, wish to study, 35 to
reform their behaviour, and to live as the Law requires.

1 All wisdom comes from the Lord,
she is with him for ever.
2 The sands of the sea, the drops of rain,
the days of eternity—who can count them?

[a] **Foreword** Ptolemy VII Euergetes Physcon (170–117 BC). So the date is 132 BC.

GREEK OLD TESTAMENT

3 ὕψος οὐρανοῦ καὶ πλάτος γῆς
καὶ ἄβυσσον καὶ σοφίαν τίς ἐξιχνιάσει;
4 προτέρα πάντων ἔκτισται σοφία
καὶ σύνεσις φρονήσεως ἐξ αἰῶνος.
6 ῥίζα σοφίας τίνι ἀπεκαλύφθη;
καὶ τὰ πανουργεύματα αὐτῆς τίς ἔγνω;
8 εἷς ἐστιν σοφός, φοβερὸς σφόδρα,
καθήμενος ἐπὶ τοῦ θρόνου αὐτοῦ.
9 κύριος αὐτὸς ἔκτισεν αὐτὴν
καὶ εἶδεν καὶ ἐξηρίθμησεν αὐτὴν
καὶ ἐξέχεεν αὐτὴν ἐπὶ πάντα τὰ ἔργα αὐτοῦ,
10 μετὰ πάσης σαρκὸς κατὰ τὴν δόσιν αὐτοῦ,
καὶ ἐχορήγησεν αὐτὴν τοῖς ἀγαπῶσιν αὐτόν.
11 Φόβος κυρίου δόξα καὶ καύχημα
καὶ εὐφροσύνη καὶ στέφανος ἀγαλλιάματος.
12 φόβος κυρίου τέρψει καρδίαν
καὶ δώσει εὐφροσύνην καὶ χαρὰν καὶ μακροημέρευσιν.
13 τῷ φοβουμένῳ τὸν κύριον εὖ ἔσται ἐπ' ἐσχάτων,
καὶ ἐν ἡμέρᾳ τελευτῆς αὐτοῦ εὐλογηθήσεται.

KING JAMES VERSION

3 Who can find out the height of heaven, and the breadth of the earth, and the deep, and wisdom?

4 Wisdom hath been created before all things, and the understanding of prudence from everlasting.

5 The word of God most high is the fountain of wisdom; and her ways are everlasting commandments.

6 To whom hath the root of wisdom been revealed? or who hath known her wise counsels?

7 [Unto whom hath the knowledge of wisdom been made manifest? and who hath understood her great experience?]

8 There is one wise and greatly to be feared, the Lord sitting upon his throne.

9 He created her, and saw her, and numbered her, and poured her out upon all his works.

10 She *is* with all flesh according to his gift, and he hath given her to them that love him.

11 The fear of the Lord is honour, and glory, and gladness, and a crown of rejoicing.

12 The fear of the Lord maketh a merry heart, and giveth joy, and gladness, and a long life.

13 Whoso feareth the Lord, it shall go well with him at the last, and he shall find favour in the day of his death.

DOUAY OLD TESTAMENT

height of heaven, and the breadth of the earth, and the depth of the abyss?

3 Who hath searched out the wisdom of God that goeth before all things?

4 Wisdom hath been created before all things, and the understanding of prudence from everlasting.

5 The word of God on high is the fountain of wisdom, and her ways are everlasting commandments.

6 To whom hath the root of wisdom been revealed, and who hath known her wise counsels?

7 To whom hath the discipline of wisdom been revealed and made manifest? and who hath understood the multiplicity of her steps?

8 There is one most high Creator Almighty, and a powerful king, and greatly to be feared, who sitteth upon his throne, and is the God of dominion.

9 He created her in the Holy Ghost, and saw her, and numbered her, and measured her.

10 And he poured her out upon all his works, and upon all flesh according to his gift, and hath given her to them that love him.

11 The fear of the Lord is honour, and glory, and gladness, and a crown of joy.

12 The fear of the Lord shall delight the heart, and shall give joy, and gladness, and length of days.

13 With him that feareth the Lord, it shall go well in the latter end, and in the day of his death he shall be blessed.

14 The love of God is honourable wisdom.

15 And they to whom she shall shew herself love her by the sight, and by the knowledge of her great works.

KNOX TRANSLATION

thou mayst measure, or the wide earth, or the depth of the
world beneath, 3 ere God's wisdom thou canst trace to her
origin, that was before all. 4 First she is of all created things;
time never was when the riddle of thought went unread.
5 (What is wisdom's fount? God's word above. What is her
course? His eternal commandments.[a]) 6 Buried her roots
beyond all search, wise her counsels beyond all knowing;
7 too high her teaching to be plainly revealed, too manifold
her movements to be understood. 8 There is but one God,
high creator of all things; sitting on his throne to govern us,
a great king, worthy of all dread; 9 he it was that created
her, through his holy Spirit. His eye took in the whole range
of her being; 10 and he has poured her out upon all his creation, upon all living things, upon all the souls that love
him, in the measure of his gift to each.
11 To fear the Lord is man's pride and boast, is joy, is a
prize proudly worn; 12 comfort it brings to the heart, happiness and content and a long life bestows; 13 well it is, at his
last hour, for the man who fears the Lord; his day of death
shall be a day of blessing. 14 Love of God is wisdom worth
the having; 15 welcome the sight when it shews itself, when
it gives proof of its wondrous power. 16 Wouldst thou be

a The words printed in brackets are not found in the Greek. There are many other differences of detail between the Greek and the Latin, too numerous to be mentioned in these notes. The Hebrew original (which has been preserved to us only in small part) must have been current in several different forms at the time when our versions were made; and it seems probable that the Latin has sometimes included two alternatives side by side (cf. verses 26 and 31, 32 of this chapter).

TODAY'S ENGLISH VERSION

[3] How high is the sky? How wide is the earth?
How deep is the ocean? How profound is Wisdom?
Can anyone find answers to these questions?
[4] Wisdom was created before anything else;
understanding has always existed.[a]
[6] Has anyone ever been shown where Wisdom
originates?
Does anyone understand her subtle cleverness?[b]
[8] There is only one who is wise,
and we must stand in awe before his throne.
[9] The Lord himself created Wisdom;
he saw her and recognized her value,
and so he filled everything he made with Wisdom.
[10] He gave some measure of Wisdom to everyone,
but poured her out on those who love him.

[11] If you fear the Lord, honor and pride will be yours;
you will be crowned with happiness and joy.
[12] To honor the Lord is a heartfelt delight;
it will give you a long and happy life,
[13] and at the end of your days all will go well for you.
God will bless you on the day of your death.

[a] *Some manuscripts add verse 5:* The source of Wisdom is the word of God on high; her ways are eternal commands. [b] *Some manuscripts add verse 7:* To whom has the knowledge of Wisdom been revealed? Who has understood her great experience?

NEW REVISED STANDARD VERSION

3 The height of heaven, the breadth of the earth,
the abyss, and wisdom[a]—who can search them out?
4 Wisdom was created before all other things,
and prudent understanding from eternity.[b]
6 The root of wisdom—to whom has it been revealed?
Her subtleties—who knows them?[c]
8 There is but one who is wise, greatly to be feared,
seated upon his throne—the Lord.
9 It is he who created her;
he saw her and took her measure;
he poured her out upon all his works,
10 upon all the living according to his gift;
he lavished her upon those who love him.[d]

11 The fear of the Lord is glory and exultation,
and gladness and a crown of rejoicing.
12 The fear of the Lord delights the heart,
and gives gladness and joy and long life.[e]
13 Those who fear the Lord will have a happy end;
on the day of their death they will be blessed.

a Other ancient authorities read *the depth of the abyss* b Other ancient authorities add as verse 5, *The source of wisdom is God's word in the highest heaven, and her ways are the eternal commandments.* c Other ancient authorities add as verse 7, *The knowledge of wisdom—to whom was it manifested? And her abundant experience—who has understood it?* d Other ancient authorities add *Love of the Lord is glorious wisdom; to those to whom he appears he apportions her, that they may see him.* e Other ancient authorities add *The fear of the Lord is a gift from the Lord; also for love he makes firm paths.*

NEW AMERICAN BIBLE

[3] Heaven's height, earth's breadth,
the depths of the abyss: who can explore these?
[4] Before all things else wisdom was created;
and prudent understanding, from eternity.
[5] To whom has wisdom's root been revealed?
Who knows her subtleties?
[6] There is but one, wise and truly awe-inspiring,
seated upon his throne:
[7] It is the LORD; he created her,
has seen her and taken note of her.
[8] He has poured her forth upon all his works,
upon every living thing according to his bounty;
he has lavished her upon his friends.
[9] Fear of the LORD is glory and splendor,
gladness and a festive crown.
[10] Fear of the LORD warms the heart,
giving gladness and joy and length of days.
[11] He who fears the LORD will have a happy end;
even on the day of his death he will be blessed.

NEW JERUSALEM BIBLE

[3] The height of the sky, the breadth of the earth,
the depth of the abyss—who can explore them?
[4] Wisdom was created before everything,
prudent understanding subsists from remotest ages.
[6] For whom has the root of wisdom ever been uncovered?
Her resourceful ways, who knows them?
[8] One only is wise, terrible indeed,
9 seated on his throne, the Lord.
It was he who created, inspected and weighed her up,
and then poured her out on all his works—
[10] as much to each living creature as he chose—
bestowing her on those who love him.
[11] The fear of the Lord is glory and pride,
happiness and a crown of joyfulness.
[12] The fear of the Lord gladdens the heart,
giving happiness, joy and long life.
[13] For those who fear the Lord, all will end well:
on their dying day they will be blessed.

GREEK OLD TESTAMENT

14 Ἀρχὴ σοφίας φοβεῖσθαι τὸν κύριον,
καὶ μετὰ πιστῶν ἐν μήτρᾳ συνεκτίσθη αὐτοῖς.
15 μετὰ ἀνθρώπων θεμέλιον αἰῶνος ἐνόσσευσεν
καὶ μετὰ τοῦ σπέρματος αὐτῶν ἐμπιστευθήσεται.
16 πλησμονὴ σοφίας φοβεῖσθαι τὸν κύριον
καὶ μεθύσκει αὐτοὺς ἀπὸ τῶν καρπῶν αὐτῆς·
17 πάντα τὸν οἶκον αὐτῶν ἐμπλήσει ἐπιθυμημάτων
καὶ τὰ ἀποδοχεῖα ἀπὸ τῶν γενημάτων αὐτῆς.
18 στέφανος σοφίας φόβος κυρίου
ἀναθάλλων εἰρήνην καὶ ὑγίειαν ἰάσεως.
19 καὶ εἶδεν καὶ ἐξηρίθμησεν αὐτήν,
ἐπιστήμην καὶ γνῶσιν συνέσεως ἐξώμβρησεν
καὶ δόξαν κρατούντων αὐτῆς ἀνύψωσεν.
20 ῥίζα σοφίας φοβεῖσθαι τὸν κύριον,
καὶ οἱ κλάδοι αὐτῆς μακροημέρευσις.
22 Οὐ δυνήσεται θυμὸς ἄδικος δικαιωθῆναι·
ἡ γὰρ ῥοπὴ τοῦ θυμοῦ αὐτοῦ πτῶσις αὐτῷ.
23 ἕως καιροῦ ἀνθέξεται μακρόθυμος,
καὶ ὕστερον αὐτῷ ἀναδώσει εὐφροσύνη·
24 ἕως καιροῦ κρύψει τοὺς λόγους αὐτοῦ,
καὶ χείλη πολλῶν ἐκδιηγήσεται σύνεσιν αὐτοῦ.

KING JAMES VERSION

14 To fear the Lord is the beginning of wisdom: and it was created with the faithful in the womb.

15 She hath built an everlasting foundation with men, and she shall continue with their seed.

16 To fear the Lord is fulness of wisdom, and filleth men with her fruits.

17 She filleth all their house with things desirable, and the garners with her increase.

18 The fear of the Lord is a crown of wisdom, making peace and perfect health to flourish; both which are the gifts of God: and it enlargeth their rejoicing that love him.

19 Wisdom raineth down skill and knowledge of understanding, and exalteth them to honour that hold her fast.

20 The root of wisdom is to fear the Lord, and the branches thereof are long life.

21 The fear of the Lord driveth away sins: and where it is present, it turneth away wrath.

22 A furious man cannot be justified; for the sway of his fury shall be his destruction.

23 A patient man will bear for a time, and afterward joy shall spring up unto him.

24 He will hide his words for a time, and the lips of many shall declare his wisdom.

DOUAY OLD TESTAMENT

16 The fear of the Lord is the beginning of wisdom, and was created with the faithful in the womb, it walketh with chosen women, and is known with the just and faithful.

17 The fear of the Lord is the religiousness of knowledge.

18 Religiousness shall keep and justify the heart, it shall give joy and gladness.

19 It shall go well with him that feareth the Lord, and in the days of his end he shall be blessed.

20 To fear God is the fulness of wisdom, and fulness is from the fruits thereof.

21 She shall fill all her house with her increase, and the storehouses with her treasures.

22 The fear of the Lord is a crown of wisdom, filling up peace and the fruit of salvation:

23 And it hath seen, and numbered her: but both are the gifts of God.

24 Wisdom shall distribute knowledge, and understanding of prudence: and exalteth the glory of them that hold her.

25 The root of wisdom is to fear the Lord: and the branches thereof are long-lived.

26 In the treasures of wisdom is understanding, and religiousness of knowledge: but to sinners wisdom is an abomination.

27 The fear of the Lord driveth out sin:

28 For he that is without fear, cannot be justified: for the wrath of his high spirits is his ruin.

29 A patient man shall bear for a time, and afterwards joy shall be restored to him.

30 A good understanding will hide his words for a time, and the lips of many shall declare his wisdom.

KNOX TRANSLATION

wise, the first step is fear of the Lord; to his chosen servants,
a gift connatural from the womb; it goes with holy mother-
hood, and where his true worshippers are, shews manifest.
17 The fear of the Lord lends wisdom that piety which is hers;
18 such piety as shall keep the heart safe and make it acceptable, bring it joy and content. 19 Well it shall be indeed for
the man who fears the Lord; at his last end he shall win
blessing. 20 The fear of the Lord is wisdom's fulfilment,
yields the deep draught that satisfies; 21 never a nook or
cranny in thy house but shall be filled with the store of its
harvesting. 22 The fear of the Lord is wisdom's crown; with
this, peace and health are thine to enjoy; 23 this fear itself is
God's gift, no less than the wisdom which is counted out
under his eye. 24 Wisdom it is that imparts to us all our
knowledge, all our powers of discernment; hold her fast, and
she will set thee on a pinnacle of renown; 25 root of her is
fear of the Lord, and long life the fruit of her.
26 True insight wisdom has in her treasure-house, and the
piety that comes of knowledge; no wonder if sinners hate the
name of her. 27 The fear of the Lord drives out sin; 28 soul
that feels no fear shall find no pardon, its own wild mood
overbalances it. 29 Patience bides her time, and with time,
content comes back to her; 30 praise shall be upon every lip
for the wise thought that checked, for a while, her utterance.

TODAY'S ENGLISH VERSION

14 To fear the Lord is the first step to Wisdom.
Wisdom is given to the faithful in their mothers' wombs.
15 She has lived with us from ancient times,
and generations to come will rely on her.
16 To fear the Lord is Wisdom at her fullest;
she satisfies us completely with her gifts
17 and fills our homes and our barns
with all that our hearts can desire.
18 To fear the Lord is the flower of Wisdom
that blossoms with peace and good health.[a]
19 She sends knowledge and understanding like the rain,
and increases the honor of those who receive her.
20 To fear the Lord is the root of Wisdom;
her branches are long life.[b]

22 There is no excuse for unjustified anger; it can bring
about your downfall. 23 Wait and be patient, and later you
will be glad you did. 24 Keep quiet until the right time to
speak, and you will gain a reputation for good sense.

[a] *Some manuscripts add:* He saw her and recognized her value *(see 1.9).*
[b] *Some manuscripts add verse 21:* Honoring the Lord takes sin away; where the fear of the Lord is found, it turns away anger.

NEW REVISED STANDARD VERSION

14 To fear the Lord is the beginning of wisdom;
she is created with the faithful in the womb.
15 She made[a] among human beings an eternal foundation,
and among their descendants she will abide faithfully.
16 To fear the Lord is fullness of wisdom;
she inebriates mortals with her fruits;
17 she fills their[b] whole house with desirable goods,
and their[c] storehouses with her produce.
18 The fear of the Lord is the crown of wisdom,
making peace and perfect health to flourish.[d]
19 She rained down knowledge and discerning comprehension,
and she heightened the glory of those who held her fast.
20 To fear the Lord is the root of wisdom,
and her branches are long life.[e]

22 Unjust anger cannot be justified,
for anger tips the scale to one's ruin.
23 Those who are patient stay calm until the right moment,
and then cheerfulness comes back to them.
24 They hold back their words until the right moment;
then the lips of many tell of their good sense.

a Gk *made as a nest* *b* Other ancient authorities read *her* *c* Other ancient authorities read *her* *d* Other ancient authorities add *Both are gifts of God for peace; glory opens out for those who love him. He saw her and took her measure.* *e* Other ancient authorities add as verse 21, *The fear of the Lord drives away sins; and where it abides, it will turn away all anger.*

NEW AMERICAN BIBLE

12 The beginning of wisdom is fear of the LORD,
which is formed with the faithful in the womb.
13 With devoted men was she created from of old,
and with their children her beneficence abides.
14 Fullness of wisdom is fear of the LORD;
she inebriates men with her fruits.
15 Her entire house she fills with choice foods,
her granaries with her harvest.
16 Wisdom's garland is fear of the LORD,
with blossoms of peace and perfect health.
17 Knowledge and full understanding she showers down;
she heightens the glory of those who possess her.
18 The root of wisdom is fear of the LORD;
her branches are length of days.

19 One cannot justify unjust anger;
anger plunges a man to his downfall.
20 A patient man need stand firm but for a time,
and then contentment comes back to him.
21 For a while he holds back his words,
then the lips of many herald his wisdom.

NEW JERUSALEM BIBLE

14 The basis of wisdom is to fear the Lord;
she was created with the faithful in their mothers' womb;
15 she has made a home in the human race, an age-old foundation,
and to their descendants will she faithfully cling.
16 The fullness of wisdom is to fear the Lord;
she intoxicates them with her fruits;
17 she fills their entire house with treasures
and their storerooms with her produce.
18 The crown of wisdom is to fear the Lord:
she makes peace and health flourish.
19 The Lord has seen and assessed her,
he has showered down knowledge and intelligence,
he has exalted the renown of those who possess her.
20 The root of wisdom is to fear the Lord,
and her branches are long life.

22 The rage of the wicked cannot put him in the right,
for the weight of his rage is his downfall.
23 A patient person puts up with things until the right time comes:
but his joy will break out in the end.
24 Till the time comes he keeps his thoughts to himself,
and many a lip will affirm how wise he is.

GREEK OLD TESTAMENT

25 Ἐν θησαυροῖς σοφίας παραβολαὶ ἐπιστήμης,
βδέλυγμα δὲ ἁμαρτωλῷ θεοσέβεια.
26 ἐπιθυμήσας σοφίαν διατήρησον ἐντολάς,
καὶ κύριος χορηγήσει σοι αὐτήν.
27 σοφία γὰρ καὶ παιδεία φόβος κυρίου,
καὶ ἡ εὐδοκία αὐτοῦ πίστις καὶ πραότης.
28 μὴ ἀπειθήσῃς φόβῳ κυρίου
καὶ μὴ προσέλθῃς αὐτῷ ἐν καρδίᾳ δισσῇ.
29 μὴ ὑποκριθῇς ἐν στόμασιν ἀνθρώπων
καὶ ἐν τοῖς χείλεσίν σου πρόσεχε.
30 μὴ ἐξύψου σεαυτόν, ἵνα μὴ πέσῃς
καὶ ἐπαγάγῃς τῇ ψυχῇ σου ἀτιμίαν,
καὶ ἀποκαλύψει κύριος τὰ κρυπτά σου
καὶ ἐν μέσῳ συναγωγῆς καταβαλεῖ σε,
ὅτι οὐ προσῆλθες φόβῳ κυρίου
καὶ ἡ καρδία σου πλήρης δόλου.

2 Τέκνον, εἰ προσέρχῃ δουλεύειν κυρίῳ,
ἑτοίμασον τὴν ψυχήν σου εἰς πειρασμόν·
2 εὔθυνον τὴν καρδίαν σου καὶ καρτέρησον
καὶ μὴ σπεύσῃς ἐν καιρῷ ἐπαγωγῆς·
3 κολλήθητι αὐτῷ καὶ μὴ ἀποστῇς,
ἵνα αὐξηθῇς ἐπ᾽ ἐσχάτων σου.
4 πᾶν, ὃ ἐὰν ἐπαχθῇ σοι, δέξαι
καὶ ἐν ἀλλάγμασιν ταπεινώσεώς σου μακροθύμησον·

KING JAMES VERSION

25 The parables of knowledge are in the treasures of wisdom: but godliness is an abomination to a sinner.

26 If thou desire wisdom, keep the commandments, and the Lord shall give her unto thee.

27 For the fear of the Lord is wisdom and instruction: and faith and meekness are his delight.

28 Distrust not the fear of the Lord when thou art poor: and come not unto him with a double heart.

29 Be not an hypocrite in the sight of men, and take good heed what thou speakest.

30 Exalt not thyself, lest thou fall, and bring dishonour upon thy soul, and so God discover thy secrets, and cast thee down in the midst of the congregation, because thou camest not in truth to the fear of the Lord, but thy heart is full of deceit.

2 My son, if thou come to serve the Lord, prepare thy soul for temptation.

2 Set thy heart aright, and constantly endure, and make not haste in time of trouble.

3 Cleave unto him, and depart not away, that thou mayest be increased at thy last end.

4 Whatsoever is brought upon thee take cheerfully, and be patient when thou art changed to a low estate.

DOUAY OLD TESTAMENT

31 In the treasures of wisdom is the signification of discipline:

32 But the worship of God is an abomination to a sinner.

33 Son, if thou desire wisdom, keep justice, and God will give her to thee.

34 For the fear of the Lord is wisdom and discipline: and that which is agreeable to him,

35 Is faith, and meekness: and he will fill up his treasures.

36 Be not incredulous to the fear of the Lord: and come not to him with a double heart.

37 Be not a hypocrite in the sight of men, and let not thy lips be a stumblingblock to thee.

38 Watch over them, lest thou fall, and bring dishonour upon thy soul,

39 And God discover thy secrets, and cast thee down in the midst of the congregation.

40 Because thou camest to the Lord wickedly, and thy heart is full of guile and deceit.

2 SON, when thou comest to the service of God, stand in justice and in fear, and prepare thy soul for temptation.

2 Humble thy heart, and endure: incline thy ear, and receive the words of understanding: and make not haste in the time of clouds.

3 Wait on God with patience: join thyself to God, and endure, that thy life may be increased in the latter end.

4 Take all that shall be brought upon thee: and in thy sorrow endure, and in thy humiliation keep patience.

KNOX TRANSLATION

31 Hidden in wisdom's treasure-house is the secret of all discernment; 32 and still sinners hate the name of piety. 33 My son, if on wisdom thy heart is set, keep the commandments, and God will grant thy wish; 34 fear of the Lord is true wisdom, true learning, and his will is to see thee 35 loyal and patient; thou shalt have no empty coffers then.

36 Let not thy fear of the Lord be overcast with doubt; never come to him with a heart that hesitates.

37 Do not play false in thy dealings with men, nor suffer thy own words to ensnare thee. 38 Watch those words well, or they may trip thee up; thou wilt have compassed thy own disgrace, 39 if God should reveal thy secret thoughts at last; wouldst thou be thrown down, in full sight of all thy neighbours assembled, 40 a heart that came to meet the Lord grudgingly, full all the while of treachery and deceit?

2 My son, if thy mind is to enter the Lord's service, wait there in his presence, with honesty of purpose and with awe, and prepare thyself to be put to the test. 2 Submissive be thy heart, and ready to bear all; to wise advice lend a ready ear, and be never hasty when ill times befall thee. 3 Wait for God, cling to God and wait for him; at the end of it, thy life shall blossom anew. 4 Accept all that comes to thee, patient in sorrow, humiliation long enduring; 5 for gold and

TODAY'S ENGLISH VERSION

25 Wisdom has a treasury of wise sayings, but sinners have
nothing but contempt for godliness. 26 If you want to be
wise, keep the Lord's commands, and he will give you
Wisdom in abundance. 27 Fearing the Lord is Wisdom and
an education in itself. He is pleased by loyalty and humility.
28 Be faithful in the practice of your religion; when you worship the Lord, do it with all your heart. 29 Be careful about
what you say, and don't be a hypocrite. 30 Don't be arrogant;
you may suffer a fall and be disgraced. The Lord will reveal
your secrets and humble you in front of everyone in the synagogue, because you did not come there with reverence for
the Lord, but with a heart full of hypocrisy.

2 My child, if you are going to serve the Lord, be prepared
for times when you will be put to the test. 2 Be sincere
and determined. Keep calm when trouble comes. 3 Stay with
the Lord; never abandon him, and you will be prosperous at
the end of your days. 4 Accept whatever happens to you.
Even if you suffer humiliation, be patient. 5 Gold is tested by

NEW REVISED STANDARD VERSION

25 In the treasuries of wisdom are wise sayings,
but godliness is an abomination to a sinner.
26 If you desire wisdom, keep the commandments,
and the Lord will lavish her upon you.
27 For the fear of the Lord is wisdom and discipline,
fidelity and humility are his delight.

28 Do not disobey the fear of the Lord;
do not approach him with a divided mind.
29 Do not be a hypocrite before others,
and keep watch over your lips.
30 Do not exalt yourself, or you may fall
and bring dishonor upon yourself.
The Lord will reveal your secrets
and overthrow you before the whole congregation,
because you did not come in the fear of the Lord,
and your heart was full of deceit.

2 My child, when you come to serve the Lord,
prepare yourself for testing.[a]
2 Set your heart right and be steadfast,
and do not be impetuous in time of calamity.
3 Cling to him and do not depart,
so that your last days may be prosperous.
4 Accept whatever befalls you,
and in times of humiliation be patient.

a Or *trials*

NEW AMERICAN BIBLE

22 Among wisdom's treasures is the paragon of prudence;
but fear of the LORD is an abomination to the sinner.
23 If you desire wisdom, keep the commandments,
and the LORD will bestow her upon you;
24 For fear of the LORD is wisdom and culture;
loyal humility is his delight.
25 Be not faithless to the fear of the LORD,
nor approach it with duplicity of heart.
26 Play not the hypocrite before men;
over your lips keep watch.
27 Exalt not yourself lest you fall
and bring upon you dishonor;
28 For then the LORD will reveal your secrets
and publicly cast you down,
29 Because you approached the fear of the LORD
with your heart full of guile.

2 My son, when you come to serve the LORD,
prepare yourself for trials.
2 Be sincere of heart and steadfast,
undisturbed in time of adversity.
3 Cling to him, forsake him not;
thus will your future be great.
4 Accept whatever befalls you,
in crushing misfortune be patient;

NEW JERUSALEM BIBLE

25 Wisdom's treasuries contain the maxims of knowledge,
the sinner, however, holds piety in abhorrence.
26 If you desire wisdom, keep the commandments,
and the Lord will bestow it on you.
27 For the fear of the Lord is wisdom and instruction,
and what pleases him is faithfulness and gentleness.
28 Do not stand out against fear of the Lord,
do not practise it with a double heart.
29 Do not act a part in public,
keep watch over your lips.
30 Do not grow too high and mighty, for fear you fall
and cover yourself in disgrace;
for the Lord would then reveal your secrets
and overthrow you before the whole community
for not having practised fear of the Lord
and for having a heart full of deceit.

2 My child, if you aspire to serve the Lord,
prepare yourself for an ordeal.
2 Be sincere of heart, be steadfast,
and do not be alarmed when disaster comes.
3 Cling to him and do not leave him,
so that you may be honoured at the end of your days.
4 Whatever happens to you, accept it,
and in the uncertainties of your humble state, be
patient,

GREEK OLD TESTAMENT

[5]ὅτι ἐν πυρὶ δοκιμάζεται χρυσὸς
καὶ ἄνθρωποι δεκτοὶ ἐν καμίνῳ ταπεινώσεως.
[6]πίστευσον αὐτῷ, καὶ ἀντιλήμψεταί σου·
εὔθυνον τὰς ὁδούς σου καὶ ἔλπισον ἐπ' αὐτόν.
7 Οἱ φοβούμενοι τὸν κύριον, ἀναμείνατε τὸ ἔλεος αὐτοῦ
καὶ μὴ ἐκκλίνητε, ἵνα μὴ πέσητε.
[8]οἱ φοβούμενοι κύριον, πιστεύσατε αὐτῷ,
καὶ οὐ μὴ πταίσῃ ὁ μισθὸς ὑμῶν.
[9]οἱ φοβούμενοι κύριον, ἐλπίσατε εἰς ἀγαθὰ
καὶ εἰς εὐφροσύνην αἰῶνος καὶ ἔλεος.
[10]ἐμβλέψατε εἰς ἀρχαίας γενεὰς καὶ ἴδετε·
τίς ἐνεπίστευσεν κυρίῳ καὶ κατῃσχύνθη;
ἢ τίς ἐνέμεινεν τῷ φόβῳ αὐτοῦ καὶ ἐγκατελείφθη;
ἢ τίς ἐπεκαλέσατο αὐτόν, καὶ ὑπερεῖδεν αὐτόν;
[11]διότι οἰκτίρμων καὶ ἐλεήμων ὁ κύριος
καὶ ἀφίησιν ἁμαρτίας καὶ σῴζει ἐν καιρῷ θλίψεως.
12 Οὐαὶ καρδίαις δειλαῖς καὶ χερσὶν παρειμέναις
καὶ ἁμαρτωλῷ ἐπιβαίνοντι ἐπὶ δύο τρίβους.
[13]οὐαὶ καρδίᾳ παρειμένῃ, ὅτι οὐ πιστεύει·
διὰ τοῦτο οὐ σκεπασθήσεται.
[14]οὐαὶ ὑμῖν τοῖς ἀπολωλεκόσιν τὴν ὑπομονήν·
καὶ τί ποιήσετε ὅταν ἐπισκέπτηται ὁ κύριος;

KING JAMES VERSION

5 For gold is tried in the fire, and acceptable men in the furnace of adversity.

6 Believe in him, and he will help thee; order thy way aright, and trust in him.

7 Ye that fear the Lord, wait for his mercy; and go not aside, lest ye fall.

8 Ye that fear the Lord, believe him; and your reward shall not fail.

9 Ye that fear the Lord, hope for good, and for everlasting joy and mercy.

10 Look at the generations of old, and see; did ever any trust in the Lord, and was confounded? or did any abide in his fear, and was forsaken? or whom did he ever despise, that called upon him?

11 For the Lord is full of compassion and mercy, longsuffering, and very pitiful, and forgiveth sins, and saveth in time of affliction.

12 Woe be to fearful hearts, and faint hands, and the sinner that goeth two ways!

13 Woe unto him that is fainthearted! for he believeth not; therefore shall he not be defended.

14 Woe unto you that have lost patience! and what will ye do when the Lord shall visit you?

DOUAY OLD TESTAMENT

5 For gold and silver are tried in the fire, but acceptable men in the furnace of humiliation.

6 Believe God, and he will recover thee: and direct thy way, and trust in him. Keep his fear, and grow old therein.

7 Ye that fear the Lord, wait for his mercy: and go not aside from him, lest ye fall.

8 Ye that fear the Lord, believe him: and your reward shall not be made void.

9 Ye that fear the Lord, hope in him: and mercy shall come to you for your delight.

10 Ye that fear the Lord, love him, and your hearts shall be enlightened.

11 My children behold the generations of men: and know ye that no one hath hoped in the Lord, and hath been confounded.

12 For who hath continued in his commandment, and hath been forsaken? or who hath called upon him, and he despised him?

13 For God is compassionate and merciful, and will forgive sins in the day of tribulation: and he is a protector to all that seek him in truth.

14 Woe to them that are of a double heart and to wicked lips, and to the hands that do evil, and to the sinner that goeth on the earth two ways.

15 Woe to them that are fainthearted, who believe not God: and therefore they shall not be protected by him.

16 Woe to them that have lost patience, and that have forsaken the right ways, and have gone aside into crooked ways.

17 And what will they do, when the Lord shall begin to examine?

KNOX TRANSLATION

silver the crucible, it is in the furnace of humiliation men
shew themselves worthy of his acceptance. [6]Trust in him,
and he will lift thee to thy feet again; go straight on thy way,
and fix in him thy hope; hold fast thy fear of him, and in
that fear to old age come thou.

[7]All you that fear the Lord, wait patiently for his mercies;
lose sight of him, and you shall fall by the way. [8]Fear him?
Ay, and trust him; you shall not miss your reward. [9]Fear
him? Ay, and fix your hope in him; his mercy you shall find,
and have great joy of it. [10]Fear him? Ay, and love him; your
hearts shall be enlightened. [11]My sons, look back on the
ages that are past; was ever man yet that trusted in the Lord,
and was disappointed? [12]Held fast to his commandments,
and was forsaken, prayed to him, and found the prayer unregarded? [13]A gracious God and a merciful; in times of affliction, he assoils us of our guilt, watches over all that with
true hearts turn to him.

[14]Out upon the false heart, the cheating lips, the hands
busy with ill-doing; upon the sinner that will go two ways at
once to enter the land of his desire. [15]Out upon the unre-
solved will, that trust in God has none, and from him shall
have no succour. [16]Out upon the men who have given up
hope, forsaking the right path, and to false paths betaking
them; [17]what shift will they make when the Lord calls them

TODAY'S ENGLISH VERSION

fire, and human character is tested in the furnace of humiliation. 6 Trust the Lord, and he will help you. Walk straight in
his ways, and put your hope in him.
7 All you that fear the Lord, wait for him to show you his
mercy. Do not turn away from him, or you will fall. 8 All you
that fear the Lord, trust him, and you will certainly be
rewarded. 9 All you that fear the Lord, look forward to his
blessings of mercy and eternal happiness.
10 Think back to the ancient generations and consider this:
has the Lord ever disappointed anyone who put his hope in
him? Has the Lord ever abandoned anyone who held him in
constant reverence? Has the Lord ever ignored anyone who
prayed to him? 11 The Lord is kind and merciful; he forgives
our sins and keeps us safe in time of trouble. 12 But those
who lose their nerve are doomed—all those sinners who try
to have it both ways! 13 Doom is sure to come for those who
lose their courage; they have no faith, and so they will have
no protection. 14 Doom is sure to come for those who lose
their hope. What will they do when the Lord comes to judge
them?

NEW REVISED STANDARD VERSION

5 For gold is tested in the fire,
and those found acceptable, in the furnace of
humiliation.[a]
6 Trust in him, and he will help you;
make your ways straight, and hope in him.

7 You who fear the Lord, wait for his mercy;
do not stray, or else you may fall.
8 You who fear the Lord, trust in him,
and your reward will not be lost.
9 You who fear the Lord, hope for good things,
for lasting joy and mercy.[b]
10 Consider the generations of old and see:
has anyone trusted in the Lord and been disappointed?
Or has anyone persevered in the fear of the Lord[c] and
been forsaken?
Or has anyone called upon him and been neglected?
11 For the Lord is compassionate and merciful;
he forgives sins and saves in time of distress.

12 Woe to timid hearts and to slack hands,
and to the sinner who walks a double path!
13 Woe to the fainthearted who have no trust!
Therefore they will have no shelter.
14 Woe to you who have lost your nerve!
What will you do when the Lord's reckoning comes?

a Other ancient authorities add *in sickness and poverty put your trust in him* *b* Other ancient authorities add *For his reward is an everlasting gift with joy.* *c* Gk *of him*

NEW AMERICAN BIBLE

5 For in fire gold is tested,
and worthy men in the crucible of humiliation.
6 Trust God and he will help you;
make straight your ways and hope in him.

7 You who fear the LORD, wait for his mercy,
turn not away lest you fall.
8 You who fear the LORD, trust him,
and your reward will not be lost.
9 You who fear the LORD, hope for good things,
for lasting joy and mercy.
10 Study the generations long past and understand;
has anyone hoped in the LORD and been
disappointed?
Has anyone persevered in his fear and been forsaken?
has anyone called upon him and been rebuffed?
11 Compassionate and merciful is the LORD;
he forgives sins, he saves in time of trouble.

12 Woe to craven hearts and drooping hands,
to the sinner who treads a double path!
13 Woe to the faint of heart who trust not,
who therefore will have no shelter!
14 Woe to you who have lost hope!
what will you do at the visitation of the LORD?

NEW JERUSALEM BIBLE

5 since gold is tested in the fire,
and the chosen in the furnace of humiliation.
6 Trust him and he will uphold you,
follow a straight path and hope in him.
7 You who fear the Lord, wait for his mercy;
do not turn aside, for fear you fall.
8 You who fear the Lord, trust him,
and you will not be robbed of your reward.
9 You who fear the Lord, hope for those good gifts of his,
everlasting joy and mercy.
10 Look at the generations of old and see:
whoever trusted in the Lord and was put to shame?
Or whoever, steadfastly fearing him, was forsaken?
Or whoever called to him and was ignored?
11 For the Lord is compassionate and merciful,
he forgives sins and saves in the time of distress.
12 Woe to faint hearts and listless hands,
and to the sinner who treads two paths.
13 Woe to the listless heart that has no faith,
for such will have no protection.
14 Woe to you who have lost the strength to endure;
what will you do at the Lord's visitation?

GREEK OLD TESTAMENT

15 οἱ φοβούμενοι κύριον οὐκ ἀπειθήσουσιν ῥημάτων αὐτοῦ,
καὶ οἱ ἀγαπῶντες αὐτὸν συντηρήσουσιν τὰς ὁδοὺς
αὐτοῦ.
16 οἱ φοβούμενοι κύριον ζητήσουσιν εὐδοκίαν αὐτοῦ,
καὶ οἱ ἀγαπῶντες αὐτὸν ἐμπλησθήσονται τοῦ νόμου.
17 οἱ φοβούμενοι κύριον ἑτοιμάσουσιν καρδίας αὐτῶν
καὶ ἐνώπιον αὐτοῦ ταπεινώσουσιν τὰς ψυχὰς αὐτῶν.
18 ἐμπεσούμεθα εἰς χεῖρας κυρίου
καὶ οὐκ εἰς χεῖρας ἀνθρώπων·
ὡς γὰρ ἡ μεγαλωσύνη αὐτοῦ,
οὕτως καὶ τὸ ἔλεος αὐτοῦ.

3 Ἐμοῦ τοῦ πατρὸς ἀκούσατε, τέκνα,
καὶ οὕτως ποιήσατε, ἵνα σωθῆτε·
2 ὁ γὰρ κύριος ἐδόξασεν πατέρα ἐπὶ τέκνοις
καὶ κρίσιν μητρὸς ἐστερέωσεν ἐφ' υἱοῖς.
3 ὁ τιμῶν πατέρα ἐξιλάσκεται ἁμαρτίας,
4 καὶ ὡς ὁ ἀποθησαυρίζων ὁ δοξάζων μητέρα αὐτοῦ.
5 ὁ τιμῶν πατέρα εὐφρανθήσεται ὑπὸ τέκνων
καὶ ἐν ἡμέρᾳ προσευχῆς αὐτοῦ εἰσακουσθήσεται.
6 ὁ δοξάζων πατέρα μακροημερεύσει,
καὶ ὁ εἰσακούων κυρίου ἀναπαύσει μητέρα αὐτοῦ·

KING JAMES VERSION

15 They that fear the Lord will not disobey his word; and they that love him will keep his ways.

16 They that fear the Lord will seek that which is wellpleasing unto him; and they that love him shall be filled with the law.

17 They that fear the Lord will prepare their hearts, and humble their souls in his sight,

18 *Saying,* We will fall into the hands of the Lord, and not into the hands of men: for as his majesty is, so is his mercy.

3 Hear me your father, O children, and do thereafter, that ye may be safe.

2 For the Lord hath given the father honour over the children, and hath confirmed the authority of the mother over the sons.

3 Whoso honoureth his father maketh an atonement for his sins:

4 And he that honoureth his mother is as one that layeth up treasure.

5 Whoso honoureth his father shall have joy of *his own* children; and when he maketh his prayer, he shall be heard.

6 He that honoureth his father shall have a long life; and he that is obedient unto the Lord shall be a comfort to his mother.

DOUAY OLD TESTAMENT

18 They that fear the Lord, will not be incredulous to his word: and they that love him, will keep his way.

19 They that fear the Lord, will seek after the things that are well pleasing to him: and they that love him, shall be filled with his law.

20 They that fear the Lord, will prepare their hearts, and in his sight will sanctify their souls.

21 They that fear the Lord, keep his commandments, and will have patience even until his visitation,

22 Saying: If we do not penance, we shall fall into the hands of the Lord, and not into the hands of men.

23 For according to his greatness, so also is his mercy with him.

3 THE sons of wisdom *are* the church of the just: and their generation, obedience and love.

2 Children, hear the judgment of your father, and so do that you may be saved.

3 For God hath made the father honourable to the children: and seeking the judgment of the mothers, hath confirmed *it* upon the children.

4 He that loveth God, shall obtain pardon for *his* sins by prayer, and shall refrain himself from them, and shall be heard in the prayer of days.

5 And he that honoureth his mother is as one that layeth up a treasure.

6 He that honoureth his father shall have joy in *his own* children, and in the day of his prayer he shall be heard.

7 He that honoureth his father shall enjoy a long life: and he that obeyeth the father, shall be a comfort to his mother.

KNOX TRANSLATION

to account? 18 Fear the Lord, and doubt his promises? Love
him, and not keep true to the way he shews us? 19 Fear the
Lord, and not study to know his will? Love him, and not find
contentment in his law? 20 Fear God, and not keep the will
alert, the heart holy in his sight? 21 Men who fear God keep
his commandments, and wait patiently until he comes to
relieve them. 22 Be this our thought, they say, that it is God's
power we have to reckon with, not man's, if there is no
penance done. 23 And he has mercy ever at his side, a God
merciful as he is great.

3 Wherever choice souls are found, wisdom is the mother
of them; all submissiveness and love their breed is.
2 Speak we now of a father's rights; do you, sons, give good
heed, and follow these counsels, if thrive you would. 3 God
will have children honour their fathers; a mother's rights are
his own strict ordinance. 4 A lover of God will fall to prayer
over his sins and sin no more; so, all his life long, his prayer
shall find audience. 5...riches he lays up for himself, that
gives his mother her due.[a] 6 As thou wouldst have joy of thy
own children, as thou wouldst be heard when thou fallest to
praying, honour thy father still. 7 A father honoured is long
life won; a father well obeyed is a mother's heart comforted.

[a] *vv.* 4, 5: The Latin version here inserts a sentence which seems out of place (perhaps belonging to the end of the foregoing chapter); it omits the words given in the Greek text: 'He who honours his father will atone for his own sins'.

TODAY'S ENGLISH VERSION

15 Those who fear the Lord do not disobey his commands;
those who love him will live as he wants them to live.
16 Those who fear and love the Lord will try to please him
and devote themselves to the Law. 17 Those who fear the
Lord are always ready to serve him. They humble themselves
before him, and say, 18 "We place our destiny in the hands of
the Lord, not in human hands, because his mercy is as great
as his majesty."

3 Children, listen to me; I am your father. Do what I tell
you and you will be safe, 2 for the Lord has given
fathers authority over their children and given children the
obligation to obey their mothers. 3 If you respect your father,
you can make up for your sins, 4 and if you honor your
mother, you are earning great wealth. 5 If you respect your
father, one day your own children will make you happy; the
Lord will hear your prayers. 6 If you obey the Lord by honoring your father and making your mother happy, you will live

NEW REVISED STANDARD VERSION

15 Those who fear the Lord do not disobey his words,
and those who love him keep his ways.
16 Those who fear the Lord seek to please him,
and those who love him are filled with his law.
17 Those who fear the Lord prepare their hearts,
and humble themselves before him.
18 Let us fall into the hands of the Lord,
but not into the hands of mortals;
for equal to his majesty is his mercy,
and equal to his name are his works.[a]

3 Listen to me your father, O children;
act accordingly, that you may be kept in safety.
2 For the Lord honors a father above his children,
and he confirms a mother's right over her children.
3 Those who honor their father atone for sins,
4 and those who respect their mother are like those
who lay up treasure.
5 Those who honor their father will have joy in their own
children,
and when they pray they will be heard.
6 Those who respect their father will have long life,
and those who honor[b] their mother obey the Lord;

a Syr: Gk lacks this line *b* Heb: Other ancient authorities read *comfort*

NEW AMERICAN BIBLE

15 Those who fear the LORD disobey not his words;
those who love him keep his ways.
16 Those who fear the LORD seek to please him,
those who love him are filled with his law.
17 Those who fear the LORD prepare their hearts
and humble themselves before him.
18 Let us fall into the hands of the LORD
and not into the hands of men,
For equal to his majesty
is the mercy that he shows.

3 Children, pay heed to a father's right;
do so that you may live.
2 For the LORD sets a father in honor over his children;
a mother's authority he confirms over her sons.
3 He who honors his father atones for sins;
4 he stores up riches who reveres his mother.
5 He who honors his father is gladdened by children,
and when he prays he is heard.
6 He who reveres his father will live a long life;
he obeys the LORD who brings comfort to his mother.

NEW JERUSALEM BIBLE

15 Those who fear the Lord do not disdain his words,
and those who love him keep his ways.
16 Those who fear the Lord do their best to please him,
and those who love him will find satisfaction in the
Law.
17 Those who fear the Lord keep their hearts prepared
and humble themselves in his presence.
18 Let us fall into the hands of the Lord, not into any
human clutches;
for as his majesty is, so too is his mercy.

3 Children, listen to me for I am your father:
do what I tell you, and so be safe;
2 for the Lord honours the father above his children
and upholds the rights of a mother over her sons.
3 Whoever respects a father expiates sins,
4 whoever honours a mother is like someone amassing
a fortune.
5 Whoever respects a father will in turn be happy with
children,
the day he prays for help, he will be heard.
6 Long life comes to anyone who honours a father,
whoever obeys the Lord makes a mother happy.

GREEK OLD TESTAMENT

7 καὶ ὡς δεσπόταις δουλεύσει ἐν τοῖς γεννήσασιν αὐτόν.
8 ἐν ἔργῳ καὶ λόγῳ τίμα τὸν πατέρα σου,
ἵνα ἐπέλθῃ σοι εὐλογία παρ᾽ αὐτοῦ·
9 εὐλογία γὰρ πατρὸς στηρίζει οἴκους τέκνων,
κατάρα δὲ μητρὸς ἐκριζοῖ θεμέλια.
10 μὴ δοξάζου ἐν ἀτιμίᾳ πατρός σου,
οὐ γάρ ἐστίν σοι δόξα πατρὸς ἀτιμία·
11 ἡ γὰρ δόξα ἀνθρώπου ἐκ τιμῆς πατρὸς αὐτοῦ,
καὶ ὄνειδος τέκνοις μήτηρ ἐν ἀδοξίᾳ.
12 τέκνον, ἀντιλαβοῦ ἐν γήρᾳ πατρός σου
καὶ μὴ λυπήσῃς αὐτὸν ἐν τῇ ζωῇ αὐτοῦ·
13 κἂν ἀπολείπῃ σύνεσιν, συγγνώμην ἔχε
καὶ μὴ ἀτιμάσῃς αὐτὸν ἐν πάσῃ ἰσχύι σου.
14 ἐλεημοσύνη γὰρ πατρὸς οὐκ ἐπιλησθήσεται
καὶ ἀντὶ ἁμαρτιῶν προσανοικοδομηθήσεταί σοι.
15 ἐν ἡμέρᾳ θλίψεώς σου ἀναμνησθήσεταί σου·
ὡς εὐδία ἐπὶ παγετῷ, οὕτως ἀναλυθήσονταί σου αἱ
ἁμαρτίαι.
16 ὡς βλάσφημος ὁ ἐγκαταλιπὼν πατέρα,
καὶ κεκατηραμένος ὑπὸ κυρίου ὁ παροργίζων μητέρα
αὐτοῦ.
17 Τέκνον, ἐν πραΰτητι τὰ ἔργα σου διέξαγε,
καὶ ὑπὸ ἀνθρώπου δεκτοῦ ἀγαπηθήσῃ.

KING JAMES VERSION

7 He that feareth the Lord will honour his father, and will do service unto his parents, as to his masters.

8 Honour thy father and mother both in word and deed, that a blessing may come upon thee from them.

9 For the blessing of the father establisheth the houses of children; but the curse of the mother rooteth out foundations.

10 Glory not in the dishonour of thy father; for thy father's dishonour is no glory unto thee.

11 For the glory of a man is from the honour of his father; and a mother in dishonour is a reproach to the children.

12 My son, help thy father in his age, and grieve him not as long as he liveth.

13 And if his understanding fail, have patience with him; and despise him not when thou art in thy full strength.

14 For the relieving of thy father shall not be forgotten: and instead of sins it shall be added to build thee up.

15 In the day of thine affliction it shall be remembered; thy sins also shall melt away, as the ice in the fair warm weather.

16 He that forsaketh his father is as a blasphemer; and he that angereth his mother is cursed of God.

17 My son, go on with thy business in meekness; so shalt thou be beloved of him that is approved.

DOUAY OLD TESTAMENT

8 He that feareth the Lord, honoureth his parents, and will serve them as his masters that brought him into the world.

9 Honour thy father, in work and word, and all patience,

10 That a blessing may come upon thee from him, and his blessing may remain in the latter end.

11 The father's blessing establisheth the houses of the children: but the mother's curse rooteth up the foundation.

12 Glory not in the dishonour of thy father: for his shame is no glory to thee.

13 For the glory of a man is from the honour of his father, and a father without honour is the disgrace of the son.

14 Son, support the old age of thy father, and grieve him not in his life;

15 And if his understanding fail, have patience with him, and despise him not when thou art in thy strength: for the relieving of the father shall not be forgotten.

16 For good shall be repaid to thee for the sin of thy mother.

17 And in justice thou shalt be built up, and in the day of affliction thou shalt be remembered: and thy sins shall melt away as the ice in the fair warm weather.

18 Of what an evil fame is he that forsaketh his father: and he is cursed of God that angereth his mother.

19 My son, do thy works in meekness, and thou shalt be beloved above the glory of men.

KNOX TRANSLATION

8 None that fears the Lord but honours the parents who gave
him life, slave to master owes no greater service. 9 Thy
father honour, in deed and in word and in all manner of forbearance; 10 so thou shalt have his blessing, a blessing that
will endure to thy life's end. 11 What is the buttress of a
man's house? A father's blessing. What tears up the foundations of it? A mother's curse. 12 Never make a boast of thy
father's ill name; what, should his discredit be thy renown?
13 Nay, for a father's good repute or ill, a son must go proudly, or hang his head. 14 My son, when thy father grows old,
take him to thyself; long as he lives, never be thou the cause
of his repining. 15 Grow he feeble of wit, make allowance for
him, nor in thy manhood's vigour despise him. The kindness
shewn to thy father will not go forgotten; 16 favour it shall
bring thee in acquittal of thy mother's guilt.[a] 17 Faithfully it
shall be made good to thee, nor shalt thou be forgotten when
the time of affliction comes; like ice in summer the record of
thy sins shall melt away. 18 Tarnished his name, that leaves
his father forsaken; God's curse rest on him, that earns a
mother's ill-will.

19 My son, do all thou dost in lowly fashion; love thou
shalt win, that is worth more than men's praise. 20 The

a In the Greek text, the giver of alms atones not for his mother's sin, but for his own. Cf. however Ps. 50. 7.

TODAY'S ENGLISH VERSION

a long life. 7 Obey your parents as if you were their slave.
8 Honor your father in everything you do and say, so that
you may receive his blessing. 9 When parents give their
blessing, they give strength to their children's homes, but
when they curse their children, they destroy the very foundations.
10 Never seek honor for yourself at your father's expense; it
is not to your credit if he is dishonored. 11 Your own honor
comes from the respect that you show to your father. If children do not honor their mothers, it is their own disgrace.
12 My child, take care of your father when he grows old; give
him no cause for worry as long as he lives. 13 Be sympathetic even if his mind fails him; don't look down on him just
because you are strong and healthy. 14 The Lord will not forget the kindness you show to your father; it will help you
make up for your sins. 15 When you are in trouble, the Lord
will remember your kindness and will help you; your sins
will melt away like frost in warm sunshine. 16 Those who
abandon their parents or give them cause for anger may as
well be cursing the Lord; they are already under the Lord's
curse.
17 My child, be humble in everything you do, and people
will appreciate it more than gifts.[a] 18 The greater you

[a] *Hebrew* people . . . gifts; *Greek* those whom the Lord approves will love you.

NEW REVISED STANDARD VERSION

7 they will serve their parents as their masters.[a]
8 Honor your father by word and deed,
that his blessing may come upon you.
9 For a father's blessing strengthens the houses of the children,
but a mother's curse uproots their foundations.
10 Do not glorify yourself by dishonoring your father,
for your father's dishonor is no glory to you.
11 The glory of one's father is one's own glory,
and it is a disgrace for children not to respect their mother.

12 My child, help your father in his old age,
and do not grieve him as long as he lives;
13 even if his mind fails, be patient with him;
because you have all your faculties do not despise him.
14 For kindness to a father will not be forgotten,
and will be credited to you against your sins;
15 in the day of your distress it will be remembered in your favor;
like frost in fair weather, your sins will melt away.
16 Whoever forsakes a father is like a blasphemer,
and whoever angers a mother is cursed by the Lord.

17 My child, perform your tasks with humility;[b]
then you will be loved by those whom God accepts.

a In other ancient authorities this line is preceded by *Those who fear the Lord honor their father,* *b* Heb: Gk *meekness*

NEW AMERICAN BIBLE

7 He who fears the LORD honors his father,
and serves his parents as rulers.
8 In word and deed honor your father
that his blessing may come upon you;
9 For a father's blessing gives a family firm roots,
but a mother's curse uproots the growing plant.
10 Glory not in your father's shame,
for his shame is no glory to you!
11 His father's honor is a man's glory;
disgrace for her children, a mother's shame.
12 My son, take care of your father when he is old;
grieve him not as long as he lives.
13 Even if his mind fail, be considerate with him;
revile him not in the fullness of your strength.
14 For kindness to a father will not be forgotten,
it will serve as a sin offering—it will take lasting root.
15 In time of tribulation it will be recalled to your advantage,
like warmth upon frost it will melt away your sins.
16 A blasphemer is he who despises his father;
accursed of his Creator, he who angers his mother.

17 My son, conduct your affairs with humility,
and you will be loved more than a giver of gifts.

NEW JERUSALEM BIBLE

7 Such a one serves parents as well as the Lord.
8 Respect your father in deed as well as word,
so that blessing may come on you from him;
9 since a father's blessing makes his children's house firm,
while a mother's curse tears up its foundations.
10 Do not make a boast of disgrace overtaking your father,
your father's disgrace reflects no honour on you;
11 for a person's own honour derives from the respect shown to his father,
and a mother held in dishonour is a reproach to her children.
12 My child, support your father in his old age,
do not grieve him during his life.
13 Even if his mind should fail, show him sympathy,
do not despise him in your health and strength;
14 for kindness to a father will not be forgotten
but will serve as reparation for your sins.
15 On your own day of ordeal God will remember you:
like frost in sunshine, your sins will melt away.
16 Whoever deserts a father is no better than a blasphemer,
and whoever distresses a mother is accursed of the Lord.
17 My child, be gentle in carrying out your business,
and you will be better loved than a lavish giver.

GREEK OLD TESTAMENT

18 ὅσῳ μέγας εἶ, τοσούτῳ ταπείνου σεαυτόν,
καὶ ἔναντι κυρίου εὑρήσεις χάριν·
20 ὅτι μεγάλη ἡ δυναστεία τοῦ κυρίου
καὶ ὑπὸ τῶν ταπεινῶν δοξάζεται.
21 χαλεπώτερά σου μὴ ζήτει
καὶ ἰσχυρότερά σου μὴ ἐξέταζε·
22 ἃ προσετάγη σοι, ταῦτα διανοοῦ,
οὐ γάρ ἐστίν σοι χρεία τῶν κρυπτῶν.
23 ἐν τοῖς περισσοῖς τῶν ἔργων σου μὴ περιεργάζου·
πλείονα γὰρ συνέσεως ἀνθρώπων ὑπεδείχθη σοι.
24 πολλοὺς γὰρ ἐπλάνησεν ἡ ὑπόλημψις αὐτῶν,
καὶ ὑπόνοια πονηρὰ ὠλίσθησεν διανοίας αὐτῶν.
26 καρδία σκληρὰ κακωθήσεται ἐπ' ἐσχάτων,
καὶ ὁ ἀγαπῶν κίνδυνον ἐν αὐτῷ ἀπολεῖται.
27 καρδία σκληρὰ βαρυνθήσεται πόνοις,
καὶ ὁ ἁμαρτωλὸς προσθήσει ἁμαρτίαν ἐφ' ἁμαρτίαις.
28 ἐπαγωγῇ ὑπερηφάνου οὐκ ἔστιν ἴασις·
φυτὸν γὰρ πονηρίας ἐρρίζωκεν ἐν αὐτῷ.
29 καρδία συνετοῦ διανοηθήσεται παραβολήν,
καὶ οὖς ἀκροατοῦ ἐπιθυμία σοφοῦ.

KING JAMES VERSION

18 The greater thou art, the more humble thyself, and thou shalt find favour before the Lord.

19 Many are in high place, and of renown: but mysteries are revealed unto the meek.

20 For the power of the Lord is great and he is honoured of the lowly.

21 Seek not out things that are too hard for thee, neither search the things that are above thy strength.

22 But what is commanded thee, think thereupon *with reverence;* for it is not needful for thee *to see with thine eyes* the things that are in secret.

23 Be not curious in unnecessary matters: for more things are shewed unto thee than men understand.

24 For many are deceived by their own vain opinion; and an evil suspicion hath overthrown their judgment.

25 Without eyes thou shalt want light: profess not the knowledge therefore that thou hast not.

26 A stubborn heart shall fare evil at the last; and he that loveth danger shall perish therein.

27 An obstinate heart shall be laden with sorrows; and the wicked man shall heap sin upon sin.

28 In the punishment of the proud there is no remedy; for the plant of wickedness hath taken root in him.

29 The heart of the prudent will understand a parable; and an attentive ear is the desire of a wise man.

DOUAY OLD TESTAMENT

20 The greater thou art, the more humble thyself in all things, and thou shalt find grace before God:

21 For great is the power of God alone, and he is honoured by the humble.

22 Seek not the things that are too high for thee, and search not into things above thy ability: but the things that God hath commanded thee, think on them always, and in many of his works be not curious.

23 For it is not necessary for thee to see with thy eyes those things that are hid.

24 In unnecessary matters be not over curious, and in many of his works thou shalt not be inquisitive.

25 For many things are shewn to thee above the understanding of men.

26 And the suspicion of them hath deceived many, and hath detained their minds in vanity.

27 A hard heart shall fear evil at the last: and he that loveth danger shall perish in it.

28 A heart that goeth two ways shall not have success, and the perverse of heart shall be scandalized therein.

29 A wicked heart shall be laden with sorrows, and the sinner will add sin to sin.

30 The congregation of the proud shall not be healed: for the plant of wickedness shall take root in them, and it shall not be perceived.

31 The heart of the wise is understood in wisdom, and a good ear will hear wisdom with all desire.

32 A wise heart, and which hath understanding, will abstain from sins, and in the works of justice shall have success.

KNOX TRANSLATION

greater thou art, the more in all things abase thyself; so thou
shalt win favour with God...[a] 21 Sovereignty belongs to God
and no other; they honour him most that most keep humility. 22 Seek not to know what is far above thee; search not
beyond thy range; let thy mind ever dwell on the duty God
has given thee to do, content to be ignorant of all his dealings besides. 23 Need is none thy eyes should see what
things lie hidden. 24 Leave off, then, thy much questioning
about such things as little concern thee, and be content with
thy ignorance; 25 more is granted to thy view than lies within human ken. 26 By such fancies, many have been led
astray, and their thoughts chained to folly.[b]

27 ...Heart that is obstinate shall thrive ill at the last; danger loved is death won. 28 Heart that will try two ways at
once shall prosper little; he falls into the snare that goes a-
straying. 29 Heart that will not mend shall be weighed down
by its own troubles; the sinner is ever ready for one sin more.
30 For one sort of men there is no remedy, the proud; too
deep a root the evil has taken, before they knew it. 31 Heart
that is wise will prove itself in wise company; ever greedy of
wise talk is the ear that knows how to listen. 32 Heart that is
wise and discerning will keep clear of wrong, and by honest
dealings prosper yet.

a Some manuscripts and versions add, at the end of this verse, 'Men's esteem and honour is to be had for the asking, but it is to the humble that hidden things are revealed'. *b* Some manuscripts and versions add, at the end of this verse, 'Want eyes, want light; boast not that thou hast knowledge, where knowledge is none'.

TODAY'S ENGLISH VERSION

become, the more humble you should be; then the Lord will
be pleased with you.[a] 20 The Lord's power is great, and he is
honored by those who are humble. 21 Don't try to understand things that are too hard for you, or investigate matters
that are beyond your power to know. 22 Concentrate on the
Law, which has been given to you. You do not need to know
about things which the Lord has not revealed, 23 so don't
concern yourself with them. After all, what has been shown
to you is beyond human power to understand. 24 Many people have been misled by their own opinions; their wrong
ideas have warped their judgment.[b]
26 Stubbornness will get you into trouble at the end. If you
live dangerously, it will kill you. 27 A stubborn person will be
burdened down with troubles. Sinners go on adding one sin
to another. 28 There is no cure for the troubles that arrogant
people have; wickedness has taken deep root in them.
29 Intelligent people will learn from proverbs and parables.
They listen well because they want to learn.

[a] *Some Greek manuscripts add verse 19:* Many are exalted and esteemed, but God's secrets are revealed to the humble; *Hebrew:* God's mercy is great, and he reveals his secrets to those who are humble.

[b] *Some Greek manuscripts add verse 25:* If you have no eyes, you cannot see; don't claim to have knowledge if you don't have it; *Hebrew has, after verse 27:* If you have no eyes, you cannot see; if you have no knowledge, you cannot have Wisdom.

NEW REVISED STANDARD VERSION

18 The greater you are, the more you must humble
yourself;
so you will find favor in the sight of the Lord.[a]
20 For great is the might of the Lord;
but by the humble he is glorified.
21 Neither seek what is too difficult for you,
nor investigate what is beyond your power.
22 Reflect upon what you have been commanded,
for what is hidden is not your concern.
23 Do not meddle in matters that are beyond you,
for more than you can understand has been shown
you.
24 For their conceit has led many astray,
and wrong opinion has impaired their judgment.

25 Without eyes there is no light;
without knowledge there is no wisdom.[b]
26 A stubborn mind will fare badly at the end,
and whoever loves danger will perish in it.
27 A stubborn mind will be burdened by troubles,
and the sinner adds sin to sins.
28 When calamity befalls the proud, there is no healing,
for an evil plant has taken root in him.
29 The mind of the intelligent appreciates proverbs,
and an attentive ear is the desire of the wise.

[a] Other ancient authorities add as verse 19, *Many are lofty and renowned, but to the humble he reveals his secrets.* [b] Heb: Other ancient authorities lack verse 25

NEW AMERICAN BIBLE

18 Humble yourself the more, the greater you are,
and you will find favor with God.
19 For great is the power of God;
by the humble he is glorified.
20 What is too sublime for you, seek not,
into things beyond your strength search not.
21 What is committed to you, attend to;
for what is hidden is not your concern.
22 With what is too much for you meddle not,
when shown things beyond human understanding.
23 Their own opinion has misled many,
and false reasoning unbalanced their judgment.
24 Where the pupil of the eye is missing, there is no light,
and where there is no knowledge, there is no
wisdom.

25 A stubborn man will fare badly in the end,
and he who loves danger will perish in it.
26 A stubborn man will be burdened with sorrow;
a sinner will heap sin upon sin.
27 For the affliction of the proud man there is no cure;
he is the offshoot of an evil plant.
28 The mind of a sage appreciates proverbs,
and an attentive ear is the wise man's joy.

29 Water quenches a flaming fire,
and alms atone for sins.

NEW JERUSALEM BIBLE

18 The greater you are, the more humbly you should
behave,
and then you will find favour with the Lord;
20 for great though the power of the Lord is,
he accepts the homage of the humble.
21 Do not try to understand things that are too difficult for
you,
or try to discover what is beyond your powers.
22 Concentrate on what has been assigned you,
you have no need to worry over mysteries.
23 Do not meddle with matters that are beyond you;
what you have been taught already exceeds the scope
of the human mind.
24 For many have been misled by their own notions,
wicked presumption having warped their judgement.

26 A stubborn heart will come to a bad end,
and whoever dallies with danger will perish in it.
27 A stubborn heart is weighed down with troubles,
the sinner heaps sin on sin.
28 For the disease of the proud there is no cure,
since an evil growth has taken root there.
29 The heart of the sensible will reflect on parables,
an attentive ear is the sage's dream.

GREEK OLD TESTAMENT

[30]πῦρ φλογιζόμενον ἀποσβέσει ὕδωρ,
καὶ ἐλεημοσύνη ἐξιλάσεται ἁμαρτίας.
[31]ὁ ἀνταποδιδοὺς χάριτας μέμνηται εἰς τὰ μετὰ ταῦτα
καὶ ἐν καιρῷ πτώσεως αὐτοῦ εὑρήσει στήριγμα.
4 Τέκνον, τὴν ζωὴν τοῦ πτωχοῦ μὴ ἀποστερήσῃς
καὶ μὴ παρελκύσῃς ὀφθαλμοὺς ἐπιδεεῖς.
[2]ψυχὴν πεινῶσαν μὴ λυπήσῃς
καὶ μὴ παροργίσῃς ἄνδρα ἐν ἀπορίᾳ αὐτοῦ.
[3]καρδίαν παρωργισμένην μὴ προσταράξῃς
καὶ μὴ παρελκύσῃς δόσιν προσδεομένου.
[4]ἱκέτην θλιβόμενον μὴ ἀπαναίνου
καὶ μὴ ἀποστρέψῃς τὸ πρόσωπόν σου ἀπὸ πτωχοῦ.
[5]ἀπὸ δεομένου μὴ ἀποστρέψῃς ὀφθαλμὸν
καὶ μὴ δῷς τόπον ἀνθρώπῳ καταράσασθαί σε·
[6]καταρωμένου γάρ σε ἐν πικρίᾳ ψυχῆς αὐτοῦ
τῆς δεήσεως αὐτοῦ ἐπακούσεται ὁ ποιήσας αὐτόν.
[7]προσφιλῆ συναγωγῇ σεαυτὸν ποίει
καὶ μεγιστᾶνι ταπείνου τὴν κεφαλήν σου.
[8]κλῖνον πτωχῷ τὸ οὖς σου
καὶ ἀποκρίθητι αὐτῷ εἰρηνικὰ ἐν πραΰτητι.
[9]ἐξελοῦ ἀδικούμενον ἐκ χειρὸς ἀδικοῦντος
καὶ μὴ ὀλιγοψυχήσῃς ἐν τῷ κρίνειν σε.
[10]γίνου ὀρφανοῖς ὡς πατὴρ
καὶ ἀντὶ ἀνδρὸς τῇ μητρὶ αὐτῶν·
καὶ ἔσῃ ὡς υἱὸς ὑψίστου,
καὶ ἀγαπήσει σε μᾶλλον ἢ μήτηρ σου.

KING JAMES VERSION

30 Water will quench a flaming fire; and alms maketh an atonement for sins.

31 And he that requiteth good turns is mindful of that which may come hereafter; and when he falleth, he shall find a stay.

4 My son, defraud not the poor of his living, and make not the needy eyes to wait long.

2 Make not an hungry soul sorrowful; neither provoke a man in his distress.

3 Add not more trouble to an heart that is vexed; and defer not to give to him that is in need.

4 Reject not the supplication of the afflicted; neither turn away thy face from a poor man.

5 Turn not away thine eye from the needy, and give him none occasion to curse thee:

6 For if he curse thee in the bitterness of his soul, his prayer shall be heard of him that made him.

7 Get thyself the love of the congregation, and bow thy head to a great man.

8 Let it not grieve thee to bow down thine ear to the poor, and give him a friendly answer with meekness.

9 Deliver him that suffereth wrong from the hand of the oppressor; and be not fainthearted when thou sittest in judgment.

10 Be as a father unto the fatherless, and instead of an husband unto their mother: so shalt thou be as the son of the most High, and he shall love thee more than thy mother doth.

DOUAY OLD TESTAMENT

33 Water quencheth a flaming fire, and alms resisteth sins:

34 And God provideth for him that sheweth favour: he remembereth him afterwards, and in the time of his fall he shall find a sure stay.

4 SON, defraud not the poor of alms, and turn not away thy eyes from the poor.

2 Despise not the hungry soul: and provoke not the poor in his want.

3 Afflict not the heart of the needy, and defer not to give to him that is in distress.

4 Reject not the petition of the afflicted: and turn not away thy face from the needy.

5 Turn not away thy eyes from the poor for fear of anger: and leave not to them that ask of thee to curse thee behind thy back.

6 For the prayer of him that curseth thee in the bitterness of *his* soul, shall be heard, for he that made him will hear him.

7 Make thyself affable to the congregation of the poor, and humble thy soul to the ancient, and bow thy head to a great man.

8 Bow down thy ear cheerfully to the poor, and pay what thou owest, and answer him peaceable words with mildness.

9 Deliver him that suffereth wrong out of the hand of the proud: and be not fainthearted in thy soul.

10 In judging be merciful to the fatherless as a father, and as a husband to their mother.

11 And thou shalt be as the obedient son of the most High, and he will have mercy on thee more than a mother.

KNOX TRANSLATION

[33]No fire burns so high but water may quench it; almsgiving was ever sin's atoning. [34]God marks the grateful eye,
and remembers it; here is sure support won against peril of
falling.
4 My son, do not cheat a poor man of the alms he asks,
nor pass him by, with averted look, in his need.
[2]Wouldst thou despise his hungry glance, and add to the
burden of his distress? [3]Wouldst thou disappoint him in his
bitter need by bidding him wait for the gift? [4]Nay, spurn
thou never the plea of the afflicted; look thy suppliant in the
face, [5]and of his poverty take good heed; shall his baffled
rage curse thee behind thy back? [6]The curse of an embittered man does not go unheard; his Maker is listening.
[7]To the common sort of men give friendly welcome; before
an elder abate thy pride; and to a man of eminence bow
meekly thy head. [8]If a poor man would speak to thee, lend
him thy ear without grudging; give him his due, and let him
have patient and friendly answer. [9]If he is wronged by
oppression, redress thou needs must win him, nor be vexed
by his importunity. [10]When thou sittest in judgement, be a
father to the orphans, a husband to the widow that bore
them; [11]so the most High an obedient son shall reckon thee,
and shew thee more than a mother's kindness.

TODAY'S ENGLISH VERSION

30 Giving to the poor can make up for sin, just as water can
put out a blazing fire. 31 Anyone who responds to others
with acts of kindness is thinking of the future, because he
will find help if he ever falls on hard times.
4 1 My child,
don't prevent the poor from making a living, or keep
them waiting in their need. 2 Never give a hungry person
any cause for resentment or anger. 3 Don't add to the troubles of someone who is already desperate. If he is in need,
don't put off giving to him. 4-5 Don't refuse to help a beggar
who is in distress. Don't turn your back on a poor person or
give him any reason to curse you. 6 If he becomes so bitter
that he does curse you, his Creator will hear his prayer.
7 Make yourself popular in the synagogue. Bow your head
to men of authority. 8 Listen to what the poor have to say,
and answer them politely. 9 Protect people from those who
want to wrong them, and be firm in your judgments. 10 Be
like a father to orphans, and provide widows with the help
their husbands can no longer give them. Then you will be
like a child of the Most High, and he will love you more than
your own mother does.

NEW REVISED STANDARD VERSION

30 As water extinguishes a blazing fire,
so almsgiving atones for sin.
31 Those who repay favors give thought to the future;
when they fall they will find support.

4 My child, do not cheat the poor of their living,
and do not keep needy eyes waiting.
2 Do not grieve the hungry,
or anger one in need.
3 Do not add to the troubles of the desperate,
or delay giving to the needy.
4 Do not reject a suppliant in distress,
or turn your face away from the poor.
5 Do not avert your eye from the needy,
and give no one reason to curse you;
6 for if in bitterness of soul some should curse you,
their Creator will hear their prayer.

7 Endear yourself to the congregation;
bow your head low to the great.
8 Give a hearing to the poor,
and return their greeting politely.
9 Rescue the oppressed from the oppressor;
and do not be hesitant in giving a verdict.
10 Be a father to orphans,
and be like a husband to their mother;
you will then be like a son of the Most High,
and he will love you more than does your mother.

NEW AMERICAN BIBLE

30 He who does a kindness is remembered afterward;
when he falls, he finds a support.

4 My son, rob not the poor man of his livelihood:
force not the eyes of the needy to turn away.
2 A hungry man grieve not,
a needy man anger not;
3 Do not exasperate the downtrodden;
delay not to give to the needy.
4 A beggar in distress do not reject;
avert not your face from the poor.
5 From the needy turn not your eyes,
give no man reason to curse you;
6 For if in the bitterness of his soul he curse you,
his Creator will hear his prayer.
7 Endear yourself to the assembly;
before a ruler bow your head.
8 Give a hearing to the poor man,
and return his greeting with courtesy;
9 Deliver the oppressed from the hand of the oppressor;
let not justice be repugnant to you.
10 To the fatherless be as a father,
and help their mother as a husband would;
Thus will you be like a son to the Most High,
and he will be more tender to you than a mother.

NEW JERUSALEM BIBLE

30 Water puts out a blazing fire,
almsgiving expiates sins.
31 Whoever gives favours in return is mindful of the
future;
at the moment of falling, such a person will find
support.

4 1 My child, do not refuse the poor a livelihood,
do not tantalise the needy.
2 Do not add to the sufferings of the hungry,
do not bait anyone in distress.
3 Do not aggravate a heart already angry,
nor keep the destitute waiting for your alms.
4 Do not repulse a hard-pressed beggar,
nor turn your face from the poor.
5 Do not avert your eyes from the needy,
give no one occasion to curse you;
6 for if someone curses you in distress,
his Maker will give ear to the imprecation.
7 Gain the love of the community,
in the presence of the great bow your head.
8 To the poor lend an ear,
and courteously return the greeting.
9 Save the oppressed from the hand of the oppressor,
and do not be mean-spirited in your judgements.
10 Be like a father to the fatherless
and as good as a husband to their mothers.
And you will be like a child to the Most High,
who will love you more than your own mother does.

GREEK OLD TESTAMENT

11 Ἡ σοφία υἱοὺς αὐτῆς ἀνύψωσεν
καὶ ἐπιλαμβάνεται τῶν ζητούντων αὐτήν.
12 ὁ ἀγαπῶν αὐτὴν ἀγαπᾷ ζωήν,
καὶ οἱ ὀρθρίζοντες πρὸς αὐτὴν ἐμπλησθήσονται
εὐφροσύνης.
13 ὁ κρατῶν αὐτῆς κληρονομήσει δόξαν,
καὶ οὗ εἰσπορεύεται, εὐλογεῖ κύριος.
14 οἱ λατρεύοντες αὐτῇ λειτουργήσουσιν ἁγίῳ,
καὶ τοὺς ἀγαπῶντας αὐτὴν ἀγαπᾷ ὁ κύριος.
15 ὁ ὑπακούων αὐτῆς κρινεῖ ἔθνη,
καὶ ὁ προσέχων αὐτῇ κατασκηνώσει πεποιθώς.
16 ἐὰν ἐμπιστεύσῃ, κατακληρονομήσει αὐτήν,
καὶ ἐν κατασχέσει ἔσονται αἱ γενεαὶ αὐτοῦ·
17 ὅτι διεστραμμένως πορεύσεται μετ' αὐτοῦ ἐν πρώτοις,
φόβον καὶ δειλίαν ἐπάξει ἐπ' αὐτὸν
καὶ βασανίσει αὐτὸν ἐν παιδείᾳ αὐτῆς,
ἕως οὗ ἐμπιστεύσῃ τῇ ψυχῇ αὐτοῦ,
καὶ πειράσει αὐτὸν ἐν τοῖς δικαιώμασιν αὐτῆς·
18 καὶ πάλιν ἐπανήξει κατ' εὐθεῖαν πρὸς αὐτὸν καὶ
εὐφρανεῖ αὐτὸν
καὶ ἀποκαλύψει αὐτῷ τὰ κρυπτὰ αὐτῆς.
19 ἐὰν ἀποπλανηθῇ, ἐγκαταλείψει αὐτὸν
καὶ παραδώσει αὐτὸν εἰς χεῖρας πτώσεως αὐτοῦ.
20 Συντήρησον καιρὸν καὶ φύλαξαι ἀπὸ πονηροῦ
καὶ περὶ τῆς ψυχῆς σου μὴ αἰσχυνθῇς·
21 ἔστιν γὰρ αἰσχύνη ἐπάγουσα ἁμαρτίαν,
καὶ ἔστιν αἰσχύνη δόξα καὶ χάρις.

KING JAMES VERSION

11 Wisdom exalteth her children, and layeth hold of them that seek her.

12 He that loveth her loveth life; and they that seek to her early shall be filled with joy.

13 He that holdeth her fast shall inherit glory; and wheresoever she entereth, the Lord will bless.

14 They that serve her shall minister to the Holy One: and them that love her the Lord doth love.

15 Whoso giveth ear unto her shall judge the nations: and he that attendeth unto her shall dwell securely.

16 If a man commit himself unto her, he shall inherit her; and his generation shall hold her in possession.

17 For at the first she will walk with him by crooked ways, and bring fear and dread upon him, and torment him with her discipline, until she may trust his soul, and try him by her laws.

18 Then will she return the straight way unto him, and comfort him, and shew him her secrets.

19 But if he go wrong, she will forsake him, and give him over to his own ruin.

20 Observe the opportunity, and beware of evil; and be not ashamed when it concerneth thy soul.

21 For there is a shame that bringeth sin; and there is a shame which is glory and grace.

DOUAY OLD TESTAMENT

12 Wisdom inspireth life into her children, and protecteth them that seek after her, and will go before *them* in the way of justice.

13 And he that loveth her, loveth life: and they that watch for her, shall embrace her sweetness.

14 They that hold her fast, shall inherit life: and whithersoever she entereth, God will give a blessing.

15 They that serve her, shall be servants to the holy one: and God loveth them that love her.

16 He that hearkeneth to her, shall judge nations: and he that looketh upon her, shall remain secure.

17 If he trust to her, he shall inherit her, and his generation shall be in assurance.

18 For she walketh with him in temptation, and at the first she chooseth him.

19 She will bring upon him fear and dread and trial: and she will scourge him with the affliction of her discipline, till she try him by her laws, and trust his soul.

20 Then she will strengthen him, and make a straight way to him, and give him joy.

21 And will disclose her secrets to him, and will heap upon him treasures of knowledge and understanding of justice.

22 But if he go astray, she will forsake him, and deliver him into the hands of his enemy.

23 Son, observe the time, and fly from evil.

24 For thy soul be not ashamed to say the truth.

25 For there is a shame that bringeth sin, and there is a shame that bringeth glory and grace.

KNOX TRANSLATION

12 New life wisdom breathes into her children, befriends all
that have recourse to her, and guides them in the right way.
13 Love her, as thou lovest life; wait early at her doors, if
thou wouldst win her sweet embrace. 14 Life the prize, if
thou hold her fast; come she in at the door, God's blessing
comes with her; 15 court paid to her, worship paid to the
Holy One; love given to her, God's love made thine in return
for it! 16 A word from her, and the world is at thy feet, a
sight of her face, and thou shalt dwell ever secure; 17 trust
her, and she will be thy inheritance, settled on the heirs of
thy body. 18 When first she chooses a man out, she does but
make trial of his company; 19 she puts him to the proof,
threatening him with her frown, teasing him with her difficult lore, until at last she has proved whether his thoughts
are hers, and can trust him perfectly. 20 Then she gives him
confidence, coming out openly to meet him; gladdens him
with her smile, and tells him all her secrets; 21 makes him
rich with store of true knowledge, and enables him to discern
the right. 22 Only if he strays away from her does she abandon him, and leave him at the mercy of his foes.

23 My son, study well what the time needs, ever on thy
guard against wrong-doing; though life itself were in peril,
24 never be ashamed to speak the truth. 25 Deference, that is
the grace and glory of a man, may yet make a sinner of him.

TODAY'S ENGLISH VERSION

11 Wisdom takes care of those who look for her; she raises
them to greatness. 12 Loving her is loving life itself; rising
early to look for her is pure joy. 13 Anyone who obtains
Wisdom will be greatly honored. Wherever he goes, the Lord
will bless him. 14 Wisdom's servants are the servants of the
Holy One, and the Lord loves everyone who loves her.
15 Those who obey her will give sound judgments;[a] those
who pay attention to her have true security. 16 Put your trust
in Wisdom, and you will possess her and pass her on to your
descendants. 17 At first, Wisdom will lead you along difficult
paths. She will make you so afraid that you will think you
cannot go on. The discipline she demands will be tormenting, and she will put you to the test with her requirements
until she trusts you[b] completely. 18 Then she will come to
you with no delay, reveal her secrets to you, and make you
happy. 19 But if you go astray, she will abandon you and let
you go to your own ruin.

20 Take advantage of opportunities, but guard yourself
against evil. Don't underrate yourself. 21 Humility deserves
honor and respect, but a low opinion of yourself leads to sin.

[a] *Hebrew* give sound judgments; *Greek* judge nations. [b] she trusts you; *or* you trust her.

NEW REVISED STANDARD VERSION

11 Wisdom teaches[a] her children
and gives help to those who seek her.
12 Whoever loves her loves life,
and those who seek her from early morning are filled
with joy.
13 Whoever holds her fast inherits glory,
and the Lord blesses the place she[b] enters.
14 Those who serve her minister to the Holy One;
the Lord loves those who love her.
15 Those who obey her will judge the nations,
and all who listen to her will live secure.
16 If they remain faithful, they will inherit her;
their descendants will also obtain her.
17 For at first she will walk with them on tortuous paths;
she will bring fear and dread upon them,
and will torment them by her discipline
until she trusts them,[c]
and she will test them with her ordinances.
18 Then she will come straight back to them again and
gladden them,
and will reveal her secrets to them.
19 If they go astray she will forsake them,
and hand them over to their ruin.

20 Watch for the opportune time, and beware of evil,
and do not be ashamed to be yourself.
21 For there is a shame that leads to sin,
and there is a shame that is glory and favor.

a Heb Syr: Gk *exalts* *b* Or *he* *c* Or *until they remain faithful in their heart*

NEW AMERICAN BIBLE

11 Wisdom instructs her children
and admonishes those who seek her.
12 He who loves her loves life;
those who seek her out win her favor.
13 He who holds her fast inherits glory;
wherever he dwells, the LORD bestows blessings.
14 Those who serve her serve the Holy One;
those who love her the LORD loves.
15 He who obeys her judges nations;
he who hearkens to her dwells in her inmost
chambers.
16 If one trusts her, he will possess her;
his descendants too will inherit her.
17 She walks with him as a stranger,
and at first she puts him to the test;
Fear and dread she brings upon him
and tries him with her discipline;
With her precepts she puts him to the proof,
until his heart is fully with her.
18 Then she comes back to bring him happiness
and reveal her secrets to him.
19 But if he fails her, she will abandon him
and deliver him into the hands of despoilers.

20 Use your time well; guard yourself from evil,
and bring upon yourself no shame.
21 There is a sense of shame laden with guilt,
and a shame that merits honor and respect.

NEW JERUSALEM BIBLE

11 Wisdom brings up her own children
and cares for those who seek her.
12 Whoever loves her loves life,
those who seek her early will be filled with joy.
13 Whoever possesses her will inherit honour,
and wherever he walks the Lord will bless him.
14 Those who serve her minister to the Holy One,
and the Lord loves those who love her.
15 Whoever obeys her rules the nations,
whoever pays attention to her dwells secure.
16 If he trusts himself to her he will inherit her,
and his descendants will remain in possession of her;
17 for though she takes him at first through winding
ways,
bringing fear and faintness on him,
trying him out with her discipline till she can trust him,
and testing him with her ordeals,
18 she then comes back to him on the straight road, makes
him happy
and reveals her secrets to him.
19 If he goes astray, however, she abandons him
and leaves him to his own destruction.

20 Take circumstances into account and beware of evil,
and have no cause to be ashamed of yourself;
21 for there is a shame that leads to sin
and a shame that is honourable and gracious.

GREEK OLD TESTAMENT

22 μὴ λάβῃς πρόσωπον κατὰ τῆς ψυχῆς σου
καὶ μὴ ἐντραπῇς εἰς πτῶσίν σου.
23 μὴ κωλύσῃς λόγον ἐν καιρῷ χρείας·
24 ἐν γὰρ λόγῳ γνωσθήσεται σοφία
καὶ παιδεία ἐν ῥήματι γλώσσης.
25 μὴ ἀντίλεγε τῇ ἀληθείᾳ
καὶ περὶ τῆς ἀπαιδευσίας σου ἐντράπηθι.
26 μὴ αἰσχυνθῇς ὁμολογῆσαι ἐφ᾽ ἁμαρτίαις σου
καὶ μὴ βιάζου ῥοῦν ποταμοῦ.
27 καὶ μὴ ὑποστρώσῃς ἀνθρώπῳ μωρῷ σεαυτὸν
καὶ μὴ λάβῃς πρόσωπον δυνάστου.
28 ἕως θανάτου ἀγώνισαι περὶ τῆς ἀληθείας,
καὶ κύριος ὁ θεὸς πολεμήσει ὑπὲρ σοῦ.
29 μὴ γίνου θρασὺς ἐν γλώσσῃ σου
καὶ νωθρὸς καὶ παρειμένος ἐν τοῖς ἔργοις σου.
30 μὴ ἴσθι ὡς λέων ἐν τῷ οἴκῳ σου
καὶ φαντασιοκοπῶν ἐν τοῖς οἰκέταις σου.
31 μὴ ἔστω ἡ χείρ σου ἐκτεταμένη εἰς τὸ λαβεῖν
καὶ ἐν τῷ ἀποδιδόναι συνεσταλμένη.

KING JAMES VERSION

22 Accept no person against thy soul, and let not the reverence of any man cause thee to fall.

23 And refrain not to speak, when there is occasion to do good, and hide not thy wisdom in her beauty.

24 For by speech wisdom shall be known: and learning by the word of the tongue.

25 In no wise speak against the truth; but be abashed of the error of thine ignorance.

26 Be not ashamed to confess thy sins; and force not the course of the river.

27 Make not thyself an underling to a foolish man; neither accept the person of the mighty.

28 Strive for the truth unto death, and the Lord shall fight for thee.

29 Be not hasty in thy tongue, and in thy deeds slack and remiss.

30 Be not as a lion in thy house, nor frantick among thy servants.

31 Let not thine hand be stretched out to receive, and shut when thou shouldest repay.

DOUAY OLD TESTAMENT

26 Accept no person against thy own person, nor against thy soul a lie.

27 Reverence not thy neighbour in his fall:

28 And refrain not to speak in the time of salvation. Hide not thy wisdom in her beauty.

29 For by the tongue wisdom is discerned: and understanding, and knowledge, and learning by the word of the wise, and steadfastness in the works of justice.

30 In nowise speak against the truth, but be ashamed of the lie of thy ignorance.

31 Be not ashamed to confess thy sins, but submit not thyself to every man for sin.

32 Resist not against the face of the mighty, and do not strive against the stream of the river.

33 Strive for justice for thy soul, and even unto death fight for justice, and God will overthrow thy enemies for thee.

34 Be not hasty in thy tongue: and slack and remiss in thy works.

35 Be not as a lion in thy house, terrifying them of thy household, and oppressing them that are under thee.

36 Let not thy hand be stretched out to receive, and shut when thou shouldst give.

KNOX TRANSLATION

26 Wouldst thou hold another man's honour dearer than thy
own, and swear the lie at thy soul's peril? 27 Nay, speak out
without shame, though thy own neighbour should be threatened with ruin. 28 Withhold not thy counsel while safety
may yet be won; thy wisdom is not to be hidden away like a
veiled beauty. 29 Wisdom still needs a tongue to disclose it;
no discernment or knowledge or shrewd counsel but waits
on the apt word; how else should men be encouraged in well
doing? 30 Speak thou never against the known truth; and if
thy ignorance has erred, own thy error. 31 Be never ashamed
to confess thy faults, nor, for thy fault, put thyself in any
man's power.

32 Wouldst thou defy, and openly, a ruler's authority? Thou hadst better swim against the stream's force.[a]

33 Do battle for the right, all thy life long, and with thy last breath do battle for the right still; God, in thy cause, will overcome thy enemies.

34 A glib tongue, and hands that hang down idle; such be not thine.

35 Lion if thou must be, let not thy own house feel the brunt of it, thy own servants harried, thy own slaves beaten to the earth.

36 Open hand when the word is Take, shut when the word is Give; such be not thine.

a *vv.* 31, 32. The Greek text here varies considerably from the Latin version. It runs: 'Be never ashamed to confess thy faults; wouldst thou swim against the stream's force? Never put thyself in the power of a fool, and never flatter a ruler's greatness'. Throughout the last fourteen verses of this chapter, the Latin and the Greek have many different twists of meaning, and neither can be interpreted with much certainty.

TODAY'S ENGLISH VERSION

22 Do not let others have their way at your expense; do not
bring on your own ruin by giving up your rights. 23 Never
hesitate to speak out when the occasion[a] calls for it. Don't
hide your wisdom.[b] 24 Your wisdom and education can be
known only by what you say. 25 Do not, however, go against
the truth, and remember that you do not know everything.
26 Don't be ashamed to confess your sins; there's no point in
trying to stop a river from flowing. 27 Don't allow yourself to
be dominated by someone who is stupid or show partiality to
influential people. 28 Stand up for what is right, even if it
costs you your life; the Lord God will be fighting on your
side.
29 Don't be quick to speak or lazy and negligent in your
work. 30 Don't act like a lion at home or be suspicious of
your servants. 31 Don't stick out your hand to get something
if you're going to be tightfisted when the time comes to pay
it back.

[a] *Probable text* the occasion; *Greek* safety. [b] *Hebrew* Don't hide your wisdom; *most Greek manuscripts do not have these words; other Greek manuscripts* Don't hide your wisdom for the sake of appearances.

NEW REVISED STANDARD VERSION

22 Do not show partiality, to your own harm,
or deference, to your downfall.
23 Do not refrain from speaking at the proper moment,[a]
and do not hide your wisdom.[b]
24 For wisdom becomes known through speech,
and education through the words of the tongue.
25 Never speak against the truth,
but be ashamed of your ignorance.
26 Do not be ashamed to confess your sins,
and do not try to stop the current of a river.
27 Do not subject yourself to a fool,
or show partiality to a ruler.
28 Fight to the death for truth,
and the Lord God will fight for you.

29 Do not be reckless in your speech,
or sluggish and remiss in your deeds.
30 Do not be like a lion in your home,
or suspicious of your servants.
31 Do not let your hand be stretched out to receive
and closed when it is time to give.

[a] Heb: Gk *at a time of salvation* [b] So some Gk Mss and Heb Syr Lat: Other Gk Mss lack *and do not hide your wisdom*

NEW AMERICAN BIBLE

22 Show no favoritism to your own discredit;
let no one intimidate you to your own downfall.
23 Refrain not from speaking at the proper time,
and hide not away your wisdom;
24 For it is through speech that wisdom becomes known,
and knowledge through the tongue's rejoinder.
25 Never gainsay the truth,
and struggle not against the rushing stream.
26 Be not ashamed to acknowledge your guilt,
but of your ignorance rather be ashamed.
27 Do not abase yourself before an impious man,
nor refuse to do so before rulers.
28 Even to the death fight for truth,
and the LORD your God will battle for you.
29 Be not surly in your speech,
nor lazy and slack in your deeds.
30 Be not a lion at home,
nor sly and suspicious at work.
31 Let not your hand be open to receive
and clenched when it is time to give.

NEW JERUSALEM BIBLE

22 Do not be too severe on yourself,
do not let shame lead you to ruin.
23 Do not refrain from speaking when it will do good,
and do not hide your wisdom;
24 for your wisdom is made known by what you say,
your erudition by the words you utter.
25 Do not contradict the truth,
rather blush for your own ignorance.
26 Do not be ashamed to confess your sins,
do not struggle against the current of the river.
27 Do not grovel to the foolish,
do not show partiality to the influential.
28 Fight to the death for truth,
and the Lord God will war on your side.
29 Do not be bold of tongue,
yet idle and slack in deed;
30 do not be like a lion at home,
or cowardly towards your servants.
31 Do not let your hands be outstretched to receive,
yet tight-fisted when the time comes to give back.

GREEK OLD TESTAMENT

5 Μὴ ἔπεχε ἐπὶ τοῖς χρήμασίν σου
καὶ μὴ εἴπῃς Αὐτάρκη μοί ἐστιν.
2 μὴ ἐξακολούθει τῇ ψυχῇ σου
καὶ τῇ ἰσχύι σου πορεύεσθαι ἐν ἐπιθυμίαις καρδίας σου·
3 καὶ μὴ εἴπῃς Τίς με δυναστεύσει;
ὁ γὰρ κύριος ἐκδικῶν ἐκδικήσει.
4 μὴ εἴπῃς Ἥμαρτον, καὶ τί μοι ἐγένετο;
ὁ γὰρ κύριός ἐστιν μακρόθυμος.
5 περὶ ἐξιλασμοῦ μὴ ἄφοβος γίνου
προσθεῖναι ἁμαρτίαν ἐφ᾽ ἁμαρτίαις·
6 καὶ μὴ εἴπῃς Ὁ οἰκτιρμὸς αὐτοῦ πολύς,
τὸ πλῆθος τῶν ἁμαρτιῶν μου ἐξιλάσεται·
ἔλεος γὰρ καὶ ὀργὴ παρ᾽ αὐτῷ,
καὶ ἐπὶ ἁμαρτωλοὺς καταπαύσει ὁ θυμὸς αὐτοῦ.
7 μὴ ἀνάμενε ἐπιστρέψαι πρὸς κύριον
καὶ μὴ ὑπερβάλλου ἡμέραν ἐξ ἡμέρας·
ἐξάπινα γὰρ ἐξελεύσεται ὀργὴ κυρίου,
καὶ ἐν καιρῷ ἐκδικήσεως ἐξολῇ.
8 Μὴ ἔπεχε ἐπὶ χρήμασιν ἀδίκοις·
οὐδὲν γὰρ ὠφελήσει σε ἐν ἡμέρᾳ ἐπαγωγῆς.
9 μὴ λίκμα ἐν παντὶ ἀνέμῳ
καὶ μὴ πορεύου ἐν πάσῃ ἀτραπῷ·
οὕτως ὁ ἁμαρτωλὸς ὁ δίγλωσσος.
10 ἴσθι ἐστηριγμένος ἐν συνέσει σου,
καὶ εἷς ἔστω σου ὁ λόγος.

KING JAMES VERSION

5 Set not thy heart upon thy goods; and say not, I have enough for my life.

2 Follow not thine own mind and thy strength, to walk in the ways of thy heart:

3 And say not, Who shall controul me for my works? for the Lord will surely revenge thy pride.

4 Say not, I have sinned, and what harm hath happened unto me? for the Lord is longsuffering, he will in no wise let thee go.

5 Concerning propitiation, be not without fear to add sin unto sin:

6 And say not, His mercy is great; he will be pacified for the multitude of my sins: for mercy and wrath come from him, and his indignation resteth upon sinners.

7 Make no tarrying to turn to the Lord, and put not off from day to day: for suddenly shall the wrath of the Lord come forth, and in thy security thou shalt be destroyed, and perish in the day of vengeance.

8 Set not thine heart upon goods unjustly gotten; for they shall not profit thee in the day of calamity.

9 Winnow not with every wind, and go not into every way: for so doth the sinner that hath a double tongue.

10 Be stedfast in thy understanding; and let thy word be the same.

DOUAY OLD TESTAMENT

5 SET not thy heart upon unjust possessions, and say not: I have enough to live on: for it shall be of no service in the time of vengeance and darkness.

2 Follow not in thy strength the desires of thy heart:

3 And say not: How mighty am I? and who shall bring me under for my deeds? for God will surely take revenge.

4 Say not: I have sinned, and what harm hath befallen me? for the most High is a patient rewarder.

5 Be not without fear about sin forgiven, and add not sin upon sin:

6 And say not: The mercy of the Lord is great, he will have mercy on the multitude of my sins.

7 For mercy and wrath quickly come from him, and his wrath looketh upon sinners.

8 Delay not to be converted to the Lord, and defer it not from day to day.

9 For his wrath shall come on a sudden, and in the time of vengeance he will destroy thee.

10 Be not anxious for goods unjustly gotten: for they shall not profit thee in the day of calamity and revenge.

11 Winnow not with every wind, and go not into every way: for so is every sinner proved by a double tongue.

12 Be steadfast in the way of the Lord, and in the truth of thy judgment, and in knowledge, and let the word of peace and justice keep with thee.

KNOX TRANSLATION

5 Wilt thou look round at ill-gotten gains, and tell thyself
thou hast enough for all thy needs? Trust me, when
vengeance finds thee out, all this shall nothing avail thee.
2 In manhood's vigour, do not follow the whim of thy heart,
3 boasting of thy strength, and asking who will call thee to
account for thy doings; God will find a way to punish thee.
4 Nor ever flatter thyself that thou hast sinned and come
away scot-free; the eternal justice waits its time. 5 Ill it were
that sin's pardon should embolden thee to sin afresh. 6 Dost
thou tell thyself God's mercies are great, and he will pardon
thy sins for all they are so many? 7 Bethink thee that his
vengeance rides swift as his mercy; it is a jealous eye that
watches the sinner. 8 Or wouldst thou make slow work of
turning to the Lord, and put it off from day to day? 9 Swift
falls his anger and perilous, when the time for vengeance is
ripe. 10 And must thy thoughts still dwell on the ill-gotten
gains, that shall nothing avail thee when vengeance finds
thee out?

11 Turn not with every wind, nor walk in every way that
offers; that sinners do, till their hypocrisy is found out.
12 Firm let thy feet be set on the path the Lord has chosen for
thee; be true to thy own thought and to the knowledge thou
hast, and ever let the counsels of peace and justice guide
thee on thy way.

TODAY'S ENGLISH VERSION

5 Don't rely on money to make you independent. 2 Don't
think you have to have everything you want, and then
spend your energy trying to get it. 3 Don't think that no one
can exercise authority over you; if you do, the Lord is certain
to punish you. 4 Don't think that you can sin and get away
with it; the Lord does not mind waiting to punish you.
5 Don't be so certain of the Lord's forgiveness that you go on
committing one sin after another. 6 Don't think that his
mercy is so great that he will forgive your sins no matter
how many they are. He does show mercy, but he also shows
his furious anger with sinners. 7 Come back to the Lord
quickly. Don't think that you can keep putting it off. His
anger can come upon you suddenly, and you will die under
his punishment. 8 Don't rely on dishonest wealth; it will do
you no good on that day of disaster.

9-10 Be certain about what you believe and consistent in
what you say. Don't try to please everyone or agree with
everything people say.[a] 11 Always be ready to listen, but

[a] *Hebrew* everything people say; *Greek adds* That is what double-tongued sinners do.

NEW REVISED STANDARD VERSION

5 Do not rely on your wealth,
or say, "I have enough."
2 Do not follow your inclination and strength
in pursuing the desires of your heart.
3 Do not say, "Who can have power over me?"
for the Lord will surely punish you.

4 Do not say, "I sinned, yet what has happened to me?"
for the Lord is slow to anger.
5 Do not be so confident of forgiveness[a]
that you add sin to sin.
6 Do not say, "His mercy is great,
he will forgive[b] the multitude of my sins,"
for both mercy and wrath are with him,
and his anger will rest on sinners.
7 Do not delay to turn back to the Lord,
and do not postpone it from day to day;
for suddenly the wrath of the Lord will come upon you,
and at the time of punishment you will perish.
8 Do not depend on dishonest wealth,
for it will not benefit you on the day of calamity.

9 Do not winnow in every wind,
or follow every path.[c]
10 Stand firm for what you know,
and let your speech be consistent.

[a] Heb: Gk *atonement* [b] Heb: Gk *he* (or *it*) *will atone for* [c] Gk adds *so it is with the double-tongued sinner* (see 6.1)

NEW AMERICAN BIBLE

5 Rely not on your wealth;
say not: "I have the power."
2 Rely not on your strength
in following the desires of your heart.
3 Say not: "Who can prevail against me?"
for the LORD will exact the punishment.
4 Say not: "I have sinned, yet what has befallen me?"
for the LORD bides his time.
5 Of forgiveness be not overconfident,
adding sin upon sin.
6 Say not: "Great is his mercy;
my many sins he will forgive."
7 For mercy and anger alike are with him;
upon the wicked alights his wrath.
8 Delay not your conversion to the LORD,
put it not off from day to day;
9 For suddenly his wrath flames forth;
at the time of vengeance, you will be destroyed.
10 Rely not upon deceitful wealth,
for it will be no help on the day of wrath.

11 Winnow not in every wind,
and start not off in every direction.
12 Be consistent in your thoughts;
steadfast be your words.

NEW JERUSALEM BIBLE

5 Do not put your confidence in your money
or say, 'With this I am self-sufficient.'
2 Do not be led by your appetites and energy
to follow the passions of your heart.
3 And do not say, 'Who has authority over me?'
for the Lord will certainly give you your deserts.
4 Do not say, 'I have sinned, but what harm has befallen
me?'
for the Lord's forbearance is long.
5 Do not be so sure of forgiveness
that you add sin to sin.
6 And do not say, 'His compassion is great,
he will forgive me my many sins';
for with him are both mercy and retribution,
and his anger does not pass from sinners.
7 Do not delay your return to the Lord,
do not put it off day after day;
for suddenly the Lord's wrath will blaze out,
and on the day of punishment you will be utterly
destroyed.
8 Do not set your heart on ill-gotten gains,
they will be of no use to you on the day of disaster.

9 Do not winnow in every wind,
or walk along every by-way
(as the double-talking sinner does).
10 Be steady in your convictions,
and be a person of your word.

GREEK OLD TESTAMENT

11 Γίνου ταχὺς ἐν ἀκροάσει σου
καὶ ἐν μακροθυμίᾳ φθέγγου ἀπόκρισιν.
12 εἰ ἔστιν σοι σύνεσις, ἀποκρίθητι τῷ πλησίον·
εἰ δὲ μή, ἡ χείρ σου ἔστω ἐπὶ τῷ στόματί σου.
13 δόξα καὶ ἀτιμία ἐν λαλιᾷ,
καὶ γλῶσσα ἀνθρώπου πτῶσις αὐτῷ.
14 Μὴ κληθῇς ψίθυρος
καὶ τῇ γλώσσῃ σου μὴ ἐνέδρευε·
ἐπὶ γὰρ τῷ κλέπτῃ ἐστὶν αἰσχύνη
καὶ κατάγνωσις πονηρὰ ἐπὶ διγλώσσου.
15 ἐν μεγάλῳ καὶ ἐν μικρῷ μὴ ἀγνόει
καὶ ἀντὶ φίλου μὴ γίνου ἐχθρός·
ὄνομα γὰρ πονηρὸν αἰσχύνην καὶ ὄνειδος κληρονομήσει·
οὕτως ὁ ἁμαρτωλὸς ὁ δίγλωσσος.
6 2 Μὴ ἐπάρῃς σεαυτὸν ἐν βουλῇ ψυχῆς σου,
ἵνα μὴ διαρπαγῇ ὡς ταῦρος ἡ ψυχή σου·
3 τὰ φύλλα σου καταφάγεσαι καὶ τοὺς καρπούς σου
ἀπολέσεις
καὶ ἀφήσεις σεαυτὸν ὡς ξύλον ξηρόν.
4 ψυχὴ πονηρὰ ἀπολεῖ τὸν κτησάμενον αὐτὴν
καὶ ἐπίχαρμα ἐχθρῶν ποιήσει αὐτόν.
5 Λάρυγξ γλυκὺς πληθυνεῖ φίλους αὐτοῦ,
καὶ γλῶσσα εὔλαλος πληθυνεῖ εὐπροσήγορα.
6 οἱ εἰρηνεύοντές σοι ἔστωσαν πολλοί,
οἱ δὲ σύμβουλοί σου εἷς ἀπὸ χιλίων.

KING JAMES VERSION

11 Be swift to hear; and let thy life be sincere; and with
patience give answer.
12 If thou hast understanding, answer thy neighbour; if
not, lay thy hand upon thy mouth.
13 Honour and shame is in talk: and the tongue of man is
his fall.
14 Be not called a whisperer, and lie not in wait with thy
tongue: for a foul shame is upon the thief, and an evil condemnation upon the double tongue.
15 Be not ignorant of any thing in a great matter or a
small.
6 Instead of a friend become not an enemy; for [thereby]
thou shalt inherit an ill name, shame, and reproach:
even so shall a sinner that hath a double tongue.
2 Extol not thyself in the counsel of thine own heart; that
thy soul be not torn in pieces as a bull [straying alone.]
3 Thou shalt eat up thy leaves, and lose thy fruit, and
leave thyself as a dry tree.
4 A wicked soul shall destroy him that hath it, and shall
make him to be laughed to scorn of his enemies.
5 Sweet language will multiply friends: and a fairspeak-
ing tongue will increase kind greetings.
6 Be in peace with many: nevertheless have but one counsellor of a thousand.

DOUAY OLD TESTAMENT

13 Be meek to hear the word, that thou mayst understand: and return a true answer with wisdom.
14 If thou have understanding, answer *thy* neighbour: but
if not, let thy hand be upon thy mouth, lest thou be surprised
in an unskilful word, and be confounded.
15 Honour and glory is in the word of the wise, but the
tongue of the fool is his ruin.
16 Be not called a whisperer, and be not taken in thy
tongue, and confounded.
17 For confusion and repentance is upon a thief, and an
evil mark of disgrace upon the double tongued, but to the
whisperer hatred, and enmity, and reproach.
18 Justify alike the small and the great.
6 INSTEAD of a friend become not an enemy to thy neighbour: for an evil man shall inherit reproach and shame,
so shall every sinner that is envious and double tongued.
2 Extol not thyself in the thoughts of thy soul like a bull:
lest thy strength be quashed by folly,
3 And it eat up thy leaves, and destroy thy fruit, and thou
be left as a dry tree in the wilderness.
4 For a wicked soul shall destroy him that hath it, and
maketh him to be a joy to his enemies, and shall lead him
into the lot of the wicked.
5 A sweet word multiplieth friends, and appeaseth enemies, and a gracious tongue in a good man aboundeth.
6 Be in peace with many, but let one of a thousand be thy
counsellor.

KNOX TRANSLATION

13 True answer and wise answer none can give but he who
listens patiently, and learns all.
14 If discernment thou hast, give thy neighbour his answer;
if none, tongue held is best, or some ill-advised word will
shame thee; 15 speech uttered was ever the wise man's pass-
port to fame, the fool's undoing.
16 Never win the name of back-biter, by thy own tongue
entrapped into shame. 17 A thief must blush and do penance,
a hypocrite men will mark and avoid; the back-biter earns
indignation and enmity and disgrace all at once.
18 To all alike, high and low, give just award.
6 Wouldst thou rather be thy neighbour's enemy than his
friend? Wouldst thou earn, by ill nature, an ill name,
and be despised for such faults as these, envy and hypocrisy?
2 Wilt thou toss thy head, bull-fashion, and glory in thy
own strength? What if that strength should be brought down
by thy own folly? 3 Then wilt thou be no better than some
dry tree-stump out in the desert, its leaves withered, its hope
of fruit all gone. 4 Ill nature brings a man to an ill end, the
scorn of his enemies and a prey to iniquity.
5 Gentleness of speech, how it wins friends everywhere,
how it disarms its enemies! Never was a good man wanting
for a gracious word. 6 Be on good terms with all, but for thy
trusted counsellor, choose one in a thousand. 7 Tried friends

TODAY'S ENGLISH VERSION

take your time in answering. 12 Answer only if you know
what to say, and if you don't know what to say, keep quiet.
13 Speaking can bring you either honor or disgrace; what you
say can ruin you.
14 Don't get a reputation for being a gossip, and don't tell
tales that will hurt people. Just as robbers will suffer disgrace,
so liars will suffer severe condemnation. 15 Do nothing
6 destructive,[a] whether it seems insignificant or not, 1 and
do not be an enemy when you should be a friend. A bad
reputation brings you the disgrace that lying sinners deserve.
2 Do not let your passions carry you away; this can tear your
soul to pieces like a bull.[b] 3 You will be left like a dead tree
without any leaves or fruit. 4 Evil desire will destroy you and
make you a joke to your enemies.
5 If you are polite and courteous, you will enjoy the friendship of many people. 6 Exchange greetings with many, but
take advice from only one person out of a thousand. 7 When

[a] *Hebrew* Do nothing destructive; *Greek* Do not be ignorant in anything.
[b] *Verse 2 in both Greek and Hebrew is unclear.*

NEW REVISED STANDARD VERSION

11 Be quick to hear,
but deliberate in answering.
12 If you know what to say, answer your neighbor;
but if not, put your hand over your mouth.

13 Honor and dishonor come from speaking,
and the tongue of mortals may be their downfall.
14 Do not be called double-tongued[a]
and do not lay traps with your tongue;
for shame comes to the thief,
and severe condemnation to the double-tongued.
15 In great and small matters cause no harm,[b]
6 1 and do not become an enemy instead of a friend;
for a bad name incurs shame and reproach;
so it is with the double-tongued sinner.

2 Do not fall into the grip of passion,[c]
or you may be torn apart as by a bull.[d]
3 Your leaves will be devoured and your fruit destroyed,
and you will be left like a withered tree.
4 Evil passion destroys those who have it,
and makes them the laughingstock of their enemies.

5 Pleasant speech multiplies friends,
and a gracious tongue multiplies courtesies.
6 Let those who are friendly with you be many,
but let your advisers be one in a thousand.

a Heb: Gk *a slanderer* *b* Heb Syr: Gk *be ignorant* *c* Heb: Meaning of Gk uncertain *d* Meaning of Gk uncertain

NEW AMERICAN BIBLE

13 Be swift to hear,
but slow to answer.
14 If you have the knowledge, answer your neighbor;
if not, put your hand over your mouth.
15 Honor and dishonor through talking!
A man's tongue can be his downfall.
16 Be not called a detractor;
use not your tongue for calumny;
17 For shame has been created for the thief,
and the reproach of his neighbor for the double-tongued.

6 Say nothing harmful, small or great;
be not a foe instead of a friend;
A bad name and disgrace will you acquire:
"That for the evil man with double tongue!"

2 Fall not into the grip of desire,
lest, like fire, it consume your strength;
3 Your leaves it will eat, your fruits destroy,
and you will be left a dry tree,
4 For contumacious desire destroys its owner
and makes him the sport of his enemies.

5 A kind mouth multiplies friends,
and gracious lips prompt friendly greetings.
6 Let your acquaintances be many,
but one in a thousand your confidant.

NEW JERUSALEM BIBLE

11 Be quick to listen,
and deliberate in giving an answer.
12 If you understand the matter, give your neighbour an answer,
if not, keep your hand over your mouth.
13 Both honour and disgrace come from talking,
the tongue is its owner's downfall.
14 Do not get a name for scandal-mongering,
do not set traps with your tongue;
for as shame lies in store for the thief,
so harsh condemnation awaits the deceitful.
15 Avoid offences in great as in small matters,
and do not exchange friendship for enmity,
6 1 for a bad name will earn you shame and reproach,
as happens to the double-talking sinner.
2 Do not get carried aloft on the wings of passion,
for fear your strength tear itself apart like a bull,
3 and you devour your own foliage and destroy your own fruit
and end by making yourself like a piece of dried-up wood.
4 An evil temper destroys the person who has it
and makes him the laughing-stock of his enemies.
5 A kindly turn of speech attracts new friends,
a courteous tongue invites many a friendly response.
6 Let your acquaintances be many,
but for advisers choose one out of a thousand.

GREEK OLD TESTAMENT

7 εἰ κτᾶσαι φίλον, ἐν πειρασμῷ κτῆσαι αὐτὸν
καὶ μὴ ταχὺ ἐμπιστεύσῃς αὐτῷ.
8 ἔστιν γὰρ φίλος ἐν καιρῷ αὐτοῦ
καὶ οὐ μὴ παραμείνῃ ἐν ἡμέρᾳ θλίψεώς σου.
9 καὶ ἔστιν φίλος μετατιθέμενος εἰς ἔχθραν
καὶ μάχην ὀνειδισμοῦ σου ἀποκαλύψει.
10 καὶ ἔστιν φίλος κοινωνὸς τραπεζῶν
καὶ οὐ μὴ παραμείνῃ ἐν ἡμέρᾳ θλίψεώς σου·
11 καὶ ἐν τοῖς ἀγαθοῖς σου ἔσται ὡς σὺ
καὶ ἐπὶ τοὺς οἰκέτας σου παρρησιάσεται·
12 ἐὰν ταπεινωθῇς, ἔσται κατὰ σοῦ
καὶ ἀπὸ τοῦ προσώπου σου κρυβήσεται.
13 ἀπὸ τῶν ἐχθρῶν σου διαχωρίσθητι
καὶ ἀπὸ τῶν φίλων σου πρόσεχε.
14 φίλος πιστὸς σκέπη κραταιά,
ὁ δὲ εὑρὼν αὐτὸν εὗρεν θησαυρόν.
15 φίλου πιστοῦ οὐκ ἔστιν ἀντάλλαγμα,
καὶ οὐκ ἔστιν σταθμὸς τῆς καλλονῆς αὐτοῦ.
16 φίλος πιστὸς φάρμακον ζωῆς,
καὶ οἱ φοβούμενοι κύριον εὑρήσουσιν αὐτόν.
17 ὁ φοβούμενος κύριον εὐθυνεῖ φιλίαν αὐτοῦ,
ὅτι κατ᾽ αὐτὸν οὕτως καὶ ὁ πλησίον αὐτοῦ.
18 Τέκνον, ἐκ νεότητός σου ἐπίλεξαι παιδείαν,
καὶ ἕως πολιῶν εὑρήσεις σοφίαν.

KING JAMES VERSION

7 If thou wouldest get a friend, prove him first, and be not hasty to credit him.

8 For some man is a friend for his own occasion, and will not abide in the day of thy trouble.

9 And there is a friend, who being turned to enmity and strife will discover thy reproach.

10 Again, some friend is a companion at the table, and will not continue in the day of thy affliction.

11 But in thy prosperity he will be as thyself, and will be bold over thy servants.

12 If thou be brought low, he will be against thee, and will hide himself from thy face.

13 Separate thyself from thine enemies, and take heed of thy friends.

14 A faithful friend is a strong defence: and he that hath found such an one hath found a treasure.

15 Nothing doth countervail a faithful friend, and his excellency is invaluable.

16 A faithful friend is the medicine of life; and they that fear the Lord shall find him.

17 Whoso feareth the Lord shall direct his friendship aright: for as he is, so shall his neighbour be also.

18 My son, gather instruction from thy youth up: so shalt thou find wisdom till thine old age.

DOUAY OLD TESTAMENT

7 If thou wouldst get a friend, try him before thou takest him, and do not credit him easily.

8 For there is a friend for his own occasion, and he will not abide in the day of thy trouble.

9 And there is a friend that turneth to enmity; and there is a friend that will disclose hatred and strife and reproaches.

10 And there is a friend a companion at the table, and he will not abide in the day of distress.

11 A friend if he continue steadfast, shall be to thee as thyself, and shall act with confidence among them of thy household.

12 If he humble himself before thee, and hide himself from thy face, thou shalt have unanimous friendship for good.

13 Separate thyself from thy enemies, and take heed of thy friends.

14 A faithful friend is a strong defence: and he that hath found him, hath found a treasure.

15 Nothing can be compared to a faithful friend, and no weight of gold and silver is able to countervail the goodness of his fidelity.

16 A faithful friend is the medicine of life and immortality: and they that fear the Lord, shall find him.

17 He that feareth God, shall likewise have good friendship: because according to him shall his friend be.

18 My son, from thy youth up receive instruction, and even to thy grey hairs thou shalt find wisdom.

KNOX TRANSLATION

be the friends thou makest; do not bestow thy confidence
lightly; 8 some men are but fair-weather friends, and will not
stand the test of adversity. 9 Some will veer from friend to
foe, and lay bare old grudges, old quarrels, to reproach thee;
10 some will be thy boon companions, but desert thee when
trouble is afoot. 11 Fast and faithful friend there is, that will
be even as thyself, and have thy servants at his beck and
call; 12 let him behave modestly, and rid thee of his presence,
and there shall be true and tried friendship between you.[a]
13 From enemies thou mayst keep thy distance; against
friends be on thy guard. 14 True friendship, sure protection
and rare treasure found; true friendship, 15 a thing beyond
compare, its tried loyalty outweighing gold and silver; 16 true
friendship, elixir of life, and of life eternal! Only those who
fear God will come by it; 17 the fear of God gives friendship
evenly shared, friend matched with friend.

18 My son, learn the lessons of youth, and garner wisdom

[a] *vv.* 11, 12: The sense of these verses is doubtful. The Greek text has, for verse 12, '(But) if thou art brought low, he will turn against thee, and hide his presence away from thee'.

TODAY'S ENGLISH VERSION

you make friends, don't be too quick to trust them; make
sure that they have proved themselves. 8 Some people will be
your friends only when it is convenient for them, but they
won't stand by you in trouble. 9 Others will fall out with you
over some argument, and then embarrass you by letting
everyone know about it. 10-11 Others will sit at your table as
long as things are going well; they will stick to you like your
shadow and give orders to your servants, but they will not
stand by you in trouble. 12 If your situation takes a turn for
the worse, they will turn against you, and you won't be able
to find them anywhere.

13 Stay away from your enemies and be on guard against
your friends. 14 A loyal friend is like a safe shelter; find one,
and you have found a treasure. 15 Nothing else is as valuable; there is no way of putting a price on it. 16 A loyal friend
is like a medicine that keeps you in good health. Only those
who fear the Lord can find such a friend. 17 A person who
fears the Lord can make real friendships, because he will
treat his friends as he does himself.[a]

18 My child, learn to value Wisdom while you are young,
and you will still be able to find her when you grow old.

[a] because . . . himself; *or* because his friends will also fear the Lord.

NEW REVISED STANDARD VERSION

7 When you gain friends, gain them through testing,
and do not trust them hastily.
8 For there are friends who are such when it suits them,
but they will not stand by you in time of trouble.
9 And there are friends who change into enemies,
and tell of the quarrel to your disgrace.
10 And there are friends who sit at your table,
but they will not stand by you in time of trouble.
11 When you are prosperous, they become your second self,
and lord it over your servants;
12 but if you are brought low, they turn against you,
and hide themselves from you.
13 Keep away from your enemies,
and be on guard with your friends.

14 Faithful friends are a sturdy shelter:
whoever finds one has found a treasure.
15 Faithful friends are beyond price;
no amount can balance their worth.
16 Faithful friends are life-saving medicine;
and those who fear the Lord will find them.
17 Those who fear the Lord direct their friendship aright,
for as they are, so are their neighbors also.

18 My child, from your youth choose discipline,
and when you have gray hair you will still find wisdom.

NEW AMERICAN BIBLE

7 When you gain a friend, first test him,
and be not too ready to trust him.
8 For one sort of friend is a friend when it suits him,
but he will not be with you in time of distress.
9 Another is a friend who becomes an enemy,
and tells of the quarrel to your shame.
10 Another is a friend, a boon companion,
who will not be with you when sorrow comes.
11 When things go well, he is your other self,
and lords it over your servants;
12 But if you are brought low, he turns against you
and avoids meeting you.
13 Keep away from your enemies;
be on your guard with your friends.
14 A faithful friend is a sturdy shelter;
he who finds one finds a treasure.
15 A faithful friend is beyond price,
no sum can balance his worth.
16 A faithful friend is a life-saving remedy,
such as he who fears God finds;
17 For he who fears God behaves accordingly,
and his friend will be like himself.

18 My son, from your youth embrace discipline;
thus will you find wisdom with graying hair.

NEW JERUSALEM BIBLE

7 If you want to make a friend, take him on trial,
and do not be in a hurry to trust him;
8 for one kind of friend is so only when it suits him
but will not stand by you in your day of trouble.
9 Another kind of friend will fall out with you
and to your dismay make your quarrel public,
10 and a third kind of friend will share your table,
but not stand by you in your day of trouble:
11 when you are doing well he will be your second self,
ordering your servants about;
12 but, if disaster befalls you, he will recoil from you
and keep out of your way.
13 Keep well clear of your enemies,
and be wary of your friends.
14 A loyal friend is a powerful defence:
whoever finds one has indeed found a treasure.
15 A loyal friend is something beyond price,
there is no measuring his worth.
16 A loyal friend is the elixir of life,
and those who fear the Lord will find one.
17 Whoever fears the Lord makes true friends,
for as a person is, so is his friend too.

18 My child, from your earliest youth choose instruction,
and till your hair is white you will keep finding wisdom.

GREEK OLD TESTAMENT

19 ὡς ὁ ἀροτριῶν καὶ ὁ σπείρων πρόσελθε αὐτῇ
καὶ ἀνάμενε τοὺς ἀγαθοὺς καρποὺς αὐτῆς·
ἐν γὰρ τῇ ἐργασίᾳ αὐτῆς ὀλίγον κοπιάσεις
καὶ ταχὺ φάγεσαι τῶν γενημάτων αὐτῆς.
20 ὡς τραχεῖά ἐστιν σφόδρα τοῖς ἀπαιδεύτοις,
καὶ οὐκ ἐμμενεῖ ἐν αὐτῇ ἀκάρδιος·
21 ὡς λίθος δοκιμασίας ἰσχυρὸς ἔσται ἐπ᾽ αὐτῷ,
καὶ οὐ χρονιεῖ ἀπορρῖψαι αὐτήν.
22 σοφία γὰρ κατὰ τὸ ὄνομα αὐτῆς ἐστιν
καὶ οὐ πολλοῖς ἐστιν φανερά.
23 Ἄκουσον, τέκνον, καὶ ἔκδεξαι γνώμην μου
καὶ μὴ ἀπαναίνου τὴν συμβουλίαν μου·
24 καὶ εἰσένεγκον τοὺς πόδας σου εἰς τὰς πέδας αὐτῆς
καὶ εἰς τὸν κλοιὸν αὐτῆς τὸν τράχηλόν σου·
25 ὑπόθες τὸν ὦμόν σου καὶ βάσταξον αὐτὴν
καὶ μὴ προσοχθίσῃς τοῖς δεσμοῖς αὐτῆς·
26 ἐν πάσῃ ψυχῇ σου πρόσελθε αὐτῇ
καὶ ἐν ὅλῃ δυνάμει σου συντήρησον τὰς ὁδοὺς αὐτῆς·
27 ἐξίχνευσον καὶ ζήτησον, καὶ γνωσθήσεταί σοι,
καὶ ἐγκρατὴς γενόμενος μὴ ἀφῇς αὐτήν·
28 ἐπ᾽ ἐσχάτων γὰρ εὑρήσεις τὴν ἀνάπαυσιν αὐτῆς,
καὶ στραφήσεταί σοι εἰς εὐφροσύνην·
29 καὶ ἔσονταί σοι αἱ πέδαι εἰς σκέπην ἰσχύος
καὶ οἱ κλοιοὶ αὐτῆς εἰς στολὴν δόξης.
30 κόσμος γὰρ χρύσεός ἐστιν ἐπ᾽ αὐτῆς,
καὶ οἱ δεσμοὶ αὐτῆς κλῶσμα ὑακίνθινον·

KING JAMES VERSION

19 Come unto her as one that ploweth and soweth, and wait for her good fruits: for thou shalt not toil much in labouring about her, but thou shalt eat of her fruits right soon.

20 She is very unpleasant to the unlearned: he that is without understanding will not remain with her.

21 She will lie upon him as a mighty stone of trial; and he will cast her from him ere it be long.

22 For wisdom is according to her name, and she is not manifest unto many.

23 Give ear, my son, receive my advice, and refuse not my counsel,

24 And put thy feet into her fetters, and thy neck into her chain.

25 Bow down thy shoulder, and bear her, and be not grieved with her bonds.

26 Come unto her with thy whole heart, and keep her ways with all thy power.

27 Search, and seek, and she shall be made known unto thee: and when thou hast got hold of her, let her not go.

28 For at the last thou shalt find her rest, and that shall be turned to thy joy.

29 Then shall her fetters be a strong defence for thee, and her chains a robe of glory.

30 For there is a golden ornament upon her, and her bands are purple lace.

DOUAY OLD TESTAMENT

19 Come to her as one that plougheth, and soweth, and wait for her good fruits:

20 For in working about her thou shalt labour a little, and shalt quickly eat of her fruits.

21 How very unpleasant is wisdom to the unlearned, and the unwise will not continue with her.

22 She shall be to them as a mighty stone of trial, and they will cast her from them before it be long.

23 For the wisdom of doctrine is according to her name, and she is not manifest unto many, but with them to whom she is known, she continueth even to the sight of God.

24 Give ear, my son, and take wise counsel, and cast not away my advice.

25 Put thy feet into her fetters, and thy neck into her chains:

26 Bow down thy shoulder, and bear her, and be not grieved with her bands.

27 Come to her with all thy mind, and keep her ways with all thy power.

28 Search for her, and she shall be made known to thee, and when thou hast gotten her, let her not go:

29 For in the latter end thou shalt find rest in her, and she shall be turned to thy joy.

30 Then shall her fetters be a strong defence for thee, and a firm foundation, and her chain a robe of glory:

31 For in her is the beauty of life, and her bands are a healthful binding.

KNOX TRANSLATION

against thy grey hairs; 19 ploughman and sower thou must
come to the task, and wait patiently for the harvest; 20 how
light the toil wisdom claims, the fruits of her how soon
enjoyed! 21 Only to undisciplined minds she seems an over-
hard task-mistress; not for long will the fool endure her company; 22 here is a weight (says he) that tries my strength too
much, and away he casts it. 23 The enlightenment which
comes with wisdom is true to its name; known to so few, yet
where men are acquainted with it, it waits to light them into
the presence of God.[a] 24 My son, give good heed to the warnings of experience, do not spurn this counsel of mine.
25 Yield foot of thine to wisdom's fetters, neck of thine to her
collar, 26 shoulder of thine to her yoke; do not chafe at her
bonds. 27 Make her thy whole heart's quest, follow, as best
thou canst, the path she makes known to thee; 28 search,
and thou wilt find her, hold fast, and never let her go; 29 in
good time, thou shalt repose in her, and find her all delight.
30 In time, those fetters of hers shall prove a strong protection, a sure support, that halter of hers a badge of honour
about thy neck; 31 there is life in those trappings, healing

a The Greek text runs, 'Wisdom is true to her name, she is revealed to few', which seems to imply a play upon words quite foreign to Hebrew vocabulary. The Latin version runs literally, 'The wisdom of doctrine is true to its name; it is revealed to few, but for those to whom it is known, it abides even to the sight of God'. There is an accidental resemblance in Hebrew between the noun 'wisdom' and the verb 'to wait'.

TODAY'S ENGLISH VERSION

19 Work as hard to find Wisdom as a farmer works to plow
and plant his fields; then you can expect a good harvest. You
will have to work at it for a while, but you will soon be
enjoying what you have earned. 20 Undisciplined people find
Wisdom's demands too hard and don't have enough determination to meet them. 21 Her requirements are a burden heavier than they are willing to bear, and they quickly lay them
aside. 22 "Discipline" means just that—discipline,[a] and not
many people are able to discipline themselves.
23 My child, listen to me and take my advice. 24 Put
Wisdom's chains around your feet and her yoke around your
neck. 25 Carry her on your shoulder and don't be resentful of
her bonds. 26 Follow Wisdom, and keep to her ways with all
your heart. 27 Go looking for her, and she will reveal herself
to you. Take hold of her and don't let go. 28 Then you will
discover the peace of mind she offers, and she will become
your joy. 29-30 The signs of slavery you wear will become
signs of royal majesty. Her chains will be your protection,

[a] *Hebrew* "Discipline" . . . discipline; *Greek* "Wisdom" . . . wisdom.

NEW REVISED STANDARD VERSION

19 Come to her like one who plows and sows,
and wait for her good harvest.
For when you cultivate her you will toil but little,
and soon you will eat of her produce.
20 She seems very harsh to the undisciplined;
fools cannot remain with her.
21 She will be like a heavy stone to test them,
and they will not delay in casting her aside.
22 For wisdom is like her name;
she is not readily perceived by many.

23 Listen, my child, and accept my judgment;
do not reject my counsel.
24 Put your feet into her fetters,
and your neck into her collar.
25 Bend your shoulders and carry her,
and do not fret under her bonds.
26 Come to her with all your soul,
and keep her ways with all your might.
27 Search out and seek, and she will become known to you;
and when you get hold of her, do not let her go.
28 For at last you will find the rest she gives,
and she will be changed into joy for you.
29 Then her fetters will become for you a strong defense,
and her collar a glorious robe.
30 Her yoke[a] is a golden ornament,
and her bonds a purple cord.

[a] Heb: Gk *Upon her*

NEW AMERICAN BIBLE

19 As though plowing and sowing, draw close to her;
then await her bountiful crops.
20 For in cultivating her you will labor but little,
and soon you will eat of her fruits.
21 How irksome she is to the unruly!
The fool cannot abide her.
22 She will be like a burdensome stone to test him,
and he will not delay in casting her aside.
23 For discipline is like her name,
she is not accessible to many.

24 Listen, my son, and heed my advice;
refuse not my counsel.
25 Put your feet into her fetters,
and your neck under her yoke.
26 Stoop your shoulders and carry her
and be not irked at her bonds.
27 With all your soul draw close to her;
with all your strength keep her ways.
28 Search her out, discover her; seek her and you will find
her.
Then when you have her, do not let her go;
29 Thus will you afterward find rest in her,
and she will become your joy.
30 Her fetters will be your throne of majesty;
her bonds, your purple cord.

NEW JERUSALEM BIBLE

19 Like ploughman and sower, cultivate her
and wait for her fine harvest,
for in tilling her you will toil a little while,
but very soon you will be eating her crops.
20 How very harsh she is to the undisciplined!
The senseless does not stay with her for long:
21 she will weigh as heavily on the senseless as a
touchstone
and such a person will lose no time in throwing her
off;
22 for Wisdom is true to her name,
she is not accessible to many.
23 Listen, my child, and take my advice,
do not reject my counsel:
24 put your feet into her fetters,
and your neck into her collar;
25 offer your shoulder to her burden,
do not be impatient of her bonds;
26 court her with all your soul,
and with all your might keep in her ways;
27 search for her, track her down: she will reveal herself;
once you hold her, do not let her go.
28 For in the end you will find rest in her
and she will take the form of joy for you:
29 her fetters you will find a mighty defence,
her collars, a precious necklace.
30 Her yoke will be a golden ornament,
and her bonds be purple ribbons;

GREEK OLD TESTAMENT

31 στολὴν δόξης ἐνδύσῃ αὐτὴν
καὶ στέφανον ἀγαλλιάματος περιθήσεις σεαυτῷ.
32 Ἐὰν θέλῃς, τέκνον, παιδευθήσῃ,
καὶ ἐὰν ἐπιδῷς τὴν ψυχήν σου, πανοῦργος ἔσῃ·
33 ἐὰν ἀγαπήσῃς ἀκούειν, ἐκδέξῃ,
καὶ ἐὰν κλίνῃς τὸ οὖς σου, σοφὸς ἔσῃ.
34 ἐν πλήθει πρεσβυτέρων στῆθι·
καὶ τίς σοφός; αὐτῷ προσκολλήθητι.
35 πᾶσαν διήγησιν θείαν θέλε ἀκροᾶσθαι,
καὶ παροιμίαι συνέσεως μὴ ἐκφευγέτωσάν σε.
36 ἐὰν ἴδῃς συνετόν, ὄρθριζε πρὸς αὐτόν,
καὶ βαθμοὺς θυρῶν αὐτοῦ ἐκτριβέτω ὁ πούς σου.
37 διανοοῦ ἐν τοῖς προστάγμασιν κυρίου
καὶ ἐν ταῖς ἐντολαῖς αὐτοῦ μελέτα διὰ παντός·
αὐτὸς στηριεῖ τὴν καρδίαν σου,
καὶ ἡ ἐπιθυμία τῆς σοφίας δοθήσεταί σοι.
7 Μὴ ποίει κακά, καὶ οὐ μή σε καταλάβῃ κακόν·
2 ἀπόστηθι ἀπὸ ἀδίκου, καὶ ἐκκλινεῖ ἀπὸ σοῦ.
3 υἱέ, μὴ σπεῖρε ἐπ' αὔλακας ἀδικίας,
καὶ οὐ μὴ θερίσῃς αὐτὰ ἑπταπλασίως.
4 μὴ ζήτει παρὰ κυρίου ἡγεμονίαν
μηδὲ παρὰ βασιλέως καθέδραν δόξης.

KING JAMES VERSION

31 Thou shalt put her on as a robe of honour, and shalt put her about thee as a crown of joy.

32 My son, if thou wilt, thou shalt be taught: and if thou wilt apply thy mind, thou shalt be prudent.

33 If thou love to hear, thou shalt receive understanding: and if thou bow thine ear, thou shalt be wise.

34 Stand in the multitude of the elders; and cleave unto him that is wise.

35 Be willing to hear every godly discourse; and let not the parables of understanding escape thee.

36 And if thou seest a man of understanding, get thee betimes unto him, and let thy foot wear the steps of his door.

37 Let thy mind be upon the ordinances of the Lord, and meditate continually in his commandments: he shall establish thine heart, and give thee wisdom at thine own desire.

7 Do no evil, so shall no harm come unto thee.

2 Depart from the unjust, and iniquity shall turn away from thee.

3 My son, sow not upon the furrows of unrighteousness, and thou shalt not reap them sevenfold.

4 Seek not of the Lord preeminence, neither of the king the seat of honour.

DOUAY OLD TESTAMENT

32 Thou shalt put her on as a robe of glory, and thou shalt set her upon thee as a crown of joy.

33 My son, if thou wilt attend to me, thou shalt learn: and if thou wilt apply thy mind, thou shalt be wise.

34 If thou wilt incline thy ear, thou shalt receive instruction: and if thou love to hear, thou shalt be wise.

35 Stand in the multitude of ancients that are wise, and join thyself from thy heart to their wisdom, that thou mayst hear every discourse of God, and the sayings of praise may not escape thee.

36 And if thou see a man of understanding, go to him early in the morning, and let thy foot wear the steps of his doors.

37 Let thy thoughts be upon the precepts of God, and meditate continually on his commandments: and he will give thee a heart, and the desire of wisdom shall be given to thee.

7 DO no evils, and no evils shall lay hold of thee.

2 Depart from the unjust, and evils shall depart from thee.

3 My son, sow not evils in the furrows of injustice, and thou shalt not reap them sevenfold.

4 Seek not of the Lord a pre-eminence, nor of the king the seat of honour.

KNOX TRANSLATION

virtue in those bonds. 32 Robe is none shall do thee more
honour, crown is none shall rest more radiant on thy brow.
33 My son, mark well and learn, take heed and be wise;
34 here is true knowledge for the listening, here is wisdom if
thou wilt lend an ear. 35 Where older men than thou are met,
and wiser, take thou thy place, and give thy whole heart to
their teaching; old tales of God's wonders thou shalt hear,
and sayings of much renown. 36 A man of discernment if
thou find, wait on him at daybreak, and wear out his doorstep with thy frequent visiting. 37 Think ever upon God's
commandments, and be constant in the following of his will;
be sure he will give thee perseverance, and all thy desire for
wisdom shall be granted thee.

7 Harm if thou do none, harm shall none befall thee;
2 clear of wrong is clear of mishap. 3 What avails it, my
son, to sow in the furrow of mischief, and reap a sevenfold
harvest?
4 Never ask of God high station, or of the king preferment.

TODAY'S ENGLISH VERSION

and you will wear her yoke like a magnificent robe. 31 You
will wear Wisdom like a splendid crown.
32 My child, you can learn if you want to. You can be clever
if you are determined to be. 33 If you are willing to listen,
you will learn and become wise. 34 Go where the old people
are; find someone who is wise, and stay with him. 35 Be
ready to listen when religious people speak, and don't miss
anything that shows insight. 36 If you find someone with
understanding, get up early to call on him; wear out his
doorstep with your visits.
37 Devote all your time to studying the Lord's commands
and thinking about them. He will give you the insight and
wisdom you are looking for.
7 1-2 If you do no wrong, no wrong will ever come to you.
3 Do not plow the ground to plant seeds of injustice; you
may reap a bigger harvest than you expect.
4 Don't ask the Lord for a place of honor or ask the king for

NEW REVISED STANDARD VERSION

31 You will wear her like a glorious robe,
and put her on like a splendid crown.[a]

32 If you are willing, my child, you can be disciplined,
and if you apply yourself you will become clever.
33 If you love to listen you will gain knowledge,
and if you pay attention you will become wise.
34 Stand in the company of the elders.
Who is wise? Attach yourself to such a one.
35 Be ready to listen to every godly discourse,
and let no wise proverbs escape you.
36 If you see an intelligent person, rise early to visit him;
let your foot wear out his doorstep.
37 Reflect on the statutes of the Lord,
and meditate at all times on his commandments.
It is he who will give insight to[b] your mind,
and your desire for wisdom will be granted.

7 Do no evil, and evil will never overtake you.
2 Stay away from wrong, and it will turn away from
you.
3 Do[c] not sow in the furrows of injustice,
and you will not reap a sevenfold crop.

4 Do not seek from the Lord high office,
or the seat of honor from the king.

a Heb: Gk *crown of gladness* b Heb: Gk *will confirm* c Gk *My child, do*

NEW AMERICAN BIBLE

31 You will wear her as your robe of glory,
bear her as your splendid crown.

32 My son, if you wish, you can be taught;
if you apply yourself, you will be shrewd.
33 If you are willing to listen, you will learn;
if you give heed, you will be wise.
34 Frequent the company of the elders;
whoever is wise, stay close to him.
35 Be eager to hear every godly discourse;
let no wise saying escape you.
36 If you see a man of prudence, seek him out;
let your feet wear away his doorstep!
37 Reflect on the precepts of the LORD,
let his commandments be your constant meditation;
Then he will enlighten your mind,
and the wisdom you desire he will grant.

7 Do no evil, and evil will not overtake you;
2 avoid wickedness, and it will turn aside from you.
3 Sow not in the furrows of injustice,
lest you harvest it sevenfold.
4 Seek not from the LORD authority,
nor from the king a place of honor.

NEW JERUSALEM BIBLE

31 you will wear her like a robe of honour,
you will put her on like a crown of joy.
32 If you wish it, my child, you can be taught;
apply yourself, and you will become intelligent.
33 If you love listening, you will learn,
if you pay attention, you will become wise.
34 Attend the gathering of elders;
if there is a wise man there, attach yourself to him.
35 Listen willingly to any discourse coming from God,
do not let wise proverbs escape you.
36 If you see a man of understanding, visit him early,
let your feet wear out his doorstep.
37 Reflect on the injunctions of the Lord,
busy yourself at all times with his commandments.
He will strengthen your mind,
and the wisdom you desire will be granted you.

7 Do no evil, and evil will not befall you;
2 shun wrong, and it will avoid you.
3 My child, do not sow in the furrows of wickedness,
for fear you have to reap them seven times over.

4 Do not ask the Lord for the highest place,
or the king for a seat of honour.

Greek Old Testament

5 μὴ δικαιοῦ ἔναντι κυρίου
καὶ παρὰ βασιλεῖ μὴ σοφίζου.
6 μὴ ζήτει γενέσθαι κριτής,
μὴ οὐκ ἰσχύσεις ἐξᾶραι ἀδικίας,
μήποτε εὐλαβηθῇς ἀπὸ προσώπου δυνάστου
καὶ θήσεις σκάνδαλον ἐν εὐθύτητί σου.
7 μὴ ἁμάρτανε εἰς πλῆθος πόλεως
καὶ μὴ καταβάλῃς σεαυτὸν ἐν ὄχλῳ.
8 μὴ καταδεσμεύσῃς δὶς ἁμαρτίαν·
ἐν γὰρ τῇ μιᾷ οὐκ ἀθῷος ἔσῃ.
9 μὴ εἴπῃς Τῷ πλήθει τῶν δώρων μου ἐπόψεται
καὶ ἐν τῷ προσενέγκαι με θεῷ ὑψίστῳ προσδέξεται.
10 μὴ ὀλιγοψυχήσῃς ἐν τῇ προσευχῇ σου
καὶ ἐλεημοσύνην ποιῆσαι μὴ παρίδῃς.
11 μὴ καταγέλα ἄνθρωπον ὄντα ἐν πικρίᾳ ψυχῆς αὐτοῦ·
ἔστιν γὰρ ὁ ταπεινῶν καὶ ἀνυψῶν.
12 μὴ ἀροτρία ψεῦδος ἐπ᾽ ἀδελφῷ σου
μηδὲ φίλῳ τὸ ὅμοιον ποίει.
13 μὴ θέλε ψεύδεσθαι πᾶν ψεῦδος·
ὁ γὰρ ἐνδελεχισμὸς αὐτοῦ οὐκ εἰς ἀγαθόν.
14 μὴ ἀδολέσχει ἐν πλήθει πρεσβυτέρων
καὶ μὴ δευτερώσῃς λόγον ἐν προσευχῇ σου.
15 μὴ μισήσῃς ἐπίπονον ἐργασίαν
καὶ γεωργίαν ὑπὸ ὑψίστου ἐκτισμένην.

King James Version

5 justify not thyself before the Lord; and boast not of thy wisdom before the king.

6 Seek not to be judge, being not able to take away iniquity; lest at any time thou fear the person of the mighty, and lay a stumblingblock in the way of thy uprightness.

7 Offend not against the multitude of a city, and then thou shalt not cast thyself down among the people.

8 Bind not one sin upon another; for in one thou shalt not be unpunished.

9 Say not, God will look upon the multitude of my oblations, and when I offer to the most high God, he will accept it.

10 Be not fainthearted when thou makest thy prayer, and neglect not to give alms.

11 Laugh no man to scorn in the bitterness of his soul: for there is one which humbleth and exalteth.

12 Devise not a lie against thy brother; neither do the like to thy friend.

13 Use not to make any manner of lie: for the custom thereof is not good.

14 Use not many words in a multitude of elders, and make not much babbling when thou prayest.

15 Hate not laborious work, neither husbandry, which the most High hath ordained.

Douay Old Testament

5 Justify not thyself before God, for he knoweth the heart: and desire not to appear wise before the king.

6 Seek not to be made a judge, unless thou have strength enough to extirpate iniquities: lest thou fear the person of the powerful, and lay a stumblingblock for thy integrity.

7 Offend not against the multitude of a city, neither cast thyself in upon the people,

8 Nor bind sin to sin: for even in one thou shalt not be unpunished.

9 Be not fainthearted in thy mind:

10 Neglect not to pray, and to give alms.

11 Say not: God will have respect to the multitude of my gifts, and when I offer to the most high God, he will accept my offerings.

12 Laugh no man to scorn in the bitterness of his soul: for there is one that humbleth and exalteth, God who seeth all.

13 Devise not a lie against thy brother: neither do the like against thy friend.

14 Be not willing to make any manner of lie: for the custom thereof is not good.

15 Be not full of words in a multitude of ancients, and repeat not the word in thy prayer.

16 Hate not laborious works, nor husbandry ordained by the most High.

Knox Translation

5 Never try to prove thy innocence before God, who knows all, nor thy subtlety before the king.

6 Do not sit in judgement, unless thou art able to crush the wrong; if thou favour the rich, what else is thy award but a snare for thy own virtue?

7 Hurt never the public weal; no need to embroil thyself with thy own neighbours.

8 Never tack sin to sin; for the first thou art in arrears.

9 Do not lose confidence 10 in thy praying, or leave almsgiving undone.

11 Do not flatter thyself that God will look favourably on thy many offerings, as if he, the most High, could not refuse thy gifts.

12 Taunt never the disconsolate; God, who sees all, casts men down and lifts them up.

13 Not against thy own brother trump up the charge; nor thy neighbour either.

14 Every breath of falsehood avoid in thy speech; so ill grows the habit of it.

15 Idle talk becomes thee not, when thou sittest with the elders in council, nor, when thou prayest, repetition of thy prayer.

16 At toil repine not; the farmer's trade is of divine appointment.

TODAY'S ENGLISH VERSION

an important position. 5 Don't try to convince the Lord that
you are righteous or make a show of your wisdom before the
king. 6 Don't set your heart on being a judge, unless you
have the strength of character it takes to put an end to injustice. If you let yourself be influenced by someone in a position of power, your integrity will be damaged. 7 Don't commit any crime against the general public, and don't disgrace
yourself among your townspeople.
8 Don't commit the same sin twice. The punishment you
get the first time ought to be enough.
9 Don't think that God Most High is going to take into
account how very generous you are and so accept any offering you decide to make.
10 Never get tired of praying, and never miss a chance to
give to the poor.
11 Don't laugh at someone who has been humiliated. It is
the Lord who humbles a person, but the Lord also raises him
up again.
12 Don't think up lies to tell about your friends. 13 Don't
tell lies at all. It never does any good.
14 In an official assembly, don't get up and talk a lot of
nonsense. And don't repeat yourself when you pray.
15 Don't try to avoid farm work or other hard labor; the
Most High has given us these jobs to do.

NEW REVISED STANDARD VERSION

5 Do not assert your righteousness before the Lord,
or display your wisdom before the king.
6 Do not seek to become a judge,
or you may be unable to root out injustice;
you may be partial to the powerful,
and so mar your integrity.
7 Commit no offense against the public,
and do not disgrace yourself among the people.

8 Do not commit a sin twice;
not even for one will you go unpunished.
9 Do not say, "He will consider the great number of my
gifts,
and when I make an offering to the Most High God,
he will accept it."
10 Do not grow weary when you pray;
do not neglect to give alms.
11 Do not ridicule a person who is embittered in spirit,
for there is One who humbles and exalts.
12 Do not devise[a] a lie against your brother,
or do the same to a friend.
13 Refuse to utter any lie,
for it is a habit that results in no good.
14 Do not babble in the assembly of the elders,
and do not repeat yourself when you pray.

15 Do not hate hard labor
or farm work, which was created by the Most High.

a Heb: Gk *plow*

NEW AMERICAN BIBLE

5 Parade not your justice before the LORD,
and before the king flaunt not your wisdom.
6 Seek not to become a judge
if you have not strength to root out crime,
Or you will show favor to the ruler
and mar your integrity.
7 Be guilty of no evil before the city's populace,
nor disgrace yourself before the assembly.
8 Do not plot to repeat a sin;
not even for one will you go unpunished.
9 Say not: "He will appreciate my many gifts;
the Most High will accept my offerings."
10 Be not impatient in prayers,
and neglect not the giving of alms.
11 Laugh not at an embittered man;
be mindful of him who exalts and humbles.
12 Plot no mischief against your brother,
nor against your friend and companion.
13 Delight not in telling lie after lie,
for it never results in good.
14 Thrust not yourself into the deliberations of princes,
and repeat not the words of your prayer.
15 Hate not laborious tasks,
nor farming, which was ordained by the Most High.

NEW JERUSALEM BIBLE

5 Do not parade your uprightness before the Lord,
or your wisdom before the king.
6 Do not scheme to be appointed judge,
for fear you should not be strong enough to stamp
out injustice,
for fear of being swayed by someone influential
and so of risking the loss of your integrity.
7 Do not wrong the general body of citizens
and so lower yourself in popular esteem.
8 Do not be drawn to sin twice over,
for you will not go unpunished even once.
9 Do not say, 'God will be impressed by my numerous
offerings;
when I sacrifice to God Most High, he is bound to
accept.'

10 Do not be hesitant in prayer;
do not neglect to give alms.

11 Do not laugh at someone who is sad of heart,
for he who brings low can lift up high.

12 Do not make up lies against your brother,
nor against a friend either.
13 Mind you tell no lies,
for no good can come of it.

14 Do not talk too much at the gathering of elders,
and do not repeat yourself at your prayers.

15 Do not shirk tiring jobs
or farm work, ordained by the Most High.

GREEK OLD TESTAMENT

16 μὴ προσλογίζου σεαυτὸν ἐν πλήθει ἁμαρτωλῶν·
μνήσθητι ὅτι ὀργὴ οὐ χρονιεῖ.
17 ταπείνωσον σφόδρα τὴν ψυχήν σου,
ὅτι ἐκδίκησις ἀσεβοῦς πῦρ καὶ σκώληξ.
18 Μὴ ἀλλάξῃς φίλον ἕνεκεν διαφόρου
μηδὲ ἀδελφὸν γνήσιον ἐν χρυσίῳ Σουφιρ.
19 μὴ ἀστόχει γυναικὸς σοφῆς καὶ ἀγαθῆς·
ἡ γὰρ χάρις αὐτῆς ὑπὲρ τὸ χρυσίον.
20 μὴ κακώσῃς οἰκέτην ἐργαζόμενον ἐν ἀληθείᾳ
μηδὲ μίσθιον διδόντα τὴν ψυχὴν αὐτοῦ·
21 οἰκέτην συνετὸν ἀγαπάτω σου ἡ ψυχή,
μὴ στερήσῃς αὐτὸν ἐλευθερίας.
22 κτήνη σοί ἐστιν; ἐπισκέπτου αὐτά·
καὶ εἰ ἔστιν σοι χρήσιμα, ἐμμενέτω σοι.
23 τέκνα σοί ἐστιν; παίδευσον αὐτὰ
καὶ κάμψον ἐκ νεότητος τὸν τράχηλον αὐτῶν.
24 θυγατέρες σοί εἰσιν; πρόσεχε τῷ σώματι αὐτῶν
καὶ μὴ ἱλαρώσῃς πρὸς αὐτὰς τὸ πρόσωπόν σου.
25 ἔκδου θυγατέρα, καὶ ἔσῃ τετελεκὼς ἔργον μέγα,
καὶ ἀνδρὶ συνετῷ δώρησαι αὐτήν.
26 γυνή σοί ἐστιν κατὰ ψυχήν; μὴ ἐκβάλῃς αὐτήν·
καὶ μισουμένῃ μὴ ἐμπιστεύσῃς σεαυτόν.

KING JAMES VERSION

16 Number not thyself among the multitude of sinners, but remember that wrath will not tarry long.

17 Humble thy soul greatly: for the vengeance of the ungodly is fire and worms.

18 Change not a friend for any good by no means; neither a faithful brother for the gold of Ophir.

19 Forego not a wise and good woman: for her grace is above gold.

20 Whereas thy servant worketh truly, entreat him not evil, nor the hireling that bestoweth himself wholly for thee.

21 Let thy soul love a good servant, and defraud him not of liberty.

22 Hast thou cattle? have an eye to them: and if they be for thy profit, keep them with thee.

23 Hast thou children? instruct them, and bow down their neck from their youth.

24 Hast thou daughters? have a care of their body, and shew not thyself cheerful toward them.

25 Marry thy daughter, and so shalt thou have performed a weighty matter: but give her to a man of understanding.

26 Hast thou a wife after thy mind? forsake her not: but give not thyself over to a light woman.

DOUAY OLD TESTAMENT

17 Number not thyself among the multitude of the disorderly.

18 Remember wrath, for it will not tarry long.

19 Humble thy spirit very much: for the vengeance on the flesh of the ungodly is fire and worms.

20 Do not transgress against thy friend deferring money, nor despise thy dear brother for the sake of gold.

21 Depart not from a wise and good wife, whom thou hast gotten in the fear of the Lord: for the grace of her modesty is above gold.

22 Hurt not the servant that worketh faithfully, nor the hired man that giveth thee his life.

23 Let a wise servant be dear to thee as thy own soul, defraud him not of liberty, nor leave him needy.

24 Hast thou cattle? have an eye to them: and if they be for thy profit, keep them with thee.

25 Hast thou children? instruct them, and bow down their neck from their childhood.

26 Hast thou daughters? have a care of their body, and shew not thy countenance gay towards them.

27 Marry thy daughter *well,* and thou shalt do a great work, and give her to a wise man.

28 If thou hast a wife according to thy soul, cast her not off: and to her that is hateful, trust not thyself. With thy whole heart,

KNOX TRANSLATION

17 When sinners abound, be not thou of their company;
18 bethink thee rather, how swiftly comes vengeance, 19 and
so curb thy unruly spirits; for sinful flesh, fire and worm.
20 Thou hast a friend who is over-long in thy debt; use no
cruelty with him; dear to thee as a brother, and shall gold
count more? 21 Thou hast a good wife, a thrifty woman that
has thrown in her lot, in the fear of the Lord, with thine; do
not leave her; that modesty of hers is a grace gold cannot
buy. 22 The slave that works for thee faithfully, the hireling
that is pledged to thy service, injure not; 23 a thrifty slave
thou shouldst love as thy own self, not baulking him of liberty or leaving him to starve. 24 Cattle thou hast; tend them
well, nor part with them while they do thee good service.
25 Thou hast sons; train them to bear the yoke from their
youth up. 26 Thou hast daughters; keep them chaste, and do
not spoil them with thy smile; 27 a daughter wed is great
good done, if a thrifty husband thou find her. 28 And thy
own wife, if thou lovest her, never do thou forsake, nor trust
thy happiness to one who is little to thy mind.

Today's English Version

16 Don't join up with a crowd of sinners; remember that the
Lord's punishment is sure to come.
17 Be very humble, because the decay of death awaits
us all.[a]
18 Don't betray a friend for money. Don't betray a real
friend for all the gold in the world.
19 Don't miss your chance to marry a wise and good
woman. A gracious wife is worth more than gold.
20 Don't mistreat servants who do their work well, or
employees who do their best for you.
21 Show the same love to wise servants that you would
show to yourself,[b] and let them have their freedom.
22 Take good care of any animals you own. If they make
money for you, keep them.
23 If you have sons, educate them. Teach them self-discipline while they are young.
24 If you have daughters, keep them virtuous, and don't be
too indulgent with them. 25 When you give your daughter in
marriage, you have finished a great task, but give her to a
sensible man.
26 If you have a good wife, do not divorce her, but do not
trust yourself to someone you don't love.

[a] *Hebrew* the decay . . . all; *Greek* the punishment of the ungodly is fire and worms. [b] *Hebrew* Show the same love . . . yourself; *Greek* Show love to a wise servant.

New Revised Standard Version

16 Do not enroll in the ranks of sinners;
remember that retribution does not delay.
17 Humble yourself to the utmost,
for the punishment of the ungodly is fire and worms.[a]

18 Do not exchange a friend for money,
or a real brother for the gold of Ophir.
19 Do not dismiss[b] a wise and good wife,
for her charm is worth more than gold.
20 Do not abuse slaves who work faithfully,
or hired laborers who devote themselves to their task.
21 Let your soul love intelligent slaves;[c]
do not withhold from them their freedom.

22 Do you have cattle? Look after them;
if they are profitable to you, keep them.
23 Do you have children? Discipline them,
and make them obedient[d] from their youth.
24 Do you have daughters? Be concerned for their chastity,[e]
and do not show yourself too indulgent with them.
25 Give a daughter in marriage, and you complete a great task;
but give her to a sensible man.
26 Do you have a wife who pleases you?[f] Do not divorce her;
but do not trust yourself to one whom you detest.

a Heb *for the expectation of mortals is worms* *b* Heb: Gk *deprive yourself of* *c* Heb *Love a wise slave as yourself* *d* Gk *bend their necks* *e* Gk *body* *f* Heb Syr lack *who pleases you*

New American Bible

16 Do not esteem yourself better than your fellows;
remember, his wrath will not delay.
17 More and more, humble your pride;
what awaits man is worms.

18 Barter not a friend for money,
nor a dear brother for the gold of Ophir.
19 Dismiss not a sensible wife;
a gracious wife is more precious than corals.
20 Mistreat not a servant who faithfully serves,
nor a laborer who devotes himself to his task.
21 Let a wise servant be dear to you as your own self;
refuse him not his freedom.
22 If you have livestock, look after them;
if they are dependable, keep them.
23 If you have sons, chastise them;
bend their necks from childhood.
24 If you have daughters, keep them chaste,
and be not indulgent to them.
25 Giving your daughter in marriage ends a great task;
but give her to a worthy man.
26 If you have a wife, let her not seem odious to you;
but where there is ill-feeling, trust her not.

New Jerusalem Bible

16 Do not swell the ranks of sinners,
remember that the retribution will not delay.
17 Be very humble,
since the recompense for the godless is fire and worms.

18 Do not barter a friend away for the sake of profit,
nor a true brother for the gold of Ophir.
19 Do not turn against a wise and good wife;
her gracious presence is worth more than gold.
20 Do not ill-treat a slave who is an honest worker,
or a wage-earner who is devoted to you.
21 Love an intelligent slave with all your heart,
and do not deny such a slave his freedom.
22 Have you cattle? Look after them;
if they are making you a profit, keep them.
23 Have you children? Educate them,
from childhood make them bow the neck.
24 Have you daughters? Take care of their bodies,
but do not be over-indulgent.
25 Marry a daughter off, and you have finished a great work;
but give her to a man of sense.
26 Have you a wife to your liking? Do not turn her out;
but if you do not love her, never trust her.

GREEK OLD TESTAMENT

27 Ἐν ὅλῃ καρδίᾳ σου δόξασον τὸν πατέρα σου
καὶ μητρὸς ὠδῖνας μὴ ἐπιλάθῃ·
28 μνήσθητι ὅτι δι᾽ αὐτῶν ἐγεννήθης,
καὶ τί ἀνταποδώσεις αὐτοῖς καθὼς αὐτοὶ σοί;
29 ἐν ὅλῃ ψυχῇ σου εὐλαβοῦ τὸν κύριον
καὶ τοὺς ἱερεῖς αὐτοῦ θαύμαζε.
30 ἐν ὅλῃ δυνάμει ἀγάπησον τὸν ποιήσαντά σε
καὶ τοὺς λειτουργοὺς αὐτοῦ μὴ ἐγκαταλίπῃς.
31 φοβοῦ τὸν κύριον καὶ δόξασον ἱερέα
καὶ δὸς τὴν μερίδα αὐτῷ, καθὼς ἐντέταλταί σοι,
ἀπαρχὴν καὶ περὶ πλημμελείας καὶ δόσιν βραχιόνων
καὶ θυσίαν ἁγιασμοῦ καὶ ἀπαρχὴν ἁγίων.
32 Καὶ πτωχῷ ἔκτεινον τὴν χεῖρά σου,
ἵνα τελειωθῇ ἡ εὐλογία σου.
33 χάρις δόματος ἔναντι παντὸς ζῶντος,
καὶ ἐπὶ νεκρῷ μὴ ἀποκωλύσῃς χάριν.
34 μὴ ὑστέρει ἀπὸ κλαιόντων
καὶ μετὰ πενθούντων πένθησον.
35 μὴ ὄκνει ἐπισκέπτεσθαι ἄρρωστον ἄνθρωπον·
ἐκ γὰρ τῶν τοιούτων ἀγαπηθήσῃ.
36 ἐν πᾶσι τοῖς λόγοις σου μιμνήσκου τὰ ἔσχατά σου,
καὶ εἰς τὸν αἰῶνα οὐχ ἁμαρτήσεις.

KING JAMES VERSION

27 Honour thy father with thy whole heart, and forget not the sorrows of thy mother.

28 Remember that thou wast begotten of them; and how canst thou recompense them the things that they have done for thee?

29 Fear the Lord with all thy soul, and reverence his priests.

30 Love him that made thee with all thy strength, and forsake not his ministers.

31 Fear the Lord, and honor the priest; and give him his portion, as it is commanded thee; the firstfruits, and the trespass offering, and the gift of the shoulders, and the sacrifice of sanctification, and the firstfruits of the holy things.

32 And stretch thine hand unto the poor, that thy blessing may be perfected.

33 A gift hath grace in the sight of every man living; and for the dead detain it not.

34 Fail not to be with them that weep, and mourn with them that mourn.

35 Be not slow to visit the sick: for that shall make thee to be beloved.

36 Whatsoever thou takest in hand, remember the end, and thou shalt never do amiss.

DOUAY OLD TESTAMENT

29 Honour thy father, and forget not the groanings of thy mother:

30 Remember that thou hadst not been born but through them: and make a return to them as they have done for thee.

31 With all thy soul fear the Lord, and reverence his priests.

32 With all thy strength love him that made thee: and forsake not his ministers.

33 Honour God with all thy soul, and give honour to the priests, and purify thyself with thy arms.

34 Give them their portion, as it is commanded thee, of the firstfruits and of purifications: and for thy negligences purify thyself with a few.

35 Offer to the Lord the gift of thy shoulders, and the sacrifice of sanctification, and the firstfruits of the holy things:

36 And stretch out thy hand to the poor, that thy expiation and thy blessing may be perfected.

37 A gift hath grace in the sight of all the living, and restrain not grace from the dead.

38 Be not wanting in comforting them that weep, and walk with them that mourn.

39 Be not slow to visit the sick: for by these things thou shalt be confirmed in love.

40 In all thy works remember thy last end, and thou shalt never sin.

KNOX TRANSLATION

29 And oh, with thy whole heart honour thy father, nor forget thy mother's pangs; 30 bethink thee, that without them
thou hadst had no being, and repay the service they have
done thee.

31 With all thy soul fear God, and reverence his priests.
32 He made thee; wilt thou not devote all thy powers to his
love? Wilt thou leave his ministers unbefriended? 33 Rather,
with all thy soul fear God, and to his priests give their due;
with gift of the consecrated shoulder clear thyself of what is
owing. 34 The priests must have their share, by law prescribed, of first-fruits and of offering for transgression; even
if thou hast committed a fault in ignorance, a little is claimed
for thy cleansing. 35 The gift of the consecrated shoulder
thou must make to the Lord, and the offering of all that is
dedicated, and the holy first-fruits; 36 moreover, thou must
open thy hand to the poor; so thy atonement shall be perfect,
and perfect thy blessing.

37 No living man but is thankful for the gift given; and it is
ill done to withhold thy favours even from the dead. 38 Fail
not to comfort the distressed, let the mourner have thee for
his escort. 39 Never tire of visiting the sick; no surer way of
winning thy neighbour's love. 40 Remember at all times what
thou must come to at the last, and thou shalt never do
amiss.

TODAY'S ENGLISH VERSION

27 Honor your father with all your heart, and never forget
how your mother suffered when you were born. 28 Remember that you owe your life to them. How can you ever repay
them for all they have done for you?

29 Fear the Lord with all your heart, and have respect for
his priests. 30 Love your Creator with all your strength, and
give his ministers your support. 31 Honor the Lord and
respect the priests. Supply them with what you have been
commanded to give: the first produce, the offering for sin,
the shoulder of the sacrificial animal—all the required sacrifices and offerings.

32 Give your help to the poor, and the Lord will give you
his perfect blessing. 33 Be generous to every living soul, and
be gracious to the memory of the dead. 34 Show sympathy to
those who have lost a loved one, and mourn with them.
35 Do not hesitate to visit the sick. You will be loved for
things like these. 36 Whatever you do, remember that some
day you must die. As long as you keep this in mind, you will
never sin.

NEW REVISED STANDARD VERSION

27 With all your heart honor your father,
and do not forget the birth pangs of your mother.
28 Remember that it was of your parents[a] you were born;
how can you repay what they have given to you?

29 With all your soul fear the Lord,
and revere his priests.
30 With all your might love your Maker,
and do not neglect his ministers.
31 Fear the Lord and honor the priest,
and give him his portion, as you have been
commanded:
the first fruits, the guilt offering, the gift of the shoulders,
the sacrifice of sanctification, and the first fruits of
the holy things.

32 Stretch out your hand to the poor,
so that your blessing may be complete.
33 Give graciously to all the living;
do not withhold kindness even from the dead.
34 Do not avoid those who weep,
but mourn with those who mourn.
35 Do not hesitate to visit the sick,
because for such deeds you will be loved.
36 In all you do, remember the end of your life,
and then you will never sin.

a Gk *them*

NEW AMERICAN BIBLE

27 With your whole heart honor your father;
your mother's birthpangs forget not.
28 Remember, of these parents you were born;
what can you give them for all they gave you?
29 With all your soul, fear God,
revere his priests.
30 With all your strength, love your Creator,
forsake not his ministers.
31 Honor God and respect the priest;
give him his portion as you have been commanded:
First fruits and contributions,
due sacrifices and holy offerings.
32 To the poor man also extend your hand,
that your blessing may be complete;
33 Be generous to all the living,
and withhold not your kindness from the dead.
34 Avoid not those who weep,
but mourn with those who mourn;
35 Neglect not to visit the sick—
for these things you will be loved.
36 In whatever you do, remember your last days,
and you will never sin.

NEW JERUSALEM BIBLE

27 With all your heart honour your father,
never forget the birthpangs of your mother.
28 Remember that you owe your birth to them;
how can you repay them for what they have done for
you?
29 With all your soul, fear the Lord
and revere his priests.
30 With all your might love him who made you,
and do not abandon his ministers.
31 Fear the Lord and honour the priest
and give him the portion enjoined on you:
first-fruits, sacrifice of reparation, shoulder-gift,
sanctification sacrifice, first-fruits of the holy things.
32 And also give generously to the poor,
so that your blessing may lack nothing.
33 Let your generosity extend to all the living,
do not withhold it even from the dead.
34 Do not turn your back on those who weep,
but share the grief of the grief-stricken.
35 Do not shrink from visiting the sick;
in this way you will make yourself loved.
36 In everything you do, remember your end,
and you will never sin.

GREEK OLD TESTAMENT

8 Μὴ διαμάχου μετὰ ἀνθρώπου δυνάστου,
μήποτε ἐμπέσῃς εἰς τὰς χεῖρας αὐτοῦ.
2 μὴ ἔριζε μετὰ ἀνθρώπου πλουσίου,
μήποτε ἀντιστήσῃ σου τὴν ὁλκήν·
πολλοὺς γὰρ ἀπώλεσεν τὸ χρυσίον
καὶ καρδίας βασιλέων ἐξέκλινεν.
3 μὴ διαμάχου μετὰ ἀνθρώπου γλωσσώδους
καὶ μὴ ἐπιστοιβάσῃς ἐπὶ τὸ πῦρ αὐτοῦ ξύλα.
4 μὴ πρόσπαιζε ἀπαιδεύτῳ,
ἵνα μὴ ἀτιμάζωνται οἱ πρόγονοί σου.
5 μὴ ὀνείδιζε ἄνθρωπον ἀποστρέφοντα ἀπὸ ἁμαρτίας·
μνήσθητι ὅτι πάντες ἐσμὲν ἐν ἐπιτίμοις.
6 μὴ ἀτιμάσῃς ἄνθρωπον ἐν γήρᾳ αὐτοῦ·
καὶ γὰρ ἐξ ἡμῶν γηράσκουσιν.
7 μὴ ἐπίχαιρε ἐπὶ νεκρῷ·
μνήσθητι ὅτι πάντες τελευτῶμεν.
8 μὴ παρίδῃς διήγημα σοφῶν
καὶ ἐν ταῖς παροιμίαις αὐτῶν ἀναστρέφου·
ὅτι παρ' αὐτῶν μαθήσῃ παιδείαν
καὶ λειτουργῆσαι μεγιστᾶσιν.
9 μὴ ἀστόχει διηγήματος γερόντων,
καὶ γὰρ αὐτοὶ ἔμαθον παρὰ τῶν πατέρων αὐτῶν·
ὅτι παρ' αὐτῶν μαθήσῃ σύνεσιν
καὶ ἐν καιρῷ χρείας δοῦναι ἀπόκρισιν.

KING JAMES VERSION

8 Strive not with a mighty man, lest thou fall into his hands.

2 Be not at variance with a rich man, lest he overweigh thee: for gold hath destroyed many, and perverted the hearts of kings.

3 Strive not with a man that is full of tongue, and heap not wood upon his fire.

4 Jest not with a rude man, lest thy ancestors be disgraced.

5 Reproach not a man that turneth from sin, but remember that we are all worthy of punishment.

6 Dishonour not a man in his old age: for even some of us wax old.

7 Rejoice not over thy greatest enemy being dead, but remember that we die all.

8 Despise not the discourse of the wise, but acquaint thyself with their proverbs: for of them thou shalt learn instruction, and how to serve great men with ease.

9 Miss not the discourse of the elders: for they also learned of their fathers, and of them thou shalt learn understanding, and to give answer as need requireth.

DOUAY OLD TESTAMENT

8 STRIVE not with a powerful man, lest thou fall into his hands.

2 Contend not with a rich man, lest he bring an action against thee.

3 For gold and silver hath destroyed many, and hath reached even to the heart of kings, and perverted them.

4 Strive not with a man that is full of tongue, and heap not wood upon his fire.

5 Communicate not with an ignorant man, lest he speak ill of thy family.

6 Despise not a man that turneth away from sin, nor reproach him therewith: remember that we are all worthy of reproof.

7 Despise not a man in his old age; for we also shall become old.

8 Rejoice not at the death of thy enemy; knowing that we all die, and are not willing that others should rejoice at our death.

9 Despise not the discourse of them that are ancient and wise, but acquaint thyself with their proverbs.

10 For of them thou shalt learn wisdom, and instruction of understanding, and to serve great men without blame.

11 Let not the discourse of the ancients escape thee, for they have learned of their fathers:

12 For of them thou shalt learn understanding, and to give an answer in time of need.

KNOX TRANSLATION

8 If quarrel thou hast, let it not be with a prince, that may
attach thy person; 2 nor with a rich man, that may
implead thee, 3 with all the power there is in silver and gold
to corrupt men, and sway even the hearts of kings; 4 nor
with a glib talker; thou dost but add fuel to his fire.
5 Be not familiar with a boor; thou wilt hear no good of thy
ancestry.
6 Scorn not the sinner that would amend his ways;
reproach comes amiss, where all stand in need of correction.
7 Nor fail in respect for the aged; it is of our stuff grey hairs
are made.[a] 8 Rejoice not over thy neighbour's death; we all
die, and would not have men rejoice over it. 9 Do not be contemptuous of what older and wiser men have to tell thee; by
their lore live thou, 10 if wise thou wouldst be, and have the
secret of discernment, and live contentedly in the service of
the great. 11 Do not let them pass thee by, these traditions
older men have inherited from their fathers; 12 they will turn
thee into a man of judgement, that answer can make when
answer is needed.

a Literally, 'men grow old out of (people like) us'.

TODAY'S ENGLISH VERSION

8 Do not challenge a person who has influence; you may
fall into his power. 2 Do not quarrel with someone rich;
he may bribe people to turn against you. Gold has destroyed
many people and corrupted kings. 3 Don't argue with someone who talks too much; you will just be adding fuel to his
fire. 4 Don't make fun of someone who has bad manners; he
may insult your ancestors. 5 Don't criticize someone if he is
already turning away from sin. Remember that we are all
guilty. 6 Never think less of someone because he is old; some
of us are growing old, too. 7 Don't be happy over the death
of anyone; remember that all of us must die.

8 Do not disregard what the wise have said. Study their
proverbs; from them you can learn to be cultured and to
serve great people. 9 Pay attention to what old people say,
for they learned from those who came before them. You can
learn from them, and they can teach you how to have an
answer ready when you need one.

NEW REVISED STANDARD VERSION

8 Do not contend with the powerful,
or you may fall into their hands.
2 Do not quarrel with the rich,
in case their resources outweigh yours;
for gold has ruined many,
and has perverted the minds of kings.
3 Do not argue with the loud of mouth,
and do not heap wood on their fire.

4 Do not make fun of one who is ill-bred,
or your ancestors may be insulted.
5 Do not reproach one who is turning away from sin;
remember that we all deserve punishment.
6 Do not disdain one who is old,
for some of us are also growing old.
7 Do not rejoice over anyone's death;
remember that we must all die.

8 Do not slight the discourse of the sages,
but busy yourself with their maxims;
because from them you will learn discipline
and how to serve princes.
9 Do not ignore the discourse of the aged,
for they themselves learned from their parents;[a]
from them you learn how to understand
and to give an answer when the need arises.

a Or *ancestors*

NEW AMERICAN BIBLE

8 Contend not with an influential man,
lest you fall into his power.
2 Quarrel not with a rich man,
lest he pay out the price of your downfall;
For gold has dazzled many,
and perverts the character of princes.
3 Dispute not with a man of railing speech,
heap no wood upon his fire.
4 Be not too familiar with an unruly man,
lest he speak ill of your forebears.
5 Shame not a repentant sinner;
remember, we all are guilty.
6 Insult no man when he is old,
for some of us, too, will grow old.
7 Rejoice not when a man dies;
remember, we are all to die.
8 Spurn not the discourse of the wise,
but acquaint yourself with their proverbs;
From them you will acquire the training
to serve in the presence of princes.
9 Reject not the tradition of old men
which they have learned from their fathers;
From it you will obtain the knowledge
how to answer in time of need.

NEW JERUSALEM BIBLE

8 Do not try conclusions with anyone influential,
in case you later fall into his clutches.
2 Do not quarrel with anyone rich,
in case he puts his weight against you;
for gold has destroyed many,
and has swayed the hearts of kings.
3 Do not argue with anyone argumentative,
do not pile wood on that fire.
4 Do not joke with anyone uncouth,
for fear of hearing your ancestors insulted.
5 Do not revile a repentant sinner;
remember that we all are guilty.
6 Do not despise anyone in old age;
after all, some of us too are growing old.
7 Do not gloat over anyone's death;
remember that we all have to die.

8 Do not scorn the discourse of the wise,
but make yourself familiar with their maxims,
since from these you will learn the theory
and the art of serving the great.
9 Do not dismiss what the old people have to say,
for they too were taught by their parents;
from them you will learn how to think,
and the art of the timely answer.

GREEK OLD TESTAMENT

10 μὴ ἔκκαιε ἄνθρακας ἁμαρτωλοῦ,
μὴ ἐμπυρισθῇς ἐν πυρὶ φλογὸς αὐτοῦ.
11 μὴ ἐξαναστῇς ἀπὸ προσώπου ὑβριστοῦ,
ἵνα μὴ ἐγκαθίσῃ ὡς ἔνεδρον τῷ στόματί σου.
12 μὴ δανείσῃς ἀνθρώπῳ ἰσχυροτέρῳ σου·
καὶ ἐὰν δανείσῃς, ὡς ἀπολωλεκὼς γίνου.
13 μὴ ἐγγυήσῃ ὑπὲρ δύναμίν σου·
καὶ ἐὰν ἐγγυήσῃ, ὡς ἀποτείσων φρόντιζε.
14 μὴ δικάζου μετὰ κριτοῦ·
κατὰ γὰρ τὴν δόξαν αὐτοῦ κρινοῦσιν αὐτῷ.
15 μετὰ τολμηροῦ μὴ πορεύου ἐν ὁδῷ,
ἵνα μὴ βαρύνηται κατὰ σοῦ·
αὐτὸς γὰρ κατὰ τὸ θέλημα αὐτοῦ ποιήσει,
καὶ τῇ ἀφροσύνῃ αὐτοῦ συναπολῇ.
16 μετὰ θυμώδους μὴ ποιήσῃς μάχην
καὶ μὴ διαπορεύου μετ᾽ αὐτοῦ τὴν ἔρημον·
ὅτι ὡς οὐδὲν ἐν ὀφθαλμοῖς αὐτοῦ αἷμα,
καὶ ὅπου οὐκ ἔστιν βοήθεια, καταβαλεῖ σε.
17 μετὰ μωροῦ μὴ συμβουλεύου·
οὐ γὰρ δυνήσεται λόγον στέξαι.
18 ἐνώπιον ἀλλοτρίου μὴ ποιήσῃς κρυπτόν·
οὐ γὰρ γινώσκεις τί τέξεται.
19 παντὶ ἀνθρώπῳ μὴ ἔκφαινε σὴν καρδίαν,
καὶ μὴ ἀναφερέτω σοι χάριν.

KING JAMES VERSION

10 Kindle not the coals of a sinner, lest thou be burnt with the flame of his fire.

11 Rise not up [in anger] at the presence of an injurious person, lest he lie in wait to entrap thee in thy words.

12 Lend not unto him that is mightier than thyself; for if thou lendest him, count it but lost.

13 Be not surety above thy power: for if thou be surety, take care to pay it.

14 Go not to law with a judge; for they will judge for him according to his honour.

15 Travel not by the way with a bold fellow, lest he become grievous unto thee: for he will do according to his own will, and thou shalt perish with him through his folly.

16 Strive not with an angry man, and go not with him into a solitary place: for blood is as nothing in his sight; and where there is no help, he will overthrow thee.

17 Consult not with a fool; for he cannot keep counsel.

18 Do no secret thing before a stranger; for thou knowest not what he will bring forth.

19 Open not thine heart to every man, lest he requite thee with a shrewd turn.

DOUAY OLD TESTAMENT

13 Kindle not the coals of sinners by rebuking them, lest thou be burnt with the flame of the fire of their sins.

14 Stand not against the face of an injurious person, lest he sit as a spy to entrap thee in thy words.

15 Lend not to a man that is mightier than thyself: and if thou lendest, count it as lost.

16 Be not surety above thy power: and if thou be surety, think as if thou wert to pay it.

17 Judge not against a judge: for he judgeth according to that which is just.

18 Go not on the way with a bold man, lest he burden thee with his evils: for he goeth according to his own will, and thou shalt perish together with his folly.

19 Quarrel not with a passionate man, and go not into the desert with a bold man: for blood is as nothing in his sight, and where there is no help he will overthrow thee.

20 Advise not with fools, for thy cannot love but such things as please them.

21 Before a stranger do no matter of counsel: for thou knowest not what he will bring forth.

22 Open not thy heart to every man: lest he repay thee with an evil turn, and speak reproachfully to thee.

KNOX TRANSLATION

13 Wouldst thou remonstrate with a sinner? Make sure thou art not fanning the flame of his passions, thyself in peril of a scorching.

14 Wouldst thou make reply to the railing accuser? Make sure he is not baiting a trap to ensnare thee.

15 Lend to one who can master thee? Then lent is lost.
16 Pledge not thyself beyond thy means; count ever thy
pledge forfeit. 17 Dispute not a judge's award; who judges by
right rule if not he? 18 Travel not with a rash companion, if
thou wouldst not shoulder all his misfortune; he will go his
own way, and thou share the reward of his folly. 19 Quarrel
not with a man of quick moods; on a desert road he is no
companion for thee; he cares nothing for bloodshed, and will
lay thee in the dust when none is by to aid thee. 20 Take not
counsel with a fool; he knows none but his own way of it.
21 Share not thy secret plans with a stranger; thou knowest
not what trouble he may breed. 22 Never open to any man
thy whole heart; an ill requital he may make, by bringing
shame on thee.

TODAY'S ENGLISH VERSION

10 You should not provide a sinner with more opportunity
to sin. You might get hurt yourself; it's as easy as getting
burned while adding logs to a fire. 11 You should not get up
and walk out on someone who is insolent. He might twist
your words and use them against you. 12 You should not
lend anything to someone more powerful than you. If you
do, you might as well consider it lost. 13 You should not
guarantee anyone else's loan to an extent that you cannot
afford. You must be prepared to pay any such guarantee.
14 You should not bring a lawsuit against a judge. He will
win because of his position. 15 You should not travel with
anyone who is reckless. It will cause you nothing but trouble. He will do any foolish thing he pleases, and you will die
with him.
16 You should not get into an argument with anyone who
has a hot temper or go to some place where the two of you
will be alone. Violence means nothing to such a person, and
he will attack you when there is no one to help you. 17 You
should not ask a stupid person for advice. He will not be able
to keep secret what you tell him. 18 You should not do anything in front of a stranger that should be kept secret. There
is no way of knowing what will happen if you do. 19 You
should not reveal your most private thoughts to anyone. If
you do, you may as well throw away any chance of happiness.[a]

[a] *Hebrew* If . . . happiness; *Greek* And don't let anyone do you a favor.

NEW REVISED STANDARD VERSION

10 Do not kindle the coals of sinners,
or you may be burned in their flaming fire.
11 Do not let the insolent bring you to your feet,
or they may lie in ambush against your words.
12 Do not lend to one who is stronger than you;
but if you do lend anything, count it as a loss.
13 Do not give surety beyond your means;
but if you give surety, be prepared to pay.

14 Do not go to law against a judge,
for the decision will favor him because of his standing.
15 Do not go traveling with the reckless,
or they will be burdensome to you;
for they will act as they please,
and through their folly you will perish with them.
16 Do not pick a fight with the quick-tempered,
and do not journey with them through lonely country,
because bloodshed means nothing to them,
and where no help is at hand, they will strike you
down.
17 Do not consult with fools,
for they cannot keep a secret.
18 In the presence of strangers do nothing that is to be
kept secret,
for you do not know what they will divulge.[a]
19 Do not reveal your thoughts to anyone,
or you may drive away your happiness.[b]

[a] Or *it will bring forth* [b] Heb: Gk *and let him not return a favor to you*

NEW AMERICAN BIBLE

10 Kindle not the coals of a sinner,
lest you be consumed in his flaming fire.
11 Let not the impious man intimidate you;
it will set him in ambush against you.
12 Lend not to one more powerful than yourself;
and whatever you lend, count it as lost.
13 Go not surety beyond your means;
think any pledge a debt you must pay.
14 Contend not at law with a judge,
for he will settle it according to his whim.
15 Travel not with a ruthless man,
lest he weigh you down with calamity;
For he will go his own way straight,
and through his folly you will perish with him.
16 Provoke no quarrel with a quick-tempered man
nor ride with him through the desert;
For bloodshed is nothing to him;
when there is no one to help you, he will destroy you.
17 Take no counsel with a fool,
for he can keep nothing to himself.
18 Before a stranger do nothing that should be kept secret,
for you know not what it will engender.
19 Open your heart to no man,
and banish not your happiness.

NEW JERUSALEM BIBLE

10 Do not kindle the coals of the sinner,
in case you scorch yourself in his blaze.
11 Refuse to be provoked by the insolent,
for fear that such a one try to trap you in your words.
12 Do not lend to anyone who is stronger than you are—
if you do lend, resign yourself to loss.
13 Do not stand surety beyond your means;
if you do stand surety, be prepared to pay up.
14 Do not go to law with a judge,
since judgement will be given in his favour.
15 Do not go travelling with a rash man,
for fear he becomes burdensome to you;
he will act as the whim takes him,
and you will both be ruined by his folly.
16 Do not argue with a quick-tempered man,
do not go with him where there are no other people,
since blood counts for nothing in his eyes,
and where no help is to be had, he will strike you
down.
17 Do not ask a fool for advice,
since a fool will not be able to keep a confidence.
18 In a stranger's presence do nothing that should be kept
secret,
since you cannot tell what use the stranger will make
of it.
19 Do not open your heart to all comers,
nor lay claim to their good offices.

GREEK OLD TESTAMENT

9 Μὴ ζήλου γυναῖκα τοῦ κόλπου σου
μηδὲ διδάξῃς ἐπὶ σεαυτὸν παιδείαν πονηράν.
2 μὴ δῷς γυναικὶ τὴν ψυχήν σου
ἐπιβῆναι αὐτὴν ἐπὶ τὴν ἰσχύν σου.
3 μὴ ὑπάντα γυναικὶ ἑταιριζομένῃ,
μήποτε ἐμπέσῃς εἰς τὰς παγίδας αὐτῆς.
4 μετὰ ψαλλούσης μὴ ἐνδελέχιζε,
μήποτε ἁλῷς ἐν τοῖς ἐπιχειρήμασιν αὐτῆς.
5 παρθένον μὴ καταμάνθανε,
μήποτε σκανδαλισθῇς ἐν τοῖς ἐπιτιμίοις αὐτῆς.
6 μὴ δῷς πόρναις τὴν ψυχήν σου,
ἵνα μὴ ἀπολέσῃς τὴν κληρονομίαν σου.
7 μὴ περιβλέπου ἐν ῥύμαις πόλεως
καὶ ἐν ταῖς ἐρήμοις αὐτῆς μὴ πλανῶ.
8 ἀπόστρεψον ὀφθαλμὸν ἀπὸ γυναικὸς εὐμόρφου
καὶ μὴ καταμάνθανε κάλλος ἀλλότριον·
ἐν κάλλει γυναικὸς πολλοὶ ἐπλανήθησαν,
καὶ ἐκ τούτου φιλία ὡς πῦρ ἀνακαίεται.
9 μετὰ ὑπάνδρου γυναικὸς μὴ κάθου τὸ σύνολον
καὶ μὴ συμβολοκοπήσῃς μετ᾽ αὐτῆς ἐν οἴνῳ,
μήποτε ἐκκλίνῃ ἡ ψυχή σου ἐπ᾽ αὐτὴν
καὶ τῷ πνεύματί σου ὀλίσθῃς εἰς ἀπώλειαν.
10 Μὴ ἐγκαταλίπῃς φίλον ἀρχαῖον,
ὁ γὰρ πρόσφατος οὐκ ἔστιν ἔφισος αὐτῷ·
οἶνος νέος φίλος νέος·
ἐὰν παλαιωθῇ, μετ᾽ εὐφροσύνης πίεσαι αὐτόν.

KING JAMES VERSION

9 Be not jealous over the wife of thy bosom, and teach her not an evil lesson against thyself.

2 Give not thy soul unto a woman to set her foot upon thy substance.

3 Meet not with an harlot, lest thou fall into her snares.

4 Use not much the company of a woman that is a singer, lest thou be taken with her attempts.

5 Gaze not on a maid, that thou fall not by those things that are precious in her.

6 Give not thy soul unto harlots, that thou lose not thine inheritance.

7 Look not round about thee in the streets of the city, neither wander thou in the solitary places thereof.

8 Turn away thine eye from a beautiful woman, and look not upon another's beauty; for many have been deceived by the beauty of a woman; for herewith love is kindled as a fire.

9 Sit not at all with another man's wife, nor sit down with her in thine arms, and spend not thy money with her at the wine; lest thine heart incline unto her, and so through thy desire thou fall into destruction.

10 Forsake not an old friend; for the new is not comparable to him: a new friend is as new wine; when it is old, thou shalt drink it with pleasure.

DOUAY OLD TESTAMENT

9 BE not jealous over the wife of thy bosom, lest she shew in thy regard the malice of a wicked lesson.

2 Give not the power of thy soul to a woman, lest she enter upon thy strength, and thou be confounded.

3 Look not upon a woman that hath a mind for many: lest thou fall into her snares.

4 Use not much the company of her that is a dancer, and hearken not to her, lest thou perish by the force of her charms.

5 Gaze not upon a maiden, lest her beauty be a stumblingblock to thee.

6 Give not thy soul to harlots in any point: lest thou destroy thyself and thy inheritance.

7 Look not round about thee in the ways of the city, nor wander up and down in the streets thereof.

8 Turn away thy face from a woman dressed up, and gaze not about upon another's beauty.

9 For many have perished by the beauty of a woman, and hereby lust is enkindled as a fire.

10 Every woman that is a harlot, shall be trodden upon as dung in the way.

11 Many by admiring the beauty of another man's wife, have become reprobate, for her conversation burneth as fire.

12 Sit not at all with another man's wife, nor repose upon the bed with her:

13 And strive not with her over wine, lest thy heart decline towards her, and by thy blood thou fall into destruction.

14 Forsake not an old friend, for the new will not be like to him.

15 A new friend is as new wine: it shall grow old, and thou shalt drink it with pleasure.

KNOX TRANSLATION

9 Never shew thyself a jealous husband to the wife thou
lovest; it may prove thou hast taught her, to thy cost, a
ruinous lesson. 2 Never give thy soul into a woman's power,
and let her command the fortress of it, to thy shame. 3 Never
turn to look at the wanton, that would catch thee in her
snare, 4 nor spend thy attentions upon some dancing
woman, that has power to be thy undoing; 5 nor let thy eyes
linger on a maid unwed, whose very beauty may take thee
unawares. 6 And for harlots, let nothing tempt thee to give
way to them, as life and patrimony thou holdest dear; 7 look
not round thee in the city streets, nor haunt the alley-ways.
8 From a woman bravely decked out turn away; have no eyes
for her beauty that is none of thine. 9 Woman's beauty has
been the ruin of many ere now, a spark to light the flame of
lust. 10 A harlot? Then trample her down like mire in thy
path. 11 The love of stolen sweets has been the undoing of
many; a word with her, and the spark is lit. 12 Sit down
never with a wedded wife, nor lean thy elbow upon table of
hers, 13 nor bandy words with her over the wine; steal she
thy heart away, thy life is forfeit.
14 An old friend leave not; the new is not his like. 15 New
friendship, new wine; it must ripen ere thou canst love the
taste of it.

TODAY'S ENGLISH VERSION

9 Don't be jealous of the wife you love. You will only be
teaching her how to do you harm. 2 Do not surrender
your dignity to any woman. 3 Keep away from other men's
wives[a] or they will trap you. 4 Don't keep company with
female musicians; they will trick you. 5 Don't look too
intently at a virgin, or you may find yourself forced to pay a
bride price. 6 Don't give yourself to prostitutes, or you may
lose everything you own. 7 So don't go looking about in the
streets or wandering around in the run-down parts of town.
8 When you see a good-looking woman, look the other way;
don't let your mind dwell on the beauty of any woman who
is not your wife. Many men have been led astray by a woman's beauty. It kindles passion as if it were fire. 9 Don't sit
down to eat with another man's wife or join her for a drink.
You may give in to the temptation of her charms and be
destroyed by your passion.
10 Never abandon old friends; you will never find a new
one who can take their place. Friendship is like wine; it gets

[a] *Hebrew* other men's wives; *Greek* immoral women.

NEW REVISED STANDARD VERSION

9 Do not be jealous of the wife of your bosom,
or you will teach her an evil lesson to your own hurt.
2 Do not give yourself to a woman
and let her trample down your strength.
3 Do not go near a loose woman,
or you will fall into her snares.
4 Do not dally with a singing girl,
or you will be caught by her tricks.
5 Do not look intently at a virgin,
or you may stumble and incur penalties for her.
6 Do not give yourself to prostitutes,
or you may lose your inheritance.
7 Do not look around in the streets of a city,
or wander about in its deserted sections.
8 Turn away your eyes from a shapely woman,
and do not gaze at beauty belonging to another;
many have been seduced by a woman's beauty,
and by it passion is kindled like a fire.
9 Never dine with another man's wife,
or revel with her at wine;
or your heart may turn aside to her,
and in blood[a] you may be plunged into destruction.

10 Do not abandon old friends,
for new ones cannot equal them.
A new friend is like new wine;
when it has aged, you can drink it with pleasure.

a Heb: Gk *by your spirit*

NEW AMERICAN BIBLE

9 Be not jealous of the wife of your bosom,
lest you teach her to do evil against you.
2 Give no woman power over you
to trample upon your dignity.
3 Be not intimate with a strange woman,
lest you fall into her snares.
4 With a singing girl be not familiar,
lest you be caught in her wiles.
5 Entertain no thoughts against a virgin,
lest you be enmeshed in damages for her.
6 Give not yourself to harlots,
lest you surrender your inheritance.
7 Gaze not about the lanes of the city
and wander not through its squares;
8 Avert your eyes from a comely woman;
gaze not upon the beauty of another's wife—
Through woman's beauty many perish,
for lust for it burns like fire.
9 With a married woman dine not,
recline not at table to drink by her side,
Lest your heart be drawn to her
and you go down in blood to the grave.

10 Discard not an old friend,
for the new one cannot equal him.
A new friend is like new wine
which you drink with pleasure only when it has
aged.

NEW JERUSALEM BIBLE

9 Do not be jealous of the wife you love,
do not teach her lessons in how to harm you.
2 Do not put yourself in a woman's hands
or she may come to dominate you completely.
3 Do not keep company with a prostitute,
in case you get entangled in her snares.
4 Do not dally with a singing girl,
in case you get caught by her wiles.
5 Do not stare at a pretty girl,
in case you and she incur the same punishment.
6 Do not give your heart to whores,
or you will ruin your inheritance.
7 Keep your eyes to yourself in the streets of a town,
do not prowl about its unfrequented quarters.
8 Turn your eyes away from a handsome woman,
do not stare at a beauty belonging to someone else.
Because of a woman's beauty, many have been undone;
this makes passion flare up like a fire.
9 Never sit down with a married woman,
or sit at table with her drinking wine,
in case you let your heart succumb to her
and you lose all self-control and slide to disaster.

10 Do not desert an old friend;
the new one will not be his match.
New friend, new wine;
when it grows old, you drink it with pleasure.

GREEK OLD TESTAMENT

11 μὴ ζηλώσῃς δόξαν ἁμαρτωλοῦ·
οὐ γὰρ οἶδας τί ἔσται ἡ καταστροφὴ αὐτοῦ.
12 μὴ εὐδοκήσῃς ἐν εὐδοκίᾳ ἀσεβῶν·
μνήσθητι ὅτι ἕως ᾅδου οὐ μὴ δικαιωθῶσιν.
13 μακρὰν ἄπεχε ἀπὸ ἀνθρώπου, ὃς ἔχει ἐξουσίαν τοῦ φονεύειν,
καὶ οὐ μὴ ὑποπτεύσῃς φόβον θανάτου·
κἂν προσέλθῃς, μὴ πλημμελήσῃς,
ἵνα μὴ ἀφέληται τὴν ζωήν σου·
ἐπίγνωθι ὅτι ἐν μέσῳ παγίδων διαβαίνεις
καὶ ἐπὶ ἐπάλξεων πόλεως περιπατεῖς.
14 κατὰ τὴν ἰσχύν σου στόχασαι τοὺς πλησίον
καὶ μετὰ σοφῶν συμβουλεύου.
15 μετὰ συνετῶν ἔστω ὁ διαλογισμός σου
καὶ πᾶσα διήγησίς σου ἐν νόμῳ ὑψίστου.
16 ἄνδρες δίκαιοι ἔστωσαν σύνδειπνοί σου,
καὶ ἐν φόβῳ κυρίου ἔστω τὸ καύχημά σου.
17 ἐν χειρὶ τεχνιτῶν ἔργον ἐπαινεσθήσεται,
καὶ ὁ ἡγούμενος λαοῦ σοφὸς ἐν λόγῳ αὐτοῦ.
18 φοβερὸς ἐν πόλει αὐτοῦ ἀνὴρ γλωσσώδης,
καὶ ὁ προπετὴς ἐν λόγῳ αὐτοῦ μισηθήσεται.

10 Κριτὴς σοφὸς παιδεύσει τὸν λαὸν αὐτοῦ,
καὶ ἡγεμονία συνετοῦ τεταγμένη ἔσται.

KING JAMES VERSION

11 Envy not the glory of a sinner: for thou knowest not what shall be his end.

12 Delight not in the thing that the ungodly have pleasure in; but remember they shall not go unpunished unto their grave.

13 Keep thee far from the man that hath power to kill; so shalt thou not doubt the fear of death: and if thou come unto him, make no fault, lest he take away thy life presently: remember that thou goest in the midst of snares, and that thou walkest upon the battlements of the city.

14 As near as thou canst, guess at thy neighbour, and consult with the wise.

15 Let thy talk be with the wise, and all thy communication in the law of the most High.

16 And let just men eat and drink with thee; and let thy glorying be in the fear of the Lord.

17 For the hand of the artificer the work shall be commended: and the wise ruler of the people for his speech.

18 A man of an ill tongue is dangerous in his city; and he that is rash in his talk shall be hated.

10 A wise judge will instruct his people; and the government of a prudent man is well ordered.

DOUAY OLD TESTAMENT

16 Envy not the glory and riches of a sinner: for thou knowest not what his ruin shall be.

17 Be not pleased with the wrong done by the unjust, knowing that even to hell the wicked shall not please.

18 Keep thee far from the man that hath power to kill, so thou shalt not suspect the fear of death.

19 And if thou come to him, commit no fault, lest he take away thy life.

20 Know it to be a communication with death: for thou art going in the midst of snares, and walking upon the arms of them that are grieved:

21 According to thy power beware of thy neighbour, and treat with the wise and prudent.

22 Let just men be thy guests, and let thy glory be in the fear of God.

23 And let the thought of God be in thy mind, and all thy discourse on the commandments of the Highest.

24 Works shall be praised for the hand of the artificers, and the prince of the people for the wisdom of his speech, but the word of the ancients for the sense.

25 A man full of tongue is terrible in his city, and he that is rash in his word shall be hateful.

10 A WISE judge shall judge his people, and the government of a prudent man shall be steady.

KNOX TRANSLATION

16 Envy not the wrong-doer his wealth and state; beyond
all expectation of thine it shall come to ruin. 17 Of his ill-gotten gains have neither love nor liking; be sure he will not die
unpunished.
18 From one that has the power of life and death keep thy
distance; so thou shalt be free from mortal alarms. 19 If dealings thou hast with him, keep clear of all offence, or thou
shalt pay for it with thy life. 20 Death has become thy familiar; pit-falls encompass thy path; thou art making the rounds
of a beleaguered city.[a]
21 Consider, as best thou mayest, thy company; be wise
and prudent men thy counsellors; 22 honest men thy guests.
23 Be the fear of God all thy boast, the thought of God all
thy thinking, the commandments of the most High all the
matter of thy discourse.
24 By skilful handiwork the artist is known, the ruler of a
people by the prudence of his counsel, the good sense of the
aged by their word spoken.
25 No such peril to a city as a great talker; for his rash
utterance, no man so well hated as he.
10 A wise ruler, a folk well disciplined; firm sits prudence on the throne. 2 Like king, like court; like

a This seems to be the meaning of the Greek, although the text is perhaps corrupt. The Latin gives no good sense: 'Thou wilt be walking on the weapons of grieving men'.

TODAY'S ENGLISH VERSION

better as it grows older. 11 Don't be jealous of a sinner's success; you don't know what kind of disaster is in store for
him. 12 Don't take pleasure in the things that make ungodly
people happy; remember that they will be held guilty as long
as they live. 13 If you keep away from someone who has the
power to put you to death, you will not have to fear for your
life; but if you must go near him, be very careful, or he may
kill you. Be conscious that you are walking among hidden
traps, that you are an easy target.
14 Get to know the people around you as well as you can,
and take advice only from those who are qualified to give it.
15 Engage in conversation with intelligent people, and let the
Law of the Most High be the topic of your discussions.
16 Choose righteous people for your dinner companions. Your
chief pride should be your fear of the Lord.
17 A skilled worker is admired for the things he makes, and
a leader's wisdom is proved by his words. 18 Someone who
speaks rashly and recklessly is feared and hated by everyone
10 in town. 1 A wise ruler will educate his people, and
his government will be orderly. 2 All the officials and

NEW REVISED STANDARD VERSION

11 Do not envy the success of sinners,
for you do not know what their end will be like.
12 Do not delight in what pleases the ungodly;
remember that they will not be held guiltless all their lives.

13 Keep far from those who have power to kill,
and you will not be haunted by the fear of death.
But if you approach them, make no misstep,
or they may rob you of your life.
Know that you are stepping among snares,
and that you are walking on the city battlements.

14 As much as you can, aim to know your neighbors,
and consult with the wise.
15 Let your conversation be with intelligent people,
and let all your discussion be about the law of the Most High.
16 Let the righteous be your dinner companions,
and let your glory be in the fear of the Lord.

17 A work is praised for the skill of the artisan;
so a people's leader is proved wise by his words.
18 The loud of mouth are feared in their city,
and the one who is reckless in speech is hated.

10 A wise magistrate educates his people,
and the rule of an intelligent person is well ordered.

NEW AMERICAN BIBLE

11 Envy not a sinner's fame,
for you know not what disaster awaits him.
12 Rejoice not at a proud man's success;
remember he will not reach death unpunished.
13 Keep far from the man who has power to kill,
and you will not be filled with the dread of death.
But if you approach him, offend him not,
lest he take away your life;
Know that you are stepping among snares
and walking over a net.
14 As best you can, take your neighbors' measure,
and associate with the wise.
15 With the learned be intimate;
let all your conversation be about the law of the LORD.
16 Have just men for your table companions;
in the fear of God be your glory.

17 Skilled artisans are esteemed for their deftness;
but the ruler of his people is the skilled sage.
18 Feared in the city is the man of railing speech,
and he who talks rashly is hated.

10 A wise magistrate lends stability to his people,
and the government of a prudent man is well ordered.

NEW JERUSALEM BIBLE

11 Do not envy the sinner his success;
you do not know how that will end.
12 Do not take pleasure in what pleases the godless;
remember they will not go unpunished here below.

13 Keep your distance from the man who has the power to put to death,
and you will not be haunted by the fear of dying.
If you do approach him, make no false move,
or he may take your life.
Realise that you are treading among trip-lines,
that you are strolling on the battlements.

14 Cultivate your neighbours to the best of your ability,
and consult with the wise.
15 For conversation seek the intelligent,
let all your discussions bear on the law of the Most High.
16 Have the upright for your table companions,
and let your pride be in fearing the Lord.
17 Work from skilled hands will earn its praise,
but a leader of the people must be skilful in words.
18 A chatterbox is a terror to his town,
a loose talker is detested.

10 A sagacious ruler educates his people,
and he makes his subjects understand order.

GREEK OLD TESTAMENT

2 κατὰ τὸν κριτὴν τοῦ λαοῦ οὕτως καὶ οἱ λειτουργοὶ
αὐτοῦ,
καὶ κατὰ τὸν ἡγούμενον τῆς πόλεως πάντες οἱ
κατοικοῦντες αὐτήν.
3 βασιλεὺς ἀπαίδευτος ἀπολεῖ τὸν λαὸν αὐτοῦ,
καὶ πόλις οἰκισθήσεται ἐν συνέσει δυναστῶν.
4 ἐν χειρὶ κυρίου ἡ ἐξουσία τῆς γῆς,
καὶ τὸν χρήσιμον ἐγερεῖ εἰς καιρὸν ἐπ᾽ αὐτῆς.
5 ἐν χειρὶ κυρίου εὐοδία ἀνδρός,
καὶ προσώπῳ γραμματέως ἐπιθήσει δόξαν αὐτοῦ.
6 Ἐπὶ παντὶ ἀδικήματι μὴ μηνιάσῃς τῷ πλησίον
καὶ μὴ πρᾶσσε μηδὲν ἐν ἔργοις ὕβρεως.
7 μισητὴ ἔναντι κυρίου καὶ ἀνθρώπων ὑπερηφανία,
καὶ ἐξ ἀμφοτέρων πλημμελὴς ἡ ἀδικία.
8 βασιλεία ἀπὸ ἔθνους εἰς ἔθνος μετάγεται
διὰ ἀδικίας καὶ ὕβρεις καὶ χρήματα.
9 τί ὑπερηφανεύεται γῆ καὶ σποδός;
ὅτι ἐν ζωῇ ἔρριψα τὰ ἐνδόσθια αὐτοῦ.
10 μακρὸν ἀρρώστημα, σκώπτει ἰατρός·
καὶ βασιλεὺς σήμερον, καὶ αὔριον τελευτήσει.
11 ἐν γὰρ τῷ ἀποθανεῖν ἄνθρωπον
κληρονομήσει ἑρπετὰ καὶ θηρία καὶ σκώληκας.
12 Ἀρχὴ ὑπερηφανίας ἀνθρώπου ἀφίστασθαι ἀπὸ κυρίου,
καὶ ἀπὸ τοῦ ποιήσαντος αὐτὸν ἀπέστη ἡ καρδία αὐτοῦ.

KING JAMES VERSION

2 As the judge of the people is himself, so are his officers; and what manner of man the ruler of the city is, such are all they that dwell therein.

3 An unwise king destroyeth his people; but through the prudence of them which are in authority the city shall be inhabited.

4 The power of the earth is in the hand of the Lord, and in due time he will set over it one that is profitable.

5 In the hand of God is the prosperity of man: and upon the person of the scribe shall he lay his honour.

6 Bear not hatred to thy neighbour for every wrong; and do nothing at all by injurious practices.

7 Pride is hateful before God and man: and by both doth one commit iniquity.

8 Because of unrighteous dealings, injuries, and riches got by deceit, the kingdom is translated from one people to another.

9 Why is earth and ashes proud? There is not a more wicked thing than a covetous man: for such an one setteth his own soul to sale; because while he liveth he casteth away his bowels.

10 The physician cutteth off a long disease; and he that is to day a king to morrow shall die.

11 For when a man is dead, he shall inherit creeping things, beasts, and worms.

12 The beginning of pride is when one departeth from God, and his heart is turned away from his Maker.

DOUAY OLD TESTAMENT

2 As the judge of the people is himself, so also are his ministers: and what manner of man the ruler of a city is, such also are they that dwell therein.

3 An unwise king shall be the ruin of his people: and cities shall be inhabited through the prudence of the rulers.

4 The power of the earth is in the hand of God, and in his time he will raise up a profitable ruler over it.

5 The prosperity of man is in the hand of God, and upon the person of the scribe he shall lay his honour.

6 Remember not any injury done thee by thy neighbour, and do thou nothing by deeds of injury.

7 Pride is hateful before God and men: and all iniquity of nations is execrable.

8 A kingdom is translated from one people to another, because of injustices, and wrongs, and injuries, and divers deceits.

9 But nothing is more wicked than the covetous man. Why is earth and ashes proud?

10 There is not a more wicked thing than to love money: for such a one setteth even his own soul to sale: because while he liveth he hath cast away his bowels.

11 All power is of short life. A long sickness is troublesome to the physician.

12 The physician cutteth off a short sickness: so also a king is to day, and to morrow he shall die.

13 For when a man shall die, he shall inherit serpents, and beasts, and worms.

14 The beginning of the pride of man, is to fall off from God:

KNOX TRANSLATION

ruler, like subjects. 3 Royal folly is a people's ruin; where
prudence reigns, there cities thrive most. 4 God's will it is,
then, that rules a nation; when the time comes, he will give
it the prince it needs, 5 granting prosperity where he will; no
scribe bears office but has divine authority stamped on his
brow.

6 Forget the wrong done, nor enrol thyself among the doers
of it.

7 Before God and man alike pride is hateful, and the wrong
the Gentiles do is foully done; 8 wrong and crime and outrage
and treacherous shift, that he punishes by passing on
the sceptre of empire into new hands; but worse sin is none
than avarice. 9 See how man, for all his pride, is but dust
and ashes! 10 This love of money is of all things the most
perverse; what does the miser but sell his own soul? As well
be bowelled alive!

11 Why be tyrannies short-lived? Why, it is a wearisome
thing to the physician, a long illness, 12 so he is fain to cut it
short, and the king that reigns to-day will be dead to-morrow.
13 And what is the new kingdom he inherits? Creeping
things, and carrion beast, and worm.[a]

14 Pride's beginning is man's revolt from God, 15 when the

a vv. 7-13: A comparison of the Latin with the Greek suggests that the order of these verses differed in different manuscripts of the original, and their sense cannot be certainly established. It seems likely that in verses 11-13 the physician referred to is Providence.

TODAY'S ENGLISH VERSION

all the citizens will be like their ruler. 3 An uneducated king
will ruin his people, but a government will grow strong if its
rulers are wise. 4 The Lord sees to the government of the
world and brings the right person to power at the right time.
5 The success of that person is in the Lord's hands. The Lord
is the source of the honor given to any official.

6 Don't be angry with someone for every little thing he does
wrong. Don't do anything out of injured pride. 7 Arrogance
and injustice are hated by both the Lord and people.
8 Injustice, arrogance, and wealth cause nations to fall from
power, and others then rise to take their place. 9 We are only
dust and ashes; what have we got to be proud of? Our body
decays even while we are alive.[a] 10 A long illness puzzles the
doctor.[b] Even a king may be alive today and dead tomorrow.
11 When a person dies, all he then possesses is worms, flies,
and maggots.

12 Pride has its beginning when a person abandons the

[a] Our body . . . alive; *this sentence in both Greek and Hebrew is unclear.*
[b] A long . . . doctor; *this sentence in both Greek and Hebrew is unclear.*

NEW REVISED STANDARD VERSION

2 As the people's judge is, so are his officials;
as the ruler of the city is, so are all its inhabitants.
3 An undisciplined king ruins his people,
but a city becomes fit to live in through the
understanding of its rulers.
4 The government of the earth is in the hand of the Lord,
and over it he will raise up the right leader for the
time.
5 Human success is in the hand of the Lord,
and it is he who confers honor upon the lawgiver.[a]

6 Do not get angry with your neighbor for every injury,
and do not resort to acts of insolence.
7 Arrogance is hateful to the Lord and to mortals,
and injustice is outrageous to both.
8 Sovereignty passes from nation to nation
on account of injustice and insolence and wealth.[b]
9 How can dust and ashes be proud?
Even in life the human body decays.[c]
10 A long illness baffles the physician;[d]
the king of today will die tomorrow.
11 For when one is dead
he inherits maggots and vermin[e] and worms.
12 The beginning of human pride is to forsake the Lord;
the heart has withdrawn from its Maker.

a Heb: Gk *scribe* *b* Other ancient authorities add here or after verse 9a, *Nothing is more wicked than one who loves money, for such a person puts his own soul up for sale.* *c* Heb: Meaning of Gk uncertain *d* Heb Lat: Meaning of Gk uncertain *e* Heb: Gk *wild animals*

NEW AMERICAN BIBLE

2 As the people's judge, so are his ministers;
as the head of a city, its inhabitants.
3 A wanton king destroys his people,
but a city grows through the wisdom of its princes.
4 Sovereignty over the earth is in the hand of God,
who raises up on it the man of the hour;
5 Sovereignty over every man is in the hand of God,
who imparts his majesty to the ruler.

6 No matter the wrong, do no violence to your neighbor,
and do not walk the path of arrogance.
7 Odious to the LORD and to men is arrogance,
and the sin of oppression they both hate.
8 Dominion is transferred from one people to another
because of the violence of the arrogant.
9 Why are dust and ashes proud?
even during life man's body decays;
10 A slight illness—the doctor jests,
a king today—tomorrow he is dead.
11 When a man dies, he inherits corruption;
worms and gnats and maggots.
12 The beginning of pride is man's stubbornness
in withdrawing his heart from his Maker;

NEW JERUSALEM BIBLE

2 As the magistrate is, so will his officials be,
as the governor is, so will be the inhabitants of his
city.
3 An undisciplined king will be the ruin of his people,
a city owes its prosperity to the intelligence of its
leading men.
4 The government of the earth is in the hands of the Lord,
he sets the right leader over it at the right time.
5 Human success is in the hands of the Lord.
He invests the scribe with honour.

6 Do not resent your neighbour's every offence,
and never act in a fit of passion.
7 Pride is hateful to God and humanity,
and injustice is abhorrent to both.

8 Sovereignty passes from nation to nation
because of injustice, arrogance and money.

9 What has dust and ashes to pride itself on?
Even in life its entrails are repellent.
10 A long illness makes a fool of the doctor;
a king today is a corpse tomorrow.
11 For in death the portion of all alike will be
insects, wild animals and worms.

12 The first stage of pride is to desert the Lord
and to turn one's heart away from one's Maker.

GREEK OLD TESTAMENT

13 ὅτι ἀρχὴ ὑπερηφανίας ἁμαρτία,
καὶ ὁ κρατῶν αὐτῆς ἐξομβρήσει βδέλυγμα·
διὰ τοῦτο παρεδόξασεν κύριος τὰς ἐπαγωγὰς
καὶ κατέστρεψεν εἰς τέλος αὐτούς.
14 θρόνους ἀρχόντων καθεῖλεν ὁ κύριος
καὶ ἐκάθισεν πραεῖς ἀντ᾽ αὐτῶν·
15 ῥίζας ἐθνῶν ἐξέτιλεν ὁ κύριος
καὶ ἐφύτευσεν ταπεινοὺς ἀντ᾽ αὐτῶν·
16 χώρας ἐθνῶν κατέστρεψεν ὁ κύριος
καὶ ἀπώλεσεν αὐτὰς ἕως θεμελίων γῆς·
17 ἐξῆρεν ἐξ αὐτῶν καὶ ἀπώλεσεν αὐτοὺς
καὶ κατέπαυσεν ἀπὸ γῆς τὸ μνημόσυνον αὐτῶν.
18 οὐκ ἔκτισται ἀνθρώποις ὑπερηφανία
οὐδὲ ὀργὴ θυμοῦ γεννήμασιν γυναικῶν.
19 Σπέρμα ἔντιμον ποῖον; σπέρμα ἀνθρώπου.
σπέρμα ἔντιμον ποῖον; οἱ φοβούμενοι τὸν κύριον.
σπέρμα ἄτιμον ποῖον; σπέρμα ἀνθρώπου.
σπέρμα ἄτιμον ποῖον; οἱ παραβαίνοντες ἐντολάς.
20 ἐν μέσῳ ἀδελφῶν ὁ ἡγούμενος αὐτῶν ἔντιμος,
καὶ οἱ φοβούμενοι κύριον ἐν ὀφθαλμοῖς αὐτοῦ.

KING JAMES VERSION

13 For pride is the beginning of sin, and he that hath it shall pour out abomination: and therefore the Lord brought upon them strange calamities, and overthrew them utterly.

14 The Lord hath cast down the thrones of proud princes, and set up the meek in their stead.

15 The Lord hath plucked up the roots of the proud nations, and planted the lowly in their place.

16 The Lord overthrew countries of the heathen, and destroyed them to the foundations of the earth.

17 He took some of them away, and destroyed them, and hath made their memorial to cease from the earth.

18 Pride was not made for men, nor furious anger for them that are born of a woman.

19 They that fear the Lord are a sure seed, and they that love him an honourable plant: they that regard not the law are a dishonourable seed; they that transgress the commandments are a deceivable seed.

20 Among brethren he that is chief is honorable; so are they that fear the Lord in his eyes.

21 The fear of the Lord goeth before the obtaining of authority: but roughness and pride is the losing thereof.

DOUAY OLD TESTAMENT

15 Because his heart is departed from him that made him: for pride is the beginning of all sin: be that holdeth it, shall be filled with maledictions, and it shall ruin him in the end.

16 Therefore hath the Lord disgraced the assemblies of the wicked, and hath utterly destroyed them.

17 God hath overturned the thrones of proud princes, and hath set up the meek in their stead.

18 God hath made the roots of proud nations to wither, and hath planted the humble of these nations.

19 The Lord hath overthrown the lands of the Gentiles, and hath destroyed them even to the foundation.

20 He hath made some of them to wither away, and hath destroyed them, and hath made the memory of them to cease from the earth.

21 God hath abolished the memory of the proud, and hath preserved the memory of them that are humble in mind.

22 Pride was not made for men: nor wrath for the race of women.

23 That seed of men shall be honoured, which feareth God: but that seed shall be dishonoured, which transgresseth the commandments of the Lord.

24 In the midst of brethren their chief is honourable: so shall they that fear the Lord, be in his eyes.

KNOX TRANSLATION

heart forgets its Maker; and of all sin pride is the root. Leave
it, or curses thou shalt have in full measure, and be ruined at
the last. 16 Such humiliation the Lord has in store; vanished
utterly is yonder confederacy; 17 proud thrones cast down, to
make room for the oppressed, 18 proud nations withered
from the root, and humbler rivals planted instead! 19 Whole
nations of the world the Lord has overthrown, rased them to
the ground; 20 shrivelled and vanished away, they have left
no trace of their passage. 21 The proud forgotten, the humble
kept in memory; such was the Lord's will. 22 Pride was never
made for man's estate; never child born of woman had
anger's mood for its birthright.

23 There are two breeds of men; one fears God and wins
renown, the other passes his commandments by, and is forgotten. 24 Let clansmen honour a chieftain's rank; it is humble fear wins the divine regard. 25 For riches and renown, as

TODAY'S ENGLISH VERSION

Lord, his maker. 13 Pride is like a fountain pouring out sin,
and whoever persists in it will be full of wickedness. That is
why the Lord brought terrible punishments on some people
and completely destroyed them. 14 The Lord has overthrown
kings and put humbler people in their place. 15 The Lord has
pulled up nations by the roots and established humbler ones
in their place. 16 The Lord has overthrown empires and completely devastated their lands. 17 He destroyed some so completely that they are not even remembered any more. 18 The
Creator never intended for human beings to be arrogant and
violent.

19 Who deserves honor? The human race does, because
people fear the Lord. Who does not deserve honor? The
human race does not, because people break the Lord's commands. 20 A leader should be honored by those who follow
him, and the Lord honors those who fear him. [a]

[a] *Some manuscripts add verse 21:* Success begins with fear of the Lord, but failure begins with stubbornness and arrogance.

NEW REVISED STANDARD VERSION

13 For the beginning of pride is sin,
and the one who clings to it pours out abominations.
Therefore the Lord brings upon them unheard-of
calamities,
and destroys them completely.
14 The Lord overthrows the thrones of rulers,
and enthrones the lowly in their place.
15 The Lord plucks up the roots of the nations, [a]
and plants the humble in their place.
16 The Lord lays waste the lands of the nations,
and destroys them to the foundations of the earth.
17 He removes some of them and destroys them,
and erases the memory of them from the earth.
18 Pride was not created for human beings,
or violent anger for those born of women.

19 Whose offspring are worthy of honor?
Human offspring.
Whose offspring are worthy of honor?
Those who fear the Lord.
Whose offspring are unworthy of honor?
Human offspring.
Whose offspring are unworthy of honor?
Those who break the commandments.
20 Among family members their leader is worthy of honor,
but those who fear the Lord are worthy of honor in
his eyes. [b]

a Other ancient authorities read *proud nations* *b* Other ancient authorities add as verse 21, *The fear of the Lord is the beginning of acceptance; obduracy and pride are the beginning of rejection.*

NEW AMERICAN BIBLE

13 For pride is the reservoir of sin,
a source which runs over with vice;
Because of it God sends unheard-of afflictions
and brings men to utter ruin.
14 The thrones of the arrogant God overturns
and establishes the lowly in their stead.
15 The roots of the proud God plucks up,
to plant the humble in their place:
16 He breaks down their stem to the level of the ground,
then digs their roots from the earth.
17 The traces of the proud God sweeps away
and effaces the memory of them from the earth.
18 Insolence is not allotted to a man,
nor stubborn anger to one born of woman.

19 Whose offspring can be in honor? Those of men.
Which offspring are in honor? Those who fear God.
Whose offspring can be in disgrace? Those of men.
Which offspring are in disgrace? Those who
transgress the commandments.
20 Among brethren their leader is in honor;
he who fears God is in honor among his people.

NEW JERUSALEM BIBLE

13 Since the first stage of pride is sin,
whoever clings to it will pour forth filth.
This is why the Lord inflicts unexpected punishments
on such people, utterly destroying them.
14 The Lord has turned mighty princes off their thrones
and seated the humble there instead.
15 The Lord has plucked up the proud by the roots,
and planted the lowly in their place.
16 The Lord has overthrown the lands of the nations
and destroyed them to the very foundations of the
earth.
17 Sometimes he has taken them away and destroyed
them,
and blotted out their memory from the earth.
18 Pride was not created for human beings,
nor furious rage for those born of woman.
19 What race deserves honour? The human race.
What race deserves honour? Those who fear the
Lord.
What race deserves contempt? The human race.
What race deserves contempt? Those who break the
Law.
20 A leader is honoured by his brothers,
and those who fear the Lord are honoured by him.

GREEK OLD TESTAMENT

22 πλούσιος καὶ ἔνδοξος καὶ πτωχός,
τὸ καύχημα αὐτῶν φόβος κυρίου.
23 οὐ δίκαιον ἀτιμάσαι πτωχὸν συνετόν,
καὶ οὐ καθήκει δοξάσαι ἄνδρα ἁμαρτωλόν.
24 μεγιστὰν καὶ κριτὴς καὶ δυνάστης δοξασθήσεται,
καὶ οὐκ ἔστιν αὐτῶν τις μείζων τοῦ φοβουμένου τὸν κύριον.
25 οἰκέτῃ σοφῷ ἐλεύθεροι λειτουργήσουσιν,
καὶ ἀνὴρ ἐπιστήμων οὐ γογγύσει.
26 Μὴ σοφίζου ποιῆσαι τὸ ἔργον σου
καὶ μὴ δοξάζου ἐν καιρῷ στενοχωρίας σου.
27 κρείσσων ἐργαζόμενος καὶ περισσεύων ἐν πᾶσιν
ἢ περιπατῶν δοξαζόμενος καὶ ἀπορῶν ἄρτων.
28 τέκνον, ἐν πραΰτητι δόξασον τὴν ψυχήν σου
καὶ δὸς αὐτῇ τιμὴν κατὰ τὴν ἀξίαν αὐτῆς.
29 τὸν ἁμαρτάνοντα εἰς τὴν ψυχὴν αὐτοῦ τίς δικαιώσει;
καὶ τίς δοξάσει τὸν ἀτιμάζοντα τὴν ζωὴν αὐτοῦ;
30 πτωχὸς δοξάζεται δι᾽ ἐπιστήμην αὐτοῦ,
καὶ πλούσιος δοξάζεται διὰ τὸν πλοῦτον αὐτοῦ.
31 ὁ δεδοξασμένος ἐν πτωχείᾳ, καὶ ἐν πλούτῳ ποσαχῶς;
καὶ ὁ ἄδοξος ἐν πλούτῳ, καὶ ἐν πτωχείᾳ ποσαχῶς;

KING JAMES VERSION

22 Whether he be rich, noble, or poor, their glory is the fear of the Lord.

23 It is not meet to despise the poor man that hath understanding; neither is it convenient to magnify a sinful man.

24 Great men, and judges, and potentates, shall be honoured; yet is there none of them greater than he that feareth the Lord.

25 Unto the servant that is wise shall they that are free do service: and he that hath knowledge will not grudge when he is reformed.

26 Be not overwise in doing thy business; and boast not thyself in the time of thy distress.

27 Better is he that laboureth, and aboundeth in all things, than he that boasteth himself, and wanteth bread.

28 My son, glorify thy soul in meekness, and give it honour according to the dignity thereof.

29 Who will justify him that sinneth against his own soul? and who will honour him that dishonoureth his own life?

30 The poor man is honoured for his skill, and the rich man is honoured for his riches.

31 He that is honoured in poverty, how much more in riches? and he that is dishonourable in riches, how much more in poverty?

DOUAY OLD TESTAMENT

25 The fear of God is the glory of the rich, *and* of the honourable, and of the poor:

26 Despise not a just man that is poor, and do not magnify a sinful man that is rich.

27 The great man, and the judge, and the mighty is in honour: and there is none greater than he that feareth God.

28 They that are free shall serve a servant that is wise: and a man that is prudent and well instructed will not murmur when he is reproved; and he that is ignorant, shall not be honoured.

29 Extol not thyself in doing thy work, and linger not in the time of distress:

30 Better is he that laboureth, and aboundeth in all things, than he that boasteth himself and wanteth bread.

31 My son, keep thy soul in meekness, and give it honour according to its desert.

32 Who will justify him that sinneth against his own soul? and who will honour him that dishonoureth his own soul?

33 The poor man is glorified by his discipline and fear: and there is a man that is honoured for his wealth.

34 But he that is glorified in poverty, how much more in wealth? and he that is glorified in wealth, let him fear poverty.

KNOX TRANSLATION

for the lowly born, there is one boast worth having, the fear
of God. 26 Honest poverty never despise, nor flatter, for all
his wealth, the evil-doer; 27 prince nor ruler nor nobleman
can win any higher title than the fear of God.

28 Of his master's sons a prudent servant shall yet be master. Only the fool, that is ill trained, takes punishment amiss;
and a fool will never rise to greatness.

29 Do not boast of thy fine craftsmanship and then, in time
of urgent need, stand idle;[a] 30 better fall to work and have a
full belly than keep thy pride and go fasting. 31 Abate thy
pride, keep body and soul together; value thy life as it
deserves. 32 There is no excusing the man who is his own
enemy, no worth in the man who thinks his life worth nothing.

33 One man, that little wealth has, may boast of his skill
and the fear of God, another man of his riches. 34 Grow he
rich, the poor man shall boast indeed; that other, grow he
poor, has good cause to fear his poverty.

a This seems, in view of the context, the best account to give of a verse which is difficult in the Latin, and in the Greek almost untranslatable.

TODAY'S ENGLISH VERSION

22 Rich people, famous people, and poor people all take
pride in their fear of the Lord. 23 It is not right to refuse
honor to a poor person who is intelligent, and it is not right
to give honor to a sinner. 24 People of influence, rulers, and
judges will be honored, but none of them is greater than a
person who fears the Lord. 25 A slave who is wise will have
free citizens serving him; and if they are sensible, they will
not resent it.

26 When you do your work, don't make a show of your
skill, and don't try to put on a show when you are in trouble.
27 It is better to work and have more than you need than to
go around boasting but hungry.

28 My child, keep your self-respect, but remain modest.
Value yourself at your true worth. 29 There is no excuse for a
person to run himself down. No one respects a person who
has no respect for himself. 30 Poor people can be honored for
their good sense, and rich people can be honored for their
wealth. 31 If someone is honored while he is poor, think how
much he will be honored if he becomes rich! If someone is
despised while he is rich, think how much more he will be

NEW REVISED STANDARD VERSION

22 The rich, and the eminent, and the poor—
their glory is the fear of the Lord.
23 It is not right to despise one who is intelligent but poor,
and it is not proper to honor one who is sinful.
24 The prince and the judge and the ruler are honored,
but none of them is greater than the one who fears
the Lord.
25 Free citizens will serve a wise servant,
and an intelligent person will not complain.

26 Do not make a display of your wisdom when you do
your work,
and do not boast when you are in need.
27 Better is the worker who has goods in plenty
than the boaster who lacks bread.

28 My child, honor yourself with humility,
and give yourself the esteem you deserve.
29 Who will acquit those who condemn[a] themselves?
And who will honor those who dishonor
themselves?[b]
30 The poor are honored for their knowledge,
while the rich are honored for their wealth.
31 One who is honored in poverty, how much more in
wealth!
And one dishonored in wealth, how much more in
poverty!

a Heb: Gk *sin against* *b* Heb Lat: Gk *their own life*

NEW AMERICAN BIBLE

21 Be it tenant or wayfarer, alien or pauper,
his glory is the fear of the LORD.
22 It is not just to despise a man who is wise but poor,
nor proper to honor any sinner.
23 The prince, the ruler, the judge are in honor;
but none is greater than he who fears God.
24 When free men serve a prudent slave,
the wise man does not complain.
25 Flaunt not your wisdom in managing your affairs,
and boast not in your time of need.
26 Better the worker who has plenty of everything
than the boaster who is without bread.
27 My son, with humility have self-esteem;
prize yourself as you deserve.
28 Who will acquit him who condemns himself?
who will honor him who discredits himself?
29 The poor man is honored for his wisdom
as the rich man is honored for his wealth;
30 Honored in poverty, how much more so in wealth!
Dishonored in wealth, in poverty how much the
more!

NEW JERUSALEM BIBLE

22 The rich, the noble, the poor,
let them pride themselves on fearing the Lord.
23 It is not right to despise one who is poor but intelligent,
and it is not good to honour one who is a sinner.
24 Magnate, magistrate, potentate, all are to be honoured,
but none is greater than the one who fears the Lord.
25 A wise slave will have free men waiting on him,
and the enlightened will not complain.

26 Do not try to be smart when you do your work,
do not put on airs when you are in difficulties.
27 Better the hardworking who has plenty of everything,
than the pretentious at a loss for a meal.
28 My child, be modest in your self-esteem,
and value yourself at your proper worth.
29 Who can justify one who inflicts injuries on himself,
or respect one who is full of self-contempt?
30 The poor is honoured for wit,
and the rich for wealth.
31 Honoured in poverty, how much the more in wealth!
Dishonoured in wealth, how much the more in
poverty!

GREEK OLD TESTAMENT

11 σοφία ταπεινοῦ ἀνυψώσει κεφαλὴν αὐτοῦ
καὶ ἐν μέσῳ μεγιστάνων καθίσει αὐτόν.
2 Μὴ αἰνέσῃς ἄνδρα ἐν κάλλει αὐτοῦ
καὶ μὴ βδελύξῃ ἄνθρωπον ἐν ὁράσει αὐτοῦ.
3 μικρὰ ἐν πετεινοῖς μέλισσα,
καὶ ἀρχὴ γλυκασμάτων ὁ καρπὸς αὐτῆς.
4 ἐν περιβολῇ ἱματίων μὴ καυχήσῃ
καὶ ἐν ἡμέρᾳ δόξης μὴ ἐπαίρου·
ὅτι θαυμαστὰ τὰ ἔργα κυρίου,
καὶ κρυπτὰ τὰ ἔργα αὐτοῦ ἀνθρώποις.
5 πολλοὶ τύραννοι ἐκάθισαν ἐπὶ ἐδάφους,
ὁ δὲ ἀνυπονόητος ἐφόρεσεν διάδημα.
6 πολλοὶ δυνάσται ἠτιμάσθησαν σφόδρα,
καὶ ἔνδοξοι παρεδόθησαν εἰς χεῖρας ἑτέρων.
7 Πρὶν ἐξετάσῃς, μὴ μέμφου·
νόησον πρῶτον καὶ τότε ἐπιτίμα.
8 πρὶν ἢ ἀκοῦσαι μὴ ἀποκρίνου
καὶ ἐν μέσῳ λόγων μὴ παρεμβάλλου.
9 περὶ πράγματος, οὗ οὐκ ἔστιν σοι χρεία, μὴ ἔριζε
καὶ ἐν κρίσει ἁμαρτωλῶν μὴ συνέδρευε.
10 Τέκνον, μὴ περὶ πολλὰ ἔστωσαν αἱ πράξεις σου·
ἐὰν πληθύνῃς, οὐκ ἀθῳωθήσῃ·
καὶ ἐὰν διώκῃς, οὐ μὴ καταλάβῃς·
καὶ οὐ μὴ ἐκφύγῃς διαδράς.

KING JAMES VERSION

11 Wisdom lifteth up the head of him that is of low degree, and maketh him to sit among great men.

2 Commend not a man for his beauty; neither abhor a man for his outward appearance.

3 The bee is little among such as fly; but her fruit is the chief of sweet things.

4 Boast not of thy clothing and raiment, and exalt not thyself in the day of honour: for the works of the Lord are wonderful, and his works among men are hidden.

5 Many kings have sat down upon the ground; and one that was never thought of hath worn the crown.

6 Many mighty men have been greatly disgraced; and the honourable delivered into other men's hands.

7 Blame not before thou hast examined the truth: understand first, and then rebuke.

8 Answer not before thou hast heard the cause: neither interrupt men in the midst of their talk.

9 Strive not in a matter that concerneth thee not; and sit not in judgment with sinners.

10 My son, meddle not with many matters: for if thou meddle much, thou shalt not be innocent; and if thou follow after, thou shalt not obtain, neither shalt thou escape by fleeing.

DOUAY OLD TESTAMENT

11 THE wisdom of the humble shall exalt his head, and shall make him sit in the midst of great men.

2 Praise not a man for his beauty, neither despise a man for his look.

3 The bee is small among flying things, but her fruit hath the chiefest sweetness.

4 Glory not in apparel at any time, and be not exalted in the day of thy honour: for the works of the Highest only are wonderful, and his works are glorious, and secret, and hidden.

5 Many tyrants have sat on the throne, and he whom no man would think on, hath worn the crown.

6 Many mighty men have been greatly brought down, and the glorious have been delivered into the hand of others.

7 Before thou inquire, blame no man: and when thou hast inquired, reprove justly.

8 Before thou hear, answer not a word: and interrupt not others in the midst of their discourse.

9 Strive not in a matter which doth not concern thee, and sit not in judgment with sinners.

10 My son, meddle not with many matters: and if thou be rich, thou shalt not be free from sin: for if thou pursue after thou shalt not overtake: and if thou run before thou shalt not escape.

KNOX TRANSLATION

11 A man may be lowly born, and yet rise high through the wisdom that is in him, till at last he takes his seat among men of rank.

2 Esteem no man for his good looks, nor for his outward
show despise him; 3 yonder bee is an inconsiderable creature, and yet there is a world of sweetness in the harvest she
wins. 4 Plume not thyself when thou goest bravely clad, nor pride thyself in thy brief hour of greatness. Of wonder and of praise what else is worthy, but the doings of the most High?
And these, how hedged about with secrecy! 5 Kings a many
have lost their thrones,[a] to pretenders they never dreamed
of; 6 great ones a many have fallen full low, and their glory has passed to others.

7 Blame not, till thou hast heard the excuse; more just thy
reproof shall be when thou hast learnt all. 8 Listen first, then answer, never breaking in when the tale is half told.

9 Quarrel not, where thou thyself art not concerned; leave judgement of the offender to others.

10 Do not be entangled, my son, in too many enterprises. The rich man pays forfeit, chasing what overtake he may not, or fleeing what he may not shun.

[a] Literally, in the Greek text, 'have sat on the ground'. The Latin version, perhaps through an error, reads 'have sat on their thrones'.

TODAY'S ENGLISH VERSION

11 despised if he becomes poor! 1 If a poor person is
wise, he has good reason to be proud, and he will be
thought of as someone great.
2 Do not compliment a person on his good looks. On the
other hand, do not look down on someone who is unattrac-
tive. 3 Compared to most flying things, a bee is very small,
but the honey it makes is the sweetest of foods. 4 Don't
make fun of someone who has fallen on hard times and is
dressed in rags.[a] The Lord does wonderful things that
human beings never notice. 5 Many are the kings who have
ended their careers sitting on the ground, while their crowns
were worn by those no one had heard of before. 6 Many are
the rulers who have suffered disgrace. Many are the famous
people who have fallen into the power of others.
7 Before you start criticizing, get your facts straight and
think the matter through. 8 Don't interrupt while someone is
speaking; hear what he has to say before you answer.
9 Don't get into an argument over something that is none of
your business. Don't take part in decisions that are being
made by sinners.
10 My child, don't get involved in too many things. If you
try to do too much, you will suffer for it. You won't be able
to finish your work, and you won't be able to get away from

[a] *Hebrew* Don't . . . rags; *Greek* Don't take pride in fine clothes, and don't let compliments go to your head.

NEW REVISED STANDARD VERSION

11 The wisdom of the humble lifts their heads high,
and seats them among the great.
2 Do not praise individuals for their good looks,
or loathe anyone because of appearance alone.
3 The bee is small among flying creatures,
but what it produces is the best of sweet things.
4 Do not boast about wearing fine clothes,
and do not exalt yourself when you are honored;
for the works of the Lord are wonderful,
and his works are concealed from humankind.
5 Many kings have had to sit on the ground,
but one who was never thought of has worn a crown.
6 Many rulers have been utterly disgraced,
and the honored have been handed over to others.

7 Do not find fault before you investigate;
examine first, and then criticize.
8 Do not answer before you listen,
and do not interrupt when another is speaking.
9 Do not argue about a matter that does not concern you,
and do not sit with sinners when they judge a case.

10 My child, do not busy yourself with many matters;
if you multiply activities, you will not be held
blameless.
If you pursue, you will not overtake,
and by fleeing you will not escape.

NEW AMERICAN BIBLE

11 The poor man's wisdom lifts his head high
and sets him among princes.
2 Praise not a man for his looks;
despise not a man for his appearance.
3 Least is the bee among winged things,
but she reaps the choicest of all harvests.
4 Mock not the worn cloak
and jibe at no man's bitter day:
For strange are the works of the LORD,
hidden from men his deeds.
5 The oppressed often rise to a throne,
and some that none would consider wear a crown.
6 The exalted often fall into utter disgrace;
the honored are given into enemy hands.

7 Before investigating, find no fault;
examine first, then criticize.
8 Before hearing, answer not,
and interrupt no one in the middle of his speech.
9 Dispute not about what is not your concern;
in the strife of the arrogant take no part.
10 My son, why increase your cares,
since he who is avid for wealth will not be
blameless?
Even if you run after it, you will never overtake it;
however you seek it, you will not find it.

NEW JERUSALEM BIBLE

11 Wisdom enables the poor to stand erect,
and gives to the poor a place with the great.
2 Do not praise anyone for good looks,
nor dislike anyone for mere appearance.
3 Small among winged creatures is the bee
but her produce is the sweetest of the sweet.

4 Do not grow proud when people honour you;
for the works of the Lord are wonderful
but hidden from human beings.
5 Many monarchs have been made to sit on the ground,
and the person nobody thought of has worn the crown.
6 Many influential people have been utterly disgraced,
and prominent people have fallen into the power of
others.
7 Do not find fault before making thorough enquiry;
first reflect, then give a reprimand.
8 Listen before you answer,
and do not interrupt a speech before it is finished.
9 Do not wrangle about something that does not concern
you,
do not interfere in the quarrels of sinners.
10 My child, do not take on a great amount of business;
if you multiply your interests, you are bound to suffer
for it;
hurry as fast as you can, yet you will never arrive,
nor will you escape by running away.

GREEK OLD TESTAMENT

11 ἔστιν κοπιῶν καὶ πονῶν καὶ σπεύδων,
καὶ τόσῳ μᾶλλον ὑστερεῖται.
12 ἔστιν νωθρὸς προσδεόμενος ἀντιλήμψεως,
ὑστερῶν ἰσχύι καὶ πτωχείᾳ περισσεύει·
καὶ οἱ ὀφθαλμοὶ κυρίου ἐπέβλεψαν αὐτῷ εἰς ἀγαθά,
καὶ ἀνώρθωσεν αὐτὸν ἐκ ταπεινώσεως αὐτοῦ
13 καὶ ἀνύψωσεν κεφαλὴν αὐτοῦ,
καὶ ἀπεθαύμασαν ἐπ' αὐτῷ πολλοί.
14 ἀγαθὰ καὶ κακά, ζωὴ καὶ θάνατος,
πτωχεία καὶ πλοῦτος παρὰ κυρίου ἐστίν.
17 δόσις κυρίου παραμένει εὐσεβέσιν,
καὶ ἡ εὐδοκία αὐτοῦ εἰς τὸν αἰῶνα εὐοδωθήσεται.
18 ἔστιν πλουτῶν ἀπὸ προσοχῆς καὶ σφιγγίας αὐτοῦ,
καὶ αὕτη ἡ μερὶς τοῦ μισθοῦ αὐτοῦ·
19 ἐν τῷ εἰπεῖν αὐτόν Εὗρον ἀνάπαυσιν
καὶ νῦν φάγομαι ἐκ τῶν ἀγαθῶν μου,
καὶ οὐκ οἶδεν τίς καιρὸς παρελεύσεται
καὶ καταλείψει αὐτὰ ἑτέροις καὶ ἀποθανεῖται.
20 Στῆθι ἐν διαθήκῃ σου καὶ ὁμίλει ἐν αὐτῇ
καὶ ἐν τῷ ἔργῳ σου παλαιώθητι.
21 μὴ θαύμαζε ἐν ἔργοις ἁμαρτωλοῦ,
πίστευε δὲ κυρίῳ καὶ ἔμμενε τῷ πόνῳ σου·
ὅτι κοῦφον ἐν ὀφθαλμοῖς κυρίου
διὰ τάχους ἐξάπινα πλουτίσαι πένητα.

KING JAMES VERSION

11 There is one that laboureth, and taketh pains, and maketh haste, and is so much the more behind.

12 Again, there is another that is slow, and hath need of help, wanting ability, and full of poverty; yet the eye of the Lord looked upon him for good, and set him up from his low estate,

13 And lifted up his head from misery; so that many that saw it marvelled at him.

14 Prosperity and adversity, life and death, poverty and riches, come of the Lord.

15 Wisdom, knowledge, and understanding of the law, are of the Lord: love, and the way of good works, are from him.

16 Error and darkness had their beginning together with sinners: and evil shall wax old with them that glory therein.

17 The gift of the Lord remaineth with the godly, and his favour bringeth prosperity for ever.

18 There is that waxeth rich by his wariness and pinching, and this is the portion of his reward:

19 Whereas he saith, I have found rest, and now will eat continually of my goods; and *yet* he knoweth not what time shall come upon him, and that he must leave those things to others, and die.

20 Be stedfast in thy covenant, and be conversant therein, and wax old in thy work.

21 Marvel not at the works of sinners; but trust in the Lord, and abide in thy labour: for it is an easy thing in the sight of the Lord on the sudden to make a poor man rich.

DOUAY OLD TESTAMENT

11 There is an ungodly man that laboureth, and maketh haste, and is in sorrow, and is so much the more in want.

12 Again, there is an inactive man that wanteth help, is very weak in ability, and full of poverty:

13 Yet the eye of God hath looked upon him for good, and hath lifted him up from his low estate, and hath exalted his head: and many have wondered at him, and have glorified God.

14 Good things and evil, life and death, poverty and riches, are from God.

15 Wisdom and discipline, and the knowledge of the law are with God. Love and the ways of good things are with him.

16 Error and darkness are created with sinners: and they that glory in evil things, grow old in evil.

17 The gift of God abideth with the just, and his advancement shall have success for ever.

18 There is one that is enriched by living sparingly, and this is the portion of his reward.

19 In that he saith: I have found me rest, and now I will eat of my goods alone:

20 And he knoweth not what time shall pass, and that death approacheth, and that he must leave all to others, and shall die.

21 Be steadfast in thy covenant, and be conversant therein, and grow old in the work of thy commandments.

22 Abide not in the works of sinners. But trust in God, and stay in thy place.

23 For it is easy in the eyes of God on a sudden to make the poor man rich.

KNOX TRANSLATION

11 Some men's lives are all toil and haste and anxiety; yet
the more they toil, the less advantage they win, for want of
piety. 12 And others are backward folk, that cannot hold
their gains, men of little power and much poverty; 13 and yet
such a man the Lord will look upon with favour, rescue him
from neglect and greatly advance him, to the world's amazement, and the greater honour of God. 14 From God all comes,
good fortune and ill, life and death, poverty and riches; 15 in
God's keeping are wisdom and temperance and knowledge of
the law, charity and the good life.
16 Error and darkness are sinful man's birthright; it is by
making evil their delight that men grow hardened in evil.
17 No momentary blessing it is, God's largesse to his faithful servants; that seed that bears an eternal crop. 18 No such
boast has the man of thrift, that by his own effort wins
wealth. 19 Does he tell himself that he has found security at
last; nothing remains but to glut, with his own earnings, his
own greed? 20 He forgets that time flies, and death draws
near; die he must, and leave all he has to another. 21 Be true
to thy covenant with God; its words to thy own ears repeat;
to that, and thy enjoined duty, inure thyself. 22 Wouldst thou
stand there gaping at the doings of sinners? Nay, trust in
God, and keep to thy appointed task. 23 Dost thou think God
finds it hard to enrich the beggar, and in a moment?

TODAY'S ENGLISH VERSION

it either. 11 For instance, here is someone who never stops
working like a slave, but gets further behind all the time.
12 On the other hand, someone else may be very poor and not
up to his task. He may be slow, and he may need help, but
the Lord is pleased with him and pulls him out of his bad situation. 13 When he is back on his feet again, everyone is
astounded.
14 Everything comes from the Lord: success and failure,
poverty and wealth, life and death. 15 Wisdom, understanding, knowledge of the Law, love, and the doing of good
deeds—all these come from the Lord. 16 Error and darkness
have been with sinners from the beginning, and those who
enjoy evil will have it with them into their old age. 17 The
Lord's gifts to religious people are gifts that endure. If he
approves of you, you will always be successful. 18 Someone
may grow rich by working hard and denying himself pleasure, but what does he get for it? 19 He says to himself,
"Now I can finally sit back and enjoy what I have worked
for." But he has no idea how long it will be before he must
die and leave his wealth to others.
20 Stand by your duty and stick to it; grow old at your
work. 21 Don't be jealous of what sinners achieve; just stick
to your own work, and trust the Lord. It is very easy for the
Lord to make a poor person suddenly rich. 22 Devout people

NEW REVISED STANDARD VERSION

11 There are those who work and struggle and hurry,
but are so much the more in want.
12 There are others who are slow and need help,
who lack strength and abound in poverty;
but the eyes of the Lord look kindly upon them;
he lifts them out of their lowly condition
13 and raises up their heads
to the amazement of the many.

14 Good things and bad, life and death,
poverty and wealth, come from the Lord.[a]
17 The Lord's gift remains with the devout,
and his favor brings lasting success.
18 One becomes rich through diligence and self-denial,
and the reward allotted to him is this:
19 when he says, "I have found rest,
and now I shall feast on my goods!"
he does not know how long it will be
until he leaves them to others and dies.

20 Stand by your agreement and attend to it,
and grow old in your work.
21 Do not wonder at the works of a sinner,
but trust in the Lord and keep at your job;
for it is easy in the sight of the Lord
to make the poor rich suddenly, in an instant.

a Other ancient authorities add as verses 15 and 16, *15 Wisdom, understanding, and knowledge of the law come from the Lord; affection and the ways of good works come from him. 16 Error and darkness were created with sinners; evil grows old with those who take pride in malice.*

NEW AMERICAN BIBLE

11 One may toil and struggle and drive,
and fall short all the more.
12 Another goes his way a weakling and a failure,
with little strength and great misery—
Yet the eyes of the LORD look favorably upon him;
he raises him free of the vile dust,
13 Lifts up his head and exalts him
to the amazement of the many.
14 Good and evil, life and death,
poverty and riches, are from the LORD.
15 Wisdom and understanding and knowledge of affairs,
love and virtuous paths are from the LORD.
16 Error and darkness were formed with sinners from their
birth,
and evil grows old with evildoers.
17 The LORD's gift remains with the just;
his favor brings continued success.
18 A man may become rich through a miser's life,
and this is his allotted reward:
19 When he says: "I have found rest,
now I will feast on my possessions,"
He does not know how long it will be
till he dies and leaves them to others.

20 My son, hold fast to your duty, busy yourself with it,
grow old while doing your task.
21 Admire not how sinners live,
but trust in the LORD and wait for his light;
For it is easy with the LORD
suddenly, in an instant, to make a poor man rich.

NEW JERUSALEM BIBLE

11 Some people work very hard at top speed,
only to find themselves falling further behind.
12 Or there is the slow kind of person, needing help,
poor in possessions and rich in poverty;
and the Lord turns a favourable eye on him,
lifts him out of his wretched condition,
13 and enables him to hold his head high,
thus causing general astonishment.
14 Good and bad, life and death,
poverty and wealth, all come from the Lord.
17 To the devout the Lord's gift remains constant,
and his favour will be there to lead them for ever.
18 Others grow rich by pinching and scraping,
and here is the reward they receive for it:
19 although they say, 'Now I can sit back
and enjoy the benefit of what I have got,'
they do not know how long this will last;
they will have to leave their goods to others and die.
20 Stick to your job, work hard at it
and grow old at your work.
21 Do not admire the achievements of sinners,
trust the Lord and mind your own business;
since it is a trifle in the eyes of the Lord,
in a moment, suddenly to make the poor rich.

GREEK OLD TESTAMENT

22 εὐλογία κυρίου ἐν μισθῷ εὐσεβοῦς,
καὶ ἐν ὥρᾳ ταχινῇ ἀναθάλλει εὐλογίαν αὐτοῦ.
23 μὴ εἴπῃς Τίς ἐστίν μου χρεία,
καὶ τίνα ἀπὸ τοῦ νῦν ἔσται μου τὰ ἀγαθά;
24 μὴ εἴπῃς Αὐτάρκη μοί ἐστιν,
καὶ τί ἀπὸ τοῦ νῦν κακωθήσομαι;
25 ἐν ἡμέρᾳ ἀγαθῶν ἀμνησία κακῶν,
καὶ ἐν ἡμέρᾳ κακῶν οὐ μνησθήσεται ἀγαθῶν·
26 ὅτι κοῦφον ἔναντι κυρίου ἐν ἡμέρᾳ τελευτῆς
ἀποδοῦναι ἀνθρώπῳ κατὰ τὰς ὁδοὺς αὐτοῦ.
27 κάκωσις ὥρας ἐπιλησμονὴν ποιεῖ τρυφῆς,
καὶ ἐν συντελείᾳ ἀνθρώπου ἀποκάλυψις ἔργων αὐτοῦ.
28 πρὸ τελευτῆς μὴ μακάριζε μηδένα,
καὶ ἐν τέκνοις αὐτοῦ γνωσθήσεται ἀνήρ.
29 Μὴ πάντα ἄνθρωπον εἴσαγε εἰς τὸν οἶκόν σου·
πολλὰ γὰρ τὰ ἔνεδρα τοῦ δολίου.
30 πέρδιξ θηρευτὴς ἐν καρτάλλῳ, οὕτως καρδία ὑπερηφάνου,
καὶ ὡς ὁ κατάσκοπος ἐπιβλέπει πτῶσιν·
31 τὰ γὰρ ἀγαθὰ εἰς κακὰ μεταστρέφων ἐνεδρεύει
καὶ ἐν τοῖς αἱρετοῖς ἐπιθήσει μῶμον.
32 ἀπὸ σπινθῆρος πυρὸς πληθύνεται ἀνθρακιά,
καὶ ἄνθρωπος ἁμαρτωλὸς εἰς αἷμα ἐνεδρεύει.

KING JAMES VERSION

22 The blessing of the Lord is in the reward of the godly, and suddenly he maketh his blessing to flourish.

23 Say not, What profit is there of my service? and what good things shall I have hereafter?

24 Again, say not, I have enough, and possess many things, and what evil can come to me hereafter?

25 In the day of prosperity there is a forgetfulness of affliction: and in the day of affliction there is no more remembrance of prosperity.

26 For it is an easy thing unto the Lord in the day of death to reward a man according to his ways.

27 The affliction of an hour maketh a man forget pleasure: and in his end his deeds shall be discovered.

28 Judge none blessed before his death: for a man shall be known in his children.

29 Bring not every man into thine house: for the deceitful man hath many trains.

30 Like as a partridge taken [and kept] in a cage, so is the heart of the proud; and like as a spy, watcheth he for thy fall:

31 For he lieth in wait, and turneth good into evil, and in things worthy praise will lay blame upon thee.

32 Of a spark of fire a heap of coals is kindled: and a sinful man layeth wait for blood.

33 Take heed of a mischievous man, for he worketh wickedness; lest he bring upon thee a perpetual blot.

DOUAY OLD TESTAMENT

24 The blessing of God maketh haste to reward the just, and in a swift hour his blessing beareth fruit.

25 Say not: What need I, and what good shall I have by this?

26 Say not: I am sufficient for myself: and what shall I be made worse by this?

27 In the day of good things be not unmindful of evils: and in the day of evils be not unmindful of good things:

28 For it is easy before God in the day of death to reward every one according to his ways.

29 The affliction of an hour maketh one forget great delights, and in the end of a man is the disclosing of his works.

30 Praise not any man before death, for a man is known by his children.

31 Bring not every man into thy house: for many are the snares of the deceitful.

32 For as corrupted bowels send forth stinking breath, and as the partridge is brought into the cage, and as the roe into the snare: so also is the heart of the proud, and as a spy that looketh on the fall of his neighbour.

33 For he lieth in wait and turneth good into evil, and on the elect he will lay a blot.

34 Of one spark cometh a great fire, and of one deceitful man much blood: and a sinful man lieth in wait for blood.

35 Take heed to thyself of a mischievous man, for he worketh evils: lest he bring upon thee reproach for ever.

KNOX TRANSLATION

24 Swift, swift comes the blessing that rewards faithful service; in one short hour its fruits ripen.
25 Never tell thyself, need thou hast none, there is no more
good can befall thee; 26 never flatter thyself, thou art master
of thy own lot, no harm can touch thee now. 27 Rather,
bethink thyself of foul weather in fair, of fair weather in foul;
28 on the very day of a man's death God can give him his
deserts. 29 One hour of misery, how it can efface in the memory long years of ease! Only a man's death-bed brings the
full history of his fortunes to light.
30 Never call a man happy until he is dead; his true epitaph
is written in his children.
31 Do not keep thy house open to every comer; knaves have
many shifts. 32 Foul breath lurks in a diseased body; the partridge a hidden lure awaits, a hidden snare the doe; so there
be unquiet hearts, ever on the watch for a neighbour's downfall, 33 ready to interpret good things amiss, and cast blame
on the innocent. 34 One spark is enough to spread a fire, and
one man's treachery may be the cause of bloodshed; such villains as these plot against life itself. 35 Against such a
plague be thou timely on thy guard, or it may prove thy

TODAY'S ENGLISH VERSION

will receive the Lord's blessing as their reward, and that
blessing can be given in a moment. 23 Don't be concerned
about what you need, or what success the future holds for
you. 24 On the other hand, don't think that you have everything you need or that nothing can go wrong for you in the
future. 25 When things are going well, people don't think
about hard times; and when things are going badly, they forget about prosperity. 26 The Lord can easily wait until the
day of our death to reward or punish us. 27 At that time our
deeds are open for all to see; all our happiness can be erased
in that one moment of misery. 28 So then, don't think of
anyone's life as happy until it is over, because all the evidence is not in until the person is dead.[a]

29 Be careful about the kind of person you invite into your
home, because clever people can fool you in many ways.
30 A proud person is a decoy to lure you into danger; like a
spy, he will look for your weaknesses.[b] 31 He will make good
appear evil and find fault with the noblest actions. 32 A single spark can set a pile of coals ablaze, and a sinner is just
waiting for a chance to do violence. 33 Watch out for such
people and their evil plans; they will ruin you permanently.

[a] *Hebrew* all . . . dead; *Greek* a man will be known by his children.
[b] *Hebrew* look . . . weaknesses; *Greek* wait for your downfall.

NEW REVISED STANDARD VERSION

22 The blessing of the Lord is[a] the reward of the pious,
and quickly God causes his blessing to flourish.
23 Do not say, "What do I need,
and what further benefit can be mine?"
24 Do not say, "I have enough,
and what harm can come to me now?"
25 In the day of prosperity, adversity is forgotten,
and in the day of adversity, prosperity is not
remembered.
26 For it is easy for the Lord on the day of death
to reward individuals according to their conduct.
27 An hour's misery makes one forget past delights,
and at the close of one's life one's deeds are revealed.
28 Call no one happy before his death;
by how he ends, a person becomes known.[b]

29 Do not invite everyone into your home,
for many are the tricks of the crafty.
30 Like a decoy partridge in a cage, so is the mind of the
proud,
and like spies they observe your weakness;[c]
31 for they lie in wait, turning good into evil,
and to worthy actions they attach blame.
32 From a spark many coals are kindled,
and a sinner lies in wait to shed blood.
33 Beware of scoundrels, for they devise evil,
and they may ruin your reputation forever.

a Heb: Gk *is in* *b* Heb: Gk *and through his children a person becomes known* *c* Heb: Gk *downfall*

NEW AMERICAN BIBLE

22 God's blessing is the lot of the just man,
and in due time his hopes bear fruit.
23 Say not: "What do I need?
What further pleasure can be mine?"
24 Say not: "I am independent.
What harm can come to me now?"
25 The day of prosperity makes one forget adversity;
the day of adversity makes one forget prosperity.
26 For it is easy with the LORD on the day of death
to repay man according to his deeds.
27 A moment's affliction brings forgetfulness of past
delights;
when a man dies, his life is revealed.
28 Call no man happy before his death,
for by how he ends, a man is known.

29 Bring not every man into your house,
for many are the snares of the crafty one;
30 Though he seem like a bird confined in a cage,
yet like a spy he will pick out the weak spots.
31 The talebearer turns good into evil;
with a spark he sets many coals afire.
32 The evil man lies in wait for blood,
and plots against your choicest possessions.
33 Avoid a wicked man, for he breeds only evil,
lest you incur a lasting stain.

NEW JERUSALEM BIBLE

22 The blessing of the Lord is the reward of the devout,
in a moment God brings his blessing to flower.
23 Do not say, 'What are my needs,
how much shall I have in the future?'
24 And do not say, 'I am self-sufficient,
what disaster can affect me now?'
25 In prosperous times, disasters are forgotten
and in times of disaster, no one remembers
prosperity.
26 Yet it is a trifle for the Lord on the day someone dies
to repay him as his conduct deserves.
27 A moment's adversity, and pleasures are forgotten;
in a person's last hour his deeds will stand revealed.
28 Call no one fortunate before his death;
it is by his end that someone will be known.

29 Do not bring everyone home with you,
for many are the traps of the crafty.
30 Like a captive partridge in a cage, so is the heart of the
proud:
like a spy he watches for your downfall,
31 ever on the look-out, turning good into bad
and finding fault with what is praiseworthy.
32 A hearthful of glowing coals starts from a single spark,
and the sinner lurks for the chance to spill blood.
33 Beware of a scoundrel and his evil contrivances,
in case he puts a smear on you for ever.

GREEK OLD TESTAMENT

33 πρόσεχε ἀπὸ κακούργου, πονηρὰ γὰρ τεκταίνει,
μήποτε μῶμον εἰς τὸν αἰῶνα δῷ σοι.
34 ἐνοίκισον ἀλλότριον, καὶ διαστρέψει σε ἐν ταραχαῖς
καὶ ἀπαλλοτριώσει σε τῶν ἰδίων σου.
12 Ἐὰν εὖ ποιῇς, γνῶθι τίνι ποιεῖς,
καὶ ἔσται χάρις τοῖς ἀγαθοῖς σου.
2 εὖ ποίησον εὐσεβεῖ, καὶ εὑρήσεις ἀνταπόδομα,
καὶ εἰ μὴ παρ' αὐτοῦ, ἀλλὰ παρὰ τοῦ ὑψίστου.
3 οὐκ ἔσται ἀγαθὰ τῷ ἐνδελεχίζοντι εἰς κακὰ
καὶ τῷ ἐλεημοσύνην μὴ χαριζομένῳ.
4 δὸς τῷ εὐσεβεῖ καὶ μὴ ἀντιλάβῃ τοῦ ἁμαρτωλοῦ.
5 εὖ ποίησον ταπεινῷ καὶ μὴ δῷς ἀσεβεῖ·
ἐμπόδισον τοὺς ἄρτους αὐτοῦ καὶ μὴ δῷς αὐτῷ,
ἵνα μὴ ἐν αὐτοῖς σε δυναστεύσῃ·
διπλάσια γὰρ κακὰ εὑρήσεις
ἐν πᾶσιν ἀγαθοῖς, οἷς ἂν ποιήσῃς αὐτῷ.
6 ὅτι καὶ ὁ ὕψιστος ἐμίσησεν ἁμαρτωλοὺς
καὶ τοῖς ἀσεβέσιν ἀποδώσει ἐκδίκησιν.
7 δὸς τῷ ἀγαθῷ καὶ μὴ ἀντιλάβῃ τοῦ ἁμαρτωλοῦ.
8 Οὐκ ἐκδικηθήσεται ἐν ἀγαθοῖς ὁ φίλος,
καὶ οὐ κρυβήσεται ἐν κακοῖς ὁ ἐχθρός.
9 ἐν ἀγαθοῖς ἀνδρὸς οἱ ἐχθροὶ αὐτοῦ ἐν λύπῃ,
καὶ ἐν τοῖς κακοῖς αὐτοῦ καὶ ὁ φίλος διαχωρισθήσεται.

KING JAMES VERSION

34 Receive a stranger into thine house, and he will disturb thee, and turn thee out of thine own.

12 When thou wilt do good, know to whom thou doest it; so shalt thou be thanked for thy benefits.

2 Do good to the godly man, and thou shalt find a recompence; and if not from him, yet from the most High.

3 There can no good come to him that is always occupied in evil, nor to him that giveth no alms.

4 Give to the godly man, and help not a sinner.

5 Do well unto him that is lowly, but give not to the ungodly: hold back thy bread, and give it not unto him, lest he overmaster thee thereby: for [else] thou shalt receive twice as much evil for all the good thou shalt have done unto him.

6 For the most High hateth sinners, and will repay vengeance unto the ungodly, and keepeth them against the mighty day of their punishment.

7 Give unto the good, and help not the sinner.

8 A friend cannot be known in prosperity: and an enemy cannot be hidden in adversity.

9 In the prosperity of a man enemies will be grieved: but in his adversity even a friend will depart.

DOUAY OLD TESTAMENT

36 Receive a stranger in, and he shall overthrow thee with a whirlwind, and shall turn thee out of thy own.

12 IF thou do good, know to whom thou dost it, and there shall be much thanks for thy good deeds.

2 Do good to the just, and thou shalt find great recompense: and if not of him, assuredly of the Lord.

3 For there is no good for him that is always occupied in evil, and that giveth no alms: for the Highest hateth sinners, and hath mercy on the penitent.

4 Give to the merciful and uphold not the sinner: God will repay vengeance to the ungodly and to sinners, and keep them against the day of vengeance.

5 Give to the good, and receive not a sinner.

6 Do good to the humble, and give not to the ungodly: hold back thy bread, and give it not to him, lest thereby he overmaster thee.

7 For thou shalt receive twice as much evil for all the good thou shalt have done to him: for the Highest also hateth sinners, and will repay vengeance to the ungodly.

8 A friend shall not be known in prosperity, and an enemy shall not be hidden in adversity.

9 In the prosperity of a man, his enemies are grieved: and a friend is known in his adversity.

KNOX TRANSLATION

eternal disgrace. 36 Alien let in is whirlwind let in, that shall
alienate from thee all thou hast.[a]

12 Favour if thou grantest, look well to whom thou
grantest it; so shall thy favours earn abundant gratitude. 2 A good turn done to an honest man is well rewarded;
if not he, then the Lord will repay thee. 3 It goes ill with the
man who spends all his time courting the wicked, and alms
gives none; does not the most High himself treat sinners as
his enemies, never sparing them till they repent? 4 ...For
rebellious sinners he has nothing but punishment, although
he may save up the day of their punishing.[b] 5 Keep thy
favours for the kind-hearted, and let the sinners go without
their welcome. 6 The friendless man deserves thy alms; to
the godless give nothing; nay, prevent food reaching him, or
he will have the mastery of thee. 7 All his gain will be doubly
thy loss; and so it is that the most High both hates sinners
and will bring retribution on their impiety.
8 Prosperity will not shew thee who are thy friends. In bad
times, thy enemies may triumph openly, 9 that till now were
grieved at thy good fortune; but it is these bad times will
shew thee try friends too.

a *vv.* 31-36: The exact bearing of these verses cannot be determined. In verse 32, 'unquiet hearts' is literally 'proud hearts'; but pride seems irrelevant to the present context, and it is likely that the original Hebrew text had 'hearts of aliens' (as in verse 36). In that case the whole passage may be a warning against undue fraternization with Gentiles. *b* At the beginning of this verse, the Latin inserts the words, 'Keep thy favours for the merciful, and let the sinners go without their entertainment', which appears to be a duplicate of verse 5, included by error. It has been omitted in the rendering given above, as fatally disturbing to the order of the sentence. There was no doubt some dislocation of the text here; the Greek, too, has a duplicate of verse 5 immediately after verse 7.

TODAY'S ENGLISH VERSION

34 If you bring a stranger home with you, it will only cause
trouble, even between you and your own family.

12 When you do a good deed, make sure you know who
is benefiting from it; then what you do will not be
wasted.[a] 2 You will be repaid for any kindness you show to
a devout person. If he doesn't repay you, the Most High will.
3 No good ever comes to a person who gives comfort to the
wicked; it is not a righteous act.[b] 4 Give to religious people,
but don't help sinners. 5 Do good to humble people, but
don't give anything to those who are not devout. Don't give
them food, or they will use your kindness against you. Every
good thing you do for such people will bring you twice as
much trouble in return. 6 The Most High himself hates sinners, and he will punish them. 7 Give to good people, but do
not help sinners.

8 When things are going well, it is hard to tell who your
real friends are, but in hard times you can recognize your
enemies; 9 even your friends will leave you then. But when
you are successful, your enemies will act like friends.[c]

[a] what you do . . . wasted; *or* you will be thanked for what you do.
[b] *Hebrew* gives . . . act; *Greek* makes evil a habit or refuses to give to the poor. [c] *Hebrew* act like friends; *Greek* be sorry.

NEW REVISED STANDARD VERSION

34 Receive strangers into your home and they will stir up
trouble for you,
and will make you a stranger to your own family.

12 If you do good, know to whom you do it,
and you will be thanked for your good deeds.
2 Do good to the devout, and you will be repaid—
if not by them, certainly by the Most High.
3 No good comes to one who persists in evil
or to one who does not give alms.
4 Give to the devout, but do not help the sinner.
5 Do good to the humble, but do not give to the
ungodly;
hold back their bread, and do not give it to them,
for by means of it they might subdue you;
then you will receive twice as much evil
for all the good you have done to them.
6 For the Most High also hates sinners
and will inflict punishment on the ungodly.[a]
7 Give to the one who is good, but do not help the sinner.
8 A friend is not known[b] in prosperity,
nor is an enemy hidden in adversity.
9 One's enemies are friendly[c] when one prospers,
but in adversity even one's friend disappears.

a Other ancient authorities add *and he is keeping them for the day of their punishment* b Other ancient authorities read *punished* c Heb: Gk *grieved*

NEW AMERICAN BIBLE

34 Lodge a stranger with you, and he will subvert your
course,
and make a stranger of you to your own household.

12 If you do good, know for whom you are doing it,
and your kindness will have its effect.
2 Do good to the just man and reward will be yours,
if not from him, from the LORD.
3 No good comes to him who gives comfort to the wicked,
nor is it an act of mercy that he does.
4 Give to the good man, refuse the sinner;
refresh the downtrodden, give nothing to the proud
man.
5 No arms for combat should you give him,
lest he use them against yourself;
6 With twofold evil you will meet
for every good deed you do for him.
7 The Most High himself hates sinners,
and upon the wicked he takes vengeance.

8 In our prosperity we cannot know our friends;
in adversity an enemy will not remain concealed.
9 When a man is successful even his enemy is friendly;
in adversity even his friend disappears.

NEW JERUSALEM BIBLE

34 Give a home to a stranger and he will start trouble
and estrange you from your own family.

12 If you mean to do a kindness, choose the right
person,
then your good deeds will not be wasted.
2 Do good to someone devout, and you will be rewarded,
if not by that person, then certainly by the Most
High.
3 No good will come to one who persists in evil,
or who refuses to give alms.
4 Give to the devout,
do not go to the help of a sinner.
5 Do good to the humble,
give nothing to the godless.
Refuse him bread, do not give him any,
it might make him stronger than you are;
then you would be repaid evil twice over
for all the good you had done him.
6 For the Most High himself detests sinners,
and will repay the wicked with what they deserve.
7 Give to the good,
and do not go to the help of a sinner.
8 In prosperity you cannot always tell a true friend,
but in adversity you cannot mistake an enemy.
9 When someone is doing well that person's enemies are
sad,
when someone is doing badly, even a friend will keep
at a distance.

GREEK OLD TESTAMENT

10 μὴ πιστεύσῃς τῷ ἐχθρῷ σου εἰς τὸν αἰῶνα·
ὡς γὰρ ὁ χαλκὸς ἰοῦται, οὕτως ἡ πονηρία αὐτοῦ·
11 καὶ ἐὰν ταπεινωθῇ καὶ πορεύηται συγκεκυφώς,
ἐπίστησον τὴν ψυχήν σου καὶ φύλαξαι ἀπ᾽ αὐτοῦ
καὶ ἔσῃ αὐτῷ ὡς ἐκμεμαχὼς ἔσοπτρον
καὶ γνώσῃ ὅτι οὐκ εἰς τέλος κατίωσεν.
12 μὴ στήσῃς αὐτὸν παρὰ σεαυτῷ,
μὴ ἀνατρέψας σε στῇ ἐπὶ τὸν τόπον σου·
μὴ καθίσῃς αὐτὸν ἐκ δεξιῶν σου,
μήποτε ζητήσῃ τὴν καθέδραν σου
καὶ ἐπ᾽ ἐσχάτων ἐπιγνώσῃ τοὺς λόγους μου
καὶ ἐπὶ τῶν ῥημάτων μου κατανυγήσῃ.
13 τίς ἐλεήσει ἐπαοιδὸν ὀφιόδηκτον
καὶ πάντας τοὺς προσάγοντας θηρίοις;
14 οὕτως τὸν προσπορευόμενον ἀνδρὶ ἁμαρτωλῷ
καὶ συμφυρόμενον ἐν ταῖς ἁμαρτίαις αὐτοῦ.
15 ὥραν μετὰ σοῦ διαμενεῖ,
καὶ ἐὰν ἐκκλίνῃς, οὐ μὴ καρτερήσῃ.
16 καὶ ἐν τοῖς χείλεσιν αὐτοῦ γλυκανεῖ ὁ ἐχθρὸς
καὶ ἐν τῇ καρδίᾳ αὐτοῦ βουλεύσεται ἀνατρέψαι σε εἰς βόθρον·
ἐν ὀφθαλμοῖς αὐτοῦ δακρύσει ὁ ἐχθρός,
καὶ ἐὰν εὕρῃ καιρόν, οὐκ ἐμπλησθήσεται ἀφ᾽ αἵματος.
17 κακὰ ἐὰν ὑπαντήσῃ σοι, εὑρήσεις αὐτὸν πρότερον ἐκεῖ σου,
καὶ ὡς βοηθῶν ὑποσχάσει πτέρναν σου·
18 τὴν κεφαλὴν αὐτοῦ κινήσει καὶ ἐπικροτήσει ταῖς χερσὶν αὐτοῦ
καὶ πολλὰ διαψιθυρίσει καὶ ἀλλοιώσει τὸ πρόσωπον αὐτοῦ.

KING JAMES VERSION

10 Never trust thine enemy: for like as iron rusteth, so is his wickedness.

11 Though he humble himself, and go crouching, yet take good heed and beware of him, and thou shalt be unto him as if thou hadst wiped a lookingglass, and thou shalt know that his rust hath not been altogether wiped away.

12 Set him not by thee, lest, when he hath overthrown thee, he stand up in thy place; neither let him sit at thy right hand, lest he seek to take thy seat, and thou at the last remember my words, and be pricked therewith.

13 Who will pity a charmer that is bitten with a serpent, or any such as come nigh wild beasts?

14 So one that goeth to a sinner, and is defiled with him in his sins, who will pity?

15 For a while he will abide with thee, but if thou begin to fall, he will not tarry.

16 An enemy speaketh sweetly with his lips, but in his heart he imagineth how to throw thee into a pit: he will weep with his eyes, but if he find opportunity, he will not be satisfied with blood.

17 If adversity come upon thee, thou shalt find him there first; and though he pretend to help thee, yet shall he undermine thee.

18 He will shake his head, and clap his hands, and whisper much, and change his countenance.

DOUAY OLD TESTAMENT

10 Never trust thy enemy: for as a brass pot his wickedness rusteth:

11 Though he humble himself and go crouching, yet take good heed and beware of him.

12 Set him not by thee, neither let him sit on thy right hand, lest he turn into thy place, and seek to take thy seat: and at the last thou acknowledge my words, and be pricked with my sayings.

13 Who will pity an enchanter struck by a serpent, or any that come near wild beasts? so is it with him that keepeth company with a wicked man, and is involved in his sins.

14 For an hour he will abide with thee: but if thou begin to decline, he will not endure it.

15 An enemy speaketh sweetly with his lips, but in his heart he lieth in wait, to throw thee into a pit.

16 An enemy weepeth with his eyes: but if he find an opportunity he will not be satisfied with blood:

17 And if evils come upon thee, thou shalt find him there first.

18 An enemy hath tears in his eyes, and while he pretendeth to help thee, will undermine thy feet.

19 He will shake his head, and clap his hands, and whisper much, and change his countenance.

KNOX TRANSLATION

10 Never trust an enemy; deep as verdigris on copper his
malice is ingrained. 11 Lout he never so low, look to it well
and be on thy guard against him; 12 never let him attend on
thee, or sit at thy right hand. His eyes are on thy place; a
time will come when he will sit where thou sittest, when
thou wilt recognize the truth of my warning, and be stung by
the memory. 13 Who shall pity snake-charmer or beast-tamer
if he takes hurt? And he deserves no less, who consorts with
rogues and is entangled in their sinful ways. 14 This false
friend will be thy companion for an hour, then, if thou art for
altering thy course, he will not hear of it; 15 all those honeyed words do but mask a plot to lure thee into some ditch.
16 How he weeps for thee, this enemy of thine! Yet, if his
chance comes, there will be no glutting him with thy blood;
17 come thou into mischief, he is there already waiting for
thee. 18 How he weeps for thee, this enemy of thine! If he
makes to aid thee, it is only to trip thy heel; 19 then what
mopping and mowing, what clapping of the hands and whispering, what a change of mien!

TODAY'S ENGLISH VERSION

10 Never trust an enemy; his wickedness is as destructive as
rust. 11 Watch out, and be on guard against him, even if he
acts ever so humble. He is like a metal mirror that rusts
away if you don't keep it polished. 12 Seat an enemy at your
right hand, and the next thing you know he'll be trying to
get your own place of honor. Put him next to you, and he
will overthrow you. Then you will realize the truth of my
words, and be stung with regret when you remember them.
13 Nobody feels sorry for snake charmers or wild animal
tamers who get bitten, 14 and nobody will feel sorry for you
if you run around with sinners and get involved in their
wrongdoing.

15 An enemy will stay with you for a while, but not when
trouble comes. 16 He will speak fine words while he plots
how to trap you. He will pretend to share your sorrows, but
he will kill you if he gets a chance. 17 If trouble comes your
way, you will find him waiting, ready to trip you up while he
pretends to help you. 18 He will be a different person then,
rubbing his hands, nodding his head, and spreading rumors
about you.

NEW REVISED STANDARD VERSION

10 Never trust your enemy,
for like corrosion in copper, so is his wickedness.
11 Even if he humbles himself and walks bowed down,
take care to be on your guard against him.
Be to him like one who polishes a mirror,
to be sure it does not become completely tarnished.
12 Do not put him next to you,
or he may overthrow you and take your place.
Do not let him sit at your right hand,
or else he may try to take your own seat,
and at last you will realize the truth of my words,
and be stung by what I have said.

13 Who pities a snake charmer when he is bitten,
or all those who go near wild animals?
14 So no one pities a person who associates with a sinner
and becomes involved in the other's sins.
15 He stands by you for a while,
but if you falter, he will not be there.
16 An enemy speaks sweetly with his lips,
but in his heart he plans to throw you into a pit;
an enemy may have tears in his eyes,
but if he finds an opportunity he will never have
enough of your blood.
17 If evil comes upon you, you will find him there ahead of
you;
pretending to help, he will trip you up.
18 Then he will shake his head, and clap his hands,
and whisper much, and show his true face.

NEW AMERICAN BIBLE

10 Never trust your enemy,
for his wickedness is like corrosion in bronze.
11 Even though he acts humbly and peaceably toward you,
take care to be on your guard against him.
Rub him as one polishes a brazen mirror,
and you will find that there is still corrosion.
12 Let him not stand near you,
lest he oust you and take your place.
Let him not sit at your right hand,
lest he then demand your seat,
And in the end you appreciate my advice,
when you groan with regret, as I warned you.
13 Who pities a snake charmer when he is bitten,
or anyone who goes near a wild beast?
14 So is it with the companion of the proud man,
who is involved in his sins:
15 While you stand firm, he makes no bold move;
but if you slip, he cannot hold back.
16 With his lips an enemy speaks sweetly,
but in his heart he schemes to plunge you into the
abyss.
Though your enemy has tears in his eyes,
if given the chance, he will never have enough of
your blood.
17 If evil comes upon you, you will find him at hand;
feigning to help, he will trip you up,
18 Then he will nod his head and clap his hands
and hiss repeatedly, and show his true face.

NEW JERUSALEM BIBLE

10 Do not ever trust an enemy;
as bronze tarnishes, so does an enemy's malice.
11 Even if he behaves humbly and comes bowing and
scraping,
maintain your reserve and be on your guard against
him.
Behave towards him as if you were polishing a mirror,
you will find that his tarnish cannot last.
12 Do not stand him beside you
in case he thrusts you out and takes your place.
Do not seat him on your right,
or he will be after your position,
and then you will remember what I have said
and sadly admit that I was right.
13 Who feels sorry for a snake-charmer bitten by a snake,
or for those who take risks with savage animals?—
14 just so for one who consorts with a sinner,
and becomes an accomplice in his sins.
15 He will stay with you for a while,
but if you once give way he will press his advantage.
16 An enemy may have sweetness on his lips,
and in his heart a scheme to throw you into the ditch.
An enemy may have tears in his eyes,
but if he gets a chance there can never be too much
blood for him.
17 If you meet with misfortune, you will find him there
before you,
and, pretending to help you, he will trip you up.
18 He will wag his head and clap his hands,
he will whisper a lot and his expression will change.

GREEK OLD TESTAMENT

13 Ὁ ἁπτόμενος πίσσης μολυνθήσεται,
καὶ ὁ κοινωνῶν ὑπερηφάνῳ ὁμοιωθήσεται αὐτῷ.
2 βάρος ὑπὲρ σὲ μὴ ἄρῃς
καὶ ἰσχυροτέρῳ σου καὶ πλουσιωτέρῳ μὴ κοινώνει.
τί κοινωνήσει χύτρα πρὸς λέβητα;
αὕτη προσκρούσει, καὶ αὕτη συντριβήσεται.
3 πλούσιος ἠδίκησεν, καὶ αὐτὸς προσενεβριμήσατο·
πτωχὸς ἠδίκηται, καὶ αὐτὸς προσδεηθήσεται.
4 ἐὰν χρησιμεύσῃς, ἐργᾶται ἐν σοί·
καὶ ἐὰν ὑστερήσῃς, καταλείψει σε.
5 ἐὰν ἔχῃς, συμβιώσεταί σοι
καὶ ἀποκενώσει σε, καὶ αὐτὸς οὐ πονέσει.
6 χρείαν ἔσχηκέν σου, καὶ ἀποπλανήσει σε
καὶ προσγελάσεταί σοι καὶ δώσει σοι ἐλπίδα·
λαλήσει σοι καλὰ καὶ ἐρεῖ Τίς ἡ χρεία σου;
7 καὶ αἰσχυνεῖ σε ἐν τοῖς βρώμασιν αὐτοῦ,
ἕως οὗ ἀποκενώσῃ σε δὶς ἢ τρίς,
καὶ ἐπ' ἐσχάτων καταμωκήσεταί σου·
μετὰ ταῦτα ὄψεταί σε καὶ καταλείψει σε
καὶ τὴν κεφαλὴν αὐτοῦ κινήσει ἐπὶ σοί.
8 πρόσεχε μὴ ἀποπλανηθῇς
καὶ μὴ ταπεινωθῇς ἐν ἀφροσύνῃ σου.

KING JAMES VERSION

13 He that toucheth pitch shall be defiled therewith; and he that hath fellowship with a proud man shall be like unto him.

2 Burden not thyself above thy power while thou livest; and have no fellowship with one that is mightier and richer than thyself: for how agree the kettle and the earthen pot together? for if the one be smitten against the other, it shall be broken.

3 The rich man hath done wrong, and yet he threateneth withal: the poor is wronged, and he must intreat also.

4 If thou be for his profit, he will use thee: but if thou have nothing, he will forsake thee.

5 If thou have any thing, he will live with thee: yea, he will make thee bare, and will not be sorry for it.

6 If he have need of thee, he will deceive thee, and smile upon thee, and put thee in hope; he will speak thee fair, and say, What wantest thou?

7 And he will shame thee by his meats, until he have drawn thee dry twice or thrice, and at the last he will laugh thee to scorn: afterward, when he seeth thee, he will forsake thee, and shake his head at thee.

8 Beware that thou be not deceived, and brought down in thy jollity.

DOUAY OLD TESTAMENT

13 HE that toucheth pitch, shall be defiled with it: and he that hath fellowship with the proud, shall put on pride.

2 He shall take a burden upon him that hath fellowship with one more honourable than himself. And have no fellowship with one that is richer than thyself.

3 What agreement shall the earthen pot have with the kettle? for if they knock one against the other, it shall be broken.

4 The rich man hath done wrong, and yet he will fume: but the poor is wronged and must hold his peace.

5 If thou give, he will make use of thee: and if thou have nothing, he will forsake thee.

6 If thou have any thing, he will live with thee, and will make thee bare, and he will not be sorry for thee.

7 If he have need of thee he will deceive thee, and smiling upon thee will put thee in hope; he will speak thee fair, and will say: What wantest thou?

8 And he will shame thee by his meats, till he have drawn thee dry twice or thrice, and at last he will laugh at thee: and afterward when he seeth thee, he will forsake thee, and shake his head at thee.

9 Humble thyself to God, and wait for his hands.

10 Beware that thou be not deceived into folly, and be humbled.

11 Be not lowly in thy wisdom, lest being humbled thou be deceived into folly.

KNOX TRANSLATION

13 Who handles pitch, with pitch is defiled; who throws
in his lot with insolence, of insolence shall have his
fill. 2 A heavy burden thou art shouldering, if thou wouldst
consort with thy betters; not for thee the company of the
rich. 3 Pot and kettle are ill matched; it is the pot breaks
when they come together; 4 rich man, that has seized all he
can, frets and fumes for more; poor man robbed may not so
much as speak. 5 If thou hast favours to bestow, thy rich
friend will make use of thee; if none, he bids thee farewell;
6 thy guest, he will eat up all thou canst give, and have no
pity to waste on thee. 7 Has he need of thee? Then, to be
sure, he will ply his arts, all smiles and fair speeches, and
eagerness to know what thy need is; 8 he encumbers thee,
now, with hospitality. So, twice and three times, he will
drain thee dry; then he will turn on thee with a laugh, and if
he meets thee again, it will be to pass thee by with a toss of
the head.

9 Learn to abase thyself before God, and wait for his hand
to beckon thee, 10 instead of courting false hopes, that bring
their own abasement. 11 For all thy wisdom, do not hold thyself too cheap, or thou wilt lower thyself to folly. 12 If a great

TODAY'S ENGLISH VERSION

13 If you touch tar, it will stick to you, and if you keep
company with arrogant people, you will come to be
just like them. 2 Don't try to lift something too heavy for
you, and don't keep company with people who are richer and
more powerful than you. You cannot keep a clay pot next to
an iron kettle; the pot will break if it hits the kettle. 3 If a
rich person wrongs someone, he can afford to add insult to
injury; but if a poor person is wronged, he is forced to apolo-
gize for himself. 4 A rich person will use you as long as he
can profit from it, but when you need him, he will leave you
helpless. 5 He will live with you as long as you have anything and will gladly drain you dry. 6 If he needs you, he will
trick you with his smiles and cheerful, kindly words. "Do you
need anything?" he will ask. 7 He will feed you until you are
embarrassed. Finally, when he has drained you two or three
times over, he will laugh at you. If you see him later, he will
pretend he doesn't know you, and will pass you by.
8 Be careful not to be misled; you can be enjoying yourself
and suddenly find yourself humiliated. 9 If you are invited to

NEW REVISED STANDARD VERSION

13 Whoever touches pitch gets dirty,
and whoever associates with a proud person
becomes like him.
2 Do not lift a weight too heavy for you,
or associate with one mightier and richer than you.
How can the clay pot associate with the iron kettle?
The pot will strike against it and be smashed.
3 A rich person does wrong, and even adds insults;
a poor person suffers wrong, and must add
apologies.
4 A rich person[a] will exploit you if you can be of use to
him,
but if you are in need he will abandon you.
5 If you own something, he will live with you;
he will drain your resources without a qualm.
6 When he needs you he will deceive you,
and will smile at you and encourage you;
he will speak to you kindly and say, "What do you
need?"
7 He will embarrass you with his delicacies,
until he has drained you two or three times,
and finally he will laugh at you.
Should he see you afterwards, he will pass you by
and shake his head at you.

8 Take care not to be led astray
and humiliated when you are enjoying yourself.[b]

a Gk *He* *b* Other ancient authorities read *in your folly*

NEW AMERICAN BIBLE

13 He who touches pitch blackens his hand;
he who associates with an impious man learns his
ways.
2 Bear no burden too heavy for you;
go with no one greater or wealthier than yourself.
How can the earthen pot go with the metal cauldron?
When they knock together, the pot will be smashed:
3 The rich man does wrong and boasts of it,
the poor man is wronged and begs forgiveness.
4 As long as the rich man can use you he will enslave
you,
but when you are exhausted, he will abandon you.
5 As long as you have anything he will speak fair words
to you,
and with smiles he will win your confidence;
6 When he needs something from you he will cajole you,
then without regret he will impoverish you.
7 While it serves his purpose he will beguile you,
then twice or three times he will terrify you;
When later he sees you he will pass you by,
and shake his head over you.
8 Guard against being presumptuous;
be not as those who lack sense.

NEW JERUSALEM BIBLE

13 Whoever touches pitch will be defiled,
and anyone who associates with the proud will
come
to be like them.
2 Do not try to carry a burden too heavy for you,
do not associate with someone more powerful and
wealthy than yourself.
Why put the clay pot next to the iron cauldron?
It will only break when they bang against each other.
3 The rich does wrong and takes a high line;
the poor is wronged and has to beg for pardon.
4 If you are useful the rich will exploit you,
if you go bankrupt he will desert you.
5 Are you well off?—he will live with you,
he will clean you out without a single qualm.
6 Does he need you?—he will hoodwink you,
smile at you and raise your hopes;
he will speak politely to you
and say, 'Is there anything you need?'
7 He will make you feel small at his dinner parties
and, having cleaned you out two or three times over,
will end by laughing at you.
Afterwards, when he sees you, he will avoid you
and shake his head about you.

8 Take care you are not hoodwinked
and thus humiliated through your own stupidity.

GREEK OLD TESTAMENT

9 Προσκαλεσαμένου σε δυνάστου ὑποχωρῶν γίνου,
καὶ τόσῳ μᾶλλόν σε προσκαλέσεται·
10 μὴ ἔμπιπτε, μὴ ἀπωσθῇς,
καὶ μὴ μακρὰν ἀφίστω, ἵνα μὴ ἐπιλησθῇς.
11 μὴ ἔπεχε ἰσηγορεῖσθαι μετ᾽ αὐτοῦ
καὶ μὴ πίστευε τοῖς πλείοσιν λόγοις αὐτοῦ·
ἐκ πολλῆς γὰρ λαλιᾶς πειράσει σε
καὶ ὡς προσγελῶν ἐξετάσει σε.
12 ἀνελεήμων ὁ μὴ συντηρῶν λόγους
καὶ οὐ μὴ φείσηται περὶ κακώσεως καὶ δεσμῶν.
13 συντήρησον καὶ πρόσεχε σφοδρῶς,
ὅτι μετὰ τῆς πτώσεώς σου περιπατεῖς.
15 Πᾶν ζῷον ἀγαπᾷ τὸ ὅμοιον αὐτῷ
καὶ πᾶς ἄνθρωπος τὸν πλησίον αὐτοῦ·
16 πᾶσα σὰρξ κατὰ γένος συνάγεται,
καὶ τῷ ὁμοίῳ αὐτοῦ προσκολληθήσεται ἀνήρ.
17 τί κοινωνήσει λύκος ἀμνῷ;
οὕτως ἁμαρτωλὸς πρὸς εὐσεβῆ.
18 τίς εἰρήνη ὑαίνῃ πρὸς κύνα;
καὶ τίς εἰρήνη πλουσίῳ πρὸς πένητα;
19 κυνήγια λεόντων ὄναγροι ἐν ἐρήμῳ·
οὕτως νομαὶ πλουσίων πτωχοί.
20 βδέλυγμα ὑπερηφάνῳ ταπεινότης·
οὕτως βδέλυγμα πλουσίῳ πτωχός.

KING JAMES VERSION

9 If thou be invited of a mighty man, withdraw thyself, and so much the more will he invite thee.

10 Press thou not upon him, lest thou be put back; stand not far off, lest thou be forgotten.

11 Affect not to be made equal unto him in talk, and believe not his many words: for with much communication will he tempt thee, and smiling upon thee will get out thy secrets:

12 But cruelly he will lay up thy words, and will not spare to do thee hurt, and to put thee in prison.

13 Observe, and take good heed, for thou walkest in peril of thy overthrowing: when thou hearest these things, awake in thy sleep.

14 Love the Lord all thy life, and call upon him for thy salvation.

15 Every beast loveth his like, and every man loveth his neighbour.

16 All flesh consorteth according to kind, and a man will cleave to his like.

17 What fellowship hath the wolf with the lamb? so the sinner with the godly.

18 What agreement is there between the hyena and a dog? and what peace between the rich and the poor?

19 As the wild ass is the lion's prey in the wilderness: so the rich eat up the poor.

20 As the proud hate humility: so doth the rich abhor the poor.

DOUAY OLD TESTAMENT

12 If thou be invited by one that is mightier, withdraw thyself: for so he will invite thee the more.

13 Be not troublesome *to him,* lest thou be put back: and keep not far from him, lest thou be forgotten.

14 Affect not to speak with him as an equal: and believe not his many words: for by much talk he will sift thee, and smiling will examine thee concerning thy secrets.

15 His cruel mind will lay up thy words: and he will not spare to do thee hurt, and to cast thee into prison.

16 Take heed to thyself, and attend diligently to what thou hearest: for thou walkest in danger of thy ruin.

17 When thou hearest those things, see as it were in sleep, and thou shalt awake.

18 Love God all thy life, and call upon him for thy salvation.

19 Every beast loveth its like: so also every man him that is nearest to himself.

20 All flesh shall consort with the like to itself, and every man shall associate himself to his like.

21 If the wolf shall at any time have fellowship with the lamb, so the sinner with the just.

22 What fellowship hath a holy man with a dog, or what part hath the rich with the poor?

23 The wild ass is the lion's prey in the desert: so also the poor are devoured by the rich.

24 And as humility is an abomination to the proud: so also the rich man abhorreth the poor.

KNOX TRANSLATION

man bids thee come close, keep try distance; he will but bid
thee the more; 13 do not court a rebuff by wearying him, nor
yet withdraw altogether, and be forgotten. 14 Affable though
he should be, treat him never familiarly; all his friendly talk
is but a lure to drag thy secrets out of thee. 15 All that thou
sayest his pitiless heart will hold against thee; never a blow,
never a chain the less. 16 Have a care of thyself, give good
heed to this warning, thou that walkest with ruin ever at thy
side; 17 wake from sleep at the hearing of it, and see thy
peril. 18 Love God all thy days, and pray that he will send
thee good deliverance.

19 Every beast consorts with its own kind, and shall not
man with his fellow? 20 Like to like is nature's rule, and for
man like to like is still the best partnership; 21 as well match
wolf with lamb as rogue with honest liver. 22 Consecrated
person[a] and prowling dog, what have they in common? And
what fellowship can there be between rich man and poor?
23 Poor man is to rich as wild ass is to lion out in the desert,
his prey; 24 wealth hates poverty, as the proud heart scorns

a Or perhaps 'holy person'. The Greek text has, 'hyena'.

TODAY'S ENGLISH VERSION

the home of someone influential, be reserved in your behavior. Then he will invite you more often. 10 If you push yourself on him, he will put you in your place. On the other hand,
if you keep your distance from him, he will forget about you.
11 Don't pretend to be his equal or trust everything he says.
In spite of all of his long and polite conversation, he is testing you.
12 If a person does not keep confidences, he is cruel; he will
not hesitate to hurt you or have you put in jail. 13 Keep your
secrets to yourself and be very careful, for you are always
walking on dangerous ground.[a]
15 Every creature prefers its own kind, and people are no
different. 16 Just as animals of the same species flock together, so people keep company with people like themselves.
17 A sinner has no more in common with a devout person
than a wolf has with a lamb. 18 Rich people have no more in
common with poor people than hyenas have with dogs.
19 The rich hunt down the poor just as lions hunt down wild
donkeys in the open country. 20 Arrogant people have nothing but scorn for the humble, and the rich think of the poor

a Some manuscripts add verses 13b-14: When you hear this in your sleep, wake up! 14 As long as you live, love the Lord and call on him to rescue you.

NEW REVISED STANDARD VERSION

9 When an influential person invites you, be reserved,
and he will invite you more insistently.
10 Do not be forward, or you may be rebuffed;
do not stand aloof, or you will be forgotten.
11 Do not try to treat him as an equal,
or trust his lengthy conversations;
for he will test you by prolonged talk,
and while he smiles he will be examining you.
12 Cruel are those who do not keep your secrets;
they will not spare you harm or imprisonment.
13 Be on your guard and very careful,
for you are walking about with your own downfall.[a]

15 Every creature loves its like,
and every person the neighbor.
16 All living beings associate with their own kind,
and people stick close to those like themselves.
17 What does a wolf have in common with a lamb?
No more has a sinner with the devout.
18 What peace is there between a hyena and a dog?
And what peace between the rich and the poor?
19 Wild asses in the wilderness are the prey of lions;
likewise the poor are feeding grounds for the rich.
20 Humility is an abomination to the proud;
likewise the poor are an abomination to the rich.

a Other ancient authorities add as verse 14, *When you hear these things in your sleep, wake up! During all your life love the Lord, and call on him for your salvation.*

NEW AMERICAN BIBLE

9 When invited by a man of influence, keep your
distance;
then he will urge you all the more.
10 Be not bold with him lest you be rebuffed,
but keep not too far away lest you be forgotten.
11 Engage not freely in discussion with him,
trust not his many words;
For by prolonged talk he will test you,
and though smiling he will probe you.
12 Mercilessly he will make of you a laughingstock,
and will not refrain from injury or chains.
13 Be on your guard and take care
never to accompany men of violence.
14 Every living thing loves its own kind,
every man a man like himself.
15 Every being is drawn to its own kind;
with his own kind every man associates.
16 Is a wolf ever allied with a lamb?
So it is with the sinner and the just.
17 Can there be peace between the hyena and the dog?
Or between the rich and the poor can there be peace?
18 Lion's prey are the wild asses of the desert;
so too the poor are feeding grounds for the rich.
19 A proud man abhors lowliness;
so does the rich man abhor the poor.

NEW JERUSALEM BIBLE

9 When an influential person invites you, show
reluctance,
and he will press his invitation all the more.
10 Do not thrust yourself forward, in case you are pushed
aside,
but do not stand aloof, or you will be overlooked.
11 Do not affect to treat him as an equal,
do not trust his flow of words;
since all this talking is expressly meant to test you,
under cover of geniality he will be weighing you up.
12 Pitiless is anyone who retails gossip;
he will not spare you either blows or chains.
13 Be wary, take very great care,
because you are walking with your own downfall.

15 Every living thing loves its own sort,
and every man his fellow.
16 Every creature mixes with its kind,
and human beings stick to their own sort.
17 How can wolf and lamb agree?—
Just so with sinner and devout.
18 What peace can there be between hyena and dog?
And what peace between rich and poor?
19 Wild desert donkeys are the prey of lions;
so too, the poor is the quarry of the rich.
20 The proud thinks humility abhorrent;
so too, the rich abominates the poor.

GREEK OLD TESTAMENT

21 πλούσιος σαλευόμενος στηρίζεται ὑπὸ φίλων,
ταπεινὸς δὲ πεσὼν προσαπωθεῖται ὑπὸ φίλων.
22 πλουσίου σφαλέντος πολλοὶ ἀντιλήμπτορες·
ἐλάλησεν ἀπόρρητα, καὶ ἐδικαίωσαν αὐτόν.
ταπεινὸς ἔσφαλεν, καὶ προσεπετίμησαν αὐτῷ·
ἐφθέγξατο σύνεσιν, καὶ οὐκ ἐδόθη αὐτῷ τόπος.
23 πλούσιος ἐλάλησεν, καὶ πάντες ἐσίγησαν
καὶ τὸν λόγον αὐτοῦ ἀνύψωσαν ἕως τῶν νεφελῶν.
πτωχὸς ἐλάλησεν καὶ εἶπαν Τίς οὗτος;
κἂν προσκόψῃ, προσανατρέψουσιν αὐτόν.
24 ἀγαθὸς ὁ πλοῦτος, ᾧ μή ἐστιν ἁμαρτία,
καὶ πονηρὰ ἡ πτωχεία ἐν στόματι ἀσεβοῦς.
25 Καρδία ἀνθρώπου ἀλλοιοῖ τὸ πρόσωπον αὐτοῦ,
ἐάν τε εἰς ἀγαθὰ ἐάν τε εἰς κακά.
26 ἴχνος καρδίας ἐν ἀγαθοῖς πρόσωπον ἱλαρόν,
καὶ εὕρεσις παραβολῶν διαλογισμοὶ μετὰ κόπων.

14 μακάριος ἀνήρ, ὃς οὐκ ὠλίσθησεν ἐν τῷ στόματι αὐτοῦ
καὶ οὐ κατενύγη ἐν λύπῃ ἁμαρτιῶν·
2 μακάριος οὗ οὐ κατέγνω ἡ ψυχὴ αὐτοῦ,
καὶ ὃς οὐκ ἔπεσεν ἀπὸ τῆς ἐλπίδος αὐτοῦ.
3 Ἀνδρὶ μικρολόγῳ οὐ καλὸς ὁ πλοῦτος,
καὶ ἀνθρώπῳ βασκάνῳ ἵνα τί χρήματα;

KING JAMES VERSION

21 A rich man beginning to fall is held up of his friends: but a poor man being down is thrust also away by his friends.

22 When a rich man is fallen, he hath many helpers: he speaketh things not to be spoken, and yet men justify him: the poor man slipped, and yet they rebuked him too; he spake wisely, and could have no place.

23 When a rich man speaketh, every man holdeth his tongue, and, look, what he saith, they extol it to the clouds: but if the poor man speak, they say, What fellow is this? and if he stumble, they will help to overthrow him.

24 Riches are good unto him that hath no sin, and poverty is evil in the mouth of the ungodly.

25 The heart of a man changeth his countenance, whether it be for good or evil: and a merry heart maketh a cheerful countenance.

26 A cheerful countenance is a token of a heart that is in prosperity; and the finding out of parables is a wearisome labour of the mind.

14 Blessed is the man that hath not slipped with his mouth, and is not pricked with the multitude of sins.

2 Blessed is he whose conscience hath not condemned him, and who is not fallen from his hope in the Lord.

3 Riches are not comely for a niggard: and what should an envious man do with money?

DOUAY OLD TESTAMENT

25 When a rich man is shaken, he is kept up by his friends: but when a poor man is fallen down, he is thrust away even by his acquaintance.

26 When a rich man hath been deceived, he hath many helpers: he hath spoken proud things, and they have justified him.

27 The poor man was deceived, and he is rebuked also: he hath spoken wisely, and could have no place.

28 The rich man spoke, and all held their peace, and what he said they extol even to the clouds.

29 The poor man spoke, and they say: Who is this? and if he stumble, they will overthrow him.

30 Riches are good to him that hath no sin in his conscience: and poverty is very wicked in the mouth of the ungodly.

31 The heart of a man changeth his countenance, either for good, or for evil.

32 The token of a good heart, and a good countenance thou shalt hardly find, and with labour.

14 BLESSED is the man that hath not slipped by a word out of his mouth, and is not pricked with the remorse of sin.

2 Happy is he that hath had no sadness of his mind, and who is not fallen from his hope.

3 Riches are not comely for a covetous man and a niggard, and what should an envious man do with gold?

KNOX TRANSLATION

humble rank. 25 Totters the lordly house, it has friends to
sustain it; the poor man in his ruin is driven from familiar
doors. 26 Trips the rich man, he has many to keep him in
countenance; his insolent talk finds acquittal; 27 trips the
poor man, he is called to account for it; even for what he
said to the purpose, no allowance is made him. 28 Speaks the
rich man, all must listen in silence, and afterwards extol his
utterance to the skies; 29 speaks the poor man, Why, say all,
who is this? And if his words offend, it is the undoing of
him.
30 Yet, where there is no sin to smite a man's conscience, a
full purse is a blessing, and poverty itself is a great evil when
it goes with a blasphemer's tongue.[a] 31 Heart of man
changes his mien, for good or ill, 32 but where that pleasant
mien is, that comes of a generous heart, no short or easy
way there is to discover.[b]

14 Blessed the man whose lips have never betrayed him
into a fault, who has never known the sting of
remorse, 2 never felt conscience condemning him, and the
hope he lived by, his no more!
3 Vain is that store the miser cherishes; wasted on his
distrustful nature, the bright gold! 4 See how he wrongs

a Literally, 'in the mouth of a sinner'. This would naturally be interpreted as meaning 'in the estimation of a sinner', but such a rendering would give no parallel of thought between the two halves of the verse. *b* Or possibly the sense is that it is difficult to find instances of the pleasant mien that results from a generous heart, because they are so rare. If so, the first two verses of ch. 14 should be taken as part of this chapter.

TODAY'S ENGLISH VERSION

in the same way. 21 When a rich person stumbles, his friends
will steady him, but if a poor person falls, his friends will
have nothing to do with him. 22 When someone rich makes a
mistake, there are many people to cover up for him and
explain away all the things he never should have said. But
let someone poor make a mistake, and he gets nothing but
criticism. Even if what he says makes good sense, nobody
will listen. 23 When a rich person speaks, everyone is silent,
and they praise him to the skies for what he says. But let a
poor person speak, and everybody says, "Who is that?" They
push him down if he so much as stumbles.

24 There is nothing wrong with being rich if you haven't
sinned to get that way. But there is nothing sinful about
being poor, either. Only the ungodly think so. 25 It's what is
in your heart that makes the expression on your face happy
or sad. 26 If you feel cheerful, you will look cheerful,
although making up proverbs calls for some intense thought.

14 If a person never says anything carelessly, he is to be
congratulated; he doesn't need to feel guilty. 2 If a
person has a clear conscience and never gives up hope, he is
certainly to be congratulated!

3 It isn't right for someone who is selfish to be rich. What
use is money to a stingy person? 4 If you deny yourself in

NEW REVISED STANDARD VERSION

21 When the rich person totters, he is supported by friends,
but when the humble[a] falls, he is pushed away even by friends.
22 If the rich person slips, many come to the rescue;
he speaks unseemly words, but they justify him.
If the humble person slips, they even criticize him;
he talks sense, but is not given a hearing.
23 The rich person speaks and all are silent;
they extol to the clouds what he says.
The poor person speaks and they say, "Who is this fellow?"
And should he stumble, they even push him down.
24 Riches are good if they are free from sin;
poverty is evil only in the opinion of the ungodly.

25 The heart changes the countenance,
either for good or for evil.[b]
26 The sign of a happy heart is a cheerful face,
but to devise proverbs requires painful thinking.

14 Happy are those who do not blunder with their lips,
and need not suffer remorse for sin.
2 Happy are those whose hearts do not condemn them,
and who have not given up their hope.

3 Riches are inappropriate for a small-minded person;
and of what use is wealth to a miser?

a Other ancient authorities read *poor* *b* Other ancient authorities add *and a glad heart makes a cheerful countenance*

NEW AMERICAN BIBLE

20 When a rich man stumbles he is supported by a friend;
when a poor man trips he is pushed down by a friend.
21 Many are the supporters for a rich man when he speaks;
though what he says is odious, it wins approval.
When a poor man speaks they make sport of him;
he speaks wisely and no attention is paid him.
22 A rich man speaks and all are silent,
his wisdom they extol to the clouds.
A poor man speaks and they say: "Who is that?"
If he slips they cast him down.
23 Wealth is good when there is no sin;
but poverty is evil by the standards of the proud.
24 The heart of a man changes his countenance,
either for good or for evil.
25 The sign of a good heart is a cheerful countenance;
withdrawn and perplexed is the laborious schemer.

14 Happy the man whose mouth brings him no grief,
who is not stung by remorse for sin.
2 Happy the man whose conscience does not reproach him,
who has not lost hope.
3 Wealth ill becomes the mean man;
and to the miser, of what use is gold?

NEW JERUSALEM BIBLE

21 When the rich stumbles he is supported by friends;
when the poor falls, his friends push him away.
22 When the rich slips, there are many hands to catch him,
if he talks nonsense he is congratulated.
The poor slips, and is blamed for it,
he may talk good sense, but no room is made for him.
23 The rich speaks and everyone stops talking,
and then they praise his discourse to the skies.
The poor speaks and people say, 'Who is this?'
and if he stumbles, they trip him up yet more.
24 Wealth is good where there is no sin,
poverty is evil, the godless say.
25 The heart moulds a person's expression
whether for better or worse.
26 Happy heart, cheerful expression;
but wearisome work, inventing proverbs.

14 Blessed is anyone who has not sinned in speech
and who needs feel no remorse for sins.
2 Blessed is anyone whose conscience brings no reproach
and who has never given up hope.
3 Wealth is not the right thing for the niggardly,
and what use are possessions to the covetous?

GREEK OLD TESTAMENT

4 ὁ συνάγων ἀπὸ τῆς ψυχῆς αὐτοῦ συνάγει ἄλλοις,
καὶ ἐν τοῖς ἀγαθοῖς αὐτοῦ τρυφήσουσιν ἕτεροι.
5 ὁ πονηρὸς ἑαυτῷ τίνι ἀγαθὸς ἔσται;
καὶ οὐ μὴ εὐφρανθήσεται ἐν τοῖς χρήμασιν αὐτοῦ.
6 τοῦ βασκαίνοντος ἑαυτὸν οὐκ ἔστιν πονηρότερος,
καὶ τοῦτο ἀνταπόδομα τῆς κακίας αὐτοῦ·
7 κἂν εὖ ποιῇ, ἐν λήθῃ ποιεῖ,
καὶ ἐπ᾽ ἐσχάτων ἐκφαίνει τὴν κακίαν αὐτοῦ.
8 πονηρὸς ὁ βασκαίνων ὀφθαλμῷ,
ἀποστρέφων πρόσωπον καὶ ὑπερορῶν ψυχάς.
9 πλεονέκτου ὀφθαλμὸς οὐκ ἐμπίπλαται μερίδι,
καὶ ἀδικία πονηρὰ ἀναξηραίνει ψυχήν.
10 ὀφθαλμὸς πονηρὸς φθονερὸς ἐπ᾽ ἄρτῳ
καὶ ἐλλιπὴς ἐπὶ τῆς τραπέζης αὐτοῦ.
11 Τέκνον, καθὼς ἐὰν ἔχῃς, εὖ ποίει σεαυτὸν
καὶ προσφορὰς κυρίῳ ἀξίως πρόσαγε·
12 μνήσθητι ὅτι θάνατος οὐ χρονιεῖ
καὶ διαθήκη ᾅδου οὐχ ὑπεδείχθη σοι·
13 πρίν σε τελευτῆσαι εὖ ποίει φίλῳ
καὶ κατὰ τὴν ἰσχύν σου ἔκτεινον καὶ δὸς αὐτῷ.
14 μὴ ἀφυστερήσῃς ἀπὸ ἀγαθῆς ἡμέρας,
καὶ μερὶς ἐπιθυμίας ἀγαθῆς μή σε παρελθάτω.
15 οὐχὶ ἑτέρῳ καταλείψεις τοὺς πόνους σου
καὶ τοὺς κόπους σου εἰς διαίρεσιν κλήρου;

KING JAMES VERSION

4 He that gathereth by defrauding his own soul gathereth for others, that shall spend his goods riotously.

5 He that is evil to himself, to whom will he be good? he shall not take pleasure in his goods.

6 There is none worse than he that envieth himself; and this is a recompence of his wickedness.

7 And if he doeth good, he doeth it unwillingly; and at the last he will declare his wickedness.

8 The envious man hath a wicked eye; he turneth away his face, and despiseth men.

9 A covetous man's eye is not satisfied with his portion; and the iniquity of the wicked drieth up his soul.

10 A wicked eye envieth [his] bread, and he is a niggard at his table.

11 My son, according to thy ability do good to thyself, and give the Lord his due offering.

12 Remember that death will not be long in coming, and that the covenant of the grave is not shewed unto thee.

13 Do good unto thy friend before thou die, and according to thy ability stretch out thy hand and give to him.

14 Defraud not thyself of the good day, and let not the part of a good desire overpass thee.

15 Shalt thou not leave thy travails unto another? and thy labours to be divided by lot?

DOUAY OLD TESTAMENT

4 He that gathereth together by wronging his own soul, gathereth for others, and another will squander away his goods in rioting.

5 He that is evil to himself, to whom will he be good? and he shall not take pleasure in his goods.

6 There is none worse than he that envieth himself, and this is the reward of his wickedness:

7 And if he do good, he doth it ignorantly, and unwillingly: and at the last he discovereth his wickedness.

8 The eye of the envious is wicked: and he turneth away his face, and despiseth his own soul.

9 The eye of the covetous man *is* insatiable in his portion of iniquity: he will not be satisfied till he consume his own soul, drying it up.

10 An evil eye is towards evil things: and he shall not have his fill of bread, but shall be needy and pensive at his own table.

11 My son, if thou have any thing, do good to thyself, and offer to God worthy offerings.

12 Remember that death is not slow, and that the covenant of hell hath been shewn to thee: for the covenant of this world shall surely die.

13 Do good to thy friend before thou die, and according to thy ability, stretching out thy hand give to the poor.

14 Defraud not thyself of the good day, and let not the part of a good gift overpass thee.

15 Shalt thou not leave to others to divide by lot thy sorrows and labours?

KNOX TRANSLATION

himself to hoard up goods for others; to let his heirs keep
high revel when he is gone! 5 Whose friend is he, that is his
own enemy, and leaves his own cheer untasted? 6 This is the
last villainy of all, that a man should grudge himself his own
happiness; 7 fit punishment for his poverty of soul that
never did good except by oversight, and to his manifest
remorse! 8 Diseased eye of the niggard, that will turn away
and let hunger go unsatisfied; 9 and restless eye of the covetous man, that craves ever more than his due, till his very
nature dries up from continual pining; 10 an eye jaundiced
with its own passions, and never a full meal, but always he
must sit hungry and pensive at his own table, and ill content!

11 My son, if wealth thou hast, regale thyself, and make
thy offering to God proportionable. 12 Bethink thee that
death waits not; there is no putting off thy tryst with the
grave; nothing in this world, but its death-warrant is out
already. 13 While life still holds, make thy friends good
cheer, and to the poor be open-handed as thy means allow
thee; 14 stint not the feast, nor any crumb put by of the
blessings granted thee; 15 wouldst thou have thy heirs
wrangling over the fruits of thy bitter toil? 16 Much give,

TODAY'S ENGLISH VERSION

order to accumulate wealth, you are only accumulating it for
someone else. Others will use your riches to live in luxury.
5 How can you be generous with others if you are stingy with
yourself, if you are not willing to enjoy your own wealth?
6 No one is worse off than someone who is stingy with himself; it is a sin that brings its own punishment. 7 When such
a person does something good, it is only by accident; his
selfishness will sooner or later be evident. 8 A selfish person
is evil; he turns his back on people's needs 9 and is never
satisfied with what he has. Greed[a] will shrivel up a person's
soul. 10 Some people are too stingy to put bread on their own
table.
11 My child, treat yourself as well as you can, and bring
worthy offerings to the Lord. 12 Remember that death is coming for you some day, and you haven't been told when that
will be. 13 Before that day comes, be kind to your friends; be
as generous as you can. 14 Don't deny yourself a single day's
happiness. If there is something you want to do and it is
lawful, go ahead! 15 Some day all that you have worked for
will be divided up and given to others. 16 So be generous;

[a] *Probable text* Greed; *Greek* Wicked injustice.

NEW REVISED STANDARD VERSION

4 What he denies himself he collects for others;
and others will live in luxury on his goods.
5 If one is mean to himself, to whom will he be generous?
He will not enjoy his own riches.
6 No one is worse than one who is grudging to himself;
this is the punishment for his meanness.
7 If ever he does good, it is by mistake;
and in the end he reveals his meanness.
8 The miser is an evil person;
he turns away and disregards people.
9 The eye of the greedy person is not satisfied with his share;
greedy injustice withers the soul.
10 A miser begrudges bread,
and it is lacking at his table.

11 My child, treat yourself well, according to your means,
and present worthy offerings to the Lord.
12 Remember that death does not tarry,
and the decree[a] of Hades has not been shown to you.
13 Do good to friends before you die,
and reach out and give to them as much as you can.
14 Do not deprive yourself of a day's enjoyment;
do not let your share of desired good pass by you.
15 Will you not leave the fruit of your labors to another,
and what you acquired by toil to be divided by lot?

a Heb Syr: Gk *covenant*

NEW AMERICAN BIBLE

4 What he denies himself he collects for others,
and in his possessions a stranger will revel.
5 To whom will he be generous who is stingy with himself
and does not enjoy what is his own?
6 None is more stingy than he who is stingy with himself;
he punishes his own miserliness.
7 If ever he is generous, it is by mistake;
and in the end he displays his greed.
8 In the miser's opinion his share is too small;
9 he refuses his neighbor and brings ruin on himself.
10 The miser's eye is rapacious for bread,
but on his own table he sets it stale.
11 My son, use freely whatever you have
and enjoy it as best you can;
12 Remember that death does not tarry,
nor have you been told the grave's appointed time.
13 Before you die, be good to your friend,
and give him a share in what you possess.
14 Deprive not yourself of present good things,
let no choice portion escape you.
15 Will you not leave your riches to others,
and your earnings to be divided by lot?

NEW JERUSALEM BIBLE

4 Whoever hoards by stinting himself is hoarding for others,
and others will live sumptuously on his riches.

5 If someone is mean to himself, whom does he benefit?
he does not even enjoy what is his own.
6 No one is meaner than the person who is mean to himself,
this is how his wickedness repays him.
7 If he does any good, he does it unintentionally,
and in the end he himself reveals his wickedness.
8 Wicked the person who has an envious eye,
averting his face, and careless of others' lives.
9 The eye of the grasping is not content with what he has,
greed shrivels up the soul.

10 The miser is grudging of bread,
there is famine at his table.
11 My child, treat yourself as well as you can afford,
and bring worthy offerings to the Lord.
12 Remember that death will not delay,
and that you have never seen Sheol's contract.
13 Be kind to your friend before you die,
treat him as generously as you can afford.
14 Do not refuse yourself the good things of today,
do not let your share of what is lawfully desired pass you by.
15 Will you not have to leave your fortune to another,
and the fruit of your labour to be divided by lot?

GREEK OLD TESTAMENT

16 δὸς καὶ λαβὲ καὶ ἀπάτησον τὴν ψυχήν σου,
ὅτι οὐκ ἔστιν ἐν ᾅδου ζητῆσαι τρυφήν.
17 πᾶσα σὰρξ ὡς ἱμάτιον παλαιοῦται·
ἡ γὰρ διαθήκη ἀπ᾽ αἰῶνος Θανάτῳ ἀποθανῇ.
18 ὡς φύλλον θάλλον ἐπὶ δένδρου δασέος,
τὰ μὲν καταβάλλει, ἄλλα δὲ φύει,
οὕτως γενεὰ σαρκὸς καὶ αἵματος,
ἡ μὲν τελευτᾷ, ἑτέρα δὲ γεννᾶται.
19 πᾶν ἔργον σηπόμενον ἐκλείπει,
καὶ ὁ ἐργαζόμενος αὐτὸ μετ᾽ αὐτοῦ ἀπελεύσεται.
20 Μακάριος ἀνήρ, ὃς ἐν σοφίᾳ μελετήσει
καὶ ὃς ἐν συνέσει αὐτοῦ διαλεχθήσεται,
21 ὁ διανοούμενος τὰς ὁδοὺς αὐτῆς ἐν καρδίᾳ αὐτοῦ
καὶ ἐν τοῖς ἀποκρύφοις αὐτῆς ἐννοηθήσεται.
22 ἔξελθε ὀπίσω αὐτῆς ὡς ἰχνευτὴς
καὶ ἐν ταῖς ὁδοῖς αὐτῆς ἐνέδρευε.
23 ὁ παρακύπτων διὰ τῶν θυρίδων αὐτῆς
καὶ ἐπὶ τῶν θυρωμάτων αὐτῆς ἀκροάσεται,
24 ὁ καταλύων σύνεγγυς τοῦ οἴκου αὐτῆς
καὶ πήξει πάσσαλον ἐν τοῖς τοίχοις αὐτῆς,
25 στήσει τὴν σκηνὴν αὐτοῦ κατὰ χεῖρας αὐτῆς
καὶ καταλύσει ἐν καταλύματι ἀγαθῶν,
26 θήσει τὰ τέκνα αὐτοῦ ἐν τῇ σκέπῃ αὐτῆς
καὶ ὑπὸ τοὺς κλάδους αὐτῆς αὐλισθήσεται,
27 σκεπασθήσεται ὑπ᾽ αὐτῆς ἀπὸ καύματος
καὶ ἐν τῇ δόξῃ αὐτῆς καταλύσει.

KING JAMES VERSION

16 Give, and take, and sanctify thy soul; for there is no seeking of dainties in the grave.

17 All flesh waxeth old as a garment: for the covenant from the beginning is, Thou shalt die the death.

18 As of the green leaves on a thick tree, some fall, and some grow; so is the generation of flesh and blood, one cometh to an end, and another is born.

19 Every work rotteth and consumeth away, and the worker thereof shall go withal.

20 Blessed is the man that doth meditate good things in wisdom, and that reasoneth of holy things by his understanding.

21 He that considereth her ways in his heart shall also have understanding in her secrets.

22 Go after her as one that traceth, and lie in wait in her ways.

23 He that prieth in at her windows shall also hearken at her doors.

24 He that doth lodge near her house shall also fasten a pin in her walls.

25 He shall pitch his tent nigh unto her, and shall lodge in a lodging where good things are.

26 He shall set his children under her shelter, and shall lodge under her branches.

27 By her he shall be covered from heat, and in her glory shall he dwell.

DOUAY OLD TESTAMENT

16 Give and take, and justify thy soul.

17 Before thy death work justice: for in hell there is no finding food.

18 All flesh shall fade as grass, and as the leaf that springeth out on a green tree.

19 Some grow, and some fall off: so is the generation of flesh and blood, one cometh to an end, and another is born.

20 Every work that is corruptible shall fail in the end: and the worker thereof shall go with it.

21 And every excellent work shall be justified: and the worker thereof shall be honoured therein.

22 Blessed is the man that shall continue in wisdom, and that shall meditate in his justice, and in his mind shall think of the all seeing eye of God.

23 He that considereth her ways in his heart, and hath understanding in her secrets, who goeth after her as one that traceth, and stayeth in her ways:

24 He who looketh in at her windows, and hearkeneth at her door:

25 He that lodgeth near her house, and fastening a pin in her walls shall set up his tent nigh unto her, where good things shall rest in his lodging for ever.

26 He shall set his children under her shelter, and shall lodge under her branches:

27 He shall be protected under her covering from the heat, and shall rest in her glory.

KNOX TRANSLATION

much take, set thy soul at ease; 17 while life still holds, do
thy duty of almsgiving; feasting there shall be none in the
grave. 18 No living thing but fades as the grass fades; as the
leaves fade, that burgeon on a growing tree, 19 some sprout-
ing fresh and some a-dying; so it is with flesh and blood,
one generation makes room for the next. 20 All the works of
man are fugitive, and must perish soon or late, and he, the
workman, goes the same way as the rest. 21 Yet shall their
choicest works win favour, and in his work he, the workman, shall live.

22 Blessed the man that dwells on wise thoughts, musing
how to acquit himself well, and remembering the all-seeing
eye of God; 23 that can plan out in his heart all wisdom's
twists and turns, fathom her secrets! Like a spy he follows
her, and lingers in her tracks, 24 peers through her window,
listens at her doors, 25 by her house takes up his abode, driving his nail into the walls of it, so as to build his cabin at her
very side, cabin that shall remain for ever a home of blessing! 26 Wisdom shall be the shade under which his children
find their appointed resting-place; her spreading boughs
27 shall protect them from the noon-day heat; wisdom shall
be the monument of his glorious repose.

TODAY'S ENGLISH VERSION

but also be willing to receive from others. Enjoy yourself, for
you will not find any pleasures in the world of the dead.
17 The human body wears out like a piece of clothing. The
ancient law decrees that we must die. 18 Human beings are
like leaves on a spreading tree. New growth takes the place
of the fallen leaves; while some of us die, others are being
born. 19 Everything made by human hands will decay and
perish, along with the person who made it.
20 It is a happy person who is concerned with Wisdom and
who uses good sense. 21 Anyone who studies the ways of
Wisdom will also learn her secrets. 22 Go after Wisdom like a
hunter looking for game. 23 Look into her windows and listen at her doors. 24 Camp as close to her house as you can
get, 25 and you will have a fine place to live. 26-27 Build your
home there, safe beneath her protecting branches, and shaded from the heat.[a]

[a] *Hebrew* Build . . . heat; *Greek* Let her protect your children. Live safe beneath her branches, shaded from the heat, surrounded by her glory.

NEW REVISED STANDARD VERSION

16 Give, and take, and indulge yourself,
because in Hades one cannot look for luxury.
17 All living beings become old like a garment,
for the decree[a] from of old is, "You must die!"
18 Like abundant leaves on a spreading tree
that sheds some and puts forth others,
so are the generations of flesh and blood:
one dies and another is born.
19 Every work decays and ceases to exist,
and the one who made it will pass away with it.

20 Happy is the person who meditates on[b] wisdom
and reasons intelligently,
21 who[c] reflects in his heart on her ways
and ponders her secrets,
22 pursuing her like a hunter,
and lying in wait on her paths;
23 who peers through her windows
and listens at her doors;
24 who camps near her house
and fastens his tent peg to her walls;
25 who pitches his tent near her,
and so occupies an excellent lodging place;
26 who places his children under her shelter,
and lodges under her boughs;
27 who is sheltered by her from the heat,
and dwells in the midst of her glory.

a Heb: Gk *covenant* *b* Other ancient authorities read *dies in*
c The structure adopted in verses 21-27 follows the Heb

NEW AMERICAN BIBLE

16 Give, take, and treat yourself well,
for in the nether world there are no joys to seek.
17 All flesh grows old, like a garment;
the age-old law is: All must die.
18 As with the leaves that grow on a vigorous tree:
one falls off and another sprouts—
So with the generations of flesh and blood:
one dies and another is born.
19 All man's works will perish in decay,
and his handiwork will follow after him.

20 Happy the man who meditates on wisdom,
and reflects on knowledge;
21 Who ponders her ways in his heart,
and understands her paths;
22 Who pursues her like a scout,
and lies in wait at her entry way;
23 Who peeps through her windows,
and listens at her doors;
24 Who encamps near her house,
and fastens his tent pegs next to her walls;
25 Who pitches his tent beside her,
and lives as her welcome neighbor;
26 Who builds his nest in her leafage,
and lodges in her branches;
27 Who takes shelter with her from the heat,
and dwells in her home.

NEW JERUSALEM BIBLE

16 Give and receive, enjoy yourself—
there are no pleasures to be found in Sheol.
17 Like clothes, every body will wear out,
the age-old law is, 'Everyone must die.'
18 Like foliage growing on a bushy tree,
some leaves falling, others growing,
so are the generations of flesh and blood:
one dies, another is born.
19 Every achievement rots away and perishes,
and with it goes its author.
20 Blessed is anyone who meditates on wisdom,
and reasons with intelligence,
21 who studies her ways in his heart,
and ponders her secrets.
22 He pursues her like a hunter,
and lies in wait by her path;
23 he peeps in at her windows,
and listens at her doors;
24 he lodges close to her house,
and fixes his peg in her walls;
25 he pitches his tent at her side,
and lodges in an excellent lodging;
26 he sets his children in her shade,
and camps beneath her branches;
27 he is sheltered by her from the heat,
and in her glory he makes his home.

GREEK OLD TESTAMENT

15 Ὁ φοβούμενος κύριον ποιήσει αὐτό,
καὶ ὁ ἐγκρατὴς τοῦ νόμου καταλήμψεται αὐτήν·
2 καὶ ὑπαντήσεται αὐτῷ ὡς μήτηρ
καὶ ὡς γυνὴ παρθενίας προσδέξεται αὐτόν·
3 ψωμιεῖ αὐτὸν ἄρτον συνέσεως
καὶ ὕδωρ σοφίας ποτίσει αὐτόν·
4 στηριχθήσεται ἐπ' αὐτὴν καὶ οὐ μὴ κλιθῇ,
καὶ ἐπ' αὐτῆς ἐφέξει καὶ οὐ μὴ καταισχυνθῇ·
5 καὶ ὑψώσει αὐτὸν παρὰ τοὺς πλησίον αὐτοῦ
καὶ ἐν μέσῳ ἐκκλησίας ἀνοίξει τὸ στόμα αὐτοῦ·
6 εὐφροσύνην καὶ στέφανον ἀγαλλιάματος εὑρήσει
καὶ ὄνομα αἰῶνος κατακληρονομήσει.
7 οὐ μὴ καταλήμψονται αὐτὴν ἄνθρωποι ἀσύνετοι,
καὶ ἄνδρες ἁμαρτωλοὶ οὐ μὴ ἴδωσιν αὐτήν·
8 μακράν ἐστιν ὑπερηφανίας,
καὶ ἄνδρες ψεῦσται οὐ μὴ μνησθήσονται αὐτῆς.
9 Οὐχ ὡραῖος αἶνος ἐν στόματι ἁμαρτωλοῦ,
ὅτι οὐ παρὰ κυρίου ἀπεστάλη·
10 ἐν γὰρ σοφίᾳ ῥηθήσεται αἶνος,
καὶ ὁ κύριος εὐοδώσει αὐτόν.
11 μὴ εἴπῃς ὅτι Διὰ κύριον ἀπέστην·
ἃ γὰρ ἐμίσησεν, οὐ ποιήσει.
12 μὴ εἴπῃς ὅτι Αὐτός με ἐπλάνησεν·
οὐ γὰρ χρείαν ἔχει ἀνδρὸς ἁμαρτωλοῦ.

KING JAMES VERSION

15 He that feareth the Lord will do good; and he that hath the knowledge of the law shall obtain her.

2 And as a mother shall she meet him, and receive him as a wife married of a virgin.

3 With the bread of understanding shall she feed him, and give him the water of wisdom to drink.

4 He shall be stayed upon her, and shall not be moved; and shall rely upon her, and shall not be confounded.

5 She shall exalt him above his neighbours, and in the midst of the congregation shall she open his mouth.

6 He shall find joy and a crown of gladness, and she shall cause him to inherit an everlasting name.

7 But foolish men shall not attain unto her, and sinners shall not see her.

8 For she is far from pride, and men that are liars cannot remember her.

9 Praise is not seemly in the mouth of a sinner, for it was not sent him of the Lord.

10 For praise shall be uttered in wisdom, and the Lord will prosper it.

11 Say not thou, It is through the Lord that I fell away: for thou oughtest not to do the things that he hateth.

12 Say not thou, He hath caused me to err: for he hath no need of the sinful man.

DOUAY OLD TESTAMENT

15 HE that feareth God, will do good: and he that possesseth justice, shall lay hold on her,

2 And she will meet him as an honourable mother, and will receive him as a wife married of a virgin.

3 With the bread of life and understanding, she shall feed him, and give him the water of wholesome wisdom to drink: and she shall be made strong in him, and he shall not be moved:

4 And she shall hold him fast, and he shall not be confounded: and she shall exalt him among his neighbours.

5 And in the midst of the church she shall open his mouth, and shall fill him with the spirit of wisdom and understanding, and shall clothe him with a robe of glory.

6 She shall heap upon him a treasure of joy and gladness, and shall cause him to inherit an everlasting name.

7 But foolish men shall not obtain her, and wise men shall meet her, foolish men shall not see her: for she is far from pride and deceit.

8 Lying men shall not be mindful of her: but men that speak truth shall be found with her, and shall advance, even till they come to the sight of God.

9 Praise is not seemly in the mouth of a sinner:

10 For wisdom came forth from God: for praise shall be with the wisdom of God, and shall abound in a faithful mouth, and the sovereign Lord will give praise unto it.

11 Say not: It is through God, that she is not with me: for do not thou the things that he hateth.

12 Say not: He hath caused me to err: for he hath no need of wicked men.

KNOX TRANSLATION

15 If a man fears the Lord, he will live an upright life. If a
man holds fast to innocence, he will find wisdom[a]
ready to his embrace, 2 welcoming him as a mother welcomes
the son who cherishes her, greeting him like a maiden bride.
3 Long life and good discernment are the bread this mother
will provide for him, truth the refreshing draught she will give
him to drink. She will take firm hold of him, 4 so that he
never wavers, restrain him, so that he is never disgraced. She
will raise him to high repute among his neighbours; 5 she will
move him to speak before the assembled people, filling him
with the spirit of wisdom and discernment, clothing him in
magnificent array. 6 Joy and triumph she has in store for him,
and will enrich him with a name that shall never be forgotten.
7 Not for the fools her embrace, only apt pupils encounter her;
how should the fools catch sight of her, that is so far removed
from proud and treacherous ways? 8 Nay, she is beyond the
deceiver's ken; true hearts alone are her company, and these
shall profit by it till they are fit for God's scrutiny. 9 Praise is
but praise deformed when it is uttered by the lips of a sinner;
10 wisdom comes from God only, and on wisdom the praise of
God needs must wait. Praise on the lips of one who trusts God
is rich in meaning; the Ruler of all inspires it.

11 This wisdom lackest thou?[b] Do not blame God for the
want of it; learn to shun the deeds God hates. 12 Do not complain that it was he led thee into false paths; what need has
God, thinkest thou, of rebels? 13 No foul misdeed there is but

a Literally, 'will find her'. Grammatically, this might refer to 'innocence', but it is fairly certain we are meant to think of Wisdom, alluded to in 14. 22 above. *b* 'This wisdom lackest thou?'; according to the Greek text, 'Hast thou rebelled against him?'

TODAY'S ENGLISH VERSION

15 If you fear the Lord, you will do this. Master his Law,
and you will find Wisdom. 2 She will come to welcome you, like a mother or a young bride. 3 She will give you
wisdom and knowledge like food and drink. 4 Rely on her for
support, and you will never know the disgrace of failure.
5 She will make you more honored than all your neighbors;
when you speak in the assembly, she will give you the right
words. 6 You will find happiness and genuine joy; your
name will be remembered forever.
7 But people who are foolish or sinful will never even catch
sight of Wisdom. 8 She will have nothing to do with conceited people; she never enters the mind of liars. 9 It is not
appropriate for a sinner to sing hymns of praise, because his
worship is insincere. 10 A hymn should be an expression of
wisdom, inspired by the Lord himself.
11 Don't blame the Lord for your sin; the Lord does not cause
what he hates.[a] 12 Don't claim that he has misled you; he
doesn't need the help of sinners to accomplish his purposes.

[a] *Hebrew* the Lord does not cause what he hates; *Greek* do not do what the Lord hates.

NEW REVISED STANDARD VERSION

15 Whoever fears the Lord will do this,
and whoever holds to the law will obtain wisdom.[a]
2 She will come to meet him like a mother,
and like a young bride she will welcome him.
3 She will feed him with the bread of learning,
and give him the water of wisdom to drink.
4 He will lean on her and not fall,
and he will rely on her and not be put to shame.
5 She will exalt him above his neighbors,
and will open his mouth in the midst of the
assembly.
6 He will find gladness and a crown of rejoicing,
and will inherit an everlasting name.
7 The foolish will not obtain her,
and sinners will not see her.
8 She is far from arrogance,
and liars will never think of her.
9 Praise is unseemly on the lips of a sinner,
for it has not been sent from the Lord.
10 For in wisdom must praise be uttered,
and the Lord will make it prosper.

11 Do not say, "It was the Lord's doing that I fell away";
for he does not do[b] what he hates.
12 Do not say, "It was he who led me astray";
for he has no need of the sinful.

[a] Gk *her* [b] Heb: Gk *you ought not to do*

NEW AMERICAN BIBLE

15 He who fears the LORD will do this;
he who is practiced in the law will come to
wisdom.
2 Motherlike she will meet him,
like a young bride she will embrace him,
3 Nourish him with the bread of understanding,
and give him the water of learning to drink.
4 He will lean upon her and not fall,
he will trust in her and not be put to shame.
5 She will exalt him above his fellows;
in the assembly she will make him eloquent.
6 Joy and gladness he will find,
an everlasting name inherit.
7 Worthless men will not attain to her,
haughty men will not behold her.
8 Far from the impious is she,
not to be spoken of by liars.
9 Unseemly is praise on a sinner's lips,
for it is not accorded to him by God.
10 But praise is offered by the wise man's tongue;
its rightful steward will proclaim it.

11 Say not: "It was God's doing that I fell away";
for what he hates he does not do.
12 Say not: "It was he who set me astray";
for he has no need of wicked man.

NEW JERUSALEM BIBLE

15 Whoever fears the Lord will act like this,
and whoever grasps the Law will obtain wisdom.
2 She will come to meet him like a mother,
and receive him like a virgin bride.
3 She will give him the bread of understanding to eat,
and the water of wisdom to drink.
4 He will lean on her and will not fall,
he will rely on her and not be put to shame.
5 She will raise him high above his neighbours,
and in full assembly she will open his mouth.
6 He will find happiness and a crown of joy,
he will inherit an everlasting name.
7 Fools will not gain possession of her,
nor will sinners set eyes on her.
8 She stands remote from pride,
and liars cannot call her to mind.
9 Praise is unseemly in a sinner's mouth,
since it has not been put there by the Lord.
10 For praise should be uttered only in wisdom,
and the Lord himself then prompts it.
11 Do not say, 'The Lord was responsible for my sinning,'
for he does not do what he hates.
12 Do not say, 'It was he who led me astray,'
for he has no use for a sinner.

GREEK OLD TESTAMENT

13 πᾶν βδέλυγμα ἐμίσησεν ὁ κύριος,
καὶ οὐκ ἔστιν ἀγαπητὸν τοῖς φοβουμένοις αὐτόν.
14 αὐτὸς ἐξ ἀρχῆς ἐποίησεν ἄνθρωπον
καὶ ἀφῆκεν αὐτὸν ἐν χειρὶ διαβουλίου αὐτοῦ.
15 ἐὰν θέλῃς, συντηρήσεις ἐντολὰς
καὶ πίστιν ποιῆσαι εὐδοκίας.
16 παρέθηκέν σοι πῦρ καὶ ὕδωρ·
οὗ ἐὰν θέλῃς, ἐκτενεῖς τὴν χεῖρά σου.
17 ἔναντι ἀνθρώπων ἡ ζωὴ καὶ ὁ θάνατος,
καὶ ὃ ἐὰν εὐδοκήσῃ, δοθήσεται αὐτῷ.
18 ὅτι πολλὴ ἡ σοφία τοῦ κυρίου·
ἰσχυρὸς ἐν δυναστείᾳ καὶ βλέπων τὰ πάντα,
19 καὶ οἱ ὀφθαλμοὶ αὐτοῦ ἐπὶ τοὺς φοβουμένους αὐτόν,
καὶ αὐτὸς ἐπιγνώσεται πᾶν ἔργον ἀνθρώπου.
20 οὐκ ἐνετείλατο οὐδενὶ ἀσεβεῖν
καὶ οὐκ ἔδωκεν ἄνεσιν οὐδενὶ ἁμαρτάνειν.

16 Μὴ ἐπιθύμει τέκνων πλῆθος ἀχρήστων
μηδὲ εὐφραίνου ἐπὶ υἱοῖς ἀσεβέσιν·
2 ἐὰν πληθύνωσιν, μὴ εὐφραίνου ἐπ' αὐτοῖς,
εἰ μή ἐστιν φόβος κυρίου μετ' αὐτῶν.
3 μὴ ἐμπιστεύσῃς τῇ ζωῇ αὐτῶν
καὶ μὴ ἔπεχε ἐπὶ τὸ πλῆθος αὐτῶν·
κρείσσων γὰρ εἷς ἢ χίλιοι
καὶ ἀποθανεῖν ἄτεκνον ἢ ἔχειν τέκνα ἀσεβῆ.

KING JAMES VERSION

13 The Lord hateth all abomination; and they that fear God love it not.

14 He himself made man from the beginning, and left him in the hand of his counsel;

15 If thou wilt, to keep the commandments, and to perform acceptable faithfulness.

16 He hath set fire and water before thee: stretch forth thy hand unto whether thou wilt.

17 Before man is life and death; and whether him liketh shall be given him.

18 For the wisdom of the Lord is great, and he is mighty in power, and beholdeth all things:

19 And his eyes are upon them that fear him, and he knoweth every work of man.

20 He hath commanded no man to do wickedly, neither hath he given any man licence to sin.

16 Desire not a multitude of unprofitable children, neither delight in ungodly sons.

2 Though they multiply, rejoice not in them, except the fear of the Lord be with them.

3 Trust not thou in their life, neither respect their multitude: for one that is just is better than a thousand; and better it is to die without children, than to have them that are ungodly.

DOUAY OLD TESTAMENT

13 The Lord hateth all abomination of error, and they that fear him shall not love it.

14 God made man from the beginning, and left him in the hand of his own counsel.

15 He added his commandments and precepts.

16 If thou wilt keep the commandments and perform acceptable fidelity for ever, they shall preserve thee.

17 He hath set water and fire before thee: stretch forth thy hand to which thou wilt.

18 Before man is life and death, good and evil, that which he shall choose shall be given him:

19 For the wisdom of God is great, and he is strong in power, seeing all men without ceasing.

20 The eyes of the Lord are towards them that fear him, and he knoweth all the work of man.

21 He hath commanded no man to do wickedly, and he hath given no man license to sin:

22 For he desireth not a multitude of faithless and unprofitable children.

16 REJOICE not in ungodly children, if they be multiplied: neither be delighted in them, if the fear of God be not with them.

2 Trust not to their life, and respect not their labours.

3 For better is one that feareth God, than a thousand ungodly children.

4 And it is better to die without children, than to leave ungodly children.

KNOX TRANSLATION

God hates it; there is no loving it and fearing him. 14 When
men first came to be, it was God made them, and, making
them, left them to the arbitrament of their own wills; 15 yet
giving them commandments to be their rule. 16 Those commandments if thou wilt observe, they in their turn shall preserve thee, and give thee warrant of his favour.[a] 17 It is as
though he offered thee fire and water, bidding thee take
which thou wouldst; 18 life and death, blessing and curse,
man finds set before him, and the gift given thee shall be the
choice thou makest; 19 so wise God is, so constraining his
power, so incessant the watch he keeps over mankind.
20 The Lord's eye is watching over the men who fear him, no
act of ours passes unobserved; 21 upon none does he enjoin
disobedience, none has leave from him to commit sin. 22 A
brood of disloyal sons and worthless, how should this be the
Lord's desire?

16 A brood of disloyal sons, let not thy eye dwell on
these with pleasure; the fear of God lacking, let not a
multitude of children be thy comfort. 2 Not on such lives as
these set thy hopes, little regard have thou for such doings as
theirs; 3 better one son who fears God than a thousand who
grow up rebellious; 4 better die childless than have rebels to

[a] The rendering given above is an attempt to combine the Greek and the Latin versions, either of which, taken by itself, is untranslatable.

TODAY'S ENGLISH VERSION

13 The Lord hates evil in all its forms, and those who fear the
Lord find nothing attractive in evil. 14 When, in the beginning,
the Lord created human beings, he left them free to do as they
wished. 15 If you want to, you can keep the Lord's commands.
You can decide whether you will be loyal to him or not. 16 He
has placed fire and water before you; reach out and take
whichever you want. 17 You have a choice between life and
death; you will get whichever you choose. 18 The Lord's wisdom and power are great and he sees everything. 19 He is
aware of everything a person does, and he takes care of those
who fear him. 20 He has never commanded anyone to be
wicked or given anyone permission to sin.

16 A large family is nothing to be desired if the children
are worthless. Godless children are nothing to be
proud of. 2 No matter how many children you have, don't
look on them with pride unless they fear the Lord. 3 Don't
put much hope in their future or expect them to live a long
time. One child who does the Lord's will is better than a
thousand who do not.[a] It is better to go to your grave with
no children at all than to have children who are godless.

[a] *Hebrew* who does . . . do not; *Greek* is better than a thousand.

NEW REVISED STANDARD VERSION

13 The Lord hates all abominations;
such things are not loved by those who fear him.
14 It was he who created humankind in the beginning,
and he left them in the power of their own free
choice.
15 If you choose, you can keep the commandments,
and to act faithfully is a matter of your own choice.
16 He has placed before you fire and water;
stretch out your hand for whichever you choose.
17 Before each person are life and death,
and whichever one chooses will be given.
18 For great is the wisdom of the Lord;
he is mighty in power and sees everything;
19 his eyes are on those who fear him,
and he knows every human action.
20 He has not commanded anyone to be wicked,
and he has not given anyone permission to sin.

16 Do not desire a multitude of worthless[a] children,
and do not rejoice in ungodly offspring.
2 If they multiply, do not rejoice in them,
unless the fear of the Lord is in them.
3 Do not trust in their survival,
or rely on their numbers;[b]
for one can be better than a thousand,
and to die childless is better than to have ungodly
children.

[a] Heb: Gk *unprofitable* [b] Other ancient authorities add *For you will groan in untimely mourning, and will know of their sudden end.*

NEW AMERICAN BIBLE

13 Abominable wickedness the LORD hates,
he does not let it befall those who fear him.
14 When God, in the beginning, created man,
he made him subject to his own free choice.
15 If you choose you can keep the commandments;
it is loyalty to do his will.
16 There are set before you fire and water;
to whichever you choose, stretch forth your hand.
17 Before man are life and death,
whichever he chooses shall be given him.
18 Immense is the wisdom of the LORD;
he is mighty in power, and all-seeing.
19 The eyes of God see all he has made;
he understands man's every deed.
20 No man does he command to sin,
to none does he give strength for lies.

16 Desire not a brood of worthless children,
nor rejoice in wicked offspring.
2 Many though they be, exult not in them
if they have not the fear of the LORD.
3 Count not on their length of life,
have no hope in their future.
For one can be better than a thousand;
rather die childless than have godless children!

NEW JERUSALEM BIBLE

13 The Lord hates all that is foul,
and no one who fears him will love it either.
14 He himself made human beings in the beginning,
and then left them free to make their own decisions.
15 If you choose, you will keep the commandments
and so be faithful to his will.
16 He has set fire and water before you;
put out your hand to whichever you prefer.
17 A human being has life and death before him;
whichever he prefers will be given him.
18 For vast is the wisdom of the Lord;
he is almighty and all-seeing.
19 His eyes are on those who fear him,
he notes every human action.
20 He never commanded anyone to be godless,
he has given no one permission to sin.

16 Do not long for a brood of worthless children,
and do not take pleasure in godless sons.
2 However many you have, take no pleasure in them,
unless the fear of the Lord lives among them.
3 Do not count on their having long life,
do not put too much faith in their number;
for better have one than a thousand,
better die childless than have children who are
godless.

GREEK OLD TESTAMENT

[4]ἀπὸ γὰρ ἑνὸς συνετοῦ συνοικισθήσεται πόλις,
φυλὴ δὲ ἀνόμων ἐρημωθήσεται.
5 Πολλὰ τοιαῦτα ἑόρακεν ὁ ὀφθαλμός μου,
καὶ ἰσχυρότερα τούτων ἀκήκοεν τὸ οὖς μου.
[6]ἐν συναγωγῇ ἁμαρτωλῶν ἐκκαυθήσεται πῦρ,
καὶ ἐν ἔθνει ἀπειθεῖ ἐξεκαύθη ὀργή.
[7]οὐκ ἐξιλάσατο περὶ τῶν ἀρχαίων γιγάντων,
οἳ ἀπέστησαν τῇ ἰσχύι αὐτῶν·
[8]οὐκ ἐφείσατο περὶ τῆς παροικίας Λωτ,
οὓς ἐβδελύξατο διὰ τὴν ὑπερηφανίαν αὐτῶν·
[9]οὐκ ἠλέησεν ἔθνος ἀπωλείας
τοὺς ἐξηρμένους ἐν ἁμαρτίαις αὐτῶν
[10]καὶ οὕτως ἑξακοσίας χιλιάδας πεζῶν
τοὺς ἐπισυναχθέντας ἐν σκληροκαρδίᾳ αὐτῶν.
11 Κἂν ᾖ εἷς σκληροτράχηλος,
θαυμαστὸν τοῦτο εἰ ἀθῳωθήσεται·
ἔλεος γὰρ καὶ ὀργὴ παρ᾽ αὐτῷ,
δυνάστης ἐξιλασμῶν καὶ ἐκχέων ὀργήν.
[12]κατὰ τὸ πολὺ ἔλεος αὐτοῦ, οὕτως καὶ πολὺς ὁ ἔλεγχος
αὐτοῦ·
ἄνδρα κατὰ τὰ ἔργα αὐτοῦ κρινεῖ.
[13]οὐκ ἐκφεύξεται ἐν ἁρπάγματι ἁμαρτωλός,
καὶ οὐ μὴ καθυστερήσει ὑπομονὴ εὐσεβοῦς.

KING JAMES VERSION

4 For by one that hath understanding shall the city be replenished: but the kindred of the wicked shall speedily become desolate.

5 Many such things have I seen with mine eyes, and mine ear hath heard greater things than these.

6 In the congregation of the ungodly shall a fire be kindled; and in a rebellious nation wrath is set on fire.

7 He was not pacified toward the old giants, who fell away in the strength of their foolishness.

8 Neither spared he the place where Lot sojourned, but abhorred them for their pride.

9 He pitied not the people of perdition, who were taken away in their sins:

10 Nor the six hundred thousand footmen, who were gathered together in the hardness of their hearts.

11 And if there be one stiffnecked among the people, it is marvel if he escape unpunished: for mercy and wrath are with him; he is mighty to forgive, and to pour out displeasure.

12 As his mercy is great, so is his correction also: he judgeth a man according to his works.

13 The sinner shall not escape with his spoils: and the patience of the godly shall not be frustrate.

DOUAY OLD TESTAMENT

5 By one that is wise a country shall be inhabited, the tribe of the ungodly shall become desolate.

6 Many such things hath my eyes seen, and greater things than these my ear hath heard.

7 In the congregation of sinners a fire shall be kindled, and in an unbelieving nation wrath shall flame out.

8 The ancient giants did not obtain pardon for their sins, who were destroyed trusting to their own strength:

9 And he spared not the place where Lot sojourned, but abhorred them for the pride of their word.

10 He had not pity on them, destroying the whole nation that extolled themselves in their sins.

11 So did he with the six hundred thousand footmen, who were gathered together in the hardness of their heart: and if one had been stiffnecked, it is a wonder if he had escaped unpunished:

12 For mercy and wrath are with him. *He is* mighty to forgive, and to pour out indignation:

13 According as his mercy is, so his correction judgeth a man according to his works.

14 The sinner shall not escape in his rapines, and the patience of him that sheweth mercy shall not be put off.

KNOX TRANSLATION

succeed thee. [5]Through one man that is well-minded a
whole country may thrive, and sinners, a whole race of
them, may be extinguished; [6]much proof of this my own
eyes have seen, and stronger proof yet are the tales that have
come to my hearing, [7]of fire breaking out where sinners
were met in company, fires of vengeance to consume a disobedient race. [8]Those giants of long ago who perished in the
pride of their strength, did they find pardon of their guilt?
[9]Lot's neighbours, did God spare them? Did he not attest his
hatred of their insolence, [10]destroying a whole nation without pity, for the sinfulness that defied him? [11]And what of
those six hundred thousand that marched out into the
desert, men of stubborn heart? Stiff-necked if he had been
like the others, Caleb himself should not have had God's pardon.[a] [12]His to pity, his to punish; intercession avails with
him, but in full flood comes his vengeance; [13]his severity,
no less than his clemency, judges men by their deeds.
[14]Never may sinner enjoy his ill-gotten gains in safety, nor
the hope of the generous be disappointed. [15]No generous act

a The words 'into the desert' have been inserted to make it clear that the Exodus is alluded to; they are not in the text. Nor is the name 'Caleb', but the grammar of the Latin version necessarily implies that one person was excepted from the general doom, cf. Num. 14. 24 and elsewhere. The Greek text has 'And if there is one stiff-necked person, it is a marvel if he escapes'.

TODAY'S ENGLISH VERSION

4 A city's population may grow because of the wisdom of
one person, while a whole tribe of lawless people disappears.
5 I have seen such things many times and have heard of even
more striking examples. 6 The Lord's flaming anger will
break out against a small gathering of sinners or a disobedient nation. 7 He did not forgive those ancient giants who
rebelled against him, confident of their own strength. 8 He
detested the arrogance of the people among whom Lot lived,
and he did not spare them. 9 He showed no mercy on that
nation which he doomed to destruction for its sins, 10 nor on
those 600,000 people on the march through the wilderness
who gathered together in stubborn rebellion. 11 Even if there
had been only one stubborn person, it would have been a
miracle if he had escaped punishment. The Lord is merciful,
but he can also become angry. He can be overwhelming in
his forgiveness or in his anger. 12 His punishment is as
severe as his mercy is great. He judges people by what they
have done. 13 No sinner can escape with what he has stolen.
The Lord will reward the patience of devout people. 14 Every

NEW REVISED STANDARD VERSION

4 For through one intelligent person a city can be filled
with people,
but through a clan of outlaws it becomes desolate.

5 Many such things my eye has seen,
and my ear has heard things more striking than
these.
6 In an assembly of sinners a fire is kindled,
and in a disobedient nation wrath blazes up.
7 He did not forgive the ancient giants
who revolted in their might.
8 He did not spare the neighbors of Lot,
whom he loathed on account of their arrogance.
9 He showed no pity on the doomed nation,
on those dispossessed because of their sins;[a]
10 or on the six hundred thousand foot soldiers
who assembled in their stubbornness.[b]
11 Even if there were only one stiff-necked person,
it would be a wonder if he remained unpunished.
For mercy and wrath are with the Lord;[c]
he is mighty to forgive—but he also pours out wrath.
12 Great as is his mercy, so also is his chastisement;
he judges a person according to his or her deeds.
13 The sinner will not escape with plunder,
and the patience of the godly will not be frustrated.

a Other ancient authorities add *All these things he did to the hard-hearted nations, and by the multitude of his holy ones he was not appeased.*
b Other ancient authorities add *Chastising, showing mercy, striking, healing, the Lord persisted in mercy and discipline.* *c* Gk *him*

NEW AMERICAN BIBLE

4 Through one wise man can a city be peopled;
through a clan of rebels it becomes desolate.
5 Many such things has my eye seen,
even more than these has my ear heard.
6 Against a sinful band fire is enkindled,
upon a godless people wrath flames out.
7 He forgave not the leaders of old
who rebelled long ago in their might;
8 He spared not the neighbors of Lot
whom he detested for their pride;
9 Nor did he spare the doomed people
who were uprooted because of their sin;
10 Nor the six hundred thousand foot soldiers
who perished for the impiety of their hearts.
11 And had there been but one stiffnecked man,
it were a wonder had he gone unpunished.
For mercy and anger alike are with him
who remits and forgives, though on the wicked
alights his wrath.
12 Great as his mercy is his punishment;
he judges men, each according to his deeds.
13 A criminal does not escape with his plunder;
a just man's hope God does not leave unfulfilled.

NEW JERUSALEM BIBLE

4 One person of sense can populate a city,
but a race of lawless people will be destroyed.
5 My eyes have seen many such things,
my ears have heard things even more impressive.
6 Fire is kindled in a sinful society,
Retribution blazes in a rebellious nation.
7 God did not pardon the giants of old
who, confident in their strength, had rebelled.
8 He did not spare the people with whom Lot lived;
he abhorred them, rather, for their pride.
9 He was pitiless to the nation of perdition—
those people who gloried in their sins—
10 as also to the six hundred thousand men on the march,
who had banded together in their obstinacy.
11 And had there been only one man stubborn,
it would have been amazing had he escaped
unpunished,
since mercy and wrath alike belong to the Lord
who is mighty to forgive and to pour out wrath.
12 As great as his mercy, so is his severity;
he judges each person as his deeds deserve:
13 the sinner will not escape with his ill-gotten gains
nor the patience of the devout go for nothing.

GREEK OLD TESTAMENT

[14]πάσῃ ἐλεημοσύνῃ ποιήσει τόπον,
ἕκαστος κατὰ τὰ ἔργα αὐτοῦ εὑρήσει.
17 Μὴ εἴπῃς ὅτι Ἀπὸ κυρίου κρυβήσομαι,
καὶ ἐξ ὕψους τίς μου μνησθήσεται;
ἐν λαῷ πλείονι οὐ μὴ γνωσθῶ,
τίς γὰρ ἡ ψυχή μου ἐν ἀμετρήτῳ κτίσει;
[18]ἰδοὺ ὁ οὐρανὸς καὶ ὁ οὐρανὸς τοῦ οὐρανοῦ,
ἄβυσσος καὶ γῆ ἐν τῇ ἐπισκοπῇ αὐτοῦ σαλευθήσονται·
[19]ἅμα τὰ ὄρη καὶ τὰ θεμέλια τῆς γῆς
ἐν τῷ ἐπιβλέψαι εἰς αὐτὰ τρόμῳ συσσείονται.
[20]καὶ ἐπ' αὐτοῖς οὐ διανοηθήσεται καρδία,
καὶ τὰς ὁδοὺς αὐτοῦ τίς ἐνθυμηθήσεται;
[21]καὶ καταιγίς, ἣν οὐκ ὄψεται ἄνθρωπος,
τὰ δὲ πλείονα τῶν ἔργων αὐτοῦ ἐν ἀποκρύφοις.
[22]ἔργα δικαιοσύνης τίς ἀναγγελεῖ;
ἢ τίς ὑπομενεῖ; μακρὰν γὰρ ἡ διαθήκη.
[23]ἐλαττούμενος καρδίᾳ διανοεῖται ταῦτα,
καὶ ἀνὴρ ἄφρων καὶ πλανώμενος διανοεῖται μωρά.
24 Ἄκουσόν μου, τέκνον, καὶ μάθε ἐπιστήμην
καὶ ἐπὶ τῶν λόγων μου πρόσεχε τῇ καρδίᾳ σου·
[25]ἐκφανῶ ἐν σταθμῷ παιδείαν
καὶ ἐν ἀκριβείᾳ ἀπαγγελῶ ἐπιστήμην.

KING JAMES VERSION

14 Make way for every work of mercy: for every man shall find according to his works.

15 The Lord hardened Pharaoh, that he should not know him, that his powerful works might be known to the world.

16 His mercy is manifest to every creature; and he hath separated his light from the darkness with an adamant.

17 Say not thou, I will hide myself from the Lord: shall any remember me from above? I shall not be remembered among so many people: for what is my soul among such an infinite number of creatures?

18 Behold, the heaven, and the heaven of heavens, the deep, and the earth, and all that therein is, shall be moved when he shall visit.

19 The mountains also and foundations of the earth shall be shaken with trembling, when the Lord looketh upon them.

20 No heart can think upon these things worthily: and who is able to conceive his ways?

21 It is a tempest which no man can see: for the most part of his works are hid.

22 Who can declare the works of his justice? or who can endure them? for his covenant is afar off, and the trial of all things is in the end.

23 He that wanteth understanding will think upon vain things: and a foolish man erring imagineth follies.

24 My son, hearken unto me, and learn knowledge, and mark my words with thy heart.

25 I will shew forth doctrine in weight, and declare his knowledge exactly.

DOUAY OLD TESTAMENT

15 All mercy shall make a place for every man according to the merit of his works, and according to the wisdom of his sojournment.

16 Say not: I shall be hidden from God, and who shall remember me from on high?

17 In such a multitude I shall not be known: for what is my soul in such an immense creation?

18 Behold the heaven, and the heavens of heavens, the deep, and all the earth, and the things that are in them, shall be moved in his sight,

19 The mountains also, and the hills, and the foundations of the earth: when God shall look upon them, they shall be shaken with trembling.

20 And in all these things the heart is senseless: and every heart is understood by him:

21 And his ways who shall understand, and the storm, which no eye of man shall see?

22 For many of his works are hidden: but the works of his justice who shall declare? or who shall endure? for the testament is far from some, and the examination of all is in the end.

23 He that wanteth understanding thinketh vain things: and the foolish, and erring man, thinketh foolish things.

24 Hearken to me, my son, and learn the discipline of understanding, and attend to my words in thy heart.

25 And I will shew forth good doctrine in equity, and will seek to declare wisdom: and attend to my words in thy heart,

KNOX TRANSLATION

but shall win God's consideration; he weighs each man's
merits, knows how each passed his time on earth.
[16]Never think to hide thyself away from God; never tell
thyself, from that great height none shall regard thee; [17]that
thou wilt pass unnoticed amidst the throng of humanity, thy
soul a mere speck in the vast fabric of creation. [18]Why, the
very heavens, and the heavens that are above the heavens,
the great deep, and the whole earth with all it contains,
shrink away at the sight of him; [19]mountains and hills and
earth's foundations tremble at his glance; [20]all these have a
heart, though it be a heart void of reason[a], and there is no
heart but its secrets are known to him. [21]There is no fathoming his ways, no piercing the dark cloud man's eyes have
never seen; [22]all but a few of his doings are hidden away.
His acts of retribution[b] who can understand, or who can
bear? Far, far removed is that covenant of his from some
men's thoughts; and yet in the end all shall undergo his
scrutiny.[c] [23]Away with these fancies of shallow minds,
these fond dreams of error!
[24]Wilt thou but listen to me, my son, thou shalt learn a
wiser lesson. Give me thy heart's heeding, [25]and instruction
thou shalt have in full measure, wisdom both profound and

a 'All these have a heart, though it be a heart void of reason'; or perhaps, 'and in all these matters, the (human) heart is powerless to reason', which is the sense of the Greek text. *b* The sense of the Greek text is probably rather 'the acts which win his approval'. *c vv.* 18-22: In the Latin version, this is apparently regarded as an answer to the notions mentioned in verses 16, 17; in the Greek text, it seems to be a continuation of them, the answer being delayed till verse 24.

TODAY'S ENGLISH VERSION

righteous person will be rewarded;[a] everyone will get what
he deserves.[b]
17 Never say, "I will hide from the Lord. Nobody up there is
going to give me a thought. How can I be noticed among so
many people? The creation is so enormous, what am I
worth? 18 When the Lord comes, everything will tremble: the
earth and the great waters beneath it, the sky and the heavens above it. 19 The mountains will shake, and the foundations of the earth will shudder when he looks at them. 20 The
Lord isn't going to give me a thought. Nobody cares what I
do. 21 If I sin and am secretly disloyal, nobody will know it.[c]
22 If I do what is right, nobody will tell the Lord about it. Who
wants to wait for him, anyway? He is too slow in doing what
he has said he would." 23 Only someone with very little
sense, and foolishly misguided, would think things like that.
24 My child, listen and pay attention to me; you will gain
knowledge if you do. 25 I will give you diligent and accurate
instruction.

[a] *Hebrew* Every . . . rewarded; *Greek* He makes room for every act of mercy.
[b] *Some manuscripts add verses 15-16:* The Lord made the king of Egypt so stubborn that he would not acknowledge the Lord, in order that the world might know the Lord's works. [16]He shows his mercy to all creation; he has divided his light from darkness with a plumb line.
[c] *Hebrew* [20-21]The Lord . . . know it; *Greek* [20]It is altogether too big for the human mind to handle. No one can understand his ways. [21]Most of his works are just as invisible as the storm wind.

NEW REVISED STANDARD VERSION

14 He makes room for every act of mercy;
everyone receives in accordance with his or her deeds.[a]
17 Do not say, "I am hidden from the Lord,
and who from on high has me in mind?
Among so many people I am unknown,
for what am I in a boundless creation?
18 Lo, heaven and the highest heaven,
the abyss and the earth, tremble at his visitation![b]
19 The very mountains and the foundations of the earth
quiver and quake when he looks upon them.
20 But no human mind can grasp this,
and who can comprehend his ways?
21 Like a tempest that no one can see,
so most of his works are concealed.[c]
22 Who is to announce his acts of justice?
Or who can await them? For his decree[d] is far off."[e]
23 Such are the thoughts of one devoid of understanding;
a senseless and misguided person thinks foolishly.

24 Listen to me, my child, and acquire knowledge,
and pay close attention to my words.
25 I will impart discipline precisely[f]
and declare knowledge accurately.

a Other ancient authorities add *[15]The Lord hardened Pharaoh so that he did not recognize him, in order that his works might be known under heaven. [16]His mercy is manifest to the whole of creation, and he divided his light and darkness with a plumb line.* *b* Other ancient authorities add *The whole world past and present is in his will.* *c* Meaning of Gk uncertain: Heb Syr *If I sin, no eye can see me, and if I am disloyal all in secret, who is to know?* *d* Heb *the decree*: Gk *the covenant* *e* Other ancient authorities add *and a scrutiny for all comes at the end* *f* Gk *by weight*

NEW AMERICAN BIBLE

14 Whoever does good has his reward,
which each receives according to his deeds.
15 Say not: "I am hidden from God;
in heaven who remembers me?
Among so many people I cannot be known;
what am I in the world of spirits?
16 Behold, the heavens, the heaven of heavens,
the earth and the abyss tremble at his visitation;
17 The roots of the mountains, the earth's foundations,
at his mere glance, quiver and quake.
18 Of me, therefore, he will take no thought;
with my ways who will concern himself?
19 If I sin, no eye will see me;
if all in secret I am disloyal, who is to know?
20 Who tells him of just deeds
and what could I expect for doing my duty?"
21 Such are the thoughts of senseless men,
which only the foolish knave will think.

22 Hearken to me, my son, take my advice,
apply your mind to my words,
23 While I propose measured wisdom,
and impart accurate knowledge.

NEW JERUSALEM BIBLE

14 He takes note of every charitable action,
and everyone is treated as he deserves.

17 Do not say, 'I shall hide from the Lord,
who is going to remember me up there?
I shall not be noticed among so many people;
what am I in the immensity of creation?'
18 For see, the sky and the heavens above the sky,
the abyss and the earth shake at his visitation.
19 The mountains and earth's foundations alike
quail and tremble when he looks at them.
20 But to all this no one gives thought.
Who keeps his movements in mind?
21 The storm wind itself is invisible,
and most of what he does goes undetected.
22 'Who will report whether justice has been done?
Who will be watching? The covenant is remote!'
23 Such are the thoughts of the person of little sense,
stupid, misguided, cherishing his folly.

24 Listen to me, my child, and learn knowledge,
and give your whole mind to my words.
25 I shall expound discipline methodically
and proclaim knowledge with precision.

GREEK OLD TESTAMENT

26 Ἐν κρίσει κυρίου τὰ ἔργα αὐτοῦ ἀπ' ἀρχῆς,
καὶ ἀπὸ ποιήσεως αὐτῶν διέστειλεν μερίδας αὐτῶν.
27 ἐκόσμησεν εἰς αἰῶνα τὰ ἔργα αὐτοῦ
καὶ τὰς ἀρχὰς αὐτῶν εἰς γενεὰς αὐτῶν·
οὔτε ἐπείνασαν οὔτε ἐκοπίασαν
καὶ οὐκ ἐξέλιπον ἀπὸ τῶν ἔργων αὐτῶν·
28 ἕκαστος τὸν πλησίον αὐτοῦ οὐκ ἐξέθλιψεν,
καὶ ἕως αἰῶνος οὐκ ἀπειθήσουσιν τοῦ ῥήματος αὐτοῦ.
29 καὶ μετὰ ταῦτα κύριος εἰς τὴν γῆν ἐπέβλεψεν
καὶ ἐνέπλησεν αὐτὴν τῶν ἀγαθῶν αὐτοῦ·
30 ψυχῇ παντὸς ζῴου ἐκάλυψεν τὸ πρόσωπον αὐτῆς,
καὶ εἰς αὐτὴν ἡ ἀποστροφὴ αὐτῶν.

17 Κύριος ἔκτισεν ἐκ γῆς ἄνθρωπον
καὶ πάλιν ἀπέστρεψεν αὐτὸν εἰς αὐτήν.
2 ἡμέρας ἀριθμοῦ καὶ καιρὸν ἔδωκεν αὐτοῖς
καὶ ἔδωκεν αὐτοῖς ἐξουσίαν τῶν ἐπ' αὐτῆς.
3 καθ' ἑαυτὸν ἐνέδυσεν αὐτοὺς ἰσχὺν
καὶ κατ' εἰκόνα αὐτοῦ ἐποίησεν αὐτούς.
4 ἔθηκεν τὸν φόβον αὐτοῦ ἐπὶ πάσης σαρκὸς
καὶ κατακυριεύειν θηρίων καὶ πετεινῶν.
6 διαβούλιον καὶ γλῶσσαν καὶ ὀφθαλμούς,
ὦτα καὶ καρδίαν ἔδωκεν διανοεῖσθαι αὐτοῖς.
7 ἐπιστήμην συνέσεως ἐνέπλησεν αὐτοὺς
καὶ ἀγαθὰ καὶ κακὰ ὑπέδειξεν αὐτοῖς.

KING JAMES VERSION

26 The works of the Lord are done in judgment from the beginning: and from the time he made them he disposed the parts thereof.
27 He garnished his works for ever, and in his hand are the chief of them unto all generations: they neither labour, nor are weary, nor cease from their works.
28 None of them hindereth another, and they shall never disobey his word.
29 After this the Lord looked upon the earth, and filled it with his blessings.
30 With all manner of living things hath he covered the face thereof; and they shall return into it again.

17 The Lord created man of the earth, and turned him into it again.
2 He gave them few days, and a short time, and power also over the things therein.
3 He endued them with strength by themselves, and made them according to his image,
4 And put the fear of man upon all flesh, and gave him dominion over beasts and fowls.
5 [They received the use of the five operations of the Lord, and in the sixth place he imparted them understanding, and in the seventh speech, an interpreter of the cogitations thereof.]
6 Counsel, and a tongue, and eyes, ears, and a heart, gave he them to understand.
7 Withal he filled them with the knowledge of understanding, and shewed them good and evil.

DOUAY OLD TESTAMENT

whilst with equity of spirit I tell thee the virtues that God hath put upon his works from the beginning, and I shew forth in truth his knowledge.
26 The works of God are done in judgment from the beginning, and from the making of them he distinguished their parts, and their beginnings in their generations.
27 He beautified their works for ever, they have neither hungered, nor laboured, and they have not ceased from their works.
28 Nor shall any of them straiten his neighbour at any time.
29 Be not thou incredulous to his word.
30 After this God looked upon the earth, and filled it with his goods.
31 The soul of every living thing hath shewn forth before the face thereof, and into it they return again.

17 GOD created man of the earth, and made him after his own image.
2 And he turned him into it again, and clothed him with strength according to himself.
3 He gave him the number of his days and time, and gave him power over all things that are upon the earth.
4 He put the fear of him upon all flesh, and he had dominion over beasts and fowls.
5 He created of him a helpmate like to himself: he gave them counsel, and a tongue, and eyes, and ears, and a heart to devise: and he filled them with the knowledge of understanding.
6 He created in them the science of the spirit, he filled their heart with wisdom, and shewed them both good and evil.

KNOX TRANSLATION

clear. Give me thy heart's heeding, and thou shalt share with
me knowledge of the wonderful endowments God gave his
creatures when first he made them; all the lore I have shall
be truly told thee. 26 From the first, all God's creatures are at
his beck and call; to each, when he first made it, he gave its
own turn of service, the principle that determines its own
nature. 27 To each, for all time, its own office is assigned,
nor lack they, nor tire they, nor cease they from work, 28 nor,
for all time, can any of them infringe upon its neighbour's
rights; 29 his word there is no gainsaying.[a] 30 This done, on
earth he let fall his regard, and filled earth with his blessings; 31 covered the face of it[b] with the living things that
breathe there, and into its bosom bade them return.

17 Man, too, God created out of the earth, fashioning
him after his own likeness, 2 and gave him, too, earth
to be his burying-place, for all the divine power that clothed
him; 3 man, too, should have his allotted toll of years, his
season of maturity, and should have power over all else on
earth; 4 no living thing, beast or bird, that should not live in
awe of him and be subject to his rule. 5 To him and to that
partner of his, created like himself and out of himself, God
gave will and speech and sight and hearing; gave them a
heart to reason with, and filled them with power of discernment; 6 spirit itself should be within their ken, their hearts
should be all sagacity. What evil was, what good, he made

a That is, according to the Greek text, the forces of nature are bound to obey it; the Latin version represents it as a warning against human disobedience.
b This is the meaning of the Greek text. The Latin version has 'denounced before the face of it', which yields no satisfactory sense.

TODAY'S ENGLISH VERSION

26 In the beginning the Lord did his work of creation,[a]
and gave everything a place of its own.
27 He arranged everything in an eternal order
and decreed that it should be that way forever.
Not one part of creation ever grows hungry;
no part grows tired or stops its work.
28 The parts do not crowd one another,
and they never disobey his word.
29 When the Lord had made all this,
he looked at the earth and filled it with good things.
30 He covered it with all kinds of creatures
that must die and return to the dust.

17 Then the Lord formed human beings from the dust
and sent each of them back to it again.
2 He gave them only a limited time to live,
but he gave them authority over everything on earth.
3 He made them to be like himself,
and gave them his[b] own strength.
4 He made all other creatures afraid of them;
he gave them authority over all the animals and birds.[c]
6 He gave them their tongues, their eyes,
their ears, their minds, and their consciences.
7 He filled them with knowledge and understanding
and showed them the difference between good and evil.

[a] *Hebrew* In . . . creation; *Greek* In the judgment of the Lord his works are from the beginning. [b] *Probable text* his; *Greek* their.
[c] *Some manuscripts add verse 5:* The Lord gave them the five senses, but he also gave them a sixth—intelligence, and a seventh—reason, which enables them to interpret what comes to them through the senses.

NEW REVISED STANDARD VERSION

26 When the Lord created[a] his works from the beginning,
and, in making them, determined their boundaries,
27 he arranged his works in an eternal order,
and their dominion[b] for all generations.
They neither hunger nor grow weary,
and they do not abandon their tasks.
28 They do not crowd one another,
and they never disobey his word.
29 Then the Lord looked upon the earth,
and filled it with his good things.
30 With all kinds of living beings he covered its surface,
and into it they must return.

17 The Lord created human beings out of earth,
and makes them return to it again.
2 He gave them a fixed number of days,
but granted them authority over everything on the
earth.[c]
3 He endowed them with strength like his own,[d]
and made them in his own image.
4 He put the fear of them[e] in all living beings,
and gave them dominion over beasts and birds.[f]
6 Discretion and tongue and eyes,
ears and a mind for thinking he gave them.
7 He filled them with knowledge and understanding,
and showed them good and evil.

a Heb: Gk *judged* *b* Or *elements* *c* Lat: Gk *it* *d* Lat: Gk *proper to them* *e* Syr: Gk *him* *f* Other ancient authorities add as verse 5, *They obtained the use of the five faculties of the Lord; as sixth he distributed to them the gift of mind, and as seventh, reason, the interpreter of one's faculties.*

NEW AMERICAN BIBLE

24 When at the first God created his works
and, as he made them, assigned their tasks,
25 He ordered for all time what they were to do
and their domains from generation to generation.
They were not to hunger, nor grow weary,
nor ever cease from their tasks.
26 Not one should ever crowd its neighbor,
nor should they ever disobey his word.
27 Then the LORD looked upon the earth,
and filled it with his blessings.
28 Its surface he covered with all manner of life
which must return into it again.

17 The LORD from the earth created man,
and in his own image he made him.
2 Limited days of life he gives him
and makes him return to earth again.
3 He endows man with a strength of his own,
and with power over all things else on earth.
4 He puts the fear of him in all flesh,
and gives him rule over beasts and birds.
5 He forms men's tongues and eyes and ears,
and imparts to them an understanding heart.
6 With wisdom and knowledge he fills them;
good and evil he shows them.

NEW JERUSALEM BIBLE

26 When God created his works in the beginning,
he assigned them their places as soon as they were
made.
27 He determined his works for all time,
from their origins to their distant generations.
They know neither hunger nor weariness,
and they never desert their duties.
28 Not one has ever got in the way of another,
and they will never disobey his word.
29 And afterwards the Lord looked at the earth,
and filled it with his good things.
30 He covered its surface with every kind of animal,
and to it they will return.

17 The Lord fashioned human beings from the earth,
to consign them back to it.
2 He gave them so many days and so much time,
he gave them authority over everything on earth.
3 He clothed them in strength, like himself,
and made them in his own image.
4 He filled all living things with dread of human beings,
making them masters over beasts and birds.
6 He made them a tongue, eyes and ears,
and gave them a heart to think with.
7 He filled them with knowledge and intelligence,
and showed them what was good and what evil.

GREEK OLD TESTAMENT

8 ἔθηκεν τὸν ὀφθαλμὸν αὐτοῦ ἐπὶ τὰς καρδίας αὐτῶν
δεῖξαι αὐτοῖς τὸ μεγαλεῖον τῶν ἔργων αὐτοῦ,
10 καὶ ὄνομα ἁγιασμοῦ αἰνέσουσιν,
ἵνα διηγῶνται τὰ μεγαλεῖα τῶν ἔργων αὐτοῦ.
11 προσέθηκεν αὐτοῖς ἐπιστήμην
καὶ νόμον ζωῆς ἐκληροδότησεν αὐτοῖς.
12 διαθήκην αἰῶνος ἔστησεν μετ᾽ αὐτῶν
καὶ τὰ κρίματα αὐτοῦ ὑπέδειξεν αὐτοῖς.
13 μεγαλεῖον δόξης εἶδον οἱ ὀφθαλμοὶ αὐτῶν,
καὶ δόξαν φωνῆς αὐτοῦ ἤκουσεν τὸ οὖς αὐτῶν.
14 καὶ εἶπεν αὐτοῖς Προσέχετε ἀπὸ παντὸς ἀδίκου·
καὶ ἐνετείλατο αὐτοῖς ἑκάστῳ περὶ τοῦ πλησίον.
15 Αἱ ὁδοὶ αὐτῶν ἐναντίον αὐτοῦ διὰ παντός,
οὐ κρυβήσονται ἀπὸ τῶν ὀφθαλμῶν αὐτοῦ.
17 ἑκάστῳ ἔθνει κατέστησεν ἡγούμενον,
καὶ μερὶς κυρίου Ισραηλ ἐστίν.
19 ἅπαντα τὰ ἔργα αὐτῶν ὡς ὁ ἥλιος ἐναντίον αὐτοῦ,
καὶ οἱ ὀφθαλμοὶ αὐτοῦ ἐνδελεχεῖς ἐπὶ τὰς ὁδοὺς αὐτῶν.
20 οὐκ ἐκρύβησαν αἱ ἀδικίαι αὐτῶν ἀπ᾽ αὐτοῦ,
καὶ πᾶσαι αἱ ἁμαρτίαι αὐτῶν ἔναντι κυρίου.

KING JAMES VERSION

8 He set his eye upon their hearts, that he might shew them the greatness of his works.

9 He gave them to glory in his marvellous acts for ever, that they might declare his works with understanding.

10 And the elect shall praise his holy name.

11 Beside this he gave them knowledge, and the law of life for an heritage.

12 He made an everlasting covenant with them, and shewed them his judgments.

13 Their eyes saw the majesty of his glory, and their ears heard his glorious voice.

14 And he said unto them, Beware of all unrighteousness; and he gave every man commandment concerning his neighbour.

15 Their ways are ever before him, and shall not be hid from his eyes.

16 Every man from his youth is given to evil; neither could they make to themselves fleshy hearts for stony.

17 For in the division of the nations of the whole earth he set a ruler over every people; but Israel is the Lord's portion:

18 Whom, being his firstborn, he nourisheth with discipline, and giving him the light of his love doth not forsake him.

19 Therefore all their works are as the sun before him, and his eyes are continually upon their ways.

20 None of their unrighteous deeds are hid from him, but all their sins are before the Lord.

21 But the Lord being gracious, and knowing his workmanship, neither left nor forsook them, but spared them.

DOUAY OLD TESTAMENT

7 He set his eye upon their hearts to shew them the greatness of his works:

8 That they might praise the name which he hath sanctified: and glory in his wondrous acts, that they might declare the glorious things of his works.

9 Moreover he gave them instructions, and the law of life for an inheritance.

10 He made an everlasting covenant with them, and he shewed them his justice and judgments.

11 And their eye saw the majesty of his glory, and their ears heard his glorious voice, and he said to them: Beware of all iniquity.

12 And he gave to every one of them commandment concerning his neighbour.

13 Their ways are always before him, they are not hidden from his eyes.

14 Over every nation he set a ruler.

15 And Israel was made the manifest portion of God.

16 And all their works are as the sun in the sight of God: and his eyes are continually upon their ways.

17 Their covenants were not hid by their iniquity, and all their iniquities are in the sight of God.

KNOX TRANSLATION

plain to them; 7 gave them his own eyes to see with, so that
they should keep his marvellous acts in view, 8 praise that
holy name of his, boast of his wonders, tell the story of his
renowned deeds. 9 Warnings, too, he gave them; the law that
brings life should be a cherished heirloom; 10 and so he made
a covenant with them which should last for ever; claim and
award of his he would make known to them. 11 Their eyes
should see him in visible majesty, their ears catch the echo of
his majestic voice. Keep your hands clear, he told them, of all
wrong-doing, 12 and gave each man a duty towards his
neighbour.

13 Ever before his eyes their doings are; nothing is hidden
from his scrutiny. 14 To every Gentile people he has given a
ruler of its own; 15 Israel alone is exempt, marked down as
God's patrimony. 16 Clear as the sun their acts shew under
his eye; over their lives, untiring his scrutiny. 17 Sin they as
they will, his covenant is still on record; no misdeed of theirs
but he is the witness of it.

TODAY'S ENGLISH VERSION

8 He gave them his own insight
to let them see the majesty of his creation.[a]
10 They will praise his holy name
and proclaim the greatness of all he does.
11 He made knowledge available to them
and gave them the Law as a source of life.
12 He made an eternal covenant with them
and revealed his commands to them.
13 They saw the splendor of his majesty
and heard the glory of his voice.
14 He warned them against unrighteousness
and taught each person how to treat others.

15 The Lord is always aware of what people do; there is no
way to hide from him.[b] 17 He gave each nation its own ruler,
but Israel is the Lord's own possession.[c] 19 The Lord is
always watching what people do; everything they do is as
clear as day to him. 20 None of their sins are hidden from
him; he is aware of them all.[d] 22 When we give to the poor,

[a] *Some manuscripts add verse 9:* and he allowed them to take pride forever in his marvelous deeds. [b] *Some manuscripts add verses 16-17a:* From childhood on they tend to be evil; their heart is like stone, and they don't seem to be able to make it more human. [17]He divided the nations of the whole earth. [c] *Some manuscripts add verse 18:* Israel is his first-born, whom he disciplines as he brings him up. He gives him the light of his love and never neglects him. [d] *Some manuscripts add verse 21:* But the Lord is gracious and knows his creatures; so he has spared them rather than abandon them.

NEW REVISED STANDARD VERSION

8 He put the fear of him into[a] their hearts
to show them the majesty of his works.[b]
10 And they will praise his holy name,
9 to proclaim the grandeur of his works.
11 He bestowed knowledge upon them,
and allotted to them the law of life.[c]
12 He established with them an eternal covenant,
and revealed to them his decrees.
13 Their eyes saw his glorious majesty,
and their ears heard the glory of his voice.
14 He said to them, "Beware of all evil."
And he gave commandment to each of them
concerning the neighbor.
15 Their ways are always known to him;
they will not be hid from his eyes.[d]
17 He appointed a ruler for every nation,
but Israel is the Lord's own portion.[e]
19 All their works are as clear as the sun before him,
and his eyes are ever upon their ways.
20 Their iniquities are not hidden from him,
and all their sins are before the Lord.[f]

a Other ancient authorities read *He set his eye upon* *b* Other ancient authorities add *and he gave them to boast of his marvels forever* *c* Other ancient authorities add *so that they may know that they who are alive now are mortal* *d* Other ancient authorities add *[16]Their ways from youth tend toward evil, and they are unable to make for themselves hearts of flesh in place of their stony hearts. [17]For in the division of the nations of the whole earth, he appointed* *e* Other ancient authorities add as verse 18, *whom, being his firstborn, he brings up with discipline, and allotting to him the light of his love, he does not neglect him.* *f* Other ancient authorities add as verse 21, *But the Lord, who is gracious and knows how they are formed, has neither left them nor abandoned them, but has spared them.*

NEW AMERICAN BIBLE

7 He looks with favor upon their hearts,
and shows them his glorious works,
8 That they may describe the wonders of his deeds
and praise his holy name.
9 He has set before them knowledge,
a law of life as their inheritance;
10 An everlasting covenant he has made with them,
his commandments he has revealed to them.
11 His majestic glory their eyes beheld,
his glorious voice their ears heard.
12 He says to them, "Avoid all evil";
each of them he gives precepts about his fellow men.
13 Their ways are ever known to him,
they cannot be hidden from his eyes.
14 Over every nation he places a ruler,
but the LORD's own portion is Israel.
15 All their actions are clear as the sun to him,
his eyes are ever upon their ways.
16 Their wickedness cannot be hidden from him;
all of their sins are before the LORD.

NEW JERUSALEM BIBLE

8 He put his own light in their hearts
to show them the magnificence of his works,
10 so that they would praise his holy name
as they told of his magnificent works.
11 He set knowledge before them,
he endowed them with the law of life.
12 He established an eternal covenant with them,
and revealed his judgements to them.
13 Their eyes saw the majesty of his glory,
and their ears heard the glory of his voice.
14 He said to them, 'Beware of all wrong-doing';
he gave each a commandment concerning his
neighbour.
15 Their ways are always under his eye,
they cannot be hidden from his sight.
17 Over each nation he has set a governor,
but Israel is the Lord's own portion.
19 Their actions are all as plain as the sun to him,
and his eyes rest constantly on their conduct.
20 Their iniquities are not hidden from him,
all their sins are before the Lord.

GREEK OLD TESTAMENT

22 ἐλεημοσύνη ἀνδρὸς ὡς σφραγὶς μετ᾽ αὐτοῦ,
καὶ χάριν ἀνθρώπου ὡς κόρην συντηρήσει.
23 μετὰ ταῦτα ἐξαναστήσεται καὶ ἀνταποδώσει αὐτοῖς
καὶ τὸ ἀνταπόδομα αὐτῶν εἰς κεφαλὴν αὐτῶν ἀποδώσει·
24 πλὴν μετανοοῦσιν ἔδωκεν ἐπάνοδον
καὶ παρεκάλεσεν ἐκλείποντας ὑπομονήν.
25 Ἐπίστρεφε ἐπὶ κύριον καὶ ἀπόλειπε ἁμαρτίας,
δεήθητι κατὰ πρόσωπον καὶ σμίκρυνον πρόσκομμα·
26 ἐπάναγε ἐπὶ ὕψιστον καὶ ἀπόστρεφε ἀπὸ ἀδικίας
καὶ σφόδρα μίσησον βδέλυγμα.
27 ὑψίστῳ τίς αἰνέσει ἐν ᾅδου
ἀντὶ ζώντων καὶ διδόντων ἀνθομολόγησιν;
28 ἀπὸ νεκροῦ ὡς μηδὲ ὄντος ἀπόλλυται ἐξομολόγησις·
ζῶν καὶ ὑγιὴς αἰνέσει τὸν κύριον.
29 ὡς μεγάλη ἡ ἐλεημοσύνη τοῦ κυρίου
καὶ ἐξιλασμὸς τοῖς ἐπιστρέφουσιν ἐπ᾽ αὐτόν.
30 οὐ γὰρ δύναται πάντα εἶναι ἐν ἀνθρώποις,
ὅτι οὐκ ἀθάνατος υἱὸς ἀνθρώπου.

KING JAMES VERSION

22 The alms of a man is as a signet with him, and he will keep the good deeds of man as the apple of the eye, and give repentance to his sons and daughters.

23 Afterwards he will rise up and reward them, and render their recompence upon their heads.

24 But unto them that repent, he granted them return, and comforted those that failed in patience.

25 Return unto the Lord, and forsake thy sins, make thy prayer before his face, and offend less.

26 Turn again to the most High, and turn away from iniquity: for he will lead thee out of darkness into the light of health, and hate thou abomination vehemently.

27 Who shall praise the most High in the grave, instead of them which live and give thanks?

28 Thanksgiving perisheth from the dead, as from one that is not: the living and sound in heart shall praise the Lord.

29 How great is the lovingkindness of the Lord our God, and his compassion unto such as turn unto him in holiness!

30 For all things cannot be in men, because the son of man is not immortal.

DOUAY OLD TESTAMENT

18 The alms of a man is as a signet with him, and shall preserve the grace of a man as the apple of the eye:

19 And afterward he shall rise up, and shall render them their reward, to every one upon their own head, and shall turn *them* down into the bowels of the earth.

20 But to the penitent he hath given the way of justice, and he hath strengthened them that were fainting in patience, and hath appointed to them the lot of truth.

21 Turn to the Lord, and forsake thy sins:

22 Make thy prayer before the face of the Lord, and offend less.

23 Return to the Lord, and turn away from thy injustice, and greatly hate abomination.

24 And know the justices and judgments of God, and stand firm in the lot set before thee, and in prayer to the most high God.

25 Go to the side of the holy age, with them that live and give praise to God.

26 Tarry not in the error of the ungodly, give glory before death. Praise perisheth from the dead as nothing.

27 Give thanks whilst thou art living, whilst thou art alive and in health thou shalt give thanks, and shalt praise God, and shalt glory in his mercies.

28 How great is the mercy of the Lord, and his forgiveness to them that turn to him!

29 For all things cannot be in men, because the son of man is not immortal, and they are delighted with the vanity of evil.

KNOX TRANSLATION

18 Alms if thou givest, thou hast the sign-manual of his
favour; treasured as the apple of his eye is the record of
man's deserving.[a]
19 ...A day will come when he rouses himself and requites
them, one by one, for their misdoing, overwhelms them in the
depths of earth. 20 Yet, to such as repent, he grants the means
of acquittal, and makes their fainting hearts strong to endure;
for them, too, he has a share in his promised reward. 21 Turn
back to the Lord, and let thy sins be; 22 make thy prayer
before him, and rid thyself of the peril in thy path. 23 Come
back to the Lord, from wrong-doing turn away, and thy foul
deeds hate; 24 in all his decrees and awards own God just,
stand in thy appointed place to make intercession to him, the
most High, 25 and take thy part with a race of men sanctified,
living men that still give thanks to God.[b] 26 Linger not in the
false path of wickedness; give thanks while breath is in thee;
the dead breathe no more, give thanks no more. 27 Thanks
while yet thou livest, thanks while health and strength are
still with thee, to praise God and to take pride in all his mercies!
28 The Lord's mercy, that is so abundant, the pardon
that is ever theirs who come back to him!
29 Think not man is the centre of all things;[c] no son of
Adam is immortal, for all the delight men take in their sinful

a It seems possible that this verse has been misplaced, since it breaks into the connexion of thought between verse 17 and verse 19. *b* vv. 24, 25: The Latin here reads very unnaturally, and is perhaps the rendering of a corrupt Hebrew original. In the first half of verse 25, the Greek text has, 'Who will give praise to the most High in the grave?' The word rendered 'give thanks', here and in the following verses, may also, according to Hebrew usage, mean 'confess'. But cf. Is. 38. 19. *c* Literally, 'it is not possible that all things should be in man'.

TODAY'S ENGLISH VERSION

the Lord considers it as precious as a valuable ring. Human
kindness is as precious to him as life itself. [23]Later he will
judge the wicked and punish them; they will get what they
deserve. [24]But the Lord will allow those who repent to
return to him. He always gives encouragement to those who
are losing hope.

[25]Come to the Lord, and leave your sin behind. Pray sincerely that he will help you live a better life. [26]Return to the
Most High and turn away from sin. Have an intense hatred
for wickedness. [27]Those who are alive can give thanks to
the Lord, but can anyone in the world of the dead sing praise
to the Most High? [28]A person who is alive and well can sing
the Lord's praises, but the dead, who no longer exist, have
no way to give him thanks. [29]How great is the Lord's merciful forgiveness of those who turn to him! [30]But this is not
the nature of human beings;[a] not one of us is immortal.

[a] But . . . human beings; *or* People cannot have everything.

NEW REVISED STANDARD VERSION

22 One's almsgiving is like a signet ring with the Lord,[a]
and he will keep a person's kindness like the apple of
his eye.[b]
23 Afterward he will rise up and repay them,
and he will bring their recompense on their heads.
24 Yet to those who repent he grants a return,
and he encourages those who are losing hope.

25 Turn back to the Lord and forsake your sins;
pray in his presence and lessen your offense.
26 Return to the Most High and turn away from iniquity,[c]
and hate intensely what he abhors.
27 Who will sing praises to the Most High in Hades
in place of the living who give thanks?
28 From the dead, as from one who does not exist,
thanksgiving has ceased;
those who are alive and well sing the Lord's praises.
29 How great is the mercy of the Lord,
and his forgiveness for those who return to him!
30 For not everything is within human capability,
since human beings are not immortal.

a Gk *him* b Other ancient authorities add *apportioning repentance to his sons and daughters* c Other ancient authorities add *for he will lead you out of darkness to the light of health.*

NEW AMERICAN BIBLE

[17]A man's goodness God cherishes like a signet ring,
a man's virtue, like the apple of his eye.
[18]Later he will rise up and repay them,
and requite each one of them as they deserve.

[19]But to the penitent he provides a way back,
he encourages those who are losing hope!
[20]Return to the LORD and give up sin,
pray to him and make your offenses few.
[21]Turn again to the Most High and away from sin,
hate intensely what he loathes;
[22]Who in the nether world can glorify the Most High
in place of the living who offer their praise?
[23]No more can the dead give praise than those who have
never lived;
they glorify the LORD who are alive and well.
[24]How great the mercy of the LORD,
his forgiveness of those who return to him!
[25]The like cannot be found in men,
for not immortal is any son of man.

NEW JERUSALEM BIBLE

[22]Almsgiving is like a signet ring to him,
he cherishes generosity like the pupil of an eye.
[23]One day he will rise and reward them,
he will repay their deserts on their own heads.
[24]But to those who repent he permits return,
and he encourages those who have lost hope.

[25]Return to the Lord and renounce your sins,
plead before his face, stop offending him.
[26]Come back to the Most High, turn away from iniquity
and hold all that is foul in abhorrence.
[27]Who is going to praise the Most High in Sheol
if we do not glorify him while we are alive?
[28]The dead can praise no more than those who do not
exist,
only those with life and health can praise the Lord.
[29]How great is the mercy of the Lord,
his pardon for those who turn to him!
[30]For we cannot have everything,
human beings are not immortal.

GREEK OLD TESTAMENT

31 τί φωτεινότερον ἡλίου; καὶ τοῦτο ἐκλείπει·
καὶ πονηρὸν ἐνθυμηθήσεται σὰρξ καὶ αἷμα.
32 δύναμιν ὕψους οὐρανοῦ αὐτὸς ἐπισκέπτεται,
καὶ ἄνθρωποι πάντες γῆ καὶ σποδός.

18 Ὁ ζῶν εἰς τὸν αἰῶνα ἔκτισεν τὰ πάντα κοινῇ·
2 κύριος μόνος δικαιωθήσεται.
4 οὐθενὶ ἐξεποίησεν ἐξαγγεῖλαι τὰ ἔργα αὐτοῦ·
καὶ τίς ἐξιχνεύσει τὰ μεγαλεῖα αὐτοῦ;
5 κράτος μεγαλωσύνης αὐτοῦ τίς ἐξαριθμήσεται;
καὶ τίς προσθήσει ἐκδιηγήσασθαι τὰ ἐλέη αὐτοῦ;
6 οὐκ ἔστιν ἐλαττῶσαι οὐδὲ προσθεῖναι,
καὶ οὐκ ἔστιν ἐξιχνιάσαι τὰ θαυμάσια τοῦ κυρίου·
7 ὅταν συντελέσῃ ἄνθρωπος, τότε ἄρχεται·
καὶ ὅταν παύσηται, τότε ἀπορηθήσεται.
8 Τί ἄνθρωπος, καὶ τί ἡ χρῆσις αὐτοῦ;
τί τὸ ἀγαθὸν αὐτοῦ, καὶ τί τὸ κακὸν αὐτοῦ;
9 ἀριθμὸς ἡμερῶν ἀνθρώπου
πολλὰ ἔτη ἑκατόν·
10 ὡς σταγὼν ὕδατος ἀπὸ θαλάσσης καὶ ψῆφος ἄμμου,
οὕτως ὀλίγα ἔτη ἐν ἡμέρᾳ αἰῶνος.
11 διὰ τοῦτο ἐμακροθύμησεν κύριος ἐπ' αὐτοῖς
καὶ ἐξέχεεν ἐπ' αὐτοὺς τὸ ἔλεος αὐτοῦ.
12 εἶδεν καὶ ἐπέγνω τὴν καταστροφὴν αὐτῶν ὅτι πονηρά·
διὰ τοῦτο ἐπλήθυνεν τὸν ἐξιλασμὸν αὐτοῦ.

KING JAMES VERSION

31 What is brighter than the sun? yet the light thereof faileth: and flesh and blood will imagine evil.

32 He vieweth the power of the height of heaven; and all men are but earth and ashes.

18 He that liveth for ever created all things in general.
2 The Lord only is righteous, and there is none other but he,

3 Who governeth the world with the palm of his hand, and all things obey his will: for he is the King of all, by his power dividing holy things among them from profane.

4 To whom hath he given power to declare his works? and who shall find out his noble acts?

5 Who shall number the strength of his majesty? and who shall also tell out his mercies?

6 As for the wondrous works of the Lord, there may nothing be taken from them, neither may any thing be put unto them, neither can the ground of them be found out.

7 When a man hath done, then he beginneth; and when he leaveth off, then he shall be doubtful.

8 What is man, and whereto serveth he? what is his good, and what is his evil?

9 The number of a man's days at the most are an hundred years.

10 As a drop of water unto the sea, and a gravelstone in comparison of the sand; so are a thousand years to the days of eternity.

11 Therefore is God patient with them, and poureth forth his mercy upon them.

12 He saw and perceived their end to be evil; therefore he multiplied his compassion.

DOUAY OLD TESTAMENT

30 What is brighter than the sun; yet it shall be eclipsed. Or what is more wicked than that which flesh and blood hath invented? and this shall be reproved.

31 He beholdeth the power of the height of heaven: and all men are earth and ashes.

18 HE that liveth for ever created all things together. God only shall be justified, and he remaineth an invincible king for ever.

2 Who is able to declare his works?

3 For who shall search out his glorious acts?

4 And who shall shew forth the power of his majesty? or who shall be able to declare his mercy?

5 Nothing may be taken away, nor added, neither is it possible to find out the glorious works of God:

6 When a man hath done, then shall he begin: and when he leaveth off, he shall be at a loss.

7 What is man, and what is his grace? and what is his good, or what is his evil?

8 The number of the days of men at the most are a hundred years: as a drop of water of the sea are they esteemed: and as a pebble of the sand, so are a few years compared to eternity.

9 Therefore God is patient in them, and poureth forth his mercy upon them.

10 He hath seen the presumption of their heart that it is wicked, and hath known their end that it is evil.

11 Therefore hath he filled up his mercy in their favour, and hath shewn them the way of justice.

KNOX TRANSLATION

follies. 30 Nought brighter than the sun, and yet its brightness shall fail; nought darker than the secret designs of flesh
and blood, yet all shall be brought to light. 31 God, that marshals the armies of high heaven, and man, all dust and
ashes!

18 Naught that is, but God made it; he, the source of all
right, the king that reigns for ever unconquerable.
2 And wouldst thou tell the number of his creatures, 3 trace
his marvellous doings to their origin, 4 set forth in words the
greatness of his power, or go further yet, and proclaim his
mercies? 5 God's wonders thou shalt learn to understand,
when thou hast learned to increase the number of them, or
diminish it. 6 Reach thou the end of thy reckoning, thou
must needs begin again; cease thou from weariness, thou
hast nothing learnt. 7 Tell me, what is man, what worth is
his, what power has he for good or ill? 8 What is his span of
life? Like a drop in the ocean, like a pebble on the beach,
seem those few years of his, a hundred at the most, matched
with eternity. 9 What wonder if God is patient with his
human creatures, lavishes mercy on them? 10 If none reads,
as he, their proud heart, none knows, as he, the cruelty of
their doom; 11 and so he has given his clemency full play,
and shewed them an even path to tread. 12 Man's mercy

TODAY'S ENGLISH VERSION

31 Nothing is brighter than the sun, but even the sun's light
fails during an eclipse. How much easier it is for human
thoughts to be eclipsed by evil! 32 The Lord can look out over
all the stars in the sky. Human beings? They are dust and
ashes.
18 The Lord, who lives forever, created the whole universe, 2 and he alone is just.[a] 4 He has given no one
enough power to describe what he has done, and no one can
investigate it completely. 5 Who can measure his majestic
power? Who can tell the whole story of his merciful actions?
6 We cannot add to them; we cannot subtract from them.
There is no way to comprehend the marvelous things the
Lord has done. 7 When we come to the end of that story, we
have not even begun; we are simply at a loss for words.
8 What are human beings? Of what use are we? The good
that we do—the evil that we do—what does it all mean? 9 If
we live a hundred years, we have lived an unusually long
time, 10 but compared with all eternity, those years are like a
drop of water in the ocean, like a single grain of sand.
11 That is why the Lord is so patient with us, why he is so
free with his mercy. 12 He looks at us and knows that we are
doomed to die; that is why he is so willing to forgive us.

[a] *Some manuscripts add verses 2b-3:* and there is no other besides him. 3 He guides the world with his hand, and everything obeys him. He is the king of all things, and his power separates what is holy from what is not.

NEW REVISED STANDARD VERSION

31 What is brighter than the sun? Yet it can be eclipsed.
So flesh and blood devise evil.
32 He marshals the host of the height of heaven;
but all human beings are dust and ashes.

18 He who lives forever created the whole universe;
2 the Lord alone is just.[a]
4 To none has he given power to proclaim his works;
and who can search out his mighty deeds?
5 Who can measure his majestic power?
And who can fully recount his mercies?
6 It is not possible to diminish or increase them,
nor is it possible to fathom the wonders of the Lord.
7 When human beings have finished, they are just
beginning,
and when they stop, they are still perplexed.
8 What are human beings, and of what use are they?
What is good in them, and what is evil?
9 The number of days in their life is great if they reach
one hundred years.[b]
10 Like a drop of water from the sea and a grain of sand,
so are a few years among the days of eternity.
11 That is why the Lord is patient with them
and pours out his mercy upon them.
12 He sees and recognizes that their end is miserable;
therefore he grants them forgiveness all the more.

[a] Other ancient authorities add *and there is no other beside him; 3 he steers the world with the span of his hand, and all things obey his will; for he is king of all things by his power, separating among them the holy things from the profane.* [b] Other ancient authorities add *but the death of each one is beyond the calculation of all*

NEW AMERICAN BIBLE

26 Is anything brighter than the sun? Yet it can be
eclipsed.
How obscure then the thoughts of flesh and blood!
27 God watches over the hosts of highest heaven,
while all men are dust and ashes.

18 The Eternal is the judge of all things without
exception;
the LORD alone is just.
2 Whom has he made equal to describing his works,
and who can probe his mighty deeds?
3 Who can measure his majestic power,
or exhaust the tale of his mercies?
4 One cannot lessen, nor increase,
nor penetrate the wonders of the LORD.
5 When a man ends he is only beginning,
and when he stops he is still bewildered.
6 What is man, of what worth is he?
the good, the evil in him, what are these?
7 The sum of a man's days is great
if it reaches a hundred years:
8 Like a drop of sea water, like a grain of sand,
so are these few years among the days of eternity.
9 That is why the LORD is patient with men
and showers upon them his mercy.
10 He sees and understands that their death is grievous,
and so he forgives them all the more.

NEW JERUSALEM BIBLE

31 What is brighter than the sun? And yet it fades.
Flesh and blood think of nothing but evil.
32 He surveys the armies of the lofty sky,
and all of us are only dust and ashes.

18 He who lives for ever has created the sum of things.
2 The Lord alone will be found just.
4 He has given no one the power to proclaim his works to
the end,
and who can fathom his magnificent deeds?
5 Who can assess his magnificent strength,
and who can go further and tell all of his mercies?
6 Nothing can be added to them, nothing subtracted,
it is impossible to fathom the marvels of the Lord.
7 When someone finishes he is only beginning,
and when he stops he is as puzzled as ever.
8 What is a human being, what purpose does he serve?
What is good and what is bad for him?
9 The length of his life: a hundred years at most.
10 Like a drop of water from the sea, or a grain of sand,
such are these few years compared with eternity.
11 This is why the Lord is patient with them
and pours out his mercy on them.
12 He sees and recognises how wretched their end is,
and so he makes his forgiveness the greater.

GREEK OLD TESTAMENT

13 ἔλεος ἀνθρώπου ἐπὶ τὸν πλησίον αὐτοῦ,
ἔλεος δὲ κυρίου ἐπὶ πᾶσαν σάρκα·
ἐλέγχων καὶ παιδεύων καὶ διδάσκων
καὶ ἐπιστρέφων ὡς ποιμὴν τὸ ποίμνιον αὐτοῦ.
14 τοὺς ἐκδεχομένους παιδείαν ἐλεᾷ
καὶ τοὺς κατασπεύδοντας ἐπὶ τὰ κρίματα αὐτοῦ.
15 Τέκνον, ἐν ἀγαθοῖς μὴ δῷς μῶμον
καὶ ἐν πάσῃ δόσει λύπην λόγων.
16 οὐχὶ καύσωνα ἀναπαύσει δρόσος;
οὕτως κρείσσων λόγος ἢ δόσις.
17 οὐκ ἰδοὺ λόγος ὑπὲρ δόμα ἀγαθόν;
καὶ ἀμφότερα παρὰ ἀνδρὶ κεχαριτωμένῳ.
18 μωρὸς ἀχαρίστως ὀνειδιεῖ,
καὶ δόσις βασκάνου ἐκτήκει ὀφθαλμούς.
19 Πρὶν ἢ λαλῆσαι μάνθανε
καὶ πρὸ ἀρρωστίας θεραπεύου.
20 πρὸ κρίσεως ἐξέταζε σεαυτόν,
καὶ ἐν ὥρᾳ ἐπισκοπῆς εὑρήσεις ἐξιλασμόν.
21 πρὶν ἀρρωστῆσαί σε ταπεινώθητι
καὶ ἐν καιρῷ ἁμαρτημάτων δεῖξον ἐπιστροφήν.
22 μὴ ἐμποδισθῇς τοῦ ἀποδοῦναι εὐχὴν εὐκαίρως
καὶ μὴ μείνῃς ἕως θανάτου δικαιωθῆναι.
23 πρὶν εὔξασθαι ἑτοίμασον σεαυτὸν
καὶ μὴ γίνου ὡς ἄνθρωπος πειράζων τὸν κύριον.

KING JAMES VERSION

13 The mercy of man is toward his neighbour; but the mercy of the Lord is upon all flesh: he reproveth, and nurtureth, and teacheth and bringeth again, as a shepherd his flock.

14 He hath mercy on them that receive discipline, and that diligently seek after his judgments.

15 My son, blemish not thy good deeds, neither use uncomfortable words when thou givest any thing.

16 Shall not the dew asswage the heat? so is a word better than a gift.

17 Lo, is not a word better than a gift? but both are with a gracious man.

18 A fool will upbraid churlishly, and a gift of the envious consumeth the eyes.

19 Learn before thou speak, and use physick or ever thou be sick.

20 Before judgment examine thyself, and in the day of visitation thou shalt find mercy.

21 Humble thyself before thou be sick, and in the time of sins shew repentance.

22 Let nothing hinder thee to pay thy vow in due time, and defer not until death to be justified.

23 Before thou prayest, prepare thyself; and be not as one that tempteth the Lord.

DOUAY OLD TESTAMENT

12 The compassion of man is toward his neighbour: but the mercy of God is upon all flesh.

13 He hath mercy, and teacheth, and correcteth, as a shepherd doth his flock.

14 He hath mercy on him that receiveth the discipline of mercy, and that maketh haste in his judgments.

15 My son, in thy good deeds, make no complaint, and when thou givest any thing, add not grief by an evil word.

16 Shall not the dew assuage the heat? so also the good word is better than the gift.

17 Lo, is not a word better than a gift? but both *are* with a justified man.

18 A fool will upbraid bitterly: and a gift of one ill taught consumeth the eyes.

19 Before judgment prepare thee justice, and learn before thou speak.

20 Before sickness take a medicine, and before judgment examine thyself, and thou shalt find mercy in the sight of God.

21 Humble thyself before thou art sick, and in the time of sickness shew thy conversation.

22 Let nothing hinder thee from praying always, and be not afraid to be justified even to death: for the reward of God continueth for ever.

23 Before prayer prepare thy soul: and be not as a man that tempteth God.

KNOX TRANSLATION

extends only to his neighbour; God has pity on all living
things. 13 He is like a shepherd who cares for his sheep,
guides and controls all alike; 14 welcome thou this merciful
discipline of his, run thou eagerly to meet his will, and he
will shew pity on thee.
15 My son, bestow thy favours ungrudgingly, nor ever mar
with harsh words the gladness of thy giving. 16 Not more welcome the dew, tempering the sun's heat, than the giver's
word, that counts for more than the gift. 17 Better the gracious word than the gracious gift; but, wouldst thou acquit
thyself perfectly, let both be thine. 18 The fool, by his scolding, mars all; never yet did eye brighten over a churl's giving.
19 First arm thyself with a just cause, then stand thy trial;
first learn, then speak. 20 Study thy health before ever thou
fallest sick, and thy own heart examine before judgement
overtakes thee; so in God's sight thou shalt find pardon.
21 While health serves thee, do penance for thy sins, and
then, when sickness comes, shew thyself the man thou art.[a]
22 From paying thy vows[b] let naught ever hinder thee; shall
death find thee still shrinking from acquitting thyself of the
task? God's award stands for ever. 23 And before ever thou
makest thy petition, count well the cost.[c] Let it not be said of
thee that thou didst invite God's anger. 24 When his

a Literally, 'shew thy conversation', or perhaps, 'shew thy conversion'—the point is the same in either case. The Greek has, 'shew thy conversion at the time of transgressions', it is not clear in what sense. *b* The Latin has simply 'praying' but this misses the emphasis of the context, this paragraph being evidently concerned with getting things done in good time.
c Literally, 'prepare thy mind' (for the fulfilment of the vow with which the petition was accompanied).

TODAY'S ENGLISH VERSION

13 We can show compassion to someone we know, but the
Lord shows compassion for all humanity. He corrects us; he
disciplines us; he teaches us. Like a shepherd tending sheep,
he brings us back to himself. 14 He will have compassion on
us if we accept his guidance and are eager for him to show
us where we are wrong.
15 My child, when you help someone, don't reprimand him
at the same time. When you make a gift, don't say anything
that hurts. 16 Your words count for more than what you
give. Even dew gives some relief during a spell of hot weather. 17 Yes, kind words are more effective than the best of
gifts, and if you are really concerned, you will give both. 18 It
is stupid to be unkind and insulting. No one's eyes are going
to sparkle at a gift that you resent giving.
19 Know what you are talking about before you speak, and
give attention to your health before you get sick. 20 Examine
your conscience before the Lord judges you; then when that
time comes, he will forgive you. 21 Humble yourself before
you are punished with sickness. When you have sinned,
show repentance. 22 If you make a promise to the Lord, keep
it as soon as you can. Don't wait until you are about to die
to set things straight. 23 But before you make such a promise, be prepared to keep it. Don't try to test the Lord's

NEW REVISED STANDARD VERSION

13 The compassion of human beings is for their neighbors,
but the compassion of the Lord is for every living
thing.
He rebukes and trains and teaches them,
and turns them back, as a shepherd his flock.
14 He has compassion on those who accept his discipline
and who are eager for his precepts.

15 My child, do not mix reproach with your good deeds,
or spoil your gift by harsh words.
16 Does not the dew give relief from the scorching heat?
So a word is better than a gift.
17 Indeed, does not a word surpass a good gift?
Both are to be found in a gracious person.
18 A fool is ungracious and abusive,
and the gift of a grudging giver makes the eyes dim.

19 Before you speak, learn;
and before you fall ill, take care of your health.
20 Before judgment comes, examine yourself;
and at the time of scrutiny you will find forgiveness.
21 Before falling ill, humble yourself;
and when you have sinned, repent.
22 Let nothing hinder you from paying a vow promptly,
and do not wait until death to be released from it.
23 Before making a vow, prepare yourself;
do not be like one who puts the Lord to the test.

NEW AMERICAN BIBLE

11 Man may be merciful to his fellow man,
but the LORD's mercy reaches all flesh,
12 Reproving, admonishing, teaching,
as a shepherd guides his flock;
13 Merciful to those who accept his guidance,
who are diligent in his precepts.

14 My son, to your charity add no reproach,
nor spoil any gift by harsh words.
15 Like dew that abates a burning wind,
so does a word improve a gift.
16 Sometimes the word means more than the gift;
both are offered by a kindly man.
17 Only a fool upbraids before giving;
a grudging gift wears out the expectant eyes.
18 Be informed before speaking;
before sickness prepare the cure.
19 Before you are judged, seek merit for yourself,
and at the time of visitation you will have a ransom.
20 Before you have fallen, humble yourself;
when you have sinned, show repentance.
21 Delay not to forsake sins,
neglect it not till you are in distress.
22 Let nothing prevent the prompt payment of your vows;
wait not to fulfill them when you are dying.
23 Before making a vow have the means to fulfill it;
be not one who tries the LORD.

NEW JERUSALEM BIBLE

13 Human compassion extends to neighbours,
but the Lord's compassion extends to everyone;
rebuking, correcting and teaching,
bringing them back as a shepherd brings his flock.
14 He has compassion on those who accept correction,
and who fervently search for his judgements.

15 My child, do not temper your favours with blame
nor any of your gifts with words that hurt.
16 Does not dew relieve the heat?
In the same way a word is worth more than a gift.
17 Why surely, a word is better than a good present,
but a generous person is ready with both.
18 A fool will offer nothing but insult,
and a grudging gift makes the eyes smart.

19 Learn before you speak,
take care of yourself before you fall ill.
20 Examine yourself before judgement comes,
and on the day of visitation you will be acquitted.
21 Humble yourself before you fall ill,
repent as soon as the sin is committed.
22 Let nothing prevent your discharging a vow in good
time,
and do not wait till death to set matters right.
23 Prepare yourself before making a vow,
and do not be like someone who tempts the Lord.

GREEK OLD TESTAMENT

24 μνήσθητι θυμοῦ ἐν ἡμέραις τελευτῆς
καὶ καιρὸν ἐκδικήσεως ἐν ἀποστροφῇ προσώπου.
25 μνήσθητι καιρὸν λιμοῦ ἐν καιρῷ πλησμονῆς,
πτωχείαν καὶ ἔνδειαν ἐν ἡμέραις πλούτου.
26 ἀπὸ πρωίθεν ἕως ἑσπέρας μεταβάλλει καιρός,
καὶ πάντα ἐστὶν ταχινὰ ἔναντι κυρίου.
27 Ἄνθρωπος σοφὸς ἐν παντὶ εὐλαβηθήσεται
καὶ ἐν ἡμέραις ἁμαρτιῶν προσέξει ἀπὸ πλημμελείας.
28 πᾶς συνετὸς ἔγνω σοφίαν
καὶ τῷ εὑρόντι αὐτὴν δώσει ἐξομολόγησιν.
29 συνετοὶ ἐν λόγοις καὶ αὐτοὶ ἐσοφίσαντο
καὶ ἀνώμβρησαν παροιμίας ἀκριβεῖς.
30 Ὀπίσω τῶν ἐπιθυμιῶν σου μὴ πορεύου
καὶ ἀπὸ τῶν ὀρέξεών σου κωλύου·
31 ἐὰν χορηγήσῃς τῇ ψυχῇ σου εὐδοκίαν ἐπιθυμίας,
ποιήσει σε ἐπίχαρμα τῶν ἐχθρῶν σου.
32 μὴ εὐφραίνου ἐπὶ πολλῇ τρυφῇ,
μὴ προσδεθῇς συμβολῇ αὐτῆς.
33 μὴ γίνου πτωχὸς συμβολοκοπῶν ἐκ δανεισμοῦ,
καὶ οὐδέν σοί ἐστιν ἐν μαρσιππίῳ.

KING JAMES VERSION

24 Think upon the wrath that shall be at the end, and the time of vengeance, when he shall turn away his face.

25 When thou hast enough, remember the time of hunger: and when thou art rich, think upon poverty and need.

26 From the morning until the evening the time is changed, and all things are soon done before the Lord.

27 A wise man will fear in every thing, and in the day of sinning he will beware of offence: but a fool will not observe time.

28 Every man of understanding knoweth wisdom, and will give praise unto him that found her.

29 They that were of understanding in sayings became also wise themselves, and poured forth exquisite parables.

30 Go not after thy lusts, but refrain thyself from thine appetites.

31 If thou givest thy soul the desires that please her, she will make thee a laughingstock to thine enemies that malign thee.

32 Take not pleasure in much good cheer, neither be tied to the expence thereof.

33 Be not made a beggar by banqueting upon borrowing, when thou hast nothing in thy purse: for thou shalt lie in wait for thine own life, and be talked on.

DOUAY OLD TESTAMENT

24 Remember the wrath that shall be at the last day, and the time of repaying when he shall turn away his face.

25 Remember poverty in the time of abundance, and the necessities of poverty in the day of riches.

26 From the morning until the evening the time shall be changed, and all these are swift in the eyes of God.

27 A wise man will fear in every thing, and in the days of sins will beware of sloth.

28 Every man of understanding knoweth wisdom, and will give praise to him that findeth her.

29 They that were of good understanding in words, have also done wisely themselves: and have understood truth and justice, and have poured forth proverbs and judgments.

30 Go not after thy lusts, but turn away from thy own will.

31 If thou give to thy soul her desires, she will make thee a joy to thy enemies.

32 Take no pleasure in riotous assemblies, be they ever so small: for their concertation is continual.

33 Make not thyself poor by borrowing to contribute to feasts when thou hast nothing in thy purse: for thou shalt be an enemy to thy own life.

KNOX TRANSLATION

vengeance is satisfied, bethink thee still of his vengeance; of
his retribution, when his glance is turned away.[a] 25 When
all abounds, bethink thee of evil times; of pinching poverty,
when thou hast wealth in store. 26 Between rise and set of
sun the face of things alters; swiftly God changes all; 27 and
he is wisest who walks timorously, shunning carelessness in
a world where sins abound.

28 They are well advised that master wisdom's secret; much
cause for thankfulness she bestows on him who finds her.
29 Wise man that has the gift of utterance does more than
wisely live; no stranger to truth and right, he is a fountain of
true sayings and of right awards.

30 Do not follow the counsel of appetite; turn thy back on
thy own liking. 31 Pamper those passions of thine, and joy it
will bring, but to thy enemies. 32 Love not the carouse,
though it be with poor men; they will be vying still one with
another in wastefulness. 33 And wouldst thou grow poor
with borrowing to pay thy shot, thou with thy empty coffers?
That were to grudge thy own life.

a Literally, this verse reads: 'Remember anger in the day of the end, and a time of retribution in the turning of the face'. It is ordinarily interpreted as meaning 'Remember the anger (which God will shew) at the end of the world (or, at the time of thy death), and the time of retribution (which will consist) in the turning away of his face'. But it is surely incredible that verse 24 should have exactly the same grammatical appearance as verse 25, and yet a totally different grammatical construction. Nor is God said to 'turn away his face' when he punishes men, but, on the contrary, when he seems to 'look the other way' and leaves them unpunished; cf. Ps. 9. 32.

TODAY'S ENGLISH VERSION

patience. 24Think! Do you want him to be angry with you
on the day you die? When you face his judgment, do you
want him to turn his back on you? 25When you have all you
want, think what it is like to be hungry, what it is to be poor.
26Things can change in a single day; the Lord can act very
quickly. 27If you are wise, you will be careful in everything
you do. When sin is all around you, be especially careful that
you do not become guilty. 28Every intelligent person can recognize wisdom and will honor anyone who shows it. 29If
you appreciate wisdom when you hear it, you will become
wise yourself, and your words will be a source of wisdom for
others.

30Don't be controlled by your lust; keep your passions in
check. 31If you allow yourself to satisfy your every desire,
you will be a joke to your enemies. 32Don't indulge in luxurious living; the expense of it will ruin you. 33Don't make
yourself a beggar by borrowing for expensive banquets when

NEW REVISED STANDARD VERSION

24 Think of his wrath on the day of death,
and of the moment of vengeance when he turns away
his face.
25 In the time of plenty think of the time of hunger;
in days of wealth think of poverty and need.
26 From morning to evening conditions change;
all things move swiftly before the Lord.

27 One who is wise is cautious in everything;
when sin is all around, one guards against
wrongdoing.
28 Every intelligent person knows wisdom,
and praises the one who finds her.
29 Those who are skilled in words become wise themselves,
and pour forth apt proverbs.[a]

SELF-CONTROL[b]

30 Do not follow your base desires,
but restrain your appetites.
31 If you allow your soul to take pleasure in base desire,
it will make you the laughingstock of your enemies.
32 Do not revel in great luxury,
or you may become impoverished by its expense.
33 Do not become a beggar by feasting with borrowed
money,
when you have nothing in your purse.[c]

a Other ancient authorities add *Better is confidence in the one Lord than clinging with a dead heart to a dead one.* b This heading is included in the Gk text. c Other ancient authorities add *for you will be plotting against your own life*

NEW AMERICAN BIBLE

24 Think of wrath and the day of death,
the time of vengeance when he will hide his face.
25 Remember the time of hunger in the time of plenty,
poverty and want in the day of wealth.
26 Between morning and evening the weather changes;
before the LORD all things are fleeting.
27 A wise man is circumspect in all things;
when sin is rife he keeps himself from wrongdoing.
28 Any learned man should make wisdom known,
and he who attains to her should declare her praise;
29 Those trained in her words must show their wisdom,
dispensing sound proverbs like life-giving waters.

30 Go not after your lusts,
but keep your desires in check.
31 If you satisfy your lustful appetites
they will make you the sport of your enemies.
32 Have no joy in the pleasures of a moment
which bring on poverty redoubled;
33 Become not a glutton and a winebibber
with nothing in your purse.

NEW JERUSALEM BIBLE

24 Bear in mind the retribution of the last days,
the time of vengeance when God averts his face.
25 In a time of plenty remember times of famine,
think of poverty and want when you are rich.
26 The time slips by between dawn and dusk,
everything passes quickly for the Lord.
27 The wise will be cautious in everything,
in sinful times will take care not to offend.
28 Every person of sense recognises wisdom,
and will respect anyone who has found her.
29 Those who understand sayings have toiled for their
wisdom
and have poured out accurate maxims.
30 Do not be governed by your passions,
restrain your desires.
31 If you allow yourself to satisfy your desires,
this will make you the laughing-stock of your
enemies.
32 Do not indulge in luxurious living,
do not get involved in such society.
33 Do not beggar yourself by banqueting on credit
when there is nothing in your pocket.

GREEK OLD TESTAMENT

19 ἐργάτης μέθυσος οὐ πλουτισθήσεται·
ὁ ἐξουθενῶν τὰ ὀλίγα κατὰ μικρὸν πεσεῖται.
2 οἶνος καὶ γυναῖκες ἀποστήσουσιν συνετούς,
καὶ ὁ κολλώμενος πόρναις τολμηρότερος ἔσται·
3 σήπη καὶ σκώληκες κληρονομήσουσιν αὐτόν,
καὶ ψυχὴ τολμηρὰ ἐξαρθήσεται.
4 Ὁ ταχὺ ἐμπιστεύων κοῦφος καρδίᾳ,
καὶ ὁ ἁμαρτάνων εἰς ψυχὴν αὐτοῦ πλημμελήσει.
5 ὁ εὐφραινόμενος καρδίᾳ καταγνωσθήσεται,
6 καὶ ὁ μισῶν λαλιὰν ἐλαττονοῦται κακίᾳ.
7 μηδέποτε δευτερώσῃς λόγον,
καὶ οὐθέν σοι οὐ μὴ ἐλαττονωθῇ.
8 ἐν φίλῳ καὶ ἐχθρῷ μὴ διηγοῦ,
καὶ εἰ μή ἐστίν σοι ἁμαρτία, μὴ ἀποκάλυπτε·
9 ἀκήκοεν γάρ σου καὶ ἐφυλάξατό σε,
καὶ ἐν καιρῷ μισήσει σε.
10 ἀκήκοας λόγον; συναποθανέτω σοι·
θάρσει, οὐ μή σε ῥήξει.
11 ἀπὸ προσώπου λόγου ὠδινήσει μωρὸς
ὡς ἀπὸ προσώπου βρέφους ἡ τίκτουσα.
12 βέλος πεπηγὸς ἐν μηρῷ σαρκός,
οὕτως λόγος ἐν κοιλίᾳ μωροῦ.

KING JAMES VERSION

19 A labouring man that is given to drunkenness shall not be rich: and he that contemneth small things shall fall by little and little.

2 Wine and women will make men of understanding to fall away: and he that cleaveth to harlots will become impudent.

3 Moths and worms shall have him to heritage, and a bold man shall be taken away.

4 He that is hasty to give credit is lightminded; and he that sinneth shall offend against his own soul.

5 Whoso taketh pleasure in wickedness shall be condemned: but he that resisteth pleasures crowneth his life.

6 He that can rule his tongue shall live without strife; and he that hateth babbling shall have less evil.

7 Rehearse not unto another that which is told unto thee, and thou shalt fare never the worse.

8 Whether it be to friend or foe, talk not of other men's lives; and if thou canst without offence, reveal them not.

9 For he heard and observed thee, and when time cometh he will hate thee.

10 If thou hast heard a word, let it die with thee; and be bold, it will not burst thee.

11 A fool travaileth with a word, as a woman in labour of a child.

12 As an arrow that sticketh in a man's thigh, so is a word within a fool's belly.

DOUAY OLD TESTAMENT

19 A WORKMAN that is a drunkard shall not be rich: and he that contemneth small things, shall fall by little and little.

2 Wine and women make wise men fall off, and shall rebuke the prudent:

3 And he that joineth himself to harlots, will be wicked. Rottenness and worms shall inherit him, and he shall be lifted up for a greater example, and his soul shall be taken away out of the number.

4 He that is hasty to give credit, is light of heart, and shall be lessened: and he that sinneth against his own soul, shall be despised.

5 He that rejoiceth in iniquity, shall be censured, and he that hateth chastisement, shall have less life: and he that hateth babbling, extinguisheth evil.

6 He that sinneth against his own soul, shall repent: and he that is delighted with wickedness, shall be condemned.

7 Rehearse not again a wicked and harsh word, and thou shalt not fare the worse.

8 Tell not thy mind to friend or foe: and if there be a sin with thee, disclose it not.

9 For he will hearken to thee, and will watch thee, and as it were defending *thy* sin he will hate thee, and so will he be with thee always.

10 Hast thou heard a word against thy neighbour? let it die within thee, trusting that it will not burst thee.

11 At the hearing of a word the fool is in travail, as a woman groaning in the bringing forth a child.

12 As an arrow that sticketh in a man's thigh: so is a word in the heart of a fool.

KNOX TRANSLATION

19 Let him toil as he will, the sot's purse is empty; little
things despise, and little by little thou shalt come to
ruin. 2 Wine and women, what a trap for the loyalty of the
wise, how hard a test of good sense! 3 He will go from bad to
worse, that clings to a harlot's love; waste and worm shall
have him for their prize; one gibbet the more, one living soul
the less.
4 Rash heart that lightly trusts shall lose all; forfeit thy
own right to live, and none will pity thee. 5 A foul blot it is,
to take pride in wrong-doing; a courting of death, to despise
reproof; a riddance of much mischief, to forswear chattering.
6 Who forfeits his own right to live, will live to rue it; who
loves cruelty, blots his own name.
7 Malicious word if thou hear, or harsh, do not repeat it;
never wilt thou be the loser. 8 Speak not out thy own
thought for friend and foe to hear alike, nor ever, if thou
hast done wrong, discover the secret. 9 He that hears it will
be on his guard, and eye thee askance, as if to avert fresh
fault of thine; such will be all his demeanour to thee thenceforward.[a] 10 Hast thou heard a tale to thy neighbour's disadvantage? Take it to the grave with thee. Courage, man! it will
not burst thee. 11 A fool with a secret labours as with child,
and groans till he is delivered of it; 12 out it must come, like
an arrow stuck in a man's thigh, from that reckless heart.

a vv. 8, 9: The sense of the Greek text is: 'Do not tell tales about friend or foe; bring nothing to light, unless it were sin in thee (to keep silent). Friend or foe will hear of it, and will keep thee under his eye, waiting for the opportunity to shew his hatred of thee'.

TODAY'S ENGLISH VERSION

19 you don't have enough money of your own. 1 If you
do, you[a] will never get rich; if you don't pay attention to small matters, you will gradually ruin yourself.
2 Wine and women make sensible men do foolish things. A
man who goes to prostitutes gets more and more careless,
3 and that carelessness will cost him his life. Worms will feed
on his decaying body.
4 It is silly to trust people too quickly. If you sin, you are
hurting yourself. 5 If wickedness makes you happy, you will
be condemned.
6 Avoid idle talk, and you will avoid a lot of trouble.
7 Never repeat what you hear, and you will have no regrets.
8 Don't tell it to your friends or your enemies unless it would
be sinful to keep it to yourself. 9 Whoever hears you will take
note of it, and sooner or later will hate you for it. 10 Have
you heard a rumor? Let it die with you. Be brave! It won't
make you explode. 11 A foolish person trying to keep a secret
suffers like a woman in labor. 12 Any time he hears a secret,
it's like an arrow stuck in his leg.

[a] *Hebrew* If you do, you; *Greek* A worker who drinks too much.

NEW REVISED STANDARD VERSION

19 The one who does this[a] will not become rich;
one who despises small things will fail little by little.
2 Wine and women lead intelligent men astray,
and the man who consorts with prostitutes is
reckless.
3 Decay and worms will take possession of him,
and the reckless person will be snatched away.

4 One who trusts others too quickly has a shallow mind,
and one who sins does wrong to himself.
5 One who rejoices in wickedness[b] will be condemned,[c]
6 but one who hates gossip has less evil.
7 Never repeat a conversation,
and you will lose nothing at all.
8 With friend or foe do not report it,
and unless it would be a sin for you, do not reveal it;
9 for someone may have heard you and watched you,
and in time will hate you.
10 Have you heard something? Let it die with you.
Be brave, it will not make you burst!
11 Having heard something, the fool suffers birth pangs
like a woman in labor with a child.
12 Like an arrow stuck in a person's thigh,
so is gossip inside a fool.

a Heb: Gk *A worker who is a drunkard* *b* Other ancient authorities read *heart* *c* Other ancient authorities add *but one who withstands pleasures crowns his life. 6One who controls the tongue will live without strife,*

NEW AMERICAN BIBLE

19 He who does so grows no richer;
he who wastes the little he has will be stripped bare.
2 Wine and women make the mind giddy,
and the companion of harlots becomes reckless.
4 He who lightly trusts in them has no sense,
and he who strays after them sins against his own
life.
3 Rottenness and worms will possess him,
for contumacious desire destroys its owner.

5 He who gloats over evil will meet with evil,
and he who repeats an evil report has no sense.
6 Never repeat gossip,
and you will not be reviled.
7 Tell nothing to friend or foe;
if you have a fault, reveal it not,
8 For he who hears it will hold it against you,
and in time become your enemy.
9 Let anything you hear die within you;
be assured it will not make you burst.
10 When a fool hears something, he is in labor,
like a woman giving birth to a child.
11 Like an arrow lodged in a man's thigh
is gossip in the breast of a fool.

NEW JERUSALEM BIBLE

19 1 A drunken workman will never grow rich,
and one who makes light of small matters will
gradually sink.
2 Wine and women corrupt intelligent men,
the customer of whores loses all sense of shame.
3 Grubs and worms will have him as their legacy,
and the man who knows no shame will lose his life.

4 Being too ready to trust shows shallowness of mind,
and sinning harms the sinner.
5 Taking pleasure in evil earns condemnation;
6 by hating gossip one avoids evil.
7 Never repeat what you are told
and you will come to no harm;
8 whether to friend or foe, do not talk about it,
unless it would be sinful not to, do not reveal it;
9 you would be heard out, then mistrusted,
and in due course you would be hated.
10 Have you heard something? Let it die with you.
Courage! It will not burst you!
11 A fool will suffer birthpangs over a piece of news,
like a woman labouring with child.
12 Like an arrow stuck in the flesh of the thigh,
so is a piece of news inside a fool.

GREEK OLD TESTAMENT

13 Ἔλεγξον φίλον, μήποτε οὐκ ἐποίησεν,
καὶ εἴ τι ἐποίησεν, μήποτε προσθῇ.
14 ἔλεγξον τὸν πλησίον, μήποτε οὐκ εἶπεν,
καὶ εἰ εἴρηκεν, ἵνα μὴ δευτερώσῃ.
15 ἔλεγξον φίλον, πολλάκις γὰρ γίνεται διαβολή,
καὶ μὴ παντὶ λόγῳ πίστευε.
16 ἔστιν ὀλισθάνων καὶ οὐκ ἀπὸ ψυχῆς,
καὶ τίς οὐχ ἥμαρτεν ἐν τῇ γλώσσῃ αὐτοῦ;
17 ἔλεγξον τὸν πλησίον σου πρὶν ἢ ἀπειλῆσαι
καὶ δὸς τόπον νόμῳ ὑψίστου.
20 Πᾶσα σοφία φόβος κυρίου,
καὶ ἐν πάσῃ σοφίᾳ ποίησις νόμου·
22 καὶ οὐκ ἔστιν σοφία πονηρίας ἐπιστήμη,
καὶ οὐκ ἔστιν ὅπου βουλὴ ἁμαρτωλῶν φρόνησις.
23 ἔστιν πανουργία καὶ αὕτη βδέλυγμα,
καὶ ἔστιν ἄφρων ἐλαττούμενος σοφίᾳ·
24 κρείττων ἡττώμενος ἐν συνέσει ἔμφοβος
ἢ περισσεύων ἐν φρονήσει καὶ παραβαίνων νόμον.

KING JAMES VERSION

13 Admonish a friend, it may be he hath not done it: and if he have done it, that he do it no more.

14 Admonish thy friend, it may be he hath not said it: and if he have, that he speak it not again.

15 Admonish a friend: for many times it is a slander, and believe not every tale.

16 There is one that slippeth in his speech, but not from his heart; and who is he that hath not offended with his tongue?

17 Admonish thy neighbour before thou threaten him; and not being angry, give place to the law of the most High.

18 The fear of the Lord is the first step to be accepted [of him,] and wisdom obtaineth his love.

19 The knowledge of the commandments of the Lord is the doctrine of life: and they that do things that please him shall receive the fruit of the tree of immortality.

20 The fear of the Lord is all wisdom; and in all wisdom is the performance of the law, and the knowledge of his omnipotency.

21 If a servant say to his master, I will not do as it pleaseth thee; though afterward he do it, he angereth him that nourisheth him.

22 The knowledge of wickedness is not wisdom, neither at any time the counsel of sinners prudence.

23 There is a wickedness, and the same an abomination; and there is a fool wanting in wisdom.

24 He that hath small understanding, and feareth God, is better than one that hath much wisdom, and transgresseth the law of the most High.

DOUAY OLD TESTAMENT

13 Reprove a friend, lest he may not have understood, and say: I did it not: or if he did it, that he may do it no more.

14 Reprove thy neighbour, for it may be he hath not said it: and if he hath said it, that he may not say it again.

15 Admonish thy friend: for there is often a fault committed.

16 And believe not every word. There is one, that slippeth with the tongue, but not from his heart.

17 For who is there that hath not offended with his tongue? Admonish thy neighbour before thou threaten him.

18 And give place to the fear of the most High: for the fear of God is all wisdom, and therein is to fear God, and the disposition of the law is in all wisdom.

19 But the learning of wickedness is not wisdom: and the device of sinners is not prudence.

20 There is a subtle wickedness, and the same is detestable: and there is a man that is foolish, wanting in wisdom.

21 Better is a man that hath less wisdom, and wanteth understanding, with the fear *of God,* than he that aboundeth in understanding, and transgresseth the law of the most High.

KNOX TRANSLATION

13 Confront thy friend with his fault; it may be he knows
nothing of the matter, and can clear himself; if not, there is
hope he will amend. 14 Confront him with the word spoken
amiss; it may be, he never said it, or if say it he did, never
again will he repeat it. 15 Be open with thy friend; tongues
will still be clattering,[a] 16 and thou dost well to believe less
than is told thee. Slips there are of the tongue when mind is
innocent; 17 what tongue was ever perfectly guarded?
Confront thy neighbour with his fault ere thou quarrellest
with him, 18 and let the fear of the most High God do its
work.

What is true wisdom? Nothing but the fear of God. And
since the fear of God is contained in all true wisdom, it must
be directed by his law; 19 wisdom is none in following the
maxims of impiety, prudence is none in scheming as the
wicked scheme. 20 Cunning rogues they may be, yet altogether abominable; a fool he must ever be called, that lacks the
true wisdom.[b] 21 Better a simpleton that wit has none, yet
knows fear, than a man of great address, that breaks the law

a Literally, 'for often there is competition', i.e., in the retailing of scandal; the same word is used by the Latin version as in 18. 32 above. The Greek text has, 'often there is slander'. *b* The first half of this verse runs, both in the Greek and in the Latin, 'There is a wickedness (or, worthlessness), and it is an abomination'; a phrase which means little and does not suit the context. Evidently the Hebrew original contained some word which might be interpreted either as 'prudence' or as 'wickedness'; e.g., the word used in the former sense by Prov. 1. 4, and in the latter sense by Jer. 11. 15.

TODAY'S ENGLISH VERSION

13 If you hear that a friend has done something wrong, ask
him about it. Maybe it isn't true. If it is true, he won't do it
again. 14 If you hear that a neighbor has said something he
shouldn't, ask him about it. Maybe he didn't say it. If he did,
he won't say it again. 15 If you hear something bad about a
friend, ask him about it. It might be a lie. Don't believe
everything you hear. 16 A person may say something carelessly and not really mean it. Everyone has sinned in this
way at one time or another. 17 If you hear something that
makes you angry with your neighbor, ask him about it
before you threaten him. Leave the matter to the Law of the
Most High.[a]

20 Fear the Lord and keep his Law; that is what Wisdom is
all about.[b] 22 You may know everything there is to know
about wickedness, but that does not make you wise. It is not
sensible to follow the advice of sinners. 23 It is possible to use
cleverness for wicked purposes, but some people act like fools
because they don't know any better. 24 A devout person, even
if he is not very intelligent, is better off than the cleverest of

[a] *Some manuscripts add verses 17c-19:* and don't be angry. [18]Fearing the Lord is the first step toward his accepting you; he will love you if you are wise. [19]Learn the Lord's commands. It is a discipline that gives life. Those who do what pleases him enjoy the fruit of the tree of immortality.

[b] *Some manuscripts add verses 20b-21:* and what the knowledge of his omnipotence means. [21]If a servant refuses to obey his master, but later does obey, the master is still angry.

NEW REVISED STANDARD VERSION

13 Question a friend; perhaps he did not do it;
or if he did, so that he may not do it again.
14 Question a neighbor; perhaps he did not say it;
or if he said it, so that he may not repeat it.
15 Question a friend, for often it is slander;
so do not believe everything you hear.
16 A person may make a slip without intending it.
Who has not sinned with his tongue?
17 Question your neighbor before you threaten him;
and let the law of the Most High take its course.[a]

20 The whole of wisdom is fear of the Lord,
and in all wisdom there is the fulfillment of the law.[b]
22 The knowledge of wickedness is not wisdom,
nor is there prudence in the counsel of sinners.
23 There is a cleverness that is detestable,
and there is a fool who merely lacks wisdom.
24 Better are the God-fearing who lack understanding
than the highly intelligent who transgress the law.

[a] Other ancient authorities add *and do not be angry.* [18]*The fear of the Lord is the beginning of acceptance, and wisdom obtains his love.* [19]*The knowledge of the Lord's commandments is life-giving discipline; and those who do what is pleasing to him enjoy the fruit of the tree of immortality.*

[b] Other ancient authorities add *and the knowledge of his omnipotence.* [21]*When a slave says to his master, "I will not act as you wish," even if later he does it, he angers the one who supports him.*

NEW AMERICAN BIBLE

12 Admonish your friend—he may not have done it;
and if he did, that he may not do it again.
13 Admonish your neighbor—he may not have said it;
and if he did, that he may not say it again.
14 Admonish your friend—often it may be slander;
every story you must not believe.
15 Then, too, a man can slip and not mean it;
who has not sinned with his tongue?
16 Admonish your neighbor before you break with him;
thus will you fulfill the law of the Most High.

17 All wisdom is fear of the LORD;
perfect wisdom is the fulfillment of the law.
18 The knowledge of wickedness is not wisdom,
nor is there prudence in the counsel of sinners.
19 There is a shrewdness that is detestable,
while the simple man may be free from sin.
20 There are those with little understanding who fear God,
and those of great intelligence who violate the law.

NEW JERUSALEM BIBLE

13 Question your friend, he may have done nothing at all;
and if he has done anything, he will not do it again.
14 Question your neighbour, he may have said nothing at all;
and if he has said anything, he will not say it again.
15 Question your friend, for slander is very common,
do not believe all you hear.
16 People sometimes make a slip, without meaning what they say;
and which of us has never sinned by speech?
17 Question your neighbour before you threaten him,
and defer to the Law of the Most High.

20 Wisdom consists entirely in fearing the Lord,
and wisdom is entirely constituted by the fulfilling of the Law.
22 Being learned in evil, however, is not wisdom,
there is no prudence in the advice of sinners.
23 There is a cleverness that is detestable;
whoever has no wisdom is a fool.
24 Better be short of sense and full of fear,
than abound in shrewdness and violate the Law.

GREEK OLD TESTAMENT

25 ἔστιν πανουργία ἀκριβὴς καὶ αὕτη ἄδικος,
καὶ ἔστιν διαστρέφων χάριν τοῦ ἐκφᾶναι κρίμα.
26 ἔστιν πονηρευόμενος συγκεκυφὼς μελανίᾳ,
καὶ τὰ ἐντὸς αὐτοῦ πλήρη δόλου·
27 συγκρύφων πρόσωπον καὶ ἐθελοκωφῶν,
ὅπου οὐκ ἐπεγνώσθη, προφθάσει σε·
28 καὶ ἐὰν ὑπὸ ἐλαττώματος ἰσχύος κωλυθῇ ἁμαρτεῖν,
ἐὰν εὕρῃ καιρόν, κακοποιήσει.
29 ἀπὸ ὁράσεως ἐπιγνωσθήσεται ἀνήρ,
καὶ ἀπὸ ἀπαντήσεως προσώπου ἐπιγνωσθήσεται
νοήμων·
30 στολισμὸς ἀνδρὸς καὶ γέλως ὀδόντων
καὶ βήματα ἀνθρώπου ἀναγγελεῖ τὰ περὶ αὐτοῦ.

20 Ἔστιν ἔλεγχος ὃς οὐκ ἔστιν ὡραῖος,
καὶ ἔστιν σιωπῶν καὶ αὐτὸς φρόνιμος.
2 ὡς καλὸν ἐλέγξαι ἢ θυμοῦσθαι,
3 καὶ ὁ ἀνθομολογούμενος ἀπὸ ἐλαττώσεως κωλυθήσεται.
4 ἐπιθυμία εὐνούχου ἀποπαρθενῶσαι νεάνιδα,
οὕτως ὁ ποιῶν ἐν βίᾳ κρίματα.
5 ἔστιν σιωπῶν εὑρισκόμενος σοφός,
καὶ ἔστιν μισητὸς ἀπὸ πολλῆς λαλιᾶς.

KING JAMES VERSION

25 There is an exquisite subtilty, and the same is unjust; and there is one that turneth aside to make judgment appear; and there is a wise man that justifieth in judgment.

26 There is a wicked man that hangeth down his head sadly; but inwardly he is full of deceit,

27 Casting down his countenance, and making as if he heard not: where he is not known, he will do thee a mischief before thou be aware.

28 And if for want of power he be hindered from sinning, yet when he findeth opportunity he will do evil.

29 A man may be known by his look, and one that hath understanding by his countenance, when thou meetest him.

30 A man's attire, and excessive laughter, and gait, shew what he is.

20 There is a reproof that is not comely: again, some man holdeth his tongue, and he is wise.

2 It is much better to reprove, than to be angry secretly: and he that confesseth his fault shall be preserved from hurt.

3 How good is it, when thou art reproved, to shew repentance! for so shalt thou escape wilful sin.

4 As is the lust of an eunuch to deflower a virgin; so is he that executeth judgment with violence.

5 There is one that keepeth silence, and is found wise: and another by much babbling becometh hateful.

DOUAY OLD TESTAMENT

22 There is an exquisite subtilty, and the same is unjust.

23 And there is one that uttereth an exact word telling the truth. There is one that humbleth himself wickedly, and his interior is full of deceit:

24 And there is one that submitteth himself exceedingly with a great lowliness: and there is one that casteth down his countenance, and maketh as if he did not see that which is unknown:

25 And if he be hindered from sinning for want of power, if he shall find opportunity to do evil, he will do it.

26 A man is known by his look, and a wise man, when thou meetest him, is known by his countenance.

27 The attire of the body, and the laughter of the teeth, and the gait of the man, shew what he is.

28 There is a lying rebuke in the anger of an injurious man: and there is a judgment that is not allowed to be good: and there is one that holdeth his peace, he is wise.

20 HOW much better is it to reprove, than to be angry, and not to hinder him that confesseth in prayer.

2 The lust of an eunuch shall deflour a young maiden:

3 So is he that by violence executeth unjust judgment.

4 How good is it, when thou art reproved, to shew repentance! for so thou shalt escape wilful sin.

5 There is one that holdeth his peace, that is found wise: and there is another that is hateful, that is bold in speech.

KNOX TRANSLATION

of the most High. 22 Exact and adroit even a rogue may be;
23 it is another thing to utter the plain word that tells the
whole truth. Here is one that wears the garb of penance for
wicked ends, his heart full of guile; 24 here is one that bows
and scrapes, and walks with bent head, feigning not to see
what is best left unnoticed, 25 and all because he is powerless to do thee a harm; if the chance of villainy comes, he
will take it. 26 Yet a man's looks betray him; a man of good
sense will make himself known to thee at first meeting;
27 the clothes he wears, the smile on his lips, his gait, will all
make thee acquainted with a man's character.
28 Reproof there is that no good brings, as the event shews;
the mistaken reproof that anger prompts in a quarrel. And a
man may shew prudence by holding his tongue.

20 Better the complaint made than the grudge secretly
nursed. When a man confesses his fault, do not cut
him short in mid utterance.
2 Redress[a] sought by violence no more content shall bring
thee 3 than eunuch's lust for maid.
4 Well it is to be reproved, and to confess thy fault, and be
rid of all such guilt as thou hast incurred knowingly.
5 A man may be the wiser for remaining dumb, where the
glib talker grows wearisome; 6 the silent man, has he nothing

[a] The Latin version substitutes 'false award' for 'redress', but it is doubtful whether this interpretation improves the sense of a passage already obscure.

TODAY'S ENGLISH VERSION

sinners. 25 It is possible to be marvelously clever and still be
dishonest, or to get what you want by being absurdly polite.
26 Then there are those wicked people who go about looking very solemn and mournful, but who are only trying to
deceive you. 27 They will turn their faces away and pretend
not to hear you, but they'll take advantage of you when you
least expect it. 28 If for some reason they are unable to sin
now, they'll get around to it at the first opportunity. 29 You
can know people by their appearance. The first time you look
at them, you can tell if they have good sense. 30 Their character shows in the way they dress, the way they laugh, and
the way they walk.

20 A person can be rebuked in the wrong way; it may be
wiser to keep quiet than to speak. 2 But it is much
better to rebuke the person than to keep your anger bottled
up. 3 Admit when you are wrong, and you will avoid embarrassment. 4 Using force to get a point across is like a castrated man trying to rape a young woman. 5 Some people are
thought to be wise because they don't talk much; others are
disliked because they talk too much. 6 Some people keep

NEW REVISED STANDARD VERSION

25 There is a cleverness that is exact but unjust,
and there are people who abuse favors to gain a verdict.
26 There is the villain bowed down in mourning,
but inwardly he is full of deceit.
27 He hides his face and pretends not to hear,
but when no one notices, he will take advantage of you.
28 Even if lack of strength keeps him from sinning,
he will nevertheless do evil when he finds the opportunity.
29 A person is known by his appearance,
and a sensible person is known when first met, face to face.
30 A person's attire and hearty laughter,
and the way he walks, show what he is.

20 There is a rebuke that is untimely,
and there is the person who is wise enough to keep silent.
2 How much better it is to rebuke than to fume!
3 And the one who admits his fault will be kept from failure.
4 Like a eunuch lusting to violate a girl
is the person who does right under compulsion.
5 Some people keep silent and are thought to be wise,
while others are detested for being talkative.

NEW AMERICAN BIBLE

21 There is a shrewdness keen but dishonest,
which by duplicity wins a judgment.
22 There is the wicked man who is bowed in grief,
but is full of guile within;
23 He bows his head and feigns not to hear,
but when not observed, he will take advantage of you:
24 Even though his lack of strength keeps him from sinning,
when he finds the opportunity, he will do harm.
25 One can tell a man by his appearance;
a wise man is known as such when first met.
26 A man's attire, his hearty laughter and his gait,
proclaim him for what he is.

20 An admonition can be inopportune,
and a man may be wise to hold his peace.
2 It is much better to admonish than to lose one's temper,
for one who admits his fault will be kept from disgrace.
3 Like a eunuch lusting for intimacy with a maiden
is he who does right under compulsion.
4 One man is silent and is thought wise,
another is talkative and is disliked.

NEW JERUSALEM BIBLE

25 There is a wickedness which is scrupulous but nonetheless dishonest,
and there are those who misuse kindness to win their case.
26 There is the person who will walk bowed down with grief,
when inwardly this is nothing but deceit:
27 he hides his face and pretends to be deaf,
if he is not unmasked, he will take advantage of you.
28 There is the person who is prevented from sinning by lack of strength,
yet he will do wrong when he gets the chance.
29 You can tell a person by his appearance,
you can tell a thinker by the look on his face.
30 The way a person dresses, the way he laughs,
the way he walks, tell you what he is.

20 There is the rebuke that is untimely,
and there is the person who keeps quiet, and he is the shrewd one.
2 But how much better to rebuke than to fume!
3 The person who acknowledges a fault wards off punishment.

4 Like a eunuch trying to take a girl's virginity
is someone who tries to impose justice by force.

5 There is the person who keeps quiet and is considered wise,
another incurs hatred for talking too much.

GREEK OLD TESTAMENT

[6]ἔστιν σιωπῶν, οὐ γὰρ ἔχει ἀπόκρισιν,
καὶ ἔστιν σιωπῶν εἰδὼς καιρόν.
[7]ἄνθρωπος σοφὸς σιγήσει ἕως καιροῦ,
ὁ δὲ λαπιστὴς καὶ ἄφρων ὑπερβήσεται καιρόν.
[8]ὁ πλεονάζων λόγῳ βδελυχθήσεται,
καὶ ὁ ἐνεξουσιαζόμενος μισηθήσεται.
9 Ἔστιν εὐοδία ἐν κακοῖς ἀνδρί,
καὶ ἔστιν εὕρεμα εἰς ἐλάττωσιν.
[10]ἔστιν δόσις, ἣ οὐ λυσιτελήσει σοι,
καὶ ἔστιν δόσις, ἧς τὸ ἀνταπόδομα διπλοῦν.
[11]ἔστιν ἐλάττωσις ἕνεκεν δόξης,
καὶ ἔστιν ὃς ἀπὸ ταπεινώσεως ἦρεν κεφαλήν.
[12]ἔστιν ἀγοράζων πολλὰ ὀλίγου
καὶ ἀποτιννύων αὐτὰ ἑπταπλάσιον.
[13]ὁ σοφὸς ἐν λόγοις ἑαυτὸν προσφιλῆ ποιήσει,
χάριτες δὲ μωρῶν ἐκχυθήσονται.
[14]δόσις ἄφρονος οὐ λυσιτελήσει σοι,
οἱ γὰρ ὀφθαλμοὶ αὐτοῦ ἀνθ' ἑνὸς πολλοί·
[15]ὀλίγα δώσει καὶ πολλὰ ὀνειδίσει
καὶ ἀνοίξει τὸ στόμα αὐτοῦ ὡς κῆρυξ·

KING JAMES VERSION

6 Some man holdeth his tongue, because he hath not to answer: and some keepeth silence, knowing his time.

7 A wise man will hold his tongue till he see opportunity: but a babbler and a fool will regard no time.

8 He that useth many words shall be abhorred; and he that taketh to himself authority therein shall be hated.

9 There is a sinner that hath good success in evil things; and there is a gain that turneth to loss.

10 There is a gift that shall not profit thee; and there is a gift whose recompence is double.

11 There is an abasement because of glory; and there is that lifteth up his head from a low estate.

12 There is that buyeth much for a little, and repayeth it sevenfold.

13 A wise man by his words maketh himself beloved: but the graces of fools shall be poured out.

14 The gift of a fool shall do thee no good when thou hast it; neither yet of the envious for his necessity: for he looketh to receive many things for one.

15 He giveth little, and upbraideth much; he openeth his

DOUAY OLD TESTAMENT

6 There is one that holdeth his peace, because he knoweth not what to say: and there is another that holdeth his peace, knowing the proper time.

7 A wise man will hold his peace till he see opportunity: but a babbler, and a fool will regard no time.

8 He that useth many words shall hurt his own soul: and he that taketh authority to himself unjustly shall be hated.

9 There is success in evil things to a man without discipline, and there is a finding that turneth to loss.

10 There is a gift that is not profitable: and there is a gift, the recompense of which is double.

11 There is an abasement because of glory: and there is one that shall lift up his head from a low estate.

12 There is that buyeth much for a small price, and restoreth the same sevenfold.

13 A man wise in words shall make himself beloved: but the graces of fools shall be poured out.

14 The gift of the fool shall do thee no good: for his eyes are sevenfold.

15 He will give a few things, and upbraid much: and the opening of his mouth is the kindling of a fire.

KNOX TRANSLATION

to say? Or is he waiting for the right time to say it? [7]Wisdom
keeps its utterance in reserve, where the fool's vanity cannot
wait. [8]The babbler cuts his own throat; claim more than thy
right, and all men are thy enemies.
[9]For a mind ill trained, success is failure, winning is losing. [10]Gift given may bring thee nothing in return, or twice
its worth. [11]Honour achieved may belittle a man, and modesty bring him renown. [12]What use to make a good bargain,
if thou must pay for it sevenfold?
[13]Word of wise man endears him; the fool spends his
favours in vain. [14]Little will the fool's gift profit thee; seven
times magnified is all he sees.[a] [15]The paltrier the gift, the
longer the admonitions that go with it, and every word of his

[a] Literally, 'his eyes are sevenfold', a phrase which is sometimes understood as meaning that be expects a sevenfold return for his gift. But this meaning does not seem to be borne out either by usage or by the context, which emphasizes only the self-importance of the clumsy giver. But it must be admitted that the interpretation of this whole paragraph cannot be reached with certainty.

TODAY'S ENGLISH VERSION

quiet because they don't have anything to say; others keep
quiet because they know the right time to speak. 7 A wise
person will not speak until the right moment, but a bragging
fool doesn't know when that time is. 8 No one can stand a
person who talks too long and will not give others a chance
to speak.

9 Bad luck can sometimes lead to success, and a stroke of
good luck can sometimes lead to loss.

10 Generosity will sometimes do you no good, but at other
times it will repay you double.

11 Honor can be followed by disgrace, but there are people
who have risen from obscurity to places of honor.

12 Sometimes what seems like a real bargain can turn out
to be a very expensive mistake.

13 When a person with good judgment speaks, he wins
friends. A stupid person, though, can shower compliments
on everybody, and it won't help him a bit. 14 If such a person
gives you something, it won't do any good; it won't be as
valuable as he thinks it is.[a] 15 He isn't generous with anything but criticism, which he will shout for all the world to

[a] it won't be . . . it is; *or* he only expects to be repaid.

NEW REVISED STANDARD VERSION

6 Some people keep silent because they have nothing to say,
while others keep silent because they know when to speak.
7 The wise remain silent until the right moment,
but a boasting fool misses the right moment.
8 Whoever talks too much is detested,
and whoever pretends to authority is hated.[a]

9 There may be good fortune for a person in adversity,
and a windfall may result in a loss.
10 There is the gift that profits you nothing,
and the gift to be paid back double.
11 There are losses for the sake of glory,
and there are some who have raised their heads from humble circumstances.
12 Some buy much for little,
but pay for it seven times over.
13 The wise make themselves beloved by only few words,[b]
but the courtesies of fools are wasted.
14 A fool's gift will profit you nothing,[c]
for he looks for recompense sevenfold.[d]
15 He gives little and upbraids much;
he opens his mouth like a town crier.

a Other ancient authorities add *How good it is to show repentance when you are reproved, for so you will escape deliberate sin!* *b* Heb: Gk *by words* *c* Other ancient authorities add *so it is with the envious who give under compulsion* *d* Syr: Gk *he has many eyes instead of one*

NEW AMERICAN BIBLE

5 One man is silent because he has nothing to say;
another is silent, biding his time.
6 A wise man is silent till the right time comes,
but a boasting fool ignores the proper time.
7 He who talks too much is detested;
he who pretends to authority is hated.

8 Some misfortunes bring success;
some things gained are a man's loss.
9 Some gifts do one no good,
and some must be paid back double.
10 Humiliation can follow fame,
while from obscurity a man can lift up his head.
11 A man may buy much for little,
but pay for it seven times over.
12 A wise man makes himself popular by a few words,
but fools pour forth their blandishments in vain.
13 A gift from a rogue will do you no good,
for in his eyes his one gift is equal to seven.
14 He gives little and criticizes often,
and like a crier he shouts aloud.

NEW JERUSALEM BIBLE

6 There is the person who keeps quiet, not knowing how to answer,
another keeps quiet, knowing when to speak.

7 The wise will keep quiet till the right moment,
but a garrulous fool will always misjudge it.
8 Someone who talks too much will earn dislike,
and someone who usurps authority will earn hatred.

9 There is the person who finds misfortune a boon,
and the piece of luck that turns to loss.
10 There is the gift that affords you no profit,
and the gift that repays you double.
11 There is the honour that leads to humiliation,
and there are people in a low state who raise their heads.

12 There is the person who buys much for little,
yet pays for it seven times over.

13 The wise wins love with words,
while fools may shower favours in vain.
14 The gift of the stupid will bring you no advantage,
his eyes look for seven times as much in return.
15 He gives little and reviles much,
he opens his mouth like the town crier,

GREEK OLD TESTAMENT

σήμερον δανιεῖ καὶ αὔριον ἀπαιτήσει,
μισητὸς ἄνθρωπος ὁ τοιοῦτος.
16 μωρὸς ἐρεῖ Οὐχ ὑπάρχει μοι φίλος,
καὶ οὐκ ἔστιν χάρις τοῖς ἀγαθοῖς μου·
17 οἱ ἔσθοντες τὸν ἄρτον αὐτοῦ φαῦλοι γλώσσῃ,
ποσάκις καὶ ὅσοι καταγελάσονται αὐτοῦ;
18 Ὀλίσθημα ἀπὸ ἐδάφους μᾶλλον ἢ ἀπὸ γλώσσης,
οὕτως πτῶσις κακῶν κατὰ σπουδὴν ἥξει.
19 ἄνθρωπος ἄχαρις, μῦθος ἄκαιρος·
ἐν στόματι ἀπαιδεύτων ἐνδελεχισθήσεται.
20 ἀπὸ στόματος μωροῦ ἀποδοκιμασθήσεται παραβολή·
οὐ γὰρ μὴ εἴπῃ αὐτὴν ἐν καιρῷ αὐτῆς.
21 Ἔστιν κωλυόμενος ἁμαρτάνειν ἀπὸ ἐνδείας,
καὶ ἐν τῇ ἀναπαύσει αὐτοῦ οὐ κατανυγήσεται.
22 ἔστιν ἀπολλύων τὴν ψυχὴν αὐτοῦ δι᾽ αἰσχύνην,
καὶ ἀπὸ ἄφρονος προσώπου ἀπολεῖ αὐτήν.
23 ἔστιν χάριν αἰσχύνης ἐπαγγελλόμενος φίλῳ,
καὶ ἐκτήσατο αὐτὸν ἐχθρὸν δωρεάν.
24 Μῶμος πονηρὸς ἐν ἀνθρώπῳ ψεῦδος,
ἐν στόματι ἀπαιδεύτων ἐνδελεχισθήσεται.
25 αἱρετὸν κλέπτης ἢ ὁ ἐνδελεχίζων ψεύδει,
ἀμφότεροι δὲ ἀπώλειαν κληρονομήσουσιν.

KING JAMES VERSION

mouth like a crier; to day he lendeth, and to morrow will he ask it again: such an one is to be hated of God and man.

16 The fool saith, I have no friends, I have no thank for all my good deeds, and they that eat my bread speak evil of me.

17 How oft, and of how many shall he be laughed to scorn! for he knoweth not aright what it is to have; and it is all one unto him as if he had it not.

18 To slip upon a pavement is better than to slip with the tongue: so the fall of the wicked shall come speedily.

19 An unseasonable tale will always be in the mouth of the unwise.

20 A wise sentence shall be rejected when it cometh out of a fool's mouth; for he will not speak it in due season.

21 There is that is hindered from sinning through want: and when he taketh rest, he shall not be troubled.

22 There is that destroyeth his own soul through bashfulness, and by accepting of persons overthroweth himself.

23 There is that for bashfulness promiseth to his friend, and maketh him his enemy for nothing.

24 A lie is a foul blot in a man, yet it is continually in the mouth of the untaught.

25 A thief is better than a man that is accustomed to lie: but they both shall have destruction to heritage.

DOUAY OLD TESTAMENT

16 To day a man lendeth, and to morrow he asketh it again: such a man as this is hateful.

17 A fool shall have no friend, and there shall be no thanks for his good deeds.

18 For they that eat his bread, are of a false tongue. How often, and how many will laugh him to scorn!

19 For he doth not distribute with right understanding that which was to be had: in like manner also that which was not to be had.

20 The slipping of a false tongue *is* as one that falleth on the pavement: so the fall of the wicked shall come speedily.

21 A man without grace is as a vain fable, it shall be continually in the mouth of the unwise.

22 A parable coming out of a fool's mouth shall be rejected: for he doth not speak it in due season.

23 There is that is hindered from sinning through want, and in his rest he shall be pricked.

24 There is that will destroy his own soul through shamefacedness, and by occasion of an unwise person he will destroy it: and by respect of person he will destroy himself.

25 There is that for bashfulness promiseth to his friend, and maketh him his enemy for nothing.

26 A lie is a foul blot in a man, and yet it will be continually in the mouth of men without discipline.

27 A thief is better than a man that is always lying: but both of them shall inherit destruction.

KNOX TRANSLATION

an incitement to anger. 16 Out upon the man who lends today, and will have the loan restored to-morrow! 17 The fool
has no friends, nor can win love by all his favours; 18 they
are but parasites that eat at his table; loud and long they will
laugh over him; 19 so injudiciously he bestows gifts worth
having, and gifts nothing worth.

20 Slip of a liar's tongue is like slip from roof to ground; a
villain's end is not long a-coming.

21 An ungracious man is no more regarded, than some idle
tale that is ever on the lips of the ill-bred.

22 No weighty saying but offends in a fool's mouth; sure it
is that he will bring it out unseasonably.

23 Some avoid wrong only because they lack the means to
do it; idle they remain, yet rest they cannot.[a]

24 Some for very shame have courted their own ruin,
resolved, though that opinion were worthless enough, to sacrifice themselves for another's good opinion. 25 Some, too,
for shame, make their friends high-sounding promises, and
thereby gain nothing, but lose a friend.

26 A lie is a foul blot upon a man's name, yet nothing so
frequent on ill-guarded lips. 27 Worse than a thief is one who
is ever lying, and to no better end may he look forward.

a Literally, 'he will be conscience-stricken in his repose'. The Greek inserts a negative.

TODAY'S ENGLISH VERSION

hear. If he lends you something today, he'll want it back
tomorrow. (Don't you hate people like that?) 16 Then that
fool will say, "Nobody likes me. Nobody appreciates what I
do for them. They'll take what I give them, but then talk
about me behind my back." 17 And he's right—he's a constant joke to everyone.

18 A slip of the tongue is worse than a slip on the pavement; the wicked will go to ruin just as suddenly as a person
slips and falls.

19 An impolite person is like one of those off-color stories
that ignorant people are always telling.

20 Nobody takes a proverb seriously when some fool quotes
it at the wrong time.

21 If a person is too poor to afford sin, he can rest without
a guilty conscience.

22 You can lose all your self-respect by being reluctant to
speak up in the presence of stupidity.

23 If you promise a friend something because you are too
bashful to say no, you're needlessly making an enemy.

24 Lying is an ugly blot on a person's character, but ignorant
people do it all the time. 25 A thief is better than a habitual

NEW REVISED STANDARD VERSION

Today he lends and tomorrow he asks it back;
such a one is hateful to God and humans.[a]

16 The fool says, "I have no friends,
and I get no thanks for my good deeds.
Those who eat my bread are evil-tongued."

17 How many will ridicule him, and how often![b]

18 A slip on the pavement is better than a slip of the tongue;
the downfall of the wicked will occur just as speedily.

19 A coarse person is like an inappropriate story,
continually on the lips of the ignorant.

20 A proverb from a fool's lips will be rejected,
for he does not tell it at the proper time.

21 One may be prevented from sinning by poverty;
so when he rests he feels no remorse.

22 One may lose his life through shame,
or lose it because of human respect.[c]

23 Another out of shame makes promises to a friend,
and so makes an enemy for nothing.

24 A lie is an ugly blot on a person;
it is continually on the lips of the ignorant.

25 A thief is preferable to a habitual liar,
but the lot of both is ruin.

a Other ancient authorities lack *to God and humans* *b* Other ancient authorities add *for he has not honestly received what he has, and what he does not have is unimportant to him* *c* Other ancient authorities read *his foolish look*

NEW AMERICAN BIBLE

He lends today, he asks it back tomorrow;
hateful indeed is such a man.

15 A fool has no friends,
nor thanks for his generosity;

16 Those who eat his bread have an evil tongue.
How many times they laugh him to scorn!

17 A fall to the ground is less sudden than a slip of the tongue;
that is why the downfall of the wicked comes so quickly.

18 Insipid food is the untimely tale;
the unruly are always ready to offer it.

19 A proverb when spoken by a fool is unwelcome,
for he does not utter it at the proper time.

20 A man through want may be unable to sin,
yet in this tranquility he cannot rest.

21 One may lose his life through shame,
and perish through a fool's intimidation.

22 A man makes a promise to a friend out of shame,
and has him for his enemy needlessly.

23 A lie is a foul blot in a man,
yet it is constantly on the lips of the unruly.

24 Better a thief than an inveterate liar,
yet both will suffer disgrace;

NEW JERUSALEM BIBLE

he lends today and demands payment tomorrow;
he is a detestable fellow.

16 The fool will say, 'I have no friends,
I get no gratitude for my good deeds;

17 those who eat my bread have malicious tongues.'
How often he will be laughed at, and by how many!

18 Better a slip on the pavement than a slip of the tongue;
this is how ruin takes the wicked by surprise.

19 A coarse-grained person is like an indiscreet story
endlessly retold by the ignorant.

20 A maxim is rejected when coming from a fool,
since the fool does not utter it on the apt occasion.

21 There is a person who is prevented from sinning by poverty;
no qualms of conscience disturb that person's rest.

22 There is a person who courts destruction out of false shame,
courts destruction for the sake of a fool's opinion.

23 There is a person who out of false shame makes promises to a friend,
and so makes an enemy for nothing.

24 Lying is an ugly blot on anyone,
and ever on the lips of the undisciplined.

25 A thief is preferable to an inveterate liar,
but both are heading for ruin.

GREEK OLD TESTAMENT

26 ἦθος ἀνθρώπου ψευδοῦς ἀτιμία,
καὶ ἡ αἰσχύνη αὐτοῦ μετ᾽ αὐτοῦ ἐνδελεχῶς.
27 Ὁ σοφὸς ἐν λόγοις προάξει ἑαυτόν,
καὶ ἄνθρωπος φρόνιμος ἀρέσει μεγιστᾶσιν.
28 ὁ ἐργαζόμενος γῆν ἀνυψώσει θιμωνιὰν αὐτοῦ,
καὶ ὁ ἀρέσκων μεγιστᾶσιν ἐξιλάσεται ἀδικίαν.
29 ξένια καὶ δῶρα ἀποτυφλοῖ ὀφθαλμοὺς σοφῶν
καὶ ὡς φιμὸς ἐν στόματι ἀποτρέπει ἐλεγμούς.
30 σοφία κεκρυμμένη καὶ θησαυρὸς ἀφανής,
τίς ὠφέλεια ἐν ἀμφοτέροις;
31 κρείσσων ἄνθρωπος ἀποκρύπτων τὴν μωρίαν αὐτοῦ
ἢ ἄνθρωπος ἀποκρύπτων τὴν σοφίαν αὐτοῦ.

21 Τέκνον, ἥμαρτες; μὴ προσθῇς μηκέτι
καὶ περὶ τῶν προτέρων σου δεήθητι.
2 ὡς ἀπὸ προσώπου ὄφεως φεῦγε ἀπὸ ἁμαρτίας·
ἐὰν γὰρ προσέλθῃς, δήξεταί σε·
ὀδόντες λέοντος οἱ ὀδόντες αὐτῆς
ἀναιροῦντες ψυχὰς ἀνθρώπων.
3 ὡς ῥομφαία δίστομος πᾶσα ἀνομία,
τῇ πληγῇ αὐτῆς οὐκ ἔστιν ἴασις.
4 καταπληγμὸς καὶ ὕβρις ἐρημώσουσιν πλοῦτον·
οὕτως οἶκος ὑπερηφάνου ἐρημωθήσεται.

KING JAMES VERSION

26 The disposition of a liar is dishonourable, and his shame is ever with him.

27 A wise man shall promote himself *to honour* with his words: and he that hath understanding will please great men.

28 He that tilleth his land shall increase his heap: and he that pleaseth great men shall get pardon for iniquity.

29 Presents and gifts blind the eyes of the wise, and stop up his mouth that he cannot reprove.

30 Wisdom that is hid, and treasure that is hoarded up, what profit is in them both?

31 Better is he that hideth his folly than a man that hideth his wisdom.

32 Necessary patience in seeking the Lord is better than he that leadeth his life without a guide.

21 My son, hast thou sinned? do so no more, but ask pardon for thy former sins.

2 Flee from sin as from the face of a serpent: for if thou comest too near it, it will bite thee: the teeth thereof are as the teeth of a lion, slaying the souls of men.

3 All iniquity is as a two edged sword, the wounds whereof cannot be healed.

4 To terrify and do wrong will waste riches: thus the house of proud men shall be made desolate.

DOUAY OLD TESTAMENT

28 The manners of lying men are without honour: and their confusion is with them without ceasing.

29 A wise man shall advance himself with his words, and a prudent man shall please the great ones.

30 He that tilleth his land shall make a high heap of corn: and he that worketh justice shall be exalted: and he that pleaseth great men shall escape iniquity.

31 Presents and gifts blind the eyes of judges, and make them dumb in the mouth, so that they cannot correct.

32 Wisdom that is hid, and treasure that is not seen: what profit is there in them both?

33 Better is he that hideth his folly, than the man that hideth his wisdom.

21 MY son, hast thou sinned? do so no more: but for thy former sins also pray that they may be forgiven thee.

2 Flee from sins as from the face of a serpent: for if thou comest near them, they will take hold of thee.

3 The teeth thereof are the teeth of a lion, killing the souls of men.

4 All iniquity is like a two-edged sword, there is no remedy for the wound thereof.

5 Injuries and wrongs will waste riches: and the house that is very rich shall be brought to nothing by pride: so the substance of the proud shall be rooted out.

KNOX TRANSLATION

28 He lives without honour that lies without scruple, and shame is at his side continually.

29 The wise word brings a man to honour; prudence will endear thee to the great. 30 Till ground, and fill barn; live uprightly, and attain honour; win prince, and escape harm.

31 Hospitality here, a gift there, how they blind the eyes of justice! No better gag to silence reproof.

32 Wisdom hidden is wasted, is treasure that never sees the light of day; 33 silence is rightly used when it masks folly, not when it is the grave of wisdom.

21 Sinned if thou hast, my son, be not emboldened to sin further; to prayer betake thee, and efface the memory of sins past. 2 Sin dread thou not less than the serpent's encounter; its fangs will not miss thee, if once thou come close. 3 Teeth so sharp no lion ever had, to catch human prey, 4 nor ever two-edged sword gave wound so incurable as the law's defiance. 5 Browbeat and oppress the poor, thy own wealth shall dwindle; riches that are grown too great the proud cannot long enjoy; pride shrivels wealth.

TODAY'S ENGLISH VERSION

liar, but both are headed for ruin. 26 A liar has no honor. He
lives in constant disgrace.
27 Speak wisely, and you will get ahead in the world.
Influential people appreciate good sense. 28 They will excuse
your errors if they like you, so cultivate the soil and reap the
harvest!
29 Gifts and bribes make even the wise blind to the truth,
and prevent them from being honest in their criticism.
30 Wisdom that is not expressed is like a treasure that has
been hidden—both are useless. 31 But a person who covers
up his foolishness is better than one who keeps his wisdom
to himself.

21 My child, have you sinned? Don't do it again, and
pray for forgiveness for what you have already done.
2 Avoid sin as if it were a snake. If you get too near, it will
sink its teeth into your soul like a lion, and destroy you.
3 Every lawless act leaves an incurable wound, like one left
by a double-edged sword.
4 If a person is insolent and arrogant, he may lose everything he has.

NEW REVISED STANDARD VERSION

26 A liar's way leads to disgrace,
and his shame is ever with him.

PROVERBIAL SAYINGS[a]

27 The wise person advances himself by his words,
and one who is sensible pleases the great.
28 Those who cultivate the soil heap up their harvest,
and those who please the great atone for injustice.
29 Favors and gifts blind the eyes of the wise;
like a muzzle on the mouth they stop reproofs.
30 Hidden wisdom and unseen treasure,
of what value is either?
31 Better are those who hide their folly
than those who hide their wisdom.[b]

21 Have you sinned, my child? Do so no more,
but ask forgiveness for your past sins.
2 Flee from sin as from a snake;
for if you approach sin, it will bite you.
Its teeth are lion's teeth,
and can destroy human lives.
3 All lawlessness is like a two-edged sword;
there is no healing for the wound it inflicts.
4 Panic and insolence will waste away riches;
thus the house of the proud will be laid waste.[c]

a This heading is included in the Gk text. *b* Other ancient authorities add 32 *Unwearied endurance in seeking the Lord is better than a masterless charioteer of one's own life.* *c* Other ancient authorities read *uprooted*

NEW AMERICAN BIBLE

25 A liar's way leads to dishonor,
his shame remains ever with him.
26 A wise man advances himself by his words,
a prudent man pleases the great.
27 He who works his land has abundant crops,
he who pleases the great is pardoned his faults.
28 Favors and gifts blind the eyes;
like a muzzle over the mouth they silence reproof.
29 Hidden wisdom and unseen treasure—
of what value is either?
30 Better the man who hides his folly
than the one who hides his wisdom.

21 My son, if you have sinned, do so no more,
and for your past sins pray to be forgiven.
2 Flee from sin as from a serpent
that will bite you if you go near it;
Its teeth are lion's teeth,
destroying the souls of men.
3 Every offense is a two-edged sword;
when it cuts, there can be no healing.
4 Violence and arrogance wipe out wealth;
so too a proud man's home is destroyed.

NEW JERUSALEM BIBLE

26 Lying is an abominable habit,
the liar's disgrace lasts for ever.

27 The wise gains advancement by words,
the shrewd wins favour from the great.
28 Whoever tills the soil will have a full harvest,
whoever wins favour from the great will secure
pardon for offences.

29 Presents and gifts blind the eyes of the wise
and stifle rebukes like a muzzle on the mouth.
30 Wisdom concealed, and treasure undiscovered,
what use is either of these?
31 Better one who conceals his folly
than one who conceals his wisdom.[a]

21 My child, have you sinned? Do so no more,
and ask forgiveness for your previous faults.
2 Flee from sin as from a snake,
if you approach it, it will bite you;
its teeth are lion's teeth,
they take human life away.
3 All law-breaking is like a two-edged sword,
the wounds it inflicts are beyond cure.

4 Terror and violence make havoc of riches,
similarly, desolation overtakes the houses of the
proud.

a **20** =41:14–15.

GREEK OLD TESTAMENT

5 δέησις πτωχοῦ ἐκ στόματος ἕως ὠτίων αὐτοῦ,
καὶ τὸ κρίμα αὐτοῦ κατὰ σπουδὴν ἔρχεται.
6 μισῶν ἐλεγμὸν ἐν ἴχνει ἁμαρτωλοῦ,
καὶ ὁ φοβούμενος κύριον ἐπιστρέψει ἐν καρδίᾳ.
7 γνωστὸς μακρόθεν ὁ δυνατὸς ἐν γλώσσῃ,
ὁ δὲ νοήμων οἶδεν ἐν τῷ ὀλισθάνειν αὐτόν.
8 ὁ οἰκοδομῶν τὴν οἰκίαν αὐτοῦ ἐν χρήμασιν ἀλλοτρίοις
ὡς συνάγων αὐτοῦ τοὺς λίθους εἰς χειμῶνα.
9 στιππύον συνηγμένον συναγωγὴ ἀνόμων,
καὶ ἡ συντέλεια αὐτῶν φλὸξ πυρός.
10 ὁδὸς ἁμαρτωλῶν ὡμαλισμένη ἐκ λίθων,
καὶ ἐπ᾽ ἐσχάτων αὐτῆς βόθρος ᾅδου.
11 Ὁ φυλάσσων νόμον κατακρατεῖ τοῦ ἐννοήματος αὐτοῦ,
καὶ συντέλεια τοῦ φόβου κυρίου σοφία.
12 οὐ παιδευθήσεται ὃς οὐκ ἔστιν πανοῦργος,
ἔστιν δὲ πανουργία πληθύνουσα πικρίαν.
13 γνῶσις σοφοῦ ὡς κατακλυσμὸς πληθυνθήσεται
καὶ ἡ βουλὴ αὐτοῦ ὡς πηγὴ ζωῆς.
14 ἔγκατα μωροῦ ὡς ἀγγεῖον συντετριμμένον
καὶ πᾶσαν γνῶσιν οὐ κρατήσει.
15 λόγον σοφὸν ἐὰν ἀκούσῃ ἐπιστήμων,
αἰνέσει αὐτὸν καὶ ἐπ᾽ αὐτὸν προσθήσει·
ἤκουσεν ὁ σπαταλῶν, καὶ ἀπήρεσεν αὐτῷ,
καὶ ἀπέστρεψεν αὐτὸν ὀπίσω τοῦ νώτου αὐτοῦ.

KING JAMES VERSION

5 A prayer out of a poor man's mouth reacheth to the ears of God, and his judgment cometh speedily.

6 He that hateth to be reproved is in the way of sinners: but he that feareth the Lord will repent from his heart.

7 An eloquent man is known far and near; but a man of understanding knoweth when he slippeth.

8 He that buildeth his house with other men's money is like one that gathereth himself stones for the tomb of his burial.

9 The congregation of the wicked is like tow wrapped together: and the end of them is a flame of fire to destroy them.

10 The way of sinners is made plain with stones, but at the end thereof is the pit of hell.

11 He that keepeth the law of the Lord getteth the understanding thereof: and the perfection of the fear of the Lord is wisdom.

12 He that is not wise will not be taught: but there is a wisdom which multiplieth bitterness.

13 The knowledge of a wise man shall abound like a flood: and his counsel is like a pure fountain of life.

14 The inner parts of a fool are like a broken vessel, and he will hold no knowledge as long as he liveth.

15 If a skilful man hear a wise word, he will commend it, and add unto it: but as soon as one of no understanding heareth it, it displeaseth him, and he casteth it behind his back.

DOUAY OLD TESTAMENT

6 The prayer out of the mouth of the poor shall reach the ears *of God,* and judgment shall come for him speedily.

7 He that hateth to be reproved *walketh in* the trace of a sinner: and he that feareth God will turn to his own heart.

8 He that is mighty by a bold tongue is known afar off, but a wise man knoweth to slip by him.

9 He that buildeth his house at other men's charges, is as he that gathereth himself stones *to build* in the winter.

10 The congregation of sinners is like tow heaped together, and the end of them is a flame of fire.

11 The way of sinners is made plain with stones, and in their end is hell, and darkness, and pains.

12 He that keepeth justice shall get the understanding thereof.

13 The perfection of the fear of God is wisdom and understanding.

14 He that is not wise in good, will not be taught.

15 But there is a wisdom that aboundeth in evil: and there is no understanding where there is bitterness.

16 The knowledge of a wise man shall abound like a flood, and his counsel continueth like a fountain of life.

17 The heart of a fool is like a broken vessel, and no wisdom at all shall it hold.

18 A man of sense will praise every wise word he shall hear, and will apply it to himself: the luxurious man hath heard it, and it shall displease him, and he will cast it behind his back.

KNOX TRANSLATION

6 Swiftly comes their doom, because the poor man's plea
reached their ears, but never their hearts.[a]
7 Where reproof is unregarded, there goes the sinner; no
God-fearing man but will come to a better mind.
8 To the glib speaker, fame comes from far and wide; only
the wise man knows the slips of his own heart.
9 Wouldst thou build thy fortunes on earnings that are
none of thine? As well mightest thou lay in stones for winter
fuel.
10 When knaves come together, it is like heaping up tow;
the flame burns all the brighter.
11 How smoothly paved is the path of sinners! Yet death
lies at the end of it, and darkness, and doom.
12 If thou wouldst be master of thy own thought, first keep
the law; 13 no wisdom or discernment but is the fruit of
God's fear. 14 Without shrewdness[b] thou wilt never advance
in the school of virtue; 15 yet shrewdness there is that breeds
abundance of mischief; where the stream runs foul, there can
be no rightness of mind. 16 Where true wisdom is, there discernment flows in full tide, there prudence springs up, an
inexhaustible fountain of life.
17 Heart of fool is leaking bucket, that loses all the wisdom
it learns. 18 Truths that wisdom will prize and cherish, the
profligate hears no less, but hearing despises, and casts them

a Literally, 'The pleas of the poor man will come from the mouth as far as his ears'. Some interpret this as meaning the ears divine justice, but there is no hint of this in the text. *b* In the Latin version, 'wisdom', in the Greek text, 'knavery'; cf. note on 19. 20.

TODAY'S ENGLISH VERSION

5 When poor people pray, God hears them and quickly
answers their prayers.
6 If you refuse to accept correction, you are committing a
sin; and if you fear the Lord, you will make a sincere change
in your ways.
7 Someone may be famous as a good speaker, but when he
is wrong, a sensible person will detect it.
8 Anyone who borrows money to build a house is just collecting stones for his own tomb.[a]
9 A group of people who have no respect for the Law is like
a pile of kindling; they will meet a fiery end. 10 The road that
sinners walk is smooth and paved, but it leads to the world
of the dead.
11 Whoever wants to keep the Law must learn what the
Law means. If you fear the Lord in every sense of the term,
you will have wisdom. 12 You have to be intelligent to learn
anything; but there is such a thing as just pretending to be
intelligent, which only makes people bitter. 13 A wise person's knowledge is like a river that never runs dry, like an
everflowing stream of good advice.
14 A fool, on the other hand, has a mind like a jar with a
hole in it; anything he learns is soon lost.
15 When an educated person hears something that shows
insight, it stimulates his mind and leads him on to other
ideas. But when someone who is satisfied with ignorance
hears it, he won't like it, and will forget it as soon as he can.

[a] his own tomb; *some manuscripts have* the winter.

NEW REVISED STANDARD VERSION

5 The prayer of the poor goes from their lips to the ears of
God,[a]
and his judgment comes speedily.
6 Those who hate reproof walk in the sinner's steps,
but those who fear the Lord repent in their heart.
7 The mighty in speech are widely known;
when they slip, the sensible person knows it.

8 Whoever builds his house with other people's money
is like one who gathers stones for his burial mound.[b]
9 An assembly of the wicked is like a bundle of tow,
and their end is a blazing fire.
10 The way of sinners is paved with smooth stones,
but at its end is the pit of Hades.

11 Whoever keeps the law controls his thoughts,
and the fulfillment of the fear of the Lord is wisdom.
12 The one who is not clever cannot be taught,
but there is a cleverness that increases bitterness.
13 The knowledge of the wise will increase like a flood,
and their counsel like a life-giving spring.
14 The mind[c] of a fool is like a broken jar;
it can hold no knowledge.

15 When an intelligent person hears a wise saying,
he praises it and adds to it;
when a fool[d] hears it, he laughs at[e] it
and throws it behind his back.

a Gk *his ears* *b* Other ancient authorities read *for the winter* *c* Syr Lat: Gk *entrails* *d* Syr: Gk *reveler* *e* Syr: Gk *dislikes*

NEW AMERICAN BIBLE

5 Prayer from a poor man's lips is heard at once,
and justice is quickly granted him.
6 He who hates correction walks the sinner's path,
but he who fears the LORD repents in his heart.
7 Widely known is the boastful speaker,
but the wise man knows his own faults.
8 He who builds his house with another's money
is collecting stones for his funeral mound.
9 A band of criminals is like a bundle of tow;
they will end in a flaming fire.
10 The path of sinners is smooth stones
that end in the depths of the nether world,

11 He who keeps the law controls his impulses;
he who is perfect in fear of the LORD has wisdom.
12 He can never be taught who is not shrewd,
but one form of shrewdness is thoroughly bitter.
13 A wise man's knowledge wells up in a flood,
and his counsel, like a living spring;
14 A fool's mind is like a broken jar—
no knowledge at all can it hold.
15 When an intelligent man hears words of wisdom,
he approves them and adds to them;
The wanton hears them with scorn
and casts them behind his back.

NEW JERUSALEM BIBLE

5 A plea from the mouth of the poor goes straight to the
ear of God,
whose judgement comes without delay.

6 Whoever resents reproof walks in the sinner's footsteps;
whoever fears the Lord is repentant of heart.

7 The glib speaker is known far and wide,
but the wary detects every slip.

8 To build your house with other people's money
is like collecting stones for your own tomb.

9 A meeting of the lawless is like a heap of tow:
they will end in a blazing fire.

10 The sinner's road is smoothly paved,
but it ends at the pit of Sheol.

11 Whoever keeps the Law will master his instincts;
the fear of the Lord is made perfect in wisdom.

12 No one who lacks aptitude can be taught,
but certain aptitudes give rise to bitterness.

13 The sage's knowledge is as rich as the abyss
and his advice is like a living spring.
14 The heart of a fool is like a broken jar,
it will not hold any knowledge.
15 If the educated hears a wise saying,
he praises it and caps it with another;
if a debauchee hears it, he does not like it
and tosses it behind his back.

GREEK OLD TESTAMENT

16 ἐξήγησις μωροῦ ὡς ἐν ὁδῷ φορτίον,
ἐπὶ δὲ χείλους συνετοῦ εὑρεθήσεται χάρις.
17 στόμα φρονίμου ζητηθήσεται ἐν ἐκκλησίᾳ,
καὶ τοὺς λόγους αὐτοῦ διανοηθήσονται ἐν καρδίᾳ.
18 Ὡς οἶκος ἠφανισμένος οὕτως μωρῷ σοφία,
καὶ γνῶσις ἀσυνέτου ἀδιεξέταστοι λόγοι.
19 πέδαι ἐν ποσὶν ἀνοήτου παιδεία
καὶ ὡς χειροπέδαι ἐπὶ χειρὸς δεξιᾶς.
20 μωρὸς ἐν γέλωτι ἀνυψοῖ φωνὴν αὐτοῦ,
ἀνὴρ δὲ πανοῦργος μόλις ἡσυχῇ μειδιάσει.
21 ὡς κόσμος χρυσοῦς φρονίμῳ παιδεία
καὶ ὡς χλιδὼν ἐπὶ βραχίονι δεξιῷ.
22 πους μωροῦ ταχὺς εἰς οἰκίαν,
ἄνθρωπος δὲ πολύπειρος αἰσχυνθήσεται ἀπὸ προσώπου.
23 ἄφρων ἀπὸ θύρας παρακύπτει εἰς οἰκίαν,
ἀνὴρ δὲ πεπαιδευμένος ἔξω στήσεται.
24 ἀπαιδευσία ἀνθρώπου ἀκροᾶσθαι παρὰ θύραν,
ὁ δὲ φρόνιμος βαρυνθήσεται ἀτιμίᾳ.
25 χείλη ἀλλοτρίων ἐν τούτοις διηγήσονται,
λόγοι δὲ φρονίμων ἐν ζυγῷ σταθήσονται.

KING JAMES VERSION

16 The talking of a fool is like a burden in the way: but grace shall be found in the lips of the wise.

17 They enquire at the mouth of the wise man in the congregation, and they shall ponder his words in their heart.

18 As is a house that is destroyed, so is wisdom to a fool: and the knowledge of the unwise is as talk without sense.

19 Doctrine unto fools is as fetters on the feet, and like manacles on the right hand.

20 A fool lifteth up his voice with laughter; but a wise man doth scarce smile a little.

21 Learning is unto a wise man as an ornament of gold, and like a bracelet upon his right arm.

22 A foolish man's foot is soon in his [neighbour's] house: but a man of experience is ashamed of him.

23 A fool will peep in at the door into the house: but he that is well nurtured will stand without.

24 It is the rudeness of a man to hearken at the door: but a wise man will be grieved with the disgrace.

25 The lips of talkers will be telling such things as pertain not unto them: but the words of such as have understanding are weighed in the balance.

DOUAY OLD TESTAMENT

19 The talking of a fool is like a burden in the way: but in the lips of the wise, grace shall be found.

20 The mouth of the prudent is sought after in the church, and they will think upon his words in their hearts.

21 As a house that is destroyed, so is wisdom to a fool: and the knowledge of the unwise is as words without sense.

22 Doctrine to a fool is as fetters on the feet, and like manacles on the right hand.

23 A fool lifteth up his voice in laughter: but a wise man will scarce laugh low to himself.

24 Learning to the prudent is as an ornament of gold, and like a bracelet upon his right arm.

25 The foot of a fool is soon in his neighbour's house: but a man of experience will be abashed at the person of the mighty.

26 A fool will peep through the window into the house: but he that is well taught will stand without.

27 It is the folly of a man to hearken at the door: and a wise man will be grieved with the disgrace.

28 The lips of the unwise will be telling foolish things: but the words of the wise shall be weighed in a balance.

KNOX TRANSLATION

to the winds. 19 Listening to a fool is like journeying with a
heavy pack; there is no pleasing the ear, where sense is none.
20 How they hang on the lips of a wise man, the folk assembled, ay, and ponder in their hearts over the word said! 21 A
fool takes refuge in wise talk as a man takes shelter in a ruin;
learning without sense, that cannot abide scrutiny. 22 To the
fool, instruction seems but a fetter to clog him, gyves that
cramp his wrist. 23 A fool laughs loud; smiling, the wise com-
press their lips. 24 Precious as an ornament of gold, close-fit-
ting as a bracelet to the right arm, is instruction to a wise
man. 25 Folly sets foot over every threshold, where the experienced mind stands, as in a royal presence, abashed; 26 folly
peeps in at windows, where experience waits patiently without; 27 listens thoughtlessly behind open doors, where prudence hangs back for very shame.[a] 28 Fools break out into
rash utterance, where the prudent are at pains to weigh their

[a] *vv.* 25-27: These verses are usually understood as an instruction in the usages of polite society. It is more probable that the sacred author is denouncing, under a metaphor, the habit of rash enquiry.

TODAY'S ENGLISH VERSION

16 Listening to a foolish person talk is like traveling with a
heavy load on your back, but it is a pleasure to hear what
intelligent people have to say. 17 The assembly will be eager
to hear from an intelligent person and will take his opinion
seriously.

18 To an ignorant person, wisdom is as useless as a house
gone to ruin. He has never even thought about the things he
is so sure of. 19 To a person without any sense, an education
is like handcuffs, 20-21 but to a sensible person, it is like gold
bracelets. An intelligent person will smile quietly while a fool
roars with laughter. 22-23 A stupid person will peep into
someone's house through the door and then march right in,
but someone with experience and good manners will have
enough respect to wait outside. 24 Eavesdropping at doors is
bad manners, and anyone with a sense of decency would be
ashamed to do it.

25 Presumptuous people talk about things that are none of
their business,[a] but the wise will consider the consequences

[a] *Probable text* Presumptuous . . . business; *Greek* The lips of strangers speak of these things.

NEW REVISED STANDARD VERSION

16 A fool's chatter is like a burden on a journey,
but delight is found in the speech of the intelligent.
17 The utterance of a sensible person is sought in the assembly,
and they ponder his words in their minds.

18 Like a house in ruins is wisdom to a fool,
and to the ignorant, knowledge is talk that has no meaning.
19 To a senseless person education is fetters on his feet,
and like manacles on his right hand.
20 A fool raises his voice when he laughs,
but the wise[a] smile quietly.
21 To the sensible person education is like a golden ornament,
and like a bracelet on the right arm.

22 The foot of a fool rushes into a house,
but an experienced person waits respectfully outside.
23 A boor peers into the house from the door,
but a cultivated person remains outside.
24 It is ill-mannered for a person to listen at a door;
the discreet would be grieved by the disgrace.

25 The lips of babblers speak of what is not their concern,[b]
but the words of the prudent are weighed in the balance.

a Syr Lat: Gk *clever* *b* Other ancient authorities read *of strangers speak of these things*

NEW AMERICAN BIBLE

16 A fool's chatter is like a load on a journey,
but there is charm to be found upon the lips of the wise.
17 The views of a prudent man are sought in an assembly,
and his words are considered with care.
18 Like a house in ruins is wisdom to a fool;
the stupid man knows it only as inscrutable words.
19 Like fetters on the legs is learning to a fool,
like a manacle on his right hand.
20 A fool raises his voice in laughter,
but a prudent man at the most smiles gently.
21 Like a chain of gold is learning to a wise man,
like a bracelet on his right arm.
22 The fool steps boldly into a house,
while the well-bred man remains outside;
23 A boor peeps through the doorway of a house,
but a cultured man keeps his glance cast down.
24 It is rude for one to listen at a door;
a cultured man would be overwhelmed by the disgrace of it.
25 The lips of the impious talk of what is not their concern,
but the words of the prudent are carefully weighed.

NEW JERUSALEM BIBLE

16 The talk of a fool is like a load on a journey,
but it is a pleasure to listen to the intelligent.
17 The utterance of the shrewd will be eagerly awaited in the assembly,
what he says will be given serious consideration.
18 The wisdom of a fool is like the wreckage of a house,
the knowledge of a dolt is incoherent talk.
19 To the senseless fellow instruction is like fetters on the feet,
like manacles on the right hand.
20 A fool laughs at the top of his voice,
but the intelligent quietly smiles.
21 To the shrewd instruction is like a golden ornament,
like a bracelet on the right arm.
22 The step of a fool goes straight into a house,
but a person of much experience makes a respectful approach;
23 the stupid peeps inside through the door,
a well-bred person waits outside.
24 Listening at doors is a sign of bad upbringing,
the perceptive would be ashamed to do so.
25 The lips of gossips repeat the words of others,
the words of the wise are carefully weighed.

GREEK OLD TESTAMENT

26 ἐν στόματι μωρῶν ἡ καρδία αὐτῶν,
καρδία δὲ σοφῶν στόμα αὐτῶν.
27 ἐν τῷ καταρᾶσθαι ἀσεβῆ τὸν σατανᾶν
αὐτὸς καταρᾶται τὴν ἑαυτοῦ ψυχήν.
28 μολύνει τὴν ἑαυτοῦ ψυχὴν ὁ ψιθυρίζων
καὶ ἐν παροικήσει μισηθήσεται.

22 Λίθῳ ἠρδαλωμένῳ συνεβλήθη ὀκνηρός,
καὶ πᾶς ἐκσυριεῖ ἐπὶ τῇ ἀτιμίᾳ αὐτοῦ.
2 βολβίτῳ κοπρίων συνεβλήθη ὀκνηρός,
πᾶς ὁ ἀναιρούμενος αὐτὸν ἐκτινάξει χεῖρα.
3 αἰσχύνη πατρὸς ἐν γεννήσει ἀπαιδεύτου,
θυγάτηρ δὲ ἐπ᾽ ἐλαττώσει γίνεται.
4 θυγάτηρ φρονίμη κληρονομήσει ἄνδρα αὐτῆς,
καὶ ἡ καταισχύνουσα εἰς λύπην γεννήσαντος.
5 πατέρα καὶ ἄνδρα καταισχύνει ἡ θρασεῖα
καὶ ὑπὸ ἀμφοτέρων ἀτιμασθήσεται.
6 μουσικὰ ἐν πένθει ἄκαιρος διήγησις,
μάστιγες δὲ καὶ παιδεία ἐν παντὶ καιρῷ σοφίας.
9 συγκολλῶν ὄστρακον ὁ διδάσκων μωρόν,
ἐξεγείρων καθεύδοντα ἐκ βαθέος ὕπνου.
10 διηγούμενος νυστάζοντι ὁ διηγούμενος μωρῷ,
καὶ ἐπὶ συντελείᾳ ἐρεῖ Τί ἐστιν;

KING JAMES VERSION

26 The heart of fools is in their mouth: but the mouth of the wise is in their heart.

27 When the ungodly curseth Satan, he curseth his own soul.

28 A whisperer defileth his own soul, and is hated wheresoever he dwelleth.

22 A slothful man is compared to a filthy stone, and every one will hiss him out to his disgrace.

2 A slothful man is compared to the filth of a dunghill: every man that takes it up will shake his hand.

3 An evilnurtured son is the dishonour of his father that begat him: and a [foolish] daughter is born to his loss.

4 A wise daughter shall bring an inheritance to her husband: but she that liveth dishonestly is her father's heaviness.

5 She that is bold dishonoureth both her father and her husband, but they both shall despise her.

6 A tale out of season [is as] musick in mourning: but stripes and correction of wisdom are never out of time.

7 Whoso teacheth a fool is as one that glueth a potsherd together, and as he that waketh one from a sound sleep.

8 He that telleth a tale to a fool speaketh to one in a slumber: when he hath told his tale, he will say, What is the matter?

9 If children live honestly, and have wherewithal, they shall cover the baseness of their parents.

10 But children, being haughty, through disdain and want of nurture do stain the nobility of their kindred.

DOUAY OLD TESTAMENT

29 The heart of fools is in their mouth: and the mouth of wise men is in their heart.

30 While the ungodly curseth the devil, he curseth his own soul.

31 The talebearer shall defile his own soul, and shall be hated by all: and he that shall abide with him shall be hateful: the silent and wise man shall be honoured.

22 THE sluggard is pelted with a dirty stone, and all men will speak of his disgrace.

2 The sluggard is pelted with the dung of oxen: and every one that toucheth him will shake his hands.

3 A son ill taught is the confusion of the father: and a *foolish* daughter shall be to his loss.

4 A wise daughter shall bring an inheritance to her husband: but she that confoundeth, becometh a disgrace to her father.

5 She that is bold shameth both her father and husband, and will not be inferior to the ungodly: and shall be disgraced by them both.

6 A tale out of time is like music in mourning: but the stripes and instruction of wisdom are never out of time.

7 He that teacheth a fool, is like one that glueth a potsherd together.

8 He that telleth a word to him that heareth not, is like one that waketh a man out of a deep sleep.

9 He speaketh with one that is asleep, who uttereth wisdom to a fool: and in the end of the discourse he saith: Who is this?

KNOX TRANSLATION

words; 29 with the one, to think is to speak, with the other, to
speak is to think.
30 Let the sinner curse the foul fiend that spites him,[a] on
his own head the curse shall recoil. 31 The tale-bearer is his
own enemy, shunned by all; court his friendship, and thou
wilt court hatred; shut lips and calm judgement shall bring
thee a good name.
22 What ill names shall we hurl at the sluggard? Stone
from the sewers, that has no man's good word;
2 dung from the midden, for all to wash their hands of him.
3 Spoilt son thou shalt beget to thy shame, spoilt daughter
to thy great loss; 4 bring she to her husband no dower of
modesty, her shame shall cost thee dear. 5 Shame the father
shall have, shame the husband; fit company for sinners, she
will have no good word from either of these.
6 Speech may be out of season, like music in time of
mourning; not so the rod, not so chastisement; there lies
ever wisdom.[b] 7 Teach a fool, and mend a pot with glue;
8 better audience thou shalt have from the sleeper thou
wouldst awake from a deep dream; 9 thy wise speech ended,
Why, what's to do?[c] ask fool and dreamer alike.

a 'The foul fiend' may, in the Hebrew text, have meant simply 'his enemy'.
b The use of words in this verse is very strained, and it is likely that the Hebrew text was corrupt. *c* The Greek text here has, 'What is it?' The Latin version ('Who is it?') would apply to the sleeper, but gives no satisfactory sense as applied to the fool.

TODAY'S ENGLISH VERSION

of what they say. 26 Fools say whatever comes to mind; wise
people think before they speak.
27 When a wicked person curses his enemy[a] he is cursing
himself.
28 A gossip ruins his own character, and everyone in the
neighborhood hates him.

22 1-2 Lazy people are no better than dung; they are
repulsive, and no one wants to get near them.
3 It is a disgrace to a father to have an undisciplined child,
especially if it is a daughter. 4 A sensible daughter will get a
husband, but a shameless daughter brings her father grief.
5 A girl with no sense of propriety will disgrace both her husband and her father; neither will have any respect for her.
6 Lecturing your children can sometimes be as out of place
as singing to people in mourning, but a whipping is a wise
choice of discipline at any time.
7 Trying to teach a fool is like gluing a broken pot back
together, like waking someone out of a deep sleep.
8 Explaining something to a fool is like explaining it to a
sleepy person; when you have finished, he'll say, "What was
that again?"[b]

[a] his enemy; *or* Satan. [b] *Some manuscripts add verses 9-10:* Children who are brought up well do not show the humble origin of their parents. 10 Children who are not brought up well, who are arrogant and conceited, are a stain on the noblest family.

NEW REVISED STANDARD VERSION

26 The mind of fools is in their mouth,
but the mouth of the wise is in[a] their mind.
27 When an ungodly person curses an adversary,[b]
he curses himself.
28 A whisperer degrades himself
and is hated in his neighborhood.

22 The idler is like a filthy stone,
and every one hisses at his disgrace.
2 The idler is like the filth of dunghills;
anyone that picks it up will shake it off his hand.

3 It is a disgrace to be the father of an undisciplined son,
and the birth of a daughter is a loss.
4 A sensible daughter obtains a husband of her own,
but one who acts shamefully is a grief to her father.
5 An impudent daughter disgraces father and husband,
and is despised by both.
6 Like music in time of mourning is ill-timed conversation,
but a thrashing and discipline are at all times wisdom.[c]

9 Whoever teaches a fool is like one who glues potsherds
together,
or who rouses a sleeper from deep slumber.
10 Whoever tells a story to a fool tells it to a drowsy man;
and at the end he will say, "What is it?"

a Other ancient authorities omit *in* *b* Or *curses Satan* *c* Other ancient authorities add *7Children who are brought up in a good life, conceal the lowly birth of their parents. 8Children who are disdainfully and boorishly haughty stain the nobility of their kindred.*

NEW AMERICAN BIBLE

26 Fools' thoughts are in their mouths,
wise men's words are in their hearts.
27 When a godless man curses his adversary,
he really curses himself.
28 A slanderer besmirches himself,
and is hated by his neighbors.

22 The sluggard is like a stone in the mud;
everyone hisses at his disgrace.
2 The sluggard is like a lump of dung;
whoever touches him wipes his hands.
3 An unruly child is a disgrace to its father;
if it be a daughter, she brings him to poverty.
4 A thoughtful daughter becomes a treasure to her
husband,
a shameless one is her father's grief.
5 A hussy shames her father and her husband;
by both she is despised.
6 Like a song in time of mourning is inopportune talk,
but lashes and discipline are at all times wisdom.
7 Teaching a fool is like gluing a broken pot,
or like disturbing a man in the depths of sleep;
8 He talks with a slumberer who talks with a fool,
for when it is over, he will say, "What was that?"

NEW JERUSALEM BIBLE

26 The heart of fools is in their mouth,
but the mouth of the wise is in their heart.

27 When the godless curses Satan,
he is cursing himself.
28 The scandal-monger sullies himself
and earns the hatred of the neighbourhood.

22 An idler is like a stone covered in filth,
everyone whistles at his disgrace.
2 An idler is like a lump of dung,
anyone picking it up shakes it off his hand.
3 It is a disgrace to have fathered a badly brought-up son,
but the birth of any daughter is a loss;
4 a sensible daughter will find a husband,
but a shameless one is a grief to her father.
5 A brazen daughter puts father and mother to shame,
and will be disowned by both.
6 An untimely remonstrance is like music at a funeral,
but a thrashing and correction are wisdom at all
times.

9 Teaching a fool is like gluing bits of pottery together—
you are rousing someone who is besotted with sleep.
10 You might as well talk to someone sound asleep;
when you have finished the fool will say, 'What's
up?'

GREEK OLD TESTAMENT

11 ἐπὶ νεκρῷ κλαῦσον, ἐξέλιπεν γὰρ φῶς,
καὶ ἐπὶ μωρῷ κλαῦσον, ἐξέλιπεν γὰρ σύνεσιν·
ἥδιον κλαῦσον ἐπὶ νεκρῷ, ὅτι ἀνεπαύσατο,
τοῦ δὲ μωροῦ ὑπὲρ θάνατον ἡ ζωὴ πονηρά.
12 πένθος νεκροῦ ἑπτὰ ἡμέραι,
μωροῦ δὲ καὶ ἀσεβοῦς πᾶσαι αἱ ἡμέραι τῆς ζωῆς αὐτοῦ.
13 μετὰ ἄφρονος μὴ πληθύνῃς λόγον
καὶ πρὸς ἀσύνετον μὴ πορεύου·
φύλαξαι ἀπ᾽ αὐτοῦ, ἵνα μὴ κόπον ἔχῃς
καὶ οὐ μὴ μολυνθῇς ἐν τῷ ἐντιναγμῷ αὐτοῦ·
ἔκκλινον ἀπ᾽ αὐτοῦ καὶ εὑρήσεις ἀνάπαυσιν
καὶ οὐ μὴ ἀκηδιάσῃς ἐν τῇ ἀπονοίᾳ αὐτοῦ.
14 ὑπὲρ μόλιβον τί βαρυνθήσεται;
καὶ τί αὐτῷ ὄνομα ἀλλ᾽ ἢ μωρός;
15 ἄμμον καὶ ἅλα καὶ βῶλον σιδήρου
εὔκοπον ὑπενεγκεῖν ἢ ἄνθρωπον ἀσύνετον.
16 Ἱμάντωσις ξυλίνη ἐνδεδεμένη εἰς οἰκοδομὴν
ἐν συσσεισμῷ οὐ διαλυθήσεται·
οὕτως καρδία ἐστηριγμένη ἐπὶ διανοήματος βουλῆς
ἐν καιρῷ οὐ δειλιάσει.
17 καρδία ἡδρασμένη ἐπὶ διανοίας συνέσεως
ὡς κόσμος ψαμμωτὸς τοίχου ξυστοῦ.
18 χάρακες ἐπὶ μετεώρου κείμενοι
κατέναντι ἀνέμου οὐ μὴ ὑπομείνωσιν·

KING JAMES VERSION

11 Weep for the dead, for he hath lost the light: and weep for the fool, for he wanteth understanding: make little weeping for the dead, for he is at rest: but the life of the fool is worse than death.

12 Seven days do men mourn for him that is dead; but for a fool and an ungodly man all the days of his life.

13 Talk not much with a fool, and go not to him that hath no understanding: beware of him, lest thou have trouble, and thou shalt never be defiled with his fooleries: depart from him, and thou shalt find rest, and never be disquieted with madness.

14 What is heavier than lead? and what is the name thereof, but a fool?

15 Sand, and salt, and a mass of iron, is easier to bear, than a man without understanding.

16 As timber girt and bound together in a building cannot be loosed with shaking: so the heart that is stablished by advised counsel shall fear at no time.

17 A heart settled upon a thought of understanding is as a fair plaistering on the wall of a gallery.

18 Pales set on an high place will never stand against the

DOUAY OLD TESTAMENT

10 Weep for the dead, for his light hath failed: and weep for the fool, for his understanding faileth.

11 Weep but a little for the dead, for he is at rest.

12 For the wicked life of a wicked fool is worse than death.

13 The mourning for the dead is seven days: but for a fool and an ungodly man all the days of their life.

14 Talk not much with a fool, and go not with him that hath no sense.

15 Keep thyself from him, that thou mayst not have trouble, and thou shalt not be defiled with his sin.

16 Turn away from him, and thou shalt find rest, and shalt not be wearied out with his folly.

17 What is heavier than lead? and what other name hath he but fool?

18 Sand and salt, and a mass of iron is easier to bear, than a man without sense, that is both foolish and wicked.

19 A frame of wood bound together in the foundation of a building, shall not be loosed: so neither shall the heart that is established by advised counsel.

20 The thought of him that is wise at all times, shall not be depraved by fear.

21 As pales set in high places, and plasterings made without cost, will not stand against the face of the wind:

KNOX TRANSLATION

10 For the dead that lacks light, for the fool that lacks wit,
never cease to mourn; 11 yet not for the dead overmuch,
since rest is his, 12 but the fool's life is empty beyond the
emptiness of death; 13 seven days the dead are mourned, but
the fool, the godless fool, all his life long.

14 Linger never with a fool in talk, nor cast in thy lot with
his; 15 keep clear of him, as thou wouldst keep clear of mischief, and of sin's pollution; 16 go thy way, and let him go
his; thou shalt sleep the sounder, for having no folly of his
to cloud thy spirits. 17 Nought like lead for heaviness? Ay,
but its name is fool. 18 With sand or salt or iron bars burden
thyself, not with rash and godless company, not with a fool.

19 Underpin the foundations with timber balks, thy house
shall withstand all shock; nor less shall he, whose heart
stands resolved in the counsels of prudence; 20 no hour of
peril can daunt that steadfast heart. 21 Palisade set on high
ground, with no better protection against the wind's fury
than cheap rubble, is but of short endurance; 22 faint heart

TODAY'S ENGLISH VERSION

11 We mourn for the dead because they have no access to
light. We ought to mourn for fools, because they have no
access to intelligence. In fact, we should go into deeper
mourning for fools, because the life they lead is worse than
death. The dead are at least at rest. 12 For seven days we
mourn the dead, but a foolish or ungodly person causes a
lifetime of grief.

13 Don't visit stupid people or spend a lot of time talking
with them. Avoid them; then they can't contaminate you,
and you can live in peace without being troubled or worn
down by their foolishness. 14 Such people are a heavier burden to bear than lead; and the only word that fits them is
"fools." 15 It is easier to carry a load of sand, salt, and iron
than to put up with a stupid person.

16 A wooden beam can be put into a building so firmly that
an earthquake cannot shake it loose; a person can be trained
to use reason and good sense so well that he keeps his head
when a crisis comes. 17 A mind that thinks things through
intelligently is like a firm wall, finely decorated. 18 Small
stones on top of a wall[a] will not stay put when the wind

[a] Small . . . wall; *some manuscripts have* A fence on top of a hill.

NEW REVISED STANDARD VERSION

11 Weep for the dead, for he has left the light behind;
and weep for the fool, for he has left intelligence
behind.
Weep less bitterly for the dead, for he is at rest;
but the life of the fool is worse than death.
12 Mourning for the dead lasts seven days,
but for the foolish or the ungodly it lasts all the days
of their lives.

13 Do not talk much with a senseless person
or visit an unintelligent person.[a]
Stay clear of him, or you may have trouble,
and be spattered when he shakes himself off.
Avoid him and you will find rest,
and you will never be wearied by his lack of sense.
14 What is heavier than lead?
And what is its name except "Fool"?
15 Sand, salt, and a piece of iron
are easier to bear than a stupid person.
16 A wooden beam firmly bonded into a building
is not loosened by an earthquake;
so the mind firmly resolved after due reflection
will not be afraid in a crisis.
17 A mind settled on an intelligent thought
is like stucco decoration that makes a wall smooth.
18 Fences[b] set on a high place
will not stand firm against the wind;

a Other ancient authorities add *For being without sense he will despise everything about you* *b* Other ancient authorities read *Pebbles*

NEW AMERICAN BIBLE

9 Weep over the dead man, for his light has gone out;
weep over the fool, for sense has left him.
10 Weep but a little over the dead man, for he is at rest;
but worse than death is the life of a fool.
11 Seven days of mourning for the dead,
but for the wicked fool a whole lifetime.

12 Speak but seldom with the stupid man,
be not the companion of a brute;
13 Beware of him lest you have trouble
and be spattered when he shakes himself;
Turn away from him and you will find rest
and not be wearied by his lack of sense.
14 What is heavier than lead,
and what is its name but "Fool"?
15 Sand and salt and an iron mass
are easier to bear than a stupid man.

16 Masonry bonded with wooden beams
is not loosened by an earthquake;
Neither is a resolve constructed with careful
deliberation
shaken in a moment of fear.
17 A resolve that is backed by prudent understanding
is like the polished surface of a smooth wall.
18 Small stones lying on an open height
will not remain when the wind blows;

NEW JERUSALEM BIBLE

11 Shed tears for the dead, who has left the light behind;
shed tears for the fool, who has left his wits behind.
Shed quieter tears for the dead who is at rest,
for the fool life is worse than death.
12 Mourning for the dead lasts seven days,
for the foolish and ungodly all the days of their lives.

13 Do not waste many words on the stupid,
do not go near a dolt.
Beware of him, or you will have trouble
and be soiled by contact with him;
keep away from him, and you will have peace of mind
and not be exasperated by his folly.

14 What is heavier than lead,
and what is its name if not 'fool'?
15 Sand and salt and a lump of iron
are a lighter burden than a dolt.

16 A tie-beam bonded into a building
will not be dislodged by an earthquake;
so too, a heart resolved after due reflection
will not flinch at the critical moment.

17 A heart founded on intelligent reflection
is like a stucco decoration on a smooth wall.

18 Pebbles placed on top of a wall
will not stand up to the wind;

GREEK OLD TESTAMENT

οὕτως καρδία δειλὴ ἐπὶ διανοήματος μωροῦ
κατέναντι παντὸς φόβου οὐ μὴ ὑπομείνῃ.
19 Ὁ νύσσων ὀφθαλμὸν κατάξει δάκρυα,
καὶ νύσσων καρδίαν ἐκφαίνει αἴσθησιν.
20 βάλλων λίθον ἐπὶ πετεινὰ ἀποσοβεῖ αὐτά,
καὶ ὁ ὀνειδίζων φίλον διαλύσει φιλίαν.
21 ἐπὶ φίλον ἐὰν σπάσῃς ῥομφαίαν,
μὴ ἀφελπίσῃς, ἔστιν γὰρ ἐπάνοδος·
22 ἐπὶ φίλον ἐὰν ἀνοίξῃς στόμα,
μὴ εὐλαβηθῇς, ἔστιν γὰρ διαλλαγή·
πλὴν ὀνειδισμοῦ καὶ ὑπερηφανίας καὶ μυστηρίου
ἀποκαλύψεως καὶ πληγῆς δολίας,
ἐν τούτοις ἀποφεύξεται πᾶς φίλος.
23 πίστιν κτῆσαι ἐν πτωχείᾳ μετὰ τοῦ πλησίον,
ἵνα ἐν τοῖς ἀγαθοῖς αὐτοῦ ὁμοῦ πλησθῇς·
ἐν καιρῷ θλίψεως διάμενε αὐτῷ,
ἵνα ἐν τῇ κληρονομίᾳ αὐτοῦ συγκληρονομήσῃς.
24 πρὸ πυρὸς ἀτμὶς καμίνου καὶ καπνός·
οὕτως πρὸ αἱμάτων λοιδορίαι.
25 φίλον σκεπάσαι οὐκ αἰσχυνθήσομαι
καὶ ἀπὸ προσώπου αὐτοῦ οὐ μὴ κρυβῶ,
26 καὶ εἰ κακά μοι συμβήσεται δι' αὐτόν,
πᾶς ὁ ἀκούων φυλάξεται ἀπ' αὐτοῦ.

KING JAMES VERSION

wind: so a fearful heart in the imagination of a fool cannot stand against any fear.

19 He that pricketh the eye will make tears to fall: and he that pricketh the heart maketh it to shew her knowledge.

20 Whoso casteth a stone at the birds frayeth them away: and he that upbraideth his friend breaketh friendship.

21 Though thou drewest a sword at thy friend, yet despair not: for there may be a returning [to favour.]

22 If thou hast opened thy mouth against thy friend, fear not; for there may be a reconciliation: except for upbraiding, or pride, or disclosing of secrets, or a treacherous wound: for for these things every friend will depart.

23 Be faithful to thy neighbour in his poverty, that thou mayest rejoice in his prosperity: abide stedfast unto him in the time of his trouble, that thou mayest be heir with him in his heritage: for a mean estate is not always to be contemned: nor the rich that is foolish to be had in admiration.

24 As the vapour and smoke of a furnace goeth before the fire; so reviling before blood.

25 I will not be ashamed to defend a friend; neither will I hide myself from him.

26 And if any evil happen unto me by him, every one that heareth it will beware of him.

DOUAY OLD TESTAMENT

22 So also a fearful heart in the imagination of a fool shall not resist against the violence of fear.

23 As a fearful heart in the thought of a fool at all times will not fear, so neither shall he that continueth always in the commandments of God.

24 He that pricketh the eye, bringeth out tears: and he that pricketh the heart, bringeth forth resentment.

25 He that flingeth a stone at birds, shall drive them away: so he that upbraideth his friend, breaketh friendship.

26 Although thou hast drawn a sword at a friend, despair not: for there may be a returning. To a friend,

27 If thou hast opened a sad mouth, fear not, for there may be a reconciliation: except upbraiding, and reproach, and pride, and disclosing of secrets, or a treacherous wound: for in all these cases a friend will flee away.

28 Keep fidelity with a friend in his poverty, that in his prosperity also thou mayst rejoice.

29 In the time of his trouble continue faithful to him, that thou mayst also be heir with him in his inheritance.

30 As the vapour of a chimney, and the smoke of the fire goeth up before the fire: so also injurious words, and reproaches, and threats, before blood.

31 I will not be ashamed to salute a friend, neither will I hide myself from his face: and if any evil happen to me by him, I will bear it.

32 But every one that shall hear it, will beware of him.

KNOX TRANSLATION

that thinks a fool's thoughts will not be proof against sudden terror. Faint heart that thinks a fool's thoughts…

23 …shall never be afraid; no more shall he, that still keeps true to God's commandments.[a]

24 Chafed eye will weep, chafed heart will shew resentment.
25 One stone flung, and the birds are all on the wing; one
taunt uttered, and the friendship is past repair. 26 Hast thou
drawn sword against thy friend? Be comforted; all may be as
it was. 27 Hast thou assailed him with angry words? Thou
mayst yet be reconciled. But the taunt, the contemptuous reproach, the secret betrayed, the covert attack, all these mean a friend lost.

28 Keep faith with a friend when his purse is empty, thou
shalt have joy of his good fortune; 29 stand by him when he
falls upon evil times, thou shalt be partner in his prosperity.

30 Chimney-fumes and smoke rising, of fire forewarn thee; curse uttered, and threat, and insult, of bloodshed.

31 Never will I be ashamed to greet friend of mine, never deny myself to him; let harm befall me for his sake, I care not.

32 …All that hear of it will keep their distance from him.[b]

a The Latin text here is evidently confused, and perhaps defective.
b *vv.* 31, 32: It is difficult to make these verses into a continuous sentence; to render 'let harm befall me through his agency' is a mistranslation of the Greek. There has perhaps been an omission in the text.

TODAY'S ENGLISH VERSION

blows, and a person whose stupid ideas have made him
timid will not be able to stand up to frightening situations.
19 If you stick something in your eye, tears will flow; and if
you hurt a person deeply, you will discover his true feelings.
20 If you throw rocks at birds, you will scare them away; and
if you insult a friend, you will break up the friendship.
21-22 Even if you have a violent argument with a friend, and
speak sharply, all is not lost. You can still make up with
him. But any friend will leave you if you insult him, if you
are arrogant, if you reveal his secrets, or if you turn on him
unexpectedly.
23 Gain the confidence of your neighbor if he is poor; then
you can share his happiness if he becomes successful. Stand
by him when he is in trouble if you want to share with him
when better times come his way.
24 Fumes and smoke appear before the flames do; insults
come before violence.
25 I will never be afraid to protect a friend, and I will never
turn a friend away if he needs me. 26 If I suffer because of
him, everyone who learns of it will be on guard against him.

NEW REVISED STANDARD VERSION

so a timid mind with a fool's resolve
will not stand firm against any fear.

19 One who pricks the eye brings tears,
and one who pricks the heart makes clear its feelings.
20 One who throws a stone at birds scares them away,
and one who reviles a friend destroys a friendship.
21 Even if you draw your sword against a friend,
do not despair, for there is a way back.
22 If you open your mouth against your friend,
do not worry, for reconciliation is possible.
But as for reviling, arrogance, disclosure of secrets, or a treacherous blow—
in these cases any friend will take to flight.

23 Gain the trust of your neighbor in his poverty,
so that you may rejoice with him in his prosperity.
Stand by him in time of distress,
so that you may share with him in his inheritance.[a]
24 The vapor and smoke of the furnace precede the fire;
so insults precede bloodshed.
25 I am not ashamed to shelter a friend,
and I will not hide from him.
26 But if harm should come to me because of him,
whoever hears of it will beware of him.

a Other ancient authorities add *For one should not always despise restricted circumstances, or admire a rich person who is stupid.*

NEW AMERICAN BIBLE

Neither can a timid resolve based on foolish plans
withstand fear of any kind.

19 One who jabs the eye brings tears;
he who pierces the heart bares its feelings.
20 He who throws stones at birds drives them away,
and he who insults a friend breaks up the friendship.
21 Should you draw a sword against a friend,
despair not, it can be undone.
22 Should you speak sharply to a friend,
fear not, you can be reconciled.
But a contemptuous insult, a confidence broken,
or a treacherous attack will drive away any friend.

23 Make fast friends with a man while he is poor;
thus will you enjoy his prosperity with him.
In time of trouble remain true to him,
so as to share in his inheritance when it comes.
24 Before flames burst forth an oven smokes;
so does abuse come before bloodshed.
25 From a friend in need of support
no one need hide in shame;
26 But from him who brings harm to his friend
all will stand aloof who hear of it.

NEW JERUSALEM BIBLE

no more can the heart of a fool frightened at his own thoughts
stand up to fear.

19 Prick an eye and you will draw a tear,
prick a heart and you reveal its feelings.

20 Throw stones at birds and you scare them away,
reproach a friend and you destroy a friendship.

21 If you have drawn your sword on a friend,
do not despair; there is a way back.
22 If you have opened your mouth against your friend,
do not worry; there is hope for reconciliation;
but insult, arrogance, betrayal of secrets, and the stab in the back—
in these cases any friend is lost.

23 Win your neighbour's confidence when he is poor,
so that you may enjoy his later good fortune with him;
stand by him in times of trouble,
in order to have your share when he comes into a legacy.

24 Fire is heralded by the reek of the furnace and smoke,
so too, bloodshed by insults.

25 I shall not be ashamed to shelter a friend
nor shall I hide away from him,
26 and if evil comes to me through him,
everyone who hears about it will beware of him.

GREEK OLD TESTAMENT

27 Τίς δώσει ἐπὶ στόμα μου φυλακὴν
καὶ ἐπὶ τῶν χειλέων μου σφραγῖδα πανοῦργον,
ἵνα μὴ πέσω ἀπ᾽ αὐτῆς
καὶ ἡ γλῶσσά μου ἀπολέσῃ με;
23 κύριε πάτερ καὶ δέσποτα ζωῆς μου,
μὴ ἐγκαταλίπῃς με ἐν βουλῇ αὐτῶν,
μὴ ἀφῇς με πεσεῖν ἐν αὐτοῖς.
2 τίς ἐπιστήσει ἐπὶ τοῦ διανοήματός μου μάστιγας
καὶ ἐπὶ τῆς καρδίας μου παιδείαν σοφίας,
ἵνα ἐπὶ τοῖς ἀγνοήμασίν μου μὴ φείσωνται
καὶ οὐ μὴ παρῇ τὰ ἁμαρτήματα αὐτῶν,
3 ὅπως μὴ πληθυνθῶσιν αἱ ἄγνοιαί μου
καὶ αἱ ἁμαρτίαι μου πλεονάσωσιν
καὶ πεσοῦμαι ἔναντι τῶν ὑπεναντίων
καὶ ἐπιχαρεῖταί μοι ὁ ἐχθρός μου;
4 κύριε πάτερ καὶ θεὲ ζωῆς μου,
μετεωρισμὸν ὀφθαλμῶν μὴ δῷς μοι
5 καὶ ἐπιθυμίαν ἀπόστρεψον ἀπ᾽ ἐμοῦ·
6 κοιλίας ὄρεξις καὶ συνουσιασμὸς μὴ καταλαβέτωσάν με,
καὶ ψυχῇ ἀναιδεῖ μὴ παραδῷς με.
7 Παιδείαν στόματος ἀκούσατε, τέκνα,
καὶ ὁ φυλάσσων οὐ μὴ ἁλῷ.
8 ἐν τοῖς χείλεσιν αὐτοῦ καταλημφθήσεται ἁμαρτωλός,
καὶ λοίδορος καὶ ὑπερήφανος σκανδαλισθήσονται ἐν αὐτοῖς.

KING JAMES VERSION

27 Who shall set a watch before my mouth, and a seal of wisdom upon my lips, that I fall not suddenly by them, and that my tongue destroy me not?

23 O Lord, Father and Governor of all my whole life, leave me not to their counsels, and let me not fall by them.

2 Who will set scourges over my thoughts, and the discipline of wisdom over mine heart? that they spare me not for mine ignorances, and it pass not by my sins:

3 Lest mine ignorances increase, and my sins abound to my destruction, and I fall before mine adversaries, and mine enemy rejoice over me, whose hope is far from thy mercy.

4 O Lord, Father and God of my life, give me not a proud look, but turn away from thy servants always a haughty mind.

5 Turn away from me vain hopes and concupiscence, and thou shalt hold him up that is desirous always to serve thee.

6 Let not the greediness of the belly nor lust of the flesh take hold of me; and give not over me thy servant into an impudent mind.

7 Hear, O ye children, the discipline of the mouth: he that keepeth it shall never be taken in his lips.

8 The sinner shall be left in his foolishness: both the evil speaker and the proud shall fall thereby.

DOUAY OLD TESTAMENT

33 Who will set a guard before my mouth, and a sure seal upon my lips, that I fall not by them, and that my tongue destroy me not?

23 O LORD, father, and sovereign ruler of my life, leave me not to their counsel: nor suffer me to fall by them.

2 Who will set scourges over my thoughts, and the discipline of wisdom over my heart, that they spare me not in their ignorances, and that their sins may not appear:

3 Lest my ignorances increase, and my offences be multiplied, and my sins abound, and I fall before my adversaries, and my enemy rejoice over me?

4 O Lord, father, and God of my life, leave me not to their devices.

5 Give me not haughtiness of my eyes, and turn away from me all coveting.

6 Take from me the greediness of the belly, and let not the lusts of the flesh take hold of me, and give me not over to a shameless and foolish mind.

7 Hear, O ye children, the discipline of the mouth: and he that will keep it shall not perish by his lips, nor be brought to fall into most wicked works.

8 A sinner is caught in his own vanity, and the proud and the evil speakers shall fall thereby.

KNOX TRANSLATION

33 Oh for a sentry to guard this mouth of mine, a seal to keep these lips inviolate! From that snare may I be safe, nor ever let my tongue betray me!

23 Lord, that gavest my life and art the ruler of it, never may these lips of mine have me at their mercy, never
let them betray me into a fall! 2 Be my thoughts ever under
the lash, my heart disciplined by true wisdom; let it never
deal gently with their unwitting offences, or gloss over the
wrong they do! 3 What if my transgressions should go, all
unobserved, from bad to worse, if I should sin ever oftener,
and add fault to fault? What humiliation were this, in full
view of my enemies; how would my ill-wishers triumph at
the sight! 4 Lord, that gavest my life and art the divine ruler
of it, let them not have me at their mercy; 5 never let
haughty looks be mine, never the assaults of passion come
near me. 6 Let the itch of gluttony pass me by, nor ever carnal lust overtake me; do not leave me, Lord, at the mercy of
a shameless, an unprofitable mind!

7 Here is the lore, my sons, of the tongue's use; hold fast by
it, and thy own lips shall never be thy undoing, to ensnare
thee in heinous wrong. 8 What is it but his lying that entraps
the sinner, what snare but their own speech catches the
proud, the slanderers? 9 That mouth of thine do not inure to

TODAY'S ENGLISH VERSION

27 I wish that a guard could be placed at my mouth, that
my lips could be wisely sealed. It would keep me from making mistakes and prevent me from destroying myself with my
own tongue!

23 O Lord, my Father and Master of my life, do not leave
me at the mercy of my own words; don't let them
cause my downfall. 2 I wish I could be whipped for my
thoughts, so that Wisdom could discipline my mind. I would
not want to be spared when I am wrong; I would not want a
single sin to be overlooked! 3 Then I would not keep on sinning, making one mistake after another. I could not fall to
my enemies and be humiliated by them.

4 O Lord, my Father, God of my life, keep me from being
arrogant; 5 protect me from evil desires. 6 Keep me from
being overcome by greed or lust; do not leave me at the
mercy of these shameless passions.

7 My children, listen to what I have to say about proper
speech; do as I teach you and you will never get trapped.
8 Sinners are caught by their own arrogant, insulting words.

NEW REVISED STANDARD VERSION

27 Who will set a guard over my mouth,
and an effective seal upon my lips,
so that I may not fall because of them,
and my tongue may not destroy me?

23 O Lord, Father and Master of my life,
do not abandon me to their designs,
and do not let me fall because of them!
2 Who will set whips over my thoughts,
and the discipline of wisdom over my mind,
so as not to spare me in my errors,
and not overlook my[a] sins?
3 Otherwise my mistakes may be multiplied,
and my sins may abound,
and I may fall before my adversaries,
and my enemy may rejoice over me.[b]
4 O Lord, Father and God of my life,
do not give me haughty eyes,
5 and remove evil desire from me.
6 Let neither gluttony nor lust overcome me,
and do not give me over to shameless passion.

DISCIPLINE OF THE TONGUE[c]

7 Listen, my children, to instruction concerning the
mouth;
the one who observes it will never be caught.
8 Sinners are overtaken through their lips;
by them the reviler and the arrogant are tripped up.

a Gk *their* b Other ancient authorities add *From them the hope of your mercy is remote* c This heading is included in the Gk text.

NEW AMERICAN BIBLE

27 Who will set a guard over my mouth,
and upon my lips an effective seal,
That I may not fail through them,
that my tongue may not destroy me?

23 LORD, Father and Master of my life,
permit me not to fall by them!
2 Who will apply the lash to my thoughts,
to my mind the rod of discipline,
That my failings may not be spared,
nor the sins of my heart overlooked;
3 Lest my failings increase,
and my sins be multiplied;
Lest I succumb to my foes,
and my enemy rejoice over me?
4 LORD, Father and God of my life,
abandon me not into their control!
5 A brazen look allow me not;
ward off passion from my heart,
6 Let not the lustful cravings of the flesh master me,
surrender me not to shameless desires.

7 Give heed, my children, to the instruction that I
pronounce,
for he who keeps it will not be enslaved.
8 Through his lips is the sinner ensnared;
the railer and the arrogant man fall thereby.

NEW JERUSALEM BIBLE

27 Who will set a guard on my mouth,
and an efficient seal on my lips,
to keep me from falling,
and my tongue from causing my ruin?

23 Lord, father and master of my life,
do not abandon me to their whims,
do not let me fall because of them.
2 Who will lay whips to my thoughts,
and the discipline of wisdom to my heart,
to be merciless to my errors
and not let my sins go unchecked,
3 for fear my errors should multiply
and my sins then abound
and I fall before my adversaries,
and my enemy gloat over me?
4 Lord, father and God of my life,
do not let my eyes be proud,
5 turn envy away from me,
6 do not let lechery and lust grip me,
do not leave me a prey to shameless desire.

7 Children, listen to what I teach,
no one who keeps it will be caught out.
8 The sinner is ensnared by his own lips,
both the abusive and the proud are tripped by them.

GREEK OLD TESTAMENT

9 ὅρκῳ μὴ ἐθίσῃς τὸ στόμα σου
καὶ ὀνομασίᾳ τοῦ ἁγίου μὴ συνεθισθῇς·
10 ὥσπερ γὰρ οἰκέτης ἐξεταζόμενος ἐνδελεχῶς
ἀπὸ μώλωπος οὐκ ἐλαττωθήσεται,
οὕτως καὶ ὁ ὀμνύων καὶ ὀνομάζων διὰ παντὸς
ἀπὸ ἁμαρτίας οὐ μὴ καθαρισθῇ.
11 ἀνὴρ πολύορκος πλησθήσεται ἀνομίας,
καὶ οὐκ ἀποστήσεται ἀπὸ τοῦ οἴκου αὐτοῦ μάστιξ·
ἐὰν πλημμελήσῃ, ἁμαρτία αὐτοῦ ἐπ' αὐτῷ,
κἂν ὑπερίδῃ, ἥμαρτεν δισσῶς·
καὶ εἰ διὰ κενῆς ὤμοσεν, οὐ δικαιωθήσεται,
πλησθήσεται γὰρ ἐπαγωγῶν ὁ οἶκος αὐτοῦ.
12 Ἔστιν λέξις ἀντιπαραβεβλημένη θανάτῳ,
μὴ εὑρεθήτω ἐν κληρονομίᾳ Ιακωβ·
ἀπὸ γὰρ εὐσεβῶν ταῦτα πάντα ἀποστήσεται,
καὶ ἐν ἁμαρτίαις οὐκ ἐγκυλισθήσονται.
13 ἀπαιδευσίαν ἀσυρῆ μὴ συνεθίσῃς τὸ στόμα σου·
ἔστιν γὰρ ἐν αὐτῇ λόγος ἁμαρτίας.
14 μνήσθητι πατρὸς καὶ μητρός σου,
ἀνὰ μέσον γὰρ μεγιστάνων συνεδρεύεις,
μήποτε ἐπιλάθῃ ἐνώπιον αὐτῶν
καὶ τῷ ἐθισμῷ σου μωρανθῇς
καὶ θελήσεις εἰ μὴ ἐγεννήθης
καὶ τὴν ἡμέραν τοῦ τοκετοῦ σου καταράσῃ.
15 ἄνθρωπος συνεθιζόμενος λόγοις ὀνειδισμοῦ
ἐν πάσαις ταῖς ἡμέραις αὐτοῦ οὐ μὴ παιδευθῇ.

KING JAMES VERSION

9 Accustom not thy mouth to swearing; neither use thyself to the naming of the Holy One.

10 For as a servant that is continually beaten shall not be without a blue mark: so he that sweareth and nameth God continually shall not be faultless.

11 A man that useth much swearing shall be filled with iniquity, and the plague shall never depart from his house: if he shall offend, his sin shall be upon him: and if he acknowledge not his sin, he maketh a double offence: and if he swear in vain, he shall not be innocent, but his house shall be full of calamities.

12 There is a word that is clothed about with death: God grant that it be not found in the heritage of Jacob; for all such things shall be far from the godly, and they shall not wallow in their sins.

13 Use not thy mouth to intemperate swearing, for therein is the word of sin.

14 Remember thy father and thy mother, when thou sittest among great men. Be not forgetful before them, and so thou by thy custom become a fool, and wish that thou hadst not been born, and curse they day of thy nativity.

15 The man that is accustomed to opprobrious words will never be reformed all the days of his life.

DOUAY OLD TESTAMENT

9 Let not thy mouth be accustomed to swearing: for in it there are many falls.

10 And let not the naming of God be usual in thy mouth, and meddle not with the names of saints, for thou shalt not escape free from them.

11 For as a slave daily put to the question, is never without a blue mark: so every one that sweareth, and nameth, shall not be wholly pure from sin.

12 A man that sweareth much, shall be filled with iniquity, and a scourge shall not depart from his house.

13 And if he make it void, his sin shall be upon him: and if he dissemble it, he offendeth double:

14 And if he swear in vain, he shall not be justified: for his house shall be filled with his punishment.

15 There is also another speech opposite to death, let it not be found in the inheritance of Jacob.

16 For from the merciful all these things shall be taken away, and they shall not wallow in sins.

17 Let not thy mouth be accustomed to indiscreet speech: for therein is the word of sin.

18 Remember thy father and thy mother, for thou sittest in the midst of great men:

19 Lest God forget thee in their sight, and thou, by thy daily custom, be infatuated and suffer reproach: and wish that thou hadst not been born, and curse the day of thy nativity.

20 The man that is accustomed to opprobrious words, will never be corrected all the days of his life.

KNOX TRANSLATION

oath-taking; therein lie many perils; 10 wilt thou take God's
name often on thy lips, and of holy titles make thy constant
invocation, thy word is forfeit to them. 11 Slave that is evermore under the lash cannot escape without bruises a many;
thy often swearing, thy often invoking, shall lead thee into
guilt at last. 12 Oaths a many, sins a many; punishment shall
be still at thy doors. 13 Forswear thyself, thou shalt be held to
account for it; forget the oath, it is at thy double peril; 14 and
though it were lightly taken, thou shalt find no excuse in
that; plague shall light on all thou hast, in amends for it.

15 Sin of speech there is, too, that has death for its counterpart; God send it be not found in Jacob's chosen race;[a]
16 from men of tender conscience every such thought is far
away, not theirs to wallow in evil-doing.

17 Beware of habituating thy tongue to lewd talk; therein is matter of offence.

18 Not thine to bring shame on father and mother. There
are great ones all around thee; 19 what if thyself God should
disregard, when thou art in their company? Then shall this
ill custom of thine strike thee dumb[b] and bring thee to great
dishonour; thou wilt wish thou hadst never been, and rue
the day of thy birth.

20 Let a man grow into a habit of railing speech, all his days there is no amending him.

a There can be little doubt that the reference is to blasphemy (see Lev. 24. 16). *b* 'What if thyself God should disregard, when thou art in their company? Then shall this ill custom of thine strike thee dumb'; literally, 'Lest by chance God should forget thee (in the Greek, thou shouldst forget) in their presence, and be made foolish by the habit'. It is difficult to be certain either of the exact meaning of the passage, or of its relevance to the context.

TODAY'S ENGLISH VERSION

9 Don't fall into the habit of taking oaths, and don't use
God's holy name too freely. 10 A slave who is constantly
beaten will never be free of bruises; someone who is always
taking an oath by the Holy Name will never be free of sin.
11 Anyone who takes oaths all the time is sinful to the core,
and punishment is never far away from his household. If he
fails to fulfill his oath, he is guilty. If he ignores his oath, he
is twice as guilty. If his oath was insincere in the first place,
he cannot be pardoned and will have a house full of trouble.
12 There is one way of speaking that is like death itself—
may no Israelite ever be guilty of it! Devout people do not
wallow in such sin, and they will keep away from such
behavior. 13 Don't fall into the habit of coarse, profane talk;
it is sinful. 14 You might forget yourself while in the company of important people and make a fool of yourself with
some foul word that comes to you naturally. Think how your
parents would feel! You would curse the day you were born
and wish you were dead! 15 If you fall into the habit of using
offensive language, you will never break yourself of it as
long as you live.

NEW REVISED STANDARD VERSION

9 Do not accustom your mouth to oaths,
nor habitually utter the name of the Holy One;
10 for as a servant who is constantly under scrutiny
will not lack bruises,
so also the person who always swears and utters the
Name
will never be cleansed[a] from sin.
11 The one who swears many oaths is full of iniquity,
and the scourge will not leave his house.
If he swears in error, his sin remains on him,
and if he disregards it, he sins doubly;
if he swears a false oath, he will not be justified,
for his house will be filled with calamities.

12 There is a manner of speaking comparable to death;[b]
may it never be found in the inheritance of Jacob!
Such conduct will be far from the godly,
and they will not wallow in sins.
13 Do not accustom your mouth to coarse, foul language,
for it involves sinful speech.
14 Remember your father and mother
when you sit among the great,
or you may forget yourself in their presence,
and behave like a fool through bad habit;
then you will wish that you had never been born,
and you will curse the day of your birth.
15 Those who are accustomed to using abusive language
will never become disciplined as long as they live.

a Syr *be free* b Other ancient authorities read *clothed about with death*

NEW AMERICAN BIBLE

9 Let not your mouth form the habit of swearing,
or becoming too familiar with the Holy Name.
10 Just as a slave that is constantly under scrutiny
will not be without welts,
So one who swears continually by the Holy Name
will not remain free from sin.
11 A man who often swears heaps up obligations;
the scourge will never be far from his house.
If he swears in error, he incurs guilt;
if he neglects his obligation, his sin is doubly great.
If he swears without reason he cannot be found just,
and all his house will suffer affliction.
12 There are words which merit death;
may they never be heard among Jacob's heirs.
For all such words are foreign to the devout,
who do not wallow in sin.
13 Let not your mouth become used to coarse talk,
for in it lies sinful matter.
14 Keep your father and mother in mind
when you sit among the mighty,
Lest in their presence you commit a blunder
and disgrace your upbringing,
By wishing you had never been born
or cursing the day of your birth.
15 A man who has the habit of abusive language
will never mature in character as long as he lives.

NEW JERUSALEM BIBLE

9 Do not get into the habit of swearing,
do not make a habit of naming the Holy One;
10 for just as a slave who is constantly overseen
will never be without bruises,
so someone who is always swearing and uttering the
Name
will not be exempt from sin.
11 A man for ever swearing is full of iniquity,
and the scourge will not depart from his house.
If he offends, his sin will be on him,
if he did it unheedingly, he has doubly sinned;
if he swears a false oath, he will not be treated as
innocent,
for his house will be filled with calamities.
12 One way of talking is like death,
let it not be found in the heritage of Jacob
since devout people have nothing to do with that:
they will not wallow in sin.
13 Do not get into the habit of using coarse and foul
language
since this involves sinful words.
14 Remember your father and mother
when you are sitting with the great,
for fear you forget yourself in their presence
and behave like a fool,
and then wish you had not been born
and curse the day of your birth.
15 No one in the habit of using shameful language
will break himself of it as long as he lives.

GREEK OLD TESTAMENT

16 Δύο εἴδη πληθύνουσιν ἁμαρτίας,
καὶ τὸ τρίτον ἐπάξει ὀργήν·
17 ψυχὴ θερμὴ ὡς πῦρ καιόμενον,
οὐ μὴ σβεσθῇ ἕως ἂν καταποθῇ·
ἄνθρωπος πόρνος ἐν σώματι σαρκὸς αὐτοῦ,
οὐ μὴ παύσηται ἕως ἂν ἐκκαύσῃ πῦρ·
ἀνθρώπῳ πόρνῳ πᾶς ἄρτος ἡδύς,
οὐ μὴ κοπάσῃ ἕως ἂν τελευτήσῃ.
18 ἄνθρωπος παραβαίνων ἀπὸ τῆς κλίνης αὐτοῦ
λέγων ἐν τῇ ψυχῇ αὐτοῦ Τίς με ὁρᾷ;
σκότος κύκλῳ μου, καὶ οἱ τοῖχοί με καλύπτουσιν,
καὶ οὐθείς με ὁρᾷ· τί εὐλαβοῦμαι;
τῶν ἁμαρτιῶν μου οὐ μὴ μνησθήσεται ὁ ὕψιστος.
19 καὶ ὀφθαλμοὶ ἀνθρώπων ὁ φόβος αὐτοῦ,
καὶ οὐκ ἔγνω ὅτι ὀφθαλμοὶ κυρίου
μυριοπλασίως ἡλίου φωτεινότεροι
ἐπιβλέποντες πάσας ὁδοὺς ἀνθρώπων
καὶ κατανοοῦντες εἰς ἀπόκρυφα μέρη.
20 πρὶν ἢ κτισθῆναι τὰ πάντα ἔγνωσται αὐτῷ,
οὕτως καὶ μετὰ τὸ συντελεσθῆναι.
21 οὗτος ἐν πλατείαις πόλεως ἐκδικηθήσεται,
καὶ οὗ οὐχ ὑπενόησεν, πιασθήσεται.
22 Οὕτως καὶ γυνὴ καταλιποῦσα τὸν ἄνδρα
καὶ παριστῶσα κληρονόμον ἐξ ἀλλοτρίου.

KING JAMES VERSION

16 Two sorts of men multiply sin, and the third will bring wrath: a hot mind is as a burning fire, it will never be quenched till it be consumed: a fornicator in the body of his flesh will never cease till he hath kindled a fire.

17 All bread is sweet to a whoremonger, he will not leave off till he die.

18 A man that breaketh wedlock, saying thus in his heart, Who seeth me? I am compassed about with darkness, the walls cover me, and no body seeth me; what need I to fear? the most High will not remember my sins:

19 Such a man only feareth the eyes of men, and knoweth not that the eyes of the Lord are ten thousand times brighter than the sun, beholding all the ways of men, and considering the most secret parts.

20 He knew all things ere ever they were created; so also after they were perfected he looked upon them all.

21 This man shall be punished in the streets of the city, and where he suspecteth not he shall be taken.

22 Thus shall it go also with the wife that leaveth her husband, and bringeth in an heir by another.

DOUAY OLD TESTAMENT

21 Two sorts of men multiply sins, and the third bringeth wrath and destruction.

22 A hot soul is a burning fire, it will never be quenched, till it devour some thing.

23 And a man that is wicked in the mouth of his flesh, will not leave off till he hath kindled a fire.

24 To a man that is a fornicator all bread is sweet, he will not be weary of sinning unto the end.

25 Every man that passeth beyond his own bed, despising his own soul, and saying: Who seeth me?

26 Darkness compasseth me about, and the walls cover me, and no man seeth me: whom do I fear? the most High will not remember my sins.

27 And he understandeth not that his eye seeth all things, for such a man's fear driveth from him the fear of God, and the eyes of men fearing him:

28 And he knoweth not that the eyes of the Lord are far brighter than the sun, beholding round about all the ways of men, and the bottom of the deep, and looking into the hearts of men, into the most hidden parts.

29 For all things were known to the Lord God, before they were created: so also after they were perfected he beholdeth all things.

30 This man shall be punished in the streets of the city, and he shall be chased as a colt: and where he suspected not, he shall be taken.

31 And he shall be in disgrace with all men, because he understood not the fear of the Lord.

32 So every woman also that leaveth her husband, and bringeth in an heir by another:

KNOX TRANSLATION

21 Two sorts of men are sinners above measure, and a third I can name that calls down vengeance. 22 There is a hot temper, all fire and fury, that cannot die down till it has had its fill. 23 A man that is corrupted by the prompting of his own lust[a] will not be content until it bursts into flame. 24 To the fornicator, one pasture-ground is as good as another; there is no wearying him till he has tried all. 25 Out on the man that takes his life in his hands and comes between another's sheets! There is none to witness it, thinks he; 26 darkness all about, and walls to shelter me, and none watching; what have I to fear? Sins like mine the most High will never mark. 27 Of that all-seeing eye no heed takes he; fear of a man has driven the fear of God from his thoughts; of human eyes only he shuns the regard.[b] 28 What, are not God's eyes a thousand times more piercing than the sun's rays? Do they not watch all the doings of men, the depths of earth, and man's heart, every secret open to their scrutiny? 29 God, that knows all he means to make, does he not watch over all he has made?

30 In full view of the open street the adulterer shall pay the penalty; loud, as for a runaway horse, the hue and cry; where he thought to escape, justice outruns him. 31 All the world shall witness his shame, that left the fear of the Lord unregarded. 32 Nor less guilty is she who plays her husband false, giving him for heir a child that is no son of his.

a Literally, 'by the mouth of his flesh'. It would be easiest to understand what are the three sins mentioned in verse 21, if we could suppose that the Hebrew text intended, in verse 23, the sin of gluttony (cf. verse 6 above). But some think that the whole passage, including verse 22, refers to sins against chastity. *b* The Latin version, evidently by an error, gives at the end of the verse 'the eyes of men fear him', instead of 'the eyes of men frighten him'.

TODAY'S ENGLISH VERSION

16 There are any number of ways to sin and bring down the
Lord's anger, but sexual passion is a hot, blazing fire that
cannot be put out at will; it can only burn itself out. A man
who lives for nothing but sexual enjoyment will keep on
until that fire destroys him. 17 To such a man all women are
desirable, and he can never get enough as long as he lives.
18 The man who is unfaithful to his wife thinks to himself,
"No one will ever know. It's dark in here, and no one sees
me. I have nothing to worry about. As for the Most High, he
won't even notice." 19 This man is only afraid of other people. He doesn't realize that the eyes of the Lord are 10,000
times brighter than the sun, that he sees everything we do,
even when we try to hide it. 20 He knew everything before he
created the world, as well as after. 21 That sinful man will be
caught when he least expects it, and punished publicly.
22 The same is true of a woman who is unfaithful to her
husband and presents him with a child by another man.

NEW REVISED STANDARD VERSION

16 Two kinds of individuals multiply sins,
and a third incurs wrath.
Hot passion that blazes like a fire
will not be quenched until it burns itself out;
one who commits fornication with his near of kin
will never cease until the fire burns him up.
17 To a fornicator all bread is sweet;
he will never weary until he dies.
18 The one who sins against his marriage bed
says to himself, "Who can see me?
Darkness surrounds me, the walls hide me,
and no one sees me. Why should I worry?
The Most High will not remember sins."
19 His fear is confined to human eyes
and he does not realize that the eyes of the Lord
are ten thousand times brighter than the sun;
they look upon every aspect of human behavior
and see into hidden corners.
20 Before the universe was created, it was known to him,
and so it is since its completion.
21 This man will be punished in the streets of the city,
and where he least suspects it, he will be seized.

22 So it is with a woman who leaves her husband
and presents him with an heir by another man.

NEW AMERICAN BIBLE

16 Two types of men multiply sins,
a third draws down wrath;
For burning passion is a blazing fire,
not to be quenched till it burns itself out:
A man given to sins of the flesh,
who never stops until the fire breaks forth;
17 The rake to whom all bread is sweet
and who is never through till he dies;
18 And the man who dishonors his marriage bed
and says to himself, "Who can see me?
Darkness surrounds me, walls hide me;
no one sees me; why should I fear to sin?"
Of the Most High he is not mindful,
19 fearing only the eyes of men;
He does not understand that the eyes of the LORD,
ten thousand times brighter than the sun,
Observe every step a man takes
and peer into hidden corners.
20 He who knows all things before they exist
still knows them all after they are made.
21 Such a man will be punished in the streets of the city;
when he least expects it, he will be apprehended.

22 So also with the woman who is unfaithful to her
husband
and offers as heir her son by a stranger.

NEW JERUSALEM BIBLE

16 There are two types of people who commit sin after sin
and a third who attracts retribution—
17 desire, blazing like a furnace,
will not die down until it has been sated—
the man who lusts after members of his own family
is not going to stop until he is quite burnt out;
every food is sweet to the promiscuous,
and he will not desist until he dies;
18 and the man who sins against the marriage bed
and says to himself, 'Who can see me?
There is darkness all round me, the walls hide me,
no one can see me, why should I worry?
The Most High will not remember my sins.'
19 What he fears are human eyes,
he does not realise that the eyes of the Lord
are ten thousand times brighter than the sun,
observing every aspect of human behaviour,
seeing into the most secret corners.
20 All things were known to him before they were created,
and are still, now that they are finished.
21 This man will be punished in view of the whole town,
and will be seized when he least expects it.

22 Similarly the woman unfaithful to her husband,
who provides him with an heir by another man:

GREEK OLD TESTAMENT

[23]πρῶτον μὲν γὰρ ἐν νόμῳ ὑψίστου ἠπείθησεν,
καὶ δεύτερον εἰς ἄνδρα αὐτῆς ἐπλημμέλησεν,
καὶ τὸ τρίτον ἐν πορνείᾳ ἐμοιχεύθη
καὶ ἐξ ἀλλοτρίου ἀνδρὸς τέκνα παρέστησεν.
[24]αὕτη εἰς ἐκκλησίαν ἐξαχθήσεται,
καὶ ἐπὶ τὰ τέκνα αὐτῆς ἐπισκοπὴ ἔσται.
[25]οὐ διαδώσουσιν τὰ τέκνα αὐτῆς εἰς ῥίζαν,
καὶ οἱ κλάδοι αὐτῆς οὐκ οἴσουσιν καρπόν.
[26]καταλείψει εἰς κατάραν τὸ μνημόσυνον αὐτῆς,
καὶ τὸ ὄνειδος αὐτῆς οὐκ ἐξαλειφθήσεται,
[27]καὶ ἐπιγνώσονται οἱ καταλειφθέντες
ὅτι οὐθὲν κρεῖττον φόβου κυρίου
καὶ οὐθὲν γλυκύτερον τοῦ προσέχειν ἐντολαῖς κυρίου.

24 Ἡ σοφία αἰνέσει ψυχὴν αὐτῆς
καὶ ἐν μέσῳ λαοῦ αὐτῆς καυχήσεται·
[2]ἐν ἐκκλησίᾳ ὑψίστου στόμα αὐτῆς ἀνοίξει
καὶ ἔναντι δυνάμεως αὐτοῦ καυχήσεται
[3]Ἐγὼ ἀπὸ στόματος ὑψίστου ἐξῆλθον
καὶ ὡς ὁμίχλη κατεκάλυψα γῆν·

KING JAMES VERSION

23 For first, she hath disobeyed the law of the most High; and secondly, she hath trespassed against her own husband; and thirdly, she hath played the whore in adultery, and brought children by another man.

24 She shall be brought out into the congregation, and inquisition shall be made of her children.

25 Her children shall not take root, and her branches shall bring forth no fruit.

26 She shall leave her memory to be cursed, and her reproach shall not be blotted out.

27 And they that remain shall know that there is nothing better than the fear of the Lord, and that there is nothing sweeter than to take heed unto the commandments of the Lord.

28 It is great glory to follow the Lord, and to be received of him is long life.

24 Wisdom shall praise herself, and shall glory in the midst of her people.

2 In the congregation of the most High shall she open her mouth, and triumph before his power.

3 I came out of the mouth of the most High, and covered the earth as a cloud.

DOUAY OLD TESTAMENT

33 For first she hath been unfaithful to the law of the most High: and secondly, she hath offended against her husband: thirdly, she hath fornicated in adultery, and hath gotten her children of another man.

34 This woman shall be brought into the assembly, and inquisition shall be made of her children.

35 Her children shall not take root, and her branches shall bring forth no fruit.

36 She shall leave her memory to be cursed, and her infamy shall not be blotted out.

37 And they that remain shall know, that there is nothing better than the fear of God: and that there is nothing sweeter than to have regard to the commandments of the Lord.

38 It is great glory to follow the Lord: for length of days shall be received from him.

24 WISDOM shall praise her own self, and shall be honoured in God, and shall glory in the midst of her people,

2 And shall open her mouth in the churches of the most High, and shall glorify herself in the sight of his power,

3 And in the midst of her own people she shall be exalted, and shall be admired in the holy assembly.

4 And in the multitude of the elect she shall have praise, and among the blessed she shall be blessed, saying:

5 I came out of the mouth of the most High, the firstborn before all creatures:

6 I made that in the heavens there should rise light that never faileth, and as a cloud I covered all the earth:

KNOX TRANSLATION

[33]Broken, the law of the most High; her plighted troth forsaken; sons borne to a paramour, has she not thrice played
the wanton? [34]Needs must she confront the folk assembled,
nor shall those sons of hers be spared; [35]such roots must
not burgeon, such boughs never bear fruit; [36]she leaves but
the memory of an accursed name, a name for ever dishonoured. [37]Warning she gives to after ages that God's fear is
best, nor sweeter lot is any than the divine law well
observed. [38]Follow the Lord, and it shall be thy renown; a
long life is the reward it shall bring thee.

24 Hear now how wisdom speaks in her own regard, of
the honour God has given her, of the boast she utters
among the nation that is hers. [2]In the court of the most
High, in the presence of all his host, she makes her boast
aloud, [3]and here, amid the holy gathering of her own people, that high renown of hers is echoed; [4]praise is hers from
God's chosen, blessing from blessed lips.

[5]I am that word, she says, that was uttered by the mouth
of the most High, the primal birth before ever creation began.
[6]Through me light rose in the heavens, inexhaustible; it was
I that covered, as with a mist, the earth. [7]In high heaven

TODAY'S ENGLISH VERSION

[23]In the first place, she has broken the Law of the Most High.
In the second place, she has wronged her husband. And in
the third place, she has made a whore of herself by committing adultery and bearing the child of a man not her husband. [24-25]The children will suffer for her sin. They will not
be able to find a place in society or establish families. She
herself will be brought before the assembly [26]and permanently disgraced. There will be a curse on her memory. After
she is gone, [27]everyone will realize that nothing is better
than fearing the Lord, nothing is sweeter than keeping his
commands.

24 Listen to Wisdom! She proudly sings her own praises
among the Israelites, her own people, [2]in the assembly of the Most High, in the presence of his power.[a]

[3]"I am the word spoken by the Most High.
I covered the earth like a mist.

[a] power; *or* angels.

NEW REVISED STANDARD VERSION

23 For first of all, she has disobeyed the law of the Most
High;
second, she has committed an offense against her
husband;
and third, through her fornication she has committed
adultery
and brought forth children by another man.
24 She herself will be brought before the assembly,
and her punishment will extend to her children.
25 Her children will not take root,
and her branches will not bear fruit.
26 She will leave behind an accursed memory
and her disgrace will never be blotted out.
27 Those who survive her will recognize
that nothing is better than the fear of the Lord,
and nothing sweeter than to heed the commandments
of the Lord.[a]

THE PRAISE OF WISDOM[b]

24 Wisdom praises herself,
and tells of her glory in the midst of her people.
2 In the assembly of the Most High she opens her mouth,
and in the presence of his hosts she tells of her glory:
3 "I came forth from the mouth of the Most High,
and covered the earth like a mist.

a Other ancient authorities add as verse 28, *It is a great honor to follow God, and to be received by him is long life.* *b* This heading is included in the Gk text.

NEW AMERICAN BIBLE

[23]First, she has disobeyed the law of the Most High;
secondly, she has wronged her husband;
Thirdly, in her wanton adultery
she has borne children by another man.
[24]Such a woman will be dragged before the assembly,
and her punishment will extend to her children;
[25]Her children will not take root;
her branches will not bring forth fruit.
[26]She will leave an accursed memory;
her disgrace will never be blotted out.
[27]Thus all who dwell on the earth shall know,
and all who inhabit the world shall understand,
That nothing is better than the fear of the LORD,
nothing more salutary than to obey his
commandments.

24 Wisdom sings her own praises,
before her own people she proclaims her glory;
[2]In the assembly of the Most High she opens her mouth,
in the presence of his hosts she declares her worth:
[3]"From the mouth of the Most High I came forth,
and mistlike covered the earth.

NEW JERUSALEM BIBLE

[23]first, she has disobeyed the Law of the Most High;
secondly, she has been false to her husband;
and thirdly, she has gone whoring in adultery
[24] and conceived children by another man.
She will be led before the assembly,
an enquiry will be held about her children.
[25]Her children will strike no root,
her branches will bear no fruit.
[26]She will leave an accursed memory behind her,
her shame will never be wiped out.
[27]And those who survive her will recognise
that nothing is better than fearing the Lord,
and nothing sweeter than adherence to the Lord's
commandments.

24 Wisdom[a] speaks her own praises,
in the midst of her people she glories in herself.
[2]She opens her mouth in the assembly of the Most High,
she glories in herself in the presence of the Mighty
One:
[3]'I came forth from the mouth of the Most High,
and I covered the earth like mist.

[a] **24** A high point: personified Wisdom shares God's throne (the cloud) but also chooses Israel for an inheritance and more specifically serves in the Temple. Sira then identifies Wisdom with the Law.

GREEK OLD TESTAMENT

[4]ἐγὼ ἐν ὑψηλοῖς κατεσκήνωσα,
καὶ ὁ θρόνος μου ἐν στύλῳ νεφέλης·
[5]γῦρον οὐρανοῦ ἐκύκλωσα μόνη
καὶ ἐν βάθει ἀβύσσων περιεπάτησα·
[6]ἐν κύμασιν θαλάσσης καὶ ἐν πάσῃ τῇ γῇ
καὶ ἐν παντὶ λαῷ καὶ ἔθνει ἐκτησάμην.
[7]μετὰ τούτων πάντων ἀνάπαυσιν ἐζήτησα
καὶ ἐν κληρονομίᾳ τίνος αὐλισθήσομαι.
[8]τότε ἐνετείλατό μοι ὁ κτίστης ἁπάντων,
καὶ ὁ κτίσας με κατέπαυσεν τὴν σκηνήν μου
καὶ εἶπεν Ἐν Ιακωβ κατασκήνωσον
καὶ ἐν Ισραηλ κατακληρονομήθητι.
[9]πρὸ τοῦ αἰῶνος ἀπ' ἀρχῆς ἔκτισέν με,
καὶ ἕως αἰῶνος οὐ μὴ ἐκλίπω.
[10]ἐν σκηνῇ ἁγίᾳ ἐνώπιον αὐτοῦ ἐλειτούργησα
καὶ οὕτως ἐν Σιων ἐστηρίχθην·
[11]ἐν πόλει ἠγαπημένῃ ὁμοίως με κατέπαυσεν,
καὶ ἐν Ιερουσαλημ ἡ ἐξουσία μου·
[12]καὶ ἐρρίζωσα ἐν λαῷ δεδοξασμένῳ,
ἐν μερίδι κυρίου, κληρονομίας αὐτοῦ.
[13]ὡς κέδρος ἀνυψώθην ἐν τῷ Λιβάνῳ
καὶ ὡς κυπάρισσος ἐν ὄρεσιν Αερμων·
[14]ὡς φοῖνιξ ἀνυψώθην ἐν Αιγγαδοις
καὶ ὡς φυτὰ ῥόδου ἐν Ιεριχω,

KING JAMES VERSION

4 I dwelt in high places, and my throne is in a cloudy pillar.

5 I alone compassed the circuit of heaven, and walked in the bottom of the deep.

6 In the waves of the sea, and in all the earth, and in every people and nation, I got a possession.

7 With all these I sought rest: and in whose inheritance shall I abide?

8 So the Creator of all things gave me a commandment, and he that made me caused my tabernacle to rest, and said, Let thy dwelling be in Jacob, and thine inheritance in Israel.

9 He created me from the beginning before the world, and I shall never fail.

10 In the holy tabernacle I served before him; and so was I established in Sion.

11 Likewise in the beloved city he gave me rest, and in Jerusalem was my power.

12 And I took root in an honourable people, even in the portion of the Lord's inheritance.

13 I was exalted like a cedar in Libanus, and as a cypress tree upon the mountains of Hermon.

14 I was exalted like a palm tree in En-gaddi, and as a

DOUAY OLD TESTAMENT

7 I dwelt in the highest places, and my throne is in a pillar of a cloud.

8 I alone have compassed the circuit of heaven, and have penetrated into the bottom of the deep, and have walked in the waves of the sea,

9 And have stood in all the earth: and in every people,

10 And in every nation I have had the chief rule:

11 And by my power I have trodden under my feet the hearts of all the high and low: and in all these I sought rest, and I shall abide in the inheritance of the Lord.

12 Then the creator of all things commanded, and said to me: and he that made me, rested in my tabernacle,

13 And he said to me: Let thy dwelling be in Jacob, and thy inheritance in Israel, and take root in my elect.

14 From the beginning, and before the world, was I created, and unto the world to come I shall not cease to be, and in the holy dwelling place I have ministered before him.

15 And so was I established in Sion, and in the holy city likewise I rested, and my power *was* in Jerusalem.

16 And I took root in an honourable people, and in the portion of my God his inheritance, and my abode is in the full assembly of saints.

17 I was exalted like a cedar in Libanus, and as a cypress tree on mount Sion.

18 I was exalted like a palm tree in Cades, and as a rose plant in Jericho:

KNOX TRANSLATION

was my dwelling-place, my throne a pillar of cloud; [8]none
but I might span the sky's vault, pierce the depth of the
abyss, walk on the sea's waves; [9]no part of earth but gave a
resting-place to my feet.

[10]People was none, nor any race of men, but I had dominion there; high and low, my power ruled over men's hearts.
[11]Yet with all these I sought rest in vain; it is among the
Lord's people that I mean to dwell. [12]He who fashioned me,
he, my own Creator, has found me a dwelling-place; [13]and
his command to me was that I should find my home in
Jacob, throw in my lot with Israel, take root among his chosen race. [14]From the beginning of time, before the worlds,
he had made me, unfailing to all eternity; in his own holy
dwelling-place I had waited on his presence; [15]and now, no
less faithfully, I made Sion my stronghold, the holy city my
resting-place, Jerusalem my throne. [16]My roots spread out
among the people that enjoys his favour, my God has granted me a share in his own domain; where his faithful servants are gathered I love to linger.

[17]I grew to my full stature as cedar grows on Lebanon, as
cypress on Sion's hill; [18]or a palm tree in Cades, or a rose-

TODAY'S ENGLISH VERSION

4 I made my home in highest heaven,
my throne on a pillar of cloud.
5 Alone I walked around the circle of the sky
and walked through the ocean beneath the earth.
6 I ruled over[a] all the earth and the ocean waves,
over every nation, over every people.
7 I looked everywhere for a place to settle,
some part of the world to make my home.
8 Then my Creator, who created the universe,
told me where I was to live.
'Make your home in Israel,' he said.
'The descendants of Jacob will be your people.'
9 He created me in eternity, before time began,
and I will exist for all eternity to come.
10 I served him in the Sacred Tent
and then made my home on Mount Zion.
11 He settled me in the Beloved City
and gave me authority over Jerusalem.
12 I put down roots among an honored people
whom the Lord had chosen as his own.
13 I grew tall, like the cedars in Lebanon,
like the cypresses on Mount Hermon,
14 like the palm trees of Engedi,[b]
like the roses of Jericho,

[a] ruled over; *some manuscripts have* gained possession of.
[b] of Engedi; *some manuscripts have* on the seashore.

NEW REVISED STANDARD VERSION

4 I dwelt in the highest heavens,
and my throne was in a pillar of cloud.
5 Alone I compassed the vault of heaven
and traversed the depths of the abyss.
6 Over waves of the sea, over all the earth,
and over every people and nation I have held sway.[a]
7 Among all these I sought a resting place;
in whose territory should I abide?

8 "Then the Creator of all things gave me a command,
and my Creator chose the place for my tent.
He said, 'Make your dwelling in Jacob,
and in Israel receive your inheritance.'
9 Before the ages, in the beginning, he created me,
and for all the ages I shall not cease to be.
10 In the holy tent I ministered before him,
and so I was established in Zion.
11 Thus in the beloved city he gave me a resting place,
and in Jerusalem was my domain.
12 I took root in an honored people,
in the portion of the Lord, his heritage.

13 "I grew tall like a cedar in Lebanon,
and like a cypress on the heights of Hermon.
14 I grew tall like a palm tree in En-gedi,[b]
and like rosebushes in Jericho;

a Other ancient authorities read *I have acquired a possession* *b* Other ancient authorities read *on the beaches*

NEW AMERICAN BIBLE

4 In the highest heavens did I dwell,
my throne on a pillar of cloud.
5 The vault of heaven I compassed alone,
through the deep abyss I wandered.
6 Over waves of the sea, over all the land,
over every people and nation I held sway.
7 Among all these I sought a resting place;
in whose inheritance should I abide?

8 "Then the Creator of all gave me his command,
and he who formed me chose the spot for my tent,
Saying, 'In Jacob make your dwelling,
in Israel your inheritance.'
9 Before all ages, in the beginning, he created me,
and through all ages I shall not cease to be.
10 In the holy tent I ministered before him,
and in Zion I fixed my abode.
11 Thus in the chosen city he has given me rest,
in Jerusalem is my domain.
12 I have struck root among the glorious people,
in the portion of the LORD, his heritage.

13 "Like a cedar on Lebanon I am raised aloft,
like a cypress on Mount Hermon,
14 Like a palm tree in Engedi,
like a rosebush in Jericho,

NEW JERUSALEM BIBLE

4 I had my tent in the heights,
and my throne was a pillar of cloud.
5 Alone, I have made the circuit of the heavens
and walked through the depths of the abyss.
6 Over the waves of the sea and over the whole earth,
and over every people and nation I have held sway.
7 Among all these I searched for rest,
and looked to see in whose territory I might pitch camp.
8 Then the Creator of all things instructed me
and he who created me fixed a place for my tent.
He said, "Pitch your tent in Jacob,
make Israel your inheritance."
9 From eternity, in the beginning, he created me,
and for eternity I shall remain.
10 In the holy tent I ministered before him
and thus became established in Zion.
11 In the beloved city he has given me rest,
and in Jerusalem I wield my authority.
12 I have taken root in a privileged people,
in the Lord's property, in his inheritance.
13 I have grown tall as a cedar on Lebanon,
as a cypress on Mount Hermon;
14 I have grown tall as a palm in En-Gedi,
as the rose bushes of Jericho;

GREEK OLD TESTAMENT

ὡς ἐλαία εὐπρεπὴς ἐν πεδίῳ,
καὶ ἀνυψώθην ὡς πλάτανος.
15 ὡς κιννάμωμον καὶ ἀσπάλαθος ἀρωμάτων δέδωκα ὀσμὴν
καὶ ὡς σμύρνα ἐκλεκτὴ διέδωκα εὐωδίαν,
ὡς χαλβάνη καὶ ὄνυξ καὶ στακτὴ
καὶ ὡς λιβάνου ἀτμὶς ἐν σκηνῇ.
16 ἐγὼ ὡς τερέμινθος ἐξέτεινα κλάδους μου,
καὶ οἱ κλάδοι μου κλάδοι δόξης καὶ χάριτος.
17 ἐγὼ ὡς ἄμπελος ἐβλάστησα χάριν,
καὶ τὰ ἄνθη μου καρπὸς δόξης καὶ πλούτου.
19 προσέλθετε πρός με, οἱ ἐπιθυμοῦντές μου,
καὶ ἀπὸ τῶν γενημάτων μου ἐμπλήσθητε·
20 τὸ γὰρ μνημόσυνόν μου ὑπὲρ τὸ μέλι γλυκύ,
καὶ ἡ κληρονομία μου ὑπὲρ μέλιτος κηρίον.
21 οἱ ἐσθίοντές με ἔτι πεινάσουσιν,
καὶ οἱ πίνοντές με ἔτι διψήσουσιν.
22 ὁ ὑπακούων μου οὐκ αἰσχυνθήσεται,
καὶ οἱ ἐργαζόμενοι ἐν ἐμοὶ οὐχ ἁμαρτήσουσιν.
23 Ταῦτα πάντα βίβλος διαθήκης θεοῦ ὑψίστου,

KING JAMES VERSION

rose plant in Jericho, as a fair olive tree in a pleasant field, and grew up as a plane tree by the water.

15 I gave a sweet smell like cinnamon and aspalathus, and I yielded a pleasant odour like the best myrrh, as galbanum, and onyx, and sweet storax, and as the fume of frankincense in the tabernacle.

16 As the turpentine tree I stretched out my branches, and my branches are the branches of honour and grace.

17 As the vine brought I forth pleasant savour, and my flowers are the fruit of honour and riches.

18 I am the mother of fair love, and fear, and knowledge, and holy hope: I therefore, being eternal, am given to all my children which are named of him.

19 Come unto me, all ye that be desirous of me, and fill yourselves with my fruits.

20 For my memorial is sweeter than honey, and mine inheritance than the honeycomb.

21 They that eat me shall yet be hungry, and they that drink me shall yet be thirsty.

22 He that obeyeth me shall never be confounded, and they that work by me shall not do amiss.

23 All these things are the book of the covenant of the

DOUAY OLD TESTAMENT

19 As a fair olive tree in the plains, and as a plane tree by the water in the streets, was I exalted.

20 I gave a sweet smell like cinnamon, and aromatical balm: I yielded a sweet odour like the best myrrh:

21 And I perfumed my dwelling as storax, and galbanum, and onyx, and aloes, and as the frankincense not cut, and my odour is as the purest balm.

22 I have stretched out my branches as the turpentine tree, and my branches are of honour and grace.

23 As the vine I have brought forth a pleasant odour: and my flowers are the fruit of honour and riches.

24 I am the mother of fair love, and of fear, and of knowledge, and of holy hope.

25 In me is all grace of the way and of the truth, in me is all hope of life and of virtue.

26 Come over to me, all ye that desire me, and be filled with my fruits.

27 For my spirit is sweet above honey, and my inheritance above honey and the honeycomb.

28 My memory is unto everlasting generations.

29 They that eat me, shall yet hunger: and they that drink me, shall yet thirst.

30 He that hearkeneth to me, shall not be confounded: and they that work by me, shall not sin.

31 They that explain me shall have life everlasting.

32 All these things are the book of life, and the covenant of the most High, and the knowledge of truth.

KNOX TRANSLATION

bush in Jericho; 19 grew like some fair olive in the valley,
some plane-tree in a well-watered street. 20 Cinnamon and
odorous balm have no scent like mine; the choicest myrrh
has no such fragrance. 21 Perfumed is all my dwelling-place
with storax, and galbanum, and onycha, and stacte, and
frankincense uncrushed; the smell of me is like pure balm.
22 Mastic-tree spread not its branches so wide, as I the hopes
I proffer of glory and of grace. 23 No vine ever yielded fruit so
fragrant; the enjoyment of honour and riches is the fruit I
bear.
24 It is I that give birth to all noble loving, all reverence, all
true knowledge, and the holy gift of hope. 25 From me comes
every grace of faithful observance, from me all promise of life
and vigour. 26 Hither turn your steps, all you that have
learned to long for me; take your fill of the increase I yield.
27 Never was honey so sweet as the influence I inspire, never
honey-comb as the gift I bring; 28 mine is a renown that
endures, age after age. 29 Eat of this fruit, and you will yet
hunger for more; drink of this wine, and your thirst for it is
still unquenched. 30 He who listens to me will never be disappointed; he who lives by me will do no wrong; 31 he who
reads my lesson aright will find in it life eternal.
32 What things are these I write of? What but the life-
giving book that is the covenant of the most High, and the

TODAY'S ENGLISH VERSION

like beautiful olive trees in the fields,
like plane trees growing by the water.
15 My breath was the spicy smell of cinnamon,
of sweet perfume and finest myrrh,
of stacte, onycha, and galbanum,
the fragrant incense in the Sacred Tent.
16 Like an oak I spread out my branches,
magnificent and graceful.
17 Like a grapevine I put out lovely shoots;
my blossoms gave way to rich and glorious fruit.[a]
19 Come to me, all you that want me,
and eat your fill of my fruit.
20 You will remember me as sweeter than honey,
better than honey from the comb.
21 Eat me, and you will hunger for more;
drink me, and you will thirst for more.
22 Obey me, and you will never have cause for
embarrassment;
do as I say, and you will be safe from sin."

23 Wisdom is the Law, the Law which Moses commanded
us to keep, the covenant of God Most High, the inheritance

[a] *Some manuscripts add verse 18:* I am the mother of beautiful love, of fear, knowledge, and holy hope. Since I am eternal, I am given to all my children, who are named by him.

NEW REVISED STANDARD VERSION

like a fair olive tree in the field,
and like a plane tree beside water[a] I grew tall.
15 Like cassia and camel's thorn I gave forth perfume,
and like choice myrrh I spread my fragrance,
like galbanum, onycha, and stacte,
and like the odor of incense in the tent.
16 Like a terebinth I spread out my branches,
and my branches are glorious and graceful.
17 Like the vine I bud forth delights,
and my blossoms become glorious and abundant
fruit.[b]

19 "Come to me, you who desire me,
and eat your fill of my fruits.
20 For the memory of me is sweeter than honey,
and the possession of me sweeter than the
honeycomb.
21 Those who eat of me will hunger for more,
and those who drink of me will thirst for more.
22 Whoever obeys me will not be put to shame,
and those who work with me will not sin."

23 All this is the book of the covenant of the Most High
God,

a Other ancient authorities omit *beside water* b Other ancient authorities add as verse 18, *I am the mother of beautiful love, of fear, of knowledge, and of holy hope; being eternal, I am given to all my children, to those who are named by him.*

NEW AMERICAN BIBLE

Like a fair olive tree in the field,
like a plane tree growing beside the water.
15 Like cinnamon, or fragrant balm, or precious myrrh,
I give forth perfume;
Like galbanum and onycha and sweet spices,
like the odor of incense in the holy place.
16 I spread out my branches like a terebinth,
my branches so bright and so graceful.
17 I bud forth delights like the vine,
my blossoms become fruit fair and rich.
18 Come to me, all you that yearn for me,
and be filled with my fruits;
19 You will remember me as sweeter than honey,
better to have than the honeycomb.
20 He who eats of me will hunger still,
he who drinks of me will thirst for more;
21 He who obeys me will not be put to shame,
he who serves me will never fail."

22 All this is true of the book of the Most High's covenant,

NEW JERUSALEM BIBLE

as a fine olive in the plain,
as a plane tree, I have grown tall.
15 Like cinnamon and acanthus, I have yielded a perfume,
like choice myrrh, have breathed out a scent,
like galbanum, onycha, labdanum,
like the smoke of incense in the tent.
16 I have spread my branches like a terebinth,
and my branches are glorious and graceful.
17 I am like a vine putting out graceful shoots,
my blossoms bear the fruit of glory and wealth.
19 Approach me, you who desire me,
and take your fill of my fruits,
20 for memories of me are sweeter than honey,
inheriting me is sweeter than the honeycomb.
21 They who eat me will hunger for more,
they who drink me will thirst for more.
22 No one who obeys me will ever have to blush,
no one who acts as I dictate will ever sin.'

23 All this is no other than the Book of the Covenant of the
Most High God,

GREEK OLD TESTAMENT

νόμον ὃν ἐνετείλατο ἡμῖν Μωυσῆς
κληρονομίαν συναγωγαῖς Ιακωβ,
25 ὁ πιμπλῶν ὡς Φισων σοφίαν
καὶ ὡς Τίγρις ἐν ἡμέραις νέων,
26 ὁ ἀναπληρῶν ὡς Εὐφράτης σύνεσιν
καὶ ὡς Ιορδάνης ἐν ἡμέραις θερισμοῦ,
27 ὁ ἐκφαίνων ὡς φῶς παιδείαν,
ὡς Γηων ἐν ἡμέραις τρυγήτου.
28 οὐ συνετέλεσεν ὁ πρῶτος γνῶναι αὐτήν,
καὶ οὕτως ὁ ἔσχατος οὐκ ἐξιχνίασεν αὐτήν·
29 ἀπὸ γὰρ θαλάσσης ἐπληθύνθη διανόημα αὐτῆς
καὶ ἡ βουλὴ αὐτῆς ἀπὸ ἀβύσσου μεγάλης.
30 Κἀγὼ ὡς διῶρυξ ἀπὸ ποταμοῦ
καὶ ὡς ὑδραγωγὸς ἐξῆλθον εἰς παράδεισον·
31 εἶπα Ποτιῶ μου τὸν κῆπον
καὶ μεθύσω μου τὴν πρασιάν·
καὶ ἰδοὺ ἐγένετό μοι ἡ διῶρυξ εἰς ποταμόν,
καὶ ὁ ποταμός μου ἐγένετο εἰς θάλασσαν.
32 ἔτι παιδείαν ὡς ὄρθρον φωτιῶ
καὶ ἐκφανῶ αὐτὰ ἕως εἰς μακράν·
33 ἔτι διδασκαλίαν ὡς προφητείαν ἐκχεῶ
καὶ καταλείψω αὐτὴν εἰς γενεὰς αἰώνων.

KING JAMES VERSION

most high God, *even* the law which Moses commanded for an heritage unto the congregations of Jacob.

24 Faint not to be strong in the Lord; that he may confirm you, cleave unto him: for the Lord Almighty is God alone, and beside him there is no other Saviour.

25 He filleth all things with his wisdom, as Phison and as Tigris in the time of the new fruits.

26 He maketh the understanding to abound like Euphrates, and as Jordan in the time of the harvest.

27 He maketh the doctrine of knowledge appear as the light, and as Geon in the time of vintage.

28 The first man knew her not perfectly: no more shall the last find her out.

29 For her thoughts are more than the sea, and her counsels profounder than the great deep.

30 I also came out as a brook from a river, and as a conduit into a garden.

31 I said, I will water my best garden, and will water abundantly my garden bed: and, lo, my brook became a river, and my river became a sea.

32 I will yet make doctrine to shine as the morning, and will send forth her light afar off.

33 I will yet pour out doctrine as prophecy, and leave it to all ages for ever.

DOUAY OLD TESTAMENT

33 Moses commanded a law in the precepts of justices, and an inheritance to the house of Jacob, and the promises to Israel.

34 He appointed to David his servant to raise up of him a most mighty king, and sitting on the throne of glory for ever.

35 Who filleth up wisdom as the Phison, and as the Tigris in the days of the new fruits.

36 Who maketh understanding to abound as the Euphrates, who multiplieth it as the Jordan in the time of harvest.

37 Who sendeth knowledge as the light, and riseth up as Gehon in the time of the vintage.

38 Who first hath perfect knowledge of her, and a weaker shall not search her out.

39 For her thoughts are more vast than the sea, and her counsels more deep than the great ocean.

40 I, wisdom, have poured out rivers.

41 I, like a brook out of a river of a mighty water; I, like a channel of a river and like an aqueduct, came out of paradise.

42 I said: I will water my garden of plants, and I will water abundantly the fruits of my meadow.

43 And behold my brook became a great river, and my river came near to a sea:

44 For I make doctrine to shine forth to all as the morning light, and I will declare it afar off.

45 I will penetrate to all the lower parts of the earth, and will behold all that sleep, and will enlighten all that hope in the Lord.

46 I will yet pour out doctrine as prophecy, and will leave it to them that seek wisdom, and will not cease to instruct their offspring even to the holy age.

KNOX TRANSLATION

revelation of all truth? 33 What but the law Moses enjoined,
with the duties it prescribes, the inheritance it bestows, the
promises it holds out? 34 Solemnly he pledged himself to
give his servant David an heir most valiant, that should hold
his royal throne for ever. 35 Who but he[a] can make wisdom
flow, deep as the stream Phison sends down, or Tigris, in the
spring; 36 make the tide of prudence run, strong as
Euphrates' own, or Jordan's tide in the month of harvest;
37 make obedience rise to its full height, like Nile[b] or Gehon
when men gather the vintage? 38 He it was that first attained
to wisdom's secret, never since made known to any less than
himself; 39 so deep are her thoughts, sea-deep, so dark her
counsels, dark as the great abyss.

40 From me rivers flow, says Wisdom, deep rivers.

41 And what am I?[c] A conduit that carries off the river's
overflow, its channel, the aqueduct that waters a park. 42 I
thought to refresh my well-set garden, give drink to the fruits
that fringe its border; 43 and all at once my channel overflowed, this stream of mine had nigh turned into a sea!
44 Teaching is here like the dawn for brightness, shedding its
rays afar. 45 Nay, I will make my way down to the depths of
earth, and visit those who sleep there, and to such as trust in
the Lord I will bring light. 46 My teaching shall yet flow on,
faithful as prophecy, heirloom to all such as make wisdom

a Some would render, 'What but this...', referring to the Law of Moses.
b Both the Latin and the Greek have, 'like the light'; but the context makes it clear that they have overlooked a single vowel in the word which must have stood in the Hebrew original. *c* *vv.* 41-46: Commentators are not agreed whether these words are to be understood as spoken by Wisdom, like verse 40, or by Ecclesiasticus himself, like verse 47 (cf. 33. 18 below).

TODAY'S ENGLISH VERSION

of the synagogues of Israel.[a] 25 The Law overflows with
Wisdom like the Pishon River, like the Tigris at fruit-picking
time. 26 The Law brims over with understanding like the
Euphrates, like the Jordan at harvest time. 27 It sparkles with
teachings like the Nile,[b] like the Gihon at grape-picking time.
28 The first human being ever created never knew Wisdom
completely, and the last person on earth will be no more successful. 29 The possibilities of Wisdom are vaster than the
ocean; her resources are more profound than the deepest
waters beneath the earth.
30 As for me, I thought of myself as an irrigation canal
bringing water from a river into a garden. 31 I only intended
to water my orchard and flower beds, but the canal soon
became a river, and the river became a sea. 32 And so I
present you with my learning; I hold it high, so that its light
can be seen everywhere, like that of the rising sun. 33 Like
an inspired prophet, I pour out my teachings, so that future
generations can benefit from them. 34 Please realize that I

[a] *Some manuscripts add verse 24:* Always be strong in the Lord; stay with him, so that he may make you strong. There is no God but the Lord Almighty, and no savior except him. [b] *One ancient translation* It sparkles . . . Nile; *Greek* It makes teachings shine like light.

NEW REVISED STANDARD VERSION

the law that Moses commanded us
as an inheritance for the congregations of Jacob.[a]
25 It overflows, like the Pishon, with wisdom,
and like the Tigris at the time of the first fruits.
26 It runs over, like the Euphrates, with understanding,
and like the Jordan at harvest time.
27 It pours forth instruction like the Nile,[b]
like the Gihon at the time of vintage.
28 The first man did not know wisdom[c] fully,
nor will the last one fathom her.
29 For her thoughts are more abundant than the sea,
and her counsel deeper than the great abyss.

30 As for me, I was like a canal from a river,
like a water channel into a garden.
31 I said, "I will water my garden
and drench my flower-beds."
And lo, my canal became a river,
and my river a sea.
32 I will again make instruction shine forth like the dawn,
and I will make it clear from far away.
33 I will again pour out teaching like prophecy,
and leave it to all future generations.

[a] Other ancient authorities add as verse 24, *"Do not cease to be strong in the Lord, cling to him so that he may strengthen you; the Lord Almighty alone is God, and besides him there is no savior."* [b] Syr: Gk *It makes instruction shine forth like light* [c] Gk *her*

NEW AMERICAN BIBLE

the law which Moses commanded us
as an inheritance for the community of Jacob.
23 It overflows, like the Pishon, with wisdom—
like the Tigris in the days of the new fruits.
24 It runs over, like the Euphrates, with understanding,
like the Jordan at harvest time.
25 It sparkles like the Nile with knowledge,
like the Gihon at vintage time.
26 The first man never finished comprehending wisdom,
nor will the last succeed in fathoming her.
27 For deeper than the sea are her thoughts;
her counsels, than the great abyss.
28 Now I, like a rivulet from her stream,
channeling the waters into a garden,
29 Said to myself, "I will water my plants,
my flower bed I will drench";
And suddenly this rivulet of mine became a river,
then this stream of mine, a sea.
30 Thus do I send my teachings forth shining like the
dawn,
to become known afar off.
31 Thus do I pour out instruction like prophecy
and bestow it on generations to come.

NEW JERUSALEM BIBLE

the Law that Moses enjoined on us,
an inheritance for the communities of Jacob.
25 This is what makes wisdom brim over like the Pishon,
like the Tigris in the season of fruit,
26 what makes intelligence overflow like the Euphrates,
like the Jordan at harvest time;
27 and makes discipline flow like the Nile,
like the Gihon when the grapes are harvested.
28 The first man did not finish discovering about her,
nor has the most recent tracked her down;
29 for her thoughts are wider than the sea,
and her designs more profound than the abyss.
30 And I, like a conduit from a river,
like a watercourse running into a garden,
31 I said, 'I am going to water my orchard,
I intend to irrigate my flower beds.'
And see, my conduit has grown into a river,
and my river has grown into a sea.
32 Making discipline shine forth from daybreak,
I shall send its light far and wide.
33 I shall pour out teaching like prophecy,
as a legacy to all future generations.

GREEK OLD TESTAMENT

34 ἴδετε ὅτι οὐκ ἐμοὶ μόνῳ ἐκοπίασα,
ἀλλ' ἅπασιν τοῖς ἐκζητοῦσιν αὐτήν.

25 Ἐν τρισὶν ὡραΐσθην καὶ ἀνέστην ὡραία
ἔναντι κυρίου καὶ ἀνθρώπων·
ὁμόνοια ἀδελφῶν, καὶ φιλία τῶν πλησίον,
καὶ γυνὴ καὶ ἀνὴρ ἑαυτοῖς συμπεριφερόμενοι.
2 τρία δὲ εἴδη ἐμίσησεν ἡ ψυχή μου
καὶ προσώχθισα σφόδρα τῇ ζωῇ αὐτῶν·
πτωχὸν ὑπερήφανον, καὶ πλούσιον ψεύστην,
γέροντα μοιχὸν ἐλαττούμενον συνέσει.
3 Ἐν νεότητι οὐ συναγείοχας,
καὶ πῶς ἂν εὕροις ἐν τῷ γήρᾳ σου;
4 ὡς ὡραῖον πολιαῖς κρίσις
καὶ πρεσβυτέροις ἐπιγνῶναι βουλήν.
5 ὡς ὡραία γερόντων σοφία
καὶ δεδοξασμένοις διανόημα καὶ βουλή.
6 στέφανος γερόντων πολυπειρία,
καὶ τὸ καύχημα αὐτῶν φόβος κυρίου.
7 Ἐννέα ὑπονοήματα ἐμακάρισα ἐν καρδίᾳ
καὶ τὸ δέκατον ἐρῶ ἐπὶ γλώσσης·
ἄνθρωπος εὐφραινόμενος ἐπὶ τέκνοις,
ζῶν καὶ βλέπων ἐπὶ πτώσει ἐχθρῶν·

KING JAMES VERSION

34 Behold that I have not laboured for myself only, but for all them that seek wisdom.

25 In three things I was beautified, and stood up beautiful both before God and men: the unity of brethren, the love of neighbours, a man and a wife that agree together.

2 Three sorts of men my soul hateth, and I am greatly offended at their life: a poor man that is proud, a rich man that is a liar, and an old adulterer that doateth.

3 If thou hast gathered nothing in thy youth, how canst thou find any thing in thine age?

4 O how comely a thing is judgment for gray hairs, and for ancient men to know counsel!

5 O how comely is the wisdom of old men, and understanding and counsel to men of honour!

6 Much experience is the crown of old men, and the fear of God is their glory.

7 There be nine things which I have judged in mine heart to be happy, and the tenth I will utter with my tongue: A man that hath joy of his children; and he that liveth to see the fall of his enemy:

DOUAY OLD TESTAMENT

47 See ye that I have not laboured for myself only, but for all that seek out the truth.

25 WITH three things my spirit is pleased, which are approved before God and men:

2 The concord of brethren, and the love of neighbours, and man and wife that agree well together.

3 Three sorts my soul hateth, and I am greatly grieved at their life:

4 A poor man that is proud: a rich man that is a liar: an old man that is a fool, and doting.

5 The things that thou hast not gathered in thy youth, how shalt thou find them in thy old age?

6 O how comely is judgment for a grey head, and for ancients to know counsel!

7 O how comely is wisdom for the aged, and understanding and counsel to men of honour!

8 Much experience is the crown of old men, and the fear of God is their glory.

9 Nine things that are not to be imagined by the heart have I magnified, and the tenth I will utter to men with my tongue.

10 A man that hath joy of his children: and he that liveth and seeth the fall of his enemies.

KNOX TRANSLATION

their quest, and to their children yet, until the holy days
come. 47 See how I have toiled, not for my own sake merely,
but for all such as covet wisdom!

25 Three sights warm my heart; God and man wish
them well: 2 peace in the clan, good will among
neighbours, man and wife well matched. 3 Three sorts of
men move my spleen, so that I am fain to grudge them life
itself: 4 poor man that is proud, rich man that is a liar, old
man that is fond and foolish.

5 The store youth never puts by, shall old age enjoy?
6 Good judgement well matches grey hairs, for still the elders
must be men of prudence; 7 wisdom for the old, discernment
for senators, and the gift of counsel! 8 No crown have old
men like their long experience, no ornament like the fear of
God.

9 Nine envious thoughts came suddenly into my mind, and
a tenth I will add for good measure. 10 Happy is he that has
joy of his children; that lives to see his enemies' downfall.

TODAY'S ENGLISH VERSION

have not done all this hard work for myself alone, but to
help anyone who wants to be wise.

25 There are three things in which I take special
delight—things that are beautiful to the Lord and
people alike:[a]
brothers who get along with each other,
neighbors who are friends,
and a married couple who are happy together.
2 There are three kinds of people I cannot stand, whose
behavior I find highly offensive:
poor people who are arrogant,
rich people who lie,
and foolish old men who commit adultery.
3 Unless you learn what you can while you are young, you
will never be wise when you reach old age. 4 Sound judgment, good advice, and gray hair go together beautifully.
5 Wisdom, understanding, and sound counsel are appropriate
to the aged and the respected. 6 Elderly people wear the
crown of long experience, and they can boast of nothing
finer than their fear of the Lord.
7 I will tell you about ten kinds of people that I feel fortunate to know, especially fortunate in the case of the tenth:
someone who takes pride in his children,
someone who lives to see his enemies fall,

[a] *Some ancient translations* There are . . . alike; *Greek* I was made beautiful in three ways and I stood before the Lord and people in beauty.

NEW REVISED STANDARD VERSION

34 Observe that I have not labored for myself alone,
but for all who seek wisdom.[a]

25 I take pleasure in three things,
and they are beautiful in the sight of God and of
mortals:[b]
agreement among brothers and sisters, friendship
among neighbors,
and a wife and a husband who live in harmony.
2 I hate three kinds of people,
and I loathe their manner of life:
a pauper who boasts, a rich person who lies,
and an old fool who commits adultery.

3 If you gathered nothing in your youth,
how can you find anything in your old age?
4 How attractive is sound judgment in the gray-haired,
and for the aged to possess good counsel!
5 How attractive is wisdom in the aged,
and understanding and counsel in the venerable!
6 Rich experience is the crown of the aged,
and their boast is the fear of the Lord.

7 I can think of nine whom I would call blessed,
and a tenth my tongue proclaims:
a man who can rejoice in his children;
a man who lives to see the downfall of his foes.

a Gk *her* *b* Syr Lat: Gk *In three things I was beautiful and I stood in beauty before the Lord and mortals.*

NEW AMERICAN BIBLE

25 With three things I am delighted,
for they are pleasing to the LORD and to men:
Harmony among brethren, friendship among neighbors,
and the mutual love of husband and wife.
2 Three kinds of men I hate;
their manner of life I loathe indeed:
A proud pauper, a rich dissembler,
and an old man lecherous in his dotage.

3 What you have not saved in your youth,
how will you acquire in your old age?
4 How becoming to the gray-haired is judgment,
and a knowledge of counsel to those on in years!
5 How becoming to the aged is wisdom,
understanding and prudence to the venerable!
6 The crown of old men is wide experience;
their glory, the fear of the LORD.

7 There are nine who come to my mind as blessed,
a tenth whom my tongue proclaims:
The man who finds joy in his children,
and he who lives to see his enemies' downfall.

NEW JERUSALEM BIBLE

34 And note, I have been working not merely for myself,
but for all who are seeking wisdom.

25 There are three things my soul delights in,
and which are delightful to God and to all people:
concord between brothers, friendship between
neighbours,
and a wife and husband who live happily together.
2 There are three sorts of people my soul hates,
and whose existence I consider an outrage:
the poor swollen with pride, the rich who is a liar
and an adulterous old man who has no sense.

3 If you have gathered nothing in your youth,
how can you discover anything in your old age?
4 How fine a thing: sound judgement with grey hairs,
and for greybeards to know how to advise!
5 How fine a thing: wisdom in the aged,
and considered advice coming from people of
distinction!
6 The crown of the aged is ripe experience,
their glory, the fear of the Lord.
7 There are nine things I can think of which strike me as
happy,
and a tenth which is now on my tongue:
the man who can be proud of his children,
he who lives to see the downfall of his enemies;

GREEK OLD TESTAMENT

8 μακάριος ὁ συνοικῶν γυναικὶ συνετῇ,
καὶ ὃς ἐν γλώσσῃ οὐκ ὠλίσθησεν,
καὶ ὃς οὐκ ἐδούλευσεν ἀναξίῳ ἑαυτοῦ·
9 μακάριος ὃς εὗρεν φρόνησιν,
καὶ ὁ διηγούμενος εἰς ὦτα ἀκουόντων·
10 ὡς μέγας ὁ εὑρὼν σοφίαν·
ἀλλ' οὐκ ἔστιν ὑπὲρ τὸν φοβούμενον τὸν κύριον·
11 φόβος κυρίου ὑπὲρ πᾶν ὑπερέβαλεν,
ὁ κρατῶν αὐτοῦ τίνι ὁμοιωθήσεται;
13 Πᾶσαν πληγὴν καὶ μὴ πληγὴν καρδίας,
καὶ πᾶσαν πονηρίαν καὶ μὴ πονηρίαν γυναικός·
14 πᾶσαν ἐπαγωγὴν καὶ μὴ ἐπαγωγὴν μισούντων,
καὶ πᾶσαν ἐκδίκησιν καὶ μὴ ἐκδίκησιν ἐχθρῶν.
15 οὐκ ἔστιν κεφαλὴ ὑπὲρ κεφαλὴν ὄφεως,
καὶ οὐκ ἔστιν θυμὸς ὑπὲρ θυμὸν ἐχθροῦ.
16 συνοικῆσαι λέοντι καὶ δράκοντι εὐδοκήσω
ἢ συνοικῆσαι μετὰ γυναικὸς πονηρᾶς.
17 πονηρία γυναικὸς ἀλλοιοῖ τὴν ὅρασιν αὐτῆς
καὶ σκοτοῖ τὸ πρόσωπον αὐτῆς ὡς ἄρκος·

KING JAMES VERSION

8 Well is him that dwelleth with a wife of understanding, and that hath not slipped with his tongue, and that hath not served a man more unworthy than himself:

9 Well is him that hath found prudence, and he that speaketh in the ears of them that will hear:

10 O how great is he that findeth wisdom! yet is there none above him that feareth the Lord.

11 But the love of the Lord passeth all things for illumination: he that holdeth it, whereto shall he be likened?

12 The fear of the Lord is the beginning of his love: and faith is the beginning of cleaving unto him.

13 [Give me] any plague, but the plague of the heart: and any wickedness, but the wickedness of a woman:

14 And any affliction, but the affliction from them that hate me: and any revenge, but the revenge of enemies.

15 There is no head above the head of a serpent; and there is no wrath above the wrath of an enemy.

16 I had rather dwell with a lion and a dragon, than to keep house with a wicked woman.

17 The wickedness of a woman changeth her face, and darkeneth her countenance like sackcloth.

DOUAY OLD TESTAMENT

11 Blessed is he that dwelleth with a wise woman, and that hath not slipped with his tongue, and that hath not served such as are unworthy of him.

12 Blessed is he that findeth a true friend, and that declareth justice to an ear that heareth.

13 How great is he that findeth wisdom and knowledge! but there is none above him that feareth the Lord.

14 The fear of God hath set itself above all things:

15 Blessed is the man, to whom it is given to have the fear of God: he that holdeth it, to whom shall he be likened?

16 The fear of God is the beginning of his love: and the beginning of faith is to be fast joined unto it.

17 The sadness of the heart is every plague: and the wickedness of a woman is all evil.

18 And a man will choose any plague, but the plague of the heart:

19 And any wickedness, but the wickedness of a woman:

20 And any affliction, but the affliction from them that hate him:

21 And any revenge, but the revenge of enemies.

22 There is no head worse than the head of a serpent:

23 And there is no anger above the anger of a woman. It will be more agreeable to abide with a lion and a dragon, than to dwell with a wicked woman.

24 The wickedness of a woman changeth her face: and she darkeneth her countenance as a bear: and sheweth it like sackcloth. In the midst of her neighbours,

KNOX TRANSLATION

11 Happiness it is to share thy home with a faithful wife; to
have a tongue that never betrays thee; to serve only thy betters. 12 Happiness it is to have a true friend...[a] and to speak
the right word to an ear that listens. 13 Happy is he that wisdom gains and skill; yet is he no match for one who fears the
Lord. 14 The fear of God, is a gift beyond all gifts; 15 blessed
the man that receives it, he has no equal. 16 Fear the Lord,
and thou shalt learn to love him; cling close, and thou shalt
learn to trust him.

17 There is no sadness but what touches the heart, no mischief but what comes from woman. 18 A man will endure
any wound but the heart's wound, 19 and any malice but a
woman's; 20 just so he will endure any annoyance but from
his ill-wishers, 21 any sentence imposed on him but by his
enemies.[b] 22 No head so venomous as the viper's, nor any
anger like a woman's. 23 Better share thy home with lion
and serpent both, than with an ill woman's company. 24 A
woman's ill will changes the very look of her; grim as a
bear's her visage, and she goes like one mourning. See

a It seems possible that one of the nine beatitudes has fallen out through a textual error, unless we reckon wisdom and skill in verse 13 as separate sources of happiness. *b* *vv.* 20, 21: It is difficult to feel certain that our versions have preserved the exact sense of the original. These two verses entirely break up the continuity of the context; in verse 23 the Greek makes matters worse by giving us 'like an enemy's' instead of 'like a woman's'. The word translated 'sentence' in verse 21 is literally 'vengeance'; and it is hard to see from what other class of people than one's enemies vengeance could reasonably be expected.

TODAY'S ENGLISH VERSION

8 a man fortunate enough to have an understanding wife,
a married couple who are well-matched, [a]
a person who never speaks sinfully,
a person who doesn't have to work for someone less competent than himself,
9 someone fortunate enough to have a real friend, [b]
a person that people are happy to listen to,
10 and the really great one: someone who is wise.
But the greatest one of all is the person who fears the Lord.
11 Such a person has no equal, because the fear of the Lord
is the most important thing in the world. [c]
13 No wound is as serious as wounded love. No troubles
are as serious as the troubles that women cause. 14 No sufferings are worse than the sufferings caused by people who
hate you. No revenge is worse than revenge taken by an
enemy. 15 No poison is deadlier than the poison of a snake,
and no anger is deadlier than the anger of a woman. [d]
16 I would rather live in the same house with a lion or a
dragon than with a bad wife. 17 When a wife is in a bad
mood, her expression changes until she looks like an angry

[a] *Hebrew and one ancient translation* a married couple . . . well-matched; *Greek does not have these words.* [b] *Some ancient translations* real friend; *Greek* good sense. [c] *Some manuscripts add verse 12:* Fearing the Lord is the first step toward loving him, and faith is the first step toward loyalty to him. [d] *Some ancient translations* woman; *Greek* enemy.

NEW REVISED STANDARD VERSION

8 Happy the man who lives with a sensible wife,
and the one who does not plow with ox and ass together. [a]
Happy is the one who does not sin with the tongue,
and the one who has not served an inferior.
9 Happy is the one who finds a friend, [b]
and the one who speaks to attentive listeners.
10 How great is the one who finds wisdom!
But none is superior to the one who fears the Lord.
11 Fear of the Lord surpasses everything;
to whom can we compare the one who has it? [c]

13 Any wound, but not a wound of the heart!
Any wickedness, but not the wickedness of a woman!
14 Any suffering, but not suffering from those who hate!
And any vengeance, but not the vengeance of enemies!
15 There is no venom [d] worse than a snake's venom, [d]
and no anger worse than a woman's [e] wrath.

16 I would rather live with a lion and a dragon
than live with an evil woman.
17 A woman's wickedness changes her appearance,
and darkens her face like that of a bear.

a Heb Syr: Gk lacks *and the one who does not plow with ox and ass together* *b* Lat Syr: Gk *good sense* *c* Other ancient authorities add as verse 12, *The fear of the Lord is the beginning of love for him, and faith is the beginning of clinging to him.* *d* Syr: Gk *head* *e* Other ancient authorities read *an enemy's*

NEW AMERICAN BIBLE

8 Happy is he who dwells with a sensible wife,
and he who plows not like a donkey yoked with an ox.
Happy is he who sins not with his tongue,
and he who serves not his inferior.
9 Happy is he who finds a friend
and he who speaks to attentive ears.
10 He who finds wisdom is great indeed,
but not greater than he who fears the LORD.
11 Fear of the LORD surpasses all else,
its possessor is beyond compare.

12 Worst of all wounds is that of the heart,
worst of all evils is that of a woman.
13 Worst of all sufferings is that from one's foes,
worst of all vengeance is that of one's enemies:
14 No poison worse than that of a serpent,
no venom greater than that of a woman.
15 With a dragon or a lion I would rather dwell
than live with an evil woman.
16 Wickedness changes a woman's looks,
and makes her sullen as a female bear.

NEW JERUSALEM BIBLE

8 happy is he who keeps house with a sensible wife;
he who does not toil with ox and donkey; [a]
he who has never sinned with his tongue;
he who does not serve a man less worthy than himself;
9 happy is he who has acquired good sense
and can find attentive ears for what he has to say;
10 how great is he who has acquired wisdom;
but unsurpassed is one who fears the Lord.
11 The fear of the Lord surpasses everything;
what can compare with someone who has mastered that?

13 Any wound rather than a wound of the heart!
Any spite rather than the spite of woman!
14 Any evil rather than an evil caused by an enemy!
Any vengeance rather than the vengeance of a foe!
15 There is no poison worse than the poison of a snake,
there is no fury worse than the fury of an enemy.
16 I would sooner keep house with a lion or a dragon
than keep house with a spiteful wife.

17 A woman's spite changes her appearance
and makes her face as grim as a bear's.

[a] **25** Such an uneven team is prohibited by Dt 22:10.

GREEK OLD TESTAMENT

18 ἀνὰ μέσον τῶν πλησίον αὐτοῦ ἀναπεσεῖται ὁ ἀνὴρ αὐτῆς
καὶ ἀκουσίως ἀνεστέναξεν πικρά.
19 μικρὰ πᾶσα κακία πρὸς κακίαν γυναικός,
κλῆρος ἁμαρτωλοῦ ἐπιπέσοι αὐτῇ.
20 ἀνάβασις ἀμμώδης ἐν ποσὶν πρεσβυτέρου,
οὕτως γυνὴ γλωσσώδης ἀνδρὶ ἡσύχῳ.
21 μὴ προσπέσῃς ἐπὶ κάλλος γυναικὸς
καὶ γυναῖκα μὴ ἐπιποθήσῃς.
22 ὀργὴ καὶ ἀναίδεια καὶ αἰσχύνη μεγάλη
γυνὴ ἐὰν ἐπιχορηγῇ τῷ ἀνδρὶ αὐτῆς.
23 καρδία ταπεινὴ καὶ πρόσωπον σκυθρωπὸν
καὶ πληγὴ καρδίας γυνὴ πονηρά·
χεῖρες παρειμέναι καὶ γόνατα παραλελυμένα
ἥτις οὐ μακαριεῖ τὸν ἄνδρα αὐτῆς.
24 ἀπὸ γυναικὸς ἀρχὴ ἁμαρτίας,
καὶ δι᾽ αὐτὴν ἀποθνῄσκομεν πάντες.
25 μὴ δῷς ὕδατι διέξοδον
μηδὲ γυναικὶ πονηρᾷ παρρησίαν·
26 εἰ μὴ πορεύεται κατὰ χεῖράς σου,
ἀπὸ τῶν σαρκῶν σου ἀπότεμε αὐτήν.

26 Γυναικὸς ἀγαθῆς μακάριος ὁ ἀνήρ,
καὶ ἀριθμὸς τῶν ἡμερῶν αὐτοῦ διπλάσιος.
2 γυνὴ ἀνδρεία εὐφραίνει τὸν ἄνδρα αὐτῆς,
καὶ τὰ ἔτη αὐτοῦ πληρώσει ἐν εἰρήνῃ.

KING JAMES VERSION

18 Her husband shall sit among his neighbours; and when he heareth it shall sigh bitterly.

19 All wickedness is but little to the wickedness of a woman: let the portion of a sinner fall upon her.

20 As the climbing up a sandy way is to the feet of the aged, so is a wife full of words to a quiet man.

21 Stumble not at the beauty of a woman, and desire her not for pleasure.

22 A woman, if she maintain her husband, is full of anger, impudence, and much reproach.

23 A wicked woman abateth the courage, maketh an heavy countenance and a wounded heart: a woman that will not comfort her husband in distress maketh weak hands and feeble knees.

24 Of the woman came the beginning of sin, and through her we all die.

25 Give the water no passage; neither a wicked woman liberty to gad abroad.

26 If she go not as thou wouldest have her, cut her off from thy flesh, and give her a bill of divorce, and let her go.

26 Blessed is the man that hath a virtuous wife, for the number of his days shall be double.

2 A virtuous woman rejoiceth her husband, and he shall fulfil the years of his life in peace.

DOUAY OLD TESTAMENT

25 Her husband groaned, and hearing he sighed a little.

26 All malice is short to the malice of a woman, let the lot of sinners fall upon her.

27 As the climbing of a sandy way is to the feet of the aged, so is a wife full of tongue to a quiet man.

28 Look not upon a woman's beauty, and desire not a woman for beauty.

29 A woman's anger, and impudence, and confusion is great.

30 A woman, if she have superiority, is contrary to her husband.

31 A wicked woman abateth the courage, and maketh a heavy countenance, and a wounded heart.

32 Feeble hands, and disjointed knees, a woman that doth not make her husband happy.

33 From the woman came the beginning of sin, and by her we all die.

34 Give no issue to thy water, no, not a little: nor to a wicked woman liberty to gad abroad.

35 If she walk not at thy hand, she will confound thee in the sight of thy enemies.

36 Cut her off from thy flesh, lest she always abuse thee.

26 HAPPY is the husband of a good wife: for the number of his years is double.

2 A virtuous woman rejoiceth her husband, and shall fulfil the years of his life in peace.

KNOX TRANSLATION

where he sits among his neighbours, 25 that husband of
hers, groaning deep and sighing as he listens to them! 26 All
other mischief is a slight thing beside the mischief an ill
woman does; may she fall to a sinner's lot! 27 Better climb
sandy cliff with the feet of old age, than be a peace-loving
man mated with a scold. 28 Let not thy eye be caught by a
woman's beauty; not for her beauty desire her; 29 think of
woman's rage, her shamelessness, the dishonour she can do
thee, 30 how hard it goes with a man if his wife will have the
uppermost. 31 Crushed spirits, a clouded brow, a heavy
heart, all this is an ill woman's work; 32 faint hand and flagging knee betoken one unblessed in his marriage. 33 Through
a woman sin first began; such fault was hers, we all must
die for it. 34 Thy cistern thou wouldst not let leak, ever so little; and wouldst thou let a wanton wife roam at large?
35 Leave she once thy side, thou shalt be the laughing-stock
of thy enemies; 36 best cut away the ill growth from thy
flesh; she will ever be taking advantage of thee.

26 Happy the man that has a faithful wife; his span of
days is doubled. 2 A wife industrious is the joy of her
husband, and crowns all his years with peace. 3 He best

TODAY'S ENGLISH VERSION

bear. [18]Her husband has to go and eat with the neighbors,
where he can't hold back his bitter sighs.
[19]Compared with the troubles caused by a woman, any
other trouble looks small. May such women suffer the fate of
sinners!
[20]A quiet man living with a nagging wife is like an old
man climbing up a sandy hill.
[21]Never lose your head over a woman's beauty, and don't
try to win a woman because she is wealthy.[a] [22]When a man
is supported by his wife, there is sure to be anger, arrogance,
and humiliation. [23]A bad wife will make her husband
gloomy and depressed, and break his heart. Show me a timid
man who can never make up his mind, and I will show you a
wife who doesn't make her husband happy. [24]Sin began
with a woman, and we must all die because of her. [25]Don't
let a bad wife have her way, any more than you would allow
water to leak from your cistern. [26]If she won't do as you tell
her, divorce her.

26 The husband of a good wife is a fortunate man; he
will live twice as long because of her. [2]A fine wife is
a joy to her husband, and he can live out his years in peace.

[a] *Hebrew* because she is wealthy; *Greek does not have these words.*

NEW REVISED STANDARD VERSION

18 Her husband sits[a] among the neighbors,
and he cannot help sighing[b] bitterly.
19 Any iniquity is small compared to a woman's iniquity;
may a sinner's lot befall her!
20 A sandy ascent for the feet of the aged—
such is a garrulous wife to a quiet husband.
21 Do not be ensnared by a woman's beauty,
and do not desire a woman for her possessions.[c]
22 There is wrath and impudence and great disgrace
when a wife supports her husband.
23 Dejected mind, gloomy face,
and wounded heart come from an evil wife.
Drooping hands and weak knees
come from the wife who does not make her husband
happy.
24 From a woman sin had its beginning,
and because of her we all die.
25 Allow no outlet to water,
and no boldness of speech to an evil wife.
26 If she does not go as you direct,
separate her from yourself.

26 Happy is the husband of a good wife;
the number of his days will be doubled.
2 A loyal wife brings joy to her husband,
and he will complete his years in peace.

a Heb Syr: Gk *loses heart* *b* Other ancient authorities read *and listening he sighs* *c* Heb Syr: Other Gk authorities read *for her beauty*

NEW AMERICAN BIBLE

[17]When her husband sits among his neighbors,
a bitter sigh escapes him unawares.
[18]There is scarce any evil like that in a woman;
may she fall to the lot of the sinner!
[19]Like a sandy hill to aged feet
is a railing wife to a quiet man.
[20]Stumble not through woman's beauty,
nor be greedy for her wealth;
[21]The man is a slave, in disgrace and shame,
when a wife supports her husband.
[22]Depressed mind, saddened face,
broken heart—this from an evil wife.
Feeble hands and quaking knees—
from a wife who brings no happiness to her husband.
[23]In woman was sin's beginning,
and because of her we all die.
[24]Allow water no outlet,
and be not indulgent to an erring wife.
[25]If she walks not by your side,
cut her away from you.

26 Happy the husband of a good wife,
twice-lengthened are his days;
[2]A worthy wife brings joy to her husband,
peaceful and full is his life.

NEW JERUSALEM BIBLE

[18]When her husband goes out to dinner with his
neighbours,
he cannot help heaving bitter sighs.
[19]No spite can approach the spite of a woman,
may a sinner's lot be hers!
[20]Like the climbing of a sandhill for elderly feet,
such is a garrulous wife for a quiet husband.
[21]Do not be taken in by a woman's beauty,
never lose your head over a woman.
[22]Bad temper, insolence and shame hold sway
where the wife supports the husband.
[23]Low spirits, gloomy face, stricken heart:
such is a spiteful wife.
Slack hands and sagging knees:
such is the wife who does not make her husband
happy.
[24]Sin began with a woman,
and thanks to her we must all die.
[25]Do not let water find a leak,
nor a spiteful woman give free rein to her tongue.
[26]If she will not do as you tell her,
get rid of her.

26 How blessed is the husband of a really good wife;
the number of his days will be doubled.
[2]A perfect wife is the joy of her husband,
he will live out the years of his life in peace.

GREEK OLD TESTAMENT

3 γυνὴ ἀγαθὴ μερὶς ἀγαθή,
ἐν μερίδι φοβουμένων κύριον δοθήσεται·
4 πλουσίου δὲ καὶ πτωχοῦ καρδία ἀγαθή,
ἐν παντὶ καιρῷ πρόσωπον ἱλαρόν.
5 Ἀπὸ τριῶν εὐλαβήθη ἡ καρδία μου,
καὶ ἐπὶ τῷ τετάρτῳ προσώπῳ ἐδεήθην·
διαβολὴν πόλεως, καὶ ἐκκλησίαν ὄχλου,
καὶ καταψευσμόν, ὑπὲρ θάνατον πάντα μοχθηρά.
6 ἄλγος καρδίας καὶ πένθος γυνὴ ἀντίζηλος ἐπὶ γυναικὶ
καὶ μάστιξ γλώσσης πᾶσιν ἐπικοινωνοῦσα.
7 βοοζύγιον σαλευόμενον γυνὴ πονηρά,
ὁ κρατῶν αὐτῆς ὡς ὁ δρασσόμενος σκορπίου.
8 ὀργὴ μεγάλη γυνὴ μέθυσος
καὶ ἀσχημοσύνην αὐτῆς οὐ συγκαλύψει.
9 πορνεία γυναικὸς ἐν μετεωρισμοῖς ὀφθαλμῶν
καὶ ἐν τοῖς βλεφάροις αὐτῆς γνωσθήσεται.
10 ἐπὶ θυγατρὶ ἀδιατρέπτῳ στερέωσον φυλακήν,
ἵνα μὴ εὑροῦσα ἄνεσιν ἑαυτῇ χρήσηται·
11 ὀπίσω ἀναιδοῦς ὀφθαλμοῦ φύλαξαι
καὶ μὴ θαυμάσῃς, ἐὰν εἰς σὲ πλημμελήσῃ·
12 ὡς διψῶν ὁδοιπόρος τὸ στόμα ἀνοίξει
καὶ ἀπὸ παντὸς ὕδατος τοῦ σύνεγγυς πίεται,
κατέναντι παντὸς πασσάλου καθήσεται
καὶ ἔναντι βέλους ἀνοίξει φαρέτραν.

KING JAMES VERSION

3 A good wife is a good portion, which shall be given in the portion of them that fear the Lord.

4 Whether a man be rich or poor, if he have a good heart toward the Lord, he shall at all times rejoice with a cheerful countenance.

5 There be three things that mine heart feareth; and for the fourth I was sore afraid: the slander of a city, the gathering together of an unruly multitude, and a false accusation: all these are worse than death.

6 But a grief of heart and sorrow is a woman that is jealous over another woman, and a scourge of the tongue which communicateth with all.

7 An evil wife is a yoke shaken to and fro: he that hath hold of her is as though he held a scorpion.

8 A drunken woman and a gadder abroad causeth great anger, and she will not cover her own shame.

9 The whoredom of a woman may be known in her haughty looks and eyelids.

10 If thy daughter be shameless, keep her in straitly, lest she abuse herself through overmuch liberty.

11 Watch over an impudent eye: and marvel not if she trespass against thee.

12 She will open her mouth, as a thirsty traveller when he hath found a fountain, and drink of every water near her: by every hedge will she sit down, and open her quiver against every arrow.

DOUAY OLD TESTAMENT

3 A good wife is a good portion, she shall be given in the portion of them that fear God, to a man for *his* good deeds.

4 Rich or poor, if his heart is good, his countenance shall be cheerful at all times.

5 Of three things my heart hath been afraid, and at the fourth my face hath trembled:

6 The accusation of a city, and the gathering together of the people:

7 And a false calumny, all *are* more grievous than death.

8 A jealous woman is the grief and mourning of the heart.

9 With a jealous woman is a scourge of the tongue which communicateth with all.

10 As a yoke of oxen that is moved to and fro, so also is a wicked woman: he that hath hold of her, is as he that taketh hold of a scorpion.

11 A drunken woman is a great wrath: and her reproach and shame shall not be hid.

12 The fornication of a woman shall be known by the haughtiness of her eyes, and by her eyelids.

13 On a daughter that turneth not away herself, set a strict watch: lest finding an opportunity she abuse herself.

14 Take heed of the impudence of her eyes, and wonder not if she slight thee.

15 She will open her mouth as a thirsty traveller to the fountain, and will drink of every water near her, and will sit down by every hedge, and open her quiver against every arrow, until she fail.

KNOX TRANSLATION

thrives that best wives; where men fear God, this is the
reward of their service, 4 good cheer given to rich and poor
alike; day in, day out, never a mournful look.
5 Three things daunt me somewhat, a fourth I dare not
face. 6 Gossip of the streets, the judgement of the rabble,
7 and the false charge preferred, all these make death itself
seem a light thing. 8 But there is no affliction wrings the
heart like a woman's jealousy; 9 once a woman grows jealous, her tongue is a scourge to all alike. 10 Easier to guide an
unsteady team of oxen than an ill woman; easier to hold a
snake than to manage her. 11 Woman that is a sot, vexation
shall bring thee, and great dishonour; there is no hiding her
shame. 12 Haughty gaze and lowered eye-lid, there goes a
wanton. 13 Headstrong daughter must be held with a tight
rein, or she will find opportunity to bestow her favours;
14 beware of that shameless eye, nor think it strange if she
defies thee. 15 Reckless thou wilt find her as thirsty traveller
that puts his mouth to the spring and drinks what water he
can get; no stake but she will make fast by it, no arrow
comes amiss to her archery, till of dalliance she has had
enough.

TODAY'S ENGLISH VERSION

3 A good wife is among the precious blessings given to those
who fear the Lord. 4 Whether such men are rich or poor, they
will be happy and always look cheerful.

5 There are four things that scare me: vicious rumors
spread around town, a gathering mob, false accusations—
these are all worse than death. 6 But a woman jealous of
another woman causes heartache and grief; her tongue
lashes out at everyone.
7 A bad wife is like a yoke that doesn't fit. Trying to control
her is like holding a scorpion. 8 A drunken woman is an
infuriating sight; she can't conceal her shameless behavior.
9 You can tell an unfaithful wife by the bold and flirting look
in her eyes.

10 If your daughter is determined to have her own way,
keep a close watch on her. If you don't, she'll take advantage
of any chance she gets. 11 If she is too self-willed, be on
guard, and don't be surprised if she disappoints you.
12 She'll spread her legs anywhere for any man who wants
her, just as a thirsty traveler will drink whatever water is
available.

NEW REVISED STANDARD VERSION

3 A good wife is a great blessing;
she will be granted among the blessings of the man
who fears the Lord.
4 Whether rich or poor, his heart is content,
and at all times his face is cheerful.
5 Of three things my heart is frightened,
and of a fourth I am in great fear:[a]
Slander in the city, the gathering of a mob,
and false accusation—all these are worse than death.
6 But it is heartache and sorrow when a wife is jealous of
a rival,
and a tongue-lashing makes it known to all.
7 A bad wife is a chafing yoke;
taking hold of her is like grasping a scorpion.
8 A drunken wife arouses great anger;
she cannot hide her shame.
9 The haughty stare betrays an unchaste wife;
her eyelids give her away.

10 Keep strict watch over a headstrong daughter,
or else, when she finds liberty, she will make use of it.
11 Be on guard against her impudent eye,
and do not be surprised if she sins against you.
12 As a thirsty traveler opens his mouth
and drinks from any water near him,
so she will sit in front of every tent peg
and open her quiver to the arrow.

a Syr: Meaning of Gk uncertain

NEW AMERICAN BIBLE

3 A good wife is a generous gift
bestowed upon him who fears the LORD;
4 Be he rich or poor, his heart is content,
and a smile is ever on his face.

5 There are three things at which my heart quakes,
a fourth before which I quail:
Though false charges in public, trial before all the
people,
and lying testimony are harder to bear than death,
6 A jealous wife is heartache and mourning
and a scourging tongue like the other three.
7 A bad wife is a chafing yoke;
he who marries her seizes a scorpion.
8 A drunken wife arouses great anger,
for she does not hide her shame.
9 By her eyelids and her haughty stare
an unchaste wife can be recognized.
10 Keep a strict watch over an unruly wife,
lest, finding an opportunity, she make use of it;
11 Follow close if her eyes are bold,
and be not surprised if she betrays you:
12 As a thirsty traveler with eager mouth
drinks from any water that he finds,
So she settles down before every tent peg
and opens her quiver for every arrow.

NEW JERUSALEM BIBLE

3 A good wife is the best of portions,
reserved for those who fear the Lord;
4 rich or poor, their hearts will be glad,
their faces cheerful, whatever the season.

5 There are three things that I dread,
and a fourth which terrifies me:
slander by a whole town, the gathering of a mob,
and a false accusation—these are all worse than
death;
6 but a woman jealous of a woman means heartbreak
and sorrow,
and all this is the scourge of the tongue.

7 A bad wife is a badly fitting ox-yoke,
trying to master her is like grasping a scorpion.
8 A drunken wife will goad anyone to fury,
she cannot conceal her own degradation.

9 A woman's wantonness shows in her wide-eyed look,
her eyelashes leave no doubt.
10 Keep a headstrong daughter under firm control,
or, feeling free, she will take advantage of it.
11 Keep a strict watch on her shameless eye,
do not be surprised if she disgraces you.
12 Like a thirsty traveller she will open her mouth
and drink any water she comes across;
she will sit down in front of every tent-peg
and open her quiver to any arrow.

GREEK OLD TESTAMENT

13 Χάρις γυναικὸς τέρψει τὸν ἄνδρα αὐτῆς,
καὶ τὰ ὀστᾶ αὐτοῦ πιανεῖ ἡ ἐπιστήμη αὐτῆς.
14 δόσις κυρίου γυνὴ σιγηρά,
καὶ οὐκ ἔστιν ἀντάλλαγμα πεπαιδευμένης ψυχῆς.
15 χάρις ἐπὶ χάριτι γυνὴ αἰσχυντηρά,
καὶ οὐκ ἔστιν σταθμὸς πᾶς ἄξιος ἐγκρατοῦς ψυχῆς·
16 ἥλιος ἀνατέλλων ἐν ὑψίστοις κυρίου
καὶ κάλλος ἀγαθῆς γυναικὸς ἐν κόσμῳ οἰκίας αὐτῆς·
17 λύχνος ἐκλάμπων ἐπὶ λυχνίας ἁγίας
καὶ κάλλος προσώπου ἐπὶ ἡλικίᾳ στασίμῃ·
18 στῦλοι χρύσεοι ἐπὶ βάσεως ἀργυρᾶς
καὶ πόδες ὡραῖοι ἐπὶ στέρνοις εὐσταθοῦς.

KING JAMES VERSION

13 The grace of a wife delighteth her husband, and her discretion will fatten his bones.

14 A silent and loving woman is a gift of the Lord; and there is nothing so much worth as a mind well instructed.

15 A shamefaced and faithful woman is a double grace, and her continent mind cannot be valued.

16 As the sun when it ariseth in the high heaven; so is the beauty of a good wife in the ordering of her house.

17 As the clear light is upon the holy candlestick; so is the beauty of the face in ripe age.

18 As the golden pillars are upon the sockets of silver; so are the fair feet with a constant heart.

19 My son, keep the flower of thine age sound; and give not thy strength to strangers.

20 When thou hast gotten a fruitful possession through all the field, sow it with thine own seed, trusting in the goodness of thy stock.

21 So thy race which thou leavest shall be magnified, having the confidence of their good descent.

22 An harlot shall be accounted as spittle; but a married woman is a tower against death to her husband.

DOUAY OLD TESTAMENT

16 The grace of a diligent woman shall delight her husband, and shall fat his bones.

17 Her discipline is the gift of God.

18 *Such is* a wise and silent woman, *and* there is nothing so much worth as a well instructed soul.

19 A holy and shamefaced woman is grace upon grace.

20 And no price is worthy of a continent soul.

21 As the sun when it riseth to the world in the high places of God, so is the beauty of a good wife for the ornament of her house.

22 As the lamp shining upon the holy candlestick, so is the beauty of the face in a ripe age.

23 As golden pillars upon bases of silver, so are the firm feet upon the soles of a steady woman.

24 As everlasting foundations upon a solid rock, so the commandments of God in the heart of a holy woman.

KNOX TRANSLATION

16 Great content an industrious wife brings to her husband;
health to every bone of his body is that good sense of hers.
17 No better gift of God to man 18 than a prudent woman that
can hold her tongue; a soul well disciplined is beyond all
price. 19 Grace so gracious is none as woman's faithfulness
and woman's modesty; 20 woman's continence there is no
valuing. 21 Sun dawning in heaven cannot match the lustre
a good wife sheds on her home, 22 and that beauty lasts into
ripe age, like the glow of lights on the holy lamp-stand.
23 Firm as golden pillar in silver socket rest the feet of steadfast woman on the ground she treads; 24 and firm as foundations built for all time on solid rock is holy woman's loyalty
to God's commandments.[a]

a A few Greek manuscripts insert here nine more verses upon the subject of women.

TODAY'S ENGLISH VERSION

13 A gracious wife is her husband's delight; her abilities
make him a stronger man.[a] 14 A wife who doesn't talk too
much is a gift from the Lord. Such restraint is admirable
beyond words. 15 A modest wife has endless charm; it is a
quality too precious to measure. 16 The beauty of a good wife
in her well-kept home is like the noonday sun shining in the
Lord's sky. 17 Her beautiful face and attractive figure are[b] as
lovely as the light from the sacred lampstand in the Temple,
18 and like its gold shaft set on its silver base are her shapely
legs and strong ankles.[c,d]

[a] her abilities . . . man; *or* she knows how to keep him well-fed.
[b] and attractive figure are; *or* as she grows older is. [c] strong ankles; *some manuscripts have* firm breasts *or* determined heart.
[d] *Some manuscripts add verses 19-27:* My child, stay healthy while you are
young, and don't give your strength to strangers. 20 Search the whole land
for a fertile field, and plant it with your own seed, trusting your own good
stock. 21 Then your children will survive and grow up confident of their good
family. 22 A prostitute is like spit; a married woman who has affairs brings
death to her lovers. 23 A lawless man will get a godless wife, as he deserves,
but a man who honors the Lord will have a devout wife. 24 A shameless wife
enjoys making a disgrace of herself, but a modest wife will act modestly
even alone with her husband. 25 A self-willed woman is a bitch, but a
woman with a sense of decency honors the Lord. 26 A wife who honors her
husband will seem wise to everyone; but if she dishonors him by her
overbearing attitude, everyone will know that she is ungodly. Fortunate is
the husband of a good wife, because he will live twice as long. 27 A loud-
mouthed, talkative woman is like a trumpet sounding the signal for attack,
and any man who has such a wife will spend his life at war.

NEW REVISED STANDARD VERSION

13 A wife's charm delights her husband,
and her skill puts flesh on his bones.
14 A silent wife is a gift from the Lord,
and nothing is so precious as her self-discipline.
15 A modest wife adds charm to charm,
and no scales can weigh the value of her chastity.
16 Like the sun rising in the heights of the Lord,
so is the beauty of a good wife in her well-ordered home.
17 Like the shining lamp on the holy lampstand,
so is a beautiful face on a stately figure.
18 Like golden pillars on silver bases,
so are shapely legs and steadfast feet.

Other ancient authorities add verses 19-27:

19 *My child, keep sound the bloom of your youth,*
and do not give your strength to strangers.
20 *Seek a fertile field within the whole plain,*
and sow it with your own seed, trusting in your fine stock.
21 *So your offspring will prosper,*
and, having confidence in their good descent, will grow great.
22 *A prostitute is regarded as spittle,*
and a married woman as a tower of death to her lovers.

NEW AMERICAN BIBLE

13 A gracious wife delights her husband,
her thoughtfulness puts flesh on his bones;
14 A gift from the LORD is her governed speech,
and her firm virtue is of surpassing worth.
15 Choicest of blessings is a modest wife,
priceless her chaste person.
16 Like the sun rising in the LORD's heavens,
the beauty of a virtuous wife is the radiance of her home.
17 Like the light which shines above the holy lampstand,
are her beauty of face and graceful figure.
18 Golden columns on silver bases
are her shapely limbs and steady feet.

Among the additions found here in some manuscripts are the following lines:

"My son, take care in the prime of life
not to surrender your strength to strangers;
Single out from the land a goodly field
and there with confidence sow the seed of your increase;
So shall you have your offspring around you,
and in confidence shall they grow up.
"Though a woman for hire be thought of as a trifle,
a married woman is a deadly snare for those who embrace her.

26, 18: In standard editions of the *New American Bible* the italicized verses that follow appear in a footnote.

NEW JERUSALEM BIBLE

13 The grace of a wife will charm her husband,
her understanding will make him the stronger.
14 A silent wife is a gift from the Lord,
no price can be put on a well-trained character.
15 A modest wife is a boon twice over,
a chaste character cannot be over-valued.
16 Like the sun rising over the mountains of the Lord,
such is the beauty of a good wife in a well-run house.
17 Like a lamp shining on the sacred lamp-stand,
such is a beautiful face on a well-proportioned body.
18 Like golden pillars on a silver base,
such are shapely legs on firm-set heels.

GREEK OLD TESTAMENT

28 Ἐπὶ δυσὶ λελύπηται ἡ καρδία μου,
καὶ ἐπὶ τῷ τρίτῳ θυμός μοι ἐπῆλθεν·
ἀνὴρ πολεμιστὴς ὑστερῶν δι' ἔνδειαν,
καὶ ἄνδρες συνετοὶ ἐὰν σκυβαλισθῶσιν,
ἐπανάγων ἀπὸ δικαιοσύνης ἐπὶ ἁμαρτίαν·
ὁ κύριος ἑτοιμάσει εἰς ῥομφαίαν αὐτόν.
29 Μόλις ἐξελεῖται ἔμπορος ἀπὸ πλημμελείας,
καὶ οὐ δικαιωθήσεται κάπηλος ἀπὸ ἁμαρτίας.

KING JAMES VERSION

23 A wicked woman is given as a portion to a wicked man: but a godly woman is given to him that feareth the Lord.

24 A dishonest woman contemneth shame: but an honest woman will reverence her husband.

25 A shameless woman shall be counted as a dog; but she that is shamefaced will fear the Lord.

26 A woman that honoureth her husband shall be judged wise of all; but she that dishonoureth him in her pride shall be counted ungodly of all.

27 A loud crying woman and a scold shall be sought out to drive away the enemies.

28 There be two things that grieve my heart; and the third maketh me angry: a man of war that suffereth poverty; and men of understanding that are not set by; and one that returneth from righteousness to sin; the Lord prepareth such an one for the sword.

29 A merchant shall hardly keep himself from doing wrong; and an huckster shall not be freed from sin.

DOUAY OLD TESTAMENT

25 At two things my heart is grieved, and the third bringeth anger upon me:

26 A man of war fainting through poverty: and a man of sense despised:

27 And he that passeth over from justice to sin, God hath prepared such an one for the sword.

28 Two sorts *of callings* have appeared to me hard and dangerous: a merchant is hardly free from negligence: and a huckster shall not be justified from the sins of the lips.

KNOX TRANSLATION

25 Two sad sights my heart knows, and one more that fills it with indignation; 26 warrior left to starve, and wise counsellor unregarded, 27 and a man that leaves right living for ill-doing, ripe for God's vengeance.

28 Two dangers I see that are hard to overcome. How shall a merchant be cured of careless dealing, or a huckster for his lying talk find pardon?

TODAY'S ENGLISH VERSION

28 There are two things that make me sad, and a third that
makes me angry:
a soldier who has become poor,
intelligent people who are not respected,
and a righteous person who turns to evil.
The Lord will punish such a person with death!
29 A merchant can hardly avoid doing wrong; every sales-

NEW REVISED STANDARD VERSION

23 *A godless wife is given as a portion to a lawless man,*
but a pious wife is given to the man who fears the
Lord.
24 *A shameless woman constantly acts disgracefully,*
but a modest daughter will even be embarrassed
before her husband.
25 *A headstrong wife is regarded as a dog,*
but one who has a sense of shame will fear the Lord.
26 *A wife honoring her husband will seem wise to all,*
but if she dishonors him in her pride she will be
known to all as ungodly.
Happy is the husband of a good wife;
for the number of his years will be doubled.
27 *A loud-voiced and garrulous wife is like a trumpet*
sounding the charge,
and every person like this lives in the anarchy of war.

---

28 At two things my heart is grieved,
and because of a third anger comes over me:
a warrior in want through poverty,
intelligent men who are treated contemptuously,
and a man who turns back from righteousness to sin—
the Lord will prepare him for the sword!

29 A merchant can hardly keep from wrongdoing,
nor is a tradesman innocent of sin.

NEW AMERICAN BIBLE

"A wife's complaint should be made in meekness,
and show itself in a slight flush;
But a loud-mouthed, scolding wife
is a trumpet signaling for battle:
Any human being who answers that challenge
will spend his life amid the turbulence of war."

---

19 These two bring grief to my heart,
and the third arouses my horror:
A wealthy man reduced to want;
illustrious men held in contempt;
And the man who passes from justice to sin,
for whom the LORD makes ready the sword.

20 A merchant can hardly remain upright,
nor a shopkeeper free from sin;

NEW JERUSALEM BIBLE

28 There are two things which grieve my heart
and a third arouses my anger:
a warrior wasting away through poverty,
the intelligent treated with contempt,
someone turning back from virtue to sin—
the Lord marks out such a person for a violent death.

29 It is difficult for a merchant to avoid doing wrong
and for a trader not to incur sin.

Greek Old Testament

27 χάριν διαφόρου πολλοὶ ἥμαρτον,
καὶ ὁ ζητῶν πληθῦναι ἀποστρέψει ὀφθαλμόν.
2 ἀνὰ μέσον ἁρμῶν λίθων παγήσεται πάσσαλος,
καὶ ἀνὰ μέσον πράσεως καὶ ἀγορασμοῦ συντριβήσεται
ἁμαρτία.
3 ἐὰν μὴ ἐν φόβῳ κυρίου κρατήσῃ κατὰ σπουδήν,
ἐν τάχει καταστραφήσεται αὐτοῦ ὁ οἶκος.
4 Ἐν σείσματι κοσκίνου διαμένει κοπρία,
οὕτως σκύβαλα ἀνθρώπου ἐν λογισμῷ αὐτοῦ.
5 σκεύη κεραμέως δοκιμάζει κάμινος,
καὶ πειρασμὸς ἀνθρώπου ἐν διαλογισμῷ αὐτοῦ.
6 γεώργιον ξύλου ἐκφαίνει ὁ καρπὸς αὐτοῦ,
οὕτως λόγος ἐνθυμήματος καρδίας ἀνθρώπου.
7 πρὸ λογισμοῦ μὴ ἐπαινέσῃς ἄνδρα·
οὗτος γὰρ πειρασμὸς ἀνθρώπων.
8 Ἐὰν διώκῃς τὸ δίκαιον, καταλήμψῃ
καὶ ἐνδύσῃ αὐτὸ ὡς ποδήρη δόξης.
9 πετεινὰ πρὸς τὰ ὅμοια αὐτοῖς καταλύσει,
καὶ ἀλήθεια πρὸς τοὺς ἐργαζομένους αὐτὴν ἐπανήξει.
10 λέων θήραν ἐνεδρεύει,
οὕτως ἁμαρτία ἐργαζομένους ἄδικα.
11 διήγησις εὐσεβοῦς διὰ παντὸς σοφία,
ὁ δὲ ἄφρων ὡς σελήνη ἀλλοιοῦται.

King James Version

27 Many have sinned for a small matter; and he that seeketh for abundance will turn his eyes away.

2 As a nail sticketh fast between the joinings of the stones; so doth sin stick close between buying and selling.

3 Unless a man hold himself diligently in the fear of the Lord, his house shall soon be overthrown.

4 As when one sifteth with a sieve, the refuse remaineth; so the filth of man in his talk.

5 The furnace proveth the potter's vessels; so the trial of man is in his reasoning.

6 The fruit declareth if the tree have been dressed; so is the utterance of a conceit in the heart of man.

7 Praise no man before thou hearest him speak; for this is the trial of men.

8 If thou followest righteousness, thou shalt obtain her, and put her on, as a glorious long robe.

9 The birds will resort unto their like; so will truth return unto them that practise in her.

10 As the lion lieth in wait for the prey; so sin for them that work iniquity.

11 The discourse of a godly man is always with wisdom; but a fool changeth as the moon.

Douay Old Testament

27 THROUGH poverty many have sinned: and he that seeketh to be enriched, turneth away his eye.

2 As a stake sticketh fast in the midst of the joining of stones, so also in the midst of selling and buying, sin shall stick fast.

3 Sin shall be destroyed with the sinner.

4 Unless thou hold thyself diligently in the fear of the Lord, thy house shall quickly be overthrown.

5 As when one sifteth with a sieve, the dust will remain: so will the perplexity of a man in his thoughts.

6 The furnace trieth the potter's vessels, and the trial of affliction just men.

7 As the dressing of a tree sheweth the fruit thereof, so a word out of the thought of the heart of man.

8 Praise not a man before he speaketh, for this is the trial of men.

9 If thou followest justice, thou shalt obtain her: and shalt put her on as a long robe of honour, and thou shalt dwell with her: and she shall protect thee for ever, and in the day of acknowledgment thou shalt find a strong foundation.

10 Birds resort unto their like: so truth will return to them that practise her.

11 The lion always lieth in wait for prey: so do sins for them that work iniquities.

12 A holy man continueth in wisdom as the sun: but a fool is changed as the moon.

Knox Translation

27 Sin comes often of an empty purse; nothing distorts
the eye like the love of riches. 2 Stake that is held
between two stones cannot escape; nor may sin be avoided
when there is seller on this side, buyer on that. 3 Wrong
done shall be undone, and the doer of it as well; 4 hold fast
to thy fear of the Lord, or thy wealth shall soon come to ruin.
5 The sieve shaken, nothing is left but refuse; so thou wilt
find a man's poverty in his thought.[a]
6 Pottery is tested in the furnace, man in the crucible of
suffering.
7 Good fruit comes from a tree well dressed, and a man will
be in word what he is in thought; 8 do not give thy opinion
of a man till he has spoken; there lies the proof.
9 Make right-doing thy quest, and thou wilt not miss the
mark; this shall be a robe of honour to clothe thee, a welcome guest in thy house, to watch over thee continually, and
to be thy stronghold at the hour when all is made known.
10 Bird mates with bird, and he that shews faithfulness
faithfulness shall meet.
11 The lion waits in ambush for his prey; leave the right
path, and sin shall be ever at thy heels.
12 Unfailing as the sun is the wisdom of a devout mind;
moon and fool change continually.

a This obscure maxim may be interpreted in several ways, none of which is quite satisfactory. There may have been an error in the text: 'poverty' is represented in the Greek by a second word for 'refuse', and in the Latin by an abstract noun which signifies 'not knowing which way to turn'.

TODAY'S ENGLISH VERSION

27 man is guilty of sin. [1]Many people have sinned
while looking for a profit; if you want to be rich you
have to keep blinders on your eyes. [2]It is hard to remove a
peg that is stuck between two stones of a house, and it is
just as hard to remove dishonesty from buying and selling.
[3]Unless you are determined in your fear of the Lord, your
house is going to come down on you.

[4]Your talk shows your faults; it is like a sieve that separates out the rubbish. [5]The way you think shows your character just as surely as a kiln shows any flaws in the pottery
being fired. [6]You can tell how well a tree has been cared for
by the fruit it bears, and you can tell a person's feelings by
the way he expresses himself. [7]Never praise anyone before
you hear him talk; that is the real test.

[8]If you try to be honest, you can be, and it will improve
your character as handsome clothing improves your appearance. [9]Birds come to roost with those of their own kind, and
the habit of honesty comes to those who try to be honest.
[10]Sin waits for those looking for a chance to sin, just as a
lion waits for prey.

[11]When devout people talk, what they say always makes
sense, but foolish people are always contradicting themselves.

NEW REVISED STANDARD VERSION

27 Many have committed sin for gain,[a]
and those who seek to get rich will avert their eyes.
2 As a stake is driven firmly into a fissure between
stones,
so sin is wedged in between selling and buying.
3 If a person is not steadfast in the fear of the Lord,
his house will be quickly overthrown.

4 When a sieve is shaken, the refuse appears;
so do a person's faults when he speaks.
5 The kiln tests the potter's vessels;
so the test of a person is in his conversation.
6 Its fruit discloses the cultivation of a tree;
so a person's speech discloses the cultivation of his
mind.
7 Do not praise anyone before he speaks,
for this is the way people are tested.

8 If you pursue justice, you will attain it
and wear it like a glorious robe.
9 Birds roost with their own kind,
so honesty comes home to those who practice it.
10 A lion lies in wait for prey;
so does sin for evildoers.

11 The conversation of the godly is always wise,
but the fool changes like the moon.

a Other ancient authorities read *a trifle*

NEW AMERICAN BIBLE

27 For the sake of profit many sin,
and the struggle for wealth blinds the eyes.
[2]Like a peg driven between fitted stones,
between buying and selling sin is wedged in.
[3]Unless you earnestly hold fast to the fear of the LORD,
suddenly your house will be thrown down.
[4]When a sieve is shaken, the husks appear;
so do a man's faults when he speaks.
[5]As the test of what the potter molds is in the furnace,
so in his conversation is the test of a man.
[6]The fruit of a tree shows the care it has had;
so too does a man's speech disclose the bent of his
mind.
[7]Praise no man before he speaks,
for it is then that men are tested.
[8]If you strive after justice you will attain it,
and put it on like a splendid robe.
[9]Birds nest with their own kind,
and fidelity comes to those who live by it.
[10]As a lion crouches in wait for prey,
so do sins for evildoers
[11]Ever wise are the discourses of the devout,
but the godless man, like the moon, is inconstant.

NEW JERUSALEM BIBLE

27 Many have sinned for the sake of profit,
one who hopes to be rich must turn a blind eye.
[2]A peg will stick in the joint between two stones,
and sin will wedge itself between selling and buying.
[3]Whoever does not firmly hold to the fear of the Lord,
his house will soon be overthrown.

[4]In a shaken sieve the rubbish is left behind,
so too the defects of a person appear in speech.
[5]The kiln tests the work of the potter,
the test of a person is in conversation.
[6]The orchard where the tree grows is judged by its fruit,
similarly words betray what a person feels.
[7]Do not praise anyone who has not yet spoken,
since this is where people are tested.

[8]If you pursue virtue, you will attain it
and put it on like a festal gown.
[9]Birds consort with their kind,
truth comes home to those who practise it.
[10]The lion lies in wait for its prey,
so does sin for those who do wrong.

[11]The conversation of the devout is wisdom at all times,
but the fool is as changeable as the moon.

GREEK OLD TESTAMENT

12 εἰς μέσον ἀσυνέτων συντήρησον καιρόν,
εἰς μέσον δὲ διανοουμένων ἐνδελέχιζε.
13 διήγησις μωρῶν προσόχθισμα,
καὶ ὁ γέλως αὐτῶν ἐν σπατάλῃ ἁμαρτίας.
14 λαλιὰ πολυόρκου ἀνορθώσει τρίχας,
καὶ ἡ μάχη αὐτῶν ἐμφραγμὸς ὠτίων.
15 ἔκχυσις αἵματος μάχη ὑπερηφάνων,
καὶ ἡ διαλοιδόρησις αὐτῶν ἀκοὴ μοχθηρά.
16 Ὁ ἀποκαλύπτων μυστήρια ἀπώλεσεν πίστιν
καὶ οὐ μὴ εὕρῃ φίλον πρὸς τὴν ψυχὴν αὐτοῦ.
17 στέρξον φίλον καὶ πιστώθητι μετ' αὐτοῦ·
ἐὰν δὲ ἀποκαλύψῃς τὰ μυστήρια αὐτοῦ, μὴ καταδιώξῃς ὀπίσω αὐτοῦ.
18 καθὼς γὰρ ἀπώλεσεν ἄνθρωπος τὸν νεκρὸν αὐτοῦ,
οὕτως ἀπώλεσας τὴν φιλίαν τοῦ πλησίον·
19 καὶ ὡς πετεινὸν ἐκ χειρός σου ἀπέλυσας,
οὕτως ἀφῆκας τὸν πλησίον καὶ οὐ θηρεύσεις αὐτόν.
20 μὴ αὐτὸν διώξῃς, ὅτι μακρὰν ἀπέστη
καὶ ἐξέφυγεν ὡς δορκὰς ἐκ παγίδος.
21 ὅτι τραῦμα ἔστιν καταδῆσαι,
καὶ λοιδορίας ἔστιν διαλλαγή,
ὁ δὲ ἀποκαλύψας μυστήρια ἀφήλπισεν.
22 Διανεύων ὀφθαλμῷ τεκταίνει κακά,
καὶ οὐδεὶς αὐτὰ ἀποστήσει ἀπ' αὐτοῦ·

KING JAMES VERSION

12 If thou be among the indiscreet, observe the time; but be continually among men of understanding.

13 The discourse of fools is irksome, and their sport is the wantonness of sin.

14 The talk of him that sweareth much maketh the hair stand upright; and their brawls make one stop his ears.

15 The strife of the proud is bloodshedding, and their revilings are grievous to the ear.

16 Whoso discovereth secrets loseth his credit; and shall never find friend to his mind.

17 Love thy friend, and be faithful unto him: but if thou betrayest his secrets, follow no more after him.

18 For as a man hath destroyed his enemy; so hast thou lost the love of thy neighbour.

19 As one that letteth a bird go out of his hand, so hast thou let thy neighbour go, and shalt not get him again.

20 Follow after him no more, for he is too far off; he is as a roe escaped out of the snare.

21 As for a wound, it may be bound up; and after reviling there may be reconcilement: but he that bewrayeth secrets is without hope.

22 He that winketh with the eyes worketh evil: and he that knoweth him will depart from him.

DOUAY OLD TESTAMENT

13 In the midst of the unwise keep in the word till its time: but be continually among men that think.

14 The discourse of sinners is hateful, and their laughter is at the pleasures of sin.

15 The speech that sweareth much shall make the hair of the head stand upright: and its irreverence shall make one stop his ears.

16 In the quarrels of the proud is the shedding of blood: and their cursing is a grievous hearing.

17 He that discloseth the secret of a friend loseth his credit, and shall never find a friend to his mind.

18 Love thy neighbour, and be joined to him with fidelity.

19 But if thou discover his secrets, follow no more after him.

20 For as a man that destroyeth his friend, so also *is* he that destroyeth the friendship of his neighbour.

21 And as one that letteth a bird go out of his hand, so hast thou let thy neighbour go, and thou shalt not get him again.

22 Follow after him no more, for he is gone afar off, he is fled, as a roe escaped out of the snare: because his soul is wounded.

23 Thou canst no more bind him up. And of a curse there is reconciliation:

24 But to disclose the secrets of a friend, leaveth no hope to an unhappy soul.

25 He that winketh with the eye forgeth wicked things, and no man will cast him off:

KNOX TRANSLATION

13 When thou hast fools for thy company, thy word can
wait; be closeted continually with the wise.
14 Out upon the wearisome talk of sinners, that of sin and
its dalliance makes a jest! 15 Out upon the man that uses
oaths lightly; hair stands upright at his blaspheming, and
ears are stopped! 16 Out upon the proud, that provoke bloodshed with their quarrelling, and by their cursing offend all
who listen!
17 Betray thy friend's secret, and all confidence is lost;
never more shalt thou have friend to comfort thee. 18 Use
such a man lovingly, and keep faith with him; 19 if once
thou hast betrayed him, court no more his company.
20 Friendship thus killed, thy friend is dead to thee; 21 bird let
go from the hand is not lost more irretrievably; 22 he is gone,
like hind released from the snare, gone beyond thy pursuit.
The wound that hurts a man's soul 23 there is no healing;
the bitter taunt may yet be unsaid, 24 but once the secret is
out all is misery, all is despair.
25 Sly glance of the false friend! How shall a man be rid of

TODAY'S ENGLISH VERSION

12 When you find yourself with stupid people, look for some
excuse to leave, but when you are with serious-minded people, stay as long as you can.
13 The stories that foolish people tell are offensive, and
they make jokes about the worst kinds of sin. 14 When such
people curse, it is enough to make your hair stand on end,
and when they start arguing among themselves, all you can
do is to stop up your ears. 15 It is painful to listen to them
insult each other, and such blustering can lead to violence.
16 If you repeat secrets that have been told to you, you are
destroying the confidence others have in you, and you will
never have a close friend. 17 Respect your friends, and keep
faith with them. If you do betray a friend's confidence, you
may as well forget you have a friend. 18 You have killed that
friendship just as surely as if you had taken a weapon and
killed an enemy. 19 Your friend is gone. You can no more get
him back than you can get a bird to come back to your hand
once you let it go. 20 Don't bother going after him. It's too
late. He is gone, like a deer escaped from a trap. 21 Wounds
can be bandaged and insults can be forgiven, but if you
betray a confidence, it is hopeless.
22 When someone starts winking at you, he has something
bad in mind, and nothing can stop him from going through

NEW REVISED STANDARD VERSION

12 Among stupid people limit your time,
but among thoughtful people linger on.
13 The talk of fools is offensive,
and their laughter is wantonly sinful.
14 Their cursing and swearing make one's hair stand on
end,
and their quarrels make others stop their ears.
15 The strife of the proud leads to bloodshed,
and their abuse is grievous to hear.

16 Whoever betrays secrets destroys confidence,
and will never find a congenial friend.
17 Love your friend and keep faith with him;
but if you betray his secrets, do not follow after him.
18 For as a person destroys his enemy,
so you have destroyed the friendship of your
neighbor.
19 And as you allow a bird to escape from your hand,
so you have let your neighbor go, and will not catch
him again.
20 Do not go after him, for he is too far off,
and has escaped like a gazelle from a snare.
21 For a wound may be bandaged,
and there is reconciliation after abuse,
but whoever has betrayed secrets is without hope.

22 Whoever winks the eye plots mischief,
and those who know him will keep their distance.

NEW AMERICAN BIBLE

12 Limit the time you spend among fools,
but frequent the company of thoughtful men.
13 The conversation of the wicked is offensive,
their laughter is wanton guilt.
14 Their oath-filled talk makes the hair stand on end,
their brawls make one stop one's ears.
15 Wrangling among the haughty ends in bloodshed,
their cursing is painful to hear.

16 He who betrays a secret cannot be trusted,
he will never find an intimate friend.
17 Cherish your friend, keep faith with him;
but if you betray his confidence, follow him not;
18 For as an enemy might kill a man,
you have killed your neighbor's friendship.
19 Like a bird released from the hand,
you have let your friend go and cannot recapture
him;
20 Follow him not, for he is far away,
he has fled like a gazelle from the trap.
21 A wound can be bound up, and an insult forgiven,
but he who betrays secrets does hopeless damage.

22 He who has shifty eyes plots mischief
and no one can ward him off;

NEW JERUSALEM BIBLE

12 When visiting stupid people, choose the right moment,
but among the thoughtful take your time.
13 The conversation of fools is disgusting,
raucous their laughter in their sinful pleasures.
14 The talk of hard-swearing people makes your hair stand
on end,
their brawling makes you stop your ears.
15 A quarrel between the proud leads to bloodshed,
and their insults are embarrassing to hear.
16 A betrayer of secrets forfeits all trust
and will never find the kind of friend he wants.
17 Be fond of a friend and keep faith with him,
but if you have betrayed his secrets, do not go after
him any more;
18 for, as one destroys a person by killing him,
so you have killed your neighbour's friendship,
19 and as you let a bird slip through your fingers,
so you have let your friend go, and will not catch
him.
20 Do not go after him—he is far away,
he has fled like a gazelle from the snare.
21 For a wound can be bandaged and abuse forgiven,
but for the betrayer of a secret there is no hope.
22 Someone with a sly wink is plotting mischief,
no one can dissuade him from it.

GREEK OLD TESTAMENT

23 ἀπέναντι τῶν ὀφθαλμῶν σου γλυκανεῖ τὸ στόμα αὐτοῦ
καὶ ἐπὶ τῶν λόγων σου ἐκθαυμάσει,
ὕστερον δὲ διαστρέψει τὸ στόμα αὐτοῦ
καὶ ἐν τοῖς λόγοις σου δώσει σκάνδαλον.
24 πολλὰ ἐμίσησα καὶ οὐχ ὡμοίωσα αὐτῷ,
καὶ ὁ κύριος μισήσει αὐτόν.
25 ὁ βάλλων λίθον εἰς ὕψος ἐπὶ κεφαλὴν αὐτοῦ βάλλει,
καὶ πληγὴ δολία διελεῖ τραύματα.
26 ὁ ὀρύσσων βόθρον εἰς αὐτὸν ἐμπεσεῖται,
καὶ ὁ ἱστῶν παγίδα ἐν αὐτῇ ἁλώσεται.
27 ὁ ποιῶν πονηρά, εἰς αὐτὸν κυλισθήσεται,
καὶ οὐ μὴ ἐπιγνῷ πόθεν ἥκει αὐτῷ.
28 ἐμπαιγμὸς καὶ ὀνειδισμὸς ὑπερηφάνῳ,
καὶ ἡ ἐκδίκησις ὡς λέων ἐνεδρεύσει αὐτόν.
29 παγίδι ἁλώσονται οἱ εὐφραινόμενοι πτώσει εὐσεβῶν,
καὶ ὀδύνη καταναλώσει αὐτοὺς πρὸ τοῦ θανάτου αὐτῶν.
30 Μῆνις καὶ ὀργή,
καὶ ταῦτά ἐστιν βδελύγματα,
καὶ ἀνὴρ ἁμαρτωλὸς ἐγκρατὴς ἔσται αὐτῶν.
28 ὁ ἐκδικῶν παρὰ κυρίου εὑρήσει ἐκδίκησιν,
καὶ τὰς ἁμαρτίας αὐτοῦ διατηρῶν διατηρήσει.
2 ἄφες ἀδίκημα τῷ πλησίον σου,
καὶ τότε δεηθέντος σου αἱ ἁμαρτίαι σου λυθήσονται.
3 ἄνθρωπος ἀνθρώπῳ συντηρεῖ ὀργήν,
καὶ παρὰ κυρίου ζητεῖ ἴασιν;

KING JAMES VERSION

23 When thou art present, he will speak sweetly, and will
admire thy words: but at the last he will writhe his mouth,
and slander thy sayings.
24 I have hated many things, but nothing like him; for the
Lord will hate him.
25 Whoso casteth a stone on high casteth it on his own
head; and a deceitful stroke shall make wounds.
26 Whoso diggeth a pit shall fall therein: and he that setteth a trap shall be taken therein.
27 He that worketh mischief, it shall fall upon him, and
he shall not know whence it cometh.
28 Mockery and reproach are from the proud; but
vengeance, as a lion, shall lie in wait for them.
29 They that rejoice at the fall of the righteous shall be
taken in the snare; and anguish shall consume them before
they die.
30 Malice and wrath, even these are abominations; and
the sinful man shall have them both.
28 He that revengeth shall find vengeance from the
Lord, and he will surely keep his sins [in remembrance.]
2 Forgive thy neighbour the hurt that he hath done unto
thee, so shall thy sins also be forgiven when thou prayest.
3 One man beareth hatred against another, and doth he
seek pardon from the Lord?

DOUAY OLD TESTAMENT

26 In the sight of thy eyes he will sweeten his mouth, and
will admire thy words: but at the last he will writhe his
mouth, and on thy words he will lay a stumblingblock.
27 I have hated many things, but not like him, and the
Lord will hate him.
28 If one cast a stone on high, it will fall upon his own
head: and the deceitful stroke will wound the deceitful.
29 He that diggeth a pit, shall fall into it: and he that setteth a stone for his neighbour, shall stumble upon it: and he
that layeth a snare for another, shall perish in it.
30 A mischievous counsel shall be rolled back upon the
author, and he shall not know from whence it cometh to
him.
31 Mockery and reproach are of the proud, and vengeance
as a lion shall lie in wait for him.
32 They shall perish in a snare that are delighted with the
fall of the just: and sorrow shall consume them before they
die.
33 Anger and fury are both of them abominable, and the
sinful man shall be subject to them.
28 HE that seeketh to revenge himself, shall find
vengeance from the Lord, and he will surely keep his
sins *in remembrance.*
2 Forgive thy neighbour if he hath hurt thee: and then
shall thy sins be forgiven to thee when thou prayest.
3 Man to man reserveth anger, and doth he seek remedy
of God?

KNOX TRANSLATION

him? 26 Here in thy presence, he smooths his brow, and is all
in wonderment at thy wise sayings; but ere long he will
change his tune, and lend thy words an ill colour. 27 Above
all else, he earns my hatred; God's hatred too, I doubt not.
28 None can throw stone in air but at his own head's peril,
nor ever was blow struck treacherously, but the traitor must
have his share of hurt; 29 a man may fall into the pit he dug,
trip on the stone he set in his neighbour's path, perish in the
snare he laid for another. 30 Plot ill, and the ill shall recoil on
thyself, springing up beyond all thy expectation.
31 For the proud, mockery and shame! Vengeance, like a
lion, couches in wait for them.
32 For all who triumph at the ill fortune of the just, a snare
to catch them, and a long remorse before death takes them!
33 Rancour and rage are detestable things both; and the
sinner has both in store.
28 He that will be avenged brings on himself the Lord's
vengeance; watch and ward shall be kept over his
sins continually. 2 Forgive thy neighbour his fault, and for
thy own sins thy prayer shall win pardon; 3 should man bear
man a grudge, and yet look to the Lord for healing? 4 Should

TODAY'S ENGLISH VERSION

with it. 23 When he's with you, his talk is so nice! He compliments you on every word you say. But behind your back it's
a different story; he will take what you have said and turn it
against you. 24 There is nothing in the world that I hate as
much as a person like that—and the Lord hates him too.
25 Throw a stone straight up in the air and it will come
down on your head. Strike a blow, and you yourself will be
wounded. 26 People who set traps fall into them themselves.
27 People who hurt others will be hurt by their own actions
and will have no idea why.
28 Arrogant people insult others and make fun of them,[a]
but someone is waiting like a lion for a chance to take
revenge on them. 29 Those who are happy to witness the
downfall of devout people are going to fall into a trap and
die a painful death.
30 Anger and a hot temper are horrible things, but sinners
28 have both. 1 The Lord is taking note of your sins,
and if you take vengeance on someone, the Lord will
take vengeance on you. 2 But if you forgive someone who
has wronged you, your sins will be forgiven when you pray.
3 You cannot expect the Lord to pardon you while you are
holding a grudge against someone else. 4 You yourself are a

[a] insult others . . . them; *or* will be insulted and mocked.

NEW REVISED STANDARD VERSION

23 In your presence his mouth is all sweetness,
and he admires your words;
but later he will twist his speech
and with your own words he will trip you up.
24 I have hated many things, but him above all;
even the Lord hates him.
25 Whoever throws a stone straight up throws it on his
own head,
and a treacherous blow opens up many wounds.
26 Whoever digs a pit will fall into it,
and whoever sets a snare will be caught in it.
27 If a person does evil, it will roll back upon him,
and he will not know where it came from.
28 Mockery and abuse issue from the proud,
but vengeance lies in wait for them like a lion.
29 Those who rejoice in the fall of the godly will be caught
in a snare,
and pain will consume them before their death.

30 Anger and wrath, these also are abominations,
yet a sinner holds on to them.

28 The vengeful will face the Lord's vengeance,
for he keeps a strict account of[a] their sins.
2 Forgive your neighbor the wrong he has done,
and then your sins will be pardoned when you pray.
3 Does anyone harbor anger against another,
and expect healing from the Lord?

[a] Other ancient authorities read *for he firmly establishes*

NEW AMERICAN BIBLE

23 In your presence he uses honeyed talk,
and admires your every word,
But later he changes his tone
and twists your words to your ruin.
24 There is nothing that I hate so much,
and the LORD hates him as well.
25 As a stone falls back on him who throws it up,
so a blow struck in treachery injures more than one.
26 As he who digs a pit falls into it,
and he who lays a snare is caught in it,
27 Whoever does harm will be involved in it
without knowing how it came upon him.

28 Mockery and abuse will be the lot of the proud,
and vengeance lies in wait for them like a lion.
29 The trap seizes those who rejoice in pitfalls,
and pain will consume them before they die;
30 Wrath and anger are hateful things,
yet the sinner hugs them tight.

28 The vengeful will suffer the LORD's vengeance,
for he remembers their sins in detail.
2 Forgive your neighbor's injustice;
then when you pray, your own sins will be forgiven.
3 Should a man nourish anger against his fellows
and expect healing from the LORD?

NEW JERUSALEM BIBLE

23 Honey-tongued to your face,
he is lost in admiration at your words;
but behind your back he has other things to say,
and turns your words into a stumbling-block.
24 I have found many things to hate, but nothing as much
as him,
and the Lord hates him too.
25 Whoever throws a stone in the air, throws it on to his
own head;
a treacherous blow cuts both ways.
26 The man who digs a pit falls into it,
whoever sets a snare will be caught by it.
27 On anyone who does evil, evil will recoil,
without his knowing where it comes from.

28 Sarcasm and abuse are the mark of the arrogant,
but vengeance lies in wait like a lion for such a one.
29 The trap will close on all who rejoice in the downfall of
the devout,
and pain will eat them up before they die.

30 Resentment and anger, these are foul things too,
and a sinner is a master at them both.
28 Whoever exacts vengeance will experience the
vengeance of the Lord,
who keeps strict account of sin.
2 Pardon your neighbour any wrongs done to you,
and when you pray, your sins will be forgiven.
3 If anyone nurses anger against another,
can one then demand compassion from the Lord?

GREEK OLD TESTAMENT

4 ἐπ' ἄνθρωπον ὅμοιον αὐτῷ οὐκ ἔχει ἔλεος,
καὶ περὶ τῶν ἁμαρτιῶν αὐτοῦ δεῖται;
5 αὐτὸς σὰρξ ὢν διατηρεῖ μῆνιν,
τίς ἐξιλάσεται τὰς ἁμαρτίας αὐτοῦ;
6 μνήσθητι τὰ ἔσχατα καὶ παῦσαι ἐχθραίνων,
καταφθορὰν καὶ θάνατον, καὶ ἔμμενε ἐντολαῖς.
7 μνήσθητι ἐντολῶν καὶ μὴ μηνίσῃς τῷ πλησίον,
καὶ διαθήκην ὑψίστου καὶ πάριδε ἄγνοιαν.
8 Ἀπόσχου ἀπὸ μάχης, καὶ ἐλαττώσεις ἁμαρτίας·
ἄνθρωπος γὰρ θυμώδης ἐκκαύσει μάχην,
9 καὶ ἀνὴρ ἁμαρτωλὸς ταράξει φίλους
καὶ ἀνὰ μέσον εἰρηνευόντων ἐμβαλεῖ διαβολήν.
10 κατὰ τὴν ὕλην τοῦ πυρὸς οὕτως ἐκκαυθήσεται,
καὶ κατὰ τὴν στερέωσιν τῆς μάχης ἐκκαυθήσεται·
κατὰ τὴν ἰσχὺν τοῦ ἀνθρώπου ὁ θυμὸς αὐτοῦ ἔσται,
καὶ κατὰ τὸν πλοῦτον ἀνυψώσει ὀργὴν αὐτοῦ.
11 ἔρις κατασπευδομένη ἐκκαίει πῦρ,
καὶ μάχη κατασπεύδουσα ἐκχέει αἷμα.
12 ἐὰν φυσήσῃς εἰς σπινθῆρα, ἐκκαήσεται,
καὶ ἐὰν πτύσῃς ἐπ' αὐτόν, σβεσθήσεται·
καὶ ἀμφότερα ἐκ τοῦ στόματός σου ἐκπορεύεται.

KING JAMES VERSION

4 He sheweth no mercy to a man, which is like himself: and doth he ask forgiveness of his own sins?

5 If he that is but flesh nourish hatred, who will intreat for pardon of his sins?

6 Remember thy end, and let enmity cease; [remember] corruption and death, and abide in the commandments.

7 Remember the commandments, and bear no malice to thy neighbour: [remember] the covenant of the Highest, and wink at ignorance.

8 Abstain from strife, and thou shalt diminish thy sins: for a furious man will kindle strife.

9 A sinful man disquieteth friends, and maketh debate among them that be at peace.

10 As the matter of the fire is, so it burneth: and as a man's strength is, so is his wrath; and according to his riches his anger riseth; and the stronger they are which contend, the more they will be inflamed.

11 An hasty contention kindleth a fire: and an hasty fighting sheddeth blood.

12 If thou blow the spark, it shall burn: if thou spit upon it, it shall be quenched: and both these come out of thy mouth.

DOUAY OLD TESTAMENT

4 He hath no mercy on a man like himself, and doth he entreat for his own sins?

5 He that is but flesh, nourisheth anger, and doth he ask forgiveness of God? who shall obtain pardon for his sins?

6 Remember thy last things, and let enmity cease:

7 For corruption and death hang over in his commandments.

8 Remember the fear of God, and be not angry with thy neighbour.

9 Remember the covenant of the most High, and overlook the ignorance of thy neighbour.

10 Refrain from strife, and thou shalt diminish *thy* sins:

11 For a passionate man kindleth strife, and a sinful man will trouble his friends, and bring in debate in the midst of them that are at peace.

12 For as the wood of the forest is, so the fire burneth: and as a man's strength is, so shall his anger be, and according to his riches he shall increase his anger.

13 A hasty contention kindleth a fire: and a hasty quarrel sheddeth blood: and a tongue that beareth witness bringeth death.

14 If thou blow the spark, it shall burn as a fire: and if thou spit upon it, it shall be quenched: both come out of the mouth.

KNOX TRANSLATION

he refuse mercy to his fellow-man, yet ask forgiveness,
5 should he think to appease God, while he, a mortal man, is
obdurate? Who shall plead for his acquittal? 6 Look to thy
last end, and leave thy quarrelling; 7 with the grave's corruption God's commandments threaten thee.[a] 8 Thy God fear,
thy neighbour forgive; 9 the covenant of the most High
remember, thy neighbour's slip forget.

10 Keep clear of quarrelling, and sin shall less abound.
11 Quick temper sets feuds a-raging, and wicked men there
are that will embroil fast friends, and stir up strife among
folk that lived at peace. 12 More fuel, more fire; strong man
will rage the more, rich man push his vengeance farther.

13 Heat is gendered by the haste of rivalry, and bloodshed by hot blood; but it is tongue of witness that brings
death. 14 Spark blown upon will blaze, spat upon will die
out; see how of both the mouth is arbiter! 15 A curse on

a Literally, in the Latin, 'Corruption and death threaten in his commandments'; in the Greek '(look to) corruption and death, and abide in his commandments'.

TODAY'S ENGLISH VERSION

sinner, and if you won't forgive another person, you have no
right to pray that the Lord will forgive your sins. 5 If you
cannot get rid of your anger, you have no hope of forgiveness—you are only a human being. 6 Think about it! Some
day you will die, and your body will decay. So give up hate
and live by the Lord's commands, 7 the commands in the
covenant of the Most High. Instead of getting upset over
your neighbor's faults, overlook them.
8 If you stay out of arguments, you will not sin so much,
because a hot temper gets them started. 9 It is sinful to break
up a friendship by creating hostility among people who get
along well together. 10 The more fuel, the hotter the fire. The
more stubbornness, the hotter the argument. And the
stronger or richer people are, the angrier they can afford to
become. 11 An argument that blazes out suddenly can lead to
violence. 12 You can blow on a spark to make it glow, or you
can spit on it to put it out. Either way, you do it with your
mouth.

NEW REVISED STANDARD VERSION

4 If one has no mercy toward another like himself,
can he then seek pardon for his own sins?
5 If a mere mortal harbors wrath,
who will make an atoning sacrifice for his sins?
6 Remember the end of your life, and set enmity aside;
remember corruption and death, and be true to the
commandments.
7 Remember the commandments, and do not be angry
with your neighbor;
remember the covenant of the Most High, and
overlook faults.

8 Refrain from strife, and your sins will be fewer;
for the hot-tempered kindle strife,
9 and the sinner disrupts friendships
and sows discord among those who are at peace.
10 In proportion to the fuel, so will the fire burn,
and in proportion to the obstinacy, so will strife
increase;[a]
in proportion to a person's strength will be his anger,
and in proportion to his wealth he will increase his
wrath.
11 A hasty quarrel kindles a fire,
and a hasty dispute sheds blood.
12 If you blow on a spark, it will glow;
if you spit on it, it will be put out;
yet both come out of your mouth.

a Other ancient authorities read *burn*

NEW AMERICAN BIBLE

4 Should a man refuse mercy to his fellows,
yet seek pardon for his own sins?
5 If he who is but flesh cherishes wrath,
who will forgive his sins?
6 Remember your last days, set enmity aside;
remember death and decay, and cease from sin!
7 Think of the commandments, hate not your neighbor;
of the Most High's covenant, and overlook faults.

8 Avoid strife and your sins will be fewer,
for a quarrelsome man kindles disputes,
9 Commits the sin of disrupting friendship
and sows discord among those at peace.
10 The more wood, the greater the fire,
the more underlying it, the fiercer the fight;
The greater a man's strength, the sterner his anger,
the greater his power, the greater his wrath.
11 Pitch and resin make fires flare up,
and insistent quarrels provoke bloodshed.

12 If you blow upon a spark, it quickens into flame,
if you spit on it, it dies out;
yet both you do with your mouth!

NEW JERUSALEM BIBLE

4 Showing no pity for someone like oneself,
can one then plead for one's own sins?
5 Mere creature of flesh, yet cherishing resentment!—
who will forgive one for sinning?
6 Remember the last things, and stop hating,
corruption and death, and be faithful to the
commandments.
7 Remember the commandments, and do not bear your
fellow ill-will,
remember the covenant of the Most High, and ignore
the offence.

8 Avoid quarrelling and you will sin less;
for the hot-tempered provokes quarrels,
9 a sinner sows trouble between friends,
introducing discord among the peaceful.
10 The way a fire burns depends on its fuel,
a quarrel spreads in proportion to its violence;
a man's rage depends on his strength,
his fury grows fiercer in proportion to his wealth.
11 A sudden quarrel kindles fire,
a hasty dispute leads to bloodshed.
12 Blow on a spark and up it flares,
spit on it and out it goes;
both are the effects of your mouth.

GREEK OLD TESTAMENT

13 Ψίθυρον καὶ δίγλωσσον καταράσασθε·
πολλοὺς γὰρ εἰρηνεύοντας ἀπώλεσεν.
14 γλῶσσα τρίτη πολλοὺς ἐσάλευσεν
καὶ διέστησεν αὐτοὺς ἀπὸ ἔθνους εἰς ἔθνος
καὶ πόλεις ὀχυρὰς καθεῖλεν
καὶ οἰκίας μεγιστάνων κατέστρεψεν.
15 γλῶσσα τρίτη γυναῖκας ἀνδρείας ἐξέβαλεν
καὶ ἐστέρεσεν αὐτὰς τῶν πόνων αὐτῶν.
16 ὁ προσέχων αὐτῇ οὐ μὴ εὕρῃ ἀνάπαυσιν
οὐδὲ κατασκηνώσει μεθ' ἡσυχίας.
17 πληγὴ μάστιγος ποιεῖ μώλωπα,
πληγὴ δὲ γλώσσης συγκλάσει ὀστᾶ.
18 πολλοὶ ἔπεσαν ἐν στόματι μαχαίρας,
καὶ οὐχ ὡς οἱ πεπτωκότες διὰ γλῶσσαν.
19 μακάριος ὁ σκεπασθεὶς ἀπ' αὐτῆς,
ὃς οὐ διῆλθεν ἐν τῷ θυμῷ αὐτῆς,
ὃς οὐχ εἵλκυσεν τὸν ζυγὸν αὐτῆς
καὶ ἐν τοῖς δεσμοῖς αὐτῆς οὐκ ἐδέθη·
20 ὁ γὰρ ζυγὸς αὐτῆς ζυγὸς σιδηροῦς,
καὶ οἱ δεσμοὶ αὐτῆς δεσμοὶ χάλκειοι·
21 θάνατος πονηρὸς ὁ θάνατος αὐτῆς,
καὶ λυσιτελὴς μᾶλλον ὁ ᾅδης αὐτῆς.
22 οὐ μὴ κρατήσῃ εὐσεβῶν,
καὶ ἐν τῇ φλογὶ αὐτῆς οὐ καήσονται.
23 οἱ καταλείποντες κύριον ἐμπεσοῦνται εἰς αὐτήν,
καὶ ἐν αὐτοῖς ἐκκαήσεται καὶ οὐ μὴ σβεσθῇ·
ἐπαποσταλήσεται αὐτοῖς ὡς λέων
καὶ ὡς πάρδαλις λυμανεῖται αὐτούς.

KING JAMES VERSION

13 Curse the whisperer and doubletongued: for such have destroyed many that were at peace.

14 A backbiting tongue hath disquieted many, and driven them from nation to nation: strong cities hath it pulled down, and overthrown the houses of great men.

15 A backbiting tongue hath cast out virtuous women, and deprived them of their labours.

16 Whoso hearkeneth unto it shall never find rest, and never dwell quietly.

17 The stroke of the whip maketh marks in the flesh: but the stroke of the tongue breaketh the bones.

18 Many have fallen by the edge of the sword: but not so many as have fallen by the tongue.

19 Well is he that is defended from it, and have not passed through the venom thereof; who hath not drawn the yoke thereof, nor hath been bound in her bands.

20 For the yoke thereof is a yoke of iron, and the bands thereof are bands of brass.

21 The death thereof is an evil death, the grave were better than it.

22 It shall not have rule over them that fear God, neither shall they be burned with the flame thereof.

23 Such as forsake the Lord shall fall into it; and it shall burn in them, and not be quenched; it shall be sent upon them as a lion, and devour them as a leopard.

DOUAY OLD TESTAMENT

15 The whisperer and the double tongued is accursed: for he hath troubled many that were at peace.

16 The tongue of a third person hath disquieted many, and scattered them from nation to nation.

17 It hath destroyed the strong cities of the rich, and hath overthrown the houses of great men.

18 It hath cut in pieces the forces of people, and undone strong nations.

19 The tongue of a third person hath cast out valiant women, and deprived them of their labours.

20 He that hearkeneth to it, shall never have rest, neither shall he have a friend in whom he may repose.

21 The stroke of a whip maketh a blue mark: but the stroke of the tongue will break the bones.

22 Many have fallen by the edge of the sword, but not so many as have perished by their own tongue.

23 Blessed is he that is defended from a wicked tongue, that hath not passed into the wrath thereof, and that hath not drawn the yoke thereof, and hath not been bound in its bands.

24 For its yoke is a yoke of iron: and its bands are bands of brass.

25 The death thereof is a most evil death: and hell is preferable to it.

26 Its continuance shall not be for a long time, but it shall possess the ways of the unjust: and the just shall not be burnt with its flame.

27 They that forsake God shall fall into it, and it shall burn in them, and shall not be quenched, and it shall be sent upon them as a lion, and as a leopard it shall tear them.

KNOX TRANSLATION

every tale-bearer and traducer that disturbs the world's
peace! 16 Tongue that comes between two friends, how
many it has exiled, sent them to wander far away, 17 how
many rich cities dismantled, great houses demolished,
18 what armies it has routed, what proud nations brought
to ruin, 19 what noble women it has driven out from their
homes, and left all their toil unrewarded! 20 Pay heed to it,
and thou shalt never rest more, never find friend in whom
thou canst trust. 21 Whip that lashes does but bruise the
skin; tongue that lashes will break bones; 22 the sword
has killed many, the tongue more.
23 Blessed is he that is preserved from the tongue's wickedness, that has never felt its fury, never borne its yoke or
worn its chains; 24 that yoke of iron, those chains of bronze!
25 Here is death worse than death itself, here is loss the grave
cannot outvie. 26 Not for ever shall its reign persist, but
where wicked men go it still follows; the just it cannot consume, 27 but if thou forsake God thou shalt encounter it, a
fire that burns thee and will not be quenched, an assault
more perilous than assault of lion or pard. 28 Fence thy ears

TODAY'S ENGLISH VERSION

13 Gossips and liars deserve to be cursed, because they
have been the ruin of many people who were minding their
own business. 14 Many have had their lives ruined and have
been driven from their homes because of people who med-
dled in their business. Such unwanted interference has
resulted in the destruction of strong cities and the homes of
respected people. 15 Meddlers have caused faithful wives to
be divorced, robbed of everything they had worked for.
16 Anyone who pays attention to slander can never find peace
of mind. 17 A whip can raise a welt, but a vicious tongue can
break bones. 18 More people have died as a result of loose
talk than were ever killed by swords. 19-20 Count yourself
lucky if you have been spared the experience of having irresponsible talk directed against you—if you have never had
that iron yoke around your neck or those heavy chains on
your legs. 21 Slander leads to a miserable death; but in fact,
you'd be better off dead.
22 Devout people, however, cannot be overcome by slander;
they cannot be burned by its flames. 23 Its victims are those
who have abandoned the Lord; once the fire of slander has
been lit among them, it cannot be put out. Slander will
pounce on them like a lion and tear them to pieces like a
leopard.

NEW REVISED STANDARD VERSION

13 Curse the gossips and the double-tongued,
for they destroy the peace of many.
14 Slander[a] has shaken many,
and scattered them from nation to nation;
it has destroyed strong cities,
and overturned the houses of the great.
15 Slander[a] has driven virtuous women from their homes,
and deprived them of the fruit of their toil.
16 Those who pay heed to slander[b] will not find rest,
nor will they settle down in peace.
17 The blow of a whip raises a welt,
but a blow of the tongue crushes the bones.
18 Many have fallen by the edge of the sword,
but not as many as have fallen because of the tongue.
19 Happy is the one who is protected from it,
who has not been exposed to its anger,
who has not borne its yoke,
and has not been bound with its fetters.
20 For its yoke is a yoke of iron,
and its fetters are fetters of bronze;
21 its death is an evil death,
and Hades is preferable to it.
22 It has no power over the godly;
they will not be burned in its flame.
23 Those who forsake the Lord will fall into its power;
it will burn among them and will not be put out.
It will be sent out against them like a lion;
like a leopard it will mangle them.

a Gk *A third tongue* b Gk *it*

NEW AMERICAN BIBLE

13 Cursed be gossips and the double-tongued,
for they destroy the peace of many.
14 A meddlesome tongue subverts many,
and makes them refugees among the peoples;
It destroys walled cities,
and overthrows powerful dynasties.
15 A meddlesome tongue can drive virtuous women from
their homes
and rob them of the fruit of their toil;
16 Whoever heeds it has no rest,
nor can he dwell in peace.

17 A blow from a whip raises a welt,
but a blow from the tongue smashes bones;
18 Many have fallen by the edge of the sword,
but not as many as by the tongue.
19 Happy he who is sheltered from it,
and has not endured its wrath;
Who has not borne its yoke
nor been fettered with its chains;
20 For its yoke is a yoke of iron
and its chains are chains of bronze!
21 Dire is the death it inflicts,
besides which even the nether world is a gain;
22 It will not take hold among the just
nor scorch them in its flame,
23 But those who forsake the LORD will fall victims to it,
as it burns among them unquenchably!
It will hurl itself against them like a lion;
like a panther, it will tear them to pieces.

NEW JERUSALEM BIBLE

13 A curse on the scandal-monger and double-talker,
such a person has ruined many who lived in concord.
14 That third tongue has shattered the peace of many
and driven them from nation to nation;
it has pulled down fortified cities,
and overthrown the houses of the great.
15 The third tongue has had upright wives divorced,
depriving them of reward for their hard work.
16 No one who listens to it will ever know peace of mind,
will ever live in peace again.
17 A stroke of the whip raises a weal,
but a stroke of the tongue breaks bones.
18 Many have fallen by the edge of the sword,
but many more have fallen by the tongue.
19 Blessed is anyone who has been sheltered from it,
and has not experienced its fury,
who has not dragged its yoke about,
or been bound in its chains;
20 for its yoke is an iron yoke,
its chains are bronze chains;
21 the death it inflicts is a miserable death,
Sheol is preferable to it.
22 It cannot gain a hold over the devout,
they are not burnt by its flames.
23 Those who desert the Lord will fall into it,
it will flare up inextinguishably among them,
it will be let loose against them like a lion,
it will tear them like a leopard.

GREEK OLD TESTAMENT

24 ἰδὲ περίφραξον τὸ κτῆμά σου ἀκάνθαις,
τὸ ἀργύριόν σου καὶ τὸ χρυσίον κατάδησον·
25 καὶ τοῖς λόγοις σου ποίησον ζυγὸν καὶ σταθμὸν
καὶ τῷ στόματί σου ποίησον θύραν καὶ μοχλόν.
26 πρόσεχε μήπως ὀλίσθῃς ἐν αὐτῇ,
μὴ πέσῃς κατέναντι ἐνεδρεύοντος.

29 Ὁ ποιῶν ἔλεος δανιεῖ τῷ πλησίον,
καὶ ὁ ἐπισχύων τῇ χειρὶ αὐτοῦ τηρεῖ ἐντολάς.
2 δάνεισον τῷ πλησίον ἐν καιρῷ χρείας αὐτοῦ
καὶ πάλιν ἀπόδος τῷ πλησίον εἰς τὸν καιρόν·
3 στερέωσον λόγον καὶ πιστώθητι μετ' αὐτοῦ,
καὶ ἐν παντὶ καιρῷ εὑρήσεις τὴν χρείαν σου.
4 πολλοὶ ὡς εὕρεμα ἐνόμισαν δάνος
καὶ παρέσχον κόπον τοῖς βοηθήσασιν αὐτοῖς.
5 ἕως οὗ λάβῃ, καταφιλήσει χεῖρας αὐτοῦ
καὶ ἐπὶ τῶν χρημάτων τοῦ πλησίον ταπεινώσει φωνήν·
καὶ ἐν καιρῷ ἀποδόσεως παρελκύσει χρόνον
καὶ ἀποδώσει λόγους ἀκηδίας
καὶ τὸν καιρὸν αἰτιάσεται.
6 ἐὰν ἰσχύσῃ, μόλις κομίσεται τὸ ἥμισυ
καὶ λογιεῖται αὐτὸ ὡς εὕρεμα·
εἰ δὲ μή, ἀπεστέρησεν αὐτὸν τῶν χρημάτων αὐτοῦ,
καὶ ἐκτήσατο αὐτὸν ἐχθρὸν δωρεάν·
κατάρας καὶ λοιδορίας ἀποδώσει αὐτῷ
καὶ ἀντὶ δόξης ἀποδώσει αὐτῷ ἀτιμίαν.

KING JAMES VERSION

24 Look that thou hedge thy possession about with thorns, and bind up thy silver and gold,

25 And weigh thy words in a balance, and make a door and bar for thy mouth.

26 Beware thou slide not by it, lest thou fall before him that lieth in wait.

29 He that is merciful will lend unto his neighbour; and he that strengtheneth his hand keepeth the commandments.

2 Lend to thy neighbour in time of his need, and pay thou thy neighbour again in due season.

3 Keep thy word, and deal faithfully with him, and thou shalt always find the thing that is necessary for thee.

4 Many, when a thing was lent them, reckoned it to be found, and put them to trouble that helped them.

5 Till he hath received, he will kiss a man's hand; and for his neighbour's money he will speak submissly: but when he should repay, he will prolong the time, and return words of grief, and complain of the time.

6 If he prevail, he shall hardly receive the half, and he will count as if he had found it: if not, he hath deprived him of his money, and he hath gotten him an enemy without cause: he payeth him with cursings and railings; and for honour he will pay him disgrace.

DOUAY OLD TESTAMENT

28 Hedge in thy ears with thorns, hear not a wicked tongue, and make doors and bars to thy mouth.

29 Melt down thy gold and silver, and make a balance for thy words, and a just bridle for thy mouth:

30 And take heed lest thou slip with thy tongue, and fall in the sight of thy enemies who lie in wait for thee, and thy fall be incurable unto death.

29 HE that sheweth mercy, lendeth to his neighbour: and he that is stronger in hand, keepeth the commandments.

2 Lend to thy neighbour in the time of his need, and pay thou thy neighbour again in due time.

3 Keep thy word, and deal faithfully with him: and thou shalt always find that which is necessary for thee.

4 Many have looked upon a thing lent as a thing found, and have given trouble to them that helped them.

5 Till they receive, they kiss the hands of the lender, and in promises they humble their voice:

6 But when they should repay, they will ask time, and will return tedious and murmuring words, and will complain of the time:

7 And if he be able to pay, he will stand off, he will scarce pay one half, and will count it as if he had found it:

8 But if not, he will defraud him of his money, and he shall get him for an enemy without cause:

9 And he will pay him with reproaches and curses, and instead of honour and good turn will repay him injuries.

KNOX TRANSLATION

about with thorns, and give the wicked tongue no hearing;
make fast thy mouth with bolt and bar. 29 Melt down gold
and silver of thine, and get thee a balance that shall weigh
thy words, a bridle that shall be the rule of thy mouth;[a]
30 do all that lies in thee to keep thy tongue from speaking
amiss, lest lurking enemies triumph over thy ruin, the fatal
and final ruin that shall be thine.

29 Heart full of kindness and hand full of comfort will
keep the commandment, Lend to thy neighbour.
2 Neighbour must borrow easily when he needs, must repay
readily when his need is over. 3 Keep thy bond, deal faithfully, and thou shalt never lack. 4 Out upon the man that treats
loan as treasure trove, and is a burden to his benefactor!
5 What, kiss the hand that gives, and make humble promises
of repayment; 6 then, when the debt falls due, ask for grace,
and complain peevishly of hard times? 7 Pay grudgingly
when pay thou canst, offer but half the sum, and count it a
windfall for the lender? 8 Or, if thou canst not, disown the
debt and make an enemy of him, 9 rewarding thy benefactor
not with due honour, but with angry curse and reproach?

a *vv.* 28, 29: The Greek here differs from the Latin considerably, but its effect is the same, and makes it clear that the sacred author is alluding, all through this paragraph, not to the danger of incurring calumny, but to the danger of falling into a habit of calumniating others.

TODAY'S ENGLISH VERSION

24 Don't you fence in your property? Don't you lock up
your money? 25 Well, be just as careful with what you say.
Weigh every word, and have a lock ready for your mouth.
26 Someone may be waiting for you to slip, and if you are not
careful, you will stumble over your own words and fall down
in front of him.

29 Be kind enough to lend to your neighbor when he
needs help. You are keeping the Lord's commands if
you help him. 2 If he needs something, lend it to him. And
when you are in debt, pay it back as soon as you can. 3 If
you meet your obligations, you will always be able to borrow
what you need. 4 Many people treat a loan as something
they found and can keep, causing embarrassment to those
who helped them. 5 Some people will speak politely, bow,
and scrape until they get the loan they want, but when the
time comes to pay it back, they'll put it off, say that it's
inconvenient, and make a lot of worthless excuses. 6 If the
lender insists on being paid, he can count himself lucky to
get back half. If he doesn't insist, the borrower has robbed
him and made an unnecessary enemy. All the lender will get
from him are curses, insults, and disrespect, but never any
gratitude.

NEW REVISED STANDARD VERSION

24a As you fence in your property with thorns,
25b so make a door and a bolt for your mouth.
24b As you lock up your silver and gold,
25a so make balances and scales for your words.
26 Take care not to err with your tongue,[a]
and fall victim to one lying in wait.

29 The merciful lend to their neighbors;
by holding out a helping hand they keep the
commandments.
2 Lend to your neighbor in his time of need;
repay your neighbor when a loan falls due.
3 Keep your promise and be honest with him,
and on every occasion you will find what you need.
4 Many regard a loan as a windfall,
and cause trouble to those who help them.
5 One kisses another's hands until he gets a loan,
and is deferential in speaking of his neighbor's money;
but at the time for repayment he delays,
and pays back with empty promises,
and finds fault with the time.
6 If he can pay, his creditor[b] will hardly get back half,
and will regard that as a windfall.
If he cannot pay, the borrower[b] has robbed the other of
his money,
and he has needlessly made him an enemy;
he will repay him with curses and reproaches,
and instead of glory will repay him with dishonor.

a Gk *with it* b Gk *he*

NEW AMERICAN BIBLE

24 As you hedge round your vineyard with thorns,
set barred doors over your mouth;
25 As you seal up your silver and gold,
so balance and weigh your words.
26 Take care not to slip by your tongue
and fall victim to your foe waiting in ambush.

29 He does a kindness who lends to his neighbor,
and he fulfills the precepts who holds out a helping
hand.
2 Lend to your neighbor in his hour of need,
and pay back your neighbor when a loan falls due;
3 Keep your promise, be honest with him,
and you will always come by what you need.
4 Many a man who asks for a loan
adds to the burdens of those who help him;
5 When he borrows, he kisses the lender's hand
and speaks with respect of his creditor's wealth;
But when payment is due he disappoints him
and says he is helpless to meet the claim.
6 If the lender is able to recover barely half,
he considers this an achievement;
If not, he is cheated of his wealth
and acquires an enemy at no extra charge;
With curses and insults the borrower pays him back,
with abuse instead of honor.

NEW JERUSALEM BIBLE

24 Be sure you put a thorn-hedge round your property,
lock away your silver and gold;
25 then make scales and weights for your words,
and put a door with bolts across your mouth.
26 Take care you take no false step through it,
in case you fall a prey to him who lies in wait.

29 Making your neighbour a loan is an act of mercy,
to lend him a helping hand is to keep the
commandments.
2 Lend to your neighbour in his time of need,
and in your turn repay your neighbour on time.
3 Be as good as your word and keep faith with him,
and you will find your needs met every time.
4 Many treat a loan as a windfall,
and embarrass those who have come to their rescue.
5 Until he gets something, a man will kiss his
neighbour's hand,
and refer diffidently to his wealth;
but when the loan falls due, he puts this off,
he repays with offhand words,
and pleads the inconvenience of the time.
6 Even if he can be made to pay, his creditor will recover
barely half,
and consider even that a windfall.
But otherwise he will be cheated of his money,
and undeservedly gain himself an enemy;
the man will pay him back in curses and abuse,
and with insults instead of honour.

GREEK OLD TESTAMENT

[7]πολλοὶ οὐ χάριν πονηρίας ἀπέστρεψαν,
ἀποστερηθῆναι δωρεὰν εὐλαβήθησαν.
[8] Πλὴν ἐπὶ ταπεινῷ μακροθύμησον
καὶ ἐπ' ἐλεημοσύνῃ μὴ παρελκύσῃς αὐτόν.
[9]χάριν ἐντολῆς ἀντιλαβοῦ πένητος
καὶ κατὰ τὴν ἔνδειαν αὐτοῦ μὴ ἀποστρέψῃς αὐτὸν κενόν.
[10]ἀπόλεσον ἀργύριον δι' ἀδελφὸν καὶ φίλον,
καὶ μὴ ἰωθήτω ὑπὸ τὸν λίθον εἰς ἀπώλειαν.
[11]θὲς τὸν θησαυρόν σου κατ' ἐντολὰς ὑψίστου,
καὶ λυσιτελήσει σοι μᾶλλον ἢ τὸ χρυσίον.
[12]σύγκλεισον ἐλεημοσύνην ἐν τοῖς ταμιείοις σου,
καὶ αὕτη ἐξελεῖταί σε ἐκ πάσης κακώσεως·
[13]ὑπὲρ ἀσπίδα κράτους καὶ ὑπὲρ δόρυ ὁλκῆς
κατέναντι ἐχθροῦ πολεμήσει ὑπὲρ σοῦ.
[14] Ἀνὴρ ἀγαθὸς ἐγγυήσεται τὸν πλησίον,
καὶ ὁ ἀπολωλεκὼς αἰσχύνην ἐγκαταλείψει αὐτόν.
[15]χάριτας ἐγγύου μὴ ἐπιλάθῃ·
ἔδωκεν γὰρ τὴν ψυχὴν αὐτοῦ ὑπὲρ σοῦ.
[16]ἀγαθὰ ἐγγύου ἀνατρέψει ἁμαρτωλός,
καὶ ἀχάριστος ἐν διανοίᾳ ἐγκαταλείψει ῥυσάμενον.

KING JAMES VERSION

7 Many therefore have refused to lend for other men's ill dealing, fearing to be defrauded.

8 Yet have thou patience with a man in poor estate, and delay not to shew him mercy.

9 Help the poor for the commandment's sake, and turn him not away because of his poverty.

10 Lose thy money for thy brother and thy friend, and let it not rust under a stone to be lost.

11 Lay up thy treasure according to the commandments of the most High, and it shall bring thee more profit than gold.

12 Shut up alms in thy storehouses: and it shall deliver thee from all affliction.

13 It shall fight for thee against thine enemies better than a mighty shield and strong spear.

14 An honest man is surety for his neighbour: but he that is impudent will forsake him.

15 Forget not the friendship of thy surety, for he hath given his life for thee.

16 A sinner will overthrow the good estate of his surety:

17 And he that is of an unthankful mind will leave him [in danger] that delivered him.

DOUAY OLD TESTAMENT

10 Many have refused to lend, not out of wickedness, but they were afraid to be defrauded without cause.

11 But yet towards the poor be thou more hearty, and delay not to shew him mercy.

12 Help the poor because of the commandment: and send him not away empty handed because of his poverty.

13 Lose thy money for thy brother and thy friend: and hide it not under a stone to be lost.

14 Place thy treasure in the commandments of the most High, and it shall bring thee more profit than gold.

15 Shut up alms in the heart of the poor, and it shall obtain help for thee against all evil.

16 Better than the shield of the mighty, and better than the spear:

17 It shall fight for thee against thy enemy.

18 A good man is surety for his neighbour: and he that hath lost shame, will leave *him* to himself.

19 Forget not the kindness of thy surety: for he hath given his life for thee.

20 The sinner and the unclean fleeth from his surety.

21 A sinner attributeth to himself the goods of his surety: and he that is of an unthankful mind will leave him that delivered him.

KNOX TRANSLATION

[10]What wonder if many refuse to lend, not churlishly but for
fear of wilful wrong? [11]Yet would have thee patient with
needy folk; do not keep them waiting for thy charity;
[12]befriend, them, as the law commands, nor ever send them
away in their misery empty-handed. [13]It is thy brother, thy
friend that asks; better lose thy money than leave it to rust
in a vault. [14]Lay up store for thyself by obeying the commandments of the most High; more than gold it shall profit
thee; [15]the good deed treasured in poor men's hearts shall
ransom thee from all harm, [16]shall more avail than stout
shield or lance [17]to ward off thy enemies.

[18]Kindness bids thee go bail for thy neighbour; he has lost
all shame if he plays thee false. [a] [19]And if another goes bail
for thee, do not forget the benefit done thee; he gave his life
for thine. [20]It is right foully done to play a surety false;
[21]wouldst thou treat his goods as if they were thy own?
Wouldst thou, ungrateful wretch, leave thy ransomer to suffer

a *vv.* 19 sqq.: In Prov. 17. 18, and elsewhere a warning is given against the folly of becoming surety for a friend, and verses 26, 27 of the present chapter seem to imply the same moral. These warnings perhaps refer to rash commercial speculations; where it is a question of charity, we may have the duty of making ourselves responsible on behalf of some poor man, at the risk of his defrauding us.

TODAY'S ENGLISH VERSION

7 Many people refuse to lend at all, not because they are
stingy, but because[a] they don't want to be cheated if they
can avoid it.
8 Nevertheless, be understanding with those who are poor.
Don't keep them waiting for your generosity. 9 The Lord has
commanded us to help the poor; don't refuse them the help
they need. 10 It is better to lose your money by helping a relative or a friend than to lose it by letting it rust away under a
rock somewhere. 11 Use your wealth as the Most High has
commanded; this will do you more good than keeping your
money for yourself. 12 Count among your treasures the fact
that you give to the poor. It will save you from all kinds of
trouble 13 and will be a better defense against your enemies
than the strongest shield or stoutest spear.
14 A good man is willing to guarantee his neighbor's debts.
Only someone who has lost all sense of decency would
refuse to do so. 15 If someone does this favor for you, don't
forget it; he has risked his good name for you. 16 There are
some ungrateful sinners who abandon those who stand
behind them, and they cause them loss of property.

[a] not because . . . stingy, but because; *some manuscripts have* therefore, because of this wickedness.

NEW REVISED STANDARD VERSION

7 Many refuse to lend, not because of meanness,
but from fear[a] of being defrauded needlessly.

8 Nevertheless, be patient with someone in humble circumstances,
and do not keep him waiting for your alms.
9 Help the poor for the commandment's sake,
and in their need do not send them away empty-handed.
10 Lose your silver for the sake of a brother or a friend,
and do not let it rust under a stone and be lost.
11 Lay up your treasure according to the commandments of the Most High,
and it will profit you more than gold.
12 Store up almsgiving in your treasury,
and it will rescue you from every disaster;
13 better than a stout shield and a sturdy spear,
it will fight for you against the enemy.

14 A good person will be surety for his neighbor,
but the one who has lost all sense of shame will fail him.
15 Do not forget the kindness of your guarantor,
for he has given his life for you.
16 A sinner wastes the property of his guarantor,
17 and the ungrateful person abandons his rescuer.

a Other ancient authorities read *many refuse to lend, therefore, because of such meanness; they are afraid*

NEW AMERICAN BIBLE

7 Many refuse to lend, not out of meanness,
but from fear of being cheated.

8 To a poor man, however, be generous;
keep him not waiting for your alms;
9 Because of the precept, help the needy,
and in their want, do not send them away empty-handed.

10 Spend your money for your brother and friend,
and hide it not under a stone to perish;
11 Dispose of your treasure as the Most High commands,
for that will profit you more than the gold.
12 Store up almsgiving in your treasure house,
and it will save you from every evil;
13 Better than a stout shield and a sturdy spear
it will fight for you against the foe.

14 A good man goes surety for his neighbor,
and only the shameless would play him false;
15 Forget not the kindness of your backer,
for he offers his very life for you.
16 The wicked turn a pledge on their behalf into misfortune,
and the ingrate abandons his protector;

NEW JERUSALEM BIBLE

7 Many, not out of malice, refuse to lend;
they are merely anxious not to be cheated for nothing.

8 Nevertheless, be patient with those who are badly off,
do not keep them waiting on your generosity.
9 In obedience to the commandment, help the poor;
do not turn the poor away empty-handed in their need.
10 Spend your money on your brother or your friend,
do not leave it under a stone to rust away.
11 Use your wealth as the Most High has decreed;
you will find that more profitable than gold.
12 Stock your store-rooms with almsgiving;
this will save you from all misfortune.
13 Better than sturdy shield or weighty spear,
this will fight for you against the enemy.

14 A good man will go surety for his neighbour;
only a shameless wretch would desert him.
15 Do not forget the favour your guarantor has done you;
he has given his life for you.
16 A sinner is careless of his guarantor's prosperity,
the ungrateful forgets his deliverer.

GREEK OLD TESTAMENT

17 ἐγγύη πολλοὺς ἀπώλεσεν κατευθύνοντας
καὶ ἐσάλευσεν αὐτοὺς ὡς κῦμα θαλάσσης·
18 ἄνδρας δυνατοὺς ἀπῴκισεν,
καὶ ἐπλανήθησαν ἐν ἔθνεσιν ἀλλοτρίοις.
19 ἁμαρτωλὸς ἐμπεσὼν εἰς ἐγγύην
καὶ διώκων ἐργολαβίας ἐμπεσεῖται εἰς κρίσεις.
20 ἀντιλαβοῦ τοῦ πλησίον κατὰ δύναμίν σου
καὶ πρόσεχε σεαυτῷ μὴ ἐμπέσῃς.
21 Ἀρχὴ ζωῆς ὕδωρ καὶ ἄρτος καὶ ἱμάτιον
καὶ οἶκος καλύπτων ἀσχημοσύνην.
22 κρείσσων βίος πτωχοῦ ὑπὸ σκέπην δοκῶν
ἢ ἐδέσματα λαμπρὰ ἐν ἀλλοτρίοις.
23 ἐπὶ μικρῷ καὶ μεγάλῳ εὐδοκίαν ἔχε,
καὶ ὀνειδισμὸν παροικίας οὐ μὴ ἀκούσῃς.
24 ζωὴ πονηρὰ ἐξ οἰκίας εἰς οἰκίαν,
καὶ οὗ παροικήσεις, οὐκ ἀνοίξεις στόμα·
25 ξενιεῖς καὶ ποτιεῖς εἰς ἀχάριστα
καὶ πρὸς ἐπὶ τούτοις πικρὰ ἀκούσῃ
26 Πάρελθε, πάροικε, κόσμησον τράπεζαν,
καὶ εἴ τι ἐν τῇ χειρί σου, ψώμισόν με·
27 ἔξελθε, πάροικε, ἀπὸ προσώπου δόξης,
ἐπεξένωταί μοι ὁ ἀδελφός, χρεία τῆς οἰκίας.
28 βαρέα ταῦτα ἀνθρώπῳ ἔχοντι φρόνησιν,
ἐπιτίμησις οἰκίας καὶ ὀνειδισμὸς δανειστοῦ.

KING JAMES VERSION

18 Suretiship hath undone many of good estate, and shaken them as a wave of the sea: mighty men hath it driven from their houses, so that they wandered among strange nations.

19 A wicked man transgressing the commandments of the Lord shall fall into suretiship: and he that undertaketh and followeth other men's business for gain shall fall into suits.

20 Help thy neighbour according to thy power, and beware that thou thyself fall not into the same.

21 The chief thing for life is water, and bread, and clothing, and an house to cover shame.

22 Better is the life of a poor man in a mean cottage, than delicate fare in another man's house.

23 Be it little or much, hold thee contented, that thou hear not the reproach of thy house.

24 For it is a miserable life to go from house to house: for where thou art a stranger, thou darest not open thy mouth.

25 Thou shalt entertain, and feast, and have no thanks: moreover thou shalt hear bitter words:

26 Come, thou stranger, and furnish a table, and feed me of that thou hast ready.

27 Give place, thou stranger, to an honourable man; my brother cometh to be lodged, and I have need of mine house.

28 These things are grievous to a man of understanding; the upbraiding of houseroom, and reproaching of the lender.

DOUAY OLD TESTAMENT

22 A man is surety for his neighbour: and when he hath lost all shame, he shall forsake him.

23 Evil suretyship hath undone many of good estate, and hath tossed them as a wave of the sea.

24 It hath made powerful men to go from place to place round about, and they have wandered in strange countries.

25 A sinner that transgresseth the commandment of the Lord, shall fall into an evil suretyship: and he that undertaketh many things, shall fall into judgment.

26 Recover thy neighbour according to thy power, and take heed to thyself that thou fall not.

27 The chief thing for man's life is water and bread, and clothing, and a house to cover shame.

28 Better is the poor man's fare under a roof of boards, than sumptuous cheer abroad in another man's house.

29 Be contented with little instead of much, and thou shalt not hear the reproach of going abroad.

30 It is a miserable life to go as a guest from house to house: for where a man is a stranger, he shall not deal confidently, nor open his mouth.

31 He shall entertain and feed, and give drink to the unthankful, and moreover he shall hear bitter words.

32 Go, stranger, and furnish the table, and give others to eat what thou hast in thy hand.

33 Give place to the honourable presence of my friends: for I want my house, my brother being to be lodged with me.

34 These things are grievous to a man of understanding: the upbraiding of houseroom, and the reproaching of the lender.

KNOX TRANSLATION

for it? 22 Men have gone bail ere now for shameless friends
that so abandoned them. 23 By going bail for scoundrels, men
of good fortune have fallen upon ruin and shipwreck; 24 men
that held their heads high must now wander far and wide,
exiles in strange countries. 25 Leave godless sinners to
become sureties to their ruin; men that take rash ventures to
fall into the law's clutches. 26 For thyself, relieve thy neighbour as thy means allow, but never to thy own entanglement.
27 What are man's first needs? Water, and bread, and
clothing, and the privacy of a home. 28 Better the poor man's
fare under his roof of bare boards, than to be guest at a
splendid banquet, and home have none. 29 Make much of
the little thou hast; never be it thine to bear the reproach of a
wanderer. 30 A wretched life it is, passing on from house to
house to find a welcome; that welcome found, thou wilt lack
all confidence, and sit there mumchance. 31 Then, when thou
hast helped to entertain, with food and drink, the guests that
owe thee no thanks, thou wilt have a poor reward for it:
32 Up, wanderer! Lay me a fresh table, and what lies before
thee hand to others; 33 I have honoured guests coming, and
thou must make way for them; a kinsman of mine stands in
need of my hospitality! 34 Bitter words for an honest man to
hear; shall he owe his bread to one that reviles him as homeless?

TODAY'S ENGLISH VERSION

17 Guaranteeing loans has ruined many prosperous people
and caused them unsettling storms of trouble. 18 Influential
people have lost their homes over it and have had to go wandering in foreign countries. 19 A sinner who hopes to make a
profit by guaranteeing a loan is going to find himself
involved in lawsuits. 20 So help your neighbor as much as
you can, but protect yourself against the dangers involved.
21 The necessities of life are water, food, clothing, and a
home where you can have privacy. 22 It is better to be poor
and live under your own crude roof than to enjoy lavish banquets in other people's homes. 23 Be happy with what you
have, even if it isn't very much, and don't listen to anyone
who would insult your home and family.[a] 24 Going from
house to house is a miserable way to live. Anywhere you go,
you don't dare speak. 25 You welcome the guests and pour
the drinks, and nobody thanks you. Instead, people humiliate you by saying things like: 26 "Stranger! Come here and
set the table! I want to eat what you've got there! Give it
here! 27 Go away, stranger! I've got an important guest! My
brother is coming to visit, and I need the room!"
28 Being denied hospitality or having a moneylender hound
you—these are hard things for any sensitive person to
endure.

[a] don't listen . . . family; *or* don't listen to insults from your family; *some manuscripts do not have these words; one ancient translation has* don't get a reputation for living off other people.

NEW REVISED STANDARD VERSION

18 Being surety has ruined many who were prosperous,
and has tossed them about like waves of the sea;
it has driven the influential into exile,
and they have wandered among foreign nations.
19 The sinner comes to grief through surety;
his pursuit of gain involves him in lawsuits.
20 Assist your neighbor to the best of your ability,
but be careful not to fall yourself.

21 The necessities of life are water, bread, and clothing,
and also a house to assure privacy.
22 Better is the life of the poor under their own crude roof
than sumptuous food in the house of others.
23 Be content with little or much,
and you will hear no reproach for being a guest.[a]
24 It is a miserable life to go from house to house;
as a guest you should not open your mouth;
25 you will play the host and provide drink without being thanked,
and besides this you will hear rude words like these:
26 "Come here, stranger, prepare the table;
let me eat what you have there."
27 "Be off, stranger, for an honored guest is here;
my brother has come for a visit, and I need the guest-room."
28 It is hard for a sensible person to bear
scolding about lodging[b] and the insults of the moneylender.

a Lat: Gk *reproach from your family*; other ancient authorities lack this line
b Or *scolding from the household*

NEW AMERICAN BIBLE

17 Going surety has ruined many prosperous men
and tossed them about like waves of the sea,
18 Has exiled men of prominence
and sent them wandering through foreign lands.
19 The sinner through surety comes to grief,
and he who undertakes too much falls into lawsuits.
20 Go surety for your neighbor according to your means,
but take care lest you fall thereby.

21 Life's prime needs are water, bread, and clothing,
a house, too, for decent privacy.
22 Better a poor man's fare under the shadow of one's own roof
than sumptuous banquets among strangers.
23 Be it little or much, be content with what you have,
and pay no heed to him who would disparage your home;
24 A miserable life it is to go from house to house,
for as a guest you dare not open your mouth.
25 The visitor has no thanks for filling the cups;
besides, you will hear these bitter words:
26 "Come here, stranger, set the table,
give me to eat the food you have!
27 Away, stranger, for one more worthy;
for my brother's visit I need the room!"
28 Painful things to a sensitive man
are abuse at home and insults from his creditors.

NEW JERUSALEM BIBLE

17 Going surety has ruined many who were prosperous,
tossing them about in a heavy sea.
18 It has driven the powerful from home
to wander among foreign nations.
19 A wicked man in a hurry to stand guarantor
in the hope of profit, is hurrying to be sentenced.
20 Come to your neighbour's help as far as you can,
but take care not to fall into the same plight.

21 The first thing in life is water, and bread, and clothing,
and a house for the sake of privacy.
22 Better the life of the poor under a roof of planks,
than lavish fare in somebody else's house.
23 Whether you have little or much, be content with it,
and you will not hear your household complaining.
24 It is a miserable life, going from house to house;
wherever you stay, you dare not open your mouth,
25 you do not belong, you receive no thanks for the drink you pour out
and hear embittering words into the bargain:
26 'Come along, stranger, lay the table,
what have you got ready? give me something to eat!'
27 'Go away, stranger, make room for someone important;
my brother is coming to stay, I need the house.'
28 It is hard for the reasonable
to be begrudged hospitality
to be shamed like a debtor.

GREEK OLD TESTAMENT

30 Ὁ ἀγαπῶν τὸν υἱὸν αὐτοῦ ἐνδελεχήσει μάστιγας αὐτῷ,
ἵνα εὐφρανθῇ ἐπ᾽ ἐσχάτων αὐτοῦ·
2 ὁ παιδεύων τὸν υἱὸν αὐτοῦ ὀνήσεται ἐπ᾽ αὐτῷ
καὶ ἀνὰ μέσον γνωρίμων ἐπ᾽ αὐτῷ καυχήσεται·
3 ὁ διδάσκων τὸν υἱὸν αὐτοῦ παραζηλώσει τὸν ἐχθρὸν
καὶ ἔναντι φίλων ἐπ᾽ αὐτῷ ἀγαλλιάσεται.
4 ἐτελεύτησεν αὐτοῦ ὁ πατήρ, καὶ ὡς οὐκ ἀπέθανεν·
ὅμοιον γὰρ αὐτῷ κατέλιπεν μετ᾽ αὐτόν.
5 ἐν τῇ ζωῇ αὐτοῦ εἶδεν καὶ εὐφράνθη
καὶ ἐν τῇ τελευτῇ αὐτοῦ οὐκ ἐλυπήθη·
6 ἐναντίον ἐχθρῶν κατέλιπεν ἔκδικον
καὶ τοῖς φίλοις ἀνταποδιδόντα χάριν.
7 περιψύχων υἱὸν καταδεσμεύσει τραύματα αὐτοῦ,
καὶ ἐπὶ πάσῃ βοῇ ταραχθήσεται σπλάγχνα αὐτοῦ.
8 ἵππος ἀδάμαστος ἐκβαίνει σκληρός,
καὶ υἱὸς ἀνειμένος ἐκβαίνει προαλής.
9 τιθήνησον τέκνον, καὶ ἐκθαμβήσει σε·
σύμπαιξον αὐτῷ, καὶ λυπήσει σε.
10 μὴ συγγελάσῃς αὐτῷ, ἵνα μὴ συνοδυνηθῇς,
καὶ ἐπ᾽ ἐσχάτων γομφιάσεις τοὺς ὀδόντας σου.
11 μὴ δῷς αὐτῷ ἐξουσίαν ἐν νεότητι·
12 θλάσον τὰς πλευρὰς αὐτοῦ, ὡς ἔστιν νήπιος,

KING JAMES VERSION

30 He that loveth his son causeth him oft to feel the rod, that he may have joy of him in the end.

2 He that chastiseth his son shall have joy in him, and shall rejoice of him among his acquaintance.

3 He that teacheth his son grieveth the enemy: and before his friends he shall rejoice of him.

4 Though his father die, yet he is as though he were not dead: for he hath left one behind him that is like himself.

5 While he lived, he saw and rejoiced in him: and when he died, he was not sorrowful.

6 He left behind him an avenger against his enemies, and one that shall requite kindness to his friends.

7 He that maketh too much of his son shall bind up his wounds; and his bowels will be troubled at every cry.

8 An horse not broken becometh headstrong: and a child left to himself will be wilful.

9 Cocker thy child, and he shall make thee afraid: play with him, and he will bring thee to heaviness.

10 Laugh not with him, lest thou have sorrow with him, and lest thou gnash thy teeth in the end.

11 Give him no liberty in his youth, and wink not at his follies.

12 Bow down his neck while he is young, and beat him

DOUAY OLD TESTAMENT

30 HE that loveth his son, frequently chastiseth him, that he may rejoice in his latter end, and not grope after the doors of his neighbours.

2 He that instructeth his son shall be praised in him, and shall glory in him in the midst of them of his household.

3 He that teacheth his son, maketh his enemy jealous, and in the midst of his friends he shall glory in him.

4 His father is dead, and he is as if he were not dead: for he hath left one behind him that is like himself.

5 While he lived he saw and rejoiced in him: and when he died he was not sorrowful, neither was he confounded before his enemies.

6 For he left behind him a defender of his house against his enemies, and one that will requite kindness to his friends.

7 For the souls of his sons he shall bind up his wounds, and at every cry his bowels shall be troubled.

8 A horse not broken becometh stubborn, and a child left to himself will become headstrong.

9 Give thy son his way, and he shall make thee afraid: play with him, and he shall make thee sorrowful.

10 Laugh not with him, lest thou have sorrow, and at the last thy teeth be set on edge.

11 Give him not liberty in his youth, and wink not at his devices.

12 Bow down his neck while he is young, and beat his

KNOX TRANSLATION

30 Inure thy son to the rod, as thou lovest him; so shalt
thou have comfort of him[a] in thy later years, nor go
about knocking softly at thy neighbour's doors. 2 Discipline
thy son, and thou shalt take pride in him; he shall be thy
boast among thy familiars. 3 Discipline thy son, if thou
wouldst make thy ill-wishers envy thee, wouldst hold thy
head high among thy friends. 4 Father that dies lives on, if a
worthy son he has begotten; 5 here is a sight to make life
joyous for him, and death not all unhappiness, and a bold
front he keeps before his ill-wishers; 6 such an heir will shew
loyalty to his race, its foes warding off, its friends requiting.
7 Let a man pamper his children, binding up every wound,[b]
his heart wrung by every cry, 8 and he shall find spoilt son
headstrong and stubborn as a horse unbroken. 9 Cosset thy
son and make a darling of him, it shall be to thy own anxiety, thy own remorse. 10 Smile at his follies now, and the bitter taste of it shall set thy teeth on edge hereafter. 11 Thou
canst not afford to give him freedom in his youth, or leave
his thoughts unchecked; 12 none is too young to be bent to
the yoke, none is too childish to be worth a drubbing, if thou

a Or possibly, 'so shall he have comfort'. *b* The sense given here is that of the Greek; the Latin version, apparently through misunderstanding a rare word in the Greek, gives us the meaningless phrase, 'he will bind up his own wounds for the souls of his sons'.

TODAY'S ENGLISH VERSION

30 A father who loves his son will whip him often, so
that he can be proud of him later. 2 If a son is disciplined, he will be of some use, and his father can boast of
him to his friends. 3 Anyone who gives good guidance to his
son cannot only take pride in him among his friends, but he
can make his enemies jealous. 4-5 While the father is alive,
the sight of his son makes him happy, and when he dies, he
has no regrets. He is not really dead, because his son is like
him. 6 He has left someone to take vengeance on his enemies and to return the favors he owes his friends.
7 But anyone who spoils his son will have to bandage his
wounds.[a] His heart will stop every time he hears a shout.
8 An untamed horse is going to be stubborn, and an undisciplined son is no different. 9 If you pamper your child and
play with him, he will be a disappointment and a source of
grief. 10 Laugh with him now, and one day you will have to
cry over him, grinding your teeth in regret. 11 Don't give him
freedom while he is young, and don't overlook what he does
wrong. 12 Whip him while he is still a child, and make him

[a] will have . . . wounds; *or* is going to be hurt.

NEW REVISED STANDARD VERSION

CONCERNING CHILDREN[a]

30 He who loves his son will whip him often,
so that he may rejoice at the way he turns out.
2 He who disciplines his son will profit by him,
and will boast of him among acquaintances.
3 He who teaches his son will make his enemies envious,
and will glory in him among his friends.
4 When the father dies he will not seem to be dead,
for he has left behind him one like himself,
5 whom in his life he looked upon with joy
and at death, without grief.
6 He has left behind him an avenger against his enemies,
and one to repay the kindness of his friends.

7 Whoever spoils his son will bind up his wounds,
and will suffer heartache at every cry.
8 An unbroken horse turns out stubborn,
and an unchecked son turns out headstrong.
9 Pamper a child, and he will terrorize you;
play with him, and he will grieve you.
10 Do not laugh with him, or you will have sorrow with
him,
and in the end you will gnash your teeth.
11 Give him no freedom in his youth,
and do not ignore his errors.
12 Bow down his neck in his youth,[b]
and beat his sides while he is young,

a This heading is included in the Gk text. *b* Other ancient authorities lack this line and the preceding line

NEW AMERICAN BIBLE

30 He who loves his son chastises him often,
that he may be his joy when he grows up.
2 He who disciplines his son will benefit from him,
and boast of him among his intimates.
3 He who educates his son makes his enemy jealous,
and shows his delight in him among his friends.
4 At the father's death, he will seem not dead,
since he leaves after him one like himself,
5 Whom he looks upon through life with joy,
and even in death, without regret:
6 The avenger he leaves against his foes,
and the one to repay his friends with kindness.

7 He who spoils his son will have wounds to bandage,
and will quake inwardly at every outcry.
8 A colt untamed turns out stubborn;
a son left to himself grows up unruly.
9 Pamper your child and he will be a terror for you,
indulge him and he will bring you grief.
10 Share not in his frivolity lest you share in his sorrow,
when finally your teeth are clenched in remorse.
11 Give him not his own way in his youth,
and close not your eyes to his follies.
12 Bend him to the yoke when he is young,
thrash his sides while he is still small,

NEW JERUSALEM BIBLE

30 Whoever loves his son will beat him frequently
so that in after years the son may be his comfort.

2 Whoever is strict with his son will reap the benefit,
and be able to boast of him to his acquaintances.
3 Whoever educates his son will be the envy of his
enemy,
and will be proud of him among his friends.
4 Even when the father dies, he might well not be dead,
since he leaves his likeness behind him.
5 In life he has had the joy of his company,
dying, he has no anxieties.
6 He leaves an avenger against his enemies
and a rewarder of favours for his friends.
7 Whoever coddles his son will bandage his wounds,
his heart will turn over at every cry.
8 A badly broken-in horse turns out stubborn,
a son left to himself turns out headstrong.
9 Pamper your child and he will terrorise you,
play along with him and he will bring you sorrow.
10 Do not laugh with him, or one day you will weep with
him
and end up gnashing your teeth.
11 While he is young, do not allow him his freedom
and do not wink at his mistakes.
12 Bend his neck in youth,
bruise his ribs while he is a child,

GREEK OLD TESTAMENT

μήποτε σκληρυνθεὶς ἀπειθήσῃ σοι.
13 παίδευσον τὸν υἱόν σου καὶ ἔργασαι ἐν αὐτῷ,
ἵνα μὴ ἐν τῇ ἀσχημοσύνῃ αὐτοῦ προσκόψῃς.
14 Κρείσσων πτωχὸς ὑγιὴς καὶ ἰσχύων τῇ ἕξει
ἢ πλούσιος μεμαστιγωμένος εἰς σῶμα αὐτοῦ.
15 ὑγίεια καὶ εὐεξία βελτίων παντὸς χρυσίου,
καὶ σῶμα εὔρωστον ἢ ὄλβος ἀμέτρητος.
16 οὐκ ἔστιν πλοῦτος βελτίων ὑγιείας σώματος,
καὶ οὐκ ἔστιν εὐφροσύνη ὑπὲρ χαρὰν καρδίας.
17 κρείσσων θάνατος ὑπὲρ ζωὴν πικρὰν
καὶ ἀνάπαυσις αἰῶνος ἢ ἀρρώστημα ἔμμονον.
18 ἀγαθὰ ἐκκεχυμένα ἐπὶ στόματι κεκλεισμένῳ
θέματα βρωμάτων παρακείμενα ἐπὶ τάφῳ.
19 τί συμφέρει κάρπωσις εἰδώλῳ;
οὔτε γὰρ ἔδεται οὔτε μὴ ὀσφρανθῇ·
οὕτως ὁ ἐκδιωκόμενος ὑπὸ κυρίου.
20 βλέπων ἐν ὀφθαλμοῖς καὶ στενάζων
ὥσπερ εὐνοῦχος περιλαμβάνων παρθένον καὶ στενάζων.

KING JAMES VERSION

on the sides while he is a child, lest he wax stubborn, and be disobedient unto thee, and so bring sorrow to thine heart.

13 Chastise thy son, and hold him to labour, lest his lewd behaviour be an offence unto thee.

14 Better is the poor, being sound and strong of constitution, than a rich man that is afflicted in his body.

15 Health and good estate of body are above all gold, and a strong body above infinite wealth.

16 There is no riches above a sound body, and no joy above the joy of the heart.

17 Death is better than a bitter life or continual sickness.

18 Delicates poured upon a mouth shut up are as messes of meat set upon a grave.

19 What good doeth the offering unto an idol? for neither can it eat nor smell: so is he that is persecuted of the Lord.

20 He seeth with his eyes and groaneth, as an eunuch that embraceth a virgin and sigheth.

DOUAY OLD TESTAMENT

sides while he is a child, lest he grow stubborn, and regard thee not, and so be a sorrow of heart to thee.

13 Instruct thy son, and labour about him, lest his lewd behaviour be an offence to thee.

14 Better is a poor man who is sound, and strong of constitution, than a rich man who is weak and afflicted with evils.

15 Health of the soul in holiness of justice, is better than all gold and silver: and a sound body, than immense revenues.

16 There is no riches above the riches of the health of the body: and there is no pleasure above the joy of the heart.

17 Better is death than a bitter life: and everlasting rest, than continual sickness.

18 Good things that are hidden in a mouth that is shut, are as messes of meat set about a grave.

19 What good shall an offering do to an idol? for it can neither eat, nor smell:

20 So is he that is persecuted by the Lord, bearing the reward of his iniquity:

21 He seeth with his eyes, and groaneth, as an eunuch embracing a virgin, and sighing.

KNOX TRANSLATION

wouldst not see him wilful and disobedient, to thy heart's
unrest. 13 Discipline thy son, be at pains with him, or his
shameless ways will be thy downfall.

14 Poor man sound and strong of body is better off than
rich man enfeebled, and racked with disease. 15 Health of the
soul, that lies in duty done faithfully, is more worth having
than gold or silver; no treasure so rare that it can match bodily strength. 16 Health is best wealth; no comfort wilt thou
find like a merry heart. 17 Better the endless repose of death,
than life by lingering sickness made irksome. 18 For mouth
that refuses nourishment what use in dainties? They are no
better than the banquet left on a tomb, 19 little availing yonder idol, that cannot taste or smell. 20 Once the Lord has laid
thee by the heels, to do penance for thy sins, 21 thou shalt
hanker and sigh for these dainties but as eunuch that fondles maid.

TODAY'S ENGLISH VERSION

respect your authority. If you don't, he will be stubborn and
disobedient and cause you nothing but sorrow. [13]So discipline your son and give him work to do, or else he will be an
embarrassment to you.
[14]It is better to be poor, but strong and healthy, than to be
rich, but in poor health. [15]A sound, healthy body and a
cheerful attitude[a] are more valuable than gold and jewels.
[16]Nothing can make you richer or give you greater happiness
than those two things. [17]It would be better to be dead,
asleep forever, than to live in the misery of chronic illness.
[18]The finest food means nothing if you are too sick to eat it;
it might as well be offered to an idol.[b] [19]But there is no
point in offering food to an idol; it can't eat it or smell it. It is
just the same with someone whom the Lord has afflicted.
[20]He looks at his food and sighs, like a castrated man hug-
ging a young woman.

[a] *Hebrew* a cheerful attitude; *Greek* a strong body. [b] *Hebrew* offered to an idol; *Greek* placed on a grave.

NEW REVISED STANDARD VERSION

or else he will become stubborn and disobey you,
and you will have sorrow of soul from him.[a]

13 Discipline your son and make his yoke heavy,[b]
so that you may not be offended by his
shamelessness.

14 Better off poor, healthy, and fit
than rich and afflicted in body.
15 Health and fitness are better than any gold,
and a robust body than countless riches.
16 There is no wealth better than health of body,
and no gladness above joy of heart.
17 Death is better than a life of misery,
and eternal sleep[c] than chronic sickness.

CONCERNING FOODS[d]

18 Good things poured out upon a mouth that is closed
are like offerings of food placed upon a grave.
19 Of what use to an idol is a sacrifice?
For it can neither eat nor smell.
So is the one punished by the Lord;
20 he sees with his eyes and groans
as a eunuch groans when embracing a girl.[e]

a Other ancient authorities lack this line *b* Heb: Gk *take pains with him* *c* Other ancient authorities lack *eternal sleep* *d* This heading is included in the Gk text; other ancient authorities place the heading before verse 16 *e* Other ancient authorities add *So is the person who does right under compulsion*

NEW AMERICAN BIBLE

Lest he become stubborn, disobey you,
and leave you disconsolate.
[13]Discipline your son, make heavy his yoke,
lest his folly humiliate you.

[14]Better a poor man strong and robust,
than a rich man with wasted frame.
[15]More precious than gold is health and well-being,
contentment of spirit than coral.
[16]No treasure greater than a healthy body;
no happiness, than a joyful heart!
[17]Preferable is death to a bitter life,
unending sleep to constant illness.
[18]Dainties set before one who cannot eat
are like the offerings placed before a tomb.
[19]What good is an offering to an idol
that can neither taste nor smell?
[20]So it is with the afflicted man
who groans at the good things his eyes behold!

NEW JERUSALEM BIBLE

or else he will grow stubborn and disobedient,
and hurt you very deeply.
[13]Be strict with your son, and persevere with him,
or you will rue his insolence.

[14]Better be poor if healthy and fit
than rich if tormented in body.
[15]Health and strength are better than any gold,
a robust body than untold wealth.
[16]No riches can outweigh bodily health,
no enjoyment surpass a cheerful heart.
[17]Better death than a wretched life,
and everlasting rest than chronic illness.
[18]Good things lavished on a closed mouth
are like food offerings put on a grave.
[19]What use is an offering to an idol
which can neither eat nor smell?
How describe someone pursued by the Lord's
displeasure?
20 He looks and sighs
like a eunuch embracing a pretty girl—how he sighs!

GREEK OLD TESTAMENT

21 Μὴ δῷς εἰς λύπην τὴν ψυχήν σου
καὶ μὴ θλίψῃς σεαυτὸν ἐν βουλῇ σου.
22 εὐφροσύνη καρδίας ζωὴ ἀνθρώπου,
καὶ ἀγαλλίαμα ἀνδρὸς μακροημέρευσις.
23 ἀπάτα τὴν ψυχήν σου καὶ παρακάλει τὴν καρδίαν σου
καὶ λύπην μακρὰν ἀπόστησον ἀπὸ σοῦ·
πολλοὺς γὰρ ἀπώλεσεν ἡ λύπη,
καὶ οὐκ ἔστιν ὠφέλεια ἐν αὐτῇ.
24 ζῆλος καὶ θυμὸς ἐλαττοῦσιν ἡμέρας,
καὶ πρὸ καιροῦ γῆρας ἄγει μέριμνα.
25 λαμπρὰ καρδία καὶ ἀγαθὴ ἐπὶ ἐδέσμασιν
τῶν βρωμάτων αὐτῆς ἐπιμελήσεται.

31 Ἀγρυπνία πλούτου ἐκτήκει σάρκας,
καὶ ἡ μέριμνα αὐτοῦ ἀφιστᾷ ὕπνον.
2 μέριμνα ἀγρυπνίας ἀποστήσει νυσταγμόν,
καὶ ἀρρώστημα βαρὺ ἐκνήψει ὕπνον.
3 ἐκοπίασεν πλούσιος ἐν συναγωγῇ χρημάτων
καὶ ἐν τῇ ἀναπαύσει ἐμπίμπλαται τῶν τρυφημάτων αὐτοῦ.
4 ἐκοπίασεν πτωχὸς ἐν ἐλαττώσει βίου
καὶ ἐν τῇ ἀναπαύσει ἐπιδεὴς γίνεται.
5 Ὁ ἀγαπῶν χρυσίον οὐ δικαιωθήσεται,
καὶ ὁ διώκων διάφορα ἐν αὐτοῖς πλανηθήσεται.
6 πολλοὶ ἐδόθησαν εἰς πτῶμα χάριν χρυσίου,
καὶ ἐγενήθη ἡ ἀπώλεια αὐτῶν κατὰ πρόσωπον αὐτῶν.

KING JAMES VERSION

21 Give not over thy mind to heaviness, and afflict not thyself in thine own counsel.

22 The gladness of the heart is the life of man, and the joyfulness of a man prolongeth his days.

23 Love thine own soul, and comfort thy heart, remove sorrow far from thee: for sorrow hath killed many, and there is no profit therein.

24 Envy and wrath shorten the life, and carefulness bringeth age before the time.

25 A cheerful and good heart will have a care of his meat and diet.

31 Watching for riches consumeth the flesh, and the care thereof driveth away sleep.

2 Watching care will not let a man slumber, as a sore disease breaketh sleep.

3 The rich hath great labour in gathering riches together; and when he resteth, he is filled with his delicates.

4 The poor laboureth in his poor estate; and when he leaveth off, he is still needy.

5 He that loveth gold shall not be justified, and he that followeth corruption shall have enough thereof.

6 Gold hath been the ruin of many, and their destruction was present.

DOUAY OLD TESTAMENT

22 Give not up thy soul to sadness, and afflict not thyself in thy own counsel.

23 The joyfulness of the heart, is the life of a man, and a never failing treasure of holiness: and the joy of a man is length of life.

24 Have pity on thy own soul, pleasing God, and contain thyself: gather up thy heart in his holiness: and drive away sadness far from thee.

25 For sadness hath killed many, and there is no profit in it.

26 Envy and anger shorten a man's days, and pensiveness will bring old age before the time.

27 A cheerful and good heart is always feasting: for his banquets are prepared with diligence.

31 WATCHING for riches consumeth the flesh, and the thought thereof driveth away sleep.

2 The thinking beforehand turneth away the understanding, and a grievous sickness maketh the soul sober.

3 The rich man hath laboured in gathering riches together, and when he resteth he shall be filled with his goods.

4 The poor man hath laboured in his low way of life, and in the end he is still poor.

5 He that loveth gold, shall not be justified: and he that followeth after corruption, shall be filled with it.

6 Many have been brought to fall for gold, and the beauty thereof hath been their ruin.

KNOX TRANSLATION

22 Nor let anxious thoughts fret thy life away; 23 a merry
heart is the true life of man, is an unfailing store of holiness;
length of years is measured by rejoicing. 24 Thy own self
befriend, doing God's will with endurance, and giving all thy
heart to the holiness he enjoins, and banish thy sad
thoughts; 25 sadness has been the death of many, and no
good ever came of it. 26 Jealousy and peevishness shorten a
man's days; cares bring old age untimely; 27 gay and gallant
heart is ever feasting, sets to and makes good cheer.

31 Wilt thou pine away with care for riches, lose thy
sleep for thinking of it? 2 These solicitudes breed a
madness in the brain, such as only grave sickness can expel.
3 Toils rich man for gain, till he can rest and enjoy what is
his; 4 toils poor man to fend off need, and when he ceases he
is a poor man still. 5 Love money, and thou shalt be called to
account for it; thy quest corruption, of corruption thou shalt
have thy fill. 6 Many have given themselves up to the lure of
gold, and in its beauty found their ruin; 7 its worship was a

TODAY'S ENGLISH VERSION

21 Don't deliberately torture yourself by giving in to depression. 22 Happiness makes for a long life and makes it worth
living. 23 Enjoy yourself and be happy; don't worry all the
time. Worry never did anybody any good, and it has
destroyed many people. 24 It will make you old before your
time. Jealousy and anger will shorten your life. 25 A cheerful
person with a good attitude will have a good appetite and
enjoy his food.

31 Worrying about money will make you lose weight
and lose sleep. 2 Worrying about business[a] will keep
you from sleeping just as surely as a serious illness does.
3 Rich people work hard to make a lot of money; then they
can sit back and live in luxury. 4 Poor people work hard and
have nothing to show for it, and when they rest, they are
still poor.
5 No one who loves money can be judged innocent; his
efforts to get rich have led him into sin.[b] 6 Many people have
been ruined because of money, brought face-to-face with

[a] *Hebrew* Worrying about business; *Greek* Sleepless worry.
[b] *Hebrew* have . . . sin; *Greek* will destroy him.

NEW REVISED STANDARD VERSION

21 Do not give yourself over to sorrow,
and do not distress yourself deliberately.
22 A joyful heart is life itself,
and rejoicing lengthens one's life span.
23 Indulge yourself[a] and take comfort,
and remove sorrow far from you,
for sorrow has destroyed many,
and no advantage ever comes from it.
24 Jealousy and anger shorten life,
and anxiety brings on premature old age.
25 Those who are cheerful and merry at table
will benefit from their food.

31 Wakefulness over wealth wastes away one's flesh,
and anxiety about it drives away sleep.
2 Wakeful anxiety prevents slumber,
and a severe illness carries off sleep.[b]
3 The rich person toils to amass a fortune,
and when he rests he fills himself with his dainties.
4 The poor person toils to make a meager living,
and if ever he rests he becomes needy.

5 One who loves gold will not be justified;
one who pursues money will be led astray[c] by it.
6 Many have come to ruin because of gold,
and their destruction has met them face to face.

a Other ancient authorities read *Beguile yourself* *b* Other ancient authorities read *sleep carries off a severe illness* *c* Heb Syr: Gk *pursues destruction will be filled*

NEW AMERICAN BIBLE

21 Do not give in to sadness,
torment not yourself with brooding;
22 Gladness of heart is the very life of man,
cheerfulness prolongs his days.
23 Distract yourself, renew your courage,
drive resentment far away from you;
For worry has brought death to many,
nor is there aught to be gained from resentment.
24 Envy and anger shorten one's life,
worry brings on premature old age.
25 One who is cheerful and gay while at table
benefits from his food.

31 Keeping watch over riches wastes the flesh,
and the care of wealth drives away rest.
2 Concern for one's livelihood banishes slumber;
more than a serious illness it disturbs repose.
3 The rich man labors to pile up wealth,
and his only rest is wanton pleasure;
4 The poor man toils for a meager subsistence,
and if ever he rests, he finds himself in want.
5 The lover of gold will not be free from sin,
for he who pursues wealth is led astray by it.
6 Many have been ensnared by gold,
though destruction lay before their eyes;

NEW JERUSALEM BIBLE

21 Do not abandon yourself to sorrow,
do not torment yourself with brooding.
22 Gladness of heart is life to anyone,
joy is what gives length of days.
23 Give your cares the slip, console your heart,
chase sorrow far away;
for sorrow has been the ruin of many,
and is no use to anybody.
24 Jealousy and anger shorten your days,
and worry brings premature old age.
25 A genial heart makes a good trencherman,
someone who enjoys a good meal.

31 The sleeplessness brought by wealth makes a person
lose weight,
the worry it causes drives away sleep.
2 The worries of the daytime prevent you from sleeping,
like a serious illness, they keep sleep at bay.
3 The rich for ever toils, piling up money,
and then, leaving off, he is gorged with luxuries;
4 the poor for ever toils, barely making a living,
and then, leaving off, is poorer than ever.

5 No one who loves money can easily avoid sinning,
whoever pursues profit will be corrupted by it.
6 Gold has been the ruin of many;
their coming destruction was self-evident,

GREEK OLD TESTAMENT

7 ξύλον προσκόμματός ἐστιν τοῖς ἐνθουσιάζουσιν αὐτῷ,
καὶ πᾶς ἄφρων ἁλώσεται ἐν αὐτῷ.
8 μακάριος πλούσιος, ὃς εὑρέθη ἄμωμος
καὶ ὃς ὀπίσω χρυσίου οὐκ ἐπορεύθη·
9 τίς ἐστιν; καὶ μακαριοῦμεν αὐτόν·
ἐποίησεν γὰρ θαυμάσια ἐν λαῷ αὐτοῦ.
10 τίς ἐδοκιμάσθη ἐν αὐτῷ καὶ ἐτελειώθη;
καὶ ἔσται αὐτῷ εἰς καύχησιν.
τίς ἐδύνατο παραβῆναι καὶ οὐ παρέβη,
καὶ ποιῆσαι κακὰ καὶ οὐκ ἐποίησεν;
11 στερεωθήσεται τὰ ἀγαθὰ αὐτοῦ,
καὶ τὰς ἐλεημοσύνας αὐτοῦ ἐκδιηγήσεται ἐκκλησία.
12 Ἐπὶ τραπέζης μεγάλης ἐκάθισας;
μὴ ἀνοίξῃς ἐπ᾽ αὐτῆς φάρυγγά σου
καὶ μὴ εἴπῃς Πολλά γε τὰ ἐπ᾽ αὐτῆς·
13 μνήσθητι ὅτι κακὸν ὀφθαλμὸς πονηρός.
πονηρότερον ὀφθαλμοῦ τί ἔκτισται;
διὰ τοῦτο ἀπὸ παντὸς προσώπου δακρύει.
14 οὗ ἐὰν ἐπιβλέψῃ, μὴ ἐκτείνῃς χεῖρα
καὶ μὴ συνθλίβου αὐτῷ ἐν τρυβλίῳ.
15 νόει τὰ τοῦ πλησίον ἐκ σεαυτοῦ
καὶ ἐπὶ παντὶ πράγματι διανοοῦ.
16 φάγε ὡς ἄνθρωπος τὰ παρακείμενά σοι
καὶ μὴ διαμασῶ, μὴ μισηθῇς.

KING JAMES VERSION

7 It is a stumblingblock unto them that sacrifice unto it, and every fool shall be taken therewith.

8 Blessed is the rich that is found without blemish, and hath not gone after gold.

9 Who is he? and we will call him blessed: for wonderful things hath he done among his people.

10 Who hath been tried thereby, and found perfect? then let him glory. Who might offend, and hath not offended? or done evil, and hath not done it?

11 His goods shall be established, and the congregation shall declare his alms.

12 If thou sit at a bountiful table, be not greedy upon it, and say not, There is much meat on it.

13 Remember that a wicked eye is an evil thing: and what is created more wicked than an eye? therefore it weepeth upon every occasion.

14 Stretch not thine hand whithersoever it looketh, and thrust it not with him into the dish.

15 Judge of thy neighbour by thyself: and be discreet in every point.

16 Eat, as it becometh a man, those things which are set before thee; and devour not, lest thou be hated.

DOUAY OLD TESTAMENT

7 Gold is a stumblingblock to them that sacrifice to it: woe to them that eagerly follow after it, and every fool shall perish by it.

8 Blessed is the rich man that is found without blemish: and that hath not gone after gold, nor put his trust in money nor in treasures.

9 Who is he, and we will praise him? for he hath done wonderful things in his life.

10 Who hath been tried thereby, and made perfect, he shall have glory everlasting. He that could have transgressed, and hath not transgressed: and could do evil things, and hath not done them:

11 Therefore are his goods established in the Lord, and all the church of the saints shall declare his alms.

12 Art thou set at a great table? be not the first to open thy mouth upon it.

13 Say not: There are many things which are upon it.

14 Remember that a wicked eye is evil.

15 What is created more wicked than an eye? therefore shall it weep over all the face when it shall see.

16 Stretch not out thy hand first, lest being disgraced with envy thou be put to confusion.

17 Be not hasty in a feast.

18 Judge of the disposition of thy neighbour by thyself.

19 Use as a frugal man the things that are set before thee: lest if thou eatest much, thou be hated.

KNOX TRANSLATION

snare to catch their feet; alas, poor fools that went searching
for it, and themselves were lost!
8 Blessed is the man who lives, for all his wealth, unreproved, who has no greed for gold and puts no trust in his
store of riches! 9 Shew us such a man, and we will be loud
in his praise; here is a life to wonder at. 10 A man so tested
and found perfect wins eternal honour; he kept clear of sin,
when sinful ways were easy, did no wrong, when wrong lay
in his power. 11 His treasure is safely preserved in the Lord's
keeping and wherever faithful men are met, his alms-deeds
will be remembered.
12 Sit thou at a rich man's table, be not quick to remark
upon it; 13 it is ill done to cry out, Here is a table well
spread! 14 Be sure a covetous eye shall do thee no good;
15 eye is a great coveter, and for that, like no other part of thy
face, condemned to weep. 16 Be not quick to reach out thy
hand, and be noted, to thy shame, for greed; 17 jostling goes
ill with a feast. 18 Learn from thy own conjecture thy neighbour's need; 19 take sparingly the good things set before
thee, nor court ill-will by thy gluttony. 20 For manners' sake,

TODAY'S ENGLISH VERSION

disaster. 7 Money is a trap for those who are fascinated by it,
a trap that every fool falls into.
8 A person who gets rich without sinfully chasing after
money is fortunate. 9 Do you know anyone like that? If so,
we will congratulate him for performing a miracle that no
one else has ever been able to do. 10 If anyone has ever
passed this test, he can well be proud. Has anyone ever
known that he could get away with cheating someone, and
not taken advantage of it? 11 If so, he deserves his wealth,
and everyone will praise him for his generosity.
12 When you sit down at a fancy banquet, don't let your
mouth hang open, and don't say, "Look at all that food!"
13 It is impolite to have a greedy eye; remember that. Nothing
in creation is greedier than the eye; that is why it sheds tears
so often.[a] 14 Don't reach out for everything you see, and
don't elbow people out of the way to get at the food. 15 Be
considerate of the other people at the table and treat them
the way you want to be treated. 16 When you get your food,
eat it like a human being. Don't smack and slurp; nobody

[a] *Hebrew* so often; *Greek* on every face.

NEW REVISED STANDARD VERSION

7 It is a stumbling block to those who are avid for it,
and every fool will be taken captive by it.
8 Blessed is the rich person who is found blameless,
and who does not go after gold.
9 Who is he, that we may praise him?
For he has done wonders among his people.
10 Who has been tested by it and been found perfect?
Let it be for him a ground for boasting.
Who has had the power to transgress and did not
transgress,
and to do evil and did not do it?
11 His prosperity will be established,[a]
and the assembly will proclaim his acts of charity.

12 Are you seated at the table of the great?[b]
Do not be greedy at it,
and do not say, "How much food there is here!"
13 Remember that a greedy eye is a bad thing.
What has been created more greedy than the eye?
Therefore it sheds tears for any reason.
14 Do not reach out your hand for everything you see,
and do not crowd your neighbor[c] at the dish.
15 Judge your neighbor's feelings by your own,
and in every matter be thoughtful.
16 Eat what is set before you like a well brought-up
person,[d]
and do not chew greedily, or you will give offense.

a Other ancient authorities add *because of this* *b* Heb Syr: Gk *at a great table* *c* Gk *him* *d* Heb: Gk *like a human being*

NEW AMERICAN BIBLE

7 It is a stumbling block to those who are avid for it,
a snare for every fool.

8 Happy the rich man found without fault,
who turns not aside after gain!
9 Who is he, that we may praise him?
he, of all his kindred, has done wonders,
10 For he has been tested by gold and come off safe,
and this remains his glory;
He could have sinned but did not,
could have done evil but would not,
11 So that his possessions are secure,
and the assembly recounts his praises.

12 If you are dining with a great man,
bring not a greedy gullet to his table,
Nor cry out, "How much food there is here?"
13 Remember that gluttony is evil.
No creature is greedier than the eye:
therefore it weeps for any cause.
15 Recognize that your neighbor feels as you do,
and keep in mind your own dislikes:
14 Toward what he eyes, do not put out a hand;
nor reach when he does for the same dish.
16 Behave at table like a favored guest,
and be not greedy, lest you be despised.

NEW JERUSALEM BIBLE

7 since it is a snare for those who sacrifice to it
and stupid people all get caught in it.
8 Happy the rich who is found to be blameless
and does not go chasing after gold.
9 Who is he, so that we can congratulate him,
for he has achieved marvels among his fellows?
10 Who has been through this test and emerged perfect?
He may well be proud of that!
Who has had the chance to sin and has not sinned,
had the chance to do wrong and has not done it?
11 His fortune will be firmly based
and the assembly will acclaim his generosity.

12 If you are sitting down to a lavish table,
do not display your greed,
do not say, 'What a lot to eat!'
13 Remember, it is bad to have a greedy eye.
Is any creature more wicked than the eye?
—That is why it is always weeping!
14 Do not reach out for anything your host has his eye on,
do not jostle him at the dish.
15 Judge your fellow-guest's needs by your own,
be thoughtful in every way.
16 Eat what is offered you like a well brought-up person,
do not wolf your food or you will earn dislike.

GREEK OLD TESTAMENT

17 παῦσαι πρῶτος χάριν παιδείας
καὶ μὴ ἀπληστεύου, μήποτε προσκόψῃς·
18 καὶ εἰ ἀνὰ μέσον πλειόνων ἐκάθισας,
πρότερος αὐτῶν μὴ ἐκτείνῃς τὴν χεῖρά σου.
19 Ὡς ἱκανὸν ἀνθρώπῳ πεπαιδευμένῳ τὸ ὀλίγον,
καὶ ἐπὶ τῆς κοίτης αὐτοῦ οὐκ ἀσθμαίνει.
20 ὕπνος ὑγιείας ἐπὶ ἐντέρῳ μετρίῳ·
ἀνέστη πρωί, καὶ ἡ ψυχὴ αὐτοῦ μετ' αὐτοῦ.
πόνος ἀγρυπνίας καὶ χολέρας
καὶ στρόφος μετὰ ἀνδρὸς ἀπλήστου·
21 καὶ εἰ ἐβιάσθης ἐν ἐδέσμασιν,
ἀνάστα ἔμεσον πόρρω, καὶ ἀναπαύσῃ.
22 ἄκουσόν μου, τέκνον, καὶ μὴ ἐξουδενήσῃς με,
καὶ ἐπ' ἐσχάτων εὑρήσεις τοὺς λόγους μου·
ἐν πᾶσι τοῖς ἔργοις σου γίνου ἐντρεχής,
καὶ πᾶν ἀρρώστημα οὐ μή σοι ἀπαντήσῃ.
23 λαμπρὸν ἐπ' ἄρτοις εὐλογήσει χείλη,
καὶ ἡ μαρτυρία τῆς καλλονῆς αὐτοῦ πιστή.
24 πονηρῷ ἐπ' ἄρτῳ διαγογγύσει πόλις,
καὶ ἡ μαρτυρία τῆς πονηρίας αὐτοῦ ἀκριβής.
25 Ἐν οἴνῳ μὴ ἀνδρίζου·
πολλοὺς γὰρ ἀπώλεσεν ὁ οἶνος.
26 κάμινος δοκιμάζει στόμωμα ἐν βαφῇ,
οὕτως οἶνος καρδίας ἐν μάχῃ ὑπερηφάνων.

KING JAMES VERSION

17 Leave off first for manners' sake; and be not unsatiable, lest thou offend.

18 When thou sittest among many, reach not thine hand out first of all.

19 A very little is sufficient for a man well nurtured, and he fetcheth not his wind short upon his bed.

20 Sound sleep cometh of moderate eating: he riseth early, and his wits are with him: but the pain of watching, and choler, and pangs of the belly, are with an unsatiable man.

21 And if thou hast been forced to eat, arise, go forth, vomit, and thou shalt have rest.

22 My son, hear me, and despise me not, and at the last thou shalt find as I told thee: in all thy works be quick, so shall there no sickness come unto thee.

23 Whoso is liberal of his meat, men shall speak well of him; and the report of his good housekeeping will be believed.

24 But against him that is a niggard of his meat the whole city shall murmur; and the testimonies of his niggardness shall not be doubted of.

25 Shew not thy valiantness in wine; for wine hath destroyed many.

26 The furnace proveth the edge by dipping: so doth wine the hearts of the proud by drunkeness.

DOUAY OLD TESTAMENT

20 Leave off first, for manners' sake: and exceed not, lest thou offend.

21 And if thou sittest among many, reach not thy hand out first of all: and be not the first to ask for drink.

22 How sufficient is a little wine for a man well taught, and in sleeping thou shalt not be uneasy with it, and thou shalt feel no pain.

23 Watching, and choler, and gripes, are with an intemperate man:

24 Sound and wholesome sleep with a moderate man: he shall sleep till morning, and his soul shall be delighted with him.

25 And if thou hast been forced to eat much, arise, go out, and vomit: and it shall refresh thee, and thou shalt not bring sickness upon thy body.

26 Hear me, my son, and despise me not: and in the end thou shalt find my words.

27 In all thy works be quick, and no infirmity shall come to thee.

28 The lips of many shall bless him that is liberal of his bread, and the testimony of his truth is faithful.

29 Against him that is niggardly of his bread, the city will murmur, and the testimony of his niggardliness is true.

30 Challenge not them that love wine: for wine hath destroyed very many.

31 Fire trieth hard iron: so wine drunk to excess shall rebuke the hearts of the proud.

KNOX TRANSLATION

leave off eating betimes, or thy greed shall give offence.
21 When there are many about thee, do not be quick to stretch
out thy hand, quick to call for wine. 22 For a man well disciplined a little wine is enough; spare thyself the uneasy sleep,
the pains that shall rack thee; 23 wakeful nights come of
excess, and bile and griping pains. 24 For the temperate man,
there is sound sleep; sleep that lasts till morning, and contents his whole being; 25 though thou have been constrained
to eat beyond thy wont, thou hast but to leave the table and
vomit, and thou shalt find relief, nor come to any bodily
harm.

26 Take good heed, my son, do not belittle this advice of
mine; thou shalt live to prove it true. 27 Put thy heart into all
thou doest, and no infirmity of purpose shall hinder thee. [a]
28 The generous host is on all men's lips; ever they bear witness to his loyal friendship; 29 the niggard has the ill word of
a whole city; men form shrewd judgement of a niggard.

30 Never challenge hard drinker to a drinking-bout; wine
has been the ruin of many. 31 Fire tests the strength of steel;
and a proud man fuddled with wine betrays his quality.

a The bearing of this maxim is very doubtful; we may translate 'sickness' instead of 'infirmity of purpose'.

TODAY'S ENGLISH VERSION

can stand that. 17 It's good manners to be the first to stop
eating; stuffing yourself is offensive. 18 If there are many
people present, don't try to be the first to be served. 19 A little
bit is plenty for anyone with good manners. Besides, you
won't be short of breath when you go to bed. 20 People who
eat too much get stomach aches and cannot sleep. If you
don't overeat, you can get a good night's sleep and wake up
early the next morning feeling fine. 21 But if you do get a
stomach ache from eating too much, go off and vomit[a] and
you will feel better. 22 My child, if you listen to what I am
saying and put it into practice, one of these days you will
thank me for it. Be moderate[b] in everything you do, and you
will never get sick.
23 People appreciate a generous host, and he deserves their
praise. 24 But everybody in town will complain about a host
who is stingy with food, and their complaints are justified.
25 Don't try to prove your manhood by how much you can
drink. Wine has been the ruin of many. 26 An arrogant person's character shows through when he is in a drunken
argument, in the same way that iron is tested when it is
heated red-hot and then dipped in water. 27 Wine can put

[a] go off and vomit; *some manuscripts have* get up in the middle of the meal.
[b] *Hebrew* moderate; *Greek* industrious.

NEW REVISED STANDARD VERSION

17 Be the first to stop, as befits good manners,
and do not be insatiable, or you will give offense.
18 If you are seated among many persons,
do not help yourself[a] before they do.

19 How ample a little is for a well-disciplined person!
He does not breathe heavily when in bed.
20 Healthy sleep depends on moderate eating;
he rises early, and feels fit.
The distress of sleeplessness and of nausea
and colic are with the glutton.
21 If you are overstuffed with food,
get up to vomit, and you will have relief.
22 Listen to me, my child, and do not disregard me,
and in the end you will appreciate my words.
In everything you do be moderate,[b]
and no sickness will overtake you.
23 People bless the one who is liberal with food,
and their testimony to his generosity is trustworthy.
24 The city complains of the one who is stingy with food,
and their testimony to his stinginess is accurate.

25 Do not try to prove your strength by wine-drinking,
for wine has destroyed many.
26 As the furnace tests the work of the smith,[c]
so wine tests hearts when the insolent quarrel.

a Gk *reach out your hand* *b* Heb Syr: Gk *industrious* *c* Heb: Gk *tests the hardening of steel by dipping*

NEW AMERICAN BIBLE

17 Be the first to stop, as befits good manners;
gorge not yourself, lest you give offense.
18 If there are many with you at table,
be not the first to reach out your hand.
19 Does not a little suffice for a well-bred man?
When he lies down, it is without discomfort.
20 Distress and anguish and loss of sleep,
and restless tossing for the glutton!
Moderate eating ensures sound slumber
and a clear mind next day on rising.
21 If perforce you have eaten too much,
once you have emptied your stomach, you will have relief.
22 Listen to me, my son, and scorn me not;
later you will find my advice good.
In whatever you do, be moderate,
and no sickness will befall you.
23 On a man generous with food, blessings are invoked,
and this testimony to his goodness is lasting;
24 He who is miserly with food is denounced in public,
and this testimony to his stinginess is lasting.
25 Let not wine-drinking be the proof of your strength,
for wine has been the ruin of many.
26 As the furnace probes the work of the smith,
so does wine the hearts of the insolent.

NEW JERUSALEM BIBLE

17 For politeness' sake be the first to stop;
do not act the glutton, or you will give offence,
18 and if you are sitting with a large party,
do not help yourself before the others do.
19 A little is quite enough for a well-bred person;
his breathing is easy when he lies in bed.
20 A moderate diet ensures sound sleep,
one gets up early, in the best of spirits.
Sleeplessness, biliousness and gripe
are what the glutton has to endure.
21 If you are forced to eat too much,
get up, go and vomit, and you will feel better.
22 Listen to me, my child, do not disregard me,
eventually you will see the force of my words.
Be moderate in all your activities
and illness will never overtake you.
23 People praise the person who keeps a splendid table,
and their opinion of his munificence is sound.
24 But a niggardly host provokes universal resentment
and people will retail instances of his meanness.

25 Do not play the valiant at your wine,
for wine has been the undoing of many.
26 The furnace proves the temper of steel,
and wine proves hearts in the drinking bouts of braggarts.

GREEK OLD TESTAMENT

27 ἔφισον ζωῆς οἶνος ἀνθρώποις,
ἐὰν πίνῃς αὐτὸν ἐν μέτρῳ αὐτοῦ.
τίς ζωὴ ἐλασσουμένῳ οἴνῳ;
καὶ αὐτὸς ἔκτισται εἰς εὐφροσύνην ἀνθρώποις.
28 ἀγαλλίαμα καρδίας καὶ εὐφροσύνη ψυχῆς
οἶνος πινόμενος ἐν καιρῷ αὐτάρκης·
29 πικρία ψυχῆς οἶνος πινόμενος πολὺς
ἐν ἐρεθισμῷ καὶ ἀντιπτώματι.
30 πληθύνει μέθη θυμὸν ἄφρονος εἰς πρόσκομμα
ἐλαττῶν ἰσχὺν καὶ προσποιῶν τραύματα.
31 ἐν συμποσίῳ οἴνου μὴ ἐλέγξῃς τὸν πλησίον
καὶ μὴ ἐξουθενήσῃς αὐτὸν ἐν εὐφροσύνῃ αὐτοῦ·
λόγον ὀνειδισμοῦ μὴ εἴπῃς αὐτῷ
καὶ μὴ αὐτὸν θλίψῃς ἐν ἀπαιτήσει.

32 Ἡγούμενόν σε κατέστησαν; μὴ ἐπαίρου·
γίνου ἐν αὐτοῖς ὡς εἷς ἐξ αὐτῶν,
φρόντισον αὐτῶν καὶ οὕτω κάθισον·
2 καὶ πᾶσαν τὴν χρείαν σου ποιήσας ἀνάπεσε,
ἵνα εὐφρανθῇς δι' αὐτοὺς
καὶ εὐκοσμίας χάριν λάβῃς στέφανον.
3 Λάλησον, πρεσβύτερε, πρέπει γάρ σοι,
ἐν ἀκριβεῖ ἐπιστήμῃ καὶ μὴ ἐμποδίσῃς μουσικά.
4 ὅπου ἀκρόαμα, μὴ ἐκχέῃς λαλιὰν
καὶ ἀκαίρως μὴ σοφίζου.

KING JAMES VERSION

27 Wine is as good as life to a man, if it be drunk moderately: what life is then to a man that is without wine? for it was made to make men glad.

28 Wine measurably drunk and in season bringeth gladness of the heart, and cheerfulness of the mind:

29 But wine drunken with excess maketh bitterness of the mind, with brawling and quarrelling.

30 Drunkenness increaseth the rage of a fool till he offend: it diminisheth strength, and maketh wounds.

31 Rebuke not thy neighbour at the wine, and despise him not in his mirth: give him no despiteful words, and press not upon him with urging him [to drink.]

32 If thou be made the master [of a feast,] lift not thyself up, but be among them as one of the rest; take diligent care for them, and so sit down.

2 And when thou hast done all thy office, take thy place, that thou mayest be merry with them, and receive a crown for thy well ordering of the feast.

3 Speak, thou that art the elder, for it becometh thee, but with sound judgment; and hinder not musick.

4 Pour not out words where there is a musician, and shew not forth wisdom out of time.

DOUAY OLD TESTAMENT

32 Wine taken with sobriety is equal life to men: if thou drink it moderately, thou shalt be sober.

33 What is his life, who is diminished with wine?

34 What taketh away life? death.

35 Wine was created from the beginning to make men joyful, and not to make them drunk.

36 Wine drunken with moderation is the joy of the soul and the heart.

37 Sober drinking is health to soul and body.

38 Wine drunken with excess raiseth quarrels, and wrath, and many ruins.

39 Wine drunken with excess is bitterness of the soul.

40 The heat of drunkenness is the stumblingblock of the fool, lessening strength and causing wounds.

41 Rebuke not thy neighbour in a banquet of wine: and despise him not in his mirth.

42 Speak not to him words of reproach: and press him not in demanding again.

32 HAVE they made thee ruler? be not lifted up: be among them as one of them.

2 Have care of them, and so sit down, and when thou hast acquitted thyself of all thy charge, take thy place:

3 That thou mayst rejoice for them, and receive a crown as an ornament of grace, and get the honour of the contribution.

4 Speak, thou that art elder: for it becometh thee,

5 To speak the first word with careful knowledge, and hinder not music.

6 Where there is no hearing, pour not out words, and be not lifted up out of season with thy wisdom.

KNOX TRANSLATION

32 Easy flow wine, easy flow life, but to men of sober habit;
sobriety must drink within measure. 33 To the drunkard,[a]
life is no life at all; 34 wine is death, when it so deprives a
man of life. 35 Wine was made for mirth, never for drunkenness; 36 drink wisely, and it shall rejoice thy heart and thy
whole being; 37 health it brings to mind and body, wine
wisely taken. 38 Wine drunk in excess brings anger and
quarrelling and calamities a many; 39 it is the poison of a
man's life. 40 What does the false courage of the drunkard?
It takes him unawares, and makes him less a man; grievous
wounds come of it. 41 When the wine goes round, do not
find fault with thy neighbour, or think the worse of him for
being merry; 42 never taunt him, never press him to repay
the debt.

32 If they will make thee master of the feast, do not give
thyself airs; bear thyself as an equal. 2 Make good provision for the guests, and so take thy place among them; thy
duty done, recline at ease, 3 and in their pleasure rejoice,
accepting the crown that marks their favour, the honour
bestowed by their gifts. 4 Speak first, as becomes thy seniority,
5 but with due choice of words; and do not break in when
music is a-playing; 6 no need for thy words to flow when none
is listening, for thy wisdom to be displayed unseasonably.

a v. 33: 'To the drunkard'; literally, 'to him who is lessened by (or, in respect of) wine'. Elsewhere in this book this verb expresses some deficit in personal qualities. The sense 'to him who must go without wine' is admissible, and if it is adopted, the next verse will refer not to immoderate drinking, but to an empty cellar.

TODAY'S ENGLISH VERSION

new life into you if you drink it in moderation. What would
life be like without it? Wine was created to make us happy.
28 If you drink it in moderation and at the right time, it can
lift your spirits and make you cheerful, 29 but if you drink
when you are angry and upset, it leads to headaches, embarrassment, and disgrace.[a] 30 A drunken fool can lose his temper and hurt himself. His drinking makes him weak and an
easy target for angry blows. 31 Never rebuke a person when
you have both been drinking. Don't hurt his feelings while
he is having a good time. It's not the time to criticize anyone,
or to ask him to pay back a debt.

32 If you are chosen to preside at a banquet, don't put
on airs. Just be like everyone else. Look after the
guests before you sit down. 2 After you have performed your
duties, you can sit down and enjoy yourself with the others.
They will respect you for doing a good job.

3 If you are older than most of the guests, you may talk;
that is your right. But you should know what you are talking
about and not interrupt the music. 4 If entertainment is
being provided, don't keep up a steady conversation; it's the
wrong time to show off your wit. 5 Music at a banquet where

[a] *Hebrew* when you are . . . disgrace; *Greek* too much, it leads to bitterness, offense, and stumbling.

NEW REVISED STANDARD VERSION

27 Wine is very life to human beings
if taken in moderation.
What is life to one who is without wine?
It has been created to make people happy.
28 Wine drunk at the proper time and in moderation
is rejoicing of heart and gladness of soul.
29 Wine drunk to excess leads to bitterness of spirit,
to quarrels and stumbling.
30 Drunkenness increases the anger of a fool to his own
hurt,
reducing his strength and adding wounds.
31 Do not reprove your neighbor at a banquet of wine,
and do not despise him in his merrymaking;
speak no word of reproach to him,
and do not distress him by making demands of him.

32 If they make you master of the feast, do not exalt
yourself;
be among them as one of their number.
Take care of them first and then sit down;
2 when you have fulfilled all your duties, take your
place,
so that you may be merry along with them
and receive a wreath for your excellent leadership.

3 Speak, you who are older, for it is your right,
but with accurate knowledge, and do not interrupt
the music.
4 Where there is entertainment, do not pour out talk;
do not display your cleverness at the wrong time.

NEW AMERICAN BIBLE

27 Wine is very life to man
if taken in moderation.
Does he really live who lacks the wine
which was created for his joy?
28 Joy of heart, good cheer and merriment
are wine drunk freely at the proper time.
29 Headache, bitterness and disgrace
is wine drunk amid anger and strife.
30 More and more wine is a snare for the fool;
it lessens his strength and multiplies his wounds.
31 Rebuke not your neighbor when wine is served,
nor put him to shame while he is merry;
Use no harsh words with him
and distress him not in the presence of others.

32 If you are chosen to preside at dinner, be not puffed
up,
but with the guests be as one of themselves;
Take care of them first before you sit down;
2 when you have fulfilled your duty, then take your
place,
To share in their joy
and win praise for your hospitality.
3 Being older, you may talk; that is only your right,
but temper your wisdom, not to disturb the singing.
4 When wine is present, do not pour out discourse,
and flaunt not your wisdom at the wrong time.

NEW JERUSALEM BIBLE

27 Wine gives life
if drunk in moderation.
What is life worth without wine?
It came into being to make people happy.
28 Drunk at the right time and in the right amount,
wine makes for a glad heart and a cheerful mind.
29 Bitterness of soul comes of wine drunk to excess
out of temper or bravado.
30 Drunkenness excites the stupid to a fury to his own
harm,
it reduces his strength while leading to blows.
31 Do not provoke your fellow-guest at a wine feast,
do not make fun of him when he is enjoying himself,
do not take him to task
or annoy him by reclaiming money owed.

32 Have they made you the presider? Do not let it go to
your head,
behave like everyone else in the party,
see that they are happy and then sit down yourself.
2 Having discharged your duties, take your place
so that your joy may be through theirs,
and you may receive the crown for your competence.
3 Speak, old man—it is proper that you should—
but with discretion: do not spoil the music.
4 If someone is singing, do not ramble on
and do not play the sage at the wrong moment.

GREEK OLD TESTAMENT

5 σφραγὶς ἄνθρακος ἐπὶ κόσμῳ χρυσῷ
σύγκριμα μουσικῶν ἐν συμποσίῳ οἴνου·
6 ἐν κατασκευάσματι χρυσῷ σφραγὶς σμαράγδου
μέλος μουσικῶν ἐφ᾽ ἡδεῖ οἴνῳ.
7 Λάλησον, νεανίσκε, εἰ χρεία σου,
μόλις δὶς ἐὰν ἐπερωτηθῇς·
8 κεφαλαίωσον λόγον, ἐν ὀλίγοις πολλά·
γίνου ὡς γινώσκων καὶ ἅμα σιωπῶν.
9 ἐν μέσῳ μεγιστάνων μὴ ἐξισάζου
καὶ ἑτέρου λέγοντος μὴ πολλὰ ἀδολέσχει.
10 πρὸ βροντῆς κατασπεύδει ἀστραπή,
καὶ πρὸ αἰσχυντηροῦ προελεύσεται χάρις.
11 ἐν ὥρᾳ ἐξεγείρου καὶ μὴ οὐράγει,
ἀπότρεχε εἰς οἶκον καὶ μὴ ῥαθύμει·
12 ἐκεῖ παῖζε καὶ ποίει τὰ ἐνθυμήματά σου
καὶ μὴ ἁμάρτῃς λόγῳ ὑπερηφάνῳ.
13 καὶ ἐπὶ τούτοις εὐλόγησον τὸν ποιήσαντά σε
καὶ μεθύσκοντά σε ἀπὸ τῶν ἀγαθῶν αὐτοῦ.
14 Ὁ φοβούμενος κύριον ἐκδέξεται παιδείαν,
καὶ οἱ ὀρθρίζοντες εὑρήσουσιν εὐδοκίαν.
15 ὁ ζητῶν νόμον ἐμπλησθήσεται αὐτοῦ,
καὶ ὁ ὑποκρινόμενος σκανδαλισθήσεται ἐν αὐτῷ.
16 οἱ φοβούμενοι κύριον εὑρήσουσιν κρίμα
καὶ δικαιώματα ὡς φῶς ἐξάψουσιν.

KING JAMES VERSION

5 A concert of musick in a banquet of wine is as a signet of carbuncle set in gold.

6 As a signet of an emerald set in a work of gold, so is the melody of musick with pleasant wine.

7 Speak, young man, if there be need of thee: and yet scarcely when thou art twice asked.

8 Let thy speech be short, comprehending much in few words; be as one that knoweth and yet holdeth his tongue.

9 If thou be among great men, make not thyself equal with them; and when ancient men are in place, use not many words.

10 Before the thunder goeth lightning; and before a shamefaced man shall go favour.

11 Rise up betimes, and be not the last; but get thee home without delay.

12 There take thy pastime, and do what thou wilt: but sin not by proud speech.

13 And for these things bless him that made thee, and hath replenished thee with his good things.

14 Whoso feareth the Lord will receive his discipline; and they that seek him early shall find favour.

15 He that seeketh the law shall be filled therewith: but the hypocrite will be offended thereat.

16 They that fear the Lord shall find judgment, and shall kindle justice as a light.

DOUAY OLD TESTAMENT

7 A concert of music in a banquet of wine is as a carbuncle set in gold.

8 As a signet of an emerald in a work of gold: so is the melody of music with pleasant and moderate wine.

9 Hear in silence, and for thy reverence good grace shall come to thee.

10 Young man, scarcely speak in thy own cause.

11 If thou be asked twice, let thy answer be short.

12 In many things be as if thou wert ignorant, and hear in silence and withal seeking.

13 In the company of great men take not upon thee: and when the ancients are present, speak not much.

14 Before a storm goeth lightning: and before shamefacedness goeth favour: and for thy reverence good grace shall come to thee.

15 And at the time of rising be not slack: but be first to run home to thy house, and there withdraw thyself, and there take thy pastime.

16 And do what thou hast a mind, but not in sin or proud speech.

17 And for all these things bless the Lord, that made thee, and that replenisheth thee with all his good things.

18 He that feareth the Lord, will receive his discipline: and they that will seek him early, shall find a blessing.

19 He that seeketh the law, shall be filled with it: and he that dealeth deceitfully, shall meet with a stumblingblock therein.

20 They that fear the Lord, shall find just judgment, and shall kindle justice as a light.

KNOX TRANSLATION

7 Music and wine, carbuncle set in gold, 8 music and wine,
signet ring of gold and emerald, so the wine be good, and
taken in due measure.

9 Keep silence, and give others a hearing; it shall win thee
a name for modesty; 10 if thou art but a young man, be loth
to speak even of what concerns thee, 11 and if thou art
pressed for an answer, give it in brief. 12 For the most part
keep thy knowledge concealed under a mask of silence and
enquiry; 13 nor ever be familiar among great men, nor garrulous among the wise. 14 Sure as the lightning is sign of a
storm, men's good word is the sign of a modest nature; they
will love thee all the better for thy bashfulness. 15 When the
time comes for going, do not Linger; get thee gone speedily
to thy home, there to divert thyself, and take thy ease, 16 and
follow the whim of thy own thoughts, yet innocently and
with no word proudly said. 17 And for all this give thanks to
God thy maker, that so contents thee with his gifts.

18 If thou fearest the Lord, thou wilt accept the schooling
he gives thee, waiting early at his door to win his blessing.
19 In the law, the law's follower finds deep content, the false
heart nothing but a snare to catch it. 20 Those who fear the
Lord will discover where right lies, the light of truth shall

TODAY'S ENGLISH VERSION

wine is served is like a ruby set in gold. 6 Good music and
good wine—an emerald set in gold.
7 If you are young, don't speak unless you have to, but
never more than twice, and only if someone speaks to you
first. 8 Come to the point and say it all in a few words. Show
that you are well-informed, but stay quiet. 9 Don't treat
important people as if you were their equal and don't make a
nuisance of yourself by asking them a lot of questions.[a]
10 The reputation of a modest person goes before him, as
lightning before thunder.
11 Leave the party at the right time and never be the last to
go. Don't linger at the door; just go straight home. 12 There
you can enjoy yourself as you wish, but don't commit the sin
of bragging. 13 And don't forget to thank your Creator for letting you enjoy so many good things.
14 If you fear the Lord, you will accept his correction. He
will bless those who get up early in the morning to pray.
15 Study his Law, and you will master it, unless you are
insincere about it, in which case you will fail. 16 If you fear
the Lord, you will know what is right, and you will be

[a] *Hebrew* make . . . questions; *Greek* keep talking when someone else is speaking.

NEW REVISED STANDARD VERSION

5 A ruby seal in a setting of gold
is a concert of music at a banquet of wine.
6 A seal of emerald in a rich setting of gold
is the melody of music with good wine.

7 Speak, you who are young, if you are obliged to,
but no more than twice, and only if asked.
8 Be brief; say much in few words;
be as one who knows and can still hold his tongue.
9 Among the great do not act as their equal;
and when another is speaking, do not babble.

10 Lightning travels ahead of the thunder,
and approval goes before one who is modest.
11 Leave in good time and do not be the last;
go home quickly and do not linger.
12 Amuse yourself there to your heart's content,
but do not sin through proud speech.
13 But above all bless your Maker,
who fills you with his good gifts.

14 The one who seeks God[a] will accept his discipline,
and those who rise early to seek him[b] will find favor.
15 The one who seeks the law will be filled with it,
but the hypocrite will stumble at it.
16 Those who fear the Lord will form true judgments,
and they will kindle righteous deeds like a light.

[a] Heb: Gk *who fears the Lord* [b] Other ancient authorities lack *to seek him*

NEW AMERICAN BIBLE

5 Like a seal of carnelian in a setting of gold
is a concert when wine is served.
6 Like a gold mounting with an emerald seal
is string music with delicious wine.
7 Young man, speak only when necessary,
when they have asked you more than once;
8 Be brief, but say much in those few words,
be like the wise man, taciturn.
9 When among your elders be not forward,
and with officials be not too insistent.
10 Like the lightning that flashes before a storm
is the esteem that shines on modesty.
11 When it is time to leave, tarry not;
be off for home! There take your ease,
12 And there enjoy doing as you wish,
but without sin or words of pride.
13 Above all, give praise to your Creator,
who showers his favors upon you.

14 He who would find God must accept discipline;
he who seeks him obtains his request.
15 He who studies the law masters it,
but the hypocrite finds it a trap.
16 His judgment is sound who fears the LORD;
out of obscurity he draws forth a clear plan.

NEW JERUSALEM BIBLE

5 An amber seal on a precious stone,
such is a concert of music at a wine feast.
6 An emerald seal in a golden setting,
such are strains of music with a vintage wine.
7 Speak, young man, when you must,
but twice at most, and then only if questioned.
8 Keep to the point, say much in few words;
give the impression of knowing but not wanting to speak.
9 Among eminent people do not behave as though you were their equal;
do not make frivolous remarks when someone else is speaking.
10 Lightning comes before the thunder,
favour goes ahead of a modest person.
11 Leave in good time, do not bring up the rear,
and hurry home without loitering.
12 There amuse yourself, and do what you have a mind to,
but do not sin by arrogant talk.
13 And for all this bless your Creator,
who intoxicates you with his favours.
14 Whoever fears the Lord will accept his correction;
those who look for him will win his favour.
15 Whoever seeks the Law will be nourished by it,
the hypocrite will find it a stumbling-block.
16 Those who fear the Lord win his approval,
their good deeds shining like a light.

GREEK OLD TESTAMENT

17 ἄνθρωπος ἁμαρτωλὸς ἐκκλινεῖ ἐλεγμὸν
καὶ κατὰ τὸ θέλημα αὐτοῦ εὑρήσει σύγκριμα.
18 Ἀνὴρ βουλῆς οὐ μὴ παρίδῃ διανόημα,
ἀλλότριος καὶ ὑπερήφανος οὐ καταπτήξει φόβον.
19 ἄνευ βουλῆς μηθὲν ποιήσῃς
καὶ ἐν τῷ ποιῆσαί σε μὴ μεταμελοῦ.
20 ἐν ὁδῷ ἀντιπτώματος μὴ πορεύου
καὶ μὴ προσκόψῃς ἐν λιθώδεσιν.
21 μὴ πιστεύσῃς ἐν ὁδῷ ἀπροσκόπῳ
22 καὶ ἀπὸ τῶν τέκνων σου φύλαξαι.
23 ἐν παντὶ ἔργῳ πίστευε τῇ ψυχῇ σου·
καὶ γὰρ τοῦτό ἐστιν τήρησις ἐντολῶν.
24 ὁ πιστεύων νόμῳ προσέχει ἐντολαῖς,
καὶ ὁ πεποιθὼς κυρίῳ οὐκ ἐλαττωθήσεται.
33 Τῷ φοβουμένῳ κύριον οὐκ ἀπαντήσει κακόν,
ἀλλ᾽ ἐν πειρασμῷ καὶ πάλιν ἐξελεῖται.
2 ἀνὴρ σοφὸς οὐ μισήσει νόμον,
ὁ δὲ ὑποκρινόμενος ἐν αὐτῷ ὡς ἐν καταιγίδι πλοῖον.

KING JAMES VERSION

17 A sinful man will not be reproved, but findeth an excuse according to his will.

18 A man of counsel will be considerate; but a strange and proud man is not daunted with fear, even when of himself he hath done without counsel.

19 Do nothing without advice; and when thou hast once done, repent not.

20 Go not in a way wherein thou mayest fall, and stumble not among the stones.

21 Be not confident in a plain way.

22 And beware of thine own children.

23 In every good work trust thy own soul; for this is the keeping of the commandments.

24 He that believeth in the Lord taketh heed to the commandment; and he that trusteth in him shall fare never the worse.

33 There shall no evil happen unto him that feareth the Lord; but in temptation even again he will deliver him.

2 A wise man hateth not the law; but he that is an hypocrite therein is as a ship in a storm.

DOUAY OLD TESTAMENT

21 A sinful man will flee reproof, and will find an excuse according to his will.

22 A man of counsel will not neglect understanding, a strange and proud man will not dread fear:

23 Even after he hath done with fear without counsel, he shall be controlled by the things of his own seeking.

24 My son, do thou nothing without counsel, and thou shalt not repent when thou hast done.

25 Go not in the way of ruin, and thou shalt not stumble against the stones: trust not thyself to a rugged way, lest thou set a stumblingblock to thy soul.

26 And beware of thy own children, and take heed of them of thy household.

27 In every work of thine regard thy soul in faith: for this is the keeping of the commandments.

28 He that believeth God, taketh heed to the commandments: and he that trusteth in him, shall fare never the worse.

33 NO evils shall happen to him that feareth the Lord, but in temptation God will keep him, and deliver him from evils.

2 A wise man hateth not the commandments and justices, and he shall not be dashed in pieces as a ship in a storm.

KNOX TRANSLATION

shine from their awards;[a] 21 the sinner fears to have his life
reproved, and will ever be finding precedents for gratifying
his own whim. 22 A man of prudence will never throw cau-
tion to the winds; his proud enemy feels no dread 23 even
upon rashly provoking him, but shall live to rue the
assault.[b] 24 Do nothing, my son, save with consideration,
and thy deeds shall not bring thee repentance. 25 Take not
some ruinous road that shall trip thee with its boulders;
some road where all journeying is difficult[c] and thou mayst
expose thy life to sudden dangers. 26 Of thy own children
beware, be on thy watch against thy own household; 27 be it
thine to trust with all thy soul's confidence,[d] and thou hast
kept the commandments. 28 Who trusts in God, keeps well
God's command; confidence in him was never disappointed.
33 If a man fears the Lord, he shall meet with no disaster; God will be watching over him, even when his
faith is put to the test, and from such disaster will preserve
him. 2 A wise man does not grow weary of the law, and the
duties it enjoins, and no shipwreck can befall him. 3 If thou

a Or perhaps 'examples of obedience' (to the Law). *b* *vv.* 22, 23: The language here is very confused, and it seems likely that the true text may have been lost. *c* In the Greek, 'where there is no danger of stumbling'. *d* Or perhaps, 'to trust with all confidence in thy own soul', that is, in thyself; this is probably the meaning of the Greek. But, in these later chapters, we have a Hebrew text to consult, which doubtless goes back (though with certain alterations) to the original manuscript from which Jesus, son of Sirach, made his Greek translation. And this, supported by the Syriac version, gives us 'keeps watch over his own soul' instead of 'trusts his own soul'.

TODAY'S ENGLISH VERSION

famous for your fairness. 17 Sinners have no use for correction, and will interpret the Law to suit themselves.

18 Sensible people will consider every opinion, but arrogant[a] people will let nothing stand in their way. 19 Never do anything without thinking it through, and once you have done something, don't look back and wish you had done something else. 20 Don't take a course of action that is dangerous, and don't make the same mistake twice.[b] 21 Don't be too sure of yourself, even when the way looks easy. 22 Always watch where you are going.[c] 23 Whatever you do be careful;[d] this is keeping the Lord's commands.

24 Believing in the Law means keeping the Lord's commands.

33 If you trust the Lord, you cannot lose. 1 No evil will ever come to a person who fears the Lord; however often danger comes, the Lord will come to the rescue. 2 A person who has no use for the Law doesn't have good sense, and anyone who is insincere about it is going to be tossed about like a boat in a storm. 3 If you are wise, you

[a] *Hebrew* arrogant; *Greek* foreign and arrogant. [b] *Hebrew* make . . . twice; *Greek* stumble on stones. [c] *Hebrew* watch . . . going; *Greek* look out for your children. [d] *Hebrew* be careful; *Greek* have confidence in yourself.

NEW REVISED STANDARD VERSION

17 The sinner will shun reproof,
and will find a decision according to his liking.

18 A sensible person will not overlook a thoughtful
suggestion;
an insolent[a] and proud person will not be deterred by
fear.[b]
19 Do nothing without deliberation,
but when you have acted, do not regret it.
20 Do not go on a path full of hazards,
and do not stumble at an obstacle twice.[c]
21 Do not be overconfident on a smooth[d] road,
22 and give good heed to your paths.[e]
23 Guard[f] yourself in every act,
for this is the keeping of the commandments.

24 The one who keeps the law preserves himself,[g]
and the one who trusts the Lord will not suffer loss.

33 No evil will befall the one who fears the Lord,
but in trials such a one will be rescued again and
again.
2 The wise will not hate the law,
but the one who is hypocritical about it is like a boat
in a storm.

[a] Heb: Gk *alien* [b] Meaning of Gk uncertain. Other ancient authorities add *and after acting, with him, without deliberation* [c] Heb: Gk *stumble on stony ground* [d] Or *an unexplored* [e] Heb Syr: Gk *and beware of your children* [f] Heb Syr: Gk *Trust* [g] Heb: Gk *who believes the law heeds the commandments*

NEW AMERICAN BIBLE

17 The sinner turns aside reproof
and distorts the law to suit his purpose.
18 The thoughtful man will not neglect direction;
the proud and insolent man is deterred by nothing.
19 Do nothing without counsel,
and then you need have no regrets.
20 Go not on a way that is set with snares,
and let not the same thing trip you twice.
21 Be not too sure even of smooth roads,
22 be careful on all your paths.
23 Whatever you do, be on your guard,
for in this way you will keep the commandments.
24 He who keeps the law preserves himself;
and he who trusts in the LORD shall not be put to
shame.

33 No evil can harm the man who fears the LORD;
through trials, again and again he is safe.
2 He who hates the law is without wisdom,
and is tossed about like a boat in a storm.

NEW JERUSALEM BIBLE

17 The sinner waves reproof aside,
he finds an excuse for headstrong behaviour.
18 A sensible person never scorns a warning;
foreigners and the proud do not know about fear.

19 Never act without reflection,
and you will not regret your actions.
20 Do not venture on a rough road,
for fear of stumbling over the stones.
21 Do not be over-confident on an even road
22 and beware of your own children.
23 Watch yourself in everything you do;
this is also the way to keep the commandments.

24 Anyone who trusts in the Law obeys its precepts,
no one who has confidence in the Lord will come to
harm.

33 No evil will befall one who fears the Lord,
such a one will be rescued even in the ordeal.
2 No one who hates the Law is wise,
one who is hypocritical about it is like a storm-tossed
ship.

GREEK OLD TESTAMENT

3 ἄνθρωπος συνετὸς ἐμπιστεύσει νόμῳ,
καὶ ὁ νόμος αὐτῷ πιστὸς ὡς ἐρώτημα δήλων.
4 ἑτοίμασον λόγον καὶ οὕτως ἀκουσθήσῃ,
σύνδησον παιδείαν καὶ ἀποκρίθητι.
5 τροχὸς ἁμάξης σπλάγχνα μωροῦ,
καὶ ὡς ἄξων στρεφόμενος ὁ διαλογισμὸς αὐτοῦ.
6 ἵππος εἰς ὀχείαν ὡς φίλος μωκός,
ὑποκάτω παντὸς ἐπικαθημένου χρεμετίζει.
7 Διὰ τί ἡμέρα ἡμέρας ὑπερέχει,
καὶ πᾶν φῶς ἡμέρας ἐνιαυτοῦ ἀφ᾽ ἡλίου;
8 ἐν γνώσει κυρίου διεχωρίσθησαν,
καὶ ἠλλοίωσεν καιροὺς καὶ ἑορτάς·
9 ἀπ᾽ αὐτῶν ἀνύψωσεν καὶ ἡγίασεν
καὶ ἐξ αὐτῶν ἔθηκεν εἰς ἀριθμὸν ἡμερῶν.
10 καὶ ἄνθρωποι πάντες ἀπὸ ἐδάφους,
καὶ ἐκ γῆς ἐκτίσθη Αδαμ·
11 ἐν πλήθει ἐπιστήμης κύριος διεχώρισεν αὐτοὺς
καὶ ἠλλοίωσεν τὰς ὁδοὺς αὐτῶν·
12 ἐξ αὐτῶν εὐλόγησεν καὶ ἀνύψωσεν
καὶ ἐξ αὐτῶν ἡγίασεν καὶ πρὸς αὐτὸν ἤγγισεν·
ἀπ᾽ αὐτῶν κατηράσατο καὶ ἐταπείνωσεν
καὶ ἀνέστρεψεν αὐτοὺς ἀπὸ στάσεως αὐτῶν.

KING JAMES VERSION

3 A man of understanding trusteth in the law; and the law is faithful unto him, as an oracle.

4 Prepare what to say, and so thou shalt be heard: and bind up instruction, and then make answer.

5 The heart of the foolish is like a cartwheel; and his thoughts are like a rolling axletree.

6 A stallion horse is as a mocking friend, he neigheth under every one that sitteth upon him.

7 Why doth one day excel another, when as all the light of every day in the year is of the sun?

8 By the knowledge of the Lord they were distinguished: and he altered seasons and feasts.

9 Some of them hath he made high days, and hallowed *them,* and some of them hath he made ordinary days.

10 And all men are from the ground, and Adam was created of earth.

11 In much knowledge the Lord hath divided them, and made their ways diverse.

12 Some of them hath he blessed and exalted, and some of them hath he sanctified, and set near himself: but some of them hath he cursed and brought low, and turned out of their places.

DOUAY OLD TESTAMENT

3 A man of understanding is faithful to the law of God, and the law is faithful to him.

4 He that cleareth up a question, shall prepare what to say, and so having prayed he shall be heard, and shall keep discipline, and then he shall answer.

5 The heart of a fool is as a wheel of a cart: and his thoughts are like a rolling axletree.

6 A friend that is a mocker, is like a stallion horse: he neigheth under every one that sitteth upon him.

7 Why doth one day excel another, and one light another, and one year another year, when all come of the sun?

8 By the knowledge of the Lord they were distinguished, the sun being made, and keeping his commandment.

9 And he ordered the seasons, and holidays of them, and in them they celebrated festivals at an hour.

10 Some of them God made high and great days, and some of them he put in the number of ordinary days. And all men are from the ground, and out of the earth, from whence Adam was created.

11 With much knowledge the Lord hath divided them and diversified their ways.

12 Some of them hath he blessed, and exalted: and some of them hath he sanctified, and set near himself: and some of them hath he cursed and brought low, and turned them from their station.

KNOX TRANSLATION

art a man of judgement, thou hast only to trust God's commandment, and it will not fail thee; ... giving a true answer
to the question asked...[a] 4 thou wilt prepare thy plea, and
find audience for thy prayer; wilt recollect the teaching given
thee, and so satisfy thy questioner. 5 A fool's heart is but a
wheel that turns; his are whirling thoughts. 6 Hast thou a
friend that will ever be mocking? Be comforted; stallion will
ever neigh, ride him who will.
7 Why is it that one day which dawns, one year, takes
precedence of another, when all come of the same sun?
8 God's wisdom it was that so set them apart when he made
the sun, and gave it a law to keep; 9 made a succession of
seasons, a succession of feast days, when at stated times
men must keep holiday. 10 To some he would assign high
dignity; others should be lost in the common rabble of days.
So it is that all men are built of the same clay; son of Adam
is son of earth; 11 yet the Lord, in the plenitude of his wisdom, has marked them off from one another, not giving the
same destiny to each. 12 For some, his blessing; he will
advance them, will set them apart and claim them as his
own. For some, his ban; he will bring them low, and single

a There may be some confusion in the text here; the words 'giving a true answer to the question asked' are connected by the Greek with what goes before, by the Latin with what follows.

TODAY'S ENGLISH VERSION

will believe in the Law; you will find it as reliable as the
sacred lots.
4 Prepare what you are going to say and people will listen
to you. Use what you have learned before you start talking.
5 A foolish person's mind works like a cartwheel, going
round and round in circles. 6 A sarcastic friend is like a wild
horse that neighs no matter who tries to ride him.
7 Why are some days holier than others, even though the
same sun rises on every day of the year? 8 It is because the
Lord made them different by setting them apart as religious
holidays and festivals. 9 He made some days holy and
important, and made other days ordinary.
10 Every human being was made from the earth, just as
Adam was. 11 But the Lord, in his wisdom, made them all
different and gave them different tasks. 12 He blessed some,
making them honored and holy, keeping them near him.
Others he cursed, humbling them and removing them from

NEW REVISED STANDARD VERSION

3 The sensible person will trust in the law;
for such a one the law is as dependable as a divine oracle.

4 Prepare what to say, and then you will be listened to;
draw upon your training, and give your answer.
5 The heart of a fool is like a cart wheel,
and his thoughts like a turning axle.
6 A mocking friend is like a stallion
that neighs no matter who the rider is.

7 Why is one day more important than another,
when all the daylight in the year is from the sun?
8 By the Lord's wisdom they were distinguished,
and he appointed the different seasons and festivals.
9 Some days he exalted and hallowed,
and some he made ordinary days.
10 All human beings come from the ground,
and humankind[a] was created out of the dust.
11 In the fullness of his knowledge the Lord distinguished them
and appointed their different ways.
12 Some he blessed and exalted,
and some he made holy and brought near to himself;
but some he cursed and brought low,
and turned them out of their place.

a Heb: Gk *Adam*

NEW AMERICAN BIBLE

3 The prudent man trusts in the word of the LORD,
and the law is dependable for him as a divine oracle.
4 Prepare your words and you will be listened to;
draw upon your training, and then give your answer.
5 Like the wheel of a cart is the mind of a fool;
his thoughts revolve in circles.
6 A fickle friend is like the stallion
that neighs, no matter who the rider.
7 Why is one day more important than another,
when it is the sun that lights up every day?
8 It is due to the LORD's wisdom that they differ;
it is through him the seasons and feasts come and go.
9 Some he dignifies and sanctifies,
and others he lists as ordinary days.
10 So too, all men are of clay,
for from earth man was formed;
11 Yet with his great knowledge the LORD makes men unlike;
in different paths he has them walk.
12 Some he blesses and makes great,
some he sanctifies and draws to himself.
Others he curses and brings low,
and expels them from their place.

NEW JERUSALEM BIBLE

3 An intelligent person will put faith in the Law,
for such a one the Law is as dependable as a prophecy.
4 Prepare what you have to say and you will get a hearing,
marshal your information before you answer.
5 The feelings of a fool are like a cart-wheel,
a fool's thought revolves like a turning axle.
6 A rutting stallion is like a sarcastic friend;
he neighs, whoever rides him.
7 Why is one day better than another,
though the sun gives the same daylight throughout the year?
8 They have been differentiated in the mind of the Lord,
who has diversified the seasons and feasts;
9 some he has made more important and has hallowed,
others he has made ordinary days.
10 Human beings come from the ground,
Adam himself was formed out of earth;
11 in the fullness of his wisdom
the Lord has made distinctions between them,
and diversified their conditions.
12 Some of them he has blessed,
hallowing and setting them near him;
others he has cursed and humiliated
by degrading them from their positions.

GREEK OLD TESTAMENT

13 ὡς πηλὸς κεραμέως ἐν χειρὶ αὐτοῦ
— πᾶσαι αἱ ὁδοὶ αὐτοῦ κατὰ τὴν εὐδοκίαν αὐτοῦ —,
οὕτως ἄνθρωποι ἐν χειρὶ τοῦ ποιήσαντος αὐτοὺς
ἀποδοῦναι αὐτοῖς κατὰ τὴν κρίσιν αὐτοῦ.
14 ἀπέναντι τοῦ κακοῦ τὸ ἀγαθόν,
καὶ ἀπέναντι τοῦ θανάτου ἡ ζωή,
οὕτως ἀπέναντι εὐσεβοῦς ἁμαρτωλός·
15 καὶ οὕτως ἔμβλεψον εἰς πάντα τὰ ἔργα τοῦ ὑψίστου,
δύο δύο, ἓν κατέναντι τοῦ ἑνός.
16 Κἀγὼ ἔσχατος ἠγρύπνησα
ὡς καλαμώμενος ὀπίσω τρυγητῶν·
17 ἐν εὐλογίᾳ κυρίου ἔφθασα
καὶ ὡς τρυγῶν ἐπλήρωσα ληνόν.
18 κατανοήσατε ὅτι οὐκ ἐμοὶ μόνῳ ἐκοπίασα,
ἀλλὰ πᾶσιν τοῖς ζητοῦσιν παιδείαν.
19 ἀκούσατέ μου, μεγιστᾶνες λαοῦ,
καὶ οἱ ἡγούμενοι ἐκκλησίας, ἐνωτίσασθε.
20 Υἱῷ καὶ γυναικί, ἀδελφῷ καὶ φίλῳ
μὴ δῷς ἐξουσίαν ἐπὶ σὲ ἐν ζωῇ σου·
καὶ μὴ δῷς ἑτέρῳ τὰ χρήματά σου,
ἵνα μὴ μεταμεληθεὶς δέῃ περὶ αὐτῶν.
21 ἕως ἔτι ζῇς καὶ πνοὴ ἐν σοί,
μὴ ἀλλάξῃς σεαυτὸν ἐν πάσῃ σαρκί·
22 κρεῖσσον γάρ ἐστιν τὰ τέκνα δεηθῆναί σου
ἢ σὲ ἐμβλέπειν εἰς χεῖρας υἱῶν σου.

KING JAMES VERSION

13 As the clay is in the potter's hand, to fashion it at his pleasure: so man is in the hand of him that made him, to render to them as liketh him best.

14 Good is set against evil, and life against death: so is the godly against the sinner, and the sinner against the godly.

15 So look upon all the works of the most High; and there are two and two, one against another.

16 I awaked up last of all, as one that gathereth after the grapegatherers: by the blessing of the Lord I profited, and filled my winepress like a gatherer of grapes.

17 Consider that I laboured not for myself only, but for all them that seek learning.

18 Hear me, O ye great men of the people, and hearken with your ears, ye rulers of the congregation.

19 Give not thy son and wife, thy brother and friend, power over thee while thou livest, and give not thy goods to another: lest it repent thee, and thou intreat for the same again.

20 As long as thou livest and hast breath in thee, give not thyself over to any.

21 For better it is that thy children should seek to thee, than that thou shouldest stand to their courtesy.

DOUAY OLD TESTAMENT

13 As the potter's clay is in his hand, to fashion and order it:

14 All his ways are according to his ordering: so man is in the hand of him that made him, and he will render to him according to his judgment.

15 Good is set against evil, and life against death: so also is the sinner against a just man. And so look upon all the works of the most High. Two and two, and one against another.

16 And I awaked last of all, and as one that gathereth after the grapegatherers.

17 In the blessing of God I also have hoped: and as one that gathereth grapes, have I filled the winepress.

18 See that I have not laboured for myself only, but for all that seek discipline.

19 Hear me, ye great men, and all ye people, and hearken with your ears, ye rulers of the church.

20 Give not to son or wife, brother or friend, power over thee while thou livest; and give not thy estate to another, lest thou repent, and thou entreat for the same.

21 As long as thou livest, and hast breath in thee, let no man change thee.

22 For it is better that thy children should ask of thee, than that thou look toward the hands of thy children.

KNOX TRANSLATION

them out no more. 13 Clay we are in the potter's hands; it is
for him who made us to dispose of us; 14 clay is what potter
wills it to be, and we are in our maker's hands, to be dealt
with at his pleasure. 15 Evil matched with good, life matched
with death, sinner matched with man of piety; so everywhere
in God's works thou wilt find pairs matched, one against the
other.

16 Think of me as one that has toiled last of all, and goes
about gleaning a fruit here, a fruit there, after the vintagers
have done. 17 Yet did I trust that I, too, might have God's
blessing, and I, too, have filled the wine-press, a vintager
like the rest. 18 See how I have toiled, not for my own sake
merely, but for all such as covet wisdom! 19 Words for the
hearing of all, high and low; you that hold high place in the
assembly, never disdain to listen.

20 Long as thou livest, do not put thyself in the power of
others, though it be son or wife, kinsman or friend; do not
make over thy goods to another; it is ill to go a-begging for
what is thy own. 21 While life and breath is in thee, never
change places with another; 22 it is for thy children to ask thee
for what they need, not to have thyself for their pensioner.

TODAY'S ENGLISH VERSION

their positions. 13 Just as clay is in the potter's hands for him
to shape as he pleases, so we are in the hands of our Creator
for him to do with as he wishes.
14 Good is the opposite of evil, life is the opposite of death,
and sin is the opposite of devotion to the Lord. 15 Think
about it: the Most High has made everything in pairs, each
thing the opposite of something else.
16 As for me, I have been the last to come on duty, as if
going through vineyards to gather whatever the grape-pickers had left behind. But the Lord blessed me, and I did well,[a]
like a grape-picker who has filled the wine press. 17 But I
want you to know that I have not done all this work for
myself alone, but for everyone who wants to learn. 18 Listen
to me, all you great leaders! All you leaders of the assemblies, hear what I have to say!
19 Never, as long as you live, give anyone power over
you—whether son, wife, brother, or friend. Don't give your
property to anyone; you might change your mind and have
to ask for it back. 20 As long as you have breath in your
body, don't let anyone lead your life for you. 21 It is better
that your children be dependent on you than the other way

[a] did well; *or* overtook the others.

NEW REVISED STANDARD VERSION

13 Like clay in the hand of the potter,
to be molded as he pleases,
so all are in the hand of their Maker,
to be given whatever he decides.

14 Good is the opposite of evil,
and life the opposite of death;
so the sinner is the opposite of the godly.
15 Look at all the works of the Most High;
they come in pairs, one the opposite of the other.

16 Now I was the last to keep vigil;
I was like a gleaner following the grape-pickers;
17 by the blessing of the Lord I arrived first,
and like a grape-picker I filled my wine press.
18 Consider that I have not labored for myself alone,
but for all who seek instruction.
19 Hear me, you who are great among the people,
and you leaders of the congregation, pay heed!

20 To son or wife, to brother or friend,
do not give power over yourself, as long as you live;
and do not give your property to another,
in case you change your mind and must ask for it.
21 While you are still alive and have breath in you,
do not let anyone take your place.
22 For it is better that your children should ask from you
than that you should look to the hand of your
children.

NEW AMERICAN BIBLE

13 Like clay in the hands of a potter,
to be molded according to his pleasure,
So are men in the hands of their Creator,
to be assigned by him their function.
14 As evil contrasts with good, and death with life,
so are sinners in contrast with the just;
15 See now all the works of the Most High:
they come in pairs, the one the opposite of the other.

16 Now I am the last to keep vigil,
like a gleaner after the vintage;
17 Since by the LORD's blessing I have made progress
till like a vintager I have filled my winepress,
18 I would inform you that not for myself only have I
toiled,
but for every seeker after wisdom.

19 Listen to me, O leaders of the multitude;
O rulers of the assembly, give ear!
20 Let neither son nor wife, neither brother nor friend,
have power over you as long as you live.
21 While breath of life is still in you,
let no man have dominion over you.
Give not to another your wealth,
lest then you have to plead with him;
22 Far better that your children plead with you
than that you should look to their generosity.

NEW JERUSALEM BIBLE

13 Like clay in the hands of the potter
to mould as it pleases him,
so are human beings in the hands of their Maker
to reward as he judges right.
14 Opposite evil stands good,
opposite death, life;
so too opposite the devout stands the sinner.
15 Contemplate all the works of the Most High,
you will find they go in pairs, by opposites.

16 Although the last to come, I have kept my eyes open
like a man picking up what the grape-pickers have
left.
17 By the blessing of the Lord I have come in first,
and like a true grape-picker have filled my winepress.
18 And note, I have not been working merely for myself,
but for all who seek instruction.

19 Listen to me, important public figures,
presidents of the assembly, give ear!

20 Neither to son nor wife, brother nor friend,
give power over yourself during your own lifetime.
And do not give your property to anyone else,
in case you regret it and have to ask for it back.
21 As long as you live and there is breath in your body,
do not yield power over yourself to anyone;
22 better for your children to come begging to you,
than for you to have to go begging to them.

GREEK OLD TESTAMENT

23 ἐν πᾶσι τοῖς ἔργοις σου γίνου ὑπεράγων,
μὴ δῷς μῶμον ἐν τῇ δόξῃ σου.
24 ἐν ἡμέρᾳ συντελείας ἡμερῶν ζωῆς σου
καὶ ἐν καιρῷ τελευτῆς διάδος κληρονομίαν.
25 Χορτάσματα καὶ ῥάβδος καὶ φορτία ὄνῳ,
ἄρτος καὶ παιδεία καὶ ἔργον οἰκέτῃ.
26 ἔργασαι ἐν παιδί, καὶ εὑρήσεις ἀνάπαυσιν·
ἄνες χεῖρας αὐτῷ, καὶ ζητήσει ἐλευθερίαν.
27 ζυγὸς καὶ ἱμὰς τράχηλον κάμψουσιν,
καὶ οἰκέτῃ κακούργῳ στρέβλαι καὶ βάσανοι·
28 ἔμβαλε αὐτὸν εἰς ἐργασίαν, ἵνα μὴ ἀργῇ,
πολλὴν γὰρ κακίαν ἐδίδαξεν ἡ ἀργία·
29 εἰς ἔργα κατάστησον, καθὼς πρέπει αὐτῷ,
κἂν μὴ πειθαρχῇ, βάρυνον τὰς πέδας αὐτοῦ.
30 καὶ μὴ περισσεύσῃς ἐπὶ πάσῃ σαρκὶ
καὶ ἄνευ κρίσεως μὴ ποιήσῃς μηδέν.
31 Εἰ ἔστιν σοι οἰκέτης, ἔστω ὡς σύ,
ὅτι ἐν αἵματι ἐκτήσω αὐτόν·
32 εἰ ἔστιν σοι οἰκέτης, ἄγε αὐτὸν ὡς ἀδελφόν,
ὅτι ὡς ἡ ψυχή σου ἐπιδεήσεις αὐτῷ·
33 ἐὰν κακώσῃς αὐτὸν καὶ ἀπάρας ἀποδρᾷ,
ἐν ποίᾳ ὁδῷ ζητήσεις αὐτόν;

34 Κεναὶ ἐλπίδες καὶ ψευδεῖς ἀσυνέτῳ ἀνδρί,
καὶ ἐνύπνια ἀναπτεροῦσιν ἄφρονας.
2 ὡς δρασσόμενος σκιᾶς καὶ διώκων ἄνεμον
οὕτως ὁ ἐπέχων ἐνυπνίοις·

KING JAMES VERSION

22 In all thy works keep to thyself the preeminence; leave not a stain in thine honour.

23 At the time when thou shalt end thy days, and finish thy life, distribute thine inheritance.

24 Fodder, a wand, and burdens, *are* for the ass; and bread, correction, and work, for a servant.

25 If thou set thy servant to labour, thou shalt find rest: but if thou let him go idle, he shall seek liberty.

26 A yoke and a collar do bow the neck: so are tortures and torments for an evil servant.

27 Send him to labour, that he be not idle; for idleness teacheth much evil.

28 Set him to work, as is fit for him: if he be not obedient, put on more heavy fetters.

29 But be not excessive toward any; and without discretion do nothing.

30 If thou have a servant, let him be unto thee as thyself, because thou hast bought him with a price.

31 If thou have a servant, entreat him as a brother: for thou hast need of him, as of thine own soul: if thou entreat him evil, and he run from thee, which way wilt thou go to seek him?

34 The hopes of a man void of understanding are vain and false: and dreams lift up fools.

2 Whoso regardeth dreams is like him that catcheth at a shadow, and followeth after the wind.

DOUAY OLD TESTAMENT

23 In all thy works keep the pre-eminence.

24 Let no stain sully thy glory. In the time when thou shalt end the days of thy life, and in the time of thy decease, distribute thy inheritance.

25 Fodder, and a wand, and a burden are for an ass: bread, and correction, and work for a slave.

26 He worketh under correction, and seeketh to rest: let his hands be idle, and he seeketh liberty.

27 The yoke and the thong bend a stiff neck, and continual labours bow a slave.

28 Torture and fetters are for a malicious slave: send him to work, that he be not idle:

29 For idleness hath taught much evil.

30 Set him to work: for so it is fit for him. And if he be not obedient, bring him down with fetters, but be not excessive towards any one: and do no grievous thing without judgment.

31 If thou have a faithful servant, let him be to thee as thy own soul: treat him as a brother: because in the blood of thy soul thou hast gotten him.

32 If thou hurt him unjustly, he will run away:

33 And if he rise up and depart, thou knowest not whom to ask, and in what way to seek him.

34 THE hopes of a man that is void of understanding are vain and deceitful: and dreams lift up fools.

2 The man that giveth heed to lying visions, is like to him that catcheth at a shadow, and followeth after the wind.

KNOX TRANSLATION

23 Be at the head of thy own affairs, 24 nor ever tarnish thy
renown, until thy days are finished; then, at the hour of thy
death, make thy bequests.
25 Fodder thy ass must have, and the whip, and a pack to
bear; thy slave, too, needs food and discipline and hard
work. 26 Under duress he toils, what marvel if ease should
tempt him? Leave his hands idle, and he will seek to be his
own master. 27 The stubborn ox yoke and rein will subdue;
slave held to his task is slave bowed to thy will; 28 keep rack
and stocks for one that is bent on mischief. To the task, no
hours of leisure! 29 Idleness is a great teacher of ill habit.
30 Toil first assign to him; toiling is his lot; then, if he disobeys thee, with the stocks thou mayst tame him. Yet do not
burden flesh and blood more than it can bear, nor inflict
more than lawful punishment while the plea is still unheard.
31 Faithful slave if thou hast, make much of him as of thy
own self; treat him as if he were thy brother, as if thy own
life were[a] the price of his purchase. 32 Wrong him, and he
may run away from thy service; 33 once he takes to his heels,
who can tell thee where or in what guise thou mayst discover him?

34 Fools are cheated by vain hopes, buoyed up with the
fancies of a dream. 2 Wouldst thou heed such lying
visions? Better clutch at shadows, or chase the wind.

a Literally, 'since thy own life is'. Different versions have different variants of the phrase, and it is not certain what meaning should be assigned to it.

TODAY'S ENGLISH VERSION

around. 22 Keep control over all that you do; don't let anything stain your reputation. 23 Wait until the last moment of
your life, when you are breathing your last, and then divide
your property among your heirs.

24 A donkey should be given its fodder and its burden, and
it should be beaten. A slave should be given food and work,
and should be disciplined. 25 If you make your slave work,
you can set your mind at ease. If you don't keep him busy,
he will be looking for freedom. 26 You can use a harness and
yoke to tame an animal, and a slave can be tortured in the
stocks. 27 Keep him at work, and don't let him be idle; idleness can only teach him how to make trouble. 28 Work is
what he needs. If he won't obey you, put him in chains.

29 But don't be too severe with anyone, and never be
unfair. 30 If you have a slave, treat him as you would want
to be treated; you bought him with your hard-earned money.
31 Treat him as a brother; you need him as you need yourself.
If you mistreat him and he runs away, where are you going
to look for him?

34 Foolish people are deceived by vain hopes, and
dreams get them all excited. 2 A person who pays
any attention at all to dreams is like someone who tries to
catch shadows or chase the wind. 3 What you see in a dream

NEW REVISED STANDARD VERSION

23 Excel in all that you do;
bring no stain upon your honor.
24 At the time when you end the days of your life,
in the hour of death, distribute your inheritance.

25 Fodder and a stick and burdens for a donkey;
bread and discipline and work for a slave.
26 Set your slave to work, and you will find rest;
leave his hands idle, and he will seek liberty.
27 Yoke and thong will bow the neck,
and for a wicked slave there are racks and tortures.
28 Put him to work, in order that he may not be idle,
29 for idleness teaches much evil.
30 Set him to work, as is fitting for him,
and if he does not obey, make his fetters heavy.
Do not be overbearing toward anyone,
and do nothing unjust.

31 If you have but one slave, treat him like yourself,
because you have bought him with blood.
If you have but one slave, treat him like a brother,
for you will need him as you need your life.
32 If you ill-treat him, and he leaves you and runs away,
33 which way will you go to seek him?

34 The senseless have vain and false hopes,
and dreams give wings to fools.
2 As one who catches at a shadow and pursues the wind,
so is anyone who believes in[a] dreams.

a Syr: Gk *pays heed to*

NEW AMERICAN BIBLE

23 Keep control over all your affairs;
let no one tarnish your glory.
24 When your few days reach their limit,
at the time of death distribute your inheritance.

25 Fodder and whip and loads for an ass;
the yoke and harness and the rod of his master.
27 Food, correction and work for a slave;
and for a wicked slave, punishment in the stocks.
26 Make a slave work and he will look for his rest;
let his hands be idle and he will seek to be free.

28 Force him to work that he be not idle,
for idleness is an apt teacher of mischief.
29 Put him to work, for that is what befits him;
if he becomes unruly, load him with chains.
30 But never lord it over any human being,
and do nothing unjust.
31 If you have but one slave, treat him like yourself,
for you have acquired him with your life's blood;
32 If you have but one slave, deal with him as a brother,
for you need him as you need your life:
33 If you mistreat him and he runs away,
in what direction will you look for him?

34 Empty and false are the hopes of the senseless,
and fools are borne aloft by dreams.
2 Like a man who catches at shadows or chases the wind,
is the one who believes in dreams.

NEW JERUSALEM BIBLE

23 In all you do be the master,
and leave a reputation unstained.
24 The day your life draws to a close,
at the hour of death, then distribute your heritage.

25 Fodder, the stick and burdens for a donkey,
bread, discipline and work for a slave.
26 Work your slave hard, and you will have peace of mind,
leave his hands idle, and he will be asking for his
freedom.
27 Yoke and harness will bow the neck,
for a bad servant, torments and the rack.
28 Set him to work, so that he will not be idle;
idleness teaches every kind of mischief.
29 Keep him at his duties, where he should be,
if he is disobedient, clap him in irons.
30 But do not be over-exacting with anyone,
and do nothing contrary to justice.

31 You have only one slave? Treat him like yourself,
since you have acquired him with blood.
32 You have only one slave? Treat him as a brother,
since you need him as you need yourself.
33 If you ill-treat him and he runs away,
which way will you go to look for him?

34 Vain and deceptive hopes are for the foolish,
and dreams lend wings to fools.
2 As well clutch at shadows and chase the wind
as put any faith in dreams.

GREEK OLD TESTAMENT

3 τοῦτο κατὰ τούτου ὅρασις ἐνυπνίων,
κατέναντι προσώπου ὁμοίωμα προσώπου.
4 ἀπὸ ἀκαθάρτου τί καθαρισθήσεται;
καὶ ἀπὸ ψευδοῦς τί ἀληθεύσει;
5 μαντεῖαι καὶ οἰωνισμοὶ καὶ ἐνύπνια μάταιά ἐστιν,
καὶ ὡς ὠδινούσης φαντάζεται καρδία·
6 ἐὰν μὴ παρὰ ὑψίστου ἀποσταλῇ ἐν ἐπισκοπῇ,
μὴ δῷς εἰς αὐτὰ τὴν καρδίαν σου·
7 πολλοὺς γὰρ ἐπλάνησεν τὰ ἐνύπνια,
καὶ ἐξέπεσον ἐλπίζοντες ἐπ' αὐτοῖς.
8 ἄνευ ψεύδους συντελεσθήσεται νόμος,
καὶ σοφία στόματι πιστῷ τελείωσις.
9 Ἀνὴρ πεπλανημένος ἔγνω πολλά,
καὶ ὁ πολύπειρος ἐκδιηγήσεται σύνεσιν·
10 ὃς οὐκ ἐπειράθη, ὀλίγα οἶδεν,
ὁ δὲ πεπλανημένος πληθυνεῖ πανουργίαν.
11 πολλὰ ἑώρακα ἐν τῇ ἀποπλανήσει μου,
καὶ πλείονα τῶν λόγων μου σύνεσίς μου·
12 πλεονάκις ἕως θανάτου ἐκινδύνευσα
καὶ διεσώθην τούτων χάριν.
13 πνεῦμα φοβουμένων κύριον ζήσεται·
ἡ γὰρ ἐλπὶς αὐτῶν ἐπὶ τὸν σῴζοντα αὐτούς.

KING JAMES VERSION

3 The vision of dreams is the resemblance of one thing to another, even as the likeness of a face to a face.

4 Of an unclean thing what can be cleansed? and from that thing which is false what truth can come?

5 Divinations, and soothsayings, and dreams, are vain: and the heart fancieth, as a woman's heart in travail.

6 If they be not sent from the most High in thy visitation, set not thy heart upon them.

7 For dreams have deceived many, and they have failed that put their trust in them.

8 The law shall be found perfect without lies: and wisdom is perfection to a faithful mouth.

9 A man that hath travelled knoweth many things; and he that hath much experience will declare wisdom.

10 He that hath no experience knoweth little: but he that hath travelled is full of prudence.

11 When I travelled, I saw many things; and I understand more than I can express.

12 I was ofttimes in danger of death: yet I was delivered because of these things.

13 The spirit of those that fear the Lord shall live; for their hope is in him that saveth them.

DOUAY OLD TESTAMENT

3 The vision of dreams is the resemblance of one thing to another: as when a man's likeness is before the face of a man.

4 What can be made clean by the unclean? and what truth can come from that which is false?

5 Deceitful divinations and lying omens and the dreams of evildoers, are vanity:

6 And the heart fancieth as that of a woman in travail: except it be a vision sent forth from the most High, set not thy heart upon them.

7 For dreams have deceived many, and they have failed that put their trust in them.

8 The word of the law shall be fulfilled without a lie, and wisdom shall be made plain in the mouth of the faithful.

9 What doth he know, that hath not been tried? A man that hath much experience, shall think of many things: and he that hath learned many things, shall shew forth understanding.

10 He that hath no experience, knoweth little: and he that hath been experienced in many things, multiplieth prudence.

11 He that hath not been tried, what manner of things doth he know? he that hath been surprised, shall abound with subtlety.

12 I have seen many things by travelling, and many customs of things.

13 Sometimes I have been in danger of death for these things, and I have been delivered by the grace of God.

14 The spirit of those that fear God, is sought after, and by his regard shall be blessed.

KNOX TRANSLATION

3 Nought thou seest in a dream but symbols; man is but face
to face with his own image. 4 As well may foul thing cleanse,
as false thing give thee a true warning. 5 Out upon the folly
of them, pretended divination, and cheating omen, and wiz-
ard's dream! 6 Heart of woman in her pangs is not more fan-
ciful. Unless it be some manifestation the most High has
sent thee, pay no heed to any such; 7 trust in dreams has
crazed the wits of many, and brought them to their ruin.
8 Believe rather the law's promises, that cannot miss their
fulfilment, the wisdom that trusty counsellors shall make
clear to thee.

9 A man will not learn until he is tested by discipline.[a] That
experience gained, he will think deeply, and the many
lessons he has learned will make him a wise talker. 10 Without experience, a man knows little; yet, if he is too venture-
some, he reaps a rich harvest of mischief... 11 A man will not
learn until he is tested by discipline...and if he is led astray
he will be full of knavery...[b] 12 I myself have seen much in
my wanderings, the customs of men more than I can tell.[c]
13 Sometimes, by this means, I have been in danger of death,
and only the divine favour has preserved me from it.

14 The life of such as fear the Lord is held precious, and
wins a blessing from his regard; 15 they have a deliverer they

a 'Tested by discipline'; some of the. Greek manuscripts have 'chastised', or perhaps simply 'schooled'; others, more plausibly, a 'travelled man'.
b *vv.* 10, 11: The Latin here seems to have suffered from much confusion. 'Mischief' and 'knavery' in the Greek are 'discernment' and 'resourcefulness'; 'if he is led astray' is 'when he has travelled'. The Latin translator seems to have given two separate renderings of the same verse, neither of them accurate. *c* In the Greek, 'I know more than I am ready to tell'.

TODAY'S ENGLISH VERSION

is no more real than the reflection of your face in a mirror.
4 What is unreal can no more produce something real than
what is dirty can produce something clean. 5 Dreams, divination, and omens are all nonsense. You see in them only what
you want to see.[a] 6 Unless the Most High has sent you the
dream, pay no attention to it. 7 Dreams have misled many
people; they put their faith in them, only to be disappointed.
8 The Law is complete without such falsehood. Wisdom, as
spoken by the righteous, is also complete without it.
9 A well-traveled[b] person with wide experience knows
many things and talks sense. 10 You can't know much if you
haven't experienced much, but travel can make you more
clever. 11 In my own travels I have seen many things and
learned more than I can put into words. 12 I have been in
danger of death many times, but I have always been able to
escape by relying on past experience.
13 Those who fear the Lord will live, because they have put
their trust in the one who can save them. 14 Fear the Lord,

[a] *Probable text* You see . . . to see; *Greek* The mind has an imagination like a woman in labor. [b] A well-traveled; *some manuscripts have* An educated.

NEW REVISED STANDARD VERSION

3 What is seen in dreams is but a reflection,
the likeness of a face looking at itself.
4 From an unclean thing what can be clean?
And from something false what can be true?
5 Divinations and omens and dreams are unreal,
and like a woman in labor, the mind has fantasies.
6 Unless they are sent by intervention from the Most
High,
pay no attention to them.
7 For dreams have deceived many,
and those who put their hope in them have perished.
8 Without such deceptions the law will be fulfilled,
and wisdom is complete in the mouth of the faithful.

9 An educated[a] person knows many things,
and one with much experience knows what he is
talking about.
10 An inexperienced person knows few things,
11 but he that has traveled acquires much cleverness.
12 I have seen many things in my travels,
and I understand more than I can express.
13 I have often been in danger of death,
but have escaped because of these experiences.

14 The spirit of those who fear the Lord will live,
15 for their hope is in him who saves them.

a Other ancient authorities read *A traveled*

NEW AMERICAN BIBLE

3 What is seen in dreams is to reality
what the reflection of a face is to the face itself.
4 Can the unclean produce the clean?
can the liar ever speak the truth?
5 Divination, omens and dreams all are unreal;
what you already expect, the mind depicts.
6 Unless it be a vision specially sent by the Most High,
fix not your heart on it;
7 For dreams have led many astray,
and those who believed in them have perished.
8 The law is fulfilled without fail,
and perfect wisdom is found in the mouth of the
faithful man.
9 A man with training gains wide knowledge;
a man of experience speaks sense.
10 One never put to the proof knows little,
whereas with travel a man adds to his
resourcefulness.
11 I have seen much in my travels,
learned more than ever I could say.
12 Often I was in danger of death,
but by these attainments I was saved.

13 Lively is the courage of those who fear the LORD,
for they put their hope in their savior;

NEW JERUSALEM BIBLE

3 Dreams are no different from mirrors;
confronting a face, the reflection of that face.
4 What can be cleansed by uncleanness,
what can be verified by falsehood?
5 Divinations, auguries and dreams are nonsense,
like the fantasies of a pregnant woman.
6 Unless sent as emissaries from the Most High,
do not give them a thought;
7 for dreams have led many astray,
and those who relied on them have come to grief.
8 Fulfilling the Law requires no such falsehood,
and wisdom is perfected in veracity.
9 A much travelled man knows many things,
and a man of great experience will talk sound sense.
10 Someone who has never had his trials knows little;
but the travelled man is master of every situation.
11 I have seen many things on my travels,
I have understood more than I can put into words.
12 I have often been in danger of death,
but I have been spared, and this is why:
13 the spirit of those who fear the Lord can survive,
for their hope is in someone with power to save
them.

GREEK OLD TESTAMENT

14 ὁ φοβούμενος κύριον οὐδὲν εὐλαβηθήσεται
καὶ οὐ μὴ δειλιάσῃ, ὅτι αὐτὸς ἐλπὶς αὐτοῦ.
15 φοβουμένου τὸν κύριον μακαρία ἡ ψυχή·
τίνι ἐπέχει; καὶ τίς αὐτοῦ στήριγμα;
16 οἱ ὀφθαλμοὶ κυρίου ἐπὶ τοὺς ἀγαπῶντας αὐτόν,
ὑπερασπισμὸς δυναστείας καὶ στήριγμα ἰσχύος,
σκέπη ἀπὸ καύσωνος καὶ σκέπη ἀπὸ μεσημβρίας,
φυλακὴ ἀπὸ προσκόμματος καὶ βοήθεια ἀπὸ πτώσεως,
17 ἀνυψῶν ψυχὴν καὶ φωτίζων ὀφθαλμούς,
ἴασιν διδούς, ζωὴν καὶ εὐλογίαν.
18 Θυσιάζων ἐξ ἀδίκου προσφορὰ μεμωμημένη,
καὶ οὐκ εἰς εὐδοκίαν δωρήματα ἀνόμων.
19 οὐκ εὐδοκεῖ ὁ ὕψιστος ἐν προσφοραῖς ἀσεβῶν
οὐδὲ ἐν πλήθει θυσιῶν ἐξιλάσκεται ἁμαρτίας.
20 θύων υἱὸν ἔναντι τοῦ πατρὸς αὐτοῦ
ὁ προσάγων θυσίαν ἐκ χρημάτων πενήτων.
21 ἄρτος ἐπιδεομένων ζωὴ πτωχῶν,
ὁ ἀποστερῶν αὐτὴν ἄνθρωπος αἱμάτων.
22 φονεύων τὸν πλησίον ὁ ἀφαιρούμενος ἐμβίωσιν,
καὶ ἐκχέων αἷμα ὁ ἀποστερῶν μισθὸν μισθίου.

KING JAMES VERSION

14 Whoso feareth the Lord shall not fear nor be afraid; for he is his hope.

15 Blessed is the soul of him that feareth the Lord: to whom doth he look? and who is his strength?

16 For the eyes of the Lord are upon them that love him, he is their mighty protection and strong stay, a defence from heat, and a cover from the sun at noon, a preservation from stumbling, and an help from falling.

17 He raiseth up the soul, and lighteneth the eyes: he giveth health, life, and blessing.

18 He that sacrificeth of a thing wrongfully gotten, his offering is ridiculous; and the gifts of unjust men are not accepted.

19 The most High is not pleased with the offerings of the wicked; neither is he pacified for sin by the multitude of sacrifices.

20 Whoso bringeth an offering of the goods of the poor doeth as one that killeth the son before his father's eyes.

21 The bread of the needy is their life: he that defraudeth him thereof is a man of blood.

22 He that taketh away his neighbour's living slayeth him; and he that defraudeth the labourer of his hire is a bloodshedder.

DOUAY OLD TESTAMENT

15 For their hope is on him that saveth them, and the eyes of God are upon them that love him.

16 He that feareth the Lord shall tremble at nothing, and shall not be afraid: for he is his hope.

17 The soul of him that feareth the Lord is blessed.

18 To whom doth he look, and who is his strength?

19 The eyes of the Lord are upon them that fear him, he is their powerful protector, and strong stay, a defence from the heat, and a cover from the sun at noon,

20 A preservation from stumbling, and a help from falling; he raiseth up the soul, and enlighteneth the eyes, and giveth health, and life, and blessing.

21 The offering of him that sacrificeth of a thing wrongfully gotten, is stained, and the mockeries of the unjust are not acceptable.

22 The Lord is only for them that wait upon him in the way of truth and justice.

23 The most High approveth not the gifts of the wicked: neither hath he respect to the oblations of the unjust, nor will he be pacified for sins by the multitude of their sacrifices.

24 He that offereth sacrifice of the goods of the poor, is as one that sacrificeth the son in the presence of his father.

25 The bread of the needy, is the life of the poor: he that defraudeth them thereof, is a man of blood.

26 He that taketh away the bread gotten by sweat, is like him that killeth his neighbour.

27 He that sheddeth blood, and he that defraudeth the labourer of his hire, are brothers.

KNOX TRANSLATION

can trust in, and God's eye watches over them in return for
their love. 16 Fear the Lord, and thou shalt never hesitate;
nothing may daunt thee, while such a hope is thine.
17 Blessed souls, that fear the Lord! 18 They know where to
look for refuge. 19 Fear the Lord, and his eyes watch over
thee; here is strong protection, here is firm support; shelter
when the hot wind blows, shade at noon-day; 20 here is reas-
surance when a man stumbles, support when he falls; soul
uplifted, eyes enlightened, health and life and blessing
bestowed.

21 Tainted is every sacrifice that comes of goods ill-gotten;
a mockery, this, of sacrifice, that shall win no favour. 22 For
those who wait upon him in loyal duty, the Lord alone is
God.[a] 23 Should the most High accept the offerings of sinners, take the gifts of the wrong-doer into his reckoning, and
pardon their sins because their sacrifices are many? 24 Who
robs the poor and then brings sacrifice, is of their fellowship
that would immolate some innocent child before the eyes of
his father. 25 Poor man's bread is poor man's life; 26 cheat
him of it, and thou hast slain him; sweat of his brow, or his
life's blood, what matters? 27 Disappoint the hireling, and
thou art own brother to a murderer. 28 Build while another

a It is difficult to see the appositeness of this phrase. The rendering 'The Lord is only (approachable) for those who wait upon him in loyal duty' does not represent the Latin.

TODAY'S ENGLISH VERSION

and you will have nothing else to fear. If your trust is in him,
you will never act like a coward. 15 People who fear the Lord
are fortunate, because they know where they can look for
help. 16 The Lord watches over those who love him; he is
their strong protection and firm support. He shelters them
from the heat, shades them from the noonday sun, and
keeps them from stumbling and falling. 17 He makes them
cheerful and puts a sparkle in their eyes. He blesses them
with life and health.

18 If you offer as a sacrifice an animal that you have
obtained dishonestly, it is defective and unacceptable. 19 The
Most High gets no pleasure from sacrifices made by ungodly
people; no amount of sacrifices can make up for their sins.
20 Anyone who steals an animal from the poor to offer as a
sacrifice is like someone who kills a boy before his father's
eyes. 21 Food means life itself to poor people, and taking it
away from them is murder. 22 It is murder to deprive someone of his living or to cheat an employee of his wages.

NEW REVISED STANDARD VERSION

16 Those who fear the Lord will not be timid,
or play the coward, for he is their hope.
17 Happy is the soul that fears the Lord!
18 To whom does he look? And who is his support?
19 The eyes of the Lord are on those who love him,
a mighty shield and strong support,
a shelter from scorching wind and a shade from
noonday sun,
a guard against stumbling and a help against falling.
20 He lifts up the soul and makes the eyes sparkle;
he gives health and life and blessing.

21 If one sacrifices ill-gotten goods, the offering is
blemished;[a]
22 the gifts[b] of the lawless are not acceptable.
23 The Most High is not pleased with the offerings of the
ungodly,
nor for a multitude of sacrifices does he forgive sins.
24 Like one who kills a son before his father's eyes
is the person who offers a sacrifice from the property
of the poor.
25 The bread of the needy is the life of the poor;
whoever deprives them of it is a murderer.
26 To take away a neighbor's living is to commit murder;
27 to deprive an employee of wages is to shed blood.

a Other ancient authorities read *is made in mockery* *b* Other ancient authorities read *mockeries*

NEW AMERICAN BIBLE

14 He who fears the LORD is never alarmed,
never afraid; for the LORD is his hope.
15 Happy the soul that fears the LORD!
In whom does he trust, and who is his support?
16 The eyes of the LORD are upon those who love him;
he is their mighty shield and strong support,
A shelter from the heat, a shade from the noonday sun,
a guard against stumbling, a help against falling.
17 He buoys up the spirits, brings a sparkle to the eyes,
gives health and life and blessing.

18 Tainted his gifts who offers in sacrifice ill-gotten goods!
Mock presents from the lawless win not God's favor.
19 The Most High approves not the gifts of the godless,
nor for their many sacrifices does he forgive their
sins.
20 Like the man who slays a son in his father's presence
is he who offers sacrifice from the possessions of the
poor.
21 The bread of charity is life itself for the needy;
he who withholds it is a man of blood.
22 He slays his neighbor who deprives him of his living;
he sheds blood who denies the laborer his wages.

NEW JERUSALEM BIBLE

14 No one who fears the Lord need ever hesitate,
or ever be daunted, since the Lord is his hope.
15 Happy the soul of one who fears the Lord.
On whom does he rely? Who supports him?
16 The eyes of the Lord watch over those who love him,
he is their powerful protection and their strong
support,
their screen from the desert wind, their shelter from the
midday sun,
a guard against stumbling, an assurance against a
fall.
17 He revives the spirit and brightens the eyes,
he gives health, life and blessing.
18 The sacrifice of an offering unjustly acquired is a
mockery;
the gifts of the impious are unacceptable.
19 The Most High takes no pleasure in offerings from the
godless,
multiplying sacrifices will not gain pardon for sin.
20 Offering sacrifice from the property of the poor
is as bad as slaughtering a son before his father's
eyes.
21 A meagre diet is the very life of the poor,
to deprive them of it is to commit murder.
22 To take away a fellow-man's livelihood is to kill him,
to deprive an employee of his wages is to shed blood.

GREEK OLD TESTAMENT

23 εἶς οἰκοδομῶν, καὶ εἶς καθαιρῶν·
τί ὠφέλησαν πλεῖον ἢ κόπους;
24 εἶς εὐχόμενος, καὶ εἶς καταρώμενος·
τίνος φωνῆς εἰσακούσεται ὁ δεσπότης;
25 βαπτιζόμενος ἀπὸ νεκροῦ καὶ πάλιν ἁπτόμενος αὐτοῦ,
τί ὠφέλησεν ἐν τῷ λουτρῷ αὐτοῦ;
26 οὕτως ἄνθρωπος νηστεύων ἐπὶ τῶν ἁμαρτιῶν αὐτοῦ
καὶ πάλιν πορευόμενος καὶ τὰ αὐτὰ ποιῶν·
τῆς προσευχῆς αὐτοῦ τίς εἰσακούσεται;
καὶ τί ὠφέλησεν ἐν τῷ ταπεινωθῆναι αὐτόν;

35 Ὁ συντηρῶν νόμον πλεονάζει προσφοράς,
θυσιάζων σωτηρίου ὁ προσέχων ἐντολαῖς.
2 ἀνταποδιδοὺς χάριν προσφέρων σεμίδαλιν,
καὶ ὁ ποιῶν ἐλεημοσύνην θυσιάζων αἰνέσεως.
3 εὐδοκία κυρίου ἀποστῆναι ἀπὸ πονηρίας,
καὶ ἐξιλασμὸς ἀποστῆναι ἀπὸ ἀδικίας.
4 μὴ ὀφθῇς ἐν προσώπῳ κυρίου κενός·
πάντα γὰρ ταῦτα χάριν ἐντολῆς.
5 προσφορὰ δικαίου λιπαίνει θυσιαστήριον,
καὶ ἡ εὐωδία αὐτῆς ἔναντι ὑψίστου.
6 θυσία ἀνδρὸς δικαίου δεκτή,
καὶ τὸ μνημόσυνον αὐτῆς οὐκ ἐπιλησθήσεται.
7 ἐν ἀγαθῷ ὀφθαλμῷ δόξασον τὸν κύριον
καὶ μὴ σμικρύνῃς ἀπαρχὴν χειρῶν σου.

KING JAMES VERSION

23 When one buildeth, and another pulleth down, what profit have they then but labour?

24 When one prayeth, and another curseth, whose voice will the Lord hear?

25 He that washeth himself after the touching of a dead body, if he touch it again, what availeth his washing?

26 So is it with a man that fasteth for his sins, and goeth again, and doeth the same: who will hear his prayer? or what doth his humbling profit him?

35 He that keepeth the law bringeth offerings enough: he that taketh heed to the commandment offereth a peace offering.

2 He that requiteth a good turn offereth fine flour; and he that giveth alms sacrificeth praise.

3 To depart from wickedness is a thing pleasing to the Lord; and to forsake unrighteousness is a propitiation.

4 Thou shalt not appear empty before the Lord.

5 For all these things [are to be done] because of the commandment.

6 The offering of the righteous maketh the altar fat, and the sweet savour thereof *is* before the most High.

7 The sacrifice of a just man is acceptable, and the memorial thereof shall never be forgotten.

8 Give the Lord his honour with a good eye, and diminish not the firstfruits of thine hands.

DOUAY OLD TESTAMENT

28 When one buildeth up, and another pulleth down: what profit have they but the labour?

29 When one prayeth, and another curseth: whose voice will God hear?

30 He that washeth himself after touching the dead, if he toucheth him again, what doth his washing avail?

31 So a man that fasteth for his sins, and doth the same again, what doth his humbling himself profit him? who will hear his prayer?

35 HE that keepeth the law, multiplieth offerings.

2 It is a wholesome sacrifice to take heed to the commandments, and to depart from all iniquity.

3 And to depart from injustice, is to offer a propitiatory sacrifice for injustices, and a begging of pardon for sins.

4 He shall return thanks, that offereth fine flour: and he that doth mercy, offereth sacrifice.

5 To depart from iniquity is that which pleaseth the Lord, and to depart from injustice, is an entreaty for sins.

6 Thou shalt not appear empty in the sight of the Lord.

7 For all these things are to be done because of the commandment of God.

8 The oblation of the just maketh the altar fat, and is an odour of sweetness in the sight of the most High.

9 The sacrifice of the just is acceptable, and the Lord will not forget the memorial thereof.

10 Give glory to God with a good heart: and diminish not the firstfruits of thy hands.

KNOX TRANSLATION

pulls down, and toil is its own reward. 29 Pray while another
curses, and which of you shall find audience with God?
30 Cleanse thyself from dead body's contamination, and touch
it again, what avails thy cleansing? 31 So it is when a man
fasts for his sins, yet will not leave his sinning; vain is the
fast, the prayer goes unanswered.

35 Live true to the law, and thou hast richly endowed
the altar. 2 Let this be thy welcome-offering, to heed
God's word and keep clear of all wickedness; 3 this thy sacrifice of amends for wrong done, of atonement for fault, to
shun wrong-doing. 4 Bloodless offering wouldst thou make,
give thanks;[a] victim wouldst thou immolate, shew mercy.
5 Wickedness and wrong-doing to shun is to win God's
favour, and pardon for thy faults.
6 Yet do not appear in the Lord's presence empty-handed;
7 due observance must be paid, because God has commanded
it. 8 If thy heart is right, thy offering shall enrich the altar;
its fragrance shall reach the presence of the most High; 9 a
just man's sacrifice the Lord accepts, and will not pass over
his claim to be remembered. 10 Generously pay the Lord his
due; do not grudge him the first-fruits of thy earnings; 11 all

a This would more naturally be rendered from the Latin, 'If thou wouldst give thanks, make a bloodless offering', but the context seems to indicate that this is a misinterpretation of the Greek.

TODAY'S ENGLISH VERSION

23 When one person builds and somebody else tears down,
has anything been accomplished but hard work? 24 When
one person blesses and somebody else curses, which one is
the Lord going to listen to? 25 If you touch a dead body and
then purify yourself by washing, but then go and touch it
again, what good did the washing do? 26 If you fast because
of your sins, and then go out and commit the same sins over
again, what have you gained by going without food? Who do
you think is going to listen to your prayers?

35 Keeping the Law is worth many offerings; it is a fellowship offering in itself. 2 Returning a kindness is
like a grain offering; giving to the poor is like a thanksgiving
offering. 3 Keeping away from sin will please the Lord and
make atonement for sin. 4 But don't come to the Temple
without an offering; 5 the Law requires that you bring one.
6 When someone righteous offers a sacrifice and the fat drips
down on the altar, a pleasant smell rises to the Most High.
7 The Lord will accept the offerings made by a righteous person and will not forget them. 8 Praise the Lord by making
generous offerings to him; don't be stingy with the first of

NEW REVISED STANDARD VERSION

28 When one builds and another tears down,
what do they gain but hard work?
29 When one prays and another curses,
to whose voice will the Lord listen?
30 If one washes after touching a corpse, and touches it
again,
what has been gained by washing?
31 So if one fasts for his sins,
and goes again and does the same things,
who will listen to his prayer?
And what has he gained by humbling himself?

35 The one who keeps the law makes many offerings;
2 one who heeds the commandments makes an
offering of well-being.
3 The one who returns a kindness offers choice flour,
4 and one who gives alms sacrifices a thank offering.
5 To keep from wickedness is pleasing to the Lord,
and to forsake unrighteousness is an atonement.
6 Do not appear before the Lord empty-handed,
7 for all that you offer is in fulfillment of the
commandment.
8 The offering of the righteous enriches the altar,
and its pleasing odor rises before the Most High.
9 The sacrifice of the righteous is acceptable,
and it will never be forgotten.
10 Be generous when you worship the Lord,
and do not stint the first fruits of your hands.

NEW AMERICAN BIBLE

23 If one man builds up and another tears down,
what do they gain but trouble?
24 If one man prays and another curses,
whose voice will the LORD hear?
25 If a man again touches a corpse after he has bathed,
what did he gain by the purification?
26 So with a man who fasts for his sins,
but then goes and commits them again:
Who will hear his prayer,
and what has he gained by his mortification?

35 To keep the law is a great oblation,
and he who observes the commandments sacrifices
a peace offering.
2 In works of charity one offers fine flour,
and when he gives alms he presents his sacrifice of
praise.
3 To refrain from evil pleases the LORD,
and to avoid injustice is an atonement.
4 Appear not before the LORD empty-handed,
for all that you offer is in fulfillment of the precepts.
5 The just man's offering enriches the altar
and rises as a sweet odor before the Most High.
6 The just man's sacrifice is most pleasing,
nor will it ever be forgotten.
7 In generous spirit pay homage to the LORD,
be not sparing of freewill gifts.

NEW JERUSALEM BIBLE

23 If one person builds while another pulls down,
what will they get out of it but trouble?
24 If one person prays and another calls down a curse,
to which one's voice is the Master going to listen?
25 If someone washes after touching a corpse, and then
touches it again,
what is the good of his washing?
26 Just so with someone who fasts for sin,
and then goes and commits it again.
Who is going to hear that person's prayer?
What is the good of the self-abasement?

35 One who keeps the Law multiplies offerings;
one who follows the commandments offers
communion sacrifices.
2 Proof of gratitude is an offering of fine flour,
almsgiving a sacrifice of praise.
3 To abandon wickedness is what pleases the Lord,
to give up wrong-doing is an expiatory sacrifice.
4 Do not appear empty-handed in the Lord's presence;
for all these things are due under the commandment.
5 The offering of the upright graces the altar,
and its savour rises before the Most High.
6 The sacrifice of the upright is acceptable,
its memorial will not be forgotten.
7 Honour the Lord with generosity,
do not stint the first-fruits you bring.

GREEK OLD TESTAMENT

8 ἐν πάσῃ δόσει ἱλάρωσον τὸ πρόσωπόν σου
καὶ ἐν εὐφροσύνῃ ἁγίασον δεκάτην.
9 δὸς ὑψίστῳ κατὰ τὴν δόσιν αὐτοῦ
καὶ ἐν ἀγαθῷ ὀφθαλμῷ καθ' εὕρεμα χειρός·
10 ὅτι κύριος ἀνταποδιδοὺς ἐστιν
καὶ ἑπταπλάσια ἀνταποδώσει σοι.
11 Μὴ δωροκόπει, οὐ γὰρ προσδέξεται,
καὶ μὴ ἔπεχε θυσίᾳ ἀδίκῳ·
12 ὅτι κύριος κριτής ἐστιν,
καὶ οὐκ ἔστιν παρ' αὐτῷ δόξα προσώπου.
13 οὐ λήμψεται πρόσωπον ἐπὶ πτωχοῦ
καὶ δέησιν ἠδικημένου εἰσακούσεται·
14 οὐ μὴ ὑπερίδῃ ἱκετείαν ὀρφανοῦ
καὶ χήραν, ἐὰν ἐκχέῃ λαλιάν·
15 οὐχὶ δάκρυα χήρας ἐπὶ σιαγόνα καταβαίνει
καὶ ἡ καταβόησις ἐπὶ τῷ καταγαγόντι αὐτά;
16 θεραπεύων ἐν εὐδοκίᾳ δεχθήσεται,
καὶ ἡ δέησις αὐτοῦ ἕως νεφελῶν συνάψει·
17 προσευχὴ ταπεινοῦ νεφέλας διῆλθεν,
καὶ ἕως συνεγγίσῃ, οὐ μὴ παρακληθῇ·
18 καὶ οὐ μὴ ἀποστῇ, ἕως ἐπισκέψηται ὁ ὕψιστος
καὶ κρινεῖ δικαίοις καὶ ποιήσει κρίσιν.
19 καὶ ὁ κύριος οὐ μὴ βραδύνῃ
οὐδὲ μὴ μακροθυμήσῃ ἐπ' αὐτοῖς,

KING JAMES VERSION

9 In all thy gifts shew a cheerful countenance, and dedicate thy tithes with gladness.

10 Give unto the most High according as he hath enriched thee; and as thou hast gotten, give with a cheerful eye.

11 For the Lord recompenseth, and will give thee seven times as much.

12 Do not think to corrupt with gifts; for such he will not receive: and trust not to unrighteous sacrifices; for the Lord is judge, and with him is no respect of persons.

13 He will not accept any person against a poor man, but will hear the prayer of the oppressed.

14 He will not despise the supplication of the fatherless; nor the widow, when she poureth out her complaint.

15 Do not the tears run down the widow's cheeks? and is not her cry against him that causeth them to fall?

16 He that serveth the Lord shall be accepted with favour, and his prayer shall reach unto the clouds.

17 The prayer of the humble pierceth the clouds: and till it come nigh, he will not be comforted; and will not depart, till the most High shall behold to judge righteously, and execute judgment.

18 For the Lord will not be slack, neither will the Mighty be patient toward them, till he have smitten in sunder the

DOUAY OLD TESTAMENT

11 In every gift shew a cheerful countenance, and sanctify thy tithes with joy.

12 Give to the most High according to what he hath given to thee, and with a good eye do according to the ability of thy hands:

13 For the Lord maketh recompense, and will give thee seven times as much.

14 Do not offer wicked gifts, for such he will not receive.

15 And look not upon an unjust sacrifice, for the Lord is judge, and there is not with him respect of person.

16 The Lord will not accept any person against a poor man, and he will hear the prayer of him that is wronged.

17 He will not despise the prayers of the fatherless; nor the widow, when she poureth out her complaint.

18 Do not the widow's tears run down the cheek, and her cry against him that causeth them to fall?

19 For from the cheek they go up even to heaven, and the Lord that heareth will not be delighted with them.

20 He that adoreth God with joy, shall be accepted, and his prayer shall approach even to the clouds.

21 The prayer of him that humbleth himself, shall pierce the clouds: and till it come nigh he will not be comforted: and he will not depart till the most High behold.

22 And the Lord will not be slack, but will judge for the just, and will do judgment: and the Almighty will not have patience with them, that he may crush their back:

KNOX TRANSLATION

thou givest, give with a smiling face, gladly bring in the
tithe. 12 In his own measure God's gift repay; grudge thou
must not what afford thou canst; 13 the Lord is a good master, and thou shalt have sevenfold in return.

14 But think not to bribe his justice; he will have none of
thy bribery. 15 Never pin thy hopes on the power of wealth
ill-gotten; the Lord is a true judge, not swayed by partiality,
16 and thou canst not win him to take thy part against the
friendless, turn him deaf to the plea of the wronged.
17 Prayer of the orphan, eloquent sigh of the widow, he will
not disregard; 18 see the tears on yonder widow's cheeks,
that accuse the author of her misery! 19 From her cheeks
they rise to heaven, where all prayers are heard, a grievous
sight. 20 None but his true worshippers he makes welcome;
for their supplication the clouds give passage. 21 Pierce those
clouds if thou wouldst, thou must humble thyself, incon-
solable till that prayer finds audience, unwearying till it wins
redress.

22 And will the Lord keep us waiting long? Hearing and
redress he will grant to the innocent; strong as of old, patient
no longer, he will crush the backs of our oppressors. 23 The

TODAY'S ENGLISH VERSION

your crops. 9 Be cheerful with every gift you make, and when
you pay your tithes, do it gladly. 10 Give to the Most High as
he has given to you, just as generously as you can. 11 The
Lord always repays and will do it many times over. 12 But
don't try to bribe him or rely on offerings that you have
obtained dishonestly. He will not accept them.

The Lord is fair[a] and does not show partiality. 13 He is not
prejudiced against the poor; when someone prays who has
been wronged, the Lord listens. 14 When orphans and widows pour out their prayers, he does not ignore them. 15 The
tears running down a widow's cheek cry out in accusation
against the one who has caused her distress.

16 Serve the Lord willingly, and the Lord will accept you;
your prayers will reach the skies. 17 The prayer of a humble
person goes past the clouds and keeps on going until it
reaches the Lord Most High, where it stays until he answers
by seeing that justice is done and that the guilty are punished.

18 And the Lord will act quickly. He will show no patience

[a] *Hebrew* fair; *Greek* judge.

NEW REVISED STANDARD VERSION

11 With every gift show a cheerful face,
and dedicate your tithe with gladness.
12 Give to the Most High as he has given to you,
and as generously as you can afford.
13 For the Lord is the one who repays,
and he will repay you sevenfold.
14 Do not offer him a bribe, for he will not accept it;
15 and do not rely on a dishonest sacrifice;
for the Lord is the judge,
and with him there is no partiality.
16 He will not show partiality to the poor;
but he will listen to the prayer of one who is wronged.
17 He will not ignore the supplication of the orphan,
or the widow when she pours out her complaint.
18 Do not the tears of the widow run down her cheek
19 as she cries out against the one who causes them to
fall?
20 The one whose service is pleasing to the Lord will be
accepted,
and his prayer will reach to the clouds.
21 The prayer of the humble pierces the clouds,
and it will not rest until it reaches its goal;
it will not desist until the Most High responds
22 and does justice for the righteous, and executes
judgment.
Indeed, the Lord will not delay,
and like a warrior[a] will not be patient

[a] Heb: Gk *and with them*

NEW AMERICAN BIBLE

8 With each contribution show a cheerful countenance,
and pay your tithes in a spirit of joy.
9 Give to the Most High as he has given to you,
generously, according to your means.

10 For the LORD is one who always repays,
and he will give back to you sevenfold.
11 But offer no bribes, these he does not accept!
Trust not in sacrifice of the fruits of extortion,
12 For he is a God of justice,
who knows no favorites.
13 Though not unduly partial toward the weak,
yet he hears the cry of the oppressed.
14 He is not deaf to the wail of the orphan,
nor to the widow when she pours out her complaint;
15 Do not the tears that stream down her cheek
cry out against him that causes them to fall?
16 He who serves God willingly is heard;
his petition reaches the heavens.
17 The prayer of the lowly pierces the clouds;
it does not rest till it reaches its goal,
18 Nor will it withdraw till the Most High responds,
judges justly and affirms the right.

19 God indeed will not delay,
and like a warrior, will not be still

NEW JERUSALEM BIBLE

8 Add a smiling face to all your gifts,
and be cheerful as you dedicate your tithes.
9 Give to the Most High as he has given to you,
as generously as your means can afford;
10 for the Lord is a good rewarder,
he will reward you seven times over.
11 Do not try to bribe him with presents, he will not accept
them,
do not put your faith in wrongly motivated sacrifices;
12 for the Lord is a judge
who is utterly impartial.
13 He never shows partiality to the detriment of the poor,
he listens to the plea of the injured party.
14 He does not ignore the orphan's supplication,
nor the widow's as she pours out her complaint.
15 Do the widow's tears not run down her cheeks,
as she accuses the man who is the cause of them?
16 Whoever wholeheartedly serves God will be accepted,
his petitions will carry to the clouds.
17 The prayer of the humble pierces the clouds:
and until it does, he is not to be consoled,
18 nor will he desist until the Most High takes notice of
him,
acquits the upright and delivers judgement.
19 And the Lord will not be slow,
nor will he be dilatory on their behalf,

GREEK OLD TESTAMENT

20 ἕως ἂν συντρίψῃ ὀσφὺν ἀνελεημόνων
καὶ τοῖς ἔθνεσιν ἀνταποδώσει ἐκδίκησιν,
21 ἕως ἐξάρῃ πλῆθος ὑβριστῶν
καὶ σκῆπτρα ἀδίκων συντρίψει,
22 ἕως ἀνταποδῷ ἀνθρώπῳ κατὰ τὰς πράξεις αὐτοῦ
καὶ τὰ ἔργα τῶν ἀνθρώπων κατὰ τὰ ἐνθυμήματα αὐτῶν,
23 ἕως κρίνῃ τὴν κρίσιν τοῦ λαοῦ αὐτοῦ
καὶ εὐφρανεῖ αὐτοὺς ἐν τῷ ἐλέει αὐτοῦ.
24 ὡραῖον ἔλεος ἐν καιρῷ θλίψεως αὐτοῦ
ὡς νεφέλαι ὑετοῦ ἐν καιρῷ ἀβροχίας.

36 Ἐλέησον ἡμᾶς, δέσποτα ὁ θεὸς πάντων,
καὶ ἐπίβλεψον
καὶ ἐπίβαλε τὸν φόβον σου ἐπὶ πάντα τὰ ἔθνη·
2 ἔπαρον τὴν χεῖρά σου ἐπὶ ἔθνη ἀλλότρια,
καὶ ἰδέτωσαν τὴν δυναστείαν σου.
3 ὥσπερ ἐνώπιον αὐτῶν ἡγιάσθης ἐν ἡμῖν,
οὕτως ἐνώπιον ἡμῶν μεγαλυνθείης ἐν αὐτοῖς·
4 καὶ ἐπιγνώτωσάν σε, καθάπερ καὶ ἡμεῖς ἐπέγνωμεν
ὅτι οὐκ ἔστιν θεὸς πλὴν σοῦ, κύριε.
5 ἐγκαίνισον σημεῖα καὶ ἀλλοίωσον θαυμάσια,
δόξασον χεῖρα καὶ βραχίονα δεξιόν·
6 ἔγειρον θυμὸν καὶ ἔκχεον ὀργήν,
ἔξαρον ἀντίδικον καὶ ἔκτριψον ἐχθρόν.
7 σπεῦσον καιρὸν καὶ μνήσθητι ὁρκισμοῦ,
καὶ ἐκδιηγησάσθωσαν τὰ μεγαλεῖά σου.

KING JAMES VERSION

loins of the unmerciful, and repayed vengeance to the heathen; till he have taken away the multitude of the proud, and broken the sceptre of the unrighteous;

19 Till he have rendered to every man according to his deeds, and to the works of men according to their devices; till he have judged the cause of his people, and made them to rejoice in his mercy.

20 Mercy is seasonable in the time of affliction, as clouds of rain in the time of drought.

36 Have mercy upon us, O Lord God of all, and behold us:

2 And send thy fear upon all the nations that seek not after thee.

3 Lift up thy hand against the strange nations, and let them see thy power.

4 As thou wast sanctified in us before them: so be thou magnified among them before us.

5 And let them know thee, as we have known thee, that there is no God but only thou, O God.

6 Shew new signs, and make other strange wonders: glorify thy hand and thy right arm, that they may set forth thy wondrous works.

7 Raise up indignation, and pour out wrath: take away the adversary, and destroy the enemy.

8 Make the time short, remember the covenant, and let them declare thy wonderful works.

DOUAY OLD TESTAMENT

23 And he will repay vengeance to the Gentiles, till he have taken away the multitude of the proud, and broken the sceptres of the unjust,

24 Till he have rendered to men according to their deeds: and according to the works of Adam, and according to his presumption,

25 Till he have judged the cause of his people, and he shall delight the just with his mercy.

26 The mercy of God is beautiful in the time of affliction, as a cloud of rain in the time of drought.

36 HAVE mercy upon us, O God of all, and behold us, and shew us the light of thy mercies:

2 And send thy fear upon the nations, that have not sought after thee: that they may know that there is no God beside thee, and that they may shew forth thy wonders.

3 Lift up thy hand over the strange nations, that they may see thy power.

4 For as thou hast been sanctified in us in their sight, so thou shalt be magnified among them in our presence,

5 That they may know thee, as we also have known thee, that there is no God beside thee, O Lord.

6 Renew thy signs, and work new miracles.

7 Glorify thy hand, and thy right arm.

8 Raise up indignation, and pour out wrath.

9 Take away the adversary, and crush the enemy.

10 Hasten the time, and remember the end, that they may declare thy wonderful works.

KNOX TRANSLATION

Gentiles punished, scattered the hordes of insolence, broken
the sceptre of wrong! 24 Men called to account everywhere
for their deeds, the harvest of their mortal pride, 25 and his
own people vindicated at last, triumphing in his mercy at
last! 26 God's mercy, welcome to the afflicted as rain-clouds
are welcome in time of drought!

36 God of all men, have mercy on us; look down, and let
us see the smile of thy favour. 2 Teach them to fear
thee, those other nations that have never looked to find thee;
let them learn to recognize thee as the only God, and to
acclaim thy wonders. 3 Lift up thy hand, to shew these
aliens thy power; 4 let us see them, as they have seen us,
humbled before thee; 5 let them learn, as we have learnt,
that there is no other God but thou. 6 Shew new marvels,
and portents stranger still; 7 win renown for that strength,
that valiant arm of thine; 8 rouse thyself to vengeance, give
thy anger free play; 9 away with the oppressors, down with
thy enemies! 10 Hasten on the time, do not forget thy purpose; make them acclaim thy wonders. 11 Let none of them

TODAY'S ENGLISH VERSION

with wicked people. He will take vengeance by crushing the
heathen. He will completely wipe out the merciless and the
arrogant, and will destroy the authority of the wicked. 19 He
will give each of us what our thoughts and actions deserve.
Because of the Lord's mercy, his people will be happy when
he has judged their case. 20 In times of trouble his mercy is
as welcome as rain after a long drought.

36 O Lord God of the universe, look upon us and have
mercy. 2 Make every nation stand in fear of you.
3 Take action against the foreign nations, and let them witness your power! 4 You have used us to show them how
holy you are; now use them to show us how great you are.
5 Let them learn, as we have learned, that there is no God,
O Lord, but you. 6 Give new signs, perform new miracles;
show us your glorious strength! 7-9 Bring on that appointed
time when everyone can talk about the great things you do.

NEW REVISED STANDARD VERSION

until he crushes the loins of the unmerciful
23 and repays vengeance on the nations;
until he destroys the multitude of the insolent,
and breaks the scepters of the unrighteous;
24 until he repays mortals according to their deeds,
and the works of all according to their thoughts;
25 until he judges the case of his people
and makes them rejoice in his mercy.
26 His mercy is as welcome in time of distress
as clouds of rain in time of drought.

36 Have mercy upon us, O God[a] of all,
2 and put all the nations in fear of you.
3 Lift up your hand against foreign nations
and let them see your might.
4 As you have used us to show your holiness to them,
so use them to show your glory to us.
5 Then they will know,[b] as we have known,
that there is no God but you, O Lord.
6 Give new signs, and work other wonders;
7 make your hand and right arm glorious.
8 Rouse your anger and pour out your wrath;
9 destroy the adversary and wipe out the enemy.
10 Hasten the day, and remember the appointed time,[c]
and let people recount your mighty deeds.

a Heb: Gk *O Master, the God* *b* Heb: Gk *And let them know you*
c Other ancient authorities read *remember your oath*

NEW AMERICAN BIBLE

20 Till he breaks the backs of the merciless
and wreaks vengeance upon the proud;
21 Till he destroys the haughty root and branch,
and smashes the scepter of the wicked;
22 Till he requites mankind according to its deeds,
and repays men according to their thoughts;
23 Till he defends the cause of his people,
and gladdens them by his mercy.
24 Welcome is his mercy in time of distress
as rain clouds in time of drought.

36 Come to our aid, O God of the universe,
and put all the nations in dread of you!
2 Raise your hand against the heathen,
that they may realize your power.
3 As you have used us to show them your holiness,
so now use them to show us your glory.
4 Thus they will know, as we know,
that there is no God but you.

5 Give new signs and work new wonders;
show forth the splendor of your right hand and arm;
6 Rouse your anger, pour out wrath,
humble the enemy, scatter the foe.
7 Hasten the day, bring on the time;
9 crush the heads of the hostile rulers.

NEW JERUSALEM BIBLE

20 until he has crushed the loins of the merciless
and exacted vengeance on the nations,
21 until he has eliminated the hordes of the arrogant
and broken the sceptres of the wicked,
22 until he has repaid all people as their deeds deserve
and human actions as their intentions merit,
23 until he has judged the case of his people
and made them rejoice in his mercy.
24 Mercy is welcome in time of trouble,
like rain clouds in time of drought.

36 Take pity on us, Master, Lord of the universe, look
at us,
spread fear of yourself throughout all other nations.
2 Raise your hand against the foreign nations
and let them see your might.
3 As, in their sight, you have proved yourself holy to us,
so now, in our sight, prove yourself great to them.
4 Let them acknowledge you, just as we have
acknowledged
that there is no God but you, Lord.
5 Send new portents, do fresh wonders,
win glory for your hand and your right arm.
6 Rouse your fury, pour out your rage,
destroy the opponent, annihilate the enemy.
7 Hasten the day, remember the oath,
and let people tell of your mighty deeds.

GREEK OLD TESTAMENT

8ἐν ὀργῇ πυρὸς καταβρωθήτω ὁ σῳζόμενος,
καὶ οἱ κακοῦντες τὸν λαόν σου εὕροισαν ἀπώλειαν.
9σύντριψον κεφαλὰς ἀρχόντων ἐχθρῶν
λεγόντων Οὐκ ἔστιν πλὴν ἡμῶν.
10συνάγαγε πάσας φυλὰς Ιακωβ
καὶ κατακληρονόμησον αὐτοὺς καθὼς ἀπ' ἀρχῆς.
11ἐλέησον λαόν, κύριε, κεκλημένον ἐπ' ὀνόματί σου
καὶ Ισραηλ, ὃν πρωτογόνῳ ὡμοίωσας.
12οἰκτίρησον πόλιν ἁγιάσματός σου,
Ιερουσαλημ τόπον καταπαύματός σου·
13πλῆσον Σιων ἀρεταλογίας σου
καὶ ἀπὸ τῆς δόξης σου τὸν λαόν σου.
14δὸς μαρτύριον τοῖς ἐν ἀρχῇ κτίσμασίν σου
καὶ ἔγειρον προφητείας τὰς ἐπ' ὀνόματί σου·
15δὸς μισθὸν τοῖς ὑπομένουσίν σε,
καὶ οἱ προφῆταί σου ἐμπιστευθήτωσαν.
16εἰσάκουσον, κύριε, δεήσεως τῶν ἱκετῶν σου
κατὰ τὴν εὐλογίαν Ααρων περὶ τοῦ λαοῦ σου,
17καὶ γνώσονται πάντες οἱ ἐπὶ τῆς γῆς
ὅτι κύριος εἶ ὁ θεὸς τῶν αἰώνων.
18 Πᾶν βρῶμα φάγεται κοιλία,
ἔστιν δὲ βρῶμα βρώματος κάλλιον.

KING JAMES VERSION

9 Let him that escapeth be consumed by the rage of the fire; and let them perish that oppress the people.

10 Smite in sunder the heads of the rulers of the heathen, that say, There is none other but we.

11 Gather all the tribes of Jacob together, and inherit thou them, as from the beginning.

12 O Lord, have mercy upon the people that is called by thy name, and upon Israel, whom thou hast named thy first-born.

13 O be merciful unto Jerusalem, thy holy city, the place of thy rest.

14 Fill Sion with thine unspeakable oracles, and thy people with thy glory.

15 Give testimony unto those that thou hast possessed from the beginning, and raise up prophets that have been in thy name.

16 Reward them that wait for thee, and let thy prophets be found faithful.

17 O Lord, hear the prayer of thy servants, according to the blessing of Aaron over thy people, that all they which dwell upon the earth may know that thou art the Lord, the eternal God.

18 The belly devoureth all meats, yet is one meat better than another.

DOUAY OLD TESTAMENT

11 Let him that escapeth be consumed by the rage of the fire: and let them perish that oppress thy people.

12 Crush the head of the princes of the enemies that say: There is no other beside us.

13 Gather together all the tribes of Jacob: that they may know that there is no God besides thee, and may declare thy great works: and thou shalt inherit them as from the beginning.

14 Have mercy on thy people, upon whom thy name is invoked: and upon Israel, whom thou hast raised up to be thy firstborn.

15 Have mercy on Jerusalem, the city which thou hast sanctified, the city of thy rest.

16 Fill Sion with thy unspeakable words, and thy people with thy glory.

17 Give testimony to them that are thy creatures from the beginning, and raise up the prophecies which the former prophets spoke in thy name.

18 Reward them that patiently wait for thee, that thy prophets may be found faithful: and hear the prayers of thy servants,

19 According to the blessing of Aaron over thy people, and direct us into the way of justice, and let all know that dwell upon the earth, that thou art God the beholder of all ages.

20 The belly will devour all meat, yet one is better than another.

KNOX TRANSLATION

escape their doom, the oppressors of thy people; let there be
a raging fire ready to devour them; 12heavy let the blow fall
on the heads of those tyrants, that no other power will recognize but their own. 13Gather anew all the tribes of Jacob; be
it theirs to know that thou alone art God, to acclaim thy
wonders; make them thy loved possession as of old. 14Have
compassion on the people that is called by thy own name, on
Israel, owned thy first-born; 15have compassion on Jerusalem, the city thou hast set apart for thy resting-place;
16fill Sion's walls, fill the hearts of thy people, with wonders
beyond all telling come true, with thy glory made manifest.
17Vindicate the race that was from the first thy chosen; old
prophecies uttered in thy name, at last fulfil; 18have we
waited for thee to no purpose? Shall thy prophets be proved
false? Listen to thy servants' plea, 19that claim the blessing
Aaron pronounced over thy people; guide us into the right
path; let all the world know that thou art God, watching us
eternally.

20Take what food thou wilt, belly is content; yet meat and

TODAY'S ENGLISH VERSION

Pour out your furious, flaming anger, and let none of our
enemies survive. Destroy those who have oppressed your
people. 10 Crush all those enemy rulers who think they are
the only people in the world who matter! 11 Gather the tribes
of Israel together again, and give them back their land as
you gave it to them long ago. 12 Lord, have mercy on Israel,
the people who are known by your name, whom you called
your first-born son. 13 Take pity on Jerusalem, your holy city,
where you chose to stay. 14 Fill your Temple[a] on Mount Zion
with your glory and with hymns of praise. 15 Testify for your
people, whom you created in the beginning; fulfill the
prophecies that have been spoken in your name. 16 Reward
those who have put their faith in you, and vindicate your
prophets. 17 You have always been gracious to your people;[b]
listen to your servants as we pray. Then everyone on earth
will recognize that you are the Lord, the God of the ages.
18 Any kind of food can be eaten, but some foods are better

[a] *Hebrew* Temple; *Greek* people. [b] *Hebrew* You have . . . people; *Greek* According to the blessing of Aaron on your people.

NEW REVISED STANDARD VERSION

11 Let survivors be consumed in the fiery wrath,
and may those who harm your people meet
destruction.
12 Crush the heads of hostile rulers
who say, "There is no one but ourselves."
13 Gather all the tribes of Jacob,[a]
16 and give them their inheritance, as at the beginning.
17 Have mercy, O Lord, on the people called by your name,
on Israel, whom you have named[b] your firstborn,
18 Have pity on the city of your sanctuary,[c]
Jerusalem, the place of your dwelling.[d]
19 Fill Zion with your majesty,[e]
and your temple[f] with your glory.
20 Bear witness to those whom you created in the beginning,
and fulfill the prophecies spoken in your name.
21 Reward those who wait for you
and let your prophets be found trustworthy.
22 Hear, O Lord, the prayer of your servants, according to
your goodwill toward[g] your people,
and all who are on the earth will know
that you are the Lord, the God of the ages.

23 The stomach will take any food,
yet one food is better than another.

[a] Owing to a dislocation in the Greek Mss of Sirach, the verse numbers 14 and 15 are not used in chapter 36, though no text is missing. [b] Other ancient authorities read *you have likened to* [c] Or *on your holy city* [d] Heb: Gk *your rest* [e] Heb Syr: Gk *the celebration of your wondrous deeds* [f] Heb Syr: Gk Lat *people* [g] Heb and two Gk witnesses: Lat and most Gk witnesses read *according to the blessing of Aaron for*

NEW AMERICAN BIBLE

8 Let raging fire consume the fugitive,
and your people's oppressors meet destruction.
10 Gather all the tribes of Jacob,
that they may inherit the land as of old.
11 Show mercy to the people called by your name;
Israel, whom you named your firstborn.
12 Take pity on your holy city,
Jerusalem, your dwelling place.
13 Fill Zion with your majesty,
your temple with your glory.
14 Give evidence of your deeds of old;
fulfill the prophecies spoken in your name,
15 Reward those who have hoped in you,
and let your prophets be proved true.
16 Hear the prayer of your servants,
for you are ever gracious to your people;
17 Thus it will be known to the very ends of the earth
that you are the eternal God.

18 The throat can swallow any food,
yet some foods are more agreeable than others;

NEW JERUSALEM BIBLE

8 Let fiery wrath swallow up the survivor,
and destruction overtake those who oppress your
people.
9 Crush the heads of hostile rulers
who say, 'There is no one else but us!'
10 Gather together all the tribes of Jacob,
restore them their heritage as at the beginning.
11 Take pity, Lord, on the people called by your name,
on Israel whom you have made your first-born.
12 Have compassion on your holy city,
on Jerusalem, the place where you rest.
13 Fill Zion with your praises
and your sanctuary with your glory.
14 Vindicate those whom you created first,
fulfil what has been prophesied in your name.
15 Give those who wait for you their reward,
let your prophets be proved true.
16 Grant, Lord, the prayer of your servants,
in the terms of Aaron's blessing on your people,
17 so that all the earth's inhabitants may acknowledge
that you are the Lord, the everlasting God.

18 The stomach takes in all kinds of food,
but some foods are better than others.

GREEK OLD TESTAMENT

19 φάρυγξ γεύεται βρώματα θήρας,
οὕτως καρδία συνετὴ λόγους ψευδεῖς.
20 καρδία στρεβλὴ δώσει λύπην,
καὶ ἄνθρωπος πολύπειρος ἀνταποδώσει αὐτῷ.
21 πάντα ἄρρενα ἐπιδέξεται γυνή,
ἔστιν δὲ θυγάτηρ θυγατρὸς κρείσσων.
22 κάλλος γυναικὸς ἱλαρύνει πρόσωπον
καὶ ὑπὲρ πᾶσαν ἐπιθυμίαν ἀνθρώπου ὑπεράγει·
23 εἰ ἔστιν ἐπὶ γλώσσης αὐτῆς ἔλεος καὶ πραΰτης,
οὐκ ἔστιν ὁ ἀνὴρ αὐτῆς καθ' υἱοὺς ἀνθρώπων.
24 ὁ κτώμενος γυναῖκα ἐνάρχεται κτήσεως,
βοηθὸν κατ' αὐτὸν καὶ στῦλον ἀναπαύσεως.
25 οὗ οὐκ ἔστιν φραγμός, διαρπαγήσεται κτῆμα·
καὶ οὗ οὐκ ἔστιν γυνή, στενάξει πλανώμενος.
26 τίς γὰρ πιστεύσει εὐζώνῳ λῃστῇ
ἀφαλλομένῳ ἐκ πόλεως εἰς πόλιν;
27 οὕτως ἀνθρώπῳ μὴ ἔχοντι νοσσιὰν
καὶ καταλύοντι οὗ ἐὰν ὀψίσῃ.

37 Πᾶς φίλος ἐρεῖ Ἐφιλίασα κἀγώ·
ἀλλ' ἔστιν φίλος ὀνόματι μόνον φίλος.
2 οὐχὶ λύπη ἔνι ἕως θανάτου ἑταῖρος
καὶ φίλος τρεπόμενος εἰς ἔχθραν;
3 ὦ πονηρὸν ἐνθύμημα, πόθεν ἐνεκυλίσθης
καλύψαι τὴν ξηρὰν ἐν δολιότητι;

KING JAMES VERSION

19 As the palate tasteth divers kinds of venison: so doth an heart of understanding false speeches.

20 A froward heart causeth heaviness: but a man of experience will recompense him.

21 A woman will receive every man, yet is one daughter better than another.

22 The beauty of a woman cheereth the countenance, and a man loveth nothing better.

23 If there be kindness, meekness, and comfort, in her tongue, then is not her husband like other men.

24 He that getteth a wife beginneth a possession, a help like unto himself, and a pillar of rest.

25 Where no hedge is, there the possession is spoiled: and he that hath no wife will wander up and down mourning.

26 Who will trust a thief well appointed, that skippeth from city to city? so [who will believe] a man that hath no house, and lodgeth wheresoever the night taketh him?

37 Every friend saith, I am his friend also: but there is a friend, which is only a friend in name.

2 Is it not a grief unto death, when a companion and friend is turned to an enemy?

3 O wicked imagination, whence camest thou in to cover the earth with deceit?

DOUAY OLD TESTAMENT

21 The palate tasteth venison and the wise heart false speeches.

22 A perverse heart will cause grief, and a man of experience will resist it.

23 A woman will receive every man: yet one daughter is better than another.

24 The beauty of a woman cheereth the countenance of her husband, and a man desireth nothing more.

25 If she have a tongue that can cure, and likewise mitigate and shew mercy: her husband is not like other men.

26 He that possesseth a good wife, beginneth a possession: she is a help like to himself, and a pillar of rest.

27 Where there is no hedge, the possession shall be spoiled: and where there is no wife, he mourneth that is in want.

28 Who will trust him that hath no rest, and that lodgeth wheresoever the night taketh him, as a robber well appointed, that skippeth from city to city.

37 EVERY friend will say: I also am his friend: but there is a friend, that is only a friend in name. Is not this a grief even to death?

2 But a companion and a friend shall be turned to an enemy.

3 O wicked presumption, whence camest thou to cover the earth with thy malice, and deceitfulness?

KNOX TRANSLATION

meat differ. 21 The savour of venison only palate can reach;
only wise heart can discern lying tongue.
22 False heart breeds dismal thoughts; mind well schooled
keeps them at bay.[a]
23 Any woman is a mate for any man; yet maid and maid
differ.
24 Fair wife, blithe husband; as no other lure, beauty draws
us. 25 What of her tongue? If that, too, has power to charm,
if that is soft and gentle, never was man so blessed. 26 Good
wife won is life well begun; a comforter thou hast, of thy
own breed, a stay to support thee. 27 No hedge, no garden;
and if wife thou hast none, thou shalt wander homeless.
28 Trust him never, that has not found a nest to dwell in, and
does but lodge where night overtakes him, cut-purse that
travels light from city to city.

37 Friends every man has that will say, I love him well;
yet friends they may be in name only. Death itself cannot match it for sadness, 2 when friend and companion
becomes thy enemy. 3 Cruel pretence, what mind first conceived thee, to turn solid earth into a morass of foul treachery?

a The meaning of this verse is uncertain.

TODAY'S ENGLISH VERSION

than others. 19 And just as the tongue can distinguish the
flavors of different kinds of meat, so a sharp mind can detect
lies. 20 A person with a warped mind causes trouble, but an
experienced person knows how to pay it back.
21 A woman has to take any man as a husband, but a man
must choose his wife carefully. 22 A woman's beauty makes
a man happy; there is no fairer sight for the human eye to
see. 23 If the woman is kind and gentle in her speech, her
husband is the most fortunate of men. 24 When a man marries, he gets the finest thing he will ever have—a wife to help
and encourage him.
25 If property is not fenced in, thieves will wander in and
help themselves. And if a man has no wife, he is a sighing
wanderer; 26 people have no more trust in a homeless person
who sleeps in a different place every night than they have in
a wandering thief who goes from town to town.

37 Anyone can claim to be your friend, but some people
are friends in name only. 2 The grief caused when a
close friendship turns sour is as bad as death. 3 This evil
impulse we have! Why was it ever formed? How did it manage to cover the earth with deceit? 4 Some people will be

NEW REVISED STANDARD VERSION

24 As the palate tastes the kinds of game,
so an intelligent mind detects false words.
25 A perverse mind will cause grief,
but a person with experience will pay him back.
26 A woman will accept any man as a husband,
but one girl is preferable to another.
27 A woman's beauty lights up a man's face,
and there is nothing he desires more.
28 If kindness and humility mark her speech,
her husband is more fortunate than other men.
29 He who acquires a wife gets his best possession,[a]
a helper fit for him and a pillar of support.[b]
30 Where there is no fence, the property will be plundered;
and where there is no wife, a man will become a
fugitive and a wanderer.[c]
31 For who will trust a nimble robber
that skips from city to city?
So who will trust a man that has no nest,
but lodges wherever night overtakes him?

37 Every friend says, "I too am a friend";
but some friends are friends only in name.
2 Is it not a sorrow like that for death itself
when a dear friend turns into an enemy?
3 O inclination to evil, why were you formed
to cover the land with deceit?

a Heb: Gk *enters upon a possession* *b* Heb: Gk *rest* *c* Heb: Gk *wander about and sigh*

NEW AMERICAN BIBLE

19 As the palate tests meat by its savor,
so does a keen mind insincere words.
20 A deceitful character causes grief,
but an experienced man can turn the tables on him.
21 Though any man may be accepted as a husband,
yet one girl will be more suitable than another:
22 A woman's beauty makes her husband's face light up,
for it surpasses all else that charms the eye;
23 And if, besides, her speech is kindly,
his lot is beyond that of mortal men.
24 A wife is her husband's richest treasure,
a helpmate, a steadying column.
25 A vineyard with no hedge will be overrun;
a man with no wife becomes a homeless wanderer.
26 Who will trust an armed band
that shifts from city to city?
27 Or a man who has no nest,
but lodges where night overtakes him?

37 Every friend declares his friendship,
but there are friends who are friends in name only.
2 Is it not a sorrow unto death
when your bosom companion becomes your enemy?
3 "Alas, my companion! Why were you created
to blanket the earth with deceit?"

NEW JERUSALEM BIBLE

19 As the palate discerns the flavour of game,
so a shrewd listener detects lying words.
20 A perverse character causes depression in others;
it needs experience to know how to repay such a one.
21 A woman will accept any husband,
but some daughters are better than others.
22 A woman's beauty delights the beholder,
a man likes nothing better.
23 If her tongue is kind and gentle,
her husband is the happiest of men.
24 The man who takes a wife has the makings of a
fortune,
a helper to match himself, a pillar of support.
25 When property has no fence, it is open to plunder,
when a man has no wife, he is aimless and
querulous.
26 Will anyone trust an armed thief
who flits from town to town?
27 So it is with the man who has no nest,
and lodges wherever night overtakes him.

37 Any friend will say, 'I am your friend too,'
but some friends are friends only in name.
2 Is it not a deadly sorrow
when a comrade or a friend turns enemy?
3 O evil inclination, why were you created,
to cover the earth with deceit?

GREEK OLD TESTAMENT

4 ἑταῖρος φίλου ἐν εὐφροσύνῃ ἥδεται
καὶ ἐν καιρῷ θλίψεως ἔσται ἀπέναντι·
5 ἑταῖρος φίλῳ συμπονεῖ χάριν γαστρός,
ἔναντι πολέμου λήμψεται ἀσπίδα.
6 μὴ ἐπιλάθῃ φίλου ἐν τῇ ψυχῇ σου
καὶ μὴ ἀμνημονήσῃς αὐτοῦ ἐν χρήμασίν σου.
7 Πᾶς σύμβουλος ἐξαίρει βουλήν,
ἀλλ' ἔστιν συμβουλεύων εἰς ἑαυτόν.
8 ἀπὸ συμβούλου φύλαξον τὴν ψυχήν σου
καὶ γνῶθι πρότερον τίς αὐτοῦ χρεία
— καὶ γὰρ αὐτὸς ἑαυτῷ βουλεύσεται —,
μήποτε βάλῃ ἐπὶ σοὶ κλῆρον
9 καὶ εἴπῃ σοι Καλὴ ἡ ὁδός σου,
καὶ στήσεται ἐξ ἐναντίας ἰδεῖν τὸ συμβησόμενόν σοι.
10 μὴ βουλεύου μετὰ τοῦ ὑποβλεπομένου σε
καὶ ἀπὸ τῶν ζηλούντων σε κρύψον βουλήν,
11 μετὰ γυναικὸς περὶ τῆς ἀντιζήλου αὐτῆς
καὶ μετὰ δειλοῦ περὶ πολέμου,
μετὰ ἐμπόρου περὶ μεταβολίας
καὶ μετὰ ἀγοράζοντος περὶ πράσεως,
μετὰ βασκάνου περὶ εὐχαριστίας
καὶ μετὰ ἀνελεήμονος περὶ χρηστοηθείας,
μετὰ ὀκνηροῦ περὶ παντὸς ἔργου
καὶ μετὰ μισθίου ἐφετίου περὶ συντελείας,
οἰκέτῃ ἀργῷ περὶ πολλῆς ἐργασίας,
μὴ ἔπεχε ἐπὶ τούτοις περὶ πάσης συμβουλίας·

KING JAMES VERSION

4 There is a companion, which rejoiceth in the prosperity of a friend, but in the time of trouble will be against him.

5 There is a companion, which helpeth his friend for the belly, and taketh up the buckler against the enemy.

6 Forget not thy friend in thy mind, and be not unmindful of him in thy riches.

7 Every counsellor extolleth counsel; but there is some that counselleth for himself.

8 Beware of a counsellor, and know before what need he hath; for he will counsel for himself; lest he cast the lot upon thee,

9 And say unto thee, Thy way is good: and afterward he stand on the other side, to see what shall befall thee.

10 Consult not with one that suspecteth thee: and hide thy counsel from such as envy thee.

11 Neither consult with a woman touching her of whom she is jealous; neither with a coward in matters of war; nor with a merchant concerning exchange; nor with a buyer of selling; nor with an envious man of thankfulness; nor with an unmerciful man touching kindness; nor with the slothful for any work; nor with an hireling for a year of finishing work; nor with an idle servant of much business: hearken not unto these in any matter of counsel.

DOUAY OLD TESTAMENT

4 There is a companion who rejoiceth with his friend in his joys, but in the time of trouble, he will be against him.

5 There is a companion who condoleth with his friend for his belly's sake, and he will take up a shield against the enemy.

6 Forget not thy friend in thy mind, and be not unmindful of him in thy riches.

7 Consult not with him that layeth a snare for thee, and hide thy counsel from them that envy thee.

8 Every counsellor giveth out counsel, but there is one that is a counsellor for himself.

9 Beware of a counsellor. And know before what need he hath: for he will devise to his own mind:

10 Lest he thrust a stake into the ground, and say to thee:

11 Thy way is good; and then stand on the other side to see what shall befall thee.

12 Treat not with a man without religion concerning holiness, nor with an unjust man concerning justice, nor with a woman touching her of whom she is jealous, nor with a coward concerning war, nor with a merchant about traffic, nor with a buyer of selling, nor with an envious man of giving thanks,

13 Nor with the ungodly of piety, nor with the dishonest of honesty, nor with the field labourer of every work,

14 Nor with him that worketh by the year of the finishing of the year, nor with an idle servant of much business: give no heed to these in any matter of counsel.

KNOX TRANSLATION

4 A companion, how he will enjoy the delights of his friend's
prosperity, and turn against him in the hour of need! 5 A companion, how he will share a friend's grief if he may share his
bake-meats; use him as a shield against some enemy![a]
6 Never let friend of thine be far from thy thoughts; in thy prosperity never forget him.
7 Never take counsel with one who may be laying a trap
for thee; from his envy hide thy purpose; 8 advice every
counsellor will give thee, but some will counsel thee for
their own ends. 9 Be on thy guard, then, against him who
advises thee; how is his own turn best served? What is his
secret mind? 10 It may be, he will hide stake in pit, for thee,
crying, 11 Thy course lies clear; then stand at a distance to
see what becomes of thee. 12 Consult, if thou wilt,[b] unbe-
liever about holiness, knave about justice, woman about her
rival, dastard about war, merchant about value, buyer about
price, cynic about gratitude, 13 scoffer about piety, rogue
about honesty, farm labourer about work to be done,
14 yearman about year's end, idle servant about great undertakings; but all the advice they give thee heed thou never.

a This is usually rendered, 'he will take up his shield against an enemy', but this, without further qualification, seems meaningless. *b* The words 'if thou wilt' are not in the original; but the context evidently demands them in the Latin version; the Greek provides no difficulty; since it gives a negative, 'Do not consult...'.

TODAY'S ENGLISH VERSION

your friend as long as things are going well, but they will
turn against you when trouble comes. 5 A real[a] friend will
help you against your enemies[b] and protect you in the fight.
6 Never forget such companions in battle;[c] share the results
of your victory with them.

7 Anyone can give advice, but some people do so only in
their own interest. 8 Be careful when somebody offers you
advice. Find out first what his interest in the matter is,
because you can be sure that he is thinking primarily of himself. Why should he come out on top instead of you?[d] 9 He
will assure you that things look good, and then stand back
to watch what happens to you.

10 Don't ask advice of anyone who doesn't trust you, and
don't give advice to anyone who is jealous of you.

11 Don't ask a woman for advice about a rival of hers,
a coward about war,
a merchant about a bargain,
a buyer about selling,
a stingy person about gratitude,
a cruel person about kindness,
a lazy person about work,
a casual worker about finishing a job,
a lazy slave about a difficult task.
Pay no attention to any advice they may give.

[a] *Hebrew* real; *Greek does not have this word.* [b] *Hebrew* against your enemies; *Greek* hoping to get a meal. [c] *Hebrew* in battle; *Greek* in your soul. [d] *Hebrew* Why . . . you?; *Greek* He may use his influence against you.

NEW REVISED STANDARD VERSION

4 Some companions rejoice in the happiness of a friend,
but in time of trouble they are against him.
5 Some companions help a friend for their stomachs' sake,
yet in battle they will carry his shield.
6 Do not forget a friend during the battle,[a]
and do not be unmindful of him when you distribute
your spoils.[b]

7 All counselors praise the counsel they give,
but some give counsel in their own interest.
8 Be wary of a counselor,
and learn first what is his interest,
for he will take thought for himself.
He may cast the lot against you
9 and tell you, "Your way is good,"
and then stand aside to see what happens to you.
10 Do not consult the one who regards you with suspicion;
hide your intentions from those who are jealous of you.
11 Do not consult with a woman about her rival
or with a coward about war,
with a merchant about business
or with a buyer about selling,
with a miser about generosity[c]
or with the merciless about kindness,
with an idler about any work
or with a seasonal laborer about completing his work,
with a lazy servant about a big task—
pay no attention to any advice they give.

a Heb: Gk *in your heart* *b* Heb: Gk *him in your wealth* *c* Heb: Gk *gratitude*

NEW AMERICAN BIBLE

4 A false friend will share your joys,
but in time of trouble he stands afar off.
5 A true friend will fight with you against the foe,
against your enemies he will be your shieldbearer.
6 Forget not your comrade during the battle,
and neglect him not when you distribute your spoils.

7 Every counselor points out a way,
but some counsel ways of their own;
8 Be on the alert when one proffers advice,
find out first of all what he wants.
For he may be thinking of himself alone;
why should the profit fall to him?
9 He may tell you how good your way will be,
and then stand by to watch your misfortune.
10 Seek no advice from one who regards you with
hostility;
from those who envy you, keep your intentions
hidden.
11 Speak not to a woman about her rival,
nor to a coward about war,
to a merchant about business,
to a buyer about value,
to a miser about generosity,
to a cruel man about mercy,
to a lazy man about work,
to a seasonal laborer about the harvest,
to an idle slave about a great task:
pay no attention to any advice they give.

NEW JERUSALEM BIBLE

4 One kind of comrade congratulates a friend in
prosperity
but in time of trouble appears on the other side.
5 One kind of comrade genuinely feels for a friend
and when it comes to a fight, springs to arms.
6 Do not forget the genuine friend,
do not push him out of mind once you are rich.

7 Any adviser will offer advice,
but some are governed by self-interest.
8 Beware of someone who offers advice;
first find out what he wants himself—
since his advice coincides with his own interest—
in case he has designs on you
9 and tells you, 'You are on the right road,'
but stands well clear to see what will happen to you.
10 Do not consult anyone who looks at you askance,
conceal your plans from people jealous of you.
11 Do not consult a woman about her rival,
or a coward about war,
a merchant about prices,
or a buyer about selling,
anyone mean about gratitude,
or anyone selfish about kindness,
a lazy fellow about any sort of work,
or a casual worker about finishing a job,
an idle servant about a major undertaking—
do not rely on these for any advice.

GREEK OLD TESTAMENT

12 ἀλλ᾽ ἢ μετὰ ἀνδρὸς εὐσεβοῦς ἐνδελέχιζε,
ὃν ἂν ἐπιγνῷς συντηροῦντα ἐντολάς,
ὃς ἐν τῇ ψυχῇ αὐτοῦ κατὰ τὴν ψυχήν σου,
καὶ ἐὰν πταίσῃς, συναλγήσει σοι.
13 καὶ βουλὴν καρδίας στῆσον,
οὐ γὰρ ἔστιν σοι πιστότερος αὐτῆς·
14 ψυχὴ γὰρ ἀνδρὸς ἀπαγγέλλειν ἐνίοτε εἴωθεν
ἢ ἑπτὰ σκοποὶ ἐπὶ μετεώρου καθήμενοι ἐπὶ σκοπῆς.
15 καὶ ἐπὶ πᾶσι τούτοις δεήθητι ὑψίστου,
ἵνα εὐθύνῃ ἐν ἀληθείᾳ τὴν ὁδόν σου.
16 Ἀρχὴ παντὸς ἔργου λόγος,
καὶ πρὸ πάσης πράξεως βουλή.
17 ἴχνος ἀλλοιώσεως καρδίας
τέσσαρα μέρη ἀνατέλλει,
18 ἀγαθὸν καὶ κακόν, ζωὴ καὶ θάνατος,
καὶ ἡ κυριεύουσα ἐνδελεχῶς αὐτῶν γλῶσσά ἐστιν.
19 ἔστιν ἀνὴρ πανοῦργος πολλῶν παιδευτής,
καὶ τῇ ἰδίᾳ ψυχῇ ἐστιν ἄχρηστος.
20 ἔστιν σοφιζόμενος ἐν λόγοις μισητός,
οὗτος πάσης τροφῆς καθυστερήσει·
21 οὐ γὰρ ἐδόθη αὐτῷ παρὰ κυρίου χάρις,
ὅτι πάσης σοφίας ἐστερήθη.
22 ἔστιν σοφὸς τῇ ἰδίᾳ ψυχῇ,
καὶ οἱ καρποὶ τῆς συνέσεως αὐτοῦ ἐπὶ στόματος
πιστοί.

KING JAMES VERSION

12 But be continually with a godly man, whom thou knowest to keep the commandments of the Lord, whose mind is according to thy mind, and will sorrow with thee, if thou shalt miscarry.

13 And let the counsel of thine own heart stand: for there is no man more faithful unto thee than it.

14 For a man's mind is sometime wont to tell him more than seven watchmen, that sit above in an high tower.

15 And above all this pray to the most High, that he will direct thy way in truth.

16 Let reason go before every enterprize, and counsel before every action.

17 The countenance is a sign of changing of the heart.

18 Four manner of things appear: good and evil, life and death: but the tongue ruleth over them continually.

19 There is one that is wise and teacheth many, and yet is unprofitable to himself.

20 There is one that sheweth wisdom in words, and is hated: he shall be destitute of all food.

21 For grace is not given him from the Lord; because he is deprived of all wisdom.

22 Another is wise to himself; and the fruits of understanding are commendable in his mouth.

DOUAY OLD TESTAMENT

15 But be continually with a holy man, whomsoever thou shalt know to observe the fear of God,

16 Whose soul is according to thy own soul: and who, when thou shalt stumble in the dark, will be sorry for thee.

17 And establish within thyself a heart of good counsel: for there is no other thing of more worth to thee than it.

18 The soul of a holy man discovereth sometimes true things, more than seven watchmen that sit in a high place to watch.

19 But above all these things pray to the most High, that he may direct thy way in truth.

20 In all thy works let the true word go before thee, and steady counsel before every action.

21 A wicked word shall change the heart: out of which four manner of things arise, good and evil, life and death: and the tongue is continually the ruler of them. There is a man that is subtle and a teacher of many, and yet is unprofitable to his own soul.

22 A skilful man hath taught many, and is sweet to his own soul.

23 He that speaketh sophistically, is hateful: he shall be destitute of every thing.

24 Grace is not given him from the Lord: for he is deprived of all wisdom.

25 There is a wise man that is wise to his own soul: and the fruit of his understanding *is* commendable.

KNOX TRANSLATION

15 Closet thyself rather with some man of holy life, known to
thee as God's worshipper, 16 some soul well matched with
thine, such as would grieve to see thee stumbling in darkness. 17 And thy own heart enthrone as thy best counsellor;
nothing may compare with that; 18 there are times when a
man of piety sees truth clearer than seven sentinels high in
a watch-tower. 19 With all this, entreat the most High to
guide thy steps in the right path.

20 For every undertaking, every act of thine let just consideration prepare thee, and trustworthy counsel. 21 Ill counsel
may make the heart veer round; four points its compass has,
good and evil, life and death; and it is ever the tongue that
sways it. [a]

Shrewdness there is that can much impart, yet is its own
enemy. 22 And there is experience that imparts much to others, and is its own friend besides. 23 There is quibbling talk
that will earn thee enemies, and an empty belly; 24 no power
to win men the Lord has given it, so empty is it of all wisdom. 25 But there is wisdom that befriends the owner of it,

a The text here is uncertain, and the meaning obscure. The Latin seems to demand some such rendering as that given above.

TODAY'S ENGLISH VERSION

12 Instead, rely on someone who is religious and known to
keep the Lord's commands, someone who is sympathetic
with you, who will be sorry to see you fail. 13 And trust your
own judgment; no one's advice is more reliable. 14 Sometimes your own intuition can tell you more than seven
watchmen on a high tower. 15 Above all, pray to the Most
High that he will show you the right thing to do.
16 Planning and thought lie behind everything that is done.
17-18 The mind concerns itself with four things: these are good
and evil, life and death. They all begin in the mind,[a] but the
tongue is their absolute ruler.
19 Someone may have the ability to teach, but still not be of
much use to himself. 20 He may be clever with words, but
end up starving because people hate him. 21 This may happen if he doesn't have good sense, if the Lord has not given
him tact. 22 Someone may consider himself wise and let you
know that he is certain about what he knows. 23 Anyone

[a] *Hebrew* The mind . . . the mind; *Greek* There are four things that show the changes of the heart: good and evil, life and death.

NEW REVISED STANDARD VERSION

12 But associate with a godly person
whom you know to be a keeper of the
commandments,
who is like-minded with yourself,
and who will grieve with you if you fail.
13 And heed[a] the counsel of your own heart,
for no one is more faithful to you than it is.
14 For our own mind sometimes keeps us better informed
than seven sentinels sitting high on a watchtower.
15 But above all pray to the Most High
that he may direct your way in truth.

16 Discussion is the beginning of every work,
and counsel precedes every undertaking.
17 The mind is the root of all conduct;
18 it sprouts four branches,[b]
good and evil, life and death;
and it is the tongue that continually rules them.
19 Some people may be clever enough to teach many,
and yet be useless to themselves.
20 A skillful speaker may be hated;
he will be destitute of all food,
21 for the Lord has withheld the gift of charm,
since he is lacking in all wisdom.
22 If a person is wise to his own advantage,
the fruits of his good sense will be praiseworthy.[c]

[a] Heb: Gk *establish* [b] Heb: Gk *As a clue to changes of heart four kinds of destiny appear* [c] Other ancient witnesses read *trustworthy*

NEW AMERICAN BIBLE

12 Instead, associate with a religious man,
who you are sure keeps the commandments;
Who is like-minded with yourself
and will feel for you if you fall.
13 Then, too, heed your own heart's counsel;
for what have you that you can depend on more?
14 A man's conscience can tell him his situation
better than seven watchmen in a lofty tower.
15 Most important of all, pray to God
to set your feet in the path of truth.

16 A word is the source of every deed;
a thought, of every act.
17 The root of all conduct is the mind;
four branches it shoots forth:
18 Good and evil, death and life,
their absolute mistress is the tongue.
19 A man may be wise and benefit many,
yet be of no use to himself.
20 Though a man may be wise, if his words are rejected
he will be deprived of all enjoyment.
21 When a man is wise to his own advantage,
the fruits of his knowledge are seen in his own
person;

NEW JERUSALEM BIBLE

12 But have constant recourse to some devout person,
whom you know to be a keeper of the
commandments,
whose soul matches your own,
and who, if you go wrong, will be sympathetic.
13 Finally, stick to the advice your own heart gives you,
no one can be truer to you than that;
14 since a person's soul often gives a clearer warning
than seven watchmen perched on a watchtower.
15 And besides all this beg the Most High
to guide your steps into the truth.

16 Reason should be the basis for every activity,
reflection must come before any undertaking.
17 Thoughts are rooted in the heart,
and this sends out four branches:
18 good and evil, life and death,
and mistress of them always is the tongue.
19 One kind of person is clever at teaching others,
yet is no good whatever to himself;
20 another, very eloquent, is detested
and ends by starving to death,
21 not having won the favour of the Lord,
and being destitute of all wisdom.
22 Another considers himself wise
and proclaims his intellectual conclusions as
certainties.

GREEK OLD TESTAMENT

23 ἀνὴρ σοφὸς τὸν ἑαυτοῦ λαὸν παιδεύσει,
καὶ οἱ καρποὶ τῆς συνέσεως αὐτοῦ πιστοί.
24 ἀνὴρ σοφὸς πλησθήσεται εὐλογίας,
καὶ μακαριοῦσιν αὐτὸν πάντες οἱ ὁρῶντες.
25 ζωὴ ἀνδρὸς ἐν ἀριθμῷ ἡμερῶν,
καὶ αἱ ἡμέραι τοῦ Ισραηλ ἀναρίθμητοι.
26 ὁ σοφὸς ἐν τῷ λαῷ αὐτοῦ κληρονομήσει πίστιν,
καὶ τὸ ὄνομα αὐτοῦ ζήσεται εἰς τὸν αἰῶνα.
27 Τέκνον, ἐν ζωῇ σου πείρασον τὴν ψυχήν σου
καὶ ἰδὲ τί πονηρὸν αὐτῇ καὶ μὴ δῷς αὐτῇ·
28 οὐ γὰρ πάντα πᾶσιν συμφέρει,
καὶ οὐ πᾶσα ψυχὴ ἐν παντὶ εὐδοκεῖ.
29 μὴ ἀπληστεύου ἐν πάσῃ τρυφῇ
καὶ μὴ ἐκχυθῇς ἐπὶ ἐδεσμάτων·
30 ἐν πολλοῖς γὰρ βρώμασιν ἔσται νόσος,
καὶ ἡ ἀπληστία ἐγγιεῖ ἕως χολέρας·
31 δι᾽ ἀπληστίαν πολλοὶ ἐτελεύτησαν,
ὁ δὲ προσέχων προσθήσει ζωήν.

38 Τίμα ἰατρὸν πρὸς τὰς χρείας αὐτοῦ τιμαῖς αὐτοῦ,
καὶ γὰρ αὐτὸν ἔκτισεν κύριος·
2 παρὰ γὰρ ὑψίστου ἐστὶν ἴασις,
καὶ παρὰ βασιλέως λήμψεται δόμα.
3 ἐπιστήμη ἰατροῦ ἀνυψώσει κεφαλὴν αὐτοῦ,
καὶ ἔναντι μεγιστάνων θαυμασθήσεται.
4 κύριος ἔκτισεν ἐκ γῆς φάρμακα,
καὶ ἀνὴρ φρόνιμος οὐ προσοχθιεῖ αὐτοῖς.

KING JAMES VERSION

23 A wise man instructeth his people; and the fruits of his understanding fail not.

24 A wise man shall be filled with blessing; and all they that see him shall count him happy.

25 The days of the life of man may be numbered: but the days of Israel are innumerable.

26 A wise man shall inherit glory among his people, and his name shall be perpetual.

27 My son, prove thy soul in thy life, and see what is evil for it, and give not that unto it.

28 For all things are not profitable for all men, neither hath every soul pleasure in every thing.

29 Be not unsatiable in any dainty thing, nor too greedy upon meats:

30 For excess of meats bringeth sickness, and surfeiting will turn into choler.

31 By surfeiting have many perished; but he that taketh heed prolongeth his life.

38 Honour a physician with the honour due unto him for the uses which ye may have of him: for the Lord hath created him.

2 For of the most High cometh healing, and he shall receive honour of the king.

3 The skill of the physician shall lift up his head: and in the sight of great men he shall be in admiration.

4 The Lord hath created medicines out of the earth; and he that is wise will not abhor them.

DOUAY OLD TESTAMENT

26 A wise man instructeth his own people, and the fruits of his understanding are faithful.

27 A wise man shall be filled with blessings, and they that see shall praise him.

28 The life of a man is in the number of his days: but the days of Israel are innumerable.

29 A wise man shall inherit honour among his people, and his name shall live for ever.

30 My son, prove thy soul in thy life: and if it be wicked, give it no power:

31 For all things are not expedient for all, and every kind pleaseth not every soul.

32 Be not greedy in any feasting, and pour not out thyself upon any meat:

33 For in many meats there will be sickness, and greediness will turn to choler.

34 By surfeiting many have perished: but he that is temperate, shall prolong life.

38 HONOUR the physician for the need thou hast of him: for the most High hath created him.

2 For all healing is from God, and he shall receive gifts of the king.

3 The skill of the physician shall lift up his head, and in the sight of great men he shall be praised.

4 The most High hath created medicines out of the earth, and a wise man will not abhor them.

KNOX TRANSLATION

earning high meed of praise; 26 if thus thou art wise, wisdom thou shalt impart to thy fellows, and shalt not miss thy
own reward; 27 blessings the wise man reaps from all
around, to see him is to praise him. 28 Man's days are numbered, Israel's none can number, 29 and among our people
the wise man wins an inheritance of honour, a deathless
renown.

30 Son, as thy life goes on, make trial of thy appetites, and
if harmful they be, give them no liberty; 31 not all things all
men suit, nor please. 32 When there is feasting, thy greed
restrain; do not fall upon all the meats thou seest; 33 much
feasting breeds infirmity, gluttony the bile, 34 and many
have died of surfeiting; the temperate live long.

38 Deny not a physician his due for thy need's sake; his
task is of divine appointment, 2 since from God all
healing comes, and kings themselves must needs bring gifts
to him. 3 High rank his skill gives him; of great men he is
the honoured guest. 4 Medicines the most High has made for
us out of earth's bounty, and shall prudence shrink from the

TODAY'S ENGLISH VERSION

who really is wise will be the teacher of his people, and they
can be certain that what he teaches is the truth. 24 Everyone
will praise such a person and speak of him as fortunate.
25 A person's life has only a limited number of days, but the
life of Israel cannot be measured in days at all. 26 The wise
will win the confidence of others, and will be remembered
forever.
27 My child, as you go through life, keep your appetite
under control, and don't eat anything that you know is bad
for you. 28 All food doesn't agree with everyone, and everyone doesn't like the same kinds of food. 29 Don't feel that
you just have to have all sorts of fancy food, and don't be a
glutton over any food. 30 If you eat too much, you'll get sick;
if you do it all the time, you'll always have stomach trouble.
31 Gluttony has been the death of many people. Avoid it and
live longer.

38 Give doctors the honor they deserve, for the Lord
gave them their work to do.[a] 2 Their skill came from
the Most High, and kings reward them for it. 3 Their knowledge gives them a position of importance, and powerful people hold them in high regard.
4 The Lord created medicines from the earth, and a sensible
person will not hesitate to use them. 5 Didn't a tree once

[a] *Hebrew* gave them their work to do; *Greek* created them.

NEW REVISED STANDARD VERSION

23 A wise person instructs his own people,
and the fruits of his good sense will endure.
24 A wise person will have praise heaped upon him,
and all who see him will call him happy.
25 The days of a person's life are numbered,
but the days of Israel are without number.
26 One who is wise among his people will inherit honor,[a]
and his name will live forever.

27 My child, test yourself while you live;
see what is bad for you and do not give in to it.
28 For not everything is good for everyone,
and no one enjoys everything.
29 Do not be greedy for every delicacy,
and do not eat without restraint;
30 for overeating brings sickness,
and gluttony leads to nausea.
31 Many have died of gluttony,
but the one who guards against it prolongs his life.

38 Honor physicians for their services,
for the Lord created them;
2 for their gift of healing comes from the Most High,
and they are rewarded by the king.
3 The skill of physicians makes them distinguished,
and in the presence of the great they are admired.
4 The Lord created medicines out of the earth,
and the sensible will not despise them.

[a] Other ancient authorities read *confidence*

NEW AMERICAN BIBLE

22 When a man is wise to his people's advantage,
the fruits of his knowledge are enduring:
23 Limited are the days of one man's life,
but the life of Israel is days without number.
24 One wise for himself has full enjoyment,
and all who see him praise him;
25 One wise for his people wins a heritage of glory,
and his name endures forever.

26 My son, while you are well, govern your appetite
so that you allow it not what is bad for you;
27 For not every food is good for everyone,
nor is everything suited to every taste.
28 Be not drawn after every enjoyment,
neither become a glutton for choice foods,
29 For sickness comes with overeating,
and gluttony brings on biliousness.
30 Through lack of self-control many have died,
but the abstemious man prolongs his life.

38 Hold the physician in honor, for he is essential to you,
and God it was who established his profession.
2 From God the doctor has his wisdom,
and the king provides for his sustenance.
3 His knowledge makes the doctor distinguished,
and gives him access to those in authority.
4 God makes the earth yield healing herbs
which the prudent man should not neglect;

NEW JERUSALEM BIBLE

23 But the truly wise instructs his people
and his intellectual conclusions are certainties.
24 The wise is showered with blessings,
and all who see him will call him happy.
25 Human life lasts a number of days,
but the days of Israel are beyond counting.
26 The wise will earn confidence among the people,
his name will live for ever.

27 During your life, my child, see what suits your
constitution,
do not give it what you find disagrees with it;
28 for not everything is good for everybody,
nor does everybody like everything.
29 Do not be insatiable for any delicacy,
do not be greedy for food,
30 for over-eating leads to illness
and excess leads to liver-attacks.
31 Many people have died from over-eating;
control yourself, and so prolong your life.

38 Treat the doctor with the honour that is his due,
in consideration of his services;
for he too has been created by the Lord.
2 Healing itself comes from the Most High,
like a gift received from a king.
3 The doctor's learning keeps his head high,
and the great regard him with awe.
4 The Lord has brought forth medicinal herbs from the
ground,
and no one sensible will despise them.

GREEK OLD TESTAMENT

5 οὐκ ἀπὸ ξύλου ἐγλυκάνθη ὕδωρ
εἰς τὸ γνωσθῆναι τὴν ἰσχὺν αὐτοῦ;
6 καὶ αὐτὸς ἔδωκεν ἀνθρώποις ἐπιστήμην
ἐνδοξάζεσθαι ἐν τοῖς θαυμασίοις αὐτοῦ·
7 ἐν αὐτοῖς ἐθεράπευσεν καὶ ἦρεν τὸν πόνον αὐτοῦ,
μυρεψὸς ἐν τούτοις ποιήσει μεῖγμα,
8 καὶ οὐ μὴ συντελεσθῇ ἔργα αὐτοῦ,
καὶ εἰρήνη παρ' αὐτοῦ ἐστιν ἐπὶ προσώπου τῆς γῆς.
9 Τέκνον, ἐν ἀρρωστήματί σου μὴ παράβλεπε,
ἀλλ' εὖξαι κυρίῳ, καὶ αὐτὸς ἰάσεταί σε·
10 ἀπόστησον πλημμέλειαν καὶ εὔθυνον χεῖρας
καὶ ἀπὸ πάσης ἁμαρτίας καθάρισον καρδίαν·
11 δὸς εὐωδίαν καὶ μνημόσυνον σεμιδάλεως
καὶ λίπανον προσφορὰν ὡς μὴ ὑπάρχων.
12 καὶ ἰατρῷ δὸς τόπον, καὶ γὰρ αὐτὸν ἔκτισεν κύριος,
καὶ μὴ ἀποστήτω σου, καὶ γὰρ αὐτοῦ χρεία.
13 ἔστιν καιρὸς ὅτε καὶ ἐν χερσὶν αὐτῶν εὐοδία·
14 καὶ γὰρ αὐτοὶ κυρίου δεηθήσονται,
ἵνα εὐοδώσῃ αὐτοῖς ἀνάπαυσιν
καὶ ἴασιν χάριν ἐμβιώσεως.

KING JAMES VERSION

5 Was not the water made sweet with wood, that the virtue thereof might be known?

6 And he hath given men skill, that he might be honoured in his marvellous works.

7 With such doth he heal [men,] and taketh away their pains.

8 Of such doth the apothecary make a confection; and of his works there is no end; and from him is peace over all the earth.

9 My son, in thy sickness be not negligent: but pray unto the Lord, and he will make thee whole.

10 Leave off from sin, and order thine hands aright, and cleanse thy heart from all wickedness.

11 Give a sweet savour, and a memorial of fine flour; and make a fat offering, as not being.

12 Then give place to the physician, for the Lord hath created him: let him not go from thee, for thou hast need of him.

13 There is a time when in their hands there is good success.

14 For they shall also pray unto the Lord, that he would prosper that, which they give for ease and remedy to prolong life.

DOUAY OLD TESTAMENT

5 Was not bitter water made sweet with wood?

6 The virtue of these things *is come* to the knowledge of men, and the most High hath given knowledge to men, that he may be honoured in his wonders.

7 By these he shall cure and shall allay their pains, and *of these* the apothecary shall make sweet confections, and shall make up ointments of health, and of his works there shall be no end.

8 For the peace of God *is* over all the face of the earth.

9 My son, in thy sickness neglect not thyself, but pray to the Lord, and he shall heal thee.

10 Turn away from sin and order thy hands aright, and cleanse thy heart from all offence.

11 Give a sweet savour, and a memorial of fine flour, and make a fat offering, and then give place to the physician.

12 For the Lord created him: and let him not depart from thee, for his works are necessary.

13 For there is a time when thou must fall into their hands:

14 And they shall beseech the Lord, that he would prosper what they give for ease and remedy, for their conversation.

KNOX TRANSLATION

use of them? 5 Were not the waters of Mara made wholesome by the touch of wood?[a] 6 Well for us men, that the
secret virtue of such remedies has been revealed; skill the
most High would impart to us, and for his marvels win
renown. 7 Thus it is that the physician cures our pain, and
the apothecary makes, not only perfumes to charm the sense,
but unguents remedial; so inexhaustible is God's creation,
8 such health comes of his gift, all the world over.
9 Son, when thou fallest sick, do not neglect thy own
needs; pray to the Lord, and thou shalt win recovery.
10 Leave off thy sinning, thy life amend, purge thee of all thy
guilt. 11 With frankincense and rich oil make bloodless offering of meal; and so leave the physician to do his work.
12 His task is of divine appointment, and thou hast need of
him; let him be ever at thy side. 13 Needs must, at times, to
physicians thou shouldst have recourse; 14 and doubt not
they will make intercession with the Lord, that they may find
a way to bring thee ease and remedy, by their often visiting

a See Ex. 15. 23.

TODAY'S ENGLISH VERSION

make bitter water fit to drink, so that the Lord's power[a]
might be known? [6]He gave medical knowledge to human
beings, so that we would praise him for the miracles he performs. [7-8]The druggist mixes these medicines, and the doctor
will use them to cure diseases and ease pain. There is no end
to the activities of the Lord, who gives health to the people of
the world.
[9]My child, when you get sick, don't ignore it. Pray to the
Lord, and he will make you well. [10]Confess all your sins and
determine that in the future you will live a righteous life.
[11]Offer incense and a grain offering, as fine as you can
afford.[b] [12]Then call the doctor—for the Lord created him—
and keep him at your side; you need him. [13]There are times
when you have to depend on his skill. [14]The doctor's prayer
is that the Lord will make him able to ease his patients' pain

[a] the Lord's power; *or* its healing properties. [b] *Hebrew* as fine as you can afford; *Greek unclear.*

NEW REVISED STANDARD VERSION

5 Was not water made sweet with a tree
in order that its[a] power might be known?
6 And he gave skill to human beings
that he[b] might be glorified in his marvelous works.
7 By them the physician[c] heals and takes away pain;
8 the pharmacist makes a mixture from them.
God's[d] works will never be finished;
and from him health[e] spreads over all the earth.

9 My child, when you are ill, do not delay,
but pray to the Lord, and he will heal you.
10 Give up your faults and direct your hands rightly,
and cleanse your heart from all sin.
11 Offer a sweet-smelling sacrifice, and a memorial portion
of choice flour,
and pour oil on your offering, as much as you can
afford.[f]
12 Then give the physician his place, for the Lord created
him;
do not let him leave you, for you need him.
13 There may come a time when recovery lies in the hands
of physicians,[g]
14 for they too pray to the Lord
that he grant them success in diagnosis[h]
and in healing, for the sake of preserving life.

a Or *his* *b* Or *they* *c* Heb: Gk *he* *d* Gk *His* *e* Or *peace*
f Heb: Lat lacks *as much as you can afford*; Meaning of Gk uncertain
g Gk *in their hands* *h* Heb: Gk *rest*

NEW AMERICAN BIBLE

[5]Was not the water sweetened by a twig
that men might learn his power?
[6]He endows men with the knowledge
to glory in his mighty works,
[7]Through which the doctor eases pain
and the druggist prepares his medicines;
[8]Thus God's creative work continues without cease
in its efficacy on the surface of the earth.

[9]My son, when you are ill, delay not,
but pray to God, who will heal you:
[10]Flee wickedness; let your hands be just,
cleanse your heart of every sin;
[11]Offer your sweet-smelling oblation and petition,
a rich offering according to your means.
[12]Then give the doctor his place
lest he leave; for you need him too.
[13]There are times that give him an advantage,
[14] and he too beseeches God
That his diagnosis may be correct
and his treatment bring about a cure.

NEW JERUSALEM BIBLE

[5]Did not a piece of wood once sweeten the water,
thus giving proof of its power?[a]
[6]He has also given some people knowledge,
so that they may draw credit from his mighty works.
[7]He uses these for healing and relieving pain;
the druggist makes up a mixture from them.
[8]Thus, there is no end to his activities;
thanks to him, well-being exists throughout the
world.

[9]My child, when you are ill, do not rebel,
but pray to the Lord and he will heal you.
[10]Renounce your faults, keep your hands unsoiled,
and cleanse your heart from all sin.
[11]Offer incense and a memorial of fine flour,
make as rich an offering as you can afford.
[12]Then let the doctor take over—the Lord created him
too—
do not let him leave you, for you need him.
[13]There are times when good health depends on doctors.
14 For they, in their turn, will pray the Lord
to grant them the grace to relieve
and to heal, and so prolong your life.

[a] **38** Ex 15:23–25.

GREEK OLD TESTAMENT

15 ὁ ἁμαρτάνων ἔναντι τοῦ ποιήσαντος αὐτὸν
ἐμπέσοι εἰς χεῖρας ἰατροῦ.
16 Τέκνον, ἐπὶ νεκρῷ κατάγαγε δάκρυα
καὶ ὡς δεινὰ πάσχων ἔναρξαι θρήνου,
κατὰ δὲ τὴν κρίσιν αὐτοῦ περίστειλον τὸ σῶμα αὐτοῦ
καὶ μὴ ὑπερίδῃς τὴν ταφὴν αὐτοῦ.
17 πίκρανον κλαυθμὸν καὶ θέρμανον κοπετὸν
καὶ ποίησον τὸ πένθος κατὰ τὴν ἀξίαν αὐτοῦ
ἡμέραν μίαν καὶ δύο χάριν διαβολῆς
καὶ παρακλήθητι λύπης ἕνεκα·
18 ἀπὸ λύπης γὰρ ἐκβαίνει θάνατος,
καὶ λύπη καρδίας κάμψει ἰσχύν.
19 ἐν ἐπαγωγῇ παραμένει καὶ λύπη,
καὶ βίος πτωχοῦ κατὰ καρδίας.
20 μὴ δῷς εἰς λύπην τὴν καρδίαν σου,
ἀπόστησον αὐτὴν μνησθεὶς τὰ ἔσχατα·
21 μὴ ἐπιλάθῃ, οὐ γάρ ἐστιν ἐπάνοδος,
καὶ τοῦτον οὐκ ὠφελήσεις καὶ σεαυτὸν κακώσεις.
22 μνήσθητι τὸ κρίμα μου, ὅτι οὕτως καὶ τὸ σόν·
ἐμοὶ ἐχθὲς καὶ σοὶ σήμερον.
23 ἐν ἀναπαύσει νεκροῦ κατάπαυσον τὸ μνημόσυνον αὐτοῦ
καὶ παρακλήθητι ἐν αὐτῷ ἐν ἐξόδῳ πνεύματος αὐτοῦ.
24 Σοφία γραμματέως ἐν εὐκαιρίᾳ σχολῆς,
καὶ ὁ ἐλασσούμενος πράξει αὐτοῦ σοφισθήσεται.

KING JAMES VERSION

15 He that sinneth before his Maker, let him fall into the hand of the physician.

16 My son, let tears fall down over the dead, and begin to lament, as if thou hadst suffered great harm thyself; and then cover his body according to the custom, and neglect not his burial.

17 Weep bitterly, and make great moan, and use lamentation, as he is worthy, and that a day or two, lest thou be evil spoken of: and then comfort thyself for thy heaviness.

18 For of heaviness cometh death, and the heaviness of the heart breaketh strength.

19 In affliction also sorrow remaineth: and the life of the poor is the curse of the heart.

20 Take no heaviness to heart: drive it away, and remember the last end.

21 Forget it not, for there is no turning again: thou shalt not do him good, but hurt thyself.

22 Remember my judgment: for thine also shall be so; yesterday for me, and to day for thee.

23 When the dead is at rest, let his remembrance rest; and be comforted for him, when his spirit is departed from him.

24 The wisdom of a learned man cometh by opportunity of leisure: and he that hath little business shall become wise.

DOUAY OLD TESTAMENT

15 He that sinneth in the sight of his Maker, shall fall into the hands of the physician.

16 My son, shed tears over the dead, and begin to lament as if thou hadst suffered some great harm, and according to judgment cover his body, and neglect not his burial.

17 And for *fear of* being ill spoken of weep bitterly for a day, and then comfort thyself in thy sadness.

18 And make mourning for him according to his merit for a day, or two, for fear of detraction.

19 For of sadness cometh death, and it overwhelmeth the strength, and the sorrow of the heart boweth down the neck.

20 In withdrawing aside sorrow remaineth: and the substance of the poor is according to his heart.

21 Give not up thy heart to sadness, but drive it from thee: and remember the latter end.

22 Forget *it* not: for there is no returning, and thou shalt do him no good, and shalt hurt thyself.

23 Remember my judgment: for thine also shall be so: yesterday for me, and to day for thee.

24 When the dead is at rest, let his remembrance rest, and comfort him in the departing of his spirit.

25 The wisdom of a scribe cometh by his time of leisure: and he that is less in action, shall receive wisdom.

KNOX TRANSLATION

thee. 15 Offend thou thy maker by wrong-doing, much
recourse thou shalt have to physicians.
16 When a man dies, let thy tears flow, and set up a great
lamenting, as for thy grievous loss; shroud him according to
his quality, and grudge him no pomp of funeral; 17 then, to
be rid of gossip, bemoan him bitterly for a day's space, ere
thou wilt be comforted in thy sorrow; 18 one day or two, as
his worth claims, bemoan him; no need to win thyself an ill
name. 19 But grief will but hasten thy own death, will be the
grave of thy own strength; where heart goes sad, back goes
bowed. 20 So long as thou withdrawest thyself, sad thy heart
will be; and what patrimony but heart's mirth is left to the
poor? 21 Why then, do not give thyself over to regrets; put
them away from thee, and bethink thee rather of thy own
end. 22 Do not fancy that the dead can return; by torturing
thyself thou canst nothing avail him. 23 Remember, he tells
thee, this doom of mine; such shall thine be; mine yesterday,
thine to-day. 24 Let his memory rest, as he rests, in death;
enough for thee that thou shouldst comfort him in the hour
when his spirit leaves him.[a]
25 The wisdom of a learned man is the fruit of leisure; he
must starve himself of doing if he is to come by it. 26 How

[a] 'Enough for thee that thou shouldst comfort him'; the meaning of the Septuagint Greek is, 'And be comforted for his loss'.

TODAY'S ENGLISH VERSION

and make them well again. 15 As for the person who sins
against his Creator, he deserves to be sick.
16 My child, when someone dies, you should mourn. Weep
and wail to show how deeply you feel the loss. Prepare the
body in the proper way, and be present at the burial. 17 Weep
bitterly and passionately; observe the proper period of
mourning for the person. Mourn for a whole day or maybe
two, to keep people from talking, but then pull yourself
together and reconcile yourself to the loss. 18 Grief can
undermine your health and even lead to your own death.
19 Grief lingers on after the death of a loved one, but it is not
wise to let it lead you into poverty.
20 Don't lose yourself in sorrow; drive it away.[a] Remember
that we must all die sometime. 21 There is no way to bring
the dead person back. All your sorrow does him no good, and
it hurts you. Don't forget that. 22 You will die, just as he did.
Today it was his turn; tomorrow it will be yours. 23 When
the dead have been laid to rest, let the memory of them fade.
Once they are gone, take courage.
24 Scholars must have time to study if they are going to be
wise; they must be relieved of other responsibilities. 25 How

[a] drive it away; *or* put the memory of the person aside.

NEW REVISED STANDARD VERSION

15 He who sins against his Maker,
will be defiant toward the physician.[a]
16 My child, let your tears fall for the dead,
and as one in great pain begin the lament.
Lay out the body with due ceremony,
and do not neglect the burial.
17 Let your weeping be bitter and your wailing fervent;
make your mourning worthy of the departed,
for one day, or two, to avoid criticism;
then be comforted for your grief.
18 For grief may result in death,
and a sorrowful heart saps one's strength.
19 When a person is taken away, sorrow is over;
but the life of the poor weighs down the heart.
20 Do not give your heart to grief;
drive it away, and remember your own end.
21 Do not forget, there is no coming back;
you do the dead[b] no good, and you injure yourself.
22 Remember his[c] fate, for yours is like it;
yesterday it was his,[d] and today it is yours.
23 When the dead is at rest, let his remembrance rest too,
and be comforted for him when his spirit has departed.

24 The wisdom of the scribe depends on the opportunity of
leisure;
only the one who has little business can become wise.

a Heb: Gk *may he fall into the hands of the physician* *b* Gk *him*
c Heb: Gk *my* *d* Heb: Gk *mine*

NEW AMERICAN BIBLE

15 He who is a sinner toward his Maker
will be defiant toward the doctor.

16 My son, shed tears for one who is dead
with wailing and bitter lament;
As is only proper, prepare the body,
absent not yourself from his burial:
17 Weeping bitterly, mourning fully,
pay your tribute of sorrow, as he deserves,
18 One or two days, to prevent gossip;
then compose yourself after your grief,
19 For grief can bring on an extremity
and heartache destroy one's health.
20 Turn not your thoughts to him again;
cease to recall him; think rather of the end.
21 Recall him not, for there is no hope of his return;
it will not help him, but will do you harm.
22 Remember that his fate will also be yours;
for him it was yesterday, for you today.
23 With the departed dead, let memory fade;
rally your courage, once the soul has left.

24 The scribe's profession increases his wisdom;
whoever is free from toil can become a wise man.

NEW JERUSALEM BIBLE

15 Whoever sins in the eyes of his Maker,
let such a one come under the care of the doctor!
16 My child, shed tears over the dead,
lament for the dead to show your sorrow,
then bury the body with due ceremony
and do not fail to honour the grave.
17 Weep bitterly, beat your breast,
observe the mourning the dead deserves
for a day or two, to avoid censorious comment,
and then be comforted in your sorrow;
18 for grief can lead to death,
a grief-stricken heart loses all energy.
19 In affliction sorrow persists,
a life of grief is hard to bear.
20 Do not abandon your heart to grief,
drive it away, bear your own end in mind.
21 Do not forget, there is no coming back;
you cannot help the dead, and you will harm
yourself.
22 'Remember my doom, since it will be yours too;
I yesterday, you today!'
23 Once the dead are laid to rest, let their memory rest,
do not fret for them, once their spirit departs.
24 Leisure gives the scribe the chance to acquire wisdom;
a man with few commitments can grow wise.

GREEK OLD TESTAMENT

25 τί σοφισθήσεται ὁ κρατῶν ἀρότρου
καὶ καυχώμενος ἐν δόρατι κέντρου,
βόας ἐλαύνων καὶ ἀναστρεφόμενος ἐν ἔργοις αὐτῶν,
καὶ ἡ διήγησις αὐτοῦ ἐν υἱοῖς ταύρων;
26 καρδίαν αὐτοῦ δώσει ἐκδοῦναι αὔλακας,
καὶ ἡ ἀγρυπνία αὐτοῦ εἰς χορτάσματα δαμάλεων.
27 οὕτως πᾶς τέκτων καὶ ἀρχιτέκτων,
ὅστις νύκτωρ ὡς ἡμέρας διάγει·
οἱ γλύφοντες γλύμματα σφραγίδων,
καὶ ἡ ἐπιμονὴ αὐτοῦ ἀλλοιῶσαι ποικιλίαν·
καρδίαν αὐτοῦ δώσει εἰς ὁμοιῶσαι ζωγραφίαν,
καὶ ἡ ἀγρυπνία αὐτοῦ τελέσαι ἔργον.
28 οὕτως χαλκεὺς καθήμενος ἐγγὺς ἄκμονος
καὶ καταμανθάνων ἔργα σιδήρου·
ἀτμὶς πυρὸς τήξει σάρκας αὐτοῦ,
καὶ ἐν θέρμῃ καμίνου διαμαχήσεται·
φωνῇ σφύρης κλινεῖ τὸ οὖς αὐτοῦ,
καὶ κατέναντι ὁμοιώματος σκεύους οἱ ὀφθαλμοὶ αὐτοῦ·
καρδίαν αὐτοῦ δώσει εἰς συντέλειαν ἔργων,
καὶ ἡ ἀγρυπνία αὐτοῦ κοσμῆσαι ἐπὶ συντελείας.
29 οὕτως κεραμεὺς καθήμενος ἐν ἔργῳ αὐτοῦ
καὶ συστρέφων ἐν ποσὶν αὐτοῦ τροχόν,
ὃς ἐν μερίμνῃ κεῖται διὰ παντὸς ἐπὶ τὸ ἔργον αὐτοῦ,
καὶ ἐναρίθμιος πᾶσα ἡ ἐργασία αὐτοῦ·
30 ἐν βραχίονι αὐτοῦ τυπώσει πηλὸν
καὶ πρὸ ποδῶν κάμψει ἰσχὺν αὐτοῦ·
καρδίαν ἐπιδώσει συντελέσαι τὸ χρῖσμα,
καὶ ἡ ἀγρυπνία αὐτοῦ καθαρίσαι κάμινον.

KING JAMES VERSION

25 How can he get wisdom that holdeth the plough, and that glorieth in the goad, that driveth oxen, and is occupied in their labours, and whose talk is of bullocks?

26 He giveth his mind to make furrows; and is diligent to give the kine fodder.

27 So every carpenter and workmaster, that laboureth night and day: and they that cut and grave seals, and are diligent to make great variety, and give themselves to counterfeit imagery, and watch to finish a work:

28 The smith also sitting by the anvil, and considering the iron work, the vapour of the fire wasteth his flesh, and he fighteth with the heat of the furnace: the noise of the hammer and the anvil is ever in his ears, and his eyes look still upon the pattern of the thing that he maketh; he setteth his mind to finish his work, and watcheth to polish it perfectly:

29 So doth the potter sitting at his work, and turning the wheel about with his feet, who is alway carefully set at his work, and maketh all his work by number;

30 He fashioneth the clay with his arm, and boweth down his strength before his feet; he applieth himself to lead it over; and he is diligent to make clean the furnace:

DOUAY OLD TESTAMENT

26 With what wisdom shall he be furnished that holdeth the plough, and that glorieth in the goad, that driveth the oxen therewith, and is occupied in their labours, and his whole talk is about the offspring of bulls?

27 He shall give his mind to turn up furrows, and his care is to give the kine fodder.

28 So every craftsman and workmaster that laboureth night and day, *he* who maketh graven seals, and by his continual diligence varieth the figure: he shall give his mind to the resemblance of the picture, and by his watching shall finish the work.

29 So doth the smith sitting by the anvil and considering the iron work. The vapour of the fire wasteth his flesh, and he fighteth with the heat of the furnace.

30 The noise of the hammer is always in his ears, and his eye is upon the pattern of the vessel he maketh.

31 He setteth his mind to finish his work, and his watching to polish *them* to perfection.

32 So doth the potter sitting at his work, turning the wheel about with his feet, who is always carefully set to his work, and maketh all his work by number:

33 He fashioneth the clay with his arm, and boweth down his strength before his feet:

34 He shall give his mind to finish the glazing, and his watching to make clean the furnace.

KNOX TRANSLATION

shall he drink full draughts of wisdom that must guide the
plough, that walks proud as any spearman while he goads
on his team, all his life taken up with their labours, all his
talk of oxen? 27 His mind all set on a straight furrow, the
feeding of his cows an anxiety to deny him sleep? 28 So it is
with every workman and master-workman, that must turn
night into day. Here is one that cuts graven seals; how he
busies himself with devising some new pattern! How the
model he works from claims his attention, while he sits late
over his craft! 29 Here is blacksmith sitting by his anvil,
intent upon his iron-work, cheeks shrivelled with the smoke,
as he battles with the heat of the furnace, 30 ears ringing
again with the hammer's clattering, eyes fixed on the design
he imitates. 31 All his heart is in the finishing of his task, all
his waking thoughts go to the perfect achieving of it. 32 Here
is potter at work, treadles flying, anxious continually over
the play of his hands, over the rhythm of his craftsmanship;
33 arms straining at the stiff clay, feet matching its strength
with theirs.[a] 34 To finish off the glaze is his nearest concern,
and long he must wake to keep his furnace clean. 35 All

[a] Literally, 'bowing down his strength before his feet', but the Greek has, 'its strength'.

TODAY'S ENGLISH VERSION

can a farm hand gain knowledge, when his only ambition is
to drive the oxen and make them work, when all he knows
to talk about is livestock? 26 He takes great pains to plow a
straight furrow and will work far into the night to feed the
animals.
27 It is the same with the artist and the craftsman, who
work night and day engraving precious stones, carefully
working out new designs. They take great pains to produce a
lifelike image, and will work far into the night to finish the
work.
28 It is the same with the blacksmith at his anvil, planning
what he will make from a piece of iron. The heat from the
fire sears his skin as he sweats away at the forge. The clanging of the hammer deafens him[a] as he carefully watches the
object he is working take shape. He takes great pains to complete his task, and will work far into the night to bring it to
perfection.
29 It is the same with the potter, sitting at his wheel and
turning it with his feet, always concentrating on his work,
concerned with how many objects he can produce. 30 He
works the clay with his feet until he can shape it with his
hands; then he takes great pains to glaze it properly, and
will work far into the night to clean out the kiln.

[a] *Probable text* deafens him; *Greek* renews his ears.

NEW REVISED STANDARD VERSION

25 How can one become wise who handles the plow,
and who glories in the shaft of a goad,
who drives oxen and is occupied with their work,
and whose talk is about bulls?
26 He sets his heart on plowing furrows,
and he is careful about fodder for the heifers.
27 So it is with every artisan and master artisan
who labors by night as well as by day;
those who cut the signets of seals,
each is diligent in making a great variety;
they set their heart on painting a lifelike image,
and they are careful to finish their work.
28 So it is with the smith, sitting by the anvil,
intent on his iron-work;
the breath of the fire melts his flesh,
and he struggles with the heat of the furnace;
the sound of the hammer deafens his ears,[a]
and his eyes are on the pattern of the object.
He sets his heart on finishing his handiwork,
and he is careful to complete its decoration.
29 So it is with the potter sitting at his work
and turning the wheel with his feet;
he is always deeply concerned over his products,
and he produces them in quantity.
30 He molds the clay with his arm
and makes it pliable with his feet;
he sets his heart to finish the glazing,
and he takes care in firing[b] the kiln.

[a] Cn: Gk *renews his ear* [b] Cn: Gk *cleaning*

NEW AMERICAN BIBLE

25 How can he become learned who guides the plow,
who thrills in wielding the goad like a lance,
Who guides the ox and urges on the bullock,
and whose every concern is for cattle?
26 His care is for plowing furrows,
and he keeps a watch on the beasts in the stalls.

27 So with every engraver and designer
who, laboring night and day,
Fashions carved seals,
and whose concern is to vary the pattern.
His care is to produce a vivid impression,
and he keeps watch till he finishes his design.

28 So with the smith standing near his anvil,
forging crude iron.
The heat from the fire sears his flesh,
yet he toils away in the furnace heat.
The clang of the hammer deafens his ears,
His eyes are fixed on the tool he is shaping.
His care is to finish his work,
and he keeps watch till he perfects it in detail.

29 So with the potter sitting at his labor
revolving the wheel with his feet.
He is always concerned for his products,
and turns them out in quantity.
30 With his hands he molds the clay,
and with his feet softens it.
His care is for proper coloring,
and he keeps watch on the fire of his kiln.

NEW JERUSALEM BIBLE

25 How can the ploughman become wise,
whose sole ambition is to wield the goad,
driving his oxen, engrossed in their work,
his conversation limited to bullocks,
26 his thoughts absorbed in the furrows he traces
and his long evenings spent in fattening heifers?
27 Similarly with all workmen and craftsmen,
toiling day and night;
those who engrave seals,
for ever trying to think of a new design,
concentrating on catching a good likeness
and staying up late to get the work done.
28 Similarly with the blacksmith sitting by his anvil;
he considers what to do with the pig-iron,
the breath of the fire scorches his skin,
as he contends with the heat of the furnace;
the noise of the hammer deafens him,
his eyes are fixed on the pattern;
he concentrates on getting the job done well
and stays up late to apply the finishing touches.
29 Similarly with the potter, sitting at his work,
turning the wheel with his feet;
constantly on the alert over his work,
each flick of the finger premeditated;
30 he pummels the clay with his arm,
and with his feet he kneads it;
he concentrates on applying the glaze right
and stays up late to clean the kiln.

GREEK OLD TESTAMENT

31 Πάντες οὗτοι εἰς χεῖρας αὐτῶν ἐνεπίστευσαν,
καὶ ἕκαστος ἐν τῷ ἔργῳ αὐτοῦ σοφίζεται·
32 ἄνευ αὐτῶν οὐκ οἰκισθήσεται πόλις,
καὶ οὐ παροικήσουσιν οὐδὲ περιπατήσουσιν.
33 ἀλλ᾽ εἰς βουλὴν λαοῦ οὐ ζητηθήσονται
καὶ ἐν ἐκκλησίᾳ οὐχ ὑπεραλοῦνται·
ἐπὶ δίφρον δικαστοῦ οὐ καθιοῦνται
καὶ διαθήκην κρίματος οὐ διανοηθήσονται.
34 οὐδὲ μὴ ἐκφάνωσιν παιδείαν καὶ κρίμα
καὶ ἐν παραβολαῖς οὐχ εὑρεθήσονται,
ἀλλὰ κτίσμα αἰῶνος στηρίσουσιν,
καὶ ἡ δέησις αὐτῶν ἐν ἐργασίᾳ τέχνης.

39 Πλὴν τοῦ ἐπιδιδόντος τὴν ψυχὴν αὐτοῦ
καὶ διανοουμένου ἐν νόμῳ ὑψίστου,
σοφίαν πάντων ἀρχαίων ἐκζητήσει
καὶ ἐν προφητείαις ἀσχοληθήσεται,
2 διήγησιν ἀνδρῶν ὀνομαστῶν συντηρήσει
καὶ ἐν στροφαῖς παραβολῶν συνεισελεύσεται,
3 ἀπόκρυφα παροιμιῶν ἐκζητήσει
καὶ ἐν αἰνίγμασι παραβολῶν ἀναστραφήσεται.
4 ἀνὰ μέσον μεγιστάνων ὑπηρετήσει
καὶ ἔναντι ἡγουμένων ὀφθήσεται·
ἐν γῇ ἀλλοτρίων ἐθνῶν διελεύσεται,
ἀγαθὰ γὰρ καὶ κακὰ ἐν ἀνθρώποις ἐπείρασεν.

KING JAMES VERSION

31 All these trust to their hands: and every one is wise in his work.

32 Without these cannot a city be inhabited: and they shall not dwell where they will, nor go up and down:

33 They shall not be sought for in publick counsel, nor sit high in the congregation: they shall not sit on the judges' seat, nor understand the sentence of judgment: they cannot declare justice and judgment; and they shall not be found where parables are spoken.

34 But they will maintain the state of the world, and [all] their desire is in the work of their craft.

39 But he that giveth his mind to the law of the most High, and is occupied in the meditation thereof, will seek out the wisdom of all the ancient, and be occupied in prophecies.

2 He will keep the sayings of the renowned men: and where subtil parables are, he will be there also.

3 He will seek out the secrets of grave sentences, and be conversant in dark parables.

4 He shall serve among great men, and appear before princes: he will travel through strange countries; for he hath tried the good and the evil among men.

DOUAY OLD TESTAMENT

35 All these trust to their hands, and every one is wise in his own art.

36 Without these a city is not built.

37 And they shall not dwell, nor walk about therein, and they shall not go up into the assembly.

38 Upon the judges' seat they shall not sit, and the ordinance of judgment they shall not understand, neither shall they declare discipline and judgment, and they shall not be found where parables are spoken:

39 But they shall strengthen the state of the world, and their prayer shall be in the work of their craft, applying their soul, and searching in the law of the most High.

39 THE wise man will seek out the wisdom of all the ancients, and will be occupied in the prophets.

2 He will keep the sayings of renowned men, and will enter withal into the subtilties of parables.

3 He will search out the hidden meanings of proverbs, and will be conversant in the secrets of parables.

4 He shall serve among great men, and appear before the governor.

5 He shall pass into strange countries: for he shall try good and evil among men.

KNOX TRANSLATION

these look to their own hands for a living, skilful each in his
own craft; 36 and without them, there is no building up a
commonwealth. 37 For them no travels abroad, no journeyings from home; they will not pass beyond their bounds to
swell the assembly,[a] 38 or to sit in the judgement-seat. Not
theirs to understand the law's awards, not theirs to impart
learning or to give judgement; they will not be known for
uttering wise sayings. 39 Theirs it is to support this unchanging world of God's creation; they ply their craft and ask for
nothing better;...lending themselves freely and making their
study in the law of the most High.[b]

39 But the wise man will be learning the lore of former
times; the prophets will be his study. 2 The tradition
handed down by famous men will be in his keeping; his to
con the niceties of every parable, 3 learn the hidden meaning
of every proverb, make himself acquainted with sayings hard
to understand. 4 To great men he will render good service,
will be summoned to the prince's own council; 5 will go
upon his travels in foreign countries, to learn by experience
what the world offers of good and of harm. 6 With dedicated

[a] Some would interpret the first part of this verse differently, taking it with verse 36 and giving it the sense 'there will be no living or going to and fro in common'. [b] The last fourteen words of the chapter really belong, as the Greek shews, to the beginning of the next chapter. As applied to the manual labourers described above, they give exactly the wrong sense.

TODAY'S ENGLISH VERSION

31 All of these people are skilled with their hands, each of
them an expert at his own craft. 32 Without such people
there could be no cities; no one would live or visit where
these services were not available. 33 These people are not
sought out to serve on the public councils, and they never
attain positions of great importance. They do not serve as
judges, and they do not understand legal matters. They have
no education and are not known for their wisdom. You never
hear them quoting proverbs. 34 But the work they do holds
this world together. When they do their work, it is the same
as offering prayer.[a]

39 But it is different with the person who devotes himself to studying the Law of the Most High. He examines the wisdom of all the ancient writers and concerns himself with the prophecies. 2 He memorizes the sayings of
famous men and is a skilled interpreter of parables. 3 He
studies the hidden meaning of proverbs and is able to discuss the obscure points of parables. 4 Great people call on
him for his services, and he is seen in the company of rulers.
He travels to foreign lands in his efforts to learn about

[a] When . . . prayer; *or* When they pray, it is about their work.

NEW REVISED STANDARD VERSION

31 All these rely on their hands,
and all are skillful in their own work.
32 Without them no city can be inhabited,
and wherever they live, they will not go hungry.[a]
Yet they are not sought out for the council of the
people,[b]
33 nor do they attain eminence in the public assembly.
They do not sit in the judge's seat,
nor do they understand the decisions of the courts;
they cannot expound discipline or judgment,
and they are not found among the rulers.[c]
34 But they maintain the fabric of the world,
and their concern is for[d] the exercise of their trade.

How different the one who devotes himself
to the study of the law of the Most High!
39 He seeks out the wisdom of all the ancients,
and is concerned with prophecies;
2 he preserves the sayings of the famous
and penetrates the subtleties of parables;
3 he seeks out the hidden meanings of proverbs
and is at home with the obscurities of parables.
4 He serves among the great
and appears before rulers;
he travels in foreign lands
and learns what is good and evil in the human lot.

a Syr: Gk *and people can neither live nor walk there* *b* Most ancient authorities lack this line *c* Cn: Gk *among parables* *d* Syr: Gk *prayer is in*

NEW AMERICAN BIBLE

31 All these men are skilled with their hands,
each one an expert at his own task;
32 Without them no city could be lived in,
and wherever they stay, they need not hunger.
33 They do not occupy the judge's bench,
nor are they prominent in the assembly;
They set forth no decisions or judgments,
nor are they found among the rulers;
34 Yet they maintain God's ancient handiwork,
and their concern is for exercise of their skill.

39 How different the man who devotes himself
to the study of the law of the Most High!
He explores the wisdom of the men of old
and occupies himself with the prophecies;
2 He treasures the discourses of famous men,
and goes to the heart of involved sayings;
3 He studies obscure parables,
and is busied with the hidden meanings of the sages.
4 He is in attendance on the great,
and has entrance to the ruler.
5 He travels among the peoples of foreign lands
to learn what is good and evil among men.

NEW JERUSALEM BIBLE

31 All these people rely on their hands
and each is skilled at his own craft.
32 A town could not be inhabited without them,
there would be no settling, no travelling.
33 But you will not find them in the parliament,
they do not hold high rank in the assembly.
They do not sit on the judicial bench,
and they do not meditate on the Law.
34 They are not remarkable for their culture or judgement,
nor are they found frequenting the philosophers.
They sustain the structure of the world,
and their prayer is concerned with their trade.

39 Not so with one who concentrates his mind
and his meditation on the Law of the Most High.
He researches into the wisdom of all the Ancients,
he occupies his time with the prophecies.
2 He preserves the discourses of famous men,
he is at home with the niceties of parables.
3 He researches into the hidden sense of proverbs,
he ponders the obscurities of parables.
4 He enters the service of princes,
he is seen in the presence of rulers.
He travels in foreign countries,
he has experienced human good and human evil.

GREEK OLD TESTAMENT

5 τὴν καρδίαν αὐτοῦ ἐπιδώσει ὀρθρίσαι
πρὸς κύριον τὸν ποιήσαντα αὐτὸν
καὶ ἔναντι ὑψίστου δεηθήσεται·
καὶ ἀνοίξει στόμα αὐτοῦ ἐν προσευχῇ
καὶ περὶ τῶν ἁμαρτιῶν αὐτοῦ δεηθήσεται.
6 ἐὰν κύριος ὁ μέγας θελήσῃ,
πνεύματι συνέσεως ἐμπλησθήσεται·
αὐτὸς ἀνομβρήσει ῥήματα σοφίας αὐτοῦ
καὶ ἐν προσευχῇ ἐξομολογήσεται κυρίῳ·
7 αὐτὸς κατευθυνεῖ βουλὴν αὐτοῦ καὶ ἐπιστήμην
καὶ ἐν τοῖς ἀποκρύφοις αὐτοῦ διανοηθήσεται·
8 αὐτὸς ἐκφανεῖ παιδείαν διδασκαλίας αὐτοῦ
καὶ ἐν νόμῳ διαθήκης κυρίου καυχήσεται.
9 αἰνέσουσιν τὴν σύνεσιν αὐτοῦ πολλοί,
καὶ ἕως τοῦ αἰῶνος οὐκ ἐξαλειφθήσεται·
οὐκ ἀποστήσεται τὸ μνημόσυνον αὐτοῦ,
καὶ τὸ ὄνομα αὐτοῦ ζήσεται εἰς γενεὰς γενεῶν·
10 τὴν σοφίαν αὐτοῦ διηγήσονται ἔθνη,
καὶ τὸν ἔπαινον αὐτοῦ ἐξαγγελεῖ ἐκκλησία·
11 ἐὰν ἐμμείνῃ, ὄνομα καταλείψει ἢ χίλιοι,
καὶ ἐὰν ἀναπαύσηται, ἐκποιεῖ αὐτῷ.
12 Ἔτι διανοηθεὶς ἐκδιηγήσομαι
καὶ ὡς διχομηνία ἐπληρώθην.
13 εἰσακούσατέ μου, υἱοὶ ὅσιοι, καὶ βλαστήσατε
ὡς ῥόδον φυόμενον ἐπὶ ῥεύματος ὑγροῦ

KING JAMES VERSION

5 He will give his heart to resort early to the Lord that made him, and will pray before the most High, and will open his mouth in prayer, and make supplication for his sins.

6 When the great Lord will, he shall be filled with the spirit of understanding: he shall pour out wise sentences, and give thanks unto the Lord in his prayer.

7 He shall direct his counsel and knowledge, and in his secrets shall he meditate.

8 He shall shew forth that which he hath learned, and shall glory in the law of the covenant of the Lord.

9 Many shall commend his understanding; and so long as the world endureth, it shall not be blotted out; his memorial shall not depart away, and his name shall live from generation to generation.

10 Nations shall shew forth his wisdom, and the congregation shall declare his praise.

11 If he die, he shall leave a greater name than a thousand: and if he live, he shall increase it.

12 Yet have I more to say, which I have thought upon; for I am filled as the moon at the full.

13 Hearken unto me, ye holy children, and bud forth as a rose growing by the brook of the field:

DOUAY OLD TESTAMENT

6 He will give his heart to resort early to the Lord that made him, and he will pray in the sight of the most High.

7 He will open his mouth in prayer, and will make supplication for his sins.

8 For if it shall please the great Lord, he will fill him with the spirit of understanding:

9 And he will pour forth the words of his wisdom as showers, and in his prayer he will confess to the Lord.

10 And he shall direct his counsel, and his knowledge, and in his secrets shall he meditate.

11 He shall shew forth the discipline he hath learned, and shall glory in the law of the covenant of the Lord.

12 Many shall praise his wisdom, and it shall never be forgotten.

13 The memory of him shall not depart away, and his name shall be in request from generation to generation.

14 Nations shall declare his wisdom, and the church shall shew forth his praise.

15 If he continue, he shall leave a name above a thousand: and if he rest, it shall be to his advantage.

16 I will yet meditate that I may declare: for I am filled as with a *holy* transport.

17 By a voice he saith: Hear me, ye divine offspring, and bud forth as the rose planted by the brooks of waters.

KNOX TRANSLATION

heart, he will keep early vigil at the Lord's gates, the Lord
that made him, to win audience for his plea from the most
High. 7 His lips will be eloquent in prayer, as he entreats
pardon for his sins. 8 At the Lord's sovereign pleasure, he
will be filled with a spirit of discernment, 9 so that he pours
out showers of wise utterance, giving thanks to the Lord in
his prayer. 10 His plans and thoughts guided from above, he
will have skill in the divine mysteries; 11 will make known to
all the tradition of teaching he has received, and take pride
in that law which is the Lord's covenant with man. 12 This
wisdom of his, extolled on every side, will never fall into
oblivion; 13 the memory of him, the renown of him, will be
held in honour from age to age. 14 His wise words will
become a legend among the nations; where faithful men
assemble, his praise will be told. 15 A life that shall leave
such fame as one man wins in a thousand; a death not unrewarded.

16 And still I have thoughts worth the telling; madman as
easily might contain himself. 17 A voice proclaims, Give heed
to me, you that are scions of the divine stock; yours to burgeon like a rose-bush that is planted by running water;

TODAY'S ENGLISH VERSION

human good and evil. 5 It is his practice to get up early and
pray aloud to the Lord his Creator, asking the Most High to
forgive his sins. 6 Then, if the great Lord is willing, he will
be filled with understanding. He will pour out a stream of
wise sayings, and give thanks to the Lord in prayer. 7 He
will have knowledge to share and good advice to give, as
well as insight into the Lord's secrets. 8 He will demonstrate
his learning in what he teaches,[a] and his pride will be in the
Lord's Law and covenant. 9 He will be widely praised for his
wisdom, and it will never be lost, because people for generations to come will remember him. 10 The Gentiles will talk
about his wisdom, and he will be praised aloud in the assembly. 11 If he lives to old age, he will die famous, but if he is
laid to rest before he is famous, he will be content.[b]

12 Like the moon, I am full—full of more ideas to be discussed. 13 Listen to me, you devout children of mine, and
blossom like a rosebush on a stream bank. 14 Bloom like a

[a] his learning . . . teaches; *or* the wisdom of what he has been taught.
[b] if he is . . . content; *Greek unclear.*

NEW REVISED STANDARD VERSION

5 He sets his heart to rise early
to seek the Lord who made him,
and to petition the Most High;
he opens his mouth in prayer
and asks pardon for his sins.

6 If the great Lord is willing,
he will be filled with the spirit of understanding;
he will pour forth words of wisdom of his own
and give thanks to the Lord in prayer.
7 The Lord[a] will direct his counsel and knowledge,
as he meditates on his mysteries.
8 He will show the wisdom of what he has learned,
and will glory in the law of the Lord's covenant.
9 Many will praise his understanding;
it will never be blotted out.
His memory will not disappear,
and his name will live through all generations.
10 Nations will speak of his wisdom,
and the congregation will proclaim his praise.
11 If he lives long, he will leave a name greater than a
thousand,
and if he goes to rest, it is enough[b] for him.

12 I have more on my mind to express;
I am full like the full moon.
13 Listen to me, my faithful children, and blossom
like a rose growing by a stream of water.

a Gk *He himself* *b* Cn: Meaning of Gk uncertain

NEW AMERICAN BIBLE

6 His care is to seek the LORD, his Maker,
to petition the Most High,
To open his lips in prayer,
to ask pardon for his sins.
Then, if it pleases the LORD Almighty,
he will be filled with the spirit of understanding;
He will pour forth his words of wisdom
and in prayer give thanks to the LORD,
7 Who will direct his knowledge and his counsel,
as he meditates upon his mysteries.
8 He will show the wisdom of what he has learned
and glory in the law of the LORD's covenant.
9 Many will praise his understanding;
his fame can never be effaced;
Unfading will be his memory,
through all generations his name will live;
10 Peoples will speak of his wisdom,
and in assembly sing his praises.
11 While he lives he is one out of a thousand,
and when he dies his renown will not cease.

12 Once more I will set forth my theme
to shine like the moon in its fullness!
13 Listen, my faithful children: open up your petals,
like roses planted near running waters;

NEW JERUSALEM BIBLE

5 At dawn and with all his heart
he turns to the Lord his Creator;
he pleads in the presence of the Most High,
he opens his mouth in prayer
and makes entreaty for his sins.
6 If such be the will of the great Lord,
he will be filled with the spirit of intelligence,
he will shower forth words of wisdom,
and in prayer give thanks to the Lord.
7 He will grow upright in purpose and learning,
he will ponder the Lord's hidden mysteries.
8 He will display the instruction he has received,
taking his pride in the Law of the Lord's covenant.
9 Many will praise his intelligence
and it will never be forgotten.
His memory will not disappear,
generation after generation his name will live.
10 Nations will proclaim his wisdom,
the assembly will celebrate his praises.[a]
11 If he lives long, his name will be more glorious than a
thousand others,
and if he dies, that will satisfy him just as well.

12 And here are some more of my reflections:
yes, I am as full as the moon at the full!
13 Listen to me, devout children, and blossom
like the rose that grows on the bank of a
watercourse.

[a] **39** =44:15.

GREEK OLD TESTAMENT

14 καὶ ὡς λίβανος εὐωδιάσατε ὀσμὴν
καὶ ἀνθήσατε ἄνθος ὡς κρίνον.
διάδοτε ὀσμὴν καὶ αἰνέσατε ᾆσμα,
εὐλογήσατε κύριον ἐπὶ πᾶσιν τοῖς ἔργοις,
15 δότε τῷ ὀνόματι αὐτοῦ μεγαλωσύνην
καὶ ἐξομολογήσασθε ἐν αἰνέσει αὐτοῦ
ἐν ᾠδαῖς χειλέων καὶ ἐν κινύραις
καὶ οὕτως ἐρεῖτε ἐν ἐξομολογήσει
16 Τὰ ἔργα κυρίου πάντα ὅτι καλὰ σφόδρα,
καὶ πᾶν πρόσταγμα ἐν καιρῷ αὐτοῦ ἔσται·
οὐκ ἔστιν εἰπεῖν Τί τοῦτο; εἰς τί τοῦτο;
πάντα γὰρ ἐν καιρῷ αὐτοῦ ζητηθήσεται.
17 ἐν λόγῳ αὐτοῦ ἔστη ὡς θιμωνιὰ ὕδωρ
καὶ ἐν ῥήματι στόματος αὐτοῦ ἀποδοχεῖα ὑδάτων.
18 ἐν προστάγματι αὐτοῦ πᾶσα ἡ εὐδοκία,
καὶ οὐκ ἔστιν ὃς ἐλαττώσει τὸ σωτήριον αὐτοῦ.
19 ἔργα πάσης σαρκὸς ἐνώπιον αὐτοῦ,
καὶ οὐκ ἔστιν κρυβῆναι ἀπὸ τῶν ὀφθαλμῶν αὐτοῦ·
20 ἀπὸ τοῦ αἰῶνος εἰς τὸν αἰῶνα ἐπέβλεψεν,
καὶ οὐθέν ἐστιν θαυμάσιον ἐναντίον αὐτοῦ.
21 οὐκ ἔστιν εἰπεῖν Τί τοῦτο; εἰς τί τοῦτο;
πάντα γὰρ εἰς χρείας αὐτῶν ἔκτισται.
22 Ἡ εὐλογία αὐτοῦ ὡς ποταμὸς ἐπεκάλυψεν
καὶ ὡς κατακλυσμὸς ξηρὰν ἐμέθυσεν·

KING JAMES VERSION

14 And give ye a sweet savour as frankincense, and flourish as a lily, send forth a smell, and sing a song of praise, bless the Lord in all his works.

15 Magnify his name, and shew forth his praise with the songs of your lips, and with harps, and in praising him ye shall say after this manner:

16 All the works of the Lord are exceeding good, and whatsoever he commandeth shall be *accomplished* in due season.

17 And none may say, What is this? wherefore is that? for at time convenient they shall all be sought out: at his commandment the waters stood as an heap, and at the words of his mouth the receptacles of waters.

18 At his commandment is done whatsoever pleaseth him; and none can hinder, when he will save.

19 The works of all flesh are before him, and nothing can be hid from his eyes.

20 He seeth from everlasting to everlasting; and there is nothing wonderful before him.

21 A man need not to say, What is this? wherefore is that? for he hath made all things for their uses.

22 His blessing covered the dry land as a river, and watered it as a flood.

DOUAY OLD TESTAMENT

18 Give ye a sweet odour as frankincense.

19 Send forth flowers, as the lily, and yield a smell, and bring forth leaves in grace, and praise with canticles, and bless the Lord in his works.

20 Magnify his name, and give glory to him with the voice of your lips, and with the canticles of your mouths, and with harps, and in praising him, you shall say in this manner:

21 All the works of the Lord are exceeding good.

22 At his word the waters stood as a heap: and at the words of his mouth the receptacles of waters:

23 For at his commandment favour is shewn, and there is no diminishing of his salvation.

24 The works of all flesh are before him, and there is nothing hid from his eyes.

25 He seeth from eternity to eternity, and there is nothing wonderful before him.

26 There is no saying: What is this, or what is that? for all things shall be sought in their time.

27 His blessing hath overflowed like a river.

KNOX TRANSLATION

18 yours to yield the fragrance of incense; 19 yours to blossom
like the lily, and smell sweet, and put forth leaves for your
adornment; yours to sing songs of praise, and bless the Lord
for all things he has made. 20 His name extol; songs of
praise let your lips utter, and let harp's melody mingle with
the song. And you shall praise him in these words following.
21 Good, wondrously good, is all the Lord has made. [a]
22 Piled high the waters stand at his command, shut in by
cisterns of his appointing. [b] 23 All-sufficient is his will,
unfailing his power to save; 24 open to his view are all deeds
of mortal men, nothing can escape that scrutiny. 25 On every
age of time his glance rests; marvel is none beyond his compass. 26 Not for man to ask what this or that may be, each
shall be needed in its turn. 27 His blessings flow like a
stream in full flood, 28 like rain pouring down to refresh the

a It is not clear how many of the remaining verses in this chapter the hymn of praise includes. *b* Cf. Ps. 32. 7 (33. 7 in the Hebrew text).

TODAY'S ENGLISH VERSION

sweet-smelling lily, and send your fragrance into the air like
incense. Sing the Lord's praises, and thank him for all that
he has done. 15 Proclaim his glory in grateful praise! To the
music of the harp, sing this song:

16 All that the Lord has done is very good;
all that he commands is sooner or later done.
17 No one should ask why things are as they are;
these questions will be answered at the right time.
He commanded, and the water piled up high,
great walls of water arose when he spoke.
18 Whatever he commands is promptly done;
there are no limits to his power to save.
19 He sees all that every human being does;
there is no way to hide from his sight.
20 He sees the whole of time, from beginning to end,
and nothing takes him by surprise.[a]
21 No one should ask why things are as they are;
everything in creation has its purpose.
22 His blessings overflow like the Nile,
enriching the world in a fertile flood.[b]

[a] takes him by surprise; *or* is too marvelous for him.
[b] *Hebrew* overflow . . . flood; *Greek* cover the dry land like a river and drench it like a flood.

NEW REVISED STANDARD VERSION

14 Send out fragrance like incense,
and put forth blossoms like a lily.
Scatter the fragrance, and sing a hymn of praise;
bless the Lord for all his works.
15 Ascribe majesty to his name
and give thanks to him with praise,
with songs on your lips, and with harps;
this is what you shall say in thanksgiving:

16 "All the works of the Lord are very good,
and whatever he commands will be done at the appointed time.
17 No one can say, 'What is this?' or 'Why is that?'—
for at the appointed time all such questions will be answered.
At his word the waters stood in a heap,
and the reservoirs of water at the word of his mouth.
18 When he commands, his every purpose is fulfilled,
and none can limit his saving power.
19 The works of all are before him,
and nothing can be hidden from his eyes.
20 From the beginning to the end of time he can see everything,
and nothing is too marvelous for him.
21 No one can say, 'What is this?' or 'Why is that?'—
for everything has been created for its own purpose.

22 "His blessing covers the dry land like a river,
and drenches it like a flood.

NEW AMERICAN BIBLE

14 Send up the sweet odor of incense,
break forth in blossoms like the lily.
Send up the sweet odor of your hymn of praise;
bless the LORD for all he has done!
15 Proclaim the greatness of his name,
loudly sing his praises,
With music on the harp and all stringed instruments;
sing out with joy as you proclaim:
16 The works of God are all of them good;
in its own time every need is supplied.
17 At his word the waters become still as in a flask;
he had but to speak and the reservoirs were made.
18 He has but to command and his will is done;
nothing can limit his achievement.
19 The works of all mankind are present to him;
not a thing escapes his eye.
20 His gaze spans all the ages;
to him there is nothing unexpected.
21 No cause then to say: "What is the purpose of this?"
Everything is chosen to satisfy a need.
22 His blessing overflows like the Nile;
like the Euphrates it enriches the surface of the earth.

NEW JERUSALEM BIBLE

14 Give off a sweet smell like incense,
flower like the lily, spread your fragrance abroad,
sing a song of praise
blessing the Lord for all his works.
15 Declare the greatness of his name,
proclaim his praise
with song and with lyre,
and this is how you must sing his praises:
16 'How wonderful, the actions of the Lord!
Whatever he orders is done at the proper time!'
You must not say, 'What is this? Why is that?'
There is a proper time for every question.
17 At his word, the water stops and piles up high,
at his voice, the watery reservoirs take shape,
18 at his command, whatever he wants is done,
no one can stop him, if he intends to save.
19 He can see whatever human beings are doing,
nothing can be hidden from his eye;
20 his gaze stretches from eternity to eternity,
and nothing can astonish him.
21 You must not say, 'What is this? Why is that?'
for everything has been made for a purpose.

22 As his blessing covers the dry land like a river
and soaks it like a flood,

GREEK OLD TESTAMENT

23 οὕτως ὀργὴν αὐτοῦ ἔθνη κληρονομήσει,
ὡς μετέστρεψεν ὕδατα εἰς ἅλμην.
24 αἱ ὁδοὶ αὐτοῦ τοῖς ὁσίοις εὐθεῖαι,
οὕτως τοῖς ἀνόμοις προσκόμματα·
25 ἀγαθὰ τοῖς ἀγαθοῖς ἔκτισται ἀπ᾽ ἀρχῆς,
οὕτως τοῖς ἁμαρτωλοῖς κακά.
26 ἀρχὴ πάσης χρείας εἰς ζωὴν ἀνθρώπου,
ὕδωρ καὶ πῦρ καὶ σίδηρος καὶ ἅλας
καὶ σεμίδαλις πυροῦ καὶ γάλα καὶ μέλι,
αἷμα σταφυλῆς καὶ ἔλαιον καὶ ἱμάτιον·
27 ταῦτα πάντα τοῖς εὐσεβέσιν εἰς ἀγαθά,
οὕτως τοῖς ἁμαρτωλοῖς τραπήσεται εἰς κακά.
28 Ἔστιν πνεύματα, ἃ εἰς ἐκδίκησιν ἔκτισται
καὶ ἐν θυμῷ αὐτοῦ ἐστερέωσεν μάστιγας αὐτῶν·
ἐν καιρῷ συντελείας ἰσχὺν ἐκχεοῦσιν
καὶ τὸν θυμὸν τοῦ ποιήσαντος αὐτοὺς κοπάσουσιν.
29 πῦρ καὶ χάλαζα καὶ λιμὸς καὶ θάνατος,
πάντα ταῦτα εἰς ἐκδίκησιν ἔκτισται·
30 θηρίων ὀδόντες καὶ σκορπίοι καὶ ἔχεις
καὶ ῥομφαία ἐκδικοῦσα εἰς ὄλεθρον ἀσεβεῖς·
31 ἐν τῇ ἐντολῇ αὐτοῦ εὐφρανθήσονται
καὶ ἐπὶ τῆς γῆς εἰς χρείας ἑτοιμασθήσονται
καὶ ἐν καιροῖς αὐτῶν οὐ παραβήσονται λόγον.

KING JAMES VERSION

23 As he hath turned the waters into saltness: so shall the heathen inherit his wrath.

24 As his ways are plain unto the holy; so are they stumblingblocks unto the wicked.

25 For the good are good things created from the beginning: so evil things for sinners.

26 The principal things for the whole use of man's life are water, fire, iron, and salt, flour of wheat, honey, milk, and the blood of the grape, and oil, and clothing.

27 All these things are for good to the godly: so to the sinners they are turned into evil.

28 There be spirits that are created for vengeance, which in their fury lay on sore strokes; in the time of destruction they pour out their force, and appease the wrath of him that made them.

29 Fire, and hail, and famine, and death, all these were created for vengeance;

30 Teeth of wild beasts, and scorpions, serpents, and the sword, punishing the wicked to destruction.

31 They shall rejoice in his commandment, and they shall be ready upon earth, when need is; and when their time is come, they shall not transgress his word.

DOUAY OLD TESTAMENT

28 And as a flood hath watered the earth; so shall his wrath inherit the nations, that have not sought after him:

29 Even as he turned the waters into a dry land, and the earth was made dry: and his ways were made plain for their journey: so to sinners *they are* stumblingblocks in his wrath.

30 Good things were created for the good from the beginning, so for the wicked, good and evil things.

31 The principal things necessary for the life of men, are water, fire, and iron, salt, milk, and bread of flour, and honey, and the cluster of the grape, and oil, and clothing.

32 All these things shall be for good to the holy, so to the sinners and the ungodly they shall be turned into evil.

33 There are spirits that are created for vengeance, and in their fury they lay on grievous torments.

34 In the time of destruction they shall pour out their force: and they shall appease the wrath of him that made them.

35 Fire, hail, famine, and death, all these were created for vengeance.

36 The teeth of beasts, and scorpions, and serpents, and the sword taking vengeance upon the ungodly unto destruction.

37 In his commandments they shall feast, and they shall be ready upon earth when need is, and when their time is come they shall not transgress his word.

KNOX TRANSLATION

parched earth. But the nations that never look to find him,
shall be the prey of his vengeance; 29 did he not turn the
waters into firm ground, and dry up the floor of them, so
that it made a path for the passage of his own people,[a] and
yet a trap to punish the wicked?
30 From the first, good things were made for good men to
enjoy; for sinners, they are good and evil at once. 31 What
are the first needs of man's life? Water, fire, iron, salt, milk,
wheat-meal, honey, the grape-cluster, oil and clothing.
32 Thereby, for just men, nought but good is intended, yet for
sinners they turn to evil. 33 Some powers[b] there be that are
created for wreaking of vengeance, and sternly they wield
the lash in their raging; 34 when the time for reckoning
comes, they will put out all their force, until their Maker's
anger is appeased. 35 Fire, hail, hunger and death, all these
were made for wreaking of vengeance; 36 ravening beasts,
too, and scorpions, and serpents, and the sword that punishes the wicked till there are none left. 37 All these hold
high revel as they perform his will; ready they stand till earth
has need of them, and when the need comes, they will obey.

a In the original, simply 'their passage'; but it seems clear that the Latin intends an allusion to the crossing of the Red Sea. The other versions would rather suggest a reference to the destruction of Sodom. *b* Literally, 'some spirits.' It may be that diabolical agencies are referred to; but the word 'spirits' may mean simply 'winds'; or (perhaps with greater probability) it may be taken as describing the forces of nature which are to be mentioned in verse 35.

TODAY'S ENGLISH VERSION

23 He turns fresh water into salt water,
and he turns his anger on the nations.
24 For the devout, his ways are straight;
for the wicked, they are laid with traps.
25 From the beginning he has made good things for the good
and terrible things for sinners.
26 The basic needs of life are these:
water, fire, iron, and salt,
flour, honey, and milk,
wine, clothing, and oil.
27 All these things are good for those who are devout,
but they turn into evils for sinners.

28 There are winds that were created to bring punishment,
fierce enough to move mountains.[a]
In times of judgment, they unleash their strength
and calm the anger of their maker.
29-30 Vicious animals, scorpions, and snakes;
the sword that destroys the wicked;
fire, hail, famine, and disease;
these have all been created as punishments.
31 They are all glad to obey the Lord's command
and are ready to serve him here on earth.
When their times of duty come,
they never disobey.

[a] *Hebrew* move mountains; *Greek* lash heavily.

NEW REVISED STANDARD VERSION

23 But his wrath drives out the nations,
as when he turned a watered land into salt.
24 To the faithful his ways are straight,
but full of pitfalls for the wicked.
25 From the beginning good things were created for the good,
but for sinners good things and bad.[a]
26 The basic necessities of human life
are water and fire and iron and salt
and wheat flour and milk and honey,
the blood of the grape and oil and clothing.
27 All these are good for the godly,
but for sinners they turn into evils.

28 "There are winds created for vengeance,
and in their anger they can dislodge mountains;[b]
on the day of reckoning they will pour out their strength
and calm the anger of their Maker.
29 Fire and hail and famine and pestilence,
all these have been created for vengeance;
30 the fangs of wild animals and scorpions and vipers,
and the sword that punishes the ungodly with destruction.
31 They take delight in doing his bidding,
always ready for his service on earth;
and when their time comes they never disobey his command."

[a] Heb Lat: Gk *sinners bad things* [b] Heb Syr: Gk *can scourge mightily*

NEW AMERICAN BIBLE

23 Again, his wrath expels the nations
and turns fertile land into a salt marsh.
24 For the virtuous his paths are level,
to the haughty they are steep;
25 Good things for the good he provided from the beginning,
but for the wicked good things and bad.
26 Chief of all needs for human life
are water and fire, iron and salt,
The heart of the wheat, milk and honey,
the blood of the grape, and oil, and cloth;
27 For the good all these are good,
but for the wicked they turn out evil.
28 There are storm winds created to punish,
which in their fury can dislodge mountains;
When destruction must be, they hurl all their force
and appease the anger of their Maker.
29 In his treasury also, kept for the proper time,
are fire and hail, famine, disease,
30 Ravenous beasts, scorpions, vipers,
and the avenging sword to exterminate the wicked;
31 In doing his bidding they rejoice,
in their assignments they disobey not his command.

NEW JERUSALEM BIBLE

23 so retribution is his legacy to the nations,
just as he has turned fresh waters to salt.
24 His ways are as smooth for the devout,
as they are full of obstacles for the wicked.
25 Good things were created from the beginning for good people,
as bad ones were for sinners.
26 The prime needs of human beings for living
are water and fire, iron and salt,
wheat-flour, milk and honey,
the juice of the grape, oil and clothing.
27 All these are good for those who are good,
but turn out bad for sinners.

28 Some winds have been created for punishing,
in his fury, he uses them as scourges;
on the day of doom, they unleash their violence
and appease the wrath of their Creator.
29 Fire and hail, famine and death,
have all been created for punishing.
30 Wild animals' fangs, scorpions, vipers,
the avenging sword for the ruin of the godless:
31 all of them exult in discharging his orders,
ready on earth whenever the need arises
and, when their time comes, not falling short of his word.

GREEK OLD TESTAMENT

32 Διὰ τοῦτο ἐξ ἀρχῆς ἐστηρίχθην
καὶ διενοήθην καὶ ἐν γραφῇ ἀφῆκα
33 Τὰ ἔργα κυρίου πάντα ἀγαθὰ
καὶ πᾶσαν χρείαν ἐν ὥρᾳ αὐτῆς χορηγήσει,
34 καὶ οὐκ ἔστιν εἰπεῖν Τοῦτο τούτου πονηρότερον,
πάντα γὰρ ἐν καιρῷ εὐδοκιμηθήσεται.
35 καὶ νῦν ἐν πάσῃ καρδίᾳ καὶ στόματι ὑμνήσατε
καὶ εὐλογήσατε τὸ ὄνομα κυρίου.

40 Ἀσχολία μεγάλη ἔκτισται παντὶ ἀνθρώπῳ
καὶ ζυγὸς βαρὺς ἐπὶ υἱοὺς Αδαμ
ἀφ' ἡμέρας ἐξόδου ἐκ γαστρὸς μητρὸς αὐτῶν
ἕως ἡμέρας ἐπιστροφῆς εἰς μητέρα πάντων·
2 τοὺς διαλογισμοὺς αὐτῶν καὶ φόβον καρδίας,
ἐπίνοια προσδοκίας, ἡμέρα τελευτῆς.
3 ἀπὸ καθημένου ἐπὶ θρόνου ἐνδόξου
καὶ ἕως τεταπεινωμένου ἐν γῇ καὶ σποδῷ,
4 ἀπὸ φοροῦντος ὑακίνθινον καὶ στέφανον
καὶ ἕως περιβαλλομένου ὠμόλινον
θυμὸς καὶ ζῆλος καὶ ταραχὴ καὶ σάλος
καὶ φόβος θανάτου καὶ μηνίαμα καὶ ἔρις.
5 καὶ ἐν καιρῷ ἀναπαύσεως ἐπὶ κοίτης
ὕπνος νυκτὸς ἀλλοιοῖ γνῶσιν αὐτοῦ·
6 ὀλίγον ὡς οὐδὲν ἐν ἀναπαύσει,
καὶ ἀπ' ἐκείνου ἐν ὕπνοις ὡς ἐν ἡμέρᾳ σκοπιᾶς
τεθορυβημένος ἐν ὁράσει καρδίας αὐτοῦ
ὡς ἐκπεφευγὼς ἀπὸ προσώπου πολέμου·

KING JAMES VERSION

32 Therefore from the beginning I was resolved, and
thought upon these things, and have left them in writing.
33 All the works of the Lord are good: and he will give
every needful thing in due season.
34 So that a man cannot say, This is worse than that: for
in time they shall all be well approved.
35 And therefore praise ye the Lord with the whole heart
and mouth, and bless the name of the Lord.

40 Great travail is created for every man, and an heavy
yoke is upon the sons of Adam, from the day that
they go out of their mother's womb, till the day that they
return to the mother of all things.
2 Their imagination of things to come, and the day of
death, [trouble] their thoughts, and [cause] fear of heart;
3 From him that sitteth on a throne of glory, unto him
that is humbled in earth and ashes;
4 From him that weareth purple and a crown, unto *him
that is clothed with a linen* frock.
5 Wrath, and envy, trouble, and unquietness, fear of
death, and anger, and strife, and in the time of rest upon his
bed his night sleep, do change his knowledge.
6 A little or nothing is his rest, and afterward he is in his
sleep, as in a day of keeping watch, troubled in the vision of
his heart, as if he were escaped out of a battle.

DOUAY OLD TESTAMENT

38 Therefore from the beginning I was resolved, and I
have meditated, and thought on these things and left them
in writing.
39 All the works of the Lord are good, and he will furnish
every work in due time.
40 It is not to be said: This is worse than that: for all shall
be well approved in their time.
41 Now therefore with the whole heart and mouth praise
ye him, and bless the name of the Lord.

40 GREAT labour is created for all men, and a heavy
yoke is upon the children of Adam, from the day of
their coming out of their mother's womb, until the day of
their burial into the mother of all.
2 Their thoughts, and fears of the heart, their imagination
of things to come, and the day of their end:
3 From him that sitteth on a glorious throne, unto him
that is humbled in earth and ashes:
4 From him that weareth purple, and beareth the crown,
even to him that is covered with rough linen: wrath, envy,
trouble, unquietness, and the fear of death, continual anger,
and strife,
5 And in the time of rest upon his bed, the sleep of the
night changeth his knowledge.
6 A little and as nothing is his rest, and afterward in
sleep, as in the day of keeping watch.
7 He is troubled in the vision of his heart, as if he had

KNOX TRANSLATION

38 From the first, all my questioning and all my thought
confirms me in what I have written, 39 all things God has
made are good, and each of them serves its turn; 40 nor ever
must we complain things have happened for the worse, since
each has its own occasion to justify it. 41 With full hearts,
then, and full voice, praise we and bless the Lord's name.

40 Great is the anxiety all men are doomed to, heavy the
yoke each son of Adam must bear, from the day
when he leaves his mother's womb to the day when he is
buried in the earth, that is mother of all. 2 What solicitude is
his, what fears catch at his heart; how quick his mind runs
out to meet coming events! And the term of it all is death.
3 What matter, whether a man sit on a throne, or grovel in
dust and ashes; 4 whether he goes clad in purple and wears
a crown, or has but coarse linen to wear? Anger he shall
know, and jealousy, and concern, and bewilderment, and the
fear of death, and the grudge that rankles, and rivalry. 5 Rest
he on his bed at night, sleep comes to fashion his thinking
anew; 6 even there, the rest he wins is but little or none at
all, and thereupon, in his dreams, he is anxious as sentry
waiting to be relieved, 7 his are such whirling thoughts as
fugitive has, just escaped from the battle. Then, at the

TODAY'S ENGLISH VERSION

([32]I was long convinced of this, so after thinking it over I
put[a] it in writing.)

[33]Everything made by the Lord is good;
he meets every need at the proper time.
[34]No one can claim that some things are worse than others,
for everything is good in its proper place.
[35]Now then, sing praises with all your heart,
and praise the name of the Lord!

40 Every person has been given a great deal of work to
do. A heavy burden lies on all of us from the day of
our birth until the day we go back to the earth, the mother of
us all. [2]We are confused and fearful, dreading the day of
our death— [3-4]all of us from the king on his splendid throne
wearing royal robes and a crown, to the humblest person
dressed in burlap and living in poverty. [5]All through our
lives we meet anger, jealousy, and trouble. Things disturb
us; we live with furious conflicts and with the fear of death.
Even when we go to bed, we think up new troubles in our
sleep. [6]We get little rest, if any at all. When we sleep, it is as
if we were awake, disturbed by our imaginations. If we
dream that we are running from an enemy, [7]just as we are

[a] put; *or* left.

NEW REVISED STANDARD VERSION

32 So from the beginning I have been convinced of all this
and have thought it out and left it in writing:
33 All the works of the Lord are good,
and he will supply every need in its time.
34 No one can say, "This is not as good as that,"
for everything proves good in its appointed time.
35 So now sing praise with all your heart and voice,
and bless the name of the Lord.

40 Hard work was created for everyone,
and a heavy yoke is laid on the children of Adam,
from the day they come forth from their mother's womb
until the day they return to[a] the mother of all the living.[b]
2 Perplexities and fear of heart are theirs,
and anxious thought of the day of their death.
3 From the one who sits on a splendid throne
to the one who grovels in dust and ashes,
4 from the one who wears purple and a crown
to the one who is clothed in burlap,
5 there is anger and envy and trouble and unrest,
and fear of death, and fury and strife.
And when one rests upon his bed,
his sleep at night confuses his mind.
6 He gets little or no rest;
he struggles in his sleep as he did by day.[c]
He is troubled by the visions of his mind
like one who has escaped from the battlefield.

a Other Gk and Lat authorities read *are buried in* *b* Heb: Gk *of all*
c Arm: Meaning of Gk uncertain

NEW AMERICAN BIBLE

[32]So from the first I took my stand,
and wrote down as my theme:
[33]The works of God are all of them good;
every need when it comes he fills.
[34]No cause then to say: "This is not as good as that";
for each shows its worth at the proper time.
[35]So now with full joy of heart proclaim
and bless the name of the Holy One.

40 A great anxiety has God allotted,
and a heavy yoke, to the sons of men;
From the day one leaves his mother's womb
to the day he returns to the mother of all the living,
[2]His thoughts, the fear in his heart,
and his troubled forebodings till the day he dies—
[3]Whether he sits on a lofty throne
or grovels in dust and ashes,
[4]Whether he bears a splendid crown
or is wrapped in the coarsest of cloaks—
[5]Are of wrath and envy, trouble and dread,
terror of death, fury and strife.
Even when he lies on his bed to rest,
his cares at night disturb his sleep.
[6]So short is his rest it seems like none,
till in his dreams he struggles as he did by day,
Terrified by what his mind's eye sees,
like a fugitive being pursued;

NEW JERUSALEM BIBLE

[32]That is why I was determined from the outset,
why I have pondered and why I have written,
[33]'The works of the Lord are all good,
when the time is right, he gives whatever is needed.
[34]You must not say, "This is worse than that,"
for, sooner or later, everything proves its worth.
[35]So now, sing with all your heart and voice,
and bless the name of the Lord!'

40 A hard lot has been created for human beings,
a heavy yoke lies on the children of Adam
from the day they come out of their mother's womb,
till the day they return to the mother of them all.
[2]What fills them with foreboding and their hearts with fear
is dread of the day of death.
[3]From the one who sits on a glorious throne
to the wretch in dust and ashes,
[4]from the one who wears purple and a crown
to the one dressed in sacking,
all is fury and jealousy, turmoil and unrest,
fear of death, rivalry, strife.
[5]And even at night while he rests on his bed
his sleep only gives a new twist to his worries:
[6]scarcely has he lain down to rest,
when in his sleep, as if in broad daylight,
he is troubled with nightmares,
like one who has escaped from a battle,

GREEK OLD TESTAMENT

7 ἐν καιρῷ χρείας αὐτοῦ ἐξηγέρθη
καὶ ἀποθαυμάζων εἰς οὐδένα φόβον.
8 μετὰ πάσης σαρκὸς ἀπὸ ἀνθρώπου ἕως κτήνους,
καὶ ἐπὶ ἁμαρτωλῶν ἑπταπλάσια πρὸς ταῦτα·
9 θάνατος καὶ αἷμα καὶ ἔρις καὶ ῥομφαία,
ἐπαγωγαί, λιμὸς καὶ σύντριμμα καὶ μάστιξ.
10 ἐπὶ τοὺς ἀνόμους ἐκτίσθη ταῦτα πάντα,
καὶ δι᾽ αὐτοὺς ἐγένετο ὁ κατακλυσμός.
11 πάντα, ὅσα ἀπὸ γῆς, εἰς γῆν ἀναστρέφει,
καὶ ἀπὸ ὑδάτων, εἰς θάλασσαν ἀνακάμπτει.
12 Πᾶν δῶρον καὶ ἀδικία ἐξαλειφθήσεται,
καὶ πίστις εἰς τὸν αἰῶνα στήσεται.
13 χρήματα ἀδίκων ὡς ποταμὸς ξηρανθήσεται
καὶ ὡς βροντὴ μεγάλη ἐν ὑετῷ ἐξηχήσει·
14 ἐν τῷ ἀνοῖξαι αὐτὸν χεῖρας εὐφρανθήσεται,
οὕτως οἱ παραβαίνοντες εἰς συντέλειαν ἐκλείψουσιν.
15 ἔκγονα ἀσεβῶν οὐ πληθυνεῖ κλάδους,
καὶ ῥίζαι ἀκάθαρτοι ἐπ᾽ ἀκροτόμου πέτρας·
16 ἄχι ἐπὶ παντὸς ὕδατος καὶ χείλους ποταμοῦ
πρὸ παντὸς χόρτου ἐκτιλήσεται.
17 χάρις ὡς παράδεισος ἐν εὐλογίαις,
καὶ ἐλεημοσύνη εἰς τὸν αἰῶνα διαμενεῖ.
18 Ζωὴ αὐτάρκους καὶ ἐργάτου γλυκανθήσεται,
καὶ ὑπὲρ ἀμφότερα ὁ εὑρίσκων θησαυρόν.

KING JAMES VERSION

7 When all is safe, he awaketh, and marvelleth that the fear was nothing.

8 [Such things happen] unto all flesh, both man and beast, and that is sevenfold more upon sinners.

9 Death, and bloodshed, strife, and sword, calamities, famine, tribulation, and the scourge;

10 These things are created for the wicked, and for their sakes came the flood.

11 All things that are of the earth shall turn to the earth again: and that which is of the waters doth return into the sea.

12 All bribery and injustice shall be blotted out: but true dealing shall endure for ever.

13 The goods of the unjust shall be dried up like a river, and shall vanish with noise, like a great thunder in rain.

14 While he openeth his hand he shall rejoice: so shall transgressors come to nought.

15 The children of the ungodly shall not bring forth many branches: but are as unclean roots upon a hard rock.

16 The weed growing upon every water and bank of a river shall be pulled up before all grass.

17 Bountifulness is as a most fruitful garden, and mercifulness endureth for ever.

18 To labour, and to be content with that a man hath, is a sweet life: but he that findeth a treasure is above them both.

DOUAY OLD TESTAMENT

escaped in the day of battle. In the time of his safety he rose up, and wondereth that there is no fear:

8 Such things happen to all flesh, from man even to beast, and upon sinners are sevenfold more.

9 Moreover, death, and bloodshed, strife, and sword, oppressions, famine, and affliction, and scourges:

10 All these things are created for the wicked, and for their sakes came the flood.

11 All things that are of the earth, shall return to the earth again, and all waters shall return to the sea.

12 All bribery, and injustice shall be blotted out, and fidelity shall stand for ever.

13 The riches of the unjust shall be dried up like a river, and shall pass away with a noise like a great thunder in rain.

14 While he openeth his hands he shall rejoice: but transgressors shall pine away in the end.

15 The offspring of the ungodly shall not bring forth many branches, and make a noise as unclean roots upon the top of a rock.

16 The weed growing over every water, and at the bank of the river, shall be pulled up before all grass.

17 Grace is like a paradise in blessings, and mercy remaineth for ever.

18 The life of a labourer that is content with what he hath, shall be sweet, and in it thou shalt find a treasure.

KNOX TRANSLATION

moment of deliverance, comes waking; and he marvels to
find his fears all vain. 8 This lot he shares with all living
things; beast has it as well as man, but for the sinner it is
multiplied sevenfold. 9 There is more besides, mortal sickness, bloodshed, quarrelling, the sword, oppression, famine,
devastation and plague; 10 all such things are designed for
the punishing of the wicked; was it not from wickedness the
flood came?

11 All that is of earth, to earth must needs return, and all
waters find their way back to the sea; 12 what shall become
of bribery and oppression? The memory of them shall vanish; faithfulness will endure for ever. 13 All the riches of the
wrong-doer will disappear, like stream that runs dry, will die
away, like roll of thunder in a storm-cloud; 14 open-handed
is merry-hearted, the sinners it is that shall pine away at the
last. 15 Never a branch will the posterity of the wicked put
forth; dead roots they are that rattle on the wind-swept rock.
16 How green yonder rushes grow by the river's bank! But
they shall be plucked up before hay-harvest. 17 But kindliness, like the garden trees, lasts on, remembered in blessing;
charity remains unforgotten.

18 Sweet is his lot, that toils and is contented; here is hidden treasure for thy finding. [a]

a The other versions assimilate this maxim to the formula observed in verses 19-25; 'Contentment and hard work (in the Hebrew, a life of wine and strong drink) may be sweet, but best of all is finding a treasure'—an observation so little worth making, that it looks as if the Latin had preserved the true text.

TODAY'S ENGLISH VERSION

about to be caught,[a] we wake up and are relieved to find
there is nothing to be afraid of.
8 Here is what all creatures, both human and animal, must
face (but it is seven times worse for sinners): 9 death, violence, conflict, murder, disaster, famine, sickness, epidemic.
10 All these things were created because of the wicked; they
are the ones who have caused destruction.[b] 11 Everything
that comes from the earth goes back to the earth, just as all
water flows into the sea.
12 Nothing that comes from bribery or injustice will last,
but the effects of loyalty will remain forever. 13 Wealth that
has been obtained dishonestly is like a stream that runs full
during a thunderstorm, 14 tumbling rocks along as it flows,
but then suddenly goes dry.[c] 15 The children of ungodly
people will not leave large families; they are like plants trying to take root on rock, 16 like reeds along a river bank,
withering[d] before any other plant. 17 Acts of kindness and
charity are as lasting as eternity.[e]
18 Being independently wealthy or working for a living—
both can make life pleasant, but it is better to find a treasure.

[a] *Probable text* caught; *Greek* rescued. [b] *Hebrew* have caused destruction; *Greek* caused the flood. [c] *Verses 13-14 are translated from Hebrew; verse 14 in Greek is unclear.* [d] *Hebrew* withering; *Greek* pulled up.
[e] *Hebrew* Acts . . . eternity; *Greek* Kindness is a blessed garden, and charity lasts forever.

NEW REVISED STANDARD VERSION

7 At the moment he reaches safety he wakes up,
astonished that his fears were groundless.
8 To all creatures, human and animal,
but to sinners seven times more,
9 come death and bloodshed and strife and sword,
calamities and famine and ruin and plague.
10 All these were created for the wicked,
and on their account the flood came.
11 All that is of earth returns to earth,
and what is from above returns above.[a]

12 All bribery and injustice will be blotted out,
but good faith will last forever.
13 The wealth of the unjust will dry up like a river,
and crash like a loud clap of thunder in a storm.
14 As a generous person has cause to rejoice,
so lawbreakers will utterly fail.
15 The children of the ungodly put out few branches;
they are unhealthy roots on sheer rock.
16 The reeds by any water or river bank
are plucked up before any grass;
17 but kindness is like a garden of blessings,
and almsgiving endures forever.

18 Wealth and wages make life sweet,[b]
but better than either is finding a treasure.

[a] Heb Syr: Gk Lat *from the waters returns to the sea* [b] Heb: Gk *Life is sweet for the self-reliant worker*

NEW AMERICAN BIBLE

7 As he reaches safety, he wakes up
astonished that there was nothing to fear.
8 So it is with all flesh, with man and with beast,
but for sinners seven times more.
9 Plague and bloodshed, wrath and the sword,
plunder and ruin, famine and death:
10 For the wicked, these were created evil,
and it is they who bring on destruction.

11 All that is of earth returns to earth,
and what is from above returns above.
12 All that comes from bribes or injustice will be wiped
out,
but loyalty remains for ages.
13 Wealth out of wickedness is like a wadi in spate:
like a mighty stream with lightning and thunder,
14 Which, in its rising, rolls along the stones,
but suddenly, once and for all, comes to an end.
15 The offshoot of violence will not flourish,
for the root of the godless is on sheer rock;
16 Or they are like reeds on the riverbank,
withered before all other plants.
17 But goodness will never be cut off,
and justice endures forever.

Wealth or wages can make life sweet,
but better than either is finding a treasure.

NEW JERUSALEM BIBLE

7 and at the moment of rescue he wakes up,
amazed that there was nothing to be afraid of!
8 For all creatures, human and animal—
and seven times more for sinners—
9 there is death and blood and strife and the sword,
disasters, famine, affliction, plague.
10 These things were all created for the wicked,
and the Flood came because of them.
11 All that comes from the earth returns to the earth,[a]
and what comes from the water returns to the sea.

12 All bribery and injustice will be blotted out,
but good faith will stand for ever.
13 Ill-gotten wealth will vanish like a torrent,
like the single thunder-clap that heralds rain.
14 When he opens his hand, he rejoices,
by the same token, sinners come to ruin.
15 The sprigs of the godless will not make many branches,
tainted roots find only hard rock.
16 The reed that grows by every lake and river's edge
is the first plant to be uprooted.
17 Charity is a very paradise of blessing
and almsgiving endures for ever.
18 For a person of private means and one who works hard,
life is pleasant,
better off than either, one who finds a treasure.

[a] **40** =41:10.

GREEK OLD TESTAMENT

[19] τέκνα καὶ οἰκοδομὴ πόλεως στηρίζουσιν ὄνομα,
καὶ ὑπὲρ ἀμφότερα γυνὴ ἄμωμος λογίζεται.
[20] οἶνος καὶ μουσικὰ εὐφραίνουσιν καρδίαν,
καὶ ὑπὲρ ἀμφότερα ἀγάπησις σοφίας.
[21] αὐλὸς καὶ ψαλτήριον ἡδύνουσιν μέλη,
καὶ ὑπὲρ ἀμφότερα γλῶσσα ἡδεῖα.
[22] χάριν καὶ κάλλος ἐπιθυμήσει ὀφθαλμὸς
καὶ ὑπὲρ ἀμφότερα χλόην σπόρου.
[23] φίλος καὶ ἑταῖρος εἰς καιρὸν ἀπαντῶντες,
καὶ ὑπὲρ ἀμφότερα γυνὴ μετὰ ἀνδρός.
[24] ἀδελφοὶ καὶ βοήθεια εἰς καιρὸν θλίψεως,
καὶ ὑπὲρ ἀμφότερα ἐλεημοσύνη ῥύσεται.
[25] χρυσίον καὶ ἀργύριον ἐπιστήσουσιν πόδα,
καὶ ὑπὲρ ἀμφότερα βουλὴ εὐδοκιμεῖται.
[26] χρήματα καὶ ἰσχὺς ἀνυψώσουσιν καρδίαν,
καὶ ὑπὲρ ἀμφότερα φόβος κυρίου·
οὐκ ἔστιν ἐν φόβῳ κυρίου ἐλάττωσις,
καὶ οὐκ ἔστιν ἐπιζητῆσαι ἐν αὐτῷ βοήθειαν·
[27] φόβος κυρίου ὡς παράδεισος εὐλογίας,
καὶ ὑπὲρ πᾶσαν δόξαν ἐκάλυψεν αὐτόν.
[28] Τέκνον, ζωὴν ἐπαιτήσεως μὴ βιώσῃς·
κρεῖσσον ἀποθανεῖν ἢ ἐπαιτεῖν.
[29] ἀνὴρ βλέπων εἰς τράπεζαν ἀλλοτρίαν,
οὐκ ἔστιν αὐτοῦ ὁ βίος ἐν λογισμῷ ζωῆς,

KING JAMES VERSION

19 Children and the building of a city continue a man's name: but a blameless wife is counted above them both.

20 Wine and musick rejoice the heart: but the love of wisdom is above them both.

21 The pipe and the psaltery make sweet melody: but a pleasant tongue is above them both.

22 Thine eye desireth favour and beauty: but more than both corn while it is green.

23 A friend and companion never meet amiss: but above both is a wife with her husband.

24 Brethren and help are against time of trouble: but alms shall deliver more than them both.

25 Gold and silver make the foot stand sure: but counsel is esteemed above them both.

26 Riches and strength lift up the heart: but the fear of the Lord is above them both: there is no want in the fear of the Lord, and it needeth not to seek help.

27 The fear of the Lord is a fruitful garden, and covereth him above all glory.

28 My son, lead not a beggar's life; for better it is to die than to beg.

29 The life of him that dependeth on another man's table is not to be counted for a life; for he polluteth himself with

DOUAY OLD TESTAMENT

19 Children, and the building of a city shall establish a name, but a blameless wife shall be counted above them both.

20 Wine and music rejoice the heart, but the love of wisdom is above them both.

21 The flute and the psaltery make a sweet melody, but a pleasant tongue is above them both.

22 Thy eye desireth favour and beauty, but more than these green sown fields.

23 A friend and companion meeting together in season, but above them both is a wife with her husband.

24 Brethren are a help in the time of trouble, but mercy shall deliver more than they.

25 Gold and silver make the feet stand sure: but wise counsel is above them both.

26 Riches and strength lift up the heart: but above these is the fear of the Lord.

27 There is no want in the fear of the Lord, and it needeth not to seek for help.

28 The fear of the Lord is like a paradise of blessing, and they have covered it above all glory.

29 My son, in thy lifetime be not indigent: for it is better to die than to want.

30 The life of him that looketh toward another man's table is not to be counted a life: for he feedeth his soul with another man's meat.

KNOX TRANSLATION

[19] Children born, and a city founded, will bring thee a great
name; best of all, a woman without spot. [20] Wine and music
make heart glad; best of all, the love of wisdom. [21] Flute and
harp make sweet melody; best of all a kindly tongue.
[22] Grace and beauty charm the eye; best of all, the green
wheat. [23] Friend and friend, gossip and gossip, are well met;
best of all, man and wife. [24] Kinsmen...[a] will help thee in
hard times; best of all thy alms-deeds to deliver thee. [25] Gold
and silver give thee sure vantage-ground; best of all, right
counsel. [26] Riches and strength make the heart beat high;
best of all, the fear of the Lord.
[27] Fear the Lord, lack thou shalt have none, help need
none; [28] the fear of the Lord is a garden that yields blessing...and in splendour above all splendour they have clothed
him.[b]
[29] Long as thou livest, my son, never turn beggar; die is
better than beg. [30] Look thou for thy meat to another's table,
I count thy life no life at all; what, owe thy very being to

a It seems clear that something has fallen out here; probably the original had 'Kinsmen and neighbours'. *b* The last clause of this verse does not fit on to what precedes it, either in sense or in grammar; once more, it seems likely that the text is defective.

TODAY'S ENGLISH VERSION

19 Your name can be preserved if you have children or if
you establish a city, but finding Wisdom is a better way.
Owning livestock and orchards will make you famous,[a]
but it is better to have a wife you love.[b]
20 Wine and music can make you happy, but a happy marriage[c] is even better.
21 Flutes and harps make fine music, but a pleasant voice
is better than either.
22 Gracefulness and beauty please the eye, but not as much
as new growth in the spring.
23 You can't go wrong with a good friend or neighbor, but
an intelligent wife is[d] better than either.
24 Relatives and helpers are good to have in times of trouble, but it will be an even greater help if you have made a
practice of giving to the poor.
25 Gold and silver provide security, but good advice is
better.
26 Wealth and strength give confidence, but the fear of the
Lord can give you even greater confidence. When you fear
the Lord you need nothing more; it is all the support you
need. 27 The fear of the Lord is like a rich garden of blessings; you could not want a more glorious shelter.
28 My child, don't live the life of a beggar; it is better to die
than to beg. 29 If you have to depend on someone else for
your food, you are not really living your own life. You pollute

[a] *Hebrew* but finding Wisdom . . . famous; *Greek does not have these words.* [b] *Hebrew* wife you love; *Greek* blameless wife. [c] *Hebrew* a happy marriage; *Greek* the love of Wisdom. [d] *Hebrew* an intelligent wife is; *Greek* a wife and a husband are.

NEW REVISED STANDARD VERSION

19 Children and the building of a city establish one's name,
but better than either is the one who finds wisdom.
Cattle and orchards make one prosperous;[a]
but a blameless wife is accounted better than either.
20 Wine and music gladden the heart,
but the love of friends[b] is better than either.
21 The flute and the harp make sweet melody,
but a pleasant voice is better than either.
22 The eye desires grace and beauty,
but the green shoots of grain more than either.
23 A friend or companion is always welcome,
but a sensible wife[c] is better than either.
24 Kindred and helpers are for a time of trouble,
but almsgiving rescues better than either.
25 Gold and silver make one stand firm,
but good counsel is esteemed more than either.
26 Riches and strength build up confidence,
but the fear of the Lord is better than either.
There is no want in the fear of the Lord,
and with it there is no need to seek for help.
27 The fear of the Lord is like a garden of blessing,
and covers a person better than any glory.

28 My child, do not lead the life of a beggar;
it is better to die than to beg.
29 When one looks to the table of another,
one's way of life cannot be considered a life.

a Heb Syr: Gk lacks *but better . . . prosperous* *b* Heb: Gk *wisdom* *c* Heb Compare Syr: Gk *wife with her husband*

NEW AMERICAN BIBLE

18 A child or a city will preserve one's name,
but better than either, attaining wisdom.
19 Sheepfolds and orchards bring flourishing health;
but better than either, a devoted wife;
20 Wine and music delight the soul,
but better than either, conjugal love.
21 The flute and the harp offer sweet melody,
but better than either, a voice that is true.
22 Charm and beauty delight the eye,
but better than either, the flowers of the field.
23 A friend, a neighbor, are timely guides,
but better than either, a prudent wife.
24 A brother, a helper, for times of stress;
but better than either, charity that rescues.
25 Gold and silver make one's way secure,
but better than either, sound judgment.
26 Wealth and vigor build up confidence,
but better than either, fear of God.
Fear of the LORD leaves nothing wanting;
he who has it need seek no other support:
27 The fear of God is a paradise of blessings;
its canopy, all that is glorious.

28 My son, live not the life of a beggar,
better to die than to beg;
29 When one has to look to another's table,
his life is not really a life.

NEW JERUSALEM BIBLE

19 Children and the founding of a city perpetuate a name:
more esteemed than either, a perfect wife.
20 Wine and music cheer the heart;
better than either, the love of wisdom.
21 Flute and harp add sweetness to a song;
better than either, a melodious voice.
22 The eye longs for grace and beauty;
better than either, the green of spring corn.
23 Friend or comrade—it is always well met;
better than either, a wife and husband.
24 Brothers and allies are good in times of trouble;
better than either, almsgiving to the rescue.
25 Gold and silver will steady your feet;
more esteemed than either, good advice.
26 Money and strength make a confident heart;
better than either, the fear of the Lord.
With fear of the Lord, nothing is lacking:
no need to seek for other help.
27 Fear of the Lord is a paradise of blessing,
a better protection than the highest reputation.

28 My child, do not live by sponging off others,
better be dead than be a sponger.
29 A life spent in eyeing someone else's table
cannot be accounted a life at all.

GREEK OLD TESTAMENT

ἀλισγήσει ψυχὴν αὐτοῦ ἐν ἐδέσμασιν ἀλλοτρίοις·
ἀνὴρ δὲ ἐπιστήμων καὶ πεπαιδευμένος φυλάξεται.
30 ἐν στόματι ἀναιδοῦς γλυκανθήσεται ἐπαίτησις,
καὶ ἐν κοιλίᾳ αὐτοῦ πῦρ καήσεται.

41 Ὦ θάνατε, ὡς πικρόν σου τὸ μνημόσυνόν ἐστιν
ἀνθρώπῳ εἰρηνεύοντι ἐν τοῖς ὑπάρχουσιν αὐτοῦ,
ἀνδρὶ ἀπερισπάστῳ καὶ εὐοδουμένῳ ἐν πᾶσιν
καὶ ἔτι ἰσχύοντι ἐπιδέξασθαι τροφήν.
2 ὦ θάνατε, καλόν σου τὸ κρίμα ἐστὶν
ἀνθρώπῳ ἐπιδεομένῳ καὶ ἐλασσουμένῳ ἰσχύι,
ἐσχατογήρῳ καὶ περισπωμένῳ περὶ πάντων
καὶ ἀπειθοῦντι καὶ ἀπολωλεκότι ὑπομονήν.
3 μὴ εὐλαβοῦ κρίμα θανάτου,
μνήσθητι προτέρων σου καὶ ἐσχάτων·
4 τοῦτο τὸ κρίμα παρὰ κυρίου πάσῃ σαρκί,
καὶ τί ἀπαναίνῃ ἐν εὐδοκίᾳ ὑψίστου;
εἴτε δέκα εἴτε ἑκατὸν εἴτε χίλια ἔτη,
οὐκ ἔστιν ἐν ᾅδου ἐλεγμὸς ζωῆς.
5 Τέκνα βδελυρὰ γίνεται τέκνα ἁμαρτωλῶν
καὶ συναναστρεφόμενα παροικίαις ἀσεβῶν·
6 τέκνων ἁμαρτωλῶν ἀπολεῖται κληρονομία,
καὶ μετὰ τοῦ σπέρματος αὐτῶν ἐνδελεχιεῖ ὄνειδος.
7 πατρὶ ἀσεβεῖ μέμψεται τέκνα,
ὅτι δι' αὐτὸν ὀνειδισθήσονται.

KING JAMES VERSION

other men's meat: but a wise man well nurtured will beware thereof.

30 Begging is sweet in the mouth of the shameless: but in his belly there shall burn a fire.

41 O death, how bitter is the remembrance of thee to a man that liveth at rest in his possessions, unto the man that hath nothing to vex him, and that hath prosperity in all things: yea, unto him that is yet able to receive meat!

2 O death, acceptable is thy sentence unto the needy, and unto him whose strength faileth, that is now in the last age, and is vexed with all things, and to him that despaireth, and hath lost patience!

3 Fear not the sentence of death, remember them that have been before thee, and that come after; for this is the sentence of the Lord over all flesh.

4 And why art thou against the pleasure of the most High? there is no inquisition in the grave, whether thou have lived ten, or an hundred, or a thousand years.

5 The children of sinners are abominable children, and they that are conversant in the dwelling of the ungodly.

6 The inheritance of sinners' children shall perish, and their posterity shall have a perpetual reproach.

7 The children will complain of an ungodly father, because they shall be reproached for his sake.

DOUAY OLD TESTAMENT

31 But a man, well instructed and taught, will look to himself.

32 Begging will be sweet in the mouth of the unwise, but in his belly there shall burn a fire.

41 O DEATH, how bitter is the remembrance of thee to a man that hath peace in his possessions!

2 To a man that is at rest, and whose ways are prosperous in all things, and that is yet able to take meat!

3 O death, thy sentence is welcome to the man that is in need, and to him whose strength faileth:

4 Who is in a decrepit age, and that is in care about all things, and to the distrustful that loseth patience!

5 Fear not the sentence of death. Remember what things have been before thee, and what shall come after thee: this sentence is from the Lord upon all flesh.

6 And what shall come upon thee by the good pleasure of the most High? whether ten, or a hundred, or a thousand years.

7 For among the dead there is no accusing of life.

8 The children of sinners become children of abominations, and they that converse near the houses of the ungodly.

9 The inheritance of the children of sinners shall perish, and with their posterity shall be a perpetual reproach.

10 The children will complain of an ungodly father, because for his sake they are in reproach.

KNOX TRANSLATION

another man's larder? 31 From such a chance, good teaching
and good training shall keep thee safe.
32 Poverty, on a fool's lips, will pass for a thing desirable;
but trust me, he has a fire raging within.

41 Out upon thee, death, how bitter is the thought of
thee to a man that lives at ease in his own home, 2 a
man untroubled by care, no difficulties in his path, that his
food still relishes! 3 Hail, death! Welcome is thy doom to a
man that is in need, and lacks vigour; 4 worn out with age
and full of anxieties, that has no confidence left in him, no
strength to endure. 5 Never fear death's doom; bethink thee
of the years that went before thee, and must come after thee.
One sentence the Lord has for all living things. 6 What the
will of the most High has in store for thee, none can tell;
what matter, whether it be ten years, or a hundred, or a
thousand? 7 Once thou art dead, thou wilt take no grudging
count of the years.
8 The children wicked men beget are born under a curse,
familiars of a godless home; 9 all they inherit is soon lost to
them; reproach dogs the footsteps of their posterity. 10 How
bitter their complaints against the father who is the author

Today's English Version

yourself by accepting food from another. Begging is torture
to the soul of any sensitive person.[a] 30 A shameless person
can make begging sound sweet, but something inside him
burns.

41 Death! The very thought of it is bitter to someone
who is prosperous, living peacefully with his possessions, free of worries, and still able to enjoy his food.
2 Death! Its sentence is welcome to someone living in
poverty, with failing health, very old, burdened with worries,
blind, and without hope.[b]
3 Do not be afraid of death's decree. Remember that it came
to those before you and will come to those after you. 4 The
Lord has decreed it for every living creature. Who are you to
object to what the Most High wishes? In the world of the
dead no one will care whether you lived ten years, a hundred, or a thousand.
5 The children of sinners, brought up in ungodly surround-
ings, turn out to be hateful people. 6 They will lose whatever
they inherit, and their own descendants will live in permanent disgrace. 7 The children will put the blame for their disgrace on their ungodly parents.

[a] *Hebrew* Begging . . . person; *Greek* An intelligent and understanding person will avoid it. [b] *Hebrew* blind, and without hope; *Greek* rebellious and without patience.

New Revised Standard Version

One loses self-respect with another person's food,
but one who is intelligent and well instructed guards against that.
30 In the mouth of the shameless begging is sweet,
but it kindles a fire inside him.

41 O death, how bitter is the thought of you
to the one at peace among possessions,
who has nothing to worry about and is prosperous in everything,
and still is vigorous enough to enjoy food!
2 O death, how welcome is your sentence
to one who is needy and failing in strength,
worn down by age and anxious about everything;
to one who is contrary, and has lost all patience!
3 Do not fear death's decree for you;
remember those who went before you and those who will come after.
4 This is the Lord's decree for all flesh;
why then should you reject the will of the Most High?
Whether life lasts for ten years or a hundred or a thousand,
there are no questions asked in Hades.

5 The children of sinners are abominable children,
and they frequent the haunts of the ungodly.
6 The inheritance of the children of sinners will perish,
and on their offspring will be a perpetual disgrace.
7 Children will blame an ungodly father,
for they suffer disgrace because of him.

New American Bible

His neighbor's delicacies bring revulsion of spirit
to one who understands inward feelings:
30 In the mouth of the shameless man begging is sweet,
but within him it burns like fire.

41 O death! how bitter the thought of you
for the man at peace amid his possessions,
For the man unruffled and always successful,
who still can enjoy life's pleasures.
2 O death! how welcome your sentence
to the weak man of failing strength,
Tottering and always rebuffed,
with no more sight, with vanished hope.
3 Fear not death's decree for you;
remember, it embraces those before you, and those after.
4 Thus God has ordained for all flesh;
why then should you reject the will of the Most High?
Whether one has lived a thousand years, a hundred, or ten,
in the nether world he has no claim on life.

5 A reprobate line are the children of sinners,
and witless offspring are in the homes of the wicked.
6 Their dominion is lost to sinners' children,
and reproach abides with their descendants.
7 Children curse their wicked father,
for they suffer disgrace through him.

New Jerusalem Bible

Other people's food defiles the gullet;
a wise, well-brought-up person will beware of doing this.
30 What a sponger says may sound very sweet
but in his belly there burns a fire.

41 O death, how bitter it is to remember you
for someone peacefully living with his possessions,
for someone with no worries and everything going well
and who can still enjoy his food!
2 O death, your sentence is welcome
to one in want, whose strength is failing,
to one worn out with age and a thousand worries,
resentful and impatient!
3 Do not dread death's sentence;
remember those who came before you and those who will come after.
4 This is the sentence passed on all living creatures by the Lord,
so why object to what seems good to the Most High?
Whether your life lasts ten or a hundred or a thousand years,
its length will not be held against you in Sheol.

5 Hateful brats, such are the children of sinners,
who foregather in the haunts of the godless.
6 The inheritance of sinners' children is doomed to perish,
their posterity will endure lasting reproach.
7 A godless father will be blamed by his children
for the reproach he has brought on them.

GREEK OLD TESTAMENT

8 οὐαὶ ὑμῖν, ἄνδρες ἀσεβεῖς,
οἵτινες ἐγκατελίπετε νόμον θεοῦ ὑψίστου·
9 καὶ ἐὰν γεννηθῆτε, εἰς κατάραν γεννηθήσεσθε,
καὶ ἐὰν ἀποθάνητε, εἰς κατάραν μερισθήσεσθε.
10 πάντα, ὅσα ἐκ γῆς, εἰς γῆν ἀπελεύσεται,
οὕτως ἀσεβεῖς ἀπὸ κατάρας εἰς ἀπώλειαν.
11 Πένθος ἀνθρώπων ἐν σώμασιν αὐτῶν,
ὄνομα δὲ ἁμαρτωλῶν οὐκ ἀγαθὸν ἐξαλειφθήσεται.
12 φρόντισον περὶ ὀνόματος, αὐτὸ γάρ σοι διαμενεῖ
ἢ χίλιοι μεγάλοι θησαυροὶ χρυσίου·
13 ἀγαθῆς ζωῆς ἀριθμὸς ἡμερῶν,
καὶ ἀγαθὸν ὄνομα εἰς αἰῶνα διαμενεῖ.
14 παιδείαν ἐν εἰρήνῃ συντηρήσατε, τέκνα·
σοφία δὲ κεκρυμμένη καὶ θησαυρὸς ἀφανής,
τίς ὠφέλεια ἐν ἀμφοτέροις;
15 κρείσσων ἄνθρωπος ἀποκρύπτων τὴν μωρίαν αὐτοῦ
ἢ ἄνθρωπος ἀποκρύπτων τὴν σοφίαν αὐτοῦ.
16 Τοιγαροῦν ἐντράπητε ἐπὶ τῷ ῥήματί μου·
οὐ γάρ ἐστιν πᾶσαν αἰσχύνην διαφυλάξαι καλόν,
καὶ οὐ πάντα πᾶσιν ἐν πίστει εὐδοκιμεῖται.

KING JAMES VERSION

8 Woe be unto you, ungodly men, which have forsaken the law of the most high God! for if ye increase, it shall be to your destruction:

9 And if ye be born, ye shall be born to a curse: and if ye die, a curse shall be your portion.

10 All that are of the earth shall turn to earth again: so the ungodly shall go from a curse to destruction.

11 The mourning of men is about their bodies: but an ill name of sinners shall be blotted out.

12 Have regard to thy name; for that shall continue with thee above a thousand great treasures of gold.

13 A good life hath but few days: but a good name endureth for ever.

14 My children, keep discipline in peace: for wisdom that is hid, and a treasure that is not seen, what profit is in them both?

15 A man that hideth his foolishness is better than a man that hideth his wisdom.

16 Therefore be shamefaced according to my word: for it is not good to retain all shamefacedness; neither is it altogether approved in every thing.

DOUAY OLD TESTAMENT

11 Woe to you, ungodly men, who have forsaken the law of the most high Lord.

12 And if you be born, you shall be born in malediction: and if you die, in malediction shall be your portion.

13 All things that are of the earth, shall return into the earth: so the ungodly shall from malediction to destruction.

14 The mourning of men is about their body, but the name of the ungodly shall be blotted out.

15 Take care of a good name: for this shall continue with thee, more than a thousand treasures precious and great.

16 A good life hath its number of days: but a good name shall continue for ever.

17 My children, keep discipline in peace: for wisdom that is hid, and a treasure that is not seen, what profit is there in them both?

18 Better is the man that hideth his folly, than the man that hideth his wisdom.

19 Wherefore have a shame of these things I am now going to speak of.

20 For it is not good to keep all shamefacedness: and all things do not please all men in opinion.

KNOX TRANSLATION

of their ill fame! 11 Woe to you, rebels, that have forsaken
the law of the Lord, the most High, 12 born of an unholy
birth, an unholy death your destiny! 13 All that is of earth, to
earth must needs return; from ban to bale is the cycle of a
life ill lived.
14 Man sighs over his body's loss; what of his name? The
wicked are lost to memory. 15 Of thy good name heed take
thou; it shall remain thine longer than a thousand heaps of
rare treasure. 16 Life is good, but its days are numbered; a
good name lasts for ever.
17 My sons, here is wholesome teaching.[a] Wisdom hidden,
I told you, is wasted, is treasure that never sees the light of
day; 18 silence is rightly used when it masks folly, not when
it is the grave of wisdom. 19 Yet sometimes bashfulness is no
fault, as I will now make known to you. 20 It is ill done to be
abashed on every occasion; but yet neither is self-confidence

a *vv.* 17-20: The order of the text here seems to be confused both in the Greek and in the Latin; they are here interpreted in the light of the Hebrew. The words, 'I told you', are not in the original, but there seems to be a deliberate quotation from 20. 32, 33.

TODAY'S ENGLISH VERSION

8 You are doomed, you irreligious people who have abandoned the Law of the Most High God. 9 When you have children, disaster will strike them and you will be left with nothing but sorrow. There will be great joy whenever you
stumble,[a] and even after your death you will be cursed.
10 What comes into being from nothing[b] will return to nothing;[b] so it will be with the godless, doomed to extinction.
11 A person's body amounts to nothing,[c] but a good reputation will last forever. 12 Protect your reputation; it will outlive you and last longer than a thousand treasures of gold.
13 A good life lasts only so long, but a good reputation will
last forever.
14 My children, do as I teach you and live at peace. Wisdom
that is not expressed is like a treasure that has been hidden—both are useless. 15 A person who covers up his foolishness is better than one who keeps his wisdom to himself.
16 My children, listen and I will teach you the circumstances when it is proper to be ashamed.[d] Sometimes it is
entirely out of place.

[a] *Hebrew* When you have . . . stumble; *Greek* You are born under a curse.
[b] *Hebrew* nothing; *Greek* earth. [c] *Hebrew* A person's . . . nothing; *Greek* The death of a person's body is mourned. [d] *Hebrew* My children . . . ashamed; *Greek* Show respect for what I say.

NEW REVISED STANDARD VERSION

8 Woe to you, the ungodly,
who have forsaken the law of the Most High God!
9 If you have children, calamity will be theirs;
you will beget them only for groaning.
When you stumble, there is lasting joy;[a]
and when you die, a curse is your lot.
10 Whatever comes from earth returns to earth;
so the ungodly go from curse to destruction.

11 The human body is a fleeting thing,
but a virtuous name will never be blotted out.[b]
12 Have regard for your name, since it will outlive you
longer than a thousand hoards of gold.
13 The days of a good life are numbered,
but a good name lasts forever.

14 My children, be true to your training and be at peace;
hidden wisdom and unseen treasure—
of what value is either?
15 Better are those who hide their folly
than those who hide their wisdom.
16 Therefore show respect for my words;
for it is not good to feel shame in every circumstance,
nor is every kind of abashment to be approved.[c]

[a] Heb: Meaning of Gk uncertain [b] Heb: Gk *People grieve over the death of the body, but the bad name of sinners will be blotted out* [c] Heb: Gk *and not everything is confidently esteemed by everyone*

NEW AMERICAN BIBLE

8 Woe to you, O sinful men,
who forsake the law of the Most High.
9 If you have children, calamity will seize them;
you will beget them only for groaning.
When you stumble, there is lasting joy;
at death, you become a curse.
10 Whatever is of nought returns to nought,
so too the godless from void to void.
11 Man's body is a fleeting thing,
but a virtuous name will never be annihilated.
12 Have a care for your name, for it will stand by you
better than precious treasures in the thousands;
13 The boon of life is for limited days,
but a good name, for days without number.

14 My children, heed my instruction about shame;
judge of disgrace only according to my rules,
For it is not always well to be ashamed,
nor is it always the proper thing to blush:

NEW JERUSALEM BIBLE

8 A bad outlook for you, godless people,
who have forsaken the Law of God Most High.
9 When you were born, you were born to be accursed,
and when you die, that curse will be your portion.
10 All that comes from the earth returns to the earth,[a]
so too the wicked proceed from curse to destruction.
11 Mourning concerns only the bodies of the dead,
but the worthless name of sinners will be blotted out.

12 Be careful of your reputation, for it will last you longer
than a thousand great hoards of gold.
13 A good life lasts a certain number of days,
but a good reputation lasts for ever.
14 Keep my instructions and be at peace, my children.
Wisdom[b] hidden away and treasure undisplayed,
what use is either of these?
15 Better someone who hides his folly
than one who hides his wisdom.
16 Preserve a sense of shame in the following matters,
for not every kind of shame is right to harbour,
nor is every situation correctly appraised by all.

[a] **41** =40:11. [b] **41** =20:30–31.

GREEK OLD TESTAMENT

17 αἰσχύνεσθε ἀπὸ πατρὸς καὶ μητρὸς περὶ πορνείας
καὶ ἀπὸ ἡγουμένου καὶ δυνάστου περὶ ψεύδους,
18 ἀπὸ κριτοῦ καὶ ἄρχοντος περὶ πλημμελείας
καὶ ἀπὸ συναγωγῆς καὶ λαοῦ περὶ ἀνομίας,
19 ἀπὸ κοινωνοῦ καὶ φίλου περὶ ἀδικίας
καὶ ἀπὸ τόπου, οὗ παροικεῖς, περὶ κλοπῆς,
20 ἀπὸ ἀληθείας θεοῦ καὶ διαθήκης
καὶ ἀπὸ πήξεως ἀγκῶνος ἐπ' ἄρτοις,
21 ἀπὸ σκορακισμοῦ λήμψεως καὶ δόσεως
καὶ ἀπὸ ἀσπαζομένων περὶ σιωπῆς,
22 ἀπὸ ὁράσεως γυναικὸς ἑταίρας
καὶ ἀπὸ ἀποστροφῆς προσώπου συγγενοῦς,
23 ἀπὸ ἀφαιρέσεως μερίδος καὶ δόσεως
καὶ ἀπὸ κατανοήσεως γυναικὸς ὑπάνδρου,
24 ἀπὸ περιεργίας παιδίσκης αὐτοῦ
καὶ μὴ ἐπιστῇς ἐπὶ τὴν κοίτην αὐτῆς,
25 ἀπὸ φίλων περὶ λόγων ὀνειδισμοῦ
καὶ μετὰ τὸ δοῦναι μὴ ὀνείδιζε,
26 ἀπὸ δευτερώσεως καὶ λόγου ἀκοῆς
καὶ ἀπὸ καλύψεως λόγων κρυφίων·
27 καὶ ἔσῃ αἰσχυντηρὸς ἀληθινῶς
καὶ εὑρίσκων χάριν ἔναντι παντὸς ἀνθρώπου.

42 Μὴ περὶ τούτων αἰσχυνθῇς
καὶ μὴ λάβῃς πρόσωπον τοῦ ἁμαρτάνειν·

KING JAMES VERSION

17 Be ashamed of whoredom before father and mother: and of a lie before a prince and a mighty man;

18 Of an offence before a judge and ruler; of iniquity before a congregation and people; of unjust dealing before thy partner and friend;

19 And of theft in regard of the place where thou sojournest, and in regard of the truth of God and his covenant; and to lean with thine elbow upon the meat; and of scorning to give and take;

20 And of silence before them that salute thee; and to look upon an harlot;

21 And to turn away thy face from thy kinsman; or to take away a portion or a gift; or to gaze upon another man's wife;

22 Or to be overbusy with his maid, and come not near her bed; or of upbraiding speeches before friends; and after thou hast given, upbraid not;

23 Or of iterating and speaking again that which thou hast heard; and of revealing of secrets.

24 So shalt thou be truly shamefaced, and find favour before all men.

42 Of these things be not thou ashamed, and accept no person to sin thereby:

DOUAY OLD TESTAMENT

21 Be ashamed of fornication before father and mother: and of a lie before a governor and a man in power:

22 Of an offence before a prince, and a judge: of iniquity before a congregation and a people:

23 Of injustice before a companion and friend: and in regard to the place where thou dwellest,

24 Of theft, and of the truth of God, and the covenant: of leaning with thy elbow over meat, and of deceit in giving and taking:

25 Of silence before them that salute thee: of looking upon a harlot: and of turning away thy face from thy kinsman.

26 Turn not away thy face from thy neighbour, and of taking away a portion and not restoring.

27 Gaze not upon another man's wife, and be not inquisitive after his handmaid, and approach not her bed.

28 *Be ashamed* of upbraiding speeches before friends: and after thou hast given, upbraid not.

42 REPEAT not the word which thou hast heard, and disclose not the thing that is secret; so shalt thou be truly without confusion, and shalt find favour before all men: be not ashamed of any of these things, and accept no person to sin thereby:

KNOX TRANSLATION

for all and every use. 21 Of these things, then, be ashamed;[a]
that thy parents should find thee a fornicator, ruler or prince
a liar, 22 magistrate or judge a wrong-doer, assembly of the
people a law-breaker, 23 partner or friend a knave, or thy
neighbour 24 a thief....concerning the faithfulness of God,
and his covenant; concerning thy sitting over meat...
Ashamed be thou of belittling the gift received, 25 of leaving
the greeting unreturned, of letting thy eyes stray after harlots, of denying thyself to kinsman 26 that has a near claim
on thy regard, of property fraudulently shared. 27 Let not thy
eye fall on woman wed to another, nor ever exchange secrets
with handmaid of hers, nor come between her sheets. 28 Be
ashamed of uttering reproach against thy friends, nor insult
the receiver of thy gift.

42 Nor ever do thou repeat gossip to the betraying of another's secret. If of such things thou art ashamed, shame thou shalt never feel, and thou shalt have all men's good word besides.

And other dealings there are over which thou must never be abashed,[b] nor, through respect for any human person

a *vv.* 21-28: There is further confusion here, as even the grammar of the sentences shews, and several phrases cannot be interpreted with certainty.
b *vv.* 1-8: Once more the text seems curiously confused. Verse 2 ought, judging by its form, to be a list of things we ought never to be ashamed of; 'Concerning the law of the most High, and his covenant, and acquitting the guilty' yields no tolerable sense. Verses 6, 7 look as if they had been displaced, and belonged to some quite different context. The explanation of verse 8 is perhaps to be found in Deut. 21. 18.

TODAY'S ENGLISH VERSION

17 Before your parents, be ashamed of immoral behavior.
Before a ruler or an important person, be ashamed of a lie.
18 Before a judge, be ashamed of criminal behavior.
Before a public assembly, be ashamed of breaking the law.
Before a friend or partner, be ashamed of dishonesty.
19 Before your neighbors, be ashamed of theft.
Be ashamed of breaking a promise,[a]
of leaning on the dinner table with your elbows,
of stinginess when you are asked for something,
20 of not returning a greeting,
of staring at a prostitute,
21 of turning down a relative's request,
of depriving someone of what is rightly his,
of staring at another man's wife,
22 of playing around with his slave woman (keep away from her bed!)
of insulting your friends,
of following up your gifts with criticism,
23 of betraying secrets.
These are times when it is proper for you to be ashamed, and people will respect you for it.

42 On the other hand, it is possible to sin by giving in to other people too much. Here are some things you should not be ashamed of:

[a] *Hebrew* of breaking a promise; *Greek* of yourself before the truth of God.

NEW REVISED STANDARD VERSION

17 Be ashamed of sexual immorality, before your father or mother;
and of a lie, before a prince or a ruler;
18 of a crime, before a judge or magistrate;
and of a breach of the law, before the congregation and the people;
of unjust dealing, before your partner or your friend;
19 and of theft, in the place where you live.
Be ashamed of breaking an oath or agreement,[a]
and of leaning on your elbow at meals;
of surliness in receiving or giving,
20 and of silence, before those who greet you;
of looking at a prostitute,
21 and of rejecting the appeal of a relative;
of taking away someone's portion or gift,
and of gazing at another man's wife;
22 of meddling with his servant-girl—
and do not approach her bed;
of abusive words, before friends—
and do not be insulting after making a gift.

42 Be ashamed of repeating what you hear,
and of betraying secrets.
Then you will show proper shame,
and will find favor with everyone.

Of the following things do not be ashamed,
and do not sin to save face:

[a] Heb: Gk *before the truth of God and the covenant*

NEW AMERICAN BIBLE

15 Before father and mother be ashamed of immorality,
before master and mistress, of falsehood;
16 Before prince and ruler, of flattery;
before the public assembly, of crime;
17 Before friend and companion, of disloyalty,
and of breaking an oath or agreement.
18 Be ashamed of theft from the people where you settle,
and of stretching out your elbow when you dine;
19 Of refusing to give when asked,
of defrauding another of his appointed share,
20 Of failing to return a greeting,
and of rebuffing a friend;
21 Of gazing at a married woman,
and of entertaining thoughts about another's wife;
Of trifling with a servant girl you have,
and of violating her couch;
22 Of using harsh words with friends,
and of following up your gifts with insults;
23 Of repeating what you hear,
and of betraying secrets—
24 These are the things you should rightly avoid as shameful
if you would be looked upon by everyone with favor.

42 But of these things be not ashamed,
lest you sin through human respect:

NEW JERUSALEM BIBLE

17 Be ashamed, before father and mother, of depraved behaviour,
and before prince or potentate of telling lies;
18 of wrong-doing before judge or magistrate,
and of impiety before the assembly of the people;
19 of sharp practice before your companion and your friend,
and of theft before the neighbourhood you live in.
20 Before the truth and covenant of God,
be ashamed of leaning elbows on the table,
21 of being ungracious when giving or receiving,
of ignoring those who greet you,
22 of gazing at a loose woman,
of repulsing your fellow-countryman,
23 of misappropriating another's portion or gift,
of paying court to another man's wife,
24 of making advances to his servant-girl
—do not go near her bed—
25 of saying disagreeable things to friends
—do not follow up a gift with a taunt—
26 of repeating everything you hear
and of betraying confidences.
27 Then you will know what true shame is,
and you will find yourself in everyone's graces.

42 The following things you should not be ashamed of,
and do not sin from fear of what others think:

GREEK OLD TESTAMENT

2 περὶ νόμου ὑψίστου καὶ διαθήκης
καὶ περὶ κρίματος δικαιῶσαι τὸν ἀσεβῆ,
3 περὶ λόγου κοινωνοῦ καὶ ὁδοιπόρων
καὶ περὶ δόσεως κληρονομίας ἑταίρων,
4 περὶ ἀκριβείας ζυγοῦ καὶ σταθμίων
καὶ περὶ κτήσεως πολλῶν καὶ ὀλίγων,
5 περὶ διαφόρου πράσεως ἐμπόρων
καὶ περὶ παιδείας τέκνων πολλῆς
καὶ οἰκέτῃ πονηρῷ πλευρὰν αἱμάξαι·
6 ἐπὶ γυναικὶ πονηρᾷ καλὸν σφραγίς,
καὶ ὅπου χεῖρες πολλαί, κλεῖσον·
7 ὃ ἐὰν παραδιδῷς, ἐν ἀριθμῷ καὶ σταθμῷ,
καὶ δόσις καὶ λῆμψις, πάντα ἐν γραφῇ·
8 περὶ παιδείας ἀνοήτου καὶ μωροῦ
καὶ ἐσχατογήρως κρινομένου πρὸς νέους·
καὶ ἔσῃ πεπαιδευμένος ἀληθινῶς
καὶ δεδοκιμασμένος ἔναντι παντὸς ζῶντος.
9 Θυγάτηρ πατρὶ ἀπόκρυφος ἀγρυπνία,
καὶ ἡ μέριμνα αὐτῆς ἀφιστᾷ ὕπνον·
ἐν νεότητι αὐτῆς, μήποτε παρακμάσῃ,
καὶ συνῳκηκυῖα, μήποτε μισηθῇ·
10 ἐν παρθενίᾳ, μήποτε βεβηλωθῇ
καὶ ἐν τοῖς πατρικοῖς αὐτῆς ἔγκυος γένηται·
μετὰ ἀνδρὸς οὖσα, μήποτε παραβῇ,
καὶ συνῳκηκυῖα, μήποτε στειρωθῇ.

KING JAMES VERSION

2 Of the law of the most High, and his covenant; and of judgment to justify the ungodly;

3 Of reckoning with thy partners and travellers; or of the gift of the heritage of friends;

4 Of exactness of balance and weights; or of getting much or little;

5 And of merchants' indifferent selling; of much correction of children; and to make the side of an evil servant to bleed.

6 Sure keeping is good, where an evil wife is; and shut up, where many hands are.

7 Deliver all things in number and weight; and put all in writing that thou givest out, or receivest in.

8 Be not ashamed to inform the unwise and foolish, and the extreme aged that contendeth with those that are young: thus shalt thou be truly learned, and approved of all men living.

9 The father waketh for the daughter, when no man knoweth; and the care for her taketh away sleep: when she is young, lest she pass away the flower of her age; and being married, lest she should be hated:

10 In her virginity, lest she should be defiled and gotten with child in her father's house; and having an husband, lest she should misbehave herself; and when she is married, lest she should be barren.

DOUAY OLD TESTAMENT

2 Of the law of the most High, and of his covenant, and of judgment to justify the ungodly:

3 Of the affair of companions and travellers, and of the gift of the inheritance of friends:

4 Of exactness of balance and weights, of getting much or little:

5 Of the corruption of buying, and of merchants, and of much correction of children, and to make the side of a wicked slave to bleed.

6 Sure keeping is good over a wicked wife.

7 Where there are many hands, shut up, and deliver all things in number, and weight: and put all in writing that thou givest out or receivest in.

8 Be not ashamed to inform the unwise and foolish, and the aged, that are judged by young men: and thou shalt be well instructed in all things, and well approved in the sight of all men living.

9 The father waketh for the daughter when no man knoweth, and the care for her taketh away his sleep, when she is young, lest she pass away the flower of her age, and when she is married, lest she should be hateful:

10 In her virginity, lest she should be corrupted, and be found with child in her father's house: and having a husband, lest she should misbehave herself, or at the least become barren.

KNOX TRANSLATION

consent to wrong. 2 Such are, the law of the most High and
his covenant; and right award, that gives the godless his
due; 3 a matter between some partner of thine and strangers
from far off, the apportioning of an inheritance among thy
friends, 4 the trueness of weight and balance, profit overmuch or too little, 5 the exchange between buyer and seller,
the strict punishing of children, the cudgelling of a wicked
slave till he bleeds… 6 Thriftless wife if thou hast, seal is
best. 7 Where many hands are at work, lock all away; part
with nothing, till it be measured and weighed, and of all thy
spending and receiving, written record kept… 8 Nor be thou
abashed, when there is question of chastising reckless folly,
and the complaints of old men against the young. So thou
shalt shew prudence in all thy dealings, and win the good
word of all.

9 Daughter to her father is ever hidden anxiety, a care that
banishes sleep. Is she young? Then how if age creep on too
soon? Is she wed? Then how if her husband should tire of
her? 10 Is she maid? Then how if she were disgraced, and in
her own father's house brought to bed? Once more, is she
wed? Then how if she were false to her husband? How if she

TODAY'S ENGLISH VERSION

2 the Law of the Most High and his covenant,
judging even godless people fairly,
3 sharing expenses with a business partner or a traveling
companion,
sharing an inheritance,
4 using accurate weights and measures,
5 making a profit, whether great or small,
bargaining with a merchant,
disciplining your children often,
beating a disloyal slave until the blood flows.

6 It is wise to lock things up if you cannot trust your wife
or if too many people are around. 7 Keep an accurate record
of any deposits you make or of anything you give or receive.
8 Don't hesitate to correct someone who is acting foolishly or
an old man who goes around with prostitutes. All of this is
worthwhile advice, and if you follow it, everyone will
approve of your behavior.

9 Although he will not let his daughter know it, a father
will lie awake at night worrying about her. If she is young,
he worries that she might not get married. If she is already
married, he worries about her happiness. 10 If she is a virgin,
he worries that she might be seduced and become pregnant
while living in his house. If she is married, he worries that
she might be unfaithful, or that she might not be able to
have children.

NEW REVISED STANDARD VERSION

2 Do not be ashamed of the law of the Most High and his
covenant,
and of rendering judgment to acquit the ungodly;
3 of keeping accounts with a partner or with traveling
companions,
and of dividing the inheritance of friends;
4 of accuracy with scales and weights,
and of acquiring much or little;
5 of profit from dealing with merchants,
and of frequent disciplining of children,
and of drawing blood from the back of a wicked slave.
6 Where there is an untrustworthy wife, a seal is a good
thing;
and where there are many hands, lock things up.
7 When you make a deposit, be sure it is counted and
weighed,
and when you give or receive, put it all in writing.
8 Do not be ashamed to correct the stupid or foolish
or the aged who are guilty of sexual immorality.
Then you will show your sound training,
and will be approved by all.

9 A daughter is a secret anxiety to her father,
and worry over her robs him of sleep;
when she is young, for fear she may not marry,
or if married, for fear she may be disliked;
10 while a virgin, for fear she may be seduced
and become pregnant in her father's house;
or having a husband, for fear she may go astray,
or, though married, for fear she may be barren.

NEW AMERICAN BIBLE

2 Of the law of the Most High and his precepts,
or of the sentence to be passed upon the sinful;
3 Of sharing the expenses of a business or a journey,
or of dividing an inheritance or property;
4 Of accuracy of scales and balances,
or of tested measures and weights;
5 Of acquiring much or little,
or of bargaining in dealing with a merchant;
Of constant training of children,
or of beating the sides of a disloyal servant;
6 Of a seal to keep an erring wife at home,
or of a lock placed where there are many hands;
7 Of numbering every deposit,
or of recording all that is given or received;
8 Of chastisement of the silly and the foolish,
or of the aged and infirm answering for wanton
conduct.
Thus you will be truly cautious
and recognized by all men as discreet.

9 A daughter is a treasure that keeps her father wakeful,
and worry over her drives away rest:
Lest she pass her prime unmarried,
or when she is married, lest she be disliked;
10 While unmarried, lest she be seduced,
or, as a wife, lest she prove unfaithful;
Lest she conceive in her father's home,
or be sterile in that of her husband.

NEW JERUSALEM BIBLE

2 of the Law of the Most High or of the covenant,
of a verdict that acquits the godless,
3 of keeping accounts with a travelling companion,
of settling property on your friends,
4 of being accurate over scales and weights,
of making small and large profits,
5 of gaining from commercial transactions,
of disciplining your children strictly,
of lashing a wicked slave till you draw blood.
6 With an interfering wife, it is as well to use your seal,
and where there are many hands, lock things up.
7 Whatever stores you issue, do it by number and weight,
spendings and takings, put everything in writing.
8 Do not be ashamed to correct a stupid person or a fool,
or an old dotard who bickers with young people.
Then you will show yourself really educated
and win the approval of everyone.

9 Unknown to her, a daughter keeps her father awake,
the worry she gives him drives away his sleep:
in her youth, in case she never marries,
married, in case she should be disliked,
10 as a virgin, in case she should be defiled
and found with child in her father's house,
having a husband, in case she goes astray,
married, in case she should be sterile!

GREEK OLD TESTAMENT

11 ἐπὶ θυγατρὶ ἀδιατρέπτῳ στερέωσον φυλακήν,
μήποτε ποιήσῃ σε ἐπίχαρμα ἐχθροῖς,
λαλιὰν ἐν πόλει καὶ ἔκκλητον λαοῦ,
καὶ καταισχύνῃ σε ἐν πλήθει πολλῶν.
12 παντὶ ἀνθρώπῳ μὴ ἔμβλεπε ἐν κάλλει
καὶ ἐν μέσῳ γυναικῶν μὴ συνέδρευε·
13 ἀπὸ γὰρ ἱματίων ἐκπορεύεται σὴς
καὶ ἀπὸ γυναικὸς πονηρία γυναικός.
14 κρείσσων πονηρία ἀνδρὸς ἢ ἀγαθοποιὸς γυνή,
καὶ γυνὴ καταισχύνουσα εἰς ὀνειδισμόν.
15 Μνησθήσομαι δὴ τὰ ἔργα κυρίου,
καὶ ἃ ἑόρακα, ἐκδιηγήσομαι·
ἐν λόγοις κυρίου τὰ ἔργα αὐτοῦ.
16 ἥλιος φωτίζων κατὰ πᾶν ἐπέβλεψεν,
καὶ τῆς δόξης κυρίου πλῆρες τὸ ἔργον αὐτοῦ.
17 οὐκ ἐξεποίησεν τοῖς ἁγίοις κυρίου
ἐκδιηγήσασθαι πάντα τὰ θαυμάσια αὐτοῦ,
ἃ ἐστερέωσεν κύριος ὁ παντοκράτωρ
στηριχθῆναι ἐν δόξῃ αὐτοῦ τὸ πᾶν.
18 ἄβυσσον καὶ καρδίαν ἐξίχνευσεν
καὶ ἐν πανουργεύμασιν αὐτῶν διενοήθη·

KING JAMES VERSION

11 Keep a sure watch over a shameless daughter, lest she make thee a laughingstock to thine enemies, and a byword in the city, and a reproach among the people, and make thee ashamed before the multitude.

12 Behold not every body's beauty, and sit not in the midst of women.

13 For from garments cometh a moth, and from women wickedness.

14 Better is the churlishness of a man than a courteous woman, a woman, *I say,* which bringeth shame and reproach.

15 I will now remember the works of the Lord, and declare the things that I have seen: In the words of the Lord are his works.

16 The sun that giveth light looketh upon all things, and the work thereof *is* full of the glory of the Lord.

17 The Lord hath not given power to the saints to declare all his marvellous works, which the Almighty Lord firmly settled, that whatsoever is might be established for his glory.

18 He seeketh out the deep, and the heart, and considereth

DOUAY OLD TESTAMENT

11 Keep a sure watch over a shameless daughter: lest at any time she make thee become a laughingstock to thy enemies, and a byword in the city, and a reproach among the people, and she make thee ashamed before all the multitude.

12 Behold not everybody's beauty: and tarry not among women.

13 For from garments cometh a moth, and from a woman the iniquity of a man.

14 For better is the iniquity of a man, than a woman doing a good turn, and a woman bringing shame and reproach.

15 I will now remember the works of the Lord, and I will declare the things I have seen. By the words of the Lord are his works.

16 The sun giving light hath looked upon all things, and full of the glory of the Lord is his work.

17 Hath not the Lord made the saints to declare all his wonderful works, which the Lord Almighty hath firmly settled to be established for his glory?

18 He hath searched out the deep, and the heart of men: and considered their crafty devices.

KNOX TRANSLATION

prove barren? 11 Over wanton daughter of thine thou canst
not keep watch too strict; else she will make thee the scorn
of thy enemies, the talk of the city; strangers will point the
finger at thee, and all the rabble know thy shame. 12 Gaze
not on the beauty of human kind, nor occupy thyself much
with women; 13 garment breeds moth, and woman wickedness in man. 14 Man's wickedness is too strong for woman
at her best;[a] and a woman that plays thee false brings thee
only disgrace.
15 Recount we now what things the Lord has made; his visible creation be our theme; nothing he has fashioned but
hangs on his word. 16 Just as yonder sun that looks down on
all gives light to all, so the glory of the Lord shines through
all his creation; 17 how should his faithful servants herald
them enough, these marvels of his, enabled by divine
omnipotence in that glory to endure? 18 Nothing is hidden
from him, the deepest depths of earth or of man's heart; he
knows our most secret designs. 19 All knowledge is his; does

a The Greek is just patient of the rendering given above; but the natural sense of all the versions is 'Man's wickedness is better than a woman who does good'—a sentiment which could have little meaning, even in the mouth of the most determined cynic. Probably the true text is lost in this passage; the Greek in verse 13 has 'wickedness in woman', and the Hebrew in verse 12 has 'let her not shew her beauty to male eyes'.

TODAY'S ENGLISH VERSION

11 Keep a close watch over your daughter if she is determined to have her own way. If you don't, she may make a
fool of you in front of your enemies. You will be a constant
joke to everyone in town, a public disgrace. Make sure that
her room has no windows or any place where she can look
out to the entrance of the house.[a] 12 Don't let her show off
her beauty in front of men, or spend her time talking with
the women.[b] 13 Women hurt other women just as moths
damage clothing.

14 A man's wickedness is better than a woman's goodness;
women bring shame and disgrace.

15 Now I will remind you of the works of the Lord
and describe the things I have seen.
The words of the Lord brought his works into being,
and the whole creation obeys his commands.
16 The light of the sun shines down on everything,
and everything is filled with the Lord's glory.
17 Not even to his holy angels has the Lord given power
to describe all his mighty deeds,
even though he has given them power
to stand unharmed in his glorious presence.[c]
18 He sees into the oceans and into the human heart,
and he knows the secrets of both.

[a] *Hebrew* Make sure . . . house; *Greek does not have these words.*
[b] *Hebrew* Don't let . . . women; *Greek unclear.* [c] *Hebrew* even though . . . presence; *Greek* which the Lord Almighty established so that everything may stand firm in his glory.

NEW REVISED STANDARD VERSION

11 Keep strict watch over a headstrong daughter,
or she may make you a laughingstock to your enemies,
a byword in the city and the assembly of[a] the people,
and put you to shame in public gatherings.[b]
See that there is no lattice in her room,
no spot that overlooks the approaches to the house.[c]
12 Do not let her parade her beauty before any man,
or spend her time among married women;[a]
13 for from garments comes the moth,
and from a woman comes woman's wickedness.
14 Better is the wickedness of a man than a woman who
does good;
it is woman who brings shame and disgrace.

15 I will now call to mind the works of the Lord,
and will declare what I have seen.
By the word of the Lord his works are made;
and all his creatures do his will.[d]
16 The sun looks down on everything with its light,
and the work of the Lord is full of his glory.
17 The Lord has not empowered even his holy ones
to recount all his marvelous works,
which the Lord the Almighty has established
so that the universe may stand firm in his glory.
18 He searches out the abyss and the human heart;
he understands their innermost secrets.

a Heb: Meaning of Gk uncertain *b* Heb: Gk *to shame before the great multitude* *c* Heb: Gk lacks *See . . . house* *d* Syr Compare Heb: most Gk witnesses lack *and all . . . will*

NEW AMERICAN BIBLE

11 Keep a close watch on your daughter,
lest she make you the sport of your enemies,
A byword in the city, a reproach among the people,
an object of derision in public gatherings.
See that there is no lattice in her room,
no place that overlooks the approaches to the house.
12 Let her not parade her charms before men,
or spend her time with married women;
13 For just as moths come from garments,
so harm to women comes from women:
14 Better a man's harshness than a woman's indulgence,
and a frightened daughter than any disgrace.

15 Now will I recall God's works;
what I have seen, I will describe.
At God's word were his works brought into being;
they do his will as he has ordained for them.
16 As the rising sun is clear to all,
so the glory of the LORD fills all his works;
17 Yet even God's holy ones must fail
in recounting the wonders of the LORD,
Though God has given these, his hosts, the strength
to stand firm before his glory.
18 He plumbs the depths and penetrates the heart;
their innermost being he understands.

NEW JERUSALEM BIBLE

11 Your daughter is headstrong? Keep a sharp look-out
that she does not make you the laughing-stock of
your enemies,
the talk of the town, the object of common gossip,
and put you to public shame.
12 Do not stare at any man for his good looks,
do not sit down with women;
13 for moth comes out of clothes,
and woman's spite out of woman.
14 Better a man's spite than a woman's kindness:
women give rise to shame and reproach.

15 Next, I shall remind you of the works of the Lord,
and tell of what I have seen.
By the words of the Lord his works come into being
and all creation obeys his will.
16 The shining sun looks down on all things,
and the work of the Lord is full of his glory.
17 The Lord has not granted the Holy Ones the power
to tell of all his marvels
which the Almighty Lord has solidly constructed
for the universe to stand firm in his glory.
18 He has fathomed both the abyss and the human heart
and seen into their devious ways;

GREEK OLD TESTAMENT

ἔγνω γὰρ ὁ ὕψιστος πᾶσαν εἴδησιν
καὶ ἐνέβλεψεν εἰς σημεῖον αἰῶνος
19 ἀπαγγέλλων τὰ παρεληλυθότα καὶ τὰ ἐσόμενα
καὶ ἀποκαλύπτων ἴχνη ἀποκρύφων·
20 οὐ παρῆλθεν αὐτὸν πᾶν διανόημα,
οὐκ ἐκρύβη ἀπ᾽ αὐτοῦ οὐδὲ εἷς λόγος.
21 τὰ μεγαλεῖα τῆς σοφίας αὐτοῦ ἐκόσμησεν,
ὡς ἔστιν πρὸ τοῦ αἰῶνος καὶ εἰς τὸν αἰῶνα·
οὔτε προσετέθη οὔτε ἠλαττώθη,
καὶ οὐ προσεδεήθη οὐδενὸς συμβούλου.
22 ὡς πάντα τὰ ἔργα αὐτοῦ ἐπιθυμητὰ
καὶ ὡς σπινθῆρός ἐστιν θεωρῆσαι·
23 πάντα ταῦτα ζῇ καὶ μένει εἰς τὸν αἰῶνα
ἐν πάσαις χρείαις, καὶ πάντα ὑπακούει.
24 πάντα δισσά, ἓν κατέναντι τοῦ ἑνός,
καὶ οὐκ ἐποίησεν οὐδὲν ἐλλεῖπον·
25 ἓν τοῦ ἑνὸς ἐστερέωσεν τὰ ἀγαθά,
καὶ τίς πλησθήσεται ὁρῶν δόξαν αὐτοῦ;

43 Γαυρίαμα ὕψους στερέωμα καθαριότητος,
εἶδος οὐρανοῦ ἐν ὁράματι δόξης.
2 ἥλιος ἐν ὀπτασίᾳ διαγγέλλων ἐν ἐξόδῳ
σκεῦος θαυμαστόν, ἔργον ὑψίστου·
3 ἐν μεσημβρίᾳ αὐτοῦ ἀναξηραίνει χώραν,
καὶ ἐναντίον καύματος αὐτοῦ τίς ὑποστήσεται;

KING JAMES VERSION

their crafty devices: for the Lord knoweth all that may be known, and he beholdeth the signs of the world.

19 He declareth the things that are past, and for to come, and revealeth the steps of hidden things.

20 No thought escapeth him, neither any word is hidden from him.

21 He hath garnished the excellent works of his wisdom, and he is from everlasting to everlasting: unto him may nothing be added, neither can he be diminished, and he hath no need of any counsellor.

22 Oh how desirable are all his works! and that a man may see even to a spark.

23 All these things live and remain for ever for all uses, and they are all obedient.

24 All things are double one against another: and he hath made nothing imperfect.

25 One thing establisheth the good of another: and who shall be filled with beholding his glory?

43 The pride of the height, the clear firmament, the beauty of heaven, with his glorious shew;

2 The sun when it appeareth, declaring at his rising a marvellous instrument, the work of the most High:

3 At noon it parcheth the country, and who can abide the burning heat thereof?

DOUAY OLD TESTAMENT

19 For the Lord knoweth all knowledge, and hath beheld the signs of the world, he declareth the things that are past, and the things that are to come, and revealeth the traces of hidden things.

20 No thought escapeth him, and no word can hide itself from him.

21 He hath beautified the glorious works of his wisdom: and he is from eternity to eternity, and to him nothing may be added,

22 Nor can he be diminished, and he hath no need of any counsellor.

23 O how desirable are all his works, and what we can know is *but* as a spark!

24 All these things live, and remain for ever, and for every use all things obey him.

25 All things are double, one against another, and he hath made nothing defective.

26 He hath established the good things of every one. And who shall be filled with beholding his glory?

43 THE firmament on high is his beauty, the beauty of heaven with its glorious shew.

2 The sun when he appeareth shewing forth at his rising, an admirable instrument, the work of the most High.

3 At noon he burneth the earth, and who can abide his burning heat? *As* one keeping a furnace in the works of heat:

KNOX TRANSLATION

he not hold the clue of eternity, making plain what has been
and what is yet to be, laying bare the track of hidden things?
20 No thought of ours escapes him, never a whisper goes
unheard. 21 How great the wisdom that so ordered all things,
his wisdom who has neither beginning nor end; nothing may
be added, 22 nothing taken away from them, nor needs he
any man's counsel. 23 How lovely is all he has made, how
dazzling to look upon![a] 24 Changeless through the ages, all
of it lives on, responsive to his calls. 25 All things he has
made in pairs, balanced against one another; never a fault of
symmetry;[b] 26 to each one its own well-being assured. His
glory contemplating, thou shalt never have thy fill.
43 Like a jewel the vault of heaven is set above us; the
sight of it is glory made visible. 2 Plain to our view is
the sun's passage as it shines out, a very masterpiece of his
workmanship, who is the most High. 3 How it burns up the
earth at noon-day! How fierce its glow, beyond all
endurance! Tend thou the furnace, heat is thy daily portion;

a Literally, 'and like a spark which is to consider'; the Greek is hardly more intelligible. *b* Cf. 33. 15.

TODAY'S ENGLISH VERSION

The Most High knows everything that can be known
and understands the signs of the ages.
19 He knows all that has ever been and all that ever
will be;
he uncovers the deepest of mysteries.
20 He takes notice of our every thought
and hears our every word.
21 The orderly world shows the greatness of his wisdom;
he is the same forever and ever.[a]
Nothing can be added to him, and nothing taken away;
he needs no one to give him advice.
22 All his works are beautiful,
down to the smallest and faintest spark of light.[b]
23 All these things go on forever,
and all of them have their purpose.
24 All things are in pairs, each the opposite of the other,
but nothing the Lord made is incomplete.
25 Everything completes the goodness of something else.
Could anyone ever see enough of this splendor?

43 How beautiful is the bright, clear sky above us!
What a glorious sight it is!
2 The sun, when it appears, proclaims as it rises
how marvelous a thing it is, made by the Most High.
3 At noon it dries up the land;
no one can stand its blazing heat.

[a] *Hebrew* he is . . . ever; *Greek* he is before eternity and is eternal.
[b] *Hebrew* down to . . . spark of light; *Greek unclear.*

NEW REVISED STANDARD VERSION

For the Most High knows all that may be known;
he sees from of old the things that are to come.[a]
19 He discloses what has been and what is to be,
and he reveals the traces of hidden things.
20 No thought escapes him,
and nothing is hidden from him.
21 He has set in order the splendors of his wisdom;
he is from all eternity one and the same.
Nothing can be added or taken away,
and he needs no one to be his counselor.
22 How desirable are all his works,
and how sparkling they are to see![b]
23 All these things live and remain forever;
each creature is preserved to meet a particular need.[c]
24 All things come in pairs, one opposite the other,
and he has made nothing incomplete.
25 Each supplements the virtues of the other.
Who could ever tire of seeing his glory?

43 The pride of the higher realms is the clear vault of
the sky,
as glorious to behold as the sight of the heavens.
2 The sun, when it appears, proclaims as it rises
what a marvelous instrument it is, the work of the
Most High.
3 At noon it parches the land,
and who can withstand its burning heat?

a Heb: Gk *he sees the sign(s) of the age* b Meaning of Gk uncertain
c Heb: Gk *forever for every need, and all are obedient*

NEW AMERICAN BIBLE

The Most High possesses all knowledge,
and sees from of old the things that are to come:
19 He makes known the past and the future,
and reveals the deepest secrets.
20 No understanding does he lack;
no single thing escapes him.
21 Perennial is his almighty wisdom;
he is from all eternity one and the same,
22 With nothing added, nothing taken away;
no need of a counselor for him!
23 How beautiful are all his works!
even to the spark and fleeting vision!
24 The universe lives and abides forever;
to meet each need, each creature is preserved.
25 All of them differ, one from another,
yet none of them has he made in vain,
For each in turn, as it comes, is good;
can one ever see enough of their splendor?

43 The clear vault of the sky shines forth
like heaven itself, a vision of glory.
2 The orb of the sun, resplendent at its rising:
what a wonderful work of the Most High!
3 At noon it seethes the surface of the earth,
and who can bear its fiery heat?

NEW JERUSALEM BIBLE

for the Most High knows all there is to know
and sees the signs of the times.
19 He declares what is past and what will be,
and reveals the trend of hidden things.
20 Not a thought escapes him,
not a single word is hidden from him.
21 He has embellished the magnificent works of his
wisdom,
he is from everlasting to everlasting,
nothing can be added to him, nothing taken away,
he needs no one's advice.
22 How lovely, all his works,
how dazzling to the eye!
23 They all live and last for ever,
and, whatever the circumstances, all obey.
24 All things go in pairs, by opposites,
he has not made anything imperfect:
25 one thing complements the excellence of another.
Who could ever grow tired of gazing at his glory?

43 Pride of the heights, a clear vault of the sky—
such is the beauty of the heavens, a glorious sight.
2 The sun, as he emerges, proclaims at his rising,
'How wonderful a thing, the work of the Most High!'
3 At his zenith, he parches the ground,
who can withstand his blaze?

GREEK OLD TESTAMENT

4 κάμινον φυσῶν ἐν ἔργοις καύματος,
τριπλασίως ἥλιος ἐκκαίων ὄρη·
ἀτμίδας πυρώδεις ἐκφυσῶν
καὶ ἐκλάμπων ἀκτῖνας ἀμαυροῖ ὀφθαλμούς.
5 μέγας κύριος ὁ ποιήσας αὐτόν,
καὶ ἐν λόγοις αὐτοῦ κατέσπευσεν πορείαν.
6 Καὶ ἡ σελήνη ἐν πᾶσιν εἰς καιρὸν αὐτῆς,
ἀνάδειξιν χρόνων καὶ σημεῖον αἰῶνος·
7 ἀπὸ σελήνης σημεῖον ἑορτῆς,
φωστὴρ μειούμενος ἐπὶ συντελείας.
8 μὴν κατὰ τὸ ὄνομα αὐτῆς ἐστιν
αὐξανόμενος θαυμαστῶς ἐν ἀλλοιώσει,
σκεῦος παρεμβολῶν ἐν ὕψει,
ἐν στερεώματι οὐρανοῦ ἐκλάμπων.
9 κάλλος οὐρανοῦ δόξα ἄστρων,
κόσμος φωτίζων ἐν ὑψίστοις κυρίου·
10 ἐν λόγοις ἁγίου στήσονται κατὰ κρίμα
καὶ οὐ μὴ ἐκλυθῶσιν ἐν φυλακαῖς αὐτῶν.
11 ἰδὲ τόξον καὶ εὐλόγησον τὸν ποιήσαντα αὐτὸ
σφόδρα ὡραῖον ἐν τῷ αὐγάσματι αὐτοῦ·
12 ἐγύρωσεν οὐρανὸν ἐν κυκλώσει δόξης,
χεῖρες ὑψίστου ἐτάνυσαν αὐτό.

KING JAMES VERSION

4 A man blowing a furnace is in works of heat, but the sun burneth the mountains three times more; breathing out fiery vapours, and sending forth bright beams, it dimmeth the eyes.

5 Great is the Lord that made it; and at his commandment it runneth hastily.

6 He made the moon also to serve in her season for a declaration of times, and a sign of the world.

7 From the moon is the sign of feasts, a light that decreaseth in her perfection.

8 The month is called after her name, increasing wonderfully in her changing, being an instrument of the armies above, shining in the firmament of heaven;

9 The beauty of heaven, the glory of the stars, an ornament giving light in the highest places of the Lord.

10 At the commandment of the Holy One they will stand in their order, and never faint in their watches.

11 Look upon the rainbow, and praise him that made it; very beautiful it is in the brightness thereof.

12 It compasseth the heaven about with a glorious circle, and the hands of the most High have bended it.

DOUAY OLD TESTAMENT

4 The sun three times as much, burneth the mountains, breathing out fiery vapours, and shining with his beams, he blindeth the eyes.

5 Great is the Lord that made him, and at his words he hath hastened his course.

6 And the moon in all in her season, is for a declaration of times and a sign of the world.

7 From the moon is the sign of the festival day, a light that decreaseth in her perfection.

8 The month is called after her name, increasing wonderfully in her perfection.

9 Being an instrument of the armies on high, shining gloriously in the firmament of heaven.

10 The glory of the stars is the beauty of heaven; the Lord enlighteneth the world on high.

11 By the words of the holy one they shall stand in judgment, and shall never fail in their watches.

12 Look upon the rainbow, and bless him that made it: it is very beautiful in its brightness.

13 It encompasseth the heaven about with the circle of its glory, the hands of the most High have displayed it.

KNOX TRANSLATION

4 yet three times hotter the sun, as it burns up the hill-side,
scorching all with its fiery breath, blinding men's eyes with
its glare. 5 Swiftly it speeds on its course, to do the bidding
of the Lord, its glorious maker. 6 The moon, too, that keeps
tryst so faithfully, ever marking how the seasons change,
7 and giving the signal when feast days come round! The
moon, whose light must decrease till it vanishes, 8 and then
increase to the full circle, the month its name-child; 9 cresset
of a watch-fire that lights up the high vault of heaven with
its radiant glow. 10 And the stars that deck the sky with their
splendour, a beacon-light the Lord kindles high above us;
11 the summons of his holy word answering so loyally,
watching so patiently at their post!
12 Look up at the rainbow, and bless the maker of it; how
fair are those bright colours 13 that span heaven with a ring
of splendour, traced by an almighty hand. 14 Swift comes the

TODAY'S ENGLISH VERSION

4 The setting sun sets fire to the hilltops,
like a metal furnace glowing from the heat.[a]
It sends out fiery rays,
blinding the eyes with its brightness.
5 The Lord, who made it, is great;
it speeds on its way at his command.

6 There is also the moon, marking the passage of time,[b]
an eternal sign of the changing seasons.
7 The moon determines the holy days.
Its light grows full and then grows dim.
8 The "month" is named after the moon,
marvelous to watch as it grows fuller each night,
a signal light for the heavenly armies,
shining out in the dome of the sky.

9 The shining stars make the night sky lovely,
brilliant ornaments in the Lord's high heavens.
10 They stay in the places assigned to them by the
Holy One
and never relax their dutiful watch.

11 Look at the rainbow and praise its Creator!
How magnificent, how radiant, its beauty!
12 Like a bow bent by the hands of the Most High,
it spans the horizon in a circle of glory.

[a] *Hebrew* The setting . . . heat; *Greek* A man at a furnace works with scorching heat, but the sun burns the hills three times as much.
[b] *Hebrew* marking . . . time; *Greek unclear.*

NEW REVISED STANDARD VERSION

4 A man tending[a] a furnace works in burning heat,
but three times as hot is the sun scorching the
mountains;
it breathes out fiery vapors,
and its bright rays blind the eyes.
5 Great is the Lord who made it;
at his orders it hurries on its course.

6 It is the moon that marks the changing seasons,[b]
governing the times, their everlasting sign.
7 From the moon comes the sign for festal days,
a light that wanes when it completes its course.
8 The new moon, as its name suggests, renews itself;[c]
how marvelous it is in this change,
a beacon to the hosts on high,
shining in the vault of the heavens!

9 The glory of the stars is the beauty of heaven,
a glittering array in the heights of the Lord.
10 On the orders of the Holy One they stand in their
appointed places;
they never relax in their watches.
11 Look at the rainbow, and praise him who made it;
it is exceedingly beautiful in its brightness.
12 It encircles the sky with its glorious arc;
the hands of the Most High have stretched it out.

a Other ancient authorities read *blowing upon* *b* Heb: Meaning of Gk uncertain *c* Heb: Gk *The month is named after the moon*

NEW AMERICAN BIBLE

4 Like a blazing furnace of solid metal,
it sets the mountains aflame with its rays;
By its fiery darts the land is consumed;
the eyes are dazzled by its light.
5 Great indeed is the LORD who made it,
at whose orders it urges on its steeds.
6 The moon, too, that marks the changing times,
governing the seasons, their lasting sign,
7 By which we know the feast days and fixed dates,
this light-giver which wanes in its course:
8 As its name says, each month it renews itself;
how wondrous in this change!
9 The beauty, the glory, of the heavens are the stars
that adorn with their sparkling the heights of God,
10 At whose command they keep their place
and never relax in their vigils.
A weapon against the flood waters stored on high,
lighting up the firmament by its brilliance,
11 Behold the rainbow! Then bless its Maker,
for majestic indeed is its splendor;
12 It spans the heavens with its glory,
this bow bent by the mighty hand of God.

NEW JERUSALEM BIBLE

4 We have to blow the furnace to produce any heat,
the sun burns the mountains three times as much;
breathing out blasts of fire,
flashing his rays, he dazzles the eyes.
5 Great is the Lord who created him
and whose word speeds him on his course.

6 And then the moon, ever punctual
to mark the times, an everlasting sign:
7 It is the moon that signals the feasts,
a luminary that wanes after being full.
8 The month derives its name from hers,
she waxes wonderfully in her phases,
banner of the hosts on high,
shining in the vault of heaven.

9 The glory of the stars makes the beauty of the sky,
a brilliant adornment of the Lord on High.
10 At the words of the Holy One they stand as he decrees,
and never grow slack at their watch.
11 See the rainbow and praise its Maker,
so superbly beautiful in its splendour.
12 Across the sky it forms a glorious arc
drawn by the hands of the Most High.

GREEK OLD TESTAMENT

13 Προστάγματι αὐτοῦ κατέσπευσεν χιόνα
καὶ ταχύνει ἀστραπὰς κρίματος αὐτοῦ·
14 διὰ τοῦτο ἠνεῴχθησαν θησαυροί,
καὶ ἐξέπτησαν νεφέλαι ὡς πετεινά·
15 ἐν μεγαλείῳ αὐτοῦ ἴσχυσεν νεφέλας,
καὶ διεθρύβησαν λίθοι χαλάζης·
16 καὶ ἐν ὀπτασίᾳ αὐτοῦ σαλευθήσεται ὄρη,
ἐν θελήματι αὐτοῦ πνεύσεται νότος.
17 φωνὴ βροντῆς αὐτοῦ ὠνείδισεν γῆν
καὶ καταιγὶς βορέου καὶ συστροφὴ πνεύματος.
18 ὡς πετεινὰ καθιπτάμενα πάσσει χιόνα,
καὶ ὡς ἀκρὶς καταλύουσα ἡ κατάβασις αὐτῆς·
κάλλος λευκότητος αὐτῆς ἐκθαυμάσει ὀφθαλμός,
καὶ ἐπὶ τοῦ ὑετοῦ αὐτῆς ἐκστήσεται καρδία.
19 καὶ πάχνην ὡς ἅλα ἐπὶ γῆς χέει,
καὶ παγεῖσα γίνεται σκολόπων ἄκρα.
20 ψυχρὸς ἄνεμος βορέης πνεύσει,
καὶ παγήσεται κρύσταλλος ἐφ᾽ ὕδατος·
ἐπὶ πᾶσαν συναγωγὴν ὕδατος καταλύσει,
καὶ ὡς θώρακα ἐνδύσεται τὸ ὕδωρ.
21 καταφάγεται ὄρη καὶ ἔρημον ἐκκαύσει
καὶ ἀποσβέσει χλόην ὡς πῦρ.
22 ἴασις πάντων κατὰ σπουδὴν ὁμίχλη,
δρόσος ἀπαντῶσα ἀπὸ καύσωνος ἱλαρώσει.
23 Λογισμῷ αὐτοῦ ἐκόπασεν ἄβυσσον
καὶ ἐφύτευσεν ἐν αὐτῇ νήσους.

KING JAMES VERSION

13 By his commandment he maketh the snow to fall apace, and sendeth swiftly the lightnings of his judgment.

14 Through this the treasures are opened: and clouds fly forth as fowls.

15 By his great power he maketh the clouds firm, and the hailstones are broken small.

16 At his sight the mountains are shaken, and at his will the south wind bloweth.

17 The noise of the thunder maketh the earth to tremble: so doth the northern storm and the whirlwind: as birds flying he scattereth the snow, and the falling down thereof is as the lighting of grasshoppers:

18 The eye marvelleth at the beauty of the whiteness thereof, and the heart is astonished at the raining of it.

19 The hoarfrost also as salt he poureth on the earth, and being congealed, it lieth on the top of sharp stakes.

20 When the cold north wind bloweth, and the water is congealed into ice, it abideth upon every gathering together of water, and clotheth the water as with a breastplate.

21 It devoureth the mountains, and burneth the wilderness, and consumeth the grass as fire.

22 A present remedy of all is a mist *coming speedily:* a dew coming after heat refresheth.

23 By his counsel he appeaseth the deep, and planteth islands therein.

DOUAY OLD TESTAMENT

14 By his commandment he maketh the snow to fall apace, and sendeth forth swiftly the lightnings of his judgment.

15 Through this are the treasures opened, and the clouds fly out like birds.

16 By his greatness he hath fixed the clouds, and the hailstones are broken.

17 At his sight shall the mountains be shaken, and at his will the south wind shall blow.

18 The noise of his thunder shall strike the earth, *so doth* the northern storm, and the whirlwind:

19 And as the birds lighting upon the earth, he scattereth snow, and the falling thereof, is as the coming down of locusts.

20 The eye admireth at the beauty of the whiteness thereof, and the heart is astonished at the shower thereof.

21 He shall pour frost as salt upon the earth: and when it freezeth, it shall become like the tops of thistles.

22 The cold north wind bloweth, and the water is congealed into crystal; upon every gathering together of waters it shall rest, and shall clothe the waters as a breastplate.

23 And it shall devour the mountains, and burn the wilderness, and consume all that is green as with fire.

24 A present remedy of all is the speedy coming of a cloud, and a dew that meeteth it, by the heat that cometh, shall overpower it.

25 At his word the wind is still, and with his thought he appeaseth the deep, and the Lord hath planted islands therein.

KNOX TRANSLATION

snow at his word, swift flashes the fire that executes his
vengeance; 15 he has but to unlock his store-house, and the
clouds hover, bird-fashion, 16 arsenals of his might, whence
the pounded hail-stones fall. 17 How his glance makes the
hills tremble! Blows the south wind at his bidding, 18 earth
echoes with the crash of his thunder; blows the north wind,
and there is whirling storm. 19 Soft as roosting bird falls the
snow, spread all around; not more silently comes locust-
swarm to earth; 20 what eye is but captivated by its pale
beauty, what heart but is filled with terror at the dark cloud
that brings it? 21 He it is pours out the frost, that lies white
as salt on the earth, the frozen earth that seems covered with
thistle-down.

22 Cold blows the north wind, and ice forms on the water;
no pool but it rests there, arming the water as with a breastplate; 23 frost gnaws at the mountain-side, parches the open
plains, strips them, as fire might have stripped them, of their
green. 24 Remedy for all these is none, but the speedy coming of the mist; frost shall be overmastered by the showers
the sirocco drives before it,[a] 25 and at the Lord's word the
chill blast dies away.

What else but divine wisdom tamed the rising of the seas,[b]
and planted the islands there? 26 Hear we what perils in the

a vv. 23, 24: It is possible, both in the Greek and in the Hebrew, to interpret verse 23 as referring to drought, with Almighty God himself as the subject of the sentence; verse 25 will then mean that the showers save the grass from the effects of the sirocco. *b* Literally, 'pacified the abyss', but it seems clear that the reference is to Gen. 1. 9 and kindred passages.

TODAY'S ENGLISH VERSION

13 He commands, and snow begins to fall;
lightning strikes to carry out his judgments.
14 The storerooms of the sky are thrown open,
and the clouds roll out like flying birds.
15 With his power he forms great masses of clouds
and shatters the ice into hailstones.
16-17 He speaks, and thunder twists the earth in pain;
the mountains are shaken by his strength.[a]
Whenever he wishes, the south wind blows,
whirlwinds come, and windstorms from the north.
He sends the snow fluttering down like birds,
like locusts lighting on the ground.
18 We marvel at its beautiful whiteness,
and in fascination we watch it fall.
19 He sprinkles frost over the ground like salt,
and it freezes into thorny flowers of ice.[b]
20 He sends the cold north wind blowing
and the water hardens into ice;
every lake and pond freezes over,
putting on a coat of icy armor.
21 He scorches the wilderness hills with drought,
and the grass turns brown from its heat;
22 but a cloudy mist restores it all to life
as the weather cools and dew appears.

23 By his wisdom he calmed the great oceans
and placed the islands there.

[a] *Hebrew* by his strength; *Greek* when he appears. [b] *Hebrew* flowers of ice; *Greek* points.

NEW REVISED STANDARD VERSION

13 By his command he sends the driving snow
and speeds the lightnings of his judgment.
14 Therefore the storehouses are opened,
and the clouds fly out like birds.
15 In his majesty he gives the clouds their strength,
and the hailstones are broken in pieces.
17a The voice of his thunder rebukes the earth;
16 when he appears, the mountains shake.
At his will the south wind blows;
17b so do the storm from the north and the whirlwind.
He scatters the snow like birds flying down,
and its descent is like locusts alighting.
18 The eye is dazzled by the beauty of its whiteness,
and the mind is amazed as it falls.
19 He pours frost over the earth like salt,
and icicles form like pointed thorns.
20 The cold north wind blows,
and ice freezes on the water;
it settles on every pool of water,
and the water puts it on like a breastplate.
21 He consumes the mountains and burns up the
wilderness,
and withers the tender grass like fire.
22 A mist quickly heals all things;
the falling dew gives refreshment from the heat.

23 By his plan he stilled the deep
and planted islands in it.

NEW AMERICAN BIBLE

13 His rebuke marks out the path for the lightning,
and speeds the arrows of his judgment to their goal.
14 At it the storehouse is opened,
and like vultures the clouds hurry forth.
15 In his majesty he gives the storm its power
and breaks off the hailstones.
16 The thunder of his voice makes the earth writhe;
before his might the mountains quake.
17 A word from him drives on the south wind,
the angry north wind, the hurricane and the storm.
18 He sprinkles the snow like fluttering birds;
it comes to settle like swarms of locusts.
19 Its shining whiteness blinds the eyes,
the mind is baffled by its steady fall.
20 He scatters frost like so much salt;
it shines like blossoms on the thornbush.
21 Cold northern blasts he sends
that turn the ponds to lumps of ice.
He freezes over every body of water,
and clothes each pool with a coat of mail.
22 When the mountain growth is scorched with heat,
and the flowering plains as though by flames,
23 The dripping clouds restore them all,
and the scattered dew enriches the parched land.
24 His is the plan that calms the deep,
and plants the islands in the sea.

NEW JERUSALEM BIBLE

13 By his command he sends the snow,
he speeds the lightning by his command.
14 In the same way, his treasuries open
and the clouds fly out like birds.
15 His great power solidifies the clouds,
then pulverises them into hail.
17a At the roar of his thunder, the earth writhes in labour,
16 at the sight of him, the mountains quake.
At his will the south wind blows,
17b or the storm from the north and the whirlwind.
18 He sprinkles snow like birds alighting,
it comes down like locusts settling.
The eye marvels at the beauty of its whiteness,
and the mind is amazed at its falling.
19 Over the earth, like salt, he also pours hoarfrost,
which, when it freezes, bristles like thorns.
20 The cold wind blows from the north,
and ice forms on the water;
it forms on every piece of standing water,
covering it like a breastplate.
21 The wind swallows up the mountains and scorches the
desert,
like a fire it consumes the vegetation.
22 But cloud brings swift healing,
and dew brings joy after the heat.
23 By his own resourcefulness he has tamed the abyss,
and planted it with islands.

GREEK OLD TESTAMENT

24 οἱ πλέοντες τὴν θάλασσαν διηγοῦνται τὸν κίνδυνον
αὐτῆς,
καὶ ἀκοαῖς ὠτίων ἡμῶν θαυμάζομεν·
25 καὶ ἐκεῖ τὰ παράδοξα καὶ θαυμάσια ἔργα,
ποικιλία παντὸς ζῴου, κτίσις κητῶν.
26 δι᾽ αὐτὸν εὐοδοῖ ἄγγελος αὐτοῦ,
καὶ ἐν λόγῳ αὐτοῦ σύγκειται τὰ πάντα.
27 Πολλὰ ἐροῦμεν καὶ οὐ μὴ ἀφικώμεθα,
καὶ συντέλεια λόγων Τὸ πᾶν ἐστιν αὐτός.
28 δοξάζοντες ποῦ ἰσχύσομεν;
αὐτὸς γὰρ ὁ μέγας παρὰ πάντα τὰ ἔργα αὐτοῦ.
29 φοβερὸς κύριος καὶ σφόδρα μέγας,
καὶ θαυμαστὴ ἡ δυναστεία αὐτοῦ.
30 δοξάζοντες κύριον ὑψώσατε
καθ᾽ ὅσον ἂν δύνησθε, ὑπερέξει γὰρ καὶ ἔτι·
καὶ ὑψοῦντες αὐτὸν πληθύνατε ἐν ἰσχύι,
μὴ κοπιᾶτε, οὐ γὰρ μὴ ἀφίκησθε.
31 τίς ἑόρακεν αὐτὸν καὶ ἐκδιηγήσεται;
καὶ τίς μεγαλυνεῖ αὐτὸν καθώς ἐστιν;
32 πολλὰ ἀπόκρυφά ἐστιν μείζονα τούτων,
ὀλίγα γὰρ ἑωράκαμεν τῶν ἔργων αὐτοῦ·
33 πάντα γὰρ ἐποίησεν ὁ κύριος
καὶ τοῖς εὐσεβέσιν ἔδωκεν σοφίαν

44 Αἰνέσωμεν δὴ ἄνδρας ἐνδόξους
καὶ τοὺς πατέρας ἡμῶν τῇ γενέσει·

KING JAMES VERSION

24 They that sail on the sea tell of the danger thereof; and when we hear it with our ears, we marvel thereat.

25 For therein be strange and wondrous works, variety of all kinds of beasts and whales created.

26 By him the end of them hath prosperous success, and by his word all things consist.

27 We may speak much, and yet come short: wherefore in sum, he is all.

28 How shall we be able to magnify him? for he is great above all his works.

29 The Lord is terrible and very great, and marvellous is his power.

30 When ye glorify the Lord, exalt him as much as ye can; for even yet will he far exceed: and when ye exalt him, put forth all your strength, and be not weary; for ye can never go far enough.

31 Who hath seen him, that he might tell us? and who can magnify him as he is?

32 There are yet hid greater things than these be, for we have seen but a few of his works.

33 For the Lord hath made all things; and to the godly hath he given wisdom.

44 Let us now praise famous men, and our fathers that begat us.

DOUAY OLD TESTAMENT

26 Let them that sail on the sea, tell the dangers thereof: and when we hear with our ears, we shall admire.

27 There are great and wonderful works: a variety of beasts, and of all living things, and the monstrous creatures of whales.

28 Through him is established the end of their journey, and by his word all things are regulated.

29 We shall say much, and yet shall want words: but the sum of our words is, He is all.

30 What shall we be able to do to glorify him? for the Almighty himself is above all his works.

31 The Lord is terrible, and exceeding great, and his power is admirable.

32 Glorify the Lord as much as ever you can, for he will yet far exceed, and his magnificence is wonderful.

33 Blessing the Lord, exalt him as much as you can: for he is above all praise.

34 When you exalt him put forth all your strength, and be not weary: for you can never go far enough.

35 Who shall see him, and declare him? and who shall magnify him as he is from the beginning?

36 There are many things hidden from us that are greater than these: for we have seen but a few of his works.

37 But the Lord hath made all things, and to the godly he hath given wisdom.

44 LET us now praise men of renown, and our fathers in their generation.

KNOX TRANSLATION

deep mariners have to tell of, and wonder at the tale; 27 of
the great marvels it contains, living things a many, both
fierce and harmless, and monstrous creatures besides.
28 Who but the Lord brought the venture to a happy issue?
His word gives all things their pattern.
29 Say we much as we will, of what needs to be said our
words come short; be this the sum of all our saying, He is in
all things.[a] 30 To what end is all our boasting?[b] He, the
Almighty, is high above all that he has made; 31 he, the
Lord, is terrible, and great beyond compare, and his power is
wonderful. 32 Glorify him as best you may, glory is still lacking, such is the marvel of his greatness; 33 praise him and
extol him as you will, he is beyond all praising; 34 summon
all your strength, the better to exalt his name, untiring still,
and you shall not reach your goal. 35 Who can tell us what
he is from sight seen of him? Who can magnify his eternal
being? 36 Much more lies beyond our ken; only the fringe of
creation meets our view; 37 and of all things the Lord is
maker. Yet, live thou in the worship of him, wisdom thou
shalt have for thy reward.

44 Speak we now in honour of famous men that were
our fathers, long ago. 2 What high achievements the

a Both the Greek and the Hebrew give, 'He is all'. *b* In the Greek and in the Hebrew, 'our glorifying of him'.

TODAY'S ENGLISH VERSION

24 Sailors tell about the dangers of the sea,
and we listen to their tales in amazement.
25 In the sea are strange and marvelous creatures:
huge monsters and all kinds of living things.
26 Each of the Lord's messengers succeeds at its task.
Everything is held together by his word.

27 We could say much more and never finish,
but it all means this: the Lord is everything.
28 How can we find the power to praise him?
He is greater than all his creation.
29 The Lord is awesome in his greatness;
his power is overwhelming.
30 Though you do your best to praise him,
he is greater than you can ever express.
Though you honor him tirelessly and with all your
strength,
you still cannot praise him enough.
31 No one has seen him, no one can describe him;
no one can praise him as he deserves.
32 Mysteries greater than these are still unknown;
we know only a fraction of his works.
33 The Lord made the universe
and then gave wisdom to devout people.

44 So let us now give praise to godly[a] men,
our ancestors of generations past,

[a] *Hebrew* godly; *Greek* famous.

NEW REVISED STANDARD VERSION

24 Those who sail the sea tell of its dangers,
and we marvel at what we hear.
25 In it are strange and marvelous creatures,
all kinds of living things, and huge sea-monsters.
26 Because of him each of his messengers succeeds,
and by his word all things hold together.

27 We could say more but could never say enough;
let the final word be: "He is the all."
28 Where can we find the strength to praise him?
For he is greater than all his works.
29 Awesome is the Lord and very great,
and marvelous is his power.
30 Glorify the Lord and exalt him as much as you can,
for he surpasses even that.
When you exalt him, summon all your strength,
and do not grow weary, for you cannot praise him
enough.
31 Who has seen him and can describe him?
Or who can extol him as he is?
32 Many things greater than these lie hidden,
for I[a] have seen but few of his works.
33 For the Lord has made all things,
and to the godly he has given wisdom.

HYMN IN HONOR OF OUR ANCESTORS[b]

44 Let us now sing the praises of famous men,
our ancestors in their generations.

[a] Heb: Gk *we* [b] This title is included in the Gk text.

NEW AMERICAN BIBLE

25 Those who go down to the sea tell part of its story,
and when we hear them we are thunderstruck;
26 In it are his creatures, stupendous, amazing,
all kinds of life, and the monsters of the deep.
27 For him each messenger succeeds,
and at his bidding accomplishes his will.
28 More than this we need not add;
let the last word be, he is all in all!
29 Let us praise him the more, since we cannot fathom
him,
for greater is he than all his works;
30 Awful indeed is the LORD's majesty,
and wonderful is his power.
31 Lift up your voices to glorify the LORD,
though he is still beyond your power to praise;
32 Extol him with renewed strength,
and weary not, though you cannot reach the end:
33 For who can see him and describe him?
or who can praise him as he is?
34 Beyond these, many things lie hid;
only a few of his works have we seen.
35 It is the LORD who has made all things,
and to those who fear him he gives wisdom.

44 Now will I praise those godly men,
our ancestors, each in his own time:

NEW JERUSALEM BIBLE

24 Those who sail the sea tell of its dangers,
their accounts fill our ears with amazement:
25 for there too exist strange and wonderful works,
animals of every kind and huge sea creatures.
26 Thanks to God, his messenger reaches port,
everything works out according to his word.

27 We could say much more and still fall short;
to put it concisely, 'He is all.'
28 Where shall we find sufficient power to glorify him,
since he is the Great One, above all his works,
29 the awe-inspiring Lord, stupendously great,
and wonderful in his power?
30 Exalt the Lord in your praises
as high as you may—still he surpasses you.
Exert all your strength when you exalt him,
do not grow tired—you will never come to the end.
31 Who has ever seen him to describe him?
Who can glorify him as he deserves?
32 Many mysteries remain even greater than these,
for we have seen only a few of his works,
33 the Lord himself having created all things
and given wisdom to those who are devout.

44 Next let us praise illustrious men,
our ancestors in their successive generations.

GREEK OLD TESTAMENT

2 πολλὴν δόξαν ἔκτισεν ὁ κύριος,
τὴν μεγαλωσύνην αὐτοῦ ἀπ' αἰῶνος.
3 κυριεύοντες ἐν ταῖς βασιλείαις αὐτῶν
καὶ ἄνδρες ὀνομαστοὶ ἐν δυνάμει·
βουλεύοντες ἐν συνέσει αὐτῶν,
ἀπηγγελκότες ἐν προφητείαις·
4 ἡγούμενοι λαοῦ ἐν διαβουλίοις
καὶ συνέσει γραμματείας λαοῦ,
σοφοὶ λόγοι ἐν παιδείᾳ αὐτῶν·
5 ἐκζητοῦντες μέλη μουσικῶν
καὶ διηγούμενοι ἔπη ἐν γραφῇ·
6 ἄνδρες πλούσιοι κεχορηγημένοι ἰσχύι,
εἰρηνεύοντες ἐν κατοικίαις αὐτῶν·
7 πάντες οὗτοι ἐν γενεαῖς ἐδοξάσθησαν,
καὶ ἐν ταῖς ἡμέραις αὐτῶν καύχημα.
8 εἰσὶν αὐτῶν οἳ κατέλιπον ὄνομα
τοῦ ἐκδιηγήσασθαι ἐπαίνους·
9 καὶ εἰσὶν ὧν οὐκ ἔστιν μνημόσυνον
καὶ ἀπώλοντο ὡς οὐχ ὑπάρξαντες
καὶ ἐγένοντο ὡς οὐ γεγονότες
καὶ τὰ τέκνα αὐτῶν μετ' αὐτούς.
10 ἀλλ' ἢ οὗτοι ἄνδρες ἐλέους,
ὧν αἱ δικαιοσύναι οὐκ ἐπελήσθησαν·
11 μετὰ τοῦ σπέρματος αὐτῶν διαμενεῖ,
ἀγαθὴ κληρονομία ἔκγονα αὐτῶν·

KING JAMES VERSION

2 The Lord hath wrought great glory by them through his great power from the beginning.

3 Such as did bear rule in their kingdoms, men renowned for their power, giving counsel by their understanding, and declaring prophecies:

4 Leaders of the people by their counsels, and by their knowledge of learning meet for the people, wise and eloquent in their instructions:

5 Such as found out musical tunes, and recited verses in writing:

6 Rich men furnished with ability, living peaceably in their habitations:

7 All these were honoured in their generations, and were the glory of their times.

8 There be of them, that have left a name behind them, that their praises might be reported.

9 And some there be, which have no memorial; who are perished, as though they had never been; and are become as though they had never been born; and their children after them.

10 But these were merciful men, whose righteousness hath not been forgotten.

11 With their seed shall continually remain a good inheritance, and their children are within the covenant.

DOUAY OLD TESTAMENT

2 The Lord hath wrought great glory through his magnificence from the beginning.

3 Such as have borne rule in their dominions, men of great power, and endued with their wisdom, shewing forth in the prophets the dignity of prophets,

4 And ruling over the present people, and by the strength of wisdom *instructing* the people in most holy words.

5 Such as by their skill sought out musical tunes, and published canticles of the scriptures.

6 Rich men in virtue, studying beautifulness: living at peace in their houses.

7 All these have gained glory in their generations, and were praised in their days.

8 They that were born of them have left a name behind them, that their praises might be related:

9 And there are some, of whom there is no memorial: who are perished, as if they had never been: and are become as if they had never been born, and their children with them.

10 But these were men of mercy, whose godly deeds have not failed:

11 Good things continue with their seed,

KNOX TRANSLATION

Lord has made known in them, ever since time began! 3 Here
were men that had power and bore rule, men that excelled in
strength, or in the wisdom that dowered them; prophets that
worthily upheld the name of prophecy, 4 issuing to the people the commands their times needed, uttering, through their
foresight, a sacred charge to the nations. 5 Here were men
that had skill to devise melodies, to make songs and set
them down in writing. 6 Here were men rich in ability, noble
of aim, that dwelt peacefully in their homes. 7 These were
the glories of their race, the ornament of their times; 8 and
the sons they begot have left a memory that adds to the
recital of their praise. 9 Not like those others, who are forgotten in death as if they had never been; nameless, they and
their children, as if they had never lived; 10 no, these were
men of tender conscience;[a] their deeds of charity will never
be forgotten. 11 Blessings abide with their posterity; 12 their

[a] Here, and in verse 27, we may translate 'men well beloved'; that is, God's favourites.

TODAY'S ENGLISH VERSION

2 those whom the Lord honored with great glory,
in whom his greatness has been seen
from the beginning of time.
3 There were some who ruled kingdoms,
and some who were known for their strength.
Some were wise advisers,
and some spoke prophecies.
4 There were statesmen whose policies governed the people,
rulers who issued decrees,[a]
scholars who spoke wise words,[b]
and those who used pointed proverbs,[c]
5 poets, and composers of music,
6 rich and powerful men living peacefully at home.
7 All of these were famous in their own times,
honored by the people of their day.
8 Some of them left a reputation,
and people still praise them today.
9 There are others who are not remembered,
as if they had never lived,
who died and were forgotten,
they, and their children after them.

10 But we will praise these godly men,
whose righteous deeds have never been forgotten.
11 Their reputations will be passed on to their descendants,
and this will be their inheritance.[d]

[a] *Probable Hebrew text* rulers who issued decrees; *Greek unclear.*
[b] *Hebrew* scholars . . . words; *Greek unclear.* [c] *Hebrew* and those . . . proverbs; *Greek does not have these words.* [d] *Verse 11 in Greek is unclear.*

NEW REVISED STANDARD VERSION

2 The Lord apportioned to them[a] great glory,
his majesty from the beginning.
3 There were those who ruled in their kingdoms,
and made a name for themselves by their valor;
those who gave counsel because they were intelligent;
those who spoke in prophetic oracles;
4 those who led the people by their counsels
and by their knowledge of the people's lore;
they were wise in their words of instruction;
5 those who composed musical tunes,
or put verses in writing;
6 rich men endowed with resources,
living peacefully in their homes—
7 all these were honored in their generations,
and were the pride of their times.
8 Some of them have left behind a name,
so that others declare their praise.
9 But of others there is no memory;
they have perished as though they had never existed;
they have become as though they had never been born,
they and their children after them.
10 But these also were godly men,
whose righteous deeds have not been forgotten;
11 their wealth will remain with their descendants,
and their inheritance with their children's children.[b]

a Heb: Gk *created* b Heb Compare Lat Syr: Meaning of Gk uncertain

NEW AMERICAN BIBLE

2 The abounding glory of the Most High's portion,
his own part, since the days of old.
Subduers of the land in kingly fashion,
men of renown for their might,
3 Or counselors in their prudence,
or seers of all things in prophecy;
4 Resolute princes of the folk,
and governors with their staves;
Authors skilled in composition,
and forgers of epigrams with their spikes;
5 Composers of melodious psalms,
or discoursers on lyric themes;
6 Stalwart men, solidly established
and at peace in their own estates—
7 All these were glorious in their time,
each illustrious in his day.
8 Some of them have left behind a name
and men recount their praiseworthy deeds;
9 But of others there is no memory,
for when they ceased, they ceased.
And they are as though they had not lived,
they and their children after them.
10 Yet these also were godly men
whose virtues have not been forgotten;
11 Their wealth remains in their families,
their heritage with their descendants;

NEW JERUSALEM BIBLE

2 The Lord has created an abundance of glory,
and displayed his greatness from earliest times.
3 Some wielded authority as kings
and were renowned for their strength;
others were intelligent advisers
and uttered prophetic sayings.
4 Others directed the people by their advice,
by their understanding of the popular mind,
and by the wise words of their teaching;
5 others composed musical melodies
and set down ballads;
6 others were rich and powerful,
living peacefully in their homes.
7 All these were honoured by their contemporaries
and were the glory of their day.
8 Some of them left a name behind them,
so that their praises are still sung.
9 While others have left no memory,
and disappeared as though they had not existed.
They are now as though they had never been,
and so too, their children after them.

10 But here is a list of illustrious men
whose good works have not been forgotten.
11 In their descendants they find
a rich inheritance, their posterity.

GREEK OLD TESTAMENT

12 ἐν ταῖς διαθήκαις ἔστη τὸ σπέρμα αὐτῶν
καὶ τὰ τέκνα αὐτῶν δι᾽ αὐτούς·
13 ἕως αἰῶνος μενεῖ σπέρμα αὐτῶν,
καὶ ἡ δόξα αὐτῶν οὐκ ἐξαλειφθήσεται·
14 τὰ σώματα αὐτῶν ἐν εἰρήνῃ ἐτάφη,
καὶ τὸ ὄνομα αὐτῶν ζῇ εἰς γενεάς·
15 σοφίαν αὐτῶν διηγήσονται λαοί,
καὶ τὸν ἔπαινον ἐξαγγέλλει ἐκκλησία.
16 Ενωχ εὐηρέστησεν κυρίῳ καὶ μετετέθη
ὑπόδειγμα μετανοίας ταῖς γενεαῖς.
17 Νωε εὑρέθη τέλειος δίκαιος,
ἐν καιρῷ ὀργῆς ἐγένετο ἀντάλλαγμα·
διὰ τοῦτον ἐγενήθη κατάλειμμα τῇ γῇ,
ὅτε ἐγένετο κατακλυσμός·
18 διαθῆκαι αἰῶνος ἐτέθησαν πρὸς αὐτόν,
ἵνα μὴ ἐξαλειφθῇ κατακλυσμῷ πᾶσα σάρξ.
19 Αβρααμ μέγας πατὴρ πλήθους ἐθνῶν,
καὶ οὐχ εὑρέθη ὅμοιος ἐν τῇ δόξῃ·
20 ὃς συνετήρησεν νόμον ὑψίστου
καὶ ἐγένετο ἐν διαθήκῃ μετ᾽ αὐτοῦ·
ἐν σαρκὶ αὐτοῦ ἔστησεν διαθήκην
καὶ ἐν πειρασμῷ εὑρέθη πιστός·

KING JAMES VERSION

12 Their seed standeth fast, and their children for their sakes.

13 Their seed shall remain for ever, and their glory shall not be blotted out.

14 Their bodies are buried in peace; but their name liveth for evermore.

15 The people will tell of their wisdom, and the congregation will shew forth their praise.

16 Enoch pleased the Lord, and was translated, being an example of repentance to all generations.

17 Noah was found perfect and righteous; in the time of wrath he was taken in exchange [for the world;] therefore was he left as a remnant unto the earth, when the flood came.

18 An everlasting covenant was made with him, that all flesh should perish no more by the flood.

19 Abraham was a great father of many people: in glory was there none like unto him;

20 Who kept the law of the most High, and was in covenant with him: he established the covenant in his flesh; and when he was proved, he was found faithful.

DOUAY OLD TESTAMENT

12 Their posterity are a holy inheritance, and their seed hath stood in the covenants.

13 And their children for their sakes remain for ever: their seed and their glory shall not be forsaken.

14 Their bodies are buried in peace, and their name liveth unto generation and generation.

15 Let the people shew forth their wisdom, and the church declare their praise.

16 Henoch pleased God, and was translated into paradise, that he may give repentance to the nations.

17 Noe was found perfect, just, and in the time of wrath he was made a reconciliation.

18 Therefore was there a remnant left to the earth, when the flood came.

19 The covenants of the world were made with him, that all flesh should no more be destroyed with the flood.

20 Abraham *was* the great father of a multitude of nations, and there was not found the like to him in glory, who kept the law of the most High, and was in covenant with him.

21 In his flesh he established the covenant, and in temptation he was found faithful.

KNOX TRANSLATION

descendants are a race set apart for God, the pledged heirs of
his promises. 13 For their sakes this line of theirs will endure
for all time; their stock, their name, will never be allowed to
die out. 14 Their bodies lie in peace; their name lasts on, age
after age. 15 Their wisdom is yet a legend among the people;
wherever faithful men assemble, their story is told.
16 Enoch there was, that did God's will, and was taken
away to Paradise, repentance his gift to mankind.[a] 17 Noe,
too, blameless lived and faithful proved; when the day of retribution came, he made amends for all;[b] 18 so it was that
earth had a remnant left when the flood came; 19 with him
God's covenant was made, never again should all living
things be drowned together. 20 What greatness was
Abraham's, to be the father of so many nations! Where shall
we find another that can boast he kept the law of the most
High as Abraham kept it? He, too, entered into a covenant
with God, 21 and was bidden to bear on his own body the
record of it. Once he had put him to the test and found him

a This is commonly interpreted by the Fathers in connexion with Apoc. 11. 3. In the Greek, Enoch is represented as an *example* of penitence; in the Hebrew, of wisdom. *b* The Greek word thus translated might also mean, 'was (allowed to survive) in exchange for all'.

TODAY'S ENGLISH VERSION

12 Their descendants continue to keep the covenant
and always will, because of what their ancestors did.
13 Their family line will go on forever,
and their fame will never fade.
14 Their bodies were laid to rest,
but their reputations will live forever.
15 Nations will tell about their wisdom,
and God's people will praise them.
16 Enoch pleased the Lord and was taken up into heaven.
He became an inspiration for repentance for all time to come.
17 Noah was a perfectly righteous man. After destruction
came, he gave the human race a new start.[a] Because of him
there were people left on earth when the flood was over.
18 The Lord made an eternal covenant with him, promising
that life would never again be destroyed by a flood.
19 Abraham was the great ancestor of many nations; his
reputation was faultless.[b] 20 He kept the Law of the Most
High and made a covenant with him, a covenant marked on
his body. When he was put to the test, he was found faithful.

[a] *Hebrew* gave . . . start; *Greek* was taken in exchange for the human race.
[b] *Hebrew* his reputation was faultless; *Greek* there was no one like him in reputation.

NEW REVISED STANDARD VERSION

12 Their descendants stand by the covenants;
their children also, for their sake.
13 Their offspring will continue forever,
and their glory will never be blotted out.
14 Their bodies are buried in peace,
but their name lives on generation after generation.
15 The assembly declares[a] their wisdom,
and the congregation proclaims their praise.

16 Enoch pleased the Lord and was taken up,
an example of repentance to all generations.

17 Noah was found perfect and righteous;
in the time of wrath he kept the race alive;[b]
therefore a remnant was left on the earth
when the flood came.
18 Everlasting covenants were made with him
that all flesh should never again be blotted out by a
flood.

19 Abraham was the great father of a multitude of nations,
and no one has been found like him in glory.
20 He kept the law of the Most High,
and entered into a covenant with him;
he certified the covenant in his flesh,
and when he was tested he proved faithful.

a Heb: Gk *Peoples declare* b Heb: Gk *was taken in exchange*

NEW AMERICAN BIBLE

12 Through God's covenant with them their family
endures,
their posterity for their sake.
13 And for all time their progeny will endure,
their glory will never be blotted out;
14 Their bodies are peacefully laid away,
but their name lives on and on.
15 At gatherings their wisdom is retold,
and the assembly proclaims their praise.

16 [ENOCH walked with the LORD and was taken up,
that succeeding generations might learn by his
example.]
17 NOAH, found just and perfect,
renewed the race in the time of devastation.
Because of his worth there were survivors,
and with a sign to him the deluge ended;
18 A lasting agreement was made with him,
that never should all flesh be destroyed.
19 ABRAHAM, father of many peoples,
kept his glory without stain:
20 He observed the precepts of the Most High,
and entered into an agreement with him;
In his own flesh he incised the ordinance,
and when tested he was found loyal.

44, 16: The present verse is an expansion of the original text.

NEW JERUSALEM BIBLE

12 Their descendants stand by the commandments
and, thanks to them, so do their children's children.
13 Their offspring will last for ever,
their glory will not fade.
14 Their bodies have been buried in peace,
and their name lives on for all generations.
15 The peoples will proclaim their wisdom,
the assembly will celebrate their praises.[a]
16 Enoch pleased the Lord and was transferred to heaven,
an example for the conversion of all generations.
17 Noah was found perfectly upright,
in the time of retribution he became the heir:
because of him a remnant was preserved for the earth
at the coming of the Flood.
18 Everlasting covenants were made with him
that never again should every living creature perish
by flood.
19 Abraham, the great ancestor of a host of nations,
no one was ever his equal in glory.
20 He observed the Law of the Most High,
and entered into a covenant with him.
He confirmed the covenant in his own flesh,
and proved himself faithful under ordeal.

[a] **44** =39:10.

GREEK OLD TESTAMENT

21 διὰ τοῦτο ἐν ὅρκῳ ἔστησεν αὐτῷ
ἐνευλογηθῆναι ἔθνη ἐν σπέρματι αὐτοῦ,
πληθῦναι αὐτὸν ὡς χοῦν τῆς γῆς
καὶ ὡς ἄστρα ἀνυψῶσαι τὸ σπέρμα αὐτοῦ
καὶ κατακληρονομῆσαι αὐτοὺς
ἀπὸ θαλάσσης ἕως θαλάσσης
καὶ ἀπὸ ποταμοῦ ἕως ἄκρου τῆς γῆς.
22 καὶ ἐν τῷ Ισαακ ἔστησεν οὕτως
δι' Αβρααμ τὸν πατέρα αὐτοῦ.
23 εὐλογίαν πάντων ἀνθρώπων καὶ διαθήκην
κατέπαυσεν ἐπὶ κεφαλὴν Ιακωβ·
ἐπέγνω αὐτὸν ἐν εὐλογίαις αὐτοῦ
καὶ ἔδωκεν αὐτῷ ἐν κληρονομίᾳ·
καὶ διέστειλεν μερίδας αὐτοῦ,
ἐν φυλαῖς ἐμέρισεν δέκα δύο.

45 Καὶ ἐξήγαγεν ἐξ αὐτοῦ ἄνδρα ἐλέους
εὑρίσκοντα χάριν ἐν ὀφθαλμοῖς πάσης σαρκὸς
ἠγαπημένον ὑπὸ θεοῦ καὶ ἀνθρώπων
Μωυσῆν, οὗ τὸ μνημόσυνον ἐν εὐλογίαις·
2 ὡμοίωσεν αὐτὸν δόξῃ ἁγίων
καὶ ἐμεγάλυνεν αὐτὸν ἐν φόβοις ἐχθρῶν·
3 ἐν λόγοις αὐτοῦ σημεῖα κατέπαυσεν,
ἐδόξασεν αὐτὸν κατὰ πρόσωπον βασιλέων·
ἐνετείλατο αὐτῷ πρὸς λαὸν αὐτοῦ
καὶ ἔδειξεν αὐτῷ τῆς δόξης αὐτοῦ·

KING JAMES VERSION

21 Therefore he assured him by an oath, that he would bless the nations in his seed, and that he would multiply him as the dust of the earth, and exalt his seed as the stars, and cause them to inherit from sea to sea, and from the river unto the utmost part of the land.

22 With Isaac did he establish likewise [for Abraham his father's sake] the blessing of all men, and the covenant,

23 And made it rest upon the head of Jacob. He acknowledged him in his blessing, and gave him an heritage, and divided his portions; among the twelve tribes did he part them.

45 And he brought out of him a merciful man, which found favour in the sight of all flesh, even Moses, beloved of God and men, whose memorial is blessed.

2 He made him like to the glorious saints, and magnified him, so that his enemies stood in fear of him.

3 By his words he caused the wonders to cease, and he made him glorious in the sight of kings, and gave him a commandment for his people, and shewed him part of his glory.

DOUAY OLD TESTAMENT

22 Therefore by an oath he gave him glory in his posterity, that he should increase as the dust of the earth,

23 And that he would exalt his seed as the stars, and they should inherit from sea to sea, and from the river to the ends of the earth.

24 And he did in like manner with Isaac for the sake of Abraham his father.

25 The Lord gave him the blessing of all nations, and confirmed his covenant upon the head of Jacob.

26 He acknowledged him in his blessings, and gave him an inheritance, and divided him his portion in twelve tribes.

27 And he preserved for him men of mercy, that found grace in the eyes of all flesh.

45 MOSES was beloved of God, and men: whose memory is in benediction.

2 He made him like the saints in glory, and magnified him in the fear of his enemies, and with his words he made prodigies to cease.

3 He glorified him in the sight of kings, and gave him commandments in the sight of his people, and shewed him his glory.

KNOX TRANSLATION

obedient, 22 God took an oath that this should be the father
of a renowned posterity; their numbers should rival the dust
on the ground, 23 should match the stars in heaven, stretching from southern to western sea, from Euphrates to the
ends of earth. 24 Isaac, the son of such a father, fared no
worse; 25 to him the Lord gave that blessing which should
extend to all nations. In Jacob's person, too, the covenant
should be revived; 26 the blessings Jacob uttered should be
ratified, and the lands promised him should be divided
among twelve tribes of his own begetting.
27 Him a posterity of famous sons awaited,[a] men of tender
conscience, that had the good word of all their fellows.
45 Well loved by God, well loved among men, on the
name of Moses a benediction rests. 2 The Lord gave
him such honour as he gives to his holy ones; gave him
renown by striking terror into his enemies, and then, at his
word, abated the prodigies that had befallen them. 3 He
made him great in the eyes of kings, entrusted commandments to him in full view of the chosen people, made a revelation to him of the divine glory. 4 The Lord set him apart,

a The Greek and the Hebrew give 'him a descendant awaited'; that is, Moses.

TODAY'S ENGLISH VERSION

21And so the Lord made him a solemn promise that his
descendants would be a blessing to the world; that their
number would be countless, like the dust of the earth; that
they would be honored more than any other people on earth;
and that their land would extend from sea to sea, from the
Euphrates to the ends of the earth.
22-23The Lord renewed that covenant with Isaac, and then
again with Jacob, repeating the promise that Abraham's
descendants would be a blessing to the whole human race.
The Lord assured Jacob that he would bless him; he gave him
the land that would be his, dividing it into twelve parts, one
for each of the tribes.

45 From Jacob's descendants the Lord raised up a godly
man who won the favor of everyone, loved by God
and people alike. This man was Moses, whose very memory
is a blessing. 2The Lord made him as glorious as the angels
and made his enemies fear him. 3There in Egypt at his command the disaster struck.[a] The Lord made kings hold him in
respect. The Lord gave him his commands for his people and
showed him the dazzling light of his presence. 4The Lord

[a] *Hebrew* struck; *Greek* stopped.

NEW REVISED STANDARD VERSION

21 Therefore the Lord[a] assured him with an oath
that the nations would be blessed through his
offspring;
that he would make him as numerous as the dust of the
earth,
and exalt his offspring like the stars,
and give them an inheritance from sea to sea
and from the Euphrates[b] to the ends of the earth.
22 To Isaac also he gave the same assurance
for the sake of his father Abraham.
The blessing of all people and the covenant
23 he made to rest on the head of Jacob;
he acknowledged him with his blessings,
and gave him his inheritance;
he divided his portions,
and distributed them among twelve tribes.

From his descendants the Lord[a] brought forth a godly
man,
who found favor in the sight of all
45 1and was beloved by God and people,
Moses, whose memory is blessed.
2 He made him equal in glory to the holy ones,
and made him great, to the terror of his enemies.
3 By his words he performed swift miracles;[c]
the Lord[a] glorified him in the presence of kings.
He gave him commandments for his people,
and revealed to him his glory.

a Gk *he* *b* Syr: Heb Gk *River* *c* Heb: Gk *caused signs to cease*

NEW AMERICAN BIBLE

21For this reason, God promised him with an oath
that in his descendants the nations would be blessed,
That he would make him numerous as the grains of
dust,
and exalt his posterity like the stars;
That he would give them an inheritance from sea to
sea,
and from the River to the ends of the earth.
22And for ISAAC he renewed the same promise
because of Abraham, his father.
The covenant with all his forebears was confirmed,
and the blessing rested upon the head of JACOB.
23God acknowledged him as the firstborn,
and gave him his inheritance.
He fixed the boundaries for his tribes,
and their division into twelve.

45 From him was to spring the man
who won the favor of all:
Dear to God and men,
MOSES, whose memory is held in benediction.
2God's honor devolved upon him,
and the Lord strengthened him with fearful powers;
3God wrought swift miracles at his words
and sustained him in the king's presence.
He gave him the commandments for his people,
and revealed to him his glory.

NEW JERUSALEM BIBLE

21The Lord therefore promised him on oath
to bless the nations through his descendants,
to multiply him like the dust on the ground,
to exalt his descendants like the stars,
and to give them the land as their heritage,
from one sea to the other,
from the River to the ends of the earth.
22To Isaac too, for the sake of Abraham his father,
he assured 23the blessing of all humanity;
he caused the covenant to rest on the head of Jacob.
He confirmed him in his blessings
and gave him the land as his inheritance;
he divided it into portions,
and shared it out among the twelve tribes.

45 From Jacob's stock he produced a generous man
who found favour in the eyes of all humanity,
beloved by God and people,
Moses, of blessed memory.
2He made him the equal of the holy ones in glory
and made him strong, to the terror of his enemies.
3By the word of Moses, he made prodigies cease
and raised him high in the respect of kings;
he gave him commandments for his people,
and showed him something of his glory.

GREEK OLD TESTAMENT

4 ἐν πίστει καὶ πραΰτητι αὐτὸν ἡγίασεν,
ἐξελέξατο αὐτὸν ἐκ πάσης σαρκός·
5 ἠκούτισεν αὐτὸν τῆς φωνῆς αὐτοῦ
καὶ εἰσήγαγεν αὐτὸν εἰς τὸν γνόφον
καὶ ἔδωκεν αὐτῷ κατὰ πρόσωπον ἐντολάς,
νόμον ζωῆς καὶ ἐπιστήμης,
διδάξαι τὸν Ιακωβ διαθήκην
καὶ κρίματα αὐτοῦ τὸν Ισραηλ.
6 Ααρων ὕψωσεν ἅγιον ὅμοιον αὐτῷ
ἀδελφὸν αὐτοῦ ἐκ φυλῆς Λευι·
7 ἔστησεν αὐτὸν διαθήκην αἰῶνος
καὶ ἔδωκεν αὐτῷ ἱερατείαν λαοῦ·
ἐμακάρισεν αὐτὸν ἐν εὐκοσμίᾳ
καὶ περιέζωσεν αὐτὸν περιστολὴν δόξης·
8 ἐνέδυσεν αὐτὸν συντέλειαν καυχήματος
καὶ ἐστερέωσεν αὐτὸν σκεύεσιν ἰσχύος,
περισκελῆ καὶ ποδήρη καὶ ἐπωμίδα·
9 καὶ ἐκύκλωσεν αὐτὸν ῥοΐσκοις,
χρυσοῖς κώδωσιν πλείστοις κυκλόθεν,
ἠχῆσαι φωνὴν ἐν βήμασιν αὐτοῦ,
ἀκουστὸν ποιῆσαι ἦχον ἐν ναῷ
εἰς μνημόσυνον υἱοῖς λαοῦ αὐτοῦ·
10 στολῇ ἁγίᾳ, χρυσῷ καὶ ὑακίνθῳ
καὶ πορφύρᾳ, ἔργῳ ποικιλτοῦ,
λογείῳ κρίσεως, δήλοις ἀληθείας,
κεκλωσμένῃ κόκκῳ, ἔργῳ τεχνίτου,

KING JAMES VERSION

4 He sanctified him *in* his faithfulness and meekness, and chose him out of all men.

5 He made him to hear his voice, and brought him into the dark cloud, and gave him commandments before his face, even the law of life and knowledge, that he might teach Jacob his covenants, and Israel his judgments.

6 He exalted Aaron, an holy man like unto him, even his brother, of the tribe of Levi.

7 An everlasting covenant he made with him, and gave him the priesthood among the people; he beautified him with comely ornaments, and clothed him with a robe of glory.

8 He put upon him perfect glory; and strengthened him with rich garments, with breeches, with a long robe, and the ephod.

9 And he compassed him with pomegranates, and with many golden bells round about, that as he went there might be a sound, and a noise made that might be heard in the temple, for a memorial to the children of his people;

10 With an holy garment, with gold, and blue silk, and purple, the work of the embroiderer, with a breastplate of judgment, and with Urim and Thummim;

11 With twisted scarlet, the work of the cunning workman,

DOUAY OLD TESTAMENT

4 He sanctified him in his faith, and meekness, and chose him out of all flesh.

5 For he heard him, and his voice, and brought him into a cloud.

6 And he gave him commandments before his face, and a law of life and instruction, that he might teach Jacob his covenant, and Israel his judgments.

7 He exalted Aaron his brother, and like to himself of the tribe of Levi:

8 He made an everlasting covenant with him, and gave him the priesthood of the nation, and made him blessed in glory,

9 And he girded him about with a glorious girdle, and clothed him with a robe of glory, and crowned him with majestic attire.

10 He put upon him a garment to the feet, and breeches, and an ephod, and he compassed him with many little bells of gold all round about,

11 That as he went there might be a sound, and a noise made that might be heard in the temple, for a memorial to the children of his people.

12 He gave him a holy robe of gold, and blue, and purple, a woven work of a wise man, endued with judgment and truth:

13 Of twisted scarlet the work of an artist, with precious

KNOX TRANSLATION

chosen out from the rest of mankind, so loyal he was and so
gentle; 5 answered his prayer by taking him up into a cloud,
6 and there, face to face, imparting commandments to him,
the law that gives life and wisdom; here, Jacob, was thy covenant, here Israel, the rule thou wast to live by.

7 Of Levite blood, too, sprang another renowned as Moses
himself, his brother Aaron. To Aaron the Lord gave high
office, 8 making an eternal covenant with him, investing
him with the priesthood of the chosen race, enriching him
with his own glory. 9 Bright was the cincture that girded
him, bright the robe that clothed him; no ornament he wore
but spoke of majesty. 10 The long tunic, the breeches, the
sacred mantle, and golden bells a many compassing him
about, 11 that tinkled still as he walked, echoing through
the temple to keep Israel's name unforgotten! 12 The hallowed robe, all gold and blue and purple, work of a master
weaver, that lacked neither skill nor faithfulness![a] 13 What
craftsmanship of twisted thread dyed scarlet, of rare stones

a The Latin translator has probably missed the meaning of the original. It seems clear from the other versions that a reference is made here to the oracular burse described in Ex. 28. 30.

TODAY'S ENGLISH VERSION

chose Moses out of the whole human race and consecrated
him because of his loyalty and humility. 5 He let him hear
his voice and led him into the dark cloud, where, face-to-
face, he gave him the commandments, the Law that gives life
and knowledge, so that Moses might teach the covenant regulations to the Israelites.
6 The Lord raised up Aaron, a holy man like his brother
Moses, of the tribe of Levi. 7 He made an eternal covenant
with him, giving him the privilege of serving as priest to the
Lord's people. He honored him by clothing him with magnificent robes and fine ornaments, 8 perfect in their splendor. He
granted him the symbols of authority: the linen shorts, the
shirt, and the robe with the pomegranates around the hem.
9 Gold bells were also around its hem, so that when he
walked, their ringing would be heard in the Temple, and the
Lord would remember his people. 10 The Lord gave Aaron the
sacred robe with the gold, blue, and purple embroidery; the
breastpiece with the Urim and Thummim;[a] 11 the red yarn,

[a] URIM AND THUMMIM: *Two objects used by the priest to determine God's will; it is not known precisely how they were used.*

NEW REVISED STANDARD VERSION

4 For his faithfulness and meekness he consecrated him,
choosing him out of all humankind.
5 He allowed him to hear his voice,
and led him into the dark cloud,
and gave him the commandments face to face,
the law of life and knowledge,
so that he might teach Jacob the covenant,
and Israel his decrees.

6 He exalted Aaron, a holy man like Moses[a]
who was his brother, of the tribe of Levi.
7 He made an everlasting covenant with him,
and gave him the priesthood of the people.
He blessed him with stateliness,
and put a glorious robe on him.
8 He clothed him in perfect splendor,
and strengthened him with the symbols of authority,
the linen undergarments, the long robe, and the
ephod.
9 And he encircled him with pomegranates,
with many golden bells all around,
to send forth a sound as he walked,
to make their ringing heard in the temple
as a reminder to his people;
10 with the sacred vestment, of gold and violet
and purple, the work of an embroiderer;
with the oracle of judgment, Urim and Thummim;
11 with twisted crimson, the work of an artisan;

[a] Gk *him*

NEW AMERICAN BIBLE

4 For his trustworthiness and meekness
God selected him from all mankind;
5 He permitted him to hear his voice,
and led him into the cloud,
Where, face to face, he gave him the commandments,
the law of life and understanding,
That he might teach his precepts to Jacob,
his judgments and decrees to Israel.

6 He raised up also, like Moses in holiness,
his brother AARON, of the tribe of Levi.
7 He made him perpetual in his office
when he bestowed on him the priesthood of his
people;
He established him in honor
and crowned him with lofty majesty;
8 He clothed him with splendid apparel,
and adorned him with the glorious vestments:
Breeches and tunic and robe
with pomegranates around the hem,
9 And a rustle of bells round about,
through whose pleasing sound at each step
He would be heard within the sanctuary,
and the children of his race would be remembered;
10 The sacred vestments of gold, of violet,
and of crimson, wrought with embroidery;
The breastpiece for decision, the ephod and cincture
11 with scarlet yarn, the work of the weaver;

NEW JERUSALEM BIBLE

4 For his loyalty and gentleness he sanctified him,
choosing him alone out of all human beings;
5 he allowed him to hear his voice,
and led him into the darkness;
6 he gave him the commandments face to face,
the law of life and knowledge,
to teach Jacob his ordinances
and Israel his decrees.

He raised up Aaron, a holy man like Moses,
his brother, of the tribe of Levi.
7 He made an everlasting covenant with him,
and gave him the priesthood of the people.
He adorned him with impressive vestments,
he dressed him in a robe of glory.
8 He clothed him in glorious perfection
and invested him with rich ornaments,
the breeches, the long robe, the *ephod*.
9 To surround the robe he gave him pomegranates,
and many gold bells all round
to chime at every step,
for their sound to be heard in the Temple
as a reminder to the children of his people;
10 and a sacred vestment of gold and aquamarine
and scarlet, the work of an embroiderer;
the pectoral of judgement, the *urim* and *thummim*,
of plaited crimson, the work of a craftsman;

GREEK OLD TESTAMENT

11 λίθοις πολυτελέσιν γλύμματος σφραγῖδος
ἐν δέσει χρυσίου, ἔργῳ λιθουργοῦ,
εἰς μνημόσυνον ἐν γραφῇ κεκολαμμένῃ
κατ' ἀριθμὸν φυλῶν Ισραηλ·
12 στέφανον χρυσοῦν ἐπάνω κιδάρεως,
ἐκτύπωμα σφραγῖδος ἁγιάσματος,
καύχημα τιμῆς, ἔργον ἰσχύος,
ἐπιθυμήματα ὀφθαλμῶν κοσμούμενα·
13 ὡραῖα πρὸ αὐτοῦ οὐ γέγονεν τοιαῦτα,
ἕως αἰῶνος οὐκ ἐνεδύσατο ἀλλογενὴς
πλὴν τῶν υἱῶν αὐτοῦ μόνον
καὶ τὰ ἔκγονα αὐτοῦ διὰ παντός.
14 θυσίαι αὐτοῦ ὁλοκαρπωθήσονται
καθ' ἡμέραν ἐνδελεχῶς δίς.
15 ἐπλήρωσεν Μωυσῆς τὰς χεῖρας
καὶ ἔχρισεν αὐτὸν ἐν ἐλαίῳ ἁγίῳ·
ἐγενήθη αὐτῷ εἰς διαθήκην αἰῶνος
καὶ τῷ σπέρματι αὐτοῦ ἐν ἡμέραις οὐρανοῦ
λειτουργεῖν αὐτῷ ἅμα καὶ ἱερατεύειν
καὶ εὐλογεῖν τὸν λαὸν αὐτοῦ ἐν τῷ ὀνόματι.
16 ἐξελέξατο αὐτὸν ἀπὸ παντὸς ζῶντος
προσαγαγεῖν κάρπωσιν κυρίῳ,
θυμίαμα καὶ εὐωδίαν εἰς μνημόσυνον,
ἐξιλάσκεσθαι περὶ τοῦ λαοῦ σου.
17 ἔδωκεν αὐτῷ ἐν ἐντολαῖς αὐτοῦ
ἐξουσίαν ἐν διαθήκαις κριμάτων
διδάξαι τὸν Ιακωβ τὰ μαρτύρια
καὶ ἐν νόμῳ αὐτοῦ φωτίσαι Ισραηλ.

KING JAMES VERSION

with precious stones graven like seals, and set in gold, the work of the jeweller, with a writing engraved for a memorial, after the number of the tribes of Israel.
12 He set a crown of gold upon the mitre, wherein was engraved Holiness, an ornament of honour, a costly work, the desires of the eyes, goodly and beautiful.
13 Before him there were none such, neither did ever any stranger put them on, but only his children and his children's children perpetually.
14 Their sacrifices shall be wholly consumed every day twice continually.
15 Moses consecrated him, and anointed him with holy oil: this was appointed unto him by an everlasting covenant, and to his seed, so long as the heavens should remain, that they should minister unto him, and execute the office of the priesthood, and bless the people in his name.
16 He chose him out of all men living to offer sacrifices to the Lord, incense, and a sweet savour, for a memorial, to make reconciliation for his people.
17 He gave unto him his commandments, and authority in the statutes of judgments, that he should teach Jacob the testimonies, and inform Israel in his laws.

DOUAY OLD TESTAMENT

stones cut and set in gold, and graven by the work of a lapidary for a memorial, according to the number of the tribes of Israel.
14 And a crown of gold upon his mitre wherein was engraved Holiness, an ornament of honour: a work of power, and delightful to the eyes for its beauty.
15 Before him there were none so beautiful, even from the beginning.
16 No stranger was ever clothed with them, but only his children alone, and his grandchildren for ever.
17 His sacrifices were consumed with fire every day.
18 Moses filled his hands and anointed him with holy oil.
19 This was made to him for an everlasting testament, and to his seed as the days of heaven, to execute the office of the priesthood, and to have praise, and to glorify his people in his name.
20 He chose him out of all men living, to offer sacrifice to God, incense, and a good savour, for a memorial to make reconciliation for his people:
21 And he gave him power in his commandments, in the covenants of his judgments, that he should teach Jacob his testimonies, and give light to Israel in his law.

KNOX TRANSLATION

in a gold setting, engraved with all the gem-cutter's art,
twelve of them to commemorate the twelve tribes of Israel!
14 The gold finishing, too, of his mitre, engraved with the
legend, Holiness; so proud an adornment, so noble a work
of art, such a lure for men's eyes in its ordered beauty!
15 Never vesture till then was seen so fair; and, from time
immemorial, 16 no other might put it on, only the sons of
Aaron's line, in undying succession.
17 Day in, day out the fire should consume his sacrifice;
18 when Moses consecrated him with the holy oil's anointing,
19 this was a right granted in perpetuity, long as the heavens
should last. His to perform the priest's office, to echo God's
praise, to bless the people in his name. 20 Alone of living
men, he was chosen out to offer sacrifice, and the sweet-
smelling incense that is a people's plea for remembrance, a
people's atonement. 21 Power was his to administer the
divine decrees, a justiciary by right, handing on to Jacob its
tradition, giving Israel the law's light to guide it. 22 Once,

TODAY'S ENGLISH VERSION

spun by an expert; the precious stones with names engraved
on them, mounted in a gold setting by a jeweler, placed on
the breastpiece to remind the Lord of the twelve tribes of
Israel. 12 He gave him the turban with the gold ornament
engraved with the words "Dedicated to the Lord." It was
expertly crafted, a beautiful work of art, and it was a high
honor to wear it. 13 Before Aaron's time such beautiful
things were never seen. No one but Aaron and his descendants ever wore them, or ever will. 14 The grain offering is to
be presented twice a day and burned completely.
15 Moses ordained Aaron to office by pouring the sacred
anointing oil over his head. An eternal covenant was made
with him and his descendants, that they would serve the
Lord as his priests and bless the people in the Lord's name.
16 The Lord chose Aaron out of the whole human race to offer
sacrifices, to burn fragrant incense to remind the Lord of his
people, and to take away their sins. 17 He entrusted the commandments to Aaron's keeping and gave him the authority
to make legal decisions and to teach Israel the Law.

NEW REVISED STANDARD VERSION

with precious stones engraved like seals,
  in a setting of gold, the work of a jeweler,
to commemorate in engraved letters
  each of the tribes of Israel;
12 with a gold crown upon his turban,
  inscribed like a seal with "Holiness,"
a distinction to be prized, the work of an expert,
  a delight to the eyes, richly adorned.
13 Before him such beautiful things did not exist.
  No outsider ever put them on,
but only his sons
  and his descendants in perpetuity.
14 His sacrifices shall be wholly burned
  twice every day continually.
15 Moses ordained him,
  and anointed him with holy oil;
it was an everlasting covenant for him
  and for his descendants as long as the heavens endure,
to minister to the Lord[a] and serve as priest
  and bless his people in his name.
16 He chose him out of all the living
  to offer sacrifice to the Lord,
incense and a pleasing odor as a memorial portion,
  to make atonement for the[b] people.
17 In his commandments he gave him
  authority and statutes and[c] judgments,
to teach Jacob the testimonies,
  and to enlighten Israel with his law.

a Gk *him*   *b* Other ancient authorities read *his* or *your*   *c* Heb: Gk *authority in covenants of*

NEW AMERICAN BIBLE

Precious stones with seal engravings
  in golden settings, the work of the jeweler,
To commemorate in incised letters
  each of the tribes of Israel;
12 On his turban the diadem of gold,
  its plate wrought with the insignia of holiness,
Majestic, glorious, renowned for splendor,
  a delight to the eyes, beauty supreme.
13 Before him, no one was adorned with these,
  nor may they ever be worn by any
Except his sons and them alone,
  generation after generation, for all time.
14 His cereal offering is wholly burnt
  with the established sacrifice twice each day;
15 For Moses ordained him
  and anointed him with the holy oil,
In a lasting covenant with him
  and with his family, as permanent as the heavens,
That he should serve God in his priesthood
  and bless his people in his name.
16 He chose him from all mankind
  to offer holocausts and choice offerings,
To burn sacrifices of sweet odor for a memorial,
  and to atone for the people of Israel.
17 He gave to him his laws,
  and authority to prescribe and to judge:
To teach the precepts to his people,
  and the ritual to the descendants of Israel.

NEW JERUSALEM BIBLE

11 precious stones cut like seals
  mounted in gold, the work of a jeweller,
as a reminder with their engraved inscriptions
  of the number of the tribes of Israel;
12 and a golden diadem on his turban,
  engraved with the seal of consecration;
superb ornamentation, magnificent work,
  adornment to delight the eye.
13 There had never been such lovely things before him,
  and no one else has ever put them on,
but only his own sons,
  and his descendants for all time.
14 His sacrifices were to be burnt entirely,
  twice each day and for ever.
15 Moses consecrated him
  and anointed him with holy oil;
and this was an everlasting covenant for him,
  and for his descendants as long as the heavens
    endure,
that he should preside over worship, act as priest,
  and bless the people in the name of the Lord.
16 He chose him out of all the living
  to offer sacrifices to the Lord,
incense and perfume as a memorial
  to make expiation for the people.
17 He entrusted him with his commandments,
  committed to him the statutes of the Law
for him to teach Jacob his decrees
  and enlighten Israel on his Law.

GREEK OLD TESTAMENT

[18]ἐπισυνέστησαν αὐτῷ ἀλλότριοι
καὶ ἐζήλωσαν αὐτὸν ἐν τῇ ἐρήμῳ,
ἄνδρες οἱ περὶ Δαθαν καὶ Αβιρων
καὶ ἡ συναγωγὴ Κορε ἐν θυμῷ καὶ ὀργῇ·
[19]εἶδεν κύριος καὶ οὐκ εὐδόκησεν,
καὶ συνετελέσθησαν ἐν θυμῷ ὀργῆς·
ἐποίησεν αὐτοῖς τέρατα
καταναλῶσαι ἐν πυρὶ φλογὸς αὐτοῦ.
[20]καὶ προσέθηκεν Ααρων δόξαν
καὶ ἔδωκεν αὐτῷ κληρονομίαν·
ἀπαρχὰς πρωτογενημάτων ἐμέρισεν αὐτῷ,
ἄρτον πρώτοις ἡτοίμασεν πλησμονήν·
[21]καὶ γὰρ θυσίας κυρίου φάγονται,
ἃς ἔδωκεν αὐτῷ τε καὶ τῷ σπέρματι αὐτοῦ.
[22]πλὴν ἐν γῇ λαοῦ οὐ κληρονομήσει,
καὶ μερὶς οὐκ ἔστιν αὐτῷ ἐν λαῷ·
αὐτὸς γὰρ μερίς σου καὶ κληρονομία.
23 Καὶ Φινεες υἱὸς Ελεαζαρ τρίτος εἰς δόξαν
ἐν τῷ ζηλῶσαι αὐτὸν ἐν φόβῳ κυρίου
καὶ στῆναι αὐτὸν ἐν τροπῇ λαοῦ
ἐν ἀγαθότητι προθυμίας ψυχῆς αὐτοῦ·
καὶ ἐξιλάσατο περὶ τοῦ Ισραηλ.
[24]διὰ τοῦτο ἐστάθη αὐτῷ διαθήκη εἰρήνης
προστατεῖν ἁγίων καὶ λαοῦ αὐτοῦ,

KING JAMES VERSION

18 Strangers conspired together against him, and maligned him in the wilderness, even the men that were of Dathan's and Abiron's side, and the congregation of Core, with fury and wrath.

19 This the Lord saw, and it displeased him, and in his wrathful indignation were they consumed: he did wonders upon them, to consume them with the fiery flame.

20 But he made Aaron more honourable, and gave him an heritage, and divided unto him the firstfruits of the increase; especially he prepared bread in abundance:

21 For they eat of the sacrifices of the Lord, which he gave unto him and his seed.

22 Howbeit in the land of the people he had no inheritance, neither had he any portion among the people: for the Lord himself is his portion and inheritance.

23 The third in glory is Phinees the son of Eleazar, because he had zeal in the fear of the Lord, and stood up with good courage of heart when the people were turned back, and made reconciliation for Israel.

24 Therefore was there a covenant of peace made with him, that he should be the chief of the sanctuary and of his

DOUAY OLD TESTAMENT

22 And strangers stood up against him, and through envy the men that were with Dathan and Abiron, compassed him about in the wilderness, and the congregation of Core in their wrath.

23 The Lord God saw and it pleased him not, and they were consumed in his wrathful indignation.

24 He wrought wonders upon them, and consumed them with a flame of fire.

25 And he added glory to Aaron, and gave him an inheritance, and divided unto him the firstfruits of the increase of the earth.

26 He prepared them bread in the first place unto fulness: for the sacrifices also of the Lord they shall eat, which he gave to him, and to his seed.

27 But he shall not inherit among the people in the land, and he hath no portion among the people: for he himself is his portion and inheritance.

28 Phinees the son of Eleazar is the third in glory, by imitating him in the fear of the Lord:

29 And he stood up in the shameful fall of the people: in the goodness and readiness of his soul he appeased God for Israel.

30 Therefore he made to him a covenant of peace, to be the prince of the sanctuary, and of his people, that the

KNOX TRANSLATION

out in the desert, that right was challenged; with envious
cries, men of another clan surrounded him, Dathan and
Abiron for their leaders, espousing Core's quarrel. [23]Ill-con-
tent was the Lord God at the sight of it; his vengeance swept
them away; [24]by no common doom, a raging flame
devoured them. [25]Fresh privileges for Aaron were kept in
store; he must share in the conquest by receiving all the
land's first-fruits; [26]his clan first of all must have bread
enough and to spare, his children should inherit the eating
of the Lord's own sacrifice. [27]But he must have no lands in
the conquered territory, no share like the rest of his race; the
Lord should be his wealth, the Lord his portion.
[28]Next to these two, Phinees the son of Eleazar won high
renown; like Aaron, with the fear of God to guide him, [29]he
stood firm while the people shrank away; a loyal and a willing heart that made amends for Israel. [30]For his reward, he
received assurance of the divine favour; command he
should have of sanctuary and of people both, and the high

TODAY'S ENGLISH VERSION

18 Once, while the people were in the wilderness, an angry
group of jealous outsiders conspired against Moses. These
were Dathan, Abiram, and Korah with their supporters.
19 The Lord saw what they were doing and became angry, so
furious that he performed a miracle and destroyed them in a
blazing fire. 20 Then he rewarded Aaron again, giving him a
special honor: the right to the offerings of the first produce,
so that the priests should have enough to eat. 21 Their food
is the sacrifices offered to the Lord; the Lord gave this to
Aaron and his descendants. 22 But Aaron, unlike the rest of
the people, was to inherit no land, no special portion of his
own. The Lord himself would be all he needed.

23 Only Moses and Aaron were more famous for their
intense devotion to the Lord than Phinehas son of Eleazar.
He brought about forgiveness for Israel's sin by standing
firm in brave determination when everyone else was in rebellion. 24 And so the Lord made a covenant with him, valid for
all time to come, that he should be in charge of the sanctuary

NEW REVISED STANDARD VERSION

18 Outsiders conspired against him,
and envied him in the wilderness,
Dathan and Abiram and their followers
and the company of Korah, in wrath and anger.
19 The Lord saw it and was not pleased,
and in the heat of his anger they were destroyed;
he performed wonders against them
to consume them in flaming fire.
20 He added glory to Aaron
and gave him a heritage;
he allotted to him the best of the first fruits,
and prepared bread of first fruits in abundance;
21 for they eat the sacrifices of the Lord,
which he gave to him and his descendants.
22 But in the land of the people he has no inheritance,
and he has no portion among the people;
for the Lord[a] himself is his[b] portion and inheritance.

23 Phinehas son of Eleazar ranks third in glory
for being zealous in the fear of the Lord,
and standing firm, when the people turned away,
in the noble courage of his soul;
and he made atonement for Israel.
24 Therefore a covenant of friendship was established with him,
that he should be leader of the sanctuary and of his people,

a Gk *he* *b* Other ancient authorities read *your*

NEW AMERICAN BIBLE

18 Men of other families were inflamed against him,
were jealous of him in the desert,
The followers of Dathan and Abiram,
and the band of Korah in their defiance.
19 But the LORD saw this and became angry,
he destroyed them in his burning wrath.
He brought down upon them a miracle,
and consumed them with his flaming fire.
20 Then he increased the glory of Aaron
and bestowed upon him his inheritance:
The sacred offerings he allotted to him,
with the showbread as his portion;
21 The oblations of the LORD are his food,
a gift to him and his descendants.
22 But he holds no land among the people
nor shares with them their heritage;
For the LORD himself is his portion,
his inheritance in the midst of Israel.

23 PHINEHAS too, the son of Eleazar,
was the courageous third of his line
When, zealous for the God of all,
he met the crisis of his people
And, at the prompting of his noble heart,
atoned for the children of Israel.
24 Therefore on him again God conferred the right,
in a covenant of friendship, to provide for the sanctuary,

NEW JERUSALEM BIBLE

18 Others plotted against him,
they were jealous of him in the desert,
Dathan and Abiram and their men,
Korah and his crew in fury and rage.
19 The Lord saw it and was displeased,
his raging fury made an end of them;
he worked miracles on them,
consuming them by his flaming fire.
20 And he added to Aaron's glory,
he gave him an inheritance;
he allotted him the offerings of the first-fruits,
before all else, as much bread as he could want.
21 Thus they eat the sacrifices of the Lord
which he gave to him and his posterity.
22 But of the people's territory he inherits nothing,
he alone of all the people has no share,
'For I myself am your share and heritage.'

23 Phinehas son of Eleazar is third in glory
because of his zeal in the fear of the Lord,
because he stood firm when the people revolted,
with a staunch and courageous heart;
and in this way made expiation for Israel.
24 Hence a covenant of peace was sealed with him,
making him governor of both sanctuary and people,

GREEK OLD TESTAMENT

ἵνα αὐτῷ ᾖ καὶ τῷ σπέρματι αὐτοῦ
ἱερωσύνης μεγαλεῖον εἰς τοὺς αἰῶνας.
25 καὶ διαθήκη τῷ Δαυιδ
υἱῷ Ιεσσαι ἐκ φυλῆς Ιουδα
κληρονομία βασιλέως υἱοῦ ἐξ υἱοῦ μόνου·
κληρονομία Ααρων καὶ τῷ σπέρματι αὐτοῦ.
26 δῴη ὑμῖν σοφίαν ἐν καρδίᾳ ὑμῶν
κρίνειν τὸν λαὸν αὐτοῦ ἐν δικαιοσύνῃ,
ἵνα μὴ ἀφανισθῇ τὰ ἀγαθὰ αὐτῶν
καὶ τὴν δόξαν αὐτῶν εἰς γενεὰς αὐτῶν.

46 Κραταιὸς ἐν πολέμῳ Ἰησοῦς Ναυη
καὶ διάδοχος Μωυσῆ ἐν προφητείαις,
ὃς ἐγένετο κατὰ τὸ ὄνομα αὐτοῦ
μέγας ἐπὶ σωτηρίᾳ ἐκλεκτῶν αὐτοῦ
ἐκδικῆσαι ἐπεγειρομένους ἐχθρούς,
ὅπως κατακληρονομήσῃ τὸν Ισραηλ.
2 ὡς ἐδοξάσθη ἐν τῷ ἐπᾶραι χεῖρας αὐτοῦ
καὶ ἐν τῷ ἐκτεῖναι ῥομφαίαν ἐπὶ πόλεις.
3 τίς πρότερος αὐτοῦ οὕτως ἔστη;
τοὺς γὰρ πολέμους κυρίου αὐτὸς ἐπήγαγεν.

KING JAMES VERSION

people, and that he and his posterity should have the dignity
of the priesthood for ever:
25 According to the covenant made with David son of
Jesse, of the tribe of Juda, that the inheritance of the king
should be to his posterity alone: so the inheritance of Aaron
should also be unto his seed.
26 God give you wisdom in your heart to judge his people
in righteousness, that their good things be not abolished,
and that their glory may endure for ever.

46 Jesus the son a Nave was valiant in the wars, and
was the successor of Moses in prophecies, who
according to his name was made great for the saving of the
elect of God, and taking vengeance of the enemies that rose
up against them, that he might set Israel in their inheritance.
2 How great glory gat he, when he did lift up his hands,
and stretched out his sword against the cities!
3 Who before him so stood to it? for the Lord himself
brought his enemies unto him.

DOUAY OLD TESTAMENT

dignity of priesthood should be to him and to his seed for
ever.
31 And a covenant to David the king, the son of Jesse of
the tribe of Juda, an inheritance to him and to his seed, that
he might give wisdom into our heart to judge his people in
justice, that their good things might not be abolished, and he
made their glory in their nation everlasting.

46 VALIANT in war was Jesus the son of Nave, who was
successor of Moses among the prophets, who was
great according to his name,
2 Very great for the saving the elect of God, to overthrow
the enemies that rose up against them, that he might get the
inheritance for Israel.
3 How great glory did he gain when he lifted up his
hands, and stretched out swords against the cities?
4 Who before him hath so resisted? for the Lord himself
brought the enemies.

KNOX TRANSLATION

priesthood that was his should descend to his heirs for ever.
31 David the son of Jesse, of Juda's tribe, should bequeath to
his children a legacy of kingship...
...with wise hearts endowing us, to preserve justice among
his people, and keep safe the blessings he has given to it;
and this pre-eminence over his people he has settled on them
in perpetuity.[a]

46 Next to Moses in the line of prophets comes Josue the
son of Nave, that fought so well. With him, name
and renown are one; 2 who is more renowned for the deliverance he brought to God's chosen people, beating down the
enemies that defied him until Israel made their land its own?
3 What fame he won by those valiant blows he dealt, hurling
his armed strength at city after city! 4 What chieftain had
ever stood his ground so manfully? And still the Lord

[a] A comparison with the other versions confirms the impression, which the incoherence of the Latin would in any case suggest, that several words have been omitted. Both the Hebrew and the Greek indicate that King David was introduced into the narrative only by way of contrast; the sacred author is pointing out an analogy between the ecclesiastical and the secular government of Israel. In the Hebrew, the concluding words of the chapter form part of a doxology, which begins, 'And now bless the Lord, that is so bountiful'.

TODAY'S ENGLISH VERSION

and of his people, that he and his descendants should hold
the office of High Priest forever. 25 Unlike the covenant made
with David son of Jesse, from the tribe of Judah, where the
kingship passed only from father to son, the priesthood was
to pass from Aaron to all his descendants.
26 Now praise the Lord, who is good, who has crowned you
with glory![a] May he give you wisdom to judge his people
fairly, so that their success and your authority[b] may continue for all time to come.

46 Joshua[c] son of Nun was a great soldier and the next
of the prophets after Moses. He lived up to the meaning of his name as the great deliverer of the Lord's chosen
people. He defeated the enemies that attacked them, so that
Israel could claim its land. 2 How magnificent it was when
he raised his arm and then led the attacks on the cities! 3 No
one could stand up to him;[d] he was fighting a holy war for

[a] *Hebrew* Now praise . . . glory; *Greek does not have these words.*
[b] *Probable Hebrew text* and your authority; *Greek unclear.*
[c] JOSHUA: *This name in Hebrew means "the Lord saves."* [d] *Hebrew* no one . . . to him; *Greek* No one before had ever been so brave.

NEW REVISED STANDARD VERSION

that he and his descendants should have
the dignity of the priesthood forever.
25 Just as a covenant was established with David
son of Jesse of the tribe of Judah,
that the king's heritage passes only from son to son,
so the heritage of Aaron is for his descendants alone.

26 And now bless the Lord
who has crowned you with glory.[a]
May the Lord[b] grant you wisdom of mind
to judge his people with justice,
so that their prosperity may not vanish,
and that their glory may endure through all their generations.

46 Joshua son of Nun was mighty in war,
and was the successor of Moses in the prophetic office.
He became, as his name implies,
a great savior of God's[c] elect,
to take vengeance on the enemies that rose against them,
so that he might give Israel its inheritance.
2 How glorious he was when he lifted his hands
and brandished his sword against the cities!
3 Who before him ever stood so firm?
For he waged the wars of the Lord.

a Heb: Gk lacks *And . . . glory* *b* Gk *he* *c* Gk *his*

NEW AMERICAN BIBLE

So that he and his descendants
should possess the high priesthood forever.
25 For even his covenant with David,
the son of Jesse of the tribe of Judah,
Was an individual heritage through one son alone;
but the heritage of Aaron is for all his descendants.

26 And now bless the LORD
who has crowned you with glory!
May he grant you wisdom of heart
to govern his people in justice,
Lest their welfare should ever be forgotten,
or your authority, throughout all time.

46 Valiant leader was JOSHUA, son of Nun
assistant to Moses in the prophetic office,
Formed to be, as his name implies,
the great savior of God's chosen ones,
To punish the enemy
and to win the inheritance for Israel.
2 What glory was his when he raised his arm,
to brandish his javelin against the city!
3 And who could withstand him
when he fought the battles of the LORD?

NEW JERUSALEM BIBLE

and securing to him and his descendants
the high priestly dignity for ever.
25 There was also a covenant with David
son of Jesse, of the tribe of Judah,
a royal succession by exclusively linear descent,
but the succession of Aaron passes to all his descendants.
26 May God endow your hearts with wisdom
to judge his people uprightly,
so that the virtues of your ancestors may never fade,
and their glory may pass to all their descendants!

46 Mighty in war was Joshua son of Nun,
successor to Moses in the prophetic office,
who well deserved his name,[a]
and was a great saviour of the chosen people,
wreaking vengeance on the enemies who opposed him,
and so bringing Israel into its inheritance.
2 How splendid he was when, arms uplifted,
he brandished his sword against cities!
3 Who had ever shown such determination as his?
He himself led the battles of the Lord.

[a] **46** *Yehoshua'* (=Joshua) means 'Yahweh saves'.

GREEK OLD TESTAMENT

4 οὐχὶ ἐν χειρὶ αὐτοῦ ἐνεποδίσθη ὁ ἥλιος
καὶ μία ἡμέρα ἐγενήθη πρὸς δύο;
5 ἐπεκαλέσατο τὸν ὕψιστον δυνάστην
ἐν τῷ θλῖψαι αὐτὸν ἐχθροὺς κυκλόθεν,
καὶ ἐπήκουσεν αὐτοῦ μέγας κύριος
ἐν λίθοις χαλάζης δυνάμεως κραταιᾶς·
6 κατέρραξεν ἐπ᾽ ἔθνος πόλεμον
καὶ ἐν καταβάσει ἀπώλεσεν ἀνθεστηκότας,
ἵνα γνῶσιν ἔθνη πανοπλίαν αὐτοῦ
ὅτι ἐναντίον κυρίου ὁ πόλεμος αὐτοῦ.
7 Καὶ γὰρ ἐπηκολούθησεν ὀπίσω δυνάστου
καὶ ἐν ἡμέραις Μωυσέως ἐποίησεν ἔλεος
αὐτὸς καὶ Χαλεβ υἱὸς Ιεφοννη
ἀντιστῆναι ἔναντι ἐκκλησίας
κωλῦσαι λαὸν ἀπὸ ἁμαρτίας
καὶ κοπάσαι γογγυσμὸν πονηρίας.
8 καὶ αὐτοὶ δύο ὄντες διεσώθησαν
ἀπὸ ἑξακοσίων χιλιάδων πεζῶν
εἰσαγαγεῖν αὐτοὺς εἰς κληρονομίαν
εἰς γῆν ῥέουσαν γάλα καὶ μέλι.
9 καὶ ἔδωκεν ὁ κύριος τῷ Χαλεβ ἰσχύν,
καὶ ἕως γήρους διέμεινεν αὐτῷ,
ἐπιβῆναι αὐτὸν ἐπὶ τὸ ὕψος τῆς γῆς,
καὶ τὸ σπέρμα αὐτοῦ κατέσχεν κληρονομίαν,
10 ὅπως ἴδωσιν πάντες οἱ υἱοὶ Ισραηλ
ὅτι καλὸν τὸ πορεύεσθαι ὀπίσω κυρίου.

KING JAMES VERSION

4 Did not the sun go back by his means? and was not one day as long as two?

5 He called upon the most high Lord, when the enemies pressed upon him on every side; and the great Lord heard him.

6 And with hailstones of mighty power he made the battle to fall violently upon the nations, and in the descent [of Beth-horon] he destroyed them that resisted, that the nations might know all their strength, because he fought in the sight of the Lord, and he followed the Mighty One.

7 In the time of Moses also he did a work of mercy, he and Caleb the son of Jephunne, in that they withstood the congregation, and withheld the people from sin, and appeased the wicked murmuring.

8 And of six hundred thousand people on foot, they two were preserved to bring them into the heritage, even unto the land that floweth with milk and honey.

9 The Lord gave strength also unto Caleb, which remained with him unto his old age: so that he entered upon the high places of the land, and his seed obtained it for an heritage:

10 That all the children of Israel might see that it is good to follow the Lord.

DOUAY OLD TESTAMENT

5 Was not the sun stopped in his anger, and one day made as two?

6 He called upon the most high Sovereign when the enemies assaulted him on every side, and the great and holy God heard him by hailstones of exceeding great force.

7 He made a violent assault against the nation of his enemies, and in the descent he destroyed the adversaries.

8 That the nations might know his power, that it is not easy to fight against God. And he followed the mighty one:

9 And in the days of Moses he did a work of mercy, he and Caleb the son of Jephone, in standing against the enemy, and withholding the people from sins, and appeasing the wicked murmuring.

10 And they two being appointed, were delivered out of the danger from among the number of six hundred thousand men on foot, to bring them into their inheritance, into the land that floweth with milk and honey.

11 And the Lord gave strength also to Caleb, and his strength continued even to his old age, so that he went up to the high places of the land, and his seed obtained it for an inheritance:

12 That all the children of Israel might see, that it is good to obey the holy God.

KNOX TRANSLATION

brought enemies to confront him. 5 On his fierce resolve the
sun itself must wait, and a whole day's length be doubled.
6 Let enemies attack him on every side, he would invoke the
most High, to whom all strength belongs, the great God, the
holy God, and his prayer was answered.[a] Hail-stones came
down in a storm of wondrous violence, 7 that fell on the
opposing army and shattered the menace of it, there on the
hill-side. 8 So the Gentiles should feel God's power, and learn
that it is a hard matter to fight against him. Ever had Josue
followed in that Prince's retinue, 9 since the days when
Moses yet lived; he it was, and Caleb the son of Jephone, that
took a generous part together; they would have engaged the
enemy, and saved their own people from guilt by hushing
the murmurs of rebellion. 10 These two alone, out of six hundred thousand warriors, survived the perils of the journey;
these two were appointed to lead Israel into the land, all
milk and honey, that was its promised home.
11 On Caleb, too, the Lord bestowed such vigour, that in his
old age he was a warrior still, and made his way up into the
hill-country, where his descendants held their lands after
him; 12 no doubt should Israel have that he is well rewarded

a *vv.* 5, 6: See Josue 10. 10-14.

TODAY'S ENGLISH VERSION

the Lord. 4 Remember how he held back the sun and made
one day as long as two? 5 When his enemies were threatening him from every side, he prayed to the mighty Lord Most
High, and his prayer was answered with a hailstorm of devastating force. 6 The Lord hurled the hail down on the
enemy[a] and destroyed them at the pass at Beth Horon, so
that the nations would realize how strong Joshua was, since
he was fighting as a devoted follower of the Lord.

7 Joshua was loyal as long as Moses lived, both he and
Caleb son of Jephunneh. They stood up to the whole community, made them stop their ungrateful complaining, and kept
them from sinning. 8 Out of the 600,000 Israelites who
marched through the wilderness, these two were the only
ones spared and allowed to enter the rich and fertile land
that was to be theirs. 9 The Lord made Caleb strong, and
when he was an old man, he was still strong enough to go
up into the hill country and capture it for himself and his
descendants. 10 Then all of Israel could see how good it is to
follow the Lord.

[a] *Probable text* The Lord hurled . . . enemy; *Greek unclear.*

NEW REVISED STANDARD VERSION

4 Was it not through him that the sun stood still
    and one day became as long as two?
5 He called upon the Most High, the Mighty One,
    when enemies pressed him on every side,
and the great Lord answered him
    with hailstones of mighty power.
6 He overwhelmed that nation in battle,
    and on the slope he destroyed his opponents,
so that the nations might know his armament,
    that he was fighting in the sight of the Lord;
    for he was a devoted follower of the Mighty One.
7 And in the days of Moses he proved his loyalty,
    he and Caleb son of Jephunneh:
they opposed the congregation,[a]
    restrained the people from sin,
    and stilled their wicked grumbling.
8 And these two alone were spared
    out of six hundred thousand infantry,
to lead the people[b] into their inheritance,
    the land flowing with milk and honey.
9 The Lord gave Caleb strength,
    which remained with him in his old age,
so that he went up to the hill country,
    and his children obtained it for an inheritance,
10 so that all the Israelites might see
    how good it is to follow the Lord.

a Other ancient authorities read *the enemy* *b* Gk *them*

NEW AMERICAN BIBLE

4 Did he not by his power stop the sun,
    so that one day became two?
5 He called upon the Most High God
    when his enemies beset him on all sides,
And God Most High gave answer to him
    in hailstones of tremendous power,
6 Which he rained down upon the hostile army
    till on the slope he destroyed the foe;
That all the doomed nations might know
    that the LORD was watching over his people's battles.
And because he was a devoted follower of God
7 and in Moses' lifetime showed himself loyal,
He and CALEB, son of Jephunneh,
    when they opposed the rebel assembly,
Averted God's anger from the people
    and suppressed the wicked complaint—
8 Because of this, they were the only two spared
    from the six hundred thousand infantry,
To lead the people into their inheritance,
    the land flowing with milk and honey.
9 And the strength he gave to Caleb
    remained with him even in his old age
Till he won his way onto the summits of the land;
    his family too received an inheritance,
10 That all the people of Jacob might know
    how good it is to be a devoted follower of the LORD.

NEW JERUSALEM BIBLE

4 Was not the sun held back by his hand,
    and one day drawn out into two?
5 He called on the Most High, the Mighty One,
    while pressing the enemies from all directions,
and the great Lord answered him
    with hard and violent hailstones.
6 He fell on that enemy nation,
    and at the Descent destroyed all resistance
to make the nations acknowledge his warlike prowess
    and that he was waging war on behalf of the Lord.
7 For he was a follower of the Mighty One,
    in the time of Moses showing his devotion,
he and Caleb son of Jephunneh,
    by opposing the whole community,
by preventing the people from sinning,
    and by silencing the mutters of rebellion.
8 Hence these two alone were preserved
    out of six hundred thousand men on the march,
and brought into their inheritance,
    into a land where milk and honey flow.
9 And the Lord conferred strength on Caleb too,
    which stayed by him into old age,
so that he could invest the highlands of the country
    which his descendants kept as their inheritance,
10 so that every Israelite might see
    that it is good to follow the Lord.

GREEK OLD TESTAMENT

11 Καὶ οἱ κριταί, ἕκαστος τῷ αὐτοῦ ὀνόματι,
ὅσων οὐκ ἐξεπόρνευσεν ἡ καρδία
καὶ ὅσοι οὐκ ἀπεστράφησαν ἀπὸ κυρίου,
εἴη τὸ μνημόσυνον αὐτῶν ἐν εὐλογίαις·
12 τὰ ὀστᾶ αὐτῶν ἀναθάλοι ἐκ τοῦ τόπου αὐτῶν
καὶ τὸ ὄνομα αὐτῶν ἀντικαταλλασσόμενον
ἐφ' υἱοῖς δεδοξασμένων αὐτῶν.
13 Ἠγαπημένος ὑπὸ κυρίου αὐτοῦ Σαμουηλ
προφήτης κυρίου κατέστησεν βασιλείαν
καὶ ἔχρισεν ἄρχοντας ἐπὶ τὸν λαὸν αὐτοῦ·
14 ἐν νόμῳ κυρίου ἔκρινεν συναγωγήν,
καὶ ἐπεσκέψατο κύριος τὸν Ιακωβ·
15 ἐν πίστει αὐτοῦ ἠκριβάσθη προφήτης
καὶ ἐγνώσθη ἐν ῥήμασιν αὐτοῦ πιστὸς ὁράσεως.
16 καὶ ἐπεκαλέσατο τὸν κύριον δυνάστην
ἐν τῷ θλῖψαι ἐχθροὺς αὐτοῦ κυκλόθεν
ἐν προσφορᾷ ἀρνὸς γαλαθηνοῦ·
17 καὶ ἐβρόντησεν ἀπ' οὐρανοῦ ὁ κύριος
καὶ ἐν ἤχῳ μεγάλῳ ἀκουστὴν ἐποίησεν τὴν φωνὴν αὐτοῦ
18 καὶ ἐξέτριψεν ἡγουμένους Τυρίων
καὶ πάντας ἄρχοντας Φυλιστιιμ.
19 καὶ πρὸ καιροῦ κοιμήσεως αἰῶνος
ἐπεμαρτύρατο ἔναντι κυρίου καὶ χριστοῦ αὐτοῦ
Χρήματα καὶ ἕως ὑποδημάτων
ἀπὸ πάσης σαρκὸς οὐκ εἴληφα·
καὶ οὐκ ἐνεκάλεσεν αὐτῷ ἄνθρωπος.

KING JAMES VERSION

11 And concerning the judges, every one by name, whose heart went not a whoring, nor departed from the Lord, let their memory be blessed.

12 Let their bones flourish out of their place, and let the name of them that were honoured be continued upon their children.

13 Samuel, the prophet of the Lord, beloved of his Lord, established a kingdom, and anointed princes over his people.

14 By the law of the Lord he judged the congregation, and the Lord had respect unto Jacob.

15 By his faithfulness he was found a true prophet, and by his word he was known to be faithful in vision.

16 He called upon the mighty Lord, when his enemies pressed upon him on every side, when he offered the sucking lamb.

17 And the Lord thundered from heaven, and with a great noise made his voice to be heard.

18 And he destroyed the rulers of the Tyrians, and all the princes of the Philistines.

19 And before his long sleep he made protestations in the sight of the Lord and his anointed, I have not taken any man's goods, so much as a shoe: and no man did accuse him.

DOUAY OLD TESTAMENT

13 Then all the judges, every one by name, whose heart was not corrupted: who turned not away from the Lord,

14 That their memory might be blessed, and their bones spring up out of their place,

15 And their name continue for ever, the glory of the holy men remaining unto their children.

16 Samuel the prophet of the Lord, the beloved of the Lord his God, established a new government, and anointed princes over his people.

17 By the law of the Lord he judged the congregation, and the God of Jacob beheld, and by his fidelity he was proved a prophet.

18 And he was known to be faithful in his words, because he saw the God of light:

19 And called upon the name of the Lord Almighty, in fighting against the enemies who beset him on every side, when he offered a lamb without blemish.

20 And the Lord thundered from heaven, and with a great noise made his voice to be heard.

21 And he crushed the princes of the Tyrians, and all the lords of the Philistines:

22 And before the time of the end of his life in the world, he protested before the Lord, and his anointed: money, or any thing else, even to a shoe, he had not taken of any man, and no man did accuse him.

KNOX TRANSLATION

who serves so holy a God. 13 The judges, too, have their glorious muster-roll, men of resolute heart, that God's cause
never forsook; 14 be their names, too, remembered in blessing, and may life spring from their bones, where they lie
buried; 15 undying be their memory, in their own posterity
continued, undying be the sacred record of their renown.
16 Dearly the Lord God loved his prophet Samuel, that
restored Israel's fortunes and anointed kings to rule over it.
17 Well was the divine law kept, when he ruled our commonwealth, and the God of Jacob was gracious to it; here was a
prophet of proved loyalty, 18 and ever his word came true,
such vision had he of the God that gives light. 19 With foes
about him on every side, he invoked the Lord, the Almighty,
with an unblemished lamb for sacrifice; 20 and therewith
came thunder, sent from heaven, loud echo of the divine
voice,[a] 21 that overthrew all the princes of the sea-coast, all
the captains of the Philistines. 22 There must be an end at
last to his life, and to the age he lived in; but first he would
make profession, with the Lord and the new-anointed king
for his witnesses, bribe he had never taken from any living
man, though it were but a gift of shoe-leather; and none
might gainsay him.[b] 23 Even when he had gone to his rest,

a See I Kg. 7. 10. *b* See I Kg. 12. 3.

TODAY'S ENGLISH VERSION

11 Then there were the judges, each of them famous in their
own right, who never fell into idolatry and never abandoned
the Lord. 12 May their memory be honored! May these whom
we honor spring from the grave to new life in their descendants!

13 Samuel was loved by the Lord. As the Lord's prophet he
established the kingdom and appointed rulers for the people.
14 He judged the nation in accordance with the Law of the
Lord, and the Lord protected Israel. 15 Because Samuel was
faithful, he was accepted as a true prophet. People trusted
him as a seer because of his words. 16 When his enemies
were threatening him from every side, he called upon the
mighty Lord and offered him a young lamb as a sacrifice.
17 Then the Lord thundered from heaven with a mighty roar
18 and destroyed all the enemy[a] rulers of Philistia. 19 When
Samuel was about to die, he gave assurances before the Lord
and the anointed king that he had never taken anyone's
property, not even so much as a pair of shoes, and no one

[a] *Hebrew* enemy; *Greek* rulers of Tyre and.

NEW REVISED STANDARD VERSION

11 The judges also, with their respective names,
whose hearts did not fall into idolatry
and who did not turn away from the Lord—
may their memory be blessed!
12 May their bones send forth new life from where they lie,
and may the names of those who have been honored
live again in their children!

13 Samuel was beloved by his Lord;
a prophet of the Lord, he established the kingdom
and anointed rulers over his people.
14 By the law of the Lord he judged the congregation,
and the Lord watched over Jacob.
15 By his faithfulness he was proved to be a prophet,
and by his words he became known as a trustworthy
seer.
16 He called upon the Lord, the Mighty One,
when his enemies pressed him on every side,
and he offered in sacrifice a suckling lamb.
17 Then the Lord thundered from heaven,
and made his voice heard with a mighty sound;
18 he subdued the leaders of the enemy[a]
and all the rulers of the Philistines.
19 Before the time of his eternal sleep,
Samuel[b] bore witness before the Lord and his anointed:
"No property, not so much as a pair of shoes,
have I taken from anyone!"
And no one accused him.

a Heb: Gk *leaders of the people of Tyre* *b* Gk *he*

NEW AMERICAN BIBLE

11 The JUDGES, too, each one of them,
whose hearts were not deceived,
Who did not abandon God:
may their memory be ever blessed,
12 Their bones return to life from their resting place,
and their names receive fresh luster in their children!
13 Beloved of his people, dear to his Maker,
dedicated from his mother's womb,
Consecrated to the LORD as a prophet,
was SAMUEL, the judge and priest.
At God's word he established the kingdom
and anointed princes to rule the people.
14 By the law of the LORD he judged the nation,
when he visited the encampments of Jacob.
15 As a trustworthy prophet he was sought out
and his words proved him true as a seer.
16 He, too, called upon God,
and offered him a suckling lamb;
17 Then the LORD thundered forth from heaven,
and the tremendous roar of his voice was heard.
18 He brought low the rulers of the enemy
and destroyed all the lords of the Philistines.
19 When Samuel approached the end of his life,
he testified before the LORD and his anointed prince,
"No bribe or secret gift have I taken from any man!"
and no one dared gainsay him.

NEW JERUSALEM BIBLE

11 The Judges too, each when he was called,
all men whose hearts were never disloyal,
who never turned their backs on the Lord—
may their memory be blessed!
12 May their bones flourish again from the tomb,
and may the names of those illustrious men
be worthily borne by their sons!

13 Samuel was the beloved of his Lord;
prophet of the Lord, he instituted the kingdom,
and anointed rulers over his people.
14 By the Law of the Lord he judged the assembly,
and the Lord watched over Jacob.
15 By his loyalty he was recognised as a prophet,
by his words he was known to be a trustworthy seer.
16 He called on the Lord, the Mighty One,
when his enemies pressed in from all directions,
by offering a sucking lamb.
17 And the Lord thundered from heaven,
and made his voice heard in a rolling peal;
18 he massacred the leaders of the enemy,
and all the rulers of the Philistines.
19 Before the time of his everlasting rest
he bore witness to the Lord and his anointed,
'Of no property, not even a pair of sandals,
have I ever deprived a soul.'
Nor did anyone accuse him.

GREEK OLD TESTAMENT

20 καὶ μετὰ τὸ ὑπνῶσαι αὐτὸν προεφήτευσεν
καὶ ὑπέδειξεν βασιλεῖ τὴν τελευτὴν αὐτοῦ
καὶ ἀνύψωσεν ἐκ γῆς τὴν φωνὴν αὐτοῦ
ἐν προφητείᾳ ἐξαλεῖψαι ἀνομίαν λαοῦ.

47 Καὶ μετὰ τοῦτον ἀνέστη Ναθαν
προφητεύειν ἐν ἡμέραις Δαυιδ.
2 ὥσπερ στέαρ ἀφωρισμένον ἀπὸ σωτηρίου,
οὕτως Δαυιδ ἀπὸ τῶν υἱῶν Ισραηλ.
3 ἐν λέουσιν ἔπαιξεν ὡς ἐν ἐρίφοις
καὶ ἐν ἄρκοις ὡς ἐν ἄρνασι προβάτων.
4 ἐν νεότητι αὐτοῦ οὐχὶ ἀπέκτεινεν γίγαντα
καὶ ἐξῆρεν ὀνειδισμὸν ἐκ λαοῦ
ἐν τῷ ἐπᾶραι χεῖρα ἐν λίθῳ σφενδόνης
καὶ καταβαλεῖν γαυρίαμα τοῦ Γολιαθ;
5 ἐπεκαλέσατο γὰρ κύριον τὸν ὕψιστον,
καὶ ἔδωκεν ἐν τῇ δεξιᾷ αὐτοῦ κράτος
ἐξᾶραι ἄνθρωπον δυνατὸν ἐν πολέμῳ
ἀνυψῶσαι κέρας λαοῦ αὐτοῦ.
6 οὕτως ἐν μυριάσιν ἐδόξασαν αὐτὸν
καὶ ᾔνεσαν αὐτὸν ἐν εὐλογίαις κυρίου
ἐν τῷ φέρεσθαι αὐτῷ διάδημα δόξης·
7 ἐξέτριψεν γὰρ ἐχθροὺς κυκλόθεν
καὶ ἐξουδένωσεν Φυλιστιιμ τοὺς ὑπεναντίους,
ἕως σήμερον συνέτριψεν αὐτῶν κέρας.

KING JAMES VERSION

20 And after his death he prophesied, and shewed the king his end, and lifted up his voice from the earth in prophecy, to blot out the wickedness of the people.

47 And after him rose up Nathan to prophesy in the time of David.

2 As is the fat taken away from the peace offering, so was David chosen out of the children of Israel.

3 He played with lions as with kids, and with bears as with lambs.

4 Slew he not a giant, when he was yet but young? and did he not take away reproach from the people, when he lifted up his hand with the stone in the sling, and beat down the boasting of Goliath?

5 For he called upon the most high Lord; and he gave him strength in his right hand to slay that mighty warrior, and set up the horn of his people.

6 So the people honoured him with ten thousands, and praised him in the blessings of the Lord, in that he gave him a crown of glory.

7 For he destroyed the enemies on every side, and brought to nought the Philistines his adversaries, and brake their horn in sunder unto this day.

DOUAY OLD TESTAMENT

23 And after this he slept, and he made known to the king, and shewed him the end of his life, and he lifted up his voice from the earth in prophecy to blot out the wickedness of the nation.

47 THEN Nathan the prophet arose in the days of David.
2 And as the fat taken away from the flesh, so was David *chosen* from among the children of Israel.

3 He played with lions as with lambs: and with bears he did in like manner as with the lambs of the flock, in his youth.

4 Did not he kill the giant, and take away reproach from his people?

5 In lifting up his hand, with the stone in the sling he beat down the boasting of Goliath:

6 For he called upon the Lord the Almighty, and he gave strength in his right hand, to take away the mighty warrior, and to set up the horn of his nation.

7 So in ten thousand did he glorify him, and praised him in the blessings of the Lord, in offering to him a crown of glory:

8 For he destroyed the enemies on every side, and extirpated the Philistines the adversaries unto this day: he broke their horn for ever.

KNOX TRANSLATION

he had a revelation for the king's ear, and gave warning of the death that awaited him; a prophet, even in the tomb, while there was yet guilt among his people to be effaced.

47 Among prophets, Nathan was the next to arise, and
it was then the reign of David began. 2 Only the fat
from the sacrifice, only David out of all Israel; the Lord must
have ever the best! 3 Here was one that would use lion or
bear as playthings for his sport, tussle with them as if they
had been yearling lambs. Such was his boyhood; 4 and who
but he should save the honour of his people, by slaying the
giant? 5 He had but to lift his hand, and the stone aimed
from his sling brought low the pride of Goliath; 6 prayer to
the Lord, the Almighty, gave him the mastery over a great
warrior, and retrieved the fortunes of his race. 7 Ere long,
they had given him the title, Slayer of ten thousand, and
sang his praises, blessing the Lord's name; kingly honours
they accorded him. 8 He it was that laid their enemies low all
about them, extirpating, to this day, the malice of the
Philistines, shattering their power for ever. 9 Yet there was

TODAY'S ENGLISH VERSION

contradicted him. 20 Even after he died, he prophesied to
King Saul how he would die. Out of the grave he spoke as a
prophet, to blot out his people's wickedness.

47 After him came Nathan, who was a prophet at the
time of David.

2 As the choice fat portion of the fellowship offering is
reserved for the Lord, so David was chosen from among the
Israelites. 3 He played with lions and bears as if they were
lambs or little goats. 4 When he was still a boy, he killed a
giant to rescue his people. He put a stone in his sling, took
aim, and put an end to Goliath's bragging. 5 He prayed to
the Lord, the Most High, and was given the strength to kill
that famous soldier, so that the nations would have respect
for the power of his people. 6 The people honored him for
killing his tens of thousands, and when he was crowned
king, they praised him for being chosen by the Lord. 7 He
wiped out all his enemies and permanently crushed the
Philistines, so that they never again became a threat.

NEW REVISED STANDARD VERSION

20 Even after he had fallen asleep, he prophesied
and made known to the king his death,
and lifted up his voice from the ground
in prophecy, to blot out the wickedness of the people.

47 After him Nathan rose up
to prophesy in the days of David.
2 As the fat is set apart from the offering of well-being,
so David was set apart from the Israelites.
3 He played with lions as though they were young goats,
and with bears as though they were lambs of the flock.
4 In his youth did he not kill a giant,
and take away the people's disgrace,
when he whirled the stone in the sling
and struck down the boasting Goliath?
5 For he called on the Lord, the Most High,
and he gave strength to his right arm
to strike down a mighty warrior,
and to exalt the power[a] of his people.
6 So they glorified him for the tens of thousands he conquered,
and praised him for the blessings bestowed by the Lord,
when the glorious diadem was given to him.
7 For he wiped out his enemies on every side,
and annihilated his adversaries the Philistines;
he crushed their power[a] to our own day.

a Gk *horn*

NEW AMERICAN BIBLE

20 Even when he lay buried, his guidance was sought;
he made known to the king his fate,
And from the grave he raised his voice
as a prophet, to put an end to wickedness.

47 After him came NATHAN
who served in the presence of David.
2 Like the choice fat of the sacred offerings,
so was DAVID in Israel.
3 He made sport of lions as though they were kids,
and of bears, like lambs of the flock.
4 As a youth he slew the giant
and wiped out the people's disgrace,
When his hand let fly the slingstone
that crushed the pride of Goliath.
5 Since he called upon the Most High God,
who gave strength to his right arm
To defeat the skilled warrior
and raise up the might of his people,
6 Therefore the women sang his praises
and ascribed to him tens of thousands.
When he assumed the royal crown, he battled
7 and subdued the enemy on every side.
He destroyed the hostile Philistines
and shattered their power till our own day.

NEW JERUSALEM BIBLE

20 And, having fallen asleep, he prophesied again,
warning the king of his end;
he spoke from the depths of the earth in prophecy,
to blot out the wickedness of the people.

47 After him arose Nathan,
to prophesy in the time of David.
2 As the fat is set apart from the communion sacrifice,
so was David chosen out of the Israelites.
3 He played with lions as though with kids,
and with bears as though with lambs.
4 While still a boy, did he not slay the giant
and take away the people's shame,
by hurling a stone from his sling
and cutting short the boasting of Goliath?
5 For he called on the Lord Most High,
who gave strength to his right arm
to put a mighty warrior to death
and assert the strength of his own people.
6 Hence they gave him credit for ten thousand,
and praised him while they blessed the Lord,
by offering him a crown of glory.
7 For he destroyed the enemies on every front,
he annihilated his foes, the Philistines,
and crushed their strength for ever.

GREEK OLD TESTAMENT

8 ἐν παντὶ ἔργῳ αὐτοῦ ἔδωκεν ἐξομολόγησιν
ἁγίῳ ὑψίστῳ ῥήματι δόξης·
ἐν πάσῃ καρδίᾳ αὐτοῦ ὕμνησεν
καὶ ἠγάπησεν τὸν ποιήσαντα αὐτόν.
9 καὶ ἔστησεν ψαλτῳδοὺς κατέναντι τοῦ θυσιαστηρίου
καὶ ἐξ ἤχους αὐτῶν γλυκαίνειν μέλη·
10 ἔδωκεν ἐν ἑορταῖς εὐπρέπειαν
καὶ ἐκόσμησεν καιροὺς μέχρι συντελείας
ἐν τῷ αἰνεῖν αὐτοὺς τὸ ἅγιον ὄνομα αὐτοῦ
καὶ ἀπὸ πρωίας ἠχεῖν τὸ ἁγίασμα.
11 κύριος ἀφεῖλεν τὰς ἁμαρτίας αὐτοῦ
καὶ ἀνύψωσεν εἰς αἰῶνα τὸ κέρας αὐτοῦ
καὶ ἔδωκεν αὐτῷ διαθήκην βασιλέων
καὶ θρόνον δόξης ἐν τῷ Ισραηλ.
12 Μετὰ τοῦτον ἀνέστη υἱὸς ἐπιστήμων
καὶ δι᾽ αὐτὸν κατέλυσεν ἐν πλατυσμῷ·
13 Σαλωμων ἐβασίλευσεν ἐν ἡμέραις εἰρήνης,
ᾧ ὁ θεὸς κατέπαυσεν κυκλόθεν,
ἵνα στήσῃ οἶκον ἐπ᾽ ὀνόματι αὐτοῦ
καὶ ἑτοιμάσῃ ἁγίασμα εἰς τὸν αἰῶνα.
14 ὡς ἐσοφίσθης ἐν νεότητί σου
καὶ ἐνεπλήσθης ὡς ποταμὸς συνέσεως.
15 γῆν ἐπεκάλυψεν ἡ ψυχή σου,
καὶ ἐνέπλησας ἐν παραβολαῖς αἰνιγμάτων·

KING JAMES VERSION

8 In all his works he praised the Holy One most high with words of glory; with his whole heart he sung songs, and loved him that made him.

9 He set singers also before the altar, that by their voices they might make sweet melody, and daily sing praises in their songs.

10 He beautified their feasts, and set in order the solemn times until the end, that they might praise his holy name, and that the temple might sound from morning.

11 The Lord took away his sins, and exalted his horn for ever: he gave him a covenant of kings, and a throne of glory in Israel.

12 After him rose up a wise son, and for his sake he dwelt at large.

13 Solomon reigned in a peaceable time, and was honoured; for God made all quiet round about him, that he might build an house in his name, and prepare his sanctuary for ever.

14 How wise wast thou in thy youth, and, as a flood, filled with understanding!

15 Thy soul covered the whole earth, and thou filledst it with dark parables.

DOUAY OLD TESTAMENT

9 In all his works he gave thanks to the holy one, and to the most High, with words of glory.

10 With his whole heart he praised the Lord, and loved God that made him: and he gave him power against his enemies:

11 And he set singers before the altar, and by their voices he made sweet melody.

12 And to the festivals he added beauty, and set in order the solemn times even to the end of his life, that they should praise the holy name of the Lord, and magnify the holiness of God in the morning.

13 The Lord took away his sins, and exalted his horn for ever: and he gave him a covenant of the kingdom, and a throne of glory in Israel.

14 After him arose up a wise son, and for his sake he cast down all the power of the enemies.

15 Solomon reigned in days of peace, and God brought all his enemies under him, that he might build a house in his name, and prepare a sanctuary for ever: O how wise wast thou in thy youth!

16 And thou wast filled as a river with wisdom, and thy soul covered the earth.

17 And thou didst multiply riddles in parables: thy name

KNOX TRANSLATION

no feat of David's but made him thank the most High, the
most Holy, and to him give the glory; 10 still with all his
heart he praised the Master he loved so well, the God who
had created him and endowed him with strength to meet his
enemies. 11 He would have musicians wait around the altar,
and rouse sweet echoes with their chant; 12 feast-days
should be kept with splendour, times and seasons duly
observed, all his life long; morning after morning the Lord's
holy name should be praised, God should receive his full tribute of worship. 13 So it was that the Lord pardoned his sins,
and bade him carry his head high evermore; his by right was
the kingship, and the proud throne of Israel.
14 To a wise son of his that throne passed; for David's sake
all the threats of the enemy were stilled, 15 and Solomon
might reign undisturbed. If God gave him mastery all
around, it was because he would have a temple built in his
honour, to be his sanctuary for all time. Ah, Solomon, how
well schooled in thy youth! 16 Deep as a river flowed thy wisdom; thy ambition it was to lay bare all the secrets of earth;
17 full scope thou wouldst have for riddle and proverb. Even

TODAY'S ENGLISH VERSION

8 In everything David did, he gave thanks and praise to the
Holy Lord, the Most High. He loved his Creator and sang
praises to him with all his heart. 9 He put singers at the altar
to provide beautiful music. 10 He set the times of the festivals throughout the year and made them splendid occasions;
the Temple rang with the Lord's praises all day long. 11 The
Lord forgave David's sin and established his power forever.
He made a covenant with him that he and his descendants
would reign in splendor over Israel.
12 David prepared the way well for his son, a wise man, to
rule after him. 13 There was no war while Solomon was king.
God gave him peace on all his borders, so that he could build
for the Lord a Temple which would stand forever. 14 How
wise you were, Solomon, when you were young! Your
knowledge was like the Nile[a] in flood. 15 Your influence
reached over all the world; your proverbs and riddles were

[a] *Hebrew* the Nile; *Greek* a river.

NEW REVISED STANDARD VERSION

8 In all that he did he gave thanks
to the Holy One, the Most High, proclaiming his glory;
he sang praise with all his heart,
and he loved his Maker.
9 He placed singers before the altar,
to make sweet melody with their voices.[a]
10 He gave beauty to the festivals,
and arranged their times throughout the year,[b]
while they praised God's[c] holy name,
and the sanctuary resounded from early morning.
11 The Lord took away his sins,
and exalted his power[d] forever;
he gave him a covenant of kingship
and a glorious throne in Israel.

12 After him a wise son rose up
who because of him lived in security:[e]
13 Solomon reigned in an age of peace,
because God made all his borders tranquil,
so that he might build a house in his name
and provide a sanctuary to stand forever.
14 How wise you were when you were young!
You overflowed like the Nile[f] with understanding.
15 Your influence spread throughout the earth,
and you filled it with proverbs having deep meaning.

a Other ancient authorities add *and daily they sing his praises* *b* Gk *to completion* *c* Gk *his* *d* Gk *horn* *e* Heb: Gk *in a broad place* *f* Heb: Gk *a river*

NEW AMERICAN BIBLE

8 With his every deed he offered thanks
to God Most High, in words of praise.
With his whole being he loved his Maker
and daily had his praises sung;
9 He added beauty to the feasts
and solemnized the seasons of each year
With string music before the altar,
providing sweet melody for the psalms
10 So that when the Holy Name was praised,
before daybreak the sanctuary would resound.
11 The LORD forgave him his sins
and exalted his strength forever;
He conferred on him the rights of royalty
and established his throne in Israel.

12 Because of his merits he had as his successor
a wise son, who lived in security:
13 SOLOMON reigned during an era of peace,
for God made tranquil all his borders.
He built a house to the name of God,
and established a lasting sanctuary.
14 How wise you were when you were young,
overflowing with instruction, like the Nile in flood!
15 Your understanding covered the whole earth,
and, like a sea, filled it with knowledge.

NEW JERUSALEM BIBLE

8 In all his activities he gave thanks
to the Holy One Most High in words of glory;
he put all his heart into his songs
out of love for his Creator.
9 He placed singers before the altar,
melodiously to sing;
10 he gave the feasts their splendour,
the festivals their solemn pomp,
causing the Lord's holy name to be praised
and the sanctuary to resound from dawn.
11 The Lord took away his sins,
making his strength ever greater;
he gave him a royal covenant,
and a glorious throne in Israel.

12 A wise son succeeded him,
who lived content, thanks to him.
13 Solomon reigned in a time of peace,
and God gave him peace all round
so that he could raise a house to his name
and prepare an everlasting sanctuary.
14 How wise you were despite your youth,
like a river, brimming over with intelligence!
15 Your mind ranged the earth,
you filled it with mysterious sayings.

GREEK OLD TESTAMENT

16 εἰς νήσους πόρρω ἀφίκετο τὸ ὄνομά σου,
καὶ ἠγαπήθης ἐν τῇ εἰρήνῃ σου·
17 ἐν ᾠδαῖς καὶ παροιμίαις καὶ παραβολαῖς
καὶ ἐν ἑρμηνείαις ἀπεθαύμασάν σε χῶραι.
18 ἐν ὀνόματι κυρίου τοῦ θεοῦ
τοῦ ἐπικεκλημένου θεοῦ Ισραηλ
συνήγαγες ὡς κασσίτερον τὸ χρυσίον
καὶ ὡς μόλιβον ἐπλήθυνας ἀργύριον.
19 παρανέκλινας τὰς λαγόνας σου γυναιξὶν
καὶ ἐνεξουσιάσθης ἐν τῷ σώματί σου·
20 ἔδωκας μῶμον ἐν τῇ δόξῃ σου
καὶ ἐβεβήλωσας τὸ σπέρμα σου
ἐπαγαγεῖν ὀργὴν ἐπὶ τὰ τέκνα σου
καὶ κατανυγῆναι ἐπὶ τῇ ἀφροσύνῃ σου
21 γενέσθαι δίχα τυραννίδα
καὶ ἐξ Εφραιμ ἄρξαι βασιλείαν ἀπειθῆ.
22 ὁ δὲ κύριος οὐ μὴ καταλίπῃ τὸ ἔλεος αὐτοῦ
καὶ οὐ μὴ διαφθείρῃ ἀπὸ τῶν λόγων αὐτοῦ
οὐδὲ μὴ ἐξαλείψῃ ἐκλεκτοῦ αὐτοῦ ἔκγονα
καὶ σπέρμα τοῦ ἀγαπήσαντος αὐτὸν οὐ μὴ ἐξάρῃ·
καὶ τῷ Ιακωβ ἔδωκεν κατάλειμμα
καὶ τῷ Δαυιδ ἐξ αὐτοῦ ῥίζαν.
23 Καὶ ἀνεπαύσατο Σαλωμων μετὰ τῶν πατέρων αὐτοῦ
καὶ κατέλιπεν μετ' αὐτὸν ἐκ τοῦ σπέρματος αὐτοῦ
λαοῦ ἀφροσύνην καὶ ἐλασσούμενον συνέσει
Ροβοαμ, ὃς ἀπέστησεν λαὸν ἐκ βουλῆς αὐτοῦ.

KING JAMES VERSION

16 Thy name went far unto the islands; and for thy peace thou wast beloved.

17 The countries marvelled at thee for thy songs, and proverbs, and parables, and interpretations.

18 By the name of the Lord God, which is called the Lord God of Israel, thou didst gather gold as tin, and didst multiply silver as lead.

19 Thou didst bow thy loins unto women, and by thy body thou wast brought into subjection.

20 Thou didst stain thy honour, and pollute thy seed: so that thou broughtest wrath upon thy children, and wast grieved for thy folly.

21 So the kingdom was divided, and out of Ephraim ruled a rebellious kingdom.

22 But the Lord will never leave off his mercy, neither shall any of his works perish, neither will he abolish the posterity of his elect, and the seed of him that loveth him he will not take away: wherefore he gave a remnant unto Jacob, and out of him a root unto David.

23 Thus rested Solomon with his fathers, and of his seed he left behind him Roboam, even the foolishness of the people, and one that had no understanding, who turned away

DOUAY OLD TESTAMENT

went abroad to the islands far off, and thou wast beloved in thy peace.

18 The countries wondered at thee for thy canticles, and proverbs, and parables, and interpretations,

19 And at the name of the Lord God, whose surname is, God of Israel.

20 Thou didst gather gold as copper, and didst multiply silver as lead,

21 And thou didst bow thyself to women: and by thy body thou wast brought under subjection.

22 Thou hast stained thy glory, and defiled thy seed so as to bring wrath upon thy children, and to have thy folly kindled,

23 That thou shouldst make the kingdom to be divided, and out of Ephraim a rebellious kingdom to rule.

24 But God will not leave off his mercy, and he will not destroy, nor abolish his own works, neither will he cut up by the roots the offspring of his elect: and he will not utterly take away the seed of him that loveth the Lord.

25 Wherefore he gave a remnant to Jacob, and to David of the same stock.

26 And Solomon had an end with his fathers.

27 And he left behind him of his seed, the folly of the nation,

28 Even Roboam that had little wisdom, who turned away the people through his counsel:

KNOX TRANSLATION

to the distant isles thy renown spread, and everywhere thy
peaceful reign made thee beloved. 18 The whole earth stood
in awe of song and proverb and parable and interpretation of
thine; 19 in awe, too, of the name of the Lord God, who is
known among men as the God of Israel. 20 Gold thou didst
amass in such plenty, as it had been only bronze; silver was
abundant in thy domains as lead. 21 Yet women bowed thee
to their will; of body's appetites thou wouldst brook no
restraint, 22 and thus thy renown was tarnished with the
gendering of a breed unhallowed. So it was that vengeance
fell upon thy children, that must rue thy folly in after times;
23 the kingdom divided, and in Ephraim a rebel dynasty exercising dominion, through thy fault.
24 Yet God is ever merciful; his own design he will not mar
fruitlessly, nor undo; should he destroy it root and branch,
the posterity of his chosen servant? Should the man that so
loved him have begotten sons in vain? 25 Jacob must have a
stock to breed from; the root of David should burgeon yet.
26 Solomon once laid to rest with his fathers, what heirs left
he? 27 A man of his own blood, born to infatuate a nation,
28 insensate Roboam, whose ill counsel drove the people to

TODAY'S ENGLISH VERSION

known everywhere. 16 You were famous everywhere, and
people loved you for bringing peace. 17 Nations around the
world held you in admiration for your songs, proverbs, parables, and witty sayings. 18 You gathered silver and gold as if
it were tin or lead, all in the name of the Lord God of Israel.
19 But your lust for women was your downfall. 20 You
stained your reputation and that of your descendants. They
suffered punishment for that foolishness of yours, which
caused them so much grief. 21 It divided the nation, and a
rival kingdom arose in northern Israel. 22 But the Lord will
always be merciful and keep all his promises.[a] He will never
destroy the descendants of David, whom he chose and who
loved him. So for Israel's sake he allowed David's family to
survive.
23 Solomon followed his ancestors in death and left one of
his sons to rule after him. This was Rehoboam, a man of little intelligence and great foolishness,[b] whose policies caused
a rebellion.

[a] *Hebrew* keep all his promises; *Greek* will not destroy what he made.
[b] *Hebrew* great foolishness; *Greek* the people's fool.

NEW REVISED STANDARD VERSION

16 Your fame reached to far-off islands,
and you were loved for your peaceful reign.
17 Your songs, proverbs, and parables,
and the answers you gave astounded the nations.
18 In the name of the Lord God,
who is called the God of Israel,
you gathered gold like tin
and amassed silver like lead.
19 But you brought in women to lie at your side,
and through your body you were brought into
subjection.
20 You stained your honor,
and defiled your family line,
so that you brought wrath upon your children,
and they were grieved[a] at your folly,
21 because the sovereignty was divided
and a rebel kingdom arose out of Ephraim.
22 But the Lord will never give up his mercy,
or cause any of his works to perish;
he will never blot out the descendants of his chosen one,
or destroy the family line of him who loved him.
So he gave a remnant to Jacob,
and to David a root from his own family.

23 Solomon rested with his ancestors,
and left behind him one of his sons,
broad in[b] folly and lacking in sense,
Rehoboam, whose policy drove the people to revolt.

a Other ancient authorities read *I was grieved* *b* Heb (with a play on the name Rehoboam) Syr: Gk *the people's*

NEW AMERICAN BIBLE

16 Your fame reached distant coasts,
and their peoples came to hear you;
17 With song and story and riddle,
and with your answers, you astounded the nations.
18 You were called by that glorious name
which was conferred upon Israel.
Gold you gathered like so much iron,
you heaped up silver as though it were lead;
19 But you abandoned yourself to women
and gave them dominion over your body.
20 You brought dishonor upon your reputation,
shame upon your marriage,
Wrath upon your descendants,
and groaning upon your domain;
21 Thus two governments came into being,
when in Ephraim kingship was usurped.
22 But God does not withdraw his mercy,
nor permit even one of his promises to fail.
He does not uproot the posterity of his chosen one,
nor destroy the offspring of his friend.
So he gave to Jacob a remnant,
to David a root from his own family.
23 Solomon finally slept with his fathers,
and left behind him one of his sons,
Expansive in folly, limited in sense,
REHOBOAM, who by his policy made the people rebel;

NEW JERUSALEM BIBLE

16 Your name reached the distant islands,
and you were loved for your peace.[a]
17 Your songs, your proverbs, your sayings
and your answers were the wonder of the world.
18 In the name of the Lord God,
of him who is called the God of Israel,
you amassed gold like so much tin,
and made silver as common as lead.
19 You abandoned your body to women,
you became the slave of your appetites.
20 You stained your honour,
you profaned your stock,
so bringing retribution on your children
and affliction for your folly:
21 the empire split in two,
from Ephraim arose a rebel kingdom.
22 But the Lord never goes back on his mercy,
never cancels any of his words,
will neither deny offspring to his elect
nor stamp out the line of the man who loved him.
And hence, he has granted a remnant to Jacob
and to David a root sprung from him.

23 Solomon rested with his ancestors,
leaving one of his stock as his successor,
the stupidest member of the nation,
brainless Rehoboam, who drove the people to rebel.

[a] **47** Solomon means 'man of peace'.

GREEK OLD TESTAMENT

24 καὶ Ιεροβοαμ υἱὸς Ναβατ, ὃς ἐξήμαρτεν τὸν Ισραηλ
καὶ ἔδωκεν τῷ Εφραιμ ὁδὸν ἁμαρτίας·
καὶ ἐπληθύνθησαν αἱ ἁμαρτίαι αὐτῶν σφόδρα
ἀποστῆσαι αὐτοὺς ἀπὸ τῆς γῆς αὐτῶν·
25 καὶ πᾶσαν πονηρίαν ἐξεζήτησαν,
ἕως ἐκδίκησις ἔλθῃ ἐπ᾽ αὐτούς.

48 Καὶ ἀνέστη Ηλιας προφήτης ὡς πῦρ,
καὶ ὁ λόγος αὐτοῦ ὡς λαμπὰς ἐκαίετο·
2 ὃς ἐπήγαγεν ἐπ᾽ αὐτοὺς λιμὸν
καὶ τῷ ζήλῳ αὐτοῦ ὠλιγοποίησεν αὐτούς·
3 ἐν λόγῳ κυρίου ἀνέσχεν οὐρανόν,
κατήγαγεν οὕτως τρὶς πῦρ.
4 ὡς ἐδοξάσθης, Ηλια, ἐν θαυμασίοις σου·
καὶ τίς ὅμοιός σοι καυχᾶσθαι;
5 ὁ ἐγείρας νεκρὸν ἐκ θανάτου
καὶ ἐξ ᾅδου ἐν λόγῳ ὑψίστου·
6 ὁ καταγαγὼν βασιλεῖς εἰς ἀπώλειαν
καὶ δεδοξασμένους ἀπὸ κλίνης αὐτῶν·
7 ἀκούων ἐν Σινα ἐλεγμὸν
καὶ ἐν Χωρηβ κρίματα ἐκδικήσεως·
8 ὁ χρίων βασιλεῖς εἰς ἀνταπόδομα
καὶ προφήτας διαδόχους μετ᾽ αὐτόν·
9 ὁ ἀναλημφθεὶς ἐν λαίλαπι πυρὸς
ἐν ἅρματι ἵππων πυρίνων·
10 ὁ καταγραφεὶς ἐν ἐλεγμοῖς εἰς καιροὺς
κοπάσαι ὀργὴν πρὸ θυμοῦ,

KING JAMES VERSION

the people through his counsel. There was also Jeroboam the son of Nebat, who caused Israel to sin, and shewed Ephraim the way of sin:

24 And their sins were multiplied exceedingly, that they were driven out of the land.

25 For they sought out all wickedness, till the vengeance came upon them.

48 Then stood up Elias the prophet as fire, and his word burned like a lamp.

2 He brought a sore famine upon them, and by his zeal he diminished their number.

3 By the word of the Lord he shut up the heaven, and also three times brought down fire.

4 O Elias, how wast thou honoured in thy wondrous deeds! and who may glory like unto thee!

5 Who didst raise up a dead man from death, and his soul from the place of the dead, by the word of the most High:

6 Who broughtest kings to destruction, and honorable men from their bed:

7 Who heardest the rebuke of the Lord in Sinai, and in Horeb the judgment of vengeance:

8 Who anointedst kings to take revenge, and prophets to succeed after him:

9 Who was taken up in a whirlwind of fire, and in a chariot of fiery horses:

10 Who wast ordained for reproofs in their times, to pacify the wrath of the Lord's judgment, before it brake forth into

DOUAY OLD TESTAMENT

29 And Jeroboam the son of Nabat, who caused Israel to sin, and shewed Ephraim the way of sin, and their sins were multiplied exceedingly.

30 They removed them far away from their land.

31 And they sought out all iniquities, till vengeance came upon them, and put an end to all their sins.

48 AND Elias the prophet stood up, as a fire, and his word burnt like a torch.

2 He brought a famine upon them, and they that provoked him in their envy, were reduced to a small number, for they could not endure the commandments of the Lord.

3 By the word of the Lord he shut up the heaven, and he brought down fire from heaven thrice.

4 Thus was Elias magnified in his wondrous works. And who can glory like to thee?

5 Who raisedst up a dead man from below, from the lot of death, by the word of the Lord God.

6 Who broughtest down kings to destruction, and brokest easily their power in pieces, and the glorious from their bed.

7 Who heardest judgment in Sina, and in Horeb the judgments of vengeance.

8 Who anointedst kings to penance, and madest prophets successors after thee.

9 Who wast taken up in a whirlwind of fire, in a chariot of fiery horses.

10 Who art registered in the judgments of times to appease

KNOX TRANSLATION

rebellion; 29 and that other, Jeroboam son of Nabat, who
taught Israel to sin. All Ephraim followed the example of his
misdoing; high rose the tide of their sins, 30 till it swept
them away altogether from their own country.
31 For all this wickedness of theirs God held them to
account, waiting till the time should come for punishing
them, and purging them of their guilt.

48 And now another prophet arose, Elias, a man of
flame; blazed, like a fire-brand, his message. 2 This
man it was brought down a famine to punish them, till few
were left of the enemies that bore him a grudge, and found
the Lord's commandment too hard for them. 3 At the Lord's
word, he laid a ban on heaven itself, and three times brought
fire down from it; 4 such was the fame of Elias' miracles.
Who else could boast, as thou, 5 of calling back the dead from
the tomb, by the power of the Lord God, and to life restoring
them; 6 of kings brought to ruin and all their power lightly
shattered, proud kings, that might leave their sick-beds no
more? 7 Sinai should tell thee, Horeb should tell thee, of
award made, and doom pronounced; 8 kings thou shouldst
anoint, to be the redressers of wrong, and prophets to come
after thee; 9 then, amidst a flaming whirlwind, in a chariot
drawn by horses of fire, thou wast taken up into heaven.
10 Of thee it was written that in time of judgement to come
thou wouldst appease the divine anger, by reconciling heart

TODAY'S ENGLISH VERSION

There was also the unspeakable[a] Jeroboam, who led northern Israel in sinful ways. 24 His people became so sinful that
they were exiled from their land. 25 They tried all kinds of
wickedness until the Lord took vengeance on them.

48 Then there arose the fiery prophet Elijah, whose
words blazed like a torch. 2 He brought a famine on
the people, and many of them died because of his persistence. 3 Speaking in the name of the Lord, he kept the rain
from coming, and on three occasions he called down fire.
4 Elijah, your miracles were marvelous! No one else can boast
of such deeds! 5 In the name of the Most High, you brought
a dead man back to life. 6 You brought a famous king down
to sickness and death. 7 At Sinai you heard the Lord rebuke
you and declare his determination to punish his enemies.
8 You anointed a king to be the instrument of that punishment, and a prophet to take your place. 9 You were taken up
to heaven in a fiery whirlwind, a chariot drawn by fiery
horses. 10 The scripture says that you are ready to appear at
the designated time,[b] to cool God's anger before it breaks out

[a] *Hebrew* the unspeakable (one); *Greek* Jeroboam son of Nebat.
[b] *Hebrew* you are . . . time; *Greek unclear.*

NEW REVISED STANDARD VERSION

Then Jeroboam son of Nebat led Israel into sin
and started Ephraim on its sinful ways.
24 Their sins increased more and more,
until they were exiled from their land.
25 For they sought out every kind of wickedness,
until vengeance came upon them.

48 Then Elijah arose, a prophet like fire,
and his word burned like a torch.
2 He brought a famine upon them,
and by his zeal he made them few in number.
3 By the word of the Lord he shut up the heavens,
and also three times brought down fire.
4 How glorious you were, Elijah, in your wondrous deeds!
Whose glory is equal to yours?
5 You raised a corpse from death
and from Hades, by the word of the Most High.
6 You sent kings down to destruction,
and famous men, from their sickbeds.
7 You heard rebuke at Sinai
and judgments of vengeance at Horeb.
8 You anointed kings to inflict retribution,
and prophets to succeed you.[a]
9 You were taken up by a whirlwind of fire,
in a chariot with horses of fire.
10 At the appointed time, it is written, you are destined[b]
to calm the wrath of God before it breaks out in fury,

a Heb: Gk *him* *b* Heb: Gk *are for reproofs*

NEW AMERICAN BIBLE

Until one arose who should not be remembered,
the sinner who led Israel into sin,
Who brought ruin to Ephraim
24 and caused them to be exiled from their land.
Their sinfulness grew more and more,
25 and they lent themselves to every evil,

48 Till like a fire there appeared the prophet
whose words were as a flaming furnace.
2 Their staff of bread he shattered,
in his zeal he reduced them to straits;
3 By God's word he shut up the heavens
and three times brought down fire.
4 How awesome are you, ELIJAH!
Whose glory is equal to yours?
5 You brought a dead man back to life
from the nether world, by the will of the LORD.
6 You sent kings down to destruction,
and nobles, from their beds of sickness.
7 You heard threats at Sinai,
at Horeb avenging judgments.
8 You anointed kings who should inflict vengeance,
and a prophet as your successor.
9 You were taken aloft in a whirlwind,
in a chariot with fiery horses.
10 You are destined, it is written, in time to come
to put an end to wrath before the day of the LORD,

NEW JERUSALEM BIBLE

24 Next, Jeroboam son of Nebat, who made Israel sin,
and set Ephraim on the way of evil;
from then on their sins multiplied so excessively
as to drive them out of their country;
25 for they tried out every kind of wickedness,
until vengeance overtook them.

48 Then the prophet Elijah arose like a fire,
his word flaring like a torch.
2 It was he who brought famine on them
and decimated them in his zeal.
3 By the word of the Lord he shut up the heavens,
three times also he brought down fire.
4 How glorious you were in your miracles, Elijah!
Has anyone reason to boast as you have?—
5 rousing a corpse from death,
from Sheol, by the word of the Most High;
6 dragging kings down to destruction,
and high dignitaries from their beds;
7 hearing a rebuke on Sinai
and decrees of punishment on Horeb;
8 anointing kings as avengers,
and prophets to succeed you;
9 taken up in the whirlwind of fire,
in a chariot with fiery horses;
10 designated in the prophecies of doom
to allay God's wrath before the fury breaks,

GREEK OLD TESTAMENT

ἐπιστρέψαι καρδίαν πατρὸς πρὸς υἱὸν
καὶ καταστῆσαι φυλὰς Ιακωβ.
11 μακάριοι οἱ ἰδόντες σε
καὶ οἱ ἐν ἀγαπήσει κεκοιμημένοι·
καὶ γὰρ ἡμεῖς ζωῇ ζησόμεθα.
12 Ηλιας ὃς ἐν λαίλαπι ἐσκεπάσθη,
καὶ Ελισαιε ἐνεπλήσθη πνεύματος αὐτοῦ·
καὶ ἐν ἡμέραις αὐτοῦ οὐκ ἐσαλεύθη ὑπὸ ἄρχοντος,
καὶ οὐ κατεδυνάστευσεν αὐτὸν οὐδείς.
13 πᾶς λόγος οὐχ ὑπερῆρεν αὐτόν,
καὶ ἐν κοιμήσει ἐπροφήτευσεν τὸ σῶμα αὐτοῦ·
14 καὶ ἐν ζωῇ αὐτοῦ ἐποίησεν τέρατα,
καὶ ἐν τελευτῇ θαυμάσια τὰ ἔργα αὐτοῦ.
15 Ἐν πᾶσιν τούτοις οὐ μετενόησεν ὁ λαὸς
καὶ οὐκ ἀπέστησαν ἀπὸ τῶν ἁμαρτιῶν αὐτῶν,
ἕως ἐπρονομεύθησαν ἀπὸ γῆς αὐτῶν
καὶ διεσκορπίσθησαν ἐν πάσῃ τῇ γῇ.
16 καὶ κατελείφθη ὁ λαὸς ὀλιγοστός,
καὶ ἄρχων ἐν τῷ οἴκῳ Δαυιδ·
τινὲς μὲν αὐτῶν ἐποίησαν τὸ ἀρεστόν,
τινὲς δὲ ἐπλήθυναν ἁμαρτίας.
17 Εζεκιας ὠχύρωσεν τὴν πόλιν αὐτοῦ
καὶ εἰσήγαγεν εἰς μέσον αὐτῆς ὕδωρ,

KING JAMES VERSION

fury, and to turn the heart of the father unto the son, and to
restore the tribes of Jacob.
11 Blessed are they that saw thee, and slept in love; for
we shall surely live.
12 Elias it was, who was covered with a whirlwind: and
Eliseus was filled with his spirit: whilst he lived, he was not
moved *with the presence* of any prince, neither could any
bring him into subjection.
13 No word could overcome him; and after his death his
body prophesied.
14 He did wonders in his life, and at his death were his
works marvellous.
15 For all this the people repented not, neither departed
they from their sins, till they were spoiled and carried out of
their land, and were scattered through all the earth: yet there
remained a small people, and a ruler in the house of David:
16 Of whom some did that which was pleasing *to God,*
and some multiplied sins.
17 Ezekias fortified his city, and brought in water into the

DOUAY OLD TESTAMENT

the wrath of the Lord, to reconcile the heart of the father to
the son, and to restore the tribes of Jacob.
11 Blessed are they that saw thee, and were honoured
with thy friendship.
12 For we live only in our life, but after death our name
shall not be such.
13 Elias was indeed covered with the whirlwind, and his
spirit was filled up in Eliseus: in his days he feared not the
prince, and no man was more powerful than he.
14 No word could overcome him, and after death his body
prophesied.
15 In his life he did great wonders, and in death he
wrought miracles.
16 For all this the people repented not, neither did they
depart from their sins till they were cast out of their land,
and were scattered through all the earth.
17 And there was left but a small people, and a prince in
the house of David.
18 Some of these did that which pleased God: but others
committed many sins.
19 Ezechias fortified his city, and brought in water into

KNOX TRANSLATION

of father to heart of son, and restore the tribes of Israel as
they were. 11 Ah, blessed souls that saw thee, and were honoured with thy friendship! 12 We live only for a life-time; and
when death comes, we shall have no such renown as thine.
13 In that whirlwind Elias was lost to view, bequeathing
his spirit of prophecy in full measure to Eliseus. Here was a
man that in all his life never held prince in awe, never made
way for human greatness. 14 For him no task too difficult;
was not his dead body prophetic still, 15 to prove him a
wonder-worker in death, that in life was marvellous? 16 Yet
the nation for whom all this was done would not amend, nor
leave its sinning, until all the inhabitants of the land were
driven out, and scattered through the world; 17 only that little kingdom remained that was ruled by the heirs of David,
18 and of these rulers, though some did God's will, there were
some that had sins a many to answer for.
19 Well did Ezechias fortify his city, and brought a running

TODAY'S ENGLISH VERSION

in fury; that you "will bring parents and children together
again," and restore the tribes of Israel. 11 Fortunate are those
who live to see you come, as well as those who have already
died in love, for we too shall live.[a]
12 When Elijah was hidden by the whirlwind, Elisha was
filled with his spirit. As long as he lived, he was not afraid of
rulers, and they could not make him do as they wished.
13 Nothing was too hard for him. Even when he was dead,
his body worked a miracle. 14 In life and in death he performed amazing miracles.
15 But in spite of all this, the people did not abandon their
sinful ways until they were taken from their land as prisoners and scattered all over the world. This left the nation few
in number, but those who remained were still ruled by the
descendants of David. 16 Some of the people did what was
pleasing to the Lord, but others committed sin after sin.
17 Hezekiah prepared his city to resist a siege and provided

[a] *Verse 11 in Greek is unclear.*

NEW REVISED STANDARD VERSION

to turn the hearts of parents to their children,
and to restore the tribes of Jacob.
11 Happy are those who saw you
and were adorned[a] with your love!
For we also shall surely live.[b]
12 When Elijah was enveloped in the whirlwind,
Elisha was filled with his spirit.
He performed twice as many signs,
and marvels with every utterance of his mouth.[c]
Never in his lifetime did he tremble before any ruler,
nor could anyone intimidate him at all.
13 Nothing was too hard for him,
and when he was dead, his body prophesied.
14 In his life he did wonders,
and in death his deeds were marvelous.
15 Despite all this the people did not repent,
nor did they forsake their sins,
until they were carried off as plunder from their land,
and were scattered over all the earth.
The people were left very few in number,
but with a ruler from the house of David.
16 Some of them did what was right,
but others sinned more and more.
17 Hezekiah fortified his city,
and brought water into its midst;

a Other ancient authorities read *and have died* *b* Text and meaning of Gk uncertain *c* Heb: Gk lacks *He performed . . . mouth*

NEW AMERICAN BIBLE

To turn back the hearts of fathers toward their sons,
and to re-establish the tribes of Jacob.
11 Blessed is he who shall have seen you before he dies,
12 O Elijah, enveloped in the whirlwind!

Then ELISHA, filled with a twofold portion of his spirit,
wrought many marvels by his mere word.
During his lifetime he feared no one,
nor was any man able to intimidate his will.
13 Nothing was beyond his power;
beneath him flesh was brought back into life.
14 In life he performed wonders,
and after death, marvelous deeds.
15 Despite all this the people did not repent,
nor did they give up their sins,
Until they were rooted out of their land
and scattered all over the earth.
But Judah remained, a tiny people,
with its rulers from the house of David.
16 Some of these did what was right,
but others were extremely sinful.
17 HEZEKIAH fortified his city
and had water brought into it;

NEW JERUSALEM BIBLE

to turn the hearts of fathers towards their children,[a]
and to restore the tribes of Jacob.
11 Blessed, those who will see you,
and those who have fallen asleep in love;
for we too shall certainly have life.
12 Such was Elijah, who was enveloped in a whirlwind;
and Elisha was filled with his spirit;
throughout his life no ruler could shake him,
and no one could subdue him.
13 No task was too hard for him,
and even in death his body prophesied.
14 In his lifetime he performed wonders,
and in death his works were marvellous.
15 Despite all this the people did not repent,
nor did they give up their sins,
until they were herded out of their country
and scattered all over the earth;
16 only a few of the people were left,
with a ruler of the House of David.
Some of them did what pleased the Lord,
others piled sin on sin.
17 Hezekiah fortified his city,
and laid on a water-supply inside it;

a **48** Ml 3:24.

GREEK OLD TESTAMENT

ὤρυξεν σιδήρῳ ἀκρότομον
καὶ ᾠκοδόμησεν κρήνας εἰς ὕδατα.
18 ἐν ἡμέραις αὐτοῦ ἀνέβη Σενναχηριμ
καὶ ἀπέστειλεν Ραψακην, καὶ ἀπῆρεν·
καὶ ἐπῆρεν χεῖρα αὐτοῦ ἐπὶ Σιων
καὶ ἐμεγαλαύχησεν ἐν ὑπερηφανίᾳ αὐτοῦ.
19 τότε ἐσαλεύθησαν καρδίαι καὶ χεῖρες αὐτῶν,
καὶ ὠδίνησαν ὡς αἱ τίκτουσαι·
20 καὶ ἐπεκαλέσαντο τὸν κύριον τὸν ἐλεήμονα
ἐκπετάσαντες τὰς χεῖρας αὐτῶν πρὸς αὐτόν.
καὶ ὁ ἅγιος ἐξ οὐρανοῦ ταχὺ ἐπήκουσεν αὐτῶν
καὶ ἐλυτρώσατο αὐτοὺς ἐν χειρὶ Ησαιου·
21 ἐπάταξεν τὴν παρεμβολὴν τῶν Ἀσσυρίων,
καὶ ἐξέτριψεν αὐτοὺς ὁ ἄγγελος αὐτοῦ.
22 ἐποίησεν γὰρ Εζεκιας τὸ ἀρεστὸν κυρίῳ
καὶ ἐνίσχυσεν ἐν ὁδοῖς Δαυιδ τοῦ πατρὸς αὐτοῦ,
ἃς ἐνετείλατο Ησαιας ὁ προφήτης
ὁ μέγας καὶ πιστὸς ἐν ὁράσει αὐτοῦ.
23 ἐν ταῖς ἡμέραις αὐτοῦ ἀνεπόδισεν ὁ ἥλιος
καὶ προσέθηκεν ζωὴν βασιλεῖ.
24 πνεύματι μεγάλῳ εἶδεν τὰ ἔσχατα
καὶ παρεκάλεσεν τοὺς πενθοῦντας ἐν Σιων.
25 ἕως τοῦ αἰῶνος ὑπέδειξεν τὰ ἐσόμενα
καὶ τὰ ἀπόκρυφα πρὶν ἢ παραγενέσθαι αὐτά.

49 Μνημόσυνον Ιωσιου εἰς σύνθεσιν θυμιάματος
ἐσκευασμένον ἔργῳ μυρεψοῦ·

KING JAMES VERSION

midst thereof: he digged the hard rock with iron, and made wells for waters.

18 In his time Sennacherib came up, and sent Rabsaces, and lifted up his hand against Sion, and boasted proudly.

19 Then trembled their hearts and hands, and they were in pain, as women in travail.

20 But they called upon the Lord which is merciful, and stretched out their hands toward him: and immediately the Holy One heard them out of heaven, and delivered them by the ministry of Esay.

21 He smote the host of the Assyrians, and his angel destroyed them.

22 For Ezekias had done the thing that pleased the Lord, and was strong in the ways of David his father, as Esay the prophet, who was great and faithful in his vision, had commanded him.

23 In his time the sun went backward, and he lengthened the king's life.

24 He saw by an excellent spirit what should come to pass at the last, and he comforted them that mourned in Sion.

25 He shewed what should come to pass for ever, and secret things or ever they came.

49 The remembrance of Josias is like the composition of the perfume that is made by the art of the apothecary:

DOUAY OLD TESTAMENT

the midst thereof, and he digged a rock with iron, and made a well for water.

20 In his days Sennacherib came up, and sent Rabsaces, and lifted up his hand against them, and he stretched out his hand against Sion, and became proud through his power.

21 Then their hearts and hands trembled, and they were in pain as women in travail.

22 And they called upon the Lord who is merciful, and spreading their hands, they lifted them up to heaven: and the holy Lord God quickly heard their voice.

23 He was not mindful of their sins, neither did he deliver them up to their enemies, but he purified them by the hand of Isaias, the holy prophet.

24 He overthrew the army of the Assyrians, and the angel of the Lord destroyed them.

25 For Ezechias did that which pleased God, and walked valiantly in the way of David his father, which Isaias, the great prophet, and faithful in the sight of God, had commanded him.

26 In his days the sun went backward, and he lengthened the king's life.

27 With a great spirit he saw the things that are to come to pass at last, and comforted the mourners in Sion.

28 He shewed what should come to pass for ever, and secret things before they came.

49 THE memory of Josias is like the composition of a sweet smell made by the art of a perfumer:

KNOX TRANSLATION

stream into the midst of it, breaking through the rock with
tools of iron, and building a cistern for the water. 20 In his
reign Sennacherib marched against the country, and sent
Rabsaces to threaten it; Sion itself he threatened with attack,
so proudly he trusted in his own strength. 21 Heart and hand
were unnerved at his coming; worse anguish woman in
labour never knew. 22 Yet they cried out upon God for pity,
with hands outstretched heavenwards; and he, the holy One,
he the Lord God, was not slow to answer them. 23 Their sins
he would remember no more; he would not leave them at the
mercy of their enemies; by means of his holy prophet Isaias
they should find release. 24 With that, the Lord's angel fell
on the camp of Assyria, and brought its armies to nothing.
25 So faithfully Ezechias did the Lord's will, following boldly
the example of his father, king David; so well he obeyed
Isaias, a great prophet and a faithful interpreter of the vision
the Lord gave him. 26 In Isaias' days it was that the sun
went back, in token that the royal life should be prolonged;
27 Isaias it was that saw things far distant, by the power of
inspiration, and comforted mourning hearts in Sion. Without
end or limit future things he foretold, that still lay hidden in
the womb of time.

49 Josias, too, is still remembered; a memory grateful as
some mingled scent, pride of the perfumer's art, 2 or

TODAY'S ENGLISH VERSION

it with a water supply. He had a tunnel built through solid
rock with iron tools and had cisterns built to hold the water.
18 During his reign Sennacherib attacked the city and sent his
chief official from Lachish. He challenged Jerusalem and
boasted arrogantly. 19 The people lost their courage and
shook with fear; they were in pain, like a woman in labor.
20 But they prayed to the merciful Lord, the Holy One in
heaven, who quickly answered their prayers and sent Isaiah
to save them. 21 The Lord struck the Assyrian camp; his
angel wiped them out. 22 Yes, Hezekiah did what was pleasing to the Lord and firmly followed the example of his ancestor David. This was what was commanded by the great
prophet Isaiah, whose visions were trusted. 23 He made the
sun move backward and lengthened the king's life. 24 He
comforted the mourners in Jerusalem. His powerful spirit
looked into the future, 25 and he predicted what was to happen before the end of time, hidden things that had not yet
occurred.

49 The memory of Josiah is as sweet as the fragrance of
expertly blended incense, sweet as honey to the

NEW REVISED STANDARD VERSION

he tunneled the rock with iron tools,
and built cisterns for the water.
18 In his days Sennacherib invaded the country;
he sent his commander[a] and departed;
he shook his fist against Zion,
and made great boasts in his arrogance.
19 Then their hearts were shaken and their hands trembled,
and they were in anguish, like women in labor.
20 But they called upon the Lord who is merciful,
spreading out their hands toward him.
The Holy One quickly heard them from heaven,
and delivered them through Isaiah.
21 The Lord[b] struck down the camp of the Assyrians,
and his angel wiped them out.
22 For Hezekiah did what was pleasing to the Lord,
and he kept firmly to the ways of his ancestor David,
as he was commanded by the prophet Isaiah,
who was great and trustworthy in his visions.
23 In Isaiah's[c] days the sun went backward,
and he prolonged the life of the king.
24 By his dauntless spirit he saw the future,
and comforted the mourners in Zion.
25 He revealed what was to occur to the end of time,
and the hidden things before they happened.

49 The name[d] of Josiah is like blended incense
prepared by the skill of the perfumer;

a Other ancient authorities add *from Lachish* *b* Gk *He* *c* Gk *his*
d Heb: Gk *memory*

NEW AMERICAN BIBLE

With iron tools he cut through the rock
and he built reservoirs for water.
18 During his reign Sennacherib led an invasion,
and sent his adjutant;
He shook his fist at Zion
and blasphemed God in his pride.
19 The people's hearts melted within them,
and they were in anguish like that of childbirth.
20 But they called upon the Most High God
and lifted up their hands to him;
He heard the prayer they uttered,
and saved them through ISAIAH.
21 God struck the camp of the Assyrians
and routed them with a plague.
22 For Hezekiah did what was right
and held fast to the paths of David,
As ordered by the illustrious prophet
Isaiah, who saw the truth in visions.
23 In his lifetime he turned back the sun
and prolonged the life of the king.
24 By his powerful spirit he looked into the future
and consoled the mourners of Zion;
25 He foretold what should be till the end of time,
hidden things yet to be fulfilled.

49 The name JOSIAH is like blended incense,
made lasting by a skilled perfumer.

NEW JERUSALEM BIBLE

with iron he tunnelled through the rock
and constructed storage-tanks.
18 In his days Sennacherib invaded
and sent Rabshakeh;
he lifted his hand against Zion,
and boasted loudly in his arrogance.
19 Then their hearts and hands trembled,
they felt the pangs of a woman in labour,
20 but they called on the merciful Lord,
stretching out their hands towards him.
Swiftly the Holy One heard them from heaven
and delivered them by the agency of Isaiah;
21 he struck the camp of the Assyrians
and his Angel annihilated them.
22 For Hezekiah did what is pleasing to the Lord,
and was steadfast[a] in the ways of David his father,
enjoined on him by the prophet Isaiah,
a great man trustworthy in his vision.
23 In his days the sun moved back;
he prolonged the life of the king.
24 In the power of the spirit he saw the last things,
he comforted the mourners of Zion,
25 he revealed the future to the end of time,
and hidden things long before they happened.

49 The memory of Josiah is like blended incense
prepared by the perfumer's art;

a **48** Word-play on 'Hezekiah' (=Yahweh makes strong).

GREEK OLD TESTAMENT

ἐν παντὶ στόματι ὡς μέλι γλυκανθήσεται
καὶ ὡς μουσικὰ ἐν συμποσίῳ οἴνου.
2 αὐτὸς κατευθύνθη ἐν ἐπιστροφῇ λαοῦ
καὶ ἐξῆρεν βδελύγματα ἀνομίας·
3 κατεύθυνεν πρὸς κύριον τὴν καρδίαν αὐτοῦ,
ἐν ἡμέραις ἀνόμων κατίσχυσεν τὴν εὐσέβειαν.
4 Πάρεξ Δαυιδ καὶ Εζεκιου καὶ Ιωσιου
πάντες πλημμέλειαν ἐπλημμέλησαν·
κατέλιπον γὰρ τὸν νόμον τοῦ ὑψίστου,
οἱ βασιλεῖς Ιουδα ἐξέλιπον·
5 ἔδωκαν γὰρ τὸ κέρας αὐτῶν ἑτέροις
καὶ τὴν δόξαν αὐτῶν ἔθνει ἀλλοτρίῳ.
6 ἐνεπύρισαν ἐκλεκτὴν πόλιν ἁγιάσματος
καὶ ἠρήμωσαν τὰς ὁδοὺς αὐτῆς
7 ἐν χειρὶ Ιερεμιου· ἐκάκωσαν γὰρ αὐτόν,
καὶ αὐτὸς ἐν μήτρᾳ ἡγιάσθη προφήτης
ἐκριζοῦν καὶ κακοῦν καὶ ἀπολλύειν,
ὡσαύτως οἰκοδομεῖν καὶ καταφυτεύειν.
8 Ιεζεκιηλ ὃς εἶδεν ὅρασιν δόξης,
ἣν ὑπέδειξεν αὐτῷ ἐπὶ ἅρματος χερουβιν·
9 καὶ γὰρ ἐμνήσθη τῶν ἐχθρῶν ἐν ὄμβρῳ
καὶ ἀγαθῶσαι τοὺς εὐθύνοντας ὁδούς.

KING JAMES VERSION

it is sweet as honey in all mouths, and as musick at a banquet of wine.

2 He behaved himself uprightly in the conversion of the people, and took away the abominations of iniquity.

3 He directed his heart unto the Lord, and in the time of the ungodly he established the worship of God.

4 All, except David and Ezekias and Josias, were defective: for they forsook the law of the most High, *even* the kings of Juda failed.

5 Therefore he gave their power unto others, and their glory to a strange nation.

6 They burnt the chosen city of the sanctuary, and made the streets desolate, according to the prophecy of Jeremias.

7 For they entreated him evil, who nevertheless was a prophet, sanctified in his mother's womb, that he might root out, and afflict, and destroy; and that he might build up also, and plant.

8 It was Ezekiel who saw the glorious vision, which was shewed him upon the chariot of the cherubims.

9 For he made mention of the enemies under *the figure of* the rain, and directed them that went right.

DOUAY OLD TESTAMENT

2 His remembrance shall be sweet as honey in every mouth, and as music at a banquet of wine.

3 He was directed by God unto the repentance of the nation, and he took away the abominations of wickedness.

4 And he directed his heart towards the Lord, and in the days of sinners he strengthened godliness.

5 Except David, and Ezechias, and Josias, all committed sin.

6 For the kings of Juda forsook the law of the most High, and despised the fear of God.

7 So they gave their kingdom to others, and their glory to a strange nation.

8 They burnt the chosen city of holiness, and made the streets thereof desolate according to the prediction of Jeremias.

9 For they treated him evil, who was consecrated a prophet from his mother's womb, to overthrow, and pluck up, and destroy, and to build again, and renew.

10 It was Ezechiel that saw the glorious vision, which was shewn him upon the chariot of cherubims.

11 For he made mention of the enemies under the figure of rain, and of doing good to them that shewed right ways.

KNOX TRANSLATION

the honey that tastes sweet in all men's mouths, or music
over the wine. 3 A king divinely ordained to make a nation's
amends, how he swept away all the foul idols of the lawbreakers; 4 how true he kept his heart to the Lord's bidding,
what comfort he gave to piety, when wickedness abounded!
5 David, Ezechias, Josias, these three only were exempt from
the guilt of their line; 6 the other kings of Juda forsook the
law of the most High, and counted the fear of God a light
matter. 7 What wonder if they were doomed to bequeath all
the glories of their kingdom to strangers, to princes of an
alien race, 8 who set fire to the city that was God's chosen
sanctuary, and left the ways unfrequented?

9 ...By means of Jeremias;[a] so ill they used him, that was
set apart to be a prophet when he was yet in his mother's
womb, empowered to overthrow, to uproot, to destroy, then
to rebuild and to plant anew. 10 And next Ezechiel, to whose
eyes God shewed the vision of glory, by wheeling cherubs
borne aloft...

11 And in storm he remembered the enemy...to reward all
such as pointed men to the right path.[b]

a It is very doubtful whether the words 'in the hand of Jeremias' can be construed so as to form a single sentence with verse 8; a gap in the text seems more probable. *b* A further gap should perhaps be indicated here; Ez. 13. 13 hardly justifies us in making Ezechiel the subject of verse 11. The Hebrew and the Syriac have 'he remembered (or, made mention of) Job', which again would not naturally apply to Ezechiel, in spite of Ez. 14. 14

TODAY'S ENGLISH VERSION

taste,[a] like music with wine at a banquet. 2 He followed the
correct policy of reforming the nation and removed the hor-
rors of idolatry. 3 He was completely loyal to the Lord and
strengthened true religion in those wicked times.
4 All the kings, except David, Hezekiah, and Josiah, were
terrible sinners, because they abandoned the Law of the Most
High to the very end of the kingdom.[b] 5 They surrendered
their power and honor to foreigners, 6 who set fire to the
holy city and left its streets deserted, just as Jeremiah had
predicted. 7 Jeremiah had been badly treated, even though he
was chosen as a prophet before he was born, "to uproot and
to pull down, to destroy and to overthrow," but also "to
build and to plant."
8 It was Ezekiel who was shown the vision of the divine
glory over the chariot and the living creatures. 9 He also
referred to the prophet Job, who always did the right thing.[c]

[a] *Hebrew* to the taste; *Greek* to everyone. [b] *Hebrew* to the very end of the kingdom; *Greek* and failed. [c] *Probable Hebrew text* He also . . . thing; *Greek unclear.*

NEW REVISED STANDARD VERSION

his memory[a] is as sweet as honey to every mouth,
and like music at a banquet of wine.
2 He did what was right by reforming the people,
and removing the wicked abominations.
3 He kept his heart fixed on the Lord;
in lawless times he made godliness prevail.

4 Except for David and Hezekiah and Josiah,
all of them were great sinners,
for they abandoned the law of the Most High;
the kings of Judah came to an end.
5 They[b] gave their power to others,
and their glory to a foreign nation,
6 who set fire to the chosen city of the sanctuary,
and made its streets desolate,
as Jeremiah had foretold.[c]
7 For they had mistreated him,
who even in the womb had been consecrated a prophet,
to pluck up and ruin and destroy,
and likewise to build and to plant.

8 It was Ezekiel who saw the vision of glory,
which God[d] showed him above the chariot of the cherubim.
9 For God[e] also mentioned Job
who held fast to all the ways of justice.[f]

a Heb: Gk *it* *b* Heb *He* *c* Gk *by the hand of Jeremiah* *d* Gk *He* *e* Gk *he* *f* Heb Compare Syr: Meaning of Gk uncertain

NEW AMERICAN BIBLE

Precious is his memory, like honey to the taste,
like music at a banquet.
2 For he grieved over our betrayals
and destroyed the abominable idols.
3 He turned to God with his whole heart,
and, though times were evil, he practiced virtue.
4 Except for David, Hezekiah and Josiah,
they all were wicked;
They abandoned the law of the Most High,
these kings of Judah, right to the very end.
5 So he gave over their power to others,
their glory to a foolish foreign nation
6 Who burned the holy city
and left its streets desolate,
As JEREMIAH had foretold; 7 for they had treated him badly
who even in the womb had been made a prophet,
To root out, pull down, and destroy,
and then to build and to plant.
8 EZEKIEL beheld the vision
and described the different creatures of the chariot;
9 He also referred to JOB,
who always persevered in the right path.

NEW JERUSALEM BIBLE

it is as sweet as honey to all mouths,
and like music at a wine feast.
2 He took the right course, of converting the people,
he rooted out the iniquitous abominations,
3 he set his heart on the Lord,
in godless times he upheld the cause of religion.

4 Apart from David, Hezekiah and Josiah,
they all heaped wrong on wrong,
they abandoned the Law of the Most High:
the kings of Judah disappeared;
5 for they handed their power over to others
and their honour to a foreign nation.
6 The holy, chosen city was burnt down,
her streets were left deserted,
7 as Jeremiah had predicted; for they had ill-treated him,
though consecrated a prophet in his mother's womb,
to tear up and afflict *and destroy*,
but also *to build up and to plant*.[a]
8 Ezekiel saw a vision of glory
which God showed to him
above the chariot of the great winged creatures,
9 for he mentioned the enemies in the downpour
to the advantage of those who follow the right way.

[a] **49** Jr 1:10.

GREEK OLD TESTAMENT

10 καὶ τῶν δώδεκα προφητῶν τὰ ὀστᾶ
ἀναθάλοι ἐκ τοῦ τόπου αὐτῶν·
παρεκάλεσαν γὰρ τὸν Ιακωβ
καὶ ἐλυτρώσαντο αὐτοὺς ἐν πίστει ἐλπίδος.
11 Πῶς μεγαλύνωμεν τὸν Ζοροβαβελ;
καὶ αὐτὸς ὡς σφραγὶς ἐπὶ δεξιᾶς χειρός,
12 οὕτως Ἰησοῦς υἱὸς Ιωσεδεκ,
οἳ ἐν ἡμέραις αὐτῶν ᾠκοδόμησαν οἶκον
καὶ ἀνύψωσαν ναὸν ἅγιον κυρίῳ
ἡτοιμασμένον εἰς δόξαν αἰῶνος.
13 καὶ Νεεμιου ἐπὶ πολὺ τὸ μνημόσυνον
τοῦ ἐγείραντος ἡμῖν τείχη πεπτωκότα
καὶ στήσαντος πύλας καὶ μοχλοὺς
καὶ ἀνεγείραντος τὰ οἰκόπεδα ἡμῶν.
14 Οὐδεὶς ἐκτίσθη ἐπὶ τῆς γῆς τοιοῦτος οἷος Ενωχ·
καὶ γὰρ αὐτὸς ἀνελήμφθη ἀπὸ τῆς γῆς.
15 οὐδὲ ὡς Ιωσηφ ἐγεννήθη ἀνὴρ
ἡγούμενος ἀδελφῶν, στήριγμα λαοῦ,
καὶ τὰ ὀστᾶ αὐτοῦ ἐπεσκέπησαν.
16 Σημ καὶ Σηθ ἐν ἀνθρώποις ἐδοξάσθησαν,
καὶ ὑπὲρ πᾶν ζῷον ἐν τῇ κτίσει Αδαμ.
50 Σιμων Ονιου υἱὸς ἱερεὺς ὁ μέγας,
ὃς ἐν ζωῇ αὐτοῦ ὑπέρραψεν οἶκον
καὶ ἐν ἡμέραις αὐτοῦ ἐστερέωσεν ναόν·

KING JAMES VERSION

10 And of the twelve prophets let the memorial be blessed, and let their bones flourish again out of their place: for they comforted Jacob, and delivered them by assured hope.
11 How shall we magnify Zorobabel? even he was as a signet on the right hand:
12 So was Jesus the son of Josedec: who in their time builded the house, and set up an holy temple to the Lord, which was prepared for everlasting glory.
13 And among the elect was Neemias, whose renown is great, who raised up for us the walls that were fallen, and set up the gates and the bars, and raised up our ruins again.
14 But upon the earth was no man created like Enoch; for he was taken from the earth.
15 Neither was there a man born like unto Joseph, a governor of his brethren, a stay of the people, whose bones were regarded of the Lord.
16 Sem and Seth were in great honour among men, and so was Adam above every living thing in the creation.
50 Simon the high priest, the son of Onias, who in his life repaired the house again, and in his days fortified the temple:

DOUAY OLD TESTAMENT

12 And may the bones of the twelve prophets spring up out of their place: for they strengthened Jacob, and redeemed themselves by strong faith.
13 How shall we magnify Zorobabel? for he was as a signet on the right hand;
14 In like manner Jesus the son of Josedec? who in their days built the house, and set up a holy temple to the Lord, prepared for everlasting glory.
15 And let Nehemias be a long time remembered, who raised up for us our walls that were cast down, and set up the gates and the bars, who rebuilt our houses.
16 No man was born upon earth like Henoch: for he also was taken up from the earth.
17 Nor as Joseph, who was a man born prince of his brethren, the support of his family, the ruler of his brethren, the stay of the people:
18 And his bones were visited, and after death they prophesied.
19 Seth and Sem obtained glory among men: and above every soul Adam in the beginning.
50 SIMON the high priest, the son of Onias, who in his life propped up the house, and in his days fortified the temple.

KNOX TRANSLATION

12 May life spring from the bones of the twelve prophets,
where they lie buried; men that put heart into the sons of
Jacob, and by trusting in God's power won deliverance.
13 The fame of Zorobabel what words of ours shall
enhance? The jewel God wore on his right hand for signet-
ring; 14 he, with Josue son of Josedec, rebuilt God's house
that then lay ruined; raised up a holy temple, of the divine
glory the. eternal dwelling-place. 15 Nor shall Nehemias be
soon forgotten, that mended these ruined walls of ours, our
gates built and barred, our homes restored to us.
16 Enoch no man born on earth can match, that from earth
was taken away; 17 nor Joseph, that was born to be his
brethren's master, and the bulwark of a great nation. Lord of
his brethren, stay of a people, 18 he left his bones to await
the day of God's deliverance, in death prophetic still. 19 Seth
and Sem are among the heroes of their race, and Adam, too,
that when earth began was made Lord of all living creatures.
50 A great priest was Simon, son of Onias;[a] in his day
the house of God was repaired, to make the temple
strong was his life's task. 2 The high part of the temple,

[a] There were two high priests who could be described as 'Simon the son of Onias'. One of these flourished about three hundred, the other about two hundred years before Christ. The former is probably the one here alluded to. We have no information elsewhere about the improvements which are described somewhat obscurely, in verses 2-5.

TODAY'S ENGLISH VERSION

10 May the bones of the twelve prophets rise to new life,
because these men encouraged the people of Israel and saved
them with confident hope.
11 How can we praise Zerubbabel? He was like a signet
ring on the Lord's right hand, 12 as was Joshua son of
Jehozadak. They rebuilt the Lord's holy Temple, destined for
eternal fame.
13 The memory of Nehemiah is also great. He rebuilt the
ruined walls of Jerusalem, installing the gates and bars. He
rebuilt our homes.
14 No one else like Enoch has ever walked the face of the
earth, for he was taken up from the earth. 15 No one else like
Joseph has ever been born;[a] even his bones were honored.[b]
16 Shem, Seth, and Enosh[c] were highly honored, but Adam's
glory was above that of any other living being.

50 The greatest of his brothers and the pride of his
people[d] was the High Priest Simon son of Onias,
who repaired the Temple 2 and laid the foundation for the

[a] *Greek adds* the greatest of his brothers and the pride of his people; *Hebrew and one ancient translation place these words in 50.1.*
[b] even . . . honored; *or* the Lord watched over his body.
[c] *Hebrew* Shem, Seth, and Enosh; *Greek* Shem and Seth among people.
[d] The greatest . . . people; *Hebrew and one ancient translation place the words at this point; Greek places them at 49.15.*

NEW REVISED STANDARD VERSION

10 May the bones of the Twelve Prophets
send forth new life from where they lie,
for they comforted the people of Jacob
and delivered them with confident hope.

11 How shall we magnify Zerubbabel?
He was like a signet ring on the right hand,
12 and so was Jeshua son of Jozadak;
in their days they built the house
and raised a temple[a] holy to the Lord,
destined for everlasting glory.
13 The memory of Nehemiah also is lasting;
he raised our fallen walls,
and set up gates and bars,
and rebuilt our ruined houses.

14 Few have[b] ever been created on earth like Enoch,
for he was taken up from the earth.
15 Nor was anyone ever born like Joseph;[c]
even his bones were cared for.
16 Shem and Seth and Enosh were honored,[d]
but above every other created living being was Adam.

50 The leader of his brothers and the pride of his people[e]
was the high priest, Simon son of Onias,
who in his life repaired the house,
and in his time fortified the temple.

a Other ancient authorities read *people* *b* Heb Syr: Gk *No one has* *c* Heb Syr: Gk adds *the leader of his brothers, the support of the people* *d* Heb: Gk *Shem and Seth were honored by people* *e* Heb Syr: Gk lacks this line. Compare 49.15

NEW AMERICAN BIBLE

10 Then, too, the TWELVE PROPHETS—
may their bones return to life from their resting
place!—
Gave new strength to Jacob
and saved him by their faith and hope.

11 How can we fittingly praise ZERUBBABEL,
who was like a signet ring on God's right hand,
12 And Jeshua, Jozadak's son?
In their time they built the house of God;
They erected the holy temple,
destined for everlasting glory.
13 Extolled be the memory of NEHEMIAH!
He rebuilt our ruined walls,
Restored our shattered defenses,
and set up gates and bars.
14 Few on earth have been made the equal of ENOCH,
for he was taken up bodily.
15 Was ever a man born like JOSEPH?
Even his dead body was provided for.
16 Glorious, too, were SHEM and SETH and ENOS;
but beyond that of any living being
was the splendor of ADAM.

50 The greatest among his brethren, the glory of his
people,
was SIMON the priest, son of Jochanan,
In whose time the house of God was renovated,
in whose days the temple was reinforced.

NEW JERUSALEM BIBLE

10 As for the twelve prophets,
may their bones flower again from the tomb,
since they have comforted Jacob
and redeemed him in faith and hope.

11 How shall we extol Zerubbabel?
He was like a signet ring on the right hand,
12 so too was Joshua son of Jozadak;
they who in their days built the Temple
and raised a sanctuary sacred to the Lord,
destined to everlasting glory.
13 Great too is the memory of Nehemiah,
who rebuilt our walls which lay in ruins,
erected the bolted gates
and rebuilt our houses.
14 No one else has ever been created on earth to equal
Enoch,
for he was taken up from earth.
15 And no one else ever born has been like Joseph,
the leader of his brothers, the prop of his people;
his bones received a visitation.
16 Shem and Seth were the most honoured of men,
but above every living creature is Adam.

50 It was the High Priest Simon son of Onias[a]
who repaired the Temple during his lifetime
and in his day fortified the sanctuary.

[a] **50** Simon II, son of Onias III, high priest *c.* 220–195 BC.

GREEK OLD TESTAMENT

2 καὶ ὑπ᾽ αὐτοῦ ἐθεμελιώθη ὕψος διπλῆς,
ἀνάλημμα ὑψηλὸν περιβόλου ἱεροῦ·
3 ἐν ἡμέραις αὐτοῦ ἐλατομήθη ἀποδοχεῖον ὑδάτων,
λάκκος ὡσεὶ θαλάσσης τὸ περίμετρον·
4 ὁ φροντίζων τοῦ λαοῦ αὐτοῦ ἀπὸ πτώσεως
καὶ ἐνισχύσας πόλιν ἐν πολιορκήσει.
5 ὡς ἐδοξάσθη ἐν περιστροφῇ λαοῦ,
ἐν ἐξόδῳ οἴκου καταπετάσματος·
6 ὡς ἀστὴρ ἑωθινὸς ἐν μέσῳ νεφελῶν,
ὡς σελήνη πλήρης ἐν ἡμέραις,
7 ὡς ἥλιος ἐκλάμπων ἐπὶ ναὸν ὑψίστου
καὶ ὡς τόξον φωτίζον ἐν νεφέλαις δόξης,
8 ὡς ἄνθος ῥόδων ἐν ἡμέραις νέων,
ὡς κρίνα ἐπ᾽ ἐξόδῳ ὕδατος,
ὡς βλαστὸς Λιβάνου ἐν ἡμέραις θέρους,
9 ὡς πῦρ καὶ λίβανος ἐπὶ πυρείου,
ὡς σκεῦος χρυσίου ὁλοσφύρητον
κεκοσμημένον παντὶ λίθῳ πολυτελεῖ,
10 ὡς ἐλαία ἀναθάλλουσα καρποὺς
καὶ ὡς κυπάρισσος ὑψουμένη ἐν νεφέλαις.
11 ἐν τῷ ἀναλαμβάνειν αὐτὸν στολὴν δόξης
καὶ ἐνδιδύσκεσθαι αὐτὸν συντέλειαν καυχήματος,
ἐν ἀναβάσει θυσιαστηρίου ἁγίου
ἐδόξασεν περιβολὴν ἁγιάσματος·
12 ἐν δὲ τῷ δέχεσθαι μέλη ἐκ χειρῶν ἱερέων,
καὶ αὐτὸς ἑστὼς παρ᾽ ἐσχάρᾳ βωμοῦ,

KING JAMES VERSION

2 And by him was built from the foundation the double height, the high fortress of the wall about the temple:

3 In his days the cistern to receive water, being in compass as the sea, was covered with plates of brass:

4 He took care of the temple that it should not fall, and fortified the city against besieging:

5 How was he honoured in the midst of the people in his coming out of the sanctuary!

6 He was as the morning star in the midst of a cloud, and as the moon at the full:

7 As the sun shining upon the temple of the most High, and as the rainbow giving light in the bright clouds:

8 And as the flower of roses in the spring of the year, as lilies by the rivers of waters, and as the branches of the frankincense tree in the time of summer:

9 As fire and incense in the censer, and as a vessel of beaten gold set with all manner of precious stones:

10 And as a fair olive tree budding forth fruit, and as a cypress tree which groweth up to the clouds.

11 When he put on the robe of honour, and was clothed with the perfection of glory, when he went up to the holy altar, he made the garment of holiness honourable.

12 When he took the portions out of the priests' hands, he himself stood by the hearth of the altar, compassed with his

DOUAY OLD TESTAMENT

2 By him also the height of the temple was founded, the double building and the high walls of the temple.

3 In his days the wells of water flowed out, and they were filled as the sea above measure.

4 He took care of his nation, and delivered it from destruction.

5 He prevailed to enlarge the city, and obtained glory in his conversation with the people: and enlarged the entrance of the house and the court.

6 He shone in his days as the morning star in the midst of a cloud, and as the moon at the full.

7 And as the sun when it shineth, so did he shine in the temple of God.

8 And as the rainbow giving light in the bright clouds, and as the flower of roses in the days of the spring, and as the lilies that are on the brink of the water, and as the sweet smelling frankincense in the time of summer.

9 As a bright fire, and frankincense burning in the fire.

10 As a massy vessel of gold, adorned with every precious stone.

11 As an olive tree budding forth, and a cypress tree rearing itself on high, when he put on the robe of glory, and was clothed with the perfection of power.

12 When he went up to the holy altar, he honoured the vesture of holiness.

13 And when he took the portions out of the hands of the priests, he himself stood by the altar. And about him was the

KNOX TRANSLATION

where the building. was of double thickness, and the towering walls about it, he underpinned; 3 in his day, too, the cisterns received their full flow of water, rose beyond all measuring, sea-deep. 4 So well he cared for his fellow-citizens;
no enemy should be able to compass our ruin; 5 nor lacked
he means to enlarge the city's span. See in what state he
comes out to meet the people; entrance of temple and of tem-
ple-court lifted high above him! 6 Bright he shone as the
day-star amid the clouds, as the full moon in her season;
7 nor sun ever shed on our own temple such generous rays as
he. 8 What shall be compared with him? Rainbow that lights
up the clouds with sudden glory, rose in spring-time, lilies by
the water-side, scent of olibanum on the summer air? 9 Fire
that glows brightly, and glow of incense on the fire?
10 Ornament of pure gold, set with whatever stones are
rarest; 11 olive-tree that burgeons, tall cypress pointing to
the sky? Such was he when he put on his robe of office, clad
himself with the full majesty of his array; 12 sacred the garments in which he went up to the sacred altar, yet were they
ennobled by the man that wore them.

13 There he stood, by the altar, with the priests handing
him their portions, every one, for sacrifice; and all these

TODAY'S ENGLISH VERSION

high double wall and the fortifications of the Temple.[a] 3The
reservoir, as big as the bronze tank, was dug[b] while he was
in office. 4He made plans to protect his people from attack
and fortified the city so that it could withstand a siege.
5How glorious he was when he came out of the Most Holy
Place![c] 6He was like the morning star shining through the
clouds, like the full moon, 7like the sun shining on the
Temple of the Most High, like the rainbow gleaming in glory
against the clouds, 8like roses in springtime, like lilies
beside a stream, like the cedars of Lebanon in summer, 9like
burning incense, like a cup made of hammered gold and decorated with all kinds of jewels, 10like an olive tree loaded
with fruit, like a cypress tree towering into the clouds.
11When Simon put on his magnificent robe and went up to
the holy altar dressed in perfect splendor, he made the
Temple courtyard a majestic sight. 12When the priests handed him the portions of the sacrifice as he stood beside the

a Verse 2 in Greek is unclear. *b Hebrew* dug; *Greek* reduced.
c Hebrew Most Holy Place; *Greek* Most Holy Place among the people.

NEW REVISED STANDARD VERSION

2 He laid the foundations for the high double walls,
the high retaining walls for the temple enclosure.
3 In his days a water cistern was dug,[a]
a reservoir like the sea in circumference.
4 He considered how to save his people from ruin,
and fortified the city against siege.
5 How glorious he was, surrounded by the people,
as he came out of the house of the curtain.
6 Like the morning star among the clouds,
like the full moon at the festal season;[a]
7 like the sun shining on the temple of the Most High,
like the rainbow gleaming in splendid clouds;
8 like roses in the days of first fruits,
like lilies by a spring of water,
like a green shoot on Lebanon on a summer day;
9 like fire and incense in the censer,
like a vessel of hammered gold
studded with all kinds of precious stones;
10 like an olive tree laden with fruit,
and like a cypress towering in the clouds.
11 When he put on his glorious robe
and clothed himself in perfect splendor,
when he went up to the holy altar,
he made the court of the sanctuary glorious.
12 When he received the portions from the hands of the
priests,
as he stood by the hearth of the altar

a Heb: Meaning of Gk uncertain

NEW AMERICAN BIBLE

2 In his time also the wall was built
with powerful turrets for the temple precincts;
3 In his time the reservoir was dug,
the pool with a vastness like the sea's.
4 He protected his people against brigands
and strengthened his city against the enemy.
5 How splendid he was as he appeared from the tent,
as he came from within the veil!
6 Like a star shining among the clouds,
like the full moon at the holyday season;
7 Like the sun shining upon the temple,
like the rainbow appearing in the cloudy sky;
8 Like the blossoms on the branches in springtime,
like a lily on the banks of a stream;
Like the trees of Lebanon in summer,
9 like the fire of incense at the sacrifice;
Like a vessel of beaten gold,
studded with precious stones;
10 Like a luxuriant olive tree thick with fruit,
like a cypress standing against the clouds;
11 Vested in his magnificent robes,
and wearing his garments of splendor,
As he ascended the glorious altar
and lent majesty to the court of the sanctuary.

12 When he received the sundered victims from the priests
while he stood before the sacrificial wood,

NEW JERUSALEM BIBLE

2 He laid the foundations of double depth,
the high buttresses of the Temple precincts.
3 In his day the pool was excavated,
a reservoir as huge as the sea.
4 Anxious to save the people from ruin,
he fortified the city against siege.
5 How splendid he was with the people thronging round
him,
when he emerged from the curtained shrine,
6 like the morning star among the clouds,
like the moon at the full,
7 like the sun shining on the Temple of the Most High,
like the rainbow gleaming against brilliant clouds,
8 like a rose in springtime,
like a lily by a spring,
like a branch of the incense tree in summer,
9 like fire and incense in the censer,
like a massive golden vessel
encrusted with every kind of precious stone,
10 like an olive tree loaded with fruit,
like a cypress soaring to the clouds;
11 when he took his ceremonial robe
and put on his magnificent ornaments,
when he went up to the holy altar
and filled the sanctuary precincts with his grandeur;
12 when he received the portions from the hands of the
priests,
himself standing by the altar hearth,

GREEK OLD TESTAMENT

κυκλόθεν αὐτοῦ στέφανος ἀδελφῶν
ὡς βλάστημα κέδρων ἐν τῷ Λιβάνῳ
καὶ ἐκύκλωσαν αὐτὸν ὡς στελέχη φοινίκων,
13 καὶ πάντες οἱ υἱοὶ Ααρων ἐν δόξῃ αὐτῶν
καὶ προσφορὰ κυρίου ἐν χερσὶν αὐτῶν
ἔναντι πάσης ἐκκλησίας Ισραηλ,
14 καὶ συντέλειαν λειτουργῶν ἐπὶ βωμῶν
κοσμῆσαι προσφορὰν ὑψίστου παντοκράτορος,
15 ἐξέτεινεν ἐπὶ σπονδείου χεῖρα αὐτοῦ
καὶ ἔσπεισεν ἐξ αἵματος σταφυλῆς,
ἐξέχεεν εἰς θεμέλια θυσιαστηρίου
ὀσμὴν εὐωδίας ὑψίστῳ παμβασιλεῖ.
16 τότε ἀνέκραγον οἱ υἱοὶ Ααρων,
ἐν σάλπιγξιν ἐλαταῖς ἤχησαν,
ἀκουστὴν ἐποίησαν φωνὴν μεγάλην
εἰς μνημόσυνον ἔναντι ὑψίστου·
17 τότε πᾶς ὁ λαὸς κοινῇ κατέσπευσαν
καὶ ἔπεσαν ἐπὶ πρόσωπον ἐπὶ τὴν γῆν
προσκυνῆσαι τῷ κυρίῳ αὐτῶν
παντοκράτορι θεῷ ὑψίστῳ·
18 καὶ ᾔνεσαν οἱ ψαλτῳδοὶ ἐν φωναῖς αὐτῶν,
ἐν πλείστῳ ἤχῳ ἐγλυκάνθη μέλος·
19 καὶ ἐδεήθη ὁ λαὸς κυρίου ὑψίστου
ἐν προσευχῇ κατέναντι ἐλεήμονος,
ἕως συντελεσθῇ κόσμος κυρίου
καὶ τὴν λειτουργίαν αὐτοῦ ἐτελείωσαν.

KING JAMES VERSION

brethren round about, as a young cedar in Libanus; and as palm trees compassed they him round about.

13 So were all the sons of Aaron in their glory, and the oblations of the Lord in their hands, before all the congregation of Israel.

14 And finishing the service at the altar, that he might adorn the offering of the most high Almighty,

15 He stretched out his hand to the cup, and poured of the blood of the grape, he poured out at the foot of the altar a sweetsmelling savour unto the most high King of all.

16 Then shouted the sons of Aaron, and sounded the silver trumpets, and made a great noise to be heard, for a remembrance before the most High.

17 Then all the people together hasted, and fell down to the earth upon their faces to worship their Lord God Almighty, the most High.

18 The singers also sang praises with their voices, with great variety of sounds was there made sweet melody.

19 And the people besought the Lord, the most High, by prayer before him that is merciful, till the solemnity of the Lord was ended, and they had finished his service.

DOUAY OLD TESTAMENT

ring of his brethren: and as the cedar planted in mount Libanus,

14 And as branches of palm trees, they stood round about him, and all the sons of Aaron in their glory.

15 And the oblation of the Lord was in their hands, before all the congregation of Israel: and finishing his service, on the altar, to honour the offering of the most high King,

16 He stretched forth his hand to make a libation, and offered of the blood of the grape.

17 He poured out at the foot of the altar a divine odour to the most high Prince.

18 Then the sons of Aaron shouted, they sounded with beaten trumpets, and made a great noise to be heard for a remembrance before God.

19 Then all the people together made haste, and fell down to the earth upon their faces, to adore the Lord their God, and to pray to the Almighty God the most High.

20 And the singers lifted up their voices, and in the great house the sound of sweet melody was increased.

21 And the people in prayer besought the Lord the most High, until the worship of the Lord was perfected, and they had finished their office.

KNOX TRANSLATION

standing about him were but Lebanon cedars standing about
Lebanon, 14 were but as palm branches growing from their
parent stem, all these sons of Aaron in the splendour of their
attire. 15 Theirs to hold out, before assembled Israel, the
offerings made to the Lord; and he, completing his task at
the altar, for the due observance of the great King's sacrifice,
16 would reach out his hand for the cup, and with the grape's
blood offer libation. 17 And as he poured out at the altar's
foot its consecrated fragrance, 18 loud shouted the sons of
Aaron, loud the silver trumpets blew; great was the cry
raised to win God's audience. 19 And with that, down fell all
the people, face to earth, worshipping the Lord their God and
pouring out their prayers to him, the Almighty, to him, the
most High. 20 The singers, too, broke out into chants of
praise; sweetly their voices echoed through the wide courts;
21 nor would the people leave off their praying to the Lord,
the most High, till the divine praise was completed, and all

TODAY'S ENGLISH VERSION

altar with his assistants circling him like a wreath, he was
like a young cedar of Lebanon surrounded by palm trees.
13 Those were the descendants of Aaron in their splendid garments, standing before the whole assembly of Israel, holding
in their hands the offering made to the Lord. 14 When he had
finished the service at the altar and had arranged the sacrifice to the Most High, the Almighty, 15 he reached for a cup
and poured out sweet-smelling wine at the foot of the altar
as an offering to the Most High, the universal King. 16 Then
the priests shouted and blew their trumpets of hammered silver. They made a loud noise that the Most High would hear.
17 All the people immediately bowed down with their faces to
the ground to worship their Lord, the Almighty, the Most
High. 18 Then the choir began to sing his praises, and the
beautiful music rang out. 19 The people kept praying to the
merciful Lord Most High until the service of worship had

NEW REVISED STANDARD VERSION

with a garland of brothers around him,
he was like a young cedar on Lebanon
surrounded by the trunks of palm trees.
13 All the sons of Aaron in their splendor
held the Lord's offering in their hands
before the whole congregation of Israel.
14 Finishing the service at the altars,[a]
and arranging the offering to the Most High, the Almighty,
15 he held out his hand for the cup
and poured a drink offering of the blood of the grape;
he poured it out at the foot of the altar,
a pleasing odor to the Most High, the king of all.
16 Then the sons of Aaron shouted;
they blew their trumpets of hammered metal;
they sounded a mighty fanfare
as a reminder before the Most High.
17 Then all the people together quickly
fell to the ground on their faces
to worship their Lord,
the Almighty, God Most High.

18 Then the singers praised him with their voices
in sweet and full-toned melody.[b]
19 And the people of the Lord Most High offered
their prayers before the Merciful One,
until the order of worship of the Lord was ended,
and they completed his ritual.

a Other ancient authorities read *altar* *b* Other ancient authorities read *in sweet melody throughout the house*

NEW AMERICAN BIBLE

His brethren ringed him about like a garland,
like a stand of cedars on Lebanon;
13 All the sons of Aaron in their dignity
clustered around him like poplars,
With the offerings to the LORD in their hands,
in the presence of the whole assembly of Israel.
14 Once he had completed the services at the altar
with the arranging of the sacrifices for the Most High,
15 And had stretched forth his hand for the cup,
to offer blood of the grape,
And poured it out at the foot of the altar,
a sweet-smelling odor to the Most High God,
16 The sons of Aaron would sound a blast,
the priests, on their trumpets of beaten metal;
A blast to resound mightily
as a reminder before the Most High.
17 Then all the people with one accord
would quickly fall prostrate to the ground
In adoration before the Most High,
before the Holy One of Israel.

18 Then hymns would re-echo,
and over the throng sweet strains of praise resound.
19 All the people of the land would shout for joy,
praying to the Merciful One,
As the high priest completed the services at the altar
by presenting to God the sacrifice due;

NEW JERUSALEM BIBLE

crowned with the circle of his brothers,
as a cedar of Lebanon is by its foliage,
as though surrounded by the trunks of palm trees.
13 When all the sons of Aaron in their glory,
with the offerings of the Lord in their hands,
stood before the whole assembly of Israel,
14 while he completed the rites at the altars,
nobly presenting the offerings to the Almighty, Most High!
15 He would reach out his hand to the cup
and pour a libation of wine,
pouring it at the foot of the altar,
a fragrance pleasing to the Most High, King of All;
16 then the sons of Aaron would shout
and blow their metal trumpets,
making a mighty sound ring out
as a reminder before the Most High;
17 and immediately the people all together
would fall on their faces to the ground,
in adoration of their Lord,
the Almighty, God Most High,
18 and with the cantors chanting their hymns of praise.
Sweet was the melody of all these voices,
19 as the people pleaded with the Lord Most High
and prayed in the presence of the Merciful,
until the service of the Lord was completed
and the ceremony at an end.

GREEK OLD TESTAMENT

20 τότε καταβὰς ἐπῆρεν χεῖρας αὐτοῦ
ἐπὶ πᾶσαν ἐκκλησίαν υἱῶν Ισραηλ
δοῦναι εὐλογίαν κυρίου ἐκ χειλέων αὐτοῦ
καὶ ἐν ὀνόματι αὐτοῦ καυχήσασθαι·
21 καὶ ἐδευτέρωσαν ἐν προσκυνήσει
ἐπιδέξασθαι τὴν εὐλογίαν παρὰ ὑψίστου.
22 Καὶ νῦν εὐλογήσατε τὸν θεὸν πάντων
τὸν μεγάλα ποιοῦντα πάντῃ,
τὸν ὑψοῦντα ἡμέρας ἡμῶν ἐκ μήτρας
καὶ ποιοῦντα μεθ' ἡμῶν κατὰ τὸ ἔλεος αὐτοῦ.
23 δῴη ἡμῖν εὐφροσύνην καρδίας
καὶ γενέσθαι εἰρήνην ἐν ἡμέραις ἡμῶν
ἐν Ισραηλ κατὰ τὰς ἡμέρας τοῦ αἰῶνος·
24 ἐμπιστεῦσαι μεθ' ἡμῶν τὸ ἔλεος αὐτοῦ
καὶ ἐν ταῖς ἡμέραις ἡμῶν λυτρωσάσθω ἡμᾶς.
25 Ἐν δυσὶν ἔθνεσιν προσώχθισεν ἡ ψυχή μου,
καὶ τὸ τρίτον οὐκ ἔστιν ἔθνος·
26 οἱ καθήμενοι ἐν ὄρει Σαμαρείας καὶ Φυλιστιιμ
καὶ ὁ λαὸς ὁ μωρὸς ὁ κατοικῶν ἐν Σικιμοις.
27 Παιδείαν συνέσεως καὶ ἐπιστήμης
ἐχάραξεν ἐν τῷ βιβλίῳ τούτῳ
Ἰησοῦς υἱὸς Σιραχ Ελεαζαρ ὁ Ιεροσολυμίτης,
ὃς ἀνώμβρησεν σοφίαν ἀπὸ καρδίας αὐτοῦ.

KING JAMES VERSION

20 Then he went down and lifted up his hands over the whole congregation of the children of Israel, to give the blessing of the Lord with his lips, and to rejoice in his name.
21 And they bowed themselves down to worship the second time, that they might receive a blessing from the most High.
22 Now therefore bless ye the God of all, which only doeth wondrous things every where, which exalteth our days from the womb, and dealeth with us according to his mercy.
23 He grant us joyfulness of heart, and that peace may be in our days in Israel for ever:
24 That he would confirm his mercy with us, and deliver us at his time!
25 There be two manner of nations which my heart abhorreth, and the third is no nation:
26 They that sit upon the mountain of Samaria, and they that dwell among the Philistines, and that foolish people that dwell in Sichem.
27 Jesus the son of Sirach of Jerusalem hath written in this book the instruction of understanding and knowledge, who out of his heart poured forth wisdom.

DOUAY OLD TESTAMENT

22 Then coming down, he lifted up his hands over all the congregation of the children of Israel, to give glory to God with his lips, and to glory in his name:
23 And he repeated his prayer, willing to shew the power of God.
24 And now pray ye to the God of all, who hath done great things in all the earth, who hath increased our days from our mother's womb, and hath done with us according to his mercy.
25 May he grant us joyfulness of heart, and that there be peace in our days in Israel for ever:
26 That Israel may believe that the mercy of God is with us, to deliver us in his days.
27 There are two nations which my soul abhorreth: and the third is no nation, which I hate:
28 They that sit on mount Seir, and the Philistines, and the foolish people that dwell in Sichem.
29 Jesus the son of Sirach, of Jerusalem, hath written in this book the doctrine of wisdom and instruction, who renewed wisdom from his heart.

KNOX TRANSLATION

their duty done. 22 And then Simon would come down, his
hand outstretched over the assembly of Israel, a blessing on
his lips, and his heart proud to serve such a Master; 23 and
so fell to prayer again, for the better manifesting of God's power.
24 Bless we now his name who is God over all;[a] wide as earth is his wondrous power, the God that has granted us life since first we were borne in the womb, and most mercifully used us. 25 Gladness of heart may he give us, and send
Israel in our time peace that shall last for ever; 26 and still
may it be Israel's faith that God's mercy is with us, ready, when his time comes, to grant us deliverance.
27 Two nations with all my heart I loathe; and a third I can
name, that nation indeed is none; 28 the hill-tribes of Edom, and the Philistines, and the miscreant folk that dwell at Sichem.
29 The lessons of discernment and of true knowledge in this book contained were written down by Jesus, the son of Sirach, of Jerusalem; his heart ever a fountain of true wisdom.

a vv. 24-26: It is not clear whether this is the formula of blessing used by Simon, or an epilogue written in the person of the author.

TODAY'S ENGLISH VERSION

come to a close. 20 Then Simon came down from the altar,
raised his hands over the whole assembly of Israel, and reverently pronounced the blessing from the Lord, 21 while the
people bowed a second time in worship to receive that blessing from the Most High.
22 Now then, give praise to the God of the universe, who
has done great things everywhere, who brings us up[a] from
the time we are born, and deals with us mercifully. 23 May
he give us happiness and allow us to have peace in Israel
forever. 24 May he continue his mercy to us and rescue us in
our time of need.
25 There are two nations that I detest, and a third that does
not even deserve to be called a nation. 26 These are the
Edomites,[b] the inhabitants of the Philistine cities, and the
stupid Samaritans.
27 I, Jesus son of Sirach Eleazar[c] of Jerusalem, put all my
wisdom into writing this book to provide instruction and

[a] brings us up; *or* honors us. [b] *Hebrew* Edomites; *Greek* Samaritans.
[c] Sirach Eleazar; *or* Sirach son of Eleazar.

NEW REVISED STANDARD VERSION

20 Then Simon[a] came down and raised his hands
over the whole congregation of Israelites,
to pronounce the blessing of the Lord with his lips,
and to glory in his name;
21 and they bowed down in worship a second time,
to receive the blessing from the Most High.

22 And now bless the God of all,
who everywhere works great wonders,
who fosters our growth from birth,
and deals with us according to his mercy.
23 May he give us[b] gladness of heart,
and may there be peace in our[c] days
in Israel, as in the days of old.
24 May he entrust to us his mercy,
and may he deliver us in our[d] days!

25 Two nations my soul detests,
and the third is not even a people:
26 Those who live in Seir,[e] and the Philistines,
and the foolish people that live in Shechem.

27 Instruction in understanding and knowledge
I have written in this book,
Jesus son of Eleazar son of Sirach[f] of Jerusalem,
whose mind poured forth wisdom.

a Gk *he* *b* Other ancient authorities read *you* *c* Other ancient authorities read *your* *d* Other ancient authorities read *his* *e* Heb Compare Lat: Gk *on the mountain of Samaria* *f* Heb: Meaning of Gk uncertain

NEW AMERICAN BIBLE

20 Then coming down he would raise his hands
over all the congregation of Israel.
The blessing of the LORD would be upon his lips,
the name of the LORD would be his glory.
21 Then again the people would lie prostrate
to receive from him the blessing of the Most High.

22 And now, bless the God of all,
who has done wondrous things on earth;
Who fosters men's growth from their mother's womb,
and fashions them according to his will!
23 May he grant you joy of heart
and may peace abide among you;
24 May his goodness toward us endure in Israel
as long as the heavens are above.

25 My whole being loathes two nations,
the third is not even a people:
26 Those who live in Seir and Philistia,
and the degenerate folk who dwell in Shechem.

27 Wise instruction, appropriate proverbs,
I have written in this book,
I, Jesus, son of Eleazar, son of Sirach,
as they gushed forth from my heart's understanding.

NEW JERUSALEM BIBLE

20 Then he would come down and raise his hands
over the whole assembly of the Israelites,
to give them the Lord's blessing from his lips,
being privileged to pronounce his name;
21 and once again the people would bow low
to receive the blessing of the Most High.

22 And now bless the God of all things,
the doer of great deeds everywhere,
who has exalted our days from the womb
and has acted mercifully towards us.
23 May he grant us cheerful hearts
and bring peace in our time,
in Israel for ages on ages.
24 May his mercy be faithfully with us,
may he redeem us in our own times!
25 There are two nations that my soul detests,
the third is not a nation at all:
26 the inhabitants of Mount Seir, the Philistines,
and the stupid people living at Shechem.

27 Instruction in wisdom and knowledge
is what has been written in this book
by Jesus son of Sira Eleazar of Jerusalem,
who has poured a rain of wisdom from his heart.

GREEK OLD TESTAMENT

28 μακάριος ὃς ἐν τούτοις ἀναστραφήσεται,
καὶ θεὶς αὐτὰ ἐπὶ καρδίαν αὐτοῦ σοφισθήσεται·
29 ἐὰν γὰρ αὐτὰ ποιήσῃ, πρὸς πάντα ἰσχύσει·
ὅτι φῶς κυρίου τὸ ἴχνος αὐτοῦ.
51 Ἐξομολογήσομαί σοι, κύριε βασιλεῦ,
καὶ αἰνέσω σε θεὸν τὸν σωτῆρά μου,
ἐξομολογοῦμαι τῷ ὀνόματί σου,
2 ὅτι σκεπαστὴς καὶ βοηθὸς ἐγένου μοι
καὶ ἐλυτρώσω τὸ σῶμά μου ἐξ ἀπωλείας
καὶ ἐκ παγίδος διαβολῆς γλώσσης,
ἀπὸ χειλέων ἐργαζομένων ψεῦδος
καὶ ἔναντι τῶν παρεστηκότων
ἐγένου βοηθὸς καὶ ἐλυτρώσω με
3 κατὰ τὸ πλῆθος ἐλέους καὶ ὀνόματός σου
ἐκ βρυγμῶν ἕτοιμον εἰς βρῶμα,
ἐκ χειρὸς ζητούντων τὴν ψυχήν μου,
ἐκ πλειόνων θλίψεων, ὧν ἔσχον,
4 ἀπὸ πνιγμοῦ πυρᾶς κυκλόθεν
καὶ ἐκ μέσου πυρός, οὗ οὐκ ἐξέκαυσα,
5 ἐκ βάθους κοιλίας ᾅδου
καὶ ἀπὸ γλώσσης ἀκαθάρτου καὶ λόγου ψευδοῦς.
6 βασιλεῖ διαβολὴ γλώσσης ἀδίκου.

KING JAMES VERSION

28 Blessed is he that shall be exercised in these things;
and he that layeth them up in his heart shall become wise.
29 For if he do them, he shall be strong to all things: for
the light of the Lord leadeth him, who giveth wisdom to the
godly. Blessed be the Lord for ever. Amen, Amen.
51 I will thank thee, O Lord and King, and praise thee, O
God my Saviour: I do give praise unto thy name:
2 For thou art my defender and helper, and hast preserved
my body from destruction, and from the snare of the slanderous tongue, and from the lips that forge lies, and hast been
mine helper against mine adversaries:
3 And hast delivered me, according to the multitude of thy
mercies and greatness of thy name, from the teeth of them
that were ready to devour me, and out of the hands of such
as sought after my life, and from the manifold afflictions
which I had;
4 From the choking of fire on every side, and from the
midst of the fire which I kindled not;
5 From the depth of the belly of hell, from an unclean
tongue, and from lying words.
6 By an accusation to the king from an unrighteous

DOUAY OLD TESTAMENT

30 Blessed is he that is conversant in these good things: and he that layeth them up in his heart, shall be wise always.

31 For if he do them, he shall be strong to do all things: because the light of God guideth his steps.

51 A PRAYER of Jesus the son of Sirach. I will give glory to thee, O Lord, O King, and I will praise thee, O God my Saviour.

2 I will give glory to thy name: for thou hast been a helper and protector to me.

3 And hast preserved my body from destruction, from the snare of an unjust tongue, and from the lips of them that forge lies, and in the sight of them that stood by, thou hast been my helper.

4 And thou hast delivered me, according to the multitude of the mercy of thy name, from them that did roar, prepared to devour.

5 Out of the hands of them that sought my life, and from the gates of afflictions, which compassed me about:

6 From the oppression of the flame which surrounded me, and in the midst of the fire I was not burnt.

7 From the depth of the belly of hell, and from an unclean tongue, and from lying words, from an unjust king, and from a slanderous tongue:

8 My soul shall praise the Lord even to death.

KNOX TRANSLATION

30 Blessed is he who lingers in these pleasant haunts, and
treasures the memory of them; wisdom he shall never lack;
31 and if by these precepts he live, nothing shall avail to daunt
him; God's beacon-light shews the track he shall tread.
51 A prayer uttered by Jesus, son of Sirach. O Lord, my
king, I give thee thanks, O God, my deliverer, I praise
thee; 2 I extol thy name, for all the succour and protection
thou hast given me, 3 saving my life from deadly peril, when
calumny lay in wait, and lying tongues assailed me. In full
sight of all that stood by thou didst come to my rescue;
4 roaring lions stood ready to devour me, and thou in that
great mercy, that renowned mercy of thine, didst deliver me.
5 I was in the hands of my mortal enemies, shut in on every
side by misfortune; 6 there were stifling flames all round me,
and I stood in the heart of the fire uninjured. 7 I looked down
into the deep womb of the grave, when foul lips brought lying
accusations, and cruel king gave unjust sentence. 8 And still I
would praise the Lord, long as I had breath to praise him,

TODAY'S ENGLISH VERSION

knowledge for others. [28] May God bless everyone who gives
attention to these teachings. Whoever takes them to heart
will become wise. [29] Whoever lives by them will be strong
enough for any occasion, because he will be walking in the
light of the Lord.

51 I give you thanks, O Lord and King;
I praise you as my God and Savior.
I give you thanks,
2 for you have helped me and protected me.
You have rescued me from death,
from dangerous lies and slander.
3 You helped me when no one else would;
in your great mercy you saved me
from the many troubles I have known:
from the glaring hatred of my enemies,
who wanted to put an end to my life;
4 from suffocation in oppressive smoke
rising from fires that I did not light;
5 from death itself;
from vicious slander reported to the king.

NEW REVISED STANDARD VERSION

28 Happy are those who concern themselves with these
things,
and those who lay them to heart will become wise.
29 For if they put them into practice, they will be equal to
anything,
for the fear[a] of the Lord is their path.

PRAYER OF JESUS SON OF SIRACH[b]

51 I give you thanks, O Lord and King,
and praise you, O God my Savior.
I give thanks to your name,
2 for you have been my protector and helper
and have delivered me from destruction
and from the trap laid by a slanderous tongue,
from lips that fabricate lies.
In the face of my adversaries
you have been my helper 3 and delivered me,
in the greatness of your mercy and of your name,
from grinding teeth about to devour me,
from the hand of those seeking my life,
from the many troubles I endured,
4 from choking fire on every side,
and from the midst of fire that I had not kindled,
5 from the deep belly of Hades,
from an unclean tongue and lying words—
6 the slander of an unrighteous tongue to the king.

a Heb: Other ancient authorities read *light* *b* This title is included in the Gk text.

NEW AMERICAN BIBLE

28 Happy the man who meditates upon these things,
wise the man who takes them to heart!
29 If he puts them into practice, he can cope with
anything,
for the fear of the LORD is his lamp.

51 I give you thanks, O God of my father;
I praise you, O God my savior!
I will make known your name, refuge of my life;
2 you have been my helper against my adversaries.
You have saved me from death,
and kept back my body from the pit,
From the clutches of the nether world you have
snatched my feet;
3 you have delivered me, in your great mercy,
From the scourge of a slanderous tongue,
and from lips that went over to falsehood;
From the snare of those who watched for my downfall,
and from the power of those who sought my life;
From many a danger you have saved me,
4 from flames that hemmed me in on every side;
From the midst of unremitting fire,
5 From the deep belly of the nether world;
From deceiving lips and painters of lies,
6 from the arrows of dishonest tongues.

NEW JERUSALEM BIBLE

28 Blessed is he who devotes his time to these
and grows wise by taking them to heart!
29 If he practises them he will be strong enough for
anything,
since the light of the Lord is his path.

51 I shall give thanks to you, Lord and King,
and praise you, God my Saviour,
I give thanks to your name;
2 for you have been my guard and support
and redeemed my body from destruction,
from the snare of the lying tongue,
from lips that fabricate falsehood;
in the presence of my assailants, you were on my side;
you have been my support, you have redeemed me,
3 true to your abounding kindness
—and the greatness of your name—you liberated me
from the fangs of those seeking to devour me,
from the clutches of those seeking my life,
from the many ordeals which I have endured,
4 from the stifling heat which hemmed me in,
from the heart of a fire which I had not kindled,
5 from deep in the belly of Sheol,
6 treacherous denunciations to the king.

GREEK OLD TESTAMENT

ἤγγισεν ἕως θανάτου ἡ ψυχή μου,
καὶ ἡ ζωή μου ἦν σύνεγγυς ᾅδου κάτω.
7 περιέσχον με πάντοθεν, καὶ οὐκ ἦν ὁ βοηθῶν·
ἐνέβλεπον εἰς ἀντίλημψιν ἀνθρώπων, καὶ οὐκ ἦν.
8 καὶ ἐμνήσθην τοῦ ἐλέους σου, κύριε,
καὶ τῆς ἐργασίας σου τῆς ἀπ' αἰῶνος,
ὅτι ἐξαιρῇ τοὺς ὑπομένοντάς σε
καὶ σῴζεις αὐτοὺς ἐκ χειρὸς ἐχθρῶν.
9 καὶ ἀνύψωσα ἀπὸ γῆς ἱκετείαν μου
καὶ ὑπὲρ θανάτου ῥύσεως ἐδεήθην·
10 ἐπεκαλεσάμην κύριον πατέρα κυρίου μου
μή με ἐγκαταλιπεῖν ἐν ἡμέραις θλίψεως,
ἐν καιρῷ ὑπερηφανιῶν ἀβοηθησίας·
αἰνέσω τὸ ὄνομά σου ἐνδελεχῶς
καὶ ὑμνήσω ἐν ἐξομολογήσει.
11 καὶ εἰσηκούσθη ἡ δέησίς μου·
ἔσωσας γάρ με ἐξ ἀπωλείας
καὶ ἐξείλου με ἐκ καιροῦ πονηροῦ.
12 διὰ τοῦτο ἐξομολογήσομαί σοι καὶ αἰνέσω σε
καὶ εὐλογήσω τῷ ὀνόματι κυρίου.

KING JAMES VERSION

tongue my soul drew near even unto death, my life was near to the hell beneath.

7 They compassed me on every side, and there was no man to help me: I looked for the succour of men, but there was none.

8 Then thought I upon thy mercy, O Lord, and upon thy acts of old, how thou deliverest such as wait for thee, and savest them out of the hands of the enemies.

9 Then lifted I up my supplication from the earth, and prayed for deliverance from death.

10 I called upon the Lord, the Father of my Lord, that he would not leave me in the days of my trouble, and in the time of the proud, when there was no help.

11 I will praise thy name continually, and will sing praise with thanksgiving; and so my prayer was heard:

12 For thou savedst me from destruction, and deliveredst me from the evil time: therefore will I give thanks, and praise thee, and bless they name, O Lord.

DOUAY OLD TESTAMENT

9 And my life was drawing near to hell beneath.

10 They compassed me on every side, and there was no one that would help me. I looked for the succour of men, and there was none.

11 I remembered thy mercy, O Lord, and thy works, which are from the beginning of the world.

12 How thou deliverest them that wait for thee, O Lord, and savest them out of the hands of the nations.

13 Thou hast exalted my dwelling place upon the earth and I have prayed for death to pass away.

14 I called upon the Lord, the father of my Lord, that he would not leave me in the day of my trouble, and in the time of the proud without help.

15 I will praise thy name continually, and will praise it with thanksgiving, and my prayer was heard.

16 And thou hast saved me from destruction, and hast delivered me from the evil time.

17 Therefore I will give thanks, and praise thee, and bless the name of the Lord.

KNOX TRANSLATION

9 though death's abyss yawned at my very feet, 10 though I
was cut off on every side, with none to aid me. Man's help I
looked for, and could not find; 11 yet I bethought me, Lord, of
thy mercy, thy deeds of long ago; 12 if men will but wait for
thee patiently, thou, Lord, dost deliver them, dost rescue them
from the power of the heathen. 13 It was thou who hadst
prospered my life on earth, and now, death ready to overwhelm me, 14 to the Lord, Father of the Master I serve,[a] I
made my plea. Would he leave me unaided when I was in distress, when my enemies were triumphing over me? 15 I will
extol thy name unceasingly, with grateful praise; my prayer
did not go unregarded. 16 Thou didst rescue me from deadly
peril, didst save me in the hour of defeat; 17 shall I not give
thanks, shall I not praise and bless thy name?

a It is not easy to see what the sacred author meant by 'the Master whom I serve'; the obscure words used in Ps. 109. 1 are only an incomplete parallel.

TODAY'S ENGLISH VERSION

6 I was once brought face-to-face with death;
7 enemies surrounded me everywhere.
I looked for someone to help me,
but there was no one there.
8 But then, O Lord, I remembered how merciful you are
and what you had done in times past.
I remembered that you rescue those who rely on you,
that you save them from their enemies.
9 Then from here on earth I prayed to you
to rescue me from death.
10 I prayed, "O Lord, you are my father;[a]
do not abandon me to my troubles
when I am helpless against arrogant enemies.
11 I will always praise you
and sing hymns of thanksgiving."
You answered my prayer,
12 and saved me from the threat of destruction.
And so I thank you and praise you.
O Lord, I praise you!

[a] *Hebrew* you are my father; *Greek* father of my Lord.

NEW REVISED STANDARD VERSION

My soul drew near to death,
and my life was on the brink of Hades below.
7 They surrounded me on every side,
and there was no one to help me;
I looked for human assistance,
and there was none.
8 Then I remembered your mercy, O Lord,
and your kindness[a] from of old,
for you rescue those who wait for you
and save them from the hand of their enemies.
9 And I sent up my prayer from the earth,
and begged for rescue from death.
10 I cried out, "Lord, you are my Father;[b]
do not forsake me in the days of trouble,
when there is no help against the proud.
11 I will praise your name continually,
and will sing hymns of thanksgiving."
My prayer was heard,
12 for you saved me from destruction
and rescued me in time of trouble.
For this reason I thank you and praise you,
and I bless the name of the Lord.

a Other ancient authorities read *work* *b* Heb: Gk *the Father of my lord*

NEW AMERICAN BIBLE

I was at the point of death,
my soul was nearing the depths of the nether world;
7 I turned every way, but there was no one to help me,
I looked for one to sustain me, but could find no one.
8 But then I remembered the mercies of the LORD,
his kindness through ages past;
For he saves those who take refuge in him,
and rescues them from every evil.
9 So I raised my voice from the very earth,
from the gates of the nether world, my cry.
10 I called out: O Lord, you are my father,
you are my champion and my savior;
Do not abandon me in time of trouble,
in the midst of storms and dangers.
11 I will ever praise your name
and be constant in my prayers to you.
Thereupon the LORD heard my voice,
he listened to my appeal;
12 He saved me from evil of every kind
and preserved me in time of trouble.
For this reason I thank him and I praise him;
I bless the name of the LORD.

51, 12: In standard editions of the *New American Bible* the italicized verses that follow appear in a footnote. (Cf Ps 148,14.)

NEW JERUSALEM BIBLE

My soul has been close to death,
my life had gone down to the brink of Sheol.
7 I was completely surrounded, there was no one to help me;
I looked for someone to help me, there was no one.
8 Then I remembered your mercy, Lord,
and your deeds from earliest times,
how you deliver those who wait for you patiently,
and save them from the clutches of their enemies.
9 And I sent up my plea from the earth,
I begged to be delivered from death.
10 I called on the Lord, the father of my Lord,
'Do not desert me in the days of ordeal,
in the days of the proud, when we are helpless.
I shall praise your name unceasingly
and gratefully sing its praises.'
11 And my plea was heard,
for you saved me from destruction,
you delivered me from that time of evil.
12 And therefore I shall thank you and praise you,
and bless the name of the Lord.

GREEK OLD TESTAMENT

KING JAMES VERSION

DOUAY OLD TESTAMENT

KNOX TRANSLATION

TODAY'S ENGLISH VERSION

NEW REVISED STANDARD VERSION

Heb adds:

Give thanks to the LORD, for he is good,
for his mercy endures forever;

Give thanks to the God of praises,
for his mercy endures forever;

Give thanks to the guardian of Israel,
for his mercy endures forever;

Give thanks to him who formed all things,
for his mercy endures forever;

Give thanks to the redeemer of Israel,
for his mercy endures forever;

Give thanks to him who gathers the dispersed of Israel,
for his mercy endures forever;

Give thanks to him who rebuilt his city and his sanctuary,
for his mercy endures forever;

Give thanks to him who makes a horn to sprout for the house of David,
for his mercy endures forever;

Give thanks to him who has chosen the sons of Zadok to be priests,
for his mercy endures forever;

NEW AMERICAN BIBLE

After verse 12 the Hebrew text gives the litany of praise contained below. It is not found in any versions and is therefore of doubtful authenticity.

Give thanks to the Lord, for he is good, for his mercy endures forever;
Give thanks to the God of glory, for his mercy endures forever;
Give thanks to the guardian of Israel, for his mercy endures forever;
Give thanks to the creator of the universe, for his mercy endures forever;
Give thanks to the redeemer of Israel, for his mercy endures forever;
Give thanks to him who gathers the dispersed of Israel, for his mercy endures forever;
Give thanks to him who builds his city and his sanctuary, for his mercy endures forever;
Give thanks to him who makes a horn to sprout forth, for the house of David, for his mercy endures forever;
Give thanks to him who has chosen for his priests the sons of Zadok, for his mercy endures forever;

NEW JERUSALEM BIBLE

GREEK OLD TESTAMENT

13 Ἔτι ὢν νεώτερος πρὶν ἢ πλανηθῆναί με
ἐζήτησα σοφίαν προφανῶς ἐν προσευχῇ μου.
14 ἔναντι ναοῦ ἠξίουν περὶ αὐτῆς
καὶ ἕως ἐσχάτων ἐκζητήσω αὐτήν.
15 ἐξ ἄνθους ὡς περκαζούσης σταφυλῆς
εὐφράνθη ἡ καρδία μου ἐν αὐτῇ.
ἐπέβη ὁ πούς μου ἐν εὐθύτητι,
ἐκ νεότητός μου ἴχνευον αὐτήν.

KING JAMES VERSION

13 When I was yet young, or ever I went abroad, I desired wisdom openly in my prayer.

14 I prayed for her before the temple, and will seek her out even to the end.

15 Even from the flower till the grape was ripe hath my heart delighted in her: my foot went the right way, from my youth up sought I after her.

DOUAY OLD TESTAMENT

18 When I was yet young, before I wandered about, I sought for wisdom openly in my prayer.

19 I prayed for her before the temple, and unto the very end I will seek after her, and she flourished as a grape soon ripe.

20 My heart delighted in her, my foot walked in the right way, from my youth up I sought after her.

KNOX TRANSLATION

18 A young man still, ere ever my wanderings began, I
made my prayer for wisdom.[a] 19 Before the temple I asked
for this, my life's quest to the end. Came early the ripening of
those grapes, and my heart rejoiced at it. 20 Down a straight

[a] It is not clear whether we are to understand the word 'wanderings' literally (cf. 34. 12) or metaphorically.

TODAY'S ENGLISH VERSION

13 When I was still young, before I started out on my travels, I boldly prayed for Wisdom. 14 I went to the Temple and
asked for her, and I will look for her as long as I live.
15 From my blossoming youth to my ripe old age she has
been my delight. I have followed directly in her path ever

NEW REVISED STANDARD VERSION

Give thanks to the shield of Abraham,
for his mercy endures forever;

Give thanks to the rock of Isaac,
for his mercy endures forever;

Give thanks to the mighty one of Jacob,
for his mercy endures forever;

Give thanks to him who has chosen Zion,
for his mercy endures forever;

Give thanks to the King of the kings of kings,
for his mercy endures forever;

He has raised up a horn for his people,
praise for all his loyal ones.

For the children of Israel, the people close to him.
Praise the LORD!

---

13 While I was still young, before I went on my travels,
I sought wisdom openly in my prayer.
14 Before the temple I asked for her,
and I will search for her until the end.

15 From the first blossom to the ripening grape
my heart delighted in her;
my foot walked on the straight path;
from my youth I followed her steps.

NEW AMERICAN BIBLE

Give thanks to the shield of Abraham, for his mercy
endures forever;
Give thanks to the rock of Isaac, for his mercy endures
forever;
Give thanks to the mighty one of Jacob, for his mercy
endures forever;
Give thanks to him who has chosen Zion, for his mercy
endures forever;
Give thanks to the king over kings of kings, for his
mercy endures forever;
He has lifted up the horn of his people, be this his praise
from all his faithful ones,
From the children of Israel, the people close to him.
Alleluia!

---

13 When I was young and innocent,
I sought wisdom.
14 She came to me in her beauty,
and until the end I will cultivate her.
15 As the blossoms yielded to ripening grapes,
the heart's joy,
My feet kept to the level path
because from earliest youth I was familiar with her.

NEW JERUSALEM BIBLE

13 When I was still a youth, before I went travelling,
in my prayers I asked outright for wisdom.
14 Outside the sanctuary I would pray for her,
and to the last I shall continue to seek her.
15 From her blossoming to the ripening of her grape
my heart has taken its delight in her.
My foot has pursued a straight path,
I have sought her ever since my youth.

GREEK OLD TESTAMENT

16 ἔκλινα ὀλίγον τὸ οὖς μου καὶ ἐδεξάμην
καὶ πολλὴν εὗρον ἐμαυτῷ παιδείαν.
17 προκοπὴ ἐγένετό μοι ἐν αὐτῇ·
τῷ διδόντι μοι σοφίαν δώσω δόξαν.
18 διενοήθην γὰρ τοῦ ποιῆσαι αὐτὴν
καὶ ἐζήλωσα τὸ ἀγαθὸν καὶ οὐ μὴ αἰσχυνθῶ.
19 διαμεμάχισται ἡ ψυχή μου ἐν αὐτῇ
καὶ ἐν ποιήσει νόμου διηκριβασάμην.
τὰς χεῖράς μου ἐξεπέτασα πρὸς ὕψος
καὶ τὰ ἀγνοήματα αὐτῆς ἐπένθησα.
20 τὴν ψυχήν μου κατεύθυνα εἰς αὐτὴν
καὶ ἐν καθαρισμῷ εὗρον αὐτήν.
καρδίαν ἐκτησάμην μετ' αὐτῆς ἀπ' ἀρχῆς·
διὰ τοῦτο οὐ μὴ ἐγκαταλειφθῶ.
21 καὶ ἡ κοιλία μου ἐταράχθη τοῦ ἐκζητῆσαι αὐτήν·
διὰ τοῦτο ἐκτησάμην ἀγαθὸν κτῆμα.
22 ἔδωκεν κύριος γλῶσσάν μοι μισθόν μου,
καὶ ἐν αὐτῇ αἰνέσω αὐτόν.
23 ἐγγίσατε πρός με, ἀπαίδευτοι,
καὶ αὐλίσθητε ἐν οἴκῳ παιδείας.
24 τί ὅτι ὑστερεῖσθαι λέγετε ἐν τούτοις
καὶ αἱ ψυχαὶ ὑμῶν διψῶσι σφόδρα;

KING JAMES VERSION

16 I bowed down mine ear a little, and received her, and gat much learning.

17 I profited therein, *therefore* will I ascribe glory unto him that giveth me wisdom.

18 For I purposed to do after her, and earnestly I followed that which is good; so shall I not be confounded.

19 My soul hath wrestled with her, and in my doings I was exact: I stretched forth my hands to the heaven above, and bewailed my ignorances of her.

20 I directed my soul unto her, and I found her in pureness: I have had my heart joined with her from the beginning, therefore shall I not be foresaken.

21 My heart was troubled in seeking her: therefore have I gotten a good possession.

22 The Lord hath given me a tongue for my reward, and I will praise him therewith.

23 Draw near unto me, ye unlearned, and dwell in the house of learning.

24 Wherefore are ye slow, and what say ye of these things, seeing your souls are very thirsty?

DOUAY OLD TESTAMENT

21 I bowed down my ear a little, and received her.

22 I found much wisdom in myself, and I profited much therein.

23 To him that giveth me wisdom, will I give glory.

24 For I have determined to follow her: I have had a zeal for good, and shall not be confounded.

25 My soul hath wrestled for her, and in doing it I have been confirmed.

26 I stretched forth my hands on high, and I bewailed my ignorance of her.

27 I directed my soul to her, and in knowledge I found her.

28 I possessed my heart with her from the beginning: therefore I shall not be forsaken.

29 My entrails were troubled in seeking her: therefore shall I possess a good possession.

30 The Lord hath given me a tongue for my reward: and with it I will praise him.

31 Draw near to me, ye unlearned, and gather yourselves together into the house of discipline.

32 Why are ye slow? and what do you say of these things? your souls are exceeding thirsty.

KNOX TRANSLATION

path I sped, the ardour of youth to aid my search. 21 Ear that
little listens shall yet hear; 22 much wisdom that little listening gave. 23 Further and further yet I travelled, thanks be to
the God that all wisdom bestows. 24 Good use to make of her
was all my love and longing; never was that hope disappointed. 25 Hardily I strove to win her, put force on myself to
keep her rule; 26 I stretched out my hands towards heaven,
and grieved for the want of her. 27 Kept I but true to the
search for her, I found and recognized her still. 28 Long since
trained by her discipline, I shall never be left forsaken.
29 Much heart-burning I had in the quest for her, but a rich
dowry she brought me. 30 Never shall this tongue, with
utterance divinely rewarded, be negligent of praise. 31 O
hearts untutored, come near, and frequent the school of
learning! 32 Parley at the gates no more, complaining of

TODAY'S ENGLISH VERSION

since I was young. 16 I received Wisdom as soon as I began
listening for her, and I have been rewarded with great
knowledge. 17 I have always been a learner and am grateful
to everyone who has been my teacher. 18 I was determined to
live wisely and was devoted to the cause of goodness. I have
no regrets. 19 I fought for Wisdom and was strict in my conduct. When I prayed, I sadly confessed how far short of
Wisdom I fell. 20 But I was determined to have her, and I
found her by keeping myself free from sin. I have grown in
Wisdom since first I found her, and I will never be without
her. 21 Because I was driven by the desire to find her, I have
been richly rewarded. 22 The Lord gave me a gift for words,
and I have used it in his praise.
23 Come to me, all you that need instruction, and learn in
my school. 24 Why do you admit that you are ignorant and

NEW REVISED STANDARD VERSION

16 I inclined my ear a little and received her,
and I found for myself much instruction.
17 I made progress in her;
to him who gives wisdom I will give glory.

18 For I resolved to live according to wisdom,[a]
and I was zealous for the good,
and I shall never be disappointed.
19 My soul grappled with wisdom,[a]
and in my conduct I was strict;[b]

I spread out my hands to the heavens,
and lamented my ignorance of her.
20 I directed my soul to her,
and in purity I found her.

With her I gained understanding from the first;
therefore I will never be forsaken.
21 My heart was stirred to seek her;
therefore I have gained a prize possession.
22 The Lord gave me my tongue as a reward,
and I will praise him with it.

23 Draw near to me, you who are uneducated,
and lodge in the house of instruction.
24 Why do you say you are lacking in these things,[c]
and why do you endure such great thirst?

a Gk *her* *b* Meaning of Gk uncertain *c* Cn Compare Heb Syr: Meaning of Gk uncertain

NEW AMERICAN BIBLE

16 In the short time I paid heed,
I met with great instruction.
17 Since in this way I have profited,
I will give my teacher grateful praise.

18 I became resolutely devoted to her—
the good I persistently strove for.
19 I burned with desire for her,
never turning back.
I became preoccupied with her,
never weary of extolling her.
My hand opened her gate
and I came to know her secrets.
20 For her I purified my hands;
in cleanness I attained to her.
At first acquaintance with her, I gained understanding
such that I will never forsake her.
21 My whole being was stirred as I learned about her;
therefore I have made her my prize possession.
22 The LORD has granted me my lips as a reward,
and my tongue will declare his praises.

23 Come aside to me, you untutored,
and take up lodging in the house of instruction;
24 How long will you be deprived of wisdom's food,
how long will you endure such bitter thirst?

NEW JERUSALEM BIBLE

16 By bowing my ear a little, I have received her,
and have found much instruction.
17 Thanks to her I have advanced;
glory be to him who has given me wisdom!
18 For I was determined to put her into practice,
have earnestly pursued the good, and shall not be
put to shame.
19 My soul has fought to possess her,
I have been scrupulous in keeping the Law;
I have stretched out my hands to heaven
and bewailed how little I knew of her;
20 I have directed my soul towards her,
and in purity I have found her;
having my heart fixed on her from the outset,
I shall never be deserted;
21 my very core having yearned to discover her,
I have now acquired a good possession.
22 In reward the Lord has given me a tongue
with which I shall sing his praises.
23 Come close to me, you ignorant,
take your place in my school.
24 Why complain about lacking these things
when your souls are so thirsty for them?

GREEK OLD TESTAMENT

25 ἤνοιξα τὸ στόμα μου καὶ ἐλάλησα
Κτήσασθε ἑαυτοῖς ἄνευ ἀργυρίου.
26 τὸν τράχηλον ὑμῶν ὑπόθετε ὑπὸ ζυγόν,
καὶ ἐπιδεξάσθω ἡ ψυχὴ ὑμῶν παιδείαν.
ἐγγύς ἐστιν εὑρεῖν αὐτήν.
27 ἴδετε ἐν ὀφθαλμοῖς ὑμῶν ὅτι ὀλίγον ἐκοπίασα
καὶ εὗρον ἐμαυτῷ πολλὴν ἀνάπαυσιν.
28 μετάσχετε παιδείας ἐν πολλῷ ἀριθμῷ ἀργυρίου
καὶ πολὺν χρυσὸν κτήσασθε ἐν αὐτῇ.
29 εὐφρανθείη ἡ ψυχὴ ὑμῶν ἐν τῷ ἐλέει αὐτοῦ,
καὶ μὴ αἰσχυνθείητε ἐν αἰνέσει αὐτοῦ.
30 ἐργάζεσθε τὸ ἔργον ὑμῶν πρὸ καιροῦ,
καὶ δώσει τὸν μισθὸν ὑμῶν ἐν καιρῷ αὐτοῦ.

KING JAMES VERSION

25 I opened my mouth, and said, Buy her for yourselves without money.

26 Put your neck under the yoke, and let your soul receive instruction: she is hard at hand to find.

27 Behold with your eyes, how that I have but little labour, and have gotten unto me much rest.

28 Get learning with a great sum of money, and get much gold by her.

29 Let your soul rejoice in his mercy, and be not ashamed of his praise.

30 Work your work betimes, and in his time he will give you your reward.

DOUAY OLD TESTAMENT

33 I have opened my mouth, and have spoken: buy her for yourselves without silver,

34 And submit your neck to the yoke, and let your soul receive discipline: for she is near at hand to be found.

35 Behold with your eyes how I have laboured a little, and have found much rest to myself.

36 Receive ye discipline as a great sum of money, and possess abundance of gold by her.

37 Let your soul rejoice in his mercy, and you shall not be confounded in his praise.

38 Work your work before the time, and he will give you your reward in his time.

KNOX TRANSLATION

thirst ever unsatisfied. 33 Rather, to my proclamation give
heed; win the treasure that is to be had without price paid.
34 Suffice it that you bow your necks to her yoke, are content
to accept her schooling. To find her, needs no distant
travel...[a] 35 Unlaborious days, as all can testify, what a harvest they have won me of repose! 36 Would you grudge free
expense of silver in the search for wisdom, that shall make
you ample returns in gold? 37 Your hearts shall yet triumph
in his mercy, nor ever rue the day when you learned to praise
him.
38 Do, while time serves, what needs doing; when the time
comes, he will reward you.

a It seems clear that some words have dropped out at the end of this verse; the Hebrew gives 'and the man who is intent upon her will discover her'.

TODAY'S ENGLISH VERSION

do nothing about it? 25 Here is what I say: It costs nothing to
be wise. 26 Put on the yoke, and be willing to learn. The
opportunity is always near. 27 See for yourselves! I have
really not studied very hard, but I have found great contentment. 28 No matter how much it costs you to get Wisdom, it
will be well worth it. 29 Be joyfully grateful for the Lord's
mercy, and never be ashamed to praise him. 30 Do your duty
at the proper time, and the Lord, at the time he thinks proper, will give you your reward.

NEW REVISED STANDARD VERSION

25 I opened my mouth and said,
Acquire wisdom[a] for yourselves without money.

26 Put your neck under her[b] yoke,
and let your souls receive instruction;
it is to be found close by.

27 See with your own eyes that I have labored but little
and found for myself much serenity.
28 Hear but a little of my instruction,
and through me you will acquire silver and gold.[c]

29 May your soul rejoice in God's[d] mercy,
and may you never be ashamed to praise him.
30 Do your work in good time,
and in his own time God[e] will give you your reward.

a Heb: Gk lacks *wisdom* *b* Heb: other ancient authorities read *the*
c Syr Compare Heb: Gk *Get instruction with a large sum of silver, and you will gain by it much gold.* *d* Gk *his* *e* Gk *he*

NEW AMERICAN BIBLE

25 I open my mouth and speak of her:
gain, at no cost, wisdom for yourselves.
26 Submit your neck to her yoke,
that your mind may accept her teaching.
For she is close to those who seek her,
and the one who is in earnest finds her.
27 See for yourselves! I have labored only a little,
but have found much.
28 Acquire but a little instruction;
you will win silver and gold through her.
29 Let your spirits rejoice in the mercy of God,
and be not ashamed to give him praise.
30 Work at your tasks in due season,
and in his own time God will give you your reward.

NEW JERUSALEM BIBLE

25 I have opened my mouth, I have said:
'Buy her without money,
26 put your necks under her yoke,
let your souls receive instruction,
she is near, within your reach.'
27 See for yourselves: how slight my efforts have been
to win so much peace.
28 Buy instruction with a large sum of silver,
thanks to her you will gain much gold.
29 May your souls rejoice in the mercy of the Lord,
may you never be ashamed of praising him.
30 Do your work before the appointed time
and at the appointed time he will give you your
reward.

(*Subscript:*) Wisdom of Jesus, son of Sira.

GREEK OLD TESTAMENT

ΒΑΡΟΥΧ

1 Καὶ οὗτοι οἱ λόγοι τοῦ βιβλίου, οὓς ἔγραψεν Βαρουχ
υἱὸς Νηριου υἱοῦ Μαασαιου υἱοῦ Σεδεκιου υἱοῦ Ασαδιου
υἱοῦ Χελκιου ἐν Βαβυλῶνι 2 ἐν τῷ ἔτει τῷ πέμπτῳ ἐν
ἑβδόμῃ τοῦ μηνὸς ἐν τῷ καιρῷ, ᾧ ἔλαβον οἱ Χαλδαῖοι τὴν
Ιερουσαλημ καὶ ἐνέπρησαν αὐτὴν ἐν πυρί. 3 καὶ ἀνέγνω
Βαρουχ τοὺς λόγους τοῦ βιβλίου τούτου ἐν ὠσὶν Ιεχονιου
υἱοῦ Ιωακιμ βασιλέως Ιουδα καὶ ἐν ὠσὶ παντὸς τοῦ λαοῦ τῶν
ἐρχομένων πρὸς τὴν βίβλον 4 καὶ ἐν ὠσὶν τῶν δυνατῶν καὶ
υἱῶν τῶν βασιλέων καὶ ἐν ὠσὶ τῶν πρεσβυτέρων καὶ ἐν ὠσὶ
παντὸς τοῦ λαοῦ ἀπὸ μικροῦ ἕως μεγάλου, πάντων τῶν
κατοικούντων ἐν Βαβυλῶνι ἐπὶ ποταμοῦ Σουδ. 5 καὶ ἔκλαιον
καὶ ἐνήστευον καὶ ηὔχοντο ἐναντίον κυρίου 6 καὶ συνήγαγον
ἀργύριον, καθὰ ἑκάστου ἠδύνατο ἡ χείρ, 7 καὶ ἀπέστειλαν
εἰς Ιερουσαλημ πρὸς Ιωακιμ υἱὸν Χελκιου υἱοῦ Σαλωμ τὸν
ἱερέα καὶ πρὸς τοὺς ἱερεῖς καὶ πρὸς πάντα τὸν λαὸν τοὺς
εὑρεθέντας μετ᾽ αὐτοῦ ἐν Ιερουσαλημ 8 ἐν τῷ λαβεῖν αὐτὸν

KING JAMES VERSION

BARUCH

1 And these are the words of the book, which Baruch the
son of Nerias, the son of Maasias, the son of Sedecias,
the son of Asadias, the son of Chelcias, wrote in Babylon,
2 In the fifth year, and in the seventh day of the month,
what time as the Chaldeans took Jerusalem, and burnt it
with fire.
3 And Baruch did read the words of this book in the hearing of Jechonias the son of Joachim king of Juda, and in the
ears of all the people that came to hear the book,
4 And in the hearing of the nobles, and of the king's sons,
and in the hearing of the elders, and of all the people, from
the lowest unto the highest, even of all them that dwelt at
Babylon by the river Sud.
5 Whereupon they wept, fasted, and prayed before the
Lord.
6 They made also a collection of money according to every
man's power:
7 And they sent it to Jerusalem unto Joachim the high
priest, the son of Chelcias, son of Salom, and to the priests,
and to all the people which were found with him at
Jerusalem,

DOUAY OLD TESTAMENT

THE PROPHECY OF BARUCH

1 AND these are the words of the book, which Baruch the
son of Nerias, the son of Maasias, the son of Sedecias,
the son of Sedei, the son of Helcias, wrote in Babylonia.
2 In the fifth year, in the seventh day of the month, at the
time that the Chaldeans took Jerusalem, and burnt it with
fire.
3 And Baruch read the words of this book in the hearing
of Jechonias the son of Joakim king of Juda, and in the hearing of all the people that came to *hear* the book.
4 And in the hearing of the nobles, the sons of the kings,
and in the hearing of the ancients, and in the hearing of the
people, from the least even to the greatest of them that dwelt
in Babylonia, by the river Sedi.
5 And when they heard it they wept, and fasted, and
prayed before the Lord.
6 And they made a collection of money according to every
man's power.
7 And they sent *it* to Jerusalem to Joakim the priest, the
son of Helcias, the son of Salom, and to the priests, and to
all the people, that were found with him in Jerusalem:

KNOX TRANSLATION

THE PROPHECY OF BARUCH

1 THE words which follow were committed to writing in
the country of Babylon. The writer of them, Baruch, was
descended from Helcias, through Nerias, Maasias, Sedecias
and Sedei, 2 and wrote in the fifth year,...on the seventh day
of the month, at the time when the Chaldaeans took
Jerusalem and burnt it to the ground.[a] 3 Baruch read this
book of his aloud to Jechonias, son of Joakim, king of Juda.
All the people, too, flocked to hear the reading of it, 4 nobles
and royal princes, and elders, and common folk high and
low; all that were then living in the country of Babylon, near
the river Sodi.
5 And as they heard it, all was weeping and fasting and
prayer offered in the Lord's presence; 6 they made a collection of money besides, each according to his means, 7 which
they sent to the chief priest, Joachim, son of Helcias, son of
Salom, and his fellow priests and fellow citizens at

a It seems almost certain that the text is defective here; to mention the day of the month and not mention which month it was, would be most unusual. But probably the omission was a more considerable one. It is difficult to see how the events referred to in verses 6-8 could have happened in or near the year 587, when Jerusalem was burnt; it had been closely besieged for two years already, It looks as if these prophecies of Baruch had been dated over a period of years, like those of his master Jeremias (Jer. 1. 2, 3), and only the earlier part of them had been sent to Jerusalem at the time indicated. The text will have run: 'in the fifth year of Sedecias' reign, right up to the eleventh year of it, the fifth month and the seventh day of the month, when the Chaldaeans took Jerusalem'. Some think, however, that the words 'at the time when' indicate an anniversary, as in Deut. 16. 6.

TODAY'S ENGLISH VERSION

THE BOOK OF BARUCH

1 This book was written by Baruch son of Neraiah, grandson of Mahseiah, and a descendant of Zedekiah, Hasadiah, and Hilkiah. It was written in Babylon 2 on the seventh
day of the month[a] in the fifth year after the Babylonians
captured Jerusalem and burned it down. 3-4 Baruch read the
book aloud to Jehoiachin son of Jehoiakim, king of Judah,
and to all the people who lived in Babylon by the Sud River.
Everyone came to hear it read—nobles, children of royal
families, elders, in fact, all the people, no matter what their
status.
5 When the book was read, everyone cried, fasted, and
prayed to the Lord. 6 Then they all gave as much money as
they could, 7 and the collection was sent to Jerusalem to
Jehoiakim the High Priest, son of Hilkiah and grandson of
Shallum, and to the other priests and to all the people who
were with him in Jerusalem.

[a] THE MONTH: *The month is probably the fifth month of the Hebrew calendar (see 2 K 25.8; Jr 52.12).*

NEW REVISED STANDARD VERSION

BARUCH

1 These are the words of the book that Baruch son of
Neriah son of Mahseiah son of Zedekiah son of Hasadiah son of Hilkiah wrote in Babylon, 2 in the fifth year, on
the seventh day of the month, at the time when the
Chaldeans took Jerusalem and burned it with fire.
3 Baruch read the words of this book to Jeconiah son of
Jehoiakim, king of Judah, and to all the people who came to
hear the book, 4 and to the nobles and the princes, and to
the elders, and to all the people, small and great, all who
lived in Babylon by the river Sud.
5 Then they wept, and fasted, and prayed before the Lord;
6 they collected as much money as each could give, 7 and
sent it to Jerusalem to the high priest[a] Jehoiakim son of
Hilkiah son of Shallum, and to the priests, and to all the people who were present with him in Jerusalem. 8 At the same

a Gk *the priest*

NEW AMERICAN BIBLE

THE BOOK OF BARUCH

1 Now these are the words of the scroll which Baruch, son
of Neriah, son of Mahseiah, son of Zedekiah, son of
Hasadiah, son of Hilkiah, wrote in Babylon, 2 in the fifth
year [on the seventh day of the month, at the time when the
Chaldeans took Jerusalem and burnt it with fire]. 3 And
Baruch read the words of this scroll for Jeconiah, son of
Jehoiakim, king of Judah, to hear it, as well as all the people
who came to the reading: 4 the nobles, the kings' sons, the
elders, and the whole people, small and great alike—all who
lived in Babylon by the river Sud.
5 They wept and fasted and prayed before the LORD, 6 and
collected such funds as each could furnish. 7 These they sent
to Jerusalem, to Jehoiakim, son of Hilkiah, son of Shallum,
the priest, and to the priests and the whole people who were
with him in Jerusalem. 8 [This was when he received the

NEW JERUSALEM BIBLE

THE BOOK OF BARUCH

1 This is the text of the book written in Babylon by Baruch
son of Neraiah, son of Mahseiah, son of Zedekiah, son
of Hasadiah, son of Hilkiah, 2 in the fifth year, on the seventh day of the month, at the time when the Chaldaeans had
captured Jerusalem and burned it down.
3 Baruch read the text of this book aloud to Jeconiah son of
Jehoiakim, king of Judah, and to all the people who had
come to hear the reading, 4 to the nobles and the sons of the
king, and to the elders; to the whole people, that is, to the
least no less than to the greatest, to all who lived in Babylon
beside the river Sud. 5 On hearing it they wept, fasted and
prayed before the Lord; 6 and they collected as much money
as each could afford 7 and sent it to Jerusalem to the priest
Jehoiakim son of Hilkiah, son of Shallum, and the other
priests, and all the people who were with him in Jerusalem.

GREEK OLD TESTAMENT

τὰ σκεύη οἴκου κυρίου τὰ ἐξενεχθέντα ἐκ τοῦ ναοῦ ἀποστρέψαι εἰς γῆν Ιουδα τῇ δεκάτῃ τοῦ Σιουαν, σκεύη ἀργυρᾶ,
ἃ ἐποίησεν Σεδεκιας υἱὸς Ιωσια βασιλεὺς Ιουδα 9 μετὰ τὸ
ἀποικίσαι Ναβουχοδονοσορ βασιλέα Βαβυλῶνος τὸν Ιεχονιαν
καὶ τοὺς ἄρχοντας καὶ τοὺς δεσμώτας καὶ τοὺς δυνατοὺς
καὶ τὸν λαὸν τῆς γῆς ἀπὸ Ιερουσαλημ καὶ ἤγαγεν αὐτὸν εἰς
Βαβυλῶνα. 10 καὶ εἶπαν Ἰδοὺ ἀπεστείλαμεν πρὸς ὑμᾶς ἀργύριον, καὶ ἀγοράσατε τοῦ ἀργυρίου ὁλοκαυτώματα καὶ περὶ
ἁμαρτίας καὶ λίβανον καὶ ποιήσατε μαννα καὶ ἀνοίσατε ἐπὶ
τὸ θυσιαστήριον κυρίου θεοῦ ἡμῶν 11 καὶ προσεύξασθε περὶ
τῆς ζωῆς Ναβουχοδονοσορ βασιλέως Βαβυλῶνος καὶ εἰς ζωὴν
Βαλτασαρ υἱοῦ αὐτοῦ, ἵνα ὦσιν αἱ ἡμέραι αὐτῶν ὡς αἱ ἡμέραι
τοῦ οὐρανοῦ ἐπὶ τῆς γῆς. 12 καὶ δώσει κύριος ἰσχὺν ἡμῖν καὶ
φωτίσει τοὺς ὀφθαλμοὺς ἡμῶν, καὶ ζησόμεθα ὑπὸ τὴν σκιὰν
Ναβουχοδονοσορ βασιλέως Βαβυλῶνος καὶ ὑπὸ τὴν σκιὰν
Βαλτασαρ υἱοῦ αὐτοῦ καὶ δουλεύσομεν αὐτοῖς ἡμέρας πολλὰς
καὶ εὑρήσομεν χάριν ἐναντίον αὐτῶν. 13 καὶ προσεύξασθε

KING JAMES VERSION

8 At the same time when he received the vessels of the house of the Lord, that were carried out of the temple, to return them into the land of Juda, the tenth day of *the month* Sivan, *namely,* silver vessels, which Sedecias the son of Josias king of Juda had made,

9 After that Nabuchodonosor king of Babylon had carried away Jechonias, and the princes, and the captives, and the mighty men, and the people of the land, from Jerusalem, and brought them unto Babylon.

10 And they said, Behold, we have sent you money to buy you burnt offerings, and sin offerings, and incense, and prepare ye manna, and offer upon the altar of the Lord our God;

11 And pray for the life of Nabuchodonosor king of Babylon, and for the life of Balthasar his son, that their days may be upon earth as the days of heaven:

12 And the Lord will give us strength, and lighten our eyes, and we shall live under the shadow of Nabuchodonosor king of Babylon, and under the shadow of Balthasar his son, and we shall serve them many days, and find favour in their sight.

DOUAY OLD TESTAMENT

8 At the time when he received the vessels of the temple of the Lord, which had been taken away out of the temple, to return them into the land of Juda the tenth day of the month Sivan, the silver vessels, which Sedecias the son of Josias king of Juda had made,

9 After that Nabuchodonosor the king of Babylon had carried away Jechonias, and the princes, and all the powerful men, and the people of the land from Jerusalem, and brought them bound to Babylon.

10 And they said: Behold we have sent you money, buy with it holocausts, and frankincense, and make meat offerings, and offerings for sin at the altar of the Lord our God:

11 And pray ye for the life of Nabuchodonosor the king of Babylon, and for the life of Balthasar his son, that their days may be upon earth as the days of heaven:

12 And that the Lord may give us strength, and enlighten our eyes, that we may live under the shadow of Nabuchodonosor the king of Babylon, and under the shadow of Balthasar his son, and may serve them many days, and may find favour in their sight.

KNOX TRANSLATION

Jerusalem. 8 ...when he[a] travelled to Juda on the tenth day of
Sivan, taking with him the sanctuary ornaments which had
been removed from the temple, and were now to be restored.
They were of silver; Sedecias, the son of Josias, that now
reigned in Juda, had had them made, 9 when Jechonias, with
the princes and all the nobles and many other citizens of
Jerusalem, was carried off by Nabuchodonosor, king of
Babylon, to his own country.
10 Here is money, they said, with which you are to buy victims for burnt-sacrifice, and incense; bloodless offerings[b] too
you must make, and amends for fault committed, at the altar
of the Lord our God. 11 You shall pray long life for king
Nabuchodonosor of Babylon, and his son Baltassar, that their
reign on earth may last as long as heaven itself. 12 May the
Lord grant courage to all of us, and send us a gleam of hope;
long thrive we under the protection of king Nabuchodonosor
and his son Baltassar, persevering loyally in their service and

a 'He' can hardly be Joakim; and the last mention of Baruch is too far away to justify a reference by pronoun. Another short deficiency in the text seems probable; the money was sent to Jerusalem 'by the hand of' some person named, Baruch or another. It is commonly assumed that Sedecias had made silver ornaments at Jerusalem, to replace the old ones which had been carried off; that these silver ones were carried off in their turn (on some unspecified occasion), and were then restored to Juda (for some unspecified reason). All this seems unduly elaborate. The gold ornaments were removed with Jechonias (IV Kg. 24. 13), and at the same time all metal-workers were exiled (ib. 16). Sedecias, who was still in favour, had to get models made *not in Jerusalem but in Babylon;* and with these silver models the prophecy of Baruch, or rather such parts of it as had already been committed to writing could conveniently be despatched. *b* Literally, 'manna', but it is clear that the Septuagint Greek has confused two separate Hebrew words, and the Latin version has come to us through the Greek.

TODAY'S ENGLISH VERSION

8 On the tenth day of the month of Sivan, Baruch took the
sacred utensils which had been carried away from the
Temple and returned them to Judah. These were the silver
utensils which Zedekiah son of King Josiah of Judah had
ordered made 9 after King Nebuchadnezzar of Babylonia had
deported Jehoiachin, the rulers, the skilled workers,[a] the
nobles, and the common people and had taken them from
Jerusalem to Babylon.
10 The people wrote:
Please use the money we are sending you to buy animals for the burnt offerings and the sin offerings, to buy
incense, and to provide the grain offerings. Offer them on
the altar of the Lord our God, 11 and pray for King Nebuchadnezzar of Babylonia and his son Belshazzar, that they
may live as long as the heavens last. 12 Then the Lord will
strengthen us and be our guide. Nebuchadnezzar and his
son Belshazzar will protect us, and we will be loyal to
them as long as we live; then they will be pleased with us.

[a] skilled workers; *Greek* prisoners.

NEW REVISED STANDARD VERSION

time, on the tenth day of Sivan, Baruch[a] took the vessels of
the house of the Lord, which had been carried away from the
temple, to return them to the land of Judah—the silver vessels that Zedekiah son of Josiah, king of Judah, had made,
9 after King Nebuchadnezzar of Babylon had carried away
from Jerusalem Jeconiah and the princes and the prisoners
and the nobles and the people of the land, and brought them
to Babylon.
10 They said: Here we send you money; so buy with the
money burnt offerings and sin offerings and incense, and
prepare a grain offering, and offer them on the altar of the
Lord our God; 11 and pray for the life of King Nebuchadnezzar of Babylon, and for the life of his son Belshazzar, so
that their days on earth may be like the days of heaven.
12 The Lord will give us strength, and light to our eyes; we
shall live under the protection[b] of King Nebuchadnezzar of
Babylon, and under the protection of his son Belshazzar, and
we shall serve them many days and find favor in their sight.

[a] Gk *he* [b] Gk *in the shadow*

NEW AMERICAN BIBLE

vessels of the house of the LORD that had been removed from
the temple, to restore them to the land of Judah, on the tenth
of Sivan. These silver vessels Zedekiah, son of Josiah, king of
Judah, had had made 9 after Nebuchadnezzar, king of
Babylon, carried off Jeconiah, and the princes, and the skilled
workers, and the nobles, and the people of the land from
Jerusalem, as captives, and brought them to Babylon.]
10 Their message was: "We send you funds, with which
you are to procure holocausts, sin offerings, and frankincense, and to prepare cereal offerings; offer these on the altar
of the LORD our God, 11 and pray for the life of Nebuchadnezzar, king of Babylon, and that of Belshazzar, his son,
that their lifetimes may equal the duration of the heavens
above the earth; 12 and that the LORD may give us strength,
and light to our eyes, that we may live under the protective
shadow of Nebuchadnezzar, king of Babylon, and that of
Belshazzar, his son, and serve them long, finding favor in
their sight.

NEW JERUSALEM BIBLE

8 Also on the tenth day of Sivan he was given the utensils of
the house of the Lord, which had been removed from the
Temple, to take them back to the land of Judah; these were
silver utensils which Zedekiah son of Josiah, king of Judah,
had had made 9 after Nebuchadnezzar king of Babylon had
deported Jeconiah from Jerusalem to Babylon, together with
the princes, the metalworkers, the nobles and the common
people.
10 Now, they wrote, we are sending you money to pay for
burnt offerings, offerings for sin, and incense. Prepare oblations and offer them on the altar of the Lord our God; 11 and
pray for the long life of Nebuchadnezzar king of Babylon,
and of his son Belshazzar, that they may endure on earth as
long as the heavens endure; 12 and that the Lord may give
us strength and enlighten our eyes, so that we may lead our
lives under the protection of Nebuchadnezzar king of
Babylon and of his son Belshazzar, and that we may serve
them for a long time and win their favour. 13 Also pray to

GREEK OLD TESTAMENT

περὶ ἡμῶν πρὸς κύριον τὸν θεὸν ἡμῶν, ὅτι ἡμάρτομεν τῷ κυρίῳ θεῷ ἡμῶν, καὶ οὐκ ἀπέστρεψεν ὁ θυμὸς κυρίου καὶ ἡ ὀργὴ αὐτοῦ ἀφ᾽ ἡμῶν ἕως τῆς ἡμέρας ταύτης. 14 καὶ ἀναγνώσεσθε τὸ βιβλίον τοῦτο, ὃ ἀπεστείλαμεν πρὸς ὑμᾶς ἐξαγορεῦσαι ἐν οἴκῳ κυρίου ἐν ἡμέρᾳ ἑορτῆς καὶ ἐν ἡμέραις καιροῦ, 15 καὶ ἐρεῖτε

Τῷ κυρίῳ θεῷ ἡμῶν ἡ δικαιοσύνη, ἡμῖν δὲ αἰσχύνη τῶν προσώπων ὡς ἡ ἡμέρα αὕτη, ἀνθρώπῳ Ιουδα καὶ τοῖς κατοικοῦσιν Ιερουσαλημ 16 καὶ τοῖς βασιλεῦσιν ἡμῶν καὶ τοῖς ἄρχουσιν ἡμῶν καὶ τοῖς ἱερεῦσιν ἡμῶν καὶ τοῖς προφήταις ἡμῶν καὶ τοῖς πατράσιν ἡμῶν, 17 ὧν ἡμάρτομεν ἔναντι κυρίου 18 καὶ ἠπειθήσαμεν αὐτῷ καὶ οὐκ ἠκούσαμεν τῆς φωνῆς κυρίου θεοῦ ἡμῶν πορεύεσθαι τοῖς προστάγμασιν κυρίου, οἷς ἔδωκεν κατὰ πρόσωπον ἡμῶν. 19 ἀπὸ τῆς ἡμέρας, ἧς ἐξήγαγεν κύριος τοὺς πατέρας ἡμῶν ἐκ γῆς Αἰγύπτου, καὶ ἕως τῆς ἡμέρας ταύτης ἤμεθα ἀπειθοῦντες πρὸς κύριον θεὸν ἡμῶν καὶ ἐσχεδιάζομεν πρὸς τὸ μὴ ἀκούειν τῆς φωνῆς αὐτοῦ. 20 καὶ ἐκολλήθη εἰς ἡμᾶς τὰ κακὰ καὶ ἡ ἀρά, ἣν συνέταξεν κύριος τῷ Μωυσῇ παιδὶ αὐτοῦ ἐν ἡμέρᾳ, ᾗ ἐξήγαγεν τοὺς πατέρας ἡμῶν ἐκ γῆς Αἰγύπτου δοῦναι ἡμῖν γῆν ῥέουσαν γάλα καὶ μέλι ὡς ἡ ἡμέρα αὕτη. 21 καὶ οὐκ ἠκούσαμεν τῆς φωνῆς κυρίου τοῦ θεοῦ ἡμῶν κατὰ πάντας τοὺς λόγους τῶν προφητῶν, ὧν ἀπέστειλεν πρὸς ἡμᾶς, 22 καὶ ᾠχόμεθα ἕκαστος ἐν διανοίᾳ καρδίας αὐτοῦ τῆς πονηρᾶς ἐργάζεσθαι θεοῖς ἑτέροις ποιῆσαι τὰ κακὰ κατ᾽ ὀφθαλμοὺς

KING JAMES VERSION

13 Pray for us also unto the Lord our God, for we have sinned against the Lord our God; and unto this day the fury of the Lord and his wrath is not turned from us.

14 And ye shall read this book which we have sent unto you, to make confession in the house of the Lord, upon the feasts and solemn days.

15 And ye shall say, To the Lord our God *belongeth* righteousness, but unto us the confusion of faces, as *it is come to pass* this day, unto them of Juda, and to the inhabitants of Jerusalem,

16 And to our kings, and to our princes, and to our priests, and to our prophets, and to our fathers:

17 For we have sinned before the Lord,

18 And disobeyed him, and have not hearkened unto the voice of the Lord our God, to walk in the commandments that he gave us openly:

19 Since the day that the Lord brought our forefathers out of the land of Egypt, unto this present day, we have been disobedient unto the Lord our God, and we have been negligent in not hearing his voice.

20 Wherefore the evils cleaved unto us, and the curse, which the Lord appointed by Moses his servant at the time that he brought our fathers out of the land of Egypt, to give us a land that floweth with milk and honey, like as *it is to see* this day.

21 Nevertheless we have not hearkened unto the voice of the Lord our God, according unto all the words of the prophets, whom he sent unto us:

22 But every man followed the imagination of his own wicked heart, to serve strange gods, and to do evil in the sight of the Lord our God.

DOUAY OLD TESTAMENT

13 And pray ye for us to the Lord our God: for we have sinned against the Lord our God, and his wrath is not turned away from us even to this day.

14 And read ye this book, which we have sent to you to be read in the temple of the Lord, on feasts, and proper days.

15 And you shall say: To the Lord our God *belongeth* justice, but to us confusion of our face: as it is come to pass at this day to all Juda, and to the inhabitants of Jerusalem,

16 To our kings, and to our princes, and to our priests, and to our prophets, and to our fathers.

17 We have sinned before the Lord our God, and have not believed him, nor put our trust in him:

18 And we were not obedient to him, and we have not hearkened to the voice of the Lord our God, to walk in his commandments, which he hath given us.

19 From the day that he brought our fathers out of the land of Egypt, even to this day, we were disobedient to the Lord our God: and going astray we turned away from hearing his voice.

20 And many evils have cleaved to us, and the curses which the Lord foretold by Moses his servant: who brought our fathers out of the land of Egypt, to give us a land flowing with milk and honey, as at this day.

21 And we have not hearkened to the voice of the Lord our God according to all the words of the prophets whom he sent to us:

22 And we have gone away every man after the inclinations of his own wicked heart, to serve strange gods, and to do evil in the sight of the Lord our God.

KNOX TRANSLATION

winning their favour! 13 And intercede with the Lord our God for us exiles; against his divine will we have rebelled, and to this hour he has not relented. 14 Scan closely, too, this book we are sending to you; it is to be read aloud on feast-days and in times of solemn assembly. 15 You shall make your prayer in these words following.

The fault was never with him, the Lord our God; ours the blush of shame, as all Juda this day and all the citizens of Jerusalem can witness. 16 With king and prince of ours, priest and prophet of ours the fault lies, and with our fathers before us. 17 We have defied the will of the Lord our God; trust and loyalty we had none to give him, 18 nor ever shewed him submission, by listening to his divine voice and following the commands he gave us. 19 Ever since the day when he rescued our fathers from Egypt we have been in rebellion against the Lord our God, straying ever further from the sound of his voice; till at last, as these times can witness, 20 bale and ban have caught us by the heels, the very same he pronounced to his servant Moses long ago, when he had rescued our fathers from Egypt and was leading them on to a land all milk and honey. 21 Unheeded, that divine voice, when message after message came to us through his prophets; 22 each must follow the whim of his own false heart, doing sacrifice to alien gods, and setting the will of the Lord, our own God, at defiance.

TODAY'S ENGLISH VERSION

13 We ask you also to pray to the Lord God for us, because
we have sinned against him, and he is still angry with us.
14 Please read this book that we are sending you and make
your own confession of sin in the Temple on the first day
of the Festival of Shelters and on other holy days of
assembly.
15 This is the confession you should make: "The Lord our
God is righteous, but we are still covered with shame. All
of us—the people of Judah, the people of Jerusalem, 16 our
kings, our rulers, our priests, our prophets, and our ancestors have been put to shame, 17 because we have sinned
against the Lord our God 18 and have disobeyed him. We
did not listen to him or live according to his commandments. 19 From the day the Lord brought our ancestors out
of Egypt until the present day, we have continued to be
unfaithful to him, and we have not hesitated to disobey
him. 20 Long ago, when the Lord led our ancestors out of
Egypt, so that he could give us a rich and fertile land, he
pronounced curses against us through his servant Moses.
And today we are suffering because of those curses. 21 We
refused to obey the word of the Lord our God which he
spoke to us through the prophets. Instead, we all did as we
pleased and went on our own evil way. We turned to other
gods and did things the Lord hates.

NEW REVISED STANDARD VERSION

13 Pray also for us to the Lord our God, for we have sinned
against the Lord our God, and to this day the anger of the
Lord and his wrath have not turned away from us. 14 And
you shall read aloud this scroll that we are sending you, to
make your confession in the house of the Lord on the days of
the festivals and at appointed seasons.
15 And you shall say: The Lord our God is in the right,
but there is open shame on us today, on the people of Judah,
on the inhabitants of Jerusalem, 16 and on our kings, our
rulers, our priests, our prophets, and our ancestors,
17 because we have sinned before the Lord. 18 We have disobeyed him, and have not heeded the voice of the Lord our
God, to walk in the statutes of the Lord that he set before us.
19 From the time when the Lord brought our ancestors out of
the land of Egypt until today, we have been disobedient to
the Lord our God, and we have been negligent, in not heeding his voice. 20 So to this day there have clung to us the
calamities and the curse that the Lord declared through his
servant Moses at the time when he brought our ancestors
out of the land of Egypt to give to us a land flowing with
milk and honey. 21 We did not listen to the voice of the Lord
our God in all the words of the prophets whom he sent to us,
22 but all of us followed the intent of our own wicked hearts
by serving other gods and doing what is evil in the sight of
the Lord our God.

NEW AMERICAN BIBLE

13 "Pray for us also to the LORD, our God; for we have
sinned against the LORD, our God, and the wrath and anger
of the LORD have not yet been withdrawn from us at the
present day. 14 And read out publicly this scroll which we
send you, in the house of the LORD, on the feast day and during the days of assembly:
15 "Justice is with the LORD, our God; and we today are
flushed with shame, we men of Judah and citizens of
Jerusalem, 16 that we, with our kings and rulers and priests
and prophets, and with our fathers, 17 have sinned in the
LORD's sight 18 and disobeyed him. We have neither heeded
the voice of the LORD, our God, nor followed the precepts
which the LORD set before us. 19 From the time the LORD led
our fathers out of the land of Egypt until the present day, we
have been disobedient to the LORD, our God, and only too
ready to disregard his voice. 20 And the evils and the curse
which the LORD enjoined upon Moses, his servant, at the time
he led our fathers forth from the land of Egypt to give us the
land flowing with milk and honey, cling to us even today.
21 For we did not heed the voice of the LORD, our God, in all
the words of the prophets whom he sent us, 22 but each one
of us went off after the devices of our own wicked hearts,
served other gods, and did evil in the sight of the LORD, our
God.

NEW JERUSALEM BIBLE

the Lord our God for us, because we have sinned against
him, and the anger, the fury of the Lord, has still not turned
away from us. 14 Lastly, you must read the booklet which we
are sending you, publicly in the house of the Lord on the
feastday and appropriate days. 15 You must say:
Saving justice is the Lord's, we have only the look of
shame we bear, as is the case today for the people of Judah
and the inhabitants of Jerusalem, 16 for our kings and
princes, our priests, our prophets, and for our ancestors,
17 because we have sinned before the Lord, 18 have disobeyed
him, and have not listened to the voice of the Lord our God
telling us to follow the commandments which the Lord had
ordained for us. 19 From the day when the Lord brought our
ancestors out of Egypt until today we have been disobedient
to the Lord our God, we have been disloyal, refusing to listen
to his voice. 20 And we are not free even today of the disasters and the curse which the Lord pronounced through his
servant Moses the day he brought our ancestors out of Egypt
to give us a land flowing with milk and honey. 21 We have
not listened to the voice of the Lord our God in all the words
of those prophets he sent us; 22 but, each following the dictates of our evil heart, we have taken to serving alien gods,
and doing what is displeasing to the Lord our God.

GREEK OLD TESTAMENT

2 κυρίου θεοῦ ἡμῶν. 1 καὶ ἔστησεν κύριος τὸν λόγον αὐτοῦ, ὃν ἐλάλησεν ἐφ' ἡμᾶς καὶ ἐπὶ τοὺς δικαστὰς ἡμῶν
τοὺς δικάσαντας τὸν Ισραηλ καὶ ἐπὶ τοὺς βασιλεῖς ἡμῶν καὶ
ἐπὶ τοὺς ἄρχοντας ἡμῶν καὶ ἐπὶ ἄνθρωπον Ισραηλ καὶ Ιουδα.
2 οὐκ ἐποιήθη ὑποκάτω παντὸς τοῦ οὐρανοῦ καθὰ ἐποίησεν
ἐν Ιερουσαλημ κατὰ τὰ γεγραμμένα ἐν τῷ νόμῳ Μωυσῆ
3 τοῦ φαγεῖν ἡμᾶς ἄνθρωπον σάρκας υἱοῦ αὐτοῦ καὶ ἄνθρωπον σάρκας θυγατρὸς αὐτοῦ. 4 καὶ ἔδωκεν αὐτοὺς ὑποχειρίους πάσαις ταῖς βασιλείαις ταῖς κύκλῳ ἡμῶν εἰς ὀνειδισμὸν
καὶ εἰς ἄβατον ἐν πᾶσι τοῖς λαοῖς τοῖς κύκλῳ, οὗ διέσπειρεν
αὐτοὺς κύριος ἐκεῖ. 5 καὶ ἐγενήθησαν ὑποκάτω καὶ οὐκ
ἐπάνω, ὅτι ἡμάρτομεν κυρίῳ θεῷ ἡμῶν πρὸς τὸ μὴ ἀκούειν
τῆς φωνῆς αὐτοῦ. — 6 τῷ κυρίῳ θεῷ ἡμῶν ἡ δικαιοσύνη, ἡμῖν
δὲ καὶ τοῖς πατράσιν ἡμῶν ἡ αἰσχύνη τῶν προσώπων ὡς ἡ
ἡμέρα αὕτη. 7 ἃ ἐλάλησεν κύριος ἐφ' ἡμᾶς, πάντα τὰ κακὰ
ταῦτα ἦλθεν ἐφ' ἡμᾶς. 8 καὶ οὐκ ἐδεήθημεν τοῦ προσώπου
κυρίου τοῦ ἀποστρέψαι ἕκαστον ἀπὸ τῶν νοημάτων τῆς καρδίας αὐτῶν τῆς πονηρᾶς. 9 καὶ ἐγρηγόρησεν κύριος ἐπὶ τοῖς
κακοῖς, καὶ ἐπήγαγε κύριος ἐφ' ἡμᾶς, ὅτι δίκαιος ὁ κύριος
ἐπὶ πάντα τὰ ἔργα αὐτοῦ, ἃ ἐνετείλατο ἡμῖν. 10 καὶ οὐκ
ἠκούσαμεν τῆς φωνῆς αὐτοῦ πορεύεσθαι τοῖς προστάγμασιν
κυρίου, οἷς ἔδωκεν κατὰ πρόσωπον ἡμῶν. — 11 καὶ νῦν, κύριε

KING JAMES VERSION

2 Therefore the Lord hath made good his word, which he pronounced against us, and against our judges that judged Israel, and against our kings, and against our princes, and against the men of Israel and Juda,

2 To bring upon us great plagues, such as never happened under the whole heaven, as it came to pass in Jerusalem, according to the things that were written in the law of Moses;

3 That a man should eat the flesh of his own son, and the flesh of his own daughter.

4 Moreover he hath delivered them to be in subjection to all the kingdoms that are round about us, to be as a reproach and desolation among all the people round about, where the Lord hath scattered them.

5 Thus we were cast down, and not exalted, because we have sinned against the Lord our God, and have not been obedient unto his voice.

6 To the Lord our God *appertaineth* righteousness: but unto us and to our fathers open shame, as *appeareth* this day.

7 *For* all these plagues are come upon us, which the Lord hath pronounced against us.

8 Yet have we not prayed before the Lord, that we might turn every one from the imaginations of his wicked heart.

9 Wherefore the Lord watched over us for evil, and the Lord hath brought it upon us: for the Lord is righteous in all his works which he hath commanded us.

10 Yet we have not hearkened unto his voice, to walk in the commandments of the Lord, that he hath set before us.

DOUAY OLD TESTAMENT

2 WHEREFORE the Lord our God hath made good his word, that he spoke to us, and to our judges that have judged Israel, and to our kings, and to our princes, and to all Israel and Juda:

2 That the Lord would bring upon us great evils, *such* as never happened under heaven, as they have come to pass in Jerusalem, according to the things that are written in the law of Moses:

3 That a man should eat the flesh of his own son, and the flesh of his own daughter.

4 And he hath delivered them up to be under the hand of all the kings that are round about us, to be a reproach, and desolation among all the people, among whom the Lord hath scattered us.

5 And we are brought under, and *are* not uppermost: because we have sinned against the Lord our God, by not obeying his voice.

6 To the Lord our God *belongeth* justice: but to us, and to our fathers confusion of face, as at this day.

7 For the Lord hath pronounced against us all these evils that are come upon us:

8 And we have not entreated the face of the Lord our God, that we might return every one of us from our most wicked ways.

9 And the Lord hath watched over us for evil, and hath brought it upon us: for the Lord is just in all his works which he hath commanded us:

10 And we have not hearkened to his voice to walk in the commandments of the Lord which he hath set before us.

KNOX TRANSLATION

2 That is why the Lord our God has made good his threats
against us; against the rulers of Israel, whether kings or
nobles, and against the common folk of Israel and Juda.
2 Here was a threat made in the law of Moses, that went
beyond all hitherto seen on earth, and yet in Jerusalem it
came true; 3 that men would be eating the flesh of their own
sons and daughters! 4 Neighbouring kings had the mastery,
and in all the far countries to which the Lord had banished
us, we became a thing of scorn and horror. 5 Slaves are we,
that might have ruled; and the reason of it? Because by sinning we offended the Lord our God, and left his voice
unheeded; 6 his was never the fault; for us and for our
fathers the blush of shame, as this day can witness. 7 No
calamity has befallen us but he, the Lord, had prophesied it;
8 and still we would not sue for the divine mercy, but each of
us went on straying by false paths. 9 That is why the Lord's
jealous care was for our undoing; he has but fulfilled what
he threatened; in all he has imposed upon us,[a] the Lord our
God is without fault. 10 It was our fault if we would not listen to his warnings, would not follow the divine commands
which he set before us.

[a] This is usually understood of God's commandments, but the context suggests rather a reference to his chastisements.

Today's English Version

2 "So the Lord carried out the threat he had made against us and against our judges, our kings, our rulers, and the people of Israel and Judah. 2 Nowhere else on earth have such things happened as happened in Jerusalem when the Lord carried out the threats written in the Law of Moses. 3 Things were so bad that we even ate the flesh of our own sons and daughters. 4 The Lord scattered our people, handing us over to the control of all the nations around us, and they looked on us with reproach and horror. 5 We sinned against the Lord our God and refused to obey him. Therefore, our nation was conquered, instead of being victorious.

6 "The Lord our God is always righteous, but we and our ancestors are still burdened with our guilt. 7 Even though the Lord punished us as he had threatened, 8 we still did not turn to him and pray that we would abandon our evil thoughts. 9-10 We did not obey him or live by his just commands, so the Lord brought on us all the punishments he had kept ready for us.

New Revised Standard Version

2 So the Lord carried out the threat he spoke against us: against our judges who ruled Israel, and against our kings and our rulers and the people of Israel and Judah. 2 Under the whole heaven there has not been done the like of what he has done in Jerusalem, in accordance with the threats that were[a] written in the law of Moses. 3 Some of us ate the flesh of their sons and others the flesh of their daughters. 4 He made them subject to all the kingdoms around us, to be an object of scorn and a desolation among all the surrounding peoples, where the Lord has scattered them. 5 They were brought down and not raised up, because our nation[b] sinned against the Lord our God, in not heeding his voice.

6 The Lord our God is in the right, but there is open shame on us and our ancestors this very day. 7 All those calamities with which the Lord threatened us have come upon us. 8 Yet we have not entreated the favor of the Lord by turning away, each of us, from the thoughts of our wicked hearts. 9 And the Lord has kept the calamities ready, and the Lord has brought them upon us, for the Lord is just in all the works that he has commanded us to do. 10 Yet we have not obeyed his voice, to walk in the statutes of the Lord that he set before us.

a Gk *in accordance with what is* *b* Gk *because we*

New American Bible

2 "And the LORD fulfilled the warning he had uttered against us: against our judges, who governed Israel, against our kings and princes, and against the men of Israel and Judah. 2 He brought down upon us evils so great that there has not been done anywhere under heaven what has been done in Jerusalem, as was written in the law of Moses: 3 that one after another of us should eat the flesh of his son or of his daughter. 4 He has made us subject to all the kingdoms round about us, a reproach and a horror among all the nations round about to which the LORD has scattered us. 5 We are brought low, not raised up, because we sinned against the LORD, our God, not heeding his voice.

6 "Justice is with the LORD, our God; and we, like our fathers, are flushed with shame even today. 7 All the evils of which the LORD had warned us have come upon us; 8 and we did not plead before the LORD, or turn, each from the figments of his evil heart. 9 And the LORD kept watch over the evils, and brought them home to us; for the LORD is just in all the works he commanded us to do, 10 but we did not heed his voice, or follow the precepts of the LORD which he set before us.

New Jerusalem Bible

2 And so the Lord has carried out the sentence which he passed on us, on our judges who governed Israel, on our kings and leaders and on the people of Israel and of Judah; 2 what he did to Jerusalem has never been paralleled under the wide heavens—in conformity with what was written in the Law of Moses; 3 we were each reduced to eating the flesh of our own sons and daughters. 4 Furthermore, he has handed them over into the power of all the kingdoms that surround us, to be the contempt and execration of all the neighbouring peoples among whom the Lord scattered them. 5 Instead of being masters, they found themselves enslaved, because we had sinned against the Lord our God by not listening to his voice.

6 Saving justice is the Lord's; we and our ancestors have only the look of shame we bear today. 7 All those disasters which the Lord pronounced against us have now befallen us. 8 And yet we have not tried to win the favour of the Lord by each of us renouncing the dictates of our own wicked heart; 9 so the Lord has been alert to our misdeeds and has brought disaster down on us, since the Lord is upright in everything he had commanded us to do, 10 and we have not listened to his voice so as to follow the commandments which the Lord had ordained for us.

GREEK OLD TESTAMENT

ὁ θεὸς Ισραηλ, ὃς ἐξήγαγες τὸν λαόν σου ἐκ γῆς Αἰγύπτου
ἐν χειρὶ κραταιᾷ καὶ ἐν σημείοις καὶ ἐν τέρασιν καὶ ἐν
δυνάμει μεγάλῃ καὶ ἐν βραχίονι ὑψηλῷ καὶ ἐποίησας σεαυτῷ
ὄνομα ὡς ἡ ἡμέρα αὕτη. 12 ἡμάρτομεν ἠσεβήσαμεν ἠδική-
σαμεν, κύριε ὁ θεὸς ἡμῶν, ἐπὶ πᾶσιν τοῖς δικαιώμασίν σου.
13 ἀποστραφήτω ὁ θυμός σου ἀφ' ἡμῶν, ὅτι κατελείφθημεν
ὀλίγοι ἐν τοῖς ἔθνεσιν, οὗ διέσπειρας ἡμᾶς ἐκεῖ. 14 εἰσάκουσον, κύριε, τῆς προσευχῆς ἡμῶν καὶ τῆς δεήσεως ἡμῶν καὶ
ἐξελοῦ ἡμᾶς ἕνεκεν σοῦ καὶ δὸς ἡμῖν χάριν κατὰ πρόσωπον
τῶν ἀποικισάντων ἡμᾶς, 15 ἵνα γνῷ πᾶσα ἡ γῆ ὅτι σὺ κύριος
ὁ θεὸς ἡμῶν, ὅτι τὸ ὄνομά σου ἐπεκλήθη ἐπὶ Ισραηλ καὶ ἐπὶ
τὸ γένος αὐτοῦ. 16 κύριε, κάτιδε ἐκ τοῦ οἴκου τοῦ ἁγίου σου
καὶ ἐννόησον εἰς ἡμᾶς. κλῖνον, κύριε, τὸ οὖς σου καὶ ἄκου-
σον· 17 ἄνοιξον, κύριε, τοὺς ὀφθαλμούς σου καὶ ἰδέ· ὅτι οὐχ
οἱ τεθνηκότες ἐν τῷ ᾅδῃ, ὧν ἐλήμφθη τὸ πνεῦμα αὐτῶν ἀπὸ
τῶν σπλάγχνων αὐτῶν, δώσουσιν δόξαν καὶ δικαίωμα τῷ
κυρίῳ, 18 ἀλλὰ ἡ ψυχὴ ἡ λυπουμένη ἐπὶ τὸ μέγεθος, ὃ βαδίζει κύπτον καὶ ἀσθενοῦν καὶ οἱ ὀφθαλμοὶ οἱ ἐκλείποντες καὶ
ἡ ψυχὴ ἡ πεινῶσα δώσουσίν σοι δόξαν καὶ δικαιοσύνην,
κύριε. 19 ὅτι οὐκ ἐπὶ τὰ δικαιώματα τῶν πατέρων ἡμῶν καὶ
τῶν βασιλέων ἡμῶν ἡμεῖς καταβάλλομεν τὸν ἔλεον ἡμῶν
κατὰ πρόσωπόν σου, κύριε ὁ θεὸς ἡμῶν, 20 ὅτι ἐνῆκας τὸν
θυμόν σου καὶ τὴν ὀργήν σου εἰς ἡμᾶς, καθάπερ ἐλάλησας ἐν
χειρὶ τῶν παίδων σου τῶν προφητῶν λέγων 21 Οὕτως εἶπεν

KING JAMES VERSION

11 And now, O Lord God of Israel, that hast brought thy people out of the land of Egypt with a mighty hand, and high arm, and with signs, and with wonders, and with great power, and hast gotten thyself a name, as *appeareth* this day:

12 O Lord our God, we have sinned, we have done ungodly, we have dealt unrighteously in all thine ordinances.

13 Let thy wrath turn from us: for we are but a few left among the heathen, where thou hast scattered us.

14 Hear our prayers, O Lord, and our petitions, and deliver us for thine own sake, and give us favour in the sight of them which have led us away:

15 That all the earth may know that thou art the Lord our God, because Israel and his posterity is called by thy name.

16 O Lord, look down from thine holy house, and consider us: bow down thine ear, O Lord, to hear us.

17 Open thine eyes, and behold; for the dead that are in the graves, whose souls are taken from their bodies, will give unto the Lord neither praise nor righteousness:

18 But the soul that is greatly vexed, which goeth stooping and feeble, and the eyes that fail, and the hungry soul, will give thee praise and righteousness, O Lord.

19 Therefore we do not make our humble supplication before thee, O Lord our God, for the righteousness of our fathers, and of our kings.

20 For thou hast sent out thy wrath and indignation upon us, as thou hast spoken by thy servants the prophets, saying,

DOUAY OLD TESTAMENT

11 And now, O Lord God of Israel, who hast brought thy people out of the land of Egypt with a strong hand, and with signs, and with wonders, and with thy great power, and with a mighty arm, and hast made thee a name as at this day,

12 We have sinned, we have done wickedly, we have acted unjustly, O Lord our God, against all thy justices.

13 Let thy wrath be turned away from us: for we are left a few among the nations where thou hast scattered us.

14 Hear, O Lord, our prayers, and our petitions, and deliver us for thy own sake: and grant that we may find favour in the sight of them that have led us away:

15 That all the earth may know that thou art the Lord our God, and that thy name is called upon Israel, and upon his posterity.

16 Look down upon us, O Lord, from thy holy house, and incline thy ear, and hear us.

17 Open thy eyes, and behold: for the dead that are in hell, whose spirit is taken away from their bowels, shall not give glory and justice to the Lord:

18 But the soul that is sorrowful for the greatness of evil *she hath done,* and goeth bowed down, and feeble, and the eyes that fail, and the hungry soul giveth glory and justice to thee the Lord.

19 For it is not for the justices of our fathers that we pour out our prayers, and beg mercy in thy sight, O Lord our God:

20 But because thou hast sent out thy wrath, and thy indignation upon us, as thou hast spoken by the hand of thy servants the prophets, saying:

KNOX TRANSLATION

11 Lord God of Israel, whose constraining hand rescued thy
people from Egypt with portents and wonders, with sovereign power signally manifested, and won thee renown that is
thine yet, 12 we are sinners! We have wronged thee, revolted
against every claim thou hast upon us. 13 But oh, would thy
vengeance give over the pursuit! So wide thou hast parted
us, and we are left so few. 14 Grant a hearing, Lord, to this
our plaint and plea; for thy own honour, be our rescuer still,
and win over the hearts of our captors; 15 prove to the whole
world that thou art the Lord our God, that it was thy name
Israel bore, and Israel's race yet bears. 16 Look down upon
us, Lord, from the sanctuary where thou dwellest; thine be
the attentive ear, 17 the watchful eye! Once breath has left
body, and a man lies in the grave, honour and devoir is none
he can pay thee; 18 but let a man be downcast over his great
misfortune, so that he goes bowed and tottering, dim eyes
and hungry belly, there, Lord, thou shalt have the honour
that is thy due.
19 Well for us, O Lord our God, as we pour out our supplications for thy mercy, if we could plead that fathers of ours,
kings of ours, did loyally thy will. 20 But no; thou hadst
given them due warning, through those prophets that were
servants of thine, before letting thy angry vengeance have its
way, and the warning went unheeded.[a] 21 Bow shoulder and

[a] 'And the warning went unheeded'; these words are not in the original, but are supplied here from the context in order to make the connexion between verses 19 and 20 intelligible.

TODAY'S ENGLISH VERSION

11 "You, O Lord, are the God of Israel who brought your people out of Egypt with great power and with signs, miracles, and wonders. You showed your mighty strength and gained a glorious reputation, which is still recognized today. 12 O Lord our God, we have sinned; we have been unfaithful; we have disobeyed all your commands. 13 But do not be angry with us any longer. Here among the nations where you have scattered us, only a few of us are left. 14 Listen to our prayer of petition, Lord, and rescue us for the sake of your own honor. Let those who have taken us into exile be pleased with us. 15 Then the whole world will know that you are the Lord our God and that you have chosen the nation of Israel to be your own people.

16 "O Lord, look down from heaven and see our misery. Listen to our prayer. 17 Open your eyes and look upon us. Those in the world of the dead with no breath left in their bodies cannot offer praises to you or proclaim how just you are. 18 Only the living, O Lord, can offer you praise and acknowledge your justice, even though they may be suffering greatly, bent and weak, hungry and with failing eyesight.

19 "O Lord our God, we pray to you for mercy, but not because of any good things done by our ancestors and our kings. 20 You turned your anger and wrath against us, just as you had threatened to do when your servants the prophets spoke your word to us and said, 21 'Bend your

NEW REVISED STANDARD VERSION

11 And now, O Lord God of Israel, who brought your people out of the land of Egypt with a mighty hand and with signs and wonders and with great power and outstretched arm, and made yourself a name that continues to this day, 12 we have sinned, we have been ungodly, we have done wrong, O Lord our God, against all your ordinances. 13 Let your anger turn away from us, for we are left, few in number, among the nations where you have scattered us. 14 Hear, O Lord, our prayer and our supplication, and for your own sake deliver us, and grant us favor in the sight of those who have carried us into exile; 15 so that all the earth may know that you are the Lord our God, for Israel and his descendants are called by your name.

16 O Lord, look down from your holy dwelling, and consider us. Incline your ear, O Lord, and hear; 17 open your eyes, O Lord, and see, for the dead who are in Hades, whose spirit has been taken from their bodies, will not ascribe glory or justice to the Lord; 18 but the person who is deeply grieved, who walks bowed and feeble, with failing eyes and famished soul, will declare your glory and righteousness, O Lord.

19 For it is not because of any righteous deeds of our ancestors or our kings that we bring before you our prayer for mercy, O Lord our God. 20 For you have sent your anger and your wrath upon us, as you declared by your servants

NEW AMERICAN BIBLE

11 "And now, LORD, God of Israel, you who led your people out of the land of Egypt with your mighty hand, with signs and wonders and great might, and with your upraised arm, so that you have made for yourself a name till the present day: 12 we have sinned, been impious, and violated, O LORD, our God, all your statutes. 13 Let your anger be withdrawn from us, for we are left few in number among the nations to which you scattered us. 14 Hear, O LORD, our prayer of supplication, and deliver us for your own sake: grant us favor in the presence of our captors, 15 that the whole earth may know that you are the LORD, our God, and that Israel and his descendants bear your name. 16 O LORD, look down from your holy dwelling and take thought of us; turn, O LORD, your ear to hear us. 17 Look directly at us, and behold: it is not the dead in the nether world, whose spirits have been taken from within them, who will give glory and vindication to the LORD. 18 He whose soul is deeply grieved, who walks bowed and feeble, with failing eyes and famished soul, will declare your glory and justice, LORD!

19 "Not on the just deeds of our fathers and our kings do we base our plea for mercy in your sight, O LORD, our God. 20 You have brought your wrath and anger down upon us, as you had warned us through your servants the prophets:

NEW JERUSALEM BIBLE

11 And now, Lord, God of Israel, who brought your people out of Egypt with a mighty hand, with signs and wonders, with great power and with outstretched arm, to win yourself a name such as you have today, 12 we have sinned, we have committed sacrilege; Lord our God, we have broken all your precepts. 13 Let your anger turn from us since we are no more than a little remnant among the nations where you have dispersed us. 14 Listen, Lord, to our prayers and our entreaties; deliver us for your own sake and let us win the favour of the people who have deported us, 15 so that the whole world may know that you are the Lord our God, since Israel and his descendants bear your name. 16 Look down, Lord, from your holy dwelling-place and think of us, bow your ear and listen, 17 open your eyes, Lord, and look; the dead down in Sheol, whose breath has been taken from their bodies, are not the ones to give glory and due recognition to the Lord; 18 whoever is overcome with affliction, who goes along bowed down and frail, with failing eyes and hungering soul, that is the one to give you glory and due recognition, Lord.

19 We do not rely on the merits of our ancestors and of our kings to offer you our humble plea, Lord our God. 20 No, you have sent down your anger and your fury on us, as you threatened through your servants the prophets when they

GREEK OLD TESTAMENT

κύριος Κλίνατε τὸν ὦμον ὑμῶν καὶ ἐργάσασθε τῷ βασιλεῖ
Βαβυλῶνος καὶ καθίσατε ἐπὶ τὴν γῆν, ἣν ἔδωκα τοῖς πατράσιν ὑμῶν· 22 καὶ ἐὰν μὴ ἀκούσητε τῆς φωνῆς κυρίου ἐργάσασθαι τῷ βασιλεῖ Βαβυλῶνος, 23 ἐκλείψειν ποιήσω ἐκ πόλεων
Ιουδα καὶ ἔξωθεν Ιερουσαλημ φωνὴν εὐφροσύνης καὶ φωνὴν
χαρμοσύνης, φωνὴν νυμφίου καὶ φωνὴν νύμφης, καὶ ἔσται
πᾶσα ἡ γῆ εἰς ἄβατον ἀπὸ ἐνοικούντων. 24 καὶ οὐκ ἠκούσαμεν τῆς φωνῆς σου ἐργάσασθαι τῷ βασιλεῖ Βαβυλῶνος, καὶ
ἔστησας τοὺς λόγους σου, οὓς ἐλάλησας ἐν χερσὶν τῶν
παίδων σου τῶν προφητῶν τοῦ ἐξενεχθῆναι τὰ ὀστᾶ βασιλέων ἡμῶν καὶ τὰ ὀστᾶ τῶν πατέρων ἡμῶν ἐκ τοῦ τόπου
αὐτῶν, 25 καὶ ἰδού ἐστιν ἐξερριμμένα τῷ καύματι τῆς ἡμέρας καὶ τῷ παγετῷ τῆς νυκτός, καὶ ἀπεθάνοσαν ἐν πόνοις
πονηροῖς, ἐν λιμῷ καὶ ἐν ῥομφαίᾳ καὶ ἐν ἀποστολῇ. 26 καὶ
ἔθηκας τὸν οἶκον, οὗ ἐπεκλήθη τὸ ὄνομά σου ἐπ' αὐτῷ, ὡς ἡ
ἡμέρα αὕτη διὰ πονηρίαν οἴκου Ισραηλ καὶ οἴκου Ιουδα. —
27 καὶ ἐποίησας εἰς ἡμᾶς, κύριε ὁ θεὸς ἡμῶν, κατὰ πᾶσαν
ἐπιείκειάν σου καὶ κατὰ πάντα οἰκτιρμόν σου τὸν μέγαν,
28 καθὰ ἐλάλησας ἐν χειρὶ παιδός σου Μωυσῆ ἐν ἡμέρᾳ
ἐντειλαμένου σου αὐτῷ γράψαι τὸν νόμον σου ἐναντίον υἱῶν
Ισραηλ λέγων 29 Ἐὰν μὴ ἀκούσητε τῆς φωνῆς μου, ἦ μὴν ἡ
βόμβησις ἡ μεγάλη ἡ πολλὴ αὕτη ἀποστρέψει εἰς μικρὰν ἐν
τοῖς ἔθνεσιν, οὗ διασπερῶ αὐτοὺς ἐκεῖ· 30 ὅτι ἔγνων ὅτι οὐ

KING JAMES VERSION

21 Thus saith the Lord, Bow down your shoulders to serve the king of Babylon: so shall ye remain in the land that I gave unto your fathers.

22 But if ye will not hear the voice of the Lord, to serve the king of Babylon,

23 I will cause to cease out of the cities of Judah, and from without Jerusalem, the voice of mirth, and the voice of joy, the voice of the bridegroom, and the voice of the bride: and the whole land shall be desolate of inhabitants.

24 But we would not hearken unto thy voice, to serve the king of Babylon: therefore hast thou made good the words that thou spakest by thy servants the prophets, namely, that the bones of our kings, and the bones of our fathers, should be taken out of their places.

25 And, lo, they are cast out to the heat of the day, and to the frost of the night, and they died in great miseries by famine, by sword, and by pestilence.

26 And the house which is called by thy name hast thou laid waste, as *it is to be seen* this day, for the wickedness of the house of Israel and the house of Juda.

27 O Lord our God, thou hast dealt with us after all thy goodness, and according to all that great mercy of thine,

28 As thou spakest by thy servant Moses in the day when thou didst command him to write the law before the children of Israel, saying,

29 If ye will not hear my voice, surely this very great multitude shall be turned into a small *number* among the nations, where I will scatter them.

DOUAY OLD TESTAMENT

21 Thus saith the Lord: Bow down your shoulder, and your neck, and serve the king of Babylon: and you shall remain in the land which I have given to your fathers.

22 But if you will not hearken to the voice of the Lord your God, to serve the king of Babylon: I will cause you to depart out of the cities of Juda, and from without Jerusalem.

23 And I will take away from you the voice of mirth, and the voice of joy, and the voice of the bridegroom, and the voice of the bride, and all the land shall be without any footstep of inhabitants.

24 And they hearkened not to thy voice, to serve the king of Babylon: and thou hast made good thy words, which thou spokest by the hands of thy servants the prophets, that the bones of our kings, and the bones of our fathers should be removed out of their place:

25 And behold they are cast out to the heat of the sun, and to the frost of the night: and they have died in grievous pains, by famine, and by the sword, and in banishment.

26 And thou hast made the temple, in which thy name was called upon, as it is at this day, for the iniquity of the house of Israel, and the house of Juda.

27 And thou hast dealt with us, O Lord our God, according to all thy goodness, and according to all that great mercy of thine:

28 As thou spokest by the hand of thy servant Moses, in the day when thou didst command him to write thy law before the children of Israel,

29 Saying: If you will not hear my voice, this great multitude shall be turned into a very small number among the nations, where I will scatter them:

KNOX TRANSLATION

bow neck, said the divine voice, and be vassals to the king of
Babylon; and the land I gave to your fathers shall still be
your home. 22 Refuse to serve the king of Babylon at my
divine bidding, and Jerusalem with her daughter cities shall
mourn their loss; 23 no more the cry of joy and mirth, no
more the voice of bridegroom and of bride; untrodden the
whole land shall be, and uninhabited. 24 But all thy threats
could not persuade them to be the king of Babylon's vassals;
thy servants prophesied in vain. And so thy threats were performed; kings of ours and fathers of ours might not rest
quiet in their graves; 25 their bones were cast out to endure
sun's heat and night frost, and great anguish they endured
in their deaths, from the sword, and famine, and pestilence.[a]
26 As for the temple that was the shrine of thy name, thou
madest it into the thing it is this day, for Israel's sin, for
Juda's sin.

27 No greater proof we could have had of thy consideration,
of that abundant mercy[b] which is thine. 28 And merciful was
the promise thou didst make to thy servant Moses, when
thou badest him write down thy law for Israel's acceptance.
29 Out of all this swarming multitude, thou didst say to him,
what a sorry remnant of scattered exiles will be left, if my

a The Greek word used here (of which the Latin gives a literal rendering) means 'a despatching of envoys', and does not justify the translation 'banishment'. It is probably used here, as in Jer. 32. 36, to represent the Hebrew word for 'pestilence', as something specially sent by Almighty God.

b In verses 19-26, the divine mercy has been shewn in the warning issued to the Jews against further resistance. In verses 27-35 the same mercy is shewn in the promise of ultimate restoration.

TODAY'S ENGLISH VERSION

backs and serve the king of Babylonia, and you can
remain in the land that I gave to your ancestors. 22 But if
you refuse to obey my command to serve him, 23 I will
bring to an end every sound of joy and celebration in the
towns of Judah and in Jerusalem. Even the happy sounds
of wedding feasts will no longer be heard. The whole land
will be desolate and uninhabited.'

24 "But we did not obey your command to serve the king
of Babylonia, so you carried out the threat that you had
made when you spoke through your servants the prophets,
when you said that the bones of our kings and of our
ancestors would be taken from their tombs and scattered.
25 And now here they lie exposed to the heat of the day and
to the frost of the night. They died in torment from famine,
war, and disease. 26 And because of the sin of the people
of Israel and Judah, you have reduced your own Temple to
ruins, even as it is today.

27 "But, Lord, you have been patient with us and have
shown us great mercy, 28 as you promised through your
servant Moses on the day you commanded him to write
your Law in the presence of the Israelites. 29 'If you do not
obey me,' you said, 'you will be reduced to a handful
among the nations where I will scatter you. 30 I know that

NEW REVISED STANDARD VERSION

the prophets, saying: 21 Thus says the Lord: Bend your
shoulders and serve the king of Babylon, and you will
remain in the land that I gave to your ancestors. 22 But if
you will not obey the voice of the Lord and will not serve the
king of Babylon, 23 I will make to cease from the towns of
Judah and from the region around Jerusalem the voice of
mirth and the voice of gladness, the voice of the bridegroom
and the voice of the bride, and the whole land will be a desolation without inhabitants.

24 But we did not obey your voice, to serve the king of
Babylon; and you have carried out your threats, which you
spoke by your servants the prophets, that the bones of our
kings and the bones of our ancestors would be brought out
of their resting place; 25 and indeed they have been thrown
out to the heat of day and the frost of night. They perished in
great misery, by famine and sword and pestilence. 26 And the
house that is called by your name you have made as it is
today, because of the wickedness of the house of Israel and
the house of Judah.

27 Yet you have dealt with us, O Lord our God, in all your
kindness and in all your great compassion, 28 as you spoke
by your servant Moses on the day when you commanded
him to write your law in the presence of the people of Israel,
saying, 29 "If you will not obey my voice, this very great multitude will surely turn into a small number among the
nations, where I will scatter them. 30 For I know that they

NEW AMERICAN BIBLE

21 'Thus says the LORD: Bend your shoulders to the service of
the king of Babylon, that you may continue in the land I
gave your fathers: 22 for if you do not hear the LORD's voice
so as to serve the king of Babylon,

23 I will make to cease from the cities of Judah
  and from the streets of Jerusalem
The sounds of joy and the sounds of gladness,
  the voice of the bridegroom
  and the voice of the bride;
And all the land shall be deserted,
  without inhabitants.'

24 But we did not heed your voice, or serve the king of
Babylon, and you fulfilled the threats you had made through
your servants the prophets, to have the bones of our kings
and the bones of our fathers brought out from their burial
places. 25 And indeed, they lie exposed to the heat of day and
the frost of night. They died in dire anguish, by hunger and
the sword and plague. 26 And you reduced the house which
bears your name to what it is today, for the wickedness of
the kingdom of Israel and the kingdom of Judah.

27 "But with us, O LORD, our God, you have dealt in all your
clemency and in all your great mercy. 28 This was your
warning through your servant Moses, the day you ordered
him to write down your law in the presence of the Israelites:
29 If you do not heed my voice, surely this great and numerous throng will dwindle away among the nations to which I

NEW JERUSALEM BIBLE

said, 21 'The Lord says this: *Bend your necks and serve the*
king of Babylon,[a] and you will remain in the country which I
gave to your ancestors. 22 But if you do not listen to the
voice of the Lord and serve the king of Babylon 23 then *I*
shall silence the shouts of rejoicing and mirth and the voices
of bridegroom and bride in the towns of Judah and the streets
of Jerusalem, and the whole country will be reduced to
desert,[b] *with no inhabitants.*' 24 But we would not listen to
your voice and serve the king of Babylon, and so you carried
out what you had threatened through your servants the
prophets: that the bones of our kings and of our ancestors
would be dragged from their resting places. 25 They were
indeed *tossed out to the heat of the day and the frost of the*
night.[c] And people died in dreadful agony, from famine,
sword and plague. 26 And so, because of the wickedness of
the House of Israel and the House of Judah, you have made
this House, that bears your name, what it is today.

27 And yet, Lord our God, you have treated us in a way
worthy of all your goodness and boundless tenderness,
28 just as you had promised through your servant Moses, the
day you told him to write your Law in the presence of the
Israelites, and said, 29 'If you do not listen to my voice, this
great and innumerable multitude will certainly be reduced to
a tiny few among the nations where I shall scatter them—

[a] **2** Jr 27:12. [b] **2** Jr 7:34. [c] **2** Jr 36:30.

GREEK OLD TESTAMENT

μὴ ἀκούσωσίν μου, ὅτι λαὸς σκληροτράχηλός ἐστιν. καὶ ἐπιστρέψουσιν ἐπὶ καρδίαν αὐτῶν ἐν γῇ ἀποικισμοῦ αὐτῶν
31 καὶ γνώσονται ὅτι ἐγὼ κύριος ὁ θεὸς αὐτῶν. καὶ δώσω αὐτοῖς καρδίαν καὶ ὦτα ἀκούοντα, 32 καὶ αἰνέσουσίν με ἐν γῇ
ἀποικισμοῦ αὐτῶν καὶ μνησθήσονται τοῦ ὀνόματός μου
33 καὶ ἀποστρέψουσιν ἀπὸ τοῦ νώτου αὐτῶν τοῦ σκληροῦ καὶ
ἀπὸ πονηρῶν πραγμάτων αὐτῶν, ὅτι μνησθήσονται τῆς ὁδοῦ
πατέρων αὐτῶν τῶν ἁμαρτόντων ἔναντι κυρίου. 34 καὶ ἀπο-
στρέψω αὐτοὺς εἰς τὴν γῆν, ἣν ὤμοσα τοῖς πατράσιν αὐτῶν
τῷ Αβρααμ καὶ τῷ Ισαακ καὶ τῷ Ιακωβ, καὶ κυριεύσουσιν
αὐτῆς. καὶ πληθυνῶ αὐτούς, καὶ οὐ μὴ σμικρυνθῶσιν· 35 καὶ
στήσω αὐτοῖς διαθήκην αἰώνιον τοῦ εἶναί με αὐτοῖς εἰς θεὸν
καὶ αὐτοὶ ἔσονταί μοι εἰς λαόν· καὶ οὐ κινήσω ἔτι τὸν λαόν
μου Ισραηλ ἀπὸ τῆς γῆς, ἧς ἔδωκα αὐτοῖς. — 3 1 κύριε
παντοκράτωρ ὁ θεὸς Ισραηλ, ψυχὴ ἐν στενοῖς καὶ πνεῦμα
ἀκηδιῶν κέκραγεν πρὸς σέ. 2 ἄκουσον, κύριε, καὶ ἐλέησον,
ὅτι ἡμάρτομεν ἐναντίον σου· 3 ὅτι σὺ καθήμενος τὸν αἰῶνα,
καὶ ἡμεῖς ἀπολλύμενοι τὸν αἰῶνα. 4 κύριε παντοκράτωρ ὁ
θεὸς Ισραηλ, ἄκουσον δὴ τῆς προσευχῆς τῶν τεθνηκότων
Ισραηλ καὶ υἱῶν τῶν ἁμαρτανόντων ἐναντίον σου, οἳ οὐκ
ἤκουσαν τῆς φωνῆς κυρίου θεοῦ αὐτῶν καὶ ἐκολλήθη ἡμῖν τὰ

KING JAMES VERSION

30 For I knew that they would not hear me, because it is a stiffnecked people: but in the land of their captivities they shall remember themselves,

31 And shall know that I am the Lord their God: for I will give them an heart, and ears to hear:

32 And they shall praise me in the land of their captivity, and think upon my name,

33 And return from their stiff neck, and from their wicked deeds: for they shall remember the way of their fathers, which sinned before the Lord.

34 And I will bring them again into the land which I promised with an oath unto their fathers, Abraham, Isaac, and Jacob, and they shall be lords of it: and I will increase them, and they shall not be diminished.

35 And I will make an everlasting covenant with them to be their God, and they shall be my people: and I will no more drive my people of Israel out of the land that I have given them.

3 O Lord Almighty, God of Israel, the soul in anguish, the troubled spirit, crieth unto thee.

2 Hear, O Lord, and have mercy; for thou art merciful: and have pity upon us, because we have sinned before thee.

3 For thou endurest for ever, and we perish utterly.

4 O Lord Almighty, thou God of Israel, hear now the prayers of the dead Israelites, and of their children, which have sinned before thee, and not hearkened unto the voice of thee their God: for the which cause these plagues cleave unto us.

DOUAY OLD TESTAMENT

30 For I know that the people will not hear me, for they are a people of a stiff neck: but they shall turn to their heart in the land of their captivity:

31 And they shall know that I am the Lord their God: and I will give them a heart, and they shall understand: and ears, and they shall hear.

32 And they shall praise me in the land of their captivity, and shall be mindful of my name.

33 And they shall turn away themselves from their stiff neck, and from their wicked deeds: for they shall remember the way of their fathers, that sinned against me.

34 And I will bring them back again into the land which I promised with an oath to their fathers, Abraham, Isaac, and Jacob, and they shall be masters thereof: and I will multiply them, and they shall not be diminished.

35 And I will make with them another covenant that *shall be* everlasting, to be their God, and they shall be my people: and I will no more remove my people, the children of Israel, out of the land that I have given them.

3 AND now, O Lord Almighty, the God of Israel, the soul in anguish, and the troubled spirit crieth to thee:

2 Hear, O Lord, and have mercy, for thou art a merciful God, and have pity on us: for we have sinned before thee.

3 For thou remainest for ever, and shall we perish everlastingly?

4 O Lord Almighty, the God of Israel, hear now the prayer of the dead of Israel, and of their children, that have sinned before thee, and have not hearkened to the voice of the Lord their God, wherefore evils have cleaved fast to us.

KNOX TRANSLATION

voice goes unheeded! 30 And go unheeded it will; this is a
race that ever spurns the yoke. What then if they come back
to a right mind, there in the country of their banishment?
31 What if they learn to recognize that I, the Lord, am their
God (the heedful heart, the listening ear, are mine to give
them); 32 what if they remember to honour me, to invoke my
name, in their exile? 33 What if they follow the example of
their fathers, that were sinners before them, repent of their
stubborn indifference and of all their ill doings? 34 Then they
shall come home again; back to the country I promised to
their fathers, Abraham, Isaac and Jacob; they shall be masters of it, and their dwindled strength shall thrive anew. 35 A
fresh covenant I will make with them, that shall last for ever;
I their God, and they my people; never again will I banish my
people, the sons of Israel, from the land I have made theirs.
3 Lord Almighty, God of Israel, here be lives in jeopardy,
here be troubled hearts, that plead with thee! 2 Listen,
Lord, and have mercy, none so merciful as thou; pardon the
sins that lie open in thy sight. 3 Thou reignest for ever; must
we for ever be lost? 4 Lord Almighty, God of Israel, listen to
the prayer Israel makes to thee from the grave![a] Our fathers
it was that defied the Lord their God, and gave no heed to
him; and to us, their sons, the punishment clings. 5 Forget

a Literally, 'the prayer of the dead of Israel'. Some think this refers to prayer offered by the dead on behalf of the living; others, that the race of Israel is, by a metaphor, described as 'dead'; others, that the Hebrew text had simply 'the folk of Israel', and that the Greek translator, having no vowel-points to guide him, was deceived by the identical form of the two words.

TODAY'S ENGLISH VERSION

you will not obey me, because you are a stubborn people.
But when you are taken into exile in another land, you
will come to your senses. 31 Then you will realize that I am
the Lord your God, and I will give you a desire to know
and a mind with which to understand. 32 There in the land
of your exile you will praise me and remember me. 33 You
will stop being so stubborn and wicked, for you will
remember what happened to your ancestors when they
sinned against the Lord. 34 Then I will bring you back to
the land that I solemnly promised to give to your ancestors, to Abraham, Isaac, and Jacob, and it will be yours
again. I will increase your population, and you will never
again be reduced to a small number. 35 I will make an
everlasting covenant with you; I will be your God and you
will be my people. I will never again remove you, the people of Israel, from the land that I gave you.'

3 "O Lord Almighty, God of Israel, from the depth of our
troubled, weary souls we cry out to you. 2 Hear us,
O Lord, and have mercy on us, because we have sinned
against you. 3 You reign as king forever, but we die and
are gone forever. 4 O Lord Almighty, God of Israel, hear
our prayer. We are no better off than the dead. Our ancestors sinned against you, the Lord their God. They refused
to obey you, and we are suffering the consequences of

NEW REVISED STANDARD VERSION

will not obey me, for they are a stiff-necked people. But in
the land of their exile they will come to themselves 31 and
know that I am the Lord their God. I will give them a heart
that obeys and ears that hear; 32 they will praise me in the
land of their exile, and will remember my name 33 and turn
from their stubbornness and their wicked deeds; for they will
remember the ways of their ancestors, who sinned before the
Lord. 34 I will bring them again into the land that I swore to
give to their ancestors, to Abraham, Isaac, and Jacob, and
they will rule over it; and I will increase them, and they will
not be diminished. 35 I will make an everlasting covenant
with them to be their God and they shall be my people; and I
will never again remove my people Israel from the land that I
have given them."

3 O Lord Almighty, God of Israel, the soul in anguish and
the wearied spirit cry out to you. 2 Hear, O Lord, and
have mercy, for we have sinned before you. 3 For you are
enthroned forever, and we are perishing forever. 4 O Lord
Almighty, God of Israel, hear now the prayer of the people[a] of
Israel, the children of those who sinned before you, who did
not heed the voice of the Lord their God, so that calamities

[a] Gk *dead*

NEW AMERICAN BIBLE

will scatter them. 30 For I know they will not heed me,
because they are a stiff-necked people. But in the land of
their captivity they shall have a change of heart; 31 they
shall know that I, the LORD, am their God. I will give them
hearts, and heedful ears; 32 and they shall praise me in the
land of their captivity, and shall invoke my name. 33 Then
they shall turn back from their stiff-necked stubbornness,
and from their evil deeds, because they shall remember the
fate of their fathers who sinned against the LORD. 34 And I
will bring them back to the land which with my oath I promised to their fathers, to Abraham, Isaac and Jacob; and they
shall rule it. I will make them increase; they shall not then
diminish. 35 And I will establish for them, as an eternal covenant, that I will be their God, and they shall be my people;
and I will not again remove my people Israel from the land I
gave them.

3 "LORD Almighty, God of Israel, afflicted souls and dismayed spirits call to you. 2 Hear, O LORD, for you are a
God of mercy; and have mercy on us, who have sinned
against you: 3 for you are enthroned forever, while we are
perishing forever. 4 LORD Almighty, God of Israel, hear the
prayer of Israel's few, the sons of those who sinned against
you; they did not heed the voice of the LORD, their God, and

NEW JERUSALEM BIBLE

30 for I knew that, being an obstinate people, they would not
listen to me. But in the country of their exile, they will come
to themselves 31 and acknowledge that I am the Lord their
God. I shall give them a heart and an attentive ear, 32 and
they will sing my praises in the country of their exile, they
will remember my name; 33 they will stop being obstinate
and, remembering what became of their ancestors who
sinned before the Lord, will turn from their evil deeds.
34 Then I shall bring them back to the country which I promised on oath to their ancestors Abraham, Isaac and Jacob,
and make them masters in it. I shall make their numbers
grow; they will not dwindle again. 35 And I shall make an
everlasting covenant with them; so that I am their God and
they are my people. And never again shall I drive my people
Israel out of the country which I have given them.'

3 Almighty Lord, God of Israel, a soul in anguish, a troubled heart now cries to you: 2 Listen and have pity,
Lord, for we have sinned before you. 3 You sit enthroned for
ever, while we are perishing for ever. 4 Almighty Lord, God
of Israel, hear the prayer of the dead of Israel, of the children
of those who have sinned against you and have not listened
to the voice of the Lord their God; hence the disasters which

GREEK OLD TESTAMENT

κακά. [5] μὴ μνησθῇς ἀδικιῶν πατέρων ἡμῶν, ἀλλὰ μνήσθητι
χειρός σου καὶ ὀνόματός σου ἐν τῷ καιρῷ τούτῳ· [6] ὅτι σὺ
κύριος ὁ θεὸς ἡμῶν, καὶ αἰνέσομέν σε, κύριε. [7] ὅτι διὰ τοῦτο
ἔδωκας τὸν φόβον σου ἐπὶ καρδίαν ἡμῶν τοῦ ἐπικαλεῖσθαι τὸ
ὄνομά σου, καὶ αἰνέσομέν σε ἐν τῇ ἀποικίᾳ ἡμῶν, ὅτι
ἀπεστρέψαμεν ἀπὸ καρδίας ἡμῶν πᾶσαν ἀδικίαν πατέρων
ἡμῶν τῶν ἡμαρτηκότων ἐναντίον σου. [8] ἰδοὺ ἡμεῖς σήμερον
ἐν τῇ ἀποικίᾳ ἡμῶν, οὗ διέσπειρας ἡμᾶς ἐκεῖ εἰς ὀνειδισμὸν
καὶ εἰς ἀρὰν καὶ εἰς ὄφλησιν κατὰ πάσας τὰς ἀδικίας πατέρων ἡμῶν, οἳ ἀπέστησαν ἀπὸ κυρίου θεοῦ ἡμῶν.

[9] Ἄκουε, Ισραηλ, ἐντολὰς ζωῆς, ἐνωτίσασθε γνῶναι φρόνησιν. [10] τί ἐστιν, Ισραηλ, τί ὅτι ἐν γῇ τῶν ἐχθρῶν εἶ, ἐπα-
λαιώθης ἐν γῇ ἀλλοτρίᾳ, [11] συνεμιάνθης τοῖς νεκροῖς, προσ-
ελογίσθης μετὰ τῶν εἰς ᾅδου; [12] ἐγκατέλιπες τὴν πηγὴν
τῆς σοφίας. [13] τῇ ὁδῷ τοῦ θεοῦ εἰ ἐπορεύθης, κατῴκεις ἂν
ἐν εἰρήνῃ τὸν αἰῶνα. [14] μάθε ποῦ ἐστιν φρόνησις, ποῦ ἐστιν
ἰσχύς, ποῦ ἐστιν σύνεσις τοῦ γνῶναι ἅμα, ποῦ ἐστιν μακρο-
βίωσις καὶ ζωή, ποῦ ἐστιν φῶς ὀφθαλμῶν καὶ εἰρήνη. —
[15] τίς εὗρεν τὸν τόπον αὐτῆς, καὶ τίς εἰσῆλθεν εἰς τοὺς

KING JAMES VERSION

5 Remember not the iniquities of our forefathers: but think upon thy power and thy name now at this time.

6 For thou art the Lord our God, and thee, O Lord, will we praise.

7 And for this cause thou hast put thy fear in our hearts, to the intent that we should call upon thy name, and praise thee in our captivity: for we have called to mind all the iniquity of our forefathers, that sinned before thee.

8 Behold, we are yet this day in our captivity, where thou hast scattered us, for a reproach and a curse, and to be subject to payments, according to all the iniquities of our fathers, which departed from the Lord our God.

9 Hear, Israel, the commandments of life: give ear to understand wisdom.

10 How happeneth it, Israel, that thou art in thine enemies' land, that thou art waxen old in a strange country, that thou art defiled with the dead,

11 That thou art counted with them that go down into the grave?

12 Thou hast forsaken the fountain of wisdom.

13 For if thou hadst walked in the way of God, thou shouldest have dwelled in peace for ever.

14 Learn where is wisdom, where is strength, where is understanding; that thou mayest know also where is length of days, and life, where is the light of the eyes, and peace.

15 Who hath found out her place? or who hath come into her treasures?

DOUAY OLD TESTAMENT

5 Remember not the iniquities of our fathers, but think upon thy hand, and upon thy name at this time:

6 For thou art the Lord our God, and we will praise thee, O Lord:

7 Because for this end thou hast put thy fear in our hearts, to the intent that we should call upon thy name, and praise thee in our captivity, for we are converted from the iniquity of our fathers, who sinned before thee.

8 And behold we are at this day in our captivity, whereby thou hast scattered us to be a reproach, and a curse, and an offence, according to all the iniquities of our fathers, who departed from thee, O Lord our God.

9 Hear, O Israel, the commandments of life: give ear, that thou mayst learn wisdom.

10 How happeneth it, O Israel, that thou art in thy enemies' land?

11 Thou art grown old in a strange country, thou art defiled with the dead: thou art counted with them that go down into hell.

12 Thou hast forsaken the fountain of wisdom:

13 For if thou hadst walked in the way of God, thou hadst surely dwelt in peace for ever.

14 Learn where is wisdom, where is strength, where is understanding: that thou mayst know also where is length of days and life, where is the light of the eyes, and peace.

15 Who hath found out her place? and who hath gone in to her treasures?

KNOX TRANSLATION

the wrong they did, those fathers of ours; remember thy
ancient power, thy own honour, this day; [6] only to thee, the
Lord our God, shall praise of ours be given. [7] Why else hast
thou inspired us with such dread of thee? Thou wouldst
have us learn to invoke thy name, to utter thy praise, here as
exiles, in proof that we disown the wrong our fathers did,
when their sins defied thee. [8] Exiles we are this day, dispersed by thee to suffer scorn and reviling, until we have
made amends for all the wrong our fathers did when they
abandoned thee, abandoned the Lord our God.

[9] Listen, Israel, to the warnings that shall bring thee life;
give attentive audience, if thou wouldst learn to be wise.
[10] What means it, Israel, that thou findest thyself in the enemy's land, [11] grown old in exile, unclean as a dead body, no
more taken into account than men who have gone down into
their graves? [12] It is because thou hast forsaken the fountains whence all wisdom comes. [13] If thou hadst but followed the path God shewed thee, thou mightest have lived in
peace eternally. [14] Learn where to find wisdom, and
strength, and discernment; so thou wilt find length of years,
too, and true life, and cheerfulness, and peace. [15] Who can
tell where wisdom dwells, who has made his way into her

TODAY'S ENGLISH VERSION

their sin. 5 Forget the sinful things that our ancestors did
in the past; at a time like this, think only of your power
and reputation, 6 for you are the Lord our God, and we
will praise you. 7 You have made us fear you, so that we
might pray to you. Here in exile we will praise you because
we have turned away from the sins of our ancestors. 8 You
have scattered us among the nations, and you have made
them despise and curse us. You are punishing us for the
sins of our ancestors when they rebelled against you, the
Lord our God."

9 Listen, Israel, to the commands that promise life; pay
attention, and you will become wise. 10 Why is it, Israel, that
you find yourself in an enemy land? Why have you grown
old in a foreign country? You are ritually unclean, like the
dead; 11 you are already counted among the dead. But why?
12 It is because you have left the source of Wisdom! 13 If you
had walked in God's ways, you would have lived in peace
forever. 14 Learn where understanding, strength, and insight
are to be found. Then you will know where to find a long
and full life, light to guide you, and peace.

15 No one has ever found where Wisdom lives or has
entered her treasure house, 16-17 and those who have tried

NEW REVISED STANDARD VERSION

have clung to us. 5 Do not remember the iniquities of our
ancestors, but in this crisis remember your power and your
name. 6 For you are the Lord our God, and it is you, O Lord,
whom we will praise. 7 For you have put the fear of you in
our hearts so that we would call upon your name; and we
will praise you in our exile, for we have put away from our
hearts all the iniquity of our ancestors who sinned against
you. 8 See, we are today in our exile where you have scattered us, to be reproached and cursed and punished for all the
iniquities of our ancestors, who forsook the Lord our God.

9 Hear the commandments of life, O Israel;
give ear, and learn wisdom!
10 Why is it, O Israel, why is it that you are in the land of
your enemies,
that you are growing old in a foreign country,
that you are defiled with the dead,
11 that you are counted among those in Hades?
12 You have forsaken the fountain of wisdom.
13 If you had walked in the way of God,
you would be living in peace forever.
14 Learn where there is wisdom,
where there is strength,
where there is understanding,
so that you may at the same time discern
where there is length of days, and life,
where there is light for the eyes, and peace.

15 Who has found her place?
And who has entered her storehouses?

NEW AMERICAN BIBLE

the evils cling to us. 5 Remember at this time not the misdeeds of our fathers, but your own hand and name: 6 for you
are the LORD our God; and you, O LORD, we praise! 7 For this,
you put into our hearts the fear of you: that we may call
upon your name, and praise you in our captivity, when we
have removed from our hearts all the wickedness of our
fathers who sinned against you. 8 Behold us today in our
captivity, where you scattered us, a reproach, a curse, and a
requital for all the misdeeds of our fathers, who withdrew
from the LORD, our God."

9 Hear, O Israel, the commandments of life:
listen, and know prudence!
10 How is it, Israel,
that you are in the land of your foes,
grown old in a foreign land,
Defiled with the dead,
11 accounted with those destined for the nether world?
12 You have forsaken the fountain of wisdom!
13 Had you walked in the way of God,
you would have dwelt in enduring peace.
14 Learn where prudence is,
where strength, where understanding;
That you may know also
where are length of days, and life,
where light of the eyes, and peace.

15 Who has found the place of wisdom,
who has entered into her treasuries?

NEW JERUSALEM BIBLE

dog us. 5 Do not call to mind the misdeeds of our ancestors,
but remember instead your power and your name. 6 You are
indeed the Lord our God and we will praise you, Lord, 7 since
you have put respect for you in our hearts to encourage us to
call on your name. We long to praise you in our exile, for we
have rid our hearts of the wickedness of our ancestors who
sinned against you. 8 Look, today we are still in exile where
you have scattered us as something contemptible, accursed,
condemned, for all the misdeeds of our ancestors who had
abandoned the Lord our God.

9 Listen, Israel, to commands that bring life;
hear, and learn what knowledge means.
10 Why, Israel, why are you in the country of your
enemies,
growing older and older in an alien land,
11 defiling yourselves with the dead,
reckoned with those who go to Sheol?
12 It is because you have forsaken the fountain of
wisdom!
13 Had you walked in the way of God,
you would be living in peace for ever.
14 Learn where knowledge is, where strength,
where understanding, and so learn
where length of days is, where life,
where the light of the eyes and where peace.

15 But who has found out where she lives,
who has entered her treasure house?

GREEK OLD TESTAMENT

θησαυροὺς αὐτῆς; 16 ποῦ εἰσιν οἱ ἄρχοντες τῶν ἐθνῶν καὶ οἱ
κυριεύοντες τῶν θηρίων τῶν ἐπὶ τῆς γῆς, 17 οἱ ἐν τοῖς
ὀρνέοις τοῦ οὐρανοῦ ἐμπαίζοντες καὶ τὸ ἀργύριον θησαυρί-
ζοντες καὶ τὸ χρυσίον, ᾧ ἐπεποίθεισαν ἄνθρωποι, καὶ οὐκ
ἔστιν τέλος τῆς κτήσεως αὐτῶν, 18 οἱ τὸ ἀργύριον τεκταί-
νοντες καὶ μεριμνῶντες, καὶ οὐκ ἔστιν ἐξεύρεσις τῶν ἔργων
αὐτῶν; 19 ἠφανίσθησαν καὶ εἰς ᾅδου κατέβησαν, καὶ ἄλλοι
ἀντανέστησαν ἀντ' αὐτῶν. 20 νεώτεροι εἶδον φῶς καὶ κατῴκησαν ἐπὶ τῆς γῆς, ὁδὸν δὲ ἐπιστήμης οὐκ ἔγνωσαν 21 οὐδὲ
συνῆκαν τρίβους αὐτῆς οὐδὲ ἀντελάβοντο αὐτῆς. οἱ υἱοὶ
αὐτῶν ἀπὸ τῆς ὁδοῦ αὐτῶν πόρρω ἐγενήθησαν. 22 οὐδὲ ἠκούσθη ἐν Χανααν οὐδὲ ὤφθη ἐν Θαιμαν, 23 οὔτε υἱοὶ Αγαρ οἱ
ἐκζητοῦντες τὴν σύνεσιν ἐπὶ τῆς γῆς, οἱ ἔμποροι τῆς
Μερραν καὶ Θαιμαν οἱ μυθολόγοι καὶ οἱ ἐκζητηταὶ τῆς
συνέσεως ὁδὸν τῆς σοφίας οὐκ ἔγνωσαν οὐδὲ ἐμνήσθησαν
τὰς τρίβους αὐτῆς. — 24 ὦ Ισραηλ, ὡς μέγας ὁ οἶκος τοῦ
θεοῦ καὶ ἐπιμήκης ὁ τόπος τῆς κτήσεως αὐτοῦ· 25 μέγας

KING JAMES VERSION

16 Where are the princes of the heathen become, and such as ruled the beasts upon the earth;

17 They that had their pastime with the fowls of the air, and they that hoarded up silver and gold, wherein men trust, and made no end of their getting?

18 For they that wrought in silver, and were so careful, and whose works are unsearchable,

19 They are vanished and gone down to the grave, and others are come up in their steads.

20 Young men have seen light, and dwelt upon the earth: but the way of knowledge have they not known,

21 Nor understood the paths thereof, nor laid hold of it: their children were far off from that way.

22 It hath not been heard of in Chanaan, neither hath it been seen in Theman.

23 The Agarenes that seek wisdom upon earth, the merchants of Meran and of Theman, the authors of fables, and searchers out of understanding; none of these have known the way of wisdom, or remember her paths.

24 O Israel, how great is the house of God! and how large is the place of his possession!

DOUAY OLD TESTAMENT

16 Where are the princes of the nations, and they that rule over the beasts that are upon the earth?

17 That take their diversion with the birds of the air.

18 That hoard up silver and gold, wherein men trust, and there is no end of their getting? who work in silver and are solicitous, and their works are unsearchable.

19 They are cut off, and are gone down to hell, and others are risen up in their place.

20 Young men have seen the light, and dwelt upon the earth: but the way of knowledge they have not known,

21 Nor have they understood the paths thereof, neither have their children received it, it is far from their face.

22 It hath not been heard of in the land of Chanaan, neither hath it been seen in Theman.

23 The children of Agar also, that search after the wisdom that is of the earth, the merchants of Merrha, and of Theman, and the tellers of fables, and searchers of prudence and understanding: but the way of wisdom they have not known, neither have they remembered her paths.

24 O Israel, how great is the house of God, and how vast is the place of his possession!

KNOX TRANSLATION

store-house? 16 What has become of those heathen princes,
who gained mastery of the beasts that roam the earth,
17 tamed the birds for their pastime; 18 heaping up silver and
gold, man's confidence, man's interminable quest? How anxiously they toiled for wealth! And now these devices of theirs
are beyond our tracing.

19 They disappeared, went to their graves, and other succeeded them; 20 a younger generation saw the light and peopled the earth in its turn; but still they could not find their
way to the true wisdom, 21 the path to it was hidden still.
Their children, too, clutched at it in vain, it was as far as
ever from their reach. 22 In Chanaan, none had heard tell of
it, in Theman none had caught sight of it; 23 even the sons
of Agar, so well schooled in earthly wisdom, even the merchants of Merrha and Theman, with all their store of legend,
their skill and cunning laboriously gained, never found the
track of true wisdom, or told us what its haunts were.

24 Israel, how wide is God's house, how spacious is his

TODAY'S ENGLISH VERSION

have vanished: the rulers of the nations, those who hunted
wild animals and birds for sport, those who accumulated
vast fortunes of silver and gold, which everyone trusts and
will do anything to get, 18 and those who worried and
schemed to make money, but who left no trace of their work
behind. 19 They have all disappeared and gone down to the
world of the dead. Others have come along to take their
place. 20 A later generation was born and lived in the land,
but they too did not discover the way to knowledge. They did
not find the path to Wisdom or ever reach her. 21 Their children also failed. 22 Wisdom was not found by the Canaanites. It has not been discovered by the Edomites 23 although
they search after knowledge. The way to Wisdom has not
been found by the merchants of Merran and Tema or by
those who relate fables or by any others who seek understanding.
24 O Israel, how great is the universe in which God dwells!
How vast is all that he possesses! 25 There is no end to it;

NEW REVISED STANDARD VERSION

16 Where are the rulers of the nations,
and those who lorded it over the animals on earth;
17 those who made sport of the birds of the air,
and who hoarded up silver and gold
in which people trust,
and there is no end to their getting;
18 those who schemed to get silver, and were anxious,
but there is no trace of their works?
19 They have vanished and gone down to Hades,
and others have arisen in their place.

20 Later generations have seen the light of day,
and have lived upon the earth;
but they have not learned the way to knowledge,
nor understood her paths,
nor laid hold of her.
21 Their descendants have strayed far from her[a] way.
22 She has not been heard of in Canaan,
or seen in Teman;
23 the descendants of Hagar, who seek for understanding
on the earth,
the merchants of Merran and Teman,
the story-tellers and the seekers for understanding,
have not learned the way to wisdom,
or given thought to her paths.

24 O Israel, how great is the house of God,
how vast the territory that he possesses!

a Other ancient authorities read *their*

NEW AMERICAN BIBLE

16 Where are the rulers of the nations,
they who lorded it over the wild beasts of the earth,
17 and made sport of the birds of the heavens:
They who heaped up the silver
and the gold in which men trust;
of whose possessions there was no end?
18 They schemed anxiously for money,
but there is no trace of their work:
19 They have vanished down into the nether world,
and others have risen up in their stead.

20 Later generations have seen the light,
have dwelt in the land,
But the way to understanding they have not known,
21 they have not perceived her paths, or reached her;
their offspring were far from the way to her.
22 She has not been heard of in Canaan,
nor seen in Teman.
23 The sons of Hagar who seek knowledge on earth,
the merchants of Midian and Teman,
the phrasemakers seeking knowledge,
These have not known the way to wisdom,
nor have they her paths in mind.

24 O Israel, how vast is the house of God,
how broad the scope of his dominion:

NEW JERUSALEM BIBLE

16 Where now are the leaders of the nations
and those who ruled even the beasts of earth,
17 those who sported with the birds of heaven,
those who accumulated silver and gold
on which all people rely,
and whose possessions had no end,
18 those who worked so carefully in silver
—but of whose works no trace is to be found?
19 They have vanished, gone down to Sheol.
Others have risen to their places,
20 more recent generations have seen the day
and peopled the earth in their turn,
but the way of knowledge they have not found;
21 they have not recognised the paths she treads.
Nor have their children had any grasp of her,
remaining far from her way.
22 Nothing has been heard of her in Canaan,
nothing has been seen of her in Teman;
23 the children of Hagar in search of worldly wisdom,
the merchants of Midian and Teman,
the tale-spinners and the philosophers have none of
them found the way to wisdom
or remembered the paths she treads.

24 How great, Israel, is the house of God,
how wide his domain,

GREEK OLD TESTAMENT

καὶ οὐκ ἔχει τελευτήν, ὑψηλὸς καὶ ἀμέτρητος. 26 ἐκεῖ ἐγεν-
νήθησαν οἱ γίγαντες οἱ ὀνομαστοὶ οἱ ἀπ' ἀρχῆς, γενόμενοι
εὐμεγέθεις, ἐπιστάμενοι πόλεμον. 27 οὐ τούτους ἐξελέξατο
ὁ θεὸς οὐδὲ ὁδὸν ἐπιστήμης ἔδωκεν αὐτοῖς. 28 καὶ ἀπώλοντο
παρὰ τὸ μὴ ἔχειν φρόνησιν, ἀπώλοντο διὰ τὴν ἀβουλίαν
αὐτῶν. — 29 τίς ἀνέβη εἰς τὸν οὐρανὸν καὶ ἔλαβεν αὐτὴν καὶ
κατεβίβασεν αὐτὴν ἐκ τῶν νεφελῶν; 30 τίς διέβη πέραν τῆς
θαλάσσης καὶ εὗρεν αὐτὴν καὶ οἴσει αὐτὴν χρυσίου ἐκλεκτοῦ; 31 οὐκ ἔστιν ὁ γινώσκων τὴν ὁδὸν αὐτῆς οὐδὲ ὁ ἐνθυμ-
ούμενος τὴν τρίβον αὐτῆς. 32 ἀλλὰ ὁ εἰδὼς τὰ πάντα
γινώσκει αὐτήν, ἐξεῦρεν αὐτὴν τῇ συνέσει αὐτοῦ· ὁ κατασκευάσας τὴν γῆν εἰς τὸν αἰῶνα χρόνον, ἐνέπλησεν αὐτὴν
κτηνῶν τετραπόδων· 33 ὁ ἀποστέλλων τὸ φῶς, καὶ πορεύεται, ἐκάλεσεν αὐτό, καὶ ὑπήκουσεν αὐτῷ τρόμῳ· 34 οἱ δὲ
ἀστέρες ἔλαμψαν ἐν ταῖς φυλακαῖς αὐτῶν καὶ εὐφράνθησαν,
35 ἐκάλεσεν αὐτοὺς καὶ εἶπον Πάρεσμεν, ἔλαμψαν μετ'
εὐφροσύνης τῷ ποιήσαντι αὐτούς. 36 οὗτος ὁ θεὸς ἡμῶν, οὐ
λογισθήσεται ἕτερος πρὸς αὐτόν. 37 ἐξεῦρεν πᾶσαν ὁδὸν

KING JAMES VERSION

25 Great, and hath none end; high, and unmeasurable.

26 There were the giants famous from the beginning, that were of so great stature, and so expert in war.

27 Those did not the Lord choose, neither gave he the way of knowledge unto them:

28 But they were destroyed, because they had no wisdom, and perished through their own foolishness.

29 Who hath gone up into heaven, and taken her, and brought her down from the clouds?

30 Who hath gone over the sea, and found her, and will bring her for pure gold?

31 No man knoweth her way, nor thinketh of her path.

32 But he that knoweth all things knoweth her, and hath found her out with his understanding: he that prepared the earth for evermore hath filled it with fourfooted beasts:

33 He that sendeth forth light, and it goeth, calleth it *again,* and it obeyeth him with fear.

34 The stars shined in their watches, and rejoiced: when he calleth them, they say, Here we be; and so with cheerfulness they shewed light unto him that made them.

35 This is our God, and there shall none other be accounted of in comparison of him.

36 He hath found out all the way of knowledge, and hath

DOUAY OLD TESTAMENT

25 It is great, and hath no end: *it is* high and immense.

26 There were the giants, those renowned men that were from the beginning, of great stature, expert in war.

27 The Lord chose not them, neither did they find the way of knowledge: therefore did they perish.

28 And because they had not wisdom, they perished through their folly.

29 Who hath gone up into heaven, and taken her, and brought her down from the clouds?

30 Who hath passed over the sea, and found her, and brought her preferably to chosen gold?

31 There is none that is able to know her ways, nor that can search out her paths:

32 But he that knoweth all things, knoweth her, and hath found her out with his understanding: he that prepared the earth for evermore, and filled it with cattle and fourfooted beasts:

33 He that sendeth forth light, and it goeth: and hath called it, and it obeyeth him with trembling.

34 And the stars have given light in their watches, and rejoiced:

35 They were called, and they said: Here we are: and with cheerfulness they have shined forth to him that made them.

36 This is our God, and there shall no other be accounted of in comparison of him.

37 He found out all the way of knowledge, and gave it to

KNOX TRANSLATION

domain, 25 large beyond all bound, high beyond all
measure![a] 26 The heroes of old were nurtured there, men
whose fame has come down to us from the beginning of
time, huge in stature, great warriors; 27 but it was not these
God had chosen; they died without ever attaining true
knowledge. 28 Not for them was the possession of wisdom,
and in their folly they perished.
29 What man ever scaled heaven, gained wisdom there, and
brought it back from the clouds? 30 What man ever crossed
the sea, and found it there, brought it back like a cargo of
pure gold? 31 The path to it none may know, the clue of it
none may find. 32 Only he who knows all things possesses
it, only his mind conceives it. He it is who framed the abiding earth, and filled it with cattle and four-footed beasts of
every kind. 33 It is on his errand that the light goes forth, his
summons that it obeys with awe; 34 joyfully the stars shine
out, keeping the watches he has appointed, 35 answer when
he calls their muster-roll, and offer their glad radiance to him
who fashioned them. 36 Such a God is ours; what rival will
be compared to him? 37 He it is who has the key to all

a v. 24 sqq. God's 'house' is usually identified as creation generally. But it must be confessed that this reference to the giants (Gen. 6. 4) belongs to a stream of tradition about which we know little.

TODAY'S ENGLISH VERSION

there is no way to measure how wide or how high it is.
26 Here in early times the famous giants were born, a mighty
race skilled in war. 27 But God did not choose them to be his
people or show them the way of knowledge. 28 They died out
because they had neither understanding nor insight.
29 No one has ever gone up into heaven to get Wisdom and
bring her down out of the clouds. 30 No one has sailed across
the seas to find Wisdom or bought her with precious gold.
31 No one knows how to get to her or how to discover the
path that leads to her.
32 The only one who knows Wisdom is God, and he knows
all things. With his understanding he found her. He established the earth for all time and filled it with all kinds of animals. 33 The light trembled and obeyed when he called. He
sent it forth, and it appeared. 34 He called the stars, and they
promptly answered; they took their places and gladly shone
to please the one who made them. 35 He is our God, and there
is none like him. 36 He discovered the entire path leading to

NEW REVISED STANDARD VERSION

25 It is great and has no bounds;
it is high and immeasurable.
26 The giants were born there, who were famous of old,
great in stature, expert in war.
27 God did not choose them,
or give them the way to knowledge;
28 so they perished because they had no wisdom,
they perished through their folly.

29 Who has gone up into heaven, and taken her,
and brought her down from the clouds?
30 Who has gone over the sea, and found her,
and will buy her for pure gold?
31 No one knows the way to her,
or is concerned about the path to her.
32 But the one who knows all things knows her,
he found her by his understanding.
The one who prepared the earth for all time
filled it with four-footed creatures;
33 the one who sends forth the light, and it goes;
he called it, and it obeyed him, trembling;
34 the stars shone in their watches, and were glad;
he called them, and they said, "Here we are!"
They shone with gladness for him who made them.
35 This is our God;
no other can be compared to him.
36 He found the whole way to knowledge,

NEW AMERICAN BIBLE

25 Vast and endless,
high and immeasurable!
26 In it were born the giants,
renowned at the first,
stalwarts, skilled in war.
27 Not these did God choose,
nor did he give them the way of understanding;
28 They perished for lack of prudence,
perished through their folly.
29 Who has gone up to the heavens and taken her,
or brought her down from the clouds?
30 Who has crossed the sea and found her,
bearing her away rather than choice gold?
31 None knows the way to her,
nor has any understood her paths.
32 Yet he who knows all things knows her;
he has probed her by his knowledge—
He who established the earth for all time,
and filled it with four-footed beasts;
33 He who dismisses the light, and it departs,
calls it, and it obeys him trembling;
34 Before whom the stars at their posts
shine and rejoice;
35 When he calls them, they answer, "Here we are!"
shining with joy for their Maker.
36 Such is our God;
no other is to be compared to him:
37 He has traced out all the way of understanding,

NEW JERUSALEM BIBLE

25 immeasurably wide,
infinitely lofty!
26 In it were born the giants, famous from the beginning,
immensely tall, expert in war;
27 God's choice did not fall on these,
he did not show them the way of knowledge;
28 they perished for lack of wisdom,
perished by their own folly.
29 Who has ever climbed the sky and seized her
to bring her down from the clouds?
30 Who has ever crossed the ocean and found her
to bring her back in exchange for the finest gold?
31 No one can learn the way to her,
no one can understand the path she treads.

32 But the One who knows all discovers her,
he has grasped her with his own intellect,
he has set the earth firm for evermore
and filled it with four-footed beasts,
33 he sends the light—and it goes,
he recalls it—and trembling it obeys;
34 the stars shine joyfully at their posts;
35 when he calls them, they answer, 'Here we are';
they shine to delight their Creator.
36 It is he who is our God,
no other can compare with him.
37 He has uncovered the whole way of knowledge

GREEK OLD TESTAMENT

ἐπιστήμης καὶ ἔδωκεν αὐτὴν Ιακωβ τῷ παιδὶ αὐτοῦ καὶ
Ισραηλ τῷ ἠγαπημένῳ ὑπ' αὐτοῦ· 38 μετὰ τοῦτο ἐπὶ τῆς γῆς
ὤφθη καὶ ἐν τοῖς ἀνθρώποις συνανεστράφη.

4 1 αὕτη ἡ
βίβλος τῶν προσταγμάτων τοῦ θεοῦ καὶ ὁ νόμος ὁ
ὑπάρχων εἰς τὸν αἰῶνα· πάντες οἱ κρατοῦντες αὐτῆς εἰς
ζωήν, οἱ δὲ καταλείποντες αὐτὴν ἀποθανοῦνται. — 2 ἐπι-
στρέφου, Ιακωβ, καὶ ἐπιλαβοῦ αὐτῆς, διόδευσον πρὸς τὴν
λάμψιν κατέναντι τοῦ φωτὸς αὐτῆς. 3 μὴ δῷς ἑτέρῳ τὴν
δόξαν σου καὶ τὰ συμφέροντά σοι ἔθνει ἀλλοτρίῳ. 4 μακάρι-
οί ἐσμεν, Ισραηλ, ὅτι τὰ ἀρεστὰ τῷ θεῷ ἡμῖν γνωστά ἐστιν

5 Θαρσεῖτε, λαός μου, μνημόσυνον Ισραηλ. 6 ἐπράθητε
τοῖς ἔθνεσιν οὐκ εἰς ἀπώλειαν, διὰ δὲ τὸ παροργίσαι ὑμᾶς
τὸν θεὸν παρεδόθητε τοῖς ὑπεναντίοις. 7 παρωξύνατε γὰρ
τὸν ποιήσαντα ὑμᾶς θύσαντες δαιμονίοις καὶ οὐ θεῷ.
8 ἐπελάθεσθε δὲ τὸν τροφεύσαντα ὑμᾶς θεὸν αἰώνιον,
ἐλυπήσατε δὲ καὶ τὴν ἐκθρέψασαν ὑμᾶς Ιερουσαλημ· 9 εἶδεν
γὰρ τὴν ἐπελθοῦσαν ὑμῖν ὀργὴν παρὰ τοῦ θεοῦ καὶ εἶπεν

KING JAMES VERSION

given it unto Jacob his servant, and to Israel his beloved.

37 Afterward did he shew himself upon earth, and conversed with men.

4 This is the book of the commandments of God, and the law that endureth for ever: all they that keep it *shall come* to life; but such as leave it shall die.

2 Turn thee, O Jacob, and take hold of it: walk in the presence of the light thereof, that thou mayest be illuminated.

3 Give not thine honour to another, nor the things that are profitable unto thee to a strange nation.

4 O Israel, happy are we: for things that are pleasing to God are made known unto us.

5 Be of good cheer, my people, the memorial of Israel.

6 Ye were sold to the nations, not for [your] destruction: but because ye moved God to wrath, ye were delivered unto the enemies.

7 For ye provoked him that made you by sacrificing unto devils, and not to God.

8 Ye have forgotten the everlasting God, that brought you up; and ye have grieved Jerusalem, that nursed you.

9 For when she saw the wrath of God coming upon you,

DOUAY OLD TESTAMENT

Jacob his servant, and to Israel his beloved.

38 Afterwards he was seen upon earth, and conversed with men.

4 THIS is the book of the commandments of God, and the law, that is for ever: all they that keep it, shall come to life: but they that have forsaken it, to death.

2 Return, O Jacob, and take hold of it, walk in the way by its brightness, in the presence of the light thereof.

3 Give not thy honour to another, nor thy dignity to a strange nation.

4 We are happy, O Israel: because the things that are pleasing to God, are made known to us.

5 Be of good comfort, O people of God, the memorial of Israel:

6 You have been sold to the Gentiles, not for your destruction: but because you provoked God to wrath, you are delivered to your adversaries.

7 For you have provoked him who made you, the eternal God, offering sacrifice to devils, and not to God.

8 For you have forgotten God, who brought you up, and you have grieved Jerusalem that nursed you.

9 For she saw the wrath of God coming upon you, and

KNOX TRANSLATION

knowledge, and gave it to his servant Jacob, to the well-loved
race of Israel; 38 not till then would he reveal himself on
earth, and hold converse with mortal men.

4 Here is the book[a] in which you may read God's commandments, that law of his which stands for ever; holding fast by it or forsaking it, a man makes life or death his
goal. 2 Jacob, thy steps retrace, and this path follow, guiding
thy steps by glow of the light that beckons thee; 3 this is thy
pride, wouldst thou yield it up to another? Thy prize, shall
an alien race enjoy it? 4 Israel, a blessed race is ours, that
has knowledge of God's will.

5 People of God, take courage, all that is left of Israel's
muster-roll! 6 Sold as slaves though you be, he does not
mean your ruin. He has given your enemies the mastery,
none the less; had you not defied his vengeance? 7 Had you
not challenged the eternal power that made you, by sacrificing to evil powers, that gods were none? 8 To God that fostered you, what ingratitude, to Jerusalem that nursed you,
what bitter pain!

9 Alas, she cried, as she saw the divine vengeance falling

a Apparently in the sense that wisdom is to be identified with the divine law.

TODAY'S ENGLISH VERSION

understanding and gave Wisdom to his servant Israel, whom
he loved. 37 From that time on, Wisdom appeared on earth
and lived among us.

4 Wisdom is the book of God's commandments, the Law
that will last forever. All who hold onto her will live, but
those who abandon her will die. 2 Turn to Wisdom, people of
Israel, and take hold of her. Make your way toward the
splendor of her light. 3 Do not surrender our glorious privileges to any other people. 4 How happy we are, people of
Israel; we have the advantage of knowing what is pleasing
to God!

5 Take courage, my people, you are the ones who keep
Israel's name alive. 6 You were sold to Gentile nations, but
not to be destroyed. Because you made God angry, he handed you over to your enemies. 7 When you offered sacrifices
to demons instead of to God, you angered the one who
made you. 8 You forgot the Eternal God, who had nourished
you as a child, and so you brought grief to Jerusalem, who
had been like a mother to you. 9 Jerusalem saw that God
was punishing you because he was angry, and she said to

NEW REVISED STANDARD VERSION

and gave her to his servant Jacob
and to Israel, whom he loved.
37 Afterward she appeared on earth
and lived with humankind.

4 She is the book of the commandments of God,
the law that endures forever.
All who hold her fast will live,
and those who forsake her will die.
2 Turn, O Jacob, and take her;
walk toward the shining of her light.
3 Do not give your glory to another,
or your advantages to an alien people.
4 Happy are we, O Israel,
for we know what is pleasing to God.

5 Take courage, my people,
who perpetuate Israel's name!
6 It was not for destruction
that you were sold to the nations,
but you were handed over to your enemies
because you angered God.
7 For you provoked the one who made you
by sacrificing to demons and not to God.
8 You forgot the everlasting God, who brought you up,
and you grieved Jerusalem, who reared you.
9 For she saw the wrath that came upon you from God,
and she said:

NEW AMERICAN BIBLE

and has given her to Jacob, his servant,
to Israel, his beloved son.

38 Since then she has appeared on earth,
and moved among men.

4 She is the book of the precepts of God,
the law that endures forever;
All who cling to her will live,
but those will die who forsake her.
2 Turn, O Jacob, and receive her:
walk by her light toward splendor.
3 Give not your glory to another,
your privileges to an alien race.
4 Blessed are we, O Israel;
for what pleases God is known to us!

5 Fear not, my people!
Remember, Israel,
6 You were sold to the nations
not for your destruction;
It was because you angered God
that you were handed over to your foes.
7 For you provoked your Maker
with sacrifices to demons, to no-gods;
8 You forsook the Eternal God who nourished you,
and you grieved Jerusalem who fostered you.
9 She indeed saw coming upon you
the anger of God; and she said:

NEW JERUSALEM BIBLE

and shown it to his servant Jacob,
to Israel his well-beloved;
38 only then did she appear on earth
and live among human beings.
4 She is the book of God's commandments,
the Law that stands for ever;
those who keep her shall live,
those who desert her shall die.
2 Turn back, Jacob, seize her,
in her radiance make your way to light:
3 do not yield your glory to another,
your privilege to a people not your own.
4 Israel, blessed are we:
what pleases God has been revealed to us!
5 Take courage, my people,
memorial of Israel!
6 You were sold to the nations,
but not for extermination.
You provoked God;
and so were delivered to your enemies,
7 since you had angered your Creator
by offering sacrifices to demons, and not to God.
8 You had forgotten the eternal God who reared you.
You had also grieved Jerusalem who nursed you,
9 for when she saw God's anger
falling on you, she said:

GREEK OLD TESTAMENT

Ἀκούσατε, αἱ πάροικοι Σιων, ἐπήγαγέν μοι ὁ θεὸς πένθος
μέγα· 10 εἶδον γὰρ τὴν αἰχμαλωσίαν τῶν υἱῶν μου καὶ τῶν
θυγατέρων, ἣν ἐπήγαγεν αὐτοῖς ὁ αἰώνιος. 11 ἔθρεψα γὰρ
αὐτοὺς μετ᾽ εὐφροσύνης, ἐξαπέστειλα δὲ μετὰ κλαυθμοῦ καὶ
πένθους. 12 μηδεὶς ἐπιχαιρέτω μοι τῇ χήρᾳ καὶ καταλει-
φθείσῃ ὑπὸ πολλῶν· ἠρημώθην διὰ τὰς ἁμαρτίας τῶν τέκνων
μου, διότι ἐξέκλιναν ἐκ νόμου θεοῦ, 13 δικαιώματα δὲ αὐτοῦ
οὐκ ἔγνωσαν οὐδὲ ἐπορεύθησαν ὁδοῖς ἐντολῶν θεοῦ οὐδὲ
τρίβους παιδείας ἐν δικαιοσύνῃ αὐτοῦ ἐπέβησαν. 14 ἐλθάτω-
σαν αἱ πάροικοι Σιων, καὶ μνήσθητε τὴν αἰχμαλωσίαν τῶν
υἱῶν μου καὶ θυγατέρων, ἣν ἐπήγαγεν αὐτοῖς ὁ αἰώνιος.
15 ἐπήγαγεν γὰρ ἐπ᾽ αὐτοὺς ἔθνος μακρόθεν, ἔθνος ἀναιδὲς
καὶ ἀλλόγλωσσον, οἳ οὐκ ᾐσχύνθησαν πρεσβύτην οὐδὲ παιδίον ἠλέησαν 16 καὶ ἀπήγαγον τοὺς ἀγαπητοὺς τῆς χήρας καὶ
ἀπὸ τῶν θυγατέρων τὴν μόνην ἠρήμωσαν. 17 ἐγὼ δὲ τί
δυνατὴ βοηθῆσαι ὑμῖν; 18 ὁ γὰρ ἐπαγαγὼν τὰ κακὰ ὑμῖν ἐξελεῖται ὑμᾶς ἐκ χειρὸς ἐχθρῶν ὑμῶν. 19 βαδίζετε, τέκνα,
βαδίζετε, ἐγὼ γὰρ κατελείφθην ἔρημος. 20 ἐξεδυσάμην τὴν

KING JAMES VERSION

she said, Hearken, O ye that dwell about Sion: God hath brought upon me great mourning;

10 For I saw the captivity of my sons and daughters, which the Everlasting brought upon them.

11 With joy did I nourish them; but sent them away with weeping and mourning.

12 Let no man rejoice over me, a widow, and forsaken of many, who for the sins of my children am left desolate; because they departed from the law of God.

13 They knew not his statutes, nor walked in the ways of his commandments, nor trod in the paths of discipline in his righteousness.

14 Let them that dwell about Sion come, and remember ye the captivity of my sons and daughters, which the Everlasting hath brought upon them.

15 For he hath brought a nation upon them from far, a shameless nation, and of a strange language, who neither reverenced old man, nor pitied child.

16 These have carried away the dear beloved children of the widow, and left her that was alone desolate without daughters.

17 But what can I help you?

18 For he that brought these plagues upon you will deliver you from the hands of your enemies.

19 Go your way, O my children, go your way: for I am left desolate.

DOUAY OLD TESTAMENT

she said: Give ear, all you that dwell near Sion, for God hath brought upon me great mourning:

10 For I have seen the captivity of my people, of my sons, and my daughters, which the Eternal hath brought upon them.

11 For I nourished them with joy: but I sent them away with weeping and mourning.

12 Let no man rejoice over me, a widow, and desolate: I am forsaken of many for the sins of my children, because they departed from the law of God.

13 And they have not known his justices, nor walked by the ways of God's commandments, neither have they entered by the paths of his truth and justice.

14 Let them that dwell about Sion come, and remember the captivity of my sons and daughters, which the Eternal hath brought upon them.

15 For he hath brought a nation upon them from afar, a wicked nation, and of a strange tongue:

16 Who have neither reverenced the ancient, nor pitied children, and have carried away the beloved of the widow, and have left *me* all alone without children.

17 But as for me, what help can I give you?

18 But he that hath brought the evils upon you, he will deliver you out of the hands of your enemies.

19 Go your way, my children, go your way: for I am left alone.

KNOX TRANSLATION

on you, listen, neighbour cities all, to my complaint; here is a
heavy load of grief God has charged me with! 10 Sentence of
banishment he, the eternal, has pronounced upon my people,
sons and daughters of mine; 11 how joyously I nurtured
them, with what tears of anguish I saw them depart! 12 And
let none boast over my widowing, that so much have lost; if I
am thus forlorn, it is because of my sons' transgression, that
refused God's will; 13 his claim disowned, his paths left
untrodden; not for them the straight road of loyal observance. 14 Come, neighbours, tell we the sad tale again, how
he, the eternal, would sentence these sons and daughters of
mine to exile. 15 A cruel race he summoned to the attack
from far away, men of an alien speech; 16 for old age they
had no reverence, for childhood no pity; robbed widow of her
darling sons, and left her desolate.

17 Alas, my children, look not to me for aid! 18 He it is
must save you from the power of your enemies, who is the
author of your calamity. 19 Go your ways, my children, go
your ways; I am left desolate; 20 the festal robe of happier

TODAY'S ENGLISH VERSION

all the neighboring cities, "Look at the great misery that God
has brought on me. 10 I saw my sons and daughters taken
into captivity, a captivity brought on them by the Eternal
God. 11 I brought up my children with great delight, but I
cried and mourned when they were taken from me. 12 Let
no one take pleasure in my suffering now that I am a widow
and so many of my children have been taken from me. They
turned away from God's Law, and their sins have made me
a deserted city. 13 They had no respect for his commandments and would not live by them; they refused to let him
guide them in the way of righteousness.

14 "All you neighboring cities, come and consider how the
Eternal God has sent my children into exile. 15 He brought
against them a nation from far away, a shameless nation
that speaks a foreign language and has no respect for the
elderly and no pity for children. 16 These people carried off
my beloved sons and took away my daughters, and I was left
a widow, completely alone.

17 "My children in exile, I can do nothing to help you.
18 Only the one who brought this punishment upon you can
rescue you from your enemies. 19 Go your own way, my children; live your own life! I am all alone. 20 I have taken off

NEW REVISED STANDARD VERSION

Listen, you neighbors of Zion,
God has brought great sorrow upon me;
10 for I have seen the exile of my sons and daughters,
which the Everlasting brought upon them.
11 With joy I nurtured them,
but I sent them away with weeping and sorrow.
12 Let no one rejoice over me, a widow
and bereaved of many;
I was left desolate because of the sins of my children,
because they turned away from the law of God.
13 They had no regard for his statutes;
they did not walk in the ways of God's
commandments,
or tread the paths his righteousness showed them.
14 Let the neighbors of Zion come;
remember the capture of my sons and daughters,
which the Everlasting brought upon them.
15 For he brought a distant nation against them,
a nation ruthless and of a strange language,
which had no respect for the aged
and no pity for a child.
16 They led away the widow's beloved sons,
and bereaved the lonely woman of her daughters.

17 But I, how can I help you?
18 For he who brought these calamities upon you
will deliver you from the hand of your enemies.
19 Go, my children, go;
for I have been left desolate.

NEW AMERICAN BIBLE

"Hear, you neighbors of Zion!
God has brought great mourning upon me,
10 For I have seen the captivity
that the Eternal God has brought
upon my sons and daughters.
11 With joy I fostered them;
but with mourning and lament I let them go.
12 Let no one gloat over me, a widow,
bereft of many:
For the sins of my children I am left desolate,
because they turned from the law of God,
13 and did not acknowledge his statutes;
In the ways of God's commandments they did not walk,
nor did they tread the disciplined paths of his justice.

14 "Let Zion's neighbors come,
to take note of the captivity of my sons and daughters,
brought upon them by the Eternal God.
15 He has brought against them a nation from afar,
a nation ruthless and of alien speech,
That has neither reverence for age
nor tenderness for childhood:
16 They have led away this widow's cherished sons,
have left me solitary, without daughters.
17 What can I do to help you?
18 He who has brought this evil upon you
must himself deliver you from your enemies' hands.
19 Farewell, my children, farewell:
I am left desolate.

NEW JERUSALEM BIBLE

Listen, you neighbours of Zion:
God has sent me great sorrow.
10 I have seen my sons and daughters taken into captivity,
which the Eternal brought down on them.
11 I had reared them joyfully;
in tears, in sorrow, I watched them go away.
12 Do not, any of you, exult over me,
a widow, deserted by so many;
I am bereaved because of the sins of my children,
who turned away from the Law of God,
13 who did not want to know his precepts
and would not follow the ways of his commandments
or tread the paths of discipline as his justice directed.
14 Come here, neighbours of Zion!
Remember my sons' and daughters' captivity,
which the Eternal brought down on them.
15 How he brought a distant nation down on them,
a ruthless nation speaking a foreign language,
they showed neither respect for the aged,
nor pity for the child;
16 they carried off the widow's cherished sons,
they left her quite alone, bereft of her daughters.
17 For my part, how could I help you?
18 He who brought those disasters down on you,
is the one to deliver you from your enemies' clutches.
19 Go, my children, go your way!
I must stay bereft and lonely;

GREEK OLD TESTAMENT

στολὴν τῆς εἰρήνης, ἐνεδυσάμην δὲ σάκκον τῆς δεήσεώς
μου, κεκράξομαι πρὸς τὸν αἰώνιον ἐν ταῖς ἡμέραις μου. —
21 θαρσεῖτε, τέκνα, βοήσατε πρὸς τὸν θεόν, καὶ ἐξελεῖται
ὑμᾶς ἐκ δυναστείας, ἐκ χειρὸς ἐχθρῶν. 22 ἐγὼ γὰρ ἤλπισα
ἐπὶ τῷ αἰωνίῳ τὴν σωτηρίαν ὑμῶν, καὶ ἦλθέν μοι χαρὰ παρὰ
τοῦ ἁγίου ἐπὶ τῇ ἐλεημοσύνῃ, ᾗ ἥξει ὑμῖν ἐν τάχει παρὰ τοῦ
αἰωνίου σωτῆρος ὑμῶν. 23 ἐξέπεμψα γὰρ ὑμᾶς μετὰ πένθους
καὶ κλαυθμοῦ, ἀποδώσει δέ μοι ὁ θεὸς ὑμᾶς μετὰ χαρμοσύνης καὶ εὐφροσύνης εἰς τὸν αἰῶνα. 24 ὥσπερ γὰρ νῦν
ἑωράκασιν αἱ πάροικοι Σιων τὴν ὑμετέραν αἰχμαλωσίαν,
οὕτως ὄψονται ἐν τάχει τὴν παρὰ τοῦ θεοῦ ὑμῶν σωτηρίαν,
ἣ ἐπελεύσεται ὑμῖν μετὰ δόξης μεγάλης καὶ λαμπρότητος
τοῦ αἰωνίου. 25 τέκνα, μακροθυμήσατε τὴν παρὰ τοῦ θεοῦ
ἐπελθοῦσαν ὑμῖν ὀργήν· κατεδίωξέν σε ὁ ἐχθρός σου, καὶ
ὄψει αὐτοῦ τὴν ἀπώλειαν ἐν τάχει καὶ ἐπὶ τραχήλους αὐτῶν
ἐπιβήσῃ. 26 οἱ τρυφεροί μου ἐπορεύθησαν ὁδοὺς τραχείας,
ἤρθησαν ὡς ποίμνιον ἡρπασμένον ὑπὸ ἐχθρῶν. —

KING JAMES VERSION

20 I have put off the clothing of peace, and put upon me the sackcloth of my prayer: I will cry unto the Everlasting in my days.

21 Be of good cheer, O my children, cry unto the Lord, and he shall deliver you from the power and hand of the enemies.

22 For my hope is in the Everlasting, that he will save you; and joy is come unto me from the Holy One, because of the mercy which shall soon come unto you from the Everlasting our Saviour.

23 For I sent you out with mourning and weeping: but God will give you to me again with joy and gladness for ever.

24 Like as now the neighbours of Sion have seen your captivity: so shall they see shortly your salvation from our God, which shall come upon you with great glory, and brightness of the Everlasting.

25 My children, suffer patiently the wrath that is come upon you from God: for thine enemy hath persecuted thee; but shortly thou shalt see his destruction, and shalt tread upon his neck.

26 My delicate ones have gone rough ways, and were taken away as a flock caught of the enemies.

DOUAY OLD TESTAMENT

20 I have put off the robe of peace, and have put upon me the sackcloth of supplication, and I will cry to the most High in my days.

21 Be of good comfort, my children, cry to the Lord, and he will deliver you out of the hand of the princes your enemies.

22 For my hope is in the Eternal that he will save you: and joy is come upon me from the Holy One, because of the mercy which shall come to you from our everlasting Saviour.

23 For I sent you forth with mourning and weeping: but the Lord will bring you back to me with joy and gladness for ever.

24 For as the neighbours of Sion have now seen your captivity from God: so shall they also shortly see your salvation from God, which shall come upon you with great honour, and everlasting glory.

25 My children, suffer patiently the wrath that is come upon you: for thy enemy hath persecuted thee, but thou shalt quickly see his destruction: and thou shalt get up upon his neck.

26 My delicate ones have walked rough ways, for they were taken away as a flock made a prey by the enemies.

KNOX TRANSLATION

times I have put aside, clothed myself in sackcloth as the
suppliants do; I will spend my days pleading with him, the
eternal. 21 Take courage, my children, and raise your voices,
too, in appeal; from the enemy's tyrant grasp the Lord shall
deliver you. 22 Upon him, the eternal, I pin evermore my
hopes of your happiness, the holy God, evermore our deliverer! Light grows my heart, to think of the mercy he has in
store for you. 23 With lamentation I bade farewell to you,
and with tears; with joy and triumph he will bring you back
to me, and for ever; 24 these neighbours of mine, that saw
you banished at his decree, shall witness ere long a divine
deliverance; what renown shall be yours when it comes,
what dawn unending! 25 Bear patiently, my children, with
the punishment that has overtaken you. What if thy enemy
hunts thee down? Ere long thou shalt see the ruin of him,
set thy foot on his neck! 26 Ah, the rough roads delicate feet
of yours have travelled! Like a plundered flock the enemy

TODAY'S ENGLISH VERSION

the robes I wore during days of peace, and I have dressed
myself like a person in mourning. I will cry out to the Eternal
God for help as long as I live.
[21] "Take courage, my children, and cry out to God for help.
He will rescue you from oppression, from the power of your
enemies. [22] I am confident that the Eternal God will soon set
you free. The Holy One, your eternal savior, will make me
happy when he shows you mercy. [23] I cried and wailed when
you were taken away, but God will bring you back and will
make me happy forever. [24] Just as the neighboring cities
watched as you were taken captive, so they will soon see the
Eternal God coming in glorious splendor to rescue you. [25] My
children, endure God's punishment with patience. Your enemies have persecuted you, but you will soon see them
destroyed and at your mercy. [26] My children, I spoiled you
with love, but you have had to follow rugged paths; you
were carried off like sheep caught in an enemy raid.

NEW REVISED STANDARD VERSION

20 I have taken off the robe of peace
and put on sackcloth for my supplication;
I will cry to the Everlasting all my days.

21 Take courage, my children, cry to God,
and he will deliver you from the power and hand of the enemy.
22 For I have put my hope in the Everlasting to save you,
and joy has come to me from the Holy One,
because of the mercy that will soon come to you
from your everlasting savior.[a]
23 For I sent you out with sorrow and weeping,
but God will give you back to me with joy and gladness forever.
24 For as the neighbors of Zion have now seen your capture,
so they soon will see your salvation by God,
which will come to you with great glory
and with the splendor of the Everlasting.
25 My children, endure with patience the wrath that has come upon you from God.
Your enemy has overtaken you,
but you will soon see their destruction
and will tread upon their necks.
26 My pampered children have traveled rough roads;
they were taken away like a flock carried off by the enemy.

[a] Or *from the Everlasting, your savior*

NEW AMERICAN BIBLE

[20] I have taken off the garment of peace,
have put on sackcloth for my prayer of supplication,
and while I live I will cry out to the Eternal God.

[21] "Fear not, my children; call upon God,
who will deliver you from oppression at enemy hands.
[22] I have trusted in the Eternal God for your welfare,
and joy has come to me from the Holy One
Because of the mercy that will swiftly reach you
from your eternal savior.
[23] With mourning and lament I sent you forth,
but God will give you back to me
with enduring gladness and joy.
[24] As Zion's neighbors lately saw you taken captive,
so shall they soon see God's salvation come to you,
with great glory and the splendor of the Eternal God.

[25] "My children, bear patiently the anger
that has come from God upon you;
Your enemies have persecuted you,
and you will soon see their destruction
and trample upon their necks.
[26] My pampered children have trodden rough roads,
carried off by their enemies like sheep in a raid.

NEW JERUSALEM BIBLE

[20] I have taken off the clothes of peace
and put on the sackcloth of entreaty;
all my life I shall cry to the Eternal.

[21] Take courage, my children, call on God:
he will deliver you from tyranny, from the clutches of your enemies;
[22] for I look to the Eternal for your rescue,
and joy has come to me from the Holy One
at the mercy soon to reach you
from your Saviour, the Eternal.
[23] In sorrow and tears I watched you go away,
but God will give you back to me in joy and gladness for ever.
[24] As the neighbours of Zion have now witnessed your captivity,
so will they soon see your rescue by God,
which will come upon you with great glory and splendour of the Eternal.
[25] My children, patiently bear the anger brought on you by God.
Your enemy has persecuted you,
but soon you will witness his destruction
and set your foot on his neck.
[26] My favourite children have travelled by rough roads,
carried off like a flock by a marauding enemy.

GREEK OLD TESTAMENT

27 θαρσήσατε, τέκνα, καὶ βοήσατε πρὸς τὸν θεόν, ἔσται γὰρ
ὑμῶν ὑπὸ τοῦ ἐπάγοντος μνεία. 28 ὥσπερ γὰρ ἐγένετο ἡ
διάνοια ὑμῶν εἰς τὸ πλανηθῆναι ἀπὸ τοῦ θεοῦ, δεκαπλασιά-
σατε ἐπιστραφέντες ζητῆσαι αὐτόν. 29 ὁ γὰρ ἐπαγαγὼν
ὑμῖν τὰ κακὰ ἐπάξει ὑμῖν τὴν αἰώνιον εὐφροσύνην μετὰ τῆς
σωτηρίας ὑμῶν.

30 Θάρσει, Ιερουσαλημ, παρακαλέσει σε ὁ ὀνομάσας σε.
31 δείλαιοι οἱ σὲ κακώσαντες καὶ ἐπιχαρέντες τῇ σῇ πτώσει,
32 δείλαιαι αἱ πόλεις αἷς ἐδούλευσαν τὰ τέκνα σου, δειλαία ἡ
δεξαμένη τοὺς υἱούς σου. 33 ὥσπερ γὰρ ἐχάρη ἐπὶ τῇ σῇ
πτώσει καὶ εὐφράνθη ἐπὶ τῷ πτώματί σου, οὕτως λυπηθήσε-
ται ἐπὶ τῇ ἑαυτῆς ἐρημίᾳ. 34 καὶ περιελῶ αὐτῆς τὸ ἀγαλλίαμα τῆς πολυοχλίας, καὶ τὸ ἀγαυρίαμα αὐτῆς ἔσται εἰς πένθος. 35 πῦρ γὰρ ἐπελεύσεται αὐτῇ παρὰ τοῦ αἰωνίου εἰς
ἡμέρας μακράς, καὶ κατοικηθήσεται ὑπὸ δαιμονίων τὸν
πλείονα χρόνον. — 36 περίβλεψαι πρὸς ἀνατολάς, Ιερουσαλημ, καὶ ἰδὲ τὴν εὐφροσύνην τὴν παρὰ τοῦ θεοῦ σοι ἐρχομένην. 37 ἰδοὺ ἔρχονται οἱ υἱοί σου, οὓς ἐξαπέστειλας,
ἔρχονται συνηγμένοι ἀπ᾽ ἀνατολῶν ἕως δυσμῶν τῷ ῥήματι

KING JAMES VERSION

27 Be of good comfort, O my children, and cry unto God: for ye shall be remembered of him that brought these things upon you.

28 For as it was your mind to go astray from God: so, being returned, seek him ten times more.

29 For he that hath brought these plagues upon you shall bring you everlasting joy again with your salvation.

30 Take a good heart, O Jerusalem: for he that gave thee that name will comfort thee.

31 Miserable are they that afflicted thee, and rejoiced at thy fall.

32 Miserable are the cities which thy children served: miserable is she that received thy sons.

33 For as she rejoiced at thy ruin, and was glad of thy fall: so shall she be grieved for her own desolation.

34 For I will take away the rejoicing of her great multitude, and her pride shall be turned into mourning.

35 For fire shall come upon her from the Everlasting, long to endure; and she shall be inhabited of devils for a great time.

36 O Jerusalem, look about thee toward the east, and behold the joy that cometh unto thee from God.

37 Lo, thy sons come, whom thou sentest away, they come gathered together from the east to the west by the word of the Holy One, rejoicing in the glory of God.

DOUAY OLD TESTAMENT

27 Be of good comfort, my children, and cry to the Lord: for you shall be remembered by him that hath led you away.

28 For as it was your mind to go astray from God; so when you return again you shall seek him ten times as much.

29 For he that hath brought evils upon you, shall bring you everlasting joy again with your salvation.

30 Be of good heart, O Jerusalem: for he exhorteth thee, that named thee.

31 The wicked that have afflicted thee, shall perish: and they that have rejoiced at thy ruin, shall be punished.

32 The cities which thy children have served, shall be punished: and she that received thy sons.

33 For as she rejoiced at thy ruin, and was glad of thy fall: so shall she be grieved for her own desolation.

34 And the joy of her multitude shall be cut off: and her gladness shall be turned to mourning.

35 For fire shall come upon her from the Eternal, long to endure, and she shall be inhabited by devils for a great time.

36 Look about thee, O Jerusalem, towards the east, and behold the joy that cometh to thee from God.

37 For behold thy children come, whom thou sentest away scattered, they come gathered together from the east even to the west, at the word of the Holy One rejoicing for the honour of God.

KNOX TRANSLATION

drove you. 27 Yet take courage, my children, and cry out
upon the Lord; he, the author of your exile, has not forgotten
you. 28 Hearts that loved to stray, ten times more eagerly
retrace your steps, and come back to him! 29 And he, that
compassed your woe, in unfading joy will compass your
deliverance.

30 Thyself, Jerusalem, take courage! He that called thee by
thy name brings thee comfort. 31 Woe to the men that
harassed thee, and triumphed in thy ruin, 32 woe to every
city that enslaved and harboured children of thine! 33 No
smile of content greeted the disaster of thy fall, but shall be
paid for with a sigh of desolation; 34 the city that was once
so populous, all its boasting gone, all its pride of yesterday
turned into lament! 35 Long shall the fires of eternal justice
smoulder there, long shall it be the haunt of devils.[a]

36 Turn thee about, Jerusalem, and look to the sun's rising;
see what rejoicing the Lord has in store for thee; 37 sons of
thine, in many lands lost to thee, gathered by his call from
east to west shall come back again, praising joyfully God's
holy will.

a The same Greek word is translated 'satyrs' in Is. 13. 21. Some think the reference is to wild goats.

TODAY'S ENGLISH VERSION

27 "Take courage, my children, and cry out to God for help.
He punished you, but he will not forget you. 28 Just as you
were once determined to turn away from God, now turn back
and serve him with ten times more determination. 29 The one
who brought these calamities upon you will rescue you and
bring you everlasting joy."

30 Take courage, Jerusalem. God, who gave you your name,
will now bring comfort to you. 31 Misery will come to those
who mistreated you and then rejoiced when you fell.
32 Misery will come to those cities that made your children
slaves. Misery will be the fate of Babylon, that city which
swallowed up your children. 33 Just as that city rejoiced
when you fell and took delight in your ruin, so now she will
mourn when she herself is deserted. 34 I will turn her proud
boastings into mourning and take away her large population
in which she took pride. 35 I, the Eternal God, will send
down fire on her, and it will burn for many days. Her ruins
will be haunted by demons for a long time to come.

36 Look to the east, Jerusalem, and see the joy that God is
bringing to you. 37 Look, your children are coming home, the
children that were taken from you. They have been gathered
together from the east and from the west by the command of
God, the Holy One. And now they are coming home, rejoicing
in the glory of God.

NEW REVISED STANDARD VERSION

27 Take courage, my children, and cry to God,
for you will be remembered by the one who brought this upon you.
28 For just as you were disposed to go astray from God,
return with tenfold zeal to seek him.
29 For the one who brought these calamities upon you
will bring you everlasting joy with your salvation.

30 Take courage, O Jerusalem,
for the one who named you will comfort you.
31 Wretched will be those who mistreated you
and who rejoiced at your fall.
32 Wretched will be the cities that your children served as slaves;
wretched will be the city that received your offspring.
33 For just as she rejoiced at your fall
and was glad for your ruin,
so she will be grieved at her own desolation.
34 I will take away her pride in her great population,
and her insolence will be turned to grief.
35 For fire will come upon her from the Everlasting for many days,
and for a long time she will be inhabited by demons.

36 Look toward the east, O Jerusalem,
and see the joy that is coming to you from God.
37 Look, your children are coming, whom you sent away;
they are coming, gathered from east and west,
at the word of the Holy One,
rejoicing in the glory of God.

NEW AMERICAN BIBLE

27 Fear not, my children; call out to God!
He who brought this upon you will remember you.
28 As your hearts have been disposed to stray from God,
turn now ten times the more to seek him;
29 For he who has brought disaster upon you
will, in saving you, bring you back enduring joy."
30 Fear not, Jerusalem!
He who gave you your name is your encouragement.
31 Fearful are those who harmed you,
who rejoiced at your downfall;
32 Fearful are the cities where your children were enslaved,
fearful the city that took your sons.
33 As that city rejoiced at your collapse,
and made merry at your downfall,
so shall she grieve over her own desolation.
34 I will take from her the joyous throngs,
and her exultation shall be turned to mourning:
35 For fire shall come upon her
from the Eternal God, for a long time,
and demons shall dwell in her from that time on.

36 Look to the east, Jerusalem!
behold the joy that comes to you from God.
37 Here come your sons whom you once let go,
gathered in from the east and from the west
By the word of the Holy One,
rejoicing in the glory of God.

NEW JERUSALEM BIBLE

27 Take courage, my children, call on God:
he who brought this on you will remember you.
28 As by your will you first strayed from God,
so now turn back and search for him ten times harder;
29 for as he has been bringing down those disasters on you,
so will he rescue you and give you eternal joy.
30 Take courage, Jerusalem:
he who gave you your name will console you.
31 Disaster will come to all who have ill-treated you
and gloated over your fall.
32 Disaster will come to the cities where your children were slaves;
disaster to whichever one received your children,
33 for just as she rejoiced at your fall
and was happy to see you ruined,
so will she grieve over her own desolation.
34 I shall deprive her of the joy of a populous city,
and her insolence will turn to mourning;
35 fire from the Eternal will befall her for many a day,
and demons will dwell in her for ages.
36 Jerusalem, turn your eyes to the east,
see the joy that is coming to you from God.
37 Look, the children you watched go away are on their way home;
reassembled from east and west, they are on their way home
at the Holy One's command, rejoicing in God's glory.

GREEK OLD TESTAMENT

5 τοῦ ἁγίου χαίροντες τῇ τοῦ θεοῦ δόξῃ. — 1 ἔκδυσαι,
Ιερουσαλημ, τὴν στολὴν τοῦ πένθους καὶ τῆς κακώσεώς
σου καὶ ἔνδυσαι τὴν εὐπρέπειαν τῆς παρὰ τοῦ θεοῦ δόξης
εἰς τὸν αἰῶνα. 2 περιβαλοῦ τὴν διπλοΐδα τῆς παρὰ τοῦ θεοῦ
δικαιοσύνης, ἐπίθου τὴν μίτραν ἐπὶ τὴν κεφαλήν σου τῆς
δόξης τοῦ αἰωνίου. 3 ὁ γὰρ θεὸς δείξει τῇ ὑπ᾿ οὐρανὸν πάσῃ
τὴν σὴν λαμπρότητα. 4 κληθήσεται γάρ σου τὸ ὄνομα παρὰ
τοῦ θεοῦ εἰς τὸν αἰῶνα Εἰρήνη δικαιοσύνης καὶ δόξα θεοσε-
βείας. — 5 ἀνάστηθι, Ιερουσαλημ, καὶ στῆθι ἐπὶ τοῦ ὑψηλοῦ
καὶ περίβλεψαι πρὸς ἀνατολὰς καὶ ἰδέ σου συνηγμένα τὰ
τέκνα ἀπὸ ἡλίου δυσμῶν ἕως ἀνατολῶν τῷ ῥήματι τοῦ ἁγίου
χαίροντας τῇ τοῦ θεοῦ μνείᾳ. 6 ἐξῆλθον γὰρ παρὰ σοῦ πεζοὶ
ἀγόμενοι ὑπὸ ἐχθρῶν, εἰσάγει δὲ αὐτοὺς ὁ θεὸς πρὸς σὲ
αἰρομένους μετὰ δόξης ὡς θρόνον βασιλείας. 7 συνέταξεν
γὰρ ὁ θεὸς ταπεινοῦσθαι πᾶν ὄρος ὑψηλὸν καὶ θῖνας ἀενάους
καὶ φάραγγας πληροῦσθαι εἰς ὁμαλισμὸν τῆς γῆς, ἵνα βαδί-
σῃ Ισραηλ ἀσφαλῶς τῇ τοῦ θεοῦ δόξῃ· 8 ἐσκίασαν δὲ καὶ οἱ
δρυμοὶ καὶ πᾶν ξύλον εὐωδίας τῷ Ισραηλ προστάγματι τοῦ
θεοῦ· 9 ἡγήσεται γὰρ ὁ θεὸς Ισραηλ μετ᾿ εὐφροσύνης τῷ
φωτὶ τῆς δόξης αὐτοῦ σὺν ἐλεημοσύνῃ καὶ δικαιοσύνῃ τῇ
παρ᾿ αὐτοῦ.

KING JAMES VERSION

5 Put off, O Jerusalem, the garment of thy mourning and affliction, and put on the comeliness of the glory that cometh from God for ever.

2 Cast about thee a double garment of the righteousness which cometh from God; and set a diadem on thine head of the glory of the Everlasting.

3 For God will shew thy brightness unto every country under heaven.

4 For thy name shall be called of God for ever The peace of righteousness, and The glory of God's worship.

5 Arise, O Jerusalem, and stand on high, and look about toward the east, and behold thy children gathered from the west unto the east by the word of the Holy One, rejoicing in the remembrance of God.

6 For they departed from thee on foot, and were led away of their enemies: but God bringeth them unto thee exalted with glory, as children of the kingdom.

7 For God hath appointed that every high hill, and banks of long continuance, should be cast down, and valleys filled up, to make even the ground, that Israel may go safely in the glory of God.

8 Moreover even the woods and every sweetsmelling tree shall overshadow Israel by the commandment of God.

9 For God shall lead Israel with joy in the light of his glory with the mercy and righteousness that cometh from him.

DOUAY OLD TESTAMENT

5 PUT off, O Jerusalem, the garment of thy mourning, and affliction: and put on the beauty, and honour of that everlasting glory which thou hast from God.

2 God will clothe thee with the double garment of justice, and will set a crown on thy head of everlasting honour.

3 For God will shew his brightness in thee, to every one under heaven.

4 For thy name shall be named to thee by God for ever: the peace of justice, and honour of piety.

5 Arise, O Jerusalem, and stand on high: and look about towards the east, and behold thy children gathered together from the rising to the setting sun, by the word of the Holy One rejoicing in the remembrance of God.

6 For they went out from thee on foot, led by the enemies: but the Lord will bring them to thee exalted with honour as children of the kingdom.

7 For God hath appointed to bring down every high mountain, and the everlasting rocks, and to fill up the valleys to make them even with the ground: that Israel may walk diligently to the honour of God.

8 Moreover the woods, and every sweet-smelling tree have overshadowed Israel by the commandment of God.

9 For God will bring Israel with joy in the light of his majesty, with mercy, and justice, that cometh from him.

KNOX TRANSLATION

5 Enough, Jerusalem; lay aside now the sad garb of thy
humiliation, and put on bright robes, befitting the eternal glory God means for thee; 2 cloak of divine protection[a]
thrown about thee, thy temples bearing a diadem of renown.
3 In thee God will manifest the splendour of his presence, for
the whole world to see; 4 and the name by which he will call
thee for ever is, Loyalty rewarded, Piety crowned.[b] 5 Up,
Jerusalem, to the heights! Look to the sun's rising, and see if
thy sons be not coming to thee, gathered from east to west,
joyfully acknowledging God's holy will! 6 Afoot they were led
off by the enemy; it is the Lord that shall lead them home,
borne aloft like royal princes. 7 He will have the ground
made level; high mountain must stoop, and immemorial hill,
and the valleys be filled up, for Israel's safe passage and
God's glory; 8 spinneys of every scented tree shall grow, by
his divine command, to give Israel shade. 9 So merciful he is,
and so faithful! In great content, their journey lit by the
majesty of his presence, Israel shall come home.

a 'Divine protection'; literally 'justice', that is, a renewal of the covenant between Israel and their God, with the obligations of it fulfilled on either side. *b* Literally, 'Prosperity (which comes) of justice (see last note), and Honour (which comes) of Piety'.

TODAY'S ENGLISH VERSION

5 Jerusalem, take off the clothes you have worn in your
mourning and distress, and put on the eternal splendor
of God's glory. 2 Put around you the cloak of God's righteousness. Place on your head the crown of the glory of the
Eternal God. 3 God will show your splendor to every nation
on earth. 4 Forever he will say to you: "Your security comes
from your righteousness, and your splendor from your devotion to me."[a]
5 Get up, Jerusalem, stand on the mountaintop; see where
God, the Holy One, is bringing your children together from
the east and from the west. They are rejoicing that God has
remembered them. 6 Jerusalem, your children were led away
by their enemies; they left you on foot, but God is bringing
them back to you, carried in royal splendor. 7 God has commanded that every high mountain and the everlasting hills
shall be made low; he has commanded that the valleys shall
be filled and the ground leveled, so that the people of Israel
may come safely home in the glory of God. 8 At the command of God, forests of fragrant trees will spring up to provide shade for the people of Israel. 9 God will lead Israel
home. They will return with great joy, guided by his mercy
and righteousness, surrounded by the light of his glorious
presence.

[a] Forever . . . devotion to me; *or* He will give you this name forever: "Peace from Righteousness and Glory from Godliness."

NEW REVISED STANDARD VERSION

5 Take off the garment of your sorrow and affliction,
O Jerusalem,
and put on forever the beauty of the glory from God.
2 Put on the robe of the righteousness that comes from God;
put on your head the diadem of the glory of the
Everlasting;
3 for God will show your splendor everywhere under
heaven.
4 For God will give you evermore the name,
"Righteous Peace, Godly Glory."

5 Arise, O Jerusalem, stand upon the height;
look toward the east,
and see your children gathered from west and east
at the word of the Holy One,
rejoicing that God has remembered them.
6 For they went out from you on foot,
led away by their enemies;
but God will bring them back to you,
carried in glory, as on a royal throne.
7 For God has ordered that every high mountain and the
everlasting hills be made low
and the valleys filled up, to make level ground,
so that Israel may walk safely in the glory of God.
8 The woods and every fragrant tree
have shaded Israel at God's command.
9 For God will lead Israel with joy,
in the light of his glory,
with the mercy and righteousness that come from
him.

NEW AMERICAN BIBLE

5 Jerusalem, take off your robe of mourning and misery;
put on the splendor of glory from God forever:
2 Wrapped in the cloak of justice from God,
bear on your head the mitre
that displays the glory of the eternal name.
3 For God will show all the earth your splendor:
4 you will be named by God forever
the peace of justice, the glory of God's worship.

5 Up, Jerusalem! stand upon the heights;
look to the east and see your children
Gathered from the east and the west
at the word of the Holy One,
rejoicing that they are remembered by God.
6 Led away on foot by their enemies they left you:
but God will bring them back to you
borne aloft in glory as on royal thrones.
7 For God has commanded
that every lofty mountain be made low,
And that the age-old depths and gorges
be filled to level ground,
that Israel may advance secure in the glory of God.
8 The forests and every fragrant kind of tree
have overshadowed Israel at God's command;
9 For God is leading Israel in joy
by the light of his glory,
with his mercy and justice for company.

NEW JERUSALEM BIBLE

5 Jerusalem, take off your dress of sorrow and distress,
put on the beauty of God's glory for evermore,
2 wrap the cloak of God's saving justice around you,
put the diadem of the Eternal One's glory on your head,
3 for God means to show your splendour to every nation
under heaven,
4 and the name God gives you for evermore will be,
'Peace-through-Justice, and Glory-through-Devotion'.
5 Arise, Jerusalem, stand on the heights
and turn your eyes to the east:
see your children reassembled from west and east
at the Holy One's command, rejoicing because God has
remembered.
6 Though they left you on foot
driven by enemies,
now God brings them back to you,
carried gloriously, like a royal throne.
7 For God has decreed the flattening
of each high mountain, of the everlasting hills,
the filling of the valleys to make the ground level
so that Israel can walk safely in God's glory.
8 And the forests and every fragrant tree will provide
shade
for Israel, at God's command;
9 for God will guide Israel in joy by the light of his glory,
with the mercy and saving justice which come from
him.

GREEK OLD TESTAMENT

ΕΠΙΣΤΟΛΗ ΙΕΡΕΜΙΟΥ

'Αντίγραφον ἐπιστολῆς, ἧς ἀπέστειλεν Ιερεμιας
πρὸς τοὺς ἀχθησομένους αἰχμαλώτους εἰς Βαβυλῶνα
ὑπὸ τοῦ βασιλέως τῶν Βαβυλωνίων ἀναγγεῖλαι αὐτοῖς
καθότι ἐπετάγη αὐτῷ ὑπὸ τοῦ θεοῦ.

[1] Διὰ τὰς ἁμαρτίας, ἃς ἡμαρτήκατε ἐναντίον τοῦ θεοῦ,
ἀχθήσεσθε εἰς Βαβυλῶνα αἰχμάλωτοι ὑπὸ Ναβουχοδονοσορ
βασιλέως τῶν Βαβυλωνίων. [2] εἰσελθόντες οὖν εἰς Βαβυλῶνα
ἔσεσθε ἐκεῖ ἔτη πλείονα καὶ χρόνον μακρὸν ἕως γενεῶν
ἑπτά, μετὰ τοῦτο δὲ ἐξάξω ὑμᾶς ἐκεῖθεν μετ' εἰρήνης.
[3] νυνὶ δὲ ὄψεσθε ἐν Βαβυλῶνι θεοὺς ἀργυροῦς καὶ χρυσοῦς
καὶ ξυλίνους ἐπ' ὤμοις αἰρομένους δεικνύντας φόβον τοῖς
ἔθνεσιν. [4] εὐλαβήθητε οὖν μὴ καὶ ὑμεῖς ἀφομοιωθέντες τοῖς
ἀλλοφύλοις ἀφομοιωθῆτε καὶ φόβος ὑμᾶς λάβη ἐπ' αὐτοῖς
[5] ἰδόντας ὄχλον ἔμπροσθεν καὶ ὄπισθεν αὐτῶν προσκυνοῦν-
τας αὐτά, εἴπατε δὲ τῇ διανοίᾳ Σοὶ δεῖ προσκυνεῖν, δέσποτα. [6] ὁ γὰρ ἄγγελός μου μεθ' ὑμῶν ἐστιν, αὐτός τε ἐκζητῶν
τὰς ψυχὰς ὑμῶν.

KING JAMES VERSION

The Letter of Jeremiah is included as Baruch ch 6 in the King James Version.

THE EPISTLE OF JEREMY

A copy of an epistle, which Jeremy sent unto them which were to be led captives into Babylon by the king of the Babylonians, to certify them, as it was commanded him of God.

Because of the sins which ye have committed before God, ye shall be led away captives into Babylon by Nabuchodonosor king of the Babylonians.

3 So when ye be come unto Babylon, ye shall remain there many years, and for a long season, namely, seven generations: and after that I will bring you away peaceably from thence.

4 Now shall ye see in Babylon gods of silver, and of gold, and of wood, borne upon shoulders, which cause the nations to fear.

5 Beware therefore that ye in no wise be like to strangers, neither be ye afraid of them, when ye see the multitude before them and behind them, worshipping them.

6 But say ye in your hearts, O Lord, we must worship thee.

7 For mine angel is with you, and I myself caring for your souls.

DOUAY OLD TESTAMENT

The Letter of Jeremiah is included as Baruch ch 6 in the Douay translation.

BARUCH 6

A COPY of the epistle that Jeremias sent to them that were to be led away captives into Babylon, by the king of Babylon, to declare to them according to what was commanded him by God.

1 FOR the sins that you have committed before God, you shall be carried away captives into Babylon by Nabuchodonosor the king of Babylon.

2 And when you are come into Babylon, you shall be there many years, and for a long time, even to seven generations: and after that I will bring you away from thence with peace.

3 But now, you shall see in Babylon gods of gold, and of silver, and of stone, and of wood borne upon shoulders, causing fear to the Gentiles.

4 Beware therefore that you imitate not the doings of others, and be afraid, and the fear of them should seize upon you.

5 But when you see the multitude behind, and before, adoring them, say you in your hearts: Thou oughtest to be adored, O Lord.

6 For my angel is with you: And I myself will demand an account of your souls.

KNOX TRANSLATION

The Letter of Jeremiah is included as Baruch ch 6 in the Knox translation.

BARUCH 6

[1] Here follows a copy of the letter Jeremias sent to the prisoners whom the king of Babylon was carrying off to his own country, with the warnings God bade him give them.

In atonement for the sins by which you have offended
God, you shall now be carried off to Babylon, by Nabuchodonosor that is king of it. [2] Babylon once reached, you shall
have a long exile there, years a many, till seven generations[a]
have passed; then I will grant you a safe return. [3] And you
must know that you will see, in that country, gods of gold
and silver, gods of stone and wood, that are carried about on
men's shoulders; to the heathen, things of great dread.
[4] Look well to it that you do not fall in with these alien customs, by the same fear overmastered. [5] What though a great
throng of worshippers attends them, before and behind? Let
your hearts whisper in adoration, To thee, Lord, all worship
belongs! [6] My angel is at your side, and your lives shall be
held to account for it.[b]

a It is not easy to see how this computation is arrived at. Notoriously the exile of Juda was expected to last seventy years. If, therefore, our versions correctly represent the figures given in the original, and the word 'generation' has its ordinary meaning, it would appear that the beginning of the exile is dated here, not by the capture of Jerusalem in B.C. 587, but by the destruction of Samaria in B.C. 722. This would give, roughly, seven generations of thirty years each down to Zorobabel, or seven generations of forty years each down to Nehemias. *b* Literally, 'I will require your lives'. Some think this means, 'I will require (or perhaps, according to the Greek, he will require) satisfaction from anyone who takes your lives'.

TODAY'S ENGLISH VERSION

THE LETTER OF JEREMIAH

1 This is a copy of the letter sent by Jeremiah to the people
of Jerusalem just before they were captured by the
Babylonian king and taken to Babylon. It contains the message that God had commanded Jeremiah to give them.
2 You have sinned against God. That is why you are about
to be taken away as prisoners to Babylon by King Nebuchadnezzar. 3 You will remain there in exile for many years, as
long as seven generations; then God will lead you peacefully
home from Babylon.
4 There in Babylon you will see gods made of wood, silver,
and gold—gods which people carry on their shoulders and
which fill the heathen with fear. 5 You must be careful never
to imitate those Gentiles. Don't let their gods fill you with
fear when you see them being carried in procession and
being worshiped. 6 Instead, say to yourselves, "It is you
alone, Lord, that we must worship." 7 God's angel will be
there with you; he will take care of you.

NEW REVISED STANDARD VERSION

THE LETTER OF JEREMIAH

6 [a] A copy of a letter that Jeremiah sent to those who were
to be taken to Babylon as exiles by the king of the
Babylonians, to give them the message that God had commanded him.
2 Because of the sins that you have committed before
God, you will be taken to Babylon as exiles by Nebuchadnezzar, king of the Babylonians. 3 Therefore when you have
come to Babylon you will remain there for many years, for a
long time, up to seven generations; after that I will bring you
away from there in peace. 4 Now in Babylon you will see
gods made of silver and gold and wood, which people carry
on their shoulders, and which cause the heathen to fear. 5 So
beware of becoming at all like the foreigners or of letting fear
for these gods[b] possess you 6 when you see the multitude
before and behind them worshiping them. But say in your
heart, "It is you, O Lord, whom we must worship." 7 For my
angel is with you, and he is watching over your lives.

a The King James Version (like the Latin Vulgate) prints The Letter of Jeremiah as Chapter 6 of the Book of Baruch, and the chapter and verse numbers are here retained. In the Greek Septuagint, the Letter is separated from Baruch by the Book of Lamentations. *b* Gk *for them*

NEW AMERICAN BIBLE

The Letter of Jeremiah is included as Baruch ch 6 in the New American Bible translation.

BARUCH 6

6 A copy of the letter which Jeremiah sent to those who
were being led captive to Babylon by the king of the
Babylonians, to convey to them what God had commanded
him:
For the sins you committed before God, you are being led
captive to Babylon by Nebuchadnezzar, king of the
Babylonians. 2 When you reach Babylon you will be there
many years, a period seven generations long; after which I
will bring you back from there in peace. 3 And now in
Babylon you will see borne upon men's shoulders gods of silver and gold and wood, which cast fear upon the pagans.
4 Take care that you yourselves do not imitate their alien
example and stand in fear of them, 5 when you see the
crowd before them and behind worshiping them. Rather, say
in your hearts, "You, O LORD, are to be worshiped!"; 6 for my
angel is with you, and he is the custodian of your lives.

NEW JERUSALEM BIBLE

The Letter of Jeremiah is included as Baruch ch 6 in the New Jerusalem Bible translation.

BARUCH 6

A copy of the letter which Jeremiah sent to those about to be led captive to Babylon by the king of the Babylonians, to tell them what he had been commanded by God:

6 'Because of the sins which you have committed before
God you are to be deported to Babylon by Nebuchadnezzar king of the Babylonians. 2 Once you have reached
Babylon you will stay there for many years, as long as seven
generations; after which I shall bring you home in peace.
3 Now in Babylon you will see gods made of silver, of gold, of
wood, being carried shoulder-high, and filling the gentiles
with fear. 4 Be on your guard! Do not imitate the foreigners,
do not have any fear of their gods 5 as you see their worshippers prostrating themselves before and behind them. Instead,
say in your hearts, "Master, it is you that we must worship."
6 For my angel is with you; your lives will be in his care.

GREEK OLD TESTAMENT

7 Γλῶσσα γὰρ αὐτῶν ἐστιν κατεξυσμένη ὑπὸ τέκτονος,
αὐτά τε περίχρυσα καὶ περιάργυρα, ψευδῆ δ' ἐστὶν καὶ οὐ
δύνανται λαλεῖν. 8 καὶ ὥσπερ παρθένῳ φιλοκόσμῳ λαμβάν-
οντες χρυσίον κατασκευάζουσιν στεφάνους ἐπὶ τὰς κεφαλὰς
τῶν θεῶν αὐτῶν· 9 ἔστι δὲ καὶ ὅτε ὑφαιρούμενοι οἱ ἱερεῖς ἀπὸ
τῶν θεῶν αὐτῶν χρυσίον καὶ ἀργύριον εἰς ἑαυτοὺς καταναλώ-
σουσιν, δώσουσιν δὲ ἀπ' αὐτῶν καὶ ταῖς ἐπὶ τοῦ τέγους πόρναις. 10 κοσμοῦσί τε αὐτοὺς ὡς ἀνθρώπους τοῖς ἐνδύμασιν,
θεοὺς ἀργυροῦς καὶ χρυσοῦς καὶ ξυλίνους. οὗτοι δὲ οὐ δια-
σῴζονται ἀπὸ ἰοῦ καὶ βρωμάτων. 11 περιβεβλημένων αὐτῶν
ἱματισμὸν πορφυροῦν, ἐκμάσσονται τὸ πρόσωπον αὐτῶν διὰ
τὸν ἐκ τῆς οἰκίας κονιορτόν, ὅς ἐστιν πλείων ἐπ' αὐτοῖς.
12 καὶ σκῆπτρον ἔχει ὡς ἄνθρωπος κριτὴς χώρας, ὃς τὸν εἰς
αὐτὸν ἁμαρτάνοντα οὐκ ἀνελεῖ. 13 ἔχει δὲ ἐγχειρίδιον ἐν
δεξιᾷ καὶ πέλεκυν, ἑαυτὸν δὲ ἐκ πολέμου καὶ λῃστῶν οὐκ ἐξελεῖται. 14 ὅθεν γνώριμοί εἰσιν οὐκ ὄντες θεοί· μὴ οὖν φοβηθῆτε αὐτούς.

15 Ὥσπερ γὰρ σκεῦος ἀνθρώπου συντριβὲν ἀχρεῖον γίνεται, τοιοῦτοι ὑπάρχουσιν οἱ θεοὶ αὐτῶν, καθιδρυμένων αὐτῶν
ἐν τοῖς οἴκοις. 16 οἱ ὀφθαλμοὶ αὐτῶν πλήρεις εἰσὶν κονιορ-
τοῦ ἀπὸ τῶν ποδῶν τῶν εἰσπορευομένων. 17 καὶ ὥσπερ τινὶ
ἠδικηκότι βασιλέα περιπεφραγμέναι εἰσὶν αἱ αὐλαὶ ὡς ἐπὶ
θανάτῳ ἀπηγμένῳ, τοὺς οἴκους αὐτῶν ὀχυροῦσιν οἱ ἱερεῖς
θυρώμασίν τε καὶ κλείθροις καὶ μοχλοῖς, ὅπως ὑπὸ τῶν
λῃστῶν μὴ συλησῶσι. 18 λύχνους καίουσιν καὶ πλείους ἢ

KING JAMES VERSION

8 As for their tongue, it is polished by the workman, and they themselves are gilded and laid over with silver; yet are they but false, and cannot speak.

9 And taking gold, as it were for a virgin that loveth to go gay, they make crowns for the heads of their gods.

10 Sometimes also the priests convey from their gods gold and silver, and bestow it upon themselves.

11 Yea, they will give thereof to the common harlots, and deck them as men with garments, [being] gods of silver, and gods of gold, and wood.

12 Yet cannot these gods save themselves from rust and moths, though they be covered with purple raiment.

13 They wipe their faces because of the dust of the temple, when there is much upon them.

14 And he that cannot put to death one that offendeth him holdeth a sceptre, as though he were a judge of the country.

15 He hath also in his right hand a dagger and an ax: but cannot deliver himself from war and thieves.

16 Whereby they are known not to be gods: therefore fear them not.

17 For like as a vessel that a man useth is nothing worth when it is broken; even so it is with their gods: when they be set up in the temple, their eyes be full of dust through the feet of them that come in.

18 And as the doors are made sure on every side upon him that offendeth the king, as being committed to suffer death: even so the priests make fast their temples with doors, with locks, and bars, lest *their gods* be spoiled with robbers.

DOUAY OLD TESTAMENT

7 For their tongue that is polished by the craftsman, and themselves laid over with gold and silver, are false things, and they cannot speak.

8 And as if it were for a maiden that loveth to go gay: so do they take gold and make them up.

9 Their gods have golden crowns upon their heads: whereof the priests secretly convey away from them gold, and silver, and bestow it on themselves.

10 Yea and they give thereof to prostitutes, and they dress out harlots: and again when they receive it of the harlots, they adorn their gods.

11 And these gods cannot defend themselves from the rust, and the moth.

12 But when they have covered them with a purple garment, they wipe their face because of the dust of the house, which is very much among them.

13 This holdeth a sceptre as a man, as a judge of the country, but cannot put to death one that offendeth him.

14 And this hath in his hand a sword, or an axe, but cannot save himself from war, or from robbers, whereby be it known to you, that they are not gods.

15 Therefore fear them not. For as a vessel that a man uses when it is broken becometh useless, even so are their gods:

16 When they are placed in the house, their eyes are full of dust by the feet of them that go in.

17 And as the gates are made sure on every side upon one that hath offended the king, or like a dead man carried to the grave, so do the priests secure the doors with bars and locks, lest they be stripped by thieves.

KNOX TRANSLATION

7 Puppets of gold and silver, speak they cannot, for all the
craftsman has given them tongues to speak with. 8 Ay, gold
must go to their fashioning, never was maid so bravely
tricked out; 9 gods they are, and must wear golden crowns.
And of this gold and silver the priests will steal some part for
their own uses, 10 and spend it on their minions; what the
gods wore, harlots wear, what harlots wore, the gods.[a]
11 From rust they cannot protect themselves, nor from the
moth; 12 alas for the purple robes that deck them! And the
temple dust lies thick upon them, so that their faces must be
wiped clean. 13 Here is an idol bearing a sceptre, human-
fashion, as though it ruled the country-side, yet has it no
power to kill the blasphemer; 14 another carries sword or
axe, yet from alarm of war or of robbers cannot defend itself;
be sure, then, gods they are not. 15 Never fear them; broken
jar a man throws away as useless can be matched with such
gods as these.

16 There they sit in their temples, with eyes full of dust
from the feet of passers-by, 17 mewed up by their priests
with bolt and bar for fear of robbery, like king's enemy in his
dungeon, dead man in his tomb; 18 of all the lights that burn

a Literally, 'They give some of it to prostitutes, and deck out harlots, and again when they have received it from harlots, they deck out their gods'. The Greek has 'They give some of it to the harlots on the roof; and they deck out the gods in clothes, like men, gods of silver and gold and wood'. Such a variation between the two versions must indicate that the Hebrew original was very obscure, or that its text had suffered from corruptions. And indeed, throughout this chapter it is impossible to feel that the versions have always caught the meaning of the original exactly.

TODAY'S ENGLISH VERSION

8 Their idols are plated with silver and gold and have
tongues that were carved by woodworkers. But they are not
real gods, and they cannot speak. 9 The people make gold
crowns and put them on the heads of their gods, as if these
idols were girls who love jewelry. 10 Sometimes the priests
steal the silver and gold from their gods and spend it on
themselves; 11 they even give some of it to the temple prostitutes. People take these gods of wood, silver, and gold, and
put clothes on them, as if they were human. 12 But even
though the gods are dressed in purple robes like kings, they
still cannot keep themselves from being tarnished or protect
themselves from termites. 13 When dust from the temple settles on their faces, someone has to wipe it off for them.
14 Like human judges they hold scepters in their hands, but
they have no power to punish anyone who wrongs them.
15 Sometimes they have daggers and axes in their hands, but
they cannot protect themselves from being destroyed in war
or from being carried off by thieves. 16 All of this proves that
they are not gods—do not worship them.
17 Those gods sitting in their temples are as useless as a
broken bowl. Their eyes are filled with the dust that people
kick up when they come in. 18 The priests fortify the temples
with doors and bars and bolts, so that thieves cannot break
in. The gods are locked up as securely as a prisoner about to
be executed for a crime against the king. 19 The priests light

NEW REVISED STANDARD VERSION

8 Their tongues are smoothed by the carpenter, and they
themselves are overlaid with gold and silver; but they are
false and cannot speak. 9 People[a] take gold and make
crowns for the heads of their gods, as they might for a girl
who loves ornaments. 10 Sometimes the priests secretly take
gold and silver from their gods and spend it on themselves,
11 or even give some of it to the prostitutes on the terrace.
They deck their gods[b] out with garments like human
beings—these gods of silver and gold and wood 12 that cannot save themselves from rust and corrosion. When they
have been dressed in purple robes, 13 their faces are wiped
because of the dust from the temple, which is thick upon
them. 14 One of them holds a scepter, like a district judge,
but is unable to destroy anyone who offends it. 15 Another
has a dagger in its right hand, and an ax, but cannot defend
itself from war and robbers. 16 From this it is evident that
they are not gods; so do not fear them.
17 For just as someone's dish is useless when it is broken,
18 so are their gods when they have been set up in the temples. Their eyes are full of the dust raised by the feet of those
who enter. And just as the gates are shut on every side
against anyone who has offended a king, as though under
sentence of death, so the priests make their temples secure
with doors and locks and bars, in order that they may not be
plundered by robbers. 19 They light more lamps for them

a Gk *They* *b* Gk *them*

NEW AMERICAN BIBLE

7 Their tongues are smoothed by woodworkers; they are
covered with gold and silver—but they are a fraud, and cannot speak. 8 People bring gold, as to a maiden in love with
ornament, 9 and furnish crowns for the heads of their gods.
Then sometimes the priests take the silver and gold from
their gods and spend it on themselves, 10 or give part of it to
the harlots on the terrace. They trick them out in garments
like men, these gods of silver and gold and wood; 11 but
though they are wrapped in purple clothing, they are not
safe from corrosion or insects. 12 They wipe their faces clean
of the house dust which is thick upon them. 13 Each has a
scepter, like the human ruler of a district; but none does
away with those that offend against it. 14 Each has in its
right hand an axe or dagger, but it cannot save itself from
war or pillage. Thus it is known they are not gods; do not
fear them.
15 As useless as one's broken tools 16 are their gods, set up
in their houses; their eyes are full of dust from the feet of
those who enter. 17 Their courtyards are walled in like those
of a man brought to execution for a crime against the king;
the priests reinforce their houses with gates and bars and
bolts, lest they be carried off by robbers. 18 They light more

NEW JERUSALEM BIBLE

7 'Overlaid with gold and silver, their tongues polished
smooth by a craftsman, they are counterfeit and have no
power to speak. 8 As though for a girl fond of finery, these
people take gold and make crowns for the heads of their
gods. 9 And sometimes, the priests filch gold and silver from
their gods to spend on themselves, even giving some of it to
the prostitutes on the terrace. 10 They dress up these gods of
silver, gold and wood, in clothes, like human beings; on their
own they cannot protect themselves from either tarnish or
woodworm; 11 when they have been dressed in purple
cloaks, their faces have to be dusted, because of the temple
dust which settles thick on them. 12 One holds a sceptre like
the governor of a province, yet is powerless to put to death
anyone who offends him; 13 another holds sword and mace
in his right hand, yet is powerless to defend himself against
war or thieves. 14 From this it is evident that they are not
gods; do not be afraid of them.
15 'Just as a pot in common use becomes useless once it is
broken, so are these gods enshrined inside their temples.
16 Their eyes are full of dust raised by the feet of those who
enter. 17 Just as the doors are locked on all sides on someone
who has offended a king and is under sentence of death, so
the priests secure the temples of these gods with gates and
bolts and bars for fear of burglary. 18 They light more lamps

GREEK OLD TESTAMENT

ἑαυτοῖς, ὧν οὐδένα δύνανται ἰδεῖν. 19 ἔστιν μὲν ὥσπερ
δοκὸς τῶν ἐκ τῆς οἰκίας, τὰς δὲ καρδίας αὐτῶν φασιν ἐκ-
λείχεσθαι, τῶν ἀπὸ τῆς γῆς ἑρπετῶν κατεσθόντων αὐτούς τε
καὶ τὸν ἱματισμὸν αὐτῶν οὐκ αἰσθάνονται. 20 μεμελανω-
μένοι τὸ πρόσωπον αὐτῶν ἀπὸ τοῦ καπνοῦ τοῦ ἐκ τῆς οἰκίας.
21 ἐπὶ τὸ σῶμα αὐτῶν καὶ ἐπὶ τὴν κεφαλὴν ἐφίπτανται
νυκτερίδες, χελιδόνες καὶ τὰ ὄρνεα, ὡσαύτως δὲ καὶ οἱ
αἴλουροι. 22 ὅθεν γνώσεσθε ὅτι οὔκ εἰσιν θεοί· μὴ οὖν
φοβεῖσθε αὐτά.
23 Τὸ γὰρ χρυσίον, ὃ περίκεινται εἰς κάλλος, ἐὰν μή τις
ἐκμάξῃ τὸν ἰόν, οὐ μὴ στίλψωσιν· οὐδὲ γάρ, ὅτε ἐχωνεύον-
το, ᾐσθάνοντο. 24 ἐκ πάσης τιμῆς ἠγορασμένα ἐστίν, ἐν οἷς
οὐκ ἔστιν πνεῦμα. 25 ἄνευ ποδῶν ἐπ' ὤμοις φέρονται
ἐνδεικνύμενοι τὴν ἑαυτῶν ἀτιμίαν τοῖς ἀνθρώποις, αἰσχύ-
νονταί τε καὶ οἱ θεραπεύοντες αὐτὰ διὰ τό, μήποτε ἐπὶ τὴν
γῆν πέσῃ, δι' αὐτῶν ἀνίστασθαι· 26 μήτε ἐάν τις αὐτὸ
ὀρθὸν στήσῃ, δι' ἑαυτοῦ κινηθήσεται, μήτε ἐὰν κλιθῇ, οὐ μὴ
ὀρθωθῇ, ἀλλ' ὥσπερ νεκροῖς τὰ δῶρα αὐτοῖς παρατίθεται.
27 τὰς δὲ θυσίας αὐτῶν ἀποδόμενοι οἱ ἱερεῖς αὐτῶν κατα-
χρῶνται· ὡσαύτως δὲ καὶ αἱ γυναῖκες αὐτῶν ἀπ' αὐτῶν
ταριχεύουσαι οὔτε πτωχῷ οὔτε ἀδυνάτῳ μεταδιδόασιν· τῶν

KING JAMES VERSION

19 They light them candles, yea, more than for themselves, whereof they cannot see one.

20 They are as one of the beams of the temple, yet they say their hearts are gnawed upon by things creeping out of the earth; and when they eat them and their clothes, they feel it not.

21 Their faces are blacked through the smoke that cometh out of the temple.

22 Upon their bodies and heads sit bats, swallows, and birds, and the cats also.

23 By this ye may know that they are no gods: therefore fear them not.

24 Notwithstanding the gold that is about them to make them beautiful, except they wipe off the rust, they will not shine: for neither when they were molten did they feel it.

25 The things wherein there is no breath are bought for a most high price.

26 They are borne upon shoulders, having no feet, whereby they declare unto men that they be nothing worth.

27 They also that serve them are ashamed: for if they fall to the ground at any time, they cannot rise up again of themselves: neither, if one set them upright, can they move of themselves: neither, if they be bowed down, can they make themselves straight: but they set gifts before them, as unto dead men.

28 As for the things that are sacrificed unto them, their priests sell and abuse; in like manner their wives lay up part thereof in salt; but unto the poor and impotent they give nothing of it.

DOUAY OLD TESTAMENT

18 They light candles to them, and in great number, of which they cannot see one: but they are like beams in the house.

19 And they say that the creeping things which are of the earth, gnaw their hearts, while they eat them and their garments, and they feel it not.

20 Their faces are black with the smoke that is made in the house.

21 Owls, and swallows, and other birds fly upon their bodies, and upon their heads, and cats in like manner.

22 Whereby you may know that they are no gods. Therefore fear them not.

23 The gold also which they have, is for shew, but except a man wipe off the rust, they will not shine: for neither when they were molten, did they feel it.

24 Men buy them at a high price, whereas there is no breath in them.

25 And having not the use of feet they are carried upon shoulders, declaring to men how vile they are. Be they confounded also that worship them.

26 Therefore if they fall to the ground, they rise not up again of themselves, nor if a man set them upright, will they stand by themselves, but their gifts shall be set before them, as to the dead.

27 The things that are sacrificed to them, their priests sell and abuse: in like manner also their wives take part of them, but give nothing of it either to the sick, or to the poor.

KNOX TRANSLATION

before them, they see none; roof-beam is not more senseless.
19 Yet men will have it that serpents creep out of the earth
and drink in the secrets of their hearts! Worms, more like,
that eat the idol up, clothes and all, and it none the wiser.[a]
20 Smoke of the temple blackens their faces; 21 about their
bodies and heads fly owl and swallow; birds hover and cats
prowl. 22 Be sure they are no gods; never fear them.
23 Fair, golden faces! Yet will they not shine on the worshipper, till he rub off the stains on them; cast once for all in
a mould, without feeling.[b] 24 Cost what they will, there is
never a breath of life in them; 25 never a pace they walk, but
must still be carried on men's shoulders, putting their own
worshippers to shame by the betrayal of their impotence.
26 Fall they to earth, they cannot rise from it, and though
they be set up again, it is in no power of their own that they
stand. As well bring gifts to dead men as to these; 27 the victim thou offerest yonder priest will sell, or put to his own
use, nor ever a slice his wife cuts shall find its way to the

a Literally, 'And they say that serpents from the earth lick out their hearts, while they eat them and their clothes, unfelt by them'. The Greek has 'creeping things' instead of serpents. If the meaning of the original has been preserved, the reference is perhaps to the belief in snakes as an incarnation of heathen divinities; cf. Aristophanes, *Plutus* 733. *b* Literally, 'The gold, too, which they have is for appearance; unless a man rubs off the stains, they will not shine, and if it comes to that, they had no feeling while they were being cast'. The Greek has, 'Unless a man rubs off the stains, they will not cause to shine the gold with which they are beautiful...' etc.

TODAY'S ENGLISH VERSION

lamps for the gods, far more than they need for their own
use, but the idols can't see even one of them. 20 Their insides
are eaten away by termites, just like the wooden beams of
the temple, and their clothing is destroyed, but they don't
even know it. 21 Their faces are blackened by the smoke in
the temple. 22 Bats, swallows, and other birds perch on
them, and even cats sit on them. 23 All of this proves that
they are not gods—do not worship them.

24 These idols have been plated with gold to make them
beautiful, but they do not shine unless someone polishes
them. When they were being poured into molds, they felt
nothing. 25 It makes no difference how high a price is paid
for them; they are still unable to breathe. 26 See how useless
they are! They can't walk on their own feet, but must be carried around. 27 Even those who take care of them are embarrassed when one of their gods falls to the ground and has to
be picked up again. When someone stands one of them in a
certain place, it cannot move, and if it is leaning over, it can
never straighten itself up. Offering gifts to them is like giving
gifts to a corpse. 28 Priests sell what is sacrificed to their
gods and use the money on themselves. And the wives of the
priests preserve the sacrifices with salt for later use, instead
of sharing them with the poor and helpless. 29 Even women

NEW REVISED STANDARD VERSION

than they light for themselves, though their gods[a] can see
none of them. 20 They are[b] just like a beam of the temple,
but their hearts, it is said, are eaten away when crawling
creatures from the earth devour them and their robes. They
do not notice 21 when their faces have been blackened by the
smoke of the temple. 22 Bats, swallows, and birds alight on
their bodies and heads; and so do cats. 23 From this you will
know that they are not gods; so do not fear them.

24 As for the gold that they wear for beauty—it[c] will not
shine unless someone wipes off the tarnish; for even when
they were being cast, they did not feel it. 25 They are bought
without regard to cost, but there is no breath in them.
26 Having no feet, they are carried on the shoulders of others,
revealing to humankind their worthlessness. And those who
serve them are put to shame 27 because, if any of these gods
falls[d] to the ground, they themselves must pick it up. If anyone sets it upright, it cannot move itself; and if it is tipped
over, it cannot straighten itself. Gifts are placed before them
just as before the dead. 28 The priests sell the sacrifices that
are offered to these gods[e] and use the money themselves.
Likewise their wives preserve some of the meat[f] with salt,
but give none to the poor or helpless. 29 Sacrifices to them

a Gk *they* *b* Gk *It is* *c* Lat Syr: Gk *they* *d* Gk *if they fall*
e Gk *to them* *f* Gk *of them*

NEW AMERICAN BIBLE

lamps for them than for themselves, yet not one of these can
they see. 19 They are like any beam in the house; it is said
their hearts are eaten away. Though the insects out of the
ground consume them and their garments, they do not feel
it. 20 Their faces are blackened by the smoke of the house.
21 Bats and swallows alight on their bodies and on their
heads; and cats as well as birds. 22 Know, therefore, that
they are not gods, and do not fear them.

23 Despite the gold that covers them for adornment, unless
someone wipes away the corrosion, they do not shine; nor
did they feel anything when they were molded. 24 They are
bought at any price, and there is no spirit in them. 25 Having
no feet, they are carried on men's shoulders, displaying their
shame to all; and those who worship them are put to confusion 26 because, if they fall to the ground, the worshipers
must raise them up. They neither move of themselves if one
sets them upright, nor come upright if they fall; but one puts
gifts beside them as beside the dead. 27 Their priests resell
their sacrifices for their own advantage. Even their wives
cure parts of the meat, but do not share it with the poor and

NEW JERUSALEM BIBLE

for them than they do for themselves, and the gods see none
of them. 19 They are like one of the temple beams, which are
said to be gnawed away from within; the termites creep out
of the ground and eat them and their clothes too, and they
feel nothing. 20 Their faces are blackened by the smoke that
rises from the temple. 21 Bats, swallows, birds of every kind
perch on their bodies and heads, and so do cats. 22 From
this, you can see for yourselves that they are not gods; do
not be afraid of them.

23 'The gold with which they are parading their futility
before the world is supposed to make them look beautiful,
but if someone does not rub off the tarnish, these gods will
not be shining much on their own, and even while they were
being cast, they felt nothing. 24 However much was paid for
them, there is still no breath of life in them. 25 Being unable
to walk, they have to be carried on men's shoulders, which
shows how futile they are. It is humiliating for their worshippers, too, who have to stand them up again if they fall over.
26 Once they have been stood up, they cannot move on their
own; if they tilt askew, they cannot right themselves; offerings made to them might as well be made to the dead.
27 Whatever is sacrificed to them, the priests re-sell and pocket the profit; while their wives salt down part of it, but give
nothing to the poor or to the helpless. As to the sacrifices

GREEK OLD TESTAMENT

θυσιῶν αὐτῶν ἀποκαθημένη καὶ λεχὼ ἅπτονται. [28] γνόντες
οὖν ἀπὸ τούτων ὅτι οὔκ εἰσιν θεοί, μὴ φοβηθῆτε αὐτούς.
[29] Πόθεν γὰρ κληθείησαν θεοί; ὅτι γυναῖκες παρατιθέασιν
θεοῖς ἀργυροῖς καὶ χρυσοῖς καὶ ξυλίνοις. [30] καὶ ἐν τοῖς
οἴκοις αὐτῶν οἱ ἱερεῖς διφρεύουσιν ἔχοντες τοὺς χιτῶνας
διερρωγότας καὶ τὰς κεφαλὰς καὶ τοὺς πώγωνας ἐξυρη-
μένους, ὧν αἱ κεφαλαὶ ἀκάλυπτοί εἰσιν, [31] ὠρύονται δὲ
βοῶντες ἐναντίον τῶν θεῶν αὐτῶν ὥσπερ τινὲς ἐν περιδεί-
πνῳ νεκροῦ. [32] ἀπὸ τοῦ ἱματισμοῦ αὐτῶν ἀφελόμενοι οἱ
ἱερεῖς ἐνδύουσιν τὰς γυναῖκας αὐτῶν καὶ τὰ παιδία. [33] οὔτε
ἐὰν κακὸν πάθωσιν ὑπό τινος οὔτε ἐὰν ἀγαθόν, δυνήσονται
ἀνταποδοῦναι· οὔτε καταστῆσαι βασιλέα δύνανται οὔτε
ἀφελέσθαι. [34] ὡσαύτως οὔτε πλοῦτον οὔτε χαλκὸν οὐ μὴ
δύνωνται διδόναι· ἐάν τις αὐτοῖς εὐχὴν εὐξάμενος μὴ
ἀποδῷ, οὐ μὴ ἐπιζητήσωσιν. [35] ἐκ θανάτου ἄνθρωπον οὐ μὴ
ῥύσωνται οὔτε ἥττονα ἀπὸ ἰσχυροῦ οὐ μὴ ἐξέλωνται.
[36] ἄνθρωπον τυφλὸν εἰς ὅρασιν οὐ μὴ περιστήσωσιν, ἐν
ἀνάγκῃ ἄνθρωπον ὄντα οὐ μὴ ἐξέλωνται. [37] χήραν οὐ μὴ
ἐλεήσωσιν οὔτε ὀρφανὸν εὖ ποιήσουσιν. [38] τοῖς ἀπὸ τοῦ
ὄρους λίθοις ὡμοιωμένοι εἰσὶν τὰ ξύλινα καὶ τὰ περίχρυσα
καὶ τὰ περιάργυρα, οἱ δὲ θεραπεύοντες αὐτὰ καταισχυνθή-
σονται. [39] πῶς οὖν νομιστέον ἢ κλητέον αὐτοὺς ὑπάρχειν
θεούς;

KING JAMES VERSION

29 Menstruous women and women in childbed eat their sacrifices: by these things ye may know that they are no gods: fear them not.

30 For how can they be called gods? because women set meat before the gods of silver, gold, and wood.

31 And the priests sit in their temples, having their clothes rent, and their heads and beards shaven, and nothing upon their heads.

32 They roar and cry before their gods, as men do at the feast when one is dead.

33 The priests also take off their garments, and clothe their wives and children.

34 Whether it be evil that one doeth unto them, or good, they are not able to recompense it: they can neither set up a king, nor put him down.

35 In like manner, they can neither give riches nor money: though a man make a vow unto them, and keep it not, they will not require it.

36 They can save no man from death, neither deliver the weak from the mighty.

37 They cannot restore a blind man to his sight, nor help any man in his distress.

38 They can shew no mercy to the widow, nor do good to the fatherless.

39 Their gods of wood, and which are overlaid with gold and silver, are like the stones that be hewn out of the mountain: they that worship them shall be confounded.

40 How should a man then think and say that they are gods, when even the Chaldeans themselves dishonour them?

DOUAY OLD TESTAMENT

28 The childbearing and menstruous women touch their sacrifices: knowing therefore by these things that they are not gods, fear them not.

29 For how can they be called gods? because women set offerings before the gods of silver, and of gold, and of wood:

30 And priests sit in their temples, having their garments rent, and their heads and beards shaven, and nothing upon their heads.

31 And they roar and cry before their gods, as men do at the feast when one is dead.

32 The priests take away their garments, and clothe their wives and their children.

33 And whether it be evil that one doth unto them, or good, they are not able to recompense it: neither can they set up a king nor put him down:

34 In like manner they can neither give riches, nor requite evil. If a man make a vow to them, and perform it not, they cannot require it.

35 They cannot deliver a man from death nor save the weak from the mighty.

36 They cannot restore the blind man to his sight: nor deliver a man from distress.

37 They shall not pity the widow, nor do good to the fatherless.

38 Their gods, of wood, and of stone, and of gold, and of silver, are like the stones that are hewn out of the mountains: and they that worship them shall be confounded.

39 How then is it to be supposed, or to be said, that they are gods?

KNOX TRANSLATION

sick and the needy. [28] Those offerings every woman may
touch if she will, child-birth and monthly times notwithstanding. And are these gods? Are these to be feared?
[29] Things of silver and gold and wood, that have women for
their ministers, shall the divine name be theirs?
[30] In their temples you shall find priests sitting by with
clothes rent, shaven and shorn, heads uncovered, [31] raising
lament over their gods as at a dead man's dirge. [32] Vestments their idols wore they will carry away, to dress their
wives and children; [33] so powerless are these gods to requite
injury or reward service done. Not theirs to make kings or
unmake them, grant riches, [34] or wreak vengeance; the
unpaid vow they cannot exact, [35] nor deliver men from
death, and the tyrant's oppression, [36] give sight to the blind,
succour in time of peril, [37] shew mercy to the widow, or
cheer the orphan's lot. [38] Things of wood and stone, gold
and silver, no more than rock on the mountain-side can they
speed their worshippers; [39] gods do we reckon them, gods do
we call them?

TODAY'S ENGLISH VERSION

who are having their monthly period or women who have
just given birth are allowed to touch the sacrifices. All of this
proves that they are not gods—do not worship them.
30 How can they ever be called gods, when women are
allowed to make offerings to these things made of wood, silver, and gold? 31 The priests even sit in the temples when
they are in mourning, with torn clothes and shaved, uncovered heads. 32 The priests roar and shout in the presence of
their gods as if they were taking part in a funeral feast.
33 They take the clothing off their gods and give it to their
wives and children. 34 It doesn't matter whether a person
helps or harms these gods, since they cannot pay him back.
They are not able to make anyone a king or to dethrone him,
35 and they cannot make a person wealthy or give him any
money. If someone makes a vow to them but does not keep
it, they will never make him pay. 36 They can never rescue a
person from death, and they never help a weak person
against one who is strong. 37 They cannot restore sight to
the blind or save anyone in distress. 38 They cannot offer any
mercy or give help to widows or orphans. 39 These things
made of wood and covered with silver and gold are as powerless as stone taken from the mountains; and the people
who worship them will be put to shame. 40 How can anyone
think that they are gods or call them gods?

NEW REVISED STANDARD VERSION

may even be touched by women in their periods or at child-
birth. Since you know by these things that they are not gods,
do not fear them.
30 For how can they be called gods? Women serve meals
for gods of silver and gold and wood; 31 and in their temples
the priests sit with their clothes torn, their heads and beards
shaved, and their heads uncovered. 32 They howl and shout
before their gods as some do at a funeral banquet. 33 The
priests take some of the clothing of their gods[a] to clothe
their wives and children. 34 Whether one does evil to them or
good, they will not be able to repay it. They cannot set up a
king or depose one. 35 Likewise they are not able to give
either wealth or money; if one makes a vow to them and
does not keep it, they will not require it. 36 They cannot save
anyone from death or rescue the weak from the strong.
37 They cannot restore sight to the blind; they cannot rescue
one who is in distress. 38 They cannot take pity on a widow
or do good to an orphan. 39 These things that are made of
wood and overlaid with gold and silver are like stones from
the mountain, and those who serve them will be put to
shame. 40 Why then must anyone think that they are gods,
or call them gods?

a Gk *some of their clothing*

NEW AMERICAN BIBLE

the weak; 28 the menstruous and women in childbed handle
their sacrifices. Knowing from this that they are not gods, do
not fear them.
29 How can they be called gods? For women bring the offerings to these gods of silver and gold and wood; 30 and in
their temples the priests squat with torn tunic and with
shaven hair and beard, and with their heads uncovered.
31 They shout and wail before their gods as others do at a
funeral banquet. 32 The priests take some of their clothing
and put it on their wives and children. 33 Whether they are
treated well or ill by anyone, they cannot requite it; they can
neither set up a king nor remove him. 34 Similarly, they cannot give anyone riches or coppers; if one fails to fulfill a vow
to them, they cannot exact it of him. 35 They neither save a
man from death, nor deliver the weak from the strong. 36 To
no blind man do they restore his sight, nor do they save any
man in an emergency. 37 They neither pity the widow nor
benefit the orphan. 38 These gilded and silvered wooden statues are like stones from the mountains; and their worshipers
will be put to shame. 39 How then can it be thought or
claimed that they are gods?

NEW JERUSALEM BIBLE

themselves, why, women during their periods and women in
childbed are not afraid to touch them! 28 From all this you
can tell that they are not gods; do not be afraid of them.
29 'Indeed, how can they even be called gods, when women
do the offering to these gods of silver, gold and wood? 30 In
their temples, the priests stay sitting down, their garments
torn, heads and beard shaved and heads uncovered; 31 they
roar and shriek before their gods as people do at funeral
feasts. 32 The priests take robes from the gods to clothe their
own wives and children. 33 Whether these gods are treated
badly or well, they are incapable of paying back either treatment; as incapable too of making or unmaking kings,
34 equally incapable of distributing wealth or money. If anyone fails to honour a vow he has made to them, they cannot
call him to account. 35 They can neither save anyone from
death nor rescue the weak from the strong, 36 nor restore
sight to the blind, nor save anyone in trouble, 37 nor take
pity on a widow, nor be generous to an orphan. 38 These
wooden gods overlaid with gold and silver are about as
much use as rocks cut out of the mountain side. Their worshippers will be confounded! 39 So how can anyone think or
say that they are gods?

GREEK OLD TESTAMENT

40 Ἔτι δὲ καὶ αὐτῶν τῶν Χαλδαίων ἀτιμαζόντων αὐτά, οἵ,
ὅταν ἴδωσιν ἐνεὸν οὐ δυνάμενον λαλῆσαι, προσενεγκάμενοι
τὸν Βῆλον ἀξιοῦσιν φωνῆσαι, ὡς δυνατοῦ ὄντος αὐτοῦ αἰσθέσθαι, 41 καὶ οὐ δύνανται αὐτοὶ νοήσαντες καταλιπεῖν αὐτά,
αἴσθησιν γὰρ οὐκ ἔχουσιν. 42 αἱ δὲ γυναῖκες περιθέμεναι
σχοινία ἐν ταῖς ὁδοῖς ἐγκάθηνται θυμιῶσαι τὰ πίτυρα·
43 ὅταν δέ τις αὐτῶν ἐφελκυσθεῖσα ὑπό τινος τῶν παρα-
πορευομένων κοιμηθῇ, τὴν πλησίον ὀνειδίζει, ὅτι οὐκ ἠξίω-
ται ὥσπερ καὶ αὐτὴ οὔτε τὸ σχοινίον αὐτῆς διερράγη.
44 πάντα τὰ γινόμενα αὐτοῖς ἐστιν ψευδῆ· πῶς οὖν νομιστέον ἢ κλητέον ὥστε θεοὺς αὐτοὺς ὑπάρχειν;
45 Ὑπὸ τεκτόνων καὶ χρυσοχόων κατεσκευασμένα εἰσίν·
οὐθὲν ἄλλο μὴ γένωνται ἢ ὃ βούλονται οἱ τεχνῖται αὐτὰ
γενέσθαι. 46 αὐτοί τε οἱ κατασκευάζοντες αὐτὰ οὐ μὴ γένωνται πολυχρόνιοι· πῶς τε δὴ μέλλει τὰ ὑπ' αὐτῶν κατα-
σκευασθέντα εἶναι θεοί; 47 κατέλιπον γὰρ ψεύδη καὶ ὄνειδος
τοῖς ἐπιγινομένοις. 48 ὅταν γὰρ ἐπέλθῃ ἐπ' αὐτὰ πόλεμος
καὶ κακά, βουλεύονται πρὸς ἑαυτοὺς οἱ ἱερεῖς ποῦ συναπο-
κρυβῶσι μετ' αὐτῶν. 49 πῶς οὖν οὐκ ἔστιν αἰσθέσθαι ὅτι οὐκ
εἰσὶν θεοί, οἳ οὔτε σῴζουσιν ἑαυτοὺς ἐκ πολέμου οὔτε ἐκ

KING JAMES VERSION

41 Who if they shall see one dumb that cannot speak, they bring him, and intreat Bel that he may speak, as though he were able to understand.

42 Yet they cannot understand this themselves, and leave them: for they have no knowledge.

43 The women also with cords about them, sitting in the ways, burn bran for perfume: but if any of them, drawn by some that passeth by, lie with him, she reproacheth her fellow, that she was not thought as worthy as herself, nor her cord broken.

44 Whatsoever is done among them is false: how may it then be thought or said that they are gods?

45 They are made of carpenters and goldsmiths: they can be nothing else than the workmen will have them to be.

46 And they themselves that made them can never continue long; how should then the things that are made of them be gods?

47 For they left lies and reproaches to them that come after.

48 For when there cometh any war or plague upon them, the priests consult with themselves, where they may be hidden with them.

49 How then cannot men perceive that they be no gods, which can neither save themselves from war, nor from plague?

DOUAY OLD TESTAMENT

40 Even the Chaldeans themselves dishonour them: who when they hear of one dumb that cannot speak, they present him to Bel, entreating him, that he may speak,

41 As though they could be sensible that have no motion themselves: and they, when they shall perceive this, will leave them: for their gods themselves have no sense.

42 The women also with cords about them, sit in the ways, burning olive stones.

43 And when any one of them, drawn away by some passenger, lieth with him, she upbraideth her neighbour, that she was not thought as worthy as herself, nor her cord broken.

44 But all things that are done about them, are false: how is it then to be thought, or to be said, that they are gods?

45 And they are made by workmen, and by goldsmiths. They shall be nothing else but what the priests will have them to be.

46 For the artificers themselves that make them, are of no long continuance. Can those things then that are made by them be gods?

47 But they have left false things and reproach to them that come after.

48 For when war cometh upon them, or evils, the priests consult with themselves where they may hide themselves with them.

49 How then can they be thought to be gods, that can neither deliver themselves from war, nor save themselves from evils?

KNOX TRANSLATION

40 And indeed the Chaldaeans themselves have but scant
reverence for these idols of theirs; hear they of a dumb child
that can utter no word, Bel's image must be brought to it and
petitioned for the gift of speech; 41 as if the senseless thing
which cannot move could yet hear them! Sense neither god
nor worshipper has, else god should find no worship.[a] 42 See
where their women sit in the streets, with ropes about them,
each before a fire of olive-stones,[b] 43 each waiting till some
passer-by drags her away and beds her, then taunting her
less coveted neighbours, that have ropes about them still!
44 All lies, the worship of them, and shall they claim the title
of gods?
45 Carpenters made them and goldsmiths, only at the
priests' whim; 46 and shall the handicraft of mortal craftsmen be divine? 47 One day, their descendants will reproach
them with a legacy of imposture. 48 Come war, come peril,
the priest thinks only of hiding himself and his gods both;
49 gods who shall think them, that from war and peril their
own selves cannot deliver? 50 Recognize it at last they will,

a *vv.* 40, 41. The meaning here is very uncertain. The Greek almost certainly implies that Bel's image was brought to the patient, not the patient to the image, and the meaning is perhaps that it was absurd to expect help from a statue which had to be carried because it could not walk (cf. verse 25). There are several differences between the Greek and the Latin; the Greek, for example, has 'sick person' in the masculine, whereas the neuter gender used in the Latin presumably implies a child in arms. *b* This ceremony of general prostitution is described by Herodotus, i. 199; he does not mention the fires of olive-stones (or bran, according to the Greek).

TODAY'S ENGLISH VERSION

The Babylonians bring dishonor on their own gods. 41 When someone cannot speak, they take him to the temple and ask Bel to give him the power of speech, as if Bel could understand anything. 42 But even when the people realize that their gods cannot help, they are stupid enough to go on worshiping them. 43 Not only that, but women wrap cords around themselves and sit alongside the road burning incense and offering themselves as prostitutes. When one of them is taken off for sex, she returns to ridicule the woman next to her who was not beautiful enough to be chosen. 44 Everything about these idols is false. How can anyone think that they are gods or call them gods?

45 Woodworkers and goldsmiths make these gods, so they can never be anything other than what these people want them to be. 46 Even their makers do not live long lives, so how are they able to create gods? 47 These people leave nothing but deceit and disgrace as an inheritance for future generations. 48 When wars and disturbances come, the priests plan where they can go into hiding with their gods. 49 These idols are helpless in the face of wars and disturbances. Why can't people realize that these idols are not gods?

NEW REVISED STANDARD VERSION

Besides, even the Chaldeans themselves dishonor them; for when they see someone who cannot speak, they bring Bel and pray that the mute may speak, as though Bel[a] were able to understand! 41 Yet they themselves cannot perceive this and abandon them, for they have no sense. 42 And the women, with cords around them, sit along the passageways, burning bran for incense. 43 When one of them is led off by one of the passers-by and is taken to bed by him, she derides the woman next to her, because she was not as attractive as herself and her cord was not broken. 44 Whatever is done for these idols[b] is false. Why then must anyone think that they are gods, or call them gods?

45 They are made by carpenters and goldsmiths; they can be nothing but what the artisans wish them to be. 46 Those who make them will certainly not live very long themselves; 47 how then can the things that are made by them be gods? They have left only lies and reproach for those who come after. 48 For when war or calamity comes upon them, the priests consult together as to where they can hide themselves and their gods.[b] 49 How then can one fail to see that these are not gods, for they cannot save themselves from war or

a Gk *he* *b* Gk *them*

NEW AMERICAN BIBLE

40 Even the Chaldeans themselves have no respect for them; for when they see a deaf mute, incapable of speech, they bring forward Bel and ask the god to make noise, as though the man could understand; 41 and they are themselves unable to reflect and abandon these gods, for they have no sense. 42 And their women, girt with cords, sit by the roads, burning chaff for incense; 43 and whenever one of them is drawn aside by some passerby who lies with her, she mocks her neighbor who has not been dignified as she has, and has not had her cord broken. 44 All that takes place around these gods is a fraud: how then can it be thought or claimed that they are gods?

45 They are produced by woodworkers and goldsmiths, and they are nothing else than what these craftsmen wish them to be. 46 Even those who produce them are not long-lived; 47 how then can what they have produced be gods? They have left frauds and opprobrium to their successors. 48 For when war or disaster comes upon them, the priests deliberate among themselves where they can hide with them. 49 How then can one not know that these are no-gods, which do not save themselves either from war or from disaster? 50 They

NEW JERUSALEM BIBLE

40 'The Chaldaeans themselves do them no honour; if they find someone who is dumb and cannot speak, they present him to Bel, entreating him for the gift of speech, as though he could perceive it! 41 And they are incapable of drawing the conclusion and abandoning those gods—such is their lack of perception. 42 Women with strings round their waists sit in the streets, burning bran like incense; 43 when one of these has been picked up by a passer-by and been to bed with him, she then gloats over her neighbour for not having been thought as worthy as herself and for not having had her string broken. 44 Whatever is done for them is spurious. So how can anyone think or say that they are gods?

45 'Made by woodworkers and goldsmiths, they are only what those workmen decide to make them. 46 Their makers have not long to live themselves, so how can the things they make be gods? 47 Their legacy to their descendants is nothing but delusion and dishonour. 48 If war or disasters befall them, the priests discuss where best to hide themselves and these gods; 49 how can anyone fail to realise that they are not gods, if they cannot save themselves from war or from

GREEK OLD TESTAMENT

κακῶν; 50 ὑπάρχοντα γὰρ ξύλινα καὶ περίχρυσα καὶ περιάργυρα γνωσθήσεται μετὰ ταῦτα ὅτι ἐστὶν ψευδῆ· τοῖς ἔθνεσι
πᾶσι τοῖς τε βασιλεῦσι φανερὸν ἔσται ὅτι οὔκ εἰσι θεοὶ ἀλλὰ
ἔργα χειρῶν ἀνθρώπων, καὶ οὐδὲν θεοῦ ἔργον ἐν αὐτοῖς
ἐστιν. 51 τίνι οὖν γνωστέον ἐστὶν ὅτι οὔκ εἰσιν θεοί;
52 Βασιλέα γὰρ χώρας οὐ μὴ ἀναστήσωσιν οὔτε ὑετὸν ἀνθρώποις οὐ μὴ δῶσιν 53 κρίσιν τε οὐ μὴ διακρίνωσιν αὐτῶν
οὐδὲ μὴ ῥύσωνται ἀδικούμενον ἀδύνατοι ὄντες. ὥσπερ γὰρ
κορῶναι ἀνὰ μέσον τοῦ οὐρανοῦ καὶ τῆς γῆς. 54 καὶ γὰρ
ὅταν ἐμπέσῃ εἰς οἰκίαν θεῶν ξυλίνων ἢ περιχρύσων ἢ περι-
αργύρων πῦρ, οἱ μὲν ἱερεῖς αὐτῶν φεύξονται καὶ διασωθή-
σονται, αὐτοὶ δὲ ὥσπερ δοκοὶ μέσοι κατακαυθήσονται.
55 βασιλεῖ δὲ καὶ πολεμίοις οὐ μὴ ἀντιστῶσιν. 56 πῶς οὖν
ἐκδεκτέον ἢ νομιστέον ὅτι εἰσὶν θεοί;
57 Οὔτε ἀπὸ κλεπτῶν οὔτε ἀπὸ λῃστῶν οὐ μὴ διασωθῶσιν
θεοὶ ξύλινοι καὶ περιάργυροι καὶ περίχρυσοι, ὧν οἱ ἰσχύοντες περιελοῦνται τὸ χρυσίον καὶ τὸ ἀργύριον καὶ τὸν
ἱματισμὸν τὸν περικείμενον αὐτοῖς ἀπελεύσονται ἔχοντες,
οὔτε ἑαυτοῖς οὐ μὴ βοηθήσωσιν· 58 ὥστε κρεῖσσον εἶναι
βασιλέα ἐπιδεικνύμενον τὴν ἑαυτοῦ ἀνδρείαν ἢ σκεῦος ἐν
οἰκίᾳ χρήσιμον, ἐφ᾽ ᾧ χρήσεται ὁ κεκτημένος, ἢ οἱ ψευδεῖς
θεοί· ἢ καὶ θύρα ἐν οἰκίᾳ διασῴζουσα τὰ ἐν αὐτῇ ὄντα ἢ οἱ
ψευδεῖς θεοί, καὶ ξύλινος στῦλος ἐν βασιλείοις ἢ οἱ ψευδεῖς

KING JAMES VERSION

50 For seeing they be but of wood, and overlaid with silver and gold, it shall be known hereafter that they are false:

51 And it shall manifestly appear to all nations and kings that they are no gods, but the works of men's hands, and that there is no work of God in them.

52 Who then may not know that they are no gods?

53 For neither can they set up a king in the land, nor give rain unto men.

54 Neither can they judge their own cause, nor redress a wrong, being unable: for they are as crows between heaven and earth.

55 Whereupon when fire falleth upon the house of gods of wood, or laid over with gold or silver, their priests will flee away, and escape; but they themselves shall be burned asunder like beams.

56 Moreover they cannot withstand any king or enemies: how can it then be thought or said that they be gods?

57 Neither are those gods of wood, and laid over with silver or gold, able to escape either from thieves or robbers.

58 Whose gold, and silver, and garments wherewith they are clothed, they that are strong do take, and go away withal: neither are they able to help themselves.

59 Therefore it is better to be a king that sheweth his power, or else a profitable vessel in an house, which the owner shall have use of, than such false gods; or to be a door in an house, to keep such things safe as be therein, than such false gods; or a pillar of wood in a palace, than such false gods.

DOUAY OLD TESTAMENT

50 For seeing they are but of wood, and laid over with gold, and with silver, it shall be known hereafter that they are false things, by all nations and kings: and it shall be manifest that they are no gods, but the work of men's hands, and that there is no work of God in them.

51 Whence therefore is it known that they are not gods, but the work of men's hands, and no work of God is in them?

52 They cannot set up a king over the land, nor give rain to men.

53 They determine no causes, nor deliver countries from oppression; because they can do nothing, and are as daws between heaven and earth.

54 For when fire shall fall upon the house of *these* gods of wood, and of silver, and of gold, their priests indeed will flee away, and be saved: but they themselves shall be burnt in the midst like beams.

55 And they cannot withstand a king and war. How then can it be supposed, or admitted that they are gods?

56 Neither are these gods of wood, and of stone, and laid over with gold, and with silver, able to deliver themselves from thieves or robbers: they that are stronger than them

57 Shall take from them the gold, and silver, and the raiment wherewith they are clothed, and shall go their way, neither shall they help themselves.

58 Therefore it is better to be a king that sheweth his power: or else a profitable vessel in the house, with which the owner thereof will be well satisfied: or a door in the house, to keep things safe that are therein, than such false gods.

KNOX TRANSLATION

kings and peoples everywhere, that gods of wood, gold and
silver are false gods, creatures of man, not creators. 51 Man's
handiwork, with nothing in them of the divine, who can
doubt it? 52 Not through them comes king to throne, comes
rain to country folk; 53 redress wrong they may not, nor rid a
people of tyranny; dead crow hung between heaven and
earth is not more powerless. 54 Does a temple catch fire? You
shall see priests taking refuge in flight, and the wooden
gods, for all the silver and gold on them, burning among the
woodwork. 55 Against the king's power, against the enemy's
attack, they can make no head; who shall reckon them or
name them divine?
56 Wood and stone, gold and silver, how to protect themselves against the superior strength of house-breaker and robber, 57 that will carry off sheathes of silver and gold, carry off
the clothes from their backs, and leave them powerless?
58 Better some golden emblem of royal prowess, cup of silver
meant for use, not only for display, door of wood that keeps
safe the treasures of a house, than these deceiving idols! [a]

[a] Literally, 'So it is better to be a king making display of his power, or a useful vessel in a house of which its owner is proud, or a door in a house which guards its contents, than false gods'. The Greek adds, 'or a wooden pillar in a palace' after the word 'contents'.

TODAY'S ENGLISH VERSION

50 These idols are nothing more than wood covered with silver and gold; one day it will be clear that they are really not gods at all. 51 All nations and kings will realize that idols are nothing more than the work of human hands. They do not have the power of a god, 52 and anyone should know that they are not really gods.

53 These gods can never make anyone a king or bring rain. 54 They can't make decisions about their own affairs or give justice to someone who has been wronged; they can do absolutely nothing. They are as useless as crows flying around in the air. 55 When a temple catches on fire, the priests run away to save themselves, while the gods made of wood and covered with silver and gold are left to burn like wooden beams. 56 They can't fight kings or go to war against enemies. How can anyone believe that they are gods?

57 These gods of wood, covered with silver and gold, cannot protect themselves from thieves and robbers 58 who take off the silver and gold and the gods' clothing and walk away with all of it. The gods can do nothing to stop them. 59 Anything from a courageous king to a useful piece of pottery is better than a false god. Even a door is better than a false god; a door at least protects the things in the house. Even a wooden pillar in a palace is better than a false god.

NEW REVISED STANDARD VERSION

calamity? 50 Since they are made of wood and overlaid with gold and silver, it will afterward be known that they are false. 51 It will be manifest to all the nations and kings that they are not gods but the work of human hands, and that there is no work of God in them. 52 Who then can fail to know that they are not gods?[a]

53 For they cannot set up a king over a country or give rain to people. 54 They cannot judge their own cause or deliver one who is wronged, for they have no power; 55 they are like crows between heaven and earth. When fire breaks out in a temple of wooden gods overlaid with gold or silver, their priests will flee and escape, but the gods[b] will be burned up like timbers. 56 Besides, they can offer no resistance to king or enemy. Why then must anyone admit or think that they are gods?

57 Gods made of wood and overlaid with silver and gold are unable to save themselves from thieves or robbers. 58 Anyone who can will strip them of their gold and silver and of the robes they wear, and go off with this booty, and they will not be able to help themselves. 59 So it is better to be a king who shows his courage, or a household utensil that serves its owner's need, than to be these false gods; better even the door of a house that protects its contents, than these false gods; better also a wooden pillar in a palace, than these false gods.

a Meaning of Gk uncertain *b* Gk *they*

NEW AMERICAN BIBLE

are wooden, gilded and silvered; they will later be known for frauds. To all peoples and kings it will be clear that they are not gods, but human handiwork; and that God's work is not in them.

51 Who does not know that they are not gods? 52 They set no king over the land, nor do they give men rain. 53 They neither vindicate their own rights, nor do they recover what is unjustly taken, for they are unable; 54 they are like crows between heaven and earth. For when fire breaks out in the temple of these wooden or gilded or silvered gods, though the priests flee and are safe, they themselves are burnt up in the fire like beams. 55 They cannot resist a king, or enemy forces. 56 How then can it be admitted or thought that they are gods?

They are safe from neither thieves nor bandits, these wooden and silvered and gilded gods; 57 those who seize them strip off the gold and the silver, and go away with the clothing that was on them, and they cannot help themselves. 58 How much better to be a king displaying his valor, or a handy tool in a house, the joy of its owner, than these false gods; or the door of a house, that keeps safe those who are within, rather than these false gods; or a wooden post in a palace, rather than these false gods! 59 The sun and moon

NEW JERUSALEM BIBLE

disasters? 50 And since they are only made of wood overlaid with gold or silver, it will later become apparent that they are spurious; it will be obvious to everyone, to nations as to kings, that they are not gods but the work of human hands, and that there is no divine activity in them. 51 Does anyone still need convincing that they are not gods?

52 'They can neither appoint a king over a country, nor give rain to humankind, 53 nor regulate their own affairs, nor rescue anyone who suffers a wrong; they are as helpless as crows between sky and ground. 54 If fire falls on the temple of these wooden gods overlaid with gold or silver, their priests fly to safety while they for their part stay there like beams, to be burnt. 55 They cannot put up any resistance to a king or to enemies. 56 So how can anyone think or say that they are gods?

57 'These wooden gods overlaid with gold or silver cannot evade thieves or marauders; strong men may rob them of their gold and silver and make off with the robes they are dressed in; yet they are powerless to help even themselves. 58 Better to be a king displaying his prowess, a household pot of use to its owner, than to be these counterfeit gods; or merely the door of a house, protecting what is inside, than these counterfeit gods; or a wooden pillar in a palace than

GREEK OLD TESTAMENT

θεοί. 59 ἥλιος μὲν γὰρ καὶ σελήνη καὶ ἄστρα ὄντα λαμπρὰ
καὶ ἀποστελλόμενα ἐπὶ χρείας εὐήκοά εἰσιν· 60 ὡσαύτως καὶ
ἀστραπή, ὅταν ἐπιφανῇ, εὔοπτός ἐστιν· τὸ δ᾽ αὐτὸ καὶ πνεῦμα ἐν πάσῃ χώρᾳ πνεῖ· 61 καὶ νεφέλαις ὅταν ἐπιταγῇ ὑπὸ
τοῦ θεοῦ ἐπιπορεύεσθαι ἐφ᾽ ὅλην τὴν οἰκουμένην, συντελοῦσι
τὸ ταχθέν· τό τε πῦρ ἐξαποσταλὲν ἄνωθεν ἐξαναλῶσαι ὄρη
καὶ δρυμοὺς ποιεῖ τὸ συνταχθέν. 62 ταῦτα δὲ οὔτε ταῖς ἰδέ-
αις οὔτε ταῖς δυνάμεσιν αὐτῶν ἀφωμοιωμένα ἐστίν. 63 ὅθεν
οὔτε νομιστέον οὔτε κλητέον ὑπάρχειν αὐτοὺς θεούς, οὐ
δυνατῶν ὄντων αὐτῶν οὔτε κρίσιν κρῖναι οὔτε εὖ ποιεῖν
ἀνθρώποις. 64 γνόντες οὖν ὅτι οὔκ εἰσιν θεοί, μὴ φοβηθῆτε
αὐτούς.

65 Οὔτε γὰρ βασιλεῦσιν οὐ μὴ καταράσωνται οὔτε μὴ εὐλο-
γήσωσι. 66 σημεῖά τε ἐν ἔθνεσιν ἐν οὐρανῷ οὐ μὴ δείξωσιν
οὐδὲ ὡς ὁ ἥλιος λάμψουσιν οὐδὲ φωτίσουσιν ὡς σελήνη.
67 τὰ θηρία ἐστὶν κρείττω αὐτῶν, ἃ δύνανται ἐκφυγόντα εἰς
σκέπην ἑαυτὰ ὠφελῆσαι. 68 κατ᾽ οὐδένα οὖν τρόπον ἐστὶν
ἡμῖν φανερὸν ὅτι εἰσὶν θεοί· διὸ μὴ φοβηθῆτε αὐτούς.

69 Ὥσπερ γὰρ ἐν σικυηράτῳ προβασκάνιον οὐδὲν φυλάσ-
σον, οὕτως οἱ θεοὶ αὐτῶν εἰσιν ξύλινοι καὶ περίχρυσοι καὶ
περιάργυροι. 70 τὸν αὐτὸν τρόπον καὶ τῇ ἐν κήπῳ ῥάμνῳ, ἐφ᾽
ἧς πᾶν ὄρνεον ἐπικάθηται, ὡσαύτως δὲ καὶ νεκρῷ ἐρριμμένῳ
ἐν σκότει ἀφωμοίωνται οἱ θεοὶ αὐτῶν ξύλινοι καὶ περίχρυσοι

KING JAMES VERSION

60 For sun, moon, and stars, being bright, and sent to do their offices, are obedient.

61 In like manner the lightning when it breaketh forth is easy to be seen; and after the same manner the wind bloweth in every country.

62 And when God commandeth the clouds to go over the whole world, they do as they are bidden.

63 And the fire sent from above to consume hills and woods doeth as it is commanded: but these are like unto them neither in shew nor power.

64 Wherefore it is neither to be supposed nor said that they are gods, seeing they are able neither to judge causes, nor to do good unto men.

65 Knowing therefore that they are no gods, fear them not.

66 For they can neither curse nor bless kings:

67 Neither can they shew signs in the heavens among the heathen, nor shine as the sun, nor give light as the moon.

68 The beasts are better than they: for they can get under a covert, and help themselves.

69 It is then by no means manifest unto us that they are gods: therefore fear them not.

70 For as a scarecrow in a garden of cucumbers keepeth nothing: so are their gods of wood, and laid over with silver and gold.

71 And likewise their gods of wood, and laid over with silver and gold, are like to a white thorn in an orchard, that every bird sitteth upon; as also to a dead body, that is cast into the dark.

DOUAY OLD TESTAMENT

59 The sun, and the moon, and the stars being bright, and sent forth for profitable uses, are obedient.

60 In like manner the lightning, when it breaketh forth, is easy to be seen: and after the same manner the wind bloweth in every country.

61 And the clouds when God commandeth them to go over the whole world, do that which is commanded them.

62 The fire also being sent from above to consume mountains and woods, doth as it is commanded. But these neither in shew, nor in power are like to any one of them.

63 Wherefore it is neither to be thought, nor to be said, that they are gods: since they are neither able to judge causes, nor to do any good to men.

64 Knowing therefore that they are not gods, fear them not.

65 For neither can they curse kings, nor bless them.

66 Neither do they shew signs in the heaven to the nations, nor shine as the sun, nor give light as the moon.

67 Beasts are better than they, which can fly under a covert, and help themselves.

68 Therefore there is no manner of appearance that they are gods: so fear them not.

69 For as a scarecrow in a garden of cucumbers keepeth nothing, so are their gods of wood, and of silver, and laid over with gold.

70 They are no better than a white thorn in a garden, upon which every bird sitteth. In like manner also their gods of wood, and laid over with gold, and with silver, are like to a dead body cast forth in the dark.

KNOX TRANSLATION

59 How fair to look upon are sun and moon and stars! Yet
theirs is loyal and useful service; 60 and so it is with yonder
lightning, that dazzles the view. Everywhere winds blowing,
61 clouds drifting across the earth as God bade them, fulfil an
appointed task; 62 an appointed task, too, has the heaven-lit
fire that burns mountain-side and forest. What beauty have
the idols, or what power, that they should be compared with
any of these? 63 Gods never think them, gods never call them,
that have no power to execute judgement, to do men good or
ill. 64 And, since gods they are not, need is none to fear them;
65 can they pronounce a curse as or a blessing on kings?
66 Can they startle the world with portents, shine like the sun,
light up darkness like the moon? 67 Why, the very beasts are
their betters, that know at least how to take shelter for their
own safety!

68 Fear we never the gods that ungod themselves so plainly! 69 Wood and silver and gold, that watch over the world
as a scare-crow over a herb-garden; 70 wood and silver and
gold, patient of the birds that perch on them as bush of
white-thorn, or corpse left to lie in a dark alley! 71 From the

TODAY'S ENGLISH VERSION

60 God provided the sun, the moon, and the stars to give
light, and they obey him. 61 The same is true of lightning
and wind. The lightning can be seen far and wide, and the
wind blows everywhere. 62 When God commands clouds to
spread out over the whole world, they obey. 63 When God
sends down fire from heaven to burn up mountains and
forests, it does what it is told. Idols cannot do these things—
they can't even do a good imitation. 64 Why should they be
called gods, when they are not able to help us or harm us in
any way? 65 You know that they are not gods—do not worship them.

66 These gods have no power over kings; they cannot pronounce curses on them or grant them blessings. 67 They cannot produce for the nations any signs in the sky; they cannot
shine like the sun or the moon. 68 Even wild animals are better off than these idols; animals can at least run from danger
to protect themselves. 69 So it is absolutely clear that they
are not gods—do not worship them.

70 These gods of theirs, made of wood and covered with silver and gold, are about as helpful as a scarecrow in a cucumber patch; they are no protection at all. 71 They do as much
good as a thorn bush in a garden; instead of keeping birds
away, they provide a perch for them. These gods are like a
dead body thrown out into the darkness. 72 The purple

NEW REVISED STANDARD VERSION

60 For sun and moon and stars are bright, and when sent
to do a service, they are obedient. 61 So also the lightning,
when it flashes, is widely seen; and the wind likewise blows
in every land. 62 When God commands the clouds to go over
the whole world, they carry out his command. 63 And the fire
sent from above to consume mountains and woods does
what it is ordered. But these idols[a] are not to be compared
with them in appearance or power. 64 Therefore one must
not think that they are gods, nor call them gods, for they are
not able either to decide a case or to do good to anyone.
65 Since you know then that they are not gods, do not fear
them.

66 They can neither curse nor bless kings; 67 they cannot
show signs in the heavens for the nations, or shine like the
sun or give light like the moon. 68 The wild animals are better than they are, for they can flee to shelter and help themselves. 69 So we have no evidence whatever that they are
gods; therefore do not fear them.

70 Like a scarecrow in a cucumber bed, which guards nothing, so are their gods of wood, overlaid with gold and silver.
71 In the same way, their gods of wood, overlaid with gold and
silver, are like a thornbush in a garden on which every bird
perches; or like a corpse thrown out in the darkness. 72 From

a Gk *these things*

NEW AMERICAN BIBLE

and stars are bright, and obedient in the service for which
they are sent. 60 Like wise the lightning, when it flashes, is a
goodly sight; and the same wind blows over all the land.
61 The clouds, too, when commanded by God to proceed
across the whole world, fulfill the order; 62 and fire, sent
from on high to burn up the mountains and the forests, does
what has been commanded. But these false gods are not
their equal, whether in beauty or in power; 63 so that it is
unthinkable, and cannot be claimed, that they are gods. They
can neither execute judgment, nor benefit man. 64 Know,
therefore, that they are not gods, and do not fear them.

65 Kings they neither curse nor bless. 66 They show the
nations no signs in the heavens, nor are they brilliant like
the sun, nor shining like the moon. 67 The beasts which can
help themselves by fleeing to shelter are better than they
are. 68 Thus in no way is it clear to us that they are gods; so
do not fear them. 69 For like a scarecrow in a cucumber
patch, that is no protection, are their wooden, gilded, silvered gods. 70 Just like a thornbush in a garden on which
perches every kind of bird, or like a corpse hurled into darkness, are their silvered and gilded wooden gods. 71 From the

NEW JERUSALEM BIBLE

these counterfeit gods. 59 The sun, the moon and the stars,
which shine and have been given work to do, are obedient;
60 similarly, the lightning, as it flashes, is a fine sight; in the
same way, the wind blows across every country, 61 the
clouds execute the order God gives them to pass over the
whole earth, and the fire, sent from above to consume mountain and forest, carries out its orders. 62 Now these gods are
not their equals, either in beauty or in power. 63 So, no one
can think or say that they are gods, powerless as they are to
administer justice or to do anyone any good. 64 Therefore,
knowing that they are not gods, do not be afraid of them.

65 'For they can neither curse nor bless kings, 66 nor produce signs in heaven for the nations, nor shine like the sun,
nor shed light like the moon. 67 The animals are better off
than they are, being able to look after themselves by making
for cover. 68 There is not the slightest shred of evidence that
they are gods; so do not be afraid of them!

69 'Their wooden gods overlaid with gold and silver are like
a scarecrow in a field of cucumbers—protecting nothing.
70 Or again, their wooden gods overlaid with gold and silver
are like a thorn-bush in a garden—any kind of bird may
perch on it—or like a corpse thrown out into the dark.

GREEK OLD TESTAMENT

καὶ περιάργυροι. 71 ἀπό τε τῆς πορφύρας καὶ τῆς μαρμάρου
τῆς ἐπ᾽ αὐτοῖς σηπομένης γνώσεσθε ὅτι οὐκ εἰσιν θεοί·
αὐτά τε ἐξ ὑστέρου βρωθήσονται, καὶ ἔσται ὄνειδος ἐν τῇ
χώρᾳ. 72 κρείσσων οὖν ἄνθρωπος δίκαιος οὐκ ἔχων εἴδωλα,
ἔσται γὰρ μακρὰν ἀπὸ ὀνειδισμοῦ.

KING JAMES VERSION

72 And ye shall know them to be no gods by the bright purple that rotteth upon then: and they themselves afterward shall be eaten, and shall be a reproach in the country.

73 Better therefore is the just man that hath none idols: for he shall be far from reproach.

DOUAY OLD TESTAMENT

71 By the purple also and the scarlet which are motheaten upon them, you shall know that they are not gods. And they themselves at last are consumed, and shall be a reproach in the country.

72 Better therefore is the just man that hath no idols: for he shall be far from reproach.

KNOX TRANSLATION

purple robes that rot on them, you may learn they are no gods; they, too, shall be eaten away when their time comes, and be a disgrace to the country-side.

72 Well it is for God's loyal servants, that eschew idolatry, and live from all censure far removed.

TODAY'S ENGLISH VERSION

linen[a] robes they wear rot away, so we know that they are not gods. Finally they will be eaten by termites, and then no one anywhere will have any use for them.
[73]The righteous person has an advantage over others; he does not own any idols, and they can never make a fool of him.

[a] linen; *Greek* marble.

NEW REVISED STANDARD VERSION

the purple and linen[a] that rot upon them you will know that they are not gods; and they will finally be consumed themselves, and be a reproach in the land. [73]Better, therefore, is someone upright who has no idols; such a person will be far above reproach.

a Cn: Gk *marble*, Syr *silk*

NEW AMERICAN BIBLE

rotting of the purple and the linen upon them, it can be known that they are not gods; they themselves will in the end be consumed, and be a disgrace in the land. [72]The better for the just man who has no idols: he shall be far from disgrace!

NEW JERUSALEM BIBLE

[71]From the purple and linen rotting on their backs you can tell that they are not gods; and in the end, eaten away, they will be the dishonour of the country. [72]Better, then, someone upright who has no idols; dishonour will never come near him.'

GREEK OLD TESTAMENT

ΔΑΝΙΗΛ 3.24–90

24 Καὶ περιεπάτουν ἐν μέσῳ τῆς φλογὸς ὑμνοῦντες τὸν
θεὸν καὶ εὐλογοῦντες τὸν κύριον. 25 καὶ συστὰς Αζαριας
προσηύξατο οὕτως καὶ ἀνοίξας τὸ στόμα αὐτοῦ ἐν μέσῳ τοῦ
πυρὸς εἶπεν

26 Εὐλογητὸς εἶ, κύριε ὁ θεὸς τῶν πατέρων ἡμῶν, καὶ αἰνετός,
καὶ δεδοξασμένον τὸ ὄνομά σου εἰς τοὺς αἰῶνας,
27 ὅτι δίκαιος εἶ ἐπὶ πᾶσιν, οἷς ἐποίησας ἡμῖν,
καὶ πάντα τὰ ἔργα σου ἀληθινά, καὶ εὐθεῖαι αἱ ὁδοί σου,
καὶ πᾶσαι αἱ κρίσεις σου ἀλήθεια,
28 καὶ κρίματα ἀληθείας ἐποίησας
κατὰ πάντα, ἃ ἐπήγαγες ἡμῖν
καὶ ἐπὶ τὴν πόλιν τὴν ἁγίαν τὴν τῶν πατέρων ἡμῶν Ιερουσαλημ,
ὅτι ἐν ἀληθείᾳ καὶ κρίσει ἐπήγαγες πάντα ταῦτα διὰ τὰς ἁμαρτίας ἡμῶν.
29 ὅτι ἡμάρτομεν καὶ ἠνομήσαμεν ἀποστῆναι ἀπὸ σοῦ
καὶ ἐξημάρτομεν ἐν πᾶσιν καὶ τῶν ἐντολῶν σου οὐκ ἠκούσαμεν

KING JAMES VERSION

THE SONG OF THE THREE HOLY CHILDREN[a]

1 And they walked in the midst of the fire, praising God, and blessing the Lord.

2 Then Azarias stood up, and prayed on this manner; and opening his mouth in the midst of the fire said,

3 Blessed art thou, O Lord God of our fathers: thy name is worthy to be praised and glorified for evermore:

4 For thou art righteous in all the things that thou hast done to us: yea, true are all thy works, thy ways are right, and all thy judgments truth.

5 In all the things that thou hast brought upon us, and upon the holy city of our fathers, *even* Jerusalem, thou hast executed true judgment: for according to truth and judgment didst thou bring all these things upon us because of our sins.

6 For we have sinned and committed iniquity, departing from thee.

a Which followeth in the third Chapter of DANIEL after this place,—*fell down bound into the midst of the burning fiery furnace.*—Verse 23. That which followeth is not in the Hebrew, to wit, *And they walked*—unto these words, *Then Nebuchadnezzar*—verse 24.

DOUAY OLD TESTAMENT

In standard editions of the Douay translation these verses are printed after Daniel 3:23.

DANIEL 3.24–90

24 And they walked in the midst of the flame, praising God and blessing the Lord.

25 Then Azarias standing up prayed in this manner, and opening his mouth in the midst of the fire, he said:

26 Blessed art thou, O Lord, the God of our fathers, and thy name is worthy of praise, and glorious for ever:

27 For thou art just in all that thou hast done to us, and all thy works are true, and thy ways right, and all thy judgments true.

28 For thou hast executed true judgments in all the things that thou hast brought upon us, and upon Jerusalem the holy city of our fathers: for according to truth and judgment, thou hast brought all these things upon us for our sins.

29 For we have sinned, and committed iniquity, departing from thee: and we have trespassed in all things:

KNOX TRANSLATION

In standard editions of the Knox translation these verses are printed after Daniel 3:23.

DANIEL 3.24–90

24 And there, in the hottest of the flames, they walked to
and fro, singing to God their praises, blessing the Lord.
25 There, as he stood in the heart of the fire, Azarias found
utterance, and thus made his prayer: 26 Blessed art thou,
Lord God of our fathers, renowned and glorious is thy name
for ever! 27 In all thy dealings with us, thou hast right on thy
side; so true to thy promises, so unswerving in thy course, so
just in thy awards! 28 No punishment thou hast inflicted
upon us, or upon Jerusalem, holy city of our fathers, but was
deserved; for sins of ours, faithfulness and justice that stroke
laid on. 29 Sinners we were, that had wronged and forsaken
thee, all was amiss with us; 30 unheard thy commandments,

TODAY'S ENGLISH VERSION

THE PRAYER OF AZARIAH AND THE SONG OF THE THREE YOUNG MEN

1 The three young men, Hananiah, Mishael, and Azariah,[a]
started walking around in the flames, singing hymns to God,
and praising him as Lord. 2 Then Azariah stood still and
there in the fire he prayed aloud: 3 "O Lord, the God of our
ancestors, we praise and adore you; may your name be honored forever. 4 You have treated us as we deserve. In everything you have done to us you are always honest, and when
you bring us to judgment, you are always fair. 5 You did
what was right when you brought disaster upon Jerusalem,
the holy city of our ancestors. We deserved that judgment
because of our sins. 6 We disobeyed you, we turned our
backs on you, and we are guilty of every sin. 7 We did not do

[a] HANANIAH, MISHAEL, AND AZARIAH: *These are the original names of Shadrach, Meshach, and Abednego (see Dn 1.6, 7).*

NEW REVISED STANDARD VERSION

THE PRAYER OF AZARIAH AND THE SONG OF THE THREE JEWS

(Additions to Daniel, inserted between 3.23 and 3.24)

1 They[a] walked around in the midst of the flames,
singing hymns to God and blessing the Lord. 2 Then Azariah
stood still in the fire and prayed aloud:

3 "Blessed are you, O Lord, God of our ancestors, and
worthy of praise;
and glorious is your name forever!
4 For you are just in all you have done;
all your works are true and your ways right,
and all your judgments are true.
5 You have executed true judgments in all you have
brought upon us
and upon Jerusalem, the holy city of our ancestors;
by a true judgment you have brought all this upon us
because of our sins.
6 For we have sinned and broken your law in turning
away from you;
in all matters we have sinned grievously.

[a] That is, Hananiah, Mishael, and Azariah (Dan 2.17), the original names of Shadrach, Meshach, and Abednego (Dan 1.6-7)

NEW AMERICAN BIBLE

In standard editions of the Douay translation these verses are printed after Daniel 3, 23.

DANIEL 3, 24–90

24 They walked about in the flames, singing to God and
blessing the Lord. 25 In the fire Azariah stood up and prayed
aloud:

26 "Blessed are you, and praiseworthy,
O Lord, the God of our fathers,
and glorious forever is your name.
27 For you are just in all you have done;
all your deeds are faultless, all your ways right,
and all your judgments proper.
28 You have executed proper judgments
in all that you have brought upon us
and upon Jerusalem, the holy city of our fathers.
By a proper judgment you have done all this
because of our sins;
29 For we have sinned and transgressed
by departing from you,
and we have done every kind of evil.

NEW JERUSALEM BIBLE

In standard editions of the New Jerusalem Bible translation these verses are printed after Daniel 3:23.

THE SONG OF AZARIAH IN THE FURNACE AND THE SONG OF THE THREE YOUNG MEN

(Daniel 3:24–90)

24[a] And they walked in the heart of the flames, praising
God and blessing the Lord. 25 Azariah stood in the heart of
the fire, praying aloud thus:

26 May you be blessed and revered, Lord, God of our
ancestors,
may your name be held glorious for ever.
27 For you are upright in all that you have done for us,
all your deeds are true,
all your ways right,
all your judgements true.
28 True is the sentence you have given
in all that you have brought down on us
and on Jerusalem, the holy city of our ancestors,
for you have treated us rightly and truly,
as our sins deserve.
29 Yes, we have sinned and committed a crime by
deserting you,
yes, we have greatly sinned;
we have not listened to your commandments,

[a] **3** The following passages are preserved only in Gk.

GREEK OLD TESTAMENT

30 οὐδὲ συνετηρήσαμεν οὐδὲ ἐποιήσαμεν
καθὼς ἐνετείλω ἡμῖν, ἵνα εὖ ἡμῖν γένηται.
31 καὶ πάντα, ὅσα ἡμῖν ἐπήγαγες, καὶ πάντα, ὅσα
ἐποίησας ἡμῖν, ἐν ἀληθινῇ κρίσει ἐποίησας
32 καὶ παρέδωκας ἡμᾶς εἰς χεῖρας ἐχθρῶν ἀνόμων
ἐχθίστων ἀποστατῶν
καὶ βασιλεῖ ἀδίκῳ καὶ πονηροτάτῳ παρὰ πᾶσαν τὴν γῆν.
33 καὶ νῦν οὐκ ἔστιν ἡμῖν ἀνοῖξαι τὸ στόμα,
αἰσχύνη καὶ ὄνειδος ἐγενήθη τοῖς δούλοις σου καὶ τοῖς
σεβομένοις σε.
34 μὴ δὴ παραδῷς ἡμᾶς εἰς τέλος διὰ τὸ ὄνομά σου
καὶ μὴ διασκεδάσῃς τὴν διαθήκην σου
35 καὶ μὴ ἀποστήσῃς τὸ ἔλεός σου ἀφ' ἡμῶν
δι' Αβρααμ τὸν ἠγαπημένον ὑπὸ σοῦ
καὶ διὰ Ισαακ τὸν δοῦλόν σου
καὶ Ισραηλ τὸν ἅγιόν σου,
36 οἷς ἐλάλησας πρὸς αὐτοὺς λέγων
πληθῦναι τὸ σπέρμα αὐτῶν ὡς τὰ ἄστρα τοῦ οὐρανοῦ
καὶ ὡς τὴν ἄμμον τὴν παρὰ τὸ χεῖλος τῆς θαλάσσης.
37 ὅτι, δέσποτα, ἐσμικρύνθημεν παρὰ πάντα τὰ ἔθνη
καί ἐσμεν ταπεινοὶ ἐν πάσῃ τῇ γῇ σήμερον διὰ τὰς
ἁμαρτίας ἡμῶν,
38 καὶ οὐκ ἔστιν ἐν τῷ καιρῷ τούτῳ ἄρχων καὶ προφήτης
καὶ ἡγούμενος
οὐδὲ ὁλοκαύτωσις οὐδὲ θυσία οὐδὲ προσφορὰ οὐδὲ
θυμίαμα,
οὐ τόπος τοῦ καρπῶσαι ἐναντίον σου καὶ εὑρεῖν ἔλεος·

KING JAMES VERSION

7 In all things have we trespassed, and not obeyed thy commandments, nor kept them, neither done as thou hast commanded us, that it might go well with us.

8 Wherefore all that thou hast brought upon us, and every thing that thou hast done to us, thou hast done in true judgment.

9 And thou didst deliver us into the hands of lawless enemies, most hateful forsakers *of God,* and to an unjust king, and the most wicked in all the world.

10 And now we cannot open our mouths, we are become a shame and reproach to thy servants, and to them that worship thee.

11 Yet deliver us not up wholly, for thy name's sake, neither disannul thou thy covenant:

12 And cause not thy mercy to depart from us, for thy beloved Abraham's sake, for thy servant Issac's sake, and for thy holy Israel's sake;

13 To whom thou hast spoken and promised, that thou wouldest multiply their seed as the stars of heaven, and as the sand that lieth upon the seashore.

14 For we, O Lord, are become less than any nation, and be kept under this day in all the world because of our sins.

15 Neither is there at this time prince, or prophet, or leader, or burnt offering, or sacrifice, or oblation, or incense, or place to sacrifice before thee, and to find mercy.

DOUAY OLD TESTAMENT

30 And we have not hearkened to thy commandments, nor have we observed nor done as thou hadst commanded us, that it might go well with us.

31 Wherefore all that thou hast brought upon us, and every thing that thou hast done to us, thou hast done in true judgment:

32 And thou hast delivered us into the hands of our enemies *that are* unjust, and most wicked, and prevaricators, and to a king unjust, and most wicked beyond all that are upon the earth.

33 And now we cannot open our mouths: we are become a shame and reproach to thy servants, and to them that worship thee.

34 Deliver us not up for ever, we beseech thee, for thy name's sake, and abolish not thy covenant.

35 And take not away thy mercy from us for the sake of Abraham thy beloved, and Isaac thy servant, and Israel thy holy one:

36 To whom thou hast spoken, promising that thou wouldst multiply their seed as the stars of heaven, and as the sand that is on the sea shore.

37 For we, O Lord, are diminished more than any nation, and are brought low in all the earth this day for our sins.

38 Neither is there at this time prince, or leader, or prophet, or holocaust, or sacrifice, or oblation, or incense, or place of firstfruits before thee,

KNOX TRANSLATION

or else unheeded, thy will neglected, and with it, our own
well-being! 31 Nothing we had not deserved, pillage of thy
contriving, plague of thy sending, 32 and at last the foul
domination of godless foes, of a tyrant that has no equal on
earth! 33 Tongue-tied we stand, that have brought disgrace
on the livery of thy true worship.
34 For thy own honour, we entreat thee not to abandon us
eternally. Do not annul thy covenant, 35 and deprive us of
thy mercy. Think of Abraham that was thy friend, of thy servant Isaac, of Jacob whom thou didst set apart for thyself;
36 the men to whom thou didst promise that thou wouldst
increase their posterity, till it was countless as the stars in
heaven, or the sand by the sea-shore. 37 Whereas now, Lord,
we are of all nations the most insignificant; all the world
over, men see us humbled for our sins. 38 In these days we
are without prince or leader or prophet, we have no burnt-
sacrifice, no victim, no offering; for us no incense burns, no
first-fruits can be brought into thy presence and win thy

Today's English Version

the things that you commanded us to do. If we had obeyed
your laws, we would have prospered, 8 but now we deserve
the judgment and punishment that you have brought upon
us. 9 You have handed us over to lawless, hateful, and defiant enemies—to the most wicked king in the world. 10 And
now all of us who worship you are humiliated; we are too
ashamed to open our mouths.
11 "Yet for the sake of your own honor, do not break your
covenant with us and abandon us forever. 12 Do not withhold your mercy from us. Keep your promises to Abraham,
whom you loved, to Isaac, your servant, and to Jacob, the
father of your holy people Israel. 13 You promised to give
them as many descendants as the stars in the sky or as the
grains of sand along the seashore. 14 But now, Lord, we are
fewer in number than any other nation; wherever we are, we
live in disgrace because of our sins. 15 We are left without a
king, without any prophets or leaders. There is no longer a
Temple where we can go to offer you burnt offerings, sacrifices, gifts, or incense, no place where we can make offerings
to you and find your mercy. 16 But we come to you with

New Revised Standard Version

7 We have not obeyed your commandments,
we have not kept them or done what you have
commanded us for our own good.
8 So all that you have brought upon us,
and all that you have done to us,
you have done by a true judgment.
9 You have handed us over to our enemies, lawless and
hateful rebels,
and to an unjust king, the most wicked in all the
world.
10 And now we cannot open our mouths;
we, your servants who worship you, have become a
shame and a reproach.
11 For your name's sake do not give us up forever,
and do not annul your covenant.
12 Do not withdraw your mercy from us,
for the sake of Abraham your beloved
and for the sake of your servant Isaac
and Israel your holy one,
13 to whom you promised
to multiply their descendants like the stars of heaven
and like the sand on the shore of the sea.
14 For we, O Lord, have become fewer than any other nation,
and are brought low this day in all the world because
of our sins.
15 In our day we have no ruler, or prophet, or leader,
no burnt offering, or sacrifice, or oblation, or incense,
no place to make an offering before you and to find
mercy.

New American Bible

30 Your commandments we have not heeded or observed,
nor have we done as you ordered us for our good.
31 Therefore all you have brought upon us,
all you have done to us,
you have done by a proper judgment.
32 You have handed us over to our enemies,
lawless and hateful rebels;
to an unjust king, the worst in all the world.
33 Now we cannot open our mouths;
we, your servants, who revere you,
have become a shame and a reproach.
34 For your name's sake, do not deliver us up forever,
or make void your covenant.
35 Do not take away your mercy from us,
for the sake of Abraham, your beloved,
Isaac your servant, and Israel your holy one,
36 To whom you promised to multiply their offspring
like the stars of heaven,
or the sand on the shore of the sea.
37 For we are reduced, O Lord, beyond any other nation,
brought low everywhere in the world this day
because of our sins.
38 We have in our day no prince, prophet, or leader,
no holocaust, sacrifice, oblation, or incense,
no place to offer first fruits, to find favor with you.

New Jerusalem Bible

30 we have not observed them,
we have not done what you commanded us to do
for our own good.
31 Yes, all that you have brought down on us,
all that you have done to us,
you have been fully justified in doing.
32 You have handed us over to our enemies,
to a lawless people, the worst of the godless,
to an unjust king, the worst in the whole world;
33 today we have no right to open our mouths,
shame and dishonour are the lot
of those who serve and worship you.

34 Do not abandon us for ever,
for the sake of your name;
do not repudiate your covenant,
35 do not withdraw your favour from us,
for the sake of Abraham, your friend,
of Isaac, your servant,
and of Israel, your holy one,
36 to whom you promised to make their descendants as
many as the stars of heaven
and as the grains of sand on the seashore.
37 Lord, we have become the least of all nations,
we are put to shame today throughout the world,
because of our sins.

38 We now have no leader, no prophet, no prince,
no burnt offering, no sacrifice, no oblation, no incense,
no place where we can make offerings to you
39 and win your favour.

GREEK OLD TESTAMENT

39 ἀλλ᾽ ἐν ψυχῇ συντετριμμένῃ καὶ πνεύματι ταπεινώσεως
προσδεχθείημεν
ὡς ἐν ὁλοκαυτώμασιν κριῶν καὶ ταύρων
καὶ ὡς ἐν μυριάσιν ἀρνῶν πιόνων·
40 οὕτως γενέσθω θυσία ἡμῶν ἐνώπιόν σου σήμερον
καὶ ἐκτελέσαι ὄπισθέν σου,
ὅτι οὐκ ἔσται αἰσχύνη τοῖς πεποιθόσιν ἐπὶ σοί.
41 καὶ νῦν ἐξακολουθοῦμεν ἐν ὅλῃ καρδίᾳ καὶ φοβούμεθά σε
καὶ ζητοῦμεν τὸ πρόσωπόν σου, μὴ καταισχύνῃς ἡμᾶς,
42 ἀλλὰ ποίησον μεθ᾽ ἡμῶν κατὰ τὴν ἐπιείκειάν σου
καὶ κατὰ τὸ πλῆθος τοῦ ἐλέους σου.
43 καὶ ἐξελοῦ ἡμᾶς κατὰ τὰ θαυμάσιά σου
καὶ δὸς δόξαν τῷ ὀνόματί σου, κύριε.
44 καὶ ἐντραπείησαν πάντες οἱ ἐνδεικνύμενοι τοῖς δούλοις
σου κακὰ
καὶ καταισχυνθείησαν ἀπὸ πάσης δυνάμεως καὶ
δυναστείας,
καὶ ἡ ἰσχὺς αὐτῶν συντριβείη·
45 γνώτωσαν ὅτι σὺ εἶ κύριος ὁ θεὸς
μόνος καὶ ἔνδοξος ἐφ᾽ ὅλην τὴν οἰκουμένην.

46 Καὶ οὐ διέλειπον οἱ ἐμβαλόντες αὐτοὺς ὑπηρέται τοῦ
βασιλέως καίοντες τὴν κάμινον νάφθαν καὶ πίσσαν καὶ
στιππύον καὶ κληματίδα. 47 καὶ διεχεῖτο ἡ φλὸξ ἐπάνω τῆς
καμίνου ἐπὶ πήχεις τεσσαράκοντα ἐννέα 48 καὶ διώδευσεν
καὶ ἐνεπύρισεν οὓς εὗρεν περὶ τὴν κάμινον τῶν Χαλδαίων.

KING JAMES VERSION

16 Nevertheless in a contrite heart and an humble spirit let us be accepted.

17 Like as in the burnt offerings of rams and bullocks, and like as in ten thousands of fat lambs: so let our sacrifice be in thy sight this day, and *grant* that we may wholly go after thee: for they shall not be confounded that put their trust in thee.

18 And now we follow thee with all our heart, we fear thee, and seek thy face.

19 Put us not to shame: but deal with us after thy lovingkindness, and according to the multitude of thy mercies.

20 Deliver us also according to thy marvellous works, and give glory to thy name, O Lord: and let all them that do thy servants hurt be ashamed;

21 And let them be confounded in all their power and might, and let their strength be broken;

22 And let them know that thou art Lord, the only God, and glorious over the whole world.

23 And the king's servants, that put them in, ceased not to make the oven hot with rosin, pitch, tow, and small wood;

24 So that the flame streamed forth above the furnace forty and nine cubits.

25 And it passed through, and burned those Chaldeans it found about the furnace.

DOUAY OLD TESTAMENT

39 That we may find thy mercy: nevertheless in a contrite heart and humble spirit let us be accepted.

40 As in holocausts of rams, and bullocks, and as in thousands of fat lambs: so let our sacrifice be made in thy sight this day, that it may please thee: for there is no confusion to them that trust in thee.

41 And now we follow thee with all our heart, and we fear thee, and seek thy face.

42 Put us not to confusion, but deal with us according to thy meekness, and according to the multitude of thy mercies.

43 And deliver us according to thy wonderful works, and give glory to thy name, O Lord:

44 And let all them be confounded that shew evils to thy servants, let them be confounded in all thy might, and let their strength be broken.

45 And let them know that thou art the Lord, the only God, and glorious over all the world.

46 Now the king's servants that had cast them in, ceased not to heat the furnace with brimstone, and tow, and pitch, and dry sticks,

47 And the flame mounted up above the furnace nine and forty cubits:

48 And it broke forth, and burnt such of the Chaldeans as it found near the furnace.

KNOX TRANSLATION

favour. 39 But oh, accept us still, hearts that are crushed,
spirits bowed down by adversity; 40 look kindly on the sacrifice we offer thee this day, as it had been burnt-sacrifice of
rams and bullocks, thousands of fattened lambs; who ever
trusted in thee and was disappointed? 41 With all our hearts,
now, we choose thy will, we reverence thee, we long after
thy presence; 42 for that clemency, that abundant mercy of
thine must we hope in vain? 43 By some wondrous deliverance vindicate thy own renown; 44 theirs be the vain hope,
that would do thy servants an injury. Fools, that would
match themselves with omnipotence! Crush down their
might; 45 teach them that in all the world Lord there is none,
God there is none, glorified as thou.

46 Meanwhile, their tormentors were not idle; naphtha and
tow, pitch and tinder must be heaped on the furnace, 47 till
the flame rose forty-nine cubits above the furnace itself,
48 breaking out and burning such Chaldaeans as stood near

TODAY'S ENGLISH VERSION

repentant hearts and humble spirits, begging you to accept
us just as if we had come with burnt offerings of rams and
bulls and thousands of fat lambs. 17 Accept our repentance
as our sacrifice to you today, so that we may obey you with
all our hearts. No one who trusts you will ever be disappointed. 18-19 Now with all our hearts we promise to obey you,
worship you, and come to you in prayer. Treat us with kindness and mercy, and let us never be put to shame. 20 O Lord,
rescue us with one of your miracles; bring honor to your
name.

21 "Bring disgrace and shame on all who harm us. Take
away their might and power and crush their strength. 22 Let
them know that you alone are Lord and God and that you
rule in majesty over the whole world."

23 The king's servants who had thrown the three men into
the furnace kept the fire hot by feeding it with oil, tar, flax,
and brushwood. 24 The flames blazed up to a height of
seventy-five feet 25 and even spread out and burned up the
Babylonians standing near the furnace. 26 But an angel of

NEW REVISED STANDARD VERSION

16 Yet with a contrite heart and a humble spirit may we be
accepted,
17 as though it were with burnt offerings of rams and
bulls,
or with tens of thousands of fat lambs;
such may our sacrifice be in your sight today,
and may we unreservedly follow you,[a]
for no shame will come to those who trust in you.
18 And now with all our heart we follow you;
we fear you and seek your presence.
19 Do not put us to shame,
but deal with us in your patience
and in your abundant mercy.
20 Deliver us in accordance with your marvelous works,
and bring glory to your name, O Lord.
21 Let all who do harm to your servants be put to shame;
let them be disgraced and deprived of all power,
and let their strength be broken.
22 Let them know that you alone are the Lord God,
glorious over the whole world."

23 Now the king's servants who threw them in kept stoking the furnace with naphtha, pitch, tow, and brushwood.
24 And the flames poured out above the furnace forty-nine
cubits, 25 and spread out and burned those Chaldeans who
were caught near the furnace. 26 But the angel of the Lord

a Meaning of Gk uncertain

NEW AMERICAN BIBLE

39 But with contrite heart and humble spirit
let us be received;
40 As though it were holocausts of rams and bullocks,
or thousands of fat lambs,
So let our sacrifice be in your presence today
as we follow you unreservedly;
for those who trust in you cannot be put to shame.
41 And now we follow you with our whole heart,
we fear you and we pray to you.
42 Do not let us be put to shame,
but deal with us in your kindness and great mercy.
43 Deliver us by your wonders,
and bring glory to your name, O Lord:
44 Let all those be routed
who inflict evils on your servants;
Let them be shamed and powerless,
and their strength broken;
45 Let them know that you alone are the Lord God,
glorious over the whole world."

46 Now the king's men who had thrown them in continued
to stoke the furnace with brimstone, pitch, tow, and faggots.
47 The flames rose forty-nine cubits above the furnace, 48 and
spread out, burning the Chaldeans nearby. 49 But the angel

NEW JERUSALEM BIBLE

But may the contrite soul, the humbled spirit, be as
acceptable to you
40 as burnt offerings of rams and bullocks,
as thousands of fat lambs:
such let our sacrifice be to you today,
and may it please you that we follow you wholeheartedly,
since those who trust in you will not be shamed.
41 And now we put our whole heart into following you,
into fearing you and seeking your face once more.
42 Do not abandon us to shame
but treat us in accordance with your gentleness,
in accordance with the greatness of your mercy.
43 Rescue us in accordance with your wonderful deeds
and win fresh glory for your name, O Lord.
44 Confusion seize all who ill-treat your servants:
may they be covered with shame,
deprived of all their power,
and may their strength be broken.
45 Let them learn that you alone are God and Lord,
glorious over the whole world.

46 All this time, the king's servants, who had thrown them
into the furnace, had been stoking it with crude oil, pitch,
tow and brushwood 47 until the flames rose forty-nine cubits
above the furnace 48 and, leaping out, burnt those Chaldaeans to death who were standing round it. 49 But the angel of

GREEK OLD TESTAMENT

[49] ὁ δὲ ἄγγελος κυρίου συγκατέβη ἅμα τοῖς περὶ τὸν Αζαριαν εἰς τὴν κάμινον καὶ ἐξετίναξεν τὴν φλόγα τοῦ πυρὸς ἐκ
τῆς καμίνου [50] καὶ ἐποίησεν τὸ μέσον τῆς καμίνου ὡς πνεῦμα δρόσου διασυρίζον, καὶ οὐχ ἥψατο αὐτῶν τὸ καθόλου τὸ
πῦρ καὶ οὐκ ἐλύπησεν οὐδὲ παρηνώχλησεν αὐτοῖς.

[51] Τότε οἱ τρεῖς ὡς ἐξ ἑνὸς στόματος ὕμνουν καὶ ἐδόξαζον
καὶ εὐλόγουν τὸν θεὸν ἐν τῇ καμίνῳ λέγοντες

[52] Εὐλογητὸς εἶ, κύριε ὁ θεὸς τῶν πατέρων ἡμῶν,
καὶ αἰνετὸς καὶ ὑπερυψούμενος εἰς τοὺς αἰῶνας,
καὶ εὐλογημένον τὸ ὄνομα τῆς δόξης σου τὸ ἅγιον
καὶ ὑπεραινετὸν καὶ ὑπερυψούμενον εἰς τοὺς αἰῶνας.
[53] εὐλογημένος εἶ ἐν τῷ ναῷ τῆς ἁγίας δόξης σου
καὶ ὑπερυμνητὸς καὶ ὑπερένδοξος εἰς τοὺς αἰῶνας.
[55] εὐλογημένος εἶ, ὁ ἐπιβλέπων ἀβύσσους καθήμενος ἐπὶ
χερουβιν,
καὶ αἰνετὸς καὶ ὑπερυψούμενος εἰς τοὺς αἰῶνας.
[54] εὐλογημένος εἶ ἐπὶ θρόνου τῆς βασιλείας σου
καὶ ὑπερυμνητὸς καὶ ὑπερυψούμενος εἰς τοὺς αἰῶνας.
[56] εὐλογημένος εἶ ἐν τῷ στερεώματι τοῦ οὐρανοῦ
καὶ ὑμνητὸς καὶ δεδοξασμένος εἰς τοὺς αἰῶνας.
[57] εὐλογεῖτε, πάντα τὰ ἔργα κυρίου, τὸν κύριον·
ὑμνεῖτε καὶ ὑπερυψοῦτε αὐτὸν εἰς τοὺς αἰῶνας.
[59] εὐλογεῖτε, οὐρανοί, τὸν κύριον·
ὑμνεῖτε καὶ ὑπερυψοῦτε αὐτὸν εἰς τοὺς αἰῶνας.
[58] εὐλογεῖτε, ἄγγελοι κυρίου, τὸν κύριον·
ὑμνεῖτε καὶ ὑπερυψοῦτε αὐτὸν εἰς τοὺς αἰῶνας.
[60] εὐλογεῖτε, ὕδατα πάντα τὰ ἐπάνω τοῦ οὐρανοῦ, τὸν
κύριον·
ὑμνεῖτε καὶ ὑπερυψοῦτε αὐτὸν εἰς τοὺς αἰῶνας.

KING JAMES VERSION

26 But the angel of the Lord came down into the oven together with Azarias and his fellows, and smote the flame of the fire out of the oven;

27 And made the midst of the furnace as it had been a moist whistling wind, so that the fire touched them not at all, neither hurt nor troubled them.

28 Then the three, as out of one mouth, praised, glorified, and blessed God in the furnace, saying,

29 Blessed art thou, O Lord God of our fathers: and to be praised and exalted above all for ever.

30 And blessed is thy glorious and holy name: and to be praised and exalted above all for ever.

31 Blessed art thou in the temple of thine holy glory: and to be praised and glorified above all for ever.

32 Blessed art thou that beholdest the depths, and sittest upon the cherubims: and to be praised and exalted above all for ever.

33 Blessed art thou on the glorious throne of thy kingdom: and to be praised and glorified above all for ever.

34 Blessed art thou in the firmament of heaven: and above all to be praised and glorified for ever.

35 O all ye works of the Lord, bless ye the Lord: praise and exalt him above all for ever.

36 O ye heavens, bless ye the Lord: praise and exalt him above all for ever.

37 O ye angels of the Lord, bless ye the Lord: praise and exalt him above all for ever.

38 O all ye waters that be above the heaven, bless ye the Lord: praise and exalt him above all for ever.

DOUAY OLD TESTAMENT

49 But the angel of the Lord went down with Azarias and his companions into the furnace: and he drove the flame of the fire out of the furnace,

50 And made the midst of the furnace like the blowing of a wind bringing dew, and the fire touched them not at all, nor troubled them, nor did them any harm.

51 Then these three as with one mouth praised, and glorified, and blessed God in the furnace, saying:

52 Blessed art thou, O Lord the God of our fathers: and worthy to be praised, and glorified, and exalted above all for ever: and blessed is the holy name of thy glory: and worthy to be praised, and exalted above all in all ages.

53 Blessed art thou in the holy temple of thy glory: and exceedingly to be praised, and exceeding glorious for ever.

54 Blessed art thou on the throne of thy kingdom, and exceedingly to be praised, and exalted above all for ever.

55 Blessed art thou, that beholdest the depths, and sittest upon the cherubims: and worthy to be praised and exalted above all for ever.

56 Blessed art thou in the firmament of heaven: and worthy of praise, and glorious for ever.

57 All ye works of the Lord, bless the Lord: praise and exalt him above all for ever.

58 O ye angels of the Lord, bless the Lord: praise and exalt him above all for ever.

59 O ye heavens, bless the Lord: praise and exalt him above all for ever.

60 O all ye waters that are above the heavens, bless the Lord: praise and exalt him above all for ever.

KNOX TRANSLATION

it. [49] But an angel of the Lord had gone down into the furnace with Azarias and his companions; and he drove the
flames away from it, [50] making a wind blow in the heart of
the furnace, like the wind that brings the dew. So that these
three were untouched, and the fire brought them neither
pain nor discomfort. [51] Whereupon all of them, as with one
mouth, began to give praise and glory and blessing to God,
there in the furnace, in these words that follow: [52] Blessed
art thou, Lord God of our fathers, praised above all,
renowned above all for ever; blessed is thy holy and glorious
name, praised above all, renowned above all for ever.
[53] Blessed art thou, whose glory fills thy holy temple, praised
above all, renowned above all for ever; [54] blessed art thou,
who reignest on thy kingly throne, praised above all,
renowned above all for ever. [55] Blessed art thou, who art
throned above the cherubim, and gazest down into the
depths, praised above all, renowned above all for ever.
[56] Blessed art thou, high in the vault of heaven, praised
above all, renowned above all for ever.

[57] Then they cried out upon all things the Lord had made,
to bless him, and praise him, and extol his name for ever. [a]
[58] Bless the Lord they should, the Lord's angels; [59] bless
him they should, the heavens, [60] and the waters above the

[a] In the original, the words 'praise him, and extol his name for ever' are repeated some thirty times in verses 58-88. Here, as in the liturgy, the passage has been abridged.

TODAY'S ENGLISH VERSION

the Lord came down into the fire where the three men were.
He pushed aside the flames 27 so that it felt as if a cool
breeze were blowing, and the fire did not touch the men at
all or hurt them in any way.
28 There in the furnace the three young men again started
singing together in praise of God:

29 "We praise you, O Lord, the God of our ancestors.
30 May your glorious, holy name
be held in honor and reverence forever.
31 May hymns be sung to your glory forever
and may your holy presence be praised in that temple,
32 where you sit on your heavenly throne above the
winged creatures
and look down to the world of the dead.
May you be praised and honored forever.
33 May you be praised as you sit on your royal throne.
May hymns be sung to your glory forever.
34 May you be praised in the dome of the heavens.
May hymns be sung to your glory forever.

35 "Praise the Lord, all creation;
sing his praise and honor him forever.
36 Praise the Lord, skies above;
sing his praise and honor him forever.
37 Praise the Lord, all angels of the Lord;
sing his praise and honor him forever.
38 Praise the Lord, all waters above the sky;
sing his praise and honor him forever.

NEW REVISED STANDARD VERSION

came down into the furnace to be with Azariah and his companions, and drove the fiery flame out of the furnace, 27 and
made the inside of the furnace as though a moist wind were
whistling through it. The fire did not touch them at all and
caused them no pain or distress.
28 Then the three with one voice praised and glorified and
blessed God in the furnace:

29 "Blessed are you, O Lord, God of our ancestors,
and to be praised and highly exalted forever;
30 And blessed is your glorious, holy name,
and to be highly praised and highly exalted forever.
31 Blessed are you in the temple of your holy glory,
and to be extolled and highly glorified forever.
32 Blessed are you who look into the depths from your
throne on the cherubim,
and to be praised and highly exalted forever.
33 Blessed are you on the throne of your kingdom,
and to be extolled and highly exalted forever.
34 Blessed are you in the firmament of heaven,
and to be sung and glorified forever.

35 "Bless the Lord, all you works of the Lord;
sing praise to him and highly exalt him forever.
36 Bless the Lord, you heavens;
sing praise to him and highly exalt him forever.
37 Bless the Lord, you angels of the Lord;
sing praise to him and highly exalt him forever.
38 Bless the Lord, all you waters above the heavens;
sing praise to him and highly exalt him forever.

NEW AMERICAN BIBLE

of the Lord went down into the furnace with Azariah and his
companions, drove the fiery flames out of the furnace, 50 and
made the inside of the furnace as though a dew-laden breeze
were blowing through it. The fire in no way touched them or
caused them pain or harm. 51 Then these three in the furnace
with one voice sang, glorifying and blessing God:

52 "Blessed are you, O Lord, the God of our fathers,
praiseworthy and exalted above all forever;
And blessed is your holy and glorious name,
praiseworthy and exalted above all for all ages.
53 Blessed are you in the temple of your holy glory,
praiseworthy and glorious above all forever.
54 Blessed are you on the throne of your kingdom,
praiseworthy and exalted above all forever.
55 Blessed are you who look into the depths
from your throne upon the cherubim,
praiseworthy and exalted above all forever.
56 Blessed are you in the firmament of heaven,
praiseworthy and glorious forever.
57 Bless the Lord, all you works of the Lord,
praise and exalt him above all forever.
58 Angels of the Lord, bless the Lord,
praise and exalt him above all forever.
59 You heavens, bless the Lord,
praise and exalt him above all forever.
60 All you waters above the heavens, bless the Lord,
praise and exalt him above all forever.

NEW JERUSALEM BIBLE

the Lord came down into the furnace beside Azariah and his
companions; he drove the flames of the fire outwards from
the furnace 50 and, in the heart of the furnace, wafted a coolness to them as of the breeze and dew, so that the fire did
not touch them at all and caused them no pain or distress.
51 Then all three in unison began to sing, glorifying and
blessing God in the furnace, with the words:

52 May you be blessed, Lord, God of our ancestors,
be praised and extolled for ever.
Blessed be your glorious and holy name,
praised and extolled for ever.
53 May you be blessed in the Temple of your sacred glory,
exalted and glorified above all for ever:
54 blessed on the throne of your kingdom,
exalted above all, glorified for ever:
55 blessed are you who fathom the abyss, enthroned on
the winged creatures,
praised and exalted above all for ever:
56 blessed in the expanse of the heavens,
exalted and glorified for ever.
57 Bless the Lord, all the Lord's creation:
praise and glorify him for ever!
58 Bless the Lord, angels of the Lord,
praise and glorify him for ever!
59 Bless the Lord, heavens,
praise and glorify him for ever!
60 Bless the Lord, all the waters above the heavens,
praise and glorify him for ever!

GREEK OLD TESTAMENT

[61]εὐλογεῖτε, πᾶσαι αἱ δυνάμεις, τὸν κύριον·
ὑμνεῖτε καὶ ὑπερυψοῦτε αὐτὸν εἰς τοὺς αἰῶνας.
[62]εὐλογεῖτε, ἥλιος καὶ σελήνη, τὸν κύριον·
ὑμνεῖτε καὶ ὑπερυψοῦτε αὐτὸν εἰς τοὺς αἰῶνας.
[63]εὐλογεῖτε, ἄστρα τοῦ οὐρανοῦ, τὸν κύριον·
ὑμνεῖτε καὶ ὑπερυψοῦτε αὐτὸν εἰς τοὺς αἰῶνας.
[64]εὐλογεῖτε, πᾶς ὄμβρος καὶ δρόσος, τὸν κύριον·
ὑμνεῖτε καὶ ὑπερυψοῦτε αὐτὸν εἰς τοὺς αἰῶνας.
[65]εὐλογεῖτε, πάντα τὰ πνεύματα, τὸν κύριον·
ὑμνεῖτε καὶ ὑπερυψοῦτε αὐτὸν εἰς τοὺς αἰῶνας.
[66]εὐλογεῖτε, πῦρ καὶ καῦμα, τὸν κύριον·
ὑμνεῖτε καὶ ὑπερυψοῦτε αὐτὸν εἰς τοὺς αἰῶνας.
[67]εὐλογεῖτε, ψῦχος καὶ καύσων, τὸν κύριον·
ὑμνεῖτε καὶ ὑπερυψοῦτε αὐτὸν εἰς τοὺς αἰῶνας.
[68]εὐλογεῖτε, δρόσοι καὶ νιφετοί, τὸν κύριον·
ὑμνεῖτε καὶ ὑπερυψοῦτε αὐτὸν εἰς τοὺς αἰῶνας.
[71]εὐλογεῖτε, νύκτες καὶ ἡμέραι, τὸν κύριον·
ὑμνεῖτε καὶ ὑπερυψοῦτε αὐτὸν εἰς τοὺς αἰῶνας.
[72]εὐλογεῖτε, φῶς καὶ σκότος, τὸν κύριον·
ὑμνεῖτε καὶ ὑπερυψοῦτε αὐτὸν εἰς τοὺς αἰῶνας.
[69]εὐλογεῖτε, πάγος καὶ ψῦχος, τὸν κύριον·
ὑμνεῖτε καὶ ὑπερυψοῦτε αὐτὸν εἰς τοὺς αἰῶνας.
[70]εὐλογεῖτε, πάχναι καὶ χιόνες, τὸν κύριον·
ὑμνεῖτε καὶ ὑπερυψοῦτε αὐτὸν εἰς τοὺς αἰῶνας.
[73]εὐλογεῖτε, ἀστραπαὶ καὶ νεφέλαι, τὸν κύριον·
ὑμνεῖτε καὶ ὑπερυψοῦτε αὐτὸν εἰς τοὺς αἰῶνας.
[74]εὐλογείτω ἡ γῆ τὸν κύριον·
ὑμνείτω καὶ ὑπερυψούτω αὐτὸν εἰς τοὺς αἰῶνας.

KING JAMES VERSION

39 O all ye powers of the Lord, bless ye the Lord: praise and exalt him above all for ever.

40 O ye sun and moon, bless ye the Lord: praise and exalt him above all for ever.

41 O ye stars of heaven, bless ye the Lord: praise and exalt him above all for ever.

42 O every shower and dew, bless ye the Lord: praise and exalt him above all for ever.

43 O all ye winds, bless ye the Lord: praise and exalt him above all for ever.

44 O ye fire and heat, bless ye the Lord: praise and exalt him above all for ever.

45 O ye winter and summer, bless ye the Lord: praise and exalt him above all for ever.

46 O ye dews and storms of snow, bless ye the Lord: praise and exalt him above all for ever.

47 O ye nights and days, bless ye the Lord: praise and exalt him above all for ever.

48 O ye light and darkness, bless ye the Lord: praise and exalt him above all for ever.

49 O ye ice and cold, bless ye the Lord: praise and exalt him above all for ever.

50 O ye frost and snow, bless ye the Lord: praise and exalt him above all for ever.

51 O ye lightnings and clouds, bless ye the Lord: praise and exalt him above all for ever.

52 O let the earth bless the Lord: praise and exalt him above all for ever.

DOUAY OLD TESTAMENT

61 O all ye powers of the Lord, bless the Lord: praise and exalt him above all for ever.

62 O ye sun and moon, bless the Lord: praise and exalt him above all for ever.

63 O ye stars of heaven, bless the Lord: praise and exalt him above all for ever.

64 O every shower and dew, bless ye the Lord: praise and exalt him above all for ever.

65 O all ye spirits of God, bless the Lord: praise and exalt him above all for ever.

66 O ye fire and heat, bless the Lord: praise and exalt him above all for ever.

67 O ye cold and heat, bless the Lord: praise and exalt him above all for ever.

68 O ye dews and hoar frosts, bless the Lord: praise and exalt him above all for ever.

69 O ye frost and cold, bless the Lord: praise and exalt him above all for ever.

70 O ye ice and snow, bless the Lord: praise and exalt him above all for ever.

71 O ye nights and days, bless the Lord: praise and exalt him above all for ever.

72 O ye light and darkness, bless the Lord: praise and exalt him above all for ever.

73 O ye lightnings and clouds, bless the Lord: praise and exalt him above all for ever.

74 O let the earth bless the Lord: let it praise and exalt him above all for ever.

KNOX TRANSLATION

heavens; [61]bless him they should, all the Lord's powers.
[62]Bless him they should, sun and moon, [63]stars of heaven,
[64]each drop of rain and moisture, [65]and all the winds of
God. [66]Bless him they should, fire and heat, [67]winter cold
and summer drought, [68]dew and rime at morning, [69]frost
and the cold air. [70]Bless him they should, ice and snow,
[71]day-time and night-time, [72]light and darkness, [73]light-
nings and storm-clouds. [74]And earth in its turn should
bless the Lord, praise him, and extol his name for ever.

TODAY'S ENGLISH VERSION

39 Praise the Lord, all heavenly powers;
sing his praise and honor him forever.
40 Praise the Lord, sun and moon;
sing his praise and honor him forever.
41 Praise the Lord, stars of heaven;
sing his praise and honor him forever.
42 Praise the Lord, rain and dew;
sing his praise and honor him forever.
43 Praise the Lord, all winds;
sing his praise and honor him forever.
44 Praise the Lord, fire and heat;
sing his praise and honor him forever.
45 Praise the Lord, bitter cold and scorching heat;
sing his praise and honor him forever.
46 Praise the Lord, dews and snows;
sing his praise and honor him forever.
47 Praise the Lord, nights and days;
sing his praise and honor him forever.
48 Praise the Lord, daylight and darkness;
sing his praise and honor him forever.
49 Praise the Lord, ice and cold;
sing his praise and honor him forever.
50 Praise the Lord, frost and snow;
sing his praise and honor him forever.
51 Praise the Lord, lightning and storm clouds;
sing his praise and honor him forever.

52 "Let the earth praise the Lord;
sing his praise and honor him forever.

NEW REVISED STANDARD VERSION

39 Bless the Lord, all you powers of the Lord;
sing praise to him and highly exalt him forever.
40 Bless the Lord, sun and moon;
sing praise to him and highly exalt him forever.
41 Bless the Lord, stars of heaven;
sing praise to him and highly exalt him forever.

42 "Bless the Lord, all rain and dew;
sing praise to him and highly exalt him forever.
43 Bless the Lord, all you winds;
sing praise to him and highly exalt him forever.
44 Bless the Lord, fire and heat;
sing praise to him and highly exalt him forever.
45 Bless the Lord, winter cold and summer heat;
sing praise to him and highly exalt him forever.
46 Bless the Lord, dews and falling snow;
sing praise to him and highly exalt him forever.
47 Bless the Lord, nights and days;
sing praise to him and highly exalt him forever.
48 Bless the Lord, light and darkness;
sing praise to him and highly exalt him forever.
49 Bless the Lord, ice and cold;
sing praise to him and highly exalt him forever.
50 Bless the Lord, frosts and snows;
sing praise to him and highly exalt him forever.
51 Bless the Lord, lightnings and clouds;
sing praise to him and highly exalt him forever.

52 "Let the earth bless the Lord;
let it sing praise to him and highly exalt him forever.

NEW AMERICAN BIBLE

61 All you hosts of the Lord, bless the Lord;
praise and exalt him above all forever.
62 Sun and moon, bless the Lord;
praise and exalt him above all forever.
63 Stars of heaven, bless the Lord;
praise and exalt him above all forever.
64 Every shower and dew, bless the Lord;
praise and exalt him above all forever.
65 All you winds, bless the Lord;
praise and exalt him above all forever.
66 Fire and heat, bless the Lord;
praise and exalt him above all forever.
67 [Cold and chill, bless the Lord;
praise and exalt him above all forever.
68 Dew and rain, bless the Lord;
praise and exalt him above all forever.]
69 Frost and chill, bless the Lord;
praise and exalt him above all forever.
70 Ice and snow, bless the Lord;
praise and exalt him above all forever.
71 Nights and days, bless the Lord;
praise and exalt him above all forever.
72 Light and darkness, bless the Lord;
praise and exalt him above all forever.
73 Lightnings and clouds, bless the Lord;
praise and exalt him above all forever.
74 Let the earth bless the Lord,
praise and exalt him above all forever.

NEW JERUSALEM BIBLE

61 Bless the Lord, powers of the Lord,
praise and glorify him for ever!
62 Bless the Lord, sun and moon,
praise and glorify him for ever!
63 Bless the Lord, stars of heaven,
praise and glorify him for ever!

64 Bless the Lord, all rain and dew,
praise and glorify him for ever!
65 Bless the Lord, every wind,
praise and glorify him for ever!
66 Bless the Lord, fire and heat,
praise and glorify him for ever!
67 Bless the Lord, cold and warmth,
praise and glorify him for ever!
68 Bless the Lord, dew and snow-storm,
praise and glorify him for ever!
69 Bless the Lord, frost and cold,
praise and glorify him for ever!
70 Bless the Lord, ice and snow,
praise and glorify him for ever!
71 Bless the Lord, nights and days,
praise and glorify him for ever!
72 Bless the Lord, light and darkness,
praise and glorify him for ever!
73 Bless the Lord, lightning and cloud,
praise and glorify him for ever!

74 Let the earth bless the Lord:
praise and glorify him for ever!

Greek Old Testament

75 εὐλογεῖτε, ὄρη καὶ βουνοί, τὸν κύριον·
ὑμνεῖτε καὶ ὑπερυψοῦτε αὐτὸν εἰς τοὺς αἰῶνας.
76 εὐλογεῖτε, πάντα τὰ φυόμενα ἐν τῇ γῇ, τὸν κύριον·
ὑμνεῖτε καὶ ὑπερυψοῦτε αὐτὸν εἰς τοὺς αἰῶνας.
78 εὐλογεῖτε, θάλασσαι καὶ ποταμοί, τὸν κύριον·
ὑμνεῖτε καὶ ὑπερυψοῦτε αὐτὸν εἰς τοὺς αἰῶνας.
77 εὐλογεῖτε, αἱ πηγαί, τὸν κύριον·
ὑμνεῖτε καὶ ὑπερυψοῦτε αὐτὸν εἰς τοὺς αἰῶνας.
79 εὐλογεῖτε, κήτη καὶ πάντα τὰ κινούμενα ἐν τοῖς ὕδασιν, τὸν κύριον·
ὑμνεῖτε καὶ ὑπερυψοῦτε αὐτὸν εἰς τοὺς αἰῶνας.
80 εὐλογεῖτε, πάντα τὰ πετεινὰ τοῦ οὐρανοῦ, τὸν κύριον·
ὑμνεῖτε καὶ ὑπερυψοῦτε αὐτὸν εἰς τοὺς αἰῶνας.
81 εὐλογεῖτε, πάντα τὰ θηρία καὶ τὰ κτήνη, τὸν κύριον·
ὑμνεῖτε καὶ ὑπερυψοῦτε αὐτὸν εἰς τοὺς αἰῶνας.
82 εὐλογεῖτε, οἱ υἱοὶ τῶν ἀνθρώπων, τὸν κύριον·
ὑμνεῖτε καὶ ὑπερυψοῦτε αὐτὸν εἰς τοὺς αἰῶνας.
83 εὐλογεῖτε, Ισραηλ, τὸν κύριον·
ὑμνεῖτε καὶ ὑπερυψοῦτε αὐτὸν εἰς τοὺς αἰῶνας.
84 εὐλογεῖτε, ἱερεῖς κυρίου, τὸν κύριον·
ὑμνεῖτε καὶ ὑπερυψοῦτε αὐτὸν εἰς τοὺς αἰῶνας.
85 εὐλογεῖτε, δοῦλοι κυρίου, τὸν κύριον·
ὑμνεῖτε καὶ ὑπερυψοῦτε αὐτὸν εἰς τοὺς αἰῶνας.
86 εὐλογεῖτε, πνεύματα καὶ ψυχαὶ δικαίων, τὸν κύριον·
ὑμνεῖτε καὶ ὑπερυψοῦτε αὐτὸν εἰς τοὺς αἰῶνας.
87 εὐλογεῖτε, ὅσιοι καὶ ταπεινοὶ τῇ καρδίᾳ, τὸν κύριον·
ὑμνεῖτε καὶ ὑπερυψοῦτε αὐτὸν εἰς τοὺς αἰῶνας.

King James Version

53 O ye mountains and little hills, bless ye the Lord: praise and exalt him above all for ever.

54 O all ye things that grow on the earth, bless ye the Lord: praise and exalt him above all for ever.

55 O ye fountains, bless ye the Lord: praise and exalt him above all for ever.

56 O ye seas and rivers, bless ye the Lord: praise and exalt him above all for ever.

57 O ye whales, and all that move in the waters, bless ye the Lord: praise and exalt him above all for ever.

58 O all ye fowls of the air, bless ye the Lord: praise and exalt him above all for ever.

59 O all ye beasts and cattle, bless ye the Lord: praise and exalt him above all for ever.

60 O ye children of men, bless ye the Lord: praise and exalt him above all for ever.

61 O Israel, bless ye the Lord: praise and exalt him above all for ever.

62 O ye priests of the Lord, bless ye the Lord: praise and exalt him above all for ever.

63 O ye servants of the Lord, bless ye the Lord: praise and exalt him above all for ever.

64 O ye spirits and souls of the righteous, bless ye the Lord: praise and exalt him above all for ever.

65 O ye holy and humble men of heart, bless ye the Lord: praise and exalt him above all for ever.

Douay Old Testament

75 O ye mountains and hills, bless the Lord: praise and exalt him above all for ever.

76 O all ye things that spring up in the earth, bless the Lord: praise and exalt him above all for ever.

77 O ye fountains, bless the Lord: praise and exalt him above all for ever.

78 O ye seas and rivers, bless the Lord: praise and exalt him above all for ever.

79 O ye whales, and all that move in the waters, bless the Lord: praise and exalt him above all for ever.

80 O all ye fowls of the air, bless the Lord: praise and exalt him above all for ever.

81 O all ye beasts and cattle, bless the Lord: praise and exalt him above all for ever.

82 O ye sons of men, bless the Lord: praise and exalt him above all for ever.

83 O let Israel bless the Lord: let them praise and exalt him above all for ever.

84 O ye priests of the Lord, bless the Lord: praise and exalt him above all for ever.

85 O ye servants of the Lord, bless the Lord: praise and exalt him above all for ever.

86 O ye spirits and souls of the just, bless the Lord: praise and exalt him above all for ever.

87 O ye holy and humble of heart, bless the Lord: praise and exalt him above all for ever.

Knox Translation

75 Bless the Lord they should, mountains and hills, 76 every
growing thing that earth yields, 77 flowing fountains,
78 seas and rivers. 79 Bless him they should, sea-monsters
and all life that is bred in the waters, 80 all the birds that fly
in heaven, 81 wild beasts and tame, 82 and the sons of men.
83 Bless him Israel should, 84 priests of the Lord bless him,
85 servants of the Lord bless him; 86 bless him they should,
spirits and souls of all faithful men; 87 bless him they
should, dedicated and humble hearts. 88 And for Ananias,

TODAY'S ENGLISH VERSION

53 Praise the Lord, mountains and hills;
sing his praise and honor him forever.
54 Praise the Lord, everything that grows;
sing his praise and honor him forever.
55 Praise the Lord, lakes and rivers;
sing his praise and honor him forever.
56 Praise the Lord, springs of water;
sing his praise and honor him forever.
57 Praise the Lord, whales and sea creatures;
sing his praise and honor him forever.
58 Praise the Lord, all birds;
sing his praise and honor him forever.
59 Praise the Lord, all cattle and wild animals;
sing his praise and honor him forever.

60 "Praise the Lord, all people on earth;
sing his praise and honor him forever.
61 Praise the Lord, people of Israel;
sing his praise and honor him forever.
62 Praise the Lord, priests of the Lord;
sing his praise and honor him forever.
63 Praise the Lord, servants of the Lord;
sing his praise and honor him forever.
64 Praise the Lord, all faithful people;
sing his praise and honor him forever.
65 Praise the Lord, all who are humble and holy;
sing his praise and honor him forever.

NEW REVISED STANDARD VERSION

53 Bless the Lord, mountains and hills;
sing praise to him and highly exalt him forever.
54 Bless the Lord, all that grows in the ground;
sing praise to him and highly exalt him forever.
55 Bless the Lord, seas and rivers;
sing praise to him and highly exalt him forever.
56 Bless the Lord, you springs;
sing praise to him and highly exalt him forever.
57 Bless the Lord, you whales and all that swim in the waters;
sing praise to him and highly exalt him forever.
58 Bless the Lord, all birds of the air;
sing praise to him and highly exalt him forever.
59 Bless the Lord, all wild animals and cattle;
sing praise to him and highly exalt him forever.

60 "Bless the Lord, all people on earth;
sing praise to him and highly exalt him forever.
61 Bless the Lord, O Israel;
sing praise to him and highly exalt him forever.
62 Bless the Lord, you priests of the Lord;
sing praise to him and highly exalt him forever.
63 Bless the Lord, you servants of the Lord;
sing praise to him and highly exalt him forever.
64 Bless the Lord, spirits and souls of the righteous;
sing praise to him and highly exalt him forever.
65 Bless the Lord, you who are holy and humble in heart;
sing praise to him and highly exalt him forever.

NEW AMERICAN BIBLE

75 Mountains and hills, bless the Lord;
praise and exalt him above all forever.
76 Everything growing from the earth, bless the Lord;
praise and exalt him above all forever.
77 You springs, bless the Lord;
praise and exalt him above all forever.
78 Seas and rivers, bless the Lord;
praise and exalt him above all forever.
79 You dolphins and all water creatures, bless the Lord;
praise and exalt him above all forever.
80 All you birds of the air, bless the Lord;
praise and exalt him above all forever.
81 All you beasts, wild and tame, bless the Lord;
praise and exalt him above all forever.
82 You sons of men, bless the Lord;
praise and exalt him above all forever.
83 O Israel, bless the Lord;
praise and exalt him above all forever.
84 Priests of the Lord, bless the Lord;
praise and exalt him above all forever.
85 Servants of the Lord, bless the Lord;
praise and exalt him above all forever.
86 Spirits and souls of the just, bless the Lord;
praise and exalt him above all forever.
87 Holy men of humble heart, bless the Lord;
praise and exalt him above all forever.

NEW JERUSALEM BIBLE

75 Bless the Lord, mountains and hills,
praise and glorify him for ever!
76 Bless the Lord, every plant that grows,
praise and glorify him for ever!
77 Bless the Lord, springs of water,
praise and glorify him for ever!
78 Bless the Lord, seas and rivers,
praise and glorify him for ever!
79 Bless the Lord, whales, and everything that moves in the waters,
praise and glorify him for ever!
80 Bless the Lord, every kind of bird,
praise and glorify him for ever!
81 Bless the Lord, all animals wild and tame,
praise and glorify him for ever!

82 Bless the Lord, all the human race:
praise and glorify him for ever!
83 Bless the Lord, O Israel,
praise and glorify him for ever!
84 Bless the Lord, priests,
praise and glorify him for ever!
85 Bless the Lord, his servants,
praise and glorify him for ever!
86 Bless the Lord, spirits and souls of the upright,
praise and glorify him for ever!
87 Bless the Lord, faithful, humble-hearted people,
praise and glorify him for ever!

GREEK OLD TESTAMENT

[88]εὐλογεῖτε, Ανανια, Αζαρια, Μισαηλ, τὸν κύριον·
ὑμνεῖτε καὶ ὑπερυψοῦτε αὐτὸν εἰς τοὺς αἰῶνας,
ὅτι ἐξείλατο ἡμᾶς ἐξ ᾅδου καὶ ἐκ χειρὸς θανάτου
ἔσωσεν ἡμᾶς
καὶ ἐρρύσατο ἡμᾶς ἐκ μέσου καμίνου καιομένης
φλογὸς
καὶ ἐκ μέσου πυρὸς ἐρρύσατο ἡμᾶς.
[89]ἐξομολογεῖσθε τῷ κυρίῳ, ὅτι χρηστός,
ὅτι εἰς τὸν αἰῶνα τὸ ἔλεος αὐτοῦ.
[90]εὐλογεῖτε, πάντες οἱ σεβόμενοι τὸν κύριον τὸν θεὸν τῶν
θεῶν·
ὑμνεῖτε καὶ ἐξομολογεῖσθε, ὅτι εἰς τὸν αἰῶνα τὸ
ἔλεος αὐτοῦ.

KING JAMES VERSION

66 O Ananias, Azarias, and Misael, bless ye the Lord: praise and exalt him above all for ever: for he hath delivered us from hell, and saved us from the hand of death, and delivered us out of the midst of the furnace *and* burning flame: even out of the midst of the fire hath he delivered us.

67 O give thanks unto the Lord, because he is gracious: for his mercy *endureth* for ever.

68 O all ye that worship the Lord, bless the God of gods, praise him, and give him thanks: for his mercy *endureth* for ever.

DOUAY OLD TESTAMENT

88 O Ananias, Azarias, and Misael, bless ye the Lord: praise and exalt him above all for ever. For he hath delivered us from hell, and saved us out of the hand of death, and delivered us out of the midst of the burning flame, and saved us out of the midst of the fire.

89 O give thanks to the Lord, because he is good: because his mercy endureth for ever and ever.

90 O all ye religious, bless the Lord the God of gods: praise him and give him thanks, because his mercy endureth for ever and ever.

KNOX TRANSLATION

Azarias and Misael, well might they bless the Lord, praise
him and extol his name for ever; here was the grave
spoiled, death robbed of its prey, and ever they were kept
safe from the furnace, let its flames rage as they would.
[89]Give thanks to the Lord, they cried, the Lord is gracious;
his mercy is eternal! [90]Bless the Lord, you that are his worshippers; he is God above all gods; praise him and give him
thanks, whose mercy is eternal.[a]

[a] Verses 24-90 are found in the Septuagint Greek, but were unknown to the Aramaic text, it seems, even in the time of St Jerome.

TODAY'S ENGLISH VERSION

66 Praise the Lord, Hananiah, Azariah, and Mishael;
sing his praise and honor him forever.
He rescued us from the world of the dead
and saved us from the power of death.
He brought us out from the burning furnace
and saved us from the fire.
67 Give thanks to the Lord, for he is good
and his mercy lasts forever.
68 Praise the Lord, all who worship him;
sing praise to the God of gods and give him thanks,
for his mercy lasts forever."

NEW REVISED STANDARD VERSION

66 "Bless the Lord, Hananiah, Azariah, and Mishael;
sing praise to him and highly exalt him forever.
For he has rescued us from Hades and saved us from
the power[a] of death,
and delivered us from the midst of the burning fiery
furnace;
from the midst of the fire he has delivered us.
67 Give thanks to the Lord, for he is good,
for his mercy endures forever.
68 All who worship the Lord, bless the God of gods,
sing praise to him and give thanks to him,
for his mercy endures forever."

a Gk *hand*

NEW AMERICAN BIBLE

88 Hananiah, Azariah, Mishael, bless the Lord;
praise and exalt him above all forever.
For he has delivered us from the nether world,
and saved us from the power of death;
He has freed us from the raging flame
and delivered us from the fire.
89 Give thanks to the Lord, for he is good,
for his mercy endures forever.
90 Bless the God of gods, all you who fear the Lord;
praise him and give him thanks,
because his mercy endures forever."

NEW JERUSALEM BIBLE

88 Hananiah, Azariah and Mishael,
bless the Lord,
praise and glorify him for ever!—
For he has rescued us from the Underworld,
he has saved us from the hand of Death,
he has snatched us
from the burning fiery furnace,
he has drawn us from the heart of the flame!
89 Give thanks to the Lord, for he is good,
for his love is everlasting.
90 Bless the Lord, the God of gods,
all who fear him,
give praise and thanks to him,
for his love is everlasting!

GREEK OLD TESTAMENT

ΣΟΥΣΑΝΝΑ

1 Καὶ ἦν ἀνὴρ οἰκῶν ἐν Βαβυλῶνι, καὶ ὄνομα αὐτῷ Ιωακιμ.
2 καὶ ἔλαβεν γυναῖκα, ᾗ ὄνομα Σουσαννα θυγάτηρ Χελκιου,
καλὴ σφόδρα καὶ φοβουμένη τὸν κύριον· 3 καὶ οἱ γονεῖς
αὐτῆς δίκαιοι καὶ ἐδίδαξαν τὴν θυγατέρα αὐτῶν κατὰ τὸν
νόμον Μωυσῆ. 4 καὶ ἦν Ιωακιμ πλούσιος σφόδρα, καὶ ἦν
αὐτῷ παράδεισος γειτνιῶν τῷ οἴκῳ αὐτοῦ· καὶ πρὸς αὐτὸν
προσήγοντο οἱ Ιουδαῖοι διὰ τὸ εἶναι αὐτὸν ἐνδοξότερον πάντων. 5 καὶ ἀπεδείχθησαν δύο πρεσβύτεροι ἐκ τοῦ λαοῦ κριταὶ ἐν τῷ ἐνιαυτῷ ἐκείνῳ, περὶ ὧν ἐλάλησεν ὁ δεσπότης ὅτι
Ἐξῆλθεν ἀνομία ἐκ Βαβυλῶνος ἐκ πρεσβυτέρων κριτῶν, οἳ
ἐδόκουν κυβερνᾶν τὸν λαόν. 6 οὗτοι προσεκαρτέρουν ἐν τῇ
οἰκίᾳ Ιωακιμ, καὶ ἤρχοντο πρὸς αὐτοὺς πάντες οἱ κρινόμενοι. 7 καὶ ἐγένετο ἡνίκα ἀπέτρεχεν ὁ λαὸς μέσον ἡμέρας,
εἰσεπορεύετο Σουσαννα καὶ περιεπάτει ἐν τῷ παραδείσῳ τοῦ
ἀνδρὸς αὐτῆς. 8 καὶ ἐθεώρουν αὐτὴν οἱ δύο πρεσβύτεροι καθ'
ἡμέραν εἰσπορευομένην καὶ περιπατοῦσαν καὶ ἐγένοντο ἐν
ἐπιθυμίᾳ αὐτῆς. 9 καὶ διέστρεψαν τὸν ἑαυτῶν νοῦν καὶ ἐξέκλιναν τοὺς ὀφθαλμοὺς αὐτῶν τοῦ μὴ βλέπειν εἰς τὸν οὐρανὸν
μηδὲ μνημονεύειν κριμάτων δικαίων. 10 καὶ ἦσαν ἀμφότεροι

KING JAMES VERSION

THE HISTORY OF SUSANNA[a]

1 There dwelt a man in Babylon, called Joacim:

2 And he took a wife, whose name was Susanna, the daughter of Chelcias, a very fair woman, and one that feared the Lord.

3 Her parents also were righteous, and taught their daughter according to the law of Moses.

4 Now Joacim was a great rich man, and had a fair garden joining unto his house: and to him resorted the Jews; because he was more honourable than all others.

5 The same year were appointed two of the ancients of the people to be judges, such as the Lord spake of, that wickedness came from Babylon from ancient judges, who seemed to govern the people.

6 These kept much at Joacim's house: and all that had any suits in law came unto them.

7 Now when the people departed away at noon, Susanna went into her husband's garden to walk.

8 And the two elders saw her going in every day, and walking; so that their lust was inflamed toward her.

9 And they perverted their own mind, and turned away their eyes, that they might not look unto heaven, nor remember just judgments.

a Set apart from the beginning of *Daniel*, because it is not in the Hebrew, as neither the Narration of *Bel and the Dragon*.

DOUAY OLD TESTAMENT

In standard editions of the Douay translation these verses are printed after Daniel 12.

DANIEL 13

1 NOW there was a man that dwelt in Babylon, and his name was Joakim:

2 And he took a wife whose name was Susanna, the daughter of Helcias, a very beautiful woman, and one that feared God.

3 For her parents being just, had instructed their daughter according to the law of Moses.

4 Now Joakim was very rich, and had an orchard near his house: and the Jews resorted to him, because he was the most honourable of them all.

5 And there were two of the ancients of the people appointed judges that year, of whom the Lord said: Iniquity came out from Babylon from the ancient judges, that seemed to govern the people.

6 These men frequented the house of Joakim, and all that had any matters of judgment came to them.

7 And when the people departed away at noon, Susanna went in, and walked in her husband's orchard.

8 And the old men saw her going in every day, and walking: and they were inflamed with lust towards her:

9 And they perverted their own mind and turned away their eyes that they might not look unto heaven, nor remember just judgments.

KNOX TRANSLATION

In standard editions of the Knox translation these verses are printed after Daniel 12.

DANIEL 13

1 There was a man called Joakim living in Babylon, 2 married to one Susanna, daughter of Helcias.[a] This was a
woman of great beauty, and one that feared God, 3 so well
had her parents, religious folk, schooled their daughter in the
law of Moses. 4 A rich man was Joakim, and had a fruit-gar-
den close to his house; and he was much visited by the Jews,
among whom there was none more honoured than he.
5 There came a year in which those two elders of the people
were appointed judges, of whom the Lord said, Wickedness
has sprung up in Babylon, and the roots of it are those elders
and judges who claim to rule the people.[b] 6 These two were
often at Joakim's house, and all those who had disputes to
settle appeared before them there.

7 At noon, when the common folk had returned home,
Susanna would walk about in her husband's garden, 8 and
these two elders, who saw her go in and walk there day after
day, fell to lusting after her. 9 Reason they dethroned, and
turned away their eyes from the sight of heaven; its just
awards they would fain have forgotten. 10 The love that

a This chapter, with chapter 14, is preserved in the Septuagint Greek, but not in the Hebrew text. *b* Some think this is an allusion to Jer. 29. 21-23.

TODAY'S ENGLISH VERSION

THE BOOK OF SUSANNA

1 In Babylon there lived a man named Joakim, 2 who was married to Susanna, daughter of Hilkiah. Susanna was a beautiful woman and deeply religious. 3 Her parents were devout Jews who had brought up their daughter to live according to the Law of Moses. 4 Her husband Joakim was very wealthy. Lovely gardens surrounded his house, and the other Jews often gathered there for meetings, because they all thought so highly of him. 5-6 Everyone who had a legal case to present would also go to Joakim's house, where two judges held court. These two leaders of the Jewish community had recently been appointed to office. They were the ones about whom the Lord said, "There is wickedness in Babylon; judges are failing to give guidance to the people."

7 Every day at noon, when all the people left for lunch, Susanna used to take a walk in the gardens. 8 The two judges were so attracted to her that they would wait around and watch for her. 9 They became so obsessed with their desire for her that they lost interest both in prayer and in their responsibility as judges. 10 They each wanted Susanna,

NEW REVISED STANDARD VERSION

SUSANNA

(Chapter 13 of the Greek version of Daniel)

1 There was a man living in Babylon whose name was Joakim. 2 He married the daughter of Hilkiah, named Susanna, a very beautiful woman and one who feared the Lord. 3 Her parents were righteous, and had trained their daughter according to the law of Moses. 4 Joakim was very rich, and had a fine garden adjoining his house; the Jews used to come to him because he was the most honored of them all.

5 That year two elders from the people were appointed as judges. Concerning them the Lord had said: "Wickedness came forth from Babylon, from elders who were judges, who were supposed to govern the people." 6 These men were frequently at Joakim's house, and all who had a case to be tried came to them there.

7 When the people left at noon, Susanna would go into her husband's garden to walk. 8 Every day the two elders used to see her, going in and walking about, and they began to lust for her. 9 They suppressed their consciences and turned away their eyes from looking to Heaven or remembering their duty

NEW AMERICAN BIBLE

In standard editions of the New American Bible translation these verses are printed after Daniel 12.

DANIEL 13

1 In Babylon there lived a man named Joakim, 2 who married a very beautiful and God-fearing woman, Susanna, the daughter of Hilkiah; 3 her pious parents had trained their daughter according to the law of Moses. 4 Joakim was very rich; he had a garden near his house, and the Jews had recourse to him often because he was the most respected of them all.

5 That year, two elders of the people were appointed judges, of whom the Lord said, "Wickedness has come out of Babylon: from the elders who were to govern the people as judges." 6 These men, to whom all brought their cases, frequented the house of Joakim. 7 When the people left at noon, Susanna used to enter her husband's garden for a walk. 8 When the old men saw her enter every day for her walk, they began to lust for her. 9 They suppressed their consciences; they would not allow their eyes to look to heaven, and did not keep in mind just judgments. 10 Though both

NEW JERUSALEM BIBLE

In standard editions of the New Jerusalem Bible translation these verses are printed after Daniel 12.

SUSANNA AND THE JUDGEMENT OF DANIEL

(Chapter 13 of the Greek Version of Daniel)

1 [a] In Babylon there lived a man named Joakim. 2 He was married to a woman called Susanna daughter of Hilkiah, a woman of great beauty; and she was God-fearing, for 3 her parents were worthy people and had instructed their daughter in the Law of Moses. 4 Joakim was a very rich man and had a garden by his house; he used to be visited by a considerable number of the Jews, since he was held in greater respect than any other man. 5 Two elderly men had been selected from the people, that year, to act as judges. Of such the Lord had said, 'Wickedness has come to Babylon through the elders and judges posing as guides to the people.' 6 These men were often at Joakim's house, and all who were engaged in litigation used to come to them. 7 At midday, when the people had gone away, Susanna would take a walk in her husband's garden. 8 The two elders, who used to watch her every day as she came in to take her walk, gradually began to desire her. 9 They threw reason aside, making no effort to turn their eyes to Heaven, and forgetting the

[a] **13** Ch. 13 occurs in Gk but not in the Hebr. text.

GREEK OLD TESTAMENT

κατανενυγμένοι περὶ αὐτῆς καὶ οὐκ ἀνήγγειλαν ἀλλήλοις
τὴν ὀδύνην αὐτῶν, 11 ὅτι ᾐσχύνοντο ἀναγγεῖλαι τὴν ἐπιθυμίαν αὐτῶν ὅτι ἤθελον συγγενέσθαι αὐτῇ. 12 καὶ παρετηρ-
οῦσαν φιλοτίμως καθ' ἡμέραν ὁρᾶν αὐτήν. 13 καὶ εἶπαν
ἕτερος τῷ ἑτέρῳ Πορευθῶμεν δὴ εἰς οἶκον, ὅτι ἀρίστου ὥρα
ἐστίν· καὶ ἐξελθόντες διεχωρίσθησαν ἀπ' ἀλλήλων· 14 καὶ
ἀνακάμψαντες ἦλθον ἐπὶ τὸ αὐτὸ καὶ ἀνετάζοντες ἀλλήλους
τὴν αἰτίαν ὡμολόγησαν τὴν ἐπιθυμίαν αὐτῶν· καὶ τότε κοινῇ
συνετάξαντο καιρὸν ὅτε αὐτὴν δυνήσονται εὑρεῖν μόνην.
15 καὶ ἐγένετο ἐν τῷ παρατηρεῖν αὐτοὺς ἡμέραν εὔθετον
εἰσῆλθέν ποτε καθὼς ἐχθὲς καὶ τρίτης ἡμέρας μετὰ δύο
μόνων κορασίων καὶ ἐπεθύμησε λούσασθαι ἐν τῷ παραδείσῳ,
ὅτι καῦμα ἦν· 16 καὶ οὐκ ἦν οὐδεὶς ἐκεῖ πλὴν οἱ δύο πρεσβύτεροι κεκρυμμένοι καὶ παρατηροῦντες αὐτήν. 17 καὶ εἶπεν
τοῖς κορασίοις Ἐνέγκατε δή μοι ἔλαιον καὶ σμῆγμα καὶ τὰς
θύρας τοῦ παραδείσου κλείσατε, ὅπως λούσωμαι. 18 καὶ ἐποίησαν καθὼς εἶπεν καὶ ἀπέκλεισαν τὰς θύρας τοῦ παραδείσου
καὶ ἐξῆλθαν κατὰ τὰς πλαγίας θύρας ἐνέγκαι τὰ προστεταγμένα αὐταῖς καὶ οὐκ εἴδοσαν τοὺς πρεσβυτέρους, ὅτι
ἦσαν κεκρυμμένοι. 19 καὶ ἐγένετο ὡς ἐξήλθοσαν τὰ κοράσια,
καὶ ἀνέστησαν οἱ δύο πρεσβῦται καὶ ἐπέδραμον αὐτῇ 20 καὶ
εἶπον Ἰδοὺ αἱ θύραι τοῦ παραδείσου κέκλεινται, καὶ οὐδεὶς
θεωρεῖ ἡμᾶς, καὶ ἐν ἐπιθυμίᾳ σού ἐσμεν· διὸ συγκατάθου ἡμῖν

KING JAMES VERSION

10 And albeit they both were wounded with her love, yet durst not one shew another his grief.

11 For they were ashamed to declare their lust, that they desired to have to do with her.

12 Yet they watched diligently from day to day to see her.

13 And the one said to the other, Let us now go home: for it is dinner time.

14 So when they were gone out, they parted the one from the other, and turning back again they came to the same place; and after that they had asked one another the cause, they acknowledged their lust: then appointed they a time both together, when they might find her alone.

15 And it fell out, as they watched a fit time, she went in as before with two maids only, and she was desirous to wash herself in the garden: for it was hot.

16 And there was no body there save the two elders, that had hid themselves, and watched her.

17 Then she said to her maids, Bring me oil and washing balls, and shut the garden doors, that I may wash me.

18 And they did as she bade them, and shut the garden doors, and went out themselves at privy doors to fetch the things that she had commanded them: but they saw not the elders, because they were hid.

19 Now when the maids were gone forth, the two elders rose up, and ran unto her, saying,

20 Behold, the garden doors are shut, that no man can see us, and we are in love with thee; therefore consent unto us, and lie with us.

DOUAY OLD TESTAMENT

10 So they were both wounded with the love of her, yet they did not make known their grief one to the other:

11 For they were ashamed to declare to one another their lust, being desirous to have to do with her.

12 And they watched carefully every day to see her. And one said to the other:

13 Let us now go home, for it is dinner time. So going out they departed one from another.

14 And turning back again, they came both to the same place: and asking one another the cause, they acknowledged their lust; and then they agreed upon a time, when they might find her alone.

15 And it fell out, as they watched a fit day, she went in on a time, as yesterday and the day before, with two maids only, and was desirous to wash herself in the orchard: for it was hot weather.

16 And there was nobody there, but the two old men that had hid themselves and were beholding her.

17 So she said to the maids: Bring me oil, and washing balls, and shut the doors of the orchard, that I may wash me.

18 And they did as she bade them: and they shut the doors of the orchard, and went out by a back door to fetch what she had commanded them, and they knew not that the elders were hid within.

19 Now when the maids were gone forth, the two elders arose, and ran to her, and said:

20 Behold the doors of the orchard are shut, and nobody seeth us, and we are in love with thee: wherefore consent to us, and lie with us.

KNOX TRANSLATION

tortured both, neither to other would disclose; 11 confess it
for very shame they might not, this hankering after a woman's favours; 12 yet day after day they seized the opportunity
to have sight of her. A day came at last when one said to the
other, 13 Home go we, it is dinner-time; and go they did, taking their several ways; 14 yet both returned hot-foot to their
watching-place, and there met one another. So there was
questioning on both sides, and out came the story of their
lust; and now they made common cause; at a suitable time
they would waylay her together, when she was alone.
15 They watched, then, for their opportunity; and she, as
her custom was, went out one day with two of her maids,
and had a mind to bathe, there in the garden, for it was summer weather, 16 and none was by except the two elders; and
they were in hiding, watching her. 17 So she bade her servants go and bring her oil and soap, and shut the garden
door while she was a-bathing. 18 Her whim was obeyed; shut
the door of the garden they did, and went out by a back
entrance to bring her what she had asked for; they knew
nothing of the elders that were hiding there within. 19 And
these two, as soon as the servants were gone, rose from their
hiding-place and ran to her side. 20 See, they told her, the
garden door is shut, and there is no witness by. We are both
smitten with a desire for thy favours; come, then, let us

TODAY'S ENGLISH VERSION

but neither told the other how he felt, 11 for each was
ashamed to admit his lust. 12 So day after day they watched
eagerly to catch sight of her.
13 One day at noon they said to each other, "It's time for
lunch; let's go home." 14 So they both left and went their
separate ways, but soon each one came back for a look at
Susanna, and by accident they met each other. At first each
tried to explain what he was doing there, but finally they
both confessed their desire for Susanna. They decided to
watch for a time when they might find her alone. 15-17 So
they kept waiting for the right opportunity.
One day Susanna went into the garden as usual with her
two servant women. No one else was there, except the two
judges, who had hidden themselves and were watching
Susanna. It was very hot and she decided to take a bath. So
she said to her servants, "Bring me some bath oil and some
perfume, and lock the gates, so that I won't be disturbed."
18 The servants locked the main gates and went out by the
side door to get what Susanna had asked for. They did not
notice the two men.
19 As soon as the servants had left, the two judges jumped
out from their hiding place, ran to Susanna, 20 and said to
her, "The gates are locked and no one will see us. We are
burning to have sex with you, so give us what we want. 21 If

NEW REVISED STANDARD VERSION

to administer justice. 10 Both were overwhelmed with passion
for her, but they did not tell each other of their distress, 11 for
they were ashamed to disclose their lustful desire to seduce
her. 12 Day after day they watched eagerly to see her.
13 One day they said to each other, "Let us go home, for it
is time for lunch." So they both left and parted from each
other. 14 But turning back, they met again; and when each
pressed the other for the reason, they confessed their lust.
Then together they arranged for a time when they could find
her alone.
15 Once, while they were watching for an opportune day,
she went in as before with only two maids, and wished to
bathe in the garden, for it was a hot day. 16 No one was
there except the two elders, who had hidden themselves and
were watching her. 17 She said to her maids, "Bring me olive
oil and ointments, and shut the garden doors so that I can
bathe." 18 They did as she told them: they shut the doors of
the garden and went out by the side doors to bring what they
had been commanded; they did not see the elders, because
they were hiding.
19 When the maids had gone out, the two elders got up
and ran to her. 20 They said, "Look, the garden doors are
shut, and no one can see us. We are burning with desire for
you; so give your consent, and lie with us. 21 If you refuse,

NEW AMERICAN BIBLE

were enamored of her, they did not tell each other their
trouble, 11 for they were ashamed to reveal their lustful
desire to have her. 12 Day by day they watched eagerly for
her. 13 One day they said to each other, "Let us be off for
home, it is time for lunch." So they went out and parted;
14 but both turned back, and when they met again, they
asked each other the reason. They admitted their lust, and
then they agreed to look for an occasion when they could
meet her alone.
15 One day, while they were waiting for the right moment,
she entered the garden as usual, with two maids only. She
decided to bathe, for the weather was warm. 16 Nobody else
was there except the two elders, who had hidden themselves
and were watching her. 17 "Bring me oil and soap," she said
to the maids, "and shut the garden doors while I bathe."
18 They did as she said; they shut the garden doors and left
by the side gate to fetch what she had ordered, unaware that
the elders were hidden inside.
19 As soon as the maids had left, the two old men got up
and hurried to her. 20 "Look," they said, "the garden doors
are shut, and no one can see us; give in to our desire, and lie

NEW JERUSALEM BIBLE

demands of virtue. 10 Both were inflamed by passion for her,
but they hid their desire from each other, 11 for they were
ashamed to admit the longing to sleep with her, 12 but they
made sure of watching her every day. 13 One day, having
parted with the words, 'Let us go home, then, it is time for
the midday meal,' they went off in different directions,
14 only to retrace their steps and find themselves face to face
again. Obliged then to explain, they admitted their desire
and agreed to look for an opportunity of surprising her
alone. 15 So they waited for a favourable moment; and one
day Susanna came as usual, accompanied only by two
young maidservants. The day was hot and she wanted to
bathe in the garden. 16 There was no one about except the
two elders, spying on her from their hiding place. 17 She said
to the servants, 'Bring me some oil and balsam and shut the
garden door while I bathe.' 18 They did as they were told,
shutting the garden door and going back to the house by a
side entrance to fetch what she had asked for; they knew
nothing about the elders, for they had concealed themselves.
19 Hardly were the maids gone than the two elders sprang
up and rushed upon her. 20 'Look,' they said, 'the garden
door is shut, no one can see us. We want to have you, so

GREEK OLD TESTAMENT

καὶ γενοῦ μεθ' ἡμῶν· 21 εἰ δὲ μή, καταμαρτυρήσομέν σου ὅτι
ἦν μετὰ σοῦ νεανίσκος καὶ διὰ τοῦτο ἐξαπέστειλας τὰ
κοράσια ἀπὸ σοῦ. 22 καὶ ἀνεστέναξεν Σουσαννα καὶ εἶπεν
Στενά μοι πάντοθεν· ἐάν τε γὰρ τοῦτο πράξω, θάνατός μοί
ἐστιν, ἐάν τε μὴ πράξω, οὐκ ἐκφεύξομαι τὰς χεῖρας ὑμῶν·
23 αἱρετόν μοί ἐστιν μὴ πράξασαν ἐμπεσεῖν εἰς τὰς χεῖρας
ὑμῶν ἢ ἁμαρτεῖν ἐνώπιον κυρίου. 24 καὶ ἀνεβόησεν φωνῇ
μεγάλῃ Σουσαννα, ἐβόησαν δὲ καὶ οἱ δύο πρεσβῦται κατέναντι αὐτῆς. 25 καὶ δραμὼν ὁ εἷς ἤνοιξεν τὰς θύρας τοῦ
παραδείσου. 26 ὡς δὲ ἤκουσαν τὴν κραυγὴν ἐν τῷ παραδείσῳ
οἱ ἐκ τῆς οἰκίας, εἰσεπήδησαν διὰ τῆς πλαγίας θύρας ἰδεῖν
τὸ συμβεβηκὸς αὐτῇ. 27 ἡνίκα δὲ εἶπαν οἱ πρεσβῦται τοὺς
λόγους αὐτῶν, κατησχύνθησαν οἱ δοῦλοι σφόδρα, ὅτι πώποτε
οὐκ ἐρρέθη λόγος τοιοῦτος περὶ Σουσαννης.

28 Καὶ ἐγένετο τῇ ἐπαύριον ὡς συνῆλθεν ὁ λαὸς πρὸς τὸν
ἄνδρα αὐτῆς Ιωακιμ, ἦλθον οἱ δύο πρεσβῦται πλήρεις τῆς
ἀνόμου ἐννοίας κατὰ Σουσαννης τοῦ θανατῶσαι αὐτὴν
29 καὶ εἶπαν ἔμπροσθεν τοῦ λαοῦ Ἀποστείλατε ἐπὶ
Σουσανναν θυγατέρα Χελκιου, ἥ ἐστιν γυνὴ Ιωακιμ· οἱ δὲ
ἀπέστειλαν. 30 καὶ ἦλθεν αὐτὴ καὶ οἱ γονεῖς αὐτῆς καὶ τὰ
τέκνα αὐτῆς καὶ πάντες οἱ συγγενεῖς αὐτῆς. 31 ἡ δὲ
Σουσαννα ἦν τρυφερὰ σφόδρα καὶ καλὴ τῷ εἴδει. 32 οἱ δὲ
παράνομοι ἐκέλευσαν ἀποκαλυφθῆναι αὐτήν, ἦν γὰρ
κατακεκαλυμμένη, ὅπως ἐμπλησθῶσιν τοῦ κάλλους αὐτῆς.

KING JAMES VERSION

21 If thou wilt not, we will bear witness against thee, that a young man was with thee: and therefore thou didst send away thy maids from thee.

22 Then Susanna sighed, and said, I am straitened on every side: for if I do this thing, it is death unto me: and if I do it not, I cannot escape your hands.

23 It is better for me to fall into your hands, and not do it, than to sin in the sight of the Lord.

24 With that Susanna cried with a loud voice: and the two elders cried out against her.

25 Then ran the one, and opened the garden door.

26 So when the servants of the house heard the cry in the garden, they rushed in at a privy door, to see what was done unto her.

27 But when the elders had declared their matter, the servants were greatly ashamed: for there was never such a report made of Susanna.

28 And it came to pass the next day, when the people were assembled to her husband Joacim, the two elders came also full of mischievous imagination against Susanna to put her to death;

29 And said before the people, Send for Susanna, the daughter of Chelcias, Joacim's wife. And so they sent.

30 So she came with her father and mother, her children, and all her kindred.

31 Now Susanna was a very delicate woman, and beauteous to behold.

32 And these wicked men commanded to uncover her *face,* (for she was covered) that they might be filled with her beauty.

DOUAY OLD TESTAMENT

21 But if thou wilt not, we will bear witness against thee, that a young man was with thee, and therefore thou didst send away thy maids from thee.

22 Susanna sighed, and said: I am straitened on every side: for if I do this thing, it is death to me: and if I do it not, I shall not escape your hands.

23 But it is better for me to fall into your hands without doing it, than to sin in the sight of the Lord.

24 With that Susanna cried out with a loud voice: and the elders also cried out against her.

25 And one *of them* ran to the door of the orchard, and opened it.

26 So when the servants of the house heard the cry in the orchard, they rushed in by the back door to see what was the matter.

27 But after the old men had spoken, the servants were greatly ashamed: for never had there been any such word said of Susanna. And on the next day,

28 When the people were come to Joakim her husband, the two elders also came full of wicked device against Susanna, to put her to death.

29 And they said before the people: Send to Susanna daughter of Helcias the wife of Joakim. And presently they sent.

30 And she came with her parents, and children, and all her kindred.

31 Now Susanna was exceeding delicate, and beautiful to behold.

32 But those wicked men commanded that her face should be uncovered, (for she was covered,) that so at least they might be satisfied with her beauty.

KNOX TRANSLATION

enjoy thee. 21 Refuse, and we will bear witness that thou
hadst a gallant here, and this was the reason thou wouldst
rid thyself of thy hand-maidens' company.
22 Whereupon Susanna groaned deeply; There is no escape
for me, she said, either way. It is death if I consent, and if I
refuse, I shall be at your mercy. 23 Let me rather fall into
your power through no act of mine, than commit sin in the
Lord's sight. 24 With that, Susanna cried aloud, and the
elders, too, began crying shame on her; 25 meanwhile, one of
them ran to the garden door and opened it. 26 And now the
servants of the house, hearing such outcry in the garden,
came running in through the back entrance to know what
was afoot; 27 and they were greatly abashed when the elders
told their story; never before had Susanna been defamed
thus.
28 When the morrow came, there was a throng of people in
Joakim's house, and the two elders were there, intent upon
their malicious design against Susanna's life. 29 They asked
publicly that Susanna, daughter of Helcias and wife to
Joakim, should be sent for; 30 sent for she was, and came out
with her parents and her children and all her kindred. 31 So
dainty she was, and so fair, 32 these two knaves would have
her let down her veil, the better to enjoy the sight of her

TODAY'S ENGLISH VERSION

you don't, we will go to court and swear that we saw you
send your servants away, so that you could be alone with a
young man."
22 "There is no way out," Susanna moaned. "If I give in to
you, I could be put to death for adultery. If I refuse, you will
still have me trapped. 23 But I would rather be your innocent
victim than sin against the Lord." 24 So she started screaming as loud as she could, and the two judges began shouting
accusations, 25 while one of them ran and unlocked the
gates.
26 As soon as the servants in the house heard all the noise,
they ran into the gardens through the side door to find out
what had happened to Susanna. 27 The judges told their
story, and the servants were shocked and ashamed. Such a
thing had never before been said about Susanna.
28 The next day, when the people assembled at Joakim's
house, the two judges arrived, fully determined to carry out
their wicked plan to have Susanna put to death. 29 In front
of all the people they said, "Send for Joakim's wife Susanna,
the daughter of Hilkiah." When she was called, 30 she came
in with her parents, her children, and all her other relatives.
31 Susanna was so graceful and beautiful 32 that the two
wicked men ordered her veil to be removed, so that they

NEW REVISED STANDARD VERSION

we will testify against you that a young man was with you,
and this was why you sent your maids away."
22 Susanna groaned and said, "I am completely trapped.
For if I do this, it will mean death for me; if I do not, I cannot
escape your hands. 23 I choose not to do it; I will fall into
your hands, rather than sin in the sight of the Lord."
24 Then Susanna cried out with a loud voice, and the two
elders shouted against her. 25 And one of them ran and
opened the garden doors. 26 When the people in the house
heard the shouting in the garden, they rushed in at the side
door to see what had happened to her. 27 And when the
elders told their story, the servants felt very much ashamed,
for nothing like this had ever been said about Susanna.
28 The next day, when the people gathered at the house
of her husband Joakim, the two elders came, full of their
wicked plot to have Susanna put to death. In the presence of
the people they said, 29 "Send for Susanna daughter of
Hilkiah, the wife of Joakim." 30 So they sent for her. And she
came with her parents, her children, and all her relatives.
31 Now Susanna was a woman of great refinement and
beautiful in appearance. 32 As she was veiled, the scoundrels
ordered her to be unveiled, so that they might feast their eyes

NEW AMERICAN BIBLE

with us. 21 If you refuse, we will testify against you that you
dismissed your maids because a young man was here with
you."
22 "I am completely trapped," Susanna groaned. "If I yield,
it will be my death; if I refuse, I cannot escape your power.
23 Yet it is better for me to fall into your power without guilt
than to sin before the Lord." 24 Then Susanna shrieked, and
the old men also shouted at her, 25 as one of them ran to
open the garden doors. 26 When the people in the house
heard the cries from the garden, they rushed in by the side
gate to see what had happened to her. 27 At the accusations
by the old men, the servants felt very much ashamed, for
never had any such thing been said about Susanna.
28 When the people came to her husband Joakim the next
day, the two wicked elders also came, fully determined to
put Susanna to death. Before all the people they ordered:
29 "Send for Susanna, the daughter of Hilkiah, the wife of
Joakim." When she was sent for, 30 she came with her parents, children and all her relatives. 31 Susanna, very delicate and beautiful, 32 was veiled; but those wicked men
ordered her to uncover her face so as to sate themselves

NEW JERUSALEM BIBLE

give in and let us! 21 Refuse, and we shall both give evidence
that a young man was with you and that this was why you
sent your maids away.' 22 Susanna sighed. 'I am trapped,'
she said, 'whatever I do. If I agree, it means death for me; if I
resist, I cannot get away from you. 23 But I prefer to fall
innocent into your power than to sin in the eyes of the Lord.'
24 She then cried out as loud as she could. The two elders
began shouting too, putting the blame on her, 25 and one of
them ran to open the garden door. 26 The household, hearing
the shouting in the garden, rushed out by the side entrance
to see what had happened to her. 27 Once the elders had told
their story, the servants were thoroughly taken aback, since
nothing of this sort had ever been said of Susanna.
28 Next day a meeting was held at the house of her husband Joakim. The two elders arrived, full of their wicked plea
against Susanna, to have her put to death. 29 They
addressed the company, 'Summon Susanna daughter of
Hilkiah and wife of Joakim.' She was sent for, 30 and came
accompanied by her parents, her children and all her relations. 31 Susanna was very graceful and beautiful to look at;
32 she was veiled, so the wretches made her unveil in order to

GREEK OLD TESTAMENT

33 ἔκλαιον δὲ οἱ παρ' αὐτῆς καὶ πάντες οἱ ἰδόντες αὐτήν.
34 ἀναστάντες δὲ οἱ δύο πρεσβῦται ἐν μέσῳ τῷ λαῷ ἔθηκαν
τὰς χεῖρας ἐπὶ τὴν κεφαλὴν αὐτῆς. 35 ἡ δὲ κλαίουσα
ἀνέβλεψεν εἰς τὸν οὐρανόν, ὅτι ἦν ἡ καρδία αὐτῆς πεποιθυῖα
ἐπὶ τῷ κυρίῳ. 36 εἶπαν δὲ οἱ πρεσβῦται Περιπατούντων ἡμῶν
ἐν τῷ παραδείσῳ μόνων εἰσῆλθεν αὕτη μετὰ δύο παιδισκῶν
καὶ ἀπέκλεισεν τὰς θύρας τοῦ παραδείσου καὶ ἀπέλυσεν τὰς
παιδίσκας. 37 καὶ ἦλθεν πρὸς αὐτὴν νεανίσκος, ὃς ἦν
κεκρυμμένος, καὶ ἀνέπεσε μετ' αὐτῆς. 38 ἡμεῖς δὲ ὄντες ἐν
τῇ γωνίᾳ τοῦ παραδείσου ἰδόντες τὴν ἀνομίαν ἐδράμομεν
ἐπ' αὐτούς. 39 καὶ ἰδόντες συγγινομένους αὐτοὺς ἐκείνου
μὲν οὐκ ἠδυνήθημεν ἐγκρατεῖς γενέσθαι διὰ τὸ ἰσχύειν
αὐτὸν ὑπὲρ ἡμᾶς καὶ ἀνοίξαντα τὰς θύρας ἐκπεπηδηκέναι,
40 ταύτης δὲ ἐπιλαβόμενοι ἐπηρωτῶμεν, τίς ἦν ὁ νεανίσκος,
41 καὶ οὐκ ἠθέλησεν ἀναγγεῖλαι ἡμῖν. ταῦτα μαρτυροῦμεν.
καὶ ἐπίστευσεν αὐτοῖς ἡ συναγωγὴ ὡς πρεσβυτέροις τοῦ
λαοῦ καὶ κριταῖς καὶ κατέκριναν αὐτὴν ἀποθανεῖν.
42 ἀνεβόησεν δὲ φωνῇ μεγάλῃ Σουσαννα καὶ εἶπεν Ὁ θεὸς ὁ
αἰώνιος ὁ τῶν κρυπτῶν γνώστης ὁ εἰδὼς τὰ πάντα πρὶν
γενέσεως αὐτῶν, 43 σὺ ἐπίστασαι ὅτι ψευδῆ μου κατεμαρ-
τύρησαν· καὶ ἰδοὺ ἀποθνήσκω μὴ ποιήσασα μηδὲν ὧν οὗτοι
ἐπονηρεύσαντο κατ' ἐμοῦ.
44 Καὶ εἰσήκουσεν κύριος τῆς φωνῆς αὐτῆς. 45 καὶ

KING JAMES VERSION

33 Therefore her friends and all that saw her wept.

34 Then the two elders stood up in the midst of the people, and laid their hands upon her head.

35 And she weeping looked up toward heaven: for her heart trusted in the Lord.

36 And the elders said, As we walked in the garden alone, this woman came in with two maids, and shut the garden doors, and sent the maids away.

37 Then a young man, who there was hid, came unto her, and lay with her.

38 Then we that stood in a corner of the garden, seeing this wickedness, ran unto them.

39 And when we saw them together, the man we could not hold: for he was stronger than we, and opened the door, and leaped out.

40 But having taken this woman, we asked who the young man was, but she would not tell us: these things do we testify.

41 Then the assembly believed them, as those that were the elders and judges of the people: so they condemned her to death.

42 Then Susanna cried out with a loud voice, and said, O everlasting God, that knowest the secrets, and knowest all things before they be:

43 Thou knowest that they have borne false witness against me, and, behold, I must die; whereas I never did such things as these men have maliciously invented against me.

44 And the Lord heard her voice.

DOUAY OLD TESTAMENT

33 Therefore her friends and all her acquaintance wept.

34 But the two elders rising up in the midst of the people, laid their hands upon her head.

35 And she weeping looked up to heaven, for her heart had confidence in the Lord.

36 And the elders said: As we walked in the orchard alone, this woman came in with two maids, and shut the doors of the orchard, and sent away the maids from her.

37 Then a young man that was there hid came to her, and lay with her.

38 But we that were in a corner of the orchard, seeing this wickedness, ran up to them, and we saw them lie together.

39 And him indeed we could not take, because he was stronger than us, and opening the doors he leaped out:

40 But having taken this woman, we asked who the young man was, but she would not tell us: of this thing we are witnesses.

41 The multitude believed them as being the elders and the judges of the people, and they condemned her to death.

42 Then Susanna cried out with a loud voice, and said: O eternal God, who knowest hidden things, who knowest all things before they come to pass,

43 Thou knowest that they have borne false witness against me: and behold I must die, whereas I have done none of these things, which these men have maliciously forged against me.

44 And the Lord heard her voice.

KNOX TRANSLATION

charms. 33 All her friends, all her acquaintances, were in
tears. 34 Then the two elders rose amidst the throng, and laid
their hands upon Susanna's head, 35 while she, weeping,
looked up to heaven, in token that her heart had not lost
confidence in the Lord. 36 We were walking in the garden
apart, said the elders, when this woman came out with two
hand-maidens. She had the garden door shut close, and sent
the maidens away; 37 whereupon a young man, who had
been in hiding till then, came out and had his will with her.
38 We, from a nook in the garden, saw what foul deed was
being done, and ran up close, so that we had full view of
their dalliance; 39 but lay hold of the man we could not; he
was too strong for us, opening the garden door and springing out. 40 The woman we caught, and asked her who her
gallant was, but she would not tell us. To all this, we bear
witness.
41 They were elders, they were judges of the people, and
they persuaded the assembly, without more ado, to pass the
death sentence. 42 Whereupon Susanna cried aloud, Eternal
God, no secret is hidden from thee, nothing comes to pass
without thy foreknowledge. 43 Thou knowest that these men
have borne false witness against me; wilt thou let me die, a
woman innocent of all the charges their malice has invented? 44 And the Lord listened to her plea; 45 even as she was

TODAY'S ENGLISH VERSION

might enjoy looking at her. 33 Her family and everyone else
were in tears.

34 Then the two judges stood up in front of the people,
placed their hands on Susanna's head, and began making
their accusations against her. 35 She was crying, but she
looked up to heaven because she trusted the Lord. 36 The
two men gave the following testimony: "We were walking in
the gardens when this woman came in with her two servant
women. She locked the main gates and asked the servants to
leave. 37 Then a young man who had been hiding in the gardens came to her, and they lay down together. 38 We were in
a corner of the gardens, and when we saw what was happening, we ran over 39 and caught them in the act. We tried
to hold on to the man, but he was too strong for us. He ran
and opened the gates and got away, 40 but we were able to
hold the woman. We asked her who the man was, but she
refused to tell us. We swear that our testimony is true."
41 Because the two men were not only leaders in the community but also judges, the people believed their story and condemned Susanna to death.

42 Then Susanna cried out in a loud voice, "Eternal God,
nothing can be kept secret from you; you know everything
before it happens. 43 Here I am about to die, but you know
that I am innocent, that these men are lying. Why must
I die?"

44 The Lord heard her prayer 45 and led a young man

NEW REVISED STANDARD VERSION

on her beauty. 33 Those who were with her and all who saw
her were weeping.

34 Then the two elders stood up before the people and
laid their hands on her head. 35 Through her tears she
looked up toward Heaven, for her heart trusted in the Lord.
36 The elders said, "While we were walking in the garden
alone, this woman came in with two maids, shut the garden
doors, and dismissed the maids. 37 Then a young man, who
was hiding there, came to her and lay with her. 38 We were
in a corner of the garden, and when we saw this wickedness
we ran to them. 39 Although we saw them embracing, we
could not hold the man, because he was stronger than we,
and he opened the doors and got away. 40 We did, however,
seize this woman and asked who the young man was, 41 but
she would not tell us. These things we testify."

Because they were elders of the people and judges, the
assembly believed them and condemned her to death.

42 Then Susanna cried out with a loud voice, and said,
"O eternal God, you know what is secret and are aware of all
things before they come to be; 43 you know that these men
have given false evidence against me. And now I am to die,
though I have done none of the wicked things that they have
charged against me!"

44 The Lord heard her cry. 45 Just as she was being led off

NEW AMERICAN BIBLE

with her beauty. 33 All her relatives and the onlookers were
weeping.

34 In the midst of the people the two elders rose up and laid
their hands on her head. 35 Through her tears she looked up
to heaven, for she trusted in the Lord wholeheartedly. 36 The
elders made this accusation: "As we were walking in the garden alone, this woman entered with two girls and shut the
doors of the garden, dismissing the girls. 37 A young man,
who was hidden there, came and lay with her. 38 When we,
in a corner of the garden, saw this crime, we ran toward
them. 39 We saw them lying together, but the man we could
not hold, because he was stronger than we; he opened the
doors and ran off. 40 Then we seized this one and asked who
the young man was, 41 but she refused to tell us. We testify
to this." The assembly believed them, since they were elders
and judges of the people, and they condemned her to death.

42 But Susanna cried aloud: "O eternal God, you know
what is hidden and are aware of all things before they come
to be: 43 you know that they have testified falsely against
me. Here I am about to die, though I have done none of the
things with which these wicked men have charged me."

44 The Lord heard her prayer. 45 As she was being led to

NEW JERUSALEM BIBLE

feast their eyes on her beauty. 33 All her own people were
weeping, and so were all the others who saw her. 34 The two
elders stood up, with all the people round them, and laid
their hands on her head. 35 Tearfully she turned her eyes to
Heaven, her heart confident in God. 36 The elders then spoke,
'While we were walking by ourselves in the garden, this
woman arrived with two maids. She shut the garden door
and then dismissed the servants. 37 A young man, who had
been hiding, went over to her and they lay together. 38 From
the end of the garden where we were, we saw this crime taking place and hurried towards them. 39 Though we saw them
together, we were unable to catch the man: he was too
strong for us; he opened the door and took to his heels.
40 We did, however, catch this woman and ask her who the
young man was. 41 She refused to tell us. That is our evidence.'

Since they were elders of the people and judges, the
assembly accepted their word: Susanna was condemned to
death. 42 She cried out as loud as she could, 'Eternal God,
you know all secrets and everything before it happens;
43 you know that they have given false evidence against me.
And now I must die, innocent as I am of everything their
malice has invented against me!'

44 The Lord heard her cry 45 and, as she was being led

GREEK OLD TESTAMENT

ἀπαγομένης αὐτῆς ἀπολέσθαι ἐξήγειρεν ὁ θεὸς τὸ πνεῦμα
τὸ ἅγιον παιδαρίου νεωτέρου, ᾧ ὄνομα Δανιηλ, 46 καὶ ἐβόησεν φωνῇ μεγάλῃ Καθαρὸς ἐγὼ ἀπὸ τοῦ αἵματος ταύτης.
47 ἐπέστρεψεν δὲ πᾶς ὁ λαὸς πρὸς αὐτὸν καὶ εἶπαν Τίς ὁ
λόγος οὗτος, ὃν σὺ λελάληκας; 48 ὁ δὲ στὰς ἐν μέσῳ αὐτῶν
εἶπεν Οὕτως μωροί, οἱ υἱοὶ Ισραηλ; οὐκ ἀνακρίναντες οὐδὲ
τὸ σαφὲς ἐπιγνόντες κατεκρίνατε θυγατέρα Ισραηλ; 49 ἀνα-
στρέψατε εἰς τὸ κριτήριον· ψευδῆ γὰρ οὗτοι κατεμαρτύρη-
σαν αὐτῆς. 50 καὶ ἀνέστρεψεν πᾶς ὁ λαὸς μετὰ σπουδῆς.
καὶ εἶπαν αὐτῷ οἱ πρεσβύτεροι Δεῦρο κάθισον ἐν μέσῳ ἡμῶν
καὶ ἀνάγγειλον ἡμῖν· ὅτι σοὶ δέδωκεν ὁ θεὸς τὸ πρεσβεῖον.
51 καὶ εἶπεν πρὸς αὐτοὺς Δανιηλ Διαχωρίσατε αὐτοὺς ἀπ'
ἀλλήλων μακράν, καὶ ἀνακρινῶ αὐτούς. 52 ὡς δὲ διεχωρίσθησαν εἷς ἀπὸ τοῦ ἑνός, ἐκάλεσεν τὸν ἕνα αὐτῶν καὶ εἶπεν
πρὸς αὐτόν Πεπαλαιωμένε ἡμερῶν κακῶν, νῦν ἥκασιν αἱ
ἁμαρτίαι σου, ἃς ἐποίεις τὸ πρότερον 53 κρίνων κρίσεις ἀδί-
κους καὶ τοὺς μὲν ἀθῴους κατακρίνων ἀπολύων δὲ τοὺς αἰτίους, λέγοντος τοῦ κυρίου Ἀθῷον καὶ δίκαιον οὐκ ἀποκτενεῖς.
54 νῦν οὖν ταύτην εἴπερ εἶδες, εἰπόν Ὑπὸ τί δένδρον εἶδες
αὐτοὺς ὁμιλοῦντας ἀλλήλοις; ὁ δὲ εἶπεν Ὑπὸ σχῖνον.
55 εἶπεν δὲ Δανιηλ Ὀρθῶς ἔψευσαι εἰς τὴν σεαυτοῦ κεφαλήν·
ἤδη γὰρ ἄγγελος τοῦ θεοῦ λαβὼν φάσιν παρὰ τοῦ θεοῦ σχίσει

KING JAMES VERSION

45 Therefore when she was led to be put to death, the Lord raised up the holy spirit of a young youth, whose name was Daniel:

46 Who cried with a loud voice, I am clear from the blood of this woman.

47 Then all the people turned them toward him, and said, What mean these words that thou hast spoken?

48 So he standing in the midst of them said, Are ye such fools, ye sons of Israel, that without examination or knowledge of the truth ye have condemned a daughter of Israel?

49 Return again to the place of judgment: for they have borne false witness against her.

50 Wherefore all the people turned again in haste, and the elders said unto him, Come, sit down among us, and shew it us, seeing God hath given thee the honour of an elder.

51 Then said Daniel unto them, Put these two aside one far from another, and I will examine them.

52 So when they were put asunder one from another, he called one of them, and said unto him, O thou that art waxen old in wickedness, now thy sins which thou hast committed aforetime are come *to light:*

53 For thou hast pronounced false judgment, and hast condemned the innocent, and hast let the guilty go free; albeit the Lord saith, The innocent and righteous shalt thou not slay.

54 Now then, if thou hast seen her, tell me, Under what tree sawest thou them companying together? Who answered, Under a mastick tree.

55 And Daniel said, Very well; thou hast lied against thine own head; for even now the angel of God hath received the sentence of God to cut thee in two.

DOUAY OLD TESTAMENT

45 And when she was led to be put to death, the Lord raised up the holy spirit of a young boy, whose name was Daniel.

46 And he cried out with a loud voice: I am clear from the blood of this woman.

47 Then all the people turning themselves towards him, said: What meaneth this word that thou hast spoken?

48 But he standing in the midst of them, said: Are ye so foolish, ye children of Israel, that without examination or knowledge of the truth, you have condemned a daughter of Israel?

49 Return to judgment, for they have borne false witness against her.

50 So all the people turned again in haste, and the old men said to him: Come, and sit thou down among us, and shew it us: seeing God hath given thee the honour of old age.

51 And Daniel said to the people: Separate these two far from one another, and I will examine them.

52 So when they were put asunder one from the other, he called one of them, and said to him: O thou that art grown old in evil days, now are thy sins come *out,* which thou hast committed before:

53 In judging unjust judgments, oppressing the innocent, and letting the guilty to go free, whereas the Lord saith: The innocent and the just thou shalt not kill.

54 Now then, if thou sawest her, tell me under what tree thou sawest them conversing together. He said: Under a mastic tree.

55 And Daniel said: Well hast thou lied against thy own head: for behold the angel of God having received the sentence of him, shall cut thee in two.

KNOX TRANSLATION

being led off to her death, all at once he roused to utterance
the holy spirit that dwelt in a young boy there, called Daniel.
46 This Daniel raised his voice and cried out, I will be no
party to the death of this woman; 47 and when all the people
turned upon him, asking what he meant, 48 he stood there in
their midst, and said, Are you such fools, men of Israel, as to
condemn an Israelite woman without trial, without investigation of the truth? 49 Go back to the place of judgement; the
witness they have borne against her is false witness.
50 Eagerly enough the people went back, and the elders
would have Daniel sit with them, such credit God had given
him beyond his years. 51 He bade them part the two men, at a
distance from each other, while he questioned them. 52 So
parted they were, and when the first was summoned, thus
Daniel greeted him: Grown so old in years, and years ill
spent! Now, that past sinning of thine has found thee out,
53 a man that perverts justice, persecutes innocence, and lets
the guilty go free. Has not the Lord said, Never shalt thou put
the innocent man, the upright man, to death? 54 Thou found-
est her; good; they met under a tree; tell us what kind of tree.
And he answered, Under a mastic-tree I surprised them.
55 The right word! cried Daniel; prized asunder thyself shall
be, when God bids his angel requite thee for this calumny.

TODAY'S ENGLISH VERSION

named Daniel to speak out, just as Susanna was being taken
away to her death. 46 He shouted, "I refuse to be a party to
her death!"
47 Everyone turned around to look at him and asked,
"What are you talking about?"
48 Daniel stood up before them and said, "People of Israel,
how foolish can you be? Are you going to condemn an
Israelite woman to death on this kind of evidence? You
haven't even tried to find out the truth. 49 Reopen the case.
The testimony these men gave was a lie."
50 So all the people hurried back to where the trial had
taken place, and the officials said to Daniel, "God has given
you wisdom beyond your years, so come and join us and
explain to us what you mean."
51 Daniel said to them, "Separate the two judges, and let
me question them one at a time." 52 Then Daniel called the
first judge and said, "You wicked old man, now you will
have to answer for all the sins you have committed. 53 You
have been giving unjust sentences. You have condemned the
innocent and released the guilty, even though the Lord has
said, 'Do not put an innocent person to death.' 54 Now if you
really did see this couple making love, tell me, what tree
were they under?"
"Under a small gum tree," he answered.
55 Daniel said, "All right! That lie will cost you your life.
God's angel has already been given orders to chop[a] you
in two."

[a] CHOP: *This word in Greek sounds like the Greek for "a small gum tree."*

NEW REVISED STANDARD VERSION

to execution, God stirred up the holy spirit of a young lad
named Daniel, 46 and he shouted with a loud voice, "I want
no part in shedding this woman's blood!"
47 All the people turned to him and asked, "What is this
you are saying?" 48 Taking his stand among them he said,
"Are you such fools, O Israelites, as to condemn a daughter
of Israel without examination and without learning the
facts? 49 Return to court, for these men have given false evidence against her."
50 So all the people hurried back. And the rest of the[a]
elders said to him, "Come, sit among us and inform us, for
God has given you the standing of an elder." 51 Daniel said
to them, "Separate them far from each other, and I will
examine them."
52 When they were separated from each other, he summoned one of them and said to him, "You old relic of wicked
days, your sins have now come home, which you have committed in the past, 53 pronouncing unjust judgments, condemning the innocent and acquitting the guilty, though the
Lord said, 'You shall not put an innocent and righteous person to death.' 54 Now then, if you really saw this woman,
tell me this: Under what tree did you see them being intimate
with each other?" He answered, "Under a mastic tree."[b]
55 And Daniel said, "Very well! This lie has cost you your
head, for the angel of God has received the sentence from
God and will immediately cut[b] you in two."

a Gk lacks *rest of the* *b* The Greek words for *mastic tree* and *cut* are similar, thus forming an ironic wordplay

NEW AMERICAN BIBLE

execution, God stirred up the holy spirit of a young boy
named Daniel, 46 and he cried aloud: "I will have no part in
the death of this woman." 47 All the people turned and asked
him, "What is this you are saying?" 48 He stood in their
midst and continued, "Are you such fools, O Israelites! To
condemn a woman of Israel without examination and without clear evidence? 49 Return to court, for they have testified
falsely against her."
50 Then all the people returned in haste. To Daniel the
elders said, "Come, sit with us and inform us, since God has
given you the prestige of old age." 51 But he replied,
"Separate these two far from one another that I may examine
them."
52 After they were separated one from the other, he called
one of them and said: "How you have grown evil with age!
Now have your past sins come to term: 53 passing unjust
sentences, condemning the innocent, and freeing the guilty,
although the Lord says, 'The innocent and the just you shall
not put to death.' 54 Now, then, if you were a witness, tell
me under what tree you saw them together." 55 "Under a
mastic tree," he answered. "Your fine lie has cost you your
head," said Daniel; "for the angel of God shall receive the
sentence from him and split you in two." 56 Putting him to

NEW JERUSALEM BIBLE

away to die, he roused the holy spirit residing in a young boy
called Daniel 46 who began to shout, 'I am innocent of this
woman's death!' 47 At this all the people turned to him and
asked, 'What do you mean by that?' 48 Standing in the middle of the crowd, he replied, 'Are you so stupid, children of
Israel, as to condemn a daughter of Israel unheard, and
without troubling to find out the truth? 49 Go back to the
scene of the trial: these men have given false evidence
against her.'
50 All the people hurried back, and the elders said to
Daniel, 'Come and sit with us and tell us what you mean,
since God has given you the gifts that elders have.' 51 Daniel
said, 'Keep the men well apart from each other, for I want to
question them.' 52 When the men had been separated, Daniel
had one of them brought to him. 'You have grown old in
wickedness,' he said, 'and now the sins of your earlier days
have overtaken you, 53 you with your unjust judgements,
your condemnation of the innocent, your acquittal of the
guilty, although the Lord has said, "You must not put the
innocent and upright to death." 54 Now then, since you saw
her so clearly, tell me what sort of tree you saw them lying
under.' He replied, 'Under an acacia tree.' 55 Daniel said,
'Indeed! Your lie recoils on your own head:[a] the angel of God
has already received from him your sentence and will cut

[a] **13** In Gk, the punishment and the tree in both cases have similar sounds: *shinos/schisei, prinos/kataprisei.*

GREEK OLD TESTAMENT

σε μέσον. 56 καὶ μεταστήσας αὐτὸν ἐκέλευσεν προσαγαγεῖν
τὸν ἕτερον· καὶ εἶπεν αὐτῷ Σπέρμα Χαναaν καὶ οὐκ Ιουδα,
τὸ κάλλος ἐξηπάτησέν σε, καὶ ἡ ἐπιθυμία διέστρεψεν τὴν
καρδίαν σου· 57 οὕτως ἐποιεῖτε θυγατράσιν Ισραηλ, καὶ
ἐκεῖναι φοβούμεναι ὡμίλουν ὑμῖν, ἀλλ᾽ οὐ θυγάτηρ Ιουδα
ὑπέμεινεν τὴν ἀνομίαν ὑμῶν· 58 νῦν οὖν λέγε μοι Ὑπὸ τί
δένδρον κατέλαβες αὐτοὺς ὁμιλοῦντας ἀλλήλοις; ὁ δὲ εἶπεν
Ὑπὸ πρῖνον. 59 εἶπεν δὲ αὐτῷ Δανιηλ Ὀρθῶς ἔψευσαι καὶ σὺ
εἰς τὴν σεαυτοῦ κεφαλήν· μένει γὰρ ὁ ἄγγελος τοῦ θεοῦ τὴν
ῥομφαίαν ἔχων πρίσαι σε μέσον, ὅπως ἐξολεθρεύσῃ ὑμᾶς.
60 καὶ ἀνεβόησεν πᾶσα ἡ συναγωγὴ φωνῇ μεγάλῃ καὶ εὐλόγησαν τῷ θεῷ τῷ σῴζοντι τοὺς ἐλπίζοντας ἐπ᾽ αὐτόν. 61 καὶ
ἀνέστησαν ἐπὶ τοὺς δύο πρεσβύτας, ὅτι συνέστησεν αὐτοὺς
Δανιηλ ἐκ τοῦ στόματος αὐτῶν ψευδομαρτυρήσαντας, καὶ
ἐποίησαν αὐτοῖς ὃν τρόπον ἐπονηρεύσαντο τῷ πλησίον,
62 ποιῆσαι κατὰ τὸν νόμον Μωυσῆ, καὶ ἀπέκτειναν αὐτούς.
καὶ ἐσώθη αἷμα ἀναίτιον ἐν τῇ ἡμέρᾳ ἐκείνῃ. 63 Χελκιας δὲ
καὶ ἡ γυνὴ αὐτοῦ ᾔνεσαν τὸν θεὸν περὶ τῆς θυγατρὸς αὐτῶν
Σουσαννας μετὰ Ιωακιμ τοῦ ἀνδρὸς αὐτῆς καὶ τῶν συγγενῶν
πάντων, ὅτι οὐχ εὑρέθη ἐν αὐτῇ ἄσχημον πρᾶγμα. 64 καὶ
Δανιηλ ἐγένετο μέγας ἐνώπιον τοῦ λαοῦ ἀπὸ τῆς ἡμέρας
ἐκείνης καὶ ἐπέκεινα.

KING JAMES VERSION

56 So he put him aside, and commanded to bring the other, and said unto him, O thou seed of Chanaan, and not of Juda, beauty hath deceived thee, and lust hath perverted thine heart.

57 Thus have ye dealt with the daughters of Israel, and they for fear companied with you: but the daughter of Juda would not abide your wickedness.

58 Now therefore tell me, Under what tree didst thou take them companying together? Who answered, Under an holm tree.

59 Then said Daniel unto him, Well; thou hast also lied against thine own head: for the angel of God waiteth with the sword to cut thee in two, that he may destroy you.

60 With that all the assembly cried out with a loud voice, and praised God, who saveth them that trust in him.

61 And they arose against the two elders, for Daniel had convicted them of false witness by their own mouth:

62 And according to the law of Moses they did unto them in such sort as they maliciously intended to do to their neighbour: and they put them to death. Thus the innocent blood was saved the same day.

63 Therefore Chelcias and his wife praised God for their daughter Susanna, with Joacim her husband, and all the kindred, because there was no dishonesty found in her.

64 From that day forth was Daniel had in great reputation in the sight of the people.

DOUAY OLD TESTAMENT

56 And having put him aside, he commanded that the other should come, and he said to him: O thou seed of Chanaan, and not of Juda, beauty hath deceived thee, and lust hath perverted thy heart:

57 Thus did you do to the daughters of Israel, and they for fear conversed with you: but a daughter of Juda would not abide your wickedness.

58 Now therefore tell me, under what tree didst thou take them conversing together. And he answered: Under a holm tree.

59 And Daniel said to him: Well hast thou also lied against thy own head: for the angel of the Lord waiteth with a sword to cut thee in two, and to destroy you.

60 With that all the assembly cried out with a loud voice, and they blessed God, who saveth them that trust in him.

61 And they rose up against the two elders, (for Daniel had convicted them of false witness by their own mouth,) and they did to them as they had maliciously dealt against their neighbour,

62 To fulfil the law of Moses: and they put them to death, and innocent blood was saved in that day.

63 But Helcias and his wife praised God, for their daughter Susanna, with Joakim her husband, and all her kindred, because there was no dishonesty found in her.

64 And Daniel became great in the sight of the people from that day, and thenceforward.

65 And king Astyages was gathered to his fathers, and Cyrus the Persian received his kingdom.

KNOX TRANSLATION

56 Then he had this one removed, and bade the other come
near. Brood of Chanaan, said he, and no true son of Juda, so
beauty ensnared thee? So lust drove thy heart astray? 57 Such
approaches you have made, long since, to women of the other
tribes, and they, from very fear, admitted your suit; but you
could not bring a woman of Juda to fall in with your wicked
design. 58 And now tell me, under what tree it was thou didst
find them talking together? Under a holm-oak, said he, I saw
them. 59 The right word again! cried Daniel. Saw thee asunder the angel of the Lord will, with the sharp blade he carries
yonder; you are both dead men.
60 And with that, the whole multitude cried aloud, blessing
God that is the deliverer of those who trust in him. 61 And
they turned on the two elders, by Daniel's questioning self-
convicted of false witness; served they must be as they
would have served others, 62 and the law of Moses obeyed;
so they put them to death. That day, an innocent life was
saved. 63 Good cause had Helcias and his wife to praise God
for their daughter Susanna, good cause had Joakim and all
his friends; no breath of suspicion assailed her now. 64 And
as for Daniel, he was in high favour with all the people from
that day forward.
65 When king Astyages became part of his line, it was
Cyrus, the Persian, succeeded him. [a]

a This verse evidently belongs to the next chapter [Daniel 14 follows as *Bel and the Dragon*]. But it only gives us a loose historical reference; it was only after he had been king of Media for twelve years that Cyrus conquered Babylon.

TODAY'S ENGLISH VERSION

56 Then the first judge was led away and the second one was brought before Daniel. "You are more like a Canaanite than a Jew," Daniel said to him. "This woman's beauty has warped your judgment, and lust has corrupted your thinking. 57 You are used to having your way with the women of Israel because they have been afraid of you, but here is a Jewish woman, and she would not give in. 58 Now, tell me what tree you saw them under."

"Under a large oak tree," he answered.

59 Daniel said, "All right! That lie will cost you your life; God's angel is waiting with his sword in his hand, ready to cut[a] you in two. Then we shall be rid of you both."

60 Then all the people shouted and praised God, who saves those who put their trust in him. 61 They turned against the two judges because Daniel had proved that they had lied under oath. 62 The Law of Moses states that people who give false testimony shall receive the same punishment that the accused person would have received. And so the two judges were put to death, and the life of an innocent woman was saved. 63 Susanna's parents, her husband, and all her relatives praised God because she had been proved innocent of the charges. 64 From that day on, Daniel was held in high regard.

[a] CUT: *This word in Greek sounds like the Greek for "a large oak tree."*

NEW REVISED STANDARD VERSION

56 Then, putting him to one side, he ordered them to bring the other. And he said to him, "You offspring of Canaan and not of Judah, beauty has beguiled you and lust has perverted your heart. 57 This is how you have been treating the daughters of Israel, and they were intimate with you through fear; but a daughter of Judah would not tolerate your wickedness. 58 Now then, tell me: Under what tree did you catch them being intimate with each other?" He answered, "Under an evergreen oak."[a] 59 Daniel said to him, "Very well! This lie has cost you also your head, for the angel of God is waiting with his sword to split[a] you in two, so as to destroy you both."

60 Then the whole assembly raised a great shout and blessed God, who saves those who hope in him. 61 And they took action against the two elders, because out of their own mouths Daniel had convicted them of bearing false witness; they did to them as they had wickedly planned to do to their neighbor. 62 Acting in accordance with the law of Moses, they put them to death. Thus innocent blood was spared that day.

63 Hilkiah and his wife praised God for their daughter Susanna, and so did her husband Joakim and all her relatives, because she was found innocent of a shameful deed. 64 And from that day onward Daniel had a great reputation among the people.

a The Greek words for *evergreen oak* and *split* are similar, thus forming an ironic wordplay

NEW AMERICAN BIBLE

one side, he ordered the other one to be brought. "Offspring of Canaan, not of Judah," Daniel said to him, "beauty has seduced you, lust has subverted your conscience. 57 This is how your acted with the daughters of Israel, and in their fear they yielded to you; but a daughter of Judah did not tolerate your wickedness. 58 Now then, tell me under what tree you surprised them together." 59 "Under an oak," he said. "Your fine lie has cost you also your head," said Daniel; "for the angel of God waits with a sword to cut you in two so as to make an end of you both."

60 The whole assembly cried aloud, blessing God who saves those that hope in him. 61 They rose up against the two elders, for by their own words Daniel had convicted them of perjury. According to the law of Moses, they inflicted on them the penalty they had plotted to impose on their neighbor: 62 they put them to death. Thus was innocent blood spared that day.

63 Hilkiah and his wife praised God for their daughter Susanna, as did Joakim her husband and all her relatives, because she was found innocent of any shameful deed. 64 And from that day onward Daniel was greatly esteemed by the people.

NEW JERUSALEM BIBLE

you in half.' 56 He dismissed the man, ordered the other to be brought and said to him, 'Son of Canaan, not of Judah, beauty has seduced you, lust has led your heart astray! 57 This is how you have been behaving with the daughters of Israel, and they have been too frightened to resist; but here is a daughter of Judah who could not stomach your wickedness! 58 Now then, tell me what sort of tree you surprised them under.' He replied, 'Under an aspen tree.' 59 Daniel said, 'Indeed! Your lie recoils on your own head: the angel of God is waiting with a sword to rend you in half, and destroy the pair of you.'

60 Then the whole assembly shouted, blessing God, the Saviour of those who trust in him. 61 And they turned on the two elders whom Daniel had convicted of false evidence out of their own mouths. 62 As the Law of Moses prescribes, they were given the same punishment as they had schemed to inflict on their neighbour. They were put to death. And thus, that day, an innocent life was saved. 63 Hilkiah and his wife gave thanks to God for their daughter Susanna, and so did her husband Joakim and all his relations, because she had been acquitted of anything dishonourable.

64 From that day onwards, Daniel's reputation stood high with the people.

GREEK OLD TESTAMENT

ΒΗΛ ΚΑΙ ΔΡΑΚΩΝ

1 Καὶ ὁ βασιλεὺς ᾿Αστυάγης προσετέθη πρὸς τοὺς πατέρας αὐτοῦ, καὶ παρέλαβεν Κῦρος ὁ Πέρσης τὴν βασιλείαν αὐτοῦ. 2 καὶ ἦν Δανιηλ συμβιωτὴς τοῦ βασιλέως καὶ
ἔνδοξος ὑπὲρ πάντας τοὺς φίλους αὐτοῦ. 3 καὶ ἦν εἴδωλον
τοῖς Βαβυλωνίοις, ᾧ ὄνομα Βηλ, καὶ ἐδαπανῶντο εἰς αὐτὸν
ἑκάστης ἡμέρας σεμιδάλεως ἀρτάβαι δώδεκα καὶ πρόβατα
τεσσαράκοντα καὶ οἴνου μετρηταὶ ἕξ. 4 καὶ ὁ βασιλεὺς ἐσέ-
βετο αὐτὸν καὶ ἐπορεύετο καθ᾿ ἑκάστην ἡμέραν προσκυνεῖν
αὐτῷ· Δανιηλ δὲ προσεκύνει τῷ θεῷ αὐτοῦ. 5 καὶ εἶπεν αὐτῷ
ὁ βασιλεύς Διὰ τί οὐ προσκυνεῖς τῷ Βηλ; ὁ δὲ εἶπεν Ὅτι οὐ
σέβομαι εἴδωλα χειροποίητα, ἀλλὰ τὸν ζῶντα θεὸν τὸν
κτίσαντα τὸν οὐρανὸν καὶ τὴν γῆν καὶ ἔχοντα πάσης σαρκὸς
κυριείαν. 6 καὶ εἶπεν αὐτῷ ὁ βασιλεύς Οὐ δοκεῖ σοι Βηλ
εἶναι ζῶν θεός; ἢ οὐχ ὁρᾷς ὅσα ἐσθίει καὶ πίνει καθ᾿
ἑκάστην ἡμέραν; 7 καὶ εἶπεν Δανιηλ γελάσας Μὴ πλανῶ,
βασιλεῦ· οὗτος γὰρ ἔσωθεν μέν ἐστι πηλὸς ἔξωθεν δὲ χαλκὸς
καὶ οὐ βέβρωκεν οὐδὲ πέπωκεν πώποτε. 8 καὶ θυμωθεὶς
ὁ βασιλεὺς ἐκάλεσεν τοὺς ἱερεῖς αὐτοῦ καὶ εἶπεν αὐτοῖς
Ἐὰν μὴ εἴπητέ μοι τίς ὁ κατέσθων τὴν δαπάνην ταύτην,

KING JAMES VERSION

THE HISTORY OF THE DESTRUCTION OF BEL AND THE DRAGON[a]

1 And king Astyages was gathered to his fathers, and Cyrus of Persia received his kingdom.

2 And Daniel conversed with the king, and was honoured above all his friends.

3 Now the Babylonians had an idol, called Bel, and there were spent upon him every day twelve great measures of fine flour, and forty sheep, and six vessels of wine.

4 And the king worshipped it, and went daily to adore it: but Daniel worshipped his own God. And the king said unto him, Why dost not thou worship Bel?

5 Who answered and said, Because I may not worship idols made with hands, but the living God, who hath created the heaven and the earth, and hath sovereignty over all flesh.

6 Then said the king unto him, Thinkest thou not that Bel is a living God? seest thou not how much he eateth and drinketh every day?

7 Then Daniel smiled, and said, O king, be not deceived: for this is but clay within, and brass without, and did never eat or drink any thing.

8 So the king was wroth, and called for his priests, and said unto them, If ye tell me not who this is that devoureth these expences, ye shall die.

a Cut off from the end of Daniel.

DOUAY OLD TESTAMENT

In standard editions of the Douay translation these verses are printed after Daniel 13.

DANIEL 14

1 AND Daniel was the king's guest, and was honoured above all his friends.

2 Now the Babylonians had an idol called Bel: and there were spent upon him every day twelve great measures of fine flour, and forty sheep, and sixty vessels of wine.

3 The king also worshipped him, and went every day to adore him: but Daniel adored his God. And the king said to him: Why dost thou not adore Bel?

4 And he answered, and said to him: Because I do not worship idols made with hands, but the living God, that created heaven and earth, and hath power over all flesh.

5 And the king said to him: Doth not Bel seem to thee to be a living god? Seest thou not how much he eateth and drinketh every day?

6 Then Daniel smiled and said: O king, be not deceived: for this is but clay within, and brass without, neither hath he eaten at any time.

7 And the king being angry called for his priests, and said to them: If you tell me not, who it is that eateth up these expenses, you shall die.

KNOX TRANSLATION

In standard editions of the Knox translation these verses are printed after Daniel 13.

DANIEL 14

1 Of this king, Daniel was the courtier, and valued above
all his other friends. 2 A great idol there was, that the men of
Babylon worshipped; Bel was the name of it, and day by day
it must be fed with thirty-two bushels of fine flour, and forty
sheep, and of wine thirty-six gallons. 3 The king himself
honoured it with the rest, and no day passed but he went to
pay it reverence. A time came when he asked Daniel, that
worshipped no God but his own, why Bel he would not worship; 4 and this answer Daniel made him, that for idols made
by men's hands worship he had none, only for that living
God that made heaven and earth, and of all mankind held
the sovereignty. 5 What, cried the king, wilt thou have it Bel
is not a living god? Hast thou no eyes for the great trencherman he is, day in, day out, of food and drink both? 6 Nay,
my lord king, Daniel answered with a smile, give no heed to
false tales. Clay he is within, and bronze without; I warrant
thee, eat he cannot. 7 Whereupon the king, in high displeasure, summoned Bel's priests. You shall give account, said
he, of yonder revenues, and that on pain of your lives. Who
is it has the eating of them? 8 Prove to me it is Bel himself,

TODAY'S ENGLISH VERSION

BEL AND THE DRAGON

1After the death of King Astyages, Cyrus of Persia took
over his kingdom. 2Daniel was one of King Cyrus' closest
companions, and the king thought more highly of Daniel
than of any other of his advisers.
3The Babylonians had an idol named Bel. Each day the
people had to provide Bel with an offering of twelve bushels
of fine flour, forty sheep, and fifty gallons of wine. 4King
Cyrus believed that Bel was a god, and each day he used to
go and worship it. But Daniel worshiped his own God.
5One day the king asked Daniel, "Why don't you
worship Bel?"
Daniel answered, "I do not worship idols made with
human hands. I worship only the living God, who created
heaven and earth and is the Lord of all human beings."
6"And don't you believe that our god Bel is really alive?"
asked the king. "Haven't you seen how much he eats and
drinks every day?"
7Daniel laughed and said, "Don't be fooled, Your Majesty.
This god you call Bel is nothing more than clay covered with
bronze; it has never eaten or drunk anything."
8-10At this the king became angry and called in all seventy
of the priests of Bel. He said to them, "I warn you that you
will be put to death, unless you can show me that it is Bel

NEW REVISED STANDARD VERSION

BEL AND THE DRAGON

(Chapter 14 of the Greek Version of Daniel)

1 When King Astyages was laid to rest with his ancestors,
Cyrus the Persian succeeded to his kingdom. 2Daniel was a
companion of the king, and was the most honored of all his
Friends.
3 Now the Babylonians had an idol called Bel, and every
day they provided for it twelve bushels of choice flour and
forty sheep and six measures[a] of wine. 4The king revered it
and went every day to worship it. But Daniel worshiped his
own God.
So the king said to him, "Why do you not worship Bel?"
5He answered, "Because I do not revere idols made with
hands, but the living God, who created heaven and earth and
has dominion over all living creatures."
6 The king said to him, "Do you not think that Bel is a living god? Do you not see how much he eats and drinks every
day?" 7And Daniel laughed, and said, "Do not be deceived,
O king, for this thing is only clay inside and bronze outside,
and it never ate or drank anything."
8 Then the king was angry and called the priests of Bel[b]
and said to them, "If you do not tell me who is eating these
provisions, you shall die. 9But if you prove that Bel is eating

a A little more than fifty gallons *b* Gk *his priests*

NEW AMERICAN BIBLE

In standard editions of the New American Bible translation these verses are printed after Daniel 13.

DANIEL 14

1After King Astyages was laid with his fathers, Cyrus the
Persian succeeded to his kingdom. 2Daniel was the king's
favorite and was held in higher esteem than any of the
friends of the king. 3The Babylonians had an idol called Bel,
and every day they provided for it six barrels of fine flour,
forty sheep, and six measures of wine. 4The king worshiped
it and went every day to adore it; but Daniel adored only his
God. 5When the king asked him, "Why do you not adore
Bel?" Daniel replied, "Because I worship not idols made with
hands, but only the living God who made heaven and earth
and has dominion over all mankind." 6Then the king continued, "You do not think Bel is a living god? Do you not see
how much he eats and drinks every day?" 7Daniel began to
laugh. "Do not be deceived, O king," he said; "it is only clay
inside and bronze outside; it has never taken any food or
drink." 8Enraged, the king called his priests and said to
them, "Unless you tell me who it is that consumes these
provisions, you shall die. 9But if you can show that Bel

NEW JERUSALEM BIBLE

In standard editions of the New American Bible translation these verses are printed after Daniel 13.

BEL AND THE DRAGON

(Chapter 14 of the Greek Version of Daniel)

1[a]When King Astyages joined his ancestors, Cyrus of
Persia succeeded him. 2Daniel was very close to the king,
who respected him more than any of his other friends.
3Now, in Babylon there was an idol called Bel,[b] to which
twelve bushels of the finest flour, forty sheep and six measures of wine were offered every day. 4The king venerated
this idol and used to go and worship it every day. Daniel,
however, worshipped his own God. 5'Why do you not worship Bel?' the king asked Daniel. 'I do not worship idols
made by human hand,' Daniel replied, 'I worship the living
God who made heaven and earth and who is lord over all living creatures.' 6'Do you not believe, then,' said the king,
'that Bel is a living god? Can you not see how much he eats
and drinks each day?' 7Daniel laughed. 'Your Majesty,' he
said, 'do not be taken in; he is clay inside, and bronze outside, and has never eaten or drunk anything.' 8This made
the king angry; he summoned his priests, 'Tell me who eats
all this food,' he said, 'or die. Prove to me that Bel really eats

a **14** Ch. 14 occurs in Gk but not in the Hebr. text. *b* **14** Another name for Marduk, chief god of Babylon.

GREEK OLD TESTAMENT

ἀποθανεῖσθε· ἐὰν δὲ δείξητε ὅτι Βηλ κατεσθίει αὐτά, ἀποθανεῖται Δανιηλ, ὅτι ἐβλασφήμησεν εἰς τὸν Βηλ. 9 καὶ εἶπεν
Δανιηλ τῷ βασιλεῖ Γινέσθω κατὰ τὸ ῥῆμά σου. καὶ ἦσαν
ἱερεῖς τοῦ Βηλ ἑβδομήκοντα ἐκτὸς γυναικῶν καὶ τέκνων.
10 καὶ ἦλθεν ὁ βασιλεὺς μετὰ Δανιηλ εἰς τὸν οἶκον τοῦ Βηλ.
11 καὶ εἶπαν οἱ ἱερεῖς τοῦ Βηλ Ἰδοὺ ἡμεῖς ἀποτρέχομεν ἔξω,
σὺ δέ, βασιλεῦ, παράθες τὰ βρώματα καὶ τὸν οἶνον κεράσας
θὲς καὶ ἀπόκλεισον τὴν θύραν καὶ σφράγισον τῷ δακτυλίῳ
σου· καὶ ἐλθὼν πρωὶ ἐὰν μὴ εὕρῃς πάντα βεβρωμένα ὑπὸ τοῦ
Βηλ, ἀποθανούμεθα ἢ Δανιηλ ὁ ψευδόμενος καθ' ἡμῶν. 12 αὐτοὶ δὲ κατεφρόνουν, ὅτι πεποιήκεισαν ὑπὸ τὴν τράπεζαν
κεκρυμμένην εἴσοδον καὶ δι' αὐτῆς εἰσεπορεύοντο διόλου καὶ
ἀνήλουν αὐτά. 13 καὶ ἐγένετο ὡς ἐξήλθοσαν ἐκεῖνοι, καὶ ὁ
βασιλεὺς παρέθηκεν τὰ βρώματα τῷ Βηλ. 14 καὶ ἐπέταξεν
Δανιηλ τοῖς παιδαρίοις αὐτοῦ καὶ ἤνεγκαν τέφραν καὶ κατέ-
σησαν ὅλον τὸν ναὸν ἐνώπιον τοῦ βασιλέως μόνου· καὶ ἐξελθόντες ἔκλεισαν τὴν θύραν καὶ ἐσφραγίσαντο ἐν τῷ δακτυλίῳ τοῦ βασιλέως, καὶ ἀπῆλθον. 15 οἱ δὲ ἱερεῖς ἦλθον τὴν
νύκτα κατὰ τὸ ἔθος αὐτῶν καὶ αἱ γυναῖκες καὶ τὰ τέκνα
αὐτῶν καὶ κατέφαγον πάντα καὶ ἐξέπιον. 16 καὶ ὤρθρισεν ὁ
βασιλεὺς τὸ πρωὶ καὶ Δανιηλ μετ' αὐτοῦ. 17 καὶ εἶπεν ὁ
βασιλεύς Σῷοι αἱ σφραγῖδες, Δανιηλ; ὁ δὲ εἶπεν Σῷοι,

KING JAMES VERSION

9 But if ye can certify me that Bel devoureth them, then Daniel shall die: for he hath spoken blasphemy against Bel. And Daniel said unto the king, Let it be according to thy word.

10 Now the priests of Bel were threescore and ten, beside their wives and children. And the king went with Daniel into the temple of Bel.

11 So Bel's priests said, Lo, we go out: but thou, O king, set on the meat, and make ready the wine, and shut the door fast, and seal it with thine own signet;

12 And to morrow when thou comest in, if thou findest not that Bel hath eaten up all, we will suffer death: or else Daniel, that speaketh falsely against us.

13 And they little regarded it: for under the table they had made a privy entrance, whereby they entered in continually, and consumed those things.

14 So when they were gone forth, the king set meats before Bel. Now Daniel had commanded his servants to bring ashes, and those they strewed throughout all the temple in the presence of the king alone: then went they out, and shut the door, and sealed it with the king's signet, and so departed.

15 Now in the night came the priests with their wives and children, as they were wont to do, and did eat and drinck up all.

16 In the morning betime the king arose, and Daniel with him.

17 And the king said, Daniel, are the seals whole? And he said, Yea, O king, they be whole.

DOUAY OLD TESTAMENT

8 But if you can shew that Bel eateth these things, Daniel shall die, because he hath blasphemed against Bel. And Daniel said to the king: Be it done according to thy word.

9 Now the priests of Bel were seventy, besides their wives, and little ones, and children. And the king went with Daniel into the temple of Bel.

10 And the priests of Bel said: Behold we go out: and do thou, O king, set on the meats, and make ready the wine, and shut the door fast, and seal it with thy own ring:

11 And when thou comest in the morning, if thou findest not that Bel hath eaten up all, we will suffer death, or else Daniel that hath lied against us.

12 And they little regarded it, because they had made under the table a secret entrance, and they always came in by it, and consumed those things.

13 So it came to pass after they were gone out, the king set the meats before Bel: and Daniel commanded his servants, and they brought ashes, and he sifted them all over the temple before the king: and going forth they shut the door, and having sealed it with the king's ring, they departed.

14 But the priests went in by night, according to their custom, with their wives and their children: and they ate and drank up all.

15 And the king arose early in the morning, and Daniel with him.

16 And the king said: Are the seals whole, Daniel? And he answered: They are whole, O king.

KNOX TRANSLATION

and Daniel shall die instead, that blasphemed him. As it
pleases the king's grace, said Daniel.
9 Seventy of these priests there were, that had wives and
children to fend for besides. And when the king reached their
temple, with Daniel in attendance, 10 this challenge they
offered: Withdraw we, as thou seest; for thee it is, lord king,
to set food, pour out wine, lock and seal door with thy own
hand. 11 To-morrow, come thou and find aught left over
from Bel's banqueting, we die for it; or else Daniel dies, that
so traduced us. 12 Lightly enough the challenge was made;
had they not provided a hidden entrance-way, close under
the god's table, by which they came in and ate what eat they
would? 13 So out they went, and the king set on Bel's viands
with his own hand; and what did Daniel? He would have his
servants bring ashes, and scatter them all over the temple
floor, there in the king's presence. Which done, all withdrew,
leaving the door locked, and the royal seal upon it. 14 And
that night in they came as came they ever, priest and priest's
wife and priest's children, and left neither bite nor sup
between them.
15 Next day, the king was early abroad, and Daniel with
him. 16 What of the seals, Daniel? the king asked. Are they
unbroken? Ay, my lord king, unbroken yet. 17 What a cry

TODAY'S ENGLISH VERSION

who is eating these offerings. If you prove to me that it is
Bel, then I will have Daniel put to death for claiming that Bel
is not a god."

Daniel agreed to this proposal.

11 Then they all went with the king into Bel's temple,
where the priests said to the king, "Your Majesty, we will go
out and let you place the food on the table and prepare the
wine. When you leave, you may lock the door behind you
and seal it with the royal seal. 12 In the morning when you
return, if you find that Bel has not eaten everything, you can
put us to death. But if he has, Daniel will die for making
false accusations against us."

13 But the priests were not worried, because they had made
a secret entrance underneath a table in the temple, so that
they could go in every night and eat the offerings.

14 When the priests had left, the king set out the food for
Bel. Then Daniel ordered his servants to bring some ashes
and scatter them all over the floor of the temple. No one
except the king saw them do this. After that they all went
out, locked the door, sealed it with the royal seal, and left.

15 That night, as usual, the priests with their wives and
children came into the temple by the secret entrance and ate
all the food and drank all the wine.

16 Early the next morning, the king and Daniel went to the
temple. 17 The king asked, "Have the seals been broken,
Daniel?"

"No, Your Majesty, they have not been broken," he replied.

NEW REVISED STANDARD VERSION

them, Daniel shall die, because he has spoken blasphemy
against Bel." Daniel said to the king, "Let it be done as you
have said."

10 Now there were seventy priests of Bel, besides their
wives and children. So the king went with Daniel into the
temple of Bel. 11 The priests of Bel said, "See, we are now
going outside; you yourself, O king, set out the food and prepare the wine, and shut the door and seal it with your signet.
12 When you return in the morning, if you do not find that
Bel has eaten it all, we will die; otherwise Daniel will, who is
telling lies about us." 13 They were unconcerned, for beneath
the table they had made a hidden entrance, through which
they used to go in regularly and consume the provisions.
14 After they had gone out, the king set out the food for Bel.
Then Daniel ordered his servants to bring ashes, and they
scattered them throughout the whole temple in the presence
of the king alone. Then they went out, shut the door and
sealed it with the king's signet, and departed. 15 During the
night the priests came as usual, with their wives and children, and they ate and drank everything.

16 Early in the morning the king rose and came, and
Daniel with him. 17 The king said, "Are the seals unbroken,
Daniel?" He answered, "They are unbroken, O king." 18 As

NEW AMERICAN BIBLE

consumes them, Daniel shall die for blaspheming Bel."
Daniel said to the king, "Let it be as you say!" 10 There were
seventy priests of Bel, besides their wives and children.

When the king went with Daniel into the temple of Bel,
11 the priests of Bel said, "See, we are going to leave. Do you,
O king, set out the food and prepare the wine; then shut the
door and seal it with your ring. 12 If you do not find that Bel
has eaten it all when you return in the morning, we are to
die; otherwise Daniel shall die for his lies against us."
13 They were not perturbed, because under the table they had
made a secret entrance through which they always came in
to consume the food. 14 After they departed the king set the
food before Bel, while Daniel ordered his servants to bring
some ashes, which they scattered through the whole temple;
the king alone was present. Then they went outside, sealed
the closed door with the king's ring, and departed. 15 The
priests entered that night as usual, with their wives and children, and they ate and drank everything.

16 Early the next morning, the king came with Daniel.
17 "Are the seals unbroken, Daniel?" he asked. And Daniel
answered, "They are unbroken, O king." 18 As soon as he

NEW JERUSALEM BIBLE

it, and I will have Daniel put to death for blaspheming him.'
9 Daniel said to the king, 'Let it be as you say.'

10 There were seventy of these priests, to say nothing of
their wives and children. The king went to the temple of Bel,
taking Daniel with him. 11 The priests of Bel said to him, 'We
shall now go out, and you, Your Majesty, will lay out the
meal and mix the wine and set it out. Then, lock the door
and seal it with your personal seal. If, when you return in
the morning, you do not find that everything has been eaten
by Bel, let us be put to death; otherwise let Daniel, that slanderer!' 12 They were thinking—hence their confidence—of a
secret entrance which they had made under the table, and by
which they came in regularly and took the offerings away.
13 When the priests had gone and the king had set out the
food for Bel, 14 Daniel made his servants bring ashes and
spread them all over the temple floor, with no other witness
than the king. They then left the building, shut the door and,
sealing it with the king's seal, went away. 15 That night, as
usual, the priests came with their wives and children; they
ate and drank everything.

16 The king was up very early next morning, and Daniel
with him. 17 'Daniel,' said the king, 'are the seals intact?'
'They are intact, Your Majesty,' he replied. 18 The king then

GREEK OLD TESTAMENT

βασιλεῦ. 18 καὶ ἐγένετο ἅμα τῷ ἀνοῖξαι τὰς θύρας ἐπι-
βλέψας ὁ βασιλεὺς ἐπὶ τὴν τράπεζαν ἐβόησεν φωνῇ μεγάλῃ
Μέγας εἶ, Βηλ, καὶ οὐκ ἔστιν παρὰ σοὶ δόλος οὐδὲ εἷς.
19 καὶ ἐγέλασεν Δανιηλ καὶ ἐκράτησεν τὸν βασιλέα τοῦ μὴ
εἰσελθεῖν αὐτὸν ἔσω καὶ εἶπεν Ἰδὲ δὴ τὸ ἔδαφος καὶ γνῶθι
τίνος τὰ ἴχνη ταῦτα. 20 καὶ εἶπεν ὁ βασιλεύς Ὁρῶ τὰ ἴχνη
ἀνδρῶν καὶ γυναικῶν καὶ παιδίων. 21 καὶ ὀργισθεὶς ὁ
βασιλεὺς τότε συνέλαβεν τοὺς ἱερεῖς καὶ τὰς γυναῖκας καὶ
τὰ τέκνα αὐτῶν, καὶ ἔδειξαν αὐτῷ τὰς κρυπτὰς θύρας, δι᾽ ὧν
εἰσεπορεύοντο καὶ ἐδαπάνων τὰ ἐπὶ τῇ τραπέζῃ. 22 καὶ
ἀπέκτεινεν αὐτοὺς ὁ βασιλεὺς καὶ ἔδωκεν τὸν Βηλ ἔκδοτον
τῷ Δανιηλ, καὶ κατέστρεψεν αὐτὸν καὶ τὸ ἱερὸν αὐτοῦ.
23 Καὶ ἦν δράκων μέγας, καὶ ἐσέβοντο αὐτὸν οἱ Βαβυλώνιοι. 24 καὶ εἶπεν ὁ βασιλεὺς τῷ Δανιηλ Οὐ δύνασαι
εἰπεῖν ὅτι οὐκ ἔστιν οὗτος θεὸς ζῶν· καὶ προσκύνησον αὐτῷ.
25 καὶ εἶπεν Δανιηλ Κυρίῳ τῷ θεῷ μου προσκυνήσω, ὅτι
οὗτός ἐστιν θεὸς ζῶν· σὺ δέ, βασιλεῦ, δός μοι ἐξουσίαν, καὶ
ἀποκτενῶ τὸν δράκοντα ἄνευ μαχαίρας καὶ ῥάβδου. 26 καὶ
εἶπεν ὁ βασιλεύς Δίδωμί σοι. 27 καὶ ἔλαβεν Δανιηλ πίσσαν
καὶ στῆρ καὶ τρίχας καὶ ἥψησεν ἐπὶ τὸ αὐτὸ καὶ ἐποίησεν
μάζας καὶ ἔδωκεν εἰς τὸ στόμα τοῦ δράκοντος, καὶ φαγὼν
διερράγη ὁ δράκων. καὶ εἶπεν Ἴδετε τὰ σεβάσματα ὑμῶν.
28 καὶ ἐγένετο ὡς ἤκουσαν οἱ Βαβυλώνιοι, ἠγανάκτησαν λίαν
καὶ συνεστράφησαν ἐπὶ τὸν βασιλέα καὶ εἶπαν Ιουδαῖος

KING JAMES VERSION

18 And as soon as he had opened the door, the king looked upon the table, and cried with a loud voice, Great art thou, O Bel, and with thee is no deceit at all.

19 Then laughed Daniel, and held the king that he should not go in, and said, Behold now the pavement, and mark well whose footsteps are these.

20 And the king said, I see the footsteps of men, women, and children. And then the king was angry,

21 And took the priests with their wives and children, who shewed him the privy doors, where they came in, and consumed such things as were upon the table.

22 Therefore the king slew them, and delivered Bel into Daniel's power, who destroyed him and his temple.

23 And in that same place there was a great dragon, which they of Babylon worshipped.

24 And the king said unto Daniel, Wilt thou also say that this is of brass? lo, he liveth, he eateth and drinketh; thou canst not say that he is no living god: therefore worship him.

25 Then said Daniel unto the king, I will worship the Lord my God: for he is the living God.

26 But give me leave, O king, and I shall slay this dragon without sword or staff. The king said, I give thee leave.

27 Then Daniel took pitch, and fat, and hair, and did seethe them together, and made lumps thereof: this he put in the dragon's mouth, and so the dragon burst in sunder: and Daniel said, Lo, these are the gods ye worship.

28 When they of Babylon heard that, they took great indignation, and conspired against the king, saying, The

DOUAY OLD TESTAMENT

17 And as soon as he had opened the door, the king looked upon the table, and cried out with a loud voice: Great art thou, O Bel, and there is not any deceit with thee.

18 And Daniel laughed: and he held the king that he should not go in: and he said: Behold the pavement, mark whose footsteps these are.

19 And the king said: I see the footsteps of men, and women, and children. And the king was angry.

20 Then he took the priests, and their wives, and their children: and they shewed him the private doors by which they came in, and consumed the things that were on the table.

21 The king therefore put them to death, and delivered Bel into the power of Daniel: who destroyed him, and his temple.

22 And there was a great dragon in that place, and the Babylonians worshipped him.

23 And the king said to Daniel: Behold thou canst not say now, that this is not a living god: adore him therefore.

24 And Daniel said: I adore the Lord my God: for he is the living God: but that is no living god.

25 But give me leave, O king, and I will kill this dragon without sword or club. And the king said: I give thee leave.

26 Then Daniel took pitch, and fat, and hair, and boiled them together: and he made lumps, and put them into the dragon's mouth, and the dragon burst asunder. And he said: Behold him whom you worshipped.

27 And when the Babylonians had heard this, they took great indignation: and being gathered together against the

KNOX TRANSLATION

was that the king gave, when he opened the door and caught
sight of the table within! A great god thou art, Bel, said he,
and no deceiver! 18 But Daniel smiled, and would not have
the king go in yet; Look about thee, he said, and ask thyself
who it was left their prints on yonder floor. 19 Why, cried the
king, these be footprints of living men, and women and children besides! With that, he fell into a rage; 20 priest and
priest's wife and priest's children must be taken into custody. And when these had shewed him the door by which
they came in and swept the table bare of its offerings, 21 he
put the whole company of them to death. And as for Bel, he
left him to Daniel's mercy, who threw down image and temple both.

22 There was a great serpent, too, in those parts that was
worshipped by the folk of Babylon; 23 and of this the king
said to Daniel, here at least was a god that lived; gainsay
that he could not, and therefore he needs must worship.
24 Nay, said Daniel, my own God I worship still; living God is
none but he. Here is no living God; 25 let me but have the
royal warrant, and I will make an end of it, and neither
sword nor club to help me. So the king gave his warrant,
26 and what did Daniel? Pitch and fat and hairs he boiled all
together, and with lumps of this fed the serpent, which
thereupon burst all to pieces; and, Here, said Daniel, is your
god.

27 Angry men were the folk of Babylon when they heard of
these doings, and they made their way into the royal

TODAY'S ENGLISH VERSION

18 As soon as the door was opened, the king saw the empty table and shouted, "You are great, O Bel! You really are a god."
19 But Daniel began to laugh and said to the king, "Before you enter the temple, look at the floor and tell me whose footprints you see there."
20 "I see the footprints of men, women, and children," said the king,
21 and he became so angry that he had the priests and their families arrested and brought to him. They showed him the secret doors through which they had come in each night to eat the food placed on the table.
22 So the king had the priests put to death, and he gave Bel to Daniel, who destroyed the idol and tore down its temple.

23 There was also a huge dragon which the Babylonians worshiped.
24 One day the king said to Daniel, "You can't tell me that this god is not alive. So worship him!"
25 "I worship the Lord," replied Daniel. "He is the only living God.
26 And if Your Majesty will give me permission, I will kill this dragon of yours without using a sword or a club."
"You have my permission," answered the king.
27 So Daniel took some tar, some fat, and some hair and boiled them all together. He made cakes out of the mixture and fed them to the dragon. When the dragon ate them, it swelled up and burst open. "That's the kind of thing you Babylonians worship," said Daniel.
28 When the people of Babylon heard what had happened, they staged an angry demonstration against the king. "The

NEW REVISED STANDARD VERSION

soon as the doors were opened, the king looked at the table, and shouted in a loud voice, "You are great, O Bel, and in you there is no deceit at all!"
19 But Daniel laughed and restrained the king from going in. "Look at the floor," he said, "and notice whose footprints these are."
20 The king said, "I see the footprints of men and women and children."
21 Then the king was enraged, and he arrested the priests and their wives and children. They showed him the secret doors through which they used to enter to consume what was on the table.
22 Therefore the king put them to death, and gave Bel over to Daniel, who destroyed it and its temple.

23 Now in that place[a] there was a great dragon, which the Babylonians revered.
24 The king said to Daniel, "You cannot deny that this is a living god; so worship him."
25 Daniel said, "I worship the Lord my God, for he is the living God.
26 But give me permission, O king, and I will kill the dragon without sword or club." The king said, "I give you permission."
27 Then Daniel took pitch, fat, and hair, and boiled them together and made cakes, which he fed to the dragon. The dragon ate them, and burst open. Then Daniel said, "See what you have been worshiping!"
28 When the Babylonians heard about it, they were very indignant and conspired against the king, saying, "The king

a Other ancient authorities lack *in that place*

NEW AMERICAN BIBLE

had opened the door, the king looked at the table and cried aloud, "Great you are, O Bel; there is no trickery in you."
19 But Daniel laughed and kept the king from entering. "Look at the floor," he said; "whose footprints are these?"
20 "I see the footprints of men, women, and children!" said the king.
21 The angry king arrested the priests, their wives, and their children. They showed him the secret door by which they used to enter to consume what was on the table.
22 He put them to death, and handed Bel over to Daniel, who destroyed it and its temple.
23 There was a great dragon which the Babylonians worshiped.
24 "Look!" said the king to Daniel, "you cannot deny that this is a living god, so adore it."
25 But Daniel answered, "I adore the Lord, my God, for he is the living God.
26 Give me permission, O king, and I will kill this dragon without sword or club." "I give you permission," the king said.
27 Then Daniel took some pitch, fat, and hair; these he boiled together and made into cakes. He but them into the mouth of the dragon, and when the dragon ate them, he burst asunder. "This," he said, "is what you worshiped."
28 When the Babylonians heard this, they were angry and

NEW JERUSALEM BIBLE

opened the door and, taking one look at the table, exclaimed, 'You are great, O Bel! There is no deception in you!'
19 But Daniel laughed; and, restraining the king from going in any further, he said, 'Look at the floor and take note whose footmarks these are!'
20 'I can see the footmarks of men, of women and of children,' said the king,
21 and angrily ordered the priests to be arrested, with their wives and children. They then showed him the secret door through which they used to come and take what was on the table.
22 The king had them put to death and handed Bel over to Daniel who destroyed both the idol and its temple.

23 There was a great dragon which the Babylonians worshipped too.
24 The king said to Daniel, 'Are you going to tell me that this is made of bronze? Look, it is alive; it eats and drinks; you cannot deny that this is a living god; worship it, then.'
25 Daniel replied, 'I will worship the Lord my God; he is the living God. With your permission, Your Majesty, without using either sword or club, I shall kill this dragon.'
26 'You have my permission,' said the king.
27 Whereupon, Daniel took some pitch, some fat and some hair and boiled them up together, rolled the mixture into balls and fed them to the dragon; the dragon swallowed them and burst. Daniel said, 'Now look at the sort of thing you worship!'
28 The Babylonians were furious when they heard about this and

GREEK OLD TESTAMENT

γέγονεν ὁ βασιλεύς· τὸν Βηλ κατέσπασεν καὶ τὸν δράκοντα
ἀπέκτεινεν καὶ τοὺς ἱερεῖς κατέσφαξεν. 29 καὶ εἶπαν
ἐλθόντες πρὸς τὸν βασιλέα Παράδος ἡμῖν τὸν Δανιηλ· εἰ δὲ
μή, ἀποκτενοῦμέν σε καὶ τὸν οἶκόν σου. 30 καὶ εἶδεν ὁ βασιλεὺς ὅτι ἐπείγουσιν αὐτὸν σφόδρα, καὶ ἀναγκασθεὶς παρέδωκεν αὐτοῖς τὸν Δανιηλ. 31 οἱ δὲ ἐνέβαλον αὐτὸν εἰς τὸν
λάκκον τῶν λεόντων, καὶ ἦν ἐκεῖ ἡμέρας ἕξ. 32 ἦσαν δὲ ἐν
τῷ λάκκῳ ἑπτὰ λέοντες, καὶ ἐδίδετο αὐτοῖς τὴν ἡμέραν δύο
σώματα καὶ δύο πρόβατα· τότε δὲ οὐκ ἐδόθη αὐτοῖς, ἵνα
καταφάγωσιν τὸν Δανιηλ. 33 καὶ ἦν Αμβακουμ ὁ προφήτης
ἐν τῇ Ιουδαίᾳ, καὶ αὐτὸς ἥψησεν ἕψεμα καὶ ἐνέθρυψεν
ἄρτους εἰς σκάφην καὶ ἐπορεύετο εἰς τὸ πεδίον ἀπενέγκαι
τοῖς θερισταῖς. 34 καὶ εἶπεν ἄγγελος κυρίου τῷ Αμβακουμ
Ἀπένεγκε τὸ ἄριστον, ὃ ἔχεις, εἰς Βαβυλῶνα τῷ Δανιηλ εἰς
τὸν λάκκον τῶν λεόντων. 35 καὶ εἶπεν Αμβακουμ Κύριε,
Βαβυλῶνα οὐχ ἑώρακα καὶ τὸν λάκκον οὐ γινώσκω. 36 καὶ
ἐπελάβετο ὁ ἄγγελος κυρίου τῆς κορυφῆς αὐτοῦ καὶ βαστά-
σας τῆς κόμης τῆς κεφαλῆς αὐτοῦ ἔθηκεν αὐτὸν εἰς Βαβυλῶνα ἐπάνω τοῦ λάκκου ἐν τῷ ῥοίζῳ τοῦ πνεύματος αὐτοῦ.
37 καὶ ἐβόησεν Αμβακουμ λέγων Δανιηλ Δανιηλ, λαβὲ τὸ ἄριστον, ὃ ἀπέστειλέν σοι ὁ θεός. 38 καὶ εἶπεν Δανιηλ Ἐμνή-
σθης γάρ μου, ὁ θεός, καὶ οὐκ ἐγκατέλιπες τοὺς ἀγαπῶντάς

KING JAMES VERSION

king is become a Jew, and he hath destroyed Bel, he hath slain the dragon, and put the priests to death.

29 So they came to the king, and said, Deliver us Daniel, or else we will destroy thee and thine house.

30 Now when the king saw that they pressed him sore, being constrained, he delivered Daniel unto them:

31 Who cast him into the lions' den: where he was six days.

32 And in the den there were seven lions, and they had given them every day two carcases, and two sheep: which then were not given to them, to the intent they might devour Daniel.

33 Now there was in Jewry a prophet, called Habbacuc, who had made pottage, and had broken bread in a bowl, and was going into the field, for to bring it to the reapers.

34 But the angel of the Lord said unto Habbacuc, Go, carry the dinner that thou hast into Babylon unto Daniel, who is in the lions' den.

35 And Habbacuc said, Lord, I never saw Babylon; neither do I know where the den is.

36 Then the angel of the Lord took him by the crown, and bare him by the hair of his head, and through the vehemency of his spirit set him in Babylon over the den.

37 And Habbacuc cried, saying, O Daniel, Daniel, take the dinner which God hath sent thee.

38 And Daniel said, Thou hast remembered me, O God: neither hast thou forsaken them that seek thee and love thee.

DOUAY OLD TESTAMENT

king, they said: The king is become a Jew. He hath destroyed Bel, he hath killed the dragon, and he hath put the priests to death.

28 And they came to the king, and said: Deliver us Daniel, or else we will destroy thee and thy house.

29 And the king saw that they pressed upon him violently: and being constrained by necessity he delivered Daniel to them.

30 And they cast him into the den of lions, and he was there six days.

31 And in the den there were seven lions, and they had given to them two carcasses every day, and two sheep: but then they were not given unto them, that they might devour Daniel.

32 Now there was in Judea a prophet called Habacuc, and he had boiled pottage, and had broken bread in a bowl: and was going into the field, to carry it to the reapers.

33 And the angel of the Lord said to Habacuc: Carry the dinner which thou hast into Babylon to Daniel, who is in the lions' den.

34 And Habacuc said: Lord, I never saw Babylon, nor do I know the den.

35 And the angel of the Lord took him by the top of his head, and carried him by the hair of his head, and set him in Babylon over the den in the force of his spirit.

36 And Habacuc cried, saying: O Daniel, thou servant of God, take the dinner that God hath sent thee.

37 And Daniel said: Thou hast remembered me, O God, and thou hast not forsaken them that love thee.

KNOX TRANSLATION

presence, crying out, Here is the king himself turned Jew!
Here is Bel overthrown, and the dragon slain, and our priests
massacred! 28 And when they found audience, Give up
Daniel to us, they said, or we will make an end of thee, and
thy household with thee. 29 The king, finding their onslaught
so determined, gave up Daniel to them against his will;
30 and they threw him into a pit in which lions were kept,
where he spent six whole days. 31 Seven lions there were in
the pit, and each day two human bodies were given them as
food, and two sheep; but now they were kept unfed, so that
Daniel might be their prey.
32 Far away, in Judaea, the prophet Habacuc had been
making broth, and crumbling bread in a great bowl, and was
even now carrying it to the reapers on the farm; 33 when
suddenly the angel of the Lord said to him, Take the dinner
thou hast with thee to Babylon, and give it to Daniel; he is in
the lion-pit. 34 Lord, said Habacuc, I was never yet in
Babylon, and know nothing of any lion-pit there. 35 Upon
which the angel of the Lord caught at his head and lifted him
by the hair of it; then by the force of his impulse, set him
down in Babylon, close to the pit. 36 So Habacuc cried out,
Daniel! Servant of God! The Lord has sent thee thy dinner;
come and take it. 37 And Daniel said, Thou wouldst not forget me, O God, wouldst not forsake such as love thee. 38 So

TODAY'S ENGLISH VERSION

king has become a Jew," they shouted. "First he destroyed
Bel and slaughtered the priests, and now he has killed our
dragon." 29 They went to the king and demanded that Daniel
be handed over to them. "If you refuse," they warned the
king, "we will put you and your family to death."
30 When the king saw that they meant what they said, he
was forced to hand Daniel over to them. 31 They threw him
into a pit of lions, where they left him for six days. 32 There
were seven lions in the pit, and normally they were fed two
human bodies and two sheep each day. But they were given
nothing to eat during these six days, in order to make sure
that Daniel would be eaten.
33 At that time the prophet Habakkuk was in the land of
Judah. He had cooked a stew and crumbled bread into it. He
was carrying a bowl of it to the workers who were out in the
fields harvesting grain, 34 when an angel of the Lord spoke
to him, "Take the food you are carrying and give it to Daniel,
who is in Babylon in a pit of lions."
35 Habakkuk answered, "Sir, I have never been to Babylon,
and I don't know where the pit of lions is."
36 So the angel grabbed the prophet by the hair and took
him to Babylon with the speed of the wind.[a] He set him
down near the pit of lions. 37 Habakkuk called out, "Daniel!
Daniel! God has sent you some food. Here, take it."
38 When Daniel heard Habakkuk, he prayed, "God, you did
remember me; you never abandon those who love you."

[a] with the speed of the wind; *or* by the power of his spirit.

NEW REVISED STANDARD VERSION

has become a Jew; he has destroyed Bel, and killed the dragon, and slaughtered the priests." 29 Going to the king, they
said, "Hand Daniel over to us, or else we will kill you and
your household." 30 The king saw that they were pressing
him hard, and under compulsion he handed Daniel over to
them.
31 They threw Daniel into the lions' den, and he was
there for six days. 32 There were seven lions in the den, and
every day they had been given two human bodies and two
sheep; but now they were given nothing, so that they would
devour Daniel.
33 Now the prophet Habakkuk was in Judea; he had made
a stew and had broken bread into a bowl, and was going
into the field to take it to the reapers. 34 But the angel of the
Lord said to Habakkuk, "Take the food that you have to
Babylon, to Daniel, in the lions' den." 35 Habakkuk said,
"Sir, I have never seen Babylon, and I know nothing about
the den." 36 Then the angel of the Lord took him by the
crown of his head and carried him by his hair; with the
speed of the wind[a] he set him down in Babylon, right over
the den.
37 Then Habakkuk shouted, "Daniel, Daniel! Take the
food that God has sent you." 38 Daniel said, "You have
remembered me, O God, and have not forsaken those who

a Or *by the power of his spirit*

NEW AMERICAN BIBLE

turned against the king. "The king has become a Jew," they
said; "he has destroyed Bel, killed the dragon, and put the
priests to death." 29 They went to the king and demanded:
"Hand Daniel over to us, or we will kill you and your family." 30 When he saw himself threatened with violence, the
king was forced to hand Daniel over to them. 31 They threw
Daniel into a lions' den, where he remained six days. 32 In
the den were seven lions, and two carcasses and two sheep
had been given to them daily. But now they were given nothing, so that they would devour Daniel.
33 In Judea there was a prophet, Habakkuk; he mixed some
bread in a bowl with the stew he had boiled, and was going
to bring it to the reapers in the field, 34 when an angel of the
Lord told him, "Take the lunch you have to Daniel in the
lions' den at Babylon." 35 But Habakkuk answered,
"Babylon, sir, I have never seen, and I do not know the den!"
36 The angel of the Lord seized him by the crown of his head
and carried him by the hair; with the speed of the wind, he
set him down in Babylon above the den. 37 "Daniel, Daniel,"
cried Habakkuk, "take the lunch God has sent you." 38 "You
have remembered me, O God," said Daniel; "you have not
forsaken those who love you." 39 While Daniel began to eat,

NEW JERUSALEM BIBLE

rose against the king. 'The king has turned Jew,' they said,
'he has allowed Bel to be overthrown, and the dragon to be
killed, and he has put the priests to death.' 29 So they went
to the king and said, 'Hand Daniel over to us or else we shall
kill you and your family.' 30 They pressed him so hard that
the king found himself forced to hand Daniel over to them.
31 They threw Daniel into the lion pit, and there he stayed
for six days. 32 In the pit were seven lions, which were given
two human bodies and two sheep every day; but for this
period they were not given anything, to make sure they
would eat Daniel.
33 Now, the prophet Habakkuk was in Judaea: he had been
making a stew and breaking up bread into a basket. He was
on his way to the fields, taking this to the harvesters,
34 when the angel of the Lord spoke to him, 'Take the meal
you are carrying to Babylon, and give it to Daniel in the lion
pit.' 35 'Lord,' replied Habakkuk, 'I have not even seen
Babylon and know nothing about this pit.' 36 The angel of
the Lord took hold of his head and carried him off by the hair
to Babylon where, with a great blast of his breath, he set
Habakkuk down on the edge of the pit. 37 'Daniel, Daniel,'
Habakkuk shouted, 'take the meal that God has sent you.'
38 And Daniel said, 'You have kept me in mind, O God; you
have not deserted those who love you.' 39 Rising to his feet,

GREEK OLD TESTAMENT

σε. 39 καὶ ἀναστὰς Δανιηλ ἔφαγεν· ὁ δὲ ἄγγελος τοῦ θεοῦ ἀπεκατέστησεν τὸν Αμβακουμ παραχρῆμα εἰς τὸν τόπον αὐτοῦ. 40 ὁ δὲ βασιλεὺς ἦλθεν τῇ ἡμέρᾳ τῇ ἑβδόμῃ πενθῆσαι τὸν Δανιηλ· καὶ ἦλθεν ἐπὶ τὸν λάκκον καὶ ἐνέβλεψεν, καὶ ἰδοὺ Δανιηλ καθήμενος. 41 καὶ ἀναβοήσας φωνῇ μεγάλῃ εἶπεν Μέγας εἶ, κύριε ὁ θεὸς τοῦ Δανιηλ, καὶ οὐκ ἔστιν πλὴν σοῦ ἄλλος. 42 καὶ ἀνέσπασεν αὐτόν, τοὺς δὲ αἰτίους τῆς ἀπωλείας αὐτοῦ ἐνέβαλεν εἰς τὸν λάκκον, καὶ κατεβρώθησαν παραχρῆμα ἐνώπιον αὐτοῦ.

KING JAMES VERSION

39 So Daniel arose, and did eat: and the angel of the Lord set Habbacuc in his own place again immediately.

40 Upon the seventh day the king went to bewail Daniel: and when he came to the den, he looked in, and, behold, Daniel was sitting.

41 Then cried the king with a loud voice, saying, Great art thou, O Lord God of Daniel, and there is none other beside thee.

42 And he drew him out, and cast those that were the cause of his destruction into the den: and they were devoured in a moment before his face.

DOUAY OLD TESTAMENT

38 And Daniel arose and ate. And the angel of the Lord presently set Habacuc again in his own place.

39 And upon the seventh day the king came to bewail Daniel: and he came to the den, and looked in, and behold Daniel was sitting in the midst of the lions.

40 And the king cried out with a loud voice, saying: Great art thou, O Lord the God of Daniel. And he drew him out of the lions' den.

41 But those that had been the cause of his destruction, he cast into the den, and they were devoured in a moment before him.

42 Then the king said: Let all the inhabitants of the whole earth fear the God of Daniel: for he is the Saviour, working signs, and wonders in the earth: who hath delivered Daniel out of the lions' den.

KNOX TRANSLATION

he rose and ate, while the angel of the Lord brought Habacuc, all at once, back to his home.
39 When the seventh day came, the king went out to mourn for Daniel; and now, reaching the pit and looking in, he saw
Daniel seated there among the lions. 40 And at that, the king
cried aloud, How great thou art, O Lord, thou who art
Daniel's God! And he took him out of the lion-pit, 41 and
shut up there instead the men who had conspired to ruin him; and in a moment, as he watched, the lions devoured
them. 42 Whereupon the king said, Well may the whole
world stand in awe of Daniel's God. What deliverance he effects, what signal proofs of his power, here on earth, the God who has rescued Daniel out of a den of lions!

Today's English Version

[39]Then he got up and ate the meal, and God's angel immediately took Habakkuk home.

[40]Seven days after Daniel had been thrown to the lions, the king went to the pit to mourn for him. When he got there and looked in, there sat Daniel. [41]The king shouted, "O Lord, the God of Daniel, how great you are. You alone are God." [42]So he pulled Daniel out of the pit and had those who had tried to kill Daniel thrown into it. And the lions ate them immediately, while the king watched.

New Revised Standard Version

love you." [39]So Daniel got up and ate. And the angel of God immediately returned Habakkuk to his own place.

40 On the seventh day the king came to mourn for Daniel. When he came to the den he looked in, and there sat Daniel! [41]The king shouted with a loud voice, "You are great, O Lord, the God of Daniel, and there is no other besides you!" [42]Then he pulled Daniel[a] out, and threw into the den those who had attempted his destruction, and they were instantly eaten before his eyes.

a Gk *him*

New American Bible

the angel of the Lord at once brought Habakkuk back to his own place.

[40]On the seventh day the king came to mourn for Daniel. As he came to the den and looked in, there was Daniel, sitting there! [41]The king cried aloud, "You are great, O Lord, the God of Daniel, and there is no other besides you!" [42]Daniel he took out, but those who had tried to destroy him he threw into the den, and they were devoured in a moment before his eyes.

New Jerusalem Bible

he ate the meal, while the angel of God carried Habakkuk back in a moment to his own country.

[40]On the seventh day, the king came to lament over Daniel; on reaching the pit he looked inside, and there sat Daniel. [41]'You are great, O Lord, God of Daniel,' he exclaimed, 'there is no god but you!' [42]He then had Daniel released from the pit and the plotters of Daniel's ruin thrown in instead, where they were instantly eaten before his eyes.

GREEK OLD TESTAMENT

ΜΑΚΚΑΒΑΙΩΝ Α΄

1 Καὶ ἐγένετο μετὰ τὸ πατάξαι Ἀλέξανδρον τὸν Φιλίπ-
που Μακεδόνα, ὃς ἐξῆλθεν ἐκ γῆς Χεττιιμ, καὶ ἐπάταξεν τὸν Δαρεῖον βασιλέα Περσῶν καὶ Μήδων καὶ ἐβασίλευσεν ἀντ᾽ αὐτοῦ, πρότερον ἐπὶ τὴν Ἑλλάδα. 2 καὶ
συνεστήσατο πολέμους πολλοὺς καὶ ἐκράτησεν ὀχυρωμάτων
καὶ ἔσφαξεν βασιλεῖς τῆς γῆς. 3 καὶ διῆλθεν ἕως ἄκρων τῆς
γῆς καὶ ἔλαβεν σκῦλα πλήθους ἐθνῶν. καὶ ἡσύχασεν ἡ γῆ
ἐνώπιον αὐτοῦ, καὶ ὑψώθη, καὶ ἐπήρθη ἡ καρδία αὐτοῦ. 4 καὶ
συνῆξεν δύναμιν ἰσχυρὰν σφόδρα καὶ ἦρξεν χωρῶν ἐθνῶν καὶ
τυράννων, καὶ ἐγένοντο αὐτῷ εἰς φόρον. 5 καὶ μετὰ ταῦτα
ἔπεσεν ἐπὶ τὴν κοίτην καὶ ἔγνω ὅτι ἀποθνῄσκει. 6 καὶ ἐκάλεσεν τοὺς παῖδας αὐτοῦ τοὺς ἐνδόξους τοὺς συνεκτρόφους
αὐτοῦ ἐκ νεότητος καὶ διεῖλεν αὐτοῖς τὴν βασιλείαν αὐτοῦ
ἔτι αὐτοῦ ζῶντος. 7 καὶ ἐβασίλευσεν Ἀλέξανδρος ἔτη δώδεκα καὶ ἀπέθανεν. 8 καὶ ἐπεκράτησαν οἱ παῖδες αὐτοῦ,
ἕκαστος ἐν τῷ τόπῳ αὐτοῦ. 9 καὶ ἐπέθεντο πάντες διαδή-
ματα μετὰ τὸ ἀποθανεῖν αὐτὸν καὶ οἱ υἱοὶ αὐτῶν ὀπίσω
αὐτῶν ἔτη πολλὰ καὶ ἐπλήθυναν κακὰ ἐν τῇ γῇ. 10 καὶ ἐξῆλθεν ἐξ αὐτῶν ῥίζα ἁμαρτωλὸς Ἀντίοχος Ἐπιφανὴς υἱὸς
Ἀντιόχου τοῦ βασιλέως, ὃς ἦν ὅμηρα ἐν Ῥώμῃ· καὶ ἐβασίλευσεν ἐν ἔτει ἑκατοστῷ καὶ τριακοστῷ καὶ ἑβδόμῳ βασιλείας Ἑλλήνων.

KING JAMES VERSION

THE FIRST BOOK OF THE MACCABEES

1 And it happened, after that Alexander *son* of Philip, the Macedonian, who came out of the land of Chettiim, had smitten Darius king of the Persians and Medes, that he reigned in his stead, the first over Greece,

2 And made many wars, and won many strong holds, and slew the kings of the earth,

3 And went through to the ends of the earth, and took spoils of many nations, insomuch that the earth was quiet before him; whereupon he was exalted, and his heart was lifted up.

4 And he gathered a mighty strong host, and ruled over countries, and nations, and kings, who became tributaries unto him.

5 And after these things he fell sick, and perceived that he should die.

6 Wherefore he called his servants, such as were honourable, and had been brought up with him from his youth, and parted his kingdom among them, while he was yet alive.

7 So Alexander reigned twelves years, and *then* died.

8 And his servants bare rule every one in his place.

9 And after his death they all put crowns *upon themselves;* so did their sons after them many years: and evils were multiplied in the earth.

10 And there came out of them a wicked root, Antiochus *surnamed* Epiphanes, son of Antiochus the king, who had been an hostage at Rome, and he reigned in the hundred and thirty and seventh year of the kingdom of the Greeks.

DOUAY OLD TESTAMENT

THE FIRST BOOK OF MACHABEES

1 NOW it came to pass, after that Alexander the *son of* Philip the Macedonian, who first reigned in Greece, coming out of the land of Cethim, had overthrown Darius king of the Persians and Medes:

2 He fought many battles, and took the strong holds of all, and slew the kings of the earth:

3 And he went through even to the ends of the earth, and took the spoils of many nations: and the earth was quiet before him.

4 And he gathered a power, and a very strong army: and his heart was exalted and lifted up.

5 And he subdued countries of nations, and princes: and they became tributaries to him.

6 And after these things, he fell down upon his bed, and knew that he should die.

7 And he called his servants the nobles that were brought up with him from his youth: and he divided his kingdom among them, while he was yet alive.

8 And Alexander reigned twelve years, and he died.

9 And his servants made themselves kings every one in his place:

10 And they all put crowns upon themselves after his death, and their sons after them many years, and evils were multiplied in the earth.

11 And there came out of them a wicked root, Antiochus the Illustrious, the son of king Antiochus, who had been a hostage at Rome: and he reigned in the hundred and thirty-seventh year of the kingdom of the Greeks.

KNOX TRANSLATION

THE FIRST BOOK OF MACHABEES

1 Now turn we to Alexander son of Philip, the Macedonian, that was the first to reign over all Greece. This
Alexander marched out from his own land of Cethim, and
overcame Darius, king of the Medes and Persians. 2 Battles
he waged a many; nor any fortress might hold out against
him, nor any king escape with his life; 3 and so he journeyed
on to the world's end, spoiling the nations everywhere; at his
coming, silence fell on the earth. 4 So great the power of
him, so valiant his armies, what wonder if his heart grew
proud? 5 All those lands conquered, all those kings his tributaries! 6 Then, all at once, he took to his bed, and the knowledge came to him he must die. 7 Whereupon he summoned
the noblest of his courtiers, men that had shared his own
upbringing, and to these, while he had life in him yet, divided up his kingdom. 8 So reigned Alexander for twelve years,
and so died.

9 And what of these courtiers turned princes, each with a
province of his own? 10 Be sure they put on royal crowns,
they and their sons after them, and so the world went from
bad to worse. 11 Burgeoned then from the stock of Antiochus
a poisoned growth, another Antiochus, he that was called
the Illustrious. He had been formerly a hostage at Rome, but
now, in the hundred and thirty-seventh year of the Grecian
empire, he came into his kingdom. 12 In his day there were

TODAY'S ENGLISH VERSION

THE FIRST BOOK OF THE MACCABEES

1 This history begins when Alexander the Great, son of
Philip of Macedonia, marched from Macedonia and
attacked Darius, king of Persia and Media. Alexander
enlarged the Greek Empire by defeating Darius and seizing
his throne. 2 He fought many battles, captured fortified cities, and put the kings of the region to death. 3 As he
advanced to the ends of the earth, he plundered many
nations; and when he had conquered the world, he became
proud and arrogant. 4 By building up a strong army, he dominated whole nations and their rulers, and forced everyone to
pay him taxes.

5-7 When Alexander had been emperor for twelve years, he
fell ill and realized that he was about to die. He called
together his generals, noblemen who had been brought up
with him since his early childhood, and he divided his
empire, giving a part to each of them. 8 After his death, the
generals took control, 9 and each had himself crowned king
of his own territory. The descendants of these kings ruled for
many generations and brought a great deal of misery on the
world.

10 The wicked ruler Antiochus Epiphanes, son of King
Antiochus the Third of Syria, was a descendant of one of
Alexander's generals. Antiochus Epiphanes had been a
hostage in Rome before he became king of Syria in the
year 137.[a]

[a] THE YEAR 137: *The dates in this book are counted from the beginning of the Syrian Kingdom in 312 B.C. The year 137 corresponds to 175 B.C.*

NEW REVISED STANDARD VERSION

1 MACCABEES

1 After Alexander son of Philip, the Macedonian, who
came from the land of Kittim, had defeated[a] King Darius
of the Persians and the Medes, he succeeded him as king.
(He had previously become king of Greece.) 2 He fought
many battles, conquered strongholds, and put to death the
kings of the earth. 3 He advanced to the ends of the earth,
and plundered many nations. When the earth became quiet
before him, he was exalted, and his heart was lifted up. 4 He
gathered a very strong army and ruled over countries,
nations, and princes, and they became tributary to him.

5 After this he fell sick and perceived that he was dying.
6 So he summoned his most honored officers, who had been
brought up with him from youth, and divided his kingdom
among them while he was still alive. 7 And after Alexander
had reigned twelve years, he died.

8 Then his officers began to rule, each in his own place.
9 They all put on crowns after his death, and so did their
descendants after them for many years; and they caused
many evils on the earth.

10 From them came forth a sinful root, Antiochus Epiphanes, son of King Antiochus; he had been a hostage in Rome.
He began to reign in the one hundred thirty-seventh year of
the kingdom of the Greeks.[b]

a Gk adds *and he defeated* *b* 175 B.C.

NEW AMERICAN BIBLE

THE FIRST BOOK OF THE MACCABEES

1 After Alexander the Macedonian, Philip's son, who came
from the land of Kittim, had defeated Darius, king of the
Persians and Medes, he became king in his place, having
first ruled in Greece. 2 He fought many campaigns, captured
fortresses, and put kings to death. 3 He advanced to the ends
of the earth, gathering plunder from many nations; the earth
fell silent before him, and his heart became proud and arrogant. 4 He collected a very strong army and conquered
provinces, nations, and rulers, and they became his tributaries. 5 But after all this he took to his bed, realizing that he
was going to die. 6 He therefore summoned his officers, the
nobles, who had been brought up with him from his youth,
to divide his kingdom among them while he was still alive.
7 Alexander had reigned twelve years when he died.

8 So his officers took over his kingdom, each in his own
territory, 9 and after his death they all put on royal crowns,
and so did their sons after them for many years, causing
much distress over the earth.

10 There sprang from these a sinful offshoot, Antiochus
Epiphanes, son of King Antiochus, once a hostage at Rome.
He became king in the year one hundred and thirty-seven of
the kingdom of the Greeks.

NEW JERUSALEM BIBLE

THE FIRST BOOK OF MACCABEES

1 Alexander of Macedon son of Philip had come from the
land of Kittim[a] and defeated Darius king of the Persians
and Medes, whom he succeeded as ruler, at first of Hellas.
2 He undertook many campaigns, gained possession of many
fortresses, and put the local kings to death. 3 So he advanced
to the ends of the earth, plundering nation after nation; the
earth grew silent before him, and his ambitious heart swelled
with pride. 4 He assembled very powerful forces and subdued
provinces, nations and princes, and they became his tributaries. 5 But the time came when Alexander took to his bed,
in the knowledge that he was dying. 6 He summoned his
officers, noblemen who had been brought up with him from
his youth, and divided his kingdom among them while he
was still alive. 7 Alexander had reigned twelve years when
he died. 8 Each of his officers established himself in his own
region. 9 All assumed crowns after his death, they and their
heirs after them for many years, bringing increasing evils on
the world.

10 From these there grew a wicked offshoot, Antiochus
Epiphanes son of King Antiochus; once a hostage in Rome,
he became king in the 107th year[b] of the kingdom of the

[a] 1 Term extended from inhabitants of Kition to all Cypriots and then to all Greeks. [b] 1 Dates in the text of 1—2 M are of the era starting with the foundation of Antioch in 312 BC.

GREEK OLD TESTAMENT

11 Ἐν ταῖς ἡμέραις ἐκείναις ἐξῆλθον ἐξ Ισραηλ υἱοὶ παράνομοι καὶ ἀνέπεισαν πολλοὺς λέγοντες Πορευθῶμεν καὶ
διαθώμεθα διαθήκην μετὰ τῶν ἐθνῶν τῶν κύκλῳ ἡμῶν, ὅτι
ἀφ᾽ ἧς ἐχωρίσθημεν ἀπ᾽ αὐτῶν, εὗρεν ἡμᾶς κακὰ πολλά.
12 καὶ ἠγαθύνθη ὁ λόγος ἐν ὀφθαλμοῖς αὐτῶν, 13 καὶ προεθυ-
μήθησάν τινες ἀπὸ τοῦ λαοῦ καὶ ἐπορεύθησαν πρὸς τὸν
βασιλέα, καὶ ἔδωκεν αὐτοῖς ἐξουσίαν ποιῆσαι τὰ δικαιώματα
τῶν ἐθνῶν. 14 καὶ ᾠκοδόμησαν γυμνάσιον ἐν Ιεροσολύμοις
κατὰ τὰ νόμιμα τῶν ἐθνῶν 15 καὶ ἐποίησαν ἑαυτοῖς ἀκροβυστίας καὶ ἀπέστησαν ἀπὸ διαθήκης ἁγίας καὶ ἐζευγίσθησαν
τοῖς ἔθνεσιν καὶ ἐπράθησαν τοῦ ποιῆσαι τὸ πονηρόν.

16 Καὶ ἡτοιμάσθη ἡ βασιλεία ἐνώπιον Ἀντιόχου, καὶ ὑπέ-
λαβεν βασιλεῦσαι γῆς Αἰγύπτου, ὅπως βασιλεύσῃ ἐπὶ τὰς
δύο βασιλείας. 17 καὶ εἰσῆλθεν εἰς Αἴγυπτον ἐν ὄχλῳ βαρεῖ,
ἐν ἅρμασιν καὶ ἐλέφασιν καὶ ἐν ἱππεῦσιν καὶ ἐν στόλῳ
μεγάλῳ 18 καὶ συνεστήσατο πόλεμον πρὸς Πτολεμαῖον
βασιλέα Αἰγύπτου· καὶ ἐνετράπη Πτολεμαῖος ἀπὸ προσώπου
αὐτοῦ καὶ ἔφυγεν, καὶ ἔπεσον τραυματίαι πολλοί. 19 καὶ
κατελάβοντο τὰς πόλεις τὰς ὀχυρὰς ἐν γῇ Αἰγύπτῳ, καὶ
ἔλαβεν τὰ σκῦλα γῆς Αἰγύπτου. 20 καὶ ἐπέστρεψεν Ἀντίοχος μετὰ τὸ πατάξαι Αἴγυπτον ἐν τῷ ἑκατοστῷ καὶ τεσσαρακοστῷ καὶ τρίτῳ ἔτει καὶ ἀνέβη ἐπὶ Ισραηλ καὶ ἀνέβη εἰς
Ιεροσόλυμα ἐν ὄχλῳ βαρεῖ. 21 καὶ εἰσῆλθεν εἰς τὸ ἁγίασμα
ἐν ὑπερηφανίᾳ καὶ ἔλαβεν τὸ θυσιαστήριον τὸ χρυσοῦν καὶ
τὴν λυχνίαν τοῦ φωτὸς καὶ πάντα τὰ σκεύη αὐτῆς 22 καὶ

KING JAMES VERSION

11 In those days went there out of Israel wicked men, who persuaded many, saying, Let us go and make a covenant with the heathen that are round about us: for since we departed from them we have had much sorrow.

12 So this device pleased them well.

13 Then certain of the people were so forward herein, that they went to the king, who gave them licence to do after the ordinances of the heathen:

14 Whereupon they built a place of exercise at Jerusalem according to the customs of the heathen:

15 And made themselves uncircumcised, and forsook the holy covenant, and joined themselves to the heathen, and were sold to do mischief.

16 Now when the kingdom was established before Antiochus, he thought to reign over Egypt, that he might have the dominion of two realms.

17 Wherefore he entered into Egypt with a great multitude, with chariots, and elephants, and horsemen, and a great navy,

18 And made war against Ptolemee king of Egypt: but Ptolemee was afraid of him, and fled; and many were wounded to death.

19 Thus they got the strong cities in the land of Egypt, and he took the spoils thereof.

20 And after that Antiochus had smitten Egypt, he returned again in the hundred forty and third year, and went up against Israel and Jerusalem with a great multitude,

21 And entered proudly into the sanctuary, and took away the golden altar, and the candlestick of light, and all the vessels thereof,

DOUAY OLD TESTAMENT

12 In those days there went out of Israel wicked men, and they persuaded many, saying: Let us go, and make a covenant with the heathens that are round about us: for since we departed from them, many evils have befallen us.

13 And the word seemed good in their eyes.

14 And some of the people determined to do this, and went to the king: and he gave them license to do after the ordinances of the heathens.

15 And they built a place of exercise in Jerusalem, according to the laws of the nations:

16 And they made themselves prepuces, and departed from the holy covenant, and joined themselves to the heathens, and were sold to do evil.

17 And the kingdom was established before Antiochus, and he had a mind to reign over the land of Egypt, that he might reign over two kingdoms.

18 And he entered into Egypt with a great multitude, with chariots and elephants, and horsemen, and a great number of ships:

19 And he made war against Ptolemee king of Egypt, but Ptolemee was afraid at his presence, and fled, and many were wounded unto death.

20 And he took the strong cities in the land of Egypt: and he took the spoils of the land of Egypt.

21 And after Antiochus had ravaged Egypt in the hundred and forty-third year, he returned and went up against Israel.

22 And he went up to Jerusalem with a great multitude.

23 And he proudly entered into the sanctuary, and took away the golden altar, and the candlestick of light, and all

KNOX TRANSLATION

godless talkers abroad in Israel, that did not want for a hearing; Come, said they, let us make terms with the heathen
that dwell about us! Ever since we forswore their company,
nought but trouble has come our way. 13 What would you?
14 Such talk gained credit, and some were at pains to ask for
the royal warrant; whereupon leave was given them, Gentile
usages they should follow if they would. 15 With that, they
must have a game-place at Jerusalem, after the Gentile fashion, 16 ay, and go uncircumcised; forgotten, their loyalty to
the holy covenant, they must throw in their lot with the heathen, and become the slaves of impiety.
17 And now that he was firmly established on his throne,
Antiochus would be lord of Egypt, and wear two crowns at
once. 18 So, with overwhelming force, with chariots and elephants and horsemen and a great array of ships, he marched
on Egypt, 19 and levied war against king Ptolemy, that could
not hold his ground, but fled away, leaving many fallen.
20 So Antiochus made himself master of all the strongholds
in Egypt, and ransacked it for spoil; 21 then, in the hundred
and forty-third year, he turned his victorious march against
Israel. 22 With all that great army of his he came to
Jerusalem 23 and entered the sanctuary in royal state; the
golden altar, the lamp-stand with its appurtenances, the

TODAY'S ENGLISH VERSION

11 At that time there appeared in the land of Israel a group
of traitorous Jews who had no regard for the Law and who
had a bad influence on many of our people. They said, "Let's
come to terms with the Gentiles, for our refusal to associate
with them has brought us nothing but trouble." 12 This proposal appealed to many people, 13 and some of them became
so enthusiastic about it that they went to the king and
received from him permission to follow Gentile customs.
14 They built in Jerusalem a stadium like those in the Greek
cities. 15 They had surgery performed to hide their circumcision, abandoned the holy covenant, started associating
with[a] Gentiles, and did all sorts of other evil things.

16 When Antiochus had firmly established himself as king,
he decided to conquer Egypt and rule that country as well as
Syria. 17 He invaded Egypt with a large fleet of ships and a
powerful army, including chariots, elephants, and cavalry.
18 When the attack came, King Ptolemy of Egypt turned and
fled, and many of his soldiers were killed. 19 Antiochus was
able to capture the fortified cities of Egypt and plunder the
whole land.

20 In the year 143,[b] after the conquest of Egypt, Antiochus
marched with a great army against the land of Israel and the
city of Jerusalem. 21 In his arrogance, he entered the Temple
and took away the gold altar, the lampstand with all its

[a] started associating with; *or* married. [b] THE YEAR 143: *This corresponds to 169 B.C.*

NEW REVISED STANDARD VERSION

11 In those days certain renegades came out from Israel
and misled many, saying, "Let us go and make a covenant
with the Gentiles around us, for since we separated from
them many disasters have come upon us." 12 This proposal
pleased them, 13 and some of the people eagerly went to the
king, who authorized them to observe the ordinances of the
Gentiles. 14 So they built a gymnasium in Jerusalem, according to Gentile custom, 15 and removed the marks of circumcision, and abandoned the holy covenant. They joined with the
Gentiles and sold themselves to do evil.

16 When Antiochus saw that his kingdom was established, he determined to become king of the land of Egypt, in
order that he might reign over both kingdoms. 17 So he
invaded Egypt with a strong force, with chariots and elephants and cavalry and with a large fleet. 18 He engaged
King Ptolemy of Egypt in battle, and Ptolemy turned and fled
before him, and many were wounded and fell. 19 They captured the fortified cities in the land of Egypt, and he plundered the land of Egypt.

20 After subduing Egypt, Antiochus returned in the one
hundred forty-third year.[a] He went up against Israel and
came to Jerusalem with a strong force. 21 He arrogantly
entered the sanctuary and took the golden altar, the lamp-
stand for the light, and all its utensils. 22 He took also the

[a] 169 B.C.

NEW AMERICAN BIBLE

11 In those days there appeared in Israel men who were
breakers of the law, and they seduced many people, saying:
"Let us go and make an alliance with the Gentiles all around
us; since we separated from them, many evils have come
upon us." 12 The proposal was agreeable; 13 some from
among the people promptly went to the king, and he authorized them to introduce the way of living of the Gentiles.
14 Thereupon they built a gymnasium in Jerusalem according
to the Gentile custom. 15 They covered over the mark of their
circumcision and abandoned the holy covenant; they allied
themselves with the Gentiles and sold themselves to wrong-
doing.

16 When his kingdom seemed secure, Antiochus proposed
to become king of Egypt, so as to rule over both kingdoms.
17 He invaded Egypt with a strong force, with chariots and
elephants, and with a large fleet, 18 to make war on Ptolemy,
king of Egypt. Ptolemy was frightened at his presence and
fled, leaving many casualties. 19 The fortified cities in the
land of Egypt were captured, and Antiochus plundered the
land of Egypt.

20 After Antiochus had defeated Egypt in the year one hundred and forty-three, he returned and went up to Israel and
to Jerusalem with a strong force. 21 He insolently invaded the
sanctuary and took away the golden altar, the lampstand for
the light with all its fixtures, 22 the offering table, the cups

NEW JERUSALEM BIBLE

Greeks. 11 It was then that there emerged from Israel a set of
renegades who led many people astray. 'Come,' they said,
'let us ally ourselves with the gentiles surrounding us, for
since we separated ourselves from them many misfortunes
have overtaken us.' 12 This proposal proved acceptable,
13 and a number of the people eagerly approached the king,
who authorised them to practise the gentiles' observances.
14 So they built a gymnasium in Jerusalem, such as the gentiles have, 15 disguised their circumcision, and abandoned
the holy covenant, submitting to gentile rule as willing
slaves of impiety.

16 Once Antiochus had seen his authority established, he
determined to make himself king of Egypt and the ruler of
both kingdoms. 17 He invaded Egypt in massive strength,
with chariots and elephants (and cavalry) and a large fleet.
18 He engaged Ptolemy king of Egypt in battle, and Ptolemy
turned back and fled before his advance, leaving many casualties. 19 The fortified cities of Egypt were captured, and
Antiochus plundered the country. 20 After his conquest of
Egypt, in the year 143, Antiochus turned about and
advanced on Israel and Jerusalem in massive strength.[a]
21 Insolently breaking into the sanctuary, he removed the
golden altar and the lamp-stand for the light with all its

[a] 1 // 2 M 5:11–16.

GREEK OLD TESTAMENT

τὴν τράπεζαν τῆς προθέσεως καὶ τὰ σπονδεῖα καὶ τὰς φιά-
λας καὶ τὰς θυΐσκας τὰς χρυσᾶς καὶ τὸ καταπέτασμα καὶ
τοὺς στεφάνους καὶ τὸν κόσμον τὸν χρυσοῦν τὸν κατὰ πρόσωπον τοῦ ναοῦ καὶ ἐλέπισεν πάντα· 23 καὶ ἔλαβεν τὸ ἀργύριον καὶ τὸ χρυσίον καὶ τὰ σκεύη τὰ ἐπιθυμητὰ καὶ ἔλαβεν
τοὺς θησαυροὺς τοὺς ἀποκρύφους, οὓς εὗρεν· 24 καὶ λαβὼν
πάντα ἀπῆλθεν εἰς τὴν γῆν αὐτοῦ. καὶ ἐποίησεν φονο-
κτονίαν καὶ ἐλάλησεν ὑπερηφανίαν μεγάλην. 25 καὶ ἐγένετο
πένθος μέγα ἐπὶ Ισραηλ ἐν παντὶ τόπῳ αὐτῶν. 26 καὶ ἐστέν-
αξαν ἄρχοντες καὶ πρεσβύτεροι, παρθένοι καὶ νεανίσκοι
ἠσθένησαν, καὶ τὸ κάλλος τῶν γυναικῶν ἠλλοιώθη. 27 πᾶς
νυμφίος ἀνέλαβεν θρῆνον, καὶ καθημένη ἐν παστῷ ἐπένθει.
28 καὶ ἐσείσθη ἡ γῆ ἐπὶ τοὺς κατοικοῦντας αὐτήν, καὶ πᾶς ὁ
οἶκος Ιακωβ ἐνεδύσατο αἰσχύνην.

29 Μετὰ δύο ἔτη ἡμερῶν ἀπέστειλεν ὁ βασιλεὺς ἄρχοντα
φορολογίας εἰς τὰς πόλεις Ιουδα, καὶ ἦλθεν εἰς Ιερουσαλημ
ἐν ὄχλῳ βαρεῖ. 30 καὶ ἐλάλησεν αὐτοῖς λόγους εἰρηνικοὺς ἐν
δόλῳ, καὶ ἐνεπίστευσαν αὐτῷ. καὶ ἐπέπεσεν ἐπὶ τὴν πόλιν
ἐξάπινα καὶ ἐπάταξεν αὐτὴν πληγὴν μεγάλην καὶ ἀπώλεσεν
λαὸν πολὺν ἐξ Ισραηλ. 31 καὶ ἔλαβεν τὰ σκῦλα τῆς πόλεως
καὶ ἐνέπρησεν αὐτὴν πυρὶ καὶ καθεῖλεν τοὺς οἴκους αὐτῆς

KING JAMES VERSION

22 And the table of the shewbread, and the pouring vessels, and the vials, and the censers of gold, and the veil, and the crowns, and the golden ornaments that were before the temple, all which he pulled off.

23 He took also the silver and the gold, and the precious vessels: also he took the hidden treasures which he found.

24 And when he had taken all away, he went into his own land, having made a great massacre, and spoken very proudly.

25 Therefore there was a great mourning in Israel, in every place where they were;

26 So that the princes and elders mourned, the virgins and young men were made feeble, and the beauty of women was changed.

27 Every bridegroom took up lamentation, and she that sat in the marriage chamber was in heaviness.

28 The land also was moved for the inhabitants thereof, and all the house of Jacob was covered with confusion.

29 And after two years fully expired the king sent his chief collector of tribute unto the cities of Juda, who came unto Jerusalem with a great multitude,

30 And spake peaceable words unto them, but *all was* deceit: for when they had given him credence, he fell suddenly upon the city, and smote it very sore, and destroyed much people of Israel.

31 And when he had taken the spoils of the city, he set it on fire, and pulled down the houses and walls thereof on every side.

DOUAY OLD TESTAMENT

the vessels thereof, and the table of proposition, and the pouring vessels, and the vials, and the little mortars of gold, and the veil, and the crowns, and the golden ornament that was before the temple: and he broke them all in pieces.

24 And he took the silver and gold, and the precious vessels: and he took the hidden treasures which he found: and when he had taken all away he departed into his own country.

25 And he made a great slaughter of men, and spoke very proudly.

26 And there was great mourning in Israel, and in every place where they were:

27 And the princes, and the ancients mourned, and the virgins and the young men were made feeble, and the beauty of the women was changed.

28 Every bridegroom took up lamentation: and the bride that sat in the marriage bed, mourned:

29 And the land was moved for the inhabitants thereof, and all the house of Jacob was covered with confusion.

30 And after two full years the king sent the chief collector of *his* tributes to the cities of Juda, and he came to Jerusalem with a great multitude.

31 And he spoke to them peaceable words in deceit: and they believed him.

32 And he fell upon the city suddenly, and struck it with a great slaughter, and destroyed much people in Israel.

33 And he took the spoils of the city, and burnt it with fire, and threw down the houses thereof, and the walls thereof round about:

KNOX TRANSLATION

table where bread was set out, beaker and goblet and golden
bowl, curtain and capital and golden facings of the temple,
all alike were stripped. 24 Silver nor gold was spared, nor
any ornament of price, nor hoarded treasures could he but
find them; and thus laden he went back to his own country,
25 first shedding a deal of blood, and speaking very blasphemously.

26 Loud mourning there was in Israel, mourning in all the
country-side; 27 wept ruler and elder, pined man and maid,
and colour fled from woman's cheeks; 28 bridegroom took up
the dirge, bride sat in her bower disconsolate; 29 here was a
land that trembled for its inhabitants, a whole race covered
with confusion.

30 Two years passed, and then the king sent his chief collector of revenue to visit the cities of Juda. To Jerusalem he
came, with a great rabble at his heels, 31 and won credence
with idle professions of friendship. 32 Then he fell suddenly
on the town and grievously mishandled it, slaying Israelites
a many, 33 plundering the city and setting fire to it. Houses
and encircling walls of it were thrown down in ruins,

TODAY'S ENGLISH VERSION

equipment, 22 the table for the bread offered to the Lord, the
cups and bowls, the gold fire pans, the curtain, and the
crowns. He also stripped all the gold from the front of the
Temple 23 and carried off the silver and gold and everything
else of value, including all the treasures that he could find
stored there. 24 Then he took it all to his own country. He
had also murdered many people and boasted arrogantly
about it. 25 There was great mourning everywhere in the
land of Israel.

26 Rulers and leaders groaned in sorrow.
Young men and young women grew weak.
The beauty of our women faded.
27 Every bridegroom sang a funeral song,
and every bride sat mourning in her room.
28 All our people were clothed with shame,
and our land trembled for them.

29 Two years later Antiochus sent a large army from
Mysia[a] against the towns of Judea. When the soldiers
entered Jerusalem, 30 their commander spoke to the people,
offering them terms of peace and completely deceiving them.
Then he suddenly launched a fierce attack on the city, dealing it a major blow and killing many of the people. 31 He
plundered the city, set it on fire, and tore down its buildings

[a] *Probable text* a large army from Mysia; *Greek* a tax collector with a large army.

NEW REVISED STANDARD VERSION

table for the bread of the Presence, the cups for drink offerings, the bowls, the golden censers, the curtain, the crowns,
and the gold decoration on the front of the temple; he
stripped it all off. 23 He took the silver and the gold, and the
costly vessels; he took also the hidden treasures that he
found. 24 Taking them all, he went into his own land.

He shed much blood,
and spoke with great arrogance.
25 Israel mourned deeply in every community,
26 rulers and elders groaned,
young women and young men became faint,
the beauty of the women faded.
27 Every bridegroom took up the lament;
she who sat in the bridal chamber was mourning.
28 Even the land trembled for its inhabitants,
and all the house of Jacob was clothed with shame.

29 Two years later the king sent to the cities of Judah a
chief collector of tribute, and he came to Jerusalem with a
large force. 30 Deceitfully he spoke peaceable words to them,
and they believed him; but he suddenly fell upon the city,
dealt it a severe blow, and destroyed many people of Israel.
31 He plundered the city, burned it with fire, and tore down
its houses and its surrounding walls. 32 They took captive

NEW AMERICAN BIBLE

and the bowls, the golden censers, the curtain, the crowns,
and the golden ornament on the façade of the temple. He
stripped off everything, 23 and took away the gold and silver
and the precious vessels; he also took all the hidden treasures he could find. 24 Taking all this, he went back to his
own country, after he had spoken with great arrogance and
shed much blood.

25 And there was great mourning for Israel, in every place
where they dwelt,
26 and the rulers and the elders groaned.
Virgins and young men languished,
and the beauty of the women was disfigured.
27 Every bridegroom took up lamentation,
she who sat in the bridal chamber mourned,
28 And the land was shaken on account of its inhabitants,
and all the house of Jacob was covered with shame.

29 Two years later, the king sent the Mysian commander to
the cities of Judah, and he came to Jerusalem with a strong
force. 30 He spoke to them deceitfully in peaceful terms, and
won their trust. Then he attacked the city suddenly, in a
great onslaught, and destroyed many of the people in Israel.
31 He plundered the city and set fire to it, demolished its
houses and its surrounding walls, 32 took captive the women

NEW JERUSALEM BIBLE

fittings, 22 together with the table for the loaves of permanent offering, the libation vessels, the cups, the golden
censers, the veil, the crowns, and the golden decoration on
the front of the Temple, which he stripped of everything.
23 He made off with the silver and gold and precious vessels;
he discovered the secret treasures and seized them 24 and,
removing all these, he went back to his own country, having
shed much blood and uttered words of extreme arrogance.

25 There was deep mourning for Israel throughout the
country:

26 Rulers and elders groaned;
girls and young men wasted away;
the women's beauty suffered a change;
27 every bridegroom took up a dirge,
the bride sat grief-stricken on her marriage-bed.
28 The earth quaked because of its inhabitants
and the whole House of Jacob was clothed with shame.

29 Two years later the king sent the Mysarch through the
cities of Judah. He came to Jerusalem with an impressive
force, 30 and addressing them with what appeared to be
peaceful words, he gained their confidence; then suddenly he
fell on the city, dealing it a terrible blow, and destroying
many of the people of Israel. 31 He pillaged the city and set it
on fire, tore down its houses and encircling wall, 32 took the

GREEK OLD TESTAMENT

καὶ τὰ τείχη κύκλῳ. 32 καὶ ᾐχμαλώτισαν τὰς γυναῖκας καὶ
τὰ τέκνα, καὶ τὰ κτήνη ἐκληρονόμησαν. 33 καὶ ᾠκοδόμησαν
τὴν πόλιν Δαυιδ τείχει μεγάλῳ καὶ ὀχυρῷ, πύργοις ὀχυροῖς,
καὶ ἐγένετο αὐτοῖς εἰς ἄκραν. 34 καὶ ἔθηκαν ἐκεῖ ἔθνος
ἁμαρτωλόν, ἄνδρας παρανόμους, καὶ ἐνίσχυσαν ἐν αὐτῇ.
35 καὶ παρέθεντο ὅπλα καὶ τροφὴν καὶ συναγαγόντες τὰ
σκῦλα Ιερουσαλημ ἀπέθεντο ἐκεῖ καὶ ἐγένοντο εἰς μεγάλην
παγίδα. 36 καὶ ἐγένετο εἰς ἔνεδρον τῷ ἁγιάσματι καὶ εἰς
διάβολον πονηρὸν τῷ Ισραηλ διὰ παντός. 37 καὶ ἐξέχεαν
αἷμα ἀθῷον κύκλῳ τοῦ ἁγιάσματος καὶ ἐμόλυναν τὸ ἁγίασμα. 38 καὶ ἔφυγον οἱ κάτοικοι Ιερουσαλημ δι' αὐτούς, καὶ
ἐγένετο κατοικία ἀλλοτρίων· καὶ ἐγένετο ἀλλοτρία τοῖς
γενήμασιν αὐτῆς, καὶ τὰ τέκνα αὐτῆς ἐγκατέλιπον αὐτήν.
39 τὸ ἁγίασμα αὐτῆς ἠρημώθη ὡς ἔρημος, αἱ ἑορταὶ αὐτῆς
ἐστράφησαν εἰς πένθος, τὰ σάββατα αὐτῆς εἰς ὀνειδισμόν,
ἡ τιμὴ αὐτῆς εἰς ἐξουδένωσιν. 40 κατὰ τὴν δόξαν αὐτῆς
ἐπληθύνθη ἡ ἀτιμία αὐτῆς, καὶ τὸ ὕψος αὐτῆς ἐστράφη εἰς
πένθος.
41 Καὶ ἔγραψεν ὁ βασιλεὺς πάσῃ τῇ βασιλείᾳ αὐτοῦ εἶναι
πάντας εἰς λαὸν ἕνα 42 καὶ ἐγκαταλιπεῖν ἕκαστον τὰ νόμιμα
αὐτοῦ. καὶ ἐπεδέξαντο πάντα τὰ ἔθνη κατὰ τὸν λόγον τοῦ
βασιλέως. 43 καὶ πολλοὶ ἀπὸ Ισραηλ εὐδόκησαν τῇ λατρείᾳ
αὐτοῦ καὶ ἔθυσαν τοῖς εἰδώλοις καὶ ἐβεβήλωσαν τὸ σάββατον.

KING JAMES VERSION

32 But the women and children took they captive, and possessed the cattle.

33 Then builded they the city of David with a great and strong wall, *and* with mighty towers, and made it a strong hold for them.

34 And they put therein a sinful nation, wicked men, and fortified *themselves* therein.

35 They stored it also with armour and victuals, and when they had gathered together the spoils of Jerusalem, they laid them up there, and so they became a sore snare:

36 For it was a place to lie in wait against the sanctuary, and an evil adversary to Israel.

37 Thus they shed innocent blood on every side of the sanctuary, and defiled it:

38 Insomuch that the inhabitants of Jerusalem fled because of them: whereupon *the city* was made an habitation of strangers, and became strange to those that were born in her; and her own children left her.

39 Her sanctuary was laid waste like a wilderness, her feasts were turned into mourning, her sabbaths into reproach, her honour into contempt.

40 As had been her glory, so was her dishonour increased, and her excellency was turned into mourning.

41 Moreover king Antiochus wrote to his whole kingdom, that all should be one people,

42 And every one should leave his laws: so all the heathen agreed according to the commandment of the king.

43 Yea, many also of the Israelites consented to his religion, and sacrificed unto idols, and profaned the sabbath.

DOUAY OLD TESTAMENT

34 And they took the women captive, and the children, and the cattle they possessed.

35 And they built the city of David with a great and strong wall, and with strong towers, and made it a fortress for them:

36 And they placed there a sinful nation, wicked men, and they fortified themselves therein: and they stored up armour, and victuals, and gathered together the spoils of Jerusalem;

37 And laid them up there: and they became a great snare.

38 And this was a place to lie in wait against the sanctuary, and an evil devil in Israel.

39 And they shed innocent blood round about the sanctuary, and defiled the holy place.

40 And the inhabitants of Jerusalem fled away by reason of them, and the city was made the habitation of strangers, and she became a stranger to her own seed, and her children forsook her.

41 Her sanctuary was desolate like a wilderness, her festival days were turned into mourning, her sabbaths into reproach, her honours were brought to nothing.

42 Her dishonour was increased according to her glory, and her excellency was turned into mourning.

43 And king Antiochus wrote to all his kingdom, that all the people should be one: and every one should leave his own law.

44 And all nations consented according to the word of king Antiochus.

45 And many of Israel consented to his service, and they sacrificed to idols, and profaned the sabbath.

KNOX TRANSLATION

34 women and children carried off into slavery, cattle driven
away. 35 And as for David's Keep, they enclosed it with high,
strong walls, and strong towers besides, to serve them for a
fortress; 36 garrisoned it with a godless crew of sinners like
themselves, and made it fast, storing it with arms and provisions, besides the plunder they had amassed in Jerusalem,
37 which they bestowed there for safety. Alas, what peril of
treachery was here, 38 what an ambush laid about the holy
place, what devil's work against Israel! 39 What a tide of
guiltless blood must flow about the sanctuary, till it was a
sanctuary no more! 40 Little wonder if the inhabitants of
Jerusalem took to flight, leaving their city to strangers; mother so unnatural her own children must forsake. 41 Her sanctuary a desert solitude, her feasts all lament, her sabbaths
derided, her greatness brought low! 42 Her pride was the
measure of that abasement, her glory of that shame.
43 And now came a letter from king Antiochus to all the subjects of his realm, bidding them leave ancestral custom of this
race or that, and become one nation instead. 44 As for the
heathen, they fell in readily enough with the royal will; 45 and
in Israel itself there were many that chose slavery, offering
sacrifice to false gods and leaving the sabbath unobserved.

TODAY'S ENGLISH VERSION

and walls. 32 He and his army took the women and children
as prisoners and seized the cattle.
33 Then Antiochus and his forces built high walls and
strong towers in the area north of the Temple, turning it into
a fort. 34 They brought in a group of traitorous Jews and
installed them there. 35 They also brought in arms and supplies and stored in the fort all the loot that they had taken in
Jerusalem. This fort became a great threat to the city.

36 The fort was a threat to the Temple,
a constant, evil menace for Israel.
37 Innocent people were murdered around the altar;
the Holy Place was defiled by murderers.
38 The people of Jerusalem fled in fear,
and the city became a colony of foreigners.
Jerusalem was foreign to its own people,
who had been forced to abandon the city.
39 Her Temple was as empty as a wilderness;
her festivals were turned into days of mourning,
her Sabbath joy into shame.
Her honor became an object of ridicule.
40 Her shame was as great as her former glory,
and her pride was turned into deepest mourning.

41-43 Antiochus now issued a decree that all nations in his
empire should abandon their own customs and become one
people. All the Gentiles and even many of the Israelites submitted to this decree. They adopted the official pagan religion,
offered sacrifices to idols, and no longer observed the Sabbath.

NEW REVISED STANDARD VERSION

the women and children, and seized the livestock. 33 Then
they fortified the city of David with a great strong wall and
strong towers, and it became their citadel. 34 They stationed
there a sinful people, men who were renegades. These
strengthened their position; 35 they stored up arms and food,
and collecting the spoils of Jerusalem they stored them there,
and became a great menace,

36 for the citadel[a] became an ambush against the
sanctuary,
an evil adversary of Israel at all times.
37 On every side of the sanctuary they shed innocent blood;
they even defiled the sanctuary.
38 Because of them the residents of Jerusalem fled;
she became a dwelling of strangers;
she became strange to her offspring,
and her children forsook her.
39 Her sanctuary became desolate like a desert;
her feasts were turned into mourning,
her sabbaths into a reproach,
her honor into contempt.
40 Her dishonor now grew as great as her glory;
her exaltation was turned into mourning.

41 Then the king wrote to his whole kingdom that all
should be one people, 42 and that all should give up their
particular customs. 43 All the Gentiles accepted the command
of the king. Many even from Israel gladly adopted his religion; they sacrificed to idols and profaned the sabbath.

a Gk *it*

NEW AMERICAN BIBLE

and children, and seized the cattle. 33 Then they built up the
City of David with a high, massive wall and strong towers,
and it became their citadel. 34 There they installed a sinful
race, perverse men, who fortified themselves inside it,
35 storing up weapons and provisions, and depositing there
the plunder they had collected from Jerusalem. And they
became a great threat.

36 The citadel became an ambush against the sanctuary,
and a wicked adversary to Israel at all times.
37 And they shed innocent blood around the sanctuary;
they defiled the sanctuary.
38 Because of them the inhabitants of Jerusalem fled
away,
and she became the abode of strangers.
She became a stranger to her own offspring,
and her children forsook her.
39 Her sanctuary was as desolate as a wilderness;
her feasts were turned into mourning,
Her sabbaths to shame,
her honor to contempt.
40 Her dishonor was as great as her glory had been,
and her exaltation was turned into mourning.

41 Then the king wrote to his whole kingdom that all
should be one people, 42 each abandoning his particular customs. All the Gentiles conformed to the command of the
king, 43 and many Israelites were in favor of his religion;
they sacrificed to idols and profaned the sabbath.

NEW JERUSALEM BIBLE

women and children captive and commandeered the cattle.
33 They then rebuilt the City of David with a great strong wall
and strong towers and made this their Citadel. 34 There they
installed a brood of sinners, of renegades, who fortified
themselves inside it, 35 storing arms and provisions, and
depositing there the loot they had collected from Jerusalem;
they were to prove a great trouble.

36 It became an ambush for the sanctuary,
an evil adversary for Israel at all times.
37 They shed innocent blood all round the sanctuary
and defiled the sanctuary itself.
38 The citizens of Jerusalem fled because of them,
she became a dwelling-place of strangers;
estranged from her own offspring,
her children forsook her.
39 Her sanctuary became as forsaken as a desert,
her feasts were turned into mourning,
her Sabbaths into a mockery,
her honour into reproach.
40 Her dishonour now fully matched her former glory,
her greatness was turned into grief.

41 The king then issued a proclamation to his whole kingdom that all were to become a single people, each nation
renouncing its particular customs. 42 All the gentiles conformed to the king's decree, 43 and many Israelites chose to
accept his religion, sacrificing to idols and profaning the

GREEK OLD TESTAMENT

[44] καὶ ἀπέστειλεν ὁ βασιλεὺς βιβλία ἐν χειρὶ ἀγγέλων εἰς
Ιερουσαλημ καὶ τὰς πόλεις Ιουδα πορευθῆναι ὀπίσω νομίμων
ἀλλοτρίων τῆς γῆς [45] καὶ κωλῦσαι ὁλοκαυτώματα καὶ θυσίαν
καὶ σπονδὴν ἐκ τοῦ ἁγιάσματος καὶ βεβηλῶσαι σάββατα καὶ
ἑορτὰς [46] καὶ μιᾶναι ἁγίασμα καὶ ἁγίους, [47] οἰκοδομῆσαι
βωμοὺς καὶ τεμένη καὶ εἰδώλια καὶ θύειν ὕεια καὶ κτήνη
κοινὰ [48] καὶ ἀφιέναι τοὺς υἱοὺς αὐτῶν ἀπεριτμήτους βδελύ-
ξαι τὰς ψυχὰς αὐτῶν ἐν παντὶ ἀκαθάρτῳ καὶ βεβηλώσει
[49] ὥστε ἐπιλαθέσθαι τοῦ νόμου καὶ ἀλλάξαι πάντα τὰ δικαιώ-
ματα· [50] καὶ ὃς ἂν μὴ ποιήσῃ κατὰ τὸν λόγον τοῦ βασιλέως,
ἀποθανεῖται. [51] κατὰ πάντας τοὺς λόγους τούτους ἔγραψεν
πάσῃ τῇ βασιλείᾳ αὐτοῦ καὶ ἐποίησεν ἐπισκόπους ἐπὶ πάντα
τὸν λαὸν καὶ ἐνετείλατο ταῖς πόλεσιν Ιουδα θυσιάζειν κατὰ
πόλιν καὶ πόλιν. [52] καὶ συνηθροίσθησαν ἀπὸ τοῦ λαοῦ πολλοὶ
πρὸς αὐτούς, πᾶς ὁ ἐγκαταλείπων τὸν νόμον, καὶ ἐποίησαν
κακὰ ἐν τῇ γῇ [53] καὶ ἔθεντο τὸν Ισραηλ ἐν κρύφοις ἐν παντὶ
φυγαδευτηρίῳ αὐτῶν. [54] καὶ τῇ πεντεκαιδεκάτῃ ἡμέρᾳ
Χασελευ τῷ πέμπτῳ καὶ τεσσαρακοστῷ καὶ ἑκατοστῷ ἔτει
ᾠκοδόμησεν βδέλυγμα ἐρημώσεως ἐπὶ τὸ θυσιαστήριον. καὶ
ἐν πόλεσιν Ιουδα κύκλῳ ᾠκοδόμησαν βωμούς. [55] καὶ ἐπὶ τῶν

KING JAMES VERSION

44 For the king had sent letters by messengers unto Jerusalem and the cities of Juda, that they should follow the strange laws of the land,

45 And forbid burnt offerings, and sacrifice, and drink offerings, in the temple; and that they should profane the sabbaths and festival days:

46 And pollute the sanctuary and holy people:

47 Set up altars, and groves, and chapels of idols, and sacrifice swine's flesh, and unclean beasts:

48 That they should also leave their children uncircumcised, and make their souls abominable with all manner of uncleanness and profanation:

49 To the end they might forget the law, and change all the ordinances.

50 And whosoever would not do according to the commandment of the king, *he said,* he should die.

51 In the selfsame manner wrote he to his whole kingdom, and appointed overseers over all the people, commanding the cities of Juda to sacrifice, city by city.

52 Then many of the people were gathered unto them, to wit, every one that forsook the law; and so they committed evils in the land;

53 And drove the Israelites into secret places, even wheresoever they could flee for succour.

54 Now the fifteenth day of *the month* Casleu, in the hundred forty and fifth year, they set up the abomination of desolation upon the altar, and builded idol altars throughout the cities of Juda on every side;

DOUAY OLD TESTAMENT

46 And the king sent letters by the hands of messengers to Jerusalem, and to all the cities of Juda: that they should follow the law of the nations of the earth,

47 And should forbid holocausts and sacrifices, and atonements to be made in the temple of God.

48 And should prohibit the sabbath, and the festival days, to be celebrated.

49 And he commanded the holy places to be profaned, and the holy people of Israel.

50 And he commanded altars to be built, and temples, and idols, and swine's flesh to be immolated, and unclean beasts.

51 And that they should leave their children uncircumcised, and let their souls be defiled with all uncleannesses, and abominations, to the end that they should forget the law, and should change all the justifications of God.

52 And that whosoever would not do according to the word of king Antiochus should be put to death.

53 According to all these words he wrote to his whole kingdom, and he appointed rulers over the people that should force them to do these things.

54 And they commanded the cities of Juda to sacrifice.

55 Then many of the people were gathered to them that had forsaken the law of the Lord: and they committed evils in the land:

56 And they drove away the people of Israel into lurking holes, and into the secret places of fugitives.

57 On the fifteenth day of the month Casleu, in the hundred and forty-fifth year, king Antiochus set up the abominable idol of desolation upon the altar of God, and they built altars throughout all the cities of Juda round about:

KNOX TRANSLATION

[46] Both in Jerusalem and in all the cities of Juda the king's
envoys published this edict; men must live by the law of the
heathen round about, [47] burnt-sacrifice, offering and atonement in God's temple should be none, [48] nor sabbath kept,
nor feast-day. [49] And, for the more profanation of the sanctuary, and of Israel's holy people, [50] altar and shrine and
idol must be set up, swine's flesh offered, and all manner of
unhallowed meat; [51] children be left uncircumcised, and
their innocent lives contaminated with rites unclean, abominable; till the law should be forgotten, and the divine precepts fashioned anew. [52] Durst any neglect the royal bidding,
he must die.
[53] Through the whole of his dominions the king's writ ran,
and commissioners were appointed besides to enforce it;
[54] no city of Juda but was ordered to do sacrifice. [55] Many
there were, traitors to the divine law, that took their part,
and much mischief they did, [56] driving the men of Israel to
seek refuge in hiding, where refuge was to be had. [57] It was
on the fifteenth of Casleu, in the hundred and forty-fifth
year, that king Antiochus set up an idol to desecrate God's
altar;[a] shrines there were in every township of Juda,

[a] Cf. Dan. 11. 31, Mt. 24. 15.

TODAY'S ENGLISH VERSION

44 The king also sent messengers with a decree to Jerusalem and all the towns of Judea, ordering the people to follow customs that were foreign to the country. 45 He ordered
them not to offer burnt offerings, grain offerings, or wine
offerings in the Temple, and commanded them to treat
Sabbaths and festivals as ordinary work days. 46 They were
even ordered to defile the Temple and the holy things in it.[a]
47 They were commanded to build pagan altars, temples, and
shrines, and to sacrifice pigs and other unclean animals
there. 48 They were forbidden to circumcise their sons and
were required to make themselves ritually unclean in every
way they could, 49 so that they would forget the Law which
the Lord had given through Moses and would disobey all its
commands. 50 The penalty for disobeying the king's decree
was death.

51 The king not only issued the same decree throughout his
whole empire, but he also appointed officials to supervise the
people and commanded each town in Judea to offer pagan
sacrifices. 52 Many of the Jews were ready to forsake the Law
and to obey these officials. They defiled the land with their
evil, 53 and their conduct forced all true Israelites to hide
wherever they could.

54 On the fifteenth day of the month of Kislev in the year
145,[b] King Antiochus set up "The Awful Horror" on the altar
of the Temple, and pagan altars were built in the towns

[a] the holy things in it; *or* the priests. [b] THE YEAR 145: *This corresponds to 167 B.C.*

NEW REVISED STANDARD VERSION

44 And the king sent letters by messengers to Jerusalem and
the towns of Judah; he directed them to follow customs
strange to the land, 45 to forbid burnt offerings and sacrifices
and drink offerings in the sanctuary, to profane sabbaths
and festivals, 46 to defile the sanctuary and the priests, 47 to
build altars and sacred precincts and shrines for idols, to sacrifice swine and other unclean animals, 48 and to leave their
sons uncircumcised. They were to make themselves abominable by everything unclean and profane, 49 so that they
would forget the law and change all the ordinances. 50 He
added,[a] "And whoever does not obey the command of the
king shall die."

51 In such words he wrote to his whole kingdom. He
appointed inspectors over all the people and commanded the
towns of Judah to offer sacrifice, town by town. 52 Many of
the people, everyone who forsook the law, joined them, and
they did evil in the land; 53 they drove Israel into hiding in
every place of refuge they had.

54 Now on the fifteenth day of Chislev, in the one hundred
forty-fifth year,[b] they erected a desolating sacrilege on the altar
of burnt offering. They also built altars in the surrounding

a Gk lacks *He added* *b* 167 B.C.

NEW AMERICAN BIBLE

44 The king sent messengers with letters to Jerusalem and
to the cities of Judah, ordering them to follow customs foreign to their land: 45 to prohibit holocausts, sacrifices, and
libations in the sanctuary, to profane the sabbaths and feast
days, 46 to desecrate the sanctuary and the sacred ministers,
to build pagan altars and temples and shrines, 47 to sacrifice
swine and unclean animals, 48 to leave their sons uncircumcised, and to let themselves be defiled with every kind of
impurity and abomination, 49 so that they might forget the
law and change all their observances. 50 Whoever refused to
act according to the command of the king should be put to
death.

51 Such were the orders he published throughout his kingdom. He appointed inspectors over all the people, and he
ordered the cities of Judah to offer sacrifices, each city in
turn. 52 Many of the people, those who abandoned the law,
joined them and committed evil in the land. 53 Israel was driven into hiding, wherever places of refuge could be found.

54 On the fifteenth day of the month Chislev, in the year
one hundred and forty-five, the king erected the horrible
abomination upon the altar of holocausts, and in the surrounding cities of Judah they built pagan altars. 55 They also

NEW JERUSALEM BIBLE

Sabbath. 44 The king also sent edicts by messenger to Jerusalem and the towns of Judah, directing them to adopt customs foreign to the country, 45 banning burnt offerings, sacrifices and libations from the sanctuary, profaning Sabbaths
and feasts, 46 defiling the sanctuary and everything holy,
47 building altars, shrines and temples for idols, sacrificing
pigs and unclean beasts, 48 leaving their sons uncircumcised, and prostituting themselves to all kinds of impurity
and abomination, 49 so that they should forget the Law and
revoke all observance of it. 50 Anyone not obeying the king's
command was to be put to death. 51 Writing in such terms to
every part of his kingdom, the king appointed inspectors for
the whole people and directed all the towns of Judah to offer
sacrifice city by city. 52 Many of the people—that is, every
apostate from the Law—rallied to them and so committed
evil in the country, 53 forcing Israel into hiding in any possible place of refuge.

54 On the fifteenth day of Chislev in the year 145 the king
built the appalling abomination[a] on top of the altar of burnt
offering; and altars were built in the surrounding towns of

[a] 1 An idolatrous altar erected on the Jewish altar of burnt-offering.

GREEK OLD TESTAMENT

θυρῶν τῶν οἰκιῶν καὶ ἐν ταῖς πλατείαις ἐθυμίων. 56 καὶ τὰ
βιβλία τοῦ νόμου, ἃ εὗρον, ἐνεπύρισαν ἐν πυρὶ κατασχί-
σαντες. 57 καὶ ὅπου εὑρίσκετο παρά τινι βιβλίον διαθήκης,
καὶ εἴ τις συνευδόκει τῷ νόμῳ, τὸ σύγκριμα τοῦ βασιλέως
ἐθανάτου αὐτόν. 58 ἐν ἰσχύι αὐτῶν ἐποίουν τῷ Ισραηλ τοῖς
εὑρισκομένοις ἐν παντὶ μηνὶ καὶ μηνὶ ἐν ταῖς πόλεσιν. 59 καὶ
τῇ πέμπτῃ καὶ εἰκάδι τοῦ μηνὸς θυσιάζοντες ἐπὶ τὸν βωμόν,
ὃς ἦν ἐπὶ τοῦ θυσιαστηρίου. 60 καὶ τὰς γυναῖκας τὰς
περιτετμηκυίας τὰ τέκνα αὐτῶν ἐθανάτωσαν κατὰ τὸ πρόσταγμα 61 καὶ ἐκρέμασαν τὰ βρέφη ἐκ τῶν τραχήλων αὐτῶν,
καὶ τοὺς οἴκους αὐτῶν καὶ τοὺς περιτετμηκότας αὐτούς.
62 καὶ πολλοὶ ἐν Ισραηλ ἐκραταιώθησαν καὶ ὠχυρώθησαν ἐν
αὐτοῖς τοῦ μὴ φαγεῖν κοινὰ 63 καὶ ἐπεδέξαντο ἀποθανεῖν,
ἵνα μὴ μιανθῶσιν τοῖς βρώμασιν καὶ μὴ βεβηλώσωσιν διαθήκην ἁγίαν, καὶ ἀπέθανον. 64 καὶ ἐγένετο ὀργὴ μεγάλη ἐπὶ
Ισραηλ σφόδρα.

2 Ἐν ταῖς ἡμέραις ἐκείναις ἀνέστη Ματταθιας υἱὸς
Ιωαννου τοῦ Συμεων ἱερεὺς τῶν υἱῶν Ιωαριβ ἀπὸ
Ιερουσαλημ καὶ ἐκάθισεν ἐν Μωδεϊν. 2 καὶ αὐτῷ υἱοὶ πέντε,
Ιωαννης ὁ ἐπικαλούμενος Γαδδι, 3 Σιμων ὁ καλούμενος
Θασσι, 4 Ιουδας ὁ καλούμενος Μακκαβαῖος, 5 Ελεαζαρ ὁ

KING JAMES VERSION

55 And burnt incense at the doors of their houses, and in the streets.

56 And when they had rent in pieces the books of the law which they found, they burnt them with fire.

57 And wheresoever was found with any the book of the testament, or if any consented to the law, the king's commandment was, that they should put him to death.

58 Thus did they by their authority unto the Israelites every month, to as many as were found in the cities.

59 Now the five and twentieth day of the month they did sacrifice upon the idol altar, which was upon the altar of God.

60 At which time according to the commandment they put to death certain women, that had caused their children to be circumcised.

61 And they hanged the infants about their necks, and rifled their houses, and slew them that had circumcised them.

62 Howbeit many in Israel were fully resolved and confirmed in themselves not to eat any unclean thing.

63 Wherefore they chose rather to die, that they might not be defiled with meats, and that they might not profane the holy covenant: so then they died.

64 And there was very great wrath upon Israel.

2 In those days arose Mattathias *the son* of John, *the son* of Simeon, a priest of the sons of Joarib, from Jerusalem, and dwelt in Modin.

2 And he had five sons, Joannan, called Caddis:

3 Simon, called Thassi:

4 Judas, who was called Maccabeus:

DOUAY OLD TESTAMENT

58 And they burnt incense, and sacrificed at the doors of the houses, and in the streets.

59 And they cut in pieces, and burnt with fire the books of the law of God:

60 And every one with whom the books of the testament of the Lord were found, and whosoever observed the law of the Lord, they put to death, according to the edict of the king.

61 Thus by their power did they deal with the people of Israel, that were found in the cities month after month.

62 And on the five and twentieth day of the month they sacrificed upon the altar of the idol that was over against the altar *of God*.

63 Now the women that circumcised their children, were slain according to the commandment of king Antiochus.

64 And they hanged the children about their necks in all their houses: and those that had circumcised them, they put to death.

65 And many of the people of Israel determined with themselves, that they would not eat unclean things: and they chose rather to die than to be defiled with unclean meats.

66 And they would not break the holy law of God, and they were put to death:

67 And there was very great wrath upon the people.

2 IN those days arose Mathathias the son of John, the son of Simeon, a priest of the sons of Joarib, from Jerusalem, and he abode in the mountain of Modin.

2 And he had five sons: John who was surnamed Gaddis:

3 And Simon, who was surnamed Thasi:

4 And Judas, who was called Machabeus:

KNOX TRANSLATION

58 offering of incense and of victims before house doors and
in the open street; 59 never a copy of the divine law but was
torn up and burned; 60 if any were found that kept the
sacred record, or obeyed the Lord's will, his life was forfeit
to the king's edict. 61 Month by month such deeds of violence were done, in all townships where men of Israel dwelt,
62 and on the twenty-fifth of the month sacrifice was made
at the shrine that overshadowed the altar. 63 Death it was
for woman to have her child circumcised in defiance of the
king; 64 there in her own house she must be hung up, with
the child about her neck, and the circumciser, too, must pay
for it with his life. 65 Many a son of Israel refused the
unclean food, preferring death to defilement; 66 and die they
must, because they would not break God's holy law.
67 Grievous, most grievous was the doom that hung then
over his people.

2 In those days it was that Mattathias came forward, son
of John, son of Simeon, a priest of Joarib's family; he was
for Jerusalem no more, but would take up his dwelling on the
hill-side at Modin. 2 Five sons he had, John, that was also
called Gaddis, 3 Simon (or Thasi), 4 Judas (or Machabaeus),

TODAY'S ENGLISH VERSION

throughout Judea. 55 Pagan sacrifices were offered in front of houses and in the streets. 56 Any books of the Law which were found were torn up and burned, 57 and anyone who was caught with a copy of the sacred books or who obeyed the Law was put to death by order of the king. 58 Month after month these wicked people used their power against the Israelites caught in the towns.

59 On the twenty-fifth of the month, these same evil people offered sacrifices on the pagan altar erected on top of the altar in the Temple. 60 Mothers who had allowed their babies to be circumcised were put to death in accordance with the king's decree. 61 Their babies were hung around their necks, and their families and those who had circumcised them were put to death. 62 But many people in Israel firmly resisted the king's decree and refused to eat food that was ritually unclean. 63 They preferred to die rather than break the holy covenant and eat unclean food—and many did die. 64 In his anger God made Israel suffer terribly.

2 During that time, a priest of the Jehoiarib family named Mattathias, who was the son of John and the grandson of Simeon, moved from Jerusalem and settled in Modein. 2 Mattathias had five sons: John (also called Gaddi), 3 Simon (also called Thassi), 4 Judas (also called Maccabeus),

NEW REVISED STANDARD VERSION

towns of Judah, 55 and offered incense at the doors of the houses and in the streets. 56 The books of the law that they found they tore to pieces and burned with fire. 57 Anyone found possessing the book of the covenant, or anyone who adhered to the law, was condemned to death by decree of the king. 58 They kept using violence against Israel, against those who were found month after month in the towns. 59 On the twenty-fifth day of the month they offered sacrifice on the altar that was on top of the altar of burnt offering. 60 According to the decree, they put to death the women who had their children circumcised, 61 and their families and those who circumcised them; and they hung the infants from their mothers' necks.

62 But many in Israel stood firm and were resolved in their hearts not to eat unclean food. 63 They chose to die rather than to be defiled by food or to profane the holy covenant; and they did die. 64 Very great wrath came upon Israel.

2 In those days Mattathias son of John son of Simeon, a priest of the family of Joarib, moved from Jerusalem and settled in Modein. 2 He had five sons, John surnamed Gaddi, 3 Simon called Thassi, 4 Judas called Maccabeus, 5 Eleazar

NEW AMERICAN BIBLE

burnt incense at the doors of houses and in the streets. 56 Any scrolls of the law which they found they tore up and burnt. 57 Whoever was found with a scroll of the covenant, and whoever observed the law, was condemned to death by royal decree. 58 So they used their power against Israel, against those who were caught, each month, in the cities. 59 On the twenty-fifth day of each month they sacrificed on the altar erected over the altar of holocausts. 60 Women who had had their children circumcised were put to death, in keeping with the decree, 61 with the babies hung from their necks; their families also and those who had circumcised them were killed. 62 But many in Israel were determined and resolved in their hearts not to eat anything unclean; 63 they preferred to die rather than to be defiled with unclean food or to profane the holy covenant; and they did die. Terrible affliction was upon Israel.

2 In those days Mattathias, son of John, son of Simeon, a priest of the family of Joarib, left Jerusalem and settled in Modein. 2 He had five sons: John, who was called Gaddi; 3 Simon, who was called Thassi; 4 Judas, who was called

NEW JERUSALEM BIBLE

Judah 55 and incense offered at the doors of houses and in the streets. 56 Any books of the Law that came to light were torn up and burned. 57 Whenever anyone was discovered possessing a copy of the covenant or practising the Law, the king's decree sentenced him to death. 58 Month after month they took harsh action against any offenders they discovered in the towns of Israel. 59 On the twenty-fifth day of each month, sacrifice was offered on the altar erected on top of the altar of burnt offering. 60 Women who had had their children circumcised were put to death according to the edict 61 with their babies hung round their necks, and the members of their household and those who had performed the circumcision were executed with them.

62 Yet there were many in Israel who stood firm and found the courage to refuse unclean food. 63 They chose death rather than contamination by such fare or profanation of the holy covenant, and they were executed. 64 It was a truly dreadful retribution that visited Israel.

2 About then, Mattathias son of John, son of Simeon, a priest of the line of Joarib, left Jerusalem and settled in Modein. 2 He had five sons, John known as Gaddi, 3 Simon called Thassi, 4 Judas called Maccabaeus, 5 Eleazar, called

GREEK OLD TESTAMENT

καλούμενος Αυαραν, Ιωναθης ὁ καλούμενος Απφους. 6 καὶ
εἶδεν τὰς βλασφημίας τὰς γινομένας ἐν Ιουδα καὶ ἐν Ιερουσαλημ 7 καὶ εἶπεν Οἴμμοι, ἵνα τί τοῦτο ἐγεννήθην ἰδεῖν τὸ
σύντριμμα τοῦ λαοῦ μου καὶ τὸ σύντριμμα τῆς ἁγίας πόλεως
καὶ καθίσαι ἐκεῖ ἐν τῷ δοθῆναι αὐτὴν ἐν χειρὶ ἐχθρῶν, τὸ
ἁγίασμα ἐν χειρὶ ἀλλοτρίων; 8 ἐγένετο ὁ ναὸς αὐτῆς ὡς
ἀνὴρ ἄδοξος, 9 τὰ σκεύη τῆς δόξης αὐτῆς αἰχμάλωτα ἀπή-
χθη, ἀπεκτάνθη τὰ νήπια αὐτῆς ἐν ταῖς πλατείαις αὐτῆς, οἱ
νεανίσκοι αὐτῆς ἐν ῥομφαίᾳ ἐχθροῦ. 10 ποῖον ἔθνος οὐκ
ἐκληρονόμησεν βασίλεια καὶ οὐκ ἐκράτησεν τῶν σκύλων
αὐτῆς; 11 πᾶς ὁ κόσμος αὐτῆς ἀφῃρέθη, ἀντὶ ἐλευθέρας ἐγένετο εἰς δούλην. 12 καὶ ἰδοὺ τὰ ἅγια ἡμῶν καὶ ἡ καλλονὴ
ἡμῶν καὶ ἡ δόξα ἡμῶν ἠρημώθη, καὶ ἐβεβήλωσαν αὐτὰ τὰ
ἔθνη. 13 ἵνα τί ἡμῖν ἔτι ζωή; 14 καὶ διέρρηξεν Ματταθιας
καὶ οἱ υἱοὶ αὐτοῦ τὰ ἱμάτια αὐτῶν καὶ περιεβάλοντο σάκκους
καὶ ἐπένθησαν σφόδρα.

15 Καὶ ἦλθον οἱ παρὰ τοῦ βασιλέως οἱ καταναγκάζοντες
τὴν ἀποστασίαν εἰς Μωδεϊν τὴν πόλιν, ἵνα θυσιάσωσιν.
16 καὶ πολλοὶ ἀπὸ Ισραηλ πρὸς αὐτοὺς προσῆλθον· καὶ Ματταθιας καὶ οἱ υἱοὶ αὐτοῦ συνήχθησαν. 17 καὶ ἀπεκρίθησαν οἱ

KING JAMES VERSION

5 Eleazar, called Avaran: and Jonathan, whose surname was Apphus.

6 And when he saw the blasphemies that were committed in Juda and Jerusalem,

7 He said, Woe is me! wherefore was I born to see this misery of my people, and of the holy city, and to dwell there, when it was delivered into the hand of the enemy, and the sanctuary into the hand of strangers?

8 Her temple is become as a man without glory.

9 Her glorious vessels are carried away into captivity, her infants are slain in the streets, her young men with the sword of the enemy.

10 What nation hath not had a part in *her* kingdom, and gotten of her spoils?

11 All her ornaments are taken away; of a free woman she is become a bondslave.

12 And, behold, our sanctuary, even our beauty and our glory, is laid waste, and the Gentiles have profaned it.

13 To what end therefore shall we live any longer?

14 Then Mattathias and his sons rent their clothes, and put on sackcloth, and mourned very sore.

15 In the mean while the king's officers, such as compelled the people to revolt, came into the city Modin, to make them sacrifice.

16 And when many of Israel came unto them, Mattathias also and his sons came together.

DOUAY OLD TESTAMENT

5 And Eleazar, who was surnamed Abaron: and Jonathan, who was surnamed Apphus.

6 These saw the evils that were done in the people of Juda, and in Jerusalem.

7 And Mathathias said: Woe is me, wherefore was I born to see the ruin of my people, and the ruin of the holy city, and to dwell there, when it is given into the hands of the enemies?

8 The holy places are come into the hands of strangers: her temple is become as a man without honour.

9 The vessels of her glory are carried away captive: her old men are murdered in the streets, and her young men are fallen by the sword of the enemies.

10 What nation hath not inherited her kingdom, and gotten of her spoils?

11 All her ornaments are taken away. She that was free is made a slave.

12 And behold our sanctuary, and our beauty, and our glory is laid waste, and the Gentiles have defiled them.

13 To what end then should we live any longer?

14 And Mathathias and his sons rent their garments, and they covered themselves with haircloth, and made great lamentation.

15 And they that were sent from king Antiochus came thither, to compel them that were fled into the city of Modin, to sacrifice, and to burn incense, and to depart from the law of God.

16 And many of the people of Israel consented, and came to them: but Mathathias and his sons stood firm.

KNOX TRANSLATION

5 Eleazar (or Abaron), and Jonathan (or Apphus) 6 and these
saw well what foul things were a-doing in Juda's country and
the city of Jerusalem. 7 Alas, what needed it, cried Mattathias,
I should have been born into such an age as this? To see my
people and the holy city alike brought to ruin, to sit by while
the enemy overcame her, 8 and in her very sanctuary the
alien had his will? Temple of hers like a churl's lot disregarded, 9 rare treasure of hers into exile carried away; young and
old, in the open streets of her, put to the sword! 10 Never a
race in heathendom but may parcel out her domains, grow
rich with the spoil of her! 11 Gone, all her fair adornment; the
mistress is turned maid; 12 laid waste, yonder sanctuary, that
was our prize and pride, by Gentile feet dishonoured! 13 And
would we live yet?

14 With that, they tore their garments about them,
Mattathias and his sons, and went clad in sackcloth, mourning right bitterly. 15 And now the pursuivants of king Antiochus came to Modin; take refuge there who might, he must
do sacrifice none the less, and burn incense, and leave the
following of God's law. 16 Out went the folk of Israel to meet
them, some complaisantly enough, but Mattathias and his

TODAY'S ENGLISH VERSION

5 Eleazar (also called Avaran), and Jonathan (also called
Apphus).
6 When Mattathias saw all the sins that were being committed in Judea and Jerusalem, 7 he said:

"Why was I born to see these terrible things,
the ruin of my people and of the holy city?
Must I sit here helpless
while the city is surrendered to enemies
and the Temple falls into the hands of foreigners?
8 The Temple is like someone without honor.
9 Its splendid furnishings
have been carried away as loot.
Our children have been killed in the streets,
and our young men by the sword of the enemy.
10 Every nation in the world has occupied the city
and robbed her of her possessions.
11 All her ornaments have been stripped away;
she is now a slave, no longer free.
12 Look at our Temple, profaned by the Gentiles,
emptied of all its splendor.
13 Why should we go on living?"

14 In their grief, Mattathias and his sons tore their clothes,
put on sackcloth, and continued in deep mourning.
15 Then the king's officials, who were forcing the people to
turn from God, came to the town of Modein to force the people there to offer pagan sacrifices. 16 Many of the Israelites
came to meet them, including Mattathias and his sons.

NEW REVISED STANDARD VERSION

called Avaran, and Jonathan called Apphus. 6 He saw the
blasphemies being committed in Judah and Jerusalem, 7 and
said,

"Alas! Why was I born to see this,
the ruin of my people, the ruin of the holy city,
and to live there when it was given over to the enemy,
the sanctuary given over to aliens?
8 Her temple has become like a person without honor;[a]
9 her glorious vessels have been carried into exile.
Her infants have been killed in her streets,
her youths by the sword of the foe.
10 What nation has not inherited her palaces[b]
and has not seized her spoils?
11 All her adornment has been taken away;
no longer free, she has become a slave.
12 And see, our holy place, our beauty,
and our glory have been laid waste;
the Gentiles have profaned them.
13 Why should we live any longer?"

14 Then Mattathias and his sons tore their clothes, put on
sackcloth, and mourned greatly.
15 The king's officers who were enforcing the apostasy
came to the town of Modein to make them offer sacrifice.
16 Many from Israel came to them; and Mattathias and his

a Meaning of Gk uncertain *b* Other ancient authorities read *has not had a part in her kingdom*

NEW AMERICAN BIBLE

Maccabeus; 5 Eleazar, who was called Avaran; and
Jonathan, who was called Apphus. 6 When he saw the sacrileges that were being committed in Judah and in Jerusalem,
7 he said: "Woe is me! Why was I born to see the ruin of my
people and the ruin of the holy city, and to sit idle while it is
given into the hands of enemies, and the sanctuary into the
hands of strangers?

8 "Her temple has become like a man disgraced,
9 her glorious ornaments have been carried off as
spoils,
Her infants have been murdered in her streets,
her young men by the sword of the enemy.
10 What nation has not taken its share of her realm,
and laid its hand on her possessions?
11 All her adornment has been taken away.
From being free, she has become a slave.
12 We see our sanctuary and our beauty
and our glory laid waste,
And the Gentiles have defiled them!
13 Why are we still alive?"

14 Then Mattathias and his sons tore their garments, put on
sackcloth, and mourned bitterly.
15 The officers of the king in charge of enforcing the apostasy came to the city of Modein to organize the sacrifices.
16 Many of Israel joined them, but Mattathias and his sons

NEW JERUSALEM BIBLE

Avaran, and Jonathan called Apphus. 6 When he saw the
blasphemies being committed in Judah and Jerusalem, 7 he
said, 'Alas that I should have been born to witness the ruin
of my people and the ruin of the Holy City, and to sit by
while she is delivered over to her enemies, and the sanctuary
into the hand of foreigners.

8 'Her Temple has become like someone of no repute,
9 the vessels that were her glory have been carried off as
booty,
her babies have been slaughtered in her streets,
her young men by the enemy's sword.
10 Is there a nation that has not claimed
a share of her royal prerogatives,
that has not taken some of her spoils?
11 All her ornaments have been snatched from her,
her former freedom has become slavery.
12 See how the Holy Place, our beauty, our glory,
is now laid waste,
see how the gentiles have profaned it!
13 What have we left to live for?'

14 Mattathias and his sons tore their garments, put on
sackcloth, and observed deep mourning.
15 The king's commissioners who were enforcing the apostasy came to the town of Modein for the sacrifices. 16 Many
Israelites gathered round them, but Mattathias and his sons

GREEK OLD TESTAMENT

παρὰ τοῦ βασιλέως καὶ εἶπον τῷ Ματταθια λέγοντες Ἄρχων
καὶ ἔνδοξος καὶ μέγας εἶ ἐν τῇ πόλει ταύτῃ καὶ ἐστηρισμέν-
ος υἱοῖς καὶ ἀδελφοῖς. 18 νῦν πρόσελθε πρῶτος καὶ ποίησον
τὸ πρόσταγμα τοῦ βασιλέως, ὡς ἐποίησαν πάντα τὰ ἔθνη
καὶ οἱ ἄνδρες Ιουδα καὶ οἱ καταλειφθέντες ἐν Ιερουσαλημ,
καὶ ἔσῃ σὺ καὶ οἱ υἱοί σου τῶν φίλων τοῦ βασιλέως, καὶ σὺ
καὶ οἱ υἱοί σου δοξασθήσεσθε ἀργυρίῳ καὶ χρυσίῳ καὶ ἀποστολαῖς πολλαῖς. 19 καὶ ἀπεκρίθη Ματταθιας καὶ εἶπεν
φωνῇ μεγάλῃ Εἰ πάντα τὰ ἔθνη τὰ ἐν οἴκῳ τῆς βασιλείας
τοῦ βασιλέως ἀκούουσιν αὐτοῦ ἀποστῆναι ἕκαστος ἀπὸ
λατρείας πατέρων αὐτοῦ καὶ ᾑρετίσαντο ἐν ταῖς ἐντολαῖς
αὐτοῦ, 20 κἀγὼ καὶ οἱ υἱοί μου καὶ οἱ ἀδελφοί μου πορευσόμεθα ἐν διαθήκῃ πατέρων ἡμῶν· 21 ἵλεως ἡμῖν καταλιπεῖν
νόμον καὶ δικαιώματα· 22 τῶν λόγων τοῦ βασιλέως οὐκ ἀκου-
σόμεθα παρελθεῖν τὴν λατρείαν ἡμῶν δεξιὰν ἢ ἀριστεράν.
23 καὶ ὡς ἐπαύσατο λαλῶν τοὺς λόγους τούτους, προσῆλθεν
ἀνὴρ Ιουδαῖος ἐν ὀφθαλμοῖς πάντων θυσιάσαι ἐπὶ τοῦ βωμοῦ
ἐν Μωδεϊν κατὰ τὸ πρόσταγμα τοῦ βασιλέως. 24 καὶ εἶδεν
Ματταθιας καὶ ἐζήλωσεν, καὶ ἐτρόμησαν οἱ νεφροὶ αὐτοῦ,
καὶ ἀνήνεγκεν θυμὸν κατὰ τὸ κρίμα καὶ δραμὼν ἔσφαξεν

KING JAMES VERSION

17 Then answered the king's officers, and said to Mattathias on this wise, Thou art a ruler, and an honourable and great man in this city, and strengthened with sons and brethren:

18 Now therefore come thou first, and fulfil the king's commandment, like as all the heathen have done, yea, and the men of Juda also, and such as remain at Jerusalem: so shalt thou and thy house be in the number of the king's friends, and thou and thy children shall be honoured with silver and gold, and many rewards.

19 Then Mattathias answered and spake with a loud voice, Though all the nations that are under the king's dominion obey him, and fall away every one from the religion of their fathers, and give consent to his commandments:

20 Yet will I and my sons and my brethren walk in the covenant of our fathers.

21 God forbid that we should forsake the law and the ordinances.

22 We will not hearken to the king's words, to go from our religion, either on the right hand, or the left.

23 Now when he had left speaking these words, there came one of the Jews in the sight of all to sacrifice on the altar which was at Modin, according to the king's commandment.

24 Which thing when Mattathias saw, he was inflamed with zeal, and his reins trembled, neither could he forbear to shew his anger according to judgment: wherefore he ran, and slew him upon the altar.

DOUAY OLD TESTAMENT

17 And they that were sent from Antiochus, answering, said to Mathathias: Thou art a ruler, and an honourable, and great man in this city, and adorned with sons, and brethren.

18 Therefore come thou first, and obey the king's commandment, as all nations have done, and the men of Juda, and they that remain in Jerusalem: and thou, and thy sons, shall be in the number of the king's friends, and enriched with gold, and silver, and many presents.

19 Then Mathathias answered, and said with a loud voice: Although all nations obey king Antiochus, so as to depart every man from the service of the law of his fathers, and consent to his commandments:

20 I and my sons, and my brethren will obey the law of our fathers.

21 God be merciful unto us: it is not profitable for us to forsake the law, and the justices of God:

22 We will not hearken to the words of king Antiochus, neither will we sacrifice, and transgress the commandments of our law, to go another way.

23 Now as he left off speaking these words, there came a certain Jew in the sight of all to sacrifice to the idols upon the altar in the city of Modin, according to the king's commandment.

24 And Mathathias saw and was grieved and his reins trembled, and his wrath was kindled according to the judgment of the law, and running upon him he slew him upon the altar:

KNOX TRANSLATION

sons firm in their resolve. 17 And they singled out Mattathias
from the rest; A man of mark, said they, and a great chieftain thou; brethren and sons thou hast a many. 18 Wilt thou
not be the first to come forward and do the king's bidding,
with the whole world, and the men of Juda everywhere, and
what is left of Jerusalem? To be the king's friend, thou and
thy sons with thee, gold and silver and much else for thy
reward! 19 Loud rang the answer of Mattathias: What
though king Antiochus have the whole world for his vassals?
Obey the edict who will, forsaking the custom his fathers
lived by, 20 both I and son of mine, both I and clansman of
mine, will obey the law handed down to us. 21 Mercy of God!
What needs it we should leave his will undone, his claims
unhonoured? 22 To deaf ears king Antiochus proclaims the
sacrifice; we swerve not from the law's path, right or left.
23 Before he had done speaking, a Jew came to offer the
false gods sacrifice, there in full view of all, before the altar
at Modin, as the king bade. 24 Mattathias took fire at the
sight of it; one heave of anger his heart gave, and his zeal
for the law could contain itself no longer; there on the altar

TODAY'S ENGLISH VERSION

17 The king's officials said to Mattathias, "You are a respected
leader in this town, and you have the support of your sons
and relatives. 18 Why not be the first one here to do what the
king has commanded? All the Gentiles, the people of Judea,
and all the people left in Jerusalem have already done so. If
you do, you and your sons will be honored with the title of
'Friends of the King,' and you will be rewarded with silver
and gold and many gifts."

19 Mattathias answered in a loud voice, "I don't care if
every Gentile in this empire has obeyed the king and yielded
to the command to abandon the religion of his ancestors.
20 My children, my relatives, and I will continue to keep the
covenant that God made with our ancestors. 21 With God's
help we will never abandon his Law or disobey his commands. 22 We will not obey the king's decree, and we will
not change our way of worship in the least."

23 Just as he finished speaking, one of the men from
Modein decided to obey the king's decree and stepped out in
front of everyone to offer a pagan sacrifice on the altar that
stood there. 24 When Mattathias saw him, he became angry
enough to do what had to be done. Shaking with rage, he
ran forward and killed the man right there on the altar. 25 He

NEW REVISED STANDARD VERSION

sons were assembled. 17 Then the king's officers spoke to
Mattathias as follows: "You are a leader, honored and great
in this town, and supported by sons and brothers. 18 Now be
the first to come and do what the king commands, as all the
Gentiles and the people of Judah and those that are left in
Jerusalem have done. Then you and your sons will be numbered among the Friends of the king, and you and your sons
will be honored with silver and gold and many gifts."

19 But Mattathias answered and said in a loud voice:
"Even if all the nations that live under the rule of the king
obey him, and have chosen to obey his commandments,
everyone of them abandoning the religion of their ancestors,
20 I and my sons and my brothers will continue to live by the
covenant of our ancestors. 21 Far be it from us to desert the
law and the ordinances. 22 We will not obey the king's words
by turning aside from our religion to the right hand or to the
left."

23 When he had finished speaking these words, a Jew
came forward in the sight of all to offer sacrifice on the altar
in Modein, according to the king's command. 24 When
Mattathias saw it, he burned with zeal and his heart was
stirred. He gave vent to righteous anger; he ran and killed

NEW AMERICAN BIBLE

gathered in a group apart. 17 Then the officers of the king
addressed Mattathias: "You are a leader, an honorable and
great man in this city, supported by sons and kinsmen.
18 Come now, be the first to obey the king's command, as all
the Gentiles and the men of Judah and those who are left in
Jerusalem have done. Then you and your sons shall be numbered among the King's Friends, and shall be enriched with
silver and gold and many gifts." 19 But Mattathias answered
in a loud voice: "Although all the Gentiles in the king's realm
obey him, so that each forsakes the religion of his fathers
and consents to the king's orders, 20 yet I and my sons and
my kinsmen will keep to the covenant of our fathers. 21 God
forbid that we should forsake the law and the commandments. 22 We will not obey the words of the king nor depart
from our religion in the slightest degree."

23 As he finished saying these words, a certain Jew came
forward in the sight of all to offer sacrifice on the altar in
Modein according to the king's order. 24 When Mattathias
saw him, he was filled with zeal; his heart was moved and
his just fury was aroused; he sprang forward and killed him

NEW JERUSALEM BIBLE

drew apart. 17 The king's commissioners then addressed
Mattathias as follows, 'You are a respected leader, a great
man in this town; you have sons and brothers to support
you. 18 Be the first to step forward and conform to the king's
decree, as all the nations have done, and the leaders of Judah
and the survivors in Jerusalem; you and your sons shall be
reckoned among the Friends of the King, you and your sons
will be honoured with gold and silver and many presents.'
19 Raising his voice, Mattathias retorted, 'Even if every
nation living in the king's dominions obeys him, each forsaking its ancestral religion to conform to his decrees, 20 I,
my sons and my brothers will still follow the covenant of our
ancestors. 21 May Heaven preserve us from forsaking the
Law and its observances. 22 As for the king's orders, we will
not follow them: we shall not swerve from our own religion
either to right or to left.' 23 As he finished speaking, a Jew
came forward in the sight of all to offer sacrifice on the altar
in Modein as the royal edict required. 24 When Mattathias
saw this, he was fired with zeal; stirred to the depth of his
being, he gave vent to his legitimate anger, threw himself on
the man and slaughtered him on the altar. 25 At the same

GREEK OLD TESTAMENT

αὐτὸν ἐπὶ τὸν βωμόν· [25] καὶ τὸν ἄνδρα τοῦ βασιλέως τὸν
ἀναγκάζοντα θύειν ἀπέκτεινεν ἐν τῷ καιρῷ ἐκείνῳ καὶ τὸν
βωμὸν καθεῖλεν. [26] καὶ ἐζήλωσεν τῷ νόμῳ, καθὼς ἐποίησεν
Φινεες τῷ Ζαμβρι υἱῷ Σαλωμ. [27] καὶ ἀνέκραξεν Ματταθιας
ἐν τῇ πόλει φωνῇ μεγάλῃ λέγων Πᾶς ὁ ζηλῶν τῷ νόμῳ καὶ
ἱστῶν διαθήκην ἐξελθέτω ὀπίσω μου. [28] καὶ ἔφυγεν αὐτὸς
καὶ οἱ υἱοὶ αὐτοῦ εἰς τὰ ὄρη καὶ ἐγκατέλιπον ὅσα εἶχον ἐν
τῇ πόλει.

[29] Τότε κατέβησαν πολλοὶ ζητοῦντες δικαιοσύνην καὶ κρίμα εἰς τὴν ἔρημον καθίσαι ἐκεῖ, [30] αὐτοὶ καὶ οἱ υἱοὶ αὐτῶν
καὶ αἱ γυναῖκες αὐτῶν καὶ τὰ κτήνη αὐτῶν, ὅτι ἐσκληρύνθη
ἐπ᾽ αὐτοὺς τὰ κακά. [31] καὶ ἀνηγγέλη τοῖς ἀνδράσιν τοῦ
βασιλέως καὶ ταῖς δυνάμεσιν, αἳ ἦσαν ἐν Ιερουσαλημ πόλει
Δαυιδ ὅτι κατέβησαν ἄνδρες, οἵτινες διεσκέδασαν τὴν ἐντολὴν τοῦ βασιλέως, εἰς τοὺς κρύφους ἐν τῇ ἐρήμῳ. [32] καὶ
ἔδραμον ὀπίσω αὐτῶν πολλοὶ καὶ κατελάβοντο αὐτοὺς καὶ
παρενέβαλον ἐπ᾽ αὐτοὺς καὶ συνεστήσαντο πρὸς αὐτοὺς πόλεμον ἐν τῇ ἡμέρᾳ τῶν σαββάτων [33] καὶ εἶπον πρὸς αὐτούς
Ἕως τοῦ νῦν· ἐξελθόντες ποιήσατε κατὰ τὸν λόγον τοῦ
βασιλέως, καὶ ζήσεσθε. [34] καὶ εἶπον Οὐκ ἐξελευσόμεθα οὐδὲ
ποιήσομεν τὸν λόγον τοῦ βασιλέως βεβηλῶσαι τὴν ἡμέραν
τῶν σαββάτων. [35] καὶ ἐτάχυναν ἐπ᾽ αὐτοὺς πόλεμον. [36] καὶ
οὐκ ἀπεκρίθησαν αὐτοῖς οὐδὲ λίθον ἐνετίναξαν αὐτοῖς οὐδὲ

KING JAMES VERSION

25 Also the king's commissioner, who compelled men to sacrifice, he killed at that time, and the altar he pulled down.

26 Thus dealt he zealously for the law of God, like as Phinees did unto Zambri the son of Salom.

27 And Mattathias cried throughout the city with a loud voice, saying, Whosoever is zealous of the law, and maintaineth the covenant, let him follow me.

28 So he and his sons fled into the mountains, and left all that ever they had in the city.

29 Then many that sought after justice and judgment went down into the wilderness, to dwell there:

30 Both they, and their children, and their wives, and their cattle; because afflictions increased sore upon them.

31 Now when it was told the king's servants, and the host that was at Jerusalem, in the city of David, that certain men, who had broken the king's commandment, were gone down into the secret places in the wilderness,

32 They pursued after them a great number, and having overtaken them, they camped against them, and made war against them on the sabbath day.

33 And they said unto them, Let that which ye have done hitherto suffice; come forth, and do according to the commandment of the king, and ye shall live.

34 But they said, We will not come forth, neither will we do the king's commandment, to profane the sabbath day.

35 So then they gave them the battle with all speed.

36 Howbeit they answered them not, neither cast they a stone at them, nor stopped the places where they lay hid;

DOUAY OLD TESTAMENT

25 Moreover the man whom king Antiochus had sent, who compelled them to sacrifice, he slew at the same time, and pulled down the altar,

26 And shewed zeal for the law, as Phinees did by Zamri the son of Salomi.

27 And Mathathias cried out in the city with a loud voice, saying: Every one that hath zeal for the law, and maintaineth the testament, let him follow me.

28 So he, and his sons fled into the mountains, and left all that they had in the city.

29 Then many that sought after judgment, and justice, went down into the desert:

30 And they abode there, they and their children, and their wives, and their cattle: because afflictions increased upon them.

31 And it was told to the king's men, and to the army that was in Jerusalem in the city of David, that certain men who had broken the king's commandment, were gone away into the secret places in the wilderness, and that many were gone after them.

32 And forthwith they went out towards them, and made war against them on the sabbath day,

33 And they said to them: Do you still resist? come forth, and do according to the edict of king Antiochus, and you shall live.

34 And they said: We will not come forth, neither will we obey the king's edict, to profane the sabbath day.

35 And they made haste to give them battle.

36 But they answered them not, neither did they cast a stone at them, nor stopped up the secret places,

KNOX TRANSLATION

the sacrificer was slain. [25] Nor spared he the pursuivant of
king Antiochus that enjoined it; the altar, too, he pulled
down. [26] Not Phinees himself struck a better blow for the
law, when he slew Zamri, the son of Salom![a] [27] And now
Mattathias raised a cry in the city, Who loves the law? Who
keeps the covenant unbroken? Out with you, and follow me!
[28] So fled he with his sons into the hill-country, leaving his
possessions behind, there in the city.

[29] Many there were that went out into the desert at this
time, for love of truth and right; [30] took children and
women-folk and cattle with them, and settled down there,
castaways in a flood of misfortune. [31] But news of it reached
Jerusalem, and the king's men that were in David's Keep;
here were rebels lurking in the waste country, and drawing
many over to their side. [32] So they went out in pursuit, and
offered battle; on a sabbath day, as it chanced.[b] [33] What,
still stubborn? cried they. Come out, and yield yourselves to
the king's pleasure; your lives shall be spared. [34] But the
Jews' answer was, come out and yield to the king's pleasure
they might not; law of the sabbath rest forbade it. [35] So the
attack began in good earnest; [36] but the Jews made no resistance, never a stone flew, never a hiding-place of theirs was

a Cf. Num. 25. 7. *b* The words 'as it chanced' are not in the original, but it does not seem to be implied that the king's men purposely chose the sabbath day for making their assault.

Today's English Version

also killed the royal official who was forcing the people to
sacrifice, and then he tore down the altar. 26 In this way
Mattathias showed his deep devotion for the Law, just as
Phinehas had done when he killed Zimri son of Salu.

27 Then Mattathias went through the town shouting,
"Everyone who is faithful to God's covenant and obeys his
Law, follow me!" 28 With this, he and his sons fled to the
mountains, leaving behind all they owned.

29-30 At that time also many of the Israelites who were seeking to be right with God through obedience to the Law went
out to live in the wilderness, taking their children, their
wives, and their livestock with them, because of the terrible
oppression they were suffering. 31 The report soon reached
the king's officials and the soldiers in the fort at Jerusalem
that some men who had defied the king's command had
gone into hiding in the wilderness. 32 A large force of soldiers pursued them, caught up with them, set up camp opposite them, and prepared to attack them on the Sabbath.
33 "There is still time," they shouted out to the Jews. "Come
out and obey the king's command, and we will spare your
lives."

34 "We will not come out," they answered. "We will not
obey the king's command, and we will not profane the
Sabbath."

35 The soldiers attacked them immediately, 36 but the Jews
did nothing to resist; they did not even throw stones or block

New Revised Standard Version

him on the altar. 25 At the same time he killed the king's
officer who was forcing them to sacrifice, and he tore down
the altar. 26 Thus he burned with zeal for the law, just as
Phinehas did against Zimri son of Salu.

27 Then Mattathias cried out in the town with a loud
voice, saying: "Let every one who is zealous for the law and
supports the covenant come out with me!" 28 Then he and
his sons fled to the hills and left all that they had in the
town.

29 At that time many who were seeking righteousness
and justice went down to the wilderness to live there,
30 they, their sons, their wives, and their livestock, because
troubles pressed heavily upon them. 31 And it was reported
to the king's officers, and to the troops in Jerusalem the city
of David, that those who had rejected the king's command
had gone down to the hiding places in the wilderness.
32 Many pursued them, and overtook them; they encamped
opposite them and prepared for battle against them on the
sabbath day. 33 They said to them, "Enough of this! Come
out and do what the king commands, and you will live."
34 But they said, "We will not come out, nor will we do what
the king commands and so profane the sabbath day."
35 Then the enemy[a] quickly attacked them. 36 But they did
not answer them or hurl a stone at them or block up their

a Gk *they*

New American Bible

upon the altar. 25 At the same time, he also killed the messenger of the king who was forcing them to sacrifice, and he
tore down the altar. 26 Thus he showed his zeal for the law,
just as Phinehas did with Zimri, son of Salu.

27 Then Mattathias went through the city shouting, "Let
everyone who is zealous for the law and who stands by the
covenant follow after me!" 28 Thereupon he fled to the
mountains with his sons, leaving behind in the city all their
possessions. 29 Many who sought to live according to righteousness and religious custom went out into the desert to
settle there, 30 they and their sons, their wives and their cattle, because misfortunes pressed so hard on them.

31 It was reported to the officers and soldiers of the king
who were in the City of David, in Jerusalem, that certain men
who had flouted the king's order had gone out to the hiding
places in the desert. 32 Many hurried out after them, and
having caught up with them, camped opposite and prepared
to attack them on the sabbath. 33 "Enough of this!" the pursuers said to them. "Come out and obey the king's command,
and your lives will be spared." 34 But they replied, "We will
not come out, nor will we obey the king's command to profane the sabbath." 35 Then the enemy attacked them at once;
36 but they did not retaliate; they neither threw stones, nor
blocked up their own hiding places. 37 They said, "Let us all

New Jerusalem Bible

time he killed the king's commissioner who was there to
enforce the sacrifice, and tore down the altar. 26 In his zeal
for the Law he acted as Phinehas had against Zimri son of
Salu.[a] 27 Then Mattathias went through the town, shouting
at the top of his voice, 'Let everyone who has any zeal for
the Law and takes his stand on the covenant come out and
follow me.' 28 Then he fled with his sons into the hills, leaving all their possessions behind in the town.

29 Many people who were concerned for virtue and justice
went down to the desert and stayed there, 30 taking with
them their sons, their wives and their cattle, so oppressive
had their sufferings become. 31 Word was brought to the
royal officials and forces stationed in Jerusalem, in the City
of David, that those who had repudiated the king's edict had
gone down to the hiding places in the desert. 32 A strong
detachment went after them, and when it came up with them
ranged itself against them in battle formation, preparing to
attack them on the Sabbath day, 33 and said, 'Enough of
this! Come out and do as the king orders and you will be
spared.' 34 The others, however, replied, 'We refuse to come
out, and we will not obey the king's orders and profane the
Sabbath day.' 35 The royal forces at once went into action,
36 but the others offered no opposition; not a stone was
thrown, there was no barricading of the hiding places.

a **2** Nb 25:6–15.

GREEK OLD TESTAMENT

ἐνέφραξαν τοὺς κρύφους 37 λέγοντες Ἀποθάνωμεν πάντες
ἐν τῇ ἁπλότητι ἡμῶν· μαρτυρεῖ ἐφ᾽ ἡμᾶς ὁ οὐρανὸς καὶ ἡ γῆ
ὅτι ἀκρίτως ἀπόλλυτε ἡμᾶς. 38 καὶ ἀνέστησαν ἐπ᾽ αὐτοὺς ἐν
πολέμῳ τοῖς σάββασιν, καὶ ἀπέθανον αὐτοὶ καὶ αἱ γυναῖκες
αὐτῶν καὶ τὰ τέκνα αὐτῶν καὶ τὰ κτήνη αὐτῶν ἕως χιλίων
ψυχῶν ἀνθρώπων.
39 Καὶ ἔγνω Ματταθιας καὶ οἱ φίλοι αὐτοῦ καὶ ἐπένθησαν
ἐπ᾽ αὐτοὺς σφόδρα. 40 καὶ εἶπεν ἀνὴρ τῷ πλησίον αὐτοῦ Ἐὰν
πάντες ποιήσωμεν ὡς οἱ ἀδελφοὶ ἡμῶν ἐποίησαν καὶ μὴ
πολεμήσωμεν πρὸς τὰ ἔθνη ὑπὲρ τῆς ψυχῆς ἡμῶν καὶ τῶν
δικαιωμάτων ἡμῶν, νῦν τάχιον ὀλεθρεύσουσιν ἡμᾶς ἀπὸ τῆς
γῆς. 41 καὶ ἐβουλεύσαντο τῇ ἡμέρᾳ ἐκείνῃ λέγοντες Πᾶς
ἄνθρωπος, ὃς ἐὰν ἔλθῃ ἐφ᾽ ἡμᾶς εἰς πόλεμον τῇ ἡμέρᾳ τῶν
σαββάτων, πολεμήσωμεν κατέναντι αὐτοῦ καὶ οὐ μὴ ἀποθάνωμεν πάντες καθὼς ἀπέθανον οἱ ἀδελφοὶ ἡμῶν ἐν τοῖς κρύφοις. 42 τότε συνήχθησαν πρὸς αὐτοὺς συναγωγὴ Ασιδαίων,
ἰσχυροὶ δυνάμει ἀπὸ Ισραηλ, πᾶς ὁ ἑκουσιαζόμενος τῷ νόμῳ·
43 καὶ πάντες οἱ φυγαδεύοντες ἀπὸ τῶν κακῶν προσετέθησαν
αὐτοῖς καὶ ἐγένοντο αὐτοῖς εἰς στήριγμα. 44 καὶ συνεστήσαντο δύναμιν καὶ ἐπάταξαν ἁμαρτωλοὺς ἐν ὀργῇ αὐτῶν καὶ
ἄνδρας ἀνόμους ἐν θυμῷ αὐτῶν· καὶ οἱ λοιποὶ ἔφυγον εἰς τὰ
ἔθνη σωθῆναι. 45 καὶ ἐκύκλωσεν Ματταθιας καὶ οἱ φίλοι αὐτοῦ καὶ καθεῖλον τοὺς βωμοὺς 46 καὶ περιέτεμον τὰ παιδάρια τὰ ἀπερίτμητα, ὅσα εὗρον ἐν ὁρίοις Ισραηλ, ἐν ἰσχύι

KING JAMES VERSION

37 But said, Let us die all in our innocency: heaven and earth shall testify for us, that ye put us to death wrongfully.

38 So they rose up against them in battle on the sabbath, and they slew them, with their wives and children, and their cattle, to the number of a thousand people.

39 Now when Mattathias and his friends understood hereof, they mourned for them right sore.

40 And one of them said to another, If we all do as our brethren have done, and fight not for our lives and laws against the heathen, they will now quickly root us out of the earth.

41 At that time therefore they decreed, saying, Whosoever shall come to make battle with us on the sabbath day, we will fight against him; neither will we die all, as our brethren that were murdered im the secret places.

42 Then came there unto him a company of Assideans, who were mighty men of Israel, even all such as were voluntarily devoted unto the law.

43 Also all they that fled for persecution joined themselves unto them, and were a stay unto them.

44 So they joined their forces, and smote sinful men in their anger, and wicked men in their wrath: but the rest fled to the heathen for succour.

45 Then Mattathias and his friends went round about, and pulled down the altars:

46 And what children soever they found within the coast of Israel uncircumcised, those they circumcised valiantly.

DOUAY OLD TESTAMENT

37 Saying: Let us all die in our innocency: and heaven and earth shall be witnesses for us, that you put us to death wrongfully.

38 So they gave them battle on the sabbath: and they were slain with their wives, and their children, and their cattle, to the number of a thousand persons.

39 And Mathathias and his friends heard of it, and they mourned for them exceedingly.

40 And every man said to his neighbour: If we shall all do as our brethren have done, and not fight against the heathens for our lives, and our justifications: they will now quickly root us out of the earth.

41 And they determined in that day, saying: Whosoever shall come up against us to fight on the sabbath day, we will fight against him: and we will not all die, as our brethren that were slain in the secret places.

42 Then was assembled to them the congregation of the Assideans, the stoutest of Israel, every one that had a good will for the law.

43 And all they that fled from the evils, joined themselves to them, and were a support to them.

44 And they gathered an army, and slew the sinners in their wrath, and the wicked men in their indignation: and the rest fled to the nations for safety.

45 And Mathathias and his friends went round about, and they threw down the altars:

46 And they circumcised all the children whom they found in the confines of Israel that were uncircumcised: and they did valiantly.

KNOX TRANSLATION

put in a state of defence; 37 Die we all, they said, innocent
men, and let heaven and earth bear witness, it was for no
fault of ours we died. 38 Thus, because it was a sabbath day
when the attack was made, these men perished, and their
wives and children and cattle with them; a thousand human
lives lost.
39 Great grief it was to Mattathias and his company when
they heard what had befallen them; 40 and now there was
high debate raised: Do we as our brethren did, forbear we to
give battle for our lives and loyalties, and they will soon
make an end of us! 41 Then and there it was resolved, if any
should attack them on the sabbath day, to engage him, else
they should be put to death all of them, like those brethren of
theirs in the covert of the hills. 42 Now it was that the
Assidaeans rallied to their side, a party that was of great consequence in Israel, lovers of the law one and all; 43 and all
who would escape from the evils of the time made common
cause with them, and came to their assistance. 44 So, mustering their forces, they wrought indignant vengeance upon sinners that were false to the law, fill they were fain to take
refuge among the heathen; 45 wherever they went, Mattathias
and his company, they threw the altars down, 46 and whatever children they found uncircumcised, from one end of Israel
to the other, they circumcised by right of conquest.[a] 47 Ere

[a] It is not clear whether we are meant to understand that Gentile as well as Jewish children were circumcised.

TODAY'S ENGLISH VERSION

the entrances to the caves where they were hiding. 37 They
said, "We will all die with a clear conscience. Let heaven and
earth bear witness that you are slaughtering us unjustly."
38 So the enemy attacked them on the Sabbath and killed the
men, their wives, their children, and their livestock. A thousand people died.
39 When Mattathias and his friends heard the news about
this, they were greatly saddened 40 and said to one another,
"If all of us do as these other Jews have done and refuse to
fight the Gentiles to defend our lives and our religion, we
will soon be wiped off the face of the earth." 41 On that day
they decided that if anyone attacked them on the Sabbath,
they would defend themselves, so that they would not all die
as other Jews had died in the caves.
42 Then Mattathias and his friends were joined by a group
of devout and patriotic Jews, the strongest and bravest men
in Israel, who had all volunteered to defend the Law. 43 In
addition, everyone who was fleeing from the persecution
joined them and strengthened their forces. 44 Now that they
had an army, they gave vent to their anger by attacking the
renegade Jews. Those who escaped were forced to flee to the
Gentiles for safety. 45 Mattathias and his friends went everywhere tearing down pagan altars 46 and circumcising by
force every uncircumcised boy they found within the borders

NEW REVISED STANDARD VERSION

hiding places, 37 for they said, "Let us all die in our innocence; heaven and earth testify for us that you are killing us
unjustly." 38 So they attacked them on the sabbath, and they
died, with their wives and children and livestock, to the
number of a thousand persons.
39 When Mattathias and his friends learned of it, they
mourned for them deeply. 40 And all said to their neighbors:
"If we all do as our kindred have done and refuse to fight
with the Gentiles for our lives and for our ordinances, they
will quickly destroy us from the earth." 41 So they made this
decision that day: "Let us fight against anyone who comes to
attack us on the sabbath day; let us not all die as our kindred died in their hiding places."
42 Then there united with them a company of Hasideans,
mighty warriors of Israel, all who offered themselves willingly for the law. 43 And all who became fugitives to escape
their troubles joined them and reinforced them. 44 They organized an army, and struck down sinners in their anger and
renegades in their wrath; the survivors fled to the Gentiles
for safety. 45 And Mattathias and his friends went around
and tore down the altars; 46 they forcibly circumcised all the
uncircumcised boys that they found within the borders of

NEW AMERICAN BIBLE

die without reproach; heaven and earth are our witnesses
that you destroy us unjustly." 38 So the officers and soldiers
attacked them on the sabbath, and they died with their
wives, their children and their cattle, to the number of a
thousand persons.
39 When Mattathias and his friends heard of it, they
mourned deeply for them. 40 "If we all do as our kinsmen
have done," they said to one another, "and do not fight
against the Gentiles for our lives and our traditions, they will
soon destroy us from the earth." 41 On that day they came to
this decision: "Let us fight against anyone who attacks us on
the sabbath, so that we may not all die as our kinsmen died
in the hiding places."
42 Then they were joined by a group of Hasideans, valiant
Israelites, all of them devout followers of the law. 43 And all
those who were fleeing from the disaster joined them and
supported them. 44 They gathered an army and struck down
sinners in their anger and lawbreakers in their wrath, and
the survivors fled to the Gentiles for safety. 45 Mattathias
and his friends went about and tore down the pagan altars;
46 they also forcibly circumcised any uncircumcised boys
whom they found in the territory of Israel. 47 They put to

NEW JERUSALEM BIBLE

37 They only said, 'Let us all die innocent; let heaven and
earth bear witness that you are massacring us with no pretence of justice.' 38 The attack was pressed home on the
Sabbath itself, and they were slaughtered, with their wives
and children and cattle, to the number of one thousand persons.
39 When the news reached Mattathias and his friends, they
mourned them bitterly 40 and said to one another, 'If we all
do as our brothers have done, and refuse to fight the gentiles
for our lives and institutions, they will only destroy us the
sooner from the earth.' 41 So then and there they came to
this decision, 'If anyone attacks us on the Sabbath day, whoever he may be, we shall resist him; we must not all be
killed, as our brothers were in the hiding places.'
42 Soon they were joined by the Hasidaean party,[a] stout
fighting men of Israel, each one a volunteer on the side of
the Law. 43 All the refugees from the persecution rallied to
them, giving them added support. 44 They organised themselves into an armed force, striking down the sinners in their
anger, and the renegades in their fury, and those who
escaped them fled to the gentiles for safety. 45 Mattathias
and his friends made a tour, overthrowing the altars 46 and
forcibly circumcising all the boys they found uncircumcised

[a] **2** lit. 'the devout'. They soon split into two groups, the Pharisees and the Essenes.

GREEK OLD TESTAMENT

47 καὶ ἐδίωξαν τοὺς υἱοὺς τῆς ὑπερηφανίας, καὶ κατευοδώθη
τὸ ἔργον ἐν χειρὶ αὐτῶν· 48 καὶ ἀντελάβοντο τοῦ νόμου ἐκ
χειρὸς τῶν ἐθνῶν καὶ τῶν βασιλέων καὶ οὐκ ἔδωκαν κέρας τῷ
ἁμαρτωλῷ.
49 Καὶ ἤγγισαν αἱ ἡμέραι Ματταθιου ἀποθανεῖν, καὶ εἶπεν
τοῖς υἱοῖς αὐτοῦ Νῦν ἐστηρίσθη ὑπερηφανία καὶ ἐλεγμὸς καὶ
καιρὸς καταστροφῆς καὶ ὀργὴ θυμοῦ. 50 νῦν, τέκνα, ζηλώ-
σατε τῷ νόμῳ καὶ δότε τὰς ψυχὰς ὑμῶν ὑπὲρ διαθήκης
πατέρων ἡμῶν 51 καὶ μνήσθητε τὰ ἔργα τῶν πατέρων, ἃ
ἐποίησαν ἐν ταῖς γενεαῖς αὐτῶν, καὶ δέξασθε δόξαν μεγάλην καὶ ὄνομα αἰώνιον. 52 Αβρααμ οὐχὶ ἐν πειρασμῷ εὑρέθη
πιστός, καὶ ἐλογίσθη αὐτῷ εἰς δικαιοσύνην; 53 Ιωσηφ ἐν
καιρῷ στενοχωρίας αὐτοῦ ἐφύλαξεν ἐντολὴν καὶ ἐγένετο
κύριος Αἰγύπτου. 54 Φινεες ὁ πατὴρ ἡμῶν ἐν τῷ ζηλῶσαι
ζῆλον ἔλαβεν διαθήκην ἱερωσύνης αἰωνίας. 55 Ἰησοῦς ἐν τῷ
πληρῶσαι λόγον ἐγένετο κριτὴς ἐν Ισραηλ. 56 Χαλεβ ἐν τῷ
μαρτύρασθαι ἐν τῇ ἐκκλησίᾳ ἔλαβεν γῆς κληρονομίαν.
57 Δαυιδ ἐν τῷ ἐλέει αὐτοῦ ἐκληρονόμησεν θρόνον βασιλείας
εἰς αἰῶνας. 58 Ηλιας ἐν τῷ ζηλῶσαι ζῆλον νόμου ἀνελήμφθη
εἰς τὸν οὐρανόν. 59 Ανανιας, Αζαριας, Μισαηλ πιστεύσαντες ἐσώθησαν ἐκ φλογός. 60 Δανιηλ ἐν τῇ ἁπλότητι αὐτοῦ

KING JAMES VERSION

47 They pursued also after the proud men, and the work prospered in their hand.

48 So they recovered the law out of the hand of the Gentiles, and out of the hand of kings, neither suffered they the sinner to triumph.

49 Now when the time drew near that Mattathias should die, he said unto his sons, Now hath pride and rebuke gotten strength, and the time of destruction, and the wrath of indignation:

50 Now therefore, my sons, be ye zealous for the law, and give your lives for the covenant of your fathers.

51 Call to remembrance what acts our fathers did in their time; so shall ye receive great honour and an everlasting name.

52 Was not Abraham found faithful in temptation, and it was imputed unto him for righteousness?

53 Joseph in the time of his distress kept the commandment, and was made lord of Egypt.

54 Phinees our father in being zealous and fervent obtained the covenant of an everlasting priesthood.

55 Jesus for fulfilling the word was made a judge in Israel.

56 Caleb for bearing witness before the congregation received the heritage of the land.

57 David for being merciful possessed the throne of an everlasting kingdom.

58 Elias for being zealous and fervent for the law was taken up into heaven.

59 Ananias, Azarias, and Misael, by believing were saved out of the flame.

DOUAY OLD TESTAMENT

47 And they pursued after the children of pride, and the work prospered in their hands:

48 And they recovered the law out of the hands of the nations, and out of the hands of the kings: and they yielded not the horn to the sinner.

49 Now the days drew near that Mathathias should die, and he said to his sons: Now hath pride and chastisement gotten strength, and the time of destruction, and the wrath of indignation:

50 Now therefore, O my sons, be ye zealous for the law, and give your lives for the covenant of your fathers.

51 And call to remembrance the works of the fathers, which they have done in their generations: and you shall receive great glory, and an everlasting name.

52 Was not Abraham found faithful in temptation, and it was reputed to him unto justice?

53 Joseph in the time of his distress kept the commandment, and he was made lord of Egypt.

54 Phinees our father, by being fervent in the zeal of God, received the covenant of an everlasting priesthood.

55 Jesus, whilst he fulfilled the word, was made ruler in Israel.

56 Caleb, for bearing witness before the congregation, received an inheritance.

57 David by his mercy obtained the throne of an everlasting kingdom.

58 Elias, while he was full of zeal for the law, was taken up into heaven.

59 Ananias and Azarias and Misael by believing, were delivered out of the flame.

KNOX TRANSLATION

long, they drove the tyrant's minions before them, and to
such good purpose 48 that Gentile was none, king though he
were, could restrain the law's observance; against their
onslaught the powers of evil could not make head.
49 Meanwhile, the life of Mattathias was drawing to an
end. And this charge he gave to his sons: Here be days
when tyrant and blasphemer have their will, when all is
calamity and bitter retribution. 50 The more reason, my
sons, why you should be jealous lovers of the law, ready to
give your lives for that covenant your fathers knew. 51 Your
fathers, what deeds they did in their time! Great glory would
you win, and a deathless name, let these be your models.
52 See how Abraham was tested, and how trustfulness of his
was counted virtue in him; 53 see how Joseph in ill fortune
was true to the commandment still, and came to be ruler of
all Egypt. 54 Here was Phinees, our own father, that grew
hot in God's cause, and earned the right of priesthood
inalienable; 55 and Josue, that for his loyalty was given
command of Israel; 56 and Caleb, that spoke out in the
assembly, what broad acres were his! 57 David, for the tender heart of him, left a dynasty that fails not; 58 for Elias
heaven opened, that was champion of the law; 59 by faith
Ananias, Azarias and Misael overcame the furnace, 60 nor

TODAY'S ENGLISH VERSION

of Israel. 47 They were also successful in hunting down the
arrogant Gentile officials. 48 They rescued the Law of Moses
from the Gentiles and their kings and broke the power of the
wicked King Antiochus.

49 When the time came for Mattathias to die, he said to his
sons, "These are times of violence and distress. Arrogant
people are in control and have made us an object of ridicule.
50 But you, my sons, must be devoted to the Law and ready
to die to defend God's covenant with our ancestors.
51 Remember what our ancestors did and how much they
accomplished in their day. Follow their example, and you
will be rewarded with great glory and undying fame.
52 Remember how Abraham put his trust in the Lord when he
was tested and how the Lord was pleased with him and
accepted him. 53 Joseph, in his time of trouble, obeyed God's
commands and became ruler over the land of Egypt.
54 Phinehas, our ancestor, because of his burning devotion,
was given the promise that his descendants would always be
priests. 55 Joshua was made a judge in Israel because he
obeyed the command of Moses. 56 Caleb brought back a good
report to the community and was given a part of the land as
a reward. 57 David was made king and was given the promise that his descendants would always be kings because of
his steadfast loyalty to God. 58 Elijah, because of his great
devotion to the Law, was taken up into heaven.
59 Hananiah, Azariah, and Mishael were saved from the
flames because they had faith. 60 Daniel was a man of

NEW REVISED STANDARD VERSION

Israel. 47 They hunted down the arrogant, and the work
prospered in their hands. 48 They rescued the law out of the
hands of the Gentiles and kings, and they never let the sinner gain the upper hand.

49 Now the days drew near for Mattathias to die, and he
said to his sons: "Arrogance and scorn have now become
strong; it is a time of ruin and furious anger. 50 Now, my
children, show zeal for the law, and give your lives for the
covenant of our ancestors.

51 "Remember the deeds of the ancestors, which they did
in their generations; and you will receive great honor and
an everlasting name. 52 Was not Abraham found faithful
when tested, and it was reckoned to him as righteousness?
53 Joseph in the time of his distress kept the commandment,
and became lord of Egypt. 54 Phinehas our ancestor,
because he was deeply zealous, received the covenant of
everlasting priesthood. 55 Joshua, because he fulfilled the
command, became a judge in Israel. 56 Caleb, because he
testified in the assembly, received an inheritance in the
land. 57 David, because he was merciful, inherited the
throne of the kingdom forever. 58 Elijah, because of great
zeal for the law, was taken up into heaven. 59 Hananiah,
Azariah, and Mishael believed and were saved from the

NEW AMERICAN BIBLE

flight the arrogant, and the work prospered in their hands.
48 They saved the law from the hands of the Gentiles and of
the kings and did not let the sinner triumph. 49 When the
time came for Mattathias to die, he said to his sons:
"Arrogance and scorn have now grown strong; it is a time of
disaster and violent anger. 50 Therefore, my sons, be zealous
for the law and give your lives for the covenant of our
fathers.

51 "Remember the deeds that our fathers did in their
times,
and you shall win great glory and an everlasting
name.
52 Was not Abraham found faithful in trial,
and it was reputed to him as uprightness?
53 Joseph, when in distress, kept the commandment,
and he became master of Egypt.
54 Phinehas our father, for his burning zeal,
received the covenant of an everlasting priesthood.
55 Joshua, for executing his commission,
became a judge in Israel.
56 Caleb, for bearing witness before the assembly,
received an inheritance in the land.
57 David, for his piety,
received as a heritage a throne of everlasting royalty.
58 Elijah, for his burning zeal for the law,
was taken up to heaven.
59 Hananiah, Azariah and Mishael, for their faith,
were saved from the fire.

NEW JERUSALEM BIBLE

in the territories of Israel. 47 They hunted down the upstarts
and managed their campaign to good effect. 48 They wrested
the Law out of the control of the gentiles and the kings and
reduced the sinners to impotence.

49 As the days of Mattathias were drawing to a close, he said
to his sons, 'Arrogance and outrage are now in the ascendant;
it is a period of turmoil and bitter hatred. 50 This is the time,
my children, for you to have a burning zeal for the Law and to
give your lives for the covenant of our ancestors.

51 Remember the deeds performed by our ancestors, each
in his generation,
and you will win great honour and everlasting renown.
52 Was not Abraham tested and found faithful,
was that not considered as justifying him?
53 Joseph in the time of his distress maintained the Law,
and so became lord of Egypt.
54 Phinehas, our father, in return for his burning zeal,
received the covenant of everlasting priesthood.
55 Joshua, for carrying out his task,
became judge of Israel.
56 Caleb, for his testimony before the assembled people,
received an inheritance in the land.
57 David for his generous heart
inherited the throne of an everlasting kingdom.
58 Elijah for his consuming fervour for the Law
was caught up to heaven itself.
59 Hananiah, Azariah and Mishael, for their fidelity,
were saved from the flame.

GREEK OLD TESTAMENT

ἐρρύσθη ἐκ στόματος λεόντων. 61 καὶ οὕτως ἐννοήθητε κατὰ
γενεὰν καὶ γενεάν, ὅτι πάντες οἱ ἐλπίζοντες ἐπ' αὐτὸν οὐκ
ἀσθενήσουσιν. 62 καὶ ἀπὸ λόγων ἀνδρὸς ἁμαρτωλοῦ μὴ φοβηθῆτε, ὅτι ἡ δόξα αὐτοῦ εἰς κόπρια καὶ εἰς σκώληκας. 63 σήμερον ἐπαρθήσεται καὶ αὔριον οὐ μὴ εὑρεθῇ, ὅτι ἐπέστρεψεν
εἰς τὸν χοῦν αὐτοῦ, καὶ ὁ διαλογισμὸς αὐτοῦ ἀπολεῖται.
64 τέκνα, ἀνδρίζεσθε καὶ ἰσχύσατε ἐν τῷ νόμῳ, ὅτι ἐν αὐτῷ
δοξασθήσεσθε. 65 καὶ ἰδοὺ Συμεων ὁ ἀδελφὸς ὑμῶν, οἶδα ὅτι
ἀνὴρ βουλῆς ἐστιν, αὐτοῦ ἀκούετε πάσας τὰς ἡμέρας, αὐτὸς
ἔσται ὑμῶν πατήρ. 66 καὶ Ιουδας Μακκαβαῖος ἰσχυρὸς δυνάμει ἐκ νεότητος αὐτοῦ, αὐτὸς ἔσται ὑμῖν ἄρχων στρατιᾶς
καὶ πολεμήσει πόλεμον λαῶν. 67 καὶ ὑμεῖς προσάξετε πρὸς
ὑμᾶς πάντας τοὺς ποιητὰς τοῦ νόμου καὶ ἐκδικήσατε ἐκδίκησιν τοῦ λαοῦ ὑμῶν· 68 ἀνταπόδοτε ἀνταπόδομα τοῖς ἔθνεσιν καὶ προσέχετε εἰς πρόσταγμα τοῦ νόμου. — 69 καὶ εὐλόγησεν αὐτούς. καὶ προσετέθη πρὸς τοὺς πατέρας αὐτοῦ.
70 καὶ ἀπέθανεν ἐν τῷ ἕκτῳ καὶ τεσσαρακοστῷ καὶ ἑκατοστῷ
ἔτει καὶ ἐτάφη ἐν τάφοις πατέρων αὐτοῦ ἐν Μωδεϊν, καὶ
ἐκόψαντο αὐτὸν πᾶς Ισραηλ κοπετὸν μέγαν.

3 Καὶ ἀνέστη Ιουδας ὁ καλούμενος Μακκαβαῖος υἱὸς
αὐτοῦ ἀντ' αὐτοῦ. 2 καὶ ἐβοήθουν αὐτῷ πάντες οἱ
ἀδελφοὶ αὐτοῦ καὶ πάντες, ὅσοι ἐκολλήθησαν τῷ πατρὶ αὐτοῦ, καὶ ἐπολέμουν τὸν πόλεμον Ισραηλ μετ' εὐφροσύνης.

KING JAMES VERSION

60 Daniel for his innocency was delivered from the mouth of lions.

61 And thus consider ye throughout all ages, that none that put their trust in him shall be overcome.

62 Fear not then the words of a sinful man: for his glory shall be dung and worms.

63 To day he shall be lifted up, and to morrow he shall not be found, because he is returned into his dust, and his thought is come to nothing.

64 Wherefore, ye my sons, be valiant, and shew yourselves men in the behalf of the law; for by it shall ye obtain glory.

65 And, behold, I know that your brother Simon is a man of counsel, give ear unto him alway: he shall be a father unto you.

66 As for Judas Maccabeus, he hath been mighty and strong, even from his youth up: let him be your captain, and fight the battle of the people.

67 Take also unto you all those that observe the law, and avenge ye the wrong of your people.

68 Recompense fully the heathen, and take heed to the commandments of the law.

69 So he blessed them, and was gathered to his fathers.

70 And he died in the hundred forty and sixth year, and his sons buried him in the sepulchres of his fathers at Modin, and all Israel made great lamentation for him.

3 Then his son Judas, called Maccabeus, rose up in his stead.

2 And all his brethren helped him, and so did all they that held with his father, and they fought with cheerfulness the battle of Israel.

DOUAY OLD TESTAMENT

60 Daniel in his innocency was delivered out of the mouth of the lions.

61 And thus consider through all generations: that none that trust in him fail in strength.

62 And fear not the words of a sinful man, for his glory is dung, and worms:

63 To day he is lifted up, and to morrow he shall not be found, because he is returned into his earth; and his thought is come to nothing.

64 You therefore, my sons, take courage, and behave manfully in the law: for by it you shall be glorious.

65 And behold, I know that your brother Simon is a man of counsel: give ear to him always, and he shall be a father to you.

66 And Judas Machabeus who is valiant and strong from his youth up, let him be the leader of your army, and he shall manage the war of the people.

67 And you shall take to you all that observe the law: and revenge ye the wrong of your people.

68 Render to the Gentiles their reward, and take heed to the precepts of the law.

69 And he blessed them, and was joined to his fathers.

70 And he died in the hundred and forty-sixth year: and he was buried by his sons in the sepulchres of his fathers in Modin, and all Israel mourned for him with great mourning.

3 THEN his son Judas, called Machabeus, rose up in his stead.

2 And all his brethren helped him, and all they that had joined themselves to his father, and they fought with cheerfulness the battle of Israel.

KNOX TRANSLATION

Daniel's innocence might ravening lions devour. 61 No generation but proves it; want they never for strength that trust
in God. 62 What, would you fear the tyrant's threats? In
dung and worms his glory shall end; 63 all royal state today, and to-morrow there shall be no news of him; gone
back to the dust he came from, and all his designs brought
to nothing!

64 Nay, my sons, take courage; in the law's cause rally you,
in the law's annals you shall win renown. 65 Here is your
brother Simon, trust me, a man of prudence; to him ever give
heed, he is your father now. 66 And here is Judas Machabaeus, from boyhood's days a warrior; let him be your
leader, and fight Israel's battles. 67 All lovers of the law
make free of your fellowship; bring your country redress,
68 and pay the Gentiles what they have earned; yet heeding
ever what the law enjoins. 69 With that, he gave them his
blessing, and became part of his race. 70 He was a hundred
and forty-six years old when he died; his sons buried him
where his fathers were buried, at Modin, and great lament all
Israel made for the loss of him.

3 And now his son Judas, that was called Machabaeus,
came forward to succeed him; 2 nor any of Judas' clan,
nor any that had taken his father's part, but lent him their
aid still; right merrily they fought Israel's battle. 3 Here was

TODAY'S ENGLISH VERSION

integrity, and the Lord rescued him from the mouth of the
lions. 61 Take each of these ancestors of ours as an example,
and you will realize that no one who puts his trust in the
Lord will ever lack strength. 62 Don't be afraid of the threats
of a wicked man. Remember that he will die and all his
splendor will end with worms feeding on his decaying body.
63 Today he may be highly honored, but tomorrow he will
disappear; his body will return to the earth and his scheming
will come to an end. 64 But you, my sons, be strong and
courageous in defending the Law, because it is through the
Law that you will earn great glory.

65 "Your brother Simon is wise, so always listen to him as
you would to me. 66 Judas Maccabeus has been strong all his
life; he will be your commander and will lead you in battle
against the enemy. 67 Call everyone who obeys God's Law to
rally around you; then avenge the wrongs done to your people. 68 Pay back the Gentiles for what they have done, and
always obey the Law and its commands."

69 Then Mattathias gave them his blessing and died. 70 He
was buried in the family tomb at Modein, and all the people
of Israel went into deep mourning for him. This happened in
the year 146.[a]

3 Judas Maccabeus took the place of his father Mattathias.
2 All his brothers and all the loyal followers of his father
gave him their support, and they were happy to carry on
Israel's war.

[a] THE YEAR 146: *This corresponds to 166 B.C.*

NEW REVISED STANDARD VERSION

flame. 60 Daniel, because of his innocence, was delivered
from the mouth of the lions.

61 "And so observe, from generation to generation, that
none of those who put their trust in him will lack strength.
62 Do not fear the words of sinners, for their splendor will
turn into dung and worms. 63 Today they will be exalted, but
tomorrow they will not be found, because they will have
returned to the dust, and their plans will have perished.
64 My children, be courageous and grow strong in the law, for
by it you will gain honor.

65 "Here is your brother Simeon who, I know, is wise in
counsel; always listen to him; he shall be your father.
66 Judas Maccabeus has been a mighty warrior from his
youth; he shall command the army for you and fight the battle against the peoples.[a] 67 You shall rally around you all
who observe the law, and avenge the wrong done to your
people. 68 Pay back the Gentiles in full, and obey the commands of the law."

69 Then he blessed them, and was gathered to his ancestors. 70 He died in the one hundred forty-sixth year[b] and was
buried in the tomb of his ancestors at Modein. And all Israel
mourned for him with great lamentation.

3 Then his son Judas, who was called Maccabeus, took
command in his place. 2 All his brothers and all who
had joined his father helped him; they gladly fought for
Israel.

a Or *of the people* *b* 166 B.C.

NEW AMERICAN BIBLE

60 Daniel, for his innocence,
was delivered from the jaws of lions.
61 And so, consider this from generation to generation,
that none who hope in him shall fail in strength.
62 Do not fear the words of a sinful man,
for his glory ends in corruption and worms.
63 Today he is exalted, and tomorrow he is not to be
found,
because he has returned to his dust,
and his schemes have perished.
64 Children! be courageous and strong in keeping the law,
for by it you shall be glorified.

65 "Here is your brother Simeon who I know is a wise man;
listen to him always, and he will be a father to you. 66 And
Judas Maccabeus, a warrior from his youth, shall be the
leader of your army and direct the war against the nations.
67 You shall also gather about you all who observe the law,
and you shall avenge the wrongs of your people. 68 Pay back
the Gentiles what they deserve, and observe the precepts of
the law."

69 Then he blessed them, and he was united with his
fathers. 70 He died in the year one hundred and forty-six,
and was buried in the tombs of his fathers in Modein, and all
Israel mourned him greatly.

3 Then his son Judas, who was called Maccabeus, took his
place. 2 All his brothers and all who had joined his
father supported him, and they carried on Israel's war joyfully.

NEW JERUSALEM BIBLE

60 Daniel for his singleness of heart
was rescued from the lion's jaws.
61 Know then that, generation after generation,
no one who hopes in him will be overcome.
62 Do not fear the threats of the sinner,
all his brave show must come to the dunghill and the
worms.
63 Exalted today, tomorrow he is nowhere to be found,
for he has returned to the dust he came from
and his scheming is brought to nothing.
64 My children, be resolute and courageous for the Law,
for it will bring you glory.

65 'Here is your brother Simeon, I know he is a man of
sound judgement. Listen to him all your lives; let him take
your father's place. 66 Judas Maccabaeus, strong and brave
from his youth, let him be your general and conduct the war
against the gentiles. 67 The rest of you are to enrol in your
ranks all those who keep the Law, and to assure the
vengeance of your people. 68 Pay back the gentiles to the full,
and hold fast to the ordinance of the Law.' 69 Then he
blessed them and was joined to his ancestors. 70 He died in
the year 146 and was buried in his ancestral tomb at
Modein, and all Israel mourned him deeply.

3 His son, Judas, known as Maccabaeus, then took his
place. 2 All his brothers, and all who had attached themselves to his father, supported him, and they fought for Israel
with a will.

GREEK OLD TESTAMENT

3 καὶ ἐπλάτυνεν δόξαν τῷ λαῷ αὐτοῦ καὶ ἐνεδύσατο θώρακα
ὡς γίγας καὶ συνεζώσατο τὰ σκεύη τὰ πολεμικὰ αὐτοῦ καὶ
πολέμους συνεστήσατο σκεπάζων παρεμβολὴν ἐν ῥομφαίᾳ.
4 καὶ ὡμοιώθη λέοντι ἐν τοῖς ἔργοις αὐτοῦ καὶ ὡς σκύμνος
ἐρευγόμενος εἰς θήραν. 5 καὶ ἐδίωξεν ἀνόμους ἐξερευνῶν
καὶ τοὺς ταράσσοντας τὸν λαὸν αὐτοῦ ἐφλόγισεν. 6 καὶ
συνεστάλησαν ἄνομοι ἀπὸ τοῦ φόβου αὐτοῦ, καὶ πάντες οἱ
ἐργάται τῆς ἀνομίας συνεταράχθησαν, καὶ εὐοδώθη σωτηρία
ἐν χειρὶ αὐτοῦ. 7 καὶ ἐπίκρανεν βασιλεῖς πολλοὺς καὶ εὔ-
φρανεν τὸν Ιακωβ ἐν τοῖς ἔργοις αὐτοῦ, καὶ ἕως τοῦ αἰῶνος
τὸ μνημόσυνον αὐτοῦ εἰς εὐλογίαν. 8 καὶ διῆλθεν ἐν πόλεσιν
Ιουδα καὶ ἐξωλέθρευσεν ἀσεβεῖς ἐξ αὐτῆς καὶ ἀπέστρεψεν
ὀργὴν ἀπὸ Ισραηλ 9 καὶ ὠνομάσθη ἕως ἐσχάτου γῆς καὶ
συνήγαγεν ἀπολλυμένους.

10 Καὶ συνήγαγεν Ἀπολλώνιος ἔθνη καὶ ἀπὸ Σαμαρείας
δύναμιν μεγάλην τοῦ πολεμῆσαι πρὸς τὸν Ισραηλ. 11 καὶ
ἔγνω Ιουδας καὶ ἐξῆλθεν εἰς συνάντησιν αὐτῷ καὶ ἐπάταξεν
αὐτὸν καὶ ἀπέκτεινεν· καὶ ἔπεσον τραυματίαι πολλοί, καὶ οἱ
ἐπίλοιποι ἔφυγον. 12 καὶ ἔλαβον τὰ σκῦλα αὐτῶν, καὶ τὴν
μάχαιραν Ἀπολλωνίου ἔλαβεν Ιουδας καὶ ἦν πολεμῶν ἐν

KING JAMES VERSION

3 So he gat his people great honour, and put on a breastplate as a giant, and girt his warlike harness about him, and he made battles, protecting the host with his sword.

4 In his acts he was like a lion, and like a lion's whelp roaring for his prey.

5 For He pursued the wicked, and sought them out, and burnt up those that vexed his people.

6 Wherefore the wicked shrunk for fear of him, and all the workers of iniquity were troubled, because salvation prospered in his hand.

7 He grieved also many kings, and made Jacob glad with his acts, and his memorial is blessed for ever.

8 Moreover he went through the cities of Juda, destroying the ungodly out of them, and turning away wrath from Israel:

9 So that he was renowned unto the utmost part of the earth, and he received unto him such as were ready to perish.

10 Then Apollonius gathered the Gentiles together, and a great host out of Samaria, to fight against Israel.

11 Which thing when Judas perceived, he went forth to meet him, and so he smote him, and slew him: many also fell down slain, but the rest fled.

12 Wherefore Judas took their spoils, and Apollonius' sword also, and therewith he fought all his life long.

DOUAY OLD TESTAMENT

3 And he got his people great honour, and put on a breastplate as a giant, and girt his warlike armour about him in battles, and protected the camp with his sword.

4 In his acts he was like a lion, and like a lion's whelp roaring for his prey.

5 And he pursued the wicked and sought them out, and them that troubled his people he burnt with fire:

6 And his enemies were driven away for fear of him, and all the workers of iniquity were troubled: and salvation prospered in his hand.

7 And he grieved many kings, and made Jacob glad with his works, and his memory is blessed for ever.

8 And he went through the cities of Juda, and destroyed the wicked out of them, and turned away wrath from Israel.

9 And he was renowned even to the utmost part of the earth, and he gathered them that were perishing.

10 And Apollonius gathered together the Gentiles, and a numerous and great army from Samaria, to make war against Israel.

11 And Judas understood it, and went forth to meet him: and he overthrew him, and killed him: and many fell down slain, and the rest fled away.

12 And he took their spoils, and Judas took the sword of Apollonius, and fought with it all his lifetime.

KNOX TRANSLATION

one that brought his race renown; as great a warrior as ever
donned breastplate, or armed himself for the fight, or drew
sword to save his camp from peril; 4 lion-hearted his deeds,
not lion itself more relentless in pursuit. 5 Traitors he ever
sought out and hunted down, ever with fire-brand the
oppressors of his people dislodged, 6 till enemy was none but
was daunted by the fear of him, traitor was none but fled in
confusion, so well sped he the work of deliverance. 7 Great
deeds, that kings rued bitterly, Jacob with exultation heard,
posterity holds blessed evermore! 8 From city to city he went,
ridding Juda of its law-breakers, averting the vengeance guilt
of theirs had deserved; 9 no corner of earth but he was
renowned there, for one that had been able to rally a doomed
people.

10 How sped Apollonius, that mustered a great force, of
Gentiles and Samaritans both, to fight against Israel? 11 No
sooner Judas heard of it, than he met and routed and slew
him; fell many and fled more, 12 leaving their spoils behind
them. The sword of Apollonius Judas himself carried away;
and this it was he evermore used in battle.

TODAY'S ENGLISH VERSION

3 Judas brought greater glory to his people.
In his armor, he was like a giant.
He took up his weapons and went to war;
with his own sword he defended his camp.
4 He was like a ferocious lion roaring as it attacks.
5 Judas hunted down those who broke the Law
and set fire to all who oppressed his people.
6 In fear of him, lawless men huddled together in terror,
not knowing which way to turn.
He advanced the cause of freedom by what he did.
7 He made life miserable for many kings,
but brought joy to the people of Israel.
We will praise him forever for what he did.
8 He went through the towns of Judea
and destroyed all the godless men.
He relieved Israel of its terrible suffering.[a]
9 His fame spread to the ends of the earth,
as he gathered together those who were threatened
with death.

10 Then Apollonius assembled a Gentile army, including a
large force from Samaria, to attack the people of Israel.
11 When Judas learned of this, he marched out to battle,
defeated the army, and killed Apollonius. Many Gentiles lost
their lives, and the rest fled. 12 When the spoils of war were
collected, Judas took the sword of Apollonius and used it in
battle until the day he died.

[a] relieved Israel of its terrible suffering; *or* saved Israel from God's anger.

NEW REVISED STANDARD VERSION

3 He extended the glory of his people.
Like a giant he put on his breastplate;
he bound on his armor of war and waged battles,
protecting the camp by his sword.
4 He was like a lion in his deeds,
like a lion's cub roaring for prey.
5 He searched out and pursued those who broke the law;
he burned those who troubled his people.
6 Lawbreakers shrank back for fear of him;
all the evildoers were confounded;
and deliverance prospered by his hand.
7 He embittered many kings,
but he made Jacob glad by his deeds,
and his memory is blessed forever.
8 He went through the cities of Judah;
he destroyed the ungodly out of the land;[a]
thus he turned away wrath from Israel.
9 He was renowned to the ends of the earth;
he gathered in those who were perishing.

10 Apollonius now gathered together Gentiles and a large
force from Samaria to fight against Israel. 11 When Judas
learned of it, he went out to meet him, and he defeated and
killed him. Many were wounded and fell, and the rest fled.
12 Then they seized their spoils; and Judas took the sword of
Apollonius, and used it in battle the rest of his life.

[a] Gk *it*

NEW AMERICAN BIBLE

3 He spread abroad the glory of his people,
and put on his breastplate like a giant.
He armed himself with weapons of war;
he planned battles and protected the camp with his
sword.
4 In his actions he was like a lion,
like a young lion roaring for prey.
5 He pursued the wicked, hunting them out,
and those who troubled his people he destroyed by
fire.
6 The lawbreakers were cowed by fear of him,
and all evildoers were dismayed.
By his hand redemption was happily achieved,
7 and he afflicted many kings;
He made Jacob glad by his deeds,
and his memory is blessed forever.
8 He went about the cities of Judah
destroying the impious there.
He turned away wrath from Israel
9 and was renowned to the ends of the earth;
he gathered together those who were perishing.

10 Then Apollonius gathered the Gentiles, together with a
large army from Samaria, to fight against Israel. 11 When
Judas learned of it, he went out to meet him and defeated
and killed him. Many fell wounded, and the rest fled.
12 Their possessions were seized and the sword of Apollonius
was taken by Judas, who fought with it the rest of his life.

NEW JERUSALEM BIBLE

3 He extended the fame of his people.
Like a giant, he put on the breastplate
and buckled on his war harness;
he engaged in battle after battle,
protecting the ranks with his sword.
4 He was like a lion in his exploits,
like a young lion roaring over its prey.
5 He pursued and tracked down the renegades,
he consigned those who troubled his people to the
flames.
6 The renegades quailed with the terror he inspired,
all evil-doers were utterly confounded,
and deliverance went forward under his leadership.
7 He brought bitterness to many a king
and rejoicing to Jacob by his deeds,
his memory is blessed for ever and ever.
8 He went through the towns of Judah
eliminating the irreligious from them,
and diverted the Retribution from Israel.
9 His name resounded to the ends of the earth,
he rallied those who were on the point of perishing.

10[a] Next, Apollonius mustered the gentiles and a large force
from Samaria to make war on Israel. 11 When Judas learned
of it, he went out to meet him and routed and killed him.
Many fell wounded, and the survivors took to flight. 12 Their
spoils were seized and the sword of Apollonius was taken by
Judas, who used it to fight with throughout his life. 13 On

[a] **3** 3:10seq. // 2 M 8.

GREEK OLD TESTAMENT

αὐτῇ πάσας τὰς ἡμέρας. 13 καὶ ἤκουσεν Σήρων ὁ ἄρχων τῆς
δυνάμεως Συρίας ὅτι ἤθροισεν Ιουδας ἄθροισμα καὶ ἐκκλησίαν πιστῶν μετ᾽ αὐτοῦ καὶ ἐκπορευομένων εἰς πόλεμον,
14 καὶ εἶπεν Ποιήσω ἐμαυτῷ ὄνομα καὶ δοξασθήσομαι ἐν τῇ
βασιλείᾳ καὶ πολεμήσω τὸν Ιουδαν καὶ τοὺς σὺν αὐτῷ τοὺς
ἐξουδενοῦντας τὸν λόγον τοῦ βασιλέως. 15 καὶ προσέθετο
καὶ ἀνέβη μετ᾽ αὐτοῦ παρεμβολὴ ἀσεβῶν ἰσχυρὰ βοηθῆσαι
αὐτῷ ποιῆσαι τὴν ἐκδίκησιν ἐν υἱοῖς Ισραηλ. 16 καὶ ἤγγισεν
ἕως ἀναβάσεως Βαιθωρων, καὶ ἐξῆλθεν Ιουδας εἰς συνάντησιν αὐτῷ ὀλιγοστός. 17 ὡς δὲ εἶδον τὴν παρεμβολὴν
ἐρχομένην εἰς συνάντησιν αὐτῶν, εἶπον τῷ Ιουδα Τί δυνησόμεθα ὀλιγοστοὶ ὄντες πολεμῆσαι πρὸς πλῆθος τοσοῦτο
ἰσχυρόν; καὶ ἡμεῖς ἐκλελύμεθα ἀσιτοῦντες σήμερον. 18 καὶ
εἶπεν Ιουδας Εὔκοπόν ἐστιν συγκλεισθῆναι πολλοὺς ἐν
χερσὶν ὀλίγων, καὶ οὐκ ἔστιν διαφορὰ ἐναντίον τοῦ οὐρανοῦ
σῴζειν ἐν πολλοῖς ἢ ἐν ὀλίγοις. 19 ὅτι οὐκ ἐν πλήθει δυνάμεως νίκη πολέμου ἐστίν, ἀλλ᾽ ἐκ τοῦ οὐρανοῦ ἡ ἰσχύς.
20 αὐτοὶ ἔρχονται ἐφ᾽ ἡμᾶς ἐν πλήθει ὕβρεως καὶ ἀνομίας
τοῦ ἐξᾶραι ἡμᾶς καὶ τὰς γυναῖκας ἡμῶν καὶ τὰ τέκνα ἡμῶν
τοῦ σκυλεῦσαι ἡμᾶς, 21 ἡμεῖς δὲ πολεμοῦμεν περὶ τῶν
ψυχῶν ἡμῶν καὶ τῶν νομίμων ἡμῶν. 22 καὶ αὐτὸς συντρίψει
αὐτοὺς πρὸ προσώπου ἡμῶν, ὑμεῖς δὲ μὴ φοβεῖσθε ἀπ᾽
αὐτῶν. 23 ὡς δὲ ἐπαύσατο λαλῶν, ἐνήλατο εἰς αὐτοὺς ἄφνω,
καὶ συνετρίβη Σήρων καὶ ἡ παρεμβολὴ αὐτοῦ ἐνώπιον αὐτοῦ.

KING JAMES VERSION

13 Now when Seron, a prince of the army of Syria, heard say that Judas had gathered unto him a multitude and company of the faithful to go out with him to war;

14 He said, I will get me a name and honour in the kingdom; for I will go fight with Judas and them that are with him, who despise the king's commandment.

15 So he made him ready to go up, and there went with him a mighty host of the ungodly to help him, and to be avenged of the children of Israel.

16 And when he came near to the going up of Bethhoron, Judas went forth to meet him with a small company:

17 Who, when they saw the host coming to meet them, said unto Judas, How shall we be able, being so few, to fight against so great a multitude *and* so strong, seeing we are ready to faint with fasting all this day?

18 Unto whom Judas answered, It is no hard matter for many to be shut up in the hands of a few; and with *the God of* heaven it is all one, to deliver with a great multitude, or a small company:

19 For the victory of battle standeth not in the multitude of an host; but strength cometh from heaven.

20 They come against us in much pride and iniquity to destroy us, and our wives and children, and to spoil us:

21 But we fight for our lives and our laws.

22 Wherefore the Lord himself will overthrow them before our face: and as for you, be ye not afraid of them.

23 Now as soon as he had left off speaking, he leapt suddenly upon them, and so Seron and his host was overthrown before him.

DOUAY OLD TESTAMENT

13 And Seron captain of the army of Syria heard that Judas had assembled a company of the faithful, and a congregation with him,

14 And he said: I will get me a name, and will be glorified in the kingdom, and will overthrow Judas, and those that are with him, that have despised the edict of the king.

15 And he made himself ready: and the host of the wicked went up with him, strong succours, to be revenged of the children of Israel.

16 And they approached even as far as Bethoron: and Judas went forth to meet him, with a small company.

17 But when they saw the army coming to meet them, they said to Judas: How shall we, being few, be able to fight against so great a multitude and so strong, and we are ready to faint with fasting to day?

18 And Judas said: It is an easy matter for many to be shut up in the hands of a few: and there is no difference in the sight of the God of heaven to deliver with a great multitude, or with a small company:

19 For the success of war is not in the multitude of the army, but strength cometh from heaven.

20 They come against us with an insolent multitude, and with pride, to destroy us, and our wives, and our children, and to take our spoils.

21 But we will fight for our lives and our laws:

22 And the Lord himself will overthrow them before our face: but as for you, fear them not.

23 And as soon as he had made an end of speaking, he rushed suddenly upon them: and Seron and his host were overthrown before him:

KNOX TRANSLATION

13 And next it was Seron, captain of the armies in Syria,
heard what a great retinue and faithful following Judas had;
14 and nothing would serve, but he must win renown and
high favour at court by crushing Judas, and all other his
companions that defied the king's edict. 15 So he made all
ready, and marched in with a strong muster of the ungodly
at his heels, to be even with the men of Israel. 16 As far as
Bethoron pass they reached, and there Judas met them with
his company, no better than a handful. 17 These, when they
saw such a host facing them, were for counsels of prudence;
What, they said to Judas, should we offer battle to foes so
many and so strong, faint as we be from a day of hungry
marching? 18 Nay, said Judas, nothing forbids great numbers
should be at the mercy of small; what matter makes it to the
God of heaven, few be his soldiers or many when he grants
deliverance? 19 Armed might avails not to win the day; victory is from above. 20 What though they come to meet us in
the proud confidence of superior strength, and think it an
easy matter to slay us, slay our wives and children, plunder
our goods? 21 Life and loyalty at stake, we will offer battle
none the less; 22 and he, the Lord, will crush them to earth
at our coming; never be afraid. 23 And with that, all
unawares, he fell upon Seron and his army, that were
crushed, sure enough, by his onslaught; 24 all down the pass

TODAY'S ENGLISH VERSION

13 Seron, the general of the Syrian forces, learned that
Judas had gathered together an army, consisting of a band of
loyal men who were ready to fight under his command.
14 Seron said to himself, "I will make a reputation for myself
throughout the empire by defeating Judas and his men, who
have no respect for the king's command." 15 Then he began
a new campaign against Judas and was joined by a strong
force of godless men who were eager to help him take
vengeance on Israel. 16 When he approached the pass at
Beth Horon, Judas went out to meet him with a small group
of men. 17 When Judas' men saw the army coming against
them, they asked, "How can our little group of men fight an
army as big as that? Besides, we have not eaten all day, and
we are tired!"

18 "It is not difficult," Judas answered, "for a small group
to overpower a large one. It makes no difference to the Lord
whether we are rescued by many people or by just a few.
19 Victory in battle does not depend on who has the largest
army; it is the Lord's power that determines the outcome.
20 Our enemies are coming against us with great violence,
intending to plunder our possessions and kill our wives and
children. 21 But we are fighting for our lives and for our religion. 22 When we attack, the Lord will crush our enemies, so
don't be afraid of them."

23 As soon as Judas had finished speaking, he and his men
made a sudden attack against Seron and his army and

NEW REVISED STANDARD VERSION

13 When Seron, the commander of the Syrian army, heard
that Judas had gathered a large company, including a body
of faithful soldiers who stayed with him and went out to battle, 14 he said, "I will make a name for myself and win honor
in the kingdom. I will make war on Judas and his companions, who scorn the king's command." 15 Once again a
strong army of godless men went up with him to help him,
to take vengeance on the Israelites.

16 When he approached the ascent of Beth-horon, Judas
went out to meet him with a small company. 17 But when
they saw the army coming to meet them, they said to Judas,
"How can we, few as we are, fight against so great and so
strong a multitude? And we are faint, for we have eaten
nothing today." 18 Judas replied, "It is easy for many to be
hemmed in by few, for in the sight of Heaven there is no difference between saving by many or by few. 19 It is not on the
size of the army that victory in battle depends, but strength
comes from Heaven. 20 They come against us in great insolence and lawlessness to destroy us and our wives and our
children, and to despoil us; 21 but we fight for our lives and
our laws. 22 He himself will crush them before us; as for you,
do not be afraid of them."

23 When he finished speaking, he rushed suddenly
against Seron and his army, and they were crushed before

NEW AMERICAN BIBLE

13 But Seron, commander of the Syrian army, heard that
Judas had gathered many about him, an assembly of faithful
men ready for war. 14 So he said, "I will make a name for
myself and win glory in the kingdom by defeating Judas and
his followers, who have despised the king's command."
15 And again a large company of renegades advanced with
him to help him take revenge on the Israelites. 16 When he
reached the ascent of Beth-horon, Judas went out to meet
him with a few men. 17 But when they saw the army coming
against them, they said to Judas: "How can we, few as we
are, fight such a mighty host as this? Besides, we are weak
today from fasting." 18 But Judas said: "It is easy for many
to be overcome by a few; in the sight of Heaven there is no
difference between deliverance by many or by few; 19 for victory in war does not depend upon the size of the army, but
on strength that comes from Heaven. 20 With great presumption and lawlessness they come against us to destroy us and
our wives and children and to despoil us; 21 but we are fighting for our lives and our laws. 22 He himself will crush them
before us; so do not be afraid of them." 23 When he finished
speaking, he rushed suddenly upon Seron and his army, who

NEW JERUSALEM BIBLE

hearing that Judas had raised a mixed force of believers and
seasoned fighters, 14 Seron, commander of the Syrian troops,
said, 'I shall make a name for myself and gain honour in the
kingdom if I fight Judas and those supporters of his who are
so contemptuous of the king's orders.' 15 He therefore
launched another expedition, with a strong army of unbelievers to support him in taking revenge on the Israelites.
16 He had nearly reached the descent of Beth-Horon when
Judas went out to confront him with a handful of men.
17 But as soon as these saw the force advancing to meet
them, they said to Judas, 'How can we, few as we are,
engage such overwhelming numbers? We are exhausted as it
is, not having had anything to eat today.' 18 'It is easy',
Judas answered, 'for a great number to be defeated by a few;
indeed, in the sight of Heaven, deliverance, whether by many
or by few, is all one; 19 for victory in war does not depend on
the size of the fighting force: Heaven accords the strength.
20 They are coming against us in full-blown insolence and
lawlessness to destroy us, our wives and our children, and to
plunder us; 21 but we are fighting for our lives and our laws,
22 and he will crush them before our eyes; do not be afraid of
them.' 23 When he had finished speaking, he made a sudden
sally against Seron and his force and overwhelmed them.

GREEK OLD TESTAMENT

24 καὶ ἐδίωκον αὐτὸν ἐν τῇ καταβάσει Βαιθωρων ἕως τοῦ
πεδίου· καὶ ἔπεσον ἀπ᾽ αὐτῶν εἰς ἄνδρας ὀκτακοσίους, οἱ δὲ
λοιποὶ ἔφυγον εἰς γῆν Φυλιστιιμ. 25 καὶ ἤρξατο ὁ φόβος
Ιουδου καὶ τῶν ἀδελφῶν αὐτοῦ καὶ ἡ πτόη ἐπέπιπτεν ἐπὶ τὰ
ἔθνη τὰ κύκλῳ αὐτῶν· 26 καὶ ἤγγισεν ἕως τοῦ βασιλέως τὸ
ὄνομα αὐτοῦ, καὶ ὑπὲρ τῶν παρατάξεων Ιουδου ἐξηγεῖτο τὰ
ἔθνη.

27 Ὡς δὲ ἤκουσεν ὁ βασιλεὺς Ἀντίοχος τοὺς λόγους τούτους, ὠργίσθη θυμῷ καὶ ἀπέστειλεν καὶ συνήγαγεν τὰς
δυνάμεις πάσας τῆς βασιλείας αὐτοῦ, παρεμβολὴν ἰσχυρὰν
σφόδρα. 28 καὶ ἤνοιξεν τὸ γαζοφυλάκιον αὐτοῦ καὶ ἔδωκεν
ὀψώνια ταῖς δυνάμεσιν εἰς ἐνιαυτὸν καὶ ἐνετείλατο αὐτοῖς
εἶναι ἑτοίμους εἰς πᾶσαν χρείαν. 29 καὶ εἶδεν ὅτι ἐξέλιπεν
τὸ ἀργύριον ἐκ τῶν θησαυρῶν καὶ οἱ φόροι τῆς χώρας ὀλίγοι
χάριν τῆς διχοστασίας καὶ πληγῆς, ἧς κατεσκεύασεν ἐν τῇ
γῇ τοῦ ἆραι τὰ νόμιμα, ἃ ἦσαν ἀφ᾽ ἡμερῶν τῶν πρώτων,
30 καὶ εὐλαβήθη μὴ οὐκ ἔχῃ ὡς ἅπαξ καὶ δὶς εἰς τὰς δαπάνας
καὶ τὰ δόματα, ἃ ἐδίδου ἔμπροσθεν δαψιλῇ χειρὶ καὶ ἐπερίσ-
σευσεν ὑπὲρ τοὺς βασιλεῖς τοὺς ἔμπροσθεν, 31 καὶ ἠπορεῖτο
τῇ ψυχῇ αὐτοῦ σφόδρα καὶ ἐβουλεύσατο τοῦ πορευθῆναι εἰς
τὴν Περσίδα καὶ λαβεῖν τοὺς φόρους τῶν χωρῶν καὶ συναγαγεῖν ἀργύριον πολύ. 32 καὶ κατέλιπεν Λυσίαν ἄνθρωπον
ἔνδοξον καὶ ἀπὸ γένους τῆς βασιλείας ἐπὶ τῶν πραγμάτων
τοῦ βασιλέως ἀπὸ τοῦ ποταμοῦ Εὐφράτου καὶ ἕως ὁρίων

KING JAMES VERSION

24 And they pursued them from the going down of Bethhoron unto the plain, where were slain about eight hundred men of them; and the residue fled into the land of the Philistines.

25 Then began the fear of Judas and his brethren, and an exceeding great dread, to fall upon the nations round about them:

26 Insomuch as his fame came unto the king, and all nations talked of the battles of Judas.

27 Now when king Antiochus heard these things, he was full of indignation: wherefore he sent and gathered together all the forces of his realm, *even* a very strong army.

28 He opened also his treasure, and gave his soldiers pay for a year, commanding them to be ready whensoever he should need them.

29 Nevertheless, when he saw that the money of his treasures failed, and that the tributes in the country were small, because of the dissension and plague, which he had brought upon the land in taking away the laws which had been of old time;

30 He feared that he should not be able to bear the charges any longer, nor to have such gifts to give so liberally as he did before: for he had abounded above the kings that were before him.

31 Wherefore, being greatly perplexed in his mind, he determined to go into Persia, there to take the tributes of the countries, and to gather much money.

32 So he left Lysias, a nobleman, and one of the blood royal, to oversee the affairs of the king from the river Euphrates unto the borders of Egypt:

DOUAY OLD TESTAMENT

24 And he pursued him by the descent of Bethoron even to the plain, and there fell of them eight hundred men, and the rest fled into the land of the Philistines.

25 And the fear of Judas and of his brethren, and the dread *of them* fell upon all the nations round about them.

26 And his fame came to the king, and all nations told of the battles of Judas.

27 Now when king Antiochus heard these words, he was angry in his mind: and he sent and gathered the forces of all his kingdom, an exceeding strong army.

28 And he opened his treasury, and gave out pay to the army for a year: and he commanded them, that they should be ready for all things.

29 And he perceived that the money of his treasures failed, and that the tributes of the country were small because of the dissension, and the evil that he had brought upon the land, that he might take away the laws of old times:

30 And he feared that he should not have as formerly enough, for charges and gifts, which he had given before with a liberal hand: for he had abounded more than the kings that had been before him.

31 And he was greatly perplexed in mind, and purposed to go into Persia, and to take tributes of the countries, and to gather much money.

32 And he left Lysias, a nobleman of the blood royal, to oversee the affairs of the kingdom, from the river Euphrates even to the river of Egypt:

KNOX TRANSLATION

of Bethoron he gave them chase, down into the plain, and
eight hundred of them had fallen before ever they took
refuge in the country of the Philistines.

25 By this, the neighbouring peoples had begun to take
alarm, so formidable did Judas and his brethren appear to
them, 26 and the renown of him reached the king's court; all
the world was talking of Judas and his victories. 27 An angry
man was king Antiochus when the news came to him; he
sent word round, and had all his army summoned together,
a brave array, be sure of it. 28 The treasury must be opened,
to provide the troops with a whole year's pay, and keep them
in readiness for every need. 29 Why, what was this? So heavily had Juda suffered, so great the discord he had aroused by
the abolishing of its ancient usages, that scant revenue had
come in from it, and the treasury was in default! 30 Whence,
now, to defray the cost of that largesse he had made so
often, and with so lavish a hand? Never was king before him
could rival his munificence.

31 Here was the king in great confusion of mind; and his
thought was, to march into Persia and take toll of those
countries; great store of money he might there amass. 32 He
left Lysias behind, that was a man of high rank and royal
blood; he was to administer all the business of the kingdom,
from Euphrates down to the Brook of Egypt, 33 and have

TODAY'S ENGLISH VERSION

crushed them. 24 They pursued them down the pass at Beth
Horon to the plain and killed about 800 men. Those who
escaped fled to Philistia. 25 After that, Gentiles everywhere
began to be afraid of Judas and his brothers. 26 His fame
reached the ears of King Antiochus, and people in every
nation talked about Judas and his victories.
27 When Antiochus heard what had happened, he was furious. He ordered all the armies of his empire to assemble in
one huge force. 28 From his treasury he paid a full year's
wages to his soldiers and ordered them to be prepared for
any emergency. 29 But then he found that the funds in his
treasury were exhausted. Income from taxes had decreased
because of the disorder and the troubles he had brought on
the world by doing away with the laws which had been in
force from the earliest times. 30 Antiochus had always given
presents more lavishly than earlier kings, but now he was
worried that he might not be able to continue this, or even to
meet expenses—this had happened once or twice before.
31 He was very disturbed; but finally he decided to go to
Persia, collect the taxes from the provinces there, and bring
together a large sum of ready cash.
32 He appointed Lysias, an important man who had been
granted the title "Relative of the King," as governor to take
care of the king's affairs in the whole territory between the
Euphrates River and the Egyptian border. 33 The king also

NEW REVISED STANDARD VERSION

him. 24 They pursued them[a] down the descent of Beth-horon
to the plain; eight hundred of them fell, and the rest fled into
the land of the Philistines. 25 Then Judas and his brothers
began to be feared, and terror fell on the Gentiles all around
them. 26 His fame reached the king, and the Gentiles talked
of the battles of Judas.
27 When King Antiochus heard these reports, he was
greatly angered; and he sent and gathered all the forces of
his kingdom, a very strong army. 28 He opened his coffers
and gave a year's pay to his forces, and ordered them to be
ready for any need. 29 Then he saw that the money in the
treasury was exhausted, and that the revenues from the
country were small because of the dissension and disaster
that he had caused in the land by abolishing the laws that
had existed from the earliest days. 30 He feared that he might
not have such funds as he had before for his expenses and
for the gifts that he used to give more lavishly than preceding kings. 31 He was greatly perplexed in mind; then he
determined to go to Persia and collect the revenues from
those regions and raise a large fund.
32 He left Lysias, a distinguished man of royal lineage, in
charge of the king's affairs from the river Euphrates to the

a Other ancient authorities read *him*

NEW AMERICAN BIBLE

were crushed before him. 24 He pursued Seron down the
descent of Beth-horon into the plain. About eight hundred of
their men fell, and the rest fled to the country of the
Philistines. 25 Then Judas and his brothers began to be
feared, and dread fell upon the Gentiles about them. 26 His
fame reached the king, and all the Gentiles talked about the
battles of Judas.
27 When Antiochus heard about these events, he was
angry; so he ordered a muster of all the forces of his kingdom, a very strong army. 28 He opened his treasure chests,
gave his soldiers a year's pay, and commanded them to be
prepared for anything. 29 He then found that this exhausted
the money in his treasury; moreover the income from the
province was small, because of the dissension and distress
he had brought upon the land by abolishing the laws which
had been in effect from of old. 30 He feared that, as had happened more than once, he would not have enough for his
expenses and for the gifts that he had previously given with
a more liberal hand than the preceding kings. 31 Greatly perplexed, he decided to go to Persia and levy tribute on those
provinces, and so raise a large sum of money. 32 He left
Lysias, a nobleman of royal blood, in charge of the king's
affairs from the Euphrates River to the frontier of Egypt,

NEW JERUSALEM BIBLE

24 Judas pursued them down from Beth-Horon as far as the
plain. About eight hundred of their men fell, and the rest
took refuge in the country of the Philistines. 25 Judas and his
brothers began to be feared, and alarm seized the surrounding peoples. 26 His name even reached the king's ears, and
among the nations there was talk of Judas and his battles.
27 The news of these events infuriated Antiochus, and he
ordered mobilisation of all the forces in his kingdom, a very
powerful army. 28 Opening his treasury, he distributed a
year's pay to his troops, telling them to be prepared for any
eventuality. 29 He then found that the money in his coffers
had run short and that the tribute of the province had
decreased, as a result of the dissension and disaster brought
on the country by his own abrogation of laws that had been
in force from antiquity. 30 He began to fear that, as had happened more than once, he would not have enough to cover
the expenses and the lavish bounties he had previously been
accustomed to make on a larger scale than his predecessors
on the throne. 31 In this grave quandary he resolved to
invade Persia, there to levy tribute on the provinces and so
accumulate substantial funds. 32 He therefore left Lysias, a
nobleman and member of the royal family, to manage the
royal affairs between the River Euphrates and the Egyptian

GREEK OLD TESTAMENT

Αἰγύπτου 33 καὶ τρέφειν Ἀντίοχον τὸν υἱὸν αὐτοῦ ἕως τοῦ
ἐπιστρέψαι αὐτόν· 34 καὶ παρέδωκεν αὐτῷ τὰς ἡμίσεις τῶν
δυνάμεων καὶ τοὺς ἐλέφαντας καὶ ἐνετείλατο αὐτῷ περὶ
πάντων, ὧν ἠβούλετο, καὶ περὶ τῶν κατοικούντων τὴν Ιουδαίαν καὶ Ιερουσαλημ 35 ἀποστεῖλαι ἐπ᾽ αὐτοὺς δύναμιν τοῦ ἐκτρῖψαι καὶ ἐξᾶραι τὴν ἰσχὺν Ισραηλ καὶ τὸ κατάλειμμα
Ιερουσαλημ καὶ ἆραι τὸ μνημόσυνον αὐτῶν ἀπὸ τοῦ τόπου
36 καὶ κατοικίσαι υἱοὺς ἀλλογενεῖς ἐν πᾶσιν τοῖς ὁρίοις
αὐτῶν καὶ κατακληροδοτῆσαι τὴν γῆν αὐτῶν. 37 καὶ ὁ βασιλεὺς παρέλαβεν τὰς ἡμίσεις τῶν δυνάμεων τὰς καταλειφθεί-
σας καὶ ἀπῆρεν ἀπὸ Ἀντιοχείας ἀπὸ πόλεως βασιλείας αὐτοῦ ἔτους ἑβδόμου καὶ τεσσαρακοστοῦ καὶ ἑκατοστοῦ καὶ
διεπέρασεν τὸν Εὐφράτην ποταμὸν καὶ διεπορεύετο τὰς
ἐπάνω χώρας.
38 Καὶ ἐπέλεξεν Λυσίας Πτολεμαῖον τὸν Δορυμένους καὶ
Νικάνορα καὶ Γοργίαν, ἄνδρας δυνατοὺς τῶν φίλων τοῦ
βασιλέως, 39 καὶ ἀπέστειλεν μετ᾽ αὐτῶν τεσσαράκοντα
χιλιάδας ἀνδρῶν καὶ ἑπτακισχιλίαν ἵππον τοῦ ἐλθεῖν εἰς γῆν
Ιουδα καὶ καταφθεῖραι αὐτὴν κατὰ τὸν λόγον τοῦ βασιλέως.
40 καὶ ἀπῆρεν σὺν πάσῃ τῇ δυνάμει αὐτῶν, καὶ ἦλθον καὶ
παρενέβαλον πλησίον Αμμαους ἐν τῇ γῇ τῇ πεδινῇ. 41 καὶ
ἤκουσαν οἱ ἔμποροι τῆς χώρας τὸ ὄνομα αὐτῶν καὶ ἔλαβον
ἀργύριον καὶ χρυσίον πολὺ σφόδρα καὶ πέδας καὶ ἦλθον εἰς
τὴν παρεμβολὴν τοῦ λαβεῖν τοὺς υἱοὺς Ισραηλ εἰς παῖδας.
καὶ προσετέθησαν πρὸς αὐτοὺς δύναμις Συρίας καὶ γῆς
ἀλλοφύλων. 42 καὶ εἶδεν Ιουδας καὶ οἱ ἀδελφοὶ αὐτοῦ ὅτι
ἐπληθύνθη τὰ κακὰ καὶ αἱ δυνάμεις παρεμβάλλουσιν ἐν τοῖς

KING JAMES VERSION

33 And to bring up his son Antiochus, until he came again.

34 Moreover he delivered unto him the half of his forces, and the elephants, and gave him charge of all things that he would have done, as also concerning them that dwelt in Juda and Jerusalem:

35 *To wit,* that he should send an army against them, to destroy and root out the strength of Israel, and the remnant of Jerusalem, and to take away their memorial from that place;

36 And that he should place strangers in all their quarters, and divide their land by lot.

37 So the king took the half of the forces that remained, and departed from Antioch, his royal city, the hundred forty and seventh year; and having passed the river Euphrates, he went through the high countries.

38 Then Lysias chose Ptolemee the *son* of Dorymenes, Nicanor, and Gorgias, mighty men of the king's friends:

39 And with them he sent forty thousand footmen, and seven thousand horsemen, to go into the land of Juda, and to destroy it, as the king commanded.

40 So they went forth with all their power, and came and pitched by Emmaus in the plain country.

41 And the merchants of the country, hearing the fame of them, took silver and gold very much, with servants, and came into the camp to buy the children of Israel for slaves: a power also of Syria and of the land of the Philistines joined themselves unto them.

42 Now when Judas and his brethren saw that miseries were multiplied, and that the forces did encamp themselves

DOUAY OLD TESTAMENT

33 And to bring up his son Antiochus, till he came again.

34 And he delivered to him half the army, and the elephants: and he gave him charge concerning all that he would have done, and concerning the inhabitants of Judea, and Jerusalem:

35 And that he should send an army against them, to destroy and root out the strength of Israel, and the remnant of Jerusalem, and to take away the memory of them from that place:

36 And that he should settle strangers to dwell in all their coasts, and divide their land by lot.

37 So the king took the half of the army that remained, and went forth from Antioch the chief city of his kingdom, in the hundred and forty-seventh year: and he passed over the river Euphrates, and went through the higher countries.

38 Then Lysias chose Ptolemee the son of Dorymenus, and Nicanor, and Gorgias, mighty men of the king's friends.

39 And he sent with them forty thousand men, and seven thousand horsemen: to go into the land of Juda, and to destroy it according to the king's orders.

40 So they went forth with all their power, and came, and pitched near Emmaus in the plain country.

41 And the merchants of the countries heard the fame of them: and they took silver and gold in abundance, and servants: and they came into the camp, to buy the children of Israel for slaves: and there were joined to them the forces of Syria, and of the land of the strangers.

42 And Judas and his brethren saw that evils were multiplied, and that the armies approached to their borders: and

KNOX TRANSLATION

charge of the young prince Antiochus, until the king's return.
34 Half his army he entrusted to Lysias, and the elephants
besides; and he signified all that he would have done, concerning Juda and Jerusalem particularly. 35 A force must be
sent to overpower all that fought for Israel, or were yet left in
Jerusalem, and make a clean riddance of them; no trace of
these must be left; 36 all through the country settlers must be
brought in from abroad, and the lands allotted between
them. 37 With that, the king left his capital of Antioch, taking the remainder of his army with him; it was the hundred
and forty-seventh year of the empire. Soon he was across
Euphrates river, and on the march through the high countries.
38 Three generals Lysias appointed for the task; Ptolemy
son of Dorymenes, Nicanor and Gorgias, nobles all that were
high in the royal favour; 39 with forty thousand foot and
seven thousand horse they were to march on Juda and make
an end of it, as the king had ordered. 40 So out they went,
with all this army at their back, marched in, and pitched
their tents near Emmaus, down in the valley. 41 Be sure the
traders all about were apprised of their coming, and made
their way into the camp with great sums of silver and gold,
and a retinue of servants besides, thinking to buy Israelite
slaves; levies, too, from Syria and Philistia made common
cause with the invader.
42 Judas, then, and his brethren found that matters had
gone from bad to worse; here were the enemy encamped

TODAY'S ENGLISH VERSION

made Lysias the guardian of his son Antiochus the Fifth
until his own return. 34 He put Lysias in charge of all the elephants and of half his army, and then gave him detailed
instructions about what he wanted done, and in particular,
what he wanted done with the inhabitants of Judea and
Jerusalem. 35 Lysias was ordered to send an army against
the Jews, especially the Jews in Jerusalem, to break their
power and destroy them, so that no trace of them would
remain. 36 He was ordered to take their land and give it to
foreigners, who would settle the whole area. 37 Taking the
other half of his army, the king set out from Antioch, his
capital city, in the year 147.[a] He crossed the Euphrates River
and marched through Mesopotamia.

38 Lysias chose Nicanor, Gorgias, and Ptolemy son of
Dorymenes as army commanders; all three were able men
who bore the title "Friend of the King." 39 He put them in
charge of 40,000 infantry and 7,000 cavalry and ordered
them to invade the land of Judea and destroy it as the king
had commanded. 40 These commanders set out with their
entire force, and when they came to the plains near
Emmaus, they made camp. 41 A force from Idumea[b] and
Philistia joined them. The merchants of the region heard
about the strength of the army, and they came to the camp
with chains and a large amount of money, hoping to buy
some Jewish slaves.

42 Judas and his brothers saw that their situation was getting more and more difficult, with foreign armies camped

[a] THE YEAR 147: *This corresponds to 165 B.C.* [b] *Probable text* Idumea; *Greek* Syria.

NEW REVISED STANDARD VERSION

borders of Egypt. 33 Lysias was also to take care of his son
Antiochus until he returned. 34 And he turned over to
Lysias[a] half of his forces and the elephants, and gave him
orders about all that he wanted done. As for the residents of
Judea and Jerusalem, 35 Lysias was to send a force against
them to wipe out and destroy the strength of Israel and the
remnant of Jerusalem; he was to banish the memory of them
from the place, 36 settle aliens in all their territory, and distribute their land by lot. 37 Then the king took the remaining
half of his forces and left Antioch his capital in the one hundred and forty-seventh year.[b] He crossed the Euphrates river
and went through the upper provinces.

38 Lysias chose Ptolemy son of Dorymenes, and Nicanor
and Gorgias, able men among the Friends of the king, 39 and
sent with them forty thousand infantry and seven thousand
cavalry to go into the land of Judah and destroy it, as the
king had commanded. 40 So they set out with their entire
force, and when they arrived they encamped near Emmaus in
the plain. 41 When the traders of the region heard what was
said to them, they took silver and gold in immense amounts,
and fetters,[c] and went to the camp to get the Israelites for
slaves. And forces from Syria and the land of the Philistines
joined with them.

42 Now Judas and his brothers saw that misfortunes had
increased and that the forces were encamped in their territory.

a Gk *him* *b* 165 B.C. *c* Syr: Gk Mss, Vg *slaves*

NEW AMERICAN BIBLE

33 and commissioned him to take care of his son Antiochus
until his own return. 34 He entrusted to him half of the
army, and the elephants, and gave him instructions concerning everything he wanted done. As for the inhabitants of
Judea and Jerusalem, 35 Lysias was to send an army against
them to crush and destroy the power of Israel and the remnant of Jerusalem and efface their memory from the land.
36 He was to settle foreigners in all their territory and distribute their land by lot.

37 The king took the remaining half of the army and set out
from Antioch, his capital, in the year one hundred and forty-
seven; he crossed the Euphrates River and advanced inland.

38 Lysias chose Ptolemy, son of Dorymenes, and Nicanor
and Gorgias, capable men among the King's Friends, 39 and
with them he sent forty thousand men and seven thousand
cavalry to invade the land of Judah and ravage it according
to the king's orders. 40 Setting out with all their forces, they
came and pitched their camp near Emmaus in the plain.
41 When the merchants of the country heard of their fame,
they came to the camp, bringing fetters and a large sum of
silver and gold, to buy the Israelites as slaves. A force from
Idumea and from Philistia joined with them.

42 Judas and his brothers saw that the situation had
become critical now that armies were encamped within their

NEW JERUSALEM BIBLE

frontier, 33 making him responsible for the education of his
son Antiochus, until he should come back. 34 To him
Antiochus made over half his forces, with the elephants, giving him instructions about what he wanted done, particularly with regard to the inhabitants of Judaea and Jerusalem,
35 against whom he was to send a force, to crush and destroy
the power of Israel and the remnant of Jerusalem, to wipe
out their very memory from the place, 36 to settle foreigners
in all parts of their territory and to distribute their land into
lots. 37 The king took the remaining half of his troops with
him and set out from Antioch, the capital of his kingdom, in
the year 147; he crossed the River Euphrates and made his
way through the Upper Provinces.

38 Lysias chose Ptolemy son of Dorymenes, with Nicanor
and Gorgias, influential men from among the Friends of the
King, 39 and, under their command, despatched forty thousand foot and seven thousand horse to invade the land of
Judah and devastate it, as the king had ordered. 40 The entire
force set out and reached the neighbourhood of Emmaus in
the lowlands, where they pitched camp. 41 The local merchants, hearing the news of this, arrived at the camp, bringing with them a large amount of gold and silver, and fetters
as well, proposing to buy the Israelites as slaves; they were
accompanied by a company from Idumaea and the Philistine
country. 42 Judas and his brothers saw that the situation was
going from bad to worse and that armies were camping in

GREEK OLD TESTAMENT

ὁρίοις αὐτῶν, καὶ ἐπέγνωσαν τοὺς λόγους τοῦ βασιλέως, οὓς
ἐνετείλατο ποιῆσαι τῷ λαῷ εἰς ἀπώλειαν καὶ συντέλειαν,
43 καὶ εἶπαν ἕκαστος πρὸς τὸν πλησίον αὐτοῦ Ἀναστήσωμεν
τὴν καθαίρεσιν τοῦ λαοῦ ἡμῶν καὶ πολεμήσωμεν περὶ τοῦ
λαοῦ ἡμῶν καὶ τῶν ἁγίων. 44 καὶ ἠθροίσθη ἡ συναγωγὴ τοῦ
εἶναι ἑτοίμους εἰς πόλεμον καὶ τοῦ προσεύξασθαι καὶ αἰτῆσαι ἔλεος καὶ οἰκτιρμούς. 45 καὶ Ιερουσαλημ ἦν ἀοίκητος ὡς
ἔρημος, οὐκ ἦν ὁ εἰσπορευόμενος καὶ ἐκπορευόμενος ἐκ τῶν
γενημάτων αὐτῆς, καὶ τὸ ἁγίασμα καταπατούμενον, καὶ υἱοὶ
ἀλλογενῶν ἐν τῇ ἄκρᾳ, κατάλυμα τοῖς ἔθνεσιν· καὶ ἐξῆρθη
τέρψις ἐξ Ιακωβ, καὶ ἐξέλιπεν αὐλὸς καὶ κινύρα. 46 καὶ συνήχθησαν καὶ ἤλθοσαν εἰς Μασσηφα κατέναντι Ιερουσαλημ,
ὅτι τόπος προσευχῆς ἦν ἐν Μασσηφα τὸ πρότερον τῷ
Ισραηλ. 47 καὶ ἐνήστευσαν τῇ ἡμέρᾳ ἐκείνῃ καὶ περιεβάλοντο σάκκους καὶ σποδὸν ἐπὶ τὴν κεφαλὴν αὐτῶν καὶ διέρρηξαν τὰ ἱμάτια αὐτῶν. 48 καὶ ἐξεπέτασαν τὸ βιβλίον τοῦ
νόμου περὶ ὧν ἐξηρεύνων τὰ ἔθνη τὰ ὁμοιώματα τῶν εἰδώλων
αὐτῶν. 49 καὶ ἤνεγκαν τὰ ἱμάτια τῆς ἱερωσύνης καὶ τὰ
πρωτογενήματα καὶ τὰς δεκάτας καὶ ἤγειραν τοὺς ναζιραί-
ους, οἳ ἐπλήρωσαν τὰς ἡμέρας, 50 καὶ ἐβόησαν φωνῇ εἰς τὸν
οὐρανὸν λέγοντες Τί ποιήσωμεν τούτοις καὶ ποῦ αὐτοὺς
ἀπαγάγωμεν, 51 καὶ τὰ ἅγιά σου καταπεπάτηνται καὶ βεβή-
λωνται καὶ οἱ ἱερεῖς σου ἐν πένθει καὶ ταπεινώσει; 52 καὶ

KING JAMES VERSION

in their borders: for they knew how the king had given commandment to destroy the people, and utterly abolish them;
43 They said one to another, Let us restore the decayed estate of our people, and let us fight for our people and the sanctuary.
44 Then was the congregation gathered together, that they might be ready for battle, and that they might pray, and ask mercy and compassion.
45 Now Jerusalem lay void as a wilderness, there was none of her children that went in or out: the sanctuary also was trodden down, and aliens kept the strong hold; the heathen had their habitation in that place; and joy was taken from Jacob, and the pipe with the harp ceased.
46 Wherefore the Israelites assembled themselves together, and came to Maspha, over against Jerusalem; for in Maspha was the place where they prayed aforetime in Israel.
47 Then they fasted that day, and put on sackcloth, and cast ashes upon their heads, and rent their clothes,
48 And laid open the book of the law, wherein the heathen had sought to paint the likeness of their images.
49 They brought also the priests' garments, and the firstfruits, and the tithes: and the Nazarites they stirred up, who had accomplished their days.
50 Then cried they with a loud voice toward heaven, saying, What shall we do with these, and whither shall we carry them away?
51 For thy sanctuary is trodden down and profaned, and thy priests are in heaviness, and brought low.

DOUAY OLD TESTAMENT

they knew the orders the king had given to destroy the people and utterly abolish them.
43 And they said every man to his neighbour: Let us raise up the low condition of our people, and let us fight for our people, and our sanctuary.
44 And the assembly was gathered that they might be ready for battle: and that they might pray, and ask mercy and compassion.
45 Now Jerusalem was not inhabited, but was like a desert: there was none of her children that went in or out: and the sanctuary was trodden down: and the children of strangers were in the castle, there was the habitation of the Gentiles: and joy was taken away from Jacob, and the pipe and harp ceased there.
46 And they assembled together, and came to Maspha over against Jerusalem: for in Maspha was a place of prayer heretofore in Israel.
47 And they fasted that day, and put on haircloth, and put ashes upon their heads: and they rent their garments:
48 And they laid open the books of the law, in which the Gentiles searched for the likeness of their idols:
49 And they brought the priestly ornaments, and the firstfruits and tithes, and stirred up the Nazarites that had fulfilled their days:
50 And they cried with a loud voice toward heaven, saying: What shall we do with these, and whither shall we carry them?
51 For thy holies are trodden down, and are profaned, and thy priests are in mourning, and are brought low.

KNOX TRANSLATION

within their frontiers; they heard, besides, what orders the
king had given for the destruction and taking away of their
people. 43 And the word went round among them, Now to
restore the lost fortunes of our race; now to do battle for people of ours, sanctuary of ours! 44 So a general assembly was
called; they must make ready for the fight, and pray besides,
to win mercy and pardon. 45 Not at Jerusalem; Jerusalem lay
there, no city but a desert waste, nor any of her sons came
and went; her sanctuary defiled, her citadel garrisoned by the
alien, she was but a haunt of the Gentiles. Sad days for the
men of Jacob; pipe nor harp sounded there now. 46 At
Maspha, then, they gathered, looking across towards Jerusalem; time was when Maspha, too, had its place of prayer.
47 All that day they fasted, and wore sackcloth, and covered
their heads with ashes, and tore their garments about them.
48 What sights were these? Here, lying open, was a copy of
the law, such as the heathen were ever making search
for,...the counterpart of their own images. [a] 49 Here they had
brought priestly vestments, and offering of first-fruits and
tithes; here Nazirites were gathered, ripe and ready for the
payment of their vows. 50 And a loud cry rose to heaven,
What shall we do for these, thy votaries? Whither escort
them now? 51 Sanctuary of thine is all profanation and
defilement, priesthood of thine all misery and despair.

a As the sentence stands, it can only mean that heathen pursuivants had confiscated the scriptures, as being objects of veneration to the Jews no less than idols were to themselves. But it seems possible that the text is deficient.

TODAY'S ENGLISH VERSION

within their own borders. They also learned that the king
had commanded the complete destruction of the people.
43 So they determined to rebuild their ruined nation and fight
for their country and the Temple. 44 Then the whole community came together to prepare for war and to pray for God's
mercy.

45 Jerusalem was as empty as a wilderness;
no citizens left or entered the city.
The holy Temple was profaned by foreigners,
and Gentiles camped in the city's fort;
so joy departed from the people of Israel,
and the sound of music was heard no more.

46 Then Judas and his men assembled and marched to
Mizpah, opposite Jerusalem, because the people of Israel had
previously had a place of worship there. 47 In deep mourning, they fasted all that day, put on sackcloth, threw ashes
on their heads, and tore their clothes. 48 The Gentiles would
have consulted their idols in such a situation, but the
Israelites unrolled the book of the Law to search for God's
guidance. 49 They brought the priests' robes, the offerings of
the first grain, and the tithes, and then they brought in some
Nazirites who had completed their vows. 50 The whole community prayed, "Lord, what shall we do with these things?
Where shall we take them, 51 now that your holy Temple has
been trampled and profaned by Gentiles, and your priests

NEW REVISED STANDARD VERSION

They also learned what the king had commanded to do to the
people to cause their final destruction. 43 But they said to one
another, "Let us restore the ruins of our people, and fight for
our people and the sanctuary." 44 So the congregation assembled to be ready for battle, and to pray and ask for mercy and
compassion.

45 Jerusalem was uninhabited like a wilderness;
not one of her children went in or out.
The sanctuary was trampled down,
and aliens held the citadel;
it was a lodging place for the Gentiles.
Joy was taken from Jacob;
the flute and the harp ceased to play.

46 Then they gathered together and went to Mizpah,
opposite Jerusalem, because Israel formerly had a place of
prayer in Mizpah. 47 They fasted that day, put on sackcloth
and sprinkled ashes on their heads, and tore their clothes.
48 And they opened the book of the law to inquire into those
matters about which the Gentiles consulted the likenesses of
their gods. 49 They also brought the vestments of the priesthood and the first fruits and the tithes, and they stirred up
the nazirites[a] who had completed their days; 50 and they
cried aloud to Heaven, saying,

"What shall we do with these?
Where shall we take them?
51 Your sanctuary is trampled down and profaned,
and your priests mourn in humiliation.

a That is *those separated* or *those consecrated*

NEW AMERICAN BIBLE

territory; they knew of the orders which the king had given
to destroy and utterly wipe out the people. 43 So they said to
one another, "Let us restore our people from their ruined
estate, and fight for our people and our sanctuary!"
44 The assembly gathered together to prepare for battle and
to pray and implore mercy and compassion.

45 Jerusalem was uninhabited, like a desert;
not one of her children entered or came out.
The sanctuary was trampled on,
and foreigners were in the citadel;
it was a habitation of Gentiles.
Joy had disappeared from Jacob,
and the flute and the harp were silent.

46 Thus they assembled and went to Mizpah near Jerusalem, because there was formerly at Mizpah a place of prayer
for Israel. 47 That day they fasted and wore sackcloth; they
sprinkled ashes on their heads and tore their clothes. 48 They
unrolled the scroll of the law, to learn about the things for
which the Gentiles consulted the images of their idols.
49 They brought with them the priestly vestments, the first
fruits, and the tithes; and they brought forward the nazirites
who had completed the time of their vows. 50 And they cried
aloud to Heaven: "What shall we do with these men, and
where shall we take them? 51 For your sanctuary has been
trampled on and profaned, and your priests are in mourning

NEW JERUSALEM BIBLE

their territory; they were also well aware that the king had
ordered the people's total destruction. 43 So they said to each
other, 'Let us restore the ruins of our people and fight for our
people and our sanctuary.' 44 The Assembly was summoned,
to prepare for war, to offer prayer and to implore compassion
and mercy.

45 Jerusalem was as empty as a desert,
none of her children to go in and out.
The sanctuary was trodden underfoot,
men of an alien race held the Citadel,
which had become a lodging for gentiles.
There was no more rejoicing for Jacob,
the flute and lyre were mute.

46 After mustering, they made their way to Mizpah, opposite Jerusalem, since Mizpah was traditionally a place of
prayer for Israel. 47 That day they fasted and put on sackcloth, covering their heads with ashes and tearing their garments. 48 For the guidance that the gentiles would have
sought from the images of their false gods, they opened the
Book of the Law. 49 They also brought out the priestly vestments, with first-fruits and tithes, and marshalled the
Nazirites who had completed the period of their vow.
50 Then, raising their voices to Heaven, they cried, 'What
shall we do with these people, and where are we to take
them? 51 Your holy place has been trampled underfoot and
defiled, your priests mourn in their humiliation, 52 and now

GREEK OLD TESTAMENT

ἰδοὺ τὰ ἔθνη συνῆκται ἐφ' ἡμᾶς τοῦ ἐξᾶραι ἡμᾶς. σὺ οἶδας ἃ
λογίζονται ἐφ' ἡμᾶς. 53 πῶς δυνησόμεθα ὑποστῆναι κατὰ
πρόσωπον αὐτῶν, ἐὰν μὴ σὺ βοηθήσῃς ἡμῖν; 54 καὶ ἐσάλπισαν ταῖς σάλπιγξιν καὶ ἐβόησαν φωνῇ μεγάλῃ. 55 καὶ
μετὰ τοῦτο κατέστησεν Ιουδας ἡγουμένους τοῦ λαοῦ, χιλιάρχους καὶ ἑκατοντάρχους καὶ πεντηκοντάρχους καὶ δεκα-
δάρχους. 56 καὶ εἶπεν τοῖς οἰκοδομοῦσιν οἰκίας καὶ μνη-
στευομένοις γυναῖκας καὶ φυτεύουσιν ἀμπελῶνας καὶ
δειλοῖς ἀποστρέφειν ἕκαστον εἰς τὸν οἶκον αὐτοῦ κατὰ τὸν
νόμον. 57 καὶ ἀπῆρεν ἡ παρεμβολή, καὶ παρενέβαλον κατὰ
νότον Αμμαους. 58 καὶ εἶπεν Ιουδας Περιζώσασθε καὶ γίνεσθε εἰς υἱοὺς δυνατοὺς καὶ γίνεσθε ἕτοιμοι εἰς πρωὶ τοῦ
πολεμῆσαι ἐν τοῖς ἔθνεσιν τούτοις τοῖς ἐπισυνηγμένοις ἐφ'
ἡμᾶς ἐξᾶραι ἡμᾶς καὶ τὰ ἅγια ἡμῶν· 59 ὅτι κρεῖσσον ἡμᾶς
ἀποθανεῖν ἐν τῷ πολέμῳ ἢ ἐπιδεῖν ἐπὶ τὰ κακὰ τοῦ ἔθνους
ἡμῶν καὶ τῶν ἁγίων. 60 ὡς δ' ἂν ᾖ θέλημα ἐν οὐρανῷ, οὕτως
ποιήσει.

4 Καὶ παρέλαβεν Γοργίας πεντακισχιλίους ἄνδρας καὶ
χιλίαν ἵππον ἐκλεκτήν, καὶ ἀπῆρεν ἡ παρεμβολὴ νυκτὸς
2 ὥστε ἐπιβαλεῖν ἐπὶ τὴν παρεμβολὴν τῶν Ιουδαίων καὶ
πατάξαι αὐτοὺς ἄφνω· καὶ υἱοὶ τῆς ἄκρας ἦσαν αὐτῷ ὁδηγοί.

KING JAMES VERSION

52 And, lo, the heathen are assembled together against us
to destroy us: what things they imagine against us, thou
knowest.
53 How shall we be able to stand against them, except
thou, *O God,* be our help?
54 Then sounded they with trumpets, and cried with a
loud voice.
55 And after this Judas ordained captains over the people,
even captains over thousands, and over hundreds, and over
fifties, and over tens.
56 But as for such as were building houses, or had
betrothed wives, or were planting vineyards, or were fearful,
those he commanded that they should return, every man to
his own house, according to the law.
57 So the camp removed, and pitched upon the south side
of Emmaus.
58 And Judas said, arm yourselves, and be valiant men,
and see that ye be in readiness against the morning, that ye
may fight with these nations, that are assembled together
against us to destroy us and our sanctuary:
59 For it is better for us to die in battle, than to behold the
calamities of our people and our sanctuary.
60 Nevertheless, as the will *of God* is in heaven, so let him
do.

4 Then took Gorgias five thousand footmen, and a thousand of the best horsemen, and removed out of the camp
by night;
2 To the end he might rush in upon the camp of the Jews,
and smite them suddenly. And the men of the fortress were
his guides.

DOUAY OLD TESTAMENT

52 And behold the nations are come together against us
to destroy us: thou knowest what they intend against us.
53 How shall we be able to stand before their face, unless
thou, O God, help us?
54 Then they sounded with trumpets, and cried out with a
loud voice.
55 And after this Judas appointed captains over the people, over thousands, and over hundreds, and over fifties, and
over tens.
56 And he said to them that were building houses, or had
betrothed wives, or were planting vineyards, or were fearful,
that they should return every man to his house, according to
the law.
57 So they removed the camp, and pitched on the south
side of Emmaus.
58 And Judas said: Gird yourselves, and be valiant men,
and be ready against the morning, that you may fight with
these nations that are assembled against us to destroy us
and our sanctuary.
59 For it is better for us to die in battle, than to see the
evils of our nation, and of the holies:
60 Nevertheless as it shall be the will *of God* in heaven so
be it done.

4 THEN Gorgias took five thousand men, and a thousand
of the best horsemen: and they removed out of the camp
by night.
2 That they might come upon the camp of the Jews, and
strike them suddenly: and the men that were of the castle
were their guides.

KNOX TRANSLATION

52 And now, see where the heathen muster their armies to
destroy us! Needs not we should tell thee, how murderous
their intent. 53 Lord, but for thy aid, how shall we resist their
onslaught? 54 Loudly their voices, and loud the trumpets
rang.
55 Thereupon Judas chose out who should be their leaders,
one with a thousand, one with a hundred, one with fifty, one
with ten men to follow him; 56 he sent home, too, all such as
the law holds exempt; all that had but just built house, or
married wife, or planted vineyard, and whoever had no
stomach to the fight.[a] 57 Then they moved camp, and
pitched their tents southward of Emmaus. 58 Now for girded
loins, cried Judas, and brave hearts! By to-morrow's light,
you must engage yonder heathen, sworn enemies to us, and
to the ground we hold sacred. 59 Better die in battle, than
live to see our race and our sanctuary overpowered. 60 Be it
what it may, heaven's will be done!

4 That night, a detachment of five thousand foot and a
thousand picked horsemen left their lines, under the
command of Gorgias, 2 thinking to reach the Jewish camp
and strike a sudden blow at it; for guides, they had men of

a See Deut. 20. 5-8.

TODAY'S ENGLISH VERSION

mourn in disgrace? 52 The Gentiles have come to attack and destroy us. You know what they plan to do! 53 If you don't help us, how can we stand up against them?" 54 Then they blew trumpets and shouted loudly.

55 After that, Judas divided his men into groups of ten, fifty, a hundred, and a thousand, placing officers in charge of each group. 56 Then, in obedience to the Law, he sent home everyone who had recently been married, built a house, or planted a vineyard, as well as anyone who was afraid. 57 Finally, the army marched out and took up positions south of Emmaus, 58 where Judas said to them: "Prepare yourselves for battle and be courageous! Be ready early tomorrow morning to fight these Gentiles who have joined forces to attack us and destroy us and our Temple. 59 It is better for us to die fighting than to stand idly by and watch the destruction of our nation and our Temple. 60 But the Lord will do what he pleases."

4 Gorgias took 5,000 infantry and 1,000 of his most experienced cavalry and left camp by night, 2 with men from the fort in Jerusalem as his guides. He had planned to make a surprise attack on the Jewish army, 3 but Judas learned of

NEW REVISED STANDARD VERSION

52 Here the Gentiles are assembled against us to destroy
us;
you know what they plot against us.
53 How will we be able to withstand them,
if you do not help us?"

54 Then they sounded the trumpets and gave a loud shout. 55 After this Judas appointed leaders of the people, in charge of thousands and hundreds and fifties and tens. 56 Those who were building houses, or were about to be married, or were planting a vineyard, or were fainthearted, he told to go home again, according to the law. 57 Then the army marched out and encamped to the south of Emmaus.

58 And Judas said, "Arm yourselves and be courageous. Be ready early in the morning to fight with these Gentiles who have assembled against us to destroy us and our sanctuary. 59 It is better for us to die in battle than to see the misfortunes of our nation and of the sanctuary. 60 But as his will in heaven may be, so shall he do."

4 Now Gorgias took five thousand infantry and one thousand picked cavalry, and this division moved out by night 2 to fall upon the camp of the Jews and attack them suddenly. Men from the citadel were his guides. 3 But Judas

NEW AMERICAN BIBLE

and humiliation. 52 Now the Gentiles are gathered together against us to destroy us. You know what they plot against us. 53 How shall we be able to resist them unless you help us?" 54 Then they blew the trumpets and cried out loudly.

55 After this Judas appointed officers among the people, over thousands, over hundreds, over fifties, and over tens. 56 He proclaimed that those who were building houses, or were just married, or were planting vineyards, and those who were afraid, could each return to his home, according to the law. 57 Then the army moved off, and they camped to the south of Emmaus. 58 Judas said: "Arm yourselves and be brave; in the morning be ready to fight these Gentiles who have assembled against us to destroy us and our sanctuary. 59 It is better for us to die in battle than to witness the ruin of our nation and our sanctuary. Whatever Heaven wills, he will do."

4 Now Gorgias took five thousand infantry and a thousand picked cavalry, and this detachment set out at night 2 in order to attack the camp of the Jews and take them by surprise. Some men from the citadel were their guides.

NEW JERUSALEM BIBLE

the gentiles are in alliance to destroy us: you know what they have in mind for us. 53 How can we stand up and face them if you do not come to our aid?' 54 Then they sounded the trumpets and raised a great shout.

55 Next, Judas appointed leaders for the people, to command a thousand, a hundred, fifty or ten men. 56 Those who were in the middle of building a house, or were about to be married, or were planting a vineyard, or were afraid, he told to go home again, as the Law allowed. 57 The column then marched off and took up a position south of Emmaus. 58 'Stand to your arms,' Judas told them, 'acquit yourselves bravely, in the morning be ready to fight these gentiles massed against us to destroy us and our sanctuary. 59 Better for us to die in battle than to watch the ruin of our nation and our Holy Place. 60 Whatever be the will of Heaven, he will perform it.'

4 Gorgias took with him five thousand foot and a thousand picked cavalry, and the force moved off by night 2 with the object of attacking the Jewish position and dealing them an unexpected blow; the men from the Citadel were

GREEK OLD TESTAMENT

3 καὶ ἤκουσεν Ιουδας καὶ ἀπῆρεν αὐτὸς καὶ οἱ δυνατοὶ πατάξαι τὴν δύναμιν τοῦ βασιλέως τὴν ἐν Αμμαους, 4 ἕως ἔτι
ἐσκορπισμέναι ἦσαν αἱ δυνάμεις ἀπὸ τῆς παρεμβολῆς. 5 καὶ
ἦλθεν Γοργίας εἰς τὴν παρεμβολὴν Ιουδου νυκτὸς καὶ οὐδένα
εὗρεν· καὶ ἐζήτει αὐτοὺς ἐν τοῖς ὄρεσιν, ὅτι εἶπεν Φεύ-
γουσιν οὗτοι ἀφ' ἡμῶν. 6 καὶ ἅμα ἡμέρᾳ ὤφθη Ιουδας ἐν τῷ
πεδίῳ ἐν τρισχιλίοις ἀνδράσιν· πλὴν καλύμματα καὶ μαχαίρας οὐκ εἶχον ὡς ἠβούλοντο. 7 καὶ εἶδον παρεμβολὴν ἐθνῶν
ἰσχυρὰν καὶ τεθωρακισμένην καὶ ἵππον κυκλοῦσαν αὐτήν, καὶ
οὗτοι διδακτοὶ πολέμου. 8 καὶ εἶπεν Ιουδας τοῖς ἀνδράσιν
τοῖς μετ' αὐτοῦ Μὴ φοβεῖσθε τὸ πλῆθος αὐτῶν καὶ τὸ ὅρμημα αὐτῶν μὴ δειλωθῆτε· 9 μνήσθητε ὡς ἐσώθησαν οἱ πατέρες ἡμῶν ἐν θαλάσσῃ ἐρυθρᾷ, ὅτε ἐδίωκεν αὐτοὺς Φαραω
ἐν δυνάμει· 10 καὶ νῦν βοήσωμεν εἰς οὐρανόν, εἰ θελήσει
ἡμᾶς καὶ μνησθήσεται διαθήκης πατέρων καὶ συντρίψει τὴν
παρεμβολὴν ταύτην κατὰ πρόσωπον ἡμῶν σήμερον, 11 καὶ
γνώσονται πάντα τὰ ἔθνη ὅτι ἔστιν ὁ λυτρούμενος καὶ σῴζων τὸν Ισραηλ. 12 καὶ ἦραν οἱ ἀλλόφυλοι τοὺς ὀφθαλμοὺς
αὐτῶν καὶ εἶδον αὐτοὺς ἐρχομένους ἐξ ἐναντίας 13 καὶ ἐξῆλθον ἐκ τῆς παρεμβολῆς εἰς πόλεμον· καὶ ἐσάλπισαν οἱ
παρὰ Ιουδου 14 καὶ συνῆψαν, καὶ συνετρίβησαν τὰ ἔθνη καὶ

KING JAMES VERSION

3 Now when Judas heard thereof, he himself removed, and the valiant men with him, that he might smite the king's army which was at Emmaus,

4 While as yet the forces were dispersed from the camp.

5 In the mean season came Gorgias by night into the camp of Judas: and when he found no man there, he sought them in the mountains: for said he, These fellows flee from us.

6 But as soon as it was day, Judas shewed himself in the plain with three thousand men, who nevertheless had neither armour nor swords to their minds.

7 And they saw the camp of the heathen, that it was strong and well harnessed, and compassed round about with horsemen; and these were expert of war.

8 Then said Judas to the men that were with him, Fear ye not their multitude, neither be ye afraid of their assault.

9 Remember how our fathers were delivered in the Red sea, when Pharaoh pursued them with an army.

10 Now therefore let us cry unto heaven, if peradventure the Lord will have mercy upon us, and remember the covenant of our fathers, and destroy this host before our face this day:

11 That so all the heathen may know that there is one who delivereth and saveth Israel.

12 Then the strangers lifted up their eyes, and saw them coming over against them.

13 Wherefore they went out of the camp to battle; but they that were with Judas sounded their trumpets.

14 So they joined battle, and the heathen being discomfited fled into the plain.

DOUAY OLD TESTAMENT

3 And Judas heard of it, and rose up, he and the valiant men, to attack the king's forces that were in Emmaus.

4 For as yet the army was dispersed from the camp.

5 And Gorgias came by night into the camp of Judas, and found no man, and he sought them in the mountains: for he said: These men flee from us.

6 And when it was day, Judas shewed himself in the plain with three thousand men only, who neither had armour nor swords.

7 And they saw the camp of the Gentiles that it was strong, and the men in breastplates, and the horsemen round about them, and these were trained up to war.

8 And Judas said to the men that were with him: Fear ye not their multitude, neither be ye afraid of their assault.

9 Remember in what manner our fathers were saved in the Red Sea, when Pharao pursued them with a great army.

10 And now let us cry to heaven: and the Lord will have mercy on us, and will remember the covenant of our fathers, and will destroy this army before our face this day:

11 And all nations shall know that there is one that redeemeth and delivereth Israel.

12 And the strangers lifted up their eyes, and saw them coming against them.

13 And they went out of the camp to battle, and they that were with Judas sounded the trumpet.

14 And they joined battle: and the Gentiles were routed, and fled into the plain.

KNOX TRANSLATION

the Jerusalem garrison. 3 But Judas had word of it; out he
went, and all his valiant company with him, to attack the
main body of the king's army at Emmaus, 4 while the
defences of the camp were yet scattered. 5 So Gorgias, making his night attack on the camp of Judas, and finding it
empty, made no doubt they had given him the slip, and fell
to scouring the hill-country for them; 6 meanwhile, came
day-break, and there was Judas down in the valley. True,
there were but three thousand at his back, for defence and
attack very ill arrayed; 7 and here was this army of heathen
folk, both strong and well protected, with cavalry circling
about them, men bred to war! 8 But Judas cried to his fellows, What, would you be daunted by the numbers of them?
Would you give ground before their attack? 9 Bethink you,
what a host it was Pharao sent in pursuit of our fathers,
there by the Red Sea, and they escaped none the less.
10 Now, as then, besiege we heaven with our cries; will not
the Lord have mercy? Will he not remember the covenant he
had with our fathers, and rout, this day, yonder army at our
coming? 11 No doubt shall the world have thenceforward,
but there is one claims Israel for his own, and grants her
deliverance.

12 And now the heathen folk caught sight of them as they
advanced to the attack, 13 and left their lines to give battle.
Thereupon Judas' men sounded with the trumpet, 14 and the
two armies met. Routed the Gentiles were, sure enough, and
took to their heels across the open country, 15 sword of the

TODAY'S ENGLISH VERSION

the plan and moved out with his men to attack the king's
army at Emmaus 4 while Gorgias and his troops were still
away from the camp. 5 When Gorgias and his army reached
Judas' camp that night, they found no one there. They
thought Judas and his men were trying to escape, so they
started looking for them in the mountains.
6 At dawn Judas appeared in the plain with 3,000 men, not
all of them as well armed as they would have liked. 7 They
saw the huge Gentile army of experienced troops wearing
armor and protected by cavalry. 8 But Judas said to his men,
"Don't worry about the size of their army, and don't be
frightened when they attack. 9 Remember how our ancestors
were saved at the Red Sea when the king of Egypt was pursuing them with his army! 10 Now let us ask the Lord to
have mercy on us. Let us pray that he will honor his covenant with our ancestors and crush this army when we
attack today. 11 Then all the Gentiles will know that Israel
has a God who rescues and saves them."
12 When the Gentiles saw Judas and his men preparing for
battle, 13 they moved out of their camp to fight. Then Judas
and his men sounded their trumpets 14 and attacked. The
Gentiles broke ranks and fled to the plain, 15 but all the

NEW REVISED STANDARD VERSION

heard of it, and he and his warriors moved out to attack the
king's force in Emmaus 4 while the division was still absent
from the camp. 5 When Gorgias entered the camp of Judas by
night, he found no one there, so he looked for them in the
hills, because he said, "These men are running away from
us."
6 At daybreak Judas appeared in the plain with three
thousand men, but they did not have armor and swords such
as they desired. 7 And they saw the camp of the Gentiles,
strong and fortified, with cavalry all around it; and these
men were trained in war. 8 But Judas said to those who were
with him, "Do not fear their numbers or be afraid when they
charge. 9 Remember how our ancestors were saved at the
Red Sea, when Pharaoh with his forces pursued them.
10 And now, let us cry to Heaven, to see whether he will favor
us and remember his covenant with our ancestors and crush
this army before us today. 11 Then all the Gentiles will know
that there is one who redeems and saves Israel."
12 When the foreigners looked up and saw them coming
against them, 13 they went out from their camp to battle.
Then the men with Judas blew their trumpets 14 and engaged
in battle. The Gentiles were crushed, and fled into the plain,

NEW AMERICAN BIBLE

3 Judas heard of it, and himself set out with his soldiers to
attack the king's army at Emmaus, 4 while the latter's forces
were still scattered away from the camp. 5 During the night
Gorgias came into the camp of Judas, and found no one
there; so he began to hunt for them in the mountains, saying, "They are fleeing from us."
6 But at daybreak Judas appeared in the plain with three
thousand men, who lacked such armor and swords as they
would have wished. 7 They saw the army of the Gentiles,
strong and breastplated, flanked with cavalry, and made up
of expert soldiers. 8 Judas said to the men with him: "Do not
be afraid of their numbers or dread their attack. 9 Remember
how our fathers were saved in the Red Sea, when Pharaoh
pursued them with an army. 10 So now let us cry to Heaven
in the hope that he will favor us, remember his covenant
with our fathers, and destroy this army before us today.
11 All the Gentiles shall know that there is One who redeems
and delivers Israel."
12 When the foreigners looked up and saw them marching
toward them, 13 they came out of their camp for battle, and
the men with Judas blew the trumpet. 14 The battle was
joined and the Gentiles were defeated and fled toward the

NEW JERUSALEM BIBLE

there to guide him. 3 Judas got wind of it and himself moved
off with his fighters to strike at the royal army at Emmaus,
4 while its fighting troops were still dispersed outside the
camp. 5 Hence, when Gorgias reached Judas' camp, he found
no one and began looking for the Jews in the mountains.
'For', he said, 'we have got them on the run.' 6 First light
found Judas in the plain with three thousand men, although
these lacked the armour and swords they would have
wished. 7 They could now see the gentile encampment with
its strong fortifications and cavalry surrounding it, clearly
people who understood warfare.
8 Judas said to his men, 'Do not be afraid of their numbers,
and do not flinch at their attack. 9 Remember how our
ancestors were delivered at the Red Sea when Pharaoh was
pursuing them in force. 10 And now let us call on Heaven: if
he cares for us, he will remember his covenant with our
ancestors and will destroy this army confronting us today;
11 then all the nations will know for certain that there is One
who ransoms and saves Israel.'
12 The foreigners looked up and, seeing the Jews advancing
against them, 13 came out of the camp to join battle. Judas'
men sounded the trumpet 14 and engaged them. The gentiles
were defeated and fled towards the plain 15 and all the

GREEK OLD TESTAMENT

ἔφυγον εἰς τὸ πεδίον, 15 οἱ δὲ ἔσχατοι πάντες ἔπεσον ἐν
ῥομφαίᾳ. καὶ ἐδίωξαν αὐτοὺς ἕως Γαζηρων καὶ ἕως τῶν πεδίων τῆς Ιδουμαίας καὶ Ἀζώτου καὶ Ιαμνείας, καὶ ἔπεσαν ἐξ
αὐτῶν εἰς ἄνδρας τρισχιλίους. 16 καὶ ἀπέστρεψεν Ιουδας
καὶ ἡ δύναμις ἀπὸ τοῦ διώκειν ὄπισθεν αὐτῶν 17 καὶ εἶπεν
πρὸς τὸν λαόν Μὴ ἐπιθυμήσητε τῶν σκύλων, ὅτι πόλεμος ἐξ
ἐναντίας ἡμῶν, 18 καὶ Γοργίας καὶ ἡ δύναμις ἐν τῷ ὄρει
ἐγγὺς ἡμῶν· ἀλλὰ στῆτε νῦν ἐναντίον τῶν ἐχθρῶν ἡμῶν καὶ
πολεμήσατε αὐτούς, καὶ μετὰ ταῦτα λάβετε τὰ σκῦλα μετὰ
παρρησίας. 19 ἔτι πληροῦντος Ιουδου ταῦτα μέρος τι ὤφθη
ἐκκύπτον ἐκ τοῦ ὄρους. 20 καὶ εἶδεν ὅτι τετρόπωνται, καὶ
ἐμπυρίζουσιν τὴν παρεμβολήν· ὁ γὰρ καπνὸς ὁ θεωρούμενος
ἐνεφάνιζεν τὸ γεγονός. 21 οἱ δὲ ταῦτα συνιδόντες ἐδειλώ-
θησαν σφόδρα· συνιδόντες δὲ καὶ τὴν Ιουδου παρεμβολὴν ἐν
τῷ πεδίῳ ἑτοίμην εἰς παράταξιν 22 ἔφυγον πάντες εἰς γῆν
ἀλλοφύλων. 23 καὶ Ιουδας ἀνέστρεψεν ἐπὶ τὴν σκυλείαν τῆς
παρεμβολῆς, καὶ ἔλαβον χρυσίον πολὺ καὶ ἀργύριον καὶ ὑά-
κινθον καὶ πορφύραν θαλασσίαν καὶ πλοῦτον μέγαν. 24 καὶ
ἐπιστραφέντες ὕμνουν καὶ εὐλόγουν εἰς οὐρανὸν ὅτι καλόν,
ὅτι εἰς τὸν αἰῶνα τὸ ἔλεος αὐτοῦ. 25 καὶ ἐγενήθη σωτηρία
μεγάλη τῷ Ισραηλ ἐν τῇ ἡμέρᾳ ἐκείνῃ.
26 Ὅσοι δὲ τῶν ἀλλοφύλων διεσώθησαν, παραγενηθέντες
ἀπήγγειλαν τῷ Λυσίᾳ πάντα τὰ συμβεβηκότα. 27 ὁ δὲ

KING JAMES VERSION

15 Howbeit all the hindmost of them were slain with the sword: for they pursued them unto Gazara, and unto the plains of Idumea, and Azotus, and Jamnia, so that there were slain of them upon a three thousand men.

16 This done, Judas returned again with his host from pursuing them,

17 And said to the people, Be not greedy of the spoils, inasmuch as there is a battle before us,

18 And Gorgias and his host are here by us in the mountain: but stand ye now against our enemies, and overcome them, and after this ye may boldly take the spoils.

19 As Judas was yet speaking these words, there appeared a part of them looking out of the mountain:

20 Who when they perceived that the Jews had put their host to flight, and were burning the tents; for the smoke that was seen declared what was done:

21 When therefore they perceived these things, they were sore afraid, and seeing also the host of Judas in the plain ready to fight,

22 They fled every one into the land of strangers.

23 Then Judas returned to spoil the tents, where they got much gold, and silver, and blue silk, and purple of the sea, and great riches.

24 After this they went home, and sung a song of thanksgiving, and praised the Lord in heaven: because it is good, because his mercy *endureth* for ever.

25 Thus Israel had a great deliverance that day.

26 Now all the strangers that had escaped came and told Lysias what had happened:

DOUAY OLD TESTAMENT

15 But all the hindmost of them fell by the sword, and they pursued them as far as Gezeron, and even to the plains of Idumea, and of Azotus, and of Jamnia: and there fell of them to the number of three thousand men.

16 And Judas returned again with his army that followed him,

17 And he said to the people: Be not greedy of the spoils: for there is war before us:

18 And Gorgias and his army are near us in the mountain: but stand ye now against our enemies, and overthrow them, and you shall take the spoils afterwards with safety.

19 And as Judas was speaking these words, behold part of them appeared looking forth from the mountain.

20 And Gorgias saw that his men were put to flight, and that they had set fire to the camp: for the smoke that was seen declared what was done.

21 And when they had seen this, they were seized with great fear, seeing at the same time Judas and his army in the plain ready to fight.

22 So they all fled away into the land of the strangers.

23 And Judas returned to take the spoils of the camp, and they got much gold, and silver, and blue silk, and purple of the sea, and great riches.

24 And returning home they sung a hymn, and blessed God in heaven, because he is good, because his mercy endureth for ever.

25 So Israel had a great deliverance that day.

26 And such of the strangers as escaped, went and told Lysias all that had happened.

KNOX TRANSLATION

pursuer ever catching the hindmost. All the way to Gezeron
they were chased, and on into the plains by Idumaea,[a]
Azotus and Jamnia, with a loss of three thousand men.
16 When Judas and his army came back from the pursuit,
17 Not yours, he told them, to run greedily after the spoils of
the camp; there is battle still awaiting us over yonder. 18 Not
far away, in the hill-country, lie Gorgias and his army; first
meet you and beat you the enemy, and then you shall fall to
your pillaging unafraid. 19 Even as he spoke, they were ware
of a company that watched them from the hill-side. 20 But by
now the camp was on fire, and it needed no more than the
smoke of it to warn Gorgias of his defeat; 21 that sight took
the heart out of Syria, the more so when it proved that Judas
and his army were in the valley, all appointed for battle,
22 and they fled for their lives, down into the plain of
Philistia. 23 So to the pillaging of the camp Judas returned;
what gold and silver they found there, what garments of blue
and sea-purple, what rich treasures! 24 Be sure there was
singing of songs on their homeward journey, as they praised
God in heaven, God who is gracious, whose mercy endures
for ever. 25 Here was a day of signal deliverance for Israel.
26 And what of Lysias? News reached him, through the survivors, of what had befallen, 27 and he was both sick and

a For 'Idumaea' some Greek manuscripts read 'Judaea'. Neither reading gives a good sense, and it seems possible that the name of Accaron, or some other Philistine town, has been accidentally miswritten.

TODAY'S ENGLISH VERSION

stragglers were killed. The Israelites pursued the enemy as
far as Gezer, the plains of Idumea, and the towns of Azotus
and Jamnia. Altogether they killed about 3,000 of the enemy.
16 When Judas and his army came back from the pursuit,
17-18 he said to his men, "Don't be greedy for loot. Gorgias
and his army are nearby in the mountains, so there is still
heavy fighting ahead of us. We must stand firm and fight.
After that, you can safely take all the loot you want."
19 Judas was just finishing his speech when an enemy patrol
on a scouting mission looked down from the mountains
20 and saw that their army had been put to flight; they could
tell from the smoke that their camp was burning. 21 When
they saw all this, they were terrified, and when they also
saw that Judas' army was in the plain ready for battle,
22 they all fled to Philistia. 23 Then Judas returned to loot the
enemy camp; he took large amounts of gold and silver, blue
and purple cloth, and other rich plunder. 24 When the Jews
came back to their own camp, they sang a hymn: "The Lord
is worthy of praise; his mercy endures forever." 25 That day
brought a great victory to the people of Israel.
26 The Gentile troops that escaped went to Lysias and
reported all that had happened. 27 When Lysias heard that

NEW REVISED STANDARD VERSION

15 and all those in the rear fell by the sword. They pursued
them to Gazara, and to the plains of Idumea, and to Azotus
and Jamnia; and three thousand of them fell. 16 Then Judas
and his force turned back from pursuing them, 17 and he
said to the people, "Do not be greedy for plunder, for there is
a battle before us; 18 Gorgias and his force are near us in the
hills. But stand now against our enemies and fight them,
and afterward seize the plunder boldly."
19 Just as Judas was finishing this speech, a detachment
appeared, coming out of the hills. 20 They saw that their
army[a] had been put to flight, and that the Jews[a] were burning the camp, for the smoke that was seen showed what had
happened. 21 When they perceived this, they were greatly
frightened, and when they also saw the army of Judas drawn
up in the plain for battle, 22 they all fled into the land of the
Philistines. 23 Then Judas returned to plunder the camp, and
they seized a great amount of gold and silver, and cloth dyed
blue and sea purple, and great riches. 24 On their return they
sang hymns and praises to Heaven—"For he is good, for his
mercy endures forever." 25 Thus Israel had a great deliverance that day.
26 Those of the foreigners who escaped went and reported
to Lysias all that had happened. 27 When he heard it, he was

a Gk *they*

NEW AMERICAN BIBLE

plain. 15 Their whole rearguard fell by the sword, and they
were pursued as far as Gazara and the plains of Judea, to
Azotus and Jamnia. About three thousand of their men fell.
16 When Judas and the army returned from the pursuit,
17 he said to the people: "Do not be greedy for the plunder,
for there is a fight ahead of us, 18 and Gorgias and his army
are near us on the mountain. But now stand firm against
our enemies and overthrow them. Afterward you can freely
take the plunder."
19 As Judas was finishing this speech, a detachment
appeared, looking down from the mountain. 20 They saw
that their army had been put to flight and their camp was
being burned. The smoke that could be seen indicated what
had happened. 21 When they realized this, they were terrified; and when they also saw the army of Judas in the plain
ready to attack, 22 they all fled to Philistine territory.
23 Then Judas went back to plunder the camp, and his men
collected much gold and silver, violet and crimson cloth, and
great treasure. 24 As they returned, they were singing hymns
and glorifying Heaven, "for he is good, for his mercy endures
forever." 25 Thus Israel had a great deliverance that day.
26 But those of the foreigners who had escaped went and
told Lysias all that had occurred. 27 When he heard it he was

NEW JERUSALEM BIBLE

stragglers fell by the sword. The pursuit continued as far as
Gezer and the plains of Idumaea, Azotus and Jamnia, and
the enemy lost about three thousand men.
16 Breaking off the pursuit, Judas returned with his men
17 and said to the people, 'Never mind the booty, for we have
another battle ahead of us. 18 Gorgias and his troops are still
near us in the mountains. First stand up to our enemies and
fight them, and then you can safely collect the booty.' 19 The
words were hardly out of Judas' mouth, when a detachment
came into view, peering down from the mountain.
20 Observing that their own troops had been routed and that
the camp had been fired—since the smoke, which they could
see, attested the fact— 21 they were panic-stricken at the
sight; and when, furthermore, they saw Judas' troops drawn
up for battle on the plain, 22 they all fled into Philistine territory. 23 Judas then turned back to plunder the camp, and a
large sum in gold and silver, with violet and sea-purple
stuffs, and many other valuables were carried off. 24 On their
return, the Jews chanted praises to Heaven, singing, 'He is
kind and his love is everlasting!' 25 That day had seen a
remarkable deliverance in Israel. 26 Those of the foreigners
who had escaped came and gave Lysias an account of all

GREEK OLD TESTAMENT

ἀκούσας συνεχύθη καὶ ἠθύμει, ὅτι οὐχ οἷα ἤθελεν, τοιαῦτα
ἐγεγόνει τῷ Ισραηλ, καὶ οὐχ οἷα αὐτῷ ἐνετείλατο ὁ βασιλεύς, ἐξέβη. 28 καὶ ἐν τῷ ἐρχομένῳ ἐνιαυτῷ συνελόχησεν
ἀνδρῶν ἐπιλέκτων ἑξήκοντα χιλιάδας καὶ πεντακισχιλίαν
ἵππον ὥστε ἐκπολεμῆσαι αὐτούς. 29 καὶ ἦλθον εἰς τὴν
Ιδουμαίαν καὶ παρενέβαλον ἐν Βαιθσουροις, καὶ συνήντησεν
αὐτοῖς Ιουδας ἐν δέκα χιλιάσιν ἀνδρῶν. 30 καὶ εἶδεν τὴν
παρεμβολὴν ἰσχυρὰν καὶ προσηύξατο καὶ εἶπεν Εὐλογητὸς
εἶ, ὁ σωτὴρ Ισραηλ ὁ συντρίψας τὸ ὅρμημα τοῦ δυνατοῦ ἐν
χειρὶ τοῦ δούλου σου Δαυιδ καὶ παρέδωκας τὴν παρεμβολὴν
τῶν ἀλλοφύλων εἰς χεῖρας Ιωναθου υἱοῦ Σαουλ καὶ τοῦ
αἴροντος τὰ σκεύη αὐτοῦ· 31 οὕτως σύγκλεισον τὴν παρεμβολὴν ταύτην ἐν χειρὶ λαοῦ σου Ισραηλ, καὶ αἰσχυνθήτωσαν
ἐπὶ τῇ δυνάμει καὶ τῇ ἵππῳ αὐτῶν· 32 δὸς αὐτοῖς δειλίαν
καὶ τῆξον θράσος ἰσχύος αὐτῶν, καὶ σαλευθήτωσαν τῇ συν-
τριβῇ αὐτῶν· 33 κατάβαλε αὐτοὺς ῥομφαίᾳ ἀγαπώντων σε,
καὶ αἰνεσάτωσάν σε πάντες οἱ εἰδότες τὸ ὄνομά σου ἐν
ὕμνοις. 34 καὶ συνέβαλλον ἀλλήλοις, καὶ ἔπεσον ἐκ τῆς
παρεμβολῆς Λυσίου εἰς πεντακισχιλίους ἄνδρας καὶ ἔπεσον
ἐξ ἐναντίας αὐτῶν. 35 ἰδὼν δὲ Λυσίας τὴν γενομένην
τροπὴν τῆς αὐτοῦ συντάξεως, τῆς δὲ Ιουδου τὸ γεγενημένον
θάρσος καὶ ὡς ἕτοιμοί εἰσιν ἢ ζῆν ἢ τεθνηκέναι γενναίως,
ἀπῆρεν εἰς Ἀντιόχειαν καὶ ἐξενολόγει πλεοναστὸν πάλιν
παραγίνεσθαι εἰς τὴν Ιουδαίαν.

KING JAMES VERSION

27 Who, when he heard thereof, was confounded and discouraged, because neither such things as he would were done unto Israel, nor such things as the king commanded him were come to pass.

28 The next year therefore following Lysias gathered together threescore thousand choice men *of foot,* and five thousand horsemen, that he might subdue them.

29 So they came into Idumea, and pitched their tents at Bethsura, and Judas met them with ten thousand men.

30 And when he saw that mighty army, he prayed and said, Blessed art thou, O Saviour of Israel, who didst quell the violence of the mighty man by the hand of thy servant David, and gavest the host of strangers into the hands of Jonathan the son of Saul, and his armourbearer;

31 Shut up this army in the hand of thy people Israel, and let them be confounded in their power and horsemen:

32 Make them to be of no courage, and cause the boldness of their strength to fall away, and let them quake at their destruction:

33 Cast them down with the sword of them that love thee, and let all those that know thy name praise thee with thanksgiving.

34 So they joined battle; and there were slain of the host of Lysias about five thousand men, even before them were they slain.

35 Now when Lysias saw his army put to flight, and the manliness of Judas' soldiers, and how they were ready either to live or die valiantly, he went into Antiochia, and gathered together a company of strangers, and having made his army greater than it was, he purposed to come again into Judea.

DOUAY OLD TESTAMENT

27 And when he heard these things, he was amazed and discouraged: because things had not succeeded in Israel according to his mind, and as the king had commanded.

28 So the year following Lysias gathered together threescore thousand chosen men, and five thousand horsemen, that he might subdue them.

29 And they came into Judea, and pitched their tents in Bethoron, and Judas met them with ten thousand men.

30 And they saw that the army was strong, and he prayed, and said: Blessed art thou, O Saviour of Israel, who didst break the violence of the mighty by the hand of thy servant David, and didst deliver up the camp of the strangers into the hands of Jonathan the son of Saul and of his armourbearer.

31 Shut up this army in the hands of thy people Israel, and let them be confounded in their host and their horsemen.

32 Strike them with fear, and cause the boldness of their strength to languish, and let them quake at their own destruction.

33 Cast them down with the sword of them that love thee: and let all that know thy name, praise thee with hymns.

34 And they joined battle: and there fell of the army of Lysias five thousand men.

35 And when Lysias saw that his men were put to flight, and how bold the Jews were, and that they were ready either to live, or to die manfully, he went to Antioch, and chose soldiers, that they might come again into Judea with greater numbers.

KNOX TRANSLATION

sorry at the hearing; his own will crossed, and his master's
command ill carried out! 28 So, in the following year, he
made a muster of sixty thousand picked men, with five thousand horse, to crush the rebellion; 29 into Judaea they
marched, and encamped at Bethoron, where Judas met them
with ten thousand.[a] 30 At the sight of their great numbers,
this was Judas' prayer: Blessed art thou, Saviour of Israel,
who didst make use of thy servant David, a giant's onset to
overthrow! Victory thou didst give, over an invading army, to
Saul's son Jonathan and the squire that bore him company!
31 So may yonder host, left at Israel's mercy, unlearn its confidence in strength and in speed; 32 strike terror into them,
let their manhood melt away, as they tremble at the
approach of doom; 33 sword of thy true lovers be their undoing, triumph-song of thy worshippers their dirge! 34 With
that, battle was joined, and of Lysias' men, five thousand
were left dead on the field. 35 What should he do? Here were
his troops fled in disorder, here was Judas in command of
brave men, that would as soon have an honourable death as
life itself. Back he went to Antioch, and there levied soldiers
for a greater expedition yet against Judaea.

[a] For 'Judaea' the Greek manuscripts have 'Idumaea', and for 'Bethoron', 'Bethsura'. Cf. verse 61 below.

TODAY'S ENGLISH VERSION

his troops had lost the battle, he was shocked and disappointed that Israel had not been defeated as the king had
commanded.
28 In the following year Lysias gathered an army of 60,000
well-trained infantry and 5,000 cavalry, intending to conquer the Jews. 29 They marched into Idumea and camped at
Bethzur. Judas came to meet them with 10,000 men.
30 When Judas saw how strong the enemy's army was, he
prayed, "We will praise you, Savior of Israel. You broke the
attack of the giant by the hand of your servant David and
you let Saul's son Jonathan and the young man who carried
his weapons defeat the entire Philistine army. 31 Now in the
same way let your people Israel defeat our enemy. Put them
to shame, in spite of all their confidence in their infantry and
cavalry. 32 Make them afraid; let their bold strength melt
away; let them tremble at the prospect of defeat. 33 We love
and worship you; so let us kill our enemies, that we may
then sing your praises."
34 The battle began, and in the hand-to-hand fighting
about 5,000 of Lysias' men were killed. 35 When Lysias saw
that his army was being defeated and when he saw the reckless courage of Judas and his men, who showed that they
were ready to live or die with honor, he returned to Antioch.
There he recruited some mercenaries and planned to return
to Judea later with a much larger army.

NEW REVISED STANDARD VERSION

perplexed and discouraged, for things had not happened to
Israel as he had intended, nor had they turned out as the
king had ordered. 28 But the next year he mustered sixty
thousand picked infantry and five thousand cavalry to subdue them. 29 They came into Idumea and encamped at Beth-
zur, and Judas met them with ten thousand men.
30 When he saw that their army was strong, he prayed,
saying, "Blessed are you, O Savior of Israel, who crushed the
attack of the mighty warrior by the hand of your servant
David, and gave the camp of the Philistines into the hands of
Jonathan son of Saul, and of the man who carried his armor.
31 Hem in this army by the hand of your people Israel, and let
them be ashamed of their troops and their cavalry. 32 Fill
them with cowardice; melt the boldness of their strength; let
them tremble in their destruction. 33 Strike them down with
the sword of those who love you, and let all who know your
name praise you with hymns."
34 Then both sides attacked, and there fell of the army of
Lysias five thousand men; they fell in action.[a] 35 When
Lysias saw the rout of his troops and observed the boldness
that inspired those of Judas, and how ready they were either
to live or to die nobly, he withdrew to Antioch and enlisted
mercenaries in order to invade Judea again with an even
larger army.

a Or *and some fell on the opposite side*

NEW AMERICAN BIBLE

disturbed and discouraged, because things in Israel had not
turned out as he intended and as the king had ordered.
28 So the following year he gathered together sixty thousand picked men and five thousand cavalry, to subdue them.
29 They came into Idumea and camped at Beth-zur, and Judas
met them with ten thousand men. 30 Seeing that the army
was strong, he prayed thus:
"Blessed are you, O Savior of Israel, who broke the rush of
the mighty one by the hand of your servant David and delivered the camp of the Philistines into the hand of Jonathan,
the son of Saul, and his armor-bearer. 31 Give this army into
the hands of your people Israel; make them ashamed of their
troops and their cavalry. 32 Strike them with fear, weaken
the boldness of their strength, and let them tremble at their
own destruction. 33 Strike them down by the sword of those
who love you, that all who know your name may hymn your
praise."
34 Then they engaged in battle, and about five thousand of
Lysias' men fell in hand-to-hand fighting. 35 When Lysias
saw his ranks beginning to give way, and the increased boldness of Judas, whose men were ready either to live or to die
bravely, he withdrew to Antioch and began to recruit mercenaries so as to return to Judea with greater numbers.

NEW JERUSALEM BIBLE

that had happened. 27 The news shocked and dismayed him,
for affairs in Israel had not gone as he intended, and the
result was quite the opposite to what the king had ordered.
28[a] The next year he mobilised sixty thousand picked
troops and five thousand cavalry with the intention of finishing off the Jews. 29 They advanced into Idumaea and made
their base at Beth-Zur, where Judas met them with ten thousand men. 30 When he saw their military strength he offered
this prayer, 'Blessed are you, Saviour of Israel, who shattered the mighty warrior's attack at the hand of your servant
David, and delivered the Philistine camp into the hands of
Jonathan son of Saul, and his armour-bearer. 31 Crush this
expedition in the same way at the hands of your people
Israel; let their troops and cavalry bring them nothing but
shame. 32 Sow panic in their ranks, confound the confidence
they put in their numbers and send them reeling in defeat.
33 Overthrow them by the sword of those who love you, and
all who acknowledge your name will sing your praises.'
34 The two forces engaged, and five thousand men of Lysias'
troops fell in hand-to-hand fighting. 35 Seeing the rout of his
army and the courage of Judas' troops and their readiness to
live or die nobly, Lysias withdrew to Antioch, where he
recruited mercenaries for a further invasion of Judaea in
even greater strength.

a **4** 4:28seq. // 2 M 11:1–12.

GREEK OLD TESTAMENT

36 Εἶπεν δὲ Ιουδας καὶ οἱ ἀδελφοὶ αὐτοῦ Ἰδοὺ συνετρίβησαν οἱ ἐχθροὶ ἡμῶν, ἀναβῶμεν καθαρίσαι τὰ ἅγια καὶ
ἐγκαινίσαι. 37 καὶ συνήχθη ἡ παρεμβολὴ πᾶσα καὶ ἀνέβησαν
εἰς ὄρος Σιων. 38 καὶ εἶδον τὸ ἁγίασμα ἠρημωμένον καὶ τὸ
θυσιαστήριον βεβηλωμένον καὶ τὰς θύρας κατακεκαυμένας
καὶ ἐν ταῖς αὐλαῖς φυτὰ πεφυκότα ὡς ἐν δρυμῷ ἢ ὡς ἐν ἑνὶ
τῶν ὀρέων καὶ τὰ παστοφόρια καθῃρημένα. 39 καὶ διέρρηξαν
τὰ ἱμάτια αὐτῶν καὶ ἐκόψαντο κοπετὸν μέγαν καὶ ἐπέθεντο
σποδὸν 40 καὶ ἔπεσαν ἐπὶ πρόσωπον ἐπὶ τὴν γῆν καὶ ἐσάλπισαν ταῖς σάλπιγξιν τῶν σημασιῶν καὶ ἐβόησαν εἰς
οὐρανόν. 41 τότε ἐπέταξεν Ιουδας ἀνδράσιν πολεμεῖν τοὺς
ἐν τῇ ἄκρᾳ, ἕως καθαρίσῃ τὰ ἅγια. 42 καὶ ἐπελέξατο ἱερεῖς
ἀμώμους θελητὰς νόμου, 43 καὶ ἐκαθάρισαν τὰ ἅγια καὶ
ἦραν τοὺς λίθους τοῦ μιασμοῦ εἰς τόπον ἀκάθαρτον. 44 καὶ
ἐβουλεύσαντο περὶ τοῦ θυσιαστηρίου τῆς ὁλοκαυτώσεως τοῦ
βεβηλωμένου, τί αὐτῷ ποιήσωσιν· 45 καὶ ἔπεσεν αὐτοῖς
βουλὴ ἀγαθὴ καθελεῖν αὐτό, μήποτε γένηται αὐτοῖς εἰς ὄνειδος ὅτι ἐμίαναν τὰ ἔθνη αὐτό· καὶ καθεῖλον τὸ θυσιαστήριον
46 καὶ ἀπέθεντο τοὺς λίθους ἐν τῷ ὄρει τοῦ οἴκου ἐν τόπῳ
ἐπιτηδείῳ μέχρι τοῦ παραγενηθῆναι προφήτην τοῦ
ἀποκριθῆναι περὶ αὐτῶν. 47 καὶ ἔλαβον λίθους ὁλοκλήρους
κατὰ τὸν νόμον καὶ ᾠκοδόμησαν θυσιαστήριον καινὸν κατὰ

KING JAMES VERSION

36 Then said Judas and his brethren, Behold, our enemies are discomfited: let us go up to cleanse and dedicate the sanctuary.

37 Upon this all the host assembled themselves together, and went up into mount Sion.

38 And when they saw the sanctuary desolate, and the altar profaned, and the gates burned up, and shrubs growing in the courts as in a forest, or in one of the mountains, yea, and the priests' chambers pulled down;

39 They rent their clothes, and made great lamentation, and cast ashes upon their heads,

40 And fell down flat to the ground upon their faces, and blew an alarm with the trumpets, and cried toward heaven.

41 Then Judas appointed certain men to fight against those that were in the fortress, until he had cleansed the sanctuary.

42 So he chose priests of blameless conversation, such as had pleasure in the law:

43 Who cleansed the sanctuary, and bare out the defiled stones into an unclean place.

44 And when as they consulted what to do with the altar of burnt offerings, which was profaned;

45 They thought it best to pull it down, lest it should be a reproach to them, because the heathen had defiled it: wherefore they pulled it down,

46 And laid up the stones in the mountain of the temple in a convenient place, until there should come a prophet to shew what should be done with them.

47 Then they took whole stones according to the law, and built a new altar according to the former;

DOUAY OLD TESTAMENT

36 Then Judas, and his brethren said: Behold our enemies are discomfited: let us go up now to cleanse the holy places and to repair them.

37 And all the army assembled together, and they went up into mount Sion.

38 And they saw the sanctuary desolate, and the altar profaned, and the gates burnt, and shrubs growing up in the courts as in a forest, or on the mountains, and the chambers joining to the temple thrown down.

39 And they rent their garments, and made great lamentation, and put ashes on their heads:

40 And they fell down to the ground on their faces, and they sounded with the trumpets of alarm, and they cried towards heaven.

41 Then Judas appointed men to fight against them that were in the castle, till they had cleansed the holy places.

42 And he chose priests without blemish, whose will was set upon the law of God:

43 And they cleansed the holy places, and took away the stones that had been defiled into an unclean place.

44 And he considered about the altar of holocausts that had been profaned, what he should do with it.

45 And a good counsel came into their minds, to pull it down: lest it should be a reproach to them, because the Gentiles had defiled it; so they threw it down.

46 And they laid up the stones in the mountain of the temple in a convenient place, till there should come a prophet, and give answer concerning them.

47 Then they took whole stones according to the law, and built a new altar according to the former:

KNOX TRANSLATION

36 And now Judas and his brethren had but one thought;
the enemy vanquished, they would betake themselves to
Jerusalem, to cleanse and restore the sanctuary. 37 So the
whole army fell into rank, and they climbed the hill of Sion
together. 38 What saw they? The holy place desolate, the
altar profaned, charred gates, courts overgrown with brushwood, like forest clearing or mountain glen, the priests' lodging in ruins. 39 Upon this, there was rending of garments,
and loud lament; dust they cast on their heads, 40 and fell
face to earth; then, as the trumpet's note gave the summons,
raised their cries to heaven.
41 And what did Judas? First, he sent a force to engage the
citadel's garrison, while the holy place was a-cleansing;
42 then he chose priests, without blot or blemish, and true
lovers of the law besides, 43 who thereupon cleansed the
sanctuary, nor any stone that was polluted with idolatry but
they had it away into a place unclean. 44 And next, he must
concern himself with the altar of burnt-sacrifice, that was
now all defiled. 45 And it was good counsel they took; the
altar must be destroyed, else the day when the Gentiles polluted it should be remembered to their shame. So destroy it
they did, 46 and laid up the stones in a place apt for their
purpose, there on the temple hill. Here they must remain,
until the coming of a prophet that should give sentence,
what was to be done with them.
47 Then they raised a new altar in place of the old, using
stones that had never felt the pick, as the law bade;[a]

[a] See Ex. 20. 25.

TODAY'S ENGLISH VERSION

36 Judas and his brothers said, "Now that our enemies have
been defeated, let's go to Jerusalem to purify the Temple and
rededicate it." 37 So the whole army was assembled and
went up to Mount Zion. 38 There they found the Temple
abandoned, the altar profaned, the gates burned down, the
courtyards grown up in a forest of weeds, and the priests'
rooms torn down. 39 In their sorrow, they tore their clothes,
cried loudly, threw ashes on their heads, 40 and fell face
down on the ground. When the signal was given on the
trumpets, everyone cried out to the Lord.

41 Then Judas ordered some of his soldiers to attack the
men in the fort, while he purified the Temple. 42 He chose
some priests who were qualified and who were devoted to
the Law. 43 They purified the Temple and took the stones
that had been defiled and put them in an unclean place.
44 They discussed what should be done with the altar of
burnt offerings, which had been desecrated 45 by the
Gentiles, and decided to tear it down, so that it would not
stand there as a monument to their shame. So they tore
down the altar 46 and put the stones in a suitable place on
the Temple hill, where they were to be kept until a prophet
should appear and decide what to do with them. 47 Then
they took uncut stones, as the Law of Moses required, and
built a new altar like the old one. 48 They repaired the

NEW REVISED STANDARD VERSION

36 Then Judas and his brothers said, "See, our enemies
are crushed; let us go up to cleanse the sanctuary and dedicate it." 37 So all the army assembled and went up to Mount
Zion. 38 There they saw the sanctuary desolate, the altar profaned, and the gates burned. In the courts they saw bushes
sprung up as in a thicket, or as on one of the mountains.
They saw also the chambers of the priests in ruins. 39 Then
they tore their clothes and mourned with great lamentation;
they sprinkled themselves with ashes 40 and fell face down
on the ground. And when the signal was given with the
trumpets, they cried out to Heaven.

41 Then Judas detailed men to fight against those in the
citadel until he had cleansed the sanctuary. 42 He chose
blameless priests devoted to the law, 43 and they cleansed
the sanctuary and removed the defiled stones to an unclean
place. 44 They deliberated what to do about the altar of burnt
offering, which had been profaned. 45 And they thought it
best to tear it down, so that it would not be a lasting shame
to them that the Gentiles had defiled it. So they tore down
the altar, 46 and stored the stones in a convenient place on
the temple hill until a prophet should come to tell what to do
with them. 47 Then they took unhewn[a] stones, as the law
directs, and built a new altar like the former one. 48 They

a Gk *whole*

NEW AMERICAN BIBLE

36 Then Judas and his brothers said, "Now that our enemies have been crushed, let us go up to purify the sanctuary
and rededicate it." 37 So the whole army assembled, and
went up to Mount Zion. 38 They found the sanctuary desolate, the altar desecrated, the gates burnt, weeds growing in
the courts as in a forest or on some mountain, and the
priests' chambers demolished. 39 Then they tore their clothes
and made great lamentation; they sprinkled their heads with
ashes 40 and fell with their faces to the ground. And when
the signal was given with trumpets, they cried out to
Heaven.

41 Judas appointed men to attack those in the citadel, while
he purified the sanctuary. 42 He chose blameless priests,
devoted to the law; 43 these purified the sanctuary and carried away the stones of the Abomination to an unclean place.
44 They deliberated what ought to be done with the altar of
holocausts that had been desecrated. 45 The happy thought
came to them to tear it down, lest it be a lasting shame to
them that the Gentiles had defiled it; so they tore down the
altar. 46 They stored the stones in a suitable place on the
temple hill, until a prophet should come and decide what to
do with them. 47 Then they took uncut stones, according to
the law, and built a new altar like the former one. 48 They

NEW JERUSALEM BIBLE

36[a] Judas and his brothers then said, 'Now that our enemies have been defeated, let us go up to purify the sanctuary
and dedicate it.' 37 So they marshalled the whole army, and
went up to Mount Zion. 38 There they found the sanctuary
deserted, the altar desecrated, the gates burnt down, and
vegetation growing in the courts as it might in a wood or on
some mountain, while the storerooms were in ruins. 39 They
tore their garments and mourned bitterly, putting dust on
their heads. 40 They prostrated themselves on the ground,
and when the trumpets gave the signal they cried aloud to
Heaven.

41 Judas then ordered his men to keep the Citadel garrison
engaged until he had purified the sanctuary. 42 Next, he
selected priests who were blameless and zealous for the Law
43 to purify the sanctuary and remove the stones of the
'Pollution' to some unclean place.

44 They discussed what should be done about the altar of
burnt offering which had been profaned, 45 and very properly
decided to pull it down, rather than later be embarrassed
about it since it had been defiled by the gentiles. They therefore demolished it 46 and deposited the stones in a suitable
place on the hill of the Dwelling to await the appearance of a
prophet who should give a ruling about them. 47 They took
unhewn stones, as the Law prescribed, and built a new altar
on the lines of the old one. 48 They restored the Holy Place

a **4** 4:36seq. // 2 M 10:1–8.

GREEK OLD TESTAMENT

τὸ πρότερον. 48 καὶ ᾠκοδόμησαν τὰ ἅγια καὶ τὰ ἐντὸς τοῦ
οἴκου καὶ τὰς αὐλὰς ἡγίασαν 49 καὶ ἐποίησαν σκεύη ἅγια
καινὰ καὶ εἰσήνεγκαν τὴν λυχνίαν καὶ τὸ θυσιαστήριον τῶν
θυμιαμάτων καὶ τὴν τράπεζαν εἰς τὸν ναόν. 50 καὶ ἐθυμί-
ασαν ἐπὶ τὸ θυσιαστήριον καὶ ἐξῆψαν τοὺς λύχνους τοὺς ἐπὶ
τῆς λυχνίας, καὶ ἔφαινον ἐν τῷ ναῷ. 51 καὶ ἐπέθηκαν ἐπὶ
τὴν τράπεζαν ἄρτους καὶ ἐξεπέτασαν τὰ καταπετάσματα.
καὶ ἐτέλεσαν πάντα τὰ ἔργα, ἃ ἐποίησαν. 52 καὶ ὤρθρισαν
τὸ πρωὶ τῇ πέμπτῃ καὶ εἰκάδι τοῦ μηνὸς τοῦ ἐνάτου [οὗτος
ὁ μὴν Χασελευ] τοῦ ὀγδόου καὶ τεσσαρακοστοῦ καὶ ἑκατοστοῦ ἔτους 53 καὶ ἀνήνεγκαν θυσίαν κατὰ τὸν νόμον ἐπὶ τὸ
θυσιαστήριον τῶν ὁλοκαυτωμάτων τὸ καινόν, ὃ ἐποίησαν.
54 κατὰ τὸν καιρὸν καὶ κατὰ τὴν ἡμέραν, ἐν ᾗ ἐβεβήλωσαν
αὐτὸ τὰ ἔθνη, ἐν ἐκείνῃ ἐνεκαινίσθη ἐν ᾠδαῖς καὶ κιθάραις
καὶ κινύραις καὶ κυμβάλοις. 55 καὶ ἔπεσεν πᾶς ὁ λαὸς ἐπὶ
πρόσωπον καὶ προσεκύνησαν καὶ εὐλόγησαν εἰς οὐρανὸν τὸν
εὐοδώσαντα αὐτοῖς. 56 καὶ ἐποίησαν τὸν ἐγκαινισμὸν τοῦ
θυσιαστηρίου ἡμέρας ὀκτὼ καὶ προσήνεγκαν ὁλοκαυτώματα
μετ᾽ εὐφροσύνης καὶ ἔθυσαν θυσίαν σωτηρίου καὶ αἰνέσεως.
57 καὶ κατεκόσμησαν τὸ κατὰ πρόσωπον τοῦ ναοῦ στεφάνοις
χρυσοῖς καὶ ἀσπιδίσκαις καὶ ἐνεκαίνισαν τὰς πύλας καὶ τὰ
παστοφόρια καὶ ἐθύρωσαν αὐτά. 58 καὶ ἐγενήθη εὐφροσύνη
μεγάλη ἐν τῷ λαῷ σφόδρα, καὶ ἀπεστράφη ὀνειδισμὸς ἐθνῶν.

KING JAMES VERSION

48 And made up the sanctuary, and the things that were within the temple, and hallowed the courts.

49 They made also new holy vessels, and into the temple they brought the candlestick, and the altar of burnt offerings, and of incense, and the table.

50 And upon the altar they burned incense, and the lamps that were upon the candlestick they lighted, that they might give light in the temple.

51 Furthermore they set the loaves upon the table, and spread out the veils, and finished all the works which they had begun to make.

52 Now on the five and twentieth day of the ninth month, which *is called* the month Casleu, in the hundred forty and eighth year, they rose up betimes in the morning,

53 And offered sacrifice according to the law upon the new altar of burnt offerings, which they had made.

54 Look, at what time and what day the heathen had profaned it, even in that was it dedicated with songs, and citherns, and harps, and cymbals.

55 Then all the people fell upon their faces, worshipping and praising the God of heaven, who had given them good success.

56 And so they kept the dedication of the altar eight days, and offered burnt offerings with gladness, and sacrificed the sacrifice of deliverance and praise.

57 They decked also the forefront of the temple with crowns of gold, and with shields; and the gates and the chambers they renewed, and hanged doors upon them.

58 Thus was there very great gladness among the people, for that the reproach of the heathen was put away.

DOUAY OLD TESTAMENT

48 And they built up the holy places, and the things that were within the temple: and they sanctified the temple, and the courts.

49 And they made new holy vessels, and brought in the candlestick, and the altar of incense, and the table into the temple.

50 And they put incense upon the altar, and lighted up the lamps that were upon the candlestick, and they gave light in the temple.

51 And they set the loaves upon the table, and hung up the veils, and finished all the works that they had begun to make.

52 And they arose before the morning on the five and twentieth day of the ninth month (which is the month of Casleu) in the hundred and forty-eighth year.

53 And they offered sacrifice according to the law upon the new altar of holocausts which they had made.

54 According to the time, and according to the day wherein the heathens had defiled it, in the same was it dedicated anew with canticles, and harps, and lutes, and cymbals.

55 And all the people fell upon their faces, and adored, and blessed up to heaven, him that had prospered them.

56 And they kept the dedication of the altar eight days, and they offered holocausts with joy, and sacrifices of salvation, and of praise.

57 And they adorned the front of the temple with crowns of gold, and escutcheons, and they renewed the gates, and the chambers, and hanged doors upon them.

58 And there was exceeding great joy among the people, and the reproach of the Gentiles was turned away.

KNOX TRANSLATION

48 repaired shrine and inner walls, and rid both temple and
temple courts of their defilement. 49 New appurtenances, too,
the temple must have, lamp-stand, incense-altar and table be
restored to it; 50 incense be put on the altar, lamps kindled to
light the holy place, 51 loaves set out on the table, and veils
hung up; then at length their task was accomplished. 52 On
the twenty-fifth of Casleu, the ninth month, in the hundred
and forty-eighth year, they rose before daybreak, 53 and
offered sacrifice, as the law bade, on the new altar they had
set up. 54 This was the very month, the very day, when it
had been polluted by the Gentiles; now, on the same day of
the same month, it was dedicated anew, with singing of
hymns, and music of harp, zither and cymbals. 55 Thereupon
all the people fell down face to earth, to adore and praise,
high as heaven, the author of their felicity; 56 and for eight
days together they celebrated the altar's renewal, burned victim and brought welcome-offering with glad and grateful
hearts.

57 They decked the front wall of the temple, at this time,
with gold crowns and escutcheons, consecrated the gates
and the priest's lodging anew, and furnished it with doors;
58 and all the while there was great rejoicing among the people; as for the taunts of the heathen, they were heard no

TODAY'S ENGLISH VERSION

Temple, inside and out, and dedicated its courtyards. 49 They
made new utensils for worship and brought the lampstand,
the altar of incense, and the table for the bread into the
Temple. 50 They burned incense on the altar and lit the
lamps on the lampstand, and there was light in the Temple!
51 They placed the loaves of bread on the table, hung the curtains, and completed all the work.
52-54 The twenty-fifth day of the ninth month, the month of
Kislev, in the year 148[a] was the anniversary of the day the
Gentiles had desecrated the altar. On that day a sacrifice was
offered on the new altar in accordance with the Law of
Moses. The new altar was dedicated and hymns were sung to
the accompaniment of harps, lutes, and cymbals. 55 All the
people bowed down with their faces to the ground and worshiped and praised the Lord for giving them victory.
56 For eight days they celebrated the rededication of the
altar. With great joy they brought burnt offerings and offered
fellowship offerings and thank offerings. 57 They decorated
the front of the Temple with gold crowns and shields, rebuilt
the gates and the priests' rooms and put doors on them.
58 Now that the Jews had removed the shame which the
Gentiles had brought, they held a great celebration. 59 Then

[a] THE YEAR 148: *This corresponds to 164 B.C.*

NEW REVISED STANDARD VERSION

also rebuilt the sanctuary and the interior of the temple, and
consecrated the courts. 49 They made new holy vessels, and
brought the lampstand, the altar of incense, and the table
into the temple. 50 Then they offered incense on the altar and
lit the lamps on the lampstand, and these gave light in the
temple. 51 They placed the bread on the table and hung up
the curtains. Thus they finished all the work they had undertaken.
52 Early in the morning on the twenty-fifth day of the
ninth month, which is the month of Chislev, in the one hundred forty-eighth year,[a] 53 they rose and offered sacrifice, as
the law directs, on the new altar of burnt offering that they
had built. 54 At the very season and on the very day that the
Gentiles had profaned it, it was dedicated with songs and
harps and lutes and cymbals. 55 All the people fell on their
faces and worshiped and blessed Heaven, who had prospered
them. 56 So they celebrated the dedication of the altar for
eight days, and joyfully offered burnt offerings; they offered
a sacrifice of well-being and a thanksgiving offering. 57 They
decorated the front of the temple with golden crowns and
small shields; they restored the gates and the chambers for
the priests, and fitted them with doors. 58 There was very
great joy among the people, and the disgrace brought by the
Gentiles was removed.

[a] 164 B.C.

NEW AMERICAN BIBLE

also repaired the sanctuary and the interior of the temple
and purified the courts. 49 They made new sacred vessels
and brought the lampstand, the altar of incense, and the
table into the temple. 50 Then they burned incense on the
altar and lighted the lamps on the lampstand, and these illuminated the temple. 51 They also put loaves on the table and
hung up the curtains. Thus they finished all the work they
had undertaken.
52 Early in the morning on the twenty-fifth day of the ninth
month, that is, the month of Chislev, in the year one hundred and forty-eight, 53 they arose and offered sacrifice
according to the law on the new altar of holocausts that they
had made. 54 On the anniversary of the day on which the
Gentiles had defiled it, on that very day it was reconsecrated
with songs, harps, flutes, and cymbals. 55 All the people
prostrated themselves and adored and praised Heaven, who
had given them success.
56 For eight days they celebrated the dedication of the altar
and joyfully offered holocausts and sacrifices of deliverance
and praise. 57 They ornamented the façade of the temple
with gold crowns and shields; they repaired the gates and
the priests' chambers and furnished them with doors.
58 There was great joy among the people now that the disgrace of the Gentiles was removed. 59 Then Judas and his

NEW JERUSALEM BIBLE

and the interior of the Dwelling, and purified the courts.
49 They made new sacred vessels, and brought the lamp-
stand, the altar of incense, and the table into the Temple.
50 They burned incense on the altar and lit the lamps on the
lamp-stand, and these shone inside the Temple. 51 They
placed the loaves on the table and hung the curtains and
completed all the tasks they had undertaken.
52 On the twenty-fifth of the ninth month, Chislev, in the
year 148 they rose at dawn 53 and offered a lawful sacrifice
on the new altar of burnt offering which they had made.
54 The altar was dedicated, to the sound of hymns, zithers,
lyres and cymbals, at the same time of year and on the same
day on which the gentiles had originally profaned it. 55 The
whole people fell prostrate in adoration and then praised
Heaven who had granted them success. 56 For eight days
they celebrated the dedication of the altar, joyfully offering
burnt offerings, communion and thanksgiving sacrifices.
57 They ornamented the front of the Temple with crowns and
bosses of gold, renovated the gates and storerooms, providing the latter with doors. 58 There was no end to the rejoicing
among the people, since the disgrace inflicted by the gentiles

GREEK OLD TESTAMENT

59 καὶ ἔστησεν Ιουδας καὶ οἱ ἀδελφοὶ αὐτοῦ καὶ πᾶσα ἡ
ἐκκλησία Ισραηλ ἵνα ἄγωνται αἱ ἡμέραι τοῦ ἐγκαινισμοῦ τοῦ
θυσιαστηρίου ἐν τοῖς καιροῖς αὐτῶν ἐνιαυτὸν κατ' ἐνιαυτὸν
ἡμέρας ὀκτὼ ἀπὸ τῆς πέμπτης καὶ εἰκάδος τοῦ μηνὸς
Χασελευ μετ' εὐφροσύνης καὶ χαρᾶς. 60 καὶ ᾠκοδόμησαν ἐν
τῷ καιρῷ ἐκείνῳ τὸ ὄρος Σιων κυκλόθεν τείχη ὑψηλὰ καὶ
πύργους ὀχυρούς, μήποτε παραγενηθέντα τὰ ἔθνη κατα-
πατήσωσιν αὐτά, ὡς ἐποίησαν τὸ πρότερον. 61 καὶ ἀπέταξεν
ἐκεῖ δύναμιν τηρεῖν αὐτὸ καὶ ὠχύρωσεν αὐτὸ τηρεῖν τὴν
Βαιθσουραν τοῦ ἔχειν τὸν λαὸν ὀχύρωμα κατὰ πρόσωπον τῆς
Ιδουμαίας.

5 Καὶ ἐγένετο ὅτε ἤκουσαν τὰ ἔθνη κυκλόθεν ὅτι ᾠκοδομήθη τὸ θυσιαστήριον καὶ ἐνεκαινίσθη τὸ ἁγίασμα ὡς
τὸ πρότερον, καὶ ὠργίσθησαν σφόδρα 2 καὶ ἐβουλεύσαντο
τοῦ ἆραι τὸ γένος Ιακωβ τοὺς ὄντας ἐν μέσῳ αὐτῶν καὶ
ἤρξαντο τοῦ θανατοῦν ἐν τῷ λαῷ καὶ ἐξαίρειν. 3 καὶ ἐπολέμει Ιουδας πρὸς τοὺς υἱοὺς Ησαυ ἐν τῇ Ιδουμαίᾳ, τὴν
Ακραβαττήνην, ὅτι περιεκάθηντο τὸν Ισραηλ, καὶ ἐπάταξεν
αὐτοὺς πληγὴν μεγάλην καὶ συνέστειλεν αὐτοὺς καὶ ἔλαβεν
τὰ σκῦλα αὐτῶν. 4 καὶ ἐμνήσθη τῆς κακίας υἱῶν Βαιαν, οἳ
ἦσαν τῷ λαῷ εἰς παγίδα καὶ σκάνδαλον ἐν τῷ ἐνεδρεύειν
αὐτοὺς ἐν ταῖς ὁδοῖς. 5 καὶ συνεκλείσθησαν ὑπ' αὐτοῦ εἰς
τοὺς πύργους, καὶ παρενέβαλεν ἐπ' αὐτοὺς καὶ ἀνεθεμάτισεν
αὐτοὺς καὶ ἐνεπύρισε τοὺς πύργους αὐτῆς ἐν πυρὶ σὺν πᾶσιν τοῖς ἐνοῦσιν. 6 καὶ διεπέρασεν ἐπὶ τοὺς υἱοὺς Αμμων
καὶ εὗρεν χεῖρα κραταιὰν καὶ λαὸν πολὺν καὶ Τιμόθεον

KING JAMES VERSION

59 Moreover Judas and his brethren with the whole congregation of Israel ordained, that the days of the dedication of the altar should be kept in their season from year to year by the space of eight days, from the five and twentieth day of the month Casleu, with mirth and gladness.

60 At that time also they builded up the mount Sion with high walls and strong towers round about, lest the Gentiles should come and tread it down, as they had done before.

61 And they set there a garrison to keep it, and fortified Bethsura to preserve it; that the people might have a defence against Idumea.

5 Now when the nations round about heard that the altar was built, and the sanctuary renewed as before, it displeased them very much.

2 Wherefore they thought to destroy the generation of Jacob that was among them, and thereupon they began to slay and destroy the people.

3 Then Judas fought against the children of Esau in Idumea at Arabattine, because they besieged Israel: and he gave them a great overthrow, and abated their courage, and took their spoils.

4 Also he remembered the injury of the children of Bean, who had been a snare and an offence unto the people, in that they lay in wait for them in the ways.

5 He shut them up therefore in the towers, and encamped against them, and destroyed them utterly, and burned the towers of that *place* with fire, and all that were therein.

6 Afterward he passed over to the children of Ammon, where he found a mighty power, and much people, with Timotheus their captain.

DOUAY OLD TESTAMENT

59 And Judas, and his brethren, and all the church of Israel decreed, that the day of the dedication of the altar should be kept in its season from year to year for eight days, from the five and twentieth day of the month of Casleu, with joy and gladness.

60 They built up also at that time mount Sion, with high walls, and strong towers round about, lest the Gentiles should at any time come, and tread it down as they did before.

61 And he placed a garrison there to keep it, and he fortified it to secure Bethsura, that the people might have a defence against Idumea.

5 NOW it came to pass, when the nations round about heard that the altar and the sanctuary were built up as before, that they were exceeding angry.

2 And they thought to destroy the generation of Jacob that were among them, and they began to kill some of the people, and to persecute them.

3 Then Judas fought against the children of Esau in Idumea, and them that were in Acrabathane: because they beset the Israelites round about, and he made a great slaughter of them.

4 And he remembered the malice of the children of Bean: who were a snare and a stumblingblock to the people, by lying in wait for them in the way.

5 And they were shut up by him in towers, and he set upon them, and devoted them to utter destruction, and burnt their towers with fire, and all that were in them.

6 Then he passed over to the children of Ammon, where he found a mighty power, and much people, and Timotheus was their captain:

KNOX TRANSLATION

more. 59 No wonder if Judas and his brethren, with the
whole assembly of Israel, made a decree that this feast
should be kept year by year for eight days together, the feast-
day of the altar's dedication.[a] Came that season, from the
twenty-fifth day of Casleu onwards, all was to be rejoicing
and holiday. 60 At this time, too, they fortified the hill of
Sion, with walls and strong towers all about; never more
should Gentile feet profane it. 61 Judas put a garrison there,
and would have it strong enough to command Bethsura; a
bulwark Israel must have against attack from the frontiers of
Edom.

5 Great indignation had the Gentiles that lived round
about, when they heard that altar and temple were
standing as of old. 2 Their first thought was to rid their own
territory of Jacob's breed, and all at once they set about to
murder and harry them. 3 So Judas must needs take arms
against them, Esau's race in Idumaea, and the men of
Acrabathane, that were keeping Israelite folk under strict
siege; and signally he defeated them. 4 Nor might he overlook Beän's tribe and the treachery they shewed, ever catching Israel at unawares by laying an ambush in his path.
5 These he chased into their strongholds and besieged them
there; laid them under a ban[b] and burned the strongholds to
the ground, with their defenders in them. 6 Then he crossed
over into Ammon, where he came upon strong resistance and
a great muster of men, that had one Timotheus for their

a Cf. Jn. 10. 22. *b* Cf. Jos. 6. 17, 18 and other passages.

TODAY'S ENGLISH VERSION

Judas, his brothers, and the entire community of Israel
decreed that the rededication of the altar should be celebrated with a festival of joy and gladness at the same time each
year, beginning on the twenty-fifth of the month of Kislev
and lasting for eight days.

60 Then they built high walls and strong towers around
Mount Zion, so that the Gentiles could not come in and
trample and defile it again. 61 Judas placed a detachment of
soldiers there to guard the Temple. He also fortified the town
of Bethzur, so that the people of Israel would have a fortress
facing Idumea.

5 When the neighboring nations heard that the Jews had
built the altar and restored the Temple as it had been
before, they were so furious 2 that they made up their minds
to destroy all the Jews who were living among them. So they
began to murder and kill our people.

3 The Idumeans were blockading the Israelites, so Judas
went to war against them at Akrabattene, crushed them, and
looted them. 4 He also dealt with the people of Baean, who
were a constant threat to the people of Israel, because they
would lie in ambush waiting to trap Israelite travelers. 5 He
shut the Baeanites up in their forts, took a solemn oath that
he would destroy them, and burned their forts with everyone
in them. 6 Then he marched against the land of Ammon,
where he met a large and powerful army under the command

NEW REVISED STANDARD VERSION

59 Then Judas and his brothers and all the assembly of
Israel determined that every year at that season the days of
dedication of the altar should be observed with joy and gladness for eight days, beginning with the twenty-fifth day of
the month of Chislev.

60 At that time they fortified Mount Zion with high walls
and strong towers all around, to keep the Gentiles from coming and trampling them down as they had done before.
61 Judas[a] stationed a garrison there to guard it; he also fortified Beth-zur to guard it, so that the people might have a
stronghold that faced Idumea.

5 When the Gentiles all around heard that the altar had
been rebuilt and the sanctuary dedicated as it was
before, they became very angry, 2 and they determined to
destroy the descendants of Jacob who lived among them. So
they began to kill and destroy among the people. 3 But Judas
made war on the descendants of Esau in Idumea, at Akrabattene, because they kept lying in wait for Israel. He dealt them
a heavy blow and humbled them and despoiled them. 4 He
also remembered the wickedness of the sons of Baean, who
were a trap and a snare to the people and ambushed them
on the highways. 5 They were shut up by him in their[b] towers; and he encamped against them, vowed their complete
destruction, and burned with fire their towers and all who
were in them. 6 Then he crossed over to attack the Ammonites, where he found a strong band and many people, with

a Gk *He*   *b* Gk *her*

NEW AMERICAN BIBLE

brothers and the entire congregation of Israel decreed that
the days of the dedication of the altar should be observed
with joy and gladness on the anniversary every year for eight
days, from the twenty-fifth day of the month Chislev.

60 At that time they built high walls and strong towers
around Mount Zion, to prevent the Gentiles from coming and
trampling over it as they had done before. 61 Judas also
placed a garrison there to protect it, and likewise fortified
Beth-zur, that the people might have a stronghold facing
Idumea.

5 When the Gentiles round about heard that the altar had
been rebuilt and the sanctuary consecrated as before,
they were very angry. 2 So they decided to destroy the
descendants of Jacob who were among them, and they began
to massacre and persecute the people. 3 Then Judas attacked
the sons of Esau at Akrabattene in Idumea, because they
were blockading Israel; he defeated them heavily, overcame
and despoiled them. 4 He also remembered the malice of the
sons of Baean, who had become a snare and a stumblingblock to the people by ambushing them along the roads. 5 He
forced them to take refuge in towers, which he besieged; he
vowed their annihilation and burned down the towers along
with all the persons in them. 6 Then he crossed over to the
Ammonites, where he found a strong army and a large body
of people with Timothy as their leader. 7 He fought many

NEW JERUSALEM BIBLE

had been effaced. 59 Judas, with his brothers and the whole
assembly of Israel, made it a law that the days of the dedication of the altar should be celebrated yearly at the proper
season, for eight days beginning on the twenty-fifth of the
month of Chislev, with rejoicing and gladness.[a]

60 They then proceeded to build high walls with strong
towers round Mount Zion, to prevent the gentiles from coming and riding roughshod over it as in the past. 61 Judas stationed a garrison there to guard it; he also fortified Beth-Zur,
so that the people would have a fortress confronting
Idumaea.

5 When the surrounding nations heard that the altar had
been rebuilt and the sanctuary restored to what it had
been before, they became very angry 2 and decided to destroy
the descendants of Jacob living among them; they began to
murder and evict our people.

3 Judas made war on the sons of Esau in Idumaea,[b] in the
region of Acrabattene where they were besieging the
Israelites. He dealt them a serious blow, drove them off and
despoiled them. 4 He also remembered the wickedness of the
sons of Baean, who were a menace and a trap for the people
with their ambushes on the roads. 5 Having blockaded them
in their town and besieged them, he put them under the
curse of destruction; he then set fire to their towers and
burned them down with everyone inside. 6 Next, he crossed
over to the Ammonites where he found a strong fighting
force and a numerous people, commanded by Timotheus.

a **4** The Feast of Hanukkah, a feast of lights.   *b* **5** // 2 M 10:15–23.

GREEK OLD TESTAMENT

ἡγούμενον αὐτῶν· 7 καὶ συνῆψεν πρὸς αὐτοὺς πολέμους
πολλούς, καὶ συνετρίβησαν πρὸ προσώπου αὐτοῦ, καὶ ἐπάταξεν αὐτούς. 8 καὶ προκατελάβετο τὴν Ιαζηρ καὶ τὰς
θυγατέρας αὐτῆς καὶ ἀνέστρεψεν εἰς τὴν Ιουδαίαν.

9 Καὶ ἐπισυνήχθησαν τὰ ἔθνη τὰ ἐν τῇ Γαλααδ ἐπὶ τὸν
Ισραηλ τοὺς ὄντας ἐπὶ τοῖς ὁρίοις αὐτῶν τοῦ ἐξᾶραι αὐτούς,
καὶ ἔφυγον εἰς Δαθεμα τὸ ὀχύρωμα 10 καὶ ἀπέστειλαν γράμματα πρὸς Ιουδαν καὶ τοὺς ἀδελφοὺς αὐτοῦ λέγοντες Ἐπισυνηγμένα ἐστὶν ἐφ᾽ ἡμᾶς τὰ ἔθνη κύκλῳ ἡμῶν τοῦ ἐξᾶραι
ἡμᾶς 11 καὶ ἑτοιμάζονται ἐλθεῖν καὶ προκαταλαβέσθαι τὸ
ὀχύρωμα, εἰς ὃ κατεφύγομεν, καὶ Τιμόθεος ἡγεῖται τῆς
δυνάμεως αὐτῶν· 12 νῦν οὖν ἐλθὼν ἐξελοῦ ἡμᾶς ἐκ χειρὸς
αὐτῶν, ὅτι πέπτωκεν ἐξ ἡμῶν πλῆθος, 13 καὶ πάντες οἱ
ἀδελφοὶ ἡμῶν οἱ ὄντες ἐν τοῖς Τουβίου τεθανάτωνται, καὶ
ᾐχμαλωτίκασιν τὰς γυναῖκας αὐτῶν καὶ τὰ τέκνα καὶ τὴν
ἀποσκευὴν καὶ ἀπώλεσαν ἐκεῖ ὡσεὶ μίαν χιλιαρχίαν ἀνδρῶν.
14 ἔτι αἱ ἐπιστολαὶ ἀνεγιγνώσκοντο, καὶ ἰδοὺ ἄγγελοι ἕτεροι
παρεγένοντο ἐκ τῆς Γαλιλαίας διερρηχότες τὰ ἱμάτια
ἀπαγγέλλοντες κατὰ τὰ ῥήματα ταῦτα 15 λέγοντες ἐπισυν-
ῆχθαι ἐπ᾽ αὐτοὺς ἐκ Πτολεμαίδος καὶ Τύρου καὶ Σιδῶνος καὶ
πᾶσαν Γαλιλαίαν ἀλλοφύλων τοῦ ἐξαναλῶσαι ἡμᾶς. 16 ὡς δὲ
ἤκουσεν Ιουδας καὶ ὁ λαὸς τοὺς λόγους τούτους, ἐπισυνήχθη
ἐκκλησία μεγάλη βουλεύσασθαι τί ποιήσωσιν τοῖς ἀδελφοῖς
αὐτῶν τοῖς οὖσιν ἐν θλίψει καὶ πολεμουμένοις ὑπ᾽ αὐτῶν.

KING JAMES VERSION

7 So he fought many battles with them, till at length they were discomfited before him; and he smote them.

8 And when he had taken Jazar, with the towns belonging thereto, he returned into Judea.

9 Then the heathen that were at Galaad assembled themselves together against the Israelites that were in their quarters, to destroy them; but they fled to the fortress of Dathema,

10 And sent letters unto Judas and his brethren, The heathen that are round about us are assembled together against us to destroy us:

11 And they are preparing to come and take the fortress whereunto we are fled, Timotheus being captain of their host.

12 Come now therefore, and deliver us from their hands, for many of us are slain:

13 Yea, all our brethren that were in the places of Tobie are put to death: their wives and their children also they have carried away captives, and borne away their stuff; and they have destroyed there about a thousand men.

14 While these letters were yet reading, behold, there came other messengers from Galilee with their clothes rent, who reported on this wise,

15 And said, They of Ptolemais, and of Tyrus, and Sidon, and all Galilee of the Gentiles, are assembled together against us to consume us.

16 Now when Judas and the people heard these words, there assembled a great congregation together, to consult what they should do for their brethren, that were in trouble, and assaulted of them.

DOUAY OLD TESTAMENT

7 And he fought many battles with them, and they were discomfited in their sight, and he smote them:

8 And he took the city of Gazer and her towns, and returned into Judea.

9 And the Gentiles that were in Galaad, assembled themselves together against the Israelites that were in their quarters to destroy them: and they fled into the fortress of Datheman.

10 And they sent letters to Judas and his brethren, saying: The heathens that are round about are gathered together against us, to destroy us:

11 And they are preparing to come, and to take the fortress into which we are fled: and Timotheus is the captain of their host.

12 Now therefore come, and deliver us out of their hands, for many of us are slain.

13 And all our brethren that were in the places of Tubin, are killed: and they have carried away their wives, and their children, captives, and taken their spoils, and they have slain there almost a thousand men.

14 And while they were yet reading these letters, behold there came other messengers out of Galilee with their garments rent, who related according to these words:

15 Saying, that they of Ptolemais, and of Tyre, and of Sidon, were assembled against them, and all Galilee is filled with strangers, in order to consume us.

16 Now when Judas and the people heard these words, a great assembly met together to consider what they should do for their brethren that were in trouble, and were assaulted by them.

KNOX TRANSLATION

leader; 7 often he engaged them, and as often put them to
rout; when he had defeated them, 8 and taken Gazer with its
daughter townships, he marched back into Judaea.

9 But by this all the heathen folk in the country of Galaad
were making common cause against the Israelites who dwelt
there, eager to be rid of them. And these, taking refuge in the
stronghold of Datheman, 10 sent dispatches to Judas and his
brethren. Here be all the neighbours, they wrote, banded
together for our destruction. 11 Even now, Timotheus at their
head, they are setting about the reduction of this our
fortress; 12 come speedily to the rescue; they have taken
cruel toll of our lives already. 13 Slain, all those clansmen of
ours that had their dwelling in the Tubin country, carried
away, their wives, their children, and their goods; nigh upon
a thousand warriors then and there have perished.
14 This letter was still in the reading, when all of a sudden
came other envoys from Galilee, their garments rent about
them; 15 their message was, Ptolemais, Tyre and Sidon were
up in arms together, and all Galilee was overrun with heathen folk, bent on massacre. 16 Grave tidings, these, for
Judas and his people; met they in high debate, and took
counsel how they might best aid their brethren in peril of

TODAY'S ENGLISH VERSION

of a man named Timothy. 7 Judas won many battles against
them and finally defeated them. 8 He captured Jazer and its
surrounding villages and then returned to Judea.
9 The Gentiles in Gilead assembled to attack and destroy
the Israelites living in their territory. But the Israelites fled to
the fortress of Dathema 10-11 and sent the following letter to
Judas and his brothers: "The Gentiles around us are joining
forces under Timothy. We have fled to this fortress for protection, and now they are getting ready to capture it and
destroy us. 12 Many of us have already been killed. Come rescue us! 13 All the Jewish men in the region of Tob[a] have
been killed, their wives and their children have been taken
captive, and their possessions have been carried off. A force
of about 1,000 men has been destroyed there."
14 This letter was still being read when other messengers,
who had torn their clothes in sorrow, arrived with a report
from Galilee. 15 They said, "An army from Ptolemais, Tyre,
Sidon, and all of Galilee has come together to destroy us."
16 When Judas and the people heard all this, a great assembly was held to decide what should be done to help these
countrymen, who were in such difficulty under enemy

[a] in the region of Tob; *or* who were fighting with Tobias.

NEW REVISED STANDARD VERSION

Timothy as their leader. 7 He engaged in many battles with
them, and they were crushed before him; he struck them
down. 8 He also took Jazer and its villages; then he returned
to Judea.
9 Now the Gentiles in Gilead gathered together against the
Israelites who lived in their territory, and planned to destroy
them. But they fled to the stronghold of Dathema, 10 and
sent to Judas and his brothers a letter that said, "The
Gentiles around us have gathered together to destroy us.
11 They are preparing to come and capture the stronghold to
which we have fled, and Timothy is leading their forces.
12 Now then, come and rescue us from their hands, for many
of us have fallen, 13 and all our kindred who were in the
land of Tob have been killed; the enemy[a] have captured their
wives and children and goods, and have destroyed about a
thousand persons there."
14 While the letter was still being read, other messengers,
with their garments torn, came from Galilee and made a similar report; 15 they said that the people of Ptolemais and Tyre
and Sidon, and all Galilee of the Gentiles,[b] had gathered
together against them "to annihilate us." 16 When Judas and
the people heard these messages, a great assembly was
called to determine what they should do for their kindred
who were in distress and were being attacked by enemies.[c]

a Gk *they* *b* Gk *aliens* *c* Gk *them*

NEW AMERICAN BIBLE

battles with them, routed them, and struck them down.
8 After seizing Jazer and its villages, he returned to Judea.
9 The Gentiles in Gilead assembled to attack and destroy
the Israelites who were in their territory; these then fled to
the stronghold of Dathema. 10 They sent a letter to Judas and
his brothers saying: "The Gentiles around us have combined
against us to destroy us, 11 and they are preparing to come
and seize this stronghold to which we have fled. Timothy is
the leader of their army. 12 Come at once and rescue us from
them, for many of us have fallen. 13 All our kinsmen who
were among the Tobiads have been killed; the Gentiles have
carried away their wives and children and their goods, and
they have slain there about a thousand men."
14 While they were reading this letter, suddenly other messengers, in torn clothes, arrived from Galilee to deliver a similar message: 15 that the inhabitants of Ptolemais, Tyre, and
Sidon, and the whole of Gentile Galilee had joined forces to
destroy them. 16 When Judas and the people heard this, a
great assembly convened to consider what they should do for
their unfortunate kinsmen who were being attacked by enemies.

NEW JERUSALEM BIBLE

7 He fought many battles with them, defeated them and cut
them to pieces. 8 Having captured Jazer and its dependent
villages, he retired to Judaea.
9 Next, the gentiles of Gilead banded together to destroy the
Israelites living in their territory. The latter, however, took
refuge in the fortress of Dathema, 10 and sent the following
letter to Judas and his brothers:

'The gentiles round us have banded themselves together
against us to destroy us, 11 and they are preparing to
storm the fortress in which we have taken refuge;
Timotheus is in command of their forces. 12 Come at once
and rescue us from their clutches, for we have already suffered great losses. 13 All our countrymen living in Tobias'
country have been killed, their women and children have
been taken into captivity, their property has been seized,
and about a thousand men have been destroyed there.'

14 While the letter was being read, other messengers
arrived from Galilee with their garments torn, bearing similar
news, 15 'The people of Ptolemais, Tyre and Sidon have
joined forces with the whole of gentile Galilee to destroy us!'
16 When Judas and the people heard this, they held a great
assembly to decide what should be done for their oppressed
countrymen who were under attack from their enemies.

GREEK OLD TESTAMENT

17 καὶ εἶπεν Ιουδας Σιμωνι τῷ ἀδελφῷ αὐτοῦ Ἐπίλεξον
σεαυτῷ ἄνδρας καὶ πορεύου καὶ ῥῦσαι τοὺς ἀδελφούς σου
τοὺς ἐν τῇ Γαλιλαίᾳ, ἐγὼ δὲ καὶ Ιωναθαν ὁ ἀδελφός μου
πορευσόμεθα εἰς τὴν Γαλααδῖτιν. 18 καὶ κατέλιπεν Ιωσηπον
τὸν τοῦ Ζαχαριου καὶ Αζαριαν ἡγούμενον τοῦ λαοῦ μετὰ τῶν
ἐπιλοίπων τῆς δυνάμεως ἐν τῇ Ιουδαίᾳ εἰς τήρησιν 19 καὶ
ἐνετείλατο αὐτοῖς λέγων Πρόστητε τοῦ λαοῦ τούτου καὶ μὴ
συνάψητε πόλεμον πρὸς τὰ ἔθνη ἕως τοῦ ἐπιστρέψαι ἡμᾶς.
20 καὶ ἐμερίσθησαν Σιμωνι ἄνδρες τρισχίλιοι τοῦ πορευθῆναι
εἰς τὴν Γαλιλαίαν, Ιουδα δὲ ἄνδρες ὀκτακισχίλιοι εἰς τὴν
Γαλααδῖτιν. 21 καὶ ἐπορεύθη Σιμων εἰς τὴν Γαλιλαίαν καὶ
συνῆψεν πολέμους πολλοὺς πρὸς τὰ ἔθνη, καὶ συνετρίβη τὰ
ἔθνη ἀπὸ προσώπου αὐτοῦ, 22 καὶ ἐδίωξεν αὐτοὺς ἕως τῆς
πύλης Πτολεμαίδος. καὶ ἔπεσον ἐκ τῶν ἐθνῶν εἰς τρισχιλίους ἄνδρας, καὶ ἔλαβεν τὰ σκῦλα αὐτῶν. 23 καὶ παρέλαβεν
τοὺς ἐκ τῆς Γαλιλαίας καὶ ἐν Αρβαττοις σὺν ταῖς γυναιξὶν
καὶ τοῖς τέκνοις καὶ πάντα, ὅσα ἦν αὐτοῖς, καὶ ἤγαγεν εἰς
τὴν Ιουδαίαν μετ' εὐφροσύνης μεγάλης. 24 καὶ Ιουδας ὁ
Μακκαβαῖος καὶ Ιωναθαν ὁ ἀδελφὸς αὐτοῦ διέβησαν τὸν
Ιορδάνην καὶ ἐπορεύθησαν ὁδὸν τριῶν ἡμερῶν ἐν τῇ ἐρήμῳ.
25 καὶ συνήντησαν τοῖς Ναβαταίοις, καὶ ἀπήντησαν αὐτοῖς
εἰρηνικῶς καὶ διηγήσαντο αὐτοῖς πάντα τὰ συμβάντα τοῖς
ἀδελφοῖς αὐτῶν ἐν τῇ Γαλααδίτιδι 26 καὶ ὅτι πολλοὶ ἐξ
αὐτῶν συνειλημμένοι εἰσὶν εἰς Βοσορρα καὶ Βοσορ ἐν
Αλεμοις, Χασφω, Μακεδ καὶ Καρναιν, πᾶσαι αἱ πόλεις αὗται

KING JAMES VERSION

17 Then said Judas unto Simon his brother, Choose thee out men, and go and deliver thy brethren that are in Galilee, for I and Jonathan my brother will go into the country of Galaad.

18 So he left Joseph the *son* of Zacharias, and Azarias, captains of the people, with the remnant of the host in Judea to keep it.

19 Unto whom he gave commandment, saying, Take ye the charge of this people, and see that ye make not war against the heathen until the time that we come again.

20 Now unto Simon were given three thousand men to go into Galilee, and unto Judas eight thousand men for the country of Galaad.

21 Then went Simon into Galilee, where he fought many battles with the heathen, so that the heathen were discomfited by him.

22 And he pursued them unto the gate of Ptolemais; and there were slain of the heathen about three thousand men, whose spoils he took.

23 And those that were in Galilee, and in Arbattis, with their wives and their children, and all that they had, took he away *with him,* and brought them into Judea with great joy.

24 Judas Maccabeus also and his brother Jonathan went over Jordan, and travelled three days' journey in the wilderness,

25 Where they met with the Nabathites, who came unto them in a peaceable manner, and told them every thing that had happened to their brethren in the land of Galaad:

26 And how that many of them were shut up in Bosora, and Bosor, and Alema, Casphor, Maked, and Carnaim; all these cities are strong and great:

DOUAY OLD TESTAMENT

17 And Judas said to Simon his brother: Choose thee men, and go, and deliver thy brethren in Galilee: and I, and my brother Jonathan will go into the country of Galaad.

18 And he left Joseph the son of Zacharias, and Azarias captains of the people with the remnant of the army in Judea to keep it:

19 And he commanded them, saying: Take ye the charge of this people: but make no war against the heathens, till we return.

20 Now three thousand men were allotted to Simon, to go into Galilee: and eight thousand to Judas to go into the land of Galaad.

21 And Simon went into Galilee, and fought many battles with the heathens: and the heathens were discomfited before his face, and he pursued them even to the gate of Ptolemais.

22 And there fell of the heathens almost three thousand men, and he took the spoils of them,

23 And he took with him those that were in Galilee and in Arbatis with their wives, and children, and all that they had, and he brought them into Judea with great joy.

24 And Judas Machabeus, and Jonathan his brother passed over the Jordan, and went three days' journey through the desert.

25 And the Nabutheans met them, and received them in a peaceable manner, and told them all that happened to their brethren in the land of Galaad,

26 And that many of them were shut up in Barasa, and in Bosor, and in Alima, and in Casphor, and in Mageth, and in Carnaim: all these strong and great cities.

KNOX TRANSLATION

assault. 17 And now Judas must share the command with his
brother Simon; Pick thy men, said he, and make for Galilee,
while Jonathan and I march into Galaad. 18 Part of his army
he left to defend Judaea, with Joseph son of Zachary and
Azarias for its captains; 19 Here is your charge, said he; and
see to it that you do not embroil yourselves with the Gentiles
while we are gone. 20 To Simon and to Galilee three thousand men were allotted; to Judas and to Galaad eight thousand. 21 As for Simon, when he reached Galilee, full many a
battle he must fight with the Gentiles, that he drove ever
before him, till he pursued them at last to the very gates of
Ptolemais. 22 Of the enemy, some three thousand fell, and
his men had the spoiling of them; 23 the Israelites that dwelt
in Galilee and Arbata he took home with him, and their
wives and children and all they had; great rejoicing there
was when he brought them back safe to Judaea.
24 Meanwhile Judas Machabaeus and his brother Jonathan
had crossed the Jordan, and marched for three days through
the desert. 25 There the Nabuthaeans came to meet them, and
gave them friendly welcome, and told them of all that had
befallen their brethren in the Galaad country; 26 how there
were many whom their fellow-citizens had brought to bay in
such great fortified cities as Barasa, Bosor, Alima, Casphor,

TODAY'S ENGLISH VERSION

attack. 17Judas said to his brother Simon, "Choose some
men and go rescue our fellow Jews in Galilee; our brother
Jonathan and I will go to Gilead." 18Judas left the rest of his
army to defend Judea and put the two leaders, Azariah and
Joseph son of Zechariah, in charge of the people. 19He told
them: "I am leaving you in command here, but don't go out
and fight the Gentiles until we get back." 20Then 3,000 men
joined Simon for the march into Galilee, and 8,000 remained
with Judas for the march into Gilead.

21Simon went into Galilee and fought many battles with
the Gentiles. He defeated them 22and pursued them all the
way to the city of Ptolemais, killing about 3,000 of them,
and taking the loot. 23Then he took the Jews who were in
Galilee and Arbatta, with their wives, their children, and all
they owned, and brought them back to Judea with him.
There was great rejoicing.

24During this time, Judas Maccabeus and his brother
Jonathan had crossed the Jordan River and had marched for
three days through the desert. 25They met some friendly
Nabateans who told them all that had happened to the Jews
in Gilead. 26They reported that many Jews were imprisoned
in the fortified cities of Bozrah, Bosor, Alema, Chaspho,

NEW REVISED STANDARD VERSION

17Then Judas said to his brother Simon, "Choose your men
and go and rescue your kindred in Galilee; Jonathan my
brother and I will go to Gilead." 18But he left Joseph, son of
Zechariah, and Azariah, a leader of the people, with the rest
of the forces, in Judea to guard it; 19and he gave them this
command, "Take charge of this people, but do not engage in
battle with the Gentiles until we return." 20Then three thousand men were assigned to Simon to go to Galilee, and eight
thousand to Judas for Gilead.

21 So Simon went to Galilee and fought many battles
against the Gentiles, and the Gentiles were crushed before
him. 22He pursued them to the gate of Ptolemais; as many
as three thousand of the Gentiles fell, and he despoiled them.
23Then he took the Jews[a] of Galilee and Arbatta, with their
wives and children, and all they possessed, and led them to
Judea with great rejoicing.

24 Judas Maccabeus and his brother Jonathan crossed the
Jordan and made three days' journey into the wilderness.
25They encountered the Nabateans, who met them peaceably
and told them all that had happened to their kindred in
Gilead: 26"Many of them have been shut up in Bozrah and
Bosor, in Alema and Chaspho, Maked and Carnaim"—all
these towns were strong and large— 27"and some have

a Gk *those*

NEW AMERICAN BIBLE

17Judas said to his brother Simon: "Choose men for yourself, and go, rescue your kinsmen in Galilee; I and my brother Jonathan will go to Gilead."

18In Judea he left Joseph, son of Zechariah, and Azariah,
leader of the people, with the rest of the army to guard it.
19"Take charge of these people," he commanded them, "but
do not fight against the Gentiles until we return." 20Three
thousand men were allotted to Simon, to go into Galilee, and
eight thousand men to Judas, for Gilead.

21Simon went into Galilee and fought many battles with
the Gentiles. They were crushed before him, 22and he pursued them to the very gate of Ptolemais. About three thousand men of the Gentiles fell, and he gathered their spoils.
23He took with him the Jews who were in Galilee and in
Arbatta, with their wives and children and all that they had,
and brought them to Judea with great rejoicing.

24Judas Maccabeus and his brother Jonathan crossed the
Jordan and marched for three days through the desert.
25There they met some Nabateans, who received them peacefully and told them all that had happened to the Jews in
Gilead: 26"Many of them have been imprisoned in Bozrah,
in Bosor near Alema, in Chaspho, Maked, and Carnaim"—all

NEW JERUSALEM BIBLE

17Judas said to his brother Simon, 'Pick your men and go
and relieve your countrymen in Galilee, while my brother
Jonathan and I make our way into Gilead.' 18He left Joseph
son of Zechariah and the people's leader Azariah with the
remainder of the army in Judaea to keep guard, and gave
them these orders, 19'You are to be responsible for our people. Do not engage the gentiles until we return.' 20Simon
was allotted three thousand men for the expedition into
Galilee, Judas eight thousand for Gilead.

21Simon advanced into Galilee, engaged the gentiles in
several battles and swept all before him; 22he pursued them
to the gate of Ptolemais, and they lost about three thousand
men, whose spoils he collected. 23With him, he took away
the Jews of Galilee and Arbatta, with their wives and children
and all their possessions, and brought them into Judaea with
great rejoicing.

24Meanwhile Judas Maccabaeus and his brother Jonathan
crossed the Jordan[a] and made a three-days' march through
the desert, 25where they encountered the Nabataeans,[b] who
gave them a friendly reception and told them everything that
had been happening to their brothers in Gilead, 26many of
whom, they said, were shut up in Bozrah and Bosor, Alema,
Chaspho, Maked and Carnaim, all large fortified towns.

a **5** // 2 M 12:10–31. *b* **5** An Arab people, centred on Petra and controlling the trade routes for 200 years.

GREEK OLD TESTAMENT

ὀχυραὶ καὶ μεγάλαι· 27 καὶ ἐν ταῖς λοιπαῖς πόλεσιν τῆς
Γαλααδίτιδός εἰσιν συνειλημμένοι, εἰς αὔριον τάσσονται
παρεμβαλεῖν ἐπὶ τὰ ὀχυρώματα καὶ καταλαβέσθαι καὶ ἐξᾶραι πάντας τούτους ἐν ἡμέρᾳ μιᾷ. 28 καὶ ἀπέστρεψεν
Ιουδας καὶ ἡ παρεμβολὴ αὐτοῦ ὁδὸν εἰς τὴν ἔρημον Βοσορρα
ἄφνω· καὶ κατελάβετο τὴν πόλιν καὶ ἀπέκτεινε πᾶν ἀρσενικὸν ἐν στόματι ῥομφαίας καὶ ἔλαβεν πάντα τὰ σκῦλα αὐτῶν
καὶ ἐνέπρησεν αὐτὴν πυρί. 29 καὶ ἀπῆρεν ἐκεῖθεν νυκτός,
καὶ ἐπορεύοντο ἕως ἐπὶ τὸ ὀχύρωμα· 30 καὶ ἐγένετο ἑωθινῇ
ἦραν τοὺς ὀφθαλμοὺς αὐτῶν καὶ ἰδοὺ λαὸς πολύς, οὗ οὐκ ἦν
ἀριθμός, αἴροντες κλίμακας καὶ μηχανὰς καταλαβέσθαι τὸ
ὀχύρωμα καὶ ἐπολέμουν αὐτούς. 31 καὶ εἶδεν Ιουδας ὅτι
ἦρκται ὁ πόλεμος καὶ ἡ κραυγὴ τῆς πόλεως ἀνέβη ἕως οὐρανοῦ σάλπιγξιν καὶ κραυγῇ μεγάλῃ, 32 καὶ εἶπεν τοῖς
ἀνδράσιν τῆς δυνάμεως Πολεμήσατε σήμερον ὑπὲρ τῶν
ἀδελφῶν ἡμῶν. 33 καὶ ἐξῆλθεν ἐν τρισὶν ἀρχαῖς ἐξόπισθεν
αὐτῶν, καὶ ἐσάλπισαν ταῖς σάλπιγξιν καὶ ἐβόησαν ἐν
προσευχῇ. 34 καὶ ἐπέγνω ἡ παρεμβολὴ Τιμοθέου ὅτι Μακκα-
βαῖός ἐστιν, καὶ ἔφυγον ἀπὸ προσώπου αὐτοῦ, καὶ ἐπάταξεν
αὐτοὺς πληγὴν μεγάλην, καὶ ἔπεσον ἐξ αὐτῶν ἐν ἐκείνῃ τῇ
ἡμέρᾳ εἰς ὀκτακισχιλίους ἄνδρας. 35 καὶ ἀπέκλινεν εἰς
Αλεμα καὶ ἐπολέμησεν αὐτὴν καὶ κατελάβετο αὐτὴν καὶ
ἀπέκτεινεν πᾶν ἀρσενικὸν αὐτῆς καὶ ἔλαβεν τὰ σκῦλα αὐτῆς
καὶ ἐνέπρησεν αὐτὴν ἐν πυρί. 36 ἐκεῖθεν ἀπῆρεν καὶ προκατελάβετο τὴν Χασφω, Μακεδ καὶ Βοσορ καὶ τὰς λοιπὰς

KING JAMES VERSION

27 And that they were shut up in the rest of the cities of the country of Galaad, and that against to morrow they had appointed to bring their host against the forts, and to take them, and to destroy them all in one day.

28 Hereupon Judas and his host turned suddenly by the way of the wilderness unto Bosora; and when he had won the city, he slew all the males with the edge of the sword, and took all their spoils, and burned the city with fire.

29 From whence he removed by night, and went till he came to the fortress.

30 And betimes in the morning they looked up, and, behold, there was an innumerable people bearing ladders and other engines of war, to take the fortress: for they assaulted them.

31 When Judas therefore saw that the battle was begun, and that the cry of the city went up to heaven, with trumpets, and a great sound,

32 He said unto his host, Fight this day for your brethren.

33 So he went forth behind them in three companies, who sounded their trumpets, and cried with prayer.

34 Then the host of Timotheus, knowing that it was Maccabeus, fled from him: wherefore he smote them with a great slaughter; so that there were killed of them that day about eight thousand men.

35 This done, Judas turned aside to Maspha; and after he had assaulted it, he took it, and slew all the males therein, and received the spoils thereof, and burnt it with fire.

36 From thence went he, and took Casphon, Maged, Bosor, and the other cities of the country of Galaad.

DOUAY OLD TESTAMENT

27 Yea, and that they were kept shut up in the rest of the cities of Galaad, and that they had appointed to bring their army on the morrow near to these cities, and to take them and to destroy them all in one day.

28 Then Judas and his army suddenly turned their march into the desert, to Bosor, and took the city: and he slew every male by the edge of the sword, and took all their spoils, and burnt it with fire.

29 And they removed from thence by night, and went till they came to the fortress.

30 And it came to pass that early in the morning, when they lifted up their eyes, behold there were people without number, carrying ladders and engines to take the fortress, and assault them.

31 And Judas saw that the fight was begun, and the cry of the battle went up to heaven like a trumpet, and a great cry out of the city:

32 And he said to his host: Fight ye to day for your brethren.

33 And he came with three companies behind them, and they sounded their trumpets, and cried out in prayer.

34 And the host of Timotheus understood that it was Machabeus, and they fled away before his face: and they made a great slaughter of them: and there fell of them in that day almost eight thousand men.

35 And Judas turned aside to Maspha, and assaulted, and took it, and he slew every male thereof, and took the spoils thereof, and burnt it with fire.

36 From thence he marched, and took Casbon, and Mageth, and Bosor, and the rest of the cities of Galaad.

KNOX TRANSLATION

Mageth and Carnaim; 27 besides many others cut off in the rest
of the Galaadite towns. And to-morrow, he was told, the heathen mean to occupy these cities with their army, seizing upon
the Israelites and making an end of them, all in one day's
work. 28 Whereupon Judas and his men suddenly turned aside
from their course into the desert of Bosor, and took the city; all
its men-folk he put to the sword, and carried off the spoil of it,
and burned it to the ground. 29 At night-fall they continued
their journey, and reached the Israelite stronghold.[a] 30 What a
sight was this that met their eyes, when day broke! A great
rabble of men past all counting, that brought up scaling-lad-
ders and engines, as if they would take the stronghold by
storm. 31 Here was the battle fairly begun; the cry of them
went up to heaven, loud as clarion-call, and a great cry, too,
was raised within the city. 32 Now, cried Judas to his men, now
to fight for your brethren's deliverance! 33 And hard at the enemy's heels he followed, with three companies of warriors that
blew trumpets as they went, and cried aloud in prayer. 34 The
name of Machabaeus once heard, how fled Timotheus' army at
his approach! How grievous the blow that fell on them, when
eight thousand fell in a single day! 35 Once more Judas turned
aside, to Maspha; took it by storm, slew men of it, took spoil of
it, burned it to the ground; 36 then on to seize Casbon, and
Mageth, and Bosor, and the remaining cities of Galaad.[b]

a The word 'Israelite' is not in the original; but evidently the stronghold was either that mentioned in verse 11 above, or else one in which the Israelites of Bosor had taken refuge. *b* There is some uncertainty about the names here; 'Casbon' is perhaps the 'Casphor' of verse 26, and 'Bosor' should perhaps be identified with the 'Barasa' (in the Greek, Bossora) of the same verse. Bosor has already been destroyed in verse 28.

TODAY'S ENGLISH VERSION

Maked, and Karnaim, 27 while others were imprisoned in the smaller towns of Gilead. They also reported that the enemy was drawn up to make an attack the next day on the Jewish fortresses, hoping to destroy all the Jews in a single day.

28 So Judas and his army suddenly turned and attacked Bozrah by the desert road, captured the town, and killed every man in it. They looted the town and set it on fire. 29 They left there and marched all night to the fortress at Dathema. 30 At dawn Judas and his men saw a vast army attacking the fortress; they were bringing up ladders, siege platforms, and battering rams in an effort to capture it. 31 When Judas heard the noise, the shouts, and the sound of trumpets coming from the city, he realized that the battle had begun, 32 so he said to his men, "Fight today for our fellow Jews!"

33 He ordered his men to march in three columns and attack the enemy from the rear. As they moved forward, they blew trumpets and shouted prayers. 34 When the army under Timothy's command saw that it was Judas Maccabeus, the soldiers turned and fled. Judas crushed them and killed about 8,000 men that day.

35 Then Judas turned aside to attack the town of Alema;[a] he captured it and killed all the men in it. He looted the town and set fire to it. 36 From there he went on and captured Chaspho, Maked, Bosor, and the other towns of Gilead.

[a] ALEMA: *The name of the town is not certain.*

NEW REVISED STANDARD VERSION

been shut up in the other towns of Gilead; the enemy[a] are getting ready to attack the strongholds tomorrow and capture and destroy all these people in a single day."

28 Then Judas and his army quickly turned back by the wilderness road to Bozrah; and he took the town, and killed every male by the edge of the sword; then he seized all its spoils and burned it with fire. 29 He left the place at night, and they went all the way to the stronghold of Dathema.[b] 30 At dawn they looked out and saw a large company, which could not be counted, carrying ladders and engines of war to capture the stronghold, and attacking the Jews within.[c] 31 So Judas saw that the battle had begun and that the cry of the town went up to Heaven, with trumpets and loud shouts, 32 and he said to the men of his forces, "Fight today for your kindred!" 33 Then he came up behind them in three companies, who sounded their trumpets and cried aloud in prayer. 34 And when the army of Timothy realized that it was Maccabeus, they fled before him, and he dealt them a heavy blow. As many as eight thousand of them fell that day.

35 Next he turned aside to Maapha,[d] and fought against it and took it; and he killed every male in it, plundered it, and burned it with fire. 36 From there he marched on and took Chaspho, Maked, and Bosor, and the other towns of Gilead.

a Gk *they* *b* Gk lacks *of Dathema*. See verse 9 *c* Gk *and they were attacking them* *d* Other ancient authorities read *Alema*

NEW AMERICAN BIBLE

of these are large, fortified cities— 27 "and some have been imprisoned in the other cities of Gilead. Tomorrow their enemies plan to attack the strongholds and to seize and destroy all these people in one day."

28 Thereupon Judas suddenly changed direction with his army, marched across the desert to Bozrah, and captured the city. He slaughtered all the male population, took all their possessions, and set fire to the city. 29 He led his army from that place by night, and they marched toward the stronghold of Dathema. 30 When morning came, they looked ahead and saw a countless multitude of people, with ladders and devices for capturing the stronghold, and beginning to attack the people within. 31 When Judas perceived that the struggle had begun and that the noise of the battle was resounding to heaven with trumpet blasts and loud shouting, 32 he said to the men of his army, "Fight for our kinsmen today."

33 He came up behind them with three columns blowing their trumpets and shouting in prayer. 34 When the army of Timothy realized that it was Maccabeus, they fell back before him, and he inflicted on them a crushing defeat. About eight thousand of their men fell that day. 35 Then he turned toward Alema and attacked and captured it; he killed all the male population, plundered the place, and burned it down. 36 From there he moved on and took Chaspho, Maked, Bosor, and the other cities of Gilead.

NEW JERUSALEM BIBLE

27 Others were blockaded in the other towns of Gilead, and the enemy planned to attack and capture these strongholds the very next day, and destroy all the people inside them on one day.

28 Judas and his army at once turned off by the desert road to Bozrah. He took the town and, having put all the males to the sword and collected the booty, burned it down. 29 When night came, he left the place, and they continued their march until they reached the fortress. 30 In the light of dawn they looked, and there was an innumerable horde, setting up ladders and engines to capture the fortress; the assault was just beginning. 31 When Judas saw that the attack had begun and that the war cry was rising to heaven from the city, mingled with trumpet calls and a great clamour, 32 he said to the men of his army, 'Into battle today for your brothers!' 33 Dividing them into three commands, he advanced on the enemy's rear, with trumpets sounding and prayers shouted aloud. 34 The troops of Timotheus, recognising that this was Maccabaeus, fled before his advance; Maccabaeus dealt them a crushing defeat; about eight thousand of their men fell that day. 35 Then, wheeling on Alema, he attacked and captured it and, having killed all the males and collected the booty, burned the place down. 36 From there he moved on and took Chaspho, Maked, Bosor and the remaining towns of Gilead.

GREEK OLD TESTAMENT

πόλεις τῆς Γαλααδίτιδος. 37 μετὰ δὲ τὰ ῥήματα ταῦτα συνήγαγεν Τιμόθεος παρεμβολὴν ἄλλην καὶ παρενέβαλεν κατὰ
πρόσωπον Ραφων ἐκ πέραν τοῦ χειμάρρου. 38 καὶ ἀπέστειλεν
Ιουδας κατασκοπεῦσαι τὴν παρεμβολήν, καὶ ἀπήγγειλαν
αὐτῷ λέγοντες Ἐπισυνηγμένα εἰσὶν πρὸς αὐτὸν πάντα τὰ
ἔθνη τὰ κύκλῳ ἡμῶν, δύναμις πολλὴ σφόδρα· 39 καὶ Ἄραβας
μεμίσθωνται εἰς βοήθειαν αὐτοῖς καὶ παρεμβάλλουσιν πέραν
τοῦ χειμάρρου ἕτοιμοι τοῦ ἐλθεῖν ἐπὶ σὲ εἰς πόλεμον. καὶ
ἐπορεύθη Ιουδας εἰς συνάντησιν αὐτῶν. 40 καὶ εἶπεν Τιμόθεος τοῖς ἄρχουσιν τῆς δυνάμεως αὐτοῦ ἐν τῷ ἐγγίζειν
Ιουδαν καὶ τὴν παρεμβολὴν αὐτοῦ ἐπὶ τὸν χειμάρρουν τοῦ
ὕδατος Ἐὰν διαβῇ πρὸς ἡμᾶς πρότερος, οὐ δυνησόμεθα
ὑποστῆναι αὐτόν, ὅτι δυνάμενος δυνήσεται πρὸς ἡμᾶς.
41 ἐὰν δὲ δειλανθῇ καὶ παρεμβάλῃ πέραν τοῦ ποταμοῦ,
διαπεράσομεν πρὸς αὐτὸν καὶ δυνησόμεθα πρὸς αὐτόν. 42 ὡς
δὲ ἤγγισεν Ιουδας ἐπὶ τὸν χειμάρρουν τοῦ ὕδατος, ἔστησεν
τοὺς γραμματεῖς τοῦ λαοῦ ἐπὶ τοῦ χειμάρρου καὶ ἐνετείλατο αὐτοῖς λέγων Μὴ ἀφῆτε πάντα ἄνθρωπον παρεμβαλεῖν,
ἀλλὰ ἐρχέσθωσαν πάντες εἰς τὸν πόλεμον. 43 καὶ διεπέρασεν ἐπ' αὐτοὺς πρότερος καὶ πᾶς ὁ λαὸς ὄπισθεν αὐτοῦ,
καὶ συνετρίβησαν πρὸ προσώπου αὐτῶν πάντα τὰ ἔθνη καὶ
ἔρριψαν τὰ ὅπλα αὐτῶν καὶ ἔφυγον εἰς τὸ τέμενος Καρναιν.
44 καὶ προκατελάβοντο τὴν πόλιν καὶ τὸ τέμενος ἐνεπύρισαν
ἐν πυρὶ σὺν πᾶσιν τοῖς ἐν αὐτῷ· καὶ ἐτροπώθη Καρναιν, καὶ
οὐκ ἠδύναντο ἔτι ὑποστῆναι κατὰ πρόσωπον Ιουδου. 45 καὶ
συνήγαγεν Ιουδας πάντα Ισραηλ τοὺς ἐν τῇ Γαλααδίτιδι ἀπὸ
μικροῦ ἕως μεγάλου καὶ τὰς γυναῖκας αὐτῶν καὶ τὰ τέκνα
αὐτῶν καὶ τὴν ἀποσκευήν, παρεμβολὴν μεγάλην σφόδρα,

KING JAMES VERSION

37 After these things gathered Timotheus another host, and encamped against Raphon beyond the brook.

38 So Judas sent *men* to espy the host, who brought him word, saying, All the heathen that be round about us are assembled unto them, even a very great host.

39 He hath also hired the Arabians to help them, and they have pitched their tents beyond the brook, ready to come and fight against thee. Upon this Judas went to meet them.

40 Then Timotheus said unto the captains of his host, When Judas and his host come near the brook, if he pass over first unto us, we shall not be able to withstand him; for he will mightily prevail against us:

41 But if he be afraid, and camp beyond the river, we shall go over unto him, and prevail against him.

42 Now when Judas came near the brook, he caused the scribes of the people to remain by the brook: unto whom he gave commandment, saying, Suffer no man to remain in the camp, but let all come to the battle.

43 So he went first over unto them, and all the people after him: then all the heathen, being discomfited before him, cast away their weapons, and fled unto the temple that was at Carnaim.

44 But they took the city, and burned the temple with all that were therein. Thus was Carnaim subdued, neither could they stand any longer before Judas.

45 Then Judas gathered together all the Israelites that were in the country of Galaad, from the least unto the greatest, even their wives, and their children, and their stuff, a very great host, to the end they might come into the land of Judea.

DOUAY OLD TESTAMENT

37 But after this Timotheus gathered another army, and camped over against Raphon beyond the torrent.

38 And Judas sent men to view the army: and they brought him word, saying: All the nations, that are round about us, are assembled unto him an army exceeding great:

39 And they have hired the Arabians to help them, and they have pitched their tents beyond the torrent, ready to come to fight against thee. And Judas went to meet them.

40 And Timotheus said to the captains of his army: When Judas and his army come near the torrent of water, if he pass over unto us first, we shall not be able to withstand him: for he will certainly prevail over us.

41 But if he be afraid to pass over, and camp on the other side of the river, we will pass over to them and shall prevail against him.

42 Now when Judas came near the torrent of water, he set the scribes of the people by the torrent, and commanded them, saying: Suffer no man to stay behind: but let all come to the battle.

43 And he passed over to them first, and all the people after him, and all the heathens were discomfited before them, and they threw away their weapons, and fled to the temple that was in Carnaim.

44 And he took that city, and the temple he burnt with fire, with all things that were therein: and Carnaim was subdued, and could not stand against the face of Judas.

45 And Judas gathered together all the Israelites that were in the land of Galaad, from the least even to the greatest, and their wives, and children, and an army exceeding great, to come into the land of Juda.

KNOX TRANSLATION

37 Yet, when all was done, Timotheus put another army
into the field, and encamped close by Raphon, across the
stream. 38 What learned Judas from the scouts he had sent
forward? Here were all the neighbouring tribes assembled in
great force, 39 with hired support from Arabia besides,
camped beyond the stream ready to engage him; so out he
marched to offer battle. 40 Wait we, said Timotheus to his
captains, till Judas and his army reach yonder stream. Cross
he and challenge us, we may not speed; beyond doubt he has
the mastery of us. 41 Fear he the passage, and encamp on
the further side, then cross we boldly, the day is ours. 42 But
Judas, when he drew near the ravine, had muster-masters in
attendance by the stream, that were charged to let none
linger behind, but send every man across into battle. 43 So
he crossed, challenging them, and all the army at his heels,
and sure enough the Gentile host was routed at their coming; threw arms away, and sought refuge in the temple at
Carnaim.[a] 44 Upon taking the city, he burned its temple to
the ground with all that were sheltered in it; so was Carnaim
vanquished, and could make head against Juda no more.
45 And now Judas gathered all the Israelites in the Galaad
country, high and low, with their wives and children, a
whole army of them, to come back with him to Juda. 46 They

a vv. 40-43. It is not clear whether Timotheus was testing the courage of his opponents, or taking an omen from the course of events (cf. I Kg. 14. 9, 10). Perhaps we are not meant to picture the crossing as taking place unopposed.

TODAY'S ENGLISH VERSION

37 After this, Timothy gathered another army and camped opposite Raphon, on the other side of a river. 38 Judas sent some men to spy on the camp, and they reported back to him that all the Gentiles in the region had joined Timothy and had formed a large army. 39 Timothy had also hired Arab mercenaries to help him, and these were camped on the other side of the river ready to attack Judas. So Judas went out to meet them in battle.

40 As Judas and his army came closer to the water, Timothy said to his officers, "If he keeps on coming and crosses the river, we won't be able to turn back his attack, and he will defeat us. 41 But if he is afraid and stops on the other side of the river, we will cross over to attack and defeat him." 42 When Judas reached the bank of the river, he gave orders to his officers to let no one stop but to push everyone forward into battle. 43 Judas was the first to cross the river against the enemy, and all his men followed him. The Gentiles broke ranks before them, threw away their arms, and fled to the pagan temple at Karnaim. 44 But Judas and his men took the city and burned down the temple with all who were in it. With Karnaim overthrown, the Gentiles could no longer offer any resistance to Judas.

45 Then Judas gathered together all the Jews in Gilead to take them back to Judea with him. It was a large group of all kinds of people, together with their wives and children and

NEW REVISED STANDARD VERSION

37 After these things Timothy gathered another army and encamped opposite Raphon, on the other side of the stream. 38 Judas sent men to spy out the camp, and they reported to him, "All the Gentiles around us have gathered to him; it is a very large force. 39 They also have hired Arabs to help them, and they are encamped across the stream, ready to come and fight against you." And Judas went to meet them.

40 Now as Judas and his army drew near to the stream of water, Timothy said to the officers of his forces, "If he crosses over to us first, we will not be able to resist him, for he will surely defeat us. 41 But if he shows fear and camps on the other side of the river, we will cross over to him and defeat him." 42 When Judas approached the stream of water, he stationed the officers[a] of the army at the stream and gave them this command, "Permit no one to encamp, but make them all enter the battle." 43 Then he crossed over against them first, and the whole army followed him. All the Gentiles were defeated before him, and they threw away their arms and fled into the sacred precincts at Carnaim. 44 But he took the town and burned the sacred precincts with fire, together with all who were in them. Thus Carnaim was conquered; they could stand before Judas no longer.

45 Then Judas gathered together all the Israelites in Gilead, the small and the great, with their wives and children and goods, a very large company, to go to the land of Judah.

a Or *scribes*

NEW AMERICAN BIBLE

37 After these events Timothy assembled another army and camped opposite Raphon, on the other side of the stream. 38 Judas sent men to spy on the camp, and they reported to him: "All the Gentiles around us have rallied to him, making a very large force; 39 they have also hired Arabs to help them, and have camped beyond the stream, ready to attack you." So Judas went forward to attack them.

40 As Judas and his army were approaching the running stream, Timothy said to the officers of his army: "If he crosses over to us first, we shall not be able to resist him; he will certainly defeat us. 41 But if he is afraid and camps on the other side of the river, we will cross over to him and defeat him."

42 But when Judas reached the running stream, he stationed the officers of the people beside the stream and gave them this order: "Do not allow any man to pitch a tent; all must go into battle." 43 He was the first to cross to the attack, with all the people behind him, and the Gentiles were crushed before them; they threw away their arms and fled to the temple enclosure at Carnaim. 44 The Jews captured that city and burnt the enclosure with all who were in it. So Carnaim was subdued, and Judas met with no more resistance.

45 Then he assembled all the Israelites, great and small, who were in Gilead, with their wives and children and their goods, a great crowd of people, to go into the land of Judah.

NEW JERUSALEM BIBLE

37 After these events, Timotheus mustered another force and pitched camp opposite Raphon, on the far side of the stream-bed. 38 Judas sent men to reconnoitre the camp, and these reported back as follows, 'With him are massed all the gentiles surrounding us, making a very numerous army, 39 with Arab mercenaries as auxiliaries; they are encamped on the far side of the stream-bed, and ready to launch an attack on you.' Judas then advanced to engage them, 40 and was approaching the watercourse with his troops when Timotheus told the commanders of his army, 'If he crosses first we shall not be able to resist him, because he will have a great advantage over us; 41 but if he is afraid and camps on the other side of the stream, we shall cross over to him and the advantage will then be ours.'

42 As soon as Judas reached the watercourse, he posted people's scribes along it, giving them this order: 'Do not let anyone pitch his tent; all are to go into battle!' 43 He was himself the first across to the enemy side, with all the people following. He defeated all the opposing gentiles, who threw down their arms and ran for refuge in the sanctuary of Carnaim. 44 The Jews first captured the town and then burned down the temple with everyone inside. And so Carnaim was overthrown, and the enemy could offer no further resistance to Judas.

45 Next, Judas assembled all the Israelites living in Gilead, from the least to the greatest, with their wives, children and belongings, an enormous muster, to take them to Judaea.

GREEK OLD TESTAMENT

ἐλθεῖν εἰς γῆν Ιουδα. 46 καὶ ἦλθον ἕως Εφρων, καὶ αὕτη πόλις μεγάλη ἐπὶ τῆς ὁδοῦ ὀχυρὰ σφόδρα, οὐκ ἦν ἐκκλῖναι ἀπ'
αὐτῆς δεξιὰν ἢ ἀριστεράν, ἀλλ' ἢ διὰ μέσου αὐτῆς πορεύ-
εσθαι· 47 καὶ ἀπέκλεισαν αὐτοὺς οἱ ἐκ τῆς πόλεως καὶ ἐνέφραξαν τὰς πύλας λίθοις. 48 καὶ ἀπέστειλεν πρὸς αὐτοὺς
Ιουδας λόγοις εἰρηνικοῖς λέγων Διελευσόμεθα διὰ τῆς γῆς
σου τοῦ ἀπελθεῖν εἰς τὴν γῆν ἡμῶν, καὶ οὐδεὶς κακοποιήσει
ὑμᾶς, πλὴν τοῖς ποσὶν παρελευσόμεθα. καὶ οὐκ ἠβούλοντο
ἀνοῖξαι αὐτῷ. 49 καὶ ἐπέταξεν Ιουδας κηρύξαι ἐν τῇ παρεμβολῇ τοῦ παρεμβαλεῖν ἕκαστον ἐν ᾧ ἐστιν τόπῳ· 50 καὶ
παρενέβαλον οἱ ἄνδρες τῆς δυνάμεως, καὶ ἐπολέμησεν τὴν
πόλιν ὅλην τὴν ἡμέραν ἐκείνην καὶ ὅλην τὴν νύκτα, καὶ
παρεδόθη ἡ πόλις ἐν χειρὶ αὐτοῦ. 51 καὶ ἀπώλεσεν πᾶν
ἀρσενικὸν ἐν στόματι ῥομφαίας καὶ ἐξερρίζωσεν αὐτὴν καὶ
ἔλαβεν τὰ σκῦλα αὐτῆς καὶ διῆλθεν διὰ τῆς πόλεως ἐπάνω
τῶν ἀπεκταμμένων. 52 καὶ διέβησαν τὸν Ιορδάνην εἰς τὸ
πεδίον τὸ μέγα κατὰ πρόσωπον Βαιθσαν. 53 καὶ ἦν Ιουδας
ἐπισυνάγων τοὺς ἐσχατίζοντας καὶ παρακαλῶν τὸν λαὸν
κατὰ πᾶσαν τὴν ὁδόν, ἕως ἦλθεν εἰς γῆν Ιουδα. 54 καὶ ἀνέβησαν εἰς ὄρος Σιων ἐν εὐφροσύνῃ καὶ χαρᾷ καὶ προσήγαγον
ὁλοκαυτώματα, ὅτι οὐκ ἔπεσεν ἐξ αὐτῶν οὐθεὶς ἕως τοῦ
ἐπιστρέψαι ἐν εἰρήνῃ.
55 Καὶ ἐν ταῖς ἡμέραις, ἐν αἷς ἦν Ιουδας καὶ Ιωναθαν ἐν
γῇ Γαλααδ καὶ Σιμων ὁ ἀδελφὸς αὐτοῦ ἐν τῇ Γαλιλαίᾳ κατὰ

KING JAMES VERSION

46 Now when they came unto Ephron, (this was a great city in the way as they should go, very well fortified) they could not turn from it, either on the right hand or the left, but must needs pass through the midst of it.

47 Then they of the city shut them out, and stopped up the gates with stones.

48 Whereupon Judas sent unto them in peaceable manner, saying, Let us pass through your land to go into our own country, and none shall do you any hurt; we will only pass through on foot: howbeit they would not open unto him.

49 Wherefore Judas commanded a proclamation to be made throughout the host, that every man should pitch his tent in the place where he was.

50 So the soldiers pitched, and assaulted the city all that day and all that night, till at the length the city was delivered into his hands:

51 Who then slew all the males with the edge of the sword, and rased the city, and took the spoils thereof, and passed through the city over them that were slain.

52 After this went they over Jordan into the great plain before Bethsan.

53 And Judas gathered together those that came behind, and exhorted the people all the way through, till they came into the land of Judea.

54 So they went up to mount Sion with joy and gladness, where they offered burnt offerings, because not one of them were slain until they had returned in peace.

55 Now what time as Judas and Jonathan were in the land of Galaad, and Simon his brother in Galilee before Ptolemais,

DOUAY OLD TESTAMENT

46 And they came as far as Ephron: now this was a great city situate in the way, strongly fortified, and there was no means to turn from it on the right hand or on the left, but the way was through the midst of it.

47 And they that were in the city, shut themselves in, and stopped up the gates with stones: and Judas sent to them with peaceable words,

48 Saying: Let us pass through your land, to go into our country: and no man shall hurt you: we will only pass through on foot. But they would not open to them.

49 Then Judas commanded proclamation to be made in the camp, that they should make an assault every man in the place where he was.

50 And the men of the army drew near, and he assaulted that city all the day, and all the night, and the city was delivered into his hands:

51 And they slew every male with the edge of the sword, and he razed the city, and took the spoils thereof, and passed through all the city over them that were slain.

52 Then they passed over the Jordan to the great plain that is over against Bethsan.

53 And Judas gathered together the hindmost, and he exhorted the people all the way through, till they came into the land of Juda.

54 And they went up to mount Sion with joy and gladness, and offered holocausts, because not one of them was slain, till they had returned in peace.

55 Now in the days that Judas and Jonathan were in the land of Galaad, and Simon his brother in Galilee before Ptolemais,

KNOX TRANSLATION

journeyed safely as far as Ephron, that was a great city and
well fortified, the very gate of Juda; turn to right or left they
might not, their road lay through the heart of it. 47 And what
must they do, the townspeople, but stand to the defence of it,
and barricade the entrance with great boulders! Thereupon
Judas made peaceful overtures to them; 48 Grant us leave,
said he, to make our way through your country to ours, nor
any harm shall befall you; we ask but the right of passage,
and on foot. But open the gates they would not; 49 so Judas
made a cry through the camp, every man should go to the
assault,[a] there where he stood; 50 and go to the assault they
did, the fighting men of his company. All day and all night
they attacked the city, and Judas was given the mastery of it.
51 Never a male creature there but was put to the sword; the
city was plundered and pulled down; and so he passed on
through the streets of it, all paved with dead men. 52 Jordan
they must still cross, there by the great plain that faces
Bethsan; 53 and to the last Judas went ever to and fro, rallying the stragglers and encouraging the people on their journey, till the land of Jude was reached. 54 Glad and merry
were men's hearts as they climbed up Sion mountain, and
there offered burnt-sacrifice in thanks for their safe homecoming, with never a life lost.[b]
55 So fought Judas and Jonathan in Galaad, and their brother Simon in Galilee at the gates of Ptolemais; 56 meanwhile,

[a] 'Go to the assault'; literally, according to the Greek, 'to encamp'; but cf. the use of the corresponding Hebrew verb in Jos. 10. 31 and elsewhere.

[b] Literally, 'Because none of them had fallen until all returned safe and sound', cf. note on Mt. 1. 25.

TODAY'S ENGLISH VERSION

all that they owned. 46 They went as far as Ephron, a large,
well-fortified town. It was impossible to go around it on
either side, and the road passed directly through the town.
47 But the people there would not let them pass and blocked
the town gates with stones. 48 Then Judas sent a friendly
message to them: "Let us pass through your territory to
return home. No one will harm you; we will just pass
through." But they still refused to open the gates.
49 So Judas told everyone in the group, except the fighting
men, to camp where they were. 50 The fighting men were
ordered to take up their positions and attack the town. They
fought all day and all night, until they had taken it. 51 Judas
had all the men of Ephron put to death, plundered the town,
and leveled it. Then he and his army marched through the
town over the dead bodies. 52 They crossed the Jordan into
the wide plain opposite Beth Shan. 53 Throughout the whole
march Judas kept gathering up the stragglers and encouraging the people until they reached the land of Judea. 54 With
thanksgiving and rejoicing, they went up to Mount Zion and
sacrificed burnt offerings because they had returned safely
without a single loss.
55 While Judas and Jonathan were in Gilead and their
brother Simon was attacking Ptolemais in Galilee, 56 Joseph

NEW REVISED STANDARD VERSION

46 So they came to Ephron. This was a large and very strong
town on the road, and they could not go around it to the
right or to the left; they had to go through it. 47 But the people of the town shut them out and blocked up the gates with
stones.
48 Judas sent them this friendly message, "Let us pass
through your land to get to our land. No one will do you
harm; we will simply pass by on foot." But they refused to
open to him. 49 Then Judas ordered proclamation to be made
to the army that all should encamp where they were. 50 So
the men of the forces encamped, and he fought against the
town all that day and all the night, and the town was delivered into his hands. 51 He destroyed every male by the edge
of the sword, and razed and plundered the town. Then he
passed through the town over the bodies of the dead.
52 Then they crossed the Jordan into the large plain
before Beth-shan. 53 Judas kept rallying the laggards and
encouraging the people all the way until he came to the land
of Judah. 54 So they went up to Mount Zion with joy and
gladness, and offered burnt offerings, because they had
returned in safety; not one of them had fallen.
55 Now while Judas and Jonathan were in Gilead and
their[a] brother Simon was in Galilee before Ptolemais,

a Gk *his*

NEW AMERICAN BIBLE

46 When they reached Ephron, a large and strongly fortified
city along the way, they found it impossible to encircle it on
either the right or the left; they would have to march right
through it. 47 But the men in the city shut them out and
blocked up the gates with stones. 48 Then Judas sent them
his peaceful message: "We wish to cross your territory in
order to reach our own; no one will harm you; we will only
march through." But they would not open to him.
49 So Judas ordered a proclamation to be made in the camp
that everyone make an attack from the place where he was.
50 When the men of the army took up their positions, he
assaulted the city all that day and night, and it was delivered
to him. 51 He slaughtered every male, razed and plundered
the city, and passed through it over the slain.
52 Then they crossed the Jordan to the great plain in front
of Beth-shan; 53 and Judas kept rounding up the stragglers
and encouraging the people the whole way, until he reached
the land of Judah. 54 They ascended Mount Zion in joy and
gladness and offered holocausts, because not one of them
had fallen; they returned in safety.
55 During the time that Judas and Jonathan were in the
land of Gilead, and Simon his brother was in Galilee opposite

NEW JERUSALEM BIBLE

46 They reached Ephron, a large town straddling the road and
strongly fortified. As it was impossible to by-pass it either to
right or to left, there was nothing for it but to march straight
through. 47 But the people of the town denied them passage
and barricaded the gates with stones. 48 Judas sent them a
conciliatory message in these terms, 'We want to pass
through your territory to reach our own; no one will do you
any harm, we only want to go through on foot.' But they
would not open up for him. 49 So Judas sent an order down
the column for everyone to halt where he stood. 50 The fighting men took up their positions; Judas attacked the town all
day and night, and the town fell to him. 51 He put all the
males to the sword, rased the town to the ground, plundered
it and marched through the town square over the bodies of
the dead. 52 They then crossed the Jordan into the Great
Plain, opposite Beth-Shean, 53 Judas all the time rallying the
stragglers and encouraging the people the whole way until
they reached Judaea. 54 They climbed Mount Zion in joy and
gladness and presented burnt offerings because they had
returned safe and sound without having lost a single man.
55 While Judas and Jonathan were in Gilead and Simon his
brother in Galilee outside Ptolemais, 56 Joseph son of

GREEK OLD TESTAMENT

πρόσωπον Πτολεμαίδος. 56 ἤκουσεν Ιωσηφ ὁ τοῦ Ζαχαριου
καὶ Αζαριας ἄρχοντες τῆς δυνάμεως τῶν ἀνδραγαθιῶν καὶ
τοῦ πολέμου, οἷα ἐποίησαν, 57 καὶ εἶπον Ποιήσωμεν καὶ αὐτοὶ ἑαυτοῖς ὄνομα καὶ πορευθῶμεν πολεμῆσαι πρὸς τὰ ἔθνη
τὰ κύκλῳ ἡμῶν. 58 καὶ παρήγγειλεν τοῖς ἀπὸ τῆς δυνάμεως
τῆς μετ᾽ αὐτῶν, καὶ ἐπορεύθησαν ἐπὶ Ιάμνειαν. 59 καὶ ἐξῆλθεν Γοργίας ἐκ τῆς πόλεως καὶ οἱ ἄνδρες αὐτοῦ εἰς συνάντησιν αὐτοῖς εἰς πόλεμον. 60 καὶ ἐτροπώθη Ιωσηπος καὶ
Αζαριας, καὶ ἐδιώχθησαν ἕως τῶν ὁρίων τῆς Ιουδαίας, καὶ
ἔπεσον ἐν τῇ ἡμέρᾳ ἐκείνῃ ἐκ τοῦ λαοῦ Ισραηλ εἰς δισχιλίους ἄνδρας. 61 καὶ ἐγενήθη τροπὴ μεγάλη ἐν τῷ λαῷ, ὅτι οὐκ
ἤκουσαν Ιουδου καὶ τῶν ἀδελφῶν αὐτοῦ οἰόμενοι ἀνδραγαθῆ-
σαι· 62 αὐτοὶ δὲ οὐκ ἦσαν ἐκ τοῦ σπέρματος τῶν ἀνδρῶν
ἐκείνων, οἷς ἐδόθη σωτηρία Ισραηλ διὰ χειρὸς αὐτῶν.

63 Καὶ ὁ ἀνὴρ Ιουδας καὶ οἱ ἀδελφοὶ αὐτοῦ ἐδοξάσθησαν
σφόδρα ἔναντι παντὸς Ισραηλ καὶ τῶν ἐθνῶν πάντων, οὗ
ἠκούετο τὸ ὄνομα αὐτῶν· 64 καὶ ἐπισυνήγοντο πρὸς αὐτοὺς
εὐφημοῦντες. 65 καὶ ἐξῆλθεν Ιουδας καὶ οἱ ἀδελφοὶ αὐτοῦ
καὶ ἐπολέμουν τοὺς υἱοὺς Ησαυ ἐν τῇ γῇ τῇ πρὸς νότον καὶ
ἐπάταξεν τὴν Χεβρων καὶ τὰς θυγατέρας αὐτῆς καὶ
καθεῖλεν τὰ ὀχυρώματα αὐτῆς καὶ τοὺς πύργους αὐτῆς
ἐνεπύρισεν κυκλόθεν. 66 καὶ ἀπῆρεν τοῦ πορευθῆναι εἰς γῆν
ἀλλοφύλων καὶ διεπορεύετο τὴν Μαρισαν. 67 ἐν τῇ ἡμέρᾳ

KING JAMES VERSION

56 Joseph the *son* of Zacharias, and Azarias, captains of the garrisons, heard of the valiant acts and warlike deeds which they had done.

57 Wherefore they said, Let us also get us a name, and go fight against the heathen that are round about us.

58 So when they had given charge unto the garrison that was with them, they went toward Jamnia.

59 Then came Gorgias and his men out of the city to fight against them.

60 And so it was, that Joseph and Azarias were put to flight, and pursued unto the borders of Judea: and there were slain that day of the people of Israel about two thousand men.

61 Thus was there a great overthrow among the children of Israel, because they were not obedient unto Judas and his brethren, but thought to do some valiant act.

62 Moreover these men came not of the seed of those, by whose hand deliverance was given unto Israel.

63 Howbeit the man Judas and his brethren were greatly renowned in the sight of all Israel, and of all the heathen, wheresoever their name was heard of;

64 Insomuch as the people assembled unto them with joyful acclamations.

65 Afterward went Judas forth with his brethren, and fought against the children of Esau in the land toward the south, where he smote Hebron, and the towns thereof, and pulled down the fortress of it, and burned the towers thereof round about.

66 From thence he removed to go into the land of the Philistines, and passed through Samaria.

DOUAY OLD TESTAMENT

56 Joseph the son of Zacharias, and Azarias captain of the soldiers, heard of the good success, and the battles that were fought.

57 And he said: Let us also get us a name, and let us go fight against the Gentiles that are round about us.

58 And he gave charge to them that were in his army, and they went towards Jamnia.

59 And Gorgias and his men went out of the city, to give them battle.

60 And Joseph and Azarias were put to flight, and were pursued unto the borders of Judea: and there fell, on that day, of the people of Israel about two thousand men, and there was a great overthrow of the people:

61 Because they did not hearken to Judas, and his brethren, thinking that they should do manfully.

62 But they were not of the seed of those men by whom salvation was brought to Israel.

63 And the men of Juda were magnified exceedingly in the sight of all Israel, and of all the nations where their name was heard.

64 And people assembled to them with joyful acclamations.

65 Then Judas and his brethren went forth and attacked the children of Esau, in the land toward the south, and he took Chebron, and her towns: and he burnt the walls thereof and the towers all round it.

66 And he removed his camp to go into the land of the aliens, and he went through Samaria.

KNOX TRANSLATION

what of Joseph son of Zachary, and Azarias, that had charge
of the garrison? News came to them of victories gained, and
great deeds done, 57 and nothing would serve but they must
make a great name for themselves too, by offering battle to
the Gentiles round about. 58 So orders went out to the army,
to march on Jamnia, 59 where Gorgias and his men came out
to meet them. 60 Back fell Joseph and Azarias to the frontiers
of Judaea in great disorder, with a loss to Israel of two thousand men; such defeat they brought on our arms, 61 because
they would not listen to Judas and his brethren, but must be
great warriors like the rest. 62 Not of that race they sprang
that should afford Israel deliverance.

63 But as for Judas and his company,[a] they were held high
in honour, both among Israelite folk, and wherever the
renown of them was heard; 64 all flocked to greet them with
cries of acclaim. 65 But still he and his brethren would be on
the march, reducing the men of Edom in the south country;
on Hebron and its daughter townships the blow fell, neither
wall nor tower of it but was burned to the ground. 66 Then
he moved camp, to march on Philistia, and would make his
way through Samaria.[b] 67 Priests there were that took up

a 'Judas and his company'; the Latin here has 'the men of Juda', which yields no good sense, 'Juda' and 'Israel' being convertible terms at this period. The Greek has, 'the man Judas and his brethren'. *b* 'Samaria' is probably a false reading for Maresa, which lay on the route between Edom and the Philistines.

TODAY'S ENGLISH VERSION

and Azariah, the commanders of the army in Judea, heard
about their brave deeds and victories. 57They said to one
another, "Let's go to war with the Gentiles around us and
win some fame for ourselves." 58So they and their men
attacked Jamnia. 59Gorgias and his men went out of the
town to meet them in battle. 60They defeated Joseph and
Azariah and pursued them as far as the borders of Judea. At
least 2,000 Israelite men were killed that day. 61This great
defeat came about because the Jewish commanders wanted
to be heroes and refused to obey Judas and his brothers.
62Besides, they did not belong to the family of the
Maccabees, whom God had chosen to bring freedom to the
people of Israel.

63But Judas Maccabeus and his brothers won great respect
among all the Israelites and all the Gentiles. When people
heard of their fame, 64large crowds gathered to praise them.
65Then Judas and his brothers went to war against the
Edomites to the south. He attacked Hebron and its surrounding towns, destroyed its fortifications, and burned down the
towers around it. 66Then he marched into the land of the
Philistines and passed through Marisa.[a] 67That day a

[a] *Some ancient translations* Marisa; *Greek* Samaria.

NEW REVISED STANDARD VERSION

56Joseph son of Zechariah, and Azariah, the commanders of
the forces, heard of their brave deeds and of the heroic war
they had fought. 57So they said, "Let us also make a name
for ourselves; let us go and make war on the Gentiles around
us." 58So they issued orders to the men of the forces that
were with them and marched against Jamnia. 59Gorgias and
his men came out of the town to meet them in battle.
60Then Joseph and Azariah were routed, and were pursued to
the borders of Judea; as many as two thousand of the people
of Israel fell that day. 61Thus the people suffered a great
rout because, thinking to do a brave deed, they did not listen
to Judas and his brothers. 62But they did not belong to the
family of those men through whom deliverance was given to
Israel.

63 The man Judas and his brothers were greatly honored
in all Israel and among all the Gentiles, wherever their name
was heard. 64People gathered to them and praised them.

65 Then Judas and his brothers went out and fought the
descendants of Esau in the land to the south. He struck
Hebron and its villages and tore down its strongholds and
burned its towers on all sides. 66Then he marched off to go
into the land of the Philistines, and passed through Marisa.[a]

[a] Other ancient authorities read *Samaria*

NEW AMERICAN BIBLE

Ptolemais, 56Joseph, son of Zechariah, and Azariah, the
leaders of the army, heard about the brave deeds and the
fighting that they were doing. 57They said, "Let us also
make a name for ourselves by going out and fighting against
the Gentiles around us."

58They gave orders to the men of their army who were
with them, and marched toward Jamnia. 59But Gorgias and
his men came out of the city to meet them in battle.
60Joseph and Azariah were beaten, and were pursued to the
frontiers of Judea, and about two thousand Israelites fell that
day. 61It was a bad defeat for the people, because they had
not obeyed Judas and his brothers, thinking that they would
do brave deeds. 62But they did not belong to the family of
those men to whom it was granted to achieve Israel's salvation. 63The valiant Judas and his brothers were greatly
renowned in all Israel and among all the Gentiles, wherever
their name was heard; 64and men gathered about them and
praised them.

65Then Judas and his brothers went out and attacked the
sons of Esau in the country toward the south; he took
Hebron and its villages, and he destroyed its strongholds and
burned the towers around it. 66He then set out for the land
of the Philistines and passed through Marisa. 67At that time

NEW JERUSALEM BIBLE

Zechariah, and Azariah, who were in command of the army,
heard of their valiant deeds and of the battles they had been
fighting, 57and said, 'Let us make a name for ourselves too
and go and fight the nations around us.' 58So they issued
orders to the men under their command and marched on
Jamnia. 59Gorgias and his men came out of the town and
gave battle. 60Joseph and Azariah were routed and pursued
as far as the frontiers of Judaea. That day about two thousand Israelites lost their lives. 61Our people thus met with a
great reverse, because they had not listened to Judas and his
brothers, thinking that they would do something equally
valiant. 62They were not, however, of the same breed of men
as those to whom the deliverance of Israel was entrusted.

63The noble Judas and his brothers, however, were held in
high honour throughout Israel and among all the nations
wherever their name was heard, 64and people thronged
round to acclaim them. 65Judas marched out with his brothers to fight the Edomites in the country towards the south;
he stormed Hebron and its dependent villages, threw down
its fortifications and burned down its encircling towers.
66Leaving there, he made for the country of the Philistines
and passed through Marisa. 67Among the fallen in that

GREEK OLD TESTAMENT

ἐκείνῃ ἔπεσον ἱερεῖς ἐν πολέμῳ βουλόμενοι ἀνδραγαθῆσαι
ἐν τῷ αὐτοὺς ἐξελθεῖν εἰς πόλεμον ἀβουλεύτως. 68 καὶ ἐξέκλινεν Ιουδας εἰς Ἄζωτον γῆν ἀλλοφύλων καὶ καθεῖλεν τοὺς
βωμοὺς αὐτῶν καὶ τὰ γλυπτὰ τῶν θεῶν αὐτῶν κατέκαυσεν
πυρὶ καὶ ἐσκύλευσεν τὰ σκῦλα τῶν πόλεων καὶ ἐπέστρεψεν
εἰς γῆν Ιουδα.

6 Καὶ ὁ βασιλεὺς Ἀντίοχος διεπορεύετο τὰς ἐπάνω χώρας καὶ ἤκουσεν ὅτι ἐστὶν Ἐλυμαΐς ἐν τῇ Περσίδι πόλις
ἔνδοξος πλούτῳ, ἀργυρίῳ καὶ χρυσίῳ· 2 καὶ τὸ ἱερὸν τὸ ἐν
αὐτῇ πλούσιον σφόδρα, καὶ ἐκεῖ καλύμματα χρυσᾶ καὶ θώρ-
ακες καὶ ὅπλα, ἃ κατέλιπεν ἐκεῖ Ἀλέξανδρος ὁ τοῦ Φιλίπ-
που ὁ βασιλεὺς ὁ Μακεδών, ὃς ἐβασίλευσεν πρῶτος ἐν τοῖς
Ἕλλησι. 3 καὶ ἦλθεν καὶ ἐζήτει καταλαβέσθαι τὴν πόλιν καὶ
προνομεῦσαι αὐτήν, καὶ οὐκ ἠδυνάσθη, ὅτι ἐγνώσθη ὁ λόγος
τοῖς ἐκ τῆς πόλεως, 4 καὶ ἀντέστησαν αὐτῷ εἰς πόλεμον,
καὶ ἔφυγεν καὶ ἀπῆρεν ἐκεῖθεν μετὰ λύπης μεγάλης
ἀποστρέψαι εἰς Βαβυλῶνα. 5 καὶ ἦλθέν τις ἀπαγγέλλων
αὐτῷ εἰς τὴν Περσίδα ὅτι τετρόπωνται αἱ παρεμβολαὶ αἱ
πορευθεῖσαι εἰς γῆν Ιουδα, 6 καὶ ἐπορεύθη Λυσίας δυνάμει
ἰσχυρᾷ ἐν πρώτοις καὶ ἐνετράπη ἀπὸ προσώπου αὐτῶν, καὶ
ἐπίσχυσαν ὅπλοις καὶ δυνάμει καὶ σκύλοις πολλοῖς, οἷς
ἔλαβον ἀπὸ τῶν παρεμβολῶν, ὧν ἐξέκοψαν, 7 καὶ καθεῖλον
τὸ βδέλυγμα, ὃ ᾠκοδόμησεν ἐπὶ τὸ θυσιαστήριον τὸ ἐν

KING JAMES VERSION

67 At that time certain priests, desirous to shew their valour, were slain in battle, for that they went out to fight unadvisedly.

68 So Judas turned to Azotus in the land of the Philistines, and when he had pulled down their altars, and burned their carved images with fire, and spoiled their cities, he returned into the land of Judea.

6 About that time king Antiochus travelling through the high countries heard say, that Elymais in the country of Persia was a city greatly renowned for riches, silver, and gold;

2 And that there was in it a very rich temple, wherein were coverings of gold, and breastplates, and shields, which Alexander, *son* of Philip, the Macedonian king, who reigned first among the Grecians, had left there.

3 Wherefore he came and sought to take the city, and to spoil it; but he was not able, because they of the city, having had warning thereof,

4 Rose up against him in battle: so he fled, and departed thence with great heaviness, and returned to Babylon.

5 Moreover there came one who brought him tidings into Persia, that the armies, which went against the land of Judea, were put to flight:

6 And that Lysias, who went forth first with a great power, was driven away of the Jews; and that they were made strong by the armour, and power, and store of spoils, which they had gotten of the armies, whom they had destroyed:

7 Also that they had pulled down the abomination, which

DOUAY OLD TESTAMENT

67 In that day some priests fell in battle, while desiring to do manfully they went out unadvisedly to fight.

68 And Judas turned to Azotus into the land of the strangers, and he threw down their altars, and he burnt the statues of their gods with fire: and he took the spoils of the cities, and returned into the land of Juda.

6 NOW king Antiochus was going through the higher countries, and he heard that the city of Elymais in Persia was greatly renowned, and abounding in silver and gold.

2 And that there was in it a temple, exceeding rich: and coverings of gold, and breastplates, and shields which king Alexander, son of Philip the Macedonian that reigned first in Greece, had left there.

3 Lo, he came, and sought to take the city and to pillage it: but he was not able, because the design was known to them that were in the city.

4 And they rose up against him in battle, and he fled away from thence, and departed with great sadness, and returned towards Babylonia.

5 And whilst he was in Persia, there came one that told him, how the armies that were in the land of Juda were put to flight:

6 And that Lysias went with a very great power, and was put to flight before the face of the Jews, and that they were grown strong by the armour, and power, and store of spoils, which they had gotten out of the camps which they had destroyed:

7 And that they had thrown down the abomination which he had set up upon the altar in Jerusalem, and that they had

KNOX TRANSLATION

arms and fell in battle that day, rashly desirous of a warrior's renown.[a] 68 And now Judas turned aside to Azotus, in
the country of the Philistines; altars he pulled down, images
of their gods burned to ashes, gave up their cities to plunder,
and so came back again to the land of Juda.

6 King Antiochus was still on his journey through the high
countries, when he heard tell of a city in Persia called
Elymais, renowned for its treasures of silver and gold; 2 here
was a temple of great magnificence, that had golden armour
in it, breastplate and shield left there by Philip's son,
Alexander of Macedon, the first overlord of Greece. 3 Thither
he marched, intent on seizing the city and plundering it; but
seize it he might not, because the townsfolk had news of his
purpose, 4 and came out to offer battle. So he was put to the
rout, and must take himself back to Babylon, grievously disappointed.

5 And here, in the Persian country, a messenger reached
him with tidings from Juda. Fled were his armies, 6 and
Lysias, that erstwhile marched out with so brave a retinue,
had left the Jews masters of the field. Now they were strong
and well-armed, such spoil they had taken from the armies
they overthrew; 7 gone was that defiling image he had set up

a Most of the Greek manuscripts have a different and very curious reading, 'Priests there were that fell in battle that day, because he (Judas?) desired to play the warrior, with which design he went into action unadvisedly'.

TODAY'S ENGLISH VERSION

number of priests were killed in battle because they wanted to be heroes and foolishly went out to fight. 68 Judas turned aside to Azotus in Philistia. He pulled down the altars, burned the images of their gods, plundered their towns, and then returned to Judea.

6 As King Antiochus the Fourth was passing through Mesopotamia, he heard of a city in Persia, named Elymais, which was famous for its riches in silver and gold. 2 The temple was very rich, containing gold shields, armor, and weapons left there by Alexander, son of King Philip of Macedonia, who was the first to rule the Greek Empire. 3 Antiochus came and tried to take the city and loot it, but he didn't succeed, because the citizens had learned what he was planning to do, 4 and they drew up their troops to resist him. In great frustration he withdrew to return to Babylonia.

5 In Persia a messenger reached him with the news that the armies he had sent into Judea had been defeated. 6 Lysias and his strong army had been forced to flee from the Jews, who were now reinforced by the additional weapons, supplies, and loot they had taken from the defeated armies. 7 The Jews had pulled down the thing they called "The Awful Horror" that Antiochus had built on the altar in Jerusalem.

NEW REVISED STANDARD VERSION

67 On that day some priests, who wished to do a brave deed, fell in battle, for they went out to battle unwisely. 68 But Judas turned aside to Azotus in the land of the Philistines; he tore down their altars, and the carved images of their gods he burned with fire; he plundered the towns and returned to the land of Judah.

6 King Antiochus was going through the upper provinces when he heard that Elymais in Persia was a city famed for its wealth in silver and gold. 2 Its temple was very rich, containing golden shields, breastplates, and weapons left there by Alexander son of Philip, the Macedonian king who first reigned over the Greeks. 3 So he came and tried to take the city and plunder it, but he could not because his plan had become known to the citizens 4 and they withstood him in battle. So he fled and in great disappointment left there to return to Babylon.

5 Then someone came to him in Persia and reported that the armies that had gone into the land of Judah had been routed; 6 that Lysias had gone first with a strong force, but had turned and fled before the Jews;[a] that the Jews[a] had grown strong from the arms, supplies, and abundant spoils that they had taken from the armies they had cut down; 7 that they had torn down the abomination that he had

[a] Gk *them*

NEW AMERICAN BIBLE

some priests fell in battle who had gone out rashly to fight in their desire to distinguish themselves. 68 Judas then turned toward Azotus in the land of the Philistines. He destroyed their altars and burned the statues of their gods; and after plundering their cities he returned to the land of Judah.

6 As King Antiochus was traversing the inland provinces, he heard that in Persia there was a city called Elymais, famous for its wealth in silver and gold, 2 and that its temple was very rich, containing gold helmets, breastplates, and weapons left there by Alexander, son of Philip, king of Macedon, the first king of the Greeks. 3 He went therefore and tried to capture and pillage the city. But he could not do so, because his plan became known to the people of the city 4 who rose up in battle against him. So he retreated and in great dismay withdrew from there to return to Babylon.

5 While he was in Persia, a messenger brought him news that the armies sent into the land of Judah had been put to flight; 6 that Lysias had gone at first with a strong army and been driven back by the Israelites; that they had grown strong by reason of the arms, men, and abundant possessions taken from the armies they had destroyed; 7 that they had pulled down the Abomination which he had built upon

NEW JERUSALEM BIBLE

day's fighting were some priests who sought to prove their courage there by joining in the battle, a foolhardy venture. 68 Judas next turned on Azotus, which belonged to the Philistines; he overthrew their altars, burned the statues of their gods and, having pillaged their towns, withdrew to Judaea.

6 [a] King Antiochus, meanwhile, was making his way through the Upper Provinces; he had heard that in Persia there was a city called Elymais, renowned for its riches, its silver and gold, 2 and its very wealthy temple containing golden armour, breastplates and weapons, left there by Alexander son of Philip, the king of Macedon, the first to reign over the Greeks. 3 He therefore went and attempted to take the city and pillage it, but without success, the citizens having been forewarned. 4 They resisted him by force of arms. He was routed, and began retreating, very gloomily, towards Babylon. 5 But, while he was still in Persia, news reached him that the armies which had invaded Judaea had been routed, 6 and that Lysias in particular had advanced in massive strength, only to be forced to turn and flee before the Jews; that the latter were now stronger than ever, thanks to the arms, supplies and abundant spoils acquired from the armies they had cut to pieces, 7 and that they had pulled down the abomination which he had erected on the altar in

[a] **6** 6:1seq. // 2 M 1:11–17; 9.

GREEK OLD TESTAMENT

Ιερουσαλημ, καὶ τὸ ἁγίασμα καθὼς τὸ πρότερον ἐκύκλωσαν
τείχεσιν ὑψηλοῖς καὶ τὴν Βαιθσουραν πόλιν αὐτοῦ. 8 καὶ
ἐγένετο ὡς ἤκουσεν ὁ βασιλεὺς τοὺς λόγους τούτους,
ἐθαμβήθη καὶ ἐσαλεύθη σφόδρα καὶ ἔπεσεν ἐπὶ τὴν κοίτην
καὶ ἐνέπεσεν εἰς ἀρρωστίαν ἀπὸ τῆς λύπης, ὅτι οὐκ ἐγένετο
αὐτῷ καθὼς ἐνεθυμεῖτο. 9 καὶ ἦν ἐκεῖ ἡμέρας πλείους, ὅτι
ἀνεκαινίσθη ἐπ᾽ αὐτὸν λύπη μεγάλη, καὶ ἐλογίσατο ὅτι
ἀποθνήσκει. 10 καὶ ἐκάλεσεν πάντας τοὺς φίλους αὐτοῦ καὶ
εἶπεν πρὸς αὐτούς Ἀφίσταται ὁ ὕπνος ἀπὸ τῶν ὀφθαλμῶν
μου, καὶ συμπέπτωκα τῇ καρδίᾳ ἀπὸ τῆς μερίμνης. 11 καὶ
εἶπα τῇ καρδίᾳ Ἕως τίνος θλίψεως ἦλθα καὶ κλύδωνος μεγάλου, ἐν ᾧ νῦν εἰμι; ὅτι χρηστὸς καὶ ἀγαπώμενος ἤμην ἐν τῇ
ἐξουσίᾳ μου. 12 νῦν δὲ μιμνῄσκομαι τῶν κακῶν, ὧν ἐποίησα
ἐν Ιερουσαλημ καὶ ἔλαβον πάντα τὰ σκεύη τὰ ἀργυρᾶ καὶ τὰ
χρυσᾶ τὰ ἐν αὐτῇ καὶ ἐξαπέστειλα ἐξᾶραι τοὺς κατοικοῦντας Ιουδα διὰ κενῆς. 13 ἔγνων ὅτι χάριν τούτων εὗρέν με τὰ
κακὰ ταῦτα· καὶ ἰδοὺ ἀπόλλυμαι λύπῃ μεγάλῃ ἐν γῇ ἀλλοτρίᾳ. 14 καὶ ἐκάλεσεν Φίλιππον ἕνα τῶν φίλων αὐτοῦ καὶ
κατέστησεν αὐτὸν ἐπὶ πάσης τῆς βασιλείας αὐτοῦ· 15 καὶ
ἔδωκεν αὐτῷ τὸ διάδημα καὶ τὴν στολὴν αὐτοῦ καὶ τὸν
δακτύλιον τοῦ ἀγαγεῖν Ἀντίοχον τὸν υἱὸν αὐτοῦ καὶ ἐκθρέψαι αὐτὸν τοῦ βασιλεύειν. 16 καὶ ἀπέθανεν ἐκεῖ Ἀντίοχος ὁ
βασιλεὺς ἔτους ἐνάτου καὶ τεσσαρακοστοῦ καὶ ἑκατοστοῦ.

KING JAMES VERSION

he had set up upon the altar in Jerusalem, and that they had compassed about the sanctuary with high walls, as before, and his city Bethsura.

8 Now when the king heard these words, he was astonished and sore moved: whereupon he laid him down upon his bed, and fell sick for grief, because it had not befallen him as he looked for.

9 And there he continued many days: for his grief was ever more and more, and he made account that he should die.

10 Wherefore he called for all his friends, and said unto them, The sleep is gone from mine eyes, and my heart faileth for very care.

11 And I thought with myself, Into what tribulation am I come, and how great a flood *of misery* is it, wherein now I am! for I was bountiful and beloved in my power.

12 But now I remember the evils that I did at Jerusalem, and that I took all the vessels of gold and silver that were therein, and sent to destroy the inhabitants of Judea without a cause.

13 I perceive therefore that for this cause these troubles are come upon me, and, behold, I perish through great grief in a strange land.

14 Then called he for Philip, one of his friends, whom he made ruler over all his realm,

15 And gave him the crown, and his robe, and his signet, to the end he should bring up his son Antiochus, and nourish him up for the kingdom.

16 So king Antiochus died there in the hundred forty and ninth year.

DOUAY OLD TESTAMENT

compassed about the sanctuary with high walls as before, and Bethsura also his city.

8 And it came to pass when the king heard these words, that he was struck with fear, and exceedingly moved: and he laid himself down upon his bed, and fell sick for grief, because it had not fallen out to him as he imagined.

9 And he remained there many days: for great grief came more and more upon him, and he made account that he should die.

10 And he called for all his friends, and said to them: Sleep is gone from my eyes, and I am fallen away, and my heart is cast down for anxiety.

11 And I said in my heart: Into how much tribulation am I come, and into what floods of sorrow, wherein now I am: I that was pleasant and beloved in my power!

12 But now I remember the evils that I have done in Jerusalem, from whence also I took away all the spoils of gold, and of silver that were in it, and I sent to destroy the inhabitants of Juda without cause.

13 I know therefore that for this cause these evils have found me: and behold I perish with great grief in a strange land.

14 Then he called Philip, one of his friends, and he made him regent over all his kingdom.

15 And he gave him the crown, and his robe, and his ring, that he should go to Antiochus his son, and should bring him up for the kingdom.

16 So king Antiochus died there in the year one hundred and forty-nine.

KNOX TRANSLATION

over the altar at Jerusalem; high walls, as of old, protected
the sanctuary; nay, they had made shift to fortify his own
stronghold of Bethsura.
8 What news was this! The king was all bewilderment and
consternation; he took to his bed, fallen into a decline for
very sadness that his hopes had failed him. 9 Long time he
languished under the double burden of his grief, and knew at
last he was a-dying. 10 So he called his friends about him,
and bade them farewell; Here is sleep quite gone from me,
said he; so dazed is this heart of mine with doubt unre-
solved. 11 Thus runs my thought: How comes it that I have
fallen upon such evil times, such a flood of calamity as now
engulfs me; I, that in the days of my greatness loved men
well, and was well beloved? 12 And now returns the memory
of all the havoc I made in Jerusalem, spoil of gold and silver I
robbed from it, doom of mine against the townsfolk, and for
no fault. 13 Past all doubt, here is the source of all those miseries that have come upon me; look you, how I die consumed
of grief, in a strange land! 14 Then he sent for Philip, one of
his trusted friends, and gave all the kingdom into his charge;
15 crown and robe and ring he delivered to him, bidding him
seek out prince Antiochus, and bring him up as heir to the
throne. 16 Then and there died king Antiochus, in the hundred and forty-ninth year of the Grecian empire. 17 And

TODAY'S ENGLISH VERSION

They had also surrounded the Temple with high walls, as it
had been before, and had taken and fortified the town of
Bethzur, one of the king's own towns.
8 When the king heard this report, he was so dumbfounded
and terribly shaken that he went to bed in a fit of deep
depression because things had not turned out as he had
hoped. 9 He remained ill for a long time, as waves of despair
swept over him, until he finally realized that he was going to
die. 10 He called together all those to whom he had given the
title "Friends of the King" and said to them, "I cannot sleep,
and my heart is broken with grief and worry. 11 At first I
asked myself why these great waves of trouble were sweeping over me, since I have been kind and well-liked during my
reign. 12 But then I remembered the wrongs I did in
Jerusalem when I took all the silver and gold objects from the
Temple and tried without any good reason to destroy the
inhabitants of Judea. 13 I know this is why all these terrible
things have happened to me and I am about to die in deep
despair here in this foreign land."
14 Then he called Philip, one of his most trusted advisers,
and put him in charge of his whole empire. 15 He gave him
his crown, robe, and official ring, and authorized him to educate his son Antiochus the Fifth and bring him up to be king.
16 King Antiochus died there in the year 149.[a]

[a] THE YEAR 149: *This corresponds to 163 B.C.*

NEW REVISED STANDARD VERSION

erected on the altar in Jerusalem; and that they had surrounded the sanctuary with high walls as before, and also
Beth-zur, his town.
8 When the king heard this news, he was astounded and
badly shaken. He took to his bed and became sick from disappointment, because things had not turned out for him as
he had planned. 9 He lay there for many days, because deep
disappointment continually gripped him, and he realized
that he was dying. 10 So he called all his Friends and said to
them, "Sleep has departed from my eyes and I am down-
hearted with worry. 11 I said to myself, 'To what distress I
have come! And into what a great flood I now am plunged!
For I was kind and beloved in my power.' 12 But now I
remember the wrong I did in Jerusalem. I seized all its vessels of silver and gold, and I sent to destroy the inhabitants
of Judah without good reason. 13 I know that it is because of
this that these misfortunes have come upon me; here I am,
perishing of bitter disappointment in a strange land."
14 Then he called for Philip, one of his Friends, and made
him ruler over all his kingdom. 15 He gave him the crown
and his robe and the signet, so that he might guide his son
Antiochus and bring him up to be king. 16 Thus King
Antiochus died there in the one hundred forty-ninth year.[a]

a 163 B.C.

NEW AMERICAN BIBLE

the altar in Jerusalem; and that they had surrounded with
high walls both the sanctuary, as it had been before, and his
city of Beth-zur.
8 When the king heard this news, he was struck with fear
and very much shaken. Sick with grief because his designs
had failed, he took to his bed. 9 There he remained many
days, overwhelmed with sorrow, for he knew he was going
to die.
10 So he called in all his Friends and said to them: "Sleep
has departed from my eyes, for my heart is sinking with anxiety. 11 I said to myself: 'Into what tribulation have I come,
and in what floods of sorrow am I now! 12 Yet I was kindly
and beloved in my rule.' But I now recall the evils I did in
Jerusalem, when I carried away all the vessels of gold and
silver that were in it, and for no cause gave orders that the
inhabitants of Judah be destroyed. 13 I know that this is why
these evils have overtaken me; and now I am dying, in bitter
grief, in a foreign land."
14 Then he summoned Philip, one of his Friends, and put
him in charge of his whole kingdom. 15 He gave him his
crown, his robe, and his signet ring, so that he might guide
the king's son Antiochus and bring him up to be king.
16 King Antiochus died in Persia in the year one hundred and
forty-nine.

NEW JERUSALEM BIBLE

Jerusalem, had encircled the sanctuary with high walls as in
the past, and had fortified Beth-Zur, one of his cities. 8 When
the king heard this news he was amazed and profoundly
shaken; he threw himself on his bed and fell sick with grief,
since things had not turned out for him as he had planned.
9 And there he remained for many days, subject to deep and
recurrent fits of melancholy, until he realised that he was
dying. 10 Then, summoning all his Friends, he said to them,
'Sleep evades my eyes, and my heart is cowed by anxiety.
11 I have been wondering how I could have come to such a
pitch of distress, so great a flood as that which now engulfs
me—I who was so generous and well-loved in my heyday.
12 But now I recall how wrongly I acted in Jerusalem when I
seized all the vessels of silver and gold there and ordered the
extermination of the inhabitants of Judah for no reason at
all. 13 This, I am convinced, is why these misfortunes have
overtaken me, and why I am dying of melancholy in a foreign land.'
14 He summoned Philip, one of his Friends, and made him
regent of the whole kingdom. 15 He entrusted him with his
diadem, his robe and his signet, on the understanding that
he was to educate his son Antiochus and train him for the
throne. 16 King Antiochus then died, in the year 149.

GREEK OLD TESTAMENT

17 καὶ ἐπέγνω Λυσίας ὅτι τέθνηκεν ὁ βασιλεύς, καὶ κατέστησεν βασιλεύειν Ἀντίοχον τὸν υἱὸν αὐτοῦ, ὃν ἐξέθρεψεν
νεώτερον, καὶ ἐκάλεσεν τὸ ὄνομα αὐτοῦ Εὐπάτωρ.

18 Καὶ οἱ ἐκ τῆς ἄκρας ἦσαν συγκλείοντες τὸν Ισραηλ κύκλῳ τῶν ἁγίων καὶ ζητοῦντες κακὰ δι' ὅλου καὶ στήριγμα
τοῖς ἔθνεσιν. 19 καὶ ἐλογίσατο Ιουδας ἐξᾶραι αὐτοὺς καὶ
ἐξεκκλησίασε πάντα τὸν λαὸν τοῦ περικαθίσαι ἐπ' αὐτούς.
20 καὶ συνήχθησαν ἅμα καὶ περιεκάθισαν ἐπ' αὐτὴν ἔτους
πεντηκοστοῦ καὶ ἑκατοστοῦ, καὶ ἐποίησεν βελοστάσεις καὶ
μηχανάς. 21 καὶ ἐξῆλθον ἐξ αὐτῶν ἐκ τοῦ συγκλεισμοῦ, καὶ
ἐκολλήθησαν αὐτοῖς τινες τῶν ἀσεβῶν ἐξ Ισραηλ, 22 καὶ
ἐπορεύθησαν πρὸς τὸν βασιλέα καὶ εἶπον Ἕως πότε οὐ ποιήσῃ κρίσιν καὶ ἐκδικήσεις τοὺς ἀδελφοὺς ἡμῶν; 23 ἡμεῖς εὐ-
δοκοῦμεν δουλεύειν τῷ πατρί σου καὶ πορεύεσθαι τοῖς ὑπ'
αὐτοῦ λεγομένοις καὶ κατακολουθεῖν τοῖς προστάγμασιν αὐτοῦ. 24 καὶ περιεκάθηντο ἐπ' αὐτὴν οἱ υἱοὶ τοῦ λαοῦ ἡμῶν
χάριν τούτου καὶ ἠλλοτριοῦντο ἀφ' ἡμῶν· πλὴν ὅσοι εὑρί-
σκοντο ἐξ ἡμῶν, ἐθανατοῦντο, καὶ αἱ κληρονομίαι ἡμῶν
διηρπάζοντο. 25 καὶ οὐκ ἐφ' ἡμᾶς μόνον ἐξέτειναν χεῖρα,
ἀλλὰ καὶ ἐπὶ πάντα τὰ ὅρια αὐτῶν· 26 καὶ ἰδοὺ παρεμβεβλή-
κασι σήμερον ἐπὶ τὴν ἄκραν ἐν Ιερουσαλημ τοῦ καταλαβέσθαι αὐτήν· καὶ τὸ ἁγίασμα καὶ τὴν Βαιθσουραν ὠχύρωσαν·
27 καὶ ἐὰν μὴ προκαταλάβῃ αὐτοὺς διὰ τάχους, μείζονα τούτων ποιήσουσιν, καὶ οὐ δυνήσῃ τοῦ κατασχεῖν αὐτῶν.

KING JAMES VERSION

17 Now when Lysias knew that the king was dead, he set up Antiochus his son, whom he had brought up being young, to reign in his stead, and his name he called Eupator.

18 About this time they that were in the tower shut up the Israelites round about the sanctuary, and sought always their hurt, and the strengthening of the heathen.

19 Wherefore Judas, purposing to destroy them, called all the people together to besiege them.

20 So they came together, and besieged them in the hundred and fiftieth year, and he made mounts for shot against them, and *other* engines.

21 Howbeit certain of them that were besieged got forth, unto whom some ungodly men of Israel joined themselves:

22 And they went unto the king, and said, How long will it be ere thou execute judgment, and avenge our brethren?

23 We have been willing to serve thy father, and to do as he would have us, and to obey his commandments;

24 For which cause they of our nation besiege the tower, and are alienated from us: moreover as many of us as they could light on they slew, and spoiled our inheritance.

25 Neither have they stretched out their hand against us only, but also against all their borders.

26 And, behold, this day are they besieging the tower at Jerusalem, to take it: the sanctuary also and Bethsura have they fortified.

27 Wherefore if thou dost not prevent them quickly, they will do greater things than these, neither shalt thou be able to rule them.

DOUAY OLD TESTAMENT

17 And Lysias understood that the king was dead, and he set up Antiochus his son to reign, whom he brought up young: and he called his name Eupator.

18 Now they that were in the castle, had shut up the Israelites round about the holy places: and they were continually seeking their hurt, and to strengthen the Gentiles.

19 And Judas purposed to destroy them: and he called together all the people, to besiege them.

20 And they came together, and besieged them in the year one hundred and fifty, and they made battering slings and engines.

21 And some of the besieged got out: and some wicked men of Israel joined themselves unto them.

22 And they went to the king, and said: How long dost thou delay to execute the judgment, and to revenge our brethren?

23 We determined to serve thy father and to do according to his orders, and obey his edicts:

24 And for this they of our nation are alienated from us, and have slain as many of us as they could find, and have spoiled our inheritances.

25 Neither have they put forth their hand against us only, but also against all our borders.

26 And behold they have approached this day to the castle of Jerusalem to take it, and they have fortified the strong hold of Bethsura:

27 And unless thou speedily prevent them, they will do greater things than these, and thou shalt not be able to subdue them.

KNOX TRANSLATION

Lysias, hearing of his death, crowned this same prince
Antiochus, that he had brought up from boyhood, giving him
the name of Eupator.

18 Meanwhile, what of the Jews that dwelt about the holy
place? Here was the garrison of the citadel hemming them
in, seeking ever to do them injury, and to sustain the Gentile
cause. 19 So Judas was fain to make an end of it, and summoned the whole people to rally for the siege. 20 Rally they
did, and began the siege in the hundred and fiftieth year,
with much contriving of catapults and engines. 21 But some
of the defenders slipped out; and these, with traitors of
Israelite stock to support them, 22 went off to gain the king's
audience. Wilt thou never bring redress, they asked, and do
our brethren right? 23 Jews are we, that resolved we would
be loyal to thy father, his policy furthering, his will obeying.
24 What came of it? Our own fellow Israelites would have no
more of our company, slew all they could lay hands on,
robbed us of our possessions. 25 Not us only, but all the
country about them, their violence threatens; 26 even now
they stand arrayed against the citadel of Jerusalem, ready to
take it by storm, and have fortified Bethsura. 27 Forestall
their plans thou must, and speedily, or they will go further
yet, and there will be no holding them.

TODAY'S ENGLISH VERSION

17 When Lysias learned that the king had died, he made the
young Antiochus king in place of his father. He had brought
up Antiochus from childhood and now gave him the name
Eupator.

18 Meanwhile, the enemies in the fort at Jerusalem had
been blockading the people of Israel in the area around the
Temple, constantly causing them trouble and giving support
to the Gentiles. 19 So Judas decided to get rid of them and
called all the people together to besiege the fort. 20 The people assembled and laid siege to the fort in the year 150.[a]
They built siege platforms and battering rams.

21 But some of the men under siege escaped, and together
with some of the renegade Jews, they went to the king and
said, 22 "How long are you going to wait before you take
revenge for what was done to our countrymen? 23 We were
willing to serve your father, follow his orders, and obey his
decrees. 24 But what good did it do us? Now our own countrymen have become our enemies.[b] In fact, they have killed
as many of us as they could find and have stolen our possessions. 25 But we are not the only ones they have harmed;
they have attacked all their neighbors. 26 And now they have
laid siege to the fort in Jerusalem and are planning to take it.
They have also fortified the Temple and Bethzur. 27 Unless
you act immediately, they will do even more, and you will
not be able to stop them."

[a] THE YEAR 150: *This corresponds to 162 B.C.*
[b] enemies; *some manuscripts add* and besieged the fort.

NEW REVISED STANDARD VERSION

17 When Lysias learned that the king was dead, he set up
Antiochus the king's[a] son to reign. Lysias[b] had brought him
up from boyhood; he named him Eupator.

18 Meanwhile the garrison in the citadel kept hemming
Israel in around the sanctuary. They were trying in every
way to harm them and strengthen the Gentiles. 19 Judas
therefore resolved to destroy them, and assembled all the
people to besiege them. 20 They gathered together and
besieged the citadel[c] in the one hundred fiftieth year;[d] and
he built siege towers and other engines of war. 21 But some
of the garrison escaped from the siege and some of the
ungodly Israelites joined them. 22 They went to the king and
said, "How long will you fail to do justice and to avenge our
kindred? 23 We were happy to serve your father, to live by
what he said, and to follow his commands. 24 For this reason the sons of our people besieged the citadel[e] and became
hostile to us; moreover, they have put to death as many of
us as they have caught, and they have seized our inheritances. 25 It is not against us alone that they have stretched
out their hands; they have also attacked all the lands on
their borders. 26 And see, today they have encamped against
the citadel in Jerusalem to take it; they have fortified both
the sanctuary and Beth-zur; 27 unless you quickly prevent
them, they will do still greater things, and you will not be
able to stop them."

a Gk *his* *b* Gk *He* *c* Gk *it* *d* 162 B.C. *e* Meaning of Gk uncertain

NEW AMERICAN BIBLE

17 When Lysias learned that the king was dead, he set up
the king's son Antiochus, whom he had reared as a child, to
be king in his place; and he gave him the title Eupator.

18 The men in the citadel were hemming in Israel around
the sanctuary, continually trying to harm them and to
strengthen the Gentiles. 19 But Judas planned to destroy
them, and called all the people together to besiege them.
20 So in the year one hundred and fifty they assembled and
stormed the citadel, for which purpose he constructed catapults and other devices. 21 Some of the besieged escaped,
joined by impious Israelites; 22 they went to the king and
said:

"How long will you fail to do justice and avenge our kinsmen? 23 We agreed to serve your father and to follow his
orders and obey his edicts. 24 And for this the sons of our
people have become our enemies; they have put to death as
many of us as they could find and have plundered our
estates. 25 They have acted aggressively not only against us,
but throughout their whole territory. 26 Look! They have
now besieged the citadel in Jerusalem in order to capture it,
and they have fortified the sanctuary and Beth-zur. 27 Unless
you quickly forestall them, they will do even worse things
than these, and you will not be able to stop them."

NEW JERUSALEM BIBLE

17 Lysias, learning that the king was dead, established on the
throne in succession to him his son Antiochus, whom he had
brought up from childhood—and styled him Eupator.

18 The people in the Citadel at the time were blockading
Israel round the sanctuary and were taking every opportunity to harm them and to support the gentiles. 19 Judas decided
that they must be destroyed, and he mobilised the whole
people to besiege them. 20 They assembled and laid siege to
the Citadel in the year 150, building batteries and siege-
engines. 21 But some of the besieged broke through the
blockade, and to these a number of renegades from Israel
attached themselves. 22 They made their way to the king and
said, 'How much longer are you going to wait before you see
justice done and avenge our fellows? 23 We were content to
serve your father, to comply with his orders, and to obey his
edicts. 24 As a result our own people will have nothing to do
with us; what is more, they have killed all those of us they
could catch, and looted our family property. 25 Nor is it on us
alone that their blows have fallen, but on all your territories.
26 At this moment, they are laying siege to the Citadel of
Jerusalem, to capture it, and they have fortified the sanctuary
and Beth-Zur. 27 Unless you forestall them at once, they will
go on to even bigger things, and then you will never be able
to control them.'

GREEK OLD TESTAMENT

28 Καὶ ὠργίσθη ὁ βασιλεύς, ὅτε ἤκουσεν, καὶ συνήγαγεν
πάντας τοὺς φίλους αὐτοῦ ἄρχοντας δυνάμεως αὐτοῦ καὶ
τοὺς ἐπὶ τῶν ἡνιῶν· 29 καὶ ἀπὸ βασιλειῶν ἑτέρων καὶ ἀπὸ
νήσων θαλασσῶν ἦλθον πρὸς αὐτὸν δυνάμεις μισθωταί·
30 καὶ ἦν ὁ ἀριθμὸς τῶν δυνάμεων αὐτοῦ ἑκατὸν χιλιάδες
πεζῶν καὶ εἴκοσι χιλιάδες ἱππέων καὶ ἐλέφαντες δύο καὶ
τριάκοντα εἰδότες πόλεμον. 31 καὶ ἦλθον διὰ τῆς Ιδουμαίας
καὶ παρενέβαλον ἐπὶ Βαιθσουραν καὶ ἐπολέμησαν ἡμέρας
πολλὰς καὶ ἐποίησαν μηχανάς. καὶ ἐξῆλθον καὶ ἐνεπύρισαν
αὐτὰς πυρὶ καὶ ἐπολέμησαν ἀνδρωδῶς. 32 καὶ ἀπῆρεν Ιουδας
ἀπὸ τῆς ἄκρας καὶ παρενέβαλεν εἰς Βαιθζαχαρια ἀπέναντι
τῆς παρεμβολῆς τοῦ βασιλέως. 33 καὶ ὤρθρισεν ὁ βασιλεὺς
τὸ πρωὶ καὶ ἀπῆρεν τὴν παρεμβολὴν ἐν ὁρμήματι αὐτῆς
κατὰ τὴν ὁδὸν Βαιθζαχαρια, καὶ διεσκευάσθησαν αἱ δυνάμεις εἰς τὸν πόλεμον καὶ ἐσάλπισαν ταῖς σάλπιγξιν. 34 καὶ
τοῖς ἐλέφασιν ἔδειξαν αἷμα σταφυλῆς καὶ μόρων τοῦ
παραστῆσαι αὐτοὺς εἰς τὸν πόλεμον. 35 καὶ διεῖλον τὰ θηρία
εἰς τὰς φάλαγγας καὶ παρέστησαν ἑκάστῳ ἐλέφαντι χιλίους
ἄνδρας τεθωρακισμένους ἐν ἁλυσιδωτοῖς, καὶ περικεφαλαῖαι
χαλκαῖ ἐπὶ τῶν κεφαλῶν αὐτῶν, καὶ πεντακοσία ἵππος
διατεταγμένη ἑκάστῳ θηρίῳ ἐκλελεγμένη· 36 οὗτοι πρὸ καιροῦ οὗ ἂν ᾖ τὸ θηρίον ἦσαν καὶ οὗ ἐὰν ἐπορεύετο ἐπορεύοντο
ἅμα, οὐκ ἀφίσταντο ἀπ᾽ αὐτοῦ. 37 καὶ πύργοι ξύλινοι ἐπ᾽
αὐτοὺς ὀχυροὶ σκεπαζόμενοι ἐφ᾽ ἑκάστου θηρίου ἐζωσμένοι
ἐπ᾽ αὐτοῦ μηχαναῖς, καὶ ἐφ᾽ ἑκάστου ἄνδρες δυνάμεως

KING JAMES VERSION

28 Now when the king heard this, he was angry, and gathered together all his friends, and the captains of his army, and those that had charge of the horse.

29 There came also unto him from other kingdoms, and from isles of the sea, bands of hired soldiers.

30 So that the number of his army was an hundred thousand footmen, and twenty thousand horsemen, and two and thirty elephants exercised in battle.

31 These went through Idumea, and pitched against Bethsura, which they assaulted many days, making engines of war; but they *of Bethsura* came out, and burned them with fire, and fought valiantly.

32 Upon this Judas removed from the tower, and pitched in Bathzacharias, over against the king's camp.

33 Then the king rising very early marched fiercely with his host toward Bathzacharias, where his armies made them ready to battle, and sounded the trumpets.

34 And to the end they might provoke the elephants to fight, they shewed them the blood of grapes and mulberries.

35 Moreover they divided the beasts among the armies, and for every elephant they appointed a thousand men, armed with coats of mail, and with helmets of brass on their heads; and beside this, for every beast were ordained five hundred horsemen of the best.

36 These were ready at every occasion: wheresoever the beast was, and whithersoever the beast went, they went also, neither departed they from him.

37 And upon the beasts were there strong towers of wood, which covered every one of them, and were girt fast unto

DOUAY OLD TESTAMENT

28 Now when the king heard this, he was angry: and he called together all his friends, and the captains of his army, and them that were over the horsemen.

29 There came also to him from other realms, and from the islands of the sea hired troops.

30 And the number of his army was an hundred thousand footmen, and twenty thousand horsemen, and thirty-two elephants, trained to battle.

31 And they went through Idumea, and approached to Bethsura, and fought many days, and they made engines: but they sallied forth and burnt them with fire, and fought manfully.

32 And Judas departed from the castle, and removed the camp to Bethzacharam, over against the king's camp.

33 And the king rose before it was light, and made his troops march on fiercely towards the way of Bethzacharam: and the armies made themselves ready for the battle, and they sounded the trumpets:

34 And they shewed the elephants the blood of grapes, and mulberries to provoke them to fight.

35 And they distributed the beasts by the legions: and there stood by every elephant a thousand men in coats of mail, and with helmets of brass on their heads: and five hundred horsemen set in order were chosen for every beast.

36 These before the time wheresoever the beast was, they were there: and whithersoever it went, they went, and they departed not from it.

37 And upon the beast, there were strong wooden towers, which covered every one of them: and engines upon them:

KNOX TRANSLATION

28 Angered by these tidings, the king sent for all his trusted
friends, for his army captains and his commanders of horse;
29 mercenaries, too, were hired from foreign countries, and
from the islands out at sea, 30 till he could put a hundred
thousand foot and twenty thousand horse into the field,
besides thirty-two elephants, inured to war. 31 Through
Edom they marched, and invested Bethsura; long they held it
besieged, and built engines to attack it, but these, by a brave
sally, the defenders burned to ashes.
32 Meanwhile, Judas drew away from the citadel, and
encamped at Bethzacharam, close to the king's army. 33 Ere
dawn broke, the king was astir, and his men marching hot-
foot towards Bethzacharam, where the armies made ready
for battle, with a great blowing of trumpets. 34 As for the elephants, they were blooded to battle with juice of grape and
mulberry, 35 and so divided here and there among the
troops. A thousand foot-soldiers were assigned to each, in
coat of mail and helmet of bronze; with each went five hundred picked horsemen; 36 these were waiting ready for every
beast at its station, and must go wherever it went, never
leaving its side. 37 On the back of every beast was a strong
protecting tower of wood, cunningly fitted; and thirty-two

TODAY'S ENGLISH VERSION

28 When the king heard this, he was furious. He brought
together all the army commanders, the cavalry officers, and
his most trusted advisers. 29 He also hired mercenary soldiers from other countries and from the Greek islands. 30 His
forces numbered 100,000 infantry, 20,000 cavalry, and 32
elephants trained for war. 31 The king and his army passed
through Idumea and laid siege to Bethzur, where they fought
for a long time. They built battering rams and siege platforms, but the defenders fought bravely and came out of the
town and burned down the platforms.

32 Then Judas withdrew his troops from the fort in
Jerusalem and set up his camp at Beth Zechariah, blocking
the advance of the king's army. 33 Early the next morning,
the king rapidly moved his army along the road to Beth
Zechariah, where his troops took up battle positions and
blew trumpets. 34 They got the elephants ready for battle by
showing them grape juice and mulberry juice. 35 The huge
animals were distributed among the infantry units. A thousand men, protected by chain armor and bronze helmets,
were stationed with each elephant. Each animal was also
accompanied by a special force of 500 cavalry, 36 which
always remained with the elephant. 37 A strong, protected
wooden platform was securely fastened by a special harness

NEW REVISED STANDARD VERSION

28 The king was enraged when he heard this. He assembled all his Friends, the commanders of his forces and those
in authority.[a] 29 Mercenary forces also came to him from
other kingdoms and from islands of the seas. 30 The number
of his forces was one hundred thousand foot soldiers, twenty
thousand horsemen, and thirty-two elephants accustomed to
war. 31 They came through Idumea and encamped against
Beth-zur, and for many days they fought and built engines of
war; but the Jews[b] sallied out and burned these with fire,
and fought courageously.

32 Then Judas marched away from the citadel and
encamped at Beth-zechariah, opposite the camp of the king.
33 Early in the morning the king set out and took his army by
a forced march along the road to Beth-zechariah, and his
troops made ready for battle and sounded their trumpets.
34 They offered the elephants the juice of grapes and mulberries, to arouse them for battle. 35 They distributed the animals among the phalanxes; with each elephant they stationed a thousand men armed with coats of mail, and with
brass helmets on their heads; and five hundred picked horsemen were assigned to each beast. 36 These took their position beforehand wherever the animal was; wherever it went,
they went with it, and they never left it. 37 On the elephants[c]
were wooden towers, strong and covered; they were fastened

a Gk *those over the reins* *b* Gk *they* *c* Gk *them*

NEW AMERICAN BIBLE

28 When the king heard this he was angry, and he called
together all his Friends, the officers of his army, and the
commanders of the cavalry. 29 Mercenary forces also came to
him from other kingdoms and from the islands of the seas.
30 His army numbered a hundred thousand foot-soldiers,
twenty thousand cavalry, and thirty-two elephants trained
for war. 31 They passed through Idumea and camped before
Beth-zur. For many days they attacked it; they constructed
siege-devices, but the besieged made a sortie and burned
these, and they fought bravely.
32 Then Judas marched away from the citadel and moved
his camp to Beth-zechariah, on the way to the king's camp.
33 The king, rising before dawn, moved his force hastily along
the road to Beth-zechariah; and the armies prepared for battle, while the trumpets sounded. 34 They made the elephants
drunk on grape and mulberry wine to provoke them to fight.
35 The beasts were distributed along the phalanxes, each
elephant having assigned to it a thousand men in coats of
mail, with bronze helmets, and five hundred picked cavalry.
36 These anticipated the beast wherever it was; and wherever
it moved, they moved too and never left it. 37 A strong wood-
en tower covering each elephant, and fastened to it by a

NEW JERUSALEM BIBLE

28 The king was furious when he heard this and summoned all his Friends, the generals of his forces and the marshals of horse. 29 He recruited mercenaries from other kingdoms and the Mediterranean islands. 30 His forces numbered
a hundred thousand foot soldiers, twenty thousand cavalry
and thirty-two elephants with experience of battle conditions. 31 They advanced through Idumaea and besieged Beth-
Zur, pressing the attack for days on end; they also constructed siege-engines, but the defenders made a sortie and set
these on fire, putting up a brave resistance.
32 At this, Judas left the Citadel and pitched camp at Beth-
Zechariah opposite the royal encampment. 33 The king rose
at daybreak and marched his army at top speed down the
road to Beth-Zechariah, where his forces took up their battle
formations and sounded the trumpets. 34 The elephants
were given a syrup of grapes and mulberries to prepare
them for the battle. 35 These animals were distributed
among the phalanxes, to each elephant being allocated a
thousand men dressed in coats of mail with bronze helmets
on their heads; five hundred picked horsemen were also
assigned to each beast. 36 The horsemen anticipated every
move their elephant made; wherever it went they went with
it, never quitting it. 37 On each elephant, to protect it, was a
stout wooden tower, kept in position by girths, each with its

GREEK OLD TESTAMENT

τέσσαρες οἱ πολεμοῦντες ἐπ' αὐτοῖς καὶ ὁ Ἰνδὸς αὐτοῦ.
38 καὶ τὴν ἐπίλοιπον ἵππον ἔνθεν καὶ ἔνθεν ἔστησεν ἐπὶ τὰ
δύο μέρη τῆς παρεμβολῆς, κατασείοντες καὶ καταφρασσό-
μενοι ἐν ταῖς φάλαγξιν. 39 ὡς δὲ ἔστιλβεν ὁ ἥλιος ἐπὶ τὰς
χρυσᾶς καὶ χαλκᾶς ἀσπίδας, ἔστιλβεν τὰ ὄρη ἀπ' αὐτῶν καὶ
κατηύγαζεν ὡς λαμπάδες πυρός. 40 καὶ ἐξετάθη μέρος τι
τῆς παρεμβολῆς τοῦ βασιλέως ἐπὶ τὰ ὑψηλὰ ὄρη καί τινες
ἐπὶ τὰ ταπεινά· καὶ ἤρχοντο ἀσφαλῶς καὶ τεταγμένως.
41 καὶ ἐσαλεύοντο πάντες οἱ ἀκούοντες φωνῆς πλήθους
αὐτῶν καὶ ὁδοιπορίας τοῦ πλήθους καὶ συγκρουσμοῦ τῶν
ὅπλων· ἦν γὰρ ἡ παρεμβολὴ μεγάλη σφόδρα καὶ ἰσχυρά.
42 καὶ ἤγγισεν Ιουδας καὶ ἡ παρεμβολὴ αὐτοῦ εἰς παράταξιν,
καὶ ἔπεσον ἀπὸ τῆς παρεμβολῆς τοῦ βασιλέως ἑξακόσιοι
ἄνδρες. 43 καὶ εἶδεν Ελεαζαρος ὁ Αυαραν ἓν τῶν θηρίων
τεθωρακισμένον θώραξιν βασιλικοῖς, καὶ ἦν ὑπεράγον πάντα
τὰ θηρία, καὶ ᾠήθη ὅτι ἐν αὐτῷ ἐστιν ὁ βασιλεύς. 44 καὶ
ἔδωκεν ἑαυτὸν τοῦ σῶσαι τὸν λαὸν αὐτοῦ καὶ περιποιῆσαι
ἑαυτῷ ὄνομα αἰώνιον· 45 καὶ ἐπέδραμεν αὐτῷ θράσει εἰς μέσον τῆς φάλαγγος καὶ ἐθανάτου δεξιὰ καὶ εὐώνυμα, καὶ
ἐσχίζοντο ἀπ' αὐτοῦ ἔνθα καὶ ἔνθα· 46 καὶ εἰσέδυ ὑπὸ τὸν
ἐλέφαντα καὶ ὑπέθηκεν αὐτῷ καὶ ἀνεῖλεν αὐτόν, καὶ ἔπεσεν
ἐπὶ τὴν γῆν ἐπάνω αὐτοῦ, καὶ ἀπέθανεν ἐκεῖ. 47 καὶ εἶδον

KING JAMES VERSION

them with devices: there were also upon every one two and thirty strong men, that fought upon them, beside the Indian that ruled him.

38 As for the remnant of the horsemen, they set them on this side and that side at the two parts of the host, giving them signs what to do, and being harnessed all over amidst the ranks.

39 Now when the sun shone upon the shields of gold and brass, the mountains glistered therewith, and shined like lamps of fire.

40 So part of the king's army being spread upon the high mountains, and part on the valleys below, they marched on safely and in order.

41 Wherefore all that heard the noise of their multitude, and the marching of the company, and the rattling of the harness, were moved: for the army was very great and mighty.

42 Then Judas and his host drew near, and entered into battle, and there were slain of the king's army six hundred men.

43 ¶ Eleazar also, *surnamed* Savaran, perceiving that one of the beasts, armed with royal harness, was higher than all the rest, and supposing that the king was upon him,

44 Put himself in jeopardy, to the end he might deliver his people, and get him a perpetual name:

45 Wherefore he ran upon him courageously through the midst of the battle, slaying on the right hand and on the left, so that they were divided from him on both sides.

46 Which done, he crept under the elephant, and thrust him under, and slew him: whereupon the elephant fell down upon him, and there he died.

DOUAY OLD TESTAMENT

and upon every one thirty-two valiant men, who fought from above; and an Indian to rule the beast.

38 And the rest of the horsemen he placed on this side and on that side at the two wings, with trumpets to stir up the army, and to hasten them forward that stood thick together in the legions thereof.

39 Now when the sun shone upon the shields of gold, and of brass, the mountains glittered therewith, and they shone like lamps of fire.

40 And part of the king's army was distinguished by the high mountains, and the other part by the low places: and they marched on warily and orderly.

41 And all the inhabitants of the land were moved at the noise of their multitude, and the marching of the company, and the rattling of the armour, for the army was exceeding great and strong.

42 And Judas and his army drew near for battle: and there fell of the king's army six hundred men.

43 And Eleazar the son of Saura saw one of the beasts harnessed with the king's harness: and it was higher than the other beasts: and it seemed to him that the king was on it:

44 And he exposed himself to deliver his people and to get himself an everlasting name.

45 And he ran up to it boldly in the midst of the legion, killing on the right hand, and on the left, and they fell by him on this side and that side.

46 And he went between the feet of the elephant, and put himself under it: and slew it, and it fell to the ground upon him, and he died there.

KNOX TRANSLATION

valiant men were appointed to do battle from this height,
over and above the Indian that was the beast's driver.[a]
38 The remainder of the cavalry were stationed on either
wing, to daunt the oncoming host with a clamour of trumpets,[b] and harass them as they stood tight packed in their
ranks. 39 Brightly the sun shone down on shield of gold,
shield of bronze, till all the mountain-side gave back the
glancing rays of them, and dazzled like points of fire. 40 Part
of the king's army was drawn up on the heights, part on the
level plain; warily they came on and in good order; 41 and
ever, as they went, murmur of voices, tramp of feet, and
clash of arms daunted the country-side around them, so
great yonder army was, and so valiant. 42 But Judas and his
men closed with them, and gave battle; and of the king's soldiers, there were six hundred that fell.
43 What did Eleazar that day, the son of Sauran?[c] Here
was one of the beasts that went decked in royal trappings,
and towered high above the rest; There rides the king,
thought he, 44 and with that, he gave his life, to win deliverance for his country, and for himself imperishable renown.
45 Bravely he ran up to it, there in the heart of the press, slaying to right and left of him, men falling on either side, 46 till
he could creep in between the very feet of the elephant;
crouched there, and dispatched it, and so, crushed by its fall
to earth, died where he lay.

a The meaning of the original is, that each elephant carried no less than thirty-two fighting men. The statement is perhaps due to some error in the copying of the Greek manuscripts. *b* There is no mention of trumpets in the Greek original. But the text is obscure, and perhaps corrupt. *c* In the Greek, 'Eleazar Sauaran', perhaps a corruption of 'Abaron' (2. 5 above).

TODAY'S ENGLISH VERSION

to the back of each elephant. Three[a] soldiers rode on each animal, in addition to the elephant driver. 38 Lysias placed the rest of the cavalry on the two flanks of the army where they could be protected by the infantry while harassing the enemy. 39 The sunlight, reflected off the bronze and gold shields, shone on the mountains and flashed like burning torches. 40 Part of the king's army was spread out over the higher ground of the mountain slopes and part over the lower land, but they all moved forward steadily and in good order. 41 All the people were terrified when they heard the noise made by the clashing of weapons and the marching of that great and powerful army.

42 Judas and his army advanced into battle, and immediately killed 600 of the king's army. 43 When Eleazar Avaran saw that one of the elephants was larger than the others and that it was covered with royal armor, he thought that the king was riding on it. 44 Eleazar sacrificed his life to save his people and to gain eternal fame. 45 He ran boldly toward the elephant, which was in the middle of a battalion of infantry. He rushed forward killing men to the right and left, so that the enemy soldiers fell back before him on both sides. 46 He slipped in under the elephant and stabbed it to death, and it fell on him and killed him. 47 But when the Jews realized

[a] *Probable text* Three; *Greek* Thirty *or* Thirty-two.

NEW REVISED STANDARD VERSION

on each animal by special harness, and on each were four[a] armed men who fought from there, and also its Indian driver. 38 The rest of the cavalry were stationed on either side, on the two flanks of the army, to harass the enemy while being themselves protected by the phalanxes. 39 When the sun shone on the shields of gold and brass, the hills were ablaze with them and gleamed like flaming torches.

40 Now a part of the king's army was spread out on the high hills, and some troops were on the plain, and they advanced steadily and in good order. 41 All who heard the noise made by their multitude, by the marching of the multitude and the clanking of their arms, trembled, for the army was very large and strong. 42 But Judas and his army advanced to the battle, and six hundred of the king's army fell. 43 Now Eleazar, called Avaran, saw that one of the animals was equipped with royal armor. It was taller than all the others, and he supposed that the king was on it. 44 So he gave his life to save his people and to win for himself an everlasting name. 45 He courageously ran into the midst of the phalanx to reach it; he killed men right and left, and they parted before him on both sides. 46 He got under the elephant, stabbed it from beneath, and killed it; but it fell to the ground upon him and he died. 47 When the Jews[b] saw the

[a] Cn: Some authorities read *thirty*; others *thirty-two* [b] Gk *they*

NEW AMERICAN BIBLE

harness, held, besides the Indian mahout, three soldiers who fought from it. 38 The remaining cavalry were stationed on one or the other of the two flanks of the army, to harass the enemy and to be protected from the phalanxes. 39 When the sun shone on the gold and bronze shields, the mountains gleamed with their brightness and blazed like flaming torches. 40 Part of the king's army extended over the heights, while some were on low ground, but they marched forward steadily and in good order. 41 All who heard the noise of their numbers, the tramp of their marching, and the clashing of the arms, trembled; for the army was very great and strong.

42 Judas with his army advanced to fight, and six hundred men of the king's army fell. 43 Eleazar, called Avaran, saw one of the beasts bigger than any of the others and covered with royal armor, and he thought the king must be on it. 44 So he gave up his life to save his people and win an everlasting name for himself. 45 He dashed up to it in the middle of the phalanx, killing men right and left, so that they fell back from him on both sides. 46 He ran right under the elephant and stabbed it in the belly, killing it. The beast fell to the ground on top of him, and he died there.

NEW JERUSALEM BIBLE

three combatants, as well as its mahout. 38 The remainder of the cavalry was stationed on one or other of the two flanks of the army, to harass the enemy and cover the phalanxes.

39 When the sun glinted on the bronze and golden shields, the mountains caught the glint and gleamed like fiery torches. 40 One part of the royal army was deployed on the upper slopes of the mountain and the other in the valley below; they advanced in solid, well-disciplined formation. 41 Everyone trembled at the noise made by this vast multitude, the thunder of the troops on the march and the clanking of their armour, for it was an immense and mighty army. 42 Judas and his army advanced to give battle, and six hundred of the king's army were killed. 43 Eleazar, called Avaran, noticing that one of the elephants was royally caparisoned and was also taller than all the others, and supposing that the king was mounted on it, 44 sacrificed himself to save his people and win an imperishable name. 45 Boldly charging towards the creature through the thick of the phalanx, dealing death to right and left, so that the enemy scattered on either side at his onslaught, 46 he darted in under the elephant, thrust at it from underneath, and killed it. The beast collapsed on top of him, and he died on the spot.

GREEK OLD TESTAMENT

τὴν ἰσχὺν τῆς βασιλείας καὶ τὸ ὅρμημα τῶν δυνάμεων καὶ
ἐξέκλιναν ἀπ᾽ αὐτῶν.
48 Οἱ δὲ ἐκ τῆς παρεμβολῆς τοῦ βασιλέως ἀνέβαινον εἰς
συνάντησιν αὐτῶν εἰς Ιερουσαλημ, καὶ παρενέβαλεν ὁ
βασιλεὺς εἰς τὴν Ιουδαίαν καὶ εἰς τὸ ὄρος Σιων. 49 καὶ ἐποίησεν εἰρήνην μετὰ τῶν ἐκ Βαιθσουρων, καὶ ἐξῆλθον ἐκ τῆς
πόλεως, ὅτι οὐκ ἦν αὐτοῖς ἐκεῖ διατροφὴ τοῦ συγκεκλεῖσθαι
ἐν αὐτῇ, ὅτι σάββατον ἦν τῇ γῇ· 50 καὶ κατελάβετο ὁ βασιλεὺς τὴν Βαιθσουραν καὶ ἀπέταξεν ἐκεῖ φρουρὰν τηρεῖν
αὐτήν. 51 καὶ παρενέβαλεν ἐπὶ τὸ ἁγίασμα ἡμέρας πολλὰς
καὶ ἔστησεν ἐκεῖ βελοστάσεις καὶ μηχανὰς καὶ πυροβόλα
καὶ λιθοβόλα καὶ σκορπίδια εἰς τὸ βάλλεσθαι βέλη καὶ
σφενδόνας. 52 καὶ ἐποίησαν καὶ αὐτοὶ μηχανὰς πρὸς τὰς
μηχανὰς αὐτῶν καὶ ἐπολέμησαν ἡμέρας πολλάς. 53 βρώματα
δὲ οὐκ ἦν ἐν τοῖς ἀγγείοις διὰ τὸ ἕβδομον ἔτος εἶναι, καὶ οἱ
ἀνασῳζόμενοι εἰς τὴν Ιουδαίαν ἀπὸ τῶν ἐθνῶν κατέφαγον τὸ
ὑπόλειμμα τῆς παραθέσεως. 54 καὶ ὑπελείφθησαν ἐν τοῖς
ἁγίοις ἄνδρες ὀλίγοι, ὅτι κατεκράτησεν αὐτῶν ὁ λιμός, καὶ
ἐσκορπίσθησαν ἕκαστος εἰς τὸν τόπον αὐτοῦ.
55 Καὶ ἤκουσεν Λυσίας ὅτι Φίλιππος, ὃν κατέστησεν ὁ
βασιλεὺς Ἀντίοχος ἔτι ζῶντος αὐτοῦ ἐκθρέψαι Ἀντίοχον
τὸν υἱὸν αὐτοῦ εἰς τὸ βασιλεῦσαι αὐτόν, 56 ἀπέστρεψεν ἀπὸ
τῆς Περσίδος καὶ Μηδίας καὶ αἱ δυνάμεις αἱ πορευθεῖσαι
μετὰ τοῦ βασιλέως μετ᾽ αὐτοῦ, καὶ ὅτι ζητεῖ παραλαβεῖν τὰ

KING JAMES VERSION

47 Howbeit *the rest of the Jews* seeing the strength of the king, and the violence of his forces, turned away from them.

48 ¶ Then the king's army went up to Jerusalem to meet them, and the king pitched his tents against Judea, and against mount Sion.

49 But with them that were in Bethsura he made peace: for they came out of the city, because they had no victuals there to endure the siege, it being a year of rest to the land.

50 So the king took Bethsura, and set a garrison there to keep it.

51 As for the sanctuary, he besieged it many days: and set there artillery with engines and instruments to cast fire and stones, and pieces to cast darts and slings.

52 Whereupon they also made engines against their engines, and held them battle a long season.

53 Yet at the last, their vessels being without victuals, (for that it was the seventh year, and they in Judea, that were delivered from the Gentiles, had eaten up the residue of the store;)

54 There were but a few left in the sanctuary, because the famine did so prevail against them, that they were fain to disperse themselves, every man to his own place.

55 At that time Lysias heard say, that Philip, whom Antiochus the king, whiles he lived, had appointed to bring up his son Antiochus, that he might be king,

56 Was returned out of Persia and Media, and the king's host also that went with him, and that he sought to take unto him the ruling of the affairs.

DOUAY OLD TESTAMENT

47 Then they seeing the strength of the king and the fierceness of his army, turned away from them.

48 But the king's army went up against them to Jerusalem: and the king's army pitched their tents against Judea and mount Sion.

49 And he made peace with them that were in Bethsura: and they came forth out of the city, because they had no victuals, being shut up there, for it was the year of rest to the land.

50 And the king took Bethsura: and he placed there a garrison to keep it.

51 And he turned his army against the sanctuary for many days: and he set up there battering slings, and engines and instruments to cast fire, and engines to cast stones and javelins, and pieces to shoot arrows, and slings.

52 And they also made engines against their engines, and they fought for many days.

53 But there were no victuals in the city, because it was the seventh year: and such as had stayed in Judea of them that came from among the nations, had eaten the residue of all that which had been stored up.

54 And there remained in the holy places but a few, for the famine had prevailed over them: and they were dispersed every man to his own place.

55 Now Lysias heard that Philip, whom king Antiochus while he lived had appointed to bring up his son Antiochus, and to reign, to be king,

56 Was returned from Persia, and Media, with the army that went with him, and that he sought to take upon him the affairs of the kingdom:

KNOX TRANSLATION

47 But now, finding the royal forces so strong, and so determined in their attack, the Jews withdrew from the encounter.
48 To Jerusalem the king's men followed them, and now here
was the king entrenched against Judaea and mount Sion
itself. 49 With the defenders of Bethsura he had made terms;
yield up the city they must, so ill were they victualled for a
siege, in a year when the land lay fallow;[a] 50 thus Bethsura
was in the king's hands, and he put a garrison there. 51 But
it was against the holy place itself that he turned his arms,
and long he beleaguered it; what catapults he brought to
bear on it, what engines! Flew fiery darts, flew stone and
javelin and arrow from mangonel and arbalest, and the
slings took their turn. 52 As for the Jews, they met engine
with engine, and fought on day after day; 53 but the seventh
year had come round, and what store was left in the city had
been eaten up by the new citizens rescued from Gentile countries, so food was none to be had. 54 Only a few defenders
were left in the holy place now; the rest, overtaken by
famine, had dispersed to their homes.
55 But Lysias could not wait; he had news from Antioch.
That same Philip, whom king Antiochus, on his death-bed,
had appointed to bring up the young prince as heir to the
throne, 56 was now returned at the head of his army from
the land of the Medes and Persians, and would fain take

a Cf. Lev. 25.4.

TODAY'S ENGLISH VERSION

how strong the royal army was and how determined it was
to fight, they retreated.
48 The king and his army advanced to fight the Jews at
Jerusalem and laid siege to the whole of Judea and
Jerusalem. 49 He made peace with the Jews of Bethzur, who
then left the town. There had not been enough food in the
town for them to withstand the siege because it was the sabbatical year, when no crops were planted. 50 The king occupied Bethzur and stationed a body of troops there to guard it.
51 Then he surrounded the Temple and besieged it for a long
time. He set up siege platforms, battering rams, catapults for
throwing fire and stones, and other weapons to throw spears
and rocks. 52 The defenders also made war machines to
oppose those of the enemy, and so the battle went on for a
long time. 53 But there was no food left in the Temple storage bins because it was the sabbatical year, and the people
who had fled from the Gentiles and taken refuge in Judea
had eaten all the food that had been stored there. 54 The
shortage of food had been so severe that many people had
scattered to their homes, and only a few men were left in the
Temple.
55 Meanwhile, Philip, who had been appointed by King
Antiochus before his death to educate his son to be king,
56 returned from Persia and Media. He had come back with the
royal army and planned to take control of the government.

NEW REVISED STANDARD VERSION

royal might and the fierce attack of the forces, they turned
away in flight.
48 The soldiers of the king's army went up to Jerusalem
against them, and the king encamped in Judea and at Mount
Zion. 49 He made peace with the people of Beth-zur, and
they evacuated the town because they had no provisions
there to withstand a siege, since it was a sabbatical year for
the land. 50 So the king took Beth-zur and stationed a guard
there to hold it. 51 Then he encamped before the sanctuary
for many days. He set up siege towers, engines of war to
throw fire and stones, machines to shoot arrows, and catapults. 52 The Jews[a] also made engines of war to match
theirs, and fought for many days. 53 But they had no food in
storage,[b] because it was the seventh year; those who had
found safety in Judea from the Gentiles had consumed the
last of the stores. 54 Only a few men were left in the sanctuary; the rest scattered to their own homes, for the famine
proved too much for them.
55 Then Lysias heard that Philip, whom King Antiochus
while still living had appointed to bring up his son
Antiochus to be king, 56 had returned from Persia and Media
with the forces that had gone with the king, and that he was
trying to seize control of the government. 57 So he quickly

a Gk *they* *b* Other ancient authorities read *in the sanctuary*

NEW AMERICAN BIBLE

47 When the Jews saw the strength of the royal army and
the ardor of its forces, they retreated from them. 48 A part of
the king's army went up to Jerusalem to attack them, and
the king established camps in Judea and at Mount Zion.
49 He made peace with the men of Beth-zur, and they evacuated the city, because they had no food there to enable them
to stand a siege, for that was a sabbath year in the land.
50 The king took Beth-zur and stationed a garrison there to
hold it. 51 For many days he besieged the sanctuary, setting
up artillery and machines, fire-throwers, catapults and
mechanical bows for shooting arrows and slingstones.
52 The Jews countered by setting up machines of their own,
and kept up the fight a long time. 53 But there were no provisions in the storerooms, because it was the seventh year, and
the tide-over provisions had been eaten up by those who had
been rescued from the Gentiles and brought to Judea. 54 Few
men remained in the sanctuary; the rest scattered, each to
his own home, for the famine was too much for them.
55 Lysias heard that Philip, whom King Antiochus, before
his death, had appointed to train his son Antiochus to be
king, 56 had returned from Persia and Media with the army
that accompanied the king, and that he was seeking to take

NEW JERUSALEM BIBLE

47 The Jews however realising how strong the king was and
how ferocious his army, retreated ahead of them.
48 The royal army moved up to encounter them outside
Jerusalem, and the king began to blockade Judaea and Mount
Zion. 49 He granted peace terms to the people of Beth-Zur,
who evacuated the town; it lacked store of provisions to
withstand a siege, since the land was enjoying a sabbatical
year. 50 Having occupied Beth-Zur, the king stationed a garrison there to hold it. 51 He besieged the sanctuary for a long
time, erecting batteries and siege-engines, flame-throwers
and ballistas, scorpions to discharge arrows, and catapults.
52 The defenders countered these by constructing their own
engines and were thus able to prolong their resistance.
53 But they had no food in their stores since it was the seventh year, and because those who had taken refuge in
Judaea from the gentiles had eaten up the last of their
reserves. 54 Only a few men were left in the Holy Place,
owing to the severity of the famine; the rest had dispersed
and gone home.
55 Meanwhile Philip, whom King Antiochus before his
death had appointed to train his son Antiochus for the
throne, 56 had returned from Persia and Media with the
forces that had accompanied the king, and was planning to

GREEK OLD TESTAMENT

τῶν πραγμάτων. 57 καὶ κατέσπευδεν καὶ ἐπένευσεν τοῦ ἀπελθεῖν καὶ εἶπεν πρὸς τὸν βασιλέα καὶ τοὺς ἡγεμόνας τῆς δυνάμεως καὶ τοὺς ἄνδρας Ἐκλείπομεν καθ᾽ ἡμέραν, καὶ ἡ τροφὴ ἡμῖν ὀλίγη, καὶ ὁ τόπος οὗ παρεμβάλλομέν ἐστιν ὀχυρός, καὶ ἐπίκειται ἡμῖν τὰ τῆς βασιλείας. 58 νῦν οὖν δῶμεν δεξιὰς τοῖς ἀνθρώποις τούτοις καὶ ποιήσωμεν μετ᾽ αὐτῶν εἰρήνην καὶ μετὰ παντὸς ἔθνους αὐτῶν 59 καὶ στήσωμεν αὐτοῖς τοῦ πορεύεσθαι τοῖς νομίμοις αὐτῶν ὡς τὸ πρότερον· χάριν γὰρ τῶν νομίμων αὐτῶν, ὧν διεσκεδάσαμεν, ὠργίσθησαν καὶ ἐποίησαν ταῦτα πάντα. 60 καὶ ἤρεσεν ὁ λόγος ἐναντίον τοῦ βασιλέως καὶ τῶν ἀρχόντων, καὶ ἀπέστειλεν πρὸς αὐτοὺς εἰρηνεῦσαι, καὶ ἐπεδέξαντο. 61 καὶ ὤμοσεν αὐτοῖς ὁ βασιλεὺς καὶ οἱ ἄρχοντες. ἐπὶ τούτοις ἐξῆλθον ἐκ τοῦ ὀχυρώματος. 62 καὶ εἰσῆλθεν ὁ βασιλεὺς εἰς ὄρος Σιων καὶ εἶδεν τὸ ὀχύρωμα τοῦ τόπου καὶ ἠθέτησεν τὸν ὁρκισμόν, ὃν ὤμοσεν, καὶ ἐνετείλατο καθελεῖν τὸ τεῖχος κυκλόθεν. 63 καὶ ἀπῆρεν κατὰ σπουδὴν καὶ ἀπέστρεψεν εἰς Ἀντιόχειαν καὶ εὗρεν Φίλιππον κυριεύοντα τῆς πόλεως καὶ ἐπολέμησεν πρὸς αὐτὸν καὶ κατελάβετο τὴν πόλιν βίᾳ.

7 Ἔτους ἑνὸς καὶ πεντηκοστοῦ καὶ ἑκατοστοῦ ἐξῆλθεν Δημήτριος ὁ τοῦ Σελεύκου ἐκ Ῥώμης καὶ ἀνέβη σὺν ἀνδράσιν ὀλίγοις εἰς πόλιν παραθαλασσίαν καὶ ἐβασίλευσεν ἐκεῖ. 2 καὶ ἐγένετο ὡς εἰσεπορεύετο εἰς οἶκον βασιλείας πατέρων αὐτοῦ, καὶ συνέλαβον αἱ δυνάμεις τὸν Ἀντίοχον καὶ τὸν Λυσίαν ἀγαγεῖν αὐτοὺς αὐτῷ. 3 καὶ ἐγνώσθη αὐτῷ

KING JAMES VERSION

57 Wherefore he went in all haste, and said to the king and the captains of the host and the company, We decay daily, and our victuals are but small, and the place we lay siege unto is strong, and the affairs of the kingdom lie upon us:

58 Now therefore let us be friends with these men, and make peace with them, and with all their nation;

59 And covenant with them, that they shall live after their laws, as they did before: for they are therefore displeased, and have done all these things, because we abolished their laws.

60 So the king and the princes were content: wherefore he sent unto them to make peace; and they accepted thereof.

61 Also the king and the princes made an oath unto them: whereupon they went out of the strong hold.

62 Then the king entered into mount Sion; but when he saw the strength of the place, he brake his oath that he had made, and gave commandment to pull down the wall round about.

63 Afterward departed he in all haste, and returned unto Antiochia, where he found Philip to be master of the city: so he fought against him, and took the city by force.

7 In the hundred and one and fiftieth year Demetrius the *son* of Seleucus departed from Rome, and came up with a few men unto a city of the sea coast, and reigned there.

2 And as he entered into the palace of his ancestors, so it was, that his forces had taken Antiochus and Lysias, to bring them unto him.

DOUAY OLD TESTAMENT

57 Wherefore he made haste to go, and say to the king and to the captains of the army: We decay daily, and our provision of victuals is small, and the place that we lay siege to is strong, and it lieth upon us to take order for the affairs of the kingdom.

58 Now therefore let us come to an agreement with these men, and make peace with them and with all their nation.

59 And let us covenant with them, that they may live according to their own laws as before. For because of our despising their laws, they have been provoked, and have done all these things.

60 And the proposal was acceptable in the sight of the king, and of the princes: and he sent to them to make peace: and they accepted of it.

61 And the king and the princes swore to them: and they came out of the strong hold.

62 Then the king entered into mount Sion, and saw the strength of the place: and he quickly broke the oath that he had taken, and gave commandment to throw down the wall round about.

63 And he departed in haste, and returned to Antioch, where he found Philip master of the city: and he fought against him, and took the city.

7 IN the hundred and fifty-first year Demetrius the son of Seleucus departed from the city of Rome, and came up with a few men into a city of the sea coast, and reigned there.

2 And it came to pass, as he entered into the house of the kingdom of his fathers, that the army seized upon Antiochus, and Lysias, to bring them unto him.

KNOX TRANSLATION

charge of the realm. 57 So Lysias must betake himself to the king and his generals, with such words as these: Our plight grows daily worse; scant food is left us, and here is a fortress well defended; all the business of the realm claims our care. 58 What remains, but to make friendly advances, offer terms to the besieged and to all their country-men? 59 Give we leave they should follow their own customs as of old, which customs neglecting, we have brought all this ill-will and all this trouble upon us. 60 King and chieftain fell in with his design; offer peace they did, and the offer was accepted. 61 So, upon terms with the king and his generals, the Jews gave up their stronghold; 62 and what must the king do, once he had set foot on mount Sion and discovered the strength of its defences, but break his oath, and have all the walls of it pulled down! 63 Then, with all haste, he took leave of it, and returned to Antioch, where he found Philip in possession, and levied war on him, taking the city by storm.

7 It was now, in the hundred and fifty-first year, that Demetrius, the son of Seleucus, escaped from Rome and landed with a small retinue at one of the sea-ports, where he was proclaimed king. 2 No sooner had he set foot in the palace of his ancestors, than his men laid hold of Antiochus and Lysias, meaning to bring them into his presence. 3 But

TODAY'S ENGLISH VERSION

When Lysias heard this news, 57 he made rapid preparations to depart. He said to the young king, to his officers, and to his men, "We are growing weaker each day; we are short of provisions, and this place we are besieging is strong. Besides, there are pressing government affairs which need our attention. 58 So now let's arrange a truce and make a peace treaty with the Jews and their whole nation. 59 We will allow them to follow their own laws and customs as they did before. All this trouble started when we provoked them by abolishing their laws and customs."

60 This recommendation was well received by the king and the officers, so Lysias proposed peace terms to the Jews, and they accepted them. 61 When the king and his officers solemnly agreed to abide by these terms, the Jews came out of their fortress. 62 But when the king entered the Temple area on Mount Zion and saw the strong fortifications, he broke his word and ordered the walls surrounding the Temple to be torn down. 63 Then he hurriedly left and returned to Antioch, where he found Philip in control of the city. The king attacked the city and took it by force.

7 In the year 151,[a] Demetrius son of Seleucus left Rome and with a few men landed at a town on the Mediterranean coast, where he proclaimed himself king. 2 As he was making his way to the royal palace of his ancestors, the soldiers arrested Antiochus the Fifth and Lysias, planning to

[a] THE YEAR 151: *This corresponds to 161 B.C.*

NEW REVISED STANDARD VERSION

gave orders to withdraw, and said to the king, to the commanders of the forces, and to the troops, "Daily we grow weaker, our food supply is scant, the place against which we are fighting is strong, and the affairs of the kingdom press urgently on us. 58 Now then let us come to terms with these people, and make peace with them and with all their nation. 59 Let us agree to let them live by their laws as they did before; for it was on account of their laws that we abolished that they became angry and did all these things."

60 The speech pleased the king and the commanders, and he sent to the Jews[a] an offer of peace, and they accepted it. 61 So the king and the commanders gave them their oath. On these conditions the Jews[b] evacuated the stronghold. 62 But when the king entered Mount Zion and saw what a strong fortress the place was, he broke the oath he had sworn and gave orders to tear down the wall all around. 63 Then he set off in haste and returned to Antioch. He found Philip in control of the city, but he fought against him, and took the city by force.

7 In the one hundred fifty-first year[c] Demetrius son of Seleucus set out from Rome, sailed with a few men to a town by the sea, and there began to reign. 2 As he was entering the royal palace of his ancestors, the army seized Antiochus and Lysias to bring them to him. 3 But when this

a Gk *them* *b* Gk *they* *c* 161 B.C.

NEW AMERICAN BIBLE

over the government. 57 So he hastily resolved to withdraw. He said to the king, the leaders of the army, and the soldiers: "We are growing weaker every day, our provisions are scanty, the place we are besieging is strong, and it is our duty to take care of the affairs of the kingdom. 58 Therefore let us now come to terms with these men, and make peace with them and all their nation. 59 Let us grant them freedom to live according to their own laws as formerly; it was on account of their laws, which we abolished, that they became angry and did all these things."

60 The proposal found favor with the king and the leaders; he sent peace terms to the Jews, and they accepted. 61 So the king and the leaders swore an oath to them, and on these terms they evacuated the fortification. 62 But when the king entered Mount Zion and saw how the place was fortified, he broke the oath he had sworn and gave orders for the encircling wall to be destroyed. 63 Then he departed in haste and returned to Antioch, where he found Philip in possession of the city. He fought against him and took the city by force.

7 In the year one hundred and fifty-one, Demetrius, son of Seleucus, set out from Rome, arrived with a few men in a city on the seacoast, and began to rule there. 2 As he was preparing to enter the royal palace of his ancestors, the soldiers seized Antiochus and Lysias to bring them to him.

NEW JERUSALEM BIBLE

seize control of affairs. 57 On hearing this, Lysias at once decided to leave,[a] and said to the king, the generals of the army and the men, 'We are growing weaker every day, we are short of food, and the place we are besieging is well fortified; moreover the affairs of the kingdom demand our attention. 58 Let us offer the hand of friendship to these men and make peace with them and with their whole nation. 59 Let us grant them permission to follow their own customs as before, since it is our abolition of these customs that has provoked them into acting like this.' 60 The king and his commanders approved this argument, and he offered the Jews peace terms, which they accepted. 61 The king and the generals ratified the treaty by oath, and the besieged accordingly left the fortress. 62 The king then entered Mount Zion, but on seeing how impregnable the place was, he broke the oath he had sworn and gave orders for the encircling wall to be demolished. 63 He then hurriedly withdrew, making off for Antioch, where he found Philip already master of the city. Antiochus gave battle and captured the city by force of arms.

7[b] In the year 151, Demetrius son of Seleucus left Rome and arrived with a few men at a town on the coast, where he inaugurated his reign. 2 It so happened that, as he was entering the royal residence of his ancestors, the army captured Antiochus and Lysias, and intended to bring them

[a] **6** // 2 M 11:13–33. [b] **7** 7:1seq. // 2 M 14:1–10.

GREEK OLD TESTAMENT

τὸ πρᾶγμα, καὶ εἶπεν Μή μοι δείξητε τὰ πρόσωπα αὐτῶν.
4 καὶ ἀπέκτειναν αὐτοὺς αἱ δυνάμεις, καὶ ἐκάθισεν Δημήτριος ἐπὶ θρόνου βασιλείας αὐτοῦ. 5 καὶ ἦλθον πρὸς αὐτὸν
πάντες ἄνδρες ἄνομοι καὶ ἀσεβεῖς ἐξ Ισραηλ, καὶ Ἄλκιμος
ἡγεῖτο αὐτῶν βουλόμενος ἱερατεύειν. 6 καὶ κατηγόρησαν
τοῦ λαοῦ πρὸς τὸν βασιλέα λέγοντες Ἀπώλεσεν Ιουδας καὶ
οἱ ἀδελφοὶ αὐτοῦ πάντας τοὺς φίλους σου, καὶ ἡμᾶς ἐσκόρπισεν ἀπὸ τῆς γῆς ἡμῶν· 7 νῦν οὖν ἀπόστειλον ἄνδρα, ᾧ
πιστεύεις, καὶ πορευθεὶς ἰδέτω τὴν ἐξολέθρευσιν πᾶσαν, ἣν
ἐποίησεν ἡμῖν καὶ τῇ χώρᾳ τοῦ βασιλέως, καὶ κολασάτω αὐτοὺς καὶ πάντας τοὺς ἐπιβοηθοῦντας αὐτοῖς. 8 καὶ ἐπέλεξεν
ὁ βασιλεὺς τὸν Βακχίδην τῶν φίλων τοῦ βασιλέως κυριεύοντα ἐν τῷ πέραν τοῦ ποταμοῦ καὶ μέγαν ἐν τῇ βασιλείᾳ καὶ
πιστὸν τῷ βασιλεῖ 9 καὶ ἀπέστειλεν αὐτὸν καὶ Ἄλκιμον τὸν
ἀσεβῆ καὶ ἔστησεν αὐτῷ τὴν ἱερωσύνην καὶ ἐνετείλατο αὐτῷ
ποιῆσαι τὴν ἐκδίκησιν ἐν τοῖς υἱοῖς Ισραηλ. 10 καὶ ἀπῆρον
καὶ ἦλθον μετὰ δυνάμεως πολλῆς εἰς γῆν Ιουδα· καὶ ἀπέστειλεν ἀγγέλους πρὸς Ιουδαν καὶ τοὺς ἀδελφοὺς αὐτοῦ λόγοις εἰρηνικοῖς μετὰ δόλου. 11 καὶ οὐ προσέσχον τοῖς λόγοις αὐτῶν· εἶδον γὰρ ὅτι ἦλθαν μετὰ δυνάμεως πολλῆς.
12 καὶ ἐπισυνήχθησαν πρὸς Ἄλκιμον καὶ Βακχίδην συναγωγὴ
γραμματέων ἐκζητῆσαι δίκαια, 13 καὶ πρῶτοι οἱ Ασιδαῖοι
ἦσαν ἐν υἱοῖς Ισραηλ καὶ ἐπεζήτουν παρ᾽ αὐτῶν εἰρήνην·

KING JAMES VERSION

3 Wherefore, when he knew it, he said, Let me not see their faces.

4 So his host slew them. Now when Demetrius was set upon the throne of his kingdom,

5 There came unto him all the wicked and ungodly men of Israel, having Alcimus, who was desirous to be high priest, for their captain:

6 And they accused the people to the king, saying, Judas and his brethren have slain all thy friends, and driven us out of our own land.

7 Now therefore send some man whom thou trustest, and let him go and see what havock he hath made among us, and in the king's land, and let him punish them with all them that aid them.

8 Then the king chose Bacchides, a friend of the king, who ruled beyond the flood, and was a great man in the kingdom, and faithful to the king.

9 And him he sent with that wicked Alcimus, whom he made high priest, and commanded that he should take vengeance of the children of Israel.

10 So they departed, and came with a great power into the land of Judea, where they sent messengers to Judas and his brethren with peaceable words deceitfully.

11 But they gave no heed to their words; for they saw that they were come with a great power.

12 Then did there assemble unto Alcimus and Bacchides a company of scribes, to require justice.

13 Now the Assideans were the first among the children of Israel that sought peace of them:

DOUAY OLD TESTAMENT

3 And when he knew it, he said: Let me not see their face.

4 So the army slew them. And Demetrius sat upon the throne of his kingdom:

5 And there came to him the wicked and ungodly men of Israel: and Alcimus was at the head of them, who desired to be made high priest.

6 And they accused the people to the king, saying: Judas and his brethren have destroyed all thy friends, and he hath driven us out of our land.

7 Now therefore send some man whom thou trustest, and let him go, and see all the havock he hath made amongst us, and in the king's lands: and let him punish all his friends and their helpers.

8 Then the king chose Bacchides, one of his friends that ruled beyond the great river in the kingdom, and was faithful to the king: and he sent him,

9 To see the havock that Judas had made: and the wicked Alcimus he made high priest, and commanded him to take revenge upon the children of Israel.

10 And they arose, and came with a great army into the land of Juda: and they sent messengers, and spoke to Judas and his brethren with peaceable words deceitfully.

11 But they gave no heed to their words: for they saw that they were come with a great army.

12 Then there assembled to Alcimus and Bacchides a company of the scribes to require things that are just:

13 And first the Assideans that were among the children of Israel, and they sought peace of them.

KNOX TRANSLATION

he was warned of it, and gave it out, sight of them he would
have none; 4 so they were dispatched by the troops, and
Demetrius established himself on the royal throne.
5 To him came certain Israelites, enemies of the law and of
religion, with Alcimus at their head, a man who coveted the
high-priestly office. 6 And thus, in the royal presence, they
defamed their own people: Here be Judas and his brethren
have made away with all thy friends, and driven us out of
our country! 7 Do but send some trusted agent to survey the
scene of it, the havoc this man has wrought upon our own
persons and upon the king's domain; ay, and to punish his
partisans, with all who comfort them. 8 The king's choice fell
on Bacchides, a courtier that was loyal to him, and had
charge now of all the realm east of Euphrates. 9 Of the havoc
wrought by Judas he should be judge, and with him went the
traitor Alcimus, now confirmed in the high priesthood; thus
should the royal vengeance fall on Israel.
10 So they took the road, and reached the land of Juda with
a great army at their heels. Envoys they sent out, to cheat
Judas and his brethren with fair promises; 11 but from these
they got no hearing; the sight of such armed strength was
enough. 12 It was a company of scribes that went out to meet
Alcimus and Bacchides, asking for honourable terms; 13 of
all Israel, the Assidaeans were foremost in demanding peace;

TODAY'S ENGLISH VERSION

take them to Demetrius. 3 When Demetrius heard about it,
he said, "I don't want to see them." 4 So the soldiers killed
them, and Demetrius took the throne.
5 Then all the godless traitorous Jews led by Alcimus, who
wanted to be High Priest, went to Demetrius. 6 They brought
accusations against the other Jews and said, "Judas and his
brothers have killed everybody who supported you, and they
have driven us out of our country. 7 We advise you to send
someone whom you can trust to go and inspect all the damage done to our property and the king's territory and to punish Judas, his brothers, and all who support them."
8 King Demetrius chose one of his advisers, a man by the
name of Bacchides, who was the governor of Greater Syria.
He was an important man in the empire and loyal to the
king. 9 He was sent along with the godless Alcimus, whom
the king had appointed High Priest; Alcimus had orders to
take revenge on the Jews. 10 They left Antioch and arrived in
Judea with a large army. Bacchides tried to trick Judas and
his brothers by sending to them messengers with offers of
peace. 11 But when Judas and his brothers saw what a large
army they had brought, they did not believe what the messengers said.
12 A group of teachers of the Law came to Alcimus and
Bacchides, asking for justice. 13 These devout and patriotic
men were the first of the Jews to try to make peace with

NEW REVISED STANDARD VERSION

act became known to him, he said, "Do not let me see their
faces!" 4 So the army killed them, and Demetrius took his
seat on the throne of his kingdom.
5 Then there came to him all the renegade and godless
men of Israel; they were led by Alcimus, who wanted to be
high priest. 6 They brought to the king this accusation
against the people: "Judas and his brothers have destroyed
all your Friends, and have driven us out of our land. 7 Now
then send a man whom you trust; let him go and see all the
ruin that Judas[a] has brought on us and on the land of the
king, and let him punish them and all who help them."
8 So the king chose Bacchides, one of the king's Friends,
governor of the province Beyond the River; he was a great
man in the kingdom and was faithful to the king. 9 He sent
him, and with him he sent the ungodly Alcimus, whom he
made high priest; and he commanded him to take vengeance
on the Israelites. 10 So they marched away and came with a
large force into the land of Judah; and he sent messengers to
Judas and his brothers with peaceable but treacherous
words. 11 But they paid no attention to their words, for they
saw that they had come with a large force.
12 Then a group of scribes appeared in a body before
Alcimus and Bacchides to ask for just terms. 13 The
Hasideans were first among the Israelites to seek peace from

a Gk *he*

NEW AMERICAN BIBLE

3 When he was informed of this, he said, "Do not show me
their faces." 4 So the soldiers killed them, and Demetrius sat
on the royal throne.
5 Then all the lawless and impious men of Israel came to
him. They were led by Alcimus, who desired to be high
priest. 6 They made this accusation to the king against the
people: "Judas and his brothers have destroyed all your
friends and have driven us out of our country. 7 So now,
send a man whom you trust to go and see all the havoc
Judas has done to us and to the king's land, and let him
punish them and all their supporters."
8 Then the king chose Bacchides, one of the King's Friends,
governor of West-of-Euphrates, a great man in the kingdom,
and faithful to the king. 9 He sent him and the impious
Alcimus, to whom he granted the high priesthood, with
orders to take revenge on the Israelites. 10 They set out and,
on arriving in the land of Judah with a great army, sent messengers who spoke deceitfully to Judas and his brothers in
peaceful terms. 11 But these paid no attention to their words,
seeing that they had come with a great army. 12 A group of
scribes, however, gathered about Alcimus and Bacchides to
ask for a just agreement. 13 The Hasideans were the first
among the Israelites to seek peace with them, 14 for they

NEW JERUSALEM BIBLE

to him. 3 On hearing this, he said, 'Keep them out of my
sight.' 4 The army put them to death, and Demetrius ascended his throne. 5 Next, all those Israelites without law or
piety, led by Alcimus, whose ambition was to become high
priest, 6 approached the king and denounced our people to
him. 'Judas and his brothers', they said, 'have killed all your
friends, and he has driven us out of our country. 7 Send
someone now whom you can trust; let him go and see the
wholesale ruin Judas has brought on us and on the king's
dominions, and let him punish the wretches and all who
assist them.'
8 The king chose Bacchides, one of the Friends of the King,
governor of Transeuphrates, an important personage in the
kingdom and loyal to the king. 9 He sent him with the godless Alcimus, whom he confirmed in the high priesthood,
with orders to exact retribution from the Israelites. 10 So they
set out with a large force and, on reaching Judaea, sent emissaries to Judas and his brothers with proposals peaceable yet
treacherous. 11 The latter, however, did not put any faith in
their words, aware that they had come with a large force.
12 Nevertheless, a commission of scribes presented themselves before Alcimus and Bacchides, to sue for just terms.
13 The first among the Israelites to ask them for peace terms

GREEK OLD TESTAMENT

14 εἶπον γάρ Ἄνθρωπος ἱερεὺς ἐκ σπέρματος Ααρων ἦλθεν
ἐν ταῖς δυνάμεσιν καὶ οὐκ ἀδικήσει ἡμᾶς. 15 καὶ ἐλάλησεν
μετ᾽ αὐτῶν λόγους εἰρηνικοὺς καὶ ὤμοσεν αὐτοῖς λέγων Οὐκ
ἐκζητήσομεν ὑμῖν κακὸν καὶ τοῖς φίλοις ὑμῶν. 16 καὶ ἐνεπίστευσαν αὐτῷ· καὶ συνέλαβεν ἐξ αὐτῶν ἑξήκοντα ἄνδρας καὶ
ἀπέκτεινεν αὐτοὺς ἐν ἡμέρᾳ μιᾷ κατὰ τὸν λόγον, ὃν
ἔγραψεν αὐτόν 17 Σάρκας ὁσίων σου καὶ αἷμα αὐτῶν ἐξέχεαν
κύκλῳ Ιερουσαλημ, καὶ οὐκ ἦν αὐτοῖς ὁ θάπτων. 18 καὶ ἐπέπεσεν αὐτῶν ὁ φόβος καὶ ὁ τρόμος εἰς πάντα τὸν λαόν, ὅτι
εἶπον Οὐκ ἔστιν ἐν αὐτοῖς ἀλήθεια καὶ κρίσις, παρέβησαν
γὰρ τὴν στάσιν καὶ τὸν ὅρκον, ὃν ὤμοσαν. 19 καὶ ἀπῆρεν
Βακχίδης ἀπὸ Ιερουσαλημ καὶ παρενέβαλεν ἐν Βηθζαιθ καὶ
ἀπέστειλεν καὶ συνέλαβεν πολλοὺς ἀπὸ τῶν μετ᾽ αὐτοῦ
αὐτομολησάντων ἀνδρῶν καί τινας τοῦ λαοῦ καὶ ἔθυσεν αὐτοὺς εἰς τὸ φρέαρ τὸ μέγα. 20 καὶ κατέστησεν τὴν χώραν τῷ
Ἀλκίμῳ καὶ ἀφῆκεν μετ᾽ αὐτοῦ δύναμιν τοῦ βοηθεῖν αὐτῷ·
καὶ ἀπῆλθεν Βακχίδης πρὸς τὸν βασιλέα. 21 καὶ ἠγωνίσατο
Ἄλκιμος περὶ τῆς ἀρχιερωσύνης, 22 καὶ συνήχθησαν πρὸς
αὐτὸν πάντες οἱ ταράσσοντες τὸν λαὸν αὐτῶν καὶ κατεκράτησαν γῆν Ιουδα καὶ ἐποίησαν πληγὴν μεγάλην ἐν Ισραηλ.
23 καὶ εἶδεν Ιουδας πᾶσαν τὴν κακίαν, ἣν ἐποίησεν Ἄλκιμος
καὶ οἱ μετ᾽ αὐτοῦ ἐν υἱοῖς Ισραηλ ὑπὲρ τὰ ἔθνη, 24 καὶ

KING JAMES VERSION

14 For said they, One that is a priest of the seed of Aaron is come with this army, and he will do us no wrong.

15 So he spake unto them peaceably, and sware unto them, saying, we will procure the harm neither of you nor your friends.

16 Whereupon they believed him: howbeit he took of them threescore men, and slew them in one day, according to the words which he wrote,

17 The flesh of thy saints *have they cast out,* and their blood have they shed round about Jerusalem, and there was none to bury them.

18 Wherefore the fear and dread of them fell upon all the people, who said, There is neither truth nor righteousness in them; for they have broken the covenant and oath that they made.

19 After this removed Bacchides from Jerusalem, and pitched his tents in Bezeth, where he sent and took many of the men that had forsaken him, and certain of the people also, and when he had slain them, *he cast them* into the great pit.

20 Then committed he the country to Alcimus, and left with him a power to aid him: so Bacchides went to the king.

21 But Alcimus contended for the high priesthood.

22 And unto him resorted all such as troubled the people, who, after they had gotten the land of Juda into their power, did much hurt in Israel.

23 Now when Judas saw all the mischief that Alcimus and his company had done among the Israelites, even above the heathen,

DOUAY OLD TESTAMENT

14 For they said: One that is a priest of the seed of Aaron is come, he will not deceive us.

15 And he spoke to them peaceably: and he swore to them, saying: We will do you no harm nor your friends.

16 And they believed him. And he took threescore of them, and slew them in one day, according to the word that is written:

17 The flesh of thy saints, and the blood of them they have shed round about Jerusalem, and there was none to bury them.

18 Then fear and trembling fell upon all the people: for they said: There is no truth, nor justice among them: for they have broken the covenant, and the oath which they made.

19 And Bacchides removed the camp from Jerusalem, and pitched in Bethzecha: and he sent, and took many of them that were fled away from him, and some of the people he killed, and threw them into a great pit.

20 Then he committed the country to Alcimus, and left with him troops to help him. So Bacchides went away to the king:

21 But Alcimus did what he could to maintain his chief priesthood.

22 And they that disturbed the people resorted to him, and they got the land of Juda into their power, and did much hurt in Israel.

23 And Judas saw all the evils that Alcimus, and they that were with him, did to the children of Israel, much more than the Gentiles.

KNOX TRANSLATION

14 Here is a priest of Aaron's line, said they, in yonder company, fear we no treachery from him. 15 Fair promises he
made them, and swore they should take no harm, nor their
friends neither; 16 and they took him at his word. And what
did he? A full sixty of them he seized and put to death in one
day. Not idly the word was written, 17 Bleeding corpses of
thy true lovers they have strewn about on every side of
Jerusalem, and there was none to bury the dead. 18 After
this, all alike dreaded the new-comers and shrank from
them; here was neither trust nor troth, when covenant and
sworn promise went for nothing. 19 So Bacchides left
Jerusalem and pitched his camp at Bethzecha, where he
made search and laid hands on many that had deserted from
his own army; some of the Jews he massacred besides, and
had their bodies thrown into the Great Cistern; 20 then he left
the whole country in Alcimus' charge, with troops to maintain him. So off went Bacchides to his master, 21 and
Alcimus remained to make the best of his high priesthood.
22 Be sure all the malcontents in Judaea rallied to his side,
and took possession of the country, to Israel's great mischief.
23 Little it liked Judas, to see Alcimus and his crew mishan-
dling the men of Israel as never the Gentiles had; 24 from

TODAY'S ENGLISH VERSION

Alcimus and Bacchides. 14 They trusted Alcimus, who was a
priest descended from Aaron, and they thought he would not
cause them any harm. 15 Alcimus assured them of his peaceful intentions and solemnly promised that no harm would
come to them or their friends. 16 But as soon as they began
to trust him, he arrested 60 of them and put them all to
death on the same day. As the scripture says,

17 "The blood of your faithful people was poured out,
their bodies were scattered around Jerusalem,
and there was no one left to bury the dead."

18 When this happened, all the people were afraid of
Alcimus and Bacchides, and they said, "They don't know
what truth or justice means. They gave their solemn word
and then broke it!" 19 Bacchides left Jerusalem and set up his
headquarters at Beth Zaith. He ordered the arrest of some of
the faithful Jews and even many of the renegades who had
willingly joined him; he had them killed and thrown into a
deep pit. 20 Bacchides put the country under the control of
Alcimus, left troops there to help him, and returned to the
king.

21 Alcimus then began his struggle to establish himself as
High Priest. 22 Every troublemaker in the country joined him.
They gained control of the land of Judea and caused great
difficulties for the Jews. 23 Judas saw that the trouble
Alcimus and his men had caused was even worse than the
damage done by the Gentiles. 24 So he went around the

NEW REVISED STANDARD VERSION

them, 14 for they said, "A priest of the line of Aaron has
come with the army, and he will not harm us." 15 Alcimus[a]
spoke peaceable words to them and swore this oath to them,
"We will not seek to injure you or your friends." 16 So they
trusted him; but he seized sixty of them and killed them in
one day, in accordance with the word that was written,

17 "The flesh of your faithful ones and their blood
they poured out all around Jerusalem,
and there was no one to bury them."

18 Then the fear and dread of them fell on all the people, for
they said, "There is no truth or justice in them, for they have
violated the agreement and the oath that they swore."

19 Then Bacchides withdrew from Jerusalem and
encamped in Beth-zaith. And he sent and seized many of the
men who had deserted to him,[b] and some of the people, and
killed them and threw them into a great pit. 20 He placed
Alcimus in charge of the country and left with him a force to
help him; then Bacchides went back to the king.

21 Alcimus struggled to maintain his high priesthood,
22 and all who were troubling their people joined him. They
gained control of the land of Judah and did great damage in
Israel. 23 And Judas saw all the wrongs that Alcimus and
those with him had done among the Israelites; it was more
than the Gentiles had done. 24 So Judas[c] went out into all

a Gk *He* *b* Or *many of his men who had deserted* *c* Gk *he*

NEW AMERICAN BIBLE

said, "A priest of the line of Aaron has come with the army,
and he will not do us any wrong." 15 He spoke with them
peacefully and swore to them, "We will not try to injure you
or your friends." 16 So they trusted him. But he arrested sixty
of them and killed them in one day, according to the text of
Scripture:

17 "The flesh of your saints they have strewn,
and their blood they have shed round about
Jerusalem,
and there was no one to bury them.

18 Then fear and dread of them came upon all the people,
who said: "There is no truth or justice among them; they violated the agreement and the oath that they swore."

19 Bacchides withdrew from Jerusalem and pitched his
camp in Beth-zaith. He had many of the men arrested who
deserted him, throwing them into the great pit. 20 He handed
the province over to Alcimus, leaving troops to help him,
while he himself returned to the king.

21 Alcimus spared no pains to maintain his high priesthood, 22 and all those who were disturbing their people gathered about him. They took possession of the land of Judah
and caused great distress in Israel. 23 When Judas saw all
the evils that Alcimus and his men were bringing upon the
Israelites, more than even the Gentiles had done, 24 he went

NEW JERUSALEM BIBLE

were the Hasidaeans, 14 who reasoned thus, 'This is a priest
of Aaron's line who has come with the armed forces; he will
not wrong us.' 15 He did in fact discuss peace terms with
them and gave them his oath, 'We shall not attempt to injure
you or your friends.' 16 They believed him, but he arrested
sixty of them and put them to death on one day, fulfilling
the words of scripture: 17 *They have scattered the bodies of
your faithful, and shed their blood all round Jerusalem, leaving no one to bury them!*[a] 18 At this, fear and dread gripped
the whole people. 'There is no truth or virtue in them,' they
said, 'they have broken their agreement and their sworn
oath.'

19 Bacchides then left Jerusalem and encamped at Beth-
Zeth, and from there sent and arrested many of the men who
had deserted him and a few of our people too; he had them
killed and thrown down the great well. 20 He then put
Alcimus in charge of the province, leaving an army with him
to support him; Bacchides himself returned to the king.
21 Alcimus continued his struggle to become high priest,
22 and all who were disturbing the peace of their own people
rallied to him, and, having won control of Judaea, did much
harm in Israel. 23 Seeing that all the wrongs done to the
Israelites by Alcimus and his supporters exceeded what the

a **7** Ps 79:2–3.

GREEK OLD TESTAMENT

ἐξῆλθεν εἰς πάντα τὰ ὅρια τῆς Ιουδαίας κυκλόθεν καὶ ἐποίησεν ἐκδίκησιν ἐν τοῖς ἀνδράσιν τοῖς αὐτομολήσασιν, καὶ
ἀνεστάλησαν τοῦ ἐκπορεύεσθαι εἰς τὴν χώραν. 25 ὡς δὲ
εἶδεν Ἄλκιμος ὅτι ἐνίσχυσεν Ιουδας καὶ οἱ μετ' αὐτοῦ, καὶ
ἔγνω ὅτι οὐ δύναται ὑποστῆναι αὐτούς, καὶ ἐπέστρεψεν
πρὸς τὸν βασιλέα καὶ κατηγόρησεν αὐτῶν πονηρά.
26 Καὶ ἀπέστειλεν ὁ βασιλεὺς Νικάνορα ἕνα τῶν ἀρχόντων
αὐτοῦ τῶν ἐνδόξων καὶ μισοῦντα καὶ ἐχθραίνοντα τῷ Ισραηλ
καὶ ἐνετείλατο αὐτῷ ἐξᾶραι τὸν λαόν. 27 καὶ ἦλθεν Νικάνωρ
εἰς Ιερουσαλημ δυνάμει πολλῇ, καὶ ἀπέστειλεν πρὸς Ιουδαν
καὶ τοὺς ἀδελφοὺς αὐτοῦ μετὰ δόλου λόγοις εἰρηνικοῖς λέγων 28 Μὴ ἔστω μάχη ἀνὰ μέσον ἐμοῦ καὶ ὑμῶν· ἥξω ἐν
ἀνδράσιν ὀλίγοις, ἵνα ἴδω ὑμῶν τὰ πρόσωπα μετ' εἰρήνης.
29 καὶ ἦλθεν πρὸς Ιουδαν, καὶ ἠσπάσαντο ἀλλήλους
εἰρηνικῶς. καὶ οἱ πολέμιοι ἕτοιμοι ἦσαν ἐξαρπάσαι τὸν
Ιουδαν. 30 καὶ ἐγνώσθη ὁ λόγος τῷ Ιουδα ὅτι μετὰ δόλου
ἦλθεν ἐπ' αὐτόν, καὶ ἐπτοήθη ἀπ' αὐτοῦ καὶ οὐκ ἐβουλήθη ἔτι
ἰδεῖν τὸ πρόσωπον αὐτοῦ. 31 καὶ ἔγνω Νικάνωρ ὅτι ἀπεκαλύφθη ἡ βουλὴ αὐτοῦ, καὶ ἐξῆλθεν εἰς συνάντησιν τῷ Ιουδα ἐν
πολέμῳ κατὰ Χαφαρσαλαμα. 32 καὶ ἔπεσον τῶν παρὰ Νικάνορος ὡσεὶ πεντακόσιοι ἄνδρες, καὶ ἔφυγον εἰς τὴν πόλιν
Δαυιδ.
33 Καὶ μετὰ τοὺς λόγους τούτους ἀνέβη Νικάνωρ εἰς ὄρος
Σιων. καὶ ἐξῆλθον ἀπὸ τῶν ἱερέων ἐκ τῶν ἁγίων καὶ ἀπὸ τῶν
πρεσβυτέρων τοῦ λαοῦ ἀσπάσασθαι αὐτὸν εἰρηνικῶς καὶ
δεῖξαι αὐτῷ τὴν ὁλοκαύτωσιν τὴν προσφερομένην ὑπὲρ τοῦ

KING JAMES VERSION

24 He went out into all the coasts of Judea round about, and took vengeance of them that had revolted from him, so that they durst no more go forth into the country.

25 On the other side, when Alcimus saw that Judas and his company had gotten the upper hand, and knew that he was not able to abide their force, he went again to the king, and said all the worst of them that he could.

26 Then the king sent Nicanor, one of his honourable princes, a man that bare deadly hate unto Israel, with commandment to destroy the people.

27 So Nicanor came to Jerusalem with a great force; and sent unto Judas and his brethren deceitfully with friendly words, saying,

28 Let there be no battle between me and you; I will come with a few men, that I may see you in peace.

29 He came therefore to Judas, and they saluted one another peaceably. Howbeit the enemies were prepared to take away Judas by violence.

30 Which thing after it was known to Judas, *to wit,* that he came unto him with deceit, he was sore afraid of him, and would see his face no more.

31 Nicanor also, when he saw that his counsel was discovered, went out to fight against Judas beside Capharsalama:

32 Where there were slain of Nicanor's side about five thousand men, and *the rest* fled into the city of David.

33 After this went Nicanor up to mount Sion, and there came out of the sanctuary certain of the priests and certain of the elders of the people, to salute him peaceably, and to shew him the burnt sacrifice that was offered for the king.

DOUAY OLD TESTAMENT

24 And he went out into all the coasts of Judea round about, and took vengeance upon the men that had revolted, and they ceased to go forth any more into the country.

25 And Alcimus saw that Judas, and they that were with him prevailed: and he knew that he could not stand against them, and he went back to the king, and accused them of many crimes.

26 And the king sent Nicanor one of his principal lords, who was a great enemy to Israel: and he commanded him to destroy the people.

27 And Nicanor came to Jerusalem with a great army, and he sent to Judas and to his brethren deceitfully with friendly words,

28 Saying: Let there be no fighting between me and you: I will come with a few men to see your faces with peace.

29 And he came to Judas, and they saluted one another peaceably: and the enemies were prepared to take away Judas by force.

30 And the thing was known to Judas that he was come to him with deceit: and he was much afraid of him, and would not see his face any more.

31 And Nicanor knew that his counsel was discovered: and he went out to fight against Judas near Capharsalama.

32 And there fell of Nicanor's army almost five thousand men, and they fled into the city of David.

33 And after this Nicanor went up into mount Sion: and some of the priests and the people came out to salute him peaceably, and to shew him the holocausts that were offered for the king.

KNOX TRANSLATION

end to end of Juda he passed, executing vengeance on such
as had left his cause, till they might take the field no longer.
25 Everywhere Judas and his company had their way, and the
sight of it warned Alcimus he was no match for them; so he,
too, went back to the king, loud in his complaints.
26 Thereupon the king sent out an army for the people's
undoing, with Nicanor at the head of it, that was one of his
most notable princes, and had a grudge against Israel to satisfy. 27 This Nicanor, reaching Jerusalem with a great array,
made peaceful overtures to Judas and his brethren, but
treacherously; 28 Need is none there should be blows given
between us, he said. Let me come with a handful of men,
and parley we together under safe conduct. 29 Come he did,
and the greeting between them was friendly enough, but
Judas was like to have been seized, then and there, by the
enemy; 30 and when he had proof of Nicanor's treachery, he
went in dread of him and would parley with him no longer.
31 Nicanor, then, his plot being now manifestly discovered,
would take to the field; it was close to Capharsalama that he
engaged Judas; 32 and his army, routed with a loss of five
thousand men, must needs take refuge in the Keep of David.[a]
33 It was after this that Nicanor made his way to mount Sion,
where some of the priests and elders came out to greet him in
friendly fashion, and shew him how burnt-sacrifice was
offered there on the king's behalf. 34 But nothing could they

a According to Josephus, who usually follows the sacred narrative closely, it was Judas who was defeated and forced to take refuge in Jerusalem; this would accord better with what follows, and it seems possible that the text has been incorrectly preserved.

TODAY'S ENGLISH VERSION

whole country of Judea taking revenge on all the men who
had willingly joined Alcimus and preventing them from leaving the towns and going into the country. 25 When Alcimus
saw that Judas and his men were growing more powerful
and when he realized that he would not be able to stand
against them, he returned to the king and accused them of
great crimes.
26 Then the king sent Nicanor, one of his most honored
officers, who hated the Jews, with orders to exterminate
them. 27 Nicanor came to Jerusalem with a big army. He tried
to trick Judas and his brothers by sending peace offers. He
said, 28 "There need not be any quarrel between you and me.
I will come to you with a small escort for a friendly private
conversation." 29 When he came to Judas, they exchanged
polite greetings, but Judas' enemies were ready to kidnap
him. 30 When Judas learned that Nicanor's visit was part of a
plot against him, he was afraid and decided not to meet him
again. 31 Nicanor realized that his plan had been discovered,
so he left Jerusalem to meet Judas in battle near Caphar-
salama. 32 About 500 of Nicanor's men were killed, and the
rest of the army escaped to the fort in Jerusalem.
33 Some time later Nicanor went to Mount Zion. Some of
the priests left the Temple and, along with some of the leaders of the people, went to welcome him with words of peace
and to show him the burnt offering that was being sacrificed

NEW REVISED STANDARD VERSION

the surrounding parts of Judea, taking vengeance on those
who had deserted and preventing those in the city[a] from
going out into the country. 25 When Alcimus saw that Judas
and those with him had grown strong, and realized that he
could not withstand them, he returned to the king and
brought malicious charges against them.
26 Then the king sent Nicanor, one of his honored
princes, who hated and detested Israel, and he commanded
him to destroy the people. 27 So Nicanor came to Jerusalem
with a large force, and treacherously sent to Judas and his
brothers this peaceable message, 28 "Let there be no fighting
between you and me; I shall come with a few men to see you
face to face in peace."
29 So he came to Judas, and they greeted one another
peaceably; but the enemy were preparing to kidnap Judas.
30 It became known to Judas that Nicanor[b] had come to him
with treacherous intent, and he was afraid of him and would
not meet him again. 31 When Nicanor learned that his plan
had been disclosed, he went out to meet Judas in battle near
Caphar-salama. 32 About five hundred of the army of
Nicanor fell, and the rest[c] fled into the city of David.
33 After these events Nicanor went up to Mount Zion.
Some of the priests from the sanctuary and some of the
elders of the people came out to greet him peaceably and to
show him the burnt offering that was being offered for the

a Gk *and they were prevented* *b* Gk *he* *c* Gk *they*

NEW AMERICAN BIBLE

about all the borders of Judea and took revenge on the men
who had deserted, preventing them from going out into the
country. 25 But when Alcimus saw that Judas and his followers were gaining strength and realized that he could not
oppose them, he returned to the king and accused them of
grave crimes.
26 Then the king sent Nicanor, one of his famous officers,
who was a bitter enemy of Israel, with orders to destroy the
people. 27 Nicanor came to Jerusalem with a large force and
deceitfully sent to Judas and his brothers this peaceable message: 28 "Let there be no fight between me and you. I will
come with a few men to meet you peaceably."
29 So he came to Judas, and they greeted one another
peaceably. But Judas' enemies were prepared to seize him.
30 When he became aware that Nicanor had come to him with
treachery in mind, Judas was afraid and would not meet him
again. 31 When Nicanor saw that his plan had been discovered, he went out to fight Judas near Caphar-salama.
32 About five hundred men of Nicanor's army fell; the rest
fled to the City of David.
33 After this, Nicanor went up to Mount Zion. Some of the
priests from the sanctuary and some of the elders of the people came out to greet him peaceably and to show him the
holocaust that was being offered for the king. 34 But he

NEW JERUSALEM BIBLE

gentiles had done, 24 Judas went right round the whole territory of Judaea to take vengeance on those who had deserted
him and to prevent their free movement about the country.
25 When Alcimus saw how strong Judas and his supporters
had grown and realised that he was powerless to resist them,
he went back to the king, to whom he made malicious accusations against them. 26 The king sent Nicanor, one of his
generals ranking as Illustrious and a bitter enemy of Israel,
with orders to exterminate the people. 27 Reaching Jerusalem
with a large force, Nicanor sent a friendly, yet treacherous,
message to Judas and his brothers, as follows: 28 'Let us
have no fighting between you and me; I shall come with a
small escort for a peaceful meeting with you.' 29 He met
Judas and they exchanged friendly greetings; the enemy,
however, had made preparations to abduct Judas. 30 When
Judas became aware of Nicanor's treacherous purpose in
coming to see him, he took fright and refused any further
meeting. 31 Nicanor then realised that his plan had been discovered, and took the field against Judas, to give battle near
Caphar-Salama. 32 About five hundred of Nicanor's men fell;
the rest took refuge in the City of David.
33 After these events Nicanor went up to Mount Zion. Some
of the priests came out of the Holy Place with some elders, to
give him a friendly welcome and show him the burnt offering

GREEK OLD TESTAMENT

βασιλέως. 34 καὶ ἐμυκτήρισεν αὐτοὺς καὶ κατεγέλασεν
αὐτῶν καὶ ἐμίανεν αὐτοὺς καὶ ἐλάλησεν ὑπερηφάνως. 35 καὶ
ὤμοσεν μετὰ θυμοῦ λέγων Ἐὰν μὴ παραδοθῇ Ιουδας καὶ ἡ
παρεμβολὴ αὐτοῦ εἰς χεῖράς μου τὸ νῦν, καὶ ἔσται ἐὰν
ἐπιστρέψω ἐν εἰρήνῃ, ἐμπυριῶ τὸν οἶκον τοῦτον. καὶ ἐξῆλθεν
μετὰ θυμοῦ μεγάλου. 36 καὶ εἰσῆλθον οἱ ἱερεῖς καὶ ἔστησαν
κατὰ πρόσωπον τοῦ θυσιαστηρίου καὶ τοῦ ναοῦ καὶ ἔκλαυσαν
καὶ εἶπον 37 Σὺ ἐξελέξω τὸν οἶκον τοῦτον ἐπικληθῆναι τὸ
ὄνομά σου ἐπ᾽ αὐτοῦ εἶναι οἶκον προσευχῆς καὶ δεήσεως τῷ
λαῷ σου· 38 ποίησον ἐκδίκησιν ἐν τῷ ἀνθρώπῳ τούτῳ καὶ ἐν
τῇ παρεμβολῇ αὐτοῦ, καὶ πεσέτωσαν ἐν ῥομφαίᾳ· μνήσθητι
τῶν δυσφημιῶν αὐτῶν καὶ μὴ δῷς αὐτοῖς μονήν. 39 καὶ ἐξῆλθεν Νικάνωρ ἐξ Ιερουσαλημ καὶ παρενέβαλεν ἐν Βαιθωρων,
καὶ συνήντησεν αὐτῷ δύναμις Συρίας. 40 καὶ Ιουδας παρενέβαλεν ἐν Αδασα ἐν τρισχιλίοις ἀνδράσιν· καὶ προσηύξατο
Ιουδας καὶ εἶπεν 41 Οἱ παρὰ τοῦ βασιλέως ὅτε ἐδυσφήμη-
σαν, ἐξῆλθεν ὁ ἄγγελός σου καὶ ἐπάταξεν ἐν αὐτοῖς ἑκατὸν
ὀγδοήκοντα πέντε χιλιάδας. 42 οὕτως σύντριψον τὴν παρεμβολὴν ταύτην ἐνώπιον ἡμῶν σήμερον, καὶ γνώτωσαν οἱ ἐπίλοιποι ὅτι κακῶς ἐλάλησεν ἐπὶ τὰ ἅγιά σου, καὶ κρῖνον
αὐτὸν κατὰ τὴν κακίαν αὐτοῦ. 43 καὶ συνῆψαν αἱ παρεμβολαὶ
εἰς πόλεμον τῇ τρισκαιδεκάτῃ τοῦ μηνὸς Αδαρ, καὶ συνετρίβη ἡ παρεμβολὴ Νικάνορος, καὶ ἔπεσεν αὐτὸς πρῶτος ἐν τῷ
πολέμῳ. 44 ὡς δὲ εἶδεν ἡ παρεμβολὴ αὐτοῦ ὅτι ἔπεσεν Νικάνωρ, ῥίψαντες τὰ ὅπλα ἔφυγον. 45 καὶ κατεδίωκον αὐτοὺς

KING JAMES VERSION

34 But he mocked them, and laughed at them, and abused them shamefully, and spake proudly,

35 And sware in his wrath, saying, Unless Judas and his host be now delivered into my hands, if ever I come again in safety, I will burn up this house: and with that he went out in a great rage.

36 Then the priests entered in, and stood before the altar and the temple, weeping, and saying,

37 Thou, *O Lord,* didst choose this house to be called by thy name, and to be a house of prayer and petition for thy people:

38 Be avenged of this man and his host, and let them fall by the sword: remember their blasphemies, and suffer them not to continue any longer.

39 So Nicanor went out of Jerusalem, and pitched his tents in Bethhoron, where an host out of Syria met him.

40 But Judas pitched in Adasa with three thousand men, and there he prayed, saying,

41 *O Lord,* when they that were sent from the king of the Assyrians blasphemed, thine angel went out, and smote an hundred fourscore and five thousand of them.

42 Even so destroy thou this host before us this day, that the rest may know that he hath spoken blasphemously against thy sanctuary, and judge thou him according to his wickedness.

43 So the thirteenth day of the month Adar the hosts joined battle: but Nicanor's host was discomfited, and he himself was first slain in the battle.

44 Now when Nicanor's host saw that he was slain, they cast away their weapons, and fled.

DOUAY OLD TESTAMENT

34 But he mocked and despised them, and abused them: and he spoke proudly,

35 And swore in anger, saying: Unless Judas and his army be delivered into my hands, as soon as ever I return in peace, I will burn this house. And he went out in a great rage.

36 And the priests went in, and stood before the face of the altar and the temple: and weeping, they said:

37 Thou, O Lord, hast chosen this house for thy name to be called upon therein, that it might be a house of prayer and supplication for thy people.

38 Be avenged of this man, and his army, and let them fall by the sword: remember their blasphemies, and suffer them not to continue any longer.

39 Then Nicanor went out from Jerusalem, and encamped near to Bethoron: and an army of Syria joined him.

40 But Judas pitched in Adarsa with three thousand men: and Judas prayed, and said:

41 O Lord, when they that were sent by king Sennacherib blasphemed thee, an angel went out, and slew of them a hundred and eighty-five thousand:

42 Even so destroy this army in our sight to day, and let the rest know that he hath spoken ill against thy sanctuary: and judge thou him according to his wickedness.

43 And the armies joined battle on the thirteenth day of the month Adar: and the army of Nicanor was defeated, and he himself was first slain in the battle.

44 And when his army saw that Nicanor was slain, they threw away their weapons, and fled:

KNOX TRANSLATION

get from him but mockery and contempt; he did despite to
their sacred persons, and sent them away with threats. 35 In
his anger, he swore to them nothing would serve but he
should have Judas and Judas' army at his mercy; if not, he
would burn the temple down, as soon as ever he returned in
safety. So, in high disdain, he left them; 36 and the priests
must take themselves back within the walls, where they stood
before altar and temple, praying very mournfully. 37 Lord,
they said, thou hast chosen this house to be the shrine of thy
name; here thy people should offer prayer, and sue for thy
favour. 38 Do thou avenge thyself on chieftain and army both;
die they at the sword's point! Wouldst thou forget their blasphemy; should they escape with their lives?

39 After this, Nicanor left Jerusalem, and pitched his camp
at Bethoron, where he was met by a fresh army from Syria;
40 Judas, in his camp at Adarsa, had but three thousand men.
And this was the prayer Judas prayed: 41 Time was, Lord,
when Sennacherib's men were loud in their blasphemy, and
thy angel must go out to smite them down, a hundred and
eighty thousand of them. 42 This day a new enemy overwhelm with our onslaught, and let all the world know what
comes of threatening thy holy place; for his ill-doing, ill
requite him!

43 It was the thirteenth of Adar when the two armies met;
sure enough, Nicanor's army was overwhelmed, and himself
the first to fall in the encounter; 44 whereupon the rest, seeing their leader gone, cast weapons away and took to their

TODAY'S ENGLISH VERSION

on behalf of the king. 34 But he ridiculed them and made
them ceremonially unclean by spitting on them. He spoke
proudly 35 and angrily threatened them with an oath,
"Unless Judas and his army are surrendered to me immediately, I will burn this Temple down as soon as I return after
my victory." And he left in a rage.
36 The priests went into the courtyard and stood facing the
altar and the Temple. They started weeping and prayed,
37 "Lord, you chose this Temple to bear your name and to be
a place of prayer and intercession for your people. 38 Now,
take vengeance on this man and his army; let them die in
battle. Remember how they spoke evil of you, and let none of
them survive."
39 Nicanor left Jerusalem and set up his headquarters at
Beth Horon, where the Syrian army joined him. 40 Meanwhile, Judas set up camp at Adasa with 3,000 men. There
Judas prayed, 41 "Lord, the Scriptures tell us that when a
king sent messengers to insult you, your angel went out and
killed 185,000 of his soldiers. 42 Now, in the same way,
crush this army before us today and let everyone know that
Nicanor is being punished because he insulted your holy
Temple. Punish him as his wickedness deserves."
43 The armies met in battle on the thirteenth day of the
month of Adar, and Nicanor's army was defeated. Nicanor
himself was the first to be killed in the battle, 44 and when
his soldiers saw that he was dead, they threw down their

NEW REVISED STANDARD VERSION

king. 34 But he mocked them and derided them and defiled
them and spoke arrogantly, 35 and in anger he swore this
oath, "Unless Judas and his army are delivered into my
hands this time, then if I return safely I will burn up this
house." And he went out in great anger. 36 At this the priests
went in and stood before the altar and the temple; they wept
and said,

37 "You chose this house to be called by your name,
and to be for your people a house of prayer and
supplication.
38 Take vengeance on this man and on his army,
and let them fall by the sword;
remember their blasphemies,
and let them live no longer."

39 Now Nicanor went out from Jerusalem and encamped
in Beth-horon, and the Syrian army joined him. 40 Judas
encamped in Adasa with three thousand men. Then Judas
prayed and said, 41 "When the messengers from the king
spoke blasphemy, your angel went out and struck down one
hundred eighty-five thousand of the Assyrians.[a] 42 So also
crush this army before us today; let the rest learn that
Nicanor[b] has spoken wickedly against the sanctuary, and
judge him according to this wickedness."
43 So the armies met in battle on the thirteenth day of the
month of Adar. The army of Nicanor was crushed, and he
himself was the first to fall in the battle. 44 When his army
saw that Nicanor had fallen, they threw down their arms and

a Gk *of them* b Gk *he*

NEW AMERICAN BIBLE

mocked and ridiculed them, defiled them, and spoke disdainfully. 35 In a rage he swore: "If Judas and his army are not
delivered to me at once, when I return victorious I will burn
this temple down." He went away in great anger. 36 The
priests, however, went in and stood before the altar and the
sanctuary. They wept and said: 37 "You have chosen this
house to bear your name, to be a house of prayer and petition for your people. 38 Take revenge on this man and his
army, and let them fall by the sword. Remember their blasphemies, and do not let them continue."
39 Nicanor left Jerusalem and pitched his camp at Beth-
horon, where the Syrian army joined him. 40 But Judas
camped in Adasa with three thousand men. Here Judas
uttered this prayer: 41 "When they who were sent by the king
blasphemed, your angel went out and killed a hundred and
eighty-five thousand of them. 42 In the same way, crush this
army before us today, and let the rest know that Nicanor
spoke wickedly against your sanctuary; judge him according
to his wickedness."
43 The armies met in battle on the thirteenth day of the
month Adar. Nicanor's army was crushed, and he himself
was the first to fall in the battle. 44 When his army saw that
Nicanor was dead, they threw down their arms and fled.

NEW JERUSALEM BIBLE

being presented for the king. 34 But he ridiculed them,
laughed at them, defiled them and used insolent language,
swearing in his rage, 35 'Unless Judas is handed over to me
this time with his army, as soon as I am safely back, I promise you, I shall burn this building down!' 36 Then he went off
in a fury. At this, the priests went in again, and stood weeping in front of the altar and the Temple, saying, 37 'You have
chosen this house to be called by your name, to be a house
of prayer and petition for your people. 38 Take vengeance on
this man and on his army, and let them fall by the sword;
remember their blasphemies and give them no respite.'
39 Nicanor left Jerusalem and encamped at Beth-Horon,
where he was joined by an army from Syria. 40 Judas, meanwhile, camped at Adasa with three thousand men, and
offered this prayer, 41 'When the king's envoys blasphemed,
your angel went out and struck down one hundred and
eighty-five thousand of his men. 42 In the same way let us
see you crush this army today, so that everyone else may
know that this man has spoken blasphemously against your
sanctuary: pass judgement on him as his wickedness
deserves!'
43 The armies met in battle on the thirteenth of the month
Adar,[a] and Nicanor's army was crushed, he himself being
the first to fall in the battle. 44 When Nicanor's soldiers saw
him fall, they threw down their arms and fled. 45 The Jews

a **7** // 2 M 15:25–36.

GREEK OLD TESTAMENT

ὁδὸν ἡμέρας μιᾶς ἀπὸ Αδασα ἕως τοῦ ἐλθεῖν εἰς Γαζηρα καὶ
ἐσάλπιζον ὀπίσω αὐτῶν ταῖς σάλπιγξιν τῶν σημασιῶν.
46 καὶ ἐξῆλθον ἐκ πασῶν τῶν κωμῶν τῆς Ιουδαίας κυκλόθεν
καὶ ὑπερεκέρων αὐτούς, καὶ ἀπέστρεφον οὗτοι πρὸς τούτους,
καὶ ἔπεσον πάντες ῥομφαίᾳ, καὶ οὐ κατελείφθη ἐξ αὐτῶν
οὐδὲ εἷς. 47 καὶ ἔλαβον τὰ σκῦλα καὶ τὴν προνομήν, καὶ τὴν
κεφαλὴν Νικάνορος ἀφεῖλον καὶ τὴν δεξιὰν αὐτοῦ, ἣν ἐξέτεινεν ὑπερηφάνως, καὶ ἤνεγκαν καὶ ἐξέτειναν παρὰ τῇ
Ιερουσαλημ. 48 καὶ ηὐφράνθη ὁ λαὸς σφόδρα καὶ ἤγαγον τὴν
ἡμέραν ἐκείνην ἡμέραν εὐφροσύνης μεγάλην· 49 καὶ ἔστησαν τοῦ ἄγειν κατ᾽ ἐνιαυτὸν τὴν ἡμέραν ταύτην τῇ τρισκαιδεκάτῃ τοῦ Αδαρ. 50 καὶ ἡσύχασεν ἡ γῆ Ιουδα ἡμέρας
ὀλίγας.

8 Καὶ ἤκουσεν Ιουδας τὸ ὄνομα τῶν Ῥωμαίων, ὅτι εἰσὶν
δυνατοὶ ἰσχύι καὶ αὐτοὶ εὐδοκοῦσιν ἐν πᾶσιν τοῖς
προστιθεμένοις αὐτοῖς, καὶ ὅσοι ἂν προσέλθωσιν αὐτοῖς,
ἱστῶσιν αὐτοῖς φιλίαν, καὶ ὅτι εἰσὶ δυνατοὶ ἰσχύι. 2 καὶ
διηγήσαντο αὐτῷ τοὺς πολέμους αὐτῶν καὶ τὰς ἀνδραγαθίας, ἃς ποιοῦσιν ἐν τοῖς Γαλάταις, καὶ ὅτι κατεκράτησαν
αὐτῶν καὶ ἤγαγον αὐτοὺς ὑπὸ φόρον, 3 καὶ ὅσα ἐποίησαν ἐν
χώρᾳ Σπανίας τοῦ κατακρατῆσαι τῶν μετάλλων τοῦ ἀργυρίου καὶ τοῦ χρυσίου τοῦ ἐκεῖ· 4 καὶ κατεκράτησαν τοῦ τόπου
παντὸς τῇ βουλῇ αὐτῶν καὶ τῇ μακροθυμίᾳ, καὶ ὁ τόπος ἦν

KING JAMES VERSION

45 Then they pursued after them a day's journey, from Adasa unto Gazera, sounding an alarm after them with their trumpets.

46 Whereupon they came forth out of all the towns of Judea round about, and closed them in; so that they, turning back upon them that pursued them, were all slain with the sword, and not one of them was left.

47 Afterwards they took the spoils, and the prey, and smote off Nicanors head, and his right hand, which he stretched out so proudly, and brought them away, and hanged them up toward Jerusalem.

48 For this cause the people rejoiced greatly, and they kept that day a day of great gladness.

49 Moreover they ordained to keep yearly this day, being the thirteenth of Adar.

50 Thus the land of Juda was in rest a little while.

8 Now Judas had heard of the fame of the Romans, that they were mighty and valiant men, and such as would lovingly accept all that joined themselves unto them, and make a league of amity with all that came unto them;

2 And that they were men of great valour. It was told him also of their wars and noble acts which they had done among the Galatians, and how they had conquered them, and brought them under tribute;

3 And what they had done in the country of Spain, for the winning of the mines of the silver and gold which is there;

4 And that by their policy and patience they had conquered all the place, though it were very far from them; and the kings

DOUAY OLD TESTAMENT

45 And they pursued after them one day's journey from Adazer, even till ye come to Gazara, and they sounded the trumpets after them with signals.

46 And they went forth out of all the towns of Judea round about, and they pushed them with the horns, and they turned again to them, and they were all slain with the sword, and there was not left of them so much as one.

47 And they took the spoils of them for a booty, and they cut off Nicanor's head, and his right hand, which he had proudly stretched out, and they brought it, and hung it up over against Jerusalem.

48 And the people rejoiced exceedingly, and they spent that day with great joy.

49 And he ordained that this day should be kept every year, being the thirteenth of the month of Adar.

50 And the land of Juda was quiet for a short time.

8 NOW Judas heard of the fame of the Romans, that they are powerful and strong, and willingly agree to all things that are requested of them: and that whosoever have come to them, they have made amity with them, and that they are mighty in power.

2 And they heard of their battles, and their noble acts, which they had done in Galatia, how they had conquered them, and brought them under tribute:

3 And how great things they had done in the land of Spain, and that they had brought under their power the mines of silver and of gold that are there, and had gotten possession of all the place by their counsel and patience:

4 And had conquered places that were very far off from

KNOX TRANSLATION

heels. 45 For a whole day the pursuit of them went on, all the
way from Adazer to the approaches of Gazara, and ever there
were trumpets sounding the hue and cry. 46 Out came Jewish
folk from all the villages round about, to head them off,[a] till
at last they turned at bay and fell at the sword's point all of
them, never a man left. 47 Spoil of them was plundered
where they lay; as for Nicanor, the Jews cut off the head from
his body, and that right hand he lifted up so defiantly, and
took them away, to be hung up in full sight of Jerusalem.
48 Glad men they were that day, and kept high festival,
49 decreeing that never thenceforward should the thirteenth
day of Adar go unobserved. 50 And for a little while the land
of Juda had peace.

8 Judas had heard tell of the Romans, and their renown.
Here was a powerful nation, that would entertain overtures none the less from such as craved their friendship,
plighting their word faithfully. 2 A powerful nation indeed;
what battles they had fought, what exploits achieved yonder
among the Galatians, their conquered vassals now! 3 In
Spain, too, they had done great feats of arms; and at last, by
policy and patient striving, won over the whole country,
made themselves masters of all the silver and gold that was
mined there. 4 Came peoples from far away, kings from the

a 'To head them off'; the Latin has 'and tossed them with the horn', probably through a misunderstanding of the word used in the Greek text.

TODAY'S ENGLISH VERSION

weapons and fled. 45 The Jews pursued them all day long
from Adasa to Gezer. As they followed, they kept sounding
the call to battle on the trumpets, 46 and from all the surrounding villages of Judea people came out and attacked the
fleeing enemy from the sides. This forced them back toward
the Jews who were chasing them, and all of the enemy were
killed in the fight. Not one of them survived.
47 The Jews took the loot and then cut off Nicanor's head
and his right arm, which he had extended so arrogantly.
They brought his head and his arm to be put on display outside Jerusalem. 48 There was great rejoicing among the Jews.
They set that day aside as a special day of celebration,
49 and decreed that the thirteenth day of Adar should be
observed as an annual day of celebration. 50 There was peace
in the land of Judea for a little while.

8 Judas had heard about the Romans and their reputation
as a military power. He knew that they welcomed all
those who joined them as allies and that those who came to
them could be sure of the friendship of Rome. 2 People had
told him about the wars the Romans had fought and their
heroic acts among the Gauls, whom they had conquered and
forced to pay taxes. 3 He had been told what they had done
in Spain when they captured the silver mines and the gold
mines there. 4 By careful planning and persistence, they had
conquered the whole country, even though it was far from

NEW REVISED STANDARD VERSION

fled. 45 The Jews[a] pursued them a day's journey, from Adasa
as far as Gazara, and as they followed they kept sounding
the battle call on the trumpets. 46 People came out of all the
surrounding villages of Judea, and they outflanked the
enemy[b] and drove them back to their pursuers,[c] so that they
all fell by the sword; not even one of them was left. 47 Then
the Jews[a] seized the spoils and the plunder; they cut off
Nicanor's head and the right hand that he had so arrogantly
stretched out, and brought them and displayed them just
outside Jerusalem. 48 The people rejoiced greatly and celebrated that day as a day of great gladness. 49 They decreed
that this day should be celebrated each year on the thirteenth
day of Adar. 50 So the land of Judah had rest for a few days.

8 Now Judas heard of the fame of the Romans, that they
were very strong and were well-disposed toward all who
made an alliance with them, that they pledged friendship to
those who came to them, 2 and that they were very strong.
He had been told of their wars and of the brave deeds that
they were doing among the Gauls, how they had defeated
them and forced them to pay tribute, 3 and what they had
done in the land of Spain to get control of the silver and gold
mines there, 4 and how they had gained control of the whole
region by their planning and patience, even though the place
was far distant from them. They also subdued the kings who

a Gk *they* b Gk *them* c Gk *these*

NEW AMERICAN BIBLE

45 The Jews pursued them a day's journey, from Adasa to
near Gazara, blowing the trumpets behind them as signals.
46 From all the surrounding villages of Judea people came out
and closed in on them. They hemmed them in, and all the
enemies fell by the sword; not a single one escaped.
47 Then the Jews collected the spoils and the booty; they
cut off Nicanor's head and his right arm, which he had lifted
up so arrogantly. These they brought to Jerusalem and displayed there. 48 The people rejoiced greatly, and observed
that day as a great festival. 49 They decreed that it should be
observed every year on the thirteenth of Adar. 50 And for a
short time the land of Judah was quiet.

8 Judas had heard of the reputation of the Romans. They
were valiant fighters and acted amiably to all who took
their side. They established a friendly alliance with all who
applied to them. 2 He was also told of their battles and the
brave deeds that they had performed against the Gauls, conquering them and forcing them to pay tribute. 3 They had
gotten possession of the silver and gold mines in Spain,
4 and by planning and persistence had conquered the whole
country, although it was very remote from their own. They

NEW JERUSALEM BIBLE

pursued them a day's journey, from Adasa to the approaches of Gezer; they sounded their trumpets in warning
as they followed them, 46 and people came out of all the
surrounding Judaean villages to encircle the fugitives, who
then turned back on their own men. All fell by the sword,
not one being left alive. 47 Having collected the spoils and
booty, they cut off Nicanor's head and the right hand he had
stretched out in a display of insolence; these were taken and
displayed within sight of Jerusalem. 48 The people were
overjoyed and kept that day as a great holiday: 49 indeed
they decided to celebrate it annually on the thirteenth of
Adar. 50 For a short while Judaea enjoyed peace.

8 Now Judas had heard of the reputation of the Romans:
how strong they were, and how well disposed towards
any who made common cause with them, making a treaty of
friendship with anyone who approached them. 2 (And,
indeed, they were extremely powerful.) He had been told of
their wars and of their prowess among the Gauls, whom they
had conquered and put under tribute; 3 and of all they had
done in the province of Spain to gain possession of the silver
and gold mines there, 4 making themselves masters of the
whole country by their determination and perseverance,
despite its great distance from their own; of the kings who

GREEK OLD TESTAMENT

ἀπέχων μακρὰν ἀπ᾽ αὐτῶν σφόδρα, καὶ τῶν βασιλέων τῶν
ἐπελθόντων ἐπ᾽ αὐτοὺς ἀπ᾽ ἄκρου τῆς γῆς, ἕως συνέτριψαν
αὐτοὺς καὶ ἐπάταξαν ἐν αὐτοῖς πληγὴν μεγάλην, καὶ οἱ ἐπίλοιποι διδόασιν αὐτοῖς φόρον κατ᾽ ἐνιαυτόν· 5 καὶ τὸν
Φίλιππον καὶ τὸν Περσέα Κιτιέων βασιλέα καὶ τοὺς ἐπηρ-
μένους ἐπ᾽ αὐτοὺς συνέτριψαν αὐτοὺς ἐν πολέμῳ καὶ κατεκράτησαν αὐτῶν· 6 καὶ Ἀντίοχον τὸν μέγαν βασιλέα τῆς
Ἀσίας τὸν πορευθέντα ἐπ᾽ αὐτοὺς εἰς πόλεμον ἔχοντα
ἑκατὸν εἴκοσι ἐλέφαντας καὶ ἵππον καὶ ἅρματα καὶ δύναμιν
πολλὴν σφόδρα, καὶ συνετρίβη ὑπ᾽ αὐτῶν, 7 καὶ ἔλαβον
αὐτὸν ζῶντα καὶ ἔστησαν αὐτοῖς διδόναι αὐτόν τε καὶ τοὺς
βασιλεύοντας μετ᾽ αὐτὸν φόρον μέγαν καὶ διδόναι ὅμηρα καὶ
διαστολὴν 8 καὶ χώραν τὴν Ἰνδικὴν καὶ Μηδίαν καὶ Λυδίαν
ἀπὸ τῶν καλλίστων χωρῶν αὐτῶν, καὶ λαβόντες αὐτὰς παρ᾽
αὐτοῦ ἔδωκαν αὐτὰς Εὐμένει τῷ βασιλεῖ· 9 καὶ ὅτι οἱ ἐκ τῆς
Ἑλλάδος ἐβουλεύσαντο ἐλθεῖν καὶ ἐξᾶραι αὐτούς, 10 καὶ
ἐγνώσθη ὁ λόγος αὐτοῖς, καὶ ἀπέστειλαν ἐπ᾽ αὐτοὺς στρατηγὸν ἕνα καὶ ἐπολέμησαν πρὸς αὐτούς, καὶ ἔπεσον ἐξ αὐτῶν
τραυματίαι πολλοί, καὶ ᾐχμαλώτισαν τὰς γυναῖκας αὐτῶν
καὶ τὰ τέκνα αὐτῶν καὶ ἐπρονόμευσαν αὐτοὺς καὶ κατεκράτησαν τῆς γῆς καὶ καθεῖλον τὰ ὀχυρώματα αὐτῶν καὶ
κατεδουλώσαντο αὐτοὺς ἕως τῆς ἡμέρας ταύτης. 11 καὶ τὰς
ἐπιλοίπους βασιλείας καὶ τὰς νήσους, ὅσοι ποτὲ ἀντέστησαν αὐτοῖς, κατέφθειραν καὶ ἐδούλωσαν αὐτούς, μετὰ δὲ
τῶν φίλων αὐτῶν καὶ τῶν ἐπαναπαυομένων αὐτοῖς συνετήρ-
ησαν φιλίαν· 12 καὶ κατεκράτησαν τῶν βασιλέων τῶν ἐγγὺς

KING JAMES VERSION

also that came against them from the uttermost part of the earth, till they had discomfited them, and given them a great overthrow, so that the rest did give them tribute every year:

5 Beside this, how they had discomfited in battle Philip, and Perseus, king of the Citims, with others that lifted up themselves against them, and had overcome them:

6 How also Antiochus the great king of Asia, that came against them in battle, having an hundred and twenty elephants, with horsemen, and chariots, and a very great army, was discomfited by them;

7 And how they took him alive, and covenanted that he and such as reigned after him should pay a great tribute, and give hostages, and that which was agreed upon,

8 And the country of India, and Media, and Lydia, and of the goodliest countries, which they took of him, and gave to king Eumenes:

9 Moreover how the Grecians had determined to come and destroy them;

10 And that they, having knowledge thereof, sent against them a certain captain, and fighting with them slew many of them, and carried away captives their wives and their children, and spoiled them, and took possession of their lands, and pulled down their strong holds, and brought them to be their servants unto this day:

11 *It was told him* besides, how they destroyed and brought under their dominion all other kingdoms and isles that at any time resisted them;

12 But with their friends and such as relied upon them they kept amity: and that they had conquered kingdoms both

DOUAY OLD TESTAMENT

them, and kings that came against them from the ends of the earth, and had overthrown them with great slaughter: and the rest pay them tribute every year.

5 And that they had defeated in battle Philip, and Perses the king of the Ceteans, and the rest that had borne arms against them, and had conquered them:

6 And how Antiochus the great king of Asia, who went to fight against them having a hundred and twenty elephants with horsemen, and chariots, and a very great army, was routed by them:

7 And how they took him alive, and appointed to him, that both he and they that should reign after him, should pay a great tribute, and that he should give hostages, and that which was agreed upon,

8 And the country of the Indians, and of the Medes, and of the Lydians, some of their best provinces: and those which they had taken from them they gave to king Eumenes.

9 And that they who were in Greece had a mind to go and to destroy them: and they had knowledge thereof,

10 And they sent a general against them, and fought with them, and many of them were slain, and they carried away their wives and their children captives, and spoiled them, and took possession of their land, and threw down their walls, and brought them to be their servants unto this day.

11 And the other kingdoms, and islands, that at any time had resisted them, they had destroyed and brought under their power.

12 But with their friends, and such as relied upon them, they kept amity, and had conquered kingdoms that were

KNOX TRANSLATION

furthest corners of earth, to offer battle, they were overwhelmed and signally defeated; those nearer at hand were
content to pay yearly tribute. 5 Had they not crushed and
conquered Philip, and Perseus king of the Greeks, and all
others that had levied war upon them? 6 And what of
Antiochus the Great, that ruled all Asia, and came against
them with a hundred and twenty elephants, with horsemen
and chariots, and a great array besides? The Romans overcame him, 7 caught him alive, and demanded both from him
and from his heirs rich tribute, and hostages, with other conditions of surrender; 8 took away from him India, Media, and
Lydia, that were his most cherished provinces, and gave
them to king Eumenes instead. 9 Later, word came that the
men of Hellas were for marching in and making an end of
them; what was the issue of it? 10 One of the Roman generals was sent out to engage them; fell many in battle, wives
and children were carried off into exile, goods plundered, the
land conquered, its fortresses destroyed, and they are slaves
to this day.

11 So it was with all the kingdoms and islands that defied
their will; the Romans crushed them and took their lands
away. 12 But to their friends, that would live at peace with
them, they were ever good friends in return. Kingdoms both

TODAY'S ENGLISH VERSION

Rome. They had overcome the kings from distant lands who had fought against them; they had defeated them so badly that the survivors had to pay annual taxes. 5 They had fought and conquered Philip and Perseus, kings of Macedonia, and all who had joined them against Rome. 6 They had even defeated Antiochus the Great, king of Syria, who had attacked them with 120 elephants, cavalry, chariots, and a powerful army. 7 They took him alive and forced him and his successors to pay heavy taxes, to give hostages, and to surrender 8 India, Media, Lydia, and some of their best lands. They took these and gave them to King Eumenes.[a]

9 When the Greeks made plans to attack and destroy them, 10 the Romans learned of the plans and sent a general to fight against them. The Romans killed many of the Greeks, took their wives and children captive, plundered their possessions, occupied their land, tore down their fortresses, and made them slaves, as they are today. 11 They also destroyed or made slaves of other kingdoms, the islands, and everyone who had ever fought against them. 12 But they maintained their friendship with their allies and those who relied on them for protection. They conquered kings near and far, and

[a] KING EUMENES: *This is King Eumenes II, king of Pergamum from 197–158 B.C.*

NEW REVISED STANDARD VERSION

came against them from the ends of the earth, until they crushed them and inflicted great disaster on them; the rest paid them tribute every year. 5 They had crushed in battle and conquered Philip, and King Perseus of the Macedonians,[a] and the others who rose up against them. 6 They also had defeated Antiochus the Great, king of Asia, who went to fight against them with one hundred twenty elephants and with cavalry and chariots and a very large army. He was crushed by them; 7 they took him alive and decreed that he and those who would reign after him should pay a heavy tribute and give hostages and surrender some of their best provinces, 8 the countries of India, Media, and Lydia. These they took from him and gave to King Eumenes. 9 The Greeks planned to come and destroy them, 10 but this became known to them, and they sent a general against the Greeks[b] and attacked them. Many of them were wounded and fell, and the Romans[c] took captive their wives and children; they plundered them, conquered the land, tore down their strongholds, and enslaved them to this day. 11 The remaining kingdoms and islands, as many as ever opposed them, they destroyed and enslaved; 12 but with their friends and those who rely on them they have kept friendship. They have subdued kings far

a Or *Kittim* *b* Gk *them* *c* Gk *they*

NEW AMERICAN BIBLE

had crushed the kings who had come against them from the far corners of the earth and had inflicted on them severe defeat, and the rest paid tribute to them every year. 5 Philip and Perseus, king of the Macedonians, and the others who opposed them in battle had been overwhelmed and subjugated. 6 Antiochus the Great, king of Asia, who had fought against them with a hundred and twenty elephants and with cavalry and chariots and a very great army, had been defeated by them. 7 They had taken him alive and obliged him and the kings who succeeded him to pay a heavy tribute, to give hostages and a section of 8 Lycia, Mysia, and Lydia from among their best provinces. The Romans took these from him and gave them to King Eumenes. 9 When the men of Greece had planned to come and destroy them, 10 the Romans discovered it, and sent against the Greeks a single general who made war on them. Many were wounded and fell, and the Romans took their wives and children captive. They plundered them, took possession of their land, tore down their strongholds and reduced them to slavery even to this day. 11 All the other kingdoms and islands that had ever opposed them they destroyed and enslaved; 12 with their friends, however, and those who relied on them, they maintained friendship. They had conquered kings both far and

NEW JERUSALEM BIBLE

came from the ends of the earth to attack them, only to be crushed by them and overwhelmed with disaster, and of others who paid them annual tribute; 5 Philip, Perseus king of the Kittim, and others who had dared to make war on them, had been defeated and reduced to subjection, 6 while Antiochus the Great, king of Asia, who had advanced to attack them with a hundred and twenty elephants, cavalry, chariots and a very large army, had also suffered defeat at their hands; 7 they had taken him alive and imposed on him and his successors, on agreed terms, the payment of an enormous tribute, the surrender of hostages, and the cession 8 of the Indian territory, with Media, Lydia, and some of their best provinces, which they took from him and gave to King Eumenes. 9 Judas had also heard how, when the Greeks planned an expedition to destroy the Romans, 10 the latter had got wind of it and, sending a single general against them, had fought a campaign in which they inflicted heavy casualties, carried their women and children away into captivity, pillaged their goods, subdued their country, tore down their fortresses and reduced them to a slavery lasting to the present day; 11 and how they had destroyed and subjugated all the other kingdoms and islands that resisted them.

12 But where their friends and those who relied on them were concerned, they had always stood by their friendship. They had subdued kings far and near, and all who heard

GREEK OLD TESTAMENT

καὶ τῶν μακράν, καὶ ὅσοι ἤκουον τὸ ὄνομα αὐτῶν, ἐφοβοῦντο
ἀπ᾽ αὐτῶν. 13 οἷς δ᾽ ἂν βούλωνται βοηθεῖν καὶ βασιλεύειν,
βασιλεύουσιν· οὓς δ᾽ ἂν βούλωνται, μεθιστῶσιν· καὶ ὑψώθησαν σφόδρα. 14 καὶ ἐν πᾶσιν τούτοις οὐκ ἐπέθεντο αὐτῶν
οὐδὲ εἷς διάδημα, οὐδὲ περιεβάλοντο πορφύραν ὥστε ἁδρυν-
θῆναι ἐν αὐτῇ· 15 καὶ βουλευτήριον ἐποίησαν ἑαυτοῖς, καὶ
καθ᾽ ἡμέραν ἐβουλεύοντο τριακόσιοι καὶ εἴκοσι βουλευόμενοι
διὰ παντὸς περὶ τοῦ πλήθους τοῦ εὐκοσμεῖν αὐτούς. 16 καὶ
πιστεύουσιν ἑνὶ ἀνθρώπῳ ἄρχειν αὐτῶν κατ᾽ ἐνιαυτὸν καὶ
κυριεύειν πάσης τῆς γῆς αὐτῶν, καὶ πάντες ἀκούουσιν τοῦ
ἑνός, καὶ οὐκ ἔστιν φθόνος οὐδὲ ζῆλος ἐν αὐτοῖς.

17 Καὶ ἐπελέξατο Ιουδας τὸν Εὐπόλεμον υἱὸν Ιωαννου τοῦ
Ακκως καὶ Ἰάσονα υἱὸν Ελεαζαρου καὶ ἀπέστειλεν αὐτοὺς
εἰς Ῥώμην στῆσαι φιλίαν καὶ συμμαχίαν 18 καὶ τοῦ ἆραι
τὸν ζυγὸν ἀπ᾽ αὐτῶν, ὅτι εἶδον τὴν βασιλείαν τῶν Ἑλλήνων
καταδουλουμένους τὸν Ισραηλ δουλείᾳ. 19 καὶ ἐπορεύθησαν
εἰς Ῥώμην, καὶ ἡ ὁδὸς πολλὴ σφόδρα, καὶ εἰσήλθοσαν εἰς τὸ
βουλευτήριον καὶ ἀπεκρίθησαν καὶ εἶπον 20 Ιουδας ὁ καὶ
Μακκαβαῖος καὶ οἱ ἀδελφοὶ αὐτοῦ καὶ τὸ πλῆθος τῶν Ιουδαίων ἀπέστειλαν ἡμᾶς πρὸς ὑμᾶς στῆσαι μεθ᾽ ὑμῶν συμμαχίαν καὶ εἰρήνην καὶ γραφῆναι ἡμᾶς συμμάχους καὶ φίλους

KING JAMES VERSION

far and nigh, insomuch as all that heard of their name were afraid of them:

13 Also that, whom they would help to a kingdom, those reign; and whom again they would, they displace: finally, that they were greatly exalted:

14 Yet for all this none of them wore a crown, or was clothed in purple, to be magnified thereby:

15 Moreover how they had made for themselves a senate house, wherein three hundred and twenty men sat in council daily, consulting alway for the people, to the end they might be well ordered:

16 And that they committed their government to one man every year, who ruled over all their country, and that all were obedient to that one, and that there was neither envy nor emulation among them.

17 In consideration of these things, Judas chose Eupolemus the son of John, *the son* of Accos, and Jason the son of Eleazar, and sent them to Rome, to make a league of amity and confederacy with them,

18 *And to intreat them* that they would take the yoke from them; for they saw that the kingdom of the Grecians did oppress Israel with servitude.

19 They went therefore to Rome, which was a very great journey, and came into the senate, where they spake and said,

20 Judas Maccabeus with his brethren, and the people of the Jews, have sent us unto you, to make a confederacy and peace with you, and that we might be registered your confederates and friends.

DOUAY OLD TESTAMENT

near, and that were far off: for all that heard their name, were afraid of them.

13 That whom they had a mind to help to a kingdom, those reigned: and whom they would, they deposed from the kingdom: and they were greatly exalted.

14 And none of all these wore a crown, or was clothed in purple, to be magnified thereby.

15 And that they had made themselves a senate house, and consulted daily three hundred and twenty men, that sat in council always for the people, that they might do the things that were right.

16 And that they committed their government to one man every year, to rule over all their country, and they all obey one, and there is no envy, nor jealousy amongst them.

17 So Judas chose Eupolemus the son of John, the son of Jacob, and Jason the son of Eleazar, and he sent them to Rome to make a league of amity and confederacy with them.

18 And that they might take off from them the yoke of the Grecians, for they saw that they oppressed the kingdom of Israel with servitude.

19 And they went to Rome, a very long journey, and they entered into the senate house, and said:

20 Judas Machabeus, and his brethren, and the people of the Jews have sent us to you, to make alliance and peace with you, and that we may be registered your confederates and friends.

KNOX TRANSLATION

far and near became their vassals, nor any that heard their
name but feared it; 13 helped they any man to a throne, the
throne was his; their good will lost, his throne was lost too;
so high was their renown.

14 Yet, with all this, was never one of them that wore
crown, or went clad in purple for his own aggrandizement.
15 A senate-house they would have, where a council of three
hundred and twenty met day by day, providing ever for the
good estate of the commonalty; 16 and every year they would
entrust one man with the rule and governance of their whole
country, the rest obeying him, without any debate or contention moved.[a]

17 So now Judas made choice of two envoys, Eupolemus,
son of John, son of Jacob, and Jason, son of Eleazar; to Rome
they should go, and there make a treaty of good will and
alliance. 18 Rome's task it should be to rid them of the
Grecian yoke; from the Greeks it was plain they could expect
nothing better than grinding slavery. 19 So, after long journeying, to Rome they came, and were admitted to the senate
house, where they gave their message as follows: 20 We have
been sent to you by Judas Machabaeus and his brethren, and
by our countrymen at large, to make a treaty of alliance with
you; fain would they be enrolled among your confederates

a These verses record only the impression which had reached Judas; it is not necessarily accurate in all points.

TODAY'S ENGLISH VERSION

everyone who heard of their reputation was afraid of them.
13 They helped some men to become kings, while they
deposed others; they had become a world power. 14 In spite
of all this, no Roman ever tried to advance his own position
by wearing a crown or putting on royal robes. 15 They created a senate, and each day 320 senators came together to
deliberate about the affairs of the people and their well-
being. 16 Each year they entrusted to one man the responsibility of governing them and controlling their whole territory.
Everyone obeyed this one man, and there was no envy or
jealousy among them.

17 Judas chose Eupolemus, the son of John and grandson of
Accos, and Jason son of Eleazar and sent them to Rome to
make a treaty of friendship and alliance with the Romans.
18 He did this to eliminate Syrian oppression, since the Jews
clearly saw that they were being reduced to slavery. 19 After
a long and difficult journey, Eupolemus and Jason reached
Rome and entered the Senate. They addressed the assembly
in these terms: 20 "Judas Maccabeus, his brothers, and the
Jewish people have sent us here to make a mutual defense
treaty with you, so that we may be officially recorded as your
friends and allies."

NEW REVISED STANDARD VERSION

and near, and as many as have heard of their fame have
feared them. 13 Those whom they wish to help and to make
kings, they make kings, and those whom they wish they
depose; and they have been greatly exalted. 14 Yet for all this
not one of them has put on a crown or worn purple as a mark
of pride, 15 but they have built for themselves a senate chamber, and every day three hundred twenty senators constantly
deliberate concerning the people, to govern them well. 16 They
trust one man each year to rule over them and to control all
their land; they all heed the one man, and there is no envy or
jealousy among them.

17 So Judas chose Eupolemus son of John son of Accos,
and Jason son of Eleazar, and sent them to Rome to establish friendship and alliance, 18 and to free themselves from
the yoke; for they saw that the kingdom of the Greeks was
enslaving Israel completely. 19 They went to Rome, a very
long journey; and they entered the senate chamber and
spoke as follows: 20 "Judas, who is also called Maccabeus,
and his brothers and the people of the Jews have sent us to
you to establish alliance and peace with you, so that we may
be enrolled as your allies and friends." 21 The proposal

NEW AMERICAN BIBLE

near, and all who heard of their fame were afraid of them.
13 In truth, those whom they desired to help to a kingdom
became kings, and those whom they wished to depose they
deposed; and they were greatly exalted. 14 Yet with all this,
none of them put on a crown or wore purple as a display of
grandeur. 15 They had made for themselves a senate house,
and every day three hundred and twenty men took counsel,
deliberating on all that concerned the people and their well-
being. 16 They entrusted their government to one man every
year, to rule over their entire country, and they all obeyed
that one, and there was no envy or jealousy among them.

17 So Judas chose Eupolemus, son of John, son of Accos,
and Jason, son of Eleazar, and sent them to Rome to establish an alliance of friendship with them. 18 He did this to get
rid of the yoke, for it was obvious that the kingdom of the
Greeks was subjecting Israel to slavery. 19 After making a
very long journey to Rome, the envoys entered the senate
and spoke as follows: 20 "Judas, called Maccabeus, and his
brothers, with the Jewish people, have sent us to you to
make a peaceful alliance with you, and to enroll ourselves
among your allies and friends." 21 The proposal pleased the

NEW JERUSALEM BIBLE

their name went in terror of them. 13 One man, if they determined to help him and advance him to a throne, would certainly occupy it, while another, if they so determined, would
find himself deposed; their influence was paramount. 14 In
spite of all this, no single one of them had assumed a crown
or put on the purple for his own aggrandisement. 15 They
had set up a senate, where three hundred and twenty councillors deliberated daily, constantly debating how best to regulate public affairs. 16 They entrusted their government to
one man for a year at a time, with absolute power over their
whole empire, and this man was obeyed by all without envy
or jealousy.

17 Having chosen Eupolemus son of John, of the family of
Accos, and Jason son of Eleazar, Judas sent them to Rome to
make a treaty of friendship and alliance with these people,
18 in the hope of being rid of the yoke, for they could see that
Greek rule was reducing Israel to slavery. 19 The envoys
made the lengthy journey to Rome and presented themselves
before the Senate with their formal proposal: 20 'Judas
Maccabaeus and his brothers, with the Jewish people, have
sent us to you to conclude a treaty of alliance and peace with
you, and to enrol ourselves as your allies and friends.'

GREEK OLD TESTAMENT

ὑμῶν. [21] καὶ ἤρεσεν ὁ λόγος ἐνώπιον αὐτῶν. [22] καὶ τοῦτο τὸ
ἀντίγραφον τῆς ἐπιστολῆς, ἧς ἀντέγραψαν ἐπὶ δέλτοις
χαλκαῖς καὶ ἀπέστειλαν εἰς Ιερουσαλημ εἶναι παρ᾽ αὐτοῖς
ἐκεῖ μνημόσυνον εἰρήνης καὶ συμμαχίας

[23] Καλῶς γένοιτο Ῥωμαίοις καὶ τῷ ἔθνει Ιουδαίων ἐν τῇ
θαλάσσῃ καὶ ἐπὶ τῆς ξηρᾶς εἰς τὸν αἰῶνα, καὶ ῥομφαία καὶ
ἐχθρὸς μακρυνθείη ἀπ᾽ αὐτῶν. [24] ἐὰν δὲ ἐνστῇ πόλεμος Ῥώμῃ προτέρᾳ ἢ πᾶσιν τοῖς συμμάχοις αὐτῶν ἐν πάσῃ τῇ
κυριείᾳ αὐτῶν, [25] συμμαχήσει τὸ ἔθνος τῶν Ιουδαίων, ὡς ἂν
ὁ καιρὸς ὑπογράφῃ αὐτοῖς, καρδίᾳ πλήρει· [26] καὶ τοῖς πολεμοῦσιν οὐ δώσουσιν οὐδὲ ἐπαρκέσουσιν σῖτον, ὅπλα, ἀργύριον, πλοῖα, ὡς ἔδοξεν Ῥώμῃ· καὶ φυλάξονται τὰ φυλάγματα
αὐτῶν οὐθὲν λαβόντες. [27] κατὰ τὰ αὐτὰ δὲ ἐὰν ἔθνει Ιουδαίων συμβῇ προτέροις πόλεμος, συμμαχήσουσιν οἱ Ῥωμαῖοι ἐκ
ψυχῆς, ὡς ἂν αὐτοῖς ὁ καιρὸς ὑπογράφῃ· [28] καὶ τοῖς συμμα-
χοῦσιν οὐ δοθήσεται σῖτος, ὅπλα, ἀργύριον, πλοῖα, ὡς ἔδοξεν
Ῥώμῃ· καὶ φυλάξονται τὰ φυλάγματα ταῦτα καὶ οὐ μετὰ δόλου. — [29] κατὰ τοὺς λόγους τούτους οὕτως ἔστησαν Ῥωμαῖοι
τῷ δήμῳ τῶν Ιουδαίων. [30] ἐὰν δὲ μετὰ τοὺς λόγους τούτους
βουλεύσωνται οὗτοι καὶ οὗτοι προσθεῖναι ἢ ἀφελεῖν, ποιή-
σονται ἐξ αἱρέσεως αὐτῶν, καὶ ὃ ἂν προσθῶσιν ἢ ἀφέλωσιν,

KING JAMES VERSION

21 So that matter pleased the Romans well.

22 And this is the copy of the epistle which *the senate* wrote back again in tables of brass, and sent to Jerusalem, that there they might have by them a memorial of peace and confederacy:

23 Good success be to the Romans, and to the people of the Jews, by sea and by land for ever: the sword also and enemy be far from them.

24 If there come first any war upon the Romans or any of their confederates throughout all their dominion,

25 The people of the Jews shall help them, as the time shall be appointed, with all their heart:

26 Neither shall they give any thing unto them that make war upon them, or aid them with victuals, weapons, money, or ships, as it hath seemed good unto the Romans; but they shall keep their covenants without taking any thing therefore.

27 In the same manner also, if war come first upon the nation of the Jews, the Romans shall help them with all their heart, according as the time shall be appointed them:

28 Neither shall victuals be given to them that take part against them, or weapons, or money, or ships, as it hath seemed good to the Romans; but they shall keep their covenants, and that without deceit.

29 According to these articles did the Romans make a covenant with the people of the Jews.

30 Howbeit if hereafter the one party or the other shall think meet to add or diminish any thing, they may do it at their pleasures, and whatsoever they shall add or take away shall be ratified.

DOUAY OLD TESTAMENT

21 And the proposal was pleasing in their sight.

22 And this is the copy of the writing that they wrote back again, graven in tables of brass, and sent to Jerusalem, that it might be with them there for a memorial of the peace and alliance.

23 GOOD SUCCESS BE TO THE ROMANS, and to the people of the Jews, by sea and by land for ever: and far be the sword and enemy from them.

24 But if there come first any war upon the Romans, or any of their confederates, in all their dominions:

25 The nation of the Jews shall help them according as the time shall direct, with all their heart:

26 Neither shall they give them, whilst they are fighting, or furnish them with wheat, or arms, or money, or ships, as it hath seemed good to the Romans: and they shall obey their orders, without taking any thing of them.

27 In like manner also if war shall come first upon the nation of the Jews, the Romans shall help them with all their heart, according as the time shall permit them.

28 And there shall not be given to them that come to their aid, either wheat, or arms, or money, or ships, as it hath seemed good to the Romans: and they shall observe their orders without deceit.

29 According to these articles did the Romans covenant with the people of the Jews.

30 And if after this one party or the other shall have a mind to add to these *articles,* or take away any thing, they may do it at their pleasure: and whatsoever they shall add, or take away, shall be ratified.

KNOX TRANSLATION

and friends. [21] This proposition liked the Romans well;
[22] and they wrote back to the Jews on tablets of bronze, that
should be kept in Jerusalem to serve them for a memorial of
treaty and alliance made, to this effect: [23] Well speed they at
all times, the Roman and the Jewish peoples, by sea and land
alike; far removed from either be alarm of war, assault of the
enemy! [24] Yet if war befall, and threaten the Romans first, or
any ally of theirs in any part of their dominions, [25] such aid
the Jewish people shall give as the occasion demands,
ungrudgingly. [26] For the needs of the enemy they shall nothing find or furnish, be it corn, or arms, or money, or ships,
according to the agreement made at Rome; and they shall
observe these undertakings with no thought of their own
advantage. [27] In like manner, if the Jews be first threatened,
it shall be for the Romans to give aid as the occasion
demands, most willingly; [28] providing neither corn nor arms,
money nor ships, to any that take part against them, according to the agreement made at Rome;[a] and they shall observe
these undertakings honourably. [29] Upon these terms the
Romans and the Jewish people are agreed; [30] if hereafter it
should be the will of both parties[b] to enlarge or to restrict
them, they may do so at their discretion, and such enlargement or restriction shall have force accordingly. [31] As for the

a The Latin has, 'according to the agreement made by the Romans'.
b 'Both parties'; according to the Latin version, 'either party', but such a stipulation would make the whole treaty ineffectual.

TODAY'S ENGLISH VERSION

21 The Romans accepted the proposal, 22 and what follows
is a copy of the letter which was engraved on bronze tablets
and sent to Jerusalem to remain there as a record of the
treaty:

23 "May things go well forever for the Romans and for
the Jewish nation on land and sea! May they never have
enemies, and may they never go to war! 24 But if war is
declared first against Rome or any of her allies anywhere,
25 the Jewish nation will come to her aid with wholehearted support, as the situation may require. 26 And to those
at war with her, the Jews shall not give or supply food,
arms, money, or ships, as was agreed in Rome. The Jews
must carry out their obligations without receiving anything in return.

27 "In the same way, if war is declared first against the
Jewish nation, the Romans will come to their aid with
hearty support, as the situation may require. 28 And to
their enemies there shall not be given or supplied food,
arms, money, or ships, as was agreed in Rome. The
Romans must carry out their obligations without deception.

29 "These are the terms of the treaty that the Romans
have made with the Jewish people. 30 But if, in the future,
both parties shall agree to add or remove anything, they
shall act on their decision, and whatever they add or
remove shall be valid.

NEW REVISED STANDARD VERSION

pleased them, 22 and this is a copy of the letter that they
wrote in reply, on bronze tablets, and sent to Jerusalem to
remain with them there as a memorial of peace and alliance:

23 "May all go well with the Romans and with the nation
of the Jews at sea and on land forever, and may sword and
enemy be far from them. 24 If war comes first to Rome or to
any of their allies in all their dominion, 25 the nation of the
Jews shall act as their allies wholeheartedly, as the occasion
may indicate to them. 26 To the enemy that makes war they
shall not give or supply grain, arms, money, or ships, just as
Rome has decided; and they shall keep their obligations
without receiving any return. 27 In the same way, if war
comes first to the nation of the Jews, the Romans shall willingly act as their allies, as the occasion may indicate to
them. 28 And to their enemies there shall not be given grain,
arms, money, or ships, just as Rome has decided; and they
shall keep these obligations and do so without deceit.
29 Thus on these terms the Romans make a treaty with the
Jewish people. 30 If after these terms are in effect both parties
shall determine to add or delete anything, they shall do so at
their discretion, and any addition or deletion that they may
make shall be valid.

NEW AMERICAN BIBLE

Romans, 22 and this is a copy of the reply they inscribed on
bronze tablets and sent to Jerusalem, to remain there with
the Jews as a record of peace and alliance:

23 "May it be well with the Romans and the Jewish nation
at sea and on land forever; may sword and enemy be far
from them. 24 But if war is first made on Rome, or any of its
allies in any of their dominions, 25 the Jewish nation will
help them wholeheartedly, as the occasion shall demand;
26 and to those who wage war they shall not give nor provide
grain, arms, money, or ships; this is Rome's decision. They
shall fulfill their obligations without receiving any recompense. 27 In the same way, if war is made first on the Jewish
nation, the Romans will help them willingly, as the occasion
shall demand, 28 and to those who are attacking them there
shall not be given grain, arms, money, or ships; this is
Rome's decision. They shall fulfill their obligations without
deception. 29 On these terms the Romans have made an
agreement with the Jewish people. 30 But if both parties
hereafter decide to add or take away anything, they shall do
as they choose, and whatever they shall add or take away
shall be valid.

NEW JERUSALEM BIBLE

21 The proposal met with the approval of the senators.
22 Here is a copy of the rescript which they engraved on
bronze tablets and sent to Jerusalem to be kept there by the
Jews as a record of peace and alliance:

23 'Good fortune attend the Romans and the Jewish nation
by sea and land for ever; may sword or enemy be far from
them!

24 'If war comes first to Rome or any of her allies
throughout her dominions, 25 the Jewish nation will take
action as her ally, as occasion may require, and do it
wholeheartedly. 26 They will not give or supply to the
enemy any grain, arms, money or ships: thus has Rome
decided, and they are to honour their obligations without
guarantees. 27 In the same way, if war comes first to the
Jewish nation, the Romans will support them energetically
as occasion may offer, 28 and the aggressor will not be furnished with grain, arms, money or ships: such is the
Roman decision, and they will honour these obligations
without treachery. 29 Such are the articles under which the
Romans have concluded their treaty with the Jewish people. 30 If, later, either party should decide to make any
addition or deletion, they will be free to do so, and any
such addition or deletion will be binding.

GREEK OLD TESTAMENT

ἔσται κύρια. 31 καὶ περὶ τῶν κακῶν, ὧν ὁ βασιλεὺς Δημήτριος συντελεῖται εἰς αὐτούς, ἐγράψαμεν αὐτῷ λέγοντες
Διὰ τί ἐβάρυνας τὸν ζυγόν σου ἐπὶ τοὺς φίλους ἡμῶν τοὺς
συμμάχους Ιουδαίους; 32 ἐὰν οὖν ἔτι ἐντύχωσιν κατὰ σοῦ,
ποιήσομεν αὐτοῖς τὴν κρίσιν καὶ πολεμήσομέν σε διὰ τῆς
θαλάσσης καὶ διὰ τῆς ξηρᾶς.

9 Καὶ ἤκουσεν Δημήτριος ὅτι ἔπεσεν Νικάνωρ καὶ ἡ δύναμις αὐτοῦ ἐν πολέμῳ, καὶ προσέθετο τὸν Βακχίδην καὶ
τὸν Ἄλκιμον ἐκ δευτέρου ἀποστεῖλαι εἰς γῆν Ιουδα καὶ τὸ
δεξιὸν κέρας μετ᾽ αὐτῶν. 2 καὶ ἐπορεύθησαν ὁδὸν τὴν εἰς
Γαλγαλα καὶ παρενέβαλον ἐπὶ Μαισαλωθ τὴν ἐν Αρβηλοις
καὶ προκατελάβοντο αὐτὴν καὶ ἀπώλεσαν ψυχὰς ἀνθρώπων
πολλάς. 3 καὶ τοῦ μηνὸς τοῦ πρώτου ἔτους τοῦ δευτέρου καὶ
πεντηκοστοῦ καὶ ἑκατοστοῦ παρενέβαλον ἐπὶ Ιερουσαλημ·
4 καὶ ἀπῆραν καὶ ἐπορεύθησαν εἰς Βερεαν ἐν εἴκοσι χιλιάσιν
ἀνδρῶν καὶ δισχιλίᾳ ἵππῳ. 5 καὶ Ιουδας ἦν παρεμβεβληκὼς
ἐν Ελασα, καὶ τρισχίλιοι ἄνδρες μετ᾽ αὐτοῦ ἐκλεκτοί. 6 καὶ
εἶδον τὸ πλῆθος τῶν δυνάμεων ὅτι πολλοί εἰσιν, καὶ ἐφοβήθησαν σφόδρα· καὶ ἐξερρύησαν πολλοὶ ἀπὸ τῆς παρεμβολῆς,
οὐ κατελείφθησαν ἐξ αὐτῶν ἀλλ᾽ ἢ ὀκτακόσιοι ἄνδρες. 7 καὶ
εἶδεν Ιουδας ὅτι ἀπερρύη ἡ παρεμβολὴ αὐτοῦ καὶ ὁ πόλεμος
ἔθλιβεν αὐτόν, καὶ συνετρίβη τῇ καρδίᾳ, ὅτι οὐκ εἶχεν
καιρὸν συναγαγεῖν αὐτούς. 8 καὶ ἐξελύθη καὶ εἶπεν τοῖς
καταλειφθεῖσιν Ἀναστῶμεν καὶ ἀναβῶμεν ἐπὶ τοὺς ὑπεναντίους ἡμῶν, ἐὰν ἄρα δυνώμεθα πολεμῆσαι πρὸς αὐτούς.

KING JAMES VERSION

31 And as touching the evils that Demetrius doeth to the Jews, we have written unto him, saying, Wherefore hast thou made thy yoke heavy upon our friends and confederates the Jews?

32 If therefore they complain any more against thee, we will do them justice, and fight with thee by sea and by land.

9 Furthermore when Demetrius heard that Nicanor and his host were slain in battle, he sent Bacchides and Alcimus into the land of Judea the second time, and with them the chief strength of his host:

2 Who went forth by the way that leadeth to Galgala, and pitched their tents before Masaloth, which is in Arbela, and after they had won it, they slew much people.

3 Also the first month of the hundred fifty and second year they encamped before Jerusalem:

4 From whence they removed, and went to Berea, with twenty thousand footmen and two thousand horsemen.

5 Now Judas had pitched his tents at Eleasa, and three thousand chosen men with him:

6 Who seeing the multitude of the other army to be so great were sore afraid; whereupon many conveyed themselves out of the host, insomuch as there abode of them no more but eight hundred men.

7 When Judas therefore saw that his host slipt away, and that the battle pressed upon him, he was sore troubled in mind, and much distressed, for that he had no time to gather them together.

8 Nevertheless unto them that remained he said, Let us arise and go up against our enemies, if peradventure we may be able to fight with them.

DOUAY OLD TESTAMENT

31 Moreover concerning the evils that Demetrius the king hath done against them, we have written to him, saying: Why hast thou made thy yoke heavy upon our friends, and allies, the Jews?

32 If therefore they come again to us complaining of thee, we will do them justice, and will make war against thee by sea and land.

9 IN the mean time when Demetrius heard that Nicanor and his army were fallen in battle, he sent again Bacchides and Alcimus into Judea; and the right wing of his army with them.

2 And they took the road that leadeth to Galgal, and they camped in Masaloth, which is in Arabella: and they made themselves masters of it, and slew many people.

3 In the first month of the hundred and fifty-second year they brought the army to Jerusalem:

4 And they arose, and went to Berea with twenty thousand men, and two thousand horsemen.

5 Now Judas had pitched his tents in Laisa, and three thousand chosen men with him:

6 And they saw the multitude of the army that they were many, and they were seized with great fear: and many withdrew themselves out of the camp, and there remained of them no more than eight hundred men.

7 And Judas saw that his army slipped away, and the battle pressed upon him, and his heart was cast down: because he had not time to gather them together, and he was discouraged.

8 Then he said to them that remained: Let us arise, and go against our enemies, if we may be able to fight against them.

KNOX TRANSLATION

wrong done by king Demetrius, we have sent him warning,
What meanest thou, to burden with so heavy a yoke the
Jewish people, our friends and allies? 32 Let them complain
of thee once more, and we will surely give them redress, by
land and sea levying war against thee.

9 While this was afoot, news came to Demetrius that
Nicanor and his men had perished in the encounter. But
he would still have his way; Bacchides and Alcimus should
be sent back to Judaea, and the northern command[a] of his
army with them. 2 Marching out along the Galgala road, they
encamped at Masaloth in Arbella; the town was surprised,
and many of its inhabitants massacred. 3 Then, in the first
month of the hundred and fifty-second year, they began an
attack on Jerusalem, 4 moving their camp to Berea. It was a
force of twenty thousand foot and two thousand horse;
5 Judas, encamped at Laisa, had three thousand picked followers with him, 6 but these were greatly daunted when they
saw what heavy odds were against them, and began to
desert their lines, till no more than eight hundred of them
were left. 7 One by one they slipped away, and raise fresh
levies he might not, with the battle so hard upon his heels;
what wonder if Judas lost heart, and was unmanned? 8 Yet
said he to the remnant that was left him, Up, go we to the
attack, and try conclusions with the enemy! 9 In vain they

a 'The northern command'; literally, 'the right wing'. Presumably this means the right extremity from Demetrius' point of view.

TODAY'S ENGLISH VERSION

31 "Furthermore, concerning the wrongs which King
Demetrius is doing against the Jews, we have written him
as follows, 'Why have you treated our friends and allies,
the Jews, so harshly? 32 If they complain to us about you
one more time, we will support their cause and go to war
against you on land and sea.' "

9 When Demetrius heard that Nicanor and his army had
been annihilated, he again sent Bacchides and Alcimus
to the land of Judea, this time with the Syrian wing of the
army. 2 They moved along Gilgal Road, laid siege to
Mesaloth in Arbela, captured it, and killed many people. 3 In
the first month of the year 152,[a] they set up camp opposite
Jerusalem. 4 From there they marched to Berea with 20,000
infantry and 2,000 cavalry.

5 Judas had camped at Elasa, with 3,000 experienced soldiers. 6 But when they saw the enormous size of the enemy
army, they were terrified. So many men deserted that only
800 Jewish soldiers were left. 7 When Judas saw that his
army was dwindling away and that the battle was about to
begin, he was worried because there was not enough time to
bring his army together. 8 He was discouraged, but he said
to those who were still with him, "Let's prepare for the
attack; maybe we can still defeat them."

[a] THE YEAR 152: *This corresponds to 160 B.C.*

NEW REVISED STANDARD VERSION

31 "Concerning the wrongs that King Demetrius is doing
to them, we have written to him as follows, 'Why have you
made your yoke heavy on our friends and allies the Jews?
32 If now they appeal again for help against you, we will
defend their rights and fight you on sea and on land.' "

9 When Demetrius heard that Nicanor and his army had
fallen in battle, he sent Bacchides and Alcimus into the
land of Judah a second time, and with them the right wing of
the army. 2 They went by the road that leads to Gilgal and
encamped against Mesaloth in Arbela, and they took it and
killed many people. 3 In the first month of the one hundred
fifty-second year[a] they encamped against Jerusalem; 4 then
they marched off and went to Berea with twenty thousand
foot soldiers and two thousand cavalry.

5 Now Judas was encamped in Elasa, and with him were
three thousand picked men. 6 When they saw the huge number of the enemy forces, they were greatly frightened, and
many slipped away from the camp, until no more than eight
hundred of them were left.

7 When Judas saw that his army had slipped away and
the battle was imminent, he was crushed in spirit, for he had
no time to assemble them. 8 He became faint, but he said to
those who were left, "Let us get up and go against our enemies. We may have the strength to fight them." 9 But they

[a] 160 B.C.

NEW AMERICAN BIBLE

31 "Moreover, concerning the wrongs that King Demetrius
has done to them, we have written to him thus: 'Why have
you made your yoke heavy upon our friends and allies the
Jews? 32 If they complain about you again, we will do them
justice and make war on you by land and sea.' "

9 When Demetrius heard that Nicanor and his army had
fallen in battle, he again sent Bacchides and Alcimus
into the land of Judah, along with the right wing of his army.
2 They took the road to Galilee, and camping opposite the
ascent at Arbela, they captured it and killed many people.
3 In the first month of the year one hundred and fifty-two,
they encamped against Jerusalem. 4 Then they set out for
Berea with twenty thousand men and two thousand cavalry.
5 Judas, with three thousand picked men, had camped at
Elasa. 6 When his men saw the great number of the troops,
they were very much afraid, and many slipped away from
the camp, until only eight hundred men remained.

7 As Judas saw that his army was melting away just when
the battle was imminent, he was panic-stricken, because he
had no time to gather them together. 8 But in spite of his dis-
couragement, he said to those who remained: "Let us go forward to meet our enemies; perhaps we can put up a good

NEW JERUSALEM BIBLE

31 'As regards the wrongs done to them by King
Demetrius, we have written to him in these terms: Why
have you made your yoke lie heavy on our friends and
allies the Jews? 32 If they appeal against you again, we
shall uphold their rights and make war on you by sea and
land.'

9 Demetrius, hearing that Nicanor and his army had fallen
in battle, sent Bacchides and Alcimus a second time into
Judaea, and with them the right wing of his army. 2 They
took the road to Galilee and besieged Mesaloth in Arbela,
and captured it, putting many people to death. 3 In the first
month of the year 152, they encamped outside Jerusalem;
4 they then moved on, making their way to Beer-Zaith with
twenty thousand foot and two thousand horse. 5 Judas lay in
camp at Elasa, with three thousand picked men. 6 When
they saw the huge size of the enemy forces they were terrified, and many slipped out of the camp, until no more than
eight hundred of the force were left. 7 With battle now
inevitable, Judas realised that his army had melted away; he
was aghast, for he had no time to rally them. 8 Yet, dismayed as he was, he said to those who were left, 'Up! Let us
face the enemy; we may yet have the strength to fight them.'

GREEK OLD TESTAMENT

9 καὶ ἀπέστρεφον αὐτὸν λέγοντες Οὐ μὴ δυνώμεθα, ἀλλ᾽ ἢ
σῴζωμεν τὰς ἑαυτῶν ψυχὰς τὸ νῦν, ἐπιστρέψωμεν καὶ οἱ
ἀδελφοὶ ἡμῶν καὶ πολεμήσωμεν πρὸς αὐτούς, ἡμεῖς δὲ ὀλίγοι. 10 καὶ εἶπεν Ιουδας Μὴ γένοιτο ποιῆσαι τὸ πρᾶγμα
τοῦτο, φυγεῖν ἀπ᾽ αὐτῶν, καὶ εἰ ἤγγικεν ὁ καιρὸς ἡμῶν, καὶ
ἀποθάνωμεν ἐν ἀνδρείᾳ χάριν τῶν ἀδελφῶν ἡμῶν καὶ μὴ
καταλίπωμεν αἰτίαν τῇ δόξῃ ἡμῶν. 11 καὶ ἀπῆρεν ἡ δύναμις
ἀπὸ τῆς παρεμβολῆς καὶ ἔστησαν εἰς συνάντησιν αὐτοῖς,
καὶ ἐμερίσθη ἡ ἵππος εἰς δύο μέρη, καὶ οἱ σφενδονῆται καὶ
οἱ τοξόται προεπορεύοντο τῆς δυνάμεως, καὶ οἱ πρωταγω-
νισταὶ πάντες οἱ δυνατοί, Βακχίδης δὲ ἦν ἐν τῷ δεξιῷ κέρα-
τι. 12 καὶ ἤγγισεν ἡ φάλαγξ ἐκ τῶν δύο μερῶν καὶ ἐφώνουν
ταῖς σάλπιγξιν, καὶ ἐσάλπισαν οἱ παρὰ Ιουδου καὶ αὐτοὶ
ταῖς σάλπιγξιν· 13 καὶ ἐσαλεύθη ἡ γῆ ἀπὸ τῆς φωνῆς τῶν
παρεμβολῶν, καὶ ἐγένετο ὁ πόλεμος συνημμένος ἀπὸ πρωίθεν ἕως ἑσπέρας. 14 καὶ εἶδεν Ιουδας ὅτι Βακχίδης καὶ τὸ
στερέωμα τῆς παρεμβολῆς ἐν τοῖς δεξιοῖς, καὶ συνῆλθον
αὐτῷ πάντες οἱ εὔψυχοι τῇ καρδίᾳ, 15 καὶ συνετρίβη τὸ
δεξιὸν μέρος ἀπ᾽ αὐτῶν, καὶ ἐδίωκεν ὀπίσω αὐτῶν ἕως
Αζωτου ὄρους. 16 καὶ οἱ εἰς τὸ ἀριστερὸν κέρας εἶδον ὅτι
συνετρίβη τὸ δεξιὸν κέρας, καὶ ἐπέστρεψαν κατὰ πόδας
Ιουδου καὶ τῶν μετ᾽ αὐτοῦ ἐκ τῶν ὄπισθεν. 17 καὶ ἐβαρύνθη ὁ
πόλεμος, καὶ ἔπεσον τραυματίαι πολλοὶ ἐκ τούτων καὶ ἐκ
τούτων, 18 καὶ Ιουδας ἔπεσεν, καὶ οἱ λοιποὶ ἔφυγον. 19 καὶ
ἦρεν Ιωναθαν καὶ Σιμων Ιουδαν τὸν ἀδελφὸν αὐτῶν καὶ
ἔθαψαν αὐτὸν ἐν τῷ τάφῳ τῶν πατέρων αὐτοῦ ἐν Μωδεϊν.

KING JAMES VERSION

9 But they dehorted him, saying, We shall never be able: let us now rather save our lives, and hereafter we will return with our brethren, and fight against them: for we are but few.

10 Then Judas said, God forbid that I should do this thing, and flee away from them: if our time be come, let us die manfully for our brethren, and let us not stain our honour.

11 With that the host *of Bacchides* removed out of their tents, and stood over against them, their horsemen being divided into two troops, and their slingers and archers going before the host, and they that marched in the foreward were all mighty men.

12 As for Bacchides, he was in the right wing: so the host drew near on the two parts, and sounded their trumpets.

13 They also of Judas' side, even they sounded their trumpets also, so that the earth shook at the noise of the armies, and the battle continued from morning till night.

14 Now when Judas perceived that Bacchides and the strength of his army were on the right side, he took with him all the hardy men,

15 Who discomfited the right wing, and pursued them unto the mount Azotus.

16 But when they of the left wing saw that they of the right wing were discomfited, they followed upon Judas and those that were with him hard at the heels from behind:

17 Whereupon there was a sore battle, insomuch as many were slain on both parts.

18 Judas also was killed, and the remnant fled.

19 Then Jonathan and Simon took Judas their brother, and buried him in the sepulchre of his fathers in Modin.

DOUAY OLD TESTAMENT

9 But they dissuaded him, saying: We shall not be able, but let us save our lives now, and return to our brethren, and then we will fight against them: for we are but few.

10 Then Judas said: God forbid we should do this thing, and flee away from them: but if our time be come, let us die manfully for our brethren, and let us not stain our glory.

11 And the army removed out of the camp, and they stood over against them: and the horsemen were divided into two troops, and the slingers, and the archers went before the army, and they that were in the front *were* all men of valour.

12 And Bacchides was in the right wing, and the legion drew near on two sides, and they sounded the trumpets:

13 And they also that were on Judas' side, even they also cried out, and the earth shook at the noise of the armies: and the battle was fought from morning even unto the evening.

14 And Judas perceived that the stronger part of the army of Bacchides was on the right side, and all the stout of heart came together with him:

15 And the right wing was discomfited by them, and he pursued them even to the mount Azotus.

16 And they that were in the left wing saw that the right wing was discomfited, and they followed after Judas, and them that were with him, at their back:

17 And the battle was hard fought, and there fell many wounded of the one side and of the other.

18 And Judas was slain, and the rest fled away.

19 And Jonathan and Simon took Judas their brother, and buried him in the sepulchre of their fathers in the city of Modin.

KNOX TRANSLATION

sought to dissuade him; Speed we may not, they said; let us
save our skins now, we may yet join hands with our
brethren, and do battle hereafter; why, we are but a handful!
10 Nay, said Judas, that may I never do; what, shew them our
backs? If our time is come, die we manfully in our brethren's
cause, nor suffer any foul blot to fall on our name!
11 By this, the opposing army had moved forward out of its
lines, and stood fronting them; here were the two bodies of
horse, the slingers and archers going on before the rest, and
the choice troops that would bear the shock of the encounter;
12 here was Bacchides himself, on the right wing. This side
and that the phalanx drew nearer, with a great blowing of
trumpets, 13 and Judas' men, they raised a great cry on their
own part, till the earth rang again with the noise of the two
armies. Thus begun, the battle went on from morning till
dusk. 14 On the right, where he saw Bacchides' army was
strongest, Judas made the attack, and all the most valiant of
his men with him; 15 broke their line, and chased them all
the way to mount Azotus. 16 But now those on the left, seeing their right wing routed, cut off Judas and his men from
the rear; 17 now indeed the battle grew fierce, and there were
many fell wounded on either part, 18 till at last Judas fell,
and with that, all the rest took to their heels.
19 As for his body, his brothers Jonathan and Simon recovered it, and so buried him where his fathers were buried, in

TODAY'S ENGLISH VERSION

9 His men tried to talk him out of it. "We are not strong
enough," they said. "Let's retreat now and save our lives.
Then we can return with reinforcements and fight the
enemy. We don't have enough men now."
10 Judas replied, "Never let it be said that I ran from a battle. If our time has come, let's die bravely for our fellow Jews
and not leave any stain on our honor."
11 The Syrian army came out of the camp and took up battle positions against the Jews. The cavalry was divided into
two parts. The shock troops were in the front lines, but the
archers and those who used slings went ahead of the main
formation. 12 Bacchides took his position on the right. The
infantry advanced, protected on both sides by the cavalry,
and the war trumpets were blown. The soldiers of Judas also
sounded their trumpets. 13 The ground shook from the noise
when the two armies met, and they fought from morning
until evening.
14 When Judas saw that Bacchides and the main force of
the Syrian army was on the right, all his bravest men joined
him, 15 and they crushed the Syrians' right wing. They pursued them as far as the foothills.[a] 16 But when the Syrians
on the left wing saw that their right wing had been crushed,
they turned to attack Judas and his men from the rear.
17 The fighting became very fierce, and many on both sides
were killed. 18 Finally Judas himself was killed. Then all his
men fled. 19 Jonathan and Simon took their brother's body
and buried it in the family tomb at Modein, 20 and there at

[a] *Probable text* the foothills; *Greek* Mount Azotus.

NEW REVISED STANDARD VERSION

tried to dissuade him, saying, "We do not have the strength.
Let us rather save our own lives now, and let us come back
with our kindred and fight them; we are too few." 10 But
Judas said, "Far be it from us to do such a thing as to flee
from them. If our time has come, let us die bravely for our
kindred, and leave no cause to question our honor."
11 Then the army of Bacchides[a] marched out from the
camp and took its stand for the encounter. The cavalry was
divided into two companies, and the slingers and the archers
went ahead of the army, as did all the chief warriors.
12 Bacchides was on the right wing. Flanked by the two companies, the phalanx advanced to the sound of the trumpets;
and the men with Judas also blew their trumpets. 13 The
earth was shaken by the noise of the armies, and the battle
raged from morning until evening.
14 Judas saw that Bacchides and the strength of his army
were on the right; then all the stouthearted men went with
him, 15 and they crushed the right wing, and he pursued
them as far as Mount Azotus. 16 When those on the left wing
saw that the right wing was crushed, they turned and followed close behind Judas and his men. 17 The battle became
desperate, and many on both sides were wounded and fell.
18 Judas also fell, and the rest fled.
19 Then Jonathan and Simon took their brother Judas and
buried him in the tomb of their ancestors at Modein, 20 and

[a] Gk lacks *of Bacchides*

NEW AMERICAN BIBLE

fight against them." 9 They tried to dissuade him, saying:
"We certainly cannot. Let us save our lives now, and come
back with our kinsmen, and then fight against them. Now
we are too few." 10 But Judas said: "Far be it from me to do
such a thing as to flee from them! If our time has come, let
us die bravely for our kinsmen and not leave a stain upon
our glory!"
11 Then the army of Bacchides moved out of camp and took
its position for combat. The cavalry were divided into two
squadrons, and the slingers and the archers came on ahead
of the army, and all the valiant men were in the front line.
12 Bacchides was on the right wing. Flanked by the two
squadrons, the phalanx attacked as they blew their trumpets.
Those who were on Judas' side also blew their trumpets.
13 The earth shook with the noise of the armies, and the battle raged from morning until evening. 14 Seeing that
Bacchides was on the right, with the main force of his army,
Judas, with all the most stouthearted rallying to him,
15 drove back the right wing and pursued them as far as the
mountain slopes. 16 But when the men on the left wing saw
that the right wing was driven back, they turned and followed Judas and his men, taking them in the rear. 17 The
battle was fought desperately, and many on both sides fell
wounded. 18 Then Judas fell, and the rest fled.
19 Jonathan and Simon took their brother Judas and buried
him in the tomb of their fathers at Modein. 20 All Israel

NEW JERUSALEM BIBLE

9 His men tried to dissuade him, declaring, 'We have no
strength for anything but to escape with our lives this time;
then we can come back with our brothers to fight them; by
ourselves we are too few.' 10 Judas retorted, 'That I should
do such a thing as run away from them! If our time has
come, at least let us die like men for our countrymen, and
leave nothing to tarnish our reputation.'
11 The army marched out of camp and drew up, facing the
enemy. The cavalry was drawn up in two squadrons; the
slingers and archers marched in the van of the army, and all
the best fighters were put in the front rank; 12 Bacchides was
on the right wing. The phalanx advanced from between the
two squadrons, sounding the trumpets; the men on Judas'
side also blew their trumpets, 13 and the earth shook with
the noise of the armies. The engagement lasted from morning until evening.
14 Judas saw that Bacchides and the main strength of his
army lay on the right; all the stout-hearted rallied to him,
15 and they crushed the right wing, pursuing them as far as
the Azara Hills. 16 But when the Syrians on the left wing
saw that the right had been broken, they turned and followed hot on the heels of Judas and his men to take them in
the rear. 17 The fight became desperate, and there were many
casualties on both sides. 18 Judas himself fell, and the remnant fled.
19 Jonathan and Simon took up their brother Judas and
buried him in his ancestral tomb at Modein. 20 All Israel

GREEK OLD TESTAMENT

[20] καὶ ἔκλαυσαν αὐτὸν καὶ ἐκόψαντο αὐτὸν πᾶς Ισραηλ κοπετὸν μέγαν καὶ ἐπένθουν ἡμέρας πολλὰς καὶ εἶπον [21] Πῶς
ἔπεσεν δυνατὸς σῴζων τὸν Ισραηλ. [22] καὶ τὰ περισσὰ τῶν
λόγων Ιουδου καὶ τῶν πολέμων καὶ τῶν ἀνδραγαθιῶν, ὧν
ἐποίησεν, καὶ τῆς μεγαλωσύνης αὐτοῦ οὐ κατεγράφη· πολλὰ
γὰρ ἦν σφόδρα.
[23] Καὶ ἐγένετο μετὰ τὴν τελευτὴν Ιουδου ἐξέκυψαν οἱ
ἄνομοι ἐν πᾶσιν τοῖς ὁρίοις Ισραηλ, καὶ ἀνέτειλαν πάντες
οἱ ἐργαζόμενοι τὴν ἀδικίαν. [24] ἐν ταῖς ἡμέραις ἐκείναις
ἐγενήθη λιμὸς μέγας σφόδρα, καὶ αὐτομόλησεν ἡ χώρα μετ'
αὐτῶν. [25] καὶ ἐξέλεξεν Βακχίδης τοὺς ἀσεβεῖς ἄνδρας καὶ
κατέστησεν αὐτοὺς κυρίους τῆς χώρας. [26] καὶ ἐξεζήτουν
καὶ ἠρεύνων τοὺς φίλους Ιουδου καὶ ἦγον αὐτοὺς πρὸς
Βακχίδην, καὶ ἐξεδίκα αὐτοὺς καὶ ἐνέπαιζεν αὐτοῖς. [27] καὶ
ἐγένετο θλῖψις μεγάλη ἐν τῷ Ισραηλ, ἥτις οὐκ ἐγένετο ἀφ'
ἧς ἡμέρας οὐκ ὤφθη προφήτης αὐτοῖς. [28] καὶ ἠθροίσθησαν
πάντες οἱ φίλοι Ιουδου καὶ εἶπον τῷ Ιωναθαν [29] Ἀφ' οὗ ὁ
ἀδελφός σου Ιουδας τετελεύτηκεν, καὶ ἀνὴρ ὅμοιος αὐτῷ οὐκ
ἔστιν ἐξελθεῖν καὶ εἰσελθεῖν πρὸς τοὺς ἐχθροὺς καὶ Βακχίδην καὶ ἐν τοῖς ἐχθραίνουσιν τοῦ ἔθνους ἡμῶν· [30] νῦν οὖν σὲ
ᾑρετισάμεθα σήμερον τοῦ εἶναι ἀντ' αὐτοῦ ἡμῖν εἰς ἄρχοντα
καὶ ἡγούμενον τοῦ πολεμῆσαι τὸν πόλεμον ἡμῶν. [31] καὶ
ἐπεδέξατο Ιωναθαν ἐν τῷ καιρῷ ἐκείνῳ τὴν ἥγησιν καὶ ἀνέστη ἀντὶ Ιουδου τοῦ ἀδελφοῦ αὐτοῦ.

KING JAMES VERSION

20 Moreover they bewailed him, and all Israel made great lamentation for him, and mourned many days, saying,

21 How is the valiant man fallen, that delivered Israel!

22 As for the other things concerning Judas and his wars, and the noble acts which he did, and his greatness, they are not written: for they were very many.

23 ¶ Now after the death of Judas the wicked began to put forth their heads in all the coasts of Israel, and there arose up all such as wrought iniquity.

24 In those days also was there a very great famine, by reason whereof the country revolted, and went with them.

25 Then Bacchides chose the wicked men, and made them lords of the country.

26 And they made enquiry and search for Judas' friends, and brought them unto Bacchides, who took vengeance of them, and used them despitefully.

27 So was there a great affliction in Israel, the like whereof was not since the time that a prophet was not seen among them.

28 For this cause all Judas' friends came together, and said unto Jonathan,

29 Since thy brother Judas died, we have no man like him to go forth against our enemies, and Bacchides, and against them of our nation that are adversaries to us.

30 Now therefore we have chosen thee this day to be our prince and captain in his stead, that thou mayest fight our battles.

31 Upon this Jonathan took the governance upon him at that time, and rose up instead of his brother Judas.

DOUAY OLD TESTAMENT

20 And all the people of Israel bewailed him with great lamentation, and they mourned for him many days.

21 And said: How is the mighty man fallen, that saved the people of Israel!

22 But the rest of the words of the wars of Judas, and of the noble acts that he did, and of his greatness, are not written: for they were very many.

23 And it came to pass after the death of Judas, that the wicked began to put forth their heads in all the confines of Israel, and all the workers of iniquity rose up.

24 In those days there was a very great famine, and they and all their country yielded to Bacchides.

25 And Bacchides chose the wicked men, and made them lords of the country:

26 And they sought out, and made diligent search after the friends of Judas, and brought them to Bacchides, and he took vengeance of them, and abused them.

27 And there was a great tribulation in Israel, such as was not since the day, that there was no prophet seen in Israel.

28 And all the friends of Judas came together, and said to Jonathan:

29 Since thy brother Judas died, there is not a man like him to go forth against our enemies, Bacchides, and them that are the enemies of our nation.

30 Now therefore we have chosen thee this day to be our prince, and captain in his stead to fight our battles.

31 So Jonathan took upon him the government at that time, and rose up in the place of Judas his brother.

KNOX TRANSLATION

the city of Modin. [20] Great lament all Israel made over him,
and long they mourned him; [21] Here is a great warrior fallen,
they said, that once brought his people deliverance! [22] What
other battles Judas fought, deeds did, greatness achieved,
you shall not find set down here; too long the record of
them.
[23] Once Judas was dead, there was no corner in Israel but
treason began to shew its face there, and lawlessness to
abound; [24] under such leadership the whole country, at this
time much distressed by famine, went over to Bacchides.
[25] Good care he took to choose out godless men, that should
have the governance of his territory; [26] and these raised a
hue and cry after Judas' partisans, haling them before
Bacchides to be punished and used despitefully; [27] never,
since prophecy died out among them, had the men of Israel
known such distress. [28] And now all that had loved Judas
rallied to Jonathan instead; [29] Since thy brother's death, they
told him, none is left to take the field against our enemies as
he did, this Bacchides and all else that bear a grudge against
our race.[a] [30] There is but one way of it; this day we have
chosen thee to be our ruler, our chieftain, to fight our battles
for us. [31] So, from that day forward, Jonathan took command, in succession to his brother Judas. [32] Bacchides no

[a] The meaning of the Greek text is, 'all those of our own race that bear a grudge against us'.

TODAY'S ENGLISH VERSION

the tomb they wept for him. All Israel mourned for him in
great sorrow for many days. They said, 21 "It can't be! The
mighty hero and savior of Israel has been killed!"
22 The other deeds of Judas, his battles, his courageous
deeds, and his great accomplishments, were too many to
write down.
23 After the death of Judas, the lawless traitors began to
reappear everywhere in Judea, and all the wicked people
returned. 24 Also at that time there was a severe famine, and
the whole country went over to the side of the renegades.
25 Bacchides deliberately appointed some renegade Jews as
rulers over the country. 26 These men hunted down the
friends of Judas and brought them all before Bacchides, and
he subjected them to torture and humiliation. 27 It was a
time of great trouble for Israel, worse than anything that had
happened to them since the time prophets ceased to appear
among them.
28 Then all the friends of Judas came together and said to
Jonathan, 29 "Since your brother Judas died, there has been
no one like him to lead us against our enemies, against
Bacchides and those of our own nation who oppose us. 30 So
today we choose you to succeed him as our ruler and commander to carry on our war." 31 Jonathan accepted the leadership that day and took the place of his brother Judas.

NEW REVISED STANDARD VERSION

wept for him. All Israel made great lamentation for him; they
mourned many days and said,
21 "How is the mighty fallen,
the savior of Israel!"
22 Now the rest of the acts of Judas, and his wars and the
brave deeds that he did, and his greatness, have not been
recorded, but they were very many.
23 After the death of Judas, the renegades emerged in all
parts of Israel; all the wrongdoers reappeared. 24 In those
days a very great famine occurred, and the country went over
to their side. 25 Bacchides chose the godless and put them in
charge of the country. 26 They made inquiry and searched for
the friends of Judas, and brought them to Bacchides, who
took vengeance on them and made sport of them. 27 So there
was great distress in Israel, such as had not been since the
time that prophets ceased to appear among them.
28 Then all the friends of Judas assembled and said to
Jonathan, 29 "Since the death of your brother Judas there has
been no one like him to go against our enemies and
Bacchides, and to deal with those of our nation who hate us.
30 Now therefore we have chosen you today to take his place
as our ruler and leader, to fight our battle." 31 So Jonathan
accepted the leadership at that time in place of his brother
Judas.

NEW AMERICAN BIBLE

bewailed him in great grief. They mourned for him many
days, and they said, 21 "How the mighty one has fallen, the
savior of Israel!" 22 The other acts of Judas, his battles, the
brave deeds he performed, and his greatness have not been
recorded; but they were very many.
23 After the death of Judas, the transgressors of the law
raised their heads in every part of Israel, and all kinds of
evildoers appeared. 24 In those days there was a very great
famine, and the country deserted to them. 25 Bacchides chose
impious men and made them masters of the country.
26 These sought out and hunted down the friends of Judas
and brought them to Bacchides, who punished and derided
them. 27 There had not been such great distress in Israel
since the time prophets ceased to appear among the people.
28 Then all the friends of Judas came together and said to
Jonathan: 29 "Since your brother Judas died, there has been
no one like him to oppose our enemies, Bacchides and those
who are hostile to our nation. 30 Now therefore we have chosen you today to be our ruler and leader in his place, and to
fight our battle." 31 From that moment Jonathan accepted the
leadership, and took the place of Judas his brother.

NEW JERUSALEM BIBLE

wept and mourned him deeply and for many days they
repeated this dirge. 21 'What a downfall for the strong man,
the man who kept Israel safe!' 22 The other deeds of Judas,
the battles he fought, the exploits he performed, and all his
titles to greatness have not been recorded; but they were very
many.
23 After the death of Judas, the renegades came out of hiding throughout Israel and all the evil-doers reappeared. 24 At
that time there was a severe famine, and the country went
over to their side. 25 Bacchides deliberately chose the enemies of religion to administer the country. 26 These traced
and searched out the friends of Judas and brought them
before Bacchides, who ill-treated and mocked them. 27 A terrible oppression began in Israel; there had been nothing like
it since the disappearance of prophecy among them.
28 The friends of Judas then all united in saying to
Jonathan, 29 'Since your brother Judas died, there has been
no one like him to head the resistance against our enemies,
people like Bacchides and others who hate our nation.
30 Accordingly, we have today chosen you to take his place as
our ruler and leader and to fight our campaigns.'
31 Whereupon, Jonathan took command, in succession to his
brother Judas.

GREEK OLD TESTAMENT

32 Καὶ ἔγνω Βακχίδης καὶ ἐζήτει αὐτὸν ἀποκτεῖναι. 33 καὶ
ἔγνω Ιωναθαν καὶ Σιμων ὁ ἀδελφὸς αὐτοῦ καὶ πάντες οἱ μετ᾽
αὐτοῦ καὶ ἔφυγον εἰς τὴν ἔρημον Θεκωε καὶ παρενέβαλον
ἐπὶ τὸ ὕδωρ λάκκου Ασφαρ. 34 καὶ ἔγνω Βακχίδης τῇ ἡμέρᾳ
τῶν σαββάτων καὶ ἦλθεν αὐτὸς καὶ πᾶν τὸ στράτευμα αὐτοῦ
πέραν τοῦ Ιορδάνου. — 35 καὶ ἀπέστειλεν τὸν ἀδελφὸν αὐτοῦ
ἡγούμενον τοῦ ὄχλου καὶ παρεκάλεσεν τοὺς Ναβαταίους φίλους αὐτοῦ τοῦ παραθέσθαι αὐτοῖς τὴν ἀποσκευὴν αὐτῶν
τὴν πολλήν. 36 καὶ ἐξῆλθον οἱ υἱοὶ Ιαμβρι οἱ ἐκ Μηδαβα καὶ
συνέλαβον Ιωαννην καὶ πάντα, ὅσα εἶχεν, καὶ ἀπῆλθον
ἔχοντες. 37 μετὰ τοὺς λόγους τούτους ἀπήγγειλαν Ιωναθαν
καὶ Σιμωνι τῷ ἀδελφῷ αὐτοῦ ὅτι Υἱοὶ Ιαμβρι ποιοῦσιν γάμον
μέγαν καὶ ἄγουσιν τὴν νύμφην ἀπὸ Ναδαβαθ, θυγατέρα ἑνὸς
τῶν μεγάλων μεγιστάνων Χανααν, μετὰ παραπομπῆς μεγάλης. 38 καὶ ἐμνήσθησαν τοῦ αἵματος Ιωαννου τοῦ ἀδελφοῦ
αὐτῶν καὶ ἀνέβησαν καὶ ἐκρύβησαν ὑπὸ τὴν σκέπην τοῦ
ὄρους. 39 καὶ ἦραν τοὺς ὀφθαλμοὺς αὐτῶν καὶ εἶδον καὶ ἰδοὺ
θροῦς καὶ ἀποσκευὴ πολλή, καὶ ὁ νυμφίος ἐξῆλθεν καὶ οἱ φίλοι αὐτοῦ καὶ οἱ ἀδελφοὶ αὐτοῦ εἰς συνάντησιν αὐτῶν μετὰ
τυμπάνων καὶ μουσικῶν καὶ ὅπλων πολλῶν. 40 καὶ ἐξανέστησαν ἐπ᾽ αὐτοὺς ἀπὸ τοῦ ἐνέδρου καὶ ἀπέκτειναν αὐτούς, καὶ
ἔπεσον τραυματίαι πολλοί, καὶ οἱ ἐπίλοιποι ἔφυγον εἰς τὸ
ὄρος. καὶ ἔλαβον πάντα τὰ σκῦλα αὐτῶν. 41 καὶ μετεστράφη
ὁ γάμος εἰς πένθος καὶ φωνὴ μουσικῶν αὐτῶν εἰς θρῆνον.

KING JAMES VERSION

32 But when Bacchides gat knowledge thereof, he sought for to slay him.

33 Then Jonathan, and Simon his brother, and all that were with him, perceiving that, fled into the wilderness of Thecoe, and pitched their tents by the water of the pool Asphar.

34 Which when Bacchides understood, he came near to Jordan with all his host upon the sabbath day.

35 Now Jonathan had sent his brother *John,* a captain of the people, to pray his friends the Nabathites, that they might leave with them their carriage, which was much.

36 But the children of Jambri came out of Medaba, and took John, and all that he had, and went their way with it.

37 After this came word to Jonathan and Simon his brother, that the children of Jambri made a great marriage, and were bringing the bride from Nadabatha with a great train, as being the daughter of one of the great princes of Chanaan.

38 Therefore they remembered John their brother, and went up, and hid themselves under the covert of the mountain:

39 Where they lifted up their eyes, and looked, and, behold, there was much ado and great carriage: and the bridegroom came forth, and his friends and brethren, to meet them with drums, and instruments of musick, and many weapons.

40 Then Jonathan and they that were with him rose up against them from the place where they lay in ambush, and made a slaughter of them in such sort, as many fell down dead, and the remnant fled into the mountain, and they took all their spoils.

41 Thus was the marriage turned into mourning, and the noise of their melody into lamentation.

DOUAY OLD TESTAMENT

32 And Bacchides had knowledge of it, and sought to kill him.

33 And Jonathan and Simon his brother, knew it, and all that were with them: and they fled into the desert of Thecua, and they pitched by the water of the lake Asphar,

34 And Bacchides understood it, and he came himself with all his army over the Jordan on the sabbath day.

35 And Jonathan sent his brother a captain of the people, to desire the Nabutheans his friends, that they would lend them their equipage, which was copious.

36 And the children of Jambri came forth out of Madaba, and took John, and all that he had, and went away with them.

37 After this it was told Jonathan, and Simon his brother, that the children of Jambri made a great marriage, and were bringing the bride out of Madaba, the daughter of one of the great princes of Chanaan, with great pomp.

38 And they remembered the blood of John their brother: and they went up, and hid themselves under the covert of the mountain.

39 And they lifted up their eyes, and saw: and behold a tumult, and great preparation: and the bridegroom came forth, and his friends, and his brethren to meet them with timbrels, and musical instruments, and many weapons.

40 And they rose up against them from the place where they lay in ambush, and slew them, and there fell many wounded, and the rest fled into the mountains, and they took all their spoils:

41 And the marriage was turned into mourning, and the noise of their musical instruments into lamentation.

KNOX TRANSLATION

sooner heard of it than he marked him down for death;
33 but of this Jonathan had warning, and took refuge, with
his brother Simon and all his company, in the desert of
Thecue. it was there, by Asphar pool, they halted; 34 and it
was there that Bacchides, well informed of their movements,
crossed Jordan at the head of his army and came upon them,
one sabbath day.
35 This was the manner of it. Jonathan had sent his brother
John, that was in command of the camp followers, on an
errand to his good friends the Nabuthaeans. They had
brought a deal of their household stuff with them; would the
Nabuthaeans take it into safe keeping? 36 But, as they went,
some of Jambri's folk came out from Madaba, seized John
and all that he had with him, and went off with them.
37 Afterwards, Jonathan and Simon heard that the men of
Jambri had a great wedding toward; they must bring home
the bride from Nadabatha,[a] and with much pomp, because
her father was a notable Chanaanite chief. 38 So, to avenge
the death of their brother John, they climbed the hill-side and
lay in ambush there. 39 What a sight was this met their eyes!
All manner of rout and display; the bridegroom, his friends
and his brethren, passing on their way to the trysting-place,
with beating of drums, and making of music, and all manner
of warlike array! 40 Then rose they up from their ambush
and laid about them, till many fell wounded, and the rest
fled into the hills, leaving all their spoil behind them. 41 So
turned they wedding mirth into funeral dirge, 42 to avenge

a 'Nadabatha'; the Latin version has 'Madaba', presumably a copyist's error.

TODAY'S ENGLISH VERSION

32 When Bacchides learned of this, he made up his mind to kill Jonathan. 33 But when this news reached Jonathan, he fled, with his brother Simon and their men, to the wilderness of Tekoa and set up camp at the pool of Asphar. (34 Bacchides learned about this on the Sabbath and crossed the Jordan with his whole army.[a]) 35 Jonathan sent his brother John, who was responsible for the soldiers' families, to ask the Nabateans, with whom he was on friendly terms, for permission to store with them the large amount of baggage they had. 36 But the Jambrites of Medeba attacked John, took him captive, and carried off all the baggage. 37 Some time later Jonathan and his brother Simon learned that the Jambrites were about to celebrate an important wedding and that there would be a bridal procession from the town of Nadabath. The bride was the daughter of one of the great princes of Canaan. 38 Jonathan and Simon had wanted revenge for the death of their brother John, so they and their men went up on one of the mountains and hid. 39 They kept watch and saw a noisy crowd loaded down with baggage. The bridegroom, his friends, and his relatives were on their way to meet the bride's party. They were heavily armed and were playing musical instruments and drums. 40 The Jews attacked from their ambush and killed many of them; the rest escaped into the mountains, while the Jews carried off all their possessions. 41 So the wedding was turned into a time of mourning and their joyful music into funeral songs. 42 Jonathan and

[a] *Verse 34 is probably misplaced and belongs with verse 43.*

NEW REVISED STANDARD VERSION

32 When Bacchides learned of this, he tried to kill him. 33 But Jonathan and his brother Simon and all who were with him heard of it, and they fled into the wilderness of Tekoa and camped by the water of the pool of Asphar. 34 Bacchides found this out on the sabbath day, and he with all his army crossed the Jordan.

35 So Jonathan[a] sent his brother as leader of the multitude and begged the Nabateans, who were his friends, for permission to store with them the great amount of baggage that they had. 36 But the family of Jambri from Medeba came out and seized John and all that he had, and left with it.

37 After these things it was reported to Jonathan and his brother Simon, "The family of Jambri are celebrating a great wedding, and are conducting the bride, a daughter of one of the great nobles of Canaan, from Nadabath with a large escort." 38 Remembering how their brother John had been killed, they went up and hid under cover of the mountain. 39 They looked out and saw a tumultuous procession with a great amount of baggage; and the bridegroom came out with his friends and his brothers to meet them with tambourines and musicians and many weapons. 40 Then they rushed on them from the ambush and began killing them. Many were wounded and fell, and the rest fled to the mountain; and the Jews[b] took all their goods. 41 So the wedding was turned into mourning and the voice of their musicians into a funeral

a Gk *he* *b* Gk *they*

NEW AMERICAN BIBLE

32 When Bacchides learned of it, he sought to kill him. 33 But Jonathan and his brother Simon and all the men with him discovered this, and they fled to the desert of Tekoa and camped by the waters of the pool of Asphar.

35 Jonathan sent his brother as leader of the convoy to ask permission of his friends, the Nabateans, to deposit with them their great quantity of baggage. 36 But the sons of Jambri from Medaba made a raid and seized and carried off John and everything he had. 37 After this, word was brought to Jonathan and his brother Simon: "The sons of Jambri are celebrating a great wedding, and with a large escort they are bringing the bride, the daughter of one of the great princes of Canaan, from Nadabath." 38 Remembering the blood of John their brother, they went up and hid themselves under cover of the mountain. 39 They watched, and suddenly saw a noisy crowd with baggage; the bridegroom and his friends and kinsmen had come out to meet the bride's party with tambourines and musicians and much equipment. 40 The Jews rose up against them from their ambush and killed them. Many fell wounded, and after the survivors fled toward the mountain, all their spoils were taken. 41 Thus the wedding was turned into mourning, and the sound of music into

9, 34: Omitted, it is a dittography of verse 43.

NEW JERUSALEM BIBLE

32 Bacchides, when he heard the news, made plans to kill Jonathan. 33 But this became known to Jonathan, his brother Simon and all his supporters, and they took refuge in the desert of Tekoa, camping by the water-supply at Asphar storage-well. 34 (Bacchides came to know of this on the Sabbath day, and he too crossed the Jordan with his entire army.)

35 Jonathan sent his brother, who was one of his commanders, to ask his friends the Nabataeans to store their considerable baggage for them. 36 The sons of Amrai, however, those of Medeba, intercepted them, captured John and everything he had and made off with their prize. 37 Later, Jonathan and his brother Simon were told that the sons of Amrai were celebrating an important wedding, and were escorting the bride, a daughter of one of the great notables of Canaan, from Nabata with a large retinue. 38 Remembering the bloody end of their brother John, they went up and hid under cover of the mountain. 39 As they were keeping watch, a noisy procession came into sight with a great deal of baggage, and the bridegroom, with his groomsmen and his family, came out to meet it with tambourines and a band, and rich, warlike display. 40 The Jews rushed down on them from their ambush and killed them, inflicting heavy casualties; the survivors escaped to the mountain, leaving their entire baggage train to be captured. 41 Thus, *the wedding was turned into mourning and the music of their band into lamentation.*[a] 42 Having in this

a **9** Am 8:10.

GREEK OLD TESTAMENT

42 καὶ ἐξεδίκησαν τὴν ἐκδίκησιν αἵματος ἀδελφοῦ αὐτῶν καὶ
ἀπέστρεψαν εἰς τὸ ἕλος τοῦ Ιορδάνου. — 43 καὶ ἤκουσεν
Βακχίδης καὶ ἦλθεν τῇ ἡμέρᾳ τῶν σαββάτων ἕως τῶν κρηπί-
δων τοῦ Ιορδάνου ἐν δυνάμει πολλῇ. 44 καὶ εἶπεν Ιωναθαν
τοῖς παρ' αὐτοῦ Ἀναστῶμεν δὴ καὶ πολεμήσωμεν περὶ τῶν
ψυχῶν ἡμῶν, οὐ γάρ ἐστιν σήμερον ὡς ἐχθὲς καὶ τρίτην
ἡμέραν· 45 ἰδοὺ γὰρ ὁ πόλεμος ἐξ ἐναντίας καὶ ἐξόπισθεν
ἡμῶν, τὸ δὲ ὕδωρ τοῦ Ιορδάνου ἔνθεν καὶ ἔνθεν καὶ ἕλος καὶ
δρυμός, οὐκ ἔστιν τόπος τοῦ ἐκκλῖναι· 46 νῦν οὖν κεκράξατε
εἰς τὸν οὐρανόν, ὅπως διασωθῆτε ἐκ χειρὸς τῶν ἐχθρῶν
ἡμῶν. 47 καὶ συνῆψεν ὁ πόλεμος. καὶ ἐξέτεινεν Ιωναθαν τὴν
χεῖρα αὐτοῦ πατάξαι τὸν Βακχίδην, καὶ ἐξέκλινεν ἀπ' αὐτοῦ
εἰς τὰ ὀπίσω. 48 καὶ ἐνεπήδησεν Ιωναθαν καὶ οἱ μετ' αὐτοῦ
εἰς τὸν Ιορδάνην καὶ διεκολύμβησαν εἰς τὸ πέραν, καὶ οὐ
διέβησαν ἐπ' αὐτοὺς τὸν Ιορδάνην. 49 ἔπεσον δὲ παρὰ
Βακχίδου τῇ ἡμέρᾳ ἐκείνῃ εἰς χιλίους ἄνδρας. 50 καὶ ἐπέστρεψεν εἰς Ιερουσαλημ, καὶ ᾠκοδόμησαν πόλεις ὀχυρὰς ἐν
τῇ Ιουδαίᾳ, τὸ ὀχύρωμα τὸ ἐν Ιεριχω καὶ τὴν Αμμαους καὶ
τὴν Βαιθωρων καὶ τὴν Βαιθηλ καὶ τὴν Θαμναθα Φαραθων καὶ
τὴν Τεφων, ἐν τείχεσιν ὑψηλοῖς καὶ πύλαις καὶ μοχλοῖς.
51 καὶ ἔθετο φρουρὰν ἐν αὐτοῖς τοῦ ἐχθραίνειν τῷ Ισραηλ.
52 καὶ ὠχύρωσεν τὴν πόλιν τὴν Βαιθσουραν καὶ Γαζαρα καὶ
τὴν ἄκραν καὶ ἔθετο ἐν αὐταῖς δυνάμεις καὶ παραθέσεις

KING JAMES VERSION

42 So when they had avenged fully the blood of their brother, they turned again to the marsh of Jordan.

43 Now when Bacchides heard hereof, he came on the sabbath day unto the banks of Jordan with a great power.

44 Then Jonathan said to his company, Let us go up now and fight for our lives, for it standeth not with us to day, as in time past:

45 For, behold, the battle is before us and behind us, and the water of Jordan on this side and that side, the marsh likewise and wood, neither is there place for us to turn aside.

46 Wherefore cry ye now unto heaven, that ye may be delivered from the hand of your enemies.

47 With that they joined battle, and Jonathan stretched forth his hand to smite Bacchides, but he turned back from him.

48 Then Jonathan and they that were with him leapt into Jordan, and swam over unto the farther bank: howbeit the other passed not over Jordan unto them.

49 So there were slain of Bacchides' side that day about a thousand men.

50 Afterward returned *Bacchides* to Jerusalem, and repaired the strong cities in Judea; the fort in Jericho, and Emmaus, and Bethhoron, and Bethel, and Thamnatha, Pharathoni, and Taphon, *these did he strengthen* with high walls, with gates, and with bars.

51 And in them he set a garrison, that they might work malice upon Israel.

52 He fortified also the city Bethsura, and Gazara, and the tower, and put forces in them, and provision of victuals.

DOUAY OLD TESTAMENT

42 And they took revenge for the blood of their brother: and they returned to the bank of the Jordan.

43 And Bacchides heard it, and he came on the sabbath day even to the bank of the Jordan with a great power.

44 And Jonathan said to his company: Let us arise, and fight against our enemies: for it is not now as yesterday, and the day before.

45 For behold the battle is before us, and the water of the Jordan on this side and on that side, and banks, and marshes, and woods: and there is no place for us to turn aside.

46 Now therefore cry ye to heaven, that ye may be delivered from the hand of your enemies. And they joined battle.

47 And Jonathan stretched forth his hand to strike Bacchides, but he turned away from him backwards.

48 And Jonathan, and they that were with him leaped into the Jordan, and swam over the Jordan to them:

49 And there fell of Bacchides' side that day a thousand men: and they returned to Jerusalem,

50 And they built strong cities in Judea, the fortress that was in Jericho, and in Ammaus, and in Bethoron, and in Bethel, and Thamnata, and Phara, and Thopo, with high walls, and gates, and bars.

51 And he placed garrisons in them, that they might wage war against Israel:

52 And he fortified the city of Bethsura, and Gazara, and the castle, and set garrisons in them, and provisions of victuals:

KNOX TRANSLATION

the murder of their brother, and withdrew to the banks of
Jordan again.[a]
43 Hearing of these alarms, Bacchides marched down to
Jordan bank one sabbath day, in great force. 44 Up now!
cried Jonathan to his men; engage our enemy we must. Gone
is the vantage we had till now; 45 here is armed force confronting us, and all around us is Jordan stream, Jordan
banks full of marshes and thickets; escape is none. 46 Cry we
rather upon heaven, for deliverance out of the enemy's hand.
So the battle was joined; 47 and here was Jonathan exerting
all his strength to deal a blow at Bacchides, who declined the
encounter! 48 What did Jonathan then? With all his company, he leapt into Jordan. So now, to reach them, the enemy
must swim for it across the stream.[b] 49 A thousand men of
his following Bacchides lost that day, and was fain to return
to Jerusalem.
50 After this, they took to fortifying the cities of Judaea with
high walls and barred gates, making strongholds at Jericho,
Ammaum, Bethoron, Bethel, Thamnata, Phara and Thopo;
51 here garrisons were set, for the harrying of Israel. 52 Bethsura, too, Bacchides fortified, and Gazara, and the Citadel
itself, keeping all of them well manned and provisioned;

a *vv.* 35-42. This incident is given by Josephus as if it followed the events described in verses 43-49; but he has probably misunderstood the sequence of the narrative. In verse 35, the Latin version seems to suggest that Jonathan asked the Nabuthaeans for the loan of their equipment, but the account given in the Greek text is more natural. *b* Literally, 'and they swam across the Jordan to them'. The Greek text has 'and they did not swim across the Jordan to them'. The meaning, in either case, can only be a matter of conjecture.

TODAY'S ENGLISH VERSION

Simon had taken full revenge for the death of their brother,
and they returned to the marshes along the Jordan.
43 Bacchides heard about this and arrived on the Sabbath
at the banks of the Jordan with a large army. 44 Jonathan
said to his men, "Now we must fight for our lives. We are in
a worse situation than we have ever been in before. 45 The
enemy is in front of us, the river is behind us, and marshes
and thickets are on both sides of us; there is no way out.
46 So pray now for the Lord to save us from our enemies."
47 The battle began and Jonathan and his men were just
about to kill Bacchides, when he escaped to the rear of the
army. 48 So Jonathan and his men jumped into the Jordan
and swam to the other side to escape, and the Syrian army
did not cross the river to follow them. 49 That day Bacchides
lost about 1,000 men.
50 After Bacchides returned to Jerusalem, the Syrians built
fortifications with high walls and barred gates for a number
of towns in Judea: Emmaus, Beth Horon, Bethel, Timnath,
Pirathon, Tephon, and the fortress in Jericho. 51 In all of
these he placed troops to harass the Jews. 52 He also
strengthened the fortifications of the towns of Bethzur and
Gezer and of the fort in Jerusalem. He placed army units in
them and stored up supplies there. 53 Then he took the sons

NEW REVISED STANDARD VERSION

dirge. 42 After they had fully avenged the blood of their
brother, they returned to the marshes of the Jordan.
43 When Bacchides heard of this, he came with a large
force on the sabbath day to the banks of the Jordan. 44 And
Jonathan said to those with him, "Let us get up now and
fight for our lives, for today things are not as they were
before. 45 For look! the battle is in front of us and behind us;
the water of the Jordan is on this side and on that, with
marsh and thicket; there is no place to turn. 46 Cry out now
to Heaven that you may be delivered from the hands of our
enemies." 47 So the battle began, and Jonathan stretched out
his hand to strike Bacchides, but he eluded him and went to
the rear. 48 Then Jonathan and the men with him leaped into
the Jordan and swam across to the other side, and the
enemy[a] did not cross the Jordan to attack them. 49 And
about one thousand of Bacchides' men fell that day.
50 Then Bacchides[b] returned to Jerusalem and built
strong cities in Judea: the fortress in Jericho, and Emmaus,
and Beth-horon, and Bethel, and Timnath, and[c] Pharathon,
and Tephon, with high walls and gates and bars. 51 And he
placed garrisons in them to harass Israel. 52 He also fortified
the town of Beth-zur, and Gazara, and the citadel, and in
them he put troops and stores of food. 53 And he took the

a Gk *they* *b* Gk *he* *c* Some authorities omit *and*

NEW AMERICAN BIBLE

lamentation. 42 Having taken their revenge for the blood of
their brother, the Jews returned to the marshes of the Jordan.
43 When Bacchides heard of it, he came on the sabbath to
the banks of the Jordan with a large force. 44 Then Jonathan
said to his companions, "Let us get up now and fight for our
lives, for today is not like yesterday and the day before.
45 The battle is before us, and behind us are the waters of the
Jordan on one side, marsh and thickets on the other, and
there is no way of escape. 46 Cry out now to Heaven for
deliverance from our enemies." 47 When they joined battle,
Jonathan raised his arm to strike Bacchides, but Bacchides
backed away from him. 48 Jonathan and his men jumped
into the Jordan and swam across to the other side, but the
enemy did not pursue them across the Jordan. 49 A thousand
men on Bacchides' side fell that day.
50 On returning to Jerusalem, Bacchides built strongholds
in Judea: the Jericho fortress, as well as Emmaus, Beth-
horon, Bethel, Timnath, Pharathon, and Tephon, with high
walls and gates and bars. 51 In each he put a garrison to
oppose Israel. 52 He fortified the city of Beth-zur, Gazara and
the citadel, and put soldiers in them and stores of provisions.

NEW JERUSALEM BIBLE

way avenged in full the blood of their brother, they returned
to the marshes of the Jordan.
43 As soon as Bacchides heard this, he came on the
Sabbath day with a considerable force to the steep banks of
the Jordan. 44 Jonathan said to his men, 'Up! Let us fight for
our lives, for today it is not as in the old days. 45 You can
see, we shall have to fight on our front and to our rear; we
have the waters of the Jordan on one side, the marsh and
scrub on the other, and we have no line of withdrawal.
46 This is the moment to call on Heaven, to deliver you from
the clutches of your enemies.' 47 The engagement was begun
by Jonathan, who aimed a blow at Bacchides, but the Syrian
disengaged himself and withdrew, 48 whereupon Jonathan
and his men leapt into the Jordan and swam to the other
bank; the enemy did not, however, cross the Jordan in pursuit. 49 That day, Bacchides lost about a thousand men.
50 Bacchides went back to Jerusalem and began fortifying
some of the Judaean towns: the fortresses of Jericho,
Emmaus, Beth-Horon, Bethel, Timnath, Pharathon and
Tephon, with high walls and barred gates, 51 and stationed a
garrison in each of them to harass Israel. 52 He also fortified
the town of Beth-Zur, Gezer and the Citadel, and placed
troops in them with supplies of provisions. 53 He took the

GREEK OLD TESTAMENT

βρωμάτων. 53 καὶ ἔλαβεν τοὺς υἱοὺς τῶν ἡγουμένων τῆς
χώρας ὅμηρα καὶ ἔθετο αὐτοὺς ἐν τῇ ἄκρᾳ ἐν Ιερουσαλημ ἐν
φυλακῇ.
54 Καὶ ἐν ἔτει τρίτῳ καὶ πεντηκοστῷ καὶ ἑκατοστῷ τῷ
μηνὶ τῷ δευτέρῳ ἐπέταξεν Ἄλκιμος καθαιρεῖν τὸ τεῖχος
τῆς αὐλῆς τῶν ἁγίων τῆς ἐσωτέρας. καὶ καθεῖλεν τὰ ἔργα
τῶν προφητῶν καὶ ἐνήρξατο τοῦ καθαιρεῖν. 55 ἐν τῷ καιρῷ
ἐκείνῳ ἐπλήγη Ἄλκιμος, καὶ ἐνεποδίσθη τὰ ἔργα αὐτοῦ, καὶ
ἀπεφράγη τὸ στόμα αὐτοῦ, καὶ παρελύθη καὶ οὐκ ἠδύνατο
ἔτι λαλῆσαι λόγον καὶ ἐντείλασθαι περὶ τοῦ οἴκου αὐτοῦ.
56 καὶ ἀπέθανεν Ἄλκιμος ἐν τῷ καιρῷ ἐκείνῳ μετὰ βασάνου
μεγάλης. 57 καὶ εἶδεν Βακχίδης ὅτι ἀπέθανεν Ἄλκιμος, καὶ
ἐπέστρεψεν πρὸς τὸν βασιλέα. καὶ ἡσύχασεν ἡ γῆ Ιουδα ἔτη
δύο.
58 Καὶ ἐβουλεύσαντο πάντες οἱ ἄνομοι λέγοντες Ἰδοὺ
Ιωναθαν καὶ οἱ παρ' αὐτοῦ ἐν ἡσυχίᾳ κατοικοῦσιν πεποιθότες. νῦν οὖν ἀνάξομεν τὸν Βακχίδην, καὶ συλλήμψεται αὐτοὺς πάντας ἐν νυκτὶ μιᾷ. 59 καὶ πορευθέντες συνεβουλεύ-
σαντο αὐτῷ. 60 καὶ ἀπῆρεν τοῦ ἐλθεῖν μετὰ δυνάμεως
πολλῆς καὶ ἀπέστειλεν λάθρᾳ ἐπιστολὰς πᾶσιν τοῖς συμμάχοις αὐτοῦ τοῖς ἐν τῇ Ιουδαίᾳ, ὅπως συλλάβωσιν τὸν
Ιωναθαν καὶ τοὺς μετ' αὐτοῦ· καὶ οὐκ ἠδύναντο, ὅτι ἐγνώσθη
ἡ βουλὴ αὐτῶν. 61 καὶ συνέλαβον ἀπὸ τῶν ἀνδρῶν τῆς χώρας
τῶν ἀρχηγῶν τῆς κακίας εἰς πεντήκοντα ἄνδρας καὶ ἀπέκτειναν αὐτούς. 62 καὶ ἐξεχώρησεν Ιωναθαν καὶ Σιμων καὶ οἱ
μετ' αὐτοῦ εἰς Βαιθβασι τὴν ἐν τῇ ἐρήμῳ καὶ ᾠκοδόμησεν τὰ
καθῃρημένα αὐτῆς, καὶ ἐστερέωσαν αὐτήν. 63 καὶ ἔγνω

KING JAMES VERSION

53 Besides, he took the chief men's sons in the country for hostages, and put them into the tower at Jerusalem to be kept.

54 Moreover in the hundred fifty and third year, in the second month, Alcimus commanded that the wall of the inner court of the sanctuary should be pulled down; he pulled down also the works of the prophets.

55 And as he began to pull down, even at that time was Alcimus plagued, and his enterprizes hindered: for his mouth was stopped, and he was taken with a palsy, so that he could no more speak any thing, nor give order concerning his house.

56 So Alcimus died at that time with great torment.

57 Now when Bacchides saw that Alcimus was dead, he returned to the king: whereupon the land of Judea was in rest two years.

58 Then all the ungodly men held a council, saying, Behold, Jonathan and his company are at ease, and dwell without care: now therefore we will bring Bacchides hither, who shall take them all in one night.

59 So they went and consulted with him.

60 Then removed he, and came with a great host, and sent letters privily to his adherents in Judea, that they should take Jonathan and those that were with him: howbeit they could not, because their counsel was known unto them.

61 Wherefore they took of the men of the country, that were authors of that mischief, about fifty persons, and slew them.

62 Afterward Jonathan, and Simon, and they that were with him, got them away to Bethbasi, which is in the wilderness, and they repaired the decays thereof, and made it strong.

DOUAY OLD TESTAMENT

53 And he took the sons of the chief men of the country for hostages, and put them in the castle in Jerusalem in custody.

54 Now in the year one hundred and fifty-three, the second month, Alcimus commanded the walls of the inner *court* of the sanctuary to be thrown down, and the works of the prophets to be destroyed: and he began to destroy.

55 At that time Alcimus was struck: and his works were hindered, and his mouth was stopped, and he was taken with a palsy, so that he could no more speak a word, nor give order concerning his house.

56 And Alcimus died at that time in great torment.

57 And Bacchides saw that Alcimus was dead: and he returned to the king, and the land was quiet for two years.

58 And all the wicked held a council, saying: Behold Jonathan, and they that are with him, dwell at ease, and without fear: now therefore let us bring Bacchides hither, and he shall take them all in one night.

59 So they went, and gave him counsel.

60 And he arose to come with a great army: and he sent secretly letters to his adherents that were in Judea, to seize upon Jonathan, and them that were with him: but they could not, for their design was known to them.

61 And he apprehended of the men of the country, that were the principal authors of the mischief, fifty men, and slew them.

62 And Jonathan, and Simon, and they that were with him retired into Bethbessen, which is in the desert: and he repaired the breaches thereof, and they fortified it.

KNOX TRANSLATION

53 ay, and the great men of all the country round must yield
up their children as hostages, to be held in Jerusalem citadel
for safe keeping. 54 Then, in the second month of the hundred and fifty-third year, came an order from Alcimus, the
dividing wall of the temple's inner court should be dismantled. The Prophets' Building[a] he had already cleared away,
and begun the dismantling, 55 when himself was smitten
down, and all his plans interrupted. Dumbstricken and
palsied, he never spoke again, even to dispose of his goods,
56 but died there and then, in great torment.
57 Alcimus dead, Bacchides was for Judaea no longer; away
he went to the king's court, and for two years the land was at
peace. 58 But ere long there was conspiracy afoot among the
godless party; here were Jonathan and his men living secure
of their safety; let Bacchides come in again, he might seize
them all, and make one night's work of it. 59 To Bacchides,
then, they went, and imparted their scheme to him; 60 whereupon he raised a great army for marching on Judaea, but first
sent word privately to his partisans there, bidding them seize
Jonathan and his company for themselves. Word went
abroad, and the plan miscarried; 61 it was Jonathan[b] seized
fifty notables of Judaea, that were the authors of the conspiracy, and put them to death. 62 Then, with Simon and the rest
of his following, he removed to Bethbessen, out in the desert,
and set about rebuilding it, to make a stronghold for them.

a The Prophet's Building (literally, Work) was presumably the name given to some part of Zorobabel's temple; no allusion is made to it elsewhere.
b The name Jonathan is not given, but it seems the natural one to supply in the context. Josephus, perhaps through a misinterpretation, attributes the massacre to Bacchides.

Today's English Version

of the leading men of the country as hostages and imprisoned them in the fort.
54 In the second month of the year 153,[a] the High Priest
Alcimus ordered that the wall of the inner court of the
Temple be torn down. This would have destroyed what the
prophets had accomplished; but just as the work began,
55 he had a stroke, and work was stopped. Paralyzed and
unable to open his mouth, he could not speak or even make
a will for his family. 56 He died in great torment. 57 When
Bacchides learned that Alcimus was dead, he returned to
King Demetrius, and the land of Judea had peace for two
years.
58 Then all the renegades got together and said, "Look,
Jonathan and his men are living in peace and security. If we
bring Bacchides here now, he can capture them all in a single
night." 59 They went to discuss the matter with Bacchides,
60 and he set out with a large army. He sent secret letters to
all his allies in Judea, asking them to seize Jonathan and his
men. But they were not able to do so because the plot was
discovered. 61 Jonathan and his men captured 50 of the traitorous leaders who had been involved in the plot and put
them to death. 62 Then Jonathan, Simon, and their forces
withdrew to Bethbasi in the wilderness. They rebuilt the fall-
en fortifications and strengthened the town's defenses.

[a] THE YEAR 153: *This corresponds to 159 B.C.*

New Revised Standard Version

sons of the leading men of the land as hostages and put
them under guard in the citadel at Jerusalem.
54 In the one hundred and fifty-third year,[a] in the second
month, Alcimus gave orders to tear down the wall of the
inner court of the sanctuary. He tore down the work of the
prophets! 55 But he only began to tear it down, for at that
time Alcimus was stricken and his work was hindered; his
mouth was stopped and he was paralyzed, so that he could
no longer say a word or give commands concerning his
house. 56 And Alcimus died at that time in great agony.
57 When Bacchides saw that Alcimus was dead, he returned
to the king, and the land of Judah had rest for two years.
58 Then all the lawless plotted and said, "See! Jonathan
and his men are living in quiet and confidence. So now let us
bring Bacchides back, and he will capture them all in one
night." 59 And they went and consulted with him. 60 He
started to come with a large force, and secretly sent letters to
all his allies in Judea, telling them to seize Jonathan and his
men; but they were unable to do it, because their plan
became known. 61 And Jonathan's men[b] seized about fifty of
the men of the country who were leaders in this treachery,
and killed them.
62 Then Jonathan with his men, and Simon, withdrew to
Bethbasi in the wilderness; he rebuilt the parts of it that had
been demolished, and they fortified it. 63 When Bacchides

a 159 B.C. *b* Gk *they*

New American Bible

53 He took as hostages the sons of the leaders of the country
and put them in custody in the citadel at Jerusalem.
54 In the year one hundred and fifty-three, in the second
month, Alcimus ordered the wall of the inner court of the
sanctuary to be torn down, thus destroying the work of the
prophets. But he only began to tear it down. 55 Just at that
time he had a stroke, and his work was interrupted; his
mouth was closed and he was paralyzed, so that he could no
longer utter a word to give orders concerning his house.
56 Finally he died in great agony. 57 Seeing that Alcimus was
dead, Bacchides returned to the king, and the land of Judah
was quiet for two years.
58 Then all the transgressors of the law held a council and
said: "Jonathan and his companions are living in peace and
security. Now then, let us have Bacchides return, and he will
capture all of them in a single night." 59 So they went and
took counsel with him. 60 When Bacchides was setting out
with a large force, he sent letters secretly to all his allies in
Judea, telling them to seize Jonathan and his companions.
They were not able to do this, however, because their plot
became known. 61 In fact, Jonathan's men seized about fifty
of the men of the country who were ring-leaders in the mischief and put them to death. 62 Then Jonathan and Simon
and their companions withdrew to Bethbasi in the desert;
they rebuilt and strengthened its fortifications that had been

New Jerusalem Bible

sons of the leading men of the country as hostages, and had
them placed under guard in the Citadel of Jerusalem.
54 In the year 153, in the second month, Alcimus ordered
the demolition of the wall of the inner court of the sanctuary,
destroying the work of the prophets. Alcimus had just begun
the demolition 55 when he suffered a stroke, and his work
was interrupted. His mouth became obstructed, and his
paralysis made him incapable of speaking at all or giving
directions to his household; 56 it was not long before he died
in great agony. 57 On the death of Alcimus, Bacchides went
back to the king, and Judaea was left in peace for two years.
58 The renegades then all agreed on a plan. 'Now is the
time,' they said, 'while Jonathan and his supporters are living in peace and are full of confidence, for us to bring back
Bacchides, and he will arrest the lot of them in one night.'
59 So they went to him and reached an understanding.
60 Bacchides at once set out with a large force, and sent
secret instructions to all his allies in Judaea to seize
Jonathan and his supporters. But they were unable to do this
because their plan became known, 61 and Jonathan and his
men arrested some fifty of the men of the country who were
ringleaders in the plot, and put them to death.
62 Jonathan and Simon then retired with their partisans to
Beth-Bassi in the desert; they rebuilt the ruinous parts of the

GREEK OLD TESTAMENT

Βακχίδης καὶ συνήγαγεν πᾶν τὸ πλῆθος αὐτοῦ καὶ τοῖς ἐκ
τῆς Ιουδαίας παρήγγειλεν· 64 καὶ ἐλθὼν παρενέβαλεν ἐπὶ
Βαιθβασι καὶ ἐπολέμησεν αὐτὴν ἡμέρας πολλὰς καὶ ἐποίησεν μηχανάς. 65 καὶ ἀπέλιπεν Ιωναθαν Σιμωνα τὸν ἀδελφὸν
αὐτοῦ ἐν τῇ πόλει καὶ ἐξῆλθεν εἰς τὴν χώραν καὶ ἦλθεν ἐν
ἀριθμῷ. 66 καὶ ἐπάταξεν Οδομηρα καὶ τοὺς ἀδελφοὺς αὐτοῦ
καὶ τοὺς υἱοὺς Φασιρων ἐν τῷ σκηνώματι αὐτῶν, καὶ ἤρξαντο τύπτειν καὶ ἀνέβαινον ἐν ταῖς δυνάμεσιν. 67 καὶ Σιμων
καὶ οἱ μετ' αὐτοῦ ἐξῆλθον ἐκ τῆς πόλεως καὶ ἐνεπύρισαν τὰς
μηχανάς. 68 καὶ ἐπολέμησαν πρὸς τὸν Βακχίδην, καὶ συνετρίβη ὑπ' αὐτῶν, καὶ ἔθλιβον αὐτὸν σφόδρα, ὅτι ἦν ἡ βουλὴ
αὐτοῦ καὶ ἡ ἔφοδος αὐτοῦ κενή. 69 καὶ ὠργίσθη ἐν θυμῷ τοῖς
ἀνδράσιν τοῖς ἀνόμοις τοῖς συμβουλεύσασιν αὐτῷ ἐλθεῖν εἰς
τὴν χώραν καὶ ἀπέκτεινεν ἐξ αὐτῶν πολλοὺς καὶ ἐβουλεύσατο τοῦ ἀπελθεῖν εἰς τὴν γῆν αὐτοῦ. 70 καὶ ἐπέγνω Ιωναθαν
καὶ ἀπέστειλεν πρὸς αὐτὸν πρέσβεις τοῦ συνθέσθαι πρὸς
αὐτὸν εἰρήνην καὶ ἀποδοῦναι αὐτοῖς τὴν αἰχμαλωσίαν.
71 καὶ ἐπεδέξατο καὶ ἐποίησεν κατὰ τοὺς λόγους αὐτοῦ καὶ
ὤμοσεν αὐτῷ μὴ ἐκζητῆσαι αὐτῷ κακὸν πάσας τὰς ἡμέρας
τῆς ζωῆς αὐτοῦ· 72 καὶ ἀπέδωκεν αὐτῷ τὴν αἰχμαλωσίαν, ἣν
ᾐχμαλώτευσεν τὸ πρότερον ἐκ γῆς Ιουδα, καὶ ἀποστρέψας
ἀπῆλθεν εἰς τὴν γῆν αὐτοῦ καὶ οὐ προσέθετο ἔτι ἐλθεῖν εἰς

KING JAMES VERSION

63 Which thing when Bacchides knew, he gathered together all his host, and sent word to them that were of Judea.

64 Then went he and laid siege against Bethbasi; and they fought against it a long season, and made engines of war.

65 But Jonathan left his brother Simon in the city, and went forth himself into the country, and with a certain number went he forth.

66 And he smote Odonarkes and his brethren, and the children of Phasiron in their tent.

67 And when he began to smite them, and came up with his forces, Simon and his company went out of the city, and burned up the engines of war,

68 And fought against Bacchides, who was discomfited by them, and they afflicted him sore: for his counsel and travail was in vain.

69 Wherefore he was very wroth at the wicked men that gave him counsel to come into the country, insomuch as he slew many of them, and purposed to return into his own country.

70 Whereof when Jonathan had knowledge, he sent ambassadors unto him, to the end he should make peace with him, and deliver them the prisoners.

71 Which thing he accepted, and did according to his demands, and sware unto him that he would never do him harm all the days of his life.

72 When therefore he had restored unto him the prisoners that he had taken aforetime out of the land of Judea, he returned and went his way into his own land, neither came he any more into their borders.

DOUAY OLD TESTAMENT

63 And when Bacchides knew it, he gathered together all his multitude: and sent word to them that were of Judea.

64 And he came, and camped above Bethbessen, and fought against it many days, and made engines.

65 But Jonathan left his brother Simon in the city, and went forth into the country: and came with a number of men.

66 And struck Odares, and his brethren, and the children of Phaseron in their tents, and he began to slay, and to increase in forces.

67 But Simon and they that were with him, sallied out of the city, and burnt the engines.

68 And they fought against Bacchides, and he was discomfited by them: and they afflicted him exceedingly, for his counsel, and his enterprise was in vain.

69 And he was angry with the wicked men that had given him counsel to come into their country, and he slew many of them: and he purposed to return with the rest into their country.

70 And Jonathan had knowledge of it and he sent ambassadors to him to make peace with him, and to restore to him the prisoners.

71 And he accepted it willingly, and did according to his words, and swore that he would do him no harm all the days of his life.

72 And he restored to him the prisoners which he before had taken out of the land of Juda: and he returned and went away into his own country, and he came no more into their borders.

KNOX TRANSLATION

63 Bacchides had news of this; mustering his whole force,
and sending word to his Jewish supporters, 64 he marched in
and pitched his camp so as to command Bethbessen. Long
time he besieged it, and brought up engines against it;
65 meanwhile, Jonathan had left his brother Simon in command of the city, and was roaming the country-side. When
he came back, it was with a band of men at his heels;
66 smote he Odares and his clan, smote he the men of
Phaseron where they lay encamped; everywhere laid about
him, and still gained strength.[a] 67 As for Simon and his company, they made a sally out of the town, and set fire to the
engines; 68 afterwards they engaged Bacchides himself, and
worsted him, so that he must pay dearly for plot and tryst of
his that came to nothing. 69 So enraged was he with the malcontents whose counsel had brought him into Judaea, he put
many of them to death, and was for marching home again
with the rest of his following, 70 when Jonathan, hearing of
it, sent envoys to offer peace, and an exchange of prisoners.
71 This offer he gladly accepted, and carried out the terms of
it, giving. his word he would do Jonathan no more injury as
long as he lived, 72 and restoring all the prisoners he had
ever taken m the land of Juda. So he took himself back to his
own country, and never came that way again. 73 Israel had a

a vv. 65, 66. The original here is strangely worded, and perhaps corrupt.

TODAY'S ENGLISH VERSION

63 When Bacchides learned about all this, he got his whole
army together and alerted his supporters in Judea. 64 He
attacked Bethbasi from all sides and built siege platforms.
After the battle had gone on for a long time, 65 Jonathan
slipped out into the country with a small body of men and
left his brother Simon in charge of the town. 66 Jonathan
defeated Odomera and his people, and then attacked and
destroyed the Phasirite camp. Once defeated, they joined
Jonathan and advanced with him in his attack against
Bacchides. 67 At the same time, Simon and his men rushed
from the town and burned the siege platforms. 68 In the battle Bacchides was pressed so hard that all his plans came to
nothing, and he was defeated. 69 He was so furious with the
traitorous Jews who had urged him to come to Judea that he
put many of them to death.

Then Bacchides decided to return to his own country,
70 but when Jonathan learned of this, he sent ambassadors to
Bacchides to arrange for peace terms and the return of
Jewish prisoners. 71 Bacchides agreed to do as Jonathan
asked and gave him his solemn promise that he would let
him live in peace the rest of his life. 72 Bacchides handed
over the prisoners and returned to his own country. Never
again did he come into Jewish territory. 73 War came to an

NEW REVISED STANDARD VERSION

learned of this, he assembled all his forces, and sent orders
to the men of Judea. 64 Then he came and encamped against
Bethbasi; he fought against it for many days and made
machines of war.

65 But Jonathan left his brother Simon in the town, while
he went out into the country; and he went with only a few
men. 66 He struck down Odomera and his kindred and the
people of Phasiron in their tents. 67 Then he[a] began to attack
and went into battle with his forces; and Simon and his men
sallied out from the town and set fire to the machines of war.
68 They fought with Bacchides, and he was crushed by them.
They pressed him very hard, for his plan and his expedition
had been in vain. 69 So he was very angry at the renegades
who had counseled him to come into the country, and he
killed many of them. Then he decided to go back to his own
land.

70 When Jonathan learned of this, he sent ambassadors
to him to make peace with him and obtain release of the
captives. 71 He agreed, and did as he said; and he swore to
Jonathan[b] that he would not try to harm him as long as he
lived. 72 He restored to him the captives whom he had taken
previously from the land of Judah; then he turned and went
back to his own land, and did not come again into their

a Other ancient authorities read *they* *b* Gk *him*

NEW AMERICAN BIBLE

demolished. 63 When Bacchides learned of this, he gathered
together his whole force and sent word to those who were in
Judea. 64 He came and pitched his camp before Bethbasi, and
constructing siege-machines, he fought against it for many
days.

65 Leaving his brother Simon in the city, Jonathan, accompanied by a small group of men, went out into the field.
66 He struck down Odomera and his kinsmen and the sons of
Phasiron in their encampment; these men had set out to go
up to the siege with their forces. 67 Simon and his men then
sallied forth from the city and set fire to the machines.
68 They fought against Bacchides, and he was beaten. This
caused him great distress. Because the enterprise he had
planned came to naught, 69 he was angry with the lawless
men who had advised him to invade the province. He killed
many of them and resolved to return to his own country.

70 Jonathan learned of this and sent ambassadors to make
peace with him and to obtain the release of the prisoners.
71 He agreed to do as Jonathan had asked. He swore an oath
to him that he would never try to injure him for the rest of
his life; 72 and he released the prisoners he had previously
taken from the land of Judah. He returned to his own country and never came into their territory again.

NEW JERUSALEM BIBLE

place and fortified it. 63 When Bacchides heard this, he mustered his whole force and notified his adherents in Judaea.
64 He then proceeded to lay siege to Beth-Bassi, the fighting
was protracted, and he constructed siege-engines.
65 Jonathan, however, leaving his brother Simon in the town,
broke out into the countryside with a handful of men. 66 He
launched a blow at Odomera and his brothers, and at the
sons of Phasiron in their encampment; whereupon, these too
came into the struggle, joining forces with him. 67 Simon
and his people, meanwhile, made a sortie from the town and
set fire to the siege-engines. 68 Taking the offensive against
Bacchides, they defeated him. He was greatly disconcerted to
find that his plan and his assault had come to nothing,
69 and vented his anger on those renegades who had induced
him to enter the country, putting many of them to death; he
then decided to take his own troops home. 70 Discovering
this, Jonathan sent envoys to negotiate peace terms and the
release of prisoners with him. 71 Bacchides agreed to this,
accepting his proposals and swearing never to seek occasion
to harm him for the rest of his life. 72 Having surrendered to
Jonathan those prisoners he had earlier taken in Judaea, he
turned about and withdrew to his own country, and never
again came near their frontiers. 73 The sword no longer hung

GREEK OLD TESTAMENT

τὰ ὅρια αὐτῶν. 73 καὶ κατέπαυσεν ῥομφαία ἐξ Ισραηλ· καὶ
ᾤκησεν Ιωναθαν ἐν Μαχμας, καὶ ἤρξατο Ιωναθαν κρίνειν τὸν
λαὸν καὶ ἠφάνισεν τοὺς ἀσεβεῖς ἐξ Ισραηλ.

10 Καὶ ἐν ἔτει ἑξηκοστῷ καὶ ἑκατοστῷ ἀνέβη Ἀλέξανδρος ὁ τοῦ Ἀντιόχου ὁ Ἐπιφανὴς καὶ κατελάβετο
Πτολεμαίδα, καὶ ἐπεδέξαντο αὐτόν, καὶ ἐβασίλευσεν ἐκεῖ.
2 καὶ ἤκουσεν Δημήτριος ὁ βασιλεὺς καὶ συνήγαγεν δυνάμεις πολλὰς σφόδρα καὶ ἐξῆλθεν εἰς συνάντησιν αὐτῷ εἰς
πόλεμον. 3 καὶ ἀπέστειλεν Δημήτριος πρὸς Ιωναθαν ἐπιστολὰς λόγοις εἰρηνικοῖς ὥστε μεγαλῦναι αὐτόν· 4 εἶπεν γάρ
Προφθάσωμεν τοῦ εἰρήνην θεῖναι μετ' αὐτῶν πρὶν ἢ θεῖναι
αὐτὸν μετὰ Ἀλεξάνδρου καθ' ἡμῶν· 5 μνησθήσεται γὰρ πάντων τῶν κακῶν, ὧν συνετελέσαμεν πρὸς αὐτὸν καὶ εἰς τοὺς
ἀδελφοὺς αὐτοῦ καὶ εἰς τὸ ἔθνος. 6 καὶ ἔδωκεν αὐτῷ ἐξουσίαν συναγαγεῖν δυνάμεις καὶ κατασκευάζειν ὅπλα καὶ εἶναι
αὐτὸν σύμμαχον αὐτοῦ, καὶ τὰ ὅμηρα τὰ ἐν τῇ ἄκρᾳ εἶπεν
παραδοῦναι αὐτῷ. 7 καὶ ἦλθεν Ιωναθαν εἰς Ιερουσαλημ καὶ
ἀνέγνω τὰς ἐπιστολὰς εἰς τὰ ὦτα παντὸς τοῦ λαοῦ καὶ τῶν
ἐκ τῆς ἄκρας. 8 καὶ ἐφοβήθησαν φόβον μέγαν, ὅτε ἤκουσαν
ὅτι ἔδωκεν αὐτῷ ὁ βασιλεὺς ἐξουσίαν συναγαγεῖν δύναμιν.
9 καὶ παρέδωκαν οἱ ἐκ τῆς ἄκρας Ιωναθαν τὰ ὅμηρα, καὶ ἀπέδωκεν αὐτοὺς τοῖς γονεῦσιν αὐτῶν. 10 καὶ ᾤκησεν Ιωναθαν ἐν
Ιερουσαλημ καὶ ἤρξατο οἰκοδομεῖν καὶ καινίζειν τὴν πόλιν.

KING JAMES VERSION

73 Thus the sword ceased from Israel: but Jonathan dwelt at Machmas, and began to govern the people; and he destroyed the ungodly men out of Israel.

10 In the hundred and sixtieth year Alexander, the *son* of Antiochus *surnamed* Epiphanes, went up and took Ptolemais: for the people had received him, by means whereof he reigned there.

2 Now when king Demetrius heard thereof, he gathered together an exceeding great host, and went forth against him to fight.

3 Moreover Demetrius sent letters unto Jonathan with loving words, so as he magnified him.

4 For said he, Let us first make peace with him, before he join with Alexander against us:

5 Else he will remember all the evils that we have done against him, and against his brethren and his people.

6 Wherefore he gave him authority to gather together an host, and to provide weapons, that he might aid him in battle: he commanded also that the hostages that were in the tower should be delivered him.

7 Then came Jonathan to Jerusalem, and read the letters in the audience of all the people, and of them that were in the tower:

8 Who were sore afraid, when they heard that the king had given him authority to gather together an host.

9 Whereupon they of the tower delivered their hostages unto Jonathan, and he delivered them unto their parents.

10 This done, Jonathan settled himself in Jerusalem, and began to build and repair the city.

DOUAY OLD TESTAMENT

73 So the sword ceased from Israel: and Jonathan dwelt in Machmas, and Jonathan began there to judge the people, and he destroyed the wicked out of Israel.

10 NOW in the hundred and sixtieth year Alexander the son of Antiochus, surnamed the Illustrious, came up and took Ptolemais, and they received him, and he reigned there.

2 And king Demetrius heard of it, and gathered together an exceeding great army, and went forth against him to fight.

3 And Demetrius sent a letter to Jonathan with peaceable words, to magnify him.

4 For he said: Let us first make a peace with him, before he make one with Alexander against us.

5 For he will remember all the evils that we have done against him, and against his brother, and against his nation.

6 And he gave him authority to gather together an army, and to make arms, and that he should be his confederate: and the hostages that were in the castle, he commanded to be delivered to him.

7 And Jonathan came to Jerusalem, and read the letters in the hearing of all the people, and of them that were in the castle.

8 And they were struck with great fear, because they heard that the king had given him authority to gather together an army.

9 And the hostages were delivered to Jonathan, and he restored them to their parents.

10 And Jonathan dwelt in Jerusalem, and began to build, and to repair the city.

KNOX TRANSLATION

respite from fighting at last, and Jonathan took up his
dwelling at Machmas, whence he ruled the people thenceforward, ridding the land of godless folk altogether.

10 And now, in the hundred and sixtieth year, came
Alexander, a son of Antiochus the Illustrious, and
took possession of Ptolemais, where he was received with
royal honours. 2 A great force king Demetrius levied, when
he heard of it, and went out to give him battle; 3 at the same
time, he wrote to Jonathan, in such loving terms as should
flatter his dignity. 4 No time to be lost, thought he, in making friends with this man, before he takes to comforting
Alexander against us; 5 for wrong done to himself, and his
brother, and all his race, he bears us a grudge yet. 6 So he
empowered Jonathan to muster an army, and to make
weapons of war, as the ally of Syria; the hostages, too, in the
citadel were to be given back to him.

7 When Jonathan came to Jerusalem, and read this letter
aloud, not to the townsfolk only, but to the citadel garrison,
8 great was the fear fell on all who listened; here was
Jonathan commissioned to levy troops by the king's own
order! 9 The hostages were surrendered without more ado,
and given back to their parents; 10 and he himself took up
his quarters in Jerusalem, where he set about building up the

TODAY'S ENGLISH VERSION

end in Israel. Jonathan settled in Michmash and began to
govern the people and to eliminate the renegade Jews from
Israel.

10 In the year 160,[a] Alexander Epiphanes,[b] son of
Antiochus the Fourth, landed at Ptolemais and captured it. The people welcomed him as their king. 2 When
King Demetrius heard of it, he gathered a large army and
went out to meet him in battle. 3 At that time Demetrius sent
Jonathan a friendly letter full of flattery, 4 in the hope of
winning Jonathan over to his side and making peace with
the Jews before Alexander made a treaty with them against
him. 5 Demetrius thought that Jonathan would certainly
remember all the wrongs he had done to him, his brothers,
and the entire Jewish nation. 6 And so Demetrius made
Jonathan his ally and gave him authority to raise an army
and equip it. He also ordered that the hostages held in the
fort at Jerusalem should be handed over to Jonathan. 7 So
Jonathan went to Jerusalem and read the letter to all the people and to the men in the fort. 8 These men were terrified
when they learned that the king had given Jonathan authority to raise an army. 9 They handed the hostages over to him,
and he returned them to their parents.

10 Jonathan set up headquarters in Jerusalem and began to
rebuild and restore the city. 11 He ordered the builders to use

[a] THE YEAR 160: *This corresponds to 152 B.C.*
[b] ALEXANDER EPIPHANES: *Alexander Epiphanes is more widely known as Alexander Balas.*

NEW REVISED STANDARD VERSION

territory. 73 Thus the sword ceased from Israel. Jonathan
settled in Michmash and began to judge the people; and he
destroyed the godless out of Israel.

10 In the one hundred sixtieth year[a] Alexander Epiphanes, son of Antiochus, landed and occupied
Ptolemais. They welcomed him, and there he began to reign.
2 When King Demetrius heard of it, he assembled a very large
army and marched out to meet him in battle. 3 Demetrius
sent Jonathan a letter in peaceable words to honor him; 4 for
he said to himself, "Let us act first to make peace with him[b]
before he makes peace with Alexander against us, 5 for he
will remember all the wrongs that we did to him and to his
brothers and his nation." 6 So Demetrius[c] gave him authority to recruit troops, to equip them with arms, and to become
his ally; and he commanded that the hostages in the citadel
should be released to him.

7 Then Jonathan came to Jerusalem and read the letter in
the hearing of all the people and of those in the citadel.
8 They were greatly alarmed when they heard that the king
had given him authority to recruit troops. 9 But those in the
citadel released the hostages to Jonathan, and he returned
them to their parents.

10 And Jonathan took up residence in Jerusalem and
began to rebuild and restore the city. 11 He directed those

a 152 B.C. b Gk *them* c Gk *he*

NEW AMERICAN BIBLE

73 Then the sword ceased in Israel. Jonathan settled in
Michmash; he began to judge the people, and he destroyed
the impious in Israel.

10 In the year one hundred and sixty, Alexander, who
was called Epiphanes, son of Antiochus, came up
and took Ptolemais. He was accepted and began to reign
there. 2 When King Demetrius heard of it, he mustered a very
large army and marched out to engage him in combat.
3 Demetrius sent a letter to Jonathan written in peaceful
terms, to pay him honor; 4 for he said: "Let us be the first to
make peace with him, before he makes peace with Alexander
against us, 5 since he will remember all the wrongs we have
done to him, his brothers, and his nation."

6 So Demetrius authorized Jonathan, as his ally, to gather
an army and procure arms; and he ordered that the hostages
in the citadel be released to him. 7 Accordingly Jonathan
went up to Jerusalem and read the letter to all the people.
The men in the citadel 8 were struck with fear when they
heard that the king had given him authority to gather an
army. 9 They released the hostages to Jonathan, and he gave
them back to their parents. 10 Thereafter Jonathan dwelt in
Jerusalem, and began to build and restore the city. 11 He

NEW JERUSALEM BIBLE

over Israel, and Jonathan settled in Michmash, where he
began to judge the people and to rid Israel of the godless.

10 In the year 160, Alexander, son of Antiochus
Epiphanes, raised an army and occupied Ptolemais.
He was well received, and there inaugurated his reign. 2 On
hearing this, King Demetrius assembled a very large army
and marched off to do battle with him. 3 Demetrius furthermore sent Jonathan a most conciliatory letter, promising to
promote him in rank, 4 for, as he said, 'We had better move
first to come to terms with these people before he makes
common cause with Alexander against us; 5 he will not have
forgotten all the wrongs we inflicted on him and his brothers, and on his nation.' 6 He even authorised him to raise an
army, to manufacture arms, and to describe himself as his
ally, and ordered the hostages in the Citadel to be surrendered to him.

7 Jonathan went straight to Jerusalem and read the letter in
the hearing of the whole people and of the men in the
Citadel. 8 They were terrified when they heard that the king
had given him authority to raise an army. 9 The men in the
Citadel surrendered the hostages to Jonathan, who handed
them back to their parents. 10 Jonathan then took up residence in Jerusalem and began the rebuilding and restoration

GREEK OLD TESTAMENT

[11] καὶ εἶπεν πρὸς τοὺς ποιοῦντας τὰ ἔργα οἰκοδομεῖν τὰ τείχη καὶ τὸ ὄρος Σιων κυκλόθεν ἐκ λίθων τετραπόδων εἰς ὀχύρ-
ωσιν, καὶ ἐποίησαν οὕτως. [12] καὶ ἔφυγον οἱ ἀλλογενεῖς οἱ
ὄντες ἐν τοῖς ὀχυρώμασιν, οἷς ᾠκοδόμησεν Βακχίδης, [13] καὶ
κατέλιπεν ἕκαστος τὸν τόπον αὐτοῦ καὶ ἀπῆλθεν εἰς τὴν
γῆν αὐτοῦ· [14] πλὴν ἐν Βαιθσουροις ὑπελείφθησάν τινες τῶν
καταλιπόντων τὸν νόμον καὶ τὰ προστάγματα· ἦν γὰρ εἰς
φυγαδευτήριον.
[15] Καὶ ἤκουσεν Ἀλέξανδρος ὁ βασιλεὺς τὰς ἐπαγγελίας,
ὅσας ἀπέστειλεν Δημήτριος τῷ Ιωναθαν, καὶ διηγήσαντο
αὐτῷ τοὺς πολέμους καὶ τὰς ἀνδραγαθίας, ἃς ἐποίησεν
αὐτὸς καὶ οἱ ἀδελφοὶ αὐτοῦ, καὶ τοὺς κόπους, οὓς ἔσχον,
[16] καὶ εἶπεν Μὴ εὑρήσομεν ἄνδρα τοιοῦτον ἕνα; καὶ νῦν
ποιήσομεν αὐτὸν φίλον καὶ σύμμαχον ἡμῶν. [17] καὶ ἔγραψεν
ἐπιστολὰς καὶ ἀπέστειλεν αὐτῷ κατὰ τοὺς λόγους τούτους
λέγων
[18] Βασιλεὺς Ἀλέξανδρος τῷ ἀδελφῷ Ιωναθαν χαίρειν.
[19] ἀκηκόαμεν περὶ σοῦ ὅτι ἀνὴρ δυνατὸς ἰσχύι καὶ ἐπιτήδειος εἶ τοῦ εἶναι ἡμῶν φίλος. [20] καὶ νῦν καθεστάκαμέν σε
σήμερον ἀρχιερέα τοῦ ἔθνους σου καὶ φίλον βασιλέως
καλεῖσθαί σε [καὶ ἀπέστειλεν αὐτῷ πορφύραν καὶ στέφανον
χρυσοῦν] καὶ φρονεῖν τὰ ἡμῶν καὶ συντηρεῖν φιλίας πρὸς
ἡμᾶς.
[21] Καὶ ἐνεδύσατο Ιωναθαν τὴν ἁγίαν στολὴν τῷ ἑβδόμῳ
μηνὶ ἔτους ἑξηκοστοῦ καὶ ἑκατοστοῦ ἐν ἑορτῇ σκηνοπηγίας
καὶ συνήγαγεν δυνάμεις καὶ κατεσκεύασεν ὅπλα πολλά.

KING JAMES VERSION

11 And he commanded the workmen to build the walls and the mount Sion round about with square stones for fortification; and they did so.

12 Then the strangers, that were in the fortresses which Bacchides had built, fled away;

13 Insomuch as every man left his place, and went into his own country.

14 Only at Bethsura certain of those that had forsaken the law and the commandments remained still: for it was their place of refuge.

15 Now when king Alexander had heard what promises Demetrius had sent unto Jonathan: when also it was told him of the battles and noble acts which he and his brethren had done, and of the pains that they had endured,

16 He said, Shall we find such another man? now therefore we will make him our friend and confederate.

17 Upon this he wrote a letter, and sent it unto him, according to these words, saying,

18 King Alexander to his brother Jonathan sendeth greeting:

19 We have heard of thee, that thou art a man of great power, and meet to be our friend.

20 Wherefore now this day we ordain thee to be the high priest of thy nation, and to be called the king's friend; (and therewithal he sent him a purple robe and a crown of gold:) and *require thee* to take our part, and keep friendship with us.

21 So in the seventh month of the hundred and sixtieth year, at the feast of the tabernacles, Jonathan put on the holy robe, and gathered together forces, and provided much armour.

DOUAY OLD TESTAMENT

11 And he ordered workmen to build the walls, and mount Sion round about with square stones for fortification: and so they did.

12 And the strangers that were in the strong holds, which Bacchides had built, fled away.

13 And every man left his place, and departed into his own country:

14 Only in Bethsura there remained some of them, that had forsaken the law, and the commandments of God: for this was a place of refuge for them.

15 And king Alexander heard of the promises that Demetrius had made Jonathan: and they told him of the battles, and the worthy acts that he, and his brethren had done, and the labours that they had endured.

16 And he said: Shall we find such another man? now therefore we will make him our friend and our confederate.

17 So he wrote a letter, and sent it to him according to these words, saying:

18 King Alexander to his brother Jonathan, greeting.

19 We have heard of thee, that thou art a man of great power, and fit to be our friend:

20 Now therefore we make thee this day high priest of thy nation, and that thou be called the king's friend, (and he sent him a purple robe, and a crown of gold,) and that thou be of one mind with us in our affairs, and keep friendship with us.

21 Then Jonathan put on the holy vestment in the seventh month, in the year one hundred and threescore, at the feast day of the tabernacles: and he gathered together an army, and made a great number of arms.

KNOX TRANSLATION

city and repairing it. [11] It was the walls needed rebuilding,
so he told his workmen; on every side, the hill of Sion must
be defended with hewn stone; and punctually they obeyed
him. [12] As for the alien folk that guarded the strongholds
Bacchides had left, they fled incontinently; [13] what matter if
their posts were abandoned? They were for home. [14] Only
Bethsura was garrisoned now, and that by traitors to God's
law and commandment; it was all the refuge they had.
[15] King Alexander heard of these overtures made by
Demetrius; heard, too, the story of Jonathan and his
brethren, battles fought, and deeds done, and labours
endured. [16] Why, said he, this man has not his match anywhere; time it is we should court his friendship and alliance.
[17] With that, he wrote him a letter, and these were the terms
of it: [18] King Alexander, to Jonathan his brother-prince,
greeting! [19] We have heard tell of thee, a man so valiant,
and so well worthy of our friendship; [20] in token whereof,
we appoint thee high priest of thy own race henceforward,
and to have the title of the King's Friend. With that, he sent
him a purple robe and a gold crown; Take ever our part, said
he, and hold fast the bond of friendship. [21] So, when the seventh month came round, in the hundred and sixtieth year,
Jonathan clad himself with the sacred vesture at the feast of
Tent-dwelling; an army he levied besides, and made
weapons of war in great abundance.

TODAY'S ENGLISH VERSION

squared stones for the city walls and for the protecting wall around Mount Zion. This was done. 12 The foreigners deserted the fortresses that Bacchides had built; 13 each man left his post and returned to his own country. 14 But some of the Jews who had abandoned the Law of Moses and its commands were still left in Bethzur, which served as their last place of refuge.

15 King Alexander learned of the promises Demetrius had made to Jonathan and he also learned about Jonathan himself, about the battles he had fought, his courageous deeds, and the troubles he and his brothers had endured. 16 He was certain that he would never find another man like Jonathan and so decided to make him his friend and ally. 17 He wrote Jonathan a letter:

18 "King Alexander to his friend Jonathan, greetings.

19 I have heard that you are a brave man who has earned the right to be a friend of the king. 20 I have this day appointed you as High Priest of your nation and conferred upon you the title of 'Friend of the King.' You are to be our ally and give us your support."

He also sent him a royal robe and a gold crown. 21 Jonathan put on the robes of the High Priest in the seventh month of the year 160[a] at the Festival of Shelters. He raised an army and stored up a large supply of weapons.

[a] THE YEAR 160: *This corresponds to 152 B.C.*

NEW REVISED STANDARD VERSION

who were doing the work to build the walls and encircle Mount Zion with squared stones, for better fortification; and they did so.

12 Then the foreigners who were in the strongholds that Bacchides had built fled; 13 all of them left their places and went back to their own lands. 14 Only in Beth-zur did some remain who had forsaken the law and the commandments, for it served as a place of refuge.

15 Now King Alexander heard of all the promises that Demetrius had sent to Jonathan, and he heard of the battles that Jonathan[a] and his brothers had fought, of the brave deeds that they had done, and of the troubles that they had endured. 16 So he said, "Shall we find another such man? Come now, we will make him our friend and ally." 17 And he wrote a letter and sent it to him, in the following words:

18 "King Alexander to his brother Jonathan, greetings. 19 We have heard about you, that you are a mighty warrior and worthy to be our friend. 20 And so we have appointed you today to be the high priest of your nation; you are to be called the king's Friend and you are to take our side and keep friendship with us." He also sent him a purple robe and a golden crown.

21 So Jonathan put on the sacred vestments in the seventh month of the one hundred sixtieth year,[b] at the festival of booths,[c] and he recruited troops and equipped them with

[a] Gk *he* [b] 152 B.C. [c] Or *tabernacles*

NEW AMERICAN BIBLE

ordered the workmen to build the walls and encircle Mount Zion with square stones for its fortification, which they did. 12 The foreigners in the strongholds that Bacchides had built, took flight; 13 each one of them left his place and returned to his own country. 14 Only in Beth-zur did some remain of those who had abandoned the law and the commandments, for they used it as a place of refuge.

15 King Alexander heard of the promises that Demetrius had made to Jonathan; he was also told of the battles and valiant deeds of Jonathan and his brothers and the troubles that they had endured. 16 He said, "Shall we ever find another man like him? Let us now make him our friend and ally." 17 So he sent Jonathan a letter written in these terms: 18 "King Alexander sends greetings to his brother Jonathan. 19 We have heard of you, that you are a mighty warrior and worthy to be our friend. 20 We have therefore appointed you today to be high priest of your nation; you are to be called the King's Friend, and you are to look after our interests and preserve amity with us." He also sent him a purple robe and a crown of gold.

21 Jonathan put on the sacred vestments in the seventh month of the year one hundred and sixty at the feast of Booths, and he gathered an army and procured many arms.

NEW JERUSALEM BIBLE

of the city. 11 He ordered those responsible for the work to build the walls and the defences round Mount Zion of squared stone blocks to make them stronger, and this was done. 12 The foreigners in the fortresses built by Bacchides abandoned them, 13 one after another leaving his post to go back to his own country. 14 Only at Beth-Zur were a few left of those who had forsaken the Law and the precepts, since this was their refuge.

15 King Alexander heard of all the promises Demetrius had sent to Jonathan, and he was also given an account of the battles and exploits of this man and his brothers and of the hardships they had endured. 16 'Shall we ever find another man like him?' he exclaimed. 'We must make him our friend and ally!' 17 He therefore wrote him a letter, addressing him in these terms:

18 'King Alexander to his brother Jonathan, greetings.

19 'You have been brought to our notice as a strong man of action and as someone who deserves to be our friend. 20 Accordingly, we have today appointed you high priest of your nation, with the title of "Friend of the King" '—he also sent him a purple robe and a golden crown—'and you are to study our interests and maintain friendly relations with us.'

21 Jonathan put on the sacred vestments in the seventh month of the year 160, on the feast of Shelters; he then set about raising troops and manufacturing arms in quantity.

GREEK OLD TESTAMENT

22 Καὶ ἤκουσεν Δημήτριος τοὺς λόγους τούτους καὶ ἐλυπήθη καὶ εἶπεν 23 Τί τοῦτο ἐποιήσαμεν ὅτι προέφθακεν ἡμᾶς
Ἀλέξανδρος τοῦ φιλίαν καταλαβέσθαι τοῖς Ιουδαίοις εἰς
στήριγμα; 24 γράψω αὐτοῖς κἀγὼ λόγους παρακλήσεως καὶ
ὕψους καὶ δομάτων, ὅπως ὦσιν σὺν ἐμοὶ εἰς βοήθειαν. 25 καὶ
ἀπέστειλεν αὐτοῖς κατὰ τοὺς λόγους τούτους
Βασιλεὺς Δημήτριος τῷ ἔθνει τῶν Ιουδαίων χαίρειν.
26 ἐπεὶ συνετηρήσατε τὰς πρὸς ἡμᾶς συνθήκας καὶ ἐνεμείν-
ατε τῇ φιλίᾳ ἡμῶν καὶ οὐ προσεχωρήσατε τοῖς ἐχθροῖς
ἡμῶν, ἠκούσαμεν καὶ ἐχάρημεν. 27 καὶ νῦν ἐμμείνατε ἔτι
τοῦ συντηρῆσαι πρὸς ἡμᾶς πίστιν, καὶ ἀνταποδώσομεν ὑμῖν
ἀγαθὰ ἀνθ' ὧν ποιεῖτε μεθ' ἡμῶν. 28 καὶ ἀφήσομεν ὑμῖν ἀφέματα πολλὰ καὶ δώσομεν ὑμῖν δόματα. 29 καὶ νῦν ἀπολύω
ὑμᾶς καὶ ἀφίημι πάντας τοὺς Ιουδαίους ἀπὸ τῶν φόρων καὶ
τῆς τιμῆς τοῦ ἁλὸς καὶ ἀπὸ τῶν στεφάνων, 30 καὶ ἀντὶ τοῦ
τρίτου τῆς σπορᾶς καὶ ἀντὶ τοῦ ἡμίσους τοῦ καρποῦ τοῦ
ξυλίνου τοῦ ἐπιβάλλοντός μοι λαβεῖν ἀφίημι ἀπὸ τῆς σήμερον καὶ ἐπέκεινα τοῦ λαβεῖν ἀπὸ γῆς Ιουδα καὶ ἀπὸ τῶν
τριῶν νομῶν τῶν προστιθεμένων αὐτῇ ἀπὸ τῆς Σαμαρίτιδος
καὶ Γαλιλαίας ἀπὸ τῆς σήμερον ἡμέρας καὶ εἰς τὸν ἅπαντα
χρόνον. 31 καὶ Ιερουσαλημ ἔστω ἁγία καὶ ἀφειμένη καὶ τὰ
ὅρια αὐτῆς, αἱ δεκάται καὶ τὰ τέλη. 32 ἀφίημι καὶ τὴν
ἐξουσίαν τῆς ἄκρας τῆς ἐν Ιερουσαλημ καὶ δίδωμι τῷ
ἀρχιερεῖ, ὅπως ἂν καταστήσῃ ἐν αὐτῇ ἄνδρας, οὓς ἂν αὐτὸς
ἐκλέξηται, τοῦ φυλάσσειν αὐτήν. 33 καὶ πᾶσαν ψυχὴν

KING JAMES VERSION

22 Whereof when Demetrius heard, he was very sorry, and said,

23 What have we done, that Alexander hath prevented us in making amity with the Jews to strengthen himself?

24 I also will write unto them words of encouragement, *and promise them* dignities and gifts, that I may have their aid.

25 He sent unto them therefore to this effect: King Demetrius unto the people of the Jews sendeth greeting:

26 Whereas ye have kept covenants with us, and continued in our friendship, not joining yourselves with our enemies, we have heard hereof, and are glad.

27 Wherefore now continue ye still to be faithful unto us, and we will well recompense you for the things ye do in our behalf,

28 And will grant you many immunities, and give you rewards.

29 And now do I free you, and for your sake I release all the Jews, from tributes, and from the customs of salt, and from crown taxes,

30 And from that which appertaineth unto me to receive for the third part of the seed, and the half of the fruit of the trees, I release it from this day forth, so that they shall not be taken of the land of Judea, nor of the three governments which are added thereunto out of the country of Samaria and Galilee, from this day forth for evermore.

31 Let Jerusalem also be holy and free, with the borders thereof, both from tenths and tributes.

32 And as for the tower which is at Jerusalem, I yield up my authority over it, and give it to the high priest, that he may set in it such men as he shall choose to keep it.

DOUAY OLD TESTAMENT

22 And Demetrius heard these words, and was exceeding sorry, and said:

23 What is this that we have done, that Alexander hath prevented us to gain the friendship of the Jews to strengthen himself?

24 I also will write to them words of request, and offer dignities, and gifts: that they may be with me to aid me.

25 And he wrote to them in these words: King Demetrius to the nation of the Jews, greeting.

26 Whereas you have kept covenant with us, and have continued in our friendship, and have not joined with our enemies, we have heard of it, and are glad.

27 Wherefore now continue still to keep fidelity towards us, and we will reward you with good things, for what you have done in our behalf.

28 And we will remit to you many charges, and will give you gifts.

29 And now I free you, and all the Jews from tributes, and I release you from the customs of salt, and remit the crowns, and the thirds of the seed:

30 And the half of the fruit of trees, which is my share, I leave to you from this day forward, so that it shall not be taken of the land of Juda, and of the three cities that are added thereto out of Samaria and Galilee, from this day forth and for ever:

31 And let Jerusalem be holy and free, with the borders thereof: and let the tenths, and tributes be for itself.

32 I yield up also the power of the castle that is in Jerusalem, and I give it to the high priest, to place therein such men as he shall choose to keep it.

KNOX TRANSLATION

22 Sick and sorry Demetrius was when he heard of these
doings; 23 Here is an ill day's work, said he, to let Alexander
forestall us in making alliance with the Jews, to his great
comfort! 24 From me, too, they shall have a message of
entreaty, they shall have honours and gifts; the Jews shall be
my good friends yet. 25 And thus he wrote: King Demetrius,
to the people of the Jews, greeting! 26 Here is welcome news
we have of you; right well you have kept troth with us, hon-
ouring the treaty when you might have taken part with our
enemies. 27 In that loyal mind continue, and your good
offices shall not go unrewarded; 28 much immunity you shall
enjoy, much largesse receive.
29 By these presents, I exempt both you and all Jews from
the poll-tax; salt-tax and coronation dues I remit and forgo,
with my right to a third part of your seed-corn, 30 and half
your fruit-crop. From this day forward, now and for ever, I
resign all this; from Juda and from the three cantons of
Samaria and Galilee[a] lately added to it, there shall be no toll
taken. 31 For Jerusalem, it shall be a place set apart, a free
city with its own confines, mistress of its own tithe and tribute; 32 nor claim I any rights over the citadel there, I make
it over to the high priest, to garrison it as he will. 33 All

a 'Samaria and Galilee', here evidently treated as a single unit; the three districts concerned had actually been Samaritan (verse 38).

TODAY'S ENGLISH VERSION

22 When Demetrius heard this, he was distressed and said,
23 "How did we manage to let Alexander get ahead of us? He
has strengthened his position by making an alliance with the
Jews. 24 I also will write them a friendly letter offering high
positions and gifts, so that they will support me."
25 He wrote:
"King Demetrius to the nation of the Jews, greetings.
26 We are delighted to learn that you have kept your obligations under our treaty, remained loyal to us, and have not
gone over to the side of our enemies. 27 Now if you continue to remain loyal to us, we will reward you well. 28 We
will grant you exemptions from many taxes and allow you
other privileges. 29 I hereby grant all the Jewish people
release and exemption from payment of regular taxes, salt
taxes, and other special taxes. 30 Furthermore, from this
day I release you from your obligation to pay me one third
of the grain harvest and one half of the fruit harvest. From
now on I will not demand these payments from Judea or
from the three districts that have been added to Judea from
Samaria and Galilee. 31 Jerusalem and its surrounding territory is to be recognized as a holy city and to be exempt
from the payment of all taxes. 32 I also give up my authority over the fort in Jerusalem and place it under the High
Priest, who may station there anyone he wishes to guard

NEW REVISED STANDARD VERSION

arms in abundance. 22 When Demetrius heard of these
things he was distressed and said, 23 "What is this that we
have done? Alexander has gotten ahead of us in forming a
friendship with the Jews to strengthen himself. 24 I also will
write them words of encouragement and promise them honor
and gifts, so that I may have their help." 25 So he sent a
message to them in the following words:
"King Demetrius to the nation of the Jews, greetings.
26 Since you have kept your agreement with us and have continued your friendship with us, and have not sided with our
enemies, we have heard of it and rejoiced. 27 Now continue
still to keep faith with us, and we will repay you with good
for what you do for us. 28 We will grant you many immunities and give you gifts.
29 "I now free you and exempt all the Jews from payment
of tribute and salt tax and crown levies, 30 and instead of
collecting the third of the grain and the half of the fruit of
the trees that I should receive, I release them from this day
and henceforth. I will not collect them from the land of Judah
or from the three districts added to it from Samaria and
Galilee, from this day and for all time. 31 Jerusalem and its
environs, its tithes and its revenues, shall be holy and free
from tax. 32 I release also my control of the citadel in
Jerusalem and give it to the high priest, so that he may station in it men of his own choice to guard it. 33 And everyone

NEW AMERICAN BIBLE

22 When Demetrius heard of these things, he was distressed
and said: 23 Why have we allowed Alexander to get ahead of
us by gaining the friendship of the Jews and thus strengthening himself? 24 I too will write them conciliatory words and
offer dignities and gifts, so that they may be an aid to me."
25 So he sent them this message: "King Demetrius sends
greetings to the Jewish nation. 26 We have heard how you
have kept the treaty with us and continued in our friendship
and not gone over to our enemies, and we are glad.
27 Continue, therefore, to keep faith with us, and we will
reward you with favors in return for what you do in our
behalf. 28 We will grant you many exemptions and will
bestow gifts on you.
29 "I now free you, as I also exempt all the Jews, from the
tribute, the salt tax, and the crown levies. 30 Instead of collecting the third of the grain and the half of the fruit of the
trees that should be my share, I renounce the right from this
day forward. Neither now nor in the future will I collect them
from the land of Judah or from the three districts annexed
from Samaria. 31 Let Jerusalem and her territory, her tithes
and her tolls, be sacred and free from tax. 32 I also yield my
authority over the citadel in Jerusalem, and I transfer it to
the high priest, that he may put in it such men as he shall

NEW JERUSALEM BIBLE

22 Demetrius was displeased when he heard what had happened. 23 'What have we been doing,' he said, 'for Alexander
to forestall us in winning the friendship of the Jews and so
improving his own position? 24 I too shall address an appeal
to them, offering them advancement and riches as an
inducement to support me.' 25 And he wrote to them as follows:

'King Demetrius to the Jewish nation, greetings.
26 'We have heard how you have kept your agreement
with us and have maintained friendly relations with us
and have not gone over to our enemies, and it has given
us great satisfaction. 27 If you now continue to keep faith
with us, we shall make you a handsome return for what
you do on our behalf. 28 We shall accord you many exemptions and grant you privileges.
29 'Henceforth I release you and exempt all the Jews from
the tribute, the salt dues and the crown levies, 30 and
whereas I am entitled to one-third of the grain and one-
half of the fruit of the trees, I release from this levy, from
today and for the future, Judaea and the three districts
annexed to it from Samaria-Galilee, from this day henceforth in perpetuity. 31 Jerusalem will be sacred and
exempt, with its territory, from tithes and dues. 32 I relinquish control of the Citadel in Jerusalem and make it over
to the high priest, so that he may man it with a garrison of

GREEK OLD TESTAMENT

Ιουδαίων τὴν αἰχμαλωτισθεῖσαν ἀπὸ γῆς Ιουδα εἰς πᾶσαν
βασιλείαν μου ἀφίημι ἐλευθέραν δωρεάν· καὶ πάντες ἀφιέτω-
σαν τοὺς φόρους καὶ τῶν κτηνῶν αὐτῶν. 34 καὶ πᾶσαι αἱ
ἑορταὶ καὶ τὰ σάββατα καὶ νουμηνίαι καὶ ἡμέραι ἀπο-
δεδειγμέναι καὶ τρεῖς ἡμέραι πρὸ ἑορτῆς καὶ τρεῖς μετὰ
ἑορτὴν ἔστωσαν πᾶσαι ἡμέραι ἀτελείας καὶ ἀφέσεως πᾶσιν
τοῖς Ιουδαίοις τοῖς οὖσιν ἐν τῇ βασιλείᾳ μου, 35 καὶ οὐχ
ἕξει ἐξουσίαν οὐδεὶς πράσσειν καὶ παρενοχλεῖν τινα αὐτῶν
περὶ παντὸς πράγματος. 36 καὶ προγραφήτωσαν τῶν Ιουδαίων εἰς τὰς δυνάμεις τοῦ βασιλέως εἰς τριάκοντα χιλιάδας
ἀνδρῶν, καὶ δοθήσεται αὐτοῖς ξένια, ὡς καθήκει πάσαις ταῖς
δυνάμεσιν τοῦ βασιλέως. 37 καὶ κατασταθήσεται ἐξ αὐτῶν
ἐν τοῖς ὀχυρώμασιν τοῦ βασιλέως τοῖς μεγάλοις, καὶ ἐκ τούτων κατασταθήσονται ἐπὶ χρειῶν τῆς βασιλείας τῶν οὐσῶν
εἰς πίστιν· καὶ οἱ ἐπ᾽ αὐτῶν καὶ οἱ ἄρχοντες ἔστωσαν ἐξ
αὐτῶν καὶ πορευέσθωσαν τοῖς νόμοις αὐτῶν, καθὰ καὶ προσέταξεν ὁ βασιλεὺς ἐν γῇ Ιουδα. 38 καὶ τοὺς τρεῖς νομοὺς
τοὺς προστεθέντας τῇ Ιουδαίᾳ ἀπὸ τῆς χώρας Σαμαρείας
προστεθήτω τῇ Ιουδαίᾳ πρὸς τὸ λογισθῆναι τοῦ γενέσθαι ὑφ᾽
ἕνα τοῦ μὴ ὑπακοῦσαι ἄλλης ἐξουσίας ἀλλ᾽ ἢ τοῦ ἀρχιερέως.
39 Πτολεμαΐδα καὶ τὴν προσκυροῦσαν αὐτῇ δέδωκα δόμα τοῖς
ἁγίοις τοῖς ἐν Ιερουσαλημ εἰς τὴν καθήκουσαν δαπάνην τοῖς
ἁγίοις. 40 κἀγὼ δίδωμι κατ᾽ ἐνιαυτὸν δέκα πέντε χιλιάδας
σίκλων ἀργυρίου ἀπὸ τῶν λόγων τοῦ βασιλέως ἀπὸ τῶν

KING JAMES VERSION

33 Moreover I freely set at liberty every one of the Jews, that were carried captives out of the land of Judea into any part of my kingdom, and *I will* that all my officers remit the tributes even of their cattle.

34 Furthermore *I will* that all the feasts, and sabbaths, and new moons, and solemn days, and the three days before the feast, and the three days after the feast, shall be all days of immunity and freedom for all the Jews in my realm.

35 Also no man shall have authority to meddle *with them,* or to molest any of them in any matter.

36 *I will* further, that there be enrolled among the king's forces about thirty thousand men of the Jews, unto whom pay shall be given, as belongeth to all the king's forces.

37 And of them *some* shall be placed in the king's strong holds, of whom also *some* shall be set over the affairs of the kingdom, which are of trust: and *I will* that their overseers and governors be of themselves, and that they live after their own laws, even as the king hath commanded in the land of Judea.

38 And concerning the three governments that are added to Judea from the country of Samaria, let them be joined with Judea, that they may be reckoned to be under one, nor bound to obey other authority than the high priest's.

39 As for Ptolemais, and the land pertaining thereto, I give it as a free gift to the sanctuary at Jerusalem for the necessary expences of the sanctuary.

40 Moreover I give every year fifteen thousand shekels of silver out of the king's accounts from the places appertaining.

DOUAY OLD TESTAMENT

33 And every soul of the Jews that hath been carried captive from the land of Juda in all my kingdom, I set at liberty freely, that all be discharged from tributes even of their cattle.

34 And I will that all the feasts, and the sabbaths, and the new moons, and the days appointed, and three days before the solemn day, and three days after the solemn day, be all *days* of immunity and freedom, for all the Jews that are in my kingdom:

35 And no man shall have power to do any thing against them, or to molest any of them, in any cause.

36 And let there be enrolled in the king's army to the number of thirty thousand of the Jews: and allowance shall be made them as is due to all the king's forces, and certain of them shall be appointed to be in the fortresses of the great king:

37 And some of them shall be set over the affairs of the kingdom, that are of trust, and let the governors be taken from among themselves, and let them walk in their own laws, as the king hath commanded in the land of Juda.

38 And the three cities that are added to Judea, out of the country of Samaria, let them be accounted with Judea: that they may be under one, and obey no other authority but that of the high priest:

39 Ptolemais, and the confines thereof, I give as a free gift to the holy places, that are in Jerusalem, for the necessary charges of the holy things.

40 And I give every year fifteen thousand sicles of silver out of the king's accounts, of what belongs to me:

KNOX TRANSLATION

persons of Jewish blood in all my realm that were taken
away as prisoners from Juda shall now be set free gratu-
itously, and no distraint made on their revenues or cattle.
34 Feast-day and new moon and sabbath, and all other such
solemnities as are appointed to be observed, with the three
days before and after the feast itself, shall be days of immunity and respite for all the Jews in my realm; 35 nor any business done or debate moved to their detriment at such times.
36 In the king's army, Jews may be enrolled up to the number
of thirty thousand, paid according to the common rate of the
royal troops; and the same shall be free to serve in all the
fortified towns of our empire. 37 Jews may be employed
besides in all positions of trust, and appointed governors,[a]
yet live still by their own laws, that have royal sanction in
the land of Juda. 38 The three cantons taken from Samaria
and added to Judaea shall be accounted part of Juda, under a
single government, with no allegiance but to the high priest.
39 Ptolemais, with all the country that lies about it, I hereby
convey as a free gift to the temple precincts at Jerusalem, to
defray the temple expenses.[b] 40 To this gift I add a sum of
fifteen thousand silver sicles yearly, out of the royal dues

[a] 'And appointed governors'; according to the Greek text, 'and let their governors be men of their own race'. [b] A fine touch; cf. verse 1.

TODAY'S ENGLISH VERSION

it. 33 I freely grant release to all Jews who are prisoners of
war anywhere in my kingdom. All of them will be exempt
from taxes, even on their cattle.[a] 34 No taxes shall be collected from any Jew anywhere in my kingdom on
Sabbaths, New Moon Festivals, and other holy days.
Furthermore, no taxes shall be collected three days before
or after the major holy days. 35 No one has the right on
any of these days to demand payment or to trouble you in
any way.
36 "Jews may be enlisted in the royal army up to a total
of 30,000 men, and they will receive the same pay as other
royal troops. 37 Some of them may be stationed in the
great royal fortresses, and others assigned to responsible
positions in the government. They shall have Jews as their
leaders and officers, and they shall be allowed to follow
their own laws and customs, just as the king has permitted for the people of Judea.
38 "The three districts added to Judea from the territory of
Samaria will be completely incorporated into Judea and
placed under the authority of the High Priest alone.
39 I give to the Temple in Jerusalem for its operating
expenses the revenues from the city of Ptolemais and the
lands belonging to it. 40 I also promise to make an annual
gift of 15,000 silver coins from appropriate accounts within

[a] *This sentence in Greek is unclear.*

NEW REVISED STANDARD VERSION

of the Jews taken as a captive from the land of Judah into
any part of my kingdom, I set free without payment; and let
all officials cancel also the taxes on their livestock.
34 "All the festivals and sabbaths and new moons and
appointed days, and the three days before a festival and the
three after a festival—let them all be days of immunity and
release for all the Jews who are in my kingdom. 35 No one
shall have authority to exact anything from them or annoy
any of them about any matter.
36 "Let Jews be enrolled in the king's forces to the number
of thirty thousand men, and let the maintenance be given
them that is due to all the forces of the king. 37 Let some of
them be stationed in the great strongholds of the king, and
let some of them be put in positions of trust in the kingdom.
Let their officers and leaders be of their own number, and let
them live by their own laws, just as the king has commanded in the land of Judah.
38 "As for the three districts that have been added to
Judea from the country of Samaria, let them be annexed to
Judea so that they may be considered to be under one ruler
and obey no other authority than the high priest.
39 Ptolemais and the land adjoining it I have given as a gift to
the sanctuary in Jerusalem, to meet the necessary expenses
of the sanctuary. 40 I also grant fifteen thousand shekels of
silver yearly out of the king's revenues from appropriate

NEW AMERICAN BIBLE

choose to guard it. 33 Every one of the Jews who has been
carried into captivity from the land of Judah into any part of
my kingdom I set at liberty without ransom; and let all their
taxes, even those on their cattle, be canceled. 34 Let all feast
days, sabbaths, new moon festivals, appointed days, and the
three days that precede each feast day, and the three days
that follow, be days of immunity and exemption for every
Jew in my kingdom. 35 Let no man have authority to exact
payment from them or to molest any of them in any matter.
36 "Let thirty thousand Jews be enrolled in the king's army
and allowances be given them, as is due to all the king's soldiers. 37 Let some of them be stationed in the king's principal strongholds, and of these let some be given positions of
trust in the affairs of the kingdom. Let their superiors and
their rulers be taken from among them, and let them follow
their own laws, as the king has commanded in the land of
Judah.
38 "Let the three districts that have been added to Judea
from the province of Samaria be incorporated with Judea so
that they may be under one man and obey no other authority
than the high priest. 39 Ptolemais and its confines I give as a
present to the sanctuary in Jerusalem for the necessary
expenses of the sanctuary. 40 I make a yearly personal grant
of fifteen thousand silver shekels out of the royal revenues,

NEW JERUSALEM BIBLE

his own choosing. 33 Every Jewish person taken from
Judaea into captivity in any part of my kingdom I set free
without ransom, and decree that all will be exempt from
taxes, even on their livestock. 34 All festivals, Sabbaths,
New Moons and days of special observance, and the three
days before and three days after a festival, will be days of
exemption and quittance for all the Jews in my kingdom,
35 and no one will have the right to exact payment from, or
to molest, any of them for any matter whatsoever.
36 'Jews will be enrolled in the king's forces to the number of thirty thousand men and receive maintenance on
the same scale as the rest of the king's forces. 37 Some of
them will be stationed in the king's major fortresses, and
from among others appointments will be made to positions
of trust in the kingdom. Their officers and commanders
will be appointed from their own number and will live
under their own laws, as the king has prescribed for
Judaea.
38 'As regards the three districts annexed to Judaea from
the province of Samaria, these will be integrated into
Judaea and considered as coming under one governor,
obeying the high priest's authority and no other.
39 Ptolemais and the land thereto pertaining I present to
the sanctuary in Jerusalem, to meet the necessary expenses
of public worship. 40 And I make a personal grant of fifteen thousand silver shekels annually chargeable to the

Greek Old Testament

τόπων τῶν ἀνηκόντων. [41] καὶ πᾶν τὸ πλεονάζον, ὃ οὐκ ἀπε-
δίδοσαν ἀπὸ τῶν χρειῶν ὡς ἐν τοῖς πρώτοις ἔτεσιν, ἀπὸ τοῦ
νῦν δώσουσιν εἰς τὰ ἔργα τοῦ οἴκου. [42] καὶ ἐπὶ τούτοις
πεντακισχιλίους σίκλους ἀργυρίου, οὓς ἐλάμβανον ἀπὸ τῶν
χρειῶν τοῦ ἁγίου ἀπὸ τοῦ λόγου κατ' ἐνιαυτόν, καὶ ταῦτα
ἀφίεται διὰ τὸ ἀνήκειν αὐτὰ τοῖς ἱερεῦσιν τοῖς λειτουρ-
γοῦσιν. [43] καὶ ὅσοι ἐὰν φύγωσιν εἰς τὸ ἱερὸν τὸ ἐν Ιεροσολύμοις καὶ ἐν πᾶσιν τοῖς ὁρίοις αὐτοῦ ὀφείλων βασιλικὰ καὶ
πᾶν πρᾶγμα, ἀπολελύσθωσαν καὶ πάντα, ὅσα ἐστὶν αὐτοῖς ἐν
τῇ βασιλείᾳ μου. [44] καὶ τοῦ οἰκοδομηθῆναι καὶ ἐπικαινισθῆ-
ναι τὰ ἔργα τῶν ἁγίων, καὶ ἡ δαπάνη δοθήσεται ἐκ τοῦ λόγου τοῦ βασιλέως. [45] καὶ τοῦ οἰκοδομηθῆναι τὰ τείχη Ιερουσαλημ καὶ ὀχυρῶσαι κυκλόθεν, καὶ ἡ δαπάνη δοθήσεται ἐκ
τοῦ λόγου τοῦ βασιλέως, καὶ τοῦ οἰκοδομηθῆναι τὰ τείχη ἐν
τῇ Ιουδαίᾳ.

[46] Ὡς δὲ ἤκουσεν Ιωναθαν καὶ ὁ λαὸς τοὺς λόγους τούτους, οὐκ ἐπίστευσαν αὐτοῖς οὐδὲ ἐπεδέξαντο, ὅτι ἐπεμνή-
σθησαν τῆς κακίας τῆς μεγάλης, ἧς ἐποίησεν ἐν Ισραηλ καὶ
ἔθλιψεν αὐτοὺς σφόδρα. [47] καὶ εὐδόκησαν ἐν Ἀλεξάνδρῳ,
ὅτι αὐτὸς ἐγένετο αὐτοῖς ἀρχηγὸς λόγων εἰρηνικῶν, καὶ
συνεμάχουν αὐτῷ πάσας τὰς ἡμέρας.

[48] Καὶ συνήγαγεν Ἀλέξανδρος ὁ βασιλεὺς δυνάμεις μεγάλας καὶ παρενέβαλεν ἐξ ἐναντίας Δημητρίου. [49] καὶ συνῆψαν πόλεμον οἱ δύο βασιλεῖς, καὶ ἔφυγεν ἡ παρεμβολὴ
Δημητρίου, καὶ ἐδίωξεν αὐτὸν ὁ Ἀλέξανδρος καὶ ἴσχυσεν ἐπ'

King James Version

41 And all the overplus, which the officers payed not in as in former time, from henceforth shall be given toward the works of the temple.

42 And beside this, the five thousand shekels of silver, which they took from the uses of the temple out of the accounts year by year, even those things shall be released, because they appertain to the priests that minister.

43 And whosoever they be that flee unto the temple at Jerusalem, or be within the liberties thereof, being indebted unto the king, or for any other matter, let them be at liberty, and all that they have in my realm.

44 For the building also and repairing of the works of the sanctuary expences shall be given of the king's accounts.

45 Yea, and for the building of the walls of Jerusalem, and the fortifying thereof round about, expences shall be given out of the king's accounts, as also for the building of the walls in Judea.

46 Now when Jonathan and the people heard these words, they gave no credit unto them, nor received them, because they remembered the great evil that he had done in Israel; for he had afflicted them very sore.

47 But with Alexander they were well pleased, because he was the first that entreated of true peace with them, and they were confederate with him always.

48 Then gathered king Alexander great forces, and camped over against Demetrius.

49 And after the two kings had joined battle, Demetrius' host fled: but Alexander followed after him, and prevailed against them.

Douay Old Testament

41 And all that is above, which they that were over the affairs the years before, had not paid, from this time they shall give it to the works of the house.

42 Moreover the five thousand sicles of silver which they received from the account of the holy places, every year, shall also belong to the priests that execute the ministry.

43 And whosoever shall flee into the temple that is in Jerusalem, and in all the borders thereof, being indebted to the king for any matter, let them be set at liberty, and all that they have in my kingdom, let them have it free.

44 For the building also, or repairing the works of the holy places, the charges shall be given out of the king's revenues:

45 For the building also of the walls of Jerusalem, and the fortifying thereof round about, the charges shall be given out of the king's account, as also for the building of the walls in Judea.

46 Now when Jonathan, and the people heard these words, they gave no credit to them nor received them: because they remembered the great evil that he had done in Israel, for he had afflicted them exceedingly.

47 And their inclinations were towards Alexander, because he had been the chief promoter of peace in their regard, and him they always helped.

48 And king Alexander gathered together a great army, and moved his camp near to Demetrius.

49 And the two kings joined battle, and the army of Demetrius fled away, and Alexander pursued after him, and pressed them close.

Knox Translation

that belong to me. [41] With this sum, arrears shall be made
good in payments for the temple building, withheld till now
by such as had charge of the matter; [42] and restitution made,
to the priests now in office, for the five thousand sicles that
were confiscated year by year from the temple treasury.[a]
[43] Debtor to the king, whatever be the charge against him,
that takes sanctuary in the temple or its precincts, shall be
left at liberty, and no distraint made upon goods of his within these dominions. [44] Payment shall be made besides from
the royal treasury for the finishing and repairing of the temple fabric; [45] as also for building up and making strong the
walls of Jerusalem, and restoring the fortresses of Judaea.
[46] But in vain were such promises made to Jonathan and
the Jewish folk, nor credence found they any nor assent.
Could they forget all the mischief Demetrius had done in
Israel, all the tyranny they had endured? [47] Alexander it was
had all their good wishes; his was the first offer of terms that
reached them, and all the while it was his cause they cherished. [48] By this, Alexander had mustered a great force, and
marched against Demetrius. [49] When the two kings met, it
was Demetrius' men took to their heels, and Alexander gave

a *vv.* 41, 42. The Latin here differs from the Greek text, which is less intelligible.

TODAY'S ENGLISH VERSION

the royal treasury. 41 The total accumulated state subsidy, which we have failed to pay in recent years, shall be paid, and the payments continued from now on for the work of the Temple. 42 In addition to this, we will no longer require the 5,000 silver coins annually from the Temple income. This money belongs to the priests serving in the Temple. 43 Whoever owes a debt to the king or any other debt and takes refuge in the Temple in Jerusalem or in any area that belongs to it may not be arrested nor may his property anywhere in my kingdom be confiscated. 44 The expenses for rebuilding and renovating the Temple shall be provided from the royal treasury. 45 Likewise, the expenses for rebuilding the walls of Jerusalem and its surrounding fortifications, as well as the walls of designated towns in Judea, shall be provided from the royal treasury."

46 When Jonathan and the people heard the proposals made by King Demetrius, they refused to believe them or accept them, because they remembered how harshly he had treated them and what terrible troubles he had caused them. 47 They preferred to give their allegiance to Alexander because he had been the first to open peace negotiations, and they remained his allies as long as he lived.

48 King Alexander raised a large army and took up battle positions facing Demetrius. 49 But when the armies of the two kings met in battle, the army of Alexander[a] turned and ran. Demetrius[b] pursued them and won the battle.

[a] Alexander; *some manuscripts have* Demetrius.
[b] Demetrius; *some manuscripts have* Alexander.

NEW REVISED STANDARD VERSION

places. 41 And all the additional funds that the government officials have not paid as they did in the first years,[a] they shall give from now on for the service of the temple.[b] 42 Moreover, the five thousand shekels of silver that my officials[c] have received every year from the income of the services of the temple, this too is canceled, because it belongs to the priests who minister there. 43 And all who take refuge at the temple in Jerusalem, or in any of its precincts, because they owe money to the king or are in debt, let them be released and receive back all their property in my kingdom.

44 "Let the cost of rebuilding and restoring the structures of the sanctuary be paid from the revenues of the king. 45 And let the cost of rebuilding the walls of Jerusalem and fortifying it all around, and the cost of rebuilding the walls in Judea, also be paid from the revenues of the king."

46 When Jonathan and the people heard these words, they did not believe or accept them, because they remembered the great wrongs that Demetrius[d] had done in Israel and how much he had oppressed them. 47 They favored Alexander, because he had been the first to speak peaceable words to them, and they remained his allies all his days.

48 Now King Alexander assembled large forces and encamped opposite Demetrius. 49 The two kings met in battle, and the army of Demetrius fled, and Alexander[e] pursued him

a Meaning of Gk uncertain *b* Gk *house* *c* Gk *they* *d* Gk *he*
e Other ancient authorities read *Alexander fled, and Demetrius*

NEW AMERICAN BIBLE

from appropriate places. 41 All the additional funds that the officials did not hand over as they had done in the first years, shall henceforth be handed over for the services of the temple. 42 Moreover, the dues of five thousand silver shekels that used to be taken from the revenue of the sanctuary every year shall be canceled, since these funds belong to the priests who perform the services. 43 Whoever takes refuge in the temple of Jerusalem or in any of its precincts, because of money he owes the king, or because of any other debt, shall be released, together with all the goods he possesses in my kingdom. 44 The cost of rebuilding and restoring the structures of the sanctuary shall be covered out of the royal revenue. 45 Likewise the cost of building the walls of Jerusalem and fortifying it all around, and of building walls in Judea, shall be donated from the royal revenue."

46 When Jonathan and the people heard these words, they neither believed nor accepted them, for they remembered the great evil that Demetrius had done in Israel, and how sorely he had afflicted them. 47 They therefore decided in favor of Alexander, for he had been the first to address them peaceably, and they remained his allies for the rest of his life.

48 King Alexander gathered together a large army and encamped opposite Demetrius. 49 The two kings joined battle, and when the army of Demetrius fled, Alexander pursued

NEW JERUSALEM BIBLE

royal revenue from appropriate places. 41 And the entire surplus, which has not been paid in by the officials as in previous years, will henceforth be paid over by them for work on the Temple. 42 In addition, the sum of five thousand silver shekels, levied annually on the profits of the sanctuary, as shown in the annual accounts, is also relinquished as the perquisite of the priests who perform the liturgy. 43 Anyone who takes refuge in the Temple in Jerusalem or any of its precincts, when in debt to the royal exchequer or otherwise, will be discharged in full possession of all the goods he owns in my kingdom. 44 As regards the building and restoration of the sanctuary, the expense of the work will be met from the royal exchequer. 45 The reconstruction of the walls of Jerusalem and the fortification of the perimeter will also be a charge on the royal exchequer, as also the reconstruction of other city walls in Judaea.'

46 When Jonathan and the people heard these proposals, they put no faith in them and refused to accept them, remembering what great wrongs Demetrius had done to Israel and how cruelly he had oppressed them. 47 They decided in favour of Alexander, since he seemed to offer the better inducements of the two, and they became his constant allies. 48 King Alexander now mustered large forces and advanced against Demetrius. 49 The two kings met in battle. Alexander's army was routed, and Demetrius pursued him and

GREEK OLD TESTAMENT

αὐτούς. 50 καὶ ἐστερέωσεν τὸν πόλεμον σφόδρα, ἕως ἔδυ ὁ
ἥλιος, καὶ ἔπεσεν ὁ Δημήτριος ἐν τῇ ἡμέρᾳ ἐκείνῃ.
51 Καὶ ἀπέστειλεν Ἀλέξανδρος πρὸς Πτολεμαῖον βασιλέα
Αἰγύπτου πρέσβεις κατὰ τοὺς λόγους τούτους λέγων
52 Ἐπεὶ ἀνέστρεψα εἰς τὴν βασιλείαν μου καὶ ἐνεκάθισα
ἐπὶ θρόνου πατέρων μου καὶ ἐκράτησα τῆς ἀρχῆς, καὶ συνέ-
τριψα τὸν Δημήτριον καὶ ἐπεκράτησα τῆς χώρας ἡμῶν
53 καὶ συνῆψα πρὸς αὐτὸν μάχην, καὶ συνετρίβη αὐτὸς καὶ ἡ
παρεμβολὴ αὐτοῦ ὑφ' ἡμῶν, καὶ ἐκαθίσαμεν ἐπὶ θρόνου
βασιλείας αὐτοῦ· 54 καὶ νῦν στήσωμεν πρὸς αὐτοὺς φιλίαν,
καὶ νῦν δός μοι τὴν θυγατέρα σου εἰς γυναῖκα, καὶ ἐπιγαμβρεύσω σοι καὶ δώσω σοι δόματα καὶ αὐτῇ ἄξιά σου.
55 Καὶ ἀπεκρίθη Πτολεμαῖος ὁ βασιλεὺς λέγων
Ἀγαθὴ ἡμέρα, ἐν ᾗ ἐπέστρεψας εἰς γῆν πατέρων σου καὶ
ἐκάθισας ἐπὶ θρόνου βασιλείας αὐτῶν. 56 καὶ νῦν ποιήσω σοι
ἃ ἔγραψας, ἀλλὰ ἀπάντησον εἰς Πτολεμαίδα, ὅπως ἴδωμεν
ἀλλήλους, καὶ ἐπιγαμβρεύσω σοι, καθὼς εἴρηκας.
57 Καὶ ἐξῆλθεν Πτολεμαῖος ἐξ Αἰγύπτου, αὐτὸς καὶ
Κλεοπάτρα ἡ θυγάτηρ αὐτοῦ, καὶ ἦλθεν εἰς Πτολεμαίδα
ἔτους δευτέρου καὶ ἑξηκοστοῦ καὶ ἑκατοστοῦ. 58 καὶ ἀπήντησεν αὐτῷ Ἀλέξανδρος ὁ βασιλεύς, καὶ ἐξέδετο αὐτῷ
Κλεοπάτραν τὴν θυγατέρα αὐτοῦ καὶ ἐποίησεν τὸν γάμον
αὐτῆς ἐν Πτολεμαίδι καθὼς οἱ βασιλεῖς ἐν δόξῃ μεγάλῃ. —
59 καὶ ἔγραψεν Ἀλέξανδρος ὁ βασιλεὺς Ιωναθη ἐλθεῖν εἰς

KING JAMES VERSION

50 And he continued the battle very sore until the sun went down: and that day was Demetrius slain.

51 Afterward Alexander sent ambassadors to Ptolemee king of Egypt with a message to this effect:

52 Forasmuch as I am come again to my realm, and am set in the throne of my progenitors, and have gotten the dominion, and overthrown Demetrius, and recovered our country;

53 For after I had joined battle with him, both he and his host was discomfited by us, so that we sit in the throne of his kingdom:

54 Now therefore let us make a league of amity together, and give me now thy daughter to wife: and I will be thy son in law, and will give both thee and her gifts as according to thy dignity.

55 Then Ptolemee the king gave answer, saying, Happy be the day wherein thou didst return into the land of thy fathers, and satest in the throne of their kingdom.

56 And now will I do to thee, as thou hast written: meet me therefore at Ptolemais, that we may see one another; for I will marry my daughter to thee according to thy desire.

57 So Ptolemee went out of Egypt with his daughter Cleopatra, and they came unto Ptolemais in the hundred threescore and second year:

58 Where king Alexander meeting him, he gave unto him his daughter Cleopatra, and celebrated her marriage at Ptolemais with great glory, as the manner of kings is.

59 Now king Alexander had written unto Jonathan, that he should come and meet him.

DOUAY OLD TESTAMENT

50 And the battle was hard fought till the sun went down: and Demetrius was slain that day.

51 And Alexander sent ambassadors to Ptolemee king of Egypt, with words to this effect, saying:

52 Forasmuch as I am returned into my kingdom, and am set in the throne of my ancestors, and have gotten the dominion, and have overthrown Demetrius, and possessed our country,

53 And have joined battle with him, and both he and his army have been destroyed by us, and we are placed in the throne of his kingdom:

54 Now therefore let us make friendship one with another: and give me now thy daughter to wife, and I will be thy son in law, and I will give both thee and her gifts worthy of thee.

55 And king Ptolemee answered, saying: Happy is the day wherein thou didst return to the land of thy fathers, and sattest in the throne of their kingdom.

56 And now I will do to thee as thou hast written: but meet me at Ptolemais, that we may see one another, and I may give her to thee as thou hast said.

57 So Ptolemee went out of Egypt, with Cleopatra his daughter, and he came to Ptolemais in the hundred and sixty-second year.

58 And king Alexander met him, and he gave him his daughter Cleopatra: and he celebrated her marriage at Ptolemais, with great glory, after the manner of kings.

59 And king Alexander wrote to Jonathan, that he should come and meet him.

KNOX TRANSLATION

chase, pressing them hard; 50 fiercely the battle raged till
sun-down, and before the day was over, Demetrius fell.
51 Hereupon Alexander sent an embassy to Ptolemy, king
of Egypt, addressing him in these terms following. 52 Take
notice I have returned to my kingdom, and sit now on the
throne of my fathers, in full possession of my princely rights.
Would I regain Syria, needs must I should overthrow
Demetrius; 53 overthrow him I did, on field of battle, with all
his army, and here I sit in his place. 54 And should we not be
upon terms of friendship, thou and I? Let me have thy
daughter to wife; a niggardly wooer thou shalt not find me,
nor she either. 55 And what answer made king Ptolemy? An
auspicious day, said he, this day of thy return to the land
and throne of thy fathers! 56 Boon thy letter asks of me thou
shalt have; but first meet we together, face to face, yonder at
Ptolemais; there will I pledge my word to the articles thou
namest. 57 So here was king Ptolemy come from Egypt, with
his daughter Cleopatra, all the way to Ptolemais, in the hundred and sixty-second year; 58 and there king Alexander met
him and took his daughter Cleopatra to wife, and they held
the wedding with great magnificence, as kings will.
59 King Alexander had sent word to Jonathan, he should
come and keep tryst with him; 60 so to Ptolemais Jonathan

TODAY'S ENGLISH VERSION

50 Alexander[a] fought bitterly until sundown, but Demetrius
was killed that day.
51 Then Alexander sent ambassadors to King Ptolemy the
Sixth of Egypt with this message:
52 "I have returned to my kingdom and taken my seat on
the throne of my ancestors. I have taken over the government, and I am now in control of the country. 53 I made
war on Demetrius, defeated him and his army, and I have
taken over his kingdom. 54 Now I am ready to make an
alliance. Give me your daughter in marriage, and I will
give both of you such gifts as you deserve."
55 King Ptolemy replied, "It was a great day when you
returned to your country and took the throne of your ancestors. 56 I agree to your proposals, but first meet me at
Ptolemais. We can get acquainted there, and I will give you
my daughter in marriage."
57 So in the year 162[b] Ptolemy and his daughter Cleopatra[c]
left Egypt and arrived at Ptolemais. 58 King Alexander met
them, and Ptolemy gave him his daughter in marriage.
The wedding was celebrated there in Ptolemais with royal
splendor.
59 King Alexander wrote asking Jonathan to come to meet

[a] Alexander; *some manuscripts have* Demetrius. [b] THE YEAR 162: *This corresponds to 150 B.C.* [c] CLEOPATRA: *This was Cleopatra Thea, also known as Cleopatra the Third, and not to be confused with Cleopatra the Seventh (69–30 B.C.), who was involved in the history of Caesar and Mark Antony.*

NEW REVISED STANDARD VERSION

and defeated them. 50 He pressed the battle strongly until the
sun set, and on that day Demetrius fell.
51 Then Alexander sent ambassadors to Ptolemy king of
Egypt with the following message: 52 "Since I have returned
to my kingdom and have taken my seat on the throne of my
ancestors, and established my rule—for I crushed Demetrius
and gained control of our country; 53 I met him in battle, and
he and his army were crushed by us, and we have taken our
seat on the throne of his kingdom— 54 now therefore let us
establish friendship with one another; give me now your
daughter as my wife, and I will become your son-in-law, and
will make gifts to you and to her in keeping with your position."
55 Ptolemy the king replied and said, "Happy was the day
on which you returned to the land of your ancestors and
took your seat on the throne of their kingdom. 56 And now I
will do for you as you wrote, but meet me at Ptolemais, so
that we may see one another, and I will become your father-
in-law, as you have said."
57 So Ptolemy set out from Egypt, he and his daughter
Cleopatra, and came to Ptolemais in the one hundred sixty-
second year.[a] 58 King Alexander met him, and Ptolemy[b]
gave him his daughter Cleopatra in marriage, and celebrated
her wedding at Ptolemais with great pomp, as kings do.
59 Then King Alexander wrote to Jonathan to come and

[a] 150 B.C. [b] Gk *he*

NEW AMERICAN BIBLE

him, and overpowered his soldiers. 50 He pressed the battle
hard until sunset, and Demetrius fell that day.
51 Alexander sent ambassadors to Ptolemy, king of Egypt,
with this message: 52 "Now that I have returned to my
realm, taken my seat on the throne of my fathers, and established my rule by crushing Demetrius and gaining control of
my country— 53 for I engaged him in battle, defeated him
and his army, and recovered the royal throne— 54 let us now
establish friendship with each other. Give me your daughter
for my wife; and as your son-in-law, I will give to you and to
her gifts worthy of you."
55 King Ptolemy answered in these words: "Happy the day
on which you returned to the land of your fathers and took
your seat on their royal throne! 56 I will do for you what you
have written; but meet me in Ptolemais, so that we may see
each other, and I will become your father-in-law as you have
proposed."
57 So Ptolemy with his daughter Cleopatra set out from
Egypt and came to Ptolemais in the year one hundred and
sixty-two. 58 There King Alexander met him, and Ptolemy
gave him his daughter Cleopatra in marriage. Their wedding
was celebrated at Ptolemais with great splendor according to
the custom of kings.
59 King Alexander also wrote to Jonathan to come and meet

NEW JERUSALEM BIBLE

defeated his troops. 50 He continued the battle with vigour
until sunset. Demetrius himself, however, was killed the
same day.
51 Alexander sent ambassadors to Ptolemy king of Egypt,
with this message:

52 'Since I have returned to my kingdom, have ascended
the throne of my ancestors, have gained control by crushing Demetrius, and so recovered our country— 53 for I
fought him and we crushed both him and his army, and I
now occupy his royal throne— 54 let us now make a treaty
of friendship. Give me your daughter in marriage: as your
son-in-law, I shall give you, and her, presents which are
worthy of you.'

55 King Ptolemy replied as follows:

'Happy the day when you returned to the land of your
ancestors and ascended their royal throne! 56 I shall at
once do for you what your letter proposes; but meet me at
Ptolemais, so that we can see one another, and I shall
become your father-in-law, as you have asked.'

57 Ptolemy left Egypt with his daughter Cleopatra and
reached Ptolemais in the year 162. 58 King Alexander went to
meet him, and Ptolemy gave him the hand of his daughter
Cleopatra and celebrated her wedding in Ptolemais with great
magnificence, as kings do. 59 King Alexander then wrote to
Jonathan to come and meet him. 60 Jonathan made his way

GREEK OLD TESTAMENT

συνάντησιν αὐτῷ. 60 καὶ ἐπορεύθη μετὰ δόξης εἰς Πτολεμαΐδα καὶ ἀπήντησεν τοῖς δυσὶν βασιλεῦσι· καὶ ἔδωκεν αὐτοῖς ἀργύριον καὶ χρυσίον καὶ τοῖς φίλοις αὐτῶν καὶ δόματα
πολλὰ καὶ εὗρεν χάριν ἐνώπιον αὐτῶν. 61 καὶ ἐπισυνήχθησαν
ἐπ' αὐτὸν ἄνδρες λοιμοὶ ἐξ Ισραηλ, ἄνδρες παράνομοι, ἐντυ-
χεῖν κατ' αὐτοῦ, καὶ οὐ προσέσχεν αὐτοῖς ὁ βασιλεύς. 62 καὶ
προσέταξεν ὁ βασιλεὺς καὶ ἐξέδυσαν Ιωναθαν τὰ ἱμάτια αὐτοῦ καὶ ἐνέδυσαν αὐτὸν πορφύραν, καὶ ἐποίησαν οὕτως.
63 καὶ ἐκάθισεν αὐτὸν ὁ βασιλεὺς μετ' αὐτοῦ καὶ εἶπεν τοῖς
ἄρχουσιν αὐτοῦ Ἐξέλθατε μετ' αὐτοῦ εἰς μέσον τῆς πόλεως
καὶ κηρύξατε τοῦ μηδένα ἐντυγχάνειν κατ' αὐτοῦ περὶ μηδενὸς πράγματος, καὶ μηδεὶς αὐτῷ παρενοχλείτω περὶ
παντὸς λόγου. 64 καὶ ἐγένετο ὡς εἶδον οἱ ἐντυγχάνοντες
τὴν δόξαν αὐτοῦ, καθὼς ἐκήρυξεν, καὶ περιβεβλημένον αὐτὸν
πορφύραν, καὶ ἔφυγον πάντες. 65 καὶ ἐδόξασεν αὐτὸν ὁ
βασιλεὺς καὶ ἔγραψεν αὐτὸν τῶν πρώτων φίλων καὶ ἔθετο
αὐτὸν στρατηγὸν καὶ μεριδάρχην. 66 καὶ ἐπέστρεψεν
Ιωναθαν εἰς Ιερουσαλημ μετ' εἰρήνης καὶ εὐφροσύνης.
67 Καὶ ἐν ἔτει πέμπτῳ καὶ ἑξηκοστῷ καὶ ἑκατοστῷ ἦλθεν
Δημήτριος υἱὸς Δημητρίου ἐκ Κρήτης εἰς τὴν γῆν τῶν πατέρων αὐτοῦ. 68 καὶ ἤκουσεν Ἀλέξανδρος ὁ βασιλεὺς καὶ
ἐλυπήθη σφόδρα καὶ ὑπέστρεψεν εἰς Ἀντιόχειαν. 69 καὶ
κατέστησεν Δημήτριος Ἀπολλώνιον τὸν ὄντα ἐπὶ Κοίλης
Συρίας, καὶ συνήγαγεν δύναμιν μεγάλην καὶ παρενέβαλεν
ἐπὶ Ιάμνειαν· καὶ ἀπέστειλεν πρὸς Ιωναθαν τὸν ἀρχιερέα
λέγων

KING JAMES VERSION

60 Who thereupon went honourably to Ptolemais, where he met the two kings, and gave them and their friends silver and gold, and many presents, and found favour in their sight.

61 At that time certain pestilent fellows of Israel, men of a wicked life, assembled themselves against him, to accuse him: but the king would not hear them.

62 Yea more than that, the king commanded to take off his garments, and clothe him in purple: and they did so.

63 And he made him sit by himself, and said into his princes, Go with him into the midst of the city, and make proclamation, that no man complain against him of any matter, and that no man trouble him for any manner of cause.

64 Now when his accusers saw that he was honored according to the proclamation, and clothed in purple, they fled all away.

65 So the king honoured him, and wrote him among his chief friends, and made him a duke, and partaker of his dominion.

66 Afterward Jonathan returned to Jerusalem with peace and gladness.

67 Furthermore in the hundred threescore and fifth year came Demetrius son of Demetrius out of Crete into the land of his fathers:

68 Whereof when king Alexander heard tell, he was right sorry, and returned into Antioch.

69 Then Demetrius made Apollonius the governor of Celosyria his general, who gathered together a great host, and camped in Jamnia, and sent unto Jonathan the high priest, saying,

DOUAY OLD TESTAMENT

60 And he went honourably to Ptolemais, and he met there the two kings, and he gave them much silver, and gold, and presents: and he found favour in their sight.

61 And some pestilent men of Israel, men of a wicked life, assembled themselves against him to accuse him: and the king gave no heed to them.

62 And he commanded that Jonathan's garments should be taken off, and that he should be clothed with purple: and they did so. And the king made him sit by himself.

63 And he said to his princes: Go out with him into the midst of the city, and make proclamation, that no man complain against him of any matter, and that no man trouble him for any manner of cause.

64 So when his accusers saw his glory proclaimed, and him clothed with purple, they all fled away.

65 And the king magnified him, and enrolled him amongst his chief friends, and made him governor and partaker of his dominion.

66 And Jonathan returned into Jerusalem with peace and joy.

67 In the year one hundred and sixty-five Demetrius the son of Demetrius came from Crete into the land of his fathers.

68 And king Alexander heard of it, and was much troubled, and returned to Antioch.

69 And king Demetrius made Apollonius his general, who was governor of Celesyria: and he gathered together a great army, and came to Jamnia: and he sent to Jonathan the high priest,

KNOX TRANSLATION

went with great state, and met the two kings there. Gifts a
many he made them, of silver and gold and much else, and
was high in favour with them. 61 It chanced that certain
Israelites, pestilent fellows of the traitorous party, came there
to bring charges against him. But to these the king would
not listen; 62 he would have Jonathan change his garments,
and go clad in purple, and when this was done, a seat he
must have beside the king himself. 63 Take him out into the
heart of the city, Alexander said to his vassals, and there
make proclamation, none may bring charge against him on
any pretext, or in any fashion molest him. 64 No thought had
his accusers, when they heard such proclamation made, and
saw Jonathan there dressed in purple, but to escape, one and
all, as best they could; 65 he himself was loaded with honours, enrolled among the king's chief friends, and made a
prince, with a share in the governance of the kingdom. 66 So
Jonathan made his way back to Jerusalem undisturbed, and
well content.
67 Then, in the hundred and sixty-fifth year, came
Demetrius, son of that other Demetrius, from the island of
Crete, and landed in his native country; 68 ill hearing indeed
for Alexander, who returned at once to Antioch.
69 Demetrius[a] gave command of his army to Apollonius, that
was governor of Coelesyria, and a great array it was he
levied. From Jamnia, where he took up his quarters, this
Apollonius sent word to the high priest Jonathan: 70 What,

[a] It seems possible that the word 'Demetrius' may have been inserted for the sake of clearness; Josephus treats Apollonius throughout as fighting on the side of Alexander (in spite of verse 88).

TODAY'S ENGLISH VERSION

him. 60 So Jonathan, in a show of splendor, went to Ptolemais and met the two kings. He presented them with gifts of
silver and gold, and he also gave many gifts to the high officials who had accompanied them. Everyone was favorably
impressed with him. 61 At the same time some traitorous
Jews who wanted to make trouble for Jonathan made accusations against him, but King Alexander paid no attention to
them. 62 He gave orders that Jonathan should be given royal
robes to wear, 63 and he honored him by letting him sit at
his side. Alexander told his officers to take Jonathan into the
center of the city and to announce that no one was to bring
charges against him for any reason and no one was to cause
him any kind of trouble. 64 When his accusers saw the honors given to him, heard the announcement, and saw him
clothed in royal robes, they all fled. 65 The king further honored Jonathan by enrolling him in the First Order of the
"Friends of the King" and by making him general and governor of his province. 66 Jonathan returned to Jerusalem
pleased and successful.
67 In the year 165[a] Demetrius the Second, the son of
Demetrius the First, left Crete and arrived in Syria, the land
of his ancestors. 68 When King Alexander heard about this,
he was worried and returned to Antioch, the capital of Syria.
69 Demetrius reappointed Apollonius governor of Greater
Syria. Apollonius raised a large army, set up camp near
Jamnia, and sent the following message to Jonathan the
High Priest:

[a] THE YEAR 165: *This corresponds to 147 B.C.*

NEW REVISED STANDARD VERSION

meet him. 60 So he went with pomp to Ptolemais and met the
two kings; he gave them and their Friends silver and gold
and many gifts, and found favor with them. 61 A group of
malcontents from Israel, renegades, gathered together
against him to accuse him; but the king paid no attention to
them. 62 The king gave orders to take off Jonathan's garments and to clothe him in purple, and they did so. 63 The
king also seated him at his side; and he said to his officers,
"Go out with him into the middle of the city and proclaim
that no one is to bring charges against him about any matter, and let no one annoy him for any reason." 64 When his
accusers saw the honor that was paid him, in accord with
the proclamation, and saw him clothed in purple, they all
fled. 65 Thus the king honored him and enrolled him among
his chief[a] Friends, and made him general and governor of
the province. 66 And Jonathan returned to Jerusalem in peace
and gladness.
67 In the one hundred sixty-fifth year[b] Demetrius son of
Demetrius came from Crete to the land of his ancestors.
68 When King Alexander heard of it, he was greatly distressed
and returned to Antioch. 69 And Demetrius appointed Apollonius the governor of Coelesyria, and he assembled a large
force and encamped against Jamnia. Then he sent the following message to the high priest Jonathan:

a Gk *first* *b* 147 B.C.

NEW AMERICAN BIBLE

him. 60 So he went with pomp to Ptolemais, where he met
the two kings and gave them and their friends silver and
gold and many gifts and thus won their favor. 61 Some pestilent Israelites, transgressors of the law, united against him
to accuse him, but the king paid no heed to them. 62 He
ordered Jonathan to be divested of his ordinary garments and
to be clothed in royal purple; and so it was done. 63 The king
also had him seated at his side. He said to his magistrates:
"Go with him to the center of the city and make a proclamation that no one is to bring charges against him on any
grounds or be troublesome to him in any way."
64 When his accusers saw the honor paid to him in the
proclamation, and the purple with which he was clothed,
they all fled. 65 The king also honored him by numbering
him among his Chief Friends and made him military commander and governor of the province. 66 So Jonathan
returned in peace and happiness to Jerusalem.
67 In the year one hundred and sixty-five, Demetrius, son
of Demetrius, came from Crete to the land of his fathers.
68 When King Alexander heard of it he was greatly troubled,
and returned to Antioch. 69 Demetrius appointed Apollonius
governor of Coelesyria. Having gathered a large army,
Apollonius pitched his camp at Jamnia. From there he sent
this message to Jonathan the high priest:

NEW JERUSALEM BIBLE

in state to Ptolemais and met the two kings; he gave them
and their friends silver and gold, and many gifts, and made a
favourable impression on them. 61 A number of scoundrels,
the pest of Israel, combined to denounce him, but the king
paid no attention to them. 62 In fact, the king commanded
that Jonathan should be divested of his own garments and
clothed in the purple, which was done. 63 The king then seated him by his side and said to his officers, 'Escort him into
the centre of the city and proclaim that no one is to bring
charges against him on any count; no one is to molest him
for any reason.' 64 And so, when his accusers saw the honour done him by this proclamation, and Jonathan himself
invested in the purple, they all fled. 65 The king did him the
honour of enrolling him among the First Friends, and
appointed him commander-in-chief and governor-general.
66 Jonathan then returned to Jerusalem in peace and gladness.
67 In the year 165, Demetrius son of Demetrius came from
Crete to the land of his ancestors. 68 When King Alexander
heard of it he was plunged into gloom, and retired to
Antioch. 69 Demetrius confirmed Apollonius as governor of
Coele-Syria; the latter assembled a large force, encamped at
Jamnia and sent the following message to Jonathan the high
priest:

GREEK OLD TESTAMENT

70 Σὺ μονώτατος ἐπαίρῃ ἐφ' ἡμᾶς, ἐγὼ δὲ ἐγενήθην εἰς καταγέλωτα καὶ εἰς ὀνειδισμὸν διὰ σέ· καὶ διὰ τί σὺ ἐξουσιάζῃ ἐφ' ἡμᾶς ἐν τοῖς ὄρεσι; 71 νῦν οὖν εἰ πέποιθας ἐπὶ ταῖς δυνάμεσίν σου, κατάβηθι πρὸς ἡμᾶς εἰς τὸ πεδίον, καὶ συγκριθῶμεν ἑαυτοῖς ἐκεῖ, ὅτι μετ' ἐμοῦ ἐστιν δύναμις τῶν πόλεων. 72 ἐρώτησον καὶ μάθε τίς εἰμι καὶ οἱ λοιποὶ οἱ βοηθοῦντες ἡμῖν, καὶ λέγουσιν Οὐκ ἔστιν ὑμῖν στάσις ποδὸς κατὰ πρόσωπον ἡμῶν, ὅτι δὶς ἐτροπώθησαν οἱ πατέρες σου ἐν τῇ γῇ αὐτῶν. 73 καὶ νῦν οὐ δυνήσῃ ὑποστῆναι τὴν ἵππον καὶ δύναμιν τοιαύτην ἐν τῷ πεδίῳ, ὅπου οὐκ ἔστιν λίθος οὐδὲ κόχλαξ οὐδὲ τόπος τοῦ φυγεῖν.

74 Ὡς δὲ ἤκουσεν Ιωναθαν τῶν λόγων Ἀπολλωνίου, ἐκινήθη τῇ διανοίᾳ καὶ ἐπέλεξεν δέκα χιλιάδας ἀνδρῶν καὶ ἐξῆλθεν ἐξ Ιερουσαλημ, καὶ συνήντησεν αὐτῷ Σιμων ὁ ἀδελφὸς αὐτοῦ ἐπὶ βοήθειαν αὐτῷ. 75 καὶ παρενέβαλεν ἐπὶ Ιοππην, καὶ ἀπέκλεισαν αὐτὴν οἱ ἐκ τῆς πόλεως, ὅτι φρουρὰ Ἀπολλωνίου ἐν Ιοππῃ· καὶ ἐπολέμησαν αὐτήν, 76 καὶ φοβηθέντες ἤνοιξαν οἱ ἐκ τῆς πόλεως, καὶ ἐκυρίευσεν Ιωναθαν Ιοππης. 77 καὶ ἤκουσεν Ἀπολλώνιος καὶ παρενέβαλεν τρισχιλίαν ἵππον καὶ δύναμιν πολλὴν καὶ ἐπορεύθη εἰς Ἄζωτον ὡς διοδεύων καὶ ἅμα προῆγεν εἰς τὸ πεδίον διὰ τὸ ἔχειν αὐτὸν πλῆθος ἵππου καὶ πεποιθέναι ἐπ' αὐτῇ. 78 καὶ κατεδίωξεν ὀπίσω αὐτοῦ εἰς Ἄζωτον, καὶ συνῆψαν αἱ παρεμβολαὶ εἰς πόλεμον. 79 καὶ

KING JAMES VERSION

70 Thou alone liftest up thyself against us, and I am laughed to scorn for thy sake, and reproached: and why dost thou vaunt thy power against us in the mountains?

71 Now therefore, if thou trustest in thine own strength, come down to us into the plain field, and there let us try the matter together: for with me is the power of the cities.

72 Ask and learn who I am, and the rest that take our part, and they shall tell thee that thy foot is not able to stand before our face; for thy fathers have been twice put to flight in their own land.

73 Wherefore now thou shalt not be able to abide the horsemen and so great a power in the plain, where is neither stone nor flint, nor place to flee unto.

74 So when Jonathan heard these words of Apollonius, he was moved in his mind, and choosing ten thousand men he went out of Jerusalem, where Simon his brother met him for to help him.

75 And he pitched his tents against Joppe: but they of Joppe shut him out of the city, because Apollonius had a garrison there.

76 Then Jonathan laid siege unto it: whereupon they of the city let him in for fear: and so Jonathan won Joppe.

77 Whereof when Apollonius heard, he took three thousand horsemen, with a great host *of footmen,* and went to Azotus as one that journeyed, and therewithal drew him forth into the plain, because he had a great number of horsemen, in whom he put his trust.

78 Then *Jonathan* followed after him to Azotus, where the armies joined battle.

DOUAY OLD TESTAMENT

70 Saying: Thou alone standest against us, and I am laughed at, and reproached, because thou shewest thy power against us in the mountains.

71 Now therefore if thou trustest in thy forces, come down to us into the plain, and there let us try one another: for with me is the strength of war.

72 Ask, and learn who I am, and the rest that help me, who also say that your foot cannot stand before our face, for thy fathers have twice been put to flight in their own land:

73 And now how wilt thou be able to abide the horsemen, and so great an army in the plain, where there is no stone, nor rock, nor place to flee to?

74 Now when Jonathan heard the words of Apollonius, he was moved in his mind: and he chose ten thousand men, and went out of Jerusalem, and Simon his brother met him to help him.

75 And they pitched their tents near Joppe, but they shut him out of the city: because a garrison of Apollonius was in Joppe, and he laid siege to it.

76 And they that were in the city being affrighted, opened the gates to him: so Jonathan took Joppe.

77 And Apollonius heard of it, and he took three thousand horsemen, and a great army.

78 And he went to Azotus as one that was making a journey, and immediately he went forth into the plain: because he had a great number of horsemen, and he trusted in them. And Jonathan followed after him to Azotus, and they joined battle.

KNOX TRANSLATION

wilt thou defy us, and all alone? Here am I mocked and flouted by the resistance offered me, up yonder in the hills! 71 Nay, if such confidence thou hast in thy own resources, come down and meet us in the plain; try we conclusions there! Trust me, I am master of the field; what I am, 72 what my troops are, thou shalt learn upon a little enquiry; stand thou canst not, they will tell thee, before onslaught of ours. Twice, on their native soil, thy fathers fled in disorder, 73 and wilt thou make head against such an array of horse and foot, here in the plain, where rock is none, nor gravel-bed, to aid thy flight?

74 Roused by this challenge, Jonathan marched out from Jerusalem with a muster of ten thousand men; his brother Simon joined hands with him; 75 and together they appeared before the gates of Joppe. Enter they might not, for Apollonius had a garrison there, but must needs attack it; 76 whereupon the citizens took alarm, and themselves opened the gates. Thus came Joppe into the power of Jonathan; 77 the news reached Apollonius, and he brought up three thousand horse, with a great array of men besides. 78 To Azotus he marched, as if he meant to pass them by, but all the while he was luring them on into the plain;[a] in horse lay his strength and his confidence. To Azotus Jonathan followed him, and battle was joined.

a 'All the time he was luring them on into the plain'; this seems to be the meaning of the Greek text, although Joppe and Azotus were both on the seaboard, far away from any hill-country. The Latin has 'immediately he went out into the plain', which yields no satisfactory sense.

TODAY'S ENGLISH VERSION

70“Because of you I am being ridiculed, but why do you,
there in your mountains, continue this rebellion when no
one supports you? 71If you really have any confidence in
your army, come down here on the plain and fight, where
we can test each other's strength. Study the situation, and
you will find that I have the support of the forces from the
cities. 72You will learn who I am and who our allies are,
and you will discover that you have no chance of standing
against us. Your predecessors have already been beaten
twice on their own ground; 73so how do you expect to
defeat my cavalry and the kind of army I have here on the
plain? Down here there is not so much as a pebble to hide
behind and no way to escape.”
74When Jonathan received this message from Apollonius,
he became angry. He took 10,000 elite troops from Jerusalem; his brother Simon also brought troops, and their two
forces 75set up camp outside of Joppa. The men of the city
refused to let them in because there was a detachment of
Apollonius' troops there, but Jonathan attacked, 76and the
men in the city became so frightened that they opened the
gates, allowing Jonathan to capture Joppa. 77When
Apollonius heard what had happened, he took 3,000 cavalry
and a large army of infantry and pretended to retreat south
toward Azotus. However, relying upon the strength of his
cavalry, he marched into the plain with his main force,
78-79positioning 1,000 cavalry where they could attack
Jonathan's forces from the rear. Jonathan continued his pursuit as far as Azotus, where the two armies met in battle.

NEW REVISED STANDARD VERSION

70 “You are the only one to rise up against us, and I have
fallen into ridicule and disgrace because of you. Why do you
assume authority against us in the hill country? 71If you
now have confidence in your forces, come down to the plain
to meet us, and let us match strength with each other there,
for I have with me the power of the cities. 72Ask and learn
who I am and who the others are that are helping us. People
will tell you that you cannot stand before us, for your ancestors were twice put to flight in their own land. 73And now
you will not be able to withstand my cavalry and such an
army in the plain, where there is no stone or pebble, or place
to flee.”
74 When Jonathan heard the words of Apollonius, his
spirit was aroused. He chose ten thousand men and set out
from Jerusalem, and his brother Simon met him to help him.
75He encamped before Joppa, but the people of the city closed
its gates, for Apollonius had a garrison in Joppa. 76So they
fought against it, and the people of the city became afraid
and opened the gates, and Jonathan gained possession of
Joppa.
77 When Apollonius heard of it, he mustered three thousand cavalry and a large army, and went to Azotus as
though he were going farther. At the same time he advanced
into the plain, for he had a large troop of cavalry and put
confidence in it. 78Jonathan[a] pursued him to Azotus, and
the armies engaged in battle. 79Now Apollonius had secretly

a Gk *he*

NEW AMERICAN BIBLE

70“You are the only one who resists us. I am laughed at
and put to shame on your account. Why are you displaying
power against us in the mountains? 71If you have confidence in your forces, come down now to us in the plain, and
let us test each other's strength there; the city forces are on
my side. 72Inquire and learn who I am and who the others
are who are helping me. Men say that you cannot make a
stand against us because your fathers were twice put to
flight in their own land. 73Now you too will be unable to
withstand our cavalry and such a force as this in the plain,
where there is not a stone or a pebble or a place to flee.”
74When Jonathan heard the message of Apollonius, he was
roused. Choosing ten thousand men, he set out from
Jerusalem, and Simon his brother joined him to help him.
75He pitched camp near Joppa, but the men in the city shut
him out because Apollonius had a garrison there. When the
Jews besieged it, 76the men of the city became afraid and
opened the gates, and so Jonathan took possession of Joppa.
77When Apollonius heard of it, he drew up three thousand
horsemen and an innumerable infantry. He marched on
Azotus as though he were going on through the country, but
at the same time he advanced into the plain, because he had
such a large number of horsemen to rely on. 78Jonathan
followed him to Azotus, and they engaged in battle.

NEW JERUSALEM BIBLE

70‘You are entirely alone in rising against us, and now I
find myself ridiculed and reproached on your account. Why
do you use your authority to our disadvantage in the
mountains? 71If you are so confident in your forces, come
down now to meet us on the plain and let us take each
other's measure there; on my side I have the strength of
the towns. 72Ask and learn who I am and who the others
supporting us are. You will hear that you cannot stand up
to us, since your ancestors were twice routed on their own
ground, 73nor will you now be able to withstand the cavalry or so great an army on the plain, where there is neither rock, nor stone, nor refuge of any kind.’

74On hearing Apollonius' words, Jonathan's spirit was
roused; he picked ten thousand men and left Jerusalem, and
his brother Simon joined him with reinforcements. 75He
drew up his forces outside Joppa, the citizens having shut
him out, since Apollonius had a garrison in Joppa. When
they began the attack, 76the citizens took fright and opened
the gates, and Jonathan occupied Joppa. 77Hearing this,
Apollonius marshalled three thousand cavalry and a large
army and made his way to Azotus as though intending to
march through, while in fact pressing on into the plain, since
he had a great number of cavalry on which he was relying.
78Jonathan pursued him as far as Azotus, where the armies

GREEK OLD TESTAMENT

ἀπέλιπεν Ἀπολλώνιος χιλίαν ἵππον κρυπτῶς κατόπισθεν
αὐτῶν. 80 καὶ ἔγνω Ιωναθαν ὅτι ἔστιν ἔνεδρον κατόπισθεν
αὐτοῦ, καὶ ἐκύκλωσαν αὐτοῦ τὴν παρεμβολὴν καὶ ἐξετίναξαν
τὰς σχίζας εἰς τὸν λαὸν ἐκ πρωίθεν ἕως δείλης. 81 ὁ δὲ λαὸς
εἱστήκει, καθὼς ἐπέταξεν Ιωναθαν, καὶ ἐκοπίασαν οἱ ἵπποι
αὐτῶν. 82 καὶ εἵλκυσεν Σιμων τὴν δύναμιν αὐτοῦ καὶ συνῆψεν πρὸς τὴν φάλαγγα, ἡ γὰρ ἵππος ἐξελύθη, καὶ συνετρίβησαν ὑπ' αὐτοῦ καὶ ἔφυγον, 83 καὶ ἡ ἵππος ἐσκορπίσθη ἐν
τῷ πεδίῳ. καὶ ἔφυγον εἰς Ἄζωτον καὶ εἰσῆλθον εἰς Βηθδα-
γων τὸ εἰδώλιον αὐτῶν τοῦ σωθῆναι.. 84 καὶ ἐνεπύρισεν Ιωναθαν τὴν Ἄζωτον καὶ τὰς πόλεις τὰς κύκλῳ αὐτῆς καὶ ἔλαβεν
τὰ σκῦλα αὐτῶν καὶ τὸ ἱερὸν Δαγων καὶ τοὺς συμφυγόντας
εἰς αὐτὸ ἐνεπύρισεν πυρί. 85 καὶ ἐγένοντο οἱ πεπτωκότες
μαχαίρᾳ σὺν τοῖς ἐμπυρισθεῖσιν εἰς ἄνδρας ὀκτακισχιλίους.
86 καὶ ἀπῆρεν ἐκεῖθεν Ιωναθαν καὶ παρενέβαλεν ἐπὶ
Ἀσκαλῶνα, καὶ ἐξῆλθον οἱ ἐκ τῆς πόλεως εἰς συνάντησιν
αὐτῷ ἐν δόξῃ μεγάλῃ. 87 καὶ ἐπέστρεψεν Ιωναθαν εἰς Ιερουσαλημ σὺν τοῖς παρ' αὐτοῦ ἔχοντες σκῦλα πολλά. 88 καὶ
ἐγένετο ὡς ἤκουσεν Ἀλέξανδρος ὁ βασιλεὺς τοὺς λόγους
τούτους, καὶ προσέθετο ἔτι δοξάσαι τὸν Ιωναθαν· 89 καὶ
ἀπέστειλεν αὐτῷ πόρπην χρυσῆν, ὡς ἔθος ἐστὶν δίδοσθαι
τοῖς συγγενέσιν τῶν βασιλέων, καὶ ἔδωκεν αὐτῷ τὴν
Ακκαρων καὶ πάντα τὰ ὅρια αὐτῆς εἰς κληροδοσίαν.

KING JAMES VERSION

79 Now Apollonius had left a thousand horsemen in ambush.

80 And Jonathan knew that there was an ambushment behind him; for they had compassed in his host, and cast darts at the people, from morning till evening.

81 But the people stood still, as Jonathan had commanded them: and so the enemies' horses were tired.

82 Then brought Simon forth his host, and set them against the footmen, (for the horsemen were spent,) who were discomfited by him, and fled.

83 The horsemen also, being scattered in the field, fled to Azotus, and went into Beth-dagon, their idol's temple, for safety.

84 But Jonathan set fire on Azotus, and the cities round about it, and took their spoils; and the temple of Dagon, with them that were fled into it, he burned with fire.

85 Thus there were burned and slain with the sword well nigh eight thousand men.

86 And from thence Jonathan removed his host, and camped against Ascalon, where the men of the city came forth, and met him with great pomp.

87 After this returned Jonathan and his host unto Jerusalem, having many spoils.

88 Now when king ALexander heard these things, he honoured Jonathan yet more,

89 And sent him a buckle of gold, as the use is to be given to such as are of the king's blood: he gave him also Accaron with the borders thereof in possession.

DOUAY OLD TESTAMENT

79 And Apollonius left privately in the camp a thousand horsemen behind them.

80 And Jonathan knew that there was an ambush behind him, and they surrounded his army, and cast darts at the people from morning till evening.

81 But the people stood still, as Jonathan had commanded them: and so their horses were fatigued.

82 Then Simon drew forth his army, and attacked the legion: for the horsemen were wearied: and they were discomfited by him, and fled.

83 And they that were scattered about the plain, fled into Azotus, and went into Bethdagon their idol's temple, there to save themselves.

84 But Jonathan set fire to Azotus, and the cities that were round about it, and took the spoils of them, and the temple of Dagon: and all them that were fled into it, he burnt with fire.

85 So they that were slain by the sword, with them that were burnt, were almost eight thousand men.

86 And Jonathan removed his army from thence, and camped against Ascalon: and they went out of the city to meet him with great honour.

87 And Jonathan returned into Jerusalem with his people, having many spoils.

88 And it came to pass: when Alexander the king heard these words, that he honoured Jonathan yet more.

89 And he sent him a buckle of gold, as the custom is, to be given to such as are of the royal blood. And he gave him Accaron and all the borders thereof in possession.

KNOX TRANSLATION

79 Apollonius, by a secret feint, had left a thousand horsemen encamped in their rear; 80 so all at once Jonathan found
himself cut off by an ambush. Round his army they rode,
casting javelins into the ranks, from morning till night-fall;
81 but ever it stood firm, at Jonathan's bidding, till the horses
were tired out at last. 82 Then, the force of the cavalry once
spent, out came Simon with his troops to attack the main
body, which thereupon broke and fled. 83 Scattered over the
open country, in vain they rallied at Azotus, and took refuge
in the precincts of their god Dagon; 84 both Azotus and all
the neighbouring cities Jonathan burnt and plundered, and
Dagon's temple, with all that took shelter there, was burnt
with the rest. 85 So perished, by sword and fire, some eight
thousand men; 86 as for Jonathan, he had no sooner
encamped before Ascalon, than the townsfolk opened the
gates to him, and gave him honourable welcome.

87 So Jonathan came back to Jerusalem, and the army
behind him, laden with spoils. 88 More than ever, when he
heard of it, did king Alexander heap honours upon him; 89 a
buckle of gold he sent him, ever the gift kings make to men
of blood royal, and Accaron, with all the country-side about
it, granted him for his domain.

TODAY'S ENGLISH VERSION

80 Not until then did Jonathan realize that he was caught in
an ambush. His army was surrounded, and enemy arrows
rained down on them from morning until evening. 81 But
Jonathan's men stood firm, as he had ordered, and the
attacking cavalry grew tired. 82 Then, when the cavalry was
exhausted, Simon appeared on the scene with his forces and
attacked and overwhelmed the enemy infantry, who broke
ranks and fled. 83 The cavalry, which by now was scattered
all over the battlefield, fled to Azotus, where they took refuge
in the temple of Dagon, their god. 84 But Jonathan set fire to
the city and to the temple of Dagon, burning to death all
those who had taken refuge there. Then he set fire to the surrounding towns and looted them. 85 That day about 8,000
were either killed in the battle or burned to death.
86 Jonathan left and set up camp at Ascalon, where the people of the city came out to welcome him with great honors.
87 Jonathan and his men returned to Jerusalem with large
quantities of loot.

88 When King Alexander heard what Jonathan had done, he
gave him even greater honors. 89 He sent him a gold shoulder buckle, which is given only to those honored with the
title "Relative of the King." He also gave him the city of
Ekron and its surrounding territory.

NEW REVISED STANDARD VERSION

left a thousand cavalry behind them. 80 Jonathan learned
that there was an ambush behind him, for they surrounded
his army and shot arrows at his men from early morning
until late afternoon. 81 But his men stood fast, as Jonathan
had commanded, and the enemy's[a] horses grew tired.

82 Then Simon brought forward his force and engaged the
phalanx in battle (for the cavalry was exhausted); they were
overwhelmed by him and fled, 83 and the cavalry was dispersed in the plain. They fled to Azotus and entered Beth-
dagon, the temple of their idol, for safety. 84 But Jonathan
burned Azotus and the surrounding towns and plundered
them; and the temple of Dagon, and those who had taken
refuge in it, he burned with fire. 85 The number of those who
fell by the sword, with those burned alive, came to eight
thousand.

86 Then Jonathan left there and encamped against
Askalon, and the people of the city came out to meet him
with great pomp.

87 He and those with him then returned to Jerusalem with
a large amount of booty. 88 When King Alexander heard of
these things, he honored Jonathan still more; 89 and he sent
to him a golden buckle, such as it is the custom to give to the
King's Kinsmen. He also gave him Ekron and all its environs
as his possession.

a Gk *their*

NEW AMERICAN BIBLE

79 Apollonius, however, had left a thousand cavalry in hiding
behind them. 80 When Jonathan discovered that there was an
ambush behind him, his army was surrounded. From morning until evening they showered his men with arrows. 81 But
his men held their ground, as Jonathan had commanded,
whereas the enemy's horses became tired out. 82 When the
horsemen were exhausted, Simon attacked the phalanx,
overwhelmed it and put it to flight. 83 The horsemen too
were scattered over the plain. The enemy fled to Azotus and
entered Beth-dagon, the temple of their idol, to save themselves. 84 But Jonathan burned and plundered Azotus with
its neighboring towns, and destroyed by fire both the temple
of Dagon and the men who had taken refuge in it. 85 Those
who fell by the sword, together with those who were burned
alive, came to about eight thousand men. 86 Then Jonathan
left there and pitched his camp at Ashkalon, and the people
of that city came out to meet him with great pomp. 87 He and
his men then returned to Jerusalem, laden with much booty.
88 When King Alexander heard of these events, he accorded
new honors to Jonathan. 89 He sent him a gold buckle, such
as is usually given to King's Kinsmen; he also gave him
Ekron and all its territory as a possession.

NEW JERUSALEM BIBLE

joined battle. 79 Now, Apollonius had left a thousand horsemen in concealment behind them. 80 Jonathan knew of this
enemy position behind him; the horsemen surrounded his
army, firing their arrows into his men from morning till
evening. 81 But the troops stood firm, as Jonathan had
ordered. Once the cavalry was exhausted, 82 Simon sent his
own troops into attack against the phalanx, which he cut to
pieces and routed. 83 The cavalry scattered over the plain
and fled to Azotus, where they took sanctuary in Beth-
Dagon, the temple of their idol. 84 Jonathan, however, set fire
to Azotus and the surrounding towns, plundered them, and
burned down the temple of Dagon, with all the fugitives who
had crowded into it. 85 The enemy losses, counting those
who fell by the sword and those burnt to death, totalled
about eight thousand men. 86 Jonathan then left and pitched
camp outside Ascalon, where the citizens came out to meet
him with great ceremony. 87 Jonathan then returned to
Jerusalem with his followers, laden with booty. 88 In the
event, when King Alexander heard what had happened, he
awarded Jonathan further honours: 89 he sent him the gold-
en brooch, of the kind customarily presented to the King's
Cousins, and gave him proprietary rights over Ekron and the
land adjoining it.

GREEK OLD TESTAMENT

11 Καὶ βασιλεὺς Αἰγύπτου ἤθροισεν δυνάμεις πολλὰς
ὡς ἡ ἄμμος ἡ παρὰ τὸ χεῖλος τῆς θαλάσσης καὶ
πλοῖα πολλὰ καὶ ἐζήτησε κατακρατῆσαι τῆς βασιλείας
Ἀλεξάνδρου δόλῳ καὶ προσθεῖναι αὐτὴν τῇ βασιλείᾳ αὐτοῦ.
2 καὶ ἐξῆλθεν εἰς Συρίαν λόγοις εἰρηνικοῖς, καὶ ἤνοιγον αὐτῷ
οἱ ἀπὸ τῶν πόλεων καὶ συνήντων αὐτῷ, ὅτι ἐντολὴ ἦν
Ἀλεξάνδρου τοῦ βασιλέως συναντᾶν αὐτῷ διὰ τὸ πενθερὸν
αὐτοῦ εἶναι· 3 ὡς δὲ εἰσεπορεύετο εἰς τὰς πόλεις Πτολεμαῖος, ἀπέτασσε τὰς δυνάμεις φρουρὰν ἐν ἑκάστῃ πόλει.
4 ὡς δὲ ἤγγισαν Ἀζώτου, ἔδειξαν αὐτῷ τὸ ἱερὸν Δαγων ἐμπε-
πυρισμένον καὶ Ἄζωτον καὶ τὰ περιπόλια αὐτῆς καθῃρημένα
καὶ τὰ σώματα ἐρριμμένα καὶ τοὺς ἐμπεπυρισμένους, οὓς
ἐνεπύρισεν ἐν τῷ πολέμῳ· ἐποίησαν γὰρ θιμωνιὰς αὐτῶν ἐν
τῇ ὁδῷ αὐτοῦ. 5 καὶ διηγήσαντο τῷ βασιλεῖ ἃ ἐποίησεν
Ιωναθαν εἰς τὸ ψογίσαι αὐτόν· καὶ ἐσίγησεν ὁ βασιλεύς.
6 καὶ συνήντησεν Ιωναθαν τῷ βασιλεῖ εἰς Ιοππην μετὰ δόξης, καὶ ἠσπάσαντο ἀλλήλους καὶ ἐκοιμήθησαν ἐκεῖ. 7 καὶ
ἐπορεύθη Ιωναθαν μετὰ τοῦ βασιλέως ἕως τοῦ ποταμοῦ τοῦ
καλουμένου Ἐλευθέρου καὶ ἐπέστρεψεν εἰς Ιερουσαλημ. 8 ὁ
δὲ βασιλεὺς Πτολεμαῖος ἐκυρίευσεν τῶν πόλεων τῆς παραλίας ἕως Σελευκείας τῆς παραθαλασσίας καὶ διελογίζετο
περὶ Ἀλεξάνδρου λογισμοὺς πονηρούς. 9 καὶ ἀπέστειλεν
πρέσβεις πρὸς Δημήτριον τὸν βασιλέα λέγων Δεῦρο συνθώ-
μεθα πρὸς ἑαυτοὺς διαθήκην, καὶ δώσω σοι τὴν θυγατέρα
μου, ἣν εἶχεν Ἀλέξανδρος, καὶ βασιλεύσεις τῆς βασιλείας
τοῦ πατρός σου· 10 μεταμεμέλημαι γὰρ δοὺς αὐτῷ τὴν
θυγατέρα μου, ἐζήτησεν γὰρ ἀποκτεῖναί με. 11 καὶ ἐψόγισεν

KING JAMES VERSION

11 And the king of Egypt gathered together a great host, like the sand that lieth upon the sea shore, and many ships, and went about through deceit to get Alexander's kingdom, and join it to his own.

2 Whereupon he took his journey into Syria in peaceable manner, so as they of the cities opened unto him, and met him: for king Alexander had commanded them so to do, because he was his father in law.

3 Now as Ptolemee entered into the cities, he set in every one of them a garrison of soldiers to keep it.

4 And when he came near to Azotus, they shewed him the temple of Dagon that was burnt, and Azotus and the suburbs thereof that were destroyed, and the bodies that were cast abroad, and them that he had burnt in the battle; for they had made heaps of them by the way where he should pass.

5 Also they told the king whatsoever Jonathan had done, to the intent he might blame him: but the king held his peace.

6 Then Jonathan met the king with great pomp at Joppe, where they saluted one another, and lodged.

7 Afterward Jonathan, when he had gone with the king to the river called Eleutherus, returned again to Jerusalem.

8 King Ptolemee therefore, having gotten the dominion of the cities by the sea unto Seleucia upon the sea coast, imagined wicked counsels against Alexander.

9 Whereupon he sent ambassadors unto king Demetrius, saying, Come, let us make a league betwixt us, and I will give thee my daughter whom Alexander hath, and thou shalt reign in thy father's kingdom:

10 For I repent that I gave my daughter unto him, for he sought to slay me.

DOUAY OLD TESTAMENT

11 AND the king of Egypt gathered together an army, like the sand that lieth upon the sea shore, and many ships: and he sought to get the kingdom of Alexander by deceit, and join it to his own kingdom.

2 And he went out into Syria with peaceable words, and they opened to him the cities, and met him: for king Alexander had ordered them to go forth to meet him, because he was his father in law.

3 Now when Ptolemee entered into the cities, he put garrisons of soldiers in every city.

4 And when he came near to Azotus, they shewed him the temple of Dagon that was burnt with fire, and Azotus, and the suburbs thereof that were destroyed, and the bodies that were cast abroad, and the graves of them that were slain in the battle, which they had made near the way.

5 And they told the king that Jonathan had done these things, to make him odious: but the king held his peace.

6 And Jonathan came to meet the king at Joppe with glory, and they saluted one another, and they lodged there.

7 And Jonathan went with the king as far as the river, called Eleutherus: and he returned into Jerusalem.

8 And king Ptolemee got the dominion of the cities by the sea side, even to Seleucia, and he devised evil designs against Alexander.

9 And he sent ambassadors to Demetrius, saying: Come, let us make a league between us, and I will give thee my daughter whom Alexander hath, and thou shalt reign in the kingdom of thy father.

10 For I repent that I have given him my daughter: for he hath sought to kill me.

KNOX TRANSLATION

11 And now Ptolemy, king of Egypt, levied a great army,
countless as sand on the beach, and a fleet besides;
to win Alexander's realm his treacherous design was, and
add it to his own. 2 To Syria he came, full of fair speeches,
and all the towns opened their gates to welcome him; such
welcome Alexander himself had prescribed; was not the king
of Egypt his father-in-law? 3 And never a town king Ptolemy
entered, but he left a guard of soldiers there. 4 When he
reached Azotus, here was Dagon's temple burnt, here was
the town itself and all its neighbourhood in ruins; the dead
lay unburied, where they fell in battle, or in heaps by the
road-side. 5 All this they shewed him, and told him, with
malicious intent, how it was Jonathan's doing; but no word
said king Ptolemy. 6 As for Jonathan, he went to meet the
king at Joppe, with a deal of pomp; there they greeted one
another, and passed the night, 7 nor would Jonathan return
to Jerusalem till he had escorted the king as far as the river
called Eleutherus.
8 All the cities of the sea-coast, as far as maritime Seleucia,
king Ptolemy occupied, and with no friendly purpose towards
Alexander; 9 it was to Demetrius he sent envoys instead.
Come, said he, a pact between us! My daughter thou shalt
have in Alexander's place, and therewithal the throne of thy
fathers; 10 here is an ill son-in-law I have chosen, that went
about but now to kill me! 11 Thus, to find pretext for

TODAY'S ENGLISH VERSION

11 King Ptolemy the Sixth of Egypt assembled an army of soldiers more numerous than the grains of sand along the seashore, and he also gathered a great fleet of ships. He intended to trap Alexander, take his kingdom, and add it to his own, 2 so he went to Syria with promises of peace, and the citizens opened their gates to him and welcomed him. King Alexander had ordered them to do this because Ptolemy was his father-in-law. 3 But as Ptolemy moved north, he stationed a detachment of troops in each town. 4 When he reached Azotus, the people there showed him the burned ruins of the temple of Dagon and all the destruction in the city and the surrounding towns. There were corpses everywhere. The bodies of the men Jonathan had burned to death during the battle were now stacked up along Ptolemy's route. 5 The people told him what Jonathan had done, hoping that he would hold him responsible, but Ptolemy said nothing. 6 Jonathan, with all the proper ceremony, went to Joppa to meet him. They exchanged greetings and spent the night there. 7 Jonathan accompanied him as far as the Eleutherus River before returning to Jerusalem. 8 In this way King Ptolemy, in his plot against Alexander, took control of the towns along the coast as far north as Seleucia-by-the-sea.

9 From there King Ptolemy sent this message to King Demetrius: "Let's make a treaty. My daughter is now Alexander's wife, but I will take her back and give her to you and let you rule over your father's kingdom. 10 I regret that I ever gave her to Alexander, because he has tried to kill me."

NEW REVISED STANDARD VERSION

11 Then the king of Egypt gathered great forces, like the sand by the seashore, and many ships; and he tried to get possession of Alexander's kingdom by trickery and add it to his own kingdom. 2 He set out for Syria with peaceable words, and the people of the towns opened their gates to him and went to meet him, for King Alexander had commanded them to meet him, since he was Alexander's[a] father-in-law. 3 But when Ptolemy entered the towns he stationed forces as a garrison in each town.

4 When he[b] approached Azotus, they showed him the burnt-out temple of Dagon, and Azotus and its suburbs destroyed, and the corpses lying about, and the charred bodies of those whom Jonathan[c] had burned in the war, for they had piled them in heaps along his route. 5 They also told the king what Jonathan had done, to throw blame on him; but the king kept silent. 6 Jonathan met the king at Joppa with pomp, and they greeted one another and spent the night there. 7 And Jonathan went with the king as far as the river called Eleutherus; then he returned to Jerusalem.

8 So King Ptolemy gained control of the coastal cities as far as Seleucia by the sea, and he kept devising wicked designs against Alexander. 9 He sent envoys to King Demetrius, saying, "Come, let us make a covenant with each other, and I will give you in marriage my daughter who was Alexander's wife, and you shall reign over your father's kingdom. 10 I now regret that I gave him my daughter, for he has tried to kill me." 11 He threw blame on Alexander[d]

a Gk *his*   *b* Other ancient authorities read *they*   *c* Gk *he*   *d* Gk *him*

NEW AMERICAN BIBLE

11 The king of Egypt gathered his forces, as numerous as the sands of the seashore, and many ships; and he sought by deceit to take Alexander's kingdom and add it to his own. 2 He entered Syria with peaceful words, and the people in the cities opened their gates to welcome him, as King Alexander had ordered them to do, since Ptolemy was his father-in-law. 3 But when Ptolemy entered the cities, he stationed garrison troops in each one. 4 When he reached Azotus, he was shown the temple of Dagon destroyed by fire, Azotus and its suburbs demolished, corpses lying about, and the charred bodies of those burned by Jonathan in the war and stacked up along his route. 5 To prejudice the king against Jonathan, he was told what the latter had done; but the king said nothing. 6 Jonathan met the king with pomp at Joppa, and they greeted each other and spent the night there. 7 Jonathan accompanied the king as far as the river called Eleutherus and then returned to Jerusalem.

8 Plotting evil against Alexander, King Ptolemy took possession of the cities along the seacoast as far as Seleucia-by-the-Sea. 9 He sent ambassadors to King Demetrius, saying: "Come, let us make a pact with each other; I will give you my daughter whom Alexander has married, and you shall reign over your father's kingdom. 10 I regret that I gave him my daughter, for he has sought to kill me." 11 His real reason for

NEW JERUSALEM BIBLE

11 The king of Egypt then assembled an army as numerous as the sands of the seashore, with many ships, and set out to take possession of Alexander's kingdom by a ruse and add it to his own kingdom. 2 He set off for Syria with protestations of peace, and the people of the towns opened their gates to him and came out to meet him, since King Alexander's orders were to welcome him, Ptolemy being his father-in-law. 3 On entering the towns, however, Ptolemy quartered troops as a garrison in each one. 4 When he reached Azotus he was shown the burnt-out temple of Dagon, with Azotus and its suburbs in ruins, corpses scattered here and there, and the charred remains of those whom Jonathan had burnt to death in the battle, piled into heaps along his route. 5 They explained to the king what Jonathan had done, hoping for his disapproval; but the king said nothing. 6 Jonathan went in state to meet the king at Joppa, where they greeted each other and spent the night. 7 Jonathan accompanied the king as far as the river called Eleutherus, and then returned to Jerusalem. 8 King Ptolemy for his part occupied the coastal towns as far as Seleucia on the coast, all the while maturing his wicked designs against Alexander. 9 He sent envoys to King Demetrius to say, 'Come and let us make a treaty; I shall give you my daughter, whom Alexander now has, and you shall rule your father's kingdom. 10 I regret having given my daughter to that man, since he has tried to kill me.' 11 He made this accusation

GREEK OLD TESTAMENT

αὐτὸν χάριν τοῦ ἐπιθυμῆσαι αὐτὸν τῆς βασιλείας αὐτοῦ·
12 καὶ ἀφελόμενος αὐτοῦ τὴν θυγατέρα ἔδωκεν αὐτὴν τῷ
Δημητρίῳ καὶ ἠλλοιώθη τῷ Ἀλεξάνδρῳ, καὶ ἐφάνη ἡ ἔχθρα
αὐτῶν. 13 καὶ εἰσῆλθεν Πτολεμαῖος εἰς Ἀντιόχειαν καὶ
περιέθετο τὸ διάδημα τῆς Ἀσίας. καὶ περιέθετο δύο διαδή-
ματα περὶ τὴν κεφαλὴν αὐτοῦ, τὸ τῆς Αἰγύπτου καὶ Ἀσίας.
14 Ἀλέξανδρος δὲ ὁ βασιλεὺς ἦν ἐν Κιλικίᾳ κατὰ τοὺς
καιροὺς ἐκείνους, ὅτι ἀπεστάτουν οἱ ἀπὸ τῶν τόπων ἐκείνων. 15 καὶ ἤκουσεν Ἀλέξανδρος καὶ ἦλθεν ἐπ' αὐτὸν ἐν
πολέμῳ. καὶ ἐξήγαγεν Πτολεμαῖος καὶ ἀπήντησεν αὐτῷ ἐν
χειρὶ ἰσχυρᾷ καὶ ἐτροπώσατο αὐτόν· 16 καὶ ἔφυγεν Ἀλέξανδρος εἰς τὴν Ἀραβίαν τοῦ σκεπασθῆναι αὐτὸν ἐκεῖ, ὁ δὲ
βασιλεὺς Πτολεμαῖος ὑψώθη. 17 καὶ ἀφεῖλεν Ζαβδιηλ ὁ
Ἄραψ τὴν κεφαλὴν Ἀλεξάνδρου καὶ ἀπέστειλεν τῷ Πτολεμαίῳ. 18 καὶ ὁ βασιλεὺς Πτολεμαῖος ἀπέθανεν ἐν τῇ ἡμέρᾳ τῇ
τρίτῃ, καὶ οἱ ὄντες ἐν τοῖς ὀχυρώμασιν αὐτοῦ ἀπώλοντο ὑπὸ
τῶν ἐν τοῖς ὀχυρώμασιν. 19 καὶ ἐβασίλευσεν Δημήτριος
ἔτους ἑβδόμου καὶ ἑξηκοστοῦ καὶ ἑκατοστοῦ.
20 Ἐν ταῖς ἡμέραις ἐκείναις συνήγαγεν Ιωναθαν τοὺς ἐκ
τῆς Ιουδαίας τοῦ ἐκπολεμῆσαι τὴν ἄκραν τὴν ἐν Ιερουσαλημ
καὶ ἐποίησεν ἐπ' αὐτὴν μηχανὰς πολλάς. 21 καὶ ἐπορεύθη-
σάν τινες μισοῦντες τὸ ἔθνος αὐτῶν ἄνδρες παράνομοι πρὸς
τὸν βασιλέα καὶ ἀπήγγειλαν αὐτῷ ὅτι Ιωναθαν περικάθηται
τὴν ἄκραν. 22 καὶ ἀκούσας ὠργίσθη· ὡς δὲ ἤκουσεν, εὐθέως
ἀναζεύξας ἦλθεν εἰς Πτολεμαίδα καὶ ἔγραψεν Ιωναθαν τοῦ

KING JAMES VERSION

11 Thus did he slander him, because he was desirous of his kingdom.

12 Wherefore he took his daughter from him, and gave her to Demetrius, and forsook Alexander, so that their hatred was openly known.

13 Then Ptolemee entered into Antioch, where he set two crowns upon his head, the crown of Asia, and of Egypt.

14 In the mean season was king Alexander in Cilicia, because those that dwelt in those parts had revolted from him.

15 But when Alexander heard of this, he came to war against him: whereupon *king* Ptolemee brought forth *his host,* and met him with a mighty power, and put him to flight.

16 So Alexander fled into Arabia, there to be defended; but king Ptolemee was exalted:

17 For Zabdiel the Arabian took off Alexander's head, and sent it unto Ptolemee.

18 King Ptolemee also died the third day after, and they that were in the strong holds were slain one of another.

19 By this means Demetrius reigned in the hundred threescore and seventh year.

20 At the same time Jonathan gathered together them that were in Judea, to take the tower that was in Jerusalem: and he made many engines of war against it.

21 Then certain ungodly persons, who hated their own people, went unto the king, and told him that Jonathan besieged the tower.

22 Whereof when he heard, he was angry, and immediately removing, he came to Ptolemais, and wrote unto Jonathan,

DOUAY OLD TESTAMENT

11 And he slandered him, because he coveted his kingdom.

12 And he took away his daughter, and gave her to Demetrius, and alienated himself from Alexander, and his enmities were made manifest.

13 And Ptolemee entered into Antioch, and set two crowns upon his head, that of Egypt, and that of Asia.

14 Now king Alexander was in Cilicia at that time: because they that were in those places had rebelled.

15 And when Alexander heard of it, he came to give him battle, and king Ptolemee brought forth his army, and met him with a strong power, and put him to flight.

16 And Alexander fled into Arabia, there to be protected: and king Ptolemee was exalted.

17 And Zabdiel the Arabian took off Alexander's head, and sent it to Ptolemee.

18 And king Ptolemee died the third day after: and they that were in the strong holds were destroyed by them that were within the camp.

19 And Demetrius reigned in the hundred and sixty-seventh year.

20 In those days Jonathan gathered together them that were in Judea, to take the castle that was in Jerusalem: and they made many engines of war against it.

21 Then some wicked men that hated their own nation, went away to king Demetrius, and told him that Jonathan was besieging the castle.

22 And when he heard it, he was angry: and forthwith he came to Ptolemais, and wrote to Jonathan, that he should

KNOX TRANSLATION

dethroning his rival, king Ptolemy defamed him; 12 took his
daughter away, and gave her to Demetrius. His estrangement
from Alexander now come to an open breach, 13 what must
he do next but enter the city of Antioch, and there assume
the double crown, as ruler of Egypt and Asia both? 14 As for
Alexander, that was then in Cilicia, quelling a revolt in those
parts, 15 he came out to do battle when the news reached
him; but Ptolemy brought up his army, met him with a superior force, and routed him. 16 Thus Egypt had the mastery;
and when Alexander fled to Arabia for refuge, 17 Zabdiel, an
Arabian, cut off his head and sent it to the conqueror.
18 Three days later, Ptolemy himself lay dead; whereupon the
garrisons he had left in the towns were massacred by the citizens, 19 and the royal power passed to Demetrius in this,
the hundred and sixty-seventh year.
20 Now it was that Jonathan mustered the men of Judaea to
deliver an attack on the Gentile citadel in Jerusalem; engines
a many they brought against it. 21 Nor wanted there Jews of
the godless party, traitors to their own race, that went off
and told Demetrius it was being attacked; 22 the news greatly angered him, and he hastened to Ptolemais, bidding

TODAY'S ENGLISH VERSION

11 Ptolemy made this accusation against Alexander because
he wanted to take over his kingdom. 12 So he took his
daughter away from Alexander and gave her to Demetrius;
he broke off all relations with Alexander, and they became
open enemies. 13 Then Ptolemy entered Antioch and
assumed the crown of Syria; so he wore both the crown of
Egypt and the crown of Syria.

14 King Alexander was in Cilicia at the time because the
people of that region were in a state of rebellion. 15 But
when he heard what Ptolemy had done, he moved to attack
him. Ptolemy met him with a large force and won a decisive
victory. 16 While Ptolemy reached the peak of his power,
Alexander fled to Arabia to find protection, 17 but an Arab
named Zabdiel cut off his head and sent it to Ptolemy.
18 Two days later Ptolemy himself died, and the troops he had
left in the fortresses were then killed by the local citizens.
19 So in the year 167[a] Demetrius the Second became king.

20 About that time Jonathan gathered the men of Judea to
attack the fort in Jerusalem. They built many siege platforms
to use in the attack. 21 But some traitorous Jews who hated
their own nation went to King Demetrius the Second and
told him that Jonathan was laying siege to the fort in
Jerusalem. 22 When Demetrius heard this, he was furious
and immediately moved his headquarters to Ptolemais. He
wrote to Jonathan and ordered him to lift the siege and to

[a] THE YEAR 167: *This corresponds to 145 B.C.*

NEW REVISED STANDARD VERSION

because he coveted his kingdom. 12 So he took his daughter
away from him and gave her to Demetrius. He was estranged
from Alexander, and their enmity became manifest.

13 Then Ptolemy entered Antioch and put on the crown of
Asia. Thus he put two crowns on his head, the crown of
Egypt and that of Asia. 14 Now King Alexander was in Cilicia
at that time, because the people of that region were in revolt.
15 When Alexander heard of it, he came against him in battle.
Ptolemy marched out and met him with a strong force, and
put him to flight. 16 So Alexander fled into Arabia to find
protection there, and King Ptolemy was triumphant.
17 Zabdiel the Arab cut off the head of Alexander and sent it
to Ptolemy. 18 But King Ptolemy died three days later, and
his troops in the strongholds were killed by the inhabitants
of the strongholds. 19 So Demetrius became king in the one
hundred sixty-seventh year.[a]

20 In those days Jonathan assembled the Judeans to
attack the citadel in Jerusalem, and he built many engines of
war to use against it. 21 But certain renegades who hated
their nation went to the king and reported to him that
Jonathan was besieging the citadel. 22 When he heard this he
was angry, and as soon as he heard it he set out and came to
Ptolemais; and he wrote Jonathan not to continue the siege,

[a] 145 B.C.

NEW AMERICAN BIBLE

accusing Alexander, however, was that he coveted
Alexander's kingdom. 12 After taking his daughter away and
giving her to Demetrius, Ptolemy broke with Alexander; their
enmity became open. 13 Then Ptolemy entered Antioch and
assumed the crown of Asia; he thus wore two crowns on his
head, that of Egypt and that of Asia.

14 King Alexander was in Cilicia at that time, because the
people of that region had revolted. 15 When Alexander heard
the news, he came to challenge Ptolemy in battle. Ptolemy
marched out and met him with a strong force and put him to
flight. 16 Alexander fled to Arabia to seek protection. King
Ptolemy's triumph was complete 17 when the Arab Zabdiel
cut off Alexander's head and sent it to Ptolemy. 18 But three
days later King Ptolemy himself died, and his men in the fortified cities were killed by the inhabitants of the strongholds.
19 Thus Demetrius became king in the year one hundred and
sixty-seven.

20 At that time Jonathan gathered together the men of
Judea to attack the citadel in Jerusalem, and they set up
many machines against it. 21 Some transgressors of the law,
enemies of their own nation, went to the king and informed
him that Jonathan was besieging the citadel. 22 When
Demetrius heard this, he was furious, and set out immediately for Ptolemais. He wrote to Jonathan to discontinue the

NEW JERUSALEM BIBLE

because he coveted his kingdom. 12 Having carried off his
daughter and bestowed her on Demetrius, he broke with
Alexander, and their enmity became open. 13 Ptolemy next
entered Antioch and assumed the crown of Asia; he now
wore on his head the two crowns of Egypt and Asia. 14 King
Alexander was in Cilicia at the time, since the people of those
parts had risen in revolt, 15 but when he heard the news, he
advanced on his rival to give battle, while Ptolemy for his
part also took the field, met him with a strong force and
routed him. 16 Alexander fled to Arabia for refuge, and King
Ptolemy reigned supreme. 17 Zabdiel the Arab cut off
Alexander's head and sent it to Ptolemy. 18 Three days later
King Ptolemy died, and the Egyptian garrisons in the strongholds were killed by the local inhabitants. 19 So Demetrius
became king in the year 167.

20 At the same time, Jonathan mustered the men of Judaea
for an assault on the Citadel of Jerusalem, and they set up
numerous siege-engines against it. 21 But some renegades
who hated their nation made their way to the king and told
him that Jonathan was besieging the Citadel. 22 The king
was angered by the news. No sooner had he been informed
than he set out and came to Ptolemais. He wrote to
Jonathan, telling him to raise the siege and to meet him for a

Greek Old Testament

μὴ περικαθῆσθαι καὶ τοῦ ἀπαντῆσαι αὐτὸν αὐτῷ συμμίσγειν
εἰς Πτολεμαίδα τὴν ταχίστην. 23 ὡς δὲ ἤκουσεν Ιωναθαν,
ἐκέλευσεν περικαθῆσθαι καὶ ἐπέλεξεν τῶν πρεσβυτέρων
Ισραηλ καὶ τῶν ἱερέων καὶ ἔδωκεν ἑαυτὸν τῷ κινδύνῳ· 24 καὶ
λαβὼν ἀργύριον καὶ χρυσίον καὶ ἱματισμὸν καὶ ἕτερα ξένια
πλείονα καὶ ἐπορεύθη πρὸς τὸν βασιλέα εἰς Πτολεμαίδα καὶ
εὗρεν χάριν ἐναντίον αὐτοῦ. 25 καὶ ἐνετύγχανον κατ' αὐτοῦ
τινες ἄνομοι τῶν ἐκ τοῦ ἔθνους. 26 καὶ ἐποίησεν αὐτῷ ὁ
βασιλεὺς καθὼς ἐποίησαν αὐτῷ οἱ πρὸ αὐτοῦ, καὶ ὕψωσεν
αὐτὸν ἐναντίον τῶν φίλων αὐτοῦ πάντων. 27 καὶ ἔστησεν
αὐτῷ τὴν ἀρχιερωσύνην καὶ ὅσα ἄλλα εἶχεν τίμια τὸ πρότερον καὶ ἐποίησεν αὐτὸν τῶν πρώτων φίλων ἡγεῖσθαι.
28 καὶ ἠξίωσεν Ιωναθαν τὸν βασιλέα ποιῆσαι τὴν Ιουδαίαν
ἀφορολόγητον καὶ τὰς τρεῖς τοπαρχίας καὶ τὴν Σαμαρῖτιν
καὶ ἐπηγγείλατο αὐτῷ τάλαντα τριακόσια. 29 καὶ εὐδόκησεν
ὁ βασιλεὺς καὶ ἔγραψεν τῷ Ιωναθαν ἐπιστολὰς περὶ πάντων
τούτων ἐχούσας τὸν τρόπον τοῦτον

30 Βασιλεὺς Δημήτριος Ιωναθαν τῷ ἀδελφῷ χαίρειν καὶ
ἔθνει Ιουδαίων. 31 τὸ ἀντίγραφον τῆς ἐπιστολῆς, ἧς ἐγράψαμεν Λασθένει τῷ συγγενεῖ ἡμῶν περὶ ὑμῶν, γεγράφαμεν
καὶ πρὸς ὑμᾶς, ὅπως εἰδῆτε. 32 Βασιλεὺς Δημήτριος
Λασθένει τῷ πατρὶ χαίρειν. 33 τῷ ἔθνει τῶν Ιουδαίων φίλοις
ἡμῶν καὶ συντηροῦσιν τὰ πρὸς ἡμᾶς δίκαια ἐκρίναμεν
ἀγαθὸν ποιῆσαι χάριν τῆς ἐξ αὐτῶν εὐνοίας πρὸς ἡμᾶς.

King James Version

that he should not lay siege to the tower, but come and speak with him at Ptolemais in great haste.

23 Nevertheless Jonathan, when he heard this, commanded to besiege it *still:* and he chose certain of the elders of Israel and the priests, and put himself in peril;

24 And took silver and gold, and raiment, and divers presents besides, and went to Ptolemais unto the king, where he found favour in his sight.

25 And though certain ungodly men of the people had made complaints against him,

26 Yet the king entreated him as his predecessors had done before, and promoted him in the sight of all his friends,

27 And confirmed him in the high priesthood, and in all the honours that he had before, and gave him preeminence among his chief friends.

28 Then Jonathan desired the king, that he would make Judea free from tribute, as also the three governments, with the country of Samaria; and he promised him three hundred talents.

29 So the king consented, and wrote letters unto Jonathan of all these things after this manner:

30 King Demetrius unto his brother Jonathan, and unto the nation of the Jews, sendeth greeting:

31 We send you here a copy of the letter which we did write unto our cousin Lasthenes concerning you, that ye might see it.

32 King Demetrius unto his father Lasthenes sendeth greeting:

33 We are determined to do good to the people of the Jews, who are our friends, and keep covenants with us, because of their good will toward us.

Douay Old Testament

not besiege the castle, but should come to him in haste, and speak to him.

23 But when Jonathan heard this, he bade them besiege it still: and he chose some of the ancients of Israel, and of the priests, and put himself in danger.

24 And he took gold, and silver, and raiment, and many other presents, and went to the king to Ptolemais, and he found favour in his sight.

25 And certain wicked men of his nation made complaints against him.

26 And the king treated him as his predecessors had done before: and he exalted him in the sight of all his friends.

27 And he confirmed him in the high priesthood, and all the honours he had before, and he made him the chief of his friends.

28 And Jonathan requested of the king that he would make Judea free from tribute, and the three governments, and Samaria, and the confines thereof: and he promised him three hundred talents.

29 And the king consented: and he wrote letters to Jonathan of all these things to this effect.

30 King Demetrius to his brother Jonathan, and to the nation of the Jews, greeting.

31 We send you here a copy of the letter, which we have written to Lasthenes our parent concerning you, that you might know it.

32 King Demetrius to Lasthenes his parent, greeting.

33 We have determined to do good to the nation of the Jews who are our friends, and keep the things that are just with us, for their good will which they bear towards us.

Knox Translation

Jonathan raise the siege and come to meet him in conference
without more ado. 23 This message notwithstanding,
Jonathan would have the siege go forward; certain elders of
Israel, and certain of the priests, he chose out to bear him
company, and so put his own life in peril, 24 going off to
meet the king at Ptolemais, with gold and silver and garments and other gifts in great number. He was received graciously enough; 25 let his own traitorous fellow-countrymen
bring what accusations they would, 26 the king would not be
behind his predecessors in making much of Jonathan, for all
his courtiers to see. 27 He was confirmed in the high priesthood, and what other high dignities he held aforetime, and
declared besides the chief of the king's friends.

28 And now Jonathan had a favour to ask; exemption from
tribute for Judaea, and the three cantons, and Samaria with
its neighbouring townships;[a] he promised in return a payment of three hundred talents. 29 To this the king agreed,
writing thus to Jonathan upon the matter raised: 30 King
Demetrius, to his brother prince Jonathan, and to the people
of the Jews, greeting. 31 We send you herewith, for your better information, a copy of the instructions we have given to
our cousin Lasthenes in your regard. 32 King Demetrius, to
Lasthenes, his good father, greeting. 33 Whereas the people
of the Jews have ever been trusty friends to us, our pleasure
it is to reward them for the loyalty they have shewn us.

a 'The three cantons, and Samaria with its neighbouring townships'; some think this is a copyist's error for 'the three cantons which had belonged to Samaria, with their neighbouring townships', cf. verse 34.

TODAY'S ENGLISH VERSION

meet him for a conference in Ptolemais without a moment's delay.

23 When Jonathan got the message, he gave orders for the siege to continue, and then chose some Jewish leaders and some priests to go with him. At the risk of his life, 24 he went to the king in Ptolemais, taking along robes, silver and gold, and many other gifts. He made a good impression on the king. 25 Although some lawless traitors of his own nation had made accusations against Jonathan, 26 the king still treated him just as his predecessors had done. He honored him in the presence of all his advisers, 27 and confirmed him as High Priest, restoring all his former honors and appointing him to the highest rank among the "Friends of the King."

28 Jonathan asked the king to release the territory of Judea and the three regions of Samaria[a] from the payment of taxes, promising that if Demetrius would do that, he would pay him a lump sum of 22,000 pounds of silver. 29 The king agreed and wrote a letter to Jonathan to confirm all this:

30 "King Demetrius to King Jonathan and to the Jewish nation, greetings.

31 "For your information I am sending a copy of the letter I have written to the Honorable Lasthenes about you:

32 " 'King Demetrius to the Honorable Lasthenes, greetings. 33 I have decided to grant the Jewish nation certain benefits because they are our loyal allies and keep their

[a] *Probable text* three regions of Samaria; *Greek* three regions and Samaria.

NEW REVISED STANDARD VERSION

but to meet him for a conference at Ptolemais as quickly as possible.

23 When Jonathan heard this, he gave orders to continue the siege. He chose some of the elders of Israel and some of the priests, and put himself in danger, 24 for he went to the king at Ptolemais, taking silver and gold and clothing and numerous other gifts. And he won his favor. 25 Although certain renegades of his nation kept making complaints against him, 26 the king treated him as his predecessors had treated him; he exalted him in the presence of all his Friends. 27 He confirmed him in the high priesthood and in as many other honors as he had formerly had, and caused him to be reckoned among his chief[a] Friends. 28 Then Jonathan asked the king to free Judea and the three districts of Samaria[b] from tribute, and promised him three hundred talents. 29 The king consented, and wrote a letter to Jonathan about all these things; its contents were as follows:

30 "King Demetrius to his brother Jonathan and to the nation of the Jews, greetings. 31 This copy of the letter that we wrote concerning you to our kinsman Lasthenes we have written to you also, so that you may know what it says. 32 'King Demetrius to his father Lasthenes, greetings. 33 We have determined to do good to the nation of the Jews, who are our friends and fulfill their obligations to us, because of the goodwill they show toward us. 34 We have confirmed as

[a] Gk *first* [b] Cn: Gk *the three districts and Samaria*

NEW AMERICAN BIBLE

siege and to meet him for a conference at Ptolemais as soon as possible.

23 On hearing this, Jonathan ordered the siege to continue. He selected some elders and priests of Israel and exposed himself to danger 24 by going to the king at Ptolemais. He brought with him silver, gold apparel, and many other presents, and found favor with the king. 25 Although some impious men of his own nation brought charges against him, 26 the king treated him just as his predecessors had done and showed him great honor in the presence of all his Friends. 27 He confirmed him in the high priesthood and in all the honors he had previously held, and had him enrolled among his Chief Friends.

28 Jonathan asked the king to exempt Judea and the three districts of Samaria from tribute, promising him in return three hundred talents. 29 The king agreed and wrote the following letter to Jonathan about all these matters:

30 "King Demetrius sends greetings to his brother Jonathan and to the Jewish nation. 31 We are sending you, for your information, a copy of the letter that we wrote to Lasthenes our kinsman concerning you. 32 'King Demetrius sends greetings to his father Lasthenes. 33 Because of the good will they show us, we have decided to bestow benefits on the Jewish nation, who are our friends and who observe their obligations

NEW JERUSALEM BIBLE

conference in Ptolemais as soon as possible. 23 When Jonathan heard this, he gave orders for the siege to continue; he then selected a deputation from the elders of Israel and the priests, and took the deliberate risk 24 of himself taking silver and gold, clothing and numerous other presents, and going to Ptolemais to face the king, whose favour he succeeded in winning; 25 and although one or two renegades of his nation brought charges against him, 26 the king treated him as his predecessors had treated him, and promoted him in the presence of all his friends. 27 He confirmed him in the high priesthood and whatever other distinctions he already held, and had him ranked among the First Friends. 28 Jonathan asked the king to exempt Judaea and the three Samaritan districts from taxation, promising him three hundred talents in return. 29 The king consented, and wrote Jonathan a rescript covering the whole matter, in these terms:

30 'King Demetrius to Jonathan his brother, and to the Jewish nation, greetings.

31 'We have written to Lasthenes our cousin concerning you, and now send you this copy of our rescript for your own information:

32 "King Demetrius to his father Lasthenes, greetings.

33 "The nation of the Jews is our ally; they fulfil their obligations to us, and in view of their goodwill towards us we have decided to show them our bounty. 34 We confirm

GREEK OLD TESTAMENT

34 ἐστάκαμεν αὐτοῖς τά τε ὅρια τῆς Ιουδαίας καὶ τοὺς τρεῖς
νομοὺς Αφαιρεμα καὶ Λυδδα καὶ Ραθαμιν· προσετέθησαν τῇ
Ιουδαίᾳ ἀπὸ τῆς Σαμαρίτιδος καὶ πάντα τὰ συγκυροῦντα
αὐτοῖς πᾶσιν τοῖς θυσιάζουσιν εἰς Ιεροσόλυμα ἀντὶ τῶν
βασιλικῶν, ὧν ἐλάμβανεν ὁ βασιλεὺς παρ' αὐτῶν τὸ πρότερον
κατ' ἐνιαυτὸν ἀπὸ τῶν γενημάτων τῆς γῆς καὶ τῶν ἀκροδρύων. 35 καὶ τὰ ἄλλα τὰ ἀνήκοντα ἡμῖν ἀπὸ τοῦ νῦν τῶν
δεκατῶν καὶ τῶν τελῶν τῶν ἀνηκόντων ἡμῖν καὶ τὰς τοῦ
ἁλὸς λίμνας καὶ τοὺς ἀνήκοντας ἡμῖν στεφάνους, πάντα
ἐπαρκέσομεν αὐτοῖς. 36 καὶ οὐκ ἀθετηθήσεται οὐδὲ ἓν τούτων ἀπὸ τοῦ νῦν εἰς τὸν ἅπαντα χρόνον. 37 νῦν οὖν ἐπιμέλ-
εσθε τοῦ ποιῆσαι τούτων ἀντίγραφον, καὶ δοθήτω Ιωναθαν
καὶ τεθήτω ἐν τῷ ὄρει τῷ ἁγίῳ ἐν τόπῳ ἐπισήμῳ.

38 Καὶ εἶδεν Δημήτριος ὁ βασιλεὺς ὅτι ἡσύχασεν ἡ γῆ ἐνώπιον αὐτοῦ καὶ οὐδὲν αὐτῷ ἀνθειστήκει, καὶ ἀπέλυσεν πάσας
τὰς δυνάμεις αὐτοῦ, ἕκαστον εἰς τὸν ἴδιον τόπον, πλὴν τῶν
ξένων δυνάμεων, ὧν ἐξενολόγησεν ἀπὸ τῶν νήσων τῶν ἐθνῶν·
καὶ ἤχθραναν αὐτῷ πᾶσαι αἱ δυνάμεις αἱ ἀπὸ τῶν πατέρων.
39 Τρύφων δὲ ἦν τῶν παρὰ Ἀλεξάνδρου τὸ πρότερον καὶ εἶδεν
ὅτι πᾶσαι αἱ δυνάμεις καταγογγύζουσιν κατὰ τοῦ Δημητρίου, καὶ ἐπορεύθη πρὸς Ιμαλκουε τὸν Ἄραβα, ὃς ἔτρεφεν
Ἀντίοχον τὸ παιδάριον τὸν τοῦ Ἀλεξάνδρου. 40 καὶ προσή-
δρευεν αὐτῷ, ὅπως παραδοῖ αὐτὸν αὐτῷ, ὅπως βασιλεύσῃ ἀντὶ
τοῦ πατρὸς αὐτοῦ· καὶ ἀπήγγειλεν αὐτῷ ὅσα συνετέλεσεν ὁ
Δημήτριος καὶ τὴν ἔχθραν, ἣν ἐχθραίνουσιν αὐτῷ αἱ δυνάμεις
αὐτοῦ, καὶ ἔμεινεν ἐκεῖ ἡμέρας πολλάς. 41 καὶ ἀπέστειλεν

KING JAMES VERSION

34 Wherefore we have ratified unto them the borders of Judea, with the three governments of Apherema and Lydda and Ramathem, that are added unto Judea from the country of Samaria, and all things appertaining unto them, for all such as do sacrifice in Jerusalem, instead of the payments which the king received of them yearly aforetime out of the fruits of the earth and of trees.

35 And as for other things that belong unto us, of the tithes and customs pertaining unto us, as also the saltpits, and the crown taxes, which are due unto us, we discharge them of them all for their relief.

36 And nothing hereof shall be revoked from this time forth for ever.

37 Now therefore see that thou make a copy of these things, and let it be delivered unto Jonathan, and set upon the holy mount in a conspicuous place.

38 After this, when king Demetrius saw that the land was quiet before him, and that no resistance was made against him, he sent away all his forces, every one to his own place, except certain bands of strangers, whom he had gathered from the isles of the heathen: wherefore all the forces of his fathers hated him.

39 Moreover there was one Tryphon, that had been of Alexander's part afore, who, seeing that all the host murmured against Demetrius, went to Simalcue the Arabian, that brought up Antiochus the young son of Alexander,

40 And lay sore upon him to deliver him *this young Antiochus,* that he might reign in his father's stead: he told him therefore all that Demetrius had done, and how his men of war were at enmity with him, and there he remained a long season.

DOUAY OLD TESTAMENT

34 We have ratified therefore unto them all the borders of Judea, and the three cities, *Apherema,* Lydda, and Ramatha, which are added to Judea, out of Samaria, and all their confines, to be set apart to all them that sacrifice in Jerusalem, instead of the payments which the king received of them every year, and for the fruits of the land, and of the trees.

35 And as for other things that belonged to us of the tithes, and of the tributes, from this time we discharge them of them: the saltpans also, and the crowns that were presented to us.

36 We give all to them, and nothing hereof shall be revoked from this time forth and for ever.

37 Now therefore see that thou make a copy of these things, and let it be given to Jonathan, and set upon the holy mountain, in a conspicuous place.

38 And king Demetrius seeing that the land was quiet before him, and nothing resisted him, sent away all his forces, every man to his own place, except the foreign army, which he had drawn together from the islands of the nations: so all the troops of his fathers hated him.

39 Now there was one Tryphon who had been of Alexander's party before: who seeing that all the army murmured against Demetrius, went to Emalchuel the Arabian, who brought up Antiochus the son of Alexander.

40 And he pressed him much to deliver him to him, that he might be king in his father's place: and he told him all that Demetrius had done, and how his soldiers hated him. And he remained there many days.

KNOX TRANSLATION

34 We therefore confirm them in the possession of all Judaea,
the three cities of Ephraim, Lydda and Ramathan, that formerly belonged to Samaria, and all their neighbouring townships…to all those who do sacrifice at Jerusalem; instead of
the yearly revenues hitherto set apart for the king from harvest and fruit-gathering.[a] 35 Tithe and tribute that was ours
we also remit to them; nor lay any claim to the salt-pits, or
the crowns which from time to time were bestowed upon us.
36 Of all this we give them a full discharge, that shall be valid
in perpetuity. 37 See to it that a copy of this decree shall be
made, and handed over to Jonathan, who shall set it up in a
public place on the holy mountain.

38 Here, then, was the whole realm at peace under Demetrius' rule, nor any rival had he; what must he do but disband all his soldiers and send them home, except the foreign
troops he had levied from the islands out at sea? Bitterly
they hated him for it, the men who had served under his
fathers; 39 and there was one Tryphon that took good note of
these discontents in the army. This Tryphon was formerly of
Alexander's faction, and now he had recourse to Emalchuel,
the Arabian, that had care of Alexander's son Antiochus.
40 Much persuasion he used with him, to let Antiochus return
to his father's throne; much told him of Demetrius, and how
the soldiers were disaffected against him.

41 Time passed, and Tryphon was in Arabia still.

a The sentence is obscure, and perhaps the text has been inaccurately transmitted. For 'Ephraim' the Greek has the form 'Aphaerema', which the Latin interprets as a common noun 'sequestration'.

TODAY'S ENGLISH VERSION

treaty obligations. 34 I confirm their rights to the land of
Judea and the three regions of Ephraim, Lydda, and
Arimathea, which are hereby annexed to Judea from
Samaria with all the lands belonging to them. This will be
of benefit to everyone who goes to Jerusalem to offer sacrifice, since payments of the annual tax on produce and
fruit from these lands will no longer be made to the king,
but to the Temple. 35 And I also grant them relief from the
payment of revenues now due me from tithes, tolls, salt
taxes, and special taxes. 36 None of the provisions mentioned in this letter shall ever be canceled in the future.
37 " 'You are required to see that a complete copy of this
decree is made and given to Jonathan, to be posted in a
prominent place on the Temple hill.' "
38 When King Demetrius saw that the land was peaceful
under his rule and there was no further resistance, he disbanded his whole army and sent everyone home, except the
soldiers he had hired from the Greek islands. This made all
the soldiers who had served under his predecessors hate him
because they had lost their source of income. 39 One of
Alexander's former supporters, Trypho, saw that all the soldiers were complaining about Demetrius, so he went to
Imalkue, the Arab who was responsible for bringing up
Alexander's young son Antiochus. 40 Trypho stayed there for
a long time and kept urging Imalkue to hand the boy over to
him, so that he could make him king in place of his father.
He also told Imalkue about the decrees of Demetrius and
how the soldiers hated him.

NEW REVISED STANDARD VERSION

their possession both the territory of Judea and the three districts of Aphairema and Lydda and Rathamin; the latter, with
all the region bordering them, were added to Judea from
Samaria. To all those who offer sacrifice in Jerusalem we have
granted release from[a] the royal taxes that the king formerly
received from them each year, from the crops of the land and
the fruit of the trees. 35 And the other payments henceforth
due to us of the tithes, and the taxes due to us, and the salt
pits and the crown taxes due to us—from all these we shall
grant them release. 36 And not one of these grants shall be
canceled from this time on forever. 37 Now therefore take care
to make a copy of this, and let it be given to Jonathan and put
up in a conspicuous place on the holy mountain.' "
38 When King Demetrius saw that the land was quiet
before him and that there was no opposition to him, he dismissed all his troops, all of them to their own homes, except
the foreign troops that he had recruited from the islands of
the nations. So all the troops who had served under his predecessors hated him. 39 A certain Trypho had formerly been
one of Alexander's supporters; he saw that all the troops
were grumbling against Demetrius. So he went to Imalkue
the Arab, who was bringing up Antiochus, the young son of
Alexander, 40 and insistently urged him to hand Antiochus[b]
over to him, to become king in place of his father. He also
reported to Imalkue[b] what Demetrius had done and told of
the hatred that the troops of Demetrius[c] had for him; and he
stayed there many days.

a Or *Samaria, for all those who offer sacrifice in Jerusalem, in place of*
b Gk *him* *c* Gk *his troops*

NEW AMERICAN BIBLE

to us. 34 Therefore we confirm their possession, not only of
the territory of Judea, but also of the three districts of
Aphairema, Lydda, and Ramathaim. These districts, together
with all their dependencies, were transferred from Samaria to
Judea in favor of all those who offer sacrifices for us in
Jerusalem instead of paying the royal taxes that formerly the
king received from them each year from the produce of the
soil and the fruit of the trees. 35 From this day on we grant
them release from payment of all other things that would
henceforth be due to us, that is, of tithes and tribute and of
the tax on the salt pans and the crown tax. 36 Henceforth
none of these provisions shall ever be revoked. 37 Be sure,
therefore, to have a copy of these instructions made and
given to Jonathan, that it may be displayed in a conspicuous
place on the holy hill.' "
38 When King Demetrius saw that the land was peaceful
under his rule and that he had no opposition, he dismissed
his entire army, every man to his home, except the foreign
troops which he had hired from the islands of the nations. So
all the soldiers who had served under his predecessors hated
him. 39 When a certain Trypho, who had previously belonged
to Alexander's party, saw that all the troops were grumbling
at Demetrius, he went to Imalkue the Arab, who was bringing
up Alexander's young son Antiochus. 40 Trypho kept urging
Imalkue to hand over the boy to him, that he might make him
king in his father's place. During his stay there of many days,
he told him of all that Demetrius had done and of the hatred
that his soldiers had for him.

NEW JERUSALEM BIBLE

them in their possession of the territory of Judaea and the
three districts of Aphairema, Lydda and Ramathaim; these
were annexed to Judaea from Samaritan territory, with all
their dependencies, in favour of all who offer sacrifice in
Jerusalem, instead of the royal dues which the king formerly received from them every year, from the yield of the
soil and the fruit crops. 35 As regards our other rights over
the tithes and taxes due to us, over the salt marshes, and
the crown taxes due to us, as from today we release them
from them all. 36 None of these grants will be revoked
henceforth or anywhere. 37 You will make yourself responsible for having a copy of this made, to be given to
Jonathan and displayed on the holy mountain in a conspicuous place." '
38 When King Demetrius saw that the country was at peace
under his rule and that no resistance was offered him, he
dismissed his forces, and sent all the men home, except for
the foreign troops that he had recruited in the foreign island,
thus incurring the enmity of the veterans who had served his
ancestors. 39 Now Trypho, one of Alexander's former supporters, noting that all the troops were muttering against
Demetrius, went to see Iamleku, the Arab who was bringing
up Antiochus, Alexander's young son, 40 and repeatedly
urged him to let him have the boy, so that he might succeed
his father as king; he told him of Demetrius' decision and of
the resentment it had aroused among his troops. He spent a

GREEK OLD TESTAMENT

Ιωναθαν πρὸς Δημήτριον τὸν βασιλέα, ἵνα ἐκβάλῃ τοὺς ἐκ
τῆς ἄκρας ἐξ Ιερουσαλημ καὶ τοὺς ἐν τοῖς ὀχυρώμασιν· ἦσαν
γὰρ πολεμοῦντες τὸν Ισραηλ. 42 καὶ ἀπέστειλεν Δημήτριος
πρὸς Ιωναθαν λέγων Οὐ ταῦτα μόνον ποιήσω σοι καὶ τῷ ἔθνει
σου, ἀλλὰ δόξῃ δοξάσω σε καὶ τὸ ἔθνος σου, ἐὰν εὐκαιρίας
τύχω· 43 νῦν οὖν ὀρθῶς ποιήσεις ἀποστείλας μοι ἄνδρας, οἳ
συμμαχήσουσίν μοι, ὅτι ἀπέστησαν πᾶσαι αἱ δυνάμεις μου.
44 καὶ ἀπέστειλεν Ιωναθαν ἄνδρας τρισχιλίους δυνατοὺς
ἰσχύι αὐτῷ εἰς Ἀντιόχειαν, καὶ ἦλθον πρὸς τὸν βασιλέα, καὶ
ηὐφράνθη ὁ βασιλεὺς ἐπὶ τῇ ἐφόδῳ αὐτῶν. 45 καὶ ἐπισυνήχθησαν οἱ ἀπὸ τῆς πόλεως εἰς μέσον τῆς πόλεως εἰς ἀνδρῶν
δώδεκα μυριάδας καὶ ἠβούλοντο ἀνελεῖν τὸν βασιλέα. 46 καὶ
ἔφυγεν ὁ βασιλεὺς εἰς τὴν αὐλήν, καὶ κατελάβοντο οἱ ἐκ τῆς
πόλεως τὰς διόδους τῆς πόλεως καὶ ἤρξαντο πολεμεῖν. 47 καὶ
ἐκάλεσεν ὁ βασιλεὺς τοὺς Ιουδαίους ἐπὶ βοήθειαν, καὶ ἐπισυνήχθησαν πρὸς αὐτὸν πάντες ἅμα καὶ διεσπάρησαν ἐν τῇ
πόλει καὶ ἀπέκτειναν ἐν τῇ ἡμέρᾳ ἐκείνῃ εἰς μυριάδας δέκα·
48 καὶ ἐνεπύρισαν τὴν πόλιν καὶ ἔλαβον σκῦλα πολλὰ ἐν ἐκείνῃ τῇ ἡμέρᾳ καὶ ἔσωσαν τὸν βασιλέα. 49 καὶ εἶδον οἱ ἀπὸ τῆς
πόλεως ὅτι κατεκράτησαν οἱ Ιουδαῖοι τῆς πόλεως ὡς ἠβούλοντο, καὶ ἠσθένησαν ταῖς διανοίαις αὐτῶν καὶ ἐκέκραξαν
πρὸς τὸν βασιλέα μετὰ δεήσεως λέγοντες 50 Δὸς ἡμῖν δεξιὰς
καὶ παυσάσθωσαν οἱ Ιουδαῖοι πολεμοῦντες ἡμᾶς καὶ τὴν

KING JAMES VERSION

41 In the mean time Jonathan sent unto king Demetrius, that he would cast those of the tower out of Jerusalem, and those also in the fortresses: for they fought against Israel.

42 So Demetrius sent unto Jonathan, saying, I will not only do this for thee and thy people, but I will greatly honour thee and thy nation, if opportunity serve.

43 Now therefore thou shalt do well, if thou send me men to help me; for all my forces are gone from me.

44 Upon this Jonathan sent him three thousand strong men unto Antioch: and when they came to the king, the king was very glad of their coming.

45 Howbeit they that were of the city gathered themselves together into the midst of the city, to the number of an hundred and twenty thousand men, and would have slain the king.

46 Wherefore the king fled into the court, but they of the city kept the passages of the city, and began to fight.

47 Then the king called to the Jews for help, who came unto him all at once, and dispersing themselves through the city slew that day in the city to the number of an hundred thousand.

48 Also they set fire on the city, and gat many spoils that day, and delivered the king.

49 So when they of the city saw that the Jews had got the city as they would, their courage was abated: wherefore they made supplication to the king, and cried, saying,

50 Grant us peace, and let the Jews cease from assaulting us and the city.

DOUAY OLD TESTAMENT

41 And Jonathan sent to king Demetrius, desiring that he would cast out them that were in the castle in Jerusalem, and those that were in the strong holds: because they fought against Israel.

42 And Demetrius sent to Jonathan, saying: I will not only do this for thee, and for thy people, but I will greatly honour thee, and thy nation, when opportunity shall serve.

43 Now therefore thou shalt do well if thou send me men to help me: for all my army is gone from me.

44 And Jonathan sent him three thousand valiant men to Antioch: and they came to the king, and the king was very glad of their coming.

45 And they that were of the city assembled themselves together, to the number of a hundred and twenty thousand men, and would have killed the king.

46 And the king fled into the palace, and they of the city kept the passages of the city, and began to fight.

47 And the king called the Jews to his assistance: and they came to him all at once, and they all dispersed themselves through the city.

48 And they slew in that day a hundred thousand men, and they set fire to the city, and got many spoils that day, and delivered the king.

49 And they that were of the city saw that the Jews had got the city as they would: and they were discouraged in their mind, and cried to the king, making supplication, and saying:

50 Grant us peace, and let the Jews cease from assaulting us, and the city.

KNOX TRANSLATION

Meanwhile, Jonathan was urgent with king Demetrius to
withdraw the garrisons from Jerusalem citadel and the other
strongholds, where they bore arms yet, and against Israel.
42 Nay answered Demetrius, that I will do and more; great
honours I have in store, for thee and for thy people both,
when the time is ripe for it. 43 For this present, it were well
done to send troops for my own protection; here is all my
army revolted from me! 44 Three thousand picked men
Jonathan dispatched to Antioch, to the king's side, and right
glad he was at their coming. 45 What though the citizens, a
hundred and twenty thousand strong, were banded together
against his royal person, 46 driving him to take refuge within
the court, and occupying the city streets in warlike fashion?
47 He had but to call the Jews to his aid, and they rallied at
his summons; posted themselves here and there about the
streets, 48 and in one day slew a hundred thousand men, setting fire to the town besides. There was spoil enough for the
winning, that day when they saved the king's life. 49 The
townsfolk, when they saw how easily the Jews got the mastery of them, had no more stomach for fighting; they were
loud in their entreaties: 50 A truce! A truce! Havoc enough
yonder Jews have made of us and of the city! 51 And so,

TODAY'S ENGLISH VERSION

41 Jonathan sent a message to King Demetrius asking him to remove his troops from the fort in Jerusalem and from the fortresses in Judea, since they kept harassing the Jews. 42 Demetrius replied: "I will do what you request, and when the opportunity presents itself, I will bestow upon you and your nation the highest honors. 43 But now you can help me by sending soldiers to fight for me, because all of my troops have revolted."

44 So Jonathan sent 3,000 trained soldiers to Antioch. The king was delighted when they arrived, 45 because a mob of 120,000 had gathered in the city determined to kill him. 46 But he escaped to the palace while the mob took control of the streets and began to riot. 47 Then the king called on the Jewish soldiers for help, and they all rushed to his aid. They went through the whole city and killed at least 100,000 people. 48 They saved the king's life, but they plundered and burned the city. 49 When the people saw that the Jews had complete control of the city, they lost courage and appealed to the king, requesting 50 him to arrange a truce and stop the

NEW REVISED STANDARD VERSION

41 Now Jonathan sent to King Demetrius the request that he remove the troops of the citadel from Jerusalem, and the troops in the strongholds; for they kept fighting against Israel. 42 And Demetrius sent this message back to Jonathan: "Not only will I do these things for you and your nation, but I will confer great honor on you and your nation, if I find an opportunity. 43 Now then you will do well to send me men who will help me, for all my troops have revolted." 44 So Jonathan sent three thousand stalwart men to him at Antioch, and when they came to the king, the king rejoiced at their arrival.

45 Then the people of the city assembled within the city, to the number of a hundred and twenty thousand, and they wanted to kill the king. 46 But the king fled into the palace. Then the people of the city seized the main streets of the city and began to fight. 47 So the king called the Jews to his aid, and they all rallied around him and then spread out through the city; and they killed on that day about one hundred thousand. 48 They set fire to the city and seized a large amount of spoil on that day, and saved the king. 49 When the people of the city saw that the Jews had gained control of the city as they pleased, their courage failed and they cried out to the king with this entreaty: 50 "Grant us peace, and make the Jews stop fighting against us and our city." 51 And they

NEW AMERICAN BIBLE

41 Meanwhile Jonathan sent the request to King Demetrius to withdraw his troops from the citadel of Jerusalem and from the other strongholds, for they were constantly hostile to Israel. 42 Demetrius, in turn, sent this word to Jonathan: "I will not only do this for you and your nation, but I will greatly honor you and your nation when I find the opportunity. 43 Do me the favor, therefore, of sending men to fight for me, because all my troops have revolted."

44 So Jonathan sent three thousand good fighting men to him at Antioch. When they came to the king, he was delighted over their arrival, 45 for the populace, one hundred and twenty thousand strong, had massed in the center of the city in an attempt to kill him. 46 But he took refuge in the palace, while the populace gained control of the main streets and began to fight. 47 So the king called the Jews to his aid. They all rallied around him and spread out through the city. On that day they killed about a hundred thousand men in the city, 48 which, at the same time, they set on fire and plundered on a large scale. Thus they saved the king's life. 49 When the populace saw that the Jews held the city at their mercy, they lost courage and cried out to the king in supplication, 50 "Give us your terms and let the Jews stop attacking

NEW JERUSALEM BIBLE

long time there. 41 Jonathan, meanwhile, sent to ask King Demetrius to withdraw the garrisons from the Citadel in Jerusalem and from the other fortresses, since they were constantly fighting Israel. 42 Demetrius sent word back to Jonathan, 'Not only will I do this for you and for your nation, but I shall heap honours on you and your nation if I find a favourable opportunity. 43 For the present, you would do well to send me reinforcements, since all my troops have deserted.' 44 Jonathan sent three thousand experienced soldiers to him in Antioch; when they reached the king, he was delighted at their arrival. 45 The citizens crowded together in the centre of the city, to the number of some hundred and twenty thousand, intending to kill the king. 46 The king took refuge in the palace, while the citizens occupied the thoroughfares of the city and began to attack. 47 The king then called on the Jews for help; and these all rallied round him, then fanned out through the city, and that day killed about a hundred thousand of its inhabitants. 48 They fired the city, seizing a great deal of plunder at the same time, and secured the king's safety. 49 When the citizens saw that the Jews had the city at their mercy, their courage failed them, and they made an abject appeal to the king, 50 'Give us the right hand of peace, and let the Jews stop their fight against us and the

GREEK OLD TESTAMENT

πόλιν. 51 καὶ ἔρριψαν τὰ ὅπλα καὶ ἐποίησαν εἰρήνην. καὶ
ἐδοξάσθησαν οἱ Ιουδαῖοι ἐναντίον τοῦ βασιλέως καὶ ἐνώπιον
πάντων τῶν ἐν τῇ βασιλείᾳ αὐτοῦ καὶ ἐπέστρεψαν εἰς Ιερουσαλημ ἔχοντες σκῦλα πολλά. 52 καὶ ἐκάθισεν Δημήτριος ὁ
βασιλεὺς ἐπὶ θρόνου τῆς βασιλείας αὐτοῦ, καὶ ἡσύχασεν ἡ γῆ
ἐνώπιον αὐτοῦ. 53 καὶ ἐψεύσατο πάντα, ὅσα εἶπεν, καὶ
ἠλλοτριώθη τῷ Ιωναθαν καὶ οὐκ ἀνταπέδωκεν τὰς εὐνοίας, ἃς
ἀνταπέδωκεν αὐτῷ, καὶ ἔθλιβεν αὐτὸν σφόδρα.

54 Μετὰ δὲ ταῦτα ἀπέστρεψεν Τρύφων καὶ Ἀντίοχος μετ'
αὐτοῦ παιδάριον νεώτερον· καὶ ἐβασίλευσεν καὶ ἐπέθετο διάδημα. 55 καὶ ἐπισυνήχθησαν πρὸς αὐτὸν πᾶσαι αἱ δυνάμεις,
ἃς ἀπεσκοράκισεν Δημήτριος, καὶ ἐπολέμησαν πρὸς αὐτόν,
καὶ ἔφυγεν καὶ ἐτροπώθη. 56 καὶ ἔλαβεν Τρύφων τὰ θηρία
καὶ κατεκράτησεν τῆς Ἀντιοχείας. 57 καὶ ἔγραψεν Ἀντίοχος ὁ νεώτερος Ιωναθη λέγων Ἵστημί σοι τὴν ἀρχιερωσύνην καὶ καθίστημί σε ἐπὶ τῶν τεσσάρων νομῶν καὶ εἶναί σε
τῶν φίλων τοῦ βασιλέως. 58 καὶ ἀπέστειλεν αὐτῷ χρυσώματα καὶ διακονίαν καὶ ἔδωκεν αὐτῷ ἐξουσίαν πίνειν ἐν
χρυσώμασιν καὶ εἶναι ἐν πορφύρᾳ καὶ ἔχειν πόρπην χρυσῆν·
59 καὶ Σιμωνα τὸν ἀδελφὸν αὐτοῦ κατέστησεν στρατηγὸν
ἀπὸ τῆς κλίμακος Τύρου ἕως τῶν ὁρίων Αἰγύπτου. 60 καὶ ἐξῆλθεν Ιωναθαν καὶ διεπορεύετο πέραν τοῦ ποταμοῦ καὶ ἐν
ταῖς πόλεσιν, καὶ ἠθροίσθησαν πρὸς αὐτὸν πᾶσα δύναμις
Συρίας εἰς συμμαχίαν· καὶ ἦλθεν εἰς Ἀσκαλῶνα, καὶ ἀπήντησαν αὐτῷ οἱ ἐκ τῆς πόλεως ἐνδόξως. 61 καὶ ἀπῆλθεν

KING JAMES VERSION

51 With that they cast away their weapons, and made peace; and the Jews were honoured in the sight of the king, and in the sight of all that were in his realm; and they returned to Jerusalem, having great spoils.

52 So king Demetrius sat on the throne of his kingdom, and the land was quiet before him.

53 Nevertheless he dissembled in all that ever he spake, and estranged himself from Jonathan, neither rewarded he him according to the benefits which he had received of him, but troubled him very sore.

54 After this returned Tryphon, and with him the young child Antiochus, who reigned, and was crowned.

55 Then there gathered unto him all the men of war, whom Demetrius had put away, and they fought against Demetrius, who turned his back and fled.

56 Moreover Tryphon took the elephants, and won Antioch.

57 At that time young Antiochus wrote unto Jonathan, saying, I confirm thee in the high priesthood, and appoint thee ruler over the four governments, and to be one of the king's friends.

58 Upon this he sent him golden vessels to be served in, and gave him leave to drink in gold, and to be clothed in purple, and to wear a golden buckle.

59 His brother Simon also he made captain from the place called The ladder of Tyrus unto the borders of Egypt.

60 Then Jonathan went forth, and passed through the cities beyond the water, and all the forces of Syria gathered themselves unto him for to help him: and when he came to Ascalon, they of the city met him honourably.

DOUAY OLD TESTAMENT

51 And they threw down their arms, and made peace, and the Jews were glorified in the sight of the king, and in the sight of all that were in his realm, and were renowned throughout the kingdom, and returned to Jerusalem with many spoils.

52 So king Demetrius sat in the throne of his kingdom: and the land was quiet before him.

53 And he falsified all whatsoever he had said, and alienated himself from Jonathan, and did not reward him according to the benefits he had received from him, but gave him great trouble.

54 And after this Tryphon returned, and with him Antiochus the young boy, who was made king, and put on the diadem.

55 And there assembled unto him all the bands which Demetrius had sent away, and they fought against Demetrius, who turned his back and fled.

56 And Tryphon took the elephants, and made himself master of Antioch.

57 And young Antiochus wrote to Jonathan, saying: I confirm thee in the high priesthood, and I appoint thee ruler over the four cities, and to be one of the king's friends.

58 And he sent him vessels of gold for his service, and he gave him leave to drink in gold, and to be clothed in purple, and to wear a golden buckle:

59 And he made his brother Simon governor from the borders of Tyre even to the confines of Egypt.

60 Then Jonathan went forth and passed through the cities beyond the river: and all the forces of Syria gathered themselves to him to help him, and he came to Ascalon, and they met him honourably out of the city.

KNOX TRANSLATION

flinging away their weapons, they came to terms. Prince and
people both had good proof, by now, of the Jews' valour;
back they went to Jerusalem high in repute among the
Syrians, and laden with spoils.
52 Demetrius, now firmly established on the throne, his
dominions all at peace, 53 recked little enough of his promises; from Jonathan he was estranged altogether, left his services unrecompensed, and much mischief did him besides.
54 It was now that Tryphon came back, and with him the
young prince Antiochus, that took the style of king and had
himself crowned; 55 all the disbanded armies of Demetrius
rallied to them, and turned upon their former master, who
fled routed before them; 56 Tryphon, meanwhile, got possession of the elephants, and Antioch fell into his hands.
57 Thereupon came a letter from the young Antiochus to
Jonathan, confirming him in the high priesthood, and in possession both of Judaea and of the three cantons; he was
acclaimed as the king's friend, 58 and a present of golden
cups sent for his use, with the right to drink out of gold
ware, to dress in purple, and to carry the golden buckle.
59 His brother Simon, too, was made lord of the sea-coast,
from Tyre to the frontiers of Egypt.

60 And now Jonathan was on the march, across the river,
patrolling the cities everywhere, with all the armies of Syria
gathered to aid him....He came to Ascalon, where the towns-

TODAY'S ENGLISH VERSION

Jewish attack. 51 The rebels threw down their arms and surrendered. The king and everyone in his kingdom now had great respect for the Jews, who returned to Jerusalem with a great deal of loot. 52 Demetrius was firmly established as king, and the country was at peace under his rule, 53 but he broke all his promises and turned against Jonathan. He did not reward him for his loyal service, but instead continued to harass him.

54 Some time later, Trypho returned with the young boy Antiochus and crowned him king. 55 All the soldiers that Demetrius had dismissed then came to the support of the young king. They defeated Demetrius, and he fled. 56 Trypho captured the elephants and took control of Antioch. 57 The young King Antiochus wrote to Jonathan and confirmed him as High Priest and as ruler over the four regions and gave him the title "Friend of the King." 58 He sent him a set of gold tableware and authorized him to drink from gold cups, to wear a royal robe, and to wear the gold shoulder buckle awarded to "Relatives of the King." 59 He also appointed Jonathan's brother Simon as governor of the territory from the Phoenician coast to the Egyptian border.

60 Jonathan then marched with his army through the towns of Greater Syria, and all the Syrian forces joined him as allies. He went to Ascalon, where the people welcomed him

NEW REVISED STANDARD VERSION

threw down their arms and made peace. So the Jews gained glory in the sight of the king and of all the people in his kingdom, and they returned to Jerusalem with a large amount of spoil.

52 So King Demetrius sat on the throne of his kingdom, and the land was quiet before him. 53 But he broke his word about all that he had promised; he became estranged from Jonathan and did not repay the favors that Jonathan[a] had done him, but treated him very harshly.

54 After this Trypho returned, and with him the young boy Antiochus who began to reign and put on the crown. 55 All the troops that Demetrius had discharged gathered around him; they fought against Demetrius,[b] and he fled and was routed. 56 Trypho captured the elephants[c] and gained control of Antioch. 57 Then the young Antiochus wrote to Jonathan, saying, "I confirm you in the high priesthood and set you over the four districts and make you one of the king's Friends." 58 He also sent him gold plate and a table service, and granted him the right to drink from gold cups and dress in purple and wear a gold buckle. 59 He appointed Jonathan's[d] brother Simon governor from the Ladder of Tyre to the borders of Egypt.

60 Then Jonathan set out and traveled beyond the river and among the towns, and all the army of Syria gathered to him as allies. When he came to Askalon, the people of the city met him and paid him honor. 61 From there he went to

a Gk *he* *b* Gk *him* *c* Gk *animals* *d* Gk *his*

NEW AMERICAN BIBLE

us and our city." So they threw down their arms and made peace. 51 The Jews thus gained glory in the eyes of the king and all his subjects, and they became renowned throughout his kingdom. Finally they returned to Jerusalem with much spoil.

52 But when King Demetrius was sure of his royal throne, and the land was peaceful under his rule, 53 he broke all his promises and became estranged from Jonathan. Instead of rewarding Jonathan for all the favors he had received from him, he caused him much trouble.

54 After this, Trypho returned and brought with him the young boy Antiochus, who became king and wore the royal crown. 55 All the soldiers whom Demetrius had discharged rallied around Antiochus and fought against Demetrius, who was routed and fled. 56 Trypho captured the elephants and occupied Antioch. 57 Then young Antiochus wrote to Jonathan: "I confirm you in the high priesthood and appoint you ruler over the four districts and wish you to be one of the King's Friends." 58 He also sent him gold dishes and a dinner service, gave him the right to drink from gold cups, to dress in royal purple, and to wear a gold buckle. 59 Likewise, he made Jonathan's brother Simon governor of the region from the Ladder of Tyre to the frontier of Egypt.

60 Jonathan set out and traveled through West-of-Euphrates and its cities, and all the forces of Syria espoused his cause as allies. When he arrived at Ashkalon, the citizens

NEW JERUSALEM BIBLE

city.' 51 They threw down their arms and made peace. The Jews were covered in glory, in the eyes of the king and of everyone else in his kingdom. Having won renown in his kingdom, they returned to Jerusalem laden with booty. 52 Thus, King Demetrius sat all the more securely on his royal throne, and the country was quiet under his government. 53 But he gave the lie to all the promises he had made, and changed his attitude to Jonathan, giving nothing in return for the services Jonathan had rendered him, but thwarting him at every turn.

54 After this, Trypho came back with the little boy Antiochus, who became king and was crowned. 55 All the troops that Demetrius had summarily dismissed rallied to Antiochus, and made war on Demetrius, who turned tail and fled. 56 Trypho captured the elephants and seized Antioch. 57 Young Antiochus then wrote as follows to Jonathan: 'I confirm you in the high priesthood and set you over the four districts and appoint you one of the Friends of the King.' 58 He sent him a service of gold plate, and granted him the right to drink from gold vessels, and to wear the purple and the golden brooch. 59 He appointed his brother Simon commander-in-chief of the region from the Ladder of Tyre to the frontiers of Egypt. 60 Jonathan then set out and made a progress through Transeuphrates and its towns, and the entire Syrian army rallied to his support. He came to Ascalon and was received in state by the inhabitants. 61 From there

GREEK OLD TESTAMENT

ἐκεῖθεν εἰς Γάζαν, καὶ ἀπέκλεισαν οἱ ἀπὸ Γάζης, καὶ
περιεκάθισεν περὶ αὐτὴν καὶ ἐνεπύρισεν τὰ περιπόλια αὐτῆς
ἐν πυρὶ καὶ ἐσκύλευσεν αὐτά. 62 καὶ ἠξίωσαν οἱ ἀπὸ Γάζης
Ιωναθαν, καὶ ἔδωκεν αὐτοῖς δεξιὰς καὶ ἔλαβεν τοὺς υἱοὺς
τῶν ἀρχόντων αὐτῶν εἰς ὅμηρα καὶ ἐξαπέστειλεν αὐτοὺς εἰς
Ιερουσαλημ· καὶ διῆλθεν τὴν χώραν ἕως Δαμασκοῦ. 63 καὶ
ἤκουσεν Ιωναθαν ὅτι παρῆσαν οἱ ἄρχοντες Δημητρίου εἰς
Κηδες τὴν ἐν τῇ Γαλιλαίᾳ μετὰ δυνάμεως πολλῆς βουλόμενοι μεταστῆσαι αὐτὸν τῆς χρείας. 64 καὶ συνήντησεν αὐτοῖς, τὸν δὲ ἀδελφὸν αὐτοῦ Σιμωνα κατέλιπεν ἐν τῇ χώρᾳ.
65 καὶ παρενέβαλεν Σιμων ἐπὶ Βαιθσουρα καὶ ἐπολέμει αὐτὴν
ἡμέρας πολλὰς καὶ συνέκλεισεν αὐτήν. 66 καὶ ἠξίωσαν αὐτὸν
τοῦ δεξιὰς λαβεῖν, καὶ ἔδωκεν αὐτοῖς. καὶ ἐξέβαλεν αὐτοὺς
ἐκεῖθεν καὶ κατελάβετο τὴν πόλιν καὶ ἔθετο ἐπ᾽ αὐτὴν
φρουράν. 67 καὶ Ιωναθαν καὶ ἡ παρεμβολὴ αὐτοῦ παρενέβαλον ἐπὶ τὸ ὕδωρ τοῦ Γεννησαρ· καὶ ὤρθρισαν τὸ πρωὶ εἰς
τὸ πεδίον Ασωρ. 68 καὶ ἰδοὺ ἡ παρεμβολὴ ἀλλοφύλων ἀπήντα
αὐτῷ ἐν τῷ πεδίῳ καὶ ἐξέβαλον ἔνεδρον ἐπ᾽ αὐτὸν ἐν τοῖς
ὄρεσιν, αὐτοὶ δὲ ἀπήντησαν ἐξ ἐναντίας. 69 τὰ δὲ ἔνεδρα
ἐξανέστησαν ἐκ τῶν τόπων αὐτῶν καὶ συνῆψαν πόλεμον.
70 καὶ ἔφυγον οἱ παρὰ Ιωναθου πάντες, οὐδὲ εἷς κατελείφθη
ἀπ᾽ αὐτῶν πλὴν Ματταθιας ὁ τοῦ Αψαλωμου καὶ Ιουδας ὁ
τοῦ Χαλφι ἄρχοντες τῆς στρατιᾶς τῶν δυνάμεων. 71 καὶ

KING JAMES VERSION

61 From whence he went to Gaza, but they of Gaza shut him out; wherefore he laid siege unto it, and burned the suburbs thereof with fire, and spoiled them.

62 Afterward, when they of Gaza made supplication unto Jonathan, he made peace with them, and took the sons of their chief men for hostages, and sent them to Jerusalem, and passed through the country unto Damascus.

63 Now when Jonathan heard that Demetrius' princes were come to Cades, which is in Galilee, with a great power, purposing to remove him out of the country,

64 He went to meet them, and left Simon his brother in the country.

65 Then Simon encamped against Bethsura, and fought against it a long season, and shut it up:

66 But they desired to have peace with him, which he granted them, and then put them out from thence, and took the city, and set a garrison in it.

67 As for Jonathan and his host, they pitched at the water of Gennesar, from whence betimes in the morning they gat them to the plain of Nasor.

68 And, behold, the host of strangers met them in the plain, who, having laid men in ambush for him in the mountains, came themselves over against him.

69 So when they that lay in ambush rose out of their places, and joined battle, all that were of Jonathan's side fled;

70 Insomuch as there was not one of them left, except Mattathias the *son* of Absalom, and Judas the *son* of Calphi, the captains of the host.

DOUAY OLD TESTAMENT

61 And he went from thence to Gaza: and they that were in Gaza shut him out: and he besieged it, and burnt all the suburbs round about, and took the spoils.

62 And the men of Gaza made supplication to Jonathan, and he gave them the right hand: and he took their sons for hostages, and sent them to Jerusalem: and he went through the country as far as Damascus.

63 And Jonathan heard that the generals of Demetrius were come treacherously to Cades, which is in Galilee, with a great army, purposing to remove him from the affairs of the kingdom:

64 And he went against them: but left his brother Simon in the country.

65 And Simon encamped against Bethsura, and assaulted it many days, and shut them up.

66 And they desired him to make peace, and he granted it them: and he cast them out from thence, and took the city, and placed a garrison in it.

67 And Jonathan, and his army encamped by the water of Genesar, and before it was light they were ready in the plain of Asor.

68 And behold the army of the strangers met him in the plain, and they laid an ambush for him in the mountains: but he went out against them.

69 And they that lay in ambush rose out of their places, and joined battle.

70 And all that were on Jonathan's side fled, and none was left of them, but Mathathias the son of Absalom, and Judas the son of Calphi, chief captain of the army.

KNOX TRANSLATION

folk welcomed him with all honour;[a] 61 came to Gaza, where
they shut the gates on him, and he must needs undertake
the siege of it. But when he had spread fire and rapine
through the country-side, 62 the men of Gaza asked for
terms, which he gave them, carrying off their sons as hostages to Jerusalem. Then he went on patrolling the country,
all the way to Damascus. 63 News reached him that the
chiefs of Demetrius' faction were making head at Cades, in
Galilee, with a whole army to support them, and their design
was to remove him from office. 64 So he went to meet them,
leaving his brother Simon in charge of Judaea.
65 As for Simon, he made an assault upon Bethsura, and
kept it for a long while besieged, 66 till at last it obtained
terms of surrender; he rid the place of its defenders and took
over the command of it, putting in a garrison of his own.
67 Meanwhile, Jonathan was encamped by the waters of
Genesar; here, on the plain of Asor, they were on the watch
before day-break, 68 when they saw the enemy's force coming to meet them over the level plain. These had an ambush
ready for him on the hill-side, and as he advanced to meet
the main body, 69 the men in ambush sprang up, and
engaged him. 70 At this, all Jonathan's supporters took to
their heels; none stood their ground but Mathathias son of

a It is hardly possible to give any satisfactory account of the text as it stands. Even if we take 'beyond' as referring to the Jewish side of the Euphrates, why should an expedition into Syria bring Jonathan down to Ascalon, some forty miles west of Jerusalem? Conceivably there has been some disturbance in the text, which may have read originally, 'And he (Antiochus) began patrolling the cities across the river, with all the armies of Syria gathered to aid him; and Jonathan marched out and came to Ascalon...'.

TODAY'S ENGLISH VERSION

with great honors. 61 Then he went to Gaza, but the people
there barred their gates against him. So he laid siege to the
city and burned and looted the surrounding area. 62 The people of Gaza then asked for peace, and Jonathan arranged a
truce. He took the sons of the leaders and sent them to
Jerusalem as hostages. After that he marched on as far as
Damascus.

63 Jonathan learned that the officers of Demetrius had come
to Kedesh in Galilee with a large army, intending to keep him
from carrying out his plan. 64 So he left his brother Simon in
Judea and set out to meet them in battle. 65 Then Simon laid
siege to Bethzur and fought against it for a long time. 66 The
people asked for peace terms, and Simon agreed. He then
took over the town, drove the people out, and stationed a
detachment of troops there.

67 Jonathan and his army set up camp by Lake Galilee.
Early the next morning he marched his troops to the plain of
Hazor, 68 where the main force of the foreign army was
advancing to meet him. Unknown to Jonathan, they had left
a detachment of troops in ambush in the mountains, 69 and
when the men in ambush came out and attacked,
70 Jonathan's entire army turned and ran. No one was left,
except two officers, Mattathias son of Absalom and Judas
son of Chalphi. 71 Jonathan was humiliated, so he tore his

NEW REVISED STANDARD VERSION

Gaza, but the people of Gaza shut him out. So he besieged it
and burned its suburbs with fire and plundered them.
62 Then the people of Gaza pleaded with Jonathan, and he
made peace with them, and took the sons of their rulers as
hostages and sent them to Jerusalem. And he passed through
the country as far as Damascus.

63 Then Jonathan heard that the officers of Demetrius had
come to Kadesh in Galilee with a large army, intending to
remove him from office. 64 He went to meet them, but left his
brother Simon in the country. 65 Simon encamped before
Beth-zur and fought against it for many days and hemmed it
in. 66 Then they asked him to grant them terms of peace, and
he did so. He removed them from there, took possession of
the town, and set a garrison over it.

67 Jonathan and his army encamped by the waters of
Gennesaret. Early in the morning they marched to the plain
of Hazor, 68 and there in the plain the army of the foreigners
met him; they had set an ambush against him in the mountains, but they themselves met him face to face. 69 Then the
men in ambush emerged from their places and joined battle.
70 All the men with Jonathan fled; not one of them was left
except Mattathias son of Absalom and Judas son of Chalphi,
commanders of the forces of the army. 71 Jonathan tore his

NEW AMERICAN BIBLE

welcomed him with pomp. 61 But when he set out for Gaza,
the people of Gaza locked their gates against him. So he
besieged it and burned and plundered its suburbs. 62 Then
the people of Gaza appealed to him for mercy, and he granted them peace. He took the sons of their chief men as hostages and sent them to Jerusalem. He then traveled on
through the province as far as Damascus.

63 Jonathan heard that the generals of Demetrius had come
with a strong force to Kadesh in Galilee, intending to remove
him from office. 64 So he went to meet them, leaving his
brother Simon in the province. 65 Simon besieged Beth-zur,
attacked it for many days, and blockaded the inhabitants.
66 When they sued for peace, he granted it to them. He
expelled them from the city, took possession of it, and put a
garrison there.

67 Meanwhile, Jonathan and his army pitched their camp
near the waters of Gennesaret, and at daybreak they went to
the plain of Hazor. 68 There, in front of him on the plain,
was the army of the foreigners. This army attacked him in
the open, having first detached an ambush against him in
the mountains. 69 Then the men in ambush rose out of their
places and joined in the battle. 70 All of Jonathan's men fled;
no one stayed except the army commanders Mattathias, son
of Absalom, and Judas, son of Chalphi. 71 Jonathan tore his

NEW JERUSALEM BIBLE

he proceeded to Gaza, but the people of Gaza shut him out,
so he laid siege to it, burning down its suburbs and plundering them. 62 The people of Gaza then pleaded with Jonathan,
and he made peace with them; but he took the sons of their
chief men as hostages and sent them away to Jerusalem. He
then travelled through the country as far as Damascus.

63 Jonathan now learned that Demetrius' generals had
arrived at Kadesh in Galilee with a large army, intending to
remove him from office, 64 and went to engage them, leaving
his brother Simon inside the country. 65 Simon laid siege to
Beth-Zur, attacking it day after day, and blockading the
inhabitants 66 till they sued for peace, which he granted
them, though he expelled them from the town and occupied
it, stationing a garrison there. 67 Jonathan and his army,
meanwhile, having pitched camp by the Lake of Gennesar,
rose early, and by morning were already in the plain of
Hazor. 68 The foreigners' army advanced to fight them on the
plain, having first positioned an ambush for him in the
mountains. While the main body was advancing directly
towards the Jews, 69 the troops in ambush broke cover and
attacked first. 70 All the men with Jonathan fled; no one was
left, except Mattathias son of Absalom and Judas son of
Chalphi, the generals of his army. 71 At this, Jonathan tore

GREEK OLD TESTAMENT

διέρρηξεν Ιωναθαν τὰ ἱμάτια αὐτοῦ καὶ ἐπέθετο γῆν ἐπὶ τὴν
κεφαλὴν αὐτοῦ καὶ προσηύξατο. 72 καὶ ὑπέστρεψεν πρὸς αὐτοὺς πολέμῳ καὶ ἐτροπώσατο αὐτούς, καὶ ἔφυγον. 73 καὶ
εἶδον οἱ φεύγοντες παρ' αὐτοῦ καὶ ἐπέστρεψαν ἐπ' αὐτὸν
καὶ ἐδίωκον μετ' αὐτοῦ ἕως Κεδες ἕως τῆς παρεμβολῆς
αὐτῶν καὶ παρενέβαλον ἐκεῖ. 74 καὶ ἔπεσον ἐκ τῶν ἀλλοφύλων ἐν τῇ ἡμέρᾳ ἐκείνῃ εἰς ἄνδρας τρισχιλίους. καὶ ἐπέστρεψεν Ιωναθαν εἰς Ιερουσαλημ.

12 Καὶ εἶδεν Ιωναθαν ὅτι ὁ καιρὸς αὐτῷ συνεργεῖ, καὶ
ἐπελέξατο ἄνδρας καὶ ἀπέστειλεν εἰς Ῥώμην στῆσαι
καὶ ἀνανεώσασθαι τὴν πρὸς αὐτοὺς φιλίαν. 2 καὶ πρὸς
Σπαρτιάτας καὶ τόπους ἑτέρους ἀπέστειλεν ἐπιστολὰς κατὰ
τὰ αὐτά. 3 καὶ ἐπορεύθησαν εἰς Ῥώμην καὶ εἰσῆλθον εἰς τὸ
βουλευτήριον καὶ εἶπον Ιωναθαν ὁ ἀρχιερεὺς καὶ τὸ ἔθνος
τῶν Ιουδαίων ἀπέστειλεν ἡμᾶς ἀνανεώσασθαι τὴν φιλίαν
ἑαυτοῖς καὶ τὴν συμμαχίαν κατὰ τὸ πρότερον. 4 καὶ ἔδωκαν
ἐπιστολὰς αὐτοῖς πρὸς αὐτοὺς κατὰ τόπον, ὅπως προπέμ-
πωσιν αὐτοὺς εἰς γῆν Ιουδα μετ' εἰρήνης.

5 Καὶ τοῦτο τὸ ἀντίγραφον τῶν ἐπιστολῶν, ὧν ἔγραψεν
Ιωναθαν τοῖς Σπαρτιάταις

6 Ιωναθαν ἀρχιερεὺς καὶ ἡ γερουσία τοῦ ἔθνους καὶ οἱ
ἱερεῖς καὶ ὁ λοιπὸς δῆμος τῶν Ιουδαίων Σπαρτιάταις τοῖς
ἀδελφοῖς χαίρειν. 7 ἔτι πρότερον ἀπεστάλησαν ἐπιστολαὶ
πρὸς Ονιαν τὸν ἀρχιερέα παρὰ Ἀρείου τοῦ βασιλεύοντος ἐν
ὑμῖν ὅτι ἐστὲ ἀδελφοὶ ἡμῶν, ὡς τὸ ἀντίγραφον ὑπόκειται.

KING JAMES VERSION

71 Then Jonathan rent his clothes, and cast earth upon his head, and prayed.

72 Afterwards turning again to battle, he put them to flight, and so they ran away.

73 Now when his own men that were fled saw this, they turned again unto him, and with him pursued them to Cades, even unto their own tents, and there they camped.

74 So there were slain of the heathen that day about three thousand men: but Jonathan returned to Jerusalem.

12 Now when Jonathan saw that time served him, he chose certain men, and sent them to Rome, for to confirm and renew the friendship that they had with them.

2 He sent letters also to the Lacedemonians, and to other places, for the same purpose.

3 So they went unto Rome, and entered into the senate, and said, Jonathan the high priest, and the people of the Jews, sent us unto you, to the end ye should renew the friendship, which ye had with them, and league, as in former time.

4 Upon this *the Romans* gave them letters unto the governors of every place, that they should bring them into the land of Judea peaceably.

5 And this is the copy of the letters which Jonathan wrote to the Lacedemonians:

6 Jonathan the high priest, and the elders of the nation, and the priests, and the other people of the Jews, unto the Lacedemonians their brethren send greeting:

7 There were letters sent in times past unto Onias the high priest from Darius, who reigned then among you, to signify that ye are our brethren, as the copy here underwritten doth specify.

DOUAY OLD TESTAMENT

71 And Jonathan rent his garments, and cast earth upon his head, and prayed.

72 And Jonathan turned again to them to battle, and he put them to flight, and they fought.

73 And they of his part that fled saw *this,* and they turned again to him, and they all with him pursued *the enemies* even to Cades to their own camp, and they came even thither.

74 And there fell of the aliens in that day three thousand men: and Jonathan returned to Jerusalem.

12 AND Jonathan saw that the time served him, and he chose certain men and sent them to Rome, to confirm and to renew the amity with them:

2 And he sent letters to the Spartans, and to other places according to the same form.

3 And they went to Rome, and entered into the senate house, and said: Jonathan the high priest, and the nation of the Jews have sent us to renew the amity, and alliance as it was before.

4 And they gave them letters to their governors in every place, to conduct them into the land of Juda with peace.

5 And this is a copy of the letters which Jonathan wrote to the Spartans:

6 Jonathan the high priest, and the ancients of the nation, and the priests, and the rest of the people of the Jews, to the Spartans, their brethren, greeting.

7 There were letters sent long ago to Onias the high priest from Arius who reigned then among you, to signify that you are our brethren, as the copy here underwritten doth specify.

KNOX TRANSLATION

Absalom and Judas son of Calphi, that had the marshalling
of his men. 71 What marvel if Jonathan tore his garments
about him, and strewed earth on his head, and betook himself to prayer? 72 Afterwards, he offered battle afresh, and
routed his enemies; as the fight went on, 73 his own men
that had deserted their ranks rallied to him, and joined in the
pursuit all the way to Cades, where they encamped once
more. 74 In that day's fighting, three thousand of the
Gentiles fell; and so Jonathan made his way back to
Jerusalem.

12 Here was a posture of affairs suited Jonathan well
enough; yet would he send delegates to confirm and
renew his alliance with the Romans; 2 Lacedaemon, too, and
other countries should have letters of the same tenour. 3 To
Rome, then, his messengers went, gained audience of the
senate, and told how the high priest Jonathan and the Jewish
people had sent them to renew their old treaty of friendship;
4 and the Romans gave them such letters of recommendation
to this country or that, as should bring them home to Juda
under safe conduct.

5 The message Jonathan sent to the men of Sparta was in
these terms following. 6 The high priest Jonathan, with the
elders and priests and all the people of the Jews, to their
brethren the Spartans, greeting. 7 Long since, your king
Arius wrote to our own high priest, Onias, claiming kinship
between us, as witness the copy here subjoined; 8 an

TODAY'S ENGLISH VERSION

clothes, threw dust on his head, and prayed. 72 Then he turned back to the battle, crushed the enemy, and put them to flight. 73 When his own fleeing soldiers saw this, they turned back and joined him in pursuit. They chased the enemy all the way back to their camp at Kedesh and then took over the camp. 74 At least 3,000 enemy soldiers were killed that day. Jonathan then returned to Jerusalem.

12 When Jonathan saw that things were working out to his advantage, he chose ambassadors and sent them to Rome to confirm and renew friendship with the Romans. 2 He also sent letters with a similar message to Sparta and other places. 3 The ambassadors went to Rome, where they were admitted to the Senate chamber, and reported that the High Priest Jonathan and the Jewish nation had sent them to renew the earlier ties of friendship and alliance with Rome. 4 The Romans provided them with letters to the authorities in each country through which they would pass, guaranteeing them safe conduct in their return to the land of Judea.

5 Here is a copy of the letter Jonathan wrote to the Spartans:

6 "Jonathan the High Priest, the national council of leaders, the priests, and the rest of the people of Judea, to our brothers in Sparta, greetings. 7 At an earlier time, your King Arius sent a letter to our High Priest Onias, stating that our two nations are related, as the attached copy

NEW REVISED STANDARD VERSION

clothes, put dust on his head, and prayed. 72 Then he turned back to the battle against the enemy[a] and routed them, and they fled. 73 When his men who were fleeing saw this, they returned to him and joined him in the pursuit as far as Kadesh, to their camp, and there they encamped. 74 As many as three thousand of the foreigners fell that day. And Jonathan returned to Jerusalem.

12 Now when Jonathan saw that the time was favorable for him, he chose men and sent them to Rome to confirm and renew the friendship with them. 2 He also sent letters to the same effect to the Spartans and to other places. 3 So they went to Rome and entered the senate chamber and said, "The high priest Jonathan and the Jewish nation have sent us to renew the former friendship and alliance with them." 4 And the Romans[b] gave them letters to the people in every place, asking them to provide for the envoys[a] safe conduct to the land of Judah.

5 This is a copy of the letter that Jonathan wrote to the Spartans: 6 "The high priest Jonathan, the senate of the nation, the priests, and the rest of the Jewish people to their brothers the Spartans, greetings. 7 Already in time past a letter was sent to the high priest Onias from Arius,[c] who was king among you, stating that you are our brothers, as the

a Gk *them* *b* Gk *they* *c* Vg Compare verse 20: Gk *Darius*

NEW AMERICAN BIBLE

clothes, threw earth on his head, and prayed. 72 Then he went back to the combat and so overwhelmed the enemy that they took to flight. 73 Those of his men who were running away saw it and returned to him; and with him they pursued the enemy as far as their camp in Kadesh, where they pitched their own camp. 74 Three thousand of the foreign troops fell on that day. Then Jonathan returned to Jerusalem.

12 When Jonathan saw that the times favored him, he sent selected men to Rome to confirm and renew his friendship with the Romans. 2 He also sent letters to Sparta and other places for the same purpose.

3 After reaching Rome, the men entered the senate chamber and said, "The high priest Jonathan and the Jewish people have sent us to renew the earlier friendship and alliance between you and them." 4 The Romans gave them letters addressed to the authorities in the various places, requesting them to provide the envoys with safe conduct to the land of Judah.

5 This is a copy of the letter that Jonathan wrote to the Spartans: 6 "Jonathan the high priest, the senate of the nation, the priests, and the rest of the Jewish people send greetings to their brothers the Spartans. 7 Long ago a letter was sent to the high priest Onias from Arius, who then reigned over you, stating that you are our brothers, as the

NEW JERUSALEM BIBLE

his garments, put dust on his head, and prayed. 72 Then he returned to the fight and routed the enemy, who fled. 73 When the fugitives from his own forces saw this, they came back to him and joined in the pursuit as far as Kadesh where the enemy encampment was, and there they themselves pitched camp. 74 About three thousand of the foreign troops fell that day. Jonathan then returned to Jerusalem.

12 When Jonathan saw that circumstances were working in his favour, he sent a select mission to Rome to confirm and renew his treaty of friendship with the Romans. 2 He also sent letters to the same effect to the Spartans and to other places. 3 The envoys made their way to Rome, entered the Senate and said, 'Jonathan the high priest and the Jewish nation have sent us to renew your treaty of friendship and alliance with them as before.' 4 The Senate gave them letters to the authorities of each place, to procure their safe conduct to Judaea.

5 The following is the copy of the letter Jonathan wrote to the Spartans:

6 'Jonathan the high priest, the senate of the nation, the priests and the rest of the Jewish people to the Spartans their brothers, greetings.

7 'In the past, a letter was sent to Onias, the high priest, from Areios, one of your kings, stating that you are indeed our brothers, as the copy subjoined attests. 8 Onias

Greek Old Testament

8 καὶ ἐπεδέξατο ὁ Ονιας τὸν ἄνδρα τὸν ἀπεσταλμένον ἐνδόξως καὶ ἔλαβεν τὰς ἐπιστολάς, ἐν αἷς διεσαφεῖτο περὶ
συμμαχίας καὶ φιλίας. 9 ἡμεῖς οὖν ἀπροσδεεῖς τούτων
ὄντες παράκλησιν ἔχοντες τὰ βιβλία τὰ ἅγια τὰ ἐν ταῖς
χερσὶν ἡμῶν 10 ἐπειράθημεν ἀποστεῖλαι τὴν πρὸς ὑμᾶς
ἀδελφότητα καὶ φιλίαν ἀνανεώσασθαι πρὸς τὸ μὴ ἐξαλλοτρι-
ωθῆναι ὑμῶν· πολλοὶ γὰρ καιροὶ διῆλθον ἀφ᾽ οὗ ἀπεστείλατε
πρὸς ἡμᾶς. 11 ἡμεῖς οὖν ἐν παντὶ καιρῷ ἀδιαλείπτως ἔν τε
ταῖς ἑορταῖς καὶ ταῖς λοιπαῖς καθηκούσαις ἡμέραις
μιμνησκόμεθα ὑμῶν ἐφ᾽ ὧν προσφέρομεν θυσιῶν καὶ ἐν ταῖς
προσευχαῖς, ὡς δέον ἐστὶν καὶ πρέπον μνημονεύειν
ἀδελφῶν. 12 εὐφραινόμεθα δὲ ἐπὶ τῇ δόξῃ ὑμῶν. 13 ἡμᾶς δὲ
ἐκύκλωσαν πολλαὶ θλίψεις καὶ πόλεμοι πολλοί, καὶ ἐπολέμησαν ἡμᾶς οἱ βασιλεῖς οἱ κύκλῳ ἡμῶν. 14 οὐκ ἠβουλόμεθα
οὖν παρενοχλῆσαι ὑμῖν καὶ τοῖς λοιποῖς συμμάχοις καὶ φίλοις ἡμῶν ἐν τοῖς πολέμοις τούτοις. 15 ἔχομεν γὰρ τὴν ἐξ
οὐρανοῦ βοήθειαν βοηθοῦσαν ἡμῖν καὶ ἐρρύσθημεν ἀπὸ τῶν
ἐχθρῶν, καὶ ἐταπεινώθησαν οἱ ἐχθροὶ ἡμῶν. 16 ἐπελέξαμεν
οὖν Νουμήνιον Ἀντιόχου καὶ Ἀντίπατρον Ἰάσονος καὶ
ἀπεστάλκαμεν πρὸς Ῥωμαίους ἀνανεώσασθαι τὴν πρὸς αὐτοὺς φιλίαν καὶ συμμαχίαν τὴν πρότερον. 17 ἐνετειλάμεθα
οὖν αὐτοῖς καὶ πρὸς ὑμᾶς πορευθῆναι καὶ ἀσπάσασθαι ὑμᾶς
καὶ ἀποδοῦναι ὑμῖν τὰς παρ᾽ ἡμῶν ἐπιστολὰς περὶ τῆς

King James Version

8 At which time Onias entreated the ambassador that was sent honourably, and received the letters, wherein declaration was made of the league and friendship.

9 Therefore we also, albeit we need none of these things, for that we have the holy books of scripture in our hands to comfort us,

10 Have nevertheless attempted to send unto you for the renewing of brotherhood and friendship, lest we should become strangers unto you altogether: for there is a long time passed since ye sent unto us.

11 We therefore at all times without ceasing, both in our feasts, and other convenient days, do remember you in the sacrifices which we offer, and in our prayers, as reason is, and as it becometh us to think upon our brethren:

12 And we are right glad of your honour.

13 As for ourselves, we have had great troubles and wars on every side, forsomuch as the kings that are round about us have fought against us.

14 Howbeit we would not be troublesome unto you, nor to others of our confederates and friends, in these wars:

15 For we have help from heaven that succoureth us, so as we are delivered from our enemies, and our enemies are brought under foot.

16 For this cause we chose Numenius *the son* of Antiochus, and Antipater *the son* of Jason, and sent them unto the Romans, to renew the amity that we had with them, and the former league.

17 We commanded them also to go unto you, and to salute you, and to deliver you our letters concerning the renewing of our brotherhood.

Douay Old Testament

8 And Onias received the ambassador with honour: and received the letters wherein there was mention made of the alliance, and amity.

9 We, though we needed none of these things, having for our comfort the holy books that are in our hands,

10 Chose rather to send to you to renew the brotherhood and friendship, lest we should become strangers to you altogether: for there is a long time passed since you sent to us.

11 We therefore at all times without ceasing, both in our festivals, and other days, wherein it is convenient, remember you in the sacrifices that we offer, and in our observances, as it is meet, and becoming to remember brethren.

12 And we rejoice at your glory.

13 But we have had many troubles and wars on every side, and the kings that are round about us, have fought against us.

14 But we would not be troublesome to you, nor to the rest of our allies and friends in these wars.

15 For we have had help from heaven, and we have been delivered, and our enemies are humbled.

16 We have chosen therefore Numenius the son of Antiochus, and Antipater the son of Jason, and have sent them to the Romans to renew with them the former amity and alliance.

17 And we have commanded them to go also to you, and to salute you, and to deliver you our letters, concerning the renewing of our brotherhood.

Knox Translation

honourable welcome Onias gave to this messenger of yours,
and accepted the proposal of friendly alliance. 9 For ourselves, we have little need of such friendship; seek we comfort, it is in the sacred books committed to our charge. 10 Yet
we thought it best to treat with you for the renewal of this
brotherly compact, before any estrangement should arise
between us; your embassy to us is of long ago. 11 Never
feast-day passes, nor day apt for remembrance, but you are
remembered, as brothers should be, in sacrifice and prayer
we offer; 12 renown of yours is pride of ours still. 13 In wars
and calamities much involved of late, powerful kings for our
neighbours and our enemies, 14 we would not embroil you,
nor other allies of ours, in these quarrels. 15 Now, by the
grace of heaven, we are delivered; our enemies lie crushed;
16 delegates of ours, Numenius son of Antiochus and Antipater son of Jason, are on their way to Rome, friendship and
alliance of former days to confirm afresh; 17 and should we
send them with no errand to you, no greeting, no word from

TODAY'S ENGLISH VERSION

shows. 8 Onias received your ambassador with full honors
and acknowledged receipt of your letter, which declared
our alliance and friendship. 9 And now, although we are
not in need of such alliances, since we find our source of
strength in the holy books we possess, 10 we have written
to renew our ties of brotherhood and friendship with you.
We do not wish to become total strangers, and it has now
been many years since your last communication.
11 Throughout the years we have taken every opportunity,
on our festival days and other suitable days, to remember
you when we have offered our sacrifices and made our
prayers, as it is fitting and proper for brothers to do. 12 We
also are pleased that fame has come to you. 13 But we
have had one series of troubles after another and have had
to fight many wars, because we have been under constant
attack by surrounding nations. 14 During this time of war,
we did not wish to trouble you or our other allies and
friends, 15 since we do have the help of the Lord, who has
defeated our enemies and rescued us from them. 16 So we
have chosen Numenius son of Antiochus together with
Antipater son of Jason and sent them as ambassadors to
Rome to renew our ties of friendship and alliance with the
Romans. 17 We have also ordered them to go to you with
our greetings and deliver this letter about the renewal of

NEW REVISED STANDARD VERSION

appended copy shows. 8 Onias welcomed the envoy with
honor, and received the letter, which contained a clear declaration of alliance and friendship. 9 Therefore, though we
have no need of these things, since we have as encouragement the holy books that are in our hands, 10 we have
undertaken to send to renew our family ties and friendship
with you, so that we may not become estranged from you,
for considerable time has passed since you sent your letter
to us. 11 We therefore remember you constantly on every
occasion, both at our festivals and on other appropriate
days, at the sacrifices that we offer and in our prayers, as it
is right and proper to remember brothers. 12 And we rejoice
in your glory. 13 But as for ourselves, many trials and many
wars have encircled us; the kings around us have waged
war against us. 14 We were unwilling to annoy you and our
other allies and friends with these wars, 15 for we have the
help that comes from Heaven for our aid, and so we were
delivered from our enemies, and our enemies were humbled. 16 We therefore have chosen Numenius son of
Antiochus and Antipater son of Jason, and have sent them
to Rome to renew our former friendship and alliance with
them. 17 We have commanded them to go also to you and
greet you and deliver to you this letter from us concerning

NEW AMERICAN BIBLE

attached copy shows. 8 Onias welcomed the envoy with
honor and received the letter, which clearly referred to
alliance and friendship. 9 Though we have no need of these
things, since we have for our encouragement the sacred
books that are in our possession, 10 we have ventured to
send word to you for the renewal of brotherhood and friendship, so as not to become strangers to you altogether; a long
time has passed since your mission to us. 11 We, on our part,
have never ceased to remember you in the sacrifices and
prayers that we offer on our feasts and other appropriate
days, as it is right and proper to remember brothers. 12 We
likewise rejoice in your renown. 13 But many hardships and
wars have beset us, and the kings around us have attacked
us. 14 We did not wish to be troublesome to you and to the
rest of our allies and friends in these wars; 15 with the help
of Heaven for our support, we have been saved from our enemies, and they have been humbled. 16 So we have chosen
Numenius, son of Antiochus, and Antipater, son of Jason,
and we have sent them to the Romans to renew our former
friendship and alliance with them. 17 We have also ordered
them to come to you and greet you, and to deliver to you our

NEW JERUSALEM BIBLE

received the envoy with honour, and accepted the letter, in
which a clear declaration was made of friendship and
alliance. 9 For our part, though we have no need of these,
having the consolation of the holy books in our possession, 10 we venture to send to renew our fraternal friendship with you, so that we may not become strangers to
you, a long time having elapsed since you last wrote to us.
11 We, for our part, on every occasion, at our festivals and
on other appointed days, unfailingly remember you in the
sacrifices we offer and in our prayers, as it is right and fitting to remember brothers. 12 We rejoice in your renown.
13 'We ourselves, however, have had many trials and
many wars, the neighbouring kings making war on us.
14 We were unwilling to trouble you or our other allies and
friends during these wars, 15 since we have the support of
Heaven to help us, thanks to which we have been delivered from our enemies, and they are the ones who have
been brought low. 16 We have therefore chosen Numenius
son of Antiochus, and Antipater son of Jason, and sent
them to the Romans to renew our former treaty of friendship and alliance, 17 and we have ordered them also to
visit you, to greet you and deliver you this letter of ours

GREEK OLD TESTAMENT

ἀνανεώσεως καὶ τῆς ἀδελφότητος ἡμῶν. 18 καὶ νῦν καλῶς
ποιήσετε ἀντιφωνήσαντες ἡμῖν πρὸς ταῦτα.
19 Καὶ τοῦτο τὸ ἀντίγραφον τῶν ἐπιστολῶν, ὧν ἀπέστειλαν Ονια
20 Ἄρειος βασιλεὺς Σπαρτιατῶν Ονια ἱερεῖ μεγάλῳ χαίρειν. 21 εὑρέθη ἐν γραφῇ περί τε τῶν Σπαρτιατῶν καὶ Ιουδαίων ὅτι εἰσὶν ἀδελφοὶ καὶ ὅτι εἰσὶν ἐκ γένους Αβρααμ. 22 καὶ
νῦν ἀφ' οὗ ἔγνωμεν ταῦτα, καλῶς ποιήσετε γράφοντες ἡμῖν
περὶ τῆς εἰρήνης ὑμῶν, 23 καὶ ἡμεῖς δὲ ἀντιγράφομεν ὑμῖν
τὰ κτήνη ὑμῶν καὶ ἡ ὕπαρξις ὑμῶν ἡμῖν ἐστιν, καὶ τὰ ἡμῶν
ὑμῖν ἐστιν. ἐντελλόμεθα οὖν ὅπως ἀπαγγείλωσιν ὑμῖν κατὰ
ταῦτα.
24 Καὶ ἤκουσεν Ιωναθαν ὅτι ἐπέστρεψαν οἱ ἄρχοντες
Δημητρίου μετὰ δυνάμεως πολλῆς ὑπὲρ τὸ πρότερον τοῦ
πολεμῆσαι πρὸς αὐτόν. 25 καὶ ἀπῆρεν ἐξ Ιερουσαλημ καὶ
ἀπήντησεν αὐτοῖς εἰς τὴν Αμαθῖτιν χώραν· οὐ γὰρ ἔδωκεν
αὐτοῖς ἀνοχὴν τοῦ ἐμβατεῦσαι εἰς τὴν χώραν αὐτοῦ. 26 καὶ
ἀπέστειλεν κατασκόπους εἰς τὴν παρεμβολὴν αὐτῶν, καὶ
ἐπέστρεψαν καὶ ἀπήγγειλαν αὐτῷ ὅτι οὕτως τάσσονται
ἐπιπεσεῖν ἐπ' αὐτοὺς τὴν νύκτα. 27 ὡς δὲ ἔδυ ὁ ἥλιος, ἐπέταξεν Ιωναθαν τοῖς παρ' αὐτοῦ γρηγορεῖν καὶ εἶναι ἐπὶ τοῖς
ὅπλοις ἑτοιμάζεσθαι εἰς πόλεμον δι' ὅλης τῆς νυκτὸς καὶ
ἐξέβαλεν προφύλακας κύκλῳ τῆς παρεμβολῆς. 28 καὶ ἤκουσαν οἱ ὑπεναντίοι ὅτι ἡτοίμασται Ιωναθαν καὶ οἱ παρ' αὐτοῦ
εἰς πόλεμον, καὶ ἐφοβήθησαν καὶ ἔπτηξαν τῇ καρδίᾳ αὐτῶν
καὶ ἀνέκαυσαν πυρὰς ἐν τῇ παρεμβολῇ αὐτῶν. 29 Ιωναθαν δὲ
καὶ οἱ παρ' αὐτοῦ οὐκ ἔγνωσαν ἕως πρωί, ἔβλεπον γὰρ τὰ

KING JAMES VERSION

18 Wherefore now ye shall do well to give us an answer thereto.

19 And this is the copy of the letters which Oniares sent.

20 Areus king of the Lacedemonians to Onias the high priest, greeting:

21 It is found in writing, that the Lacedemonians and Jews are brethren, and that they are of the stock of Abraham:

22 Now therefore, since this is come to our knowledge, ye shall do well to write unto us of your prosperity.

23 We do write back again to you, that your cattle and goods are our's, and our's are your's. We do command therefore *our ambassadors* to make report unto you on this wise.

24 Now when Jonathan heard that Demetrius' princes were come to fight against him with a greater host than afore,

25 He removed from Jerusalem, and met them in the land of Amathis: for he gave them no respite to enter his country.

26 He sent spies also unto their tents, who came again, and told him that they were appointed to come upon them in the night season.

27 Wherefore so soon as the sun was down, Jonathan commanded his men to watch, and to be in arms, that all the night long they might be ready to fight: also he sent forth centinels round about the host.

28 But when the adversaries heard that Jonathan and his men were ready for battle, they feared, and trembled in their hearts, and they kindled fires in their camp.

29 Howbeit Jonathan and his company knew it not till the morning: for they saw the lights burning.

DOUAY OLD TESTAMENT

18 And now you shall do well to give us an answer hereto.

19 And this is the copy of the letter which he had sent to Onias:

20 Arius king of the Spartans to Onias the high priest, greeting.

21 It is found in writing concerning the Spartans, and the Jews, that they are brethren, and that they are of the stock of Abraham.

22 And now since this is come to our knowledge, you do well to write to us of your prosperity.

23 And we also have written back to you: That our cattle, and our possessions are yours: and yours, ours. We therefore have commanded that these things should be told you.

24 Now Jonathan heard that the generals of Demetrius were come again with a greater army than before to fight against him.

25 So he went out from Jerusalem, and met them in the land of Amath: for he gave them no time to enter into his country.

26 And he sent spies into their camp, and they came back and brought him word that they designed to come upon them in the night.

27 And when the sun was set, Jonathan commanded his men to watch, and to be in arms all night long ready to fight, and he set sentinels round about the camp.

28 And the enemies heard that Jonathan and his men were ready for battle, and they were struck with fear, and dread in their heart: and they kindled fires in their camp.

29 But Jonathan and they that were with him knew it not till the morning: for they saw the lights burning.

KNOX TRANSLATION

us of brotherhood revived? 18 Pray you, send us fair answer
in your turn.
19 And, for Arius' letter to Onias, thus the copy of it ran,
20 Arius, king of the Spartans, to the high priest Onias, greeting. 21 Spartan and Jew, written record shews it, come of one
blood, Abraham's. 22 Apprised of this, we would fain know
how you do; pray tell us. 23 And take this message in return,
Cattle and whatever else is ours, is yours, and yours ours; of
that, the bearer of this letter brings you assurance.
24 Then came news to Jonathan that the chiefs of
Demetrius' faction were returning to the attack, and in
greater force than ever; 25 so out he marched, and met them
in the Amathite country; respite he would not give them, to
invade his own. 26 Spies of his went out into the enemy's
camp, and reported, all was ready for a night attack; 27 so,
when the sun was down, Jonathan would have his men keep
watch, ready armed all night for battle, and posted sentries
round his lines. 28 The enemy, hearing of such preparedness
on their part, took alarm and let cowardly counsels prevail;[a]
they were at pains to leave watchfires burning in their camp,
29 so that Jonathan and his men, deceived by the glow of
light, knew nothing of their plans till morning; 30 and when

a 'Let cowardly counsels prevail'; literally, 'were dismayed in their hearts', but the context shews that in fact they beat a retreat.

TODAY'S ENGLISH VERSION

our ties of brotherhood. 18 And now we request an answer
to this letter.
19 "The following is a copy of the earlier letter:
20 " 'King Arius of Sparta to Onias the High Priest, greetings. 21 We have found a document about the Spartans
and the Jews indicating that we are related and that both
of our nations are descended from Abraham. 22 Now that
we have discovered this, please send us a report about
your situation. 23 In reply, we will send you a letter indicating that we are willing to share our possessions, including cattle and property, if you will do the same. We have
given orders to our ambassadors to give you a full report
about these matters.' "
24 Jonathan learned that the officers of Demetrius had
returned to attack him with an even larger army than before.
25 Jonathan did not want to give them an opportunity to penetrate his own territory, so he left Jerusalem and went to meet
them in the region of Hamath. 26 Jonathan sent spies into the
enemy camp, who reported to him that the enemy forces were
making plans to attack the Jews by night. 27 At sunset
Jonathan ordered all his soldiers to be on the alert and to
have their weapons ready for a surprise attack any time during the night. He also stationed guards all around the camp.
28 When the enemy soldiers learned that Jonathan and his
men were ready for battle, they were panic-stricken and fled,
leaving their campfires burning. 29 Jonathan and his men
saw the campfires but did not realize what had happened

NEW REVISED STANDARD VERSION

the renewal of our family ties. 18 And now please send us a
reply to this."
19 This is a copy of the letter that they sent to Onias:
20 "King Arius of the Spartans, to the high priest Onias, greetings. 21 It has been found in writing concerning the Spartans
and the Jews that they are brothers and are of the family of
Abraham. 22 And now that we have learned this, please write
us concerning your welfare; 23 we on our part write to you
that your livestock and your property belong to us, and ours
belong to you. We therefore command that our envoys[a]
report to you accordingly."
24 Now Jonathan heard that the commanders of Demetrius had returned, with a larger force than before, to wage
war against him. 25 So he marched away from Jerusalem and
met them in the region of Hamath, for he gave them no
opportunity to invade his own country. 26 He sent spies to
their camp, and they returned and reported to him that the
enemy[a] were being drawn up in formation to attack the
Jews[b] by night. 27 So when the sun had set, Jonathan commanded his troops to be alert and to keep their arms at hand
so as to be ready all night for battle, and he stationed outposts around the camp. 28 When the enemy heard that
Jonathan and his troops were prepared for battle, they were
afraid and were terrified at heart; so they kindled fires in
their camp and withdrew.[c] 29 But Jonathan and his troops
did not know it until morning, for they saw the fires burning.

a Gk *they* *b* Gk *them* *c* Other ancient authorities omit *and withdrew*

NEW AMERICAN BIBLE

letter about the renewal of our brotherhood. 18 Therefore
kindly send us an answer on this matter."
19 This is a copy of the letter that was sent to Onias:
20 "Arius, king of the Spartans, sends greetings to Onias the
high priest. 21 A document has been found stating that the
Spartans and the Jews are brothers; both nations descended
from Abraham. 22 Now that we have learned this, kindly
write to us about your welfare. 23 We, on our part, are
informing you that your cattle and your possessions are
ours, and ours are yours. We have, therefore, given orders
that you should be told of this."
24 Jonathan heard that the generals of Demetrius had
returned to attack him with a stronger army than before.
25 He set out from Jerusalem and went into the country of
Hamath to meet them, giving them no time to enter his province. 26 The spies he had sent into their camp came back and
reported that the enemy had made ready to attack the Jews
that very night. 27 Therefore, when the sun set, Jonathan
ordered his men to be on guard and to remain armed, ready
for combat, throughout the night. He also set outposts all
around the camp. 28 When the enemy heard that Jonathan
and his men were ready for battle, their hearts sank with fear
and dread. They lighted fires and then withdrew. 29 But
because Jonathan and his men were watching the lights burning, they did not know what had happened until morning.

NEW JERUSALEM BIBLE

concerning the renewal of our brotherhood; 18 we shall be
grateful for an answer to it.'

19 The following is the copy of the letter sent to Onias:
20 'Areios king of the Spartans, to Onias the high priest,
greetings.
21 'It has been discovered in records regarding the
Spartans and Jews that they are brothers, and of the race
of Abraham. 22 Now that this has come to our knowledge,
we shall be obliged if you will send us news of your welfare. 23 Our own message to you is this: your flocks and
your possessions are ours, and ours are yours, and we are
instructing our envoys to give you a message to this
effect.'

24 Jonathan learned that Demetrius' generals had returned
with a larger army than before to make war on him. 25 He
therefore left Jerusalem and went to engage them in the area
of Hamath, not giving them the time to invade his own territory. 26 He sent spies into their camp, who told him on their
return that the enemy were taking up positions for a night
attack on the Jews. 27 At sunset, Jonathan ordered his men
to keep watch with their weapons at hand, in readiness to
fight at any time during the night, and posted advance
guards all round the camp. 28 On learning that Jonathan and
his men were ready to fight, the enemy took fright and, with
quaking hearts, lit fires in their bivouac and decamped.
29 Jonathan and his men, watching the glow of the fires, were
unaware of their withdrawal until morning, 30 and although

GREEK OLD TESTAMENT

φῶτα καιόμενα. 30 καὶ κατεδίωξεν Ιωναθαν ὀπίσω αὐτῶν καὶ
οὐ κατέλαβεν αὐτούς, διέβησαν γὰρ τὸν Ἐλεύθερον ποταμόν.
31 καὶ ἐξέκλινεν Ιωναθαν ἐπὶ τοὺς Ἄραβας τοὺς καλου-
μένους Ζαβαδαίους καὶ ἐπάταξεν αὐτοὺς καὶ ἔλαβεν τὰ
σκῦλα αὐτῶν. 32 καὶ ἀναζεύξας ἦλθεν εἰς Δαμασκὸν καὶ διώδευσεν ἐν πάσῃ τῇ χώρᾳ. 33 καὶ Σιμων ἐξῆλθεν καὶ διώδευσεν ἕως Ἀσκαλῶνος καὶ τὰ πλησίον ὀχυρώματα καὶ ἐξέκλινεν εἰς Ιοππην καὶ προκατελάβετο αὐτήν· 34 ἤκουσεν γὰρ
ὅτι βούλονται τὸ ὀχύρωμα παραδοῦναι τοῖς παρὰ Δημητρίου·
καὶ ἔθετο ἐκεῖ φρουράν, ὅπως φυλάσσωσιν αὐτήν. 35 καὶ ἐπέστρεψεν Ιωναθαν καὶ ἐξεκκλησίασεν τοὺς πρεσβυτέρους τοῦ
λαοῦ καὶ ἐβουλεύετο μετ᾽ αὐτῶν τοῦ οἰκοδομῆσαι ὀχυρώματα
ἐν τῇ Ιουδαίᾳ 36 καὶ προσυψῶσαι τὰ τείχη Ιερουσαλημ καὶ
ὑψῶσαι ὕψος μέγα ἀνὰ μέσον τῆς ἄκρας καὶ τῆς πόλεως εἰς
τὸ διαχωρίζειν αὐτὴν τῆς πόλεως, ἵνα ᾖ αὕτη κατὰ μόνας,
ὅπως μήτε ἀγοράζωσιν μήτε πωλῶσιν. 37 καὶ συνήχθησαν
τοῦ οἰκοδομεῖν τὴν πόλιν, καὶ ἔπεσεν τοῦ τείχους τοῦ
χειμάρρου τοῦ ἐξ ἀπηλιώτου, καὶ ἐπεσκεύασεν τὸ καλούμενον Χαφεναθα. 38 καὶ Σιμων ᾠκοδόμησεν τὴν Αδιδα ἐν τῇ
Σεφηλα καὶ ὠχύρωσεν αὐτὴν καὶ ἐπέστησεν θύρας καὶ
μοχλούς.
39 Καὶ ἐζήτησεν Τρύφων βασιλεῦσαι τῆς Ἀσίας καὶ
περιθέσθαι τὸ διάδημα καὶ ἐκτεῖναι χεῖρα ἐπ᾽ Ἀντίοχον τὸν
βασιλέα. 40 καὶ εὐλαβήθη μήποτε οὐκ ἐάσῃ αὐτὸν Ιωναθαν

KING JAMES VERSION

30 Then Jonathan pursued after them, but overtook them not: for they were gone over the river Eleutherus.

31 Wherefore Jonathan turned to the Arabians, who were called Zabadeans, and smote them, and took their spoils.

32 And removing thence, he came to Damascus, and so passed through all the country.

33 Simon also went forth, and passed through the country unto Ascalon, and the holds there adjoining, from whence he turned aside to Joppe, and won it.

34 For he had heard that they would deliver the hold unto them that took Demetrius' part; wherefore he set a garrison there to keep it.

35 After this came Jonathan home again, and calling the elders of the people together, he consulted with them about building strong holds in Judea,

36 And making the walls of Jerusalem higher, and raising a great mount between the tower and the city, for to separate it from the city, that so it might be alone, that men might neither sell nor buy in it.

37 Upon this they came together to build up the city, forasmuch as *part of* the wall toward the brook on the east side was fallen down, and they repaired that which was called Caphenatha.

38 Simon also set up Adida in Sephela, and made it strong with gates and bars.

39 Now Tryphon went about to get the kingdom of Asia, and to kill Antiochus the king, that he might set the crown upon his own head.

40 Howbeit he was afraid that Jonathan would not suffer

DOUAY OLD TESTAMENT

30 And Jonathan pursued after them, but overtook them not: for they had passed the river Eleutherus.

31 And Jonathan turned upon the Arabians that are called Zabadeans: and he defeated them, and took the spoils of them.

32 And he went forward, and came to Damascus, and passed through all that country.

33 Simon also went forth, and came as far as Ascalon, and the neighbouring fortresses, and he turned aside to Joppe, and took possession of it,

34 (For he heard that they designed to deliver the hold to them that took part with Demetrius,) and he put a garrison there to keep it.

35 And Jonathan came back, and called together the ancients of the people, and he took a resolution with them to build fortresses in Judea,

36 And to build up walls in Jerusalem, and raise a mount between the castle and the city, to separate it from the city, that so it might have no communication, and that they might neither buy nor sell.

37 And they came together to build up the city: for the wall that was upon the brook towards the east was broken down, and he repaired that which is called Caphetetha:

38 And Simon built Adiada in Sephela, and fortified it, and set up gates and bars.

39 Now when Tryphon had conceived a design to make himself king of Asia, and to take the crown, and to stretch out his hand against king Antiochus:

40 Fearing lest Jonathan would not suffer him, but would

KNOX TRANSLATION

he gave chase, it was too late to catch them; already they
had crossed the river Eleutherus. 31 Thereupon he turned his
attack against the Zabadeans, an Arabian tribe, defeating
them and taking spoils from them; 32 and so, harnessing his
waggons, pressed on to Damascus, patrolling all the country
round about. 33 Meanwhile, Simon had marched out to
Ascalon and the neighbouring strongholds; thence he turned
aside to Joppe, and took possession of it; 34 rumour had
reached him, the townsfolk would yield the citadel to
Demetrius' party, and he must have a garrison there of his
own.
35 When Jonathan returned, he summoned the elders of the
people, and took counsel with them, how best to raise
strongholds in Judaea, 36 and build up walls in Jerusalem
itself. Height these must have, above all, between the Citadel
and the rest of the town; he would have it cut off from the
rest, standing by itself, with no opportunity to buy and sell.
37 A great muster there was for the city's rebuilding; and
where the wall had tumbled down, over the ravine on the
east, he made it good; it is the part called Caphetetha.
38 Meanwhile, Simon rebuilt Adiada in the Sephela and fortified it; bolt and bar it should have thenceforward.
39 And what of Tryphon? Lordship of all Asia he coveted,
and a royal crown; it should be Antiochus' turn next. 40 The
danger was, Jonathan would refuse his assent, and resort to

TODAY'S ENGLISH VERSION

until the next morning. [30]Jonathan then set out after them,
but he could not overtake them because they had already
crossed the Eleutherus River. [31]Then Jonathan turned aside
and attacked a tribe of Arabs called Zabadeans. He defeated
them and plundered their possessions. [32]Then he broke camp
and went to Damascus, inspecting the entire area along
the way.
[33]Meanwhile, Simon had also set out on a campaign and
had advanced as far as Ascalon and the neighboring fortresses. Then he turned aside to Joppa [34]and stationed a detachment of soldiers there because he had heard that the people
were planning to hand over the fortress of Joppa to the soldiers of Demetrius.
[35]When Jonathan returned, he called the council of the
leaders together and made plans with them to build fortresses in Judea, [36]to increase the height of the walls of
Jerusalem, and to build a high wall to separate the fort from
the city. This would isolate the fort, making it impossible for
the enemy to buy or sell anything. [37]The people worked
together to strengthen the city's defenses because a part of
the east wall along the Kidron Valley had collapsed and the
Chaphenatha section was in need of repair. [38]Simon also
rebuilt the town of Adida in the foothills. He fortified it and
constructed barred gates for it.
[39]Then Trypho plotted a rebellion against King Antiochus
so that he could make himself king of Syria. [40]He was
afraid, however, that Jonathan would not agree to this and

NEW REVISED STANDARD VERSION

[30]Then Jonathan pursued them, but he did not overtake
them, for they had crossed the Eleutherus river. [31]So
Jonathan turned aside against the Arabs who are called
Zabadeans, and he crushed them and plundered them.
[32]Then he broke camp and went to Damascus, and marched
through all that region.
33 Simon also went out and marched through the country
as far as Askalon and the neighboring strongholds. He
turned aside to Joppa and took it by surprise, [34]for he had
heard that they were ready to hand over the stronghold to
those whom Demetrius had sent. And he stationed a garrison
there to guard it.
35 When Jonathan returned he convened the elders of the
people and planned with them to build strongholds in Judea,
[36]to build the walls of Jerusalem still higher, and to erect a
high barrier between the citadel and the city to separate it
from the city, in order to isolate it so that its garrison[a] could
neither buy nor sell. [37]So they gathered together to rebuild
the city; part of the wall on the valley to the east had fallen,
and he repaired the section called Chaphenatha. [38]Simon
also built Adida in the Shephelah; he fortified it and installed
gates with bolts.
39 Then Trypho attempted to become king in Asia and put
on the crown, and to raise his hand against King Antiochus.
[40]He feared that Jonathan might not permit him to do so, but

a Gk *they*

NEW AMERICAN BIBLE

[30]Then Jonathan pursued them, but he could not overtake
them, for they had crossed the river Eleutherus. [31]So
Jonathan turned aside against the Arabs who are called
Zabadeans, overwhelming and plundering them. [32]Then he
marched on to Damascus and traversed that whole region.
[33]Simon also set out and went as far as Ashkalon and its
neighboring strongholds. He then turned to Joppa and occupied it, [34]for he heard that its men had intended to hand
over this stronghold to the supporters of Demetrius. He left a
garrison there to guard it.
[35]When Jonathan returned, he assembled the elders of the
people, and with them he made plans for building strongholds in Judea, [36]for making the walls of Jerusalem still
higher, and for erecting a high barrier between the citadel
and the city, that would isolate the citadel and so prevent its
garrison from commerce with the city. [37]The people therefore worked together on building up the city, for part of the
east wall above the ravine had collapsed. The quarter called
Chaphenatha was also repaired. [38]Simon likewise built up
Adida in the Shephelah, and strengthened its fortifications
by providing them with gates and bars.
[39]Trypho was determined to become king of Asia, assume
the crown, and do away with King Antiochus. [40]But he was
afraid that Jonathan would not permit him, but would fight

NEW JERUSALEM BIBLE

Jonathan pursued them, he failed to overtake them, for they
had already crossed the river Eleutherus. [31]So Jonathan
wheeled round on the Arabs called Zabadaeans, beat them
and plundered them; [32]then, breaking camp, he went to
Damascus, thus crossing the whole province. [33]Simon,
meanwhile, had also set out and had penetrated as far as
Ascalon and the neighbouring towns. He then turned on
Joppa and moved quickly to occupy it, [34]for he had heard of
their intention to hand over this strong point to the supporters of Demetrius; he stationed a garrison there to hold it.
[35]Jonathan, on his return, called a meeting of the elders of
the people and decided with them to build fortresses in
Judaea [36]and to heighten the walls of Jerusalem and erect a
high barrier between the Citadel and the city, to cut the former off from the city and isolate it, to prevent the occupants
from buying or selling. [37]Rebuilding the city was a co-opera-
tive effort: part of the wall over the eastern ravine had fallen
down; he restored the quarter called Chaphenatha. [38]Simon,
meanwhile, rebuilt Adida in the lowlands, fortifying it, and
erecting gates with bolts.
[39]Trypho's ambition was to become king of Asia, assume
the crown, and overpower King Antiochus. [40]He was appre-
hensive that Jonathan might not allow him to do this, and

Greek Old Testament

καὶ μήποτε πολεμήσῃ πρὸς αὐτόν, καὶ ἐζήτει συλλαβεῖν
αὐτὸν τοῦ ἀπολέσαι, καὶ ἀπάρας ἦλθεν εἰς Βαιθσαν. 41 καὶ
ἐξῆλθεν Ιωναθαν εἰς ἀπάντησιν αὐτῷ ἐν τεσσαράκοντα
χιλιάσιν ἀνδρῶν ἐπιλελεγμέναις εἰς παράταξιν καὶ ἦλθεν
εἰς Βαιθσαν. 42 καὶ εἶδεν Τρύφων ὅτι ἦλθεν μετὰ δυνάμεως
πολλῆς, καὶ ἐκτεῖναι χεῖρας ἐπ' αὐτὸν εὐλαβήθη. 43 καὶ
ἐπεδέξατο αὐτὸν ἐνδόξως καὶ συνέστησεν αὐτὸν πᾶσιν τοῖς
φίλοις αὐτοῦ καὶ ἔδωκεν αὐτῷ δόματα καὶ ἐπέταξεν τοῖς φίλοις αὐτοῦ καὶ ταῖς δυνάμεσιν αὐτοῦ ὑπακούειν αὐτοῦ ὡς
αὐτοῦ. 44 καὶ εἶπεν τῷ Ιωναθαν Ἵνα τί ἐκόπωσας πάντα τὸν
λαὸν τοῦτον πολέμου μὴ ἐνεστηκότος ἡμῖν; 45 καὶ νῦν ἀπόστειλον αὐτοὺς εἰς τοὺς οἴκους αὐτῶν, ἐπίλεξαι δὲ σεαυτῷ
ἄνδρας ὀλίγους, οἵτινες ἔσονται μετὰ σοῦ, καὶ δεῦρο μετ'
ἐμοῦ εἰς Πτολεμαίδα, καὶ παραδώσω σοι αὐτὴν καὶ τὰ λοιπὰ
ὀχυρώματα καὶ τὰς δυνάμεις τὰς λοιπὰς καὶ πάντας τοὺς
ἐπὶ τῶν χρειῶν, καὶ ἐπιστρέψας ἀπελεύσομαι· τούτου γὰρ
χάριν πάρειμι. 46 καὶ ἐμπιστεύσας αὐτῷ ἐποίησεν καθὼς
εἶπεν, καὶ ἐξαπέστειλεν τὰς δυνάμεις, καὶ ἀπῆλθον εἰς γῆν
Ιουδα. 47 κατέλιπεν δὲ μεθ' ἑαυτοῦ ἄνδρας τρισχιλίους, ὧν
δισχιλίους ἀφῆκεν ἐν τῇ Γαλιλαίᾳ, χίλιοι δὲ συνῆλθον αὐτῷ.
48 ὡς δὲ εἰσῆλθεν Ιωναθαν εἰς Πτολεμαίδα, ἀπέκλεισαν οἱ
Πτολεμαεῖς τὰς πύλας καὶ συνέλαβον αὐτόν, καὶ πάντας
τοὺς συνεισελθόντας μετ' αὐτοῦ ἀπέκτειναν ἐν ῥομφαίᾳ.
49 καὶ ἀπέστειλεν Τρύφων δυνάμεις καὶ ἵππον εἰς τὴν
Γαλιλαίαν καὶ τὸ πεδίον τὸ μέγα τοῦ ἀπολέσαι πάντας
τοὺς παρὰ Ιωναθου. 50 καὶ ἐπέγνωσαν ὅτι συνελήμφθη καὶ

King James Version

him, and that he would fight against him; wherefore he
sought a way how to take Jonathan, that he might kill him.
So he removed, and came to Bethsan.
41 Then Jonathan went out to meet him with forty thousand men chosen for the battle, and came to Bethsan.
42 Now when Tryphon saw that Jonathan came with so
great a force, he durst not stretch his hand against him;
43 But received him honourably, and commended him
unto all his friends, and gave him gifts, and commanded his
men of war to be as obedient unto him, as to himself.
44 Unto Jonathan also he said, Why hast thou put all this
people to so great trouble, seeing there is no war betwixt us?
45 Therefore send them now home again, and choose a
few men to wait on thee, and come thou with me to
Ptolemais, for I will give it thee, and the rest of the strong
holds and forces, and all that have any charge: as for me, I
will return and depart: for this is the cause of my coming.
46 So Jonathan believing him did as he bade him, and
sent away his host, who went into the land of Judea.
47 And with himself he retained but three thousand men,
of whom he sent two thousand into Galilee, and one thousand went with him.
48 Now as soon as Jonathan entered into Ptolemais, they
of Ptolemais shut the gates, and took him, and all them that
came with him they slew with the sword.
49 Then sent Tryphon an host of footmen and horsemen
into Galilee, and into the great plain, to destroy all Jonathan's
company.
50 But when they knew that Jonathan and they that were

Douay Old Testament

fight against him: he sought to seize upon him, and to kill
him. So he rose up and came to Bethsan.
41 And Jonathan went out to meet him with forty thousand men chosen for battle, and came to Bethsan.
42 Now when Tryphon saw that Jonathan came with a
great army, he durst not stretch forth his hand against him,
43 But received him with honour, and commended him to
all his friends, and gave him presents: and he commanded
his troops to obey him, as himself.
44 And he said to Jonathan: Why hast thou troubled all
the people, whereas we have no war?
45 Now therefore send them back to their own houses:
and choose thee a few men that may be with thee, and come
with me to Ptolemais, and I will deliver it to thee, and the
rest of the strong holds, and the army, and all that have any
charge, and I will return and go away: for this is the cause of
my coming.
46 And Jonathan believed him, and did as he said: and
sent away his army, and they departed into the land of Juda:
47 But he kept with him three thousand men: of whom he
sent two thousand into Galilee, and one thousand went with
him.
48 Now as soon as Jonathan entered into Ptolemais, they
of Ptolemais shut the gates of the city, and took him: and all
them that came in with him they slew with the sword.
49 Then Tryphon sent an army and horsemen into Galilee,
and into the great plain to destroy all Jonathan's company.
50 But they, when they understood that Jonathan and all

Knox Translation

arms; Jonathan first he must seize and put to death. So he
moved his quarters to Bethsan, 41 where Jonathan came out
to meet him with forty thousand men, picked warriors all of
them, at his back. 42 Here was a great retinue; and Tryphon,
daunted by this show of force, 43 was fain to give him an
honourable welcome. He would admit Jonathan among his
closest friends, and bestow gifts on him; let Jonathan give
orders, and Tryphon's soldiers would obey. 44 Then he
asked, What needs it, such a host of men should go campaigning, when threat of war is none? 45 It were better to
disband them, and choose out a few for thy own retinue.
That done, bear me company to Ptolemais; city and strongholds and troops and officers I will hand over into thy charge
and so get me gone home; it was on that errand I came.
46 What did Jonathan? He fell into the trap, sent his men
back to Juda, 47 and kept but three thousand under arms; of
these, he left two thousand in Galilee, and took but a thousand in his company. 48 No sooner had he entered Ptolemais
than the townsfolk shut the gates behind him, secured his
person, and put his retinue to the sword. 49 Horse and foot
Tryphon sent out to Galilee, to find the rest of his followers
in the Great Plain, and make an end of them; 50 but these,
hearing that Jonathan and his men had been caught and

TODAY'S ENGLISH VERSION

would go to war against him to prevent it. So Trypho got his
army ready and went to Beth Shan in the hope of capturing
Jonathan and putting him to death. 41 But Jonathan also
came to Beth Shan with 40,000 well-trained soldiers.
42 When Trypho saw how large an army Jonathan had
brought with him, he was afraid to take action. 43 So he
received Jonathan with all honors, presented him to all his
advisers, gave him gifts, and ordered his advisers and soldiers to obey Jonathan as they would him. 44 He asked
Jonathan, "Why have you put these soldiers to so much trouble when we are not at war? 45 Why don't you send them
home? Choose a few men to stay with you, and then accompany me to Ptolemais. I will hand the city over to you, as
well as the rest of the fortresses, the troops, and all the officials. Then I will turn around and leave. In fact, that's why I
am here." 46 Jonathan believed him, and following his
advice, sent his soldiers back to Judea. 47 He took 3,000 men
with him, but left 2,000 of them in Galilee, while only 1,000
accompanied him the rest of the way. 48 But when Jonathan
entered Ptolemais, the people of the city locked the gates,
arrested him, and killed everyone who had come with him.

49 Trypho sent infantry and cavalry units to Galilee and
Jezreel Valley to kill the rest of Jonathan's soldiers. 50 The
Jewish troops thought that Jonathan had been captured and

NEW REVISED STANDARD VERSION

might make war on him, so he kept seeking to seize and kill
him, and he marched out and came to Beth-shan.
41 Jonathan went out to meet him with forty thousand picked
warriors, and he came to Beth-shan. 42 When Trypho saw
that he had come with a large army, he was afraid to raise
his hand against him. 43 So he received him with honor and
commended him to all his Friends, and he gave him gifts and
commanded his Friends and his troops to obey him as they
would himself. 44 Then he said to Jonathan, "Why have you
put all these people to so much trouble when we are not at
war? 45 Dismiss them now to their homes and choose for
yourself a few men to stay with you, and come with me to
Ptolemais. I will hand it over to you as well as the other
strongholds and the remaining troops and all the officials,
and will turn around and go home. For that is why I am
here."

46 Jonathan[a] trusted him and did as he said; he sent
away the troops, and they returned to the land of Judah.
47 He kept with himself three thousand men, two thousand of
whom he left in Galilee, while one thousand accompanied
him. 48 But when Jonathan entered Ptolemais, the people of
Ptolemais closed the gates and seized him, and they killed
with the sword all who had entered with him.

49 Then Trypho sent troops and cavalry into Galilee and
the Great Plain to destroy all Jonathan's soldiers. 50 But they
realized that Jonathan had been seized and had perished

a Gk *he*

NEW AMERICAN BIBLE

against him. Looking for a way to seize and kill him, he set
out and reached Beth-shan. 41 Jonathan marched out against
him with forty thousand picked fighting men and came to
Beth-shan. 42 But when Trypho saw that Jonathan had
arrived with a large army, he was afraid to offer him violence. 43 Instead, he received him with honor, introduced
him to all his friends, and gave him presents. He also
ordered his friends and soldiers to obey him as they would
himself. 44 Then he said to Jonathan: "Why have you put all
your soldiers to so much trouble when we are not at war?
45 Pick out a few men to stay with you, send the rest back
home, and then come with me to Ptolemais. I will hand it
over to you together with other strongholds and their garrisons, as well as the officials, then I will leave and go home.
That is why I came here."

46 Jonathan believed him and did as he said. He dismissed
his troops, and they returned to the land of Judah. 47 But he
kept with him three thousand men, of whom he sent two
thousand to Galilee while one thousand accompanied him.
48 Then as soon as Jonathan had entered Ptolemais, the men
of the city closed the gates and seized him; all who had
entered with him, they killed with the sword.

49 Trypho sent soldiers and cavalry to Galilee and the Great
Plain to destroy all Jonathan's men. 50 These, upon learning
that Jonathan had been captured and his companions killed,

NEW JERUSALEM BIBLE

might even make war on him, so he set out and came to
Beth-Shean, in the hopes of finding some pretext for having
him arrested and put to death.

41 Jonathan went out to intercept him, with forty thousand
picked men in battle order, and arrived at Beth-Shean.
42 When Trypho saw him there with a large force, he hesitated to make any move against him. 43 He even received him
with honour, commended him to all his friends, gave him
presents and ordered his friends and his troops to obey him
as they would himself. 44 He said to Jonathan, 'Why have
you given all these people so much trouble, when there is no
threat of war between us? 45 Send them back home; pick
yourself a few men as your bodyguard, and come with me to
Ptolemais, which I am going to hand over to you, with the
other fortresses and the remaining troops and all the officials; after which, I shall take the road for home. This was
my purpose in coming here.' 46 Jonathan trusted him and did
as he said; he dismissed his forces, who went back to
Judaea. 47 With him he retained three thousand men, of
whom he left two thousand in Galilee, while a thousand
accompanied him. 48 But as soon as Jonathan had entered
Ptolemais, the people of Ptolemais closed the gates, seized
him, and put all those who had entered with him to the
sword. 49 Trypho sent troops and cavalry into Galilee and the
Great Plain to destroy all Jonathan's supporters. 50 These,
concluding that he had been taken and had perished with his

GREEK OLD TESTAMENT

ἀπόλωλεν καὶ οἱ μετ᾽ αὐτοῦ, καὶ παρεκάλεσαν ἑαυτοὺς καὶ
ἐπορεύοντο συνεστραμμένοι ἕτοιμοι εἰς πόλεμον. 51 καὶ
εἶδον οἱ διώκοντες ὅτι περὶ ψυχῆς αὐτοῖς ἐστιν, καὶ ἐπέστρεψαν. 52 καὶ ἦλθον πάντες μετ᾽ εἰρήνης εἰς γῆν Ιουδα
καὶ ἐπένθησαν τὸν Ιωναθαν καὶ τοὺς μετ᾽ αὐτοῦ καὶ ἐφοβήθησαν σφόδρα· καὶ ἐπένθησεν πᾶς Ισραηλ πένθος μέγα.
53 καὶ ἐζήτησαν πάντα τὰ ἔθνη τὰ κύκλῳ αὐτῶν ἐκτρῖψαι
αὐτούς. εἶπον γάρ Οὐκ ἔχουσιν ἄρχοντα καὶ βοηθοῦντα· νῦν
οὖν πολεμήσωμεν αὐτοὺς καὶ ἐξάρωμεν ἐξ ἀνθρώπων τὸ
μνημόσυνον αὐτῶν.

13 Καὶ ἤκουσεν Σιμων ὅτι συνήγαγεν Τρύφων δύναμιν
πολλὴν τοῦ ἐλθεῖν εἰς γῆν Ιουδα καὶ ἐκτρῖψαι αὐτήν.
2 καὶ εἶδεν τὸν λαόν, ὅτι ἔντρομός ἐστιν καὶ ἔκφοβος, καὶ
ἀνέβη εἰς Ιερουσαλημ καὶ ἤθροισεν τὸν λαὸν 3 καὶ παρεκάλεσεν αὐτοὺς καὶ εἶπεν αὐτοῖς Αὐτοὶ οἴδατε ὅσα ἐγὼ καὶ οἱ
ἀδελφοί μου καὶ ὁ οἶκος τοῦ πατρός μου ἐποιήσαμεν περὶ
τῶν νόμων καὶ τῶν ἁγίων, καὶ τοὺς πολέμους καὶ τὰς
στενοχωρίας, ἃς εἴδομεν. 4 τούτου χάριν ἀπώλοντο οἱ ἀδελφοί μου πάντες χάριν τοῦ Ισραηλ, καὶ κατελείφθην ἐγὼ
μόνος. 5 καὶ νῦν μή μοι γένοιτο φείσασθαί μου τῆς ψυχῆς
ἐν παντὶ καιρῷ θλίψεως. οὐ γάρ εἰμι κρείσσων τῶν ἀδελφῶν
μου. 6 πλὴν ἐκδικήσω περὶ τοῦ ἔθνους μου καὶ περὶ τῶν
ἁγίων καὶ περὶ τῶν γυναικῶν καὶ τέκνων ὑμῶν, ὅτι συνήχθησαν πάντα τὰ ἔθνη ἐκτρῖψαι ἡμᾶς ἔχθρας χάριν. 7 καὶ

KING JAMES VERSION

with him were taken and slain, they encouraged one another, and went close together, prepared to fight.

51 They therefore that followed upon them, perceiving that they were ready to fight for their lives, turned back again.

52 Whereupon they all came into the land of Judea peaceably, and there they bewailed Jonathan, and them that were with him, and they were sore afraid; wherefore all Israel made great lamentation.

53 Then all the heathen that were round about then sought to destroy them: for said they, They have no captain, nor any to help them: now therefore let us make war upon them, and take away their memorial from among men.

13 Now when Simon heard that Tryphon had gathered together a great host to invade the land of Judea, and destroy it,

2 And saw that the people was in great trembling and fear, he went up to Jerusalem, and gathered the people together,

3 And gave them exhortation, saying, Ye yourselves know what great things I, and my brethren, and my father's house, have done for the laws and the sanctuary, the battles also and troubles which we have seen,

4 By reason whereof all my brethren are slain for Israel's sake, and I am left alone.

5 Now therefore be it far from me, that I should spare mine own life in any time of trouble: for I am no better than my brethren.

6 Doubtless I will avenge my nation, and the sanctuary, and our wives, and our children: for all the heathen are gathered to destroy us of very malice.

DOUAY OLD TESTAMENT

that were with him were taken and slain, encouraged one another, and went out ready for battle.

51 Then they that had come after them, seeing that they stood for their lives, returned back.

52 Whereupon they all came peaceably into the land of Juda. And they bewailed Jonathan, and them that had been with him, exceedingly: and Israel mourned with great lamentation.

53 Then all the heathens that were round about them, sought to destroy them. For they said:

54 They have no prince, nor any to help them: now therefore let us make war upon them, and take away the memory of them from amongst men.

13 NOW Simon heard that Tryphon was gathering together a very great army, to invade the land of Juda, and to destroy it.

2 And seeing that the people was in dread, and in fear, he went up to Jerusalem, and assembled the people:

3 And exhorted them, saying: You know what great battles I and my brethren, and the house of my father, have fought for the laws, and the sanctuary, and the distresses that we have seen:

4 By reason whereof all my brethren have lost their lives for Israel's sake, and I am left alone.

5 And now far be it from me to spare my life in any time of trouble: for I am not better than my brethren.

6 I will avenge then my nation and the sanctuary, and our children, and wives: for all the heathens are gathered together to destroy us out of mere malice.

KNOX TRANSLATION

murdered, resolved to put a bold front on it, and marched in
battle array. 51 Finding them ready to sell their lives dearly,
their pursuers abandoned the chase, 52 and all reached Juda
safe and sound. For Jonathan and his companions they
made great dole, and loudly all Israel echoed their lament.
53 Neighbouring people was none but went about to overthrow them, and no wonder; 54 their chieftain, their champion gone, now was the time to fall upon them, and rid earth
of their memory.

13 And what did Simon, when he heard that Tryphon
had levied a strong force, for Juda's invasion and
overthrow? 2 Here was all the people in a great taking of
fear; so he made his way to Jerusalem and there gathered
them to meet him. 3 And thus, to put heart into them, he
spoke: Need is none to tell you what battles we have fought,
what dangers endured, I and my brethren and all my father's
kin, law and sanctuary to defend. 4 In that cause, and for the
love of Israel, my brothers have died, one and all, till I only
am left; 5 never be it said of me, in the hour of peril I held
life dear, more precious than theirs! 6 Nay, come the whole
world against us, to glut its malice with our ruin, race and
sanctuary, wives and children of ours shall find me their

TODAY'S ENGLISH VERSION

killed, along with all those who had accompanied him, so they encouraged one another and marched out in battle formation. 51 When the approaching enemy forces saw that the Jews were ready to fight for their lives, they turned back. 52 Then the Jewish soldiers returned to Judea safely, but terribly afraid. The whole nation was in deep mourning, assuming that Jonathan and all his men had been killed. 53 All the surrounding nations now tried to destroy them. They thought that the Jews had no leaders or allies and that the time was ripe to annihilate them and put an end to their history.

13 Simon learned that Trypho had assembled a large army and that he had plans to invade Judea and devastate it. 2 He realized that this news had brought panic and fear to the people, so he went to Jerusalem, called the people together, 3 and tried to encourage them by saying, "You know how much my father's family, my brothers, and I have done for the sake of the Law of Moses and the Temple. You also know about the wars we have fought and the troubles we have had. 4 All my brothers have been killed fighting for our Law, our Temple, and our nation, and I am the only one left. 5 But never let it be said that I tried to save my own life in a time of danger; I do not consider myself better than my brothers. 6 Not in the least! It is true that in their hatred all the Gentile nations have gathered together to destroy us, but I will fight to defend my nation, the Temple, and your loved ones."

NEW REVISED STANDARD VERSION

along with his men, and they encouraged one another and kept marching in close formation, ready for battle. 51 When their pursuers saw that they would fight for their lives, they turned back. 52 So they all reached the land of Judah safely, and they mourned for Jonathan and his companions and were in great fear; and all Israel mourned deeply. 53 All the nations around them tried to destroy them, for they said, "They have no leader or helper. Now therefore let us make war on them and blot out the memory of them from humankind."

13 Simon heard that Trypho had assembled a large army to invade the land of Judah and destroy it, 2 and he saw that the people were trembling with fear. So he went up to Jerusalem, and gathering the people together 3 he encouraged them, saying to them, "You yourselves know what great things my brothers and I and the house of my father have done for the laws and the sanctuary; you know also the wars and the difficulties that my brothers and I have seen. 4 By reason of this all my brothers have perished for the sake of Israel, and I alone am left. 5 And now, far be it from me to spare my life in any time of distress, for I am not better than my brothers. 6 But I will avenge my nation and the sanctuary and your wives and children, for all the nations have gathered together out of hatred to destroy us."

NEW AMERICAN BIBLE

encouraged one another and went out in compact body ready to fight. 51 As their pursuers saw that they were ready to fight for their lives, they turned back. 52 Thus all these men of Jonathan came safely into the land of Judah. They mourned over Jonathan and his men, and were in great fear, and all Israel fell into deep mourning.

53 All the nations round about sought to destroy them. They said, "Now that they have no leader to help them, let us make war on them and wipe out their memory from among men."

13 When Simon heard that Trypho was gathering a large army to invade and ravage the land of Judah, 2 and saw that the people were in dread and terror, he went up to Jerusalem. There he assembled the people 3 and exhorted them in these words: "You know what I, my brothers, and my father's house have done for the laws and the sanctuary; what battles and disasters we have been through. 4 It was for the sake of these, for the sake of Israel, that all my brothers have perished, and I alone am left. 5 Far be it from me, then, to save my own life in any time of distress, for I am not better than my brothers. 6 Rather will I avenge my nation and the sanctuary, as well as your wives and children, for all the nations out of hatred have united to destroy us."

NEW JERUSALEM BIBLE

companions, encouraged one another, marching with closed ranks and ready to give battle, 51 and when their pursuers saw that they would fight for their lives, they turned back. 52 All reached Judaea safe and sound, and there they lamented Jonathan and his companions, being very frightened indeed; all Israel was plunged into mourning. 53 The surrounding nations were all now looking for ways of destroying them: 'They have no leader,' they said, 'no ally; we have only to attack them now, and we shall blot out their very memory from all peoples.'

13 Simon heard that Trypho had collected a large army to invade and devastate Judaea, 2 and when he saw how the people were quaking with fear, he went up to Jerusalem, called the people together, 3 and exhorted them thus, 'You know yourselves how much I and my brothers and my father's family have done for the laws and the sanctuary; you know what wars and hardships we have experienced. 4 That is why my brothers are all dead, for Israel's sake, and I am the only one left. 5 Far be it from me, then, to be sparing of my own life in any time of oppression, for I am not worth more than my brothers. 6 Rather will I avenge my nation and the sanctuary and your wives and children, now that the foreigners are all united in malice to destroy us.'

GREEK OLD TESTAMENT

ἀνεζωπύρησεν τὸ πνεῦμα τοῦ λαοῦ ἅμα τοῦ ἀκοῦσαι τῶν λόγων τούτων, 8 καὶ ἀπεκρίθησαν φωνῇ μεγάλῃ λέγοντες Σὺ εἶ
ἡμῶν ἡγούμενος ἀντὶ Ιουδου καὶ Ιωναθου τοῦ ἀδελφοῦ σου·
9 πολέμησον τὸν πόλεμον ἡμῶν, καὶ πάντα, ὅσα ἂν εἴπῃς
ἡμῖν, ποιήσομεν. 10 καὶ συνήγαγεν πάντας τοὺς ἄνδρας
τοὺς πολεμιστὰς καὶ ἐτάχυνεν τοῦ τελέσαι τὰ τείχη Ιερουσαλημ καὶ ὠχύρωσεν αὐτὴν κυκλόθεν. 11 καὶ ἀπέστειλεν
Ιωναθαν τὸν τοῦ Αψαλωμου καὶ μετ᾽ αὐτοῦ δύναμιν ἱκανὴν
εἰς Ιοππην, καὶ ἐξέβαλεν τοὺς ὄντας ἐν αὐτῇ καὶ ἔμεινεν
ἐκεῖ ἐν αὐτῇ.

12 Καὶ ἀπῆρεν Τρύφων ἀπὸ Πτολεμαίδος μετὰ δυνάμεως
πολλῆς ἐλθεῖν εἰς γῆν Ιουδα, καὶ Ιωναθαν μετ᾽ αὐτοῦ ἐν
φυλακῇ. 13 Σιμων δὲ παρενέβαλεν ἐν Αδιδοις κατὰ πρόσωπον
τοῦ πεδίου. 14 καὶ ἐπέγνω Τρύφων ὅτι ἀνέστη Σιμων ἀντὶ
Ιωναθου τοῦ ἀδελφοῦ αὐτοῦ καὶ ὅτι συνάπτειν αὐτῷ μέλλει
πόλεμον, καὶ ἀπέστειλεν πρὸς αὐτὸν πρέσβεις λέγων
15 Περὶ ἀργυρίου, οὗ ὤφειλεν Ιωναθαν ὁ ἀδελφός σου εἰς τὸ
βασιλικὸν δι᾽ ἃς εἶχεν χρείας, συνέχομεν αὐτόν· 16 καὶ νῦν
ἀπόστειλον ἀργυρίου τάλαντα ἑκατὸν καὶ δύο τῶν υἱῶν αὐτοῦ ὅμηρα, ὅπως μὴ ἀφεθεὶς ἀποστατήσῃ ἀφ᾽ ἡμῶν, καὶ ἀφήσομεν αὐτόν. 17 καὶ ἔγνω Σιμων ὅτι δόλῳ λαλοῦσιν πρὸς
αὐτόν, καὶ πέμπει τοῦ λαβεῖν τὸ ἀργύριον καὶ τὰ παιδάρια,
μήποτε ἔχθραν ἄρῃ μεγάλην πρὸς τὸν λαὸν 18 λέγοντες Ὅτι

KING JAMES VERSION

7 Now as soon as the people heard these words, their spirit revived.

8 And they answered with a loud voice, saying, Thou shalt be our leader instead of Judas and Jonathan thy brother.

9 Fight thou our battles, and whatsoever thou commandest us, that will we do.

10 So then he gathered together all the men of war, and made haste to finish the walls of Jerusalem, and he fortified it round about.

11 Also he sent Jonathan the *son* of Absolom, and with him a great power, to Joppe: who casting out them that were therein remained there in it.

12 So Tryphon removed from Ptolemaus with a great power to invade the land of Judea, and Jonathan was with him in ward.

13 But Simon pitched his tents at Adida, over against the plain.

14 Now when Tryphon knew that Simon was risen up instead of his brother Jonathan, and meant to join battle with him, he sent messengers unto him, saying,

15 Whereas we have Jonathan thy brother in hold, it is for money that he is owing unto the king's treasure, concerning the business that was committed unto him.

16 Wherefore now send an hundred talents of silver, and two of his sons for hostages, that when he is at liberty he may not revolt from us, and we will let him go.

17 Hereupon Simon, albeit he perceived that they spake deceitfully unto him, yet sent he the money and the children, lest peradventure he should procure to himself great hatred of the people:

DOUAY OLD TESTAMENT

7 And the spirit of the people was enkindled as soon as they heard these words.

8 And they answered with a loud voice, saying: Thou art our leader in the place of Judas, and Jonathan thy brother.

9 Fight thou our battles, and we will do whatsoever thou shalt say to us.

10 So gathering together all the men of war, he made haste to finish all the walls of Jerusalem, and he fortified it round about.

11 And he sent Jonathan the son of Absalom, and with him a new army into Joppe, and he cast out them that were in it, and himself remained there.

12 And Tryphon removed from Ptolemais with a great army, to invade the land of Juda, and Jonathan was with him in custody.

13 But Simon pitched in Addus, over against the plain.

14 And when Tryphon understood that Simon was risen up in the place of his brother Jonathan, and that he meant to join battle with him, he sent messengers to him,

15 Saying: We have detained thy brother Jonathan for the money that he owed in the king's account, by reason of the affairs which he had the management of.

16 But now send a hundred talents of silver, and his two sons for hostages, that when he is set at liberty he may not revolt from us, and we will release him.

17 Now Simon knew that he spoke deceitfully to him, nevertheless he ordered the money, and the children to be sent: lest he should bring upon himself a great hatred of the people of Israel, who might have said:

KNOX TRANSLATION

champion yet. 7 At these words, the spirit of the whole people revived; 8 loud came their answer, Brother of Judas and
Jonathan, thine to lead us now! 9 Thine to sustain our cause;
and never word of thine shall go unheeded!
10 Thereupon, he summoned all the fighting men together,
and pressed on to have the walls of Jerusalem finished, till it
was fortified all about; 11 and he sent Jonathan, son of
Absalom, to Joppe, at the head of a force newly raised; the
garrison was disbanded, and a new captain held it now.
12 Meanwhile, Tryphon had left Ptolemais, with a great army
at his heels, marching on Juda; and with him went Jonathan,
his prisoner. 13 He found Simon encamped at Addus, that
looks out over the plain; 14 here was Jonathan's brother
Simon taking his place, and offering battle. Envoys were sent
out to make his excuses: 15 Hold we the person of thy brother Jonathan, it is because he is in default to the royal treasury over his dealings with it. 16 Thou hast but to send a
hundred talents of silver, and his two sons, to be surety he
will not play us false when we release him, and he is a free
man. 17 Well Simon knew it was treacherously spoken; yet
he gave orders, both money and hostages should be surrendered. A bitter grudge Israel's people would bear him, if they

TODAY'S ENGLISH VERSION

7 These words immediately revived the morale of the people, 8 and they answered with a loud shout, "You are now
our leader in place of your brothers Judas and Jonathan.
9 Fight our wars, and we will do whatever you ask." 10 So
Simon gathered together all the soldiers and hurried to complete the walls of Jerusalem and to strengthen all its
defenses. 11 He sent Jonathan son of Absalom to Joppa with
a large army. This Jonathan drove out the people who were
there and occupied the town.

12 Trypho left Ptolemais with a large army to invade Judea,
taking Simon's brother Jonathan along with him as a prisoner. 13 Simon set up camp at Adida at the edge of the plain.
14 When Trypho learned that Simon had succeeded his brother Jonathan and that he was ready to meet him in battle, he
sent this message to him: 15 "I am holding your brother
Jonathan under arrest because while he was in office he did
not pay his debts to the royal treasury. 16 However, I will
release him if you will pay me 6,000 pounds of silver and
send two of his sons as hostages to guarantee that he will
not revolt against us when he is released."

17 Although Simon knew that they were deceiving him, he
sent for the money and the two sons because he did not
want to arouse the hostility of the Jews. 18 He was afraid

NEW REVISED STANDARD VERSION

7 The spirit of the people was rekindled when they heard
these words, 8 and they answered in a loud voice, "You are
our leader in place of Judas and your brother Jonathan.
9 Fight our battles, and all that you say to us we will do."
10 So he assembled all the warriors and hurried to complete
the walls of Jerusalem, and he fortified it on every side. 11 He
sent Jonathan son of Absalom to Joppa, and with him a considerable army; he drove out its occupants and remained
there.

12 Then Trypho left Ptolemais with a large army to invade
the land of Judah, and Jonathan was with him under guard.
13 Simon encamped in Adida, facing the plain. 14 Trypho
learned that Simon had risen up in place of his brother
Jonathan, and that he was about to join battle with him, so
he sent envoys to him and said, 15 "It is for the money that
your brother Jonathan owed the royal treasury, in connection
with the offices he held, that we are detaining him. 16 Send
now one hundred talents of silver and two of his sons as
hostages, so that when released he will not revolt against us,
and we will release him."

17 Simon knew that they were speaking deceitfully to
him, but he sent to get the money and the sons, so that he
would not arouse great hostility among the people, who

NEW AMERICAN BIBLE

7 As the people heard these words, their spirit was rekindled. 8 They shouted in reply: "You are our leader in place of
your brothers Judas and Jonathan. 9 Fight our battles, and
we will do everything that you tell us." 10 So Simon mustered all the men able to fight, and quickly completing the
walls of Jerusalem, fortified it on every side. 11 He sent
Jonathan, son of Absalom, to Joppa with a large force;
Jonathan drove out the occupants and remained there.

12 Then Trypho moved from Ptolemais with a large army to
invade the land of Judah, bringing Jonathan with him as
prisoner. 13 But Simon pitched his camp at Adida, facing the
plain. 14 When Trypho learned that Simon had succeeded his
brother Jonathan, and that he intended to fight him, he sent
envoys to him with this message: 15 "We have detained your
brother Jonathan on account of the money that he owed the
royal treasury in connection with the offices that he held.
16 Therefore, if you send us a hundred talents of silver, and
two of his sons as hostages to guarantee that when he is set
free he will not revolt against us, we will release him."

17 Although Simon knew that they were speaking deceitfully to him, he gave orders to get the money and the boys, for
fear of provoking much hostility among the people, who

NEW JERUSALEM BIBLE

7 The people's spirit rekindled as they listened to his words,
8 and they shouted back at him, 'You are our leader in place
of Judas and your brother Jonathan. 9 Fight our battles for
us, and we will do whatever you tell us.' 10 So he assembled
all the fighting men and hurried on with completing the
walls of Jerusalem, fortifying the whole perimeter. 11 He sent
a considerable force to Joppa under Jonathan son of Absalom
who drove out the inhabitants and remained there in occupa-
tion.

12 Trypho now left Ptolemais with a large army to invade
Judaea, taking Jonathan with him under guard. 13 Simon
pitched camp in Adida, facing the plain. 14 When Trypho
learned that Simon had taken the place of his brother
Jonathan and that he intended to join battle with him, he
sent envoys to him with this message, 15 'Your brother
Jonathan was in debt to the royal exchequer for the offices he
held; that is why we are detaining him. 16 If you send a hundred talents of silver and two of his sons as hostages, to
make sure that on his release he does not revolt against us,
we shall release him.' 17 Although Simon was aware that the
message was a ruse, he sent for the money and the boys for
fear of incurring great hostility from the people, 18 who

GREEK OLD TESTAMENT

οὐκ ἀπέστειλα αὐτῷ τὸ ἀργύριον καὶ τὰ παιδάρια, ἀπώλετο.
19 καὶ ἀπέστειλεν τὰ παιδάρια καὶ τὰ ἑκατὸν τάλαντα, καὶ
διεψεύσατο καὶ οὐκ ἀφῆκεν τὸν Ιωναθαν. 20 καὶ μετὰ ταῦτα
ἦλθεν Τρύφων τοῦ ἐμβατεῦσαι εἰς τὴν χώραν καὶ ἐκτρῖψαι
αὐτήν, καὶ ἐκύκλωσαν ὁδὸν τὴν εἰς Αδωρα. καὶ Σιμων καὶ ἡ
παρεμβολὴ αὐτοῦ ἀντιπαρῆγεν αὐτῷ εἰς πάντα τόπον, οὗ ἂν
ἐπορεύετο. 21 οἱ δὲ ἐκ τῆς ἄκρας ἀπέστελλον πρὸς Τρύφωνα
πρεσβευτὰς κατασπεύδοντας αὐτὸν τοῦ ἐλθεῖν πρὸς αὐτοὺς
διὰ τῆς ἐρήμου καὶ ἀποστεῖλαι αὐτοῖς τροφάς. 22 καὶ ἡτοίμασεν Τρύφων πᾶσαν τὴν ἵππον αὐτοῦ ἐλθεῖν, καὶ ἐν τῇ νυκτὶ
ἐκείνῃ ἦν χιὼν πολλὴ σφόδρα, καὶ οὐκ ἦλθεν διὰ τὴν χιόνα.
καὶ ἀπῆρεν καὶ ἦλθεν εἰς τὴν Γαλααδῖτιν. 23 ὡς δὲ ἤγγισεν
τῆς Βασκαμα, ἀπέκτεινεν τὸν Ιωναθαν, καὶ ἐτάφη ἐκεῖ.
24 καὶ ἐπέστρεψεν Τρύφων καὶ ἀπῆλθεν εἰς τὴν γῆν αὐτοῦ.

25 Καὶ ἀπέστειλεν Σιμων καὶ ἔλαβεν τὰ ὀστᾶ Ιωναθου τοῦ
ἀδελφοῦ αὐτοῦ καὶ ἔθαψεν αὐτὸν ἐν Μωδεϊν πόλει τῶν πατέρων αὐτοῦ. 26 καὶ ἐκόψαντο αὐτὸν πᾶς Ισραηλ κοπετὸν μέγαν καὶ ἐπένθησαν αὐτὸν ἡμέρας πολλάς. 27 καὶ ᾠκοδόμησεν
Σιμων ἐπὶ τὸν τάφον τοῦ πατρὸς αὐτοῦ καὶ τῶν ἀδελφῶν αὐτοῦ καὶ ὕψωσεν αὐτὸν τῇ ὁράσει λίθῳ ξεστῷ ἐκ τῶν ὄπισθεν
καὶ ἔμπροσθεν. 28 καὶ ἔστησεν ἑπτὰ πυραμίδας, μίαν κατέναντι τῆς μιᾶς, τῷ πατρὶ καὶ τῇ μητρὶ καὶ τοῖς τέσσαρσιν

KING JAMES VERSION

18 Who might have said, Because I sent him not the money and the children, therefore is *Jonathan* dead.

19 So he sent them the children and the hundred talents: howbeit *Tryphon* dissembled, neither would he let Jonathan go.

20 And after this came Tryphon to invade the land, and destroy it, going round about by the way that leadeth unto Adora: but Simon and his host marched against him in every place, wheresoever he went.

21 Now they that were in the tower sent messengers unto Tryphon, to the end that he should hasten his coming unto them by the wilderness, and send them victuals.

22 Wherefore Tryphon made ready all his horsemen to come that night: but there fell a very great snow, by reason whereof he came not. So he departed, and came into the country of Galaad.

23 And when he came near to Bascama, he slew Jonathan, who was buried there.

24 Afterward Tryphon returned and went into his own land.

25 Then sent Simon, and took the bones of Jonathan his brother, and buried them in Modin, the city of his fathers.

26 And all Israel made great lamentation for him, and bewailed him many days.

27 Simon also built a monument upon the sepulchre of his father and his brethren, and raised it aloft to the sight, with hewn stone behind and before.

28 Moreover he set up seven pyramids, one against another, for his father, and his mother, and his four brethren.

DOUAY OLD TESTAMENT

18 Because he sent not the money, and the children, therefore is he lost.

19 So he sent the children, and the hundred talents: and he lied, and did not let Jonathan go.

20 And after this Tryphon entered within the country, to destroy it: and they went about by the way that leadeth to Ador: and Simon and his army marched to every place whithersoever they went.

21 And they that were in the castle, sent messengers to Tryphon, that he should make haste to come through the desert, and send them victuals.

22 And Tryphon made ready all his horsemen to come that night: but there fell a very great snow, and he came not into the country of Galaad.

23 And when he approached to Bascama, he slew Jonathan and his sons there.

24 And Tryphon returned, and went into his own country.

25 And Simon sent, and took the bones of Jonathan his brother, and buried them in Modin, in the city of his fathers.

26 And all Israel bewailed him with great lamentation: and they mourned for him many days.

27 And Simon built over the sepulchre of his father and of his brethren, a building lofty to the sight, of polished stone behind and before:

28 And he set up seven pyramids one against another for his father and his mother, and his four brethren:

KNOX TRANSLATION

had cause to say, 18 For want of money paid over and surety
given, Jonathan must die! 19 Sent they were, the boys and
the money both, but all was treachery; Jonathan never came
back.

20 And now Tryphon invaded Juda, bent on its undoing; his
troops must fetch a compass by the road that leads round to
Ador, and, march they where they would, Simon and his
army were at their heels. 21 Word came to Tryphon from the
defenders of Jerusalem citadel, he should make his way
across the desert without more ado, and bring them supplies;
22 and that same night he had all his cavalry in readiness for
the march, but there was a great fall of snow, and come he
might not...into the country of Galaad.[a] 23 When he reached
Bascaman, then and there he put Jonathan and his sons to
death; 24 and with that, he turned about, and went back to
his own country.

25 There lay the bones of Simon's brother Jonathan, till he
sent to fetch them, and gave them burial at Modin, the city of
his fathers. 26 Loud lament all Israel made for him, and long
they bemoaned him. 27 Over the graves of his father and his
brethren Simon raised a towering monument, of dressed
stone behind and before; 28 then, with father and mother
and his four brethren in mind, he built seven pyramids, in

a It seems clear from the context that some words have dropped out. The Greek text has, 'and come he might not, because of the snow. So he moved camp and went into the country of Galaad'. But the passage may originally have indicated what reasons Tryphon had for abandoning his campaign in Judaea.

TODAY'S ENGLISH VERSION

that they might later say that Jonathan was put to death
because Simon would not send the money and the boys.
19 So he did as Trypho had demanded, but Trypho broke his
promise and did not release Jonathan.

20 Then Trypho made his move to invade the land and
destroy it, circling around by the road to Adora. But Simon
and his army moved along facing him wherever he went.
21 The enemy soldiers in the fort in Jerusalem kept sending
messengers to Trypho urging him to come to them quickly by
way of the desert and to send them supplies. 22 Trypho got
all his cavalry ready for the invasion, but that night there
was a heavy snowstorm, and he was not able to move up
into the hills. So he withdrew and went into Gilead. 23 When
he was near Baskama, he had Jonathan put to death and his
body buried there. 24 Then Trypho turned and went back to
his own country.

25 Simon had the body of his brother Jonathan brought to
Modein, to be buried in the town of their ancestors.
26 Everyone in Israel was in deep sorrow at the loss of
Jonathan, and they mourned for him a long time. 27 Over the
tomb of his father and his brothers Simon built a high monument that could be seen from a great distance. It was covered
front and back with polished stone. 28 He constructed seven
pyramids side by side for his father, his mother, and his four

NEW REVISED STANDARD VERSION

might say, 18 "It was because Simon[a] did not send him the
money and the sons, that Jonathan[b] perished." 19 So he sent
the sons and the hundred talents, but Trypho[b] broke his
word and did not release Jonathan.

20 After this Trypho came to invade the country and
destroy it, and he circled around by the way to Adora. But
Simon and his army kept marching along opposite him to
every place he went. 21 Now the men in the citadel kept
sending envoys to Trypho urging him to come to them by
way of the wilderness and to send them food. 22 So Trypho
got all his cavalry ready to go, but that night a very heavy
snow fell, and he did not go because of the snow. He
marched off and went into the land of Gilead. 23 When he
approached Baskama, he killed Jonathan, and he was buried
there. 24 Then Trypho turned and went back to his own land.

25 Simon sent and took the bones of his brother
Jonathan, and buried him in Modein, the city of his ancestors. 26 All Israel bewailed him with great lamentation, and
mourned for him many days. 27 And Simon built a monument over the tomb of his father and his brothers; he made it
high so that it might be seen, with polished stone at the
front and back. 28 He also erected seven pyramids, opposite
one another, for his father and mother and four brothers.

a Gk *I* b Gk *he*

NEW AMERICAN BIBLE

might say 18 that Jonathan perished because Simon would
not send Trypho the money and the boys. 19 So he sent the
boys and the hundred talents; but Trypho broke his promise
and would not let Jonathan go. 20 Next he began to invade
and ravage the country. His troops went around by the road
that leads to Adora, but Simon and his army moved along
opposite him everywhere he went. 21 The men in the citadel
sent messengers to Trypho, urging him to come to them by
way of the desert, and to send them provisions. 22 Although
Trypho got all his cavalry ready to go, there was a heavy fall
of snow that night, and he could not go. So he left for Gilead.
23 When he was approaching Baskama, he had Jonathan
killed and buried there. 24 Then Trypho returned to his own
country.

25 Simon sent for the remains of his brother Jonathan, and
buried him in Modein, the city of his fathers. 26 All Israel
bewailed him with solemn lamentation, mourning over him
for many days. 27 Then Simon erected over the tomb of his
father and his brothers a monument of stones, polished front
and back, and raised high enough to be seen at a distance.
28 He set up seven pyramids facing one another for his father
and his mother and his four brothers. 29 For the pyramids he

NEW JERUSALEM BIBLE

would have said that Jonathan had died because Simon
would not send Trypho the money and the children. 19 He
therefore sent both the boys and the hundred talents, but
Trypho broke his word and did not release Jonathan. 20 Next,
Trypho set about the invasion and devastation of the country; he made a detour along the Adora road, but Simon and
his army confronted him wherever he attempted to go.
21 The men in the Citadel kept sending messengers to Trypho,
urging him to get through to them by way of the desert and
send them supplies. 22 Trypho organised his entire cavalry to
go, but that night it snowed so heavily that he could not get
through for the snow, so he left there and moved off into
Gilead. 23 As he approached Baskama he killed Jonathan,
who was buried there. 24 Trypho turned back and regained
his own country.

25 Simon sent and recovered the bones of his brother
Jonathan, and buried him in Modein, the town of his ancestors. 26 All Israel kept solemn mourning for him and long
bewailed him. 27 Over the tomb of his father and brothers,
Simon raised a monument high enough to catch the eye,
using dressed stone back and front. 28 He erected seven
pyramids facing each other, for his father and mother and

GREEK OLD TESTAMENT

ἀδελφοῖς. [29]καὶ ταύταις ἐποίησεν μηχανήματα περιθεὶς
στύλους μεγάλους καὶ ἐποίησεν ἐπὶ τοῖς στύλοις πανοπλίας
εἰς ὄνομα αἰώνιον καὶ παρὰ ταῖς πανοπλίαις πλοῖα
ἐγγεγλυμμένα εἰς τὸ θεωρεῖσθαι ὑπὸ πάντων τῶν πλεόντων
τὴν θάλασσαν. [30]οὗτος ὁ τάφος, ὃν ἐποίησεν ἐν Μωδεϊν,
ἕως τῆς ἡμέρας ταύτης.

[31]Ὁ δὲ Τρύφων ἐπορεύετο δόλῳ μετὰ Ἀντιόχου τοῦ
βασιλέως τοῦ νεωτέρου καὶ ἀπέκτεινεν αὐτὸν [32]καὶ ἐβασίλευσεν ἀντ' αὐτοῦ καὶ περιέθετο τὸ διάδημα τῆς Ἀσίας καὶ
ἐποίησεν πληγὴν μεγάλην ἐπὶ τῆς γῆς. [33]καὶ ᾠκοδόμησεν
Σιμων τὰ ὀχυρώματα τῆς Ιουδαίας καὶ περιετείχισεν πύργοις ὑψηλοῖς καὶ τείχεσιν μεγάλοις καὶ πύλαις καὶ μοχλοῖς
καὶ ἔθετο βρώματα ἐν τοῖς ὀχυρώμασιν. [34]καὶ ἐπέλεξεν
Σιμων ἄνδρας καὶ ἀπέστειλεν πρὸς Δημήτριον τὸν βασιλέα
τοῦ ποιῆσαι ἄφεσιν τῇ χώρᾳ, ὅτι πᾶσαι αἱ πράξεις Τρύ-
φωνος ἦσαν ἁρπαγαί. [35]καὶ ἀπέστειλεν αὐτῷ Δημήτριος ὁ
βασιλεὺς κατὰ τοὺς λόγους τούτους καὶ ἀπεκρίθη αὐτῷ καὶ
ἔγραψεν αὐτῷ ἐπιστολὴν τοιαύτην

[36]Βασιλεὺς Δημήτριος Σιμωνι ἀρχιερεῖ καὶ φίλῳ βασιλέων
καὶ πρεσβυτέροις καὶ ἔθνει Ιουδαίων χαίρειν. [37]τὸν στέφανον τὸν χρυσοῦν καὶ τὴν βαΐνην, ἣν ἀπεστείλατε, κεκομί-
σμεθα καὶ ἕτοιμοί ἐσμεν τοῦ ποιεῖν ὑμῖν εἰρήνην μεγάλην
καὶ γράφειν τοῖς ἐπὶ τῶν χρειῶν τοῦ ἀφιέναι ὑμῖν τὰ ἀφέματα. [38]καὶ ὅσα ἐστήσαμεν πρὸς ὑμᾶς, ἕστηκεν, καὶ τὰ
ὀχυρώματα, ἃ ᾠκοδομήσατε, ὑπαρχέτω ὑμῖν. [39]ἀφίεμεν δὲ

KING JAMES VERSION

29 And in these he made cunning devices, about the which he set great pillars, and upon the pillars he made all their armour for a perpetual memory, and by the armour ships carved, that they might be seen of all that sail on the sea.

30 This is the sepulchre which he made at Modin, and it standeth yet unto this day.

31 Now Tryphon dealt deceitfully with the young king Antiochus, and slew him.

32 And he reigned in his stead, and crowned himself king of Asia, and brought a great calamity upon the land.

33 Then Simon built up the strong holds in Judea, and fenced them about with high towers, and great walls, and gates, and bars, and laid up victuals therein.

34 Moreover Simon chose men, and sent to king Demetrius, to the end he should give the land an immunity, because all that Tryphon did was to spoil.

35 Unto whom king Demetrius answered and wrote after this manner:

36 King Demetrius unto Simon the high priest, and friend of kings, as also unto the elders and nation of the Jews, sendeth greeting:

37 The golden crown, and the scarlet robe, which ye sent unto us, we have received: and we are ready to make a stedfast peace with you, yea, and to write unto our officers, to confirm the immunities which we have granted.

38 And whatsoever covenants we have made with you shall stand; and the strong holds, which ye have builded, shall be your own.

DOUAY OLD TESTAMENT

29 And round about these he set great pillars: and upon the pillars arms for a perpetual memory: and by the arms ships carved, which might be seen by all that sailed on the sea.

30 This is the sepulchre that he made in Modin even unto this day.

31 But Tryphon when he was upon a journey with the young king Antiochus, treacherously slew him.

32 And he reigned in his place, and put on the crown of Asia: and brought great evils upon the land.

33 And Simon built up the strong holds of Judea, fortifying them with high towers, and great walls, and gates, and bars: and he stored up victuals in the fortresses.

34 And Simon chose men and sent to king Demetrius, to the end that he should grant an immunity to the land: for all that Tryphon did was to spoil.

35 And king Demetrius in answer to this request, wrote a letter in this manner:

36 King Demetrius to Simon the high priest, and friend of kings, and to the ancients, and to the nation of the Jews, greeting.

37 The golden crown, and the palm, which you sent, we have received: and we are ready to make a firm peace with you, and to write to the king's chief officers to release you the things that we have released.

38 For all that we have decreed in your favour, shall stand in force. The strong holds that you have built, shall be your own.

KNOX TRANSLATION

rows; [29]and all about were great columns, carved with
armour and ships; an abiding memorial, and a land mark to
mariners at sea. [30]Such was the tomb he raised at Modin,
and it may be seen to this day. [31]Meanwhile, as they were
journeying together, Tryphon murdered the young king
Antiochus by artifice, [32]and succeeded to his throne, wearing the crown of all Asia; great mischief it was he did to his
country.

[33]All the fortresses of Judaea Simon repaired, building
them up with high tower and stout wall, with bolt and bar;
and never a garrison but had provisions laid up in store.
[34]Then he chose out envoys and sent them to king
Demetrius, praying that the land might enjoy immunity after
the tyrannous actions of Tryphon.[a] [35]When king Demetrius
answered the request, he wrote in these terms following.
[36]King Demetrius to the high priest Simon, the friend of
kings, and to all the elders and people of the Jews, greeting.
[37]Crown of gold and robe of scarlet you sent us were faithfully delivered. Great favour we mean to shew you, by sending word to the king's officers to respect the remissions
granted you. [38]The decrees we made concerning you are yet
in force; and, for the strongholds you have built, they shall

a 'After the tyrannous actions of Tryphon'; literally (in the Greek text), 'because all the actions of Tryphon were seizures'. The meaning is perhaps that Simon now recognized all the actions of Tryphon as usurpations of power; it is evident from what follows that he was not sure of his position; had the Jews, by their support of a pretender, forfeited the privileges granted in 11. 33-37?

TODAY'S ENGLISH VERSION

brothers. 29 For the pyramids he created a setting of tall
columns on which there were carvings. Some of these carvings were of suits of armor and some were of ships. It was a
monument to their victories, which travelers from overseas
could visit.[a] 30 The tomb which he built in Modein is still
there today.

31 Meanwhile, Trypho assassinated the young king,
Antiochus the Sixth, 32 and took over his kingdom in Syria.
He brought that country great troubles.

33 Simon rebuilt the fortresses of Judea with high towers,
strong walls, and barred gates; then he placed stores of supplies there. 34 He sent ambassadors to King Demetrius the
Second to ask for tax relief for the land, since Trypho was
doing nothing but robbing them. 35 King Demetrius sent the
following letter in reply:

36 "King Demetrius to the High Priest Simon, the friend of
kings, to the Jewish nation, and to their leaders, greetings.
37 I have received the gold crown and the gold palm branch
which you sent, and I am prepared to make a peace treaty
with you and to instruct our tax officials to grant you exemptions. 38 Our previous agreements with you are confirmed,
and the fortresses which you have built are to remain yours.

[a] *Verses 28-29 in Greek are unclear.*

NEW REVISED STANDARD VERSION

29 For the pyramids[a] he devised an elaborate setting, erecting
about them great columns, and on the columns he put suits
of armor for a permanent memorial, and beside the suits of
armor he carved ships, so that they could be seen by all who
sail the sea. 30 This is the tomb that he built in Modein; it
remains to this day.

31 Trypho dealt treacherously with the young King
Antiochus; he killed him 32 and became king in his place,
putting on the crown of Asia; and he brought great calamity
on the land. 33 But Simon built up the strongholds of Judea
and walled them all around, with high towers and great
walls and gates and bolts, and he stored food in the strongholds. 34 Simon also chose emissaries and sent them to King
Demetrius with a request to grant relief to the country, for all
that Trypho did was to plunder. 35 King Demetrius sent him
a favorable reply to this request, and wrote him a letter as
follows, 36 "King Demetrius to Simon, the high priest and
friend of kings, and to the elders and nation of the Jews,
greetings. 37 We have received the gold crown and the palm
branch that you[b] sent, and we are ready to make a general
peace with you and to write to our officials to grant you
release from tribute. 38 All the grants that we have made to
you remain valid, and let the strongholds that you have built

a Gk *For these* *b* The word *you* in verses 37-40 is plural

NEW AMERICAN BIBLE

devised a setting of big columns, on which he carved suits of
armor as a perpetual memorial, and next to the armor he
placed carved ships, which could be seen by all who sailed
the sea. 30 This tomb which he built at Modein is there to the
present day.

31 Trypho dealt treacherously with the young King
Antiochus. He killed him 32 and assumed the kingship in his
place, putting on the crown of Asia. Thus he brought much
evil on the land. 33 Simon, on his part, built up the strongholds of Judea, strengthening their fortifications with high
towers, thick walls, and gates with bars, and he stored up
provisions in the fortresses. 34 Simon also sent chosen men
to King Demetrius with the request that he grant the land a
release from taxation, for all that Trypho did was to plunder
the land. 35 In reply, King Demetrius sent him the following
letter:

36 "King Demetrius sends greetings to Simon the high
priest, the friend of kings, and to the elders and the Jewish
people. 37 We have received the gold crown and the palm
branch that you sent. We are willing to be on most peaceful
terms with you and to write to our official to grant you
release from tribute. 38 Whatever we have guaranteed to you
remains in force, and the strongholds that you have built

NEW JERUSALEM BIBLE

his four brothers, 29 surrounding them with a structure consisting of tall columns surmounted by trophies of arms to
their everlasting memory and, beside the trophies of arms,
ships sculpted on a scale to be seen by all who sail the sea.
30 Such was the monument he constructed at Modein, and it
is still there today.

31 Now Trypho, betraying the trust of young King
Antiochus, put him to death. 32 He usurped his throne,
assuming the crown of Asia, and brought great havoc on the
country. 33 Simon built up the fortresses of Judaea, surrounding them with high towers, great walls and gates with
bolts, and stocked these fortresses with food. 34 He also sent
a delegation to King Demetrius, to get him to grant the province a remission, since all Trypho did was to despoil. 35 King
Demetrius replied to his request in a letter framed as follows:

36 'King Demetrius to Simon, high priest and Friend of
Kings, and to the elders and nation of the Jews, greetings.
37 'It has pleased us to accept the golden crown and the
palm you have sent us, and we are disposed to make a
general peace with you, and to write to the officials to
grant you remissions. 38 Everything that we have decreed
concerning you remains in force, and the fortresses you
have built may remain in your hands. 39 We pardon all

GREEK OLD TESTAMENT

ἀγνοήματα καὶ τὰ ἁμαρτήματα ἕως τῆς σήμερον ἡμέρας καὶ
τὸν στέφανον, ὃν ὠφείλετε, καὶ εἴ τι ἄλλο ἐτελωνεῖτο ἐν
Ιερουσαλημ, μηκέτι τελωνείσθω. 40 καὶ εἴ τινες ἐπιτήδειοι
ὑμῶν γραφῆναι εἰς τοὺς περὶ ἡμᾶς, ἐγγραφέσθωσαν, καὶ
γινέσθω ἀνὰ μέσον ἡμῶν εἰρήνη.
41 Ἔτους ἑβδομηκοστοῦ καὶ ἑκατοστοῦ ἤρθη ὁ ζυγὸς τῶν
ἐθνῶν ἀπὸ τοῦ Ισραηλ, 42 καὶ ἤρξατο ὁ λαὸς γράφειν ἐν ταῖς
συγγραφαῖς καὶ συναλλάγμασιν Ἔτους πρώτου ἐπὶ Σιμωνος
ἀρχιερέως μεγάλου καὶ στρατηγοῦ καὶ ἡγουμένου Ιουδαίων.
43 Ἐν ταῖς ἡμέραις ἐκείναις παρενέβαλεν ἐπὶ Γαζαρα καὶ
ἐκύκλωσεν αὐτὴν παρεμβολαῖς καὶ ἐποίησεν ἑλεόπολιν καὶ
προσήγαγεν τῇ πόλει καὶ ἐπάταξεν πύργον ἕνα καὶ κατελάβετο. 44 καὶ ἐξήλλοντο οἱ ἐν τῇ ἑλεοπόλει εἰς τὴν πόλιν, καὶ
ἐγένετο κίνημα μέγα ἐν τῇ πόλει. 45 καὶ ἀνέβησαν οἱ ἐν τῇ
πόλει σὺν γυναιξὶν καὶ τοῖς τέκνοις ἐπὶ τὸ τεῖχος διερρηχότες τὰ ἱμάτια αὐτῶν καὶ ἐβόησαν φωνῇ μεγάλῃ ἀξιοῦντες
Σιμωνα δεξιὰς αὐτοῖς δοῦναι 46 καὶ εἶπαν Μὴ ἡμῖν χρήσῃ
κατὰ τὰς πονηρίας ἡμῶν, ἀλλὰ κατὰ τὸ ἔλεός σου. 47 καὶ
συνελύθη αὐτοῖς Σιμων καὶ οὐκ ἐπολέμησεν αὐτούς, καὶ ἐξέβαλεν αὐτοὺς ἐκ τῆς πόλεως, καὶ ἐκαθάρισεν τὰς οἰκίας, ἐν
αἷς ἦν τὰ εἴδωλα, καὶ οὕτως εἰσῆλθεν εἰς αὐτὴν ὑμνῶν καὶ
εὐλογῶν. 48 καὶ ἐξέβαλεν ἐξ αὐτῆς πᾶσαν ἀκαθαρσίαν καὶ
κατῴκισεν ἐν αὐτῇ ἄνδρας, οἵτινες τὸν νόμον ποιήσωσιν,
καὶ προσωχύρωσεν αὐτὴν καὶ ᾠκοδόμησεν ἑαυτῷ ἐν αὐτῇ
οἴκησιν.

KING JAMES VERSION

39 As for any oversight or fault committed unto this day, we forgive it, and the crown tax also, which ye owe us: and if there were any other tribute paid in Jerusalem, it shall no more be paid.

40 And look who are meet among you to be in our court, let them be enrolled, and let there be peace betwixt us.

41 Thus the yoke of the heathen was taken away from Israel in the hundred and seventieth year.

42 Then the people of Israel began to write in their instruments and contracts, In the first year of Simon the high priest, the governor and leader of the Jews.

43 In those days Simon camped against Gaza, and besieged it round about; he made also an engine of war, and set it by the city, and battered a certain tower, and took it.

44 And they that were in the engine leaped into the city; whereupon there was a great uproar in the city:

45 Insomuch as the people of the city rent their clothes, and climbed upon the walls with their wives and children, and cried with a loud voice, beseeching Simon to grant them peace.

46 And they said, Deal not with us according to our wickedness, but according to thy mercy.

47 So Simon was appeased toward them, and fought no more against them, but put them out of the city, and cleansed the houses wherein the idols were, and so entered into it with songs and thanksgiving.

48 Yea, he put all uncleanness out of it, and placed such men there as would keep the law, and made it stronger than it was before, and built therein a dwellingplace for himself.

DOUAY OLD TESTAMENT

39 And as for any oversight or fault committed unto this day, we forgive it, and the crown which you owed: and if any other thing were taxed in Jerusalem, now let it not be taxed.

40 And if any of you be fit to be enrolled among ours, let them be enrolled, and let there be peace between us.

41 In the year one hundred and seventy the yoke of the Gentiles was taken off from Israel.

42 And the people of Israel began to write in the instruments, and public records, The first year under Simon the high priest, the great captain and prince of the Jews.

43 In those days Simon besieged Gaza, and camped round about it, and he made engines, and set them to the city, and he struck one tower, and took it.

44 And they that were within the engine leaped into the city: and there was a great uproar in the city.

45 And they that were in the city went up with their wives and children upon the wall, with their garments rent, and they cried with a loud voice, beseeching Simon to grant them peace.

46 And they said: Deal not with us according to our evil deeds, but according to thy mercy.

47 And Simon being moved, did not destroy them: but yet he cast them out of the city, and cleansed the houses wherein there had been idols, and then he entered into it with hymns, blessing the Lord.

48 And having cast out of it all uncleanness, he placed in it men that should observe the law: and he fortified it, and made it his habitation.

KNOX TRANSLATION

be yours. 39 Fault of yours in the past, witting or unwitting,
is condoned; coronation tax you owed, and all other tribute
that was due from Jerusalem, is due no longer. 40 Fit be they
for such enrolment, Jews shall be enrolled in our armies, and
ever between us and you let there be peace!
41 Thus, in the hundred and seventieth year, Israel was free
of the Gentile yoke at last; 42 and this style the people began
to use, were it private bond or public instrument they indit-
ed, In the first year of Simon's high priesthood, chief paramount and governor of the Jews.
43 Then it was that Simon marched on Gaza,[a] and beleaguered it with his army; built engines, and forced an entry
into one of the towers. 44 Out into the streets they sallied,
that manned the engine, and there was a fine commotion in
the city; 45 here were the townsfolk, with their wives and
children, mounting the walls with their garments rent about
them, and crying aloud, Simon should give them quarter;
46 great were their fault, greater still his clemency! 47 At that,
Simon relented; harry them to the death he would not, but
he drove them out of the city, and cleansed all the houses
where idols had stood; then, with singing of psalms and giving of thanks, he made his entry; 48 and now all defilement
must be put away, and such citizens it must have as did
what the law commanded. After that, he fortified it, and
made his own dwelling there.

[a] Josephus is perhaps right in reading 'Gazara' (less than twenty miles from Jerusalem) instead of 'Gaza'; cf. 14. 7.

TODAY'S ENGLISH VERSION

39 I grant you pardon for treaty violations committed up to
the present date, and I release you from payment of the special tax still due and any other taxes that have been collected
up to this time in Jerusalem. 40 All Jews who are qualified
may enroll in the royal service. Let us have peace."
41 So in the year 170[a] the yoke of the Gentile oppressors
was removed from the Jews. 42 People began to date their
documents and contracts with these words: "In the first year
of Simon, the great High Priest, commander and leader of the
Jews."
43 At that time Simon laid siege to Gezer and surrounded it
with his army. He built a movable siege platform, brought it
up to the town wall, attacked one of the towers, and captured
it. 44 The men who had been on the siege platform then moved
rapidly into the town, and this created great confusion. 45 The
men of the town, their wives, and their children tore their
clothes in distress and climbed up on the top of the town wall.
They pleaded loudly with Simon for a truce. 46 "Have mercy
on us," they begged. "Don't punish us as we deserve!"
47 So Simon came to terms with them and ended the fighting. He made the people leave the town; then he purified the
houses in which there had been idols. When that was done,
he and his men entered the town singing hymns and songs
of praise. 48 He eliminated everything that would make the
town ritually unclean and settled it with people who would
obey every command contained in the Law of Moses. He
strengthened the defenses of the town and built himself a
palace there.

[a] THE YEAR 170: *This corresponds to 142 B.C.*

NEW REVISED STANDARD VERSION

be your possession. 39 We pardon any errors and offenses
committed to this day, and cancel the crown tax that you
owe; and whatever other tax has been collected in Jerusalem
shall be collected no longer. 40 And if any of you are qualified to be enrolled in our bodyguard,[a] let them be enrolled,
and let there be peace between us."
41 In the one hundred seventieth year[b] the yoke of the
Gentiles was removed from Israel, 42 and the people began to
write in their documents and contracts, "In the first year of
Simon the great high priest and commander and leader of
the Jews."
43 In those days Simon[c] encamped against Gazara[d] and
surrounded it with troops. He made a siege engine, brought
it up to the city, and battered and captured one tower. 44 The
men in the siege engine leaped out into the city, and a great
tumult arose in the city. 45 The men in the city, with their
wives and children, went up on the wall with their clothes
torn, and they cried out with a loud voice, asking Simon to
make peace with them; 46 they said, "Do not treat us according to our wicked acts but according to your mercy." 47 So
Simon reached an agreement with them and stopped fighting
against them. But he expelled them from the city and
cleansed the houses in which the idols were located, and
then entered it with hymns and praise. 48 He removed all
uncleanness from it, and settled in it those who observed the
law. He also strengthened its fortifications and built in it a
house for himself.

a Or *court* *b* 142 B.C. *c* Gk *he* *d* Cn: Gk *Gaza*

NEW AMERICAN BIBLE

shall remain yours. 39 We remit any oversights and defaults
incurred up to now, as well as the crown tax that you owe.
Any other tax that may have been collected in Jerusalem
shall no longer be collected there. 40 If any of you are qualified for enrollment in our service, let them be enrolled. Let
there be peace between us."
41 Thus in the year one hundred and seventy, the yoke of
the Gentiles was removed from Israel, 42 and the people
began to write in their records and contracts, "In the first
year of Simon, high priest, governor, and leader of the Jews."
43 In those days Simon besieged Gazara and surrounded it
with troops. He made a siege machine, pushed it up against
the city, and attacked and captured one of the towers. 44 The
men who had been on the siege machine jumped down into
the city and caused a great tumult there. 45 The men of the
city, joined by their wives and children, went up on the wall,
with their garments rent, and cried out in loud voices, begging Simon to grant them peace. 46 "Do not treat us according to our evil deeds," they said, "but according to your
mercy."
47 So Simon came to terms with them and did not destroy
them. He made them leave the city, however, and he purified
the houses in which there were idols. Then he entered the
city with hymns and songs of praise. 48 After removing from
it everything that was impure, he settled there men who
observed the law. He improved its fortifications and built
himself a residence.

NEW JERUSALEM BIBLE

offences, unwitting or intentional, hitherto committed, and
remit the crown tax you now owe us; and whatever other
taxes were levied in Jerusalem are no longer to be levied.
40 If any of you are suitable for enrolment in our bodyguard, let them be enrolled, and let there be peace between
us.'
41 The gentile yoke was thus lifted from Israel in the year
170, 42 when our people began engrossing their documents
and contracts: 'In the first year of Simon, eminent high
priest, commander-in-chief and ethnarch of the Jews'.
43 About that time Simon laid siege to Gezer, surrounding
it with his troops. He constructed a mobile tower, brought it
up to the city, opened a breach in one of the bastions and
took it. 44 The men in the mobile tower sprang out into the
city, where great confusion ensued. 45 The citizens, accompanied by their wives and children, mounted the ramparts with
their garments torn and loudly implored Simon to make
peace with them: 46 'Treat us', they said, 'not as our wickedness deserves, but as your mercy prompts you.' 47 Simon
came to terms with them and stopped the fighting; but he
expelled them from the city, purified the houses which contained idols, and then made his entry with songs of praise.
48 He banished all impurity from it, settled in it people who
observed the Law, and having fortified it, built a residence
there for himself.

GREEK OLD TESTAMENT

49 Οἱ δὲ ἐκ τῆς ἄκρας ἐν Ιερουσαλημ ἐκωλύοντο ἐκπορεύεσθαι καὶ εἰσπορεύεσθαι εἰς τὴν χώραν ἀγοράζειν καὶ
πωλεῖν καὶ ἐπείνασαν σφόδρα, καὶ ἀπώλοντο ἐξ αὐτῶν ἱκανοὶ
τῷ λιμῷ. 50 καὶ ἐβόησαν πρὸς Σιμωνα δεξιὰς λαβεῖν, καὶ
ἔδωκεν αὐτοῖς. καὶ ἐξέβαλεν αὐτοὺς ἐκεῖθεν καὶ ἐκαθάρισεν
τὴν ἄκραν ἀπὸ τῶν μιασμάτων. 51 καὶ εἰσῆλθον εἰς αὐτὴν τῇ
τρίτῃ καὶ εἰκάδι τοῦ δευτέρου μηνὸς ἔτους πρώτου καὶ
ἑβδομηκοστοῦ καὶ ἑκατοστοῦ μετὰ αἰνέσεως καὶ βαΐων καὶ
ἐν κινύραις καὶ ἐν κυμβάλοις καὶ ἐν νάβλαις καὶ ἐν ὕμνοις
καὶ ἐν ᾠδαῖς, ὅτι συνετρίβη ἐχθρὸς μέγας ἐξ Ισραηλ. 52 καὶ
ἔστησεν κατ' ἐνιαυτὸν τοῦ ἄγειν τὴν ἡμέραν ταύτην μετὰ
εὐφροσύνης. καὶ προσωχύρωσεν τὸ ὄρος τοῦ ἱεροῦ τὸ παρὰ
τὴν ἄκραν· καὶ ᾤκει ἐκεῖ αὐτὸς καὶ οἱ παρ' αὐτοῦ. 53 καὶ
εἶδεν Σιμων τὸν Ιωαννην υἱὸν αὐτοῦ ὅτι ἀνήρ ἐστιν, καὶ
ἔθετο αὐτὸν ἡγούμενον τῶν δυνάμεων πασῶν· καὶ ᾤκει ἐν
Γαζαροις.

14 Καὶ ἐν ἔτει δευτέρῳ καὶ ἑβδομηκοστῷ καὶ ἑκατοστῷ
συνήγαγεν Δημήτριος ὁ βασιλεὺς τὰς δυνάμεις αὐτοῦ καὶ ἐπορεύθη εἰς Μηδίαν τοῦ ἐπισπάσασθαι βοήθειαν
ἑαυτῷ, ὅπως πολεμήσῃ τὸν Τρύφωνα. 2 καὶ ἤκουσεν Ἀρσά-
κης ὁ βασιλεὺς τῆς Περσίδος καὶ Μηδίας ὅτι εἰσῆλθεν
Δημήτριος εἰς τὰ ὅρια αὐτοῦ, καὶ ἀπέστειλεν ἕνα τῶν
ἀρχόντων αὐτοῦ συλλαβεῖν αὐτὸν ζῶντα. 3 καὶ ἐπορεύθη καὶ
ἐπάταξεν τὴν παρεμβολὴν Δημητρίου καὶ συνέλαβεν αὐτὸν
καὶ ἤγαγεν αὐτὸν πρὸς Ἀρσάκην, καὶ ἔθετο αὐτὸν ἐν
φυλακῇ.

KING JAMES VERSION

49 They also of the tower in Jerusalem were kept so strait, that they could neither come forth, nor go into the country, nor buy, nor sell: wherefore they were in great distress for want of victuals, and a great number of them perished through famine.

50 Then cried they to Simon, beseeching him to be at one with them: which thing he granted them; and when he had put them out from thence, he cleansed the tower from pollutions:

51 And entered into it the three and twentieth day of the second month, in the hundred seventy and first year, with thanksgiving, and branches of palm trees, and with harps, and cymbals, and with viols, and hymns, and songs: because there was destroyed a great enemy out of Israel.

52 He ordained also that that day should be kept every year with gladness. Moreover the hill of the temple that was by the tower he made stronger than it was, and there he dwelt himself with his company.

53 And when Simon saw that John his son was a valiant man, he made him captain of all the hosts: and he dwelt in Gazara.

14 Now in the hundred threescore and twelfth year king Demetrius gathered his forces together, and went into Media, to get him help to fight against Tryphon.

2 But when Arsaces, the king of Persia and Media, heard that Demetrius was entered within his borders, he sent one of his princes to take him alive:

3 Who went and smote the host of Demetrius, and took him, and brought him to Arsaces, by whom he was put in ward.

DOUAY OLD TESTAMENT

49 But they that were in the castle of Jerusalem were hindered from going out and coming into the country, and from buying and selling: and they were straitened with hunger, and many of them perished through famine.

50 And they cried to Simon for peace, and he granted it to them: and he cast them out from thence, and cleansed the castle from uncleannesses.

51 And they entered into it the three and twentieth day of the second month, in the year one hundred and seventy-one, with thanksgiving, and branches of palm trees, and harps, and cymbals, and psalteries, and hymns, and canticles, because the great enemy was destroyed out of Israel.

52 And he ordained that these days should be kept every year with gladness.

53 And he fortified the mountain of the temple that was near the castle, and he dwelt there himself, and they that were with him.

54 And Simon saw that John his son was a valiant man for war: and he made him captain of all the forces: and he dwelt in Gazara.

14 IN the year one hundred and seventy-two, king Demetrius assembled his army, and went into Media to get him succours to fight against Tryphon.

2 And Arsaces the king of Persia and Media heard that Demetrius was entered within his borders, and he sent one of his princes to take him alive, and bring him to him.

3 And he went and defeated the army of Demetrius: and took him, and brought him to Arsaces, and he put him into custody.

KNOX TRANSLATION

49 And what of the Gentiles that were left in Jerusalem
citadel? Enter Jewish territory or leave it they might not, buy
or sell they might not, so that they were hard put to it for
food, and many died of famine. 50 At last they cried out to
Simon, he should give them quarter, and give them quarter
he did, but drove them out, and cleansed the citadel of its
pollution. 51 On the twenty-third day of the second month, in
the hundred and seventy-first year, in came the Jewish folk
singing praise and bearing palm-branches, with music of
harp, and cymbals, and zither, and chanting of psalms; of
such ill neighbours Israel was now rid. 52 Every year, Simon
proclaimed, holiday should be kept at this time; 53 and he
fortified that part of the temple mountain which was close by
the citadel; here he dwelt, and his followers with him. 54 And
now here was his son John grown into a brave warrior; him
Simon put at the head of the whole army, with his quarters
at Gazara.

14 The year following, what must Demetrius do but
muster his army and betake himself to Media, where
he would raise levies for the war against Tryphon? 2 When
Arsaces, king of the Medes and Persians, had news of it, he
gave orders to one of his chieftains, the invader must be
taken alive and brought into his presence. 3 The order was
obeyed; the Syrian king, routed and captured, was brought
before Arsaces, who put him safely in prison.

TODAY'S ENGLISH VERSION

49 Those in the fort in Jerusalem were now prevented from leaving to buy or sell anything. They were suffering from severe hunger and many of them had died of starvation. 50 Finally they appealed to Simon for a truce. He agreed, removed them from the fort, and purified it. 51 On the twenty-third day of the second month, in the year 171,[a] there was a great celebration in the city because this terrible threat to the security of Israel had come to an end. Simon and his men entered the fort singing hymns of praise and thanksgiving, while carrying palm branches and playing harps, cymbals, and lyres. 52 Simon issued a decree that the day should be joyfully celebrated every year. He strengthened the defenses of the Temple hill on the side facing the fort, and he and his men made their headquarters there. 53 Simon's son John was now a grown man, so Simon made him commander of the whole army, and John set up headquarters at Gezer.

14 In the year 172[b] King Demetrius the Second gathered his army and went to Media to seek additional help for his war against Trypho. 2 When King Arsaces the Sixth of Persia and Media heard that Demetrius had entered his territory, he sent one of his commanders with some troops to capture Demetrius alive. 3 They attacked and defeated the army of Demetrius, took him captive, and brought him back to King Arsaces, who threw him in prison.

[a] THE YEAR 171: *This corresponds to 141 B.C.* [b] THE YEAR 172: *This corresponds to 140 B.C.*

NEW REVISED STANDARD VERSION

49 Those who were in the citadel at Jerusalem were prevented from going in and out to buy and sell in the country. So they were very hungry, and many of them perished from famine. 50 Then they cried to Simon to make peace with them, and he did so. But he expelled them from there and cleansed the citadel from its pollutions. 51 On the twenty-third day of the second month, in the one hundred seventy-first year,[a] the Jews[b] entered it with praise and palm branches, and with harps and cymbals and stringed instruments, and with hymns and songs, because a great enemy had been crushed and removed from Israel. 52 Simon[c] decreed that every year they should celebrate this day with rejoicing. He strengthened the fortifications of the temple hill alongside the citadel, and he and his men lived there. 53 Simon saw that his son John had reached manhood, and so he made him commander of all the forces; and he lived at Gazara.

14 In the one hundred seventy-second year[d] King Demetrius assembled his forces and marched into Media to obtain help, so that he could make war against Trypho. 2 When King Arsaces of Persia and Media heard that Demetrius had invaded his territory, he sent one of his generals to take him alive. 3 The general[c] went and defeated the army of Demetrius, and seized him and took him to Arsaces, who put him under guard.

a 141 B.C. *b* Gk *they* *c* Gk *He* *d* 140 B.C.

NEW AMERICAN BIBLE

49 The men in the citadel in Jerusalem were prevented from going out into the country and back for the purchase of food; they suffered greatly from hunger, and many of them died of starvation. 50 They finally cried out to Simon for peace, and he gave them peace. He expelled them from the citadel and cleansed it of impurities. 51 On the twenty-third day of the second month, in the year one hundred and seventy-one, the Jews entered the citadel with shouts of jubilation, waving of palm branches, the music of harps and cymbals and lyres, and the singing of hymns and canticles, because a great enemy of Israel had been destroyed. 52 Simon decreed that this day should be celebrated every year with rejoicing. He also strengthened the fortifications of the temple hill alongside the citadel, and he and his companions dwelt there. 53 Seeing that his son John was now a grown man, Simon made him commander of all his soldiers, with his residence in Gazara.

14 In the year one hundred and seventy-two, King Demetrius assembled his army and marched into Media to obtain help so that he could fight Trypho. 2 When Arsaces, king of Persia and Media, heard that Demetrius had invaded his territory, he sent one of his generals to take him alive. 3 The general went forth and defeated the army of Demetrius; he captured him and brought him to Arsaces, who put him in prison.

NEW JERUSALEM BIBLE

49 The occupants of the Citadel in Jerusalem, prevented as they were from coming out and going into the countryside to buy and sell, were in desperate need of food, and numbers of them were being carried off by starvation. 50 They begged Simon to make peace with them, and he granted this, though he expelled them and purified the Citadel from its pollutions. 51 The Jews made their entry on the twenty-third day of the second month in the year 171, with acclamations and carrying palms, to the sound of lyres, cymbals and harps, chanting hymns and canticles, since a great enemy had been crushed and thrown out of Israel. Simon made it a day of annual rejoicing. 52 He fortified the Temple hill on the Citadel side, and took up residence there with his men. 53 Since his son John had come to manhood, Simon appointed him general-in-chief, with his residence in Gezer.

14 In the year 172, King Demetrius assembled his forces and marched into Media to raise help for the fight against Trypho. 2 When Arsaces king of Persia and Media heard that Demetrius had entered his territory, he sent one of his generals to capture him alive. 3 The general defeated the army of Demetrius, seized him and brought him to Arsaces,

GREEK OLD TESTAMENT

4 Καὶ ἡσύχασεν ἡ γῆ Ιουδα πάσας τὰς ἡμέρας Σιμωνος,
καὶ ἐζήτησεν ἀγαθὰ τῷ ἔθνει αὐτοῦ, καὶ ἤρεσεν αὐτοῖς ἡ
ἐξουσία αὐτοῦ καὶ ἡ δόξα αὐτοῦ πάσας τὰς ἡμέρας. 5 καὶ
μετὰ πάσης τῆς δόξης αὐτοῦ ἔλαβεν τὴν Ιοππην εἰς λιμένα
καὶ ἐποίησεν εἴσοδον ταῖς νήσοις τῆς θαλάσσης. 6 καὶ
ἐπλάτυνεν τὰ ὅρια τῷ ἔθνει αὐτοῦ καὶ ἐκράτησεν τῆς χώρας.
7 καὶ συνήγαγεν αἰχμαλωσίαν πολλὴν καὶ ἐκυρίευσεν
Γαζαρων καὶ Βαιθσουρων καὶ τῆς ἄκρας. καὶ ἐξῆρεν τὰς
ἀκαθαρσίας ἐξ αὐτῆς, καὶ οὐκ ἦν ὁ ἀντικείμενος αὐτῷ. 8 καὶ
ἦσαν γεωργοῦντες τὴν γῆν αὐτῶν μετ᾽ εἰρήνης, καὶ ἡ γῆ
ἐδίδου τὰ γενήματα αὐτῆς καὶ τὰ ξύλα τῶν πεδίων τὸν
καρπὸν αὐτῶν. 9 πρεσβύτεροι ἐν ταῖς πλατείαις ἐκάθηντο,
πάντες περὶ ἀγαθῶν ἐκοινολογοῦντο, καὶ οἱ νεανίσκοι ἐνεδύ-
σαντο δόξας καὶ στολὰς πολέμου. 10 ταῖς πόλεσιν ἐχορήγησεν βρώματα καὶ ἔταξεν αὐτὰς ἐν σκεύεσιν ὀχυρώσεως,
ἕως ὅτου ὠνομάσθη τὸ ὄνομα τῆς δόξης αὐτοῦ ἕως ἄκρου
γῆς. 11 ἐποίησεν εἰρήνην ἐπὶ τῆς γῆς, καὶ εὐφράνθη Ισραηλ
εὐφροσύνην μεγάλην. 12 καὶ ἐκάθισεν ἕκαστος ὑπὸ τὴν
ἄμπελον αὐτοῦ καὶ τὴν συκῆν αὐτοῦ, καὶ οὐκ ἦν ὁ ἐκφοβῶν
αὐτούς. 13 καὶ ἐξέλιπεν πολεμῶν αὐτοὺς ἐπὶ τῆς γῆς, καὶ οἱ
βασιλεῖς συνετρίβησαν ἐν ταῖς ἡμέραις ἐκείναις. 14 καὶ

KING JAMES VERSION

4 As for the land *of Judea,* that was quiet all the days of Simon; for he sought the good of his nation in such wise, as that evermore his authority and honour pleased them well.

5 And as he was honourable in all his acts, so in this, that he took Joppe for an haven, and made an entrance to the isles of the sea,

6 And enlarged the bounds of his nation, and recovered the country,

7 And gathered together a great number of captives, and had the dominion of Gazara, and Bethsura, and the tower, out of the which he took all uncleanness, neither was there any that resisted him.

8 Then did they till their ground in peace, and the earth gave her increase, and the trees of the field their fruit.

9 The ancient men sat all in the streets, communing together of good things, and the young men put on glorious and warlike apparel.

10 He provided victuals for the cities, and set in them all manner of munition, so that his honourable name was renowned unto the end of the world.

11 He made peace in the land, and Israel rejoiced with great joy:

12 For every man sat under his vine and his fig tree, and there was none to fray them:

13 Neither was there any left in the land to fight against them: yea, the kings themselves were overthrown in those days.

DOUAY OLD TESTAMENT

4 And all the land of Juda was at rest all the days of Simon, and he sought the good of his nation: and his power, and his glory pleased them well all *his* days.

5 And with all his glory he took Joppe for a haven, and made an entrance to the isles of the sea.

6 And he enlarged the bounds of his nation, and made himself master of the country.

7 And he gathered together a great number of captives, and had the dominion of Gazara, and of Bethsura, and of the castle: and took away all uncleanness out of it, and there was none that resisted him.

8 And every man tilled his land with peace: and the land of Juda yielded her increase, and the trees of the fields their fruit.

9 The ancient men sat all in the streets, and treated together of the good things of the land, and the young men put on them glory, and the robes of war.

10 And he provided victuals for the cities, and he appointed that they should be furnished with ammunition, so that the fame of his glory was renowned even to the end of the earth.

11 He made peace in the land, and Israel rejoiced with great joy.

12 And every man sat under his vine, and under his fig tree: and there was none to make them afraid.

13 There was none left in the land to fight against them: kings were discomfited in those days.

KNOX TRANSLATION

4 Thus, during Simon's days, the whole land of Juda was at
peace. Ever his people's good sought he, and ever by willing
hearts was obeyed and honoured. 5 With great state he took
possession of Joppe as a harbour,[a] and so found access to
the islands out at sea. 6 How wide spread he the frontiers of
Israel, how firmly held its possessions, 7 captured how many
of its foes! Gazara and Bethsura he won, ay, and the Citadel
itself, ridding it of all defilement; there was no resisting his
power. 8 In his day, every man farmed his own lands in
security, soil of Juda yielded its crops, and the trees their
fruit; 9 sat old men in the market-place, busy over the common weal, and young men wore the livery of their glorious
campaigning. 10 Never a city but he furnished it with store of
provisions; a bulwark each of them should be of sturdy
defence. What wonder if the story of his renown was noised
to the world's end? 11 Such peaceful times brought he to his
country, when all Israel kept high holiday, 12 every man with
his own vine and fig-tree for shade, and enemy was none to
daunt them; 13 domestic malice undone, foreign tyranny
shattered all around! 14 Among his own folk, what comfort

a This is perhaps the best interpretation of a difficult phrase, 'With all his glory he received Joppe to be a harbour'. For the language used, cf. 10. 58, II Mac. 5. 20. Joppe had been captured by Jonathan (10. 76), and remained at least nominally in Jewish possession (12. 33; 13. 11); Simon's achievement, according to verse 34 below, was to fortify it.

TODAY'S ENGLISH VERSION

4 The land of Judea was at peace as long as Simon lived.
During his entire reign, he used his position of power and
influence to do what was good for his people, and they were
always pleased with him as their ruler. 5 He added to his
reputation when he captured the port of Joppa and opened
up the route to the Greek islands. 6 He not only enlarged the
territory of his nation and gained control of the whole country, 7 but he brought back many prisoners of war and captured Gezer, Bethzur, and the fort in Jerusalem. He purified
the fort, and there was no one to oppose him.
8 The Jews farmed their land in peace; the land produced
its crops and the trees bore fruit. 9 The young men showed
off their splendid military uniforms, while the old men sat
around the city squares and talked about the great things
that had happened. 10 Simon supplied the cities with food
and provided them with weapons of defense. His fame
spread everywhere. 11 He brought peace to the country, and
Israel's joy knew no bounds. 12 Everyone lived in peace
among his own grapevines and fig trees, and no one made
them afraid. 13 In those days all the enemy kings had been
defeated, and there was no one left in the land to fight the

NEW REVISED STANDARD VERSION

4 The land[a] had rest all the days of Simon.
He sought the good of his nation;
his rule was pleasing to them,
as was the honor shown him, all his days.
5 To crown all his honors he took Joppa for a harbor,
and opened a way to the isles of the sea.
6 He extended the borders of his nation,
and gained full control of the country.
7 He gathered a host of captives;
he ruled over Gazara and Beth-zur and the citadel,
and he removed its uncleanness from it;
and there was none to oppose him.
8 They tilled their land in peace;
the ground gave its increase,
and the trees of the plains their fruit.
9 Old men sat in the streets;
they all talked together of good things,
and the youths put on splendid military attire.
10 He supplied the towns with food,
and furnished them with the means of defense,
until his renown spread to the ends of the earth.
11 He established peace in the land,
and Israel rejoiced with great joy.
12 All the people sat under their own vines and fig trees,
and there was none to make them afraid.
13 No one was left in the land to fight them,
and the kings were crushed in those days.

a Other ancient authorities add *of Judah*

NEW AMERICAN BIBLE

4 The land was at rest all the days of Simon,
who sought the good of his nation.
His people were delighted with his power
and his magnificence throughout his reign.
5 As his crowning glory he captured the port of Joppa
and made it a gateway to the isles of the sea.
6 He enlarged the borders of his nation
and gained control of the country.
7 He took many enemies prisoners of war
and made himself master of Gazara, Beth-zur, and
the citadel.

He cleansed the citadel of its impurities;
there was no one to withstand him.
8 The people cultivated their land in peace;
the land yielded its produce
and the trees of the field their fruit.
9 Old men sat in the squares,
all talking about the good times,
while the young men wore the glorious apparel of war.
10 He supplied the cities with food
and equipped them with means of defense,
till his glorious name reached the ends of the earth.
11 He brought peace to the land,
and Israel was filled with happiness.
12 Every man sat under his vine and his fig tree,
with no one to disturb him.
13 No one was left to attack them in their land;
the kings in those days were crushed.

NEW JERUSALEM BIBLE

who imprisoned him. 4 The country was at peace throughout
the days of Simon.

He sought the good of his nation
and they were well pleased with his authority,
as with his magnificence, throughout his life.
5 To crown his titles to glory,
he took Joppa and made it a harbour,
gaining access to the Mediterranean Isles.
6 He enlarged the frontiers of his nation,
keeping his mastery over the homeland,
7 resettling a host of captives.
He conquered Gezer, Beth-Zur and the Citadel,
ridding them of every impurity,
and no one could resist him.
8 The people farmed their land in peace,
the land gave its produce,
the trees of the plain their fruit.
9 The elders sat at ease in the squares,
all their talk was of their prosperity;
the young men wore splendid armour.
10 He kept the towns supplied with provisions
and furnished with fortifications,
until his fame resounded to the ends of the earth.
11 He established peace in the land,
and Israel knew great joy.
12 Each man sat under his own vine and his own fig tree,
and there was no one to make them afraid.
13 No enemy was left in the land to fight them,
the very kings of those times had been crushed.

GREEK OLD TESTAMENT

ἐστήρισεν πάντας τοὺς ταπεινοὺς τοῦ λαοῦ αὐτοῦ· τὸν νόμον ἐξεζήτησεν καὶ ἐξῆρεν πάντα ἄνομον καὶ πονηρόν· [15] τὰ ἅγια ἐδόξασεν καὶ ἐπλήθυνεν τὰ σκεύη τῶν ἁγίων.

[16] Καὶ ἠκούσθη ἐν Ῥώμῃ ὅτι ἀπέθανεν Ιωναθαν καὶ ἕως Σπάρτης, καὶ ἐλυπήθησαν σφόδρα. [17] ὡς δὲ ἤκουσαν ὅτι Σιμων ὁ ἀδελφὸς αὐτοῦ γέγονεν ἀρχιερεὺς ἀντ' αὐτοῦ καὶ αὐτὸς ἐπικρατεῖ τῆς χώρας καὶ τῶν πόλεων τῶν ἐν αὐτῇ, [18] ἔγραψαν πρὸς αὐτὸν δέλτοις χαλκαῖς τοῦ ἀνανεώσασθαι πρὸς αὐτὸν φιλίαν καὶ συμμαχίαν, ἣν ἔστησαν πρὸς Ιουδαν καὶ Ιωναθαν τοὺς ἀδελφοὺς αὐτοῦ. [19] καὶ ἀνεγνώσθησαν ἐνώπιον τῆς ἐκκλησίας ἐν Ιερουσαλημ. [20] καὶ τοῦτο τὸ ἀντίγραφον τῶν ἐπιστολῶν, ὧν ἀπέστειλαν οἱ Σπαρτιᾶται

Σπαρτιατῶν ἄρχοντες καὶ ἡ πόλις Σιμωνι ἱερεῖ μεγάλῳ καὶ τοῖς πρεσβυτέροις καὶ τοῖς ἱερεῦσιν καὶ τῷ λοιπῷ δήμῳ τῶν Ιουδαίων ἀδελφοῖς χαίρειν. [21] οἱ πρεσβευταὶ οἱ ἀποσταλέντες πρὸς τὸν δῆμον ἡμῶν ἀπήγγειλαν ἡμῖν περὶ τῆς δόξης ὑμῶν καὶ τιμῆς, καὶ ηὐφράνθημεν ἐπὶ τῇ ἐφόδῳ αὐτῶν. [22] καὶ ἀνεγράψαμεν τὰ ὑπ' αὐτῶν εἰρημένα ἐν ταῖς βουλαῖς τοῦ δήμου οὕτως Νουμήνιος Ἀντιόχου καὶ Ἀντίπατρος Ἰάσονος πρεσβευταὶ Ιουδαίων ἦλθον πρὸς ἡμᾶς ἀνανεούμενοι τὴν πρὸς ἡμᾶς φιλίαν. [23] καὶ ἤρεσεν τῷ δήμῳ ἐπιδέξασθαι τοὺς ἄνδρας ἐνδόξως καὶ τοῦ θέσθαι τὸ ἀντίγραφον τῶν λόγων αὐτῶν ἐν τοῖς ἀποδεδειγμένοις τῷ δήμῳ βιβλίοις

KING JAMES VERSION

14 Moreover he strengthened all those of his people that were brought low: the law he searched out; and every contemner of the law and wicked person he took away.

15 He beautified the sanctuary, and multiplied the vessels of the temple.

16 Now when it was heard at Rome, and as far as Sparta, that Jonathan was dead, they were very sorry.

17 But as soon as they heard that his brother Simon was made high priest in his stead, and ruled the country, and the cities therein:

18 They wrote unto him in tables of brass, to renew the friendship and league which they had made with Judas and Jonathan his brethren:

19 Which writings were read before the congregation at Jerusalem.

20 And this is the copy of the letters that the Lacedemonians sent; The rulers of the Lacedemonians, with the city, unto Simon the high priest, and the elders, and priests, and residue of the people of the Jews, our brethren, *send* greeting:

21 The ambassadors that were sent unto our people certified us of your glory and honour: wherefore we were glad of their coming,

22 And did register the things that they spake in the council of the people in this manner; Numenius *son* of Antiochus, and Antipater *son* of Jason, the Jews' ambassadors, came unto us to renew the friendship they had with us.

23 And it pleased the people to entertain the men honourably, and to put the copy of their ambassage in publick records, to the end the people of the Lacedemonians might

DOUAY OLD TESTAMENT

14 And he strengthened all those of his people that were brought low, and he sought the law, and took away every unjust and wicked man.

15 He glorified the sanctuary, and multiplied the vessels of the holy places.

16 And it was heard at Rome, and as far as Sparta, that Jonathan was dead: and they were very sorry.

17 But when they heard that Simon his brother was made high priest in his place, and was possessed of all the country, and the cities therein:

18 They wrote to him in tables of brass, to renew the friendship and alliance which they had made with Judas, and with Jonathan his brethren.

19 And they were read before the assembly in Jerusalem. And this is the copy of the letters that the Spartans sent.

20 The princes and the cities of the Spartans to Simon the high priest, and to the ancients, and the priests, and the rest of the people of the Jews their brethren, greeting.

21 The ambassadors that were sent to our people, have told us of your glory, and honour, and joy: and we rejoiced at their coming.

22 And we registered what was said by them in the councils of the people in this manner: Numenius the son of Antiochus, and Antipater the son of Jason, ambassadors of the Jews, came to us to renew the former friendship with us.

23 And it pleased the people to receive the men honourably, and to put a copy of their words in the public

KNOX TRANSLATION

he gave the friendless, how scrutinized the law, what short work made of traitor and malcontent; [15] how adorned the sanctuary, how increased the number of its treasures!

[16] To Rome, to Sparta itself, came tidings of Jonathan's death, and was heard right sorrowfully. [17] When they learned that his brother Simon had been made high priest instead, master now of the land and all its cities, [18] they wrote to him on tablets made of bronze, to renew the treaty of friendship they had with his brethren, Judas and Jonathan, before him;[a] [19] and their letters were read out before the whole assembly at Jerusalem. The Spartans wrote in these words following: [20] The rulers and commonalty of Sparta, to the high priest Simon, the elders and priests and all the people of the Jews, greeting. [21] Welcome news your ambassadors have brought us, of fame and credit and prosperity you enjoy. [22] And their errand stands recorded in our public annals; how Numenius son of Antiochus and Antipater son of Jason came on the Jews' part to renew our old treaty of friendship with you; [23] how the people resolved to give them fair greeting, and to lay up a copy of their report in the public archives, that should preserve the memory of it

a The implication appears to be that both Rome and Sparta sent answers in the manner described.

TODAY'S ENGLISH VERSION

Jews. 14 Simon provided help for all the poor among his people, and guided by the Law of Moses, he eliminated all
wicked and lawless men. 15 He provided the Temple with
splendid furnishings and added a large number of utensils
for use in worship.

16 When the news that Jonathan had died reached Rome
and Sparta, it brought great sorrow. 17 But when the
Spartans heard that Simon had succeeded his brother as
High Priest and that he was in control of the country and its
towns, 18 they engraved on bronze tablets a renewal of the
treaty of friendship which they had made with his brothers
Judas and Jonathan and sent the tablets to him. 19 These
were read to the assembly in Jerusalem. 20 What follows is a
copy of the letter sent by the Spartans:

"The people of Sparta and their rulers to Simon the High
Priest, to the leaders and the priests of the Jews, and to all
our Jewish brothers, greetings. 21 The delegation that you
sent to our people has told us how respected and
renowned you are. Their visit has been a source of joy for
us, 22 and a report of their visit has been written down in
our public records, as follows: 'Numenius son of Antiochus
and Antipater son of Jason, honored representatives of the
Jews, appeared before us to renew their treaty of friendship. 23 The assembly of the people was pleased to receive
these men with all honors and to place a copy of their
report in the public archives, so that the people of Sparta

NEW REVISED STANDARD VERSION

14 He gave help to all the humble among his people;
he sought out the law,
and did away with all the renegades and outlaws.
15 He made the sanctuary glorious,
and added to the vessels of the sanctuary.

16 It was heard in Rome, and as far away as Sparta, that
Jonathan had died, and they were deeply grieved. 17 When
they heard that his brother Simon had become high priest in
his stead, and that he was ruling over the country and the
towns in it, 18 they wrote to him on bronze tablets to renew
with him the friendship and alliance that they had established with his brothers Judas and Jonathan. 19 And these
were read before the assembly in Jerusalem.

20 This is a copy of the letter that the Spartans sent:
"The rulers and the city of the Spartans to the high priest
Simon and to the elders and the priests and the rest of the
Jewish people, our brothers, greetings. 21 The envoys who
were sent to our people have told us about your glory and
honor, and we rejoiced at their coming. 22 We have recorded
what they said in our public decrees, as follows, 'Numenius
son of Antiochus and Antipater son of Jason, envoys of the
Jews, have come to us to renew their friendship with us. 23 It
has pleased our people to receive these men with honor and
to put a copy of their words in the public archives, so that

NEW AMERICAN BIBLE

14 He strengthened all the lowly among his people
and was zealous for the law;
he suppressed all the lawless and the wicked.
15 He made the temple splendid
and enriched its equipment.

16 When people heard in Rome and even in Sparta that
Jonathan had died, they were deeply grieved. 17 But when
the Romans heard that his brother Simon had been made
high priest in his place and was master of the country and
the cities, 18 they sent him inscribed tablets of bronze to
renew with him the friendship and alliance that they had
established with his brothers Judas and Jonathan. 19 These
were read before the assembly in Jerusalem.

20 This is a copy of the letter that the Spartans sent: "The
rulers and the citizens of Sparta send greetings to Simon the
high priest, the elders, the priests, and the rest of the Jewish
people, our brothers. 21 The envoys you sent to our people
have informed us of your glory and fame, and we were
happy that they came. 22 In accordance with what they said
we have recorded the following in the public decrees: Since
Numenius, son of Antiochus, and Antipater, son of Jason,
envoys of the Jews, have come to us to renew their friendship with us, 23 the people have voted to receive the men
with honor, and to deposit a copy of their words in the public

NEW JERUSALEM BIBLE

14 He encouraged the afflicted members of his people,
suppressing every wicked man and renegade.
He strove to observe the Law,
15 and gave new splendour to the Temple,
enriching it with many sacred vessels.

16 When it became known in Rome and as far as Sparta
that Jonathan was dead, people were deeply grieved. 17 But
as soon as they heard that his brother Simon had succeeded
him as high priest and was master of the country and the cities in it, 18 they wrote to him on bronze tablets to renew the
treaty of friendship and alliance which they had made with
his brothers, Judas and Jonathan, 19 and the document was
read out before the assembly in Jerusalem.

20 This is the copy of the letter sent by the Spartans:

'The rulers and the city of Sparta, to Simon the high priest
and to the elders and priests and the rest of the people of
the Jews, greetings.

21 'The ambassadors whom you sent to our people have
informed us of your glory and prosperity, and we are
delighted with their visit. 22 We have recorded their declarations in the minutes of our public assemblies, as follows,
"Numenius son of Antiochus, and Antipater son of Jason,
ambassadors of the Jews, came to us to renew their friendship with us. 23 And it was the people's pleasure to receive
these personages with honour and to deposit a copy of
their statements in the public archives, so that the people

GREEK OLD TESTAMENT

τοῦ μνημόσυνον ἔχειν τὸν δῆμον τῶν Σπαρτιατῶν. τὸ δὲ
ἀντίγραφον τούτων ἔγραψαν Σιμωνι τῷ ἀρχιερεῖ.
24 Μετὰ ταῦτα ἀπέστειλεν Σιμων τὸν Νουμήνιον εἰς Ῥώμην ἔχοντα ἀσπίδα χρυσῆν μεγάλην ὁλκὴν μνῶν χιλίων εἰς τὸ
στῆσαι πρὸς αὐτοὺς τὴν συμμαχίαν.
25 Ὡς δὲ ἤκουσεν ὁ δῆμος τῶν λόγων τούτων, εἶπαν Τίνα
χάριν ἀποδώσομεν Σιμωνι καὶ τοῖς υἱοῖς αὐτοῦ; 26 ἐστήρισεν γὰρ αὐτὸς καὶ οἱ ἀδελφοὶ αὐτοῦ καὶ ὁ οἶκος τοῦ πατρὸς
αὐτοῦ καὶ ἐπολέμησεν τοὺς ἐχθροὺς Ισραηλ ἀπ᾽ αὐτῶν καὶ
ἔστησαν αὐτῷ ἐλευθερίαν. καὶ κατέγραψαν ἐν δέλτοις
χαλκαῖς καὶ ἔθεντο ἐν στήλαις ἐν ὄρει Σιων. 27 καὶ τοῦτο τὸ
ἀντίγραφον τῆς γραφῆς

Ὀκτωκαιδεκάτῃ Ελουλ ἔτους δευτέρου καὶ ἑβδομηκοστοῦ
καὶ ἑκατοστοῦ — καὶ τοῦτο τρίτον ἔτος ἐπὶ Σιμωνος
ἀρχιερέως μεγάλου ἐν ασαραμελ, — 28 ἐπὶ συναγωγῆς μεγάλης ἱερέων καὶ λαοῦ καὶ ἀρχόντων ἔθνους καὶ τῶν πρεσβυτέρων τῆς χώρας ἐγνώρισεν ἡμῖν· 29 ἐπεὶ πολλάκις ἐγενήθησαν πόλεμοι ἐν τῇ χώρᾳ, Σιμων δὲ υἱὸς Ματταθιου ἱερεὺς
τῶν υἱῶν Ιωαριβ καὶ οἱ ἀδελφοὶ αὐτοῦ ἔδωκαν αὐτοὺς τῷ
κινδύνῳ καὶ ἀντέστησαν τοῖς ὑπεναντίοις τοῦ ἔθνους αὐτῶν,
ὅπως σταθῇ τὰ ἅγια αὐτῶν καὶ ὁ νόμος, καὶ δόξῃ μεγάλῃ
ἐδόξασαν τὸ ἔθνος αὐτῶν. 30 καὶ ἤθροισεν Ιωναθαν τὸ ἔθνος
αὐτῶν καὶ ἐγενήθη αὐτοῖς ἀρχιερεὺς καὶ προσετέθη πρὸς

KING JAMES VERSION

have a memorial thereof: furthermore we have written a
copy thereof unto Simon the high priest.
24 After this Simon sent Numenius to Rome with a great
shield of gold of a thousand pound weight, to confirm the
league with them.
25 Whereof when the people heard, they said, What
thanks shall we give to Simon and his sons?
26 For he and his brethren and the house of his father
have established Israel, and chased away in fight their enemies from them, and confirmed their liberty.
27 So then they wrote *it* in tables of brass, which they set
upon pillars in mount Sion: and this is the copy of the writing; The eighteenth day of *the month* Elul, in the hundred
threescore and twelfth year, being the third year of Simon
the high priest,
28 At Saramel in the great congregation of the priests,
and people, and rulers of the nation, and elders of the country, were these things notified unto us.
29 Forasmuch as oftentimes there have been wars in the
country, wherein for the maintenance of their sanctuary, and
the law, Simon the son of Mattathias, of the posterity of
Jarib, together with his brethren, put themselves in jeopardy,
and resisting the enemies of their nation did their nation
great honour:
30 (For after that Jonathan, having gathered his nation
together, and been their high priest, was added to his people,

DOUAY OLD TESTAMENT

records, to be a memorial to the people of the Spartans. And
we have written a copy of them to Simon the high priest.
24 And after this Simon sent Numenius to Rome, with a
great shield of gold of the weight of a thousand pounds, to
confirm the league with them. And when the people of Rome
had heard
25 These words, they said: What thanks shall we give to
Simon, and his sons?
26 For he hath restored his brethren, and hath driven
away in fight the enemies of Israel from them: and they
decreed him liberty, and registered it in tables of brass, and
set it upon pillars in mount Sion.
27 And this is a copy of the writing: The eighteenth day of
the month Elul, in the year one hundred and seventy-two,
being the third year under Simon the high priest at Asaramel,
28 In a great assembly of the priests, and of the people,
and the princes of the nation, and the ancients of the country, these things were notified: Forasmuch as there have
often been wars in our country,
29 And Simon the son of Mathathias of the children of
Jarib, and his brethren have put themselves in danger, and
resisted the enemies of their nation, for the maintenance of
their holy places, and the law: and have raised their nation
to great glory.
30 And Jonathan gathered together his nation, and was
made their high priest, and he was laid to his people.

KNOX TRANSLATION

among the Spartan people; and how an account of all this
was sent to the high priest Simon.
24 Numenius was sent on a further mission to Rome, bearing a great target of gold, a thousand minas in weight, to
renew the alliance there. And when all this reached the ears
of the people...[a]
25 ...Men began to ask, how they could shew their gratitude to Simon, and to his sons? 26 Here was one that had
restored the fortunes of his race, and rid Israel of its foes. So
they gave him exemption from public burdens, and inscribed
their decree on tablets of bronze, fastened to pillars which
were set up on mount Sion.
27 And thus the inscription ran: On this eighteenth day of
Elul, in the hundred and seventy-second year of the Greek
empire, the third of Simon's high priesthood, 28 there was a
high assembly held at Saramel[b] of priests and people, clan-
chiefs and elders of the whole nation, that had before them
these considerations following. All through the long wars of
our country, 29 Simon and his brethren, sons of Mattathias,
of Jarib's clan, put their lives in peril, and fought for law and
sanctuary against the common enemy, much glory winning
for their own nation. 30 When Jonathan, that had rallied the
people and been their high priest, became a part of his race,

a v. 24. It would be natural to assume that the end of this verse refers to the Roman people; and the Clementine Vulgate, without any manuscript authority, actually inserts the word 'Roman'. But the proceedings of verses 25 sqq. are evidently those of the Jewish people. There is a want of sequence in the narrative as it stands, and it seems possible that verses 15-24 of chapter 15 originally stood here, and were accidentally misplaced; if so, 'all this' will refer to the Roman dispatches. *b* This name is not found elsewhere, and probably conceals some error in the text.

TODAY'S ENGLISH VERSION

may have it on record. A copy of this document has been made for the High Priest Simon.' "
24 Later, Simon sent Numenius to Rome with the gift of a large gold shield weighing half a ton, to confirm the Jews' alliance with the Romans.
25 When the people of Israel heard about all this, they asked themselves, "How can we express our thanks to Simon and his sons? 26 He, his brothers, and his father's whole family have been towers of strength for our nation. They have fought off our enemies and set the nation free."

So they recorded this on bronze tablets and set them up on columns on Mount Zion. 27 The inscription read as follows:

"On the eighteenth day of the month of Elul in the year 172,[a] that is, in the third year of Simon, the High Priest,[b]
28 at a great assembly of priests, people, officials, and national leaders the following facts were made known to
us: 29 Often when wars broke out in the country, Simon son of Mattathias, a priest of the Jehoiarib family, and his brothers risked their lives in protecting our nation, our Temple, and our Law against our enemies. They have brought great glory to our nation. 30 Jonathan united our
people and became the High Priest before he died. 31 The

[a] THE YEAR 172: *This corresponds to 140 B.C.* [b] *Greek has an additional word, the meaning of which is unclear.*

NEW REVISED STANDARD VERSION

the people of the Spartans may have a record of them. And they have sent a copy of this to the high priest Simon.' "
24 After this Simon sent Numenius to Rome with a large gold shield weighing one thousand minas, to confirm the alliance with the Romans.[a]
25 When the people heard these things they said, "How
shall we thank Simon and his sons? 26 For he and his brothers and the house of his father have stood firm; they have fought and repulsed Israel's enemies and established its freedom." 27 So they made a record on bronze tablets and put it on pillars on Mount Zion.

This is a copy of what they wrote: "On the eighteenth day of Elul, in the one hundred seventy-second year,[b] which is
the third year of the great high priest Simon, 28 in
Asaramel,[c] in the great assembly of the priests and the people and the rulers of the nation and the elders of the country, the following was proclaimed to us:
29 "Since wars often occurred in the country, Simon son of Mattathias, a priest of the sons[d] of Joarib, and his brothers, exposed themselves to danger and resisted the enemies of their nation, in order that their sanctuary and the law might be preserved; and they brought great glory to their
nation. 30 Jonathan rallied the[e] nation, became their high
priest, and was gathered to his people. 31 When their

a Gk *them* *b* 140 B.C. *c* This word resembles the Hebrew words for *the court of the people of God* or *the prince of the people of God*
d Meaning of Gk uncertain *e* Gk *their*

NEW AMERICAN BIBLE

archives, so that the people of Sparta may have a record of them. A copy of this decree has been made for Simon the high priest."
24 After this, Simon sent Numenius to Rome with a great gold shield weighing a thousand minas, to confirm the alliance with the Romans.
25 When the people heard of these things, they said, "How
can we thank Simon and his sons? 26 He and his brothers and his father's house have stood firm and repulsed Israel's enemies. They have thus preserved its liberty." So they made an inscription on bronze tablets, which they affixed to pillars
on Mount Zion. 27 The following is a copy of the inscription:

"On the eighteenth day of Elul, in the year one hundred and seventy-two, that is, the third year under Simon the high
priest in Asaramel, 28 in a great assembly of priests, people, rulers of the nation, and elders of the country, the following proclamation was made:
29 " 'Since there have often been wars in our country, Simon, son of the priest Mattathias, descendant of Joarib, and his brothers have put themselves in danger and resisted the enemies of their nation, so that their sanctuary and law might be maintained, and they have thus brought great glory
to their nation. 30 After Jonathan had rallied his nation and become their high priest, he was gathered to his kinsmen.

NEW JERUSALEM BIBLE

of Sparta might preserve a record of them. A copy was also made for Simon the high priest." '

24 After this, Simon sent Numenius to Rome as the bearer of a large golden shield weighing a thousand *mina*, to confirm the alliance with them.

25 When these events were reported to our people, they
said, 'What mark of appreciation shall we give to Simon and
his sons? 26 He stood firm, he and his brothers and his father's house: he fought off the enemies of Israel and secured its freedom.' So they recorded an inscription on
bronze tablets and set it up on pillars on Mount Zion. 27 This
is a copy of the text:

'The eighteenth of Elul, in the year 172, being the third year of Simon, eminent high priest:

28 'In Asaramel, in the Grand Assembly of priests and people, of princes of the nation and of elders of the country:

'We are acquainted with the matters following:

29 'When there was almost incessant fighting in the country Simon, son of Mattathias, a priest of the line of Joarib, and his brothers courted danger and withstood their nation's enemies to safeguard the integrity of their sanctuary and of the Law, and so brought their nation great glory;

30 'For when, Jonathan having rallied his nation and become its high priest and having then been gathered to

GREEK OLD TESTAMENT

τὸν λαὸν αὐτοῦ, 31 καὶ ἐβουλήθησαν οἱ ἐχθροὶ αὐτῶν ἐμβατεῦσαι εἰς τὴν χώραν αὐτῶν καὶ ἐκτεῖναι χεῖρας ἐπὶ τὰ
ἅγια αὐτῶν· 32 τότε ἀντέστη Σιμων καὶ ἐπολέμησε περὶ τοῦ
ἔθνους αὐτοῦ καὶ ἐδαπάνησεν χρήματα πολλὰ τῶν ἑαυτοῦ
καὶ ὁπλοδότησεν τοὺς ἄνδρας τῆς δυνάμεως τοῦ ἔθνους αὐτοῦ καὶ ἔδωκεν αὐτοῖς ὀψώνια 33 καὶ ὠχύρωσεν τὰς πόλεις
τῆς Ιουδαίας καὶ τὴν Βαιθσουραν τὴν ἐπὶ τῶν ὁρίων τῆς
Ιουδαίας, οὗ ἦν τὰ ὅπλα τῶν πολεμίων τὸ πρότερον, καὶ
ἔθετο ἐκεῖ φρουρὰν ἄνδρας Ιουδαίους. 34 καὶ Ιοππην ὠχύρωσεν τὴν ἐπὶ τῆς θαλάσσης καὶ τὴν Γαζαραν τὴν ἐπὶ τῶν
ὁρίων Ἀζώτου, ἐν ᾗ ᾤκουν οἱ πολέμιοι τὸ πρότερον, καὶ
κατῴκισεν ἐκεῖ Ιουδαίους, καὶ ὅσα ἐπιτήδεια ἦν πρὸς τῇ
τούτων ἐπανορθώσει, ἔθετο ἐν αὐτοῖς. 35 καὶ εἶδεν ὁ λαὸς
τὴν πίστιν τοῦ Σιμωνος καὶ τὴν δόξαν, ἣν ἐβουλεύσατο ποιῆσαι τῷ ἔθνει αὐτοῦ, καὶ ἔθεντο αὐτὸν ἡγούμενον αὐτῶν καὶ
ἀρχιερέα διὰ τὸ αὐτὸν πεποιηκέναι πάντα ταῦτα καὶ τὴν
δικαιοσύνην καὶ τὴν πίστιν, ἣν συνετήρησεν τῷ ἔθνει αὐτοῦ,
καὶ ἐξεζήτησεν παντὶ τρόπῳ ὑψῶσαι τὸν λαὸν αὐτοῦ. 36 καὶ
ἐν ταῖς ἡμέραις αὐτοῦ εὐοδώθη ἐν ταῖς χερσὶν αὐτοῦ τοῦ
ἐξαρθῆναι τὰ ἔθνη ἐκ τῆς χώρας αὐτῶν καὶ τοὺς ἐν τῇ πόλει
Δαυιδ τοὺς ἐν Ιερουσαλημ, οἳ ἐποίησαν αὐτοῖς ἄκραν, ἐξ ἧς
ἐξεπορεύοντο καὶ ἐμίαινον κύκλῳ τῶν ἁγίων καὶ ἐποίουν
πληγὴν μεγάλην ἐν τῇ ἁγνείᾳ. 37 καὶ κατῴκισεν ἐν αὐτῇ
ἄνδρας Ιουδαίους καὶ ὠχύρωσεν αὐτὴν πρὸς ἀσφάλειαν τῆς
χώρας καὶ τῆς πόλεως καὶ ὕψωσεν τὰ τείχη τῆς Ιερουσαλημ.
38 καὶ ὁ βασιλεὺς Δημήτριος ἔστησεν αὐτῷ τὴν ἀρχιερωσύνην κατὰ ταῦτα 39 καὶ ἐποίησεν αὐτὸν τῶν φίλων αὐτοῦ καὶ

KING JAMES VERSION

31 Their enemies purposed to invade their country, that they might destroy it, and lay hands on the sanctuary:

32 At which time Simon rose up, and fought for his nation, and spent much of his own substance, and armed the valiant men of his nation and gave them wages,

33 And fortified the cities of Judea, together with Bethsura, that lieth upon the borders of Judea, where the armour of the enemies had been before; but he set a garrison of Jews there:

34 Moreover he fortified Joppe, which lieth upon the sea, and Gazara, that bordereth upon Azotus, where the enemies had dwelt before: but he placed Jews there, and furnished them with all things convenient for the reparation thereof.)

35 The people therefore, seeing the acts of Simon, and unto what glory he thought to bring his nation, made him their governor and chief priest, because he had done all these things, and for the justice and faith which he kept to his nation, and for that he sought by all means to exalt his people.

36 For in his time things prospered in his hands, so that the heathen were taken out of their country, and they also that were in the city of David in Jerusalem, who had made themselves a tower, out of which they issued, and polluted all about the sanctuary, and did much hurt in the holy place:

37 But he placed Jews therein, and fortified it for the safety of the country and the city, and raised up the walls of Jerusalem.

38 King Demetrius also confirmed him in the high priesthood according to those things,

39 And made him one of his friends, and honoured him with great honour.

DOUAY OLD TESTAMENT

31 And their enemies desired to tread down and destroy their country, and to stretch forth their hands against their holy places.

32 Then Simon resisted and fought for his nation, and laid out much of his money, and armed the valiant men of his nation, and gave them wages:

33 And he fortified the cities of Judea, and Bethsura that lieth in the borders of Judea, where the armour of the enemies was before: and he placed there a garrison of Jews.

34 And he fortified Joppe which lieth by the sea: and Gazara, which bordereth upon Azotus, wherein the enemies dwelt before, and he placed Jews here: and furnished them with all things convenient for their reparation.

35 And the people seeing the acts of Simon, and to what glory he meant to bring his nation, made him their prince, and high priest, because he had done all these things, and for the justice, and faith, which he kept to his nation, and for that he sought by all means to advance his people.

36 And in his days things prospered in his hands, so that the heathens were taken away out of their country, and they also that were in the city of David in Jerusalem in the castle, out of which they issued forth, and profaned all places round about the sanctuary, and did much evil to its purity.

37 And he placed therein Jews for the defence of the country, and of the city, and he raised up the walls of Jerusalem.

38 And king Demetrius confirmed him in the high priesthood.

39 According to these things he made him his friend, and glorified him with great glory.

KNOX TRANSLATION

31 enemies thought to invade the country and crush the power
of it, violate its holy places; 32 and Simon it was withstood
them. Champion of his people's cause, much he spent to arm
its warriors, and furnish them with pay. 33 Juda's cities he
fortified, and others besides; Bethsura on the frontiers, once a
stronghold of the enemy, garrisoned now by Jews, 34 Joppe on
the sea-coast, and Gazara in the Azotus region; Gazara, too,
once hostile, with Jewish troops manned he, and in each
town made provision for repairs to be done.
35 The people, seeing him so loyal a lover of his country's
renown, made him their ruler and high priest; no less was
due to such exploits, public service so faithfully done, such
constant ambition for his people's honour. 36 In his days it
was, and by his means, the land was rid at last of Gentile
intruders; not least the garrison of David's own Keep at
Jerusalem, that by their sallying out profaned the sacred
precincts, and much defiled their purity; 37 a Jewish garrison
he set there, to guard both city and country-side, and built
Jerusalem walls yet higher. 38 High priesthood of his, king
Demetrius must needs acknowledge, 39 bestowing on him
the title of king's friend, and loading him with honours.

TODAY'S ENGLISH VERSION

enemies of the Jews plotted to invade the land and defile
the Temple. 32 Then Simon assumed command and fought
for his country. He spent a large amount of his own money
to provide weapons and wages for his nation's armed
forces. 33 He fortified the towns of Judea, and especially
Bethzur on the border, where enemy weapons had previously been stored. He stationed a detachment of soldiers
there. 34 He fortified the seaport of Joppa and the city of
Gezer on the border of Azotus, which was previously occupied by enemy soldiers. He settled Jews there and provided
the towns with everything that the people needed.[a]
35 When the people saw Simon's patriotism and how he
wanted to bring glory to his nation, they made him their
leader and High Priest. They did this because of all that he
had accomplished through his loyalty and because he had
brought about justice and had tried in every way to bring
glory to his nation.
36 "Under his leadership the Gentiles were driven out of
the land. Enemy soldiers were forced out of the area north
of the Temple, where they had built the fort, from which
the soldiers used to go out and defile the holy Temple.
37 Simon settled Jews in the fort, strengthened it for the
security of the country and the city of Jerusalem, and
increased the height of the city walls. 38 As a result, King
Demetrius confirmed him as High Priest, 39 gave him the
title of "Friend of the King," and treated him with great

[a] that the people needed; *or* that was needed to keep them in repair.

NEW REVISED STANDARD VERSION

enemies decided to invade their country and lay hands on
their sanctuary, 32 then Simon rose up and fought for his
nation. He spent great sums of his own money; he armed the
soldiers of his nation and paid them wages. 33 He fortified
the towns of Judea, and Beth-zur on the borders of Judea,
where formerly the arms of the enemy had been stored, and
he placed there a garrison of Jews. 34 He also fortified Joppa,
which is by the sea, and Gazara, which is on the borders of
Azotus, where the enemy formerly lived. He settled Jews
there, and provided in those towns[a] whatever was necessary
for their restoration.
35 "The people saw Simon's faithfulness[b] and the glory
that he had resolved to win for his nation, and they made
him their leader and high priest, because he had done all
these things and because of the justice and loyalty that he
had maintained toward his nation. He sought in every way
to exalt his people. 36 In his days things prospered in his
hands, so that the Gentiles were put out of the[c] country, as
were also those in the city of David in Jerusalem, who had
built themselves a citadel from which they used to sally forth
and defile the environs of the sanctuary, doing great damage
to its purity. 37 He settled Jews in it and fortified it for the
safety of the country and of the city, and built the walls of
Jerusalem higher.
38 "In view of these things King Demetrius confirmed him
in the high priesthood, 39 made him one of his Friends, and

[a] Gk *them* [b] Other ancient authorities read *conduct* [c] Gk *their*

NEW AMERICAN BIBLE

31 When the enemies of the Jews sought to invade and devastate their country and to lay hands on their temple, 32 Simon
rose up and fought for his nation, spending large sums of his
own money to equip the men of his nation's armed forces
and giving them their pay. 33 He fortified the cities of Judea,
especially the frontier city of Beth-zur, where he stationed a
garrison of Jewish soldiers, and where previously the enemy's arms had been stored. 34 He also fortified Joppa by the
sea and Gazara on the border of Azotus, a place previously
occupied by the enemy; these cities he resettled with Jews,
and furnished them with all that was necessary for their
restoration. 35 When the Jewish people saw Simon's loyalty
and the glory he planned to bring to his nation, they made
him their leader and high priest because of all he had accomplished and the loyalty and justice he had shown his nation.
In every way he sought to exalt his people.
36 " 'In his time and under his guidance they succeeded in
driving the Gentiles out of their country, especially those in
the City of David in Jerusalem, who had built for themselves
a citadel from which they used to sally forth to defile the
environs of the temple and inflict grave injury on its purity.
37 In this citadel he stationed Jewish soldiers, and he
strengthened its fortifications for the defense of the land and
the city, while he also raised the wall of Jerusalem to a
greater height. 38 Consequently, King Demetrius confirmed
him in the high priesthood, 39 made him one of his Friends,
and conferred the highest honors on him. 40 He had indeed

NEW JERUSALEM BIBLE

his ancestors, 31 the enemy planned to invade the country,
intending to devastate their territory and to lay hands on
their sanctuary, 32 Simon next came forward to fight for
his nation: spending much of his personal wealth on arming his nation's fighting men and on providing their pay;
33 fortifying the towns of Judaea, as well as Beth-Zur on
the Judaean frontier where the enemy arsenal had formerly
been, and stationing in it a garrison of Jewish soldiers;
34 fortifying Joppa on the coast, and Gezer on the borders
of Azotus, a place formerly inhabited by the enemy, founding a Jewish colony there, and providing the settlers with
everything they needed to set them on their feet;
35 'In consequence of which, the people, aware of Simon's
loyalty and of the glory which he was determined to win for
his nation, have made him their ethnarch and high priest,
for all his services and for the integrity and loyalty which
he has shown towards his nation, and for having by every
means sought to enhance his people's power;
36 'It has fallen to him in his time to expel the foreigners
from his country, including those in the City of David in
Jerusalem, who had converted it into a citadel for their
own use, from which they would sally out to defile the sur-
roundings of the sanctuary and to violate its sacred character; 37 to station Jewish soldiers there instead for the
security of the country and the city; and to heighten the
walls of Jerusalem;
38 'And since King Demetrius has heard that the Romans
call the Jews their friends, allies and brothers, 39 and that
they have given an honourable reception to Simon's

GREEK OLD TESTAMENT

ἐδόξασεν αὐτὸν δόξῃ μεγάλῃ. 40 ἤκουσεν γὰρ ὅτι προσηγόρ-
ευνται οἱ Ιουδαῖοι ὑπὸ Ῥωμαίων φίλοι καὶ σύμμαχοι καὶ
ἀδελφοί, καὶ ὅτι ἀπήντησαν τοῖς πρεσβευταῖς Σιμωνος ἐνδόξως, 41 καὶ ὅτι οἱ Ιουδαῖοι καὶ οἱ ἱερεῖς εὐδόκησαν τοῦ εἶναι
αὐτῶν Σιμωνα ἡγούμενον καὶ ἀρχιερέα εἰς τὸν αἰῶνα ἕως
τοῦ ἀναστῆναι προφήτην πιστὸν 42 καὶ τοῦ εἶναι ἐπ' αὐτῶν
στρατηγόν, καὶ ὅπως μέλῃ αὐτῷ περὶ τῶν ἁγίων καθιστάναι
δι' αὐτοῦ ἐπὶ τῶν ἔργων αὐτῶν καὶ ἐπὶ τῆς χώρας καὶ ἐπὶ
τῶν ὅπλων καὶ ἐπὶ τῶν ὀχυρωμάτων, 43 καὶ ὅπως μέλῃ αὐτῷ
περὶ τῶν ἁγίων, καὶ ὅπως ἀκούηται ὑπὸ πάντων, καὶ ὅπως
γράφωνται ἐπὶ τῷ ὀνόματι αὐτοῦ πᾶσαι συγγραφαὶ ἐν τῇ
χώρᾳ, καὶ ὅπως περιβάλληται πορφύραν καὶ χρυσοφορῇ·
44 καὶ οὐκ ἐξέσται οὐθενὶ τοῦ λαοῦ καὶ τῶν ἱερέων ἀθετῆσαί
τι τούτων καὶ ἀντειπεῖν τοῖς ὑπ' αὐτοῦ ῥηθησομένοις καὶ
ἐπισυστρέψαι συστροφὴν ἐν τῇ χώρᾳ ἄνευ αὐτοῦ καὶ περι-
βάλλεσθαι πορφύραν καὶ ἐμπορποῦσθαι πόρπην χρυσῆν·
45 ὃς δ' ἂν παρὰ ταῦτα ποιήσῃ ἢ ἀθετήσῃ τι τούτων, ἔνοχος
ἔσται. 46 καὶ εὐδόκησεν πᾶς ὁ λαὸς θέσθαι Σιμωνι ποιῆσαι
κατὰ τοὺς λόγους τούτους. 47 καὶ ἐπεδέξατο Σιμων καὶ
εὐδόκησεν ἀρχιερατεύειν καὶ εἶναι στρατηγὸς καὶ ἐθνάρχης
τῶν Ιουδαίων καὶ ἱερέων καὶ τοῦ προστατῆσαι πάντων.
48 καὶ τὴν γραφὴν ταύτην εἶπον θέσθαι ἐν δέλτοις χαλκαῖς
καὶ στῆσαι αὐτὰς ἐν περιβόλῳ τῶν ἁγίων ἐν τόπῳ ἐπισήμῳ,

KING JAMES VERSION

40 For he had heard say, that the Romans had called the Jews their friends and confederates and brethren; and that they had entertained the ambassadors of Simon honourably;

41 Also that the Jews and priests were well pleased that Simon should be their governor and high priest for ever, until there should arise a faithful prophet;

42 Moreover that he should be their captain, and should take charge of the sanctuary, to set them over their works, and over the country, and over the armour, and over the fortresses, that, *I say,* he should take charge of the sanctuary;

43 Beside this, that he should be obeyed of every man, and that all the writings in the country should be made in his name, and that he should be clothed in purple, and wear gold:

44 Also that it should be lawful for none of the people or priests to break any of these things, or to gainsay his words, or to gather an assembly in the country without him, or to be clothed in purple, or wear a buckle of gold:

45 And whosoever should do otherwise, or break any of these things, he should be punished.

46 Thus it liked all the people to deal with Simon, and to do as hath been said.

47 Then Simon accepted hereof, and was well pleased to be high priest, and captain and governor of the Jews and priests, and to defend them all.

48 So they commanded that this writing should be put in tables of brass, and that they should be set up within the compass of the sanctuary in a conspicuous place;

DOUAY OLD TESTAMENT

40 For he had heard that the Romans had called the Jews their friends, and confederates, and brethren, and that they had received Simon's ambassadors with honour:

41 And that the Jews, and their priests, had consented that he should be their prince, and high priest for ever, till there should arise a faithful prophet:

42 And that he should be chief over them, and that he should have the charge of the sanctuary, and that he should appoint rulers over their works, and over the country, and over the armour, and over the strong holds.

43 And that he should have care of the holy places: and that he should be obeyed by all, and that all the writings in the country should be made in his name: and that he should be clothed with purple, and gold:

44 And that it should not be lawful for any of the people, or of the priests, to disannul any of these things, or to gainsay his words, or to call together an assembly in the country without him: or to be clothed with purple, or to wear a buckle of gold:

45 And whosoever shall do otherwise, or shall make void any of these things shall be punished.

46 And it pleased all the people to establish Simon, and to do according to these words.

47 And Simon accepted thereof, and was well pleased to execute the office of the high priesthood, and to be captain, and prince of the nation of the Jews, and of the priests, and to be chief over all.

48 And they commanded that this writing should be put in tables of brass, and that they should be set up within the compass of the sanctuary, in a conspicuous place:

KNOX TRANSLATION

What could he do else? 40 Here was Rome itself greeting the
Jewish folk as allies, good friends, and kinsmen, welcoming
the envoys of Simon with civic state. 41 Here were the Jews,
priests and people both, agreed that he should rule them,
granting him the high priesthood[a] by right inalienable, until
true prophet they should have once more. 42 Their ruler he
should be, and guardian of their temple; appoint officer and
magistrate, master of ordnance and captain of garrison,
43 and have charge of the sanctuary besides. Him all must
obey, in his name deeds be drawn up, all the country
through; of purple and gold should be his vesture. 44 Of the
rest, both priests and people, none should retrench these
privileges, nor gainsay Simon's will, nor convoke assembly
in the country without him; garment of purple, buckle of
gold none should wear; 45 nor any man defy or void this
edict, but at his peril.
46 The people's pleasure it was to ennoble Simon after this
sort; 47 and Simon, he would not say them nay; high priest,
and of priests and people leader, governor and champion, he
would be henceforward. 48 So they had the decree inscribed
on tablets of bronze, and set up plain to view in the temple

a The Machabaean high priesthood seems to have been regarded as an emergency dispensation. For the mention of the prophet, cf. 4. 46.

TODAY'S ENGLISH VERSION

honor. 40 Demetrius did this because he had heard that the
Romans were calling the Jews their friends, allies, and
brothers and that they had received Simon's delegation
with full honors.

41 "Therefore,[a] the Jews and their priests are happy to
have Simon and his descendants as their leaders and High
Priests, until a true prophet appears. 42 Simon shall govern
their country, have charge of the Temple, and shall be their
military commander. He shall be in charge of military supplies, fortifications, and public works. 43 The people must
obey him in everything. All government contracts shall be
drawn up in his name. He shall have the right to wear
royal robes with the gold shoulder buckle.

44 "No one, priest or people, shall have the legal right to
annul any of these decisions, to alter or change any of
Simon's orders, to convene any assembly in the country
without his permission, or to wear royal robes with the
gold shoulder buckle. 45 Anyone who disobeys or disregards these regulations shall be subject to punishment.

46 "The people gave their unanimous approval to grant
Simon the right to act in accordance with these regulations. 47 Simon consented and agreed to be supreme
leader: High Priest, commander of the armies, and governor of the Jews and the priests."

48 It was decided that this declaration should be engraved
on bronze tablets and set up in a prominent place within the

[a] Therefore; *some manuscripts have* and that.

NEW REVISED STANDARD VERSION

paid him high honors. 40 For he had heard that the Jews
were addressed by the Romans as friends and allies and
brothers, and that the Romans[a] had received the envoys of
Simon with honor.

41 "The Jews and their priests have resolved that Simon
should be their leader and high priest forever, until a trustworthy prophet should arise, 42 and that he should be governor over them and that he should take charge of the sanctuary and appoint officials over its tasks and over the country
and the weapons and the strongholds, and that he should
take charge of the sanctuary, 43 and that he should be
obeyed by all, and that all contracts in the country should be
written in his name, and that he should be clothed in purple
and wear gold.

44 "None of the people or priests shall be permitted to
nullify any of these decisions or to oppose what he says, or
to convene an assembly in the country without his permission, or to be clothed in purple or put on a gold buckle.
45 Whoever acts contrary to these decisions or rejects any of
them shall be liable to punishment."

46 All the people agreed to grant Simon the right to act in
accordance with these decisions. 47 So Simon accepted and
agreed to be high priest, to be commander and ethnarch of
the Jews and priests, and to be protector of them all.[b] 48 And
they gave orders to inscribe this decree on bronze tablets, to
put them up in a conspicuous place in the precincts of the

[a] Gk *they* [b] Or *to preside over them all*

NEW AMERICAN BIBLE

heard that the Romans had addressed the Jews as friends,
allies, and brothers and that they had received Simon's
envoys with honor.

41 " 'The Jewish people and their priest have, therefore,
made the following decisions. Simon shall be their permanent leader and high priest until a true prophet arises. 42 He
shall act as governor general over them, and shall have
charge of the temple, to make regulations concerning its
functions and concerning the country, its weapons and
strongholds; 43 he shall be obeyed by all. All contracts made
in the country shall be dated by his name. He shall have the
right to wear royal purple and gold ornaments. 44 It shall not
be lawful for any of the people or priests to nullify any of
these decisions, or to contradict the orders given by him, or
to convene an assembly in the country without his consent,
to be clothed in royal purple or wear an official gold brooch.
45 Whoever acts otherwise or violates any of these prescriptions shall be liable to punishment.

46 " 'All the people approved of granting Simon the right to
act in accord with these decisions, 47 and Simon accepted
and agreed to act as high priest, governor general, and ethnarch of the Jewish people and priests and to exercise
supreme authority over all.' "

48 It was decreed that this inscription should be engraved
on bronze tablets, to be set up in a conspicuous place in the

NEW JERUSALEM BIBLE

ambassadors, and, furthermore, 40 that the Jews and
priests are happy that Simon should, pending the advent
of a genuine prophet, be their ethnarch and high priest for
life 41 therefore he has confirmed him in the high-priestly
office, has raised him to the rank of Friend and has showered great honours on him, also confirming him as their
commander-in-chief, 42 with the right to appoint officials
to oversee the fabric of the sanctuary and to administer the
country, munitions and fortresses; 43 he is to have personal charge of the sanctuary, and to be obeyed by all; all official documents in the country must be drawn up in his
name; and he may assume the purple and may wear gold-
en ornaments;

44 'Furthermore, it is against the law for any member of
the public or of the priesthood to contravene any of these
enactments or to contest his decisions, or to convene a
meeting anywhere in the country without his permission,
or to assume the purple or wear the golden brooch; 45 and
anyone acting contrary to, or rejecting any article of, these
enactments is liable to punishment;

46 'And since the people have unanimously agreed to
grant Simon the right to act as aforesaid, and 47 since
Simon, for his part, has given his assent, and has consented to assume the high-priestly office and to be commander-in-chief and ethnarch of the Jews and their priests,
and to preside over all:

48 'So, be it now enacted: that this record be inscribed on
bronze tablets and be erected at some conspicuous place

GREEK OLD TESTAMENT

[49] τὰ δὲ ἀντίγραφα αὐτῶν θέσθαι ἐν τῷ γαζοφυλακίῳ, ὅπως
ἔχῃ Σιμων καὶ οἱ υἱοὶ αὐτοῦ.

15 Καὶ ἀπέστειλεν Ἀντίοχος υἱὸς Δημητρίου τοῦ βασιλέως ἐπιστολὰς ἀπὸ τῶν νήσων τῆς θαλάσσης
Σιμωνι ἱερεῖ καὶ ἐθνάρχῃ τῶν Ιουδαίων καὶ παντὶ τῷ ἔθνει,
[2] καὶ ἦσαν περιέχουσαι τὸν τρόπον τοῦτον

Βασιλεὺς Ἀντίοχος Σίμωνι ἱερεῖ μεγάλῳ καὶ ἐθνάρχῃ καὶ
ἔθνει Ιουδαίων χαίρειν. [3] ἐπεί τινες λοιμοὶ κατεκράτησαν
τῆς βασιλείας τῶν πατέρων ἡμῶν, βούλομαι δὲ ἀντιποιή-
σασθαι τῆς βασιλείας, ὅπως ἀποκαταστήσω αὐτὴν ὡς ἦν τὸ
πρότερον, ἐξενολόγησα δὲ πλῆθος δυνάμεων καὶ κατεσκεύ-
ασα πλοῖα πολεμικά, [4] βούλομαι δὲ ἐκβῆναι κατὰ τὴν χώραν,
ὅπως μετέλθω τοὺς κατεφθαρκότας τὴν χώραν ἡμῶν καὶ
τοὺς ἠρημωκότας πόλεις πολλὰς ἐν τῇ βασιλείᾳ μου, [5] νῦν
οὖν ἵστημί σοι πάντα τὰ ἀφέματα, ἃ ἀφῆκάν σοι οἱ πρὸ ἐμοῦ
βασιλεῖς, καὶ ὅσα ἄλλα δόματα ἀφῆκάν σοι. [6] καὶ ἐπέτρεψά
σοι ποιῆσαι κόμμα ἴδιον, νόμισμα τῇ χώρᾳ σου, [7] Ιερουσαλημ δὲ καὶ τὰ ἅγια εἶναι ἐλεύθερα· καὶ πάντα τὰ ὅπλα,
ὅσα κατεσκεύασας, καὶ τὰ ὀχυρώματα, ἃ ᾠκοδόμησας, ὧν
κρατεῖς, μενέτω σοι. [8] καὶ πᾶν ὀφείλημα βασιλικὸν καὶ τὰ
ἐσόμενα βασιλικὰ ἀπὸ τοῦ νῦν καὶ εἰς τὸν ἅπαντα χρόνον
ἀφιέσθω σοι· [9] ὡς δ' ἂν κρατήσωμεν τῆς βασιλείας ἡμῶν,
δοξάσομέν σε καὶ τὸ ἔθνος σου καὶ τὸ ἱερὸν δόξῃ μεγάλῃ
ὥστε φανερὰν γενέσθαι τὴν δόξαν ὑμῶν ἐν πάσῃ τῇ γῇ.

KING JAMES VERSION

49 Also that the copies thereof should be laid up in the treasury, to the end that Simon and his sons might have them.

15 Moreover Antiochus son of Demetrius the king sent letters from the isles of the sea unto Simon the priest and prince of the Jews, and to all the people;

2 The contents whereof were these: King Antiochus to Simon the high priest and prince of his nation, and to the people of the Jews, greeting:

3 Forasmuch as certain pestilent men have usurped the kingdom of our fathers, and my purpose is to challenge it again, that I may restore it to the old estate, and to that end have gathered a multitude of foreign soldiers together, and prepared ships of war;

4 My meaning also being to go through the country, that I may be avenged of them that have destroyed it, and made many cities in the kingdom desolate:

5 Now therefore I confirm unto thee all the oblations which the kings before me granted thee, and whatsoever gifts besides they granted.

6 I give thee leave also to coin money for thy country with thine own stamp.

7 And as concerning Jerusalem and the sanctuary, let them be free; and all the armour that thou hast made, and fortresses that thou hast built, and keepest in thine hands, let them remain unto thee.

8 And if anything be, or shall be, owing to the king, let it be forgiven thee from this time forth for evermore.

9 Furthermore, when we have obtained our kingdom, we will honour thee, and thy nation, and thy temple, with great honour, so that your honour shall be known throughout the world.

DOUAY OLD TESTAMENT

49 And that a copy thereof should be put in the treasury, that Simon and his sons may have it.

15 AND king Antiochus the son of Demetrius sent letters from the isles of the sea to Simon the priest, and prince of the nation of the Jews, and to all the people:

2 And the contents were these: King Antiochus to Simon the high priest, and to the nation of the Jews, greeting.

3 Forasmuch as certain pestilent men have usurped the kingdom of our fathers, and my purpose is to challenge the kingdom, and to restore it to its former estate: and I have chosen a great army, and have built ships of war.

4 And I design to go through the country that I may take revenge of them that have destroyed our country, and that have made many cities desolate in my realm.

5 Now therefore I confirm unto thee all the oblations which all the kings before me remitted to thee, and what other gifts soever they remitted to thee:

6 And I give thee leave to coin thy own money in thy country:

7 And let Jerusalem be holy and free, and all the armour that hath been made, and the fortresses which thou hast built, and which thou keepest in thy hands, let them remain to thee.

8 And all that is due to the king, and what should be the king's hereafter, from this present and for ever, is forgiven thee.

9 And when we shall have recovered our kingdom, we will glorify thee, and thy nation, and the temple with great glory, so that your glory shall be made manifest in all the earth.

KNOX TRANSLATION

precincts; [49] and a copy of it they put by in the treasury, in
the safe keeping of Simon and his heirs.[a]

15 Now turn we to Demetrius' other son, Antiochus.[b]
He it was directed a letter, from the islands over sea,
to Simon, high priest and ruler of the Jews, and to the whole
nation; [2] and this was the tenour of it. King Antiochus, to
the high priest Simon and to the people of the Jews, greeting.
[3] Here is the kingdom of my fathers overrun by ill folk; I
mean to challenge them, and bring back the old ways. To
this end, I have made a great levy of mercenaries, and built
ships of war; [4] passage I needs must have through yonder
territory, ere I can take vengeance for lands of mine ravaged,
cities of mine laid waste. [5] This grant, then, I make thee;
exemption, such as thou hadst, in the name of former kings,
from public offerings and all other payment due to me; [6] the
right of minting money within thy own borders; [7] for
Jerusalem, enjoyment of her sacred liberties; of weapons
thou hast made, strongholds thou hast built, the undisturbed
possession. [8] Never a claim the king has, or shall have hereafter, on his subjects, but to thee it is remitted; [9] and, when
the kingdom is ours, such honours we will bestow as shall
make thee, and thy race, and its sanctuary, renowned all the
world over.

a *vv.* 45-49. We should perhaps take these verses as part of the decree itself; otherwise verse 48 seems a needless repetition of verse 26.

b Antiochus was son to the Demetrius whose death is recorded in 10. 50, brother to the Demetrius first mentioned in 10. 67.

TODAY'S ENGLISH VERSION

Temple area 49 and that copies should be placed in the
Temple treasury, where Simon and his sons would have
access to them.

15 From the Greek islands Antiochus son of King
Demetrius wrote the following letter to Simon the
High Priest and governor of the Jews and to the whole
nation:

2 "King Antiochus to Simon, the High Priest and governor, and to the Jewish nation, greetings. 3 As you know,
the kingdom of my ancestors has been seized by traitors. I
have decided to reclaim it and restore its former greatness.
I have raised a large army of mercenary troops and have
fitted out warships. 4 I plan to invade the land and to
attack those who have destroyed many of the towns and
ruined the country.

5 "Now therefore, I confirm all exemptions from taxes
and payments granted you by former kings. 6 I authorize
you to mint your own coins as legal currency in your own
country. 7 Jerusalem and the Temple shall be free of taxation. All the weapons that you have manufactured and the
defenses you have built and now occupy shall remain
yours. 8 In addition, all debts now owed to the royal treasury, or which may in the future fall due, are permanently
canceled. 9 As soon as I have regained control of my kingdom, I will confer upon you, your nation, and the Temple
such great honors that the glory of your country will be
evident to the whole world."

NEW REVISED STANDARD VERSION

sanctuary, 49 and to deposit copies of them in the treasury,
so that Simon and his sons might have them.

15 Antiochus, son of King Demetrius, sent a letter from
the islands of the sea to Simon, the priest and ethnarch of the Jews, and to all the nation; 2 its contents were
as follows: "King Antiochus to Simon the high priest and
ethnarch and to the nation of the Jews, greetings. 3 Whereas
certain scoundrels have gained control of the kingdom of our
ancestors, and I intend to lay claim to the kingdom so that I
may restore it as it formerly was, and have recruited a host
of mercenary troops and have equipped warships, 4 and
intend to make a landing in the country so that I may proceed against those who have destroyed our country and
those who have devastated many cities in my kingdom,
5 now therefore I confirm to you all the tax remissions that
the kings before me have granted you, and a release from all
the other payments from which they have released you. 6 I
permit you to mint your own coinage as money for your
country, 7 and I grant freedom to Jerusalem and the sanctuary. All the weapons that you have prepared and the strongholds that you have built and now hold shall remain yours.
8 Every debt you owe to the royal treasury and any such
future debts shall be canceled for you from henceforth and
for all time. 9 When we gain control of our kingdom, we will
bestow great honor on you and your nation and the temple,
so that your glory will become manifest in all the earth."

NEW AMERICAN BIBLE

precincts of the temple, 49 and that copies of it should be
deposited in the treasury, where they would be available to
Simon and his sons.

15 Antiochus, son of King Demetrius, sent a letter from
the islands of the sea to Simon, the priest and ethnarch of the Jews, and to all the nation, 2 which read as follows:

"King Antiochus sends greetings to Simon, the priest and
ethnarch, and to the Jewish nation. 3 Whereas certain villains have gained control of the kingdom of my ancestors, I
intend to reclaim it, that I may restore it to its former state. I
have recruited a large number of mercenary troops and
equipped warships 4 to make a landing in my country and
take revenge on those who have ruined it and laid waste
many cities in my realm.

5 "Now, therefore, I confirm to you all the tax exemptions
that the kings before me granted you and whatever other
privileges they conferred on you. 6 I authorize you to coin
your own money, as legal tender in your country. 7 Jerusalem and its temple shall be free. All the weapons you have
prepared and all the strongholds you have built and now
occupy shall remain in your possession. 8 All debts, present
or future, due to the royal treasury shall be canceled for you,
now and for all time. 9 When we recover our kingdom, we
will greatly honor you and your nation and the temple, so
that your glory will be manifest in all the earth."

NEW JERUSALEM BIBLE

within the precincts of the Temple, 49 and that copies be
deposited in the Treasury for Simon and his descendants.'

15 Antiochus son of King Demetrius addressed a letter
from the Mediterranean Isles to Simon, priest and
ethnarch of the Jews, and to the whole nation; 2 this was
how it read:

'King Antiochus to Simon, high priest and ethnarch, and
to the Jewish nation, greetings.

3 'Whereas certain scoundrels have seized control of the
kingdom of our fathers, and I propose to claim back the
kingdom so that I may re-establish it as it was before, and
whereas I have accordingly recruited very large forces and
fitted out warships, 4 intending to make a landing in the
country and to hunt down the men who have ruined it and
laid waste many towns in my kingdom;

5 'I now, therefore, confirm in your favour all remissions
of taxes granted to you by the kings my predecessors, as
well as the waiving of whatever presents they may have
conceded. 6 I hereby authorise you to mint your own
coinage as legal tender for your own country. 7 I declare
Jerusalem and the sanctuary to be free; all the arms you
have manufactured and the fortresses you have built and
now occupy may remain yours. 8 All debts to the royal
treasury, present or future, are cancelled henceforth in perpetuity. 9 Furthermore, when we have won back our kingdom, we shall bestow such great honour on yourself, your
nation and the sanctuary as will make your glory known
throughout the world.'

GREEK OLD TESTAMENT

10 Ἔτους τετάρτου καὶ ἑβδομηκοστοῦ καὶ ἑκατοστοῦ ἐξῆλθεν Ἀντίοχος εἰς τὴν γῆν τῶν πατέρων αὐτοῦ, καὶ συνῆλθον πρὸς αὐτὸν πᾶσαι αἱ δυνάμεις ὥστε ὀλίγους εἶναι σὺν
Τρύφωνι. 11 καὶ ἐδίωξεν αὐτὸν Ἀντίοχος, καὶ ἦλθεν εἰς
Δωρα φεύγων τὴν ἐπὶ θαλάσσης. 12 ᾔδει γὰρ ὅτι ἐπισυνῆ-
κται ἐπ᾽ αὐτὸν τὰ κακά, καὶ ἀφῆκαν αὐτὸν αἱ δυνάμεις.
13 καὶ παρενέβαλεν Ἀντίοχος ἐπὶ Δωρα, καὶ σὺν αὐτῷ δώδεκα μυριάδες ἀνδρῶν πολεμιστῶν καὶ ὀκτακισχιλία ἵππος.
14 καὶ ἐκύκλωσεν τὴν πόλιν, καὶ τὰ πλοῖα ἀπὸ θαλάσσης συνῆψαν, καὶ ἔθλιβε τὴν πόλιν ἀπὸ τῆς γῆς καὶ τῆς θαλάσσης,
καὶ οὐκ εἴασεν οὐδένα ἐκπορεύεσθαι οὐδὲ εἰσπορεύεσθαι.

15 Καὶ ἦλθεν Νουμήνιος καὶ οἱ παρ᾽ αὐτοῦ ἐκ Ῥώμης
ἔχοντες ἐπιστολὰς τοῖς βασιλεῦσιν καὶ ταῖς χώραις, ἐν αἷς
ἐγέγραπτο τάδε

16 Λεύκιος ὕπατος Ῥωμαίων Πτολεμαίῳ βασιλεῖ χαίρειν.
17 οἱ πρεσβευταὶ τῶν Ιουδαίων ἦλθον πρὸς ἡμᾶς φίλοι ἡμῶν
καὶ σύμμαχοι ἀνανεούμενοι τὴν ἐξ ἀρχῆς φιλίαν καὶ
συμμαχίαν ἀπεσταλμένοι ἀπὸ Σιμωνος τοῦ ἀρχιερέως καὶ
τοῦ δήμου τῶν Ιουδαίων, 18 ἤνεγκαν δὲ ἀσπίδα χρυσῆν ἀπὸ
μνῶν χιλίων. 19 ἤρεσεν οὖν ἡμῖν γράψαι τοῖς βασιλεῦσιν καὶ
ταῖς χώραις ὅπως μὴ ἐκζητήσωσιν αὐτοῖς κακὰ καὶ μὴ
πολεμήσωσιν αὐτοὺς καὶ τὰς πόλεις αὐτῶν καὶ τὴν χώραν
αὐτῶν καὶ ἵνα μὴ συμμαχῶσιν τοῖς πολεμοῦσιν πρὸς αὐτούς.
20 ἔδοξεν δὲ ἡμῖν δέξασθαι τὴν ἀσπίδα παρ᾽ αὐτῶν. 21 εἴ

KING JAMES VERSION

10 In the hundred threescore and fourteenth year went Antiochus into the land of his fathers: at which time all the forces came together unto him, so that few were left with Tryphon.

11 Wherefore being pursued by king Antiochus, he fled unto Dora, which lieth by the sea side:

12 For he saw that troubles came upon him all at once, and that his forces had forsaken him.

13 Then camped Antiochus against Dora, having with him an hundred and twenty thousand men of war, and eight thousand horsemen.

14 And when he had compassed the city round about, and joined ships close to the town on the sea side, he vexed the city by land and by sea, neither suffered he any to go out or in.

15 In the mean season came Numenius and his company from Rome, having letters to the kings and countries; wherein were written these things:

16 Lucius, consul of the Romans unto king Ptolemee, greeting:

17 The Jews' ambassadors, our friends and confederates, came unto us to renew the old friendship and league, being sent from Simon the high priest, and from the people of the Jews:

18 And they brought a shield of gold of a thousand pound.

19 We thought it good therefore to write unto the kings and countries, that they should do them no harm, nor fight against them, their cities, or countries, nor yet aid their enemies against them.

20 It seemed also good to us to receive the shield of them.

DOUAY OLD TESTAMENT

10 In the year one hundred and seventy-four Antiochus entered into the land of his fathers, and all the forces assembled to him, so that few were left with Tryphon.

11 And king Antiochus pursued after him, and he fled along by the sea coast and came to Dora.

12 For he perceived that evils were gathered together upon him, and his troops had forsaken him.

13 And Antiochus camped above Dora with a hundred and twenty thousand men of war, and eight thousand horsemen:

14 And he invested the city, and the ships drew near by sea: and they annoyed the city by land, and by sea, and suffered none to come in, or to go out.

15 And Numenius, and they that had been with him, came from the city of Rome, having letters written to the kings, and countries, the contents whereof were these:

16 Lucius the consul of the Romans, to king Ptolemee, greeting.

17 The ambassadors of the Jews our friends came to us, to renew the former friendship and alliance, being sent from Simon the high priest, and the people of the Jews.

18 And they brought also a shield of gold of a thousand pounds.

19 It hath seemed good therefore to us to write to the kings, and countries, that they should do them no harm, nor fight against them, their cities, or countries: and that they should give no aid to them that fight against them.

20 And it hath seemed good to us to receive the shield of them.

KNOX TRANSLATION

10 So, in the hundred and seventy-fourth year, Antiochus
returned to his native country, and the armies rallied to him,
until Tryphon had but a small following left; 11 all down the
sea-coast he fled, with Antiochus at his heels, till he reached
Dora; 12 and ever he saw the toils closing round him, now
his troops had played him false. 13 With a hundred and
twenty thousand foot, and eight thousand horse, Antiochus
came to the gates of Dora 14 and began the siege of it; his
ships, too, blockaded the coast, so that it was cut off by land
and sea alike; enter it none might, nor leave it...

15 And now here were Numenius and his fellow envoys
come back from Rome,[a] with a copy of despatches sent out
to kings and nations everywhere, and this was the tenour of
them. 16 Lucius, the Roman consul, to king Ptolemy, greeting. 17 Envoys we have but now received in audience from a
friendly country, to wit, Judaea; the people of the Jews, with
their high priest Simon, had sent to renew their old treaty of
alliance with us, 18 and had made us a present besides, a
golden target of a thousand minas weight. 19 Agreed we
then to warn kings and nations everywhere, they should not
hurt or assault the Jewish people, its cities and country-side,
nor comfort its enemies; 20 and for the target of gold, our
pleasure was to accept the gift of it. 21 If then there be

[a] *vv.* 15-24. See note on 14. 24.

TODAY'S ENGLISH VERSION

10 In the year 174[a] Antiochus invaded the land of his
ancestors. Most of the soldiers came over to his side, so that
there were very few left with Trypho. 11 Trypho, pursued by
Antiochus, fled to the coastal city of Dor, 12 realizing that he
was in a desperate situation, now that all his troops had
deserted him. 13 Then Antiochus laid siege to Dor with
120,000 well-trained soldiers and 8,000 cavalry. 14 With his
ships joining the attack, he completely surrounded the town
and brought such pressure on it that no one was able to
enter or leave.

15 Meanwhile, Numenius and those with him arrived in
Jerusalem from Rome with the following letter addressed to
various kings and countries:

16 "From Lucius, consul of the Romans, to King Ptolemy,
greetings. 17 A delegation from our friends and allies the
Jews has come to us to renew the earlier treaty of friendship and alliance. They were sent by the High Priest Simon
and the Jewish people, 18 and they have brought as a gift a
gold shield weighing half a ton. 19 So we have decided to
write to various kings and countries urging them not to
harm the Jews, their towns, or their country in any way.
They must not make war against the Jews or give support
to those who attack them. 20 We have decided to accept
the shield and grant them protection. 21 Therefore if any

[a] THE YEAR 174: *This corresponds to 138 B.C.*

NEW REVISED STANDARD VERSION

10 In the one hundred seventy-fourth year[a] Antiochus set
out and invaded the land of his ancestors. All the troops rallied to him, so that there were only a few with Trypho.
11 Antiochus pursued him, and Trypho[b] came in his flight to
Dor, which is by the sea; 12 for he knew that troubles had
converged on him, and his troops had deserted him. 13 So
Antiochus encamped against Dor, and with him were one
hundred twenty thousand warriors and eight thousand cavalry. 14 He surrounded the town, and the ships joined battle
from the sea; he pressed the town hard from land and sea,
and permitted no one to leave or enter it.

15 Then Numenius and his companions arrived from
Rome, with letters to the kings and countries, in which the
following was written: 16 "Lucius, consul of the Romans, to
King Ptolemy, greetings. 17 The envoys of the Jews have
come to us as our friends and allies to renew our ancient
friendship and alliance. They had been sent by the high
priest Simon and by the Jewish people 18 and have brought a
gold shield weighing one thousand minas. 19 We therefore
have decided to write to the kings and countries that they
should not seek their harm or make war against them and
their cities and their country, or make alliance with those
who war against them. 20 And it has seemed good to us to
accept the shield from them. 21 Therefore if any scoundrels

a 138 B.C. *b* Gk *he*

NEW AMERICAN BIBLE

10 In the year one hundred and seventy-four, Antiochus
invaded the land of his ancestors, and all the troops rallied
to him, so that few were left with Trypho. 11 Pursued by
Antiochus, Trypho fled to Dor, by the sea, 12 realizing what a
mass of troubles had come upon him now that his soldiers
had deserted him. 13 Antiochus encamped before Dor with a
hundred and twenty thousand infantry and eight thousand
horsemen. 14 While he invested the city, his ships closed in
along the coast, so that he blockaded it by land and sea and
let no one go in or out.

15 Meanwhile, Numenius and his companions left Rome
with letters such as this addressed to various kings and
countries:

16 "Lucius, Consul of the Romans, sends greetings to King
Ptolemy. 17 Certain envoys of the Jews, our friends and allies,
have come to us to renew their earlier alliance of friendship.
They had been sent by Simon the high priest and the Jewish
people, 18 and they brought with them a gold shield worth a
thousand minas. 19 Therefore we have decided to write to
various kings and countries, that they are not to harm them,
or wage war against them or their cities or their country, and
are not to assist those who fight against them. 20 We have
also decided to accept the shield from them. 21 If, then, any

NEW JERUSALEM BIBLE

10 Antiochus invaded the land of his ancestors in the year
174 and, since the troops all rallied to him, Trypho was left
with few supporters. 11 Antiochus pursued the usurper, who
took refuge in Dora on the coast, 12 knowing that misfortunes were piling up on him and that his troops had deserted
him. 13 Antiochus pitched camp outside Dora with a hundred
and twenty thousand fighting men and eight thousand cavalry. 14 He laid siege to the city while the ships closed in
from the sea, so that he had the city under attack from land
and sea, and allowed no one to go in or come out.

15 Numenius and his companions, meanwhile, arrived from
Rome, bringing letters addressed to various kings and states,
in the following terms:

16 'Lucius, consul of the Romans, to King Ptolemy, greetings.

17 'The Jewish ambassadors have come to us as our
friends and allies to renew our original friendship and
alliance in the name of the high priest Simon and the
Jewish people. 18 They have brought a golden shield worth
a thousand *mina*. 19 Accordingly, we have seen fit to write
to various kings and states, warning them neither to
molest the Jewish people nor to attack either them or their
towns or their country, nor to ally themselves with any
such aggressors. 20 We have seen fit to accept the shield

Greek Old Testament

τινες οὖν λοιμοὶ διαπεφεύγασιν ἐκ τῆς χώρας αὐτῶν πρὸς
ὑμᾶς, παράδοτε αὐτοὺς Σιμωνι τῷ ἀρχιερεῖ, ὅπως ἐκδικήσῃ
αὐτοὺς κατὰ τὸν νόμον αὐτῶν.
22 Καὶ ταὐτὰ ἔγραψεν Δημητρίῳ τῷ βασιλεῖ καὶ Ἀττάλῳ
καὶ Ἀριαράθῃ καὶ Ἀρσάκῃ 23 καὶ εἰς πάσας τὰς χώρας καὶ
Σαμψάμῃ καὶ Σπαρτιάταις καὶ εἰς Δῆλον καὶ εἰς Μύνδον καὶ
εἰς Σικυῶνα καὶ εἰς τὴν Καρίαν καὶ εἰς Σάμον καὶ εἰς τὴν
Παμφυλίαν καὶ εἰς Λυκίαν καὶ εἰς Ἁλικαρνασσὸν καὶ εἰς
Ῥόδον καὶ εἰς Φασηλίδα καὶ εἰς Κῶ καὶ εἰς Σίδην καὶ εἰς
Ἄραδον καὶ Γόρτυναν καὶ Κνίδον καὶ Κύπρον καὶ Κυρήνην.
24 τὸ δὲ ἀντίγραφον τούτων ἔγραψαν Σιμωνι τῷ ἀρχιερεῖ.
25 Ἀντίοχος δὲ ὁ βασιλεὺς παρενέβαλεν ἐπὶ Δωρα ἐν τῇ
δευτέρᾳ προσάγων διὰ παντὸς αὐτῇ τὰς χεῖρας καὶ μηχανὰς
ποιούμενος καὶ συνέκλεισεν τὸν Τρύφωνα τοῦ ἐκπορεύεσθαι
καὶ εἰσπορεύεσθαι. 26 καὶ ἀπέστειλεν αὐτῷ Σιμων δισχιλίους ἄνδρας ἐκλεκτοὺς συμμαχῆσαι αὐτῷ καὶ ἀργύριον καὶ
χρυσίον καὶ σκεύη ἱκανά. 27 καὶ οὐκ ἠβούλετο αὐτὰ δέξασθαι, ἀλλὰ ἠθέτησεν πάντα, ὅσα συνέθετο αὐτῷ τὸ πρότερον, καὶ ἠλλοτριοῦτο αὐτῷ. 28 καὶ ἀπέστειλεν πρὸς αὐτὸν
Ἀθηνόβιον ἕνα τῶν φίλων αὐτοῦ κοινολογησόμενον αὐτῷ λέγων Ὑμεῖς κατακρατεῖτε τῆς Ιοππης καὶ Γαζαρων καὶ τῆς
ἄκρας τῆς ἐν Ιερουσαλημ, πόλεις τῆς βασιλείας μου. 29 τὰ
ὅρια αὐτῶν ἠρημώσατε καὶ ἐποιήσατε πληγὴν μεγάλην ἐπὶ
τῆς γῆς καὶ ἐκυριεύσατε τόπων πολλῶν ἐν τῇ βασιλείᾳ μου.

King James Version

21 If therefore there be any pestilent fellows, that have fled from their country unto you, deliver them unto Simon the high priest, that he may punish them according to their own law.

22 The same things wrote he likewise unto Demetrius the king, and Attalus, to Ariarathes, and Arsaces,

23 And to all the countries, and to Sampsames, and the Lacedemonians, and to Delus, and Myndus, and Sicyon, and Caria, and Samos, and Pamphylia, and Lycia, and Halicarnassus, and Rhodus, and Phaselis, and Cos, and Side, and Aradus, and Gortyna, and Cnidus, and Cyprus, and Cyrene.

24 And the copy hereof they wrote to Simon the high priest.

25 So Antiochus the king camped against Dora the second *day*, assaulting it continually, and making engines, by which means he shut up Tryphon, that he could neither go out nor in.

26 At that time Simon sent him two thousand chosen men to aid him; silver also, and gold, and much armour.

27 Nevertheless he would not receive them, but brake all the covenants which he had made with him afore, and became strange unto him.

28 Furthermore he sent unto him Athenobius, one of his friends, to commune with him, and say, Ye withhold Joppe and Gazara, with the tower that is in Jerusalem, which are cities of my realm.

29 The borders thereof ye have wasted, and done great hurt in the land, and got the dominion of many places within my kingdom.

Douay Old Testament

21 If therefore any pestilent men are fled out of their country to you, deliver them to Simon the high priest, that he may punish them according to their law.

22 These same things were written to king Demetrius, and to Attalus, and to Ariarathes, and to Arsaces,

23 And to all the countries; and to Lampsacus, and to the Spartans, and to Delus, and Myndus, and Sicyon, and Caria, and Samus, and Pamphylia, and Lycia, and Alicarnassus, and Cos, and Side, and Aradus, and Rhodes, and Phaselis, and Gortyna, and Gnidus, and Cyprus, and Cyrene.

24 And they wrote a copy thereof to Simon the high priest, and to the people of the Jews.

25 But king Antiochus moved his camp to Dora the second time, assaulting it continually, and making engines: and he shut up Tryphon, that he could not go out.

26 And Simon sent to him two thousand chosen men to aid him, silver also, and gold, and abundance of furniture.

27 And he would not receive them, but broke all the covenant that he had made with him before, and alienated himself from him.

28 And he sent to him Athenobius one of his friends, to treat with him, saying: You hold Joppe, and Gazara, and the castle that is in Jerusalem, which are cities of my kingdom:

29 Their borders you have wasted, and you have made great havock in the land, and have got the dominion of many places in my kingdom.

Knox Translation

malcontents from Judaea sheltering among you, our
bidding is you should hand them over to the high priest
Simon, for such punishment as the Jewish law prescribes.
22 Copies of this decree have been sent to Demetrius, Attalus,
Ariarathes and Arsaces, 23 and to these countries following:
Lampsacus, Sparta, Delos, Myndos, Sicyon, Caria, Samos,
Pamphylia, Lycia, Halicarnassus, Coös, Side, Arados,
Rhodes, Phaselis, Gortyna, Cnidus, Cyprus and Cyrene. 24 A
further copy has been sent to the high priest Simon and to
the Jewish people…
25 Once again[a] king Antiochus laid siege to Dora, bringing
fresh force to bear, and devising fresh engines; and ever he
kept Tryphon hemmed in, so that escape was none.
26 Thereupon Simon despatched two thousand picked men to
aid in the siege, with silver and gold and a deal of tackle
besides; 27 but accept them the king would not; all his promises were forgot, and Simon a stranger now. 28 Athenobius it
was, one of the king's friends, that came to treat with him,
and this was the message he bore: Cities of mine you hold,
Joppe, and Gazara, and Jerusalem citadel; 29 lands about
them you have laid waste, and done Syria much mischief
besides, encroaching everywhere on my domain. 30 Needs

a Some Greek manuscripts have 'on the second day', instead of 'once again', but this is probably a correction, designed to clear up a difficulty. Nothing has been said which implies that the siege described in verse 14 had come to an end; and it is not easy to account for the mention of a second siege, unless we suppose a gap in the manuscript which has been accidentally filled up by verses 15-24.

TODAY'S ENGLISH VERSION

traitors escape from Judea and seek refuge in your land,
hand them over to Simon the High Priest, so that he may
punish them according to Jewish law."
22 Lucius wrote the same letter to King Demetrius, to
Attalus, Ariarathes, and Arsaces, 23 and to all the following
countries: Sampsames, Sparta, Delos, Myndos, Sicyon, Caria,
Samos, Pamphylia, Lycia, Halicarnassus, Rhodes, Phaselis,
Cos, Side, Aradus, Gortyna, Cnidus, Cyprus, and Cyrene.
24 A copy of the letter was also sent to Simon the High Priest.
25 King Antiochus laid siege to Dor for a second time, keeping it under constant attack. He built siege platforms, and
his blockade kept Trypho and his men from going in or out.
26 Simon sent 2,000 well-trained soldiers to help Antiochus,
as well as silver and gold and a great deal of equipment.
27 But Antiochus refused to accept them, canceled all the previous agreements that he had made with Simon, and became
his enemy. 28 Then Antiochus sent his trusted official
Athenobius to negotiate with Simon. He told Simon, "You
are occupying Joppa, Gezer, and the fort in Jerusalem, cities
that belong to my kingdom. 29 You have devastated those
regions and brought great trouble to the country. You have
seized control of many places in my kingdom. 30 Now you

NEW REVISED STANDARD VERSION

have fled to you from their country, hand them over to the
high priest Simon, so that he may punish them according to
their law."
22 The consul[a] wrote the same thing to King Demetrius
and to Attalus and Ariarathes and Arsaces, 23 and to all the
countries, and to Sampsames,[b] and to the Spartans, and to
Delos, and to Myndos, and to Sicyon, and to Caria, and to
Samos, and to Pamphylia, and to Lycia, and to Halicarnassus, and to Rhodes, and to Phaselis, and to Cos, and to Side,
and to Aradus and Gortyna and Cnidus and Cyprus and
Cyrene. 24 They also sent a copy of these things to the high
priest Simon.
25 King Antiochus besieged Dor for the second time, continually throwing his forces against it and making engines
of war; and he shut Trypho up and kept him from going out
or in. 26 And Simon sent to Antiochus[c] two thousand picked
troops, to fight for him, and silver and gold and a large
amount of military equipment. 27 But he refused to receive
them, and broke all the agreements he formerly had made
with Simon, and became estranged from him. 28 He sent to
him Athenobius, one of his Friends, to confer with him, saying, "You hold control of Joppa and Gazara and the citadel
in Jerusalem; they are cities of my kingdom. 29 You have
devastated their territory, you have done great damage in
the land, and you have taken possession of many places in

a Gk *He* *b* The name is uncertain *c* Gk *him*

NEW AMERICAN BIBLE

troublemakers from their country take refuge with you, hand
them over to Simon the high priest, so that he may punish
them according to their law."
22 The consul sent similar letters to Kings Demetrius,
Attalus, Ariarthes and Arsaces; 23 to all the countries—
Sampsames, Sparta, Delos, Myndos, Sicyon, Caria, Samos,
Pamphylia, Lycia, Halicarnassus, Rhodes, Phaselis, Cos,
Side, Aradus, Gortyna, Cnidus, Cyprus, and Cyrene. 24 A copy
of the letter was also sent to Simon the high priest.
25 When King Antiochus was encamped before Dor, he
assaulted it continuously both with troops and with the siege
machines he had made. He blockaded Trypho by preventing
anyone from going in or out. 26 Simon sent to Antiochus'
support two thousand elite troops, together with gold and
silver and much equipment. 27 But he refused to accept the
aid; in fact, he broke all the agreements he had previously
made with Simon and became hostile toward him.
28 He sent Athenobius, one of his Friends, to confer with
Simon and say: "You are occupying Joppa and Gazara and
the citadel of Jerusalem; these are cities of my kingdom.
29 You have laid waste their territories, done great harm to
the land, and taken possession of many districts in my

NEW JERUSALEM BIBLE

from them. 21 If, therefore, any scoundrels have fled their
country to take refuge with you, hand them over to Simon
the high priest, to be punished by him according to their
law.'
22 The consul sent the same letter to King Demetrius, to
Attalus, Ariarathes and Arsaces, 23 and to all states, including Sampsames, the Spartans, Delos, Myndos, Sicyon, Caria,
Samos, Pamphylia, Lycia, Halicarnassus, Rhodes, Phaselis,
Cos, Side, Arados, Gortyn, Cyprus and Cyrene. 24 They also
drew up a copy for Simon the high priest.
25 Antiochus, meanwhile, from his positions on the out-
skirts of Dora, was continually throwing detachments
against the town. He constructed siege-engines, and blockaded Trypho, preventing movement in or out. 26 Simon sent
him two thousand picked men to support him in the fight,
with silver and gold and plenty of equipment. 27 But
Antiochus would not accept them; instead, he repudiated all
his previous agreements with Simon and completely changed
his attitude to him. 28 He sent him Athenobius, one of his
Friends, to confer with him and say, 'You are now occupying
Joppa and Gezer and the Citadel in Jerusalem, which are
towns in my kingdom. 29 You have laid waste their territory
and done immense harm to the country; and you have seized
control of many places properly in my kingdom. 30 Either

GREEK OLD TESTAMENT

30 νῦν οὖν παράδοτε τὰς πόλεις, ἃς κατελάβεσθε, καὶ τοὺς
φόρους τῶν τόπων, ὧν κατεκυριεύσατε ἐκτὸς τῶν ὁρίων τῆς
Ιουδαίας. 31 εἰ δὲ μή, δότε ἀντ᾽ αὐτῶν πεντακόσια τάλαντα
ἀργυρίου καὶ τῆς καταφθορᾶς, ἧς κατεφθάρκατε, καὶ τῶν
φόρων τῶν πόλεων ἄλλα τάλαντα πεντακόσια· εἰ δὲ μή,
παραγενόμενοι ἐκπολεμήσομεν ὑμᾶς. 32 καὶ ἦλθεν Ἀθηνό-
βιος ὁ φίλος τοῦ βασιλέως εἰς Ιερουσαλημ καὶ εἶδεν τὴν δόξαν Σιμωνος καὶ κυλικεῖον μετὰ χρυσωμάτων καὶ ἀργυρωμά-
των καὶ παράστασιν ἱκανὴν καὶ ἐξίστατο καὶ ἀπήγγειλεν
αὐτῷ τοὺς λόγους τοῦ βασιλέως. 33 καὶ ἀποκριθεὶς Σιμων
εἶπεν αὐτῷ Οὔτε γῆν ἀλλοτρίαν εἰλήφαμεν οὔτε ἀλλοτρίων
κεκρατήκαμεν, ἀλλὰ τῆς κληρονομίας τῶν πατέρων ἡμῶν,
ὑπὸ δὲ ἐχθρῶν ἡμῶν ἀκρίτως ἔν τινι καιρῷ κατεκρατήθη·
34 ἡμεῖς δὲ καιρὸν ἔχοντες ἀντεχόμεθα τῆς κληρονομίας τῶν
πατέρων ἡμῶν. 35 περὶ δὲ Ιοππης καὶ Γαζαρων, ὧν αἰτεῖς,
αὗται ἐποίουν ἐν τῷ λαῷ πληγὴν μεγάλην καὶ τὴν χώραν
ἡμῶν, τούτων δώσομεν τάλαντα ἑκατόν. 36 καὶ οὐκ ἀπεκρίθη
αὐτῷ λόγον, ἀπέστρεψεν δὲ μετὰ θυμοῦ πρὸς τὸν βασιλέα
καὶ ἀπήγγειλεν αὐτῷ τοὺς λόγους τούτους καὶ τὴν δόξαν
Σιμωνος καὶ πάντα, ὅσα εἶδεν, καὶ ὠργίσθη ὁ βασιλεὺς
ὀργὴν μεγάλην.

37 Τρύφων δὲ ἐμβὰς εἰς πλοῖον ἔφυγεν εἰς Ὀρθωσίαν.
38 καὶ κατέστησεν ὁ βασιλεὺς τὸν Κενδεβαῖον ἐπιστράτηγον
τῆς παραλίας καὶ δυνάμεις πεζικὰς καὶ ἱππικὰς ἔδωκεν
αὐτῷ· 39 καὶ ἐνετείλατο αὐτῷ παρεμβάλλειν κατὰ πρόσωπον

KING JAMES VERSION

30 Now therefore deliver the cities which ye have taken, and the tributes of the places, whereof ye have gotten dominion without the borders of Judea:

31 Or else give me for them five hundred talents of silver; and for the harm that ye have done, and the tributes of the cities, other five hundred talents: if not, we will come and fight against you.

32 So Athenobius the king's friend came to Jerusalem: and when he saw the glory of Simon, and the cupboard of gold and silver plate, and his great attendance, he was astonished, and told him the king's message.

33 Then answered Simon, and said unto him, We have neither taken other men's land, nor holden that which appertaineth to others, but the inheritance of our fathers, which our enemies had wrongfully in possession a certain time.

34 Wherefore we, having opportunity, hold the inheritance of our fathers.

35 And whereas thou demandest Joppe and Gazara, albeit they did great harm unto the people in our country, yet will we give an hundred talents for them. Hereunto Athenobius answered him not a word;

36 But returned in a rage to the king, and made report unto him of these speeches, and of the glory of Simon, and of all that he had seen: whereupon the king was exceeding wroth.

37 In the mean time fled Tryphon by ship unto Orthosias.

38 Then the king made Cendebeus captain of the sea coast, and gave him an host of footmen and horsemen,

39 And commanded him to remove his host toward Judea:

DOUAY OLD TESTAMENT

30 Now therefore deliver up the cities that you have taken, and the tributes of the places whereof you have gotten the dominion without the borders of Judea.

31 But if not, give me for them five hundred talents of silver, and for the havock that you have made, and the tributes of the cities other five hundred talents: or else we will come and fight against you.

32 So Athenobius the king's friend came to Jerusalem, and saw the glory of Simon and his magnificence in gold, and silver, and his great equipage, and he was astonished, and told him the king's words.

33 And Simon answered him, and said to him: We have neither taken other men's land, neither do we hold that which is other men's: but the inheritance of our fathers, which was for some time unjustly possessed by our enemies.

34 But we having opportunity claim the inheritance of our fathers.

35 And as to thy complaints concerning Joppe and Gazara, they did great harm to the people, and to our country: *yet* for these we will give a hundred talents. And Athenobius answered him not a word:

36 But returning in a rage to the king, made report to him of these words, and of the glory of Simon, and of all that he had seen, and the king was exceeding angry.

37 And Tryphon fled away by ship to Orthosias.

38 And the king appointed Cendebeus captain of the sea coast, and gave him an army of footmen and horsemen.

39 And he commanded him to march with his army

KNOX TRANSLATION

must you should hand over cities you have occupied, revenues of Gentile lands you have detained, 31 or else five hundred talents of silver in exchange, and five hundred more to
compensate for damage done and revenue lost; if not, we
will come and overpower you by force of arms.
32 So came Athenobius, the king's friend, to Jerusalem,
where he saw what state Simon kept, much display of gold
and silver, and a great throng of attendants, till he was dazzled at the sight. Yet delivered he his errand; 33 to which
Simon made this answer: Other men's fief seized we never,
nor other men's rights detain; here be lands that were our
fathers' once, by enemies of ours for some while wrongfully
held; 34 opportunity given us, should we not claim the patrimony we had lost? 35 As for thy talk of Joppe and Gazara,
these were cities did much mischief to people and land of
ours; for the worth of them, thou shalt have a hundred talents if thou wilt. Never a word said Athenobius, 36 but went
back to the king very ill pleased, and told him what answer
was given; of Simon's court, too, and of all else he had seen.
Antiochus was in a great taking of anger; 37 here was
Tryphon newly escaped by ship to Orthosias! 38 He must
needs leave the sea-coast in charge of Cendebaeus, with a
strong command both of horse and foot, while himself gave
Tryphon chase. 39 This Cendebaeus had orders to advance and

TODAY'S ENGLISH VERSION

must hand back these cities that you have captured, and you
must give me the tax money that you have taken from places
that you occupied outside the territory of Judea. 31 If you are
unwilling to do this, then you must pay me 30,000 pounds
of silver, and 30,000 additional pounds of silver to compensate me for damages and for lost taxes. If you refuse to do
either of these, we will go to war against you."

32 When Athenobius came to Jerusalem and saw the splendor of Simon's court, the gold and silver tableware in his
banquet hall, and the rest of the display of great wealth, he
was amazed. He delivered the king's message to Simon,
33 and Simon answered, "We have never taken land away
from other nations or confiscated anything that belonged to
other people. On the contrary, we have simply taken back
property that we inherited from our ancestors, land that had
been unjustly taken away from us by our enemies at one
time or another. 34 We are now only making use of this
opportunity to recover our ancestral heritage. 35 As for Joppa
and Gezer, which you claim, we will give you 6,000 pounds
of silver, in spite of the fact that the people of those cities
have done great harm to our nation."

Athenobius made no reply, 36 but he returned to the king
in a rage. When he told the king what Simon had said, and
reported on the splendor of Simon's court and all that he had
seen, the king became violently angry.

37 In the meantime, Trypho had boarded a ship and
escaped to the town of Orthosia. 38 King Antiochus appointed Cendebeus as commander of the coastal area, provided
him with infantry and cavalry, 39 and gave him orders to

NEW REVISED STANDARD VERSION

my kingdom. 30 Now then, hand over the cities that you
have seized and the tribute money of the places that you
have conquered outside the borders of Judea; 31 or else pay
me five hundred talents of silver for the destruction that you
have caused and five hundred talents more for the tribute
money of the cities. Otherwise we will come and make war
on you."

32 So Athenobius, the king's Friend, came to Jerusalem,
and when he saw the splendor of Simon, and the sideboard
with its gold and silver plate, and his great magnificence, he
was amazed. When he reported to him the king's message,
33 Simon said to him in reply: "We have neither taken foreign
land nor seized foreign property, but only the inheritance of
our ancestors, which at one time had been unjustly taken by
our enemies. 34 Now that we have the opportunity, we are
firmly holding the inheritance of our ancestors. 35 As for
Joppa and Gazara, which you demand, they were causing
great damage among the people and to our land; for them we
will give you one hundred talents."

Athenobius[a] did not answer him a word, 36 but returned
in wrath to the king and reported to him these words, and
also the splendor of Simon and all that he had seen. And the
king was very angry.

37 Meanwhile Trypho embarked on a ship and escaped to
Orthosia. 38 Then the king made Cendebeus commander-in-
chief of the coastal country, and gave him troops of infantry
and cavalry. 39 He commanded him to encamp against

a Gk *He*

NEW AMERICAN BIBLE

realm. 30 Therefore, give up the cities you have seized and
the tribute money of the districts outside the territory of
Judea of which you have taken possession; 31 or instead, pay
me five hundred talents of silver for the devastation you
have caused and five hundred talents more for the tribute
money of the cities. If you do not do this, we will come and
make war on you."

32 So Athenobius, the king's Friend, came to Jerusalem,
and on seeing the splendor of Simon's court, the gold and
silver plate on the sideboard, and the rest of his rich display,
he was amazed. When he gave him the king's message,
33 Simon said to him in reply:

"We have not seized any foreign land; what we took is not
the property of others, but our ancestral heritage which for a
time had been unjustly held by our enemies. 34 Now that we
have the opportunity, we are holding on to the heritage of
our ancestors. 35 As for Joppa and Gazara, which you
demand, the men of these cities were doing great harm to
our people and laying waste our country; however, we are
willing to pay you a hundred talents for these cities."

36 Athenobius made no reply, but returned to the king in
anger. When he told him of Simon's words, of his splendor,
and of all he had seen, the king fell into a violent rage.

37 Trypho had gotten aboard a ship and escaped to
Orthosia. 38 Then the king appointed Cendebeus commander
in chief of the seacoast, and gave him infantry and cavalry
forces. 39 He ordered him to move his troops against Judea

NEW JERUSALEM BIBLE

now surrender the towns you have taken and the taxes from
the places you have seized outside the frontiers of Judaea,
31 or else pay me five hundred talents of silver in compensa-
tion for them and for the destruction you have done, and
another five hundred talents for the taxes from the towns;
otherwise we shall come and make war on you.' 32 When the
King's Friend, Athenobius, reached Jerusalem and saw
Simon's magnificence, his cabinet of gold and silver plate
and the state he kept, he was dumbfounded. He delivered the
king's message, 33 but Simon gave him this answer, 'We
have not taken foreign territory or any alien property but
have occupied our ancestral heritage, for some time unjustly
wrested from us by our enemies; 34 now that we have a
favourable opportunity, we are merely recovering our ancestral heritage. 35 As regards Joppa and Gezer, which you
claim, these were towns that did great harm to our people
and laid waste our country; we are prepared to give a hundred talents for them.' Without so much as a word in
answer, 36 the envoy went back to the king in a rage and
reported on Simon's answer and his magnificence, and on
everything he had seen, at which the king fell into a fury.

37 Trypho now boarded a ship and escaped to Orthosia.
38 The king appointed Cendebaeus military governor of the
coastal region and allotted him a force of infantry and cavalry. 39 He ordered him to deploy his men facing Judaea, and

GREEK OLD TESTAMENT

τῆς Ιουδαίας καὶ ἐνετείλατο αὐτῷ οἰκοδομῆσαι τὴν Κεδρων
καὶ ὀχυρῶσαι τὰς πύλας καὶ ὅπως πολεμῇ τὸν λαόν· ὁ δὲ
βασιλεὺς ἐδίωκε τὸν Τρύφωνα. 40 καὶ παρεγενήθη Κενδεβαῖος εἰς Ιάμνειαν καὶ ἤρξατο τοῦ ἐρεθίζειν τὸν λαὸν καὶ
ἐμβατεύειν εἰς τὴν Ιουδαίαν καὶ αἰχμαλωτίζειν τὸν λαὸν καὶ
φονεύειν. 41 καὶ ᾠκοδόμησεν τὴν Κεδρων καὶ ἀπέταξεν ἐκεῖ
ἱππεῖς καὶ δυνάμεις, ὅπως ἐκπορευόμενοι ἐξοδεύωσιν τὰς
ὁδοὺς τῆς Ιουδαίας, καθὰ συνέταξεν αὐτῷ ὁ βασιλεύς.
16 Καὶ ἀνέβη Ιωαννης ἐκ Γαζαρων καὶ ἀπήγγειλεν
Σιμωνι τῷ πατρὶ αὐτοῦ ἃ συνετέλεσεν Κενδεβαῖος.
2 καὶ ἐκάλεσεν Σιμων τοὺς δύο υἱοὺς αὐτοῦ τοὺς πρεσβυτέρους Ιουδαν καὶ Ιωαννην καὶ εἶπεν αὐτοῖς Ἐγὼ καὶ οἱ
ἀδελφοί μου καὶ ὁ οἶκος τοῦ πατρός μου ἐπολεμήσαμεν τοὺς
πολέμους Ισραηλ ἀπὸ νεότητος ἕως τῆς σήμερον ἡμέρας,
καὶ εὐοδώθη ἐν ταῖς χερσὶν ἡμῶν ῥύσασθαι τὸν Ισραηλ
πλεονάκις. 3 νυνὶ δὲ γεγήρακα, καὶ ὑμεῖς δὲ ἐν τῷ ἐλέει
ἱκανοί ἐστε ἐν τοῖς ἔτεσιν· γίνεσθε ἀντ' ἐμοῦ καὶ τοῦ
ἀδελφοῦ μου καὶ ἐξελθόντες ὑπερμαχεῖτε ὑπὲρ τοῦ ἔθνους
ἡμῶν, ἡ δὲ ἐκ τοῦ οὐρανοῦ βοήθεια ἔστω μεθ' ὑμῶν. 4 καὶ
ἐπέλεξεν ἐκ τῆς χώρας εἴκοσι χιλιάδας ἀνδρῶν πολεμιστῶν
καὶ ἱππεῖς, καὶ ἐπορεύθησαν ἐπὶ τὸν Κενδεβαῖον καὶ ἐκοιμήθησαν ἐν Μωδειν. 5 καὶ ἀναστάντες τὸ πρωὶ ἐπορεύθησαν
εἰς τὸ πεδίον, καὶ ἰδοὺ δύναμις πολλὴ εἰς συνάντησιν αὐτοῖς, πεζικὴ καὶ ἱππεῖς, καὶ χειμάρρους ἦν ἀνὰ μέσον
αὐτῶν. 6 καὶ παρενέβαλε κατὰ πρόσωπον αὐτῶν αὐτὸς καὶ ὁ
λαὸς αὐτοῦ. καὶ εἶδεν τὸν λαὸν δειλούμενον διαπερᾶσαι τὸν

KING JAMES VERSION

also he commanded him to build up Cedron, and to fortify the gates, and to war against the people; but as for the king *himself,* he pursued Tryphon.

40 So Cendebeus came to Jamnia, and began to provoke the people, and to invade Judea, and to take the people prisoners, and slay them.

41 And when he had built up Cedron, he set horsemen there, and an host *of footmen,* to the end that issuing out they might make outroads upon the ways of Judea, as the king had commanded him.

16 Then came up John from Gazara, and told Simon his father what Cendebeus had done.

2 Wherefore Simon called his two eldest sons, Judas and John, and said unto them, I, and my brethren, and my father's house, have ever from our youth unto this day fought against the enemies of Israel; and things have prospered so well in our hands, that we have delivered Israel oftentimes.

3 But now I am old, and ye, by *God's* mercy, are of a sufficient age: be ye instead of me and my brother, and go and fight for our nation, and the help from heaven be with you.

4 So he chose out of the country twenty thousand men of war with horsemen, who went out against Cendebeus, and rested that night at Modin.

5 And when as they rose in the morning, and went into the plain, behold, a mighty great host both of footmen and horsemen came against them: howbeit there was a water brook betwixt them.

6 So he and his people pitched over against them: and when he saw that the people were afraid to go over the water

DOUAY OLD TESTAMENT

towards Judea: and he commanded him to build up Gedor, and to fortify the gates of the city, and to war against the people. But the king himself pursued after Tryphon.

40 And Cendebeus came to Jamnia, and began to provoke the people, and to ravage Judea, and to take the people prisoners, and to kill, and to build Gedor.

41 And he placed there horsemen, and an army: that they might issue forth, and make incursions upon the ways of Judea, as the king had commanded him.

16 THEN John came up from Gazara, and told Simon his father what Cendebeus had done against their people.

2 And Simon called his two eldest sons, Judas and John, and said to them: I and my brethren, and my father's house, have fought against the enemies of Israel from our youth even to this day: and things have prospered so well in our hands that we have delivered Israel oftentimes.

3 And now I am old, but be you instead of me, and my brethren, and go out, and fight for our nation: and the help from heaven be with you.

4 Then he chose out of the country twenty thousand fighting men, and horsemen, and they went forth against Cendebeus: and they rested in Modin.

5 And they arose in the morning, and went into the plain: and behold a very great army of footmen and horsemen came against them, and there was a running river between them.

6 And he and his people pitched their camp over against them, and he saw that the people were afraid to go over the

KNOX TRANSLATION

threaten Judaea; Gedor[a] he should fortify, and there make
himself fast, the better to levy war on Juda. 40 So he marched
away to Jamnia, and set about harassing the Jews; now it was
an inroad, with prisoners carried away, now a massacre; and
all the while he was fortifying Gedor. 41 Cavalry he quartered
there, and other troops besides, to sally out and patrol the
roads into Judaea; the king would have it so.
16 It was not long before John came up from Gazara, to
tell his father Simon how ill Cendebaeus was using
their fellow-countrymen. 2 And at that, Simon must have his
two elder sons present, Judas and John both, and made the
command over to them. Still young we were, he said, I and
my brothers and my father's kin, when we began that war
on Israel's enemies which is being fought yet; under our ban-
ners once and again came victory, and the day was saved for
Israel. 3 I am an old man now, and it is yours to do what I
and brother of mine did; march out, fight in our people's
cause, and heaven's aid be with you!
4 Twenty thousand warriors John[b] chose out from the rest,
and cavalry to support them, and away they went to fight
Cendebaeus. That night they spent at Modin, 5 and on the
morrow, when they left it for the valley, what a huge array
was this, both of horse and foot, encountering them! And a
mountain torrent flowed in between. 6 When John brought
his army to the opposite bank, and found his men had little

a 'Gedor' is 'Cedron' in the Greek text, here and in verse 40 below, to correspond with verse 9 of the following chapter. *b* The name John is not mentioned in the original, either here or in verses 6 and 7 below. But it is plain that either John or Judas is meant, and 13. 54 seems to give the best grounds for a decision.

TODAY'S ENGLISH VERSION

move against Judea. He also ordered him to rebuild the town
of Kedron and fortify its gates, so that he could fight against
the Jewish people. The king himself continued to pursue
Trypho.
40 Cendebeus then came to Jamnia and began to harass the
Jews by invading Judea, capturing people, and murdering
them. 41 He rebuilt Kedron and stationed some cavalry and
infantry units there, so that they could make attacks and
patrol the roads of Judea, as the king had ordered.
16 Simon's son John left Gezer and went to report to his
father what Cendebeus had done. 2 Simon said to
John and Judas, his two oldest sons, "All my father's family,
my brothers, and I have fought Israel's battles all our lives,
and many times we have been successful in saving Israel.
3 I am old now, but you, thanks to God, are in the prime of
life. You must take my place and that of my brother in fighting for our nation. And may God himself be with you."
4 Then John raised an Israelite army of 20,000 trained soldiers and cavalry and marched out against Cendebeus. They
spent the night in Modein, 5 and then early the next morning
they moved into the plain. There a large army of infantry and
cavalry moved to meet them, but there was a river between
the two armies. 6 John and his army took up battle positions
facing the enemy, but when John saw that his soldiers were

NEW REVISED STANDARD VERSION

Judea, to build up Kedron and fortify its gates, and to make
war on the people; but the king pursued Trypho. 40 So
Cendebeus came to Jamnia and began to provoke the people
and invade Judea and take the people captive and kill them.
41 He built up Kedron and stationed horsemen and troops
there, so that they might go out and make raids along the
highways of Judea, as the king had ordered him.
16 John went up from Gazara and reported to his father
Simon what Cendebeus had done. 2 And Simon
called in his two eldest sons Judas and John, and said to
them: "My brothers and I and my father's house have fought
the wars of Israel from our youth until this day, and things
have prospered in our hands so that we have delivered Israel
many times. 3 But now I have grown old, and you by
Heaven's[a] mercy are mature in years. Take my place and my
brother's, and go out and fight for our nation, and may the
help that comes from Heaven be with you."
4 So John[b] chose out of the country twenty thousand warriors and cavalry, and they marched against Cendebeus and
camped for the night in Modein. 5 Early in the morning they
started out and marched into the plain, where a large force
of infantry and cavalry was coming to meet them; and a
stream lay between them. 6 Then he and his army lined up
against them. He saw that the soldiers were afraid to cross

a Gk *his* *b* Other ancient authorities read *he*

NEW AMERICAN BIBLE

and to fortify Kedron and strengthen its gates, so that he
could launch attacks against the Jewish people. Meanwhile
the king went in pursuit of Trypho. 40 When Cendebeus came
to Jamnia, he began to harass the people and to make incursions into Judea, where he took people captive or massacred
them. 41 As the king ordered, he fortified Kedron and stationed horsemen and infantry there, so that they could go
out and patrol the roads of Judea.
16 John then went up from Gazara and told his father
Simon what Cendebeus was doing. 2 Simon called
his two oldest sons, Judas and John, and said to them: "I and
my brothers and my father's house have fought the battles of
Israel from our youth until today, and many times we succeeded in saving Israel. 3 I have now grown old, but you, by
the mercy of Heaven, have come to man's estate. Take my
place and my brother's, and go out and fight for our nation;
and may the help of Heaven be with you!"
4 John then mustered in the land twenty thousand warriors
and horsemen. Setting out against Cendebeus, they spent the
night at Modein, 5 rose early, and marched into the plain.
There, facing them, was an immense army of foot soldiers
and horsemen, and between the two armies was a stream.
6 John and his men took their position against the enemy.
Seeing that his men were afraid to cross the stream, John

NEW JERUSALEM BIBLE

instructed him to rebuild Kedron and fortify its gates, and to
make war on our people, while the king himself went in pursuit of Trypho. 40 Cendebaeus arrived at Jamnia and began to
provoke our people forthwith, invading Judaea, taking prisoners, and massacring. 41 Having rebuilt Kedron, he stationed cavalry and troops there to make sorties and patrol
the roads of Judaea, as the king had ordered.
16 John then went up from Gezer and reported to his
father Simon what Cendebaeus was busy doing. 2 At
this, Simon summoned his two elder sons, Judas and John,
and said to them, 'My brothers and I, and my father's House,
have fought the enemies of Israel from our youth until today,
and many a time we have been successful in rescuing Israel.
3 But now I am an old man, while you, by the mercy of
Heaven, are the right age; take the place of my brother and
myself, go out and fight for our nation, and may Heaven's
aid be with you.' 4 He then selected twenty thousand of the
country's fighting men and cavalry, and these marched
against Cendebaeus, spending the night at Modein. 5 Making
an early start, they marched into the plain, to find a large
army opposing them, both infantry and cavalry; there was,
however, a stream-bed in between. 6 John drew up facing
them, he and his army and, seeing that the men were afraid

GREEK OLD TESTAMENT

χειμάρρουν καὶ διεπέρασεν πρῶτος. καὶ εἶδον αὐτὸν οἱ
ἄνδρες καὶ διεπέρασαν κατόπισθεν αὐτοῦ. 7 καὶ διεῖλεν τὸν
λαὸν καὶ τοὺς ἱππεῖς ἐν μέσῳ τῶν πεζῶν· ἦν δὲ ἵππος τῶν
ὑπεναντίων πολλὴ σφόδρα. 8 καὶ ἐσάλπισαν ταῖς σάλπιγξιν,
καὶ ἐτροπώθη Κενδεβαῖος καὶ ἡ παρεμβολὴ αὐτοῦ, καὶ
ἔπεσον ἐξ αὐτῶν τραυματίαι πολλοί· οἱ δὲ καταλειφθέντες
ἔφυγον εἰς τὸ ὀχύρωμα. 9 τότε ἐτραυματίσθη Ιουδας ὁ
ἀδελφὸς Ιωαννου· Ιωαννης δὲ κατεδίωξεν αὐτούς, ἕως ἦλθεν
εἰς Κεδρων, ἣν ᾠκοδόμησεν. 10 καὶ ἔφυγον εἰς τοὺς πύργους
τοὺς ἐν τοῖς ἀγροῖς Ἀζώτου, καὶ ἐνεπύρισεν αὐτὴν ἐν πυρί,
καὶ ἔπεσον ἐξ αὐτῶν εἰς ἄνδρας δισχιλίους. καὶ ἀπέστρεψεν
εἰς τὴν Ιουδαίαν μετὰ εἰρήνης.
11 Καὶ Πτολεμαῖος ὁ τοῦ Ἀβούβου ἦν καθεσταμένος
στρατηγὸς εἰς τὸ πεδίον Ιεριχω καὶ ἔσχεν ἀργύριον καὶ
χρυσίον πολύ· 12 ἦν γὰρ γαμβρὸς τοῦ ἀρχιερέως. 13 καὶ
ὑψώθη ἡ καρδία αὐτοῦ, καὶ ἐβουλήθη κατακρατῆσαι τῆς
χώρας καὶ ἐβουλεύετο δόλῳ κατὰ Σιμωνος καὶ τῶν υἱῶν αὐτοῦ ἆραι αὐτούς. 14 Σιμων δὲ ἦν ἐφοδεύων τὰς πόλεις τὰς
ἐν τῇ χώρᾳ καὶ φροντίζων τῆς ἐπιμελείας αὐτῶν· καὶ κατέβη
εἰς Ιεριχω αὐτὸς καὶ Ματταθιας καὶ Ιουδας οἱ υἱοὶ αὐτοῦ
ἔτους ἑβδόμου καὶ ἑβδομηκοστοῦ καὶ ἑκατοστοῦ ἐν μηνὶ
ἑνδεκάτῳ [οὗτος ὁ μὴν Σαβατ]. 15 καὶ ὑπεδέξατο αὐτοὺς ὁ

KING JAMES VERSION

brook, he went first over himself, and then the men seeing him passed through after him.

7 *That done,* he divided his men, and set the horsemen in the midst of the footmen: for the enemies' horsemen were very many.

8 Then sounded they with the holy trumpets: whereupon Cendebeus and his host were put to flight, so that many of them were slain, and the remnant gat them to the strong hold.

9 At that time was Judas John's brother wounded; but John still followed after them, until he came to Cedron, which *Cendebeus* had built.

10 So they fled even unto the towers in the fields of Azotus; wherefore he burned it with fire: so that there were slain of them about two thousand men. Afterward he returned into the land of Judea in peace.

11 Moreover in the plain of Jericho was Ptolemeus the son of Abubus made captain, and he had abundance of silver and gold:

12 For he was the high priest's son in law.

13 Wherefore his heart being lifted up, he thought to get the country to himself, and thereupon consulted deceitfully against Simon and his sons to destroy them.

14 Now Simon was visiting the cities that were in the country, and taking care for the good ordering of them; at which time he came down himself to Jericho with his sons, Mattathias and Judas, in the hundred threescore and seventeenth year, in the eleventh month, called Sabat:

DOUAY OLD TESTAMENT

river, so he went over first: then the men seeing him, passed over after him.

7 And he divided the people, and set the horsemen in the midst of the footmen: but the horsemen of the enemies were very numerous.

8 And they sounded the holy trumpets: and Cendebeus and his army were put to flight: and there fell many of them wounded, and the rest fled into the strong hold.

9 At that time Judas John's brother was wounded: but John pursued after them, till he came to Cedron, which he had built:

10 And they fled even to the towers that were in the fields of Azotus, and he burnt them with fire. And there fell of them two thousand men, and he returned into Judea in peace.

11 Now Ptolemee the son of Abobus was appointed captain in the plain of Jericho, and he had abundance of silver and gold,

12 For he was son in law of the high priest.

13 And his heart was lifted up, and he designed to make himself master of the country, and he purposed treachery against Simon, and his sons, to destroy them.

14 Now Simon, as he was going through the cities that were in the country of Judea, and taking care for the good ordering of them, went down to Jericho, he and Mathathias and Judas his sons, in the year one hundred and seventy-seven, the eleventh month: the same is the month Sabath.

KNOX TRANSLATION

stomach for the crossing, he made the passage first, leaving
the rest to follow at his heels; 7 then drew them up by companies, with the cavalry in between, so greatly did the enemy's cavalry outnumber them. 8 And now the sacred trumpets sounded the charge; fled Cendebaeus, fled his army at
their onslaught, and many were left dead on the field; for the
rest, they were fain to take refuge behind their walls again.
9 John went in pursuit, for all his brother Judas had been
wounded in the battle, and chased them as far as the walls
of Cedron...which he had fortified.[a] 10 Nor might they find
shelter in the strongholds of the Azotus territory; he burnt
these to the ground; a toll of two thousand men he had
taken before he returned victorious to Judaea.
11 Turn we now to Ptolemy, son of Abobus, that was in
charge of all Jericho plain, and had a purse well lined with silver and gold; 12 was he not the son-in-law of a high priest?[b]
13 But higher still his ambition ran; he would make himself
master of the whole country; murder he plotted for Simon and
his sons together. 14 It was in Sabath, the eleventh month, of
the hundred and seventy-seventh year, that Simon came
down to Jericho, as ever he visited all the cities of Judaea in
his great care for them; and his sons Mattathias and Judas

a v. 9. It is grammatically impossible to make Cendebaeus the subject of the verb 'he had fortified', as the sentence stands. It seems likely that there is some slight error or omission in the manuscripts. *b* 'Of a high priest'; Josephus understands this as referring to Simon himself. But it does not seem likely that the author should have suppressed his name in verse 12, only to mention it in verse 13; nor does he mention the circumstances of affinity as adding to the heinousness of the crime (cf. verse 17). Possibly some other name has dropped out, e.g. that of Alcimus.

TODAY'S ENGLISH VERSION

afraid to cross the river, he crossed ahead of them, and his
men saw him and followed. 7 John divided his army and
placed his cavalry in the middle of the infantry, because
there was a large number of enemy cavalry. 8 The trumpets
sounded the attack, and Cendebeus and his army were
defeated, and many of them were killed. The rest ran back to
their fortress at Kedron. 9 Judas was wounded in the battle,
but his brother John continued to pursue the enemy as far as
Kedron, which Cendebeus had rebuilt. 10 The escaping soldiers fled to the towers in the fields at Azotus, and John set
fire to the city. On that day, 2,000 enemy soldiers were
killed, and John returned safely to Judea.
11 Simon the High Priest had appointed Ptolemy son of
Abubus commander for the Plain of Jericho. Ptolemy was
very rich, 12 because he was Simon's son-in-law. 13 But he
became too ambitious and wanted to take over the country.
So he devised a plan to assassinate Simon and his sons.
14 Simon, together with his sons Mattathias and Judas, was
visiting the towns in the area, in order to take care of their
needs. They arrived in Jericho in the month of Shebat, the
eleventh month, in the year 177.[a] 15 Ptolemy, still plotting to

[a] THE YEAR 177: *This corresponds to 134 B.C.*

NEW REVISED STANDARD VERSION

the stream, so he crossed over first; and when his troops saw
him, they crossed over after him. 7 Then he divided the army
and placed the cavalry in the center of the infantry, for the
cavalry of the enemy were very numerous. 8 They sounded
the trumpets, and Cendebeus and his army were put to flight;
many of them fell wounded and the rest fled into the stronghold. 9 At that time Judas the brother of John was wounded,
but John pursued them until Cendebeus[a] reached Kedron,
which he had built. 10 They also fled into the towers that
were in the fields of Azotus, and John[a] burned it with fire,
and about two thousand of them fell. He then returned to
Judea safely.
11 Now Ptolemy son of Abubus had been appointed governor over the plain of Jericho; he had a large store of silver
and gold, 12 for he was son-in-law of the high priest. 13 His
heart was lifted up; he determined to get control of the country, and made treacherous plans against Simon and his sons,
to do away with them. 14 Now Simon was visiting the towns
of the country and attending to their needs, and he went
down to Jericho with his sons Mattathias and Judas, in the
one hundred seventy-seventh year,[b] in the eleventh month,
which is the month of Shebat. 15 The son of Abubus received

a Gk *he* *b* 134 B.C.

NEW AMERICAN BIBLE

crossed first. When his men saw this, they crossed over after
him. 7 Then he divided his infantry into two corps and put
his cavalry between them, for the enemy's horsemen were
very numerous. 8 They blew the trumpets, and Cendebeus
and his army were put to flight; many of them fell wounded,
and the rest fled toward the stronghold. 9 It was then that
John's brother Judas fell wounded; but John pursued them
until Cendebeus reached Kidron, which he had fortified.
10 Some took refuge in the towers on the plain of Azotus, but
John set fire to these, and about two thousand of the enemy
perished. He then returned to Judea in peace.
11 Ptolemy, son of Abubus, had been appointed governor of
the plain of Jericho, and he had much silver and gold,
12 being the son-in-law of the high priest. 13 But he became
ambitious and sought to get control of the country. So he
made treacherous plans to do away with Simon and his
sons. 14 As Simon was inspecting the cities of the country
and providing for their needs, he and his sons Mattathias
and Judas went down to Jericho in the year one hundred and
seventy-seven, in the eleventh month (that is, the month

NEW JERUSALEM BIBLE

to cross the stream-bed, crossed over first himself. When his
men saw this, they too crossed after him. 7 He divided his
army into two, with the cavalry in the centre and the
infantry on either flank, as the opposing cavalry was very
numerous. 8 The trumpets rang out; Cendebaeus and his
army were put to flight, many of them falling mortally
wounded and the rest of them fleeing to the fortress. 9 Then
it was that Judas, John's brother, was wounded, but John
pursued them until Cendebaeus reached Kedron, which he
had rebuilt. 10 Their flight took them as far as the towers in
the countryside of Azotus, and John burnt these down. The
enemy losses amounted to ten thousand men; John returned
safely to Judaea.
11 Ptolemy son of Abubos had been appointed general in
command of the Plain of Jericho; he owned a great deal of
silver and gold, 12 and was the high priest's son-in-law.
13 His ambition was fired; he hoped to make himself master
of the whole country and therefore treacherously began to
plot the destruction of Simon and his sons. 14 Simon, who
was inspecting the towns up and down the country and
attending to their administration, had come down to Jericho
with his sons Mattathias and Judas, in the year 172, in the
eleventh month, the month of Shebat. 15 The son of Abubos

GREEK OLD TESTAMENT

τοῦ Ἀβούβου εἰς τὸ ὀχυρωμάτιον τὸ καλούμενον Δωκ μετὰ
δόλου, ὃ ᾠκοδόμησεν, καὶ ἐποίησεν αὐτοῖς πότον μέγαν καὶ
ἐνέκρυψεν ἐκεῖ ἄνδρας. 16 καὶ ὅτε ἐμεθύσθη Σιμων καὶ οἱ
υἱοὶ αὐτοῦ, ἐξανέστη Πτολεμαῖος καὶ οἱ παρ᾽ αὐτοῦ καὶ
ἔλαβον τὰ ὅπλα αὐτῶν καὶ ἐπεισῆλθον τῷ Σιμωνι εἰς τὸ
συμπόσιον καὶ ἀπέκτειναν αὐτὸν καὶ τοὺς δύο υἱοὺς αὐτοῦ
καί τινας τῶν παιδαρίων αὐτοῦ. 17 καὶ ἐποίησεν ἀθεσίαν
μεγάλην καὶ ἀπέδωκεν κακὰ ἀντὶ ἀγαθῶν. 18 καὶ ἔγραψεν
ταῦτα Πτολεμαῖος καὶ ἀπέστειλεν τῷ βασιλεῖ, ὅπως ἀποστείλῃ αὐτῷ δυνάμεις εἰς βοήθειαν καὶ παραδῷ τὴν χώραν
αὐτῶν καὶ τὰς πόλεις. 19 καὶ ἀπέστειλεν ἑτέρους εἰς
Γαζαρα ἆραι τὸν Ιωαννην, καὶ τοῖς χιλιάρχοις ἀπέστειλεν
ἐπιστολὰς παραγενέσθαι πρὸς αὐτόν, ὅπως δῷ αὐτοῖς ἀργύριον καὶ χρυσίον καὶ δόματα, 20 καὶ ἑτέρους ἀπέστειλεν
καταλαβέσθαι τὴν Ιερουσαλημ καὶ τὸ ὄρος τοῦ ἱεροῦ. 21 καὶ
προδραμών τις ἀπήγγειλεν Ιωαννῃ εἰς Γαζαρα ὅτι ἀπώλετο
ὁ πατὴρ αὐτοῦ καὶ οἱ ἀδελφοὶ αὐτοῦ, καὶ ὅτι Ἀπέσταλκεν
καὶ σὲ ἀποκτεῖναι. 22 καὶ ἀκούσας ἐξέστη σφόδρα καὶ συνέλαβεν τοὺς ἄνδρας τοὺς ἐλθόντας ἀπολέσαι αὐτὸν καὶ ἀπέκτεινεν αὐτούς. ἐπέγνω γὰρ ὅτι ἐζήτουν αὐτὸν ἀπολέσαι.
23 Καὶ τὰ λοιπὰ τῶν λόγων Ιωαννου καὶ τῶν πολέμων
αὐτοῦ καὶ τῶν ἀνδραγαθιῶν αὐτοῦ, ὧν ἠνδραγάθησεν, καὶ
τῆς οἰκοδομῆς τῶν τειχῶν, ὧν ᾠκοδόμησεν, καὶ τῶν πράξεων
αὐτοῦ, 24 ἰδοὺ ταῦτα γέγραπται ἐπὶ βιβλίῳ ἡμερῶν ἀρχιερωσύνης αὐτοῦ, ἀφ᾽ οὗ ἐγενήθη ἀρχιερεὺς μετὰ τὸν πατέρα
αὐτοῦ.

KING JAMES VERSION

15 Where the *son* of Abubus receiving them deceitfully into a little hold, called Docus, which he had built, made them a great banquet: howbeit he had hid men there.

16 So when Simon and his sons had drunk largely, Ptolemee and his men rose up, and took their weapons, and came upon Simon into the banqueting place, and slew him, and his two sons, and certain of his servants.

17 In which doing he committed a great treachery, and recompensed evil for good.

18 Then Ptolemee wrote these things, and sent to the king, that he should send him an host to aid him, and he would deliver him the country and cities.

19 He sent others also to Gazara to kill John: and unto the tribunes he sent letters to come unto him, that he might give them silver, and gold, and rewards.

20 And others he sent to take Jerusalem, and the mountain of the temple.

21 Now one had run afore to Gazara, and told John that his father and brethren were slain, and, *quoth he, Ptolemee* hath sent to slay thee also.

22 Hereof when he heard, he was sore astonished: so he laid hands on them that were come to destroy him, and slew them; for he knew that they sought to make him away.

23 As concerning the rest of the acts of John, and his wars, and worthy deeds which he did, and the building of the walls which he made, and his doings,

24 Behold, these are written in the chronicles of his priesthood, from the time he was made high priest after his father.

DOUAY OLD TESTAMENT

15 And the son of Abobus received them deceitfully into a little fortress, that is called Doch which he had built: and he made them a great feast, and hid men there.

16 And when Simon and his sons had drunk plentifully, Ptolemee and his men rose up and took their weapons, and entered into the banqueting place, and slew him, and his two sons, and some of his servants.

17 And he committed a great treachery in Israel, and rendered evil for good.

18 And Ptolemee wrote these things and sent to the king that he should send him an army to aid him, and he would deliver him the country, and their cities, and tributes.

19 And he sent others to Gazara to kill John: and to the tribunes he sent letters to come to him, and that he would give them silver, and gold, and gifts.

20 And he sent others to take Jerusalem, and the mountain of the temple.

21 Now one running before, told John in Gazara, that his father and his brethren were slain, and that he hath sent men to kill thee also.

22 But when he heard it he was exceedingly afraid: and he apprehended the men that came to kill him, and he put them to death: for he knew that they sought to make him away.

23 And as concerning the rest of the acts of John, and his wars, and the worthy deeds, which he bravely achieved, and the building of the walls, which he made, and the things that he did:

24 Behold these are written in the book of the days of his priesthood, from the time that he was made high priest after his father.

KNOX TRANSLATION

went with him. 15 And there, in a castle he had built for himself, Doch is the name of it, the son of Abobus gave them
treacherous welcome. A great feast he made, but he had men
waiting in readiness, 16 and with these, when Simon and his
sons had drunk deep, he took arms, broke into the banquet-
ing-chamber, and slew both father and sons, with certain of
their retinue. 17 Never saw Israel so treacherous a deed, or
good service so ill rewarded.
18 News of all this was sent by Ptolemy to the king, and in
writing; his plea was, an army should be sent out in support
of him, and the country, with all its cities and all the tribute
that came from them, given into his charge. 19 Others of his
men he despatched to Gazara; John must be put to death, he
wrote, and for the captains, they should have silver and gold
and good recompense, would they but rally to his side;
20 others again were to take possession of Jerusalem, and of
the temple hill. 21 But too late; a messenger had reached
John at Gazara, telling him his father and brothers were
dead, and himself too marked down for slaughter; 22 whereupon he took alarm in good earnest; their murderous errand
known, he seized his executioners and made an end of them.
23 What else John did, and how fought he, brave deeds
done, and strong walls built, and all his history, 24 you may
read in the annals of his time, that were kept faithfully since
the day when he succeeded his father as high priest.

TODAY'S ENGLISH VERSION

murder Simon and his two sons, received them in a small
fortress called Dok, which he had built. He gave a great banquet for them, but he had men hidden within the fortress.
16 When Simon and his sons were drunk, Ptolemy and his
men came out of hiding and with swords in hand rushed
into the banquet hall, where they killed Simon, his two sons,
and some of the servants. 17 With this horrible act of treachery, Ptolemy returned evil for good.

18 Then Ptolemy wrote a report of what he had done and
sent it to the king. In the letter he requested that troops be
sent to help him and that the country and the cities be
turned over to him. 19 He wrote a letter to the army officers
inviting them to join him and promising them silver, gold,
and gifts. Then he sent some of his men to Gezer to kill John,
20 and others to take control of Jerusalem and the Temple
hill. 21 But someone ran to Gezer ahead of Ptolemy's men
and reported to John that his father and his brothers had
been killed and that Ptolemy was sending his soldiers to kill
him. 22 John was horrified at this news, but, because he had
been warned in advance, he was able to capture and put to
death the men who had been sent to kill him.

23 Now the rest of what John did from the time he succeeded his father: his wars, his deeds of courage, his rebuilding
of walls, and his other accomplishments, 24 are all written in
the chronicles of his reign as High Priest.

NEW REVISED STANDARD VERSION

them treacherously in the little stronghold called Dok, which
he had built; he gave them a great banquet, and hid men
there. 16 When Simon and his sons were drunk, Ptolemy and
his men rose up, took their weapons, rushed in against
Simon in the banquet hall and killed him and his two sons,
as well as some of his servants. 17 So he committed an act of
great treachery and returned evil for good.

18 Then Ptolemy wrote a report about these things and
sent it to the king, asking him to send troops to aid him and
to turn over to him the towns and the country. 19 He sent
other troops to Gazara to do away with John; he sent letters
to the captains asking them to come to him so that he might
give them silver and gold and gifts; 20 and he sent other
troops to take possession of Jerusalem and the temple hill.
21 But someone ran ahead and reported to John at Gazara
that his father and brothers had perished, and that "he has
sent men to kill you also." 22 When he heard this, he was
greatly shocked; he seized the men who came to destroy him
and killed them, for he had found out that they were seeking
to destroy him.

23 The rest of the acts of John and his wars and the brave
deeds that he did, and the building of the walls that he completed, and his achievements, 24 are written in the annals of
his high priesthood, from the time that he became high priest
after his father.

NEW AMERICAN BIBLE

Shebat). 15 The son of Abubus gave them a deceitful welcome in the little stronghold called Dok which he had built.
While serving them a sumptuous banquet, he had his men
hidden there. 16 Then, when Simon and his sons had drunk
freely, Ptolemy and his men sprang up, weapons in hand,
rushed upon Simon in the banquet hall, and killed him, his
two sons, and some of his servants. 17 By this vicious act of
treason he repaid good with evil.

18 Then Ptolemy wrote an account of this and sent it to the
king, asking that troops be sent to help him and that the
country be turned over to him. 19 He sent other men to
Gazara to do away with John. To the army officers he sent
letters inviting them to come to him so that he might present
them with silver, gold, and gifts. 20 He also sent others to
seize Jerusalem and the mount of the temple. 21 But someone ran ahead and brought word to John at Gazara that his
father and his brothers had perished, and that Ptolemy had
sent men to kill him also. 22 On hearing this, John was utterly astounded. When the men came to kill him, he had them
arrested and put to death, for he knew what they meant to
do. 23 Now the rest of the history of John, his wars and the
brave deeds he performed, his rebuilding of the walls, and
his other achievements— 24 these things are recorded in the
chronicle of his pontificate, from the time that he succeeded
his father as high priest.

NEW JERUSALEM BIBLE

lured them into a small fortress called Dok, which he had
built, where he offered them a great banquet, having previously hidden men in the place. 16 When Simon and his sons
were drunk, Ptolemy and his men reached for their weapons,
rushed on Simon in the banqueting hall and killed him with
his two sons and some of his servants. 17 He thus committed
a great act of treachery and rendered evil for good.

18 Ptolemy wrote a report of the affair and sent it to the
king, in the expectation of being sent reinforcements and of
having the cities and the province made over to him. 19 He
also sent people to Gezer to murder John, and sent written
orders to the military commanders to come to him so that he
could give them silver, gold and presents; 20 and he also sent
others to seize control of Jerusalem and the Temple mount.
21 But someone had been too quick for him and had already
informed John in Gezer that his father and brothers had perished, adding, 'He is sending someone to kill you too!'
22 Overcome as John was by the news, he arrested the men
who had come to kill him and put them to death, being forewarned of their murderous design. 23 The rest of John's acts,
the battles he fought and the exploits he performed, the city
walls he built, and all his other achievements, 24 from the
day he succeeded his father as high priest, are recorded in
the annals of his pontificate.

GREEK OLD TESTAMENT

ΜΑΚΚΑΒΑΙΩΝ Β´

1 Τοῖς ἀδελφοῖς τοῖς κατ' Αἴγυπτον Ιουδαίοις χαίρειν οἱ
ἀδελφοὶ οἱ ἐν Ιεροσολύμοις Ιουδαῖοι καὶ οἱ ἐν τῇ χώρᾳ
τῆς Ιουδαίας εἰρήνην ἀγαθήν· 2 καὶ ἀγαθοποιήσαι ὑμῖν ὁ
θεὸς καὶ μνησθείη τῆς διαθήκης αὐτοῦ τῆς πρὸς Αβρααμ καὶ
Ισαακ καὶ Ιακωβ τῶν δούλων αὐτοῦ τῶν πιστῶν· 3 καὶ δῴη
ὑμῖν καρδίαν πᾶσιν εἰς τὸ σέβεσθαι αὐτὸν καὶ ποιεῖν αὐτοῦ
τὰ θελήματα καρδίᾳ μεγάλῃ καὶ ψυχῇ βουλομένῃ· 4 καὶ
διανοίξαι τὴν καρδίαν ὑμῶν ἐν τῷ νόμῳ αὐτοῦ καὶ ἐν τοῖς
προστάγμασιν καὶ εἰρήνην ποιήσαι 5 καὶ ἐπακούσαι ὑμῶν
τῶν δεήσεων καὶ καταλλαγείη ὑμῖν καὶ μὴ ὑμᾶς ἐγκαταλίποι
ἐν καιρῷ πονηρῷ. 6 καὶ νῦν ὧδέ ἐσμεν προσευχόμενοι περὶ
ὑμῶν. 7 βασιλεύοντος Δημητρίου ἔτους ἑκατοστοῦ
ἑξηκοστοῦ ἐνάτου ἡμεῖς οἱ Ιουδαῖοι γεγράφαμεν ὑμῖν ἐν τῇ
θλίψει καὶ ἐν τῇ ἀκμῇ τῇ ἐπελθούσῃ ἡμῖν ἐν τοῖς ἔτεσιν
τούτοις ἀφ' οὗ ἀπέστη Ἰάσων καὶ οἱ μετ' αὐτοῦ ἀπὸ τῆς
ἁγίας γῆς καὶ τῆς βασιλείας 8 καὶ ἐνεπύρισαν τὸν πυλῶνα
καὶ ἐξέχεαν αἷμα ἀθῷον· καὶ ἐδεήθημεν τοῦ κυρίου καὶ
εἰσηκούσθημεν καὶ προσηνέγκαμεν θυσίαν καὶ σεμίδαλιν καὶ
ἐξήψαμεν τοὺς λύχνους καὶ προεθήκαμεν τοὺς ἄρτους. 9 καὶ
νῦν ἵνα ἄγητε τὰς ἡμέρας τῆς σκηνοπηγίας τοῦ Χασελευ
μηνός. ἔτους ἑκατοστοῦ ὀγδοηκοστοῦ καὶ ὀγδόου.

KING JAMES VERSION

THE SECOND BOOK OF THE MACCABEES

1 The brethren, the Jews that be at Jerusalem and in the
land of Judea, wish unto the brethren, the Jews that are
throughout Egypt, health and peace:
2 God be gracious unto you, and remember his covenant
that he made with Abraham, Isaac, and Jacob, his faithful
servants;
3 And give you all an heart to serve him, and to do his
will, with a good courage and a willing mind;
4 And open your hearts in his law and commandments,
and send you peace,
5 And hear your prayers, and be at one with you, and
never forsake you in time of trouble.
6 And now we be here praying for you.
7 What time as Demetrius reigned, in the hundred threescore and ninth year, we the Jews wrote unto you in the
extremity of trouble that came upon us in those years, from
the time that Jason and his company revolted from the holy
land and kingdom,
8 And burned the porch, and shed innocent blood: then
we prayed unto the Lord, and were heard; we offered also
sacrifices and fine flour, and lighted the lamps, and set forth
the loaves.
9 And now see that ye keep the feast of tabernacles in the
month Casleu.
10 In the hundred fourscore and eighth year, the people

DOUAY OLD TESTAMENT

THE SECOND BOOK OF MACHABEES

1 TO the brethren the Jews that are throughout Egypt, the
brethren, the Jews that are in Jerusalem, and in the land
of Judea, send health, and good peace.
2 May God be gracious to you, and remember his covenant that he made with Abraham, and Isaac, and Jacob, his
faithful servants:
3 And give you all a heart to worship him, and to do his
will with a great heart, and a willing mind.
4 May he open your heart in his law, and in his commandments, and send you peace.
5 May he hear your prayers, and be reconciled unto you,
and never forsake you in the evil time.
6 And now here we are praying for you.
7 When Demetrius reigned, in the year one hundred and
sixty-nine, we Jews wrote to you, in the trouble, and violence, that came upon us in those years, after Jason withdrew himself from the holy land, and from the kingdom.
8 They burnt the gate, and shed innocent blood: then we
prayed to the Lord, and were heard, and we offered sacrifices, and fine flour, and lighted the lamps, and set forth the
loaves.
9 And now celebrate ye the days of Scenopegia in the
month of Casleu.
10 In the year one hundred and eighty-eight, the people

KNOX TRANSLATION

THE SECOND BOOK OF MACHABEES

1 To their brethren, the Jews of Egypt, those of Jerusalem
and Judaea send brotherly greeting and good health.[a]
2 God speed you well, the covenant he made with his true
worshippers, Abraham, Isaac and Jacob, never forgetting;
3 reverent hearts may he give to all of you, brave and generous to perform his will; 4 with law and precept of his enlarge
your thoughts, and send you happiness; 5 may he listen to
your prayer, and be gracious, and in the hour of peril never
forsake you! 6 Take courage, then; we in this land are praying for you. 7 Time was, in the hundred and sixty-ninth year,
when Demetrius was a-reigning, we ourselves were writing
to you in the midst of suffering and alarms. Much had we to
undergo, when Jason would betray his own country, his own
people; 8 here was the gateway burnt to the ground, here
were innocent lives forfeited. Cried we upon the Lord, and all
our prayers were answered; burnt-sacrifice and bloodless
offering were made, lamps lighted, and loaves set forth in
the temple as of old! 9 Look to it, then, you make bowers
and keep holiday in this month of Casleu.[b] 10 Written in the
hundred and eighty-eighth year.

a vv. 1-9. The first, it would seem, of a series of fragments prefixed to the book proper. If the date given at the end belongs to it, it must have been written about the year 125 before Christ, after the death of Simon.
b Here and in verse 18 the feast alluded to is not the feast of Tent-dwelling (Lev. 23. 34), but that of the Dedication (I Mac. 4. 59, Jn. 10. 22) at which it appears that the same ceremonies were used.

TODAY'S ENGLISH VERSION

THE SECOND BOOK OF THE MACCABEES

1 "From the Jews of Jerusalem and Judea to those in
Egypt, warm greetings.
2 "May God be good to you and keep the covenant he made
with Abraham, Isaac, and Jacob, his faithful servants. 3 May
he fill each of you with the desire to worship him and to do
his will eagerly with all your heart and soul. 4 May he enable
you to understand his Law and his commands. May he give
you peace, 5 answer your prayers, forgive your sins, and
never abandon you in times of trouble. 6 Here in Judah we
are now praying for you.
7 "In the year 169,[a] when Demetrius the Second was king
of Syria, we wrote to tell you about the persecution and the
hard times that came upon us in the years after Jason revolted against authority in the Holy Land. 8 Jason and his men
set fire to the Temple gates and slaughtered innocent people.
Then we prayed to the Lord and he answered our prayers. So
we sacrificed animals, gave offerings of grain, lit the lamps
in the Temple, and set out the sacred loaves. 9 This is why
we urge you to celebrate in the month of Kislev a festival
similar to the Festival of Shelters. Written in the year 188."[b]

[a] THE YEAR 169: *This corresponds to 143 B.C.* [b] THE YEAR 188: *This corresponds to 124 B.C.*

NEW REVISED STANDARD VERSION

2 MACCABEES

1 The Jews in Jerusalem and those in the land of Judea,
To their Jewish kindred in Egypt,
Greetings and true peace.
2 May God do good to you, and may he remember his covenant with Abraham and Isaac and Jacob, his faithful servants. 3 May he give you all a heart to worship him and to
do his will with a strong heart and a willing spirit. 4 May he
open your heart to his law and his commandments, and may
he bring peace. 5 May he hear your prayers and be reconciled
to you, and may he not forsake you in time of evil. 6 We are
now praying for you here.
7 In the reign of Demetrius, in the one hundred sixty-
ninth year,[a] we Jews wrote to you, in the critical distress
that came upon us in those years after Jason and his company revolted from the holy land and the kingdom 8 and
burned the gate and shed innocent blood. We prayed to the
Lord and were heard, and we offered sacrifice and grain
offering, and we lit the lamps and set out the loaves. 9 And
now see that you keep the festival of booths in the month of
Chislev, in the one hundred eighty-eighth year.[b]

a 143 B.C. *b* 124 B.C.

NEW AMERICAN BIBLE

THE SECOND BOOK OF MACCABEES

1 The Jews in Jerusalem and in the land of Judea send
greetings to their brethren, the Jews in Egypt, and wish
them true peace! 2 May God bless you and remember his covenant with his faithful servants, Abraham, Isaac and Jacob.
3 May he give to all of you a heart to worship him and to do
his will readily and generously. 4 May he open your heart to
his law and his commandments and grant you peace. 5 May
he hear your prayers, and be reconciled to you, and never
forsake you in time of adversity. 6 Even now we are praying
for you here.
7 In the reign of Demetrius, the year one hundred and
sixty-nine, we Jews wrote to you during the trouble and violence that overtook us in those years after Jason and his followers had revolted against the holy land and the kingdom,
8 setting fire to the gatehouse and shedding innocent blood.
But we prayed to the LORD, and our prayer was heard; we
offered sacrifices and fine flour; we lighted the lamps and set
out the loaves of bread. 9 We are now reminding you to celebrate the feast of Booths in the month of Chislev. 10 Dated in
the year one hundred and eighty-eight.

NEW JERUSALEM BIBLE

THE SECOND BOOK OF MACCABEES

1 'To their brothers, the Jews living in Egypt, from their
brothers, the Jews in Jerusalem and Judaea, greetings
and untroubled peace.
2 'May God prosper you, remembering his covenant with
Abraham, Isaac and Jacob, his faithful servants. 3 May he
give you all a heart to worship him and to do his will with a
generous mind and a willing spirit. 4 May he open your
hearts to his Law and his precepts, and give you peace.
5 May he hear your prayers and be reconciled with you, and
not abandon you in time of evil. 6 Such is our prayer for you.
7 'During the reign of Demetrius, in the year 169, we Jews
wrote to you as follows, "In the extremity of trouble that
befell us in the years after Jason and his associates had
betrayed the Holy Land and the kingdom, 8 burning down
the Temple gateway and shedding innocent blood, we prayed
to the Lord and were then heard. And we then offered a sacrifice, with wheat-flour, we lit the lamps and we set out the
loaves."
9 'And we now recommend you too to keep the feast of
Shelters in the month of Chislev, in the year one hundred
and eighty-eight.'

GREEK OLD TESTAMENT

10 Οἱ ἐν Ιεροσολύμοις καὶ οἱ ἐν τῇ Ιουδαίᾳ καὶ ἡ γερουσία
καὶ Ιουδας Ἀριστοβούλῳ διδασκάλῳ Πτολεμαίου τοῦ βασιλέως, ὄντι δὲ ἀπὸ τοῦ τῶν χριστῶν ἱερέων γένους, καὶ τοῖς ἐν
Αἰγύπτῳ Ιουδαίοις χαίρειν καὶ ὑγιαίνειν. 11 ἐκ μεγάλων
κινδύνων ὑπὸ τοῦ θεοῦ σεσῳσμένοι μεγάλως εὐχαριστοῦμεν
αὐτῷ ὡς ἂν πρὸς βασιλέα παρατασσόμενοι· 12 αὐτὸς γὰρ
ἐξέβρασεν τοὺς παραταξαμένους ἐν τῇ ἁγίᾳ πόλει. 13 εἰς
τὴν Περσίδα γενόμενος γὰρ ὁ ἡγεμὼν καὶ ἡ περὶ αὐτὸν
ἀνυπόστατος δοκοῦσα εἶναι δύναμις κατεκόπησαν ἐν τῷ τῆς
Ναναίας ἱερῷ, παραλογισμῷ χρησαμένων τῶν περὶ τὴν
Ναναίαν ἱερέων. 14 ὡς γὰρ συνοικήσων αὐτῇ παρεγένετο εἰς
τὸν τόπον ὅ τε Ἀντίοχος καὶ οἱ σὺν αὐτῷ φίλοι χάριν τοῦ
λαβεῖν τὰ χρήματα πλείονα εἰς φερνῆς λόγον 15 καὶ προθέν-
των αὐτὰ τῶν ἱερέων τοῦ Ναναίου κἀκείνου προσελθόντος
μετ' ὀλίγων εἰς τὸν περίβολον τοῦ τεμένους, συγκλείσαντες
τὸ ἱερόν, ὡς εἰσῆλθεν Ἀντίοχος, 16 ἀνοίξαντες τὴν τοῦ
φατνώματος κρυπτὴν θύραν βάλλοντες πέτρους συνεκεραύν-
ωσαν τὸν ἡγεμόνα καὶ μέλη ποιήσαντες καὶ τὰς κεφαλὰς
ἀφελόντες τοῖς ἔξω παρέρριψαν. 17 κατὰ πάντα εὐλογητὸς

KING JAMES VERSION

that were at Jerusalem and in Judea, and the council, and Judas, sent greeting and health unto Aristobulus, king Ptolemeus' master, who was of the stock of the anointed priests, and to the Jews that were in Egypt:

11 Insomuch as God hath delivered us from great perils, we thank him highly, as having been in battle against a king.

12 For he cast them out that fought within the holy city.

13 For when the leader was come into Persia, and the army with him that seemed invincible, they were slain in the temple of Nanea by the deceit of Nanea's priests.

14 For Antiochus, as though he would marry her, came into the place, and his friends that were with him, to receive money in name of a dowry.

15 Which when the priests of Nanea had set forth, and he was entered with a small company into the compass of the temple, they shut the temple as soon as Antiochus was come in:

16 And opening a privy door of the roof, they threw stones like thunderbolts, and struck down the captain, hewed them in pieces, smote off their heads, and cast them to those that were without.

DOUAY OLD TESTAMENT

that is at Jerusalem, and in Judea, and the senate, and Judas, to Aristobulus, the preceptor of king Ptolemee, who is of the stock of the anointed priests, and to the Jews that are in Egypt, health and welfare.

11 Having been delivered by God out of great dangers, we give him great thanks, forasmuch as we have been in war with such a king.

12 For he made numbers of men swarm out of Persia that have fought against us, and the holy city.

13 For when the leader himself was in Persia, and with him a very great army, he fell in the temple of Nanea, being deceived by the counsel of the priests of Nanea.

14 For Antiochus, with his friends, came to the place as though he would marry her, and that he might receive great sums of money under the title of a dowry.

15 And when the priests of Nanea had set it forth, and he with a small company had entered into the compass of the temple, they shut the temple,

16 When Antiochus was come in: and opening a secret entrance of the temple, they cast stones and slew the leader, and them that were with him, and hewed them in pieces, and cutting off their heads they threw them forth.

KNOX TRANSLATION

The common folk of Jerusalem and Judaea,[a] their council of
elders, and I, Judas, to Aristobulus, of the anointed priestly
race, that was master of king Ptolemy, and to the Jews of
Egypt, greeting and health. 11 Great thanks we owe to God,
that from the extreme of peril has delivered us; ay, though we
had such a king for our adversary, 12 as could bring in hordes
of men from Persia, both us and our holy city to subdue.[b]
13 What became of him, think you, the general that marched
away into Persia with a countless army at his heels?[c] He met
his end in the temple of Nanea, through guile of the priests that
served it. 14 Thither Antiochus had come with his friends,
putting it about that he would wed the goddess, and laying
claim to a great part of her treasures under the title of dowry.
15 The priests, then, had the money laid out in readiness; into
the precincts he came, with a meagre retinue, and they, now
that Antiochus was within, shut the temple gates. 16 Thereupon, letting themselves in by their secret door, they killed the
general and his company with throwing of stones, cut them
limb from limb, and threw them down headless to the populace

a vv. 10-18. The date mentioned in verse 10 probably belongs to the earlier fragment, since the ancients usually dated their letters at the end, cf. 11. 21, 33, 38 below. If so, this second fragment, undated, will have been written by Judas Machabaeus to Aristobulus, tutor of the Egyptian king Ptolemy Philometor, some forty years earlier than verses 1-9. *b vv.* 11, 12. The Latin here seems designed to make sense of a passage untranslatable, and probably corrupt, in the Greek text. *c vv.* 13-16. If Antiochus Epiphanes is meant, the description of him as 'the general' is highly suspicious. It seems possible that no name was mentioned in the original, and that the word 'Antiochus' was twice introduced by a copyist, mistakenly anxious to identify the unnamed figure. If so, the fate we are concerned with is that of some general in command of Antiochus's army; his own is described, quite differently, in 9. 5 below.

TODAY'S ENGLISH VERSION

10 "From the Jews of Jerusalem and Judea, the Jewish Senate, and Judas, to Aristobulus, a descendant of priests and the teacher of King Ptolemy, and to the Jews in Egypt, greetings and good health.

11 "We thank God because he saved us from great danger. We were like men ready to fight against a king, 12 but God drove the enemy from our holy city. 13 When King Antiochus arrived in Persia, his army seemed impossible to defeat, but they were cut to pieces in the temple of the goddess Nanea by an act of treachery on the part of her priests. 14 King Antiochus had gone to the temple with some of his most trusted advisers, so that he might marry the goddess and then take away most of the temple treasures as a wedding gift. 15 After the priests had laid out the treasure, he and a few of his men went into the temple to collect it. But the priests closed the doors behind him 16 and stoned him and his men from trap doors hidden in the ceiling. Then they cut up the bodies and threw the heads to the people outside.

NEW REVISED STANDARD VERSION

10 The people of Jerusalem and of Judea and the senate and Judas,

To Aristobulus, who is of the family of the anointed priests, teacher of King Ptolemy, and to the Jews in Egypt,

Greetings and good health.

11 Having been saved by God out of grave dangers we thank him greatly for taking our side against the king,[a] 12 for he drove out those who fought against the holy city. 13 When the leader reached Persia with a force that seemed irresistible, they were cut to pieces in the temple of Nanea by a deception employed by the priests of the goddess[b] Nanea. 14 On the pretext of intending to marry her, Antiochus came to the place together with his Friends, to secure most of its treasures as a dowry. 15 When the priests of the temple of Nanea had set out the treasures and Antiochus had come with a few men inside the wall of the sacred precinct, they closed the temple as soon as he entered it. 16 Opening a secret door in the ceiling, they threw stones and struck down the leader and his men; they dismembered them and cut off their heads and threw them to the people outside. 17 Blessed

a Cn: Gk *as those who array themselves against a king* *b* Gk lacks *the goddess*

NEW AMERICAN BIBLE

The people of Jerusalem and Judea, the senate, and Judas send greetings and good wishes to Aristobulus, counselor of King Ptolemy and member of the family of the anointed priests, and to the Jews in Egypt. 11 Since we have been saved by God from grave dangers, we give him great thanks for having fought on our side against the king; 12 it was he who drove out those who fought against the holy city. 13 When their leader arrived in Persia with his seemingly irresistible army, they were cut to pieces in the temple of the goddess Nanea through a deceitful stratagem employed by Nanea's priests. 14 On the pretext of marrying the goddess, Antiochus with his Friends had come to the place to get its great treasures by way of dowry. 15 When the priests of the Nanaeon had displayed the treasures, Antiochus with a few attendants came to the temple precincts. As soon as he entered the temple, the priests locked the doors. 16 Then they opened a hidden trapdoor in the ceiling, hurled stones at the leader and his companions and struck them down. They dismembered the bodies, cut off their heads and tossed them to

NEW JERUSALEM BIBLE

10 'The people of Jerusalem and of Judaea, the senate and Judas, to Aristobulus, tutor to King Ptolemy and one of the family of the anointed priests, and to the Jews in Egypt, greetings and good health.

11 'Since we have been rescued by God from great danger, we give him great thanks for championing our cause against the king, 12 for he it was who carried off those who had taken up arms against the Holy City. 13 For when their leader reached Persia with his seemingly irresistible army, he was cut to pieces in the temple of Nanaea, as the result of a ruse employed by the priests who served that goddess. 14 On the pretext of marrying Nanaea, Antiochus came to the place with his friends, intending to take its many treasures as a dowry. 15 The priests of Nanaea had put these on display, and he for his part had entered the temple precincts with only a small retinue. As soon as Antiochus had gone inside the temple, the priests shut him in, 16 opened a trap-door hidden in the ceiling and struck the leader down by hurling stones like thunderbolts. They then cut him into pieces and threw his head to those who were waiting outside.

Greek Old Testament

ἡμῶν ὁ θεός, ὃς παρέδωκεν τοὺς ἀσεβήσαντας. [18] μέλλοντες ἄγειν ἐν τῷ Χασελευ πέμπτῃ καὶ εἰκάδι τὸν καθαρισμὸν τοῦ ἱεροῦ δέον ἡγησάμεθα διασαφῆσαι ὑμῖν, ἵνα καὶ αὐτοὶ ἄγητε σκηνοπηγίας καὶ τοῦ πυρός, ὅτε Νεεμιας ὁ οἰκοδομήσας τό τε ἱερὸν καὶ τὸ θυσιαστήριον ἀνήνεγκεν θυσίας. [19] καὶ γὰρ ὅτε εἰς τὴν Περσικὴν ἤγοντο ἡμῶν οἱ πατέρες, οἱ τότε εὐσεβεῖς ἱερεῖς λαβόντες ἀπὸ τοῦ πυρὸς τοῦ θυσιαστηρίου λαθραίως κατέκρυψαν ἐν κοιλώματι φρέατος τάξιν ἔχοντος ἄνυδρον, ἐν ᾧ κατησφαλίσαντο ὥστε πᾶσιν ἄγνωστον εἶναι τὸν τόπον. [20] διελθόντων δὲ ἐτῶν ἱκανῶν, ὅτε ἔδοξεν τῷ θεῷ, ἀποσταλεὶς Νεεμιας ὑπὸ τοῦ βασιλέως τῆς Περσίδος τοὺς ἐκγόνους τῶν ἱερέων τῶν ἀποκρυψάντων ἔπεμψεν ἐπὶ τὸ πῦρ· ὡς δὲ διεσάφησαν ἡμῖν μὴ εὑρηκέναι πῦρ, ἀλλὰ ὕδωρ παχύ, ἐκέλευσεν αὐτοὺς ἀποβάψαντας φέρειν. [21] ὡς δὲ

King James Version

17 Blessed be our God in all things, who hath delivered up the ungodly.

18 Therefore whereas we are now purposed to keep the purification of the temple upon the five and twentieth day of *the month* Casleu, we thought it necessary to certify you thereof, that ye also might keep *it, as the feast* of the tabernacles, and of the fire, *which was given us* when Neemias offered sacrifice, after that he had builded the temple and the altar.

19 For when our fathers were led into Persia, the priests that were then devout took the fire of the altar privily, and hid it in an hollow place of a pit without water, where they kept *it* sure, so that the place was unknown to all men.

20 Now after many years, when it pleased God, Neemias, being sent from the king of Persia, did send of the posterity of those priests that had hid it to the fire: but when they told us they found no fire, but thick water;

21 Then commanded he them to draw it up, and to bring

Douay Old Testament

17 Blessed be God in all things, who hath delivered up the wicked.

18 Therefore whereas we purpose to keep the purification of the temple on the five and twentieth day of the month of Casleu, we thought it necessary to signify it to you: that you also may keep the day of Scenopegia, and the day of the fire, that was given when Nehemias offered sacrifice, after the temple and the altar was built.

19 For when our fathers were led into Persia, the priests that then were worshippers of God took privately the fire from the altar, and hid it in a valley where there was a deep pit without water, and there they kept it safe, so that the place was unknown to all men.

20 But when many years had passed, and it pleased God that Nehemias should be sent by the king of Persia, he sent some of the posterity of those priests that had hid it, to seek for the fire: and as they told us, they found no fire, but thick water.

21 Then he bade them draw it up, and bring it to him: and

Knox Translation

without. [17] Blessed, upon every account, be this God of ours, that denies protection to the sinner! [18] We, then, on this twenty-fifth day of Casleu, mean to solemnize the purification of the temple, and hold ourselves bound to notify you of it, so that you too may keep holiday, with making of bowers….

…And of the fire imparted to us, when Nehemias offered sacrifice at the rebuilding of temple and altar.[a] [19] Long ago, when our fathers were being carried off into the Persian country, such priests of the true God as held office in those days took away the fire from the altar, and hid it down in the valley, in a pit both deep and dry, so well guarding their secret that none might know where it was to be found. [20] Years passed, and God's will was that Nehemias should come back, holding the Persian king's warrant. Nehemias it was that had search made for the fire, and by the grandsons of those very priests that hid it; but they made report, fire they could find none, only a puddle of water.[b] [21] And what

a The Latin makes a single sentence of the whole verse, but by dint of concealing what is evidently a gap in the Greek text. The end of the second fragment seems to have been lost; and also the beginning of this third fragment, which occupies the rest of the chapter. The identity of Nehemias seems doubtful; the well-known governor of that name restored the walls of Jerusalem nearly a century after the rebuilding of the Temple. But a Nehemias is mentioned in I Esd. 2. 2, Neh. 7. 7, among the exiles who returned with Zorobabel. The description 'Nehemias the priest' in verse 21 is probably due to an error in our present Latin text. *b* The 'fire' hidden in the pit was presumably a smouldering log, such as might be buried away at night to be re-lit in the morning. The 'puddle of water' (literally, 'thick water') found on the site was evidently something different, and there is no reason to think that its properties, natural or supernatural, belonged to the 'fire' originally deposited there.

TODAY'S ENGLISH VERSION

17 Praise God for punishing those evil men! Praise him for
everything!
18 "On the twenty-fifth day of the month of Kislev we will
celebrate the Festival of Rededication just as we celebrate the
Festival of Shelters. We thought it important to remind you
of this, so that you too may celebrate this festival. In this
way you will remember how fire appeared when Nehemiah
offered sacrifices after he had rebuilt the Temple and the
altar. 19 At the time when our ancestors were being taken to
exile in Persia, a few devout priests took some fire from the
altar and secretly hid it in the bottom of a dry cistern. They
hid the fire so well that no one ever discovered it. 20 Years
later, when it pleased God, the Persian emperor sent
Nehemiah back to Jerusalem, and Nehemiah told the descendants of those priests to find the fire. They reported to us
that they had found no fire but only some oily liquid.
Nehemiah then told them to scoop some up and bring it to

NEW REVISED STANDARD VERSION

in every way be our God, who has brought judgment on
those who have behaved impiously.
18 Since on the twenty-fifth day of Chislev we shall celebrate the purification of the temple, we thought it necessary
to notify you, in order that you also may celebrate the festival of booths and the festival of the fire given when
Nehemiah, who built the temple and the altar, offered sacrifices.
19 For when our ancestors were being led captive to
Persia, the pious priests of that time took some of the fire of
the altar and secretly hid it in the hollow of a dry cistern,
where they took such precautions that the place was
unknown to anyone. 20 But after many years had passed,
when it pleased God, Nehemiah, having been commissioned
by the king of Persia, sent the descendants of the priests who
had hidden the fire to get it. And when they reported to us
that they had not found fire but only a thick liquid, he
ordered them to dip it out and bring it. 21 When the materials

NEW AMERICAN BIBLE

the people outside. 17 Forever blessed be our God, who has
thus punished the wicked!
18 We shall be celebrating the purification of the temple on
the twenty-fifth day of the month Chislev, so we thought it
right to inform you that you too may celebrate the feast of
Booths and of the fire that appeared when Nehemiah, the
rebuilder of the temple and the altar, offered sacrifices.
19 When our fathers were being exiled to Persia, devout priests
of the time took some of the fire from the altar and hid it
secretly in the hollow of a dry cistern, making sure that the
place would be unknown to anyone. 20 Many years later,
when it so pleased God, Nehemiah, commissioned by the king
of Persia, sent the descendants of the priests who had hidden
the fire to look for it. 21 When they informed us that they
could not find any fire, but only muddy water, he ordered
them to scoop some out and bring it. After the material for the

NEW JERUSALEM BIBLE

17 Blessed in all things be our God, who has delivered the
sacrilegious over to death!
18 'As we shall be celebrating the purification of the Temple
on the twenty-fifth of Chislev, we consider it proper to notify
you, so that you too may celebrate it, as you do the feast of
Shelters and the fire that appeared when Nehemiah, the
builder of the Temple and the altar, offered sacrifice. 19 For
when our ancestors were being deported to Persia, the
devout priests of the time took some of the fire from the altar
and hid it secretly in a hole like a dry well, where they concealed it in such a way that the place was unknown to anyone. 20 When some years had elapsed, in God's good time,
Nehemiah, commissioned by the king of Persia, sent the
descendants of the priests who had hidden the fire to look
for it. When they reported that in fact they had found not fire
but a thick liquid, Nehemiah ordered them to draw some out

GREEK OLD TESTAMENT

ἀνηνέχθη τὰ τῶν θυσιῶν, ἐκέλευσεν τοὺς ἱερεῖς Νεεμιας
ἐπιρρᾶναι τῷ ὕδατι τά τε ξύλα καὶ τὰ ἐπικείμενα. 22 ὡς δὲ
ἐγένετο τοῦτο καὶ χρόνος διῆλθεν ὅ τε ἥλιος ἀνέλαμψεν
πρότερον ἐπινεφὴς ὤν, ἀνήφθη πυρὰ μεγάλη ὥστε θαυμάσαι
πάντας. 23 προσευχὴν δὲ ἐποιήσαντο οἱ ἱερεῖς δαπανωμένης
τῆς θυσίας, οἵ τε ἱερεῖς καὶ πάντες, καταρχομένου Ιωναθου,
τῶν δὲ λοιπῶν ἐπιφωνούντων ὡς Νεεμιου· 24 ἦν δὲ ἡ
προσευχὴ τὸν τρόπον ἔχουσα τοῦτον
Κύριε κύριε ὁ θεός, ὁ πάντων κτίστης, ὁ φοβερὸς καὶ
ἰσχυρὸς καὶ δίκαιος καὶ ἐλεήμων, ὁ μόνος βασιλεὺς καὶ χρηστός, 25 ὁ μόνος χορηγός, ὁ μόνος δίκαιος καὶ παντοκράτωρ
καὶ αἰώνιος, ὁ διασῴζων τὸν Ισραηλ ἐκ παντὸς κακοῦ, ὁ
ποιήσας τοὺς πατέρας ἐκλεκτοὺς καὶ ἁγιάσας αὐτούς,
26 πρόσδεξαι τὴν θυσίαν ὑπὲρ παντὸς τοῦ λαοῦ σου Ισραηλ
καὶ διαφύλαξον τὴν μερίδα σου καὶ καθαγίασον. 27 ἐπισυν-
άγαγε τὴν διασπορὰν ἡμῶν, ἐλευθέρωσον τοὺς δουλεύοντας
ἐν τοῖς ἔθνεσιν, τοὺς ἐξουθενημένους καὶ βδελυκτοὺς ἔπιδε,
καὶ γνώτωσαν τὰ ἔθνη ὅτι σὺ εἶ ὁ θεὸς ἡμῶν. 28 βασάνισον
τοὺς καταδυναστεύοντας καὶ ἐξυβρίζοντας ἐν ὑπερηφανίᾳ.
29 καταφύτευσον τὸν λαόν σου εἰς τὸν τόπον τὸν ἅγιόν σου,
καθὼς εἶπεν Μωυσῆς.

30 Οἱ δὲ ἱερεῖς ἐπέψαλλον τοὺς ὕμνους. 31 καθὼς δὲ
ἀνηλώθη τὰ τῆς θυσίας, καὶ τὸ περιλειπόμενον ὕδωρ ὁ Νεεμιας ἐκέλευσεν λίθους μείζονας καταχεῖν. 32 ὡς δὲ τοῦτο

KING JAMES VERSION

it; and when the sacrifices were laid on, Neemias commanded the priests to sprinkle the wood and the things laid thereupon with the water.

22 When this was done, and the time came that the sun shone, which afore was hid in the cloud, there was a great fire kindled, so that every man marvelled.

23 And the priests made a prayer whilst the sacrifice was consuming, *I say,* both the priests, and all *the rest,* Jonathan beginning, and the rest answering thereunto, as Neemias did.

24 And the prayer was after this manner; O Lord, Lord God, Creator of all things, who art fearful and strong, and righteous, and merciful, and the only and gracious King,

25 The only giver of all things, the only just, almighty, and everlasting, thou that deliverest Israel from all trouble, and didst choose the fathers, and sanctify them:

26 Receive the sacrifice for thy whole people Israel, and preserve thine own portion, and sanctify it.

27 Gather those together that are scattered from us, deliver them that serve among the heathen, look upon them that are despised and abhorred, and let the heathen know that thou art our God.

28 Punish them that oppress us, and with pride do us wrong.

29 Plant thy people again in thy holy place, as Moses hath spoken.

30 And the priests sung psalms of thanksgiving.

31 Now when the sacrifice was consumed, Neemias commanded the water that was left to be poured on the great stones.

DOUAY OLD TESTAMENT

the priest Nehemias commanded the sacrifices that were laid on, to be sprinkled with the same water, both the wood, and the things that were laid upon it.

22 And when this was done, and the time came that the sun shone out, which before was in a cloud, there was a great fire kindled, so that all wondered.

23 And all the priests made prayer, while the sacrifice was consuming, Jonathan beginning, and the rest answering.

24 And the prayer of Nehemias was after this manner: O Lord God, Creator of all things, dreadful and strong, just and merciful, who alone art the good king,

25 Who alone art gracious, who alone art just, and almighty, and eternal, who deliverest Israel from all evil, who didst choose the fathers and didst sanctify them:

26 Receive the sacrifice for all thy people Israel, and preserve thy own portion, and sanctify it.

27 Gather together our scattered people, deliver them that are slaves to the Gentiles, and look upon them that are despised and abhorred: that the Gentiles may know that thou art our God.

28 Punish them that oppress us, and that treat us injuriously with pride.

29 Establish thy people in thy holy place, as Moses hath spoken.

30 And the priests sung hymns till the sacrifice was consumed.

31 And when the sacrifice was consumed, Nehemias commanded the water that was left to be poured out upon the great stones.

KNOX TRANSLATION

did Nehemias? He would have some of the water drawn and
fetched to him; with this water, once the sacrifice was laid
on the altar, both the wood and the offerings themselves
must be sprinkled. 22 Sprinkled they were, and when the sun
shone out, that till now was hidden by a cloud, all at once a
great fire blazed up, astonishing the beholders.
23 To prayer fell the priests all around, while sacrifice was
done, Jonathan to lead them,[a] and the rest answering; 24 to
prayer fell Nehemias, and this was the manner of his praying: Lord God, that all things madest, the terrible, the strong,
the just, the merciful, King gracious as none else; 25 none
else so kindly, none else so just, as thou, the almighty, the
eternal! Israel from all peril thou deliverest, thou didst make
choice of our fathers, and set them apart for thyself. 26 For
the whole nation of Israel receive our sacrifice; all are thine;
thy own domain keep inviolate. 27 Bring home the exiles;
captives of the heathen conquer or set free; to the despised,
the outcast grant redress; let the world know what a God is
ours! 28 Crush the oppressor, the tyrant that so mishandles
us, 29 and to thy own sanctuary, as Moses foretold, thy own
people restore!
30 Then, till the sacrifice was consumed, the priests went
on with their singing of hymns; 31 and when all was finished, Nehemias would have them drench great stones with
the water that was left. 32 Thereupon, a flame broke out

[a] Jonathan was not the high priest, but the leader of a course of priests (Neh. 12. 14).

TODAY'S ENGLISH VERSION

him. 21 When everything for the sacrifice had been placed on
the altar, he told the priests to pour the liquid over both the
wood and the sacrifice. 22 After this was done and some time
had passed, the sun appeared from behind the clouds, and
suddenly everything on the altar burst into flames. Everyone
looked on in amazement. 23 Then, while the fire was consuming the sacrifice, Jonathan the High Priest led the people
in prayer, and Nehemiah and all the people responded.

24 "Nehemiah's prayer went something like this: 'Lord God,
Creator of all things, you are awesome and strong, yet merciful and just. You alone are king. No one but you is kind;
25 no one but you is gracious and just. You are almighty and
eternal, forever ready to rescue Israel from trouble. You chose
our ancestors to be your own special people. 26 Accept this
sacrifice which we offer on behalf of all Israel; protect your
chosen people and make us holy. 27 Free those who are
slaves in foreign lands and gather together our scattered people. Have mercy on our people, who are mistreated and
despised, so that all other nations will know that you are our
God. 28 Punish the brutal and arrogant people who have
oppressed us, 29 and then establish your people in your holy
land, as Moses said you would.'

30 "Then the priests sang hymns. 31 After the sacrifices had
been consumed, Nehemiah gave orders for the rest of the liquid to be poured over some large stones. 32 Immediately a

NEW REVISED STANDARD VERSION

for the sacrifices were presented, Nehemiah ordered the
priests to sprinkle the liquid on the wood and on the things
laid upon it. 22 When this had been done and some time had
passed, and when the sun, which had been clouded over,
shone out, a great fire blazed up, so that all marveled. 23 And
while the sacrifice was being consumed, the priests offered
prayer—the priests and everyone. Jonathan led, and the rest
responded, as did Nehemiah. 24 The prayer was to this effect:

"O Lord, Lord God, Creator of all things, you are awe-
inspiring and strong and just and merciful, you alone are
king and are kind, 25 you alone are bountiful, you alone are
just and almighty and eternal. You rescue Israel from every
evil; you chose the ancestors and consecrated them.
26 Accept this sacrifice on behalf of all your people Israel and
preserve your portion and make it holy. 27 Gather together
our scattered people, set free those who are slaves among the
Gentiles, look on those who are rejected and despised, and
let the Gentiles know that you are our God. 28 Punish those
who oppress and are insolent with pride. 29 Plant your people in your holy place, as Moses promised."

30 Then the priests sang the hymns. 31 After the materials
of the sacrifice had been consumed, Nehemiah ordered that
the liquid that was left should be poured on large stones.

NEW AMERICAN BIBLE

sacrifices had been prepared, Nehemiah ordered the priests to
sprinkle with the water the wood and what lay on it. 22 When
this was done and in time the sun, which had been clouded
over, began to shine, a great fire blazed up, so that everyone
marveled. 23 While the sacrifice was being burned, the priests
recited a prayer, and all present joined in with them, Jonathan
leading and the rest responding with Nehemiah.

24 The prayer was as follows: "LORD, LORD God, creator of
all things, awesome and strong, just and merciful, the only
king and benefactor, 25 who alone are gracious, just,
almighty, and eternal, Israel's savior from all evil, who chose
our forefathers and sanctified them: 26 accept this sacrifice
on behalf of all your people Israel and guard and sanctify
your heritage. 27 Gather together our scattered people, free
those who are the slaves of the Gentiles, look kindly on
those who are despised and detested, and let the Gentiles
know that you are our God. 28 Punish those who tyrannize
over us and arrogantly mistreat us. 29 Plant your people in
your holy place, as Moses promised."

30 Then the priests began to sing hymns. 31 After the sacrifice was burned, Nehemiah ordered the rest of the liquid to
be poured upon large stones. 32 As soon as this was done, a

NEW JERUSALEM BIBLE

and bring it back. 21 When they had done this, Nehemiah
ordered the priests to pour this liquid over the sacrificial
materials, that is, the wood and what lay on it. 22 When this
had been done, and when in due course the sun, which had
previously been clouded over, shone out, a great fire flared
up, to the astonishment of all. 23 While the sacrifice was
being burned, the priests offered prayer, Jonathan intoning
with all the priests, and the rest responding with Nehemiah.
24 The prayer took this form, "Lord, Lord God, Creator of all
things, awesome, strong, just, merciful, the only king and
benefactor, 25 the only provider, who alone are just, almighty
and everlasting, the deliverer of Israel from every evil, who
made our fathers your chosen ones and sanctified them,
26 accept this sacrifice on behalf of all your people Israel, and
protect your heritage and consecrate it. 27 Bring together
those of us who are dispersed, set free those in slavery
among the heathen, look favourably on those held in contempt or abhorrence, and let the heathen know that you are
our God. 28 Punish those who oppress us and affront us by
their insolence, 29 and plant your people firmly in your Holy
Place, as Moses promised."

30 'The priests then chanted hymns accompanied by the
harp. 31 When the sacrifice had been burnt, Nehemiah
ordered the remaining liquid to be poured over large stones,

GREEK OLD TESTAMENT

ἐγενήθη, φλὸξ ἀνήφθη· τοῦ δὲ ἀπὸ τοῦ θυσιαστηρίου ἀντιλάμψαντος φωτὸς ἐδαπανήθη. 33 ὡς δὲ φανερὸν ἐγενήθη τὸ πρᾶγμα, καὶ διηγγέλη τῷ βασιλεῖ τῶν Περσῶν ὅτι εἰς τὸν τόπον, οὗ τὸ πῦρ ἔκρυψαν οἱ μεταχθέντες ἱερεῖς, τὸ ὕδωρ ἐφάνη, ἀφ' οὗ καὶ οἱ περὶ τὸν Νεεμιαν ἥγνισαν τὰ τῆς θυσίας, 34 περιφράξας δὲ ὁ βασιλεὺς ἱερὸν ἐποίησεν δοκιμάσας τὸ πρᾶγμα. 35 καὶ οἷς ἐχαρίζετο ὁ βασιλεύς, πολλὰ διάφορα ἐλάμβανεν καὶ μετεδίδου. 36 προσηγόρευσαν δὲ οἱ περὶ τὸν Νεεμιαν τοῦτο νεφθαρ, ὃ διερμηνεύεται καθαρισμός. καλεῖται δὲ παρὰ τοῖς πολλοῖς νεφθαι.

2 Εὑρίσκεται δὲ ἐν ταῖς ἀπογραφαῖς Ιερεμιας ὁ προφήτης ὅτι ἐκέλευσεν τοῦ πυρὸς λαβεῖν τοὺς μεταγενομένους, ὡς σεσήμανται, 2 καὶ ὡς ἐνετείλατο τοῖς μεταγενομένοις ὁ προφήτης δοὺς αὐτοῖς τὸν νόμον, ἵνα μὴ ἐπιλάθωνται τῶν προσταγμάτων τοῦ κυρίου, καὶ ἵνα μὴ ἀποπλανηθῶσιν ταῖς διανοίαις βλέποντες ἀγάλματα χρυσᾶ καὶ ἀργυρᾶ καὶ τὸν περὶ αὐτὰ κόσμον· 3 καὶ ἕτερα τοιαῦτα λέγων παρεκάλει μὴ ἀποστῆναι τὸν νόμον ἀπὸ τῆς καρδίας αὐτῶν. 4 ἦν δὲ ἐν τῇ γραφῇ ὡς τὴν σκηνὴν καὶ τὴν κιβωτὸν ἐκέλευσεν ὁ προφήτης χρηματισμοῦ γενηθέντος αὐτῷ συνακολουθεῖν· ὡς δὲ ἐξῆλθεν εἰς τὸ ὄρος, οὗ ὁ Μωυσῆς ἀναβὰς ἐθεάσατο τὴν τοῦ

KING JAMES VERSION

32 When this was done, there was kindled a flame: but it was consumed by the light that shined from the altar.

33 So when this matter was known, it was told the king of Persia, that in the place, where the priests that were led away had hid the fire, there appeared water, and that Neemias had purified the sacrifices therewith.

34 Then the king, inclosing the place, made it holy, after he had tried the matter.

35 And the king took many gifts, and bestowed thereof on those whom he would gratify.

36 And Neemias called this thing Naphthar, which is as much as to say, a cleansing: but many men call it Nephi.

2 It is also found in the records, that Jeremy the prophet commanded them that were carried away to take of the fire, as it hath been signified:

2 And how that the prophet, having given them the law, charged them not to forget the commandments of the Lord, and that they should not err in their minds, when they see images of silver and gold, with their ornaments.

3 And with other such speeches exhorted he them, that the law should not depart from their hearts.

4 It was also contained in the same writing, that the prophet, being warned of God, commanded the tabernacle and the ark to go with him, as he went forth into the

DOUAY OLD TESTAMENT

32 Which being done, there was kindled a flame from them: but it was consumed by the light that shined from the altar.

33 And when this matter became public, it was told to the king of Persia, that in the place where the priests that were led away, had hid the fire, there appeared water, with which Nehemias and they that were with him had purified the sacrifices.

34 And the king considering, and diligently examining the matter, made a temple for it, that he might prove what had happened.

35 And when he had proved it, he gave the priests many goods, and divers presents, and he took and distributed them to them with his own hand.

36 And Nehemias called this place Nephthar, which is interpreted purification. But many call it Nephi.

2 NOW it is found in the descriptions of Jeremias the prophet, that he commanded them that went into captivity, to take the fire, as it hath been signified, and how he gave charge to them that were carried away into captivity.

2 And how he gave them the law that they should not forget the commandments of the Lord, and that they should not err in their minds, seeing the idols of gold, and silver, and the ornaments of them.

3 And with other such like speeches, he exhorted them that they would not remove the law from their heart.

4 It was also contained in the same writing, how the prophet, being warned by God, commanded that the tabernacle and the ark should accompany him, till he came forth to

KNOX TRANSLATION

from them, but died away when the altar fires blazed up again over yonder.[a] 33 The news travelled, till the Persian king himself was told how water appeared where exiled priests had hidden the fire, how, with this water, Nehemias and his company had bathed the sacrifice. 34 Good heed he gave to the matter, and after due examination fenced the ground in with a shrine, in witness of what befell there. 35 Largesse the priests had, and many were the gifts passed from hand to hand, when the truth of the matter was proved.[b] 36 As for the place, Nehemias himself called it Nephthar, which means Purification; but the vulgar call it Nephi.

2 You shall also find it set down in the dispositions made by the prophet Jeremias, that he bade the exiles rescue the sacred fire, in the manner aforesaid.[c] 2 Strict charge he gave them, the Lord's commandments they should keep ever in mind, nor let false gods, all gold and silver and fine array, steal away their hearts; 3 with much else to confirm them in their regard for the law. 4 And here, in this same document, the story was told, how a divine oracle came to Jeremias, and he must needs go out, with tabernacle and ark to bear him company, to the very mountain Moses climbed long ago,

a *vv.* 31, 32. The Greek text here is very doubtful, and perhaps indicates, not that the water was poured out on stones, but that stones were used to block up the hidden pool. *b* In the Greek text, no mention is made of the priests; the Persian king exchanged gifts with his favourites, by way of celebrating the event (cf. Apoc. 11. 10). *c* *vv.* 1-19. These verses seem to be a continuation of the third fragment preserved in the foregoing chapter. Nothing in the prophecy of Jeremias, as we have it, relates the circumstances here mentioned, although verse 2 is possibly a reference to Bar. 6.

TODAY'S ENGLISH VERSION

fire blazed up, but it was extinguished by a flame from the
fire on the altar.
33 "News of what had happened spread everywhere. The
Persian emperor heard that a liquid had been found in the
place where the priests had hidden the altar fire, just before
they were taken into exile. He also heard that Nehemiah and
his friends had used this liquid to burn the sacrifice on the
altar. 34 When the emperor investigated the matter and
found out that this was true, he had the area fenced off and
made into a shrine. 35 It became a substantial source of
income for him, and he used the money for gifts to anyone
who was in his good favor. 36 Nehemiah and his friends
called the liquid *nephthar,* which means 'purification,' but
most people call it 'naphtha.'

2 "We know from the records that Jeremiah the prophet
instructed the people who were being taken into exile to
hide some of the fire from the altar, as we have just mentioned. 2 We also know that he taught them God's Law and
warned them not to be deceived by the ornamented gold and
silver idols which they would see in the land of their exile.
3 And then he urged them never to abandon the Law.
4 "These same records also tell us that Jeremiah, acting
under divine guidance, commanded the Tent of the Lord's
Presence and the Covenant Box to follow him to the mountain where Moses had looked down on the land which God

NEW REVISED STANDARD VERSION

32 When this was done, a flame blazed up; but when the light
from the altar shone back, it went out. 33 When this matter
became known, and it was reported to the king of the
Persians that, in the place where the exiled priests had hidden the fire, the liquid had appeared with which Nehemiah
and his associates had burned the materials of the sacrifice,
34 the king investigated the matter, and enclosed the place
and made it sacred. 35 And with those persons whom the
king favored he exchanged many excellent gifts. 36 Nehemiah and his associates called this "nephthar," which means
purification, but by most people it is called naphtha.[a]

2 One finds in the records that the prophet Jeremiah
ordered those who were being deported to take some of
the fire, as has been mentioned, 2 and that the prophet, after
giving them the law, instructed those who were being deported not to forget the commandments of the Lord, or to be led
astray in their thoughts on seeing the gold and silver statues
and their adornment. 3 And with other similar words he
exhorted them that the law should not depart from their
hearts.
4 It was also in the same document that the prophet,
having received an oracle, ordered that the tent and the ark
should follow with him, and that he went out to the mountain where Moses had gone up and had seen the inheritance

[a] Gk *nephthai*

NEW AMERICAN BIBLE

flame blazed up, but its light was lost in the brilliance cast
from a light on the altar. 33 When the event became known
and the king of the Persians was told that, in the very place
where the exiled priests had hidden the fire, a liquid was
found with which Nehemiah and his people had burned the
sacrifices, 34 the king, after verifying the fact, fenced the
place off and declared it sacred. 35 To those on whom the
king wished to bestow favors he distributed the large revenues he received there. 36 Nehemiah and his companions
called the liquid nephthar, meaning purification, but most
people name it naphtha.

2 You will find in the records, not only that Jeremiah the
prophet ordered the deportees to take some of the aforementioned fire with them, 2 but also that the prophet, in
giving them the law, admonished them not to forget the
commandments of the LORD or be led astray in their
thoughts, when seeing the gold and silver idols and their
ornaments. 3 With other similar words he urged them not to
let the law depart from their hearts. 4 The same document
also tells how the prophet, following a divine revelation,
ordered that the tent and the ark should accompany him
and how he went off to the mountain which Moses climbed

NEW JERUSALEM BIBLE

32 and when this was done a flame flared up, to be absorbed
in a corresponding blaze of light from the altar. 33 When the
matter became known and the king of the Persians heard
that, in the place where the exiled priests had hidden the fire,
a liquid had appeared, with which Nehemiah and his people
had purified the sacrificial offerings, 34 the king, after verifying the facts, had the place enclosed and pronounced sacred.
35 To the people on whom the king bestowed it, he granted a
part of the considerable revenue he derived from it.
36 Nehemiah and his people termed this stuff "nephtar",
which means "purification", but it is commonly called
"naphta".

2 'It is on record that the prophet Jeremiah ordered the
deportees to take the fire, as we have described, 2 and
how, having given them the Law, the prophet warned the
deportees never to forget the Lord's precepts, nor to let their
thoughts be tempted by the sight of gold and silver statues or
the finery adorning them. 3 Among other similar admonitions, he urged them not to let the Law depart from their
hearts.
4 'The same document also describes how the prophet,
warned by an oracle, gave orders for the tent and the ark to
go with him, when he set out for the mountain which Moses

GREEK OLD TESTAMENT

θεοῦ κληρονομίαν. 5 καὶ ἐλθὼν ὁ Ιερεμιας εὗρεν οἶκον
ἀντρώδη καὶ τὴν σκηνὴν καὶ τὴν κιβωτὸν καὶ τὸ θυσιαστήριον τοῦ θυμιάματος εἰσήνεγκεν ἐκεῖ καὶ τὴν θύραν ἐνέφραξεν. 6 καὶ προσελθόντες τινὲς τῶν συνακολουθούντων
ὥστε ἐπισημάνασθαι τὴν ὁδὸν καὶ οὐκ ἐδυνήθησαν εὑρεῖν.
7 ὡς δὲ ὁ Ιερεμιας ἔγνω, μεμψάμενος αὐτοῖς εἶπεν ὅτι Καὶ
ἄγνωστος ὁ τόπος ἔσται, ἕως ἂν συναγάγῃ ὁ θεὸς ἐπισυνα-
γωγὴν τοῦ λαοῦ καὶ ἵλεως γένηται· 8 καὶ τότε ὁ κύριος
ἀναδείξει ταῦτα, καὶ ὀφθήσεται ἡ δόξα τοῦ κυρίου καὶ ἡ
νεφέλη, ὡς ἐπὶ Μωυσῆ ἐδηλοῦτο, ὡς καὶ ὁ Σαλωμων ἠξίωσεν
ἵνα ὁ τόπος καθαγιασθῇ μεγάλως. 9 διεσαφεῖτο δὲ καὶ ὡς
σοφίαν ἔχων ἀνήνεγκεν θυσίαν ἐγκαινισμοῦ καὶ τῆς τελειώ-
σεως τοῦ ἱεροῦ. 10 καθὼς καὶ Μωυσῆς προσηύξατο πρὸς κύριον, καὶ κατέβη πῦρ ἐκ τοῦ οὐρανοῦ καὶ τὰ τῆς θυσίας ἐδαπάνησεν, οὕτως καὶ Σαλωμων προσηύξατο, καὶ καταβὰν τὸ
πῦρ ἀνήλωσεν τὰ ὁλοκαυτώματα. 11 καὶ εἶπεν Μωυσῆς Διὰ
τὸ μὴ βεβρῶσθαι τὸ περὶ τῆς ἁμαρτίας ἀνηλώθη. 12 ὡσαύτως
καὶ ὁ Σαλωμων τὰς ὀκτὼ ἡμέρας ἤγαγεν. 13 ἐξηγοῦντο δὲ καὶ
ἐν ταῖς ἀναγραφαῖς καὶ ἐν τοῖς ὑπομνηματισμοῖς τοῖς κατὰ
τὸν Νεεμιαν τὰ αὐτὰ καὶ ὡς καταβαλλόμενος βιβλιοθήκην

KING JAMES VERSION

mountain, where Moses climbed up, and saw the heritage of God.

5 And when Jeremy came thither, he found an hollow cave, wherein he laid the tabernacle, and the ark, and the altar of incense, and so stopped the door.

6 And some of those that followed him came to mark the way, but they could not find it.

7 Which when Jeremy perceived, he blamed them, saying, As for that place, it shall be unknown until the time that God gather his people again together, and receive them unto mercy.

8 Then shall the Lord shew them these things, and the glory of the Lord shall appear, and the cloud also, as it was shewed under Moses, and as when Solomon desired that the place might be honourably sanctified.

9 It was also declared, that he being wise offered the sacrifice of dedication, and of the finishing of the temple.

10 And as when Moses prayed unto the Lord, the fire came down from heaven, and consumed the sacrifices: even so prayed Solomon also, and the fire came down from heaven, and consumed the burnt offerings.

11 And Moses said, Because the sin offering was not to be eaten, it was consumed.

12 So Solomon kept those eight days.

13 The same things also were reported in the writings and commentaries of Neemias; and how he founding a library

DOUAY OLD TESTAMENT

the mountain where Moses went up, and saw the inheritance of God.

5 And when Jeremias came thither he found a hollow cave: and he carried in thither the tabernacle, and the ark, and the altar of incense, and so stopped the door.

6 Then some of them that followed him, came up to mark the place: but they could not find it.

7 And when Jeremias perceived it, he blamed them, saying: The place shall be unknown, till God gather together the congregation of the people, and receive them to mercy.

8 And then the Lord will shew these things, and the majesty of the Lord shall appear, and there shall be a cloud as it was also shewed to Moses, and he shewed it when Solomon prayed that the place might be sanctified to the great God.

9 For he treated wisdom in a magnificent manner: and like a wise man, he offered the sacrifice of the dedication, and of the finishing of the temple.

10 And as Moses prayed to the Lord, and fire came down from heaven, and consumed the holocaust: so Solomon also prayed, and fire came down from heaven and consumed the holocaust.

11 And Moses said: Because the sin offering was not eaten, it was consumed.

12 So Solomon also celebrated the dedication eight days.

13 And these same things were set down in the memoirs and commentaries of Nehemias: and how he made a library,

KNOX TRANSLATION

when he had sight of God's domain.[a] 5 A cave Jeremias found
there, in which he set down tabernacle and ark and incense-
altar, and stopped up the entrance behind him. 6 There were
some that followed; no time they lost in coming up to mark
the spot, but find it they could not. 7 He, when they told him
of it, rebuked their eagerness; Nay, said he, the place must
remain ever unknown, till the day when God brings his people together once more, and is reconciled; 8 then, divinely, the
secret shall be made manifest. Then once again the Lord's
majesty shall be seen, and the cloud that enshrines it; the
same vision that was granted to Moses, and to Solomon
when he prayed that the great God would have his temple on
earth; 9 Solomon, the master of wisdom, that in his wisdom
offered sacrifice to hallow the temple he had made.
10 Prayed Moses, prayed Solomon, and fire came down
from heaven to consume the burnt-sacrifice....
11 ...Uneaten, Moses said, the victim for fault, and so the
fire must consume it....
12 ...No other mind had king Solomon, that for eight days
would continue his dedication feast.[b]
13 With all this, dispositions Nehemias made, records Nehemias kept, are in full agreement. He it was founded a library,

a Some of the actions described by the Hebrew prophets may have taken place only in a vision, not in actual life, cf. e.g. Jer. 13. 1-7. The mountain is no doubt Phasga (Deut. 34). *b* vv. 10-12. It is difficult to make any continuous sense out of these verses as they have come down to us, and it seems possible that a considerable portion of the letter has here been lost. The missing part might have explained what was the relevance of this long excursion into past history, which has no immediate bearing on Judas and the re-dedication of the temple.

TODAY'S ENGLISH VERSION

had promised our people. 5 When Jeremiah got to the mountain, he found a huge cave and there he hid the Tent of the
Lord's Presence, the Covenant Box, and the altar of incense.
Then he sealed up the entrance.
6 "Some of Jeremiah's friends tried to follow him and mark
the way, but they could not find the cave. 7 When Jeremiah
learned what they had done, he reprimanded them, saying,
'No one must know about this place until God gathers his
people together again and shows them mercy. 8 At that time
he will reveal where these things are hidden, and the dazzling light of his presence will be seen in the cloud, as it was
in the time of Moses and on the occasion when Solomon
prayed that the Temple might be dedicated in holy splendor.'
9 "We are also told how the wise King Solomon offered a
sacrifice of dedication at the completion of the Temple,
10 and that when he prayed, fire came down from heaven and
consumed the sacrifices, just as it had done earlier when
Moses prayed. 11 Moses had explained that the sin offering
was consumed by fire because it was not eaten. 12 Solomon
celebrated the festival for eight days.
13 "These same facts are found in the royal records and in
the memoirs of Nehemiah, who established a library and

NEW REVISED STANDARD VERSION

of God. 5 Jeremiah came and found a cave-dwelling, and he
brought there the tent and the ark and the altar of incense;
then he sealed up the entrance. 6 Some of those who followed him came up intending to mark the way, but could
not find it. 7 When Jeremiah learned of it, he rebuked them
and declared: "The place shall remain unknown until God
gathers his people together again and shows his mercy.
8 Then the Lord will disclose these things, and the glory of
the Lord and the cloud will appear, as they were shown in
the case of Moses, and as Solomon asked that the place
should be specially consecrated."
9 It was also made clear that being possessed of wisdom
Solomon[a] offered sacrifice for the dedication and completion
of the temple. 10 Just as Moses prayed to the Lord, and fire
came down from heaven and consumed the sacrifices, so
also Solomon prayed, and the fire came down and consumed
the whole burnt offerings. 11 And Moses said, "They were
consumed because the sin offering had not been eaten."
12 Likewise Solomon also kept the eight days.
13 The same things are reported in the records and in the
memoirs of Nehemiah, and also that he founded a library

a Gk *he*

NEW AMERICAN BIBLE

to see God's inheritance. 5 When Jeremiah arrived there, he
found a room in a cave in which he put the tent, the ark,
and the altar of incense; then he blocked up the entrance.
6 Some of those who followed him came up intending to
mark the path, but they could not find it. 7 When Jeremiah
heard of this, he reproved them: "The place is to remain
unknown until God gathers his people together again and
shows them mercy. 8 Then the LORD will disclose these
things, and the glory of the LORD will be seen in the cloud,
just as it appeared in the time of Moses and when Solomon
prayed that the Place might be gloriously sanctified."
9 It is also related how Solomon in his wisdom offered a
sacrifice at the dedication and the completion of the temple.
10 Just as Moses prayed to the LORD and fire descended from
the sky and consumed the sacrifices, so Solomon also prayed
and fire came down and burned up the holocausts. 11 Moses
had said, "Because it had not been eaten, the sin offering
was burned up." 12 Solomon also celebrated the feast in the
same way for eight days.
13 Besides these things, it is also told in the records and in
Nehemiah's Memoirs how he collected the books about the

NEW JERUSALEM BIBLE

had climbed to survey God's heritage. 5 On his arrival,
Jeremiah found a cave-dwelling, into which he put the tent,
the ark and the altar of incense, afterwards blocking up the
entrance. 6 Some of his companions went back later to mark
out the path but were unable to find it. 7 When Jeremiah
learned this, he reproached them, "The place is to remain
unknown", he said, "until God gathers his people together
again and shows them his mercy. 8 Then the Lord will bring
these things once more to light, and the glory of the Lord will
be seen, and so will the cloud, as it was revealed in the time
of Moses[a] and when Solomon[b] prayed that the holy place
might be gloriously hallowed."
9 'It was also recorded how Solomon in his wisdom offered
the sacrifice of the dedication and completion of the sanctuary. 10 As Moses had prayed to the Lord and fire had come
down from heaven and burned up the sacrifice, so Solomon
also prayed, and the fire from above consumed the burnt
offerings. 11 Moses[c] had said, "Because the sacrifice for sin
had not been eaten, it was burnt instead." 12 Solomon[d] similarly observed the eight-day festival.
13 'In addition to the above, it was also recorded, both in
these writings and in the *Memoirs of Nehemiah*, how Nehemiah founded a library and made a collection of the books

a **2** Ex 24:16. *b* **2** 1 K 8:10–11. *c* **2** Lv 10:16–17. *d* **2** 1 K 8:65–66.

GREEK OLD TESTAMENT

ἐπισυνήγαγεν τὰ περὶ τῶν βασιλέων βιβλία καὶ προφητῶν
καὶ τὰ τοῦ Δαυιδ καὶ ἐπιστολὰς βασιλέων περὶ ἀναθεμάτων.
14 ὡσαύτως δὲ καὶ Ιουδας τὰ διαπεπτωκότα διὰ τὸν γεγονότα πόλεμον ἡμῖν ἐπισυνήγαγεν πάντα, καὶ ἔστιν παρ᾽ ἡμῖν·
15 ὧν οὖν ἐὰν χρείαν ἔχητε, τοὺς ἀποκομιοῦντας ὑμῖν
ἀποστέλλετε.
16 Μέλλοντες οὖν ἄγειν τὸν καθαρισμὸν ἐγράψαμεν ὑμῖν·
καλῶς οὖν ποιήσετε ἄγοντες τὰς ἡμέρας. 17 ὁ δὲ θεὸς ὁ
σώσας τὸν πάντα λαὸν αὐτοῦ καὶ ἀποδοὺς τὴν κληρονομίαν
πᾶσιν καὶ τὸ βασίλειον καὶ τὸ ἱεράτευμα καὶ τὸν ἁγιασμόν,
18 καθὼς ἐπηγγείλατο διὰ τοῦ νόμου· ἐλπίζομεν γὰρ ἐπὶ τῷ
θεῷ ὅτι ταχέως ἡμᾶς ἐλεήσει καὶ ἐπισυνάξει ἐκ τῆς ὑπὸ τὸν
οὐρανὸν εἰς τὸν ἅγιον τόπον· ἐξείλετο γὰρ ἡμᾶς ἐκ μεγάλων
κακῶν καὶ τὸν τόπον ἐκαθάρισεν.
19 Τὰ δὲ κατὰ τὸν Ιουδαν τὸν Μακκαβαῖον καὶ τοὺς τούτου
ἀδελφοὺς καὶ τὸν τοῦ ἱεροῦ τοῦ μεγίστου καθαρισμὸν καὶ
τὸν τοῦ βωμοῦ ἐγκαινισμὸν 20 ἔτι τε τοὺς πρὸς Ἀντίοχον
τὸν Ἐπιφανῆ καὶ τὸν τούτου υἱὸν Εὐπάτορα πολέμους 21 καὶ
τὰς ἐξ οὐρανοῦ γενομένας ἐπιφανείας τοῖς ὑπὲρ τοῦ
Ιουδαϊσμοῦ φιλοτίμως ἀνδραγαθήσασιν, ὥστε τὴν ὅλην χώραν ὀλίγους ὄντας λεηλατεῖν καὶ τὰ βάρβαρα πλήθη διώκειν,
22 καὶ τὸ περιβόητον καθ᾽ ὅλην τὴν οἰκουμένην ἱερὸν

KING JAMES VERSION

gathered together the acts of the kings, and the prophets, and of David, and the epistles of the kings concerning the holy gifts.

14 In like manner also Judas gathered together all those things that were lost by reason of the war we had, and they remain with us.

15 Wherefore if ye have need thereof, send some to fetch them unto you.

16 Whereas we then are about to celebrate the purification, we have written unto you, and ye shall do well, if ye keep the same days.

17 We hope also, that the God, that delivered all his people, and gave them all an heritage, and the kingdom, and the priesthood, and the sanctuary,

18 As he promised in the law, will shortly have mercy upon us, and gather us together out of every land under heaven into the holy place: for he hath delivered us out of great troubles, and hath purified the place.

19 Now as concerning Judas Maccabeus, and his brethren, and the purification of the great temple, and the dedication of the altar,

20 And the wars against Antiochus Epiphanes, and Eupator his son,

21 And the manifest signs that came from heaven unto those that behaved themselves manfully to their honour for Judaism: so that, being but a few, they overcame the whole country, and chased barbarous multitudes,

22 And recovered again the temple renowned all the world

DOUAY OLD TESTAMENT

and gathered together out of the countries, the books both of the prophets, and of David, and the epistles of the kings, and concerning the holy gifts.

14 And in like manner Judas also gathered together all such things as were lost by the war we had, and they are in our possession.

15 Wherefore if you want these things, send some that may fetch them to you.

16 As we are then about to celebrate the purification, we have written unto you: and you shall do well, if you keep the same days.

17 And we hope that God who hath delivered his people, and hath rendered to all the inheritance, and the kingdom, and the priesthood, and the sanctuary,

18 As he promised in the law, will shortly have mercy upon us, and will gather us together from every land under heaven into the holy place.

19 For he hath delivered us out of great perils, and hath cleansed the place.

20 Now as concerning Judas Machabeus, and his brethren, and the purification of the great temple, and the dedication of the altar:

21 As also the wars against Antiochus the Illustrious, and his son Eupator:

22 And the manifestations that came from heaven to them, that behaved themselves manfully on the behalf of the Jews, so that, being but a few, they made themselves masters of the whole country, and put to flight the barbarous multitude:

23 And recovered again the most renowned temple in all the

KNOX TRANSLATION

and there collected histories of king and prophet, and of
David himself; dispatches, too, the kings had sent, and
inventories of gifts made. 14 And now Judas in his turn has
recovered all such records as were lost to us through the late
wars, and they are here in our keeping; 15 would you be in
possession of these, you have but to send and fetch them.
16 Meanwhile, we notify you by these presents of that
cleansing ceremony we mean to perform; do us the courtesy
to keep holiday on your part. 17 See what deliverance God has
sent to his people, restoring to us our common domain, our
sovereignty, our priesthood, our temple's sanctity! 18 Think
you not he will fulfil, ere long, the promise made in his law;
take pity on us, that are scattered wide as heaven, and on
this hallowed soil reunite us? 19 What meant they else, those
great perils overcome, that sanctuary purified at last?…
20 Speak we of Judas Machabaeus and his brethren, and
how the great temple was purified, and the altar hallowed
anew;[a] 21 of the battles they fought against Antiochus,
called the Illustrious, and Eupator, that was his son.
22 Speak we of heavenly manifestations, sent to encourage
the champions of Jewry, till at last, though so few, they won
back their country, and put the hordes of heathendom to
flight. 23 Speak we of that temple, the most famous in all the

a vv. 20-33. The book proper begins with this preamble, in which the author is concerned, not to shift the responsibility for his statements on to Jason of Cyrene, but to justify himself in selecting certain incidents for recital, and omitting the rest. The exact sense of the Latin is hard to determine; it is here interpreted in conformity with the Greek text.

TODAY'S ENGLISH VERSION

collected the writings of David, letters of the kings concerning offerings, and books about the kings and prophets.
14 Judas also collected the books that had been scattered
because of the war, and we still have them. 15 If you ever
need any of these books, let us know, and we will send
them.

16 "Since we are about to celebrate the Festival of Rededication, we are writing to you, advising you to celebrate it
as well. 17 God has saved all his people and has restored to
all of us our holy land, the kingship, the priesthood, and the
Temple services, 18 just as he promised in his Law. He has
rescued us from terrible evils and has purified the Temple,
and we are confident that in his mercy he will soon gather us
to his holy Temple from every nation under the sun."

19 Jason of Cyrene has recorded in five volumes the story of
Judas Maccabeus and his brothers, the purification of the
great Temple, and the dedication of its altar. 20 He has
described the battles with Antiochus Epiphanes and with his
son Eupator, 21 and he has told of the heavenly visions that
appeared to those who fought bravely and enthusiastically to
defend Judaism. Our forces were few in number, but they
plundered the entire country and routed the heathen forces.
22 They recaptured the Temple famous throughout the world,

NEW REVISED STANDARD VERSION

and collected the books about the kings and prophets, and
the writings of David, and letters of kings about votive offerings. 14 In the same way Judas also collected all the books
that had been lost on account of the war that had come upon
us, and they are in our possession. 15 So if you have need of
them, send people to get them for you.

16 Since, therefore, we are about to celebrate the purification, we write to you. Will you therefore please keep the
days? 17 It is God who has saved all his people, and has
returned the inheritance to all, and the kingship and the
priesthood and the consecration, 18 as he promised through
the law. We have hope in God that he will soon have mercy
on us and will gather us from everywhere under heaven into
his holy place, for he has rescued us from great evils and has
purified the place.

19 The story of Judas Maccabeus and his brothers, and
the purification of the great temple, and the dedication of the
altar, 20 and further the wars against Antiochus Epiphanes
and his son Eupator, 21 and the appearances that came from
heaven to those who fought bravely for Judaism, so that
though few in number they seized the whole land and pursued the barbarian hordes, 22 and regained possession of the
temple famous throughout the world, and liberated the city,

NEW AMERICAN BIBLE

kings, the writings of the prophets and of David, and the
royal letters about sacred offerings. 14 In like manner Judas
also collected for us the books that had been scattered
because of the war, and we now have them in our possession. 15 If you need them, send messengers to get them for
you.

16 As we are about to celebrate the feast of the purification
of the temple, we are writing to you requesting you also to
please celebrate the feast. 17 It is God who has saved all his
people and has restored to all of them their heritage, the
kingdom, the priesthood, and the sacred rites, 18 as he promised through the law. We trust in God, that he will soon have
mercy on us and gather us together from everywhere under
the heavens to his holy Place, for he has rescued us from
great perils and has purified his Place.

19 This is the story of Judas Maccabeus and his brothers, of
the purification of the great temple, the dedication of the
altar, 20 the campaigns against Antiochus Epiphanes and his
son Eupator, 21 and of the heavenly manifestations accorded
to the heroes who fought bravely for Judaism, so that, few as
they were, they seized the whole land, put to flight the barbarian hordes, 22 regained possession of the world-famous

NEW JERUSALEM BIBLE

dealing with the kings and the prophets, the writings of
David and the letters of the kings on the subject of offerings.
14 Similarly, Judas made a complete collection of the books
dispersed in the late war, and these we still have. 15 If you
need any of them, send someone to fetch them.

16 'Since we are about to celebrate the purification, we now
write, requesting you to observe the same days. 17 God, who
has saved his whole people, conferring heritage, kingdom,
priesthood and sanctification on all of us, 18 as he has promised in the Law, will surely, as our hope is in him, be swift to
show us mercy and gather us together from everywhere
under heaven to the holy place, since he has rescued us from
great evils and has purified it.'

19 The story of Judas Maccabaeus and his brothers, the
purification of the great Temple, the dedication of the altar,
20 together with the wars against Antiochus Epiphanes and
his son Eupator, 21 and the celestial manifestations that came
to hearten the brave champions of Judaism, so that, few
though they were, they pillaged the whole country, routed the
barbarian hordes, 22 recovered the sanctuary renowned the

GREEK OLD TESTAMENT

ἀνακομίσασθαι καὶ τὴν πόλιν ἐλευθερῶσαι καὶ τοὺς μέλ-
λοντας καταλύεσθαι νόμους ἐπανορθῶσαι, τοῦ κυρίου μετὰ
πάσης ἐπιεικείας ἵλεω γενομένου αὐτοῖς, 23 ὑπὸ Ἰάσωνος
τοῦ Κυρηναίου δεδηλωμένα διὰ πέντε βιβλίων πειρασόμεθα
δι' ἑνὸς συντάγματος ἐπιτεμεῖν. 24 συνορῶντες γὰρ τὸ χύ-
μα τῶν ἀριθμῶν καὶ τὴν οὖσαν δυσχέρειαν τοῖς θέλουσιν
εἰσκυκλεῖσθαι τοῖς τῆς ἱστορίας διηγήμασιν διὰ τὸ πλῆθος
τῆς ὕλης 25 ἐφροντίσαμεν τοῖς μὲν βουλομένοις ἀναγινώσκειν ψυχαγωγίαν, τοῖς δὲ φιλοφρονοῦσιν εἰς τὸ διὰ μνήμης
ἀναλαβεῖν εὐκοπίαν, πᾶσιν δὲ τοῖς ἐντυγχάνουσιν ὠφέλειαν.
26 καὶ ἡμῖν μὲν τοῖς τὴν κακοπάθειαν ἐπιδεδεγμένοις τῆς
ἐπιτομῆς οὐ ῥᾴδιον, ἱδρῶτος δὲ καὶ ἀγρυπνίας τὸ πρᾶγμα,
27 καθάπερ τῷ παρασκευάζοντι συμπόσιον καὶ ζητοῦντι τὴν
ἑτέρων λυσιτέλειαν οὐκ εὐχερές, ὅμως διὰ τὴν τῶν πολλῶν
εὐχαριστίαν ἡδέως τὴν κακοπάθειαν ὑποίσομεν 28 τὸ μὲν
διακριβοῦν περὶ ἑκάστων τῷ συγγραφεῖ παραχωρήσαντες, τὸ
δὲ ἐπιπορεύεσθαι τοῖς ὑπογραμμοῖς τῆς ἐπιτομῆς διαπον-
οῦντες. 29 καθάπερ γὰρ τῆς καινῆς οἰκίας ἀρχιτέκτονι τῆς
ὅλης καταβολῆς φροντιστέον, τῷ δὲ ἐγκαίειν καὶ Ζωγραφεῖν
ἐπιχειροῦντι τὰ ἐπιτήδεια πρὸς διακόσμησιν ἐξεταστέον,
οὕτως δοκῶ καὶ ἐπὶ ἡμῶν. 30 τὸ μὲν ἐμβατεύειν καὶ περίπα-
τον ποιεῖσθαι λόγων καὶ πολυπραγμονεῖν ἐν τοῖς κατὰ μέρος
τῷ τῆς ἱστορίας ἀρχηγέτῃ καθήκει· 31 τὸ δὲ σύντομον τῆς
λέξεως μεταδιώκειν καὶ τὸ ἐξεργαστικὸν τῆς πραγματείας
παραιτεῖσθαι τῷ τὴν μετάφρασιν ποιουμένῳ συγχωρητέον.

KING JAMES VERSION

over, and freed the city, and upheld the laws which were going down, the Lord being gracious unto them with all favour:

23 *All these things, I say,* being declared by Jason of Cyrene in five books, we will assay to abridge in one volume.

24 For considering the infinite number, and the difficulty which they find that desire to look into the narrations of the story, for the variety of the matter,

25 We have been careful, that they that will read may have delight, and that they that are desirous to commit to memory might have ease, and that all into whose hands it comes might have profit.

26 Therefore to us, that have taken upon us this painful labour of abridging, it was not easy, but a matter of sweat and watching;

27 Even as it is no ease unto him that prepareth a banquet, and seeketh the benefit of others: yet for the pleasuring of many we will undertake gladly this great pains;

28 Leaving to the author the exact handling of every particular, and labouring to follow the rules of an abridgement.

29 For as the master builder of a new house must care for the whole building; but he that undertaketh to set it out, and paint it, must seek out fit things for the adorning thereof: even so I think it is with us.

30 To stand upon every point, and go over things at large, and to be curious in particulars, belongeth to the first author of the story:

31 But to use brevity, and avoid much labouring of the work, is to be granted to him that will make an abridgment.

DOUAY OLD TESTAMENT

world, and delivered the city, and restored the laws that were abolished, the Lord with all clemency shewing mercy to them.

24 And all such things as have been comprised in five books by Jason of Cyrene, we have attempted to abridge in one book.

25 For considering the multitude of books, and the difficulty that they find that desire to undertake the narrations of histories, because of the multitude of the matter,

26 We have taken care for those indeed that are willing to read, that it might be a pleasure of mind: and for the studious, that they may more easily commit to memory: and that all that read might receive profit.

27 And as to ourselves indeed, in undertaking this work of abridging, we have taken in hand no easy task, yea rather a business full of watching and sweat.

28 But as they that prepare a feast, and seek to satisfy the will of others: for the sake of many, we willingly undergo the labour.

29 Leaving to the authors the exact handling of every particular, and as for ourselves, according to the plan proposed, studying to be brief.

30 For as the master builder of a new house must have care of the whole building: but he that taketh care to paint it, must seek out fit things for the adorning of it: so must it be judged for us.

31 For to collect all that is to be known, to put the discourse in order, and curiously to discuss every particular point, is the duty of the author of a history:

32 But to pursue brevity of speech, and to avoid nice declarations of things, is to be granted to him that maketh an abridgment.

KNOX TRANSLATION

world, by their means recovered, of a city set free, of forgotten laws re-established, and how the Lord, in his great com-
plaisance, shewed them mercy. 24 All this, the argument of
five books Jason of Cyrene wrote, we have been at pains to
abridge within the compass of a single volume.
25 What would you? There be books a many, and they are
hard put to it that would trace the course of history, for the
abundance of the matter therein comprised. 26 And my aim
was, if a man would read, read he should and with relish;
would a man study, without great ado he should be able to
commit all to memory; and so I would serve every man's
turn. 27 But for me, that undertook the business of abridgement, think you it was light labour? Nay, here was a task all
watching and sweat; 28 yet shoulder the burden I would;
host that prepares a banquet must work for other men's
pleasure, and earn nothing but their thanks. 29 Full information would you have about this or that, I remit you to my
author; for myself, I will be true to my own pattern of shortness. 30 When a house is first in building, the architect must
needs bestow pains on every part of it; not such the painter's
care, he will pick out the surfaces that are most apt for
adornment. 31 And so, methinks, it is here; to expatiate, to
digress, to indulge curiosity on every point, is for the arch-
historian; 32 your epitomist will ask leave to study brevity,
and let long disquisitions be. 33 And now, to our matter!

TODAY'S ENGLISH VERSION

liberated Jerusalem, and restored the laws that were in danger of being abolished. They were able to do all these things because the Lord was merciful and kind to them.

23 I will now try to summarize in a single book the five volumes written by Jason. 24 The number of details and the bulk of material can be overwhelming for anyone who wants to read an account of the events. 25 But I have attempted to simplify it for all readers; those who read for sheer pleasure will find enjoyment and those who want to memorize the facts will not find it difficult. 26 Writing such a summary is a difficult task, demanding hard work and sleepless nights. 27 It is as difficult as preparing a banquet that people of different tastes will enjoy. But I am happy to undergo this hardship in order to please my readers. 28 I will leave the matter of details to the original author and attempt to give only a summary of the events. 29 I am not the builder of a new house who is concerned with every detail of the structure, but simply a painter whose only concern is to make the house look attractive. 30 The historian must master his subject, examine every detail, and then explain it carefully, 31 but whoever is merely writing a summary should be permitted to give a brief account without going into a detailed discussion. 32 So then, without any further comment, I will

NEW REVISED STANDARD VERSION

and re-established the laws that were about to be abolished, while the Lord with great kindness became gracious to them— 23 all this, which has been set forth by Jason of Cyrene in five volumes, we shall attempt to condense into a single book. 24 For considering the flood of statistics involved and the difficulty there is for those who wish to enter upon the narratives of history because of the mass of material, 25 we have aimed to please those who wish to read, to make it easy for those who are inclined to memorize, and to profit all readers. 26 For us who have undertaken the toil of abbreviating, it is no light matter but calls for sweat and loss of sleep, 27 just as it is not easy for one who prepares a banquet and seeks the benefit of others. Nevertheless, to secure the gratitude of many we will gladly endure the uncomfortable toil, 28 leaving the responsibility for exact details to the compiler, while devoting our effort to arriving at the outlines of the condensation. 29 For as the master builder of a new house must be concerned with the whole construction, while the one who undertakes its painting and decoration has to consider only what is suitable for its adornment, such in my judgment is the case with us. 30 It is the duty of the original historian to occupy the ground, to discuss matters from every side, and to take trouble with details, 31 but the one who recasts the narrative should be allowed to strive for brevity of expression and to forego exhaustive treatment. 32 At this point therefore let us begin

NEW AMERICAN BIBLE

temple, liberated the city, and reestablished the laws that were in danger of being abolished, while the LORD favored them with all his generous assistance. 23 All this, which Jason of Cyrene set forth in detail in five volumes, we will try to condense into a single book.

24 In view of the flood of statistics, and the difficulties encountered by those who wish to plunge into historical narratives where the material is abundant, 25 we have aimed to please those who prefer simple reading, as well as to make it easy for the studious who wish to commit things to memory, and to be helpful to all. 26 For us who have taken upon ourselves the labor of making this digest, the task, far from being easy, is one of sweat and of sleepless nights, 27 just as the preparation of a festive banquet is no light matter for one who thus seeks to give enjoyment to others. Similarly, to win the gratitude of many we will gladly endure these inconveniences, 28 while we leave the responsibility for exact details to the original author, and confine our efforts to giving only a summary outline. 29 As the architect of a new house must give his attention to the whole structure, while the man who undertakes the decoration and the frescoes has only to concern himself with what is needed for ornamentation, so I think it is with us. 30 To enter into questions and examine them thoroughly from all sides is the task of the professional historian; 31 but the man who is making an adaptation should be allowed to aim at brevity of expression and to omit detailed treatment of the matter. 32 Here, then, we shall

NEW JERUSALEM BIBLE

whole world over, liberated the city and re-established the laws by then all but abolished, the Lord showing his favour by all his gracious help to them— 23 all this, already related in five books by Jason of Cyrene, we shall attempt to condense into a single work. 24 Considering the spate of figures and the difficulty encountered, because of the mass of material, by those who wish to immerse themselves in historical records, 25 we have aimed at providing diversion for those who merely want something to read, a saving of labour for those who enjoy committing things to memory, and profit for each and all. 26 For us who have undertaken the drudgery of this abridgement, it has been no easy task but a matter of sweat and midnight oil, 27 comparable to the exacting task of someone organising a banquet, whose aim is to satisfy a variety of tastes. Nevertheless, for the sake of rendering a general service, we remain glad to endure this drudgery, 28 leaving accuracy of detail to the historian, and concentrating our effort on tracing the outlines in this condensed version. 29 Just as the architect of a new house is responsible for the construction as a whole, while the man undertaking the ceramic painting has to take into consideration only the decorative requirements, so, I think, it is with us. 30 To make the subject his own, to explore its by-ways, to be meticulous about details, is the business of the original historian, 31 but the person making the adaptation must be allowed to aim at conciseness of expression and to forgo any exhaustive treatment of his subject.

GREEK OLD TESTAMENT

32 ἐντεῦθεν οὖν ἀρξώμεθα τῆς διηγήσεως τοῖς προειρημένοις
τοσοῦτον ἐπιζεύξαντες. εὔηθες γὰρ τὸ μὲν πρὸ τῆς ἱστορίας
πλεονάζειν, τὴν δὲ ἱστορίαν ἐπιτεμεῖν.

3 Τῆς ἁγίας πόλεως κατοικουμένης μετὰ πάσης εἰρήνης
καὶ τῶν νόμων ὅτι κάλλιστα συντηρουμένων διὰ τὴν
Ονιου τοῦ ἀρχιερέως εὐσέβειάν τε καὶ μισοπονηρίαν 2 συνέ-
βαινεν καὶ αὐτοὺς τοὺς βασιλεῖς τιμᾶν τὸν τόπον καὶ τὸ
ἱερὸν ἀποστολαῖς ταῖς κρατίσταις δοξάζειν 3 ὥστε καὶ Σέλευκον τὸν τῆς Ἀσίας βασιλέα χορηγεῖν ἐκ τῶν ἰδίων προσόδων πάντα τὰ πρὸς τὰς λειτουργίας τῶν θυσιῶν ἐπιβάλ-
λοντα δαπανήματα. 4 Σιμων δέ τις ἐκ τῆς Βενιαμιν φυλῆς
προστάτης τοῦ ἱεροῦ καθεσταμένος διηνέχθη τῷ ἀρχιερεῖ
περὶ τῆς κατὰ τὴν πόλιν ἀγορανομίας. 5 καὶ νικῆσαι τὸν
Ονιαν μὴ δυνάμενος ἦλθεν πρὸς Ἀπολλώνιον Θαρσεου τὸν
κατ᾽ ἐκεῖνον τὸν καιρὸν Κοίλης Συρίας καὶ Φοινίκης
στρατηγὸν 6 καὶ προσήγγειλεν περὶ τοῦ χρημάτων ἀμυθή-
των γέμειν τὸ ἐν Ιεροσολύμοις γαζοφυλάκιον ὥστε τὸ πλῆθος τῶν διαφόρων ἀναρίθμητον εἶναι, καὶ μὴ προσήκειν αὐτὰ
πρὸς τὸν τῶν θυσιῶν λόγον, εἶναι δὲ δυνατὸν ὑπὸ τὴν τοῦ
βασιλέως ἐξουσίαν πεσεῖν ταῦτα. 7 συμμείξας δὲ ὁ Ἀπολλώνιος τῷ βασιλεῖ περὶ τῶν μηνυθέντων αὐτῷ χρημάτων
ἐνεφάνισεν· ὁ δὲ προχειρισάμενος Ἡλιόδωρον τὸν ἐπὶ τῶν
πραγμάτων ἀπέστειλεν δοὺς ἐντολὰς τὴν τῶν προειρημένων
χρημάτων ἐκκομιδὴν ποιήσασθαι. 8 εὐθέως δὲ ὁ Ἡλιόδωρος
ἐποιεῖτο τὴν πορείαν, τῇ μὲν ἐμφάσει ὡς τὰς κατὰ Κοίλην
Συρίαν καὶ Φοινίκην πόλεις ἐφοδεῦσαι, τῷ πράγματι δὲ τὴν
τοῦ βασιλέως πρόθεσιν ἐπιτελεῖν. 9 παραγενηθεὶς δὲ εἰς

KING JAMES VERSION

32 Here then will we begin the story: only adding thus much to that which hath been said, that it is a foolish thing to make a long prologue, and to be short in the story itself.

3 Now when the holy city was inhabited with all peace, and the laws were kept very well, because of the godliness of Onias the high priest, and his hatred of wickedness,

2 It came to pass that even the kings themselves did honour the place, and magnify the temple with their best gifts;

3 Insomuch that Seleucus king of Asia of his own revenues bare all the costs belonging to the service of the sacrifices.

4 But one Simon of the tribe of Benjamin, who was made governor of the temple, fell out with the high priest about disorder in the city.

5 And when he could not overcome Onias, he gat him to Apollonius *the son* of Thraseas, who then was governor of Celosyria and Phenice,

6 And told him that the treasury in Jerusalem was full of infinite sums of money, so that the multitude of their riches, which did not pertain to the account of the sacrifices, was innumerable, and that it was possible to bring all into the king's hand.

7 Now when Apollonius came to the king, and had shewed him of the money whereof he was told, the king chose out Heliodorus his treasurer, and sent him with a commandment to bring him the foresaid money.

8 So forthwith Heliodorus took his journey, under a colour of visiting the cities of Celosyria and Phenice, but indeed to fulfil the king's purpose.

DOUAY OLD TESTAMENT

33 Here then we will begin the narration: let this be enough by way of a preface: for it is a foolish thing to make a long prologue, and to be short in the story itself.

3 THEREFORE when the holy city was inhabited with all peace, and the laws as yet were very well kept, because of the godliness of Onias the high priest, and the hatred his soul had of evil,

2 It came to pass that even the kings themselves, and the princes esteemed the place worthy of the highest honour, and glorified the temple with very great gifts:

3 So that Seleucus king of Asia allowed out of his revenues all the charges belonging to the ministry of the sacrifices.

4 But one Simon of the tribe of Benjamin, who was appointed overseer of the temple, strove in opposition to the high priest, to bring about some unjust thing in the city.

5 And when he could not overcome Onias he went to Apollonius the son of Tharseas, who at that time was governor of Celesyria and Phenicia:

6 And told him, that the treasury in Jerusalem was full of immense sums of money, and the common store was infinite, which did not belong to the account of the sacrifices: and that it was possible to bring all into the king's hands.

7 Now when Apollonius had given the king notice concerning the money that he was told of, he called for Heliodorus, who had the charge over his affairs, and sent him with commission to bring him the foresaid money.

8 So Heliodorus forthwith began his journey, under a colour of visiting the cities of Celesyria and Phenicia, but indeed to fulfil the king's purpose.

KNOX TRANSLATION

Here is preface enough; it were ill done to draw out the preamble, and leave our story cramped for room.

3 Time was, the holy city was a home of content; ever the
laws of it were well kept; such a high priest they had,
Onias, a devout man, and one that hated evil. 2 In those
days, king and chieftain held the place much in reverence,
and with rich gifts endowed the temple; 3 did not Seleucus,
king of Asia, defray all the cost of maintaining its sacrifices?
4 Yet one citizen there was, Simon the Benjamite, the temple
governor, that had lawless schemes afoot, do the high priest
what he would to gainsay him. 5 And at last, when overcome
Onias he might not, what did he? To Apollonius he betook
himself, the son of Tharseas, that was then in charge of
Coelesyria and Phoenice, 6 and gave him great news indeed;
here was the treasury at Jerusalem stocked with treasures
innumerable, here was vast public wealth, unclaimed by the
needs of the altar, and nothing prevented but it should fall
into the king's hands.

7 No sooner did Apollonius find himself in the royal presence than he told the story of the rumoured treasure; and at
that, the king sent for Heliodorus, that had charge of his
affairs, and despatched him with orders to fetch the said
money away. 8 This Heliodorus set out on his journey without more ado, under colour of making a progress through
the towns of Coelesyria and Phoenice, but with the king's

TODAY'S ENGLISH VERSION

begin my story. It would be foolish to write such a long
introduction that the story itself would have to be cut short.

3 When Onias[a] was High Priest in Jerusalem, the holy city
enjoyed peace and prosperity, and its laws were strictly
obeyed, because he was devout and hated evil. 2 The kings
of Syria and Egypt honored the Temple and presented it with
expensive gifts, 3 and King Seleucus,[b] ruler of all Asia, even
used to pay the costs of the Temple sacrifices from the revenues he collected.
4 But a man by the name of Simon, of the tribe of Bilgah,[c]
the chief administrative official of the Temple, lost an argument he had with Onias over the regulations governing the
city market. 5 At this time Apollonius son of Thraseus was
the governor of Greater Syria. Simon went to him 6 and said
that there was so much money in the Temple treasury that it
could not be counted, and since the money was not needed
for sacrifices, it might as well be placed under the king's
control.
7 When Apollonius met with the king, he told him about
the money, and the king ordered Heliodorus, his chief minister, to get it for him. 8 Heliodorus set out at once on his mission, but he claimed that he was only making a tour of
inspection of the cities of Greater Syria. 9 After he had

[a] ONIAS: *This is Onias the Third, son of Simon the Second (see 4.4-6; Si 50.1-21).* [b] SELEUCUS: *This is Seleucus the Fourth, known as Philopator, son of Antiochus the Third, 187–175 B.C.* [c] *Some ancient translations* Bilgah *(see Ne 12.5,18); Greek* Benjamin.

NEW REVISED STANDARD VERSION

our narrative, without adding any more to what has already
been said; for it would be foolish to lengthen the preface
while cutting short the history itself.

3 While the holy city was inhabited in unbroken peace and
the laws were strictly observed because of the piety of
the high priest Onias and his hatred of wickedness, 2 it came
about that the kings themselves honored the place and glorified the temple with the finest presents, 3 even to the extent
that King Seleucus of Asia defrayed from his own revenues
all the expenses connected with the service of the sacrifices.
4 But a man named Simon, of the tribe of Benjamin, who
had been made captain of the temple, had a disagreement
with the high priest about the administration of the city market. 5 Since he could not prevail over Onias, he went to
Apollonius of Tarsus,[a] who at that time was governor of
Coelesyria and Phoenicia, 6 and reported to him that the
treasury in Jerusalem was full of untold sums of money, so
that the amount of the funds could not be reckoned, and that
they did not belong to the account of the sacrifices, but that
it was possible for them to fall under the control of the king.
7 When Apollonius met the king, he told him of the money
about which he had been informed. The king[b] chose Heliodorus, who was in charge of his affairs, and sent him with
commands to effect the removal of the reported wealth.
8 Heliodorus at once set out on his journey, ostensibly to
make a tour of inspection of the cities of Coelesyria and
Phoenicia, but in fact to carry out the king's purpose.

a Gk *Apollonius son of Tharseas* *b* Gk *He*

NEW AMERICAN BIBLE

begin our account without further ado; it would be nonsense
to write a long preface to a story and then abbreviate the
story itself.

3 While the holy city lived in perfect peace and the laws
were strictly observed because of the piety of the high
priest Onias and his hatred of evil, 2 the kings themselves
honored the Place and glorified the temple with the most
magnificent gifts. 3 Thus Seleucus, king of Asia, defrayed
from his own revenues all the expenses necessary for the
sacrificial services. 4 But a certain Simon, of the priestly
course of Bilgah, who had been appointed superintendent of
the temple, had a quarrel with the high priest about the
supervision of the city market. 5 Since he could not prevail
against Onias, he went to Apollonius of Tarsus, who at that
time was governor of Coelesyria and Phoenicia, 6 and reported to him that the treasury in Jerusalem was so full of untold
riches that the total sum of money was incalculable and out
of all proportion to the cost of the sacrifices, and that it
would be possible to bring it all under the control of the
king.
7 When Apollonius had an audience with the king, he
informed him about the riches that had been reported to him.
The king chose his minister Heliodorus and sent him with
instructions to expropriate the aforesaid wealth. 8 So
Heliodorus immediately set out on his journey, ostensibly to
visit the cities of Coelesyria and Phoenicia, but in reality to
carry out the king's purpose. 9 When he arrived in Jerusalem

NEW JERUSALEM BIBLE

32 So now let us begin our narrative, without adding any
more to what has been said above; there would be no sense
in expanding the preface to the history and curtailing the
history itself.

3 While the holy city was inhabited in all peace and the
laws were observed as perfectly as possible, owing to the
piety of Onias the high priest and his hatred of wickedness,
2 it came about that the kings themselves honoured the holy
place and enhanced the glory of the Temple with the most
splendid offerings, 3 even to the extent that Seleucus king of
Asia defrayed from his own revenues all the expenses arising
out of the sacrificial liturgy. 4 But a certain Simon, of the
tribe of Bilgah, on being appointed administrator of the
Temple, came into conflict with the high priest over the regu-
lation of the city markets. 5 Unable to get the better of Onias,
he went off to Apollonius, son of Thraseos, who was at that
time commander-in-chief of Coele-Syria and Phoenicia, 6 and
made out to him that the Treasury in Jerusalem was groaning
with untold wealth, that the amount contributed was incalculable and out of all proportion to expenditure on the sacrifice,
but that it could all be brought under the control of the king.
7 Apollonius met the king and told him about the wealth that
had been disclosed to him; whereupon the king selected
Heliodorus, his chancellor, and sent him with instructions to
effect the removal of the reported wealth. 8 Heliodorus lost no
time in setting out, ostensibly to inspect the towns of Coele-
Syria and Phoenicia, but in fact to accomplish the king's

GREEK OLD TESTAMENT

Ιεροσόλυμα καὶ φιλοφρόνως ὑπὸ τοῦ ἀρχιερέως τῆς πόλεως
ἀποδεχθεὶς ἀνέθετο περὶ τοῦ γεγονότος ἐμφανισμοῦ, καὶ
τίνος ἕνεκεν πάρεστιν διεσάφησεν· ἐπυνθάνετο δὲ εἰ ταῖς
ἀληθείαις ταῦτα οὕτως ἔχοντα τυγχάνει. 10 τοῦ δὲ ἀρχιερέως ὑποδείξαντος παρακαταθήκας εἶναι χηρῶν τε καὶ ὀρ-
φανῶν, 11 τινὰ δὲ καὶ Ὑρκανοῦ τοῦ Τωβιου σφόδρα ἀνδρὸς
ἐν ὑπεροχῇ κειμένου — οὕτως ἦν διαβάλλων ὁ δυσσεβὴς
Σιμων —, τὰ δὲ πάντα ἀργυρίου τετρακόσια τάλαντα, χρυσίου δὲ διακόσια· 12 ἀδικηθῆναι δὲ τοὺς πεπιστευκότας τῇ
τοῦ τόπου ἁγιωσύνῃ καὶ τῇ τοῦ τετιμημένου κατὰ τὸν σύμ-
παντα κόσμον ἱεροῦ σεμνότητι καὶ ἀσυλίᾳ παντελῶς ἀμή-
χανον εἶναι. 13 ὁ δὲ Ἡλιόδωρος, δι᾽ ἃς εἶχεν βασιλικὰς
ἐντολάς, πάντως ἔλεγεν εἰς τὸ βασιλικὸν ἀναλημπτέα ταῦτα
εἶναι. 14 ταξάμενος δὲ ἡμέραν εἰσῄει τὴν περὶ τούτων ἐπίσκεψιν οἰκονομήσων· ἦν δὲ οὐ μικρὰ καθ᾽ ὅλην τὴν πόλιν
ἀγωνία. 15 οἱ δὲ ἱερεῖς πρὸ τοῦ θυσιαστηρίου ἐν ταῖς
ἱερατικαῖς στολαῖς ῥίψαντες ἑαυτοὺς ἐπεκαλοῦντο εἰς οὐρανὸν τὸν περὶ παρακαταθήκης νομοθετήσαντα τοῖς παρα-
καταθεμένοις ταῦτα σῶα διαφυλάξαι. 16 ἦν δὲ ὁρῶντα τὴν
τοῦ ἀρχιερέως ἰδέαν τιτρώσκεσθαι τὴν διάνοιαν· ἡ γὰρ ὄψις
καὶ τὸ τῆς χρόας παρηλλαγμένον ἐνέφαινεν τὴν κατὰ ψυχὴν

KING JAMES VERSION

9 And when he was come to Jerusalem, and had been courteously received of the high priest of the city, he told him what intelligence was given of the money, and declared wherefore he came, and asked if these things were so indeed.

10 Then the high priest told him that there was such money laid up for the relief of widows and fatherless children:

11 And that some of it belonged to Hircanus *son* of Tobias, a man of great dignity, and not as that wicked Simon had misinformed: the sum whereof in all was four hundred talents of silver, and two hundred of gold:

12 And that it was altogether impossible that such wrongs should be done unto them, that had committed it to the holiness of the place, and to the majesty and inviolable sanctity of the temple, honoured over all the world.

13 But Heliodorus, because of the king's commandment given him, said, That in any wise it must be brought into the king's treasury.

14 So at the day which he appointed he entered in to order this matter: wherefore there was no small agony throughout the whole city.

15 But the priests, prostrating themselves before the altar in their priests' vestments, called unto heaven upon him that made a law concerning things given to he kept, that they should safely be preserved for such as had committed them to be kept.

16 Then whoso had looked the high priest in the face, it would have wounded his heart: for his countenance and the changing of his colour declared the inward agony of his mind.

DOUAY OLD TESTAMENT

9 And when he was come to Jerusalem, and had been courteously received in the city by the high priest, he told him what information had been given concerning the money: and declared the cause for which he was come: and asked if these things were so indeed.

10 Then the high priest told him that these were sums deposited, and provisions for the subsistence of the widows and the fatherless.

11 And that some part of that which wicked Simon had given intelligence of, belonged to Hircanus *son* of Tobias, a man of great dignity: and that the whole was four hundred talents of silver, and two hundred of gold:

12 But that to deceive them who had trusted to the place and temple which is honoured throughout the whole world, for the reverence and holiness of it, was a thing which could not by any means be done.

13 But he, by reason of the orders he had received from the king, said that by all means the money must be carried to the king.

14 So on the day he had appointed, Heliodorus entered in to order this matter. But there was no small terror throughout the whole city.

15 And the priests prostrated themselves before the altar in their priests' vestments, and called upon him from heaven, who made the law concerning things given to be kept, that he would preserve them safe, for them that had deposited them.

16 Now whosoever saw the countenance of the high priest, was wounded in heart: for his face, and the changing of his colour declared the inward sorrow of his mind.

KNOX TRANSLATION

business still in mind. 9 And when he reached Jerusalem,
and there received a gracious welcome from the high priest,
he made no secret of the information he possessed, or of his
errand, and he would know the truth about these moneys.
10 A plain account the high priest gave him; some were moneys deposited on trust, for the maintenance of widows and
orphans; 11 there were some, too, belonging to Hyrcanus
son of Tobias, a man of repute. The information was maliciously laid, nor did the whole sum amount to more than
four hundred talents of silver, and two hundred of gold.
12 Men had reposed their confidence in a city and a temple
renowned throughout the world, for the high opinion they
had of its sanctity; and should he play them false? It was
not to be thought of. 13 But Heliodorus stood upon the terms
of his commission; delivered to the king the money must be,
there was no other way of it.
14 So the appointed day came, when he would visit the
temple and take order in the matter; what a stir there was
then in the city! 15 Priests, in their sacred vesture, cast themselves down before the altar, and cried out upon heaven;
would not he, whose law enjoined safe-keeping, keep property safe for its rightful owners? 16 And for the high priest
himself, the very aspect of him was heart-rending; such a
change of look and colour betrayed his inward feelings;

TODAY'S ENGLISH VERSION

arrived in Jerusalem and had been warmly received by the
High Priest, he explained the real reason for his visit and
asked if what he had been told was true. 10-11 The High Priest
then stated that Simon, that devil of a man, had not been
telling the truth. There was indeed some money in the
Temple treasury, but part of it was set aside for widows and
orphans and part of it belonged to Hyrcanus son of Tobias, a
very important man. He also pointed out that the total
amount was only 30,000 pounds of silver and 15,000
pounds of gold. 12 He added that it was absolutely impossible that anyone should be permitted to take the money of
those people who had placed their trust in the sanctity and
safety of this world-famous Temple.

13 But Heliodorus insisted that the money should be taken
for the royal treasury, as the king had ordered. 14 So he set a
day and went into the Temple to supervise the counting of
the money. This caused an uproar throughout the entire city.
15 Priests, wearing their priestly robes, threw themselves face
downward before the altar and begged God to keep the
money safe, since he had given the laws designed to protect
the money that people deposited in the Temple. 16 It was
heartbreaking to see the High Priest. His face turned pale,

NEW REVISED STANDARD VERSION

9 When he had arrived at Jerusalem and had been kindly
welcomed by the high priest of[a] the city, he told about the
disclosure that had been made and stated why he had come,
and he inquired whether this really was the situation. 10 The
high priest explained that there were some deposits belonging to widows and orphans, 11 and also some money of
Hyrcanus son of Tobias, a man of very prominent position,
and that it totaled in all four hundred talents of silver and
two hundred of gold. To such an extent the impious Simon
had misrepresented the facts. 12 And he said that it was
utterly impossible that wrong should be done to those people
who had trusted in the holiness of the place and in the sanctity and inviolability of the temple that is honored throughout the whole world.

13 But Heliodorus, because of the orders he had from the
king, said that this money must in any case be confiscated
for the king's treasury. 14 So he set a day and went in to
direct the inspection of these funds.

There was no little distress throughout the whole city.
15 The priests prostrated themselves before the altar in their
priestly vestments and called toward heaven upon him who
had given the law about deposits, that he should keep them
safe for those who had deposited them. 16 To see the appearance of the high priest was to be wounded at heart, for his
face and the change in his color disclosed the anguish of his

a Other ancient authorities read *and*

NEW AMERICAN BIBLE

and had been graciously received by the high priest of the
city, he told him about the information that had been given,
and explained the reason for his presence, and he asked if
these things were really true. 10 The high priest explained
that part of the money was a care fund for widows and
orphans, 11 and a part was the property of Hyrcanus, son of
Tobias, a man who occupied a very high position. Contrary
to the calumnies of the impious Simon, the total amounted
to four hundred talents of silver and two hundred of gold.
12 He added that it was utterly unthinkable to defraud those
who had placed their trust in the sanctity of the Place and in
the sacred inviolability of a temple venerated all over the
world. 13 But because of the orders he had from the king,
Heliodorus said that in any case the money must be confiscated for the royal treasury. 14 So on the day he had set he
went in to take an inventory of the funds.

There was great distress throughout the city. 15 Priests
prostrated themselves in their priestly robes before the altar,
and loudly begged him in heaven who had given the law
about deposits to keep the deposits safe for those who had
made them. 16 Whoever saw the appearance of the high
priest was pierced to the heart, for the changed color of his
face manifested the anguish of his soul. 17 The terror and

NEW JERUSALEM BIBLE

purpose. 9 On his arrival in Jerusalem, and after a hospitable
reception from the high priest and the city, he announced
what had been disclosed, thus revealing the reason for his
presence, and asked if this was indeed the true situation.
10 The high priest explained that there were funds set aside for
widows and orphans, 11 with some belonging to Hyrcanus
son of Tobias, a man occupying a very exalted position, and
that the whole sum, in contrast to what the evil Simon had
alleged, amounted to four hundred talents of silver and two
hundred of gold. 12 He also added that it was entirely out of
the question that an injustice should be done to those who
had put their trust in the sanctity of the place and in the inviolable majesty of a Temple venerated throughout the entire
world.

13 But Heliodorus, because of his instructions from the
king, peremptorily insisted that the funds must be confiscated for the royal exchequer. 14 Fixing a day for the purpose,
he went in to draw up an inventory of the funds. There was
no little consternation throughout the city; 15 the priests in
their sacred vestments prostrated themselves before the altar
and prayed to Heaven, to the Author of the law governing
deposits, to preserve these funds intact for the depositors.
16 The appearance of the high priest was enough to pierce the
heart of the beholder, his expression and his altered colour

GREEK OLD TESTAMENT

ἀγωνίαν· 17 περιεκέχυτο γὰρ περὶ τὸν ἄνδρα δέος τι καὶ
φρικασμὸς σώματος, δι' ὧν πρόδηλον ἐγίνετο τοῖς θεωροῦσιν
τὸ κατὰ καρδίαν ἐνεστὸς ἄλγος. 18 ἔτι δὲ ἐκ τῶν οἰκιῶν
ἀγεληδὸν ἐξεπήδων ἐπὶ πάνδημον ἱκετείαν διὰ τὸ μέλλειν
εἰς καταφρόνησιν ἔρχεσθαι τὸν τόπον. 19 ὑπεζωσμέναι δὲ
ὑπὸ τοὺς μαστοὺς αἱ γυναῖκες σάκκους κατὰ τὰς ὁδοὺς
ἐπλήθυνον· αἱ δὲ κατάκλειστοι τῶν παρθένων, αἱ μὲν συνέ-
τρεχον ἐπὶ τοὺς πυλῶνας, αἱ δὲ ἐπὶ τὰ τείχη, τινὲς δὲ διὰ
τῶν θυρίδων διεξέκυπτον· 20 πᾶσαι δὲ προτείνουσαι τὰς
χεῖρας εἰς τὸν οὐρανὸν ἐποιοῦντο τὴν λιτανείαν· 21 ἐλεεῖν
δ' ἦν τὴν τοῦ πλήθους παμμιγῆ πρόπτωσιν τήν τε τοῦ μεγάλως ἀγωνιῶντος ἀρχιερέως προσδοκίαν. 22 οἱ μὲν οὖν ἐπεκαλοῦντο τὸν παγκρατῆ κύριον τὰ πεπιστευμένα τοῖς πεπι-
στευκόσιν σῶα διαφυλάσσειν μετὰ πάσης ἀσφαλείας. 23 ὁ
δὲ Ἡλιόδωρος τὸ διεγνωσμένον ἐπετέλει. 24 αὐτόθι δὲ αὐτοῦ
σὺν τοῖς δορυφόροις κατὰ τὸ γαζοφυλάκιον ἤδη παρόντος ὁ
τῶν πνευμάτων καὶ πάσης ἐξουσίας δυνάστης ἐπιφάνειαν
μεγάλην ἐποίησεν ὥστε πάντας τοὺς κατατολμήσαντας
συνελθεῖν καταπλαγέντας τὴν τοῦ θεοῦ δύναμιν εἰς ἔκλυσιν
καὶ δειλίαν τραπῆναι· 25 ὤφθη γάρ τις ἵππος αὐτοῖς
φοβερὸν ἔχων τὸν ἐπιβάτην καὶ καλλίστῃ σαγῇ διακεκοσμη-
μένος, φερόμενος δὲ ῥύδην ἐνέσεισεν τῷ Ἡλιοδώρῳ τὰς
ἐμπροσθίους ὁπλάς. ὁ δὲ ἐπικαθήμενος ἐφαίνετο χρυσῆν

KING JAMES VERSION

17 For the man was so compassed with fear and horror of the body, that it was manifest to them that looked upon him, what sorrow he had now in his heart.

18 Others ran flocking out of their houses to the general supplication, because the place was like to come into contempt.

19 And the women, girt with sackcloth under their breasts, abounded in the streets, and the virgins that were kept in ran, some to the gates, and some to the walls, and others looked out of the windows.

20 And all, holding their hands toward heaven, made supplication.

21 Then it would have pitied a man to see the falling down of the multitude of all sorts, and the fear of the high priest, being in such an agony.

22 They then called upon the Almighty Lord to keep the things committed of trust safe and sure for those that had committed them.

23 Nevertheless Heliodorus executed that which was decreed.

24 Now as he was there present himself with his guard about the treasury, the Lord of spirits, and the Prince of all power, caused a great apparition, so that all that presumed to come in with him were astonished at the power of God, and fainted, and were sore afraid.

25 For there appeared unto them an horse with a terrible rider upon him, and adorned with a very fair covering, and he ran fiercely, and smote at Heliodorus with his forefeet, and it seemed that he that sat upon the horse had complete harness of gold.

DOUAY OLD TESTAMENT

17 For the man was so compassed with sadness and horror of the body, that it was manifest to them that beheld him, what sorrow he had in his heart.

18 Others also came flocking together out of their houses, praying and making public supplication, because the place was like to come into contempt.

19 And the women, girded with haircloth about their breasts, came together in the streets. And the virgins also that were shut up, came forth, some to Onias, and some to the walls, and others looked out of the windows.

20 And all holding up their hands towards heaven, made supplication.

21 For the expectation of the mixed multitude, and of the high priest who was in an agony, would have moved any one to pity.

22 And these indeed called upon almighty God, to preserve the things that had been committed to them, safe and sure for those that had committed them.

23 But Heliodorus executed that which he had resolved on, himself being present in the same place with his guard about the treasury.

24 But the spirit of the almighty God gave a great evidence of his presence, so that all that had presumed to obey him, falling down by the power of God, were struck with fainting and dread.

25 For there appeared to them a horse with a terrible rider upon him, adorned with a very rich covering: and he ran fiercely and struck Heliodorus with his fore feet, and he that sat upon him seemed to have armour of gold.

KNOX TRANSLATION

17 grief and horror were stamped on his features, and to all
that saw him he seemed a broken man. 18 Folk streamed out
of their houses in droves, to make public intercession over
the affront that should be put on the holy place; 19 sackcloth
about their waists, the women thronged the streets, and
maids that might not go abroad must yet run to the housetops, or peer out at windows, to see Onias pass.
20 Heavenward they raised their hands, each one of them, in
prayer; 21 and pity it was to see how common folk about him
were sharing the high priest's agony of suspense.
22 Here, then, was a whole city praying Almighty God, no
loss might befall the men who had trusted them; 23 and here
was Heliodorus carrying out his design, already arrived at
the treasury with his body-guard in attendance. 24 All at
once the spirit of God, the omnipotent, gave signal proof of
its presence; daunted by the divine power they trembled and
stood irresolute, these ministers of wrong. 25 What saw
they? A horse, royally caparisoned, that charged upon
Heliodorus and struck him down with its fore-feet; terrible of
aspect its rider was, and his armour seemed all of gold.

TODAY'S ENGLISH VERSION

revealing the agony of his soul, 17 and his body was trembling with fear, reflecting the pain in his heart. 18 People ran
from their houses to join together in prayer that the Temple
might not be defiled. 19 Women, wearing nothing but skirts
of sackcloth, crowded the streets. Young girls whose parents
had never allowed them to be seen in public ran to the gates
or to the walls of the city, or just stared out of their windows. 20 But wherever they went, they lifted their hands to
God in prayer. 21 What a pitiful sight it was to see the High
Priest in such great agony and frustration and to see everyone in the city confused and lying face down on the ground.
22 While everyone was begging the Lord Almighty to protect the money that had been entrusted to his care, 23 Heliodorus went on with his plan. 24 But at the very moment that
he and his bodyguards arrived at the treasury, the Lord of all
supernatural powers caused such a vision to appear that
everyone who had dared to enter with Heliodorus was panic-
stricken and weak with fear at this display of the Lord's
power. 25 In the vision they saw a horse and a rider. The
horse had a richly decorated bridle, and its rider, dressed in
gold armor, was frightening. Suddenly the horse rushed at
Heliodorus, then reared up and struck at him with its hoofs.

NEW REVISED STANDARD VERSION

soul. 17 For terror and bodily trembling had come over the
man, which plainly showed to those who looked at him the
pain lodged in his heart. 18 People also hurried out of their
houses in crowds to make a general supplication because the
holy place was about to be brought into dishonor.
19 Women, girded with sackcloth under their breasts,
thronged the streets. Some of the young women who were
kept indoors ran together to the gates, and some to the
walls, while others peered out of the windows. 20 And holding up their hands to heaven, they all made supplication.
21 There was something pitiable in the prostration of the
whole populace and the anxiety of the high priest in his
great anguish.
22 While they were calling upon the Almighty Lord that
he would keep what had been entrusted safe and secure for
those who had entrusted it, 23 Heliodorus went on with what
had been decided. 24 But when he arrived at the treasury
with his bodyguard, then and there the Sovereign of spirits
and of all authority caused so great a manifestation that all
who had been so bold as to accompany him were astounded
by the power of God, and became faint with terror. 25 For
there appeared to them a magnificently caparisoned horse,
with a rider of frightening mien; it rushed furiously at
Heliodorus and struck at him with its front hoofs. Its rider
was seen to have armor and weapons of gold. 26 Two young

NEW AMERICAN BIBLE

bodily trembling that had come over the man clearly showed
those who saw him the pain that lodged in his heart.
18 People rushed out of their houses in crowds to make public
supplication, because the Place was in danger of being profaned. 19 Women, girded with sackcloth below their breasts,
filled the streets; maidens secluded indoors ran together,
some to the gates, some to the walls, others peered through
the windows, 20 all of them with hands raised toward heav-
en, making supplication. 21 It was pitiful to see the populace
variously prostrated in prayer and the high priest full of
dread and anguish.
22 While they were imploring the almighty LORD to keep the
deposits safe and secure for those who had placed them in
trust, 23 Heliodorus went on with his plan. 24 But just as he
was approaching the treasury with his bodyguards, the LORD
of spirits who holds all power manifested himself in so striking a way that those who had been bold enough to follow
Heliodorus were panic-stricken at God's power and fainted
away in terror. 25 There appeared to them a richly caparisoned horse, mounted by a dreadful rider. Charging furiously, the horse attacked Heliodorus with its front hoofs. The
rider was seen to be wearing golden armor. 26 Then two

NEW JERUSALEM BIBLE

betraying the anguish of his soul; 17 the man was so overwhelmed by fear and bodily trembling that those who saw
him could not possibly mistake the distress he was suffering.
18 People rushed headlong from the houses, intent on making
public supplication because of the indignity threatening the
holy place. 19 Women thronged the streets swathed in sackcloth below their breasts; girls secluded indoors came running, some to the doorways, some to the city walls, while
others leaned out of the windows, 20 all stretching out their
hands to Heaven in entreaty. 21 It was pitiful to see the people crowding together to prostrate themselves, and the foreboding of the high priest in his deep anguish. 22 While they
were calling on the all-powerful Lord to preserve the deposits
intact for the depositors, in full security, 23 Heliodorus set
about his appointed task.
24 He had already arrived with his bodyguard near the
Treasury, when the Sovereign of spirits and of every power
caused so great an apparition that all who had dared to
accompany Heliodorus were dumbfounded at the power of
God and reduced to abject terror. 25 Before their eyes
appeared a horse richly caparisoned and carrying a fearsome
rider. Rearing violently, it struck at Heliodorus with its
forefeet. The rider was seen to be accoutred entirely in gold.

GREEK OLD TESTAMENT

πανοπλίαν ἔχων. 26 ἕτεροι δὲ δύο προσεφάνησαν αὐτῷ
νεανίαι τῇ ῥώμῃ μὲν ἐκπρεπεῖς, κάλλιστοι δὲ τὴν δόξαν,
διαπρεπεῖς δὲ τὴν περιβολήν, οἳ καὶ περιστάντες ἐξ ἑκατέρου μέρους ἐμαστίγουν αὐτὸν ἀδιαλείπτως πολλὰς ἐπιρρι-
πτοῦντες αὐτῷ πληγάς. 27 ἄφνω δὲ πεσόντα πρὸς τὴν γῆν
καὶ πολλῷ σκότει περιχυθέντα συναρπάσαντες καὶ εἰς φο-
ρεῖον ἐνθέντες 28 τὸν ἄρτι μετὰ πολλῆς παραδρομῆς καὶ πάσης δορυφορίας εἰς τὸ προειρημένον εἰσελθόντα γαζοφυλάκιον ἔφερον ἀβοήθητον ἑαυτῷ καθεστῶτα φανερῶς τὴν τοῦ
θεοῦ δυναστείαν ἐπεγνωκότες. 29 καὶ ὁ μὲν διὰ τὴν θείαν
ἐνέργειαν ἄφωνος καὶ πάσης ἐστερημένος ἐλπίδος καὶ σωτηρίας ἔρριπτο, 30 οἱ δὲ τὸν κύριον εὐλόγουν τὸν παραδοξά-
ζοντα τὸν ἑαυτοῦ τόπον, καὶ τὸ μικρῷ πρότερον δέους καὶ
ταραχῆς γέμον ἱερὸν τοῦ παντοκράτορος ἐπιφανέντος κυρίου χαρᾶς καὶ εὐφροσύνης ἐπεπλήρωτο. 31 ταχὺ δέ τινες τῶν
τοῦ Ἡλιοδώρου συνήθων ἠξίουν τὸν Ονιαν ἐπικαλέσασθαι
τὸν ὕψιστον καὶ τὸ ζῆν χαρίσασθαι τῷ παντελῶς ἐν ἐσχάτῃ
πνοῇ κειμένῳ. 32 ὕποπτος δὲ γενόμενος ὁ ἀρχιερεὺς μήποτε
διάλημψιν ὁ βασιλεὺς σχῇ κακουργίαν τινὰ περὶ τὸν Ἡλιόδωρον ὑπὸ τῶν Ιουδαίων συντετελέσθαι προσήγαγεν θυσίαν
ὑπὲρ τῆς τοῦ ἀνδρὸς σωτηρίας. 33 ποιουμένου δὲ τοῦ ἀρχιερέως τὸν ἱλασμὸν οἱ αὐτοὶ νεανίαι πάλιν ἐφάνησαν τῷ
Ἡλιοδώρῳ ἐν ταῖς αὐταῖς ἐσθήσεσιν ἐστολισμένοι καὶ στάντες εἶπον Πολλὰς Ονια τῷ ἀρχιερεῖ χάριτας ἔχε, διὰ γὰρ
αὐτόν σοι κεχάρισται τὸ ζῆν ὁ κύριος. 34 σὺ δὲ ἐξ οὐρανοῦ

KING JAMES VERSION

26 Moreover two other young men appeared before him, notable in strength, excellent in beauty, and comely in apparel, who stood by him on either side, and scourged him continually, and gave him many sore stripes.

27 And Heliodorus fell suddenly unto the ground, and was compassed with great darkness: but they that were with him took him up, and put him into a litter.

28 Thus him, that lately came with a great train and with all his guard into the said treasury, they carried out, being unable to help himself with his weapons: and manifestly they acknowledged the power of God:

29 For he by the hand of God was cast down, and lay speechless without all hope of life.

30 But they praised the Lord, that had miraculously honoured his own place: for the temple, which a little afore was full of fear and trouble, when the Almighty Lord appeared, was filled with joy and gladness.

31 Then straightways certain of Heliodorus' friends prayed Onias, that he would call upon the most High to grant him his life, who lay ready to give up the ghost.

32 So the high priest, suspecting lest the king should misconceive that some treachery had been done to Heliodorus by the Jews, offered a sacrifice for the health of the man.

33 Now as the high priest was making an atonement, the same young men in the same clothing appeared and stood beside Heliodorus, saying, Give Onias the high priest great thanks, insomuch as for his sake the Lord hath granted thee life:

34 And seeing that thou hast been scourged from heaven,

DOUAY OLD TESTAMENT

26 Moreover there appeared two other young men beautiful and strong, bright and glorious, and in comely apparel: who stood by him, on either side, and scourged him without ceasing with many stripes.

27 And Heliodorus suddenly fell to the ground, and they took him up covered with great darkness, and having put him into a litter they carried him out.

28 So he that came with many servants, and all his guard into the aforesaid treasury, was carried out, no one being able to help him, the manifest power of God being known.

29 And he indeed by the power of God lay speechless, and without all hope of recovery.

30 But they praised the Lord because he had glorified his place: and the temple, that a little before was full of fear and trouble, when the almighty Lord appeared, was filled with joy and gladness.

31 Then some of the friends of Heliodorus forthwith begged of Onias, that he would call upon the most High to grant him his life, who was ready to give up the ghost.

32 So the high priest considering that the king might perhaps suspect that some mischief had been done to Heliodorus by the Jews, offered a sacrifice of health for the recovery of the man.

33 And when the high priest was praying, the same young men in the same clothing stood by Heliodorus, and said to him: Give thanks to Onias the priest: because for his sake the Lord hath granted thee life.

34 And thou having been scourged by God, declare unto

KNOX TRANSLATION

26 Two other warriors they saw, how strong of limb, how
dazzling of mien, how bravely clad! These stood about
Heliodorus and fell to scourging him, this side and that,
blow after blow, without respite. 27 With the suddenness of
his fall to the ground, darkness had closed about him; hastily they caught him up and carried him out in his litter; 28 a
helpless burden now, that entered yonder treasury with such
a rabble of tipstaves and halberdiers! Here was proof of
God's power most manifest. 29 There he lay, by heaven's
decree speechless and beyond hope of recovery; 30 and all
around men were praising the Lord, for thus vindicating the
honour of his sanctuary. In the temple, where all had been
anxiety and turmoil until heaven showed its almighty power,
all was rejoicing and contentment now.
31 It was not long before friends of Heliodorus were
entreating Onias to call down mercy from the most High, on
one that was now at death's door. 32 This was anxious news
for the high priest; what if the king should suspect the Jews
of foul play? Offer sacrifice he did for the man's recovery,
and with good effect. 33 He was yet at his prayers, when
those two warriors, in the same brave attire, stood by
Heliodorus again; Thanks thou owest, they said, to the high
priest Onias; at his instance, the Lord grants thee life;
34 God's scourge thou hast felt, God's wondrous power be

TODAY'S ENGLISH VERSION

26 Heliodorus also saw two unusually strong and handsome young men, wearing very fine clothes. They stood on either side of him and beat him unmercifully. 27 He immediately fell to the ground unconscious, and his men put him on a stretcher 28 and carried him out. Only a moment earlier this man had entered the treasury with a large group of men, including all his bodyguards, but now he was being carried away helpless. So they all[a] openly acknowledged the mighty power of God.

29 Heliodorus lay there unable to speak and without hope of recovery from this demonstration of God's power. 30 But the Jews praised Almighty God because he had miraculously protected his Temple and had brought great happiness where only minutes before there had been fear and confusion. 31 Some of Heliodorus' friends quickly asked Onias the High Priest to pray that the Most High would spare the life of this man who was at the point of death. 32 So the High Priest offered a sacrifice in the hope that God would save Heliodorus, for he did not want the king to think that the Jews had done this to the man he had sent. 33 While Onias was offering the sacrifice, the two young men, wearing the same clothes as before, again appeared to Heliodorus and said, "Be grateful to the High Priest; the Lord has spared your life because of him. 34 Remember that it was the Lord of heaven

[a] they all; *some manuscripts have* he.

NEW REVISED STANDARD VERSION

men also appeared to him, remarkably strong, gloriously beautiful and splendidly dressed, who stood on either side of him and flogged him continuously, inflicting many blows on him. 27 When he suddenly fell to the ground and deep darkness came over him, his men took him up, put him on a stretcher, 28 and carried him away—this man who had just entered the aforesaid treasury with a great retinue and all his bodyguard but was now unable to help himself. They recognized clearly the sovereign power of God.

29 While he lay prostrate, speechless because of the divine intervention and deprived of any hope of recovery, 30 they praised the Lord who had acted marvelously for his own place. And the temple, which a little while before was full of fear and disturbance, was filled with joy and gladness, now that the Almighty Lord had appeared.

31 Some of Heliodorus's friends quickly begged Onias to call upon the Most High to grant life to one who was lying quite at his last breath. 32 So the high priest, fearing that the king might get the notion that some foul play had been perpetrated by the Jews with regard to Heliodorus, offered sacrifice for the man's recovery. 33 While the high priest was making an atonement, the same young men appeared again to Heliodorus dressed in the same clothing, and they stood and said, "Be very grateful to the high priest Onias, since for his sake the Lord has granted you your life. 34 And see that you, who have been flogged by heaven, report to all

NEW AMERICAN BIBLE

other young men, remarkably strong, strikingly beautiful, and splendidly attired, appeared before him. Standing on each side of him, they flogged him unceasingly until they had given him innumerable blows. 27 Suddenly he fell to the ground, enveloped in great darkness. Men picked him up and laid him on a stretcher. 28 The man who a moment before had entered that treasury with a great retinue and his whole bodyguard was carried away helpless, having clearly experienced the sovereign power of God. 29 While he lay speechless and deprived of all hope of aid, due to an act of God's power, 30 the Jews praised the LORD who had marvelously glorified his holy Place; and the temple, charged so shortly before with fear and commotion, was filled with joy and gladness, now that the almighty LORD had manifested himself.

31 Soon some of the companions of Heliodorus begged Onias to invoke the Most High, praying that the life of the man who was about to expire might be spared. 32 Fearing that the king might think that Heliodorus had suffered some foul play at the hands of the Jews, the high priest offered a sacrifice for the man's recovery. 33 While the high priest was offering the sacrifice of atonement, the same young men in the same clothing again appeared and stood before Heliodorus. "Be very grateful to the high priest Onias," they told him. "It is for his sake that the LORD has spared your life. 34 Since you have been scourged by Heaven, proclaim to

NEW JERUSALEM BIBLE

26 Two other young men of outstanding strength and radiant beauty, magnificently apparelled, appeared to him at the same time and, taking their stand on each side of him, flogged him unremittingly, inflicting stroke after stroke. 27 Suddenly Heliodorus fell to the ground, enveloped in thick darkness. His men came to his rescue and placed him in a litter, 28 this man who but a moment before had made his way into the Treasury, as we said above, with a great retinue and his whole bodyguard; and as they carried him away, powerless to help himself, they openly acknowledged the sovereign power of God.

29 While Heliodorus lay prostrate under the divine visitation, speechless and bereft of all hope of deliverance, 30 the Jews blessed the Lord who had miraculously glorified his own holy place. And the Temple, which a little while before had been filled with terror and commotion, now overflowed with joy and gladness at the manifestation of the almighty Lord. 31 Some of Heliodorus' companions quickly begged Onias to entreat the Most High to grant the man his life, lying as he did at the very point of death.

32 The high priest, afraid that the king might suspect the Jews of some foul play concerning Heliodorus, did indeed offer a sacrifice for the man's recovery. 33 And while the high priest was performing the rite of expiation, the same young men again appeared to Heliodorus, wearing the same apparel and, standing beside him, said, 'Be very grateful to Onias the high priest, since it is for his sake that the Lord has granted you your life. 34 As for you, who have been scourged

GREEK OLD TESTAMENT

μεμαστιγωμένος διάγγελλε πᾶσι τὸ μεγαλεῖον τοῦ θεοῦ κράτος. ταῦτα δὲ εἰπόντες ἀφανεῖς ἐγένοντο. 35 ὁ δὲ Ἡλιόδωρος θυσίαν ἀνενέγκας τῷ κυρίῳ καὶ εὐχὰς μεγίστας εὐξάμενος τῷ τὸ ζῆν περιποιήσαντι καὶ τὸν Ονιαν ἀποδεξάμενος
ἀνεστρατοπέδευσεν πρὸς τὸν βασιλέα. 36 ἐξεμαρτύρει δὲ
πᾶσιν ἅπερ ἦν ὑπ' ὄψιν τεθεαμένος ἔργα τοῦ μεγίστου θεοῦ.
37 τοῦ δὲ βασιλέως ἐπερωτήσαντος τὸν Ἡλιόδωρον ποῖός τις
εἴη ἐπιτήδειος ἔτι ἅπαξ διαπεμφθῆναι εἰς Ιεροσόλυμα,
ἔφησεν 38 Εἴ τινα ἔχεις πολέμιον ἢ πραγμάτων ἐπίβουλον,
πέμψον αὐτὸν ἐκεῖ, καὶ μεμαστιγωμένον αὐτὸν προσδέξῃ,
ἐάνπερ καὶ διασωθῇ, διὰ τὸ περὶ τὸν τόπον ἀληθῶς εἶναί
τινα θεοῦ δύναμιν· 39 αὐτὸς γὰρ ὁ τὴν κατοικίαν ἐπουράνιον
ἔχων ἐπόπτης ἐστὶν καὶ βοηθὸς ἐκείνου τοῦ τόπου καὶ τοὺς
παραγινομένους ἐπὶ κακώσει τύπτων ἀπολλύει. 40 καὶ τὰ
μὲν κατὰ Ἡλιόδωρον καὶ τὴν τοῦ γαζοφυλακίου τήρησιν
οὕτως ἐχώρησεν.

4 Ὁ δὲ προειρημένος Σιμων ὁ τῶν χρημάτων καὶ τῆς
πατρίδος ἐνδείκτης γεγονὼς ἐκακολόγει τὸν Ονιαν, ὡς
αὐτός τε εἴη τὸν Ἡλιόδωρον ἐπισεσεικὼς καὶ τῶν κακῶν
δημιουργὸς καθεστηκώς, 2 καὶ τὸν εὐεργέτην τῆς πόλεως
καὶ τὸν κηδεμόνα τῶν ὁμοεθνῶν καὶ ζηλωτὴν τῶν νόμων ἐπίβουλον τῶν πραγμάτων ἐτόλμα λέγειν. 3 τῆς δὲ ἔχθρας ἐπὶ
τοσοῦτον προβαινούσης ὥστε καὶ διά τινος τῶν ὑπὸ τοῦ
Σιμωνος δεδοκιμασμένων φόνους συντελεῖσθαι, 4 συνορῶν ὁ
Ονιας τὸ χαλεπὸν τῆς φιλονεικίας καὶ Ἀπολλώνιον

KING JAMES VERSION

declare unto all men the mighty power of God. And when they had spoken these words, they appeared no more.

35 So Heliodorus, after he had offered sacrifice unto the Lord, and made great vows unto him that had saved his life, and saluted Onias, returned with his host to the king.

36 Then testified he to all men the works of the great God, which he had seen with his eyes.

37 And when the king asked Heliodorus, who might be a fit man to be sent yet once again to Jerusalem, he said,

38 If thou hast any enemy or traitor, send him thither, and thou shalt receive him well scourged, if he escape with his life: for in that place, no doubt, there is an especial power of God.

39 For he that dwelleth in heaven hath his eye on that place, and defendeth it; and he beateth and destroyeth them that come to hurt it.

40 And the things concerning Heliodorus, and the keeping of the treasury, fell out on this sort.

4 This Simon now, of whom we spake afore, having been a bewrayer of the money, and of his country, slandered Onias, as if he had terrified Heliodorus, and been the worker of these evils.

2 Thus was he bold to call him a traitor, that had deserved well of the city, and tendered his own nation, and was so zealous of the laws.

3 But when their hatred went so far, that by one of Simon's faction murders were committed,

4 Onias seeing the danger of this contention, and that

DOUAY OLD TESTAMENT

all men the great works and the power of God. And having spoken thus, they appeared no more.

35 So Heliodorus after he had offered a sacrifice to God, and made great vows to him, that had granted him life, and given thanks to Onias, taking his troops with him, returned to the king.

36 And he testified to all men the works of the great God, which he had seen with his own eyes.

37 And when the king asked Heliodorus, who might be a fit man to be sent yet once more to Jerusalem, he said:

38 If thou hast any enemy or traitor to thy kingdom, send him thither, and thou shalt receive him again scourged, if so be he escape: for there is undoubtedly in that place a certain power of God.

39 For he that hath his dwelling in the heavens, is the visitor, and protector of that place, and he striketh and destroyeth them that come to do evil to it.

40 And the things concerning Heliodorus, and the keeping of the treasury fell out in this manner.

4 BUT Simon, of whom we spoke before, who was the betrayer of the money, and of his country, spoke ill of Onias, as though he had incited Heliodorus to do these things, and had been the promoter of evils:

2 And he presumed to call him a traitor to the kingdom, who provided for the city, and defended his nation, and was zealous for the law of God.

3 But when the enmities proceeded so far, that murders also were committed by some of Simon's friends:

4 Onias considering the danger of this contention, and

KNOX TRANSLATION

ever on thy lips. And with that, they were seen no more.
35 Be sure this Heliodorus offered God sacrifice; ay, and made
vows a many for his preservation, and thanked Onias
besides; then he marched his army back to the king.
36 Everywhere he testified how great a God was this, what
strange things his own eyes had witnessed; 37 and when the
king himself asked what manner of emissary he should next
send to Jerusalem, Why, said he, 38 some enemy of thine,
some rebel that plots against the kingdom. Escape he with
his life, I warrant he will come back to thee soundly beaten.
Past doubt, there is some divine influence haunts yonder
place; 39 watch and ward he keeps over it, that has his
dwelling in heaven, to be the plague and the undoing of all
who come that way upon an errand of mischief.
40 Such is the tale of Heliodorus, and of the treasury's preserving.

4 And now, what must Simon do, the same that had
drawn men's eyes to his country with stories of treasure,
but fall to slandering Onias? Onias it was, by his way of it,
had egged Heliodorus on,[a] and been the author of the mischief. 2 So true a patriot, that well loved his race, well guarded the divine law, and he must be branded with the name of
traitor! 3 The feud grew worse, till at last there were murders
done, and Simon's faction answerable for it. 4 Here was the
public peace much endangered; here was Apollonius, the

a 'Egged Heliodorus on'; some think the word used in the Greek has a quite different meaning from the usual, and that Onias was accused of having attacked Heliodorus with violence (cf. 3. 32).

TODAY'S ENGLISH VERSION

who punished you. Now go and tell everyone of his great power." When they had said this, they disappeared.

35 So Heliodorus offered a sacrifice to the Lord and made many promises, because the Lord had spared his life. Then he said good-bye to Onias and returned with his army to the king. 36 There he told everyone what the Lord, the most powerful of all gods, had done.

37 When the king asked Heliodorus who would be the best man to send on the next mission to Jerusalem, Heliodorus replied, 38 "If you have an enemy or know of someone plotting against your government, send him. He will come back badly beaten, if he comes back at all, for some strange power from God is at work there. 39 The God of heaven watches over the Temple; he strikes down and destroys anyone who comes to harm it." 40 That is the story of how the Temple treasury was protected from Heliodorus.

4 But Simon (mentioned earlier as the one who informed Apollonius about the money and brought trouble on the nation) also lied about Onias, claiming that he was responsible for the attack on Heliodorus and for the difficulties that followed. 2 He dared to accuse Onias of plotting against the government—Onias who not only had made donations to Jerusalem and had protected the Temple, but who was eager to see that all our laws were obeyed. 3-4 Apollonius son of

NEW REVISED STANDARD VERSION

people the majestic power of God." Having said this they vanished.

35 Then Heliodorus offered sacrifice to the Lord and made very great vows to the Savior of his life, and having bidden Onias farewell, he marched off with his forces to the king. 36 He bore testimony to all concerning the deeds of the supreme God, which he had seen with his own eyes. 37 When the king asked Heliodorus what sort of person would be suitable to send on another mission to Jerusalem, he replied, 38 "If you have any enemy or plotter against your government, send him there, for you will get him back thoroughly flogged, if he survives at all; for there is certainly some power of God about the place. 39 For he who has his dwelling in heaven watches over that place himself and brings it aid, and he strikes and destroys those who come to do it injury." 40 This was the outcome of the episode of Heliodorus and the protection of the treasury.

4 The previously mentioned Simon, who had informed about the money against[a] his own country, slandered Onias, saying that it was he who had incited Heliodorus and had been the real cause of the misfortune. 2 He dared to designate as a plotter against the government the man who was the benefactor of the city, the protector of his compatriots, and a zealot for the laws. 3 When his hatred progressed to such a degree that even murders were committed by one of Simon's approved agents, 4 Onias recognized that the rivalry

a Gk *and*

NEW AMERICAN BIBLE

all men the majesty of God's power." When they had said this, they disappeared.

35 After Heliodorus had offered a sacrifice to the LORD and made most solemn vows to him who had spared his life, he bade Onias farewell, and returned with his soldiers to the king. 36 Before all men he gave witness to the deeds of the most high God that he had seen with his own eyes. 37 When the king asked Heliodorus who would be a suitable man to be sent to Jerusalem next, he answered: 38 "If you have an enemy or a plotter against the government, send him there, and you will receive him back well-flogged, if indeed he survives at all; for there is certainly some special divine power about the Place. 39 He who has his dwelling in heaven watches over that Place and protects it, and he strikes down and destroys those who come to harm it." 40 This was how the matter concerning Heliodorus and the preservation of the treasury turned out.

4 The Simon mentioned above as the informer about the funds against his own country, made false accusations that it was Onias who threatened Heliodorus and instigated the whole miserable affair. 2 He dared to brand as a plotter against the government the man who was a benefactor of the city, a protector of his compatriots, and a zealous defender of the laws. 3 When Simon's hostility reached such a point that murders were being committed by one of his henchmen, 4 Onias saw that the opposition was serious and that

NEW JERUSALEM BIBLE

by Heaven, you must proclaim to everyone the grandeur of God's power.' So saying, they vanished.

35 Heliodorus offered sacrifice to the Lord and made most solemn vows to the preserver of his life, and then took courteous leave of Onias and marched his forces back to the king. 36 He openly testified to everyone about the works of the supreme God which he had seen with his own eyes. 37 When the king asked Heliodorus what sort of man would be the right person to send to Jerusalem on a second occasion, he replied, 38 'If you have some enemy or anyone disloyal to the state, send him there, and you will get him back well flogged, if he survives at all, since some peculiarly divine power attaches to the holy place. 39 He who has his dwelling in heaven watches over the place and defends it, and he strikes down and destroys those who come to harm it.' 40 This was the outcome of the affair of Heliodorus and the preservation of the Treasury.

4 The Simon mentioned above as the informer against the funds and against his country began slandering Onias, insinuating that the latter had been responsible for the assault on Heliodorus and himself had contrived this misfortune. 2 Simon now had the effrontery to name this benefactor of the city, this protector of his compatriots, this zealot for the laws, as an enemy of the public good. 3 This hostility reached such proportions that murders were actually committed by some of Simon's agents, 4 and at this point Onias,

Greek Old Testament

Μενεσθέως τὸν Κοίλης Συρίας καὶ Φοινίκης στρατηγὸν συν-
αύξοντα τὴν κακίαν τοῦ Σιμωνος, 5 πρὸς τὸν βασιλέα διεκομίσθη οὐ γινόμενος τῶν πολιτῶν κατήγορος, τὸ δὲ σύμφορον
κοινῇ καὶ κατ' ἰδίαν παντὶ τῷ πλήθει σκοπῶν· 6 ἑώρα γὰρ
ἄνευ βασιλικῆς προνοίας ἀδύνατον εἶναι τυχεῖν εἰρήνης ἔτι
τὰ πράγματα καὶ τὸν Σιμωνα παῦλαν οὐ λημψόμενον τῆς
ἀνοίας.

7 Μεταλλάξαντος δὲ τὸν βίον Σελεύκου καὶ παραλαβόντος
τὴν βασιλείαν Ἀντιόχου τοῦ προσαγορευθέντος Ἐπιφανοῦς
ὑπενόθευσεν Ἰάσων ὁ ἀδελφὸς Ονιου τὴν ἀρχιερωσύνην
8 ἐπαγγειλάμενος τῷ βασιλεῖ δι' ἐντεύξεως ἀργυρίου τάλαντα ἑξήκοντα πρὸς τοῖς τριακοσίοις καὶ προσόδου τινὸς
ἄλλης τάλαντα ὀγδοήκοντα. 9 πρὸς δὲ τούτοις ὑπισχνεῖτο
καὶ ἕτερα διαγράφειν πεντήκοντα πρὸς τοῖς ἑκατόν, ἐὰν
ἐπιχωρηθῇ διὰ τῆς ἐξουσίας αὐτοῦ γυμνάσιον καὶ ἐφηβεῖον
αὐτῷ συστήσασθαι καὶ τοὺς ἐν Ιεροσολύμοις Ἀντιοχεῖς
ἀναγράψαι. 10 ἐπινεύσαντος δὲ τοῦ βασιλέως καὶ τῆς ἀρχῆς
κρατήσας εὐθέως πρὸς τὸν Ἑλληνικὸν χαρακτῆρα τοὺς
ὁμοφύλους μετέστησε. 11 καὶ τὰ κείμενα τοῖς Ιουδαίοις
φιλάνθρωπα βασιλικὰ διὰ Ιωάννου τοῦ πατρὸς Εὐπολέμου
τοῦ ποιησαμένου τὴν πρεσβείαν ὑπὲρ φιλίας καὶ συμμαχίας
πρὸς τοὺς Ῥωμαίους παρώσας καὶ τὰς μὲν νομίμους καταλύων πολιτείας παρανόμους ἐθισμοὺς ἐκαίνιζεν. 12 ἀσμένως
γὰρ ὑπ' αὐτὴν τὴν ἀκρόπολιν γυμνάσιον καθίδρυσεν καὶ τοὺς

King James Version

Apollonius, as being the governor of Celosyria and Phenice, did rage, and increase Simon's malice,

5 He went to the king, not to be an accuser of his countrymen, but seeking the good of all, both publick and private:

6 For he saw that it was impossible that the state should continue quiet, and Simon leave his folly, unless the king did look thereunto.

7 But after the death of Seleucus, when Antiochus, called Epiphanes, took the kingdom, Jason the brother of Onias laboured underhand to be high priest,

8 Promising unto the king by intercession three hundred and threescore talents of silver, and of another revenue eighty talents:

9 Beside this, he promised to assign an hundred and fifty more, if he might have licence to set him up a place for exercise, and for the training up of youth in the fashions of the heathen, and to write them of Jerusalem *by the name of* Antiochians.

10 Which when the king had granted, and he had gotten into his hand the rule, he forthwith brought his own nation to the Greekish fashion.

11 And the royal privileges granted of special favour to the Jews by the means of John the father of Eupolemus, who went ambassador to Rome for amity and aid, he took away; and putting down the governments which were according to the law, he brought up new customs against the law:

12 For he built gladly a place of exercise under the tower

Douay Old Testament

that Apollonius, who was the governor of Celesyria and Phenicia, was outrageous, which increased the malice of Simon, went to the king,

5 Not to be an accuser of his countrymen, but with a view to the common good of all the people.

6 For he saw that, except the king took care, it was impossible that matters should be settled in peace, or that Simon would cease from his folly.

7 But after the death of Seleucus, when Antiochus, who was called the Illustrious, had taken possession of the kingdom, Jason the brother of Onias ambitiously sought the high priesthood:

8 And went to the king, promising him three hundred and sixty talents of silver, and out of other revenues fourscore talents.

9 Besides this he promised also a hundred and fifty more, if he might have license to set him up a place for exercise, and a place for youth, and to entitle them, that were at Jerusalem, Antiochians.

10 Which when the king had granted, and he had gotten the rule into his hands, forthwith he began to bring over his countrymen to the fashion of the heathens.

11 And abolishing those things, which had been decreed of special favour by the kings in behalf of the Jews, by the means of John the father of that Eupolemus, who went ambassador to Rome to make amity and alliance, he disannulled the lawful ordinances of the citizens, and brought in fashions that were perverse.

12 For he had the boldness to set up, under the very castle,

Knox Translation

governor of Coelesyria and Phoenice, adding fuel to the flame
of Simon's malice;[a] what marvel if Onias had recourse to the
king? 5 Little enough it liked him to bring an ill name on his
fellow-citizens; yet common good of the Jewish folk he must
needs have in mind; 6 how should quiet times return, or
Simon's madness be cooled, unless the king took order in the
matter?

7 But king Seleucus was done with life now, and the throne
passed to Antiochus, called the Illustrious. And here was a
brother Onias had, called Jason, that coveted the office of
high priest. 8 This Jason went to the new king, and made
him an offer of three hundred and sixty talents of silver out
of its revenue, besides eighty from other incomings. 9 Let
leave be granted him to set up a game-place for the training
of youth, and enrol the men of Jerusalem as citizens of
Antioch, he would give his bond for a hundred and fifty
more. 10 To this the king assented; high priest he became,
and straightway set about perverting his fellow-countrymen
to the Gentile way of living. 11 Till now, the Jews had followed their own customs, by grace of a royal privilege; it was
John that won it for them, father of that Eupolemus, who
afterwards went in embassage to Rome, to make a treaty of
alliance. But Jason would abrogate these customs; common
right should be none, and great wrong should find acceptance instead. 12 This game-place of his he did not scruple to

a v. 4. 'Adding fuel to the flame of Simon's malice'; literally, 'raving to increase Simon's malice', but this curious phrase is probably due to a copyist's mistake.

TODAY'S ENGLISH VERSION

Menestheus, the governor of Greater Syria, encouraged
Simon in every evil thing he did, and Simon's opposition
finally grew so strong that one of his trusted followers committed several murders. Onias realized how dangerous the
situation had become, 5 so he went to the king, not for the
purpose of making accusations against his own people, but
for the common good of all Jews, both in their private and
public lives. 6 He realized that without the king's cooperation there was no hope for peace, and Simon would keep on
with his foolishness.

7 Later, when King Seleucus died and Antiochus (known as
Epiphanes) became king, Jason the brother of Onias became
High Priest by corrupt means. 8 He went to see[a] the king and
offered him 27,000 pounds of silver with 6,000 more pounds
to be paid later. 9 Jason also offered him an additional
11,250 pounds of silver for the authority to establish a stadium where young men could train and to enroll the people of
Jerusalem as citizens of Antioch.[b]

10 The king gave his approval, and just as soon as Jason
took over the office of High Priest, he made the people of Jerusalem change to the Greek way of life. 11 He began by abolishing the favors that John had secured for the Jews from previous Syrian kings. (John was the father of the Eupolemus
who later went to Rome to make an alliance and to establish
ties of friendship.) Jason also did away with our Jewish customs and introduced new customs that were contrary to our
Law. 12 With great enthusiasm he built a stadium near the

[a] went to see; *or* wrote to. [b] the people . . . Antioch; *or* the men of Jerusalem as supporters of King Antiochus.

NEW REVISED STANDARD VERSION

was serious and that Apollonius son of Menestheus,[a] and
governor of Coelesyria and Phoenicia, was intensifying the
malice of Simon. 5 So he appealed to the king, not accusing
his compatriots but having in view the welfare, both public
and private, of all the people. 6 For he saw that without the
king's attention public affairs could not again reach a peaceful settlement, and that Simon would not stop his folly.

7 When Seleucus died and Antiochus, who was called
Epiphanes, succeeded to the kingdom, Jason the brother of
Onias obtained the high priesthood by corruption, 8 promising the king at an interview[b] three hundred sixty talents of
silver, and from another source of revenue eighty talents.
9 In addition to this he promised to pay one hundred fifty
more if permission were given to establish by his authority a
gymnasium and a body of youth for it, and to enroll the people of Jerusalem as citizens of Antioch. 10 When the king
assented and Jason[c] came to office, he at once shifted his
compatriots over to the Greek way of life.

11 He set aside the existing royal concessions to the Jews,
secured through John the father of Eupolemus, who went on
the mission to establish friendship and alliance with the
Romans; and he destroyed the lawful ways of living and
introduced new customs contrary to the law. 12 He took
delight in establishing a gymnasium right under the citadel,

a Vg Compare verse 21: Meaning of Gk uncertain *b* Or *by a petition*
c Gk *he*

NEW AMERICAN BIBLE

Apollonius, son of Menestheus, the governor of Coelesyria
and Phoenicia, was abetting Simon's wickedness. 5 So he
had recourse to the king, not as an accuser of his countrymen, but as a man looking to the general and particular
good of all the people. 6 He saw that, unless the king intervened, it would be impossible to have a peaceful government, and that Simon would not desist from his folly.

7 But Seleucus died, and when Antiochus surnamed
Epiphanes succeeded him on the throne, Onias' brother
Jason obtained the high priesthood by corrupt means: 8 in an
interview, he promised the king three hundred and sixty talents of silver, as well as eighty talents from another source
of income. 9 Besides this he agreed to pay a hundred and
fifty more, if he were given authority to establish a gymnasium and a youth club for it and to enroll men in Jerusalem as
Antiochians.

10 When Jason received the king's approval and came into
office, he immediately initiated his countrymen into the
Greek way of life. 11 He set aside the royal concessions
granted to the Jews through the mediation of John, father of
Eupolemus (that Eupolemus who would later go on an
embassy to the Romans to establish a treaty of friendship
with them); he abrogated the lawful institutions and introduced customs contrary to the law. 12 He quickly established
a gymnasium at the very foot of the acropolis, where he

NEW JERUSALEM BIBLE

recognising how mischievous this rivalry was, and aware
that Apollonius son of Menestheus, the general commanding
Coele-Syria and Phoenicia, was encouraging Simon in his
malice, 5 went to see the king, not to play the accuser of his
fellow-citizens, but having the public and private welfare of
the entire people at heart. 6 He saw that, without some intervention by the king, an orderly administration would no
longer be possible, nor would Simon put a stop to his folly.

7 When Seleucus had departed this life and Antiochus
styled Epiphanes had succeeded to the kingdom, Jason,
brother of Onias, usurped the high priesthood: 8 he
approached the king with a promise of three hundred and
sixty talents of silver, with eighty talents to come from some
other source of revenue. 9 He further committed himself to
paying another hundred and fifty, if the king would empow-
er him to set up a gymnasium and youth centre, and to register the Antiochists of Jerusalem. 10 When the king gave his
assent, Jason, as soon as he had seized power, imposed the
Greek way of life on his fellow-countrymen. 11 He suppressed the liberties which the kings had graciously granted
to the Jews at the instance of John, father of that Eupolemus
who was later to be sent on an embassy to negotiate a treaty
of friendship and alliance with the Romans and, overthrowing the lawful institutions, introduced new usages contrary
to the Law. 12 He went so far as to found a gymnasium at
the very foot of the Citadel, and to fit out the noblest of his

Greek Old Testament

κρατίστους τῶν ἐφήβων ὑποτάσσων ὑπὸ πέτασον ἤγαγεν.
13 ἦν δ᾽ οὕτως ἀκμή τις Ἑλληνισμοῦ καὶ πρόσβασις ἀλλοφυ-
λισμοῦ διὰ τὴν τοῦ ἀσεβοῦς καὶ οὐκ ἀρχιερέως Ἰάσωνος
ὑπερβάλλουσαν ἀναγνείαν 14 ὥστε μηκέτι περὶ τὰς τοῦ
θυσιαστηρίου λειτουργίας προθύμους εἶναι τοὺς ἱερεῖς, ἀλλὰ
τοῦ μὲν νεὼ καταφρονοῦντες καὶ τῶν θυσιῶν ἀμελοῦντες
ἔσπευδον μετέχειν τῆς ἐν παλαίστρῃ παρανόμου χορηγίας
μετὰ τὴν τοῦ δίσκου πρόσκλησιν, 15 καὶ τὰς μὲν πατρῴους
τιμὰς ἐν οὐδενὶ τιθέμενοι, τὰς δὲ Ἑλληνικὰς δόξας καλλί-
στας ἡγούμενοι. 16 ὧν καὶ χάριν περιέσχεν αὐτοὺς χαλεπὴ
περίστασις, καὶ ὧν ἐζήλουν τὰς ἀγωγὰς καὶ καθ᾽ ἅπαν
ἤθελον ἐξομοιοῦσθαι, τούτους πολεμίους καὶ τιμωρητὰς
ἔσχον· 17 ἀσεβεῖν γὰρ εἰς τοὺς θείους νόμους οὐ ῥᾴδιον,
ἀλλὰ ταῦτα ὁ ἀκόλουθος καιρὸς δηλώσει.
18 Ἀγομένου δὲ πενταετηρικοῦ ἀγῶνος ἐν Τύρῳ καὶ τοῦ
βασιλέως παρόντος 19 ἀπέστειλεν Ἰάσων ὁ μιαρὸς θεωροὺς
ὡς ἀπὸ Ιεροσολύμων Ἀντιοχεῖς ὄντας παρακομίζοντας
ἀργυρίου δραχμὰς τριακοσίας εἰς τὴν τοῦ Ἡρακλέους θυσίαν, ἃς καὶ ἠξίωσαν οἱ παρακομίσαντες μὴ χρῆσθαι εἰς θυσίαν διὰ τὸ μὴ καθήκειν, εἰς ἑτέραν δὲ καταθέσθαι δαπάνην.
20 ἔπεσε μὲν οὖν ταῦτα διὰ μὲν τὸν ἀποστείλαντα εἰς τὴν
τοῦ Ἡρακλέους θυσίαν, ἕνεκεν δὲ τῶν παρακομιζόντων εἰς
τὰς τῶν τριηρέων κατασκευάς.

King James Version

itself, and brought the chief young men under his subjection, and made them wear a hat.

13 Now such was the height of Greek fashions, and increase of heathenish manners, through the exceeding profaneness of Jason, that ungodly wretch, and no high priest;

14 That the priests had no courage to serve any more at the altar, but despising the temple, and neglecting the sacrifices, hastened to be partakers of the unlawful allowance in the place of exercise, after the game of Discus called them forth;

15 Not setting by the honours of their fathers, but liking the glory of the Grecians best of all.

16 By reason whereof sore calamity came upon them: for they had them to be their enemies and avengers, whose custom they followed so earnestly, and unto whom they desired to be like in all things.

17 For it is not a light thing to do wickedly against the laws of God: but the time following shall declare these things.

18 Now when the game that was used every fifth year was kept at Tyrus, the king being present,

19 This ungracious Jason sent special messengers from Jerusalem, who were Antiochians, to carry three hundred drachms of silver to the sacrifice of Hercules, which even the bearers thereof thought fit not to bestow upon the sacrifice, because it was not convenient, but to be reserved for other charges.

20 This money then, in regard of the sender, was appointed to Hercules' sacrifice; but because of the bearers thereof, it was employed to the making of gallies.

Douay Old Testament

a place of exercise, and to put all the choicest youths in brothel houses.

13 Now this was not the beginning, but an increase, and progress of heathenish and foreign manners, through the abominable and unheard of wickedness of Jason, that impious wretch and no priest.

14 Insomuch that the priests were not now occupied about the offices of the altar, but despising the temple and neglecting the sacrifices, hastened to be partakers of the games, and of the unlawful allowance thereof, and of the exercise of the discus.

15 And setting nought by the honours of their fathers, they esteemed the Grecian glories for the best:

16 For the sake of which they incurred a dangerous contention, and followed earnestly their ordinances, and in all things they coveted to be like them, who were their enemies and murderers.

17 For acting wickedly against the laws of God doth not pass unpunished: but this the time following will declare.

18 Now when the game that was used every fifth year was kept at Tyre, the king being present,

19 The wicked Jason sent from Jerusalem sinful men to carry three hundred didrachmas of silver for the sacrifice of Hercules; but the bearers thereof desired it might not be bestowed on the sacrifices, because it was not necessary, but might be deputed for other charges.

20 So the money was appointed by him that sent it to the sacrifice of Hercules: but because of them that carried it was employed for the making of galleys.

Knox Translation

set up in the very shadow of the Citadel, and debauch[a] all
that was noblest of Judaea's youth.
13 Mischief in the bud, think you, when such alien Gentile
ways came in? Nay, here was flower and fruit of it; and all
through the unexampled villainy of one man, this Jason, that
high priest was none, but rather an arch-traitor. 14 Why, the
priests themselves had no more stomach for serving the altar;
temple scorned, and sacrifice unheeded, off they went to the
wrestling-ground, there to enter their names and win unhallowed prizes, soon as ever the first quoit was thrown! 15 What
glory their fathers had handed down to them! And fame such
as the Greeks covet was all their ambition now. 16 Alas, here
was a perilous contest awaiting them; Greek fashions they
would follow, and Greeks would be, that ere long should have
Greeks for their enemies, ay, and conquerors. 17 There is no
breaking God's laws without paying the price; time will show
that. 18 When the quinquennial games were being held at
Tyre, in the king's presence, 19 this vile Jason it was sent some
of his wretches[b] with a gift of three hundred silver pieces to do
honour to Hercules. True it is, the bearers of them asked they
should not be spent on sacrifice, but on some other need that
was more befitting; 20 yet Jason's meaning was, Hercules
should have them, and if they went to the building of the fleet,
it was thanks to Jason's envoys.

a 'Debauch'; the Latin says he exposed them in brothels, but the obscure phrase used in the Greek, 'he brought them under the hat' is usually interpreted as meaning that he encouraged them to wear the broad-brimmed Greek *petasus* as a symbol of devotion to Hermes, the patron deity of athletics. *b* 'Wretches'; the word found in our Latin text is probably a copyist's error for 'supplicators', i.e. religious representatives.

TODAY'S ENGLISH VERSION

Temple hill and led our finest young men to adopt the Greek
custom of participating in athletic events. 13 Because of the
unrivaled wickedness of Jason, that ungodly and illegitimate
High Priest, the craze for the Greek way of life and for foreign
customs reached such a point 14 that even the priests lost all
interest in their sacred duties. They lost interest in the Temple
services and neglected the sacrifices. Just as soon as the signal was given, they would rush off to take part in the games
that were forbidden by our Law. 15 They did not care about
anything their ancestors had valued; they prized only Greek
honors. 16 And this turned out to be the source of all their
troubles, for the very people whose ways they admired and
whose customs they tried to imitate became their enemies
and oppressed them. 17 It is a serious thing to disregard God's
Law, as you will see from the following events.

18 Once when the king was present for the athletic games
that were held every five[a] years in the city of Tyre, 19 that
worthless Jason sent some men there from Jerusalem, who
were also enrolled as citizens of Antioch, to take 22,500
pounds of silver to pay for a sacrifice to the god Hercules.
But even these men did not think it was fitting to use such a
large sum of money for a sacrifice, and 20 so the money originally intended as a sacrifice to Hercules was used for the
construction of warships.

[a] five; *or* four.

NEW REVISED STANDARD VERSION

and he induced the noblest of the young men to wear the
Greek hat. 13 There was such an extreme of Hellenization
and increase in the adoption of foreign ways because of the
surpassing wickedness of Jason, who was ungodly and no
true[a] high priest, 14 that the priests were no longer intent
upon their service at the altar. Despising the sanctuary and
neglecting the sacrifices, they hurried to take part in the
unlawful proceedings in the wrestling arena after the signal
for the discus-throwing, 15 disdaining the honors prized by
their ancestors and putting the highest value upon Greek
forms of prestige. 16 For this reason heavy disaster overtook
them, and those whose ways of living they admired and
wished to imitate completely became their enemies and punished them. 17 It is no light thing to show irreverence to the
divine laws—a fact that later events will make clear.

18 When the quadrennial games were being held at Tyre
and the king was present, 19 the vile Jason sent envoys, chosen as being Antiochian citizens from Jerusalem, to carry
three hundred silver drachmas for the sacrifice to Hercules.
Those who carried the money, however, thought best not to
use it for sacrifice, because that was inappropriate, but to
expend it for another purpose. 20 So this money was intended by the sender for the sacrifice to Hercules, but by the decision of its carriers it was applied to the construction of
triremes.

a Gk lacks *true*

NEW AMERICAN BIBLE

induced the noblest young men to wear the Greek hat. 13 The
craze for Hellenism and foreign customs reached such a
pitch, through the outrageous wickedness of the ungodly
pseudo-highpriest Jason, 14 that the priests no longer cared
about the service of the altar. Disdaining the temple and
neglecting the sacrifices, they hastened, at the signal for the
discus-throwing, to take part in the unlawful exercises on
the athletic field. 15 They despised what their ancestors had
regarded as honors, while they highly prized what the Greeks
esteemed as glory. 16 Precisely because of this, they found
themselves in serious trouble: the very people whose manner
of life they emulated, and whom they desired to imitate in
everything, became their enemies and oppressors. 17 It is no
light matter to flout the laws of God, as the following period
will show.

18 When the quinquennial games were held at Tyre in the
presence of the king, 19 the vile Jason sent envoys as representatives of the Antiochians of Jerusalem, to bring there
three hundred silver drachmas for the sacrifice to Hercules.
But the bearers themselves decided that the money should
not be spent on a sacrifice, as that was not right, but should
be used for some other purpose. 20 So the contribution destined by the sender for the sacrifice to Hercules was in fact
applied, by those who brought it, to the construction of
triremes.

NEW JERUSALEM BIBLE

young men in the petasos. 13 Godless wretch that he was
and no true high priest, Jason set no bounds to his impiety;
indeed the hellenising process reached such a pitch 14 that
the priests ceased to show any interest in serving the altar;
but, scorning the Temple and neglecting the sacrifices, they
would hurry, on the stroke of the gong, to take part in the
distribution, forbidden by the Law, of the oil on the exercise
ground; 15 setting no store by the honours of their fatherland, they esteemed hellenic glories best of all. 16 But all this
brought its own retribution; the very people whose way of
life they envied, whom they sought to resemble in everything, proved to be their enemies and executioners. 17 It is
no small thing to violate the divine laws, as the period that
followed will demonstrate.

18 On the occasion of the quadrennial games at Tyre in the
presence of the king, 19 the vile Jason sent an embassy of
Antiochists from Jerusalem, taking with them three hundred
silver drachmas for the sacrifice to Hercules. But even those
who brought the money did not think it would be right to
spend it on the sacrifice and decided to reserve it for some
other item of expenditure; 20 and so what the sender had
intended for the sacrifice to Hercules was in fact applied, at
the suggestion of those who brought it, to the construction
of triremes.

GREEK OLD TESTAMENT

21 Ἀποσταλέντος δὲ εἰς Αἴγυπτον Ἀπολλωνίου τοῦ Μενεσθέως διὰ τὰ πρωτοκλίσια τοῦ Φιλομήτορος βασιλέως μεταλαβὼν Ἀντίοχος ἀλλότριον αὐτὸν τῶν αὐτοῦ γεγονέναι
πραγμάτων τῆς καθ' αὐτὸν ἀσφαλείας ἐφρόντιζεν· ὅθεν εἰς
Ιοππην παραγενόμενος κατήντησεν εἰς Ιεροσόλυμα.
22 μεγαλομερῶς δὲ ὑπὸ τοῦ Ἰάσωνος καὶ τῆς πόλεως ἀποδεχθεὶς μετὰ δᾳδουχίας καὶ βοῶν εἰσεδέχθη, εἶθ' οὕτως εἰς
τὴν Φοινίκην κατεστρατοπέδευσεν.
23 Μετὰ δὲ τριετῆ χρόνον ἀπέστειλεν Ἰάσων Μενέλαον
τὸν τοῦ προσημαινομένου Σιμωνος ἀδελφὸν παρακομίζοντα
τὰ χρήματα τῷ βασιλεῖ καὶ περὶ πραγμάτων ἀναγκαίων
ὑπομνηματισμοὺς τελέσοντα. 24 ὁ δὲ συσταθεὶς τῷ βασιλεῖ
καὶ δοξάσας αὐτὸν τῷ προσώπῳ τῆς ἐξουσίας εἰς ἑαυτὸν
κατήντησεν τὴν ἀρχιερωσύνην ὑπερβαλὼν τὸν Ἰάσωνα τάλαντα ἀργυρίου τριακόσια. 25 λαβὼν δὲ τὰς βασιλικὰς ἐντολὰς παρεγένετο τῆς μὲν ἀρχιερωσύνης οὐδὲν ἄξιον φέρων,
θυμοὺς δὲ ὠμοῦ τυράννου καὶ θηρὸς βαρβάρου ὀργὰς ἔχων.
26 καὶ ὁ μὲν Ἰάσων ὁ τὸν ἴδιον ἀδελφὸν ὑπονοθεύσας
ὑπονοθευθεὶς ὑφ' ἑτέρου φυγὰς εἰς τὴν Αμμανῖτιν χώραν
συνήλαστο. 27 ὁ δὲ Μενέλαος τῆς μὲν ἀρχῆς ἐκράτει, τῶν
δὲ ἐπηγγελμένων τῷ βασιλεῖ χρημάτων οὐδὲν εὐτάκτει·
28 ποιουμένου δὲ τὴν ἀπαίτησιν Σωστράτου τοῦ τῆς ἀκροπό-
λεως ἐπάρχου, πρὸς τοῦτον γὰρ ἦν ἡ τῶν διαφόρων πρᾶξις.
δι' ἣν αἰτίαν οἱ δύο ὑπὸ τοῦ βασιλέως προσεκλήθησαν, 29 καὶ

KING JAMES VERSION

21 Now when Apollonius the *son* of Menestheus was sent into Egypt for the coronation of king *Ptolemeus* Philometor, Antiochus, understanding him not to be well affected to his affairs, provided for his own safety: whereupon he came to Joppe, and from thence to Jerusalem:

22 Where he was honourably received of Jason, and of the city, and was brought in with torch light, and with great shoutings: and so afterward went with his host unto Phenice.

23 Three years afterward Jason sent Menelaus, the aforesaid Simon's brother, to bear the money unto the king, and to put him in mind of certain necessary matters.

24 But he being brought to the presence of the king, when he had magnified him for the glorious appearance of his power, got the priesthood to himself, offering more than Jason by three hundred talents of silver.

25 So he came with the king's mandate, bringing nothing worthy the high priesthood, but having the fury of a cruel tyrant, and the rage of a savage beast.

26 Then Jason, who had undermined his own brother, being undermined by another, was compelled to flee into the country of the Ammonites.

27 So Menelaus got the principality: but as for the money that he had promised unto the king, he took no good order for it, albeit Sostratus the ruler of the castle required it:

28 For unto him appertained the gathering of the customs. Wherefore they were both called before the king.

DOUAY OLD TESTAMENT

21 Now when Apollonius the son of Mnestheus was sent into Egypt to treat with the nobles of king Philometor, and Antiochus understood that he was wholly excluded from the affairs of the kingdom, consulting his own interest, he departed thence and came to Joppe, and from thence to Jerusalem:

22 Where he was received in a magnificent manner by Jason, and the city, and came in with torch lights, and with praises, and from thence he returned with his army into Phenicia.

23 Three years afterwards Jason sent Menelaus, brother of the aforesaid Simon, to carry money to the king, and to bring answers from him concerning certain necessary affairs.

24 But he being recommended to the king, when he had magnified the appearance of his power, got the high priesthood for himself, by offering more than Jason by three hundred talents of silver.

25 So having received the king's mandate, he returned bringing nothing worthy of the high priesthood: but having the mind of a cruel tyrant, and the rage of a savage beast.

26 Then Jason, who had undermined his own brother, being himself undermined, was driven out a fugitive into the country of the Ammonites.

27 So Menelaus got the principality: but as for the money he had promised to the king he took no care, when Sostratus the governor of the castle called for it.

28 For to him appertained the gathering of the taxes: wherefore they were both called before the king.

KNOX TRANSLATION

21 Afterwards, Apollonius the son of Menestheus was
despatched to Egypt, for the enthroning of king Ptolemy
Philometor. Well Antiochus knew that he was disaffected
towards the royal policy, and there was his own safety to be
considered…He passed on to Joppe, and so to Jerusalem,[a]
22 where Jason and the whole city welcomed him in state,
with carrying of torches and great huzza'ing. And so he led
his army back to Phoenice.
23 Three years later, Jason would send to the king certain
moneys, together with a report on affairs of moment; and for
this errand he chose Menelaus, brother to that Simon we
have before mentioned. 24 Access thus gained to the king's
person, Menelaus was careful to flatter his self-conceit; then,
outbidding Jason by three hundred talents of silver, diverted
the high-priestly succession to himself. 25 Back he came to
Jerusalem, with the royal warrant to maintain him, yet all
unworthy, with a tyrant's cruel heart, more wild beast than
high priest. 26 Thus was Jason supplanted, that had supplanted his own brother, and was driven to take refuge in
the Ammonite country; 27 as for Menelaus, he got the office
he coveted, but never a penny paid the king of all he had
promised, however urgent Sostratus might be, that was in
command of the citadel. 28 For all exaction of tribute this fellow was answerable; and so it fell out that both of them

a This sentence, in the original, is of unexampled obscurity. It runs, 'And when Apollonius son of Menestheus had been sent to Egypt for the enthroning of king Ptolemy Philometor, Antiochus, realizing that he (who?) was estranged from his (whose?) past deeds, felt anxious for his own safety. And for that reason (what reason? Or perhaps, 'from that place', but what place?) he (who?) came to Joppe, and then rounded up at Jerusalem'. It seems possible that the text has been inaccurately transmitted.

TODAY'S ENGLISH VERSION

21 When Apollonius son of Menestheus was sent to Egypt to attend the crowning of Philometor as king, Antiochus learned that Philometor was opposed to his policies. Antiochus became concerned about the security of his own kingdom, so he went to Joppa and then on to Jerusalem. 22 There he was welcomed with great splendor by Jason and the people of the city who went out to greet him, shouting and carrying torches. From Jerusalem Antiochus led his army to Phoenicia.

23 Three years later, Jason sent Menelaus (brother of the Simon[a] mentioned earlier) to take some money to the king and to get his decision on several important matters. 24 But when he stood before the king, Menelaus impressed him with his show of authority and offered 22,500 pounds of silver more than Jason had offered for his appointment to the office of High Priest. 25 As a result Menelaus returned to Jerusalem with papers from the king, confirming him as High Priest. But he possessed no other qualifications; he had the temper of a cruel tyrant and could be as fierce as a wild animal. 26 So Jason, who had cheated his own brother out of the office of High Priest, was now forced to flee to the land of Ammon. 27 Menelaus continued to be High Priest, but he never paid any of the money he had promised the king. 28 However, Sostratus, the captain of the fort in Jerusalem, kept demanding the money, since it was his responsibility to collect it. So finally, the two men were summoned to appear before the king concerning the matter. 29 Menelaus left his

[a] SIMON: *See 3.4.*

NEW REVISED STANDARD VERSION

21 When Apollonius son of Menestheus was sent to Egypt for the coronation[a] of Philometor as king, Antiochus learned that Philometor[b] had become hostile to his government, and he took measures for his own security. Therefore upon arriving at Joppa he proceeded to Jerusalem. 22 He was welcomed magnificently by Jason and the city, and ushered in with a blaze of torches and with shouts. Then he marched his army into Phoenicia.

23 After a period of three years Jason sent Menelaus, the brother of the previously mentioned Simon, to carry the money to the king and to complete the records of essential business. 24 But he, when presented to the king, extolled him with an air of authority, and secured the high priesthood for himself, outbidding Jason by three hundred talents of silver. 25 After receiving the king's orders he returned, possessing no qualification for the high priesthood, but having the hot temper of a cruel tyrant and the rage of a savage wild beast. 26 So Jason, who after supplanting his own brother was supplanted by another man, was driven as a fugitive into the land of Ammon. 27 Although Menelaus continued to hold the office, he did not pay regularly any of the money promised to the king. 28 When Sostratus the captain of the citadel kept requesting payment—for the collection of the revenue was his responsibility—the two of them were summoned by the king on account of this issue. 29 Menelaus left his own

a Meaning of Gk uncertain *b* Gk *he*

NEW AMERICAN BIBLE

21 When Apollonius, son of Menestheus, was sent to Egypt for the coronation of King Philometor, Antiochus learned that the king was opposed to his policies; so he took measures for his own security. 22 After going to Joppa, he proceeded to Jerusalem. There he was received with great pomp by Jason and the people of the city, who escorted him with torchlights and acclamations; following this, he led his army into Phoenicia.

23 Three years later Jason sent Menelaus, brother of the aforementioned Simon, to deliver the money to the king, and to obtain decisions on some important matters. 24 When he had been introduced to the king, he flattered him with such an air of authority that he secured the high priesthood for himself, outbidding Jason by three hundred talents of silver. 25 He returned with the royal commission, but with nothing that made him worthy of the high priesthood; he had the temper of a cruel tyrant and the rage of a wild beast. 26 Then Jason, who had cheated his own brother and now saw himself cheated by another man, was driven out as a fugitive to the country of the Ammonites.

27 Although Menelaus had obtained the office, he did not make any payments of the money he had promised to the king, 28 in spite of the demand of Sostratus, the commandant of the citadel, whose duty it was to collect the taxes. For this reason, both were summoned before the king.

NEW JERUSALEM BIBLE

21 Apollonius son of Menestheus had been sent to Egypt to attend the wedding of King Philometor. Antiochus, having learnt that the latter had become hostile to his affairs, began thinking about his own safety: that was why he had come to Joppa. He then moved to Jerusalem, 22 where he was given a magnificent welcome by Jason and the city, and escorted in by torchlight with acclamation. After which, he marched his army into Phoenicia.

23 When three years had passed, Jason sent Menelaus, brother of the Simon mentioned above, to convey the money to the king and to complete negotiations on various essential matters. 24 But Menelaus, on being presented to the king, flattered him by his own appearance of authority, and so secured the high priesthood for himself, outbidding Jason by three hundred talents of silver. 25 He returned with the royal mandate, bringing nothing worthy of the high priesthood and supported only by the fury of a cruel tyrant and the rage of a savage beast. 26 Thus Jason, who had supplanted his own brother, was in turn supplanted by a third, and obliged to take refuge in Ammanitis. 27 As for Menelaus, he secured the office, but defaulted altogether on the sums promised to the king, 28 although Sostratus, the commandant of the Citadel, whose business it was to collect the revenue, kept demanding payment. The pair of them in consequence were summoned before the king, 29 Menelaus leaving his brother

GREEK OLD TESTAMENT

ὁ μὲν Μενέλαος ἀπέλιπεν τῆς ἀρχιερωσύνης διάδοχον Λυσίμαχον τὸν ἑαυτοῦ ἀδελφόν, Σώστρατος δὲ Κράτητα τὸν ἐπὶ
τῶν Κυπρίων.
30 Τοιούτων δὲ συνεστηκότων συνέβη Ταρσεῖς καὶ Μαλλώ-
τας στασιάζειν διὰ τὸ Ἀντιοχίδι τῇ παλλακῇ τοῦ βασιλέως
ἐν δωρεᾷ δεδόσθαι. 31 θᾶττον οὖν ὁ βασιλεὺς ἧκεν
καταστεῖλαι τὰ πράγματα καταλιπὼν τὸν διαδεχόμενον
Ἀνδρόνικον τῶν ἐν ἀξιώματι κειμένων. 32 νομίσας δὲ ὁ
Μενέλαος εἰληφέναι καιρὸν εὐφυῆ χρυσώματά τινα τῶν τοῦ
ἱεροῦ νοσφισάμενος ἐχαρίσατο τῷ Ἀνδρονίκῳ καὶ ἕτερα
ἐτύγχανεν πεπρακὼς εἴς τε Τύρον καὶ τὰς κύκλῳ πόλεις.
33 ἃ καὶ σαφῶς ἐπεγνωκὼς ὁ Ονιας ἀπήλεγχεν
ἀποκεχωρηκὼς εἰς ἄσυλον τόπον ἐπὶ Δάφνης τῆς πρὸς
Ἀντιόχειαν κειμένης. 34 ὅθεν ὁ Μενέλαος λαβὼν ἰδίᾳ τὸν
Ἀνδρόνικον παρεκάλει χειρώσασθαι τὸν Ονιαν· ὁ δὲ
παραγενόμενος ἐπὶ τὸν Ονιαν καὶ πεισθεὶς ἐπὶ δόλῳ καὶ
δεξιασθεὶς μεθ᾽ ὅρκων δοὺς δεξιάν, καίπερ ἐν ὑποψίᾳ κείμενος, ἔπεισεν ἐκ τοῦ ἀσύλου προελθεῖν, ὃν καὶ παραχρῆμα
παρέκλεισεν οὐκ αἰδεσθεὶς τὸ δίκαιον. 35 δι᾽ ἣν αἰτίαν οὐ
μόνον Ιουδαῖοι, πολλοὶ δὲ καὶ τῶν ἄλλων ἐθνῶν ἐδείναζον καὶ
ἐδυσφόρουν ἐπὶ τῷ τοῦ ἀνδρὸς ἀδίκῳ φόνῳ. 36 τοῦ δὲ βασιλέως ἐπανελθόντος ἀπὸ τῶν κατὰ Κιλικίαν τόπων ἐνετύγχανον
οἱ κατὰ πόλιν Ιουδαῖοι συμμισοπονηρούντων καὶ τῶν Ἑλλήνων ὑπὲρ τοῦ παρὰ λόγον τὸν Ονιαν ἀπεκτονῆσθαι.
37 ψυχικῶς οὖν ὁ Ἀντίοχος ἐπιλυπηθεὶς καὶ τραπεὶς ἐπὶ

KING JAMES VERSION

29 Now Menelaus left his brother Lysimachus in his stead in the priesthood; and Sostratus *left* Crates, who was governor of the Cyprians.

30 While those things were in doing, they of Tarsus and Mallos made insurrection, because they were given to the king's concubine, called Antiochus.

31 Then came the king in all haste to appease matters, leaving Andronicus, a man in authority, for his deputy.

32 Now Menelaus, supposing that he had gotten a convenient time, stole certain vessels of gold out of the temple, and gave some of them to Andronicus, and some he sold into Tyrus and the cities round about.

33 Which when Onias knew of a surety, he reproved him, and withdrew himself into a sanctuary at Daphne, that lieth by Antiochia.

34 Wherefore Menelaus, taking Andronicus apart, prayed him to get Onias into his hands; who being persuaded thereunto, and coming to Onias in deceit, gave him his right hand with oaths; and though he were suspected *by him,* yet persuaded he him to come forth of the sanctuary: whom forthwith he shut up without regard of justice.

35 For the which cause not only the Jews, but many also of other nations, took great indignation, and were much grieved for the unjust murder of the man.

36 And when the king was come again from the places about Cilicia, the Jews that were in the city, and certain of the Greeks that abhorred the fact also, complained because Onias was slain without cause.

37 Therefore Antiochus was heartily sorry, and moved to

DOUAY OLD TESTAMENT

29 And Menelaus was removed from the priesthood, Lysimachus his brother succeeding: and Sostratus was made governor of the Cyprians.

30 When these things were in doing, it fell out that they of Tharsus and Mallos raised a sedition, because they were given for a gift to Antiochis, the king's concubine.

31 The king therefore went in all haste to appease them, leaving Andronicus, one of his nobles, for his deputy.

32 Then Menelaus supposing that he had found a convenient time, having stolen certain vessels of gold out of the temple, gave them to Andronicus, and others he had sold at Tyre, and in the neighbouring cities.

33 Which when Onias understood most certainly, he reproved him, keeping himself in a safe place at Antioch beside Daphne.

34 Whereupon Menelaus coming to Andronicus, desired him to kill Onias. And he went to Onias, and gave him his right hand with an oath, and (though he were suspected by him) persuaded him to come forth out of the sanctuary, and immediately slew him, without any regard to justice.

35 For which cause not only the Jews, but also the other nations, conceived indignation, and were much grieved for the unjust murder of so great a man.

36 And when the king was come back from the places of Cilicia, the Jews that were at Antioch, and also the Greeks went to him: complaining of the unjust murder of Onias.

37 Antiochus therefore was grieved in his mind for Onias,

KNOX TRANSLATION

were summoned to court, 29 Menelaus leaving his high
priesthood to his own brother, Lysimachus, and for Sostratus...he became governor of Cyprus.[a]
30 It befell at this very time that the men of Tharsus and
Mallus made an insurrection; so little it liked them that a gift
should be made of their cities to Antiochis, the king's paramour. 31 Post-haste the king went off to appease them, leaving one of his courtiers, Andronicus, to be viceroy. 32 Here
was Menelaus' opportunity; he had gold ornaments with him,
that he had stolen out of the temple, and now, giving some of
these as a present to Andronicus, he sold the rest at Tyre and
other cities in the neighbourhood. 33 Of these doings, one
man had clear proof, and thereupon denounced him: Onias,
that had now taken refuge in Daphne sanctuary, close by
Antioch. 34 What did Menelaus? He gained the ear of
Andronicus and demanded that Onias should pay for it with
his life. So the viceroy himself paid Onias a visit, swore
friendship and overcame his suspicions; then, when he had
left sanctuary, without scruple of conscience put him to
death. 35 Here was great matter of indignation, and not
among the Jews only; the very heathen took it amiss, so great
a man should meet so unworthy an end. 36 No sooner was
the king back from Cilicia than the citizens of Antioch, Jew
and Gentile both, assailed him with complaints about the
murder of an innocent man; 37 whereat Antiochus himself

a According to the Greek text, Sostratus left his own office in charge of Crates, 'who was (afterwards?) over the Cyprians'. The island of Cyprus belonged at this time to Egypt, and only came into the Seleucid empire some years later.

TODAY'S ENGLISH VERSION

brother Lysimachus as acting High Priest, while Sostratus left the fort under the command of Crates, the commander of the mercenary troops from Cyprus.

30 Meanwhile, there was a revolt in the Cilician cities of Tarsus and Mallus, because the king had given those cities to Antiochis, his mistress. 31 So the king left Andronicus, one of his high officials, in command, while he hurried off to Cilicia to restore order. 32 Menelaus took advantage of this opportunity and presented Andronicus with some of the gold objects he had removed from the Temple in Jerusalem. He had already sold some of them to the city of Tyre and to other nearby cities. 33 When Onias heard about this, he fled for safety to a temple at Daphne near the city of Antioch and openly accused Menelaus. 34 Then Menelaus secretly persuaded Andronicus to kill Onias. So Andronicus went to Onias and deceived him with a friendly greeting and with promises of safety. Although Onias was suspicious, Andronicus finally lured him away from the safety of the temple and immediately murdered him in cold blood.

35 The Jews and Gentiles were very angry because Onias had been murdered. 36 So when the king returned from the territory of Cilicia, the Jews of Antioch went to him and protested against this senseless killing. Many Gentiles felt the same way about the crime. 37 King Antiochus was deeply

NEW REVISED STANDARD VERSION

brother Lysimachus as deputy in the high priesthood, while Sostratus left Crates, the commander of the Cyprian troops.

30 While such was the state of affairs, it happened that the people of Tarsus and of Mallus revolted because their cities had been given as a present to Antiochis, the king's concubine. 31 So the king went hurriedly to settle the trouble, leaving Andronicus, a man of high rank, to act as his deputy. 32 But Menelaus, thinking he had obtained a suitable opportunity, stole some of the gold vessels of the temple and gave them to Andronicus; other vessels, as it happened, he had sold to Tyre and the neighboring cities. 33 When Onias became fully aware of these acts, he publicly exposed them, having first withdrawn to a place of sanctuary at Daphne near Antioch. 34 Therefore Menelaus, taking Andronicus aside, urged him to kill Onias. Andronicus[a] came to Onias, and resorting to treachery, offered him sworn pledges and gave him his right hand; he persuaded him, though still suspicious, to come out from the place of sanctuary; then, with no regard for justice, he immediately put him out of the way.

35 For this reason not only Jews, but many also of other nations, were grieved and displeased at the unjust murder of the man. 36 When the king returned from the region of Cilicia, the Jews in the city[b] appealed to him with regard to the unreasonable murder of Onias, and the Greeks shared their hatred of the crime. 37 Therefore Antiochus was grieved

a Gk *He* *b* Or *in each city*

NEW AMERICAN BIBLE

29 Menelaus left his brother Lysimachus as his substitute in the high priesthood, while Sostratus left Crates, commander of the Cypriots, as his substitute.

30 While these things were taking place, the people of Tarsus and Mallus rose in revolt, because their cities had been given as a gift to Antiochis, the king's mistress. 31 The king, therefore, went off in haste to settle the affair, leaving Andronicus, one of his nobles, as his deputy. 32 Then Menelaus, thinking this a good opportunity, stole some gold vessels from the temple and presented them to Andronicus; he had already sold some other vessels in Tyre and in the neighboring cities. 33 When Onias had clear evidence of the facts, he made a public protest, after withdrawing to the inviolable sanctuary at Daphne, near Antioch. 34 Thereupon Menelaus approached Andronicus privately and asked him to lay hands on Onias. So Andronicus went to Onias, and by treacherously reassuring him through sworn pledges with right hands joined, persuaded him, in spite of his suspicions, to leave the sanctuary. Then, without any regard for justice, he immediately put him to death.

35 As a result, not only the Jews, but many people of other nations as well, were indignant and angry over the unjust murder of the man. 36 When the king returned from the region of Cilicia, the Jews of the city, together with the Greeks who detested the crime, went to see him about the murder of Onias. 37 Antiochus was deeply grieved and full of

NEW JERUSALEM BIBLE

Lysimachus as deputy high priest, while Sostratus left Crates, the commander of the Cypriots, to act for him.

30 While all this was going on, it happened that the people of Tarsus and Mallus revolted, because their towns had been given as a present to Antiochis, the king's concubine. 31 The king therefore hurried off to settle the affair, leaving Andronicus, one of his dignitaries, to act as his deputy. 32 Thinking he had found a favourable opportunity, Menelaus abstracted a number of golden vessels from the Temple and presented them to Andronicus, and managed to sell others to Tyre and the surrounding cities. 33 On receiving clear evidence to this effect, Onias retired to a place of sanctuary at Daphne near Antioch and then taxed him with it. 34 Menelaus then had a quiet word with Andronicus, urging him to get rid of Onias. Andronicus sought out Onias and, resorting to the trick of offering him his right hand on oath, succeeded in persuading him, despite the latter's lingering suspicions, to leave sanctuary; whereupon, in defiance of all justice, he immediately put him to death. 35 The result was that not only Jews but many people of other nationalities were appalled and outraged by the unjust murder of this man.

36 On the king's return from the region of Cilicia, the Jews of the capital, and those Greeks who shared their hatred of the crime, appealed to him about the unjustified murder of Onias. 37 Antiochus was profoundly grieved and filled with

GREEK OLD TESTAMENT

ἔλεος καὶ δακρύσας διὰ τὴν τοῦ μετηλλαχότος σωφροσύνην
καὶ πολλὴν εὐταξίαν [38] καὶ πυρωθεὶς τοῖς θυμοῖς παραχρῆμα τὴν τοῦ Ἀνδρονίκου πορφύραν περιελόμενος καὶ τοὺς
χιτῶνας περιρρήξας περιαγαγὼν καθ' ὅλην τὴν πόλιν ἐπ'
αὐτὸν τὸν τόπον, οὗπερ τὸν Ονιαν ἠσέβησεν, ἐκεῖ τὸν
μιαιφόνον ἀπεκόσμησεν τοῦ κυρίου τὴν ἀξίαν αὐτῷ κόλασιν
ἀποδόντος.
[39] Γενομένων δὲ πολλῶν ἱεροσυλημάτων κατὰ τὴν πόλιν
ὑπὸ τοῦ Λυσιμάχου μετὰ τῆς τοῦ Μενελάου γνώμης καὶ
διαδοθείσης ἔξω τῆς φήμης ἐπισυνήχθη τὸ πλῆθος ἐπὶ τὸν
Λυσίμαχον χρυσωμάτων ἤδη πολλῶν διενηνεγμένων.
[40] ἐπεγειρομένων δὲ τῶν ὄχλων καὶ ταῖς ὀργαῖς
διεμπιπλαμένων καθοπλίσας ὁ Λυσίμαχος πρὸς τρισχιλίους
κατῆρξατο χειρῶν ἀδίκων προηγησαμένου τινὸς Αυρανου
προβεβηκότος τὴν ἡλικίαν, οὐδὲν δὲ ἧττον καὶ τὴν ἄνοιαν·
[41] συνιδόντες δὲ καὶ τὴν ἐπίθεσιν τοῦ Λυσιμάχου συναρπάσαντες οἱ μὲν πέτρους, οἱ δὲ ξύλων πάχη, τινὲς δὲ ἐκ τῆς
παρακειμένης σποδοῦ δρασσόμενοι φύρδην ἐνετίνασσον εἰς
τοὺς περὶ τὸν Λυσίμαχον· [42] δι' ἣν αἰτίαν πολλοὺς μὲν
αὐτῶν τραυματίας ἐποίησαν, τινὰς δὲ καὶ κατέβαλον, πάντας δὲ εἰς φυγὴν συνήλασαν, αὐτὸν δὲ τὸν ἱερόσυλον παρὰ
τὸ γαζοφυλάκιον ἐχειρώσαντο. [43] περὶ δὲ τούτων ἐνέστη
κρίσις πρὸς τὸν Μενέλαον. [44] καταντήσαντος δὲ τοῦ
βασιλέως εἰς Τύρον ἐπ' αὐτοῦ τὴν δικαιολογίαν ἐποιήσαντο
οἱ πεμφθέντες τρεῖς ἄνδρες ὑπὸ τῆς γερουσίας. [45] ἤδη δὲ
λελειμμένος ὁ Μενέλαος ἐπηγγείλατο χρήματα ἱκανὰ τῷ
Πτολεμαίῳ Δορυμένους πρὸς τὸ πεῖσαι τὸν βασιλέα. [46] ὅθεν
ἀπολαβὼν ὁ Πτολεμαῖος εἴς τι περίστυλον ὡς ἀναψύξοντα
τὸν βασιλέα μετέθηκεν, [47] καὶ τὸν μὲν τῆς ὅλης κακίας

KING JAMES VERSION

pity, and wept, because of the sober and modest behaviour of him that was dead.

38 And being kindled with anger, forthwith he took away Andronicus his purple, and rent off his clothes, and leading him through the whole city unto that very place, where he had committed impiety against Onias, there slew he the cursed murderer. Thus the Lord rewarded him his punishment, as he had deserved.

39 Now when many sacrileges had been committed in the city by Lysimachus with the consent of Menelaus, and the bruit thereof was spread abroad, the multitude gathered themselves together against Lysimachus, many vessels of gold being already carried away.

40 Whereupon the common people rising, and being filled with rage, Lysimachus armed about three thousand men, and began first to offer violence; one Auranus being the leader, a man far gone in years, and no less in folly.

41 They then seeing the attempt of Lysimachus, some of them caught stones, some clubs, others taking handfuls of dust, that was next at hand, cast them all together upon Lysimachus, and those that set upon them.

42 Thus many of them they wounded, and some they struck to the ground, and all *of them* they forced to flee: but as for the churchrobber himself, him they killed beside the treasury.

43 Of these matters therefore there was an accusation laid against Menelaus.

44 Now when the king came to Tyrus, three men that were sent from the senate pleaded the cause before him:

DOUAY OLD TESTAMENT

and being moved to pity, shed tears, remembering the sobriety and modesty of the deceased.

38 And being inflamed to anger, he commanded Andronicus to be stripped of his purple, and to be led about through all the city: and that in the same place wherein he had committed the impiety against Onias, the sacrilegious wretch should be put to death, the Lord repaying him his deserved punishment.

39 Now when many sacrileges had been committed by Lysimachus in the temple by the counsel of Menelaus, and the rumour of it was spread abroad, the multitude gathered themselves together against Lysimachus, a great quantity of gold being already carried away.

40 Wherefore the multitude making an insurrection, and their minds being filled with anger, Lysimachus armed about three thousand men, and began to use violence, one Tyrannus being captain, a man far gone both in age, and in madness.

41 But when they perceived the attempt of Lysimachus, some caught up stones, some strong clubs: and some threw ashes upon Lysimachus,

42 And many of them were wounded, and some struck down to the ground, but all were put to flight: and as for the sacrilegious fellow himself, they slew him beside the treasury.

43 Now concerning these matters, an accusation was laid against Menelaus.

44 And when the king was come to Tyre, three men were sent from the ancients to plead the cause before him.

KNOX TRANSLATION

was heartily grieved, ay, and moved to tears of pity, such
memories he had of Onias' well-ordered, honourable life.
[38] Anon he fell into a rage, stripped Andronicus of his purple,
and would have him led away all through the streets, till he
reached the very spot where he had lifted his impious hand
against Onias. There the sacrilegious wretch perished, by the
divine vengeance worthily requited.
[39] Meanwhile, word had gone abroad at Jerusalem, how
Lysimachus was ever robbing the temple, by Menelaus' con-
trivance. Great store of gold was lost already; [40] but now
there was a rising of the common folk against Lysimachus,
whose numbers and their rage increasing, he was fain to put
some three thousand men under arms, with one Tyrannus at
their head, that was far gone in years, and no less in folly.
[41] Lysimachus it was that first resorted to violence; but the
rabble, when they saw what he would be at, caught up
stones or stout clubs for the attack, and some of them pelted
him with cinders. [42] When they had wounded some of his
retinue, and felled others to earth, the rest took to their
heels; and there, close beside the treasury, this robber of the
temple was done to death.
[43] And next, they must implead Menelaus himself on the
same charge. [44] Three envoys from the council of elders
brought the whole matter before the king, when he visited

TODAY'S ENGLISH VERSION

grieved and was so filled with sorrow that he was moved to
tears when he recalled the wisdom and self-control that
Onias had shown throughout his life. 38 Antiochus became
so angry that he tore off Andronicus' royal robe, stripped him
naked, and marched him around the city to the very spot
where Onias had been murdered. Then Antiochus had this
bloodthirsty murderer put to death. This was how the Lord
gave him the punishment he deserved.

39 Meanwhile, with the support of his brother Menelaus,
Lysimachus had on numerous occasions robbed the Jerusalem Temple and had taken many of its gold objects. When
word of this spread around, crowds began to gather in
protest against Lysimachus. 40 Finally, the crowds were
becoming dangerous and were beginning to get out of control, so Lysimachus sent 3,000 armed men to attack them.
They were led by Auranus, a man as stupid as he was old.
41 When the Jews in the Temple courtyard realized what was
happening, they picked up rocks, pieces of wood, or simply
handfuls of ashes from the altar and threw them at
Lysimachus and his men in the confusion. 42 They killed a
few of Lysimachus' men, wounded many of them, and all the
rest ran for their lives. Lysimachus himself, that temple robber, was killed near the Temple treasury.

43 Because of this incident Menelaus was brought to trial.
44 When the king came to the city of Tyre, the Jewish authorities in Jerusalem sent three men to bring charges against

NEW REVISED STANDARD VERSION

at heart and filled with pity, and wept because of the moderation and good conduct of the deceased. 38 Inflamed with
anger, he immediately stripped off the purple robe from
Andronicus, tore off his clothes, and led him around the
whole city to that very place where he had committed the
outrage against Onias, and there he dispatched the bloodthirsty fellow. The Lord thus repaid him with the punishment he deserved.

39 When many acts of sacrilege had been committed in
the city by Lysimachus with the connivance of Menelaus,
and when report of them had spread abroad, the populace
gathered against Lysimachus, because many of the gold vessels had already been stolen. 40 Since the crowds were
becoming aroused and filled with anger, Lysimachus armed
about three thousand men and launched an unjust attack,
under the leadership of a certain Auranus, a man advanced
in years and no less advanced in folly. 41 But when the
Jews[a] became aware that Lysimachus was attacking them,
some picked up stones, some blocks of wood, and others
took handfuls of the ashes that were lying around, and
threw them in wild confusion at Lysimachus and his men.
42 As a result, they wounded many of them, and killed some,
and put all the rest to flight; the temple robber himself they
killed close by the treasury.

43 Charges were brought against Menelaus about this
incident. 44 When the king came to Tyre, three men sent by
the senate presented the case before him. 45 But Menelaus,

a Gk *they*

NEW AMERICAN BIBLE

pity; he wept as he recalled the prudence and noble conduct
of the deceased. 38 Inflamed with anger, he immediately
stripped Andronicus of his purple robe, tore off his other garments, and had him led through the whole city to the very
place where he had committed the outrage against Onias;
and there he put the murderer to death. Thus the LORD rendered him the punishment he deserved.

39 Many sacrilegious thefts had been committed by Lysimachus in the city with the connivance of Menelaus. When
word was spread that a large number of gold vessels had
been stolen, the people assembled in protest against
Lysimachus. 40 As the crowds, now thoroughly enraged,
began to riot, Lysimachus launched an unjustified attack
against them with about three thousand armed men under
the leadership of Auranus, a man as advanced in folly as he
was in years. 41 Reacting against Lysimachus' attack, the
people picked up stones or pieces of wood or handfuls of the
ashes lying there and threw them in wild confusion at
Lysimachus and his men. 42 As a result, they wounded many
of them and even killed a few, while they put all the rest to
flight. The sacrilegious thief himself they slew near the treasury.

43 Charges about this affair were brought against
Menelaus. 44 When the king came to Tyre, three men sent by
the senate presented to him the justice of their cause. 45 But

NEW JERUSALEM BIBLE

pity, and he wept for the prudence and moderation of the
dead man. 38 Burning with indignation, he immediately
stripped Andronicus of the purple, tore his garments off him
and, parading him through the length of the city, rid the
world of the assassin on the very spot where he had laid
impious hands on Onias, the Lord dealing out to him the
punishment he deserved.

39 Now Lysimachus with the connivance of Menelaus had
committed many sacrilegious thefts in the city, and when the
facts became widely known, the populace rose against
Lysimachus, who had already disposed of many pieces of
gold plate. 40 The infuriated mob was becoming menacing,
and Lysimachus armed nearly three thousand men and took
aggressive action; the troops were led by a certain Auranus,
a man advanced in years and no less in folly. 41 Recognising
this act of aggression as the work of Lysimachus, some
snatched up stones, others cudgels, while others scooped up
handfuls of ashes lying at hand, and all hurled everything
indiscriminately at Lysimachus' men, 42 to such effect that
they wounded many of them, even killing a few, and routed
them all; the sacrilegious thief himself they killed near the
Treasury.

43 As a result of this, legal proceedings were taken against
Menelaus. 44 When the king came down to Tyre, three men
deputed by the Senate pleaded their case before him.

GREEK OLD TESTAMENT

αἴτιον Μενέλαον ἀπέλυσεν τῶν κατηγορημένων, τοῖς δὲ
ταλαιπώροις, οἵτινες, εἰ καὶ ἐπὶ Σκυθῶν ἔλεγον, ἀπελύθησαν
ἀκατάγνωστοι, τούτοις θάνατον ἐπέκρινεν. 48 ταχέως οὖν
τὴν ἄδικον ζημίαν ὑπέσχον οἱ περὶ πόλεως καὶ δήμων καὶ
τῶν ἱερῶν σκευῶν προηγορήσαντες. 49 δι᾽ ἣν αἰτίαν καὶ Τύρ-
ιοι μισοπονηρήσαντες τὰ πρὸς τὴν κηδείαν αὐτῶν μεγαλοπρεπῶς ἐχορήγησαν. 50 ὁ δὲ Μενέλαος διὰ τὰς τῶν κρατούντων πλεονεξίας ἔμενεν ἐπὶ τῇ ἀρχῇ ἐπιφυόμενος τῇ
κακίᾳ μέγας τῶν πολιτῶν ἐπίβουλος καθεστώς.

5 Περὶ δὲ τὸν καιρὸν τοῦτον τὴν δευτέραν ἔφοδον ὁ Ἀντίοχος εἰς Αἴγυπτον ἐστείλατο. 2 συνέβη δὲ καθ᾽ ὅλην
τὴν πόλιν σχεδὸν ἐφ᾽ ἡμέρας τεσσαράκοντα φαίνεσθαι διὰ
τῶν ἀέρων τρέχοντας ἱππεῖς διαχρύσους στολὰς ἔχοντας
καὶ λόγχας σπειρηδὸν ἐξωπλισμένους καὶ μαχαιρῶν σπα-
σμοὺς 3 καὶ ἴλας ἵππων διατεταγμένας καὶ προσβολὰς
γινομένας καὶ καταδρομὰς ἑκατέρων καὶ ἀσπίδων κινήσεις
καὶ καμάκων πλήθη καὶ βελῶν βολὰς καὶ χρυσέων κόσμων
ἐκλάμψεις καὶ παντοίους θωρακισμούς. 4 διὸ πάντες ἠξίουν

KING JAMES VERSION

45 But Menelaus, being now convicted, promised Ptolemee the *son* of Dorymenes to give him much money, if he would pacify the king toward him.

46 Whereupon Ptolemee taking the king aside into a certain gallery, as it were to take the air, brought him to be of another mind:

47 Insomuch that he discharged Menelaus from the accusations, who notwithstanding was cause of all the mischief: and those poor men, who, if they had told their cause, yea, before the Scythians, should have been judged innocent, them he condemned to death.

48 Thus they that followed the matter for the city, and for the people, and for the holy vessels, did soon suffer unjust punishment.

49 Wherefore even they of Tyrus, moved with hatred of that wicked deed, caused them to be honourably buried.

50 And so through the covetousness of them that were of power Menelaus remained still in authority, increasing in malice, and being a great traitor to the citizens.

5 About the same time Antiochus prepared his second voyage into Egypt:

2 And then it happened, that through all the city, for the space almost of forty days, there were seen horsemen running in the air, in cloth of gold, and armed with lances, like a band of soldiers,

3 And troops of horsemen in array, encountering and running one against another, with shaking of shields, and multitude of pikes, and drawing of swords, and casting of darts, and glittering of golden ornaments, and harness of all sorts.

DOUAY OLD TESTAMENT

45 But Menelaus being convicted, promised Ptolemee to give him much money to persuade the king to favour him.

46 So Ptolemee went to the king in a certain court where he was, as it were to cool himself, and brought him to be of another mind:

47 So Menelaus who was guilty of all the evil, was acquitted by him of the accusations: and those poor men, who, if they had pleaded their cause even before Scythians, should have been judged innocent, were condemned to death.

48 Thus they that prosecuted the cause for the city, and for the people, and the sacred vessels, did soon suffer unjust punishment.

49 Wherefore even the Tyrians being moved with indignation, were liberal towards their burial.

50 And so through the covetousness of them that were in power, Menelaus continued in authority, increasing in malice to the betraying of the citizens.

5 AT the same time Antiochus prepared for a second journey into Egypt.

2 And it came to pass that through the whole city of Jerusalem for the space of forty days there were seen horsemen running in the air, in gilded raiment, and armed with spears, like bands of soldiers.

3 And horses set in order by ranks, running one against another, with the shakings of shields, and a multitude of men in helmets, with drawn swords, and casting of darts, and glittering of golden armour, and of harnesses of all sorts.

KNOX TRANSLATION

Tyre, 45 and Menelaus was as good as lost. What did he?
With the promise of a great bribe he secured the good word
of Ptolemy, son of Dorymenes;[a] 46 Ptolemy it was waylaid
the king, as he rested from the heat in a covered walk of his,
and put him from his purpose. 47 So now Menelaus, that
was at the root of all the mischief, must go scot free, and his
unhappy accusers, that might have cleared themselves easily
enough before a court of bloodthirsty Scythians,[b] with their
lives must pay for it. 48 Here were men come to plead for
their own city, their own people, their own temple treasures,
and must they be hurried off to undeserved punishment?
49 Even the Tyrians thought shame of it, and in princely fashion gave them burial. 50 So, through the avarice of the great,
throve Menelaus still, and his wickedness went from bad to
worse, to his countrymen's undoing.

5 At this time Antiochus was preparing once more for a
campaign against Egypt. 2 And all about the city of
Jerusalem, by the space of forty days together, there were
strange sights appearing. High up in air, horsemen were
seen riding this way and that, in vesture of gold, and spears
they carried as if they went to battle; 3 now riding in ordered
ranks, now engaged in close combat. In long array they
moved past, shields and helmeted heads and drawn swords;
flew javelin and flashed golden harness, a whole armoury of

a v. 45. The words 'son of Dorymenes' appear in the Greek text, but not in the Latin; they are inserted here to distinguish this Ptolemy (cf. I Mac. 3. 38) from the king of Egypt mentioned in verse 21 above. *b* 'Scythians', a barbarous race then inhabiting Russia.

TODAY'S ENGLISH VERSION

Menelaus. 45 When Menelaus saw that he was losing the case, he offered Ptolemy son of Dorymenes a large bribe to persuade the king to decide in his favor. 46 Ptolemy then asked the king to go outside the courtroom with him, as though to get some fresh air, and there he persuaded him to change his mind 47 and declare Menelaus innocent of the charges against him. So Menelaus was set free, although he had caused the trouble; but the three men, whom even the cruel Scythians would have declared innocent, were sentenced to death. 48 The three men had spoken in defense of Jerusalem, its people,[a] and the sacred objects stolen from the Temple, but they were quickly and unjustly executed. 49 Some of the people of Tyre, however, showed their disgust with this crime and their respect for these men by giving them a splendid funeral. 50 Menelaus stayed on in his position because of the greed of those in power. He grew more evil every day and became the worst enemy of his own people.

5 About this time Antiochus the Fourth made a second attack against Egypt. 2 For nearly forty days people all over Jerusalem saw visions of cavalry troops in gold armor charging across the sky. The riders were armed with spears and their swords were drawn. 3 They were lined up in battle against one another, attacking and counterattacking. Shields were clashing, there was a rain of spears, and arrows flew through the air. All the different kinds of armor and the gold

[a] its people; *some manuscripts also have* the surrounding villages.

NEW REVISED STANDARD VERSION

already as good as beaten, promised a substantial bribe to Ptolemy son of Dorymenes to win over the king. 46 Therefore Ptolemy, taking the king aside into a colonnade as if for refreshment, induced the king to change his mind. 47 Menelaus, the cause of all the trouble, he acquitted of the charges against him, while he sentenced to death those unfortunate men, who would have been freed uncondemned if they had pleaded even before Scythians. 48 And so those who had spoken for the city and the villages[a] and the holy vessels quickly suffered the unjust penalty. 49 Therefore even the Tyrians, showing their hatred of the crime, provided magnificently for their funeral. 50 But Menelaus, because of the greed of those in power, remained in office, growing in wickedness, having become the chief plotter against his compatriots.

5 About this time Antiochus made his second invasion of Egypt. 2 And it happened that, for almost forty days, there appeared over all the city golden-clad cavalry charging through the air, in companies fully armed with lances and drawn swords— 3 troops of cavalry drawn up, attacks and counterattacks made on this side and on that, brandishing of shields, massing of spears, hurling of missiles, the flash of golden trappings, and armor of all kinds. 4 Therefore

[a] Other ancient authorities read *the people*

NEW AMERICAN BIBLE

Menelaus, seeing himself on the losing side, promised Ptolemy, son of Dorymenes, a substantial sum of money if he would win the king over. 46 So Ptolemy retired with the king under a colonnade, as if to get some fresh air, and persuaded him to change his mind. 47 Menelaus, who was the cause of all the trouble, the king acquitted of the charges, while he condemned to death those poor men who would have been declared innocent even if they had pleaded their case before Scythians. 48 Thus, those who had prosecuted the case for the city, for the people, and for the sacred vessels, quickly suffered unjust punishment. 49 For this reason, even some Tyrians were indignant over the crime and provided sumptuously for their burial. 50 But Menelaus, thanks to the covetousness of the men in power, remained in office, where he grew in wickedness and became the chief plotter against his fellow citizens.

5 About this time Antiochus sent his second expedition into Egypt. 2 It then happened that all over the city, for nearly forty days, there appeared horsemen charging in midair, clad in garments interwoven with gold—companies fully armed with lances 3 and drawn swords; squadrons of cavalry in battle array, charges and countercharges on this side and that, with brandished shields and bristling spears, flights of arrows and flashes of gold ornaments, together

NEW JERUSALEM BIBLE

45 Menelaus, seeing the case had gone against him, promised a substantial sum to Ptolemy son of Dorymenes if he would influence the king in his favour. 46 Ptolemy then took the king aside into a colonnade, as though for a breath of fresh air, and persuaded him to change his mind; 47 the king then dismissed the charges against Menelaus, the cause of all this evil, while he condemned to death the other poor wretches who, had they pleaded even before Scythians, would have been let off scot-free. 48 No time was lost in carrying out this unjust punishment on those who had championed the cause of the city, the townships and the sacred vessels. 49 Some Tyrians even were so outraged by the crime that they provided sumptuously for their funeral, 50 while, as a result of the greed of the powerful, Menelaus remained in power, growing more wicked than ever and establishing himself as the chief enemy of his fellow-citizens.

5 At about this time, Antiochus was preparing for his second attack on Egypt. 2 It then happened that all over the city for nearly forty days there were apparitions of horsemen galloping through the air in cloth of gold, troops of lancers fully armed, 3 squadrons of cavalry in order of battle, attacks and charges this way and that, a flourish of shields, a forest of pikes, a brandishing of swords, a hurling of missiles, a glittering of golden accoutrements and armour of all kinds.

GREEK OLD TESTAMENT

ἐπ' ἀγαθῷ τὴν ἐπιφάνειαν γεγενῆσθαι. 5 γενομένης δὲ
λαλιᾶς ψευδοῦς ὡς μετηλλαχότος Ἀντιόχου τὸν βίον παραλαβὼν ὁ Ἰάσων οὐκ ἐλάττους τῶν χιλίων αἰφνιδίως ἐπὶ τὴν
πόλιν συνετελέσατο ἐπίθεσιν· τῶν δὲ ἐπὶ τῷ τείχει συνελα-
σθέντων καὶ τέλος ἤδη καταλαμβανομένης τῆς πόλεως ὁ
Μενέλαος εἰς τὴν ἀκρόπολιν ἐφυγάδευσεν. 6 ὁ δὲ Ἰάσων
ἐποιεῖτο σφαγὰς τῶν πολιτῶν τῶν ἰδίων ἀφειδῶς οὐ συννοῶν
τὴν εἰς τοὺς συγγενεῖς εὐημερίαν δυσημερίαν εἶναι τὴν
μεγίστην, δοκῶν δὲ πολεμίων καὶ οὐχ ὁμοεθνῶν τρόπαια
καταβάλλεσθαι. 7 τῆς μὲν ἀρχῆς οὐκ ἐκράτησεν, τὸ δὲ τέλος
τῆς ἐπιβουλῆς αἰσχύνην λαβὼν φυγὰς πάλιν εἰς τὴν Αμμανῖτιν ἀπῆλθεν. 8 πέρας οὖν κακῆς καταστροφῆς ἔτυχεν.
ἐγκληθεὶς πρὸς Ἀρέταν τὸν τῶν Ἀράβων τύραννον πόλιν ἐκ
πόλεως φεύγων διωκόμενος ὑπὸ πάντων στυγούμενος ὡς τῶν
νόμων ἀποστάτης καὶ βδελυσσόμενος ὡς πατρίδος καὶ
πολιτῶν δήμιος εἰς Αἴγυπτον ἐξεβράσθη, 9 καὶ ὁ συχνοὺς
τῆς πατρίδος ἀποξενώσας ἐπὶ ξένης ἀπώλετο πρὸς
Λακεδαιμονίους ἀναχθεὶς ὡς διὰ τὴν συγγένειαν τευξό-
μενος σκέπης. 10 καὶ ὁ πλῆθος ἀτάφων ἐκρίψας ἀπένθητος
ἐγενήθη καὶ κηδείας οὐδ' ἡστινοσοῦν οὔτε πατρῴου τάφου
μετέσχεν.

11 Προσπεσόντων δὲ τῷ βασιλεῖ περὶ τῶν γεγονότων διέ-
λαβεν ἀποστατεῖν τὴν Ιουδαίαν· ὅθεν ἀναζεύξας ἐξ Αἰγύπτου
τεθηριωμένος τῇ ψυχῇ ἔλαβεν τὴν μὲν πόλιν δοριάλωτον

KING JAMES VERSION

4 Wherefore every man prayed that that apparition might turn to good.

5 Now when there was gone forth a false rumour, as though Antiochus had been dead, Jason took at the least a thousand men, and suddenly made an assault upon the city; and they that were upon the walls being put back, and the city at length taken, Menelaus fled into the castle:

6 But Jason slew his own citizens without mercy, not considering that to get the day of them of his own nation would be a most unhappy day for him; but thinking they had been *his* enemies, and not *his* countrymen, whom he conquered.

7 Howbeit for all this he obtained not the principality, but at the last received shame for the reward of his treason, and fled again into the country of the Ammonites.

8 In the end therefore he had an unhappy return, being accused before Aretas the king of the Arabians, fleeing from city to city, pursued of all men, hated as a forsaker of the laws, and being had in abomination as an open enemy of his country and countrymen, he was cast out into Egypt.

9 Thus he that had driven many out of their country perished in a strange land, retiring to the Lacedemonians, and thinking *there* to find succour by reason of his kindred:

10 And he that had cast out many unburied had none to mourn for him, nor any solemn funerals at all, nor sepulchre with his fathers.

11 Now when this that was done came to the king's ear, he thought that Judea had revolted: whereupon removing out of Egypt in a furious mind, he took the city by force of arms,

DOUAY OLD TESTAMENT

4 Wherefore all men prayed that these prodigies might turn to good.

5 Now when there was gone forth a false rumour, as though Antiochus had been dead, Jason taking with him no fewer than a thousand men, suddenly assaulted the city: and though the citizens ran together to the wall, the city at length was taken, and Menelaus fled into the castle.

6 But Jason slew his countrymen without mercy, not considering that prosperity against one's own kindred is a very great evil, thinking they had been enemies, and not citizens, whom he conquered.

7 Yet he did not get the principality, but received confusion at the end, for the reward of his treachery, and fled again into the country of the Ammonites.

8 At the last having been shut up by Aretas the king of the Arabians, in order for his destruction, flying from city to city, hated by all men, as a forsaker of the laws, and execrable, as an enemy of his country and countrymen, he was thrust out into Egypt:

9 And he that had driven many out of their country, perished in a strange land, going to Lacedemon, as if for kindred sake he should have refuge there:

10 But he that had cast out many unburied, was himself cast forth both unlamented and unburied, neither having foreign burial, nor being partaker of the sepulchre of his fathers.

11 Now when these things were done, the king suspected that the Jews would forsake the alliance: whereupon departing out of Egypt with a furious mind, he took the city by force of arms.

KNOX TRANSLATION

shining mail. 4 No wonder if the prayer was on all men's
lips, good not ill such high visions might portend.
5 And now a false rumour went abroad, Antiochus had
come by his death. Jason's ears it reached, and all at once,
with full a thousand men at his back, he delivered an assault
upon the city. Let the townsfolk man the walls as they
would, at last it fell, and Menelaus must take refuge within
the citadel. 6 As for Jason, he fell upon his own fellow-countrymen, and that without mercy. His own flesh and blood to
vanquish, what was this but shameful defeat? Ay, but to him
friend was foe, were there spoil for the winning! 7 Yet high
priesthood he got none; disappointed of his scheming, back
he must go to the Ammonite country, 8 and there, marked
down for death by king Aretas of the Arabians, fled from city
to city. An outlaw, hated and shunned by his kind, of a
whole land, of a whole race, the common foe, he was driven
out into Egypt; 9 and so making his way to Lacedaemon, as
if to find refuge there by right of kinship, died miserably. In
exile he died, that had brought exile on so many; 10 cast
away without dole or tomb, that left so many tombless; in a
strange land unburied, that might have rested in his fathers'
grave.

11 Here was news to make the king doubt whether the Jews
were loyal to him, and back he came from Egypt in a great
taking of rage. He occupied the city, and that by force of

TODAY'S ENGLISH VERSION

bridles on the horses flashed in the sunlight. 4 Everyone in
the city prayed that these visions might be a good sign.
5 When a false report began to spread that Antiochus had
died, Jason took more than a thousand men and suddenly
attacked Jerusalem. They drove back those stationed on the
city walls and finally captured the city. Menelaus fled for
safety to the fort, near the Temple hill, 6 while Jason and his
men went on slaughtering their fellow Jews without mercy.
Jason did not realize that success against one's own people
is the worst kind of failure. He even considered his success a
victory over enemies, rather than a defeat of his own people.
7 But Jason did not take over the government. Instead he was
forced to flee once again to the territory of the Ammonites,
and in the end his evil plot brought him nothing but shame
and disgrace, 8 and he died in misery. Aretas, the ruler of the
Arabs, imprisoned him; he was looked upon as a criminal
and despised because he had betrayed his own people; everyone was hunting for him, and he had to run from town to
town. He fled to Egypt for safety, 9 then to Greece, hoping to
find refuge among the Spartans, who were related to the
Jews. Finally, this man, who had forced so many others to
flee from their own country, died as a fugitive in a foreign
land. 10 Jason had killed many people and left their bodies
unburied, but now his own death was unmourned. He was
not given a funeral or even buried with his ancestors.
11 When the news of what had happened in Jerusalem
reached Antiochus, he thought the whole country of Judea
was in revolt, and he became as furious as a wild animal. So
he left Egypt and took Jerusalem by storm, 12 giving his men

NEW REVISED STANDARD VERSION

everyone prayed that the apparition might prove to have
been a good omen.
5 When a false rumor arose that Antiochus was dead,
Jason took no fewer than a thousand men and suddenly
made an assault on the city. When the troops on the wall
had been forced back and at last the city was being taken,
Menelaus took refuge in the citadel. 6 But Jason kept relentlessly slaughtering his compatriots, not realizing that success at the cost of one's kindred is the greatest misfortune,
but imagining that he was setting up trophies of victory over
enemies and not over compatriots. 7 He did not, however,
gain control of the government; in the end he got only disgrace from his conspiracy, and fled again into the country of
the Ammonites. 8 Finally he met a miserable end. Accused[a]
before Aretas the ruler of the Arabs, fleeing from city to city,
pursued by everyone, hated as a rebel against the laws, and
abhorred as the executioner of his country and his compatriots, he was cast ashore in Egypt. 9 There he who had driven
many from their own country into exile died in exile, having
embarked to go to the Lacedaemonians in hope of finding
protection because of their kinship. 10 He who had cast out
many to lie unburied had no one to mourn for him; he had
no funeral of any sort and no place in the tomb of his ancestors.
11 When news of what had happened reached the king,
he took it to mean that Judea was in revolt. So, raging
inwardly, he left Egypt and took the city by storm. 12 He

a Cn: Gk *Imprisoned*

NEW AMERICAN BIBLE

with armor of every sort. 4 Therefore all prayed that this
vision might be a good omen.
5 But when a false rumor circulated that Antiochus was
dead, Jason gathered fully a thousand men and suddenly
attacked the city. As the defenders on the walls were forced
back and the city was finally being taken, Menelaus took
refuge in the citadel. 6 Jason then slaughtered his fellow citizens without mercy, not realizing that triumph over one's
own kindred was the greatest failure, but imagining that he
was winning a victory over his enemies, not his fellow countrymen. 7 Even so, he did not gain control of the government, but in the end received only disgrace for his treachery,
and once again took refuge in the country of the Ammonites.
8 At length he met a miserable end. Called to account before
Aretas, king of the Arabs, he fled from city to city, hunted by
all men, hated as a transgressor of the laws, abhorred as the
butcher of his country and his countrymen. After being driv-
en into Egypt, 9 he crossed the sea to the Spartans, among
whom he hoped to find protection because of his relations
with them. There he who had exiled so many from their
country perished in exile; 10 and he who had cast out so
many to lie unburied went unmourned himself with no
funeral of any kind or any place in the tomb of his ancestors.
11 When these happenings were reported to the king, he
thought that Judea was in revolt. Raging like a wild animal,
he set out from Egypt and took Jerusalem by storm. 12 He

NEW JERUSALEM BIBLE

4 So everyone prayed that this manifestation might prove a
good omen.
5 Then, on the strength of a false report that Antiochus was
dead, Jason took at least a thousand men and launched an
unexpected attack on the city. When the walls had been
breached and the city was finally on the point of being taken,
Menelaus took refuge in the Citadel. 6 Jason, however, made
a pitiless slaughter of his fellow-citizens, oblivious of the fact
that success against his own countrymen was the greatest of
disasters, but rather picturing himself as winning trophies
from some enemy, and not from his fellow-countrymen.
7 Even so, he did not manage to seize power; and, in the end,
his machinations brought him nothing but shame, and he
took refuge once more in Ammanitis. 8 His career of wickedness was thus brought to a halt: imprisoned by Aretas, the
Arab despot, escaping from his town, hunted by everyone,
detested for having overthrown the laws, abhorred as the
butcher of his country and his countrymen, he drifted to
Egypt. 9 He who had exiled so many from their fatherland,
himself perished on foreign soil, having travelled to Sparta,
hoping that, for kinship's sake, he might find harbour there.
10 So many carcases he had thrust out to lie unburied; now
he himself had none to mourn him, no funeral rites, no place
in the tomb of his ancestors.
11 When the king came to hear of what had happened, he
concluded that Judaea was in revolt. He therefore marched
from Egypt, raging like a wild beast, and began by storming

GREEK OLD TESTAMENT

12 καὶ ἐκέλευσεν τοῖς στρατιώταις κόπτειν ἀφειδῶς τοὺς
ἐμπίπτοντας καὶ τοὺς εἰς τὰς οἰκίας ἀναβαίνοντας κατασφάζειν. 13 ἐγίνετο δὲ νέων καὶ πρεσβυτέρων ἀναίρεσις,
ἀνήβων τε καὶ γυναικῶν καὶ τέκνων ἀφανισμός, παρθένων τε
καὶ νηπίων σφαγαί. 14 ὀκτὼ δὲ μυριάδες ἐν ταῖς πάσαις
ἡμέραις τρισὶν κατεφθάρησαν, τέσσαρες μὲν ἐν χειρῶν
νομαῖς, οὐχ ἧττον δὲ τῶν ἐσφαγμένων ἐπράθησαν. 15 οὐκ
ἀρκεσθεὶς δὲ τούτοις κατετόλμησεν εἰς τὸ πάσης τῆς γῆς
ἁγιώτατον ἱερὸν εἰσελθεῖν ὁδηγὸν ἔχων τὸν Μενέλαον τὸν
καὶ τῶν νόμων καὶ τῆς πατρίδος προδότην γεγονότα 16 καὶ
ταῖς μιαραῖς χερσὶν τὰ ἱερὰ σκεύη λαμβάνων καὶ τὰ ὑπ'
ἄλλων βασιλέων ἀνατεθέντα πρὸς αὔξησιν καὶ δόξαν τοῦ τόπου καὶ τιμὴν ταῖς βεβήλοις χερσὶν συσσύρων. 17 καὶ
ἐμετεωρίζετο τὴν διάνοιαν ὁ Ἀντίοχος οὐ συνορῶν ὅτι διὰ
τὰς ἁμαρτίας τῶν τὴν πόλιν οἰκούντων ἀπώργισται βραχέως
ὁ δεσπότης, διὸ γέγονεν περὶ τὸν τόπον παρόρασις. 18 εἰ δὲ
μὴ συνέβη προσενέχεσθαι πολλοῖς ἁμαρτήμασιν, καθάπερ ἦν
ὁ Ἡλιόδωρος ὁ πεμφθεὶς ὑπὸ Σελεύκου τοῦ βασιλέως ἐπὶ τὴν
ἐπίσκεψιν τοῦ γαζοφυλακίου, οὗτος προαχθεὶς παραχρῆμα
μαστιγωθεὶς ἀνετράπη τοῦ θράσους. 19 ἀλλ' οὐ διὰ τὸν τόπον
τὸ ἔθνος, ἀλλὰ διὰ τὸ ἔθνος τὸν τόπον ὁ κύριος ἐξελέξατο.
20 διόπερ καὶ αὐτὸς ὁ τόπος συμμετασχὼν τῶν τοῦ ἔθνους
δυσπετημάτων γενομένων ὕστερον εὐεργετημάτων ἐκοινώνησεν, καὶ ὁ καταλειφθεὶς ἐν τῇ τοῦ παντοκράτορος ὀργῇ πάλιν
ἐν τῇ τοῦ μεγάλου δεσπότου καταλλαγῇ μετὰ πάσης δόξης
ἐπανωρθώθη.

KING JAMES VERSION

12 And commanded his men of war not to spare such as they met, and to slay such as went up upon the houses.

13 Thus there was killing of young and old, making away of men, women, and children, slaying of virgins and infants.

14 And there were destroyed within the space of three whole days fourscore thousand, whereof forty thousand were slain in the conflict; and no fewer sold than slain.

15 Yet was he not content with this, but presumed to go into the most holy temple of all the world; Menelaus, that traitor to the laws, and to his own country, being his guide:

16 And taking the holy vessels with polluted hands, and with profane hands pulling down the things that were dedicated by other kings to the augmentation and glory and honour of the place, he gave them away.

17 And so haughty was Antiochus in mind, that he considered not that the Lord was angry for a while for the sins of them that dwelt in the city, and therefore his eye was not upon the place.

18 For had they not been formerly wrapped in many sins, this man, as soon as he had come, had forthwith been scourged, and put back from his presumption, as Heliodorus was, whom Seleucus the king sent to view the treasury.

19 Nevertheless God did not choose the people for the place's sake, but the place for the people's sake.

20 And therefore the place itself, that was partaker with them of the adversity that happened to the nation, did afterward communicate in the benefits sent from the Lord: and as it was forsaken in the wrath of the Almighty, so again, the great Lord being reconciled, it was set up with all glory.

DOUAY OLD TESTAMENT

12 And commanded the soldiers to kill, and not to spare any that came in their way, and to go up into the houses to slay.

13 Thus there was a slaughter of young and old, a destruction of women and children, and killing of virgins and infants.

14 And there were slain in the space of three whole days fourscore thousand, forty thousand were made prisoners, and as many sold.

15 But this was not enough; he presumed also to enter into the temple, the most holy in all the world, Menelaus, that traitor to the laws, and to his country, being his guide.

16 And taking in his wicked hands the holy vessels, which were given by other kings and cities, for the ornament and the glory of the place, he unworthily handled and profaned them.

17 Thus Antiochus going astray in mind, did not consider that God was angry for a while, because of the sins of the inhabitants of the city: and therefore this contempt had happened to the place:

18 Otherwise had they not been involved in many sins, as Heliodorus, who was sent by king Seleucus to rob the treasury, so this man also, as soon as he had come, had been forthwith scourged, and put back from his presumption.

19 But God did not choose the people for the place's sake, but the place for the people's sake.

20 And therefore the place also itself was made partaker of the evils of the people: but afterward shall communicate in the good things thereof, and as it was forsaken in the wrath of Almighty God, shall be exalted again with great glory, when the great Lord shall be reconciled.

KNOX TRANSLATION

arms; 12 then he bade his troops go about killing, with no
quarter for any they met; let a man but shew his face on the
house-top, he must be slaughtered with the rest. 13 Fell
young and old alike; children with their mothers must die,
nor maidenhood was spared, nor helpless infancy. 14 By the
end of three days, eighty thousand had been massacred,
forty thousand held as prisoners, and as many more sold
into slavery.
15 Nor might all this content him; with Menelaus for his
guide, that was traitor to faith and folk, what must he do but
make his way into God's temple, holier in all the world is
none? 16 What, should those sacred ornaments, dedicated by
kings and peoples for the more splendour and worthiness of
it, be caught up in his impious hands, pawed and defiled by
his touch? 17 Surely he had taken leave of his wits, this
Antiochus; how should he know that this sanctuary, for
once, would lack the divine protection? And only because,
for a little, God's anger was provoked by sins of the men that
dwelt there! 18 Free had they been from the meshes of such
guilt, Antiochus, too, should have been greeted with a drubbing, as Heliodorus was, the man king Seleucus sent to rob
the treasury, and should have learned to leave his rash purpose. 19 But what would you? People it was God chose, and
city for people's sake; 20 chastisement that fell on the people,
city must rue, and anon share its good fortune. He, the
omnipotent, the ruler of all, would leave Jerusalem forlorn in
his anger, would raise her to heights of glory, his anger once
appeased.

Today's English Version

orders to cut down without mercy everyone they met and to
slaughter anyone they found hiding in the houses. 13 They
murdered everyone—men and women, boys and girls; even
babies were butchered. 14 Three days later Jerusalem had lost
80,000 people: 40,000 killed in the attack and at least that
many taken away to be sold as slaves.
15 But Antiochus was still not satisfied. He even dared to
enter the holiest Temple in all the world, guided by Menelaus, who had become a traitor both to his religion and to his
people. 16 With his filthy and unholy hands, Antiochus
swept away the sacred objects of worship and the gifts which
other kings had given to increase the glory and honor of the
Temple. 17 He was so thrilled with his conquest that he did
not realize that the Lord had let his holy Temple be defiled
because the sin of the people of Jerusalem had made him
angry for a while. 18 If the people of Jerusalem had not been
involved in so many sins, Antiochus would have been punished immediately and prevented from taking such a foolish
action. He would have suffered the same fate as Heliodorus,
who was sent by King Seleucus to inspect the treasury.
19 But the Lord did not choose his people for the sake of his
Temple; he established his Temple for the sake of his people.
20 So the Temple shared in the people's suffering but also
later shared in their prosperity. The Lord abandoned it when
he became angry, but restored it when his anger had cooled
down.

New Revised Standard Version

commanded his soldiers to cut down relentlessly everyone
they met and to kill those who went into their houses.
13 Then there was massacre of young and old, destruction of
boys, women, and children, and slaughter of young girls and
infants. 14 Within the total of three days eighty thousand
were destroyed, forty thousand in hand-to-hand fighting,
and as many were sold into slavery as were killed.
15 Not content with this, Antiochus[a] dared to enter the
most holy temple in all the world, guided by Menelaus, who
had become a traitor both to the laws and to his country.
16 He took the holy vessels with his polluted hands, and
swept away with profane hands the votive offerings that
other kings had made to enhance the glory and honor of the
place. 17 Antiochus was elated in spirit, and did not perceive
that the Lord was angered for a little while because of the
sins of those who lived in the city, and that this was the reason he was disregarding the holy place. 18 But if it had not
happened that they were involved in many sins, this man
would have been flogged and turned back from his rash act
as soon as he came forward, just as Heliodorus had been,
whom King Seleucus sent to inspect the treasury. 19 But the
Lord did not choose the nation for the sake of the holy place,
but the place for the sake of the nation. 20 Therefore the
place itself shared in the misfortunes that befell the nation
and afterward participated in its benefits; and what was forsaken in the wrath of the Almighty was restored again in all
its glory when the great Lord became reconciled.

a Gk *he*

New American Bible

ordered his soldiers to cut down without mercy those whom
they met and to slay those who took refuge in their houses.
13 There was a massacre of young and old, a killing of
women and children, a slaughter of virgins and infants. 14 In
the space of three days, eighty thousand were lost, forty
thousand meeting a violent death, and the same number
being sold into slavery. 15 Not satisfied with this, the king
dared to enter the holiest temple in the world; Menelaus, that
traitor both to the laws and to his country, served as guide.
16 He laid his impure hands on the sacred vessels and gathered up with profane hands the votive offerings made by
other kings for the advancement, the glory, and the honor of
the Place. 17 Puffed up in spirit, Antiochus did not realize
that it was because of the sins of the city's inhabitants that
the Lord was angry for a little while and hence disregarded
the holy Place. 18 If they had not become entangled in so
many sins, this man, like Heliodorus, who was sent by King
Seleucus to inspect the treasury, would have been flogged
and turned back from his presumptuous action as soon as he
approached. 19 The Lord, however, had not chosen the people for the sake of the Place, but the Place for the sake of the
people. 20 Therefore, the Place itself, having shared in the
people's misfortunes, afterward participated in their good
fortune; and what the Almighty had forsaken in his anger
was restored in all its glory, once the great Sovereign became
reconciled.

New Jerusalem Bible

the city. 12 He then ordered his soldiers to cut down without
mercy everyone they encountered, and to butcher all who
took refuge in their houses. 13 It was a massacre of young
and old, a slaughter of women and children, a butchery of
young girls and infants. 14 There were eighty thousand victims in the course of those three days, forty thousand dying
by violence and as many again being sold into slavery.
15[a] Not content with this, he had the audacity to enter the
holiest Temple in the entire world, with Menelaus, that traitor to the laws and to his country, as his guide; 16 with
impure hands he seized the sacred vessels; with impious
hands he seized the offerings presented by other kings for
the aggrandisement, glory and dignity of the holy place.
17 Holding so high an opinion of himself, Antiochus did
not realise that the Lord was temporarily angry at the sins of
the inhabitants of the city, hence his unconcern for the holy
place. 18 Had they not been entangled in many sins,
Antiochus too, like Heliodorus when King Seleucus sent him
to inspect the Treasury, would have been flogged the
moment he arrived and checked in his presumption. 19 The
Lord, however, had not chosen the people for the sake of the
holy place, but the holy place for the sake of the people;
20 and so the holy place itself, having shared the disasters
that befell the people, in due course also shared their good
fortune; having been abandoned by the Almighty in his
anger, once the great Sovereign was placated it was reinstat-
ed in all its glory.

a **5** 5:15seq. // 1 M 1:20–24.

Greek Old Testament

21 Ὁ γοῦν Ἀντίοχος ὀκτακόσια πρὸς τοῖς χιλίοις ἀπεν-
εγκάμενος ἐκ τοῦ ἱεροῦ τάλαντα θᾶττον εἰς τὴν Ἀντιόχειαν
ἐχωρίσθη οἰόμενος ἀπὸ τῆς ὑπερηφανίας τὴν μὲν γῆν πλω-
τὴν καὶ τὸ πέλαγος πορευτὸν θέσθαι διὰ τὸν μετεωρισμὸν
τῆς καρδίας. 22 κατέλιπεν δὲ καὶ ἐπιστάτας τοῦ κακοῦν τὸ
γένος, ἐν μὲν Ιεροσολύμοις Φίλιππον, τὸ μὲν γένος Φρύγα,
τὸν δὲ τρόπον βαρβαρώτερον ἔχοντα τοῦ καταστήσαντος,
23 ἐν δὲ Γαριζιν Ἀνδρόνικον, πρὸς δὲ τούτοις Μενέλαον, ὃς
χείριστα τῶν ἄλλων ὑπερῄρετο τοῖς πολίταις, ἀπεχθῆ δὲ
πρὸς τοὺς πολίτας Ιουδαίους ἔχων διάθεσιν. 24 ἔπεμψεν δὲ
τὸν Μυσάρχην Ἀπολλώνιον μετὰ στρατεύματος, δισμυρίους
δὲ πρὸς τοῖς δισχιλίοις, προστάξας τοὺς ἐν ἡλικίᾳ πάντας
κατασφάξαι, τὰς δὲ γυναῖκας καὶ τοὺς νεωτέρους πωλεῖν.
25 οὗτος δὲ παραγενόμενος εἰς Ιεροσόλυμα καὶ τὸν εἰρηνικὸν
ὑποκριθεὶς ἐπέσχεν ἕως τῆς ἁγίας ἡμέρας τοῦ σαββάτου καὶ
λαβὼν ἀργοῦντας τοὺς Ιουδαίους τοῖς ὑφ᾽ ἑαυτὸν ἐξοπλη-
σίαν παρήγγειλεν 26 καὶ τοὺς ἐξελθόντας πάντας ἐπὶ τὴν
θεωρίαν συνεξεκέντησεν καὶ εἰς τὴν πόλιν σὺν τοῖς ὅπλοις
εἰσδραμὼν ἱκανὰ κατέστρωσεν πλήθη.

27 Ιουδας δὲ ὁ καὶ Μακκαβαῖος δέκατός που γενηθεὶς καὶ
ἀναχωρήσας εἰς τὴν ἔρημον θηρίων τρόπον ἐν τοῖς ὄρεσιν
διέζη σὺν τοῖς μετ᾽ αὐτοῦ, καὶ τὴν χορτώδη τροφὴν σιτού-
μενοι διετέλουν πρὸς τὸ μὴ μετασχεῖν τοῦ μολυσμοῦ.

6 Μετ᾽ οὐ πολὺν δὲ χρόνον ἐξαπέστειλεν ὁ βασιλεὺς γέροντα Ἀθηναῖον ἀναγκάζειν τοὺς Ιουδαίους μεταβαίνειν
ἀπὸ τῶν πατρίων νόμων καὶ τοῖς τοῦ θεοῦ νόμοις μὴ

King James Version

21 So when Antiochus had carried out of the temple a thousand and eight hundred talents, he departed in all haste unto Antiochia, weening in his pride to make the land navigable, and the sea passable by foot: such was the haughtiness of his mind.

22 And he left governors to vex the nation: at Jerusalem, Philip, for his country a Phrygian, and for manners more barbarous than he that set him there;

23 And at Garizim, Andronicus; and besides, Menelaus, who worse than all the rest bare an heavy hand over the citizens, having a malicious mind against his countrymen the Jews.

24 He sent also that detestable ringleader Apollonius with an army of two and twenty thousand, commanding him to slay all those that were in their best age, and to sell the women and the younger sort:

25 Who coming to Jerusalem, and pretending peace, did forbear till the holy day of the sabbath, when taking the Jews keeping holy day, he commanded his men to arm themselves.

26 And so he slew all them that were gone to the celebrating of the sabbath, and running through the city with weapons slew great multitudes.

27 But Judas Maccabeus with nine others, or thereabout, withdrew himself into the wilderness, and lived in the mountains after the manner of beasts, with his company, who fed on herbs continually, lest they should be partakers of the pollution.

6 Not long after this the king sent an old man of Athens to compel the Jews to depart from the laws of their fathers, and not to live after the laws of God:

Douay Old Testament

21 So when Antiochus had taken away out of the temple a thousand and eight hundred talents, he went back in all haste to Antioch, thinking through pride, that he might now make the land navigable, and the sea passable on foot: such was the haughtiness of his mind.

22 He left also governors to afflict the people: at Jerusalem, Philip, a Phrygian by birth, but in manners more barbarous than he that set him there:

23 And in Gazarim, Andronicus and Menelaus, who bore a more heavy hand upon the citizens than the rest.

24 And whereas he was set against the Jews, he sent that hateful prince Apollonius with an army of two and twenty thousand men, commanding him to kill all that were of perfect age, and to sell the women and the younger sort.

25 Who when he was come to Jerusalem, pretending peace, rested till the holy day of the sabbath: and then the Jews keeping holiday, he commanded his men to take arms.

26 And he slew all that were come forth to see: and running through the city with armed men, he destroyed a very great multitude.

27 But Judas Machabeus, who was the tenth, had withdrawn himself into a desert place, and there lived amongst wild beasts in the mountains with his company: and they continued feeding on herbs, that they might not be partakers of the pollution.

6 BUT not long after the king sent a certain old man of Antioch, to compel the Jews to depart from the laws of their fathers and of God:

Knox Translation

21 Antiochus, then, came away from the temple a thousand
and eight hundred talents the richer; and back he went to
Antioch, all at reckless speed; he had a mind to sail his fleet
over the plain, march his troops across the sea, his heart so
swelled with pride in his doings. 22 As for the Jewish folk, he
left viceroys of his own to harry them; in Jerusalem Philip,
that was a Phrygian born, and outdid his own master in cruelty; 23 at Garizim Andronicus and Menelaus, heaviest burden of all for the folk to bear. 24 But he would do worse by
the Jews yet; or why did he send out Apollonius, the arch-
enemy, and a force of twenty-two thousand, to cut off manhood in its flower, women and children to sell for slaves?
25 This Apollonius, when he reached Jerusalem, was all professions of friendship, and nothing did until the sabbath
came round, when the Jews kept holiday. Then he put his
men under arms, 26 and butchered all that went out to keep
festival; to and fro he went about the streets, with armed fellows at his heels, and made a great massacre.

27 Meanwhile Judas Machabaeus, and nine others with
him, went out into the desert, where they lived like wild
beasts on the mountain-side; better lodge there with herbs
for food, than be party to the general defilement.

6 Not long after, the king despatched one of the senators at
Antioch, with orders he should compel the Jewish people,
custom of their fathers and law of their God to forsake. 2 The

TODAY'S ENGLISH VERSION

21 Antiochus took 135,000 pounds of silver from the
Temple and hurried off to Antioch. Such was his arrogance
that he felt he could make ships sail across dry land or
troops march across the sea. 22 He appointed governors to
cause trouble for the people. In Jerusalem he placed Philip, a
man from Phrygia who was more evil than Antiochus himself. 23 At Mount Gerizim he placed Andronicus. In addition
to these, there was Menelaus, who mistreated his fellow Jews
far worse than the governors did. Antiochus hated the Jews
so much 24 that he sent an army of 22,000 mercenary troops
from Mysia to Jerusalem under the command of a man
named Apollonius, with orders to kill every man in the city
and to sell the women and boys as slaves. 25 Apollonius
arrived in Jerusalem, pretending to be on a peace mission.
Then on a Sabbath, when all the Jews were observing the
day of rest, he led his troops, who were fully armed, in a
parade outside the city. 26 Suddenly he commanded his men
to kill everyone who had come out to see them. They rushed
into the city and murdered a great many people.
27 But Judas Maccabeus and about nine others escaped into
the barren mountains, where they lived like wild animals. In
order not to defile themselves, they ate only plants which
they found growing there.

6 Not long after that, the king sent an elderly Athenian[a] to
force the Jews to abandon their religion and the customs

[a] elderly Athenian; *or* an elder of Athens, *or* Athenaios the elder, *or* Geron an Athenian; *some manuscripts have* an elderly Antiochean; *or* an elder of Antioch.

NEW REVISED STANDARD VERSION

21 So Antiochus carried off eighteen hundred talents from
the temple, and hurried away to Antioch, thinking in his
arrogance that he could sail on the land and walk on the sea,
because his mind was elated. 22 He left governors to oppress
the people: at Jerusalem, Philip, by birth a Phrygian and in
character more barbarous than the man who appointed him;
23 and at Gerizim, Andronicus; and besides these Menelaus,
who lorded it over his compatriots worse than the others did.
In his malice toward the Jewish citizens,[a] 24 Antiochus[b] sent
Apollonius, the captain of the Mysians, with an army of
twenty-two thousand, and commanded him to kill all the
grown men and to sell the women and boys as slaves.
25 When this man arrived in Jerusalem, he pretended to be
peaceably disposed and waited until the holy sabbath day;
then, finding the Jews not at work, he ordered his troops to
parade under arms. 26 He put to the sword all those who
came out to see them, then rushed into the city with his
armed warriors and killed great numbers of people.
27 But Judas Maccabeus, with about nine others, got
away to the wilderness, and kept himself and his companions alive in the mountains as wild animals do; they continued to live on what grew wild, so that they might not share
in the defilement.

6 Not long after this, the king sent an Athenian[c] senator[d]
to compel the Jews to forsake the laws of their ancestors
and no longer to live by the laws of God; 2 also to pollute the

a Or *worse than the others did in his malice toward the Jewish citizens*
b Gk *he* *c* Other ancient authorities read *Antiochian* *d* Or *Geron an Athenian*

NEW AMERICAN BIBLE

21 Antiochus carried off eighteen hundred talents from the
temple, and hurried back to Antioch. In his arrogance he
planned to make the land navigable and the sea passable on
foot, so carried away was he with pride. 22 But he left governors to harass the nation: at Jerusalem, Philip, a Phrygian by
birth, and in character more cruel than the man who
appointed him; 23 at Mount Gerizim, Andronicus; and
besides these, Menelaus, who lorded it over his fellow citizens worse than the others did. Out of hatred for the Jewish
citizens, 24 the king sent Apollonius, commander of the
Mysians, at the head of an army of twenty-two thousand
men, with orders to kill all the grown men and sell the
women and young men into slavery. 25 When this man
arrived in Jerusalem, he pretended to be peacefully disposed
and waited until the holy day of the sabbath; then, finding
the Jews refraining from work, he ordered his men to parade
fully armed. 26 All those who came out to watch, he massacred, and running through the city with armed men, he cut
down a large number of people.
27 But Judas Maccabeus with about nine others withdrew
to the wilderness where he and his companions lived like
wild animals in the hills, continuing to eat what grew wild to
avoid sharing the defilement.

6 Not long after this the king sent an Athenian senator to
force the Jews to abandon the customs of their ancestors
and live no longer by the laws of God; 2 also to profane the

NEW JERUSALEM BIBLE

21 Antiochus, having extracted eighteen hundred talents
from the Temple, hurried back to Antioch; in his pride he
would have undertaken to make the dry land navigable and
the sea passable on foot, so high his arrogance soared.
22 But he left officials behind to plague the nation: in
Jerusalem, Philip, a Phrygian by race, and by nature more
barbarous than the man who appointed him; 23 on Mount
Gerizim, Andronicus; and, besides these, Menelaus, who
lorded it over his countrymen worse than all the others.
In his rooted hostility to the Jews, 24 the king also sent the
Mysarch Apollonius at the head of an army twenty-two thousand strong, with orders to put to death all men in their
prime and to sell the women and children. 25 Arriving in
Jerusalem and posing as a man of peace, this man waited
until the holy day of the Sabbath and then, taking advantage
of the Jews as they rested from work, ordered his men to
parade fully armed; 26 all those who came out to watch he
put to the sword; then, rushing into the city with his armed
troops, he cut down an immense number of people.
27 Judas, also known as Maccabaeus, however, with about
nine others, withdrew into the desert. He lived like the wild
animals in the hills with his companions, eating nothing but
wild plants to avoid contracting defilement.

6 [a] Shortly afterwards, the king sent Gerontes the Athenian
to force the Jews to violate their ancestral customs and
live no longer by the laws of God; 2 and to profane the

[a] **6** 6:1seq. // 1 M 1:45–51, 60–61; 2:32–38.

Greek Old Testament

πολιτεύεσθαι, 2 μολῦναι δὲ καὶ τὸν ἐν Ἱεροσολύμοις νεὼ καὶ
προσονομάσαι Διὸς Ὀλυμπίου καὶ τὸν ἐν Γαριζιν, καθὼς
ἐτύγχανον οἱ τὸν τόπον οἰκοῦντες, Διὸς Ξενίου. 3 χαλεπὴ
δὲ καὶ τοῖς ὅλοις ἦν δυσχερὴς ἡ ἐπίτασις τῆς κακίας. 4 τὸ
μὲν γὰρ ἱερὸν ἀσωτίας καὶ κώμων ὑπὸ τῶν ἐθνῶν ἐπεπληροῦ-
το ῥᾳθυμούντων μεθ᾽ ἑταιρῶν καὶ ἐν τοῖς ἱεροῖς περιβόλοις
γυναιξὶ πλησιαζόντων, ἔτι δὲ τὰ μὴ καθήκοντα ἔνδον
εἰσφερόντων. 5 τὸ δὲ θυσιαστήριον τοῖς ἀποδιεσταλμένοις
ἀπὸ τῶν νόμων ἀθεμίτοις ἐπεπλήρωτο. 6 ἦν δ᾽ οὔτε σαββατί-
ζειν οὔτε πατρῴους ἑορτὰς διαφυλάττειν οὔτε ἁπλῶς
Ἰουδαῖον ὁμολογεῖν εἶναι, 7 ἤγοντο δὲ μετὰ πικρᾶς ἀνάγκης
εἰς τὴν κατὰ μῆνα τοῦ βασιλέως γενέθλιον ἡμέραν ἐπὶ
σπλαγχνισμόν, γενομένης δὲ Διονυσίων ἑορτῆς ἠναγκάζοντο
κισσοὺς ἔχοντες πομπεύειν τῷ Διονύσῳ. 8 ψήφισμα δὲ ἐξέ-
πεσεν εἰς τὰς ἀστυγείτονας Ἑλληνίδας πόλεις Πτολεμαίου
ὑποθεμένου τὴν αὐτὴν ἀγωγὴν κατὰ τῶν Ιουδαίων ἄγειν καὶ
σπλαγχνίζειν, 9 τοὺς δὲ μὴ προαιρουμένους μεταβαίνειν
ἐπὶ τὰ Ἑλληνικὰ κατασφάζειν. παρῆν οὖν ὁρᾶν τὴν ἐνεστῶ-
σαν ταλαιπωρίαν. 10 δύο γὰρ γυναῖκες ἀνήχθησαν περιτε-
τμηκυῖαι τὰ τέκνα· τούτων δὲ ἐκ τῶν μαστῶν κρεμάσαντες
τὰ βρέφη καὶ δημοσίᾳ περιαγαγόντες αὐτὰς τὴν πόλιν κατὰ

King James Version

2 And to pollute also the temple in Jerusalem, and to call it the temple of Jupiter Olympius; and that in Garizim, of Jupiter the Defender of strangers, as they did desire that dwelt in the place.

3 The coming in of this mischief was sore and grievous to the people:

4 For the temple was filled with riot and revelling by the Gentiles, who dallied with harlots, and had to do with women within the circuit of the holy places, and besides that brought in things that were not lawful.

5 The altar also was filled with profane things, which the law forbiddeth.

6 Neither was it lawful for a man to keep sabbath days or ancient feasts, or to profess himself at all to be a Jew.

7 And in the day of the king's birth every month they were brought by bitter constraint to eat of the sacrifices; and when the feast of Bacchus was kept, the Jews were compelled to go in procession to Bacchus, carrying ivy.

8 Moreover there went out a decree to the neighbour cities of the heathen, by the suggestion of Ptolemee, against the Jews, that they should observe the same fashions, and be partakers of their sacrifices:

9 And whoso would not conform themselves to the manners of the Gentiles should be put to death. Then might a man have seen the present misery.

10 For there were two women brought, who had circumcised their children; whom when they had openly led round about the city, the babes hanging at their breasts, they cast them down headlong from the wall.

Douay Old Testament

2 And to defile the temple that was in Jerusalem, and to call it the temple of Jupiter Olympius: and that in Gazarim of Jupiter Hospitalis, according as they were that inhabited the place.

3 And very bad was this invasion of evils and grievous to all.

4 For the temple was full of the riot and revellings of the Gentiles: and of men lying with lewd women. And women trust themselves of their accord into the holy places, and brought in things that were not lawful.

5 The altar also was filled with unlawful things, which were forbidden by the laws.

6 And neither were the sabbaths kept, nor the solemn days of the fathers observed, neither did any man plainly profess himself to be a Jew.

7 But they were led by bitter constraint on the king's birthday to the sacrifices: and when the feast of Bacchus was kept, they were compelled to go about crowned with ivy in honour of Bacchus.

8 And there went out a decree into the neighbouring cities of the Gentiles, by the suggestion of the Ptolemeans, that they also should act in like manner against the Jews, to oblige them to sacrifice:

9 And whosoever would not conform themselves to the ways of the Gentiles, should be put to death: then was misery to be seen.

10 For two women were accused to have circumcised their children: whom, when they had openly led about through the city with the infants hanging at their breasts, they threw down headlong from the walls.

Knox Translation

temple at Jerusalem must be profaned, and dedicated now to
Jupiter Olympius; as for the temple on Garizim, the
Samaritans were to call it, as well they might,[a] after Jupiter
the god of strangers. 3 What a storm of troubles broke then
upon the commonwealth, most grievous to be borne! 4 All riot
and revelry the temple became, once the Gentiles had it; here
was dallying with harlots, and women making their way into
the sacred precincts, and bringing in of things abominable;
5 with forbidden meats, to the law's injury, the very altar
groaned. 6 Sabbath none would observe, nor keep holiday his
fathers kept; even the name of Jew was disclaimed. 7 Instead,
they went to sacrifice on the king's birthday, though it were
ruefully and under duress; and when the feast of Liber came
round, make procession they must in Liber's honour, garlanded with ivy each one. 8 And now, among all the neighbouring
cities, a decree went out, wherein the Ptolemies[b] were the
prime movers; all alike should constrain the Jews to do sacrifice, 9 and those that would not fall in with Gentile ways,
with their lives must pay for it.

Here were sights to be seen most pitiable. 10 Two mothers
there were, denounced for the circumcision of their own
sons; what, think you, befell them? Both must be driven
through the streets, with the children hung about their
breasts, and cast headlong from the battlements! 11 At

a 'As well they might'; literally, 'according as they were'. The author seems to be taunting the Samaritans with their Gentile origin. But the Greek might mean 'according as they gained their request'; Josephus alleges that the Samaritans themselves asked leave of the king to re-dedicate their temple.
b 'The Ptolemies'; the Greek has 'Ptolemy', cf. note on 4. 45.

TODAY'S ENGLISH VERSION

of their ancestors. 2 He was also to defile their Temple by
dedicating it to the Olympian god Zeus.[a] The temple on
Mount Gerizim was to be officially named "Temple of Zeus
the God of Hospitality," as the people who lived there had
requested.
3 The oppression was harsh and almost intolerable.
4 Gentiles filled the Temple with drinking parties and all
sorts of immorality. They even had intercourse with prostitutes there. Forbidden objects were brought into the Temple,
5 and the altar was covered with detestable sacrifices prohibited by our Law. 6 It was impossible to observe the Sabbath,
to celebrate any of the traditional festivals, or even so much
as to admit to being a Jew. 7 Each month when the king's
birthday was celebrated, the Jews were compelled by brute
force to eat the intestines of sacrificial animals. Then, during the festival in honor of the wine god Dionysus, they
were required to wear ivy wreaths on their heads and march
in procession. 8 On the advice of Ptolemy,[b] the neighboring
Greek cities were also instructed to require Jews to eat the
sacrifices; 9 they were told to put to death every Jew who
refused to adopt the Greek way of life. It was easy to see
that hard times were ahead. 10 For example, two women
were arrested for having their babies circumcised. They were
paraded around the city with their babies hung from their
breasts; then they were thrown down from the city wall.

[a] ZEUS: *The supreme god of the Greeks; Mount Olympus was thought to be his home.* [b] Ptolemy *(see 4.45); some manuscripts have* the people of Ptolemais.

NEW REVISED STANDARD VERSION

temple in Jerusalem and to call it the temple of Olympian
Zeus, and to call the one in Gerizim the temple of Zeus-the-
Friend-of-Strangers, as did the people who lived in that
place.
3 Harsh and utterly grievous was the onslaught of evil.
4 For the temple was filled with debauchery and reveling by
the Gentiles, who dallied with prostitutes and had intercourse with women within the sacred precincts, and besides
brought in things for sacrifice that were unfit. 5 The altar
was covered with abominable offerings that were forbidden
by the laws. 6 People could neither keep the sabbath, nor
observe the festivals of their ancestors, nor so much as confess themselves to be Jews.
7 On the monthly celebration of the king's birthday, the
Jews[a] were taken, under bitter constraint, to partake of the
sacrifices; and when a festival of Dionysus was celebrated,
they were compelled to wear wreaths of ivy and to walk in
the procession in honor of Dionysus. 8 At the suggestion of
the people of Ptolemais[b] a decree was issued to the neighboring Greek cities that they should adopt the same policy
toward the Jews and make them partake of the sacrifices,
9 and should kill those who did not choose to change over to
Greek customs. One could see, therefore, the misery that had
come upon them. 10 For example, two women were brought
in for having circumcised their children. They publicly paraded them around the city, with their babies hanging at their
breasts, and then hurled them down headlong from the wall.

[a] Gk *they* [b] Cn: Gk *suggestion of the Ptolemies* (or *of Ptolemy*)

NEW AMERICAN BIBLE

temple in Jerusalem and dedicate it to Olympian Zeus, and
that on Mount Gerizim to Zeus the Hospitable, as the inhabitants of the place requested. 3 This intensified the evil in an
intolerable and utterly disgusting way. 4 The Gentiles filled
the temple with debauchery and revelry; they amused themselves with prostitutes and had intercourse with women even
in the sacred court. They also brought into the temple things
that were forbidden, 5 so that the altar was covered with
abominable offerings prohibited by the laws.
6 A man could not keep the sabbath or celebrate the traditional feasts, nor even admit that he was a Jew. 7 Moreover,
at the monthly celebration of the king's birthday the Jews
had, from bitter necessity, to partake of the sacrifices, and
when the festival of Dionysus was celebrated, they were
compelled to march in his procession, wearing wreaths of
ivy.
8 At the suggestion of the citizens of Ptolemais, a decree
was issued ordering the neighboring Greek cities to act in the
same way against the Jews: oblige them to partake of the
sacrifices, 9 and put to death those who would not consent
to adopt the customs of the Greeks. It was obvious, therefore,
that disaster was impended. 10 Thus, two women who were
arrested for having circumcised their children were publicly
paraded about the city with their babies hanging at their
breasts and then thrown down from the top of the city wall.

NEW JERUSALEM BIBLE

Temple in Jerusalem and dedicate it to Olympian Zeus, and
the one on Mount Gerizim to Zeus, Patron of Strangers, as
the inhabitants of the latter place had requested. 3 The
advent of these evils was painfully hard for all the people to
bear. 4 The Temple was filled with revelling and debauchery
by the gentiles, who took their pleasure with prostitutes and
had intercourse with women in the sacred precincts, introducing other indecencies besides. 5 The altar of sacrifice was
loaded with victims proscribed by the law as profane. 6 No
one might either keep the Sabbath or observe the traditional
feasts, or so much as admit to being a Jew. 7 People were
driven by harsh compulsion to take part in the monthly ritual meal commemorating the king's birthday; and when a
feast of Dionysus occurred, they were forced to wear ivy
wreaths and walk in the Dionysiac procession. 8 A decree
was issued at the instance of the people of Ptolemais for the
neighbouring Greek cities, enforcing the same conduct on the
Jews there, obliging them to share in the sacrificial meals,
9 and ordering the execution of those who would not voluntarily conform to Greek customs. So it became clear that
disaster was imminent.
10 For example, two women were charged with having circumcised their children. They were paraded publicly round
the town, with their babies hung at their breasts, and then

Greek Old Testament

τοῦ τείχους ἐκρήμνισαν. [11] ἕτεροι δὲ πλησίον συνδραμόντες
εἰς τὰ σπήλαια λεληθότως ἄγειν τὴν ἑβδομάδα μηνυθέντες
τῷ Φιλίππῳ συνεφλογίσθησαν διὰ τὸ εὐλαβῶς ἔχειν βοηθῆσαι ἑαυτοῖς κατὰ τὴν δόξαν τῆς σεμνοτάτης ἡμέρας.
[12] Παρακαλῶ οὖν τοὺς ἐντυγχάνοντας τῇδε τῇ βίβλῳ μὴ
συστέλλεσθαι διὰ τὰς συμφοράς, λογίζεσθαι δὲ τὰς τιμωρίας μὴ πρὸς ὄλεθρον, ἀλλὰ πρὸς παιδείαν τοῦ γένους ἡμῶν
εἶναι· [13] καὶ γὰρ τὸ μὴ πολὺν χρόνον ἐᾶσθαι τοὺς δυσσε-
βοῦντας, ἀλλ' εὐθέως περιπίπτειν ἐπιτίμοις, μεγάλης εὐεργεσίας σημεῖόν ἐστιν. [14] οὐ γὰρ καθάπερ καὶ ἐπὶ τῶν ἄλλων
ἐθνῶν ἀναμένει μακροθυμῶν ὁ δεσπότης μέχρι τοῦ καταντή-
σαντας αὐτοὺς πρὸς ἐκπλήρωσιν ἁμαρτιῶν κολάσαι, οὕτως
καὶ ἐφ' ἡμῶν ἔκρινεν εἶναι, [15] ἵνα μὴ πρὸς τέλος ἀφι-
κομένων ἡμῶν τῶν ἁμαρτιῶν ὕστερον ἡμᾶς ἐκδικᾷ. [16] διόπερ
οὐδέποτε μὲν τὸν ἔλεον ἀφ' ἡμῶν ἀφίστησιν, παιδεύων δὲ
μετὰ συμφορᾶς οὐκ ἐγκαταλείπει τὸν ἑαυτοῦ λαόν. [17] πλὴν
ἕως ὑπομνήσεως ταῦθ' ἡμῖν εἰρήσθω· δι' ὀλίγων δ' ἐλευστέον
ἐπὶ τὴν διήγησιν.
[18] Ελεάζαρός τις τῶν πρωτευόντων γραμματέων, ἀνὴρ ἤδη
προβεβηκὼς τὴν ἡλικίαν καὶ τὴν πρόσοψιν τοῦ προσώπου
κάλλιστος, ἀναχανὼν ἠναγκάζετο φαγεῖν ὕειον κρέας. [19] ὁ
δὲ τὸν μετ' εὐκλείας θάνατον μᾶλλον ἢ τὸν μετὰ μύσους βίον ἀναδεξάμενος, αὐθαιρέτως ἐπὶ τὸ τύμπανον προσῆγεν,
[20] προπτύσας δὲ καθ' ὃν ἔδει τρόπον προσέρχεσθαι τοὺς
ὑπομένοντας ἀμύνασθαι ὧν οὐ θέμις γεύσασθαι διὰ τὴν πρὸς

King James Version

11 And others, that had run together into caves near by, to keep the sabbath day secretly, being discovered to Philip, were all burnt together, because they made a conscience to help themselves for the honour of the most sacred day.

12 Now I beseech those that read this book, that they be not discouraged for these calamities, but that they judge those punishments not to be for destruction, but for a chastening of our nation.

13 For it is a token of his great goodness, when wicked doers are not suffered any long time, but forthwith punished.

14 For not as with other nations, whom the Lord patiently forbeareth to punish, till they be come to the fulness of their sins, so dealeth he with us,

15 Lest that, being come to the height of sin, afterwards he should take vengeance of us.

16 And therefore he never withdraweth his mercy from us: and though he punish with adversity, yet doth he never forsake his people.

17 But let this that we at spoken be for a warning unto us. And now will we come to the declaring of the matter in a few words.

18 Eleazar, one of the principal scribes, an aged man, and of a well favoured countenance, was constrained to open his mouth, and to eat swine's flesh.

19 But he, choosing rather to die gloriously, than to live stained with such an abomination, spit it forth, and came of his own accord to the torment,

20 As it behoved them to come, that are resolute to stand out against such things, as are not lawful for love of life to be tasted.

Douay Old Testament

11 And others that had met together in caves that were near, and were keeping the sabbath day privately, being discovered by Philip, were burnt with fire, because they made a conscience to help themselves with their hands, by reason of the religious observance of the day.

12 Now I beseech those that shall read this book, that they be not shocked at these calamities, but that they consider the things that happened, not as being for the destruction, but for the correction of our nation.

13 For it is a token of great goodness when sinners are not suffered to go on in their ways for a long time, but are presently punished.

14 For, not as with other nations (whom the Lord patiently expecteth, that when the day of judgment shall come, he may punish them in the fulness of their sins:)

15 Doth he also deal with us, so as to suffer our sins to come to their height, and then take vengeance on us.

16 And therefore he never withdraweth his mercy from us: but though he chastise his people with adversity, he forsaketh them not.

17 But let this suffice in a few words for a warning to the readers. And now we must come to the narration.

18 Eleazar one of the chief of the scribes, a man advanced in years, and of a comely countenance, was pressed to open his mouth to eat swine's flesh.

19 But he, choosing rather a most glorious death than a hateful life, went forward voluntarily to the torment.

20 And considering in what manner he was come to it, patiently bearing, he determined not to do any unlawful things for the love of life.

Knox Translation

another time, Philip had information that certain Jews were
meeting in caves near at hand, to keep the sabbath there
without remark. Not one of these would lift a hand to help
himself, so great care they had of the day's observance, and
all were burned to death.
[12] Reader, by these tales of ill fortune be not too much dismayed; bethink thee, all this came about for the punishment
of our race, not for its undoing. [13] A mark of signal favour it
is, when the Lord is quick to chastise, nor lets the sinner sin
on unreproved. [14] See how he deals with other nations, waiting patiently to take full toll when the hour comes for judgement! [15] Not so with us; for our guilt he will not delay reckoning, and claim strict vengeance at last. [16] Towards us, his
mercy is inalienable; chastise us he will with adversity, but
forsake us never. [17] So much, reader, for thy warning; and
now go we back to our history.
[18] Here was Eleazar, one of the chief scribes, a man of
great age and of noble features, being required to eat swine's
flesh; but though they held his mouth open they could not
force him to eat. [19] He would rather die gloriously than live
defiled; on he went, of his own accord, to the place of torture, [20] scanning every step of the path that lay before him.
He must endure all in patience, rather than taste, for love of

TODAY'S ENGLISH VERSION

11 On another occasion, Philip was told that some Jews had
gathered in a nearby cave to observe the Sabbath in secret.
Philip attacked and burned them all alive. They had such
respect for the Sabbath that they would not fight to defend
themselves.

12 I beg you not to become discouraged as you read about
the terrible things that happened. Consider that this was the
Lord's way of punishing his people, not of destroying them.
13 In fact, it is a sign of kindness to punish a person immediately for his sins, rather than to wait a long time. 14 The
Lord does not treat us as he does other nations: he waits
patiently until they have become deeply involved in sin
before he punishes them, 15 but he punishes us before we
have sinned too much. 16 So the Lord is always merciful to
us, his own people. Although he punishes us with disasters,
he never abandons us. 17 I have made these few observa-
tions by way of reminder. We will now get on with the story.

18 There was an elderly and highly respected teacher of the
Law by the name of Eleazar, whose mouth was being forced
open to make him eat pork. 19-20 But he preferred an honorable death rather than a life of disgrace. So he spit out the
meat and went willingly to the place of torture, showing how
people should have courage to refuse unclean food, even if it

NEW REVISED STANDARD VERSION

11 Others who had assembled in the caves nearby, in order to
observe the seventh day secretly, were betrayed to Philip and
were all burned together, because their piety kept them from
defending themselves, in view of their regard for that most
holy day.

12 Now I urge those who read this book not to be
depressed by such calamities, but to recognize that these
punishments were designed not to destroy but to discipline
our people. 13 In fact, it is a sign of great kindness not to let
the impious alone for long, but to punish them immediately.
14 For in the case of the other nations the Lord waits patiently to punish them until they have reached the full measure of
their sins; but he does not deal in this way with us, 15 in
order that he may not take vengeance on us afterward when
our sins have reached their height. 16 Therefore he never
withdraws his mercy from us. Although he disciplines us
with calamities, he does not forsake his own people. 17 Let
what we have said serve as a reminder; we must go on
briefly with the story.

18 Eleazar, one of the scribes in high position, a man now
advanced in age and of noble presence, was being forced to
open his mouth to eat swine's flesh. 19 But he, welcoming
death with honor rather than life with pollution, went up to
the rack of his own accord, spitting out the flesh, 20 as all
ought to go who have the courage to refuse things that it is
not right to taste, even for the natural love of life.

NEW AMERICAN BIBLE

11 Others, who had assembled in nearby caves to observe the
sabbath in secret, were betrayed to Philip and all burned to
death. In their respect for the holiness of that day, they had
scruples about defending themselves.

12 Now I beg those who read this book not to be disheartened by these misfortunes, but to consider that these chastisements were meant not for the ruin but for the correction
of our nation. 13 It is, in fact, a sign of great kindness to
punish sinners promptly instead of letting them go for long.
14 Thus, in dealing with other nations, the LORD patiently
waits until they reach the full measure of their sins before he
punishes them; but with us he has decided to deal differently, 15 in order that he may not have to punish us more
severely later, when our sins have reached their fullness.
16 He never withdraws his mercy from us. Although he disciplines us with misfortunes, he does not abandon his own
people. 17 Let these words suffice for recalling this truth.
Without further ado we must go on with our story.

18 Eleazar, one of the foremost scribes, a man of advanced
age and noble appearance, was being forced to open his
mouth to eat pork. 19 But preferring a glorious death to a
life of defilement, he spat out the meat, and went forward of
his own accord to the instrument of torture, 20 as men
ought to do who have the courage to reject the food which it
is unlawful to taste even for love of life. 21 Those in charge

NEW JERUSALEM BIBLE

hurled over the city wall. 11 Other people, who had assembled in some near-by caves to keep the seventh day without
attracting attention, were denounced to Philip, and were
then all burnt to death together, since their consciences
would not allow them to defend themselves, out of respect
for the holiness of the day.

12 Now, I urge anyone who may read this book not to be
dismayed at these calamities, but to reflect that such visita-
tions are intended not to destroy our race but to discipline it.
13 Indeed, when evil-doers are not left for long to their own
devices but incur swift retribution, it is a sign of great benevolence. 14 In the case of other nations, the Master waits
patiently for them to attain the full measure of their sins
before he punishes them, but with us he has decided to deal
differently, 15 rather than have to punish us later, when our
sins come to full measure. 16 And so he never entirely withdraws his mercy from us; he may discipline us by some
disaster, but he does not desert his own people. 17 Let this be
said simply by way of reminder; we must return to our story
without more ado.

18 Eleazar, one of the foremost teachers of the Law, a man
already advanced in years and of most noble appearance,
had his mouth forced open, to make him eat a piece of pork.
19 But he, resolving to die with honour rather than to live disgraced, walked of his own accord to the torture of the wheel,
20 having spat the stuff out, as befits those with the courage
to reject what is not lawful to taste, rather than live. 21 The

GREEK OLD TESTAMENT

τὸ ζῆν φιλοστοργίαν. 21 οἱ δὲ πρὸς τῷ παρανόμῳ σπλαγχνι-
σμῷ τεταγμένοι διὰ τὴν ἐκ τῶν παλαιῶν χρόνων πρὸς τὸν
ἄνδρα γνῶσιν ἀπολαβόντες αὐτὸν κατ' ἰδίαν παρεκάλουν
ἐνέγκαντα κρέα, οἷς καθῆκον αὐτῷ χρᾶσθαι, δι' αὐτοῦ παρα-
σκευασθέντα, ὑποκριθῆναι δὲ ὡς ἐσθίοντα τὰ ὑπὸ τοῦ βασιλέως προστεταγμένα τῶν ἀπὸ τῆς θυσίας κρεῶν, 22 ἵνα τοῦτο πράξας ἀπολυθῇ τοῦ θανάτου καὶ διὰ τὴν ἀρχαίαν πρὸς
αὐτοὺς φιλίαν τύχῃ φιλανθρωπίας. 23 ὁ δὲ λογισμὸν ἀστεῖον
ἀναλαβὼν καὶ ἄξιον τῆς ἡλικίας καὶ τῆς τοῦ γήρως ὑπερο-
χῆς καὶ τῆς ἐπικτήτου καὶ ἐπιφανοῦς πολιᾶς καὶ τῆς ἐκ
παιδὸς καλλίστης ἀναστροφῆς, μᾶλλον δὲ τῆς ἁγίας καὶ
θεοκτίστου νομοθεσίας ἀκολούθως ἀπεφήνατο ταχέως λέγων
προπέμπειν εἰς τὸν ᾅδην. 24 Οὐ γὰρ τῆς ἡμετέρας ἡλικίας
ἄξιόν ἐστιν ὑποκριθῆναι, ἵνα πολλοὶ τῶν νέων ὑπολαβόντες
Ελεαζαρον τὸν ἐνενηκονταετῆ μεταβεβηκέναι εἰς ἀλλοφυλι-
σμὸν 25 καὶ αὐτοὶ διὰ τὴν ἐμὴν ὑπόκρισιν καὶ διὰ τὸ μικρὸν
καὶ ἀκαριαῖον ζῆν πλανηθῶσιν δι' ἐμέ, καὶ μύσος καὶ κηλῖδα
τοῦ γήρως κατακτήσωμαι. 26 εἰ γὰρ καὶ ἐπὶ τοῦ παρόντος
ἐξελοῦμαι τὴν ἐξ ἀνθρώπων τιμωρίαν, ἀλλὰ τὰς τοῦ παντοκράτορος χεῖρας οὔτε ζῶν οὔτε ἀποθανὼν ἐκφεύξομαι.
27 διόπερ ἀνδρείως μὲν νῦν διαλλάξας τὸν βίον τοῦ μὲν
γήρως ἄξιος φανήσομαι, 28 τοῖς δὲ νέοις ὑπόδειγμα γεν-
ναῖον καταλελοιπὼς εἰς τὸ προθύμως καὶ γενναίως ὑπὲρ τῶν
σεμνῶν καὶ ἁγίων νόμων ἀπευθανατίζειν. τοσαῦτα δὲ εἰπὼν
ἐπὶ τὸ τύμπανον εὐθέως ἦλθεν. 29 τῶν δὲ ἀγόντων πρὸς

KING JAMES VERSION

21 But they that had the charge of that wicked feast, for the old acquaintance they had with the man, taking him aside, besought him to bring flesh of his own provision, such as was lawful for him to use, and make as if he did eat of the flesh taken from the sacrifice commanded by the king;

22 That in so doing he might be delivered from death, and for the old friendship with them find favour.

23 But he began to consider discreetly, and as became his age, and the excellency of his ancient years, and the honour of his gray head, whereunto was come, and his most honest education from a child, or rather the holy law made and given by God: therefore he answered accordingly, and willed them straightways to send him to the grave.

24 For it becometh not our age, *said he,* in any wise to dissemble, whereby many young persons might think that Eleazar, being fourscore years old and ten, were now gone to a strange religion;

25 And so they through mine hypocrisy, and desire to live a little time and a moment longer, should be deceived by me, and I get a stain to mine old age, and make it abominable.

26 For though for the present time I should be delivered from the punishment of men: yet should I not escape the hand of the Almighty, neither alive, nor dead.

27 Wherefore now, manfully changing this life, I will shew myself such an one as mine age requireth,

28 And leave a notable example to such as be young to die willingly and courageously for the honourable and holy laws. And when he had said these words, immediately he went to the torment:

DOUAY OLD TESTAMENT

21 But they that stood by, being moved with wicked pity, for the old friendship they had with the man, taking him aside, desired that flesh might be brought, which it was lawful for him to eat, that he might make as if he had eaten, as the king had commanded of the flesh of the sacrifice:

22 That by so doing he might be delivered from death: and for the sake of their old friendship with the man they did him this courtesy.

23 But he began to consider the dignity of his age, and his ancient years, and the inbred honour of his grey head, and his good life and conversation from a child: and he answered without delay, according to the ordinances of the holy law made by God, saying, that he would rather be sent into the other world.

24 For it doth not become our age, said he, to dissemble: whereby many young persons might think that Eleazar, at the age of fourscore and ten years, was gone over to the life of the heathens:

25 And so they, through my dissimulation, and for a little time of a corruptible life, should be deceived, and hereby I should bring a stain and a curse upon my old age.

26 For though, for the present time, I should be delivered from the punishments of men, yet should I not escape the hand of the Almighty neither alive nor dead.

27 Wherefore by departing manfully out of this life, I shall shew myself worthy of my old age:

28 And I shall leave an example of fortitude to young men, if with a ready mind and constancy I suffer an honourable death, for the most venerable and most holy laws. And having spoken thus, he was forthwith carried to execution.

KNOX TRANSLATION

life, the forbidden meat. 21 Old friends among the bystanders, out of misplaced kindness, took him aside and urged
him to let meat of some other kind be brought, which he
could taste without scruple; he could pretend to have obeyed
the king's will by eating the sacrilegious food, 22 and his life
should no longer be forfeit. Such kind offices old friendship
claimed; 23 but he thought rather of the reverence that was
due to his great age, of his venerable grey hairs, of a life
blamelessly lived from childhood onwards. True to the precepts of God's holy law, he answered that they would do better to send him to his grave and have done with it. 24 It does
not suit my time of life, said he, to play a part. What of
many that stand here, younger than myself, who would
think that Eleazar, at the age of ninety, had turned Gentile?
25 To gain a brief hour of this perishable life, shall I play a
trick on them, shall I disgrace this hoary head of mine and
bring down a curse on it? 26 Man's sentence here I may
avoid if I will, but God's almighty hand, living or dead,
escape I may not. 27 Let me take leave of life with a good
grace, as best suits my years, 28 bequeathing to men younger
than myself an example of courage; meeting, with ready
resolve, an honourable death, for the sake of laws holy and
august as ours are. And so without more ado he was led

TODAY'S ENGLISH VERSION

costs them their lives. 21-22Those in charge of the sacrifice
had been friends of Eleazar for a long time, and because of
this friendship they told him privately to bring meat that was
lawful for him to eat. He need only pretend to eat the pork,
they said, and in this way he would not be put to death.
23But Eleazar made a decision worthy of his gray hair and
advanced age. All his life he had lived in perfect obedience to
God's holy laws, so he replied, "Kill me, here and now.
24Such deception is not worthy of a man of my years. Many
young people would think that I had denied my faith after I
was ninety years old. 25If I pretended to eat this meat, just
to live a little while longer, it would bring shame and disgrace on me and lead many young people astray. 26For the
present I might be able to escape what you could do to me,
but whether I live or die, I cannot escape Almighty God. 27If
I die bravely now, it will show that I deserved my long life.
28It will also set a good example of the way young people
should be willing and glad to die for our sacred and respected laws."

As soon as he said these things, he went[a] off to be tortured,

[a] went; *some manuscripts have* was dragged.

NEW REVISED STANDARD VERSION

21 Those who were in charge of that unlawful sacrifice
took the man aside because of their long acquaintance with
him, and privately urged him to bring meat of his own providing, proper for him to use, and to pretend that he was eating the flesh of the sacrificial meal that had been commanded by the king, 22so that by doing this he might be saved
from death, and be treated kindly on account of his old
friendship with them. 23But making a high resolve, worthy
of his years and the dignity of his old age and the gray hairs
that he had reached with distinction and his excellent life
even from childhood, and moreover according to the holy
God-given law, he declared himself quickly, telling them to
send him to Hades.

24 "Such pretense is not worthy of our time of life," he
said, "for many of the young might suppose that Eleazar in
his ninetieth year had gone over to an alien religion, 25and
through my pretense, for the sake of living a brief moment
longer, they would be led astray because of me, while I defile
and disgrace my old age. 26Even if for the present I would
avoid the punishment of mortals, yet whether I live or die I
will not escape the hands of the Almighty. 27Therefore, by
bravely giving up my life now, I will show myself worthy of
my old age 28and leave to the young a noble example of
how to die a good death willingly and nobly for the revered
and holy laws."

When he had said this, he went[a] at once to the rack.

[a] Other ancient authorities read *was dragged*

NEW AMERICAN BIBLE

of that unlawful ritual meal took the man aside privately,
because of their long acquaintance with him, and urged him
to bring meat of his own providing, such as he could legiti-
mately eat, and to pretend to be eating some of the meat of
the sacrifice prescribed by the king; 22in this way he would
escape the death penalty, and be treated kindly because of
their old friendship with him. 23But he made up his mind
in a noble manner, worthy of his years, the dignity of his
advanced age, the merited distinction of his gray hair, and
of the admirable life he had lived from childhood; and so he
declared that above all he would be loyal to the holy laws
given by God.

He told them to send him at once to the abode of the dead,
explaining: 24"At our age it would be unbecoming to make
such a pretense; many young men would think the ninety-
year-old Eleazar had gone over to an alien religion.
25Should I thus dissimulate for the sake of a brief moment of
life, they would be led astray by me, while I would bring
shame and dishonor on my old age. 26Even if, for the time
being, I avoid the punishment of men, I shall never, whether
alive or dead, escape the hands of the Almighty. 27There-
fore, by manfully giving up my life now, I will prove myself
worthy of my old age, 28and I will leave to the young a
noble example of how to die willingly and generously for the
revered and holy laws."

He spoke thus, and went immediately to the instrument of

NEW JERUSALEM BIBLE

people supervising the ritual meal, forbidden by the Law,
because of the length of time for which they had known him,
took him aside and privately urged him to have meat
brought of a kind he could properly use, prepared by himself,
and only pretend to eat the portions of sacrificial meat as
prescribed by the king; 22this action would enable him to
escape death, by availing himself of an act of kindness
prompted by their long friendship. 23But having taken a
noble decision worthy of his years and the dignity of his
great age and the well-earned distinction of his grey hairs,
worthy too of his impeccable conduct from boyhood, and
above all of the holy legislation established by God himself,
he answered accordingly, telling them to send him at once to
Hades. 24'Pretence', he said, 'does not befit our time of life;
many young people would suppose that Eleazar at the age of
ninety had conformed to the foreigners' way of life 25and,
because I had played this part for the sake of a paltry brief
spell of life, might themselves be led astray on my account; I
should only bring defilement and disgrace on my old age.
26Even though for the moment I avoid execution by man, I
can never, living or dead, elude the grasp of the Almighty.
27Therefore if I am man enough to quit this life here and
now, I shall prove myself worthy of my old age, 28and I
shall have left the young a noble example of how to make a
good death, eagerly and generously, for the venerable and
holy laws.'

So saying, he walked straight to the wheel, 29while those

GREEK OLD TESTAMENT

αὐτὸν τὴν μικρῷ πρότερον εὐμένειαν εἰς δυσμένειαν μετα-
βαλόντων διὰ τὸ τοὺς προειρημένους λόγους, ὡς αὐτοὶ διε-
λάμβανον, ἀπόνοιαν εἶναι, 30 μέλλων δὲ ταῖς πληγαῖς τελευτᾶν ἀναστενάξας εἶπεν Τῷ κυρίῳ τῷ τὴν ἁγίαν γνῶσιν
ἔχοντι φανερόν ἐστιν ὅτι δυνάμενος ἀπολυθῆναι τοῦ θανάτου σκληρὰς ὑποφέρω κατὰ τὸ σῶμα ἀλγηδόνας μαστιγού-
μενος, κατὰ ψυχὴν δὲ ἡδέως διὰ τὸν αὐτοῦ φόβον ταῦτα
πάσχω. 31 καὶ οὗτος οὖν τοῦτον τὸν τρόπον μετήλλαξεν οὐ
μόνον τοῖς νέοις, ἀλλὰ καὶ τοῖς πλείστοις τοῦ ἔθνους τὸν
ἑαυτοῦ θάνατον ὑπόδειγμα γενναιότητος καὶ μνημόσυνον
ἀρετῆς καταλιπών.

7 Συνέβη δὲ καὶ ἑπτὰ ἀδελφοὺς μετὰ τῆς μητρὸς συλλημ-
φθέντας ἀναγκάζεσθαι ὑπὸ τοῦ βασιλέως ἀπὸ τῶν
ἀθεμίτων ὑείων κρεῶν ἐφάπτεσθαι μάστιξιν καὶ νευραῖς
αἰκιζομένους. 2 εἷς δὲ αὐτῶν γενόμενος προήγορος οὕτως
ἔφη Τί μέλλεις ἐρωτᾶν καὶ μανθάνειν ἡμῶν; ἕτοιμοι γὰρ
ἀποθνῄσκειν ἐσμὲν ἢ παραβαίνειν τοὺς πατρίους νόμους.
3 ἔκθυμος δὲ γενόμενος ὁ βασιλεὺς προσέταξεν τήγανα καὶ
λέβητας ἐκπυροῦν. 4 τῶν δὲ παραχρῆμα ἐκπυρωθέντων τὸν
γενόμενον αὐτῶν προήγορον προσέταξεν γλωσσοτομεῖν καὶ
περισκυθίσαντας ἀκρωτηριάζειν τῶν λοιπῶν ἀδελφῶν καὶ
τῆς μητρὸς συνορώντων. 5 ἄχρηστον δὲ αὐτὸν τοῖς ὅλοις
γενόμενον ἐκέλευσεν τῇ πυρᾷ προσάγειν ἔμπνουν καὶ τηγα-
νίζειν. τῆς δὲ ἀτμίδος ἐφ᾿ ἱκανὸν διαδιδούσης τοῦ τηγάνου
ἀλλήλους παρεκάλουν σὺν τῇ μητρὶ γενναίως τελευτᾶν

KING JAMES VERSION

29 They that led him changing the good will they bare him a little before into hatred, because the foresaid speeches proceeded, as they thought, from a desperate mind.

30 But when he was ready to die with stripes, he groaned, and said, It is manifest unto the Lord, that hath the holy knowledge, that whereas I might have been delivered from death, I *now* endure sore pains in body by being beaten: but in soul am well content to suffer these things, because I fear him.

31 And thus this man died, leaving his death for an example of a noble courage, and a memorial of virtue, not only unto young men, but unto all his nation.

7 It came to pass also, that seven brethren with their mother were taken, and compelled by the king against the law to taste swine's flesh, and were tormented with scourges and whips.

2 But one of them that spake first said thus, What wouldest thou ask or learn of us? we are ready to die, rather than to transgress the laws of our fathers.

3 Then the king, being in a rage, commanded pans and caldrons to be made hot:

4 Which forthwith being heated, he commanded to cut out the tongue of him that spake first, and to cut off the utmost parts of his body, the rest of his brethren and his mother looking on.

5 Now when he was thus maimed in all his members, he commanded him being yet alive to be brought to the fire, and to be fried in the pan: and as the vapour of the pan was for a good space dispersed, they exhorted one another with the mother to die manfully, saying thus,

DOUAY OLD TESTAMENT

29 And they that led him, and had been a little before more mild, were changed to wrath for the words he had spoken, which they thought were uttered out of arrogancy.

30 But when he was now ready to die with the stripes, he groaned, and said: O Lord, who hast the holy knowledge, thou knowest manifestly that whereas I might be delivered from death, I suffer grevious pains in body: but in soul am well content to suffer these things because I fear thee.

31 Thus did this man die, leaving not only to young men, but also to the whole nation, the memory of his death for an example of virtue and fortitude.

7 IT came to pass also, that seven brethren, together with their mother, were apprehended, and compelled by the king to eat swine's flesh against the law, for which end they were tormented with whips and scourges.

2 But one of them, who was the eldest, said thus: What wouldst thou ask, or learn of us? we are ready to die rather than to transgress the laws of God, received from our fathers.

3 Then the king being angry commanded fryingpans, and brazen caldrons to be made hot: which forthwith being heated,

4 He commanded to cut out the tongue of him that had spoken first: and the skin of his head being drawn off, to chop off also the extremities of his hands and feet, the rest of his brethren, and his mother, looking on.

5 And when he was now maimed in all parts, he commanded him, being yet alive, to be brought to the fire, and to be fried in the fryingpan: and while he was suffering therein long torments, the rest, together with the mother, exhorted one another to die manfully,

KNOX TRANSLATION

away to his torturing; 29 his executioners were in a rage,
that but now had been gentle with him; pride, they would
have it, spoke here. 30 And this was the last sigh he uttered,
as he lay there dying under the lash, Lord, in thy holy wisdom this thou well knowest; I might have had life if I would,
yet never a cruel pang my body endures, but my soul suffers
it gladly for thy reverence. 31 Thus he died, not only to those
younger men he spoke of, but to our whole race, leaving the
pattern of a brave and honourable death.

7 Seven brothers there were, that lay under arrest, and
their mother with them; these too were tortured at the
king's command, to see if whip and thong would not make
them eat swine's flesh, for all their scruples. 2 And thus
spoke out one of them in the name of the rest: Why dost
thou put us to the question? What secret wouldst thou
learn? Of this be sure, we had rather die than break the
divine law given to our fathers. 3 The king, in a rage, would
have fire-pan heated, and caldron of bronze; heated they
were, 4 and then he passed judgement upon this same
spokesman. Tongue of him should be cut out, scalp torn off,
hands and feet mutilated, while mother and brethren stood
by to see it; 5 then, so maimed, he was for the fire; they
should roast him alive in a caldron. Long time he suffered,
and there stood the rest with their mother, each heartening

TODAY'S ENGLISH VERSION

29 and the very people who had treated him kindly a few minutes before, now turned against him, because they thought he
had spoken like a madman. 30 When they had beaten him
almost to the point of death, he groaned and said, "The Lord
possesses all holy knowledge. He knows I could have escaped
these terrible sufferings and death, yet he also knows that I
gladly suffer these things, because I fear him."
31 So Eleazar died. But his courageous death was remembered as a glorious example, not only by young people, but
by the entire nation as well.

7 On another occasion a Jewish mother and her seven
sons were arrested. The king was having them beaten to
force them to eat pork. 2 Then one of the young men said,
"What do you hope to gain by doing this? We would rather
die than abandon the traditions of our ancestors."
3 This made the king so furious that he gave orders for
huge pans and kettles to be heated red hot, 4 and it was
done immediately. Then he told his men to cut off the tongue
of the one who had spoken and to scalp him and chop off his
hands and feet, while his mother and six brothers looked on.
5 After the young man had been reduced to a helpless mass
of breathing flesh, the king gave orders for him to be carried
over and thrown into one of the pans. As a cloud of smoke
streamed up from the pan, the brothers and their mother
encouraged one another to die bravely, saying, 6 "The Lord

NEW REVISED STANDARD VERSION

29 Those who a little before had acted toward him with goodwill now changed to ill will, because the words he had
uttered were in their opinion sheer madness.[a] 30 When he
was about to die under the blows, he groaned aloud and
said: "It is clear to the Lord in his holy knowledge that,
though I might have been saved from death, I am enduring
terrible sufferings in my body under this beating, but in my
soul I am glad to suffer these things because I fear him."
31 So in this way he died, leaving in his death an example of nobility and a memorial of courage, not only to the
young but to the great body of his nation.

7 It happened also that seven brothers and their mother
were arrested and were being compelled by the king,
under torture with whips and thongs, to partake of unlawful
swine's flesh. 2 One of them, acting as their spokesman, said,
"What do you intend to ask and learn from us? For we are
ready to die rather than transgress the laws of our ancestors."
3 The king fell into a rage, and gave orders to have pans
and caldrons heated. 4 These were heated immediately, and
he commanded that the tongue of their spokesman be cut out
and that they scalp him and cut off his hands and feet, while
the rest of the brothers and the mother looked on. 5 When he
was utterly helpless, the king[b] ordered them to take him to
the fire, still breathing, and to fry him in a pan. The smoke
from the pan spread widely, but the brothers[c] and their
mother encouraged one another to die nobly, saying, 6 "The

a Meaning of Gk uncertain *b* Gk *he* *c* Gk *they*

NEW AMERICAN BIBLE

torture. 29 Those who shortly before had been kindly disposed, now became hostile toward him because what he had
said seemed to them utter madness. 30 When he was about
to die under the blows, he groaned and said: "The LORD in
his holy knowledge knows full well that, although I could
have escaped death, I am not only enduring terrible pain in
my body from this scourging, but also suffering it with joy in
my soul because of my devotion to him." 31 This is how he
died, leaving in his death a model of courage and an unfor-
gettable example of virtue not only for the young but for the
whole nation.

7 It also happened that seven brothers with their mother
were arrested and tortured with whips and scourges by
the king, to force them to eat pork in violation of God's law.
2 One of the brothers, speaking for the others, said: "What do
you expect to achieve by questioning us? We are ready to die
rather than transgress the laws of our ancestors." 3 At that
the king, in a fury, gave orders to have pans and caldrons
heated. 4 While they were being quickly heated, he commanded his executioners to cut out the tongue of the one
who had spoken for the others, to scalp him and cut off his
hands and feet, while the rest of his brothers and his mother
looked on. 5 When he was completely maimed but still
breathing, the king ordered them to carry him to the fire and
fry him. As a cloud of smoke spread from the pan, the brothers and their mother encouraged one another to die bravely,

NEW JERUSALEM BIBLE

who were escorting him, recently so well disposed towards
him, turned against him after this declaration, which they
regarded as sheer madness. 30 He for his part, just before he
died under the blows, gave a sigh and said, 'The Lord whose
knowledge is holy sees clearly that, though I might have
escaped death, from awe of him I gladly endure these agonies of body under the lash, and that in my soul I am glad to
suffer.'
31 This was how he died, leaving his death as an example
of nobility and a record of virtue not only for the young but
for the greater part of the nation.

7 It also happened that seven brothers were arrested with
their mother. The king tried to force them to taste some
pork, which the Law forbids, by torturing them with whips
and scourges. 2 One of them, acting as spokesman for the
others, said, 'What are you trying to find out from us? We
are prepared to die rather than break the laws of our ancestors.' 3 The king, in a fury, ordered pans and cauldrons to be
heated over a fire. 4 As soon as these were red-hot, he commanded that their spokesman should have his tongue cut
out, his head scalped and his extremities cut off, while the
other brothers and his mother looked on. 5 When he had
been rendered completely helpless, the king gave orders for
him to be brought, still breathing, to the fire and fried alive
in a pan. As the smoke from the pan drifted about, his mother and the rest encouraged one another to die nobly, with

GREEK OLD TESTAMENT

λέγοντες οὕτως 6 Ὁ κύριος ὁ θεὸς ἐφορᾷ καὶ ταῖς ἀληθείαις
ἐφ' ἡμῖν παρακαλεῖται, καθάπερ διὰ τῆς κατὰ πρόσωπον
ἀντιμαρτυρούσης ᾠδῆς διεσάφησεν Μωυσῆς λέγων Καὶ ἐπὶ
τοῖς δούλοις αὐτοῦ παρακληθήσεται.
7 Μεταλλάξαντος δὲ τοῦ πρώτου τὸν τρόπον τοῦτον τὸν
δεύτερον ἦγον ἐπὶ τὸν ἐμπαιγμὸν καὶ τὸ τῆς κεφαλῆς δέρμα
σὺν ταῖς θριξὶν περισύραντες ἐπηρώτων Εἰ φάγεσαι πρὸ τοῦ
τιμωρηθῆναι τὸ σῶμα κατὰ μέλος; 8 ὁ δὲ ἀποκριθεὶς τῇ
πατρίῳ φωνῇ προσεῖπεν Οὐχί. διόπερ καὶ οὗτος τὴν ἑξῆς
ἔλαβεν βάσανον ὡς ὁ πρῶτος. 9 ἐν ἐσχάτῃ δὲ πνοῇ γενόμενος εἶπεν Σὺ μέν, ἀλάστωρ, ἐκ τοῦ παρόντος ἡμᾶς ζῆν
ἀπολύεις, ὁ δὲ τοῦ κόσμου βασιλεὺς ἀποθανόντας ἡμᾶς ὑπὲρ
τῶν αὐτοῦ νόμων εἰς αἰώνιον ἀναβίωσιν ζωῆς ἡμᾶς ἀνα-
στήσει.
10 Μετὰ δὲ τοῦτον ὁ τρίτος ἐνεπαίζετο καὶ τὴν γλῶσσαν
αἰτηθεὶς ταχέως προέβαλεν καὶ τὰς χεῖρας εὐθαρσῶς προέ-
τεινεν 11 καὶ γενναίως εἶπεν Ἐξ οὐρανοῦ ταῦτα κέκτημαι
καὶ διὰ τοὺς αὐτοῦ νόμους ὑπερορῶ ταῦτα καὶ παρ' αὐτοῦ
ταῦτα πάλιν ἐλπίζω κομίσασθαι· 12 ὥστε αὐτὸν τὸν βασιλέα
καὶ τοὺς σὺν αὐτῷ ἐκπλήσσεσθαι τὴν τοῦ νεανίσκου ψυχήν,
ὡς ἐν οὐδενὶ τὰς ἀλγηδόνας ἐτίθετο.
13 Καὶ τούτου δὲ μεταλλάξαντος τὸν τέταρτον ὡσαύτως
ἐβασάνιζον αἰκιζόμενοι. 14 καὶ γενόμενος πρὸς τὸ τελευτᾶν
οὕτως ἔφη Αἱρετὸν μεταλλάσσοντας ὑπ' ἀνθρώπων τὰς ὑπὸ
τοῦ θεοῦ προσδοκᾶν ἐλπίδας πάλιν ἀναστήσεσθαι ὑπ' αὐτοῦ·
σοὶ μὲν γὰρ ἀνάστασις εἰς ζωὴν οὐκ ἔσται.

KING JAMES VERSION

6 The Lord God looketh upon us, and in truth hath comfort in us, as Moses in his song, which witnessed to their faces, declared, saying, And he shall be comforted in his servants.

7 So when the first was dead after this manner, they brought the second to make him a mocking stock: and when they had pulled off the skin of his head with the hair, they asked him, Wilt thou eat, before thou be punished throughout every member of thy body?

8 But he answered in his own language, and said, No. Wherefore he also received the next torment in order, as the former did.

9 And when he was at the last gasp, he said, Thou like a fury takest us out of this present life, but the King of the world shall raise us up, who have died for his laws, unto everlasting life.

10 After him was the third made a mocking stock: and when he was required, he put out his tongue, and that right soon, holding forth his hands manfully,

11 And said courageously, These I had from heaven; and for his laws I despise them; and from him I hope to receive them again.

12 Insomuch that the king, and they that were with him, marvelled at the young man's courage, for that he nothing regarded the pains.

13 Now when this man was dead also, they tormented and mangled the fourth in like manner.

14 So when he was ready to die he said thus, It is good, being put to death by men, to look for hope from God to be raised up again by him: as for thee, thou shalt have no resurrection to life.

DOUAY OLD TESTAMENT

6 Saying: The Lord God will look upon the truth, and will take pleasure in us, as Moses declared in the profession of the canticle: And in his servants he will take pleasure.

7 So when the first was dead after this manner, they brought the next to make him a mocking stock: and when they had pulled off the skin of his head with the hair, they asked him if he would eat, before he were punished throughout the whole body in every limb.

8 But he answered in his own language, and said: I will not do it. Wherefore he also in the next place, received the torments of the first:

9 And when he was at the last gasp, he said thus: Thou indeed, O most wicked man, destroyest us out of this present life: but the King of the world will raise us up, who die for his laws, in the resurrection of eternal life.

10 After him the third was made a mocking stock, and when he was required, he quickly put forth his tongue, and courageously stretched out his hands:

11 And said with confidence: These I have from heaven, but for the laws of God I now despise them: because I hope to receive them again from him.

12 So that the king, and they that were with him, wondered at the young man's courage, because he esteemed the torments as nothing.

13 And after he was thus dead, they tormented the fourth in the like manner.

14 And when he was now ready to die, he spoke thus: It is better, being put to death by men, to look for hope from God, to be raised up again by him: for, as to thee thou shalt have no resurrection unto life.

KNOX TRANSLATION

other to die bravely; 6 God sees true, said they, and will not
allow us to go uncomforted. Did not Moses prophesy as
much, even in his song of remonstrance, He will comfort his
servants?[a]
7 So died the first, and now the second must make sport for
them. When the hair was torn from his head and the skin
with it, they asked, Would he eat, or must his whole body
pay for it, limb by limb? 8 And he answered in good round
Hebrew,[b] eat he would not; whereupon he, in his turn, suffered like the first. 9 Ay, miscreant, he said with his last
breath, of this present life it lies in thy power to rob us; but
he, who is ruler of the whole world, he, for whose laws we
perish, will raise us up again, and to life everlasting. 10 And
now they had their will with the third, who was no sooner
bidden than he put forth tongue and hands very courageously; 11 Heaven's gift these be, he said, and for God's law I
make light account of them, well assured he will give them
back to me. 12 Well might they marvel, king and courtiers
both, at one so young that recked so little of his sufferings.
13 Such was the manner of his passing; the fourth, too, when
with like tortures they assailed him, 14 died with these words
on his lips: Man's sentence of death, what matters it, so
there be hope in God, that shall raise up the dead? For thee,
resurrection to new life shall be none. 15 And when the fifth

a Deut. 32. 36. *b* 'In good round Hebrew', that is, in the Aramaic dialect, as if to clinch his attitude of defiance by refusing to address his persecutors in Greek.

TODAY'S ENGLISH VERSION

God is looking on and understands our suffering. Moses
made this clear when he wrote a song condemning those
who had abandoned the Lord. He said, 'The Lord will have
mercy on those who serve him.' "
7 After the first brother had died in this way, the soldiers
started amusing themselves with the second one by tearing
the hair and skin from his head. Then they asked him, "Now
will you eat this pork, or do you want us to chop off your
hands and feet one by one?"
8 He replied in his native language, "I will never eat it!" So
the soldiers tortured him, just as they had the first one, 9 but
with his dying breath he cried out to the king, "You butcher!
You may kill us, but the King of the universe will raise us
from the dead and give us eternal life, because we have
obeyed his laws."
10 The soldiers began entertaining themselves with the
third brother. When he was ordered to stick out his tongue,
he quickly did so. Then he bravely held out his hands 11 and
courageously said, "God gave these to me. But his laws
mean more to me than my hands, and I know God will give
them back to me again." 12 The king and those with him
were amazed at his courage and at his willingness to suffer.
13 After he had died, the soldiers tortured the fourth one in
the same cruel way, 14 but his final words were, "I am glad
to die at your hands, because we have the assurance that
God will raise us from death. But there will be no resurrection to life for you, Antiochus!"

NEW REVISED STANDARD VERSION

Lord God is watching over us and in truth has compassion
on us, as Moses declared in his song that bore witness
against the people to their faces, when he said, 'And he will
have compassion on his servants.' "[a]
7 After the first brother had died in this way, they brought
forward the second for their sport. They tore off the skin of
his head with the hair, and asked him, "Will you eat rather
than have your body punished limb by limb?" 8 He replied in
the language of his ancestors and said to them, "No."
Therefore he in turn underwent tortures as the first brother
had done. 9 And when he was at his last breath, he said,
"You accursed wretch, you dismiss us from this present life,
but the King of the universe will raise us up to an everlasting
renewal of life, because we have died for his laws."
10 After him, the third was the victim of their sport. When
it was demanded, he quickly put out his tongue and courageously stretched forth his hands, 11 and said nobly, "I got
these from Heaven, and because of his laws I disdain them,
and from him I hope to get them back again." 12 As a result
the king himself and those with him were astonished at the
young man's spirit, for he regarded his sufferings as nothing.
13 After he too had died, they maltreated and tortured the
fourth in the same way. 14 When he was near death, he said,
"One cannot but choose to die at the hands of mortals and to
cherish the hope God gives of being raised again by him. But
for you there will be no resurrection to life!"

a Gk *slaves*

NEW AMERICAN BIBLE

saying such words as these: 6 "The LORD God is looking on,
and he truly has compassion on us, as Moses declared in his
canticle, when he protested openly with the words, 'And he
will have pity on his servants.' "
7 When the first brother had died in this manner, they
brought the second to be made sport of. After tearing off the
skin and hair of his head, they asked him, "Will you eat the
pork rather than have your body tortured limb by limb?"
8 Answering in the language of his forefathers, he said,
"Never!" So he too in turn suffered the same tortures as the
first. 9 At the point of death he said: "You accursed fiend,
you are depriving us of this present life, but the King of the
world will raise us up to live again forever. It is for his laws
that we are dying."
10 After him the third suffered their cruel sport. He put out
his tongue at once when told to do so, and bravely held out
his hands, 11 as he spoke these noble words: "It was from
Heaven that I received these; for the sake of his laws I disdain them; from him I hope to receive them again." 12 Even
the king and his attendants marveled at the young man's
courage, because he regarded his sufferings as nothing.
13 After he had died, they tortured and maltreated the
fourth brother in the same way. 14 When he was near death,
he said, "It is my choice to die at the hands of men with the
God-given hope of being restored to life by him; but for you,
there will be no resurrection to life."

NEW JERUSALEM BIBLE

such words as these, 6 'The Lord God is watching and certainly feels sorry for us, as Moses declared in his song, which
clearly states that "he will take pity on his servants." '
7 When the first had left the world in this way, they
brought the second forward to be tortured. After stripping the
skin from his head, hair and all, they asked him, 'Will you
eat some pork, before your body is tortured limb by limb?'
8 Replying in his ancestral tongue, he said, 'No!' So he too
was put to the torture in his turn. 9 With his last breath he
exclaimed, 'Cruel brute, you may discharge us from this
present life, but the King of the world will raise us up, since
we die for his laws, to live again for ever.'
10 After him, they tortured the third, who on being asked
for his tongue promptly thrust it out and boldly held out his
hands, 11 courageously saying, 'Heaven gave me these
limbs; for the sake of his laws I have no concern for them;
from him I hope to receive them again.' 12 The king and his
attendants were astounded at the young man's courage and
his utter indifference to suffering.
13 When this one was dead they subjected the fourth to the
same torments and tortures. 14 When he neared his end he
cried, 'Ours is the better choice, to meet death at men's
hands, yet relying on God's promise that we shall be raised
up by him; whereas for you there can be no resurrection to
new life.'

GREEK OLD TESTAMENT

15 Ἐχομένως δὲ τὸν πέμπτον προσάγοντες ᾐκίζοντο. 16 ὁ
δὲ πρὸς αὐτὸν ἰδὼν εἶπεν Ἐξουσίαν ἐν ἀνθρώποις ἔχων
φθαρτὸς ὢν ὃ θέλεις ποιεῖς. μὴ δόκει δὲ τὸ γένος ἡμῶν ὑπὸ
τοῦ θεοῦ καταλελεῖφθαι· 17 σὺ δὲ καρτέρει καὶ θεώρει τὸ
μεγαλεῖον αὐτοῦ κράτος, ὡς σὲ καὶ τὸ σπέρμα σου βασανιεῖ.
18 Μετὰ δὲ τοῦτον ἦγον τὸν ἕκτον, καὶ μέλλων ἀποθνήσκειν ἔφη Μὴ πλανῶ μάτην, ἡμεῖς γὰρ δι' ἑαυτοὺς ταῦτα
πάσχομεν ἁμαρτόντες εἰς τὸν ἑαυτῶν θεόν, ἄξια θαυμασμοῦ
γέγονεν· 19 σὺ δὲ μὴ νομίσῃς ἀθῷος ἔσεσθαι θεομαχεῖν
ἐπιχειρήσας.
20 Ὑπεραγόντως δὲ ἡ μήτηρ θαυμαστὴ καὶ μνήμης ἀγαθῆς
ἀξία, ἥτις ἀπολλυμένους υἱοὺς ἑπτὰ συνορῶσα μιᾶς ὑπὸ
καιρὸν ἡμέρας εὐψύχως ἔφερεν διὰ τὰς ἐπὶ κύριον ἐλπίδας.
21 ἕκαστον δὲ αὐτῶν παρεκάλει τῇ πατρίῳ φωνῇ γενναίῳ
πεπληρωμένη φρονήματι καὶ τὸν θῆλυν λογισμὸν ἄρσενι
θυμῷ διεγείρασα λέγουσα πρὸς αὐτούς 22 Οὐκ οἶδ' ὅπως εἰς
τὴν ἐμὴν ἐφάνητε κοιλίαν, οὐδὲ ἐγὼ τὸ πνεῦμα καὶ τὴν ζωὴν
ὑμῖν ἐχαρισάμην, καὶ τὴν ἑκάστου στοιχείωσιν οὐκ ἐγὼ
διερρύθμισα· 23 τοιγαροῦν ὁ τοῦ κόσμου κτίστης ὁ πλάσας
ἀνθρώπου γένεσιν καὶ πάντων ἐξευρὼν γένεσιν καὶ τὸ πνεῦμα καὶ τὴν ζωὴν ὑμῖν πάλιν ἀποδίδωσιν μετ' ἐλέους, ὡς νῦν
ὑπεροράτε ἑαυτοὺς διὰ τοὺς αὐτοῦ νόμους.
24 Ὁ δὲ Ἀντίοχος οἰόμενος καταφρονεῖσθαι καὶ τὴν ὀνει-
δίζουσαν ὑφορώμενος φωνὴν ἔτι τοῦ νεωτέρου περιόντος οὐ

KING JAMES VERSION

15 Afterward they brought the fifth also, and mangled him.

16 Then looked he unto the king, and said, Thou hast power over men, thou art corruptible, thou doest what thou wilt; yet think not that our nation is forsaken of God;

17 But abide a while, and behold his great power, how he will torment thee and thy seed.

18 After him also they brought the sixth, who being ready to die said, Be not deceived without cause: for we suffer these things for ourselves, having sinned against our God: therefore marvellous things are done *unto us.*

19 But think not thou, that takest in hand to strive against God, that thou shalt escape unpunished.

20 But the mother was marvellous above all, and worthy of honourable memory: for when she saw her seven sons slain within the space of one day, she bare it with a good courage, because of the hope that she had in the Lord.

21 Yea, she exhorted every one of them in her own language, filled with courageous spirits; and stirring up her womanish thoughts with a manly stomach, she said unto them,

22 I cannot tell how ye came into my womb; for I neither gave you breath nor life, neither was it I that formed the members of every one of you;

23 But doubtless the Creator of the world, who formed the generation of man, and found out the beginning of all things, will also of his own mercy give you breath and life again, as ye now regard not your own selves for his laws' sake.

24 Now Antiochus, thinking himself despised, and suspecting it to be a reproachful speech, whilst the youngest

DOUAY OLD TESTAMENT

15 And when they had brought the fifth, they tormented him. But he looking upon the king,

16 Said: Whereas thou hast power among men, though thou art corruptible, thou dost what thou wilt: but think not that our nation is forsaken by God.

17 But stay patiently a while, and thou shalt see his great power, in what manner he will torment thee and thy seed.

18 After him they brought the sixth, and he being ready to die spoke thus: Be not deceived without cause: for we suffer these things for ourselves, having sinned against our God, and things worthy of admiration are done to us:

19 But do not think that thou shalt escape unpunished, for that thou hast attempted to fight against God.

20 Now the mother was to be admired above measure, and worthy to be remembered by good men, who beheld her seven sons slain in the space of one day, and bore it with a good courage, for the hope that she had in God:

21 And she bravely exhorted every one of them in her own language, being filled with wisdom: and joining a man's heart to a woman's thought,

22 She said to them: I know not how you were formed in my womb: for I neither gave you breath, nor soul, nor life, neither did I frame the limbs of every one of you.

23 But the Creator of the world, that formed the nativity of man, and that found out the origin of all, he will restore to you again in his mercy, both breath and life, as now you despise yourselves for the sake of his laws.

24 Now Antiochus, thinking himself despised, and withal despising the voice of the upbraider, when the youngest was

KNOX TRANSLATION

was put to the question, he looked Antiochus in the face,
16 thus warning him: Mortal, at thy own whim free to govern
thy fellow men, think not God has abandoned this race of
ours! 17 Wait but a little, and good proof thou shalt have of
his sovereign power, such torment thee and thine awaits.
18 So they came to the sixth, and this was his dying utterance: Never flatter thyself with vain hope; speed we amiss, it
was our own doing, that sinned against our God. 19 Strange
be his dealings with us, yet think not thou to defy God
unpunished.
20 And here was the greatest marvel of all, by honest folk
ever to be kept in mind, that the mother of seven children
should be content to lose them all in one day, for the hope
she had in God's mercy. 21 What generosity of mind was
this, that could temper her womanly feelings with a man's
thoughts! One by one, in the speech of her own country, she
put heart into them; 22 Into this womb you came, she told
them, who knows how? Not I quickened, not I the breath of
life gave you, nor fashioned the bodies of you one by one!
23 Man's birth, and the origin of all things, he devised who is
the whole world's Maker; and shall he not mercifully give the
breath of life back to you, that for his law's sake hold your
lives so cheap?
24 What should Antiochus do? Here was defiance of his
authority, here were tones of remonstrance that liked him

TODAY'S ENGLISH VERSION

15 When the soldiers took the fifth boy and began torturing
him, 16 he looked the king squarely in the eye and said, "You
have the power to do whatever you want with us, even
though you also are mortal. But do not think that God has
abandoned our people. 17 Just wait. God will use his great
power to torture you and your descendants."
18 Then the soldiers took the sixth boy, and just before he
died he said, "Make no mistake. We are suffering what we
deserve, because we have sinned against our God. That's
why all these terrible things are happening to us. 19 But
don't think for a minute that you will avoid being punished
for fighting against God."
20 The mother was the most amazing one of them all, and
she deserves a special place in our memory. Although she
saw her seven sons die in a single day, she endured it with
great courage because she trusted in the Lord. 21 She combined womanly emotion with manly courage and spoke
words of encouragement to each of her sons in their native
language. 22 "I do not know how your life began in my
womb," she would say, "I was not the one who gave you life
and breath and put together each part of your body. 23 It was
God who did it, God who created the universe, the human
race, and all that exists. He is merciful and he will give you
back life and breath again, because you love his laws more
than you love yourself."
24 Antiochus was sure that the mother was making fun of

NEW REVISED STANDARD VERSION

15 Next they brought forward the fifth and maltreated
him. 16 But he looked at the king,[a] and said, "Because you
have authority among mortals, though you also are mortal,
you do what you please. But do not think that God has forsaken our people. 17 Keep on, and see how his mighty power
will torture you and your descendants!"
18 After him they brought forward the sixth. And when he
was about to die, he said, "Do not deceive yourself in vain.
For we are suffering these things on our own account,
because of our sins against our own God. Therefore[b]
astounding things have happened. 19 But do not think that
you will go unpunished for having tried to fight against God!"
20 The mother was especially admirable and worthy of
honorable memory. Although she saw her seven sons perish
within a single day, she bore it with good courage because of
her hope in the Lord. 21 She encouraged each of them in the
language of their ancestors. Filled with a noble spirit, she
reinforced her woman's reasoning with a man's courage, and
said to them, 22 "I do not know how you came into being in
my womb. It was not I who gave you life and breath, nor I
who set in order the elements within each of you. 23 Therefore the Creator of the world, who shaped the beginning of
humankind and devised the origin of all things, will in his
mercy give life and breath back to you again, since you now
forget yourselves for the sake of his laws."
24 Antiochus felt that he was being treated with contempt, and he was suspicious of her reproachful tone. The

a Gk *at him* *b* Lat: Other ancient authorities lack *Therefore*

NEW AMERICAN BIBLE

15 They next brought forward the fifth brother and maltreated him. 16 Looking at the king, he said: "Since you have
power among men, mortal though you are, do what you
please. But do not think that our nation is forsaken by God.
17 Only wait, and you will see how his great power will torment you and your descendants."
18 After him they brought the sixth brother. When he was
about to die, he said: "Have no vain illusions. We suffer
these things on our own account, because we have sinned
against our God; that is why such astonishing things have
happened to us. 19 Do not think, then, that you will go
unpunished for having dared to fight against God."
20 Most admirable and worthy of everlasting remembrance
was the mother, who saw her seven sons perish in a single
day, yet bore it courageously because of her hope in the
LORD. 21 Filled with a noble spirit that stirred her womanly
heart with manly courage, she exhorted each of them in the
language of their forefathers with these words: 22 "I do not
know how you came into existence in my womb; it was not I
who gave you the breath of life, nor was it I who set in order
the elements of which each of you is composed. 23 Therefore,
since it is the Creator of the universe who shapes each man's
beginning, as he brings about the origin of everything, he, in
his mercy, will give you back both breath and life, because
you now disregard yourselves for the sake of his law."
24 Antiochus, suspecting insult in her words, thought he

NEW JERUSALEM BIBLE

15 Next they brought forward the fifth and began torturing
him. 16 But he looked at the king and said, 'You have power
over human beings, mortal as you are, and can act as you
please. But do not think that our race has been deserted by
God. 17 Only wait, and you will see in your turn how his
mighty power will torment you and your descendants.'
18 After him, they led out the sixth, and his dying words
were these, 'Do not delude yourself: we are suffering like this
through our own fault, having sinned against our own God;
hence, appalling things have befallen us— 19 but do not
think you yourself will go unpunished for attempting to
make war on God.'
20 But the mother was especially admirable and worthy of
honourable remembrance, for she watched the death of
seven sons in the course of a single day, and bravely
endured it because of her hopes in the Lord. 21 Indeed she
encouraged each of them in their ancestral tongue; filled
with noble conviction, she reinforced her womanly argument
with manly courage, saying to them, 22 'I do not know how
you appeared in my womb; it was not I who endowed you
with breath and life, I had not the shaping of your every
part. 23 And hence, the Creator of the world, who made
everyone and ordained the origin of all things, will in his
mercy give you back breath and life, since for the sake of his
laws you have no concern for yourselves.'
24 Antiochus thought he was being ridiculed, suspecting
insult in the tone of her voice; and as the youngest was still

GREEK OLD TESTAMENT

μόνον διὰ λόγων ἐποιεῖτο τὴν παράκλησιν, ἀλλὰ καὶ δι᾽ ὅρκων ἐπίστου ἅμα πλουτιεῖν καὶ μακαριστὸν ποιήσειν μεταθέμενον ἀπὸ τῶν πατρίων καὶ φίλον ἕξειν καὶ χρείας ἐμπιστεύσειν. 25 τοῦ δὲ νεανίου μηδαμῶς προσέχοντος προσκαλεσάμενος ὁ βασιλεὺς τὴν μητέρα παρῄνει γενέσθαι τοῦ μειρακίου σύμβουλον ἐπὶ σωτηρίᾳ. 26 πολλὰ δὲ αὐτοῦ παραινέσαντος ἐπεδέξατο πείσειν τὸν υἱόν· 27 προσκύψασα δὲ αὐτῷ χλευάσασα τὸν ὠμὸν τύραννον οὕτως ἔφησεν τῇ πατρίῳ φωνῇ Υἱέ, ἐλέησόν με τὴν ἐν γαστρὶ περιενέγκασάν σε μῆνας ἐννέα καὶ θηλάσασάν σε ἔτη τρία καὶ ἐκθρέψασάν σε καὶ ἀγαγοῦσαν εἰς τὴν ἡλικίαν ταύτην καὶ τροφοφορήσασαν. 28 ἀξιῶ σε, τέκνον, ἀναβλέψαντα εἰς τὸν οὐρανὸν καὶ τὴν γῆν καὶ τὰ ἐν αὐτοῖς πάντα ἰδόντα γνῶναι ὅτι οὐκ ἐξ ὄντων ἐποίησεν αὐτὰ ὁ θεός, καὶ τὸ τῶν ἀνθρώπων γένος οὕτω γίνεται. 29 μὴ φοβηθῇς τὸν δήμιον τοῦτον, ἀλλὰ τῶν ἀδελφῶν ἄξιος γενόμενος ἐπίδεξαι τὸν θάνατον, ἵνα ἐν τῷ ἐλέει σὺν τοῖς ἀδελφοῖς σου κομίσωμαί σε.

30 Ἔτι δὲ ταύτης καταληγούσης ὁ νεανίας εἶπεν Τίνα μένετε; οὐχ ὑπακούω τοῦ προστάγματος τοῦ βασιλέως, τοῦ δὲ προστάγματος ἀκούω τοῦ νόμου τοῦ δοθέντος τοῖς πατράσιν ἡμῶν διὰ Μωυσέως. 31 σὺ δὲ πάσης κακίας εὑρετὴς γενόμενος εἰς τοὺς Εβραίους οὐ μὴ διαφύγῃς τὰς χεῖρας τοῦ θεοῦ. 32 ἡμεῖς γὰρ διὰ τὰς ἑαυτῶν ἁμαρτίας πάσχομεν.

KING JAMES VERSION

was yet alive, did not only exhort him by words, but also assured him with oaths, that he would make him both a rich and a happy man, if he would turn from the laws of his fathers; and that also he would take him for his friend, and trust him with affairs.

25 But when the young man would in no case hearken unto him, the king called his mother, and exhorted her that she would counsel the young man to save his life.

26 And when he had exhorted her with many words, she promised him that she would counsel her son.

27 But she bowing herself toward him, laughing the cruel tyrant to scorn, spake in her country language on this manner; O my son, have pity upon me that bare thee nine months in my womb, and gave thee suck three years, and nourished thee, and brought thee up unto this age, and endured the troubles of education.

28 I beseech thee, my son, look upon the heaven and the earth, and all that is therein, and consider that God made them of things that were not; and so was mankind made likewise.

29 Fear not this tormentor, but, being worthy of thy brethren, take thy death, that I may receive thee again in mercy with thy brethren.

30 Whiles she was yet speaking these words, the young man said, Whom wait ye for? I will not obey the king's commandment: but I will obey the commandment of the law that was given unto our fathers by Moses.

31 And thou, that hast been the author of all mischief against the Hebrews, shalt not escape the hands of God.

32 For we suffer because of our sins.

DOUAY OLD TESTAMENT

yet alive, did not only exhort him by words, but also assured him with an oath, that he would make him a rich and a happy man, and, if he would turn from the laws of his fathers, would take him for a friend, and furnish him with things necessary.

25 But when the young man was not moved with these things, the king called the mother, and counselled her to deal with the young man to save his life.

26 And when he had exhorted her with many words, she promised that she would counsel her son.

27 So bending herself towards him, mocking the cruel tyrant, she said in her own language: My son, have pity upon me, that bore thee nine months in my womb, and gave thee suck three years, and nourished thee, and brought thee up unto this age.

28 I beseech *thee,* my son, look upon heaven and earth, and all that is in them: and consider that God made them out of nothing, and mankind also:

29 So thou shalt not fear this tormentor, but being made a worthy partner with thy brethren, receive death, that in that mercy I may receive thee again with thy brethren.

30 While she was yet speaking these words, the young man said: For whom do you stay? I will not obey the commandment of the king, but the commandment of the law, which was given us by Moses.

31 But thou that hast been the author of all mischief against the Hebrews, shalt not escape the hand of God.

32 For we suffer thus for our sins.

KNOX TRANSLATION

little. The youngest son lived yet; for him, what encouragement, what royal assurances of wealth and happiness! Would he but leave the law of his fathers, he should be the king's friend, and have weighty matters entrusted to him. 25 But yield the boy would not; till at last the king beckoned the mother apart; mother of son should be the saviour yet. 26 Much ado he had to win her, but she agreed at last, counsel her son she would. 27 And a fine trick she played on the bloodthirsty tyrant, leaning over her son and counselling him in her own native speech, to this effect: Nine months in the womb I bore thee, three years at the breast fed thee, reared thee to be what thou art; and now, my son, this boon grant me. 28 Look round at heaven and earth and all they contain; bethink thee that all this, and mankind too, God made out of nothing. 29 Of this butcher have thou no fear; claim rightful share among thy brethren in yonder inheritance of death; so shall the divine mercy give me back all my sons at once.

30 Before ever she had finished speaking, the boy cried out, What dallying is this? To the king's law I own no allegiance; rule I live by is the law we had through Moses. 31 Archenemy of the Jewish race, thinkest thou to escape from God's hand? 32 Grievously if we suffer, grievously we have sinned;

TODAY'S ENGLISH VERSION

him, so he did his best to convince her youngest son to abandon the traditions of his ancestors. He promised not only to make the boy rich and famous, but to place him in a position of authority and to give him the title "Friend of the King." 25 But the boy paid no attention to him, so Antiochus tried to persuade the boy's mother to talk him into saving his life, 26 and after much persuasion she agreed to do so. 27 Leaning over her son, she fooled the cruel tyrant by saying in her native language, "My son, have pity on me. Remember that I carried you in my womb for nine months and nursed you for three years. I have taken care of you and looked after all your needs up to the present day. 28 So I urge you, my child, to look at the sky and the earth. Consider everything you see there, and realize that God made it all from nothing, just as he made the human race. 29 Don't be afraid of this butcher. Give up your life willingly and prove yourself worthy of your brothers, so that by God's mercy I may receive you back with them at the resurrection."

30 Before she could finish speaking, the boy said, "King Antiochus, what are you waiting for? I refuse to obey your orders. I only obey the commands in the Law which Moses gave to our ancestors. 31 You have thought up all kinds of cruel things to do to our people, but you won't escape the punishment that God has in store for you. 32-33 It is true that our living Lord is angry with us and is making us suffer

NEW REVISED STANDARD VERSION

youngest brother being still alive, Antiochus[a] not only appealed to him in words, but promised with oaths that he would make him rich and enviable if he would turn from the ways of his ancestors, and that he would take him for his Friend and entrust him with public affairs. 25 Since the young man would not listen to him at all, the king called the mother to him and urged her to advise the youth to save himself. 26 After much urging on his part, she undertook to persuade her son. 27 But, leaning close to him, she spoke in their native language as follows, deriding the cruel tyrant: "My son, have pity on me. I carried you nine months in my womb, and nursed you for three years, and have reared you and brought you up to this point in your life, and have taken care of you.[b] 28 I beg you, my child, to look at the heaven and the earth and see everything that is in them, and recognize that God did not make them out of things that existed.[c] And in the same way the human race came into being. 29 Do not fear this butcher, but prove worthy of your brothers. Accept death, so that in God's mercy I may get you back again along with your brothers."

30 While she was still speaking, the young man said, "What are you[d] waiting for? I will not obey the king's command, but I obey the command of the law that was given to our ancestors through Moses. 31 But you,[e] who have contrived all sorts of evil against the Hebrews, will certainly not escape the hands of God. 32 For we are suffering because of

a Gk *he* *b* Or *have borne the burden of your education* *c* Or *God made them out of things that did not exist* *d* The Gk here for *you* is plural *e* The Gk here for *you* is singular

NEW AMERICAN BIBLE

was being ridiculed. As the youngest brother was still alive, the king appealed to him, not with mere words, but with promises on oath, to make him rich and happy if he would abandon his ancestral customs: he would make him his Friend and entrust him with high office. 25 When the youth paid no attention to him at all, the king appealed to the mother, urging her to advise her boy to save his life. 26 After he had urged her for a long time, she went through the motions of persuading her son. 27 In derision of the cruel tyrant, she leaned over close to her son and said in their native language: "Son, have pity on me, who carried you in my womb for nine months, nursed you for three years, brought you up, educated and supported you to your present age. 28 I beg you, child, to look at the heavens and the earth and see all that is in them; then you will know that God did not make them out of existing things; and in the same way the human race came into existence. 29 Do not be afraid of this executioner, but be worthy of your brothers and accept death, so that in the time of mercy I may receive you again with them."

30 She had scarcely finished speaking when the youth said: "What are you waiting for? I will not obey the king's command. I obey the command of the law given to our forefathers through Moses. 31 But you, who have contrived every kind of affliction for the Hebrews, will not escape the hands of God. 32 We, indeed, are suffering because of our sins.

NEW JERUSALEM BIBLE

alive he appealed to him not with mere words but with promises on oath to make him both rich and happy if he would abandon the traditions of his ancestors; he would make him his Friend and entrust him with public office. 25 The young man took no notice at all, and so the king then appealed to the mother, urging her to advise the youth to save his life. 26 After a great deal of urging on his part she agreed to try persuasion on her son. 27 Bending over him, she fooled the cruel tyrant with these words, uttered in their ancestral tongue, 'My son, have pity on me; I carried you nine months in my womb and suckled you three years, fed you and reared you to the age you are now, and provided for you. 28 I implore you, my child, look at the earth and sky and everything in them, and consider how God made them out of what did not exist, and that human beings come into being in the same way. 29 Do not fear this executioner, but prove yourself worthy of your brothers and accept death, so that I may receive you back with them in the day of mercy.'

30 She had hardly finished, when the young man said, 'What are you all waiting for? I will not comply with the king's ordinance; I obey the ordinance of the Law given to our ancestors through Moses. 31 As for you, who have contrived every kind of evil against the Hebrews, you will certainly not escape the hands of God. 32 We are suffering for

GREEK OLD TESTAMENT

33 εἰ δὲ χάριν ἐπιπλήξεως καὶ παιδείας ὁ ζῶν κύριος ἡμῶν
βραχέως ἐπώργισται, καὶ πάλιν καταλλαγήσεται τοῖς ἑαυτοῦ δούλοις. 34 σὺ δέ, ὦ ἀνόσιε καὶ πάντων ἀνθρώπων μιαρώτατε, μὴ μάτην μετεωρίζου φρυαττόμενος ἀδήλοις ἐλπίσιν
ἐπὶ τοὺς οὐρανίους παῖδας ἐπαιρόμενος χεῖρα· 35 οὔπω γὰρ
τὴν τοῦ παντοκράτορος ἐπόπτου θεοῦ κρίσιν ἐκπέφευγας.
36 οἱ μὲν γὰρ νῦν ἡμέτεροι ἀδελφοὶ βραχὺν ὑπενέγκαντες
πόνον ἀενάου ζωῆς ὑπὸ διαθήκην θεοῦ πεπτώκασιν· σὺ δὲ τῇ
τοῦ θεοῦ κρίσει δίκαια τὰ πρόστιμα τῆς ὑπερηφανίας ἀποί-
σῃ. 37 ἐγὼ δέ, καθάπερ οἱ ἀδελφοί, καὶ σῶμα καὶ ψυχὴν
προδίδωμι περὶ τῶν πατρίων νόμων ἐπικαλούμενος τὸν θεὸν
ἵλεως ταχὺ τῷ ἔθνει γενέσθαι καὶ σὲ μετὰ ἐτασμῶν καὶ
μαστίγων ἐξομολογήσασθαι διότι μόνος αὐτὸς θεός ἐστιν,
38 ἐν ἐμοὶ δὲ καὶ τοῖς ἀδελφοῖς μου στῆσαι τὴν τοῦ παντοκράτορος ὀργὴν τὴν ἐπὶ τὸ σύμπαν ἡμῶν γένος δικαίως
ἐπηγμένην.

39 Ἔκθυμος δὲ γενόμενος ὁ βασιλεὺς τούτῳ παρὰ τοὺς
ἄλλους χειρίστως ἀπήντησεν πικρῶς φέρων ἐπὶ τῷ μυκτηρι-
σμῷ. 40 καὶ οὗτος οὖν καθαρὸς μετήλλαξεν παντελῶς ἐπὶ τῷ
κυρίῳ πεποιθώς.

41 Ἐσχάτη δὲ τῶν υἱῶν ἡ μήτηρ ἐτελεύτησεν.

42 Τὰ μὲν οὖν περὶ τοὺς σπλαγχνισμοὺς καὶ τὰς ὑπερ-
βαλλούσας αἰκίας ἐπὶ τοσοῦτον δεδηλώσθω.

8 Ιουδας δὲ ὁ καὶ Μακκαβαῖος καὶ οἱ σὺν αὐτῷ παρεισ-
πορευόμενοι λεληθότως εἰς τὰς κώμας προσεκαλοῦντο

KING JAMES VERSION

33 And though the living Lord be angry with us a little while for our chastening and correction, yet shall he be at one again with his servants.

34 But thou, O godless man, and of all other most wicked, be not lifted up without a cause, nor puffed up with uncertain hopes, lifting up thy hand against the servants of God:

35 For thou hast not yet escaped the judgment of Almighty God, who seeth all things.

36 For our brethren, who now have suffered a short pain, are dead under God's covenant of everlasting life: but thou, through the judgment of God, shalt receive just punishment for thy pride.

37 But I, as my brethren, offer up my body and life for the laws of our fathers, beseeching God that he would speedily be merciful unto our nation; and that thou by torments and plagues mayest confess, that he alone is God;

38 And that in me and my brethren the wrath of the Almighty, which is justly brought upon all our nation, may cease.

39 Than the king, being in a rage, handled him worse than all the rest, and took it grievously that he was mocked.

40 So this man died undefiled, and put his whole trust in the Lord.

41 Last of all after the sons the mother died.

42 Let this be enough now to have spoken concerning the idolatrous feasts, and the extreme tortures.

8 Then Judas Maccabeus, and they that were with him, went privily into the towns, and called their kinsfolks

DOUAY OLD TESTAMENT

33 And though the Lord our God is angry with us a little while for our chastisement and correction: yet he will be reconciled again to his servants.

34 But thou, O wicked and of all men most flagitious, be not lifted up without cause with vain hopes, whilst thou art raging against his servants.

35 For thou hast not yet escaped the judgment of the almighty God, who beholdeth all things.

36 For my brethren, having now undergone a short pain, are under the covenant of eternal life: but thou by the judgment of God shalt receive just punishment for thy pride.

37 But I, like my brethren, offer up my life and my body for the laws of our fathers: calling upon God to be speedily merciful to our nation, and that thou by torments and stripes mayst confess that he alone is God.

38 But in me and in my brethren the wrath of the Almighty, which hath justly been brought upon all our nation, shall cease.

39 Then the king being incensed with anger, raged against him more cruelly than all the rest, taking it grievously that he was mocked.

40 So this man also died undefiled, wholly trusting in the Lord.

41 And last of all after the sons the mother also was consumed.

42 But now there is enough said of the sacrifices, and of the excessive cruelties.

8 BUT Judas Machabeus, and they that were with him, went privately into the towns: and calling together their

KNOX TRANSLATION

33 chides he for a little, the Lord our God, he does but school,
does but correct us; to us, his worshippers, he will be reconciled again. 34 But thou, miserable wretch, viler on earth is
none, wouldst thou vent thy rage on those worshippers of
his, and flatter thyself with vain hopes none the less?
35 Trust me, thou shalt yet abide his judgement, who is God
almighty and all-seeing. 36 Brief pains, that under his warrant have seised my brethren of eternal life! And shalt not
thou, by his sentence, pay the deserved penalty of thy pride?
37 As my brethren, so I for our country's laws both soul and
body forfeit; my prayer is, God will early relent towards this
nation, while thou dost learn, under the lash of his torments,
that he alone is God. 38 And may the divine anger, that has
justly fallen on our race, with me and these others be laid to
rest!

39 No wonder if this last, that so baffled the king's rage,
was more barbarously used than all the others; 40 yet kept
he ever his confidence in the Lord, and made a clean end of
it. 41 And at length, when all her sons were gone, it was the
mother's turn to die.

42 Enough! Of idolatrous sacrifice and inhuman cruelty you
shall hear no more.

8 Now turn we to Judas Machabaeus and his company.
Secretly they made entry into the villages, whence they
summoned both kinsman and friend of theirs; ay, and rallied

TODAY'S ENGLISH VERSION

because of our sins, in order to correct and discipline us. But
this will last only a short while, for we are still his servants,
and he will forgive us. 34 But you are the cruelest and most
disgusting thing that ever lived. So don't fool yourself with
illusions of greatness while you punish God's people.
35 There is no way for you to escape punishment at the hands
of the almighty and all-seeing God. 36 My brothers suffered
briefly because of our faithfulness to God's covenant, but
now they have entered eternal life.[a] But you will fall under
God's judgment and be punished as you deserve for your
arrogance. 37 I now give up my body and my life for the laws
of our ancestors, just as my brothers did. But I also beg God
to show mercy to his people quickly and to torture you until
you are forced to acknowledge that he alone is God. 38 May
my brothers and I be the last to suffer the anger of Almighty
God, which he has justly brought upon our entire nation."
39 These words of ridicule made Antiochus so furious that
he had the boy tortured even more cruelly than his brothers.
40 And so the boy died, with absolute trust in the Lord, never
unfaithful for a minute.
41 Last of all, the mother was put to death.
42 But I have said enough about the Jews being tortured
and being forced to eat the intestines of sacrificial animals.

8 Judas Maccabeus and his friends went secretly from village to village until they had gathered a force of about

[a] briefly . . . life; *or* briefly, but now they have entered eternal life because of our covenant with God.

NEW REVISED STANDARD VERSION

our own sins. 33 And if our living Lord is angry for a little
while, to rebuke and discipline us, he will again be reconciled with his own servants.[a] 34 But you, unholy wretch, you
most defiled of all mortals, do not be elated in vain and
puffed up by uncertain hopes, when you raise your hand
against the children of heaven. 35 You have not yet escaped
the judgment of the almighty, all-seeing God. 36 For our
brothers after enduring a brief suffering have drunk[b] of ever-
flowing life, under God's covenant; but you, by the judgment
of God, will receive just punishment for your arrogance. 37 I,
like my brothers, give up body and life for the laws of our
ancestors, appealing to God to show mercy soon to our
nation and by trials and plagues to make you confess that he
alone is God, 38 and through me and my brothers to bring to
an end the wrath of the Almighty that has justly fallen on
our whole nation."
39 The king fell into a rage, and handled him worse than
the others, being exasperated at his scorn. 40 So he died in
his integrity, putting his whole trust in the Lord.
41 Last of all, the mother died, after her sons.
42 Let this be enough, then, about the eating of sacrifices
and the extreme tortures.

8 Meanwhile Judas, who was also called Maccabeus, and
his companions secretly entered the villages and summoned their kindred and enlisted those who had continued

a Gk *slaves* *b* Cn: Gk *fallen*

NEW AMERICAN BIBLE

33 Though our living LORD treats us harshly for a little while
to correct us with chastisements, he will again be reconciled
with his servants. 34 But you, wretch, vilest of all men! do
not, in your insolence, concern yourself with unfounded
hopes, as you raise your hand against the children of
Heaven. 35 You have not yet escaped the judgment of the
almighty and all-seeing God. 36 My brothers, after enduring
brief pain, have drunk of never-failing life, under God's covenant, but you, by the judgment of God, shall receive just
punishments for your arrogance. 37 Like my brothers, I offer
up my body and my life for our ancestral laws, imploring
God to show mercy soon to our nation, and by afflictions
and blows to make you confess that he alone is God.
38 Through me and my brothers, may there be an end to the
wrath of the Almighty that has justly fallen on our whole
nation." 39 At that, the king became enraged and treated him
even worse than the others, since he bitterly resented the
boy's contempt. 40 Thus he too died undefiled, putting all his
trust in the LORD. 41 The mother was last to die, after her
sons.
42 Enough has been said about the sacrificial meals and the
excessive cruelties.

8 Judas Maccabeus and his companions entered the villages secretly, summoned their kinsmen, and by also

NEW JERUSALEM BIBLE

our own sins; 33 and if, to punish and discipline us, our living Lord is briefly angry with us, he will be reconciled with
us in due course. 34 But you, unholy wretch and wickedest of
villains, what cause have you for pride, nourishing vain
hopes and raising your hand against his servants?— 35 for
you have not yet escaped the judgement of God the almighty,
the all-seeing. 36 Our brothers, having endured brief pain, for
the sake of ever-flowing life have died for the covenant of
God, while you, by God's judgement, will have to pay the
just penalty for your arrogance. 37 I too, like my brothers,
surrender my body and life for the laws of my ancestors, begging God quickly to take pity on our nation, and by trials and
afflictions to bring you to confess that he alone is God, 38 so
that with my brothers and myself there may be an end to the
wrath of the Almighty, rightly let loose on our whole nation.'
39 The king fell into a rage and treated this one more cruelly than the others, for he was himself smarting from the
young man's scorn. 40 And so the last brother met his end
undefiled and with perfect trust in the Lord. 41 The mother
was the last to die, after her sons.
42 But let this be sufficient account of the ritual meals and
monstrous tortures.

8 Judas, otherwise known as Maccabaeus, and his companions made their way secretly among the villages, rallying their fellow-countrymen; they recruited those who

GREEK OLD TESTAMENT

τοὺς συγγενεῖς καὶ τοὺς μεμενηκότας ἐν τῷ Ιουδαϊσμῷ
προσλαμβανόμενοι συνήγαγον εἰς ἑξακισχιλίους. 2 καὶ ἐπεκαλοῦντο τὸν κύριον ἐπιδεῖν τὸν ὑπὸ πάντων καταπατούμενον λαόν, οἰκτῖραι δὲ καὶ τὸν ναὸν τὸν ὑπὸ τῶν ἀσεβῶν
ἀνθρώπων βεβηλωθέντα, 3 ἐλεῆσαι δὲ καὶ τὴν καταφθειρο-
μένην πόλιν καὶ μέλλουσαν ἰσόπεδον γίνεσθαι καὶ τῶν κατα-
βοώντων πρὸς αὐτὸν αἱμάτων εἰσακοῦσαι, 4 μνησθῆναι δὲ
καὶ τῆς τῶν ἀναμαρτήτων νηπίων παρανόμου ἀπωλείας καὶ
περὶ τῶν γενομένων εἰς τὸ ὄνομα αὐτοῦ βλασφημιῶν καὶ
μισοπονηρῆσαι. 5 γενόμενος δὲ ὁ Μακκαβαῖος ἐν συστέματι
ἀνυπόστατος ἤδη τοῖς ἔθνεσιν ἐγίνετο τῆς ὀργῆς τοῦ κυρίου
εἰς ἔλεον τραπείσης. 6 πόλεις δὲ καὶ κώμας ἀπροσδοκήτως
ἐρχόμενος ἐνεπίμπρα καὶ τοὺς ἐπικαίρους τόπους ἀπολαμ-
βάνων οὐκ ὀλίγους τῶν πολεμίων τροπούμενος 7 μάλιστα
τὰς νύκτας πρὸς τὰς τοιαύτας ἐπιβολὰς συνεργοὺς ἐλάμβανεν. καὶ λαλιὰ τῆς εὐανδρίας αὐτοῦ διηχεῖτο πανταχῇ.
8 Συνορῶν δὲ ὁ Φίλιππος κατὰ μικρὸν εἰς προκοπὴν ἐρχόμενον τὸν ἄνδρα, πυκνότερον δὲ ἐν ταῖς εὐημερίαις προβαί-
νοντα, πρὸς Πτολεμαῖον τὸν Κοίλης Συρίας καὶ Φοινίκης
στρατηγὸν ἔγραψεν ἐπιβοηθεῖν τοῖς τοῦ βασιλέως πράγμασιν. 9 ὁ δὲ ταχέως προχειρισάμενος Νικάνορα τὸν τοῦ
Πατρόκλου τῶν πρώτων φίλων ἀπέστειλεν ὑποτάξας παμφύ-
λων ἔθνη οὐκ ἐλάττους τῶν δισμυρίων τὸ σύμπαν τῆς Ιουδαίας ἐξᾶραι γένος. συνέστησεν δὲ αὐτῷ καὶ Γοργίαν ἄνδρα
στρατηγὸν καὶ ἐν πολεμικαῖς χρείαις πεῖραν ἔχοντα.
10 διεστήσατο δὲ ὁ Νικάνωρ τὸν φόρον τῷ βασιλεῖ τοῖς
Ῥωμαίοις ὄντα ταλάντων δισχιλίων ἐκ τῆς τῶν Ιουδαίων

KING JAMES VERSION

together, and took unto them all such as continued in the Jews' religion, and assembled about six thousand men.

2 And they called upon the Lord, that he would look upon the people that was trodden down of all; and also pity the temple profaned of ungodly men;

3 And that he would have compassion upon the city, sore defaced, and ready to be made even with the ground; and hear the blood that cried unto him,

4 And remember the wicked slaughter of harmless infants, and the blasphemies committed against his name; and that he would shew his hatred against the wicked.

5 Now when Maccabeus had his company about him, he could not be withstood by the heathen: for the wrath of the Lord was turned into mercy.

6 Therefore he came at unawares, and burnt up towns and cities, and got into his hands the most commodious places, and overcame and put to flight no small number of his enemies.

7 But specially took he advantage of the night for such privy attempts, insomuch that the fruit of his manliness was spread every where.

8 So when Philip saw that this man increased by little and little, and that things prospered with him still more and more, he wrote unto Ptolemeus, the governor of Celosyria and Phenice, to yield more aid to the king's affairs.

9 Then forthwith choosing Nicanor the *son* of Patroclus, one of his special friends, he sent him with no fewer than twenty thousand of all nations under him, to root out the whole generation of the Jews; and with him he joined also Gorgias a captain, who in matters of war had great experience.

DOUAY OLD TESTAMENT

kinsmen and friends, and taking unto them such as continued in the Jews' religion, they assembled six thousand men.

2 And they called upon the Lord that he would look upon his people that was trodden down by all, and would have pity on the temple, that was defiled by the wicked:

3 That he would have pity also upon the city that was destroyed, that was ready to be made even with the ground, and would hear the voice of the blood that cried to him:

4 That he would remember also the most unjust deaths of innocent children, and the blasphemies offered to his name, and would shew his indignation on this occasion.

5 Now when Machabeus had gathered a multitude, he could not be withstood by the heathens: for the wrath of the Lord was turned into mercy.

6 So coming unawares upon the towns and cities, he set them on fire, and taking possession of the most commodious places, he made no small slaughter of the enemies:

7 And especially in the nights he went upon these expeditions, and the fame of his valour was spread abroad every where.

8 Then Philip, seeing that the man gained ground by little and little, and that things for the most part succeeded prosperously with him, wrote to Ptolemee the governor of Celesyria and Phenicia, to send aid to the king's affairs.

9 And he with all speed sent Nicanor the son of Patroclus, one of his special friends, giving him no fewer than twenty thousand armed men of different nations, to root out the whole race of the Jews, joining also with him Gorgias, a good soldier, and of great experience in matters of war.

KNOX TRANSLATION

many more, that were yet true to the Jewish faith, till they
had mustered an army of six thousand men. 2 And ever they
besought the Lord, he would look with favour on a race
down-trodden, have pity on a temple defiled by the heathen.
3 Their city was like to be razed to the ground; would he
watch the ruin of it unmoved? Would he be deaf, while
bloodshed cried out for vengeance? 4 Cruel murders of innocent childhood, his own honour dragged in the dust, would
he not mark all this, and be roused to indignation?
5 By this, the divine anger had given place to clemency;
and to all the heathen round about Machabaeus and his
company were an infliction past bearing. 6 On village or
town of theirs he would fall suddenly, and burn it to the
ground; by seizing some point of vantage, once and again he
put their forces to the rout; 7 going about these forays at
night-time for the most part, till the fame of his valour
spread far and wide. 8 What was to be done? Here was a
man that grew ever in strength, and still his enterprises
throve. At last Philip was fain to send dispatches, calling on
Ptolemy, the governor of Coelesyria and Phoenice, to further
the king's business. 9 And he, without more ado, chose one
of his best friends, Nicanor son of Patroclus, and sent him
out to exterminate the Jewish race altogether. For which purpose, he armed full twenty thousand men, a rabble of all
nations; and Gorgias should be at Nicanor's side, a soldier
that had much experience in the wars.

Today's English Version

6,000 Jewish men who had remained faithful to their religion. 2 They begged the Lord to help his people, now trampled under foot by all nations, to take pity on the Temple, now defiled by pagans, 3 and to have mercy on Jerusalem, now destroyed and almost leveled to the ground. 4 They also asked the Lord to show his hatred of evil by taking revenge on those who were murdering his people, mercilessly slaughtering innocent children, and saying evil things against the Lord.

5 When Judas had finally organized his forces, the Gentiles were unable to stand against him, because the Lord's anger against Israel had now turned to mercy. 6-7 Judas would make sudden attacks on towns and villages and burn them. He captured strategic positions and routed many enemy troops, finding that he was most successful at night. People everywhere spoke of his bravery.

8 When Philip, governor of Jerusalem, realized that Judas was gaining ground little by little and that his victories were becoming more and more frequent, he wrote a letter to Ptolemy, governor of Greater Syria, requesting his help in defending the royal interests. 9 Ptolemy immediately appointed Nicanor son of Patroclus, who was also in the closest circle of the King's Friends, and sent him with more than 20,000 troops of various nationalities to wipe out the entire Jewish race. Ptolemy also appointed Gorgias, a general of wide military experience, to go with him. 10 King

New Revised Standard Version

in the Jewish faith, and so they gathered about six thousand. 2 They implored the Lord to look upon the people who were oppressed by all; and to have pity on the temple that had been profaned by the godless; 3 to have mercy on the city that was being destroyed and about to be leveled to the ground; to hearken to the blood that cried out to him; 4 to remember also the lawless destruction of the innocent babies and the blasphemies committed against his name; and to show his hatred of evil.

5 As soon as Maccabeus got his army organized, the Gentiles could not withstand him, for the wrath of the Lord had turned to mercy. 6 Coming without warning, he would set fire to towns and villages. He captured strategic positions and put to flight not a few of the enemy. 7 He found the nights most advantageous for such attacks. And talk of his valor spread everywhere.

8 When Philip saw that the man was gaining ground little by little, and that he was pushing ahead with more frequent successes, he wrote to Ptolemy, the governor of Coelesyria and Phoenicia, to come to the aid of the king's government. 9 Then Ptolemy[a] promptly appointed Nicanor son of Patroclus, one of the king's chief[b] Friends, and sent him, in command of no fewer than twenty thousand Gentiles of all nations, to wipe out the whole race of Judea. He associated with him Gorgias, a general and a man of experience in military

a Gk *he* *b* Gk *one of the first*

New American Bible

enlisting others who remained faithful to Judaism, assembled about six thousand men. 2 They implored the Lord to look kindly upon his people, who were being oppressed on all sides; to have pity on the temple, which was profaned by godless men; 3 to have mercy on the city, which was being destroyed and about to be leveled to the ground; to hearken to the blood that cried out to him; 4 to remember the criminal slaughter of innocent children and the blasphemies uttered against his name; and to manifest his hatred of evil. 5 Once Maccabeus got his men organized, the Gentiles could not withstand him, for the Lord's wrath had now changed to mercy. 6 Coming unexpectedly upon towns and villages, he would set them on fire. He captured strategic positions, and put to flight a large number of the enemy. 7 He preferred the nights as being especially helpful for such attacks. Soon the fame of his valor spread everywhere.

8 When Philip saw that Judas was gaining ground little by little and that his successful advances were becoming more frequent, he wrote to Ptolemy, governor of Coelesyria and Phoenicia, to come to the aid of the king's government. 9 Ptolemy promptly selected Nicanor, son of Patroclus, one of the Chief Friends, and sent him at the head of at least twenty thousand armed men of various nations to wipe out the entire Jewish race. With him he associated Gorgias, a professional military commander, well-versed in the art of war.

New Jerusalem Bible

remained loyal to Judaism and assembled about six thousand. 2 They called on the Lord to have regard for the people oppressed on all sides, to take pity on the Temple profaned by the godless, 3 to have mercy on the city now being destroyed and levelled to the ground, to hear the blood of the victims that cried aloud to him, 4 to remember too the criminal slaughter of innocent babies and to avenge the blasphemies perpetrated against his name. 5 As soon as Maccabaeus had an organised force, he at once proved invincible to the foreigners, the Lord's anger having turned into compassion. 6 Making surprise attacks on towns and villages, he fired them; he captured favourable positions and inflicted very heavy losses on the enemy, 7 generally availing himself of the cover of night for such enterprises. The fame of his valour spread far and wide.

8[a] When Philip saw Judas was making steady progress and winning more and more frequent successes, he wrote to Ptolemy, the general officer commanding Coele-Syria and Phoenicia, asking for reinforcements in the royal interest. 9 Ptolemy chose Nicanor son of Patroclus, one of the king's First Friends, and sent him without delay at the head of an international force of at least twenty thousand men to exterminate the entire Jewish race. As his associate he appointed Gorgias, a professional general of wide military experience.

a **8** 8:8seq. // 1 M 3:38—4:25.

GREEK OLD TESTAMENT

αἰχμαλωσίας ἐκπληρώσειν. [11] εὐθέως δὲ εἰς τὰς παραθαλασσίους πόλεις ἀπέστειλεν προκαλούμενος ἐπ᾽ ἀγορασμὸν Ιουδαίων σωμάτων ὑπισχνούμενος ἐνενήκοντα σώματα ταλάντου παραχωρήσειν οὐ προσδεχόμενος τὴν παρὰ τοῦ παντοκράτορος μέλλουσαν παρακολουθήσειν ἐπ᾽ αὐτῷ δίκην. [12] τῷ δὲ Ιουδα προσέπεσεν περὶ τῆς τοῦ Νικάνορος ἐφόδου, καὶ μεταδόντος τοῖς σὺν αὐτῷ τὴν παρουσίαν τοῦ στρατοπέδου [13] οἱ δειλανδροῦντες καὶ ἀπιστοῦντες τὴν τοῦ θεοῦ δίκην διεδίδρασκον ἑαυτοὺς καὶ ἐξετόπιζον. [14] οἱ δὲ τὰ περιλελειμμένα πάντα ἐπώλουν, ὁμοῦ δὲ τὸν κύριον ἠξίουν ῥύσασθαι τοὺς ὑπὸ τοῦ δυσσεβοῦς Νικάνορος πρὶν συντυχεῖν πεπραμένους. [15] καὶ εἰ μὴ δι᾽ αὐτούς, ἀλλὰ διὰ τὰς πρὸς τοὺς πατέρας αὐτῶν διαθήκας καὶ ἕνεκα τῆς ἐπ᾽ αὐτοὺς ἐπικλήσεως τοῦ σεμνοῦ καὶ μεγαλοπρεποῦς ὀνόματος αὐτοῦ. [16] συναγαγὼν δὲ ὁ Μακκαβαῖος τοὺς περὶ αὐτὸν ὄντας ἀριθμὸν ἑξακισχιλίους παρεκάλει μὴ καταπλαγῆναι τοῖς πολεμίοις μηδὲ εὐλαβεῖσθαι τὴν τῶν ἀδίκως παραγινομένων ἐπ᾽ αὐτοὺς ἐθνῶν πολυπλήθειαν, ἀγωνίσασθαι δὲ γενναίως [17] πρὸ ὀφθαλμῶν λαβόντας τὴν ἀνόμως εἰς τὸν ἅγιον τόπον συντετελεσμένην ὑπ᾽ αὐτῶν ὕβριν καὶ τὸν τῆς ἐμπεπαιγμένης πόλεως αἰκισμόν, ἔτι δὲ τὴν τῆς προγονικῆς πολιτείας κατάλυσιν. [18] οἱ μὲν γὰρ ὅπλοις πεποίθασιν ἅμα καὶ τόλμαις, ἔφησεν, ἡμεῖς δὲ ἐπὶ τῷ παντοκράτορι θεῷ, δυναμένῳ καὶ

KING JAMES VERSION

10 So Nicanor undertook to make so much money of the captive Jews, as should defray the tribute of two thousand talents, which the king was to pay to the Romans.

11 Wherefore immediately he sent to the cities upon the sea coast, proclaiming a sale of the captive Jews, and promising that they should have fourscore and ten bodies for one talent, not expecting the vengeance that was to follow upon him from the Almighty God.

12 Now when word was brought unto Judas of Nicanor's coming, and he had imparted unto those that were with him that the army was at hand,

13 They that were fearful, and distrusted the justice of God, fled, and conveyed themselves away.

14 Others sold all that they had left, and withal besought the Lord to deliver them, being sold by the wicked Nicanor before they met together:

15 And if not for their own sakes, yet for the covenants he had made with their fathers, and for his holy and glorious name's sake, by which they were called.

16 So Maccabeus called his men together unto the number of six thousand, and exhorted them not to be stricken with terror of the enemy, nor to fear the great multitude of the heathen, who came wrongfully against them; but to fight manfully,

17 And to set before their eyes the injury that they had unjustly done to the holy place, and the cruel handling of the city, whereof they made a mockery, and also the taking away of the government of their forefathers:

18 For they, said he, trust in their weapons and boldness; but our confidence is in the Almighty God, who at a beck can

DOUAY OLD TESTAMENT

10 And Nicanor purposed to raise for the king the tribute of two thousand talents, that was to be given to the Romans, by making so much money of the captive Jews:

11 Wherefore he sent immediately to the cities upon the sea coast, to invite men together to buy up the Jewish slaves, promising that they should have ninety slaves for one talent, not reflecting on the vengeance, which was to follow him from the Almighty.

12 Now when Judas found that Nicanor was coming, he imparted to the Jews that were with him, that the enemy was at hand.

13 And some of them being afraid, and distrusting the justice of God, fled away:

14 Others sold all that they had left, and withal besought the Lord, that he would deliver them from the wicked Nicanor, who had sold them before he came near them:

15 And if not for their sakes, yet for the covenant that he had made with their fathers, and for the sake of his holy and glorious name that was invoked upon them.

16 But Machabeus calling together seven thousand that were with him, exhorted them not to be reconciled to the enemies, nor to fear the multitude of the enemies who came wrongfully against them, but to fight manfully:

17 Setting before their eyes the injury they had unjustly done the holy place, and also the injury they had done to the city, which had been shamefully abused, besides their destroying the ordinances of the fathers.

18 For, said he, they trust in their weapons, and in their boldness: but we trust in the Almighty Lord, who at a beck

KNOX TRANSLATION

[10] Nicanor's purpose it was, to sell the Jewish people for slaves, and thereby reimburse the king for a tribute of two thousand talents he must needs pay to Rome. [11] So, before aught else was done, he sent word to the towns on the seacoast, crying a sale of Jewish captives, and offering them at ninety for the talent; so little did he guess what divine vengeance was to overtake him. [12] No sooner did Judas hear of Nicanor's coming, than he gave warning of it to the Jews who bore him company. [13] Some of these, cowardly souls that put no trust in God's awarding, took refuge in flight; [14] the rest made shift to sell all the goods they yet had, crying out upon the Lord to deliver them from such an impious wretch as would sell them first, and conquer them after. [15] Themselves if he nothing regarded, let him remember at least the covenant made with their fathers; the renown, too, of that holy name they bore!

[16] As for Machabaeus, he called together the seven thousand[a] that followed him, and warned them they should make no terms with the enemy, nor be affrighted by a great rabble of men coming against them in so ill a cause. [17] Courage! he said; bethink you of the sanctuary their insults have outraged, of a city wronged and mocked, of immemorial traditions overthrown! [18] What gives them confidence? Weapons of war, and their own daring. Ours to trust in his omnipotence, who with a single nod both these

[a] This seems to be a slip in the Latin version; the Greek has 'six thousand' here, as in verse 1 above.

TODAY'S ENGLISH VERSION

Antiochus owed the Romans 150,000 pounds of silver;
Nicanor planned to pay off the debt by selling Jewish prisoners of war as slaves.
11 So he at once sent word to the towns along the coast,
informing them that he would be selling Jews for less than a
pound of silver each. But he did not know of the judgment
that Almighty God had in store for him.
12 Judas learned that Nicanor was advancing with his army
toward Judea, so he informed his men. 13 Some were cowardly and did not believe in the justice of God, and they ran
away as fast as they could. 14 But others sold all their
remaining possessions so that the Lord would consider them
worthy to be saved from the godless Nicanor, who had sold
them as slaves even before the battle had taken place.
15 They prayed that if God was not willing to do this for their
sake alone, he might be willing to rescue them because of the
covenants he had made with their ancestors, and because he,
the great and wonderful God, had called them to be his people. 16 Judas brought together all 6,000 of his men and
encouraged them not to be frightened or to flee in panic at
the sight of the large number of Gentile troops who were
marching against them without cause. Instead they should
fight bravely, 17 never forgetting the crimes the Gentiles had
committed against the Temple and how they had made
Jerusalem suffer terribly and had done away with Jewish traditions. 18 "They rely on their weapons and their daring,"
Judas said, "but we trust in Almighty God, who is able to

NEW REVISED STANDARD VERSION

service. 10 Nicanor determined to make up for the king the
tribute due to the Romans, two thousand talents, by selling
the captured Jews into slavery. 11 So he immediately sent to
the towns on the seacoast, inviting them to buy Jewish slaves
and promising to hand over ninety slaves for a talent, not
expecting the judgment from the Almighty that was about to
overtake him.
12 Word came to Judas concerning Nicanor's invasion;
and when he told his companions of the arrival of the army,
13 those who were cowardly and distrustful of God's justice
ran off and got away. 14 Others sold all their remaining property, and at the same time implored the Lord to rescue those
who had been sold by the ungodly Nicanor before he ever
met them, 15 if not for their own sake, then for the sake of
the covenants made with their ancestors, and because he
had called them by his holy and glorious name. 16 But
Maccabeus gathered his forces together, to the number six
thousand, and exhorted them not to be frightened by the
enemy and not to fear the great multitude of Gentiles who
were wickedly coming against them, but to fight nobly,
17 keeping before their eyes the lawless outrage that the
Gentiles[a] had committed against the holy place, and the torture of the derided city, and besides, the overthrow of their
ancestral way of life. 18 "For they trust to arms and acts of
daring," he said, "but we trust in the Almighty God, who is

a Gk *they*

NEW AMERICAN BIBLE

10 Nicanor planned to raise the two thousand talents of tribute owed by the king to the Romans by selling captured Jews
into slavery. 11 So he immediately sent word to the coastal
cities, inviting them to buy Jewish slaves and promising to
deliver ninety slaves for a talent—little did he dream of the
punishment that was to fall upon him from the Almighty.
12 When Judas learned of Nicanor's advance and informed
his companions about the approach of the army, 13 the cowardly and those who lacked faith in God's justice deserted
and got away. 14 But the others sold everything they had
left, and at the same time besought the LORD to deliver those
whom the ungodly Nicanor had sold before even meeting
them. 15 They begged the LORD to do this, if not for their
sake, at least for the sake of the covenants made with their
forefathers, and because they themselves bore his holy, glorious name. 16 Maccabeus assembled his men, six thousand
strong, and exhorted them not be panicstricken before the
enemy, nor to fear the large number of the Gentiles attacking
them unjustly, but to fight courageously, 17 keeping before
their eyes the lawless outrage perpetrated by the Gentiles
against the holy Place and the affliction of the humiliated
city, as well as the subversion of their ancestral way of life.
18 "They trust in weapons and acts of daring," he said, "but
we trust in almighty God, who can by a mere nod destroy not

NEW JERUSALEM BIBLE

10 Nicanor for his part proposed, by the sale of Jewish prisoners of war, to raise the two thousand talents of tribute
money owed by the king to the Romans. 11 He lost no time
in sending the seaboard towns an invitation to come and
buy Jewish manpower, promising delivery of ninety head for
one talent; but he did not reckon on the judgement from the
Almighty that was soon to overtake him.
12 When news reached Judas of Nicanor's advance, he
warned his men of the enemy's approach, 13 whereupon the
cowardly ones and those who lacked confidence in the justice of God took to their heels and ran away. 14 The rest sold
all their remaining possessions, at the same time praying the
Lord to deliver them from the godless Nicanor, who had sold
them even in advance of any encounter— 15 if not for their
own sakes, then at least out of consideration for the covenants made with their ancestors, and because they themselves bore his sacred and majestic name.
16 Maccabaeus marshalled his men, who numbered about
six thousand, and exhorted them not to be dismayed at the
enemy or discouraged at the vast horde of gentiles wickedly
advancing against them, but to fight bravely, 17 keeping
before their eyes the outrage committed by them against the
holy place and the infamous and scornful treatment inflicted
on the city, not to mention the destruction of their traditional
way of life. 18 'They may put their trust in their weapons and
their exploits,' he said, 'but our confidence is in almighty

GREEK OLD TESTAMENT

τοὺς ἐρχομένους ἐφ᾽ ἡμᾶς καὶ τὸν ὅλον κόσμον ἑνὶ νεύματι
καταβαλεῖν, πεποίθαμεν. 19 προσαναλεξάμενος δὲ αὐτοῖς καὶ
τὰς ἐπὶ τῶν προγόνων γενομένας ἀντιλήμψεις καὶ τὴν ἐπὶ
Σενναχηριμ, ἑκατὸν ὀγδοήκοντα πέντε χιλιάδες ὡς ἀπώλοντο, 20 καὶ τὴν ἐν τῇ Βαβυλωνίᾳ τὴν πρὸς τοὺς Γαλάτας
παράταξιν γενομένην, ὡς οἱ πάντες ἐπὶ τὴν χρείαν ἦλθον
ὀκτακισχίλιοι σὺν Μακεδόσιν τετρακισχιλίοις, τῶν Μακεδόν-
ων ἀπορουμένων οἱ ὀκτακισχίλιοι τὰς δώδεκα μυριάδας ἀπώλεσαν διὰ τὴν γινομένην αὐτοῖς ἀπ᾽ οὐρανοῦ βοήθειαν καὶ
ὠφέλειαν πολλὴν ἔλαβον. 21 ἐφ᾽ οἷς εὐθαρσεῖς αὐτοὺς παρα-
στήσας καὶ ἑτοίμους ὑπὲρ τῶν νόμων καὶ τῆς πατρίδος ἀποθνῄσκειν τετραμερές τι τὸ στράτευμα ἐποίησεν. 22 τάξας
καὶ τοὺς ἀδελφοὺς αὐτοῦ προηγουμένους ἑκατέρας τάξεως,
Σιμωνα καὶ Ιωσηπον καὶ Ιωναθην, ὑποτάξας ἑκάστῳ χιλίους
πρὸς τοῖς πεντακοσίοις, 23 ἔτι δὲ καὶ Ελεαζαρον, παραναγ-
νοὺς τὴν ἱερὰν βίβλον καὶ δοὺς σύνθημα θεοῦ βοηθείας τῆς
πρώτης σπείρας αὐτὸς προηγούμενος συνέβαλε τῷ Νικάνορι.
24 γενομένου δὲ αὐτοῖς τοῦ παντοκράτορος συμμάχου κατέσφαξαν τῶν πολεμίων ὑπὲρ τοὺς ἐνακισχιλίους, τραυματίας
δὲ καὶ τοῖς μέλεσιν ἀναπείρους τὸ πλεῖον μέρος τῆς τοῦ
Νικάνορος στρατιᾶς ἐποίησαν, πάντας δὲ φυγεῖν ἠνάγκασαν.
25 τὰ δὲ χρήματα τῶν παραγεγονότων ἐπὶ τὸν ἀγορασμὸν
αὐτῶν ἔλαβον· συνδιώξαντες δὲ αὐτοὺς ἐφ᾽ ἱκανὸν ἀνέλυσαν
ὑπὸ τῆς ὥρας συγκλειόμενοι· 26 ἦν γὰρ ἡ πρὸ τοῦ σαββάτου,
δι᾽ ἣν αἰτίαν οὐκ ἐμακροτόνησαν κατατρέχοντες αὐτούς.

KING JAMES VERSION

cast down both them that come against us, and also all the world.

19 Moreover he recounted unto them what helps their forefathers had found, and how they were delivered, when under Sennacherib an hundred fourscore and five thousand perished.

20 And he told them of the battle that they had in Babylon with the Galatians, how they came but eight thousand in all to the business, with four thousand Macedonians, and that the Macedonians being perplexed, the eight thousand destroyed an hundred and twenty thousand because of the help that they had from heaven, and so received a great booty.

21 Thus when he had made them bold with these words, and ready to die for the laws and the country, he divided his army into four parts;

22 And joined with himself his own brethren, leaders of each band, *to wit,* Simon, and Joseph, and Jonathan, giving each one fifteen hundred men.

23 Also *he appointed* Eleazar to read the holy book: and when he had given them this watchword, The help of God; himself leading the first band, he joined battle with Nicanor.

24 And by the help of the Almighty they slew above nine thousand of their enemies, and wounded and maimed the most part of Nicanor's host, and so put all to flight;

25 And took their money that came to buy them, and pursued them far: but lacking time they returned:

26 For it was the day before the sabbath, and therefore they would no longer pursue them.

DOUAY OLD TESTAMENT

can utterly destroy both them that come against us, and the whole world.

19 Moreover he put them in mind also of the helps their fathers had received from God: and how under Sennacherib a hundred and eighty-five thousand had been destroyed.

20 And of the battle that they had fought against the Galatians in Babylonia, how they, being in all but six thousand, when it came to the point, and the Macedonians their companions were at a stand, slew a hundred and twenty thousand, because of the help they had from heaven, and for this they received many favours.

21 With these words they were greatly encouraged, and disposed even to die for the laws and their country.

22 So he appointed his brethren captains over each division of his army, Simon, and Joseph, and Jonathan, giving to each one fifteen hundred men.

23 And after the holy Book had been read to them by Esdras, and he had given them for a watchword, The help of God: himself leading the first band, he joined battle with Nicanor:

24 And the Almighty being their helper, they slew above nine thousand men: and having wounded and disabled the greater part of Nicanor's army, they obliged them to fly.

25 And they took the money of them that came to buy them, and they pursued them on every side.

26 But they came back for want of time: for it was the day before the sabbath: and therefore they did not continue the pursuit.

KNOX TRANSLATION

our adversaries and the whole world besides can undo. 19 He
put them in mind, moreover, of God's signal mercy shewed
to their forefathers; how Sennacherib's army perished, a
hundred and eighty-five thousand strong; 20 how they
fought the Galatians at Babylon, with Macedonian allies
whose heart failed them at the encounter, and six thousand
Jews, alone but for heaven's aid, made havoc of a hundred
and twenty thousand men, much to the common advantage.[a] 21 With such words as these he put heart into them,
till they were ready to die for law and country's sake.
22 And now he put the several commands of his army in
charge of his brethren, Simon, Joseph and Jonathan, entrust-
ing one thousand five hundred men to each; 23 Esdras[b] was
bidden read aloud from the sacred writings, and the watchword was given, God's Aid. And with that, out went Judas at
the head of his army, and engaged the enemy. 24 Such help
the Almighty gave them, they cut down more than nine thousand men; and the rest of Nicanor's disabled forces must
needs take to their heels. 25 All the money that had been
paid for their enslaving fell into Jewish hands, and they gave
the enemy chase far and wide, 26 only time hindering them;
the sabbath was coming on, and pursue further they might

a No other record of this engagement has been preserved to us. *b* For 'Esdras' the Greek text has 'Eleazar', meaning presumably Judas' brother. If the Latin reading is right, Esdras must be some person not elsewhere mentioned.

TODAY'S ENGLISH VERSION

destroy not only these troops, but, if necessary, the entire
world, with a mere nod of his head."
19 Then Judas went on to remind them of the ways God had
helped their ancestors: during the time of Sennacherib
185,000 of the enemy had been destroyed; 20 and once in
Babylonia 8,000 Jews came to the aid of 4,000 Macedonians,
defeating 120,000 Galatians and taking a great deal of loot,
all because of God's help.
21 Judas' words encouraged his men and made them willing to die for their religion and their country. He then divided
his army into four divisions 22 of about 1,500 men each,
with himself and his brothers Simon, Joseph, and Jonathan
each in charge of a division. 23 After ordering Eleazar to read
aloud[a] from the holy book, he gave his men the battle cry:
"God will help us," and personally led the attack against
Nicanor.
24 Almighty God fought on their side, and they killed more
than 9,000 of the enemy. They wounded many others and
put the entire enemy army to flight. 25 They seized the
money from the people who had come to buy them as slaves.
Then they pursued the enemy a long way, until they had to
return, 26 because it was almost time for the Sabbath to

[a] *Probable text* After . . . aloud; *Greek unclear.*

NEW REVISED STANDARD VERSION

able with a single nod to strike down those who are coming
against us, and even, if necessary, the whole world."
19 Moreover, he told them of the occasions when help
came to their ancestors; how, in the time of Sennacherib,
when one hundred eighty-five thousand perished, 20 and the
time of the battle against the Galatians that took place in
Babylonia, when eight thousand Jews[a] fought along with
four thousand Macedonians; yet when the Macedonians
were hard pressed, the eight thousand, by the help that came
to them from heaven, destroyed one hundred twenty thousand Galatians[b] and took a great amount of booty.
21 With these words he filled them with courage and
made them ready to die for their laws and their country; then
he divided his army into four parts. 22 He appointed his
brothers also, Simon and Joseph and Jonathan, each to command a division, putting fifteen hundred men under each.
23 Besides, he appointed Eleazar to read aloud[c] from the holy
book, and gave the watchword, "The help of God"; then,
leading the first division himself, he joined battle with
Nicanor.
24 With the Almighty as their ally, they killed more than
nine thousand of the enemy, and wounded and disabled
most of Nicanor's army, and forced them all to flee. 25 They
captured the money of those who had come to buy them as
slaves. After pursuing them for some distance, they were
obliged to return because the hour was late. 26 It was the day
before the sabbath, and for that reason they did not continue

a Gk lacks *Jews* *b* Gk lacks *Galatians* *c* Meaning of Gk uncertain

NEW AMERICAN BIBLE

only those who attack us, but the whole world." 19 He went
on to tell them of the times when help had been given their
ancestors: both the time of Sennacherib, when a hundred
and eighty-five thousand of his men were destroyed, 20 and
the time of the battle in Babylonia against the Galatians,
when only eight thousand Jews fought along with four thousand Macedonians; yet when the Macedonians were hard
pressed, the eight thousand routed one hundred and twenty
thousand and took a great quantity of booty, because of the
help they received from Heaven. 21 With such words he
encouraged them and made them ready to die for their laws
and their country.
Then Judas divided his army into four, 22 placing his
brothers, Simon, Joseph, and Jonathan, each over a division,
assigning to each fifteen hundred men. 23 (There was also
Eleazar.) After reading to them from the holy book and giving them the watchword, "The Help of God," he himself took
charge of the first division and joined in battle with Nicanor.
24 With the Almighty as their ally, they killed more than nine
thousand of the enemy, wounded and disabled the greater
part of Nicanor's army, and put all of them to flight. 25 They
also seized the money of those who had come to buy them as
slaves. When they had pursued the enemy for some time,
26 they were obliged to return by reason of the late hour. It
was the day before the sabbath, and for that reason they
could not continue the pursuit. 27 They collected the enemy's

NEW JERUSALEM BIBLE

God, who is able with a single nod to overthrow both those
marching on us and the whole world with them.' 19 He
reminded them of the occasions on which their ancestors had
received help: that time when, under Sennacherib, a hundred
and eighty-five thousand men had perished;[a] 20 that time in
Babylonia when in the battle with the Galatians the Jewish
combatants numbered only eight thousand, with four thousand Macedonians, yet when the Macedonians were hard
pressed, the eight thousand had destroyed a hundred and
twenty thousand, thanks to the help they had received from
Heaven, and had taken great booty as a result.
21 Having so roused their courage by these words that they
were ready to die for the laws and their country, he then
divided his army into four, 22 putting his brothers, Simon,
Joseph and Jonathan in command of one division each, and
assigning them fifteen hundred men apiece. 23 Next, he
ordered Esdrias to read the Holy Book aloud and gave them
their watchword 'Help from God'. Then, putting himself at
the head of the first division, he attacked Nicanor. 24 With
the Almighty for their ally they slaughtered over nine thousand of the enemy, wounded and crippled the greater part of
Nicanor's army and put them all to flight. 25 The money of
their prospective purchasers fell into their hands. After pursuing them for a good while, they turned back, since time
was pressing: 26 it was the eve of the Sabbath, and for that
reason they did not prolong their pursuit. 27 They collected

[a] **8** 2 K 19:35. The next incident is non-biblical.

Greek Old Testament

[27] ὁπλολογήσαντες δὲ αὐτοὺς καὶ τὰ σκῦλα ἐκδύσαντες τῶν
πολεμίων περὶ τὸ σάββατον ἐγίνοντο περισσῶς εὐλογοῦντες
καὶ ἐξομολογούμενοι τῷ κυρίῳ τῷ διασώσαντι εἰς τὴν ἡμέραν
ταύτην, ἀρχὴν ἐλέους τάξαντος αὐτοῖς. [28] μετὰ δὲ τὸ σάββατον τοῖς ᾐκισμένοις καὶ ταῖς χήραις καὶ ὀρφανοῖς μερί-
σαντες ἀπὸ τῶν σκύλων τὰ λοιπὰ αὐτοὶ καὶ τὰ παιδία
διεμερίσαντο. [29] ταῦτα δὲ διαπραξάμενοι καὶ κοινὴν ἱκετείαν ποιησάμενοι τὸν ἐλεήμονα κύριον ἠξίουν εἰς τέλος καταλ-
λαγῆναι τοῖς αὐτοῦ δούλοις.

[30] Καὶ τοῖς περὶ Τιμόθεον καὶ Βακχίδην συνερίσαντες
ὑπὲρ τοὺς δισμυρίους αὐτῶν ἀνεῖλον καὶ ὀχυρωμάτων
ὑψηλῶν εὖ μάλα ἐγκρατεῖς ἐγένοντο καὶ λάφυρα πλείονα
ἐμερίσαντο ἰσομοίρους αὐτοῖς καὶ τοῖς ᾐκισμένοις καὶ ὀρφανοῖς καὶ χήραις, ἔτι δὲ καὶ πρεσβυτέροις ποιήσαντες.
[31] ὁπλολογήσαντες δὲ αὐτοὺς ἐπιμελῶς πάντα συνέθηκαν εἰς
τοὺς ἐπικαίρους τόπους, τὰ δὲ λοιπὰ τῶν σκύλων ἤνεγκαν
εἰς Ἱεροσόλυμα. [32] τὸν δὲ φυλάρχην τῶν περὶ Τιμόθεον ἀνεῖλον, ἀνοσιώτατον ἄνδρα καὶ πολλὰ τοὺς Ἰουδαίους ἐπιλελυ-
πηκότα. [33] ἐπινίκια δὲ ἄγοντες ἐν τῇ πατρίδι τοὺς ἐμπρή-
σαντας τοὺς ἱεροὺς πυλῶνας καὶ Καλλισθένην ὑφῆψαν εἰς ἓν
οἰκίδιον πεφευγότα, καὶ τὸν ἄξιον τῆς δυσσεβείας ἐκομίσατο μισθόν. [34] ὁ δὲ τρισαλιτήριος Νικάνωρ ὁ τοὺς χιλίους
ἐμπόρους ἐπὶ τὴν πρᾶσιν τῶν Ἰουδαίων ἀγαγὼν [35] ταπεινω-
θεὶς ὑπὸ τῶν κατ᾽ αὐτὸν νομιζομένων ἐλαχίστων εἶναι τῇ
τοῦ κυρίου βοηθείᾳ τὴν δοξικὴν ἀποθέμενος ἐσθῆτα διὰ τῆς

King James Version

27 So when they had gathered their armour together, and spoiled their enemies, they occupied themselves about the sabbath, yielding exceeding praise and thanks to the Lord, who had preserved them unto that day, which was the beginning of mercy distilling upon them.

28 And after the sabbath, when they had given part of the spoils to the maimed, and the widows, and orphans, the residue they divided among themselves and their servants.

29 When this was done, and they had made a common supplication, they besought the merciful Lord to be reconciled with his servants for ever.

30 Moreover of those that were with Timotheus and Bacchides, who fought against them, they slew above twenty thousand, and very easily got high and strong holds, and divided among themselves many spoils more, and made the maimed, orphans, widows, yea, and the aged also, equal in spoils with themselves.

31 And when they had gathered their armour together, they laid them up all carefully in convenient places, and the remnant of the spoils they brought to Jerusalem.

32 They slew also Philarches, that wicked person, who was with Timotheus, and had annoyed the Jews many ways.

33 Furthermore at such time as they kept the feast for the victory in their country they burnt Callisthenes, that had set fire upon the holy gates, who had fled into a little house; and so he received a reward meet for his wickedness.

34 As for that most ungracious Nicanor, who had brought a thousand merchants to buy the Jews,

35 He was through the help of the Lord brought down by them, of whom he made least account; and putting off his

Douay Old Testament

27 But when they had gathered together their arms and their spoils, they kept the sabbath: blessing the Lord who had delivered them that day, distilling the beginning of mercy upon them.

28 Then after the sabbath they divided the spoils to the feeble and the orphans, and the widows: and the rest they took for themselves and their servants.

29 When this was done, and they had all made a common supplication, they besought the merciful Lord to be reconciled to his servants unto the end.

30 Moreover they slew above twenty thousand of them that were with Timotheus and Bacchides who fought against them, and they made themselves masters of the high strong holds: and they divided amongst them many spoils, giving equal portions to the feeble, the fatherless and the widows, yea and the aged also.

31 And when they had carefully gathered together their arms, they laid them all up in convenient places, and the residue of their spoils they carried to Jerusalem:

32 They slew also Philarches who was with Timotheus, a wicked man, who had many ways afflicted the Jews.

33 And when they kept the feast of the victory at Jerusalem, they burnt Callisthenes, that had set fire to the holy gates, who had taken refuge in a certain house, rendering to him a worthy reward for his impieties:

34 But as for that most wicked man Nicanor, who had brought a thousand merchants to the sale of the Jews,

35 Being through the help of the Lord brought down by them, of whom he had made no account, laying aside his

Knox Translation

not. [27] Arms and spoils of the fallen they gathered in, and so
fell to keeping the sabbath, blessing the Lord for the deliverance he had sent that day, the first refreshing dew of his
mercy. [28] The sabbath day over, they gave a share of the
spoils to crippled folk, orphans and widows; they and theirs
should have the rest. [29] And when this was done, they made
public intercession, beseeching the Lord, that was so merciful, to be reconciled with his servants for good and all.

[30] Other invaders they slew, twenty thousand of them and
more, under Bacchides and Timotheus; and when they seized
their high fortresses, and had spoil to divide in plenty, once
more cripples and orphans and widows, and the aged folk
too, must have a share to match their own. [31] Weapons of
war they gathered with all care, and bestowed where they
were most needed; it was the rest of the spoil they carried
back to Jerusalem. [32] At this time they slew Philarches, that
had been of Timotheus' company, a man stained with crime,
and many ways a persecutor of the Jewish people. [33] There
was Callisthenes, too, that had burnt down the gates of the
sanctuary; when all Jerusalem was rejoicing over the victory,
he took refuge within doors, and they burnt the place down
about his ears; he too was served right for his godless
doings. [34] As for Nicanor, that was the arch-villain of all,
and would have sold the Jews to a thousand slave-dealers,
[35] the very men whose lives he held so cheap had now, by
divine aid, humbled him to the dust. Robe of office he must

TODAY'S ENGLISH VERSION

begin. 27 When they had collected the enemy's weapons and
looted the dead, they celebrated the Sabbath, praising the
Lord and giving thanks to him, because he had brought them
safely to that day and had given them the first sign of his
mercy. 28 When the Sabbath was over, they gave some of the
loot to the victims of persecution and to the widows and
orphans; then they divided the rest among their own families. 29 Afterward they joined together in prayer to the merciful Lord, asking him to look favorably upon his servants.
30 The Jews later fought against the forces of Timothy and
Bacchides and killed more than 20,000 of them. They captured some very high fortresses and took a lot of loot, which
they divided equally among themselves and the widows,
orphans, old men, and the victims of persecution. 31 They
carefully collected all the enemy's weapons and stored them
in strategic places, but the rest of the loot was taken to
Jerusalem. 32 They executed the commanding officer of
Timothy's forces, a godless man who had caused the Jews
much suffering. 33 While celebrating their victory in the city
of their ancestors, they burned alive those men who had set
fire to the Temple gates. The dead included Callisthenes, who
had hidden in a small house; and so he received the punishment he deserved for his evil deeds.
34 In this way, the evil Nicanor, who had brought a thousand merchants to buy the Jews, 35 was defeated with the
help of the Lord by the very people he despised so much. He

NEW REVISED STANDARD VERSION

their pursuit. 27 When they had collected the arms of the
enemy and stripped them of their spoils, they kept the sabbath, giving great praise and thanks to the Lord, who had
preserved them for that day and allotted it to them as the
beginning of mercy. 28 After the sabbath they gave some of
the spoils to those who had been tortured and to the widows
and orphans, and distributed the rest among themselves and
their children. 29 When they had done this, they made common supplication and implored the merciful Lord to be wholly reconciled with his servants.[a]
30 In encounters with the forces of Timothy and Bacchides
they killed more than twenty thousand of them and got possession of some exceedingly high strongholds, and they divided a very large amount of plunder, giving to those who had
been tortured and to the orphans and widows, and also to the
aged, shares equal to their own. 31 They collected the arms of
the enemy,[b] and carefully stored all of them in strategic
places; the rest of the spoils they carried to Jerusalem. 32 They
killed the commander of Timothy's forces, a most wicked
man, and one who had greatly troubled the Jews. 33 While
they were celebrating the victory in the city of their ancestors,
they burned those who had set fire to the sacred gates,
Callisthenes and some others, who had fled into one little
house; so these received the proper reward for their impiety.[c]
34 The thrice-accursed Nicanor, who had brought the
thousand merchants to buy the Jews, 35 having been humbled with the help of the Lord by opponents whom he regarded as of the least account, took off his splendid uniform and

a Gk *slaves* *b* Gk *their arms* *c* Meaning of Gk uncertain

NEW AMERICAN BIBLE

arms and stripped them of their spoils, and then observed
the sabbath with fervent praise and thanks to the LORD who
kept them safe for that day on which he let descend on them
the first dew of his mercy. 28 After the sabbath, they gave a
share of the booty to the persecuted and to widows and
orphans; the rest they divided among themselves and their
children. 29 When this was done, they made supplication in
common, imploring the merciful LORD to be completely reconciled with his servants.
30 They also challenged the forces of Timothy and Bacchides, killed more than twenty thousand of them, and captured some very high fortresses. They divided the enormous
plunder, allotting half to themselves and the rest to the persecuted, to orphans, widows, and the aged. 31 They collected
the enemies' weapons and carefully stored them in suitable
places; the rest of the spoils they carried to Jerusalem.
32 They also killed the commander of Timothy's forces, a
most wicked man, who had done great harm to the Jews.
33 While celebrating the victory in their ancestral city, they
burned both those who had set fire to the sacred gates and
Callisthenes, who had taken refuge in a little house; so he
received the reward his wicked deeds deserved.
34 The accursed Nicanor, who had brought the thousand
slave dealers to buy the Jews, 35 after being humbled
through the LORD's help by those whom he had thought of no
account, laid aside his fine clothes and fled alone across

NEW JERUSALEM BIBLE

the enemy's weapons and stripped them of their spoils, and
because of the Sabbath even more heartily blessed and
praised the Lord, who had saved them and who had chosen
that day for the first manifestation of his compassion.
28 When the Sabbath was over, they distributed some of the
booty among the victims of the persecution and the widows
and orphans; the rest they divided among themselves and
their children. 29 They then joined in public supplication,
imploring the merciful Lord to be fully reconciled with his
servants.
30 They also challenged the forces of Timotheus and
Bacchides and destroyed over twenty thousand of them,
gaining possession of several high fortresses. They divided
their enormous booty into two equal shares, one for themselves, the other for the victims of the persecution and the
orphans and widows, not forgetting the aged. 31 They carefully collected the enemy's weapons and stored them in suitable places. The rest of the spoils they took to Jerusalem.
32 They killed the tribal chieftain on Timotheus' staff, an
extremely wicked man who had done great harm to the Jews.
33 In the course of their victory celebrations in Jerusalem,
they burned the men who had fired the Holy Gates; with
Callisthenes they had taken refuge in one small house; so
these received a fitting reward for their sacrilege.
34 The triple-dyed scoundrel Nicanor, who had brought the
thousand merchants to buy the Jews, 35 finding himself with
the Lord's help humbled by men he had himself reckoned as
of very little account, stripped off his robes of state, and

GREEK OLD TESTAMENT

μεσογείου δραπέτου τρόπον ἔρημον ἑαυτὸν ποιήσας ἧκεν
εἰς Ἀντιόχειαν ὑπὲρ ἅπαν εὐημερηκὼς ἐπὶ τῇ τοῦ στρατοῦ
διαφθορᾷ. 36 καὶ ὁ τοῖς Ῥωμαίοις ἀναδεξάμενος φόρον ἀπὸ
τῆς τῶν ἐν Ιεροσολύμοις αἰχμαλωσίας κατορθώσασθαι
κατήγγελλεν ὑπέρμαχον ἔχειν τοὺς Ιουδαίους καὶ διὰ τὸν
τρόπον τοῦτον ἀτρώτους εἶναι τοὺς Ιουδαίους διὰ τὸ
ἀκολουθεῖν τοῖς ὑπ᾽ αὐτοῦ προτεταγμένοις νόμοις.

9 Περὶ δὲ τὸν καιρὸν ἐκεῖνον ἐτύγχανεν Ἀντίοχος ἀναλε-
λυκὼς ἀκόσμως ἐκ τῶν περὶ τὴν Περσίδα τόπων. 2 εἰσε-
ληλύθει γὰρ εἰς τὴν λεγομένην Περσέπολιν καὶ ἐπεχείρησεν
ἱεροσυλεῖν καὶ τὴν πόλιν συνέχειν· διὸ δὴ τῶν πληθῶν
ὁρμησάντων ἐπὶ τὴν τῶν ὅπλων βοήθειαν ἐτράπησαν, καὶ
συνέβη τροπωθέντα τὸν Ἀντίοχον ὑπὸ τῶν ἐγχωρίων ἀσχή-
μονα τὴν ἀναζυγὴν ποιήσασθαι. 3 ὄντι δὲ αὐτῷ κατ᾽ Ἐκβάτανα προσέπεσεν τὰ κατὰ Νικάνορα καὶ τοὺς περὶ Τιμόθεον
γεγονότα. 4 ἐπαρθεὶς δὲ τῷ θυμῷ ᾤετο καὶ τὴν τῶν πεφυγα-
δευκότων αὐτὸν κακίαν εἰς τοὺς Ιουδαίους ἐναπερείσασθαι,
διὸ συνέταξεν τὸν ἁρματηλάτην ἀδιαλείπτως ἐλαύνοντα
κατανύειν τὴν πορείαν τῆς ἐξ οὐρανοῦ δὴ κρίσεως συνούσης
αὐτῷ· οὕτως γὰρ ὑπερηφάνως εἶπεν Πολυάνδριον Ιουδαίων
Ιεροσόλυμα ποιήσω παραγενόμενος ἐκεῖ. 5 ὁ δὲ παντεπό-
πτης κύριος ὁ θεὸς τοῦ Ισραηλ ἐπάταξεν αὐτὸν ἀνιάτῳ καὶ
ἀοράτῳ πληγῇ· ἄρτι δὲ αὐτοῦ καταλήξαντος τὸν λόγον
ἔλαβεν αὐτὸν ἀνήκεστος τῶν σπλάγχνων ἀλγηδὼν καὶ πικραὶ
τῶν ἔνδον βάσανοι 6 πάνυ δικαίως τὸν πολλαῖς καὶ ξενιζούσαις συμφοραῖς ἑτέρων σπλάγχνα βασανίσαντα. 7 ὁ δ᾽

KING JAMES VERSION

glorious apparel, and discharging his company, he came like a fugitive servant through the midland unto Antioch, having very great dishonour, for that his host was destroyed.

36 Thus he, that took upon him to make good to the Romans their tribute by means of the captives in Jerusalem, told abroad, that the Jews had God to fight for them, and therefore they could not be hurt, because they followed the laws that he gave them.

9 About that time came Antiochus with dishonour out of the country of Persia.

2 For he had entered the *city* called Persepolis, and went about to rob the temple, and to hold the city; whereupon the multitude running to defend themselves with their weapons put them to flight; and so it happened, that Antiochus being put to flight of the inhabitants returned with shame.

3 Now when he came to Ecbatane, news was brought him what had happened unto Nicanor and Timotheus.

4 Then swelling with anger, he thought to avenge upon the Jews the disgrace done unto him by those that made him flee. Therefore commanded he his chariotman to drive without ceasing, and to dispatch the journey, the judgment of GOd now following him. For he had spoken proudly in this sort, That he would come to Jerusalem, and make it a common burying place of the Jews.

5 But the Lord Almighty, the God of Israel, smote him with an incurable and invisible plague: for as soon as he had spoken these words, a pain of the bowels that was remediless came upon him, and sore torments of the inner parts;

6 And that most justly: for he had tormented other men's bowels with many and strange torments.

DOUAY OLD TESTAMENT

garment of glory, fleeing through the midland country, he came alone to Antioch, being rendered very unhappy by the destruction of his army.

36 And he that had promised to levy the tribute for the Romans by the means of the captives of Jerusalem, now professed that the Jews had God for their protector, and therefore they could not be hurt, because they followed the laws appointed by him.

9 AT that time Antiochus returned with dishonour out of Persia.

2 For he had entered into the city called Persepolis, and attempted to rob the temple, and to oppress the city: but the multitude running together to arms, put them to flight: and so it fell out that Antiochus being put to flight returned with disgrace.

3 Now when he was come about Ecbatana, he received the news of what had happened to Nicanor and Timotheus.

4 And swelling with anger he thought to revenge upon the Jews the injury done by them that had put him to flight. And therefore he commanded his chariot to be driven, without stopping in his journey, the judgment of heaven urging him forward, because he had spoken so proudly, that he would come to Jerusalem, and make it a common burying place of the Jews.

5 But the Lord the God of Israel, that seeth all things, struck him with an incurable and an invisible plague. For as soon as he had ended these words, a dreadful pain in his bowels came upon him, and bitter torments of the inner parts.

6 And indeed very justly, seeing he had tormented the bowels of others with many and new torments, albeit he by no means ceased from his malice.

KNOX TRANSLATION

lay by, and slink by country ways all unattended to Antioch.
A fine homecoming, this, with the loss of a whole army!
36 Where were the Jewish captives that should have paid off
the tribute to Rome? He was fain to confess, now, that the
Jews had God himself for their protector, and, would they but
keep his laws, there was no conquering them!

9 Antiochus himself, at this time, had a sorry home-com-
ing from Persia. 2 He had made his way into the city
they call Persepolis, thinking to plunder its temple and of
itself have the mastery; but the common folk ran to arms
and routed him. So he was a man defeated and disgraced
3 when he reached Ecbatana, and there news came to him of
how Nicanor had fared, and Timotheus. 4 And now, in a
great taking of rage, he would make the Jews suffer for the
ignominy of his own defeat; on, on his chariot must be driv-
en, and never a halt in the journey, with the divine
vengeance ever at his heels. Had he not boasted, Jerusalem
was his goal, and he would bury the Jewish race under the
ruins of it?

5 The Lord, Israel's God, how should aught escape his
scrutiny? The words were barely uttered, when he smote
Antiochus with such a hurt, there was neither remedying nor
discovering it. A deadly griping it was that took him, with
cruel torment of the bowels; 6 fitting reward for one that had
often tortured his fellows, and to the marrow, in unexampled
fashion. Even so, he would not leave his wicked purpose;

TODAY'S ENGLISH VERSION

threw off his splendid uniform and fled all alone like a runaway slave, until he reached Antioch. He had succeeded only in destroying his entire army. 36 This man, who had tried to pay a debt to Rome by selling the people of Jerusalem, showed that the Jews could not be defeated. God was their mighty Defender, because they obeyed the laws he had given them.

9 About this time Antiochus was retreating in disorder from Persia, 2 where he had entered the city of Persepolis and had attempted to rob a temple and take control of the city. The people took up arms and attacked Antiochus, forcing his army to retreat in disgrace. 3 When he reached Ecbatana, he was told what had happened to the forces of Nicanor and Timothy. 4 He became furious and decided to make the Jews pay for the defeat he had suffered. So he ordered his chariot driver not to stop until they reached Jerusalem. With great arrogance he said, "I will turn Jerusalem into a graveyard full of Jews."

But he did not know that he was heading straight for God's judgment. 5 In fact, as soon as he had said these words, the all-seeing Lord, the God of Israel, struck him down with an invisible but fatal blow. He was seized with sharp intestinal pains for which there was no relief— 6 a fitting punishment for the man who had tortured others in so

NEW REVISED STANDARD VERSION

made his way alone like a runaway slave across the country until he reached Antioch, having succeeded chiefly in the destruction of his own army! 36 So he who had undertaken to secure tribute for the Romans by the capture of the people of Jerusalem proclaimed that the Jews had a Defender, and that therefore the Jews were invulnerable, because they followed the laws ordained by him.

9 About that time, as it happened, Antiochus had retreated in disorder from the region of Persia. 2 He had entered the city called Persepolis and attempted to rob the temples and control the city. Therefore the people rushed to the rescue with arms, and Antiochus and his army were defeated,[a] with the result that Antiochus was put to flight by the inhabitants and beat a shameful retreat. 3 While he was in Ecbatana, news came to him of what had happened to Nicanor and the forces of Timothy. 4 Transported with rage, he conceived the idea of turning upon the Jews the injury done by those who had put him to flight; so he ordered his charioteer to drive without stopping until he completed the journey. But the judgment of heaven rode with him! For in his arrogance he said, "When I get there I will make Jerusalem a cemetery of Jews."

5 But the all-seeing Lord, the God of Israel, struck him with an incurable and invisible blow. As soon as he stopped speaking he was seized with a pain in his bowels, for which there was no relief, and with sharp internal tortures— 6 and that very justly, for he had tortured the bowels of others with

a Gk *they were defeated*

NEW AMERICAN BIBLE

country like a runaway slave, until he reached Antioch. He was eminently successful in destroying his own army. 36 So he who had promised to provide tribute for the Romans by the capture of the people of Jerusalem testified that the Jews had a champion, and that they were invulnerable for the very reason that they followed the laws laid down by him.

9 About that time Antiochus retreated in disgrace from the region of Persia. 2 He had entered the city called Persepolis and attempted to rob the temple and gain control of the city. Thereupon the people had swift recourse to arms, and Antiochus' men were routed, so that in the end Antiochus was put to flight by the natives and forced to beat a shameful retreat. 3 On his arrival in Ecbatana, he learned what had happened to Nicanor and to Timothy's forces. 4 Overcome with anger, he planned to make the Jews suffer for the injury done by those who had put him to flight. Therefore he ordered his charioteer to drive without stopping until he finished the journey.

Yet the condemnation of Heaven rode with him, since he said in his arrogance, "I will make Jerusalem the common graveyard of the Jews as soon as I arrive there." 5 So the all-seeing LORD, the God of Israel, struck him down with an unseen but incurable blow; for scarcely had he uttered those words when he was seized with excruciating pains in his bowels and sharp internal torment, 6 a fit punishment for him who had tortured the bowels of others with many

NEW JERUSALEM BIBLE

made his way across country unaccompanied, like a runaway slave, reaching Antioch by a singular stroke of fortune, since his army had been destroyed. 36 Thus the man who had promised the Romans to make good their tribute money by selling the prisoners from Jerusalem, bore witness that the Jews had a defender and that they were in consequence invulnerable, since they followed the laws which that defender had ordained.

9 [a]At about the same time, Antiochus was beating a disorderly retreat from Persia. 2 He had entered the city called Persepolis, planning to rob the temple and occupy the city; but the population at once sprang to arms to defend themselves, with the result that Antiochus was routed by the inhabitants and forced to beat a humiliating retreat. 3 On his arrival in Ecbatana he learned what had happened to Nicanor and to Timotheus' forces. 4 Flying into a passion, he resolved to make the Jews pay for the disgrace inflicted by those who had routed him, and with this in mind he ordered his charioteer to drive without stopping and get the journey over. But the sentence of Heaven was already hanging over him. In his pride, he had said, 'When I reach Jerusalem, I shall turn it into a mass grave for the Jews.' 5 But the all-seeing Lord, the God of Israel, struck him with an incurable and unseen complaint. The words were hardly out of his mouth when he was seized with an incurable pain in his bowels and with excruciating internal torture; 6 and this was only right, since he had inflicted many barbaric tortures on

a **9** 9:1seq. // 1 M 6:1–16.

GREEK OLD TESTAMENT

οὐδαμῶς τῆς ἀγερωχίας ἔληγεν, ἔτι δὲ καὶ τῆς ὑπερηφανίας
ἐπεπλήρωτο πῦρ πνέων τοῖς θυμοῖς ἐπὶ τοὺς Ιουδαίους καὶ
κελεύων ἐποξύνειν τὴν πορείαν. συνέβη δὲ καὶ πεσεῖν αὐτὸν
ἀπὸ τοῦ ἅρματος φερομένου ῥοίζῳ καὶ δυσχερεῖ πτώματι
περιπεσόντα πάντα τὰ μέλη τοῦ σώματος ἀποστρεβλοῦσθαι.
8 ὁ δ᾽ ἄρτι δοκῶν τοῖς τῆς θαλάσσης κύμασιν ἐπιτάσσειν διὰ
τὴν ὑπὲρ ἄνθρωπον ἀλαζονείαν καὶ πλάστιγγι τὰ τῶν ὀρέων
οἰόμενος ὕψη στήσειν κατὰ γῆν γενόμενος ἐν φορείῳ
παρεκομίζετο φανερὰν τοῦ θεοῦ πᾶσιν τὴν δύναμιν ἐνδεικνύ-
μενος, 9 ὥστε καὶ ἐκ τοῦ σώματος τοῦ δυσσεβοῦς σκώληκας
ἀναζεῖν, καὶ ζῶντος ἐν ὀδύναις καὶ ἀλγηδόσιν τὰς σάρκας
αὐτοῦ διαπίπτειν, ὑπὸ δὲ τῆς ὀσμῆς αὐτοῦ πᾶν τὸ στρατόπεδον βαρύνεσθαι τὴν σαπρίαν. 10 καὶ τὸν μικρῷ πρότερον
τῶν οὐρανίων ἄστρων ἅπτεσθαι δοκοῦντα παρακομίζειν
οὐδεὶς ἐδύνατο διὰ τὸ τῆς ὀσμῆς ἀφόρητον βάρος. 11 ἐνταῦθα οὖν ἤρξατο τὸ πολὺ τῆς ὑπερηφανίας λήγειν
τεθραυσμένος καὶ εἰς ἐπίγνωσιν ἔρχεσθαι θείᾳ μάστιγι
κατὰ στιγμὴν ἐπιτεινόμενος ταῖς ἀλγηδόσιν. 12 καὶ μηδὲ
τῆς ὀσμῆς αὐτοῦ δυνάμενος ἀνέχεσθαι ταῦτ᾽ ἔφη Δίκαιον
ὑποτάσσεσθαι τῷ θεῷ καὶ μὴ θνητὸν ὄντα ἰσόθεα φρονεῖν.
13 ηὔχετο δὲ ὁ μιαρὸς πρὸς τὸν οὐκέτι αὐτὸν ἐλεήσοντα
δεσπότην οὕτως λέγων 14 τὴν μὲν ἁγίαν πόλιν, ἣν σπεύδων
παρεγίνετο ἰσόπεδον ποιῆσαι καὶ πολυάνδριον οἰκοδομῆσαι,

KING JAMES VERSION

7 Howbeit he nothing at all ceased from his bragging, but still was filled with pride, breathing out fire in his rage against the Jews, and commanding to haste the journey: but it came to pass that he fell down from his chariot, carried violently; so that having a sore fall, all the members of his body were much pained.

8 And thus he that a little afore thought he might command the waves of the sea, (so proud was he beyond the condition of man) and weigh the high mountains in a balance, was now cast on the ground, and carried in an horselitter, shewing forth unto all the manifest power of God.

9 So that the worms rose up out of the body of this wicked man, and whiles he lived in sorrow and pain, his flesh fell away, and the filthiness of his smell was noisome to all his army.

10 And the man, that thought a little afore he could reach to the stars of heaven, no man could endure to carry for his intolerable stink.

11 Here therefore, being plagued, he began to leave off his great pride, and to come to the knowledge *of himself* by the scourge of God, his pain increasing every moment.

12 And when he himself could not abide his own smell, he said these words, It is meet to be subject unto God, and that a man that is mortal should not proudly think of himself, as if he were God.

13 This wicked person vowed also unto the Lord, who now no more would have mercy upon him, saying thus,

14 That the holy city (to the which he was going in haste, to lay it even with the ground, and to make it a common buryingplace,) he would set at liberty:

DOUAY OLD TESTAMENT

7 Moreover being filled with pride, breathing out fire in his rage against the Jews, and commanding the matter to be hastened, it happened as he was going with violence that he fell from the chariot, so that his limbs were much pained by a grievous bruising of the body.

8 Thus he that seemed to himself to command even the waves of the sea, being proud above the condition of man, and to weigh the heights of the mountains in a balance, now being cast down to the ground, was carried in a litter, bearing witness to the manifest power of God in himself:

9 So that worms swarmed out of the body of this man, and whilst he lived in sorrow and pain, his flesh fell off, and the filthiness of his smell was noisome to the army.

10 And the man that thought a little before he could reach to the stars of heaven, no man could endure to carry, for the intolerable stench.

11 And by this means, being brought from his great pride, he began to come to the knowledge of himself, being admonished by the scourge of God, his pains increasing every moment.

12 And when he himself could not now abide his own stench, he spoke thus: It is just to be subject to God, and that a mortal man should not equal himself to God.

13 Then this wicked man prayed to the Lord, of whom he was not like to obtain mercy.

14 And the city, to which he was going in haste to lay it even with the ground, and to make it a common burying place, he now desireth to make free.

KNOX TRANSLATION

7 with pride undiminished, still breathing out fiery threats
against the Jewish folk, he pressed forward on his errand, till
of a sudden, in full career, down fell he from his chariot, and
never a limb but was racked grievously by the fall. 8 What a
living proof was this of God's power, when he was struck to
earth, and must finish his journey by litter, one that boasted,
till now, he could rise beyond man's measure, the sea's
waves govern, and weigh mountains in the balance! 9 Bred
worms at last in that sinful body, and he lived yet, though
miserably enough, to see his own flesh rot away, till his own
men could not bear the foul stench of him; 10 it was but yesterday the very stars seemed within his reach, and never a
man now would carry so foul a burden.
11 What marvel, if the swelling pride of him ebbed away,
and heaven's judgements brought him to himself? With
every moment his anguish grew, 12 and the foul breath of
his disease was past his own bearing. Alas, said he, to God
all must bow; mortals we are, and god ourselves we may
not. 13 Nay, he made suit to the Lord, vile wretch though he
were, hoping all in vain to win mercy. 14 Forgotten, his haste
to lay Jerusalem in ruins, and make a cemetery of it; a free
city it should be thenceforward. 15 Grudge the Jewish folk

TODAY'S ENGLISH VERSION

many terrible ways! 7But this in no way caused him to give up his pride. Instead he became more arrogant than ever, and breathing out fiery threats against the Jews, he gave orders to drive even faster. As a result he fell out of his chariot with such a thud that it made every bone in his body ache. 8His arrogant pride made him think he had the superhuman strength to make ocean waves obey him and to weigh high mountains on a pair of scales. But suddenly he fell flat on the ground and had to be carried off on a stretcher, a clear sign to everyone of God's power. 9Even the eyes of this godless man were crawling with worms and he lived in terrible pain and agony. The stink was so bad that his entire army was sickened, 10and no one was able to come close enough to carry him around. Yet only a short while before, he thought he could take hold of the stars.

11Antiochus was deeply depressed and suffered constant pain because of the punishment that God had brought on him, so he finally came to his senses and gave up his arrogant pride. 12Then, when he could no longer endure his own stink, he said, "It is right that all mortals should be subject to God and not think that they are his equal." 13The time of the Lord's mercy had come to an end for Antiochus, but this worthless man made the Lord a promise: 14"I once intended to level Jerusalem to the ground and make that holy city a graveyard full of Jews," he said, "but now I declare it a free

NEW REVISED STANDARD VERSION

many and strange inflictions. 7Yet he did not in any way stop his insolence, but was even more filled with arrogance, breathing fire in his rage against the Jews, and giving orders to drive even faster. And so it came about that he fell out of his chariot as it was rushing along, and the fall was so hard as to torture every limb of his body. 8Thus he who only a little while before had thought in his superhuman arrogance that he could command the waves of the sea, and had imagined that he could weigh the high mountains in a balance, was brought down to earth and carried in a litter, making the power of God manifest to all. 9And so the ungodly man's body swarmed with worms, and while he was still living in anguish and pain, his flesh rotted away, and because of the stench the whole army felt revulsion at his decay. 10Because of his intolerable stench no one was able to carry the man who a little while before had thought that he could touch the stars of heaven. 11Then it was that, broken in spirit, he began to lose much of his arrogance and to come to his senses under the scourge of God, for he was tortured with pain every moment. 12And when he could not endure his own stench, he uttered these words, "It is right to be subject to God; mortals should not think that they are equal to God."[a]

13 Then the abominable fellow made a vow to the Lord, who would no longer have mercy on him, stating 14that the holy city, which he was hurrying to level to the ground and to make a cemetery, he was now declaring to be free; 15and

a Or *not think thoughts proper only to God*

NEW AMERICAN BIBLE

barbarous torments. 7Far from giving up his insolence, he was all the more filled with arrogance. Breathing fire in his rage against the Jews, he gave orders to drive even faster. As a result he hurtled from the dashing chariot, and every part of his body was racked by the violent fall. 8Thus he who previously, in his superhuman presumption, thought he could command the waves of the sea, and imagined he could weigh the mountaintops in his scales, was now thrown to the ground and had to be carried on a litter, clearly manifesting to all the power of God. 9The body of this impious man swarmed with worms, and while he was still alive in hideous torments, his flesh rotted off, so that the entire army was sickened by the stench of his corruption. 10Shortly before, he had thought that he could reach the stars of heaven, and now, no one could endure to transport the man because of this intolerable stench.

11At last, broken in spirit, he began to give up his excessive arrogance, and to gain some understanding, under the scourge of God, for he was racked with pain unceasingly. 12When he could no longer bear his own stench, he said, "It is right to be subject to God, and not to think one's mortal self divine." 13Then this vile man vowed to the LORD, who would no longer have mercy on him, 14that he would set free the holy city, toward which he had been hurrying with the intention of leveling it to the ground and making it a

NEW JERUSALEM BIBLE

the bowels of others. 7Even so, he in no way diminished his arrogance; still bursting with pride, breathing fire in his wrath against the Jews, he was in the act of ordering an even keener pace when the chariot gave a sudden lurch and out he fell and, in this serious fall, was dragged along, every joint of his body wrenched out of place. 8He who only a little while before had thought in his superhuman boastfulness he could command the waves of the sea, he who had imagined he could weigh mountain peaks in a balance, found himself flat on the ground and then being carried in a litter, a visible demonstration to all of the power of God, 9in that the very eyes of this godless man teemed with worms and his flesh rotted away while he lingered on in agonising pain, and the stench of his decay sickened the whole army. 10A short while before, he had thought to grasp the stars of heaven; now no one could bring himself to act as his bearer, for the stench was intolerable.

11Then and there, as a consequence, in his shattered state, he began to shed his excessive pride and come to his senses under the divine lash, spasms of pain overtaking him. 12His stench being unbearable even to himself, he exclaimed, 'It is right to submit to God; no mortal should aspire to equality with the Godhead.' 13The wretch began to pray to the Master, who would never take pity on him now, declaring 14that the holy city, towards which he had been speeding to rase it to the ground and turn it into a mass grave, should be

GREEK OLD TESTAMENT

ἐλευθέραν ἀναδεῖξαι, 15 τοὺς δὲ Ιουδαίους, οὓς διεγνώκει
μηδὲ ταφῆς ἀξιῶσαι, οἰωνοβρώτους δὲ σὺν τοῖς νηπίοις
ἐκρίψειν θηρίοις, πάντας αὐτοὺς ἴσους Ἀθηναίοις ποιήσειν·
16 ὃν δὲ πρότερον ἐσκύλευσεν ἅγιον νεὼ καλλίστοις ἀναθήμασιν κοσμήσειν καὶ τὰ ἱερὰ σκεύη πολυπλάσια πάντα ἀπο-
δώσειν, τὰς δὲ ἐπιβαλλούσας πρὸς τὰς θυσίας συντάξεις ἐκ
τῶν ἰδίων προσόδων χορηγήσειν· 17 πρὸς δὲ τούτοις καὶ
Ιουδαῖον ἔσεσθαι καὶ πάντα τόπον οἰκητὸν ἐπελεύσεσθαι
καταγγέλλοντα τὸ τοῦ θεοῦ κράτος. 18 οὐδαμῶς δὲ ληγόντων
τῶν πόνων, ἐπεληλύθει γὰρ ἐπ' αὐτὸν δικαία ἡ τοῦ θεοῦ κρίσις, τὰ κατ' αὐτὸν ἀπελπίσας ἔγραψεν πρὸς τοὺς Ιουδαίους
τὴν ὑπογεγραμμένην ἐπιστολὴν ἱκετηρίας τάξιν ἔχουσαν,
περιέχουσαν δὲ οὕτως
19 Τοῖς χρηστοῖς Ιουδαίοις τοῖς πολίταις πολλὰ χαίρειν
καὶ ὑγιαίνειν καὶ εὖ πράττειν βασιλεὺς καὶ στρατηγὸς Ἀντίοχος. 20 εἰ ἔρρωσθε καὶ τὰ τέκνα καὶ τὰ ἴδια κατὰ γνώμην
ἐστὶν ὑμῖν· εἰς οὐρανὸν τὴν ἐλπίδα ἔχων 21 ὑμῶν τὴν τιμὴν
καὶ τὴν εὔνοιαν ἐμνημόνευον φιλοστόργως. ἐπανάγων ἐκ τῶν
κατὰ τὴν Περσίδα τόπων καὶ περιπεσὼν ἀσθενείᾳ δυσχέρειαν
ἐχούσῃ ἀναγκαῖον ἡγησάμην φροντίσαι τῆς κοινῆς πάντων
ἀσφαλείας. 22 οὐκ ἀπογινώσκων τὰ κατ' ἐμαυτόν, ἀλλὰ ἔχων
πολλὴν ἐλπίδα ἐκφεύξεσθαι τὴν ἀσθένειαν, 23 θεωρῶν δὲ ὅτι
καὶ ὁ πατήρ, καθ' οὓς καιροὺς εἰς τοὺς ἄνω τόπους ἐστρα-
τοπέδευσεν, ἀνέδειξεν τὸν διαδεξάμενον, 24 ὅπως, ἐάν τι

KING JAMES VERSION

15 And as touching the Jews, whom he had judged not worthy so much as to be buried, but to be cast out with their children to be devoured of the fowls and wild beasts, he would make them all equals to the citizens of Athens:

16 And the holy temple, which before he had spoiled, he would garnish with goodly gifts, and restore all the holy vessels with many more, and out of his own revenue defray the charges belonging to the sacrifices:

17 Yea, and that also he would become a Jew himself, and go through all the world that was inhabited, and declare the power of God.

18 But for all this his pains would not cease: for the just judgment of God was come upon him: therefore despairing of his health, he wrote unto the Jews the letter underwritten, containing the form of a supplication, after this manner:

19 Antiochus, king and governor, to the good Jews his citizens wisheth much joy, health, and prosperity:

20 If ye and your children fare well, and your affairs be to your contentment, I give very great thanks to God, having my hope in heaven.

21 As for me, I was weak, or else I would have remembered kindly your honour and good will. Returning out of Persia, and being taken with a grievous disease, I thought it necessary to care for the common safety of all:

22 Not distrusting mine health, but having great hope to escape this sickness.

23 But considering that even my father, at what time he led an army into the high countries, appointed a successor,

DOUAY OLD TESTAMENT

15 And the Jews whom he said he would not account worthy to be so much as buried, but would give them up to be devoured by the birds and wild beasts, and would utterly destroy them with their children, he now promiseth to make equal with the Athenians.

16 The holy temple also which before he had spoiled, he promiseth to adorn with goodly gifts, and to multiply the holy vessels, and to allow out of his revenues the charges pertaining to the sacrifices.

17 Yea also, that he would become a Jew himself, and would go through every place of the earth, and declare the power of God.

18 But his pains not ceasing (for the just judgment of God was come upon him) despairing *of life* he wrote to the Jews in the manner of a supplication, a letter in these words:

19 To his very good subjects the Jews, Antiochus king and ruler wisheth much health and welfare, and happiness.

20 If you and your children are well, and if all matters go with you to your mind, we give very great thanks.

21 As for me, being infirm, but yet kindly remembering you, returning out of the places of Persia, and being taken with a grievous disease, I thought it necessary to take care for the common good:

22 Not distrusting my life, but having great hope to escape the sickness.

23 But considering that my father also, at what time he led an army into the higher countries, appointed who should reign after him:

KNOX TRANSLATION

burial, give their carrion to bird and beast, make an end of
them, children and all? Nay, such high privileges they should
have as the townsfolk of Athens itself. 16 And for that sacred
temple he had stripped bare, with choice gifts he would
enrich it, furnishing it as never before, and defraying, from
his own purse, all the cost of its sacrifices. 17 Stay, he would
become a Jew himself, would go the rounds of earth, proclaiming everywhere the divine power!
18 But all to no avail; the vengeance of God, well earned,
had overtaken him, and find relief he might not. So now,
despairing of that, he wrote to the Jews in very humble fashion, as here follows.[a] 19 To his loyal Jewish subjects Antiochus, their king and general, sends greeting, health, and
happiness! 20 Thrive you and yours, and fare prosperously, I
am well content. 21 For myself, I am in ill case, yet think ever
kindly of you. On my way home from Persia, so grievous a
distemper has fallen upon me, needs must I should take
order for the public safety. 22 Despair I will not; there is good
hope yet of my recovery. 23 But this thought weighs with me;
when he went a-campaigning in the high countries, my
father gave out who was to succeed him; 24 should aught go

a *vv.* 18-27. It seems probable that this proclamation was sent to all Antiochus' subjects, the Jews receiving it among others. The document referred to at the end of verse 25 is no longer extant.

TODAY'S ENGLISH VERSION

city. 15 I had planned to throw out the dead bodies of the
Jews and their children for the wild animals and the birds to
eat, for I did not consider them worth burying. But now I
intend to grant them the same privileges as the citizens of
Athens enjoy. 16 I once looted the Temple and took its sacred
utensils, but I will fill it with splendid gifts and with better
utensils than before, and I will pay the cost of the sacrifices
from my own resources. 17 Besides all this, I will become a
Jew myself and go wherever people live, telling them of God's
power."

18 Antiochus was in despair and could find no relief from
his pain, because God was punishing him as he deserved, so
he wrote the following letter to the Jews:

19 "King Antiochus to the Jews, my most distinguished
subjects. Warm greetings and best wishes for your health
and prosperity.

20 "I hope that you and your families are in good health
and that all goes well with you. My hope is in God, 21 and
I remember with a deep sense of joy the respect and kindness that you have shown me.

"On my way home from Persia I fell violently ill, and so I
thought it best to begin making plans for the general welfare of the people. 22 I have not given up hopes of getting
well; in fact I am fully confident that I will recover. 23 But I
recall that my father used to appoint a successor whenever
he went on a military campaign east of the Euphrates.

NEW REVISED STANDARD VERSION

the Jews, whom he had not considered worth burying but
had planned to throw out with their children for the wild
animals and for the birds to eat, he would make, all of them,
equal to citizens of Athens; 16 and the holy sanctuary, which
he had formerly plundered, he would adorn with the finest
offerings; and all the holy vessels he would give back, many
times over; and the expenses incurred for the sacrifices he
would provide from his own revenues; 17 and in addition to
all this he also would become a Jew and would visit every
inhabited place to proclaim the power of God. 18 But when
his sufferings did not in any way abate, for the judgment of
God had justly come upon him, he gave up all hope for himself and wrote to the Jews the following letter, in the form of
a supplication. This was its content:

19 "To his worthy Jewish citizens, Antiochus their king
and general sends hearty greetings and good wishes for their
health and prosperity. 20 If you and your children are well
and your affairs are as you wish, I am glad. As my hope is in
heaven, 21 I remember with affection your esteem and goodwill. On my way back from the region of Persia I suffered an
annoying illness, and I have deemed it necessary to take
thought for the general security of all. 22 I do not despair of
my condition, for I have good hope of recovering from my illness, 23 but I observed that my father, on the occasions
when he made expeditions into the upper country, appointed

NEW AMERICAN BIBLE

common graveyard; 15 he would put on perfect equality with
the Athenians all the Jews, whom he had judged not even
worthy of burial, but fit only to be thrown out with their children to be eaten by vultures and wild animals; 16 he would
adorn with the finest offerings the holy temple which he had
previously despoiled; he would restore all the sacred vessels
many times over; and would provide from his own revenues
the expenses required for the sacrifices. 17 Besides all this, he
would become a Jew himself and visit every inhabited place
to proclaim there the power of God. 18 But since God's punishment had justly come upon him, his sufferings were not
lessened, so he lost hope for himself and wrote the following
letter to the Jews in the form of a supplication. It read thus:

19 "To my esteemed Jewish citizens, Antiochus, their king
and general, sends hearty greetings and best wishes for their
health and happiness. 20 If you and your children are well
and your affairs are going as you wish, I thank God very
much, for my hopes are in heaven. 21 Now that I am ill, I
recall with affection the esteem and good will you bear me.
On returning from the regions of Persia, I fell victim to a
troublesome illness; so I thought it necessary to form plans
for the general welfare of all. 22 Actually, I do not despair
about my health, since I have great hopes of recovering from
my illness. 23 Nevertheless, I know that my father, whenever
he went on campaigns in the hinterland, would name his

NEW JERUSALEM BIBLE

declared free; 15 as for the Jews, whom he had considered as
not even worth burying, so much carrion to be thrown out
with their children for birds and beasts to prey on, he would
give them all equal rights with the Athenians; 16 the holy
Temple which he had once plundered he would now adorn
with the finest offerings; he would restore all the sacred vessels many times over; he would defray from his personal revenue the expenses incurred for the sacrifices; 17 and, to
crown all, he would himself turn Jew and visit every inhabited place, proclaiming the power of God.

18 Finding no respite at all from his suffering, God's just
sentence having overtaken him, he abandoned all hope for
himself and wrote the Jews the letter transcribed below,
which takes the form of an appeal in these terms:

19 'To the excellent Jews, to the citizens, Antiochus, king
and commander-in-chief, sends hearty greetings, wishing
them all health and prosperity.

20 'If you and your children are well and your affairs as
you would wish, we are profoundly thankful. 21 For my
part, I cherish affectionate memories of you.

'On my return from the country of Persia I fell seriously
ill, and thought it necessary to make provision for the
common security of all. 22 Not that I despair of my condition, for I have great hope of shaking off the malady,
23 but considering how my father, whenever he was making an expedition into the uplands, would designate his

GREEK OLD TESTAMENT

παράδοξον ἀποβαίνῃ ἢ καὶ προσαγγελθῇ τι δυσχερές, εἰδότες
οἱ κατὰ τὴν χώραν ᾧ καταλέλειπται τὰ πράγματα μὴ ἐπι-
ταράσσωνται· 25 πρὸς δὲ τούτοις κατανοῶν τοὺς παρακειμένους δυνάστας καὶ γειτνιῶντας τῇ βασιλείᾳ τοῖς καιροῖς
ἐπέχοντας καὶ προσδοκῶντας τὸ ἀποβησόμενον, ἀναδέδειχα
τὸν υἱὸν Ἀντίοχον βασιλέα, ὃν πολλάκις ἀνατρέχων εἰς τὰς
ἐπάνω σατραπείας τοῖς πλείστοις ὑμῶν παρεκατετιθέμην καὶ
συνίστων· γέγραφα δὲ πρὸς αὐτὸν τὰ ὑπογεγραμμένα.
26 παρακαλῶ οὖν ὑμᾶς καὶ ἀξιῶ μεμνημένους τῶν εὐεργεσιῶν
κοινῇ καὶ κατ' ἰδίαν ἕκαστον συντηρεῖν τὴν οὖσαν εὔνοιαν
εἰς ἐμὲ καὶ τὸν υἱόν· 27 πέπεισμαι γὰρ αὐτὸν ἐπιεικῶς καὶ
φιλανθρώπως παρακολουθοῦντα τῇ ἐμῇ προαιρέσει συμπερι-
ενεχθήσεσθαι ὑμῖν.

28 Ὁ μὲν οὖν ἀνδροφόνος καὶ βλάσφημος τὰ χείριστα
παθών, ὡς ἑτέρους διέθηκεν, ἐπὶ ξένης ἐν τοῖς ὄρεσιν οἰκτί-
στῳ μόρῳ κατέστρεψεν τὸν βίον. 29 παρεκομίζετο δὲ τὸ
σῶμα Φίλιππος ὁ σύντροφος αὐτοῦ, ὃς καὶ διευλαβηθεὶς τὸν
υἱὸν Ἀντιόχου πρὸς Πτολεμαῖον τὸν Φιλομήτορα εἰς Αἴγυπτον διεκομίσθη.

10 Μακκαβαῖος δὲ καὶ οἱ σὺν αὐτῷ τοῦ κυρίου προά-
γοντος αὐτοὺς τὸ μὲν ἱερὸν ἐκομίσαντο καὶ τὴν πόλιν, 2 τοὺς δὲ κατὰ τὴν ἀγορὰν βωμοὺς ὑπὸ τῶν ἀλλοφύλων
δεδημιουργημένους, ἔτι δὲ τεμένη καθεῖλαν 3 καὶ τὸν νεὼ
καθαρίσαντες ἕτερον θυσιαστήριον ἐποίησαν καὶ πυρώσαντες λίθους καὶ πῦρ ἐκ τούτων λαβόντες ἀνήνεγκαν θυσίας

KING JAMES VERSION

24 To the end that, if any thing fell out contrary to expectation, or if any tidings were brought that were grievous, they of the land, knowing to whom the state was left, might not be troubled:

25 Again, considering how that the princes that are borderers and neighbours unto my kingdom wait for opportunities, and expect what shall be the event, I have appointed my son Antiochus king, whom I often committed and commended unto many of you, when I went up into the high provinces; to whom I have written as followeth:

26 Therefore I pray and request you to remember the benefits that I have done unto you generally, and in special, and that every man will be still faithful to me and my son.

27 For I am persuaded that he understanding my mind will favourably and graciously yield to your desires.

28 Thus the murderer and blasphemer having suffered most grievously, as he entreated other men, so died he a miserable death in a strange country in the mountains.

29 And Philip, that was brought up with him, carried away his body, who also fearing the son of Antiochus went into Egypt to Ptolemeus Philometor.

10 Now Maccabeus and his company, the Lord guiding them, recovered the temple and the city:

2 But the altars which the heathen had built in the open street, and also the chapels, they pulled down.

3 And having cleansed the temple they made another altar, and striking stones they took fire out of them, and

DOUAY OLD TESTAMENT

24 To the end that if any thing contrary to expectation should fall out, or any bad tidings should be brought, they that were in the countries, knowing to whom the whole government was left, might not be troubled.

25 Moreover, considering that neighbouring princes and borderers wait for opportunities, and expect what shall be the event, I have appointed my son Antiochus king, whom I often recommended to many of you, when I went into the higher provinces: and I have written to him what I have joined here below.

26 I pray you therefore, and request of you, that remembering favours both public and private, you will every man of you continue to be faithful to me and to my son.

27 For I trust that he will behave with moderation and humanity, and following my intentions, will be gracious unto you.

28 Thus the murderer and blasphemer, being grievously struck, as himself had treated others, died a miserable death in a strange country among the mountains.

29 But Philip that was brought up with him, carried away his body: and out of fear of the son of Antiochus, went into Egypt to Ptolemee Philometor.

10 BUT Machabeus, and they that were with him, by the protection of the Lord, recovered the temple and the city again.

2 But he threw down the altars, which the heathens had set up in the streets, as also the temples of the idols.

3 And having purified the temple, they made another altar: and taking fire out of the fiery stones, they offered sacrifices

KNOX TRANSLATION

amiss, and ill tidings come, every governor in his own province must know his duty without fear of confusion. 25 And
here be princes all about, I know it well, waiting upon events
and ready to go with the times. Heir to the throne, then, I
needs must designate. Again and again, when I set out for
the high countries, I entrusted my son Antiochus to the general care. And now this written commission I have sent
him... 26 As you love me, then, bethink you of those benefits
you have received, both publicly and in private; keep faith,
each and all of you, with me and with my son. 27 I doubt not
he will shew himself his father's true heir, ever courteous,
and kindly, and easy of approach.

28 So died he, wretchedly enough, the murderer, the blasphemer, out in the hill-country far away from home. Cruel
the blow that struck him down, as he had ever been cruel in
his dealings. 29 His body was brought home again; Philip,
his foster-brother, came back with it, and then took refuge in
Egypt with Ptolemy Philometor, so little he trusted the young
prince Antiochus.

10 Meanwhile, God aiding, Machabaeus and his followers had recovered both temple and city. 2 Down came
the altars Gentile folk had set up in the open streets, down
came the shrines, 3 and the temple was purged of its defilement. They made a fresh altar, struck fire from flint, and

TODAY'S ENGLISH VERSION

24 He did this so that if something unexpected happened,
or if some bad news came back, then his subjects would
not be afraid, for they knew who had been left in command. 25 Also, I know how the rulers along the frontiers of
my kingdom are constantly on the lookout for any opportunity that may come along. That is why I have appointed
my son Antiochus to succeed me as king. I have frequently
entrusted him to your care and recommended him to you
when I went on my regular visits to the provinces east of
the Euphrates. (He is receiving a copy of the letter which
follows.) 26 Now I strongly urge each of you to keep in
mind the good things that I have done for you, both individually and as a nation, and to continue in your good will
toward me and my son. 27 I am confident that he will treat
you with fairness and kindness, just as I have always
done."

28 And so, this murderer, who had cursed God, suffered the
same terrible agonies he had brought on others, and then
died a miserable death in the mountains of a foreign land.
29 One of his close friends, Philip, took his body home; but,
because he was afraid of Antiochus' son, he went on to King
Ptolemy Philometor of Egypt.

10 Judas Maccabeus and his followers, under the leadership of the Lord, recaptured the Temple and the city
of Jerusalem. 2 They tore down the altars which foreigners
had set up in the marketplace and destroyed the other places
of worship that had been built. 3 They purified the Temple
and built a new altar. Then, with new fire started by striking

NEW REVISED STANDARD VERSION

his successor, 24 so that, if anything unexpected happened or
any unwelcome news came, the people throughout the realm
would not be troubled, for they would know to whom the
government was left. 25 Moreover, I understand how the
princes along the borders and the neighbors of my kingdom
keep watching for opportunities and waiting to see what will
happen. So I have appointed my son Antiochus to be king,
whom I have often entrusted and commended to most of you
when I hurried off to the upper provinces; and I have written
to him what is written here. 26 I therefore urge and beg you
to remember the public and private services rendered to you
and to maintain your present goodwill, each of you, toward
me and my son. 27 For I am sure that he will follow my policy and will treat you with moderation and kindness."

28 So the murderer and blasphemer, having endured the
more intense suffering, such as he had inflicted on others,
came to the end of his life by a most pitiable fate, among the
mountains in a strange land. 29 And Philip, one of his
courtiers, took his body home; then, fearing the son of Antiochus, he withdrew to Ptolemy Philometor in Egypt.

10 Now Maccabeus and his followers, the Lord leading
them on, recovered the temple and the city; 2 they
tore down the altars that had been built in the public square
by the foreigners, and also destroyed the sacred precincts.
3 They purified the sanctuary, and made another altar of sacrifice; then, striking fire out of flint, they offered sacrifices,

NEW AMERICAN BIBLE

successor, 24 so that, if anything unexpected happened or
any unwelcome news came, the people throughout the realm
would know to whom the government had been entrusted,
and so not be disturbed. 25 I am also bearing in mind that
the neighboring rulers, especially those on the borders of our
kingdom, are on the watch for opportunities and waiting to
see what will happen. I have therefore appointed as king my
son Antiochus, whom I have often before entrusted and commended to most of you, when I made hurried visits to the
outlying provinces. I have written to him the letter copied
below. 26 Therefore I beg and entreat each of you to remember the general and individual benefits you have received,
and to continue to show good will toward me and my son.
27 I am confident that, following my policy, he will treat you
with mildness and kindness in his relations with you."

28 So this murderer and blasphemer, after extreme sufferings, such as he had inflicted on others, died a miserable
death in the mountains of a foreign land. 29 His foster brother Philip brought the body home; but fearing Antiochus' son,
he later withdrew into Egypt, to Ptolemy Philometor.

10 When Maccabeus and his companions, under the
LORD's leadership, had recovered the temple and
the city, 2 they destroyed the altars erected by the Gentiles
in the marketplace and the sacred enclosures. 3 After purifying the temple, they made a new altar. Then, with fire struck

NEW JERUSALEM BIBLE

successor 24 so that, in case of any unforeseen event or disquieting rumour, the people of the provinces might know to
whom he had left the conduct of affairs, and thus remain
undisturbed; 25 furthermore, being well aware that the sov-
ereigns on our frontiers and the neighbours of our realm
are watching for opportunities and waiting to see what will
happen, I have designated as king my son Antiochus,
whom I have more than once entrusted and commended to
most of you when I was setting out for the upland
satrapies; a transcript of my letter to him is appended hereto. 26 I therefore urge and require you, being mindful of the
benefits both public and personal received from me, that
you each persist in those sentiments of goodwill that you
harbour towards me. 27 I am confident that he will pursue
my own policy with benevolence and humanity, and will
prove accommodating to your interests.'

28 And so this murderer and blasphemer, having endured
sufferings as terrible as those which he had made others
endure, met his pitiable fate, and ended his life in the mountains far from his home. 29 His comrade Philip brought back
his body, and then, fearing Antiochus' son, withdrew to
Egypt, to the court of Ptolemy Philometor.

10 [a] Maccabaeus and his companions, under the Lord's
guidance, restored the Temple and the city, 2 and
pulled down the altars erected by the foreigners in the market place, as well as the shrines. 3 They purified the sanctuary and built another altar; then, striking fire from flints and

[a] 10 10:1seq. // 1 M 4:36–61.

GREEK OLD TESTAMENT

μετὰ διετῆ χρόνον καὶ θυμίαμα καὶ λύχνους καὶ τῶν ἄρτων
τὴν πρόθεσιν ἐποιήσαντο. 4 ταῦτα δὲ ποιήσαντες ἠξίωσαν
τὸν κύριον πεσόντες ἐπὶ κοιλίαν μηκέτι περιπεσεῖν τοιού-
τοις κακοῖς, ἀλλ' ἐάν ποτε καὶ ἁμάρτωσιν, ὑπ' αὐτοῦ μετὰ
ἐπιεικείας παιδεύεσθαι καὶ μὴ βλασφήμοις καὶ βαρβάροις
ἔθνεσιν παραδίδοσθαι. 5 ἐν ᾗ δὲ ἡμέρᾳ ὁ νεὼς ὑπὸ ἀλλοφύλων ἐβεβηλώθη, συνέβη κατὰ τὴν αὐτὴν ἡμέραν τὸν καθαρισμὸν γενέσθαι τοῦ ναοῦ, τῇ πέμπτῃ καὶ εἰκάδι τοῦ αὐτοῦ
μηνός, ὅς ἐστιν Χασελευ. 6 καὶ μετ' εὐφροσύνης ἦγον ἡμέρας ὀκτὼ σκηνωμάτων τρόπον μνημονεύοντες ὡς πρὸ μικροῦ
χρόνου τὴν τῶν σκηνῶν ἑορτὴν ἐν τοῖς ὄρεσιν καὶ ἐν τοῖς
σπηλαίοις θηρίων τρόπον ἦσαν νεμόμενοι. 7 διὸ θύρσους καὶ
κλάδους ὡραίους, ἔτι δὲ καὶ φοίνικας ἔχοντες ὕμνους ἀνέφερον τῷ εὐοδώσαντι καθαρισθῆναι τὸν ἑαυτοῦ τόπον.
8 ἐδογμάτισαν δὲ μετὰ κοινοῦ προστάγματος καὶ ψηφίσμα-
τος παντὶ τῷ τῶν Ιουδαίων ἔθνει κατ' ἐνιαυτὸν ἄγειν τάσδε
τὰς ἡμέρας. 9 καὶ τὰ μὲν τῆς Ἀντιόχου τοῦ προσαγορευθέντος Ἐπιφανοῦς τελευτῆς οὕτως εἶχεν.

10 Νυνὶ δὲ τὰ κατὰ τὸν Εὐπάτορα Ἀντίοχον, υἱὸν δὲ τοῦ
ἀσεβοῦς γενόμενον, δηλώσομεν αὐτὰ συντέμνοντες τὰ συνέ-
χοντα τῶν πολέμων κακά. 11 οὗτος γὰρ παραλαβὼν τὴν
βασιλείαν ἀνέδειξεν ἐπὶ τῶν πραγμάτων Λυσίαν τινά, Κοίλης δὲ Συρίας καὶ Φοινίκης στρατηγὸν πρώταρχον. 12 Πτολεμαῖος γὰρ ὁ καλούμενος Μάκρων τὸ δίκαιον συντηρεῖν

KING JAMES VERSION

offered a sacrifice after two years, and set forth incense, and lights, and shewbread.

4 When that was done, they fell flat down, and besought the Lord that they might come no more into such troubles; but if they sinned any more against him, that he himself would chasten them with mercy, and that they might not be delivered unto the blasphemous and barbarous nations.

5 Now upon the same day that the strangers profaned the temple, on the very same day it was cleansed again, even the five and twentieth day of the same month, which is Casleu.

6 And they kept eight days with gladness, as in the feast of the tabernacles, remembering that not long afore they had held the feast of the tabernacles, when as they wandered in the mountains and dens like beasts.

7 Therefore they bare branches, and fair boughs, and palms also, and sang psalms unto him that had given them good success in cleansing his place.

8 They ordained also by a common statute and decree, That every year those days should be kept of the whole nation of the Jews.

9 And this was the end of Antiochus, called Epiphanes.

10 Now will we declare the acts of Antiochus Eupator, who was the son of this wicked man, gathering briefly the calamities of the wars.

11 So when he was come to the crown, he set one Lysias over the affairs of his realm, and *appointed him* chief governor of Celosyria and Phenice.

12 For Ptolemeus, that was called Macron, choosing rather

DOUAY OLD TESTAMENT

after two years, and set forth incense, and lamps, and the loaves of proposition.

4 And when they had done these things, they besought the Lord, lying prostrate on the ground, that they might no more fall into such evils; but if they should at any time sin, that they might be chastised by him more gently, and not be delivered up to barbarians and blasphemous men.

5 Now upon the same day that the temple had been polluted by the strangers, on the very same day it was cleansed again, to wit, on the five and twentieth day of the month of Casleu.

6 And they kept eight days with joy, after the manner of the feast of the tabernacles, remembering that not long before they had kept the feast of the tabernacles when they were in the mountains, and in dens like wild beasts.

7 Therefore they *now* carried boughs, and green branches, and palms for Him that had given them good success in cleansing his place.

8 And they ordained by a common statute, and decree, that all the nation of the Jews should keep those days every year.

9 And this was the end of Antiochus that was called the Illustrious.

10 But now we will relate the acts of Eupator the son of that wicked Antiochus, abridging the account of the evils that happened in the wars.

11 For when he was come to the crown, he appointed over the affairs of his realm one Lysias, general of the army of Phenicia and Syria.

12 For Ptolemee that was called Macer, was determined to

KNOX TRANSLATION

offered sacrifice again after two years' intermission; rose
incense, burned lamp, loaves were set out on the sacred table
once more. 4 Then, bowing down to earth, they made petition to the Lord, never again such calamity might overtake
them; sin if they did, himself in his great mercy should chastise them, not hand them over into the cruel power of blasphemous enemies. 5 It so fell out, that the temple was purified on the twenty-fifth day of Casleu, the very time of its
profanation by the Gentiles. 6 Eight days of rejoicing they
kept, with such ceremonies as belong to the feast of Tent-
dwelling; it was a feast of tent-dwelling indeed they had kept
a while back, when they lodged like beasts among the hill-
side caverns! 7 Now that God had made the way clear for his
temple's cleansing, what wonder if they set up in his honour
branches, and green boughs, and arbours of palm? 8 What
wonder if a decree was passed, by common consent, all
Jewry should keep the festival year by year?

9 Now the story is told, how Antiochus called the
Illustrious came by his end, 10 turn we to his son, Antiochus
Eupator, that was born of a very ill father;[a] record we in
brief the history of his reign, and the hazards of war that
went with it. 11 Upon his accession, this king entrusted all
the business of the realm to one Lysias, commander of the
forces in Phoenice and Coelesyria. 12 With Ptolemy, that was
called Macer, we are concerned no more; fain would he have

a The Greek word 'Eupator' means 'born of a noble father'.

TODAY'S ENGLISH VERSION

flint, they offered sacrifice for the first time in two years,
burned incense, lighted the lamps, and set out the sacred
loaves. 4 After they had done all this, they lay face down on
the ground and prayed that the Lord would never again let
such disasters strike them. They begged him to be merciful
when he punished them for future sins and not hand them
over any more to barbaric, pagan Gentiles. 5 They rededicated the Temple on the twenty-fifth day of the month of Kislev,
the same day of the same month on which the Temple had
been desecrated by the Gentiles. 6 The happy celebration lasted eight days, like the Festival of Shelters, and the people
remembered how only a short time before, they had spent
the Festival of Shelters wandering like wild animals in the
mountains and living in caves. 7 But now, carrying green
palm branches and sticks decorated with ivy, they paraded
around, singing grateful praises to him who had brought
about the purification of his own Temple. 8 Everyone agreed
that the entire Jewish nation should celebrate this festival
each year.

9 The days of Antiochus Epiphanes had come to an end.
10 Now we will tell about Antiochus Eupator, the son of this
godless man, and give a summary of the evil effects of his
wars. 11 When he became king he appointed a man by the
name of Lysias to be in charge of the affairs of state and to
be chief governor of Greater Syria, 12 replacing Ptolemy
Macron, who had been the first governor to treat the Jews

NEW REVISED STANDARD VERSION

after a lapse of two years, and they offered incense and lighted lamps and set out the bread of the Presence. 4 When they
had done this, they fell prostrate and implored the Lord that
they might never again fall into such misfortunes, but that,
if they should ever sin, they might be disciplined by him with
forbearance and not be handed over to blasphemous and
barbarous nations. 5 It happened that on the same day on
which the sanctuary had been profaned by the foreigners, the
purification of the sanctuary took place, that is, on the twenty-fifth day of the same month, which was Chislev. 6 They
celebrated it for eight days with rejoicing, in the manner of
the festival of booths, remembering how not long before,
during the festival of booths, they had been wandering in the
mountains and caves like wild animals. 7 Therefore, carrying
ivy-wreathed wands and beautiful branches and also fronds
of palm, they offered hymns of thanksgiving to him who had
given success to the purifying of his own holy place. 8 They
decreed by public edict, ratified by vote, that the whole
nation of the Jews should observe these days every year.
9 Such then was the end of Antiochus, who was called
Epiphanes.

10 Now we will tell what took place under Antiochus
Eupator, who was the son of that ungodly man, and will
give a brief summary of the principal calamities of the wars.
11 This man, when he succeeded to the kingdom, appointed
one Lysias to have charge of the government and to be chief
governor of Coelesyria and Phoenicia. 12 Ptolemy, who was

NEW AMERICAN BIBLE

from flint, they offered sacrifice for the first time in two
years, burned incense, and lighted lamps. They also set out
the showbread. 4 When they had done this, they prostrated
themselves and begged the LORD that they might never again
fall into such misfortunes, and that if they should sin at any
time, he might chastise them with moderation and not hand
them over to blasphemous and barbarous Gentiles. 5 On the
anniversary of the day on which the temple had been profaned by the Gentiles, that is, the twenty-fifth of the same
month Chislev, the purification of the temple took place.
6 The Jews celebrated joyfully for eight days as on the feast of
Booths, remembering how, a little while before, they had
spent the feast of Booths living like wild animals in caves on
the mountains. 7 Carrying rods entwined with leaves, green
branches and palms, they sang hymns of grateful praise to
him who had brought about the purification of his own
Place. 8 By public edict and decree they prescribed that the
whole Jewish nation should celebrate these days every year.

9 Such was the end of Antiochus surnamed Epiphanes.
10 Now we shall relate what happened under Antiochus
Eupator, the son of that godless man, and shall give a summary of the chief evils caused by the wars. 11 When Eupator
succeeded to the kingdom, he put a certain Lysias in charge
of the government as commander in chief of Coelesyria and
Phoenicia. 12 Ptolemy, surnamed Macron, had taken the lead

NEW JERUSALEM BIBLE

using this fire, they offered the first sacrifice for two years,
burning incense, lighting the lamps and setting out the
loaves. 4 When they had done this, prostrating themselves
on the ground, they implored the Lord never again to let
them fall into such adversity, but if they should ever sin, to
correct them with moderation and not to deliver them over to
blasphemous and barbarous nations. 5 This day of the purification of the Temple fell on the very day on which the
Temple had been profaned by the foreigners, the twenty-fifth
of the same month, Chislev. 6 They kept eight festal days
with rejoicing, in the manner of the feast of Shelters, remembering how, not long before at the time of the feast of
Shelters, they had been living in the mountains and caverns
like wild beasts. 7 Then, carrying thyrsuses, leafy boughs
and palms, they offered hymns to him who had brought the
cleansing of his own holy place to a happy outcome. 8 They
also decreed by public edict, ratified by vote, that the whole
Jewish nation should celebrate those same days every year.

9 Such were the circumstances attending the death of
Antiochus styled Epiphanes. 10 Our task now is to unfold the
history of Antiochus Eupator, son of that godless man, and
briefly to relate the evil effects of the wars. 11 On coming to
the throne, this prince put at the head of affairs a certain
Lysias, the general officer commanding Coele-Syria and
Phoenicia, 12 whereas Ptolemy, known as Macron, and the

Greek Old Testament

προηγούμενος πρὸς τοὺς Ιουδαίους διὰ τὴν γεγονυῖαν εἰς
αὐτοὺς ἀδικίαν ἐπειρᾶτο τὰ πρὸς αὐτοὺς εἰρηνικῶς διεξά-
γειν· 13 ὅθεν κατηγορούμενος ὑπὸ τῶν φίλων πρὸς τὸν
Εὐπάτορα καὶ προδότης παρ᾽ ἕκαστα ἀκούων διὰ τὸ τὴν Κύπρον ἐμπιστευθέντα ὑπὸ τοῦ Φιλομήτορος ἐκλιπεῖν καὶ πρὸς
᾽Αντίοχον τὸν ᾽Επιφανῆ ἀναχωρῆσαι μήτε εὐγενῆ τὴν
ἐξουσίαν εὐγενίσας φαρμακεύσας ἑαυτὸν ἐξέλιπεν τὸν βίον.
14 Γοργίας δὲ γενόμενος στρατηγὸς τῶν τόπων ἐξενοτρό-
φει καὶ παρ᾽ ἕκαστα πρὸς τοὺς Ιουδαίους ἐπολεμοτρόφει.
15 ὁμοῦ δὲ τούτῳ καὶ οἱ Ιδουμαῖοι ἐγκρατεῖς ἐπικαίρων
ὀχυρωμάτων ὄντες ἐγύμναζον τοὺς Ιουδαίους καὶ τοὺς
φυγαδεύσαντας ἀπὸ Ιεροσολύμων προσλαβόμενοι πολεμοτρο-
φεῖν ἐπεχείρουν. 16 οἱ δὲ περὶ τὸν Μακκαβαῖον ποιησάμενοι
λιτανείαν καὶ ἀξιώσαντες τὸν θεὸν σύμμαχον αὐτοῖς γενέσθαι ἐπὶ τὰ τῶν Ιδουμαίων ὀχυρώματα ὥρμησαν, 17 οἷς καὶ
προσβαλόντες εὐρώστως ἐγκρατεῖς ἐγένοντο τῶν τόπων
πάντας τε τοὺς ἐπὶ τῷ τείχει μαχομένους ἠμύναντο κατέ-
σφαζόν τε τοὺς ἐμπίπτοντας, ἀνεῖλον δὲ οὐχ ἧττον τῶν
δισμυρίων. 18 συμφυγόντων δὲ οὐκ ἔλαττον τῶν ἐνακισχιλί-
ων εἰς δύο πύργους ὀχυροὺς εὖ μάλα καὶ πάντα τὰ πρὸς
πολιορκίαν ἔχοντας 19 ὁ Μακκαβαῖος εἰς ἐπείγοντας τόπους ἀπολιπὼν Σιμωνα καὶ Ιωσηπον, ἔτι δὲ καὶ Ζακχαῖον καὶ
τοὺς σὺν αὐτῷ ἱκανοὺς πρὸς τὴν τούτων πολιορκίαν αὐτὸς
ἐχωρίσθη. 20 οἱ δὲ περὶ τὸν Σιμωνα φιλαργυρήσαντες ὑπό
τινων τῶν ἐν τοῖς πύργοις ἐπείσθησαν ἀργυρίῳ, ἑπτάκις δὲ

King James Version

to do justice unto the Jews for the wrong that had been done unto them, endeavoured to continue peace with them.

13 Whereupon being accused of *the king's* friends before Eupator, and called traitor at every word, because he had left Cyprus, that Philometor had committed unto him, and departed to Antiochus Epiphanes, and seeing that he was in no honourable place, he was so discouraged, that he poisoned himself and died.

14 But when Gorgias was governor of the holds, he hired soldiers, and nourished war continually with the Jews:

15 And therewithall the Idumeans, having gotten into their hands the most commodious holds, kept the Jews occupied, and receiving those that were banished from Jerusalem, they went about to nourish war.

16 Then they that were with Maccabeus made supplication, and besought God that he would be their helper; and so they ran with violence upon the strong holds of the Idumeans,

17 And assaulting them strongly, they won the holds, and kept off all that fought upon the wall, and slew all that fell into their hands, and killed no fewer than twenty thousand.

18 And because certain, who were no less than nine thousand, were fled together into two very strong castles, having all manner of things convenient to *sustain* the siege,

19 Maccabeus left Simon and Joseph, and Zaccheus also, and them that were with him, who were enough to besiege them, and departed himself unto those places which more needed his help.

20 Now they that were with Simon, being led with covetousness, were persuaded for money through certain of

Douay Old Testament

be strictly just to the Jews, and especially by reason of the wrong that had been done them, and to deal peaceably with them.

13 But being accused for this to Eupator by his friends, and being oftentimes called traitor, because he had left Cyprus which Philometor had committed to him, and coming over to Antiochus the Illustrious, had revolted also from him, he put an end to his life by poison.

14 But Gorgias, who was governor of the holds, taking with him the strangers, often fought against the Jews.

15 And the Jews that occupied the most commodious hold, received those that were driven out of Jerusalem, and attempted to make war.

16 Then they that were with Machabeus, beseeching the Lord by prayers to be their helper, made a strong attack upon the strong holds of the Idumeans:

17 And assaulting them with great force, won the holds, killed them that came in the way, and slew altogether no fewer than twenty thousand.

18 And whereas some were fled into very strong towers, having all manner of provision to sustain a siege,

19 Machabeus left Simon and Joseph, and Zacheus, and them that were with them in sufficient number to besiege them, and departed to those expeditions which urged more.

20 Now they that were with Simon, being led with covetousness, were persuaded for the sake of money by some

Knox Translation

made amends to the Jews for the wrong done them, and kept
their friendship, 13 but for that very reason he was
denounced to Eupator by his courtiers. He was a traitor, they
said, twice over, false to his trust, when Philometor left him
in charge of Cyprus, and now weary of his new allegiance to
Antiochus the Illustrious! Whereupon he put an end to his
own life by poison. 14 When Gorgias was given command of
the district, he was for ever making war on the Jews, with
mercenaries to aid him; 15 and there were natives of the
country besides,[a] well entrenched in their strongholds, that
gave welcome to deserters from Jerusalem, and so fanned the
flames of enmity.
16 And now the followers of Machabaeus, after prayer
made for the divine assistance, delivered an attack upon the
Edomite strongholds. 17 These, by a very courageous assault,
they occupied, and cut down all they met, putting not less
than twenty thousand men to the sword; 18 but there were
two fortresses yet remaining, into which the survivors threw
themselves, well provided with means of defence. 19 Machabaeus himself went off to fight other battles of greater
moment, leaving Simon, Joseph and Zacchaeus, with a
strong force under their command, to carry on the siege.
20 And here the avarice of Simon's men was their undoing;

a 'Natives of the country'; literally, in the Latin version, 'Jews', but this is probably a copyist's mistake for 'Edomites', the reading found in the Greek text.

TODAY'S ENGLISH VERSION

fairly. Macron had established peaceful relations with them
in an attempt to make up for the wrongs they had suffered.
13 As a result the King's Friends went to Eupator and accused
Macron of treachery, because he had abandoned the island of
Cyprus, which King Philometor of Egypt had placed under his
command, and had gone over to Antiochus Epiphanes. In
fact, everyone called Macron a traitor. No longer able to
maintain the respect that his office demanded, he committed
suicide by taking poison.

14 When Gorgias became governor of Idumea, he kept a
force of mercenaries and attacked the Jews at every opportunity. 15 Not only this, but the Idumeans themselves controlled certain strategic fortresses and were constantly
harassing the Jews. They welcomed those who fled from
Jerusalem and did everything they could to keep the country
in a perpetual state of war. 16 So Judas Maccabeus and his
men, after offering prayers for God's help, rushed out and
made a vigorous attack against the Idumean fortresses.
17 They beat back those who were defending the walls and
captured the fortresses, killing everyone they found, a total
of about 20,000 people.

18 About 9,000 of the enemy, however, managed to take
refuge in two easily defended forts, with everything they
needed to withstand a siege. 19 Judas had to go on to some
other places in the country, where he was more urgently
needed, but he left behind Simon and Joseph, together with
Zacchaeus and his men. This force was large enough to continue the siege, 20 but some of Simon's men were greedy,

NEW REVISED STANDARD VERSION

called Macron, took the lead in showing justice to the Jews
because of the wrong that had been done to them, and
attempted to maintain peaceful relations with them. 13 As a
result he was accused before Eupator by the king's Friends.
He heard himself called a traitor at every turn, because he
had abandoned Cyprus, which Philometor had entrusted to
him, and had gone over to Antiochus Epiphanes. Unable to
command the respect due his office,[a] he took poison and
ended his life.

14 When Gorgias became governor of the region, he maintained a force of mercenaries, and at every turn kept attacking the Jews. 15 Besides this, the Idumeans, who had control
of important strongholds, were harassing the Jews; they
received those who were banished from Jerusalem, and
endeavored to keep up the war. 16 But Maccabeus and his
forces, after making solemn supplication and imploring God
to fight on their side, rushed to the strongholds of the
Idumeans. 17 Attacking them vigorously, they gained possession of the places, and beat off all who fought upon the wall,
and slaughtered those whom they encountered, killing no
fewer than twenty thousand.

18 When at least nine thousand took refuge in two very
strong towers well equipped to withstand a siege, 19 Maccabeus left Simon and Joseph, and also Zacchaeus and his
troops, a force sufficient to besiege them; and he himself set
off for places where he was more urgently needed. 20 But
those with Simon, who were money-hungry, were bribed by

a Cn: Meaning of Gk uncertain

NEW AMERICAN BIBLE

in treating the Jews fairly because of the previous injustice
that had been done them, and he endeavored to have peaceful relations with them. 13 As a result, he was accused before
Eupator by the King's Friends. In fact, on all sides he heard
himself called a traitor for having abandoned Cyprus, which
Philometor had entrusted to him, and for having gone over
to Antiochus Epiphanes. Since he could not command the
respect due to his high office, he ended his life by taking poison.

14 When Gorgias became governor of the region, he
employed foreign troops and used every opportunity to
attack the Jews. 15 At the same time the Idumeans, who held
some important strongholds, were harassing the Jews; they
welcomed fugitives from Jerusalem and endeavored to continue the war. 16 Maccabeus and his companions, after public prayers asking God to be their ally, moved quickly against
the strongholds of the Idumeans. 17 Attacking vigorously,
they gained control of the places, drove back all who manned
the walls, and cut down those who opposed them, killing as
many as twenty thousand men. 18 When at least nine thousand took refuge in two very strong towers, containing
everything necessary to sustain a siege, 19 Maccabeus left
Simon and Joseph, along with Zacchaeus and his men, in
sufficient numbers to besiege them, while he himself went
off to places where he was more urgently needed. 20 But
some of the men in Simon's force who were money lovers let
themselves be bribed by some of the men in the towers; on

NEW JERUSALEM BIBLE

first person to govern the Jews justly, had done his best to
govern them peacefully to make up for the wrongs inflicted on
them in the past. 13 Denounced, in consequence, to Eupator
by the Friends of the King, he heard himself called traitor at
every turn: for having abandoned Cyprus, which had been
entrusted to him by Philometer, for having gone over to
Antiochus Epiphanes, and for having shed no lustre on his
illustrious office: he committed suicide by poisoning himself.

14 Gorgias now became general of the area; he maintained
a force of mercenaries and a continual state of war with the
Jews.[a] 15 At the same time, the Idumaeans, who controlled
important fortresses, were harassing the Jews, welcoming
outlaws from Jerusalem and endeavouring to maintain a
state of war. 16 Maccabaeus and his men, after making public supplication to God, entreating him to support them,
began operations against the Idumaean fortresses.
17 Vigorously pressing home their attack, they seized possession of these vantage points, beating off all who fought on
the ramparts; they slaughtered all who fell into their hands,
accounting for no fewer than twenty thousand. 18 Nine thousand at least took refuge in two exceptionally strong towers
with everything they needed to withstand a siege, 19 whereupon, Maccabaeus left Simon and Joseph, with Zacchaeus
and his forces, in sufficient numbers to besiege them, and
himself went off to other places requiring his attention.
20 But Simon's men were greedy for money and allowed
themselves to be bribed by some of the men in the towers;

a **10** // 1 M 5:1–8.

GREEK OLD TESTAMENT

μυρίας δραχμὰς λαβόντες εἴασάν τινας διαρρυῆναι.
21 προσαγγελέντος δὲ τῷ Μακκαβαίῳ περὶ τοῦ γεγονότος
συναγαγὼν τοὺς ἡγουμένους τοῦ λαοῦ κατηγόρησεν ὡς
ἀργυρίου πέπρακαν τοὺς ἀδελφοὺς τοὺς πολεμίους κατ'
αὐτῶν ἀπολύσαντες. 22 τούτους μὲν οὖν προδότας γενομένους ἀπέκτεινεν, καὶ παραχρῆμα τοὺς δύο πύργους κατελάβετο. 23 τοῖς δὲ ὅπλοις τὰ πάντα ἐν ταῖς χερσὶν εὐοδού-
μενος ἀπώλεσεν ἐν τοῖς δυσὶν ὀχυρώμασιν πλείους τῶν
δισμυρίων.

24 Τιμόθεος δὲ ὁ πρότερον ἡττηθεὶς ὑπὸ τῶν Ιουδαίων
συναγαγὼν ξένας δυνάμεις παμπληθεῖς καὶ τοὺς τῆς Ἀσίας
γενομένους ἵππους συναθροίσας οὐκ ὀλίγους παρῆν ὡς
δοριάλωτον λημψόμενος τὴν Ιουδαίαν. 25 οἱ δὲ περὶ τὸν
Μακκαβαῖον συνεγγίζοντος αὐτοῦ πρὸς ἱκετείαν τοῦ θεοῦ
γῇ τὰς κεφαλὰς καταπάσαντες καὶ τὰς ὀσφύας σάκκοις ζώ-
σαντες 26 ἐπὶ τὴν ἀπέναντι τοῦ θυσιαστηρίου κρηπῖδα
προσπεσόντες ἠξίουν ἵλεως αὐτοῖς γενόμενον ἐχθρεῦσαι
τοῖς ἐχθροῖς αὐτῶν καὶ ἀντικεῖσθαι τοῖς ἀντικειμένοις,
καθὼς ὁ νόμος διασαφεῖ. 27 γενόμενοι δὲ ἀπὸ τῆς δεήσεως
ἀναλαβόντες τὰ ὅπλα προῆγον ἀπὸ τῆς πόλεως ἐπὶ πλεῖον·
συνεγγίσαντες δὲ τοῖς πολεμίοις ἐφ' ἑαυτῶν ἦσαν. 28 ἄρτι
δὲ τῆς ἀνατολῆς διαχεομένης προσέβαλον ἑκάτεροι, οἱ μὲν
ἔγγυον ἔχοντες εὐημερίας καὶ νίκης μετὰ ἀρετῆς τὴν ἐπὶ
τὸν κύριον καταφυγήν, οἱ δὲ καθηγεμόνα τῶν ἀγώνων
ταττόμενοι τὸν θυμόν. 29 γενομένης δὲ καρτερᾶς μάχης

KING JAMES VERSION

those that were in the castle, and took seventy thousand drachms, and let some of them escape.

21 But when it was told Maccabeus what was done, he called the governors of the people together, and accused those men, that they had sold their brethren for money, and set their enemies free to fight against them.

22 So he slew those that were found traitors, and immediately took the two castles.

23 And having good success with his weapons in all things he took in hand, he slew in the two holds more than twenty thousand.

24 Now Timotheus, whom the Jews had overcome before, when he had gathered a great multitude of foreign forces, and horses out of Asia not a few, came as though he would take Jewry by force of arms.

25 But when he drew near, they that were with Maccabeus turned themselves to pray unto God, and sprinkled earth upon their heads, and girded their loins with sackcloth,

26 And fell down at the foot of the altar, and besought him to be merciful to them, and to be an enemy to their enemies, and an adversary to their adversaries, as the law declareth.

27 So after the prayer they took their weapons, and went on further from the city: and when they drew near to their enemies, they kept by themselves.

28 Now the sun being newly risen, they joined both together; the one part having together with their virtue their refuge also unto the Lord for a pledge of their success and victory: the other side making their rage leader of their battle.

29 But when the battle waxed strong, there appeared unto

DOUAY OLD TESTAMENT

that were in the towers: and taking seventy thousand didrachmas, let some of them escape.

21 But when it was told Machabeus what was done, he assembled the rulers of the people, and accused those men that they had sold their brethren for money, having let their adversaries escape.

22 So he put these traitors to death, and forthwith took the two towers.

23 And having good success in arms and in all things he took in hand, he slew more than twenty thousand in the two holds.

24 But Timotheus who before had been overcome by the Jews, having called together a multitude of foreign troops, and assembled horsemen out of Asia, came as though he would take Judea by force of arms.

25 But Machabeus and they that were with him, when he drew near, prayed to the Lord, sprinkling earth upon their heads and girding their loins with haircloth,

26 And lying prostrate at the foot of the altar, besought him to be merciful to them, and to be an enemy to their enemies, and an adversary to their adversaries, as the law saith.

27 And so after prayer taking their arms, they went forth further from the city, and when they were come very near the enemies they rested.

28 But as soon as the sun was risen both sides joined battle: the one part having with their valour the Lord for a surety of victory and success: but the other side making their rage their leader in battle.

29 But when they were in the heat of the engagement

KNOX TRANSLATION

for a bribe of seventy thousand silver pieces, they allowed
some of the defenders to escape. 21 Machabaeus no sooner
heard of it, than he summoned the leaders of the people, and
arraigned the guilty men in their presence; what, would they
sell their brethren's lives, by letting the enemies of their race
go free? 22 So he put these traitors to death; and for the
strongholds, he conquered both of them at a blow, 23 so carrying all before him by force of arms, that more than twenty
thousand of the defenders perished.

24 But Timotheus could not be content with one defeat at
the hands of the Jews; he would bring in hordes of foreign
soldiery, and cavalry from Asia, threatening Judaea with
slavery. 25 At his coming, the party of Machabaeus fell to
prayer; earth on their heads, sackcloth about their loins,
26 they lay prostrate at the altar's foot, entreating the Lord he
would espouse their quarrel, and their foes should be his; the
law had promised it. 27 Then, this supplication made, they
took up arms and marched out, leaving the city far away in
their rear, nor ever halted till they were close to the enemy's
lines. 28 Soon as the dawn broke, they engaged; on the one
side, all trust in the Lord, valour's best pledge of victory and
fairer times; on the other, naught but human eagerness to
inspire courage. 29 Hard went the day, and, so it seemed to

TODAY'S ENGLISH VERSION

and when they were offered 140 pounds of silver, they let
some of the enemy escape from the forts. 21When Judas
heard what had happened, he called together the leaders of
his troops and accused those men of selling their brothers by
setting their enemies free to fight against them. 22Then he
executed the traitors and immediately captured the two forts.
23Judas was always successful in battle, and in his assault
on those two forts he killed more than 20,000 men.

24Timothy, who had been defeated by the Jews once
before, had gathered a large number of cavalry from Asia
and a tremendous force of mercenary troops and was now
advancing to take Judea by armed attack. 25But as the
enemy forces were approaching, Judas and his men prayed to
God. They put on sackcloth, threw dirt on their heads, 26and
lay face downward on the steps of the altar, begging God to
help them by fighting against their enemies, as he had promised in his Law.

27When they had finished praying, they took up their
weapons, went out a good distance from Jerusalem, and
stopped for the night not far from the enemy. 28At daybreak
the two armies joined in battle. The Jewish forces depended
upon both their bravery and their trust in the Lord for victory, while the enemy relied only on their ability to fight fiercely. 29When the fighting was at its worst, the enemy saw five

NEW REVISED STANDARD VERSION

some of those who were in the towers, and on receiving seventy thousand drachmas let some of them slip away.
21When word of what had happened came to Maccabeus, he
gathered the leaders of the people, and accused these men of
having sold their kindred for money by setting their enemies
free to fight against them. 22Then he killed these men who
had turned traitor, and immediately captured the two towers.
23Having success at arms in everything he undertook, he
destroyed more than twenty thousand in the two strongholds.

24 Now Timothy, who had been defeated by the Jews
before, gathered a tremendous force of mercenaries and collected the cavalry from Asia in no small number. He came
on, intending to take Judea by storm. 25As he drew near,
Maccabeus and his men sprinkled dust on their heads and
girded their loins with sackcloth, in supplication to God.
26Falling upon the steps before the altar, they implored him
to be gracious to them and to be an enemy to their enemies
and an adversary to their adversaries, as the law declares.
27And rising from their prayer they took up their arms and
advanced a considerable distance from the city; and when
they came near the enemy they halted. 28Just as dawn was
breaking, the two armies joined battle, the one having as
pledge of success and victory not only their valor but also
their reliance on the Lord, while the other made rage their
leader in the fight.

29 When the battle became fierce, there appeared to the

NEW AMERICAN BIBLE

receiving seventy thousand drachmas, they allowed a number of them to escape. 21When Maccabeus was told what
had happened, he assembled the rulers of the people and
accused those men of having sold their kinsmen for money
by setting their enemies free to fight against them. 22So he
put them to death as traitors, and without delay captured the
two towers. 23As he was successful at arms in all his undertakings, he destroyed more than twenty thousand men in the
two strongholds.

24Timothy, who had previously been defeated by the Jews,
gathered a tremendous force of foreign troops and collected a
large number of cavalry from Asia; then he appeared in
Judea, ready to conquer it by force. 25At his approach,
Maccabeus and his men made supplication to God, sprinkling earth upon their heads and girding their loins in sackcloth. 26Lying prostrate at the foot of the altar, they begged
him to be gracious to them, and to be an enemy to their enemies, and a foe to their foes, as the law declares.

27After the prayer, they took up their arms and advanced a
considerable distance from the city, halting when they were
close to the enemy. 28As soon as dawn broke, the armies
joined battle, the one having as pledge of success and victory
not only their valor but also their reliance on the LORD, and
the other taking fury as their leader in the fight.

29In the midst of the fierce battle, there appeared to the

NEW JERUSALEM BIBLE

accepting seventy thousand drachmas, they let a number of
them escape. 21When Maccabaeus was told what had happened, he summoned the people's commanders and accused
the offenders of having sold their brothers for money by
releasing their enemies to fight them. 22Having executed
them as traitors, he at once proceeded to capture both towers. 23Successful in all that he undertook by force of arms,
in these two fortresses he slaughtered more than twenty
thousand men.

24Timotheus, who had been beaten by the Jews once
before, now assembled an enormous force of mercenaries,
mustering cavalry from Asia in considerable numbers, and
soon appeared in Judaea, expecting to conquer it by force of
arms. 25At his approach, Maccabaeus and his men made
their supplications to God, sprinkling earth on their heads
and putting sackcloth round their waists. 26Prostrating
themselves on the terrace before the altar, they begged him
to support them and to show himself the enemy of their enemies, the adversary of their adversaries, as the Law clearly
states.

27After these prayers, they armed themselves and
advanced a fair distance from the city, halting when they
were close to the enemy. 28As the first light of dawn began
to spread, the two sides joined battle, the one having as their
pledge of success and victory not only their own valour but
their recourse to the Lord, the other making their own ardour
their mainstay in the fight. 29When the battle was at its

GREEK OLD TESTAMENT

ἐφάνησαν τοῖς ὑπεναντίοις ἐξ οὐρανοῦ ἐφ᾽ ἵππων
χρυσοχαλίνων ἄνδρες πέντε διαπρεπεῖς, καὶ ἀφηγούμενοι
τῶν Ιουδαίων, 30 οἳ καὶ τὸν Μακκαβαῖον μέσον λαβόντες καὶ
σκεπάζοντες ταῖς ἑαυτῶν πανοπλίαις ἄτρωτον διεφύλαττον,
εἰς δὲ τοὺς ὑπεναντίους τοξεύματα καὶ κεραυνοὺς ἐξερρί-
πτουν, διὸ συγχυθέντες ἀορασίᾳ διεκόπτοντο ταραχῆς
πεπληρωμένοι. 31 κατεσφάγησαν δὲ δισμύριοι πρὸς τοῖς
πεντακοσίοις, ἱππεῖς δὲ ἑξακόσιοι. 32 αὐτὸς δὲ ὁ Τιμόθεος
συνέφυγεν εἰς Γαζαρα λεγόμενον ὀχύρωμα, εὖ μάλα φρούριον, στρατηγοῦντος ἐκεῖ Χαιρεου. 33 οἱ δὲ περὶ τὸν Μακκαβαῖον ἄσμενοι περιεκάθισαν τὸ φρούριον ἡμέρας τέσσαρας.
34 οἱ δὲ ἔνδον τῇ ἐρυμνότητι τοῦ τόπου πεποιθότες ὑπερά-
γαν ἐβλασφήμουν καὶ λόγους ἀθεμίτους προΐεντο. 35 ὑποφαινούσης δὲ τῆς πέμπτης ἡμέρας εἴκοσι νεανίαι τῶν περὶ
τὸν Μακκαβαῖον πυρωθέντες τοῖς θυμοῖς διὰ τὰς βλασφημίας προσβαλόντες τῷ τείχει ἀρρενωδῶς καὶ θηριώδει θυμῷ
τὸν ἐμπίπτοντα ἔκοπτον· 36 ἕτεροι δὲ ὁμοίως προσαναβάν-
τες ἐν τῷ περισπασμῷ πρὸς τοὺς ἔνδον ἐνεπίμπρων τοὺς
πύργους καὶ πυρὰς ἀνάπτοντες ζῶντας τοὺς βλασφήμους
κατέκαιον· οἱ δὲ τὰς πύλας διέκοπτον, εἰσδεξάμενοι δὲ τὴν
λοιπὴν τάξιν προκατελάβοντο τὴν πόλιν. 37 καὶ τὸν Τιμόθεον ἀποκεκρυμμένον ἔν τινι λάκκῳ κατέσφαξαν καὶ τὸν
τούτου ἀδελφὸν Χαιρέαν καὶ τὸν Ἀπολλοφάνην. 38 ταῦτα δὲ
διαπραξάμενοι μεθ᾽ ὕμνων καὶ ἐξομολογήσεων εὐλόγουν τῷ
κυρίῳ τῷ μεγάλως εὐεργετοῦντι τὸν Ισραηλ καὶ τὸ νῖκος
αὐτοῖς διδόντι.

KING JAMES VERSION

the enemies from heaven five comely men upon horses, with bridles of gold, and two of them led the Jews,

30 And took Maccabeus betwixt them, and covered him on every side with their weapons, and kept him safe, but shot arrows and lightnings against the enemies: so that being confounded with blindness, and full of trouble, they were killed.

31 And there were slain *of footmen* twenty thousand and five hundred, and six hundred horsemen.

32 As for Timotheus himself, he fled into a very strong hold, called Gazara, where Chereas was governor.

33 But they that were with Maccabeus laid siege against the fortress courageously four days.

34 And they that were within, trusting to the strength of the place, blasphemed exceedingly, and uttered wicked words.

35 Nevertheless upon the fifth day early twenty young men of Maccabeus' company, inflamed with anger because of the blasphemies, assaulted the wall manly, and with a fierce courage killed all that they met withal.

36 Others likewise ascending after them, whiles they were busied with them that were within, burnt the towers, and kindling fires burnt the blasphemers alive; and others broke open the gates, and, having received in the rest of the army, took the city,

37 And killed Timotheus, that was hid in a certain pit, and Chereas his brother, with Apollophanes.

38 When this was done, they praised the Lord with psalms and thanksgiving, who had done so great things for Israel, and given them the victory.

DOUAY OLD TESTAMENT

there appeared to the enemies from heaven five men upon horses, comely with golden bridles, conducting the Jews:

30 Two of whom took Machabeus between them, and covered him on every side with their arms, and kept him safe: but cast darts and fireballs against the enemy, so that they fell down, being both confounded with blindness, and filled with trouble.

31 And there were slain twenty thousand five hundred, and six hundred horsemen.

32 But Timotheus fled into Gazara a strong hold, where Chereas was governor.

33 Then Machabeus, and they that were with him, cheerfully laid siege to the fortress four days.

34 But they that were within, trusting to the strength of the place, blasphemed exceedingly, and cast forth abominable words.

35 But when the fifth day appeared, twenty young men of them that were with Machabeus, inflamed in their minds because of the blasphemy, approached manfully to the wall, and pushing forward with fierce courage got up upon it.

36 Moreover others also getting up after them, went to set fire to the towers and the gates, and to burn the blasphemers alive.

37 And having for two days together pillaged and sacked the fortress, they killed Timotheus, who was found hid in a certain place: they slew also his brother Chereas, and Apollophanes.

38 And when this was done, they blessed the Lord with hymns and thanksgiving, who had done great things in Israel, and given them the victory.

KNOX TRANSLATION

the enemy, heaven itself took part. Five horsemen came riding, with splendid trappings of gold, to lead the Jews
onward; 30 and two of these served Machabaeus for escort,
covering him with their shields to keep all hurt away from
him. With shaft of theirs, lightning of theirs, dazzled and
dismayed, the enemy fell to earth; 31 twenty thousand and
five hundred of them perished that day, besides six hundred
of the cavalry.

32 As for Timotheus, he took refuge in Gazara, a strong
fortress that was under the command of Chaereas. 33 Four
days together, Machabaeus and his men eagerly pressed on
the siege of it; 34 but the defenders were confident in its
strength; loud their defiance was, and very blasphemous the
words they uttered. 35 Stung by these taunts, twenty warriors of Machabaeus' company made a bold attack on the
wall as the fifth day was dawning, and, by the fierceness of
their onslaught, made shift to climb it; 36 others, following
at their heels, fell to burning tower and gateway alike, and
made a bonfire of the blasphemers. 37 For two whole days
they ransacked the fort, and at last came upon Timotheus[a]
in his hiding-place; so they made an end of him, his brother
Chaereas and Apollophanes perishing with him. 38 When all
was over, they sang hymns of praise and gave thanks to the
Lord, that had done marvellous things for Israel, and granted
them victory.

a If the text here is sound, the Timotheus mentioned in 12. 2 is a different person.

TODAY'S ENGLISH VERSION

handsome men riding on horses with gold bridles and leading the Jewish forces. 30 These five men surrounded Judas,
protecting him with their own armor and showering the
enemy with arrows and thunderbolts. The enemy forces then
became so confused and bewildered that they broke ranks,
and the Jews cut them to pieces, 31 slaughtering 20,500
infantry and 600 cavalry.

32 Timothy himself escaped to the strongly defended fort of
Gezer, where his brother Chaereas was in command. 33 Judas
and his men besieged the fort for four days with great enthusiasm, 34 but those inside trusted to the security of their
positions and shouted all sorts of terrible insults against the
Jews and their God. 35 At dawn on the fifth day, twenty of
Judas' men, burning with anger at these insults, bravely
climbed the wall and with savage fury chopped down everyone they met. 36 At the same time, others climbed the walls
on the other side of the fort and set the towers on fire. Many
of the enemy were burned to death as the flames spread. A
third force broke down the gates and let in the rest of Judas'
men to capture the city. 37 Timothy had hidden in a cistern,
but they killed him, as well as his brother Chaereas and
Apollophanes.

38 When it was over, the Jews celebrated by singing hymns
and songs of thanksgiving to the Lord, who had shown them
great kindness and had given them victory.

NEW REVISED STANDARD VERSION

enemy from heaven five resplendent men on horses with
golden bridles, and they were leading the Jews. 30 Two of
them took Maccabeus between them, and shielding him with
their own armor and weapons, they kept him from being
wounded. They showered arrows and thunderbolts on the
enemy, so that, confused and blinded, they were thrown into
disorder and cut to pieces. 31 Twenty thousand five hundred
were slaughtered, besides six hundred cavalry.

32 Timothy himself fled to a stronghold called Gazara,
especially well garrisoned, where Chaereas was commander.
33 Then Maccabeus and his men were glad, and they besieged
the fort for four days. 34 The men within, relying on the
strength of the place, kept blaspheming terribly and uttering
wicked words. 35 But at dawn of the fifth day, twenty young
men in the army of Maccabeus, fired with anger because of
the blasphemies, bravely stormed the wall and with savage
fury cut down everyone they met. 36 Others who came up in
the same way wheeled around against the defenders and set
fire to the towers; they kindled fires and burned the blasphemers alive. Others broke open the gates and let in the rest
of the force, and they occupied the city. 37 They killed
Timothy, who was hiding in a cistern, and his brother
Chaereas, and Apollophanes. 38 When they had accomplished these things, with hymns and thanksgivings they
blessed the Lord who shows great kindness to Israel and
gives them the victory.

NEW AMERICAN BIBLE

enemy from the heavens five majestic men riding on golden-
bridled horses, who led the Jews on. 30 They surrounded
Maccabeus, and shielding him with their own armor, kept
him from being wounded. They shot arrows and hurled
thunderbolts at the enemy, who were bewildered and blinded, thrown into confusion and routed. 31 Twenty-five hundred of their foot soldiers and six hundred of their horsemen
were slain. 32 Timothy, however, fled to a well-fortified
stronghold called Gazara, where Chaereas was in command.
33 For four days Maccabeus and his men eagerly besieged the
fortress. 34 Those inside, relying on the strength of the place,
kept repeating outrageous blasphemies and uttering abominable words. 35 When the fifth day dawned, twenty young
men in the army of Maccabeus, angered over such blasphemies, bravely stormed the wall and with savage fury cut
down everyone they encountered. 36 Others who climbed up
the same way swung around on the defenders, taking the
besieged in the rear; they put the towers to the torch, spread
the fire and burned the blasphemers alive. Still others broke
down the gates and let in the rest of the troops, who took
possession of the city. 37 Timothy had hidden in a cistern,
but they killed him, along with his brother Chaereas, and
Apollophanes. 38 On completing these exploits, they blessed,
with hymns of grateful praise, the LORD who shows great
kindness to Israel and grants them victory.

NEW JERUSALEM BIBLE

height, the enemy saw five magnificent men appear from
heaven on horses with golden bridles and put themselves at
the head of the Jews; 30 surrounding Maccabaeus and
screening him with their own armour, they kept him
unscathed, while they rained arrows and thunderbolts on the
enemy until, blinded and confused, they scattered in complete disorder. 31 Twenty thousand five hundred infantry and
six hundred cavalry were slaughtered. 32 Timotheus himself
fled to a strongly guarded citadel called Gezer, where
Chaereas was in command. 33 For four days Maccabaeus and
his men eagerly besieged the fortress, 34 while the defenders,
confident in the security of the place, hurled fearful blasphemies and godless insults at them. 35 At daybreak on the fifth
day, twenty young men of Maccabaeus' forces, fired with
indignation at the blasphemies, manfully assaulted the wall,
with wild courage cutting down everyone they encountered.
36 Others, in a similar scaling operation, took the defenders
in the rear, and set fire to the towers, lighting pyres on
which they burned the blasphemers alive. The first, meanwhile, breaking open the gates, let the rest of the army in
and, at their head, captured the town. 37 Timotheus had hidden in a storage-well, but they killed him, with his brother
Chaereas, and Apollophanes. 38 When all this was over, with
hymns and thanksgiving they blessed the Lord, who had
shown such great kindness to Israel and given them the
victory.

GREEK OLD TESTAMENT

11 Μετ᾽ ὀλίγον δὲ παντελῶς χρονίσκον Λυσίας ἐπίτρο-
πος τοῦ βασιλέως καὶ συγγενὴς καὶ ἐπὶ τῶν πραγμάτων λίαν βαρέως φέρων ἐπὶ τοῖς γεγονόσι 2 συναθροίσας
περὶ τὰς ὀκτὼ μυριάδας καὶ τὴν ἵππον ἅπασαν παρεγίνετο
ἐπὶ τοὺς Ιουδαίους λογιζόμενος τὴν μὲν πόλιν Ἕλλησιν
οἰκητήριον ποιήσειν, 3 τὸ δὲ ἱερὸν ἀργυρολόγητον, καθὼς τὰ
λοιπὰ τῶν ἐθνῶν τεμένη, πρατὴν δὲ κατὰ ἔτος τὴν ἀρχιερωσύνην ποιήσειν, 4 οὐδαμῶς ἐπιλογιζόμενος τὸ τοῦ θεοῦ κράτος, πεφρενωμένος δὲ ταῖς μυριάσιν τῶν πεζῶν καὶ ταῖς
χιλιάσιν τῶν ἱππέων καὶ τοῖς ἐλέφασιν τοῖς ὀγδοήκοντα.
5 εἰσελθὼν δὲ εἰς τὴν Ιουδαίαν καὶ συνεγγίσας Βαιθσουρα
ὄντι μὲν ἐρυμνῷ χωρίῳ, Ιεροσολύμων δὲ ἀπέχοντι ὡσεὶ
σταδίους πέντε τοῦτο ἔθλιβεν. 6 ὡς δὲ μετέλαβον οἱ περὶ
τὸν Μακκαβαῖον πολιορκοῦντα αὐτὸν τὰ ὀχυρώματα, μετὰ
ὀδυρμῶν καὶ δακρύων ἱκέτευον σὺν τοῖς ὄχλοις τὸν κύριον
ἀγαθὸν ἄγγελον ἀποστεῖλαι πρὸς σωτηρίαν τῷ Ισραηλ.
7 αὐτὸς δὲ πρῶτος ὁ Μακκαβαῖος ἀναλαβὼν τὰ ὅπλα προετρέψατο τοὺς ἄλλους ἅμα αὐτῷ διακινδυνεύοντας ἐπιβοηθεῖν
τοῖς ἀδελφοῖς αὐτῶν· ὁμοῦ δὲ καὶ προθύμως ἐξώρμησαν.
8 αὐτόθι δὲ πρὸς τοῖς Ιεροσολύμοις ὄντων ἐφάνη προηγούμενος αὐτῶν ἔφιππος ἐν λευκῇ ἐσθῆτι πανοπλίαν χρυσῆν
κραδαίνων. 9 ὁμοῦ δὲ πάντες εὐλόγησαν τὸν ἐλεήμονα θεὸν
καὶ ἐπερρώσθησαν ταῖς ψυχαῖς οὐ μόνον ἀνθρώπους, θῆρας
δὲ τοὺς ἀγριωτάτους καὶ σιδηρᾶ τείχη τιτρώσκειν ὄντες

KING JAMES VERSION

11 Not long after this, Lysias the king's protector and cousin, who also managed the affairs, took sore displeasure for the things that were done.

2 And when he had gathered about fourscore thousand with all the horsemen, he came against the Jews, thinking to make the city an habitation of the Gentiles,

3 And to make a gain of the temple, as of the other chapels of the heathen, and to set the high priesthood to sale every year:

4 Not at all considering the power of God, but puffed up with his ten thousands of footmen, and his thousands of horsemen, and his fourscore elephants.

5 So he came to Judea, and drew near to Bethsura, which was a strong town, but distant from Jerusalem about five furlongs, and he laid sore siege unto it.

6 Now when they that were with Maccabeus heard that he besieged the holds, they and all the people with lamentation and tears besought the Lord that he would send a good angel to deliver Israel.

7 Then Maccabeus himself first of all took weapons, exhorting the other that they would jeopard themselves together with him to help their brethren: so they went forth together with a willing mind.

8 And as they were at Jerusalem, there appeared before them on horseback one in white clothing, shaking his armour of gold.

9 Then they praised the merciful God all together, and took heart, insomuch that they were ready not only to fight with men, but with most cruel beasts, and to pierce through walls of iron.

DOUAY OLD TESTAMENT

11 A SHORT time after this Lysias the king's lieutenant, and cousin, and who had chief charge over all the affairs, being greatly displeased with what had happened,

2 Gathered together fourscore thousand men, and all the horsemen, and came against the Jews, thinking to take the city, and make it a habitation of the Gentiles:

3 And to make a gain of the temple, as of the other temples of the Gentiles, and to set the high priesthood to sale every year:

4 Never considering the power of God, but puffed up in mind, and trusting in the multitude of his foot soldiers, and the thousands of his horsemen, and his fourscore elephants.

5 So he came into Judea, and approaching to Bethsura, which was in a narrow place, the space of five furlongs from Jerusalem, he laid siege to that fortress.

6 But when Machabeus and they that were with him, understood that the strong holds were besieged, they and all the people besought the Lord with lamentations and tears, that he would send a good angel to save Israel.

7 Then Machabeus himself, first taking his arms, exhorted the rest to expose themselves together with him, to the danger, and to succour their brethren.

8 And when they were going forth together with a willing mind, there appeared at Jerusalem a horseman going before them in white clothing, with golden armour, shaking a spear.

9 Then they all together blessed the merciful Lord, and took great courage, being ready to break through not only men, but also the fiercest beasts, and walls of iron.

KNOX TRANSLATION

11 It was but a short respite they had; Lysias, a kinsman
of Antiochus that was regent and managed his affairs
for him, was not a little concerned over these happenings,
2 and he marched on Judaea at the head of eighty thousand
men, with all the cavalry he could muster. Here was a city
worth the capture, for Gentile folk to dwell in; 3 here was a
temple that would yield a fine spoil, as temples did everywhere; a priesthood, too, that might be put up for sale year
after year. 4 Of all this he bethought him, never of God's
avenging power; blindly he trusted in his foot-soldiers by the
ten thousand, his horsemen by the thousand, in his elephants
that numbered four score. 5 Upon marching into Judaea he
first reached Bethsura, that stood in a narrow pass five furlongs away from Jerusalem,[a] and laid siege to the citadel of it.
6 What did Machabaeus and his fellows, when they learned
that the siege of the fortress was already begun? Most
piteously they besought the Lord, amid the tears of a whole
populace, a gracious angel he would send out for Israel's
deliverance. 7 Then they armed for battle, Machabaeus himself the first of all, as he summoned the rest to share with
him the hour of danger, for the relief of their brethren. 8 So,
in good heart, they set out together, and before they left
Jerusalem a vision came to them; of a rider that went before
them in white array, with armour of gold, brandishing his
spear. 9 How they blessed God's mercy, all of them, at the
sight! How their courage rose, a match for all it should
encounter, men or wild beast or walls of iron! 10 They

a A more probable reading in the Greek makes the distance not five furlongs, but about twenty miles, which would be a just estimate.

TODAY'S ENGLISH VERSION

11 Not long after Timothy was defeated, Lysias, the King's guardian and relative, and head of the government, heard what had happened. He became angry 2 and led 80,000 infantry and all his cavalry against the Jews with the intention of turning Jerusalem into a Greek city. 3 The Temple would be taxed, as were all Gentile places of worship, and the office of High Priest would be up for sale each year. 4 Lysias was so pleased with his tens of thousands of infantry, his thousands of cavalry, and his eighty elephants that he failed to take into account the power of God. 5 He invaded Judea and attacked the fort of Bethzur, about twenty miles south of Jerusalem.

6 When Judas and his men heard that Lysias was laying siege to their forts, they and all the people cried and wept, begging the Lord to send a good angel to save them. 7 Judas was the first to take up his weapons, and he urged the others to join him in risking their lives to help the other Jews. So with great eagerness they all set out together. 8 But they had not gone far from Jerusalem, when suddenly they noticed they were being led by a horseman dressed in white and carrying gold weapons. 9 Immediately all of them together thanked God for his mercy; he had made them brave enough to attack not only men, but even the most savage animals or

NEW REVISED STANDARD VERSION

11 Very soon after this, Lysias, the king's guardian and kinsman, who was in charge of the government, being vexed at what had happened, 2 gathered about eighty thousand infantry and all his cavalry and came against the Jews. He intended to make the city a home for Greeks, 3 and to levy tribute on the temple as he did on the sacred places of the other nations, and to put up the high priesthood for sale every year. 4 He took no account whatever of the power of God, but was elated with his ten thousands of infantry, and his thousands of cavalry, and his eighty elephants. 5 Invading Judea, he approached Beth-zur, which was a fortified place about five stadia[a] from Jerusalem, and pressed it hard.

6 When Maccabeus and his men got word that Lysias[b] was besieging the strongholds, they and all the people, with lamentations and tears, prayed the Lord to send a good angel to save Israel. 7 Maccabeus himself was the first to take up arms, and he urged the others to risk their lives with him to aid their kindred. Then they eagerly rushed off together. 8 And there, while they were still near Jerusalem, a horseman appeared at their head, clothed in white and brandishing weapons of gold. 9 And together they all praised the merciful God, and were strengthened in heart, ready to assail not only humans but the wildest animals or walls of iron. 10 They

a Meaning of Gk uncertain *b* Gk *he*

NEW AMERICAN BIBLE

11 Very soon afterward, Lysias, guardian and kinsman of the king and head of the government, being greatly displeased at what had happened, 2 mustered about eighty thousand infantry and all his cavalry and marched against the Jews. His plan was to make Jerusalem a Greek settlement; 3 to levy tribute on the temple, as he did on the sanctuaries of the other nations; and to put the high priesthood up for sale every year. 4 He did not take God's power into account at all, but felt exultant confidence in his myriads of foot soldiers, his thousands of horsemen, and his eighty elephants. 5 So he invaded Judea, and when he reached Beth-zur, a fortified place about twenty miles from Jerusalem, launched a strong attack against it. 6 When Maccabeus and his men learned that Lysias was besieging the strongholds, they and all the people begged the LORD with lamentations and tears to send a good angel to save Israel. 7 Maccabeus himself was the first to take up arms, and he exhorted the others to join him in risking their lives to help their kinsmen. Then they resolutely set out together. 8 Suddenly, while they were still near Jerusalem, a horseman appeared at their head, clothed in white garments and brandishing gold weapons. 9 Then all of them together thanked God for his mercy, and their hearts were filled with such courage that they were ready to assault not only men, but the most savage beasts,

NEW JERUSALEM BIBLE

11 [a]Almost immediately afterwards, Lysias, the king's tutor and cousin, chief minister of the realm, much disturbed at the turn of events, 2 mustered about eighty thousand foot soldiers and his entire cavalry and advanced against the Jews, intending to make the city a place for Greeks to live in, 3 to levy a tax on the Temple as on other national shrines, and to put the office of high priest up for sale every year; 4 he took no account at all of the power of God, being sublimely confident in his tens of thousands of infantrymen, his thousands of cavalry, and his eighty elephants.

5 Invading Judaea, he approached Beth-Zur, a fortified position about twenty miles from Jerusalem, and began to subject it to strong pressure. 6 When Maccabaeus and his men learned that Lysias was besieging the fortresses, they and the populace with them begged the Lord with lamentation and tears to send a good angel to save Israel. 7 Maccabaeus himself was the first to take up his weapons, and he urged the rest to risk their lives with him in support of their brothers; so they sallied out resolutely, as one man. 8 They were still near Jerusalem when a rider attired in white appeared at their head, brandishing golden weapons. 9 With one accord they all blessed the God of mercy, and found themselves filled with such courage that they were ready to lay low not men only but the fiercest beasts and walls of

a **11** 11:1seq. // 1 M 4:26–35.

Greek Old Testament

ἕτοιμοι. 10 προῆγον ἐν διασκευῇ τὸν ἀπ᾿ οὐρανοῦ σύμμαχον
ἔχοντες ἐλεήσαντος αὐτοὺς τοῦ κυρίου. 11 λεοντηδὸν δὲ
ἐντινάξαντες εἰς τοὺς πολεμίους κατέστρωσαν αὐτῶν χιλίους πρὸς τοῖς μυρίοις, ἱππεῖς δὲ ἑξακοσίους πρὸς τοῖς χιλίοις. τοὺς δὲ πάντας ἠνάγκασαν φεύγειν. 12 οἱ πλείονες δὲ
αὐτῶν τραυματίαι γυμνοὶ διεσώθησαν· καὶ αὐτὸς δὲ ὁ Λυσίας αἰσχρῶς φεύγων διεσώθη. 13 οὐκ ἄνους δὲ ὑπάρχων πρὸς
ἑαυτὸν ἀντιβάλλων τὸ γεγονὸς περὶ αὐτὸν ἐλάττωμα καὶ
συννοήσας ἀνικήτους εἶναι τοὺς Εβραίους τοῦ δυναμένου
θεοῦ συμμαχοῦντος αὐτοῖς 14 προσαποστείλας ἔπεισεν
συλλύεσθαι ἐπὶ πᾶσι τοῖς δικαίοις, καὶ διότι καὶ τὸν βασιλέα πείσει φίλον αὐτοῖς ἀναγκάζων γενέσθαι. 15 ἐπένευσεν
δὲ ὁ Μακκαβαῖος ἐπὶ πᾶσιν, οἷς ὁ Λυσίας παρεκάλει, τοῦ
συμφέροντος φροντίζων· ὅσα γὰρ ὁ Μακκαβαῖος ἐπέδωκεν
τῷ Λυσίᾳ διὰ γραπτῶν περὶ τῶν Ιουδαίων, συνεχώρησεν ὁ
βασιλεύς.

16 Ἦσαν γὰρ αἱ γεγραμμέναι τοῖς Ιουδαίοις ἐπιστολαὶ
παρὰ μὲν Λυσίου περιέχουσαι τὸν τρόπον τοῦτον

Λυσίας τῷ πλήθει τῶν Ιουδαίων χαίρειν. 17 Ιωαννης καὶ
Αβεσσαλωμ οἱ πεμφθέντες παρ᾿ ὑμῶν ἐπιδόντες τὸν
ὑπογεγραμμένον χρηματισμὸν ἠξίουν περὶ τῶν δι᾿ αὐτοῦ
σημαινομένων. 18 ὅσα μὲν οὖν ἔδει καὶ τῷ βασιλεῖ προσενεχθῆναι, διεσάφησα· ἃ δὲ ἦν ἐνδεχόμενα, συνεχώρησεν.
19 ἐὰν μὲν οὖν συντηρήσητε τὴν εἰς τὰ πράγματα εὔνοιαν,
καὶ εἰς τὸ λοιπὸν πειράσομαι παραίτιος ἀγαθῶν γενέσθαι.

King James Version

10 Thus they marched forward in their armour, having an helper from heaven: for the Lord was merciful unto them.

11 And giving a charge upon their enemies like lions, they slew eleven thousand *footmen,* and sixteen hundred horsemen, and put all the other to flight.

12 Many of them also being wounded escaped naked; and Lysias himself fled away shamefully, and so escaped.

13 Who, as he was a man of understanding, casting with himself what loss he had had, and considering that the Hebrews could not be overcome, because the Almighty God helped them, he sent unto them,

14 And persuaded them to agree to all reasonable *conditions,* and *promised* that he would persuade the king that he must needs be a friend unto them.

15 Then Maccabeus consented to all that Lysias desired, being careful of the common good; and whatsoever Maccabeus wrote unto Lysias concerning the Jews, the king granted it.

16 For there were letters written unto the Jews from Lysias to this effect: Lysias unto the people of the Jews *sendeth* greeting:

17 John and Absolon, who were sent from you, delivered me the petition subscribed, and made request for the performance of the contents thereof.

18 Therefore what things soever were meet to be reported to the king, I have declared them, and he hath granted as much as might be.

19 If then ye will keep yourselves loyal to the state, hereafter also will I endeavour to be a means of your good.

Douay Old Testament

10 So they went on courageously, having a helper from heaven, and the Lord who shewed mercy to them.

11 And rushing violently upon the enemy, like lions, they slew of them eleven thousand footmen, and one thousand six hundred horsemen:

12 And put all the rest to flight: and many of them being wounded, escaped naked: yea and Lysias himself fled away shamefully, and escaped.

13 And as he was a man of understanding, considering with himself, the loss he had suffered, and perceiving that the Hebrews could not be overcome, because they relied upon the help of the Almighty God, he sent to them:

14 And promised that he would agree to all things that are just, and that he would persuade the king to be their friend.

15 Then Machabeus consented to the request of Lysias, providing for the common good in all things, and whatsoever Machabeus wrote to Lysias concerning the Jews, the king allowed of.

16 For there were letters written to the Jews from Lysias, to this effect: Lysias to the people of the Jews, greeting.

17 John and Abesalom who were sent from you, delivering your writings, requested that I would accomplish those things which were signified by them.

18 Therefore whatsoever things could be reported to the king I have represented to him: and he hath granted as much as the matter permitted.

19 If therefore you will keep yourselves loyal in affairs, hereafter also I will endeavour to be a means of your good.

Knox Translation

marched on, ready for battle, sure now of a heavenly champion, and of the Lord's favour; 11 and when they charged the
enemy, they were very lions for valour. At their onslaught,
fell eleven thousand of the foot, fell a thousand and six hundred of the horse; 12 and the whole army took to its heels,
for the most part wounded and disarmed; Lysias himself,
ingloriously enough, turned and fled.

13 Yet good sense he lacked not; great loss he had sustained, and, let the Hebrews continue to rely for aid upon
divine Omnipotence, he saw there was no conquering them.
14 So he wrote, offering to conclude honourable terms with
them, and secure them the king's friendship. 15 As for
Machabaeus, he consented to what Lysias asked, having no
thought but for the common good; and the written terms he
proposed to Lysias in the Jewish people's name received the
royal assent.

16 The letter sent to the Jews by Lysias was after this manner: Lysias, to the people of the Jews, all health! 17 Your
envoys, John and Abesalom, handed me a written petition,
and desired that I would give effect to the terms of it. 18 All
that needed to be known, I have made clear to the king's
grace, and he has granted what grant he could. 19 Doubt not
I will be a good suitor in your cause hereafter, so you abide

TODAY'S ENGLISH VERSION

even walls of iron. 10 So they marched in battle formation,
and with them went the one whom the Lord in his mercy had
sent to fight on their side. 11 Then they charged into the
enemy like lions, killing 11,000 infantry and 1,600 cavalry,
and forcing the rest to run for their lives. 12 Most of those
who ran were wounded and had lost their weapons, and
Lysias himself managed to escape only because he ran away
like a coward.

13 Lysias was no fool. As he thought about the defeat he
had suffered, he realized it was because the mighty God had
fought for the Jews, making it impossible for them to be
defeated. So he sent a message to the Jews, 14 trying to persuade them to agree to a just settlement and promising to do
all he could to make the king friendly toward them.[a]
15 Judas Maccabeus considered what would be best for the
people, and so he agreed to all the proposals Lysias had
made, since the king had granted every written request that
Judas had presented to Lysias.[b]

16 Here is a copy of the letter which Lysias wrote to the Jews:

"Lysias to the Jewish people, greetings. 17 Your representatives John and Absalom have delivered to me the official
document you sent with them, and they have asked me to
agree to what is contained in it. 18 I have informed the
king of the matters that needed to be brought to his attention, and he has agreed to do whatever is possible. 19 If
you continue to be loyal to the government, I will do everything I can in the future to benefit your nation. 20 I have

[a] to do . . . them; *Greek unclear.* [b] since . . . Lysias; *or* and the king granted every written request that Judas presented to Lysias.

NEW REVISED STANDARD VERSION

advanced in battle order, having their heavenly ally, for the
Lord had mercy on them. 11 They hurled themselves like
lions against the enemy, and laid low eleven thousand of
them and sixteen hundred cavalry, and forced all the rest to
flee. 12 Most of them got away stripped and wounded, and
Lysias himself escaped by disgraceful flight.

13 As he was not without intelligence, he pondered over
the defeat that had befallen him, and realized that the
Hebrews were invincible because the mighty God fought on
their side. So he sent to them 14 and persuaded them to settle everything on just terms, promising that he would persuade the king, constraining him to be their friend.[a] 15 Maccabeus, having regard for the common good, agreed to all
that Lysias urged. For the king granted every request in
behalf of the Jews which Maccabeus delivered to Lysias in
writing.

16 The letter written to the Jews by Lysias was to this
effect:

"Lysias to the people of the Jews, greetings. 17 John and
Absalom, who were sent by you, have delivered your signed
communication and have asked about the matters indicated
in it. 18 I have informed the king of everything that needed
to be brought before him, and he has agreed to what was
possible. 19 If you will maintain your goodwill toward the
government, I will endeavor in the future to help promote

a Meaning of Gk uncertain

NEW AMERICAN BIBLE

yes, even walls of iron. 10 Now that the LORD had shown his
mercy toward them, they advanced in battle order with the
aid of their heavenly ally. 11 Hurling themselves upon the
enemy like lions, they laid low eleven thousand foot soldiers
and sixteen hundred horsemen, and put all the rest to flight.
12 Most of those who got away were wounded and stripped of
their arms, while Lysias himself escaped only by shameful
flight.

13 But Lysias was not a stupid man. He reflected on the
defeat he had suffered, and came to realize that the Hebrews
were invincible because the mighty God was their ally. He
therefore sent a message 14 persuading them to settle everything on just terms, and promising to persuade the king also,
and to induce him to become their friend. 15 Maccabeus,
solicitous for the common good, agreed to all that Lysias proposed; and the king, on his part, granted in behalf of the
Jews all the written requests of Maccabeus to Lysias.

16 These are the terms of the letter which Lysias wrote to
the Jews: "Lysias sends greetings to the Jewish people.
17 John and Absalom, your envoys, have presented your
signed communication and asked about the matters contained in it. 18 Whatever had to be referred to the king I
called to his attention, and the things that were acceptable
he has granted. 19 If you maintain your loyalty to the government, I will endeavor to further your interests in the

NEW JERUSALEM BIBLE

iron. 10 They advanced in battle order with the aid of their
celestial ally, the Lord having had mercy on them.
11 Charging like lions on the enemy, they laid low eleven
thousand of the infantry and sixteen hundred horsemen, and
routed all the rest. 12 Of those, the majority got away,
wounded and weaponless. Lysias himself escaped only by
ignominious flight.

13[a] Now Lysias was not lacking in intelligence and, as he
reflected on the reverse he had just suffered, he realised that
the Hebrews were invincible because the mighty God fought
for them. He therefore sent them a delegation 14 to persuade
them to accept reasonable terms all round, and promised to
compel the king to become their friend. 15 Maccabaeus,
thinking only of the common good, agreed to all that Lysias
proposed, and whatever Maccabaeus submitted to Lysias in
writing concerning the Jews was granted by the king.

16 Here is the text of the letter Lysias wrote to the Jews:

'Lysias to the Jewish people, greetings.

17 'John and Absalom, your envoys, have delivered to me
the communication transcribed below, requesting me to
approve its provisions. 18 Anything requiring the king's
attention I have put before him; whatever was possible, I
have granted. 19 Provided you maintain your goodwill
towards the interests of the State, I shall do my best in the
future to promote your well-being. 20 As regards the

[a] 11 11:13seq. // 1 M 6:57.

GREEK OLD TESTAMENT

20 ὑπὲρ δὲ τούτων καὶ τῶν κατὰ μέρος ἐντέταλμαι τούτοις
τε καὶ τοῖς παρ᾽ ἐμοῦ διαλεχθῆναι ὑμῖν. 21 ἔρρωσθε. ἔτους
ἑκατοστοῦ τεσσαρακοστοῦ ὀγδόου, Διὸς Κορινθίου τετράδι
καὶ εἰκάδι.

22 Ἡ δὲ τοῦ βασιλέως ἐπιστολὴ περιεῖχεν οὕτως

Βασιλεὺς Ἀντίοχος τῷ ἀδελφῷ Λυσίᾳ χαίρειν. 23 τοῦ
πατρὸς ἡμῶν εἰς θεοὺς μεταστάντος βουλόμενοι τοὺς ἐκ
τῆς βασιλείας ἀταράχους ὄντας γενέσθαι πρὸς τὴν τῶν ἰδίων ἐπιμέλειαν 24 ἀκηκοότες τοὺς Ιουδαίους μὴ συνευδοκοῦν-
τας τῇ τοῦ πατρὸς ἐπὶ τὰ Ἑλληνικὰ μεταθέσει, ἀλλὰ τὴν
ἑαυτῶν ἀγωγὴν αἱρετίζοντας ἀξιοῦντας συγχωρηθῆναι αὐτοῖς τὰ νόμιμα, 25 αἱρούμενοι οὖν καὶ τοῦτο τὸ ἔθνος ἐκτὸς
ταραχῆς εἶναι κρίνομεν τό τε ἱερὸν ἀποκατασταθῆναι αὐτοῖς καὶ πολιτεύεσθαι κατὰ τὰ ἐπὶ τῶν προγόνων αὐτῶν ἔθη.
26 εὖ οὖν ποιήσεις διαπεμψάμενος πρὸς αὐτοὺς καὶ δοὺς
δεξιάς, ὅπως εἰδότες τὴν ἡμετέραν προαίρεσιν εὔθυμοί τε
ὦσιν καὶ ἡδέως διαγίνωνται πρὸς τῇ τῶν ἰδίων ἀντιλήμψει.

27 Πρὸς δὲ τὸ ἔθνος ἡ τοῦ βασιλέως ἐπιστολὴ τοιάδε ἦν

Βασιλεὺς Ἀντίοχος τῇ γερουσίᾳ τῶν Ιουδαίων καὶ τοῖς
ἄλλοις Ιουδαίοις χαίρειν. 28 εἰ ἔρρωσθε, εἴη ἂν ὡς βουλό-
μεθα· καὶ αὐτοὶ δὲ ὑγιαίνομεν. 29 ἐνεφάνισεν ἡμῖν Μενέλαος βούλεσθαι κατελθόντας ὑμᾶς γίνεσθαι πρὸς τοῖς ἰδίοις.
30 τοῖς οὖν καταπορευομένοις μέχρι τριακάδος Ξανθικοῦ
ὑπάρξει δεξιὰ μετὰ τῆς ἀδείας 31 χρῆσθαι τοὺς Ιουδαίους

KING JAMES VERSION

20 But of the particulars I have given order both to these, and the other that came from me, to commune with you.

21 Fare ye well. The hundred and eight and fortieth year, the four and twentieth day of *the month* Dioscorinthius.

22 Now the king's letter contained these words: King Antiochus unto his brother Lysias *sendeth* greeting:

23 Since our father is translated unto the gods, our will is, that they that are in our realm live quietly, that every one may attend upon his own affairs.

24 We understand also that the Jews would not consent to our father, for to be brought unto the custom of the Gentiles, but had rather keep their own manner of living: for the which cause they require of us, that we should suffer them to live after their own laws.

25 Wherefore our mind is, that this nation shall be in rest, and we have determined to restore them their temple, that they may live according to the customs of their forefathers.

26 Thou shalt do well therefore to send unto them, and grant them peace, that when they are certified of our mind, they may be of good comfort, and ever go cheerfully about their own affairs.

27 And the letter of the king unto the nation of the Jews was after this manner: King Antiochus *sendeth* greeting unto the council, and the rest of the Jews:

28 If ye fare well, we have our desire; we are also in good health.

29 Menelaus declared unto us, that your desire was to return home, and to follow your own business:

30 Wherefore they that will depart shall have safe conduct till the thirtieth day of Xanthicus with security.

DOUAY OLD TESTAMENT

20 But as concerning other particulars, I have given orders by word both to these, and to them that are sent by me, to commune with you.

21 Fare ye well. In the year one hundred and forty-eight, the four and twentieth day of the month of Dioscorus.

22 But the king's letter contained these words: King Antiochus to Lysias his brother, greeting.

23 Our father being translated amongst the gods, we are desirous that they that are in our realm should live quietly, and apply themselves diligently to their own concerns,

24 And we have heard that the Jews would not consent to my father to turn to the rites of the Greeks, but that they would keep to their own manner of living, and therefore that they request us to allow them to live after their own laws.

25 Wherefore being desirous that this nation also should be at rest, we have ordained and decreed, that the temple should be restored to them, and that they may live according to the custom of their ancestors.

26 Thou shalt do well therefore to send to them, and grant them peace, that our pleasure being known, they may be of good comfort, and look to their own affairs.

27 But the king's letter to the Jews was in this manner: King Antiochus to the senate of the Jews, and to the rest of the Jews, greeting.

28 If you are well, you are as we desire, we ourselves also are well.

29 Menelaus came to us, saying that you desired to come down to your countrymen, that are with us.

30 We grant therefore a safe conduct to all that come and go, until the thirtieth day of the month of Xanthicus,

KNOX TRANSLATION

loyal to the king's interest. 20 Meanwhile I have given a ver-
bal message to your envoys and mine, which they will
impart to you. 21 Farewell. Given on this twenty-fourth day
of Dioscorus, in the hundred and forty-eighth year.

22 And of the king's own letter, the tenour was this: King
Antiochus, to his good cousin Lysias, all health! 23 Now that
our father has found his place among the gods, it is for us to
see that our subjects live at peace, and go quietly about their
business. 24 But of one nation, the Jews, we hear that they
resisted our father's will, who would have had them conform
to the Greek way of living; to their own tradition they hold
fast, and their plea is, we should grant them the enjoyment
of their rights in the matter. 25 And whereas we would have
this nation live peaceably like the rest, we enact and decree
that their temple should be restored to them, and that they
should follow the custom of their forefathers. 26 Do us the
kindness, then, to send word and give them assurance of
this; our will made known, let them take heart, and order
their own affairs contentedly.

27 To the Jews themselves the king wrote as follows: King
Antiochus, to the elders and people of the Jews, all health!
28 Thrive you as well as ourselves, we are well content.
29 Menelaus has brought us word, you would fain have free
intercourse with the men of your race who dwell in these
parts;[a] 30 and we hereby grant safe conduct to all of you that

[a] *vv.* 29-31. The situation is not made fully clear, either in the Greek text or in the Latin. There seems to be a gap between verses 30 and 31, perhaps due to a mistake in the manuscripts. The allusion to faults committed 'through inadvertence' is perhaps only a diplomatic formula for granting a general amnesty.

TODAY'S ENGLISH VERSION

instructed your representatives and mine to meet with you
to discuss the details of these matters. 21 May all go well
with you. Dated the twenty-fourth day of the month of
Dioscorinthius in the year 148."[a]
22 Here is a copy of the King's letter:
"King Antiochus to the honorable Lysias, greetings.
23 Now that my father has gone to be with the gods, I want
the subjects of my kingdom to conduct their own affairs
without interference. 24 I understand that the Jews do not
wish to adopt the Greek way of life, as my father had
intended, but prefer their own way of life and have
requested that they be allowed to live according to their
own customs. 25 Since I desire that they live undisturbed
like the other nations in my empire, I hereby decree that
their Temple be restored to them and that they be allowed
to live according to the customs of their ancestors.
26 Please inform them of this decision and assure them of
my friendship, so that they may conduct their own affairs
in peace, without anything to worry about."
27 Here is a copy of the king's letter to the Jewish people:
"King Antiochus to the Jewish leaders and all the Jews,
greetings. 28 I hope that all is going well for you. I am in
good health. 29 Menelaus has informed me of your desire to
return home and attend to your own affairs. 30 So then,
those of you who return home by the thirtieth of the month
of Xanthicus may rest assured that you have nothing to

[a] THE YEAR 148: *This corresponds to 164 B.C.*

NEW REVISED STANDARD VERSION

your welfare. 20 And concerning such matters and their
details, I have ordered these men and my representatives to
confer with you. 21 Farewell. The one hundred forty-eighth
year,[a] Dioscorinthius twenty-fourth."
22 The king's letter ran thus:
"King Antiochus to his brother Lysias, greetings. 23 Now
that our father has gone on to the gods, we desire that the
subjects of the kingdom be undisturbed in caring for their
own affairs. 24 We have heard that the Jews do not consent
to our father's change to Greek customs, but prefer their own
way of living and ask that their own customs be allowed
them. 25 Accordingly, since we choose that this nation also
should be free from disturbance, our decision is that their
temple be restored to them and that they shall live according
to the customs of their ancestors. 26 You will do well, therefore, to send word to them and give them pledges of friendship, so that they may know our policy and be of good cheer
and go on happily in the conduct of their own affairs."
27 To the nation the king's letter was as follows:
"King Antiochus to the senate of the Jews and to the other
Jews, greetings. 28 If you are well, it is as we desire. We also
are in good health. 29 Menelaus has informed us that you
wish to return home and look after your own affairs.
30 Therefore those who go home by the thirtieth of Xanthicus
will have our pledge of friendship and full permission 31 for

a 164 B.C.

NEW AMERICAN BIBLE

future. 20 On the details of these matters I have authorized
my representatives, as well as your envoys, to confer with
you. 21 Farewell." The year one hundred and forty-eight, the
twenty-fourth of Dioscorinthius.
22 The king's letter read thus: "King Antiochus sends greetings to his brother Lysias. 23 Now that our father has taken
his place among the gods, we wish the subjects of our kingdom to be undisturbed in conducting their own affairs. 24 We
understand that the Jews do not agree with our father's policy concerning Greek customs but prefer their own way of life.
They are petitioning us to let them retain their own customs.
25 Since we desire that this people too should be undisturbed,
our decision is that their temple be restored to them and that
they live in keeping with the customs of their ancestors.
26 Accordingly, please send them messengers to give them
our assurances of friendship, so that, when they learn of our
decision, they may have nothing to worry about but may
contentedly go about their own business."
27 The king's letter to the people was as follows: "King
Antiochus sends greetings to the Jewish senate and to the
rest of the Jews. 28 If you are well, it is what we desire. We
too are in good health. 29 Menelaus has told us of your wish
to return home and attend to your own affairs. 30 Therefore,
those who return by the thirtieth of Xanthicus will have our
assurance of full permission 31 to observe their dietary laws

NEW JERUSALEM BIBLE

details, I have given orders for your envoys and my own
officials to discuss these with you. 21 May you prosper.
'The twenty-fourth day of Dioscorus, in the year one
hundred and forty-eight.'

22 The king's letter ran as follows:
'King Antiochus to his brother Lysias, greetings.
23 'Now that our father has taken his place among the
gods, our will is that the subjects of the realm be left
undisturbed to attend to their own affairs. 24 We understand that the Jews do not approve our father's policy, the
adoption of Greek customs, but prefer their own way of life
and ask to be allowed to observe their own laws.
25 Accordingly, since we intend this people to be free from
vexation like any other, our ruling is that the Temple be
restored to them and that they conduct their affairs according to the customs of their ancestors.
26 'It will therefore be your concern to send them a mission of friendship, so that on learning our policy they may
have confidence and happily go about their business.'
27 The king's letter to the Jewish nation was in these terms:
'King Antiochus to the Jewish Senate and the rest of the
Jews, greetings.
28 'If you are well, that is as we would wish; we ourselves are in good health.
29 'Menelaus informs us that you wish to return home
and attend to your own affairs. 30 Accordingly, all those
who return before the thirtieth day of Xanthicus may rest

GREEK OLD TESTAMENT

τοῖς ἑαυτῶν δαπανήμασιν καὶ νόμοις, καθὰ καὶ τὸ πρότερον,
καὶ οὐδεὶς αὐτῶν κατ᾽ οὐδένα τρόπον παρενοχληθήσεται
περὶ τῶν ἠγνοημένων. 32 πέπομφα δὲ καὶ τὸν Μενέλαον
παρακαλέσοντα ὑμᾶς. 33 ἔρρωσθε. ἔτους ἑκατοστοῦ τεσσαρακοστοῦ ὀγδόου, Ξανθικοῦ πεντεκαιδεκάτῃ.
34 Ἔπεμψαν δὲ καὶ οἱ Ῥωμαῖοι πρὸς αὐτοὺς ἐπιστολὴν
ἔχουσαν οὕτως

Κόιντος Μέμμιος, Τίτος Μάνιος, πρεσβῦται Ῥωμαίων, τῷ
δήμῳ τῶν Ιουδαίων χαίρειν. 35 ὑπὲρ ὧν Λυσίας ὁ συγγενὴς
τοῦ βασιλέως συνεχώρησεν ὑμῖν, καὶ ἡμεῖς συνευδοκοῦμεν.
36 ἃ δὲ ἔκρινεν προσανενεχθῆναι τῷ βασιλεῖ, πέμψατέ τινα
παραχρῆμα ἐπισκεψάμενοι περὶ τούτων, ἵνα ἐκθῶμεν ὡς
καθήκει ὑμῖν· ἡμεῖς γὰρ προσάγομεν πρὸς Ἀντιόχειαν.
37 διὸ σπεύσατε καὶ πέμψατέ τινας, ὅπως καὶ ἡμεῖς ἐπιγνῶ-
μεν ὁποίας ἐστὲ γνώμης. 38 ὑγιαίνετε. ἔτους ἑκατοστοῦ
τεσσαρακοστοῦ ὀγδόου, Ξανθικοῦ πεντεκαιδεκάτῃ.

12 Γενομένων δὲ τῶν συνθηκῶν τούτων ὁ μὲν Λυσίας
ἀπῄει πρὸς τὸν βασιλέα, οἱ δὲ Ιουδαῖοι περὶ τὴν
γεωργίαν ἐγίνοντο. 2 τῶν δὲ κατὰ τόπον στρατηγῶν Τιμόθεος καὶ Ἀπολλώνιος ὁ τοῦ Γενναίου, ἔτι δὲ Ἱερώνυμος καὶ
Δημοφῶν, πρὸς δὲ τούτοις Νικάνωρ ὁ Κυπριάρχης οὐκ εἴων
αὐτοὺς εὐσταθεῖν καὶ τὰ τῆς ἡσυχίας ἄγειν. 3 Ἰοππῖται δὲ

KING JAMES VERSION

31 And the Jews shall use their own kind of meats and laws, as before; and none of them any manner of ways shall be molested for things ignorantly done.

32 I have sent also Menelaus, that he may comfort you.

33 Fare ye well. In the hundred forty and eighth year, *and* the fifteenth day of *the month* Xanthicus.

34 The Romans also sent unto them a letter containing these words: Quintus Memmius and Titus Manlius, ambassadors of the Romans, *send* greeting unto the people of the Jews.

35 Whatsoever Lysias the king's cousin hath granted, therewith we also are well pleased.

36 But touching such things as he judged to be referred to the king, after ye have advised thereof, send one forthwith, that we may declare as it is convenient for you: for we are now going to Antioch.

37 Therefore send some with speed, that we may know what is your mind.

38 Farewell. This hundred and eight and fortieth year, the fifteenth day of *the month* Xanthicus.

12 When these covenants were made, Lysias went unto the king, and the Jews were about their husbandry.

2 But of the governours of several places, Timotheus, and Apollonius the *son* of Genneus, also Hieronymus, and Demophon, and beside them Nicanor the governor of Cyprus, would not suffer them to be quiet, and live in peace.

DOUAY OLD TESTAMENT

31 That the Jews may use their own kind of meats, and their own laws as before, and that none of them any manner of ways be molested for things which have been done by ignorance.

32 And we have sent also Menelaus to speak to you.

33 Fare ye well. In the year one hundred and forty-eight, the fifteenth day of the month of Xanthicus.

34 The Romans also sent them a letter, to this effect. Quintus Memmius, and Titus Manilius, ambassadors of the Romans, to the people of the Jews, greeting.

35 Whatsoever Lysias the king's cousin hath granted you, we also have granted.

36 But touching such things as he thought should be referred to the king, after you have diligently conferred among yourselves, send some one forthwith, that we may decree as it is convenient for you: for we are going to Antioch.

37 And therefore make haste to write back, that we may know of what mind you are.

38 Fare ye well. In the year one hundred and forty-eight, the fifteenth day of the month of Xanthicus.

12 WHEN these covenants were made, Lysias went to the king, and the Jews gave themselves to husbandry.

2 But they that were behind, namely, Timotheus and Apollonius the son of Genneus, also Hieronymus, and Demophon, and besides them Nicanor the governor of Cyprus, would not suffer them to live in peace, and to be quiet.

KNOX TRANSLATION

would travel here, up to the thirtieth day of Xanthicus...
31 That the Jewish folk may eat what food they will, use what
laws they will, according to their ancient custom; and if
aught has been done amiss through inadvertence, none of
them, for that cause, shall be molested. 32 We are sending
Menelaus besides, to give a charge to you. 33 Farewell. Given
on the fifteenth day of Xanthicus, in the hundred and forty-
eighth year.
34 The Romans, too, wrote to them after the manner following; Quintus Memmius and Titus Manlius, envoys of
Rome, to the Jewish people, all health! 35 The privileges
Lysias has granted you in the name of his royal cousin, we
hereby ratify. 36 Other matters he has remitted to the king's
decision; take counsel among yourselves, and let us know at
once what your mind is, if you would have us order all to
your liking. Even now we are on the road to Antioch;
37 write speedily, to let us know how you are minded.
38 Farewell. Given on the twenty-fifth day of Xanthicus, in
the hundred and forty-eighth year.

12 So all was agreed upon; Lysias was for the court
again, and the Jewish folk went back to their farms.
2 But neither rest nor respite might they have while
Timotheus[a] and Apollonius, son of Gennaeus, were left at
their posts; Hieronymus, too, and Demophon, and Nicanor
that ruled in Cyprus.

[a] For Timotheus, see note on 10. 37.

TODAY'S ENGLISH VERSION

fear. 31 You may continue to observe your food laws and
other laws, as you used to do, and no Jew will be punished
for any crime done in ignorance. 32 I am sending Menelaus
to set your minds at ease. 33 May all go well with you.
Dated the fifteenth day of the month of Xanthicus in the
year 148."[a]
34 The Romans also sent the Jews the following letter:
"Quintus Memmius and Titus Manius, representatives of
the Romans, to the Jews, greetings. 35 We are in complete
agreement with all that has been granted to you by the
honorable Lysias. 36 We are now on our way to Antioch,
so please examine carefully those matters that Lysias
referred to the king. Then send a reply to us immediately
so that we can represent your best interests before him. Do
this as soon as you can, 37 without delay, so that we may
know what you have decided. 38 May all go well with you.
Dated the fifteenth day of the month of Xanthicus in the
year 148."

12 When the peace agreement between the Jews and the
Syrians was completed, Lysias returned to the king,
and the Jews went back to their farming. 2 But some of the
local governors, Timothy and Apollonius son of Gennaeus,
as well as Hieronymus and Demophon, would not let them
live in peace; and neither would Nicanor, the commander of
the mercenaries from Cyprus.

[a] THE YEAR 148: *This corresponds to 164 B.C.*

NEW REVISED STANDARD VERSION

the Jews to enjoy their own food and laws, just as formerly,
and none of them shall be molested in any way for what
may have been done in ignorance. 32 And I have also sent
Menelaus to encourage you. 33 Farewell. The one hundred
forty-eighth year,[a] Xanthicus fifteenth."
34 The Romans also sent them a letter, which read thus:
"Quintus Memmius and Titus Manius, envoys of the
Romans, to the people of the Jews, greetings. 35 With regard
to what Lysias the kinsman of the king has granted you, we
also give consent. 36 But as to the matters that he decided
are to be referred to the king, as soon as you have considered
them, send some one promptly so that we may make proposals appropriate for you. For we are on our way to Antioch.
37 Therefore make haste and send messengers so that we
may have your judgment. 38 Farewell. The one hundred
forty-eighth year,[a] Xanthicus fifteenth."

12 When this agreement had been reached, Lysias
returned to the king, and the Jews went about their
farming.
2 But some of the governors in various places, Timothy
and Apollonius son of Gennaeus, as well as Hieronymus and
Demophon, and in addition to these Nicanor the governor of
Cyprus, would not let them live quietly and in peace. 3 And

[a] 164 B.C.

NEW AMERICAN BIBLE

and other laws, just as before, and none of the Jews shall be
molested in any way for faults committed through ignorance.
32 I have also sent Menelaus to reassure you. 33 Farewell." In
the year one hundred and forty-eight, the fifteenth of
Xanthicus.
34 The Romans also sent them a letter as follows: "Quintus
Memmius and Titus Manius, legates of the Romans, send
greetings to the Jewish people. 35 Whatever Lysias, kinsman
of the king, has granted you, we also approve. 36 But the
matters on which he passed judgment should be submitted
to the king. As soon as you have considered them, send
someone to us with your decisions so that we may present
them to your advantage, for we are on our way to Antioch.
37 Make haste, then, to send us those who can inform us of
your intentions. 38 Farewell." In the year one hundred and
forty-eight, the fifteenth of Xanthicus.

12 After these agreements were made, Lysias returned
to the king, and the Jews went about their farming.
2 But some of the local governors, Timothy and Apollonius,
son of Gennaeus, as also Hieronymus and Demophon, to say
nothing of Nicanor, the commander of the Cyprians, would
not allow them to live in peace.

NEW JERUSALEM BIBLE

assured that they have nothing to fear. 31 The Jews may
make use of their own kind of food and their own laws as
formerly, and none of them is to be molested in any way
for any unwitting offences. 32 I am in fact sending
Menelaus to set your minds at rest. 33 Farewell.
'The fifteenth day of Xanthicus in the year one hundred
and forty-eight.'

34 The Romans also sent the Jews a letter, which read as follows:
'Quintus Memmius, Titus Manilius, Manius Sergius,
legates of the Romans, to the people of the Jews, greetings.
35 'Whatever Lysias, the king's Cousin, has granted you
we also approve. 36 As for the matters he decided to refer
to the king, consider them carefully and send someone
without delay, if we are to interpret them to your advantage, because we are leaving for Antioch. 37 Lose no time,
therefore, in sending us those who can tell us what your
intentions are. 38 Farewell.
'The fifteenth day of Dioscorus in the year one hundred
and forty-eight.'

12 These agreements once concluded, Lysias returned to
the king and the Jews went back to their farming.
2 Among the local generals, Timotheus and Apollonius son of
Gennaeus, as also Hieronymus and Demophon, and Nicanor
the Cypriarch as well, would not allow the Jews to live in
peace and quiet.

Greek Old Testament

τηλικοῦτο συνετέλεσαν τὸ δυσσέβημα· παρακαλέσαντες
τοὺς σὺν αὐτοῖς οἰκοῦντας Ιουδαίους ἐμβῆναι εἰς τὰ παρα-
κατασταθέντα ὑπ᾽ αὐτῶν σκάφη σὺν γυναιξὶν καὶ τέκνοις ὡς
μηδεμιᾶς ἐνεστώσης πρὸς αὐτοὺς δυσμενείας, 4 κατὰ δὲ τὸ
κοινὸν τῆς πόλεως ψήφισμα· καὶ τούτων ἐπιδεξαμένων ὡς
ἂν εἰρηνεύειν θελόντων καὶ μηδὲν ὕποπτον ἐχόντων ἐπανα-
χθέντας αὐτοὺς ἐβύθισαν ὄντας οὐκ ἔλαττον τῶν διακοσίων.
5 μεταλαβὼν δὲ Ιουδας τὴν γεγονυῖαν εἰς τοὺς ὁμοεθνεῖς
ὠμότητα παραγγείλας τοῖς περὶ αὐτὸν ἀνδράσιν 6 καὶ ἐπι-
καλεσάμενος τὸν δίκαιον κριτὴν θεὸν παρεγένετο ἐπὶ τοὺς
μιαιφόνους τῶν ἀδελφῶν καὶ τὸν μὲν λιμένα νύκτωρ ἐνέπρησεν καὶ τὰ σκάφη κατέφλεξεν, τοὺς δὲ ἐκεῖ συμφυγόντας
ἐξεκέντησεν. 7 τοῦ δὲ χωρίου συγκλεισθέντος ἀνέλυσεν ὡς
πάλιν ἥξων καὶ τὸ σύμπαν τῶν Ιοππιτῶν ἐκριζῶσαι πολί-
τευμα. 8 μεταλαβὼν δὲ καὶ τοὺς ἐν Ιαμνείᾳ τὸν αὐτὸν
ἐπιτελεῖν βουλομένους τρόπον τοῖς παροικοῦσιν Ιουδαίοις,
9 καὶ τοῖς Ιαμνίταις νυκτὸς ἐπιβαλὼν ὑφῆψεν τὸν λιμένα
σὺν τῷ στόλῳ ὥστε φαίνεσθαι τὰς αὐγὰς τοῦ φέγγους εἰς
τὰ Ιεροσόλυμα σταδίων ὄντων διακοσίων τεσσαράκοντα.

10 Ἐκεῖθεν δὲ ἀποσπάσαντες σταδίους ἐννέα, ποιουμένων
τὴν πορείαν ἐπὶ τὸν Τιμόθεον, προσέβαλον Ἄραβες αὐτῷ
οὐκ ἐλάττους τῶν πεντακισχιλίων, ἱππεῖς δὲ πεντακόσιοι.
11 γενομένης δὲ καρτερᾶς μάχης καὶ τῶν περὶ τὸν Ιουδαν
διὰ τὴν παρὰ τοῦ θεοῦ βοήθειαν εὐημερησάντων ἐλαττονω-
θέντες οἱ νομάδες ἠξίουν δοῦναι τὸν Ιουδαν δεξιὰς αὐτοῖς

King James Version

3 The men of Joppe also did such an ungodly deed: they prayed the Jews that dwelt among them to go with their wives and children into the boats which they had prepared, as though they had meant them no hurt.

4 Who accepted of it according to the common decree of the city, as being desirous to live in peace, and suspecting nothing: but when they were gone forth into the deep, they drowned no less than two hundred of them.

5 When Judas heard of this cruelty done unto his countrymen, he commanded those that were with him *to make them ready.*

6 And calling upon God the righteous Judge, he came against those murderers of his brethren, and burnt the haven by night, and set the boats on fire, and those that fled thither he slew.

7 And when the town was shut up, he went backward, as if he would return to root out all them of the city of Joppe.

8 But when he heard that the Jamnites were minded to do in like manner unto the Jews that dwelt among them,

9 He came upon the Jamnites also by night, and set fire on the haven and the navy, so that the light of the fire was seen at Jerusalem two hundred and forty furlongs off.

10 Now when they were gone from thence nine furlongs in their journey toward Timotheus, no fewer than five thousand *men on foot* and five hundred horsemen of the Arabians set upon him.

11 Whereupon there was a very sore battle; but Judas' side by the help of God got the victory; so that the Nomades

Douay Old Testament

3 The men of Joppe also were guilty of this kind of wickedness: they desired the Jews who dwelt among them to go with their wives and children into the boats, which they had prepared, as though they had no enmity to them.

4 Which when they had consented to, according to the common decree of the city, suspecting nothing, because of the peace: when they were gone forth into the deep, they drowned no fewer than two hundred of them.

5 But as soon as Judas heard of this cruelty done to his countrymen, he commanded the men that were with him: and after having called upon God the just judge,

6 He came against those murderers of his brethren, and set the haven on fire in the night, burnt the boats, and slew with the sword them that escaped from the fire.

7 And when he had done these things in this manner, he departed as if he would return again, and root out all the Joppites.

8 But when he understood that the men of Jamnia also designed to do in like manner to the Jews that dwelt among them,

9 He came upon the Jamnites also by night, and set the haven on fire with the ships, so that the light of the fire was seen at Jerusalem two hundred and forty furlongs off.

10 And when they were now gone from thence nine furlongs, and were marching towards Timotheus, five thousand footmen and five hundred horsemen of the Arabians set upon them.

11 And after a hard fight, in which by the help of God they got the victory, the rest of the Arabians being overcome,

Knox Translation

3 This was a very foul deed done by the men of Joppe; they
fitted out certain vessels of theirs, and would have the neighbouring Jews go aboard, with their wives and children, for all
the world as if there were no grudge between them. 4 It was
the common wish of their fellow-citizens; how should the
Jews gainsay it? They were lovers of peace, and cause for
suspicion had none. Yet once they were on the high seas,
they were cast overboard and drowned, a full two hundred of
them. 5 Such tidings of cruel murder done upon men of his
own race, Judas could not hear unmoved; mustering his followers, and calling upon God, that judges aright, to speed
him, 6 he marched out against the slayers of his brethren; at
dead of night he burned down their wharves, and set all the
ships ablaze, nor any man that escaped the fire but was put
to the sword. 7 This done, he left them, but threatening he
would return, and leave none alive in Joppe. 8 He had word,
too, that the men of Jamnia meant to do the same by the
Jews in their part; 9 so he fell on Jamnia, too, by night, and
burnt both wharves and ships there; the light of that blaze
was seen at Jerusalem, thirty miles off....
10 Nine furlongs they had marched, on their way to meet
Timotheus, when an Arab force engaged them, of five thousand foot and five hundred horse.[a] 11 Stern was the
encounter, but with God's help they won the day; and the
defeated remnant of the Arabs asked Judas for quarter,

a The mention of Timotheus and of the Arabs would suggest that this incident took place beyond Jordan, rather than in the Jamnia neighbourhood. It seems possible there is a gap in the text.

TODAY'S ENGLISH VERSION

3 About this time, the people of Joppa did a cruel thing to
the Jews of their city. They pretended to be friendly to the
Jews and invited them and their families to go sailing with
them on ships they had provided. 4 Since all the people of
the town had decided to do this, the Jews suspected nothing
and accepted the invitation out of a feeling of good will. But
when they were out at sea, the people of Joppa drowned all
two hundred of them.

5 As soon as Judas heard of this inhuman thing that had
been done to those Jews, he informed his men. 6 After they
had prayed to God, the just judge, they attacked the murderers. Under cover of darkness they set fire to the harbor, burning all the ships, and killing everyone they found hiding
there. 7 The gates of the city were locked, so Judas withdrew;
but he was determined to return at some other time and wipe
out everyone living there.

8 Judas heard that the people of Jamnia had plans to kill
the Jews of their city also. 9 So he attacked Jamnia at night,
setting fire to its harbor and the ships there. The flames
could be seen as far as Jerusalem, thirty miles away.

10 When Judas and his men were about a mile away from
Jamnia on their way to meet Timothy in battle, they were
attacked by more than 5,000 Arabs, supported by 500 cavalry. 11 It was a hard fight, but with the help of God they
defeated these desert tribesmen, who then asked to be on

NEW REVISED STANDARD VERSION

the people of Joppa did so ungodly a deed as this: they invited the Jews who lived among them to embark, with their
wives and children, on boats that they had provided, as
though there were no ill will to the Jews;[a] 4 and this was
done by public vote of the city. When they accepted, because
they wished to live peaceably and suspected nothing, the
people of Joppa[b] took them out to sea and drowned them, at
least two hundred. 5 When Judas heard of the cruelty visited
on his compatriots, he gave orders to his men 6 and, calling
upon God, the righteous judge, attacked the murderers of his
kindred. He set fire to the harbor by night, burned the boats,
and massacred those who had taken refuge there. 7 Then,
because the city's gates were closed, he withdrew, intending
to come again and root out the whole community of Joppa.
8 But learning that the people in Jamnia meant in the same
way to wipe out the Jews who were living among them, 9 he
attacked the Jamnites by night and set fire to the harbor and
the fleet, so that the glow of the light was seen in Jerusalem,
thirty miles[c] distant.

10 When they had gone more than a mile[d] from there, on
their march against Timothy, at least five thousand Arabs
with five hundred cavalry attacked them. 11 After a hard
fight, Judas and his companions, with God's help, were victorious. The defeated nomads begged Judas to grant them

a Gk *to them* *b* Gk *they* *c* Gk *two hundred forty stadia* *d* Gk *nine stadia*

NEW AMERICAN BIBLE

3 Some people of Joppa also committed this outrage: they
invited the Jews who lived among them, together with their
wives and children, to embark on boats which they had provided. There was no hint of enmity toward them: 4 this was
done by public vote of the city. When the Jews, not suspecting treachery and wishing to live on friendly terms, accepted
the invitation, the people of Joppa took them out to sea and
drowned at least two hundred of them.

5 As soon as Judas heard of the barbarous deed perpetrated
against his countrymen, he summoned his men; 6 and after
calling upon God, the just judge, he marched against the
murderers of his kinsmen. In a night attack he set the harbor
on fire, burnt the boats, and put to the sword those who had
taken refuge there. 7 When the gates of the town were shut,
he withdrew, intending to come back later and wipe out the
entire population of Joppa.

8 On hearing that the men of Jamnia planned to give like
treatment to the Jews who lived among them, 9 he attacked
the Jamnian populace by night, setting fire to the harbor and
the fleet, so that the glow of the flames was visible as far as
Jerusalem, thirty miles away.

10 When the Jews had gone about a mile from there in the
campaign against Timothy, they were attacked by Arabs
numbering at least five thousand foot soldiers, and five hundred horsemen. 11 After a hard fight, Judas and his companions, with God's help, were victorious. The defeated nomads

NEW JERUSALEM BIBLE

3 The people of Joppa committed a particularly wicked
crime: they invited the Jews living among them to go aboard
some boats they had lying ready, taking their wives and children. There was no hint of any intention to harm them;
4 there had been a public vote by the citizens, and the Jews
accepted, as well they might, being peaceable people with no
reason to suspect anything. But once out in the open sea
they were all sent to the bottom, a company of at least two
hundred.

5 When Judas heard of the cruel fate of his countrymen, he
issued his orders to his men 6 and after invoking God, the
just judge, he attacked his brothers' murderers. Under cover
of dark he set fire to the port, burned the boats and put to
the sword everyone who had taken refuge there. 7 As the
town gates were closed, he withdrew, intending to come back
and wipe out the whole community of Joppa. 8 But hearing
that the people of Jamnia were planning to treat their resident Jews in the same way, 9 he made a night attack on the
Jamnites and fired the port with its fleet; the glow of the
flames was seen as far off as Jerusalem, thirty miles away.

10[a] When they had left the town barely a mile behind them
in their advance on Timotheus, Judas was attacked by an
Arab force of at least five thousand foot soldiers, with five
hundred cavalry. 11 A fierce engagement followed, and with
God's help Judas' men won the day; the defeated nomads

a **12** 12:10seq. // 1 M 5:24–54.

GREEK OLD TESTAMENT

ὑπισχνούμενοι καὶ βοσκήματα δώσειν καὶ ἐν τοῖς λοιποῖς
ὠφελήσειν αὐτούς. 12 Ιουδας δὲ ὑπολαβὼν ὡς ἀληθῶς ἐν πολλοῖς αὐτοὺς χρησίμους ἐπεχώρησεν εἰρήνην ἄξειν πρὸς
αὐτούς. καὶ λαβόντες δεξιὰς εἰς τὰς σκηνὰς ἐχωρίσθησαν.
13 Ἐπέβαλεν δὲ καὶ ἐπί τινα πόλιν γεφύραις ὀχυρὰν καὶ
τείχεσιν περιπεφραγμένην καὶ παμμειγέσιν ἔθνεσιν κατοι-
κουμένην, ὄνομα δὲ Κασπιν. 14 οἱ δὲ ἔνδον πεποιθότες τῇ
τῶν τειχέων ἐρυμνότητι τῇ τε τῶν βρωμάτων παραθέσει
ἀναγωγότερον ἐχρῶντο τοῖς περὶ τὸν Ιουδαν λοιδοροῦντες
καὶ προσέτι βλασφημοῦντες καὶ λαλοῦντες ἃ μὴ θέμις. 15 οἱ
δὲ περὶ τὸν Ιουδαν ἐπικαλεσάμενοι τὸν μέγαν τοῦ κόσμου
δυνάστην τὸν ἄτερ κριῶν καὶ μηχανῶν ὀργανικῶν κατακρη-
μνίσαντα τὴν Ιεριχω κατὰ τοὺς Ἰησοῦ χρόνους ἐνέσεισαν
θηριωδῶς τῷ τείχει. 16 καταλαβόμενοί τε τὴν πόλιν τῇ τοῦ
θεοῦ θελήσει ἀμυθήτους ἐποιήσαντο σφαγὰς ὥστε τὴν παρα-
κειμένην λίμνην τὸ πλάτος ἔχουσαν σταδίους δύο κατάρ-
ρυτον αἵματι πεπληρωμένην φαίνεσθαι.

17 Ἐκεῖθεν δὲ ἀποσπάσαντες σταδίους ἑπτακοσίους
πεντήκοντα διήνυσαν εἰς τὸν Χάρακα πρὸς τοὺς λεγομένους
Τουβιανοὺς Ιουδαίους. 18 καὶ Τιμόθεον μὲν ἐπὶ τῶν τόπων οὐ
κατέλαβον ἄπρακτον τότε ἀπὸ τῶν τόπων ἐκλελυκότα,
καταλελοιπότα δὲ φρουρὰν ἔν τινι τόπῳ καὶ μάλα ὀχυράν.

KING JAMES VERSION

of Arabia, being overcome, besought Judas for peace, promising both to give him cattle, and to pleasure him otherwise.

12 Then Judas, thinking indeed that they would be profitable in many things, granted them peace: whereupon they shook hands, and so they departed to their tents.

13 He went also about to make a bridge to a certain strong city, which was fenced about with walls, and inhabited by people of divers countries; and the name of it was Caspis.

14 But they that were within it put such trust in the strength of the walls and provision of victuals, that they behaved themselves rudely toward them that were with Judas, railing and blaspheming, and uttering such words as were not to be spoken.

15 Wherefore Judas with his company, calling upon the great Lord of the world, who without any rams or engines of war did cast down Jericho in the time of Joshua, gave a fierce assault against the walls,

16 And took the city by the will of God, and made unspeakable slaughters, insomuch that a lake two furlongs broad near adjoining thereunto, being filled full, was seen running with blood.

17 Then departed they from thence seven hundred and fifty furlongs, and came to Characa unto the Jews that are called Tubieni.

18 But as for Timotheus, they found him not in the places: for before he had dispatched any thing, he departed from thence, having left a very strong garrison in a certain hold.

DOUAY OLD TESTAMENT

besought Judas for peace, promising to give him pastures, and to assist him in other things.

12 And Judas thinking that they might be profitable indeed in many things, promised them peace, and after having joined hands, they departed to their tents.

13 He also laid siege to a certain strong city, encompassed with bridges and walls, and inhabited by multitudes of different nations, the name of which is Casphin.

14 But they that were within it, trusting in the strength of the walls, and the provision of victuals, behaved in a more negligent manner, and provoked Judas with railing and blaspheming, and uttering such words as were not to be spoken.

15 But Machabeus calling upon the great Lord of the world, who without any rams or engines of war threw down the walls of Jericho in the time of Josue, fiercely assaulted the walls.

16 And having taken the city by the will of the Lord, he made an unspeakable slaughter, so that a pool adjoining of two furlongs broad seemed to run with the blood of the slain.

17 From thence they departed seven hundred and fifty furlongs, and came to Characa to the Jews that are called Tubianites.

18 But as for Timotheus, they found him not in those places, for before he had dispatched any thing he went back, having left a very strong garrison in a certain hold:

KNOX TRANSLATION

promising a grant of pasture-lands, with other advantages.
12 And, beyond doubt, they could be many ways serviceable
to him; so he made terms with them. They swore friendship,
and the Arabs went back to their tents.
13 A city there was called Casphin, moated and walled
about for its defence, and held by a rabble of many races;
this, too, Judas attacked. 14 Such trust the defenders had in
the strength of their ramparts, and their plentiful supplies of
food, they carried themselves recklessly, hurling taunts at
Judas, with blasphemies and other talk little fit to be uttered.
15 But Machabaeus to that King made appeal, who needed
neither engine nor battering-ram, in Josue's day, to bring
Jericho down in ruins; a fierce attack he delivered upon the
walls, 16 and, so God willed, became master of the city. The
slaughter in it was past reckoning; there was a pool hard by,
of two furlongs' breadth, that seemed as if it ran in full tide
with the blood of slain men.
17 It needed a march of ninety-five miles to bring them to
Charax, where the Jews were whom they call Tubianaeans.
18 Yet could they not come up with Timotheus; he had retired,
with nothing achieved, leaving a strong garrison in one of

Today's English Version

friendly terms with the Jews, promising to give them some
livestock and offering to help them in other ways as well.
12 Judas thought their friendship might prove useful in many
ways, so he agreed to make peace with them; after that the
Arabs returned to their tents.

13 Judas also attacked the heavily fortified walled city of
Caspin. The people who lived there were a mixed population
of Gentiles 14 who relied on the strength of their walls and
felt confident that they had enough food stored up to last
through a siege. So they made fun of Judas and his men,
shouting out insults against them and profanities against
their God. 15 But the Jews prayed to the Almighty Lord of the
universe, who had torn down the walls of Jericho in the days
of Joshua without using battering rams or siege weapons.
Then they made a fierce attack against the wall 16 and
because it was God's will, they captured the city. The Jews
slaughtered so many people that a nearby lake, which was
about a quarter of a mile wide, seemed to be overflowing
with blood.

17 From the city of Caspin, Judas and his men marched
about 95 miles, until they came to the Jewish settlement of
Charax, near the city of Tob. 18 But they did not find
Timothy there, because he had already left the region. He
had been able to do nothing there except leave behind a

New Revised Standard Version

pledges of friendship, promising to give him livestock and to
help his people[a] in all other ways. 12 Judas, realizing that
they might indeed be useful in many ways, agreed to make
peace with them; and after receiving his pledges they went
back to their tents.

13 He also attacked a certain town that was strongly fortified with earthworks[b] and walls, and inhabited by all sorts
of Gentiles. Its name was Caspin. 14 Those who were within,
relying on the strength of the walls and on their supply of
provisions, behaved most insolently toward Judas and his
men, railing at them and even blaspheming and saying
unholy things. 15 But Judas and his men, calling upon the
great Sovereign of the world, who without battering rams or
engines of war overthrew Jericho in the days of Joshua,
rushed furiously upon the walls. 16 They took the town by
the will of God, and slaughtered untold numbers, so that the
adjoining lake, a quarter of a mile[c] wide, appeared to be running over with blood.

17 When they had gone ninety-five miles[d] from there,
they came to Charax, to the Jews who are called Toubiani.
18 They did not find Timothy in that region, for he had by
then left there without accomplishing anything, though in
one place he had left a very strong garrison. 19 Dositheus

a Gk *them* b Meaning of Gk uncertain c Gk *two stadia*
d Gk *seven hundred fifty stadia*

New American Bible

begged Judas to make friends with them and promised to
supply the Jews with cattle and to help them in every other
way. 12 Realizing that they could indeed be useful in many
respects, Judas agreed to make peace with them. After the
pledge of friendship had been exchanged, the Arabs withdrew to their tents.

13 He also attacked a certain city called Caspin, fortified
with earthworks and ramparts and inhabited by a mixed
population of Gentiles. 14 Relying on the strength of their
walls and their supply of provisions, the besieged treated
Judas and his men with contempt, insulting them and even
uttering blasphemies and profanity. 15 But Judas and his
men invoked the aid of the great Sovereign of the world,
who, in the day of Joshua, overthrew Jericho without battering-ram or siege machine; then they furiously stormed the
ramparts. 16 Capturing the city by the will of God, they
inflicted such indescribable slaughter on it that the adjacent
pool, which was about a quarter of a mile wide, seemed to be
filled with the blood that flowed into it.

17 When they had gone on some ninety miles, they reached
Charax, where there were certain Jews known as Toubiani.
18 But they did not find Timothy in that region, for he had
already departed from there without having done anything
except to leave behind in one place a very strong garrison.

New Jerusalem Bible

begged Judas to offer them the right hand of friendship, and
promised to surrender their herds and make themselves generally useful to him. 12 Realising that they might indeed
prove valuable in many ways, Judas consented to make
peace with them and after an exchange of pledges the Arabs
withdrew to their tents.

13 Judas also attacked a certain fortified town, closed by
ramparts and inhabited by a medley of races; its name was
Caspin. 14 Confident in the strength of their walls and their
stock of provisions, the besieged adopted an insolent attitude
to Judas and his men, reinforcing their insults with blasphemies and profanity. 15 But Judas and his men invoked the
great Sovereign of the world who without battering-ram or
siege-engine had overthrown Jericho in the days of Joshua;
they then made a fierce assault on the wall. 16 By God's will,
having captured the town, they made such indescribable
slaughter that the nearby lake, a quarter of a mile across,
seemed filled to overflowing with blood.

17[a] Ninety-five miles further on from there, they reached
the Charax, in the country of Jews known as Tubians.
18 They did not find Timotheus himself in that neighbourhood; he had already left the district, having achieved nothing apart from leaving a very strong garrison at one point.

a **12** 12:17seq. // 1 M 5:37–44.

GREEK OLD TESTAMENT

19 Δοσίθεος δὲ καὶ Σωσίπατρος τῶν περὶ τὸν Μακκαβαῖον
ἡγεμόνων ἐξοδεύσαντες ἀπώλεσαν τοὺς ὑπὸ Τιμοθέου κατα-
λειφθέντας ἐν τῷ ὀχυρώματι πλείους τῶν μυρίων ἀνδρῶν.
20 ὁ δὲ Μακκαβαῖος διατάξας τὴν περὶ αὐτὸν στρατιὰν
σπειρηδὸν κατέστησεν αὐτοὺς ἐπὶ τῶν σπειρῶν καὶ ἐπὶ τὸν
Τιμόθεον ὥρμησεν ἔχοντα περὶ αὐτὸν μυριάδας δώδεκα
πεζῶν, ἱππεῖς δὲ δισχιλίους πρὸς τοῖς πεντακοσίοις. 21 τὴν
δὲ ἔφοδον μεταλαβὼν Ιουδου προεξαπέστειλεν ὁ Τιμόθεος
τὰς γυναῖκας καὶ τὰ τέκνα καὶ τὴν ἄλλην ἀποσκευὴν εἰς τὸ
λεγόμενον Καρνιον· ἦν γὰρ δυσπολιόρκητον καὶ δυσπρόσιτον
τὸ χωρίον διὰ τὴν πάντων τῶν τόπων στενότητα.
22 ἐπιφανείσης δὲ τῆς Ιουδου σπείρας πρώτης καὶ γενομένου
δέους ἐπὶ τοὺς πολεμίους φόβου τε ἐκ τῆς τοῦ τὰ πάντα
ἐφορῶντος ἐπιφανείας γενομένης ἐπ᾽ αὐτοὺς εἰς φυγὴν
ὥρμησαν ἄλλος ἀλλαχῇ φερόμενος ὥστε πολλάκις ὑπὸ τῶν
ἰδίων βλάπτεσθαι καὶ ταῖς τῶν ξιφῶν ἀκμαῖς ἀναπείρεσθαι.
23 ἐποιεῖτο δὲ τὸν διωγμὸν εὐτονώτερον ὁ Ιουδας συγκεντῶν
τοὺς ἀλιτηρίους διέφθειρέν τε εἰς μυριάδας τρεῖς ἀνδρῶν.
24 αὐτὸς δὲ ὁ Τιμόθεος ἐμπεσὼν τοῖς περὶ τὸν Δοσίθεον καὶ
Σωσίπατρον ἠξίου μετὰ πολλῆς γοητείας ἐξαφεῖναι σῶον
αὐτὸν διὰ τὸ πλειόνων μὲν γονεῖς, ὧν δὲ ἀδελφοὺς ἔχειν καὶ
τούτους ἀλογηθῆναι συμβήσεται. 25 πιστώσαντος δὲ αὐτοῦ
διὰ πλειόνων τὸν ὁρισμὸν ἀποκαταστῆσαι τούτους ἀπημάν-
τους ἀπέλυσαν αὐτὸν ἕνεκα τῆς τῶν ἀδελφῶν σωτηρίας.

KING JAMES VERSION

19 Howbeit Dositheus and Sosipater, who were of Maccabeus' captains, went forth, and slew those that Timotheus had left in the fortress, above ten thousand men.

20 And Maccabeus ranged his army by bands, and set them over the bands, and went against Timotheus, who had about him an hundred and twenty thousand men of foot, and two thousand and five hundred horsemen.

21 Now when Timotheus had knowledge of Judas' coming, he sent the women and children and the other baggage unto a fortress called Carnion: for the town was hard to besiege, and uneasy to come unto, by reason of the straitness of all the places.

22 But when Judas his first band came in sight, the enemies, being smitten with fear and terror through the appearing of him who seeth all things, fled amain, one running this way, another that way, so as that they were often hurt of their own men, and wounded with the points of their own swords.

23 Judas also was very earnest in pursuing them, killing those wicked wretches, of whom he slew about thirty thousand men.

24 Moreover Timotheus himself fell into the hands of Dositheus and Sosipater, whom he besought with much craft to let him go with his life, because he had many of the Jews' parents, and the brethren of some of them, who, if they put him to death, should not be regarded.

25 So when he had assured them with many words that he would restore them without hurt, according to the agreement, they let him go for the saving of their brethren.

DOUAY OLD TESTAMENT

19 But Dositheus, and Sosipater, who were captains with Machabeus, slew them that were left by Timotheus in the hold, to the number of ten thousand men.

20 And Machabeus having set in order about him six thousand men, and divided them by bands, went forth against Timotheus, who had with him a hundred and twenty thousand footmen, and two thousand five hundred horsemen.

21 Now when Timotheus had knowledge of the coming of Judas, he sent the women and children, and the other baggage before him into a fortress, called Carnion: for it was impregnable and hard to come at, by reason of the straitness of the places.

22 But when the first band of Judas came in sight, the enemies were struck with fear, by the presence of God, who seeth all things, and they were put to flight one from another, so that they were often thrown down by their own companions, and wounded with the strokes of their own swords.

23 But Judas was vehemently earnest in punishing the profane, of whom he slew thirty thousand men.

24 And Timotheus himself fell into the hands of the band of Dositheus and Sosipater, and with many prayers he besought them to let him go with his life, because he had the parents and brethren of many of the Jews, who, by his death, might happen to be deceived.

25 And when he had given his faith that he would restore them according to the agreement, they let him go without hurt, for the saving of their brethren.

KNOX TRANSLATION

the forts there; 19 which garrison of his, ten thousand
strong, was destroyed by two of Machabaeus' captains,
Dositheus and Sosipater. 20 Machabaeus himself, with six
thousand men at his heels, divided into companies, pressed
on against Timotheus, that had a hundred and twenty thousand foot, and two thousand five hundred horse, under his
command. 21 At the news of Judas' coming, Timotheus was
fain to send on women, children, and stores, to Carnion, an
impregnable fortress and one difficult of approach, so narrow the pass was. 22 And now the first of Judas' companies
came in sight, and with it the presence of the all-seeing
God.[a] What fear fell upon the enemy, how they scattered in
flight, stumbling over their own fellows, wounded by the
point of their own swords! 23 And all the while Judas pressed
them hard, the scourge of ill-doers; thirty thousand of them
that day he slaughtered. 24 As for Timotheus, he fell into the
hands of another force, under Dositheus and Sosipater; of
these he begged earnestly for his life, telling them of Jewish
hostages in his keeping, their own fathers and brothers, that
would get no quarter if he came by his death. 25 Many were
the pledges he gave, covenanting for the restoration of these
hostages, and at last, for love of their brethren, they let him
go free.

[a] The Greek implies that the divine presence was in some way visibly manifested.

TODAY'S ENGLISH VERSION

strong garrison in one place. 19 Two of Judas' generals,
Dositheus and Sosipater, attacked the garrison and killed all
10,000 men stationed there. 20 Then Judas divided his army
into several divisions, placing Dositheus and Sosipater each
in command of a division, and hurried after Timothy, who
had a force of 120,000 infantry and 2,500 cavalry. 21 When
Timothy found out that Judas was coming after him, he sent
the women and the children on ahead with the baggage to
the city of Karnaim, which was almost impossible to besiege
or even to reach, because of the narrow passes that led up
to it. 22 But at the moment that Judas' first division came
into sight, the enemy forces were thrown into panic by a
vision sent by God, who sees everything. In terror they
began to run wildly about and many of them were wounded
by the swords of their own men. 23 So Judas and his men
pursued them as hard as they could, killing at least 30,000
of the enemy. 24 Timothy himself was captured by the
troops of Dositheus and Sosipater. But he was very shrewd
and managed to convince them that many of their relatives
were his prisoners and would be put to death if anything
happened to him. 25 Finally, after he had promised to send
their relatives home safely, they let him go free.

NEW REVISED STANDARD VERSION

and Sosipater, who were captains under Maccabeus,
marched out and destroyed those whom Timothy had left in
the stronghold, more than ten thousand men. 20 But Maccabeus arranged his army in divisions, set men[a] in command
of the divisions, and hurried after Timothy, who had with
him one hundred twenty thousand infantry and two thousand five hundred cavalry. 21 When Timothy learned of the
approach of Judas, he sent off the women and the children
and also the baggage to a place called Carnaim; for that place
was hard to besiege and difficult of access because of the
narrowness of all the approaches. 22 But when Judas's first
division appeared, terror and fear came over the enemy at
the manifestation to them of him who sees all things. In
their flight they rushed headlong in every direction, so that
often they were injured by their own men and pierced by the
points of their own swords. 23 Judas pressed the pursuit with
the utmost vigor, putting the sinners to the sword, and
destroyed as many as thirty thousand.

24 Timothy himself fell into the hands of Dositheus and
Sosipater and their men. With great guile he begged them to
let him go in safety, because he held the parents of most of
them, and the brothers of some, to whom no consideration
would be shown. 25 And when with many words he had confirmed his solemn promise to restore them unharmed, they
let him go, for the sake of saving their kindred.

a Gk *them*

NEW AMERICAN BIBLE

19 But Dositheus and Sosipater, two of Maccabeus' captains,
marched out and destroyed the force of more than ten thousand men that Timothy had left in the stronghold. 20 Meanwhile, Maccabeus divided his army into cohorts, with a commander over each cohort, and went in pursuit of Timothy,
who had a force of a hundred and twenty thousand foot soldiers and twenty-five hundred horsemen. 21 When Timothy
learned of the approach of Judas, he sent on ahead of him
the women and children, as well as the baggage, to a place
called Karnion, which was hard to besiege and even hard to
reach because of the difficult terrain of that region. 22 But
when Judas' first cohort appeared, the enemy was overwhelmed with fear and terror at the manifestation of the All-
seeing. Scattering in every direction, they rushed away in
such headlong flight that in many cases they wounded one
another, pierced by the swords of their own men. 23 Judas
pressed the pursuit vigorously, putting the sinners to the
sword and destroying as many as thirty thousand men.

24 Timothy himself fell into the hands of the men under
Dositheus and Sosipater; but with great cunning, he asked
them to spare his life and let him go, because he had in his
power the parents and relatives of many of them, and could
make these suffer. 25 When he had fully confirmed his
solemn pledge to restore them unharmed, they let him go for
the sake of saving their brethren.

NEW JERUSALEM BIBLE

19 Dositheus and Sosipater, two of the Maccabaean generals,
marched out and destroyed the force Timotheus had left
behind in the fortress, amounting to more than ten thousand
men. 20 Maccabaeus himself divided his army into cohorts to
which he assigned commanders, and then hurried in pursuit
of Timotheus, whose troops numbered one hundred and
twenty thousand infantry and two thousand five hundred
cavalry. 21 Timotheus' first move on learning of Judas'
advance was to send away the women and children and the
rest of the baggage train to the place called the Carnaim,
since it was an impregnable position, difficult of access
owing to the narrowness of all the approaches. 22 Judas'
cohort came into sight first. The enemy, seized with fright
and panic-stricken by the manifestation of the All-seeing,
began to flee, one running this way, one running that, often
wounding one another in consequence and running on the
points of one another's swords. 23 Judas pursued them with
a will, cutting the sinners to pieces and killing something
like thirty thousand men. 24 Timotheus himself, having fall-
en into the hands of Dositheus and Sosipater and their men,
very craftily pleaded with them to let him go with his life, on
the grounds that he had the relatives and even the brothers
of many of them in his power, and that these could otherwise expect short shrift. 25 When at long last he convinced
them that he would honour his promise and return these
people safe and sound, they let him go for the sake of saving
their brothers.

GREEK OLD TESTAMENT

26 Ἐξελθὼν δὲ ἐπὶ τὸ Καρνιον καὶ τὸ Ατεργατειον κατέσφαξεν μυριάδας σωμάτων δύο καὶ πεντακισχιλίους. 27 μετὰ δὲ τὴν τούτων τροπὴν καὶ ἀπώλειαν ἐπεστράτευσεν καὶ ἐπὶ Εφρων πόλιν ὀχυράν, ἐν ᾗ κατῴκει Λυσίας καὶ πάμφυλα πλήθη, νεανίαι δὲ ῥωμαλέοι πρὸ τῶν τειχέων καθεστῶτες εὐρώστως ἀπεμάχοντο, ἔνθα δὲ ὀργάνων καὶ βελῶν πολλαὶ παραθέσεις ὑπῆρχον. 28 ἐπικαλεσάμενοι δὲ τὸν δυνάστην τὸν μετὰ κράτους συντρίβοντα τὰς τῶν πολεμίων ἀλκὰς ἔλαβον τὴν πόλιν ὑποχείριον, κατέστρωσαν δὲ τῶν ἔνδον εἰς μυριάδας δύο πεντακισχιλίους. 29 ἀναζεύξαντες δὲ ἐκεῖθεν ὥρμησαν ἐπὶ Σκυθῶν πόλιν ἀπέχουσαν ἀπὸ Ιεροσολύμων σταδίους ἑξακοσίους. 30 ἀπομαρτυρησάντων δὲ τῶν ἐκεῖ καθεστώτων Ιουδαίων, ἣν οἱ Σκυθοπολῖται ἔσχον πρὸς αὐτοὺς εὔνοιαν καὶ ἐν τοῖς τῆς ἀτυχίας καιροῖς ἥμερον ἀπάντησιν, 31 εὐχαριστήσαντες καὶ προσπαρακαλέσαντες καὶ εἰς τὰ λοιπὰ πρὸς τὸ γένος εὐμενεῖς εἶναι παρεγενήθησαν εἰς Ιεροσόλυμα τῆς τῶν ἑβδομάδων ἑορτῆς οὔσης ὑπογύου.

32 Μετὰ δὲ τὴν λεγομένην πεντηκοστὴν ὥρμησαν ἐπὶ Γοργίαν τὸν τῆς Ιδουμαίας στρατηγόν. 33 ἐξῆλθεν δὲ μετὰ πεζῶν τρισχιλίων, ἱππέων δὲ τετρακοσίων. 34 παραταξαμένους δὲ συνέβη πεσεῖν ὀλίγους τῶν Ιουδαίων. 35 Δοσίθεός δέ τις τῶν τοῦ Βακήνορος, ἔφιππος ἀνὴρ καὶ καρτερός, εἴχετο τοῦ Γοργίου καὶ λαβόμενος τῆς χλαμύδος ἦγεν αὐτὸν εὐρώστως καὶ βουλόμενος τὸν κατάρατον λαβεῖν ζωγρίαν,

KING JAMES VERSION

26 Then Maccabeus marched forth to Carnion, and to the temple of Atargatis, and there he slew five and twenty thousand persons.

27 And after he had put to flight and destroyed them, Judas removed the host toward Ephron, a strong city, wherein Lysias abode, and a great multitude of divers nations, and the strong young men kept the walls, and defended them mightily: wherein also was great provision of engines and darts.

28 But when Judas and his company had called upon Almighty God, who with his power breaketh the strength of his enemies, they won the city, and slew twenty and five thousand of them that were within.

29 From thence they departed to Scythopolis, which lieth six hundred furlongs from Jerusalem.

30 But when the Jews that dwelt there had testified that the Scythopolitans dealt lovingly with them, and entreated them kindly in the time of their adversity;

31 They gave them thanks, desiring them to be friendly still unto them: and so they came to Jerusalem, the feast of the weeks approaching.

32 And after the *feast,* called Pentecost, they went forth against Gorgias the governor of Idumea,

33 Who came out with three thousand men of foot and four hundred horsemen.

34 And it happened that in their fighting together a few of the Jews were slain.

35 At which time Dositheus, one of Bacenor's company, who was on horseback, and a strong man, was still upon Gorgias, and taking hold of his coat drew him by force; and

DOUAY OLD TESTAMENT

26 Then Judas went away to Carnion, where he slew five and twenty thousand persons.

27 And after he had put to flight and destroyed these, he removed his army to Ephron, a strong city, wherein there dwelt a multitude of divers nations: and stout young men standing upon the walls made a vigorous resistance: and in this place there were many engines of war, and a provision of darts.

28 But when they had invocated the Almighty, who with his power breaketh the strength of the enemies, they took the city; and slew five and twenty thousand of them that were within.

29 From thence they departed to Scythopolis, which lieth six hundred furlongs from Jerusalem.

30 But the Jews that were among the Scythopolitans testifying that they were used kindly by them, and that even in the times of their adversity they had treated them with humanity:

31 They gave them thanks exhorting them to be still friendly to their nation, and so they came to Jerusalem, the feast of the weeks being at hand.

32 And after Pentecost they marched against Gorgias the governor of Idumea.

33 And he came out with three thousand footmen, and four hundred horsemen.

34 And when they had joined battle, it happened that a few of the Jews were slain.

35 But Dositheus, a horseman, one of Bacenor's *band,* a valiant man, took hold of Gorgias: and when he would have

KNOX TRANSLATION

26 Judas went on to Carnion, where the enemy lost twenty-five thousand men, routed and slain; 27 thence to Ephron, a fortified city, where stout warriors of many different breeds manned the walls most valiantly, well provided with engines and weapons. 28 Yet strength is none can hold its own against the Omnipotent; to him the Jews made appeal, and so took the city, killing twenty-five thousand of the defenders. 29 And thence to Scythopolis, at seventy-five miles' distance from Jerusalem; 30 but here the Jews themselves bore witness, how kindly their neighbours used them, and how honourably they carried themselves even in troublous times. 31 Thanking all such, and desiring them they would continue their good offices towards the Jewish folk, the army returned to Jerusalem, to keep the festival of the Weeks.

32 Then, after-Pentecost, they marched away to meet Gorgias, that was in command of Idumaea;[a] 33 it was but a muster of three thousand foot and four hundred horse.[b] 34 Battle was joined, and some few Jews fell. 35 As for Gorgias, one Dositheus, a great warrior that was in Bacenor's company of horse, kept close on his heels and would

a 'Idumaea' is probably a copyist's error for 'Jamnia'; the context seems to indicate that this engagement was fought in the Philistine country.

b 'It was but a muster of'; literally, 'And he marched out with', but who? Grammatically, it should be Gorgias, but most commentators think Judas is referred to.

TODAY'S ENGLISH VERSION

26 Next, Judas attacked the city of Karnaim and the temple of the goddess Atargatis there, killing 25,000 people 27 and completely destroying both the city and the temple. Then he attacked the fortified city of Ephron where Lysias and[a] people of all nationalities were living. Strong young men took up their positions in front of the walls and fought bravely, while inside the city were stored large quantities of military supplies and weapons. 28 But the Jews prayed for help to the Lord, who crushes the power of his enemies. So they captured the city and killed about 25,000 people. 29 From there they hurried on to the city of Beth Shan, seventy-five miles north of Jerusalem. 30 The Jews there told Judas how kindly the people of the city had treated them, especially during hard times. 31 So Judas and his men thanked the people and urged them to show the same good will toward the Jews in the future. Then they left for Jerusalem, where they arrived shortly before the Harvest Festival.

32 After Pentecost (as the Harvest Festival is called in Greek) Judas and his men quickly marched out against Gorgias, the governor of Idumea, 33 who met them with 3,000 infantry and 400 cavalry. 34 In the battle that followed, a few Jews were killed. 35 Then a Jew from the city of Tob,[b] a powerful cavalry soldier by the name of Dositheus, grabbed Gorgias by his cloak and started dragging him away by brute force, intending to take the worthless man alive. But

[a] Lysias and; *some manuscripts do not have these words.* [b] a Jew from the city of Tob; *some manuscripts have* one of Bacenor's men.

NEW REVISED STANDARD VERSION

26 Then Judas[a] marched against Carnaim and the temple of Atargatis, and slaughtered twenty-five thousand people. 27 After the rout and destruction of these, he marched also against Ephron, a fortified town where Lysias lived with multitudes of people of all nationalities.[b] Stalwart young men took their stand before the walls and made a vigorous defense; and great stores of war engines and missiles were there. 28 But the Jews[c] called upon the Sovereign who with power shatters the might of his enemies, and they got the town into their hands, and killed as many as twenty-five thousand of those who were in it.

29 Setting out from there, they hastened to Scythopolis, which is seventy-five miles[d] from Jerusalem. 30 But when the Jews who lived there bore witness to the goodwill that the people of Scythopolis had shown them and their kind treatment of them in times of misfortune, 31 they thanked them and exhorted them to be well disposed to their race in the future also. Then they went up to Jerusalem, as the festival of weeks was close at hand.

32 After the festival called Pentecost, they hurried against Gorgias, the governor of Idumea, 33 who came out with three thousand infantry and four hundred cavalry. 34 When they joined battle, it happened that a few of the Jews fell. 35 But a certain Dositheus, one of Bacenor's men, who was on horseback and was a strong man, caught hold of Gorgias, and grasping his cloak was dragging him off by main strength, wishing to take the accursed man alive, when one of the

a Gk *he* b Meaning of Gk uncertain c Gk *they* d Gk *six hundred stadia*

NEW AMERICAN BIBLE

26 Judas then marched to Karnion and the shrine of Atargatis, where he killed twenty-five thousand people. 27 After the defeat and destruction of these, he moved his army to Ephron, a fortified city inhabited by people of many nationalities. Robust young men took up their posts in defense of the walls, from which they fought valiantly; inside were large supplies of machines and missiles. 28 But the Jews, invoking the Sovereign who forcibly shatters the might of his enemies, got possession of the city and slaughtered twenty-five thousand of the people in it. 29 Then they set out from there and hastened on to Scythopolis, seventy-five miles from Jerusalem. 30 But when the Jews who lived there testified to the good will shown by the Scythopolitans and to their kind treatment even in times of adversity, 31 Judas and his men thanked them and exhorted them to be well disposed to their race in the future also. Finally they arrived in Jerusalem, shortly before the feast of Weeks.

32 After this feast called Pentecost, they lost no time in marching against Gorgias, governor of Idumea, 33 who opposed them with three thousand foot soldiers and four hundred horsemen. 34 In the ensuing battle, a few of the Jews were slain. 35 A man called Dositheus, a powerful horseman and one of Bacenor's men, caught hold of Gorgias, grasped his military cloak and dragged him along by main strength, intending to capture the vile wretch alive, when a

NEW JERUSALEM BIBLE

26 Reaching the Carnaim and the Atargateion, Judas slaughtered twenty-five thousand men.

27 Having defeated and destroyed them, he led his army against Ephron, a fortified town, where Lysanias was living. Stalwart young men drawn up outside the walls offered vigorous resistance, while inside there were quantities of war-engines and missiles in reserve. 28 But the Jews, having invoked the Sovereign who by his power shatters enemies' defences, gained control of the town and cut down nearly twenty-five thousand of the people inside. 29 Moving off from there, they pressed on to Scythopolis, 30 seventy-five miles from Jerusalem. But as the Jews who had settled there assured Judas that the people of Scythopolis had always treated them well and had been particularly kind to them when times were at their worst, 31 he and his men thanked them and urged them to extend the same friendship to his race in the future.

They reached Jerusalem shortly before the feast of Weeks.

32 After Pentecost, as it is called, they marched against Gorgias, the general commanding Idumaea. 33 He came out at the head of three thousand infantry and four hundred cavalry; 34 in the course of the ensuing battle a few Jews lost their lives.

35 A man called Dositheus, a horseman of the Tubian contingent, a valiant man, overpowered Gorgias and, gripping him by the cloak, was forcibly dragging him along, intending to take the accursed man alive, but one of the Thracian

GREEK OLD TESTAMENT

τῶν ἱππέων τινὸς Θρᾳκῶν ἐπενεχθέντος αὐτῷ καὶ τὸν ὦμον
καθελόντος διέφυγεν ὁ Γοργίας εἰς Μαρισα. 36 τῶν δὲ περὶ
τὸν Εσδριν ἐπὶ πλεῖον μαχομένων καὶ κατακόπων ὄντων ἐπι-
καλεσάμενος Ιουδας τὸν κύριον σύμμαχον φανῆναι καὶ προ-
οδηγὸν τοῦ πολέμου· 37 καταρξάμενος τῇ πατρίῳ φωνῇ τὴν
μεθ᾽ ὕμνων κραυγὴν ἐνσείσας ἀπροσδοκήτως τοῖς περὶ τὸν
Γοργίαν, τροπὴν αὐτῶν ἐποιήσατο.
38 Ιουδας δὲ ἀναλαβὼν τὸ στράτευμα ἧκεν εἰς Οδολλαμ
πόλιν· τῆς δὲ ἑβδομάδος ἐπιβαλλούσης κατὰ τὸν ἐθισμὸν
ἁγνισθέντες αὐτόθι τὸ σάββατον διήγαγον. 39 τῇ δὲ ἐχομέ-
νῃ ἦλθον οἱ περὶ τὸν Ιουδαν καθ᾽ ὃν χρόνον τὸ τῆς χρείας
ἐγεγόνει, τὰ σώματα τῶν προπεπτωκότων ἀνακομίσασθαι
καὶ μετὰ τῶν συγγενῶν ἀποκαταστῆσαι εἰς τοὺς πατρῴους
τάφους. 40 εὗρον δὲ ἑκάστου τῶν τεθνηκότων ὑπὸ τοὺς χιτῶνας ἱερώματα τῶν ἀπὸ Ιαμνείας εἰδώλων, ἀφ᾽ ὧν ὁ νόμος
ἀπείργει τοὺς Ιουδαίους. τοῖς δὲ πᾶσι σαφὲς ἐγένετο διὰ
τήνδε τὴν αἰτίαν τούσδε πεπτωκέναι. 41 πάντες οὖν εὐλογή-
σαντες τὰ τοῦ δικαιοκρίτου κυρίου τὰ κεκρυμμένα φανερὰ
ποιοῦντος 42 εἰς ἱκετείαν ἐτράπησαν ἀξιώσαντες τὸ γεγονὸς ἁμάρτημα τελείως ἐξαλειφθῆναι. ὁ δὲ γενναῖος
Ιουδας παρεκάλεσε τὸ πλῆθος συντηρεῖν αὑτοὺς ἀναμαρτή-
τους εἶναι ὑπ᾽ ὄψιν ἑωρακότας τὰ γεγονότα διὰ τὴν τῶν
προπεπτωκότων ἁμαρτίαν. 43 ποιησάμενός τε κατ᾽ ἀνδρο-
λογίαν εἰς ἀργυρίου δραχμὰς δισχιλίας ἀπέστειλεν εἰς

KING JAMES VERSION

when he would have taken that cursed man alive, a horseman of Thracia coming upon him smote off his shoulder, so
that Gorgias fled unto Marisa.
36 Now when they that were with Gorgias had fought
long, and were weary, Judas called upon the Lord, that he
would shew himself to be their helper and leader of the battle.
37 And with that he began in his own language, and sung
psalms with a loud voice, and rushing unawares upon
Gorgias' men, he put them to flight.
38 So Judas gathered his host, and came into the city of
Odollam. And when the seventh day came, they purified
themselves, as the custom was, and kept the sabbath in the
same place.
39 And upon the day following, as the use had been,
Judas and his company came to take up the bodies of them
that were slain, and to bury them with their kinsmen in their
fathers' graves.
40 Now under the coats of every one that was slain they
found things consecrated to the idols of the Jamnites, which
is forbidden the Jews by the law. Then every man saw that
this was the cause wherefore they were slain.
41 All men therefore praising the Lord, the righteous
Judge, who had opened the things that were hid,
42 Betook themselves unto prayer, and besought him that
the sin committed might wholly be put out of remembrance.
Besides, that noble Judas exhorted the people to keep themselves from sin, forsomuch as they saw before their eyes the
things that came to pass for the sins of those that were slain.
43 And when he had made a gathering throughout the

DOUAY OLD TESTAMENT

taken him alive, a certain horseman of the Thracians came
upon him, and cut off his shoulder: and so Gorgias escaped
to Maresa.
36 But when they that were with Esdrin had fought long,
and were weary, Judas called upon the Lord to be their
helper, and leader of the battle:
37 Then beginning in his own language, and singing
hymns with a loud voice, he put Gorgias' soldiers to flight.
38 So Judas having gathered together his army, came into
the city Odollam: and when the seventh day came, they purified themselves according to the custom, and kept the sabbath in the same place.
39 And the day following Judas came with his company,
to take away the bodies of them that were slain, and to bury
them with their kinsmen, in the sepulchres of their fathers.
40 And they found under the coats of the slain some of
the donaries of the idols of Jamnia, which the law forbiddeth
to the Jews: so that all plainly saw, that for this cause they
were slain.
41 Then they all blessed the just judgment of the Lord,
who had discovered the things that were hidden.
42 And so betaking themselves to prayers, they besought
him, that the sin which had been committed might be forgotten. But the most valiant Judas exhorted the people to keep
themselves from sin, forasmuch as they saw before their eyes
what had happened, because of the sins of those that were
slain.
43 And making a gathering, he sent twelve thousand

KNOX TRANSLATION

have taken him alive; but one of the Thracian horsemen fell
upon him and cut off his arm at the shoulder, so Gorgias
escaped safe to Maresa. 36 A long fight Esdrin's company
had of it, and were full weary, when Judas called upon the
Lord to succour them and lead them onwards, 37 battle-
hymn and battle-cry raising in his own language; and so he
put Gorgias' army to the rout.
38 And now, recalling his men from the pursuit, he made
his way to the city of Adollam; the week had gone round,
and here, duly cleansed from defilement, they kept the sabbath. 39 Next day, with Judas at their head, they went back
to recover the bodies of the slain, for burial among their own
folk in their fathers' graves; 40 and what found they? Each of
the fallen was wearing, under his shirt, some token carried
away from the false gods of Jamnia. Here was defiance of the
Jewish law, and none doubted it was the cause of their undoing; 41 none but praised the Lord for his just retribution, that
had brought hidden things to light; 42 and so they fell to
prayer, pleading that the sin might go unremembered. Judas
himself, their gallant commander, gave public warning to his
men, of fault they should evermore keep clear, with the fate
of these transgressors under their eyes. 43 Then he would
have contribution made; a sum of twelve thousand silver

TODAY'S ENGLISH VERSION

suddenly one from the Thracian cavalry rushed at Dositheus
and chopped off his arm, allowing Gorgias to escape to the
city of Marisa.
36 By now the Jewish men under the command of Esdrias
had been fighting for a long time and were exhausted. So
Judas prayed that the Lord would show that he was on their
side and in command of their troops. 37 Then, while Judas
sang a hymn in his native language as a battle cry, the Jews
made a surprise attack against Gorgias and his men and put
them to flight.
38 After the battle Judas led his men to the town of
Adullam. It was the day before the Sabbath, so they purified
themselves according to Jewish custom and then observed
the holy day. 39 By the following day it was urgent that they
gather up the bodies of the men who had been killed in battle and bury them in their family tombs. 40 But on each of
the dead, hidden under their clothes, they found small
images of the gods worshiped in Jamnia, which the Law forbids Jews to wear. Everyone then knew why these men had
been killed. 41 So they praised the ways of the Lord, the just
judge, who reveals what is hidden, 42 and they begged him
that this sin might be completely blotted out. Then, Judas,
that great man, urged the people to keep away from sin,
because they had seen for themselves what had happened to
those men who had sinned. 43 He also took up a collection
from all his men, totaling about four pounds of silver, and

NEW REVISED STANDARD VERSION

Thracian cavalry bore down on him and cut off his arm; so
Gorgias escaped and reached Marisa.
36 As Esdris and his men had been fighting for a long
time and were weary, Judas called upon the Lord to show
himself their ally and leader in the battle. 37 In the language
of their ancestors he raised the battle cry, with hymns; then
he charged against Gorgias's troops when they were not
expecting it, and put them to flight.
38 Then Judas assembled his army and went to the city of
Adullam. As the seventh day was coming on, they purified
themselves according to the custom, and kept the sabbath
there.
39 On the next day, as had now become necessary, Judas
and his men went to take up the bodies of the fallen and to
bring them back to lie with their kindred in the sepulchres of
their ancestors. 40 Then under the tunic of each one of the
dead they found sacred tokens of the idols of Jamnia, which
the law forbids the Jews to wear. And it became clear to all
that this was the reason these men had fallen. 41 So they all
blessed the ways of the Lord, the righteous judge, who
reveals the things that are hidden; 42 and they turned to supplication, praying that the sin that had been committed
might be wholly blotted out. The noble Judas exhorted the
people to keep themselves free from sin, for they had seen
with their own eyes what had happened as the result of the
sin of those who had fallen. 43 He also took up a collection,
man by man, to the amount of two thousand drachmas of

NEW AMERICAN BIBLE

Thracian horseman attacked Dositheus and cut off his arm at
the shoulder. Then Gorgias fled to Marisa. 36 After Esdris
and his men had been fighting for a long time and were
weary, Judas called upon the LORD to show himself their ally
and leader in the battle. 37 Then, raising a battle cry in his
ancestral language, and with songs, he charged Gorgias'
men when they were not expecting it and put them to flight.
38 Judas rallied his army and went to the city of Adullam.
As the week was ending, they purified themselves according
to custom and kept the sabbath there. 39 On the following
day, since the task had now become urgent, Judas and his
men went to gather up the bodies of the slain and bury them
with their kinsmen in their ancestral tombs. 40 But under the
tunic of each of the dead they found amulets sacred to the
idols of Jamnia, which the law forbids the Jews to wear. So it
was clear to all that this was why these men had been slain.
41 They all therefore praised the ways of the LORD, the just
judge who brings to light the things that are hidden.
42 Turning to supplication, they prayed that the sinful deed
might be fully blotted out. The noble Judas warned the soldiers to keep themselves free from sin, for they had seen
with their own eyes what had happened because of the sin of
those who had fallen. 43 He then took up a collection among
all his soldiers, amounting to two thousand silver drachmas,

NEW JERUSALEM BIBLE

cavalry, hurling himself on Dositheus, slashed his shoulder,
and Gorgias escaped to Marisa. 36 Meanwhile, since Esdrias
and his men had been fighting for a long time and were
exhausted, Judas called on the Lord to show himself their
ally and leader in battle.
37 Then, chanting the battle cry and hymns at the top of his
voice in his ancestral tongue, by a surprise attack he routed
Gorgias' troops.
38 Judas then rallied his army and moved on to the town of
Adullam where, as it was the seventh day of the week, they
purified themselves according to custom and kept the Sabbath. 39 Next day, they came to find Judas (since the necessity was by now urgent) to have the bodies of the fallen taken
up and laid to rest among their relatives in their ancestral
tombs. 40 But when they found on each of the dead men,
under their tunics, objects dedicated to the idols of Jamnia,
which the Law prohibits to Jews, it became clear to everyone
that this was why these men had lost their lives. 41 All then
blessed the ways of the Lord, the upright judge who brings
hidden things to light, 42 and gave themselves to prayer,
begging that the sin committed might be completely forgiven.
Next, the valiant Judas urged the soldiers to keep themselves
free from all sin, having seen with their own eyes the effects
of the sin of those who had fallen; 43 after this he took a
collection from them individually, amounting to nearly two

GREEK OLD TESTAMENT

Ιεροσόλυμα προσαγαγεῖν περὶ ἁμαρτίας θυσίαν πάνυ καλῶς καὶ ἀστείως πράττων ὑπὲρ ἀναστάσεως διαλογιζόμενος. 44 εἰ μὴ γὰρ τοὺς προπεπτωκότας ἀναστῆναι προσεδόκα, περισσὸν καὶ ληρῶδες ὑπὲρ νεκρῶν εὔχεσθαι· 45 εἴτε' ἐμβλέπων τοῖς μετ' εὐσεβείας κοιμωμένοις κάλλιστον ἀποκείμενον χαριστήριον, ὁσία καὶ εὐσεβὴς ἡ ἐπίνοια· ὅθεν περὶ τῶν τεθνηκότων τὸν ἐξιλασμὸν ἐποιήσατο τῆς ἁμαρτίας ἀπολυθῆναι.

13 Τῷ δὲ ἐνάτῳ καὶ τεσσαρακοστῷ καὶ ἑκατοστῷ ἔτει προσέπεσεν τοῖς περὶ τὸν Ιουδαν Ἀντίοχον τὸν Εὐπάτορα παραγενέσθαι σὺν πλήθεσιν ἐπὶ τὴν Ιουδαίαν 2 καὶ σὺν αὐτῷ Λυσίαν τὸν ἐπίτροπον καὶ ἐπὶ τῶν πραγμάτων, ἕκαστον ἔχοντα δύναμιν Ἑλληνικὴν πεζῶν μυριάδας ἕνδεκα καὶ ἱππέων πεντακισχιλίους τριακοσίους καὶ ἐλέφαντας εἴκοσι δύο, ἅρματα δὲ δρεπανηφόρα τριακόσια. 3 συνέμειξεν δὲ αὐτοῖς καὶ Μενέλαος καὶ παρεκάλει μετὰ πολλῆς εἰρωνείας τὸν Ἀντίοχον, οὐκ ἐπὶ σωτηρίᾳ τῆς πατρίδος, οἰόμενος δὲ ἐπὶ τῆς ἀρχῆς κατασταθήσεσθαι. 4 ὁ δὲ βασιλεὺς τῶν βασιλέων ἐξήγειρεν τὸν θυμὸν τοῦ Ἀντιόχου ἐπὶ τὸν ἀλιτήριον, καὶ Λυσίου ὑποδείξαντος τοῦτον αἴτιον εἶναι πάντων τῶν κακῶν, προσέταξεν, ὡς ἔθος ἐστὶν ἐν τῷ τόπῳ, προσαπολέσαι ἀγαγόντας εἰς Βέροιαν. 5 ἔστιν δὲ ἐν τῷ τόπῳ πύργος πεντήκοντα πήχεων πλήρης σποδοῦ, οὗτος δὲ ὄργανον εἶχεν περιφερὲς πάντοθεν ἀπόκρημνον εἰς

KING JAMES VERSION

company to the sum of two thousand drachms of silver, he sent it to Jerusalem to offer a sin offering, doing therein very well and honestly, in that he was mindful of the resurrection:

44 For if he had not hoped that they that were slain should have risen again, it had been superfluous and vain to pray for the dead.

45 And also in that he perceived that there was great favour laid up for those that died godly, it was an holy and good thought. Whereupon he made a reconciliation for the dead, that they might be delivered from sin.

13 In the hundred forty and ninth year it was told Judas, that Antiochus Eupator was coming with a great power into Judea,

2 And with him Lysias his protector, and ruler of his affairs, having either of them a Grecian power of footmen, an hundred and ten thousand, and horsemen five thousand and three hundred, and elephants two and twenty, and three hundred chariots armed with hooks.

3 Menelaus also joined himself with them, and with great dissimulation encouraged Antiochus, not for the safeguard of the country, but because he thought to have been made governor.

4 But the King of kings moved Antiochus' mind against this wicked wretch, and Lysias informed the king that this man was the cause of all mischief, so that the king commanded to bring him unto Berea, and to put him to death, as the manner is in that place.

5 Now there was in that place a tower of fifty cubits high, full of ashes, and it had a round instrument, which on every side hanged down into the ashes.

DOUAY OLD TESTAMENT

drachms of silver to Jerusalem for sacrifice to be offered for the sins of the dead, thinking well and religiously concerning the resurrection,

44 (For if he had not hoped that they that were slain should rise again, it would have seemed superfluous and vain to pray for the dead,)

45 And because he considered that they who had fallen asleep with godliness, had great grace laid up for them.

46 It is therefore a holy and wholesome thought to pray for the dead, that they may be loosed from sins.

13 IN the year one hundred and forty-nine, Judas understood that Antiochus Eupator was coming with a multitude against Judea,

2 And with him Lysias the regent, who had charge over the affairs *of the realm,* having with him a hundred and ten thousand footmen, five thousand horsemen, twenty-two elephants, *and* three hundred chariots armed with hooks.

3 Menelaus also joined himself with them: and with great deceitfulness besought Antiochus, not for the welfare of his country, but in hopes that he should be appointed chief ruler.

4 But the King of kings stirred up the mind of Antiochus against the sinner, and upon Lysias suggesting that he was the cause of all the evils, he commanded (as the custom is with them) that he should be apprehended and put to death in the same place.

5 Now there was in that place a tower fifty cubits high, having a heap of ashes on every side: this had a prospect steep down.

KNOX TRANSLATION

pieces he levied, and sent it to Jerusalem, to have sacrifice made there for the guilt of their dead companions. Was not this well done and piously? Here was a man kept the resurrection ever in mind; 44 he had done fondly and foolishly indeed, to pray for the dead, if these might rise no more, that once were fallen! 45 And these had made a godly end; could he doubt, a rich recompense awaited them? 46 A holy and wholesome thought it is to pray for the dead, for their guilt's undoing.

13 It was in the hundred and forty-ninth year news came to Judas that Antiochus Eupator was marching on Judaea in great force. 2 Lysias was at his side, that was lord protector and managed the affairs of the realm, and with him were a hundred and ten thousand foot, five thousand horse, twenty-two elephants, and three hundred scythed chariots. 3 Menelaus, too, must be of their company, and ever it was treacherous advice he gave to Antiochus; not that he cared for his country's safety, but he had designs upon the high priesthood still. 4 And hereupon the King of all kings brought this guilty wretch into ill favour with his master Antiochus, who (upon Lysias' averring, here was the true source of all their misadventures) would have him apprehended and put to death according to the custom of the place where they were quartered. 5 There is here a tower fifty cubits in height, rising sheer above a heap of ashes that

TODAY'S ENGLISH VERSION

sent it to Jerusalem to provide for a sin offering. Judas did
this noble thing because he believed in the resurrection of
the dead. 44 If he had not believed that the dead would be
raised, it would have been foolish and useless to pray for
them. 45 In his firm and devout conviction that all of God's
faithful people would receive a wonderful reward, Judas
made provision for a sin offering to set free from their sin
those who had died.

13 In the year 149[a] Judas Maccabeus and his followers
found out that Antiochus Eupator was marching
against Judea with a large army 2 and that Lysias, the young
king's guardian and the head of his government, was with
him. They[b] had a force of Greek troops consisting of 110,000
infantry, 5,300 cavalry, 22 elephants, and 300 chariots with
sharp blades attached to their wheels.

3 Menelaus, trying to take advantage of the situation, went
over to their side and urged them on, not because he was
concerned for the country, but because he hoped to be confirmed as High Priest. 4 But God, the King of kings, made
Antiochus furious with Menelaus. Lysias proved to Antiochus that this criminal had been the source of all his troubles, so Antiochus ordered him to be taken to the city of
Berea and put to death in the way that it was done there.
5 In that city there is a tower about 75 feet high. It is filled
with ashes, and all around the inside of the tower is a platform sloping down into the ashes. 6 People accused of crimes

[a] THE YEAR 149: *This corresponds to 163 B.C.* [b] They; *Greek unclear.*

NEW REVISED STANDARD VERSION

silver, and sent it to Jerusalem to provide for a sin offering.
In doing this he acted very well and honorably, taking
account of the resurrection. 44 For if he were not expecting
that those who had fallen would rise again, it would have
been superfluous and foolish to pray for the dead. 45 But if
he was looking to the splendid reward that is laid up for
those who fall asleep in godliness, it was a holy and pious
thought. Therefore he made atonement for the dead, so that
they might be delivered from their sin.

13 In the one hundred forty-ninth year[a] word came to
Judas and his men that Antiochus Eupator was coming with a great army against Judea, 2 and with him Lysias,
his guardian, who had charge of the government. Each of
them had a Greek force of one hundred ten thousand
infantry, five thousand three hundred cavalry, twenty-two
elephants, and three hundred chariots armed with scythes.

3 Menelaus also joined them and with utter hypocrisy
urged Antiochus on, not for the sake of his country's welfare,
but because he thought that he would be established in
office. 4 But the King of kings aroused the anger of Antiochus against the scoundrel; and when Lysias informed him
that this man was to blame for all the trouble, he ordered
them to take him to Beroea and to put him to death by the
method that is customary in that place. 5 For there is a tower
there, fifty cubits high, full of ashes, and it has a rim running around it that on all sides inclines precipitously into the

a 163 B.C.

NEW AMERICAN BIBLE

which he sent to Jerusalem to provide for an expiatory sacrifice. In doing this he acted in a very excellent and noble way,
inasmuch as he had the resurrection of the dead in view;
44 for if he were not expecting the fallen to rise again, it
would have been useless and foolish to pray for them in
death. 45 But if he did this with a view to the splendid
reward that awaits those who had gone to rest in godliness,
it was a holy and pious thought. 46 Thus he made atonement
for the dead that they might be freed from this sin.

13 In the year one hundred and forty-nine, Judas and
his men learned that Antiochus Eupator was invading Judea with a large force, 2 and that with him was Lysias,
his guardian, who was in charge of the government. They led
a Greek army of one hundred and ten thousand foot soldiers,
fifty-three hundred horsemen, twenty-two elephants, and
three hundred chariots armed with scythes.

3 Menelaus also joined them, and with great duplicity kept
urging Antiochus on, not for the welfare of his country, but
in the hope of being established in office. 4 But the King of
kings aroused the anger of Antiochus against the scoundrel.
When the king was shown by Lysias that Menelaus was to
blame for all the trouble, he ordered him to be taken to
Beroea and executed there in the customary local method.
5 There is at that place a tower seventy-five feet high, full of
ashes, with a circular rim sloping down steeply on all sides

NEW JERUSALEM BIBLE

thousand drachmas, and sent it to Jerusalem to have a sacrifice for sin offered, an action altogether fine and noble,
prompted by his belief in the resurrection. 44 For had he not
expected the fallen to rise again, it would have been superfluous and foolish to pray for the dead, 45 whereas if he had
in view the splendid recompense reserved for those who
make a pious end, the thought was holy and devout. Hence,
he had this expiatory sacrifice offered for the dead, so that
they might be released from their sin.

13 In the year one hundred and forty-nine, Judas and
his men discovered that Antiochus Eupator was
advancing in force against Judaea, 2 and with him Lysias his
tutor and chief minister; he had moreover a Greek force of
one hundred and ten thousand infantry, five thousand three
hundred cavalry, twenty-two elephants, and three hundred
chariots fitted with scythes.

3 Menelaus, too, joined them and very craftily kept urging
Antiochus on, not for the welfare of his own country but in
the hope of being restored to office. 4 But the King of kings
stirred up the anger of Antiochus against the guilty wretch,
and when Lysias made it clear to the king that Menelaus was
the cause of all the troubles, Antiochus gave orders for him to
be taken to Beroea and there put to death by the local method
of execution. 5 In that place there is a tower fifty cubits high,
full of ash, with an internal lip all round overhanging the

GREEK OLD TESTAMENT

τὴν σποδόν. 6 ἐνταῦθα τὸν ἱεροσυλίας ἔνοχον ἤ καί τινων
ἄλλων κακῶν ὑπεροχὴν πεποιημένον ἅπαντες προσωθοῦσιν
εἰς ὄλεθρον. 7 τοιούτῳ μόρῳ τὸν παράνομον συνέβη θανεῖν
μηδὲ τῆς γῆς τυχόντα Μενέλαον· 8 πάνυ δικαίως. ἐπεὶ γὰρ
συνετελέσατο πολλὰ περὶ τὸν βωμὸν ἁμαρτήματα, οὗ τὸ πῦρ
ἁγνὸν ἦν καὶ ἡ σποδός, ἐν σποδῷ τὸν θάνατον ἐκομίσατο.
9 Τοῖς δὲ φρονήμασιν ὁ βασιλεὺς βεβαρβαρωμένος ἤρχετο
τὰ χείριστα τῶν ἐπὶ τοῦ πατρὸς αὐτοῦ γεγονότων ἐνδειξό-
μενος τοῖς Ιουδαίοις. 10 μεταλαβὼν δὲ Ιουδας ταῦτα παρήγγειλεν τῷ πλήθει δι' ἡμέρας καὶ νυκτὸς ἐπικαλεῖσθαι τὸν
κύριον, εἴ ποτε καὶ ἄλλοτε, καὶ νῦν ἐπιβοηθεῖν τοῖς τοῦ νόμου καὶ πατρίδος καὶ ἱεροῦ ἁγίου στερεῖσθαι μέλλουσιν 11 καὶ
τὸν ἄρτι βραχέως ἀνεψυχότα λαὸν μὴ ἐᾶσαι τοῖς δυσφήμοις
ἔθνεσιν ὑποχειρίους γενέσθαι. 12 πάντων δὲ τὸ αὐτὸ ποιη-
σάντων ὁμοῦ καὶ καταξιωσάντων τὸν ἐλεήμονα κύριον μετὰ
κλαυθμοῦ καὶ νηστειῶν καὶ προπτώσεως ἐπὶ ἡμέρας τρεῖς
ἀδιαλείπτως παρακαλέσας αὐτοὺς ὁ Ιουδας ἐκέλευσεν παραγίνεσθαι. 13 καθ' ἑαυτὸν δὲ σὺν τοῖς πρεσβυτέροις γενόμενος ἐβουλεύσατο πρὶν εἰσβαλεῖν τοῦ βασιλέως τὸ στράτευμα εἰς τὴν Ιουδαίαν καὶ γενέσθαι τῆς πόλεως ἐγκρατεῖς
ἐξελθόντας κρῖναι τὰ πράγματα τῇ τοῦ θεοῦ βοηθείᾳ.
14 δοὺς δὲ τὴν ἐπιτροπὴν τῷ κτίστῃ τοῦ κόσμου παρακαλέσας τοὺς σὺν αὐτῷ γενναίως ἀγωνίσασθαι μέχρι θανάτου
περὶ νόμων, ἱεροῦ, πόλεως, πατρίδος, πολιτείας, περὶ δὲ
Μωδεϊν ἐποιήσατο τὴν στρατοπεδείαν. 15 ἀναδοὺς δὲ τοῖς

KING JAMES VERSION

6 And whosoever was condemned of sacrilege, or had committed any other grievous crime, there did all men thrust him unto death.

7 Such a death it happened that wicked man to die, not having so much as burial in the earth; and that most justly:

8 For inasmuch as he had committed many sins about the altar, whose fire and ashes were holy, he received his death in ashes.

9 Now the king came with a barbarous and haughty mind to do far worse to the Jews, than had been done in his father's time.

10 Which things when Judas perceived, he commanded the multitude to call upon the Lord night and day, that if ever at any other time, he would now also help them, being at the point to be put from their law, from their country, and from the holy temple:

11 And that he would not suffer the people, that had even now been but a little refreshed, to be in subjection to the blasphemous nations.

12 So when they had all done this together, and besought the merciful Lord with weeping and fasting, and lying flat upon the ground three days long, Judas, having exhorted them, commanded they should be in a readiness.

13 And Judas, being apart with the elders, determined, before the king's host should enter into Judea, and get the city, to go forth and try the matter *in fight* by the help of the Lord.

14 So when he had committed *all* to the Creator of the world, and exhorted his soldiers to fight manfully, even unto death, for the laws, the temple, the city, the country, and the commonwealth, he camped by Modin:

DOUAY OLD TESTAMENT

6 From thence he commanded the sacrilegious wretch to be thrown down into the ashes, all men thrusting him forward unto death.

7 And by such a law it happened that Menelaus the transgressor of the law was put to death: not having so much as burial in the earth.

8 And indeed very justly, for insomuch as he had committed many sins against the altar of God, the fire and ashes of which were holy: he was condemned to die in ashes.

9 But the king, with his mind full of rage, came on to shew himself worse to the Jews than his father was.

10 Which, when Judas understood, he commanded the people to call upon the Lord day and night, that as he had always done, so now also he would help them:

11 Because they were afraid to be deprived of the law, and of their country, and of the holy temple: and that he would not suffer the people, that had of late taken breath for a little while, to be again in subjection to blasphemous nations.

12 So when they had all done this together, and had craved mercy of the Lord with weeping and fasting, lying prostrate on the ground for three days continually, Judas exhorted them to make themselves ready.

13 But he with the ancients determined, before the king should bring his army into Judea, and make himself master of the city, to go out, and to commit the event of the thing to the judgment of the Lord.

14 So committing all to God, the creator of the world, and having exhorted his people to fight manfully, and to stand up even to death for the laws, the temple, the city, their country, and citizens: he placed his army about Modin.

KNOX TRANSLATION

surrounds it; 6 from its walls the author of sacrilege is thrust
forward to his death by the common impulse of the
bystanders. 7 This, then, was the doom of Menelaus; by this
law the law-breaker met his end, and lay there unburied. 8 A
fitting reward, this, for one that had done so many outrages
upon God's altar; fire of it and ashes of it are sacred, and it
was by ashes Menelaus went to his death.
9 Yet still the king pressed forward on his mad career, as if
he would prove himself a worse enemy of Jewry than his
father; 10 and Judas, when the news came to him, bade the
people entreat God night and day he would come to their
rescue, as ever he was wont hitherto. 11 Here was great
peril, they should be deprived at one blow of law, of country,
and of sanctuary; would he allow blaspheming Gentiles to
lord it again over his people, that had but now won a little
breathing-space? 12 Entreat the Lord they did, and with one
accord, for his mercy; wept they and fasted, and kept on
their knees for three days together. Then Judas gave them
the word to arm, 13 and himself called the elders to a council; his plan was, he told them, to march out and engage the
king before he could reach Judaea and overpower the city,
and the issue of it he would leave to the Lord's good pleasure. 14 So, committing all to God, the world's creator, and
bidding his men fight bravely, even to the death, for law,
temple, city, country and kinsmen, he pitched his camp at

TODAY'S ENGLISH VERSION

against the gods or of any other serious crime are taken
there and thrown down to their death. 7 Menelaus was put
to death in that way, without even having the privilege of a
burial, 8 and that was just what he deserved. He had often
profaned the sacred ashes of the altar fire in the Temple, and
now he met his death in ashes.

9 King Antiochus arrogantly continued his barbaric invasion of Judah, intending to deal with the Jews more harshly
than his father had ever done. 10 When Judas learned of this,
he told the people to pray to the Lord day and night, because
they were in danger of losing their Law, their country, and
their holy Temple. As never before, they needed his help and
protection 11 to keep their newly restored country from
falling into the hands of godless Gentiles. 12 For three days
the people did nothing but lie face down on the ground, fasting and crying, begging the merciful Lord for his help. Then
Judas spoke words of encouragement to the people, urging
them to get ready for action.

13 Afterward, Judas met privately with the Jewish leaders
and decided to march out with God's help to battle against
the king, rather than to wait for Antiochus to invade Judea
and besiege Jerusalem. 14 Then, leaving the outcome of the
battle to the Creator of the world, Judas encouraged his men
to fight bravely and to be willing to die for their laws, the
Temple, Jerusalem, their country, and their whole way of life.
They set up camp near the city of Modein. 15 Judas gave his

NEW REVISED STANDARD VERSION

ashes. 6 There they all push to destruction anyone guilty of
sacrilege or notorious for other crimes. 7 By such a fate it
came about that Menelaus the lawbreaker died, without even
burial in the earth. 8 And this was eminently just; because
he had committed many sins against the altar whose fire and
ashes were holy, he met his death in ashes.

9 The king with barbarous arrogance was coming to show
the Jews things far worse than those that had been done[a] in
his father's time. 10 But when Judas heard of this, he ordered
the people to call upon the Lord day and night, now if ever to
help those who were on the point of being deprived of the
law and their country and the holy temple, 11 and not to let
the people who had just begun to revive fall into the hands
of the blasphemous Gentiles. 12 When they had all joined in
the same petition and had implored the merciful Lord with
weeping and fasting and lying prostrate for three days without ceasing, Judas exhorted them and ordered them to stand
ready.

13 After consulting privately with the elders, he determined to march out and decide the matter by the help of God
before the king's army could enter Judea and get possession
of the city. 14 So, committing the decision to the Creator of
the world and exhorting his troops to fight bravely to the
death for the laws, temple, city, country, and commonwealth, he pitched his camp near Modein. 15 He gave his

a Or *the worst of the things that had been done*

NEW AMERICAN BIBLE

toward the ashes. 6 A man guilty of sacrilege or notorious for
certain other crimes is brought up there and then hurled
down to destruction. 7 In such a manner was Menelaus, the
transgressor of the law, fated to die; he was deprived even of
decent burial. 8 It was altogether just that he who had committed so many sins against the altar with its pure fire and
ashes should meet his death in ashes.

9 The king was advancing, his mind full of savage plans
for inflicting on the Jews worse things than those they suffered in his father's time. 10 When Judas learned of this, he
urged the people to call upon the LORD night and day, to help
them now, if ever, 11 when they were about to be deprived of
their law, their country, and their holy temple; and not to
allow this nation, which had just begun to revive, to be subjected again to blasphemous Gentiles. 12 When they had all
joined in doing this, and had implored the merciful LORD continuously with weeping and fasting and prostrations for
three days, Judas encouraged them and told them to stand
ready. 13 After a private meeting with the elders, he decided
that, before the king's army could invade Judea and take
possession of the city, the Jews should march out and settle
the matter with God's help. 14 Leaving the outcome to the
Creator of the world, and exhorting his followers to fight
nobly to death for the laws, the temple, the city, the country,
and the government, he pitched his camp near Modein.

NEW JERUSALEM BIBLE

ashes. 6 If anyone is convicted of sacrilegious theft or of some
other heinous crime, he is taken up to the top and pushed
over to perish. 7 In such a manner was the renegade fated to
die; Menelaus had not even the privilege of burial. 8 Deserved
justice, this; since he had committed many sins against the
altar, the fire and ashes of which were holy, it was in ashes
that he met his death.

9 The king, then, was advancing, his mind filled with barbarous designs, to give the Jews a demonstration of far
worse things than anything that had happened under his
father. 10 When Judas heard of this, he ordered the people
day and night to call on the Lord as never before, to come to
the help of those who were in peril of being deprived of the
Law, their fatherland and the holy Temple, 11 and not to
allow the people, just when they were beginning to breathe
again, to fall into the power of ill-famed foreigners. 12 When
they had all, with one voice, obeyed his instructions and had
made their petitions to the merciful Lord, weeping, fasting
and prostrating themselves for three days continuously,
Judas spoke words of encouragement and told them to keep
close to him. 13 After separate consultation with the elders,
he resolved not to wait for the king's army to invade Judaea
and take possession of the city, but to march out and settle
the whole matter with the Lord's help.

14 Having thus committed the outcome to the Creator of the
world, and having exhorted his soldiers to fight bravely to
the death for the laws, the Temple, the city, their country and
their way of life, he encamped his army near Modein.

GREEK OLD TESTAMENT

περὶ αὐτὸν σύνθημα ϛθεοῦ νίκηνς μετὰ νεανίσκων ἀρίστων
κεκριμένων ἐπιβαλὼν νύκτωρ ἐπὶ τὴν βασιλικὴν αὐλὴν τὴν
παρεμβολὴν ἀνεῖλεν εἰς ἄνδρας δισχιλίους, καὶ τὸν πρωτεύ-
οντα τῶν ἐλεφάντων σὺν τῷ κατ' οἰκίαν ὄντι συνεκέντησεν
[16] καὶ τὸ τέλος τὴν παρεμβολὴν δέους καὶ ταραχῆς ἐπλήρωσαν καὶ ἐξέλυσαν εὐημεροῦντες. [17] ὑποφαινούσης δὲ ἤδη
τῆς ἡμέρας τοῦτο ἐγεγόνει διὰ τὴν ἐπαρήγουσαν αὐτῷ τοῦ
κυρίου σκέπην.

[18] Ὁ δὲ βασιλεὺς εἰληφὼς γεῦμα τῆς τῶν Ιουδαίων
εὐτολμίας κατεπείρασεν διὰ μεθόδων τοὺς τόπους. [19] καὶ
ἐπὶ Βαιθσουρα φρούριον ὀχυρὸν τῶν Ιουδαίων προσῆγεν,
ἐτροποῦτο, προσέκρουεν, ἠλαττονοῦτο· [20] τοῖς δὲ ἔνδον Ιουδας τὰ δέοντα εἰσέπεμψεν. [21] προσήγγειλεν δὲ τὰ μυστήρια
τοῖς πολεμίοις Ροδοκος ἐκ τῆς Ιουδαϊκῆς τάξεως. ἀνεζητήθη
καὶ κατελήμφθη καὶ κατεκλείσθη. [22] ἐδευτερολόγησεν ὁ
βασιλεὺς τοῖς ἐν Βαιθσουροις, δεξιὰν ἔδωκεν, ἔλαβεν, ἀπῄει,
προσέβαλεν τοῖς περὶ τὸν Ιουδαν, ἥττων ἐγένετο, [23] μετέ-
λαβεν ἀπονενοῆσθαι τὸν Φίλιππον ἐν Ἀντιοχείᾳ τὸν ἀπολε-
λειμμένον ἐπὶ τῶν πραγμάτων, συνεχύθη, τοὺς Ιουδαίους
παρεκάλεσεν, ὑπετάγη καὶ ὤμοσεν ἐπὶ πᾶσι τοῖς δικαίοις,
συνελύθη καὶ θυσίαν προσήγαγεν, ἐτίμησεν τὸν νεὼ καὶ τὸν
τόπον ἐφιλανθρώπησεν· [24] καὶ τὸν Μακκαβαῖον ἀπεδέξατο,
κατέλιπεν στρατηγὸν ἀπὸ Πτολεμαίδος ἕως τῶν Γερρηνῶν

KING JAMES VERSION

15 And having given the watchword to them that were about him, Victory is of God; with the most valiant and choice young men he went in into the king's tent by night, and slew in the camp about four thousand men, and the chiefest of the elephants, with all that were upon him.

16 And at last they filled the camp with fear and tumult, and departed with good success.

17 This was done in the break of the day, because the protection of the Lord did help him.

18 Now when the king had taken a taste of the manliness of the Jews, he went about to take the holds by policy,

19 And marched toward Bethsura, which was a strong hold of the Jews: but he was put to flight, failed, and lost of his men:

20 For Judas had conveyed unto them that were in it such things as were necessary.

21 But Rhodocus, who was in the Jews' host, disclosed the secrets to the enemies; therefore he was sought out, and when they had gotten him, they put him in prison.

22 The king treated with them in Bethsura the second time, gave his hand, took their's, departed, fought with Judas, was overcome;

23 Heard that Philip, who was left over the affairs in Antioch, was desperately bent, confounded, intreated the Jews, submitted himself, and sware to all equal conditions, agreed with them, and offered sacrifice, honoured the temple, and dealt kindly with the place,

24 And accepted well of Maccabeus, made him principal governor from Ptolemais unto the Gerrhenians;

DOUAY OLD TESTAMENT

15 And having given his company for a watchword, The victory of God, with most valiant chosen young men, he set upon the king's quarter by night, and slew four thousand men in the camp, and the greatest of the elephants, with them that had been upon him,

16 And having filled the camp of the enemies with exceeding great fear and tumult, they went off with good success.

17 Now this was done at the break of day, by the protection and help of the Lord.

18 But the king having taken a taste of the hardiness of the Jews, attempted to take the strong places by policy:

19 And he marched with his army to Bethsura, which was a strong hold of the Jews: but he was repulsed, he failed, he lost his men.

20 Now Judas sent necessaries to them that were within.

21 But Rhodocus, one of the Jews' army, disclosed the secrets to the enemies, so he was sought out, and taken up, and put in prison.

22 Again the king treated with them that were in Bethsura: gave his right hand: took theirs: and went away.

23 He fought with Judas: and was overcome. And when he understood that Philip, who had been left over the affairs, had rebelled at Antioch, he was in a consternation of mind, and entreating the Jews, and yielding to them, he swore to all things that seemed reasonable, and, being reconciled, offered sacrifices, honoured the temple, and left gifts.

24 He embraced Machabeus, and made him governor and prince from Ptolemais unto the Gerrenians.

KNOX TRANSLATION

Modin. [15] The watchword he gave them was, Victory lies
with God; and now, choosing out the best of his fighting
men, he made a night attack upon the royal quarters. Four
thousand men they slew in the camp, and the greatest of all
the elephants, with the crew that rode him, [16] and so went
back in triumph, leaving the camp all confusion and dismay.
[17] After this daybreak victory, won under God's protection,
[18] the king had taste enough of Jewish valour, and set about
to reduce the strongholds by policy. [19] And first he would
deliver an attack upon Bethsura, a fortress of the Jews, but
ever he was thrown back and repulsed with great loss, [20] so
well did Judas supply the garrison with all they needed.
[21] There was one Rhodocus in the Jewish army that betrayed
secrets to the enemy, but, upon enquiry made, he was apprehended and put under arrest; [22] so the king was fain to parley with the defenders of Bethsura, and, upon agreed terms,
the siege of it was raised. [23] Thus did he try conclusions with
Judas, and had the worst of it; news came to him besides
that Philip, whom he had left in charge at Antioch, was levying revolt against him. So, in great consternation of mind, he
must needs throw himself on the mercy of the Jews, submitting under oath to the just terms they imposed on him. In
token of this reconciliation, he offered sacrifice, paying the
temple much reverence and offering gifts there; [24] as for
Machabaeus, the king made a friend of him, and appointed
him both governor and commander of all the territory from
Ptolemais to the Gerrenes.[a] [25] When he reached Ptolemais,

a The Greek text here seems to include a proper name, so that the sense would be 'and appointed Hegemonides commander of all the territory from Ptolemais to the Gerrenes'. Nothing is known about Hegemonides.

TODAY'S ENGLISH VERSION

men the battle cry, "Victory comes from God," and that night,
with a picked force of his bravest young men, he attacked the
area near the king's tent and killed as many as 2,000 men.
They also stabbed to death[a] the lead elephant and its keeper.
16 Everyone in camp was terrified and in panic when Judas
and his men finally left victoriously 17 just before dawn. The
help and protection of the Lord had made all this possible.
18 This taste of Jewish daring was enough to convince King
Antiochus that he had to find some better way of capturing
the Jewish positions. 19 He attacked the strong Jewish fort of
Bethzur, but was repeatedly beaten back and finally defeated. 20 Judas sent supplies to the men who were defending
the fort, 21 but a Jewish soldier by the name of Rhodocus
gave some secret information to the enemy. He was found
out, however, caught, and put to death. 22 The king made a
second attempt to come to terms with the people of Bethzur,
and when he had reached an agreement with them, he withdrew his forces. Then he went to attack Judas, but again he
was defeated. 23 Meanwhile, Philip had been left at Antioch
in charge of the government, but King Antiochus learned
that he had revolted. The king did not know what to do, so
he initiated peace talks with the Jews, agreed to their terms,
and promised to be just in his treatment of them. To put the
treaty into effect, he offered a sacrifice, gave a generous gift
to show his respect for the Temple, 24 and graciously
received Judas Maccabeus. After that, the king appointed
Hegemonides to be governor of the territory between the
cities of Ptolemais and Gerar, 25 and then he himself went on

[a] *Probable text* stabbed to death; *Greek unclear.*

NEW REVISED STANDARD VERSION

troops the watchword, "God's victory," and with a picked
force of the bravest young men, he attacked the king's pavilion at night and killed as many as two thousand men in the
camp. He stabbed[a] the leading elephant and its rider. 16 In
the end they filled the camp with terror and confusion and
withdrew in triumph. 17 This happened, just as day was
dawning, because the Lord's help protected him.
18 The king, having had a taste of the daring of the Jews,
tried strategy in attacking their positions. 19 He advanced
against Beth-zur, a strong fortress of the Jews, was turned
back, attacked again,[b] and was defeated. 20 Judas sent in to
the garrison whatever was necessary. 21 But Rhodocus, a
man from the ranks of the Jews, gave secret information to
the enemy; he was sought for, caught, and put in prison.
22 The king negotiated a second time with the people in Beth-
zur, gave pledges, received theirs, withdrew, attacked Judas
and his men, was defeated; 23 he got word that Philip, who
had been left in charge of the government, had revolted in
Antioch; he was dismayed, called in the Jews, yielded and
swore to observe all their rights, settled with them and
offered sacrifice, honored the sanctuary and showed generosity to the holy place. 24 He received Maccabeus, left Hegemonides as governor from Ptolemais to Gerar, 25 and went to

a Meaning of Gk uncertain *b* Or *faltered*

NEW AMERICAN BIBLE

15 Giving his men the battle cry "God's Victory," he made a
night attack on the king's pavilion with a picked force of the
bravest young men and killed about two thousand in the
camp. They also slew the lead elephant and its rider.
16 Finally they withdrew in triumph, having filled the camp
with terror and confusion. 17 Day was just breaking when
this was accomplished with the help and protection of the
LORD.
18 The king, having had a taste of the Jews' daring, tried to
take their positions by a stratagem. 19 So he marched
against Beth-zur, a strong fortress of the Jews; but he was
driven back, checked, and defeated. 20 Judas then sent supplies to the men inside, 21 but Rhodocus, of the Jewish army,
betrayed military secrets to the enemy. He was found out,
arrested, and imprisoned. 22 The king made a second attempt
by negotiating with the men of Beth-zur. After giving them
his pledge and receiving theirs, he withdrew 23 and attacked
Judas and his men. But he was defeated. Next he heard that
Philip, who was left in charge of the government in Antioch,
had rebelled. Dismayed, he parleyed with the Jews, submitted
to their terms, and swore to observe their rights. Having
come to this agreement, he offered a sacrifice, and honored
the temple with a generous donation. 24 He approved of
Maccabeus and left him as military and civil governor of the
territory from Ptolemais to the region of the Gerrenes.

NEW JERUSALEM BIBLE

15 Giving his men the password 'Victory from God', he made
a night attack on the king's pavilion with a picked band of
the bravest young men. Inside the camp he destroyed about
two thousand, and his men cut down the largest of the elephants with its mahout; 16 having eventually filled the camp
with terror and confusion, they successfully withdrew,
17 just as dawn was breaking. This was achieved, thanks to
the protection which the Lord granted Judas.
18[a] The king, having had a taste of Jewish daring, now
tried to capture their positions by trickery. 19 He advanced on
Beth-Zur, a strong fortress of the Jews, but was checked,
overcome and so repulsed.
20 Judas supplied the garrison with what they needed,
21 but Rhodocus, of the Jewish army, supplied the enemy
with secret information; the man was identified, arrested,
and dealt with. 22 A second time, the king parleyed with the
garrison of Beth-Zur; he offered and accepted pledges of
friendship, retired, then attacked Judas and his men, but lost
the battle. 23 He was then told that Philip, left in charge of
affairs, had rebelled in Antioch. He was stunned by this,
opened negotiations with the Jews, came to an agreement,
and swore to abide by all reasonable conditions. Agreement
reached, he offered a sacrifice, honoured the Temple, and
made generous gifts to the holy place.
24 He received Maccabaeus kindly and, leaving Hegemonides to exercise command from Ptolemais to the territory of

[a] **13** 13:18seq. // 1 M 6:48–63.

GREEK OLD TESTAMENT

Ἡγεμονίδην. 25 ἦλθεν εἰς Πτολεμαίδα· ἐδυσφόρουν περὶ τῶν
συνθηκῶν οἱ Πτολεμαεῖς, ἐδείναζον γὰρ ὑπὲρ ὧν ἠθέλησαν
ἀθετεῖν τὰς διαστάλσεις. 26 προσῆλθεν ἐπὶ τὸ βῆμα Λυσίας,
ἀπελογήσατο ἐνδεχομένως, συνέπεισεν, κατεπράυνεν, εὐμενεῖς ἐποίησεν, ἀνέζευξεν εἰς Ἀντιόχειαν. οὕτω τὰ τοῦ
βασιλέως τῆς ἐφόδου καὶ τῆς ἀναζυγῆς ἐχώρησεν.

14 Μετὰ δὲ τριετῆ χρόνον προσέπεσεν τοῖς περὶ τὸν
Ιουδαν Δημήτριον τὸν τοῦ Σελεύκου διὰ τοῦ κατὰ
Τρίπολιν λιμένος εἰσπλεύσαντα μετὰ πλήθους ἰσχυροῦ καὶ
στόλου 2 κεκρατηκέναι τῆς χώρας ἐπανελόμενον Ἀντίοχον
καὶ τὸν τούτου ἐπίτροπον Λυσίαν. 3 Ἄλκιμος δέ τις προγε-
γονὼς ἀρχιερεύς, ἑκουσίως δὲ μεμολυσμένος ἐν τοῖς τῆς
ἀμειξίας χρόνοις, συννοήσας ὅτι καθ' ὀντιναοῦν τρόπον οὐκ
ἔστιν αὐτῷ σωτηρία οὐδὲ πρὸς τὸ ἅγιον θυσιαστήριον ἔτι
πρόσοδος, 4 ἧκεν πρὸς τὸν βασιλέα Δημήτριον ὡς πρώτῳ καὶ
πεντηκοστῷ καὶ ἑκατοστῷ ἔτει προσάγων αὐτῷ στέφανον
χρυσοῦν καὶ φοίνικα, πρὸς δὲ τούτοις τῶν νομιζομένων
θαλλῶν τοῦ ἱεροῦ, καὶ τὴν ἡμέραν ἐκείνην ἡσυχίαν ἔσχεν.
5 καιρὸν δὲ λαβὼν τῆς ἰδίας ἀνοίας συνεργὸν προσκληθεὶς
εἰς συνέδριον ὑπὸ τοῦ Δημητρίου καὶ ἐπερωτηθείς, ἐν τίνι
διαθέσει καὶ βουλῇ καθέστηκαν οἱ Ιουδαῖοι, πρὸς ταῦτα ἔφη

KING JAMES VERSION

25 Came to Ptolemais: the people there were grieved for
the covenants; for they stormed, because they would make
their covenants void:

26 Lysias went up to the judgment seat, said as much as
could be in defence of the cause, persuaded, pacified, made
them well affected, returned to Antioch. Thus it went touching the king's coming and departing.

14 After three years was Judas informed, that Demetrius
the *son* of Seleucus, having entered by the haven of
Tripolis with a great power and navy,

2 Had taken the country, and killed Antiochus, and Lysias
his protector.

3 Now one Alcimus, who had been high priest, and had
defiled himself wilfully in the times of their mingling *with
the Gentiles,* seeing that by no means he could save himself,
nor have any more access to the holy altar,

4 Came to king Demetrius in the hundred and one and
fiftieth year, presenting unto him a crown of gold, and a
palm, and also of the boughs which were used solemnly in
the temple: and so that day he held his peace.

5 Howbeit, having gotten opportunity to further his foolish enterprize, *and* being called into counsel by Demetrius,
and asked how the Jews stood affected, and what they
intended, he answered thereunto:

DOUAY OLD TESTAMENT

25 But when he was come to Ptolemais, the men of that
city were much displeased with the conditions of the peace,
being angry for fear they should break the covenant.

26 Then Lysias went up to the judgment seat, and set
forth the reason, and appeased the people, and returned to
Antioch: and thus matters went with regard to the king's
coming and his return.

14 BUT after the space of three years Judas, and they
that were with him, understood that Demetrius the
son of Seleucus was come up with a great power, and a navy
by the haven of Tripolis to places proper for his purpose.

2 And had made himself master of the countries against
Anthiochus, and his general Lysias.

3 Now one Alcimus, who had been chief priest, but had
wilfully defiled himself in the time of mingling *with the heathens,* seeing that there was no safety for him, nor access to
the altar,

4 Came to king Demetrius in the year one hundred and
fifty, presenting unto him a crown of gold, and a palm, and
besides these, some boughs which seemed to belong to the
temple. And that day indeed he held his peace.

5 But having gotten a convenient time to further his madness, being called to counsel by Demetrius, and asked what
the Jews relied upon, and what were their counsels,

KNOX TRANSLATION

he found the citizens much incensed over this treaty made,
and angrily averring the terms of it would never be kept;
26 until at last Lysias must go up to an open stage, and give
his reasons; whereby he calmed the indignation of the people, and so returned to Antioch. Such was the king's march
upon Judaea, and such his homecoming.

14 Three years later, came tidings to Judas and his company that Demetrius, son of Seleucus, was on the
throne. This Demetrius, with a body of resolute followers and
with ships to support him, had landed at Tripolis, in a part of
the country well suited to his purpose, 2 and had wrested the
whole kingdom from Antiochus, and from Lysias his general.
3 Now turn we to one Alcimus, that had been high priest
formerly, but had wilfully incurred defilement in the days
when folk began consorting with the Gentiles.[a] Little hope
was left him, he should live to present himself at the altar
again; 4 and now he had recourse to king Demetrius, in the
hundred and fiftieth year. He came with gifts, a gold crown
and a palm branch, and wreaths that had been better
employed in the service of the temple.[b] No word said he on
the first day of his arriving; 5 but ere long opportunity was
given him of carrying out his impious design. He was called
into counsel by Demetrius himself, and asked what resources
the Jews had, or what purposes in view, that gave them such

a 'Began consorting'; the Greek text has, 'refused to consort'. *b* 'That had been better employed in the service of the temple'; literally, 'that seemed to belong to the temple'. The sense of the Greek text is probably 'such as were customarily used in the service of the temple'.

TODAY'S ENGLISH VERSION

to Ptolemais. The people there were angry because of the
treaty he had made with the Jews—so angry, in fact, that
they wanted the treaty canceled. 26 But Lysias made a public
speech, defending the treaty as well as he could. After he had
calmed the people down and convinced them that he was
right, he returned to Antioch.

In this way King Antiochus' invasion was turned into a
retreat.

14 Three years later, Judas and his men learned that
Demetrius son of Seleucus had sailed into the port of
Tripolis with a powerful army and a fleet. 2 It was reported
that he had killed King Antiochus and his guardian Lysias
and had taken over the country.

3 There was a man by the name of Alcimus, who had formerly been High Priest but who had gladly adopted the Greek
way of life during the revolt. Realizing that he could never
again be High Priest and fearful of what the Jews might do to
him, 4 he went to see King Demetrius in the year 151.[a] On
this occasion he presented the king with a gold crown and a
palm branch, together with some olive branches traditionally
presented to the Temple, but he said nothing about his
plans. 5 Later, however, he got the chance to put his foolish
plans into effect when Demetrius summoned him to a meeting of his advisers and asked him what the Jews were
intending to do.

[a] THE YEAR 151: *This corresponds to 161 B.C.*

NEW REVISED STANDARD VERSION

Ptolemais. The people of Ptolemais were indignant over the
treaty; in fact they were so angry that they wanted to annul
its terms.[a] 26 Lysias took the public platform, made the best
possible defense, convinced them, appeased them, gained
their goodwill, and set out for Antioch. This is how the
king's attack and withdrawal turned out.

14 Three years later, word came to Judas and his men
that Demetrius son of Seleucus had sailed into the
harbor of Tripolis with a strong army and a fleet, 2 and had
taken possession of the country, having made away with
Antiochus and his guardian Lysias.

3 Now a certain Alcimus, who had formerly been high
priest but had willfully defiled himself in the times of separa-
tion,[b] realized that there was no way for him to be safe or to
have access again to the holy altar, 4 and went to King
Demetrius in about the one hundred fifty-first year,[c] presenting to him a crown of gold and a palm, and besides these
some of the customary olive branches from the temple.
During that day he kept quiet. 5 But he found an opportunity
that furthered his mad purpose when he was invited by
Demetrius to a meeting of the council and was asked about
the attitude and intentions of the Jews. He answered:

a Meaning of Gk uncertain *b* Other ancient authorities read *of mixing*
c 161 B.C.

NEW AMERICAN BIBLE

25 When he came to Ptolemais, the people of that city were
angered by the peace treaty; in fact they were so indignant
that they wanted to annul its provisions. 26 But Lysias took
the platform, defended the treaty as well as he could, and
won them over by persuasion. After calming them and gaining their good will, he returned to Antioch.

That is how the king's attack and withdrawal went.

14 Three years later, Judas and his men learned that
Demetrius, son of Seleucus, had sailed into the port
of Tripolis with a powerful army and a fleet, 2 and that he
had occupied the country, after doing away with Antiochus
and his guardian Lysias.

3 A certain Alcimus, a former high priest, who had willfully
incurred defilement at the time of the revolt, realized that
there was no way for him to salvage his position and regain
access to the holy altar. 4 So he went to King Demetrius in
the year one hundred and fifty-one and presented him with a
gold crown and a palm branch, as well as some of the customary olive branches from the temple. On that occasion he
kept quiet. 5 But he found an opportunity to further his mad
scheme when he was invited to the council by Demetrius and
questioned about the dispositions and intentions of the Jews.

NEW JERUSALEM BIBLE

the Gerrenians, 25 went to Ptolemais. The inhabitants of the
place disapproved of the treaty; they complained furiously
and wanted to annul its provisions. 26 Lysias mounted the
rostrum and made a convincing defence of the provisions
which convinced and calmed them and won their goodwill.
He then withdrew to Antioch.

So much for the episode of the king's offensive and retreat.

14 [a] Three years after this, Judas and his men learned
that Demetrius son of Seleucus had landed at the
port of Tripolis with a strong army and a fleet, 2 and that he
had occupied the country and had killed Antiochus and his
tutor Lysias. 3 A certain Alcimus, a former high priest, had
wilfully incurred defilement at the time of the insurrection;
realising that whichever way he turned there was no security
for him, nor any further access to the holy altar, 4 he went to
King Demetrius in about the year one hundred and fifty-one
and presented him with a golden crown and a palm, together
with the traditional olive branches from the Temple; there,
for that day, he let the matter rest.

5 Presently he found an opportunity to further his mad
plan. When Demetrius called him into his council and questioned him about the dispositions and intentions of the Jews,

[a] **14** 14:1seq. // 1 M 7.

GREEK OLD TESTAMENT

6 Οἱ λεγόμενοι τῶν Ιουδαίων Ασιδαῖοι, ὧν ἀφηγεῖται Ιουδας ὁ Μακκαβαῖος, πολεμοτροφοῦσιν καὶ στασιάζουσιν οὐκ ἐῶντες τὴν βασιλείαν εὐσταθείας τυχεῖν. 7 ὅθεν ἀφελόμενος τὴν προγονικὴν δόξαν [λέγω δὴ τὴν ἀρχιερωσύνην] δεῦρο νῦν ἐλήλυθα 8 πρῶτον μὲν ὑπὲρ τῶν ἀνηκόντων τῷ βασιλεῖ γνησίως φρονῶν, δεύτερον δὲ καὶ τῶν ἰδίων πολιτῶν στοχαζόμενος. τῇ μὲν γὰρ τῶν προειρημένων ἀλογιστίᾳ τὸ σύμπαν ἡμῶν γένος οὐ μικρῶς ἀκληρεῖ. 9 ἕκαστα δὲ τούτων ἐπεγνωκὼς σύ, βασιλεῦ, καὶ τῆς χώρας καὶ τοῦ περιισταμένου γένους ἡμῶν προνοήθητι καθ' ἣν ἔχεις πρὸς ἅπαντας εὐαπάντητον φιλανθρωπίαν. 10 ἄχρι γὰρ Ιουδας περίεστιν, ἀδύνατον εἰρήνης τυχεῖν τὰ πράγματα. 11 τοιούτων δὲ ῥηθέντων ὑπὸ τούτου θᾶττον οἱ λοιποὶ φίλοι δυσμενῶς ἔχοντες τὰ πρὸς τὸν Ιουδαν προσεπύρωσαν τὸν Δημήτριον. 12 προχειρισάμενος δὲ εὐθέως Νικάνορα τὸν γενόμενον ἐλεφαντάρχην καὶ στρατηγὸν ἀναδείξας τῆς Ιουδαίας ἐξαπέστειλεν 13 δοὺς ἐντολὰς αὐτὸν μὲν τὸν Ιουδαν ἐπανελέσθαι, τοὺς δὲ σὺν αὐτῷ σκορπίσαι, καταστῆσαι δὲ Ἄλκιμον ἀρχιερέα τοῦ μεγίστου ἱεροῦ. 14 οἱ δὲ ἐπὶ τῆς Ιουδαίας πεφυγαδευκότες τὸν Ιουδαν ἔθνη συνέμισγον ἀγεληδὸν τῷ Νικάνορι τὰς τῶν Ιουδαίων ἀτυχίας καὶ συμφορὰς ἰδίας εὐημερίας δοκοῦντες ἔσεσθαι.

15 Ἀκούσαντες δὲ τὴν τοῦ Νικάνορος ἔφοδον καὶ τὴν ἐπίθεσιν τῶν ἐθνῶν καταπασάμενοι γῆν ἐλιτάνευον τὸν ἄχρι

KING JAMES VERSION

6 Those of the Jews that he called Assideans, whose captain is Judas Maccabeus, nourish war, and are seditious, and will not let the realm be in peace.

7 Therefore I, being deprived of mine ancestors' honour, I mean the high priesthood, am now come hither:

8 First, verily for the unfeigned care I have of things pertaining to the king; and secondly, even for that I intend the good of mine own countrymen: for all our nation is in no small misery through the unadvised dealing of them aforesaid.

9 Wherefore, O king, seeing thou knowest all these things, be careful for the country, and our nation, which is pressed on every side, according to the clemency that thou readily shewest unto all.

10 For as long as Judas liveth, it is not possible that the state should be quiet.

11 This was no sooner spoken of him, but others of the king's friends, being maliciously set against Judas, did more incense Demetrius.

12 And forthwith calling Nicanor, who had been master of the elephants, and making him governor over Judea, he sent him forth,

13 Commanding him to slay Judas, and to scatter them that were with him, and to make Alcimus high priest of the great temple.

14 Then the heathen, that had fled out of Judea from Judas, came to Nicanor by flocks, thinking the harm and calamities of the Jews to be their welfare.

15 Now when the Jews heard of Nicanor's coming, and that the heathen were up against them, they cast earth upon

DOUAY OLD TESTAMENT

6 He answered thereunto: They among the Jews that are called Assideans, of whom Judas Machabeus is captain, nourish wars, and raise seditions, and will not suffer the realm to be in peace.

7 For I also being deprived of my ancestors' glory (I mean of the high priesthood) am now come hither:

8 Principally indeed out of fidelity to the king's interests, but in the next place also to provide for the good of my countrymen: for all our nation suffereth much from the evil proceedings of those men.

9 Wherefore, O king, seeing thou knowest all these things, take care, I beseech thee, both of the country, and of our nation, according to thy humanity which is known to all men,

10 For as long as Judas liveth, it is not possible that the state should be quiet.

11 Now when this man had spoken to this effect, the rest also of the *king's* friends, who were enemies of Judas, incensed Demetrius against him.

12 And forthwith he sent Nicanor, the commander over the elephants, governor into Judea:

13 Giving him in charge, to take Judas himself: and disperse all them that were with him, and to make Alcimus the high priest of the great temple.

14 Then the Gentiles who had fled out of Judea from Judas, came to Nicanor by flocks, thinking the miseries and calamities of the Jews to be the welfare of their affairs.

15 Now when the Jews heard of Nicanor's coming, and that the nations were assembled against them, they cast

KNOX TRANSLATION

confidence. 6 And this was his answer: It is the faction of the
Assideans, with Judas Machabaeus at their head, that will
ever be fanning the flames of war, and moving revolt, and
destroying the peace of the realm. 7 Thou seest here a man
robbed of the high priesthood, his rightful inheritance. And
the cause of my coming is, 8 first, the loyalty I have to the
king's own interest, but not less, the love of nay own fellow-
countrymen; by the false aims of a faction the whole of our
race is brought into utter misery, 9 Do but satisfy thyself, my
lord king, that all is as I have said, and then, with that kindliness the world knows so well, take order concerning the
country and its inhabitants. 10 No peace the commonwealth
may have, while Judas lives.

11 Such was the opinion he gave, and the courtiers, that
had little love for Judas, fell to egging Demetrius on; 12 he,
with all haste, despatched one of his generals to Judaea,
Nicanor, that was in command of the elephants. 13 His
orders were, to take Judas alive, to disperse his company,
and of our glorious temple to make Alcimus high priest.
14 The Gentiles whom Judas had chased out of the country
flocked, now, to Nicanor's side, confident that the miserable
ruin of the Jews would be the foundation of their own prosperity. 15 As for the Jews, when they heard Nicanor was on
the march, with all this rabble of alien folk, they cast earth

TODAY'S ENGLISH VERSION

Alcimus said, 6 "The followers of Judas Maccabeus think of themselves as devout and patriotic; they love war and are constantly inciting the people to rebellion and will never leave the nation in peace. 7 It is their fault that I no longer hold the glorious position of High Priest, to which I am entitled by birth. And so I have come here, 8 primarily out of a genuine concern for your interests as king, but also out of consideration for my own people, for the foolish policies of Judas and his followers have brought terrible suffering on our entire nation. 9 When Your Majesty has examined all the details of these matters, please act in your usual kind and generous manner to relieve the oppression of our nation and its people. 10 As long as Judas is alive, it will be impossible for our nation to enjoy peace."

11 As soon as Alcimus had finished his speech, the other advisers quickly seized this opportunity to arouse Demetrius' anger against Judas, because they also hated him. 12 So King Demetrius immediately appointed Nicanor, who was the commander of his elephant forces, to be governor of Judea, and sent him there 13 with orders to kill Judas, scatter his followers, and make Alcimus High Priest of the greatest Temple in all the world. 14 All the foreigners in Judea, who had fled from Judas' attacks, now rushed to join forces with Nicanor, because they thought that any defeat or trouble that came to the Jews would be to their own advantage.

15 The Jews heard that Nicanor was attacking and that the foreigners in their country were giving him their support. So they threw dirt on themselves and prayed to their God, who

NEW REVISED STANDARD VERSION

6 "Those of the Jews who are called Hasideans, whose leader is Judas Maccabeus, are keeping up war and stirring up sedition, and will not let the kingdom attain tranquility. 7 Therefore I have laid aside my ancestral glory—I mean the high priesthood—and have now come here, 8 first because I am genuinely concerned for the interests of the king, and second because I have regard also for my compatriots. For through the folly of those whom I have mentioned our whole nation is now in no small misfortune. 9 Since you are acquainted, O king, with the details of this matter, may it please you to take thought for our country and our hard-pressed nation with the gracious kindness that you show to all. 10 For as long as Judas lives, it is impossible for the government to find peace." 11 When he had said this, the rest of the king's Friends,[a] who were hostile to Judas, quickly inflamed Demetrius still more. 12 He immediately chose Nicanor, who had been in command of the elephants, appointed him governor of Judea, and sent him off 13 with orders to kill Judas and scatter his troops, and to install Alcimus as high priest of the great[b] temple. 14 And the Gentiles throughout Judea, who had fled before[c] Judas, flocked to join Nicanor, thinking that the misfortunes and calamities of the Jews would mean prosperity for themselves.

15 When the Jews[d] heard of Nicanor's coming and the gathering of the Gentiles, they sprinkled dust on their heads

a Gk *of the Friends* *b* Gk *greatest* *c* Meaning of Gk uncertain
d Gk *they*

NEW AMERICAN BIBLE

He replied: 6 "Those Jews called Hasideans, led by Judas Maccabeus, are warmongers, who stir up sedition and keep the kingdom from enjoying peace and quiet. 7 For this reason, now that I am deprived of my ancestral dignity, that is to say, the high priesthood, I have come here— 8 first, out of my genuine concern for the king's interests, and secondly, out of consideration for my own countrymen, since our entire nation is suffering great affliction from the unreasonable conduct of the people just mentioned. 9 When you have informed yourself in detail on these matters, O king, act in the interest of our country and its hard-pressed people with the same gracious consideration that you show toward all. 10 As long as Judas is around, it is impossible for the state to enjoy peace." 11 When he had said this, the other Friends who were hostile to Judas quickly added fuel to Demetrius' indignation.

12 The king immediately chose Nicanor, who had been in command of the elephants, and appointed him governor of Judea. He sent him off 13 with orders to put Judas to death, to disperse his followers, and to set up Alcimus as high priest of the great temple. 14 The Gentiles from Judea, who would have banished Judas, came flocking to Nicanor, thinking that the misfortunes and calamities of the Jews would mean prosperity for themselves. 15 When the Jews heard of Nicanor's coming, and that the Gentiles were rallying to him, they sprinkled themselves with earth and prayed to him who

NEW JERUSALEM BIBLE

he replied, 6 'Those Jews called Hasidaeans, who are led by Judas Maccabaeus, are war-mongers and rebels who are preventing the kingdom from finding stability. 7 That is why, after being deprived of my hereditary dignity—I mean the high priesthood—I have come here now, 8 first out of genuine concern for the king's interests, and secondly, out of a regard for our own fellow-citizens, because the irresponsible behaviour of those I have mentioned has brought no slight misery on our entire race. 9 When your majesty has taken note of all these points, may it please you to make provision for the welfare of our country and our oppressed nation, as befits the gracious benevolence you extend to all; 10 for, as long as Judas remains alive, the State will never enjoy peace.'

11 No sooner had he spoken thus than the rest of the King's Friends, who were hostile to Judas' activities, stoked Demetrius' anger. 12 The latter at once selected Nicanor, then commander of the elephants, promoted him to the command of Judaea and despatched him 13 with instructions to dispose of Judas, disperse his followers and instal Alcimus as high priest of the greatest of temples. 14 The foreigners in Judaea, who had fled before Judas, flocked to join Nicanor, thinking that the misfortunes and troubles of the Jews would be to their own advantage.

15 When the Jews heard that Nicanor was coming and that the foreigners were about to attack, they sprinkled dust over

GREEK OLD TESTAMENT

αἰῶνος συστήσαντα τὸν αὐτοῦ λαόν, ἀεὶ δὲ μετ᾽ ἐπιφανείας
ἀντιλαμβανόμενον τῆς ἑαυτοῦ μερίδος. 16 προστάξαντος δὲ
τοῦ ἡγουμένου ἐκεῖθεν εὐθέως ἀναζεύξας συμμίσγει αὐτοῖς
ἐπὶ κώμην Δεσσαου. 17 Σιμων δὲ ὁ ἀδελφὸς Ιουδου συμβε-
βληκὼς ἦν τῷ Νικάνορι, βραδέως δὲ διὰ τὴν αἰφνίδιον τῶν
ἀντιπάλων ἀφασίαν ἐπταικώς. 18 ὅμως δὲ ἀκούων ὁ Νικάνωρ
ἣν εἶχον οἱ περὶ τὸν Ιουδαν ἀνδραγαθίαν καὶ ἐν τοῖς περὶ
τῆς πατρίδος ἀγῶσιν εὐψυχίαν, ὑπευλαβεῖτο τὴν κρίσιν δι᾽
αἱμάτων ποιήσασθαι. 19 διόπερ ἔπεμψεν Ποσιδώνιον καὶ
Θεόδοτον καὶ Ματταθιαν δοῦναι καὶ λαβεῖν δεξιάς. 20 πλεί-
ονος δὲ γενομένης περὶ τούτων ἐπισκέψεως καὶ τοῦ ἡγουμένου τοῖς πλήθεσιν ἀνακοινωσαμένου καὶ φανείσης ὁμοψήφου
γνώμης ἐπένευσαν ταῖς συνθήκαις. 21 ἐτάξαντο δὲ ἡμέραν
ἐν ᾗ κατ᾽ ἰδίαν ἥξουσιν εἰς τὸ αὐτό· καὶ προῆλθεν παρ᾽ ἑκάστου δίφραξ, ἔθεσαν δίφρους. 22 διέταξεν Ιουδας ἐνόπλους
ἑτοίμους ἐν τοῖς ἐπικαίροις τόποις, μήποτε ἐκ τῶν πολεμίων αἰφνιδίως κακουργία γένηται· τὴν ἁρμόζουσαν ἐποιήσαντο κοινολογίαν. 23 διέτριβεν ὁ Νικάνωρ ἐν Ιεροσολύμοις
καὶ ἔπραττεν οὐθὲν ἄτοπον, τοὺς δὲ συναχθέντας ἀγελαίους
ὄχλους ἀπέλυσεν. 24 καὶ εἶχεν τὸν Ιουδαν διὰ παντὸς ἐν
προσώπῳ, ψυχικῶς τῷ ἀνδρὶ προσεκέκλιτο. 25 παρεκάλεσεν

KING JAMES VERSION

their heads, and made supplication to him that had established his people for ever, and who always helpeth his portion with manifestation of his presence.

16 So at the commandment of the captain they removed straightways from thence, and came near unto them at the town of Dessau.

17 Now Simon, Judas' brother, had joined battle with Nicanor, but was somewhat discomfited through the sudden silence of his enemies.

18 Nevertheless Nicanor, hearing of the manliness of them that were with Judas, and the courageousness that they had to fight for their country, durst not try the matter by the sword.

19 Wherefore he sent Posidonius, and Theodotus, and Mattathias, to make peace.

20 So when they had taken long advisement thereupon, and the captain had made the multitude acquainted therewith, and it appeared that they were all of one mind, they consented to the covenants,

21 And appointed a day to meet in together by themselves: and when the day came, and stools were set for either of them,

22 Judas placed armed men ready in convenient places, lest some treachery should be suddenly practised by the enemies: so they made a peaceable conference.

23 Now Nicanor abode in Jerusalem, and did no hurt, but sent away the people that came flocking unto him.

24 And he would not willingly have Judas out of his sight: for he love the man from his heart.

DOUAY OLD TESTAMENT

earth upon their heads, and made supplication to him, who chose his people to keep them for ever, and who protected his portion by evident signs.

16 Then at the commandment of their captain, they forthwith removed from the place where they were, and went to the town of Dessau, to meet them.

17 Now Simon the brother of Judas had joined battle with Nicanor, but was frightened with the sudden coming of the adversaries.

18 Nevertheless Nicanor hearing of the valour of Judas' companions, and the greatness of courage with which they fought for their country, was afraid to try the matter by the sword.

19 Wherefore he sent Posidonius, and Theodotius, and Matthias before to present and receive the right hands.

20 And when there had been a consultation thereupon, and the captain had acquainted the multitude with it, they were all of one mind to consent to covenants.

21 So they appointed a day upon which they might commune together by themselves: and seats were brought out, and set for each one.

22 But Judas ordered men to be ready in convenient places, lest some mischief might be suddenly practised by the enemies: so they made an agreeable conference.

23 And Nicanor abode in Jerusalem, and did no wrong, but sent away the flocks of the multitudes that had been gathered together.

24 And Judas was always dear to him from the heart, and he was well affected to the man.

KNOX TRANSLATION

on their heads and betook themselves to prayer. Was it not
God's appointment, his people he should evermore preserve?
Was he not wont to protect them with signal marks of his
favour? 16 And now orders came to them from their leader;
they must be on the march. Their mustering-place was a
fortress called Dessau, 17 to which Simon, Judas' brother,
had withdrawn after a brush with the enemy, who daunted
him by the suddenness of their advance.[a]
18 But Nicanor had heard much about the valour of Judas'
men, and how nobly they fought in their country's quarrel;
no wonder if he shrank from the arbitrament of the sword,
19 and sent envoys to meet them, Posidonius, Theodotius
and Matthias, with an offer of terms. 20 After a deal of nego-
tiation, Judas referred the matter to the general voice, and
all were agreed upon accepting the offer of friendship. 21 So
the day was fixed for a secret conference to be held between
them; thrones of honour were brought out and set ready,
22 and you may be sure Judas had armed men posted in
waiting, to forestall any sudden treachery on the enemy's
part; but their parleys ended happily enough. 23 Nicanor
was now lodged in Jerusalem, and did there no manner of
hurt; all the rabble he had brought with him were dispersed
to their homes. 24 Towards Judas he shewed unaffected
friendship, such a liking he had taken for the man; 25 ay,

a vv. 16, 17. There is perhaps some fault here in the manuscripts; the Greek text reads literally, 'And, the leader having commanded it, he (who?) immediately moved his camp from there (from where?), and made contact with them (with whom?) at the village of Dessau. But Simon, the brother of Judas, had engaged Nicanor, but slowly, having come to grief through the sudden silence of the enemy.'

TODAY'S ENGLISH VERSION

had chosen their nation as his possession forever and had
never failed to help them in time of need. 16 Then Judas,
their leader, gave the orders, and they immediately marched
out to engage the enemy in battle near the village of Adasa.[a]
17 Judas' brother Simon was fighting Nicanor but was gradually losing the battle because of an unexpected move on the
part of the enemy. 18 However, when Nicanor heard how
bravely and courageously Judas and his men were fighting
for their country, he decided not to settle the matter in battle.
19 Instead, he sent Posidonius, Theodotus, and Mattathias to
make a treaty with the Jews.

20 After the terms of the treaty had been worked out in
detail, Nicanor informed his troops, and they unanimously
agreed. 21 Then a day was set on which the leaders would
meet in private. Ceremonial chairs were brought out from
each camp and set up. 22 Judas had taken the precaution of
placing battle-ready troops in strategic places, in case of sudden treachery on the part of the enemy. But the two leaders
had a friendly meeting. 23 Nicanor stayed on in Jerusalem for
some time after that. He did not mistreat the Jews in any
way, and even sent away the people who had come over to
his side. 24 The two men became the best of friends, and
Judas was Nicanor's constant companion. 25 Nicanor urged

[a] *Probable text* Adasa; *Greek* Dessau.

NEW REVISED STANDARD VERSION

and prayed to him who established his own people forever
and always upholds his own heritage by manifesting himself. 16 At the command of the leader, they[a] set out from
there immediately and engaged them in battle at a village
called Dessau.[b] 17 Simon, the brother of Judas, had encountered Nicanor, but had been temporarily[c] checked because of
the sudden consternation created by the enemy.

18 Nevertheless Nicanor, hearing of the valor of Judas and
his troops and their courage in battle for their country,
shrank from deciding the issue by bloodshed. 19 Therefore he
sent Posidonius, Theodotus, and Mattathias to give and
receive pledges of friendship. 20 When the terms had been
fully considered, and the leader had informed the people, and
it had appeared that they were of one mind, they agreed to
the covenant. 21 The leaders[d] set a day on which to meet by
themselves. A chariot came forward from each army; seats of
honor were set in place; 22 Judas posted armed men in readiness at key places to prevent sudden treachery on the part of
the enemy; so they duly held the consultation.

23 Nicanor stayed on in Jerusalem and did nothing out of
the way, but dismissed the flocks of people that had gathered. 24 And he kept Judas always in his presence; he was
warmly attached to the man. 25 He urged him to marry and

a Gk *he* *b* Meaning of Gk uncertain *c* Other ancient authorities read *slowly* *d* Gk *They*

NEW AMERICAN BIBLE

established his people forever, and who always comes to the
aid of his heritage. 16 At their leader's command, they set out
at once and came upon the enemy at the village of Adasa.
17 Judas' brother Simon had engaged Nicanor, but because of
the sudden appearance of the enemy suffered a slight
repulse. 18 However, when Nicanor heard of the valor of
Judas and his men, and the great courage with which they
fought for their country, he shrank from deciding the issue
by bloodshed. 19 So he sent Posidonius, Theodotus and
Mattathias to arrange an agreement. 20 After a long discussion of the terms, each leader communicated them to his
troops; and when general agreement was expressed, they
assented to the treaty. 21 A day was set on which the leaders
would meet by themselves. From each side a chariot came
forward and thrones were set in place. 22 Judas had posted
armed men in readiness at suitable points for fear that the
enemy might suddenly carry out some treacherous plan. But
the conference was held in the proper way. 23 Nicanor stayed
on in Jerusalem, where he did nothing out of place. He got
rid of the throngs of ordinary people who gathered around
him; 24 but he always kept Judas in his company, for he had
a cordial affection for the man. 25 He urged him to marry

NEW JERUSALEM BIBLE

themselves and made supplication to him who had established his people for ever and who never failed to support his
own heritage by direct manifestations. 16 On their leader's
orders, they at once left the place where they were and confronted the enemy at the village of Dessau. 17 Simon, brother
of Judas, engaged Nicanor but, owing to the sudden arrival
of the enemy, suffered a slight reverse. 18 Nicanor, however,
had heard how brave Judas and his men were and how resolutely they always fought for their country, and he did not
dare allow bloodshed to decide the issue. 19 And so he sent
Posidonius, Theodotus and Mattathias to offer the Jews
pledges of friendship and to accept theirs.

20 After careful consideration of his terms, the leader communicated them to his troops, and since they were all clearly
of one mind they agreed to the treaty. 21 A day was fixed on
which the respective leaders were to meet as individuals. A
litter came out from either side and seats were set up.
22 Judas had posted armed men in strategic positions, in case
of a sudden treacherous move by the enemy. The leaders
held their conference and reached agreement. 23 Nicanor
took up residence in Jerusalem and did nothing out of place
there; indeed, he sent away the crowds that had flocked to
join him. 24 He kept Judas constantly with him, becoming
deeply attached to him 25 and encouraged him to marry and

Greek Old Testament

αὐτὸν γῆμαι καὶ παιδοποιήσασθαι· ἐγάμησεν, εὐστάθησεν,
ἐκοινώνησεν βίου.
[26] Ὁ δὲ Ἄλκιμος συνιδὼν τὴν πρὸς ἀλλήλους εὔνοιαν καὶ
τὰς γενομένας συνθήκας λαβὼν ἧκεν πρὸς τὸν Δημήτριον
καὶ ἔλεγεν τὸν Νικάνορα ἀλλότρια φρονεῖν τῶν πραγμάτων·
τὸν γὰρ ἐπίβουλον τῆς βασιλείας Ιουδαν αὐτοῦ διάδοχον
ἀναδεῖξαι. [27] ὁ δὲ βασιλεὺς ἔκθυμος γενόμενος καὶ ταῖς
τοῦ παμπονήρου διαβολαῖς ἐρεθισθεὶς ἔγραψεν Νικάνορι
φάσκων ὑπὲρ μὲν τῶν συνθηκῶν βαρέως φέρειν, κελεύων δὲ
τὸν Μακκαβαῖον δέσμιον ἐξαποστέλλειν εἰς Ἀντιόχειαν
ταχέως. [28] προσπεσόντων δὲ τούτων τῷ Νικάνορι συνεκέ-
χυτο καὶ δυσφόρως ἔφερεν, εἰ τὰ διεσταλμένα ἀθετήσει
μηδὲν τἀνδρὸς ἠδικηκότος. [29] ἐπεὶ δὲ τῷ βασιλεῖ ἀντι-
πράττειν οὐκ ἦν, εὔκαιρον ἐτήρει στρατηγήματι τοῦτ᾽ ἐπιτελέσαι. [30] ὁ δὲ Μακκαβαῖος αὐστηρότερον διεξαγαγόντα
συνιδὼν τὸν Νικάνορα τὰ πρὸς αὐτὸν καὶ τὴν εἰθισμένην
ἀπάντησιν ἀγροικότερον ἐσχηκότα νοήσας οὐκ ἀπὸ τοῦ
βελτίστου τὴν αὐστηρίαν εἶναι συστρέψας οὐκ ὀλίγους τῶν
περὶ αὐτὸν συνεκρύπτετο τὸν Νικάνορα. [31] συγγνοὺς δὲ ὁ
ἕτερος ὅτι γενναίως ὑπὸ τοῦ ἀνδρὸς ἐστρατήγηται, παραγενόμενος ἐπὶ τὸ μέγιστον καὶ ἅγιον ἱερὸν τῶν ἱερέων τὰς
καθηκούσας θυσίας προσαγόντων ἐκέλευσεν παραδιδόναι
τὸν ἄνδρα. [32] τῶν δὲ μεθ᾽ ὅρκων φασκόντων μὴ γινώσκειν
ποῦ ποτ᾽ ἔστιν ὁ ζητούμενος, [33] προτείνας τὴν δεξιὰν ἐπὶ

King James Version

25 He prayed him also to take a wife, and to beget children: so he married, was quiet, and took part of this life.

26 But Alcimus, perceiving the love that was betwixt them, and considering the covenants that were made, came to Demetrius, and told him that Nicanor was not well affected toward the state; for that he had ordained Judas, a traitor to his realm, to be the king's successor.

27 Then the king being in a rage, and provoked with the accusations of the most wicked man, wrote to Nicanor, signifying that he was much displeased with the covenants, and commanding him that he should send Maccabeus prisoner in all haste unto Antioch.

28 When this came to Nicanor's hearing, he was much confounded in himself, and took it grievously that he should make void the articles which were agreed upon, the man being in no fault.

29 But because there was no dealing against the king, he watched his time to accomplish this thing by policy.

30 Notwithstanding, when Maccabeus saw that Nicanor began to be churlish unto him, and that he entreated him more roughly than he was wont, perceiving that such sour behaviour came not of good, he gathered together not a few of his men, and withdrew himself from Nicanor.

31 But the other, knowing that he was notably prevented by Judas' policy, came into the great and holy temple, and commanded the priests, that were offering their usual sacrifices, to deliver him the man.

32 And when they sware that they could not tell where the man was whom he sought,

Douay Old Testament

25 And he desired him to marry a wife, and to have children. So he married: he lived quietly, and they lived in common.

26 But Alcimus seeing the love they had one to another, and the covenants, came to Demetrius, and told him that Nicanor assented to the foreign interest, for that he meant to make Judas, who was a traitor to the kingdom, his successor.

27 Then the king being in a rage and provoked with this man's wicked accusations, wrote to Nicanor, signifying, that he was greatly displeased with the covenant of friendship: and that he commanded him nevertheless to send Machabeus prisoner in all haste to Antioch.

28 When this was known, Nicanor was in a consternation, and took it grievously that he should make void the articles that were agreed upon, having received no injury from the man.

29 But because he could not oppose the king, he watched an opportunity to comply with the orders.

30 But when Machabeus perceived that Nicanor was more stern to him, and that when they met together as usual he behaved himself in a rough manner: and was sensible that this rough behaviour came not of good, he gathered together a few of his men, and hid himself from Nicanor.

31 But he finding himself notably prevented by the man, came to the great and holy temple: and commanded the priests that were offering the accustomed sacrifices, to deliver him the man.

32 And when they swore unto him, that they knew not where the man was whom he sought, he stretched out his hand to the temple,

Knox Translation

and encouraged him to take a wife and beget children; so
Judas married, and took his ease, and ever he lived on close
terms with Nicanor.
[26] And what of Alcimus? Little it liked him to see all this
good-will between the two of them, and their treaty-making;
to Demetrius he betook him, and charged Nicanor with disaf-
fection; was he not purposing to hand over his command to
Judas, a traitor against the realm? [27] Vile accusations, that
threw Demetrius into a great taking of fury; he wrote to
Nicanor, he was very ill content with the peace made, and
would have Machabaeus sent to Antioch in chains without
more ado. [28] Here was Nicanor left in great confusion of
mind; it went against the grain with him to cancel the treaty
with Judas, that had nothing wronged him, [29] yet run
counter to the king's will he might not. So he began looking
for an opportunity of carrying out his orders; [30] and
Machabaeus, remarking that a coolness had sprung up, and
their meetings were less courteous than hitherto, made sure
this behaviour of his boded no good. Whereupon he gathered
some of his company, and went into concealment.
[31] So Nicanor found himself quite outwitted; and he must
needs make his way into the high and holy precincts of the
temple, where even then the priests were offering their accustomed sacrifice. Judas, he said, must be handed over to him;
[32] and when they, upon oath, denied all knowledge of his hiding-place, what did Nicanor? He pointed to the temple, [33] and

TODAY'S ENGLISH VERSION

him to marry and start a family. So Judas did this and settled
down to a peaceful life.
26 When Alcimus noticed how well Nicanor and Judas were
getting along, he obtained a copy of the treaty and went to
see King Demetrius. He told the king that Nicanor was disloyal to the government, because he had appointed the traitor Judas to be his successor. 27 These false accusations infuriated the king, and in his anger he wrote to Nicanor, informing him that he was dissatisfied with the treaty and ordering
him to arrest Judas Maccabeus and send him to Antioch at
once.
28 When this message reached Nicanor, he was hurt and
didn't know what to do, because he did not like having to
break an agreement with a man who had kept his part of the
bargain. 29 Yet it was impossible for him to ignore the king's
command, so he began looking for a way to trap Judas.
30 Judas, however, noticed that Nicanor was becoming hostile
and rude toward him, and he knew that this was a bad sign.
So he gathered a large number of his followers and went into
hiding.
31 When Nicanor realized that Judas had outsmarted him,
he went to the great and holy Temple at the time when the
priests were offering sacrifice and ordered them to surrender
Judas to him. 32 But the priests declared under oath that they
had no idea where Judas was hiding. 33 Then Nicanor raised

NEW REVISED STANDARD VERSION

have children; so Judas[a] married, settled down, and shared
the common life.
26 But when Alcimus noticed their goodwill for one
another, he took the covenant that had been made and went
to Demetrius. He told him that Nicanor was disloyal to the
government, since he had appointed that conspirator against
the kingdom, Judas, to be his successor. 27 The king became
excited and, provoked by the false accusations of that
depraved man, wrote to Nicanor, stating that he was displeased with the covenant and commanding him to send
Maccabeus to Antioch as a prisoner without delay.
28 When this message came to Nicanor, he was troubled
and grieved that he had to annul their agreement when the
man had done no wrong. 29 Since it was not possible to
oppose the king, he watched for an opportunity to accomplish this by a stratagem. 30 But Maccabeus, noticing that
Nicanor was more austere in his dealings with him and was
meeting him more rudely than had been his custom, concluded that this austerity did not spring from the best motives.
So he gathered not a few of his men, and went into hiding
from Nicanor. 31 When the latter became aware that he had
been cleverly outwitted by the man, he went to the great[b]
and holy temple while the priests were offering the customary sacrifices, and commanded them to hand the man over.
32 When they declared on oath that they did not know where
the man was whom he wanted, 33 he stretched out his right

a Gk *he* *b* Gk *greatest*

NEW AMERICAN BIBLE

and have children; so Judas married, settled down, and
shared the common life.
26 When Alcimus saw their friendship for each other, he
took the treaty that had been made, went to Demetrius, and
said that Nicanor was plotting against the state, and that he
had appointed Judas, the conspirator against the kingdom, to
be his successor. 27 Stirred up by the villain's calumnies, the
king became enraged. He wrote to Nicanor, stating that he
was displeased with the treaty, and ordering him to send
Maccabeus as a prisoner to Antioch without delay. 28 When
this message reached Nicanor he was dismayed, for he hated
to break his agreement with a man who had done no wrong.
29 However, there was no way of opposing the king, so he
watched for an opportunity to carry out this order by a stratagem. 30 But Maccabeus noticed that Nicanor was becoming
cool in his dealings with him, and acting with unaccustomed
rudeness when they met; he concluded that this coldness
betokened no good. So he gathered together a large number
of his men, and went into hiding from Nicanor.
31 When Nicanor realized that he had been disgracefully
outwitted by the man, he went to the great and holy temple,
at a time when the priests were offering the customary sacrifices, and ordered them to surrender Judas. 32 As they
declared under oath that they did not know where the wanted man was, 33 he raised his right hand toward the temple

NEW JERUSALEM BIBLE

have children. Judas married, settled down and led a normal
life.
26 When Alcimus saw how friendly the two men had
become, he went to Demetrius with a copy of the treaty they
had signed and told him that Nicanor was harbouring
thoughts against the interests of the State, and was planning
that Judas, an enemy of the realm, should fill the next
vacancy among the Friends of the King.
27 The king flew into a rage; roused by the slanders of this
villain, he wrote to Nicanor, telling him of his strong displeasure at these agreements and ordering him immediately to
send Maccabaeus to Antioch in chains.
28 When the letter reached Nicanor, he was very much
upset, for he disliked the prospect of breaking an agreement
with a man who had done nothing wrong. 29 Since, however, there was no way of opposing the king, he waited for an
opportunity to carry out the order by a stratagem.
30 Maccabaeus began to notice that Nicanor was treating him
more sharply and that his manner of speaking to him was
more abrupt than it had been, and he concluded that such
sharpness could have no very good motive. He therefore collected a considerable number of his followers and got away
from Nicanor. 31 The latter, realising that the man had well
and truly outmanoeuvred him, went to the greatest and holiest of Temples when the priests were offering the customary
sacrifices, and ordered them to surrender Judas. 32 When
they protested on oath that they did not know where the
wanted man could be, 33 he stretched out his right hand

GREEK OLD TESTAMENT

τὸν νεὼ ταῦτ' ὤμοσεν Ἐὰν μὴ δέσμιόν μοι τὸν Ιουδαν παραδῶτε, τόνδε τὸν τοῦ θεοῦ σηκὸν εἰς πεδίον ποιήσω καὶ τὸ θυσιαστήριον κατασκάψω καὶ ἱερὸν ἐνταῦθα τῷ Διονύσῳ ἐπιφανὲς ἀναστήσω. 34 τοσαῦτα δὲ εἰπὼν ἀπῆλθεν· οἱ δὲ ἱερεῖς προτείναντες τὰς χεῖρας εἰς τὸν οὐρανὸν ἐπεκαλοῦντο τὸν διὰ παντὸς ὑπέρμαχον τοῦ ἔθνους ἡμῶν ταῦτα λέγοντες 35 Σὺ κύριε τῶν ὅλων ἀπροσδεὴς ὑπάρχων ηὐδόκησας ναὸν τῆς σῆς σκηνώσεως ἐν ἡμῖν γενέσθαι· 36 καὶ νῦν, ἅγιε παντὸς ἁγιασμοῦ κύριε, διατήρησον εἰς αἰῶνα ἀμίαντον τόνδε τὸν προσφάτως κεκαθαρισμένον οἶκον.

37 Ραζις δέ τις τῶν ἀπὸ Ιεροσολύμων πρεσβυτέρων ἐμηνύθη τῷ Νικάνορι ἀνὴρ φιλοπολίτης καὶ σφόδρα καλῶς ἀκούων καὶ κατὰ τὴν εὔνοιαν πατὴρ τῶν Ιουδαίων προσαγορευόμενος. 38 ἦν γὰρ ἐν τοῖς ἔμπροσθεν χρόνοις τῆς ἀμειξίας κρίσιν εἰσενηνεγμένος Ιουδαϊσμοῦ, καὶ σῶμα καὶ ψυχὴν ὑπὲρ τοῦ Ιουδαϊσμοῦ παραβεβλημένος μετὰ πάσης ἐκτενίας. 39 βουλόμενος δὲ Νικάνωρ πρόδηλον ποιῆσαι ἣν εἶχεν πρὸς τοὺς Ιουδαίους δυσμένειαν, ἀπέστειλεν στρατιώτας ὑπὲρ τοὺς πεντακοσίους συλλαβεῖν αὐτόν· 40 ἔδοξεν γὰρ ἐκεῖνον συλλαβὼν τούτοις ἐνεργάσασθαι συμφοράν. 41 τῶν δὲ πληθῶν μελλόντων τὸν πύργον καταλαβέσθαι καὶ τὴν αὐλαίαν θύραν βιαζομένων καὶ κελευόντων πῦρ προσάγειν καὶ τὰς θύρας ὑφάπτειν, περικατάλημπτος γενόμενος ὑπέθηκεν

KING JAMES VERSION

33 He stretched out his right hand toward the temple, and made an oath in this manner: If ye will not deliver me Judas as a prisoner, I will lay this temple of God even with the ground, and I will break down the altar, and erect a notable temple unto Bacchus.

34 After these words he departed. Then the priests lifted up their hands toward heaven, and besought him that was ever a defender of their nation, saying in this manner;

35 Thou, O Lord of all things, who hast need of nothing, wast pleased that the temple of thine habitation should be among us:

36 Therefore now, O holy Lord of all holiness, keep this house ever undefiled, which lately was cleansed, and stop every unrighteous mouth.

37 Now was there accused unto Nicanor one Razis, one of the elders of Jerusalem, a lover of his countrymen, and a man of very good report, who for his kindness was called a father of the Jews.

38 For in the former times, when they mingled not themselves with the Gentiles, he had been accused of Judaism, and did boldly jeopard his body and life with all vehemency for the religion of the Jews.

39 So Nicanor, willing to declare the hate that he bare unto the Jews, sent above five hundred men of war to take him:

40 For he thought by taking him to do the Jews much hurt.

41 Now when the multitude would have taken the tower, and violently broken into the outer door, and bade that fire should be brought to burn it, he being ready to be taken on every side fell upon his sword;

DOUAY OLD TESTAMENT

33 And swore, saying: Unless you deliver Judas prisoner to me, I will lay this temple of God even with the ground, and will beat down the altar, and I will dedicate this temple to Bacchus.

34 And when he had spoken thus he departed. But the priests stretching forth their hands to heaven, called upon him that was ever the defender of their nation, saying in this manner:

35 Thou, O Lord of all things, who wantest nothing, wast pleased that the temple of thy habitation should be amongst us.

36 Therefore now, O Lord the holy of all holies, keep this house for ever undefiled which was lately cleansed.

37 Now Razias, one of the ancients of Jerusalem, was accused to Nicanor, a man that was a lover of the city, and of good report, who for his affection was called the father of the Jews.

38 This man, for a long time, had held fast his purpose of keeping himself pure in the Jews' religion, and was ready to expose his body and life, that he might persevere therein.

39 So Nicanor being willing to declare the hatred that he bore the Jews, sent five hundred soldiers to take him.

40 For he thought by insnaring him to hurt the Jews very much.

41 Now as the multitude sought to rush into his house, and to break open the door, and to set fire to it, when he was ready to be taken, he struck himself with his sword:

KNOX TRANSLATION

swore that if Judas were not handed over to him in chains he would raze yonder sanctuary to the ground, demolish the altar, and consecrate its precincts anew to Bacchus. 34 With that, he left them; and the priests, lifting up their hands to heaven, called upon the God that was ever the champion of their race, with such prayer as this: 35 Lord of all, that need of thy creatures hast none, thy will it was to have thy dwelling-place among us! 36 Holy thou art, and of all holy things the master; this house, that was so lately cleansed of its defilement, keep thou for ever undefiled.

37 It was this Nicanor that received information against one of the elders at Jerusalem, named Razias, a true patriot and a man of good repute; for the love he bore it, men called him the father of the Jewish people. 38 Long time this man had held to his resolve of keeping aloof from the Gentiles, ready to put life and limb in jeopardy, so he might persevere. 39 And now, as if to give public proof of hatred towards the Jews, Nicanor sent five hundred men to take him alive; 40 shrewder blow was none he could deal them, than to beguile such a man as this. 41 And when this great company set about to force an entry into his dwelling, breaking down the door and calling out for firebrands, cut off from all escape, what did Razias? He thrust a sword into his own body, 42 counting it

TODAY'S ENGLISH VERSION

his right arm in the direction of the Temple and made a
solemn threat: "If you do not hand Judas over to me as a
prisoner, I will level God's Temple to the ground, demolish
this altar, and on this spot build a glorious temple to
Dionysus." 34 Then he left, and immediately the priests lifted
their arms toward heaven and prayed to God, the faithful
Defender of our nation: 35 "Lord, you are in need of nothing,
yet it has pleased you to place your Temple here and to live
among us. 36 You alone are holy, and your Temple has only
recently been purified, so now protect its holiness forever."

37 One of the leaders in Jerusalem, a man by the name of
Razis, was denounced to Nicanor. It was said that he had
helped his people in many ways and was so highly respected
by them that he was known as "the Father of the Jews."
38 During the early days of the revolution he had risked his
life for Judaism and had been brought to trial because of his
loyalty. 39 Wanting to show clearly how much he disliked
the Jews, Nicanor sent more than 500 soldiers to arrest
Razis, 40 because he thought his arrest would be a crippling
blow to the Jews. 41 The soldiers were about to capture the
tower where Razis had gone. They were forcing open the
gates to the courtyard, and the order had been given to set
the door on fire. Razis realized there was no escape, so he
tried to commit suicide with his sword, 42 preferring to die

NEW REVISED STANDARD VERSION

hand toward the sanctuary, and swore this oath: "If you do
not hand Judas over to me as a prisoner, I will level this
shrine of God to the ground and tear down the altar, and
build here a splendid temple to Dionysus."

34 Having said this, he went away. Then the priests
stretched out their hands toward heaven and called upon the
constant Defender of our nation, in these words: 35 "O Lord
of all, though you have need of nothing, you were pleased
that there should be a temple for your habitation among us;
36 so now, O holy One, Lord of all holiness, keep undefiled
forever this house that has been so recently purified."

37 A certain Razis, one of the elders of Jerusalem, was
denounced to Nicanor as a man who loved his compatriots
and was very well thought of and for his goodwill was called
father of the Jews. 38 In former times, when there was no
mingling with the Gentiles, he had been accused of Judaism,
and he had most zealously risked body and life for Judaism.
39 Nicanor, wishing to exhibit the enmity that he had for the
Jews, sent more than five hundred soldiers to arrest him;
40 for he thought that by arresting[a] him he would do them an
injury. 41 When the troops were about to capture the tower
and were forcing the door of the courtyard, they ordered that
fire be brought and the doors burned. Being surrounded,
Razis[b] fell upon his own sword, 42 preferring to die nobly

a Meaning of Gk uncertain *b* Gk *he*

NEW AMERICAN BIBLE

and swore this oath: "If you do not hand Judas over to me as
prisoner, I will level this shrine of God to the ground; I will
tear down the altar, and erect here a splendid temple to
Dionysus." 34 With these words he went away. The priests
stretched out their hands toward heaven, calling upon the
unfailing defender of our nation in these words: 35 "LORD of
all, though you are in need of nothing, you have approved of
a temple for your dwelling place among us. 36 Therefore, O
holy One, LORD of all holiness, preserve forever undefiled this
house, which has been so recently purified." 37 A certain
Razis, one of the elders of Jerusalem, was denounced to
Nicanor as a patriot. A man highly regarded, he was called a
father of the Jews because of his love for them. 38 In the
early days of the revolt, he had been convicted of Judaism,
and had risked body and life in his ardent zeal for it.
39 Nicanor, to show his detestation of the Jews, sent more
than five hundred soldiers to arrest him. 40 He thought that
by arresting such a man he would deal the Jews a hard blow.
41 But when these troops, on the point of capturing the
tower, were forcing the outer gate and calling for fire to set
the door ablaze, Razis, now caught on all sides, turned his

NEW JERUSALEM BIBLE

towards the Temple and swore this oath, 'If you do not hand
Judas over to me as prisoner, I shall rase this dwelling of God
to the ground, I shall demolish the altar, and on this very
spot I shall erect a splendid temple to Dionysus.' 34 With
these words he left them. The priests stretched out their
hands to heaven, calling on him who has at all times done
battle for our nation; this was their prayer: 35 'O Lord in
need of nothing, it has pleased you that the Temple where
you dwell should be here with us. 36 Now, therefore, holy
Lord of all holiness, preserve for ever from all profanation
this House, so newly purified.'

37 Now, a man called Razis, one of the elders of Jerusalem,
was denounced to Nicanor. He was a man who loved his
countrymen and stood high in their esteem, and he was
known as the father of the Jews because of his kindness.
38 In the earlier days of the insurrection he had been convicted of Judaism, and he had risked both life and limb for
Judaism with the utmost zeal. 39 Nicanor, by way of demonstrating the enmity he had for the Jews, sent over five hundred soldiers to arrest him, 40 reckoning that if he eliminated
this man he would be dealing them a severe blow. 41 When
the troops were on the point of capturing the tower and were
forcing the outer door and calling for fire to set the doors
alight, Razis, finding himself completely surrounded, fell on

GREEK OLD TESTAMENT

ἑαυτῷ τὸ ξίφος 42 εὐγενῶς θέλων ἀποθανεῖν ἤπερ τοῖς
ἀλιτηρίοις ὑποχείριος γενέσθαι καὶ τῆς ἰδίας εὐγενείας
ἀναξίως ὑβρισθῆναι. 43 τῇ δὲ πληγῇ μὴ κατευθικτήσας διὰ
τὴν τοῦ ἀγῶνος σπουδὴν καὶ τῶν ὄχλων ἔσω τῶν θυρωμάτων
εἰσβαλλόντων ἀναδραμὼν γενναίως ἐπὶ τὸ τεῖχος κατεκρη-
μνισεν ἑαυτὸν ἀνδρωδῶς εἰς τοὺς ὄχλους. 44 τῶν δὲ ταχέως
ἀναποδισάντων γενομένου διαστήματος ἦλθεν κατὰ μέσον
τὸν κενεῶνα. 45 ἔτι δὲ ἔμπνους ὑπάρχων καὶ πεπυρωμένος
τοῖς θυμοῖς ἐξαναστὰς φερομένων κρουνηδὸν τῶν αἱμάτων
καὶ δυσχερῶν τῶν τραυμάτων ὄντων δρόμῳ τοὺς ὄχλους
διελθὼν καὶ στὰς ἐπί τινος πέτρας ἀπορρῶγος 46 παντελῶς
ἔξαιμος ἤδη γινόμενος προβαλὼν τὰ ἔντερα καὶ λαβὼν
ἑκατέραις ταῖς χερσὶν ἐνέσεισε τοῖς ὄχλοις καὶ ἐπικαλεσά-
μενος τὸν δεσπόζοντα τῆς ζωῆς καὶ τοῦ πνεύματος ταῦτα
αὐτῷ πάλιν ἀποδοῦναι τόνδε τὸν τρόπον μετήλλαξεν.

15 Ὁ δὲ Νικάνωρ μεταλαβὼν τοὺς περὶ τὸν Ιουδαν ὄντας
ἐν τοῖς κατὰ Σαμάρειαν τόποις ἐβουλεύσατο τῇ τῆς
καταπαύσεως ἡμέρᾳ μετὰ πάσης ἀσφαλείας αὐτοῖς ἐπιβαλεῖν. 2 τῶν δὲ κατὰ ἀνάγκην συνεπομένων αὐτῷ Ιουδαίων
λεγόντων Μηδαμῶς οὕτως ἀγρίως καὶ βαρβάρως ἀπολέσῃς,
δόξαν δὲ ἀπομέρισον τῇ προτετιμημένῃ ὑπὸ τοῦ πάντα ἐφορῶντος μεθ' ἁγιότητος ἡμέρᾳ· 3 ὁ δὲ τρισαλιτήριος ἐπηρώτησεν εἰ ἔστιν ἐν οὐρανῷ δυνάστης ὁ προστεταχὼς ἄγειν
τὴν τῶν σαββάτων ἡμέραν· 4 τῶν δ' ἀποφηναμένων Ἔστιν ὁ
κύριος ζῶν αὐτὸς ἐν οὐρανῷ δυνάστης ὁ κελεύσας ἀσκεῖν τὴν

KING JAMES VERSION

42 Choosing rather to die manfully, than to come into the hands of the wicked, to be abused otherwise than beseemed his noble birth:

43 But missing his stroke through haste, the multitude also rushing within the doors, he ran boldly up to the wall, and cast himself down manfully among the thickest of them.

44 But they quickly giving back, and a space being made, he fell down into the midst of the void place.

45 Nevertheless, while there was yet breath within him, being inflamed with anger, he rose up; and though his blood gushed out like spouts of water, and his wounds were grievous, yet he ran through the midst of the throng; and standing upon a steep rock,

46 When as his blood was now quite gone, he plucked out his bowels, and taking them in both his hands, he cast them upon the throng, and calling upon the Lord of life and spirit to restore him those again, he thus died.

15 But Nicanor, hearing that Judas and his company were in the strong places about Samaria, resolved without any danger to set upon them on the sabbath day.

2 Nevertheless the Jews that were compelled to go with him said, O destroy not so cruelly and barbarously, but give honour to that day, which he, that seeth all things, hath honoured with holiness above *other days*.

3 Then the most ungracious wretch demanded, if there were a Mighty one in heaven, that had commanded the sabbath day to be kept.

4 And when they said, There is in heaven a living Lord, and mighty, who commanded the seventh day to be kept:

DOUAY OLD TESTAMENT

42 Choosing to die nobly rather than to fall into the hands of the wicked, and to suffer abuses unbecoming his noble birth.

43 But whereas through haste he missed of giving himself a sure wound, and the crowd was breaking into the doors, he ran boldly to the wall, and manfully threw himself down to the crowd:

44 But they quickly making room for his fall, he came upon the midst of the neck.

45 And as he had yet breath in him, being inflamed in mind he arose: and while his blood ran down with a great stream, and he was grievously wounded, he ran through the crowd:

46 And standing upon a steep rock, when he was now almost without blood, grasping his bowels with both hands, he cast them upon the throng, calling upon the Lord of life and spirit, to restore these to him again: and so he departed this life.

15 BUT when Nicanor understood that Judas was in the places of Samaria, he purposed to set upon him with all violence on the sabbath day.

2 And when the Jews that were constrained to follow him, said: Do not act so fiercely and barbarously, but give honour to the day that is sanctified: and reverence him that beholdeth all things:

3 That unhappy man asked, if there were a mighty One in heaven, that had commanded the sabbath day to be kept.

4 And when they answered: There is the living Lord himself in heaven, the mighty One, that commanded the seventh day to be kept,

KNOX TRANSLATION

better to die honourably than to fall into the hands of sinners,
and suffer outrage unworthy of a free-born man.[a] 43 The
hasty blow missed its aim; and now, with a rabble of men
pouring in through the doors he made gallantly for the outer
wall, and never hesitated to cast himself down, there in the
heart of the crowd. 44 You may be sure they made room for
his coming, and he fell on the very joints of his neck;[b] 45 yet,
breathing still, he rose to his feet undaunted; blood streaming
from his mortal wounds, he made his way through the press
of men, 46 till he stood on a sheer rock above them. And
there, for now he had no blood left in him, he laid hold of his
own entrails, and with both hands cast them into the crowd
beneath, calling upon the Lord, giver of life and breath, to
restore these same to his body; and so died.

15 When Nicanor was told, Judas was in the Samaritan
country, he would have pressed home the attack
against him, there and then, on the sabbath day. 2 But the
Jews gainsaid him; for there were Jews that fought, unwillingly enough, under his orders. What, said they, wouldst
thou fight beast-fashion, without mercy? This holy day
respect thou needs must, in his honour that is God all-seeing. 3 Why, where is he then, said the impious wretch, this
God who would have sabbath kept? In the heavens? 4 In
heaven he is, sure enough, they answered, the living Lord
our master, that gave orders the seventh day should be

a Some have attributed this action of Razias to a special inspiration; but we are at liberty to suppose he was not conscious of a divine law against self-destruction, and to admire his courage accordingly. *b* 'He fell on the very joints of his neck'; the Greek text may also be interpreted as meaning 'he fell in the midst of the empty space'.

TODAY'S ENGLISH VERSION

with honor rather than suffer humiliation at the hands of
evil men.
43 Under the pressure of the moment, Razis misjudged the
thrust of the sword, and it did not kill him. So, while the soldiers were swarming into the room, he rushed to the wall
and jumped off like a brave hero into the crowd below.
44 The crowd quickly moved back, and he fell in the space
they left. 45 Still alive, and burning with courage, he got up,
and with blood gushing from his wounds, he ran through
the crowd and finally climbed a steep rock. 46 Now completely drained of blood, he tore out his intestines with both
hands and threw them at the crowd, and as he did so, he
prayed for the Lord of life and breath to give them back to
him. That was how he died.
15 Nicanor learned that Judas and his men were in the
region of Samaria, and so he decided to attack them
on a Sabbath, when he could do so without any danger to
himself. 2 The Jews who were forced to accompany his army
begged him not to do such a cruel and savage thing, but to
respect the day that the all-seeing God had honored and
made the most holy of all days. 3 Then Nicanor, the lowest
creature on earth, asked if there was some sovereign ruler in
heaven who had commanded them to honor the Sabbath.
4 And the Jews replied, "Yes; the living Lord, who rules in
heaven, commanded us to honor the Sabbath."

NEW REVISED STANDARD VERSION

rather than to fall into the hands of sinners and suffer outrages unworthy of his noble birth. 43 But in the heat of the
struggle he did not hit exactly, and the crowd was now rushing in through the doors. He courageously ran up on the
wall, and bravely threw himself down into the crowd. 44 But
as they quickly drew back, a space opened and he fell in the
middle of the empty space. 45 Still alive and aflame with
anger, he rose, and though his blood gushed forth and his
wounds were severe he ran through the crowd; and standing
upon a steep rock, 46 with his blood now completely drained
from him, he tore out his entrails, took them in both hands
and hurled them at the crowd, calling upon the Lord of life
and spirit to give them back to him again. This was the manner of his death.
15 When Nicanor heard that Judas and his troops were
in the region of Samaria, he made plans to attack
them with complete safety on the day of rest. 2 When the
Jews who were compelled to follow him said, "Do not destroy
so savagely and barbarously, but show respect for the day
that he who sees all things has honored and hallowed above
other days," 3 the thrice-accursed wretch asked if there were
a sovereign in heaven who had commanded the keeping of
the sabbath day. 4 When they declared, "It is the living Lord
himself, the Sovereign in heaven, who ordered us to observe

NEW AMERICAN BIBLE

sword against himself, 42 preferring to die nobly rather than
fall into the hands of vile men and suffer outrages unworthy
of his noble birth. 43 In the excitement of the struggle he
failed to strike exactly. So while the troops rushed in through
the doors, he gallantly ran up to the top of the wall and with
manly courage threw himself down into the crowd. 44 But as
they quickly drew back and left an opening, he fell into the
middle of the empty space. 45 Still breathing, and inflamed
with anger, he got up and ran through the crowd, with blood
gushing from his frightful wounds. 46 Then, standing on a
steep rock, as he lost the last of his blood, he tore out his
entrails and flung them with both hands into the crowd, calling upon the LORD of life and of spirit to give these back to
him again. Such was the manner of his death.
15 When Nicanor learned that Judas and his companions were in the territory of Samaria, he decided to
attack them in all safety on the day of rest. 2 The Jews who
were forced to follow him pleaded, "Do not massacre them in
that way, like a savage barbarian, but show respect for the
day which the All-seeing has exalted with holiness above all
other days." 3 At this the thrice-sinful wretch asked if there
was a ruler in heaven who prescribed the keeping of the sabbath day. 4 When they replied that there was indeed such a
ruler in heaven, the living LORD himself, who commanded the

NEW JERUSALEM BIBLE

his own sword, 42 nobly resolving to die rather than fall into
the clutches of these villains and suffer outrages unworthy
of his noble birth. 43 But in the heat of conflict he missed his
thrust, and while the troops swarmed in through the doorways, he ran nimbly upstairs to the parapet and manfully
threw himself down among the troops. 44 But, as they immediately drew back, he fell into the middle of the empty space.
45 Still breathing, and blazing with anger, he struggled to his
feet, blood spurting in all directions, and despite his terrible
wounds ran right through the crowd; then, taking his stand
on a steep rock, 46 although he had now lost every drop of
blood, he tore out his entrails and taking them in both hands
flung them down on the crowd, calling on the Master of his
life and spirit to give them back to him one day. Thus he
died.
15 Nicanor heard that Judas and his men were in the
neighbourhood of Samaria, so he decided to attack
them, at no risk to himself, on the day of rest. 2 Those Jews
who had been compelled to follow him, said, 'Do not massacre them in such a savage, barbarous way. Respect the day
on which the All-seeing has conferred a special holiness.'
3 At this the triple-dyed scoundrel asked if there were in
heaven a sovereign who had ordered the keeping of the
Sabbath day. 4 When they answered, 'The living Lord himself, the Heavenly Sovereign, has ordered the observance of

GREEK OLD TESTAMENT

ἑβδομάδα· 5 ὁ δὲ ἕτερος Κἀγώ φησιν δυνάστης ἐπὶ τῆς γῆς
ὁ προστάσσων αἴρειν ὅπλα καὶ τὰς βασιλικὰς χρείας ἐπιτελεῖν. ὅμως οὐ κατέσχεν ἐπιτελέσαι τὸ σχέτλιον αὐτοῦ βού-
λημα.
6 Καὶ ὁ μὲν Νικάνωρ μετὰ πάσης ἀλαζονείας ὑψαυχενῶν
διεγνώκει κοινὸν τῶν περὶ τὸν Ιουδαν συστήσασθαι τρό-
παιον. 7 ὁ δὲ Μακκαβαῖος ἦν ἀδιαλείπτως πεποιθὼς μετὰ
πάσης ἐλπίδος ἀντιλήμψεως τεύξασθαι παρὰ τοῦ κυρίου
8 καὶ παρεκάλει τοὺς σὺν αὐτῷ μὴ δειλιᾶν τὴν τῶν ἐθνῶν
ἔφοδον ἔχοντας δὲ κατὰ νοῦν τὰ προγεγονότα αὐτοῖς ἀπ'
οὐρανοῦ βοηθήματα καὶ τὰ νῦν προσδοκᾶν τὴν παρὰ τοῦ
παντοκράτορος ἐσομένην αὐτοῖς νίκην. 9 καὶ παραμυθού-
μενος αὐτοὺς ἐκ τοῦ νόμου καὶ τῶν προφητῶν, προσυπομνή-
σας δὲ αὐτοὺς καὶ τοὺς ἀγῶνας, οὓς ἦσαν ἐκτετελεκότες,
προθυμοτέρους αὐτοὺς κατέστησεν. 10 καὶ τοῖς θυμοῖς
διεγείρας αὐτοὺς παρήγγειλεν ἅμα παρεπιδεικνὺς τὴν τῶν
ἐθνῶν ἀθεσίαν καὶ τὴν τῶν ὅρκων παράβασιν. 11 ἕκαστον δὲ
αὐτῶν καθοπλίσας οὐ τὴν ἀσπίδων καὶ λογχῶν ἀσφάλειαν,
ὡς τὴν ἐν τοῖς ἀγαθοῖς λόγοις παράκλησιν καὶ προσεξηγη-
σάμενος ὄνειρον ἀξιόπιστον ὕπαρ τι πάντας ηὔφρανεν.
12 ἦν δὲ ἡ τούτου θεωρία τοιάδε· Ονιαν τὸν γενόμενον
ἀρχιερέα, ἄνδρα καλὸν καὶ ἀγαθόν, αἰδήμονα μὲν τὴν ἀπάντησιν, πρᾶον δὲ τὸν τρόπον καὶ λαλιὰν προϊέμενον πρεπόν-
τως καὶ ἐκ παιδὸς ἐκμεμελετηκότα πάντα τὰ τῆς ἀρετῆς
οἰκεῖα, τοῦτον τὰς χεῖρας προτείναντα κατεύχεσθαι τῷ
παντὶ τῶν Ιουδαίων συστήματι. 13 εἶθ' οὕτως ἐπιφανῆναι

KING JAMES VERSION

5 Then said the other, And I also am mighty upon earth, and I command to take arms, and to do the king's business. Yet he obtained not to have his wicked will done.

6 So Nicanor in exceeding pride and haughtiness determined to set up a publick monument of his victory over Judas and them that were with him.

7 But Maccabeus had ever sure confidence that the Lord would help him:

8 Wherefore he exhorted his people not to fear the coming of the heathen against them, but to remember the help which in former times they had received from heaven, and now to expect the victory and aid, which should come unto them from the Almighty.

9 And so comforting them out of the law and the prophets, and withal putting them in mind of the battles that they won afore, he made them more cheerful.

10 And when he had stirred up their minds, he gave them their charge, shewing them therewithall the falsehood of the heathen, and the breach of oaths.

11 Thus he armed every one of them, not so much with defence of shields and spears, as with comfortable and good words: and beside that, he told them a dream worthy to be believed, as if it had been so indeed, which did not a little rejoice them.

12 And this was his vision: That Onias, who had been high priest, a virtuous and a good man, reverend in conversation, gentle in condition, well spoken also, and exercised from a child in all points of virtue, holding up his hands prayed for the whole body of the Jews.

DOUAY OLD TESTAMENT

5 Then he said: And I am mighty upon the earth, and I command to take arms, and to do the king's business. Nevertheless he prevailed not to accomplish his design.

6 So Nicanor being puffed up with exceeding great pride, thought to set up a public monument of his victory over Judas.

7 But Machabeus ever trusted with all hope that God would help them.

8 And he exhorted his people not to fear the coming of the nations, but to remember the help they had before received from heaven, and now to hope for victory from the Almighty.

9 And speaking to them out of the law, and the prophets, and withal putting them in mind of the battles they had fought before, he made them more cheerful:

10 Then after he had encouraged them, he shewed withal the falsehood of the Gentiles, and their breach of oaths.

11 So he armed every one of them, not with defence of shield and spear, but with very good speeches and exhortations, and told them a dream worthy to be believed, whereby he rejoiced them all.

12 Now the vision was in this manner: Onias who had been high priest, a good and virtuous man, modest in his looks, gentle in his manners, and graceful in his speech, and who from a child was exercised in virtues, holding up his hands, prayed for all the people of the Jews:

KNOX TRANSLATION

observed. 5 So be it, said he, and I am your master on earth,
and my orders are, To arms, and despatch the king's business! Yet carry out his design they would not.
6 Such an empty braggart was this Nicanor, he thought to
make a single victory of it, over all the Jews at once;
7 Machabaeus on his side kept ever his confidence, yet with
the sure hope, God would bring him aid. 8 And for his men
he had the same encouragement; let them never be daunted
by the onslaught of the heathen, but rather bethink them of
heaven's mercies in time past, and look to God Omnipotent
for victory. 9 Of the law and the prophets he spoke to them,
and reminded them of their old battles, till all were eager for
the fight; 10 nor was it enough to arouse their ardour; he
shewed them, too, how treacherous the heathen had proved,
and how forsworn. 11 Thus it was his care to arm them, not
with shield or spear for their defence, but with excellent
words of good cheer.
A dream of his he told them, most worthy of credence,
that brought comfort to one and all. 12 And what saw he?
Onias, that had once been high priest, appeared to him; an
excellent good man this, modest of mien, courteous, well-
spoken, and from his boyhood schooled in all the virtues.
With hands outstretched, he stood there praying for the

TODAY'S ENGLISH VERSION

5 But Nicanor answered, "I am the ruler on earth, and I order you to take up your weapons and to do what the king commands." However, he did not succeed in carrying out his cruel plan.

6 In his arrogance Nicanor had boasted that he would set up a monument in honor of his victory over Judas. 7 But Judas was fully confident that the Lord would help him, 8 so he urged his men not to be afraid of the enemy. He encouraged them to remember how the Almighty had helped them in times past and to rest assured that he would give them victory this time also. 9 He renewed their hope by reading to them from the Law and the Prophets and by reminding them of the battles they had already won. 10 When his men were ready for battle, he gave them their orders and at the same time pointed out how the Gentiles could not be trusted, because they never kept their treaties. 11 He armed all his men, not by encouraging them to trust in shields and spears, but by inspiring them with courageous words. He also lifted their morale by telling them about his dream, a kind of vision that they could trust in.

12 He told them that he had seen a vision of Onias, the former High Priest, that great and wonderful man of humble and gentle disposition, who was an outstanding orator and who had been taught from childhood how to live a virtuous life. With outstretched arms Onias was praying for the entire

NEW REVISED STANDARD VERSION

the seventh day," 5 he replied, "But I am a sovereign also, on earth, and I command you to take up arms and finish the king's business." Nevertheless, he did not succeed in carrying out his abominable design.

6 This Nicanor in his utter boastfulness and arrogance had determined to erect a public monument of victory over Judas and his forces. 7 But Maccabeus did not cease to trust with all confidence that he would get help from the Lord. 8 He exhorted his troops not to fear the attack of the Gentiles, but to keep in mind the former times when help had come to them from heaven, and so to look for the victory that the Almighty would give them. 9 Encouraging them from the law and the prophets, and reminding them also of the struggles they had won, he made them the more eager. 10 When he had aroused their courage, he issued his orders, at the same time pointing out the perfidy of the Gentiles and their violation of oaths. 11 He armed each of them not so much with confidence in shields and spears as with the inspiration of brave words, and he cheered them all by relating a dream, a sort of vision,[a] which was worthy of belief.

12 What he saw was this: Onias, who had been high priest, a noble and good man, of modest bearing and gentle manner, one who spoke fittingly and had been trained from childhood in all that belongs to excellence, was praying with outstretched hands for the whole body of the Jews. 13 Then

a Meaning of Gk uncertain

NEW AMERICAN BIBLE

observance of the sabbath day, 5 he said, "I, on my part, am ruler on earth, and my orders are that you take up arms and carry out the king's business." Nevertheless he did not succeed in carrying out his cruel plan.

6 In his utter boastfulness and arrogance Nicanor had determined to erect a public monument of victory over Judas and his men. 7 But Maccabeus remained confident, fully convinced that he would receive help from the LORD. 8 He urged his men not to fear the enemy, but mindful of the help they had received from Heaven in the past, to expect that now, too, victory would be given them by the Almighty. 9 By encouraging them with words from the law and the prophets, and by reminding them of the battles they had already won, he filled them with fresh enthusiasm. 10 Having stirred up their courage, he gave his orders and pointed out at the same time the perfidy of the Gentiles and their violation of oaths. 11 When he had armed each of them, not so much with the safety of shield and spear as with the encouragement of noble words, he cheered them all by relating a dream, a kind of vision, worthy of belief.

12 What he saw was this: Onias, the former high priest, a good and virtuous man, modest in appearance, gentle in manners, distinguished in speech, and trained from childhood in every virtuous practice, was praying with outstretched arms for the whole Jewish community. 13 Then in

NEW JERUSALEM BIBLE

the seventh day,' 5 he retorted, 'And I, as sovereign on earth, order you to take up arms and do the king's business.' For all that, he did not manage to carry out his wicked plan.

6 While Nicanor, in his unlimited boastfulness and pride, was planning to erect a general trophy with the spoils taken from Judas and his men, 7 Maccabaeus remained firm in his confident conviction that the Lord would stand by him. 8 He urged his men not to be dismayed by the foreigners' attacks but, keeping in mind the help that had come to them from Heaven in the past, to be confident that this time too victory would be theirs with the help of the Almighty. 9 He put fresh heart into them by citing the Law and the Prophets and, by stirring up memories of the battles they had already won, he filled them with new enthusiasm. 10 Having thus aroused their courage, he ended his exhortation by demonstrating the treachery of the foreigners and how they had violated their oaths.

11 Having armed each one of them not so much with the safety given by shield and lance as with that confidence which springs from noble language, he encouraged them all by describing to them a convincing dream—a vision, as it were. 12 What he had seen was this: Onias, the former high priest, that paragon of men, modest of bearing and gentle of manners, suitably eloquent and trained from boyhood in the practice of every virtue—Onias was stretching out his hands and praying for the whole Jewish community. 13 Next, there

GREEK OLD TESTAMENT

ἄνδρα πολιᾷ καὶ δόξῃ διαφέροντα, θαυμαστὴν δέ τινα καὶ
μεγαλοπρεπεστάτην εἶναι τὴν περὶ αὐτὸν ὑπεροχήν. [14] ἀπο-
κριθέντα δὲ τὸν Ονιαν εἰπεῖν Ὁ φιλάδελφος οὗτός ἐστιν ὁ
πολλὰ προσευχόμενος περὶ τοῦ λαοῦ καὶ τῆς ἁγίας πόλεως
Ιερεμιας ὁ τοῦ θεοῦ προφήτης. [15] προτείναντα δὲ Ιερεμιαν
τὴν δεξιὰν παραδοῦναι τῷ Ιουδα ῥομφαίαν χρυσῆν, διδόντα
δὲ προσφωνῆσαι τάδε [16] Λαβὲ τὴν ἁγίαν ῥομφαίαν δῶρον
παρὰ τοῦ θεοῦ, δι᾽ ἧς θραύσεις τοὺς ὑπεναντίους.

[17] Παρακληθέντες δὲ τοῖς Ιουδου λόγοις πάνυ καλοῖς καὶ
δυναμένοις ἐπ᾽ ἀρετὴν παρορμῆσαι καὶ ψυχὰς νέων ἐπαν-
δρῶσαι διέγνωσαν μὴ στρατεύεσθαι, γενναίως δὲ ἐμφέρε-
σθαι καὶ μετὰ πάσης εὐανδρίας ἐμπλακέντες κρῖναι τὰ πράγματα διὰ τὸ καὶ τὴν πόλιν καὶ τὰ ἅγια καὶ τὸ ἱερὸν
κινδυνεύειν· [18] ἦν γὰρ ὁ περὶ γυναικῶν καὶ τέκνων, ἔτι δὲ
ἀδελφῶν καὶ συγγενῶν ἐν ἥττονι μέρει κείμενος αὐτοῖς, μέ-
γιστος δὲ καὶ πρῶτος ὁ περὶ τοῦ καθηγιασμένου ναοῦ φόβος.
[19] ἦν δὲ καὶ τοῖς ἐν τῇ πόλει κατειλημμένοις οὐ πάρεργος
ἀγωνία ταρασσομένοις τῆς ἐν ὑπαίθρῳ προσβολῆς. [20] καὶ
πάντων ἤδη προσδοκώντων τὴν ἐσομένην κρίσιν καὶ ἤδη
προσμειξάντων τῶν πολεμίων καὶ τῆς στρατιᾶς ἐκταγείσης
καὶ τῶν θηρίων ἐπὶ μέρος εὔκαιρον ἀποκατασταθέντων τῆς
τε ἵππου κατὰ κέρας τεταγμένης [21] συνιδὼν ὁ Μακκαβαῖος
τὴν τῶν πληθῶν παρουσίαν καὶ τῶν ὅπλων τὴν ποικίλην
παρασκευὴν τήν τε τῶν θηρίων ἀγριότητα ἀνατείνας τὰς
χεῖρας εἰς τὸν οὐρανὸν ἐπεκαλέσατο τὸν τερατοποιὸν κύριον

KING JAMES VERSION

13 This done, in like manner there appeared a man with gray hairs, and exceeding glorious, who was of a wonderful and excellent majesty.

14 Then Onias answered, saying, This is a lover of the brethren, who prayeth much for the people, and for the holy city, *to wit,* Jeremias the prophet of God.

15 Whereupon Jeremias holding forth his right hand gave to Judas a sword of gold, and in giving it spake thus,

16 Take this holy sword, a gift from God, with the which thou shalt wound the adversaries.

17 Thus being well comforted by the words of Judas, which were very good, and able to stir them up to valour, and to encourage the hearts of the young men, they determined not to pitch camp, but courageously to set upon them, and manfully to try the matter by conflict, because the city and the sanctuary and the temple were in danger.

18 For the care that they took for their wives, and their children, their brethren, and kinsfolks, was in least account with them: but the greatest and principal fear was for the holy temple.

19 Also they that were in the city took not the least care, being troubled for the conflict abroad.

20 And now, when as all looked what should be the trial, and the enemies were already come near, and the army was set in array, and the beasts conveniently placed, and the horsemen set in wings,

21 Maccabeus seeing the coming of the multitude, and the divers preparations of armour, and the fierceness of the beasts, stretched out his hands toward heaven, and called

DOUAY OLD TESTAMENT

13 After this there appeared also another man, admirable for age, and glory, and environed with great beauty and majesty:

14 Then Onias answering, said: This is a lover of his brethren, and of the people of Israel: this is he that prayeth much for the people, and for all the holy city, Jeremias the prophet of God.

15 Whereupon Jeremias stretched forth his right hand, and gave to Judas a sword of gold, saying:

16 Take this holy sword a gift from God, wherewith thou shalt overthrow the adversaries of my people Israel.

17 Thus being exhorted with the words of Judas, which were very good, and proper to stir up the courage, and strengthen the hearts of the young men, they resolved to fight, and to set upon them manfully: that valour might decide the matter, because the holy city and the temple were in danger.

18 For their concern was less for their wives, and children, and for their brethren, and kinsfolks: but their greatest and principal fear was for the holiness of the temple.

19 And they also that were in the city, had no little concern for them that were to be engaged in battle.

20 And now when all expected what judgment would be given, and the enemies were at hand, and the army was set in array, the beasts and the horsemen ranged in convenient places,

21 Machabeus considering the coming of the multitude, and the divers preparations of armour, and the fierceness of the beasts, stretching out his hands to heaven, called upon

KNOX TRANSLATION

Jewish folk. [13] Then he was ware of another, a man of great
age and reverence, nothing about him but was most wor-
shipful; [14] who this might be, Onias told him forthwith: Here
is one that loves our brethren, the people of Israel, well; one
that for Israel and for every stone of the holy city prays
much; God's prophet Jeremias. [15] And with that, Jeremias
reached forward to Judas, and gave him a golden sword;
[16] This holy sword take thou, he said, God's gift; this wielding, all the enemies of my people Israel thou shalt lay low.

[17] A most noble harangue, and one very apt to rouse the
emulation of his followers, and to stiffen their courage. No
wonder if they resolved they would put it to the touch, and
manfully engage the enemy; valour should decide all. Was
not the holy city, was not the temple itself in jeopardy?
[18] For wives and children, for brethren and kindred, their
concern was less; of the perils they dreaded, profanation of
the temple was first and foremost. [19] And what of those who
were left in the city? No common anxiety they felt for these
others that were going into battle. [20] Now was the hour of
decision; the enemy was at the gates, drawn up in full array;
here were the elephants, here was the cavalry, posted at
points of vantage. [21] Judas, when he saw the number of his
assailants, how manifold were their appointments, how
fierce the temper of the beasts, was fain to lift hands heavenward, and to the Lord make his appeal; the Lord, that is

TODAY'S ENGLISH VERSION

Jewish nation. 13 Judas then saw an impressive white-haired man of great dignity and authority. 14 Onias said: "This is God's prophet Jeremiah, who loves the Jewish people and offers many prayers for us and for Jerusalem, the holy city."

15 Then Jeremiah stretched out his right hand and gave Judas a gold sword, saying as he did so, 16 "This holy sword is a gift from God. Take it and destroy your enemies."

17 The eloquent words that Judas spoke encouraged everyone to be brave, and inspired boys to fight like men. Their city, their religion, and their Temple were in danger. So the Jews made up their minds not to waste any time, but to make a daring attack against the enemy and bravely decide their fate in hand-to-hand combat. 18 They were not so concerned about their own families and relatives as they were about their sacred Temple. 19 And the people who had to stay in Jerusalem were deeply concerned about how a battle on open ground would turn out.

20 Everyone was waiting to see who would win the battle. The enemy troops were already moving forward, with their cavalry on each side of them, and their elephants placed in strategic positions. 21 Judas Maccabeus looked at the huge enemy force, the variety of their weapons, and their fierce elephants. Then he raised his hands toward heaven and prayed to the Lord, who works miracles, because he knew

NEW REVISED STANDARD VERSION

in the same fashion another appeared, distinguished by his gray hair and dignity, and of marvelous majesty and authority. 14 And Onias spoke, saying, "This is a man who loves the family of Israel and prays much for the people and the holy city—Jeremiah, the prophet of God." 15 Jeremiah stretched out his right hand and gave to Judas a golden sword, and as he gave it he addressed him thus: 16 "Take this holy sword, a gift from God, with which you will strike down your adversaries."

17 Encouraged by the words of Judas, so noble and so effective in arousing valor and awaking courage in the souls of the young, they determined not to carry on a campaign[a] but to attack bravely, and to decide the matter by fighting hand to hand with all courage, because the city and the sanctuary and the temple were in danger. 18 Their concern for wives and children, and also for brothers and sisters[b] and relatives, lay upon them less heavily; their greatest and first fear was for the consecrated sanctuary. 19 And those who had to remain in the city were in no little distress, being anxious over the encounter in the open country.

20 When all were now looking forward to the coming issue, and the enemy was already close at hand with their army drawn up for battle, the elephants[c] strategically stationed and the cavalry deployed on the flanks, 21 Maccabeus, observing the masses that were in front of him and the varied supply of arms and the savagery of the elephants, stretched out his hands toward heaven and called upon the

a Or *to remain in camp* *b* Gk *for brothers* *c* Gk *animals*

NEW AMERICAN BIBLE

the same way another man appeared, distinguished by his white hair and dignity, and with an air about him of extraordinary, majestic authority. 14 Onias then said of him, "This is God's prophet Jeremiah, who loves his brethren and fervently prays for his people and their holy city." 15 Stretching out his right hand, Jeremiah presented a gold sword to Judas. As he gave it to him he said, 16 "Accept this holy sword as a gift from God; with it you shall crush your adversaries."

17 Encouraged by Judas' noble words, which had power to instill valor and stir young hearts to courage, the Jews determined not to delay, but to charge gallantly and decide the issue by hand-to-hand combat with the utmost courage, since their city and its temple with the sacred vessels were in danger. 18 They were not so much concerned about their wives and children or their brothers and kinsmen; their first and foremost fear was for the consecrated sanctuary. 19 Those who remained in the city suffered a like agony, anxious as they were about the battle in the open country.

20 Everyone now awaited the decisive moment. The enemy were already drawing near with their troops drawn up in battle line, their elephants placed in strategic positions, and their cavalry stationed on the flanks. 21 Maccabeus, contemplating the hosts before him, their elaborate equipment, and the fierceness of their elephants, stretched out his hands toward heaven and called upon the LORD who works

NEW JERUSALEM BIBLE

appeared a man equally remarkable for his great age and dignity and invested with a marvellous and impressive air of majesty. 14 Onias began to speak: 'This is a man', he said, 'who loves his brothers and prays much for the people and the holy city—Jeremiah, the prophet of God.' 15 Jeremiah then stretched out his right hand and presented Judas with a golden sword, saying as he gave it, 16 'Take this holy sword as a gift from God; with it you will shatter the enemy.'

17 Encouraged by the noble words of Judas, which had the power to inspire valour and give the young the spirit of mature men, they decided not to entrench themselves in a camp, but bravely to take the offensive and, in hand-to-hand fighting, to commit the result to the fortune of war, since the city, their holy religion and the Temple were in danger. 18 Their concern for their wives and children, their brothers and relatives, had shrunk to minute importance; their chief and greatest fear was for the consecrated Temple. 19 Those left behind in the city felt a similar anxiety, alarmed as they were about the forthcoming encounter in the open country. 20 Everyone now awaited the coming issue. The enemy had already concentrated their forces and stood formed up in order of battle, with the elephants drawn up in a strategic position and the cavalry disposed on the wings. 21 Maccabaeus took note of these masses confronting him, the glittering array of armour and the fierce aspect of the elephants; then, raising his hands to heaven, he called on the

GREEK OLD TESTAMENT

γινώσκων ὅτι οὐκ ἔστιν δι᾽ ὅπλων, καθὼς δὲ ἐὰν αὐτῷ κριθῇ,
τοῖς ἀξίοις περιποιεῖται τὴν νίκην. 22 ἔλεγεν δὲ ἐπικαλούμενος τόνδε τὸν τρόπον Σύ, δέσποτα, ἀπέστειλας τὸν
ἄγγελόν σου ἐπὶ Εζεκιου τοῦ βασιλέως τῆς Ιουδαίας, καὶ
ἀνεῖλεν ἐκ τῆς παρεμβολῆς Σενναχηριμ εἰς ἑκατὸν ὀγδοήκοντα πέντε χιλιάδας. 23 καὶ νῦν, δυνάστα τῶν οὐρανῶν,
ἀπόστειλον ἄγγελον ἀγαθὸν ἔμπροσθεν ἡμῶν εἰς δέος καὶ
τρόμον· 24 μεγέθει βραχίονός σου καταπλαγείησαν οἱ μετὰ
βλασφημίας παραγινόμενοι ἐπὶ τὸν ἅγιόν σου λαόν. καὶ
οὗτος μὲν ἐν τούτοις ἔληξεν.

25 Οἱ δὲ περὶ τὸν Νικάνορα μετὰ σαλπίγγων καὶ παιάνων
προσῆγον. 26 οἱ δὲ περὶ τὸν Ιουδαν μετὰ ἐπικλήσεως καὶ
εὐχῶν συνέμειξαν τοῖς πολεμίοις. 27 καὶ ταῖς μὲν χερσὶν
ἀγωνιζόμενοι, ταῖς δὲ καρδίαις πρὸς τὸν θεὸν εὐχόμενοι
κατέστρωσαν οὐδὲν ἧττον μυριάδων τριῶν καὶ πεντακισχιλίων τῇ τοῦ θεοῦ μεγάλως εὐφρανθέντες ἐπιφανείᾳ. 28 γενόμενοι δὲ ἀπὸ τῆς χρείας καὶ μετὰ χαρᾶς ἀναλύοντες ἐπέγνωσαν προπεπτωκότα Νικάνορα σὺν τῇ πανοπλίᾳ. 29 γενομένης δὲ κραυγῆς καὶ ταραχῆς εὐλόγουν τὸν δυνάστην τῇ
πατρίῳ φωνῇ. 30 καὶ προσέταξεν ὁ καθ᾽ ἅπαν σώματι καὶ
ψυχῇ πρωταγωνιστὴς ὑπὲρ τῶν πολιτῶν ὁ τὴν τῆς ἡλικίας
εὔνοιαν εἰς ὁμοεθνεῖς διαφυλάξας τὴν τοῦ Νικάνορος
κεφαλὴν ἀποτεμόντας καὶ τὴν χεῖρα σὺν τῷ ὤμῳ φέρειν εἰς

KING JAMES VERSION

upon the Lord that worketh wonders, knowing that victory
cometh not by arms, but even as it seemeth good to him, he
giveth it to such as are worthy:

22 Therefore in his prayer he said after this manner; O
Lord, thou didst send thine angel in the time of Ezekias king
of Judea, and didst slay in the host of Sennacherib an hundred fourscore and five thousand:

23 Wherefore now also, O Lord of heaven, send a good
angel before us for a fear and dread unto them;

24 And through the might of thine arm let those be strick-
en with terror, that come against thy holy people to blaspheme. And he ended thus.

25 Then Nicanor and they that were with him came forward with trumpets and songs.

26 But Judas and his company encountered the enemies
with invocation and prayer.

27 So that fighting with their hands, and praying unto
God with their hearts, they slew no less than thirty and five
thousand men: for through the appearance of God they were
greatly cheered.

28 Now when the battle was done, returning again with
joy, they knew that Nicanor lay dead in his harness.

29 Then they made a great shout and a noise, praising the
Almighty in their own language.

30 And *Judas,* who was ever the chief defender of the citizens both in body and mind, and who continued his love
toward his countrymen all his life, commanded to strike off
Nicanor's head, and his hand with his shoulder, and bring
them to Jerusalem.

DOUAY OLD TESTAMENT

the Lord, that worketh wonders, who giveth victory to them
that are worthy, not according to the power of their arms,
but according as it seemeth good to him.

22 And in his prayer he said after this manner: Thou, O
Lord, who didst send thy angel in the time of Ezechias king
of Juda, and didst kill a hundred and eighty-five thousand of
the army of Sennacherib:

23 Send now also, O Lord of heaven, thy good angel
before us, for the fear and dread of the greatness of thy arm,

24 That they may be afraid, who come with blasphemy
against thy holy people. And thus he concluded his prayer.

25 But Nicanor, and they that were with him came forward, with trumpets and songs.

26 But Judas, and they that were with him, encountered
them, calling upon God by prayers:

27 So fighting with their hands, but praying to the Lord
with their hearts, they slew no less than five and thirty thousand, being greatly cheered with the presence of God.

28 And when the battle was over, and they were returning
with joy, they understood that Nicanor was slain in his
armour.

29 Then making a shout, and a great noise, they blessed
the Almighty Lord in their own language.

30 And Judas, who was altogether ready, in body and
mind, to die for his countrymen, commanded that Nicanor's
head, and his hand with the shoulder should be cut off, and
carried to Jerusalem.

KNOX TRANSLATION

wondrous in his doings, and at his own pleasure crowns
right, not might, with victory. 22 And this was the manner of
his praying: Lord, in the days of Ezechias thou didst send
thy angel, and take toll of a hundred and eighty-five thousand in the camp of Sennacherib! 23 Ruler of heaven, some
friendly angel of thine this day escort us; 24 dread and dismay let thy outstretched hand inspire, to the confusion of
yonder blasphemers that levy war on thy holy people! And so
he brought his prayer to an end.

25 By this, Nicanor's army was coming forward to the
attack, with blowing of trumpets and with songs of battle.
26 But Judas and his company went to meet them calling still
upon God for his succour; 27 and ever while hand fought,
heart prayed. Such joy had they of God's present assistance,
they cut down a full thirty-five thousand of the enemy;
28 when they let be, and returned in triumph from the pursuit, news greeted them Nicanor himself had armed for the
fight, and lay there dead. 29 What a cry was then raised,
what a stir, what hymns they sang, in the speech of their
own country, to God Omnipotent!

30 And Judas? Not for nothing had he devoted body and
soul, this long while, to the service of his fellow countrymen!
Nicanor's head, and one of his arms cut off from the shoulder downwards, he bade them carry to Jerusalem; 31 and

TODAY'S ENGLISH VERSION

that the Lord gives victory to those who deserve it, not to
those who have a strong army. 22 Judas said: "Lord, when
Hezekiah was king of Judah, you sent your angel, who killed
185,000 of King Sennacherib's men. 23 Now once again,
Lord of heaven, send your good angel to make our enemies
shake and tremble with fear. 24 With your great power,
destroy these people who have slandered you and have come
out to attack your chosen people." So Judas ended his prayer.
25 Nicanor and his army moved forward to the sound of
trumpets and battle songs, 26 but Judas and his men went
into battle calling on God for help. 27 So by fighting with
their hands and praying to God in their hearts, the Jews
killed more than 35,000 of the enemy. How grateful they
were for the help they had received from God! 28 When the
battle was over and they were going home celebrating their
victory, they noticed Nicanor in full armor lying dead on the
battlefield. 29 Then with loud shouts they praised the Lord in
their native language.
30 Judas Maccabeus, who had always fought with all his
body and soul for his own people, never losing the patriotism of his youth, ordered his men to cut off Nicanor's head
and right arm and to take them to Jerusalem. 31 When they

NEW REVISED STANDARD VERSION

Lord who works wonders; for he knew that it is not by arms,
but as the Lord[a] decides, that he gains the victory for those
who deserve it. 22 He called upon him in these words:
"O Lord, you sent your angel in the time of King Hezekiah of
Judea, and he killed fully one hundred eighty-five thousand
in the camp of Sennacherib. 23 So now, O Sovereign of the
heavens, send a good angel to spread terror and trembling
before us. 24 By the might of your arm may these blasphemers who come against your holy people be struck
down." With these words he ended his prayer.
25 Nicanor and his troops advanced with trumpets and
battle songs, 26 but Judas and his troops met the enemy in
battle with invocations to God and prayers. 27 So, fighting
with their hands and praying to God in their hearts, they laid
low at least thirty-five thousand, and were greatly gladdened
by God's manifestation.
28 When the action was over and they were returning
with joy, they recognized Nicanor, lying dead, in full armor.
29 Then there was shouting and tumult, and they blessed the
Sovereign Lord in the language of their ancestors. 30 Then
the man who was ever in body and soul the defender of his
people, the man who maintained his youthful goodwill
toward his compatriots, ordered them to cut off Nicanor's
head and arm and carry them to Jerusalem. 31 When he
arrived there and had called his compatriots together and
stationed the priests before the altar, he sent for those who

a Gk *he*

NEW AMERICAN BIBLE

miracles; for he knew that it is not through arms but through
the LORD's decision that victory is won by those who deserve
it. 22 He prayed to him thus: "You, O LORD, sent your angel
in the days of King Hezekiah of Judea, and he slew a hundred and eighty-five thousand men of Sennacherib's army.
23 Sovereign of the heavens, send a good angel now to spread
fear and dread before us. 24 By the might of your arm may
those be struck down who have blasphemously come against
your holy people!" With this he ended his prayer.
25 Nicanor and his men advanced to the sound of trumpets
and battle songs. 26 But Judas and his men met the army
with supplication and prayers. 27 Fighting with their hands
and praying to God with their hearts, they laid low at least
thirty-five thousand, and rejoiced greatly over this manifestation of God's power. 28 When the battle was over and they
were joyfully departing, they discovered Nicanor lying there
in all his armor; 29 so they raised tumultuous shouts in their
native tongue in praise of the divine Sovereign.
30 Then Judas, who was ever in body and soul the chief
defender of his fellow citizens, and had maintained from
youth his affection for his countrymen, ordered Nicanor's
head and whole right arm to be cut off and taken to

NEW JERUSALEM BIBLE

Lord who works miracles, in the knowledge that it is not by
force of arms but as he sees fit to decide, that victory is
granted by him to such as deserve it. 22 His prayer was
worded thus: 'You, Master, sent your angel in the days of
Hezekiah king of Judaea, and he destroyed no less than one
hundred and eighty-five thousand of Sennacherib's army;
23 now, once again, Sovereign of heaven, send a good angel
before us to spread terror and dismay. 24 May these men be
struck down by the might of your arm, since they have come
with blasphemy on their lips to attack your holy people.' And
on these words he finished.
25[a] Nicanor and his men advanced to the sound of trumpets and war songs, 26 but the men of Judas closed with the
enemy uttering invocations and prayers. 27 Fighting with
their hands and praying to God in their hearts, they cut
down at least thirty-five thousand men and were greatly
cheered by this manifestation of God. 28 When the engagement was over and they were withdrawing in triumph, they
recognised Nicanor, lying dead in full armour.
29 With shouting and confusion all around, they blessed
the sovereign Master in their ancestral tongue. 30 He who, as
protagonist, had devoted himself, body and soul, to his fellow-citizens, and had preserved the love he felt even in youth
for those of his own race, gave orders for Nicanor's head to
be cut off, with his arm up to the shoulder, and taken to

a **15** 15:25seq. // 1 M 7:43–50.

GREEK OLD TESTAMENT

Ιεροσόλυμα. 31 παραγενόμενος δὲ ἐκεῖ καὶ συγκαλέσας τοὺς
ὁμοεθνεῖς καὶ τοὺς ἱερεῖς πρὸ τοῦ θυσιαστηρίου στήσας
μετεπέμψατο τοὺς ἐκ τῆς ἄκρας. 32 καὶ ἐπιδειξάμενος τὴν
τοῦ μιαροῦ Νικάνορος κεφαλὴν καὶ τὴν χεῖρα τοῦ δυσφήμου,
ἣν ἐκτείνας ἐπὶ τὸν ἅγιον τοῦ παντοκράτορος οἶκον ἐμεγαλαύχησεν, 33 καὶ τὴν γλῶσσαν τοῦ δυσσεβοῦς Νικάνορος ἐκ-
τεμὼν ἔφη κατὰ μέρος δώσειν τοῖς ὀρνέοις, τὰ δ᾽ ἐπίχειρα
τῆς ἀνοίας κατέναντι τοῦ ναοῦ κρεμάσαι. 34 οἱ δὲ πάντες
εἰς τὸν οὐρανὸν εὐλόγησαν τὸν ἐπιφανῆ κύριον λέγοντες
Εὐλογητὸς ὁ διατηρήσας τὸν ἑαυτοῦ τόπον ἀμίαντον.
35 ἐξέδησεν δὲ τὴν τοῦ Νικάνορος προτομὴν ἐκ τῆς ἄκρας
ἐπίδηλον πᾶσιν καὶ φανερὸν τῆς τοῦ κυρίου βοηθείας
σημεῖον. 36 ἐδογμάτισαν δὲ πάντες μετὰ κοινοῦ ψηφί-
σματος μηδαμῶς ἐᾶσαι ἀπαρασήμαντον τήνδε τὴν ἡμέραν,
ἔχειν δὲ ἐπίσημον τὴν τρισκαιδεκάτην τοῦ δωδεκάτου μηνὸς
— Αδαρ λέγεται τῇ Συριακῇ φωνῇ — πρὸ μιᾶς ἡμέρας τῆς
Μαρδοχαϊκῆς ἡμέρας.
37 Τῶν οὖν κατὰ Νικάνορα χωρησάντων οὕτως καὶ ἀπ᾽
ἐκείνων τῶν καιρῶν κρατηθείσης τῆς πόλεως ὑπὸ τῶν Εβραίων καὶ αὐτὸς αὐτόθι τὸν λόγον καταπαύσω. 38 καὶ εἰ μὲν
καλῶς εὐθίκτως τῇ συντάξει, τοῦτο καὶ αὐτὸς ἤθελον· εἰ δὲ
εὐτελῶς καὶ μετρίως, τοῦτο ἐφικτὸν ἦν μοι. 39 καθάπερ γὰρ
οἶνον κατὰ μόνας πίνειν, ὡσαύτως δὲ καὶ ὕδωρ πάλιν πο-
λέμιον· ὃν δὲ τρόπον οἶνος ὕδατι συγκερασθεὶς ἡδὺς καὶ
ἐπιτερπῆ τὴν χάριν ἀποτελεῖ, οὕτως καὶ τὸ τῆς κατασκευῆς
τοῦ λόγου τέρπει τὰς ἀκοὰς τῶν ἐντυγχανόντων τῇ συντάξει. ἐνταῦθα δὲ ἔσται ἡ τελευτή.

KING JAMES VERSION

31 So when he was there, and had called them of his nation together, and set the priests before the altar, he sent for them that were of the tower,

32 And shewed them vile Nicanor's head, and the hand of that blasphemer, which with proud brags he had stretched out against the holy temple of the Almighty.

33 And when he had cut out the tongue of that ungodly Nicanor, he commanded that they should give it by pieces unto the fowls, and hang up the reward of his madness before the temple.

34 So every man praised toward the heaven the glorious Lord, saying, Blessed be he that hath kept his own place undefiled.

35 He hanged also Nicanor's head upon the tower, an evident and manifest sign unto all of the help of the Lord.

36 And they ordained all with a common decree in no case to let that day pass without solemnity, but to celebrate the thirteenth day of the twelfth month, which in the Syrian tongue is called Adar, the day before Mardocheus' day.

37 Thus went it with Nicanor: and from that time forth the Hebrews had the city in their power. And here will I make an end.

38 And if *I have done* well, and as is fitting the story, it is that which I desired: but if slenderly and meanly, it is that which I could attain unto.

39 For as it is hurtful to drink wine or water alone; and as wine mingled with water is pleasant, and delighteth the taste: even so speech finely framed delighteth the ears of them that read the story. And here shall be an end.

DOUAY OLD TESTAMENT

31 And when he was come thither, having called together his countrymen, and the priests to the altar, he sent also for them that were in the castle,

32 And shewing them the head of Nicanor, and the wicked hand, which he had stretched out, with proud boasts, against the holy house of the Almighty God,

33 He commanded also, that the tongue of the wicked Nicanor, should be cut out and given by pieces to birds, and the hand of the furious man to be hanged up over against the temple.

34 Then all blessed the Lord of heaven, saying: Blessed be he that hath kept his own place undefiled.

35 And he hung up Nicanor's head in the top of the castle, that it might be an evident and manifest sign of the help of God.

36 And they all ordained by a common decree, by no means to let this day pass without solemnity:

37 But to celebrate the thirteenth day of the month of Adar, called, in the Syrian language, the day before Mardochias' day.

38 So these things being done with relation to Nicanor, and from that time the city being possessed by the Hebrews, I also will here make an end of my narration.

39 Which if I have done well, and as it becometh the history, it is what I desired: but if not so perfectly, it must be pardoned me.

40 For as it is hurtful to drink always wine, or always water, but pleasant to use sometimes the one, and sometimes the other: so if the speech be always nicely framed, it will not be grateful to the readers. But here it shall be ended.

KNOX TRANSLATION

there he called the tribesmen together, ranged the priests
about the altar, and sent his summons to the heathen that
garrisoned the citadel. 32 Head and hand he shewed them of
the godless Nicanor, the hand that was stretched out so
boastfully against the holy temple of the Almighty, 33 bidding them cut the blaspheming tongue in pieces and cast it
to the birds, nail the rash hand to the temple's face. 34 None
but praised the Lord of heaven at the sight; Blessed be the
Lord, they cried, that has kept his house undefiled still! 35 As
for Nicanor's head, Judas hung it at the top of the citadel, to
be a clear and evident token, how God gives aid. 36 And all
with one consent made a decree, never should that day pass
unobserved; 37 they would keep holiday on the thirteenth of
the Syrian month Adar, which is the eve of Mardochaeus'
feast.[a]
38 Such was the history of Nicanor; and since that time the
city has been in Jewish possession. Here, then, I will make
an end of writing; 39 if it has been done workmanly, and in
historian's fashion, none better pleased than I; if it is of little
merit, I must be humoured none the less.[b] 40 Nothing but
wine to take, nothing but water, thy health forbids; vary thy
drinking,[c] and thou shalt find content. So it is with reading;
if the book be too nicely polished at every point, it grows
wearisome. So here we will have done with it.

a See Est. 9. 17 and 18. *b* 'I must be humoured none the less'; according to the Greek text, 'I have done as well as I could'. Divine inspiration is something superadded to, not a substitute for, human labour and human self-criticism. *c* For 'vary thy drinking' the Greek text has 'mix both together'; and the rest of the sentence is a (somewhat obscure) recommendation of style.

TODAY'S ENGLISH VERSION

arrived in the city, he called together all the people, stationed
the priests before the altar, and sent for the men in the fort.
32 He showed them the head of the evil Nicanor and the arm
which that wicked man had arrogantly stretched out against
the sacred Temple of the Almighty God. 33 Then he cut out
the tongue of that godless man, promising to feed it bit by bit
to the birds and to hang up his head opposite the Temple, as
evidence of what his foolishness did for him. 34 Everyone
there looked up to heaven and praised the Lord, who had
revealed his power and had kept his Temple from being
defiled. 35 Judas hung Nicanor's head from the wall of the
fort, as a clear proof to everyone of the Lord's help. 36 By
unanimous vote it was decided that this day would never be
forgotten, but would be celebrated each year on the eve of
Mordecai's Day,[a] which is the thirteenth day of the twelfth
month, called Adar in Aramaic.

37 That is how things turned out for Nicanor. The city of
Jerusalem remained in the possession of the Jewish people
from that time on, so I will end my story here. 38 If it is well
written and to the point, I am pleased; if it is poorly written
and uninteresting, I have still done my best. 39 We know it is
unhealthy to drink wine or water alone, whereas wine mixed
with water makes a delightfully tasty drink. So also a good
story skillfully written gives pleasure to those who read it.
With this I conclude.

[a] MORDECAI'S DAY: *The Festival of Purim (see Es 9.17-22).*

NEW REVISED STANDARD VERSION

were in the citadel. 32 He showed them the vile Nicanor's
head and that profane man's arm, which had been boastfully
stretched out against the holy house of the Almighty. 33 He
cut out the tongue of the ungodly Nicanor and said that he
would feed it piecemeal to the birds and would hang up
these rewards of his folly opposite the sanctuary. 34 And they
all, looking to heaven, blessed the Lord who had manifested
himself, saying, "Blessed is he who has kept his own place
undefiled!" 35 Judas[a] hung Nicanor's head from the citadel,
a clear and conspicuous sign to everyone of the help of the
Lord. 36 And they all decreed by public vote never to let this
day go unobserved, but to celebrate the thirteenth day of the
twelfth month—which is called Adar in the Aramaic language—the day before Mordecai's day.

37 This, then, is how matters turned out with Nicanor,
and from that time the city has been in the possession of the
Hebrews. So I will here end my story.

38 If it is well told and to the point, that is what I myself
desired; if it is poorly done and mediocre, that was the best I
could do. 39 For just as it is harmful to drink wine alone, or,
again, to drink water alone, while wine mixed with water is
sweet and delicious and enhances one's enjoyment, so also
the style of the story delights the ears of those who read the
work. And here will be the end.

a Gk *He*

NEW AMERICAN BIBLE

Jerusalem. 31 When he arrived there, he assembled his countrymen, stationed the priests before the altar, and sent for
those in the citadel. 32 He showed them the vile Nicanor's
head and the wretched blasphemer's arm that had been
boastfully stretched out against the holy dwelling of the
Almighty. 33 He cut out the tongue of the godless Nicanor,
saying he would feed it piecemeal to the birds and would
hang up the other wages of his folly opposite the temple.
34 At this, everyone looked toward heaven and praised the
LORD who manifests his divine power, saying, "Blessed be he
who has kept his own Place undefiled!"

35 Judas hung up Nicanor's head on the wall of the citadel,
a clear and evident proof to all of the Lord's help. 36 By public vote it was unanimously decreed never to let this day pass
unobserved, but to celebrate it on the thirteenth day of the
twelfth month, called Adar in Aramaic, the eve of Mordecai's
Day.

37 Since Nicanor's doings ended in this way, with the city
remaining in possession of the Hebrews from that time on, I
will bring my own story to an end here too. 38 If it is well
written and to the point, that is what I wanted; if it is poorly
done and mediocre, that is the best I could do. 39 Just as it is
harmful to drink wine alone or water alone, whereas mixing
wine with water makes a more pleasant drink that increases
delight, so a skillfully composed story delights the ears of
those who read the work. Let this, then, be the end.

NEW JERUSALEM BIBLE

Jerusalem. 31 When he arrived there himself, he called his
countrymen together, stationed the priests in front of the
altar and then sent for the people from the Citadel. 32 He
showed them the head of the abominable Nicanor, and the
hand which this infamous man had stretched out so insolently against the holy House of the Almighty. 33 Then, cutting out godless Nicanor's tongue, he gave orders for it to be
fed piecemeal to the birds, and for the salary of his folly to be
hung up in front of the Temple. 34 At this, everyone sent
blessings heavenwards to the glorious Lord, saying, 'Blessed
be he who has preserved his holy place from pollution!'

35 He hung Nicanor's head from the Citadel, a clear and
evident sign to all of the help of the Lord. 36 They all decreed
by public vote never to let that day go by unobserved, but to
celebrate the thirteenth day of the twelfth month, called Adar
in Aramaic, the eve of what is called the Day of Mordecai.

37 So ends the episode of Nicanor, and as, since then, the
city has remained in the possession of the Hebrews, I shall
bring my own work to an end here too. 38 If it is well composed and to the point, that is just what I wanted. If it is
worthless and mediocre, that is all I could manage. 39 Just as
it is injurious to drink wine by itself, or again water alone,
whereas wine mixed with water is pleasant and produces a
delightful sense of well-being, so skill in presenting the incidents is what delights the understanding of those who read
the book. And here I close.

GREEK OLD TESTAMENT

1 Esdras is included only in the Greek Old Testament, the King James Version, Today's English Version, and the New Revised Standard Version.

ΕΣΔΡΑΣ Α΄

1 Καὶ ἤγαγεν Ιωσιας τὸ πασχα ἐν Ιερουσαλημ τῷ κυρίῳ
αὐτοῦ καὶ ἔθυσεν τὸ πασχα τῇ τεσσαρεσκαιδεκάτῃ
ἡμέρᾳ τοῦ μηνὸς τοῦ πρώτου 2 στήσας τοὺς ἱερεῖς κατ'
ἐφημερίας ἐστολισμένους ἐν τῷ ἱερῷ τοῦ κυρίου. 3 καὶ εἶπεν
τοῖς Λευίταις, ἱεροδούλοις τοῦ Ισραηλ, ἁγιάσαι ἑαυτοὺς τῷ
κυρίῳ ἐν τῇ θέσει τῆς ἁγίας κιβωτοῦ τοῦ κυρίου ἐν τῷ οἴκῳ,
ᾧ ᾠκοδόμησεν Σαλωμων ὁ τοῦ Δαυιδ ὁ βασιλεύς Οὐκ ἔσται
ὑμῖν ἆραι ἐπ' ὤμων αὐτήν· 4 καὶ νῦν λατρεύετε τῷ κυρίῳ θεῷ
ὑμῶν καὶ θεραπεύετε τὸ ἔθνος αὐτοῦ Ισραηλ καὶ ἑτοιμάσατε
κατὰ τὰς πατριὰς καὶ τὰς φυλὰς ὑμῶν κατὰ τὴν γραφὴν
Δαυιδ βασιλέως Ισραηλ καὶ κατὰ τὴν μεγαλειότητα Σαλωμων
τοῦ υἱοῦ αὐτοῦ 5 καὶ στάντες ἐν τῷ ἱερῷ κατὰ τὴν μεριδαρχίαν τὴν πατρικὴν ὑμῶν τῶν Λευιτῶν τῶν ἔμπροσθεν τῶν
ἀδελφῶν ὑμῶν υἱῶν Ισραηλ ἐν τάξει 6 θύσατε τὸ πασχα καὶ
τὰς θυσίας ἑτοιμάσατε τοῖς ἀδελφοῖς ὑμῶν καὶ ποιήσατε τὸ
πασχα κατὰ τὸ πρόσταγμα τοῦ κυρίου τὸ δοθὲν τῷ Μωυσῇ.
7 καὶ ἐδωρήσατο Ιωσιας τῷ λαῷ τῷ εὑρεθέντι ἀρνῶν καὶ
ἐρίφων τριάκοντα χιλιάδας, μόσχους τρισχιλίους. ταῦτα ἐκ
τῶν βασιλικῶν ἐδόθη κατ' ἐπαγγελίαν τῷ λαῷ καὶ τοῖς
ἱερεῦσιν καὶ Λευίταις. 8 καὶ ἔδωκεν Χελκιας καὶ Ζαχαριας
καὶ Ησυηλος οἱ ἐπιστάται τοῦ ἱεροῦ τοῖς ἱερεῦσιν εἰς
πασχα πρόβατα δισχίλια ἑξακόσια, μόσχους τριακοσίους.
9 καὶ Ιεχονιας καὶ Σαμαιας καὶ Ναθαναηλ ὁ ἀδελφὸς καὶ
Ασαβιας καὶ Οχιηλος καὶ Ιωραμ χιλίαρχοι ἔδωκαν τοῖς Λευίταις εἰς πασχα πρόβατα πεντακισχίλια, μόσχους ἑπτακοσίους. 10 καὶ ταῦτα τὰ γενόμενα· εὐπρεπῶς ἔστησαν οἱ ἱερεῖς
καὶ οἱ Λευῖται 11 ἔχοντες τὰ ἄζυμα κατὰ τὰς φυλὰς 12 καὶ
κατὰ τὰς μεριδαρχίας τῶν πατέρων ἔμπροσθεν τοῦ λαοῦ
προσενεγκεῖν τῷ κυρίῳ κατὰ τὰ γεγραμμένα ἐν βιβλίῳ
Μωυσῆ, καὶ οὕτω τὸ πρωινόν. 13 καὶ ὤπτησαν τὸ πασχα πυρὶ
ὡς καθήκει καὶ τὰς θυσίας ἥψησαν ἐν τοῖς χαλκείοις καὶ λέβησιν μετ' εὐωδίας καὶ ἀπήνεγκαν πᾶσι τοῖς ἐκ τοῦ λαοῦ.
14 μετὰ δὲ ταῦτα ἡτοίμασαν ἑαυτοῖς τε καὶ τοῖς ἱερεῦσιν
ἀδελφοῖς αὐτῶν υἱοῖς Ααρων· οἱ γὰρ ἱερεῖς ἀνέφερον τὰ
στέατα ἕως ἀωρίας, καὶ οἱ Λευῖται ἡτοίμασαν ἑαυτοῖς καὶ
τοῖς ἱερεῦσιν ἀδελφοῖς αὐτῶν υἱοῖς Ααρων. 15 καὶ οἱ ἱεροψάλται υἱοὶ Ασαφ ἦσαν ἐπὶ τῆς τάξεως αὐτῶν κατὰ τὰ ὑπὸ
Δαυιδ τεταγμένα καὶ Ασαφ καὶ Ζαχαριας καὶ Εδδινους οἱ
παρὰ τοῦ βασιλέως, καὶ οἱ θυρωροὶ ἐφ' ἑκάστου πυλῶνος. οὐκ
ἔστιν παραβῆναι ἕκαστον τὴν ἑαυτοῦ ἐφημερίαν, οἱ γὰρ
ἀδελφοὶ αὐτῶν οἱ Λευῖται ἡτοίμασαν αὐτοῖς. 16 καὶ συνετελέσθη τὰ τῆς θυσίας τοῦ κυρίου ἐν ἐκείνῃ τῇ ἡμέρᾳ, ἀχθῆναι

KING JAMES VERSION

1 Esdras is included only in the Greek Old Testament, the King James Version, Today's English Version, and the New Revised Standard Version.

1 ESDRAS

1 And Josias held the feast of the passover in Jerusalem unto his Lord, and offered the passover the fourteenth day of the first month;

2 Having set the priests according to their daily courses, being arrayed in long garments, in the temple of the Lord.

3 And he spake unto the Levites, the holy ministers of Israel, that they should hallow themselves unto the Lord, to set the holy ark of the Lord in the house that king Solomon the son of David had built:

4 *And said,* Ye shall no more bear the ark upon your shoulders: now therefore serve the Lord your God, and minister unto his people Israel, and prepare you after your families and kindreds,

5 According as David the king of Israel prescribed, and according to the magnificence of Solomon his son: and standing in the temple according to the several dignity of the families of you the Levites, who minister in the presence of your brethren the children of Israel,

6 Offer the passover in order, and make ready the sacrifices for your brethren, and keep the passover according to the commandment of the Lord, which was given unto Moses.

7 And unto the people that was found there Josias gave thirty thousand lambs and kids, and three thousand calves: these things were given of the king's allowance, according as he promised, to the people, to the priests, and to the Levites.

8 And Helkias, Zacharias, and Syelus, the governors of the temple, gave to the priests for the passover two thousand and six hundred sheep, and three hundred calves.

9 And Jeconias, and Samaias, and Nathanael his brother, and Assabias, and Ochiel, and Joram, captains over thousands, gave to the Levites for the passover five thousand sheep, and seven hundred calves.

10 And when these things were done, the priests and Levites, having the unleavened bread, stood in very comely order according to the kindreds,

11 And according to the several dignities of the fathers, before the people, to offer to the Lord, as it is written in the book of Moses: and thus did they in the morning.

12 And they roasted the passover with fire, as appertaineth: as for the sacrifices, they sod them in brass pots and pans with a good savour,

13 And set them before all the people: and afterward they prepared for themselves, and for the priests their brethren, the sons of Aaron.

14 For the priests offered the fat until night: and the Levites prepared for themselves, and the priests their brethren, the sons of Aaron.

15 The holy singers also, the sons of Asaph, were in their order, according to the appointment of David, to wit, Asaph, Zacharias, and Jeduthun, who was of the king's retinue.

16 Moreover the porters were at every gate; it was not

TODAY'S ENGLISH VERSION

1 Esdras is included only in the Greek Old Testament, the King James Version, Today's English Version, and the New Revised Standard Version.

THE FIRST BOOK OF ESDRAS

1 King Josiah celebrated the Passover at Jerusalem in honor of the Lord; on the fourteenth day of the first month they killed the animals for the festival. 2 Josiah assigned the priests, dressed in their priestly robes, to serve in the Temple according to the daily order. 3 He also instructed the Levites, the Temple servants, to purify themselves for the Lord's service, so that they could put the sacred Covenant Box of the Lord in the Temple that King Solomon, the son of David, had built. 4 Josiah said to them, "You must no longer carry it from place to place, but you are to serve the Lord your God and minister to his people Israel. Get ready by family and clan to carry out your duties 5 according to the directions given by King David and the splendid way that they were carried out by his son King Solomon. Take your places in the Temple in proper order according to your family divisions as Levites serving the Lord for the people of Israel. 6 Kill the Passover lambs and goats and prepare the sacrifices for your people. Then celebrate the Passover according to the instructions that the Lord gave to Moses."

7 Josiah gave to the people who were present 30,000 young sheep and goats and 3,000 calves. These were a gift from the royal estates to carry out the promise he had made to the people, the priests, and the Levites. 8 The officials in charge of the Temple—Hilkiah, Zechariah, and Jehiel—also gave the priests 2,600 sheep and 300 calves for the sacrifices during the festival. 9 And the army commanders—Conaniah, Shemaiah and his brother Nethanel, Hashabiah, Ochiel, and Joram—contributed 5,000 sheep and 700 calves for the Levites to offer as sacrifices.

10-11 Here is what happened. The priests and the Levites, dressed in the proper manner and carrying the unleavened bread, came that morning to present the offerings to the Lord according to the instructions in the Law of Moses. They took their positions in front of the people in the order of tribal and family divisions. 12 The Levites roasted the Passover sacrifices and then boiled them in pots and kettles, making a pleasant smell. 13 Then they distributed the meat to all the people. After that was done, they took meat for themselves and for the priests, the descendants of Aaron, 14 because the priests were kept busy until night burning the fat of the sacrifices. 15-16 The guards at the Temple gates and the Temple singers of the Levite clan of Asaph (with Asaph, Zechariah, and Eddinus, who were representatives of the king) remained at the places assigned to them by King David's

NEW REVISED STANDARD VERSION

(b) The books from 1 Esdras through 3 Maccabees are recognized as Deuterocanonical Scripture by the Greek and the Russian Orthodox Churches. They are not so recognized by the Roman Catholic Church, but 1 Esdras and the Prayer of Manasseh (together with 2 Esdras) are placed in an appendix to the Latin Vulgate Bible.

1 Esdras is included only in the Greek Old Testament, the King James Version, Today's English Version, and the New Revised Standard Version.

1 ESDRAS

1 Josiah kept the passover to his Lord in Jerusalem; he killed the passover lamb on the fourteenth day of the first month, 2 having placed the priests according to their divisions, arrayed in their vestments, in the temple of the Lord. 3 He told the Levites, the temple servants of Israel, that they should sanctify themselves to the Lord and put the holy ark of the Lord in the house that King Solomon, son of David, had built; 4 and he said, "You need no longer carry it on your shoulders. Now worship the Lord your God and serve his people Israel; prepare yourselves by your families and kindred, 5 in accordance with the directions of King David of Israel and the magnificence of his son Solomon. Stand in order in the temple according to the groupings of the ancestral houses of you Levites, who minister before your kindred the people of Israel, 6 and kill the passover lamb and prepare the sacrifices for your kindred, and keep the passover according to the commandment of the Lord that was given to Moses."

7 To the people who were present Josiah gave thirty thousand lambs and kids, and three thousand calves; these were given from the king's possessions, as he promised, to the people and the priests and Levites. 8 Hilkiah, Zechariah, and Jehiel,[a] the chief officers of the temple, gave to the priests for the passover two thousand six hundred sheep and three hundred calves. 9 And Jeconiah and Shemaiah and his brother Nethanel, and Hashabiah and Ochiel and Joram, captains over thousands, gave the Levites for the passover five thousand sheep and seven hundred calves.

10 This is what took place. The priests and the Levites, having the unleavened bread, stood in proper order according to kindred 11 and the grouping of the ancestral houses, before the people, to make the offering to the Lord as it is written in the book of Moses; this they did in the morning. 12 They roasted the passover lamb with fire, as required; and they boiled the sacrifices in bronze pots and caldrons, with a pleasing odor, 13 and carried them to all the people. Afterward they prepared the passover for themselves and for their kindred the priests, the sons of Aaron, 14 because the priests were offering the fat until nightfall; so the Levites prepared it for themselves and for their kindred the priests, the sons of Aaron. 15 The temple singers, the sons of Asaph, were in their place according to the arrangement made by David, and also Asaph, Zechariah, and Eddinus, who represented the king. 16 The gatekeepers were at each gate; no one needed to

a Gk *Esyelus*

τὸ πασχα καὶ προσενεχθῆναι τὰς θυσίας ἐπὶ τὸ τοῦ κυρίου
θυσιαστήριον κατὰ τὴν ἐπιταγὴν τοῦ βασιλέως Ιωσιου.
17 καὶ ἠγάγοσαν οἱ υἱοὶ Ισραηλ οἱ εὑρεθέντες ἐν τῷ καιρῷ
τούτῳ τὸ πασχα καὶ τὴν ἑορτὴν τῶν ἀζύμων ἡμέρας ἑπτά.
18 καὶ οὐκ ἤχθη τὸ πασχα τοιοῦτο ἐν τῷ Ισραηλ ἀπὸ τῶν
χρόνων Σαμουηλ τοῦ προφήτου, 19 καὶ πάντες οἱ βασιλεῖς
τοῦ Ισραηλ οὐκ ἠγάγοσαν πασχα τοιοῦτον, οἷον ἤγαγεν
Ιωσιας καὶ οἱ ἱερεῖς καὶ οἱ Λευῖται καὶ οἱ Ιουδαῖοι καὶ πᾶς
Ισραηλ οἱ εὑρεθέντες ἐν τῇ κατοικήσει αὐτῶν ἐν Ιερου-
σαλημ· 20 ὀκτωκαιδεκάτῳ ἔτει βασιλεύοντος Ιωσιου ἤχθη τὸ
πασχα τοῦτο. — 21 καὶ ὠρθώθη τὰ ἔργα Ιωσιου ἐνώπιον τοῦ
κυρίου αὐτοῦ ἐν καρδίᾳ πλήρει εὐσεβείας. 22 καὶ τὰ κατ᾽
αὐτὸν δὲ ἀναγέγραπται ἐν τοῖς ἔμπροσθεν χρόνοις, περὶ
τῶν ἡμαρτηκότων καὶ ἠσεβηκότων εἰς τὸν κύριον παρὰ πᾶν
ἔθνος καὶ βασιλείαν, καὶ ἃ ἐλύπησαν αὐτὸν ἐν αἰσθήσει, καὶ
οἱ λόγοι τοῦ κυρίου ἀνέστησαν ἐπὶ Ισραηλ.
23 Καὶ μετὰ πᾶσαν τὴν πρᾶξιν ταύτην Ιωσιου συνέβη
Φαραω βασιλέα Αἰγύπτου ἐλθόντα πόλεμον ἐγεῖραι ἐν
Χαρκαμυς ἐπὶ τοῦ Εὐφράτου, καὶ ἐξῆλθεν εἰς ἀπάντησιν
αὐτῷ Ιωσιας. 24 καὶ διεπέμψατο βασιλεὺς Αἰγύπτου πρὸς
αὐτὸν λέγων Τί ἐμοὶ καὶ σοί ἐστιν, βασιλεῦ τῆς Ιουδαίας;
25 οὐχὶ πρὸς σὲ ἐξαπέσταλμαι ὑπὸ κυρίου τοῦ θεοῦ, ἐπὶ γὰρ
τοῦ Εὐφράτου ὁ πόλεμός μού ἐστιν. καὶ νῦν κύριος μετ᾽ ἐμοῦ
ἐστιν, καὶ κύριος μετ᾽ ἐμοῦ ἐπισπεύδων ἐστίν· ἀπόστηθι καὶ
μὴ ἐναντιοῦ τῷ κυρίῳ. 26 καὶ οὐκ ἀπέστρεψεν ἑαυτὸν Ιωσιας
ἐπὶ τὸ ἅρμα αὐτοῦ, ἀλλὰ πολεμεῖν αὐτὸν ἐπιχειρεῖ οὐ προσέχων ῥήμασιν Ιερεμιου προφήτου ἐκ στόματος κυρίου·
27 ἀλλὰ συνεστήσατο πρὸς αὐτὸν πόλεμον ἐν τῷ πεδίῳ
Μαγεδδαους, καὶ κατέβησαν οἱ ἄρχοντες πρὸς τὸν βασιλέα
Ιωσιαν. 28 καὶ εἶπεν ὁ βασιλεὺς τοῖς παισὶν αὐτοῦ Ἀποστή-
σατέ με ἀπὸ τῆς μάχης, ἠσθένησα γὰρ λίαν. καὶ εὐθέως
ἀπέστησαν αὐτὸν οἱ παῖδες αὐτοῦ ἀπὸ τῆς παρατάξεως,
29 καὶ ἀνέβη ἐπὶ τὸ ἅρμα τὸ δευτέριον αὐτοῦ· καὶ ἀποκατα-
σταθεὶς εἰς Ιερουσαλημ μετήλλαξεν τὸν βίον αὐτοῦ καὶ
ἐτάφη ἐν τῷ πατρικῷ τάφῳ. 30 καὶ ἐν ὅλῃ τῇ Ιουδαίᾳ ἐπένθησαν τὸν Ιωσιαν, καὶ ἐθρήνησεν Ιερεμιας ὁ προφήτης ὑπὲρ
Ιωσιου, καὶ οἱ προκαθήμενοι σὺν γυναιξὶν ἐθρηνοῦσαν αὐτὸν
ἕως τῆς ἡμέρας ταύτης, καὶ ἐξεδόθη τοῦτο γίνεσθαι αἰεὶ εἰς
ἅπαν τὸ γένος Ισραηλ. 31 ταῦτα δὲ ἀναγέγραπται ἐν τῇ βύ-
βλῳ τῶν ἱστορουμένων περὶ τῶν βασιλέων τῆς Ιουδαίας. καὶ
τὸ καθ᾽ ἓν πραχθὲν τῆς πράξεως Ιωσιου καὶ τῆς δόξης αὐτοῦ
καὶ τῆς συνέσεως αὐτοῦ ἐν τῷ νόμῳ κυρίου, τά τε προπρα-
χθέντα ὑπ᾽ αὐτοῦ καὶ τὰ νῦν, ἱστόρηται ἐν τῷ βυβλίῳ τῶν
βασιλέων Ισραηλ καὶ Ιουδα.
32 Καὶ ἀναλαβόντες οἱ ἐκ τοῦ ἔθνους τὸν Ιεχονιαν υἱὸν
Ιωσιου ἀνέδειξαν βασιλέα ἀντὶ Ιωσιου τοῦ πατρὸς αὐτοῦ
ὄντα ἐτῶν εἴκοσι τριῶν. 33 καὶ ἐβασίλευσεν ἐν Ιουδα καὶ
Ιερουσαλημ μῆνας τρεῖς. καὶ ἀπεκατέστησεν αὐτὸν
βασιλεὺς Αἰγύπτου βασιλεύειν ἐν Ιερουσαλημ 34 καὶ ἐζημίω-
σεν τὸ ἔθνος ἀργυρίου ταλάντοις ἑκατὸν καὶ χρυσίου ταλάν-
τῳ ἑνί. 35 καὶ ἀνέδειξεν ὁ βασιλεὺς Αἰγύπτου βασιλέα
Ιωακιμ τὸν ἀδελφὸν αὐτοῦ, βασιλέα τῆς Ιουδαίας καὶ

lawful for any to go from his ordinary service: for their brethren the Levites prepared for them.

17 Thus were the things that belonged to the sacrifices of the Lord accomplished in that day, that they might hold the passover,

18 And offer sacrifices upon the altar of the Lord, according to the commandment of king Josias.

19 So the children of Israel which were present held the passover at that time, and the feast of sweet bread seven days.

20 And such a passover was not kept in Israel since the time of the prophet Samuel.

21 Yea, all the kings of Israel held not such a passover as Josias, and the priests, and the Levites, and the Jews, held with all Israel that were found dwelling at Jerusalem.

22 In the eighteenth year of the reign of Josias was this passover kept.

23 And the works or Josias were upright before his Lord with an heart full of godliness.

24 As for the things that came to pass in his time, they were written in former times, concerning those that sinned, and did wickedly against the Lord above all people and kingdoms, and how they grieved him exceedingly, so that the words of the Lord rose up against Israel.

25 Now after all these acts of Josias it came to pass, that Pharaoh the king of Egypt came to raise war at Carchamis upon Euphrates: and Josias went out against him.

26 But the king of Egypt sent to him, saying, What have I to do with thee, O king of Judea?

27 I am not sent out from the Lord God against thee; for my war is upon Euphrates: and now the Lord is with me, yea, the Lord is with me hasting me forward: depart from me, and be not against the Lord.

28 Howbeit Josias did not turn back his chariot from him, but undertook to fight with him, not regarding the words of the prophet Jeremy spoken by the mouth of the Lord:

29 But joined battle with him in the plain of Magiddo, and the princes came against king Josias.

30 Then said the king unto his servants, Carry me away out of the battle; for I am very weak. And immediately his servants took him away out of the battle.

31 Then gat he up upon his second chariot; and being brought back to Jerusalem died, and was buried in his father's sepulchre.

32 And in all Jewry they mourned for Josias, yea, Jeremy the prophet lamented for Josias, and the chief men with the women made lamentation for him unto this day: and this was given out for an ordinance to be done continually in all the nation of Israel.

33 These things are written in the book of the stories of the kings of Judah, and every one of the acts that Josias did, and his glory, and his understanding in the law of the Lord, and the things that he had done before, and the things now recited, are reported in the book of the kings of Israel and Judea.

34 And the people took Joachaz the son of Josias, and made him king instead of Josias his father, when he was twenty and three years old.

35 And he reigned in Judea and in Jerusalem three months: and then the king of Egypt deposed him from reigning in Jerusalem.

Today's English Version

instructions. They did not need to leave their posts, because
the other Levites prepared the Passover for them.
17-18 So, as King Josiah had commanded, everything that
related to the sacrifices offered to the Lord was done that
day; the Passover Festival was celebrated, and the sacrifices
were offered on the altar. 19 All the people of Israel who were
present at that time kept the Passover and observed the
Festival of Unleavened Bread for seven days. 20 Since the
days of the prophet Samuel, the Passover had never been celebrated so well. 21-22 None of the former kings of Israel had
ever celebrated a Passover like this one celebrated by King
Josiah in Jerusalem in the eighteenth year of his reign; it was
celebrated by the priests, the Levites, and all the people of
Judah and Israel.
23 The Lord was pleased with everything Josiah did, for he
was a very religious man. 24 But the ancient records also tell
the story of those who sinned and rebelled against the Lord
during Josiah's reign. They sinned more than any other
nation or kingdom and did things that offended the Lord so
much that his judgment fell on the people of Israel.
25 After Josiah had done all these things, the king of Egypt
led an army to fight at Carchemish on the Euphrates River.
Josiah tried to stop him, 26 but the king of Egypt sent Josiah
this message: "The war I am fighting does not concern you,
King of Judah. 27 The Lord God did not send me to fight you;
my battle is on the Euphrates River. The Lord is with me,
and he is urging me on; so withdraw your troops and don't
oppose the Lord." 28 But Josiah did not go back to his chariot
and withdraw. He refused to listen to what the Lord had said
through the prophet Jeremiah and decided to fight. 29 He
went into battle on the plain of Megiddo, and the Egyptian
commanders attacked him.
30 King Josiah ordered his servants, "Take me off the battlefield; I'm badly hurt." So they took him out of the line of battle immediately, 31 and he got into a second chariot and was
taken back to Jerusalem. There he died and was buried in the
royal tomb. 32 All the people of Judah mourned his death.

The prophet Jeremiah composed a lament for King Josiah.
It has become a custom in Israel for the leaders and their
wives to sing this song when they mourn for him. 33 These
things are recorded in *The History of the Kings of Judah*.
Everything that Josiah did, how he gained his fame and his
understanding of the Law, what he did earlier and what is
told here, is all recorded in *The History of the Kings of Israel
and Judah*.
34 The people of Judah chose Josiah's son Joahaz[a] and
made him king. Joahaz was twenty-three years old, 35 and
he ruled Judah and Jerusalem for three months. Then the
king of Egypt deposed him 36 and made the nation pay

[a] Joahaz; *some manuscripts have* Jeconiah.

New Revised Standard Version

interrupt his daily duties, for their kindred the Levites prepared the passover for them.
17 So the things that had to do with the sacrifices to the
Lord were accomplished that day: the passover was kept
18 and the sacrifices were offered on the altar of the Lord,
according to the command of King Josiah. 19 And the people
of Israel who were present at that time kept the passover and
the festival of unleavened bread seven days. 20 No passover
like it had been kept in Israel since the times of the prophet
Samuel; 21 none of the kings of Israel had kept such a
passover as was kept by Josiah and the priests and Levites
and the people of Judah and all of Israel who were living in
Jerusalem. 22 In the eighteenth year of the reign of Josiah
this passover was kept.
23 And the deeds of Josiah were upright in the sight of the
Lord, for his heart was full of godliness. 24 In ancient times
the events of his reign have been recorded—concerning those
who sinned and acted wickedly toward the Lord beyond any
other people or kingdom, and how they grieved the Lord[a]
deeply, so that the words of the Lord fell upon Israel.
25 After all these acts of Josiah, it happened that Pharaoh,
king of Egypt, went to make war at Carchemish on the
Euphrates, and Josiah went out against him. 26 And the king
of Egypt sent word to him saying, "What have we to do with
each other, O king of Judea? 27 I was not sent against you by
the Lord God, for my war is at the Euphrates. And now the
Lord is with me! The Lord is with me, urging me on! Stand
aside, and do not oppose the Lord."
28 Josiah, however, did not turn back to his chariot, but
tried to fight with him, and did not heed the words of the
prophet Jeremiah from the mouth of the Lord. 29 He joined
battle with him in the plain of Megiddo, and the commanders came down against King Josiah. 30 The king said to his
servants, "Take me away from the battle, for I am very
weak." And immediately his servants took him out of the
line of battle. 31 He got into his second chariot; and after he
was brought back to Jerusalem he died, and was buried in
the tomb of his ancestors.
32 In all Judea they mourned for Josiah. The prophet
Jeremiah lamented for Josiah, and the principal men, with
the women,[b] have made lamentation for him to this day; it
was ordained that this should always be done throughout
the whole nation of Israel. 33 These things are written in the
book of the histories of the kings of Judea; and every one of
the acts of Josiah, and his splendor, and his understanding
of the law of the Lord, and the things that he had done
before, and these that are now told, are recorded in the book
of the kings of Israel and Judah.
34 The men of the nation took Jeconiah[c] son of Josiah,
who was twenty-three years old, and made him king in succession to his father Josiah. 35 He reigned three months in
Judah and Jerusalem. Then the king of Egypt deposed him

a Gk *him* *b* Or *their wives* *c* 2 Kings 23.30; 2 Chr 36.1 *Jehoahaz*

Greek Old Testament

Ιερουσαλημ. 36 καὶ ἔδησεν Ιωακιμ τοὺς μεγιστᾶνας, Ζαριον
δὲ τὸν ἀδελφὸν αὐτοῦ συλλαβὼν ἀνήγαγεν ἐξ Αἰγύπτου.
37 Ἐτῶν δὲ ἦν εἴκοσι πέντε Ιωακιμ, ὅτε ἐβασίλευσεν τῆς
Ιουδαίας καὶ Ιερουσαλημ, καὶ ἐποίησεν τὸ πονηρὸν ἐνώπιον
κυρίου. 38 ἐπ᾽ αὐτὸν δὲ ἀνέβη Ναβουχοδονοσορ βασιλεὺς
Βαβυλῶνος καὶ δήσας αὐτὸν ἐν χαλκείῳ δεσμῷ ἀπήγαγεν εἰς
Βαβυλῶνα. 39 καὶ ἀπὸ τῶν ἱερῶν σκευῶν τοῦ κυρίου λαβὼν
Ναβουχοδονοσορ καὶ ἀπενέγκας ἀπηρείσατο ἐν τῷ ναῷ αὐτοῦ ἐν Βαβυλῶνι. 40 τὰ δὲ ἱστορηθέντα περὶ αὐτοῦ καὶ τῆς
αὐτοῦ ἀκαθαρσίας καὶ δυσσεβείας ἀναγέγραπται ἐν τῇ βίβλῳ τῶν χρόνων τῶν βασιλέων.
41 Καὶ ἐβασίλευσεν ἀντ᾽ αὐτοῦ Ιωακιμ ὁ υἱὸς αὐτοῦ· ὅτε
γὰρ ἀνεδείχθη, ἦν ἐτῶν δέκα ὀκτώ, 42 βασιλεύει δὲ μῆνας
τρεῖς καὶ ἡμέρας δέκα ἐν Ιερουσαλημ καὶ ἐποίησεν τὸ
πονηρὸν ἔναντι κυρίου.
43 Καὶ μετ᾽ ἐνιαυτὸν ἀποστείλας Ναβουχοδονοσορ μετήγαγεν αὐτὸν εἰς Βαβυλῶνα ἅμα τοῖς ἱεροῖς σκεύεσιν τοῦ
κυρίου 44 καὶ ἀνέδειξε Σεδεκιαν βασιλέα τῆς Ιουδαίας καὶ
Ιερουσαλημ, Σεδεκιαν ὄντα ἐτῶν εἴκοσι ἑνός, βασιλεύει δὲ
ἔτη ἕνδεκα. 45 καὶ ἐποίησεν τὸ πονηρὸν ἐνώπιον κυρίου καὶ
οὐκ ἐνετράπη ἀπὸ τῶν ῥηθέντων λόγων ὑπὸ Ιερεμιου τοῦ
προφήτου ἐκ στόματος τοῦ κυρίου. 46 καὶ ὁρκισθεὶς ἀπὸ τοῦ
βασιλέως Ναβουχοδονοσορ τῷ ὀνόματι τοῦ κυρίου ἐπιορ-
κήσας ἀπέστη καὶ σκληρύνας αὐτοῦ τὸν τράχηλον καὶ τὴν
καρδίαν αὐτοῦ παρέβη τὰ νόμιμα κυρίου θεοῦ Ισραηλ. 47 καὶ
οἱ ἡγούμενοι δὲ τοῦ λαοῦ καὶ τῶν ἱερέων πολλὰ ἠσέβησαν
καὶ ἠνόμησαν ὑπὲρ πάσας τὰς ἀκαθαρσίας πάντων τῶν ἐθνῶν καὶ ἐμίαναν τὸ ἱερὸν τοῦ κυρίου τὸ ἁγιαζόμενον ἐν
Ιεροσολύμοις. 48 καὶ ἀπέστειλεν ὁ θεὸς τῶν πατέρων αὐτῶν
διὰ τοῦ ἀγγέλου αὐτοῦ μετακαλέσαι αὐτούς, καθὸ ἐφείδετο
αὐτῶν καὶ τοῦ σκηνώματος αὐτοῦ. 49 αὐτοὶ δὲ ἐξεμυκτήρι-
σαν ἐν τοῖς ἀγγέλοις αὐτοῦ, καὶ ᾗ ἡμέρᾳ ἐλάλησεν κύριος,
ἦσαν ἐκπαίζοντες τοὺς προφήτας αὐτοῦ ἕως τοῦ θυμωθέντα
αὐτὸν ἐπὶ τῷ ἔθνει αὐτοῦ διὰ τὰ δυσσεβήματα προστάξαι
ἀναβιβάσαι ἐπ᾽ αὐτοὺς τοὺς βασιλεῖς τῶν Χαλδαίων.
50 οὗτοι ἀπέκτειναν τοὺς νεανίσκους αὐτῶν ἐν ῥομφαίᾳ
περικύκλῳ τοῦ ἁγίου αὐτῶν ἱεροῦ καὶ οὐκ ἐφείσαντο νεανίσκου καὶ παρθένου καὶ πρεσβύτου καὶ νεωτέρου, ἀλλὰ πάντας παρέδωκεν εἰς τὰς χεῖρας αὐτῶν. 51 καὶ πάντα τὰ ἱερὰ
σκεύη τοῦ κυρίου τὰ μεγάλα καὶ τὰ μικρὰ καὶ τὰς κιβωτοὺς
τοῦ κυρίου καὶ τὰς βασιλικὰς ἀποθήκας ἀναλαβόντες ἀπήνεγκαν εἰς Βαβυλῶνα. 52 καὶ ἐνεπύρισαν τὸν οἶκον τοῦ κυρίου
καὶ ἔλυσαν τὰ τείχα Ιεροσολύμων καὶ τοὺς πύργους αὐτῶν
ἐνεπύρισαν ἐν πυρὶ 53 καὶ συνετέλεσαν πάντα τὰ ἔνδοξα
αὐτῆς ἀχρεῶσαι· καὶ τοὺς ἐπιλοίπους ἀπήγαγεν μετὰ
ῥομφαίας εἰς Βαβυλῶνα. 54 καὶ ἦσαν παῖδες αὐτῷ καὶ τοῖς

King James Version

36 And he set a tax upon the land of an hundred talents of silver and one talent of gold.

37 The king of Egypt also made king Joacim his brother king of Judea and Jerusalem.

38 And he bound Joacim and the nobles: but Zaraces his brother he apprehended, and brought him out of Egypt.

39 Five and twenty years old was Joacim when he was made king in the land of Judea and Jerusalem; and he did evil before the Lord.

40 Wherefore against him Nabuchodonosor the king of Babylon came up, and bound him with a chain of brass, and carried him into Babylon.

41 Nabuchodonosor also took of the holy vessels of the Lord, and carried them away, and set them in his own temple at Babylon.

42 But those things that are recorded of him, and of his uncleaness and impiety, are written in the chronicles of the kings.

43 And Joacim his son reigned in his stead: he was made king being eighteen years old;

44 And reigned but three months and ten days in Jerusalem; and did evil before the Lord.

45 So after a year Nabuchodonosor sent and caused him to be brought into Babylon with the holy vessels of the Lord;

46 And made Zedechias king of Judea and Jerusalem, when he was one and twenty years old; and he reigned eleven years:

47 And he did evil also in the sight of the Lord, and cared not for the words that were spoken unto him by the prophet Jeremy from the mouth of the Lord.

48 And after that king Nabuchodonosor had made him to swear by the name of the Lord, he forswore himself, and rebelled; and hardening his neck, and his heart, he transgressed the laws of the Lord God of Israel.

49 The governors also of the people and of the priests did many things against the laws, and passed all the pollutions of all nations, and defiled the temple of the Lord, which was sanctified in Jerusalem.

50 Nevertheless the God of their fathers sent by his messenger to call them back, because he spared them and his tabernacle also.

51 But they had his messengers in derision; and, look, when the Lord spake unto them, they made a sport of his prophets:

52 So far forth, that he, being wroth with his people for their great ungodliness, commanded the kings of the Chaldees to come up against them;

53 Who slew their young men with the sword, yea, even within the compass of their holy temple, and spared neither young man nor maid, old man nor child, among them; for he delivered all into their hands.

54 And they took all the holy vessels of the Lord, both great and small, with the vessels of the ark of God, and the king's treasures, and carried them away into Babylon.

55 As for the house of the Lord, they burnt it, and brake down the walls of Jerusalem, and set fire upon her towers:

56 And as for her glorious things, they never ceased till they had consumed and brought them all to nought: and the people that were not slain with the sword he carried unto Babylon:

57 Who became servants to him and his children, till the

TODAY'S ENGLISH VERSION

7,500 pounds of silver and 75 pounds of gold as tribute. 37 The king of Egypt appointed Joahaz's brother Jehoiakim king of Judah and Jerusalem. 38 Jehoiakim put the leading men of the nation in prison, then had his brother Zarius arrested and brought back from Egypt.

39 Jehoiakim was twenty-five years old when he became king of Judah and Jerusalem. He sinned against the Lord. 40 King Nebuchadnezzar of Babylonia invaded Judah, captured Jehoiakim, and took him to Babylonia in bronze chains. 41 Nebuchadnezzar also carried off some of the sacred utensils from the Temple and put them in his own temple in Babylon. 42 The stories about Jehoiakim, his depravity, and the godless way he lived are recorded in *The Chronicles of the Kings.*

43 Jehoiachin was eighteen years old when he succeeded his father Jehoiakim as king, 44 and he ruled in Jerusalem for three months and ten days. He too sinned against the Lord. 45 A year later King Nebuchadnezzar had Jehoiachin taken to Babylonia as a prisoner; Nebuchadnezzar also carried off sacred utensils from the Temple. 46 Then he made Zedekiah king of Judah and Jerusalem.

Zedekiah was then twenty-one years old, and he ruled for eleven years. 47 He sinned against the Lord and refused to listen to the prophet Jeremiah, who spoke the word of the Lord.

48 Although King Nebuchadnezzar had forced Zedekiah to swear in the Lord's name that he would be loyal to him, Zedekiah broke his oath and rebelled against him. He stubbornly refused to obey the commands of the Lord, the God of Israel. 49 In addition, the leaders of the people and even the chief priests did more godless and lawless things than all the corrupt heathen; they defiled the Temple of the Lord, which he had made holy. 50 The God of their ancestors had continued to send prophets to call them back from their sins, because he wanted to spare them and the Temple. 51 But when the Lord spoke through his prophets, the people made fun of them and laughed. 52 At last the Lord became so angry with his people and their depraved ways that he ordered the kings of Babylonia to attack them. 53 The Babylonians killed the young men of Judah all around the Temple and did not spare anyone, young or old, man or woman. The Lord handed them all over to their enemies. 54 The Babylonians carried off all the sacred utensils from the Temple, the treasure chests,[a] and the wealth of the king; they took everything away to Babylon, leaving nothing behind. 55 They burned down the Temple, broke down the city wall, set fire to its towers, 56 and completely destroyed all its beauty. Nebuchadnezzar forced all the survivors to be led away to Babylon, 57 where they served him and his

[a] treasure chests; *some manuscripts have* the equipment of the Covenant Box.

NEW REVISED STANDARD VERSION

from reigning in Jerusalem, 36 and fined the nation one hundred talents of silver and one talent of gold. 37 The king of Egypt made his brother Jehoiakim king of Judea and Jerusalem. 38 Jehoiakim put the nobles in prison, and seized his brother Zarius and brought him back from Egypt.

39 Jehoiakim was twenty-five years old when he began to reign in Judea and Jerusalem; he did what was evil in the sight of the Lord. 40 King Nebuchadnezzar of Babylon came up against him; he bound him with a chain of bronze and took him away to Babylon. 41 Nebuchadnezzar also took some holy vessels of the Lord, and carried them away, and stored them in his temple in Babylon. 42 But the things that are reported about Jehoiakim,[a] and his uncleanness and impiety, are written in the annals of the kings.

43 His son Jehoiachin[b] became king in his place; when he was made king he was eighteen years old, 44 and he reigned three months and ten days in Jerusalem. He did what was evil in the sight of the Lord. 45 A year later Nebuchadnezzar sent and removed him to Babylon, with the holy vessels of the Lord, 46 and made Zedekiah king of Judea and Jerusalem.

Zedekiah was twenty-one years old, and he reigned eleven years. 47 He also did what was evil in the sight of the Lord, and did not heed the words that were spoken by the prophet Jeremiah from the mouth of the Lord. 48 Although King Nebuchadnezzar had made him swear by the name of the Lord, he broke his oath and rebelled; he stiffened his neck and hardened his heart and transgressed the laws of the Lord, the God of Israel. 49 Even the leaders of the people and of the priests committed many acts of sacrilege and lawlessness beyond all the unclean deeds of all the nations, and polluted the temple of the Lord in Jerusalem—the temple that God had made holy. 50 The God of their ancestors sent his messenger to call them back, because he would have spared them and his dwelling place. 51 But they mocked his messengers, and whenever the Lord spoke, they scoffed at his prophets, 52 until in his anger against his people because of their ungodly acts he gave command to bring against them the kings of the Chaldeans. 53 These killed their young men with the sword around their holy temple, and did not spare young man or young woman,[c] old man or child, for he gave them all into their hands. 54 They took all the holy vessels of the Lord, great and small, the treasure chests of the Lord, and the royal stores, and carried them away to Babylon. 55 They burned the house of the Lord, broke down the walls of Jerusalem, burned their towers with fire, 56 and utterly destroyed all its glorious things. The survivors he led away to Babylon with the sword, 57 and they were servants to him

a Gk *him* *b* Gk *Jehoiakim* *c* Gk *virgin*

υἱοῖς αὐτοῦ μέχρι τοῦ βασιλεῦσαι Πέρσας εἰς ἀναπλήρωσιν τοῦ ῥήματος τοῦ κυρίου ἐν στόματι Ιερεμιου 55 Ἕως τοῦ εὐδοκῆσαι τὴν γῆν τὰ σάββατα αὐτῆς, πάντα τὸν χρόνον τῆς ἐρημώσεως αὐτῆς, σαββατιεῖ εἰς συμπλήρωσιν ἐτῶν ἑβδομήκοντα.

2 Βασιλεύοντος Κύρου Περσῶν ἔτους πρώτου εἰς συντέλειαν ῥήματος κυρίου ἐν στόματι Ιερεμιου ἤγειρεν κύριος τὸ πνεῦμα Κύρου βασιλέως Περσῶν, καὶ ἐκήρυξεν ἐν ὅλῃ τῇ βασιλείᾳ αὐτοῦ καὶ ἅμα διὰ γραπτῶν λέγων 2 Τάδε λέγει ὁ βασιλεὺς Περσῶν Κῦρος Ἐμὲ ἀνέδειξεν βασιλέα τῆς οἰκουμένης ὁ κύριος τοῦ Ισραηλ, κύριος ὁ ὕψιστος, καὶ ἐσήμηνέν μοι οἰκοδομῆσαι αὐτῷ οἶκον ἐν Ιερουσαλημ τῇ ἐν τῇ Ιουδαίᾳ. 3 εἴ τίς ἐστιν οὖν ὑμῶν ἐκ τοῦ ἔθνους αὐτοῦ, ἔστω ὁ κύριος αὐτοῦ μετ᾽ αὐτοῦ, καὶ ἀναβὰς εἰς τὴν Ιερουσαλημ τὴν ἐν τῇ Ιουδαίᾳ οἰκοδομείτω τὸν οἶκον τοῦ κυρίου τοῦ Ισραηλ (οὗτος ὁ κύριος ὁ κατασκηνώσας ἐν Ιερουσαλημ). 4 ὅσοι οὖν κατὰ τόπους οἰκοῦσιν, βοηθείτωσαν αὐτῷ οἱ ἐν τῷ τόπῳ αὐτοῦ ἐν χρυσίῳ καὶ ἐν ἀργυρίῳ ἐν δόσεσιν μεθ᾽ ἵππων καὶ κτηνῶν σὺν τοῖς ἄλλοις τοῖς κατ᾽ εὐχὰς προστεθειμένοις εἰς τὸ ἱερὸν τοῦ κυρίου τὸ ἐν Ιερουσαλημ. — 5 καὶ καταστάντες οἱ ἀρχίφυλοι τῶν πατριῶν τῆς Ιουδα καὶ Βενιαμιν φυλῆς καὶ οἱ ἱερεῖς καὶ οἱ Λευῖται καὶ πάντων ὧν ἤγειρεν κύριος τὸ πνεῦμα ἀναβῆναι οἰκοδομῆσαι οἶκον τῷ κυρίῳ τὸν ἐν Ιερουσαλημ, 6 καὶ οἱ περικύκλῳ αὐτῶν ἐβοήθησαν ἐν πᾶσιν, ἀργυρίῳ καὶ χρυσίῳ, ἵπποις καὶ κτήνεσιν καὶ εὐχαῖς ὡς πλείσταις πολλῶν, ὧν ὁ νοῦς ἠγέρθη. 7 καὶ ὁ βασιλεὺς Κῦρος ἐξήνεγκεν τὰ ἱερὰ σκεύη τοῦ κυρίου, ἃ μετήγαγεν Ναβουχοδονοσορ ἐξ Ιερουσαλημ καὶ ἀπηρείσατο αὐτὰ ἐν τῷ ἑαυτοῦ εἰδωλίῳ· 8 ἐξενέγκας δὲ αὐτὰ Κῦρος ὁ βασιλεὺς Περσῶν παρέδωκεν αὐτὰ Μιθριδάτῃ τῷ ἑαυτοῦ γαζοφύλακι, διὰ δὲ τούτου παρεδόθησαν Σαναβασσάρῳ προστάτῃ τῆς Ιουδαίας. 9 ὁ δὲ τούτων ἀριθμὸς ἦν· σπονδεῖα χρυσᾶ χίλια, σπονδεῖα ἀργυρᾶ χίλια, θυίσκαι ἀργυραῖ εἴκοσι ἐννέα, 10 φιάλαι χρυσαῖ τριάκοντα, ἀργυραῖ δισχίλιαι τετρακόσιαι δέκα καὶ ἄλλα σκεύη χίλια. 11 τὰ δὲ πάντα σκεύη διεκομίσθη, χρυσᾶ καὶ ἀργυρᾶ, πεντακισχίλια τετρακόσια ἑξήκοντα ἐννέα, ἀνηνέχθη δὲ ὑπὸ Σαναβασσάρου ἅμα τοῖς ἐκ τῆς αἰχμαλωσίας ἐκ Βαβυλῶνος εἰς Ιεροσόλυμα.

12 Ἐν δὲ τοῖς ἐπὶ Ἀρταξέρξου τοῦ Περσῶν βασιλέως χρόνοις κατέγραψεν αὐτῷ κατὰ τῶν κατοικούντων ἐν τῇ Ιουδαίᾳ καὶ Ιερουσαλημ Βεσλεμος καὶ Μιθραδάτης καὶ Ταβελλιος καὶ Ραουμος καὶ Βεελτέεμος καὶ Σαμσαῖος ὁ γραμματεὺς καὶ οἱ λοιποὶ οἱ τούτοις συντασσόμενοι, οἰκοῦντες δὲ ἐν Σαμαρείᾳ καὶ τοῖς ἄλλοις τόποις, τὴν ὑπογεγραμμένην ἐπιστολήν 13 Βασιλεῖ Ἀρταξέρξῃ κυρίῳ οἱ παῖδές σου Ραουμος ὁ τὰ προσπίπτοντα καὶ Σαμσαῖος ὁ γραμματεὺς καὶ οἱ ἐπίλοιποι τῆς βουλῆς αὐτῶν κριταὶ οἱ ἐν Κοίλῃ Συρίᾳ καὶ Φοινίκῃ· 14 καὶ νῦν γνωστὸν ἔστω τῷ κυρίῳ βασιλεῖ διότι οἱ Ιουδαῖοι ἀναβάντες παρ᾽ ὑμῶν πρὸς ἡμᾶς, ἐλθόντες εἰς

Persians reigned, to fulfil the word of the Lord spoken by the mouth of Jeremy:

58 Until the land had enjoyed her sabbaths, the whole time of her desolation shall she rest, until the full term of seventy years.

2 In the first year of Cyrus king of the Persians, that the word of the Lord might be accomplished, that he had promised by the mouth of Jeremy;

2 The Lord raised up the spirit of Cyrus the king of the Persians, and he made proclamation through all his kingdom, and also by writing,

3 Saying, Thus saith Cyrus king of the Persians; The Lord of Israel, the most high Lord, hath made me king of the whole world,

4 And commanded me to build him an house at Jerusalem in Jewry.

5 If therefore there be any of you that are of his people, let the Lord, even his Lord, be with him, and let him go up to Jerusalem that is in Judea, and build the house of the Lord of Israel: for he is the Lord that dwelleth in Jerusalem.

6 Whosoever then dwell in the places about, let them help him, those, I say, that are his neighbours, with gold, and with silver,

7 With gifts, with horses, and with cattle, and other things, which have been set forth by vow, for the temple of the Lord at Jerusalem.

8 ¶ Then the chief of the families of Judea and of the tribe of Benjamin stood up; the priests also, and the Levites, and all they whose mind the Lord had moved to go up, and to build an house for the Lord at Jerusalem,

9 And they that dwelt round about them, and helped them in all things with silver and gold, with horses and cattle, and with very many free gifts of a great number whose minds were stirred up thereto.

10 King Cyrus also brought forth the holy vessels, which Nabuchodonosor had carried away from Jerusalem, and had set up in his temple of idols.

11 Now when Cyrus king of the Persians had brought them forth, he delivered them to Mithridates his treasurer:

12 And by him they were delivered to Sanabassar the governor of Judea.

13 And this was the number of them; A thousand golden cups, and a thousand of silver, censers of silver twenty nine, vials of gold thirty, and of silver two thousand four hundred and ten, and a thousand other vessels.

14 So all the vessels of gold and of silver, which were carried away, were five thousand four hundred threescore and nine.

15 These were brought back by Sanabassar, together with them of the captivity, from Babylon to Jerusalem.

16 But in the time of Artaxerxes king of the Persians Belemus, and Mithridates, and Tabellius, and Rathumus, and Beeltethmus, and Semellius the secretary, with others that were in commission with them, dwelling in Samaria and other places, wrote unto him against them that dwelt in Judea and Jerusalem these letters following;

17 To king Artaxerxes our lord, Thy servants, Rathumus the storywriter, and Semellius the scribe, and the rest of their council, and the judges that are in Celosyria and Phenice.

18 Be it now known to the lord the king, that the Jews that are come up from you to us, being come into Jerusalem,

Today's English Version

descendants as slaves until the rise of the Persian Empire.
And so what the Lord had foretold through the prophet
Jeremiah was fulfilled: 58 "The land will lie desolate for seventy years to make up for the Sabbath rest[a] that has not
been observed."

2 In the first year that Cyrus of Persia was emperor,[b] the
Lord made come true what he had said through the
prophet Jeremiah. 2 He prompted Cyrus to issue the following command and send it out in writing to be read aloud
everywhere in his empire:

3 "This is the command of Cyrus, emperor of Persia. The
Lord of Israel, the Lord Most High, has appointed me ruler
over the whole world 4 and has given me the responsibility
of building a Temple for him in Jerusalem in Judah. 5 May
the Lord be with those of you who are his people. You are
to go to Jerusalem and rebuild the Temple of the Lord of
Israel, the Lord who lives in Jerusalem. 6 If any of his people in exile need help to return, their neighbors must give
them this help, providing them with silver and gold 7 and
other gifts, with horses and pack animals, as well as anything else offered for the Temple of the Lord in Jerusalem
in fulfillment of a vow."

8 Then the heads of the clans of the tribes of Judah and
Benjamin, the priests and the Levites, and everyone else
whose heart the Lord had moved, got ready to go and rebuild
the Lord's Temple in Jerusalem. 9 Their neighbors helped
them with everything, giving them silver, gold, horses, and
pack animals. Many of their neighbors were also led to give
a large number of other things, in fulfillment of vows.

10 Emperor Cyrus gave them back the sacred utensils that
King Nebuchadnezzar had taken from Jerusalem and had put
in the temple of his idols. 11 He brought them out and handed them over to Mithredath, chief of the royal treasury,
12 who delivered them to Sheshbazzar, the governor of Judah.
13 Here is the inventory of the utensils:

gold bowls for offerings	1,000
silver bowls for offerings	1,000
silver fire pans	29
small gold bowls	30
small silver bowls	2,410
other utensils	1,000

14 In all there were 5,469 gold and silver bowls and other
utensils, 15 and Sheshbazzar took these with him when he
and the other exiles went from Babylon to Jerusalem.

16 In the reign of Emperor Artaxerxes of Persia, Bishlam,
Mithredath, Tabeel, Rehum, Beltethmus, Shimshai the secretary of the province, and their associates who lived in
Samaria and elsewhere wrote the following letter in protest
against the Jews who were living in Judah and Jerusalem:

17 "To Your Majesty Emperor Artaxerxes from your servants, the official correspondent Rehum, the secretary
Shimshai, the other members of the council, and the
judges of Greater Syria and Phoenicia.

18 "We want Your Majesty to know that the Jews who
came here from your other territories have settled in

[a] SABBATH REST: *A reference to the requirement of the Law that every seventh year the land was not to be farmed (see Lv 25.1-7).* [b] EMPEROR: *King Cyrus of Persia occupied the city of Babylon in 539 B.C. and began to reign as the emperor of Babylonia.*

New Revised Standard Version

and to his sons until the Persians began to reign, in fulfillment of the word of the Lord by the mouth of Jeremiah,
58 saying, "Until the land has enjoyed its sabbaths, it shall
keep sabbath all the time of its desolation until the completion of seventy years."

2 In the first year of Cyrus as king of the Persians, so that
the word of the Lord by the mouth of Jeremiah might be
accomplished— 2 the Lord stirred up the spirit of King Cyrus
of the Persians, and he made a proclamation throughout all
his kingdom and also put it in writing:

3 "Thus says Cyrus king of the Persians: The Lord of
Israel, the Lord Most High, has made me king of the world,
4 and he has commanded me to build him a house at
Jerusalem, which is in Judea. 5 If any of you, therefore, are of
his people, may your Lord be with you; go up to Jerusalem,
which is in Judea, and build the house of the Lord of Israel—
he is the Lord who dwells in Jerusalem— 6 and let each of
you, wherever you may live, be helped by the people of your
place with gold and silver, 7 with gifts and with horses and
cattle, besides the other things added as votive offerings for
the temple of the Lord that is in Jerusalem."

8 Then arose the heads of families of the tribes of Judah
and Benjamin, and the priests and the Levites, and all whose
spirit the Lord had stirred to go up to build the house in
Jerusalem for the Lord; 9 their neighbors helped them with
everything, with silver and gold, with horses and cattle, and
with a very great number of votive offerings from many
whose hearts were stirred.

10 King Cyrus also brought out the holy vessels of the
Lord that Nebuchadnezzar had carried away from Jerusalem
and stored in his temple of idols. 11 When King Cyrus of the
Persians brought these out, he gave them to Mithridates, his
treasurer, 12 and by him they were given to Sheshbazzar,[a]
the governor of Judea. 13 The number of these was: one
thousand gold cups, one thousand silver cups, twenty-nine
silver censers, thirty gold bowls, two thousand four hundred
ten silver bowls, and one thousand other vessels. 14 All the
vessels were handed over, gold and silver, five thousand four
hundred sixty-nine, 15 and they were carried back by Sheshbazzar with the returning exiles from Babylon to Jerusalem.

16 In the time of King Artaxerxes of the Persians,
Bishlam, Mithridates, Tabeel, Rehum, Beltethmus, the scribe
Shimshai, and the rest of their associates, living in Samaria
and other places, wrote him the following letter, against
those who were living in Judea and Jerusalem:

17 "To King Artaxerxes our lord, your servants the
recorder Rehum and the scribe Shimshai and the other members of their council, and the judges in Coelesyria and
Phoenicia: 18 Let it now be known to our lord the king that
the Jews who came up from you to us have gone to

[a] Gk *Sanabassaros*

Greek Old Testament

Ιερουσαλημ, τὴν πόλιν τὴν ἀποστάτιν καὶ πονηρὰν οἰκοδομοῦσιν, τάς τε ἀγορὰς αὐτῆς καὶ τὰ τείχη θεραπεύουσιν καὶ
ναὸν ὑποβάλλονται. 15 ἐὰν οὖν ἡ πόλις αὕτη οἰκοδομηθῇ καὶ
τὰ τείχη συντελεσθῇ, φορολογίαν οὐ μὴ ὑπομείνωσιν δοῦναι,
ἀλλὰ καὶ βασιλεῦσιν ἀντιστήσονται. 16 καὶ ἐπεὶ ἐνεργεῖται
τὰ κατὰ τὸν ναόν, καλῶς ἔχειν ὑπολαμβάνομεν μὴ ὑπεριδεῖν
τὸ τοιοῦτο, ἀλλὰ προσφωνῆσαι τῷ κυρίῳ βασιλεῖ, ὅπως, ἂν
φαίνηταί σοι, ἐπισκεφθῇ ἐν τοῖς ἀπὸ τῶν πατέρων σου βιβλίοις. 17 καὶ εὑρήσεις ἐν τοῖς ὑπομνηματισμοῖς τὰ γεγραμμένα περὶ τούτων καὶ γνώσῃ ὅτι ἡ πόλις ἦν ἐκείνη ἀπο-
στάτις καὶ βασιλεῖς καὶ πόλεις ἐνοχλοῦσα καὶ οἱ Ιουδαῖοι
ἀποστάται καὶ πολιορκίας συνιστάμενοι ἐν αὐτῇ ἔτι ἐξ
αἰῶνος, δι' ἣν αἰτίαν καὶ ἡ πόλις αὕτη ἠρημώθη. 18 νῦν οὖν
ὑποδεικνυμέν σοι, κύριε βασιλεῦ, διότι, ἐὰν ἡ πόλις αὕτη
οἰκοδομηθῇ καὶ τὰ ταύτης τείχη ἀνασταθῇ, κάθοδός σοι
οὐκέτι ἔσται εἰς Κοίλην Συρίαν καὶ Φοινίκην. — 19 τότε
ἀντέγραψεν ὁ βασιλεὺς Ραούμῳ τῷ γράφοντι τὰ προσπίπτοντα καὶ Βεελτεέμῳ καὶ Σαμσαίῳ γραμματεῖ καὶ τοῖς
λοιποῖς τοῖς συντασσομένοις καὶ οἰκοῦσιν ἐν τῇ Σαμαρείᾳ
καὶ Συρίᾳ καὶ Φοινίκῃ τὰ ὑπογεγραμμένα 20 Ἀνέγνων τὴν
ἐπιστολήν, ἣν πεπόμφατε πρός με. 21 ἐπέταξα οὖν ἐπισκέψασθαι, καὶ εὑρέθη ὅτι ἐστὶν ἡ πόλις ἐκείνη ἐξ αἰῶνος
βασιλεῦσιν ἀντιπαρατάσσουσα καὶ οἱ ἄνθρωποι ἀποστάσεις
καὶ πολέμους ἐν αὐτῇ συντελοῦντες 22 καὶ βασιλεῖς ἰσχυροὶ
καὶ σκληροὶ ἦσαν ἐν Ιερουσαλημ κυριεύοντες καὶ φορολο-
γοῦντες Κοίλην Συρίαν καὶ Φοινίκην. 23 νῦν οὖν ἐπέταξα
ἀποκωλῦσαι τοὺς ἀνθρώπους ἐκείνους τοῦ οἰκοδομῆσαι τὴν
πόλιν 24 καὶ προνοηθῆναι ὅπως μηθὲν παρὰ ταῦτα γένηται
καὶ μὴ προβῇ ἐπὶ πλεῖον τὰ τῆς κακίας εἰς τὸ βασιλεῖς ἐνο-
χλῆσαι. — 25 τότε ἀναγνωσθέντων τῶν παρὰ τοῦ βασιλέως
Ἀρταξέρξου γραφέντων ὁ Ραουμος καὶ Σαμσαῖος ὁ γραμματεὺς καὶ οἱ τούτοις συντασσόμενοι ἀναζεύξαντες κατὰ
σπουδὴν εἰς Ιερουσαλημ μεθ' ἵππου καὶ ὄχλου παρατάξεως
ἤρξαντο κωλύειν τοὺς οἰκοδομοῦντας. 26 καὶ ἤργει ἡ οἰκοδομὴ τοῦ ἱεροῦ τοῦ ἐν Ιερουσαλημ μέχρι τοῦ δευτέρου ἔτους
τῆς βασιλείας Δαρείου τοῦ Περσῶν βασιλέως.

3 Καὶ βασιλεὺς Δαρεῖος ἐποίησεν δοχὴν μεγάλην πᾶσιν
τοῖς ὑπ' αὐτὸν καὶ πᾶσιν τοῖς οἰκογενέσιν αὐτοῦ καὶ
πᾶσιν τοῖς μεγιστᾶσιν τῆς Μηδίας καὶ τῆς Περσίδος 2 καὶ
πᾶσιν τοῖς σατράπαις καὶ στρατηγοῖς καὶ τοπάρχαις τοῖς
ὑπ' αὐτὸν ἀπὸ τῆς Ἰνδικῆς μέχρι τῆς Αἰθιοπίας ἐν ταῖς
ἑκατὸν εἴκοσι ἑπτὰ σατραπείαις. 3 καὶ ἐφάγοσαν καὶ ἔπί-
οσαν καὶ ἐμπλησθέντες ἀνέλυσαν, ὁ δὲ Δαρεῖος ὁ βασιλεὺς
ἀνέλυσεν εἰς τὸν κοιτῶνα καὶ ἐκοιμήθη καὶ ἔξυπνος ἐγένετο.
4 τότε οἱ τρεῖς νεανίσκοι οἱ σωματοφύλακες οἱ φυλάσσοντες
τὸ σῶμα τοῦ βασιλέως εἶπαν ἕτερος πρὸς τὸν ἕτερον
5 Εἴπωμεν ἕκαστος ἡμῶν ἕνα λόγον, ὃς ὑπερισχύσει· καὶ οὗ
ἂν φανῇ τὸ ῥῆμα αὐτοῦ σοφώτερον τοῦ ἑτέρου, δώσει αὐτῷ
Δαρεῖος ὁ βασιλεὺς δωρεὰς μεγάλας καὶ ἐπινίκια μεγάλα
6 καὶ πορφύραν περιβαλέσθαι καὶ ἐν χρυσώμασιν πίνειν καὶ

King James Version

that rebellious and wicked city, do build the marketplaces, and repair the walls of it, and do lay the foundation of the temple.

19 Now if this city and the walls thereof be made up again, they will not only refuse to give tribute, but also rebel against kings.

20 And forasmuch as the things pertaining to the temple are now in hand, we think it meet not to neglect such a matter,

21 But to speak unto our lord the king, to the intent that, if it be thy pleasure, it may be sought out in the books of thy fathers:

22 And thou shalt find in the chronicles what is written concerning these things, and shalt understand that that city was rebellious, troubling both kings and cities:

23 And that the Jews were rebellious, and raised always wars therein; for the which cause even this city was made desolate.

24 Wherefore now we do declare unto thee, O lord the king, that if this city be built again, and the walls thereof set up anew, thou shalt from henceforth have no passage into Celosyria and Phenice.

25 Then the king wrote back again to Rathumus the storywriter, to Beeltethmus, to Semellius the scribe, and to the rest that were in commission, and dwellers in Samaria and Syria and Phenice, after this manner;

26 I have read the epistle which ye have sent unto me: therefore I commanded to make diligent search, and it hath been found that that city was from the beginning practising against kings;

27 And the men therein were given to rebellion and war: and that mighty kings and fierce were in Jerusalem, who reigned and exacted tributes in Celosyria and Phenice.

28 Now therefore I have commanded to hinder those men from building the city, and heed to be taken that there be no more done in it;

29 And that those wicked workers proceed no further to the annoyance of kings.

30 Then king Artaxerxes his letters being read, Rathumus, and Semellius the scribe, and the rest that were in commission with them, removing in haste toward Jerusalem with a troop of horsemen and a multitude of people in battle array, began to hinder the builders; and the building of the temple in Jerusalem ceased until the second year of the reign of Darius king of the Persians.

3 Now when Darius reigned, he made a great feast unto all his subjects, and unto all his household, and unto all the princes of Media and Persia,

2 And to all the governors and captains and lieutenants that were under him, from India unto Ethiopia, of an hundred twenty and seven provinces.

3 And when they had eaten and drunken, and being satisfied were gone home, then Darius the king went into his bedchamber, and slept, and soon after awaked.

4 Then three young men, that were of the guard that kept the king's body, spake one to another;

5 Let every one of us speak a sentence: he that shall overcome, and whose sentence shall seem wiser than the others, unto him shall the king Darius give great gifts, and great things in token of victory:

6 As, to be clothed in purple, to drink in gold, and to sleep

Today's English Version

Jerusalem and are rebuilding that evil and rebellious city.
They are restoring the marketplaces, repairing the walls,
and laying the foundations for a Temple. 19 If this city is
rebuilt and its walls are completed, the people will stop
paying taxes and will even rebel against royal authority.
20 Since work on the Temple has already begun, we consider it appropriate not to overlook such an important matter
21 but to bring it to the attention of Your Majesty. Then, if
it seems proper to you, a search may be made in the
records your ancestors kept. 22 You will find information
about these matters in the historical records, and you will
discover that this city has always been rebellious and
given trouble to other cities and kings. 23 The Jews have
used it from ancient times as a base for rebellions and
wars. That is why the city was destroyed. 24 We therefore
declare to you that if this city is rebuilt and its walls are
restored, Your Majesty will no longer be able to enter
Greater Syria and Phoenicia."

25 The emperor sent the following answer to the official
correspondent Rehum, Beltethmus, the secretary Shimshai,
and their associates who lived in Samaria, Syria, and
Phoenicia:

26 "After reading the letter which you sent me, I gave
orders for an investigation to be made, and it has indeed
been found that from ancient times Jerusalem has revolted
against royal authority, 27 and its people have been
involved in insurrections and wars. Powerful and cruel
kings have reigned there and have ruled over Greater Syria
and Phoenicia, from which they collected taxes. 28 Therefore I am now issuing orders that those men be prevented
from rebuilding the city and that necessary steps be taken
to insure that these orders will not be disobeyed, 29 so that
this trouble spot will no longer be a threat to the royal
interests."

30 As soon as this letter from Emperor Artaxerxes was read,
Rehum, Shimshai the secretary, and their associates hurried
to Jerusalem with a force of cavalry and a large number of
armed troops and began interfering with the rebuilding of
the Temple. The work had to stop, and no more was done
until the second year of the reign of Emperor Darius of
Persia.

3 The Emperor Darius gave a great banquet for all those
under him, all the members of his family and staff, all
the leading officials of Persia and Media, 2 all his chief officers, administrators, and the governors of the 127 provinces
stretching from India to Ethiopia.[a] 3 When everyone had
enough to eat and drink, they left, and Darius went to bed.
He fell asleep but soon awoke.

4 Then the three young men who served Emperor Darius as
his personal bodyguard said to one another, 5 "Let each one
of us name the one thing that he considers the strongest
thing in the world. The emperor will decide who has given
the wisest answer to this question and will give magnificent
gifts and prizes to the winner. 6 He will wear royal robes,
drink from a gold cup, and sleep in a gold bed. He will have

[a] *Greek* Ethiopia: *Ethiopia is the name given in Graeco-Roman times to the extensive territory south of the First Cataract of the Nile River. Cush was the ancient (Hebrew) name of this region which included within its borders most of modern Sudan and some of present-day Ethiopia (Abyssinia).*

New Revised Standard Version

Jerusalem and are building that rebellious and wicked city,
repairing its market places and walls and laying the foundations for a temple. 19 Now if this city is built and the walls
finished, they will not only refuse to pay tribute but will even
resist kings. 20 Since the building of the temple is now going
on, we think it best not to neglect such a matter, 21 but to
speak to our lord the king, in order that, if it seems good to
you, search may be made in the records of your ancestors.
22 You will find in the annals what has been written about
them, and will learn that this city was rebellious, troubling
both kings and other cities, 23 and that the Jews were rebels
and kept setting up blockades in it from of old. That is why
this city was laid waste. 24 Therefore we now make known
to you, O lord and king, that if this city is built and its walls
finished, you will no longer have access to Coelesyria and
Phoenicia."

25 Then the king, in reply to the recorder Rehum,
Beltethmus, the scribe Shimshai, and the others associated
with them and living in Samaria and Syria and Phoenicia,
wrote as follows:

26 "I have read the letter that you sent me. So I ordered
search to be made, and it has been found that this city from
of old has fought against kings, 27 that the people in it were
given to rebellion and war, and that mighty and cruel kings
ruled in Jerusalem and exacted tribute from Coelesyria and
Phoenicia. 28 Therefore I have now issued orders to prevent
these people from building the city and to take care that
nothing more be done 29 and that such wicked proceedings
go no further to the annoyance of kings."

30 Then, when the letter from King Artaxerxes was read,
Rehum and the scribe Shimshai and their associates went
quickly to Jerusalem, with cavalry and a large number of
armed troops, and began to hinder the builders. And the
building of the temple in Jerusalem stopped until the second
year of the reign of King Darius of the Persians.

3 Now King Darius gave a great banquet for all that were
under him, all that were born in his house, and all the
nobles of Media and Persia, 2 and all the satraps and generals and governors that were under him in the hundred twenty-seven satrapies from India to Ethiopia. 3 They ate and
drank, and when they were satisfied they went away, and
King Darius went to his bedroom; he went to sleep, but woke
up again.

4 Then the three young men of the bodyguard, who kept
guard over the person of the king, said to one another, 5 "Let
each of us state what one thing is strongest; and to the one
whose statement seems wisest, King Darius will give rich
gifts and great honors of victory. 6 He shall be clothed in
purple, and drink from gold cups, and sleep on a gold bed,[a]

[a] Gk *on gold*

ἐπὶ χρυσῷ καθεύδειν καὶ ἅρμα χρυσοχάλινον καὶ κίδαριν βυσσίνην καὶ μανιάκην περὶ τὸν τράχηλον, 7 καὶ δεύτερος καθιεῖται Δαρείου διὰ τὴν σοφίαν αὐτοῦ καὶ συγγενὴς Δαρείου κληθήσεται. 8 καὶ τότε γράψαντες ἕκαστος τὸν ἑαυτοῦ λόγον ἐσφραγίσαντο καὶ ἔθηκαν ὑπὸ τὸ προσκεφάλαιον Δαρείου τοῦ βασιλέως καὶ εἶπαν 9 Ὅταν ἐγερθῇ ὁ βασιλεύς, δώσουσιν αὐτῷ τὸ γράμμα, καὶ ὃν ἂν κρίνῃ ὁ βασιλεὺς καὶ οἱ τρεῖς μεγιστᾶνες τῆς Περσίδος ὅτι ὁ λόγος αὐτοῦ σοφώτερος, αὐτῷ δοθήσεται τὸ νῖκος καθὼς γέγραπται. 10 ὁ εἷς ἔγραψεν Ὑπερισχύει ὁ οἶνος. 11 ὁ ἕτερος ἔγραψεν Ὑπερισχύει ὁ βασιλεύς. 12 ὁ τρίτος ἔγραψεν Ὑπερισχύουσιν αἱ γυναῖκες, ὑπὲρ δὲ πάντα νικᾷ ἡ ἀλήθεια. 13 καὶ ὅτε ἐξηγέρθη ὁ βασιλεύς, λαβόντες τὸ γράμμα ἔδωκαν αὐτῷ, καὶ ἀνέγνω. 14 καὶ ἐξαποστείλας ἐκάλεσεν πάντας τοὺς μεγιστᾶνας τῆς Περσίδος καὶ τῆς Μηδίας καὶ σατράπας καὶ στρατηγοὺς καὶ τοπάρχας καὶ ὑπάτους καὶ ἐκάθισεν ἐν τῷ χρηματιστηρίῳ, καὶ ἀνεγνώσθη τὸ γράμμα ἐνώπιον αὐτῶν. 15 καὶ εἶπεν Καλέσατε τοὺς νεανίσκους, καὶ αὐτοὶ δηλώσουσιν τοὺς λόγους αὐτῶν· καὶ ἐκλήθησαν καὶ εἰσήλθοσαν. 16 καὶ εἶπαν αὐτοῖς Ἀπαγγείλατε ἡμῖν περὶ τῶν γεγραμμένων.

17 Καὶ ἤρξατο ὁ πρῶτος ὁ εἴπας περὶ τῆς ἰσχύος τοῦ οἴνου καὶ ἔφη οὕτως 18 Ἄνδρες, πῶς ὑπερισχύει ὁ οἶνος; πάντας τοὺς ἀνθρώπους τοὺς πίνοντας αὐτὸν πλανᾷ τὴν διάνοιαν. 19 τοῦ τε βασιλέως καὶ τοῦ ὀρφανοῦ ποιεῖ τὴν διάνοιαν μίαν, τήν τε τοῦ οἰκέτου καὶ τὴν τοῦ ἐλευθέρου, τήν τε τοῦ πένητος καὶ τὴν τοῦ πλουσίου. 20 καὶ πᾶσαν διάνοιαν μεταστρέφει εἰς εὐωχίαν καὶ εὐφροσύνην καὶ οὐ μέμνηται πᾶσαν λύπην καὶ πᾶν ὀφείλημα. 21 καὶ πάσας καρδίας ποιεῖ πλουσίας καὶ οὐ μέμνηται βασιλέα οὐδὲ σατράπην καὶ πάντα διὰ ταλάντων ποιεῖ λαλεῖν. 22 καὶ οὐ μέμνηται, ὅταν πίνωσιν, φιλιάζειν φίλοις καὶ ἀδελφοῖς, καὶ μετ᾽ οὐ πολὺ σπῶνται μαχαίρας. 23 καὶ ὅταν ἀπὸ τοῦ οἴνου γενηθῶσιν, οὐ μέμνηται ἃ ἔπραξαν. 24 ὦ ἄνδρες, οὐχ ὑπερισχύει ὁ οἶνος, ὅτι οὕτως ἀναγκάζει ποιεῖν; καὶ ἐσίγησεν οὕτως εἴπας.

4 Καὶ ἤρξατο ὁ δεύτερος λαλεῖν ὁ εἴπας περὶ τῆς ἰσχύος τοῦ βασιλέως 2 Ὦ ἄνδρες, οὐχ ὑπερισχύουσιν οἱ ἄνθρωποι τὴν γῆν καὶ τὴν θάλασσαν κατακρατοῦντες καὶ πάντα τὰ ἐν αὐτοῖς; 3 ὁ δὲ βασιλεὺς ὑπερισχύει καὶ κυριεύει αὐτῶν καὶ δεσπόζει αὐτῶν, καὶ πᾶν, ὃ ἐὰν εἴπῃ αὐτοῖς, ἐνακούουσιν. 4 ἐὰν εἴπῃ αὐτοῖς ποιῆσαι πόλεμον ἕτερος πρὸς τὸν ἕτερον, ποιοῦσιν· ἐὰν δὲ ἐξαποστείλῃ αὐτοὺς πρὸς τοὺς πολεμίους, βαδίζουσιν καὶ κατεργάζονται τὰ ὄρη καὶ τὰ τείχη καὶ τοὺς πύργους. 5 φονεύουσιν καὶ φονεύονται καὶ τὸν λόγον τοῦ βασιλέως οὐ παραβαίνουσιν· ἐὰν δὲ νικήσωσιν, τῷ βασιλεῖ κομίζουσιν πάντα, καὶ ὅσα ἐὰν προνομεύσωσιν, καὶ τὰ ἄλλα πάντα. 6 καὶ ὅσοι οὐ στρατεύονται οὐδὲ πολεμοῦσιν, ἀλλὰ γεωργοῦσιν τὴν γῆν, πάλιν ὅταν σπείρωσι, θερίσαντες ἀναφέρουσιν τῷ βασιλεῖ· καὶ ἕτερος τὸν ἕτερον ἀναγκάζοντες ἀναφέρουσι τοὺς φόρους τῷ βασιλεῖ. 7 καὶ

upon gold, and a chariot with bridles of gold, and an headtire of fine linen, and a chain about his neck:

7 And he shall sit next to Darius because of his wisdom, and shall be called Darius his cousin.

8 And then every one wrote his sentence, sealed it, and laid it under king Darius his pillow;

9 And said that, when the king is risen, some will give him the writings; and of whose side the king and the three princes of Persia shall judge that his sentence is the wisest, to him shall the victory be given, as was appointed.

10 The first wrote, Wine is the strongest.

11 The second wrote, The king is strongest.

12 The third wrote, Women are strongest: but above all things Truth beareth away the victory.

13 ¶ Now when the king was risen up, they took their writings, and delivered them unto him, and so he read them:

14 And sending forth he called all the princes of Persia and Media, and the governors, and the captains, and the lieutenants, and the chief officers;

15 And sat him down in the royal seat of judgment; and the writings were read before them.

16 And he said, Call the young men, and they shall declare their own sentences. So they were called, and came in.

17 And he said unto them, Declare unto us your mind concerning the writings. Then began the first, who had spoken of the strength of wine;

18 And he said thus, O ye men, how exceeding strong is wine! it causeth all men to err that drink it:

19 It maketh the mind of the king and of the fatherless child to be all one; of the bondman and of the freeman, of the poor man and of the rich:

20 It turneth also every thought into jollity and mirth, so that a man remembereth neither sorrow nor debt:

21 And it maketh every heart rich, so that a man remembereth neither king nor governor; and it maketh to speak all things by talents:

22 And when they are in their cups, they forget their love both to friends and brethren, and a little after draw out swords:

23 But when they are from the wine, they remember not what they have done.

24 O ye men, is not wine the strongest, that enforceth to do thus? And when he had so spoken, he held his peace.

4 Then the second, that had spoken of the strength of the king, began to say,

2 O ye men, do not men excel in strength, that bear rule over sea and land, and all things in them?

3 But yet the king is more mighty: for he is lord of all these things, and hath dominion over them; and whatsoever he commandeth them they do.

4 If he bid them make war the one against the other, they do it: if he send them out against the enemies, they go, and break down mountains, walls, and towers.

5 They slay and are slain, and transgress not the king's commandment: if they get the victory, they bring all to the king, as well the spoil, as all things else.

6 Likewise for those that are no soldiers, and have not to do with wars, but use husbundry, when they have reaped again that which they had sown, they bring it to the king, and compel one another to pay tribute unto the king.

TODAY'S ENGLISH VERSION

a chariot with gold-studded bridles, wear a fine linen turban,
and have a gold necklace. 7 Because of his wisdom he will be
an adviser to the emperor and will be given the title "Relative
of the Emperor."

8 Then each of them wrote down the best answer he could
think of, sealed it, and put it under the emperor's pillow.
They said to one another, 9 "When the emperor wakes up,
the statements will be given to him. He and the three leading
officials of Persia will decide who gave the wisest answer.
The winner will be given the prize on the basis of what he
has written." 10 The first wrote, "There is nothing stronger
than wine." 11 The second wrote, "There is nothing stronger
than the emperor." 12 And the third wrote, "There is nothing
stronger than a woman, but truth can conquer anything."

13 When the emperor woke up, the written statements were
given to him, and he read them. 14 Then he sent messengers
and called together all the leading officials of Persia and
Media, including the chief officers, administrators, governors, and commissioners. 15 He took his seat in the council
chamber and had the three statements read aloud. 16 "Bring
in the three young men," he said, "and let them explain their
answers." So when they were brought in, 17 they were asked
to explain what they had written.

The bodyguard who had written about the strength of
wine spoke first: 18 "Gentlemen," he began, "wine is clearly
the strongest thing in the world. It confuses the mind of
everyone who drinks it. 19 It has exactly the same effect on
everyone: king or orphan, slave or free, rich or poor. 20 It
makes every thought happy and carefree, and makes one forget every sorrow and responsibility. 21 It makes everyone feel
rich, ignore the power of kings and officials, and talk as if he
owned the whole world. 22 When men drink wine, they forget who their friends and neighbors are, and then they are
soon drawing their swords to fight them. 23 Then, when they
sober up, they don't remember what they have done.
24 Gentlemen," he concluded, "if wine makes men act in this
way, it certainly must be the strongest thing in the world."

4 The bodyguard who had written about the strength of
the emperor spoke next. 2 "Gentlemen," he began,
"nothing in the world is stronger than men, since they rule
over land and sea and, in fact, over everything in the world.
3 But the emperor is the strongest of them all; he is their lord
and master, and men obey him, no matter what he commands. 4 If he tells them to make war on one another, they
do it. If he sends them out against his enemies, they go, even
if they have to break down mountains, walls, or towers.
5 They may kill or be killed, but they never disobey the
emperor's orders. If they are victorious, they bring him all
their loot and everything else they have taken in battle.
6 Farmers do not go out to war, but even they bring to the
emperor a part of everything that they harvest, and they
compel one another to pay taxes to the emperor. 7 Although

NEW REVISED STANDARD VERSION

and have a chariot with gold bridles, and a turban of fine
linen, and a necklace around his neck; 7 and because of his
wisdom he shall sit next to Darius and shall be called
Kinsman of Darius."

8 Then each wrote his own statement, and they sealed
them and put them under the pillow of King Darius, 9 and
said, "When the king wakes, they will give him the writing;
and to the one whose statement the king and the three
nobles of Persia judge to be wisest the victory shall be given
according to what is written." 10 The first wrote, "Wine is
strongest." 11 The second wrote, "The king is strongest."
12 The third wrote, "Women are strongest, but above all
things truth is victor."[a]

13 When the king awoke, they took the writing and gave
it to him, and he read it. 14 Then he sent and summoned all
the nobles of Persia and Media and the satraps and generals
and governors and prefects, 15 and he took his seat in the
council chamber, and the writing was read in their presence.
16 He said, "Call the young men, and they shall explain their
statements." So they were summoned, and came in. 17 They
said to them, "Explain to us what you have written."

Then the first, who had spoken of the strength of wine,
began and said: 18 "Gentlemen, how is wine the strongest? It
leads astray the minds of all who drink it. 19 It makes equal
the mind of the king and the orphan, of the slave and the
free, of the poor and the rich. 20 It turns every thought to
feasting and mirth, and forgets all sorrow and debt. 21 It
makes all hearts feel rich, forgets kings and satraps, and
makes everyone talk in millions.[b] 22 When people drink they
forget to be friendly with friends and kindred, and before
long they draw their swords. 23 And when they recover from
the wine, they do not remember what they have done.
24 Gentlemen, is not wine the strongest, since it forces people
to do these things?" When he had said this, he stopped
speaking.

4 Then the second, who had spoken of the strength of the
king, began to speak: 2 "Gentlemen, are not men
strongest, who rule over land and sea and all that is in
them? 3 But the king is stronger; he is their lord and master,
and whatever he says to them they obey. 4 If he tells them to
make war on one another, they do it; and if he sends them
out against the enemy, they go, and conquer mountains,
walls, and towers. 5 They kill and are killed, and do not disobey the king's command; if they win the victory, they bring
everything to the king—whatever spoil they take and everything else. 6 Likewise those who do not serve in the army or
make war but till the soil; whenever they sow and reap, they
bring some to the king; and they compel one another to pay

a Or *but truth is victor over all things* b Gk *talents*

Greek Old Testament

αὐτὸς εἷς μόνος ἐστίν· ἐὰν εἴπῃ ἀποκτεῖναι, ἀποκτέννουσιν·
εἶπεν ἀφεῖναι, ἀφίουσιν· 8 εἶπε πατάξαι, τύπτουσιν· εἶπεν
ἐρημῶσαι, ἐρημοῦσιν· εἶπεν οἰκοδομῆσαι, οἰκοδομοῦσιν·
9 εἶπεν ἐκκόψαι, ἐκκόπτουσιν· εἶπεν φυτεῦσαι, φυτεύουσιν.
10 καὶ πᾶς ὁ λαὸς αὐτοῦ καὶ αἱ δυνάμεις αὐτοῦ ἐνακούουσιν.
11 πρὸς δὲ τούτοις αὐτὸς ἀνάκειται, ἐσθίει καὶ πίνει καὶ
καθεύδει, αὐτοὶ δὲ τηροῦσιν κύκλῳ περὶ αὐτὸν καὶ οὐ δύνανται ἕκαστος ἀπελθεῖν καὶ ποιεῖν τὰ ἔργα αὐτοῦ οὐδὲ
παρακούουσιν αὐτοῦ. 12 ὦ ἄνδρες, πῶς οὐχ ὑπερισχύει ὁ
βασιλεύς, ὅτι οὕτως ἐπακουστός ἐστιν; καὶ ἐσίγησεν.
13 Ὁ δὲ τρίτος ὁ εἴπας περὶ τῶν γυναικῶν καὶ τῆς ἀληθείας — οὗτός ἐστιν Ζοροβαβελ — ἤρξατο λαλεῖν 14 Ἄνδρες,
οὐ μέγας ὁ βασιλεὺς καὶ πολλοὶ οἱ ἄνθρωποι καὶ ὁ οἶνος
ἰσχύει; τίς οὖν ὁ δεσπόζων αὐτῶν ἢ τίς ὁ κυριεύων αὐτῶν;
οὐχ αἱ γυναῖκες; 15 αἱ γυναῖκες ἐγέννησαν τὸν βασιλέα καὶ
πάντα τὸν λαόν, ὃς κυριεύει τῆς θαλάσσης καὶ τῆς γῆς.
16 καὶ ἐξ αὐτῶν ἐγένοντο, καὶ αὗται ἐξέθρεψαν αὐτοὺς τοὺς
φυτεύοντας τοὺς ἀμπελῶνας, ἐξ ὧν ὁ οἶνος γίνεται. 17 καὶ
αὗται ποιοῦσιν τὰς στολὰς τῶν ἀνθρώπων, καὶ αὗται
ποιοῦσιν δόξαν τοῖς ἀνθρώποις, καὶ οὐ δύνανται οἱ ἄνθρωποι
εἶναι χωρὶς τῶν γυναικῶν. 18 ἐὰν δὲ συναγάγωσιν χρυσίον
καὶ ἀργύριον καὶ πᾶν πρᾶγμα ὡραῖον καὶ ἴδωσιν γυναῖκα
μίαν καλὴν τῷ εἴδει καὶ τῷ κάλλει, 19 καὶ ταῦτα πάντα
ἀφέντες εἰς αὐτὴν ἐγκέχηναν καὶ χάσκοντες τὸ στόμα θεωροῦσιν αὐτήν, καὶ πάντες αὐτὴν αἱρετίζουσιν μᾶλλον ἢ τὸ
χρυσίον καὶ τὸ ἀργύριον καὶ πᾶν πρᾶγμα ὡραῖον. 20 ἄνθρωπος τὸν ἑαυτοῦ πατέρα ἐγκαταλείπει, ὃς ἐξέθρεψεν αὐτόν,
καὶ τὴν ἰδίαν χώραν καὶ πρὸς τὴν ἰδίαν γυναῖκα κολλᾶται·
21 καὶ μετὰ τῆς γυναικὸς ἀφίησι τὴν ψυχὴν καὶ οὔτε τὸν
πατέρα μέμνηται οὔτε τὴν μητέρα οὔτε τὴν χώραν. 22 καὶ
ἐντεῦθεν δεῖ ὑμᾶς γνῶναι ὅτι αἱ γυναῖκες κυριεύουσιν ὑμῶν·
οὐχὶ πονεῖτε καὶ μοχθεῖτε καὶ πάντα ταῖς γυναιξὶν δίδοτε
καὶ φέρετε; 23 καὶ λαμβάνει ἄνθρωπος τὴν ῥομφαίαν αὐτοῦ
καὶ ἐκπορεύεται ἐξοδεύειν καὶ λῃστεύειν καὶ κλέπτειν καὶ
εἰς τὴν θάλασσαν πλεῖν καὶ ποταμούς. 24 καὶ τὸν λέοντα
θεωρεῖ καὶ ἐν σκότει βαδίζει, καὶ ὅταν κλέψῃ καὶ ἁρπάσῃ καὶ
λωποδυτήσῃ, τῇ ἐρωμένῃ ἀποφέρει. 25 καὶ πλεῖον ἀγαπᾷ
ἄνθρωπος τὴν ἰδίαν γυναῖκα μᾶλλον ἢ τὸν πατέρα καὶ τὴν
μητέρα· 26 καὶ πολλοὶ ἀπενοήθησαν ταῖς ἰδίαις διανοίαις
διὰ τὰς γυναῖκας καὶ δοῦλοι ἐγένοντο δι᾽ αὐτάς, 27 καὶ πολλοὶ ἀπώλοντο καὶ ἐσφάλησαν καὶ ἡμάρτοσαν διὰ τὰς γυναῖκας. 28 καὶ νῦν οὐ πιστεύετέ μοι; οὐχὶ μέγας ὁ βασιλεὺς τῇ
ἐξουσίᾳ αὐτοῦ; οὐχὶ πᾶσαι αἱ χῶραι εὐλαβοῦνται ἅψασθαι
αὐτοῦ; 29 ἐθεώρουν αὐτὸν καὶ Ἀπάμην τὴν θυγατέρα Βαρ-
τάκου τοῦ θαυμαστοῦ τὴν παλλακὴν τοῦ βασιλέως καθημένην
ἐν δεξιᾷ τοῦ βασιλέως 30 καὶ ἀφαιροῦσαν τὸ διάδημα ἀπὸ
τῆς κεφαλῆς τοῦ βασιλέως καὶ ἐπιτιθοῦσαν ἑαυτῇ καὶ ἐρρά-
πιζεν τὸν βασιλέα τῇ ἀριστερᾷ. 31 καὶ πρὸς τούτοις ὁ βασιλεὺς χάσκων τὸ στόμα ἐθεώρει αὐτήν· καὶ ἐὰν προσγελάσῃ

King James Version

7 And yet he is but one man: if he command to kill, they kill; if he command to spare, they spare;

8 If he command to smite, they smite; if he command to make desolate, they make desolate; if he command to build, they build;

9 If he command to cut down, they cut down; if he command to plant, they plant.

10 So all his people and his armies obey him: furthermore he lieth down, he eateth and drinketh, and taketh his rest:

11 And these keep watch round about him, neither may any one depart, and do his own business, neither disobey they him in any thing.

12 O ye men, how should not the king be mightiest, when in such sort he is obeyed? And he held his tongue.

13 ¶ Then the third, who had spoken of women, and of the truth, (this was Zorobabel) began to speak.

14 O ye men, it is not the great king, nor the multitude of men, neither is it wine, that excelleth; who is it then that ruleth them, or hath the lordship over them? are they not women?

15 Women have borne the king and all the people that bear rule by sea and land.

16 Even of them came they: and they nourished them up that planted the vineyards, from whence the wine cometh.

17 These also make garments for men; these bring glory unto men; and without women cannot men be.

18 Yea, and if men have gathered together gold and silver, or any other goodly thing, do they not love a woman which is comely in favour and beauty?

19 And letting all those things go, do they not gape, and even with open mouth fix their eyes fast on her; and have not all men more desire unto her than unto silver or gold, or any goodly thing whatsoever?

20 A man leaveth his own father that brought him up, and his own country, and cleaveth unto his wife.

21 He sticketh not to spend his life with his wife, and remembereth neither father, nor mother, nor country.

22 By this also ye must know that women have dominion over you: do ye not labour and toil, and give and bring all to the woman?

23 Yea, a man taketh his sword, and goeth his way to rob and to steal, to sail upon the sea and upon rivers;

24 And looketh upon a lion, and goeth in the darkness; and when he hath stolen, spoiled, and robbed, he bringeth it to his love.

25 Wherefore a man loveth his wife better than father or mother.

26 Yea, many there be that have run out of their wits for women, and become servants for their sakes.

27 Many also have perished, have erred, and sinned, for women.

28 And now do ye not believe me? is not the king great in his power? do not all regions fear to touch him?

29 Yet did I see him and Apame the king's concubine, the daughter of the admirable Bartacus, sitting at the right hand of the king,

30 And taking the crown from the king's head, and setting it upon her own head; she also struck the king with her left hand.

31 And yet for all this the king gaped and gazed upon her with open mouth: if she laughed upon him, he laughed also:

Today's English Version

the emperor is only one man, if he orders people to kill, they
kill; if he orders them to set prisoners free, they do it; 8 if he
orders them to attack, they do; if he orders destruction, they
destroy; if he orders them to build, they build; 9 if he orders
crops to be destroyed or fields to be planted, it is done.
10 Everybody, soldier or civilian, obeys the emperor. And
when he sits down to eat or drink and then falls asleep,
11 his servants stand guard around him, without being able
to go and take care of their own affairs, for they never disobey him. 12 Gentlemen," he concluded, "since people obey
the emperor like this, certainly nothing in the world is
stronger than he is."

13 The bodyguard who had written about women and the
truth—it was Zerubbabel—spoke last. 14 "Gentlemen," he
began, "the emperor is certainly powerful, men are numerous, and wine is strong, but who rules and controls them
all? It is women! 15 Women gave birth to the emperor and all
the men who rule over land and sea. 16 Women brought
them into the world. Women brought up the men who planted the vineyards from which wine comes. 17 Women make
the clothes that men wear; women bring honor to men; in
fact, without women, men couldn't live.

18 "Men may accumulate silver or gold or other beautiful
things, but if they see a woman with a pretty face or a good
figure, 19 they will leave it all to gape and stare, and they
will desire her more than their wealth. 20 A man will leave
his own father, who brought him up, and leave his own
country to get married. 21 He will forget his father, his mother, and his country to spend the rest of his life with his wife.
22 So you must recognize that women are your masters.
Don't you work and sweat and then take all that you have
earned and give it to your wives? 23 A man will take his
sword and go out to attack, rob and steal, and sail the seas
and rivers. 24 He may have to face lions or travel in the dark,
but when he has robbed, stolen, and plundered, he will bring
the loot home to the woman he loves.

25 "A man loves his wife more than his parents. 26 Some
men are driven out of their minds on account of a woman,
and others become slaves for the sake of a woman. 27 Others
have been put to death, have ruined their lives, or have committed crimes because of a woman. 28 So now do you
believe me?

"The emperor's power is certainly great—no nation has
the courage to attack him. 29 But once I saw him with
Apame, his concubine, the daughter of the famous Bartacus.
While sitting at the emperor's right, 30 she took his crown off
his head, put it on her own, and then slapped his face with
her left hand. 31 All the emperor did was look at her with his
mouth open. Whenever she smiles at him, he smiles back;

New Revised Standard Version

taxes to the king. 7 And yet he is only one man! If he tells
them to kill, they kill; if he tells them to release, they release;
8 if he tells them to attack, they attack; if he tells them to lay
waste, they lay waste; if he tells them to build, they build;
9 if he tells them to cut down, they cut down; if he tells them
to plant, they plant. 10 All his people and his armies obey
him. Furthermore, he reclines, he eats and drinks and sleeps,
11 but they keep watch around him, and no one may go away
to attend to his own affairs, nor do they disobey him.
12 Gentlemen, why is not the king the strongest, since he is to
be obeyed in this fashion?" And he stopped speaking.

13 Then the third, who had spoken of women and truth
(and this was Zerubbabel), began to speak: 14 "Gentlemen, is
not the king great, and are not men many, and is not wine
strong? Who is it, then, that rules them, or has the mastery
over them? Is it not women? 15 Women gave birth to the
king and to every people that rules over sea and land.
16 From women they came; and women brought up the very
men who plant the vineyards from which comes wine.
17 Women make men's clothes; they bring men glory; men
cannot exist without women. 18 If men gather gold and silver or any other beautiful thing, and then see a woman lovely in appearance and beauty, 19 they let all those things go,
and gape at her, and with open mouths stare at her, and all
prefer her to gold or silver or any other beautiful thing. 20 A
man leaves his own father, who brought him up, and his
own country, and clings to his wife. 21 With his wife he ends
his days, with no thought of his father or his mother or his
country. 22 Therefore you must realize that women rule over
you!

"Do you not labor and toil, and bring everything and give
it to women? 23 A man takes his sword, and goes out to
travel and rob and steal and to sail the sea and rivers; 24 he
faces lions, and he walks in darkness, and when he steals
and robs and plunders, he brings it back to the woman he
loves. 25 A man loves his wife more than his father or his
mother. 26 Many men have lost their minds because of
women, and have become slaves because of them. 27 Many
have perished, or stumbled, or sinned because of women.
28 And now do you not believe me?

"Is not the king great in his power? Do not all lands fear to
touch him? 29 Yet I have seen him with Apame, the king's
concubine, the daughter of the illustrious Bartacus; she
would sit at the king's right hand 30 and take the crown
from the king's head and put it on her own, and slap the
king with her left hand. 31 At this the king would gaze at her
with mouth agape. If she smiles at him, he laughs; if she

αὐτῷ, γελᾷ· ἐὰν δὲ πικρανθῇ ἐπ᾿ αὐτόν, κολακεύει αὐτήν,
ὅπως διαλλαγῇ αὐτῷ. 32 ὦ ἄνδρες, πῶς οὐχὶ ἰσχυραὶ αἱ
γυναῖκες, ὅτι οὕτως πράσσουσιν; 33 καὶ τότε ὁ βασιλεὺς καὶ
οἱ μεγιστᾶνες ἐνέβλεπον ἕτερος πρὸς τὸν ἕτερον. — 34 καὶ
ἤρξατο λαλεῖν περὶ τῆς ἀληθείας Ἄνδρες, οὐχὶ ἰσχυραὶ αἱ
γυναῖκες; μεγάλη ἡ γῆ, καὶ ὑψηλὸς ὁ οὐρανός, καὶ ταχὺς τῷ
δρόμῳ ὁ ἥλιος, ὅτι στρέφεται ἐν τῷ κύκλῳ τοῦ οὐρανοῦ καὶ
πάλιν ἀποτρέχει εἰς τὸν ἑαυτοῦ τόπον ἐν μιᾷ ἡμέρᾳ. 35 οὐχὶ
μέγας ὃς ταῦτα ποιεῖ; καὶ ἡ ἀλήθεια μεγάλη καὶ ἰσχυροτέρα
παρὰ πάντα. 36 πᾶσα ἡ γῆ τὴν ἀλήθειαν καλεῖ, καὶ ὁ οὐρανὸς αὐτὴν εὐλογεῖ, καὶ πάντα τὰ ἔργα σείεται καὶ τρέμει,
καὶ οὐκ ἔστιν μετ᾿ αὐτοῦ ἄδικον οὐθέν. 37 ἄδικος ὁ οἶνος,
ἄδικος ὁ βασιλεύς, ἄδικοι αἱ γυναῖκες, ἄδικοι πάντες οἱ υἱοὶ
τῶν ἀνθρώπων, καὶ ἄδικα πάντα τὰ ἔργα αὐτῶν, πάντα τὰ
τοιαῦτα· καὶ οὐκ ἔστιν ἐν αὐτοῖς ἀλήθεια, καὶ ἐν τῇ ἀδικίᾳ
αὐτῶν ἀπολοῦνται. 38 ἡ δὲ ἀλήθεια μένει καὶ ἰσχύει εἰς τὸν
αἰῶνα καὶ ζῇ καὶ κρατεῖ εἰς τὸν αἰῶνα τοῦ αἰῶνος. 39 καὶ
οὐκ ἔστιν παρ᾿ αὐτῇ λαμβάνειν πρόσωπα οὐδὲ διάφορα, ἀλλὰ
τὰ δίκαια ποιεῖ ἀπὸ πάντων τῶν ἀδίκων καὶ πονηρῶν· καὶ
πάντες εὐδοκοῦσι τοῖς ἔργοις αὐτῆς, καὶ οὐκ ἔστιν ἐν τῇ
κρίσει αὐτῆς οὐθὲν ἄδικον. 40 καὶ αὐτῇ ἡ ἰσχὺς καὶ τὸ βασίλειον καὶ ἡ ἐξουσία καὶ ἡ μεγαλειότης τῶν πάντων αἰώνων.
εὐλογητὸς ὁ θεὸς τῆς ἀληθείας. 41 καὶ ἐσιώπησεν τοῦ
λαλεῖν· καὶ πᾶς ὁ λαὸς τότε ἐφώνησεν, καὶ τότε εἶπον
Μεγάλη ἡ ἀλήθεια καὶ ὑπερισχύει.

42 Τότε ὁ βασιλεὺς εἶπεν αὐτῷ Αἴτησαι ὃ θέλεις πλείω τῶν
γεγραμμένων, καὶ δώσομέν σοι, ὃν τρόπον εὑρέθης σοφώτερος. καὶ ἐχόμενός μου καθήσῃ καὶ συγγενής μου κληθήσῃ.
43 τότε εἶπεν τῷ βασιλεῖ Μνήσθητι τὴν εὐχήν, ἣν ηὔξω
οἰκοδομῆσαι τὴν Ιερουσαλημ ἐν τῇ ἡμέρᾳ, ᾗ τὸ βασίλειόν
σου παρέλαβες, 44 καὶ πάντα τὰ σκεύη τὰ λημφθέντα ἐξ
Ιερουσαλημ ἐκπέμψαι, ἃ ἐξεχώρισεν Κῦρος, ὅτε ηὔξατο
ἐκκόψαι Βαβυλῶνα, καὶ ηὔξατο ἐξαποστεῖλαι ἐκεῖ. 45 καὶ σὺ
εὔξω οἰκοδομῆσαι τὸν ναόν, ὃν ἐνεπύρισαν οἱ Ιδουμαῖοι, ὅτε
ἠρημώθη ἡ Ιουδαία ὑπὸ τῶν Χαλδαίων. 46 καὶ νῦν τοῦτό
ἐστιν, ὅ σε ἀξιῶ, κύριε βασιλεῦ, καὶ ὃ αἰτοῦμαί σε, καὶ αὕτη
ἐστὶν ἡ μεγαλωσύνη ἡ παρὰ σοῦ· δέομαι οὖν ἵνα ποιήσῃς
τὴν εὐχήν, ἣν ηὔξω τῷ βασιλεῖ τοῦ οὐρανοῦ ποιῆσαι ἐκ στόματός σου. — 47 τότε ἀναστὰς Δαρεῖος ὁ βασιλεὺς κατεφίλησεν αὐτὸν καὶ ἔγραψεν αὐτῷ τὰς ἐπιστολὰς πρὸς πάντας
τοὺς οἰκονόμους καὶ τοπάρχας καὶ στρατηγοὺς καὶ σατράπας, ἵνα προπέμψωσιν αὐτὸν καὶ τοὺς μετ᾿ αὐτοῦ πάντας
ἀναβαίνοντας οἰκοδομῆσαι τὴν Ιερουσαλημ. 48 καὶ πᾶσι τοῖς
τοπάρχαις ἐν Κοίλῃ Συρίᾳ καὶ Φοινίκῃ καὶ τοῖς ἐν τῷ
Λιβάνῳ ἔγραψεν ἐπιστολὰς μεταφέρειν ξύλα κέδρινα ἀπὸ
τοῦ Λιβάνου εἰς Ιερουσαλημ καὶ ὅπως οἰκοδομήσωσιν μετ᾿
αὐτοῦ τὴν πόλιν. 49 καὶ ἔγραψεν πᾶσι τοῖς Ιουδαίοις τοῖς
ἀναβαίνουσιν ἀπὸ τῆς βασιλείας εἰς τὴν Ιουδαίαν ὑπὲρ τῆς
ἐλευθερίας, πάντα δυνατὸν καὶ σατράπην καὶ τοπάρχην καὶ
οἰκονόμον μὴ ἐπελεύσεσθαι ἐπὶ τὰς θύρας αὐτῶν, 50 καὶ

but if she took any displeasure at him, the king was fain to flatter, that she might be reconciled to him again.

32 O ye men, how can it be but women should be strong, seeing they do thus?

33 Then the king and the princes looked one upon another: so he began to speak of the truth.

34 O ye men, are not women strong? great is the earth, high is the heaven, swift is the sun in his course, for he compasseth the heavens round about, and fetcheth his course again to his own place in one day.

35 Is he not great that maketh these things? therefore great is the truth, and stronger than all things.

36 All the earth calleth upon the truth, and the heaven blesseth it: all works shake and tremble at it, and with it is no unrighteous thing.

37 Wine is wicked, the king is wicked, women are wicked, all the children of men are wicked, and such are all their wicked works; and there is no truth in them; in their unrighteousness also they shall perish.

38 As for the truth, it endureth, and is always strong; it liveth and conquereth for evermore.

39 With her there is no accepting of persons or rewards; but she doeth the things that are just, and refraineth from all unjust and wicked things; and all men do well like of her works.

40 Neither in her judgment is any unrighteousness; and she is the strength, kingdom, power, and majesty, of all ages. Blessed be the God of truth.

41 And with that he held his peace. And all the people then shouted, and said, Great is Truth, and mighty above all things.

42 Then said the king unto him, Ask what thou wilt more than is appointed in the writing, and we will give it thee, because thou art found wisest; and thou shalt sit next me, and shalt be called my cousin.

43 Then said he unto the king, Remember thy vow, which thou hast vowed to build Jerusalem, in the day when thou camest to thy kingdom,

44 And to send away all the vessels that were taken away out of Jerusalem, which Cyrus set apart, when he vowed to destroy Babylon, and to send them again thither.

45 Thou also hast vowed to build up the temple, which the Edomites burned when Judea was made desolate by the Chaldees.

46 And now, O lord the king, this is that which I require, and which I desire of thee, and this is the princely liberality proceeding from thyself: I desire therefore that thou make good the vow, the performance whereof with thine own mouth thou hast vowed to the King of heaven.

47 Then Darius the king stood up, and kissed him, and wrote letters for him unto all the treasurers and lieutenants and captains and governors, that they should safely convey on their way both him, and all those that go up with him to build Jerusalem.

48 He wrote letters also unto the lieutenants that were in Celosyria and Phenice, and unto them in Libanus, that they should bring cedar wood from Libanus unto Jerusalem, and that they should build the city with him.

49 Moreover he wrote for all the Jews that went out of his realm up into Jewry, concerning their freedom, that no officer, no ruler, no lieutenant, nor treasurer, should forcibly enter into their doors;

Today's English Version

and when she gets angry with him, he flatters her and teases her until she is in a good mood again. 32 Gentlemen, if women can do all that, surely there can be nothing stronger in the world." 33 The emperor and his officials just looked at one another.

Then Zerubbabel began to speak about truth. 34 "Yes, gentlemen," he said, "women are very strong. But think of how big the earth is, how high the sky is; think how fast the sun moves, as it rapidly circles the whole sky in a single day. 35 If the sun can do this, it is certainly great. But truth is greater and stronger than all of these things. 36 Everyone on earth honors truth; heaven praises it; all creation trembles in awe before it.

"There is not the slightest injustice in truth.[a] 37 You will find injustice in wine, the emperor, women, all human beings, in all they do, and in everything else. There is no truth in them; they are unjust and they will perish. 38 But truth endures and is always strong; it will continue to live and reign forever. 39 Truth shows no partiality or favoritism; it does what is right, rather than what is unjust or evil. Everyone approves what truth does; 40 its decisions are always fair. Truth is strong, royal, powerful, and majestic forever. Let all things praise the God of truth!"

41 When Zerubbabel had finished speaking, all the people shouted, "Truth is great—there is nothing stronger!"

42 Then the emperor said to him, "You may ask anything you want, even more than what was agreed, and I will give it to you. You will be my adviser, and you will be granted the title 'Relative of the Emperor.' "

43 Zerubbabel replied, "Your Majesty, permit me to remind you of the solemn vow you took on the day you became emperor. You promised to rebuild Jerusalem 44 and to send back all the treasures that had been taken from the city. Remember that when Cyrus made a vow to destroy Babylon, he set these things aside and solemnly promised to send them back to Jerusalem. 45 You also promised to rebuild the Temple, which the Edomites burned down when the Babylonians devastated the land of Judah. 46 So, Your Majesty, because you are a man of generosity, I beg you to fulfill the solemn promise you made to the King of heaven."

47 Then Emperor Darius stood up, kissed Zerubbabel, and wrote letters for him to all the treasurers, governors, and administrators in the provinces, ordering them to provide safe conduct for him and all those going with him to rebuild Jerusalem. 48 He also wrote letters to all the governors in Greater Syria and Phoenicia, with special instructions to those in Lebanon, to transport cedar logs to Jerusalem and help Zerubbabel rebuild the city.

49 The emperor also provided letters for all the Jews who wished to return to Jerusalem. These letters guaranteed their freedom and ordered all governors, treasurers, and other administrators not to interfere with them in any way. 50 All

[a] in truth; *some manuscripts have* with God.

New Revised Standard Version

loses her temper with him, he flatters her, so that she may be reconciled to him. 32 Gentlemen, why are not women strong, since they do such things?"

33 Then the king and the nobles looked at one another; and he began to speak about truth: 34 "Gentlemen, are not women strong? The earth is vast, and heaven is high, and the sun is swift in its course, for it makes the circuit of the heavens and returns to its place in one day. 35 Is not the one who does these things great? But truth is great, and stronger than all things. 36 The whole earth calls upon truth, and heaven blesses it. All God's works[a] quake and tremble, and with him there is nothing unrighteous. 37 Wine is unrighteous, the king is unrighteous, women are unrighteous, all human beings are unrighteous, all their works are unrighteous, and all such things. There is no truth in them and in their unrighteousness they will perish. 38 But truth endures and is strong forever, and lives and prevails forever and ever. 39 With it there is no partiality or preference, but it does what is righteous instead of anything that is unrighteous or wicked. Everyone approves its deeds, 40 and there is nothing unrighteous in its judgment. To it belongs the strength and the kingship and the power and the majesty of all the ages. Blessed be the God of truth!" 41 When he stopped speaking, all the people shouted and said, "Great is truth, and strongest of all!"

42 Then the king said to him, "Ask what you wish, even beyond what is written, and we will give it to you, for you have been found to be the wisest. You shall sit next to me, and be called my Kinsman." 43 Then he said to the king, "Remember the vow that you made on the day when you became king, to build Jerusalem, 44 and to send back all the vessels that were taken from Jerusalem, which Cyrus set apart when he began[b] to destroy Babylon, and vowed to send them back there. 45 You also vowed to build the temple, which the Edomites burned when Judea was laid waste by the Chaldeans. 46 And now, O lord the king, this is what I ask and request of you, and this befits your greatness. I pray therefore that you fulfill the vow whose fulfillment you vowed to the King of heaven with your own lips."

47 Then King Darius got up and kissed him, and wrote letters for him to all the treasurers and governors and generals and satraps, that they should give safe conduct to him and to all who were going up with him to build Jerusalem. 48 And he wrote letters to all the governors in Coelesyria and Phoenicia and to those in Lebanon, to bring cedar timber from Lebanon to Jerusalem, and to help him build the city. 49 He wrote in behalf of all the Jews who were going up from his kingdom to Judea, in the interest of their freedom, that no officer or satrap or governor or treasurer should forcibly

[a] Gk *All the works* [b] Cn: Gk *vowed*

πᾶσαν τὴν χώραν, ἣν κρατήσουσιν, ἀφορολόγητον αὐτοῖς
ὑπάρχειν, καὶ ἵνα οἱ Ιδουμαῖοι ἀφιῶσι τὰς κώμας ἃς διακρα-
τοῦσιν τῶν Ιουδαίων, 51 καὶ εἰς τὴν οἰκοδομὴν τοῦ ἱεροῦ
δοθῆναι κατ᾽ ἐνιαυτὸν τάλαντα εἴκοσι μέχρι τοῦ οἰκοδομηθῆναι, 52 καὶ ἐπὶ τὸ θυσιαστήριον ὁλοκαυτώματα καρποῦσθαι
καθ᾽ ἡμέραν, καθὰ ἔχουσιν ἐντολὴν ἑπτακαίδεκα προσφέρειν,
ἄλλα τάλαντα δέκα κατ᾽ ἐνιαυτόν, 53 καὶ πᾶσιν τοῖς
προσβαίνουσιν ἀπὸ τῆς Βαβυλωνίας κτίσαι τὴν πόλιν ὑπάρχειν τὴν ἐλευθερίαν, αὐτοῖς τε καὶ τοῖς τέκνοις αὐτῶν καὶ
πᾶσι τοῖς ἱερεῦσι τοῖς προσβαίνουσιν. 54 ἔγραψεν δὲ καὶ
τὴν χορηγίαν καὶ τὴν ἱερατικὴν στολήν, ἐν τίνι λατρεύουσιν
ἐν αὐτῇ. 55 καὶ τοῖς Λευίταις ἔγραψεν δοῦναι τὴν χορηγίαν
ἕως ἧς ἡμέρας ἐπιτελεσθῇ ὁ οἶκος καὶ Ιερουσαλημ
οἰκοδομηθῆναι, 56 καὶ πᾶσι τοῖς φρουροῦσι τὴν πόλιν,
ἔγραψε δοῦναι αὐτοῖς κλήρους καὶ ὀψώνια. 57 καὶ ἐξαπέστειλεν πάντα τὰ σκεύη, ἃ ἐξεχώρισεν Κῦρος ἀπὸ Βαβυλῶνος. καὶ πάντα, ὅσα εἶπεν Κῦρος ποιῆσαι, καὶ αὐτὸς ἐπέταξεν ποιῆσαι καὶ ἐξαποστεῖλαι εἰς Ιερουσαλημ.

58 Καὶ ὅτε ἐξῆλθεν ὁ νεανίσκος, ἄρας τὸ πρόσωπον εἰς τὸν
οὐρανὸν ἐναντίον Ιερουσαλημ εὐλόγησεν τῷ βασιλεῖ τοῦ
οὐρανοῦ λέγων 59 Παρὰ σοῦ ἡ νίκη, καὶ παρὰ σοῦ ἡ σοφία,
καὶ σὴ ἡ δόξα, καὶ ἐγὼ σὸς οἰκέτης. 60 εὐλογητὸς εἶ, ὃς
ἔδωκάς μοι σοφίαν· καὶ σοὶ ὁμολογῶ, δέσποτα τῶν πατέρων.
61 καὶ ἔλαβεν τὰς ἐπιστολὰς καὶ ἐξῆλθεν εἰς Βαβυλῶνα καὶ
ἀπήγγειλεν τοῖς ἀδελφοῖς αὐτοῦ πᾶσιν. 62 καὶ εὐλόγησαν
τὸν θεὸν τῶν πατέρων αὐτῶν, ὅτι ἔδωκεν αὐτοῖς ἄνεσιν καὶ
ἄφεσιν 63 ἀναβῆναι καὶ οἰκοδομῆσαι Ιερουσαλημ καὶ τὸ
ἱερόν, οὗ ὠνομάσθη τὸ ὄνομα αὐτοῦ ἐπ᾽ αὐτῷ, καὶ ἐκωθωνίζοντο μετὰ μουσικῶν καὶ χαρᾶς ἡμέρας ἑπτά.

5 Μετὰ δὲ ταῦτα ἐξελέγησαν ἀναβῆναι ἀρχηγοὶ οἴκου
πατριῶν κατὰ φυλὰς αὐτῶν καὶ αἱ γυναῖκες αὐτῶν καὶ οἱ
υἱοὶ καὶ αἱ θυγατέρες καὶ οἱ παῖδες αὐτῶν καὶ αἱ παιδίσκαι
καὶ τὰ κτήνη αὐτῶν. 2 καὶ Δαρεῖος συναπέστειλεν μετ᾽
αὐτῶν ἱππεῖς χιλίους ἕως τοῦ ἀποκαταστῆσαι αὐτοὺς εἰς
Ιερουσαλημ μετ᾽ εἰρήνης καὶ μετὰ μουσικῶν, τυμπάνων καὶ
αὐλῶν· 3 καὶ πάντες οἱ ἀδελφοὶ αὐτῶν παίζοντες, καὶ ἐποίησεν αὐτοὺς συναναβῆναι μετ᾽ ἐκείνων.

4 Καὶ ταῦτα τὰ ὀνόματα τῶν ἀνδρῶν τῶν ἀναβαινόντων
κατὰ πατριὰς αὐτῶν εἰς τὰς φυλὰς ἐπὶ τὴν μεριδαρχίαν
αὐτῶν. 5 οἱ ἱερεῖς υἱοὶ Φινεες υἱοῦ Ααρων· Ἰησοῦς ὁ τοῦ
Ιωσεδεκ τοῦ Σαραιου καὶ Ιωακιμ ὁ τοῦ Ζοροβαβελ τοῦ Σαλαθιηλ ἐκ τοῦ οἴκου τοῦ Δαυιδ ἐκ τῆς γενεᾶς Φαρες, φυλῆς δὲ
Ιουδα, 6 ὃς ἐλάλησεν ἐπὶ Δαρείου τοῦ βασιλέως Περσῶν
λόγους σοφοὺς ἐν τῷ δευτέρῳ ἔτει τῆς βασιλείας αὐτοῦ
μηνὶ Νισαν τοῦ πρώτου μηνός. — 7 εἰσὶν δὲ οὗτοι ἐκ τῆς
Ιουδαίας οἱ ἀναβάντες ἐκ τῆς αἰχμαλωσίας τῆς παροικίας,
οὓς μετῴκισεν Ναβουχοδονοσορ βασιλεὺς Βαβυλῶνος εἰς
Βαβυλῶνα 8 καὶ ἐπέστρεψαν εἰς Ιερουσαλημ καὶ τὴν λοιπὴν
Ιουδαίαν ἕκαστος εἰς τὴν ἰδίαν πόλιν, οἱ ἐλθόντες μετὰ
Ζοροβαβελ καὶ Ἰησοῦ, Νεεμιου, Ζαραιου, Ρησαιου, Ενηνιος,

50 And that all the country which they hold should be free without tribute; and that the Edomites should give over the villages of the Jews which then they held:

51 Yea, that there should be yearly given twenty talents to the building of the temple, until the time that it were built;

52 And other ten talents yearly, to maintain the burnt offerings upon the altar every day, as they had a commandment to offer seventeen:

53 And that all they that went from Babylon to build the city should have free liberty, as well they as their posterity, and all the priests that went away.

54 He wrote also concerning the charges, and the priests' vestments wherein they minister;

55 And likewise for the charges of the Levites, to be given them until the day that the house were finished, and Jerusalem builded up.

56 And he commanded to give to all that kept the city pensions and wages.

57 He sent away also all the vessels from Babylon, that Cyrus had set apart; and all that Cyrus had given in commandment, the same charged he also to be done, and sent unto Jerusalem.

58 Now when this young man was gone forth, he lifted up his face to heaven toward Jerusalem, and praised the King of heaven,

59 And said, From thee cometh victory, from thee cometh wisdom, and thine is the glory, and I am thy servant.

60 Blessed art thou, who hast given me wisdom: for to thee I give thanks, O Lord of our fathers.

61 And so he took the letters, and went out, and came unto Babylon, and told it all his brethren.

62 And they praised the God of their fathers, because he had given them freedom and liberty

63 To go up, and to build Jerusalem, and the temple which is called by his name: and they feasted with instruments of musick and gladness seven days.

5 After this were the principal men of the families chosen according to their tribes, to go up with their wives and sons and daughters, with their menservants and maidservants, and their cattle.

2 And Darius sent with them a thousand horsemen, till they had brought them back to Jerusalem safely, and with musical [instruments] tabrets and flutes.

3 And all their brethren played, and he made them go up together with them.

4 And these are the names of the men which went up, according to their families among their tribes, after their several heads.

5 The priests, the sons of Phinees the son of Aaron: Jesus the son of Josedec, the son of Saraias, and Joacim the son of Zorobabel, the son of Salathiel, of the house of David, out of the kindred of Phares, of the tribe of Judah;

6 Who spake wise sentences before Darius the king of Persia in the second year of his reign, in the month Nisan, which is the first month.

7 And these are they of Jewry that came up from the captivity, where they dwelt as strangers, whom Nabuchodonosor the king of Babylon had carried away unto Babylon.

8 And they returned unto Jerusalem, and to the other parts of Jewry, every man to his own city, who came with Zorobabel, with Jesus, Nehemias, and Zacharias, and

Today's English Version

the land that they acquired was to be exempt from taxation,
and the Edomites were to surrender the villages they had
taken from the Jews. 51 Each year 1,500 pounds of silver
would be given for the construction of the Temple until it
was finished. 52 In addition, 750 pounds of silver would be
given each year to provide for the seventeen burnt offerings
to be offered in the Temple each day. 53 All the Jews who left
Babylonia to build the city of Jerusalem would be granted
their freedom, together with their children and the priests.
54 The emperor's orders gave specific instructions, as follows: the priests must be supported, their robes for the
Temple service must be provided, 55 the Levites must be supported until the Temple and Jerusalem are completely rebuilt,
56 and land and wages must be provided for all the guards of
the city. 57 He also reaffirmed Cyrus' instructions that all the
small utensils and Temple treasures that Cyrus had set aside
should be returned to Jerusalem.
58 Then the young man Zerubbabel left the council chamber, turned toward Jerusalem, looked up to heaven, and
praised the King of heaven: 59 "Lord, all praise belongs to
you; you are the source of all victory and wisdom, 60 and I
thank you, O Lord of our ancestors, for giving wisdom to me,
your servant."
61 Zerubbabel took the emperor's letters and went to
Babylon, where he told the other Jews everything that had
happened. 62 They praised the God of their ancestors because
he had made it possible for them 63 to go and rebuild
Jerusalem and the Temple which bears his name. For seven
days they held a joyful celebration, accompanied by music.

5 After this, the heads of clans were chosen, tribe by tribe,
to go to Jerusalem with their wives, children, slaves, and
animals. 2 Emperor Darius sent a thousand cavalry troops to
escort them safely back to Jerusalem. 3 He sent them off to
the music of drums and flutes, while all the rest of the
Jewish people danced for joy.
4 These are the names, by tribes, clans, and families, of the
men who returned: 5 Among the priests, descendants of
Phinehas son of Aaron, was Joshua, son of Jozadak and
grandson of Seraiah. He was accompanied by Zerubbabel,[a]
who was the son of Shealtiel of the family of David, of the
line of Perez, of the tribe of Judah. 6 He was the one who had
spoken the wise words before Emperor Darius of Persia. They
left Babylon in the second year of his reign in Nisan, the first
month.
7 These are the Jewish men who returned from exile. Their
families had been living in Babylonia since King Nebuchadnezzar had taken them there as prisoners. 8 They returned to
Jerusalem and the rest of Judah, each to his own hometown.
Their leaders were Zerubbabel, Joshua, Nehemiah, Seraiah,

[a] *Probable text* He was accompanied by Zerubbabel; *Greek* and Joakim son of Zerubbabel.

New Revised Standard Version

enter their doors; 50 that all the country that they would
occupy should be theirs without tribute; that the Idumeans
should give up the villages of the Jews that they held; 51 that
twenty talents a year should be given for the building of the
temple until it was completed, 52 and an additional ten talents a year for burnt offerings to be offered on the altar every
day, in accordance with the commandment to make seventeen offerings; 53 and that all who came from Babylonia to
build the city should have their freedom, they and their children and all the priests who came. 54 He wrote also concerning their support and the priests' vestments in which[a] they
were to minister. 55 He wrote that the support for the Levites
should be provided until the day when the temple would be
finished and Jerusalem built. 56 He wrote that land and
wages should be provided for all who guarded the city.
57 And he sent back from Babylon all the vessels that Cyrus
had set apart; everything that Cyrus had ordered to be done,
he also commanded to be done and to be sent to Jerusalem.
58 When the young man went out, he lifted up his face to
heaven toward Jerusalem, and praised the King of heaven,
saying, 59 "From you comes the victory; from you comes wisdom, and yours is the glory. I am your servant. 60 Blessed
are you, who have given me wisdom; I give you thanks,
O Lord of our ancestors."
61 So he took the letters, and went to Babylon and told
this to all his kindred. 62 And they praised the God of their
ancestors, because he had given them release and permission
63 to go up and build Jerusalem and the temple that is called
by his name; and they feasted, with music and rejoicing, for
seven days.

5 After this the heads of ancestral houses were chosen to
go up, according to their tribes, with their wives and
sons and daughters, and their male and female servants, and
their livestock. 2 And Darius sent with them a thousand cavalry to take them back to Jerusalem in safety, with the music
of drums and flutes; 3 all their kindred were making merry.
And he made them go up with them.
4 These are the names of the men who went up, according
to their ancestral houses in the tribes, over their groups:
5 the priests, the descendants of Phinehas son of Aaron;
Jeshua son of Jozadak son of Seraiah and Joakim son of
Zerubbabel son of Shealtiel, of the house of David, of the lineage of Phares, of the tribe of Judah, 6 who spoke wise words
before King Darius of the Persians, in the second year of his
reign, in the month of Nisan, the first month.
7 These are the Judeans who came up out of their sojourn
in exile, whom King Nebuchadnezzar of Babylon had carried
away to Babylon 8 and who returned to Jerusalem and the
rest of Judea, each to his own town. They came with
Zerubbabel and Jeshua, Nehemiah, Seraiah, Resaiah,

[a] Gk *in what priestly vestments*

Μαρδοχαιου, Βεελσαρου, Ασφαρασου, Βορολιου, Ροϊμου,
Βαανα τῶν προηγουμένων αὐτῶν. 9 ἀριθμὸς τῶν ἀπὸ τοῦ
ἔθνους καὶ οἱ προηγούμενοι αὐτῶν· υἱοὶ Φορος δύο χιλιάδες
καὶ ἑκατὸν ἑβδομήκοντα δύο. 10 υἱοὶ Σαφατ τετρακόσιοι
ἑβδομήκοντα δύο. υἱοὶ Αρεε ἑπτακόσιοι πεντήκοντα ἕξ.
11 υἱοὶ Φααθμωαβ εἰς τοὺς υἱοὺς Ἰησοῦ καὶ Ιωαβ δισχίλιοι
ὀκτακόσιοι δέκα δύο. 12 υἱοὶ Ωλαμου χίλιοι διακόσιοι
πεντήκοντα τέσσαρες. υἱοὶ Ζατου ἐννακόσιοι τεσσαράκοντα πέντε. υἱοὶ Χορβε ἑπτακόσιοι πέντε. υἱοὶ Βανι ἑξακόσιοι τεσσαράκοντα ὀκτώ. 13 υἱοὶ Βηβαι ἑξακόσιοι εἴκοσι
τρεῖς. υἱοὶ Ασγαδ χίλιοι τριακόσιοι εἴκοσι δύο. 14 υἱοὶ
Αδωνικαμ ἑξακόσιοι ἑξήκοντα ἑπτά. υἱοὶ Βαγοι δισχίλιοι
ἑξήκοντα ἕξ. υἱοὶ Αδινου τετρακόσιοι πεντήκοντα τέσσαρες. 15 υἱοὶ Ατηρ Εζεκιου ἐνενήκοντα δύο. υἱοὶ Κιλαν καὶ
Αζητας ἑξήκοντα ἑπτά. υἱοὶ Αζουρου τετρακόσιοι τριάκοντα δύο. 16 υἱοὶ Αννιας ἑκατὸν εἷς. υἱοὶ Αρομ υἱοὶ
Βασσαι τριακόσιοι εἴκοσι τρεῖς. υἱοὶ Αριφου ἑκατὸν δέκα
δύο. 17 υἱοὶ Βαιτηρους τρισχίλιοι πέντε. υἱοὶ ἐκ Βαιθλωμων
ἑκατὸν εἴκοσι τρεῖς. 18 οἱ ἐκ Νετεβας πεντήκοντα πέντε.
οἱ ἐξ Ενατου ἑκατὸν πεντήκοντα ὀκτώ. οἱ ἐκ Βαιτασμων
τεσσαράκοντα δύο. 19 οἱ ἐκ Καριαθιαριος εἴκοσι πέντε. οἱ
ἐκ Καπιρας καὶ Βηροτ ἑπτακόσιοι τεσσαράκοντα τρεῖς.
20 οἱ Χαδιασαι καὶ Αμμιδιοι τετρακόσιοι εἴκοσι δύο. οἱ ἐκ
Κιραμας καὶ Γαββης ἑξακόσιοι εἴκοσι εἷς. 21 οἱ ἐκ Μακα-
λων ἑκατὸν εἴκοσι δύο. οἱ ἐκ Βαιτολιω πεντήκοντα δύο. υἱοὶ
Νιφις ἑκατὸν πεντήκοντα ἕξ. 22 υἱοὶ Καλαμω ἄλλου καὶ
Ωνους ἑπτακόσιοι εἴκοσι πέντε. υἱοὶ Ιερεχου τριακόσιοι
τεσσαράκοντα πέντε. 23 υἱοὶ Σαναας τρισχίλιοι τριακόσιοι
τριάκοντα. — 24 οἱ ἱερεῖς. υἱοὶ Ιεδδου τοῦ υἱοῦ Ἰησοῦ εἰς
τοὺς υἱοὺς Ανασιβ ἐννακόσιοι ἑβδομήκοντα δύο. υἱοὶ
Εμμηρου χίλιοι πεντήκοντα δύο. 25 υἱοὶ Φασσουρου χίλιοι
διακόσιοι τεσσαράκοντα ἑπτά. υἱοὶ Χαρμη χίλιοι δέκα
ἑπτά. — 26 οἱ δὲ Λευῖται· υἱοὶ Ἰησοῦ καὶ Καδμιηλου καὶ
Βαννου καὶ Σουδιου ἑβδομήκοντα τέσσαρες. 27 οἱ ἱεροψάλ-
ται· υἱοὶ Ασαφ ἑκατὸν εἴκοσι ὀκτώ. 28 οἱ θυρωροί· υἱοὶ
Σαλουμ, υἱοὶ Αταρ, υἱοὶ Τολμαν, υἱοὶ Ακουβ, υἱοὶ Ατητα,
υἱοὶ Σωβαι, οἱ πάντες ἑκατὸν τριάκοντα ἐννέα. — 29 οἱ ἱερό-
δουλοι· υἱοὶ Ησαυ, υἱοὶ Ασιφα, υἱοὶ Ταβαωθ, υἱοὶ Κηρας, υἱοὶ
Σουα, υἱοὶ Φαδαιου, υἱοὶ Λαβανα, υἱοὶ Αγγαβα, 30 υἱοὶ
Ακουδ, υἱοὶ Ουτα, υἱοὶ Κηταβ, υἱοὶ Αγαβα, υἱοὶ Συβαϊ, υἱοὶ
Αναν, υἱοὶ Καθουα, υἱοὶ Γεδδουρ, 31 υἱοὶ Ιαϊρου, υἱοὶ

Reesaias, Enenius, Mardocheus, Beelsarus, Aspharasus, Reelius, Roimus, and Baana, their guides.

9 The number of them of the nation, and their governors, sons of Phoros, two thousand an hundred seventy and two; the sons of Saphat, four hundred seventy and two:

10 The sons of Ares, seven hundred fifty and six:

11 The sons of Phaath Moab, two thousand eight hundred and twelve:

12 The sons of Elam, a thousand two hundred fifty and four: the sons of Zathui, nine hundred forty and five: the sons of Corbe, seven hundred and five: the sons of Bani, six hundred forty and eight:

13 The sons of Bebai, six hundred twenty and three: the sons of Sadas, three thousand two hundred twenty and two:

14 The sons of Adonikam, six hundred sixty and seven: the sons of Bagoi, two thousand sixty and six: the sons of Adin, four hundred fifty and four:

15 The sons of Aterezias, ninety and two: the sons of Ceilan and Azetas, threescore and seven: the sons of Azuran, four hundred thirty and two:

16 The sons of Ananias, an hundred and one: the sons of Arom, thirty two: and the sons of Bassa, three hundred twenty and three: the sons of Azephurith, an hundred and two:

17 The sons of Meterus, three thousand and five: the sons of Bethlomon, an hundred twenty and three:

18 They of Netophah, fifty and five: they of Anathoth, an hundred fifty and eight: they of Bethsamos, forty and two:

19 They of Kiriathiarius, twenty and five: they of Caphira and Beroth, seven hundred forty and three: they of Pira, seven hundred:

20 They of Chadias and Ammidoi, four hundred twenty and two: they of Cirama and Gabdes, six hundred twenty and one:

21 They of Macalon, an hundred twenty and two: they of Betolius, fifty and two: the sons of Nephis, an hundred fifty and six:

22 The sons of Calamolalus and Onus, seven hundred twenty and five: the sons of Jerechus, two hundred forty and five:

23 The sons of Annaas, three thousand three hundred and thirty.

24 The priests: the sons of Jeddu, the son of Jesus, among the sons of Sanasib, nine hundred seventy and two: the sons of Meruth, a thousand fifty and two:

25 The sons of Phassaron, a thousand forty and seven: the sons of Carme, a thousand and seventeen.

26 The Levites: the sons of Jessue, and Cadmiel, and Banuas, and Sudias, seventy and four.

27 The holy singers: the sons of Asaph, an hundred twenty and eight.

28 The porters: the sons of Salum, the sons of Jatal, the sons of Talmon, the sons of Dacobi, the sons of Teta, the sons of Sami, in all an hundred thirty and nine.

29 The servants of the temple: the sons of Esau, the sons of Asipha, the sons of Tabaoth, the sons of Ceras, the sons of Sud, the sons of Phaleas, the sons of Labana, the sons of Graba,

30 The sons of Acua, the sons of Uta, the sons of Cetab, the sons of Agaba, the sons of Subai, the sons of Anan, the sons of Cathua, the sons of Geddur,

TODAY'S ENGLISH VERSION

Resaiah, Eneneus, Mordecai, Beelsarus, Aspharasus, Reeliah, Rehum, and Baanah.

9-17a The following is a list of the clans of Israel, with the number of those from each clan who returned with their leaders from exile:

Parosh	2,172
Shephatiah	472
Arah	756
Pahath Moab (descendants of Jeshua and Joab)	2,812
Elam	1,254
Zattu	945
Chorbe	705
Bani	648
Bebai	623
Azgad	1,322
Adonikam	667
Bigvai	2,066
Adin	454
Ater (also called Hezekiah)	92
Kilan and Azetas	67
Azaru	432
Annias	101
Arom	—
Bezai	323
Arsiphurith	112
Baiterus	3,005

17b-23 People whose ancestors had lived in the following towns also returned:

Bethlehem	123
Netophah	55
Anathoth	158
Beth Azmaveth	42
Kiriath Jearim	25
Chephirah and Beeroth	743
the towns of the Chadiasans and the Ammidians	422
Ramah and Geba	621
Michmash	122
Bethel	52
Magbish	156
The other Elam and Ono	725
Jericho	345
Senaah	3,330

24-25 The following is the list of the priestly clans that returned from exile:

Jedaiah (descendants of Jeshua and Anasib)	972
Immer	1,052
Pashhur	1,247
Harim	1,017

26-28 Clans of Levites who returned from exile:

Jeshua, Kadmiel, Bannas, and Sudias	74
Temple musicians (descendants of Asaph)	128
Temple guards (descendants of Shallum, Ater, Talmon, Akkub, Hatita, and Shobai)	139

29-32 Clans of Temple workmen who returned from exile:

Esau, Hasupha, Tabbaoth,
Keros, Siaha, Padon,
Lebanah, Hagabah, Akkub,
Uthai, Ketab, Hagab,
Shamlai, Hanan, Cathua,

NEW REVISED STANDARD VERSION

Eneneus, Mordecai, Beelsarus, Aspharasus, Reeliah, Rehum,
and Baanah, their leaders.
9 The number of those of the nation and their leaders: the
descendants of Parosh, two thousand one hundred seventy-
two. The descendants of Shephatiah, four hundred seventy-
two. 10 The descendants of Arah, seven hundred fifty-six.
11 The descendants of Pahath-moab, of the descendants of
Jeshua and Joab, two thousand eight hundred twelve. 12 The
descendants of Elam, one thousand two hundred fifty-four.
The descendants of Zattu, nine hundred forty-five. The
descendants of Chorbe, seven hundred five. The descendants
of Bani, six hundred forty-eight. 13 The descendants of
Bebai, six hundred twenty-three. The descendants of Azgad,
one thousand three hundred twenty-two. 14 The descendants
of Adonikam, six hundred sixty-seven. The descendants of
Bigvai, two thousand sixty-six. The descendants of Adin,
four hundred fifty-four. 15 The descendants of Ater, namely
of Hezekiah, ninety-two. The descendants of Kilan and
Azetas, sixty-seven. The descendants of Azaru, four hundred
thirty-two. 16 The descendants of Annias, one hundred one.
The descendants of Arom. The descendants of Bezai, three
hundred twenty-three. The descendants of Arsiphurith, one
hundred twelve. 17 The descendants of Baiterus, three thousand five. The descendants of Bethlomon, one hundred twenty-three. 18 Those from Netophah, fifty-five. Those from
Anathoth, one hundred fifty-eight. Those from Bethasmoth,
forty-two. 19 Those from Kiriatharim, twenty-five. Those
from Chephirah and Beeroth, seven hundred forty-three.
20 The Chadiasans and Ammidians, four hundred twenty-two.
Those from Kirama and Geba, six hundred twenty-one.
21 Those from Macalon, one hundred twenty-two. Those from
Betolio, fifty-two. The descendants of Niphish, one hundred
fifty-six. 22 The descendants of the other Calamolalus and
Ono, seven hundred twenty-five. The descendants of
Jerechus, three hundred forty-five. 23 The descendants of
Senaah, three thousand three hundred thirty.
24 The priests: the descendants of Jedaiah son of Jeshua,
of the descendants of Anasib, nine hundred seventy-two. The
descendants of Immer, one thousand and fifty-two. 25 The
descendants of Pashhur, one thousand two hundred forty-
seven. The descendants of Charme, one thousand seventeen.
26 The Levites: the descendants of Jeshua and Kadmiel
and Bannas and Sudias, seventy-four. 27 The temple singers:
the descendants of Asaph, one hundred twenty-eight. 28 The
gatekeepers: the descendants of Shallum, the descendants of
Ater, the descendants of Talmon, the descendants of Akkub,
the descendants of Hatita, the descendants of Shobai, in all
one hundred thirty-nine.
29 The temple servants: the descendants of Esau, the
descendants of Hasupha, the descendants of Tabbaoth, the
descendants of Keros, the descendants of Sua, the descen-
dants of Padon, the descendants of Lebanah, the descen-
dants of Hagabah, 30 the descendants of Akkub, the descen-
dants of Uthai, the descendants of Ketab, the descendants of
Hagab, the descendants of Subai, the descendants of Hana,
the descendants of Cathua, the descendants of Geddur, 31 the

Δαισαν, υἱοὶ Νοεβα, υἱοὶ Χασεβα, υἱοὶ Γαζηρα, υἱοὶ Οζιου,
υἱοὶ Φινοε, υἱοὶ Ασαρα, υἱοὶ Βασθαι, υἱοὶ Ασανα, υἱοὶ
Μαανι, υἱοὶ Ναφισι, υἱοὶ Ακουφ, υἱοὶ Αχιβα, υἱοὶ Ασουρ,
υἱοὶ Φαρακιμ, υἱοὶ Βασαλωθ, 32 υἱοὶ Μεεδδα, υἱοὶ Κουθα,
υἱοὶ Χαρεα, υἱοὶ Βαρχους, υἱοὶ Σεραρ, υἱοὶ Θομοι, υἱοὶ Νασι,
υἱοὶ Ατιφα. 33 υἱοὶ παίδων Σαλωμων· υἱοὶ Ασσαφιωθ, υἱοὶ
Φαριδα, υἱοὶ Ιεηλι, υἱοὶ Λοζων, υἱοὶ Ισδαηλ, υἱοὶ Σαφυθι,
34 υἱοὶ Αγια, υἱοὶ Φακαρεθ-σαβιη, υἱοὶ Σαρωθιε, υἱοὶ
Μασιας, υἱοὶ Γας, υἱοὶ Αδδους, υἱοὶ Σουβας, υἱοὶ Αφερρα,
υἱοὶ Βαρωδις, υἱοὶ Σαφατ, υἱοὶ Αμων. 35 πάντες οἱ ἱερόδουλοι καὶ οἱ υἱοὶ τῶν παίδων Σαλωμων τριακόσιοι ἑβδομήκοντα δύο. — 36 οὗτοι ἀναβάντες ἀπὸ Θερμελεθ καὶ Θελερ-
σας, ἡγούμενος αὐτῶν Χαρααθ, Αδαν καὶ Αμαρ, 37 καὶ οὐκ
ἠδύναντο ἀπαγγεῖλαι τὰς πατριὰς αὐτῶν καὶ γενεὰς ὡς ἐκ
τοῦ Ισραηλ εἰσίν· υἱοὶ Δαλαν τοῦ υἱοῦ Τουβαν, υἱοὶ
Νεκωδαν, ἑξακόσιοι πεντήκοντα δύο. 38 καὶ ἐκ τῶν ἱερέων
οἱ ἐμποιούμενοι ἱερωσύνης καὶ οὐχ εὑρέθησαν· υἱοὶ Οββια,
υἱοὶ Ακκως, υἱοὶ Ιοδδους τοῦ λαβόντος Αυγιαν γυναῖκα τῶν
θυγατέρων Φαρζελλαιου καὶ ἐκλήθη ἐπὶ τῷ ὀνόματι αὐτοῦ·
39 καὶ τούτων ζητηθείσης τῆς γενικῆς γραφῆς ἐν τῷ κατα-
λοχισμῷ καὶ μὴ εὑρεθείσης ἐχωρίσθησαν τοῦ ἱερατεύειν,
40 καὶ εἶπεν αὐτοῖς Νεεμιας καὶ Ατθαριας μὴ μετέχειν τῶν
ἁγίων αὐτούς, ἕως ἀναστῇ ἀρχιερεὺς ἐνδεδυμένος τὴν δή-
λωσιν καὶ τὴν ἀλήθειαν. — 41 οἱ δὲ πάντες ἦσαν· Ισραηλ
ἀπὸ δωδεκαετοῦς χωρὶς παίδων καὶ παιδισκῶν μυριάδες
τέσσαρες δισχίλιοι τριακόσιοι ἑξήκοντα· παῖδες τούτων καὶ
παιδίσκαι ἑπτακισχίλιοι τριακόσιοι τριάκοντα ἑπτά· ψάλται καὶ ψαλτῳδοὶ διακόσιοι τεσσαράκοντα πέντε· 42 κάμηλοι τετρακόσιοι τριάκοντα πέντε, καὶ ἵπποι ἑπτακισχίλιοι
τριάκοντα ἕξ, ἡμίονοι διακόσιοι τεσσαράκοντα πέντε, ὑπο-
ζύγια πεντακισχίλια πεντακόσια εἴκοσι πέντε. — 43 καὶ ἐκ
τῶν ἡγουμένων κατὰ τὰς πατριὰς ἐν τῷ παραγίνεσθαι αὐτοὺς εἰς τὸ ἱερὸν τοῦ θεοῦ τὸ ἐν Ιερουσαλημ εὔξαντο
ἐγεῖραι τὸν οἶκον ἐπὶ τοῦ τόπου αὐτοῦ κατὰ τὴν αὐτῶν δύναμιν 44 καὶ δοῦναι εἰς τὸ ἱερὸν γαζοφυλάκιον τῶν ἔργων
χρυσίου μνᾶς χιλίας καὶ ἀργυρίου μνᾶς πεντακισχιλίας καὶ
στολὰς ἱερατικὰς ἑκατόν. — 45 καὶ κατῳκίσθησαν οἱ ἱερεῖς
καὶ οἱ Λευῖται καὶ οἱ ἐκ τοῦ λαοῦ ἐν Ιερουσαλημ καὶ τῇ χώρᾳ, οἵ τε ἱεροψάλται καὶ οἱ θυρωροὶ καὶ πᾶς Ισραηλ ἐν ταῖς
κώμαις αὐτῶν.

46 Ἐνστάντος δὲ τοῦ ἑβδόμου μηνὸς καὶ ὄντων τῶν υἱῶν
Ισραηλ ἑκάστου ἐν τοῖς ἰδίοις συνήχθησαν ὁμοθυμαδὸν εἰς
τὸ εὐρύχωρον τοῦ πρώτου πυλῶνος τοῦ πρὸς τῇ ἀνατολῇ.

31 The sons of Airus, the sons of Daisan, the sons of Noeba, the sons of Chaseba, the sons of Gazera, the sons of Azia, the sons of Phinees, the sons of Azara, the sons of Bastai, the sons of Asana, the sons of Meani, the sons of Naphisi, the sons of Acub, the sons of Acipha, the sons of Assur, the sons of Pharacim, the sons of Basaloth,

32 The sons of Meeda, the sons of Coutha, the sons of Charea, the sons of Charcus, the sons of Aserer, the sons of Thomoi, the sons of Nasith, the sons of Atipha.

33 The sons of the servants of Solomon: the sons of Azaphion, the sons of Pharira, the sons of Jeeli, the sons of Lozon, the sons of Isdael, the sons of Sapheth,

34 The sons of Hagia, the sons of Pharacareth, the sons of Sabi, the sons of Sarothie, the sons of Masias, the sons of Gar, the sons of Addus, the sons of Suba, the sons of Apherra, the sons of Barodis, the sons of Sabat, the sons of Allom.

35 All the ministers of the temple, and the sons of the servants of Solomon, were three hundred seventy and two.

36 These came up from Thermeleth and Thelersas, Charaathalar leading them, and Aalar;

37 Neither could they shew their families, nor their stock, how they were of Israel: the sons of Ladan, the son of Ban, the sons of Necodan, six hundred fifty and two.

38 And of the priests that usurped the office of the priesthood, and were not found: the sons of Obdia, the sons of Accoz, the sons of Addus, who married Augia one of the daughters of Barzelus, and was named after his name.

39 And when the description of the kindred of these men was sought in the register, and was not found, they were removed from executing the office of the priesthood:

40 For unto them said Nehemias and Atharias, that they should not be partakers of the holy things, till there arose up an high priest clothed with doctrine and truth.

41 So of Israel, from them of twelve years old and upward, they were all in number forty thousand, beside menservants and womenservants two thousand three hundred and sixty.

42 Their menservants and handmaids were seven thousand three hundred forty and seven: the singing men and singing women, two hundred forty and five:

43 Four hundred thirty and five camels, seven thousand thirty and six horses, two hundred forty and five mules, five thousand five hundred twenty and five beasts used to the yoke.

44 And certain of the chief of their families, when they came to the temple of God that is in Jerusalem, vowed to set up the house again in his own place according to their ability,

45 And to give into the holy treasury of the works a thousand pounds of gold, five thousand of silver, and an hundred priestly vestments.

46 And so dwelt the priests and the Levites and the people in Jerusalem, and in the country, the singers also and the porters; and all Israel in their villages.

47 But when the seventh month was at hand, and when the children of Israel were every man in his own place, they came all together with one consent into the open place of the first gate which is toward the east.

TODAY'S ENGLISH VERSION

Geddur, Jairus, Daisan,
Noeba, Chaseba, Gazera,
Uzza, Phinoe, Asara,
Besai, Asnah, Meunim,
Nephisim, Akub, Hakupha,
Asur, Pharakim, Bazluth,
Mehida, Cutha, Charea,
Barkos, Sisera, Temah,
Neziah, Hatipha

33-34 Clans of Solomon's servants who returned from exile:
Hassophereth, Peruda, Jaalah,
Lozon, Giddel, Shephatiah,
Agia, Phochereth Hazzebaim,
Sarothie, Masiah, Gas,
Addus, Subas, Apherra,
Barodis, Shaphat, Adlon

35 The total number of descendants of the Temple workmen
and of Solomon's servants who returned from exile was 372.

36-37 There were 652 belonging to the clans of Delaiah
(descendants of Tobiah) and Nekoda who returned from the
towns of Tel Melah and Tel Harsha, with their leaders
Cherub, Addan, and Immer; but these could not prove that
they were descendants of Israelites.

38-39 The following clans, who claimed to be priestly clans,
could find no record to prove their ancestry: Habaiah,
Hakkoz, Jaddus (the ancestor of the clan of Jaddus had married Agia, one of the daughters of Barzillai, and had taken
the name of his father-in-law's clan). Since they were unable
to prove who their ancestors were, they were not allowed to
function as priests. 40 Nehemiah the governor[a] told them
that they could not eat the food offered to God until there
was a High Priest who could use the Revelation and Truth.[b]

41-43 The total number of Israelites (twelve years old or older, not counting servants) 42,360

Male and female servants	7,337
Male and female musicians	245
Camels	435
Horses	7,036
Mules	245
Donkeys	5,525

44 When the exiles arrived at the place of God's Temple in
Jerusalem, some of the leaders of the clans took a vow to
rebuild the Temple on its old site, to the best of their ability.
45 They promised to contribute for the rebuilding and the service of the Temple 1,000 pounds of gold, 5,000 pounds of
silver, and 100 robes for priests.

46 The priests, the Levites, and some of the people settled
in or near Jerusalem; the musicians and the Temple guards
settled in nearby towns; and the rest of the Israelites settled
in the towns where their ancestors had lived.

47 By the seventh month the people of Israel were all settled in their towns. Then they all assembled in the open
square in front of the first gate on the east side of the Temple

[a] *Probable meaning* the governor; *Greek* and Attharias.
[b] REVELATION AND TRUTH: *This is the Greek translation of Urim and Thummim, two objects used by the priest to determine God's will; it is not known precisely how they were used.*

NEW REVISED STANDARD VERSION

descendants of Jairus, the descendants of Daisan, the descendants of Noeba, the descendants of Chezib, the descendants
of Gazera, the descendants of Uzza, the descendants of
Phinoe, the descendants of Hasrah, the descendants
of Basthai, the descendants of Asnah, the descendants of
Maani, the descendants of Nephisim, the descendants of
Acuph,[a] the descendants of Hakupha, the descendants
of Asur, the descendants of Pharakim, the descendants of
Bazluth, 32 the descendants of Mehida, the descendants
of Cutha, the descendants of Charea, the descendants of
Barkos, the descendants of Serar, the descendants of Temah,
the descendants of Neziah, the descendants of Hatipha.

33 The descendants of Solomon's servants: the descendants
of Assaphioth, the descendants of Peruda, the descendants of
Jaalah, the descendants of Lozon, the descendants of Isdael,
the descendants of Shephatiah, 34 the descendants of Agia, the
descendants of Pochereth-hazzebaim, the descendants of
Sarothie, the descendants of Masiah, the descendants of Gas,
the descendants of Addus, the descendants of Subas, the
descendants of Apherra, the descendants of Barodis, the
descendants of Shaphat, the descendants of Allon.

35 All the temple servants and the descendants of
Solomon's servants were three hundred seventy-two.

36 The following are those who came up from Tel-melah
and Tel-harsha, under the leadership of Cherub, Addan, and
Immer, 37 though they could not prove by their ancestral
houses or lineage that they belonged to Israel: the descendants of Delaiah son of Tobiah, and the descendants of
Nekoda, six hundred fifty-two.

38 Of the priests the following had assumed the priesthood
but were not found registered: the descendants of Habaiah,
the descendants of Hakkoz, and the descendants of Jaddus
who had married Agia, one of the daughters of Barzillai, and
was called by his name. 39 When a search was made in the
register and the genealogy of these men was not found, they
were excluded from serving as priests. 40 And Nehemiah and
Attharias[b] told them not to share in the holy things until a
high priest should appear wearing Urim and Thummim.[c]

41 All those of Israel, twelve or more years of age, besides
male and female servants, were forty-two thousand three
hundred sixty; 42 their male and female servants were seven
thousand three hundred thirty-seven; there were two hundred forty-five musicians and singers. 43 There were four
hundred thirty-five camels, and seven thousand thirty-six
horses, two hundred forty-five mules, and five thousand five
hundred twenty-five donkeys.

44 Some of the heads of families, when they came to the
temple of God that is in Jerusalem, vowed that, to the best of
their ability, they would erect the house on its site, 45 and
that they would give to the sacred treasury for the work a
thousand minas of gold, five thousand minas of silver, and
one hundred priests' vestments.

46 The priests, the Levites, and some of the people[d] settled in Jerusalem and its vicinity; and the temple singers, the
gatekeepers, and all Israel in their towns.

47 When the seventh month came, and the Israelites were
all in their own homes, they gathered with a single purpose
in the square before the first gate toward the east. 48 Then

[a] Other ancient authorities read *Acub* or *Acum* [b] Or *the governor*
[c] Gk *Manifestation and Truth* [d] Or *those who were of the people*

Greek Old Testament

47 καὶ καταστὰς Ἰησοῦς ὁ τοῦ Ιωσεδεκ καὶ οἱ ἀδελφοὶ αὐτοῦ
οἱ ἱερεῖς καὶ Ζοροβαβελ ὁ τοῦ Σαλαθιηλ καὶ οἱ τούτου
ἀδελφοὶ ἡτοίμασαν τὸ θυσιαστήριον τοῦ θεοῦ τοῦ Ισραηλ
48 προσενέγκαι ἐπ᾽ αὐτοῦ ὁλοκαυτώσεις ἀκολούθως τοῖς ἐν
τῇ Μωυσέως βίβλῳ τοῦ ἀνθρώπου τοῦ θεοῦ διηγορευμένοις.
49 καὶ ἐπισυνήχθησαν αὐτοῖς ἐκ τῶν ἄλλων ἐθνῶν τῆς γῆς.
καὶ κατώρθωσαν τὸ θυσιαστήριον ἐπὶ τοῦ τόπου αὐτοῦ, ὅτι
ἐν ἔχθρᾳ ἦσαν αὐτοῖς καὶ κατίσχυσαν αὐτοὺς πάντα τὰ ἔθνη
τὰ ἐπὶ τῆς γῆς, καὶ ἀνέφερον θυσίας κατὰ τὸν καιρὸν καὶ
ὁλοκαυτώματα τῷ κυρίῳ τὸ πρωινὸν καὶ τὸ δειλινὸν 50 καὶ
ἠγάγοσαν τὴν τῆς σκηνοπηγίας ἑορτήν, ὡς ἐπιτέτακται ἐν
τῷ νόμῳ, καὶ θυσίας καθ᾽ ἡμέραν, ὡς προσῆκον ἦν, 51 καὶ
μετὰ ταῦτα προσφορὰς ἐνδελεχισμοῦ καὶ θυσίας σαββάτων
καὶ νουμηνιῶν καὶ ἑορτῶν πασῶν ἡγιασμένων. 52 καὶ ὅσοι
εὔξαντο εὐχὴν τῷ θεῷ, ἀπὸ τῆς νουμηνίας τοῦ ἑβδόμου
μηνὸς ἤρξαντο προσφέρειν θυσίας τῷ θεῷ, καὶ ὁ ναὸς τοῦ
θεοῦ οὔπω ᾠκοδόμητο. 53 καὶ ἔδωκαν ἀργύριον τοῖς λατόμοις
καὶ τέκτοσι καὶ βρωτὰ καὶ ποτὰ καὶ χαρα τοῖς Σιδωνίοις καὶ
Τυρίοις εἰς τὸ παράγειν αὐτοὺς ἐκ τοῦ Λιβάνου ξύλα κέδρινα διαφέρειν σχεδίας εἰς τὸν Ιοππης λιμένα κατὰ τὸ
πρόσταγμα τὸ γραφὲν αὐτοῖς παρὰ Κύρου τοῦ Περσῶν
βασιλέως. — 54 καὶ τῷ δευτέρῳ ἔτει παραγενόμενος εἰς τὸ
ἱερὸν τοῦ θεοῦ εἰς Ιερουσαλημ μηνὸς δευτέρου ἤρξατο
Ζοροβαβελ ὁ τοῦ Σαλαθιηλ καὶ Ἰησοῦς ὁ τοῦ Ιωσεδεκ καὶ οἱ
ἀδελφοὶ αὐτῶν καὶ οἱ ἱερεῖς οἱ Λευῖται καὶ πάντες οἱ
παραγενόμενοι ἐκ τῆς αἰχμαλωσίας εἰς Ιερουσαλημ 55 καὶ
ἐθεμελίωσαν τὸν ναὸν τοῦ θεοῦ τῇ νουμηνίᾳ τοῦ δευτέρου
μηνὸς τοῦ δευτέρου ἔτους ἐν τῷ ἐλθεῖν εἰς τὴν Ιουδαίαν καὶ
Ιερουσαλημ. 56 καὶ ἔστησαν τοὺς Λευίτας ἀπὸ εἰκοσαετοῦς
ἐπὶ τῶν ἔργων τοῦ κυρίου, καὶ ἔστη Ἰησοῦς καὶ οἱ υἱοὶ καὶ οἱ
ἀδελφοὶ καὶ Καδμιηλ ὁ ἀδελφὸς καὶ οἱ υἱοὶ Ἰησοῦ Ημαδα-
βουν καὶ οἱ υἱοὶ Ιωδα τοῦ Ιλιαδουν σὺν τοῖς υἱοῖς καὶ
ἀδελφοῖς, πάντες οἱ Λευῖται, ὁμοθυμαδὸν ἐργοδιῶκται
ποιοῦντες εἰς τὰ ἔργα ἐν τῷ οἴκῳ τοῦ θεοῦ. 57 καὶ ᾠκοδόμησαν οἱ οἰκοδόμοι τὸν ναὸν τοῦ κυρίου, καὶ ἔστησαν οἱ ἱερεῖς
ἐστολισμένοι μετὰ μουσικῶν καὶ σαλπίγγων καὶ οἱ Λευῖται
υἱοὶ Ασαφ ἔχοντες τὰ κύμβαλα ὑμνοῦντες τῷ κυρίῳ καὶ εὐλογοῦντες κατὰ Δαυιδ βασιλέα τοῦ Ισραηλ 58 καὶ ἐφώνησαν
δι᾽ ὕμνων ὁμολογοῦντες τῷ κυρίῳ, ὅτι ἡ χρηστότης αὐτοῦ
καὶ ἡ δόξα εἰς τοὺς αἰῶνας παντὶ Ισραηλ. 59 καὶ πᾶς ὁ λαὸς
ἐσάλπισαν καὶ ἐβόησαν φωνῇ μεγάλῃ ὑμνοῦντες τῷ κυρίῳ
ἐπὶ τῇ ἐγέρσει τοῦ οἴκου τοῦ κυρίου. 60 καὶ ἦλθοσαν ἐκ τῶν
ἱερέων τῶν Λευιτῶν καὶ τῶν προκαθημένων κατὰ τὰς πατριὰς αὐτῶν οἱ πρεσβύτεροι οἱ ἑωρακότες τὸν πρὸ τούτου
οἶκον πρὸς τὴν τούτου οἰκοδομὴν μετὰ κραυγῆς καὶ κλαυθμοῦ μεγάλου 61 καὶ πολλοὶ διὰ σαλπίγγων καὶ χαρᾶς
μεγάλῃ τῇ φωνῇ 62 ὥστε τὸν λαὸν μὴ ἀκούειν τῶν σαλπίγγων διὰ τὸν κλαυθμὸν τοῦ λαοῦ, ὁ γὰρ ὄχλος ἦν ὁ σαλπίζων
μεγαλωστὶ ὥστε μακρόθεν ἀκούεσθαι.

63 Καὶ ἀκούσαντες οἱ ἐχθροὶ τῆς φυλῆς Ιουδα καὶ Βενιαμιν
ἦλθοσαν ἐπιγνῶναι τίς ἡ φωνὴ τῶν σαλπίγγων. 64 καὶ

King James Version

48 Then stood up Jesus the son of Josedec, and his brethren the priests, and Zorobabel the son of Salathiel, and his brethren, and made ready the altar of the God of Israel,

49 To offer burnt sacrifices upon it, according as it is expressly commanded in the book of Moses the man of God.

50 And there were gathered unto them out of the other nations of the land, and they erected the altar upon his own place, because all the nations of the land were at enmity with them, and oppressed them; and they offered sacrifices according to the time, and burnt offerings to the Lord both morning and evening.

51 Also they held the feast of tabernacles, as it is commanded in the law, and *offered* sacrifices daily, as was meet:

52 And after that, the continual oblations, and the sacrifice of the sabbaths, and of the new moons, and of all holy feasts.

53 And all they that had made any vow to God began to offer sacrifices to God from the first day of the seventh month, although the temple of the Lord was not yet built.

54 And they gave unto the masons and carpenters money, meat, and drink, with cheerfulness.

55 Unto them of Zidon also and Tyre they gave carrs, that they should bring cedar trees from Libanus, which should be brought by floats to the haven of Joppe, according as it was commanded them by Cyrus king of the Persians.

56 And in the second year and second month after his coming to the temple of God at Jerusalem began Zorobabel the son of Salathiel, and Jesus the son of Josedec, and their brethren, and the priests, and the Levites, and all they that were come unto Jerusalem out of the captivity:

57 And they laid the foundation of the house of God in the first day of the second month, in the second year after they were come to Jewry and Jerusalem.

58 And they appointed the Levites from twenty years old over the works of the Lord. Then stood up Jesus, and his sons and brethren, and Cadmiel his brother, and the sons of Madiabun, with the sons of Joda the son of Eliadun, with their sons and brethren, all Levites, with one accord setters forward of the business, labouring to advance the works in the house of God. So the workmen built the temple of the Lord.

59 And the priests stood arrayed in their vestments with musical instruments and trumpets; and the Levites the sons of Asaph had cymbals,

60 Singing songs of thanksgiving, and praising the Lord, according as David the king of Israel had ordained.

61 And they sung *with* loud voices songs to the praise of the Lord, because his mercy and glory is for ever in all Israel.

62 And all the people sounded trumpets, and shouted with a loud voice, singing songs of thanksgiving unto the Lord for the rearing up of the house of the Lord.

63 Also of the priests and Levites, and of the chief of their families, the ancients who had seen the former house came to the building of this with weeping and great crying.

64 But many with trumpets and joy shouted with loud voice,

65 Insomuch that the trumpets might not be heard for the weeping of the people: yet the multitude sounded marvellously, so that it was heard afar off.

66 Wherefore when the enemies of the tribe of Judah and Benjamin heard it, they came to know what that noise of trumpets should mean.

Today's English Version

area. 48Joshua son of Jehozadak, his fellow priests, and Zerubbabel son of Shealtiel, together with his relatives, prepared the altar of the God of Israel, 49so that they could burn sacrifices on it according to the instructions written in the Law of Moses, the man of God. 50Some of the local people, even though they were stronger than the Jews and opposed to them, joined them[a] in rebuilding the altar where it had stood before. Then the Jews began once again to burn the regular morning and evening sacrifices on the altar. 51They celebrated the Festival of Shelters, according to the regulations, each day offering the sacrifices required for that day. 52They also offered the normal daily sacrifices, as well as those required for the Sabbath, the New Moon Festival, and the other regular assemblies for worship. 53Although the people had not yet rebuilt God's Temple, everyone who had made a vow to God began to offer sacrifices on the first day of the seventh month.

54The people gave money to pay the stonemasons and the carpenters; they gave food, drink, 55and carts to be sent to the cities of Tyre and Sidon in exchange for cedar logs from Lebanon, which were to be floated to the harbor at Joppa. All of this was done according to the orders given by Emperor Cyrus of Persia.

56-57So in the second month of the year after they came back to the site of the Temple in Jerusalem, they started the work and began laying the foundation. Zerubbabel, Joshua, and the rest of the Jewish people, the priests, and the Levites—in fact, all the exiles who had come back to Jerusalem, joined in the work. 58The Levites twenty years of age or older were put in charge of rebuilding the Temple for the Lord. The Levite Jeshua and his sons and relatives, his brother Kadmiel, the sons of Jeshua Emadabun, the sons of Joda son of Iliadun, and all their sons and relatives—in fact, all the Levites joined together to take charge of the rebuilding of the Temple.

While the workers were building the Temple of the Lord, 59the priests in their robes took their places with trumpets and other musical instruments in their hands, and the Levites of the clan of Asaph stood there with cymbals. 60They praised the Lord and gave thanks to him according to the instructions handed down from the time of King David. 61They sang psalms praising the Lord, repeating the refrain: "The goodness of the Lord and his glorious presence are with all Israel forever." 62All the people blew trumpets and shouted with all their might, praising the Lord because the Temple was being rebuilt. 63Some of the older priests, Levites, and heads of clans had seen the first Temple, and when they came and saw the building of this Temple, they cried and wailed. 64Others who were there blew trumpets and shouted for joy. 65The crowd blew the trumpets so loud that the blast could be heard far away, but no one nearby could hear the blast of the trumpets because the sound made by those who were crying and wailing was so loud.

66The enemies of the tribes of Judah and Benjamin heard the sound of the trumpets and came to see what it meant.

[a] Some of . . . joined them; *Greek unclear.*

New Revised Standard Version

Jeshua son of Jozadak, with his fellow priests, and Zerubbabel son of Shealtiel, with his kinsmen, took their places and prepared the altar of the God of Israel, 49to offer burnt offerings upon it, in accordance with the directions in the book of Moses the man of God. 50And some joined them from the other peoples of the land. And they erected the altar in its place, for all the peoples of the land were hostile to them and were stronger than they; and they offered sacrifices at the proper times and burnt offerings to the Lord morning and evening. 51They kept the festival of booths, as it is commanded in the law, and offered the proper sacrifices every day, 52and thereafter the regular offerings and sacrifices on sabbaths and at new moons and at all the consecrated feasts. 53And all who had made any vow to God began to offer sacrifices to God, from the new moon of the seventh month, though the temple of God was not yet built. 54They gave money to the masons and the carpenters, and food and drink 55and carts[a] to the Sidonians and the Tyrians, to bring cedar logs from Lebanon and convey them in rafts to the harbor of Joppa, according to the decree that they had in writing from King Cyrus of the Persians.

56 In the second year after their coming to the temple of God in Jerusalem, in the second month, Zerubbabel son of Shealtiel and Jeshua son of Jozadak made a beginning, together with their kindred and the levitical priests and all who had come back to Jerusalem from exile; 57and they laid the foundation of the temple of God on the new moon of the second month in the second year after they came to Judea and Jerusalem. 58They appointed the Levites who were twenty or more years of age to have charge of the work of the Lord. And Jeshua arose, and his sons and kindred and his brother Kadmiel and the sons of Jeshua Emadabun and the sons of Joda son of Iliadun, with their sons and kindred, all the Levites, pressing forward the work on the house of God with a single purpose.

So the builders built the temple of the Lord. 59And the priests stood arrayed in their vestments, with musical instruments and trumpets, and the Levites, the sons of Asaph, with cymbals, 60praising the Lord and blessing him, according to the directions of King David of Israel; 61they sang hymns, giving thanks to the Lord, "For his goodness and his glory are forever upon all Israel." 62And all the people sounded trumpets and shouted with a great shout, praising the Lord for the erection of the house of the Lord. 63Some of the levitical priests and heads of ancestral houses, old men who had seen the former house, came to the building of this one with outcries and loud weeping, 64while many came with trumpets and a joyful noise, 65so that the people could not hear the trumpets because of the weeping of the people.

For the multitude sounded the trumpets loudly, so that the sound was heard far away; 66and when the enemies of the tribe of Judah and Benjamin heard it, they came to find out what the sound of the trumpets meant. 67They learned that

a Meaning of Gk uncertain

Greek Old Testament

ἐπέγνωσαν ὅτι οἱ ἐκ τῆς αἰχμαλωσίας οἰκοδομοῦσιν τὸν
ναὸν τῷ κυρίῳ θεῷ Ισραηλ, 65 καὶ προσελθόντες τῷ Ζοροβαβελ καὶ Ἰησοῦ καὶ τοῖς ἡγουμένοις τῶν πατριῶν λέγουσιν
αὐτοῖς Συνοικοδομήσομεν ὑμῖν· 66 ὁμοίως γὰρ ὑμῖν ἀκού-
ομεν τοῦ κυρίου ὑμῶν καὶ αὐτῷ ἐπιθύομεν ἀπὸ ἡμερῶν
Ασβασαρεθ βασιλέως Ἀσσυρίων, ὃς μετήγαγεν ἡμᾶς ἐνταῦθα. 67 καὶ εἶπεν αὐτοῖς Ζοροβαβελ καὶ Ἰησοῦς καὶ οἱ
ἡγούμενοι τῶν πατριῶν τοῦ Ισραηλ Οὐχ ὑμῖν καὶ ἡμῖν τοῦ
οἰκοδομῆσαι τὸν οἶκον κυρίῳ τῷ θεῷ ἡμῶν· 68 ἡμεῖς γὰρ
μόνοι οἰκοδομήσομεν τῷ κυρίῳ τοῦ Ισραηλ ἀκολούθως οἷς
προσέταξεν ἡμῖν Κῦρος ὁ βασιλεὺς Περσῶν. 69 τὰ δὲ ἔθνη
τῆς γῆς ἐπικείμενα τοῖς ἐν τῇ Ιουδαίᾳ καὶ πολιορκοῦντες
εἶργον τοῦ οἰκοδομεῖν 70 καὶ ἐπιβουλὰς καὶ δημαγωγίας καὶ
ἐπισυστάσεις ποιούμενοι ἀπεκώλυσαν τοῦ ἐπιτελεσθῆναι
τὴν οἰκοδομὴν πάντα τὸν χρόνον τῆς ζωῆς τοῦ βασιλέως Κύρου. 71 καὶ εἴρχθησαν τῆς οἰκοδομῆς ἔτη δύο ἕως τῆς
Δαρείου βασιλείας.

6 Ἐν δὲ τῷ δευτέρῳ ἔτει τῆς τοῦ Δαρείου βασιλείας ἐπροφήτευσεν Αγγαιος καὶ Ζαχαριας ὁ τοῦ Εδδι οἱ προφῆται
ἐπὶ τοὺς Ιουδαίους τοὺς ἐν τῇ Ιουδαίᾳ καὶ Ιερουσαλημ ἐπὶ
τῷ ὀνόματι κυρίου θεοῦ Ισραηλ ἐπ' αὐτούς. 2 τότε στὰς
Ζοροβαβελ ὁ τοῦ Σαλαθιηλ καὶ Ἰησοῦς ὁ τοῦ Ιωσεδεκ ἤρξαντο οἰκοδομεῖν τὸν οἶκον τοῦ κυρίου τὸν ἐν Ιερουσαλημ
συνόντων τῶν προφητῶν τοῦ κυρίου βοηθούντων αὐτοῖς. 3 ἐν
αὐτῷ τῷ χρόνῳ παρῆν πρὸς αὐτοὺς Σισίννης ὁ ἔπαρχος
Συρίας καὶ Φοινίκης καὶ Σαθραβουζάνης καὶ οἱ συνέταιροι
καὶ εἶπαν αὐτοῖς 4 Τίνος ὑμῖν συντάξαντος τὸν οἶκον τοῦτον οἰκοδομεῖτε καὶ τὴν στέγην ταύτην καὶ τἆλλα πάντα
ἐπιτελεῖτε; καὶ τίνες εἰσὶν οἱ οἰκοδόμοι οἱ ταῦτα ἐπιτελοῦν-
τες; 5 καὶ ἔσχοσαν χάριν ἐπισκοπῆς γενομένης ἐπὶ τὴν
αἰχμαλωσίαν παρὰ τοῦ κυρίου οἱ πρεσβύτεροι τῶν Ιουδαίων
6 καὶ οὐκ ἐκωλύθησαν τῆς οἰκοδομῆς μέχρι τοῦ ὑποσημαν-
θῆναι Δαρείῳ περὶ αὐτῶν καὶ προσφωνηθῆναι.
7 Ἀντίγραφον ἐπιστολῆς, ἧς ἔγραψεν Δαρείῳ καὶ ἀπέστειλεν Σισίννης ὁ ἔπαρχος Συρίας καὶ Φοινίκης καὶ Σαθραβουζάνης καὶ οἱ συνέταιροι οἱ ἐν Συρίᾳ καὶ Φοινίκῃ
ἡγεμόνες 8 Βασιλεῖ Δαρείῳ χαίρειν. πάντα γνωστὰ ἔστω τῷ
κυρίῳ ἡμῶν τῷ βασιλεῖ, ὅτι παραγενόμενοι εἰς τὴν χώραν
τῆς Ιουδαίας καὶ ἐλθόντες εἰς Ιερουσαλημ τὴν πόλιν κατε-
λάβομεν τῆς αἰχμαλωσίας τοὺς πρεσβυτέρους τῶν Ιουδαίων
ἐν Ιερουσαλημ τῇ πόλει οἰκοδομοῦντας οἶκον τῷ κυρίῳ μέγαν καινὸν διὰ λίθων ξυστῶν πολυτελῶν ξύλων τιθεμένων ἐν
τοῖς τοίχοις 9 καὶ τὰ ἔργα ἐκεῖνα ἐπὶ σπουδῆς γιγνόμενα
καὶ εὐοδούμενον τὸ ἔργον ἐν ταῖς χερσὶν αὐτῶν καὶ ἐν πάσῃ
δόξῃ καὶ ἐπιμελείᾳ συντελούμενα. 10 τότε ἐπυνθανόμεθα
τῶν πρεσβυτέρων τούτων λέγοντες Τίνος ὑμῖν προστάξαντος οἰκοδομεῖτε τὸν οἶκον τοῦτον καὶ τὰ ἔργα ταῦτα θεμε-
λιοῦτε; 11 ἐπηρωτήσαμεν οὖν αὐτοὺς εἵνεκεν τοῦ γνωρίσαι
σοι καὶ γράψαι σοι τοὺς ἀνθρώπους τοὺς ἀφηγουμένους καὶ
τὴν ὀνοματογραφίαν ᾐτοῦμεν αὐτοὺς τῶν προκαθηγουμένων.

King James Version

67 And they perceived that they that were of the captivity did build the temple unto the Lord God of Israel.

68 So they went to Zorobabel and Jesus, and to the chief of the families, and said unto them, We will build together with you.

69 For we likewise, as ye, do obey your Lord, and do sacrifice unto him from the days of Azbazareth the king of the Assyrians, who brought us hither.

70 Then Zorobabel and Jesus and the chief of the families of Israel said unto them, It is not for us and you to build together an house unto the Lord our God.

71 We ourselves alone will build unto the Lord of Israel, according as Cyrus the king of the Persians hath commanded us.

72 But the heathen of the land lying heavy upon the inhabitants of Judea, and holding them strait, hindered their building;

73 And by their secret plots, and popular persuasions and commotions, they hindered the finishing of the building all the time that king Cyrus lived: so they were hindered from building for the space of two years, until the reign of Darius.

6 Now in the second year of the reign of Darius Aggeus and Zacharias the son of Addo, the prophets, prophesied unto the Jews in Jewry and Jerusalem in the name of the Lord God of Israel, which was upon them.

2 Then stood up Zorobabel the son of Salatiel, and Jesus the son of Josedec, and began to build the house of the Lord at Jerusalem, the prophets of the Lord being with them, *and* helping them.

3 At the same time came unto them Sisinnes the governor of Syria and Phenice, with Sathrabuzanes and his companions, and said unto them,

4 By whose appointment do ye build this house and this roof, and perform all the other things? and who are the workmen that perform these things?

5 Nevertheless the elders of the Jews obtained favour, because the Lord had visited the captivity;

6 And they were not hindered from building, until such time as signification was given unto Darius concerning them, and an answer received.

7 The copy of the letters which Sisinnes, governor of Syria and Phenice, and Sathrabuzanes, with their companions, rulers in Syria and Phenice, wrote and sent unto Darius; To king Darius, greeting:

8 Let all things be known unto our lord the king, that being come into the country of Judea, and entered into the city of Jerusalem, we found in the city of Jerusalem the ancients of the Jews that were of the captivity

9 Building an house unto the Lord, great *and* new, of hewn and costly stones, and the timber already laid upon the walls.

10 And those works are done with great speed, and the work goeth on prosperously in their hands, and with all glory and diligence is it made.

11 Then asked we these elders, saying, By whose commandment build ye this house, and lay the foundations of these works?

12 Therefore to the intent that we might give knowledge unto thee by writing, we demanded of them who were the chief doers, and we required of them the names in writing of their principal men.

TODAY'S ENGLISH VERSION

67 When they learned that those who had returned from exile
were rebuilding the Temple of the Lord, the God of Israel,
68 they went to Zerubbabel, Joshua, and the heads of the
clans and said, "Let us join you in building the Temple.
69 We worship the same Lord you worship and we have been
offering sacrifices to him ever since Emperor Esarhaddon[a] of
Assyria sent us here to live."

70 Zerubbabel, Joshua, and the heads of the clans told
them, "We don't need your help in building the Temple for
the Lord our God. 71 We will build it ourselves, just as
Emperor Cyrus of Persia commanded us."

72 Then the people who had been living in the land began
to harass[b] the Jews; they cut off their supplies and kept them
from building. 73 These people plotted, agitated, and rioted
so much that they prevented the Temple from being completed during the reign of Emperor Cyrus. The work was halted
until Darius became emperor, two years later.

6 In the second year of the reign of Emperor Darius, the
two prophets, Haggai and Zechariah son of Iddo, began
to speak in the name of the Lord God of Israel to the Jews
who lived in Judah and Jerusalem. 2 When Zerubbabel son of
Shealtiel and Joshua son of Jehozadak heard their messages,
they began to rebuild the Temple in Jerusalem, and the two
prophets helped them.

3 Almost at once Governor Sisinnes of Greater Syria and
Phoenicia, with Shethar Bozenai and the other officials,
came to Jerusalem and demanded: 4 "Who gave you orders
to build this Temple and complete this roof and everything
else? Who is doing this work?" 5 But the Lord was with the
people who had returned from exile and was watching over
the Jewish leaders, 6 and they were allowed to continue
building until Emperor Darius could be informed and his
reply received. 7 Here is the report that the Persian officials
sent to the emperor:

8 "To Emperor Darius, greetings.

"Your Majesty should know that we went to Judah and
to Jerusalem and there we found the leaders of the Jews
who have returned from exile 9 building a large new
Temple for the Lord with expensive, shaped stone blocks
and with wooden beams set in the walls. 10 The work is
being done rapidly and is moving ahead steadily; yet they
are taking great care and doing their work beautifully.

11 "We then asked the leaders of the people to tell us
who had given them orders to rebuild the Temple and lay
the foundations for the buildings. 12 We also asked them
who their leaders were and demanded a list of their
names, so that we could inform you.

[a] ESARHADDON: *Greek* Asbasareth. [b] *Probable text* harass; *Greek unclear.*

NEW REVISED STANDARD VERSION

those who had returned from exile were building the temple
for the Lord God of Israel. 68 So they approached Zerubbabel
and Jeshua and the heads of the ancestral houses and said to
them, "We will build with you. 69 For we obey your Lord just
as you do and we have been sacrificing to him ever since the
days of King Esar-haddon[a] of the Assyrians, who brought us
here." 70 But Zerubbabel and Jeshua and the heads of the
ancestral houses in Israel said to them, "You have nothing to
do with us in building the house for the Lord our God, 71 for
we alone will build it for the Lord of Israel, as Cyrus, the king
of the Persians, has commanded us." 72 But the peoples of
the land pressed hard[b] upon those in Judea, cut off their supplies, and hindered their building; 73 and by plots and dema-
goguery and uprisings they prevented the completion of the
building as long as King Cyrus lived. They were kept from
building for two years, until the reign of Darius.

6 Now in the second year of the reign of Darius, the
prophets Haggai and Zechariah son of Iddo prophesied
to the Jews who were in Judea and Jerusalem; they prophesied to them in the name of the Lord God of Israel. 2 Then
Zerubbabel son of Shealtiel and Jeshua son of Jozadak began
to build the house of the Lord that is in Jerusalem, with the
help of the prophets of the Lord who were with them.

3 At the same time Sisinnes the governor of Syria and
Phoenicia and Sathrabuzanes and their associates came to
them and said, 4 "By whose order are you building this
house and this roof and finishing all the other things? And
who are the builders that are finishing these things?" 5 Yet
the elders of the Jews were dealt with kindly, for the providence of the Lord was over the captives; 6 they were not prevented from building until word could be sent to Darius concerning them and a report made.

7 A copy of the letter that Sisinnes the governor of Syria
and Phoenicia, and Sathrabuzanes, and their associates the
local rulers in Syria and Phoenicia, wrote and sent to Darius:

8 "To King Darius, greetings. Let it be fully known to our
lord the king that, when we went to the country of Judea and
entered the city of Jerusalem, we found the elders of the
Jews, who had been in exile, 9 building in the city of Jerusalem a great new house for the Lord, of hewn stone, with
costly timber laid in the walls. 10 These operations are going
on rapidly, and the work is prospering in their hands and
being completed with all splendor and care. 11 Then we
asked these elders, 'At whose command are you building this
house and laying the foundations of this structure?' 12 In
order that we might inform you in writing who the leaders
are, we questioned them and asked them for a list of the
names of those who are at their head. 13 They answered us,

[a] Gk *Asbasareth* [b] Meaning of Gk uncertain

Greek Old Testament

12 οἱ δὲ ἀπεκρίθησαν ἡμῖν λέγοντες Ἡμεῖς ἐσμεν παῖδες τοῦ
κυρίου τοῦ κτίσαντος τὸν οὐρανὸν καὶ τὴν γῆν. 13 καὶ
ᾠκοδόμητο ὁ οἶκος ἔμπροσθεν ἐτῶν πλειόνων διὰ βασιλέως
τοῦ Ισραηλ μεγάλου καὶ ἰσχυροῦ καὶ ἐπετελέσθη. 14 καὶ ἐπεὶ
οἱ πατέρες ἡμῶν παραπικράναντες ἥμαρτον εἰς τὸν κύριον
τοῦ Ισραηλ τὸν οὐράνιον, παρέδωκεν αὐτοὺς εἰς χεῖρας
Ναβουχοδονοσορ βασιλέως Βαβυλῶνος βασιλέως τῶν Χαλ-
δαίων· 15 τόν τε οἶκον καθελόντες ἐνεπύρισαν καὶ τὸν λαὸν
ᾐχμαλώτευσαν εἰς Βαβυλῶνα. 16 ἐν δὲ τῷ πρώτῳ ἔτει βασιλεύοντος Κύρου χώρας Βαβυλωνίας ἔγραψεν ὁ βασιλεὺς
Κῦρος οἰκοδομῆσαι τὸν οἶκον τοῦτον· 17 καὶ τὰ ἱερὰ σκεύη
τὰ χρυσᾶ καὶ τὰ ἀργυρᾶ, ἃ ἐξήνεγκεν Ναβουχοδονοσορ ἐκ
τοῦ οἴκου τοῦ ἐν Ιερουσαλημ καὶ ἀπηρείσατο αὐτὰ ἐν τῷ
ἑαυτοῦ ναῷ, πάλιν ἐξήνεγκεν αὐτὰ Κῦρος ὁ βασιλεὺς ἐκ τοῦ
ναοῦ τοῦ ἐν Βαβυλῶνι, καὶ παρεδόθη Ζοροβαβελ καὶ Σαναβασσάρῳ τῷ ἐπάρχῳ, 18 καὶ ἐπετάγη αὐτῷ ἀπενέγκαντι πάντα τὰ σκεύη ταῦτα ἀποθεῖναι ἐν τῷ ναῷ τῷ ἐν Ιερουσαλημ
καὶ τὸν ναὸν τοῦ κυρίου τοῦτον οἰκοδομηθῆναι ἐπὶ τοῦ τόπου. 19 τότε ὁ Σαναβάσσαρος ἐκεῖνος παραγενόμενος ἐνεβά-
λετο τοὺς θεμελίους τοῦ οἴκου κυρίου τοῦ ἐν Ιερουσαλημ, καὶ
ἀπ' ἐκείνου μέχρι τοῦ νῦν οἰκοδομούμενος οὐκ ἔλαβεν συντέλειαν. 20 νῦν οὖν, εἰ κρίνεται, βασιλεῦ, ἐπισκεπήτω ἐν τοῖς
βασιλικοῖς βιβλιοφυλακίοις τοῦ κυρίου βασιλέως τοῖς ἐν
Βαβυλῶνι· 21 καὶ ἐὰν εὑρίσκηται μετὰ τῆς γνώμης Κύρου
τοῦ βασιλέως γενομένην τὴν οἰκοδομὴν τοῦ οἴκου κυρίου τοῦ
ἐν Ιερουσαλημ καὶ κρίνηται τῷ κυρίῳ βασιλεῖ ἡμῶν, προσ-
φωνησάτω ἡμῖν περὶ τούτων.

22 Τότε ὁ βασιλεὺς Δαρεῖος προσέταξεν ἐπισκέψασθαι ἐν
τοῖς βασιλικοῖς βιβλιοφυλακίοις τοῖς κειμένοις ἐν Βαβυλῶνι,
καὶ εὑρέθη ἐν Ἐκβατάνοις τῇ βάρει τῇ ἐν Μηδίᾳ χώρᾳ τόμος
εἷς, ἐν ᾧ ὑπεμνημάτιστο τάδε 23 Ἔτους πρώτου βασιλεύοντος Κύρου· βασιλεὺς Κῦρος προσέταξεν τὸν οἶκον τοῦ
κυρίου τὸν ἐν Ιερουσαλημ οἰκοδομῆσαι, ὅπου ἐπιθύουσιν διὰ
πυρὸς ἐνδελεχοῦς, 24 οὗ τὸ ὕψος πήχεων ἑξήκοντα, πλάτος
πήχεων ἑξήκοντα, διὰ δόμων λιθίνων ξυστῶν τριῶν καὶ δόμου
ξυλίνου ἐγχωρίου καινοῦ ἑνός, καὶ τὸ δαπάνημα δοθῆναι ἐκ
τοῦ οἴκου Κύρου τοῦ βασιλέως. 25 καὶ τὰ ἱερὰ σκεύη τοῦ
οἴκου κυρίου, τά τε χρυσᾶ καὶ τὰ ἀργυρᾶ, ἃ ἐξήνεγκεν
Ναβουχοδονοσορ ἐκ τοῦ οἴκου τοῦ ἐν Ιερουσαλημ καὶ ἀπήν-
εγκεν εἰς Βαβυλῶνα, ἀποκατασταθῆναι εἰς τὸν οἶκον τὸν ἐν
Ιερουσαλημ, οὗ ἦν κείμενα, ὅπως τεθῇ ἐκεῖ. 26 προσέταξεν
δὲ ἐπιμεληθῆναι Σισίννῃ ἐπάρχῳ Συρίας καὶ Φοινίκης καὶ
Σαθραβουζάνῃ καὶ τοῖς συνεταίροις καὶ τοῖς ἀποτεταγμέ-
νοις ἐν Συρίᾳ καὶ Φοινίκῃ ἡγεμόσιν ἀπέχεσθαι τοῦ τόπου,
ἐᾶσαι δὲ τὸν παῖδα τοῦ κυρίου Ζοροβαβελ, ἔπαρχον δὲ τῆς
Ιουδαίας, καὶ τοὺς πρεσβυτέρους τῶν Ιουδαίων τὸν οἶκον τοῦ
κυρίου ἐκεῖνον οἰκοδομεῖν ἐπὶ τοῦ τόπου. 27 κἀγὼ δὲ ἐπέταξα ὁλοσχερῶς οἰκοδομῆσαι καὶ ἀτενίσαι ἵνα συμποιῶσιν
τοῖς ἐκ τῆς αἰχμαλωσίας τῆς Ιουδαίας μέχρι τοῦ ἐπιτελεσθῆναι τὸν οἶκον τοῦ κυρίου· 28 καὶ ἀπὸ τῆς φορολογίας
Κοίλης Συρίας καὶ Φοινίκης ἐπιμελῶς σύνταξιν δίδοσθαι
τούτοις τοῖς ἀνθρώποις εἰς θυσίας τῷ κυρίῳ, Ζοροβαβελ

King James Version

13 So they gave us this answer, We are the servants of the Lord which made heaven and earth.

14 And as for this house, it was builded many years ago by a king of Israel great and strong, and was finished.

15 But when our fathers provoked God unto wrath, and sinned against the Lord of Israel which is in heaven, he gave them over into the power of Nabuchodonosor king of Babylon, of the Chaldees;

16 Who pulled down the house, and burned it, and carried away the people captives unto Babylon.

17 But in the first year that king Cyrus reigned over the country of Babylon Cyrus the king wrote to build up this house.

18 And the holy vessels of gold and of silver, that Nabuchodonosor had carried away out of the house at Jerusalem, and had set them in his own temple, those Cyrus the king brought forth again out of the temple at Babylon, and they were delivered to Zorobabel and to Sanabassarus the ruler,

19 With commandment that he should carry away the same vessels, and put them in the temple at Jerusalem; and that the temple of the Lord should be built in his place.

20 Then the same Sanabassarus, being come hither, laid the foundations of the house of the Lord at Jerusalem; and from that time to this being still a building, it is not yet fully ended.

21 Now therefore, if it seem good unto the king, let search be made among the records of king Cyrus:

22 And if it be found that the building of the house of the Lord at Jerusalem hath been done with the consent of king Cyrus, and if our lord the king be so minded, let him signify unto us thereof.

23 Then commanded king Darius to seek among the records at Babylon: and so at Ecbatana the palace, which is in the country of Media, there was found a roll wherein these things were recorded.

24 In the first year of the reign of Cyrus king Cyrus commanded that the house of the Lord at Jerusalem should be built again, where they do sacrifice with continual fire:

25 Whose height shall be sixty cubits, and the breadth sixty cubits, with three rows of hewn stones, and one row of new wood of that country; and the expences thereof to be given out of the house of king Cyrus:

26 And that the holy vessels of the house of the Lord, both of gold and silver, that Nabuchodonosor took out of the house at Jerusalem, and brought to Babylon, should be restored to the house at Jerusalem, and be set in the place where they were before.

27 And also he commanded that Sisinnes the governor of Syria and Phenice, and Sathrabuzanes, and their companions, and those which were appointed rulers in Syria and Phenice, should be careful not to meddle with the place, but suffer Zorobabel, the servant of the Lord, and governor of Judea, and the elders of the Jews, to build the house of the Lord in that place.

28 I have commanded also to have it built up whole again; and that they look diligently to help those that be of the captivity of the Jews, till the house of the Lord be finished:

29 And out of the tribute of Celosyria and Phenice a portion carefully to be given these men for the sacrifices of the

Today's English Version

13 "They answered, 'We are servants of the Lord who created heaven and earth. 14 This Temple was built and
equipped many years ago by a very powerful king of Israel.
15 But because our ancestors sinned against Israel's Lord in
heaven and made him angry, he let them be conquered by
King Nebuchadnezzar of Babylonia, a king of the Chaldean
dynasty. 16 The Temple was demolished and burned, and
the people were taken into exile in Babylonia. 17 Then, in
the first year of his reign as emperor of Babylonia, Cyrus
issued orders for the Temple to be rebuilt. 18 He gave back
the sacred gold and silver utensils which Nebuchadnezzar
had taken from the Temple in Jerusalem and had placed in
his own temple in Babylon. Emperor Cyrus turned these
utensils over to Zerubbabel and the governor, Sheshbazzar. 19 The Emperor told Sheshbazzar to take them and
return them to the Temple in Jerusalem, and to rebuild the
Temple where it had stood before. 20 So Sheshbazzar came
and laid its foundation, and construction has continued
from then until the present, but the Temple is still not finished.'

21 "Now, if it please Your Majesty, have a search made in
the royal records in Babylon 22 to find whether or not the
building of this Temple in Jerusalem had the approval of
Emperor Cyrus, and then, if it please Your Majesty, inform
us what your will is in this matter."

23 So Emperor Darius ordered a search to be made in the
royal records that were kept in Babylon. It was, however, in
the fortress of Ecbatana in the province of Media that a scroll
was found, containing the following record:

24 "In the first year of his reign Emperor Cyrus ordered
the rebuilding of the Temple in Jerusalem, where sacrifices
are continually offered. 25 The Temple is to be 90 feet high
and 90 feet wide. The walls must be built with one layer of
new local wood on top of each three layers of shaped
stone. All expenses are to be paid by the royal treasury.
26 Also the gold and silver utensils which King
Nebuchadnezzar brought to Babylon from the Temple in
Jerusalem are to be returned to their proper place in the
Jerusalem Temple."

27 Then Emperor Darius gave strict orders to Sisinnes, governor of Greater Syria and Phoenicia, Shethar Bozenai, the
other officials, and the local officials to stay away from
Jerusalem and let Zerubbabel, the servant of the Lord and
governor of Judah, and the other Jewish leaders rebuild the
Temple of the Lord where it stood before. 28 "And I also command," he continued, "that it be completely rebuilt and that,
until it is finished, every effort be made to help the Jews who
have returned from exile. 29 From the taxes received in
Greater Syria and Phoenicia a contribution shall be made on

New Revised Standard Version

'We are the servants of the Lord who created the heaven and
the earth. 14 The house was built many years ago by a king
of Israel who was great and strong, and it was finished.
15 But when our ancestors sinned against the Lord of Israel
who is in heaven, and provoked him, he gave them over into
the hands of King Nebuchadnezzar of Babylon, king of the
Chaldeans; 16 and they pulled down the house, and burned
it, and carried the people away captive to Babylon. 17 But in
the first year that Cyrus reigned over the country of
Babylonia, King Cyrus wrote that this house should be
rebuilt. 18 And the holy vessels of gold and of silver, which
Nebuchadnezzar had taken out of the house in Jerusalem
and stored in his own temple, these King Cyrus took out
again from the temple in Babylon, and they were delivered to
Zerubbabel and Sheshbazzar[a] the governor 19 with the command that he should take all these vessels back and put
them in the temple at Jerusalem, and that this temple of the
Lord should be rebuilt on its site. 20 Then this Sheshbazzar,
after coming here, laid the foundations of the house of the
Lord that is in Jerusalem. Although it has been in process of
construction from that time until now, it has not yet reached
completion.' 21 Now therefore, O king, if it seems wise to do
so, let search be made in the royal archives of our lord[b] the
king that are in Babylon; 22 if it is found that the building of
the house of the Lord in Jerusalem was done with the consent of King Cyrus, and if it is approved by our lord the king,
let him send us directions concerning these things."

23 Then Darius commanded that search be made in the
royal archives that were deposited in Babylon. And in
Ecbatana, the fortress that is in the country of Media, a
scroll[c] was found in which this was recorded: 24 "In the first
year of the reign of King Cyrus, he ordered the building of the
house of the Lord in Jerusalem, where they sacrifice with perpetual fire; 25 its height to be sixty cubits and its width sixty
cubits, with three courses of hewn stone and one course of
new native timber; the cost to be paid from the treasury of
King Cyrus; 26 and that the holy vessels of the house of the
Lord, both of gold and of silver, which Nebuchadnezzar took
out of the house in Jerusalem and carried away to Babylon,
should be restored to the house in Jerusalem, to be placed
where they had been."

27 So Darius[d] commanded Sisinnes the governor of Syria
and Phoenicia, and Sathrabuzanes, and their associates, and
those who were appointed as local rulers in Syria and
Phoenicia, to keep away from the place, and to permit
Zerubbabel, the servant of the Lord and governor of Judea,
and the elders of the Jews to build this house of the Lord on
its site. 28 "And I command that it be built completely, and
that full effort be made to help those who have returned from
the exile of Judea, until the house of the Lord is finished;
29 and that out of the tribute of Coelesyria and Phoenicia a
portion be scrupulously given to these men, that is, to

a Gk *Sanabassarus* *b* Other ancient authorities read *of Cyrus* *c* Other authorities read *passage* *d* Gk *he*

ἐπάρχῳ, εἰς ταύρους καὶ κριοὺς καὶ ἄρνας, 29 ὁμοίως δὲ καὶ πυρὸν καὶ ἅλα καὶ οἶνον καὶ ἔλαιον ἐνδελεχῶς κατ᾽ ἐνιαυτόν, καθὼς ἂν οἱ ἱερεῖς οἱ ἐν Ιερουσαλημ ὑπαγορεύσωσιν ἀναλίσκεσθαι καθ᾽ ἡμέραν ἀναμφισβητήτως, 30 ὅπως προσφέρωνται σπονδαὶ τῷ θεῷ τῷ ὑψίστῳ ὑπὲρ τοῦ βασιλέως καὶ τῶν παίδων καὶ προσεύχωνται περὶ τῆς αὐτῶν ζωῆς. 31 καὶ προσέταξεν ἵνα ὅσοι ἐὰν παραβῶσίν τι τῶν προειρημένων καὶ τῶν προσγεγραμμένων ἢ καὶ ἀκυρώσωσιν, λημφθῆναι ξύλον ἐκ τῶν ἰδίων αὐτοῦ καὶ ἐπὶ τούτου κρεμασθῆναι καὶ τὰ ὑπάρχοντα αὐτοῦ εἶναι βασιλικά. 32 διὰ ταῦτα καὶ ὁ κύριος, οὗ τὸ ὄνομα αὐτοῦ ἐπικέκληται ἐκεῖ, ἀφανίσαι πάντα βασιλέα καὶ ἔθνος, ὃς ἐκτενεῖ τὴν χεῖρα αὐτοῦ κωλῦσαι ἢ κακοποιῆσαι τὸν οἶκον τοῦ κυρίου ἐκεῖνον τὸν ἐν Ιερουσαλημ. 33 ἐγὼ βασιλεὺς Δαρεῖος δεδογμάτικα ἐπιμελῶς κατὰ ταῦτα γίγνεσθαι.

7 Τότε Σισίννης ὁ ἔπαρχος Κοίλης Συρίας καὶ Φοινίκης καὶ Σαθραβουζάνης καὶ οἱ συνέταιροι κατακολουθήσαντες τοῖς ὑπὸ τοῦ βασιλέως Δαρείου προσταγεῖσιν 2 ἐπεστάτουν τῶν ἱερῶν ἔργων ἐπιμελέστερον συνεργοῦντες τοῖς πρεσβυτέροις τῶν Ιουδαίων καὶ ἱεροστάταις. 3 καὶ εὔοδα ἐγίνετο τὰ ἱερὰ ἔργα προφητευόντων Αγγαιου καὶ Ζαχαριου τῶν προφητῶν, 4 καὶ συνετέλεσαν ταῦτα διὰ προστάγματος τοῦ κυρίου θεοῦ Ισραηλ, 5 καὶ μετὰ τῆς γνώμης Κύρου καὶ Δαρείου καὶ Ἀρταξέρξου βασιλέως Περσῶν συνετελέσθη ὁ οἶκος ὁ ἅγιος ἕως τρίτης καὶ εἰκάδος μηνὸς Αδαρ τοῦ ἕκτου ἔτους βασιλέως Δαρείου. 6 καὶ ἐποίησαν οἱ υἱοὶ Ισραηλ καὶ οἱ ἱερεῖς καὶ οἱ Λευῖται καὶ οἱ λοιποὶ οἱ ἐκ τῆς αἰχμαλωσίας οἱ προστεθέντες ἀκολούθως τοῖς ἐν τῇ Μωυσέως βίβλῳ· 7 καὶ προσήνεγκαν εἰς τὸν ἐγκαινισμὸν τοῦ ἱεροῦ τοῦ κυρίου ταύρους ἑκατόν, κριοὺς διακοσίους, ἄρνας τετρακοσίους, 8 χιμάρους ὑπὲρ ἁμαρτίας παντὸς τοῦ Ισραηλ δώδεκα πρὸς ἀριθμὸν ἐκ τῶν φυλάρχων τοῦ Ισραηλ δώδεκα· 9 καὶ ἔστησαν οἱ ἱερεῖς καὶ οἱ Λευῖται ἐστολισμένοι κατὰ φυλὰς ἐπὶ τῶν ἔργων τοῦ κυρίου θεοῦ Ισραηλ ἀκολούθως τῇ Μωυσέως βίβλῳ καὶ οἱ θυρωροὶ ἐφ᾽ ἑκάστου πυλῶνος.

10 Καὶ ἠγάγοσαν οἱ υἱοὶ Ισραηλ τῶν ἐκ τῆς αἰχμαλωσίας τὸ πασχα ἐν τῇ τεσσαρεσκαιδεκάτῃ τοῦ πρώτου μηνός. ὅτι ἡγνίσθησαν οἱ ἱερεῖς καὶ οἱ Λευῖται ἅμα, 11 καὶ πάντες οἱ υἱοὶ τῆς αἰχμαλωσίας οὐχ ἡγνίσθησαν, ὅτι οἱ Λευῖται ἅμα πάντες ἡγνίσθησαν 12 καὶ ἔθυσαν τὸ πασχα πᾶσιν τοῖς υἱοῖς τῆς αἰχμαλωσίας καὶ τοῖς ἀδελφοῖς αὐτῶν τοῖς ἱερεῦσιν καὶ ἑαυτοῖς. 13 καὶ ἐφάγοσαν οἱ υἱοὶ Ισραηλ οἱ ἐκ τῆς αἰχμαλωσίας, πάντες οἱ χωρισθέντες ἀπὸ τῶν βδελυγμάτων τῶν ἐθνῶν τῆς γῆς, ζητοῦντες τὸν κύριον. 14 καὶ ἠγάγοσαν τὴν ἑορτὴν τῶν ἀζύμων ἑπτὰ ἡμέρας εὐφραινόμενοι ἔναντι τοῦ κυρίου, 15 ὅτι μετέστρεψεν τὴν βουλὴν τοῦ βασιλέως Ἀσσυρίων ἐπ᾽ αὐτοὺς κατισχῦσαι τὰς χεῖρας αὐτῶν ἐπὶ τὰ ἔργα κυρίου θεοῦ Ισραηλ.

Lord, *that is,* to Zorobabel the governor, for bullocks, and rams, and lambs;

30 And also corn, salt, wine, and oil, and that continually every year without further question, according as the priests that be in Jerusalem shall signify to be daily spent:

31 That offerings may be made to the most high God for the king and for his children, and that they may pray for their lives.

32 And he commanded that whosoever should transgress, yea, or make light of any thing afore spoken or written, out of his own house should a tree be taken, and he thereon be hanged, and all his goods seized for the king.

33 The Lord therefore, whose name is there called upon, utterly destroy every king and nation, that stretcheth out his hand to hinder or endamage that house of the Lord in Jerusalem.

34 I Darius the king have ordained that according unto these things it be done with diligence.

7 Then Sisinnes the governor of Celosyria and Phenice, and Sathrabuzanes, with their companions, following the commandments of king Darius,

2 Did very carefully oversee the holy works, assisting the ancients of the Jews and governors of the temple.

3 And so the holy works prospered, when Aggeus and Zacharias the prophets prophesied.

4 And they finished these things by the commandment of the Lord God of Israel, and with the consent of Cyrus, Darius, and Artaxerxes, kings of Persia.

5 And thus was the holy house finished in the three and twentieth day of the month Adar, in the sixth year of Darius king of the Persians.

6 And the children of Israel, the priests, and the Levites, and others that were of the captivity, that were added unto them, did according to the things written in the book of Moses.

7 And to the dedication of the temple of the Lord they offered an hundred bullocks, two hundred rams, four hundred lambs;

8 And twelve goats for the sin of all Israel, according to the number of the chief of the tribes of Israel.

9 The priests also and the Levites stood arrayed in their vestments, according to their kindreds, in the service of the Lord God of Israel, according to the book of Moses: and the porters at every gate.

10 And the children of Israel that were of the captivity held the passover the fourteenth day of the first month, after that the priests and the Levites were sanctified.

11 They that were of the captivity were not all sanctified together: but the Levites were all sanctified together.

12 And so they offered the passover for all them of the captivity, and for their brethren the priests, and for themselves.

13 And the children of Israel that came out of the captivity did eat, even all they that had separated themselves from the abominations of the people of the land, and sought the Lord.

14 And they kept the feast of unleavened bread seven days, making merry before the Lord,

15 For that he had turned the counsel of the king of Assyria toward them, to strengthen their hands in the works of the Lord God of Israel.

Today's English Version

a regular basis to these men, payable to Governor Zerubbabel, for bulls, sheep, and lambs to be used in their sacrifices to the Lord. 30 In the same way, each year and without further question, wheat, salt, wine, and olive oil are to be supplied, according to the daily needs indicated by the priests. 31 This must be done so that they can make wine offerings to God Most High for me and my children and pray for his blessing on our lives." 32 He also gave these orders: "If anyone disobeys the commands as written above or fails to carry them out, he is to be hanged on a wooden beam taken from his own house, and his property is to be turned over to the emperor. 33 May the Lord who is worshiped at Jerusalem destroy any king or nation that tries to stop the work or damage the Temple there. 34 I, Emperor Darius, issue the command that these orders be carried out in every detail."

7 Then Governor Sisinnes, Shethar Bozenai, and the other officials did exactly as the emperor had commanded 2 and gave careful supervision to the work on the Temple, helping the Jewish leaders and Temple officials. 3 The workers made good progress with the building of the Temple, encouraged by the prophets Haggai and Zechariah. 4 The Jews completed the building according to the command of the Lord, the God of Israel, and with the permission of Cyrus, Darius, and Artaxerxes, emperors of Persia. 5 The Temple was completed on the twenty-third day of the month of Adar in the sixth year of the reign of Emperor Darius. 6 Then the people of Israel—the priests, the Levites, and all the others who had returned from exile and joined them—carried out all the commands in the Law of Moses. 7 For the dedication they offered 100 bulls, 200 sheep, and 400 lambs as sacrifices, 8 and 12 goats as offerings for sin, one goat for the leader of each tribe of Israel. 9 The priests in their robes and the Levites took their positions, family by family, for the Temple services of the Lord, the God of Israel, according to the instructions contained in the book of Moses. The Temple guards stood at each gate.

10 The people of Israel who had returned from exile celebrated the Passover on the fourteenth day of the first month of the following year. The priests and Levites had purified themselves at the same time. 11 Not all the Jews who had returned purified themselves at that time, but the Levites did.[a] 12 The Levites killed the animals for the Passover sacrifices for all the people who had returned, for the priests, and for themselves. 13 The sacrifices were eaten by all the Israelites who had returned from exile; they worshiped the Lord and rejected the pagan ways of the other people who were living in the land. 14 For seven days they celebrated the Festival of Unleavened Bread. They rejoiced in the presence of the Lord, 15 the God of Israel, because he had made the plans of the emperor of Assyria[b] favorable to them and had supported them in their work.

[a] Verse 11 in Greek is unclear. *[b]* EMPEROR OF ASSYRIA: *Apparently a reference to the Persian emperor who then also ruled the territory once occupied by Assyria, Israel's ancient enemy.*

New Revised Standard Version

Zerubbabel the governor, for sacrifices to the Lord, for bulls and rams and lambs, 30 and likewise wheat and salt and wine and oil, regularly every year, without quibbling, for daily use as the priests in Jerusalem may indicate, 31 in order that libations may be made to the Most High God for the king and his children, and prayers be offered for their lives."

32 He commanded that if anyone should transgress or nullify any of the things herein written,[a] a beam should be taken out of the house of the perpetrator, who then should be impaled upon it, and all property forfeited to the king.

33 "Therefore may the Lord, whose name is there called upon, destroy every king and nation that shall stretch out their hands to hinder or damage that house of the Lord in Jerusalem.

34 "I, King Darius, have decreed that it be done with all diligence as here prescribed."

7 Then Sisinnes the governor of Coelesyria and Phoenicia, and Sathrabuzanes, and their associates, following the orders of King Darius, 2 supervised the holy work with very great care, assisting the elders of the Jews and the chief officers of the temple. 3 The holy work prospered, while the prophets Haggai and Zechariah prophesied; 4 and they completed it by the command of the Lord God of Israel. So with the consent of Cyrus and Darius and Artaxerxes, kings of the Persians, 5 the holy house was finished by the twenty-third day of the month of Adar, in the sixth year of King Darius. 6 And the people of Israel, the priests, the Levites, and the rest of those who returned from exile who joined them, did according to what was written in the book of Moses. 7 They offered at the dedication of the temple of the Lord one hundred bulls, two hundred rams, four hundred lambs, 8 and twelve male goats for the sin of all Israel, according to the number of the twelve leaders of the tribes of Israel; 9 and the priests and the Levites stood arrayed in their vestments, according to kindred, for the services of the Lord God of Israel in accordance with the book of Moses; and the gatekeepers were at each gate.

10 The people of Israel who came from exile kept the passover on the fourteenth day of the first month, after the priests and the Levites were purified together. 11 Not all of the returned captives were purified, but the Levites were all purified together,[b] 12 and they sacrificed the passover lamb for all the returned captives and for their kindred the priests and for themselves. 13 The people of Israel who had returned from exile ate it, all those who had separated themselves from the abominations of the peoples of the land and sought the Lord. 14 They also kept the festival of unleavened bread seven days, rejoicing before the Lord, 15 because he had changed the will of the king of the Assyrians concerning them, to strengthen their hands for the service of the Lord God of Israel.

[a] Other authorities read *stated above* or *added in writing* [b] Meaning of Gk uncertain

Greek Old Testament

8 Καὶ μεταγενέστερος τούτων βασιλεύοντος Ἀρταξέρξου
τοῦ Περσῶν βασιλέως προσέβη Εσδρας Σαραιου τοῦ
Εζεριου τοῦ Χελκιου τοῦ Σαλημου 2 τοῦ Σαδδουκου τοῦ
Αχιτωβ τοῦ Αμαριου τοῦ Οζιου τοῦ Βοκκα τοῦ Αβισουε τοῦ
Φινεες τοῦ Ελεαζαρ τοῦ Ααρων τοῦ πρώτου ἱερέως. 3 οὗτος
Εσδρας ἀνέβη ἐκ Βαβυλῶνος ὡς γραμματεὺς εὐφυὴς ὢν ἐν
τῷ Μωυσέως νόμῳ τῷ ἐκδεδομένῳ ὑπὸ τοῦ θεοῦ τοῦ Ισραηλ,
4 καὶ ἔδωκεν αὐτῷ ὁ βασιλεὺς δόξαν, εὑρόντος χάριν ἐναντίον αὐτοῦ ἐπὶ πάντα τὰ ἀξιώματα αὐτοῦ. 5 καὶ συνανέ-
βησαν ἐκ τῶν υἱῶν Ισραηλ καὶ τῶν ἱερέων καὶ Λευιτῶν καὶ
ἱεροψαλτῶν καὶ θυρωρῶν καὶ ἱεροδούλων εἰς Ιεροσόλυμα
ἔτους ἑβδόμου βασιλεύοντος Ἀρταξέρξου ἐν τῷ πέμπτῳ
μηνί (οὗτος ἐνιαυτὸς ἕβδομος τῷ βασιλεῖ)· 6 ἐξελθόντες
γὰρ ἐκ Βαβυλῶνος τῇ νουμηνίᾳ τοῦ πρώτου μηνὸς ἐν τῇ
νουμηνίᾳ τοῦ πέμπτου μηνὸς παρεγένοντο εἰς Ιεροσόλυμα
κατὰ τὴν δοθεῖσαν αὐτοῖς εὐοδίαν παρὰ τοῦ κυρίου ἐπ᾽ αὐτῷ.
7 ὁ γὰρ Εσδρας πολλὴν ἐπιστήμην περιεῖχεν εἰς τὸ μηδὲν
παραλιπεῖν τῶν ἐκ τοῦ νόμου κυρίου καὶ ἐκ τῶν ἐντολῶν
διδάξαι τὸν πάντα Ισραηλ πάντα τὰ δικαιώματα καὶ τὰ κρίματα.

8 Προσπεσόντος δὲ τοῦ γραφέντος προστάγματος παρὰ
Ἀρταξέρξου τοῦ βασιλέως πρὸς Εσδραν τὸν ἱερέα καὶ
ἀναγνώστην τοῦ νόμου κυρίου, οὗ ἐστιν ἀντίγραφον τὸ
ὑποκείμενον 9 Βασιλεὺς Ἀρταξέρξης Εσδρα τῷ ἱερεῖ καὶ
ἀναγνώστῃ τοῦ νόμου κυρίου χαίρειν. 10 καὶ τὰ φιλάνθρωπα
ἐγὼ κρίνας προσέταξα τοὺς βουλομένους ἐκ τοῦ ἔθνους τῶν
Ιουδαίων αἱρετίζοντας καὶ τῶν ἱερέων καὶ τῶν Λευιτῶν, καὶ
τῶν δὲ ἐν τῇ ἡμετέρᾳ βασιλείᾳ, συμπορεύεσθαί σοι εἰς
Ιερουσαλημ. 11 ὅσοι οὖν ἐνθυμοῦνται, συνεξορμάτωσαν,
καθάπερ δέδοκται ἐμοί τε καὶ τοῖς ἑπτὰ φίλοις συμβουλευ-
ταῖς, 12 ὅπως ἐπισκέψωνται τὰ κατὰ τὴν Ιουδαίαν καὶ
Ιερουσαλημ ἀκολούθως ᾧ ἔχει ἐν τῷ νόμῳ τοῦ κυρίου, 13 καὶ
ἀπενεγκεῖν δῶρα τῷ κυρίῳ τοῦ Ισραηλ, ἃ ηὐξάμην ἐγώ τε καὶ
οἱ φίλοι, εἰς Ιερουσαλημ καὶ πᾶν χρυσίον καὶ ἀργύριον, ὃ ἐὰν
εὑρεθῇ ἐν τῇ χώρᾳ τῆς Βαβυλωνίας, τῷ κυρίῳ εἰς Ιερουσαλημ
σὺν τῷ δεδωρημένῳ ὑπὸ τοῦ ἔθνους εἰς τὸ ἱερὸν τοῦ κυρίου
αὐτῶν τὸ ἐν Ιερουσαλημ 14 συναχθῆναι τό τε χρυσίον καὶ
ἀργύριον εἰς ταύρους καὶ κριοὺς καὶ ἄρνας καὶ τὰ τούτοις
ἀκόλουθα 15 ὥστε προσενεγκεῖν θυσίας ἐπὶ τὸ θυσιαστήριον
τοῦ κυρίου αὐτῶν τὸ ἐν Ιερουσαλημ. 16 καὶ πάντα, ὅσα ἂν
βούλῃ μετὰ τῶν ἀδελφῶν σου ποιῆσαι χρυσίῳ καὶ ἀργυρίῳ,
ἐπιτέλει κατὰ τὸ θέλημα τοῦ θεοῦ σου 17 καὶ τὰ ἱερὰ σκεύη
τοῦ κυρίου τὰ διδόμενά σοι εἰς τὴν χρείαν τοῦ ἱεροῦ τοῦ
θεοῦ σου τοῦ ἐν Ιερουσαλημ. 18 καὶ τὰ λοιπά, ὅσα ἂν ὑποπί-
πτῃ σοι εἰς τὴν χρείαν τοῦ ἱεροῦ τοῦ θεοῦ σου, δώσεις ἐκ
τοῦ βασιλικοῦ γαζοφυλακίου· 19 κἀγὼ δὲ Ἀρταξέρξης ὁ
βασιλεὺς προσέταξα τοῖς γαζοφύλαξι Συρίας καὶ Φοινίκης,
ἵνα ὅσα ἂν ἀποστείλῃ Εσδρας ὁ ἱερεὺς καὶ ἀναγνώστης τοῦ
νόμου τοῦ θεοῦ τοῦ ὑψίστου, ἐπιμελῶς διδῶσιν αὐτῷ ἕως ἀργυρίου ταλάντων ἑκατόν, 20 ὁμοίως δὲ καὶ ἕως πυροῦ κόρων

King James Version

8 And after these things, when Artaxerxes the king of the Persians reigned, came Esdras the son of Saraias, the son of Ezerias, the son of Helchiah, the son of Salum,

2 The son of Sadduc, the son of Achitob, the son of Amarias, the son of Ezias, the son of Meremoth, the son of Zaraias, the son of Savias, the son of Boccas, the son of Abisum, the son of Phinees, the son of Eleazar, the son of Aaron the chief priest.

3 This Esdras went up from Babylon, as a scribe, being very ready in the law of Moses, that was given by the God of Israel.

4 And the king did him honour: for he found grace in his sight in all his requests.

5 There went up with him also certain of the children of Israel, of the priests, of the Levites, of the holy singers, porters, and ministers of the temple, unto Jerusalem,

6 In the seventh year of the reign of Artaxerxes, in the fifth month, this was the king's seventh year; for they went from Babylon in the first day of the first month, and came to Jerusalem, according to the prosperous journey which the Lord gave them.

7 For Esdras had very great skill, so that he omitted nothing of the law and commandments of the Lord, but taught all Israel the ordinances and judgments.

8 Now the copy of the commission, which was written from Artaxerxes the king, and came to Esdras the priest and reader of the law of the Lord, is this that followeth;

9 King Artaxerxes unto Esdras the priest and reader of the law of the Lord sendeth greeting:

10 Having determined to deal graciously, I have given order, that such of the nation of the Jews, and of the priests and Levites, being within our realm, as are willing and desirous, should go with thee unto Jerusalem.

11 As many therefore as have a mind thereunto, let them depart with thee, as it hath seemed good both to me and my seven friends the counsellors;

12 That they may look unto the affairs of Judea and Jerusalem, agreeably to that which is in the law of the Lord;

13 And carry the gifts unto the Lord of Israel to Jerusalem, which I and my friends have vowed, and all the gold and silver that in the country of Babylon can be found, to the Lord in Jerusalem,

14 With that also which is given of the people for the temple of the Lord their God at Jerusalem: and that silver and gold may be collected for bullocks, rams, and lambs, and things thereunto appertaining;

15 To the end that they may offer sacrifices unto the Lord upon the altar of the Lord their God, which is in Jerusalem.

16 And whatsoever thou and thy brethren will do with the silver and gold, that do, according to the will of thy God.

17 And the holy vessels of the Lord, which are given thee for the use of the temple of thy God, which is in Jerusalem, thou shalt set before thy God in Jerusalem.

18 And whatsoever thing else thou shalt remember for the use of the temple of thy God, thou shalt give it out of the king's treasury.

19 And I king Artaxerxes have also commanded the keepers of the treasures in Syria and Phenice, that whatsoever Esdras the priest and the reader of the law of the most high God shall send for, they should give it him with speed,

20 To the sum of an hundred talents of silver, likewise

TODAY'S ENGLISH VERSION

8 Many years later, when Artaxerxes was emperor of Persia, a man named Ezra came from Babylon. He traced his ancestry back to Aaron, the High Priest, as follows: Ezra was the son of Seraiah, son of Azariah, son of Hilkiah, son of Shallum, 2 son of Zadok, son of Ahitub, son of Amariah, son of Azariah, son of Bukki, son of Abishua, son of Phinehas, son of Eleazar, son of Aaron.

3-4 Ezra was a scholar with a thorough knowledge of the Law, which the God of Israel had given to Moses. The emperor had a high regard for him and approved all the requests he made. Ezra set out from Babylonia 5 for Jerusalem with a group of Israelites which included priests, Levites, Temple musicians, Temple guards, and workmen. 6 They left Babylonia on the first day of the first month in the seventh year of the reign of Artaxerxes. God gave them a safe journey, and they arrived in Jerusalem on the first day of the fifth month. 7 Ezra had a thorough knowledge of the Law of the Lord and neglected none of its details. As a result he could teach all its laws and regulations to all the people of Israel.

8 The following is a copy of the decree that Emperor Artaxerxes gave to Ezra, the priest and scholar of the Law of the Lord:

9 "From Emperor Artaxerxes to the priest Ezra, scholar of the Law of the Lord, greetings.

10 "In my generosity I have decided to decree that throughout my empire any of the Jews who so desire, including priests and Levites, may go with you to Jerusalem. 11 I and the seven counselors who have the title 'Friends of the Emperor' have decided that all who wish to do so may go with you. 12 Let them investigate the conditions in Jerusalem and Judah to see how well the Law of the Lord is being obeyed. 13 Let them also take with them to Jerusalem the gifts which I and my counselors have vowed to give to the Lord of Israel, including all the silver and gold belonging to the Lord which may be found in Babylonia, 14 and all that is given by the people of Israel for the Temple of their Lord. The silver and gold are to be collected to buy bulls, rams, lambs, and everything else that is necessary, 15 so that sacrifices may be offered on the altar of the Lord in Jerusalem.

16 "You may use the silver and gold for whatever you and the rest of your people desire, in accordance with the will of your God. 17-18 You may obtain from the royal treasury the sacred vessels of the Lord that are being entrusted to you for use in the Temple of your God in Jerusalem, as well as anything else you may need for the Temple service.

19 "I command all the treasury officials in Greater Syria and Phoenicia to provide promptly for Ezra, the priest and scholar of the Law of God Most High, everything he asks for, 20 up to a limit of 7,500 pounds of silver, 500 bushels

NEW REVISED STANDARD VERSION

8 After these things, when Artaxerxes, the king of the Persians, was reigning, Ezra came, the son of Seraiah, son of Azariah, son of Hilkiah, son of Shallum, 2 son of Zadok, son of Ahitub, son of Amariah, son of Uzzi, son of Bukki, son of Abishua, son of Phineas, son of Eleazar, son of Aaron the high[a] priest. 3 This Ezra came up from Babylon as a scribe skilled in the law of Moses, which was given by the God of Israel; 4 and the king showed him honor, for he found favor before the king[b] in all his requests. 5 There came up with him to Jerusalem some of the people of Israel and some of the priests and Levites and temple singers and gatekeepers and temple servants, 6 in the seventh year of the reign of Artaxerxes, in the fifth month (this was the king's seventh year); for they left Babylon on the new moon of the first month and arrived in Jerusalem on the new moon of the fifth month, by the prosperous journey that the Lord gave them.[c] 7 For Ezra possessed great knowledge, so that he omitted nothing from the law of the Lord or the commandments, but taught all Israel all the ordinances and judgments.

8 The following is a copy of the written commission from King Artaxerxes that was delivered to Ezra the priest and reader of the law of the Lord:

9 "King Artaxerxes to Ezra the priest and reader of the law of the Lord, greeting. 10 In accordance with my gracious decision, I have given orders that those of the Jewish nation and of the priests and Levites and others in our realm, those who freely choose to do so, may go with you to Jerusalem. 11 Let as many as are so disposed, therefore, leave with you, just as I and the seven Friends who are my counselors have decided, 12 in order to look into matters in Judea and Jerusalem, in accordance with what is in the law of the Lord, 13 and to carry to Jerusalem the gifts for the Lord of Israel that I and my Friends have vowed, and to collect for the Lord in Jerusalem all the gold and silver that may be found in the country of Babylonia, 14 together with what is given by the nation for the temple of their Lord that is in Jerusalem, both gold and silver for bulls and rams and lambs and what goes with them, 15 so as to offer sacrifices on the altar of their Lord that is in Jerusalem. 16 Whatever you and your kindred are minded to do with the gold and silver, perform it in accordance with the will of your God; 17 deliver the holy vessels of the Lord that are given you for the use of the temple of your God that is in Jerusalem. 18 And whatever else occurs to you as necessary for the temple of your God, you may provide out of the royal treasury.

19 "I, King Artaxerxes, have commanded the treasurers of Syria and Phoenicia that whatever Ezra the priest and reader of the law of the Most High God sends for, they shall take care to give him, 20 up to a hundred talents of silver, and

a Gk *the first* *b* Gk *him* *c* Other authorities add *for him* or *upon him*

ἑκατὸν καὶ οἴνου μετρητῶν ἑκατὸν καὶ ἄλα ἐκ πλήθους.
21 πάντα τὰ κατὰ τὸν τοῦ θεοῦ νόμον ἐπιτελεσθήτω ἐπιμελῶς τῷ θεῷ τῷ ὑψίστῳ ἕνεκα τοῦ μὴ γενέσθαι ὀργὴν εἰς τὴν
βασιλείαν τοῦ βασιλέως καὶ τῶν υἱῶν. 22 καὶ ὑμῖν δὲ λέγεται
ὅπως πᾶσι τοῖς ἱερεῦσιν καὶ τοῖς Λευίταις καὶ ἱεροψάλταις
καὶ θυρωροῖς καὶ ἱεροδούλοις καὶ πραγματικοῖς τοῦ ἱεροῦ
τούτου μηδεμία φορολογία μηδὲ ἄλλη ἐπιβολὴ γίγνηται, καὶ
ἐξουσίαν μηδένα ἔχειν ἐπιβαλεῖν τι τούτοις. 23 καὶ σύ,
Εσδρα, κατὰ τὴν σοφίαν τοῦ θεοῦ ἀνάδειξον κριτὰς καὶ
δικαστάς, ὅπως δικάζωσιν ἐν ὅλῃ Συρίᾳ καὶ Φοινίκῃ πάντας
τοὺς ἐπισταμένους τὸν νόμον τοῦ θεοῦ σου· καὶ τοὺς μὴ
ἐπισταμένους δὲ διδάξεις. 24 καὶ πάντες, ὅσοι ἐὰν παρα-
βαίνωσι τὸν νόμον τοῦ θεοῦ σου καὶ τὸν βασιλικόν, ἐπιμελῶς
κολασθήσονται, ἐάν τε καὶ θανάτῳ ἐάν τε καὶ τιμωρίᾳ ἢ ἀρ-
γυρικῇ ζημίᾳ ἢ ἀπαγωγῇ.
25 Εὐλογητὸς μόνος ὁ κύριος ὁ δοὺς ταῦτα εἰς τὴν καρδίαν
τοῦ βασιλέως, δοξάσαι τὸν οἶκον αὐτοῦ τὸν ἐν Ιερουσαλημ,
26 καὶ ἐμὲ ἐτίμησεν ἔναντι τοῦ βασιλέως καὶ τῶν συμβου-
λευόντων καὶ πάντων τῶν φίλων καὶ μεγιστάνων αὐτοῦ.
27 καὶ ἐγὼ εὐθαρσὴς ἐγενόμην κατὰ τὴν ἀντίλημψιν κυρίου
τοῦ θεοῦ μου καὶ συνήγαγον ἐκ τοῦ Ισραηλ ἄνδρας ὥστε
συναναβῆναί μοι.
28 Καὶ οὗτοι οἱ προηγούμενοι κατὰ τὰς πατριὰς αὐτῶν καὶ
τὰς μεριδαρχίας οἱ ἀναβάντες μετ' ἐμοῦ ἐκ Βαβυλῶνος ἐν
τῇ βασιλείᾳ Ἀρταξέρξου τοῦ βασιλέως. 29 ἐκ τῶν υἱῶν
Φινεες Γαρσομος. ἐκ τῶν υἱῶν Ιεταμαρου Γαμηλος. ἐκ τῶν
υἱῶν Δαυιδ Αττους ὁ Σεχενιου· 30 ἐκ τῶν υἱῶν Φορος
Ζαχαριας καὶ μετ' αὐτοῦ ἀπὸ γραφῆς ἄνδρες ἑκατὸν πεντή-
κοντα· 31 ἐκ τῶν υἱῶν Φααθμωαβ Ελιαωνιας Ζαραιου καὶ
μετ' αὐτοῦ ἄνδρες διακόσιοι· 32 ἐκ τῶν υἱῶν Ζαθοης Σεχεν-
ιας Ιεζηλου καὶ μετ' αὐτοῦ ἄνδρες τριακόσιοι· ἐκ τῶν υἱῶν
Αδινου Βην-Ιωναθου καὶ μετ' αὐτοῦ ἄνδρες διακόσιοι πεντή-
κοντα· 33 ἐκ τῶν υἱῶν Ηλαμ Ιεσιας Γοθολιου καὶ μετ' αὐτοῦ
ἄνδρες ἑβδομήκοντα· 34 ἐκ τῶν υἱῶν Σαφατιου Ζαραιας
Μιχαηλου καὶ μετ' αὐτοῦ ἄνδρες ἑβδομήκοντα· 35 ἐκ τῶν
υἱῶν Ιωαβ Αβαδιας Ιεζηλου καὶ μετ' αὐτοῦ ἄνδρες διακόσιοι
δέκα δύο· 36 ἐκ τῶν υἱῶν Βανι Ασσαλιμωθ Ιωσαφιου καὶ μετ'
αὐτοῦ ἄνδρες ἑκατὸν ἑξήκοντα· 37 ἐκ τῶν υἱῶν Βαβι Ζαχαριας Βηβαι καὶ μετ' αὐτοῦ ἄνδρες εἴκοσι ὀκτώ· 38 ἐκ τῶν υἱῶν
Ασγαθ Ιωανης Ακαταν καὶ μετ' αὐτοῦ ἄνδρες ἑκατὸν δέκα·
39 ἐκ τῶν υἱῶν Αδωνικαμ οἱ ἔσχατοι, καὶ ταῦτα τὰ ὀνόματα
αὐτῶν· Ελιφαλατος, Ιεουηλ καὶ Σαμαιας, καὶ μετ' αὐτῶν
ἄνδρες ἑβδομήκοντα· 40 ἐκ τῶν υἱῶν Βαγο Ουθι ὁ τοῦ
Ισταλκουρου καὶ μετ' αὐτοῦ ἄνδρες ἑβδομήκοντα.
41 Καὶ συνήγαγον αὐτοὺς ἐπὶ τὸν λεγόμενον Θεραν ποταμόν, καὶ παρενεβάλομεν αὐτόθι ἡμέρας τρεῖς, καὶ κατέμαθον
αὐτούς. 42 καὶ ἐκ τῶν υἱῶν τῶν ἱερέων καὶ ἐκ τῶν Λευιτῶν
οὐχ εὑρὼν ἐκεῖ 43 ἀπέστειλα πρὸς Ελεαζαρον καὶ Ιδουηλον

also of wheat even to an hundred cors, and an hundred pieces of wine, and other things in abundance.

21 Let all things be performed after the law of God diligently unto the most high God, that wrath come not upon the kingdom of the king and his sons.

22 I command you also, that ye require no tax, nor any other imposition, of any of the priests, or Levites, or holy singers, or porters, or ministers of the temple, or of any that have doings in this temple, and that no man have authority to impose any thing upon them.

23 And thou, Esdras, according to the wisdom of God ordain judges and justices, that they may judge in all Syria and Phenice all those that know the law of thy God; and those that know it not thou shalt teach.

24 And whosoever shall transgress the law of thy God, and of the king, shall be punished diligently, whether it be by death, or other punishment, by penalty of money, or by imprisonment.

25 ¶ Then said Esdras the scribe, Blessed be the only Lord God of my fathers, who hath put these things into the heart of the king, to glorify his house that is in Jerusalem:

26 And hath honoured me in the sight of the king, and his counsellors, and all his friends and nobles.

27 Therefore was I encouraged by the help of the Lord my God, and gathered together men of Israel to go up with me.

28 And these are the chief according to their families and several dignities, that went up with me from Babylon in the reign of king Artaxerxes:

29 Of the sons of Phinees, Gerson: of the sons of Ithamar, Gamael: of the sons of David, Lettus the son of Sechenias:

30 Of the sons of Pharez, Zacharias; and with him were counted an hundred and fifty men:

31 Of the sons of Pahath Moab, Eliaonias, the son of Zaraias, and with him two hundred men:

32 Of the sons of Zathoe, Sechenias the son of Jezelus, and with him three hundred men: of the sons of Adin, Obeth the son of Jonathan, and with him two hundred and fifty men:

33 Of the sons of Elam, Josias son of Gotholias, and with him seventy men:

34 Of the sons of Saphatias, Zaraias son of Michael, and with him threescore and ten men:

35 Of the sons of Joab, Abadias son of Jezelus, and with him two hundred and twelve men:

36 Of the sons of Banid, Assalimoth son of Josaphias, and with him an hundred and threescore men:

37 Of the sons of Babi, Zacharias son of Bebai, and with him twenty and eight men:

38 Of the sons of Astath, Johannes *son of* Acatan, and with him an hundred and ten men:

39 Of the sons of Adonikam the last, and these are the names of them, Eliphalet, Jeuel, and Samaias, and with them seventy men:

40 Of the sons of Bago, Uthi the son of Istalcurus, and with him seventy men.

41 And these I gathered together to the river called Theras, where we pitched our tents three days: and then I surveyed them.

42 But when I had found there none of the priests and Levites,

43 Then sent I unto Eleazar, and Iduel, and Masman,

TODAY'S ENGLISH VERSION

of wheat, 550 gallons of wine, and as much salt as may be
needed. 21 You must be careful to do everything that the
Law requires in order to honor God Most High and so
make sure that he is never angry with me or with those
who reign after me. 22 You are forbidden to collect any
taxes from the priests, Levites, musicians, guards, workmen, or anyone else connected with this Temple. No one
has the right to impose any burden on them.

23 "You, Ezra, using the wisdom that comes from God,
shall appoint administrators and judges to govern all the
people in Greater Syria and Phoenicia who live by the Law
of your God. You must teach that Law to anyone who does
not know it. 24 If anyone disobeys the laws of your God or
the laws of the empire, he is to be punished promptly: by
death, by fine, by exile, or by some other punishment."

25 Ezra said, "Praise the Lord, the Lord alone! He has made
the emperor willing to restore the glory of the Temple of the
Lord in Jerusalem. 26 By God's grace, I have won the respect
of the emperor, his counselors, all his Friends, and all his
powerful officials. 27 The Lord my God has given me
courage, and I have been able to persuade many men to
return with me."

28 This is the list of the leaders of the clans and families
who had been in exile in Babylonia and returned with Ezra
to Jerusalem when Artaxerxes was emperor:

29-40 Gershom, of the clan of Phinehas
Gamael, of the clan of Ithamar
Hattush son of Shecaniah, of the clan of David
Zechariah, of the clan of Parosh, with 150 men of his clan
(there were records of their family line)
Eliehoenai son of Zechariah, of the clan of Pahath Moab,
with 200 men
Shecaniah son of Jehaziel, of the clan of Zattu, with
300 men
Ebed son of Jonathan, of the clan of Adin, with 250 men
Jeshaiah son of Gotholiah, of the clan of Elam, with
70 men
Zeraiah son of Michael, of the clan of Shephatiah, with
70 men
Obadiah son of Jehiel, of the clan of Joab, with 212 men
Shelomith son of Josiphiah, of the clan of Bani, with
160 men
Zechariah son of Bebai, of the clan of Bebai, with 28 men
Johanan son of Hakkatan, of the clan of Azgad, with
110 men
Eliphelet, Jeuel, and Shemaiah, of the clan of Adonikam,
with 70 men (they returned at a later date)
Uthai son of Istalcurus, of the clan of Bigvai, with 70 men

41 I assembled the entire group at Theras River, and we
camped there for three days. I inspected them 42 and found
that there were no priests or Levites in the group, 43-44 so I
sent a message to ten of the leaders who were competent
men: Eliezer, Iduel, Maasmas, Elnathan, Shemaiah, Jarib,

NEW REVISED STANDARD VERSION

likewise up to a hundred cors of wheat, a hundred baths of
wine, and salt in abundance. 21 Let all things prescribed in
the law of God be scrupulously fulfilled for the Most High
God, so that wrath may not come upon the kingdom of the
king and his sons. 22 You are also informed that no tribute
or any other tax is to be laid on any of the priests or Levites
or temple singers or gatekeepers or temple servants or persons employed in this temple, and that no one has authority
to impose any tax on them.

23 "And you, Ezra, according to the wisdom of God,
appoint judges and justices to judge all those who know the
law of your God, throughout all Syria and Phoenicia; and
you shall teach it to those who do not know it. 24 All who
transgress the law of your God or the law of the kingdom
shall be strictly punished, whether by death or some other
punishment, either fine or imprisonment."

25 Then Ezra the scribe said,[a] "Blessed be the Lord alone,
who put this into the heart of the king, to glorify his house
that is in Jerusalem, 26 and who honored me in the sight of
the king and his counselors and all his Friends and nobles.
27 I was encouraged by the help of the Lord my God, and I
gathered men from Israel to go up with me."

28 These are the leaders, according to their ancestral
houses and their groups, who went up with me from Babylon, in the reign of King Artaxerxes: 29 Of the descendants
of Phineas, Gershom. Of the descendants of Ithamar,
Gamael. Of the descendants of David, Hattush son of
Shecaniah. 30 Of the descendants of Parosh, Zechariah, and
with him a hundred fifty men enrolled. 31 Of the descendants
of Pahath-moab, Eliehoenai son of Zerahiah, and with him
two hundred men. 32 Of the descendants of Zattu, Shecaniah
son of Jahaziel, and with him three hundred men. Of the
descendants of Adin, Obed son of Jonathan, and with him
two hundred fifty men. 33 Of the descendants of Elam,
Jeshaiah son of Gotholiah, and with him seventy men. 34 Of
the descendants of Shephatiah, Zeraiah son of Michael, and
with him seventy men. 35 Of the descendants of Joab,
Obadiah son of Jehiel, and with him two hundred twelve
men. 36 Of the descendants of Bani, Shelomith son of
Josiphiah, and with him a hundred sixty men. 37 Of the
descendants of Bebai, Zechariah son of Bebai, and with him
twenty-eight men. 38 Of the descendants of Azgad, Johanan
son of Hakkatan, and with him a hundred ten men. 39 Of the
descendants of Adonikam, the last ones, their names being
Eliphelet, Jeuel, and Shemaiah, and with them seventy men.
40 Of the descendants of Bigvai, Uthai son of Istalcurus, and
with him seventy men.

41 I assembled them at the river called Theras, and we
encamped there three days, and I inspected them. 42 When
I found there none of the descendants of the priests or of
the Levites, 43 I sent word to Eliezar, Iduel, Maasmas,

a Other ancient authorities lack *Then Ezra the scribe said*

καὶ Μαασμαν καὶ Ελναταν καὶ Σαμαιαν καὶ Ιωριβον, Ναθαν,
Ενναταν, Ζαχαριαν καὶ Μεσολαμον τοὺς ἡγουμένους καὶ
ἐπιστήμονας 44 καὶ εἶπα αὐτοῖς ἐλθεῖν πρὸς Αδδαιον τὸν
ἡγούμενον τὸν ἐν τῷ τόπῳ τοῦ γαζοφυλακίου 45 ἐντειλά-
μενος αὐτοῖς διαλεγῆναι Αδδαιω καὶ τοῖς ἀδελφοῖς αὐτοῦ
καὶ τοῖς ἐν τῷ τόπῳ γαζοφύλαξιν ἀποστεῖλαι ἡμῖν τοὺς
ἱερατεύσοντας ἐν τῷ οἴκῳ τοῦ κυρίου ἡμῶν. 46 καὶ ἤγαγον
ἡμῖν κατὰ τὴν κραταιὰν χεῖρα τοῦ κυρίου ἡμῶν ἄνδρας
ἐπιστήμονας τῶν υἱῶν Μοολι τοῦ Λευι τοῦ Ισραηλ· Ασεβη-
βιαν καὶ τοὺς υἱοὺς καὶ τοὺς ἀδελφούς, δέκα ὀκτώ· 47 καὶ
Ασεβιαν καὶ Αννουνον καὶ Ωσαιαν ἀδελφὸν ἐκ τῶν υἱῶν
Χανουναιου καὶ οἱ υἱοὶ αὐτῶν, ἄνδρες εἴκοσι· 48 καὶ ἐκ τῶν
ἱεροδούλων, ὧν ἔδωκεν Δαυιδ καὶ οἱ ἡγούμενοι εἰς τὴν ἐργασίαν τῶν Λευιτῶν, ἱερόδουλοι διακόσιοι εἴκοσι· πάντων ἐση-
μάνθη ἡ ὀνοματογραφία. 49 καὶ εὐξάμην ἐκεῖ νηστείαν τοῖς
νεανίσκοις ἔναντι τοῦ κυρίου ἡμῶν 50 ζητῆσαι παρ᾽ αὐτοῦ
εὐοδίαν ἡμῖν τε καὶ τοῖς συνοῦσιν ἡμῖν τέκνοις ἡμῶν καὶ
κτήνεσιν. 51 ἐνετράπην γὰρ αἰτῆσαι τὸν βασιλέα πεζούς τε
καὶ ἱππεῖς καὶ προπομπὴν ἕνεκεν ἀσφαλείας τῆς πρὸς τοὺς
ἐναντιουμένους ἡμῖν· 52 εἴπαμεν γὰρ τῷ βασιλεῖ ὅτι Ἰσχὺς
τοῦ κυρίου ἡμῶν ἔσται μετὰ τῶν ἐπιζητούντων αὐτὸν εἰς
πᾶσαν ἐπανόρθωσιν. 53 καὶ πάλιν ἐδεήθημεν τοῦ κυρίου
ἡμῶν κατὰ ταῦτα καὶ εὐιλάτου ἐτύχομεν. 54 καὶ ἐχώρισα
τῶν φυλάρχων τῶν ἱερέων ἄνδρας δέκα δύο, καὶ Σερεβιαν καὶ
Ασαβιαν καὶ μετ᾽ αὐτῶν ἐκ τῶν ἀδελφῶν αὐτῶν ἄνδρας δέκα,
55 καὶ ἔστησα αὐτοῖς τὸ ἀργύριον καὶ τὸ χρυσίον καὶ τὰ ἱερὰ
σκεύη τοῦ οἴκου τοῦ κυρίου ἡμῶν, ἃ αὐτὸς ἐδωρήσατο ὁ
βασιλεὺς καὶ οἱ σύμβουλοι αὐτοῦ καὶ οἱ μεγιστᾶνες καὶ πᾶς
Ισραηλ. 56 καὶ στήσας παρέδωκα αὐτοῖς ἀργυρίου τάλαντα
ἑξακόσια πεντήκοντα καὶ σκεύη ἀργυρᾶ ταλάντων ἑκατὸν
καὶ χρυσίου τάλαντα ἑκατὸν καὶ χρυσώματα εἴκοσι καὶ
σκεύη χαλκᾶ ἀπὸ χρηστοῦ χαλκοῦ στίλβοντα χρυσοειδῆ
σκεύη δώδεκα. 57 καὶ εἶπα αὐτοῖς Καὶ ὑμεῖς ἅγιοί ἐστε τῷ
κυρίῳ, καὶ τὰ σκεύη ἅγια, καὶ τὸ ἀργύριον καὶ τὸ χρυσίον
εὐχὴ τῷ κυρίῳ κυρίῳ τῶν πατέρων ἡμῶν· 58 ἀγρυπνεῖτε καὶ
φυλάσσετε ἕως τοῦ παραδοῦναι αὐτὰ ὑμᾶς τοῖς φυλάρχοις
τῶν ἱερέων καὶ τῶν Λευιτῶν καὶ τοῖς ἡγουμένοις τῶν πατριῶν τοῦ Ισραηλ ἐν Ιερουσαλημ ἐν τοῖς παστοφορίοις τοῦ
οἴκου τοῦ κυρίου ἡμῶν. 59 καὶ οἱ παραλαβόντες οἱ ἱερεῖς καὶ
οἱ Λευῖται τὸ ἀργύριον καὶ τὸ χρυσίον καὶ τὰ σκεύη τὰ ἐν
Ιερουσαλημ εἰσήνεγκαν εἰς τὸ ἱερὸν τοῦ κυρίου.

60 Καὶ ἀναζεύξαντες ἀπὸ τοῦ ποταμοῦ Θερα τῇ δωδεκάτῃ
τοῦ πρώτου μηνὸς εἰσήλθομεν εἰς Ιερουσαλημ κατὰ τὴν
κραταιὰν χεῖρα τοῦ κυρίου ἡμῶν τὴν ἐφ᾽ ἡμῖν· καὶ ἐρρύσατο
ἡμᾶς ἐπὶ τῆς εἰσόδου ἀπὸ παντὸς ἐχθροῦ, καὶ ἤλθομεν εἰς
Ιερουσαλημ. 61 καὶ γενομένης αὐτόθι ἡμέρας τρίτης σταθὲν
τὸ ἀργύριον καὶ τὸ χρυσίον παρεδόθη ἐν τῷ οἴκῳ τοῦ κυρίου
ἡμῶν Μαρμωθι Ουρια ἱερεῖ 62 — καὶ μετ᾽ αὐτοῦ Ελεαζαρ ὁ

44 And Alnathan, and Mamaias, and Joribas, and Nathan, Eunatan, Zacharias, and Mosollamon, principal men and learned.

45 And I bade them that they should go unto Saddeus the captain, who was in the place of the treasury:

46 And commanded them that they should speak unto Daddeus, and to his brethren, and to the treasurers in that place, to send us such men as might execute the priests' office in the house of the Lord.

47 And by the mighty hand of our Lord they brought unto us skilful men of the sons of Moli the son of Levi, the son of Israel, Asebebia, and his sons, and his brethren, who were eighteen.

48 And Asebia, and Annuus, and Osaias his brother, of the sons of Channuneus, and their sons, were twenty men.

49 And of the servants of the temple whom David had ordained, and the principal men for the service of the Levites, to wit, the servants of the temple, two hundred and twenty, the catalogue of whose names were shewed.

50 And there I vowed a fast unto the young men before our Lord, to desire of him a prosperous journey both for us and them that were with us, for our children, and for the cattle:

51 For I was ashamed to ask the king footmen, and horsemen, and conduct for safeguard against our adversaries.

52 For we had said unto the king, that the power of the Lord our God should be with them that seek him, to support them in all ways.

53 And again we besought our Lord as touching these things, and found him favourable unto us.

54 Then I separated twelve of the chief of the priests, Esebrias, and Assanias, and ten men of their brethren with them:

55 And I weighed them the gold, and the silver, and the holy vessels of the house of our Lord, which the king, and his council, and the princes, and all Israel, had given.

56 And when I had weighed it, I delivered unto them six hundred and fifty talents of silver, and silver vessels of an hundred talents, and an hundred talents of gold,

57 And twenty golden vessels, and twelve vessels of brass, even of fine brass, glittering like gold.

58 And I said unto them, Both ye are holy unto the Lord, and the vessels are holy, and the gold and the silver is a vow unto the Lord, the Lord of our fathers.

59 Watch ye, and keep them till ye deliver them to the chief of the priests and Levites, and to the principal men of the families of Israel, in Jerusalem, into the chambers of the house of our God.

60 So the priests and the Levites, who had received the silver and the gold and the vessels, brought them unto Jerusalem, into the temple of the Lord.

61 And from the river Theras we departed the twelfth day of the first month, and came to Jerusalem by the mighty hand of our Lord, which was with us: and from the beginning of our journey the Lord delivered us from every enemy, and *so* we came to Jerusalem.

62 And when we had been there three days, the gold and silver that was weighed was delivered in the house of our Lord on the fourth day unto Marmoth the priest the son of Iri.

63 And with him was Eleazar the son of Phinees, and

Today's English Version

Nathan, Elnathan, Zechariah, and Meshullam. 45 I told them
to go to Iddo, the chief official at the treasury, 46 and ask
him, his associates, and the treasury officials to send us
priests to serve in the Temple of our Lord. 47 With God's
help, they sent us some able men: Sherebiah, a Levite from
the clan of Mahli, with eighteen of his sons and relatives,
48 and Hashabiah, Annunus, and his brother Jeshaiah of the
clan of Hananiah, with twenty of their sons. 49 There were
also 220 Temple workmen whose ancestors had been designated by King David and his officials to assist the Levites.
They were all listed in the register by name.

50 There by Theras River I made a vow that the young men
should fast in the presence of our Lord and ask him for a
safe journey for us, our children, and our animals. 51 I would
have been ashamed to ask the emperor for infantry and cavalry to accompany us and protect us from our enemies,
52 because I had told him that our Lord by his strength
blesses and protects those who trust him. 53 So once again
we prayed for our Lord to protect us, and he answered our
prayers.

54 From among the leading priests I chose Sherebiah,
Hashabiah, and ten others. 55 Then I weighed out the silver,
the gold, and the sacred utensils which the emperor, his
advisers and officials, and the people of Israel had given to
be used in the Temple, and I gave it to the priests. 56-57 This
is what I gave them:

silver	25	tons
silver utensils	7,500	pounds
gold	7,500	pounds
gold bowls	20	
fine bronze bowls that looked like gold	12	

58 I said to the priests, "You are sacred to the Lord, the
Lord of our ancestors, and so are the utensils and the silver
and gold brought to him in fulfillment of a vow. 59 Guard
them carefully until you reach the Temple. There in the
priests' rooms, turn them over to the leaders of the priests
and the Levites and to the leaders of the people of Israel in
Jerusalem." 60 So the priests and the Levites took charge of
the silver, the gold, and the utensils for Jerusalem and
brought them to the Temple.

61 It was on the twelfth day of the first month that we left
Theras River, and with the Lord's presence and protection we
reached Jerusalem. He protected us from all our enemies on
our journey, and we arrived safely. 62 After we had been
there three days, we went to the Temple, weighed the silver
and gold and turned it all over to Meremoth the priest, son of
Uriah. 63 With him were Eleazar son of Phinehas and two

New Revised Standard Version

44 Elnathan, Shemaiah, Jarib, Nathan, Elnathan, Zechariah,
and Meshullam, who were leaders and men of understanding; 45 I told them to go to Iddo, who was the leading man at
the place of the treasury, 46 and ordered them to tell Iddo
and his kindred and the treasurers at that place to send us
men to serve as priests in the house of our Lord. 47 And by
the mighty hand of our Lord they brought us competent men
of the descendants of Mahli son of Levi, son of Israel, namely Sherebiah[a] with his descendants and kinsmen, eighteen;
48 also Hashabiah and Annunus and his brother Jeshaiah, of
the descendants of Hananiah, and their descendants, twenty
men; 49 and of the temple servants, whom David and the
leaders had given for the service of the Levites, two hundred
twenty temple servants; the list of all their names was
reported.

50 There I proclaimed a fast for the young men before our
Lord, to seek from him a prosperous journey for ourselves
and for our children and the livestock that were with us.
51 For I was ashamed to ask the king for foot soldiers and
cavalry and an escort to keep us safe from our adversaries;
52 for we had said to the king, "The power of our Lord will be
with those who seek him, and will support them in every
way." 53 And again we prayed to our Lord about these
things, and we found him very merciful.

54 Then I set apart twelve of the leaders of the priests,
Sherebiah and Hashabiah, and ten of their kinsmen with
them; 55 and I weighed out to them the silver and the gold
and the holy vessels of the house of our Lord, which the king
himself and his counselors and the nobles and all Israel had
given. 56 I weighed and gave to them six hundred fifty talents of silver, and silver vessels worth a hundred talents,
and a hundred talents of gold, 57 and twenty golden bowls,
and twelve bronze vessels of fine bronze that glittered like
gold. 58 And I said to them, "You are holy to the Lord, and
the vessels are holy, and the silver and the gold are vowed to
the Lord, the Lord of our ancestors. 59 Be watchful and on
guard until you deliver them to the leaders of the priests and
the Levites, and to the heads of the ancestral houses of
Israel, in Jerusalem, in the chambers of the house of our
Lord." 60 So the priests and the Levites who took the silver
and the gold and the vessels that had been in Jerusalem carried them to the temple of the Lord.

61 We left the river Theras on the twelfth day of the first
month; and we arrived in Jerusalem by the mighty hand of
our Lord, which was upon us; he delivered us from every
enemy on the way, and so we came to Jerusalem. 62 When
we had been there three days, the silver and the gold were
weighed and delivered in the house of our Lord to the priest
Meremoth son of Uriah; 63 with him was Eleazar son of

a Gk *Asbebias*

τοῦ Φινεες, καὶ ἦσαν μετ᾽ αὐτῶν Ιωσαβδος Ἰησοῦ καὶ Μωεθ
Σαβαννου οἱ Λευῖται — πρὸς ἀριθμὸν καὶ ὁλκὴν ἅπαντα, καὶ
ἐγράφη πᾶσα ἡ ὁλκὴ αὐτῶν αὐτῇ τῇ ὥρᾳ. 63 οἱ δὲ παραγενόμενοι ἐκ τῆς αἰχμαλωσίας προσήνεγκαν θυσίας τῷ θεῷ τοῦ
Ισραηλ κυρίῳ ταύρους δώδεκα ὑπὲρ παντὸς Ισραηλ, κριοὺς
ἐνενήκοντα ἕξ, ἄρνας ἑβδομήκοντα δύο, τράγους ὑπὲρ
σωτηρίου δέκα δύο· ἅπαντα θυσίαν τῷ κυρίῳ. 64 καὶ ἀπέδωκαν τὰ προστάγματα τοῦ βασιλέως τοῖς βασιλικοῖς οἰκονόμοις καὶ τοῖς ἐπάρχοις Κοίλης Συρίας καὶ Φοινίκης, καὶ
ἐδόξασαν τὸ ἔθνος καὶ τὸ ἱερὸν τοῦ κυρίου.
65 Καὶ τούτων τελεσθέντων προσήλθοσάν μοι οἱ ἡγούμενοι
λέγοντες 66 Οὐκ ἐχώρισαν τὸ ἔθνος τοῦ Ισραηλ καὶ οἱ
ἄρχοντες καὶ οἱ ἱερεῖς καὶ οἱ Λευῖται τὰ ἀλλογενῆ ἔθνη τῆς
γῆς καὶ τὰς ἀκαθαρσίας αὐτῶν, Χαναναίων καὶ Χετταίων
καὶ Φερεζαίων καὶ Ιεβουσαίων καὶ Μωαβιτῶν καὶ Αἰγυπτίων
καὶ Ιδουμαίων· 67 συνῴκησαν γὰρ μετὰ τῶν θυγατέρων
αὐτῶν καὶ αὐτοὶ καὶ οἱ υἱοὶ αὐτῶν, καὶ ἐπεμίγη τὸ σπέρμα
τὸ ἅγιον εἰς τὰ ἀλλογενῆ ἔθνη τῆς γῆς, καὶ μετεῖχον οἱ
προηγούμενοι καὶ οἱ μεγιστᾶνες τῆς ἀνομίας ταύτης ἀπὸ
τῆς ἀρχῆς τοῦ πράγματος. 68 καὶ ἅμα τῷ ἀκοῦσαί με ταῦτα
διέρρηξα τὰ ἱμάτια καὶ τὴν ἱερὰν ἐσθῆτα καὶ κατέτιλα τοῦ
τριχώματος τῆς κεφαλῆς καὶ τοῦ πώγωνος καὶ ἐκάθισα σύν-
νους καὶ περίλυπος. 69 καὶ ἐπισυνήχθησαν πρός με ὅσοι
ποτὲ ἐπεκινοῦντο τῷ ῥήματι κυρίου τοῦ Ισραηλ, ἐμοῦ πεν-
θοῦντος ἐπὶ τῇ ἀνομίᾳ, καὶ ἐκαθήμην περίλυπος ἕως τῆς
δειλινῆς θυσίας. 70 καὶ ἐξεγερθεὶς ἐκ τῆς νηστείας διερρηγ-
μένα ἔχων τὰ ἱμάτια καὶ τὴν ἱερὰν ἐσθῆτα κάμψας τὰ γόνατα καὶ ἐκτείνας τὰς χεῖρας πρὸς τὸν κύριον ἔλεγον
71 Κύριε, ᾔσχυμμαι, ἐντέτραμμαι κατὰ πρόσωπόν σου· 72 αἱ
γὰρ ἁμαρτίαι ἡμῶν ἐπλεόνασαν ὑπὲρ τὰς κεφαλὰς ἡμῶν, αἱ
δὲ ἄγνοιαι ἡμῶν ὑπερήνεγκαν ἕως τοῦ οὐρανοῦ 73 ἀπὸ τῶν
χρόνων τῶν πατέρων ἡμῶν, καί ἐσμεν ἐν μεγάλῃ ἁμαρτίᾳ
ἕως τῆς ἡμέρας ταύτης. 74 καὶ διὰ τὰς ἁμαρτίας ἡμῶν καὶ
τῶν πατέρων ἡμῶν παρεδόθημεν σὺν τοῖς ἀδελφοῖς ἡμῶν καὶ
σὺν τοῖς βασιλεῦσιν ἡμῶν καὶ σὺν τοῖς ἱερεῦσιν ἡμῶν τοῖς
βασιλεῦσιν τῆς γῆς εἰς ῥομφαίαν καὶ αἰχμαλωσίαν καὶ
προνομὴν μετὰ αἰσχύνης μέχρι τῆς σήμερον ἡμέρας. 75 καὶ
νῦν κατὰ πόσον τι ἐγενήθη ἡμῖν ἔλεος παρὰ σοῦ, κύριε,
καταλειφθῆναι ἡμῖν ῥίζαν καὶ ὄνομα ἐν τῷ τόπῳ τοῦ ἁγιάσματός σου 76 καὶ τοῦ ἀνακαλύψαι φωστῆρα ἡμῶν ἐν τῷ
οἴκῳ τοῦ κυρίου ἡμῶν δοῦναι ἡμῖν τροφὴν ἐν τῷ καιρῷ τῆς
δουλείας ἡμῶν· 77 καὶ ἐν τῷ δουλεύειν ἡμᾶς οὐκ ἐγκατελεί-
φθημεν ὑπὸ τοῦ κυρίου ἡμῶν, ἀλλὰ ἐποίησεν ἡμᾶς ἐν χάριτι
ἐνώπιον τῶν βασιλέων Περσῶν 78 δοῦναι ἡμῖν τροφὴν καὶ
δοξάσαι τὸ ἱερὸν τοῦ κυρίου ἡμῶν καὶ ἐγεῖραι τὴν ἔρημον
Σιων δοῦναι ἡμῖν στερέωμα ἐν τῇ Ιουδαίᾳ καὶ Ιερουσαλημ.
79 καὶ νῦν τί ἐροῦμεν, κύριε, ἔχοντες ταῦτα; παρέβημεν γὰρ
τὰ προστάγματά σου, ἃ ἔδωκας ἐν χειρὶ τῶν παίδων σου τῶν

with them were Josabad the son of Jesu and Moeth the son of Sabban, Levites: all was *delivered them* by number and weight.

64 And all the weight of them was written up the same hour.

65 Moreover they that were come out of the captivity offered sacrifice unto the Lord God of Israel, even twelve bullocks for all Israel, fourscore and sixteen rams,

66 Threescore and twelve lambs, goats for a peace offering, twelve; all of them a sacrifice to the Lord.

67 And they delivered the king's commandments unto the king's stewards, and to the governors of Celosyria and Phenice; and they honoured the people and the temple of God.

68 Now when these things were done, the rulers came unto me, and said,

69 The nation of Israel, the princes, the priests and Levites, have not put away from them the strange people of the land, nor the pollutions of the Gentiles, *to wit,* of the Canaanites, Hittites, Pheresites, Jebusites, and the Moabites, Egyptians, and Edomites.

70 For both they and their sons have married with their daughters, and the holy seed is mixed with the strange people of the land; and from the beginning of this matter the rulers and the great men have been partakers of this iniquity.

71 And as soon as I had heard these things, I rent my clothes, and the holy garment, and pulled off the hair from off my head and beard, and sat me down sad and very heavy.

72 So all they that were then moved at the word of the Lord God of Israel assembled unto me, whilst I mourned for the iniquity: but I sat still full of heaviness until the evening sacrifice.

73 Then rising up from the fast with my clothes and the holy garment rent, and bowing my knees, and stretching forth my hands unto the Lord,

74 I said, O Lord, I am confounded and ashamed before thy face;

75 For our sins are multiplied above our heads, and our ignorances have reached up unto heaven.

76 For ever since the time of our fathers we *have been* and are in great sin, even unto this day.

77 And for our sins and our fathers' we with our brethren and our kings and our priests were given up unto the kings of the earth, to the sword, and to captivity, and for a prey with shame, unto this day.

78 And now in some measure hath mercy been shewed unto us from thee, O Lord, that there should be left us a root and a name in the place of thy sanctuary;

79 And to discover unto us a light in the house of the Lord our God, and to give us food in the time of our servitude.

80 Yea, when we were in bondage, we were not forsaken of our Lord; but he made us gracious before the kings of Persia, so that they gave us food;

81 Yea, and honoured the temple of our Lord, and raised up the desolate Sion, that they have given us a sure abiding in Jewry and Jerusalem.

82 And now, O Lord, what shall we say, having these things? for we have transgressed thy commandments, which

TODAY'S ENGLISH VERSION

Levites, Jozabad son of Jeshua and Moeth son of Sabannus. 64 Everything was counted and weighed, and a complete record was made at the same time.

65 All those who had returned from exile then offered sacrifices to the Lord, the God of Israel. They offered 12 bulls for all Israel, 96 rams, 66 and 72 lambs; they also offered 12 goats as a fellowship offering. They sacrificed all these animals to the Lord. 67 Then they took the decree the emperor had given them and gave it to the governors and officials of Greater Syria and Phoenicia, who then honored the Jewish people and the Temple of the Lord.

68 After all this had been done, some of the leaders of the people of Israel came and told me that 69 the people, the leaders, the priests, and the Levites had not kept themselves separate from the people in the neighboring countries of Edom, Moab, and Egypt, or from the Canaanites, Hittites, Perizzites, and Jebusites. They were doing the same disgusting things which those people did. 70 God's holy people had become contaminated because Jewish men were marrying foreign women. Even the leaders and the officials had taken part in this breaking of the Law from the very beginning. 71 As soon as I heard this, I tore my clothes and my sacred robe in despair. I also tore my hair and my beard, and sat down crushed with anxiety and grief. 72 I sat there grieving about this sin until it was time for the evening sacrifice to be offered, when people began to gather around me—all those who were disturbed by what the Lord of Israel had said.

73 Then I got up from where I had been fasting, and still wearing my torn clothes, I knelt in prayer and stretched out my hands to the Lord. 74 I said, "O Lord, I am ashamed and confused in your presence. 75 Our sins tower over our heads; they reach as high as the heavens. 76 This has been true from the days of our ancestors until now; we, your people, have sinned greatly. 77 Because of our sins and the sins of our ancestors, we and our relatives, our kings, and our priests have fallen into the hands of foreign kings, and we have been slaughtered, robbed, and carried away as prisoners. We have been totally disgraced, as we still are today. 78 Now, Lord, for a short time you have shown us great mercy. You have allowed just a few of us to survive in order to carry on the name Israel here in your holy Temple. 79 You have let the light of our nation shine again, after feeding us and taking care of us during the time of our slavery. 80 Even when we were slaves you did not abandon us; you made the emperors of Persia favor us, so that they gave us food, 81 restored the glory of your Temple, rebuilt the city of Jerusalem out of its ruins, and gave us a place of security here in Judah and Jerusalem.

82 "But now, Lord, what can we say, after you have done all this for us? We have again disobeyed the commands that

NEW REVISED STANDARD VERSION

Phinehas, and with them were Jozabad son of Jeshua and Moeth son of Binnui,[a] the Levites. 64 The whole was counted and weighed, and the weight of everything was recorded at that very time. 65 And those who had returned from exile offered sacrifices to the Lord, the God of Israel, twelve bulls for all Israel, ninety-six rams, 66 seventy-two lambs, and as a thank offering twelve male goats—all as a sacrifice to the Lord. 67 They delivered the king's orders to the royal stewards and to the governors of Coelesyria and Phoenicia; and these officials[b] honored the people and the temple of the Lord.

68 After these things had been done, the leaders came to me and said, 69 "The people of Israel and the rulers and the priests and the Levites have not put away from themselves the alien peoples of the land and their pollutions, the Canaanites, the Hittites, the Perizzites, the Jebusites, the Moabites, the Egyptians, and the Edomites. 70 For they and their descendants have married the daughters of these people,[c] and the holy race has been mixed with the alien peoples of the land; and from the beginning of this matter the leaders and the nobles have been sharing in this iniquity."

71 As soon as I heard these things I tore my garments and my holy mantle, and pulled out hair from my head and beard, and sat down in anxiety and grief. 72 And all who were ever moved at[d] the word of the Lord of Israel gathered around me, as I mourned over this iniquity, and I sat grief-stricken until the evening sacrifice. 73 Then I rose from my fast, with my garments and my holy mantle torn, and kneeling down and stretching out my hands to the Lord 74 I said,

"O Lord, I am ashamed and confused before your face. 75 For our sins have risen higher than our heads, and our mistakes have mounted up to heaven 76 from the times of our ancestors, and we are in great sin to this day. 77 Because of our sins and the sins of our ancestors, we with our kindred and our kings and our priests were given over to the kings of the earth, to the sword and exile and plundering, in shame until this day. 78 And now in some measure mercy has come to us from you, O Lord, to leave to us a root and a name in your holy place, 79 and to uncover a light for us in the house of the Lord our God, and to give us food in the time of our servitude. 80 Even in our bondage we were not forsaken by our Lord, but he brought us into favor with the kings of the Persians, so that they have given us food 81 and glorified the temple of our Lord, and raised Zion from desolation, to give us a stronghold in Judea and Jerusalem.

82 "And now, O Lord, what shall we say, when we have these things? For we have transgressed your commandments,

a Gk *Sabannus* *b* Gk *they* *c* Gk *their daughters* *d* Or *zealous for*

προφητῶν λέγων ὅτι 80 Ἡ γῆ, εἰς ἣν εἰσέρχεσθε κληρονομῆσαι, ἔστιν γῆ μεμολυσμένη μολυσμῷ τῶν ἀλλογενῶν τῆς
γῆς, καὶ τῆς ἀκαθαρσίας αὐτῶν ἐνέπλησαν αὐτήν· 81 καὶ νῦν
τὰς θυγατέρας ὑμῶν μὴ συνοικίσητε τοῖς υἱοῖς αὐτῶν καὶ
τὰς θυγατέρας αὐτῶν μὴ λάβητε τοῖς υἱοῖς ὑμῶν· 82 καὶ οὐ
ζητήσετε εἰρηνεῦσαι τὰ πρὸς αὐτοὺς τὸν ἅπαντα χρόνον,
ἵνα ἰσχύσαντες φάγητε τὰ ἀγαθὰ τῆς γῆς καὶ κατακληρονο-
μήσητε τοῖς υἱοῖς ὑμῶν ἕως αἰῶνος. 83 καὶ τὰ συμβαίνοντα
πάντα ἡμῖν γίγνεται διὰ τὰ ἔργα ἡμῶν τὰ πονηρὰ καὶ τὰς
μεγάλας ἁμαρτίας ἡμῶν. 84 σὺ γάρ, κύριε, ἐκούφισας τὰς
ἁμαρτίας ἡμῶν καὶ ἔδωκας ἡμῖν τοιαύτην ῥίζαν· πάλιν
ἀνεκάμψαμεν παραβῆναι τὸν νόμον σου εἰς τὸ ἐπιμιγῆναι
τῇ ἀκαθαρσίᾳ τῶν ἐθνῶν τῆς γῆς. 85 οὐχὶ ὠργίσθης ἡμῖν
ἀπολέσαι ἡμᾶς ἕως τοῦ μὴ καταλιπεῖν ῥίζαν καὶ σπέρμα καὶ
ὄνομα ἡμῶν; 86 κύριε τοῦ Ισραηλ, ἀληθινὸς εἶ· κατελείφθημεν γὰρ ῥίζα ἐν τῇ σήμερον. 87 ἰδοὺ νῦν ἐσμεν ἐνώπιόν
σου ἐν ταῖς ἀνομίαις ἡμῶν· οὐ γὰρ ἔστιν στῆναι ἔτι
ἔμπροσθέν σου ἐπὶ τούτοις.

88 Καὶ ὅτε προσευχόμενος Εσδρας ἀνθωμολογεῖτο κλαίων
χαμαιπετὴς ἔμπροσθεν τοῦ ἱεροῦ, ἐπισυνήχθησαν πρὸς
αὐτὸν ἀπὸ Ιερουσαλημ ὄχλος πολὺς σφόδρα, ἄνδρες καὶ
γυναῖκες καὶ νεανίαι· κλαυθμὸς γὰρ ἦν μέγας ἐν τῷ πλήθει.
89 καὶ φωνήσας Ιεχονιας Ιεηλου τῶν υἱῶν Ισραηλ εἶπεν
Εσδρα Ἡμεῖς ἡμάρτομεν εἰς τὸν κύριον καὶ συνῳκίσαμεν
γυναῖκας ἀλλογενεῖς ἐκ τῶν ἐθνῶν τῆς γῆς. καὶ νῦν ἐστιν
ἐλπὶς τῷ Ισραηλ. 90 ἐν τούτῳ γενέσθω ἡμῖν ὁρκωμοσία πρὸς
τὸν κύριον, ἐκβαλεῖν πάσας τὰς γυναῖκας ἡμῶν τὰς ἐκ τῶν
ἀλλογενῶν σὺν τοῖς τέκνοις αὐτῶν, ὡς ἐκρίθη σοι καὶ ὅσοι
πειθαρχοῦσιν τῷ νόμῳ τοῦ κυρίου. 91 ἀναστὰς ἐπιτέλει·
πρὸς σὲ γὰρ τὸ πρᾶγμα, καὶ ἡμεῖς μετὰ σοῦ ἰσχὺν ποιεῖν.
92 καὶ ἀναστὰς Εσδρας ὥρκισεν τοὺς φυλάρχους τῶν ἱερέων
καὶ Λευιτῶν παντὸς τοῦ Ισραηλ ποιῆσαι κατὰ ταῦτα· καὶ
9 ὤμοσαν. 1 καὶ ἀναστὰς Εσδρας ἀπὸ τῆς αὐλῆς τοῦ ἱεροῦ
ἐπορεύθη εἰς τὸ παστοφόριον Ιωαναν τοῦ Ελιασιβου
2 καὶ αὐλισθεὶς ἐκεῖ ἄρτου οὐκ ἐγεύσατο οὐδὲ ὕδωρ ἔπιεν
πενθῶν ὑπὲρ τῶν ἀνομιῶν τῶν μεγάλων τοῦ πλήθους. 3 καὶ
ἐγένετο κήρυγμα ἐν ὅλῃ τῇ Ιουδαίᾳ καὶ Ιερουσαλημ πᾶσι
τοῖς ἐκ τῆς αἰχμαλωσίας συναχθῆναι εἰς Ιερουσαλημ· 4 καὶ
ὅσοι ἂν μὴ ἀπαντήσωσιν ἐν δυσὶν ἢ τρισὶν ἡμέραις κατὰ τὸ
κρίμα τῶν προκαθημένων πρεσβυτέρων, ἀνιερωθήσονται τὰ
κτήνη αὐτῶν, καὶ αὐτὸς ἀλλοτριωθήσεται ἀπὸ τοῦ πλήθους
τῆς αἰχμαλωσίας.

5 Καὶ ἐπισυνήχθησαν οἱ ἐκ τῆς φυλῆς Ιουδα καὶ Βενιαμιν
ἐν τρισὶν ἡμέραις εἰς Ιερουσαλημ (οὗτος ὁ μὴν ἔνατος τῇ
εἰκάδι τοῦ μηνός), 6 καὶ συνεκάθισαν πᾶν τὸ πλῆθος ἐν τῇ
εὐρυχώρῳ τοῦ ἱεροῦ τρέμοντες διὰ τὸν ἐνεστῶτα χειμῶνα.
7 καὶ ἀναστὰς Εσδρας εἶπεν αὐτοῖς Ὑμεῖς ἠνομήσατε καὶ
συνῳκίσατε γυναῖκας ἀλλογενεῖς τοῦ προσθεῖναι ἁμαρτίαν

thou gavest by the hand of thy servants the prophets, saying,

83 That the land, which ye enter into to possess as an heritage, is a land polluted with the pollutions of the strangers of the land, and they have filled it with their uncleanness.

84 Therefore now shall ye not join your daughters unto their sons, neither shall ye take their daughters unto your sons.

85 Moreover ye shall never seek to have peace with them, that ye may be strong, and eat the good things of the land, and that ye may leave the inheritance of the land unto your children for evermore.

86 And all that is befallen is done unto us for our wicked works and great sins: for thou, O Lord, didst make our sins light,

87 And didst give unto us such a root: but we have turned back again to transgress thy law, and to mingle ourselves with the uncleanness of the nations of the land.

88 Mightest not thou be angry with us to destroy us, till thou hadst left us neither root, seed, nor name?

89 O Lord of Israel, thou art true: for we are left a root this day.

90 Behold, now are we before thee in our iniquities, for we cannot stand any longer by reason of these things before thee.

91 And as Esdras in his prayer made his confession, weeping, and lying flat upon the ground before the temple, there gathered unto him from Jerusalem a very great multitude of men and women and children: for there was great weeping among the multitude.

92 Then Jechonias the son of Jeelus, one of the sons of Israel, called out, and said, O Esdras, we have sinned against the Lord God, we have married strange women of the nations of the land, and now is all Israel aloft.

93 Let us make an oath to the Lord, that we will put away all our wives, which we have taken of the heathen, with their children,

94 Like as thou hast decreed, and as many as do obey the law of the Lord.

95 Arise, and put in execution: for to thee doth this matter appertain, and we will be with thee: do valiantly.

96 So Esdras arose, and took an oath of the chief of the priests and Levites of all Israel to do after these things; and *so* they sware.

9 Then Esdras rising from the court of the temple went to the chamber of Joanan the son of Eliasib,

2 And remained there, and did eat no meat nor drink water, mourning for the great iniquities of the multitude.

3 And there was a proclamation in all Jewry and Jerusalem to all them that were of the captivity, that they should be gathered together at Jerusalem:

4 And that whosoever met not there within two or three days, according as the elders that bare rule appointed, their cattle should be seized to the use of the temple, and himself cast out from them that were of the captivity.

5 And in three days were all they of the tribe of Judah and Benjamin gathered together at Jerusalem the twentieth day of the ninth month.

6 And all the multitude sat trembling in the broad court of the temple because of the present foul weather.

7 So Esdras arose up, and said unto them, Ye have transgressed the law in marrying strange wives, thereby to increase the sins of Israel.

Today's English Version

you gave us through your servants, the prophets. They told
us that 83 the land we were to occupy was an impure land
because the heathen people who lived in it filled it with their
disgusting deeds. 84 They told us that we should never inter-
marry with those people 85 and never seek peaceful relations
with them if we wanted to be strong and enjoy the land and
pass it on to our descendants forever. 86 Even after everything that has happened to us in punishment for our sins,
we know that you, Lord, have punished us less than we
deserve 87 and have allowed us to survive. But we have
rebelled again, broken your Law, and intermarried with these
wicked people. 88 Yet you were not angry enough to destroy
us completely and leave none of us alive, with no descendants and without our name. 89 Lord of Israel, you are faithful; you have allowed us to survive. 90 We confess our guilt
to you; we have no right to come into your presence."
91 While Ezra was bowing in prayer in front of the Temple,
weeping and confessing these sins, a large group of people
from Jerusalem—men, women, and children—gathered
around him, all of them weeping bitterly. 92 Then Shecaniah
son of Jehiel, one of the Israelites, said to Ezra, "We have
sinned against the Lord by marrying foreign women, but
even so, there is still hope for Israel. 93 Now we must make a
solemn promise to the Lord that we will send all these foreign women and their children away. 94 We will do what you
and the others who obey the Law of the Lord advise us to do.
95 It is your responsibility to act. We are behind you, so go
ahead and get it done."
96 So Ezra began by making the leaders of the priests, of
the Levites, and of the rest of the people take an oath that
they would divorce their foreign wives.

9 Then Ezra went from the court of the Temple into the
living quarters of Jehohanan son of Eliashib 2 and spent
the night there grieving over the people's terrible violation of
the Law. He did not eat or drink anything.
3 A message was sent throughout Jerusalem and Judah,
calling all those who had returned from exile to meet in
Jerusalem, 4 by order of the leaders of the people. If anyone
failed to come within two or three days, his cattle would be
confiscated, and he would lose his right to be a member of
the community.
5 Within the three days, on the twentieth day of the ninth
month, all the men of the tribes of Judah and Benjamin came
to Jerusalem 6 and assembled in the Temple square. Everyone was shivering from the cold because it was wintertime.
7 Then Ezra stood up and spoke to them, "You have broken
the Law and brought guilt on Israel by marrying foreign

New Revised Standard Version

which you gave by your servants the prophets, saying,
83 'The land that you are entering to take possession of is a
land polluted with the pollution of the aliens of the land, and
they have filled it with their uncleanness. 84 Therefore do not
give your daughters in marriage to their descendants, and do
not take their daughters for your descendants; 85 do not seek
ever to have peace with them, so that you may be strong and
eat the good things of the land and leave it for an inheritance
to your children forever.' 86 And all that has happened to us
has come about because of our evil deeds and our great sins.
For you, O Lord, lifted the burden of our sins 87 and gave us
such a root as this; but we turned back again to transgress
your law by mixing with the uncleanness of the peoples of
the land. 88 Were you not angry enough with us to destroy us
without leaving a root or seed or name? 89 O Lord of Israel,
you are faithful; for we are left as a root to this day. 90 See,
we are now before you in our iniquities; for we can no longer
stand in your presence because of these things."
91 While Ezra was praying and making his confession,
weeping and lying on the ground before the temple, there
gathered around him a very great crowd of men and women
and youths from Jerusalem; for there was great weeping
among the multitude. 92 Then Shecaniah son of Jehiel, one
of the men of Israel, called out, and said to Ezra, "We have
sinned against the Lord, and have married foreign women
from the peoples of the land; but even now there is hope for
Israel. 93 Let us take an oath to the Lord about this, that we
will put away all our foreign wives, with their children, 94 as
seems good to you and to all who obey the law of the Lord.
95 Rise up[a] and take action, for it is your task, and we are
with you to take strong measures." 96 Then Ezra rose up and
made the leaders of the priests and Levites of all Israel swear
that they would do this. And they swore to it.

9 Then Ezra set out and went from the court of the temple
to the chamber of Jehohanan son of Eliashib, 2 and
spent the night there; and he did not eat bread or drink
water, for he was mourning over the great iniquities of the
multitude. 3 And a proclamation was made throughout Judea
and Jerusalem to all who had returned from exile that they
should assemble at Jerusalem, 4 and that if any did not meet
there within two or three days, in accordance with the decision of the ruling elders, their livestock would be seized for
sacrifice and the men themselves[b] expelled from the multitude of those who had returned from the captivity.
5 Then the men of the tribe of Judah and Benjamin assembled at Jerusalem within three days; this was the ninth
month, on the twentieth day of the month. 6 All the multitude sat in the open square before the temple, shivering
because of the bad weather that prevailed. 7 Then Ezra stood
up and said to them, "You have broken the law and married
foreign women, and so have increased the sin of Israel.

a Other ancient authorities read *as seems good to you." And all who obeyed the law of the Lord rose and said to Ezra, 95 "Rise up* *b* Gk *he himself*

τῷ Ισραηλ· 8 καὶ νῦν δότε ὁμολογίαν δόξαν τῷ κυρίῳ θεῷ τῶν πατέρων ἡμῶν 9 καὶ ποιήσατε τὸ θέλημα αὐτοῦ καὶ χωρίσθητε ἀπὸ τῶν ἐθνῶν τῆς γῆς καὶ ἀπὸ τῶν γυναικῶν τῶν ἀλλογενῶν. 10 καὶ ἐφώνησαν ἅπαν τὸ πλῆθος καὶ εἶπον μεγάλῃ τῇ φωνῇ Οὕτως ὡς εἴρηκας ποιήσομεν· 11 ἀλλὰ τὸ πλῆθος πολὺ καὶ ἡ ὥρα χειμερινή, καὶ οὐκ ἰσχύομεν στῆναι αἴθριοι καὶ οὐχ εὕρομεν, καὶ τὸ ἔργον ἡμῖν οὐκ ἔστιν ἡμέρας μιᾶς οὐδὲ δύο· ἐπὶ πλεῖον γὰρ ἡμάρτομεν ἐν τούτοις. 12 στήτωσαν δὲ οἱ προηγούμενοι τοῦ πλήθους, καὶ πάντες οἱ ἐκ τῶν κατοικιῶν ἡμῶν, ὅσοι ἔχουσιν γυναῖκας ἀλλογενεῖς, παραγενηθήτωσαν λαβόντες χρόνον· 13 καὶ ἑκάστου δὲ τόπου τοὺς πρεσβυτέρους καὶ τοὺς κριτὰς ἕως τοῦ λῦσαι τὴν ὀργὴν τοῦ κυρίου ἀφ᾽ ἡμῶν τοῦ πράγματος τούτου. 14 Ιωναθας Αζαηλου καὶ Ιεζιας Θοκανου ἐπεδέξαντο κατὰ ταῦτα, καὶ Μοσολλαμος καὶ Λευις καὶ Σαββαταιος συνεβράβευσαν αὐτοῖς. 15 καὶ ἐποίησαν κατὰ πάντα ταῦτα οἱ ἐκ τῆς αἰχμαλωσίας. 16 καὶ ἐπελέξατο ἑαυτῷ Εσδρας ὁ ἱερεὺς ἄνδρας ἡγουμένους τῶν πατριῶν αὐτῶν, κατ᾽ ὄνομα πάντας, καὶ συνεκάθισαν τῇ νουμηνίᾳ τοῦ μηνὸς τοῦ δεκάτου ἐτάσαι τὸ πρᾶγμα. 17 καὶ ἤχθη ἐπὶ πέρας τὰ κατὰ τοὺς ἄνδρας τοὺς ἐπισυνέχοντας γυναῖκας ἀλλογενεῖς ἕως τῆς νουμηνίας τοῦ πρώτου μηνός.

18 Καὶ εὑρέθησαν τῶν ἱερέων οἱ ἐπισυναχθέντες ἀλλογενεῖς γυναῖκας ἔχοντες. 19 ἐκ τῶν υἱῶν Ἰησοῦ τοῦ Ιωσεδεκ καὶ τῶν ἀδελφῶν Μασηας καὶ Ελεαζαρος καὶ Ιωριβος καὶ Ιωδανος. 20 καὶ ἐπέβαλον τὰς χεῖρας ἐκβαλεῖν τὰς γυναῖκας αὐτῶν, καὶ εἰς ἐξιλασμὸν κριοὺς ὑπὲρ τῆς ἀγνοίας αὐτῶν. 21 καὶ ἐκ τῶν υἱῶν Εμμηρ Ανανιας καὶ Ζαβδαιος καὶ Μανης καὶ Σαμαιος καὶ Ιιηλ καὶ Αζαριας. 22 καὶ ἐκ τῶν υἱῶν Φαισουρ Ελιωναις, Μασσιας, Ισμαηλος καὶ Ναθαναηλος καὶ Ωκιδηλος καὶ Σαλθας. — 23 καὶ ἐκ τῶν Λευιτῶν· Ιωζαβδος καὶ Σεμεῒς καὶ Κωλιος (οὗτος Καλιτας) καὶ Παθαιος καὶ Ωουδας καὶ Ιωανας. 24 ἐκ τῶν ἱεροψαλτῶν Ελιασιβος, Βακχουρος. 25 ἐκ τῶν θυρωρῶν Σαλλουμος καὶ Τολβανης. — 26 ἐκ τοῦ Ισραηλ· ἐκ τῶν υἱῶν Φορος Ιερμας καὶ Ιεζιας καὶ Μελχιας καὶ Μιαμινος καὶ Ελεαζαρος καὶ Ασιβιας καὶ Βανναιας. 27 ἐκ τῶν υἱῶν Ηλαμ Ματανιας καὶ Ζαχαριας, Ιεζριηλος καὶ Ωβαδιος καὶ Ιερεμωθ καὶ Ηλιας. 28 καὶ ἐκ τῶν υἱῶν Ζαμοθ Ελιαδας, Ελιασιμος, Οθονιας, Ιαριμωθ καὶ Σαβαθος καὶ Ζερδαιας. 29 καὶ ἐκ τῶν υἱῶν Βηβαι Ιωαννης καὶ Ανανιας καὶ Ζαβδος καὶ Εμαθις. 30 καὶ ἐκ τῶν υἱῶν Μανι Ωλαμος, Μαμουχος, Ιεδαιος, Ιασουβος καὶ Ασαηλος καὶ Ιερεμωθ· 31 καὶ ἐκ τῶν υἱῶν Αδδι Ναаθος καὶ Μοοσσιας, Λακκουνος καὶ Ναϊδος καὶ Βεσκασπασμυς καὶ Σεσθηλ καὶ Βαλνουος καὶ Μανασσηας. 32 καὶ ἐκ τῶν υἱῶν Ανναν Ελιωνας καὶ Ασαιας καὶ Μελχιας καὶ Σαββαιας καὶ Σιμων Χοσαμαιος. 33 καὶ ἐκ τῶν υἱῶν Ασομ Μαλταννaιος καὶ Ματταθιας καὶ Σαβανναιους καὶ Ελιφαλατ καὶ Μανασσης καὶ Σεμεϊ· 34 καὶ

8 And now by confessing give glory unto the Lord God of our fathers,

9 And do his will, and separate yourselves from the heathen of the land, and from the strange women.

10 Then cried the whole multitude, and said with a loud voice, Like as thou hast spoken, so will we do.

11 But forasmuch as the people are many, and it is foul weather, so that we cannot stand without, and this is not a work of a day or two, seeing our sin in these things is spread far:

12 Therefore let the rulers of the multitude stay, and let all them of our habitations that have strange wives come at the time appointed,

13 And with them the rulers and judges of every place, till we turn away the wrath of the Lord from us for this matter.

14 Then Jonathan the son of Azael and Ezechias the son of Theocanus accordingly took this matter upon them: and Mosollam and Levis and Sabbatheus helped them.

15 And they that were of the captivity did according to all these things.

16 And Esdras the priest chose unto him the principal men of their families, all by name: and in the first day of the tenth month they sat together to examine the matter.

17 So their cause that held strange wives was brought to an end in the first day of the first month.

18 And of the priests that were come together, and had strange wives, there were found;

19 Of the sons of Jesus the son of Josedec, and his brethren; Matthelas, and Eleazar, and Joribus, and Joadanus.

20 And they gave their hands to put away their wives, and to offer rams to make reconcilement for their errors.

21 And of the sons of Emmer; Ananias, and Zabdeus, and Eanes, and Sameius, and Hiereel, and Azarias.

22 And of the sons of Phaisur; Elionas, Massias, Ismael, and Nathanael, and Ocidelus, and Talsas.

23 And of the Levites; Jozabad, and Semis, and Colius, who was called Calitas, and Patheus, and Judas, and Jonas.

24 Of the holy singers; Eleazurus, Bacchurus.

25 Of the porters; Sallumus, and Tolbanes.

26 Of them of Israel, of the sons of Phoros; Hiermas, and Eddias, and Melchias, and Maelus, and Eleazar, and Asibias, and Baanias.

27 Of the sons of Ela; Matthanias, Zacharias, and Hierielus, and Hieremoth, and Aedias.

28 And of the sons of Zamoth; Eliadas, Elisimus, Othonias, Jarimoth, and Sabatus, and Sardeus.

29 Of the sons of Bebai; Johannes, and Ananias, and Josabad, and Amatheis.

30 Of the sons of Mani; Olamus, Mamuchus, Jedeus, Jasubus, Jasael, and Hieremoth.

31 And of the sons of Addi; Naathus, and Moosias, Lacunus, and Naidus, and Mathanias, and Sesthel, Balnuus, and Manasseas.

32 And of the sons of Annas; Elionas, and Aseas, and Melchias, and Sabbeus, and Simon Chosameus.

33 And of the sons of Asom; Altaneus, and Matthias, and Bannaia, Eliphalat, and Manasses, and Semei.

TODAY'S ENGLISH VERSION

women. [8]Now then, tell the truth and confess your sins to the Lord, the God of our ancestors, [9]and do what he requires. Separate yourselves from the foreigners living in our land and get rid of your foreign wives."

[10]The people shouted in reply, "We will do whatever you say." [11]But they added, "The crowd is too big, and it's wintertime. We can't stand here in the open like this. This isn't something that can be settled in one or two days, since so many of us are involved in this sin. [12]Let our officials stay in Jerusalem and take charge of the matter. Then let anyone who has a foreign wife come at an appointed time, [13]together with the leaders and the judges of his city. In this way God's anger over this situation will be turned away." [14]Jonathan son of Asahel and Jahzeiah son of Tikvah assumed responsibility for the plan; and Meshullam, Levi, and Shabbethai served with them as judges.

[15]The returned exiles carried out the investigation in full. [16]Ezra the priest appointed men from among the heads of the clans and recorded their names. On the first day of the tenth month they began their investigation. [17]And within the next three months they investigated all the cases of men with foreign wives.

[18]The following is a list of the men who had foreign wives:

Priests, listed by clans:

[19]Clan of Joshua and his brothers, sons of Jozadak: Maaseiah, Eliezar, Jarib, and Jodan. [20]They promised to divorce their wives, and they offered rams as a sacrifice for their sins.

[21]Clan of Immer: Hanani, Zebadiah, Manes, Shemaiah, Jehiel, and Azariah

[22]Clan of Pashhur: Elioenai, Maaseiah, Ishmael, Nathanael, Okidelus, and Elasah

[23]*Levites:*

Jozabad, Shimei, Kelaiah (also called Kelita), Pethahiah, Judah, and Jonah

[24]*Musicians:*

Eliashib and Bacchurus

[25]*Temple guards:*

Shallum and Telem

[26]*Others:*

Clan of Parosh: Ramiah, Izziah, Malchijah, Milelos, Eleazar, Asebiah, Benaiah

[27]Clan of Elam: Mattaniah, Zechariah, Jezriel, Abdi, Jeremoth, and Elijah

[28]Clan of Zattu: Elioenai, Eliashib, Othoniah, Jeremoth, Zabad, and Zerdaiah

[29]Clan of Bebai: Jehohanan, Hananiah, Zabbai, and Emathis

[30]Clan of Bani: Meshullam, Malluch, Adaiah, Jashub, Sheal, and Jeremoth

[31]Clan of Addi: Naathus, Moossias, Laccunus, Naidus, Bescaspasmys, Sesthel, Belnuus, and Manasseas

[32]Clan of Annan: Elionas, Asiah, Melchiah, Sabbaiah, and Simon Chosamaeus

[33]Clan of Hashum: Mattenai, Mattattah, Zabad, Eliphelet, Manasseh, and Shimei

NEW REVISED STANDARD VERSION

[8]Now then make confession and give glory to the Lord the God of our ancestors, [9]and do his will; separate yourselves from the peoples of the land and from your foreign wives."

10 Then all the multitude shouted and said with a loud voice, "We will do as you have said. [11]But the multitude is great and it is winter, and we are not able to stand in the open air. This is not a work we can do in one day or two, for we have sinned too much in these things. [12]So let the leaders of the multitude stay, and let all those in our settlements who have foreign wives come at the time appointed, [13]with the elders and judges of each place, until we are freed from the wrath of the Lord over this matter."

14 Jonathan son of Asahel and Jahzeiah son of Tikvah[a] undertook the matter on these terms, and Meshullam and Levi and Shabbethai served with them as judges. [15]And those who had returned from exile acted in accordance with all this.

16 Ezra the priest chose for himself the leading men of their ancestral houses, all of them by name; and on the new moon of the tenth month they began their sessions to investigate the matter. [17]And the cases of the men who had foreign wives were brought to an end by the new moon of the first month.

18 Of the priests, those who were brought in and found to have foreign wives were: [19]of the descendants of Jeshua son of Jozadak and his kindred, Maaseiah, Eliezar, Jarib, and Jodan. [20]They pledged themselves to put away their wives, and to offer rams in expiation of their error. [21]Of the descendants of Immer: Hanani and Zebadiah and Maaseiah and Shemaiah and Jehiel and Azariah. [22]Of the descendants of Pashhur: Elioenai, Maaseiah, Ishmael, and Nathanael, and Gedaliah, and Salthas.

23 And of the Levites: Jozabad and Shimei and Kelaiah, who was Kelita, and Pethahiah and Judah and Jonah. [24]Of the temple singers: Eliashib and Zaccur.[b] [25]Of the gatekeepers: Shallum and Telem.[c]

26 Of Israel: of the descendants of Parosh: Ramiah, Izziah, Malchijah, Mijamin, and Eleazar, and Asibias, and Benaiah. [27]Of the descendants of Elam: Mattaniah and Zechariah, Jezrielus and Abdi, and Jeremoth and Elijah. [28]Of the descendants of Zamoth: Eliadas, Eliashib, Othoniah, Jeremoth, and Zabad and Zerdaiah. [29]Of the descendants of Bebai: Jehohanan and Hananiah and Zabbai and Emathis. [30]Of the descendants of Mani: Olamus, Mamuchus, Adaiah, Jashub, and Sheal and Jeremoth. [31]Of the descendants of Addi: Naathus and Moossias, Laccunus and Naidus, and Bescaspasmys and Sesthel, and Belnuus and Manasseas. [32]Of the descendants of Annan, Elionas and Asaias and Melchias and Sabbaias and Simon Chosamaeus. [33]Of the descendants of Hashum: Mattenai and Mattattah and Zabad and Eliphelet and Manasseh and

a Gk *Thocanos* *b* Gk *Bacchurus* *c* Gk *Tolbanes*

ἐκ τῶν υἱῶν Βαανι Ιερεμιας, Μομδιος, Μαηρος, Ιουηλ,
Μαμδαι καὶ Πεδιας καὶ Ανως, Καραβασιων καὶ Ελιασιβος
καὶ Μαμνιταναιμος, Ελιασις, Βαννους, Ελιαλις, Σομεϊς,
Σελεμιας, Ναθανιας. καὶ ἐκ τῶν υἱῶν Εζωρα Σεσσις, Εζριλ,
Αζαηλος, Σαματος, Ζαμβρις, Ιωσηπος. 35 καὶ ἐκ τῶν υἱῶν
Νοομα Μαζιτιας, Ζαβαδαιας, Ηδαις, Ιουηλ, Βαναιας. —
36 πάντες οὗτοι συνῴκισαν γυναῖκας ἀλλογενεῖς. καὶ ἀπέ-
λυσαν αὐτὰς σὺν τέκνοις.

37 Καὶ κατῴκησαν οἱ ἱερεῖς καὶ οἱ Λευῖται καὶ οἱ ἐκ τοῦ
Ισραηλ ἐν Ιερουσαλημ καὶ ἐν τῇ χώρᾳ. τῇ νουμηνίᾳ τοῦ
ἑβδόμου μηνός — καὶ οἱ υἱοὶ Ισραηλ ἐν ταῖς κατοικίαις
αὐτῶν, — 38 καὶ συνήχθη πᾶν τὸ πλῆθος ὁμοθυμαδὸν ἐπὶ τὸ
εὐρύχωρον τοῦ πρὸς ἀνατολὰς τοῦ ἱεροῦ πυλῶνος 39 καὶ
εἶπον Εσδρα τῷ ἀρχιερεῖ καὶ ἀναγνώστῃ κομίσαι τὸν νόμον
Μωυσέως τὸν παραδοθέντα ὑπὸ τοῦ κυρίου θεοῦ Ισραηλ.
40 καὶ ἐκόμισεν Εσδρας ὁ ἀρχιερεὺς τὸν νόμον παντὶ τῷ
πλήθει ἀπὸ ἀνθρώπου ἕως γυναικὸς καὶ πᾶσιν τοῖς ἱερεῦσιν
ἀκοῦσαι τοῦ νόμου νουμηνίᾳ τοῦ ἑβδόμου μηνός. 41 καὶ
ἀνεγίγνωσκεν ἐν τῷ πρὸ τοῦ ἱεροῦ πυλῶνος εὐρυχώρῳ ἀπὸ
ὄρθρου ἕως μεσημβρινοῦ ἐνώπιον ἀνδρῶν τε καὶ γυναικῶν,
καὶ ἐπέδωκαν πᾶν τὸ πλῆθος τὸν νοῦν εἰς τὸν νόμον. 42 καὶ
ἔστη Εσδρας ὁ ἱερεὺς καὶ ἀναγνώστης τοῦ νόμου ἐπὶ τοῦ
ξυλίνου βήματος τοῦ κατασκευασθέντος, 43 καὶ ἔστησαν
παρ' αὐτῷ Ματταθιας, Σαμμους, Ανανιας, Αζαριας, Ουριας,
Εζεκιας, Βααλσαμος ἐκ δεξιῶν, 44 καὶ ἐξ εὐωνύμων Φαδαι-
ος, Μισαηλ, Μελχιας, Λωθασουβος, Ναβαριας, Ζαχαριας.
45 καὶ ἀναλαβὼν Εσδρας τὸ βιβλίον τοῦ νόμου ἐνώπιον τοῦ
πλήθους — προεκάθητο γὰρ ἐπιδόξως ἐνώπιον πάντων —
46 καὶ ἐν τῷ λῦσαι τὸν νόμον πάντες ὀρθοὶ ἔστησαν. καὶ
εὐλόγησεν Εσδρας τῷ κυρίῳ θεῷ ὑψίστῳ θεῷ σαβαωθ παντοκράτορι, 47 καὶ ἐπεφώνησεν πᾶν τὸ πλῆθος Αμην, καὶ
ἄραντες ἄνω τὰς χεῖρας προσπεσόντες ἐπὶ τὴν γῆν προσεκύνησαν τῷ κυρίῳ. 48 Ἰησοῦς καὶ Αννιουθ καὶ Σαραβιας,
Ιαδινος, Ιακουβος, Σαββαταιος, Αυταιας, Μαιαννας καὶ
Καλιτας, Αζαριας καὶ Ιωζαβδος, Ανανιας, Φαλιας οἱ
Λευῖται ἐδίδασκον τὸν νόμον κυρίου καὶ πρὸς τὸ πλῆθος
ἀνεγίνωσκον τὸν νόμον τοῦ κυρίου ἐμφυσιοῦντες ἅμα τὴν
ἀνάγνωσιν. — 49 καὶ εἶπεν Ατταρατης Εσδρα τῷ ἀρχιερεῖ
καὶ ἀναγνώστῃ καὶ τοῖς Λευίταις τοῖς διδάσκουσι τὸ πλῆθος
ἐπὶ πάντας 50 Ἡ ἡμέρα αὕτη ἐστὶν ἁγία τῷ κυρίῳ — καὶ
πάντες ἔκλαιον ἐν τῷ ἀκοῦσαι τοῦ νόμου —· 51 βαδίσαντες
οὖν φάγετε λιπάσματα καὶ πίετε γλυκάσματα καὶ ἀποστείλατε ἀποστολὰς τοῖς μὴ ἔχουσιν, 52 ἁγία γὰρ ἡ ἡμέρα τῷ
κυρίῳ· καὶ μὴ λυπεῖσθε, ὁ γὰρ κύριος δοξάσει ὑμᾶς. 53 καὶ οἱ
Λευῖται ἐκέλευον τῷ δήμῳ παντὶ λέγοντες Ἡ ἡμέρα αὕτη
ἁγία, μὴ λυπεῖσθε. 54 καὶ ᾤχοντο πάντες φαγεῖν καὶ πιεῖν
καὶ εὐφραίνεσθαι καὶ δοῦναι ἀποστολὰς τοῖς μὴ ἔχουσιν καὶ
εὐφρανθῆναι μεγάλως, 55 ὅτι καὶ ἐνεφυσιώθησαν ἐν τοῖς ῥήμασιν, οἷς ἐδιδάχθησαν. — καὶ ἐπισυνήχθησαν.

34 And of the sons of Maani; Jeremias, Momdis, Omaerus, Juel, Mabdai, and Pelias, and Anos, Carabasion, and Enasibus, and Mamnitanaimus, Eliasis, Bannus, Eliali, Samis, Selemias, Nathanias: and of the sons of Ozora; Sesis, Esril, Azaelus, Samatus, Zambis, Josephus.

35 And of the sons of Ethma; Mazitias, Zabadaias, Edes, Juel, Banaias.

36 All these had taken strange wives, and they put them away with their children.

37 And the priests and Levites, and they that were of Israel, dwelt in Jerusalem, and in the country, in the first day of the seventh month: so the children of Israel were in their habitations.

38 And the whole multitude came together with one accord into the broad place of the holy porch toward the east:

39 And they spake unto Esdras the priest and reader, that he would bring the law of Moses, that was given of the Lord God of Israel.

40 So Esdras the chief priest brought the law unto the whole multitude from man to woman, and to all the priests, to hear the law in the first day of the seventh month.

41 And he read in the broad court before the holy porch from morning unto midday, before both men and women; and all the multitude gave heed unto the law.

42 And Esdras the priest and reader of the law stood up upon a pulpit of wood, which was made *for that purpose.*

43 And there stood up by him Mattathias, Sammus, Ananias, Azarias, Urias, Ezecias, Balasamus, upon the right hand:

44 And upon his left hand stood Phaldaius, Misael, Melchias, Lothasubus, and Nabarias.

45 Then took Esdras the book of the law before the multitude: for he sat honourably in the first place in the sight of them all.

46 And when he opened the law, they stood all straight up. So Esdras blessed the Lord God most High, the God of hosts, Almighty.

47 And all the people answered, Amen; and lifting up their hands they fell to the ground, and worshipped the Lord.

48 Also Jesus, Anus, Sarabias, Adinus, Jacubus, Sabateas, Auteas, Maianeas, and Calitas, Azarias, and Joazabdus, and Ananias, Biatas, the Levites, taught the law of the Lord, making them withal to understand it.

49 Then spake Attharates unto Esdras the chief priest and reader, and to the Levites that taught the multitude, even to all, saying,

50 This day is holy unto the Lord; (for they all wept when they heard the law:)

51 Go then, and eat the fat, and drink the sweet, and send part to them that have nothing;

52 For this day is holy unto the Lord: and be not sorrowful; for the Lord will bring you to honour.

53 So the Levites published all things to the people, saying, This day is holy to the Lord; be not sorrowful.

54 Then went they their way, every one to eat and drink, and make merry, and to give part to them that had nothing, and to make great cheer;

55 Because they understood the words wherein they were instructed, and for the which they had been assembled.

TODAY'S ENGLISH VERSION

34 Clan of Bani: Jeremai, Maadai, Amram, Joel, Mamdai, Bedeiah, Vaniah, Carabasion, Eliashib, Machnadebai, Eliasis, Binnui, Elialis, Shimei, Shelemiah, and Nathaniah

Clan of Ezora: Shashai, Azarel, Azael, Shemaiah, Amariah, and Joseph

35 Clan of Nebo: Mattithiah, Zabad, Iddo, Joel, and Benaiah

36 All these men had foreign wives. They divorced them and sent them and their children away.

37 The priests, the Levites, and many of the ordinary people of Israel settled in Jerusalem and its vicinity. By the seventh month the other Israelites were all settled in their towns. On the first day of that month 38 they all assembled in Jerusalem in the square just inside the east gate of the Temple. 39 They asked Ezra, the High Priest and scholar of the Law which the Lord had given Israel through Moses, to bring the book of the Law. 40 So Ezra brought it to the place where all the people—men, women, and all the priests—had gathered to hear it. 41 There in the square by the gate he read the Law to them from dawn until noon, and they all listened attentively.

42 Ezra was standing on a wooden platform that had been built for the occasion. 43 The following men stood at his right: Mattathiah, Shema, Ananiah, Azariah, Uriah, Hezekiah, and Baalsamos; 44 and the following stood at his left: Pedaiah, Mishael, Malchijah, Lothasubus, Nabariah, and Zechariah.

45 Ezra took his seat on the platform in a prominent place where everyone could see him. As soon as he took the book of the Law 46 and opened it, all the people stood up. Ezra said, "Praise the Lord, God Most High, God Almighty, Ruler of all."

47 All the people raised their arms in the air and answered, "Amen!" They knelt down in worship, with their faces to the ground.

48 The following Levites taught the Law of the Lord to the people: Jeshua, Anniuth, Sherebiah, Jamin, Akkub, Shabbethai, Hodiah, Maiannas, Kelita, Azariah, Jozabad, Hanan, and Peliah. They read the Law to the people and explained what was read.

49-50 When the people heard what the Law required, they were so moved that they began to weep. The governor[a] said to Ezra, the priest and scholar of the Law, and to all the Levites who were teaching the people, "This day is holy to the Lord; 51 go home and have a feast. Share your food and wine with those who don't have any. 52 Today is holy to the Lord, so don't be sad. He will restore your former glory."

53 The Levites gave the command to all the people: "This day is holy; do not be sad." 54 So all the people went home and joyfully ate and drank and shared what they had with those who had nothing. They celebrated 55 because they understood what had been read to them.

Then they assembled. . . .[b]

[a] *Probable meaning* The governor; *Greek* Atharates. [b] *Originally the Greek text must have continued (see Ne 8.13).*

NEW REVISED STANDARD VERSION

Shimei. 34 Of the descendants of Bani: Jeremai, Momdius, Maerus, Joel, Mamdai and Bedeiah and Vaniah, Carabasion and Eliashib and Mamitanemus, Eliasis, Binnui, Elialis, Shimei, Shelemiah, Nethaniah. Of the descendants of Ezora: Shashai, Azarel, Azael, Samatus, Zambris, Joseph. 35 Of the descendants of Nooma: Mazitias, Zabad, Iddo, Joel, Benaiah. 36 All these had married foreign women, and they put them away together with their children.

37 The priests and the Levites and the Israelites settled in Jerusalem and in the country. On the new moon of the seventh month, when the people of Israel were in their settlements, 38 the whole multitude gathered with one accord in the open square before the east gate of the temple; 39 they told Ezra the chief priest and reader to bring the law of Moses that had been given by the Lord God of Israel. 40 So Ezra the chief priest brought the law, for all the multitude, men and women, and all the priests to hear the law, on the new moon of the seventh month. 41 He read aloud in the open square before the gate of the temple from early morning until midday, in the presence of both men and women; and all the multitude gave attention to the law. 42 Ezra the priest and reader of the law stood on the wooden platform that had been prepared; 43 and beside him stood Mattathiah, Shema, Ananias, Azariah, Uriah, Hezekiah, and Baalsamus on his right, 44 and on his left Pedaiah, Mishael, Malchijah, Lothasubus, Nabariah, and Zechariah. 45 Then Ezra took up the book of the law in the sight of the multitude, for he had the place of honor in the presence of all. 46 When he opened the law, they all stood erect. And Ezra blessed the Lord God Most High, the God of hosts, the Almighty, 47 and the multitude answered, "Amen." They lifted up their hands, and fell to the ground and worshiped the Lord. 48 Jeshua and Anniuth and Sherebiah, Jadinus, Akkub, Shabbethai, Hodiah, Maiannas and Kelita, Azariah and Jozabad, Hanan, Pelaiah, the Levites, taught the law of the Lord,[a] at the same time explaining what was read.

49 Then Attharates[b] said to Ezra the chief priest and reader, and to the Levites who were teaching the multitude, and to all, 50 "This day is holy to the Lord"—now they were all weeping as they heard the law— 51 "so go your way, eat the fat and drink the sweet, and send portions to those who have none; 52 for the day is holy to the Lord; and do not be sorrowful, for the Lord will exalt you." 53 The Levites commanded all the people, saying, "This day is holy; do not be sorrowful." 54 Then they all went their way, to eat and drink and enjoy themselves, and to give portions to those who had none, and to make great rejoicing; 55 because they were inspired by the words which they had been taught. And they came together.[c]

[a] Other ancient authorities add *and read the law of the Lord to the multitude* [b] Or *the governor* [c] The Greek text ends abruptly: compare Neh 8.13

GREEK OLD TESTAMENT

The Prayer of Manasseh is included only in the Greek Old Testament, King James Version, Today's English Version, and New Revised Standard Version.

ΩΙΔΗ ΙΒ΄
ΠΡΟΣΕΥΧΗ ΜΑΝΑΣΣΗ

1 Κύριε παντοκράτωρ,
ὁ θεὸς τῶν πατέρων ἡμῶν,
τοῦ Αβρααμ καὶ Ισαακ καὶ Ιακωβ
καὶ τοῦ σπέρματος αὐτῶν τοῦ δικαίου,
2 ὁ ποιήσας τὸν οὐρανὸν καὶ τὴν γῆν σὺν παντὶ τῷ κόσμῳ αὐτῶν,
3 ὁ πεδήσας τὴν θάλασσαν τῷ λόγῳ τοῦ προστάγματός σου,
ὁ κλείσας τὴν ἄβυσσον καὶ σφραγισάμενος τῷ φοβερῷ καὶ ἐνδόξῳ ὀνόματί σου·
4 ὃν πάντα φρίττει καὶ τρέμει ἀπὸ προσώπου δυνάμεώς σου,
5 ὅτι ἄστεκτος ἡ μεγαλοπρέπεια τῆς δόξης σου,
καὶ ἀνυπόστατος ἡ ὀργὴ τῆς ἐπὶ ἁμαρτωλοὺς ἀπειλῆς σου,
6 ἀμέτρητόν τε καὶ ἀνεξιχνίαστον τὸ ἔλεος τῆς ἐπαγγελίας σου,
7 ὅτι σὺ εἶ κύριος ὕψιστος,
εὔσπλαγχνος, μακρόθυμος καὶ πολυέλεος
καὶ μετανοῶν ἐπὶ κακίαις ἀνθρώπων·
8 σὺ οὖν, κύριε ὁ θεὸς τῶν δικαίων,
οὐκ ἔθου μετάνοιαν δικαίοις,
τῷ Αβρααμ καὶ Ισαακ καὶ Ιακωβ τοῖς οὐχ ἡμαρτηκόσιν σοι,
ἀλλ᾽ ἔθου μετάνοιαν ἐμοὶ τῷ ἁμαρτωλῷ,
9 διότι ἥμαρτον ὑπὲρ ἀριθμὸν ψάμμου θαλάσσης,
ἐπλήθυναν αἱ ἀνομίαι μου, κύριε, ἐπλήθυναν,
καὶ οὐκ εἰμὶ ἄξιος ἀτενίσαι καὶ ἰδεῖν τὸ ὕψος τοῦ οὐρανοῦ
ἀπὸ πλήθους τῶν ἀδικιῶν μου
10 κατακαμπτόμενος πολλῷ δεσμῷ σιδήρου
εἰς τὸ ἀνανεῦσαί με ὑπὲρ ἁμαρτιῶν μου,
καὶ οὐκ ἔστιν μοι ἄνεσις,
διότι παρώργισα τὸν θυμόν σου
καὶ τὸ πονηρὸν ἐνώπιόν σου ἐποίησα
στήσας βδελύγματα καὶ πληθύνας προσοχθίσματα.
11 καὶ νῦν κλίνω γόνυ καρδίας δεόμενος τῆς παρὰ σοῦ χρηστότητος
12 Ἡμάρτηκα, κύριε, ἡμάρτηκα
καὶ τὰς ἀνομίας μου ἐγὼ γινώσκω.
13 αἰτοῦμαι δεόμενός σου
Ἄνες μοι, κύριε, ἄνες μοι,
μὴ συναπολέσῃς με ταῖς ἀνομίαις μου
μηδὲ εἰς τὸν αἰῶνα μηνίσας τηρήσῃς τὰ κακά μοι

KING JAMES VERSION

The Prayer of Manasseh is included only in the Greek Old Testament, King James Version, Today's English Version, and New Revised Standard Version.

THE PRAYER OF MANASSES

1[a] O Lord, Almighty God of our fathers, Abraham, Isaac, and Jacob, and of their righteous seed;
2 Who hast made heaven and earth, with all the ornament thereof;
3 Who hast bound the sea by the word of thy commandment; who hast shut up the deep, and sealed it by thy terrible and glorious name;
4 Whom all men fear, and tremble before thy power;
5 For the majesty of thy glory cannot be borne, and thine angry threatening toward sinners is importable:
6 But thy merciful promise is unmeasurable and unsearchable;
7 For thou art the most high Lord, of great compassion, longsuffering, very merciful, and repentest of the evils of men. Thou, O Lord, according to thy great goodness hast promised repentance and forgiveness to them that have sinned against thee: and of thine infinite mercies hast appointed repentance unto sinners, that they may be saved.
8 Thou therefore, O Lord, that art the God of the just, hast not appointed repentance to the just, as to Abraham, and Isaac, and Jacob, which have not sinned against thee; but thou hast appointed repentance unto me that am a sinner:
9 For I have sinned above the number of the sands of the sea. My transgressions, O Lord, are multiplied: my transgressions are multiplied, and I am not worthy to behold and see the height of heaven for the multitude of mine iniquities.
10 I am bowed down with many iron bands, that I cannot lift up mine head, neither have any release: for I have provoked thy wrath, and done evil before thee: I did not thy will, neither kept I thy commandments: I have set up abominations, and have multiplied offences.
11 Now therefore I bow the knee of mine heart, beseeching thee of grace.
12 I have sinned, O Lord, I have sinned, and I acknowledge mine iniquities:
13 Wherefore, I humbly beseech thee, forgive me, O Lord, forgive me, and destroy me not with mine iniquites. Be not angry with me for ever, by reserving evil for me; neither

a Verse breaks and numbers, which are not used in other settings of the KJV, have been added to faciliate comparison with the parallel versions.

TODAY'S ENGLISH VERSION

The Prayer of Manasseh is included only in the Greek Old Testament, King James Version, Today's English Version, and New Revised Standard Version.

THE PRAYER OF MANASSEH

1 Lord Almighty, God of our ancestors,
God of Abraham, Isaac, and Jacob,
God of their righteous descendants,
2 you created the universe
and all the splendor that fills it.
3 The sea obeys your command
and never overflows its bounds.
The power of your wonderful, glorious name
keeps the ocean depths in their place.
4 When you show your power,
all creation trembles.
5 Your glorious splendor is overwhelming,
and your anger is more than sinners can endure.
6 But the mercy you promise is also greater
than we can understand or measure.
7 For you are the Lord Most High;
you are patient and show mercy and compassion.
You make our punishment easier to bear
when we suffer for our sins.
O Lord, in your great goodness and mercy
you promise forgiveness and salvation
to those who repent of their sin against you.[a]
8 You, Lord, are the God of righteous people.
Repentance was not necessary
for Abraham, Isaac, and Jacob,
for they did not sin against you.
But for sinners like me
you have made repentance possible.
9 I have committed more sins
than there are grains of sand along the seashore.
They are so many, Lord, they are so many.
I have done so much that is wrong
that I am not worthy to turn my face toward heaven.
10 I am crushed beneath the weight of my sin;[b]
I am bowed down by its heavy iron chain.
I can find no relief,
for I have made you angry.
I have set up idols everywhere;
I have done what you hate.
11 But now I bow in deep humility,
praying for your mercy.
12 I have sinned, Lord, I have sinned;
I confess the wicked things I have done.
13 I beg you, Lord, I earnestly pray:
forgive me, forgive me.
Do not destroy me because of my sins;
do not stay angry with me forever
or store up punishment for me.

[a] O Lord . . . against you; *some manuscripts do not have these words.*
[b] *crushed* . . . my sin; *Greek unclear.*

NEW REVISED STANDARD VERSION

The Prayer of Manasseh is included only in the Greek Old Testament, King James Version, Today's English Version, and New Revised Standard Version.

THE PRAYER OF MANASSEH

1 O Lord Almighty,
God of our ancestors,
of Abraham and Isaac and Jacob
and of their righteous offspring;
2 you who made heaven and earth
with all their order;
3 who shackled the sea by your word of command,
who confined the deep
and sealed it with your terrible and glorious name;
4 at whom all things shudder,
and tremble before your power,
5 for your glorious splendor cannot be borne,
and the wrath of your threat to sinners is unendurable;
6 yet immeasurable and unsearchable
is your promised mercy,
7 for you are the Lord Most High,
of great compassion, long-suffering, and very merciful,
and you relent at human suffering.
O Lord, according to your great goodness
you have promised repentance and forgiveness
to those who have sinned against you,
and in the multitude of your mercies
you have appointed repentance for sinners,
so that they may be saved.[a]
8 Therefore you, O Lord, God of the righteous,
have not appointed repentance for the righteous,
for Abraham and Isaac and Jacob, who did not sin
against you,
but you have appointed repentance for me, who am a
sinner.
9 For the sins I have committed are more in number than
the sand of the sea;
my transgressions are multiplied, O Lord, they are
multiplied!
I am not worthy to look up and see the height of
heaven
because of the multitude of my iniquities.
10 I am weighted down with many an iron fetter,
so that I am rejected[b] because of my sins,
and I have no relief;
for I have provoked your wrath
and have done what is evil in your sight,
setting up abominations and multiplying offenses.
11 And now I bend the knee of my heart,
imploring you for your kindness.
12 I have sinned, O Lord, I have sinned,
and I acknowledge my transgressions.
13 I earnestly implore you,
forgive me, O Lord, forgive me!
Do not destroy me with my transgressions!
Do not be angry with me forever or store up evil for me;

[a] Other ancient authorities lack *O Lord, according . . . be saved* [b] Other ancient authorities read *so that I cannot lift up my head*

GREEK OLD TESTAMENT

μηδὲ καταδικάσῃς με ἐν τοῖς κατωτάτοις τῆς γῆς.
ὅτι σὺ εἶ, κύριε, ὁ θεὸς τῶν μετανοούντων,
14 καὶ ἐν ἐμοὶ δείξῃς τὴν ἀγαθωσύνην σου·
ὅτι ἀνάξιον ὄντα σώσεις με κατὰ τὸ πολὺ ἔλεός σου,
15 καὶ αἰνέσω σε διὰ παντὸς ἐν ταῖς ἡμέραις τῆς ζωῆς μου.
ὅτι σὲ ὑμνεῖ πᾶσα ἡ δύναμις τῶν οὐρανῶν,
καὶ σοῦ ἐστιν ἡ δόξα εἰς τοὺς αἰῶνας. αμην.

KING JAMES VERSION

condemn me into the lower parts of the earth. For thou art
the God, *even* the God of them that repent;
14 And in me thou wilt shew all thy goodness: for thou
wilt save me, that am unworthy, according to thy great
mercy.
15 Therefore I will praise thee for ever all the days of my
life: for all the powers of the heavens do praise thee, and
thine is the glory for ever and ever. Amen.

Psalm 151 is included only in the Greek Old Testament and New Revised Standard Version.

ΨΑΛΜΟΣ 151

1 Οὗτος ὁ ψαλμὸς ἰδιόγραφος εἰς Δαυιδ
καὶ ἔξωθεν τοῦ ἀριθμοῦ·
ὅτε ἐμονομάχησεν τῷ Γολιαδ.
Μικρὸς ἤμην ἐν τοῖς ἀδελφοῖς μου
καὶ νεώτερος ἐν τῷ οἴκῳ τοῦ πατρός μου·
ἐποίμαινον τὰ πρόβατα τοῦ πατρός μου.
2 αἱ χεῖρές μου ἐποίησαν ὄργανον,
οἱ δάκτυλοί μου ἥρμοσαν ψαλτήριον.
3 καὶ τίς ἀναγγελεῖ τῷ κυρίῳ μου;
αὐτὸς κύριος, αὐτὸς εἰσακούει.
4 αὐτὸς ἐξαπέστειλεν τὸν ἄγγελον αὐτοῦ
καὶ ἦρέν με ἐκ τῶν προβάτων τοῦ πατρός μου
καὶ ἔχρισέν με ἐν τῷ ἐλαίῳ τῆς χρίσεως αὐτοῦ.
5 οἱ ἀδελφοί μου καλοὶ καὶ μεγάλοι,
καὶ οὐκ εὐδόκησεν ἐν αὐτοῖς κύριος.
6 ἐξῆλθον εἰς συνάντησιν τῷ ἀλλοφύλῳ,
καὶ ἐπικατηράσατό με ἐν τοῖς εἰδώλοις αὐτοῦ·
7 ἐγὼ δὲ σπασάμενος τὴν παρ' αὐτοῦ μάχαιραν
ἀπεκεφάλισα αὐτὸν καὶ ἦρα ὄνειδος ἐξ υἱῶν Ισραηλ.

TODAY'S ENGLISH VERSION

Do not condemn me to the world of the dead,
for you, O Lord, forgive those who repent.
14 Show me all your mercy and kindness and save me,
even though I do not deserve it.
15 Then I will go on praising you as long as I live.
All the heavenly powers sing your praises,
and your glory endures forever. Amen.

NEW REVISED STANDARD VERSION

do not condemn me to the depths of the earth.
For you, O Lord, are the God of those who repent,
14 and in me you will manifest your goodness;
for, unworthy as I am, you will save me according to
your great mercy,
15 and I will praise you continually all the days of my life.
For all the host of heaven sings your praise,
and yours is the glory forever. Amen.

Psalm 151 is included only in the Greek Old Testament and New Revised Standard Version.

PSALM 151

This psalm is ascribed to David as his own composition (though it is outside the number[a]), after he had fought in single combat with Goliath.

1 I was small among my brothers,
and the youngest in my father's house;
I tended my father's sheep.

2 My hands made a harp;
my fingers fashioned a lyre.

3 And who will tell my Lord?
The Lord himself; it is he who hears.[b]

4 It was he who sent his messenger[c]
and took me from my father's sheep,
and anointed me with his anointing oil.

5 My brothers were handsome and tall,
but the Lord was not pleased with them.

6 I went out to meet the Philistine,[d]
and he cursed me by his idols.

7 But I drew his own sword;
I beheaded him, and took away disgrace from the
people of Israel.

a Other ancient authorities add *of the one hundred fifty* (psalms) *b* Other ancient authorities add *everything*; others add *me*; others read *who will hear me* *c* Or *angel* *d* Or *foreigner*

GREEK OLD TESTAMENT

3 Maccabees is included only in the Greek Old Testament and New Revised Standard Version.

ΜΑΚΚΑΒΑΙΩΝ Γʹ

1 Ὁ δὲ Φιλοπάτωρ παρὰ τῶν ἀνακομισθέντων μαθὼν τὴν
γενομένην τῶν ὑπ' αὐτοῦ κρατουμένων τόπων ἀφαίρεσιν
ὑπὸ Ἀντιόχου παραγγείλας ταῖς πάσαις δυνάμεσιν πεζι-
καῖς τε καὶ ἱππικαῖς καὶ τὴν ἀδελφὴν Ἀρσινόην συμπαρα-
λαβὼν ἐξώρμησεν μέχρι τῶν κατὰ Ῥαφίαν τόπων, ὅπου
παρεμβεβλήκεισαν οἱ περὶ Ἀντίοχον. 2 Θεόδοτος δέ τις ἐκ-
πληρῶσαι τὴν ἐπιβουλὴν διανοηθεὶς παραλαβὼν τῶν
προϋποτεταγμένων αὐτῷ ὅπλων Πτολεμαϊκῶν τὰ κράτιστα
διεκομίσθη νύκτωρ ἐπὶ τὴν τοῦ Πτολεμαίου σκηνὴν ὡς μόνος
κτεῖναι αὐτὸν καὶ ἐν τούτῳ διαλῦσαι τὸν πόλεμον. 3 τοῦτον
δὲ διαγαγὼν Δοσίθεος ὁ Δριμύλου λεγόμενος, τὸ γένος
Ιουδαῖος, ὕστερον δὲ μεταβαλὼν τὰ νόμιμα καὶ τῶν πατρίων
δογμάτων ἀπηλλοτριωμένος, ἄσημόν τινα κατέκλινεν ἐν τῇ
σκηνῇ, ὃν συνέβη κομίσασθαι τὴν ἐκείνου κόλασιν. 4 γενομένης δὲ καρτερᾶς μάχης καὶ τῶν πραγμάτων μᾶλλον ἐρρω-
μένων τῷ Ἀντιόχῳ ἱκανῶς ἡ Ἀρσινόη ἐπιπορευσαμένη τὰς
δυνάμεις παρεκάλει μετὰ οἴκτου καὶ δακρύων τοὺς πλοκά-
μους λελυμένη βοηθεῖν ἑαυτοῖς τε καὶ τοῖς τέκνοις καὶ
γυναιξὶν θαρραλέως ἐπαγγελλομένη δώσειν νικήσασιν ἑκάστῳ δύο μνᾶς χρυσίου. 5 καὶ οὕτως συνέβη τοὺς ἀντιπάλους
ἐν χειρονομίαις διαφθαρῆναι, πολλοὺς δὲ καὶ δοριαλώτους
συλλημφθῆναι. 6 κατακρατήσας δὲ τῆς ἐπιβουλῆς ἔκρινεν
τὰς πλησίον πόλεις ἐπελθὼν παρακαλέσαι. 7 ποιήσας δὲ
τοῦτο καὶ τοῖς τεμένεσι δωρεὰς ἀπονείμας εὐθαρσεῖς τοὺς
ὑποτεταγμένους κατέστησεν.

8 Τῶν δὲ Ιουδαίων διαπεμψαμένων πρὸς αὐτὸν ἀπὸ τῆς
γερουσίας καὶ τῶν πρεσβυτέρων τοὺς ἀσπασομένους αὐτὸν
καὶ ξένια κομιοῦντας καὶ ἐπὶ τοῖς συμβεβηκόσιν χαρισομέ-
νους συνέβη μᾶλλον αὐτὸν προθυμηθῆναι ὡς τάχιστα πρὸς
αὐτοὺς παραγενέσθαι. 9 διακομισθεὶς δὲ εἰς Ιεροσόλυμα καὶ
θύσας τῷ μεγίστῳ θεῷ καὶ χάριτας ἀποδοὺς καὶ τῶν ἑξῆς τι
τῷ τόπῳ ποιήσας καὶ δὴ παραγενόμενος εἰς τὸν τόπον καὶ
τῇ σπουδαιότητι καὶ εὐπρεπείᾳ καταπλαγείς, 10 θαυμάσας
δὲ καὶ τὴν τοῦ ἱεροῦ εὐταξίαν ἐνεθυμήθη βουλεύσασθαι εἰς
τὸν ναὸν εἰσελθεῖν. 11 τῶν δὲ εἰπόντων μὴ καθήκειν γίνεσθαι τοῦτο διὰ τὸ μηδὲ τοῖς ἐκ τοῦ ἔθνους ἐξεῖναι εἰσιέναι
μηδὲ πᾶσιν τοῖς ἱερεῦσιν, ἀλλ' ἢ μόνῳ τῷ προηγουμένῳ πάντων ἀρχιερεῖ, καὶ τούτῳ κατ' ἐνιαυτὸν ἅπαξ, ὁ δὲ οὐδαμῶς
ἐπείθετο. 12 τοῦ τε νόμου παραναγνωσθέντος οὐδ' ὧς
ἀπέλιπεν προφερόμενος ἑαυτὸν δεῖν εἰσελθεῖν λέγων Καὶ εἰ
ἐκεῖνοι ἐστέρηνται ταύτης τῆς τιμῆς, ἐμὲ δὲ οὐ δεῖ. 13 καὶ
ἐπυνθάνετο διὰ τίνα αἰτίαν εἰσερχόμενον αὐτὸν εἰς πᾶν
τέμενος οὐθεὶς ἐκώλυσεν τῶν παρόντων. 14 καί τις ἀπρονοή-
τως ἔφη κακῶς αὐτὸ τοῦτο τερατεύεσθαι. 15 γενομένου δέ,
φησιν, τούτου διὰ τίνα αἰτίαν, οὐχὶ πάντως εἰσελεύσεσθαι
καὶ θελόντων αὐτῶν καὶ μή; 16 τῶν δὲ ἱερέων ἐν πάσαις ταῖς
ἐσθήσεσιν προσπεσόντων καὶ δεομένων τοῦ μεγίστου θεοῦ
βοηθεῖν τοῖς ἐνεστῶσιν καὶ τὴν ὁρμὴν τοῦ κακῶς ἐπιβαλλο-
μένου μεταθεῖναι κραυγῆς τε μετὰ δακρύων τὸ ἱερὸν ἐμπλη-
σάντων 17 οἱ κατὰ τὴν πόλιν ἀπολειπόμενοι ταραχθέντες

NEW REVISED STANDARD VERSION

3 Maccabees is included only in the Greek Old Testament and New Revised Standard Version.

3 MACCABEES

1 When Philopator learned from those who returned that
the regions that he had controlled had been seized by
Antiochus, he gave orders to all his forces, both infantry and
cavalry, took with him his sister Arsinoë, and marched out to
the region near Raphia, where the army of Antiochus was
encamped. 2 But a certain Theodotus, determined to carry
out the plot he had devised, took with him the best of the
Ptolemaic arms that had been previously issued to him,[a] and
crossed over by night to the tent of Ptolemy, intending sin-
gle-handed to kill him and thereby end the war. 3 But
Dositheus, known as the son of Drimylus, a Jew by birth who
later changed his religion and apostatized from the ancestral
traditions, had led the king away and arranged that a certain
insignificant man should sleep in the tent; and so it turned
out that this man incurred the vengeance meant for the
king.[b] 4 When a bitter fight resulted, and matters were turning out rather in favor of Antiochus, Arsinoë went to the
troops with wailing and tears, her locks all disheveled, and
exhorted them to defend themselves and their children and
wives bravely, promising to give them each two minas of
gold if they won the battle. 5 And so it came about that the
enemy was routed in the action, and many captives also
were taken. 6 Now that he had foiled the plot, Ptolemy[c]
decided to visit the neighboring cities and encourage them.
7 By doing this, and by endowing their sacred enclosures
with gifts, he strengthened the morale of his subjects.

8 Since the Jews had sent some of their council and elders
to greet him, to bring him gifts of welcome, and to congratulate him on what had happened, he was all the more eager to
visit them as soon as possible. 9 After he had arrived in
Jerusalem, he offered sacrifice to the supreme God[d] and
made thank offerings and did what was fitting for the holy
place.[e] Then, upon entering the place and being impressed
by its excellence and its beauty, 10 he marveled at the good
order of the temple, and conceived a desire to enter the sanctuary. 11 When they said that this was not permitted,
because not even members of their own nation were allowed
to enter, not even all of the priests, but only the high priest
who was pre-eminent over all—and he only once a year—the
king was by no means persuaded. 12 Even after the law had
been read to him, he did not cease to maintain that he ought
to enter, saying, "Even if those men are deprived of this
honor, I ought not to be." 13 And he inquired why, when he
entered every other temple,[f] no one there had stopped him.
14 And someone answered thoughtlessly that it was wrong to
take that as a portent.[g] 15 "But since this has happened,"
the king[c] said, "why should not I at least enter, whether they
wish it or not?"

16 Then the priests in all their vestments prostrated themselves and entreated the supreme God[d] to aid in the present
situation and to avert the violence of this evil design, and
they filled the temple with cries and tears; 17 those who

a Or *the best of the Ptolemaic soldiers previously put under his command*
b Gk *that one* *c* Gk *he* *d* Gk *the greatest God* *e* Gk *the place*
f Or *entered the temple precincts* *g* Or *to boast of this*

ἐξεπήδησαν ἄδηλον τιθέμενοι τὸ γινόμενον. 18 αἵ τε κατάκλειστοι παρθένοι ἐν θαλάμοις σὺν ταῖς τεκούσαις ἐξώρμησαν καὶ ἀπέδωκαν κόνει τὰς κόμας πασάμεναι γόου τε καὶ στεναγμῶν ἐνεπίμπλων τὰς πλατείας. 19 αἱ δὲ καὶ προσαρτίως ἐσταλμέναι τοὺς πρὸς ἀπάντησιν διατεταγμένους παστοὺς καὶ τὴν ἁρμόζουσαν αἰδῶ παραλείπουσαι δρόμον ἄτακτον ἐν τῇ πόλει συνίσταντο. 20 τὰ δὲ νεογνὰ τῶν τέκνων αἱ πρὸς τούτοις μητέρες καὶ τιθηνοὶ παραλείπουσαι ἄλλως καὶ ἄλλως, αἱ μὲν κατ' οἴκους, αἱ δὲ κατὰ τὰς ἀγυιάς, ἀνεπιστρέπτως εἰς τὸ πανυπέρτατον ἱερὸν ἠθροίζοντο. 21 ποικίλη δὲ ἦν τῶν εἰς τοῦτο συλλεγέντων ἡ δέησις ἐπὶ τοῖς ἀνοσίως ὑπ' ἐκείνου κατεγχειρουμένοις. 22 σύν τε τούτοις οἱ περὶ τῶν πολιτῶν θρασυνθέντες οὐκ ἠνείχοντο τέλεον αὐτοῦ ἐπικειμένου καὶ τὸ τῆς προθέσεως ἐκπληροῦν διανοουμένου, 23 φωνήσαντες δὲ τὴν ὁρμὴν ἐπὶ τὰ ὅπλα ποιήσασθαι καὶ θαρραλέως ὑπὲρ τοῦ πατρῴου νόμου τελευτᾶν ἱκανὴν ἐποίησαν ἐν τῷ τόπῳ τραχύτητα, μόλις δὲ ὑπό τε τῶν γεραιῶν καὶ τῶν πρεσβυτέρων ἀποτραπέντες ἐπὶ τὴν αὐτὴν τῆς δεήσεως παρῆσαν στάσιν. 24 καὶ τὸ μὲν πλῆθος ὡς ἔμπροσθεν ἐν τούτοις ἀνεστρέφετο δεόμενον. 25 οἱ δὲ περὶ τὸν βασιλέα πρεσβύτεροι πολλαχῶς ἐπειρῶντο τὸν ἀγέρωχον αὐτοῦ νοῦν ἐξιστάνειν τῆς ἐντεθυμημένης ἐπιβουλῆς. 26 θρασυνθεὶς δὲ καὶ πάντα παραπέμψας ἤδη καὶ πρόσβασιν ἐποιεῖτο τέλος ἐπιθήσειν δοκῶν τῷ προειρημένῳ. 27 ταῦτα οὖν καὶ οἱ περὶ αὐτὸν ὄντες θεωροῦντες ἐτράπησαν εἰς τὸ σὺν τοῖς ἡμετέροις ἐπικαλεῖσθαι τὸν πᾶν κράτος ἔχοντα τοῖς παροῦσιν ἐπαμῦναι μὴ παριδόντα τὴν ἄνομον καὶ ὑπερήφανον πρᾶξιν. 28 ἐκ δὲ τῆς πυκνοτάτης τε καὶ ἐμπόνου τῶν ὄχλων συναγομένης κραυγῆς ἀνείκαστός τις ἦν βοή· 29 δοκεῖν γὰρ ἦν μὴ μόνον τοὺς ἀνθρώπους, ἀλλὰ καὶ τὰ τείχη καὶ τὸ πᾶν ἔδαφος ἠχεῖν ἅτε δὴ τῶν πάντων τότε θάνατον ἀλλασσομένων ἀντὶ τῆς τοῦ τόπου βεβηλώσεως.

2 Ὁ μὲν οὖν ἀρχιερεὺς Σιμων ἐξ ἐναντίας τοῦ ναοῦ κάμψας τὰ γόνατα καὶ τὰς χεῖρας προτείνας εὐτάκτως ἐποιήσατο τὴν δέησιν τοιαύτην 2 Κύριε κύριε, βασιλεῦ τῶν οὐρανῶν καὶ δέσποτα πάσης κτίσεως, ἅγιε ἐν ἁγίοις, μόναρχε, παντοκράτωρ, πρόσχες ἡμῖν καταπονουμένοις ὑπὸ ἀνοσίου καὶ βεβήλου θράσει καὶ σθένει πεφρυαγμένου. 3 σὺ γὰρ ὁ κτίσας τὰ πάντα καὶ τῶν ὅλων ἐπικρατῶν δυνάστης δίκαιος εἶ καὶ τοὺς ὕβρει καὶ ἀγερωχίᾳ τι πράσσοντας κρίνεις. 4 σὺ τοὺς ἔμπροσθεν ἀδικίαν ποιήσαντας, ἐν οἷς καὶ γίγαντες ἦσαν ῥώμῃ καὶ θράσει πεποιθότες, διέφθειρας ἐπαγαγὼν αὐτοῖς ἀμέτρητον ὕδωρ. 5 σὺ τοὺς ὑπερηφανίαν ἐργαζομένους Σοδομίτας διαδήλους ταῖς κακίαις γενομένους πυρὶ καὶ θείῳ κατέφλεξας παράδειγμα τοῖς ἐπιγινομένοις καταστήσας. 6 σὺ τὸν θρασὺν Φαραω καταδουλωσάμενον τὸν λαόν σου τὸν ἅγιον Ισραηλ ποικίλαις καὶ πολλαῖς δοκιμάσας τιμωρίαις ἐγνώρισας τὴν σὴν δύναμιν, ἐφ' οἷς ἐγνώρισας τὸ μέγα σου κράτος. 7 καὶ ἐπιδιώξαντα αὐτὸν σὺν ἅρμασιν καὶ ὄχλων πλήθει ἐπέκλυσας βάθει θαλάσσης, τοὺς δὲ ἐμπιστεύσαντας ἐπὶ σοὶ τῷ τῆς ἁπάσης κτίσεως δυναστεύοντι σώους διεκόμισας, 8 οἳ καὶ συνιδόντες ἔργα

remained behind in the city were agitated and hurried out, supposing that something mysterious was occurring. 18 Young women who had been secluded in their chambers rushed out with their mothers, sprinkled their hair with dust,[a] and filled the streets with groans and lamentations. 19 Those women who had recently been arrayed for marriage abandoned the bridal chambers[b] prepared for wedded union, and, neglecting proper modesty, in a disorderly rush flocked together in the city. 20 Mothers and nurses abandoned even newborn children here and there, some in houses and some in the streets, and without a backward look they crowded together at the most high temple. 21 Various were the supplications of those gathered there because of what the king was profanely plotting. 22 In addition, the bolder of the citizens would not tolerate the completion of his plans or the fulfillment of his intended purpose. 23 They shouted to their compatriots to take arms and die courageously for the ancestral law, and created a considerable disturbance in the holy place;[c] and being barely restrained by the old men and the elders,[d] they resorted to the same posture of supplication as the others. 24 Meanwhile the crowd, as before, was engaged in prayer, 25 while the elders near the king tried in various ways to change his arrogant mind from the plan that he had conceived. 26 But he, in his arrogance, took heed of nothing, and began now to approach, determined to bring the aforesaid plan to a conclusion. 27 When those who were around him observed this, they turned, together with our people, to call upon him who has all power to defend them in the present trouble and not to overlook this unlawful and haughty deed. 28 The continuous, vehement, and concerted cry of the crowds[e] resulted in an immense uproar; 29 for it seemed that not only the people but also the walls and the whole earth around echoed, because indeed all at that time[f] preferred death to the profanation of the place.

2 Then the high priest Simon, facing the sanctuary, bending his knees and extending his hands with calm dignity, prayed as follows:[g] 2 "Lord, Lord, king of the heavens, and sovereign of all creation, holy among the holy ones, the only ruler, almighty, give attention to us who are suffering grievously from an impious and profane man, puffed up in his audacity and power. 3 For you, the creator of all things and the governor of all, are a just Ruler, and you judge those who have done anything in insolence and arrogance. 4 You destroyed those who in the past committed injustice, among whom were even giants who trusted in their strength and boldness, whom you destroyed by bringing on them a boundless flood. 5 You consumed with fire and sulfur the people of Sodom who acted arrogantly, who were notorious for their vices;[h] and you made them an example to those who should come afterward. 6 You made known your mighty power by inflicting many and varied punishments on the audacious Pharaoh who had enslaved your holy people Israel. 7 And when he pursued them with chariots and a mass of troops, you overwhelmed him in the depths of the sea, but carried through safely those who had put their confidence in you, the Ruler over the whole creation. 8 And when they had seen

a Other ancient authorities add *and ashes* *b* Or *the canopies* *c* Gk *the place* *d* Other ancient authorities read *priests* *e* Other ancient authorities read *vehement cry of the assembled crowds* *f* Other ancient authorities lack *at that time* *g* Other ancient authorities lack verse 1 *h* Other ancient authorities read *secret in their vices*

σῆς χειρὸς ᾔνεσάν σε τὸν παντοκράτορα. 9 σύ, βασιλεῦ,
κτίσας τὴν ἀπέραντον καὶ ἀμέτρητον γῆν ἐξελέξω τὴν πόλιν
ταύτην καὶ ἡγίασας τὸν τόπον τοῦτον εἰς ὄνομά σοι τῷ τῶν
ἁπάντων ἀπροσδεεῖ καὶ παρεδόξασας ἐν ἐπιφανείᾳ μεγαλο-
πρεπεῖ σύστασιν ποιησάμενος αὐτοῦ πρὸς δόξαν τοῦ μεγάλου καὶ ἐντίμου ὀνόματός σου. 10 καὶ ἀγαπῶν τὸν οἶκον τοῦ
Ισραηλ ἐπηγγείλω διότι, ἐὰν γένηται ἡμῶν ἀποστροφὴ καὶ
καταλάβῃ ἡμᾶς στενοχωρία καὶ ἐλθόντες εἰς τὸν τόπον τοῦτον δεηθῶμεν, εἰσακούσῃ τῆς δεήσεως ἡμῶν. 11 καὶ δὴ
πιστὸς εἶ καὶ ἀληθινός. 12 ἐπεὶ δὲ πλεονάκις θλιβέντων τῶν
πατέρων ἡμῶν ἐβοήθησας αὐτοῖς ἐν τῇ ταπεινώσει καὶ ἐρρύσω αὐτοὺς ἐκ μεγάλων κακῶν, 13 ἰδοὺ δὲ νῦν, ἅγιε βασιλεῦ,
διὰ τὰς πολλὰς καὶ μεγάλας ἡμῶν ἁμαρτίας καταπονούμεθα
καὶ ὑπετάγημεν τοῖς ἐχθροῖς ἡμῶν καὶ παρείμεθα ἐν
ἀδυναμίαις. 14 ἐν δὲ τῇ ἡμετέρᾳ καταπτώσει ὁ θρασὺς καὶ
βέβηλος οὗτος ἐπιτηδεύει καθυβρίσαι τὸν ἐπὶ τῆς γῆς ἀνα-
δεδειγμένον τῷ ὀνόματι τῆς δόξης σου ἅγιον τόπον. 15 τὸ
μὲν γὰρ κατοικητήριόν σου οὐρανὸς τοῦ οὐρανοῦ ἀνέφικτος
ἀνθρώποις ἐστίν. 16 ἀλλὰ ἐπεὶ εὐδοκήσας τὴν δόξαν σου ἐν
τῷ λαῷ σου Ισραηλ ἡγίασας τὸν τόπον τοῦτον, 17 μὴ ἐκδικήσῃς ἡμᾶς ἐν τῇ τούτων ἀκαθαρσίᾳ μηδὲ εὐθύνῃς ἡμᾶς ἐν
βεβηλώσει, ἵνα μὴ καυχήσωνται οἱ παράνομοι ἐν θυμῷ αὐτῶν
μηδὲ ἀγαλλιάσωνται ἐν ὑπερηφανίᾳ γλώσσης αὐτῶν λέγοντες 18 Ἡμεῖς κατεπατήσαμεν τὸν οἶκον τοῦ ἁγιασμοῦ, ὡς
καταπατοῦνται οἱ οἶκοι τῶν προσοχθισμάτων. 19 ἀπάλειψον
τὰς ἁμαρτίας ἡμῶν καὶ διασκέδασον τὰς ἀμβλακίας ἡμῶν
καὶ ἐπίφανον τὸ ἔλεός σου κατὰ τὴν ὥραν ταύτην. 20 ταχὺ
προκαταλαβέτωσαν ἡμᾶς οἱ οἰκτιρμοί σου, καὶ δὸς αἰνέσεις
ἐν τῷ στόματι τῶν καταπεπτωκότων καὶ συντετριμμένων
τὰς ψυχὰς ποιήσας ἡμῖν εἰρήνην.

21 Ἐνταῦθα ὁ πάντων ἐπόπτης θεὸς καὶ προπάτωρ ἅγιος
ἐν ἁγίοις εἰσακούσας τῆς ἐνθέσμου λιτανείας, τὸν ὕβρει καὶ
θράσει μεγάλως ἐπηρμένον ἐμάστιξεν αὐτὸν 22 ἔνθεν καὶ
ἔνθεν κραδάνας αὐτὸν ὡς κάλαμον ὑπὸ ἀνέμου ὥστε κατ᾽
ἐδάφους ἄπρακτον, ἔτι καὶ τοῖς μέλεσιν παραλελυμένον
μηδὲ φωνῆσαι δύνασθαι δικαίᾳ περιπεπληγμένον κρίσει.
23 ὅθεν οἵ τε φίλοι καὶ σωματοφύλακες ὀξεῖαν ἰδόντες τὴν
καταλαβοῦσαν αὐτὸν εὔθυναν φοβούμενοι μὴ καὶ τὸ ζῆν ἐκ-
λείπῃ, ταχέως αὐτὸν ἐξείλκυσαν ὑπερβάλλοντι καταπεπληγ-
μένοι φόβῳ. 24 ἐν χρόνῳ δὲ ὕστερον ἀναλεξάμενος αὐτὸν οὐδαμῶς εἰς μετάμελον ἦλθεν ἐπιτιμηθείς, ἀπειλὰς δὲ πικρὰς
θέμενος ἀνέλυσεν.

25 Διακομισθεὶς δὲ εἰς τὴν Αἴγυπτον καὶ τὰ τῆς κακίας
ἐπαύξων διά τε τῶν προαποδεδειγμένων συμποτῶν καὶ
ἑταίρων τοῦ παντὸς δικαίου κεχωρισμένων 26 οὐ μόνον ταῖς
ἀναριθμήτοις ἀσελγείαις διηρκέσθη, ἀλλὰ καὶ ἐπὶ τοσοῦτον
θράσους προῆλθεν ὥστε δυσφημίας ἐν τοῖς τόποις συνί-
στασθαι καὶ πολλοὺς τῶν φίλων ἀτενίζοντας εἰς τὴν τοῦ
βασιλέως πρόθεσιν καὶ αὐτοὺς ἕπεσθαι τῇ ἐκείνου θελήσει.
27 προέθετο δημοσίᾳ κατὰ τοῦ ἔθνους διαδοῦναι ψόγον· ἐπὶ
τοῦ κατὰ τὴν αὐλὴν πύργου στήλην ἀναστήσας ἐκόλαψεν
γραφὴν 28 μηδένα τῶν μὴ θυόντων εἰς τὰ ἱερὰ αὐτῶν εἰσιέναι, πάντας δὲ τοὺς Ιουδαίους εἰς λαογραφίαν καὶ οἰκετικὴν
διάθεσιν ἀχθῆναι, τοὺς δὲ ἀντιλέγοντας βίᾳ φερομένους τοῦ
ζῆν μεταστῆσαι, 29 τούς τε ἀπογραφομένους χαράσσεσθαι
καὶ διὰ πυρὸς εἰς τὸ σῶμα παρασήμῳ Διονύσου κισσοφύλλῳ,

works of your hands, they praised you, the Almighty. 9 You,
O King, when you had created the boundless and immeasurable earth, chose this city and sanctified this place for your
name, though you have no need of anything; and when you
had glorified it by your magnificent manifestation,[a] you
made it a firm foundation for the glory of your great and
honored name. 10 And because you love the house of Israel,
you promised that if we should have reverses and tribulation
should overtake us, you would listen to our petition when
we come to this place and pray. 11 And indeed you are faithful and true. 12 And because oftentimes when our fathers
were oppressed you helped them in their humiliation, and
rescued them from great evils, 13 see now, O holy King, that
because of our many and great sins we are crushed with suffering, subjected to our enemies, and overtaken by helplessness. 14 In our downfall this audacious and profane man
undertakes to violate the holy place on earth dedicated to
your glorious name. 15 For your dwelling is the heaven of
heavens, unapproachable by human beings. 16 But because
you graciously bestowed your glory on your people Israel,
you sanctified this place. 17 Do not punish us for the defilement committed by these men, or call us to account for this
profanation, otherwise the transgressors will boast in their
wrath and exult in the arrogance of their tongue, saying,
18 'We have trampled down the house of the sanctuary as the
houses of the abominations are trampled down.' 19 Wipe
away our sins and disperse our errors, and reveal your mercy
at this hour. 20 Speedily let your mercies overtake us, and
put praises in the mouth of those who are downcast and broken in spirit, and give us peace."

21 Thereupon God, who oversees all things, the first
Father of all, holy among the holy ones, having heard the
lawful supplication, scourged him who had exalted himself
in insolence and audacity. 22 He shook him on this side and
that as a reed is shaken by the wind, so that he lay helpless
on the ground and, besides being paralyzed in his limbs, was
unable even to speak, since he was smitten[b] by a righteous
judgment. 23 Then both friends and bodyguards, seeing the
severe punishment that had overtaken him, and fearing that
he would lose his life, quickly dragged him out, panic-strick-
en in their exceedingly great fear. 24 After a while he recovered, and though he had been punished, he by no means
repented, but went away uttering bitter threats.

25 When he arrived in Egypt, he increased in his deeds of
malice, abetted by the previously mentioned drinking companions and comrades, who were strangers to everything
just. 26 He was not content with his uncounted licentious
deeds, but even continued with such audacity that he framed
evil reports in the various localities; and many of his friends,
intently observing the king's purpose, themselves also followed his will. 27 He proposed to inflict public disgrace on
the Jewish community,[c] and he set up a stone[d] on the tower
in the courtyard with this inscription: 28 "None of those who
do not sacrifice shall enter their sanctuaries, and all Jews
shall be subjected to a registration involving poll tax and to
the status of slaves. Those who object to this are to be taken
by force and put to death; 29 those who are registered are
also to be branded on their bodies by fire with the ivy-leaf

a Or *epiphany* *b* Other ancient authorities read *pierced* *c* Gk *the nation* *d* Gk *stele*

οὓς καὶ καταχωρίσαι εἰς τὴν προσυνεσταλμένην αὐθεντίαν.
30 ἵνα δὲ μὴ τοῖς πᾶσιν ἀπεχθόμενος φαίνηται, ὑπέγραψεν
Ἐὰν δέ τινες ἐξ αὐτῶν προαιρῶνται ἐν τοῖς κατὰ τὰς τελετὰς μεμυημένοις ἀναστρέφεσθαι, τούτους ἰσοπολίτας
Ἀλεξανδρεῦσιν εἶναι.

31 Ἔνιοι μὲν οὖν ἐπιπολαίως τὰς τῆς πόλεως εὐσεβείας
ἐπιβάθρας στυγοῦντες εὐχερῶς ἑαυτοὺς ἐδίδοσαν ὡς μεγάλης τινὸς κοινωνήσοντες εὐκλείας ἀπὸ τῆς ἐσομένης τῷ
βασιλεῖ συναναστροφῆς. 32 οἱ δὲ πλεῖστοι γενναίᾳ ψυχῇ
ἐνίσχυσαν καὶ οὐ διέστησαν τῆς εὐσεβείας τά τε χρήματα
περὶ τοῦ ζῆν ἀντικαταλλασσόμενοι ἀδεῶς ἐπειρῶντο
ἑαυτοὺς ῥύσασθαι ἐκ τῶν ἀπογραφῶν· 33 εὐέλπιδές τε καθειστήκεισαν ἀντιλήμψεως τεύξασθαι καὶ τοὺς ἀποχωροῦντας
ἐξ αὐτῶν ἐβδελύσσοντο καὶ ὡς πολεμίους τοῦ ἔθνους ἔκρινον
καὶ τῆς κοινῆς συναναστροφῆς καὶ εὐχρηστίας ἐστέρουν.

3 Ἃ καὶ μεταλαμβάνων ὁ δυσσεβὴς ἐπὶ τοσοῦτον ἐξε-
χόλησεν ὥστε οὐ μόνον τοῖς κατὰ Ἀλεξάνδρειαν διοργί-
ζεσθαι, ἀλλὰ καὶ τοῖς ἐν τῇ χώρᾳ βαρυτέρως ἐναντιωθῆναι
καὶ προστάξαι σπεύσαντας συναγαγεῖν πάντας ἐπὶ τὸ αὐτὸ
καὶ χειρίστῳ μόρῳ τοῦ ζῆν μεταστῆσαι. 2 τούτων δὲ οἰκον-
ομουμένων φήμη δυσμενὴς ἐξηχεῖτο κατὰ τοῦ γένους ἀνθρώποις συμφρονοῦσιν εἰς κακοποίησιν ἀφορμῆς διδομένης εἰς
διάθεσιν ὡς ἂν ἀπὸ τῶν νομίμων αὐτοὺς κωλυόντων. 3 οἱ δὲ
Ιουδαῖοι τὴν μὲν πρὸς τοὺς βασιλεῖς εὔνοιαν καὶ πίστιν
ἀδιάστροφον ἦσαν φυλάσσοντες, 4 σεβόμενοι δὲ τὸν θεὸν
καὶ τῷ τούτου νόμῳ πολιτευόμενοι χωρισμὸν ἐποίουν ἐπὶ τῷ
κατὰ τὰς τροφάς, δι' ἣν αἰτίαν ἐνίοις ἀπεχθεῖς ἐφαίνοντο.
5 τῇ δὲ τῶν δικαίων εὐπραξίᾳ κοσμοῦντες τὴν συνανα-
στροφὴν ἅπασιν ἀνθρώποις εὐδόκιμοι καθειστήκεισαν. 6 τὴν
μὲν οὖν περὶ τοῦ γένους ἐν πᾶσιν θρυλουμένην εὐπραξίαν οἱ
ἀλλόφυλοι οὐδαμῶς διηριθμήσαντο, 7 τὴν δὲ περὶ τῶν προσ-
κυνήσεων καὶ τροφῶν διάστασιν ἐθρύλουν φάσκοντες μήτε
τῷ βασιλεῖ μήτε ταῖς δυνάμεσιν ὁμοσπόνδους τοὺς ἀνθρώπους γίνεσθαι, δυσμενεῖς δὲ εἶναι καὶ μέγα τι τοῖς πράγμασιν ἐναντιουμένους. καὶ οὐ τῷ τυχόντι περιῆψαν ψόγῳ. 8 οἱ
δὲ κατὰ τὴν πόλιν Ἕλληνες οὐδὲν ἠδικημένοι ταραχὴν
ἀπροσδόκητον περὶ τοὺς ἀνθρώπους θεωροῦντες καὶ συνδρο-
μὰς ἀπροσκόπους γινομένας βοηθεῖν μὲν οὐκ ἔσθενον,
τυραννικὴ γὰρ ἦν ἡ διάθεσις, παρεκάλουν δὲ καὶ δυσφόρως
εἶχον καὶ μεταπεσεῖσθαι ταῦτα ὑπελάμβανον· 9 μὴ γὰρ
οὕτω παροραθήσεσθαι τηλικοῦτο σύστεμα μηδὲν ἠγνοηκός.
10 ἤδη δὲ καί τινες γείτονές τε καὶ φίλοι καὶ συμπραγμα-
τευόμενοι μυστικῶς τινας ἐπισπώμενοι πίστεις ἐδίδουν
συνασπιεῖν καὶ πᾶν ἐκτενὲς προσοίσεσθαι πρὸς ἀντίλημψιν.

11 Ἐκεῖνος μὲν οὖν τῇ κατὰ τὸ παρὸν εὐημερίᾳ γεγαυρω-
μένος καὶ οὐ καθορῶν τὸ τοῦ μεγίστου θεοῦ κράτος,
ὑπολαμβάνων δὲ διηνεκῶς ἐν τῇ αὐτῇ διαμενεῖν βουλῇ,
ἔγραψεν κατ' αὐτῶν ἐπιστολὴν τήνδε 12 Βασιλεὺς Πτολεμαῖος Φιλοπάτωρ τοῖς κατ' Αἴγυπτον καὶ κατὰ τόπον στρατηγοῖς καὶ στρατιώταις χαίρειν καὶ ἐρρῶσθαι· 13 ἔρρωμαι δὲ
καὶ αὐτὸς ἐγὼ καὶ τὰ πράγματα ἡμῶν. 14 τῆς εἰς τὴν Ἀσίαν

symbol of Dionysus, and they shall also be reduced to their
former limited status." 30 In order that he might not appear
to be an enemy of all, he inscribed below: "But if any of them
prefer to join those who have been initiated into the mysteries, they shall have equal citizenship with the Alexandrians."

31 Now some, however, with an obvious abhorrence of
the price to be exacted for maintaining the religion of their
city,[a] readily gave themselves up, since they expected to
enhance their reputation by their future association with the
king. 32 But the majority acted firmly with a courageous spirit and did not abandon their religion; and by paying money
in exchange for life they confidently attempted to save themselves from the registration. 33 They remained resolutely
hopeful of obtaining help, and they abhorred those who separated themselves from them, considering them to be enemies of the Jewish nation,[b] and depriving them of companionship and mutual help.

3 When the impious king comprehended this situation, he
became so infuriated that not only was he enraged
against those Jews who lived in Alexandria, but was still
more bitterly hostile toward those in the countryside; and he
ordered that all should promptly be gathered into one place,
and put to death by the most cruel means. 2 While these
matters were being arranged, a hostile rumor was circulated
against the Jewish nation by some who conspired to do them
ill, a pretext being given by a report that they hindered
others[c] from the observance of their customs. 3 The Jews,
however, continued to maintain goodwill and unswerving
loyalty toward the dynasty; 4 but because they worshiped
God and conducted themselves by his law, they kept their
separateness with respect to foods. For this reason they
appeared hateful to some; 5 but since they adorned their
style of life with the good deeds of upright people, they were
established in good repute with everyone. 6 Nevertheless
those of other races paid no heed to their good service to
their nation, which was common talk among all; 7 instead
they gossiped about the differences in worship and foods,
alleging that these people were loyal neither to the king nor
to his authorities, but were hostile and greatly opposed to his
government. So they attached no ordinary reproach to them.

8 The Greeks in the city, though wronged in no way,
when they saw an unexpected tumult around these people
and the crowds that suddenly were forming, were not strong
enough to help them, for they lived under tyranny. They did
try to console them, being grieved at the situation, and
expected that matters would change; 9 for such a great community ought not be left to its fate when it had committed no
offense. 10 And already some of their neighbors and friends
and business associates had taken some of them aside privately and were pledging to protect them and to exert more
earnest efforts for their assistance.

11 Then the king, boastful of his present good fortune,
and not considering the might of the supreme God,[d] but
assuming that he would persevere constantly in his same
purpose, wrote this letter against them:

12 "King Ptolemy Philopator to his generals and soldiers
in Egypt and all its districts, greetings and good health:

13 "I myself and our government are faring well. 14 When

a Meaning of Gk uncertain *b* Gk *the nation* *c* Gk *them* *d* Gk *the greatest God*

GREEK OLD TESTAMENT

γενομένης ἡμῖν ἐπιστρατείας, ἧς ἴστε καὶ αὐτοί, τῇ τῶν θεῶν ἀπροπτώτῳ συμμαχίᾳ κατὰ λόγον ἐπὶ τέλος ἀχθείσης 15 ἡγησάμεθα μὴ βίᾳ δόρατος, ἐπιεικείᾳ δὲ καὶ πολλῇ φιλανθρωπίᾳ τιθηνήσασθαι τὰ κατοικοῦντα Κοίλην Συρίαν καὶ Φοινίκην ἔθνη εὖ ποιῆσαί τε ἀσμένως. 16 καὶ τοῖς κατὰ πόλιν ἱεροῖς ἀπονείμαντες προσόδους πλείστας προήχθημεν καὶ εἰς τὰ Ιεροσόλυμα ἀναβάντες τιμῆσαι τὸ ἱερὸν τῶν ἀλιτηρίων καὶ μηδέποτε ληγόντων τῆς ἀνοίας. 17 οἱ δὲ λόγῳ μὲν τὴν ἡμετέραν ἀποδεξάμενοι παρουσίαν, τῷ δὲ πράγματι νόθως, προθυμηθέντων ἡμῶν εἰσελθεῖν εἰς τὸν ναὸν αὐτῶν καὶ τοῖς ἐκπρεπέσιν καὶ καλλίστοις ἀναθήμασιν τιμῆσαι 18 τύφοις φερόμενοι παλαιοτέροις εἶρξαν ἡμᾶς τῆς εἰσόδου λειπόμενοι τῆς ἡμετέρας ἀλκῆς δι' ἣν ἔχομεν πρὸς ἅπαντας ἀνθρώπους φιλανθρωπίαν. 19 τὴν δὲ αὐτῶν εἰς ἡμᾶς δυσμένειαν ἔκδηλον καθιστάντες ὡς μονώτατοι τῶν ἐθνῶν βασιλεῦσιν καὶ τοῖς ἑαυτῶν εὐεργέταις ὑψαυχενοῦντες οὐδὲν γνήσιον βούλονται φέρειν. 20 ἡμεῖς δὲ τῇ τούτων ἀνοίᾳ συμπεριενεχθέντες καὶ μετὰ νίκης διακομισθέντες εἰς τὴν Αἴγυπτον τοῖς πᾶσιν ἔθνεσιν φιλανθρώπως ἀπαντήσαντες καθὼς ἔπρεπεν ἐποιήσαμεν, 21 ἐν δὲ τούτοις πρὸς τοὺς ὁμοφύλους αὐτῶν ἀμνησικακίαν ἅπασιν γνωρίζοντες. διά τε τὴν συμμαχίαν καὶ τὰ πεπιστευμένα μετὰ ἁπλότητος αὐτοῖς ἀρχῆθεν μύρια πράγματα τολμήσαντες ἐξαλλοιῶσαι ἐβουλήθημεν καὶ πολιτείας αὐτοὺς Ἀλεξανδρέων καταξιῶσαι καὶ μετόχους τῶν ἀεὶ ἱερῶν καταστῆσαι. 22 οἱ δὲ τοὐναντίον ἐκδεχόμενοι καὶ τῇ συμφύτῳ κακοηθείᾳ τὸ καλὸν ἀπωσάμενοι, διηνεκῶς δὲ εἰς τὸ φαῦλον ἐκνεύοντες 23 οὐ μόνον ἀπεστρέψαντο τὴν ἀτίμητον πολιτείαν, ἀλλὰ καὶ βδελύσσονται λόγῳ τε καὶ σιγῇ τοὺς ἐν αὐτοῖς ὀλίγους πρὸς ἡμᾶς γνησίως διακειμένους παρ' ἕκαστα ὑφορώμενοι μετὰ τῆς δυσκλεεστάτης ἐμβιώσεως διὰ τάχους ἡμᾶς καταστρέψαι τὰ πράγματα. 24 διὸ καὶ τεκμηρίοις καλῶς πεπεισμένοι τούτους κατὰ πάντα δυσνοεῖν ἡμῖν τρόπον καὶ προνοούμενοι μήποτε αἰφνιδίου μετέπειτα ταραχῆς ἐνστάσης ἡμῖν τοὺς δυσσεβεῖς τούτους κατὰ νώτου προδότας καὶ βαρβάρους ἔχωμεν πολεμίους 25 προστετάχαμεν ἅμα τῷ προσπεσεῖν τὴν ἐπιστολὴν τήνδε αὐθωρὶ τοὺς ἐννεμομένους σὺν γυναιξὶ καὶ τέκνοις μετὰ ὕβρεων καὶ σκυλμῶν ἀποστεῖλαι πρὸς ἡμᾶς ἐν δεσμοῖς σιδηροῖς πάντοθεν κατακεκλεισμένους, εἰς ἀνήκεστον καὶ δυσκλεῆ πρέποντα δυσμενέσι φόνον. 26 τούτων γὰρ ὁμοῦ κολασθέντων διειλήφαμεν εἰς τὸν ἐπίλοιπον χρόνον τελείως ἡμῖν τὰ πράγματα ἐν εὐσταθείᾳ καὶ τῇ βελτίστῃ διαθέσει κατασταθήσεσθαι. 27 ὃς δ' ἂν σκεπάσῃ τινὰ τῶν Ιουδαίων ἀπὸ γεραιοῦ μέχρι νηπίου καὶ μέχρι τῶν ὑπομαστιδίων, αἰσχίσταις βασάνοις ἀποτυμπανισθήσεται πανοικίᾳ. 28 μηνύειν δὲ τὸν βουλόμενον, ἐφ' ᾧ τὴν οὐσίαν τοῦ ἐμπίπτοντος ὑπὸ τὴν εὔθυναν λήμψεται καὶ ἐκ τοῦ βασιλικοῦ ἀργυρίου δραχμὰς δισχιλίας καὶ τῇ ἐλευθερίᾳ στεφανωθήσεται. 29 πᾶς δὲ τόπος, οὗ ἐὰν φωραθῇ τὸ σύνολον σκεπαζόμενος Ιουδαῖος, ἄβατος καὶ πυριφλεγὴς γινέσθω καὶ πάσῃ θνητῇ φύσει καθ' ἅπαν ἄχρηστος φανήσεται εἰς τὸν ἀεὶ χρόνον.

30 Καὶ ὁ μὲν τῆς ἐπιστολῆς τύπος οὕτως ἐγέγραπτο.

NEW REVISED STANDARD VERSION

our expedition took place in Asia, as you yourselves know, it was brought to conclusion, according to plan, by the gods' deliberate alliance with us in battle, 15 and we considered that we should not rule the nations inhabiting Coelesyria and Phoenicia by the power of the spear, but should cherish them with clemency and great benevolence, gladly treating them well. 16 And when we had granted very great revenues to the temples in the cities, we came on to Jerusalem also, and went up to honor the temple of those wicked people, who never cease from their folly. 17 They accepted our presence by word, but insincerely by deed, because when we proposed to enter their inner temple and honor it with magnificent and most beautiful offerings, 18 they were carried away by their traditional arrogance, and excluded us from entering; but they were spared the exercise of our power because of the benevolence that we have toward all. 19 By maintaining their manifest ill-will toward us, they become the only people among all nations who hold their heads high in defiance of kings and their own benefactors, and are unwilling to regard any action as sincere.

20 "But we, when we arrived in Egypt victorious, accommodated ourselves to their folly and did as was proper, since we treat all nations with benevolence. 21 Among other things, we made known to all our amnesty toward their compatriots here, both because of their alliance with us and the myriad affairs liberally entrusted to them from the beginning; and we ventured to make a change, by deciding both to deem them worthy of Alexandrian citizenship and to make them participants in our regular religious rites.[a] 22 But in their innate malice they took this in a contrary spirit, and disdained what is good. Since they incline constantly to evil, 23 they not only spurn the priceless citizenship, but also both by speech and by silence they abominate those few among them who are sincerely disposed toward us; in every situation, in accordance with their infamous way of life, they secretly suspect that we may soon alter our policy. 24 Therefore, fully convinced by these indications that they are ill-disposed toward us in every way, we have taken precautions so that, if a sudden disorder later arises against us, we shall not have these impious people behind our backs as traitors and barbarous enemies. 25 Therefore we have given orders that, as soon as this letter arrives, you are to send to us those who live among you, together with their wives and children, with insulting and harsh treatment, and bound securely with iron fetters, to suffer the sure and shameful death that befits enemies. 26 For when all of these have been punished, we are sure that for the remaining time the government will be established for ourselves in good order and in the best state. 27 But those who shelter any of the Jews, whether old people or children or even infants, will be tortured to death with the most hateful torments, together with their families. 28 Any who are willing to give information will receive the property of those who incur the punishment, and also two thousand drachmas from the royal treasury, and will be awarded their freedom.[b] 29 Every place detected sheltering a Jew is to be made unapproachable and burned with fire, and shall become useless for all time to any mortal creature." 30 The letter was written in the above form.

a Other ancient authorities read *partners of our regular priests*
b Gk *crowned with freedom*

Greek Old Testament

4 Πάντῃ δέ, ὅπου προσέπιπτεν τοῦτο τὸ πρόσταγμα, δημοτελὴς συνίστατο τοῖς ἔθνεσιν εὐωχία μετὰ ἀλαλαγμῶν καὶ χαρᾶς ὡς ἂν τῆς προκατεσκιρωμένης αὐτοῖς πάλαι κατὰ διάνοιαν μετὰ παρρησίας νῦν ἐκφαινομένης ἀπεχθείας. [2] τοῖς δὲ Ιουδαίοις ἄληκτον πένθος ἦν καὶ πανόδυρτος μετὰ δακρύων βοὴ στεναγμοῖς πεπυρωμένης πάντοθεν αὐτῶν τῆς καρδίας ὀλοφυρομένων τὴν ἀπροσδόκητον ἐξαίφνης αὐτοῖς ἐπικριθεῖσαν ὀλεθρίαν. [3] τίς νομὸς ἢ πόλις ἢ τίς τὸ σύνολον οἰκητὸς τόπος ἢ τίνες ἀγυιαὶ κοπετοῦ καὶ γόων ἐπ᾽ αὐτοῖς οὐκ ἐνεπιπλῶντο; [4] οὕτως γὰρ μετὰ πικρίας ἀνοίκτου ψυχῆς ὑπὸ τῶν κατὰ πόλιν στρατηγῶν ὁμοθυμαδὸν ἐξαπεστέλλοντο ὥστε ἐπὶ ταῖς ἐξάλλοις τιμωρίαις καί τινας τῶν ἐχθρῶν λαμβάνοντας πρὸ τῶν ὀφθαλμῶν τὸν κοινὸν ἔλεον καὶ λογιζομένους τὴν ἄδηλον τοῦ βίου καταστροφὴν δακρύειν αὐτῶν τὴν δυσάθλιον ἐξαποστολήν. [5] ἤγετο γὰρ γεραιῶν πλῆθος πολιᾷ πεπυκασμένων, τὴν ἐκ τοῦ γήρως νωθρότητα ποδῶν ἐπίκυφον ἀνατροπῆς ὁρμῇ βιαίας ἁπάσης αἰδοῦς ἄνευ πρὸς ὀξεῖαν καταχρωμένων πορείαν. [6] αἱ δὲ ἄρτι πρὸς βίου κοινωνίαν γαμικὸν ὑπεληλυθυῖαι παστὸν νεάνιδες ἀντὶ τέρψεως μεταλαβοῦσαι γόους καὶ κόνει τὴν μυροβρεχῆ πεφυρμέναι κόμην, ἀκαλύπτως δὲ ἀγόμεναι θρῆνον ἀνθ᾽ ὑμεναίων ὁμοθυμαδὸν ἐξῆρχον ὡς ἐσπαραγμέναι σκυλμοῖς ἀλλοεθνέσιν· [7] δέσμιαι δὲ δημοσίᾳ μέχρι τῆς εἰς τὸ πλοῖον ἐμβολῆς εἵλκοντο μετὰ βίας. [8] οἵ τε τούτων συνζυγεῖς βρόχοις ἀντὶ στεφέων τοὺς αὐχένας περιπεπλεγμένοι μετὰ ἀκμαίας νεανικῆς ἡλικίας ἀντὶ εὐωχίας καὶ νεωτερικῆς ῥᾳθυμίας τὰς ἐπιλοίπους τῶν γάμων ἡμέρας ἐν θρήνοις διῆγον παρὰ πόδας ἤδη τὸν ᾅδην ὁρῶντες κείμενον. [9] κατήχθησαν δὲ θηρίων τρόπον ἀγόμενοι σιδηροδέσμοις ἀνάγκαις, οἱ μὲν τοῖς ζυγοῖς τῶν πλοίων προσηλωμένοι τοὺς τραχήλους, οἱ δὲ τοὺς πόδας ἀρρήκτοις κατησφαλισμένοι πέδαις, [10] ἔτι καὶ τῷ καθύπερθε πυκνῷ σανιδώματι διακειμένῳ, ὅπως πάντοθεν ἐσκοτισμένοι τοὺς ὀφθαλμοὺς ἀγωγὴν ἐπιβούλων ἐν παντὶ τῷ κατάπλῳ λαμβάνωσιν.

[11] Τούτων δὲ ἐπὶ τὴν λεγομένην Σχεδίαν ἀχθέντων καὶ τοῦ παράπλου περανθέντος, καθὼς ἦν δεδογματισμένον τῷ βασιλεῖ, προσέταξεν αὐτοὺς ἐν τῷ πρὸ τῆς πόλεως ἱπποδρόμῳ παρεμβαλεῖν ἀπλάτῳ καθεστῶτι περιμέτρῳ καὶ πρὸς παραδειγματισμὸν ἄγαν εὐκαιροτάτῳ καθεστῶτι πᾶσι τοῖς καταπορευομένοις εἰς τὴν πόλιν καὶ τοῖς ἐκ τούτων εἰς τὴν χώραν στελλομένοις πρὸς ἐκδημίαν πρὸς τὸ μηδὲ ταῖς δυνάμεσιν αὐτοῦ κοινωνεῖν μηδὲ τὸ σύνολον καταξιῶσαι περιβόλων. [12] ὡς δὲ τοῦτο ἐγενήθη, ἀκούσας τοὺς ἐκ τῆς πόλεως ὁμοεθνεῖς κρυβῇ ἐκπορευομένους πυκνότερον ἀποδύρεσθαι τὴν ἀκλεῆ τῶν ἀδελφῶν ταλαιπωρίαν [13] διοργισθεὶς προσέταξεν καὶ τούτοις ὁμοῦ τὸν αὐτὸν τρόπον ἐπιμελῶς ὡς ἐκείνοις ποιῆσαι μὴ λειπομένοις κατὰ μηδένα τρόπον τῆς ἐκείνων τιμωρίας, [14] ἀπογραφῆναι δὲ πᾶν τὸ φῦλον ἐξ ὀνόματος, οὐκ εἰς τὴν ἔμπροσθεν βραχεῖ προδεδηλωμένην τῶν ἔργων κατάπονον λατρείαν, στρεβλωθέντας δὲ ταῖς παρηγγελμέναις αἰκίαις τὸ τέλος ἀφανίσαι μιᾶς ὑπὸ καιρὸν ἡμέρας. [15] ἐγίνετο μὲν οὖν ἡ τούτων ἀπογραφὴ μετὰ πικρᾶς σπουδῆς καὶ φιλοτίμου προσεδρείας ἀπὸ

New Revised Standard Version

4 In every place, then, where this decree arrived, a feast at public expense was arranged for the Gentiles with shouts and gladness, for the inveterate enmity that had long ago been in their minds was now made evident and outspoken. [2] But among the Jews there was incessant mourning, lamentation, and tearful cries; everywhere their hearts were burning, and they groaned because of the unexpected destruction that had suddenly been decreed for them. [3] What district or city, or what habitable place at all, or what streets were not filled with mourning and wailing for them? [4] For with such a harsh and ruthless spirit were they being sent off, all together, by the generals in the several cities, that at the sight of their unusual punishments, even some of their enemies, perceiving the common object of pity before their eyes, reflected on the uncertainty of life and shed tears at the most miserable expulsion of these people. [5] For a multitude of gray-headed old men, sluggish and bent with age, was being led away, forced to march at a swift pace by the violence with which they were driven in such a shameful manner. [6] And young women who had just entered the bridal chamber[a] to share married life exchanged joy for wailing, their myrrh-perfumed hair sprinkled with ashes, and were carried away unveiled, all together raising a lament instead of a wedding song, as they were torn by the harsh treatment of the heathen.[b] [7] In bonds and in public view they were violently dragged along as far as the place of embarkation. [8] Their husbands, in the prime of youth, their necks encircled with ropes instead of garlands, spent the remaining days of their marriage festival in lamentations instead of good cheer and youthful revelry, seeing death immediately before them.[c] [9] They were brought on board like wild animals, driven under the constraint of iron bonds; some were fastened by the neck to the benches of the boats, others had their feet secured by unbreakable fetters, [10] and in addition they were confined under a solid deck, so that, with their eyes in total darkness, they would undergo treatment befitting traitors during the whole voyage.

11 When these people had been brought to the place called Schedia, and the voyage was concluded as the king had decreed, he commanded that they should be enclosed in the hippodrome that had been built with a monstrous perimeter wall in front of the city, and that was well suited to make them an obvious spectacle to all coming back into the city and to those from the city[d] going out into the country, so that they could neither communicate with the king's forces nor in any way claim to be inside the circuit of the city.[e] [12] And when this had happened, the king, hearing that the Jews' compatriots from the city frequently went out in secret to lament bitterly the ignoble misfortune of their kindred, [13] ordered in his rage that these people be dealt with in precisely the same fashion as the others, not omitting any detail of their punishment. [14] The entire race was to be registered individually, not for the hard labor that has been briefly mentioned before, but to be tortured with the outrages that he had ordered, and at the end to be destroyed in the space of a single day. [15] The registration of these people was therefore conducted with bitter haste and zealous intensity

a Or *the canopy* b Other ancient authorities read *as though torn by heathen whelps* c Gk *seeing Hades already lying at their feet* d Gk *those of them* e Or *claim protection of the walls*; meaning of Gk uncertain

ἀνατολῶν ἡλίου μέχρι δυσμῶν ἀνήνυτον λαμβάνουσα τὸ τέλος ἐπὶ ἡμέρας τεσσαράκοντα.

16 Μεγάλως δὲ καὶ διηνεκῶς ὁ βασιλεὺς χαρᾷ πεπληρωμένος συμπόσια ἐπὶ πάντων τῶν εἰδώλων συνιστάμενος πεπλανημένῃ πόρρω τῆς ἀληθείας φρενὶ καὶ βεβήλῳ στόματι τὰ μὲν κωφὰ καὶ μὴ δυνάμενα αὐτοῖς λαλεῖν ἢ ἀρήγειν ἐπαινῶν, εἰς δὲ τὸν μέγιστον θεὸν τὰ μὴ καθήκοντα λαλῶν. 17 μετὰ δὲ τὸ προειρημένον τοῦ χρόνου διάστημα προσηνέγκαντο οἱ γραμματεῖς τῷ βασιλεῖ μηκέτι ἰσχύειν τὴν τῶν Ιουδαίων ἀπογραφὴν ποιεῖσθαι διὰ τὴν ἀμέτρητον αὐτῶν πληθὺν 18 καίπερ ὄντων ἔτι κατὰ τὴν χώραν τῶν πλειόνων, τῶν μὲν κατὰ τὰς οἰκίας ἔτι συνεστηκότων, τῶν δὲ καὶ κατὰ τόπον, ὡς ἀδυνάτου καθεστῶτος πᾶσιν τοῖς ἐπ' Αἴγυπτον στρατηγοῖς. 19 ἀπειλήσαντος δὲ αὐτοῖς σκληρότερον ὡς δεδωροκοπημένοις εἰς μηχανὴν τῆς ἐκφυγῆς συνέβη σαφῶς αὐτὸν περὶ τούτου πιστωθῆναι 20 λεγόντων μετὰ ἀποδείξεως καὶ τὴν χαρτηρίαν ἤδη καὶ τοὺς γραφικοὺς καλάμους, ἐν οἷς ἐχρῶντο, ἐκλελοιπέναι. 21 τοῦτο δὲ ἦν ἐνέργεια τῆς τοῦ βοηθοῦντος τοῖς Ιουδαίοις ἐξ οὐρανοῦ προνοίας ἀνικήτου.

5 Τότε προσκαλεσάμενος Ἕρμωνα τὸν πρὸς τῇ τῶν ἐλεφάντων ἐπιμελείᾳ βαρείᾳ μεμεστωμένος ὀργῇ καὶ χόλῳ κατὰ πᾶν ἀμετάθετος 2 ἐκέλευσεν ὑπὸ τὴν ἐπερχομένην ἡμέραν δαψιλέσι δράκεσι λιβανωτοῦ καὶ οἴνῳ πλείονι ἀκράτῳ ἅπαντας τοὺς ἐλέφαντας ποτίσαι ὄντας τὸν ἀριθμὸν πεντακοσίους καὶ ἀγριωθέντας τῇ τοῦ πόματος ἀφθόνῳ χορηγίᾳ εἰσαγαγεῖν πρὸς συνάντησιν τοῦ μόρου τῶν Ιουδαίων. 3 ὁ μὲν τάδε προστάσσων ἐτρέπετο πρὸς τὴν εὐωχίαν συναγαγὼν τοὺς μάλιστα τῶν φίλων καὶ τῆς στρατιᾶς ἀπεχθῶς ἔχοντας πρὸς τοὺς Ιουδαίους. 4 ὁ δὲ ἐλεφαντάρχης τὸ προσταγὲν ἀραρότως Ἕρμων συνετέλει. 5 οἵ τε πρὸς τούτοις λειτουργοὶ κατὰ τὴν ἑσπέραν ἐξιόντες τὰς τῶν ταλαιπωρούντων ἐδέσμευον χεῖρας τήν τε λοιπὴν ἐμηχανῶντο περὶ αὐτοὺς ἀσφάλειαν ἔννυχον δόξαντες ὁμοῦ λήμψεσθαι τὸ φῦλον πέρας τῆς ὀλεθρίας. 6 οἱ δὲ πάσης σκέπης ἔρημοι δοκοῦντες εἶναι τοῖς ἔθνεσιν Ιουδαῖοι διὰ τὴν πάντοθεν περιέχουσαν αὐτοὺς μετὰ δεσμῶν ἀνάγκην 7 τὸν παντοκράτορα κύριον καὶ πάσης δυνάμεως δυναστεύοντα, ἐλεήμονα θεὸν αὐτῶν καὶ πατέρα, δυσκαταπαύστῳ βοῇ πάντες μετὰ δακρύων ἐπεκαλέσαντο δεόμενοι 8 τὴν κατ' αὐτῶν μεταστρέψαι βουλὴν ἀνοσίαν καὶ ῥύσασθαι αὐτοὺς μετὰ μεγαλομεροῦς ἐπιφανείας ἐκ τοῦ παρὰ πόδας ἐν ἑτοίμῳ μόρου. 9 τούτων μὲν οὖν ἐκτενῶς ἡ λιτανεία ἀνέβαινεν εἰς τὸν οὐρανόν.

10 Ὁ δὲ Ἕρμων τοὺς ἀνηλεεῖς ἐλέφαντας ποτίσας πεπληρωμένους τῆς τοῦ οἴνου πολλῆς χορηγίας καὶ τοῦ λιβάνου μεμεστωμένους ὄρθριος ἐπὶ τὴν αὐλὴν παρῆν περὶ τούτων προσαγγεῖλαι τῷ βασιλεῖ. 11 τὸ δὲ ἀπ' αἰῶνος χρόνου κτίσμα καλὸν ἐν νυκτὶ καὶ ἡμέρᾳ ἐπιβαλλόμενον ὑπὸ τοῦ χαριζομένου πᾶσιν, οἷς ἂν αὐτὸς θελήσῃ, ὕπνου μέρος ἀπέστειλεν εἰς τὸν βασιλέα, 12 καὶ ἡδίστῳ καὶ βαθεῖ κατεσχέθη τῇ ἐνεργείᾳ τοῦ δεσπότου τῆς ἀθέσμου μὲν προθέσεως πολὺ διεσφαλμένος, τοῦ δὲ ἀμεταθέτου λογισμοῦ μεγάλως διεψευσμένος. 13 οἵ τε Ιουδαῖοι τὴν προσημανθεῖσαν ὥραν διαφυγόντες τὸν ἅγιον ᾔνουν θεὸν αὐτῶν καὶ πάλιν ἠξίουν τὸν εὐκατάλλακτον δεῖξαι μεγαλοσθενοῦς ἑαυτοῦ χειρὸς κράτος ἔθνεσιν ὑπερηφάνοις. 14 μεσούσης δὲ ἤδη δεκάτης ὥρας σχεδὸν ὁ πρὸς ταῖς κλήσεσιν τεταγμένος ἀθρόους

from the rising of the sun until its setting, coming to an end after forty days but still uncompleted.

16 The king was greatly and continually filled with joy, organizing feasts in honor of all his idols, with a mind alienated from truth and with a profane mouth, praising speechless things that are not able even to communicate or to come to one's help, and uttering improper words against the supreme God.[a] 17 But after the previously mentioned interval of time the scribes declared to the king that they were no longer able to take the census of the Jews because of their immense number, 18 though most of them were still in the country, some still residing in their homes, and some at the place;[b] the task was impossible for all the generals in Egypt. 19 After he had threatened them severely, charging that they had been bribed to contrive a means of escape, he was clearly convinced about the matter 20 when they said and proved that both the paper[c] and the pens they used for writing had already given out. 21 But this was an act of the invincible providence of him who was aiding the Jews from heaven.

5 Then the king, completely inflexible, was filled with overpowering anger and wrath; so he summoned Hermon, keeper of the elephants, 2 and ordered him on the following day to drug all the elephants—five hundred in number—with large handfuls of frankincense and plenty of unmixed wine, and to drive them in, maddened by the lavish abundance of drink, so that the Jews might meet their doom. 3 When he had given these orders he returned to his feasting, together with those of his Friends and of the army who were especially hostile toward the Jews. 4 And Hermon, keeper of the elephants, proceeded faithfully to carry out the orders. 5 The servants in charge of the Jews[d] went out in the evening and bound the hands of the wretched people and arranged for their continued custody through the night, convinced that the whole nation would experience its final destruction. 6 For to the Gentiles it appeared that the Jews were left without any aid, 7 because in their bonds they were forcibly confined on every side. But with tears and a voice hard to silence they all called upon the Almighty Lord and Ruler of all power, their merciful God and Father, praying 8 that he avert with vengeance the evil plot against them and in a glorious manifestation rescue them from the fate now prepared for them. 9 So their entreaty ascended fervently to heaven.

10 Hermon, however, when he had drugged the pitiless elephants until they had been filled with a great abundance of wine and satiated with frankincense, presented himself at the courtyard early in the morning to report to the king about these preparations. 11 But the Lord[e] sent upon the king a portion of sleep, that beneficence that from the beginning, night and day, is bestowed by him who grants it to whomever he wishes. 12 And by the action of the Lord he was overcome by so pleasant and deep a sleep[f] that he quite failed in his lawless purpose and was completely frustrated in his inflexible plan. 13 Then the Jews, since they had escaped the appointed hour, praised their holy God and again implored him who is easily reconciled to show the might of his all-powerful hand to the arrogant Gentiles.

14 But now, since it was nearly the middle of the tenth hour, the person who was in charge of the invitations, seeing

a Gk *the greatest God* *b* Other ancient authorities read *on the way*
c Or *paper factory* *d* Gk *them* *e* Gk *he* *f* Other ancient authorities add *from evening until the ninth hour*

GREEK OLD TESTAMENT

τοὺς κλητοὺς ἰδὼν ἔνυξεν προσελθὼν τὸν βασιλέα. 15 καὶ
μόλις διεγείρας ὑπέδειξε τὸν τῆς συμποσίας καιρὸν ἤδη
παρατρέχοντα τὸν περὶ τούτων λόγον ποιούμενος. 16 ὃν ὁ
βασιλεὺς λογισάμενος καὶ τραπεὶς εἰς τὸν πότον ἐκέλευσεν
τοὺς παραγεγονότας ἐπὶ τὴν συμποσίαν ἄντικρυς ἀνακλῖναι
αὐτοῦ. 17 οὗ καὶ γενομένου παρῄνει εἰς εὐωχίαν δόντας
ἑαυτοὺς τὸ παρὸν τῆς συμποσίας ἐπὶ πολὺ γεραιρομένους
εἰς εὐφροσύνην καταθέσθαι μέρος. 18 ἐπὶ πλεῖον δὲ προβαινούσης τῆς ὁμιλίας τὸν Ἕρμωνα προσκαλεσάμενος ὁ
βασιλεὺς μετὰ πικρᾶς ἀπειλῆς ἐπυνθάνετο, τίνος ἕνεκεν αἰτίας εἰάθησαν οἱ Ιουδαῖοι τὴν περιοῦσαν ἡμέραν περιβεβιω-
κότες. 19 τοῦ δὲ ὑποδείξαντος ἔτι νυκτὸς τὸ προσταγὲν ἐπὶ
τέλος ἀγειοχέναι καὶ τῶν φίλων αὐτῷ προσμαρτυρησάντων
20 τὴν ὠμότητα χείρονα Φαλάριδος ἐσχηκὼς ἔφη τῷ τῆς
σήμερον ὕπνῳ χάριν ἔχειν αὐτούς. ἀνυπερθέτως δὲ εἰς τὴν
ἐπιτελοῦσαν ἡμέραν κατὰ τὸ ὅμοιον ἑτοίμασον τοὺς ἐλέφαντας ἐπὶ τὸν τῶν ἀθεμίτων Ιουδαίων ἀφανισμόν. 21 εἰπόντος
δὲ τοῦ βασιλέως ἀσμένως πάντες μετὰ χαρᾶς οἱ παρόντες
ὁμοῦ συναινέσαντες εἰς τὸν ἴδιον οἶκον ἕκαστος ἀνέλυσεν.
22 καὶ οὐχ οὕτως εἰς ὕπνον κατεχρήσαντο τὸν χρόνον τῆς
νυκτός, ὡς εἰς τὸ παντοίους μηχανᾶσθαι τοῖς ταλαιπώροις
δοκοῦσιν ἐμπαιγμούς.

23 Ἄρτι δὲ ἀλεκτρυὼν ἐκέκραγεν ὄρθριος, καὶ τὰ θηρία
καθωπλικὼς ὁ Ἕρμων ἐν τῷ μεγάλῳ περιστύλῳ διεκίνει.
24 τὰ δὲ κατὰ τὴν πόλιν πλήθη συνήθροιστο πρὸς τὴν οἰκτρο-
τάτην θεωρίαν προσδοκῶντα τὴν πρωίαν μετὰ σπουδῆς. 25 οἱ
δὲ Ιουδαῖοι κατὰ τὸν ἀμερῆ ψυχουλκούμενοι χρόνον πολύ-
δακρυν ἱκετείαν ἐν μέλεσιν γοεροῖς τείνοντες τὰς χεῖρας
εἰς τὸν οὐρανὸν ἐδέοντο τοῦ μεγίστου θεοῦ πάλιν αὐτοῖς
βοηθῆσαι συντόμως. 26 οὔπω δὲ ἡλίου βολαὶ κατεσπείροντο,
καὶ τοῦ βασιλέως τοὺς φίλους ἐκδεχομένου ὁ Ἕρμων παρα-
στὰς ἐκάλει πρὸς τὴν ἔξοδον ὑποδεικνύων τὸ πρόθυμον τοῦ
βασιλέως ἐν ἑτοίμῳ κεῖσθαι. 27 τοῦ δὲ ἀποδεξαμένου καὶ
καταπλαγέντος ἐπὶ τῇ παρανόμῳ ἐξόδῳ κατὰ πᾶν ἀγνωσίᾳ
κεκρατημένος ἐπυνθάνετο, τί τὸ πρᾶγμα, ἐφ᾽ οὗ τοῦτο αὐτῷ
μετὰ σπουδῆς τετέλεσται· 28 τοῦτο δὲ ἦν ἡ ἐνέργεια τοῦ
πάντα δεσποτεύοντος θεοῦ τῶν πρὶν αὐτῷ μεμηχανημένων
λήθην κατὰ διάνοιαν ἐντεθεικότος. 29 ὑπεδείκνυεν ὁ Ἕρμων
καὶ πάντες οἱ φίλοι τὰ θηρία καὶ τὰς δυνάμεις ἡτοιμάσθαι,
βασιλεῦ, κατὰ τὴν σὴν ἐκτενῆ πρόθεσιν. 30 ὁ δὲ ἐπὶ τοῖς
ῥηθεῖσιν πληρωθεὶς βαρεῖ χόλῳ διὰ τὸ περὶ τούτων προνοίᾳ
θεοῦ διεσκεδάσθαι πᾶν αὐτοῦ τὸ νόημα ἐνατενίσας μετὰ
ἀπειλῆς εἶπεν 31 Ὅσοι γονεῖς παρῆσαν ἢ παίδων γόνοι,
τήνδε θηρσὶν ἀγρίοις ἐσκεύασα ἂν δαψιλῆ θοῖναν ἀντὶ τῶν
ἀνεγκλήτων ἐμοὶ καὶ προγόνοις ἐμοῖς ἀποδεδειγμένων
ὁλοσχερῆ βεβαίαν πίστιν ἐξόχως Ιουδαίων. 32 καίπερ εἰ μὴ
διὰ τὴν τῆς συντροφίας στοργὴν καὶ τῆς χρείας, τὸ ζῆν
ἀντὶ τούτων ἐστερήθης. 33 οὕτως ὁ Ἕρμων ἀπροσδόκητον

NEW REVISED STANDARD VERSION

that the guests were assembled, approached the king and
nudged him. 15 And when he had with difficulty roused him,
he pointed out that the hour of the banquet was already slipping by, and he gave him an account of the situation. 16 The
king, after considering this, returned to his drinking, and
ordered those present for the banquet to recline opposite
him. 17 When this was done he urged them to give themselves over to revelry and to make the present[a] portion of the
banquet joyful by celebrating all the more. 18 After the party
had been going on for some time, the king summoned
Hermon and with sharp threats demanded to know why the
Jews had been allowed to remain alive through the present
day. 19 But when he, with the corroboration of the king's[b]
Friends, pointed out that while it was still night he had carried out completely the order given him, 20 the king,[c] possessed by a savagery worse than that of Phalaris, said that
the Jews[d] were benefited by today's sleep, "but," he added,
"tomorrow without delay prepare the elephants in the same
way for the destruction of the lawless Jews!" 21 When the
king had spoken, all those present readily and joyfully with
one accord gave their approval, and all went to their own
homes. 22 But they did not so much employ the duration of
the night in sleep as in devising all sorts of insults for those
they thought to be doomed.

23 Then, as soon as the cock had crowed in the early
morning, Hermon, having equipped[e] the animals, began to
move them along in the great colonnade. 24 The crowds of
the city had been assembled for this most pitiful spectacle
and they were eagerly waiting for daybreak. 25 But the Jews,
at their last gasp—since the time had run out—stretched
their hands toward heaven and with most tearful supplication and mournful dirges implored the supreme God[f] to help
them again at once. 26 The rays of the sun were not yet shed
abroad, and while the king was receiving his Friends,
Hermon arrived and invited him to come out, indicating that
what the king desired was ready for action. 27 But he, on
receiving the report and being struck by the unusual invitation to come out—since he had been completely overcome by
incomprehension—inquired what the matter was for which
this had been so zealously completed for him. 28 This was
the act of God who rules over all things, for he had implanted in the king's mind a forgetfulness of the things he had
previously devised. 29 Then Hermon and all the king's
Friends[g] pointed out that the animals and the armed forces
were ready, "O king, according to your eager purpose."[h]
30 But at these words he was filled with an overpowering
wrath, because by the providence of God his whole mind had
been deranged concerning these matters; and with a threatening look he said, 31 "If your parents or children were
present, I would have prepared them to be a rich feast for the
savage animals instead of the Jews, who give me no ground
for complaint and have exhibited to an extraordinary degree
a full and firm loyalty to my ancestors. 32 In fact you would
have been deprived of life instead of these, if it were not for
an affection arising from our nurture in common and your
usefulness." 33 So Hermon suffered an unexpected and

a Other ancient authorities read *delayed* (Gk *untimely*) *b* Gk *his*
c Gk *he* *d* Gk *they* *e* Or *armed* *f* Gk *the greatest God* *g* Gk *all the Friends* *h* Other ancient authorities read *pointed to the beasts and the armed forces, saying, "They are ready, O king, according to your eager purpose."*

Greek Old Testament

ἐπικίνδυνον ὑπήνεγκεν ἀπειλὴν καὶ τῇ ὁράσει καὶ τῷ προσώπῳ συνεστάλη. 34 ὁ καθεῖς δὲ τῶν φίλων σκυθρωπῶς ὑπεκρέ-
ων τοὺς συνηθροισμένους ἀπέλυσαν ἕκαστον ἐπὶ τὴν ἰδίαν
ἀσχολίαν. 35 οἵ τε Ιουδαῖοι τὰ παρὰ τοῦ βασιλέως ἀκούσαντες τὸν ἐπιφανῆ θεὸν κύριον βασιλέα τῶν βασιλέων ᾔνουν
καὶ τῆσδε τῆς βοηθείας αὐτοῦ τετευχότες.
36 Κατὰ δὲ τοὺς αὐτοὺς νόμους ὁ βασιλεὺς συστησάμενος
πᾶν τὸ συμπόσιον εἰς εὐφροσύνην τραπῆναι παρεκάλει.
37 τὸν δὲ Ἕρμωνα προσκαλεσάμενος μετὰ ἀπειλῆς εἶπεν
Ποσάκις δὲ δεῖ σοι περὶ τούτων αὐτῶν προστάττειν, ἀθλιώ-
τατε; 38 τοὺς ἐλέφαντας ἔτι καὶ νῦν καθόπλισον εἰς τὴν
αὔριον ἐπὶ τὸν τῶν Ιουδαίων ἀφανισμόν. 39 οἱ δὲ συνανακεί-
μενοι συγγενεῖς τὴν ἀσταθῆ διάνοιαν αὐτοῦ θαυμάζοντες
προεφέροντο τάδε 40 Βασιλεῦ, μέχρι τίνος ὡς ἀλόγους ἡμᾶς
διαπειράζεις προστάσσων ἤδη τρίτον αὐτοὺς ἀφανίσαι καὶ
πάλιν ἐπὶ τῶν πραγμάτων ἐκ μεταβολῆς ἀναλύων τὰ σοὶ
δεδογμένα; 41 ὧν χάριν ἡ πόλις διὰ τὴν προσδοκίαν ὀχλεῖ
καὶ πληθύουσα συστροφαῖς ἤδη καὶ κινδυνεύει πολλάκις
διαρπασθῆναι. 42 ὅθεν ὁ κατὰ πάντα Φάλαρις βασιλεὺς ἐμ-
πληθυνθεὶς ἀλογιστίας καὶ τὰς γινομένας πρὸς ἐπισκοπὴν
τῶν Ιουδαίων ἐν αὐτῷ μεταβολὰς τῆς ψυχῆς παρ᾽ οὐδὲν
ἡγούμενος ἀτελέστατον βεβαίως ὅρκον ὁρισάμενος τούτους
μὲν ἀνυπερθέτως πέμψειν εἰς ᾅδην ἐν γόνασιν καὶ ποσὶν
θηρίων ᾐκισμένους, 43 ἐπιστρατεύσαντα δὲ ἐπὶ τὴν Ιουδαίαν
ἰσόπεδον πυρὶ καὶ δόρατι θήσεσθαι διὰ τάχους καὶ τὸν
ἄβατον ἡμῖν αὐτῶν ναὸν πυρὶ πρηνέα ἐν τάχει τῶν συν-
τελούντων ἐκεῖ θυσίας ἔρημον εἰς τὸν ἅπαντα χρόνον κατα-
στήσειν. 44 τότε περιχαρεῖς ἀναλύσαντες οἱ φίλοι καὶ συγγενεῖς μετὰ πίστεως διέτασσον τὰς δυνάμεις ἐπὶ τοὺς
εὐκαιροτάτους τόπους τῆς πόλεως πρὸς τὴν τήρησιν. 45 ὁ
δὲ ἐλεφαντάρχης τὰ θηρία σχεδὸν ὡς εἰπεῖν εἰς κατάστεμα
μανιῶδες ἀγειοχὼς εὐωδεστάτοις πόμασιν οἴνου λελιβανω-
μένου φοβερῶς κεκοσμημένα κατασκευαῖς 46 περὶ τὴν ἕω
τῆς πόλεως ἤδη πλήθεσιν ἀναριθμήτοις κατὰ τοῦ ἱπποδρό-
μου καταμεμεστωμένης εἰσελθὼν εἰς τὴν αὐλὴν ἐπὶ τὸ προκείμενον ὤτρυνε τὸν βασιλέα. 47 ὁ δὲ ὀργῇ βαρείᾳ γεμίσας
δυσσεβῆ φρένα παντὶ τῷ βάρει σὺν τοῖς θηρίοις ἐξώρμησε
βουλόμενος ἀτρώτῳ καρδίᾳ καὶ κόραις ὀφθαλμῶν θεάσασθαι
τὴν ἐπίπονον καὶ ταλαίπωρον τῶν προσεσημαμμένων κατα-
στροφήν. 48 ὡς δὲ τῶν ἐλεφάντων ἐξιόντων περὶ πύλην καὶ
τῆς συνεπομένης ἐνόπλου δυνάμεως τῆς τε τοῦ πλήθους
πορείας κονιορτὸν ἰδόντες καὶ βαρυηχῆ θόρυβον ἀκούσαντες
οἱ Ιουδαῖοι 49 ὑστάτην βίου ῥοπὴν αὐτοῖς ἐκείνην δόξαντες
εἶναι τὸ τέλος τῆς ἀθλιωτάτης προσδοκίας εἰς οἶκτον καὶ
γόους τραπέντες κατεφίλουν ἀλλήλους περιπλεκόμενοι τοῖς
συγγενέσιν ἐπὶ τοὺς τραχήλους ἐπιπίπτοντες, γονεῖς παισὶν καὶ μητέρες νεάνισιν, ἕτεραι δὲ νεογνὰ πρὸς μαστοὺς
ἔχουσαι βρέφη τελευταῖον ἕλκοντα γάλα. 50 οὐ μὴν δὲ ἀλλὰ
καὶ τὰς ἔμπροσθεν αὐτῶν γεγενημένας ἀντιλήμψεις ἐξ
οὐρανοῦ συνιδόντες πρηνεῖς ὁμοθυμαδὸν ῥίψαντες ἑαυτοὺς
καὶ τὰ νήπια χωρίσαντες τῶν μαστῶν 51 ἀνεβόησαν φωνῇ
μεγάλῃ σφόδρα τὸν τῆς ἁπάσης δυνάμεως δυνάστην ἱκετεύοντες οἰκτῖραι μετὰ ἐπιφανείας αὐτοὺς ἤδη πρὸς πύλαις
ᾅδου καθεστῶτας.

New Revised Standard Version

dangerous threat, and his eyes wavered and his face fell.
34 The king's Friends one by one sullenly slipped away and
dismissed[a] the assembled people to their own occupations.
35 Then the Jews, on hearing what the king had said, praised
the manifest Lord God, King of kings, since this also was his
aid that they had received.
36 The king, however, reconvened the party in the same
manner and urged the guests to return to their celebrating.
37 After summoning Hermon he said in a threatening tone,
"How many times, you poor wretch, must I give you orders
about these things? 38 Equip[b] the elephants now once more
for the destruction of the Jews tomorrow!" 39 But the officials
who were at table with him, wondering at his instability of
mind, remonstrated as follows: 40 "O king, how long will
you put us to the test, as though we are idiots, ordering now
for a third time that they be destroyed, and again revoking
your decree in the matter?[c] 41 As a result the city is in a
tumult because of its expectation; it is crowded with masses
of people, and also in constant danger of being plundered."
42 At this the king, a Phalaris in everything and filled
with madness, took no account of the changes of mind that
had come about within him for the protection of the Jews,
and he firmly swore an irrevocable oath that he would send
them to death[d] without delay, mangled by the knees and feet
of the animals, 43 and would also march against Judea and
rapidly level it to the ground with fire and spear, and by
burning to the ground the temple inaccessible to him[e] would
quickly render it forever empty of those who offered sacrifices there. 44 Then the Friends and officers departed with
great joy, and they confidently posted the armed forces at the
places in the city most favorable for keeping guard.
45 Now when the animals had been brought virtually to a
state of madness, so to speak, by the very fragrant draughts
of wine mixed with frankincense and had been equipped with
frightful devices, the elephant keeper 46 entered at about
dawn into the courtyard—the city now being filled with
countless masses of people crowding their way into the hippodrome—and urged the king on to the matter at hand. 47 So
he, when he had filled his impious mind with a deep rage,
rushed out in full force along with the animals, wishing to
witness, with invulnerable heart and with his own eyes, the
grievous and pitiful destruction of the aforementioned people.
48 When the Jews saw the dust raised by the elephants
going out at the gate and by the following armed forces, as
well as by the trampling of the crowd, and heard the loud
and tumultuous noise, 49 they thought that this was their
last moment of life, the end of their most miserable suspense, and giving way to lamentation and groans they
kissed each other, embracing relatives and falling into one
another's arms[f]—parents and children, mothers and daughters, and others with babies at their breasts who were drawing their last milk. 50 Not only this, but when they considered the help that they had received before from heaven, they
prostrated themselves with one accord on the ground, removing the babies from their breasts, 51 and cried out in a very
loud voice, imploring the Ruler over every power to manifest
himself and be merciful to them, as they stood now at the
gates of death.[g]

a Other ancient authorities read *he dismissed* *b* Or *Arm* *c* Other ancient authorities read *when the matter is in hand* *d* Gk *Hades* *e* Gk *us* *f* Gk *falling upon their necks* *g* Gk *Hades*

GREEK OLD TESTAMENT

6 Ελεαζαρος δέ τις ἀνὴρ ἐπίσημος τῶν ἀπὸ τῆς χώρας
ἱερέων, ἐν πρεσβείῳ τὴν ἡλικίαν ἤδη λελογχὼς καὶ πάσῃ
τῇ κατὰ τὸν βίον ἀρετῇ κεκοσμημένος, τοὺς περὶ αὐτὸν
καταστείλας πρεσβυτέρους ἐπικαλεῖσθαι τὸν ἅγιον θεὸν
προσηύξατο τάδε 2 Βασιλεῦ μεγαλοκράτωρ, ὕψιστε παντοκράτωρ θεὲ τὴν πᾶσαν διακυβερνῶν ἐν οἰκτιρμοῖς κτίσιν,
3 ἔπιδε ἐπὶ Αβρααμ σπέρμα, ἐπὶ ἡγιασμένου τέκνα Ιακωβ,
μερίδος ἡγιασμένης σου λαὸν ἐν ξένῃ γῇ ξένον ἀδίκως ἀπολ-
λύμενον, πάτερ. 4 σὺ Φαραω πληθύνοντα ἅρμασιν, τὸν πρὶν
Αἰγύπτου ταύτης δυνάστην, ἐπαρθέντα ἀνόμῳ θράσει καὶ
γλώσσῃ μεγαλορρήμονι, σὺν τῇ ὑπερηφάνῳ στρατιᾷ ποντο-
βρόχους ἀπώλεσας φέγγος ἐπιφάνας ἐλέους Ισραηλ γένει.
5 σὺ τὸν ἀναριθμήτοις δυνάμεσιν γαυρωθέντα Σενναχηριμ,
βαρὺν Ἀσσυρίων βασιλέα, δόρατι τὴν πᾶσαν ὑποχείριον ἤδη
λαβόντα γῆν καὶ μετεωρισθέντα ἐπὶ τὴν ἁγίαν σου πόλιν,
βαρέα λαλοῦντα κόμπῳ καὶ θράσει σύ, δέσποτα, ἔθραυσας
ἔκδηλον δεικνὺς ἔθνεσιν πολλοῖς τὸ σὸν κράτος. 6 σὺ τοὺς
κατὰ τὴν Βαβυλωνίαν τρεῖς ἑταίρους πυρὶ τὴν ψυχὴν αὐθαιρέτως δεδωκότας εἰς τὸ μὴ λατρεῦσαι τοῖς κενοῖς
διάπυρον δροσίσας κάμινον ἐρρύσω μέχρι τριχὸς ἀπημάν-
τους φλόγα πᾶσιν ἐπιπέμψας τοῖς ὑπεναντίοις. 7 σὺ τὸν
διαβολαῖς φθόνου λέουσι κατὰ γῆς ῥιφέντα θηρσὶν βορὰν
Δανιηλ εἰς φῶς ἀνήγαγες ἀσινῆ. 8 τόν τε βυθοτρεφοῦς ἐν
γαστρὶ κήτους Ιωναν τηκόμενον ἀφιδὼν ἀπήμαντον πᾶσιν
οἰκείοις ἀνέδειξας, πάτερ. 9 καὶ νῦν, μίσυβρι πολυέλεε τῶν
ὅλων σκεπαστά, τὸ τάχος ἐπιφάνηθι τοῖς ἀπὸ Ισραηλ γένους
ὑπὸ ἐβδελυγμένων ἀνόμων ἐθνῶν ὑβριζομένοις. 10 εἰ δὲ ἀσε-
βείαις κατὰ τὴν ἀποικίαν ὁ βίος ἡμῶν ἐνέσχηται, ῥυσάμενος
ἡμᾶς ἀπὸ ἐχθρῶν χειρός, ᾧ προαιρῇ, δέσποτα, ἀπόλεσον
ἡμᾶς μόρῳ. 11 μὴ τοῖς ματαίοις οἱ ματαιόφρονες εὐλογη-
σάτωσαν ἐπὶ τῇ τῶν ἠγαπημένων σου ἀπωλείᾳ λέγοντες
Οὐδὲ ὁ θεὸς αὐτῶν ἐρρύσατο αὐτούς. 12 σὺ δέ, ὁ πᾶσαν
ἀλκὴν καὶ δυναστείαν ἔχων ἅπασαν αἰώνιε, νῦν ἔπιδε· ἐλέησον ἡμᾶς τοὺς καθ' ὕβριν ἀνόμων ἀλόγιστον ἐκ τοῦ ζῆν
μεθισταμένους ἐν ἐπιβούλων τρόπῳ. 13 πτηξάτω δὲ ἔθνη σὴν
δύναμιν ἀνίκητον σήμερον, ἔντιμε δύναμιν ἔχων ἐπὶ σωτηρίᾳ Ιακωβ γένους. 14 ἱκετεύει σε τὸ πᾶν πλῆθος τῶν νηπίων
καὶ οἱ τούτων γονεῖς μετὰ δακρύων. 15 δειχθήτω πᾶσιν
ἔθνεσιν ὅτι μεθ' ἡμῶν εἶ, κύριε, καὶ οὐκ ἀπέστρεψας τὸ
πρόσωπόν σου ἀφ' ἡμῶν, ἀλλὰ καθὼς εἶπας ὅτι Οὐδὲ ἐν τῇ
γῇ τῶν ἐχθρῶν αὐτῶν ὄντων ὑπερεῖδον αὐτούς, οὕτως ἐπι-
τέλεσον, κύριε.

16 Τοῦ δὲ Ελεαζαρου λήγοντος ἄρτι τῆς προσευχῆς ὁ
βασιλεὺς σὺν τοῖς θηρίοις καὶ παντὶ τῷ τῆς δυνάμεως φρυ-
άγματι κατὰ τὸν ἱππόδρομον παρῆγεν. 17 καὶ θεωρήσαντες
οἱ Ιουδαῖοι μέγα εἰς οὐρανὸν ἀνέκραξαν ὥστε καὶ τοὺς
παρακειμένους αὐλῶνας συνηχήσαντας ἀκατάσχετον πτόην
ποιῆσαι παντὶ τῷ στρατοπέδῳ. 18 τότε ὁ μεγαλόδοξος παντοκράτωρ καὶ ἀληθινὸς θεὸς ἐπιφάνας τὸ ἅγιον αὐτοῦ
πρόσωπον ἠνέῳξεν τὰς οὐρανίους πύλας, ἐξ ὧν δεδοξασμένοι
δύο φοβεροειδεῖς ἄγγελοι κατέβησαν φανεροὶ πᾶσιν πλὴν
τοῖς Ιουδαίοις 19 καὶ ἀντέστησαν καὶ τὴν δύναμιν τῶν
ὑπεναντίων ἐπλήρωσαν ταραχῆς καὶ δειλίας καὶ ἀκινήτοις

NEW REVISED STANDARD VERSION

6 Then a certain Eleazar, famous among the priests of the
country, who had attained a ripe old age and throughout
his life had been adorned with every virtue, directed the
elders around him to stop calling upon the holy God, and he
prayed as follows: 2 "King of great power, Almighty God
Most High, governing all creation with mercy, 3 look upon
the descendants of Abraham, O Father, upon the children of
the sainted Jacob, a people of your consecrated portion who
are perishing as foreigners in a foreign land. 4 Pharaoh with
his abundance of chariots, the former ruler of this Egypt,
exalted with lawless insolence and boastful tongue, you
destroyed together with his arrogant army by drowning them
in the sea, manifesting the light of your mercy on the nation
of Israel. 5 Sennacherib exulting in his countless forces,
oppressive king of the Assyrians, who had already gained
control of the whole world by the spear and was lifted up
against your holy city, speaking grievous words with boasting and insolence, you, O Lord, broke in pieces, showing
your power to many nations. 6 The three companions in
Babylon who had voluntarily surrendered their lives to the
flames so as not to serve vain things, you rescued
unharmed, even to a hair, moistening the fiery furnace with
dew and turning the flame against all their enemies.
7 Daniel, who through envious slanders was thrown down
into the ground to lions as food for wild animals, you
brought up to the light unharmed. 8 And Jonah, wasting
away in the belly of a huge, sea-born monster, you, Father,
watched over and restored[a] unharmed to all his family.
9 And now, you who hate insolence, all-merciful and protector of all, reveal yourself quickly to those of the nation of
Israel[b]—who are being outrageously treated by the abominable and lawless Gentiles.

10 "Even if our lives have become entangled in impieties
in our exile, rescue us from the hand of the enemy, and
destroy us, Lord, by whatever fate you choose. 11 Let not the
vain-minded praise their vanities[c] at the destruction of your
beloved people, saying, 'Not even their god has rescued
them.' 12 But you, O Eternal One, who have all might and all
power, watch over us now and have mercy on us who by the
senseless insolence of the lawless are being deprived of life
in the manner of traitors. 13 And let the Gentiles cower today
in fear of your invincible might, O honored One, who have
power to save the nation of Jacob. 14 The whole throng of
infants and their parents entreat you with tears. 15 Let it be
shown to all the Gentiles that you are with us, O Lord, and
have not turned your face from us; but just as you have said,
'Not even when they were in the land of their enemies did I
neglect them,' so accomplish it, O Lord."

16 Just as Eleazar was ending his prayer, the king arrived
at the hippodrome with the animals and all the arrogance of
his forces. 17 And when the Jews observed this they raised
great cries to heaven so that even the nearby valleys
resounded with them and brought an uncontrollable terror
upon the army. 18 Then the most glorious, almighty, and
true God revealed his holy face and opened the heavenly
gates, from which two glorious angels of fearful aspect
descended, visible to all but the Jews. 19 They opposed the
forces of the enemy and filled them with confusion and

a Other ancient authorities read *rescued and restored*; others, *mercifully restored* *b* Other ancient authorities read *to the saints of Israel*
c Or *bless their vain gods*

ἔδησαν πέδαις. 20 καὶ ὑπόφρικον καὶ τὸ τοῦ βασιλέως σῶμα
ἐγενήθη, καὶ λήθη τὸ θράσος αὐτοῦ τὸ βαρύθυμον ἔλαβεν.
21 καὶ ἀπέστρεψαν τὰ θηρία ἐπὶ τὰς συνεπομένας ἐνόπλους
δυνάμεις καὶ κατεπάτουν αὐτὰς καὶ ὠλέθρευον.

22 Καὶ μετεστράφη τοῦ βασιλέως ἡ ὀργὴ εἰς οἶκτον καὶ
δάκρυα ὑπὲρ τῶν ἔμπροσθεν αὐτῷ μεμηχανευμένων. 23 ἀκούσας γὰρ τῆς κραυγῆς καὶ συνιδὼν πρηνεῖς ἅπαντας εἰς τὴν
ἀπώλειαν δακρύσας μετ᾽ ὀργῆς τοῖς φίλοις διηπειλεῖτο λέγων 24 Παραβασιλεύετε καὶ τυράννους ὑπερβεβήκατε ὠμό-
τητι καὶ ἐμὲ αὐτὸν τὸν ὑμῶν εὐεργέτην ἐπιχειρεῖτε τῆς
ἀρχῆς ἤδη καὶ τοῦ πνεύματος μεθιστᾶν λάθρᾳ μηχανώμενοι
τὰ μὴ συμφέροντα τῇ βασιλείᾳ. 25 τίς τοὺς κρατήσαντας
ἡμῶν ἐν πίστει τὰ τῆς χώρας ὀχυρώματα τῆς οἰκίας
ἀποστήσας ἕκαστον ἀλόγως ἤθροισεν ἐνθάδε; 26 τίς τοὺς ἐξ
ἀρχῆς εὐνοίᾳ πρὸς ἡμᾶς κατὰ πάντα διαφέροντας πάντων
ἐθνῶν καὶ τοὺς χειρίστους πλεονάκις ἀνθρώπων ἐπιδεδεγμέ-
νους κινδύνους οὕτως ἀθέσμως περιέβαλεν αἰκίαις; 27 λύσα-
τε ἐκλύσατε ἄδικα δεσμά· εἰς τὰ ἴδια μετ᾽ εἰρήνης ἐξαπο-
στείλατε τὰ προπεπραγμένα παραιτησάμενοι. 28 ἀπολύσατε
τοὺς υἱοὺς τοῦ παντοκράτορος ἐπουρανίου θεοῦ ζῶντος, ὃς
ἀφ᾽ ἡμετέρων μέχρι τοῦ νῦν προγόνων ἀπαραπόδιστον μετὰ
δόξης εὐστάθειαν παρέχει τοῖς ἡμετέροις πράγμασιν. 29 ὁ
μὲν οὖν ταῦτα ἔλεξεν· οἱ δὲ ἐν ἀμερεῖ χρόνῳ λυθέντες τὸν
ἅγιον σωτῆρα θεὸν αὐτῶν εὐλόγουν ἄρτι τὸν θάνατον ἐκπε-
φευγότες.

30 Εἶτα ὁ βασιλεὺς εἰς τὴν πόλιν ἀπαλλαγεὶς τὸν ἐπὶ τῶν
προσόδων προσκαλεσάμενος ἐκέλευσεν οἴνους τε καὶ τὰ
λοιπὰ πρὸς εὐωχίαν ἐπιτήδεια τοῖς Ιουδαίοις χορηγεῖν ἐπὶ
ἡμέρας ἑπτὰ κρίνας αὐτοὺς ἐν ᾧ τόπῳ ἔδοξαν τὸν ὄλεθρον
ἀναλαμβάνειν, ἐν τούτῳ ἐν εὐφροσύνῃ πάσῃ σωτήρια ἀγαγεῖν. 31 τότε οἱ τὸ πρὶν ἐπονείδιστοι καὶ πλησίον τοῦ ᾅδου,
μᾶλλον δὲ ἐπ᾽ αὐτῷ βεβηκότες ἀντὶ πικροῦ καὶ δυσαιάκτου
μόρου κώθωνα σωτήριον συστησάμενοι τὸν εἰς πτῶσιν αὐτοῖς καὶ τάφον ἡτοιμασμένον τόπον κλισίαις κατεμερίσαντο
πλήρεις χαρμονῆς. 32 καταλήξαντες δὲ θρήνων πανόδυρτον
μέλος ἀνέλαβον ᾠδὴν πάτριον τὸν σωτῆρα καὶ τερατοποιὸν
αἰνοῦντες θεόν· οἰμωγήν τε πᾶσαν καὶ κωκυτὸν ἀπωσάμενοι
χοροὺς συνίσταντο εὐφροσύνης εἰρηνικῆς σημεῖον.
33 ὡσαύτως δὲ καὶ ὁ βασιλεὺς περὶ τούτων συμπόσιον βαρὺ
συναγαγὼν ἀδιαλείπτως εἰς οὐρανὸν ἀνθωμολογεῖτο μεγαλομερῶς ἐπὶ τῇ παραδόξῳ γενηθείσῃ αὐτῷ σωτηρίᾳ. 34 οἵ τε
πρὶν εἰς ὄλεθρον καὶ οἰωνοβρώτους αὐτοὺς ἔσεσθαι τιθέμενοι
καὶ μετὰ χαρᾶς ἀπογραψάμενοι κατεστέναξαν αἰσχύνην ἐφ᾽
ἑαυτοῖς περιβαλόμενοι καὶ τὴν πυρόπνουν τόλμαν ἀκλεῶς
ἐσβεσμένοι. 35 οἵ τε Ιουδαῖοι, καθὼς προειρήκαμεν, συστησάμενοι τὸν προειρημένον χορὸν μετ᾽ εὐωχίας ἐν ἐξομολογήσεσιν ἱλαραῖς καὶ ψαλμοῖς διῆγον. 36 καὶ κοινὸν ὁρισά-
μενοι περὶ τούτων θεσμὸν ἐπὶ πᾶσαν τὴν παροικίαν αὐτῶν
εἰς γενεὰς τὰς προειρημένας ἡμέρας ἄγειν ἔστησαν εὐφροσύνους, οὐ πότου χάριν καὶ λιχνείας, σωτηρίας δὲ τῆς διὰ

terror, binding them with immovable shackles. 20 Even the
king began to shudder bodily, and he forgot his sullen insolence. 21 The animals turned back upon the armed forces following them and began trampling and destroying them.

22 Then the king's anger was turned to pity and tears
because of the things that he had devised beforehand. 23 For
when he heard the shouting and saw them all fallen headlong to destruction, he wept and angrily threatened his
Friends, saying, 24 "You are committing treason and surpassing tyrants in cruelty; and even me, your benefactor, you
are now attempting to deprive of dominion and life by secretly devising acts of no advantage to the kingdom. 25 Who has
driven from their homes those who faithfully kept our country's fortresses, and foolishly gathered every one of them
here? 26 Who is it that has so lawlessly encompassed with
outrageous treatment those who from the beginning differed
from[a] all nations in their goodwill toward us and often have
accepted willingly the worst of human dangers? 27 Loose
and untie their unjust bonds! Send them back to their homes
in peace, begging pardon for your former actions![b]
28 Release the children of the almighty and living God of
heaven, who from the time of our ancestors until now has
granted an unimpeded and notable stability to our government." 29 These then were the things he said; and the Jews,
immediately released, praised their holy God and Savior,
since they now had escaped death.

30 Then the king, when he had returned to the city, summoned the official in charge of the revenues and ordered him
to provide to the Jews both wines and everything else needed
for a festival of seven days, deciding that they should celebrate their rescue with all joyfulness in that same place in
which they had expected to meet their destruction.
31 Accordingly those disgracefully treated and near to death,[c]
or rather, who stood at its gates, arranged for a banquet of
deliverance instead of a bitter and lamentable death, and full
of joy they apportioned to celebrants the place that had been
prepared for their destruction and burial. 32 They stopped
their chanting of dirges and took up the song of their ancestors, praising God, their Savior and worker of wonders.[d]
Putting an end to all mourning and wailing, they formed
choruses[e] as a sign of peaceful joy. 33 Likewise also the
king, after convening a great banquet to celebrate these
events, gave thanks to heaven unceasingly and lavishly for
the unexpected rescue that he[f] had experienced. 34 Those
who had previously believed that the Jews would be
destroyed and become food for birds, and had joyfully registered them, groaned as they themselves were overcome by
disgrace, and their fire-breathing boldness was ignominiously[g] quenched.

35 The Jews, as we have said before, arranged the aforementioned choral group[h] and passed the time in feasting to
the accompaniment of joyous thanksgiving and psalms.
36 And when they had ordained a public rite for these things
in their whole community and for their descendants, they
instituted the observance of the aforesaid days as a festival,
not for drinking and gluttony, but because of the deliverance

a Or *excelled above* *b* Other ancient authorities read *revoking your former commands* *c* Gk *Hades* *d* Other ancient authorities read *praising Israel and the wonder-working God*; or *praising Israel's Savior, the wonder-working God* *e* Or *dances* *f* Other ancient authorities read *they* *g* Other ancient authorities read *completely* *h* Or *dance*

θεὸν γενομένης αὐτοῖς. 37 ἐνέτυχον δὲ τῷ βασιλεῖ τὴν ἀπό-
λυσιν αὐτῶν εἰς τὰ ἴδια αἰτούμενοι. 38 ἀπογράφονται δὲ αὐτοὺς ἀπὸ πέμπτης καὶ εἰκάδος τοῦ Παχων ἕως τῆς τετάρ-
της τοῦ Επιφι ἐπὶ ἡμέρας τεσσαράκοντα, συνίστανται δὲ
αὐτῶν τὴν ἀπώλειαν ἀπὸ πέμπτης τοῦ Επιφι ἕως ἑβδόμης
ἡμέραις τρισίν, 39 ἐν αἷς καὶ μεγαλοδόξως ἐπιφάνας τὸ
ἔλεος αὐτοῦ ὁ τῶν πάντων δυνάστης ἀπταίστους αὐτοὺς ἐρρύσατο ὁμοθυμαδόν. 40 εὐωχοῦντο δὲ πάνθ᾽ ὑπὸ τοῦ βασιλέως χορηγούμενοι μέχρι τῆς τεσσαρεσκαιδεκάτης, ἐν ᾗ καὶ
τὴν ἐντυχίαν ἐποιήσαντο περὶ τῆς ἀπολύσεως αὐτῶν.
41 συναινέσας δὲ αὐτοῖς ὁ βασιλεὺς ἔγραψεν αὐτοῖς τὴν
ὑπογεγραμμένην ἐπιστολὴν πρὸς τοὺς κατὰ πόλιν στρατηγοὺς μεγαλοψύχως τὴν ἐκτενίαν ἔχουσαν

7 Βασιλεὺς Πτολεμαῖος Φιλοπάτωρ τοῖς κατ᾽ Αἴγυπτον
στρατηγοῖς καὶ πᾶσιν τοῖς τεταγμένοις ἐπὶ πραγμάτων
χαίρειν καὶ ἐρρῶσθαι· 2 ἐρρώμεθα δὲ καὶ αὐτοὶ καὶ τὰ τέκνα
ἡμῶν κατευθύναντος ἡμῖν τοῦ μεγάλου θεοῦ τὰ πράγματα,
καθὼς προαιρούμεθα. 3 τῶν φίλων τινὲς κατὰ κακοήθειαν
πυκνότερον ἡμῖν παρακείμενοι συνέπεισαν ἡμᾶς εἰς τὸ τοὺς
ὑπὸ τὴν βασιλείαν Ιουδαίους συναθροίσαντας σύστημα
κολάσασθαι ξενιζούσαις ἀποστατῶν τιμωρίαις 4 προφερόμενοι μηδέποτε εὐσταθήσειν τὰ πράγματα ἡμῶν δι᾽ ἣν
ἔχουσιν οὗτοι πρὸς πάντα τὰ ἔθνη δυσμένειαν, μέχρι ἂν
συντελεσθῇ τοῦτο. 5 οἳ καὶ δεσμίους καταγαγόντες αὐτοὺς
μετὰ σκυλμῶν ὡς ἀνδράποδα, μᾶλλον δὲ ὡς ἐπιβούλους, ἄνευ
πάσης ἀνακρίσεως καὶ ἐξετάσεως ἐπεχείρησαν ἀνελεῖν νόμου Σκυθῶν ἀγριωτέραν ἐμπεπορπημένοι ὠμότητα. 6 ἡμεῖς
δὲ ἐπὶ τούτοις σκληρότερον διαπειλησάμενοι καθ᾽ ἣν ἔχομεν
πρὸς ἅπαντας ἀνθρώπους ἐπιείκειαν μόγις τὸ ζῆν αὐτοῖς
χαρισάμενοι καὶ τὸν ἐπουράνιον θεὸν ἐγνωκότες ἀσφαλῶς
ὑπερησπικότα τῶν Ιουδαίων ὡς πατέρα ὑπὲρ υἱῶν διὰ
παντὸς συμμαχοῦντα 7 τήν τε τοῦ φίλου ἣν ἔχουσιν βεβαίαν
πρὸς ἡμᾶς καὶ τοὺς προγόνους ἡμῶν εὔνοιαν ἀναλογισά-
μενοι δικαίως ἀπολελύκαμεν πάσης καθ᾽ ὁντινοῦν αἰτίας
τρόπον 8 καὶ προστετάχαμεν ἑκάστῳ πάντας εἰς τὰ ἴδια
ἐπιστρέφειν ἐν παντὶ τόπῳ μηθενὸς αὐτοὺς τὸ σύνολον
καταβλάπτοντος μήτε ὀνειδίζειν περὶ τῶν γεγενημένων
παρὰ λόγον. 9 γινώσκετε γὰρ ὅτι κατὰ τούτων ἐάν τι κακο-
τεχνήσωμεν πονηρὸν ἢ ἐπιλυπήσωμεν αὐτοὺς τὸ σύνολον,
οὐκ ἄνθρωπον, ἀλλὰ τὸν πάσης δεσπόζοντα δυνάμεως θεὸν
ὕψιστον ἀντικείμενον ἡμῖν ἐπ᾽ ἐκδικήσει τῶν πραγμάτων
κατὰ πᾶν ἀφεύκτως διὰ παντὸς ἕξομεν. ἔρρωσθε.

10 Λαβόντες δὲ τὴν ἐπιστολὴν ταύτην οὐκ ἐσπούδασαν
εὐθέως γενέσθαι περὶ τὴν ἄφοδον, ἀλλὰ τὸν βασιλέα προση-
ξίωσαν τοὺς ἐκ τοῦ γένους τῶν Ιουδαίων τὸν ἅγιον θεὸν
αὐθαιρέτως παραβεβηκότας καὶ τοῦ θεοῦ τὸν νόμον τυχεῖν
δι᾽ αὐτῶν τῆς ὀφειλομένης κολάσεως 11 προφερόμενοι τοὺς
γαστρὸς ἕνεκεν τὰ θεῖα παραβεβηκότας προστάγματα μηδέποτε εὐνοήσειν μηδὲ τοῖς τοῦ βασιλέως πράγμασιν. 12 ὁ δὲ
τἀληθὲς αὐτοὺς λέγειν παραδεξάμενος καὶ παραινέσας
ἔδωκεν αὐτοῖς ἄδειαν πάντων, ὅπως τοὺς παραβεβηκότας
τοῦ θεοῦ τὸν νόμον ἐξολεθρεύσωσιν κατὰ πάντα τὸν ὑπὸ τὴν
βασιλείαν αὐτοῦ τόπον μετὰ παρρησίας ἄνευ πάσης βασιλικῆς ἐξουσίας καὶ ἐπισκέψεως. 13 τότε κατευφημήσαντες αὐτόν, ὡς πρέπον ἦν, οἱ τούτων ἱερεῖς καὶ πᾶν τὸ πλῆθος ἐπι-
φωνήσαντες τὸ αλληλουια μετὰ χαρᾶς ἀνέλυσαν. 14 οὕτως
τε τὸν ἐμπεσόντα τῶν μεμιαμμένων ὁμοεθνῆ κατὰ τὴν ὁδὸν

that had come to them through God. 37 Then they petitioned
the king, asking for dismissal to their homes. 38 So their registration was carried out from the twenty-fifth of Pachon to
the fourth of Epeiph,[a] for forty days; and their destruction
was set for the fifth to the seventh of Epeiph,[b] the three days
39 on which the Lord of all most gloriously revealed his mercy
and rescued them all together and unharmed. 40 Then they
feasted, being provided with everything by the king, until the
fourteenth day,[c] on which also they made the petition for
their dismissal. 41 The king granted their request at once and
wrote the following letter for them to the generals in the cities, magnanimously expressing his concern:

7 "King Ptolemy Philopator to the generals in Egypt and
all in authority in his government, greetings and good
health:

2 "We ourselves and our children are faring well, the great
God guiding our affairs according to our desire. 3 Certain of
our friends, frequently urging us with malicious intent, persuaded us to gather together the Jews of the kingdom in a
body and to punish them with barbarous penalties as traitors; 4 for they declared that our government would never be
firmly established until this was accomplished, because of
the ill-will that these people had toward all nations. 5 They
also led them out with harsh treatment as slaves, or rather
as traitors, and, girding themselves with a cruelty more savage than that of Scythian custom, they tried without any
inquiry or examination to put them to death. 6 But we very
severely threatened them for these acts, and in accordance
with the clemency that we have toward all people we barely
spared their lives. Since we have come to realize that the God
of heaven surely defends the Jews, always taking their part
as a father does for his children, 7 and since we have taken
into account the friendly and firm goodwill that they had
toward us and our ancestors, we justly have acquitted them
of every charge of whatever kind. 8 We also have ordered all
people to return to their own homes, with no one in any
place[d] doing them harm at all or reproaching them for the
irrational things that have happened. 9 For you should know
that if we devise any evil against them or cause them any
grief at all, we always shall have not a mortal but the Ruler
over every power, the Most High God, in everything and
inescapably as an antagonist to avenge such acts. Farewell."

10 On receiving this letter the Jews[e] did not immediately
hurry to make their departure, but they requested of the king
that at their own hands those of the Jewish nation who had
willfully transgressed against the holy God and the law of
God should receive the punishment they deserved. 11 They
declared that those who for the belly's sake had transgressed
the divine commandments would never be favorably disposed toward the king's government. 12 The king[f] then,
admitting and approving the truth of what they said, granted
them a general license so that freely, and without royal
authority or supervision, they might destroy those everywhere in his kingdom who had transgressed the law of God.
13 When they had applauded him in fitting manner, their
priests and the whole multitude shouted the Hallelujah and
joyfully departed. 14 And so on their way they punished and
put to a public and shameful death any whom they met of

a July 7—August 15 *b* August 16—18 *c* August 25 *d* Other ancient authorities read *way* *e* Gk *they* *f* Gk *He*

ἐκολάζοντο καὶ μετὰ παραδειγματισμῶν ἀνῄρουν. 15 ἐκείνῃ δὲ τῇ ἡμέρᾳ ἀνεῖλον ὑπὲρ τοὺς τριακοσίους ἄνδρας, ἣν καὶ ἤγαγον εὐφροσύνην μετὰ χαρᾶς βεβήλους χειρωσάμενοι. 16 αὐτοὶ δὲ οἱ μέχρι θανάτου τὸν θεὸν ἐσχηκότες παντελῆ σωτηρίας ἀπόλαυσιν εἰληφότες ἀνέζευξαν ἐκ τῆς πόλεως παντοίοις εὐωδεστάτοις ἄνθεσιν κατεστεμμένοι μετ' εὐφροσύνης καὶ βοῆς ἐν αἴνοις καὶ παμμελέσιν ὕμνοις εὐχαριστοῦντες τῷ θεῷ τῶν πατέρων αὐτῶν αἰωνίῳ σωτῆρι τοῦ Ισραηλ.

17 Παραγενηθέντες δὲ εἰς Πτολεμαίδα τὴν ὀνομαζομένην διὰ τὴν τοῦ τόπου ἰδιότητα ῥοδοφόρον, ἐν ᾗ προσέμεινεν αὐτοὺς ὁ στόλος κατὰ κοινὴν αὐτῶν βουλὴν ἡμέρας ἑπτά, 18 ἐκεῖ ἐποίησαν πότον σωτήριον τοῦ βασιλέως χορηγήσαντος αὐτοῖς εὐψύχως τὰ πρὸς τὴν ἄφιξιν πάντα ἑκάστῳ ἕως εἰς τὴν ἰδίαν οἰκίαν. 19 καταχθέντες δὲ μετ' εἰρήνης ἐν ταῖς πρεπούσαις ἐξομολογήσεσιν ὡσαύτως κἀκεῖ ἔστησαν καὶ ταύτας ἄγειν τὰς ἡμέρας ἐπὶ τὸν τῆς παροικίας αὐτῶν χρόνον εὐφροσύνους. 20 ἃς καὶ ἀνιερώσαντες ἐν στήλῃ κατὰ τὸν τῆς συμποσίας τόπον προσευχῆς καθιδρύσαντες ἀνέλυσαν ἀσινεῖς, ἐλεύθεροι, ὑπερχαρεῖς, διά τε γῆς καὶ θαλάσσης καὶ ποταμοῦ ἀνασῳζόμενοι τῇ τοῦ βασιλέως ἐπιταγῇ, ἕκαστος εἰς τὴν ἰδίαν, 21 καὶ πλείστην ἢ ἔμπροσθεν ἐν τοῖς ἐχθροῖς ἐξουσίαν ἐσχηκότες μετὰ δόξης καὶ φόβου, τὸ σύνολον ὑπὸ μηδενὸς διασεισθέντες τῶν ὑπαρχόντων. 22 καὶ πάντα τὰ ἑαυτῶν πάντες ἐκομίσαντο ἐξ ἀπογραφῆς ὥστε τοὺς ἔχοντάς τι μετὰ φόβου μεγίστου ἀποδοῦναι αὐτοῖς, τὰ μεγαλεῖα τοῦ μεγίστου θεοῦ ποιήσαντος τελείως ἐπὶ σωτηρίᾳ αὐτῶν. 23 εὐλογητὸς ὁ ῥύστης Ισραηλ εἰς τοὺς ἀεὶ χρόνους. αμην.

their compatriots who had become defiled. 15 In that day they put to death more than three hundred men; and they kept the day as a joyful festival, since they had destroyed the profaners. 16 But those who had held fast to God even to death and had received the full enjoyment of deliverance began their departure from the city, crowned with all sorts of very fragrant flowers, joyfully and loudly giving thanks to the one God of their ancestors, the eternal Savior[a] of Israel, in words of praise and all kinds of melodious songs.

17 When they had arrived at Ptolemais, called "rose-bearing" because of a characteristic of the place, the fleet waited for them, in accordance with the common desire, for seven days. 18 There they celebrated their deliverance,[b] for the king had generously provided all things to them for their journey until all of them arrived at their own houses. 19 And when they had all landed in peace with appropriate thanksgiving, there too in like manner they decided to observe these days as a joyous festival during the time of their stay. 20 Then, after inscribing them as holy on a pillar and dedicating a place of prayer at the site of the festival, they departed unharmed, free, and overjoyed, since at the king's command they had all of them been brought safely by land and sea and river to their own homes. 21 They also possessed greater prestige among their enemies, being held in honor and awe; and they were not subject at all to confiscation of their belongings by anyone. 22 Besides, they all recovered all of their property, in accordance with the registration, so that those who held any of it restored it to them with extreme fear.[c] So the supreme God perfectly performed great deeds for their deliverance. 23 Blessed be the Deliverer of Israel through all times! Amen.

a Other ancient authorities read *the holy Savior*; others, *the holy one*
b Gk *they made a cup of deliverance* *c* Other ancient authorities read *with a very large supplement*

LATIN VULGATE

Second Esdras is included only in the Latin Vulgate, King James Version, Today's English Version, and New Revised Standard Version.

LIBER IIII EZRAE

1 liber Ezrae prophetae, filii Sarei, filii Azarei, filii
Helchiae, filii Salame, filii Sadoch, filii Acitob, 2 filii
Achiae, filii Finees, filii Heli, filii Ameriae, filii Aziei, filii
Marimoth, filii Arna, filii Oziae, filii Borith, filii Abissei, filii
Finees, filii Eleazar, 3 filii Aaron ex tribu Levi, qui fuit cap-
tivus in regione Medorum, in regno Artaxersis regis
Persarum.

4 Et factum est verbum Domini ad me dicens: 5 Vade
adnuntia populo meo facinora ipsorum et filiis eorum iniquitates, quas in me admiserunt, ut nuntient filiis filiorum suorum, 6 quia peccata parentum illorum in illis creverunt; obliti enim me sacrificaverunt diis alienis. 7 Nonne ego eos
eduxi de terra Aegypti de domo servitutis? Ipsi autem inri-
taverunt me et consilia mea spreverunt. 8 Tu autem excute
comam capitis tui et proice omnia mala super illos, quoniam
non oboedierunt legi meae; populus autem indisciplinatus.
9 Usquequo eos sustinebo, quibus tanta beneficia contuli?
10 Reges multos propter eos subverti, Pharaonem cum pueris
suis et omnem exercitum eius percussi. 11 Omnes gentes a
facie eorum perdidi et in oriente provinciarum duarum populos Tyri et Sidonis dissipavi et omnes adversarios eorum
interfeci.

12 Tu vero loquere ad eos dicens: Haec dicit Dominus:
13 Nempe ego vos mare traieci et plateas vobis in invio muni-
tas exhibui; ducem vobis dedi Moysen et Aaron sacerdotem.
14 Lucem vobis per columnam ignis praestiti et magna
mirabilia feci in vobis. Vos autem mei obliti estis, dicit
Dominus.

15 Haec dicit Dominus omnipotens: Coturnix vobis in signo
fuit, castra vobis ad tutelam dedi, et illic murmurastis. 16 Et
non triumphastis in nomine meo de perditione inimicorum
vestrorum, sed adhuc nunc usque murmuratis. 17 Ubi sunt
beneficia quae praestiti vobis? Nonne in deserto cum
esuriretis et sitiretis proclamastis ad me 18 dicentes: Ut quid
nos in desertum istud adduxisti interficere nos? Melius nobis
fuerat servire Agyptiis quam mori in deserto hoc. 19 Ego
dolui gemitos vestros et dedi mannam vobis in escam,
panem angelorum manducastis. 20 Nonne cum sitiretis

KING JAMES VERSION

Second Esdras is included only in the Latin Vulgate, King James Version, Today's English Version, and New Revised Standard Version.

2 ESDRAS

1 The second book of the prophet Esdras, the son of Saraias, the son of Azarias, the son of Helchias, the son of Sadamias, the son of Sadoc, the son of Achitob,

2 The son of Achias, the son of Phinees, the son of Heli, the son of Amarias, the son of Aziei, the son of Marimoth, the son of Arna, the son of Ozias, the son of Borith, the son of Abisei, the son of Phinees, the son of Eleazar,

3 The son of Aaron, of the tribe of Levi; which was captive in the land of the Medes, in the reign of Artaxerxes king of the Persians.

4 And the word of the Lord came unto me, saying,

5 Go thy way, and shew my people their sinful deeds, and their children their wickedness which they have done against me; that they may tell their children's children:

6 Because the sins of their fathers are increased in them: for they have forgotten me, and have offered unto strange gods.

7 Am not I even he that brought them out of the land of Egypt, from the house of bondage? but they have provoked me unto wrath, and despised my counsels.

8 Pull thou off then the hair of thy head, and cast all evil upon them, for they have not been obedient unto my law, but it is a rebellious people.

9 How long shall I forbear them, unto whom I have done so much good?

10 Many kings have I destroyed for their sakes; Pharaoh with his servants and all his power have I smitten down.

11 All the nations have I destroyed before them, and in the east I have scattered the people of two provinces, even of Tyrus and Sidon, and have slain all their enemies.

12 Speak thou therefore unto them, saying, Thus saith the Lord,

13 I led you through the sea, and in the beginning gave you a large and safe passage; I gave you Moses for a leader, and Aaron for a priest.

14 I gave you light in a pillar of fire, and great wonders have I done among you; yet have ye forgotten me, saith the Lord.

15 Thus saith the Almighty Lord, The quails were as a token to you; I gave you tents for your safeguard: nevertheless ye murmured there,

16 And triumphed not in my name for the destruction of your enemies, but ever to this day do ye yet murmur.

17 Where are the benefits that I have done for you? when ye were hungry and thirsty in the wilderness, did ye not cry unto me,

18 Saying, Why hast thou brought us into this wilderness to kill us? it had been better for us to have served the Egyptians, than to die in this wilderness.

19 Then had I pity upon your mournings, and gave you manna to eat; so ye did eat angels' bread.

TODAY'S ENGLISH VERSION

Second Esdras is included only in the Latin Vulgate, King James Version,
Today's English Version, and New Revised Standard Version.

THE SECOND BOOK OF ESDRAS

1 This is the second book of the prophet Ezra. He was the
son of Seraiah, the grandson of Azariah, and a descendant of Hilkiah, Shallum, Zadok, Ahitub, 2 Ahijah, Phinehas,
Eli, Amariah, Azariah, Meraioth, Arna, Uzzi, Borith, Abishua,
Phinehas, Eleazar, 3 and Aaron, of the tribe of Levi.

When I, Ezra, was a captive in Media during the reign of
Artaxerxes, king of Persia, 4 the Lord said to me, 5 "Go and
remind my people and their children of the sins they have
committed against me, and let them tell their grandchildren.
6 My people have sinned even more than their ancestors, for
they have forgotten me and offered sacrifices to foreign gods.
7 I rescued them from Egypt, where they were slaves, but they
have done things that made me angry and have refused to
listen to my warnings.

8 "Ezra, tear your hair in grief and call down on these people all the disasters they deserve. They are rebellious and
refuse to obey my Law. 9 How much longer can I tolerate
these people for whom I have done so much? 10 For their
sake I overthrew many kings and crushed the king of Egypt
together with his officials and all his army. 11 I destroyed all
the nations that opposed them, and in the east I scattered
the people of the provinces of Tyre and Sidon and killed all
the enemies of Israel.

12 "Ezra, tell them that the Lord says: 13 I brought you
across the Red Sea and made safe roads for you where there
were none. I made Moses your leader and gave you Aaron as
your priest. 14 I provided you with light from a pillar of fire
and performed great miracles among you, but you have forgotten me. I, the Lord, have spoken.

15 "The Lord Almighty says: I sent you quails as a sign of
my care for you. I provided you with camps where you could
be safe, but all you did there was complain. 16 Even when I
destroyed your enemies, you did not appreciate what I had
done. You have never done anything but complain. 17 Have
you forgotten the blessings I gave you? There in the desert
when you were hungry and thirsty you cried out to me:
18 'Why have you brought us out to this desert to kill us?
Being slaves to the Egyptians was better than coming here to
die.' 19 I was moved by your bitter groans and gave you
manna, the bread of angels. 20 When you were thirsty, I split

NEW REVISED STANDARD VERSION

(c) The following book is included in the Slavonic Bible as 3 Esdras, but is
not found in the Greek. It is included in the Appendix to the Latin Vulgate
Bible as 4 Esdras.

Second Esdras is included only in the Latin Vulgate, King James Version,
Today's English Version, and New Revised Standard Version.

2 ESDRAS

Comprising what is sometimes called 5 Ezra (chapters 1-2),
4 Ezra (chapters 3-14), and 6 Ezra (chapters 15-16)

1 The book[a] of the prophet Ezra son of Seraiah, son of
Azariah, son of Hilkiah, son of Shallum, son of Zadok,
son of Ahitub, 2 son of Ahijah, son of Phinehas, son of Eli,
son of Amariah, son of Azariah, son of Meraimoth, son of
Arna, son of Uzzi, son of Borith, son of Abishua, son of
Phinehas, son of Eleazar, 3 son of Aaron, of the tribe of Levi,
who was a captive in the country of the Medes in the reign of
Artaxerxes, king of the Persians.[b]

4 The word of the Lord came to me, saying, 5 "Go, declare
to my people their evil deeds, and to their children the iniquities that they have committed against me, so that they may
tell[c] their children's children 6 that the sins of their parents
have increased in them, for they have forgotten me and have
offered sacrifices to strange gods. 7 Was it not I who brought
them out of the land of Egypt, out of the house of bondage?
But they have angered me and despised my counsels. 8 Now
you, pull out the hair of your head and hurl[d] all evils upon
them, for they have not obeyed my law—they are a rebellious people. 9 How long shall I endure them, on whom I
have bestowed such great benefits? 10 For their sake I have
overthrown many kings; I struck down Pharaoh with his servants and all his army. 11 I destroyed all nations before
them, and scattered in the east the peoples of two
provinces,[e] Tyre and Sidon; I killed all their enemies.

12 "But speak to them and say, Thus says the Lord:
13 Surely it was I who brought you through the sea, and
made safe highways for you where there was no road; I gave
you Moses as leader and Aaron as priest; 14 I provided light
for you from a pillar of fire, and did great wonders among
you. Yet you have forgotten me, says the Lord.

15 "Thus says the Lord Almighty:[f] The quails were a sign
to you; I gave you camps for your protection, and in them
you complained. 16 You have not exulted in my name at the
destruction of your enemies, but to this day you still complain.[g] 17 Where are the benefits that I bestowed on you?
When you were hungry and thirsty in the wilderness, did
you not cry out to me, 18 saying, 'Why have you led us into
this wilderness to kill us? It would have been better for us to
serve the Egyptians than to die in this wilderness.' 19 I pitied
your groanings and gave you manna for food; you ate the
bread of angels. 20 When you were thirsty, did I not split the

a Other ancient authorities read *The second book* *b* Other ancient authorities, which place chapters 1 and 2 after 16.78, lack verses 1-3 and begin the chapter: *The word of the Lord that came to Ezra son of Chusi in the days of King Nebuchadnezzar, saying, "Go,* *c* Other ancient authorities read *nourish* *d* Other ancient authorities read *and shake out* *e* Other ancient authorities read *Did I not destroy the city of Bethsaida because of you, and to the south burn two cities . . . ?* *f* Other ancient authorities lack *Almighty* *g* Other ancient authorities read verse 16, *Your pursuer with his army I sank in the sea, but still the people complain also concerning their own destruction.*

LATIN VULGATE

petram excidi, et fluxerunt aquae in satietatem? Propter aes-
tus folia arborum vos texi. 21 Divisi vobis terras pingues,
Chananeos et Ferezeos et Philistheos a facie vestra proieci.
Quid faciam vobis adhuc? dicit Dominus.
22 Haec dicit Dominus omnipotens: In deserto cum essetis
in flumine amaro sitientes et blasphemantes nomen meum,
23 non ignem vobis pro blasphemiis dedi, sed mittens lignum
in aqua dulce feci flumen. 24 Quid tibi faciam, Iacob?
Noluisti me obaudire, Iuda. Transferam me ad alias gentes et
dabo eis nomen meum, ut custodiant legitima mea.
25 Quoniam me dereliquistis, et ego vos derelinquam; peten-
tibus vobis a me misericordiam, non miserebor vestri.
26 Quando invocabitis me, ego non exaudiam vos. Maculastis
enim manus vestras sanguine, et pedes vestri impigri sunt
ad committenda homicidia. 27 Non quasi me dereliquistis,
sed vos ipsos, dicit Dominus.
28 Haec dicit Dominus omnipotens: Nonne ego vos rogavi
ut pater filios et ut mater filias et nutrix parvulos suos, 29 ut
essetis mihi in populo et ego vobis in Deum, et vos mihi in
filios et ego vobis in patrem? 30 Ita vos collegi ut gallina filios suos sub alas suas. Modo autem quid faciam vobis?
Proiciam vos a facie mea. 31 Oblationes mihi cum obtuleritis,
avertam faciem meam a vobis; dies enim festos vestros et
neomenias et circumcisiones carnis repudiavi. 32 Ego misi
pueros meos prophetas ad vos, quos acceptos interfecistis et
laniastis corpora illorum, quorum sanguinem exquiram, dicit
Dominus.
33 Haec dicit Dominus omnipotens: Domus vestra deserta
est, proiciam vos sicut ventus stipulam. 34 Et filii procre-
ationem non facient, quoniam mandatum meum vobiscum
neglexerunt et quod malum est coram me fecerunt.
35 Tradam domus vestras populo venienti. Qui me non audi-
entes credunt; quibus signa non ostendi, facient quae praecepi. 36 Prophetas non viderunt et memorabuntur antiqui-
tatum eorum. 37 Testor populi venientis gratiam, cuius
parvuli exultant cum laetitia, me non videntes oculis carnal-
ibus, sed spiritu credent quae dixi. 38 Et nunc, pater, aspice
cum gloria et vide populum venientem ab oriente. 39 Quibus
dabo ducatum Abraham, Isaac et Iacob et Osee et Amos et
Michae et Iohelis et Abdiae et Ionae 40 et Naum et Abacuc,

KING JAMES VERSION

20 When ye were thirsty, did I not cleave the rock, and waters flowed out to your fill? for the heat I covered you with the leaves of the trees.

21 I divided among you a fruitful land, I cast out the Canaanites, the Pherezites, and the Philistines, before you: what shall I yet do more for you? saith the Lord.

22 Thus saith the Almighty Lord, When ye were in the wilderness, in the river of the Amorites, being athirst, and blaspheming my name,

23 I gave you not fire for your blasphemies, but cast a tree in the water, and made the river sweet.

24 What shall I do unto thee, O Jacob? thou, Juda, wouldest not obey me: I will turn me to other nations, and unto those will I give my name, that they may keep my statutes.

25 Seeing ye have forsaken me, I will forsake you also; when ye desire me to be gracious unto you, I shall have no mercy upon you.

26 Whensoever ye shall call upon me, I will not hear you: for ye have defiled your hands with blood, and your feet are swift to commit manslaughter.

27 Ye have not as it were forsaken me, but your own selves, saith the Lord.

28 Thus saith the Almighty Lord, Have I not prayed you as a father his sons, as a mother her daughters, and a nurse her young babes,

29 That ye would be my people, and I should be your God; that ye would be my children, and I should be your father?

30 I gathered you together, as a hen gathereth her chickens under her wings: but now, what shall I do unto you? I will cast you out from my face.

31 When ye offer unto me, I will turn my face from you: for your solemn feastdays, your new moons, and your circumcisions, have I forsaken.

32 I sent unto you my servants the prophets, whom ye have taken and slain, and torn their bodies in pieces, whose blood I will require of your hands, saith the Lord.

33 Thus saith the Almighty Lord, Your house is desolate, I will cast you out as the wind doth stubble.

34 And your children shall not be fruitful; for they have despised my commandment, and done the thing that is evil before me.

35 Your houses will I give to a people that shall come; which not having heard of me yet shall believe me; to whom I have shewed no signs, yet they shall do that I have commanded them.

36 They have seen no prophets, yet they shall call their sins to remembrance, and acknowledge them.

37 I take to witness the grace of the people to come, whose little ones rejoice in gladness: and though they have not seen me with bodily eyes, yet in spirit they believe the thing that I say.

38 And now, brother, behold what glory; and see the people that come from the east:

39 Unto whom I will give for leaders, Abraham, Isaac, and Jacob, Oseas, Amos, and Micheas, Joel, Abdias, and Jonas,

the rock and all the water you needed flowed out. To protect
you from the heat, I provided you with shade trees.
21 I divided fertile lands among you and drove out the
Canaanites, the Perizzites, and the Philistines who opposed
your advance. What more could I have done for you?
22 "The Lord Almighty says: There in the desert by the river
of bitter water when you were thirsty and cursed me, 23 in
spite of your insults I did not send fire upon you. Instead, I
made the water fit to drink by throwing wood into the river.
24 People of Israel, what can I do with you? People of Judah,
you refuse to obey me. So I will turn to other nations and
make them my people. They will keep my laws. 25 Because
you have abandoned me, I will abandon you. You will beg
me for mercy, but I will show you none. 26 When you pray to
me, I will not hear you. You never hesitate to commit murder;
your hands are stained with the blood of those you have
killed. 27 It is not me that you have betrayed; you have
betrayed yourselves.
28 "The Lord Almighty says: I have pleaded with you as a
father pleads with his sons, as a mother pleads with her
daughters, or as a nursemaid pleads with her small children.
29 I begged you to be my people so that I could be your God,
to be my children so that I could be your father. 30 I gathered
you together as a hen gathers her chicks under her wings.
But now what can I do with you? I will banish you from my
sight; 31 and even when you offer sacrifices to me, I will turn
away from you. Your religious festivals, your New Moon celebrations,
or your circumcision ceremonies mean nothing to
me. 32 I sent to you my servants, the prophets, but you killed
them and mutilated their corpses. I will make you pay for
murdering them.
33 "The Lord Almighty says: Your Temple is abandoned. I
will scatter you like straw blown away by the wind. 34 Your
children will have no descendants because they rejected my
commandments and did what I hated, just as you did. 35 I
will give your home to a people that is about to appear. They
will believe me, even though they have not yet heard of me.
They will do what I command, even though I never performed
any miracles for them. 36 They have not seen the
prophets, but they will live by their ancient teachings.
37 I give my solemn promise that I will bless those people,
and their little children will laugh and shout for joy. Those
people have never seen me, but deep within them they will
believe my words.
38 "Now, Father Ezra, look with pride at the people you see
coming from the east. 39 Look at the leaders I have given
them: Abraham, Isaac, Jacob, Hosea, Amos, Micah, Joel,
Obadiah, Jonah, 40 Nahum, Habakkuk, Zephaniah, Haggai,

rock so that waters flowed in abundance? Because of the
heat I clothed you with the leaves of trees.[a] 21 I divided fertile
lands among you; I drove out the Canaanites, the
Perizzites, and the Philistines[b] before you. What more can I
do for you? says the Lord. 22 Thus says the Lord Almighty:[c]
When you were in the wilderness, at the bitter stream, thirsty
and blaspheming my name, 23 I did not send fire on you for
your blasphemies, but threw a tree into the water and made
the stream sweet.
24 "What shall I do to you, O Jacob? You, Judah, would
not obey me. I will turn to other nations and will give them
my name, so that they may keep my statutes. 25 Because you
have forsaken me, I also will forsake you. When you beg
mercy of me, I will show you no mercy. 26 When you call to
me, I will not listen to you; for you have defiled your hands
with blood, and your feet are swift to commit murder. 27 It is
not as though you had forsaken me; you have forsaken yourselves,
says the Lord.
28 "Thus says the Lord Almighty: Have I not entreated
you as a father entreats his sons or a mother her daughters
or a nurse her children, 29 so that you should be my people
and I should be your God, and that you should be my children
and I should be your father? 30 I gathered you as a hen
gathers her chicks under her wings. But now, what shall I do
to you? I will cast you out from my presence. 31 When you
offer oblations to me, I will turn my face from you; for I have
rejected your[d] festal days, and new moons, and circumcisions
of the flesh.[e] 32 I sent you my servants the prophets,
but you have taken and killed them and torn their bodies[f] in
pieces; I will require their blood of you, says the Lord.[g]
33 "Thus says the Lord Almighty: Your house is desolate;
I will drive you out as the wind drives straw; 34 and your
sons will have no children, because with you[h] they have
neglected my commandment and have done what is evil in
my sight. 35 I will give your houses to a people that will
come, who without having heard me will believe. Those to
whom I have shown no signs will do what I have commanded.
36 They have seen no prophets, yet will recall their former
state.[i] 37 I call to witness the gratitude of the people that is
to come, whose children rejoice with gladness;[j] though they
do not see me with bodily eyes, yet with the spirit they will
believe the things I have said.
38 "And now, father,[k] look with pride and see the people
coming from the east; 39 to them I will give as leaders Abraham,
Isaac, and Jacob, and Hosea and Amos and Micah and
Joel and Obadiah and Jonah 40 and Nahum and Habakkuk,

a Other ancient authorities read *I made for you trees with leaves* b Other ancient authorities read *Perizzites and their children* c Other ancient authorities lack *Almighty* d Other ancient authorities read *I have not commanded for you* e Other ancient authorities lack *of the flesh* f Other ancient authorities read *the bodies of the apostles* g Other ancient authorities add *Thus says the Lord Almighty: Recently you also laid hands on me, crying out before the judge's seat for him to deliver me to you. You took me as a sinner, not as a father who freed you from slavery, and you delivered me to death by hanging me on the tree; these are the things you have done. Therefore, says the Lord, let my Father and his angels return and judge between you and me; if I have not kept the commandment of the Father, if I have not nourished you, if I have not done the things my Father commanded, I will contend in judgment with you, says the Lord.* h Other ancient authorities lack *with you* i Other ancient authorities read *their iniquities* j Other ancient authorities read *The apostles bear witness to the coming people with joy* k Other ancient authorities read *brother*

Latin Vulgate

Sofoniae, Aggei, Zacchariae et Malachiae, qui et angelus
Domini vocatus est.

2 Haec dicit Dominus: Ego eduxi populum istum de servi-
tute, quibus mandata dedi per pueros meos prophetas,
quos audire noluerunt, sed irrita fecerunt mea consilia.
2 Mater quae eos generavit dicit illis: Ite, filii, quia ego vidua
sum et derelicta. 3 Educavi vos cum laetitia et amisi vos cum
luctu et tristitia, quoniam peccastis coram Domino Deo et
quod malum est coram me fecistis. 4 Modo autem quid faciam vobis? Ego enim vidua sum et derelicta. Ite, filii, et petite
a Domino misericordiam. 5 Ego autem te, pater, testem invo-
co super matrem filiorum, quia noluerunt testamentum
meum servare, 6 ut des eis confusionem et matrem eorum in
direptionem, ne generatio eorum fiat. 7 Dispergantur in
gentes, nomina eorum deleantur a terra, quoniam spreverunt
testamentum meum.

8 Vae tibi, Assur, qui abscondis iniquos penes te. Gens
mala, memorare quid fecerim Sodomae et Gomorrae, 9 quorum terra iacet in piceis glebis et aggeribus cinerum. Sic dabo
eos qui me non audierunt, dicit Dominus omnipotens.

10 Haec dicit Dominus ad Ezram: Adnuntia populo meo,
quoniam dabo eis regnum Hierusalem, quod daturus eram
Israhel. 11 Et sumam mihi gloriam illorum et dabo eis taber-
nacula aeterna, quae praeparaveram illis. 12 Lignum vitae
erit illis in odore unguenti, et non laborabunt neque fatiga-
buntur. 13 Ite et accipietis, rogate vobis dies paucos ut
minorentur; iam paratum est vobis regnum, vigilate.
14 Testare, testare caelum et terram, omisi enim malum et
creavi bonum, quia vivo ego, dicit Dominus. 15 Mater, con-
plectere filios tuos, educa illos cum laetitia sicut columba,
confirma pedes eorum, quoniam te elegi, dicit Dominus.
16 Et resuscitabo mortuos de locis suis et de monumentis
educam illos, quoniam cognovi nomen meum in illis. 17 Noli
timere, mater filiorum, quoniam te elegi, dicit Dominus.
18 Mittam tibi adiutorium pueros meos Esaiam et Hieremiam,
ad quorum consilium sanctificavi et paravi tibi arbores
duodecim gravatas variis fructibus 19 et totidem fontes flu-
entes lac et mel et montes inmensos septem habentes rosam
et lilium, in quibus gaudio replebo filios tuos.

20 Viduam iustifica, pupillo iudica, egenti da, orfanum
tuere, nudum vesti, 21 confractum et debilem cura, claudum
inridere noli, tutare mancum, et caecum ad visionem claritatis meae admitte, 22 senem et iuvenem intra muros tuos

King James Version

40 Nahum, and Abacuc, Sophonias, Aggeus, Zachary, and Malachy, which is called also an angel of the Lord.

2 Thus saith the Lord, I brought this people out of bondage, and I gave them my commandments by my servants the prophets; whom they would not hear, but despised my counsels.

2 The mother that bare them saith unto them, Go your way, ye children; for I am a widow and forsaken.

3 I brought you up with gladness; but with sorrow and heaviness have I lost you: for ye have sinned before the Lord your God, and done that thing that is evil before him.

4 But what shall I now do unto you? I am a widow and forsaken: go your way, O my children, and ask mercy of the Lord.

5 As for me, O father, I call upon thee for a witness over the mother of these children, which would not keep my covenant,

6 That thou bring them to confusion, and their mother to a spoil, that there may be no offspring of them.

7 Let them be scattered abroad among the heathen, let their names be put out of the earth: for they have despised my covenant.

8 Woe be unto thee, Assur, thou that hidest the unrighteous in thee! O thou wicked people, remember what I did unto Sodom and Gomorrha;

9 Whose land lieth in clods of pitch and heaps of ashes: even so also will I do unto them that hear me not, saith the Almighty Lord.

10 Thus saith the Lord unto Esdras, Tell my people that I will give them the kingdom of Jerusalem, which I would have given unto Israel.

11 Their glory also will I take unto me, and give these the everlasting tabernacles, which I had prepared for them.

12 They shall have the tree of life for an ointment of sweet savour; they shall neither labour, nor be weary.

13 Go, and ye shall receive: pray for few days unto you, that they may be shortened: the kingdom is already prepared for you: watch.

14 Take heaven and earth to witness; for I have broken the evil in pieces, and created the good: for I live, saith the Lord.

15 Mother, embrace thy children, and bring them up with gladness, make their feet as fast as a pillar: for I have chosen thee, saith the Lord.

16 And those that be dead will I raise up again from their places, and bring them out of the graves: for I have known my name in Israel.

17 Fear not, thou mother of the children: for I have chosen thee, saith the Lord.

18 For thy help will I send my servants Esay and Jeremy, after whose counsel I have sanctified and prepared for thee twelve trees laden with divers fruits,

19 And as many fountains flowing with milk and honey, and seven mighty mountains, whereupon there grow roses and lilies, whereby I will fill thy children with joy.

20 Do right to the widow, judge for the fatherless, give to the poor, defend the orphan, clothe the naked,

21 Heal the broken and the weak, laugh not a lame man to scorn, defend the maimed, and let the blind man come into the sight of my clearness.

22 Keep the old and young within thy walls.

Today's English Version

Zechariah, and Malachi (who is also called the Lord's messenger).

2 "The Lord says: I led my people out of slavery in Egypt; I
gave them commandments through my servants, the
prophets, but they refused to listen and ignored my teachings.
2 Jerusalem, the mother who brought them into the world,
says to them, 'Go your own way, my children; I am now a
widow left completely alone. 3 I took great delight in bringing
you up, but you sinned against the Lord God and did what I
knew was wrong, so I mourned in deep grief when I lost you.
4 What can I do for you, now that I am a widow and left completely alone? Go, my children, and ask the Lord for mercy.'
5 "Father Ezra, I call on you to testify against these people
as their mother has done, because they have refused to keep
my covenant. 6 Now bring confusion on them and ruin on
their mother, so that they will have no descendants. 7 They
will be scattered among the nations, and no one on earth
will remember them any longer, for they have despised my
covenant.
8 "How terrible will be your punishment, Assyria. You have
let wicked people hide within your borders. Remember, sinful
nation, what I did to Sodom and Gomorrah. 9 Their land
now lies covered with lumps of tar and heaps of ashes. That
is what I do to people who do not obey me.
10 "The Lord says to Ezra: Announce to my new people that
I will give them the kingdom of Jerusalem, which I had
planned to give to Israel. 11 I will take the dazzling light of
my presence away from Israel and will give to my new people the eternal Temple that I had prepared for Israel. 12 The
tree of life will fill the air around them with its fragrance.
They will never have to work; they will never grow tired.
13 Ask, and you will receive. Pray that the number of the days
you have to wait will be reduced. Even now the kingdom has
been prepared for you, so stay alert. 14 Call heaven and earth
to witness that I, the living God, have abolished evil and created good.
15 "Mother Jerusalem, take your children in your arms.
Guide their steps in safe paths; raise them with the same
delight that a dove has in raising her young. I, the Lord,
have chosen you. 16 I will raise your dead from their graves
because I recognize them as my people. 17 Jerusalem, mother
of these people, do not be afraid; I, the Lord, have
chosen you.
18 "I will send my servants Isaiah and Jeremiah to help
you. At their request I have consecrated and prepared for you
twelve trees, heavy with different kinds of fruit, 19 twelve
fountains flowing with milk and honey, and seven high
mountains covered with roses and lilies. I will make your
children very happy there. 20 Now, Jerusalem, come to the
defense of widows, take the side of the fatherless, give to the
poor, protect orphans, give clothing to those who have none,
21 take care of those who are broken and weak, do not make
fun of those who are crippled, protect the disabled, and help
the blind to catch a vision of my dazzling splendor. 22 Keep
both the old and the young safe within your walls.

New Revised Standard Version

Zephaniah, Haggai, Zechariah and Malachi, who is also
called the messenger of the Lord.[a]

2 "Thus says the Lord: I brought this people out of
bondage, and I gave them commandments through my
servants the prophets; but they would not listen to them,
and made my counsels void. 2 The mother who bore them[b]
says to them, 'Go, my children, because I am a widow and
forsaken. 3 I brought you up with gladness; but with mourning and sorrow I have lost you, because you have sinned
before the Lord God and have done what is evil in my sight.[c]
4 But now what can I do for you? For I am a widow and forsaken. Go, my children, and ask for mercy from the Lord.'
5 Now I call upon you, father, as a witness in addition to the
mother of the children, because they would not keep my covenant, 6 so that you may bring confusion on them and bring
their mother to ruin, so that they may have no offspring.
7 Let them be scattered among the nations; let their names be
blotted out from the earth, because they have despised my
covenant.
8 "Woe to you, Assyria, who conceal the unrighteous
within you! O wicked nation, remember what I did to Sodom
and Gomorrah, 9 whose land lies in lumps of pitch and
heaps of ashes.[d] That is what I will do to those who have
not listened to me, says the Lord Almighty."
10 Thus says the Lord to Ezra: "Tell my people that I will
give them the kingdom of Jerusalem, which I was going to
give to Israel. 11 Moreover, I will take back to myself their
glory, and will give to these others the everlasting habitations, which I had prepared for Israel.[e] 12 The tree of life
shall give them fragrant perfume, and they shall neither toil
nor become weary. 13 Go[f] and you will receive; pray that
your days may be few, that they may be shortened. The kingdom is already prepared for you; be on the watch! 14 Call,
O call heaven and earth to witness: I set aside evil and created good; for I am the Living One, says the Lord.
15 "Mother, embrace your children; bring them up with
gladness, as does a dove; strengthen their feet, because I
have chosen you, says the Lord. 16 And I will raise up the
dead from their places, and bring them out from their tombs,
because I recognize my name in them. 17 Do not fear, mother
of children, for I have chosen you, says the Lord. 18 I will
send you help, my servants Isaiah and Jeremiah. According
to their counsel I have consecrated and prepared for you
twelve trees loaded with various fruits, 19 and the same
number of springs flowing with milk and honey, and seven
mighty mountains on which roses and lilies grow; by these I
will fill your children with joy.
20 "Guard the rights of the widow, secure justice for the
ward, give to the needy, defend the orphan, clothe the naked,
21 care for the injured and the weak, do not ridicule the lame,
protect the maimed, and let the blind have a vision of my
splendor. 22 Protect the old and the young within your walls.

a Other ancient authorities read *and Jacob, Elijah and Enoch, Zechariah and Hosea, Amos, Joel, Micah, Obadiah, Zephaniah, 40Nahum, Jonah, Mattia* (or *Mattathias*), *Habakkuk, and twelve angels with flowers* *b* Other ancient authorities read *They begat for themselves a mother who* *c* Other ancient authorities read *in his sight* *d* Other ancient authorities read *Gomorrah, whose land descends to hell* *e* Lat *for those* *f* Other ancient authorities read *Seek*

Latin Vulgate

serva, 23 mortuos ubi inveneris signans commenda sepul-
chro, et dabo tibi primam sessionem in resurrectione mea.
24 Pausa et quiesce, populus meus, quia veniet requies tua.
25 Nutrix bona, nutri filios tuos, confirma pedes eorum.
26 Servos quos tibi dedi, nemo ex eis interiet, ego enim eos
requiram de numero tuo. 27 Noli satagere, cum venerit enim
dies pressurae et angustiae, alii plorabunt et tristes erunt, tu
autem hilaris et copiosa eris. 28 Zelabunt gentes et nihil
adversum te poterunt, dicit Dominus. 29 Manus meae tegent
te, ne filii tui gehennam videant. 30 Iucundare, mater, cum
filiis tuis, quia ego te eripiam, dicit Dominus. 31 Filios tuos
dormientes memorare, quoniam ego eos educam de latibulis
terrae et misericordiam cum illis faciam, quoniam misericors
sum, dicit Dominus omnipotens. 32 Amplectere natos tuos
usque dum venio et praedica illis misericordiam, quoniam
exuberant fontes mei et gratia mea non deficiet.
33 Ego Ezra accepi praeceptum a Domino in monte Horeb,
ut irem ad Israhel. Ad quos cum venirem, reprobaverunt me
et respuerunt mandatum Domini. 34 Ideoque vobis dico,
gentes quae auditis et intellegitis: Expectate pastorem
vestrum, requiem aeternitatis dabit vobis, quoniam in proximo est ille, qui in finem saeculi adveniet. 35 Parati estote ad
praemia regni, quia lux perpetua lucebit vobis per aeterni-
tatem temporis. 36 Fugite umbram saeculi huius, accipite
iucunditatem gloriae vestrae. Ego testor palam salvatorem
meum. 37 Commendatum Domini accipite et iucundamini
gratias agentes ei qui vos ad caelestia regna vocavit.
38 Surgite et state et videte numerum signatorum in convivio
Domini. 39 Qui se de umbra saeculi transtulerunt, splendidas
tunicas a Domino acceperunt. 40 Recipe, Sion, numerum
tuum et conclude candidatos tuos, qui legem Domini con-
pleverunt. 41 Filiorum tuorum, quos optabas, plenus est
numerus; roga imperium Domini, ut sanctificetur populus
tuus, qui vocatus est ab initio.
42 Ego Ezra vidi in monte Sion turbam magnam, quam
numerare non potui, et omnes canticis conlaudabant Dominum. 43 Et in medio eorum erat iuvenis statura celsus, emi-
nentior omnibus illis, et singulis eorum capitibus inponebat
coronas, et magis exaltabatur; ego autem miraculo tenebar.
44 Tunc interrogavi angelum et dixi: Qui sunt hii, domine?
45 Qui respondens dixit mihi: Hii sunt qui mortalem tunicam
deposuerunt et inmortalem sumpserunt et confessi sunt
nomen Dei; modo coronantur et accipiunt palmas. 46 Et dixi

King James Version

23 Wheresoever thou findest the dead, take them and bury them, and I will give thee the first place in my resurrection.

24 Abide still, O my people, and take thy rest, for thy quietness shall come.

25 Nourish thy children, O thou good nurse; stablish their feet.

26 As for the servants whom I have given thee, there shall not one of them perish; for I will require them from among thy number.

27 Be not weary: for when the day of trouble and heaviness cometh, others shall weep and be sorrowful, but thou shalt be merry and have abundance.

28 The heathen shall envy thee, but they shall be able to do nothing against thee, saith the Lord.

29 My hands shall cover thee, so that thy children shall not see hell.

30 Be joyful, O thou mother, with thy children; for I will deliver thee, saith the Lord.

31 Remember thy children that sleep, for I shall bring them out of the sides of the earth, and shew mercy unto them: for I am merciful, saith the Lord Almighty.

32 Embrace thy children until I come and shew mercy unto them: for my wells run over, and my grace shall not fail.

33 I Esdras received a charge of the Lord upon the mount Oreb, that I should go unto Israel; but when I came unto them, they set me at nought, and despised the commandment of the Lord.

34 And therefore I say unto you, O ye heathen, that hear and understand, look for your Shepherd, he shall give you everlasting rest; for he is nigh at hand, that shall come in the end of the world.

35 Be ready to the reward of the kingdom, for the everlasting light shall shine upon you for evermore.

36 Flee the shadow of this world, receive the joyfulness of your glory: I testify my Saviour openly.

37 O receive the gift that is given you, and be glad, giving thanks unto him that hath called you to the heavenly kingdom.

38 Arise up and stand, behold the number of those that be sealed in the feast of the Lord;

39 Which are departed from the shadow of the world, and have received glorious garments of the Lord.

40 Take thy number, O Sion, and shut up those of thine that are clothed in white, which have fulfilled the law of the Lord.

41 The number of thy children, whom thou longedst for, is fulfilled: beseech the power of the Lord, that thy people, which have been called from the beginning, may be hallowed.

42 I Esdras saw upon the mount Sion a great people, whom I could not number, and they all praised the Lord with songs.

43 And in the midst of them there was a young man of a high stature, taller than all the rest, and upon every one of their heads he set crowns, and was more exalted; which I marvelled at greatly.

44 So I asked the angel, and said, Sir, what are these?

45 He answered and said unto me, These be they that have put off the mortal clothing, and put on the immortal, and have confessed the name of God: now are they crowned, and receive palms.

Today's English Version

23 Whenever you find a dead body, bury it and mark the
grave, and I will give you a place of honor when I raise the
dead.
24 "Be calm, my people; your time to rest will come. 25 Take
care of your children like a faithful nursemaid and guide
their steps in safe paths, 26 so that none of them will be lost.
When the time comes, I will hold you responsible for them.
27 Don't worry; when the day of trouble and distress comes,
others will cry and mourn, but you will be happy and rich.
28 The other nations will be jealous of you, but they will not
be able to harm you.
29 "I will protect you with my power and save your children
from hell. 30 Be happy, Jerusalem, you and your children,
because I, the Lord, will rescue you. 31 Remember your children who are asleep in their graves; I, the Lord Almighty, am
merciful, and I will bring them out from the place where they
lie hidden in the earth. 32 Until I come, hold your children
close and tell them about my grace and mercy, which are like
a spring that never runs dry."
33 I, Ezra, was on Mount Sinai when the Lord ordered me
to go to the people of Israel. But when I went to them, they
rejected me and refused to listen to what the Lord commanded. 34 That is why I am speaking to you Gentiles. You are
ready to listen and understand: "Wait for your shepherd who
is coming very soon, at the end of the age, to give you eternal rest. 35 Be ready to receive the blessings of the kingdom,
for eternal light will shine on you forever. 36 Flee from the
darkness of this present age and accept the joyful splendor
prepared for you. I testify publicly for my savior. 37 The Lord
has appointed him, so accept him and be happy. Give thanks
to God, who has called you into his heavenly kingdom.
38 Stand up and see the number of those who have received
the Lord's mark and who share in his banquet. 39 They have
left the darkness of this age and have received shining white
robes from the Lord. 40 So now, Jerusalem, welcome these
people who have kept the Law of the Lord, and this will complete the list of those whom God has assigned to you. 41 The
children you longed for have returned; their number is now
complete. So pray that the Lord's kingdom may come and
that your people, whom God chose before he created the
world, may become holy."
42 I, Ezra, saw an enormous crowd on Mount Zion, too
many people to count. They were all singing and praising the
Lord. 43 Standing in the middle of this crowd was a very tall
young man, taller than any of the others. He was placing a
crown on the head of each person, but he towered above
them all. I was spellbound by the sight, 44 and I asked the
angel, "Who are these people, sir?"
45 He replied, "These are people who have taken off their
mortal robes and have put on immortal ones. They have confessed their faith in God, and now they are being given
crowns and palm branches as symbols of their victory."

New Revised Standard Version

23 When you find any who are dead, commit them to the
grave and mark it,[a] and I will give you the first place in my
resurrection. 24 Pause and be quiet, my people, because your
rest will come.
25 "Good nurse, nourish your children; strengthen their
feet. 26 Not one of the servants[b] whom I have given you will
perish, for I will require them from among your number.
27 Do not be anxious, for when the day of tribulation and
anguish comes, others shall weep and be sorrowful, but you
shall rejoice and have abundance. 28 The nations shall envy
you, but they shall not be able to do anything against you,
says the Lord. 29 My power will protect[c] you, so that your
children may not see hell.[d]
30 "Rejoice, O mother, with your children, because I will
deliver you, says the Lord. 31 Remember your children that
sleep, because I will bring them out of the hiding places of
the earth, and will show mercy to them; for I am merciful,
says the Lord Almighty. 32 Embrace your children until I
come, and proclaim mercy to them; because my springs run
over, and my grace will not fail."

33 I, Ezra, received a command from the Lord on Mount
Horeb to go to Israel. When I came to them they rejected me
and refused the Lord's commandment. 34 Therefore I say to
you, O nations that hear and understand, "Wait for your
shepherd; he will give you everlasting rest, because he who
will come at the end of the age is close at hand. 35 Be ready
for the rewards of the kingdom, because perpetual light will
shine on you forevermore. 36 Flee from the shadow of this
age, receive the joy of your glory; I publicly call on my savior
to witness.[e] 37 Receive what the Lord has entrusted to you
and be joyful, giving thanks to him who has called you to
the celestial kingdoms. 38 Rise, stand erect and see the number of those who have been sealed at the feast of the Lord.
39 Those who have departed from the shadow of this age
have received glorious garments from the Lord. 40 Take
again your full number, O Zion, and close the list of your
people who are clothed in white, who have fulfilled the law
of the Lord. 41 The number of your children, whom you
desired, is now complete; implore the Lord's authority that
your people, who have been called from the beginning, may
be made holy."
42 I, Ezra, saw on Mount Zion a great multitude that I
could not number, and they all were praising the Lord with
songs. 43 In their midst was a young man of great stature,
taller than any of the others, and on the head of each of
them he placed a crown, but he was more exalted than they.
And I was held spellbound. 44 Then I asked an angel, "Who
are these, my lord?" 45 He answered and said to me, "These
are they who have put off mortal clothing and have put on
the immortal, and have confessed the name of God. Now
they are being crowned, and receive palms." 46 Then I said to

a Or *seal it*; or *mark them and commit them to the grave* *b* Or *slaves*
c Lat *hands will cover* *d* Lat *Gehenna* *e* Other ancient authorities
read *I testify that my savior has been commissioned by the Lord*

LATIN VULGATE

ad angelum: Ille iuvenis quis est, qui eis coronas inponit et
palmas in manus tradit? 47 Qui respondens dixit mihi: Ipse
est Filius Dei, quem in saeculo confessi sunt. Ego autem
magnificare eos coepi, qui fortiter pro nomine Domini
steterunt. 48 Tunc dixit mihi angelus: Vade et adnuntia populo meo, qualia et quanta mirabilia Domini Dei vidisti.

3 Anno tricesimo ruinae civitatis eram in Babylone, ego
Salathihel qui et Ezras, et conturbatus sum super cubili
meo recumbens, et cogitationes meae ascendebant super cor
meum, 2 quoniam vidi desertionem Sion et abundantiam
eorum qui habitabant in Babylone.

3 Et ventilatus est spiritus meus valde, et coepi loqui ad
Altissimum verba timorata, 4 et dixi: O Domine Dominator,
tu dixisti ab initio, quando plantasti terram, et hoc solus, et
imperasti pulveri, 5 et dedit Adam corpus mortuum. Sed et
ipsum figmentum manuum tuarum erat, et insuflasti in eum
spiritum vitae, et factus est vivens coram te. 6 Et induxisti
eum in paradisum, quem plantavit dextera tua antequam
terra adventaret. 7 Et huic mandasti diligentiam unam tuam,
et praeterivit eam, et statim instituisti in eum mortem et in
nationibus eius. Et natae sunt ex eo gentes et tribus, populi
et cognationes, quorum non est numerus. 8 Et ambulavit
unaquaque gens in voluntate sua, et impie agebant coram te
et spernebant praecepta tua, et tu non prohibuisti eos.
9 Iterum autem in tempore induxisti diluvium super habitantes saeculum et perdidisti eos. 10 Et factum est in uno
casui eorum, sicut Adae mors sic et his diluvium.

11 Dereliquisti autem ex his unum Noe cum domo sua; ex
eo iustos omnes. 12 Et factum est cum coepissent multiplicari qui habitabant super terram, et multiplicaverunt filios et
populos et gentes multas, et coeperunt iterato impietatem
facere plus quam priores. 13 Et factum est cum iniquitatem
facerent coram te, elegisti tibi ex his unum, cui nomen erat
Abraham. 14 Et dilexisti eum et demonstrasti ei temporum
finem solo secrete noctu. 15 Et disposuisti ei testamentum
aeternum et dixisti ei, ut non umquam derelinquas semen
eius. Et dedisti ei Isaac, et Isaac dedisti Iacob et Esau. 16 Et
segregasti tibi Iacob, Esau autem separasti, et factus est
Iacob in multitudine magna.

17 Et factum est cum educeres semen eius ex Aegypto, et
adduxisti eos super montem Sina. 18 Et inclinasti caelos et
statuisti terram et commovisti orbem et tremere fecisti
abyssos et conturbasti saeculum. 19 Et transiit gloria tua
portas quattuor, ignis et terraemotus et spiritus et gelu, ut
dares semini Iacob legem et generationi Israhel diligentiam.

KING JAMES VERSION

46 Then said I unto the angel, What young person is it that crowneth them, and giveth them palms in their hands?

47 So he answered and said unto me, It is the Son of God, whom they have confessed in the world. Then began I greatly to commend them that stood so stiffly for the name of the Lord.

48 Then the angel said unto me, Go thy way, and tell my people what manner of things, and how great wonders of the Lord thy God, thou hast seen.

3 In the thirtieth year after the ruin of the city I was in Babylon, and lay troubled upon my bed, and my thoughts came up over my heart:

2 For I saw the desolation of Sion, and the wealth of them that dwelt at Babylon.

3 And my spirit was sore moved, so that I began to speak words full of fear to the most High, and said,

4 O Lord, who bearest rule, thou spakest at the beginning, when thou didst plant the earth, and that thyself alone, and commandedst the people,

5 And gavest a body unto Adam without soul, which was the workmanship of thine hands, and didst breathe into him the breath of life, and he was made living before thee.

6 And thou leadest him into paradise, which thy right hand had planted, before ever the earth came forward.

7 And unto him thou gavest commandment to love thy way: which he transgressed, and immediately thou appointedst death in him and in his generations, of whom came nations, tribes, people, and kindreds, out of number.

8 And every people walked after their own will, and did wonderful things before thee, and despised thy commandments.

9 And again in process of time thou broughtest the flood upon those that dwelt in the world, and destroyedst them.

10 And it came to pass in every of them, that as death was to Adam, so was the flood to these.

11 Nevertheless one of them thou leftest, namely, Noah with his household, of whom came all righteous men.

12 And it happened, that when they that dwelt upon the earth began to multiply, and had gotten them many children, and were a great people, they began again to be more ungodly than the first.

13 Now when they lived so wickedly before thee, thou didst choose thee a man from among them, whose name was Abraham.

14 Him thou lovedst, and unto him only thou shewedst thy will:

15 And madest an everlasting covenant with him, promising him that thou wouldest never forsake his seed.

16 And unto him thou gavest Isaac, and unto Isaac also thou gavest Jacob and Esau. As for Jacob, thou didst choose him to thee, and put by Esau: and so Jacob became a great multitude.

17 And it came to pass, that when thou leddest his seed out of Egypt, thou broughtest them up to the mount Sinai.

18 And bowing the heavens, thou didst set fast the earth, movedst the whole world, and madest the depths to tremble, and troubledst the men of that age.

19 And thy glory went through four gates, of fire, and of earthquake, and of wind, and of cold; that thou mightest give the law unto the seed of Jacob, and diligence unto the generation of Israel.

TODAY'S ENGLISH VERSION

46 Then I asked the angel, "Who is the young man who is
putting the crowns on their heads and giving them the
palms?"
47 "He is the Son of God," the angel replied, "and all these
people confessed their faith in him while they lived on
earth." Then I began to praise those who had stood for the
Lord so bravely. 48 And the angel said to me, "Go and tell my
people what you have seen, the many marvelous wonders of
the Lord."

3 Thirty years after the fall of Jerusalem, I, Shealtiel (also
known as Ezra), was in Babylon. I was lying on my bed,
troubled and disturbed, 2 as I thought about the ruins of
Jerusalem and the prosperity of those who lived in Babylon.
3 I was deeply disturbed and began to express my fears to
God Most High. 4 "O Lord and Master," I said, "you, and you
alone, spoke the word at the beginning of creation and
formed the world. At your command the dust 5 produced the
lifeless body of Adam. Then with your hands you shaped it,
you breathed into it the breath of life, and he began to live.
6 You brought him into the Garden of Eden, which you yourself had planted before the earth was made. 7 You gave him
just one commandment, but he disobeyed it, and you immediately made him and his descendants subject to death.
"From Adam were born more nations, tribes, clans, and
families than can be counted. 8 All the nations did whatever
they wished; they sinned against you and rejected your commands. But you did nothing to stop them. 9 Then again,
after a while, you brought on the flood and destroyed the
world's population. 10 They all suffered the same fate: as
death had come to Adam, so now death came to a whole
generation in the flood. 11 But you spared one man, Noah,
with his family and all his righteous descendants.
12 "The number of people living on earth began to increase,
and the number of families, tribes, and nations grew. They
too fell into sin and were worse than the generations before
them. 13 But then you chose Abraham. 14 You loved him,
and to him alone in the dead of night, you secretly disclosed
how the world would end. 15 You made an everlasting covenant with him and promised him that you would never
abandon his descendants. You gave him Isaac, and to Isaac
you gave Jacob and Esau. 16 You chose Jacob, and his
descendants became a great nation, but you rejected Esau.
17 "You rescued the descendants of Jacob from Egypt and
led them to Mount Sinai. 18 There you bent down the skies,
shook[a] the earth, moved the world, made the waters beneath
the earth tremble, and brought disorder to the universe.
19 The dazzling light of your presence passed through the
four gates of fire, earthquake, wind, and frost, in order to
give the Law and its commandments to Jacob's descendants,

[a] *Some ancient translations* shook; *Latin* steadied.

NEW REVISED STANDARD VERSION

the angel, "Who is that young man who is placing crowns on
them and putting palms in their hands?" 47 He answered
and said to me, "He is the Son of God, whom they confessed
in the world." So I began to praise those who had stood
valiantly for the name of the Lord.[a] 48 Then the angel said to
me, "Go, tell my people how great and how many are the
wonders of the Lord God that you have seen."

3 In the thirtieth year after the destruction of the city, I
was in Babylon—I, Salathiel, who am also called Ezra. I
was troubled as I lay on my bed, and my thoughts welled up
in my heart, 2 because I saw the desolation of Zion and the
wealth of those who lived in Babylon. 3 My spirit was greatly
agitated, and I began to speak anxious words to the Most
High, and said, 4 "O sovereign Lord, did you not speak at the
beginning when you planted[b] the earth—and that without
help—and commanded the dust[c] 5 and it gave you Adam, a
lifeless body? Yet he was the creation of your hands, and you
breathed into him the breath of life, and he was made alive
in your presence. 6 And you led him into the garden that
your right hand had planted before the earth appeared.
7 And you laid upon him one commandment of yours; but he
transgressed it, and immediately you appointed death for
him and for his descendants. From him there sprang nations
and tribes, peoples and clans without number. 8 And every
nation walked after its own will; they did ungodly things in
your sight and rejected your commands, and you did not hinder them. 9 But again, in its time you brought the flood upon
the inhabitants of the world and destroyed them. 10 And the
same fate befell all of them: just as death came upon Adam,
so the flood upon them. 11 But you left one of them, Noah
with his household, and all the righteous who have descended from him.
12 "When those who lived on earth began to multiply,
they produced children and peoples and many nations, and
again they began to be more ungodly than were their ancestors. 13 And when they were committing iniquity in your
sight, you chose for yourself one of them, whose name was
Abraham; 14 you loved him, and to him alone you revealed
the end of the times, secretly by night. 15 You made an everlasting covenant with him, and promised him that you
would never forsake his descendants; and you gave him
Isaac, and to Isaac you gave Jacob and Esau. 16 You set apart
Jacob for yourself, but Esau you rejected; and Jacob became a
great multitude. 17 And when you led his descendants out of
Egypt, you brought them to Mount Sinai. 18 You bent down
the heavens and shook[d] the earth, and moved the world,
and caused the depths to tremble, and troubled the times.
19 Your glory passed through the four gates of fire and earthquake and wind and ice, to give the law to the descendants
of Jacob, and your commandment to the posterity of Israel.

a Other ancient authorities read *to praise and glorify the Lord* *b* Other ancient authorities read *formed* *c* Syr Ethiop: Lat *people* or *world* *d* Syr Ethiop Arab 1 Georg: Lat *set fast*

Latin Vulgate

20 Et non abstulisti ab eis cor malignum, ut faceret lex tua in
eis fructum. 21 Cor enim malignum baiulans primus Adam
transgressus et victus est, sed et omnes qui ex eo nati sunt.
22 Et facta est permanens infirmitas et lex cum corde populi
cum malignitate radicis, et discessit quod bonum est et man-
sit malignum.

23 Et transierunt tempora et finiti sunt anni, et suscitasti
tibi servum nomine David. 24 Et dixisti ei aedificare civitatem nominis tui et offerre tibi in ea de tuis oblationes.
25 Et factum est hoc annis multis. Et dereliquerunt qui habitabant civitatem, 26 in omnibus facientes sicut fecit Adam et
omnes generationes eius; utebantur enim et ipsi cor
malignum. 27 Et tradidisti civitatem tuam in manus inimicorum tuorum. 28 Et dixi ego tunc in corde meo: Numquid
meliora faciunt qui habitant in Babylone, et propter hoc
dominabit Sion?

29 Factum est autem cum venissem huc, et vidi impietates
quorum non est numerus, et delinquentes multos vidit
anima mea hoc tricesimo anno. Et excessit cor meum,
30 quoniam vidi quomodo sustines eos peccantes et pepercisti
impie agentibus, et perdidisti populum tuum et conservasti
inimicos tuos, et non significasti 31 nihil nemini quomodo
debeat derelinqui via haec. Numquid meliora facit Babylon
quam Sion, 32 aut alia gens cognovit te praeter Israhel? Aut
quae tribus crediderunt testamentis sicut haec Iacob,
33 quarum merces non conparuit neque labor fructificavit?
Pertransiens enim pertransivi in gentibus, et vidi abundantes
eas et non memorantes mandatorum tuorum. 34 Nunc ergo
pondera in statera nostras iniquitates et eorum qui habitant
in saeculo, et invenietur momentum puncti ubi declinet.
35 Aut quando non peccaverunt in conspectu tuo qui habitant terram, aut quae gens sic observavit mandata tua?
36 Homines quidem per nomina invenies servasse mandata
tua, gentes autem non invenies.

4 Et respondit ad me angelus qui missus est ad me, cui
nomen Urihel, 2 et dixit mihi: Excedens excessit cor
tuum in saeculo hoc, et conprehendere cogitas viam
Altissimi? 3 Et dixi: Ita, domine meus. Et respondit mihi et
dixit: Tres vias missus sum ostendere tibi et tres simili-
tudines proponere coram te. 4 De quibus si mihi renunti-
averis unam ex his, et ego tibi demonstrabo viam quam
desideras videre, et doceam te quare cor malignum. 5 Et dixi:
Loquere, domine meus. Et dixit ad me: Vade, pondera mihi
ignis pondus, aut mensura mihi flatum venti, aut revoca
mihi diem quae praeteriit. 6 Et respondi et dixi: Quis natorum poterit facere, ut me interroges de his? 7 Et dixit ad me:

King James Version

20 And yet tookest thou not away from them a wicked heart, that thy law might bring forth fruit in them.

21 For the first Adam bearing a wicked heart transgressed, and was overcome; and so be all they that are born of him.

22 Thus infirmity was made permanent; and the law (also) in the heart of the people with the malignity of the root; so that the good departed away, and the evil abode still.

23 So the times passed away, and the years were brought to an end: then didst thou raise thee up a servant, called David:

24 Whom thou commandedst to build a city unto thy name, and to offer incense and oblations unto thee therein.

25 When this was done many years, then they that inhabited the city forsook thee,

26 And in all things did even as Adam and all his generations had done: for they also had a wicked heart:

27 And so thou gavest thy city over into the hands of thine enemies.

28 Are their deeds then any better that inhabit Babylon, that they should therefore have the dominion over Sion?

29 For when I came thither, and had seen impieties without number, then my soul saw many evildoers in this thirtieth year, so that my heart failed me.

30 For I have seen how thou sufferest them sinning, and hast spared wicked doers: and hast destroyed thy people, and hast preserved thine enemies, and hast not signified it.

31 I do not remember how this way may be left: Are they then of Babylon better than they of Sion?

32 Or is there any other people that knoweth thee beside Israel? or what generation hath so believed thy covenants as Jacob?

33 And yet their reward appeareth not, and their labour hath no fruit: for I have gone here and there through the heathen, and I see that they flow in wealth, and think not upon thy commandments.

34 Weigh thou therefore our wickedness now in the balance, and their's also that dwell the world; and so shall thy name no where be found but in Israel.

35 Or when was it that they which dwell upon the earth have not sinned in thy sight? or what people have so kept thy commandments?

36 Thou shalt find that Israel by name hath kept thy precepts; but not the heathen.

4 And the angel that was sent unto me, whose name was Uriel, gave me an answer,

2 And said, Thy heart hath gone too far in this world, and thinkest thou to comprehend the way of the most High?

3 Then said I, Yea, my lord. And he answered me, and said, I am sent to shew thee three ways, and to set forth three similitudes before thee:

4 Whereof if thou canst declare me one, I will shew thee also the way that thou desirest to see, and I shall shew thee from whence the wicked heart cometh.

5 And I said, Tell on, my lord. Then said he unto me, Go thy way, weigh me the weight of the fire, or measure me the blast of the wind, or call me again the day that is past.

6 Then answered I and said, What man is able to do that, that thou shouldest ask such things of me?

7 And he said unto me, If I should ask thee how great

TODAY'S ENGLISH VERSION

the people of Israel. 20 Yet you did not remove their evil impulse, but let your Law guide their lives. 21 The first man, Adam, weighed down with an evil impulse, sinned and was defeated, and the same was true of all of his descendants. 22 So the disease became permanent, and although the Law was in the hearts of the people, so also was the root of evil! That is why what was good passed away, while what was evil continued.

23 "Many years later you sent your servant David 24 and told him to build a city which would bear your name and in which sacrifices would be offered to you. 25 This was done for many years, but then the inhabitants of the city disobeyed you 26 and sinned just like Adam and all his descendants, because they had the same evil impulse. 27 So you handed over your own city to your enemies.

28 "I said to myself, 'Perhaps Babylon has been allowed to conquer Jerusalem because the people who live there are better than we are.' 29 But when I got to Babylon, I saw more sins than I could count, and now for thirty years I have seen many sinners here. So I was perplexed 30 when I saw how you tolerate sinners and do not punish them, how you protect your enemies and yet destroy your own people. 31 You haven't given the faintest hint as to how these ways of yours can be changed. Surely Babylon is no better than Jerusalem. 32 No other nation, except Israel, has ever known you or accepted your covenants. 33 But Israel was never rewarded, and never profited from its labor. I have traveled widely in the other nations, and I have seen how prosperous they are, although they don't keep your commands. 34 Now then, Lord, if you would just weigh our sins on the scales against those of the rest of the world, it would be perfectly clear that their sins are heavier. 35 There has never been a time when the people of the world did not sin against you; but has any other nation kept your commands as well as Israel has? 36 You may find individuals who have, but you won't find a nation that has done so."

4 The angel Uriel, who had been sent to me, replied, 2 "You can't even understand what happens in this world. Do you think you can understand the ways of God Most High?"

3 "Yes, sir, I do!" I answered.

The angel continued, "I have been sent to ask you to solve three riddles about what happens in this world. 4 If you can explain even one of them to me, I will answer your questions about God's ways and teach you why the human race has an evil impulse."

5 "I agree, sir," I said.

Then he said to me, "Good! How do you weigh out a pound of fire? How do you measure a bushel[a] of wind? How do you bring back a day that has passed?"

6 I answered, "Why do you ask me such questions? No human being could answer them."

7 Then he said, "What if I had asked you how many

[a] *Some ancient translations* bushel; *Latin* blast.

NEW REVISED STANDARD VERSION

20 "Yet you did not take away their evil heart from them, so that your law might produce fruit in them. 21 For the first Adam, burdened with an evil heart, transgressed and was overcome, as were also all who were descended from him. 22 Thus the disease became permanent; the law was in the hearts of the people along with the evil root; but what was good departed, and the evil remained. 23 So the times passed and the years were completed, and you raised up for yourself a servant, named David. 24 You commanded him to build a city for your name, and there to offer you oblations from what is yours. 25 This was done for many years; but the inhabitants of the city transgressed, 26 in everything doing just as Adam and all his descendants had done, for they also had the evil heart. 27 So you handed over your city to your enemies.

28 "Then I said in my heart, Are the deeds of those who inhabit Babylon any better? Is that why it has gained dominion over Zion? 29 For when I came here I saw ungodly deeds without number, and my soul has seen many sinners during these thirty years.[a] And my heart failed me, 30 because I have seen how you endure those who sin, and have spared those who act wickedly, and have destroyed your people, and protected your enemies, 31 and have not shown to anyone how your way may be comprehended.[b] Are the deeds of Babylon better than those of Zion? 32 Or has another nation known you besides Israel? Or what tribes have so believed the covenants as these tribes of Jacob? 33 Yet their reward has not appeared and their labor has borne no fruit. For I have traveled widely among the nations and have seen that they abound in wealth, though they are unmindful of your commandments. 34 Now therefore weigh in a balance our iniquities and those of the inhabitants of the world; and it will be found which way the turn of the scale will incline. 35 When have the inhabitants of the earth not sinned in your sight? Or what nation has kept your commandments so well? 36 You may indeed find individuals who have kept your commandments, but nations you will not find."

4 Then the angel that had been sent to me, whose name was Uriel, answered 2 and said to me, "Your understanding has utterly failed regarding this world, and do you think you can comprehend the way of the Most High?" 3 Then I said, "Yes, my lord." And he replied to me, "I have been sent to show you three ways, and to put before you three problems. 4 If you can solve one of them for me, then I will show you the way you desire to see, and will teach you why the heart is evil."

5 I said, "Speak, my lord."

And he said to me, "Go, weigh for me the weight of fire, or measure for me a blast[c] of wind, or call back for me the day that is past."

6 I answered and said, "Who of those that have been born can do that, that you should ask me about such things?"

7 And he said to me, "If I had asked you, 'How many

[a] Ethiop Arab 1 Arm: Lat Syr *in this thirtieth year* [b] Syr; compare Ethiop: Lat *how this way should be forsaken* [c] Syr Ethiop Arab 1 Arab 2 Georg *a measure*

Latin Vulgate

Si eram interrogans te dicens: Quantae habitationes sunt in
corde maris, aut quantae venae sunt in principio abyssi, aut
quantae venae sunt super firmamentum, aut qui sint exitus
paradisi, 8 dicebas fortassis mihi: In abyssum non descendi
neque in infernum adhuc, neque in caelis umquam ascendi.
9 Nunc autem non interrogavi te nisi de igne et vento et diem
per quem transisti, et sine quibus separari non potes, et non
respondisti mihi de eis. 10 Et dixit mihi: Tu quae tua sunt
tecum coadulescentia non potes cognoscere, 11 et quomodo
poterit vas tuum capere Altissimi viam? ... Et iam exterritus
corrupto saeculo intellegere incorruptionem?

Et cum haec audissem, cecidi in faciem meam 12 et dixi
illi: Melius erat nos non adesse, quam advenientes vivere in
impietatibus et pati et non intellegere de qua re. 13 Et
respondit ad me et dixit: Proficiscens profectus sum ad silvam lignorum campi, et cogitaverunt cogitationem 14 et
dixerunt: Venite et eamus et faciamus ad mare bellum, ut
recedat coram nos, et faciamus nobis alias silvas. 15 Et
similiter fluctus maris et ipsi cogitaverunt cogitationem et
dixerunt: Venite ascendentes debellemus silvam campi, ut et
ibi consummemus nobismet ipsis aliam regionem. 16 Et factus est cogitatus silvae in vano, venit enim ignis et consump-
sit eam. 17 Similiter et cogitatus fluctuum maris, stetit enim
harena et prohibuit eam. 18 Si enim eras iudex horum, quem
incipiebas iustificare aut quem condemnare? 19 Et respondi
et dixi: Utrique vanam cogitationem cogitaverunt, terra enim
data est silvae, et maris locus portare fluctus suos. 20 Et
respondit ad me et dixit: Bene tu iudicasti, et quare non iudicasti tibimet ipso? 21 Quemadmodum enim terra silvae data
est et mare fluctibus suis, et qui super terram inhabitant
quae sunt super terram intellegere solummodo possunt, et
qui super caelos super altitudinem caelorum.

22 Et respondi et dixi: Deprecor te, domine, ut mihi datus
est sensus intellegendi. 23 Non enim volui interrogare de
superioribus viis, sed de his quae pertranseunt per nos coti-
die, propter quod Israhel datus est in obprobrium gentibus,
quem dilexisti populum datus est tribubus impiis, et lex
patrum nostrorum in interitum deducta est, et dispositiones
scriptae nusquam sunt. 24 Et pertransivimus de saeculo ut
lucustae, et vita nostra ut vapor, et nec digni sumus misericordiam consequi. 25 Sed quid faciet nomini suo quod invo-
catum est super nos? Et his interrogavi.

26 Et respondit ad me et dixit: Si fueris videbis, et si vixeris
frequenter miraberis, quoniam festinans festinat saeculum

King James Version

dwellings are in the midst of the sea, or how many springs are in the beginning of the deep, or how many springs are above the firmament, or which are the outgoings of paradise:

8 Peradventure thou wouldest say unto me, I never went down into the deep, nor as yet into hell, neither did I ever climb up into heaven.

9 Nevertheless now have I asked thee but only of the fire and wind, and of the day wherethrough thou hast passed, and of things from which thou canst not be separated, and yet canst thou give me no answer of them.

10 He said moreover unto me, Thine own things, and such as are grown up with thee, canst thou not know;

11 How should thy vessel then be able to comprehend the way of the Highest, and, the world being now outwardly corrupted, to understand the corruption that is evident in my sight?

12 Then said I unto him, It were better that we were not at all, than that we should live still in wickedness, and to suffer, and not to know wherefore.

13 He answered me, and said, I went into a forest into a plain, and the trees took counsel,

14 And said, Come, let us go and make war against the sea, that it may depart away before us, and that we may make us more woods.

15 The floods of the sea also in like manner took counsel, and said, Come, let us go up and subdue the woods of the plain, that there also we may make us another country.

16 The thought of the wood was in vain, for the fire came and consumed it.

17 The thought of the floods of the sea came likewise to nought, for the sand stood up and stopped them.

18 If thou wert judge now betwixt these two, whom wouldest thou begin to justify? or whom wouldest thou condemn?

19 I answered and said, Verily it is a foolish thought that they both have devised, for the ground is given unto the wood, and the sea also hath his place to bear his floods.

20 Then answered he me, and said, Thou hast given a right judgment, but why judgest thou not thyself also?

21 For like as the ground is given unto the wood, and the sea to his floods: even so they that dwell upon the earth may understand nothing but that which is upon the earth: and he that dwelleth above the heavens may only understand the things that are above the height of the heavens.

22 Then answered I and said, I beseech thee, O Lord, let me have understanding:

23 For it was not my mind to be curious of the high things, but of such as pass by us daily, namely, wherefore Israel is given up as a reproach to the heathen, and for what cause the people whom thou hast loved is given over unto ungodly nations, and why the law of our forefathers is brought to nought, and the written covenants come to none effect,

24 And we pass away out of the world as grasshoppers, and our life is astonishment and fear, and we are not worthy to obtain mercy.

25 What will he then do unto his name whereby we are called? of these things have I asked.

26 Then answered he me, and said, The more thou searchest, the more thou shalt marvel; for the world hasteth fast to pass away,

TODAY'S ENGLISH VERSION

dwelling places there are at the bottom of the sea? How
many rivers flow into the waters beneath the earth? How
many rivers are there above the dome of the sky? Where are
the exits from the world of the dead? Where are the
entrances to[a] Paradise? 8 If I had asked you these questions,
you might have answered, 'I have never gone down into the
waters beneath the earth, and I have not yet entered the
world of the dead. I have never gone up to heaven.' 9 But all
I have asked you about is fire, wind, and the day that has
just passed—things that you have experienced. Yet you have
given me no answer. 10 You can't even understand things
that you have been familiar with since you were a child.
11 How then can your little mind understand the ways of God
Most High? Can someone already worn down by this corrupt
world understand the ways of the incorruptible God?"

When I heard this, I fell face downward on the ground[b]
12 and said to him, "It would have been better if we had
never been born than to have to live in a world of sin and
suffering without understanding why things happen as
they do."

13 The angel Uriel answered, "I once went into the woods
and heard the trees plotting together. 14 They were saying,
'Let's go to war against the sea and push it back, so that we
may have more room.' 15 But the waves of the sea also plotted together and said, 'Let's conquer the woods and extend
our territory.' 16 But all the plotting of the trees was useless
because fire came and destroyed them. 17 And the plotting of
the sea was just as useless because the sand stood firm and
blocked its advance. 18 Now, if you were the judge and had
to decide between them, which would you pronounce right?"

19 I replied, "They were both wrong, because trees belong
on the land, and waves belong in the sea."

20 "You have given the right answer," he said. "So why
can't you see the answer to your own problems? 21 For just
as trees have their place on land, and waves have their place
in the sea, so the people of this world can understand only
what goes on in this world, and only heavenly beings can
understand what goes on in heaven."

22 "Please tell me, sir," I asked, "why then was I given the
ability to understand anything? 23 I am not interested in asking questions about what goes on in the heavens; I am only
concerned about things that go on around us. Why has God
allowed Israel to be disgraced by foreign nations? Why has
he let the nation he loves be handed over to the power of
godless nations? Why do the Law and the covenant that
were given to our ancestors mean nothing any more? 24 Why
do we die as quickly as insects? Why is our life shorter than
a breath? Why does God think us unworthy of his mercy?
25 Why doesn't God do something to help his own people?
These are the questions that I want to ask."

26 Uriel answered, "If you live long enough, you will be
surprised at what you will see, because this age is rapidly

[a] *Some ancient translations* exits from . . . entrances to; *Latin* exits from.
[b] *Verse 11 in Latin is unclear.*

NEW REVISED STANDARD VERSION

dwellings are in the heart of the sea, or how many streams
are at the source of the deep, or how many streams are
above the firmament, or which are the exits of Hades, or
which are the entrances[a] of paradise?' 8 perhaps you would
have said to me, 'I never went down into the deep, nor as yet
into Hades, neither did I ever ascend into heaven.' 9 But now
I have asked you only about fire and wind and the day—
things that you have experienced and from which you cannot be separated, and you have given me no answer about
them." 10 He said to me, "You cannot understand the things
with which you have grown up; 11 how then can your mind
comprehend the way of the Most High? And how can one
who is already worn out[b] by the corrupt world understand
incorruption?"[c] When I heard this, I fell on my face[d] 12 and
said to him, "It would have been better for us not to be here
than to come here and live in ungodliness, and to suffer and
not understand why."

13 He answered me and said, "I went into a forest of trees
of the plain, and they made a plan 14 and said, 'Come, let us
go and make war against the sea, so that it may recede
before us and so that we may make for ourselves more
forests.' 15 In like manner the waves of the sea also made a
plan and said, 'Come, let us go up and subdue the forest of
the plain so that there also we may gain more territory for
ourselves.' 16 But the plan of the forest was in vain, for the
fire came and consumed it; 17 likewise also the plan of the
waves of the sea was in vain,[e] for the sand stood firm and
blocked it. 18 If now you were a judge between them, which
would you undertake to justify, and which to condemn?"

19 I answered and said, "Each made a foolish plan, for
the land has been assigned to the forest, and the locale of the
sea a place to carry its waves."

20 He answered me and said, "You have judged rightly,
but why have you not judged so in your own case? 21 For as
the land has been assigned to the forest and the sea to its
waves, so also those who inhabit the earth can understand
only what is on the earth, and he who is[f] above the heavens
can understand what is above the height of the heavens."

22 Then I answered and said, "I implore you, my lord,
why[g] have I been endowed with the power of understanding? 23 For I did not wish to inquire about the ways above,
but about those things that we daily experience: why Israel
has been given over to the Gentiles in disgrace; why the people whom you loved has been given over to godless tribes,
and the law of our ancestors has been brought to destruction
and the written covenants no longer exist. 24 We pass from
the world like locusts, and our life is like a mist,[h] and we are
not worthy to obtain mercy. 25 But what will he do for his[i]
name that is invoked over us? It is about these things that I
have asked."

26 He answered me and said, "If you are alive, you will
see, and if you live long,[j] you will often marvel, because the
age is hurrying swiftly to its end. 27 It will not be able to

a Syr Compare Ethiop Arab 2 Arm: Lat lacks *of Hades, or which are the entrances* *b* Meaning of Lat uncertain *c* Syr Ethiop *the way of the incorruptible?* *d* Syr Ethiop Arab 1: Meaning of Lat uncertain
e Lat lacks *was in vain* *f* Or *those who are* *g* Syr Ethiop Arm: Meaning of Lat uncertain *h* Syr Ethiop Arab Georg: Lat *a trembling*
i Ethiop adds *holy* *j* Syr: Lat *live*

pertransire. 27 Non capiet portare quae in temporibus iustis
repromissa sunt, quoniam plenum maestitia est saeculum hoc
et infirmitatibus. 28 Seminatum est enim malum, de quibus
me interrogas de ea, et necdum venit destrictio ipsius. 29 Si
ergo non messum fuerit quod seminatum est, et discesserit
locus ubi seminatum est malum, non veniet ager ubi seminatum est bonum. 30 Quoniam granum seminis mali seminatum est in corde Adam ab initio, et quantum impietatis generavit usque nunc et generabit usque cum veniat area.
31 Aestima autem apud te, granum mali seminis quantum
fructum impietatis generaverit. 32 Quando seminatae fuerint
spicae quarum non est numerus, quam magnam aream incipient facere.

33 Et respondi et dixi: Quo et quando haec? Quare modici
et mali anni nostri? 34 Et respondit ad me et dixit: Non festina spiritu super Altissimum; tu enim festinas propter temet
ipsum spiritum, nam Excelsus pro multis. 35 Nonne de his
interrogaverunt animae iustorum in promptuariis suis
dicentes: Usquequo spero sic? Et quando venit fructus areae
mercedis nostrae? 36 Et respondit ad ea Hieremihel
archangelus et dixit: Quando impletus fuerit numerus simili-
um vobis, quoniam in statera ponderavit saeculum 37 et
mensura mensuravit tempora et numero numeravit tempora,
et non commovet nec excitabit usque dum impleatur praedicta mensura. 38 Et respondi et dixi: O dominator domine, sed
et nos omnes pleni sumus impietate. 39 Et ne forte propter
nos inpediatur iustorum area, propter peccata inhabitantium
super terram. 40 Et respondit ad me et dixit: Vade et interroga praegnantem, si quando impleverit novem menses suos,
adhuc poterit matrix eius retinere fetus in semet ipsa. 41 Et
dixi: Non potest, domine. Et dixit ad me: In inferno promptuaria animarum matrici adsimilata sunt. 42 Quemadmodum
enim festinavit quae parit effugere necessitatem partus, sic et
haec festinat reddere ea quae commendata sunt 43 ab initio.
Tunc tibi demonstrabitur de his quae concupiscis videre.

44 Et respondi et dixi: Si inveni gratiam ante oculos tuos,
et si possibile est, et si idoneus sum, 45 demonstra mihi et
hoc, si plus quam praeteriti habet venire aut plura pertran-
sierunt super nos, 46 quoniam quod pertransivit scio, quid
autem futuri sit ignoro. 47 Et dixit ad me: Sta super dexteram partem et demonstrabo tibi interpretationem similitudi-
nis. 48 Et steti et vidi, et ecce fornax ardens transiit coram
me; et factum est cum transiret flamma, et vidi et ecce superavit fumus. 49 Et post hoc transiit coram me nubes plena

27 And cannot comprehend the things that are promised to the righteous in time to come: for this world is full of unrighteousness and infirmities.

28 But as concerning the things whereof thou askest me, I will tell thee; for the evil is sown, but the destruction thereof is not yet come.

29 If therefore that which is sown be not turned upside down, and if the place where the evil is sown pass not away, then cannot it come that is sown with good.

30 For the grain of evil seed hath been sown in the heart of Adam from the beginning, and how much ungodliness hath it brought up unto this time? and how much shall it yet bring forth until the time of threshing come?

31 Ponder now by thyself, how great fruit of wickedness the grain of evil seed hath brought forth.

32 And when the ears shall be cut down, which are without number, how great a floor shall they fill?

33 Then I answered and said, How, and when shall these things come to pass? wherefore are our years few and evil?

34 And he answered me, saying, Do not thou hasten above the most Highest: for thy haste is in vain to be above him, for thou hast much exceeded.

35 Did not the souls also of the righteous ask question of these things in their chambers, saying, How long shall I hope on this fashion? when cometh the fruit of the floor of our reward?

36 And unto these things Uriel the archangel gave them answer, and said, Even when the number of seeds is filled in you: for he hath weighed the world in the balance.

37 By measure hath he measured the times, and by number hath he numbered the times; and he doth not move nor stir them, until the said measure be fulfilled.

38 Then answered I and said, O Lord that bearest rule, even we all are full of impiety.

39 And for our sakes peradventure it is that the floors of the righteous are not filled, because of the sins of them that dwell upon the earth.

40 So he answered me, and said, Go thy way to a woman with child, and ask of her when she hath fulfilled her nine months, if her womb may keep the birth any longer within her.

41 Then said I, No, Lord, that can she not. And he said unto me, In the grave the chambers of souls are like the womb of a woman:

42 For like as a woman that travaileth maketh haste to escape the necessity of the travail: even so do these places haste to deliver those things that are committed unto them.

43 From the beginning, look, what thou desirest to see, it shall be shewed thee.

44 Then answered I and said, If I have found favour in thy sight, and if it be possible, and if I be meet therefore,

45 Shew me then whether there be more to come than is past, or more past than is to come.

46 What is past I know, but what is for to come I know not.

47 And he said unto me, Stand up upon the right side, and I shall expound the similitude unto thee.

48 So I stood, and saw, and, behold, an hot burning oven passed by before me: and it happened that when the flame was gone by I looked, and, behold, the smoke remained still.

49 After this there passed by before me a watery cloud,

TODAY'S ENGLISH VERSION

passing away. 27 This age is so full of misery and imperfection that it cannot hold all the blessings that God has promised the righteous in the time to come. 28 The evil about which you have asked me has already been planted, but the time for its harvesting has not yet arrived. 29 This evil must be harvested, and this world where it was planted must be removed, before the new age where the good is to be planted can appear. 30 At the beginning of time one grain of evil seed was sown in the heart of Adam. See how much wickedness it has already produced! Think of how much more it will produce before it is cut down and threshed out at Judgment Day. 31 You can see for yourself what a big crop this one evil seed has produced. 32 How terrible will be the harvest on Judgment Day when these countless heads of grain are threshed out!"

33 Then I asked, "How long do we have to wait before this happens? Why are our lives so short and so full of misery?"

34 Uriel answered, "Don't be in a greater hurry than God Most High! You are thinking only of yourself, but God has to be concerned about everybody.[a] 35 Your questions are the same ones asked by the souls of the righteous dead in the places where God is keeping them waiting: 'How long must we wait here? When will the day of judgment come, when we will get our reward?' 36 The archangel Jeremiel answers them, 'It will happen as soon as the complete number of those who have suffered as you have are here. For God has weighed this age, 37 measured the years, and numbered the days. Nothing will be changed until time has run its predetermined course.' "

38 "But, sir," I replied, "all of us here on earth are such wicked sinners. 39 Is it possible that because of our sin the righteous dead are having to wait for their reward?"

40 His answer was, "Can a pregnant woman keep her child from being born after her nine months are up?"

41 "No, sir, she cannot," I answered.

And he continued, "In the world of the dead, the place where God has stored the souls is like a womb. 42 It is as eager to return the souls entrusted to it from the beginning of the world as a woman is to end her labor pains. 43 When that happens, you will have the answer to all your questions."

44 "Please, sir," I asked, "if you think I am able to understand it, can you 45 tell me one more thing? Is the time that is still to come longer than the past that has already gone by? 46 I know how long the past has been, but I don't know the future."

47 "Come here and stand at my right," he commanded, "and I will show you a vision and explain its meaning." 48 So I stood by him and looked, and I saw a blazing fire pass by in front of me, and when it was gone, I saw that smoke was still there. 49 Then a rain cloud passed by in front of me,

a *Verse 34 in Latin is unclear.*

NEW REVISED STANDARD VERSION

bring the things that have been promised to the righteous in their appointed times, because this age is full of sadness and infirmities. 28 For the evil about which[a] you ask me has been sown, but the harvest of it has not yet come. 29 If therefore that which has been sown is not reaped, and if the place where the evil has been sown does not pass away, the field where the good has been sown will not come. 30 For a grain of evil seed was sown in Adam's heart from the beginning, and how much ungodliness it has produced until now—and will produce until the time of threshing comes! 31 Consider now for yourself how much fruit of ungodliness a grain of evil seed has produced. 32 When heads of grain without number are sown, how great a threshing floor they will fill!"

33 Then I answered and said, "How long?[a] When will these things be? Why are our years few and evil?" 34 He answered me and said, "Do not be in a greater hurry than the Most High. You, indeed, are in a hurry for yourself,[b] but the Highest is in a hurry on behalf of many. 35 Did not the souls of the righteous in their chambers ask about these matters, saying, 'How long are we to remain here?[c] And when will the harvest of our reward come?' 36 And the archangel Jeremiel answered and said, 'When the number of those like yourselves is completed;[d] for he has weighed the age in the balance, 37 and measured the times by measure, and numbered the times by number; and he will not move or arouse them until that measure is fulfilled.' "

38 Then I answered and said, "But, O sovereign Lord, all of us also are full of ungodliness. 39 It is perhaps on account of us that the time of threshing is delayed for the righteous—on account of the sins of those who inhabit the earth."

40 He answered me and said, "Go and ask a pregnant woman whether, when her nine months have been completed, her womb can keep the fetus within her any longer."

41 And I said, "No, lord, it cannot."

He said to me, "In Hades the chambers of the souls are like the womb. 42 For just as a woman who is in labor makes haste to escape the pangs of birth, so also do these places hasten to give back those things that were committed to them from the beginning. 43 Then the things that you desire to see will be disclosed to you."

44 I answered and said, "If I have found favor in your sight, and if it is possible, and if I am worthy, 45 show me this also: whether more time is to come than has passed, or whether for us the greater part has gone by. 46 For I know what has gone by, but I do not know what is to come."

47 And he said to me, "Stand at my right side, and I will show you the interpretation of a parable."

48 So I stood and looked, and lo, a flaming furnace passed by before me, and when the flame had gone by I looked, and lo, the smoke remained. 49 And after this a cloud

a Syr Ethiop: Meaning of Lat uncertain *b* Syr Ethiop Arab Arm: Meaning of Lat uncertain *c* Syr Ethiop Arab 2 Georg: Lat *How long do I hope thus?* *d* Syr Ethiop Arab 2: Lat *number of seeds is completed for you*

LATIN VULGATE

aquae et inmisit pluviam impetu multam; et cum transisset
impetus pluviae, et superaverunt in ea guttae. 50 Et dixit ad
me: Cogita tibi. Sicut enim crescit pluvia amplius quam guttae, et ignis amplius quam fumus, sic superabundavit quae
transivit mensura, superaverunt autem guttae et fumus.
51 Et oravi et dixi: Putas vivo usque in diebus illis, vel quis
erit in diebus illis? 52 Respondit ad me et dixit: De signis de
quibus me perrogas, ex parte possum tibi dicere, de vita
autem tua non sum missus dicere tibi, sed nescio.

5 De signis autem: Ecce dies venient, et adprehendentur
qui inhabitant super terram in excessu multo, et abscondetur veritatis via, et sterilis erit a fide regio. 2 Et multiplicabitur iniustitia super hanc quam ipse tu vides et super
quam audisti olim. 3 Et erit inconposita vestigio quam nunc
vides regnare regionem, et videbunt eam desertam. 4 Si
autem tibi dederit Altissimus vivere, et videbis post tertiam
turbatam, et relucescet subito sol noctu et luna interdie. 5 Et
de ligno sanguis stillabit, et lapis dabit vocem suam; et populi commovebuntur, et gressus commutabuntur. 6 Et regnabit quem non sperant qui inhabitant super terram; et
volatilia conmigrationem facient. 7 Et mare Sodomitum
pisces reiciet. Et dabit vocem noctu quem non noverant
multi, omnes autem audient vocem eius. 8 Et chaus fiet per
loca multa, et ignis frequenter emittetur, et bestiae agrestes
transmigrabunt regionem suam, et mulieres parient menstru-
atae monstra, 9 et in dulcibus aquis salsae invenientur. Et
amici omnes semet ipsos expugnabunt; et abscondetur tunc
sensus, et intellectus separabitur in promptuarium suum.
10 Et quaeretur a multis et non invenietur, et multiplicabitur
iniustitia et incontinentia super terram. 11 Et interrogabit
regio proximam suam et dicet: Numquid per te pertransiit
iustitia iustum faciens? Et haec negabit. 12 Et erit in illo
tempore, et sperabunt homines et non inpetrabunt, laborabunt et non dirigentur viae eorum. 13 Haec signa dicere
tibi permissum est mihi. Et si oraveris iterum et ploraveris
sicut et nunc et ieiunaveris septem diebus, audies iterato
horum maiora.
14 Et evigilavi, et corpus meum horruit valde, et anima
mea laboravit ut deficeret. 15 Et tenuit me qui venit angelus,
qui loquebatur in me, et confortavit me et statuit me super
pedes. 16 Et factum est in nocte secunda, et venit ad me
Phalthihel dux populi et dixit mihi: Ubi eras et quare vultus
tuus tristis? 17 Aut nescis quoniam tibi creditus est Israhel
in regione transmigrationis eorum? 18 Exsurge ergo et gusta
panem alicuius, et non derelinquas nos sicut pastor gregem
suum in manibus luporum malignorum. 19 Et dixi ei: Vade a

KING JAMES VERSION

and sent down much rain with a storm; and when the stormy rain was past, the drops remained still.

50 Then said he unto me, Consider with thyself; as the rain is more than the drops, and as the fire is greater than the smoke; but the drops and the smoke remain behind: so the quantity which is past did more exceed.

51 Then I prayed, and said, May I live, thinkest thou, until that time? or what shall happen in those days?

52 He answered me, and said, As for the tokens whereof thou askest me, I may tell thee of them in part: but as touching thy life, I am not sent to shew thee; for I do not know it.

5 Nevertheless as concerning the tokens, behold, the days shall come, that they which dwell upon earth shall be taken in a great number, and the way of truth shall be hidden, and the land shall be barren of faith.

2 But iniquity shall be increased above that which now thou seest, or that thou hast heard long ago.

3 And the land, that thou seest now to have root, shalt thou see wasted suddenly.

4 But if the most High grant thee to live, thou shalt see after the third trumpet that the sun shall suddenly shine again in the night, and the moon thrice in the day:

5 And blood shall drop out of wood, and the stone shall give his voice, and the people shall be troubled:

6 And even he shall rule, whom they look not for that dwell upon the earth, and the fowls shall take their flight away together:

7 And the Sodomitish sea shall cast out fish, and make a noise in the night, which many have not known: but they shall all hear the voice thereof.

8 There shall be a confusion also in many places, and the fire shall be oft sent out again, and the wild beasts shall change their places, and menstruous women shall bring forth monsters:

9 And salt waters shall be found in the sweet, and all friends shall destroy one another; then shall wit hide itself, and understanding withdraw itself into his secret chamber,

10 And shall be sought of many, and yet not be found: then shall unrighteousness and incontinency be multiplied upon earth.

11 One land also shall ask another, and say, Is righteousness that maketh a man righteous gone through thee? And it shall say, No.

12 At the same time shall men hope, but nothing obtain: they shall labour, but their ways shall not prosper.

13 To shew thee such tokens I have leave; and if thou wilt pray again, and weep as now, and fast seven days, thou shalt hear yet greater things.

14 Then I awaked, and an extreme fearfulness went through all my body, and my mind was troubled, so that it fainted.

15 So the angel that was come to talk with me held me, comforted me, and set me up upon my feet.

16 And in the second night it came to pass, that Salathiel the captain of the people came unto me, saying, Where hast thou been? and why is thy countenance so heavy?

17 Knowest thou not that Israel is committed unto thee in the land of their captivity?

18 Up then, and eat bread, and forsake us not, as the shepherd that leaveth his flock in the hands of cruel wolves.

TODAY'S ENGLISH VERSION

bringing a heavy downpour of rain; and when the downpour
was over, there was still a light rain. 50 "Think about this,"
said Uriel. "Just as the downpour was greater than the light
rain that followed it and the fire was greater than the smoke
left behind, in the same way the time that has passed is
much longer than the time to come. The time that is left is
like the light rain and the smoke."

51 "Please tell me," I asked, "do you think I will live until
that time? If not, who will be alive when it happens?"

52 He answered, "I can tell you some of the signs of the
end, if that is what you are asking about; but I am not here
to tell you how long you will live, and in any case, I don't
know.

5 "But these are the signs: The time will come when all
people on earth will be in the grip of great confusion.[a]
The way of truth will be hidden, and no faith will be left in
the land. 2 Wickedness will increase until it has become
worse than you have ever known it to be. 3 The country that
you now see ruling the world will lie in ruins, with no inhabitant or traveler there. 4 After that,[b] if God Most High lets
you live long enough, you will see that country in confusion.
The sun will suddenly start shining at night, and the moon
in the daytime. 5 Blood will drip from trees; stones will
speak; nations will be in confusion; the movement of the
stars will be changed. 6 A king unwanted by anyone will
begin to rule, and the birds will fly away. 7 Fish will be
washed up on the shores of the Dead Sea. The voice of one
whom many do not know will be heard at night; everyone
will hear it. 8 The earth will break open[c] in many places and
begin spouting out flames. Wild animals will leave the fields
and forests. At their monthly periods women will bear monsters. 9 Fresh water will become salty. Friends everywhere
will attack one another. Then understanding will disappear,
and reason will go into hiding, 10 and they will not be found
even though many may look for them. Everywhere on earth
wickedness and violence will increase. 11 One country will
ask a neighboring country if justice or anyone who does
right has come that way, but the answer will always be 'No.'
12 At that time people will hope for much, but will get nothing; they will work hard, but will never succeed at anything.
13 These are the signs of the end that I am permitted to show
you. But if you begin to pray again and continue to weep
and fast for seven more days, you will hear even greater
things."

14 Then I woke up, and I was trembling violently. I was so
disturbed that I was about to faint, 15 but the angel that had
come to talk with me took hold of me, strengthened me, and
set me on my feet.

16 The next night, Phaltiel, who was a leader of the people,
came to me and asked, "Where have you been? And why do
you look so sad? 17 Don't you know that the people of Israel
in the land of their exile have been put in your care? 18 So
get up and eat. Do not abandon us like a shepherd leaving
his flock to the attacks of savage wolves."

[a] *Some ancient translations* confusion; *Latin unclear.* [b] After that; *Latin unclear.* [c] *One ancient translation* The earth will break open; *Latin* Chaos will appear.

NEW REVISED STANDARD VERSION

full of water passed before me and poured down a heavy and
violent rain, and when the violent rainstorm had passed,
drops still remained in the cloud.[a]

50 He said to me, "Consider it for yourself; for just as the
rain is more than the drops, and the fire is greater than the
smoke, so the quantity that passed was far greater; but drops
and smoke remained."

51 Then I prayed and said, "Do you think that I shall live
until those days? Or who will be alive in those days?"

52 He answered me and said, "Concerning the signs about
which you ask me, I can tell you in part; but I was not sent
to tell you concerning your life, for I do not know.

5 "Now concerning the signs: lo, the days are coming
when those who inhabit the earth shall be seized with
great terror,[b] and the way of truth shall be hidden, and the
land shall be barren of faith. 2 Unrighteousness shall be
increased beyond what you yourself see, and beyond what
you heard of formerly. 3 And the land that you now see ruling shall be a trackless waste, and people shall see it desolate. 4 But if the Most High grants that you live, you shall
see it thrown into confusion after the third period;[c]

and the sun shall suddenly begin to shine at night,
and the moon during the day.
5 Blood shall drip from wood,
and the stone shall utter its voice;
the peoples shall be troubled,
and the stars shall fall.[d]

6 And one shall reign whom those who inhabit the earth do
not expect, and the birds shall fly away together; 7 and the
Dead Sea[e] shall cast up fish; and one whom the many do not
know shall make his voice heard by night, and all shall hear
his voice.[f] 8 There shall be chaos also in many places, fire
shall often break out, the wild animals shall roam beyond
their haunts, and menstruous women shall bring forth monsters. 9 Salt waters shall be found in the sweet, and all
friends shall conquer one another; then shall reason hide
itself, and wisdom shall withdraw into its chamber, 10 and it
shall be sought by many but shall not be found, and unrighteousness and unrestraint shall increase on earth. 11 One
country shall ask its neighbor, 'Has righteousness, or anyone
who does right, passed through you?' And it will answer,
'No.' 12 At that time people shall hope but not obtain; they
shall labor, but their ways shall not prosper. 13 These are the
signs that I am permitted to tell you, and if you pray again,
and weep as you do now, and fast for seven days, you shall
hear yet greater things than these."

14 Then I woke up, and my body shuddered violently, and
my soul was so troubled that it fainted. 15 But the angel who
had come and talked with me held me and strengthened me
and set me on my feet.

16 Now on the second night Phaltiel, a chief of the people,
came to me and said, "Where have you been? And why is
your face sad? 17 Or do you not know that Israel has been
entrusted to you in the land of their exile? 18 Rise therefore
and eat some bread, and do not forsake us, like a shepherd
who leaves the flock in the power of savage wolves."

[a] Lat *in it* [b] Syr Ethiop: Meaning of Lat uncertain [c] Literally *after the third*; Ethiop *after three months*; Arm *after the third vision*; Georg *after the third day* [d] Ethiop Compare Syr and Arab: Meaning of Lat uncertain [e] Lat *Sea of Sodom* [f] Cn: Lat *fish; and it shall make its voice heard by night, which the many have not known, but all shall hear its voice.*

me et non ad me accedas usque diebus septem, et tunc
venies ad me. Et audivit ut dixi et recessit a me. 20 Et ego
ieiunavi diebus septem ululans et plorans, sicut mihi mandavit Urihel angelus.

21 Et factum est post dies septem, et iterum cogitationes
cordis mei molestae erant mihi valde. 22 Et resumpsit anima
mea spiritum intellectus, et iterum coepi loqui coram
Altissimo sermones 23 et dixi: Dominator Domine, ex omni
silva terrae et ex omnium arborum eius elegisti vineam
unam, 24 et ex omnium terrarum orbis elegisti tibi foveam
unam, et ex omnibus floribus orbis elegisti tibi lilium unum,
25 et ex omnibus abyssis maris replesti tibi rivum unum, et
ex omnibus aedificatis civitatibus sanctificasti tibimet ipsi
Sion, 26 et ex omnibus creatis volatilibus nominasti tibi
columbam unam, et ex omnibus plasmatis pecoribus pro-
vidisti tibi ovem unam, 27 et ex omnibus multiplicatis pop-
ulis adquisisti tibi populum unum, et ab omnibus probatam
legem donasti huic quem desiderasti populo. 28 Et nunc
Domine, ut quid tradidisti unum plurimis et praeparasti
unam radicem super alias et dispersisti unicum tuum in multis? 29 Et conculcaverunt qui contradicebant sponsionibus
tuis quique tuis testamentis credebant. 30 Et si odiens odisti
populum tuum; tuis manibus debet castigari.

31 Et factum est, cum locutus essem sermones istos, et
missus est angelus ad me qui ante venerat ad me praeterita
nocte, 32 et dixit mihi: Audi me et instruam te, et intende
mihi et adiciam coram te. 33 Et dixi: Loquere, dominus
meus. Et dixit ad me: Valde in excessu mentis factus es in
Israhel; aut plus dilexisti eum super eum qui fecit eum?
34 Et dixi: Non, domine, sed dolens locutus sum, torquent
enim me renes mei per omnem horam quaerentem adprehen-
dere semitam Altissimi et investigare partem iudicii eius.
35 Et dixit ad me: Non potes. Et dixi: Quare, domine, aut quid
nascebar, aut quare non fiebat matrix matris meae mihi
sepulchrum, ut non viderem laborem Iacob et defatigationem
generis Israhel?

36 Et dixit ad me: Numera mihi qui necdum venerunt, et
collige mihi dispersas guttas, et revirida mihi aridos flores,
37 et aperi mihi clausa promptuaria et produc mihi inclusos
in eis flatus, aut monstra mihi vocis imaginem, et tunc
ostendam tibi eum laborem quem rogas videre. 38 Et dixi:
Dominator domine, quis enim est qui potest haec scire, nisi
qui cum hominibus habitationem non habet? 39 Ego autem
insipiens, et quomodo potero dicere de his quibus me interro-
gasti? 40 Et dixit ad me: Quomodo non potes facere unum de
his quae dicta sunt, sic non poteris invenire iudicium meum
aut finem caritatis quem pro populo meo promisi.

19 Then said I unto him, Go thy ways from me, and come not nigh me. And he heard what I said, and went from me.

20 And so I fasted seven days, mourning and weeping, like as Uriel the angel commanded me.

21 And after seven days so it was, that the thoughts of my heart were very grievous unto me again,

22 And my soul recovered the spirit of understanding, and I began to talk with the most High again,

23 And said, O Lord that bearest rule, of every wood of the earth, and of all the trees thereof, thou hast chosen thee one only vine:

24 And of all lands of the whole world thou hast chosen thee one pit: and of all the flowers thereof one lily:

25 And of all the depths of the sea thou hast filled thee one river: and of all builded cities thou hast hallowed Sion unto thyself:

26 And of all the fowls that are created thou hast named thee one dove: and of all the cattle that are made thou hast provided thee one sheep:

27 And among all the multitudes of people thou hast gotten thee one people: and unto this people, whom thou lovedst, thou gavest a law that is approved of all.

28 And now, O Lord, why hast thou given this one people over unto many? and upon the one root hast thou prepared others, and why hast thou scattered thy only one people among many?

29 And they which did gainsay thy promises, and believed not thy covenants, have trodden them down.

30 If thou didst so much hate thy people, yet shouldest thou punish them with thine own hands.

31 Now when I had spoken these words, the angel that came to me the night afore was sent unto me,

32 And said unto me, Hear me, and I will instruct thee; hearken to the thing that I say, and I shall tell thee more.

33 And I said, Speak on, my Lord. Then said he unto me, Thou art sore troubled in mind for Israel's sake: lovest thou that people better than he that made them?

34 And I said, No, Lord: but of very grief have I spoken: for my reins pain me every hour, while I labour to comprehend the way of the most High, and to seek out part of his judgment.

35 And he said unto me, Thou canst not. And I said, Wherefore, Lord? whereunto was I born then? or why was not my mother's womb then my grave, that I might not have seen the travail of Jacob, and the wearisome toil of the stock of Israel?

36 And he said unto me, Number me the things that are not yet come, gather me together the drops that are scattered abroad, make me the flowers green again that are withered,

37 Open me the places that are closed, and bring me forth the winds that in them are shut up, shew me the image of a voice: and then I will declare to thee the thing that thou labourest to know.

38 And I said, O Lord that bearest rule, who may know these things, but he that hath not his dwelling with men?

39 As for me, I am unwise: how may I then speak of these things whereof thou askest me?

40 Then said he unto me, Like as thou canst do none of these things that I have spoken of, even so canst thou not find out my judgment, or in the end the love that I have promised unto my people.

TODAY'S ENGLISH VERSION

19 "Leave me alone," I answered, "do not come near me for
the next seven days. Then come back." So he left.

20 Then, crying and mourning, I fasted seven days, as the
angel Uriel had commanded me to do. 21 At the end of the
seven days, I was again deeply troubled, 22 but I recovered
my ability to think, and again I began to speak with God
Most High. 23 "Lord and Master," I said, "from all the forests
and plants on earth you have chosen this one vine. 24 From
all the countries of the world, you have chosen this one
small land. From all the flowers in the world, you have chosen this one lily. 25 From all the water in the deep oceans,
you have filled up this one river. From all the cities that have
ever been built, you have set apart this one city, Jerusalem,
as your own. 26 From all the birds that were created, you
chose this one dove. From all the animals that were made,
you chose this one lamb. 27 From all the nations of the
world, you chose this one nation to be your own, and you
gave its people your Law, which is honored by people everywhere.

28 "And now, Lord, since all of this is true, why have you
dishonored[a] this one people more than all others by handing
them over to many nations? Why have you scattered your
own people, 29 who believed in your covenants? Why have
you let them be trampled by people who rejected your promises? 30 If you are so angry with your own people, you yourself ought to punish them."

31 When I had finished speaking, the angel who had come
to me on a previous night was sent to me again. 32 He said,
"Listen carefully to me, and I will teach you more."

33 "Please go on, sir," I said.

So he continued, "Are you worried about the people of
Israel? Do you think you love them more than God, who
made them?"

34 "No, sir," I replied. "I spoke as I did because I was so
confused and upset. I am always troubled whenever I try to
think about the ways of God Most High or to understand
even a small part of what he does."

35 "You cannot understand!" he answered.

And I asked, "Why not, sir? In that case, why was I born?
Why didn't I die before I was born? Then I wouldn't have
seen the sufferings and troubles of the people of Israel."

36 The angel said to me, "I will answer you if you can do
the following things: Tell me how many people are yet to be
born; collect scattered raindrops for me; make dead flowers
bloom again; 37 open the rooms where the winds are locked
up and make them blow for me; show me the picture of a
sound. If you can do these things, I will answer your questions about the sufferings of the people of Israel."

38 I answered, "Lord and master, no one can do these
things, except God, who is not confined to this world.
39 How can I give you any kind of answer? What do I know?"

40 He continued, "You could not do even one of the things
that I asked you to do. How can you expect to understand
God's judgments or why God has promised his love to his
people?"

[a] *Some ancient translations* dishonored; *Latin* prepared.

NEW REVISED STANDARD VERSION

19 Then I said to him, "Go away from me and do not
come near me for seven days; then you may come to me."
He heard what I said and left me. 20 So I fasted seven
days, mourning and weeping, as the angel Uriel had commanded me.

21 After seven days the thoughts of my heart were very
grievous to me again. 22 Then my soul recovered the spirit of
understanding, and I began once more to speak words in the
presence of the Most High. 23 I said, "O sovereign Lord, from
every forest of the earth and from all its trees you have chosen one vine, 24 and from all the lands of the world you have
chosen for yourself one region,[a] and from all the flowers of
the world you have chosen for yourself one lily, 25 and from
all the depths of the sea you have filled for yourself one
river, and from all the cities that have been built you have
consecrated Zion for yourself, 26 and from all the birds that
have been created you have named for yourself one dove,
and from all the flocks that have been made you have provided for yourself one sheep, 27 and from all the multitude of
peoples you have gotten for yourself one people; and to this
people, whom you have loved, you have given the law that is
approved by all. 28 And now, O Lord, why have you handed
the one over to the many, and dishonored[b] the one root
beyond the others, and scattered your only one among the
many? 29 And those who opposed your promises have trampled on those who believed your covenants. 30 If you really
hate your people, they should be punished at your own
hands."

31 When I had spoken these words, the angel who had
come to me on a previous night was sent to me. 32 He said to
me, "Listen to me, and I will instruct you; pay attention to
me, and I will tell you more."

33 Then I said, "Speak, my lord." And he said to me, "Are
you greatly disturbed in mind over Israel? Or do you love
him more than his Maker does?"

34 I said, "No, my lord, but because of my grief I have
spoken; for every hour I suffer agonies of heart, while I strive
to understand the way of the Most High and to search out
some part of his judgment."

35 He said to me, "You cannot." And I said, "Why not, my
lord? Why then was I born? Or why did not my mother's
womb become my grave, so that I would not see the travail
of Jacob and the exhaustion of the people of Israel?"

36 He said to me, "Count up for me those who have not
yet come, and gather for me the scattered raindrops, and
make the withered flowers bloom again for me; 37 open for
me the closed chambers, and bring out for me the winds shut
up in them, or show me the picture of a voice; and then I will
explain to you the travail that you ask to understand."[c]

38 I said, "O sovereign Lord, who is able to know these
things except him whose dwelling is not with mortals? 39 As
for me, I am without wisdom, and how can I speak concerning the things that you have asked me?"

40 He said to me, "Just as you cannot do one of the things
that were mentioned, so you cannot discover my judgment,
or the goal of the love that I have promised to my people."

a Ethiop: Lat *pit* *b* Syr Ethiop Arab: Lat *prepared* *c* Lat *see*

Latin Vulgate

41 Et dixi: Sed ecce, domine, tu praees his qui in fine sunt,
et quid facient qui ante me sunt aut nos aut hii qui post nos?
42 Et dixit ad me: Coronae adsimilabo iudicium meum. Sicut
non novissimorum tarditas, sic nec priorum velocitas. 43 Et
respondi et dixi: Nec enim poteras facere qui facti sunt et qui
sunt et qui futuri sunt in unum, ut celerius iudicium tuum
ostendas? 44 Et respondit ad me et dixit: Non potest fes-
tinare creatura super creatorem, nec sustinere saeculum qui
in eo creati sunt in unum. 45 Et dixi: Quomodo dixisti servo
tuo, quoniam vivificans vivificabis a te creatam creaturam in
unum? Si ergo viventes vivent in unum et sustinebit creatura, poterit et nunc portare praesentes in unum. 46 Et dixit ad
me: Interroga matricem mulieris et dices ad eam: Decem si
paris, quare per tempus? Roga ergo eam, ut det decem in
unum. 47 Et dixi: Non utique poterit, sed secundum tempus.
48 Et dixit ad me: Et ego dedi matricem terrae his qui seminati sunt super eam per tempus. 49 Quemadmodum enim
infans non parit nec ea quae senuit adhuc, sic ego disposui a
me creatum saeculum.

50 Et interrogavi et dixi: Cum iam dederis mihi viam,
loquar coram te; nam mater nostra, de qua dixisti mihi,
adhuc iuvenis est, iam ad senectutem adpropinquat? 51 Et
respondit ad me et dixit: Interroga quae parit, et dicet tibi.
52 Dices enim ei: Quare quos peperisti nunc non sunt similes
his qui ante, sed minores statu? 53 Et dicet tibi et ipsa: Alii
sunt qui in iuventute virtutis nati sunt, et alii qui sub tempus senectutis deficiente matrice sunt nati. 54 Considera ergo
et tu, quoniam minores statu estis prae his qui ante vos,
55 et qui post vos quam ut vos, quasi iam senescentis creaturae et fortitudinem iuventutis praeterientis.

Et dixi: Rogo domine, si inveni gratiam ante oculos tuos,
demonstra servo tuo per quem visitas creaturam tuam.

6 1 Et dixit ad me: Initium terreni orbis, et antequam star-
ent exitus saeculi, et antequam spirarent conventiones
ventorum, 2 et antequam sonarent voces tonitruum, et antequam splenderent nitores coruscuum, et antequam confirmarentur fundamenta paradisi, 3 et antequam viderentur
decores flores, et antequam confirmarentur motuum virtutes,
et antequam colligerentur innumerabiles militiae angelorum,
4 et antequam extollerentur altitudines aerum, et antequam

King James Version

41 And I said, Behold, O Lord, yet art thou nigh unto them that be reserved till the end: and what shall they do that have been before me, or we that be now, or they that shall come after us?

42 And he said unto me, I will liken my judgment unto a ring: like as there is no slackness of the last, even so there is no swiftness of the first.

43 So I answered and said, Couldest thou not make those that have been made, and be now, and that are for to come, at once; that thou mightest shew thy judgment the sooner?

44 Then answered he me, and said, The creature may not haste above the maker; neither may the world hold them at once that shall be created therein.

45 And I said, As thou hast said unto thy servant, that thou, which givest life to all, hast given life at once to the creature that thou hast created, and the creature bare it: even so it might now also bear them that now be present at once.

46 And he said unto me, Ask the womb of a woman, and say unto her, If thou bringest forth children, why dost thou it not together, but one after another? pray her therefore to bring forth ten children at once.

47 And I said, She cannot: but must do it by distance of time.

48 Then said he unto me, Even so have I given the womb of the earth to those that be sown in it in their times.

49 For like as a young child may not bring forth the things that belong to the aged, even so have I disposed the world which I created.

50 And I asked, and said, Seeing thou hast now given me the way, I will *proceed to* speak before thee: for our mother, of whom thou hast told me that she is young, draweth now nigh unto age.

51 He answered me, and said, Ask a woman that beareth children, and she shall tell thee.

52 Say unto her, Wherefore are not they whom thou hast now brought forth like those that were before, but less of stature?

53 And she shall answer thee, They that be born in the the strength of youth are of one fashion, and they that are born in the time of age, when the womb faileth, are otherwise.

54 Consider thou therefore also, how that ye are less of stature than those that were before you.

55 And so are they that come after you less than ye, as the creatures which now begin to be old, and have passed over the strength of youth.

56 Then said I, Lord, I beseech thee, if I have found favour in thy sight, shew thy servant by whom thou visitest thy creature.

6 And he said unto me, In the beginning, when the earth was made, before the borders of the world stood, or ever the winds blew,

2 Before it thundered and lightened, or ever the foundations of paradise were laid,

3 Before the fair flowers were seen, or ever the moveable powers were established, before the innumerable multitude of angels were gathered together,

4 Or ever the heights of the air were lifted up, before the

TODAY'S ENGLISH VERSION

41 Then I said, "But, Lord God, your concern is with the
people who will be alive at the end of the world. What will
happen to those who live before that time? What about us?
What about those who came before us, and those who will
live after us?"
42 He answered me, "The final judgment can be compared
to a circle, and just as a circle has no beginning or end, so
those who come early will not be too early, and those who
come late will not be too late."
43 I replied, "But couldn't you have created all human
beings, those of the past, the present, and the future, so that
they would all live at the same time? In that way, you could
have had your final judgment sooner."
44 He answered, "The creation cannot move faster than the
Creator. And besides, the world wouldn't have been able to
hold all the people if everyone had been created at the same
time."
45 "Why, then," I asked, "did you just now tell me that one
day you would bring back to life at the same time every creature that ever lived? If the world can hold them all then, it
can hold them now."
46 He answered, "That would be like asking a woman who
has given birth to ten children why she didn't have them all
at once, instead of one at a time."
47 "That would be impossible," I answered. "She can't have
them all at once."
48 "In the same way," he continued, "I have made the
world like a womb so that it produces human beings at regular intervals. 49 The rule that neither a young child nor an
old woman can give birth to a baby also applies to the world
that I have created."
50 Then I said, "Since you have brought up the subject,
may I ask if the world you have been talking about is still
young or is it approaching old age?"
51 He replied, "You can learn the answer from any woman
who has given birth to several children. 52 Ask her why her
younger children do not grow as tall as her older children.
53 She will tell you that those born while she was young and
healthy are much stronger than those born when she was
getting old and becoming weak. 54 You will notice that you
are smaller than people of earlier generations; 55 those who
come later will be smaller still. This shows you that creation
is already getting old and losing the strength of her youth."
56 "If you please, Lord," I asked, "will you show me the one
through whom you will bring judgment on your creation?"
6 He said to me, "I made this decision before I created the
world: before the gates of the world were standing;
before the winds were brought together to blow, 2 or the
lightning flashed, or the thunder rolled; before the foundations of Paradise were laid, 3 or the beautiful flowers
appeared; before the powers that move the stars were established, or the armies of angels assembled; 4 before the air
was piled up high, or the divisions of the heavens given their

NEW REVISED STANDARD VERSION

41 I said, "Yet, O Lord, you have charge of those who are
alive at the end, but what will those do who lived before me,
or we, ourselves, or those who come after us?"
42 He said to me, "I shall liken my judgment to a circle;[a]
just as for those who are last there is no slowness, so for
those who are first there is no haste."
43 Then I answered and said, "Could you not have created
at one time those who have been and those who are and
those who will be, so that you might show your judgment
the sooner?"
44 He replied to me and said, "The creation cannot move
faster than the Creator, nor can the world hold at one time
those who have been created in it."
45 I said, "How have you said to your servant that you[b]
will certainly give life at one time to your creation? If therefore all creatures will live at one time[c] and the creation will
sustain them, it might even now be able to support all of
them present at one time."
46 He said to me, "Ask a woman's womb, and say to it, 'If
you bear ten[d] children, why one after another?' Request it
therefore to produce ten at one time."
47 I said, "Of course it cannot, but only each in its own
time."
48 He said to me, "Even so I have given the womb of the
earth to those who from time to time are sown in it. 49 For as
an infant does not bring forth, and a woman who has
become old does not bring forth any longer, so I have made
the same rule for the world that I created."
50 Then I inquired and said, "Since you have now given
me the opportunity, let me speak before you. Is our mother,
of whom you have told me, still young? Or is she now
approaching old age?"
51 He replied to me, "Ask a woman who bears children,
and she will tell you. 52 Say to her, 'Why are those whom
you have borne recently not like those whom you bore
before, but smaller in stature?' 53 And she herself will
answer you, 'Those born in the strength of youth are different from those born during the time of old age, when the
womb is failing.' 54 Therefore you also should consider that
you and your contemporaries are smaller in stature than
those who were before you, 55 and those who come after you
will be smaller than you, as born of a creation that already is
aging and passing the strength of youth."
56 I said, "I implore you, O Lord, if I have found favor in
your sight, show your servant through whom you will visit
your creation."
6 He said to me, "At the beginning of the circle of the
earth, before[e] the portals of the world were in place, and
before the assembled winds blew, 2 and before the rumblings
of thunder sounded, and before the flashes of lightning
shone, and before the foundations of paradise were laid,
3 and before the beautiful flowers were seen, and before the
powers of movements[f] were established, and before the
innumerable hosts of angels were gathered together, 4 and
before the heights of the air were lifted up, and before the

a Or *crown* *b* Syr Ethiop Arab 1: Meaning of Lat uncertain
c Lat lacks *If . . . one time* *d* Syr Ethiop Arab 2 Arm: Meaning of Lat
uncertain *e* Meaning of Lat uncertain: Compare Syr *The beginning by the
hand of humankind, but the end by my own hands. For as before the land of
the world existed there, and before*; Ethiop: *At first by the Son of Man, and
afterwards I myself. For before the earth and the lands were created, and
before* *f* Or *earthquakes*

LATIN VULGATE

nominarentur mensurae firmamentorum, et antequam aesti-
maretur scabillum Sion, 5 et antequam investigarentur praesentes anni, et antequam abalienarentur eorum qui nunc
peccant adinventiones et consignarentur qui fidem thesaur-
izaverunt, 6 tunc cogitavi, et facta sunt haec per me solum
et non per alium, ut et finis per me et non per alium.
7 Et respondi et dixi: Quae erit separatio temporum, aut
quando prioris finis aut sequentis initium? 8 Et dixit ad me:
Ab Abraham usque ad Abraham, quoniam ab eo natus est
Iacob et Esau, manus enim Iacob tenebat ab initio calcaneum
Esau. 9 Finis enim huius saeculi Esau, et principium sequentis Iacob. 10 Finis enim hominis calcaneum et principium
hominis manus, inter calcaneum et manum aliud noli
quaerere, Ezra.
11 Et respondi et dixi: O dominator domine, si inveni gratiam ante oculos tuos, 12 ut demonstres servo tuo finem signorum tuorum, quorum ex parte mihi demonstrasti nocte
praecedente. 13 Et respondit et dixit ad me: Surge super
pedes tuos et audies vocem plenissimam sonus. 14 Et erit, si
commotione commovebitur locus, in quo stas super eum,
15 in eo cum loqueretur, tu non expaveas, quoniam de fine
verbum. Et fundamenta terrae intellegetur, 16 quoniam de
ipsis sermo, tremescet et commovebitur; scit enim, quoniam
finem eorum oportet commutari. 17 Et factum est cum audissem, et surrexi super pedes meos et audivi, et ecce vox
loquens, et sonus eius sicut sonus aquarum multarum.
18 Et dixit: Ecce dies veniunt, et erit quando adpropinquare
incipio, ut visitem habitantes in terram, 19 et quando
inquirere incipiam ab eis qui iniuste nocuerunt iniustitia
sua, et quando suppleta fuerit humilitas Sion, 20 et cum
supersignabitur saeculum quod incipiet pertransire, haec
signa faciam: Libri aperientur ante faciem firmamenti et
omnes videbunt simul, 21 et anniculi infantes loquentur
vocibus suis, et praegnantes inmaturos parient infantes
trium et quattuor mensuum et vivent et scirtabuntur, 22 et
subito apparebunt seminata loca non seminata, et plena
promptuaria subito invenientur vacua, 23 et tuba canet cum
sono, quam cum omnes audierint subito expavescent. 24 Et
erit in illo tempore, debellabunt amici amicos ut inimici, et
expavescet terra cum his qui inhabitant in eam, et venae
fontium stabunt ut non decurrant in horis tribus. 25 Et erit,
omnis qui derelictus fuerit ex omnibus istis quibus praedixi
tibi, ipse salvabitur et videbit salutare meum et finem saeculi
mei. 26 Et videbunt qui recepti sunt homines, qui mortem

KING JAMES VERSION

measures of the firmament were named, or ever the chimneys in Sion were hot,

5 And ere the present years were sought out, and or ever the inventions of them that now sin were turned, before they were sealed that have gathered faith for a treasure:

6 Then did I consider these things, and they all were made through me alone, and through none other: by me also they shall be ended, and by none other.

7 Then answered I and said, What shall be the parting asunder of the times? or when shall be the end of the first, and the beginning of it that followeth?

8 And he said unto me, From Abraham unto Isaac, when Jacob and Esau were born of him, Jacob's hand held first the heel of Esau.

9 For Esau is the end of the world, and Jacob is the beginning of it that followeth.

10 The hand of man is betwixt the heel and the hand: other question, Esdras, ask thou not.

11 I answered then and said, O Lord that bearest rule, if I have found favour in thy sight,

12 I beseech thee, shew thy servant the end of thy tokens, whereof thou shewedst me part the last night.

13 So he answered and said unto me, Stand up upon thy feet, and hear a mighty sounding voice.

14 And it shall be as it were a great motion; but the place where thou standest shall not be moved.

15 And therefore when it speaketh be not afraid: for the word is of the end, and the foundation of the earth is understood.

16 And why? because the speech of these things trembleth and is moved: for it knoweth that the end of these things must be changed.

17 And it happened, that when I had heard it I stood up upon my feet, and hearkened, and, behold, there was a voice that spake, and the sound of it was like the sound of many waters.

18 And it said, Behold, the days come, that I will begin to draw nigh, and to visit them that dwell upon the earth,

19 And will begin to make inquisition of them, what they be that have hurt unjustly with their unrighteousness, and when the affliction of Sion shall be fulfilled;

20 And when the world, that shall begin to vanish away, shall be finished, then will I shew these tokens: the books shall be opened before the firmament, and they shall see all together:

21 And the children of a year old shall speak with their voices, the women with child shall bring forth untimely children of three or four months old, and they shall live, and be raised up.

22 And suddenly shall the sown places appear unsown, the full storehouses shall suddenly be found empty:

23 And the trumpet shall give a sound, which when every man heareth, they shall be suddenly afraid.

24 At that time shall friends fight one against another like enemies, and the earth shall stand in fear with those that dwell therein, the springs of the fountains shall stand still, and in three hours they shall not run.

25 Whosoever remaineth from all these that I have told thee shall escape, and see my salvation, and the end of your world.

26 And the men that are received shall see it, who have

TODAY'S ENGLISH VERSION

names; before I chose Mount Zion as my footstool; 5 before
the present age was planned, or the scheming of its sinners
was rejected, or my seal was placed on those who obeyed the
Law and laid up a treasure of faithfulness. 6 Even then, I
decided that since I, and I alone, had created the world, I,
and I alone, would bring it to an end."

7 Then I asked, "How long a period of time will divide the
ages? When will the first age end and the next age begin?"

8 He answered, "The interval will be no longer than that
between Abraham and Abraham.[a] He was the grandfather of
both Jacob and Esau, and when they were born, Jacob was
holding Esau's heel. 9 Esau represents the end of this age,
and Jacob represents the beginning of the new age. 10 So, if
Jacob's hand is the beginning and Esau's heel is the end,[b] do
not try to find a space in between."

11 "Lord and Master," I said, "please hear my request.
12 On that earlier night you showed me some of the signs of
the end; now please show me the rest."

13 "Stand up," he said, "and you will hear a very loud
voice. 14 If the place where you are standing is violently
shaken 15 while the voice is speaking, don't be afraid. The
message will be about the end of the world, and the foundations of the world will understand 16 that the voice is speaking about them. They will tremble and quake because they
know that they will undergo a change when the end comes."

17 When he said this, I stood up and listened. I heard a
voice that sounded like a roaring river. 18 It said, "The time
is near when I will come to judge the people living on the
earth. 19 I will punish those who have hurt others with their
injustice. Jerusalem's humiliation will come to an end,
20 and this age which is about to pass away will have the
final seal put on it. Then I will give the following signs: the
books will be opened across the sky for all to see. 21 Children
only a year old will speak. Pregnant women will give birth
after only three or four months, and their premature babies
will live and run about. 22 Planted fields will suddenly
become bare, and full barns will suddenly become empty.
23 Then the trumpet will sound, and sudden terror will grip
the heart of everyone when they hear it. 24 Friends will fight
like enemies, and the earth and its people will be terrified.
Rivers will stop flowing and stand still for three hours.

25 "Those who survive all these things that I have predicted
will be rescued when I bring to an end this world that I created. 26 They will see those who never died but were taken up

[a] Abraham; *some manuscripts have* Isaac. [b] *Some ancient translations* So . . . end; *Latin unclear.*

NEW REVISED STANDARD VERSION

measures of the firmaments were named, and before the
footstool of Zion was established, 5 and before the present
years were reckoned and before the imaginations of those
who now sin were estranged, and before those who stored
up treasures of faith were sealed— 6 then I planned these
things, and they were made through me alone and not
through another; just as the end shall come through me
alone and not through another."

7 I answered and said, "What will be the dividing of the
times? Or when will be the end of the first age and the beginning of the age that follows?"

8 He said to me, "From Abraham to Isaac,[a] because from
him were born Jacob and Esau, for Jacob's hand held Esau's
heel from the beginning. 9 Now Esau is the end of this age,
and Jacob is the beginning of the age that follows. 10 The
beginning of a person is the hand, and the end of a person is
the heel;[b] seek for nothing else, Ezra, between the heel and
the hand, Ezra!"

11 I answered and said, "O sovereign Lord, if I have found
favor in your sight, 12 show your servant the last of your
signs of which you showed me a part on a previous night."

13 He answered and said to me, "Rise to your feet and
you will hear a full, resounding voice. 14 And if the place
where you are standing is greatly shaken 15 while the voice
is speaking, do not be terrified; because the word concerns
the end, and the foundations of the earth will understand
16 that the speech concerns them. They will tremble and be
shaken, for they know that their end must be changed."

17 When I heard this, I got to my feet and listened; a
voice was speaking, and its sound was like the sound of
mighty[c] waters. 18 It said, "The days are coming when I
draw near to visit the inhabitants of the earth, 19 and when I
require from the doers of iniquity the penalty of their iniquity, and when the humiliation of Zion is complete. 20 When
the seal is placed upon the age that is about to pass away,
then I will show these signs: the books shall be opened
before the face of the firmament, and all shall see my judgment[d] together. 21 Children a year old shall speak with their
voices, and pregnant women shall give birth to premature
children at three and four months, and these shall live and
leap about. 22 Sown places shall suddenly appear unsown,
and full storehouses shall suddenly be found to be empty;
23 the trumpet shall sound aloud, and when all hear it, they
shall suddenly be terrified. 24 At that time friends shall make
war on friends like enemies, the earth and those who inhabit
it shall be terrified, and the springs of the fountains shall
stand still, so that for three hours they shall not flow.

25 "It shall be that whoever remains after all that I have
foretold to you shall be saved and shall see my salvation and
the end of my world. 26 And they shall see those who were

[a] Other ancient authorities read *to Abraham* [b] Syr: Meaning of Lat uncertain [c] Lat *many* [d] Syr: Lat lacks *my judgment*

LATIN VULGATE

non gustaverunt a nativitate sua, et mutabitur cor inhabitantium et convertetur in sensum alium. 27 Delebitur enim
malum et extinguetur dolus. 28 Florebit autem fides et vince-
tur corruptela, et ostendebitur veritas quae sine fructu fuit
tantis temporibus.

29 Et factum est cum loqueretur mihi, et ecce paulatim
movebatur locus super quem stabam super eum. 30 Et dixit
ad me: Haec veni tibi ostendere et venturae nocti. 31 Si ergo
iterum rogaveris et iterum ieiunaveris septem diebus, iterum
tibi renuntiabo horum maiora per diem, 32 quoniam auditu
audita est vox tua apud Altissimum. Vidit enim Fortis direc-
tionem tuam et providit pudicitiam quam a iuventute tua
habuisti. 33 Et propter hoc misit me demonstrare tibi haec
omnia et dicere tibi: Confide et noli timere, 34 et noli fes-
tinare in prioribus temporibus cogitare vana, ut non properes
a novissimis temporibus.

35 Et factum est post haec, et flevi iterum et similiter ieiunavi septem diebus, ut suppleam tres ebdomadas quae dictae
sunt mihi. 36 Et factum est in octava nocte, et cor meum iterato turbabatur in me et coepi loqui coram Altissimo.
37 Inflammabatur enim spiritus meus valde et anima mea
anxiabatur.

38 Et dixi: O Domine, loquens locutus es ab initio creaturae
in primo die dicens: Fiat caelum et terra, et tuum verbum
opus perfecit. 39 Et erat tunc spiritus volans, et tenebrae cir-
cumferebantur et silentium, sonus vocis hominis nondum
erat abs te. 40 Tunc dixisti de thesauris tuis proferri lumen
quod luminis, ut apparerent tunc opera tua. 41 Et in die
secundo iterum creasti spiritum firmamenti et imperasti ei,
ut divideret et divisionem faceret inter aquas, ut pars quidem
sursum recederet, pars vero deorsum maneret. 42 Et tertio
die imperasti aquis congregari in septima parte terrae, sex
vero partes siccasti et conservasti, ut ex his sint coram te
ministrantia seminata adeo et culta. 43 Verbum enim tuum
processit, et opus statim fiebat. 44 Processit enim subito
fructus multitudinis inmensus et concupiscentia gustus mul-
tiformis et flores colore inimitabili et odores odoramentis
investigabiles. Et die tertio haec facta sunt. 45 Quarta autem
die imperasti fieri solis splendorem, lunae lumen, stellarum
dispositionem, 46 et imperasti eis, ut deservirent futuro plas-
mato homini. 47 Quinto autem die dixisti septimae parti ubi
erat aqua congregata, ut procrearet animalia, volatilia et
pisces, et ita fiebat 48 aqua muta et sine anima, quod ei
iubebatur, animalia faciens, ut ex hoc mirabilia tua nationes

KING JAMES VERSION

not tasted death from their birth: and the heart of the inhabitants shall be changed, and turned into another meaning.

27 For evil shall be put out, and deceit shall be quenched.

28 As for faith, it shall flourish, corruption shall be overcome, and the truth, which hath been so long without fruit, shall be declared.

29 And when he talked with me, behold, I looked by little and little upon him before whom I stood.

30 And these words said he unto me; I am come to shew thee the time of the night to come.

31 If thou wilt pray yet more, and fast seven days again, I shall tell thee greater things by day than I have heard.

32 For thy voice is heard before the most High: for the Mighty hath seen thy righteous dealing, he hath seen also thy chastity, which thou hast had ever since thy youth.

33 And therefore hath he sent me to shew thee all these things, and to say unto thee, Be of good comfort, and fear not.

34 And hasten not with the times that are past, to think vain things, that thou mayest not hasten from the latter times.

35 And it came to pass after this, that I wept again, and fasted seven days in like manner, that I might fulfil the three weeks which he told me.

36 And in the eighth night was my heart vexed within me again, and I began to speak before the most High.

37 For my spirit was greatly set on fire, and my soul was in distress.

38 And I said, O Lord, thou spakest from the beginning of the creation, even the first day, and saidst thus; Let heaven and earth be made; and thy word was a perfect work.

39 And then was the spirit, and darkness and silence were on every side; the sound of man's voice was not yet formed.

40 Then commandedst thou a fair light to come forth of thy treasures, that thy work might appear.

41 Upon the second day thou madest the spirit of the firmament, and commandedst it to part asunder, and to make a division betwixt the waters, that the one part might go up, and the other remain beneath.

42 Upon the third day thou didst command that the waters should be gathered in the seventh part of the earth: six parts hast thou dried up, and kept them, to the intent that of these some being planted of God and tilled might serve thee.

43 For as soon as thy word went forth the work was made.

44 For immediately there was great and innumerable fruit, and many and divers pleasures for the taste, and flowers of unchangeable colour, and odours of wonderful smell: and this was done the third day.

45 Upon the fourth day thou commandedst that the sun should shine, and the moon give her light, and the stars should be in order:

46 And gavest them a charge to do service unto man, that was to be made.

47 Upon the fifth day thou saidst unto the seventh part, where the waters were gathered, that it should bring forth living creatures, fowls and fishes: and so it came to pass.

48 For the dumb water and without life brought forth living things at the commandment of God, that all people might praise thy wondrous works.

TODAY'S ENGLISH VERSION

alive into heaven. The hearts and minds of people on earth
will be changed. 27 Evil will be destroyed and deceit eliminated. 28 Faith will grow strong, corruption will be overcome,
and truth, which has not produced fruit for so long, will
make itself felt again."
29 While the voice was speaking, the ground beneath me
began to rock back and forth.[a] 30 Then the angel said to me,
"These are the things that I have come to show you tonight.[b]
31 Now if you will pray and fast for seven more days, I will
come back and tell you even greater things,[c] 32 because God
Most High has heard your prayer; the Mighty God has seen
the pure and righteous life that you have lived since your
youth. 33 That is why he has sent me to show you all these
things and to tell you not to be afraid but to trust him. 34 Do
not be so quick to raise useless questions in the present age;
then you will not be so quick to do so in the final age."

35 After that, I mourned and fasted for seven more days, as
I had done before, and so I completed the three weeks of
fasting that I had been commanded to observe. 36 On the
eighth night I was again deeply troubled, and I began to
speak to God Most High. 37 I was very tense and my heart
was uneasy, 38 but I said, "O Lord, at the beginning of creation you spoke the word. On the first day you commanded,
'Let the universe be made,' and your word carried out that
command. 39 At that time the spirit was moving, darkness
and silence were everywhere, and no human voice was yet
heard.[d] 40 Then you commanded that a ray of light shine out
of the room where it was stored, so that your works could be
seen. 41 On the second day you created the angel of the sky
and commanded him to separate the water, so that part of it
would move up above the dome of the sky and part remain
below. 42 On the third day you commanded the water that
covered the earth to come together in one place and cover
one-seventh of the earth's surface. Then you dried out the
rest of the earth's surface to make dry land, so that it might
be cultivated and planted and used in your service. 43 Your
word went out and completed the work immediately. 44 In an
instant all kinds of fruits and vegetables appeared, enough
kinds to satisfy every taste. There were flowers of indescribable fragrances and of the most magnificent colors. These
things were made on the third day. 45 On the fourth day the
bright-shining sun, the light of the moon, and the arrangement of the stars were created by your command. 46 You
commanded them to serve the human race, which would
soon be created. 47 On the fifth day you commanded the part
of the earth covered by water to produce birds and fish; and
it was done. 48 At your command, the still and lifeless water
brought forth living creatures, so that the nations might proclaim your wonderful works. 49 Then you singled out two of

[a] *Some ancient translations* the ground . . . forth; *Latin unclear.*
[b] *One ancient translation* tonight; *Latin unclear.*
[c] *Some ancient translations* things; *Latin adds* in the daytime.
[d] *Some ancient translations* yet heard; *Latin adds* from you.

NEW REVISED STANDARD VERSION

taken up, who from their birth have not tasted death; and
the heart of the earth's[a] inhabitants shall be changed and
converted to a different spirit. 27 For evil shall be blotted out,
and deceit shall be quenched; 28 faithfulness shall flourish,
and corruption shall be overcome, and the truth, which has
been so long without fruit, shall be revealed."
29 While he spoke to me, little by little the place where I
was standing began to rock to and fro.[b] 30 And he said to
me, "I have come to show you these things this night.[c] 31 If
therefore you will pray again and fast again for seven days, I
will again declare to you greater things than these,[d]
32 because your voice has surely been heard by the Most
High; for the Mighty One has seen your uprightness and has
also observed the purity that you have maintained from your
youth. 33 Therefore he sent me to show you all these things,
and to say to you: 'Believe and do not be afraid! 34 Do not be
quick to think vain thoughts concerning the former times;
then you will not act hastily in the last times.' "
35 Now after this I wept again and fasted seven days in
the same way as before, in order to complete the three weeks
that had been prescribed for me. 36 Then on the eighth night
my heart was troubled within me again, and I began to
speak in the presence of the Most High. 37 My spirit was
greatly aroused, and my soul was in distress.
38 I said, "O Lord, you spoke at the beginning of creation,
and said on the first day, 'Let heaven and earth be made,'
and your word accomplished the work. 39 Then the spirit
was blowing, and darkness and silence embraced everything;
the sound of human voices was not yet there.[e] 40 Then you
commanded a ray of light to be brought out from your store-
chambers, so that your works could be seen.
41 "Again, on the second day, you created the spirit of the
firmament, and commanded it to divide and separate the
waters, so that one part might move upward and the other
part remain beneath.
42 "On the third day you commanded the waters to be
gathered together in a seventh part of the earth; six parts
you dried up and kept so that some of them might be planted
and cultivated and be of service before you. 43 For your word
went forth, and at once the work was done. 44 Immediately
fruit came forth in endless abundance and of varied appeal
to the taste, and flowers of inimitable color, and odors of
inexpressible fragrance. These were made on the third day.
45 "On the fourth day you commanded the brightness of
the sun, the light of the moon, and the arrangement of the
stars to come into being; 46 and you commanded them to
serve humankind, about to be formed.
47 "On the fifth day you commanded the seventh part,
where the water had been gathered together, to bring forth
living creatures, birds, and fishes; and so it was done. 48 The
dumb and lifeless water produced living creatures, as it was
commanded, so that therefore the nations might declare your
wondrous works.

a Syr Compare Ethiop Arab 1 Arm: Lat lacks *earth's* *b* Syr Ethiop Compare Arab Arm: Meaning of Lat uncertain *c* Syr Compare Ethiop: Meaning of Lat uncertain *d* Syr Ethiop Arab 1 Arm: Lat adds *by day* *e* Syr Ethiop: Lat *was not yet from you*

LATIN VULGATE

enarrent. 49 Et tunc conservasti duas animas, nomen uni
vocasti Enoch et nomen secundi vocasti Leviathan. 50 Et
separasti ea ab alterutro; non enim poterat septima pars ubi
erat aqua congregata capere ea. 51 Et dedisti Enoch unam
partem quae siccata est tertio die, ut inhabitet in ea, ubi sunt
montes mille. 52 Leviathae autem dedisti septimam partem
humidam. Et servasti ea, ut fiant in devorationem quibus vis
et quando vis. 53 Sexto autem die imperasti terrae, ut crearet
coram te iumenta et bestias et reptilia, 54 et super his Adam,
quem constituisti ducem super omnibus factis quae fecisti, et
ex eo educimur nos omnes quem elegisti populum. 55 Haec
autem omnia dixi coram te, Domine, quoniam dixisti quia
propter nos creasti primogenitum saeculum. 56 Residuas
autem gentes ab Adam natas dixisti eas nihil esse, et quoniam salivae adsimilatae sunt, et sicut stillicidium de vaso
similasti abundantiam eorum. 57 Et nunc, Domine, ecce
istae gentes quae in nihilum deputatae sunt dominari nostri
et devorare nos. 58 Nos autem populus tuus quem vocasti
primogenitum, unigenitum, aemulatorem, carissimum, tradi-
ti sumus in manibus eorum. 59 Et si propter nos creatum est
saeculum, quare non hereditatem possidemus nostrum
saeculum? Usquequo haec?

7 Et factum est cum finissem loqui verba haec, et missus
est ad me angelus, qui missus fuerat ad me primis
noctibus, 2 et dixit ad me: Surge, Ezra, et audi sermones
quos veni loqui ad te. 3 Et dixi: Loquere, dominus meus. Et
dixit ad me: Mare positum est in spatioso loco, ut esset
altum et inmensum. 4 Erit autem ei introitus in angusto loco
positus, ut esset similis fluminis. 5 Si quis enim volens
voluerit ingredi mare videre eum vel dominari eius, si non
transierit angustum, in latitudinem venire quomodo poterit?
6 Item aliud: Civitas est aedificata et posita in loco campestri,
est autem plena omnium bonorum. 7 Introitus autem eius
angustus et in praecipiti positus, ut esset a dextris quidem
ignis, a sinistris vero aqua alta. 8 Semita autem est una sola
inter eos posita, hoc est ignis et aqua, ut non capiat semita
nisi solummodo vestigium hominis. 9 Si autem data dabitur
civitas homini in hereditatem, si non heres antepositum periculum pertransierit, quomodo accipiet hereditatem suam?
10 Et dixi: Sic, domine. Et dixit ad me: Sic est et Israhel pars.
11 Propter eos enim feci saeculum, et quando transgressus
est Adam constitutiones meas, iudicatum est quod factum

KING JAMES VERSION

49 Then didst thou ordain two living creatures, the one thou calledst Enoch, and the other Leviathan;

50 And didst separate the one from the other: for the seventh part, namely, where the water was gathered together, might not hold them both.

51 Unto Enoch thou gavest one part, which was dried up the third day, that he should dwell in the same part, wherein are a thousand hills:

52 But unto Leviathan thou gavest the seventh part, namely, the moist; and hast kept him to be devoured of whom thou wilt, and when.

53 Upon the sixth day thou gavest commandment unto the earth, that before thee it should bring forth beasts, cattle, and creeping things:

54 And after these, Adam also, whom thou madest lord of all thy creatures: of him come we all, and the people also whom thou hast chosen.

55 All this have I spoken before thee, O Lord, because thou madest the world for our sakes.

56 As for the other people, which also come of Adam, thou hast said that they are nothing, but be like unto spittle: and hast likened the abundance of them unto a drop that falleth from a vessel.

57 And now, O Lord, behold, these heathen, which have ever been reputed as nothing, have begun to be lords over us, and to devour us.

58 But we thy people, whom thou hast called thy firstborn, thy only begotten, and thy fervent lover, are given into their hands.

59 If the world now be made for our sakes, why do we not possess an inheritance with the world? how long shall this endure?

7 And when I had made an end of speaking these words, there was sent unto me the angel which had been sent unto me the nights afore:

2 And he said unto me, Up, Esdras, and hear the words that I am come to tell thee.

3 And I said, Speak on, my God. Then said he unto me, The sea is set in a wide place, that it might be deep and great.

4 But put the case the entrance were narrow, and like a river;

5 Who then could go into the sea to look upon it, and to rule it? if he went not through the narrow, how could he come into the broad?

6 There is also another thing; A city is builded, and set upon a broad field, and is full of all good things:

7 The entrance thereof is narrow, and is set in a dangerous place to fall, like as if there were a fire on the right hand, and on the left a deep water:

8 And one only path between them both, even between the fire and the water, *so small* that there could but one man go there at once.

9 If this city now were given unto a man for an inheritance, if he never shall pass the danger set before it, how shall he receive this inheritance?

10 And I said, It is so, Lord. Then said he unto me, Even so also is Israel's portion.

11 Because for their sakes I made the world: and when Adam transgressed my statutes, then was decreed that now is done.

TODAY'S ENGLISH VERSION

the living creatures; you named one of them Behemoth and
the other Leviathan. 50 You separated them from each other
because the sea wasn't big enough to hold them both. 51 You
let Behemoth live on a part of the land that you dried up on
the third day of creation; it is a land of a thousand mountains. 52 You let Leviathan live in the sea. You kept them
both alive, so that your chosen people may feast on them at
the time you choose. 53 On the sixth day you commanded the
earth to produce the animals, domestic and wild, large and
small. 54 More important than all of these, you created Adam
and put him in charge of everything that you had made. And
all of us, the people you have chosen, are descended
from him.

55 "O Lord, I have told you all this because you said that
you created this first world for the sake of your people.
56 You said that, in spite of their great numbers, all the other
nations which descended from Adam are nothing, worth no
more than a drop of water, no more than spit. 57 But now,
Lord, those nations that are considered as nothing are ruling
over us and destroying us. 58 We are your people, and you
have called us your first-born, your only child, your witness,
your loved one, but we have been handed over to the power
of these other nations. 59 If this world was really created for
the sake of your people, why don't we have possession of it?
How much longer must we wait?"

7 When I had finished speaking, the same angel that had
been sent to me on the earlier nights appeared again.
2 He said, "Stand up, Ezra, and listen to what I have come to
tell you."

3 "Go ahead, sir," I said.

He continued, "Picture in your mind a broad,[a] immense
sea spreading over a vast area, 4 but with an entrance no
wider than a river. 5 No one who wishes to enter that sea,
whether to visit it or control it, can reach its broad expanse
of water without passing through the narrow entrance. 6 Or
take another example: Picture a city built on a plain. The city
is full of all kinds of good things, 7 but the entrance to it is
narrow and steep, with fire on one side and deep water on
the other. 8 The one path between the fire and the water is
so narrow that only one person at a time may walk on it. 9 If
anyone inherits this city, he cannot take possession of his
inheritance without passing through this dangerous
entrance."

10 "That is right, sir," I said.

"That is how it is with the people of Israel," he added. 11 "I
made this world for their sake, but when Adam broke my
commands, the world came under my judgment. 12 Then the

[a] *Some ancient translations* broad; *Latin* deep.

NEW REVISED STANDARD VERSION

49 "Then you kept in existence two living creatures;[a] the
one you called Behemoth[b] and the name of the other Leviathan. 50 And you separated one from the other, for the seventh part where the water had been gathered together could
not hold them both. 51 And you gave Behemoth[b] one of the
parts that had been dried up on the third day, to live in it,
where there are a thousand mountains; 52 but to Leviathan
you gave the seventh part, the watery part; and you have
kept them to be eaten by whom you wish, and when you
wish.

53 "On the sixth day you commanded the earth to bring
forth before you cattle, wild animals, and creeping things;
54 and over these you placed Adam, as ruler over all the
works that you had made; and from him we have all come,
the people whom you have chosen.

55 "All this I have spoken before you, O Lord, because you
have said that it was for us that you created this world.[c]
56 As for the other nations that have descended from Adam,
you have said that they are nothing, and that they are like
spittle, and you have compared their abundance to a drop
from a bucket. 57 And now, O Lord, these nations, which are
reputed to be as nothing, domineer over us and devour us.
58 But we your people, whom you have called your firstborn,
only begotten, zealous for you,[d] and most dear, have been
given into their hands. 59 If the world has indeed been created for us, why do we not possess our world as an inheritance? How long will this be so?"

7 When I had finished speaking these words, the angel
who had been sent to me on the former nights was sent
to me again. 2 He said to me, "Rise, Ezra, and listen to the
words that I have come to speak to you."

3 I said, "Speak, my lord." And he said to me, "There is a
sea set in a wide expanse so that it is deep and vast, 4 but it
has an entrance set in a narrow place, so that it is like a
river. 5 If there are those who wish to reach the sea, to look
at it or to navigate it, how can they come to the broad part
unless they pass through the narrow part? 6 Another example: There is a city built and set on a plain, and it is full of all
good things; 7 but the entrance to it is narrow and set in a
precipitous place, so that there is fire on the right hand and
deep water on the left. 8 There is only one path lying
between them, that is, between the fire and the water, so
that only one person can walk on the path. 9 If now the city
is given to someone as an inheritance, how will the heir
receive the inheritance unless by passing through the
appointed danger?"

10 I said, "That is right, lord." He said to me, "So also is
Israel's portion. 11 For I made the world for their sake, and
when Adam transgressed my statutes, what had been made

a Syr Ethiop: Lat *two souls* *b* Other Lat authorities read *Enoch*
c Syr Ethiop Arab 2: Lat *the firstborn world* Compare Arab 1 *first world*
d Meaning of Lat uncertain

Latin Vulgate

est. 12 Et facti sunt introitus huius saeculi angusti et
dolentes et laboriosi, paucae autem et malae et periculorum
plenae et laborum magnorum fultae. 13 Nam maioris saeculi
introitus spatiosi et securi et facientes inmortalitatis fructum.
14 Si ergo non ingredientes ingressi fuerint qui vivunt angusta et vana haec, non poterunt recipere quae sunt reposita.
15 Nunc ergo tu quare conturbaris, corruptibilis cum sis? Et
quid moveris tu, cum sis mortalis? 16 Et quare non accepisti
in corde tuo quod futurum, sed quod in praesenti?

17 Et respondi et dixi: Dominator domine, ecce disposuisti
in lege tua, quoniam iusti hereditabunt haec, impii autem
peribunt. 18 Iusti autem ferent angusta sperantes spatiosa;
qui enim impie gesserunt, et angustiam passi sunt et spatiosa non viderunt. 19 Et dixit ad me: Non es iudex super
Dominum neque intellegens super Altissimum. 20 Pereant
enim multi praesentes, quam neglegatur quae anteposita est
Dei lex. 21 Mandans enim mandavit Dominus venientibus
quando venerunt, quid facientes viverent, et quid observantes non punirentur. 22 Hii autem non sunt persuasi et
contradixerunt ei. Et constituerunt sibi cogitamenta vanitatis
23 et proposuerunt sibi circumventiones delictorum. Et
superdixerunt Altissimum non esse, et vias eius non cognoverunt. 24 Et legem eius spreverunt et sponsiones eius
abnegaverunt et legitimis eius fidem non habuerunt et opera
eius non perfecerunt. 25 Propter hoc, Ezra, vacua vacuis et
plena plenis.

26 Ecce enim tempus veniet, et erit quando venient signa
quae praedixi tibi, et apparebit sponsa et apparescens civitas
et ostendetur quae nunc subducitur terra. 27 Et omnis qui
liberatus est de praedictis malis, ipse videbit mirabilia mea.
28 Revelabitur enim Filius meus Iesus cum his qui cum eo, et
iucundabit qui relicti sunt annis quadringentis. 29 Et erit
post annos hos, et morietur Filius meus Christus et omnes
qui spiramentum habent hominis. 30 Et convertetur saeculum in antiquum silentium diebus septem sicut in prioribus
initiis, ita ut nemo derelinquatur. 31 Et erit post dies septem,
et excitabitur qui nondum vigilat saeculum et morietur corruptum. 32 Et terra reddet qui in eam dormiunt, et pulvis qui
in eo silentio habitant, et promptuaria reddent quae eis com-
mendatae sunt animae. 33 Et revelabitur Altissimus super
sedem iudicii, et pertransibunt misericordiae, et longanimitas
congregabitur, 34 iudicium autem solum remanebit. Et
veritas stabit et fides convalescet, 35 et opus subsequetur et

King James Version

12 Then were the entrances of this world made narrow, full of sorrow and travail: they are but few and evil, full of perils, and very painful.

13 For the entrances of the elder world were wide and sure, and brought immortal fruit.

14 If then they that live labour not to enter these strait and vain things, they can never receive those that are laid up for them.

15 Now therefore why disquietest thou thyself, seeing thou art but a corruptible man? and why art thou moved, whereas thou art but mortal?

16 Why hast thou not considered in thy mind this thing that is to come, rather than that which is present?

17 Then answered I and said, O Lord that bearest rule, thou hast ordained in thy law, that the righteous should inherit these things, but that the ungodly should perish.

18 Nevertheless the righteous shall suffer strait things, and hope for wide: for they that have done wickedly have suffered the strait things, and yet shall not see the wide.

19 And he said unto me, There is no judge above God, and none that hath understanding above the Highest.

20 For there be many that perish in this life, because they despise the law of God that is set before them.

21 For God hath given strait commandment to such as came, what they should do to live, even as they came, and what they should observe to avoid punishment.

22 Nevertheless they were not obedient unto him; but spake against him, and imagined vain things;

23 And deceived themselves by their wicked deeds; and said of the most High, that he is not; and knew not his ways:

24 But his law have they despised, and denied his covenants; in his statutes have they not been faithful, and have not performed his works.

25 And therefore, Esdras, for the empty are empty things, and for the full are the full things.

26 Behold, the time shall come, that these tokens which I have told thee shall come to pass, and the bride shall appear, and she coming forth shall be seen, that now is withdrawn from the earth.

27 And whosoever is delivered from the foresaid evils shall see my wonders.

28 For my son Jesus shall be revealed with those that be with him, and they that remain shall rejoice within four hundred years.

29 After these years shall my son Christ die, and all men that have life.

30 And the world shall be turned into the old silence seven days, like as in the former judgments: so that no man shall remain.

31 And after seven days the world, that yet awaketh not, shall be raised up, and that shall die that is corrupt.

32 And the earth shall restore those that are asleep in her, and so shall the dust those that dwell in silence, and the secret places shall deliver those souls that were committed unto them.

33 And the most High shall appear upon the seat of judgment, and misery shall pass away, and the long suffering shall have an end:

34 But judgment only shall remain, truth shall stand, and faith shall wax strong:

TODAY'S ENGLISH VERSION

entrances into this world were made narrow and difficult to
travel. They were rough, dangerous, and few in number.
13 But the entrances to the great world to come are wide and
safe and lead to immortality. 14 Everyone who lives must
walk the narrow and meaningless ways of this world in
order to receive the blessings stored up in the world to come.
15 So, Ezra, why are you upset and disturbed by the thought
that[a] you are mortal and must die? 16 Why don't you think
about the age to come, rather than the present age?"

17 I answered, "Lord and master, in your Law you said that
the righteous would receive all these blessings, but that the
wicked would perish. 18 The righteous then can endure all
the difficulties of this narrow way because they look forward
to the broad and open life of the future, but the wicked must
pass through the narrow way without any hope of seeing the
broad open life."

19 The angel replied, "Do you think you are a better judge
than God? Do you think you are wiser than God Most High?
20 It is better to let many people of the present age perish
than to allow them to neglect the Law that God has given
them. 21 God has given clear commandments to everyone
coming into this world, telling them what they should do to
obtain life and to avoid punishment. 22 But the wicked
would not listen and refused to obey him. In their foolishness 23 they have made their own wicked and deceitful
plans. They denied the existence of God Most High and
refused to follow his ways. 24 They have rejected his Law,
refused to accept his promises, disobeyed his decrees, and
failed to do what he commanded. 25 That's the reason, Ezra,
that there is emptiness for the empty and fullness for the
full.

26 "The time is coming when these signs will take place.
The invisible city will appear,[b] and the land that is now hidden will be seen. 27 Everyone who survives the calamities I
have predicted will also see the wonderful things I will do.
28 My son the Messiah[c] will be revealed, together with those
who come with him. He will bring four hundred years of
happiness to all these survivors. 29 At the end of that time,
my son the Messiah and all human beings will die. 30 Then
the world will return to its original silence, and for seven
days it will be like it was at the beginning. No one will be left
alive. 31 After seven days this corrupt age will pass out of
existence and a new age will be awakened. 32 The ground
will give up the dead who sleep there in silence, and the
souls of the dead will be released from the places where they
have been kept. 33 God Most High will appear on his judgment seat. Mercy and patience will vanish completely 34 and
be replaced by judgment. Truth and faithfulness will once

[a] by the thought that; *or* since. [b] *Some ancient translations* The invisible city will appear; *Latin* The bride will appear and the appearing city.
[c] *Some ancient translations* the Messiah; *Latin* Jesus.

NEW REVISED STANDARD VERSION

was judged. 12 And so the entrances of this world were made
narrow and sorrowful and toilsome; they are few and evil,
full of dangers and involved in great hardships. 13 But the
entrances of the greater world are broad and safe, and yield
the fruit of immortality. 14 Therefore unless the living pass
through the difficult and futile experiences, they can never
receive those things that have been reserved for them.
15 Now therefore why are you disturbed, seeing that you are
to perish? Why are you moved, seeing that you are mortal?
16 Why have you not considered in your mind what is to
come, rather than what is now present?"

17 Then I answered and said, "O sovereign Lord, you
have ordained in your law that the righteous shall inherit
these things, but that the ungodly shall perish. 18 The righteous, therefore, can endure difficult circumstances while
hoping for easier ones; but those who have done wickedly
have suffered the difficult circumstances and will never see
the easier ones."

19 He said to me, "You are not a better judge than the
Lord,[a] or wiser than the Most High! 20 Let many perish who
are now living, rather than that the law of God that is set
before them be disregarded! 21 For the Lord[b] strictly commanded those who came into the world, when they came,
what they should do to live, and what they should observe to
avoid punishment. 22 Nevertheless they were not obedient,
and spoke against him;

they devised for themselves vain thoughts,
23 and proposed to themselves wicked frauds;
they even declared that the Most High does not exist,
and they ignored his ways.
24 They scorned his law,
and denied his covenants;
they have been unfaithful to his statutes,
and have not performed his works.

25 That is the reason, Ezra, that empty things are for the
empty, and full things are for the full.

26 "For indeed the time will come, when the signs that I
have foretold to you will come to pass, that the city that now
is not seen shall appear,[c] and the land that now is hidden
shall be disclosed. 27 Everyone who has been delivered from
the evils that I have foretold shall see my wonders. 28 For my
son the Messiah[d] shall be revealed with those who are with
him, and those who remain shall rejoice four hundred years.
29 After those years my son the Messiah shall die, and all
who draw human breath.[e] 30 Then the world shall be turned
back to primeval silence for seven days, as it was at the first
beginnings, so that no one shall be left. 31 After seven days
the world that is not yet awake shall be roused, and that
which is corruptible shall perish. 32 The earth shall give up
those who are asleep in it, and the dust those who rest there
in silence; and the chambers shall give up the souls that
have been committed to them. 33 The Most High shall be
revealed on the seat of judgment, and compassion shall pass
away, and patience shall be withdrawn.[f] 34 Only judgment
shall remain, truth shall stand, and faithfulness shall grow

[a] Other ancient authorities read *God*; Ethiop Georg *the only One* [b] Other ancient authorities read *God* [c] Arm: Lat Syr *that the bride shall appear, even the city appearing* [d] Syr Arab 1: Ethiop *my Messiah*; Arab 2 *the Messiah*; Arm *the Messiah of God*; Lat *my son Jesus* [e] Arm *all who have continued in faith and in patience* [f] Lat *shall gather together*

LATIN VULGATE

merces ostendetur, et iustitiae vigilabunt et iniustitiae non
dormibunt. 36 Et apparebit lacus tormenti et contra illum erit
locus requietionis, et clibanus gehennae ostendetur et contra
eam iucunditatis paradisus. 37 Et dicet tunc Altissimus ad
excitatas gentes: Videte et intellegite quem negastis vel cui
non servistis vel cuius diligentias sprevistis. 38 Videte contra
et in contra, hic iucunditas et requies, et ibi ignis et tormenta. Haec autem loquetur ad eos in die iudicii. 39 Haec talis
quae neque solem habet neque lunam neque stellas,
40 neque nubem neque tonitruum neque coruscationem,
neque ventum neque aquam neque aerem, neque tenebras
neque sero neque mane, 41 neque aestatem neque ver neque
aestum, neque hiemem neque gelum neque frigus, neque
grandinem neque pluviam neque ros, 42 neque meridiem
neque noctem neque ante lucem, neque nitorem neque claritatem neque lucem, nisi solummodo splendorem claritatis
Altissimi, unde omnes incipiant videre quae anteposita sunt.
43 Spatium enim habebit sicut ebdomada annorum. 44 Hoc
est iudicium meum et constitutio eius, tibi autem soli ostendi
haec.

45 Et respondi: Tunc et dixi, domine, et nunc dico: Beati
praesentes et observantes quae a te constituta sunt. 46 Sed
de quibus erat oratio mea, quis enim est de praesentibus qui
non peccavit, vel quis natorum qui non praeterivit spon-
sionem tuam? 47 Et nunc video, quoniam ad paucos per-
tinebit futurum saeculum iucunditatem facere, multis autem
tormenta. 48 Increvit enim in nos cor malum, quod nos
abalienavit ab his et deduxit nos in corruptionem, et itinera
mortis ostendit nobis, semitas perditionis, et longe fecit nos
a vita; et hoc non paucos, sed paene omnes qui creati sunt.

49 Et respondit ad me et dixit: Audi me et instruam te et de
sequenti corripiam te. 50 Propter hoc non fecit Altissimus
unum saeculum sed duo. 51 Tu enim quia dixisti non esse
multos iustos sed paucos, impios vero multiplicari, audi ad
haec. 52 Lapides electos si habueris paucos valde, ad
numerum eorum conpones eos tibi, plumbum autem et fictile
abundat. 53 Et dixi: Domine, quomodo poterit? 54 Et dixit ad
me: Non hoc solummodo, sed interroga terram et dicet tibi,
adulare ei et narrabit tibi. 55 Dices enim ei: Aurum creas et
argentum et aeramentum et ferrum quoque et plumbum et
fictile. 56 Multiplicatur autem argentum super aurum, et
aeramentum super argentum, et ferrum super aeramentum,
plumbum super ferrum, et fictile super plumbum. 57 Aestima
ergo tu quae haec sint pretiosa et desiderabilia, quod multiplicatur aut quod rarum nascitur. 58 Et dixi: Dominator
domine, quod abundat vilius, quod enim rarius pretiosius
est. 59 Et respondit ad me et dixit: In te ista pondera quae
cogitasti, quoniam qui habet quod difficile est, gaudet super
eum qui habet abundantia. 60 Sic et a me repromissa creatura. Iucundabor enim super paucis qui salvabuntur, propterea

KING JAMES VERSION

35 And the work shall follow, and the reward shall be
shewed, and the good deeds shall be of force, and wicked
deeds shall bear no rule.[a]

[a] *Verses 36-105 in the Latin Vulgate, Today's English Version, and the New Revised Standard Version are not found in the King James Version, as they were not in the texts and manuscripts available to the translators.*

TODAY'S ENGLISH VERSION

again stand firm. 35 The good and bad that people have done will be fully revealed, and reward and punishment will follow immediately.[a] 36 The pit of torment, the fires of hell, will appear, and opposite them the Paradise of joy and rest.

37 "Then God Most High will say to the nations that have been raised from the dead, 'Look! I am the one whom you have denied and refused to serve; it is my commands that you have rejected. 38 Look around you; there is joy and peace in one direction, fire and torment in the other.' That's what he will say to them on Judgment Day.

39 "On Judgment Day there will be no sun, moon, or stars; 40 no cloud, thunder, or lightning; no wind, water, or air; no darkness, evening, or morning; 41 no summer, spring, or winter; no heat, frost, or cold; no hail, rain, or dew; 42 no noon, night, or dawn; no daylight, brightness, or light. The only light will be the dazzling brightness of God Most High, making it possible for everyone to see. 43 The judgment will last seven years. 44 That's the arrangement I have made for Judgment Day, but I have revealed these things only to you."

45 Then I said, "Lord, I repeat what I said earlier: How fortunate are the people who can live now and obey your commands! 46 But what about those for whom I have been praying? There is no one in the present generation who has not sinned, no one who has not broken your covenant. 47 Now I understand that the world to come will bring joy to only a few, but torment to many. 48 The evil impulse within us has grown and it has led us away from God's ways, brought us to ruin, put us on the way to death and destruction, and taken us far from life. It has destroyed not only a few, but almost everyone who was ever created."

49 "Listen to me," the angel said, "and I will teach you further and correct your thinking. 50 Because only a few will be saved, God created two worlds, instead of only one. 51 As you say, only a few people are righteous, but there are large numbers of wicked people. But listen: 52 If you had only a few precious stones, would you add lumps of lead and clay to them in order to have more?"[b]

53 "Surely no one would do that, sir," I answered.

54 "Take another illustration," he continued. "The earth itself will give you an answer if you humbly ask it 55 whether it produces more gold, silver, copper, iron, lead, or clay. 56 There is more silver than gold, more copper than silver, more iron than copper, more lead than iron, and more clay than lead. 57 So judge for yourself which are more desirable and valuable, common things or rare things."

58 I answered, "Lord and master, the common things are cheap; it is the rare things that are valuable."

59 "All right," he replied, "so draw the logical conclusion: the person who has what is scarce has more reason to be pleased than the person who has what is plentiful. 60 It's the same with the judgment[c] that I have promised: I will be pleased with the few who will be saved, because they are the

[a] *Verses 36-105 are not found in the King James Version, but they have been restored from ancient sources.* [b] *One ancient translation* would you . . . more; *Latin unclear.* [c] *Some ancient translations* judgment; *Latin* creation.

NEW REVISED STANDARD VERSION

strong. 35 Recompense shall follow, and the reward shall be manifested; righteous deeds shall awake, and unrighteous deeds shall not sleep.[a] 36 The pit[b] of torment shall appear, and opposite it shall be the place of rest; and the furnace of hell[c] shall be disclosed, and opposite it the paradise of delight. 37 Then the Most High will say to the nations that have been raised from the dead, 'Look now, and understand whom you have denied, whom you have not served, whose commandments you have despised. 38 Look on this side and on that; here are delight and rest, and there are fire and torments.' Thus he will[d] speak to them on the day of judgment— 39 a day that has no sun or moon or stars, 40 or cloud or thunder or lightning, or wind or water or air, or darkness or evening or morning, 41 or summer or spring or heat or winter[e] or frost or cold, or hail or rain or dew, 42 or noon or night, or dawn or shining or brightness or light, but only the splendor of the glory of the Most High, by which all shall see what has been destined. 43 It will last as though for a week of years. 44 This is my judgment and its prescribed order; and to you alone I have shown these things."

45 I answered and said, "O sovereign Lord, I said then and[f] I say now: Blessed are those who are alive and keep your commandments! 46 But what of those for whom I prayed? For who among the living is there that has not sinned, or who is there among mortals that has not transgressed your covenant? 47 And now I see that the world to come will bring delight to few, but torments to many. 48 For an evil heart has grown up in us, which has alienated us from God,[g] and has brought us into corruption and the ways of death, and has shown us the paths of perdition and removed us far from life—and that not merely for a few but for almost all who have been created."

49 He answered me and said, "Listen to me, Ezra,[h] and I will instruct you, and will admonish you once more. 50 For this reason the Most High has made not one world but two. 51 Inasmuch as you have said that the righteous are not many but few, while the ungodly abound, hear the explanation for this.

52 "If you have just a few precious stones, will you add to them lead and clay?"[i] 53 I said, "Lord, how could that be?" 54 And he said to me, "Not only that, but ask the earth and she will tell you; defer to her, and she will declare it to you. 55 Say to her, 'You produce gold and silver and bronze, and also iron and lead and clay; 56 but silver is more abundant than gold, and bronze than silver, and iron than bronze, and lead than iron, and clay than lead.' 57 Judge therefore which things are precious and desirable, those that are abundant or those that are rare?"

58 I said, "O sovereign Lord, what is plentiful is of less worth, for what is more rare is more precious."

59 He answered me and said, "Consider within yourself[j] what you have thought, for the person who has what is hard to get rejoices more than the person who has what is plentiful. 60 So also will be the judgment[k] that I have promised; for I will rejoice over the few who shall be saved, because it

a The passage from verse *36* to verse *105*, formerly missing, has been restored to the text *b* Syr Ethiop: Lat *place* *c* Lat Syr Ethiop *Gehenna* *d* Syr Ethiop Arab 1: Lat *you shall* *e* Or *storm* *f* Syr: Lat *And I answered, "I said then, O Lord, and* *g* Cn: Lat Syr Ethiop *from these* *h* Syr Arab 1 Georg: Lat Ethiop lack *Ezra* *i* Arab 1: Meaning of Lat Syr Ethiop uncertain *j* Syr Ethiop Arab 1: Meaning of Lat uncertain *k* Syr Arab 1: Lat *creation*

quod ipsi sunt qui gloriam meam nunc dominationem
fecerunt et per quos nunc nomen meum nominatum est.
61 Et non contristabor super multitudinem eorum qui
perierunt, ipsi enim sunt qui vapori nunc adsimilati sunt et
flammae ac fumo adaequati sunt et exarserunt et ferverunt
et extincti sunt.

62 Et respondi et dixi: O tu terra, quid peperisti? Si sensus
factus est de pulvere sicut et cetera creatura, 63 melius enim
erat et ipsum pulverem non esse natum, ut non sensus inde
fieret. 64 Nunc autem nobiscum crescit sensus, et propter
hoc torquemur, quoniam scientes perimus. 65 Lugeat
hominum genus et agrestes bestiae laetentur; lugeant omnes
qui nati sunt, quadrupedia vero et pecora iucundentur.
66 Multum enim melius est illis quam nobis. Non enim sperant iudicium, nec enim sciunt cruciamenta nec salutem post
mortem repromissam sibi. 67 Nobis autem quid prodest, quoniam salvati salvabimur sed tormento tormentabimur?
68 Omnes enim qui nati sunt commixti sunt iniquitatibus et
pleni sunt peccatis et gravati delictis. 69 Et si non essemus
post mortem in iudicio venientes, melius fortassis nobis
venisset.

70 Et respondit ad me et dixit: Et quando Altissimus faciens
faciebat saeculum et Adam et omnes qui ex eo venerunt, primum praeparavit iudicium et quae sunt iudicii. 71 Et nunc de
sermonibus tuis intellege, quoniam dixisti quia sensus nobiscum crescit. 72 Qui ergo commorantes sunt in terra hinc cruciabuntur, quoniam sensum habentes iniquitatem fecerunt,
et mandata accipientes non servaverunt ea, et legem consecuti fraudaverunt eam quam acceperunt. 73 Et quid habebunt
dicere in iudicio vel quomodo respondebunt in novissimis
temporibus? 74 Quantum enim tempus, ex quo longanimitatem habuit Altissimus his qui inhabitant saeculum, et non
propter eos, sed propter ea quae providit tempora.

75 Et respondi et dixi: Si inveni gratiam coram te, domine,
demonstra et hoc servo tuo, si post mortem vel nunc quando
reddemus unusquisque animam suam, si conservati conserv-
abimur in requie, donec veniant tempora illa in quibus incipies creaturam renovare, aut amodo cruciabimur? 76 Et
respondit ad me et dixit: Ostendam tibi et hoc. Tu autem noli
commisceri cum eis qui spreverunt, neque connumeres te
cum his qui cruciantur. 77 Etenim est tibi thesaurus operum
repositus apud Altissimum, sed non tibi demonstrabitur
usque in novissimis temporibus.

78 Nam de morte sermo: Quando profectus fuerit terminus
sententiae ab Altissimo ut homo moriatur, recedente inspira-
tione de corpore ut dimittatur iterum ad eum qui dedit, ado-
rare gloriam Altissimi primum. 79 Et si quidem esset eorum
qui spreverunt et non servaverunt viam Altissimi et eorum
qui contempserunt legem eius et eorum qui oderunt eos qui
timent Deum, 80 haec inspirationes inhabitationes non
ingredientur, sed vagantes erunt amodo in cruciamentis,
dolentes semper et tristes, per septem vias. 81 Via prima,
quia spreverunt legem Altissimi. 82 Secunda via, quia iam
non possunt reversionem bonam facere, ut vivant. 83 Tertia

TODAY'S ENGLISH VERSION

ones who now praise and honor me and make my name
known. 61 I will not be sad about the large number of people
who will be lost, because even now they last no longer than
a vapor; they disappear like fire and smoke; they catch fire,
blaze up, and quickly go out."

62 Then I said to the earth, "Look at what you have done!
When you gave birth to the rest of creation you gave birth to
reason. 63 It would have been better if you had never been
created. Then we humans would never have had the power
of reasoning! 64 But as it is now, our reason grows up with
us and then torments us, because we realize that we are
going to die! 65 Compared to us who must bear this sorrow,
the dumb animals must be happy. 66 They are much better
off than we are. They do not have to look forward to the
judgment; they are not aware of any torment or salvation
that is promised to them after death. 67 What good is it to us
that we are going to be given life in the future if it is to be a
life of terrible torment? 68 Everyone who is born is caught in
the web of sin, is full of wickedness and burdened with guilt.
69 I think it would be better if after death we did not have to
face judgment."

70 The angel replied, "When God Most High was creating
the world, as well as Adam and his descendants, the first
thing he did was to get everything ready for the judgment.
71 So you ought to learn from your own words. You said that
your reason grows up with you, 72 and that's the point. The
people of this world used their reason and sinned; they
received God's commands but did not keep them; they
accepted the Law and then disobeyed it. And that's why they
will suffer torment. 73 What excuse can they offer at the
judgment? How can they answer at the last day? 74 God
Most High has been very patient with the people of this
world for a long time, but it has not been for their sake. He
has done it for the sake of the age to come."

75 Then I said, "Sir, may I ask you, please, to explain to me
what happens when we die, when each of us must give back
our soul? Will we be kept at rest until the time when you
begin to make your new creation, or will our torment begin
immediately?"

76 "I will answer that question also," he replied, "but do
not include yourself among those who will be tormented
because they have no use for religion. 77 After all, you have
a treasure of good works stored up with God Most High,
which will not be shown to you until the last days. 78 But to
answer your question about death: When God Most High has
pronounced the final decree that a person shall die, the soul
leaves the body to return to the one who gave it. Immediately
it praises the glory of God Most High. 79 Let me explain first
about people who had no use for the ways of God Most High
and hated those who worshiped him. 80 There is no place
where their souls can go for rest; they must wander around
forever in torment, grief, and sorrow. Their torment will
progress in seven stages. 81 First, they ignore the Law of God
Most High. 82 Second, they can no longer make a sincere
repentance and obtain life. 83 Third, they see the reward

NEW REVISED STANDARD VERSION

is they who have made my glory to prevail now, and through
them my name has now been honored. 61 I will not grieve
over the great number of those who perish; for it is they who
are now like a mist, and are similar to a flame and smoke—
they are set on fire and burn hotly, and are extinguished."

62 I replied and said, "O earth, what have you brought
forth, if the mind is made out of the dust like the other created things? 63 For it would have been better if the dust itself
had not been born, so that the mind might not have been
made from it. 64 But now the mind grows with us, and therefore we are tormented, because we perish and we know it.
65 Let the human race lament, but let the wild animals of the
field be glad; let all who have been born lament, but let the
cattle and the flocks rejoice. 66 It is much better with them
than with us; for they do not look for a judgment, and they
do not know of any torment or salvation promised to them
after death. 67 What does it profit us that we shall be preserved alive but cruelly tormented? 68 For all who have been
born are entangled in[a] iniquities, and are full of sins and
burdened with transgressions. 69 And if after death we were
not to come into judgment, perhaps it would have been better for us."

70 He answered me and said, "When the Most High made
the world and Adam and all who have come from him, he
first prepared the judgment and the things that pertain to the
judgment. 71 But now, understand from your own words—
for you have said that the mind grows with us. 72 For this
reason, therefore, those who live on earth shall be tormented, because though they had understanding, they committed
iniquity; and though they received the commandments, they
did not keep them; and though they obtained the law, they
dealt unfaithfully with what they received. 73 What, then,
will they have to say in the judgment, or how will they
answer in the last times? 74 How long the Most High has
been patient with those who inhabit the world!—and not for
their sake, but because of the times that he has fore-
ordained."

75 I answered and said, "If I have found favor in your
sight, O Lord, show this also to your servant: whether after
death, as soon as everyone of us yields up the soul, we shall
be kept in rest until those times come when you will renew
the creation, or whether we shall be tormented at once?"

76 He answered me and said, "I will show you that also,
but do not include yourself with those who have shown
scorn, or number yourself among those who are tormented.
77 For you have a treasure of works stored up with the Most
High, but it will not be shown to you until the last times.
78 Now concerning death, the teaching is: When the decisive
decree has gone out from the Most High that a person shall
die, as the spirit leaves the body to return again to him who
gave it, first of all it adores the glory of the Most High. 79 If it
is one of those who have shown scorn and have not kept the
way of the Most High, who have despised his law and hated
those who fear God— 80 such spirits shall not enter into
habitations, but shall immediately wander about in torments, always grieving and sad, in seven ways. 81 The first
way, because they have scorned the law of the Most High.
82 The second way, because they cannot now make a good
repentance so that they may live. 83 The third way, they

a Syr *defiled with*

via, vident repositam mercedem his qui testamentis Altissimi
crediderunt. 84 Quarta via, considerabunt sibi in novissimis
repositum cruciamentum. 85 Quinta via, videntes aliorum
habitacula ab angelis conservari cum silentio magno.
86 Sexta via, videntes quemadmodum de eis pertransientem
cruciamentum. 87 Septima via, quae omnium supradictarum
viarum maior est, quoniam detabescent in confusione et consumentur inhonoribus et marcescent in timoribus, videntes
gloriam Altissimi coram quem viventes peccaverunt et coram
quem incipient in novissimis temporibus iudicari.

88 Nam eorum qui servaverunt vias Altissimi ordo hic est,
quando separari incipient a vaso corruptibili. 89 In eo tempore commoratae servierunt cum labore Altissimo et omni
hora sustinuerunt periculum, uti perfecte custodirent legisla-
toris legem. 90 Propter quod hic de his sermo: 91 In primis
vident cum exultatione multa gloriam eius qui suscipit eas,
requiescent enim per septem ordines. 92 Ordo primus, quoniam cum labore multo certati sunt, ut vincerent cum eis plasmatum cogitamentum malum, ut non eas seducat a vita ad
mortem. 93 Secundus ordo, quoniam vident conplicationem
in qua vagantur impiorum animae et quae in eis manet puni-
tio. 94 Tertius ordo, videntes testimonium quod testificatus
est eis qui plasmavit eas, quoniam viventes servaverunt
quae per fidem data est lex. 95 Quartus ordo, intellegentes
requiem quam nunc in promptuariis eorum congregati requiescent cum silentio multo ab angelis conservati, et quae in
novissimis eorum manet gloriam. 96 Quintus ordo, exul-
tantes quomodo corruptibile effugerunt nunc, et futurum
quomodo hereditatem possidebunt, adhuc autem videntes
angustum et labore plenum quo iam liberati sunt et spatio-
sum incipiunt recipere, frunescentes et inmortales. 97 Sextus
ordo, quando eis ostendetur quomodo incipiet vultus eorum
fulgere sicut sol, et quomodo incipient stellis adsimilari lumi-
ni, amodo non corrupti. 98 Septimus ordo, qui est omnibus
supradictis maior, quoniam exultabunt cum fiducia et quoniam confidebunt non confusi et gaudebunt non reverentes;
festinant enim videre vultum eius cui serviunt viventes et a
quo incipiunt gloriosi mercedem recipere. 99 Hic ordo animarum iustorum, ut amodo adnuntiatur; praedictae viae cru-
ciatus quas patiuntur amodo qui neglexerint.

100 Et respondi et dixi: Ergo dabitur tempus animabus,
postquam separatae fuerint de corporibus, ut videant de quo
mihi dixisti? 101 Et dixit mihi: Septem diebus erit libertas
earum, ut videant in septem diebus qui praedicti sunt sermones, et postea congregabuntur in habitaculis suis.

102 Et respondi et dixi: Si inveni gratiam ante oculos tuos,
demonstra mihi adhuc servo tuo, si in die iudicii iusti impios

TODAY'S ENGLISH VERSION

stored up for those who put their faith in the covenants of God Most High. 84 Fourth, they think about the torment that has been stored up for them in the last days. 85 Fifth, they see angels guarding the homes of other souls in complete silence. 86 Sixth, they recognize that they must soon be tormented.[a] 87 Seventh, and worst of all, when they see the glory of God Most High, they are sick with remorse and shame. They cringe in fear, because while they were living they sinned against him. And now they are about to come before him to be judged on the last day.

88 "Now let me explain about those who followed the ways of God Most High and what will happen when the time comes for them to leave their mortal bodies. 89 While they lived on earth, through constant difficulty and danger, they served God Most High and carefully kept the Law given by the Lawgiver. 90 This is what they will receive: 91 They will rejoice when they see the great glory of God. He will receive them, and they will enter their rest in seven stages of joy. 92 The first joy is to have struggled hard and won the victory over the evil impulse which was formed in them, but which did not succeed in leading them from life into death. 93 The second is to see the endless wandering of the souls of the wicked and the punishment that is waiting for them. 94 The third is to know what a good report their Maker has given about them, that during their lifetime they kept the Law that was entrusted to them. 95 The fourth is to appreciate the rest that they are to enjoy in the places where they have been brought together, guarded by angels, in complete silence, and with the glory that is waiting for them at the last day. 96 The fifth is to rejoice that they have now escaped the corrupt world and that they will receive the future life as their possession. They can see both the narrow, troubled[b] world from which they have been freed and the spacious world they will receive and enjoy forever. 97 The sixth is to be shown how their faces will shine like the sun and how they are to be like the light of the stars that never die. 98 The seventh joy, and best of all, is when they rush to meet God face-to-face, with perfect trust and happiness, without any fear or shame. They served him during their lifetime and now they will receive from him their reward in glory. 99 These rewards that I have been telling you about are those that have been prepared for the souls of the righteous. I described to you earlier the torment that the rebellious will suffer."

100 Then I asked, "When the souls of the righteous are separated from their bodies, will they be given time to see what you have told me about?"

101 "They will be free for seven days," he answered, "and during that time they will be able to see the things I have told you about. After that they will be brought together with the other souls in their homes."

102 Then I said, "Sir, please tell me whether the righteous will be able to ask God Most High to show mercy on the

a Verse 86 in Latin is unclear. *b Some ancient translations* troubled; *Latin unclear.*

NEW REVISED STANDARD VERSION

shall see the reward laid up for those who have trusted the covenants of the Most High. *84* The fourth way, they shall consider the torment laid up for themselves in the last days. *85* The fifth way, they shall see how the habitations of the others are guarded by angels in profound quiet. *86* The sixth way, they shall see how some of them will cross over[a] into torments. *87* The seventh way, which is worse[b] than all the ways that have been mentioned, because they shall utterly waste away in confusion and be consumed with shame,[c] and shall wither with fear at seeing the glory of the Most High in whose presence they sinned while they were alive, and in whose presence they are to be judged in the last times.

88 "Now this is the order of those who have kept the ways of the Most High, when they shall be separated from their mortal body.[d] *89* During the time that they lived in it,[c] they laboriously served the Most High, and withstood danger every hour so that they might keep the law of the Lawgiver perfectly. *90* Therefore this is the teaching concerning them: *91* First of all, they shall see with great joy the glory of him who receives them, for they shall have rest in seven orders. *92* The first order, because they have striven with great effort to overcome the evil thought that was formed with them, so that it might not lead them astray from life into death. *93* The second order, because they see the perplexity in which the souls of the ungodly wander and the punishment that awaits them. *94* The third order, they see the witness that he who formed them bears concerning them, that throughout their life they kept the law with which they were entrusted. *95* The fourth order, they understand the rest that they now enjoy, being gathered into their chambers and guarded by angels in profound quiet, and the glory waiting for them in the last days. *96* The fifth order, they rejoice that they have now escaped what is corruptible and shall inherit what is to come; and besides they see the straits and toil[e] from which they have been delivered, and the spacious liberty that they are to receive and enjoy in immortality. *97* The sixth order, when it is shown them how their face is to shine like the sun, and how they are to be made like the light of the stars, being incorruptible from then on. *98* The seventh order, which is greater than all that have been mentioned, because they shall rejoice with boldness, and shall be confident without confusion, and shall be glad without fear, for they press forward to see the face of him whom they served in life and from whom they are to receive their reward when glorified. *99* This is the order of the souls of the righteous, as henceforth is announced;[f] and the previously mentioned are the ways of torment that those who would not give heed shall suffer hereafter."

100 Then I answered and said, "Will time therefore be given to the souls, after they have been separated from the bodies, to see what you have described to me?"

101 He said to me, "They shall have freedom for seven days, so that during these seven days they may see the things of which you have been told, and afterwards they shall be gathered in their habitations."

102 I answered and said, "If I have found favor in your sight, show further to me, your servant, whether on the day

a Cn: Meaning of Lat uncertain *b* Lat Syr Ethiop *greater*
c Syr Ethiop: Meaning of Lat uncertain *d* Lat *the corruptible vessel*
e Syr Ethiop: Lat *fullness* *f* Syr: Meaning of Lat uncertain

Latin Vulgate

excusare poterint vel deprecari pro eis Altissimum, 103 si
patres pro filiis vel filii pro parentibus, si fratres pro
fratribus, si adfines pro proximis, si fidentes pro carissimis.
104 Et respondit ad me et dixit: Quoniam invenisti gratiam
coram oculis meis, et hoc tibi demonstrabo. Dies iudicii
audax est et omnibus signaculum veritatis demonstrans.
Quemadmodum nunc non mittit pater filium vel filius
patrem aut dominus servum vel fidus carissimum, ut pro eo
intellegat aut dormiat aut manducet aut curetur, 105 sic
numquam nemo pro aliquo rogabit; omnes enim portabunt
unusquisque tunc iniustitias suas aut iustitias.

106 Et respondi et dixi: Et quomodo invenimus modo, quoniam rogavit primus Abraham propter Sodomitas, et Moyses
pro patribus qui in deserto peccaverunt, 107 et Iesus qui post
eum pro Israhel in diebus Achar, et Samuhel in diebus Saul,
108 et David pro confractione, et Salomon pro eis qui in sanctificationem, 109 et Helias pro his qui pluviam acceperunt et
pro mortuo ut viveret, 110 et Ezechias pro populo in diebus
Sennacherib, et multi pro multis? 111 Si ergo modo, quando
corruptibile increvit et iniustitia multiplicata est, exoraverunt
iusti pro impiis, quare et tunc sic non erit? 112 Et respondit
ad me et dixit: Praesens saeculum non est finis, gloria in eo
non frequens manet, propter hoc oraverunt qui potuerunt
pro invalidis. 113 Dies enim iudicii erit finis temporis huius
et initium futuri inmortalis temporis, in quo pertransivit corruptela, 114 soluta est intemperantia, abscisa est increduli-
tas, crevit autem iustitia, orta est veritas. 115 Tunc ergo
nemo poterit misereri eius qui in iudicio victus fuerit, neque
demergere eum qui vicerit.

116 Et respondi et dixi: Hic sermo meus primus et novis-
simus, quoniam melius erat non dare terram Adam vel, cum
iam dedisset, coercere eum ut non peccaret. 117 Quid enim
prodest omnibus in praesenti vivere in tristitia et mortuos
sperare punitionem? 118 O tu quid fecisti, Adam? Si enim tu
peccasti, non est factum solius tuus casus sed et nostrum qui
ex te advenimus. 119 Quid enim nobis prodest, si promissum
est nobis inmortale tempus, nos vero mortalia opera egimus?
120 Et quoniam praedicta est nobis perennis spes, nos vero
pessime vani facti sumus? 121 Et quoniam reposita sunt
habitacula sanitatis et securitatis, nos vero male conversati
sumus? 122 Et quoniam incipiet gloria Altissimi protegere eos
qui caste conversati sunt, nos autem pessimis viis ambulav-
imus? 123 Et quoniam ostendetur paradisus, cuius fructus
incorruptus perseverat, in quo est saturitas et medella,

King James Version

36[a] Then said I, Abraham prayed first for the Sodomites, and Moses for the fathers that sinned in the wilderness:

37 And Jesus after him for Israel in the time of Achan:

38 And Samuel and David for the destruction: and Solomon for them that should come to the sanctuary:

39 And Helias for those that received rain; and for the dead, that he might live:

40 And Ezechias for the people in the time of Sennacherib: and many for many.

41 Even so now, seeing corruption is grown up, and wickedness increased, and the righteous have prayed for the ungodly: wherefore shall it not be so now also?

42 He answered me, and said, This present life is not the end where much glory doth abide; therefore have they prayed for the weak.

43 But the day of doom shall be the end of this time, and the beginning of the immortality for to come, wherein corruption is past,

44 Intemperance is at an end, infidelity is cut off, righteousness is grown, and truth is sprung up.

45 Then shall no man be able to save him that is destroyed, nor to oppress him that hath gotten the victory.

46 I answered then and said, This is my first and last saying, that it had been better not to have given the earth unto Adam: or else, when it was given him, to have restrained him from sinning.

47 For what profit is it for men now in this present time to live in heaviness, and after death to look for punishment?

48 O thou Adam, what hast thou done? for though it was thou that sinned, thou art not fallen alone, but we all that come of thee.

49 For what profit is it unto us, if there be promised us an immortal time, whereas we have done the works that bring death?

50 And that there is promised us an everlasting hope, whereas ourselves being most wicked are made vain?

51 And that there are laid up for us dwellings of health and safety, whereas we have lived wickedly?

52 And that the glory of the most High is kept to defend them which have led a wary life, whereas we have walked in the most wicked ways of all?

53 And that there should be shewed a paradise, whose fruit endureth for ever, wherein is security and medicine, since we shall not enter into it?

a Verses 36–70 in the King James Version correspond to 106–140 in the Latin Vulgate and Today's English Version; the New Revised Standard Version has both versification systems.

Today's English Version

unrighteous on Judgment Day. 103 Will fathers be able to
pray for their children, children for parents, brothers for
brothers, relatives for those near to them, and friends[a] for
those dear to them?"

104 "I will be happy to tell you," he replied. "Judgment Day
is final[b] and sets the final seal on truth for all to see. You
know that in this age a father cannot send his son to be
sick[c] for him or sleep or eat or be healed for him. An owner
cannot send his slave to do these things for him, nor can a
person send his best friend. 105 In the same way, on that day,
no one will be able to pray for another person. Each person
will receive the punishment or reward for his own sinfulness
or righteousness."[d]

106 "If that is so," I answered, "how can we explain what
we find in the Scriptures? Abraham prayed for the people of
Sodom, and Moses for our ancestors who sinned in the
desert. 107 Later, Joshua prayed for the people of Israel in the
time of Achan, 108 and Samuel prayed for them in the days of
Saul.[e] David prayed at the time of the epidemic, and
Solomon prayed for those who were going to worship in the
Temple. 109 Elijah prayed that the people might have rain
and for a dead person to come back to life. 110 Hezekiah
prayed for the people during the time of Sennacherib. And
there are many other examples. 111 If righteous people
prayed for the unrighteous during such times when corruption increased and injustice multiplied, why won't the same
thing happen at the Judgment Day?"

112 "The present age is not the end of everything," the angel
answered. "Even in this age, the glorious presence of God is
not[f] always seen. That is why the strong have prayed for the
weak during this age. 113 But the Judgment Day will be the
end of the present age and the beginning of the future age.
Then all corruption will end, 114 self-indulgence and disloyalty will be eliminated. Righteousness and truth will reach
their full maturity. 115 So on Judgment Day, no one will be
able to have mercy on those who have been condemned, and
no one will be able to harm those who have been acquitted."

116 I answered, "I made this point before, and I will make it
again. It would have been better if the earth had never produced Adam, or when it had done so, if it had made him so
that he could not sin. 117 What good is it for any of us to
have life in the present age, when it is full of misery and
when all we can look forward to after death is punishment?
118 O Adam, what have you done? Your sin was not only your
own downfall; it was also the downfall of all of us who are
your descendants. 119 What good is it to us that we have the
promise of immortal life, when we have committed sins that
condemn us to death? 120 What good is the hope of eternity,
when we find ourselves in such a completely hopeless situation? 121 What good is it that safe and secure homes have
been prepared for us in the future world, when we have lived
such wicked lives? 122 What good is the promise that the glorious presence of God Most High will protect those who have
lived pure lives, when our own lives have been so full of sin?
123 What good is it that Paradise is shown to us, that its
imperishable fruit can heal us and provide all we need? We

[a] *Some ancient translations* friends; *Latin* the confident.
[b] *One ancient translation* final; *Latin* bold. [c] *Some ancient translations* be sick; *Latin* understand. [d] *Verses 106-140 are the equivalent of verses 36-70 in the King James Version.* [e] *Some ancient translations* in the days of Saul; *Latin does not have these words.* [f] *Some ancient translations* is not; *Latin* is.

New Revised Standard Version

of judgment the righteous will be able to intercede for the
ungodly or to entreat the Most High for them— *103* fathers
for sons or sons for parents, brothers for brothers, relatives
for their kindred, or friends for those who are most dear."

104 He answered me and said, "Since you have found
favor in my sight, I will show you this also. The day of judgment is decisive[a] and displays to all the seal of truth. Just as
now a father does not send his son, or a son his father, or a
master his servant, or a friend his dearest friend, to be ill[b] or
sleep or eat or be healed in his place, *105* so no one shall ever
pray for another on that day, neither shall anyone lay a burden on another;[c] for then all shall bear their own righteousness and unrighteousness."

36 *106* I answered and said, "How then do we find that
first Abraham prayed for the people of Sodom, and Moses for
our ancestors who sinned in the desert, 37 *107* and Joshua
after him for Israel in the days of Achan, 38 *108* and Samuel
in the days of Saul,[d] and David for the plague, and Solomon
for those at the dedication, 39 *109* and Elijah for those who
received the rain, and for the one who was dead, that he
might live, 40 *110* and Hezekiah for the people in the days of
Sennacherib, and many others prayed for many? 41 *111* So if
now, when corruption has increased and unrighteousness
has multiplied, the righteous have prayed for the ungodly,
why will it not be so then as well?"

42 *112* He answered me and said, "This present world is
not the end; the full glory does not[e] remain in it;[f] therefore
those who were strong prayed for the weak. 43 *113* But the
day of judgment will be the end of this age and the
beginning[g] of the immortal age to come, in which corruption
has passed away, 44 *114* sinful indulgence has come to an
end, unbelief has been cut off, and righteousness has
increased and truth has appeared. 45 *115* Therefore no one
will then be able to have mercy on someone who has been
condemned in the judgment, or to harm[h] someone who is
victorious."

46 *116* I answered and said, "This is my first and last
comment: it would have been better if the earth had not produced Adam, or else, when it had produced him, had
restrained him from sinning. 47 *117* For what good is it to all
that they live in sorrow now and expect punishment after
death? 48 *118* O Adam, what have you done? For though it
was you who sinned, the fall was not yours alone, but ours
also who are your descendants. 49 *119* For what good is it to
us, if an immortal time has been promised to us, but we
have done deeds that bring death? 50 *120* And what good is it
that an everlasting hope has been promised to us, but we
have miserably failed? 51 *121* Or that safe and healthful habitations have been reserved for us, but we have lived wickedly? 52 *122* Or that the glory of the Most High will defend
those who have led a pure life, but we have walked in
the most wicked ways? 53 *123* Or that a paradise shall
be revealed, whose fruit remains unspoiled and in which
are abundance and healing, but we shall not enter it

[a] Lat *bold* [b] Syr Ethiop Arm: Lat *to understand* [c] Syr Ethiop: Lat lacks *on that . . . another* [d] Syr Ethiop Arab 1: Lat Arab 2 Arm lack *in the days of Saul* [e] Lat lacks *not* [f] Or *the glory does not continuously abide in it* [g] Syr Ethiop: Lat lacks *the beginning* [h] Syr Ethiop: Lat *overwhelm*

Latin Vulgate

124 nos vero non ingrediemur, ingratis enim locis conversati
sumus? 125 Et quoniam super stellas fulgebunt facies eorum
qui abstinentiam habuerunt, nostrae vero facies super tenebras nigrae? 126 Non enim cogitavimus viventes quando iniquitatem faciebamus, quid incipientes post mortem pati.

127 Et respondit et dixit: Hoc est cogitamentum certaminis,
quem certavit qui super terram natus est homo, 128 ut si victus fuerit patiatur quod dixisti, si autem vicerit recipiet quod
dico, 129 quoniam haec est via, quam Moyses dixit cum
viveret ad populum dicens: Elige tibi vitam ut vivas. 130 Non
crediderunt autem ei, sed nec post eum prophetis, sed nec
mihi qui locutus sum ad eos, 131 quoniam non esset tristitia
in perditione eorum, sicut et futurum est gaudium super eos
quibus persuasa est salus.

132 Et respondi et dixi: Scio, domine, quoniam nunc vocatus est Altissimus misericors, in eo quod misereatur qui nondum in saeculo advenerunt, 133 et miserator, in eo quod mis-
eretur illis qui conversionem faciunt in lege eius, 134 et lon-
ganimis, quoniam longanimitatem praestat his qui peccaverunt quasi suis operibus, 135 et munificus, quoniam quidem donare vult pro exigere, 136 et multae misericordiae,
quoniam multiplicat magis misericordias his qui praesentes
sunt et qui praeterierunt et qui futuri sunt. 137 Si enim non
multiplicaverit, non vivificabitur saeculum cum his qui habitant in eo. 138 Et donator, quoniam si non donaverit de boni-
tate sua, ut adleventur hii qui iniquitates fecerunt de suis
iniquitatibus, non poterit decies millesima pars hominum
vivificari, 139 et iudex, si non ignoverit his qui creati sunt
verbo eius et deleverit multitudinem contemptionum, non
fortassis derelinquentur innumerabilem multitudinem nisi
pauci valde.

8 Et respondit ad me et dixit: Hoc saeculum fecit
Altissimus propter multos, futurum autem propter paucos. 2 Dicam autem coram te similitudinem, Ezra. Quomodo
autem interrogabis terram et dicet tibi, quoniam dabit terram
multam magis unde fiat fictile, parvum autem pulverem
unde aurum fit, sic et actus praesentis saeculi. 3 Multi quidem creati sunt, pauci autem salvabuntur.

4 Et respondi et dixi: Absolve ergo anima sensum et
devoret quod sapit. 5 Convenisti inobaudire et profecta es
nolens, nec enim tibi est datum spatium nisi solum modicum
vivere. 6 O Domine super nos, si permittes servo tuo, ut ore-
mus coram te et des nobis semen cordis et sensui culturam
unde fructum fiat, unde vivere possit omnis corruptus qui
portabit locum hominis. 7 Solus enim es, et una plasmatio
nos sumus manuum tuarum, sicut locutus es.

King James Version

54 (For we have walked in unpleasant places.)

55 And that the faces of them which have used abstinence shall shine above the stars, whereas our faces shall be blacker than darkness?

56 For while we lived and committed iniquity, we considered not that we should begin to suffer for it after death.

57 Then answered he me, and said, This is the condition of the battle, which man that is born upon the earth shall fight;

58 That, if he be overcome, he shall suffer as thou hast said: but if he get the victory, he shall receive the thing that I say.

59 For this is the life whereof Moses spake unto the people while he lived, saying, Choose thee life, that thou mayest live.

60 Nevertheless they believed not him, nor yet the prophets after him, no nor me which have spoken unto them,

61 That there should not be such heaviness in their destruction, as shall be joy over them that are persuaded to salvation.

62 I answered then, and said, I know, Lord, that the most High is called merciful, in that he hath mercy upon them which are not yet come into the world,

63 And upon those also that turn to his law;

64 And that he is patient, and long suffereth those that have sinned, as his creatures;

65 And that he is bountiful, for he is ready to give where it needeth;

66 And that he is of great mercy, for he multiplieth more and more mercies to them that are present, and that are past, and also to them which are to come.

67 For if he shall not multiply his mercies, the world would not continue with them that inherit therein.

68 And he pardoneth; for if he did not so of his goodness, that they which have committed iniquities might be eased of them, the ten thousandth part of men should not remain living.

69 And being judge, if he should not forgive them that are cured with his word, and put out the multitude of contentions,

70 There should be very few left peradventure in an innumerable multitude.

8 And he answered me, saying, The most High hath made this world for many, but the world to come for few.

2 I will tell thee a similitude, Esdras; As when thou askest the earth, it shall say unto thee, that it giveth much mould whereof earthen vessels are made, but little dust that gold cometh of: even so is the course of this present world.

3 There be many created, but few shall be saved.

4 So answered I and said, Swallow then down, O my soul, understanding, and devour wisdom.

5 For thou hast agreed to give ear, and art willing to prophesy: for thou hast no longer space than only to live.

6 O Lord, if thou suffer not thy servant, that we may pray before thee, and thou give us seed unto our heart, and culture to our understanding, that there may come fruit of it; how shall each man live that is corrupt, who beareth the place of a man?

7 For thou art alone, and we all one workmanship of thine hands, like as thou hast said.

TODAY'S ENGLISH VERSION

can never go there 124 because we have lived unacceptable lives.[a] 125 What good is it that the faces of those who practice self-control will shine more brightly than the stars, when our own faces will be blacker than the night? 126 Never in our whole lives, when we sinned, did we think about what we would have to suffer after death."

127 The angel replied, "Here is the meaning of the conflict that every person on earth must endure: 128 If he is defeated, he must suffer the things you have just told me about, but if he is victorious, he will receive the rewards that I have just mentioned. 129 That is why Moses long ago urged the people to choose life so that they might live. 130 But they did not believe him or the prophets who came after him, and they did not believe me when I spoke to them. 131 So the sadness over their destruction is nothing compared to the great joy over the salvation of those who believe."

132 I answered, "Sir, I know that God Most High is spoken of as merciful because he shows mercy to those who have not yet entered this world. 133 He is called compassionate because he shows compassion to those who repent and obey his Law. 134 He is thought of as patient because he is patient with his own creatures who have sinned. 135 He is known as generous because he prefers to give rather than to demand. 136 And he is known as very forgiving because he continues to forgive sinners of the past, present, and future. 137 If he did not continue to forgive, there would be no life for this world or the people in it. 138 He is spoken of as pardoning because, if it were not for his goodness in pardoning sinners, not one person in ten thousand would gain life. 139 He is called judge because he pardons and blots out the many sins of those who were created by his word. 140 If he did not, only a handful of the whole human race would be left."[b]

8 The angel replied, "God Most High made this world for many people, but the future world for only a few. 2 Ezra, let me give you an illustration. If you ask the earth, it will tell you that it produces a large amount of clay for pots but only a small amount of gold dust. And that's the way it is with the present world: 3 many have been created, but only a few will be saved."

4 I said to myself, "I must search for wisdom and try to understand. 5 I was brought into this world without my consent,[c] and I will leave it against my will. God has given me only a few short years as my span of life."

6 Then I prayed, "O Lord above, permit me, your humble servant, to offer this prayer: Plant a seed within us, and let it grow until it produces new hearts and minds, so that sinful humanity may have life. 7 For you alone are God, and you created all of us, as the scripture says. 8 You give life and

[a] *Probable text* unacceptable lives; *Latin* in unacceptable places.
[b] *Verses 106-140 are the equivalent of verses 36-70 in the King James Version.* [c] *One ancient translation* without my consent; *Latin* to obey.

NEW REVISED STANDARD VERSION

54 *124* because we have lived in perverse ways?[a] 55 *125* Or that the faces of those who practiced self-control shall shine more than the stars, but our faces shall be blacker than darkness? 56 *126* For while we lived and committed iniquity we did not consider what we should suffer after death."

57 *127* He answered and said, "This is the significance of the contest that all who are born on earth shall wage: 58 *128* if they are defeated they shall suffer what you have said, but if they are victorious they shall receive what I have said.[b] 59 *129* For this is the way of which Moses, while he was alive, spoke to the people, saying, 'Choose life for yourself, so that you may live!' 60 *130* But they did not believe him or the prophets after him, or even myself who have spoken to them. 61 *131* Therefore there shall not be[c] grief at their destruction, so much as joy over those to whom salvation is assured."

62 *132* I answered and said, "I know, O Lord, that the Most High is now called merciful, because he has mercy on those who have not yet come into the world; 63 *133* and gracious, because he is gracious to those who turn in repentance to his law; 64 *134* and patient, because he shows patience toward those who have sinned, since they are his own creatures; 65 *135* and bountiful, because he would rather give than take away;[d] 66 *136* and abundant in compassion, because he makes his compassions abound more and more to those now living and to those who are gone and to those yet to come— 67 *137* for if he did not make them abound, the world with those who inhabit it would not have life— 68 *138* and he is called the giver, because if he did not give out of his goodness so that those who have committed iniquities might be relieved of them, not one ten-thousandth of humankind could have life; 69 *139* and the judge, because if he did not pardon those who were created by his word and blot out the multitude of their sins,[e] 70 *140* there would probably be left only very few of the innumerable multitude."

8 He answered me and said, "The Most High made this world for the sake of many, but the world to come for the sake of only a few. 2 But I tell you a parable, Ezra. Just as, when you ask the earth, it will tell you that it provides a large amount of clay from which earthenware is made, but only a little dust from which gold comes, so is the course of the present world. 3 Many have been created, but only a few shall be saved."

4 I answered and said, "Then drink your fill of understanding,[f] O my soul, and drink wisdom, O my heart. 5 For not of your own will did you come into the world,[g] and against your will you depart, for you have been given only a short time to live. 6 O Lord above us, grant to your servant that we may pray before you, and give us a seed for our heart and cultivation of our understanding so that fruit may be produced, by which every mortal who bears the likeness[h] of a human being may be able to live. 7 For you alone exist, and we are a work of your hands, as you have declared.

a Cn: Lat Syr *places* *b* Syr Ethiop Arab 1: Lat *what I say* *c* Syr: Lat *there was not* *d* Or *he is ready to give according to requests* *e* Lat *contempts* *f* Syr: Lat *Then release understanding* *g* Syr: Meaning of Lat uncertain *h* Syr: Lat *place*

Latin Vulgate

8 Et quoniam vivificas nunc in matrice plasmatum corpus
et praestas membra, conservatur in igne et aqua tua creatio
et novem mensibus patitur tua plasmatio tuae creaturae
quae in eo creata est. 9 Ipsum autem quod servat et quod
servatur utraque servabuntur servatione tua. Et quando
iterum reddit matrix quae in ea creverint, 10 imperasti ut ex
ipsis membris, hoc est mamillis, praebere lac, fructum
mamillarum, 11 ut nutriatur id quod plasmatum est usque in
tempus aliquem. Et postea dispones eum tuae misericordiae,
12 enutristi eum tuae iustitiae, et erudisti eum in lege tua et
corripuisti eum tuo intellectu, 13 et mortificabis eum ut tuam
creaturam et vivificabis eum ut tuum opus. 14 Si ergo per-
dideris qui tantis laboribus plasmatus est tuo iussu, facili
ordine, et ut quid fiebat?

15 Et nunc dicens dicam: De omni homine tu magis scis, de
populo autem tuo quod mihi dolet, 16 et de hereditate tua
propter quam lugeo, et de Israhel propter quem tristis sum, et
de semine Iacob propter quod conturbor. 17 Ideo incipiam
orare coram te pro me et pro eis, quoniam video lapsos nos-
tros qui inhabitamus terram, 18 sed audivi celeritatem iudicii
quod futurum est. 19 Ideo audi meam vocem et intellege ser-
monum meorum, et loquar coram te.

20 Initium verborum Ezrae priusquam adsumeretur, et
dixit: Domine qui habitas in saeculum, cuius oculi elati et
superna in aerem, 21 et cuius thronus inaestimabilis et gloria inconprehensibilis, cui adstat exercitus angelorum cum
tremore, 22 quorum servatio in vento et igni convertitur,
cuius verbum verum et dicta perseverantia, 23 cuius iussio
fortis et dispositio terribilis, cuius aspectus arefecit abyssos
et indignatio tabescere facit montes et veritas testificatur.
24 Exaudi, Domine, orationem servi tui et auribus percipe
precationem figmenti tui, intende verba mea. 25 Dum enim
vivo loquar et dum sapio respondeam. 26 Ne aspicias populi
tui delicta, sed qui tibi in veritate serviunt. 27 Nec adtendas
impie agentium studia, sed qui tua testimonia cum doloribus
custodierunt. 28 Neque cogites qui in conspectu tuo false
conversati sunt, sed memorare qui ex voluntate tuum timo-
rem cognoverunt. 29 Neque volueris perdere qui pecorum
mores habuerunt, sed respicias eos qui legem tuam splendide
docuerunt. 30 Neque indigneris eis qui bestiis peius sunt
iudicati, sed diligas eos qui semper in tua gloria confiderunt.

King James Version

8 For when the body is fashioned now in the mother's womb, and thou givest it members, thy creature is preserved in fire and water, and nine months doth thy workmanship endure thy creature which is created in her.

9 But that which keepeth and is kept shall both be preserved: and when the time cometh, the womb preserved delivereth up the things that grew in it.

10 For thou hast commanded out of the parts of the body, that is to say, out of the breasts, milk to be given, which is the fruit of the breasts,

11 That the thing which is fashioned may be nourished for a time, till thou disposest it to thy mercy.

12 Thou broughtest it up with thy righteousness, and nurturedst it in thy law, and reformedst it with thy judgment.

13 And thou shalt mortify it as thy creature, and quicken it as thy work.

14 If therefore thou shalt destroy him which with so great labour was fashioned, it is an easy thing to be ordained by thy commandment, that the thing which was made might be preserved.

15 Now therefore, Lord, I will speak; touching man in general, thou knowest best; but touching thy people, for whose sake I am sorry;

16 And for thine inheritance, for whose cause I mourn; and for Israel, for whom I am heavy; and for Jacob, for whose sake I am troubled;

17 Therefore will I begin to pray before thee for myself and for them: for I see the falls of us that dwell in the land.

18 But I have heard the swiftness of the judge which is to come.

19 Therefore hear my voice, and understand my words, and I shall speak before thee. This is the beginning of the words of Esdras, before he was taken up: and I said,

20 O Lord, thou that dwellest in everlastingness, which beholdest from above things in the heaven and in the air;

21 Whose throne is inestimable; whose glory may not be comprehended; before whom the hosts of angels stand with trembling,

22 Whose service is conversant in wind and fire; whose word is true, and sayings constant; whose commandment is strong, and ordinance fearful;

23 Whose look drieth up the depths, and indignation maketh the mountains to melt away; which the truth witnesseth:

24 O hear the prayer of thy servant, and give ear to the petition of thy creature.

25 For while I live I will speak, and so long as I have understanding I will answer.

26 O look not upon the sins of thy people; but on them which serve thee in truth.

27 Regard not the wicked inventions of the heathen, but the desire of those that keep thy testimonies in afflictions.

28 Think not upon those that have walked feignedly before thee: but remember them, which according to thy will have known thy fear.

29 Let it not be thy will to destroy them which have lived like beasts; but to look upon them that have clearly taught thy law.

30 Take thou no indignation at them which are deemed worse than beasts; but love them that alway put their trust in thy righteousness and glory.

TODAY'S ENGLISH VERSION

provide arms and legs to the body formed in the womb,
where it is kept safe in the elements of fire and water. The
body which you form is carried in the womb for nine
months, 9 and you alone provide safety for the protecting
womb and the protected body. Then when the womb delivers
what was created in it, 10 your command produces milk from
the breasts of the human body. 11 The infant you created is
fed in this way for a while, and then you continue to provide
your mercy. 12 You raise the person on your righteousness,
teach him your Law, and discipline him with your wisdom.
13 You are his Creator and, as you wish, you can take away
his life or allow him to live. 14 But if you are so ready to
destroy a person that was so carefully created at your command, why was he created in the first place?

15 "Now, Lord, I must say this: You may know what is best
in regard to the rest of the human race, but I mourn for your
own people— 16 I am disturbed and grieved for your own
nation Israel, the descendants of Jacob. 17 So I want to pray
for them and for myself, because I can see how all of us who
live on this earth have failed, 18 and I know that judgment
will soon come upon us. 19 So please hear me and listen to
my prayer."

The prayer that Ezra prayed before he was taken up into
heaven begins here. He prayed, 20 "O Lord, you live forever,
and the highest heavens are yours. 21 Your throne is more
wonderful than anything we can imagine; your glory surpasses our understanding; the heavenly army of angels
stands trembling before you. 22 They are ready to turn themselves into wind or fire at your command. Your word is everlastingly true. 23 Your mighty commands accomplish fearful
things. With one look, you dry up the deep oceans, and you
can melt the mountains with your anger. Your truth lasts
forever.[a] 24 O Lord, you created me, and I am your servant,
so listen to my prayer. 25 As long as I have life and understanding, I cannot keep silent.

26 "Do not take account of the sins of your people; rather,
consider those who have served you faithfully. 27 Pay no
attention to godless people and what they do, but take into
account those who have kept your covenant in spite of all
their sufferings. 28 Do not think about those who have lived
wicked lives, but remember those who have gladly confessed
you as God. 29 Do not destroy your people because of those
who have lived like animals, but be mindful of those who
have taught your Law in such a wonderful way. 30 Do not be
angry with those you consider worse than animals, but show
your love to those who have always trusted in your glorious
presence.

[a] *Some ancient translations* lasts forever; *Latin* testifies.

NEW REVISED STANDARD VERSION

8 And because you give life to the body that is now fashioned
in the womb, and furnish it with members, what you have
created is preserved amid fire and water, and for nine
months the womb[a] endures your creature that has been created in it. 9 But that which keeps and that which is kept
shall both be kept by your keeping.[b] And when the womb
gives up again what has been created in it, 10 you have commanded that from the members themselves (that is, from the
breasts) milk, the fruit of the breasts, should be supplied,
11 so that what has been fashioned may be nourished for a
time; and afterwards you will still guide it in your mercy.
12 You have nurtured it in your righteousness, and instructed
it in your law, and reproved it in your wisdom. 13 You put it
to death as your creation, and make it live as your work.
14 If then you will suddenly and quickly[c] destroy what with
so great labor was fashioned by your command, to what purpose was it made? 15 And now I will speak out: About all
humankind you know best; but I will speak about your people, for whom I am grieved, 16 and about your inheritance,
for whom I lament, and about Israel, for whom I am sad, and
about the seed of Jacob, for whom I am troubled.
17 Therefore I will pray before you for myself and for them,
for I see the failings of us who inhabit the earth; 18 and now
also[d] I have heard of the swiftness of the judgment that is to
come. 19 Therefore hear my voice and understand my words,
and I will speak before you."

The beginning of the words of Ezra's prayer,[e] before he
was taken up. He said: 20 "O Lord, you who inhabit eternity,[f] whose eyes are exalted[g] and whose upper chambers
are in the air, 21 whose throne is beyond measure and whose
glory is beyond comprehension, before whom the hosts of
angels stand trembling 22 and at whose command they are
changed to wind and fire,[h] whose word is sure and whose
utterances are certain, whose command is strong and whose
ordinance is terrible, 23 whose look dries up the depths and
whose indignation makes the mountains melt away, and
whose truth is established[i] forever— 24 hear, O Lord, the
prayer of your servant, and give ear to the petition of your
creature; attend to my words. 25 For as long as I live I will
speak, and as long as I have understanding I will answer.
26 O do not look on the sins of your people, but on those who
serve you in truth. 27 Do not take note of the endeavors of
those who act wickedly, but of the endeavors of those who
have kept your covenants amid afflictions. 28 Do not think of
those who have lived wickedly in your sight, but remember
those who have willingly acknowledged that you are to be
feared. 29 Do not will the destruction of those who have the
ways of cattle, but regard those who have gloriously taught
your law.[j] 30 Do not be angry with those who are deemed
worse than wild animals, but love those who have always
put their trust in your glory. 31 For we and our ancestors

a Lat *what you have formed* *b* Syr: Meaning of Lat uncertain
c Syr: Lat *will with a light command* *d* Syr: Lat *but* *e* Syr Ethiop; Lat
beginning of Ezra's words *f* Or *you who abide forever* *g* Another Lat
text reads *whose are the highest heavens* *h* Syr: Lat *they whose service
takes the form of wind and fire* *i* Arab 2: Other authorities read *truth
bears witness* *j* Syr *have received the brightness of your law*

LATIN VULGATE

31 Quoniam nos et patres nostri mortalibus moribus egimus,
tu autem propter nos peccatores misericors vocaberis. 32 Si
enim desideraveris ut nostri miserearis, tunc misericors
vocaberis, nobis enim non habentibus opera iustitiae.
33 Iusti enim, quibus sunt operae multae repositae apud te,
ex propriis operibus recipient mercedem. 34 Quid est enim
homo, ut ei indigneris, aut genus corruptibile, ut ita
amariceris de ipso? 35 In veritate enim nemo de genitis est
qui non impie gessit, et de confitentibus qui non deliquit.
36 In hoc enim adnuntiabitur iustitia tua et bonitas tua,
Domine, cum misertus fueris eis qui non habent substantiam
operum bonorum.

37 Et respondit ad me et dixit: Recte locutus es aliqua, et
iuxta sermones tuos sic et fiet, 38 quoniam vere non cog-
itabo super plasma eorum qui peccaverunt aut mortem aut
iudicium aut perditionem, 39 sed iucundabor super iustorum
figmentum, peregrinationes quoque et salvationes et mercedis receptiones. 40 Quomodo ergo locutus sum, sic et est.
41 Sicut enim agricola serit super terram semina multa et
plantationis multitudinem plantat, sed non in tempore non
omnia quae seminata sunt salvabuntur, sed nec omnia quae
plantata sunt radicabunt, sic et qui in saeculo seminati sunt
non omnes salvabuntur.

42 Et respondi et dixi: Si inveni gratiam loquar, 43 quoniam semen agricolae, si non ascenderit — non enim accepit
pluviam tuam in tempore — et si corruptum fuerit multitudine pluviae, 44 hoc perit; sed homo qui manibus tuis plasmatus est et tuae imagini nominatus, quoniam similatus est
per quem omnia plasmasti, et similasti eum semini agricolae.
45 Non super nos, sed parce populo tuo et miserere hereditati
tuae, tuae enim creaturae misereris.

46 Et respondit ad me et dixit: Quae sunt praesentia praesentibus et quae futura futuris. 47 Multum enim tibi restat,
ut possis diligere meam creaturam super me. Tu autem frequenter te et ipsum proximasti iniustis numquam. 48 Sed et
in hoc mirabilis eris coram Altissimo, 49 quoniam humiliasti
te, sicut decet te, et non iudicasti te inter iustos. Plurimum
glorificeris, 50 propter quod miseriae multae miserabiles effi-
cientur qui inhabitant saeculum in novissimis, quia in multa
superbia ambulaverunt. 51 Tu autem pro te intellege et de
similibus tuis inquire gloriam. 52 Vobis enim apertus est paradisus, plantata est arbor vitae, praeparatum est futurum
tempus, praeparata est abundantia, aedificata est civitas,
probata est requies, perfecta est bonitas, ante perfecta sapientia. 53 Radix signata est a vobis, infirmitas extincta est a

KING JAMES VERSION

31 For we and our fathers do languish of such diseases: but because of us sinners thou shalt be called merciful.

32 For if thou hast a desire to have mercy upon us, thou shalt be called merciful, to us namely, that have no works of righteousness.

33 For the just, which have many good works laid up with thee, shall out of their own deeds receive reward.

34 For what is man, that thou shouldest take displeasure at him? or what is a corruptible generation, that thou shouldest be so bitter toward it?

35 For in truth there is no man among them that be born, but he hath dealt wickedly; and among the faithful there is none which hath not done amiss.

36 For in this, O Lord, thy righteousness and thy goodness shall be declared, if thou be merciful unto them which have not the confidence of good works.

37 Then answered he me, and said, Some things hast thou spoken aright, and according unto thy words it shall be.

38 For indeed I will not think on the disposition of them which have sinned before death, before judgment, before destruction:

39 But I will rejoice over the disposition of the righteous, and I will remember also their pilgrimage, and the salvation, and the reward, that they shall have.

40 Like as I have spoken now, so shall it come to pass.

41 For as the husbandman soweth much seed upon the ground, and planteth many trees, and yet the thing that is sown good in his season cometh not up, neither doth all that is planted take root: even so is it of them that are sown in the world; they shall not all be saved.

42 I answered then and said, If I have found grace, let me speak.

43 Like as the husbandman's seed perisheth, if it come not up, and receive not thy rain in due season; or if there come too much rain, and corrupt it:

44 Even so perisheth man also, which is formed with thy hands, and is called thine own image, because thou art like unto him, for whose sake thou hast made all things, and likened him unto the husbandman's seed.

45 Be not wroth with us, but spare thy people, and have mercy upon thine own inheritance: for thou art merciful unto thy creature.

46 Then answered he me, and said, Things present are for the present, and things to come for such as be to come.

47 For thou comest far short that thou shouldest be able to love my creature more than I: but I have ofttimes drawn nigh unto thee, and unto it, but never to the unrighteous.

48 In this also thou art marvellous before the most High:

49 In that thou hast humbled thyself, as it becometh thee, and hast not judged thyself worthy to be much glorified among the righteous.

50 For many great miseries shall be done to them that in the latter time shall dwell in the world, because they have walked in great pride.

51 But understand thou for thyself, and seek out the glory for such as be like thee.

52 For unto you is paradise opened, the tree of life is planted, the time to come is prepared, plenteousness is made ready, a city is builded, and rest is allowed, yea, perfect goodness and wisdom.

53 The root of evil is sealed up from you, weakness and

TODAY'S ENGLISH VERSION

31 "It is true that we and our ancestors have lived our lives
in ways that bring death, but it is because of us who are sinners that you are called merciful. 32 You will surely be called
merciful if you choose to take pity on us—we are sinners
without any righteous deeds to our credit. 33 Those who are
righteous will receive their reward on the basis of the many
good works that they have stored up with you.

34 "What are human beings that you should be angry with
them? What is this mortal race that you should be so bitter
against it? 35 To speak the truth, no person was ever born
who did not sin; there is no one living who is not guilty.
36 Therefore, Lord, your righteousness and goodness will certainly be made known when you show your mercy to those
who have no treasure of good deeds."

37 The Lord answered me, "Part of what you have said is
correct, and things will happen as you have indicated. 38 You
can be sure that I will give no thought to those who have
sinned or to their creation, death, judgment, or destruction.
39 Instead, I will find my joy in the creation of the righteous,
their earthly journey, their salvation, and their final reward.
40 Things will happen just as I have said. 41 The farmer
plants many seeds and puts out many plants, but not all of
them take root or come up at the right time. That's the way it
is with this world. Not everyone who has been placed in this
world will be saved."

42 Then I said, "Please let me speak. 43 The farmer's seed
may not come up because you did not send rain at the right
time, or it may be ruined by too much rain. 44 But people are
different. You formed them with your own hands; you created them to be like you; and you made everything for their
benefit. How can you compare them to a farmer's seed?
45 It's impossible, O Lord[a] above! Spare the people who are
your own. Have pity on them. Show your mercy to the people
you have created."

46 He answered, "The present is for those who live now,
and the future for those who are to come. 47 You are certainly not able to love what I have created more than I do. Never
again consider yourself among the unrighteous, as you have
done so often. 48 Yet I am very pleased 49 that you have
shown proper humility and not boasted by thinking of yourself as righteous. 50 The people of this world who have lived
their lives in pride and arrogance will suffer many things in
the last days. 51 But, Ezra, you should be thinking about the
glory that is waiting for you and those like you. 52 For all of
you, Paradise has been opened, the tree of life has been
planted, the world to come has been made ready, all your
needs have been provided, the heavenly city has been built,
full rest from your labors has been offered, goodness and
wisdom have been perfected. 53 The source of evil has been
sealed off, so that it cannot reach you; all sickness has been

[a] *Some ancient translations* O Lord; *Latin does not have these words.*

NEW REVISED STANDARD VERSION

have passed our lives in ways that bring death;[a] but it is
because of us sinners that you are called merciful. 32 For if
you have desired to have pity on us, who have no works of
righteousness, then you will be called merciful. 33 For the
righteous, who have many works laid up with you, shall
receive their reward in consequence of their own deeds.
34 But what are mortals, that you are angry with them; or
what is a corruptible race, that you are so bitter against it?
35 For in truth there is no one among those who have been
born who has not acted wickedly; among those who have
existed[b] there is no one who has not done wrong. 36 For in
this, O Lord, your righteousness and goodness will be
declared, when you are merciful to those who have no store
of good works."

37 He answered me and said, "Some things you have spoken rightly, and it will turn out according to your words.
38 For indeed I will not concern myself about the fashioning
of those who have sinned, or about their death, their judgment, or their destruction; 39 but I will rejoice over the creation of the righteous, over their pilgrimage also, and their
salvation, and their receiving their reward. 40 As I have spoken, therefore, so it shall be.

41 "For just as the farmer sows many seeds in the ground
and plants a multitude of seedlings, and yet not all that have
been sown will come up[c] in due season, and not all that
were planted will take root; so also those who have been
sown in the world will not all be saved."

42 I answered and said, "If I have found favor in your
sight, let me speak. 43 If the farmer's seed does not come up,
because it has not received your rain in due season, or if it
has been ruined by too much rain, it perishes.[d] 44 But people, who have been formed by your hands and are called
your own image because they are made like you, and for
whose sake you have formed all things—have you also made
them like the farmer's seed? 45 Surely not, O Lord[e] above!
But spare your people and have mercy on your inheritance,
for you have mercy on your own creation."

46 He answered me and said, "Things that are present are
for those who live now, and things that are future are for
those who will live hereafter. 47 For you come far short of
being able to love my creation more than I love it. But you
have often compared yourself[f] to the unrighteous. Never do
so! 48 But even in this respect you will be praiseworthy before
the Most High, 49 because you have humbled yourself, as is
becoming for you, and have not considered yourself to be
among the righteous. You will receive the greatest glory,
50 for many miseries will affect those who inhabit the world in
the last times, because they have walked in great pride.
51 But think of your own case, and inquire concerning the
glory of those who are like yourself, 52 because it is for you
that paradise is opened, the tree of life is planted, the age to
come is prepared, plenty is provided, a city is built, rest is
appointed,[g] goodness is established and wisdom perfected
beforehand. 53 The root of evil[h] is sealed up from you, illness

a Syr Ethiop: Meaning of Lat uncertain *b* Syr: Meaning of Lat uncertain
c Syr Ethiop *will live*; Lat *will be saved* *d* Cn: Compare Syr Arab 1 Arm
Georg 2: Meaning of Lat uncertain *e* Ethiop Arab Compare Syr: Lat lacks
O Lord *f* Syr Ethiop: Lat *brought yourself near* *g* Syr Ethiop: Lat
allowed *h* Lat lacks *of evil*

LATIN VULGATE

vobis et mors absconsa est, infernum fugit et corruptio in
oblivionem. 54 Transierunt dolores et ostensus est in finem
thesaurus inmortalitatis. 55 Noli ergo adicere inquirendo de
multitudine eorum qui pereunt. 56 Nam et ipsi accipientes
libertatem spreverunt Altissimum et legem eius contempserunt et vias eius dereliquerunt. 57 Adhuc autem et
iustos eius conculcaverunt. 58 Et dixerunt in corde suo non
esse Deum, et quidem scientes quoniam moriuntur. 59 Sicut
enim vos suscipient quae praedicta sunt, sic eos sitis et cru-
ciatus quae praeparata sunt, non enim Altissimus voluit
hominem disperdi, 60 sed ipsi qui creati sunt coin-
quinaverunt nomen eius qui fecit eos, et ingrati fuerunt ei
qui praeparavit eis nunc vitam. 61 Quapropter iudicium
meum modo adpropinquat, 62 quod non omnibus demonstravi nisi tibi et tibi similibus paucis.

Et respondi et dixi: 63 Ecce nunc, Domine, demonstrasti
mihi multitudinem signorum quae incipies facere in novissimis, sed non demonstrasti mihi quo tempore.

9 Et respondit ad me et dixit: Metiens metire in temet ipso,
et erit cum videris, quoniam transivit pars quaedam signorum quae praedicta sunt, 2 tunc intelleges, quoniam ipsud
est tempus, in quo incipiet Altissimus visitare saeculum qui
ab eo factus est. 3 Et quando videbitur in saeculo motio
locorum, populorum turbatio, gentium cogitationes, ducum
inconstantia, principum turbatio, 4 et tunc intelleges, quoniam de his erat Altissimus locutus a diebus qui fuerunt ante
ab initio. 5 Sicut enim omne quod factum est in saeculo, initium per consummationem et consummatio manifesta, 6 sic
et Altissimi tempora, initia manifesta in prodigiis et vir-
tutibus, et consummatio in actu et in signis. 7 Et erit, omnis
qui salvus factus fuerit et qui poterit effugere per opera sua
vel per fidem in qua credidit, is 8 relinquetur de praedictis
periculis et videbit salutare meum in terra mea et in finibus
meis, quae sanctificavi mihi a saeculo. 9 Et tunc mirabuntur
qui nunc abusi sunt vias meas, et in cruciamentis com-
morabuntur hii qui eos proiecerunt in contemptu.
10 Quotquot enim non cognoverunt me viventes beneficia
consecuti, 11 et quotquot fastidierunt legem meam, cum
adhuc erant habentes libertatem, 12 et cum adhuc esset eis
apertum paenitentiae locus non intellexerunt sed spreverunt,
hos oportet post mortem in cruciamento cognoscere. 13 Tu
ergo adhuc noli curiosus esse quomodo impii cruciabuntur,
sed inquire quomodo iusti salvabuntur, et quorum saeculum
et propter quos saeculum et quando.

14 Respondi et dixi: 15 Olim locutus sum et nunc dico et
postea dicam, quoniam plures sunt qui pereunt quam qui
salvabuntur, 16 sicut multiplicat fluctus super guttam. Et

KING JAMES VERSION

the moth is hid from you, and corruption is fled into hell to be forgotten:

54 Sorrows are passed, and in the end is shewed the treasure of immortality.

55 And therefore ask thou no more questions concerning the multitude of them that perish.

56 For when they had taken liberty, they despised the most High, thought scorn of his law, and forsook his ways.

57 Moreover they have trodden down his righteous,

58 And said in their heart, that there is no God; yea, and that knowing they must die.

59 For as the things aforesaid shall receive you, so thirst and pain are prepared for them: for it was not his will that men should come to nought:

60 But they which be created have defiled the name of him that made them, and were unthankful unto him which prepared life for them.

61 And therefore is my judgment now at hand.

62 These things have I not shewed unto all men, but unto thee, and a few like thee. Then answered I and said,

63 Behold, O Lord, now hast thou shewed me the multitude of the wonders, which thou wilt begin to do in the last times: but at what time, thou hast not shewed me.

9 He answered me then, and said, Measure thou the time diligently in itself: and when thou seest part of the signs past, which I have told thee before,

2 Then shalt thou understand, that it is the very same time, wherein the Highest will begin to visit the world which he made.

3 Therefore when there shall be seen earthquakes and uproars of the people in the world:

4 Then shalt thou well understand, that the most High spake of those things from the days that were before thee, even from the beginning.

5 For like as all that is made in the world hath a beginning and an end, and the end is manifest:

6 Even so the times also of the Highest have plain beginnings in wonders and powerful works, and endings in effects and signs.

7 And every one that shall be saved, and shall be able to escape by his works, and by faith, whereby ye have believed,

8 Shall be preserved from the said perils, and shall see my salvation in my land, and within my borders: for I have sanctified them for me from the beginning.

9 Then shall they be in pitiful case, which now have abused my ways: and they that have cast them away despitefully shall dwell in torments.

10 For such as in their life have received benefits, and have not known me;

11 And they that have loathed my law, while they had yet liberty, and, when as yet place of repentance was open unto them, understood not, but despised it;

12 The same must know it after death by pain.

13 And therefore be thou not curious how the ungodly shall be punished, and when: but enquire how the righteous shall be saved, whose the world is, and for whom the world is created.

14 Then answered I and said,

15 I have said before, and now do speak, and will speak it also hereafter, that there be many more of them which perish, than of them which shall be saved:

16 Like as a wave is greater than a drop.

TODAY'S ENGLISH VERSION

removed, death[a] has been taken away, hell is gone, and corruption has disappeared. 54 All suffering has been taken away, and the treasure of immortality is at last revealed.

55 "So don't ask any more questions about the large number of people who are lost. 56 For when they had the opportunity to choose, they despised God Most High, had contempt for his Law, and refused to follow his ways. 57 In addition, they mistreated the righteous servants of God. 58 They even said to themselves that there was no God, although they knew that they must die. 59 So the joys I have described are waiting for you, while thirst and torment are in store for them. But God Most High did not want anyone to perish. 60 He created everyone and prepared life for everyone, but those he created dishonored the name of their Creator and were ungrateful to the one who offered them life. 61 That is why the day on which I will judge them is near. 62 I have made this known to you and a few others like you, but not to everyone."

I answered, 63 "Sir, you have shown me many signs which you will perform in the last days, but you have not told me how I can know when this will happen."

9 He answered, "Consider all these things very carefully. When you see that some of the signs I have told you about have appeared, 2 you will know that the time has come when God Most High will bring judgment on the world he has created. 3 There will be earthquakes, national rebellions, international intrigues, unstable leaders, and confused rulers. When you see these things happening, 4 you will know that they are what God Most High has spoken about since the beginning of creation. 5 The beginning and the end[b] of everything that happens in this world are clear. 6 The same is true in the world above:[c] wonders and miracles show the beginning of events, and mighty signs show when they end.

7 "Some people will escape destruction and be saved by their good works or by their faith. All of them 8 will survive the dangers I have described and will enjoy the salvation provided in the land that I have set apart from eternity as my own. 9 Then those who have ignored my ways and held them in contempt will be surprised when they find themselves in continual torment. 10 This will include all those who ignored me while they were alive, even though they accepted the blessings I gave them. 11 It will include all those who scorned my Law during the time they were free to do so and all those who refused to repent when they still had the chance. 12 The torment they will have to suffer after death will force them to recognize the truth. 13 Therefore, Ezra, you should stop asking questions about how the wicked will be punished. Instead, be concerned about how and when the righteous will be saved. The world was created for them and belongs to them."

14 I said, 15 "I must repeat what I said before. The lost far outnumber those who are saved— 16 it is like a wave compared with a drop of water."

[a] *Some ancient translations* death; *Latin does not have this word.*
[b] *One ancient translation* The beginning and the end; *Latin unclear.*
[c] The same . . . above; *Latin unclear.*

NEW REVISED STANDARD VERSION

is banished from you, and death[a] is hidden; Hades has fled and corruption has been forgotten;[b] 54 sorrows have passed away, and in the end the treasure of immortality is made manifest. 55 Therefore do not ask any more questions about the great number of those who perish. 56 For when they had opportunity to choose, they despised the Most High, and were contemptuous of his law, and abandoned his ways. 57 Moreover, they have even trampled on his righteous ones, 58 and said in their hearts that there is no God—though they knew well that they must die. 59 For just as the things that I have predicted await[c] you, so the thirst and torment that are prepared await them. For the Most High did not intend that anyone should be destroyed; 60 but those who were created have themselves defiled the name of him who made them, and have been ungrateful to him who prepared life for them now. 61 Therefore my judgment is now drawing near; 62 I have not shown this to all people, but only to you and a few like you."

Then I answered and said, 63 "O Lord, you have already shown me a great number of the signs that you will do in the last times, but you have not shown me when you will do them."

9 He answered me and said, "Measure carefully in your mind, and when you see that some of the predicted signs have occurred, 2 then you will know that it is the very time when the Most High is about to visit the world that he has made. 3 So when there shall appear in the world earthquakes, tumult of peoples, intrigues of nations, wavering of leaders, confusion of princes, 4 then you will know that it was of these that the Most High spoke from the days that were of old, from the beginning. 5 For just as with everything that has occurred in the world, the beginning is evident,[d] and the end manifest; 6 so also are the times of the Most High: the beginnings are manifest in wonders and mighty works, and the end in penalties[e] and in signs.

7 "It shall be that all who will be saved and will be able to escape on account of their works, or on account of the faith by which they have believed, 8 will survive the dangers that have been predicted, and will see my salvation in my land and within my borders, which I have sanctified for myself from the beginning. 9 Then those who have now abused my ways shall be amazed, and those who have rejected them with contempt shall live in torments. 10 For as many as did not acknowledge me in their lifetime, though they received my benefits, 11 and as many as scorned my law while they still had freedom, and did not understand but despised it[f] while an opportunity of repentance was still open to them, 12 these must in torment acknowledge it[f] after death. 13 Therefore, do not continue to be curious about how the ungodly will be punished; but inquire how the righteous will be saved, those to whom the age belongs and for whose sake the age was made."[g]

14 I answered and said, 15 "I said before, and I say now, and will say it again: there are more who perish than those who will be saved, 16 as a wave is greater than a drop of water."

a Syr Ethiop Arm: Lat lacks *death* *b* Syr: Lat *Hades and corruption have fled into oblivion*; or *corruption has fled into Hades to be forgotten*
c Syr: Lat *will receive* *d* Syr: Ethiop *is in the word*; Meaning of Lat uncertain *e* Syr: Lat Ethiop *in effects* *f* Or *me* *g* Syr: Lat *saved, and whose is the age and for whose sake the age was made and when*

LATIN VULGATE

respondit ad me et dixit: 17 Qualis ager, talia et semina, et
quales flores, tales et tincturae, et qualis opera, talis et creatio, et qualis agricola, talis et area. Quoniam tempus erat
saeculi, 18 et tunc cum essem parans eis, his qui nunc, antequam fieret illis saeculum in quo inhabitarent, et nemo con-
tradixit mihi 19 tunc, nec enim erat quisquam, et nunc creati
in hoc mundo parato et mensa indeficienti et lege investiga-
bili, corrupti sunt moribus eorum. 20 Et consideravi saeculum meum, et ecce erat perditum, et orbem meum, et ecce
erat periculi propter cogitationes quae in eo advenerunt.
21 Et vidi et peperci eis vix valde, et salvavi mihi acinum de
botru et plantationem de tribu multa. 22 Pereat ergo multitudo quae sine causa nata est, et servetur acinus meus et plan-
tatio mea, quia cum multo labore perfeci haec.

23 Tu autem si adhuc intermittas septem dies alios, sed
non ieiunabis in eis, 24 ibis autem in campum florum, ubi
domus non est aedificata, et manduca solummodo de
floribus campi, et carnem non gustabis et vinum non bibes
sed solummodo flores, 25 et deprecare Altissimum sine intermissione, et veniam et loquar tecum.

26 Et profectus sum, sicut dixit mihi, in campum quod
vocatur Ardat, et sedi ibi in floribus et de herbis agri mandu-
cavi et facta est esca earum mihi in saturitatem. 27 Et factum est post dies septem, et ego discumbebam supra faenum
et cor meum iterum turbabatur sicut et ante.

28 Et apertum est os meum et inchoavi dicere coram
Altissimo et dixi: 29 O Domine, in nobis ostendens ostensus
es patribus nostris in deserto, quando erant exientes de
Aegypto et quando veniebant in deserto quod non calcatur et
infructuoso, et dicens dixisti: 30 Tu Israhel audi me, et
semen Iacob intendite sermonibus meis. 31 Ecce enim ego
semino in vobis legem meam, et faciet in vobis fructum, et
glorificamini in eo per saeculum. 32 Nam patres nostri accipientes legem non servaverunt et legitima mea non custodierunt. Et factum est fructum legis non periens; nec enim
poterat, quoniam tuus erat. 33 Nam qui acceperunt
perierunt, non custodientes quod in eis seminatum fuerat.
34 Et ecce consuetudo est ut, cum acceperit terra semen vel
navem mare vel vas aliud escas vel potus, et cum fuerit ut
exterminetur 35 quod seminatum est vel quod missum est
vel quae suscepta sunt, exterminentur haec, susceptoria vero
manent. Apud nos si enim non sic factum est. 36 Nos quidem qui legem accepimus peccantes peribimus et cor nostrum quod suscepit eam, 37 nam lex non perit sed permanet
in suo honore.

38 Et cum loquor haec in corde meo, et respexi oculis meis
et vidi mulierem in dextera parte, et ecce haec lugebat et
plorabat cum voce magna, et animo dolebat valde, et vesti-
menta eius discisa, et cinis super caput eius. 39 Et dimisi

KING JAMES VERSION

17 And he answered me, saying, Like as the field is, so is also the seed; as the flowers be, such are the colours also; such as the workman is, such also is the work; and as the husbandman is himself, so is his husbandry also: for it was the time of the world.

18 And now when I prepared the world, which was not yet made, even for them to dwell in that now live, no man spake against me.

19 For then every one obeyed: but now the manners of them which are created in this world that is made are corrupted by a perpetual seed, and by a law which is unsearchable rid themselves.

20 So I considered the world, and, behold, there was peril because of the devices that were come into it.

21 And I saw, and spared it greatly, and have kept me a grape of the cluster, and a plant of a great people.

22 Let the multitude perish then, which was born in vain; and let my grape be kept, and my plant; for with great labour have I made it perfect.

23 Nevertheless, if thou wilt cease yet seven days more, (but thou shalt not fast in them,

24 But go into a field of flowers, where no house is builded, and eat only the flowers of the field; taste no flesh, drink no wine, but eat flowers only;)

25 And pray unto the Highest continually, then will I come and talk with thee.

26 So I went my way into the field which is called Ardath, like as he commanded me; and there I sat among the flowers, and did eat of the herbs of the field, and the meat of the same satisfied me.

27 After seven days I sat upon the grass, and my heart was vexed within me, like as before:

28 And I opened my mouth, and began to talk before the most High, and said,

29 O Lord, thou that shewest thyself unto us, thou wast shewed unto our fathers in the wilderness, in a place where no man treadeth, in a barren place, when they came out of Egypt.

30 And thou spakest, saying, Hear me, O Israel; and mark my words, thou seed of Jacob.

31 For, behold, I sow my law in you, and it shall bring fruit in you, and ye shall be honoured in it for ever.

32 But our fathers, which received the law, kept it not, and observed not thy ordinances: and though the fruit of thy law did not perish, neither could it, for it was thine;

33 Yet they that received it perished, because they kept not the thing that was sown in them.

34 And, lo, it is a custom, when the ground hath received seed, or the sea a ship, or any vessel meat or drink, that, that being perished wherein it was sown or cast into,

35 That thing also which was sown, or cast therein, or received, doth perish, and remaineth not with us: but with us it hath not happened so.

36 For we that have received the law perish by sin, and our heart also which received it.

37 Notwithstanding the law perisheth not, but remaineth in his force.

38 And when I spake these things in my heart, I looked back with mine eyes, and upon the right side I saw a woman, and, behold, she mourned and wept with a loud voice, and was much grieved in heart, and her clothes were rent, and she had ashes upon her head.

TODAY'S ENGLISH VERSION

17 He answered, "The seed to be planted depends on the soil; the color of the flower depends on the kind of flower; the quality of a product depends on the skill of the worker; and the size of the harvest depends on how hard the farmer has worked. 18 Before I created this world or the people who would live in it, no one opposed me, because no one existed. 19 When I had created the world, I supplied it with an abundance of food and a Law of profound wisdom, but the people I created lived corrupt lives. 20 I looked at my world and saw that it was ruined. I saw that my earth was in danger of being destroyed by the wicked plans of the people who had come into it. 21 When I saw this, I found it very difficult to spare them, but I saved a few for myself, one grape out of a bunch and one tree out of a great forest.[a] 22 So let them perish—all those people who were born only to be lost. But let my chosen people be kept safe—those for whom I worked so hard to bring to perfection.

23 "And now, Ezra, you must wait seven more days, but do not fast this time. 24 Go to a field of wild flowers where no one has ever lived and eat nothing but the flowers—do not eat any meat or drink any wine. 25 Pray the whole time to God Most High. Then I will come and talk with you again."

26 I obeyed the angel's command and went to a field called Ardat. I sat there among the flowers and ate the wild plants, and that was enough food for me. 27 After seven days I was lying on the grass, and once again my thoughts began to trouble me. 28 Then I began to speak and said to God Most High, 29 "O Lord, you revealed yourself to our ancestors when they were traveling through the trackless, barren desert after they had left Egypt. You said to them, 30 'Listen to me, people of Israel. 31 I am giving you my Law. It will be like a seed planted among you that produces fruit, and it will be your crowning glory forever.' 32 Our ancestors received the Law, but they disobeyed its commands. Yet the fruit of the Law was not destroyed—it could not be destroyed because it was yours. 33 Those who had received the Law were destroyed because they did not guard the good seed that was sown in them. 34-35 The usual thing is that the container remains after its contents have been destroyed, for example, seed in the ground, a ship on the sea, or food in a bowl. But this is not the case with us sinners. 36 The Law was placed in our hearts, and we are the ones who will be destroyed because we have sinned. 37 The Law will not be destroyed; it will remain in all its glory."

38 While I was saying these things to myself, I looked around and saw a woman on my right. She was weeping and wailing, terribly upset; her clothes were torn, and there

[a] *Some ancient translations* a great forest; *Latin* great tribes.

NEW REVISED STANDARD VERSION

17 He answered me and said, "As is the field, so is the seed; and as are the flowers, so are the colors; and as is the work, so is the product; and as is the farmer, so is the threshing floor. 18 For there was a time in this age when I was preparing for those who now exist, before the world was made for them to live in, and no one opposed me then, for no one existed; 19 but now those who have been created in this world, which is supplied both with an unfailing table and an inexhaustible pasture,[a] have become corrupt in their ways. 20 So I considered my world, and saw that it was lost. I saw that my earth was in peril because of the devices of those who[b] had come into it. 21 And I saw and spared some[c] with great difficulty, and saved for myself one grape out of a cluster, and one plant out of a great forest.[d] 22 So let the multitude perish that has been born in vain, but let my grape and my plant be saved, because with much labor I have perfected them.

23 "Now, if you will let seven days more pass—do not, however, fast during them, 24 but go into a field of flowers where no house has been built, and eat only of the flowers of the field, and taste no meat and drink no wine, but eat only flowers— 25 and pray to the Most High continually, then I will come and talk with you."

26 So I went, as he directed me, into the field that is called Ardat;[e] there I sat among the flowers and ate of the plants of the field, and the nourishment they afforded satisfied me. 27 After seven days, while I lay on the grass, my heart was troubled again as it was before. 28 Then my mouth was opened, and I began to speak before the Most High, and said, 29 "O Lord, you showed yourself among us, to our ancestors in the wilderness when they came out from Egypt and when they came into the untrodden and unfruitful wilderness; 30 and you said, 'Hear me, O Israel, and give heed to my words, O descendants of Jacob. 31 For I sow my law in you, and it shall bring forth fruit in you, and you shall be glorified through it forever.' 32 But though our ancestors received the law, they did not keep it and did not observe the[f] statutes; yet the fruit of the law did not perish—for it could not, because it was yours. 33 Yet those who received it perished, because they did not keep what had been sown in them. 34 Now this is the general rule that, when the ground has received seed, or the sea a ship, or any dish food or drink, and when it comes about that what was sown or what was launched or what was put in is destroyed, 35 they are destroyed, but the things that held them remain; yet with us it has not been so. 36 For we who have received the law and sinned will perish, as well as our hearts that received it; 37 the law, however, does not perish but survives in its glory."

38 When I said these things in my heart, I looked around,[g] and on my right I saw a woman; she was mourning and weeping with a loud voice, and was deeply grieved at heart; her clothes were torn, and there were ashes on her

a Cn: Lat *law* *b* Cn: Lat *devices that* *c* Lat *them* *d* Syr Ethiop Arab 1: Lat *tribe* *e* Syr Ethiop *Arpad*; Arm *Ardab* *f* Lat *my* *g* Syr Arab Arm: Lat *I looked about me with my eyes*

cogitatus in quibus eram cogitans et conversus sum ad eam
et dixi ei: 40 Ut quid fles et quid doles animo? Et dixit ad
me: 41 Dimitte me, dominus meus, ut defleam me et adiciam dolorem, quoniam valde amara sum animo et humiliata
sum valde. 42 Et dixi ei: Quid passa es, dic mihi.

Et dixit ad me: 43 Sterilis fui ego famula tua et non peperi
habens maritum annis triginta. 44 Ego enim per singulas
horas et per singulos dies in annis triginta his deprecabar
Altissimum nocte ac die. 45 Et factum est post triginta
annos, exaudivit me Deus ancillae tuae et pervidit humili-
tatem meam et adtendit tribulationi meae et dedit mihi filium. Et iucundata sum super eum valde ego et vir meus et
omnes cives mei, et honorificabamus valde Fortem. 46 Et
nutrivi eum cum labore multo. 47 Et factum est cum crevis-
set et venissem accipere illi uxorem, et feci diem epuli.

10 1 Et factum est cum introisset filius meus in thalamo
suo, cecidit et mortuus est. 2 Et evertimus omnes
lumina, et surrexerunt omnes cives mei ad consolandam me,
et quievi usque in alium diem usque noctem. 3 Et factum est
cum omnes quievissent ut me consolarentur ut quiescerem,
et surrexi nocte et fugi et veni, sicut vides, in hoc campo.
4 Et cogito iam non reverti in civitatem sed hic consistere, et
neque manducabo neque bibam, sed sine intermissione
lugere et ieiunare, usque dum moriar.

5 Et dereliqui adhuc sermones in quibus eram et respondi
cum iracundia ad eam et dixi: 6 Stulta super omnes
mulieres, non vides luctum nostrum et quae nobis contigerunt? 7 Quoniam Sion mater nostra omnium in tristitia
contristatur et humilitate humiliata est. Lugete validissime
8 et nunc quoniam omnes lugemus, et tristes este quoniam
omnes contristati sumus. Tu autem contristaris in uno filio.
9 Interroga enim terram et dicet tibi, quoniam haec est quae
debeat lugere tantorum superstes germinantium. 10 Et ex
ipsa initio omnes nati et alii venient, et ecce paene omnes in
perditionem ambulant et in exterminium fit multitudo
eorum. 11 Et quis ergo debet lugere magis nisi haec quae
tam magnam multitudinem perdidit, quam tu quae pro uno
doles? Si autem dices mihi 12 quoniam non est similis planc-
tus meus terrae, quoniam fructum ventris mei perdidi, quem
cum maeroribus peperi et cum doloribus genui, 13 terra
autem secundum viam terrae, abiit quae in ea multitudo
praesens quomodo et venit, et ego tibi dico: 14 Sicut tu cum
dolore peperisti, sic et terra dedit fructum suum hominem ab
initio ei qui fecit eam. 15 Nunc ergo retine apud temet ipsam
dolorem tuum et fortiter fer quae tibi contigerunt casus. 16 Si
enim iustificaveris terminum Dei, et filium tuum recipies in

39 Then let I my thoughts go that I was in, and turned me unto her,

40 And said unto her, Wherefore weepest thou? why art thou so grieved in thy mind?

41 And she said unto me, Sir, let me alone, that I may bewail myself, and add unto my sorrow, for I am sore vexed in my mind, and brought very low.

42 And I said unto her, What aileth thee? tell me.

43 She said unto me, I thy servant have been barren, and had no child, though I had an husband thirty years.

44 And those thirty years I did nothing else day and night, and every hour, but make my prayer to the Highest.

45 After thirty years God heard me thine handmaid, looked upon my misery, considered my trouble, and gave me a son: and I was very glad of him, so was my husband also, and all my neighbours: and we gave great honour unto the Almighty.

46 And I nourished him with great travail.

47 So when he grew up, and came to the time that he should have a wife, I made a feast.

10 And it so came to pass, that when my son was entered into his wedding chamber, he fell down, and died.

2 Then we all overthrew the lights, and all my neighbours rose up to comfort me: so I took my rest unto the second day at night.

3 And it came to pass, when they had all left off to comfort me, to the end I might be quiet; then rose I up by night, and fled, and came hither into this field, as thou seest.

4 And I do now purpose not to return into the city, but here to stay, and neither to eat nor drink, but continually to mourn and to fast until I die.

5 Then left I the meditations wherein I was, and spake to her in anger, saying,

6 Thou foolish woman above all other, seest thou not our mourning, and what happeneth unto us?

7 How that Sion our mother is full of all heaviness, and much humbled, mourning very sore?

8 And now, seeing we all mourn and are sad, for we are all in heaviness, art thou grieved for one son?

9 For ask the earth, and she shall tell thee, that it is she which ought to mourn for the fall of so many that grow upon her.

10 For out of her came all at the first, and out of her shall all others come, and, behold, they walk almost all into destruction, and a multitude of them is utterly rooted out.

11 Who then should make more mourning than she, that hath lost so great a multitude; and not thou, which art sorry but for one?

12 But if thou sayest unto me, My lamentation is not like the earth's, because I have lost the fruit of my womb, which I brought forth with pains, and bare with sorrows;

13 But the earth *not so:* for the multitude present in it according to the course of the earth is gone, as it came:

14 Then say I unto thee, Like as thou hast brought forth with labour; even so the earth also hath given her fruit, namely, man, ever since the beginning unto him that made her.

15 Now therefore keep thy sorrow to thyself, and bear with a good courage that which hath befallen thee.

16 For if thou shalt acknowledge the determination of

TODAY'S ENGLISH VERSION

were ashes on her head. 39 I immediately put my own troubles out of my mind, turned to the woman, 40 and asked, "Why are you crying? Why are you so upset?"

41 "Please, sir," she answered, "leave me alone and let me go on crying and mourning; I am bitter and depressed."

42 "Tell me what's wrong," I said.

43 She answered, "Sir, I was married for thirty years, but I was never able to have a child. 44 During those thirty years I prayed every day and every hour, day and night, to God Most High for a child. 45 After thirty years God answered my prayer; he saw my suffering, took away my distress, and gave me a son. What great joy this brought to my husband and me and to all our neighbors! We sang the praises of the Almighty. 46 I brought our son up with the greatest care, 47 and when he was grown, I chose a wife for him and prepared for the wedding.

10 "On the wedding night when my son entered the bedroom, he dropped dead. 2 So we put out all the wedding lamps, and all my neighbors came to comfort me. I remained in control of myself until the evening of the second day, 3 when they all left. That night I got up and came out to this field, as you see. 4 I have decided never to return to that town. I am going to stay here in constant mourning, neither eating nor drinking anything until I die."

5 When she told me this, I put aside my own thoughts and spoke sharply to her: 6 "You are the most foolish woman I ever met. Don't you see what our people are suffering? Don't you know all that has happened to us? 7 Jerusalem, the mother of us all, is overcome with grief and shame. You ought to be mourning for her 8 and sharing the grief and sorrow of all of us. But you are mourning for that one son of yours. 9 Ask the earth; let her tell you that she is the one who ought to be mourning for the vast multitudes of people that she has brought to birth. 10 All of us who are living came originally from her, and there are more to come. Almost all of us go straight to destruction—the vast multitude of earth's children are lost. 11 So who has more right to mourn, you for your one son, or the earth, which has lost so many? 12-13 I know what you are thinking; you think that your sorrow is worse than the earth's. You think that it is only natural for earth's multitudes to live and then die, but you have lost your own flesh and blood which you brought to birth with such trouble and pain. But let me tell you 14 that from the time God created the earth she has suffered as much in producing human beings for God as you did in childbirth. 15 So keep your tears to yourself, and be brave about what has happened to you. 16 If you will accept God's

NEW REVISED STANDARD VERSION

head. 39 Then I dismissed the thoughts with which I had been engaged, and turned to her 40 and said to her, "Why are you weeping, and why are you grieved at heart?"

41 She said to me, "Let me alone, my lord, so that I may weep for myself and continue to mourn, for I am greatly embittered in spirit and deeply distressed."

42 I said to her, "What has happened to you? Tell me."

43 And she said to me, "Your servant was barren and had no child, though I lived with my husband for thirty years. 44 Every hour and every day during those thirty years I prayed to the Most High, night and day. 45 And after thirty years God heard your servant, and looked upon my low estate, and considered my distress, and gave me a son. I rejoiced greatly over him, I and my husband and all my neighbors;[a] and we gave great glory to the Mighty One. 46 And I brought him up with much care. 47 So when he grew up and I came to take a wife for him, I set a day for the marriage feast.

10 "But it happened that when my son entered his wedding chamber, he fell down and died. 2 So all of us put out our lamps, and all my neighbors[a] attempted to console me; I remained quiet until the evening of the second day. 3 But when all of them had stopped consoling me, encouraging me to be quiet, I got up in the night and fled, and I came to this field, as you see. 4 And now I intend not to return to the town, but to stay here; I will neither eat nor drink, but will mourn and fast continually until I die."

5 Then I broke off the reflections with which I was still engaged, and answered her in anger and said, 6 "You most foolish of women, do you not see our mourning, and what has happened to us? 7 For Zion, the mother of us all, is in deep grief and great distress. 8 It is most appropriate to mourn now, because we are all mourning, and to be sorrowful, because we are all sorrowing; you are sorrowing for one son, but we, the whole world, for our mother.[b] 9 Now ask the earth, and she will tell you that it is she who ought to mourn over so many who have come into being upon her. 10 From the beginning all have been born of her, and others will come; and, lo, almost all go[c] to perdition, and a multitude of them will come to doom. 11 Who then ought to mourn the more, she who lost so great a multitude, or you who are grieving for one alone? 12 But if you say to me, 'My lamentation is not like the earth's, for I have lost the fruit of my womb, which I brought forth in pain and bore in sorrow; 13 but it is with the earth according to the way of the earth—the multitude that is now in it goes as it came'; 14 then I say to you, 'Just as you brought forth in sorrow, so the earth also has from the beginning given her fruit, that is, humankind, to him who made her.' 15 Now, therefore, keep your sorrow to yourself, and bear bravely the troubles that have come upon you. 16 For if you acknowledge the decree of God to be

a Literally *all my citizens* *b* Compare Syr: Meaning of Lat uncertain
c Literally *walk*

Latin Vulgate

tempore et in mulieribus conlaudaberis. 17 Ingredere ergo in
civitatem ad virum tuum.
Et dixit ad me: 18 Non faciam neque ingrediar civitatem,
sed hic moriar. 19 Et adposui adhuc loqui ad eam et dixi:
20 Noli facere sermonem hunc, sed consenti persuaderi —
quid enim casus Sion — et consolare propter dolorem
Hierusalem. 21 Vides enim, quoniam sanctificatio nostra
deserta effecta est et altare nostrum demolitum est et tem-
plum nostrum destructum est, 22 et psalterium nostrum
humiliatum est et hymnus noster conticuit et exultatio nostra dissoluta est, et lumen candelabri nostri extinctum est et
arca testamenti nostri direpta est et sancta nostra contami-
nata sunt, et nomen quod nominatum est super nos paene
profanatum est, et liberi nostri contumeliam passi sunt, et
sacerdotes nostri succensi sunt et Levitae nostri in captivitate abierunt, et virgines nostrae coinquinatae sunt et
mulieres nostrae vim passae sunt, et iusti nostri rapti sunt et
parvuli nostri proditi sunt, et iuvenes nostri servierunt et
fortes nostri invalidi facti sunt. 23 Et quod omnium maius,
signaculum Sion, quoniam resignata est de gloria sua nunc
et tradita est in manibus eorum qui nos oderunt. 24 Tu ergo
excute tuam multam tristitiam et depone abs te multitudinem dolorum, ut tibi repropitietur Fortis et requiem faci-
at tibi Altissimus, requietionem laborum.
25 Et factum est cum loquebar ad eam, et ecce facies eius
fulgebat valde subito, et species coruscus fiebat visus eius, ut
etiam paverem valde ad eam et cogitarem, quid esset hoc.
26 Et ecce subito emisit sonum vocis magnum timore
plenum, ut commoveretur terra a sono. Et vidi, 27 et ecce
amplius mulier non conparebat mihi, sed civitas aedifica-
batur et locus demonstrabatur de fundamentis magnis. Et
timui et clamavi voce magna et dixi: 28 Ubi est Urihel
angelus, qui a principio venit ad me? Quoniam ipse me fecit
venire in multitudinem excessus mentis huius, et factus est
finis meus in corruptionem et oratio mea in inproperium.
29 Et cum essem loquens ego haec, et ecce venit ad me
angelus qui in principio venerat ad me et vidit me, 30 et ecce
eram positus ut mortuus et intellectus meus alienatus erat,
et tenuit dexteram meam et confortavit me et statuit me
super pedes meos et dixit mihi: 31 Quid tibi est et quare conturbaris et quid conturbatum est intellectum tuum et sensus
cordis tui? Et dixi: 32 Quoniam derelinquens dereliquisti me.
Ego quidem feci secundum sermones tuos et exivi in campum, et ecce vidi et video quod non possum enarrare. Et dixit
ad me: 33 Sta ut vir, et commonebo te. Et dixi: 34 Loquere,
dominus meus, tantum me noli derelinquere, ut non frustra
moriar, 35 quoniam vidi quae non sciebam, et audio quae
non scio. 36 Aut numquid sensus meus fallitur et anima mea
somniat? 37 Nunc ergo deprecor te, ut demonstres servo tuo
de excessu hoc.

King James Version

God to be just, thou shalt both receive thy son in time, and shalt be commended among women.

17 Go thy way then into the city to thine husband.

18 And she said unto me, That will I not do: I will not go into the city, but here will I die.

19 So I proceeded to speak further unto her, and said,

20 Do not so, but be counselled by me: for how many are the adversities of Sion? be comforted in regard of the sorrow of Jerusalem.

21 For thou seest that our sanctuary is laid waste, our altar broken down, our temple destroyed;

22 Our psaltery is laid on the ground, our song is put to silence, our rejoicing is at an end, the light of our candlestick is put out, the ark of our covenant is spoiled, our holy things are defiled, and the name that is called upon us is almost profaned: our children are put to shame, our priests are burnt, our Levites are gone into captivity, our virgins are defiled, and our wives ravished; our righteous men carried away, our little ones destroyed, our young men are brought in bondage, and our strong men are become weak;

23 And, which is the greatest of all, the seal of Sion hath now lost her honour; for she is delivered into the hands of them that hate us.

24 And therefore shake off thy great heaviness, and put away the multitude of sorrows, that the Mighty may be merciful unto thee again, and the Highest shall give thee rest and ease from thy labour.

25 And it came to pass, while I was talking with her, behold, her face upon a sudden shined exceedingly, and her countenance glistered, so that I was afraid of her, and mused what it might be.

26 And, behold, suddenly she made a great cry very fearful: so that the earth shook at the noise of the woman.

27 And I looked, and, behold, the woman appeared unto me no more, but there was a city builded, and a large place shewed itself from the foundations: then was I afraid, and cried with a loud voice, and said,

28 Where is Uriel the angel, who came unto me at the first? for he hath caused me to fall into many trances, and mine end is turned into corruption, and my prayer to rebuke.

29 And as I was speaking these words, behold, he came unto me, and looked upon me.

30 And, lo, I lay as one that had been dead, and mine understanding was taken from me: and he took me by the right hand, and comforted me, and set me upon my feet, and said unto me,

31 What aileth thee? and why art thou so disquieted? and why is thine understanding troubled, and the thoughts of thine heart?

32 And I said, Because thou hast forsaken me, and yet I did according to thy words, and I went into the field, and, lo, I have seen, and yet see, that I am not able to express.

33 And he said unto me, Stand up manfully, and I will advise thee.

34 Then said I, Speak on, my lord, in me; only forsake me not, lest I die frustrate of my hope.

35 For I have seen that I knew not, and hear that I do not know.

36 Or is my sense deceived, or my soul in a dream?

37 Now therefore I beseech thee that thou wilt shew thy servant of this vision.

Today's English Version

decision as just, you will get your son back at the right time,
and you will receive the praise due a mother. 17 Go back to
the city and to your husband."
18 "No," she answered, "I will never go back; I am going to
stay here and die."
19-20 "Don't do that," I continued. "Consider the misfortunes
and sorrows of Jerusalem, and you won't feel so sorry for
yourself. 21 You can see that our place of worship is in ruins,
our altar has been torn down, our Temple has been
destroyed, 22 our musical instruments lie quiet, our hymns
have been silenced, our joy has ended, the light of the sacred
lamp has been put out, our Covenant Box has been carried
off, our sacred utensils have been desecrated, the name of
our God has been profaned, our leaders have been dishonored, our priests have been burned to death, our Levites have
been taken captive, our virgins have been raped, our wives
have been violated, our devout men have been carried off,
our children have been abandoned, our young people have
been made slaves, and our strong soldiers have been made
helpless. 23 Worst of all, Jerusalem, once marked as God's
own city, has lost its glory and has been handed over to our
enemies. 24 So put aside all your sorrow and grief. May God
Most High, the Almighty, be merciful to you and give you
peace. May he give you rest from your troubles."
25 While I was speaking to the woman, her face suddenly
began to shine with a light that flashed like lightning. I was
afraid to stand near her and wondered what all this meant.
26 Suddenly she let out a loud and terrifying cry that shook
the earth. 27 When I looked up, I could no longer see the
woman, but there was a city built[a] on huge foundations. I
was afraid and shouted, 28 "Where is the angel Uriel, who
came to me earlier? It is his fault that I am so confused. My
prayer is useless, and I have nothing to hope for but death."
29 I was still speaking when the angel Uriel appeared
again. He saw me 30 lying there unconscious like a corpse,
so he took hold of my right hand, gave me strength, and
stood me on my feet. Then he asked, 31 "What's the matter?
Why are you so disturbed and confused?"
32 I answered, "You abandoned me completely! I did as you
told me and came out to this field, but I cannot explain what
I am seeing."
33 "Stand up straight," he answered, "and I will explain it
to you."
34 "Sir," I answered, "please explain it to me. I will die in
my frustration if you leave me, 35 for I cannot understand
what I have seen and heard. 36 Or is my mind playing tricks
on me, and is this just a bad dream? 37 I beg you, sir, tell me
what this vision means."

a *Some ancient translations* built; *Latin* being built.

New Revised Standard Version

just, you will receive your son back in due time, and will be
praised among women. 17 Therefore go into the town to your
husband."
18 She said to me, "I will not do so; I will not go into the
city, but I will die here."
19 So I spoke again to her, and said, 20 "Do not do that,
but let yourself be persuaded—for how many are the adversities of Zion?—and be consoled because of the sorrow of
Jerusalem. 21 For you see how our sanctuary has been laid
waste, our altar thrown down, our temple destroyed; 22 our
harp has been laid low, our song has been silenced, and our
rejoicing has been ended; the light of our lampstand has
been put out, the ark of our covenant has been plundered,
our holy things have been polluted, and the name by which
we are called has been almost profaned; our children[a] have
suffered abuse, our priests have been burned to death, our
Levites have gone into exile, our virgins have been defiled,
and our wives have been ravished; our righteous men[b] have
been carried off, our little ones have been cast out, our
young men have been enslaved and our strong men made
powerless. 23 And, worst of all, the seal of Zion has been
deprived of its glory, and given over into the hands of those
that hate us. 24 Therefore shake off your great sadness and
lay aside your many sorrows, so that the Mighty One may be
merciful to you again, and the Most High may give you rest,
a respite from your troubles."
25 While I was talking to her, her face suddenly began to
shine exceedingly; her countenance flashed like lightning, so
that I was too frightened to approach her, and my heart was
terrified. While[c] I was wondering what this meant, 26 she
suddenly uttered a loud and fearful cry, so that the earth
shook at the sound. 27 When I looked up, the woman was no
longer visible to me, but a city was being built,[d] and a place
of huge foundations showed itself. I was afraid, and cried
with a loud voice and said, 28 "Where is the angel Uriel, who
came to me at first? For it was he who brought me into this
overpowering bewilderment; my end has become corruption,
and my prayer a reproach."
29 While I was speaking these words, the angel who had
come to me at first came to me, and when he saw me
30 lying there like a corpse, deprived of my understanding, he
grasped my right hand and strengthened me and set me on
my feet, and said to me, 31 "What is the matter with you?
And why are you troubled? And why are your understanding
and the thoughts of your mind troubled?"
32 I said, "It was because you abandoned me. I did as you
directed, and went out into the field, and lo, what I have
seen and can still see, I am unable to explain."
33 He said to me, "Stand up like a man, and I will instruct
you."
34 I said, "Speak, my lord; only do not forsake me, so that
I may not die before my time.[e] 35 For I have seen what I did
not know, and I hear[f] what I do not understand 36 —or is
my mind deceived, and my soul dreaming? 37 Now therefore
I beg you to give your servant an explanation of this bewildering vision."

a Ethiop *free men* b Syr *our seers* c Syr Ethiop Arab 1: Lat lacks *I was too . . . terrified. While* d Lat: Syr Ethiop Arab 1 Arab 2 Arm *but there was an established city* e Syr Ethiop Arab: Lat *die to no purpose* f Other ancient authorities read *have heard*

LATIN VULGATE

Et respondit ad me et dixit: 38 Audi me, et doceam te et
dicam tibi de quibus times, quoniam Altissimus revelavit tibi
mysteria multa. 39 Vidit rectam viam tuam, quoniam sine
intermissione contristabaris pro populo tuo et valde lugebas
propter Sion. 40 Hic ergo intellectus visionis: Mulier quae tibi
apparuit ante paululum, 41 quam vidisti lugentem et
inchoasti consolare eam, 42 nunc autem iam non speciem
mulieris vides, sed apparuit tibi civitas aedificari. 43 Et quoniam enarrabat tibi de casu filii sui, haec absolutio est:
44 Haec mulier quam vidisti haec est Sion, quam nunc con-
spicis ut civitatem aedificatam. 45 Et quoniam dixit tibi, quia
sterilis fuit annis triginta, propter quod erant anni saeculo
tria milia, quando non erat in ea adhuc oblatio oblata. 46 Et
factum est post annos tres, et aedificavit Salomon civitatem
et obtulit oblationes. Tunc fuit quando peperit sterilis filium.
47 Et quod tibi dixit quoniam nutrivi eum cum labore, haec
erat habitatio Hierusalem. 48 Et quoniam dixit tibi quod filius meus veniens in suo thalamo mortuus esset et contigis-
set ei casus, haec erat quae facta est ruina Hierusalem. 49 Et
ecce vidisti similitudinem eius, quomodo filium luget, et tu
inchoasti consolare eam de his quae contigerunt. Haec erant
tibi aperienda.

50 Et nunc videns Altissimus, quoniam ex animo contrista-
tus es et quoniam ex toto corde pateris pro ea, ostendit tibi
claritatem gloriae eius et pulchritudinem decoris eius.
51 Propterea enim dixi tibi, ut maneres in campo, ubi domus
non est aedificata. 52 Sciebam enim ego, quoniam
Altissimus incipiebat tibi ostendere haec. 53 Propterea dixi
tibi, ut venires in agrum, ubi non est fundamentum aedificii.
54 Nec enim poterat opus aedificii hominis sustinere in loco,
ubi incipiebat Altissimi civitas ostendi. 55 Tu ergo noli timere
neque expavescat cor tuum, sed ingredere et vide splendorem
vel magnitudinem aedificii, quantum capax est tibi visu ocu-
lorum videre. 56 Et post haec audies, quantum capit auditus
aurium tuarum audire. 57 Tu enim beatus es prae multis et
vocatus es apud Altissimum sicut et pauci. 58 Nocte autem
quae in crastinum futura est manebis hic, 59 et ostendet tibi
Altissimus eas visiones somniorum, quae faciet Altissimus
his qui inhabitant super terram a novissimis diebus.

60 Et dormivi illam noctem et aliam sicut dixerat mihi.

11 1 Et factum est secunda nocte, et vidi somnium, et
ecce ascendebat de mari aquila, cui erant duodecim
alae pinnarum et capita tria. 2 Et vidi, et ecce expandebat
alas suas in omnem terram, et omnes venti caeli insuflabant
ad eam et nubes ad eam colligebantur. 3 Et vidi, et de pinnis eius nascebantur contrariae pinnae, et ipsae fiebant in

KING JAMES VERSION

38 He answered me then, and said, Hear me, and I shall inform thee, and tell thee wherefore thou art afraid: for the Highest will reveal many secret things unto thee.

39 He hath seen that thy way is right: for that thou sorrowest continually for thy people, and makest great lamentation for Sion.

40 This therefore is the meaning of the vision which thou lately sawest:

41 Thou sawest a woman mourning, and thou begannest to comfort her:

42 But now seest thou the likeness of the woman no more, but there appeared unto thee a city builded.

43 And whereas she told thee of the death of her son, this is the solution:

44 This woman, whom thou sawest, is Sion: and whereas she said unto thee, even she whom thou seest as a city builded,

45 Whereas, *I say,* she said unto thee, that she hath been thirty years barren: those are the thirty years wherein there was no offering made in her.

46 But after thirty years Solomon builded the city, and offered offerings: and then bare the barren a son.

47 And whereas she told thee that she nourished him with labour: that was the dwelling in Jerusalem.

48 But whereas she said unto thee, That my son coming into his marriage chamber happened to have a fall, and died: this was the destruction that came to Jerusalem.

49 And, behold, thou sawest her likeness, and because she mourned for her son, thou begannest to comfort her: and of these things which have chanced, these are to be opened unto thee.

50 For now the most High seeth that thou art grieved unfeignedly, and sufferest from thy whole heart for her, so hath he shewed thee the brightness of her glory, and the comeliness of her beauty:

51 And therefore I bade thee remain in the field where no house was builded:

52 For I knew that the Highest would shew this unto thee.

53 Therefore I commanded thee to go into the field, where no foundation of any building was.

54 For in the place wherein the Highest beginneth to shew his city, there can no man's building be able to stand.

55 And therefore fear not, let not thine heart be affrighted, but go thy way in, and see the beauty and greatness of the building, as much as thine eyes be able to see:

56 And then shalt thou hear as much as thine eyes may comprehend.

57 For thou art blessed above many other, and art called with the Highest; and so are but few.

58 But to morrow at night thou shalt remain here;

59 And so shall the Highest shew thee visions of the high things, which the most High will do unto them that dwell upon the earth in the last days. So I slept that night and another, like as he commanded me.

11 Then saw I a dream, and, behold, there came up from the sea an eagle, which had twelve feathered wings, and three heads.

2 And I saw, and, behold, she spread her wings over all the earth, and all the winds of the air blew on her, and were gathered together.

3 And I beheld, and out of her feathers there grew other contrary feathers; and they became little feathers and small.

Today's English Version

38 The angel said, "Now listen closely, and I will explain
the meaning of these things that you fear. God Most High
has revealed many secrets to you 39 because he has seen that
you have lived a righteous life and have always grieved and
mourned for your people and for Jerusalem. 40 This is what
the vision means: A woman appeared to you a little while
ago, 41 and when you saw that she was mourning, you tried
to console her. 42-43 The woman told you about the death of
her son. Then she vanished from your sight, and a whole
city[a] appeared. This is the meaning: 44 The woman you saw
is Jerusalem, which you now see as a completed city.
45 When she told you that for thirty years she had had no
children, it meant that for three thousand[b] years no offerings
had yet been made there. 46 Then Solomon built the city, and
sacrifices began to be offered there. At that time the childless
woman gave birth to her son. 47 When she told you that she
took great care in bringing the son up, that referred to the
period when Jerusalem was inhabited. 48 When she told you
of the death of her son on his wedding day, that meant the
destruction of Jerusalem. 49 So in the vision you saw how
she mourned for her son, and you tried to console her for
what had happened—this is what was to be revealed to you.
50 When God Most High saw that you were grieving for the
woman with all your heart and soul, he showed you all her
glory and majestic beauty. 51 That is why I told you to go
and stay in the field where no one had ever lived, 52 for I
knew that God Most High was going to show you these
things. 53 I told you to go to the field where no foundation
had ever been built, 54 because nothing built by human
hands could stand in the place where the city of God Most
High was about to be revealed.

55 "So don't be afraid. Go into the city and look at its beautiful and majestic buildings. See as much as you can. 56 After
that, you will hear as much as you can. 57 You are more fortunate than most people, and only a few have the reputation
with God Most High that you have. 58 Remain here until
tomorrow night, 59 and he will show you in dreams and
visions what he plans to do for those who will be living on
the earth in the last days." So I slept there that night and the
next, as I had been told.

11 The second night I had a dream. I saw an eagle coming up out of the sea. It had twelve wings and three
heads. 2 As I looked, it spread out its wings over the whole
world. Winds blew on it from every direction, and clouds[c]
gathered over it. 3 Then from its wings I saw rival wings
begin to grow, but they were small and insignificant. 4 All

[a] *Some ancient translations* whole city; *Latin* city being built.
[b] *Some ancient translations* three thousand; *Latin* three.
[c] *Some ancient translations* clouds; *Latin does not have this word.*

New Revised Standard Version

38 He answered me and said, "Listen to me, and I will
teach you, and tell you about the things that you fear; for the
Most High has revealed many secrets to you. 39 He has seen
your righteous conduct, and that you have sorrowed continually for your people and mourned greatly over Zion. 40 This
therefore is the meaning of the vision. 41 The woman who
appeared to you a little while ago, whom you saw mourning
and whom you began to console 42 (you do not now see the
form of a woman, but there appeared to you a city being
built)[a] 43 and who told you about the misfortune of her
son—this is the interpretation: 44 The woman whom you
saw is Zion, which you now behold as a city being built.[b]
45 And as for her telling you that she was barren for thirty
years, the reason is that there were three thousand[c] years in
the world before any offering was offered in it.[d] 46 And after
three thousand[e] years Solomon built the city, and offered
offerings; then it was that the barren woman bore a son.
47 And as for her telling you that she brought him up with
much care, that was the period of residence in Jerusalem.
48 And as for her saying to you, 'My son died as he entered
his wedding chamber,' and that misfortune had overtaken
her,[f] this was the destruction that befell Jerusalem. 49 So
you saw her likeness, how she mourned for her son, and you
began to console her for what had happened.[g] 50 For now
the Most High, seeing that you are sincerely grieved and profoundly distressed for her, has shown you the brilliance of
her glory, and the loveliness of her beauty. 51 Therefore I told
you to remain in the field where no house had been built,
52 for I knew that the Most High would reveal these things to
you. 53 Therefore I told you to go into the field where there
was no foundation of any building, 54 because no work of
human construction could endure in a place where the city of
the Most High was to be revealed.

55 "Therefore do not be afraid, and do not let your heart
be terrified; but go in and see the splendor or[h] the vastness
of the building, as far as it is possible for your eyes to see it,
56 and afterward you will hear as much as your ears can
hear. 57 For you are more blessed than many, and you have
been called to be with[i] the Most High as few have been.
58 But tomorrow night you shall remain here, 59 and the Most
High will show you in those dream visions what the Most
High will do to those who inhabit the earth in the last days."

So I slept that night and the following one, as he had told
me.

11 On the second night I had a dream: I saw rising from
the sea an eagle that had twelve feathered wings and
three heads. 2 I saw it spread its wings over[j] the whole
earth, and all the winds of heaven blew upon it, and the
clouds were gathered around it.[k] 3 I saw that out of its
wings there grew opposing wings; but they became little,

[a] Lat: Syr Ethiop Arab 1 Arab 2 Arm *an established city* [b] Cn: Lat *an established city* [c] Most Lat Mss read *three* [d] Cn: Lat Syr Arab Arm *her* [e] Syr Ethiop Arab Arm: Lat *three* [f] Or *him* [g] Most Lat Mss and Arab 1 add *These were the things to be opened to you* [h] Other ancient authorities read *and* [i] Or *been named by* [j] Arab 2 Arm: Lat Syr Ethiop *in* [k] Syr: Compare Ethiop Arab: Lat lacks *the clouds* and *around it*

LATIN VULGATE

pinnaculis minutis et modicis. 4 Nam capita eius erant quiescentia, et de medium caput erat maius aliorum capitum,
sed et ipsa quiescebat cum eis. 5 Et vidi, et ecce aquila
volavit in pinnis suis et regnavit super terram et super eos
qui inhabitant in ea. 6 Et vidi, quomodo subiecta erant ei
omnia quae sub caelo, et nemo illi contradicebat, neque
unus de creatura quae est super terram. 7 Et vidi, et ecce
surrexit aquila super ungues suos et emisit vocem pinnis
suis dicens: 8 Nolite omnes simul vigilare, dormite
unusquisque in loco suo et per tempus vigilate, 9 capita
autem in novissimo serventur. 10 Et vidi, et ecce vox non
exiebat de capitibus eius, sed de medietate corporis eius.
11 Et numeravi contrarias pinnas eius, et ecce ipsae erant
octo.

12 Et vidi, et ecce a dextera parte surrexit una pinna et regnavit super omnem terram. 13 Et factum est cum regnaret, et
venit ei finis et non apparuit, ita ut non appareret locus eius.
Et sequens exsurrexit et regnabat et ipsa multum tenuit tempus. 14 Et factum est cum regnaret, et veniebat finis eius, ut
non appareret sicut prior. 15 Et ecce vox emissa est illi
dicens: 16 Audi, tu quae toto tempore tenuisti terram, hoc
adnuntii, antequam incipias non parere: 17 Nemo post te
tenebit tempus tuum, sed nec dimidium eius. 18 Et levavit se
tertia et tenuit principatum sicut priores, et non apparuit et
ipsa. 19 Et sic contingebat omnibus alis singillatim principatum gerere et iterum nusquam conparere. 20 Et vidi, et ecce
in tempore sequentes pinnae erigebantur et ipsae a dextera
parte, ut tenerent et ipsae principatum, et ex his erant quae
tenebant, sed tamen statim non conparescebant. 21 Nam et
aliquae ex eis erigebantur, sed non tenebant principatum.
22 Et vidi post haec, et ecce non conparuerunt duodecim pinnae et duo pinnacula. 23 Et nihil superavit in corpore aquilae
nisi tria capita quiescentia et sex pinnacula.

24 Et vidi, et ecce de sex pinnaculis divisa sunt duo et
manserunt sub capite quod est ad dexteram partem; nam
quattuor manserunt in loco suo. 25 Et vidi, et ecce hae subalares cogitabant se erigere et tenere principatus. 26 Et vidi,
et ecce una erecta est, sed statim non conparuit. 27 Et secunda, et haec velocius quam prior non conparuit. 28 Et vidi, et
ecce duae quae superaverunt apud semet ipsas cogitabant et
ipsae regnare. 29 Et in eo cum cogitarent, et ecce unum de
quiescentium capitum, quod erat medium, evigilabat, hoc
enim erat duorum capitum maior. 30 Et vidi, quomodo con-
plexa est duo capita secum, 31 et ecce conversum est caput
cum his qui cum ea erant et comedit duas subalares quae

KING JAMES VERSION

4 But her heads were at rest: the head in the midst was greater than the other, yet rested it with the residue.

5 Moreover I beheld, and, lo, the eagle flew with her feathers, and reigned upon earth, and over them that dwelt therein.

6 And I saw that all things under heaven were subject unto her, and no man spake against her, no, not one creature upon earth.

7 And I beheld, and, lo, the eagle rose upon her talons, and spake to her feathers, saying,

8 Watch not all at once: sleep every one in his own place, and watch by course:

9 But let the heads be preserved for the last.

10 And I beheld, and, lo, the voice went not out of her heads, but from the midst of her body.

11 And I numbered her contrary feathers, and, behold, there were eight of them.

12 And I looked, and, behold, on the right side there arose one feather, and reigned over all the earth;

13 And so it was, that when it reigned, the end of it came, and the place thereof appeared no more: so the next following stood up, and reigned, and had a great time;

14 And it happened, that when it reigned, the end of it came also, like as the first, so that it appeared no more.

15 Then came there a voice unto it, and said,

16 Hear thou that hast borne rule over the earth so long: this I say unto thee, before thou beginnest to appear no more,

17 There shall none after thee attain unto thy time, neither unto the half thereof.

18 Then arose the third, and reigned as the other before, and appeared no more also.

19 So went it with all the residue one after another, as that every one reigned, and then appeared no more.

20 Then I beheld, and, lo, in process of time the feathers that followed stood up upon the right side, that they might rule also; and some of them ruled, but within a while they appeared no more:

21 For some of them were set up, but ruled not.

22 After this I looked, and, behold, the twelve feathers appeared no more, nor the two little feathers:

23 And there was no more upon the eagle's body, but three heads that rested, and six little wings.

24 Then saw I also that two little feathers divided themselves from the six, and remained under the head that was upon the right side: for the four continued in their place.

25 And I beheld, and, lo, the feathers that were under the wing thought to set up themselves, and to have the rule.

26 And I beheld, and, lo, there was one set up, but shortly it appeared no more.

27 And the second was sooner away than the first.

28 And I beheld, and, lo, the two that remained thought also in themselves to reign:

29 And when they so thought, behold, there awaked one of the heads that were at rest, namely, it that was in the midst; for that was greater than the two other heads.

30 And then I saw that the two other heads were joined with it.

31 And, behold, the head was turned with them that were with it, and did eat up the two feathers under the wing that would have reigned.

TODAY'S ENGLISH VERSION

three heads of the eagle were asleep, even the middle one,
which was larger than the others. 5While I was watching,
the eagle flew up in the air and became ruler of the whole
earth and all its people. 6I saw how everything on earth was
brought under the eagle's control—no one on earth was able
to oppose it. 7Then I saw the eagle stand up on its claws
and say to its wings, 8"Not all of you are to wake up at the
same time; you must sleep where you are and wake up when
your turn comes, 9and the heads must wake up last."
10I looked again and saw that the voice was not coming
from any of the eagle's heads but from the middle of its
body. 11I counted its rival wings, and there were eight of
them.

12I saw one of the wings on the right side rise up and govern the whole world. 13After its rule came to an end, it vanished so completely that it left no trace. Then the next wing
rose up and governed for a long time. 14When its rule was
coming to an end and it was about to vanish like the first
wing, 15a voice said to it, 16"Listen, you have ruled the
world for a long time, and I want you to hear this message
before you disappear: 17No one after you will rule as long as
you did—not even half as long." 18The third wing rose up
and governed as the earlier ones had done; then it also vanished. 19The same thing happened to all the other wings:
one after the other they rose to power and then vanished.

20I kept looking, and after a while the other small wings
on the right side rose up to seize power. Some of them governed briefly and quickly disappeared, 21while others rose
up but were never able to govern. 22Then I noticed that the
twelve large wings and two of the small wings had disappeared. 23Nothing was left on the eagle's body except the
three sleeping heads and the six small wings. 24I kept
watching, and suddenly two of the six small wings left the
others and moved under the head on the right side, while the
other four remained where they were. 25Then I saw that
these four small wings were plotting to rise up and seize
power. 26One of them rose up, but it quickly disappeared.
27The second one also rose up, but it disappeared even more
quickly than the first. 28I saw that the two remaining small
wings were also plotting to seize control for themselves.
29While they were making their plans, one of the sleeping
heads suddenly awoke. It was the one in the middle, the one
that was larger than the other two. 30Then I saw that it was
joined by the other heads, 31and when it turned to eat up
the two little wings that were planning to seize power, the
other two heads helped it. 32This head gained power over

NEW REVISED STANDARD VERSION

puny wings. 4But its heads were at rest; the middle head
was larger than the other heads, but it too was at rest with
them. 5Then I saw that the eagle flew with its wings, and it
reigned over the earth and over those who inhabit it. 6And I
saw how all things under heaven were subjected to it, and
no one spoke against it—not a single creature that was on
the earth. 7Then I saw the eagle rise upon its talons, and it
uttered a cry to its wings, saying, 8"Do not all watch at the
same time; let each sleep in its own place, and watch in its
turn; 9but let the heads be reserved for the last."

10 I looked again and saw that the voice did not come
from its heads, but from the middle of its body. 11I counted
its rival wings, and there were eight of them. 12As I
watched, one wing on the right side rose up, and it reigned
over all the earth. 13And after a time its reign came to an
end, and it disappeared, so that even its place was no longer
visible. Then the next wing rose up and reigned, and it continued to reign a long time. 14While it was reigning its end
came also, so that it disappeared like the first. 15And a voice
sounded, saying to it, 16"Listen to me, you who have ruled
the earth all this time; I announce this to you before you disappear. 17After you no one shall rule as long as you have
ruled, not even half as long."

18 Then the third wing raised itself up, and held the rule
as the earlier ones had done, and it also disappeared. 19And
so it went with all the wings; they wielded power one after
another and then were never seen again. 20I kept looking,
and in due time the wings that followed[a] also rose up on the
right[b] side, in order to rule. There were some of them that
ruled, yet disappeared suddenly; 21and others of them rose
up, but did not hold the rule.

22 And after this I looked and saw that the twelve wings
and the two little wings had disappeared, 23and nothing
remained on the eagle's body except the three heads that
were at rest and six little wings.

24 As I kept looking I saw that two little wings separated
from the six and remained under the head that was on the
right side; but four remained in their place. 25Then I saw
that these little wings[c] planned to set themselves up and
hold the rule. 26As I kept looking, one was set up, but suddenly disappeared; 27a second also, and this disappeared
more quickly than the first. 28While I continued to look the
two that remained were planning between themselves to
reign together; 29and while they were planning, one of the
heads that were at rest (the one that was in the middle) suddenly awoke; it was greater than the other two heads. 30And
I saw how it allied the two heads with itself, 31and how the
head turned with those that were with it and devoured the
two little wings[c] that were planning to reign. 32Moreover

a Syr Arab 2 *the little wings* *b* Some Ethiop Mss read *left* *c* Syr: Lat *underwings*

Latin Vulgate

cogitabant regnare. 32 Hoc autem caput percontinuit omnem
terram et dominavit qui inhabitant in ea cum labore multo,
et potentatum tenuit orbem terrarum super omnes alas quae
fuerunt. 33 Et vidi post haec, et ecce medium caput subito
non conparuit, et hoc sicut alae. 34 Superaverunt autem duo
capita, quae et ipsa similiter regnaverunt super terram et
super eos qui habitant in ea. 35 Et vidi, et ecce devoravit
caput a dextera parte illud quod est a leva.

36 Et audivi vocem dicentem mihi: Conspice contra te et
considera quod vides. 37 Et vidi, et ecce sicut leo suscitatus
de silva mugiens, et audivi quomodo emisit vocem hominis
ad aquilam et dixit dicens: 38 Audi tu, et loquar ad te, et dicit
Altissimus tibi: 39 Nonne tu es, quae superasti de quattuor
animalibus quae feceram regnare saeculi mei, et ut per eos
veniret finis temporum meorum? 40 Et quartus veniens devic-
it omnia animalia quae transierunt, et potentatum tenens
saeculum cum tremore multo et omnem orbem cum labore
pessimo, et inhabitabant tot temporibus orbem terrarum cum
dolo. 41 Et iudicasti terram non cum veritate. 42 Tribulasti
enim mansuetos et laesisti quiescentes, odisti verum dicentes
et dilexisti mendaces, et destruxisti habitationes eorum qui
fructificabant, et humiliasti muros eorum qui te non
nocuerunt. 43 Et ascendit contumelia ad Altissimum et superbia tua ad Fortem. 44 Et respexit Altissimus super sua tempora, et ecce finita sunt et saecula eius conpleta sunt.
45 Propterea non apparens non appareas, tu aquila et alae
tuae horribiles et pinnacula tua pessima et capita tua maligna
et ungues tui pessimi et omne corpus tuum vanum, 46 uti
refrigeret omnis terra et relevetur liberata de tua vi et speret
iudicium et misericordiam eius qui fecit eam.

12 Et factum est dum loqueretur leo verba haec ad
aquilam, et vidi, 2 et ecce quod superaverat caput et
non conparuit, et alae duae quae ad eum transierunt et erec-
tae sunt ut regnarent, et erat regnum eorum exile et tumultu
plenum. 3 Et vidi, et ecce ipsa non apparescebant, et omne
corpus aquilae incendebatur, et expavescebat terra valde.

Et ego a multo excessu mentis et a magno timore vigilavi,
et dixi spiritui meo: 4 Ecce tu mihi praestitisti haec, in eo
quod scrutas vias Altissimi. 5 Ecce adhuc fatigatus sum
animo et spiritu meo invalidus sum valde, et nec modica est
in me virtus a multo timore quem expavi nocte hac. 6 Nunc
ergo orabo Altissimum, ut me confortet usque in finem. 7 Et
dixi: Dominator Domine, si inveni gratiam ante oculos tuos,
et si iustificatus sum apud te prae multis, et si certum ascendit deprecatio mea ante faciem tuam, 8 conforta me et

King James Version

32 But this head put the whole earth in fear, and bare rule in it over all those that dwelt upon the earth with much oppression; and it had the governance of the world more than all the wings that had been.

33 And after this I beheld, and, lo, the head that was in the midst suddenly appeared no more, like as the wings.

34 But there remained the two heads, which also in like sort ruled upon the earth, and over those that dwelt therein.

35 And I beheld, and, lo, the head upon the right side devoured it that was upon the left side.

36 Then I heard a voice, which said unto me, Look before thee, and consider the thing that thou seest.

37 And I beheld, and lo as it were a roaring lion chased out of the wood: and I saw that he sent out a man's voice unto the eagle, and said,

38 Hear thou, I will talk with thee, and the Highest shall say unto thee,

39 Art not thou it that remainest of the four beasts, whom I made to reign in my world, that the end of their times might come through them?

40 And the fourth came, and overcame all the beasts that were past, and had power over the world with great fearfulness, and over the whole compass of the earth with much wicked oppression; and so long time dwelt he upon the earth with deceit.

41 For the earth hast thou not judged with truth.

42 For thou hast afflicted the meek, thou hast hurt the peaceable, thou hast loved liars, and destroyed the dwellings of them that brought forth fruit, and hast cast down the walls of such as did thee no harm.

43 Therefore is thy wrongful dealing come up unto the Highest, and thy pride unto the Mighty.

44 The Highest also hath looked upon the proud times, and, behold, they are ended, and his abominations are fulfilled.

45 And therefore appear no more, thou eagle, nor thy horrible wings, nor thy wicked feathers, nor thy malicious heads, nor thy hurtful claws, nor all thy vain body:

46 That all the earth may be refreshed, and may return, being delivered from thy violence, and that she may hope for the judgment and mercy of him that made her.

12 And it came to pass, whiles the lion spake these words unto the eagle, I saw,

2 And, behold, the head that remained and the four wings appeared no more, and the two went unto it, and set themselves up to reign, and their kingdom was small, and fill of uproar.

3 And I saw, and, behold, they appeared no more, and the whole body of the eagle was burnt, so that the earth was in great fear: then awaked I out of the trouble and trance of my mind, and from great fear, and said unto my spirit,

4 Lo, this hast thou done unto me, in that thou searchest out the ways of the Highest.

5 Lo, yet am I weary in my mind, and very weak in my spirit; and little strength is there in me, for the great fear wherewith I was affrighted this night.

6 Therefore will I now beseech the Highest, that he will comfort me unto the end.

7 And I said, Lord that bearest rule, if I have found grace before thy sight, and if I am justified with thee before many others, and if my prayer indeed be come up before thy face;

TODAY'S ENGLISH VERSION

the whole world, established an oppressive rule over people everywhere, and exercised more power over the world than any of the other wings had done before. 33 Then, as I watched, the middle head disappeared just as suddenly as the wings had done. 34 Two heads were left, and they also gained power over the earth and its people; 35 but while I was still watching, the head on the right ate up the head on the left.

36 Then I heard a voice which said, "Ezra, look straight ahead and think about what you see."

37 I looked and saw what appeared to be an angry lion come roaring out of the forest. I heard it speak in human language to the eagle and say, 38 "Listen, Eagle, to what I have to say to you; it is the message of God Most High: 39 You are the only one left of the four animals that I appointed to govern my world and to bring the ages of this world to an end. 40 You are the fourth animal and you have conquered all the animals that came before you. As long as you have been in this world, you have ruled it through terror, oppression, and deceit, 41 with a total disregard for truth. 42 You have viciously attacked harmless people who were living in peace; you have hated those who spoke the truth, and you have loved liars. You have destroyed the homes of those who were prosperous and have torn down the walls of those who did you no harm. 43 God Most High knows how proud and arrogant you are. The Almighty One 44 has looked back over the world he established. The end has come; the final age is over. 45 So, Eagle, the time has come for you to vanish, along with your big, terrible wings, your small, wicked wings, your evil heads, your awful claws, and your whole worthless body. 46 The entire world will be set free from your violence and renewed as it sets its hope on the judgment and mercy of God, who created it."

12 While the lion was speaking in this way to the eagle, I looked 2 and saw that the last head of the eagle was gone. Then the two small wings that had moved over to that head rose up to govern, but their rule was short and full of trouble. 3 They disappeared before my eyes, and the whole body of the eagle burst into flames, and the world was terrified.

I was so disturbed and so afraid that I woke up. I said, 4 "I have brought this on myself, because I have tried to study the ways of God Most High. 5 I am mentally exhausted and completely worn out. The terrible fears I have experienced this night have taken my last bit of strength. 6 All I can do now is pray to God Most High to give me strength until the end." 7 Then I prayed, "Master and Lord, if it is true that you consider me more righteous than many others and if you

NEW REVISED STANDARD VERSION

this head gained control of the whole earth, and with much oppression dominated its inhabitants; it had greater power over the world than all the wings that had gone before.

33 After this I looked again and saw the head in the middle suddenly disappear, just as the wings had done. 34 But the two heads remained, which also in like manner ruled over the earth and its inhabitants. 35 And while I looked, I saw the head on the right side devour the one on the left.

36 Then I heard a voice saying to me, "Look in front of you and consider what you see." 37 When I looked, I saw what seemed to be a lion roused from the forest, roaring; and I heard how it uttered a human voice to the eagle, and spoke, saying, 38 "Listen and I will speak to you. The Most High says to you, 39 'Are you not the one that remains of the four beasts that I had made to reign in my world, so that the end of my times might come through them? 40 You, the fourth that has come, have conquered all the beasts that have gone before; and you have held sway over the world with great terror, and over all the earth with grievous oppression; and for so long you have lived on the earth with deceit.[a] 41 You have judged the earth, but not with truth, 42 for you have oppressed the meek and injured the peaceable; you have hated those who tell the truth, and have loved liars; you have destroyed the homes of those who brought forth fruit, and have laid low the walls of those who did you no harm. 43 Your insolence has come up before the Most High, and your pride to the Mighty One. 44 The Most High has looked at his times; now they have ended, and his ages have reached completion. 45 Therefore you, eagle, will surely disappear, you and your terrifying wings, your most evil little wings, your malicious heads, your most evil talons, and your whole worthless body, 46 so that the whole earth, freed from your violence, may be refreshed and relieved, and may hope for the judgment and mercy of him who made it.' "

12 While the lion was saying these words to the eagle, I looked 2 and saw that the remaining head had disappeared. The two wings that had gone over to it rose up and[b] set themselves up to reign, and their reign was brief and full of tumult. 3 When I looked again, they were already vanishing. The whole body of the eagle was burned, and the earth was exceedingly terrified.

Then I woke up in great perplexity of mind and great fear, and I said to my spirit, 4 "You have brought this upon me, because you search out the ways of the Most High. 5 I am still weary in mind and very weak in my spirit, and not even a little strength is left in me, because of the great fear with which I have been terrified tonight. 6 Therefore I will now entreat the Most High that he may strengthen me to the end."

7 Then I said, "O sovereign Lord, if I have found favor in your sight, and if I have been accounted righteous before you beyond many others, and if my prayer has indeed come up

a Syr Arab Arm: Lat Ethiop *The fourth came, however, and conquered . . . and held sway . . . and for so long lived* *b* Ethiop: Lat lacks *rose up and*

LATIN VULGATE

ostende servo tuo mihi interpretationem et distinctionem
visus horribilis huius, ut plenissime consoles animam meam.
9 Dignum enim me habuisti ostendere mihi temporum finem
et temporum novissima.
Et dixit ad me: 10 Haec est interpretatio visionis huius
quam vidisti: 11 Aquilam quam vidisti ascendentem de mari,
hoc est regnum quartum, quod visum est in visu Danihelo
fratri tuo, 12 sed non est illi interpretatum, quomodo ego
nunc tibi interpretor vel interpretavi. 13 Ecce dies veniunt, et
exsurget regnum super terram et erit timoratior omnium reg-
norum quae fuerunt ante eam. 14 Regnabunt autem in ea
duodecim reges, unus post unum. 15 Nam secundus qui
incipiet regnare, ipse tenebit amplius tempus prae duodecim.
16 Haec est interpretatio duodecim alarum quas vidisti. 17 Et
quoniam audisti vocem quae locuta est non de capitibus eius
exientem, sed de medio corpore eius, 18 haec est interpretatio, quoniam post tempus regni illius nascentur contentiones
non modicae, et periclitabitur ut cadat, et non cadet tunc, sed
iterum constituetur in suum initium. 19 Et quoniam vidisti
subalares octo coherentes alis eius, 20 haec est interpretatio:
Exsurgent enim in ipso octo reges, quorum erunt tempora
levia et anni citati, et duo quidem ex ipsis perient
21 adpropinquante tempore medio, quattuor autem servabuntur in tempore, cum incipiet adpropinquare tempus eius ut
finiatur, duo vero in finem servabuntur.
22 Et quoniam vidisti tria capita quiescentia, 23 haec est
interpretatio: In novissimis eius suscitabit Altissimus tria
regna et renovabit in ea multa, et dominabunt terram 24 et
qui inhabitant in ea cum labore multo super omnes qui
fuerunt ante hos. Propter hoc ipsi vocati sunt capita aquilae.
25 Isti enim erunt qui recapitulabunt impietates eius et qui
perficient novissima eius. 26 Et quoniam vidisti caput maius
non apparescentem, quoniam unus ex eis super lectum suum
morietur, et tamen cum tormentis. 27 Nam duo qui persever-
averunt, gladius eos comedet. 28 Unius enim gladius
comedet qui cum eo, sed tamen et hic gladio in novissimis
cadet. 29 Et quoniam vidisti duas subalares treicientes super
caput quod est a dextera parte, 30 haec est interpretatio: Hii
sunt quos conservavit Altissimus in finem suam, hoc erat
regnum exile et turbationis plenum, 31 sicut vidisti.
Et leonem quem vidisti de silva evigilantem mugientem et
loquentem ad aquilam et arguentem eam iniustitias ipsius
per omnes sermones eius, sicut audisti, 32 hic est unctus,
quem reservavit Altissimus in finem ad eos et impietates
ipsorum. Arguet illos de iniustitiis ipsorum et infulciet coram

KING JAMES VERSION

8 Comfort me then, and shew me thy servant the interpretation and plain difference of this fearful vision, that thou mayest perfectly comfort my soul.

9 For thou hast judged me worthy to shew me the last times.

10 And he said unto me, This is the interpretation of the vision:

11 The eagle, whom thou sawest come up from the sea, is the kingdom which was seen in the vision of thy brother Daniel.

12 But it was not expounded unto him, therefore now I declare it unto thee.

13 Behold, the days will come, that there shall rise up a kingdom upon earth, and it shall be feared above all the kingdoms that were before it.

14 In the same shall twelve kings reign, one after another:

15 Whereof the second shall begin to reign, and shall have more time than any of the twelve.

16 And this do the twelve wings signify, which thou sawest.

17 As for the voice which thou heardest speak, and that thou sawest not to go out from the heads, but from the midst of the body thereof, this is the interpretation:

18 That after the time of that kingdom there shall arise great strivings, and it shall stand in peril of falling: nevertheless it shall not then fall, but shall be restored again to his beginning.

19 And whereas thou sawest the eight small under feathers sticking to her wings, this is the interpretation:

20 That in him there shall arise eight kings, whose times shall be but small, and their years swift.

21 And two of them shall perish, the middle time approaching: four shall be kept until their end begin to approach: but two shall be kept unto the end.

22 And whereas thou sawest three heads resting, this is the interpretation:

23 In his last days shall the most High raise up three kingdoms, and renew many things therein, and they shall have the dominion of the earth,

24 And of those that dwell therein, with much oppression, above all those that were before them: therefore are they called the heads of the eagle.

25 For these are they that shall accomplish his wickedness, and that shall finish his last end.

26 And whereas thou sawest that the great head appeared no more, it signifieth that one of them shall die upon his bed, and yet with pain.

27 For the two that remain shall be slain with the sword.

28 For the sword of the one shall devour the other: but at the last shall he fall through the sword himself.

29 And whereas thou sawest two feathers under the wings passing over the head that is on the right side;

30 It signifieth that these are they, whom the Highest hath kept unto their end: this is the small kingdom and full of trouble, as thou sawest.

31 And the lion, whom thou sawest rising up out of the wood, and roaring, and speaking to the eagle, and rebuking her for her unrighteousness with all the words which thou hast heard;

32 This is the anointed, which the Highest hath kept for them and for their wickedness unto the end: he shall reprove them, and shall upbraid them with their cruelty.

TODAY'S ENGLISH VERSION

hear my prayers, then I beg you, 8 give me strength. Show me, O Lord, the full meaning of this terrifying vision, and set my mind at ease. 9 After all, you did consider me worthy to be shown the end of this age."

10 God's angel said to me, "Here is the interpretation of the vision you saw. 11 The eagle you saw coming up out of the sea represents the fourth kingdom in the vision that your brother Daniel saw. 12 But he was not given the same interpretation of it that I am giving you. 13 The time is coming when an empire will be established on earth that is more terrible than any before it. 14 Twelve kings will rule over it, one after the other. 15 The second king will rule longer than any of the others. 16 That is the meaning of the twelve wings that you saw.

17 "You heard the voice speaking from the middle of the eagle's body, instead of from its heads. 18 That means that after the rule of the second king, a great struggle for power will take place, and the empire will be in danger of breaking up. But that will not happen, and the empire will regain its earlier power.

19 "You saw the eight small wings growing out of the eagle's big wings. That means 20 that eight kings will rise up in the empire, but their rule will be brief and unimportant. 21 Two of them will appear briefly near the middle of the period, four of them will not appear until near the end, and two will be left until the very end.

22 "You saw the three heads that were asleep. That means 23 that in the last days of the empire, God Most High will raise up three kings; they[a] will restore much of the empire and rule over the world 24 and its people with more harshness than any before them. The reason they are called the eagle's heads 25 is that these three kings will bring to a head and complete the godless work of the eagle. 26 You saw the largest head disappear. This means that one of the kings will die in his bed, in great agony. 27 The other two will die in battle. 28 One of them will kill the other; then he also will be killed in battle at the end of time.

29 "You saw the two small wings moving under the head on the right side. 30 That means that God Most High has kept them until the end, but their rule was short and full of trouble, as you saw.

31 "You saw the angry lion come roaring out of the forest, and you heard it speak to the eagle and rebuke it for the evil that it had done and for all that it had said. 32 The lion represents the Messiah, whom God Most High has held back until the end. He will be a descendant of David and will come and speak[b] to the rulers. He will rebuke them for their wickedness, their sinfulness, and their contempt for God's

[a] *Some ancient translations* they; *Latin* he. [b] *Some ancient translations* He will . . . speak; *Latin does not have these words.*

NEW REVISED STANDARD VERSION

before your face, 8 strengthen me and show me, your servant, the interpretation and meaning of this terrifying vision so that you may fully comfort my soul. 9 For you have judged me worthy to be shown the end of the times and the last events of the times."

10 He said to me, "This is the interpretation of this vision that you have seen: 11 The eagle that you saw coming up from the sea is the fourth kingdom that appeared in a vision to your brother Daniel. 12 But it was not explained to him as I now explain to you or have explained it. 13 The days are coming when a kingdom shall rise on earth, and it shall be more terrifying than all the kingdoms that have been before it. 14 And twelve kings shall reign in it, one after another. 15 But the second that is to reign shall hold sway for a longer time than any other one of the twelve. 16 This is the interpretation of the twelve wings that you saw.

17 "As for your hearing a voice that spoke, coming not from the eagle's[a] heads but from the midst of its body, this is the interpretation: 18 In the midst of[b] the time of that kingdom great struggles shall arise, and it shall be in danger of falling; nevertheless it shall not fall then, but shall regain its former power.[c] 19 As for your seeing eight little wings[d] clinging to its wings, this is the interpretation: 20 Eight kings shall arise in it, whose times shall be short and their years swift; 21 two of them shall perish when the middle of its time draws near; and four shall be kept for the time when its end approaches, but two shall be kept until the end.

22 "As for your seeing three heads at rest, this is the interpretation: 23 In its last days the Most High will raise up three kings,[e] and they[f] shall renew many things in it, and shall rule the earth 24 and its inhabitants more oppressively than all who were before them. Therefore they are called the heads of the eagle, 25 because it is they who shall sum up his wickedness and perform his last actions. 26 As for your seeing that the large head disappeared, one of the kings[g] shall die in his bed, but in agonies. 27 But as for the two who remained, the sword shall devour them. 28 For the sword of one shall devour him who was with him; but he also shall fall by the sword in the last days.

29 "As for your seeing two little wings[h] passing over to[i] the head which was on the right side, 30 this is the interpretation: It is these whom the Most High has kept for the eagle's[a] end; this was the reign which was brief and full of tumult, as you have seen.

31 "And as for the lion whom you saw rousing up out of the forest and roaring and speaking to the eagle and reproving him for his unrighteousness, and as for all his words that you have heard, 32 this is the Messiah[j] whom the Most High has kept until the end of days, who will arise from the offspring of David, and will come and speak[k] with them. He will denounce them for their ungodliness and for their wickedness, and will display before them their contemptuous

a Lat *his* *b* Syr Arm: Lat *After* *c* Ethiop Arab 1 Arm: Lat Syr *its beginning* *d* Syr: Lat *underwings* *e* Syr Ethiop Arab Arm: Lat *kingdoms* *f* Syr Ethiop Arm: Lat *he* *g* Lat *them* *h* Arab 1: Lat *underwings* *i* Syr Ethiop: Lat lacks *to* *j* Literally *anointed one* *k* Syr: Lat lacks *of days . . . and speak*

Latin Vulgate

ipsis spretiones eorum. 33 Statuet enim eos primum in iudicium vivos, et erit cum arguerit eos, tunc corrumpet eos.
34 Nam residuum populum meum liberabit cum misericordia,
qui salvati sunt super fines meos, et iucundabit eos, quoadusque veniat finis, dies iudicii, de quo locutus sum tibi ab
initio. 35 Hoc somnium quod vidisti, et haec interpretatio
eius.

36 Tu ergo solus dignus fuisti scire Altissimi secretum hoc.
37 Scribe ergo omnia ista in libro quae vidisti, et pones ea in
loco abscondito. 38 Et docebis ea sapientes de populo tuo,
quorum scis corda posse capere et servare secreta haec.
39 Tu autem adhuc sustine hic alios dies septem, ut tibi
ostendatur quicquid visum fuerit Altissimo ostendere tibi.
40 Et profectus est a me.

Et factum est cum audisset omnis populus, quoniam per-
transierunt septem dies, et ego non fuissem reversus in civitatem, et congregavit se omnis a minimo usque ad maximum
et venit ad me, et dixerunt mihi dicentes: 41 Quid peccav-
imus tibi et quid iniuste egimus in te, quoniam derelinquens
nos sedisti in loco hoc? 42 Tu enim nobis superasti ex
omnibus prophetis, sicut botrus de vindemia, et sicut lucerna
in loco obscuro, et sicut portus navi salvatae a tempestate.
43 Aut non sufficiunt nobis mala quae contigerunt? 44 Si
ergo tu nos dereliqueris, quanto erat nobis melius, si essemus succensi et nos incendio Sion. 45 Nec enim nos meliores
sumus eorum, qui ibi mortui sunt. Et ploraverunt voce
magna.

Et respondi ad eos et dixi: 46 Confide, Israhel, et noli tris-
tari, tu domus Iacob. 47 Est enim memoria vestri coram
Altissimo, et Fortis non est oblitus vestri in contentione.
48 Ego enim non dereliqui vos neque excessi a vobis, sed veni
in hunc locum, ut deprecarer pro desolatione Sion, et ut
quaererem misericordiam pro humilitate sanctificationis vestrae. 49 Et nunc ite unusquisque vestrum in domum suam,
et ego veniam ad vos post dies istos. 50 Et profectus est populus, sicut dixi ei, in civitatem.

51 Ego autem sedi in campo septem diebus, sicut mihi
mandavit, et manducabam de floribus solummodo agri, de
13 herbis facta est mihi esca in diebus illis. 1 Et factum
est post dies septem, et somniavi somnium nocte.

2 Et ecce de mari ventus exsurgebat, ut conturbaret omnes
fluctus eius. 3 Et vidi, et ecce convolabat ipse homo cum
nubibus caeli. Et ubi vultum suum convertebat ut consider-
aret, tremebant omnia quae sub eo videbantur. 4 Et
ubicumque exiebat vox de ore eius, ardescebant omnes qui
audiebant voces eius, sicut liquescit cera quando senserit
ignem. 5 Et vidi post haec, et ecce congregabatur multitudo
hominum, quorum non erat numerus, de quattuor ventis

King James Version

33 For he shall set them before him alive in judgment, and shall rebuke them, and correct them.

34 For the rest of my people shall he deliver with mercy, those that have been preserved upon my borders, and he shall make them joyful until the coming of the day of judgment, whereof I have spoken unto thee from the the beginning.

35 This is the dream that thou sawest, and these are the interpretations.

36 Thou only hast been meet to know this secret of the Highest.

37 Therefore write all these things that thou hast seen in a book, and hide them:

38 And teach them to the wise of the people, whose hearts thou knowest may comprehend and keep these secrets.

39 But wait thou here thyself yet seven days more, that it may be shewed thee, whatsoever it pleaseth the Highest to declare unto thee. And with that he went his way.

40 And it came to pass, when all the people saw that the seven days were past, and I not come again into the city, they gathered them all together, from the least unto the greatest, and came unto me, and said,

41 What have we offended thee? and what evil have we done against thee, that thou forsakest us, and sittest here in this place?

42 For of all the prophets thou only art left us, as a cluster of the vintage, and as a candle in a dark place, and as a haven or ship preserved from the tempest.

43 Are not the evils which are come to us sufficient?

44 If thou shalt forsake us, how much better had it been for us, if we also had been burned in the midst of Sion?

45 For we are not better than they that died there. And they wept with a loud voice. Then answered I them, and said,

46 Be of good comfort, O Israel; and be not heavy, thou house of Jacob:

47 For the Highest hath you in remembrance, and the Mighty hath not forgotten you in temptation.

48 As for me, I have not forsaken you, neither am I departed from you: but am come into this place, to pray for the desolation of Sion, and that I might seek mercy for the low estate of your sanctuary.

49 And now go your way home every man, and after these days will I come unto you.

50 So the people went their way into the city, like as I commanded them:

51 But I remained still in the field seven days, as the angel commanded me; and did eat only in those days of the flowers of the field, and had my meat of the herbs.

13 And it came to pass after seven days, I dreamed a dream by night:

2 And, lo, there arose a wind from the sea, that it moved all the waves thereof.

3 And I beheld, and, lo, that man waxed strong with the thousands of heaven: and when he turned his countenance to look, all the things trembled that were seen under him.

4 And whensoever the voice went out of his mouth, all they burned that heard his voice, like as the earth faileth when it feeleth the fire.

5 And after this I beheld, and, lo, there was gathered together a multitude of men, out of number, from the four

TODAY'S ENGLISH VERSION

ways. 33 While they are still living, he will bring them to
judgment, condemn them for their sin, and destroy them.
34 But he will have mercy on the rest of my people, those who
are left in my land; he will set them free and make them
happy until the end comes, the Judgment Day about which I
told you at the beginning.

35 "That is the dream you had, and that is its interpretation. 36 But you are the only one that God Most High has
considered worthy to reveal this secret to. 37 So write in a
book everything you saw, and put it in a safe hiding place.
38 Then teach these secrets to those who are wise among
your people, those who will be able to understand them and
keep them secret. 39 But you must stay here seven more
days, so that God Most High may reveal to you whatever he
wishes." Then the angel left me.

40 When the seven days had passed and all the people
heard that I had not yet returned to the city, all of them, rich
and poor, came and asked me, 41 "What wrong have we
done to you? How have we mistreated you? Why have you
abandoned us and settled down in this place? 42 You are the
only one of all our prophets who is left. You are like the last
bunch of grapes in a vineyard, like a lantern in a dark place,
like a safe harbor for a ship in a storm. 43 Haven't we suffered enough already? 44 If you abandon us, it would have
been better if we had died like the others in the fire that
destroyed Jerusalem. 45 We are no better than those who
died." Then they all started crying loudly.

I answered, 46 "Be brave, Israel, put away your sorrow.
47 God Most High will keep you in mind; the Almighty One
has not forgotten you in all your troubles. 48 And I haven't
left you or abandoned you. I came here to pray for Jerusalem
in her time of trouble and to ask mercy for her and for your
Temple, now in disgrace. 49 Please return to your homes, all
of you. I will come back to you in a few days." 50 So they left
me and went back to the city.

51 I stayed in the field for seven days, as the angel had
commanded me. I ate nothing but wild flowers; I was a vege-
tarian in those days.

13 The seven days passed, and the following night I had
a dream. 2 In my dream I saw a wind coming up out
of the sea and stirring up great waves. 3 As I watched, the
wind brought with it out of the sea what looked like a man,[a]
and he was flying[b] on the clouds. When he turned his face,
everything he looked at began to tremble, 4 and when he
spoke, everyone who heard his voice melted like wax in a
fire.

5 I looked again and saw a crowd too large to count. They
were people gathered together from all parts of the world to

[a] *Some ancient translations* the wind . . . man; *Latin does not have these words.* [b] *Some ancient translations* flying; *Latin* growing strong.

NEW REVISED STANDARD VERSION

dealings. 33 For first he will bring them alive before his judgment seat, and when he has reproved them, then he will
destroy them. 34 But in mercy he will set free the remnant of
my people, those who have been saved throughout my borders, and he will make them joyful until the end comes, the
day of judgment, of which I spoke to you at the beginning.
35 This is the dream that you saw, and this is its interpretation. 36 And you alone were worthy to learn this secret of the
Most High. 37 Therefore write all these things that you have
seen in a book, put it[a] in a hidden place; 38 and you shall
teach them to the wise among your people, whose hearts you
know are able to comprehend and keep these secrets. 39 But
as for you, wait here seven days more, so that you may be
shown whatever it pleases the Most High to show you."
Then he left me.

40 When all the people heard that the seven days were
past and I had not returned to the city, they all gathered
together, from the least to the greatest, and came to me and
spoke to me, saying, 41 "How have we offended you, and
what harm have we done you, that you have forsaken us
and sit in this place? 42 For of all the prophets you alone are
left to us, like a cluster of grapes from the vintage, and like a
lamp in a dark place, and like a haven for a ship saved from
a storm. 43 Are not the disasters that have befallen us
enough? 44 Therefore if you forsake us, how much better it
would have been for us if we also had been consumed in the
burning of Zion. 45 For we are no better than those who died
there." And they wept with a loud voice.

Then I answered them and said, 46 "Take courage,
O Israel; and do not be sorrowful, O house of Jacob; 47 for
the Most High has you in remembrance, and the Mighty One
has not forgotten you in your struggle. 48 As for me, I have
neither forsaken you nor withdrawn from you; but I have
come to this place to pray on account of the desolation of
Zion, and to seek mercy on account of the humiliation of
our[b] sanctuary. 49 Now go to your homes, every one of you,
and after these days I will come to you." 50 So the people
went into the city, as I told them to do. 51 But I sat in the
field seven days, as the angel[c] had commanded me; and I ate
only of the flowers of the field, and my food was of plants
during those days.

13 After seven days I dreamed a dream in the night.
2 And lo, a wind arose from the sea and stirred up[d]
all its waves. 3 As I kept looking the wind made something
like the figure of a man come up out of the heart of the sea.
And I saw[e] that this man flew[f] with the clouds of heaven;
and wherever he turned his face to look, everything under
his gaze trembled, 4 and whenever his voice issued from his
mouth, all who heard his voice melted as wax melts[g] when
it feels the fire.

5 After this I looked and saw that an innumerable multitude of people were gathered together from the four winds of

[a] Ethiop Arab 1 Arab 2 Arm: Lat Syr *them* [b] Syr Ethiop: Lat *your* [c] Literally *he* [d] Other ancient authorities read *I saw a wind arise from the sea and stir up* [e] Syr: Lat lacks *the wind . . . I saw* [f] Syr Ethiop Arab Arm: Lat *grew strong* [g] Syr: Lat *burned as the earth rests*

caeli, ut debellarent hominem qui ascenderat de mari. 6 Et
vidi, et ecce sibimet ipso sculpsit montem magnum et volavit
super eum. 7 Ego autem quaesivi videre regionem vel locum,
unde sculptus esset mons, et non potui.

8 Et post haec vidi, et ecce omnes, qui congregati sunt ad
eum ut expugnarent eum, timebant valde, tamen audebant
pugnare. 9 Et ecce ut vidit impetum multitudinis venientis,
non levavit manum suam neque frameam tenebat neque
aliquod vas bellicosum, nisi solummodo vidi, 10 quomodo
emittit de ore suo sicut fluctum ignis, et de labiis eius spiritum flammae, et de lingua eius emittebat scintillas tempestatis. Et commixta sunt simul omnia haec, fluctus ignis et spiritus flammae et multitudo tempestatis. 11 Et concidit super
multitudinis impetum quod paratum erat pugnare, et succen-
dit omnes, ut subito nihil videretur de innumerabili multitudine nisi solummodo pulvis cineris et fumi odor. Et vidi et
extiti.

12 Et post haec vidi ipsum hominem descendentem de
monte et advocantem ad se multitudinem aliam pacificam.
13 Et accedebant ad eum vultus hominum multorum, quorumdam gaudentium, quorumdam tristantium, aliqui vero
alligati, aliqui adducentes ex eis qui offerebantur. Et ego a
multitudine pavoris expergefactus sum et deprecatus sum
Altissimum et dixi:

14 Tu ab initio demonstrasti servo tuo mirabilia haec et
dignum me habuisti, ut susciperes deprecationem meam.
15 Et nunc demonstra mihi adhuc et interpretationem somnii
huius. 16 Sicut enim existimo in sensu meo, vae qui derelicti
fuerint in diebus illis, et multo plus vae his qui non sunt
derelicti. 17 Qui enim non sunt derelicti, tristes erunt
18 intellegentes quae sunt reposita in novissimis diebus, et
non occurrentes eis. Sed et qui derelicti sunt 19 propter hoc
vae, viderunt enim pericula magna et necessitates multas,
sicut ostendunt somnia haec. 20 Attamen facilius est pericli-
tantem venire in haec, quam pertransire sicut nubem a
saeculo et non videre quae contigerunt in novissimo.

Et respondit ad me et dixit: 21 Et visionis interpretationem
dicam tibi, sed et de quibus locutus es adaperiam tibi.
22 Quoniam dixisti de his qui derelicti sunt et de his qui non
derelicti sunt, haec interpretatio: 23 Qui adferet periculum in
illo tempore, ipse custodibit qui in periculo inciderint, qui
habent operas et fidem ad Fortissimum. 24 Scito ergo, quoniam magis beatificati sunt qui derelicti super eos qui mortui
sunt.

25 Interpretatio enim visionis haec: Quia vidisti virum
ascendentem de corde maris, 26 ipse est quem conservat
Altissimus multis temporibus, qui per semet ipsum liberabit
creaturam suam, et ipse disponet qui derelicti sunt. 27 Et
quoniam vidisti de ore eius exire ut spiritum et ignem et tem-
pestatem, 28 et quoniam non tenebat frameam neque vas

winds of the heaven, to subdue the man that came out of the sea.

6 But I beheld, and, lo, he had graved himself a great mountain, and flew up upon it.

7 But I would have seen the region or place whereout the hill was graven, and I could not.

8 And after this I beheld, and, lo, all they which were gathered together to subdue him were sore afraid, and yet durst fight.

9 And, lo, as he saw the violence of the multitude that came, he neither lifted up his hand, nor held sword, nor any instrument of war:

10 But only I saw that he sent out of his mouth as it had been a blast of fire, and out of his lips a flaming breath, and out of his tongue he cast out sparks and tempests.

11 And they were all mixed together; the blast of fire, the flaming breath, and the great tempest; and fell with violence upon the multitude which was prepared to fight, and burned them up every one, so that upon a sudden of an innumerable multitude nothing was to be perceived, but only dust and smell of smoke: when I saw this I was afraid.

12 Afterward saw I the same man come down from the mountain, and call unto him another peaceable multitude.

13 And there came much people unto him, whereof some were glad, some were sorry, some of them were bound, and other some brought of them that were offered: then was I sick through great fear, and I awaked, and said,

14 Thou hast shewed thy servant these wonders from the beginning, and hast counted me worthy that thou shouldest receive my prayer:

15 Shew me now yet the interpretation of this dream.

16 For as I conceive in mine understanding, woe unto them that shall be left in those days! and much more woe unto them that are not left behind!

17 For they that were not left were in heaviness.

18 Now understand I the things that are laid up in the latter days, which shall happen unto them, and to those that are left behind.

19 Therefore are they come into great perils and many necessities, like as these dreams declare.

20 Yet is it easier for him that is in danger to come into these things, than to pass away as a cloud out of the world, and not to see the things that happen in the last days. And he answered unto me, and said,

21 The interpretation of the vision shall I shew thee, and I will open unto thee the thing that thou hast required.

22 Whereas thou hast spoken of them that are left behind, this is the interpretation:

23 He that shall endure the peril in that time hath kept himself: they that be fallen into danger are such as have works, and faith toward the Almighty.

24 Know this therefore, that they which be left behind are more blessed than they that be dead.

25 This is the meaning of the vision: Whereas thou sawest a man coming up from the midst of the sea:

26 The same is he whom God the Highest hath kept a great season, which by his own self shall deliver his creature: and he shall order them that are left behind.

27 And whereas thou sawest, that out of his mouth there came as a blast of wind, and fire, and storm;

28 And that he held neither sword, nor any instrument of

TODAY'S ENGLISH VERSION

fight against the man who had come up out of the sea.
6 Then I watched the man carve out a high mountain and fly
up on it. 7 I tried to see the place or the region from which
the mountain was carved, but I couldn't. 8 Then I saw that
all the people who had come together to make war against
him were terrified, but they still prepared to fight him.
9 When the man saw the great crowd advancing to attack
him, he did not take up any weapons. 10 The only thing I
saw was what looked like a stream of fire coming out of his
mouth. He sent a flaming wind from his lips and a storm of
sparks from his tongue. The stream of fire, the flaming wind,
and the great storm combined 11 and swept down on the
crowd that was coming to attack him, and burned them all
up. In a single moment, that crowd too large to count vanished, and there was nothing left but powdery ashes and the
smell of smoke. I was shocked when I saw what had happened.

12 Then I saw the man come down from the mountain and
call another large crowd to come to him—this was a peace-
loving crowd. 13 All sorts of people came: some were happy,
some were sad, some had their hands and feet tied, and
some brought others as a gift to the Lord.

I was so frightened that I woke up. I prayed to God Most
High and said, 14 "Lord, you have been showing me all these
marvelous things. You have considered me worthy and have
heard my prayers. 15 Now please show me the meaning of
this dream also. 16 I have been thinking how terrible it will
be for the people who will be living in those days, but how
much worse for those who do not survive. 17 They will be in
great sorrow 18 because they will not enjoy any of the pleasures reserved for the last days. 19 But how terrible also for
those who do survive; they will have to face great dangers
and many troubles, as these dreams have shown. 20 Nevertheless, it is better to pass through these dangers and reach
the end than to disappear like a cloud from this world and
never see what takes place in the last days."

He answered, 21 "I will explain to you the meaning of the
vision and answer the questions you have asked. 22 You
have raised questions about those who will survive until the
end. The answer is that 23 the one who brings the dangers in
those days will also protect from danger the people who have
stored up good works and faithfulness with God the
Almighty One. 24 You may be certain that those who survive
are far more fortunate than those who die.

25 "This is the meaning of the vision. The man you saw
coming up out of the sea 26 represents the one whom God
Most High has kept ready for many ages. He will free the
world he created and establish the new order for those who
survive. 27 You saw the wind, fire, and storm going out of
the man's mouth, 28 and you saw that without the use of a

NEW REVISED STANDARD VERSION

heaven to make war against the man who came up out of
the sea. 6 And I looked and saw that he carved out for himself a great mountain, and flew up on to it. 7 And I tried to
see the region or place from which the mountain was carved,
but I could not.

8 After this I looked and saw that all who had gathered
together against him, to wage war with him, were filled with
fear, and yet they dared to fight. 9 When he saw the onrush
of the approaching multitude, he neither lifted his hand nor
held a spear or any weapon of war; 10 but I saw only how he
sent forth from his mouth something like a stream of fire,
and from his lips a flaming breath, and from his tongue he
shot forth a storm of sparks.[a] 11 All these were mingled
together, the stream of fire and the flaming breath and the
great storm, and fell on the onrushing multitude that was
prepared to fight, and burned up all of them, so that suddenly nothing was seen of the innumerable multitude but only
the dust of ashes and the smell of smoke. When I saw it, I
was amazed.

12 After this I saw the same man come down from the
mountain and call to himself another multitude that was
peaceable. 13 Then many people[b] came to him, some of
whom were joyful and some sorrowful; some of them were
bound, and some were bringing others as offerings.

Then I woke up in great terror, and prayed to the Most
High, and said, 14 "From the beginning you have shown
your servant these wonders, and have deemed me worthy to
have my prayer heard by you; 15 now show me the interpretation of this dream also. 16 For as I consider it in my mind,
alas for those who will be left in those days! And still more,
alas for those who are not left! 17 For those who are not left
will be sad 18 because they understand the things that are
reserved for the last days, but cannot attain them. 19 But
alas for those also who are left, and for that very reason! For
they shall see great dangers and much distress, as these
dreams show. 20 Yet it is better[c] to come into these things,[d]
though incurring peril, than to pass from the world like a
cloud, and not to see what will happen in the last days."

He answered me and said, 21 "I will tell you the interpretation of the vision, and I will also explain to you the things
that you have mentioned. 22 As for what you said about
those who survive, and concerning those who do not
survive,[e] this is the interpretation: 23 The one who brings
the peril at that time will protect those who fall into peril,
who have works and faith toward the Almighty. 24 Understand therefore that those who are left are more blessed than
those who have died.

25 "This is the interpretation of the vision: As for your
seeing a man come up from the heart of the sea, 26 this is he
whom the Most High has been keeping for many ages, who
will himself deliver his creation; and he will direct those who
are left. 27 And as for your seeing wind and fire and a storm
coming out of his mouth, 28 and as for his not holding a

a Meaning of Lat uncertain *b* Lat Syr Arab 2 literally *the faces of many people* *c* Ethiop Compare Arab 2: Lat *easier* *d* Syr: Lat *this* *e* Syr Arab 1: Lat lacks *and . . . not survive*

Latin Vulgate

bellicosum, corrumpit enim impetum eius multitudinis quae
venerat ad expugnare eum, haec interpretatio: 29 Ecce dies
veniunt, quando incipiet Altissimus liberare eos qui super
terram sunt. 30 Et veniet excessus mentis super eos qui
inhabitant terram. 31 Et in alisalio cogitabunt bellare, civitates civitatem et locus locum et gens ad gentem et regnum
adversus regnum.
32 Et erit cum fient haec et contingent signa quae ante
ostendi tibi, et tunc revelabitur Filius meus quem vidisti
virum ascendentem. 33 Et erit quando audierint omnes
gentes vocem eius, et derelinquet unusquisque regionem
suam et bellum quod habent in alterutro, 34 et colligetur in
unum multitudo innumerabilis, sicut vidisti volentes venire
et expugnare eum. 35 Ipse autem stabit super cacumen mon-
tis Sion. 36 Sion autem veniet et ostendetur omnibus parata
et aedificata, sicut vidisti montem sculpi sine manibus.
37 Ipse autem Filius meus arguet quae advenerunt gentes
impietates eorum, has quae tempestati adpropiaverunt, et
inproperabit coram eis mala cogitamenta eorum et cruciamenta quibus incipient cruciari, 38 quae adsimilatae sunt
flammae, et perdet eos sine labore et legem quae igni adsimilata est.
39 Et quoniam vidisti eum colligentem ad se aliam multitudinem pacificam, 40 haec sunt novem tribus, quae captivae
factae sunt de terra sua in diebus Iosiae regis, quem cap-
tivum duxit Salmanassar rex Assyriorum, et transtulit eos
trans Flumen, et translati sunt in terram aliam. 41 Ipsi
autem sibi dederunt consilium hoc, ut derelinquerent multitudinem gentium, et proficiscerentur in ulteriorem regionem,
ubi numquam quisquam inhabitavit ibi genus humanum,
42 ut vel ibi observarent legitima sua, quae non fuerant ser-
vantes in regione sua. 43 Per introitus autem angustos fluminis Eufraten introierunt. 44 Fecit enim eis tunc Altissimus
signa, et statuit venas Fluminis usquequo transirent. 45 Per
eam enim regionem erat via multa itineris anni unius et
dimidii, nam regio illa vocatur Arzar, et 46 tunc inhab-
itaverunt ibi usque in novissimo tempore. Et nunc iterum
coeperunt venire, 47 iterum Altissimus statuit venas
Fluminis, ut possint transire, propter hoc vidisti multitudinem collectam cum pace, 48 sed et qui derelicti sunt de
populo tuo, qui invenientur intra terminum meum 49 sanctum. Erit ergo quando incipiet perdere multitudinem earum
quae collectae sunt gentes, proteget qui superaverit populum. 50 Et tunc ostendet eis multa plurima portenta.
51 Et dixi ego: Dominator Domine, hoc mihi ostende,
propter quod vidi virum ascendentem de corde maris. Et dixit

King James Version

war, but that the rushing in of him destroyed the whole multitude that came to subdue him; this is the interpretation:

29 Behold, the days come, when the most High will begin to deliver them that are upon the earth.

30 And he shall come to the astonishment of them that dwell on the earth.

31 And one shall undertake to fight against another, one city against another, one place against another, one people against another, and one realm against another.

32 And the time shall be when these things shall come to pass, and the signs shall happen which I shewed thee before, and then shall my Son be declared, whom thou sawest as a man ascending.

33 And when all the people hear his voice, every man shall in their own land leave the battle they have one against another.

34 And an innumerable multitude shall be gathered together, as thou sawest them, willing to come, and to overcome him by fighting.

35 But he shall stand upon the top of the mount Sion.

36 And Sion shall come, and shall be shewed to all men, being prepared and builded, like as thou sawest the hill graven without hands.

37 And this my Son shall rebuke the wicked inventions of those nations, which for their wicked life are fallen into the tempest;

38 And shall lay before them their evil thoughts, and the torments wherewith they shall begin to be tormented, which are like unto a flame: and he shall destroy them without labour by the law which is like unto fire.

39 And whereas thou sawest that he gathered another peaceable multitude unto him;

40 Those are the ten tribes, which were carried away prisoners out of their own land in the time of Osea the king, whom Salmanasar the king of Assyria led away captive, and he carried them over the waters, and so came they into another land.

41 But they took this counsel among themselves, that they would leave the multitude of the heathen, and go forth into a further country, where never mankind dwelt,

42 That they might there keep their statutes, which they never kept in their own land.

43 And they entered into Euphrates by the narrow passages of the river.

44 For the most High then shewed signs for them, and held still the flood, till they were passed over.

45 For through that country there was a great way to go, namely, of a year and a half: and the same region is called Arsareth.

46 Then dwelt they there until the latter time; and now when they shall begin to come,

47 The Highest shall stay the springs of the stream again, that they may go through: therefore sawest thou the multitude with peace.

48 But those that be left behind of thy people are they that are found within my borders.

49 Now when he destroyeth the multitude of the nations that are gathered together, he shall defend his people that remain.

50 And then shall he shew them great wonders.

51 Then said I, O Lord that bearest rule, shew me this: Wherefore have I seen the man coming up from the midst of the sea?

TODAY'S ENGLISH VERSION

spear or any other weapon he destroyed the great crowd that
was advancing to attack him. This means that 29 the time is
near when God Most High will begin to free the people on
earth. 30 At that time everyone will be close to panic. 31 They
will begin to make war against one another, city against city,
region against region, nation against nation, and kingdom
against kingdom. 32 When that happens, the signs I told you
about earlier will take place, and then I will reveal my son,
whom you saw as a man coming out of the sea. 33 When
they hear his voice, all the nations will leave their own territory, forget their wars with one another, 34 and come together in one great crowd too large to count, as you saw in your
dream. The nations will unite with the single purpose of
making war on my son. 35 He will take his stand on the top
of Mount Zion, 36 and the new Jerusalem will be seen by
everyone. It will be completed and fully built, just as in your
dream you saw the mountain carved out, but not by human
hands. 37 Then my son will condemn the assembled nations
for their godlessness. That is what the storm meant. 38 He
will confront them with the wicked plans they have made
and also with the torments they must endure. That is what
the flames meant. Then he will easily destroy them by means
of[a] the Law. That is what the fire meant.

39 "You saw him gather another great crowd of peace-loving people. 40 These are the ten tribes of Israel who were
taken away into captivity in the time of King Hoshea. King
Shalmaneser of Assyria captured them and deported them to
a foreign land east of the Euphrates River. 41 But the ten
tribes decided not to stay in that land among the many
Gentiles, so they moved farther east to a country where no
human beings had ever lived before. 42 There they hoped to
keep their laws, which they had failed to keep in their own
country. 43 When they had to make the difficult passage
across the Euphrates, 44 God Most High performed miracles
for them and blocked the channels of the river until they had
crossed over. 45 Their long journey through that region,
which is named Arzareth, took a year and a half, 46 and they
have lived there ever since. Now in these last days they are
coming back home, 47 and once again God Most High will
block the channels of the river, so that they may cross over.
That is the meaning of the great crowd of peace-loving people you saw. 48 But they will also have with them all of your
own people who are left and who are found within the borders of my holy land. 49 When the time comes for my son to
destroy the crowd that has gathered from every nation, he
will protect his people who are left 50 and perform many
great miracles for them."

51 Then I said, "Lord and Master, please tell me why the
man came up out of the sea."

[a] *One ancient translation* by means of; *Latin* and.

NEW REVISED STANDARD VERSION

spear or weapon of war, yet destroying the onrushing multitude that came to conquer him, this is the interpretation:
29 The days are coming when the Most High will deliver those
who are on the earth. 30 And bewilderment of mind shall
come over those who inhabit the earth. 31 They shall plan to
make war against one another, city against city, place
against place, people against people, and kingdom against
kingdom. 32 When these things take place and the signs
occur that I showed you before, then my Son will be
revealed, whom you saw as a man coming up from the sea.[a]

33 "Then, when all the nations hear his voice, all the
nations shall leave their own lands and the warfare that they
have against one another; 34 and an innumerable multitude
shall be gathered together, as you saw, wishing to come and
conquer him. 35 But he shall stand on the top of Mount Zion.
36 And Zion shall come and be made manifest to all people,
prepared and built, as you saw the mountain carved out
without hands. 37 Then he, my Son, will reprove the assembled nations for their ungodliness (this was symbolized by
the storm), 38 and will reproach them to their face with their
evil thoughts and the torments with which they are to be tortured (which were symbolized by the flames), and will
destroy them without effort by means of the law[b] (which
was symbolized by the fire).

39 "And as for your seeing him gather to himself another
multitude that was peaceable, 40 these are the nine[c] tribes
that were taken away from their own land into exile in the
days of King Hoshea, whom Shalmaneser, king of the
Assyrians, made captives; he took them across the river, and
they were taken into another land. 41 But they formed this
plan for themselves, that they would leave the multitude of
the nations and go to a more distant region, where no
human beings had ever lived, 42 so that there at least they
might keep their statutes that they had not kept in their own
land. 43 And they went in by the narrow passages of the
Euphrates river. 44 For at that time the Most High performed
signs for them, and stopped the channels of the river until
they had crossed over. 45 Through that region there was a
long way to go, a journey of a year and a half; and that
country is called Arzareth.[d]

46 "Then they lived there until the last times; and now,
when they are about to come again, 47 the Most High will
stop[e] the channels of the river again, so that they may be
able to cross over. Therefore you saw the multitude gathered
together in peace. 48 But those who are left of your people,
who are found within my holy borders, shall be saved.[f]
49 Therefore when he destroys the multitude of the nations
that are gathered together, he will defend the people who
remain. 50 And then he will show them very many wonders."

51 I said, "O sovereign Lord, explain this to me: Why did I
see the man coming up from the heart of the sea?"

a Syr and most Lat Mss lack *from the sea* *b* Syr: Lat *effort and the law*
c Other Lat Mss *ten*; Syr Ethiop Arab 1 Arm *nine and a half* *d* That is
Another Land *e* Syr: Lat *stops* *f* Syr: Lat lacks *shall be saved*

Latin Vulgate

mihi: [52] Sicut non potest hoc vel scrutinare vel scire quis,
quid sit in profundo maris, sic non poterit quisquam super
terram videre Filium meum vel eos qui cum eo sunt nisi in
tempore diei. [53] Haec est interpretatio somnii quem vidisti,
et propter quod inluminatus es haec solus. [54] Dereliquisti
enim tua et circa mea vacasti et legem meam exquisisti.
[55] Vitam enim tuam disposuisti in sapientiam, et sensum
tuum vocasti matrem. [56] Et propter hoc ostendi tibi haec,
merces apud Altissimum. Erit enim post alios tres dies, ad te
alia loquar et exponam tibi gravia et mirabilia.

[57] Et profectus sum et transii in campum, multum glorifi-
cans et laudans Altissimum de mirabilibus, quae per tempus
faciebat, [58] et quoniam gubernat tempora et quae sunt in
temporibus inlata. Et sedi ibi tribus diebus.

14 [1] Et fac-
tum est tertio die, et ego sedebam sub quercu, [2] et
ecce vox exivit contra me de rubo et dixit: Ezra, Ezra. Et dixi:
Ecce ego, Domine. Et surrexi super pedes meos. Et dixit ad
me:

[3] Revelans revelatus sum super rubum et locutus sum
Moysi, quando populus meus serviebat in Aegypto. [4] Et misi
eum et eduxi populum meum de Aegypto, et adduxi eum
super montem Sina et detinebam eum apud me diebus multis, [5] et enarravi ei mirabilia multa, et ostendi ei temporum
secreta et temporum finem. Et praecepi ei dicens: [6] Haec in
palam facies verba et haec abscondes. [7] Et nunc tibi dico:
[8] Signa quae demonstravi et somnia quae vidisti et interpre-
tationes quas tu audisti, in corde tuo repone ea. [9] Tu enim
recipieris ab hominibus, et converteris residuum cum Filio
meo et cum similibus tuis, usquequo finiantur tempora,
[10] quoniam saeculum perdidit iuventutem suam et tempora
adpropinquant senescere. [11] Duodecim enim partibus divi-
sum est saeculum, et transierunt eius decem iam et dimidium decimae partis, [12] superant autem eius duae prae medium decimae partis [13] Nunc ergo dispone domum tuam, et
corripe populum tuum, et consolare humiles eorum, et
renuntia iam corruptae vitae, [14] et dimitte abs te mortales
cogitationes, et proice abs te pondera humana, et exue te iam
infirmam naturam, et repone in unam partem molestissima
tibi cogitamenta, et festina transmigrare a temporibus his.
[15] Quae enim vidisti nunc contigisse mala, iterum horum
deteriora facientur, [16] quantum enim invalidum fieri saeculum a senectute, tantum multiplicabunt super inhabitantes
mala. [17] Prolongavit enim magis veritas et adpropinquavit
mendacium. Iam enim festinat aquila venire, quam vidisti in
visionem.

[18] Et respondi: Dixi coram te, Domine. [19] Ecce enim ego

King James Version

52 And he said unto me, Like as thou canst neither seek out nor know the things that are in the deep of the sea: even so can no man upon earth see my Son, or those that be with him, but in the day time.

53 This is the interpretation of the dream which thou sawest, and whereby thou only art here lightened.

54 For thou hast forsaken thine own way, and applied thy diligence unto my law, and sought it.

55 Thy life hast thou ordered in wisdom, and hast called understanding thy mother.

56 And therefore have I shewed thee the treasures of the Highest: after other three days I will speak other things unto thee, and declare unto thee mighty and wondrous things.

57 Then went I forth into the field, giving praise and thanks greatly unto the most High because of his wonders, which he did in time;

58 And because he governeth the same, and such things as fall in their seasons: and there I sat three days.

14 And it came to pass upon the third day, I sat under an oak, and, behold, there came a voice out of a bush over against me, and said, Esdras, Esdras.

2 And I said, Here am I, Lord. And I stood up upon my feet.

3 Then said he unto me, In the bush I did manifestly reveal myself unto Moses, and talked with him, when my people served in Egypt:

4 And I sent him, and led my people out of Egypt, and brought him up to the mount of Sinai, where I held him by me a long season,

5 And told him many wondrous things, and shewed him the secrets of the times, and the end; and commanded him, saying,

6 These words shalt thou declare, and these shalt thou hide.

7 And now I say unto thee,

8 That thou lay up in thy heart the signs that I have shewed, and the dreams that thou hast seen, and the interpretations which thou hast heard:

9 For thou shalt be taken away from all, and from henceforth thou shalt remain with my Son, and with such as be like thee, until the times be ended.

10 For the world hath lost his youth, and the times begin to wax old.

11 For the world is divided into twelve parts, and the ten parts of it are gone already, and half of a tenth part:

12 And there remaineth that which is after the half of the tenth part.

13 Now therefore set thine house in order, and reprove thy people, comfort such of them as be in trouble, and now renounce corruption,

14 Let go from thee mortal thoughts, cast away the burdens of man, put off now the weak nature,

15 And set aside the thoughts that are most heavy unto thee, and haste thee to flee from these times.

16 For yet greater evils than those which thou hast seen happen shall be done hereafter.

17 For look how much the world shall be weaker through age, so much the more shall evils increase upon them that dwell therein.

18 For the truth is fled far away, and leasing is hard at hand: for now hasteth the vision to come, which thou hast seen.

Today's English Version

52 He answered, "No one can explore the bottom of the sea to find out what is there. In the same way, no human being can see my son or those who come with him until the day that has been fixed. 53 That is the meaning of your dream. You alone have been given this information, 54 because you have given up your own interests to devote yourself to mine and to the study of my Law. 55 You have dedicated your life to wisdom, and understanding has been like a mother to you. 56 That is why God Most High has rewarded you by showing you these things. After three days, I will come back and tell you about other profound wonders."

57 I went for a walk in the field, worshiping and praising God Most High for the miracles he performs in his own good time. 58 For he controls the ages and what happens in them. I remained there for three days.

14 On the third day, while I was sitting under an oak tree, 2 suddenly a voice came out of a bush near me and called, "Ezra! Ezra!"

I stood up and answered, "Here I am, Lord."

3 The voice continued, "I revealed myself from a bush and spoke to Moses when my people were slaves in Egypt. 4 I sent him to lead them out of Egypt, and I brought them to Mount Sinai. I kept Moses with me there on the mountain for a long time, 5 while I told him the secrets about the ages and the end of time. I told him 6 what to make public and what to keep secret. 7 Now I command you 8 to memorize the signs, visions, and interpretations that I have given you. 9 You will be taken out of this world into the heavenly world where you and others like you will live with my son until the end of time. 10 The world is no longer young; it is rapidly approaching old age. 11 The whole history of the world is divided into twelve periods, and the tenth period has already arrived 12 and it is half over; only two and a half parts remain. 13 So set your house in order, warn your people, comfort those who are humble, and teach those who are wise.[a] Then say good-bye to this mortal life. 14 Put earthly cares away from you, throw down your human burdens, and lay aside your weak human nature. 15 Put all your anxieties aside, and get ready to leave this world quickly. 16 You have seen many evil things already, but far worse things are about to happen. 17 As the world grows older and weaker, the evils that will come upon its people will multiply. 18 Truth will depart and falsehood will draw ever nearer. The eagle you saw in your vision is just about to arrive."

a Some ancient translations teach . . . wise; *Latin does not have these words.*

New Revised Standard Version

52 He said to me, "Just as no one can explore or know what is in the depths of the sea, so no one on earth can see my Son or those who are with him, except in the time of his day.[a] 53 This is the interpretation of the dream that you saw. And you alone have been enlightened about this, 54 because you have forsaken your own ways and have applied yourself to mine, and have searched out my law; 55 for you have devoted your life to wisdom, and called understanding your mother. 56 Therefore I have shown you these things; for there is a reward laid up with the Most High. For it will be that after three more days I will tell you other things, and explain weighty and wondrous matters to you."

57 Then I got up and walked in the field, giving great glory and praise to the Most High for the wonders that he does[b] from time to time, 58 and because he governs the times and whatever things come to pass in their seasons. And I stayed there three days.

14 On the third day, while I was sitting under an oak, suddenly a voice came out of a bush opposite me and said, "Ezra, Ezra!" 2 And I answered, "Here I am, Lord," and I rose to my feet. 3 Then he said to me, "I revealed myself in a bush and spoke to Moses when my people were in bondage in Egypt; 4 and I sent him and led[c] my people out of Egypt; and I led him up on Mount Sinai, where I kept him with me many days. 5 I told him many wondrous things, and showed him the secrets of the times and declared to him[d] the end of the times. Then I commanded him, saying, 6 'These words you shall publish openly, and these you shall keep secret.' 7 And now I say to you: 8 Lay up in your heart the signs that I have shown you, the dreams that you have seen, and the interpretations that you have heard; 9 for you shall be taken up from among humankind, and henceforth you shall live with my Son and with those who are like you, until the times are ended. 10 The age has lost its youth, and the times begin to grow old. 11 For the age is divided into twelve parts, and nine[e] of its parts have already passed, 12 as well as half of the tenth part; so two of its parts remain, besides half of the tenth part.[f] 13 Now therefore, set your house in order, and reprove your people; comfort the lowly among them, and instruct those that are wise.[g] And now renounce the life that is corruptible, 14 and put away from you mortal thoughts; cast away from you the burdens of humankind, and divest yourself now of your weak nature; 15 lay to one side the thoughts that are most grievous to you, and hurry to escape from these times. 16 For evils worse than those that you have now seen happen shall take place hereafter. 17 For the weaker the world becomes through old age, the more shall evils be increased upon its inhabitants. 18 Truth shall go farther away, and falsehood shall come near. For the eagle[h] that you saw in the vision is already hurrying to come."

a Syr: Ethiop *except when his time and his day have come.* Lat lacks *his*
b Lat *did* *c* Syr Arab 1 Arab 2 *he led* *d* Syr Ethiop Arab Arm: Lat lacks *declared to him* *e* Cn: Lat Ethiop *ten* *f* Syr lacks verses 11, 12: Ethiop *For the world is divided into ten parts, and has come to the tenth, and half of the tenth remains. Now . . .* *g* Lat lacks *and . . . wise*
h Syr Ethiop Arab Arm: Meaning of Lat uncertain

Latin Vulgate

abibo sicut praecepisti mihi, et corripiam praesentem populum. Qui autem iterum nati fuerint, quis commonebit? 20 Positum est ergo saeculum in tenebris, et qui inhabitant in eo sine lumine, 21 quoniam lex tua incensa est, propter quod nemo scit quae a te facta sunt vel quae incipient operae. 22 Si enim inveni gratiam coram te, inmitte in me spiritum sanctum, et scribam omne quod factum est in saeculo ab initio, quae erant in lege tua scripta, ut possint homines invenire semitam, et qui voluerint vivere in novissimis vivant.

23 Et respondit ad me et dixit: Vadens congrega populum et dices ad eos, ut non te quaerant diebus quadraginta. 24 Tu autem praepara tibi buxos multos et accipe tecum Saream, Dabriam, Selemiam, Ethanum et Asihel, quinque hos qui parati sunt ad scribendum velociter. 25 Et venies hic, et ego accendam in corde tuo lucernam intellectus, quae non extinguetur quoadusque finiantur quae incipies scribere. 26 Et cum perfeceris, quaedam palam facies, quaedam sapientibus absconse trades. In crastinum enim hac hora incipies scribere.

27 Et profectus sum, sicut mihi praecepit, et congregavi omnem populum et dixi: 28 Audi, Israhel, verba haec: 29 Peregrinantes peregrinati sunt patres nostri ab initio in Aegypto, et liberati sunt inde. 30 Et acceperunt legem vitae, quem non custodierunt, quem et vos post eos transgressi estis. 31 Et data est vobis terra in sortem in terra Sion, et vos et patres vestri iniquitatem fecistis et non servastis vias, quas vobis praecepit Altissimus. 32 Iustus iudex cum sit, abstulit a vobis in tempore quod donaverat. 33 Et nunc vos hic estis, et fratres vestri introrsus vestrum sunt. 34 Si ergo imperaveritis sensui vestro et erudieritis cor vestrum, vivi conservati eritis et post mortem misericordiam consequemini. 35 Iudicium enim post mortem veniet, quando iterum revivescemus, et tunc iustorum nomina parebunt et impiorum facta ostendentur. 36 Ad me autem nemo accedat nunc, neque requirent me usque diebus quadraginta.

37 Et accepi quinque viros, sicut mandavit mihi, et profecti sumus in campo et mansimus ibi. 38 Et factus sum in crastinum, et ecce vox vocavit me dicens: Ezra, aperi os tuum et bibe quod te potiono. 39 Et aperui os meum, et ecce calix plenus porrigebatur mihi; hoc erat plenum sicut aqua, color autem eius ut ignis similis. 40 Et accepi et bibi, et in eo cum bibissem cor meum eructabatur intellectum et in pectus meum increscebat sapientia. Nam spiritus meus conservabat memoriam, 41 et apertum est os meum et non est clausum amplius.

42 Altissimus autem dedit intellectum quinque viris, et scripserunt quae dicebantur ex successione notis quas non sciebant, et sederunt quadraginta diebus. Ipsi autem per

King James Version

19 Then answered I before thee, and said,

20 Behold, Lord, I will go, as thou hast commanded me, and reprove the people which are present: but they that shall be born afterward, who shall admonish them? thus the world is set in darkness, and they that dwell therein are without light.

21 For thy law is burnt, therefore no man knoweth the things that are done of thee, or the works that shall begin.

22 But if I have found grace before thee, send the Holy Ghost into me, and I shall write all that hath been done in the world since the beginning, which were written in thy law, that men may find thy path, and that they which will live in the latter days may live.

23 And he answered me, saying, Go thy way, gather the people together, and say unto them, that they seek thee not for forty days.

24 But look thou prepare thee many box trees, and take with thee Sarea, Dabria, Selemia, Ecanus, and Asiel, these five which are ready to write swiftly;

25 And come hither, and I shall light a candle of understanding in thine heart, which shall not be put out, till the things be performed which thou shalt begin to write.

26 And when thou hast done, some things shalt thou publish, and some things shalt thou shew secretly to the wise: to morrow this hour shalt thou begin to write.

27 Then went I forth, as he commanded, and gathered all the people together, and said,

28 Hear these words, O Israel.

29 Our fathers at the beginning were strangers in Egypt, from whence they were delivered:

30 And received the law of life, which they kept not, which ye also have transgressed after them.

31 Then was the land, even the land of Sion, parted among you by lot: but your fathers, and ye yourselves, have done unrighteousness, and have not kept the ways which the Highest commanded you.

32 And forasmuch as he is a righteous judge, he took from you in time the thing that he had given you.

33 And now are ye here, and your brethren among you.

34 Therefore if so be that ye will subdue your own understanding, and reform your hearts, ye shall be kept alive, and after death ye shall obtain mercy.

35 For after death shall the judgment come, when we shall live again: and then shall the names of the righteous be manifest, and the works of the ungodly shall be declared.

36 Let no man therefore come unto me now, nor seek after me these forty days.

37 So I took the five men, as he commanded me, and we went into the field, and remained there.

38 And the next day, behold, a voice called me, saying, Esdras, open thy mouth, and drink that I give thee to drink.

39 Then opened I my mouth, and, behold, he reached me a full cup, which was full as it were with water, but the colour of it was like fire.

40 And I took it, and drank: and when I had drunk of it, my heart uttered understanding, and wisdom grew in my breast, for my spirit strengthened my memory:

41 And my mouth was opened, and shut no more.

42 The Highest gave understanding unto the five men, and they wrote the wonderful visions of the night that were told, which they knew not: and they sat forty days, and they wrote in the day, and at night they ate bread.

Today's English Version

19 I replied, "Let me speak[a] in your presence, Lord. 20 I am ready to depart, as you have commanded, and I will warn the present generation; but who will warn the people who have not yet been born? This world is a dark place, and its people have no light. 21 Your Law has been destroyed by fire, so no one can know what you have done in the past or what you are planning to do in the future. 22 Please send your holy spirit to me, so that I can write down everything that has been done in this world from the beginning, everything that was written in your Law. Then in these last days, people will be able to find the right way and obtain life if they want to."

23 He answered, "Go and call the people together and tell them not to look for you for forty days. 24 Prepare a large number of writing tablets, and take with you these five men who can write fast: Seraiah, Dabriah, Shelemiah, Ethan, and Asiel. 25 Then come here, and I will light the lamp of understanding in your heart, and it will not go out until you have finished what you are supposed to write. 26 When you have finished your work, you will make some of it public, and you will give the rest to some wise people, who will keep it secret. Tomorrow at this time you will begin to write."

27 I did as I was commanded and called all the people together. I said, 28 "Listen to what I have to say, people of Israel. 29 At first our ancestors lived as foreigners in Egypt, but then they were set free 30 and received from God the life-giving Law. But they did not keep it, and when your turn came, you did not keep it either. 31 God gave you the holy land as your own possession, but you were as sinful as your ancestors and did not follow the ways that God Most High had commanded. 32 God is a just judge, so after a while he took away what he had given you. 33 Now you are in exile here, but you are closer to Jerusalem than some of your own people.[b] 34 But if you will discipline your thoughts and be willing to learn, you will be kept safe in this life and will be granted mercy after death, 35 for Judgment Day comes after death. We will be brought back to life, and the righteous people will be made known, while what the godless have done will be exposed. 36 But now for forty days, no one is to come near me or try to find me."

37 As I had been commanded, I took the five men, and we went to the field and stayed there. 38 On the next day I suddenly heard a voice saying, "Ezra, open your mouth and drink what I am giving you." 39 So I opened my mouth, and I was handed a cup full of a fiery-colored liquid, 40 which I took and drank. When I had drunk it, my mind overflowed with understanding, and wisdom increased within me as my memory became perfect. 41 I began to speak and went on talking without stopping. 42 God Most High also gave wisdom to the five men with me, and they took turns writing down what I said. They used an alphabet[c] that they had not known before, and worked for forty days, writing in the

[a] *Some ancient translations* Let me speak; *Latin does not have these words.*
[b] but . . . own people; *Latin unclear.* [c] *Some ancient translations* an alphabet; *Latin unclear.*

New Revised Standard Version

19 Then I answered and said, "Let me speak[a] in your presence, Lord. 20 For I will go, as you have commanded me, and I will reprove the people who are now living; but who will warn those who will be born hereafter? For the world lies in darkness, and its inhabitants are without light. 21 For your law has been burned, and so no one knows the things which have been done or will be done by you. 22 If then I have found favor with you, send the holy spirit into me, and I will write everything that has happened in the world from the beginning, the things that were written in your law, so that people may be able to find the path, and that those who want to live in the last days may do so."

23 He answered me and said, "Go and gather the people, and tell them not to seek you for forty days. 24 But prepare for yourself many writing tablets, and take with you Sarea, Dabria, Selemia, Ethanus, and Asiel—these five, who are trained to write rapidly; 25 and you shall come here, and I will light in your heart the lamp of understanding, which shall not be put out until what you are about to write is finished. 26 And when you have finished, some things you shall make public, and some you shall deliver in secret to the wise; tomorrow at this hour you shall begin to write."

27 Then I went as he commanded me, and I gathered all the people together, and said, 28 "Hear these words, O Israel. 29 At first our ancestors lived as aliens in Egypt, and they were liberated from there 30 and received the law of life, which they did not keep, which you also have transgressed after them. 31 Then land was given to you for a possession in the land of Zion; but you and your ancestors committed iniquity and did not keep the ways that the Most High commanded you. 32 And since he is a righteous judge, in due time he took from you what he had given. 33 And now you are here, and your people[b] are farther in the interior.[c] 34 If you, then, will rule over your minds and discipline your hearts, you shall be kept alive, and after death you shall obtain mercy. 35 For after death the judgment will come, when we shall live again; and then the names of the righteous shall become manifest, and the deeds of the ungodly shall be disclosed. 36 But let no one come to me now, and let no one seek me for forty days."

37 So I took the five men, as he commanded me, and we proceeded to the field, and remained there. 38 And on the next day a voice called me, saying, "Ezra, open your mouth and drink what I give you to drink." 39 So I opened my mouth, and a full cup was offered to me; it was full of something like water, but its color was like fire. 40 I took it and drank; and when I had drunk it, my heart poured forth understanding, and wisdom increased in my breast, for my spirit retained its memory, 41 and my mouth was opened and was no longer closed. 42 Moreover, the Most High gave understanding to the five men, and by turns they wrote what was dictated, using characters that they did not know.[d] They sat forty days; they wrote during the daytime, and ate their

a Most Lat Mss lack *Let me speak* *b* Lat *brothers* *c* Syr Ethiop Arm: Lat *are among you* *d* Syr Compare Ethiop Arab 2 Arm: Meaning of Lat uncertain

Latin Vulgate

diem scribebant, 43 nocte autem manducabant panem; ego
autem per diem loquebar et nocte non tacebam. 44 Scripti
sunt autem in quadraginta diebus libri nongenti quattuor.
45 Et factum est cum conpleti essent quadraginta dies, et
locutus est Altissimus dicens: Priora quae scripsisti in palam
pone, et legant digni et indigni. 46 Novissimos autem septuaginta conservabis, ut tradas eos sapientibus de populo tuo.
47 In his enim est vena intellectus et sapientiae fons et scien-
tiae flumen. Et feci sic.

15 Ecce loquere in aures plebi meae sermones propheti-
ae quos inmisero in os tuum, dicit Dominus, 2 et fac
in carta scribi eos, quoniam fideles et veri sunt. 3 Ne timeas
a cogitationibus adversum te, nec conturbent te increduli-
tates dicentium, 4 quoniam omnis incredulus in increduli-
tate sua morietur.
5 Ecce ego induco, dicit Dominus, super orbem terrarum
mala, gladium et famem et mortem et interitum, 6 propter
quod superposuit iniquitas omnem terram et adimpletae sunt
operationes eorum. 7 Propterea dicit Dominus: 8 Iam non
silebo impietates eorum quae inreligiose agunt, nec
sustinebo in his quae inique exercent. Ecce sanguis innoxius
et iustus clamat ad me, et animae iustorum clamant perse-
veranter. 9 Vindicans vindicabo illos, dicit Dominus, et
accipiam omnem sanguinem innocuum ex illis ad me.
10 Ecce populus meus quasi grex ad occisionem ducitur. Iam
non patiar illum habitare in terra Aegypti, 11 sed educam
eum in manu potenti et brachio excelso, et percutiam
Aegyptum plaga sicut prius, et corrumpam terram omnem
eius.
12 Lugeat Aegyptus et fundamenta eius a plaga verberati et
mastigati quam inducet Dominus. 13 Lugeant cultores oper-
antes terram, quoniam deficient semina eorum et vastabun-
tur ligna eorum ab uredine et grandine et a sidus terribile.
14 Vae saeculo et qui habitant in eum, 15 quia adpropinquavit gladius et extritio illorum, et exsurget gens contra gentem
ad pugnam, et romphea in manibus eorum. 16 Erit enim con-
stabilitio hominibus, alisalios supervalescentes non curabunt
regem suum et principem megestanorum suorum in potentia
sua. 17 Concupiscet enim homo in civitatem ire et non poterit. 18 Propter superbiam enim eorum civitates turbabuntur,
domus exterentur, homines metuent. 19 Non miserebitur
homo proximo suo ad irritum faciendum in domos eorum in
gladium, ad diripiendas substantias eorum propter famem
panis et tribulationem multam.
20 Ecce ego convoco, dicit Deus, omnes reges terrae ad
movendum, qui sunt a borea et a noto et ab euro et a libano,

King James Version

43 As for me, I spake in the day, and I held not my tongue by night.

44 In forty days they wrote two hundred and four books.

45 And it came to pass, when the forty days were fulfilled, that the Highest spake, saying, The first that thou hast written publish openly, that the worthy and unworthy may read it:

46 But keep the seventy last, that thou mayest deliver them only to such as be wise among the people:

47 For in them is the spring of understanding, the fountain of wisdom, and the stream of knowledge.

48 And I did so.

15 Behold, speak thou in the ears of my people the words of prophecy, which I will put in thy mouth, saith the Lord:

2 And cause them to be written in paper: for they are faithful and true.

3 Fear not the imaginations against thee, let not the incredulity of them trouble thee, that speak against thee.

4 For all the unfaithful shall die in their unfaithfulness.

5 Behold, saith the Lord, I will bring plagues upon the world; the sword, famine, death, and destruction.

6 For wickedness hath exceedingly polluted the whole earth, and their hurtful works are fulfilled.

7 Therefore saith the Lord,

8 I will hold my tongue no more as touching their wickedness, which they profanely commit, neither will I suffer them in those things, in which they wickedly exercise themselves: behold, the innocent and righteous blood crieth unto me, and the souls of the just complain continually.

9 And therefore, saith the Lord, I will surely avenge them, and receive unto me all the innocent blood from among them.

10 Behold, my people is led as a flock to the slaughter: I will not suffer them now to dwell in the land of Egypt:

11 But I will bring them with a mighty hand and a stretched out arm, and smite Egypt with plagues, as before, and will destroy all the land thereof.

12 Egypt shall mourn, and the foundation of it shall be smitten with the plague and punishment that God shall bring upon it.

13 They that till the ground shall mourn: for their seeds shall fail through the blasting and hail, and with a fearful constellation.

14 Woe to the world and them that dwell therein!

15 For the sword and their destruction draweth nigh, and one people shall stand up to fight against another, and swords in their hands.

16 For there shall be sedition among men, and invading one another; they shall not regard their kings nor princes, and the course of their actions shall stand in their power.

17 A man shall desire to go into a city, and shall not be able.

18 For because of their pride the cities shall be troubled, the houses shall be destroyed, and men shall be afraid.

19 A man shall have no pity upon his neighbour, but shall destroy their houses with the sword, and spoil their goods, because of the lack of bread, and for great tribulation.

20 Behold, saith God, I will call together all the kings of the earth to reverence me, which are from the rising of the sun, from the south, from the east, and Libanus; to turn

TODAY'S ENGLISH VERSION

daytime and eating at night. 43 I spoke all day long, and I
was not silent even at night. 44 During the forty days,
ninety-four[a] books were written.
45 At the end of the forty days, God Most High said to me,
"You are now to make public the first twenty-four[b] books[c]
that you wrote, so that everyone, whether they are worthy or
not, may read them. 46 But the last seventy books that you
wrote are to be held back and to be given only to those who
are wise among your people, 47 because these books contain
a flood of understanding, a fountain of wisdom, and a river
of knowledge." 48 Then I did as I was told.

15 The Lord says, "Proclaim to my people the prophetic
messages that I will give you, 2 and then have them
written down, because they are true and will be fulfilled.
3 Do not be afraid of those who plot against you or be disturbed by their unbelief. 4 All unbelievers will die because of
their unbelief."
5 The Lord says, "I am going to bring terrible disasters on
the whole world—war and famine, death and destruction,
6 because wickedness has spread everywhere, and evil has
reached its limit."
7 "Therefore," the Lord says, 8 "I will no longer remain
silent about the wickedness of these godless people; I will no
longer tolerate it. They have murdered innocent people, and
the blood they have spilled cries out to me for revenge; the
souls of the righteous are constantly pleading for vengeance.
9 Let there be no doubt," says the Lord, "I will hear the plea
of all the innocent people who have been murdered and I will
take vengeance for what has been done to them.
10 "My people are being led to the slaughter like a flock of
sheep. They will no longer have to live in Egypt; 11 I will use
all my strength and power to bring them out of that land. I
will bring disasters upon the Egyptians, as I did earlier, and I
will destroy their country. 12 The whole land will be in
mourning; it will be shaken to its foundations when I, the
Lord, strike it and pound on it. 13 The farmers will mourn
because their seed will fail to sprout, and their trees will be
destroyed by blight, hail, and terrible storms.
14 "The world and the people in it are doomed. 15 The war
that will bring their destruction is very near. Nations will
arm themselves and fight against other nations. 16 There will
be great political turmoil, with one group trying to overpower
another and gain control, while ignoring the legitimate government. 17 There will no longer be free access to the cities,
18 because the struggle for power will bring destruction, terror, and total confusion wherever people live. 19 Driven by
famine and terrible suffering, people will assault their neighbors and mercilessly plunder their possessions."
20 God says, "I am calling together all the kings of the earth
to come from north, south, east, and west to turn back and

[a] *Some ancient translations* ninety-four; *Latin unclear.*
[b] *Some ancient translations* twenty-four; *Latin does not have this word.*
[c] TWENTY-FOUR BOOKS: *The Hebrew Bible contains twenty-four books, corresponding to the thirty-nine books of the Christian Old Testament.*

NEW REVISED STANDARD VERSION

bread at night. 43 But as for me, I spoke in the daytime and
was not silent at night. 44 So during the forty days, ninety-
four[a] books were written. 45 And when the forty days were
ended, the Most High spoke to me, saying, "Make public the
twenty-four[b] books that you wrote first, and let the worthy
and the unworthy read them; 46 but keep the seventy that
were written last, in order to give them to the wise among
your people. 47 For in them is the spring of understanding,
the fountain of wisdom, and the river of knowledge." 48 And
I did so.[c]

15 [d] Speak in the ears of my people the words of the
prophecy that I will put in your mouth, says the
Lord, 2 and cause them to be written on paper; for they are
trustworthy and true. 3 Do not fear the plots against you,
and do not be troubled by the unbelief of those who oppose
you. 4 For all unbelievers shall die in their unbelief.[e]
5 Beware, says the Lord, I am bringing evils upon the
world, the sword and famine, death and destruction,
6 because iniquity has spread throughout every land, and
their harmful doings have reached their limit. 7 Therefore,
says the Lord, 8 I will be silent no longer concerning their
ungodly acts that they impiously commit, neither will I tolerate their wicked practices. Innocent and righteous blood cries
out to me, and the souls of the righteous cry out continually.
9 I will surely avenge them, says the Lord, and will receive to
myself all the innocent blood from among them. 10 See, my
people are being led like a flock to the slaughter; I will not
allow them to live any longer in the land of Egypt, 11 but I
will bring them out with a mighty hand and with an uplifted
arm, and will strike Egypt with plagues, as before, and will
destroy all its land.
12 Let Egypt mourn, and its foundations, because of the
plague of chastisement and castigation that the Lord will
bring upon it. 13 Let the farmers that till the ground mourn,
because their seed shall fail to grow[f] and their trees shall be
ruined by blight and hail and by a terrible tempest. 14 Alas
for the world and for those who live in it! 15 For the sword
and misery draw near them, and nation shall rise up to fight
against nation, with swords in their hands. 16 For there shall
be unrest among people; growing strong against one another, they shall in their might have no respect for their king or
the chief of their leaders. 17 For a person will desire to go
into a city, and shall not be able to do so. 18 Because of their
pride the cities shall be in confusion, the houses shall be
destroyed, and people shall be afraid. 19 People shall have no
pity for their neighbors, but shall make an assault upon[g]
their houses with the sword, and plunder their goods,
because of hunger for bread and because of great tribulation.
20 See how I am calling together all the kings of the earth
to turn to me, says God, from the rising sun and from the
south, from the east and from Lebanon; to turn and repay

a Syr Ethiop Arab 1 Arm: Meaning of Lat uncertain *b* Syr Arab 1: Lat lacks *twenty-four* *c* Syr adds *in the seventh year of the sixth week, five thousand years and three months and twelve days after creation. At that time Ezra was caught up, and taken to the place of those who are like him, after he had written all these things. And he was called the scribe of the knowledge of the Most High for ever and ever.* Ethiop Arab 1 Arm have a similar ending *d* Chapters 15 and 16 (except 15.57-59, which has been found in Greek) are extant only in Lat *e* Other ancient authorities add *and all who believe shall be saved by their faith* *f* Lat lacks *to grow* *g* Cn: Lat *shall empty*

Latin Vulgate

ad convertendos in se et reddere quae dederunt illis. 21 Sicut
faciunt usque hodie electis meis, sic faciam et reddam in
sinum ipsorum. Haec dicit Dominus Deus: 22 Non parcet
dextera mea super peccantes nec cessabit romphea super
effundentes sanguinem innocuum super terram. 23 Et exiit
ignis ab ira eius et devoravit fundamenta terrae et peccatores
quasi stramen incensum. 24 Vae eis qui peccant et non
observant mandata mea, dicit Dominus, 25 non parcam illis.
Discedite, filii apostatae, nolite contaminare sanctificationem
meam. 26 Novit Deus qui peccant in eum, propterea tradet
eos in mortem et in occisionem. 27 Iam enim venerunt super
orbem terrarum mala, et manebitis in illis; non enim liberabit vos Deus, propter quod peccastis in eum.

28 Ecce visio horribilis, et facies illius ab oriente. 29 Et
exient nationes draconum Arabum in curris multis, et sibila-
tus eorum a die itineris fertur super terram, ut etiam timeant
et trepidentur omnes qui illos audient. 30 Carmonii
insanientes in ira exient de silva et advenient in virtute
magna et constabunt in pugnam cum illis et vastabunt portionem terrae Assyriorum in dentibus suis. 31 Et post haec
supervalescet draco nativitatis memoria suae, et si convert-
erint se conspirantes in virtute magna ad persequendos eos,
32 et isti turbabuntur et silebunt in virtute illorum et conver-
tent pedes suos in fugam, 33 et a territorio Assyriorum sub-
sessor subsedebit eos et consumet unum ex illis, et erit timor
et tremor in exercitum illorum et inconstabilitio in regno illorum.

34 Ecce nubs ab oriente et a septentrione usque ad meridi-
anum, et facies illorum horrida valde, plena irae et procellae.
35 Et conlident se invicem et effundent sidus copiosum super
terram et sidus illorum, et erit sanguis a gladio usque ad
ventrem equi 36 et femur hominis et suffraginem cameli. Et
erit timor et tremor multus super terram, 37 et horrebunt qui
videbunt iram illam, et tremor adprehendet illos. Et post haec
movebuntur nimbi copiosi 38 a meridiano et septentrione, et
portio alia ab occidente. 39 Et superinvalescent venti ab oriente et recludent eum et nubem quam suscitavit in ira, et
sidus ad faciendam exteritionem ab orientalem notum et
occidentem violabitur. 40 Et exaltabuntur nubes magnae et
validae plenae irae et sidus, ut exterant omnem terram et
inhabitantes eam, et fundent super omnem altum et eminen-
tem sidus terribile, 41 ignem et grandinem et rompheas
volantes et aquas multas, ut etiam impleantur omnes campi
et omnes rivi a plenitudine aquarum illarum. 42 Et demolient

King James Version

themselves one against another, and repay the things that they have done to them.

21 Like as they do yet this day unto my chosen, so will I do also, and recompense in their bosom. Thus saith the Lord God;

22 My right hand shall not spare the sinners, and my sword shall not cease over them that shed innocent blood upon the earth.

23 The fire is gone forth from his wrath, and hath consumed the foundations of the earth, and the sinners, like the straw that is kindled.

24 Woe to them that sin, and keep not my commandments! saith the Lord.

25 I will not spare them: go your way, ye children, from the power, defile not my sanctuary.

26 For the Lord knoweth all them that sin against him, and therefore delivereth he them unto death and destruction.

27 For now are the plagues come upon the whole earth, and ye shall remain in them: for God shall not deliver you, because ye have sinned against him.

28 Behold an horrible vision, and the appearance thereof from the east:

29 Where the nations of the dragons of Arabia shall come out with many chariots, and the multitude of them shall be carried as the wind upon earth, that all they which hear them may fear and tremble.

30 Also the Carmanians raging in wrath shall go forth as the wild boars of the wood, and with great power shall they come, and join battle with them, and shall waste a portion of the land of the Assyrians.

31 And then shall the dragons have the upper hand, remembering their nature; and if they shall turn themselves, conspiring together in great power to persecute them,

32 Then these shall be troubled, and keep silence through their power, and shall flee.

33 And from the land of the Assyrians shall the enemy besiege them, and consume some of them, and in their host shall be fear and dread, and strife among their kings.

34 Behold clouds from the east and from the north unto the south, and they are very horrible to look upon, full of wrath and storm.

35 They shall smite one upon another, and they shall smite down a great multitude of stars upon the earth, even their own star; and blood shall be from the sword unto the belly,

36 And dung of men unto the camel's hough.

37 And there shall be great fearfulness and trembling upon earth: and they that see the wrath shall be afraid, and trembling shall come upon them.

38 And then shall there come great storms from the south, and from the north, and another part from the west.

39 And strong winds shall arise from the east, and shall open it; and the cloud which he raised up in wrath, and the star stirred to cause fear toward the east and west wind, shall be destroyed.

40 The great and mighty clouds shall be lifted up full of wrath, and the star, that they may make all the earth afraid, and them that dwell therein; and they shall pour out over every high and eminent place an horrible star,

41 Fire, and hail, and flying swords, and many waters, that all fields may be full, and all rivers, with the abundance of great waters.

TODAY'S ENGLISH VERSION

restore what they have taken. 21 I will pay them back with the same harsh treatment they have always given to my chosen people." The Lord says, 22 "I will use my power, and there will be no mercy for sinners; I will put to death all who have murdered innocent people. 23 My anger has become so fierce that fire has blazed out to burn up the foundations of the earth and to burn up sinners like straw. 24 Sinners who do not keep my commands are doomed," says the Lord. 25 "I will have no mercy on them! Out of my sight, you rebels! Do not defile my holy Temple."

26 God is aware of all those who sin against him, and he will hand them over to death and destruction. 27 Terrible disasters have already come upon the world, and there is no escape. You have sinned against God, and he will not rescue you.

28 Then in the east you will suddenly see a fearsome sight. 29 Arab armies with many chariots will advance like dragons. As soon as they start out, the sound of their hissing will spread across the world and bring fear and trembling to everyone who hears it. 30 The Carmonians will come out of the forest in a fierce rage like wild boars advancing in full strength to attack the dragons. With their tusks they will tear up a large part of Assyria, 31 but the dragons will unite their forces, regain their former strength, and win the victory. They will turn and pursue the wild boars, 32 who will be thrown into panic, beaten into silence, and forced to turn and run. 33 The wild boars will be ambushed in Assyria, and one of them will be killed. This will bring fear and panic to their army and indecision to their kings.

34 Then suddenly clouds—terrible, angry storm clouds—will cover the sky from one end to the other. 35 They will collide head-on and release their violence upon the earth. The blood of war will be as deep as a horse's belly 36 or someone's thigh or a camel's knee. 37 Everywhere on earth people will tremble in fear at the horrible sight. 38 Then great storm clouds will move in from the north and the south, and others from the west. 39 But the winds from the east will prevail and push back those angry storm clouds that were about to bring destruction.[a] 40-41 Huge, powerful, angry storm clouds will arise and ruin the whole world and its people. A terrible storm of fire, hail, and flashing swords will come sweeping down on those who have power and authority.[b] Every river will overflow into the fields, and the floods 42 will demolish

[a] *Verse 39 in Latin is unclear.* [b] those who have power and authority; *or* every hill and mountain.

NEW REVISED STANDARD VERSION

what they have given them. 21 Just as they have done to my elect until this day, so I will do, and will repay into their bosom. Thus says the Lord God: 22 My right hand will not spare the sinners, and my sword will not cease from those who shed innocent blood on earth. 23 And a fire went forth from his wrath, and consumed the foundations of the earth and the sinners, like burnt straw. 24 Alas for those who sin and do not observe my commandments, says the Lord;[a] 25 I will not spare them. Depart, you faithless children! Do not pollute my sanctuary. 26 For God[b] knows all who sin against him; therefore he will hand them over to death and slaughter. 27 Already calamities have come upon the whole earth, and you shall remain in them; God[b] will not deliver you, because you have sinned against him.

28 What a terrifying sight, appearing from the east! 29 The nations of the dragons of Arabia shall come out with many chariots, and from the day that they set out, their hissing shall spread over the earth, so that all who hear them will fear and tremble. 30 Also the Carmonians, raging in wrath, shall go forth like wild boars[c] from the forest, and with great power they shall come and engage them in battle, and with their tusks they shall devastate a portion of the land of the Assyrians with their teeth. 31 And then the dragons,[d] remembering their origin, shall become still stronger; and if they combine in great power and turn to pursue them, 32 then these shall be disorganized and silenced by their power, and shall turn and flee.[e] 33 And from the land of the Assyrians an enemy in ambush shall attack them and destroy one of them, and fear and trembling shall come upon their army, and indecision upon their kings.

34 See the clouds from the east, and from the north to the south! Their appearance is exceedingly threatening, full of wrath and storm. 35 They shall clash against one another and shall pour out a heavy tempest on the earth, and their own tempest;[f] and there shall be blood from the sword as high as a horse's belly 36 and a man's thigh and a camel's hock. 37 And there shall be fear and great trembling on the earth; those who see that wrath shall be horror-stricken, and they shall be seized with trembling. 38 After that, heavy storm clouds shall be stirred up from the south, and from the north, and another part from the west. 39 But the winds from the east shall prevail over the cloud that was[g] raised in wrath, and shall dispel it; and the tempest[f] that was to cause destruction by the east wind shall be driven violently toward the south and west. 40 Great and mighty clouds, full of wrath and tempest, shall rise and destroy all the earth and its inhabitants, and shall pour out upon every high and lofty place[h] a terrible tempest, 41 fire and hail and flying swords and floods of water, so that all the fields and all the streams shall be filled with the abundance of those waters. 42 They

[a] Other ancient authorities read *God* [b] Other ancient authorities read *the Lord* [c] Other ancient authorities lack *like wild boars* [d] Cn: Lat *dragon* [e] Other ancient authorities read *turn their face to the north* [f] Meaning of Lat uncertain [g] Literally *that he* [h] Or *eminent person*

LATIN VULGATE

civitates et muros et montes et colles et ligna silvarum et
faena pratorum et frumenta eorum. 43 Et transibunt con-
stanter usque Babylonem et exterent eam. 44 Convenient ad
ipsam et circuibunt eam et effundent sidus et omnem iram
super eam, et subibit pulvis et fumus usque ad caelum, et
omnes in circuitu lugebunt eam, 45 et qui subremanserint
servientes his qui eam exteruerunt.
46 Et tu Asia, consors in specie Babylonis et gloria person-
ae eius, 47 vae tibi, misera, propter quod adsimilasti ei,
ornasti filias tuas in fornicatione ad placendum et glorian-
dum in amatoribus tuis, qui te cupierunt semper fornicari.
48 Odibilem imitata es in omnibus operibus eius et adinven-
tionibus eius. Propterea dicit Deus: 49 Inmittam tibi mala,
viduitatem, paupertatem et famem et gladium et pestem ad
devastandas domos tuas, ad violationem et mortem. Et gloria virtutis tuae 50 sicut flos siccabitur, cum exsurget ardor
qui emissus est super te. 51 Et infirmaberis et paupera a
plaga et mastigata a vulneribus, ut non possis tuos suscipere
potentes et amatores. 52 Numquid ego sic zelabo te, dicit
Dominus, 53 nisi occidisses electos meos in omni tempore,
exultans percussione manuum et dicens, super mortem
eorum cum inebriata es: 54 Exorna speciem vultus tui?
55 Merces fornicariae in sinus tuos, propterea redditionem
percipies. 56 Sicut facies electis meis, dicit Dominus, sic faciet tibi Deus et tradet te in malis. 57 Et nati tui fame interient,
et tu romphea cades, et civitates tuae conterentur, et omnes
tui in campo gladio cadent. 58 Et qui sunt in montibus fame
peribunt, et manducabunt carnes suas et sanguinem bibent a
fame panis et siti aquae. 59 Propter priora misera es et
iterum excipies mala. 60 Et in transitum adlident civitatem
oditam et exterent eam, portionem aliquam gloriae tuae et
territorii tui, dum revertuntur a Babylonia. 61 Extrita illis
eris in stramine, et ipsi tibi erunt ignis. 62 Omnes hii come-
dunt te et civitates tuas et territoria tua et montes, et omnem
silvam tuam et ligna pomifera igne consument. 63 Et natos
tuos captivabunt et honestatem tuam spoliabunt et gloriam
faciei tuae exterminabunt.

16 Vae tibi, Babylon et Asia, vae tibi, Aegypte et Syria.
2 Praecingite vos saccos, plangite filios vestros et
dolete de his, quia adpropinquavit contritio vestra.

KING JAMES VERSION

42 And they shall break down the cities and walls, mountains and hills, trees of the wood, and grass of the meadows, and their corn.

43 And they shall go stedfastly unto Babylon, and make her afraid.

44 They shall come to her, and besiege her, the star and all wrath shall they pour out upon her: then shall the dust and smoke go up unto the heaven, and all they that be about her shall bewail her.

45 And they that remain under her shall do service unto them that have put her in fear.

46 And thou, Asia, that art partaker of the hope of Babylon, and art the glory of her person:

47 Woe be unto thee, thou wretch, because thou hast made thyself like unto her; and hast decked thy daughters in whoredom, that they might please and glory in thy lovers, which have alway desired to commit whoredom with thee!

48 Thou hast followed her that is hated in all her works and inventions: therefore saith God,

49 I will send plagues upon thee; widowhood, poverty, famine, sword, and pestilence, to waste thy houses with destruction and death.

50 And the glory of thy Power shall be dried up as a flower, when the heat shall arise that is sent over thee.

51 Thou shalt be weakened as a poor woman with stripes, and as one chastised with wounds, so that the mighty and lovers shall not be able to receive thee.

52 Would I with jealousy have so proceeded against thee, saith the Lord,

53 If thou hadst not always slain my chosen, exalting the stroke of thine hands, and saying over their dead, when thou wast drunken,

54 Set forth the beauty of thy countenance?

55 The reward of thy whoredom shall be in thy bosom, therefore shalt thou receive recompence.

56 Like as thou hast done unto my chosen, saith the Lord, even so shall God do unto thee, and shall deliver thee into mischief.

57 Thy children shall die of hunger, and thou shalt fall through the sword: thy cities shall be broken down, and all thine shall perish with the sword in the field.

58 They that be in the mountains shall die of hunger, and eat their own flesh, and drink their own blood, for very hunger of bread, and thirst of water.

59 Thou as unhappy shalt come through the sea, and receive plagues again.

60 And in the passage they shall rush on the idle city, and shall destroy some portion of thy land, and consume part of thy glory, and shall return to Babylon that was destroyed.

61 And thou shalt be cast down by them as stubble, and they shall be unto thee as fire;

62 And shall consume thee, and thy cities, thy land, and thy mountains; all thy woods and thy fruitful trees shall they burn up with fire.

63 Thy children shall they carry away captive, and, look, what thou hast, they shall spoil it, and mar the beauty of thy face.

16 Woe be unto thee, Babylon, and Asia! woe be unto thee, Egypt, and Syria!

2 Gird up yourselves with cloths of sack and hair, bewail your children, and be sorry; for your destruction is at hand.

TODAY'S ENGLISH VERSION

cities, walls, mountains, hills, forests, and crops. 43-44 This destruction will press on until it reaches Babylon and engulfs it in a raging storm of ruin. The dust and the smoke will form a great cloud reaching to the sky, and all the neighboring cities will mourn for Babylon. 45 Anyone who survives will become a slave to those who destroyed the city.

46-47 You, Asia, are to be pitied. You are doomed! You have enjoyed the splendor and glory of Babylon. You have imitated her and dressed up your daughters to look like prostitutes to please and gratify your lovers, who have always lusted for you. 48 Because you have imitated that vile prostitute in everything she has done or planned, God has this to say: 49 "I will send disasters upon you. I will make you a widow and send poverty, famine, war, and epidemics to destroy your homes and bring ruin and death. 50 The power of which you boast will wither like a flower when the burning heat is sent upon you. 51 You will be a wretched, weak woman so bruised, beaten, and wounded that you will no longer attract your wealthy lovers. 52 I would not punish you so severely," says the Lord, 53 "if you had not murdered my chosen people. But you took great delight in striking them, and when you were drunk, you boasted about killing them.

54 "Paint your face! 55 You will be paid for your work as a prostitute; you will get what you have earned. 56 I will pay you back," says the Lord, "for what you have done to my chosen people. I will bring disaster on you. 57 You will be put to death, and your children will starve. Your cities will be torn down, and the people out in the country will be killed. 58 Those in the mountains will starve; their hunger and thirst will drive them to eat their own flesh and drink their own blood. 59 You will be more miserable than anyone has ever been, but there will be still more punishment to come. 60 The army that destroyed Babylon will march back through your country and devastate your peaceful city; they will destroy your beautiful country and leave most of it in ruins. 61 Your country will be destroyed like straw in a fire. 62 They will burn up all your forests and orchards. All over your land, your cities and mountains will be covered with ruins. 63 Your splendor will vanish; your children will be carried off as prisoners; your possessions will be plundered."

16 Babylonia, Asia, Egypt, and Syria, you are doomed! 2 Put on your clothes of mourning, your sackcloth and goat's hair. Cry and wail for your children because the time for your destruction is near. 3 I am sending war on you,

NEW REVISED STANDARD VERSION

shall destroy cities and walls, mountains and hills, trees of the forests, and grass of the meadows, and their grain. 43 They shall go on steadily to Babylon and blot it out. 44 They shall come to it and surround it; they shall pour out on it the tempest[a] and all its fury;[b] then the dust and smoke shall reach the sky, and all who are around it shall mourn for it. 45 And those who survive shall serve those who have destroyed it.

46 And you, Asia, who share in the splendor of Babylon and the glory of her person— 47 woe to you, miserable wretch! For you have made yourself like her; you have decked out your daughters for prostitution to please and glory in your lovers, who have always lusted after you. 48 You have imitated that hateful one in all her deeds and devices.[c] Therefore God[d] says, 49 I will send evils upon you: widowhood, poverty, famine, sword, and pestilence, bringing ruin to your houses, bringing destruction and death. 50 And the glory of your strength shall wither like a flower when the heat shall rise that is sent upon you. 51 You shall be weakened like a wretched woman who is beaten and wounded, so that you cannot receive your mighty lovers. 52 Would I have dealt with you so violently, says the Lord, 53 if you had not killed my chosen people continually, exulting and clapping your hands and talking about their death when you were drunk?

54 Beautify your face! 55 The reward of a prostitute is in your lap; therefore you shall receive your recompense. 56 As you will do to my chosen people, says the Lord, so God will do to you, and will hand you over to adversities. 57 Your children shall die of hunger, and you shall fall by the sword; your cities shall be wiped out, and all your people who are in the open country shall fall by the sword. 58 Those who are in the mountains and highlands[e] shall perish of hunger, and they shall eat their own flesh in hunger for bread and drink their own blood in thirst for water. 59 Unhappy above all others, you shall come and suffer fresh miseries. 60 As they pass by they shall crush the hateful[f] city, and shall destroy a part of your land and abolish a portion of your glory, when they return from devastated Babylon. 61 You shall be broken down by them like stubble,[g] and they shall be like fire to you. 62 They shall devour you and your cities, your land and your mountains; they shall burn with fire all your forests and your fruitful trees. 63 They shall carry your children away captive, plunder your wealth, and mar the glory of your countenance.

16 Woe to you, Babylon and Asia! Woe to you, Egypt and Syria! 2 Bind on sackcloth and cloth of goats' hair,[h] and wail for your children, and lament for them; for your destruction is at hand. 3 The sword has been sent upon

a Meaning of Lat uncertain *b* Other ancient authorities add *until they destroy it to its foundations* *c* Other ancient authorities read *devices, and you have followed after that one about to gratify her magnates and leaders so that you may be made proud and be pleased by her fornications* *d* Other ancient authorities read *the Lord* *e* Gk: Lat omits *and highlands* *f* Another reading is *idle* or *unprofitable* *g* Other ancient authorities read *like dry straw* *h* Other ancient authorities lack *cloth of goats' hair*

LATIN VULGATE

3 Inmissus est gladius vobis, et quis est qui avertat eum?
4 Inmissus est vobis ignis, et quis est qui extinguat eum?
5 Inmissa sunt vobis mala, et quis est qui recutiet ea?
6 Numquid recutiet aliquis leonem esurientem in silva? Aut
numquid extinguet ignem, cum stramen incensum fuerit?
7 Aut numquid recutiet sagittam inmissam a sagittario forte?
8 Dominus Deus mittit mala, et quis recutiet ea? 9 Et exiet
ignis ex iracundia eius, et quis est qui extinguat eum?
10 Coruscabit, et quis non timebit? Tonabit, et quis non hor-
rebit? 11 Dominus comminatur, quis non conterretur a facie
eius? 12 Tremet terra a fundamento eius, mare fluctuatur de
profundo, et fluctus eius turbabuntur et pisces eius a facie
Domini et a gloria virtutis eius, 13 quoniam fortis gloriae qui
tendit sagittam, et acumen eius acutum, quae dimissa est ab
eo, non deficiet missa super fines terrae. 14 Ecce mittuntur
mala et non revertentur, donec venient super terram. 15 Et
ignis incendetur et non extinguetur, donec excomedat frumenta terrae. 16 Quomodo non revertitur sagitta missa a
sagittario valido, sic non revertentur mala quae fuerint emissa in terram.

17 Vae mihi, vae mihi, quis me liberabit in diebus illis?
18 Initium gemitus et copiosi suspirantium, initium famis et
multi disperient, initium belli et timebunt potestates, initium
malorum et trepidabunt 19 ab eis; quid facient, cum venerint
mala? 20 Ecce famis plaga dimissa est, et tribulatio eius
tamquam mastix, castigatio in disciplina. 21 Et super his
omnibus non se avertent ab iniquitatibus suis nec super has
plagas memorantur sempiterna. 22 Ecce erit annonae vilitas
in brevi super terram, ut putent sibi esse directam pacem.
Tunc superflorescent mala super terram, gladius et famis.
23 Et aporiant vitam super terram, et gladius dispersit quae
superaverint a fame. 24 Et mortui quasi stercora proicientur,
et non habent qui consolentur eos. Et derelinquetur deserta
terra, et civitates eius demolientur. 25 Non derelinquetur
agricola, qui colit terram et qui seminat eam. 26 Ligna fruc-
tiferabunt, et quis vindemiet illa? 27 Et uva tradet se ad vindemiam, et quis adligabit eam? Erit enim et locis desertio
multa. 28 Concupiscet enim homo hominem videre vel certe
vocem eius audire. 29 Relinquentur enim decem de civitate et
duo ex agro, qui absconderint se in silva et in fissuras

KING JAMES VERSION

3 A sword is sent upon you, and who may turn it back?

4 A fire is sent among you, and who may quench it?

5 Plagues are sent unto you, and what is he that may drive them away?

6 May any man drive away an hungry lion in the wood? or may any one quench the fire in stubble, when it hath begun to burn?

7 May one turn again the arrow that is shot of a strong archer?

8 The mighty Lord sendeth the plagues, and who is he that can drive them away?

9 A fire shall go forth from his wrath, and who is he that may quench it?

10 He shall cast lightnings, and who shall not fear? he shall thunder, and who shall not be afraid?

11 The Lord shall threaten, and who shall not be utterly beaten to powder at his presence?

12 The earth quaketh, and the foundations thereof; the sea ariseth up with waves from the deep, and the waves of it are troubled, and the fishes thereof also, before the Lord, and before the glory of his power:

13 For strong is his right hand that bendeth the bow, his arrows that he shooteth are sharp, and shall not miss, when they begin to be shot into the ends of the world.

14 Behold, the plagues are sent, and shall not return again, until they come upon the earth.

15 The fire is kindled, and shall not be put out, till it consume the foundation of the earth.

16 Like as an arrow which is shot of a mighty archer returneth not backward: even so the plagues that shall be sent upon earth shall not return again.

17 Woe is me! woe is me! who will deliver me in those days?

18 The beginning of sorrows and great mournings; the beginning of famine and great death; the beginning of wars, and the powers shall stand in fear; the beginning of evils! what shall I do when these evils shall come?

19 Behold, famine and plague, tribulation and anguish, are sent as scourges for amendment.

20 But for all these things they shall not turn from their wickedness, nor be alway mindful of the scourges.

21 Behold, victuals shall be so good cheap upon earth, that they shall think themselves to be in good case, and even then shall evils grow upon earth, sword, famine, and great confusion.

22 For many of them that dwell upon earth shall perish of famine; and the other, that escape the hunger, shall the sword destroy.

23 And the dead shall be cast out as dung, and there shall be no man to comfort them: for the earth shall be wasted, and the cities shall be cast down.

24 There shall be no man left to till the earth, and to sow it.

25 The trees shall give fruit, and who shall gather them?

26 The grapes shall ripen, and who shall tread them? for all places shall be desolate of men:

27 So that one man shall desire to see another, and to hear his voice.

28 For of a city there shall be ten left, and two of the field, which shall hide themselves in the thick groves, and in the clefts of the rocks.

Today's English Version

and no one can stop it. 4I am sending fire on you, and no one can put it out. 5I am sending disasters on you, and no one can stop them from coming. 6Can anyone stop a hungry lion in the forest or put out a fire that is burning in straw 7or turn back an arrow shot by a strong archer? 8When the Lord God sends disaster, no one can hold it back. 9No one can escape the blazing anger of the Lord. 10When he sends lightning, no one can keep from trembling; and when it thunders, everyone is afraid. 11When the Lord makes his threats, no one can keep from falling to the ground in his presence. 12The foundations of the earth tremble. There is violent churning in the deepest part of the sea. Even the creatures in the sea are in turmoil when the Lord makes his glorious power felt. 13He is like a mighty archer whose strong right arm bends the bow. His arrows are sharp and never miss their mark once they are shot out toward any part of the earth. 14He has already sent out his disasters toward the earth, and they will not miss their target. 15The fire has been lit, and it cannot be put out until it burns up the foundations of the earth. 16The disasters are on their way toward the earth, and like an arrow shot by a strong archer, they cannot be turned back.

17I'm doomed! I'm doomed! Who will rescue me in those days? 18Troubles will come, and many people will groan. Famine will come, and many will die. Wars will come, and the world powers will tremble. Disasters will come, and everyone will be terrified. What will people do when these disasters come? 19Famine, epidemics, troubles, and suffering are sent to punish and correct people. 20But in spite of all this, they will not turn away from their sins; they soon forget their punishment. 21The time is coming when food will be so cheap that people will think a time of peace and plenty has arrived. But then disasters will spring up everywhere—wars, famine, and great confusion. 22Many people on earth will starve to death, and those who escape starvation will be killed in war. 23Their corpses will be thrown out like garbage, and there will be no one left to comfort the living. The earth will be deserted and its cities demolished. 24There will be no one left to plow the land or plant it. 25Trees will bear their fruit, but there will be no one left to pick it. 26Grapes will ripen, but there will be no one left to make wine. There will be desolation everywhere, 27and a person will long to see the face of another human being or even to hear another person's voice. 28Only ten will be left out of a whole city, and in the countryside, only two, who have hidden in the forest or in caves. 29When an olive grove

New Revised Standard Version

you, and who is there to turn it back? 4A fire has been sent upon you, and who is there to quench it? 5Calamities have been sent upon you, and who is there to drive them away? 6Can one drive off a hungry lion in the forest, or quench a fire in the stubble once it has started to burn?[a] 7Can one turn back an arrow shot by a strong archer? 8The Lord God sends calamities, and who will drive them away? 9Fire will go forth from his wrath, and who is there to quench it? 10He will flash lightning, and who will not be afraid? He will thunder, and who will not be terrified? 11The Lord will threaten, and who will not be utterly shattered at his presence? 12The earth and its foundations quake, the sea is churned up from the depths, and its waves and the fish with them shall be troubled at the presence of the Lord and the glory of his power. 13For his right hand that bends the bow is strong, and his arrows that he shoots are sharp and when they are shot to the ends of the world will not miss once. 14Calamities are sent forth and shall not return until they come over the earth. 15The fire is kindled, and shall not be put out until it consumes the foundations of the earth. 16Just as an arrow shot by a mighty archer does not return, so the calamities that are sent upon the earth shall not return. 17Alas for me! Alas for me! Who will deliver me in those days?

18 The beginning of sorrows, when there shall be much lamentation; the beginning of famine, when many shall perish; the beginning of wars, when the powers shall be terrified; the beginning of calamities, when all shall tremble. What shall they do, when the calamities come? 19Famine and plague, tribulation and anguish are sent as scourges for the correction of humankind. 20Yet for all this they will not turn from their iniquities, or ever be mindful of the scourges. 21Indeed, provisions will be so cheap upon earth that people will imagine that peace is assured for them, and then calamities shall spring up on the earth—the sword, famine, and great confusion. 22For many of those who live on the earth shall perish by famine; and those who survive the famine shall die by the sword. 23And the dead shall be thrown out like dung, and there shall be no one to console them; for the earth shall be left desolate, and its cities shall be demolished. 24No one shall be left to cultivate the earth or to sow it. 25The trees shall bear fruit, but who will gather it? 26The grapes shall ripen, but who will tread them? For in all places there shall be great solitude; 27a person will long to see another human being, or even to hear a human voice. 28For ten shall be left out of a city; and two, out of the field, those who have hidden themselves in thick groves and clefts in the

a Other ancient authorities read *fire when dry straw has been set on fire*

LATIN VULGATE

petrarum. 30 Quemadmodum relinquentur in oliveto tres vel
quattuor olivae, 31 aut sicut in vinea vindemiata et subre-
manet racemus patens ab scrutantibus vindemiam diligenter,
32 sic remanebunt in diebus illis tres vel quattuor ab scrutantibus domos eorum in romphea. 33 Et relinquetur deserta
terra, et agri eius inveteraverunt, et viae eius et omnes semi-
tae germinabunt spinas, eo quod non transient oves per eam.
34 Lugebunt virgines non habentes sponsos, lugebunt
mulieres non habentes viros, lugebunt filiae earum non
habentes adiutorium. 35 Sponsi earum in bello consumentur,
et viri earum in fame exterentur.

36 Audite vero ista et cognoscite ea, servi Domini. 37 Ecce
verbum Domini, excipite eum, ne discredatis de quibus dicit
Dominus: 38 Ecce adpropinquant mala et non tardantur.
39 Quemadmodum praegnans in nono mense filium suum in
adpropinquante hora partus eius, ante horas duas vel tres
gementes dolores circum ventrem eius, et prodiente infante
de ventre non tardabit uno puncto, 40 sic non morabuntur
mala ad prodiendum super terram, et saeculum gemet et
dolores circumtenent illum.

41 Audite verbum, plebs mea, parate vos ad pugnam in
malis. Sic estote quasi advenae terrae: 42 Qui vendit, quasi
qui fugiet; et qui emit, quasi qui perditurus; 43 qui mercatur,
quasi qui fructum non capiat; et qui aedificat, quasi non
habitaturus; 44 qui seminat, quasi non messem facturus; et
qui putat, quasi non vindemiaturus; 45 qui nubunt, sic quasi
filios non facturi; et qui non nubunt, sic quasi vidui.
46 Propter quod qui laborant sine causa laborant, 47 fructus
enim illorum alienigenae metent et substantiam illorum rapient et domos evertent et filios eorum captivabunt, quia in
captivitate et fame generant natos suos 48 et qui negotiantur
negotiantur in rapina. Quamdiu exornant civitates et domos
suas et possessiones et personas suas, 49 tanto magis adze-
labor eos super peccata, dicit Dominus. 50 Quomodo zelatur
fornicaria mulierem idoneam et bonam valde, 51 sic
zelabitur iustitia iniquitatem cum exornat se, et accusat eam
in faciem, cum venerit qui defendat exquirentem omnem pec-
catum super terram. 52 Propterea nolite similari eam nec
operibus eius, 53 quoniam ecce adhuc pusillum, et tolletur
iniquitas a terra et iustitia regnabit in nos. 54 Non dicat pec-
cator non se peccasse, quoniam carbones ignis conburet
super caput eius qui dicit: Non peccavi coram Deo et gloria
ipsius.

55 Ecce Dominus cognoscit omnia opera hominis et adinventiones illorum et cogitatum illorum et corda illorum.

KING JAMES VERSION

29 As in an orchard of olives upon every tree there are left three or four olives;

30 Or as when a vineyard is gathered, there are left some clusters of them that diligently seek through the vineyard:

31 Even so in those days there shall be three or four left by them that search their houses with the sword.

32 And the earth shall be laid waste, and the fields thereof shall wax old, and her ways and all her paths shall grow full of thorns, because no man shall travel therethrough.

33 The virgins shall mourn, having no bridegrooms; the women shall mourn, having no husbands; their daughters shall mourn, having no helpers.

34 In the wars shall their bridegrooms be destroyed, and their husbands shall perish of famine.

35 Hear now these things, and understand them, ye servants of the Lord.

36 Behold the word of the Lord, receive it: believe not the gods of whom the Lord spake.

37 Behold, the plagues draw nigh, and are not slack.

38 As when a woman with child in the ninth month bringeth forth her son, with two or three hours of her birth great pains compass her womb, which pains, when the child cometh forth, they slack not a moment:

39 Even so shall not the plagues be slack to come upon the earth, and the world shall mourn, and sorrows shall come upon it on every side.

40 O my people, hear my word: make you ready to the battle, and in those evils be even as pilgrims upon the earth.

41 He that selleth, let him be as he that fleeth away: and he that buyeth, as one that will lose:

42 He that occupieth merchandise, as he that hath no profit by it: and he that buildeth, as he that shall not dwell therein:

43 He that soweth, as if he should not reap: so also he that planteth the vineyard, as he that shall not gather the grapes:

44 They that marry, as they that shall get no children; and they that marry not, as the widowers.

45 And therefore they that labour labour in vain:

46 For strangers shall reap their fruits, and spoil their goods, overthrow their houses, and take their children captives, for in captivity and famine shall they get children.

47 And they that occupy their merchandise with robbery, the more they deck their cities, their houses, their possessions, and their own persons:

48 The more will I be angry with them for their sin, saith the Lord.

49 Like as a whore envieth a right honest and virtuous woman:

50 So shall righteousness hate iniquity, when she decketh herself, and shall accuse her to her face, when he cometh that shall defend him that diligently searcheth out every sin upon earth.

51 And therefore be ye not like thereunto, nor to the works thereof.

52 For yet a little, and iniquity shall be taken away out of the earth, and righteousness shall reign among you.

53 Let not the sinner say that he hath not sinned: for God shall burn coals of fire upon his head, which saith before the Lord God and his glory, I have not sinned.

54 Behold, the Lord knoweth all the works of men, their imaginations, their thoughts, and their hearts:

TODAY'S ENGLISH VERSION

is harvested, three or four olives may be left on each tree.
30 When grapes in a vineyard are picked, a few bunches may
be left even by those who look carefully. 31 That is how it
will be in those days. Three or four will be missed by the soldiers who search through the houses to kill everyone. 32 The
land will be left empty; the fields will be overgrown with
briers; the roads and paths will be covered with weeds and
thorns because there will be no sheep to graze along them.
33 Young women will be in mourning because there is no one
to marry them; wives will be in mourning because they have
lost their husbands; daughters will be in mourning because
there is no one to help them. 34 All the young men will be
killed in the war, and all the married men will die in the
famine.

35 Now listen to my message, you people who serve the
Lord. 36 It is the Lord's message, so receive it and believe
what he says. 37 The disasters are approaching rapidly, and
they will not be delayed. 38 A woman in the ninth month of
pregnancy may suffer labor pains for several hours, but
when the time comes for the baby to be born, there is no
longer any delay. 39 In the same way, the disasters that are
coming on the earth will not be delayed, and the world will
groan when it is caught in its labor pains.

40 Listen to my message, my people, and get ready for the
battle. When the disasters come, you must live as people
whose home is not in this world. 41-42 Merchants must not
expect to make a profit from what they sell; they must be
ready to run for their lives. Their customers must expect to
lose whatever they buy. Whoever builds a house should not
plan to live in it. 43 Farmers should not expect to harvest
their crops or pick their grapes. 44 Those who marry must
not expect to have children, and those who don't marry must
live as if they had been widowed. 45 Anything that is done
will be useless. 46 Foreigners will harvest the crops, seize the
wealth, tear down the houses, and carry off the children as
slaves. Anyone who has children will be bringing them up to
be slaves or to die of starvation. 47 Anyone who makes
money will do so only to see it violently taken away. The
more possessions people gather, the more they spend on
their cities and houses, the more attention they give to their
personal appearance, 48 the more angry the Lord will become
with them because of their sin. This is what the Lord says.
49 Just as a respectable woman despises a prostitute, 50 so
righteousness despises sinfulness, no matter how attractive
it may look. Righteousness will expose every sin in the world
and condemn it face-to-face when her Defender comes. 51 So
do not imitate sinfulness or what it does, 52 for in a very
short time sinfulness will be swept out of the world and righteousness will rule among us.

53 Sinners must not deny their sins. Those who say that
they have not sinned against God and his majesty are only
bringing fiery shame upon themselves. 54 The Lord certainly
knows everything that people do; he knows their plans and
innermost thoughts. 55 When the Lord said, "Let the world

NEW REVISED STANDARD VERSION

rocks. 29 Just as in an olive orchard three or four olives may
be left on every tree, 30 or just as, when a vineyard is gathered, some clusters may be left[a] by those who search carefully through the vineyard, 31 so in those days three or four
shall be left by those who search their houses with the
sword. 32 The earth shall be left desolate, and its fields shall
be plowed up,[b] and its roads and all its paths shall bring
forth thorns, because no sheep will go along them. 33 Virgins
shall mourn because they have no bridegrooms; women shall
mourn because they have no husbands; their daughters shall
mourn, because they have no help. 34 Their bridegrooms
shall be killed in war, and their husbands shall perish of
famine.

35 Listen now to these things, and understand them, you
who are servants of the Lord. 36 This is the word of the Lord;
receive it and do not disbelieve what the Lord says.[c] 37 The
calamities draw near, and are not delayed. 38 Just as a pregnant woman, in the ninth month when the time of her delivery draws near, has great pains around her womb for two or
three hours beforehand, but when the child comes forth from
the womb, there will not be a moment's delay, 39 so the
calamities will not delay in coming upon the earth, and the
world will groan, and pains will seize it on every side.

40 Hear my words, O my people; prepare for battle, and in
the midst of the calamities be like strangers on the earth.
41 Let the one who sells be like one who will flee; let the one
who buys be like one who will lose; 42 let the one who does
business be like one who will not make a profit; and let the
one who builds a house be like one who will not live in it;
43 let the one who sows be like one who will not reap; so also
the one who prunes the vines, like one who will not gather
the grapes; 44 those who marry, like those who will have no
children; and those who do not marry, like those who are
widowed. 45 Because of this, those who labor, labor in vain;
46 for strangers shall gather their fruits, and plunder their
goods, overthrow their houses, and take their children captive; for in captivity and famine they will produce their children.[d] 47 Those who conduct business, do so only to have it
plundered; the more they adorn their cities, their houses and
possessions, and their persons, 48 the more angry I will be
with them for their sins, says the Lord. 49 Just as a
respectable and virtuous woman abhors a prostitute, 50 so
righteousness shall abhor iniquity, when she decks herself
out, and shall accuse her to her face when he comes who will
defend the one who searches out every sin on earth.

51 Therefore do not be like her or her works. 52 For in a
very short time iniquity will be removed from the earth, and
righteousness will reign over us. 53 Sinners must not say
that they have not sinned;[e] for God[f] will burn coals of fire
on the head of everyone who says, "I have not sinned before
God and his glory." 54 The Lord[g] certainly knows everything
that people do; he knows their imaginations and their
thoughts and their hearts. 55 He said, "Let the earth be

a Other ancient authorities read *a cluster may remain exposed* *b* Other ancient authorities read *be for briers* *c* Cn: Lat *do not believe the gods of whom the Lord speaks* *d* Other ancient authorities read *therefore those who are married may know that they will produce children for captivity and famine* *e* Other ancient authorities add *or the unjust done injustice* *f* Lat *for he* *g* Other ancient authorities read *Lord God*

LATIN VULGATE

56 Qui dixit: Fiat terra, et facta est, fiat caelum, et factum est,
57 et in verbo illius stellae fundatae sunt, et novit numerum
stellarum, 58 qui scrutat abyssum et thesauros illorum, qui
metitus est mare et conceptum eius, 59 qui conclusit mare in
medio aquarum et suspendit terram super aquam verbo suo,
60 qui extendit caelum quasi cameram et super aquas fun-
davit eum, 61 qui posuit in deserto fontes aquarum et super
vertices montium lacus ad emittendum flumina ab eminenti
ut potaret terra, 62 qui finxit hominem et posuit cor in medio
corporis et misit ei spiritum et vitam et intellectum 63 et spiramentum Dei omnipotentis, qui fecit omnia et scrutinat
absconsa in absconsis; certe 64 hic novit adinventionem ves-
tram et quae cogitatis in cordibus vestris.

Vae peccantibus et volentibus occultare peccata sua.
65 Propter quod Dominus scrutinando scrutinabit omnia
opera eorum et traducet vos omnes. 66 Et vos confusi eritis,
cum processerint peccata vestra coram hominibus, et iniquitates erint quae accusatores stabunt in die illo. 67 Quid faci-
etis aut quomodo abscondetis peccata vestra coram Domino
et gloria eius? 68 Ecce iudex Deus, timete eum, et desinite a
peccatis vestris et obliviscimini iniquitates vestras iam agere
eas sempiterno, et Deus educabit vos et liberabit de omni
tribulatione. 69 Ecce enim incenditur ardor super vos turbae
copiosae, et rapient quosdam ex vobis et cibabunt idolis
occisam. 70 Et qui consenserint eis, erunt illis in derisum et
in inproperium et in conculcationem. 71 Erit enim Lociis et
in vicinas civitates exsurrectio multa super timentes
Dominum. 72 Erunt quasi insani neminem parcentes ad
diripiendum et devastandum adhuc timentes Dominum,
73 quia devastabunt et diripient substantias eorum et de
domo sua eos eicient,

74 Tunc parebit probatio electorum meorum, ut aurum
quod probatur ab igne. 75 Audite, electi mei, dicit Dominus,
ecce adsunt dies tribulationis, et de his liberabo vos. 76 Ne
timeatis nec haesitemini, quoniam Deus dux vester est. 77 Et
qui servatis mandata et praecepta mea, dicit Dominus Deus,
ne praeponderent vos peccata vestra nec superelevent se
iniquitates vestrae. 78 Vae qui constringuntur a peccatis suis
et obteguntur ab iniquitatibus suis, quemadmodum ager con-
stringitur a silva et spinis tegitur semita eius, per quam non
transiet homo, et excluditur et mittitur ad devorationem
ignis.

KING JAMES VERSION

55 Which spake but the word, Let the earth be made; and it was made: Let the heaven be made; and it was created.

56 In his word were the stars made, and he knoweth the number of them.

57 He searcheth the deep, and the treasures thereof; he hath measured the sea, and what it containeth.

58 He hath shut the sea in the midst of the waters, and with his word hath he hanged the earth upon the waters.

59 He spreadeth out the heavens like a vault; upon the waters hath he founded it.

60 In the desert hath he made springs of water, and pools upon the tops of the mountains, that the floods might pour down from the high rocks to water the earth.

61 He made man, and put his heart in the midst of the body, and gave him breath, life, and understanding.

62 Yea, and the Spirit of Almighty God, which made all things, and searcheth out all hidden things in the secrets of the earth,

63 Surely he knoweth your inventions, and what ye think in your hearts, even them that sin, and would hide their sin.

64 Therefore hath the Lord exactly searched out all your works, and he will put you all to shame.

65 And when your sins are brought forth, ye shall be ashamed before men, and your own sins shall be your accusers in that day.

66 What will ye do? or how will ye hide your sins before God and his angels?

67 Behold, God himself is the judge, fear him: leave off from your sins, and forget your iniquities, to meddle no more with them for ever: so shall God lead you forth, and deliver you from all trouble.

68 For, behold, the burning wrath of a great multitude is kindled over you, and they shall take away certain of you, and feed you, being idle, with things offered unto idols.

69 And they that consent unto them shall be had in derision and in reproach, and trodden under foot.

70 For there shall be in every place, and in the next cities, a great insurrection upon those that fear the Lord.

71 They shall be like mad men, sparing none, but still spoiling and destroying those that fear the Lord.

72 For they shall waste and take away their goods, and cast them out of their houses.

73 Then shall they be known, who are my chosen; and they shall be tried as the gold in the fire.

74 Hear, O ye my beloved, saith the Lord: behold, the days of trouble are at hand, but I will deliver you from the same.

75 Be ye not afraid, neither doubt; for God is your guide,

76 And the guide of them who keep my commandments and precepts, saith the Lord God: let not your sins weigh you down, and let not your iniquities lift up themselves.

77 Woe be unto them that are bound with their sins, and covered with their iniquities, like as a field is covered over with bushes, and the path thereof covered with thorns, that no man may travel through!

78 It is left undressed, and is cast into the fire to be consumed therewith.

TODAY'S ENGLISH VERSION

be created," it was done! When he said, "Let the sky be created," that was done too. 56 He set the stars in place by his
command, and he knows how many of them there are. 57 He
knows what is in the deepest part of the sea and the treasures that are there. He has measured the sea and everything
that is in it. 58 By his word he confined the sea to its place
and put the land on top of the water. 59 The Lord stretched
out the sky and fixed it firmly over the water like a dome.
60 He put springs of water in the desert and lakes in the high
mountains, so that water could flow down in the rivers and
water the land. 61 The Lord created human beings and gave
each one of them a heart. He gave them life, breath, and
understanding, 62 which is the spirit of God the Almighty,
who created everything and who knows all secrets and sees
into all hidden places. 63 My people, the Lord knows everything you plan and the secret thoughts of your heart. Sinners
who try to hide their sins are doomed. 64 The Lord will carefully examine everything you have done and bring you to
judgment. 65 On that day you will be thrown into utter confusion; all your sins will be publicly exposed and the wicked
things you have done will witness against you. 66 What will
you do then? How will you hide your sins from God and his
angels? 67 God is your judge, so fear him! Abandon your
sins, put away the evil you have done, and never sin again.
Then God will save you from all these disasters.

68 A vast mob of people is ready now to descend on you
and devour you like flames. They will drag some of you off
and force you to eat pagan sacrifices. 69 If you give in to
them, they will ridicule you, mock you, and humiliate you.
70 In many places near the cities[a] there will be violent persecution against those who fear the Lord. 71 The attackers will
act like wild people; they will plunder and destroy without
pity all those who still fear the Lord. 72 They will turn them
out of their homes and take away all their possessions.
73 This will be the time of testing for my chosen people, and
they will prove to be as pure as refined gold.

74 But listen to what the Lord says: "My chosen people, the
time of terrible suffering is near, but I will rescue you.
75 Don't be afraid or have any doubts; I am your God and I
will lead you. 76 If you keep my laws and commands," says
the Lord, "you must not let your sins weigh you down or
control you. 77 Those who are chained by their sins, overwhelmed by the evil they have done, are doomed. They will
be like a field overgrown with brush, with the path across it
so choked with thorns that no one can get through. 78 It is
abandoned and doomed to be destroyed by fire."

[a] In . . . cities; *Latin unclear.*

NEW REVISED STANDARD VERSION

made," and it was made, and "Let the heaven be made," and
it was made. 56 At his word the stars were fixed in their
places, and he knows the number of the stars. 57 He searches
the abyss and its treasures; he has measured the sea and its
contents; 58 he has confined the sea in the midst of the
waters;[a] and by his word he has suspended the earth over
the water. 59 He has spread out the heaven like a dome and
made it secure upon the waters; 60 he has put springs of
water in the desert, and pools on the tops of the mountains,
so as to send rivers from the heights to water the earth.
61 He formed human beings and put a heart in the midst of
each body, and gave each person breath and life and understanding 62 and the spirit[b] of Almighty God,[c] who surely
made all things and searches out hidden things in hidden
places. 63 He knows your imaginations and what you think
in your hearts! Woe to those who sin and want to hide their
sins! 64 The Lord will strictly examine all their works, and
will make a public spectacle of all of you. 65 You shall be put
to shame when your sins come out before others, and your
own iniquities shall stand as your accusers on that day.
66 What will you do? Or how will you hide your sins before
the Lord and his glory? 67 Indeed, God[d] is the judge; fear
him! Cease from your sins, and forget your iniquities, never
to commit them again; so God[d] will lead you forth and deliver you from all tribulation.

68 The burning wrath of a great multitude is kindled over
you; they shall drag some of you away and force you to eat
what was sacrificed to idols. 69 And those who consent to eat
shall be held in derision and contempt, and shall be trampled
under foot. 70 For in many places[e] and in neighboring cities
there shall be a great uprising against those who fear the
Lord. 71 They shall[f] be like maniacs, sparing no one, but
plundering and destroying those who continue to fear the
Lord.[g] 72 For they shall destroy and plunder their goods, and
drive them out of house and home. 73 Then the tested quality
of my elect shall be manifest, like gold that is tested by fire.

74 Listen, my elect ones, says the Lord; the days of tribulation are at hand, but I will deliver you from them. 75 Do
not fear or doubt, for God[d] is your guide. 76 You who keep
my commandments and precepts, says the Lord God, must
not let your sins weigh you down, or your iniquities prevail
over you. 77 Woe to those who are choked by their sins and
overwhelmed by their iniquities! They are like a field choked
with underbrush and its path[h] overwhelmed with thorns, so
that no one can pass through. 78 It is shut off and given up
to be consumed by fire.

a Other ancient authorities read *confined the world between the waters and the waters* *b* Or *breath* *c* Other ancient authorities read *of the Lord Almighty* *d* Other ancient authorities read *the Lord* *e* Meaning of Lat uncertain *f* Other ancient authorities read *For people, because of their misfortunes, shall* *g* Other ancient authorities read *fear God* *h* Other ancient authorities read *seed*

GREEK OLD TESTAMENT

Fourth Maccabees is included only in the Greek Old Testament and New Revised Standard Version.

ΜΑΚΚΑΒΑΙΩΝ Δ´

1 Φιλοσοφώτατον λόγον ἐπιδείκνυσθαι μέλλων, εἰ αὐτοδέσποτός ἐστιν τῶν παθῶν ὁ εὐσεβὴς λογισμός, συμβουλεύσαιμ᾽ ἂν ὑμῖν ὀρθῶς ὅπως προσέχητε προθύμως τῇ φιλοσοφίᾳ. 2 καὶ γὰρ ἀναγκαῖος εἰς ἐπιστήμην παντὶ ὁ λόγος καὶ ἄλλως τῆς μεγίστης ἀρετῆς, λέγω δὴ φρονήσεως, περιέχει ἔπαινον. 3 εἰ ἄρα τῶν σωφροσύνης κωλυτικῶν παθῶν ὁ λογισμὸς φαίνεται ἐπικρατεῖν, γαστριμαργίας τε καὶ ἐπιθυμίας, 4 ἀλλὰ καὶ τῶν τῆς δικαιοσύνης ἐμποδιστικῶν παθῶν κυριεύειν ἀναφαίνεται, οἷον κακοηθείας, καὶ τῶν τῆς ἀνδρείας ἐμποδιστικῶν παθῶν, θυμοῦ τε καὶ φόβου καὶ πόνου. 5 πῶς οὖν, ἴσως εἴποιεν ἄν τινες, εἰ τῶν παθῶν ὁ λογισμὸς κρατεῖ, λήθης καὶ ἀγνοίας οὐ δεσπόζει; γελοῖον ἐπιχειροῦντες λέγειν. 6 οὐ γὰρ τῶν αὐτοῦ παθῶν ὁ λογισμὸς κρατεῖ, ἀλλὰ τῶν τῆς δικαιοσύνης καὶ ἀνδρείας καὶ σωφροσύνης ἐναντίων, καὶ τούτων οὐχ ὥστε αὐτὰ καταλῦσαι, ἀλλ᾽ ὥστε αὐτοῖς μὴ εἶξαι. 7 πολλαχόθεν μὲν οὖν καὶ ἀλλαχόθεν ἔχοιμ᾽ ἂν ὑμῖν ἐπιδεῖξαι ὅτι αὐτοκράτωρ ἐστὶν τῶν παθῶν ὁ λογισμός, 8 πολὺ δὲ πλέον τοῦτο ἀποδείξαιμι ἀπὸ τῆς ἀνδραγαθίας τῶν ὑπὲρ ἀρετῆς ἀποθανόντων, Ελεαζαρου τε καὶ τῶν ἑπτὰ ἀδελφῶν καὶ τῆς τούτων μητρός. 9 ἅπαντες γὰρ οὗτοι τοὺς ἕως θανάτου πόνους ὑπεριδόντες ἐπεδείξαντο ὅτι περικρατεῖ τῶν παθῶν ὁ λογισμός. 10 τῶν μὲν οὖν ἀρετῶν ἔπεστί μοι ἐπαινεῖν τοὺς κατὰ τοῦτον τὸν καιρὸν ὑπὲρ τῆς καλοκἀγαθίας ἀποθανόντας μετὰ τῆς μητρὸς ἄνδρας, τῶν δὲ τιμῶν μακαρίσαιμ᾽ ἄν. 11 θαυμασθέντες γὰρ οὐ μόνον ὑπὸ πάντων ἀνθρώπων ἐπὶ τῇ ἀνδρείᾳ καὶ ὑπομονῇ, ἀλλὰ καὶ ὑπὸ τῶν αἰκισαμένων, αἴτιοι κατέστησαν τοῦ καταλυθῆναι τὴν κατὰ τοῦ ἔθνους τυραννίδα νικήσαντες τὸν τύραννον τῇ ὑπομονῇ ὥστε καθαρισθῆναι δι᾽ αὐτῶν τὴν πατρίδα. 12 ἀλλὰ καὶ περὶ τούτου νῦν αὐτίκα δὴ λέγειν ἐξέσται ἀρξαμένῳ τῆς ὑποθέσεως, ὅπερ εἴωθα ποιεῖν, καὶ οὕτως εἰς τὸν περὶ αὐτῶν τρέψομαι λόγον δόξαν διδοὺς τῷ πανσόφῳ θεῷ.

13 Ζητοῦμεν δὴ τοίνυν εἰ αὐτοκράτωρ ἐστὶν τῶν παθῶν ὁ λογισμός. 14 διακρίνομεν τί ποτέ ἐστιν λογισμὸς καὶ τί πάθος, καὶ πόσαι παθῶν ἰδέαι, καὶ εἰ πάντων ἐπικρατεῖ τούτων ὁ λογισμός. 15 λογισμὸς μὲν δὴ τοίνυν ἐστὶν νοῦς μετὰ ὀρθοῦ λόγου προτιμῶν τὸν σοφίας βίον. 16 σοφία δὴ τοίνυν ἐστὶν γνῶσις θείων καὶ ἀνθρωπίνων πραγμάτων καὶ τῶν τούτων αἰτιῶν. 17 αὕτη δὴ τοίνυν ἐστὶν ἡ τοῦ νόμου παιδεία, δι᾽ ἧς τὰ θεῖα σεμνῶς καὶ τὰ ἀνθρώπινα συμφερόντως μανθάνομεν. 18 τῆς δὲ σοφίας ἰδέαι καθεστήκασιν φρόνησις καὶ δικαιοσύνη καὶ ἀνδρεία καὶ σωφροσύνη· 19 κυριωτάτη δὲ πάντων ἡ φρόνησις, ἐξ ἧς δὴ τῶν παθῶν ὁ λογισμὸς ἐπικρατεῖ. 20 παθῶν δὲ φύσεις εἰσὶν αἱ περιεκτικώταται δύο ἡδονή τε καὶ πόνος. τούτων δὲ ἑκάτερον καὶ περὶ τὸ σῶμα καὶ περὶ τὴν ψυχὴν πέφυκεν. 21 πολλαὶ δὲ καὶ περὶ τὴν ἡδονὴν καὶ τὸν πόνον παθῶν εἰσιν ἀκολουθίαι. 22 πρὸ μὲν οὖν τῆς ἡδονῆς ἐστιν ἐπιθυμία, μετὰ δὲ τὴν ἡδονὴν χαρά. 23 πρὸ δὲ τοῦ πόνου ἐστὶν φόβος, μετὰ δὲ τὸν πόνον λύπη. 24 θυμὸς δὲ

NEW REVISED STANDARD VERSION

(d) The following book appears in an appendix to the Greek Bible.

Fourth Maccabees is included only in the Greek Old Testament and New Revised Standard Version.

4 MACCABEES

1 The subject that I am about to discuss is most philosophical, that is, whether devout reason is sovereign over the emotions. So it is right for me to advise you to pay earnest attention to philosophy. 2 For the subject is essential to everyone who is seeking knowledge, and in addition it includes the praise of the highest virtue—I mean, of course, rational judgment. 3 If, then, it is evident that reason rules over those emotions that hinder self-control, namely, gluttony and lust, 4 it is also clear that it masters the emotions that hinder one from justice, such as malice, and those that stand in the way of courage, namely anger, fear, and pain. 5 Some might perhaps ask, "If reason rules the emotions, why is it not sovereign over forgetfulness and ignorance?" Their attempt at argument is ridiculous![a] 6 For reason does not rule its own emotions, but those that are opposed to justice, courage, and self-control;[b] and it is not for the purpose of destroying them, but so that one may not give way to them.

7 I could prove to you from many and various examples that reason[c] is dominant over the emotions, 8 but I can demonstrate it best from the noble bravery of those who died for the sake of virtue, Eleazar and the seven brothers and their mother. 9 All of these, by despising sufferings that bring death, demonstrated that reason controls the emotions. 10 On this anniversary[d] it is fitting for me to praise for their virtues those who, with their mother, died for the sake of nobility and goodness, but I would also call them blessed for the honor in which they are held. 11 All people, even their torturers, marveled at their courage and endurance, and they became the cause of the downfall of tyranny over their nation. By their endurance they conquered the tyrant, and thus their native land was purified through them. 12 I shall shortly have an opportunity to speak of this; but, as my custom is, I shall begin by stating my main principle, and then I shall turn to their story, giving glory to the all-wise God.

13 Our inquiry, accordingly, is whether reason is sovereign over the emotions. 14 We shall decide just what reason is and what emotion is, how many kinds of emotions there are, and whether reason rules over all these. 15 Now reason is the mind that with sound logic prefers the life of wisdom. 16 Wisdom, next, is the knowledge of divine and human matters and the causes of these. 17 This, in turn, is education in the law, by which we learn divine matters reverently and human affairs to our advantage. 18 Now the kinds of wisdom are rational judgment, justice, courage, and self-control. 19 Rational judgment is supreme over all of these, since by means of it reason rules over the emotions. 20 The two most comprehensive types[e] of the emotions are pleasure and pain; and each of these is by nature concerned with both body and soul. 21 The emotions of both pleasure and pain have many consequences. 22 Thus desire precedes pleasure and delight follows it. 23 Fear precedes pain and sorrow comes after.

a Or *They are attempting to make my argument ridiculous!* *b* Other ancient authorities add *and rational judgment* *c* Other ancient authorities read *devout reason* *d* Gk *At this time* *e* Or *sources*

GREEK OLD TESTAMENT

κοινὸν πάθος ἐστὶν ἡδονῆς καὶ πόνου, ἐὰν ἐννοηθῇ τις ὅτι
αὐτῷ περιέπεσεν. 25 ἐν τῇ ἡδονῇ δὲ ἔνεστιν καὶ ἡ κακοήθης
διάθεσις, πολυτροπωτάτη πάντων οὖσα τῶν παθῶν, 26 καὶ τὰ
μὲν ψυχῆς ἀλαζονεία καὶ φιλαργυρία καὶ φιλοδοξία καὶ
φιλονεικία καὶ βασκανία, 27 κατὰ δὲ τὸ σῶμα παντοφαγία
καὶ λαιμαργία καὶ μονοφαγία. 28 καθάπερ οὖν δυεῖν τοῦ σώματος καὶ τῆς ψυχῆς φυτῶν ὄντων ἡδονῆς τε καὶ πόνου πολλαὶ τούτων τῶν φυτῶν εἰσιν παραφυάδες, 29 ὧν ἑκάστην ὁ
παγγέωργος λογισμὸς περικαθαίρων καὶ ἀποκνίζων καὶ
περιπλέκων καὶ ἐπάρδων καὶ πάντα τρόπον μεταχέων ἐξη-
μεροῖ τὰς τῶν ἠθῶν καὶ παθῶν ὕλας. 30 ὁ γὰρ λογισμὸς τῶν
μὲν ἀρετῶν ἐστιν ἡγεμών, τῶν δὲ παθῶν αὐτοκράτωρ.

Ἐπιθεωρεῖτε τοίνυν πρῶτον διὰ τῶν κωλυτικῶν τῆς
σωφροσύνης ἔργων ὅτι αὐτοδέσποτός ἐστιν τῶν παθῶν ὁ
λογισμός. 31 σωφροσύνη δὴ τοίνυν ἐστὶν ἐπικράτεια τῶν
ἐπιθυμιῶν, 32 τῶν δὲ ἐπιθυμιῶν αἱ μέν εἰσιν ψυχικαί, αἱ δὲ
σωματικαί, καὶ τούτων ἀμφοτέρων ἐπικρατεῖν ὁ λογισμὸς
φαίνεται. 33 ἐπεὶ πόθεν κινούμενοι πρὸς τὰς ἀπειρημένας
τροφὰς ἀποστρεφόμεθα τὰς ἐξ αὐτῶν ἡδονάς; οὐχ ὅτι δύναται τῶν ὀρέξεων ἐπικρατεῖν ὁ λογισμός; ἐγὼ μὲν οἶμαι.
34 τοιγαροῦν ἐνύδρων ἐπιθυμοῦντες καὶ ὀρνέων καὶ τετραπόδων καὶ παντοίων βρωμάτων τῶν ἀπηγορευμένων ἡμῖν
κατὰ τὸν νόμον ἀπεχόμεθα διὰ τὴν τοῦ λογισμοῦ ἐπικρά-
τειαν. 35 ἀνέχεται γὰρ τὰ τῶν ὀρέξεων πάθη ὑπὸ τοῦ σώφρονος νοὸς ἀνακοπτόμενα, καὶ φιμοῦται πάντα τὰ τοῦ σώματος κινήματα ὑπὸ τοῦ λογισμοῦ.

2 Καὶ τί θαυμαστόν, εἰ αἱ τῆς ψυχῆς ἐπιθυμίαι πρὸς τὴν
τοῦ κάλλους μετουσίαν ἀκυροῦνται; 2 ταύτῃ γοῦν ὁ σώφρων Ιωσηφ ἐπαινεῖται, ὅτι διανοίᾳ περιεκράτησεν τῆς
ἡδυπαθείας. 3 νέος γὰρ ὢν καὶ ἀκμάζων πρὸς συνουσιασμὸν
ἠκύρωσε τῷ λογισμῷ τὸν τῶν παθῶν οἶστρον. 4 καὶ οὐ μόνον
δὲ τὴν τῆς ἡδυπαθείας οἰστρηλασίαν ὁ λογισμὸς ἐπικρατεῖν
φαίνεται, ἀλλὰ καὶ πάσης ἐπιθυμίας. 5 λέγει γοῦν ὁ νόμος
Οὐκ ἐπιθυμήσεις τὴν γυναῖκα τοῦ πλησίον σου οὐδὲ ὅσα τῷ
πλησίον σού ἐστιν. 6 καίτοι ὅτε μὴ ἐπιθυμεῖν εἴρηκεν ἡμᾶς
ὁ νόμος, πολὺ πλέον πείσαιμ' ἂν ὑμᾶς ὅτι τῶν ἐπιθυμιῶν
κρατεῖν δύναται ὁ λογισμός.

Ὥσπερ καὶ τῶν κωλυτικῶν τῆς δικαιοσύνης παθῶν· 7 ἐπεὶ
τίνα τις τρόπον μονοφάγος ὢν τὸ ἦθος καὶ γαστρίμαργος ἢ
καὶ μέθυσος μεταπαιδεύεται, εἰ μὴ δῆλον ὅτι κύριός ἐστιν
τῶν παθῶν ὁ λογισμός; 8 αὐτίκα γοῦν τῷ νόμῳ πολιτευόμενος, κἂν φιλάργυρός τις ᾖ, βιάζεται τὸν αὑτοῦ τρόπον
τοῖς δεομένοις δανείζων χωρὶς τόκων καὶ τὸ δάνειον τῶν
ἑβδομάδων ἐνστασῶν χρεοκοπούμενος. 9 κἂν φειδωλός τις ᾖ,
ὑπὸ τοῦ νόμου κρατεῖται διὰ τὸν λογισμὸν μήτε ἐπικαρπο-
λογούμενος τοὺς ἀμητοὺς μήτε ἐπιρρωγολογούμενος τοὺς
ἀμπελῶνας.

Καὶ ἐπὶ τῶν ἑτέρων δὲ ἔστιν ἐπιγνῶναι τοῦτο, ὅτι τῶν
παθῶν ἐστιν ὁ λογισμὸς κρατῶν· 10 ὁ γὰρ νόμος καὶ τῆς
πρὸς γονεῖς εὐνοίας κρατεῖ μὴ καταπροδιδοὺς τὴν ἀρετὴν
δι' αὐτοὺς 11 καὶ τῆς πρὸς γαμετὴν φιλίας ἐπικρατεῖ διὰ
τὴν παρανομίαν αὐτὴν ἀπελέγχων 12 καὶ τῆς τέκνων φιλίας
κυριεύει διὰ κακίαν αὐτὰ κολάζων 13 καὶ τῆς φίλων συνηθείας δεσπόζει διὰ πονηρίαν αὐτοὺς ἐξελέγχων. 14 καὶ μὴ
νομίσητε παράδοξον εἶναι, ὅπου καὶ ἔχθρας ἐπικρατεῖν ὁ
λογισμὸς δύναται διὰ τὸν νόμον μήτε δενδροτομῶν τὰ

NEW REVISED STANDARD VERSION

24 Anger, as a person will see by reflecting on this experience,
is an emotion embracing pleasure and pain. 25 In pleasure
there exists even a malevolent tendency, which is the most
complex of all the emotions. 26 In the soul it is boastfulness,
covetousness, thirst for honor, rivalry, and malice; 27 in the
body, indiscriminate eating, gluttony, and solitary gorman-
dizing.

28 Just as pleasure and pain are two plants growing from
the body and the soul, so there are many offshoots of these
plants,[a] 29 each of which the master cultivator, reason,
weeds and prunes and ties up and waters and thoroughly
irrigates, and so tames the jungle of habits and emotions.
30 For reason is the guide of the virtues, but over the emotions it is sovereign.

Observe now, first of all, that rational judgment is sovereign over the emotions by virtue of the restraining power of
self-control. 31 Self-control, then, is dominance over the
desires. 32 Some desires are mental, others are physical, and
reason obviously rules over both. 33 Otherwise, how is it that
when we are attracted to forbidden foods we abstain from
the pleasure to be had from them? Is it not because reason is
able to rule over appetites? I for one think so. 34 Therefore
when we crave seafood and fowl and animals and all sorts of
foods that are forbidden to us by the law, we abstain because
of domination by reason. 35 For the emotions of the appetites
are restrained, checked by the temperate mind, and all the
impulses of the body are bridled by reason.

2 And why is it amazing that the desires of the mind for
the enjoyment of beauty are rendered powerless? 2 It is
for this reason, certainly, that the temperate Joseph is
praised, because by mental effort[b] he overcame sexual
desire. 3 For when he was young and in his prime for intercourse, by his reason he nullified the frenzy[c] of the passions.
4 Not only is reason proved to rule over the frenzied urge of
sexual desire, but also over every desire.[d] 5 Thus the law
says, "You shall not covet your neighbor's wife or anything
that is your neighbor's." 6 In fact, since the law has told us
not to covet, I could prove to you all the more that reason is
able to control desires.

Just so it is with the emotions that hinder one from justice.
7 Otherwise how could it be that someone who is habitually a
solitary gormandizer, a glutton, or even a drunkard can learn
a better way, unless reason is clearly lord of the emotions?
8 Thus, as soon as one adopts a way of life in accordance
with the law, even though a lover of money, one is forced to
act contrary to natural ways and to lend without interest to
the needy and to cancel the debt when the seventh year
arrives. 9 If one is greedy, one is ruled by the law through
reason so that one neither gleans the harvest nor gathers the
last grapes from the vineyard.

In all other matters we can recognize that reason rules the
emotions. 10 For the law prevails even over affection for parents, so that virtue is not abandoned for their sakes. 11 It is
superior to love for one's wife, so that one rebukes her when
she breaks the law. 12 It takes precedence over love for children, so that one punishes them for misdeeds. 13 It is sovereign over the relationship of friends, so that one rebukes
friends when they act wickedly. 14 Do not consider it para-
doxical when reason, through the law, can prevail even over

a Other ancient authorities read *these emotions* *b* Other ancient
authorities add *in reasoning* *c* Or *gadfly* *d* Or *all covetousness*

ἥμερα τῶν πολεμίων φυτά, τὰ δὲ τῶν ἐχθρῶν τοῖς ἀπολέσασι διασῴζων καὶ τὰ πεπτωκότα συνεγείρων.

15 Καὶ τῶν βιαιοτέρων δὲ παθῶν κρατεῖν ὁ λογισμὸς φαίνεται, φιλαρχίας καὶ κενοδοξίας καὶ ἀλαζονείας καὶ μεγαλαυχίας καὶ βασκανίας. 16 πάντα γὰρ ταῦτα τὰ κακοήθη πάθη ὁ σώφρων νοῦς ἀπωθεῖται, ὥσπερ καὶ τὸν θυμόν· καὶ γὰρ τούτου δεσπόζει. 17 θυμούμενός γέ τοι Μωυσῆς κατὰ Δαθαν καὶ Αβιρων οὐ θυμῷ τι κατ' αὐτῶν ἐποίησεν, ἀλλὰ λογισμῷ τὸν θυμὸν διῄτησεν. 18 δυνατὸς γὰρ ὁ σώφρων νοῦς, ὡς ἔφην, κατὰ τῶν παθῶν ἀριστεῦσαι καὶ τὰ μὲν αὐτῶν μεταθεῖναι, τὰ δὲ καὶ ἀκυρῶσαι. 19 ἐπεὶ διὰ τί ὁ πάνσοφος ἡμῶν πατὴρ Ιακωβ τοὺς περὶ Συμεων καὶ Λευιν αἰτιᾶται μὴ λογισμῷ τοὺς Σικιμίτας ἐθνηδὸν ἀποσφάξαντας λέγων Ἐπικατάρατος ὁ θυμὸς αὐτῶν; 20 εἰ μὴ γὰρ ἐδύνατο τοῦ θυμοῦ ὁ λογισμὸς κρατεῖν, οὐκ ἂν εἶπεν οὕτως. 21 ὁπηνίκα γὰρ ὁ θεὸς τὸν ἄνθρωπον κατεσκεύασεν, τὰ πάθη αὐτοῦ καὶ τὰ ἤθη περιεφύτευσεν· 22 ἡνίκα δὲ ἐπὶ πάντων τὸν ἱερὸν ἡγεμόνα νοῦν διὰ τῶν αἰσθητηρίων ἐνεθρόνισεν, 23 καὶ τούτῳ νόμον ἔδωκεν, καθ' ὃν πολιτευόμενος βασιλεύσει βασιλείαν σώφρονά τε καὶ δικαίαν καὶ ἀγαθὴν καὶ ἀνδρείαν.

24 Πῶς οὖν, εἴποι τις ἄν, εἰ τῶν παθῶν δεσπότης ἐστὶν ὁ

3 λογισμός, λήθης καὶ ἀγνοίας οὐ κρατεῖ; 1 ἔστιν δὲ κομιδῇ γελοῖος ὁ λόγος. οὐ γὰρ τῶν ἑαυτοῦ παθῶν ὁ λογισμὸς ἐπικρατεῖν φαίνεται, ἀλλὰ τῶν σωματικῶν. 2 οἷον ἐπιθυμίαν τις οὐ δύναται ἐκκόψαι ἡμῶν, ἀλλὰ μὴ δουλωθῆναι τῇ ἐπιθυμίᾳ δύναται ὁ λογισμὸς παρασχέσθαι. 3 θυμόν τις οὐ δύναται ἐκκόψαι ὑμῶν τῆς ψυχῆς, ἀλλὰ τῷ θυμῷ δυνατὸν τὸν λογισμὸν βοηθῆσαι. 4 κακοήθειάν τις ἡμῶν οὐ δύναται ἐκκόψαι, ἀλλὰ τὸ μὴ καμφθῆναι τῇ κακοηθείᾳ δύναιτ' ἂν ὁ λογισμὸς συμμαχῆσαι· 5 οὐ γὰρ ἐκριζωτὴς τῶν παθῶν ὁ λογισμός ἐστιν, ἀλλὰ ἀνταγωνιστής.

6 Ἔστιν γοῦν τοῦτο διὰ τῆς Δαυιδ τοῦ βασιλέως δίψης σαφέστερον ἐπιλογίσασθαι. 7 ἐπεὶ γὰρ δι' ὅλης ἡμέρας προσβαλὼν τοῖς ἀλλοφύλοις ὁ Δαυιδ πολλοὺς αὐτῶν ἀπέκτεινεν μετὰ τῶν τοῦ ἔθνους στρατιωτῶν, 8 τότε δὴ γενομένης ἑσπέρας ἱδρῶν καὶ σφόδρα κεκμηκὼς ἐπὶ τὴν βασίλειον σκηνὴν ἦλθεν, περὶ ἣν ὁ πᾶς τῶν προγόνων στρατὸς ἐστρατοπεδεύκει. 9 οἱ μὲν οὖν ἄλλοι πάντες ἐπὶ τὸ δεῖπνον ἦσαν, 10 ὁ δὲ βασιλεὺς ὡς μάλιστα διψῶν, καίπερ ἀφθόνους ἔχων πηγάς, οὐκ ἠδύνατο δι' αὐτῶν ἰάσασθαι τὴν δίψαν, 11 ἀλλά τις αὐτὸν ἀλόγιστος ἐπιθυμία τοῦ παρὰ τοῖς πολεμίοις ὕδατος ἐπιτείνουσα συνέφρυγεν καὶ λύουσα κατέφλεγεν. 12 ὅθεν τῶν ὑπασπιστῶν ἐπὶ τῇ τοῦ βασιλέως ἐπιθυμίᾳ σχετλιαζόντων δύο νεανίσκοι στρατιῶται καρτεροὶ καταιδεσθέντες τὴν τοῦ βασιλέως ἐπιθυμίαν τὰς παντευχίας καθωπλίσαντο καὶ κάλπην λαβόντες ὑπερέβησαν τοὺς τῶν πολεμίων χάρακας 13 καὶ λαθόντες τοὺς τῶν πυλῶν ἀκροφύλακας διεξῄεσαν ἀνερευνώμενοι κατὰ πᾶν τὸ τῶν πολεμίων στρατόπεδον 14 καὶ ἀνευράμενοι τὴν πηγὴν ἐξ αὐτῆς θαρραλέως ἐκόμισαν τῷ βασιλεῖ τὸ ποτόν· 15 ὁ δὲ καίπερ τῇ δίψῃ διαπυρούμενος ἐλογίσατο πάνδεινον εἶναι κίνδυνον ψυχῇ λογισθὲν ἰσοδύναμον ποτὸν αἵματι, 16 ὅθεν ἀντιθεὶς τῇ ἐπιθυμίᾳ τὸν λογισμὸν ἔσπεισεν τὸ πόμα τῷ θεῷ. 17 δυνατὸς γὰρ ὁ σώφρων νοῦς νικῆσαι τὰς τῶν παθῶν ἀνάγκας καὶ σβέσαι τὰς τῶν οἴστρων φλεγμονὰς 18 καὶ τὰς τῶν σωμάτων ἀλγηδόνας καθ' ὑπερβολὴν οὔσας καταπαλαῖσαι καὶ τῇ καλοκἀγαθίᾳ τοῦ λογισμοῦ ἀποπτύσαι πάσας τὰς τῶν παθῶν ἐπικρατείας.

enmity. The fruit trees of the enemy are not cut down, but one preserves the property of enemies from marauders and helps raise up what has fallen.[a]

15 It is evident that reason rules even[b] the more violent emotions: lust for power, vainglory, boasting, arrogance, and malice. 16 For the temperate mind repels all these malicious emotions, just as it repels anger—for it is sovereign over even this. 17 When Moses was angry with Dathan and Abiram, he did nothing against them in anger, but controlled his anger by reason. 18 For, as I have said, the temperate mind is able to get the better of the emotions, to correct some, and to render others powerless. 19 Why else did Jacob, our most wise father, censure the households of Simeon and Levi for their irrational slaughter of the entire tribe of the Shechemites, saying, "Cursed be their anger"? 20 For if reason could not control anger, he would not have spoken thus. 21 Now when God fashioned human beings, he planted in them emotions and inclinations, 22 but at the same time he enthroned the mind among the senses as a sacred governor over them all. 23 To the mind he gave the law; and one who lives subject to this will rule a kingdom that is temperate, just, good, and courageous.

24 How is it then, one might say, that if reason is master of the emotions, it does not control forgetfulness and

3 ignorance? 1 But this argument is entirely ridiculous; for it is evident that reason rules not over its own emotions, but over those of the body. 2 No one of us[c] can eradicate that kind of desire, but reason can provide a way for us not to be enslaved by desire. 3 No one of us can eradicate anger from the mind, but reason can help to deal with anger. 4 No one of us can eradicate malice, but reason can fight at our side so that we are not overcome by malice. 5 For reason does not uproot the emotions but is their antagonist.

6 Now this can be explained more clearly by the story of King David's thirst. 7 David had been attacking the Philistines all day long, and together with the soldiers of his nation had killed many of them. 8 Then when evening fell, he[d] came, sweating and quite exhausted, to the royal tent, around which the whole army of our ancestors had encamped. 9 Now all the rest were at supper, 10 but the king was extremely thirsty, and though springs were plentiful there, he could not satisfy his thirst from them. 11 But a certain irrational desire for the water in the enemy's territory tormented and inflamed him, undid and consumed him. 12 When his guards complained bitterly because of the king's craving, two staunch young soldiers, respecting[e] the king's desire, armed themselves fully, and taking a pitcher climbed over the enemy's ramparts. 13 Eluding the sentinels at the gates, they went searching throughout the enemy camp 14 and found the spring, and from it boldly brought the king a drink. 15 But David,[f] though he was burning with thirst, considered it an altogether fearful danger to his soul to drink what was regarded as equivalent to blood. 16 Therefore, opposing reason to desire, he poured out the drink as an offering to God. 17 For the temperate mind can conquer the drives of the emotions and quench the flames of frenzied desires; 18 it can overthrow bodily agonies even when they are extreme, and by nobility of reason spurn all domination by the emotions.

a Or *the beasts that have fallen* *b* Other ancient authorities read *through*
c Gk *you* *d* Other ancient authorities read *he hurried and*
e Or *embarrassed because of* *f* Gk *he*

GREEK OLD TESTAMENT

19 Ἤδη δὲ καὶ ὁ καιρὸς ἡμᾶς καλεῖ ἐπὶ τὴν ἀπόδειξιν τῆς
ἱστορίας τοῦ σώφρονος λογισμοῦ.

20 Ἐπειδὴ γὰρ βαθεῖαν εἰρήνην διὰ τὴν εὐνομίαν οἱ πατέρες ἡμῶν εἶχον καὶ ἔπραττον καλῶς ὥστε καὶ τὸν τῆς
Ἀσίας βασιλέα Σέλευκον τὸν Νικάνορα καὶ χρήματα εἰς τὴν
ἱερουργίαν αὐτοῖς ἀφορίσαι καὶ τὴν πολιτείαν αὐτῶν ἀποδέ-
χεσθαι, 21 τότε δή τινες πρὸς τὴν κοινὴν νεωτερίσαντες
ὁμόνοιαν πολυτρόποις ἐχρήσαντο συμφοραῖς.

4 Σιμων γάρ τις πρὸς Ονιαν ἀντιπολιτευόμενος τόν ποτε
τὴν ἀρχιερωσύνην ἔχοντα διὰ βίου, καλὸν καὶ ἀγαθὸν
ἄνδρα, ἐπειδὴ πάντα τρόπον διαβάλλων ὑπὲρ τοῦ ἔθνους οὐκ
ἴσχυσεν κακῶσαι, φυγὰς ᾤχετο τὴν πατρίδα προδώσων.
2 ὅθεν ἥκων πρὸς Ἀπολλώνιον τὸν Συρίας τε καὶ Φοινίκης
καὶ Κιλικίας στρατηγὸν ἔλεγεν 3 Εὔνους ὢν τοῖς τοῦ βασιλέως πράγμασιν ἥκω μηνύων πολλὰς ἰδιωτικῶν χρημάτων
μυριάδας ἐν τοῖς Ἱεροσολύμων γαζοφυλακίοις τεθησαυρίσθαι
τοῖς ἱεροῖς μὴ ἐπικοινωνούσας, καὶ προσήκειν ταῦτα Σελεύ-
κῳ τῷ βασιλεῖ. 4 τούτων ἕκαστα γνοὺς ὁ Ἀπολλώνιος τὸν
μὲν Σιμωνα τῆς εἰς τὸν βασιλέα κηδεμονίας ἐπαινεῖ, πρὸς
δὲ τὸν Σέλευκον ἀναβὰς κατεμήνυσε τὸν τῶν χρημάτων
θησαυρόν. 5 καὶ λαβὼν τὴν περὶ αὐτῶν ἐξουσίαν ταχὺ εἰς
τὴν πατρίδα ἡμῶν μετὰ τοῦ καταράτου Σιμωνος καὶ βαρυ-
τάτου στρατοῦ 6 προσελθὼν ταῖς τοῦ βασιλέως ἐντολαῖς
ἥκειν ἔλεγεν ὅπως τὰ ἰδιωτικὰ τοῦ γαζοφυλακίου λάβοι χρήματα. 7 καὶ τοῦ ἔθνους πρὸς τὸν λόγον σχετλιάζοντος
ἀντιλέγοντός τε, πάνδεινον εἶναι νομίσαντες εἰ οἱ τὰς
παρακαταθήκας πιστεύσαντες τῷ ἱερῷ θησαυρῷ στερηθή-
σονται, ὡς οἷόν τε ἦν ἐκώλυον. 8 μετὰ ἀπειλῶν δὲ ὁ Ἀπολλώνιος ἀπῄει εἰς τὸ ἱερόν. 9 τῶν δὲ ἱερέων μετὰ γυναικῶν
καὶ παιδίων ἐν τῷ ἱερῷ ἱκετευσάντων τὸν θεὸν ὑπερασπίσαι
τοῦ ἱεροῦ καταφρονουμένου τόπου 10 ἀνιόντος τε μετὰ
καθωπλισμένης τῆς στρατιᾶς τοῦ Ἀπολλωνίου πρὸς τὴν τῶν
χρημάτων ἁρπαγὴν οὐρανόθεν ἔφιπποι προυφάνησαν ἄγγελοι
περιαστράπτοντες τοῖς ὅπλοις καὶ πολὺν αὐτοῖς φόβον τε
καὶ τρόμον ἐνιέντες. 11 καταπεσών γέ τοι ἡμιθανὴς ὁ
Ἀπολλώνιος ἐπὶ τὸν πάμφυλον τοῦ ἱεροῦ περίβολον τὰς
χεῖρας ἐξέτεινεν εἰς τὸν οὐρανὸν καὶ μετὰ δακρύων τοὺς
Εβραίους παρεκάλει ὅπως περὶ αὐτοῦ προσευξάμενοι τὸν
οὐράνιον ἐξευμενίσωνται στρατόν. 12 ἔλεγεν γὰρ ἡμαρτηκὼς
ὥστε καὶ ἀποθανεῖν ἄξιος ὑπάρχειν πᾶσίν τε ἀνθρώποις
ὑμνήσειν σωθεὶς τὴν τοῦ ἱεροῦ τόπου μακαριότητα. 13 τούτοις ὑπαχθεὶς τοῖς λόγοις Ονιας ὁ ἀρχιερεύς, καίπερ ἄλλως
εὐλαβηθείς, μήποτε νομίσειεν ὁ βασιλεὺς Σέλευκος ἐξ
ἀνθρωπίνης ἐπιβουλῆς καὶ μὴ θείας δίκης ἀνῃρῆσθαι τὸν
Ἀπολλώνιον ηὔξατο περὶ αὐτοῦ. 14 καὶ ὁ μὲν παραδόξως
διασωθεὶς ᾤχετο δηλώσων τῷ βασιλεῖ τὰ συμβάντα αὐτῷ.

15 Τελευτήσαντος δὲ Σελεύκου τοῦ βασιλέως διαδέχεται
τὴν ἀρχὴν ὁ υἱὸς αὐτοῦ Ἀντίοχος ὁ Ἐπιφανής, ἀνὴρ ὑπερήφανος καὶ δεινός, 16 ὃς καταλύσας τὸν Ονιαν τῆς ἀρχιερωσύνης Ιασονα τὸν ἀδελφὸν αὐτοῦ κατέστησεν ἀρχιερέα
17 συνθέμενον δώσειν, εἰ ἐπιτρέψειεν αὐτῷ τὴν ἀρχήν, κατ'
ἐνιαυτὸν τρισχίλια ἑξακόσια ἑξήκοντα τάλαντα. 18 ὁ δὲ
ἐπέτρεψεν αὐτῷ καὶ ἀρχιερᾶσθαι καὶ τοῦ ἔθνους ἀφηγεῖ-
σθαι· 19 καὶ ἐξεδιῄτησεν τὸ ἔθνος καὶ ἐξεπολίτευσεν ἐπὶ
πᾶσαν παρανομίαν 20 ὥστε μὴ μόνον ἐπ' αὐτῇ τῇ ἄκρᾳ τῆς

NEW REVISED STANDARD VERSION

19 The present occasion now invites us to a narrative
demonstration of temperate reason.

20 At a time when our ancestors were enjoying profound
peace because of their observance of the law and were prospering, so that even Seleucus Nicanor, king of Asia, had both
appropriated money to them for the temple service and recognized their commonwealth— 21 just at that time certain
persons attempted a revolution against the public harmony
and caused many and various disasters.

4 Now there was a certain Simon, a political opponent of
the noble and good man, Onias, who then held the high
priesthood for life. When despite all manner of slander he
was unable to injure Onias in the eyes of the nation, he fled
the country with the purpose of betraying it. 2 So he came to
Apollonius, governor of Syria, Phoenicia, and Cilicia, and
said, 3 "I have come here because I am loyal to the king's
government, to report that in the Jerusalem treasuries there
are deposited tens of thousands in private funds, which are
not the property of the temple but belong to King Seleucus."
4 When Apollonius learned the details of these things, he
praised Simon for his service to the king and went up to
Seleucus to inform him of the rich treasure. 5 On receiving
authority to deal with this matter, he proceeded quickly to
our country accompanied by the accursed Simon and a very
strong military force. 6 He said that he had come with the
king's authority to seize the private funds in the treasury.
7 The people indignantly protested his words, considering it
outrageous that those who had committed deposits to the
sacred treasury should be deprived of them, and did all that
they could to prevent it. 8 But, uttering threats, Apollonius
went on to the temple. 9 While the priests together with
women and children were imploring God in the temple to
shield the holy place that was being treated so contemptuously, 10 and while Apollonius was going up with his armed
forces to seize the money, angels on horseback with lightning flashing from their weapons appeared from heaven,
instilling in them great fear and trembling. 11 Then Apollonius fell down half dead in the temple area that was open
to all, stretched out his hands toward heaven, and with tears
begged the Hebrews to pray for him and propitiate the wrath
of the heavenly army. 12 For he said that he had committed a
sin deserving of death, and that if he were spared he would
praise the blessedness of the holy place before all people.
13 Moved by these words, the high priest Onias, although otherwise he had scruples about doing so, prayed for him so
that King Seleucus would not suppose that Apollonius had
been overcome by human treachery and not by divine justice.
14 So Apollonius,[a] having been saved beyond all expectations, went away to report to the king what had happened to
him.

15 When King Seleucus died, his son Antiochus Epiphanes succeeded to the throne, an arrogant and terrible man,
16 who removed Onias from the priesthood and appointed
Onias's[b] brother Jason as high priest. 17 Jason[c] agreed that if
the office were conferred on him he would pay the king three
thousand six hundred sixty talents annually. 18 So the king
appointed him high priest and ruler of the nation. 19 Jason[c]
changed the nation's way of life and altered its form of government in complete violation of the law, 20 so that not only

a Gk *he* b Gk *his* c Gk *He*

πατρίδος ἡμῶν γυμνάσιον κατασκευάσαι, ἀλλὰ καὶ καταλῦσαι τὴν τοῦ ἱεροῦ κηδεμονίαν. 21 ἐφ᾽ οἷς ἀγανακτήσασα ἡ
θεία δίκη αὐτὸν αὐτοῖς τὸν Ἀντίοχον ἐπολέμωσεν. 22 ἐπειδὴ γὰρ πολεμῶν ἦν κατ᾽ Αἴγυπτον Πτολεμαίῳ, ἤκουσέν τε
ὅτι φήμης διαδοθείσης περὶ τοῦ τεθνάναι αὐτὸν ὡς ἔνι μάλιστα χαίροιεν οἱ Ιεροσολυμῖται, ταχέως ἐπ᾽ αὐτοὺς ἀνέζευξεν, 23 καὶ ὡς ἐπόρθησεν αὐτούς, δόγμα ἔθετο ὅπως, εἴ
τινες αὐτῶν φάνοιεν τῷ πατρίῳ πολιτευόμενοι νόμῳ, θά-
νοιεν. 24 καὶ ἐπεὶ κατὰ μηδένα τρόπον ἴσχυεν καταλῦσαι
διὰ τῶν δογμάτων τὴν τοῦ ἔθνους εὐνομίαν, ἀλλὰ πάσας τὰς
ἑαυτοῦ ἀπειλὰς καὶ τιμωρίας ἑώρα καταλυομένας 25 ὥστε
καὶ γυναῖκας, ὅτι περιέτεμον τὰ παιδία, μετὰ τῶν βρεφῶν
κατακρημνισθῆναι προειδυίας ὅτι τοῦτο πείσονται· 26 ἐπεὶ
οὖν τὰ δόγματα αὐτοῦ κατεφρονεῖτο ὑπὸ τοῦ λαοῦ, αὐτὸς
διὰ βασάνων ἕνα ἕκαστον τοῦ ἔθνους ἠνάγκαζεν μιαρῶν
ἀπογευομένους τροφῶν ἐξόμνυσθαι τὸν Ιουδαϊσμόν.

5 Προκαθίσας γέ τοι μετὰ τῶν συνέδρων ὁ τύραννος
Ἀντίοχος ἐπί τινος ὑψηλοῦ τόπου καὶ τῶν στρατευ-
μάτων αὐτῷ παρεστηκότων κυκλόθεν ἐνόπλων 2 παρεκέλευεν
τοῖς δορυφόροις ἕνα ἕκαστον Εβραῖον ἐπισπᾶσθαι καὶ κρεῶν
ὑείων καὶ εἰδωλοθύτων ἀναγκάζειν ἀπογεύεσθαι· 3 εἰ δέ
τινες μὴ θέλοιεν μιαροφαγῆσαι, τούτους τροχισθέντας ἀναι-
ρεθῆναι. 4 πολλῶν δὲ συναρπασθέντων εἷς πρῶτος ἐκ τῆς
ἀγέλης ὀνόματι Ελεαζαρος, τὸ γένος ἱερεύς, τὴν ἐπιστήμην
νομικὸς καὶ τὴν ἡλικίαν προήκων καὶ πολλοῖς τῶν περὶ τὸν
τύραννον διὰ τὴν ἡλικίαν γνώριμος, παρήχθη πλησίον αὐτοῦ.
5 Καὶ αὐτὸν ἰδὼν ὁ Ἀντίοχος ἔφη 6 Ἐγὼ πρὶν ἄρξασθαι
τῶν κατὰ σοῦ βασάνων, ὦ πρεσβῦτα, συμβουλεύσαιμ᾽ ἄν σοι
ταῦτα, ὅπως ἀπογευσάμενος τῶν ὑείων σῴζοιο· 7 αἰδοῦμαι
γάρ σου τὴν ἡλικίαν καὶ τὴν πολιάν, ἣν μετὰ τοσοῦτον ἔχων
χρόνον οὔ μοι δοκεῖς φιλοσοφεῖν τῇ Ιουδαίων χρώμενος
θρησκείᾳ. 8 διὰ τί γὰρ τῆς φύσεως κεχαρισμένης καλλίστην
τὴν τοῦδε τοῦ ζῴου σαρκοφαγίαν βδελύττῃ; 9 καὶ γὰρ ἀνόη-
τον τοῦτο, τὸ μὴ ἀπολαύειν τῶν χωρὶς ὀνείδους ἡδέων, καὶ
ἄδικον ἀποστρέφεσθαι τὰς τῆς φύσεως χάριτας. 10 σὺ δέ
μοι καὶ ἀνοητότερον ποιήσειν δοκεῖς, εἰ κενοδοξῶν περὶ τὸ
ἀληθὲς ἔτι κἀμοῦ καταφρονήσεις ἐπὶ τῇ ἰδίᾳ τιμωρίᾳ. 11 οὐκ
ἐξυπνώσεις ἀπὸ τῆς φλυάρου φιλοσοφίας ὑμῶν καὶ
ἀποσκεδάσεις τῶν λογισμῶν σου τὸν λῆρον καὶ ἄξιον τῆς
ἡλικίας ἀναλαβὼν νοῦν φιλοσοφήσεις τὴν τοῦ συμφέροντος
ἀλήθειαν 12 καὶ προσκυνήσας μου τὴν φιλάνθρωπον παρη-
γορίαν οἰκτιρήσεις τὸ σεαυτοῦ γῆρας; 13 καὶ γὰρ ἐνθυμή-
θητι ὡς, εἰ καί τίς ἐστιν τῆσδε τῆς θρησκείας ὑμῶν ἐποπτι-
κὴ δύναμις, συγγνωμονήσειεν ἄν σοι ἐπὶ πάσῃ δι᾽ ἀνάγκην
παρανομίᾳ γινομένῃ.

14 Τοῦτον τὸν τρόπον ἐπὶ τὴν ἔκθεσμον σαρκοφαγίαν
ἐποτρύνοντος τοῦ τυράννου λόγον ᾔτησεν ὁ Ελεαζαρος
15 καὶ λαβὼν τοῦ λέγειν ἐξουσίαν ἤρξατο δημηγορεῖν οὕτως
16 Ἡμεῖς, Ἀντίοχε, θείῳ πεπεισμένοι νόμῳ πολιτεύεσθαι
οὐδεμίαν ἀνάγκην βιαιοτέραν εἶναι νομίζομεν τῆς πρὸς τὸν
νόμον ἡμῶν εὐπειθείας. 17 διὸ δὴ κατ᾽ οὐδένα τρόπον παρανομεῖν ἀξιοῦμεν. 18 καίτοι εἰ κατὰ ἀλήθειαν μὴ ἦν ὁ νόμος
ἡμῶν, ὡς ὑπολαμβάνεις, θεῖος, ἄλλως δὲ ἐνομίζομεν αὐτὸν
εἶναι θεῖον, οὐδὲ οὕτως ἐξὸν ἦν ἡμῖν τὴν ἐπὶ τῇ εὐσεβείᾳ

was a gymnasium constructed at the very citadel[a] of our
native land, but also the temple service was abolished.
21 The divine justice was angered by these acts and caused
Antiochus himself to make war on them. 22 For when he was
warring against Ptolemy in Egypt, he heard that a rumor of
his death had spread and that the people of Jerusalem had
rejoiced greatly. He speedily marched against them, 23 and
after he had plundered them he issued a decree that if any of
them were found observing the ancestral law they should
die. 24 When, by means of his decrees, he had not been able
in any way to put an end to the people's observance of the
law, but saw that all his threats and punishments were
being disregarded 25—even to the extent that women,
because they had circumcised their sons, were thrown headlong from heights along with their infants, though they had
known beforehand that they would suffer this— 26 when, I
say, his decrees were despised by the people, he himself tried
through torture to compel everyone in the nation to eat defiling foods and to renounce Judaism.

5 The tyrant Antiochus, sitting in state with his counselors
on a certain high place, and with his armed soldiers
standing around him, 2 ordered the guards to seize each and
every Hebrew and to compel them to eat pork and food sacrificed to idols. 3 If any were not willing to eat defiling food,
they were to be broken on the wheel and killed. 4 When
many persons had been rounded up, one man, Eleazar by
name, leader of the flock, was brought[b] before the king. He
was a man of priestly family, learned in the law, advanced in
age, and known to many in the tyrant's court because of his
philosophy.[c]

5 When Antiochus saw him he said, 6 "Before I begin to
torture you, old man, I would advise you to save yourself by
eating pork, 7 for I respect your age and your gray hairs.
Although you have had them for so long a time, it does not
seem to me that you are a philosopher when you observe the
religion of the Jews. 8 When nature has granted it to us, why
should you abhor eating the very excellent meat of this animal? 9 It is senseless not to enjoy delicious things that are
not shameful, and wrong to spurn the gifts of nature. 10 It
seems to me that you will do something even more senseless
if, by holding a vain opinion concerning the truth, you continue to despise me to your own hurt. 11 Will you not awak-
en from your foolish philosophy, dispel your futile reasonings, adopt a mind appropriate to your years, philosophize
according to the truth of what is beneficial, 12 and have compassion on your old age by honoring my humane advice?
13 For consider this: if there is some power watching over this
religion of yours, it will excuse you from any transgression
that arises out of compulsion."

14 When the tyrant urged him in this fashion to eat meat
unlawfully, Eleazar asked to have a word. 15 When he had
received permission to speak, he began to address the people
as follows: 16 "We, O Antiochus, who have been persuaded
to govern our lives by the divine law, think that there is no
compulsion more powerful than our obedience to the law.
17 Therefore we consider that we should not transgress it in
any respect. 18 Even if, as you suppose, our law were not
truly divine and we had wrongly held it to be divine, not
even so would it be right for us to invalidate our reputation

a Or *high place* *b* Or *was the first of the flock to be brought* *c* Other ancient authorities read *his advanced age*

GREEK OLD TESTAMENT

δόξαν ἀκυρῶσαι. 19 μὴ μικρὰν οὖν εἶναι νομίσῃς ταύτην, εἰ μιαροφαγήσαιμεν, ἁμαρτίαν· 20 τὸ γὰρ ἐπὶ μικροῖς καὶ μεγάλοις παρανομεῖν ἰσοδύναμόν ἐστιν, 21 δι᾽ ἑκατέρου γὰρ ὡς ὁμοίως ὁ νόμος ὑπερηφανεῖται. 22 χλευάζεις δὲ ἡμῶν τὴν φιλοσοφίαν ὥσπερ οὐ μετὰ εὐλογιστίας ἐν αὐτῇ βιούντων· 23 σωφροσύνην τε γὰρ ἡμᾶς ἐκδιδάσκει ὥστε πασῶν τῶν ἡδονῶν καὶ ἐπιθυμιῶν κρατεῖν καὶ ἀνδρείαν ἐξασκεῖ ὥστε πάντα πόνον ἑκουσίως ὑπομένειν 24 καὶ δικαιοσύνην παιδεύει ὥστε· διὰ πάντων τῶν ἠθῶν ἰσονομεῖν καὶ εὐσέβειαν ἐκδιδάσκει ὥστε μόνον τὸν ὄντα θεὸν σέβειν μεγαλοπρεπῶς. 25 διὸ οὐ μιαροφαγοῦμεν· πιστεύοντες γὰρ θεοῦ καθεστάναι τὸν νόμον οἴδαμεν ὅτι κατὰ φύσιν ἡμῖν συμπαθεῖ νομοθετῶν ὁ τοῦ κόσμου κτίστης. 26 τὰ μὲν οἰκειωθησόμενα ἡμῶν ταῖς ψυχαῖς ἐπέτρεψεν ἐσθίειν, τὰ δὲ ἐναντιωθησόμενα ἐκώλυσεν σαρκοφαγεῖν. 27 τυραννικὸν δὲ οὐ μόνον ἀναγκάζειν ἡμᾶς παρανομεῖν, ἀλλὰ καὶ ἐσθίειν, ὅπως τῇ ἐχθίστῃ ἡμῶν μιαροφαγίᾳ ταύτῃ ἐπεγγελάσῃς. 28 ἀλλ᾽ οὐ γελάσεις κατ᾽ ἐμοῦ τοῦτον τὸν γέλωτα, 29 οὔτε τοὺς ἱεροὺς τῶν προγόνων περὶ τοῦ φυλάξαι τὸν νόμον ὅρκους οὐ παρήσω, 30 οὐδ᾽ ἂν ἐκκόψειάς μου τὰ ὄμματα καὶ τὰ σπλάγχνα μου τήξειας. 31 οὐχ οὕτως εἰμὶ γέρων ἐγὼ καὶ ἄνανδρος ὥστε μοι διὰ τὴν εὐσέβειαν μὴ νεάζειν τὸν λογισμόν. 32 πρὸς ταῦτα τροχοὺς εὐτρέπιζε καὶ τὸ πῦρ ἐκφύσα σφοδρότερον. 33 οὐχ οὕτως οἰκτίρομαι τὸ ἐμαυτοῦ γῆρας ὥστε δι᾽ ἐμαυτοῦ τὸν πάτριον καταλῦσαι νόμον. 34 οὐ ψεύσομαί σε, παιδευτὰ νόμε, οὐδὲ ἐξομοῦμαί σε, φίλη ἐγκράτεια, 35 οὐδὲ καταισχυνῶ σε, φιλόσοφε λόγε, οὐδὲ ἐξαρνήσομαί σε, ἱερωσύνη τιμία καὶ νομοθεσίας ἐπιστήμη· 36 οὐδὲ μιανεῖς μου τὸ σεμνὸν γήρως στόμα οὐδὲ νομίμου βίου ἡλικίαν. 37 ἁγνόν με οἱ πατέρες εἰσδέξονται μὴ φοβηθέντα σου τὰς μέχρι θανάτου ἀνάγκας. 38 ἀσεβῶν μὲν γὰρ τυραννήσεις, τῶν δὲ ἐμῶν ὑπὲρ τῆς εὐσεβείας λογισμῶν οὔτε λόγοις δεσπόσεις οὔτε δι᾽ ἔργων.

6 Τοῦτον τὸν τρόπον ἀντιρρητορεύσαντα ταῖς τοῦ τυράννου παρηγορίαις παραστάντες οἱ δορυφόροι πικρῶς ἔσυραν ἐπὶ τὰ βασανιστήρια τὸν Ελεαζαρον. 2 καὶ πρῶτον μὲν περιέδυσαν τὸν γεραιὸν ἐγκοσμούμενον τῇ περὶ τὴν εὐσέβειαν εὐσχημοσύνῃ· 3 ἔπειτα περιαγκωνίσαντες ἑκατέρωθεν μάστιξιν κατῄκιζον, 4 Πείσθητι ταῖς τοῦ βασιλέως ἐντολαῖς, ἑτέρωθεν κήρυκος ἐπιβοῶντος. 5 ὁ δὲ μεγαλόφρων καὶ εὐγενὴς ὡς ἀληθῶς Ελεαζαρος ὥσπερ ἐν ὀνείρῳ βασανιζόμενος κατ᾽ οὐδένα τρόπον μετετρέπετο, 6 ἀλλὰ ὑψηλοὺς ἀνατείνας εἰς οὐρανὸν τοὺς ὀφθαλμοὺς ἀπεξαίνετο ταῖς μάστιξιν τὰς σάρκας ὁ γέρων καὶ κατερρεῖτο τῷ αἵματι καὶ τὰ πλευρὰ κατετιτρώσκετο. 7 καὶ πίπτων εἰς τὸ ἔδαφος ἀπὸ τοῦ μὴ φέρειν τὸ σῶμα τὰς ἀλγηδόνας ὀρθὸν εἶχεν καὶ ἀκλινῆ τὸν λογισμόν. 8 λὰξ γέ τοι τῶν πικρῶν τις δορυφόρων εἰς τοὺς κενεῶνας ἐναλλόμενος ἔτυπτεν, ὅπως ἐξανίσταιτο πίπτων. 9 ὁ δὲ ὑπέμενε τοὺς πόνους καὶ περιεφρόνει τῆς ἀνάγκης καὶ διεκαρτέρει τοὺς αἰκισμούς, 10 καὶ καθάπερ γενναῖος ἀθλητὴς τυπτόμενος ἐνίκα τοὺς βασανίζοντας ὁ γέρων· 11 ἱδρῶν γέ τοι τὸ πρόσωπον καὶ ἐπασθμαίνων σφοδρῶς καὶ ὑπ᾽ αὐτῶν τῶν βασανιζόντων ἐθαυμάζετο ἐπὶ τῇ εὐψυχίᾳ.

NEW REVISED STANDARD VERSION

for piety. 19 Therefore do not suppose that it would be a petty sin if we were to eat defiling food; 20 to transgress the law in matters either small or great is of equal seriousness, 21 for in either case the law is equally despised. 22 You scoff at our philosophy as though living by it were irrational, 23 but it teaches us self-control, so that we master all pleasures and desires, and it also trains us in courage, so that we endure any suffering willingly; 24 it instructs us in justice, so that in all our dealings we act impartially,[a] and it teaches us piety, so that with proper reverence we worship the only living God.

25 "Therefore we do not eat defiling food; for since we believe that the law was established by God, we know that in the nature of things the Creator of the world in giving us the law has shown sympathy toward us. 26 He has permitted us to eat what will be most suitable for our lives,[b] but he has forbidden us to eat meats that would be contrary to this. 27 It would be tyrannical for you to compel us not only to transgress the law, but also to eat in such a way that you may deride us for eating defiling foods, which are most hateful to us. 28 But you shall have no such occasion to laugh at me, 29 nor will I transgress the sacred oaths of my ancestors concerning the keeping of the law, 30 not even if you gouge out my eyes and burn my entrails. 31 I am not so old and cowardly as not to be young in reason on behalf of piety. 32 Therefore get your torture wheels ready and fan the fire more vehemently! 33 I do not so pity my old age as to break the ancestral law by my own act. 34 I will not play false to you, O law that trained me, nor will I renounce you, beloved self-control. 35 I will not put you to shame, philosophical reason, nor will I reject you, honored priesthood and knowledge of the law. 36 You, O king,[c] shall not defile the honorable mouth of my old age, nor my long life lived lawfully. 37 My ancestors will receive me as pure, as one who does not fear your violence even to death. 38 You may tyrannize the ungodly, but you shall not dominate my religious principles, either by words or through deeds."

6 When Eleazar in this manner had made eloquent response to the exhortations of the tyrant, the guards who were standing by dragged him violently to the instruments of torture. 2 First they stripped the old man, though he remained adorned with the gracefulness of his piety. 3 After they had tied his arms on each side they flogged him, 4 while a herald who faced him cried out, "Obey the king's commands!" 5 But the courageous and noble man, like a true Eleazar, was unmoved, as though being tortured in a dream; 6 yet while the old man's eyes were raised to heaven, his flesh was being torn by scourges, his blood flowing, and his sides were being cut to pieces. 7 Although he fell to the ground because his body could not endure the agonies, he kept his reason upright and unswerving. 8 One of the cruel guards rushed at him and began to kick him in the side to make him get up again after he fell. 9 But he bore the pains and scorned the punishment and endured the tortures. 10 Like a noble athlete the old man, while being beaten, was victorious over his torturers; 11 in fact, with his face bathed in sweat, and gasping heavily for breath, he amazed even his torturers by his courageous spirit.

a Or *so that we hold in balance all our habitual inclinations* *b* Or *souls*
c Gk lacks *O king*

GREEK OLD TESTAMENT

12 Ὅθεν τὰ μὲν ἐλεῶντες τὰ τοῦ γήρως αὐτοῦ, 13 τὰ δὲ ἐν
συμπαθείᾳ τῆς συνηθείας ὄντες, τὰ δὲ ἐν θαυμασμῷ τῆς
καρτερίας προσιόντες αὐτῷ τινες τοῦ βασιλέως ἔλεγον
14 Τί τοῖς κακοῖς τούτοις σεαυτὸν ἀλογίστως ἀπόλλεις,
Ελεαζαρ; 15 ἡμεῖς μέν τοι τῶν ἡψημένων βρωμάτων παραθή-
σομεν, σὺ δὲ ὑποκρινόμενος τῶν ὑείων ἀπογεύεσθαι σώθητι.

16 Καὶ ὁ Ελεαζαρος ὥσπερ πικρότερον διὰ τῆς συμβουλίας
αἰκισθεὶς ἀνεβόησεν 17 Μὴ οὕτως κακῶς φρονήσαιμεν οἱ
Αβρααμ παῖδες ὥστε μαλακοψυχήσαντας ἀπρεπὲς ἡμῖν δρᾶ-
μα ὑποκρίνασθαι. 18 καὶ γὰρ ἀλόγιστον εἰ πρὸς ἀλήθειαν
ζήσαντες τὸν μέχρι γήρως βίον καὶ τὴν ἐπ᾽ αὐτῷ δόξαν
νομίμως φυλάσσοντες νῦν μεταβαλοίμεθα 19 καὶ αὐτοὶ μὲν
ἡμεῖς γενοίμεθα τοῖς νέοις ἀσεβείας τύπος, ἵνα παράδειγμα
γενώμεθα τῆς μιαροφαγίας. 20 αἰσχρὸν δὲ εἰ ἐπιβιώσομεν
ὀλίγον χρόνον καὶ τοῦτον καταγελώμενοι πρὸς ἁπάντων ἐπὶ
δειλίᾳ 21 καὶ ὑπὸ μὲν τοῦ τυράννου καταφρονηθῶμεν ὡς
ἄνανδροι, τὸν δὲ θεῖον ἡμῶν νόμον μέχρι θανάτου μὴ προα-
σπίσαιμεν. 22 πρὸς ταῦτα ὑμεῖς μέν, ὦ Αβρααμ παῖδες, εὐγενῶς ὑπὲρ τῆς εὐσεβείας τελευτᾶτε. 23 οἱ δὲ τοῦ τυράννου
δορυφόροι, τί μέλλετε;

24 Πρὸς τὰς ἀνάγκας οὕτως μεγαλοφρονοῦντα αὐτὸν
ἰδόντες καὶ μηδὲ πρὸς τὸν οἰκτιρμὸν αὐτῶν μεταβαλλόμενον
ἐπὶ τὸ πῦρ αὐτὸν ἀνῆγον· 25 ἔνθα διὰ κακοτέχνων ὀργάνων
καταφλέγοντες αὐτὸν ὑπερρίπτοσαν, καὶ δυσώδεις χυλοὺς
εἰς τοὺς μυκτῆρας αὐτοῦ κατέχεον. 26 ὁ δὲ μέχρι τῶν
ὀστέων ἤδη κατακεκαυμένος καὶ μέλλων λιποθυμεῖν ἀνέτεινε
τὰ ὄμματα πρὸς τὸν θεὸν καὶ εἶπεν 27 Σὺ οἶσθα, θεέ, παρόν
μοι σῴζεσθαι βασάνοις καυστικαῖς ἀποθνῄσκω διὰ τὸν νόμον. 28 ἵλεως γενοῦ τῷ ἔθνει σου ἀρκεσθεὶς τῇ ἡμετέρᾳ ὑπὲρ
αὐτῶν δίκῃ. 29 καθάρσιον αὐτῶν ποίησον τὸ ἐμὸν αἷμα καὶ
ἀντίψυχον αὐτῶν λαβὲ τὴν ἐμὴν ψυχήν. 30 καὶ ταῦτα εἰπὼν
ὁ ἱερὸς ἀνὴρ εὐγενῶς ταῖς βασάνοις ἐναπέθανεν καὶ μέχρι
τῶν τοῦ θανάτου βασάνων ἀντέστη τῷ λογισμῷ διὰ τὸν
νόμον.

31 Ὁμολογουμένως οὖν δεσπότης τῶν παθῶν ἐστιν ὁ
εὐσεβὴς λογισμός. 32 εἰ γὰρ τὰ πάθη τοῦ λογισμοῦ κεκρατή-
κει, τούτοις ἂν ἀπέδομεν τὴν τῆς ἐπικρατείας μαρτυρίαν·
33 νυνὶ δὲ τοῦ λογισμοῦ τὰ πάθη νικήσαντος αὐτῷ προσηκόν-
τως τὴν τῆς ἡγεμονίας προσνέμομεν ἐξουσίαν. 34 καὶ δί-
καιόν ἐστιν ὁμολογεῖν ἡμᾶς τὸ κράτος εἶναι τοῦ λογισμοῦ,
ὅπου γε καὶ τῶν ἔξωθεν ἀλγηδόνων ἐπικρατεῖ, ἐπεὶ καὶ
γελοῖον. 35 καὶ οὐ μόνον τῶν ἀλγηδόνων ἐπιδείκνυμι κεκρατηκέναι τὸν λογισμόν, ἀλλὰ καὶ τῶν ἡδονῶν κρατεῖν καὶ
μηδὲν αὐταῖς ὑπείκειν.

7 Ὥσπερ γὰρ ἄριστος κυβερνήτης ὁ τοῦ πατρὸς ἡμῶν
Ελεαζαρου λογισμὸς πηδαλιουχῶν τὴν τῆς εὐσεβείας
ναῦν ἐν τῷ τῶν παθῶν πελάγει 2 καὶ καταικιζόμενος ταῖς
τοῦ τυράννου ἀπειλαῖς καὶ καταντλούμενος ταῖς τῶν βασάνων τρικυμίαις 3 κατ᾽ οὐδένα τρόπον ἔτρεψε τοὺς τῆς εὐσεβείας οἴακας, ἕως οὗ ἔπλευσεν ἐπὶ τὸν τῆς ἀθανάτου νίκης
λιμένα. 4 οὐχ οὕτως πόλις πολλοῖς καὶ ποικίλοις μηχανή-
μασιν ἀντέσχε ποτὲ πολιορκουμένη, ὡς ὁ πανάγιος ἐκεῖνος.
τὴν ἱερὰν ψυχὴν αἰκισμοῖς τε καὶ στρέβλαις πυρπολούμενος
ἐνίκησεν τοὺς πολιορκοῦντας διὰ τὸν ὑπερασπίζοντα τῆς
εὐσεβείας λογισμόν. 5 ὥσπερ γὰρ πρόκρημνον ἄκραν τὴν
ἑαυτοῦ διάνοιαν ὁ πατὴρ Ελεαζαρ ἐκτείνας περιέκλασεν
τοὺς ἐπιμαινομένους τῶν παθῶν κλύδωνας. 6 ὦ ἄξιε τῆς
ἱερωσύνης ἱερεῦ, οὐκ ἐμίανας τοὺς ἱεροὺς ὀδόντας οὐδὲ τὴν
θεοσέβειαν καὶ καθαρισμὸν χωρήσασαν γαστέρα ἐκοίνωσας

NEW REVISED STANDARD VERSION

12 At that point, partly out of pity for his old age, 13 partly out of sympathy from their acquaintance with him, partly
out of admiration for his endurance, some of the king's retinue came to him and said, 14 "Eleazar, why are you so irra-
tionally destroying yourself through these evil things? 15 We
will set before you some cooked meat; save yourself by pretending to eat pork."

16 But Eleazar, as though more bitterly tormented by this
counsel, cried out: 17 "Never may we, the children of Abraham,[a] think so basely that out of cowardice we feign a role
unbecoming to us! 18 For it would be irrational if having
lived in accordance with truth up to old age and having
maintained in accordance with law the reputation of such a
life, we should now change our course 19 and ourselves
become a pattern of impiety to the young by setting them an
example in the eating of defiling food. 20 It would be shameful if we should survive for a little while and during that
time be a laughingstock to all for our cowardice, 21 and be
despised by the tyrant as unmanly by not contending even to
death for our divine law. 22 Therefore, O children of Abraham, die nobly for your religion! 23 And you, guards of the
tyrant, why do you delay?"

24 When they saw that he was so courageous in the face
of the afflictions, and that he had not been changed by their
compassion, the guards brought him to the fire. 25 There
they burned him with maliciously contrived instruments,
threw him down, and poured stinking liquids into his nostrils. 26 When he was now burned to his very bones and
about to expire, he lifted up his eyes to God and said,
27 "You know, O God, that though I might have saved myself,
I am dying in burning torments for the sake of the law. 28 Be
merciful to your people, and let our punishment suffice for
them. 29 Make my blood their purification, and take my life
in exchange for theirs." 30 After he said this, the holy man
died nobly in his tortures; even in the tortures of death he
resisted, by virtue of reason, for the sake of the law.

31 Admittedly, then, devout reason is sovereign over the
emotions. 32 For if the emotions had prevailed over reason,
we would have testified to their domination. 33 But now that
reason has conquered the emotions, we properly attribute to
it the power to govern. 34 It is right for us to acknowledge
the dominance of reason when it masters even external agonies. It would be ridiculous to deny it.[b] 35 I have proved not
only that reason has mastered agonies, but also that it masters pleasures and in no respect yields to them.

7 For like a most skillful pilot, the reason of our father
Eleazar steered the ship of religion over the sea of the
emotions, 2 and though buffeted by the stormings of the
tyrant and overwhelmed by the mighty waves of tortures,
3 in no way did he turn the rudder of religion until he sailed
into the haven of immortal victory. 4 No city besieged with
many ingenious war machines has ever held out as did that
most holy man. Although his sacred life was consumed by
tortures and racks, he conquered the besiegers with the
shield of his devout reason. 5 For in setting his mind firm
like a jutting cliff, our father Eleazar broke the maddening
waves of the emotions. 6 O priest, worthy of the priesthood,
you neither defiled your sacred teeth nor profaned your
stomach, which had room only for reverence and purity, by

a Or *O children of Abraham* *b* Syr: Meaning of Gk uncertain

μιαροφαγία. 7 ὦ σύμφωνε νόμου καὶ φιλόσοφε θείου βίου. 8 τοιούτους δεῖ εἶναι τοὺς δημιουργοῦντας τὸν νόμον ἰδίῳ αἵματι καὶ γενναίῳ ἱδρῶτι τοῖς μέχρι θανάτου πάθεσιν ὑπερασπίζοντας. 9 σύ, πάτερ, τὴν εὐνομίαν ἡμῶν διὰ τῶν ὑπομονῶν εἰς δόξαν ἐκύρωσας καὶ τὴν ἁγιαστίαν σεμνολογήσας οὐ κατέλυσας καὶ διὰ τῶν ἔργων ἐπιστοποίησας τοὺς τῆς θείας φιλοσοφίας σου λόγους, 10 ὦ βασάνων βιαιότερε γέρων καὶ πυρὸς εὐτονώτερε πρεσβῦτα καὶ παθῶν μέγιστε βασιλεῦ Ελεαζαρ. 11 ὥσπερ γὰρ ὁ πατὴρ Ααρων τῷ θυμιατηρίῳ καθωπλισμένος διὰ τοῦ ἐθνοπλήθους ἐπιτρέχων τὸν ἐμπυριστὴν ἐνίκησεν ἄγγελον, 12 οὕτως ὁ Ααρωνίδης Ελεαζαρ διὰ τοῦ πυρὸς ὑπερτηκόμενος οὐ μετετράπη τὸν λογισμόν. 13 καίτοι τὸ θαυμασιώτατον, γέρων ὢν λελυμένων μὲν ἤδη τῶν τοῦ σώματος τόνων, περικεχαλασμένων δὲ τῶν σαρκῶν, κεκμηκότων δὲ καὶ τῶν νεύρων ἀνενέασεν 14 τῷ πνεύματι διὰ τοῦ λογισμοῦ καὶ τῷ Ισακίῳ λογισμῷ τὴν πολυκέφαλον στρέβλαν ἠκύρωσεν. 15 ὦ μακαρίου γήρως καὶ σεμνῆς πολιᾶς καὶ βίου νομίμου, ὃν πιστὴ θανάτου σφραγὶς ἐτελείωσεν.

16 Εἰ δὴ τοίνυν γέρων ἀνὴρ τῶν μέχρι θανάτου βασάνων περιεφρόνει δι᾽ εὐσέβειαν, ὁμολογουμένως ἡγεμών ἐστιν τῶν παθῶν ὁ εὐσεβὴς λογισμός. 17 ἴσως δ᾽ ἂν εἴποιέν τινες Τῶν παθῶν οὐ πάντες περικρατοῦσιν, ὅτι οὐδὲ πάντες φρόνιμον ἔχουσιν τὸν λογισμόν. 18 ἀλλ᾽ ὅσοι τῆς εὐσεβείας προνοοῦσιν ἐξ ὅλης καρδίας, οὗτοι μόνοι δύνανται κρατεῖν τῶν τῆς σαρκὸς παθῶν 19 πιστεύοντες ὅτι θεῷ οὐκ ἀποθνήσκουσιν, ὥσπερ οὐδὲ οἱ πατριάρχαι ἡμῶν Αβρααμ καὶ Ισαακ καὶ Ιακωβ, ἀλλὰ ζῶσιν τῷ θεῷ. 20 οὐδὲν οὖν ἐναντιοῦται τὸ φαίνεσθαί τινας παθοκρατεῖσθαι διὰ τὸν ἀσθενῆ λογισμόν· 21 ἐπεὶ τίς πρὸς ὅλον τὸν τῆς φιλοσοφίας κανόνα φιλοσοφῶν καὶ πεπιστευκὼς θεῷ 22 καὶ εἰδὼς ὅτι διὰ τὴν ἀρετὴν πάντα πόνον ὑπομένειν μακάριόν ἐστιν, οὐκ ἂν περικρατήσειεν τῶν παθῶν διὰ τὴν θεοσέβειαν; 23 μόνος γὰρ ὁ σοφὸς καὶ ἀνδρεῖός ἐστιν τῶν παθῶν κύριος.

8 Διὰ τοῦτό γέ τοι καὶ μειρακίσκοι τῷ τῆς εὐσεβείας λογισμῷ φιλοσοφοῦντες χαλεπωτέρων βασανιστηρίων ἐπεκράτησαν. 2 ἐπειδὴ γὰρ κατὰ τὴν πρώτην πεῖραν ἐνικήθη περιφανῶς ὁ τύραννος μὴ δυνηθεὶς ἀναγκάσαι γέροντα μιαροφαγῆσαι, τότε δὴ σφόδρα περιπαθῶς ἐκέλευσεν ἄλλους ἐκ τῆς λείας τῶν Εβραίων ἀγαγεῖν, καὶ εἰ μὲν μιαροφαγήσαιεν, ἀπολύειν φαγόντας, εἰ δ᾽ ἀντιλέγοιεν, πικρότερον βασανίζειν. 3 ταῦτα διαταξαμένου τοῦ τυράννου, παρῆσαν ἀγόμενοι μετὰ γεραιᾶς μητρὸς ἑπτὰ ἀδελφοὶ καλοί τε καὶ αἰδήμονες καὶ γενναῖοι καὶ ἐν παντὶ χαρίεντες. 4 οὓς ἰδὼν ὁ τύραννος καθάπερ ἐν χορῷ μέσην τὴν μητέρα περιέχοντας ἥσθετο ἐπ᾽ αὐτοῖς καὶ τῆς εὐπρεπείας ἐκπλαγεὶς καὶ τῆς εὐγενείας προσεμειδίασεν αὐτοῖς καὶ πλησίον καλέσας ἔφη 5 Ὦ νεανίαι, φιλοφρόνως ἐγὼ καθ᾽ ἑνὸς ἑκάστου ὑμῶν θαυμάζω, τὸ κάλλος καὶ τὸ πλῆθος τοσούτων ἀδελφῶν ὑπερτιμῶν οὐ μόνον συμβουλεύω μὴ μανῆναι τὴν αὐτὴν τῷ προβασανισθέντι γέροντι μανίαν, ἀλλὰ καὶ παρακαλῶ συνείξαντάς μοι τῆς ἐμῆς ἀπολαύειν φιλίας. 6 δυναίμην δ᾽ ἂν ὥσπερ κολάζειν τοὺς ἀπειθοῦντάς μου τοῖς ἐπιτάγμασιν, οὕτω καὶ εὐεργετεῖν τοὺς εὐπειθοῦντάς μοι. 7 πιστεύσατε οὖν καὶ

eating defiling foods. 7 O man in harmony with the law and philosopher of divine life! 8 Such should be those who are administrators of the law, shielding it with their own blood and noble sweat in sufferings even to death. 9 You, father, strengthened our loyalty to the law through your glorious endurance, and you did not abandon the holiness that you praised, but by your deeds you made your words of divine[a] philosophy credible. 10 O aged man, more powerful than tortures; O elder, fiercer than fire; O supreme king over the passions, Eleazar! 11 For just as our father Aaron, armed with the censer, ran through the multitude of the people and conquered the fiery[b] angel, 12 so the descendant of Aaron, Eleazar, though being consumed by the fire, remained unmoved in his reason. 13 Most amazing, indeed, though he was an old man, his body no longer tense and firm,[c] his muscles flabby, his sinews feeble, he became young again 14 in spirit through reason; and by reason like that of Isaac he rendered the many-headed rack ineffective. 15 O man of blessed age and of venerable gray hair and of law-abiding life, whom the faithful seal of death has perfected!

16 If, therefore, because of piety an aged man despised tortures even to death, most certainly devout reason is governor of the emotions. 17 Some perhaps might say, "Not all have full command of their emotions, because not all have prudent reason." 18 But as many as attend to religion with a whole heart, these alone are able to control the passions of the flesh, 19 since they believe that they, like our patriarchs Abraham and Isaac and Jacob, do not die to God, but live to God. 20 No contradiction therefore arises when some persons appear to be dominated by their emotions because of the weakness of their reason. 21 What person who lives as a philosopher by the whole rule of philosophy, and trusts in God, 22 and knows that it is blessed to endure any suffering for the sake of virtue, would not be able to overcome the emotions through godliness? 23 For only the wise and courageous are masters of their emotions.

8 For this is why even the very young, by following a philosophy in accordance with devout reason, have prevailed over the most painful instruments of torture. 2 For when the tyrant was conspicuously defeated in his first attempt, being unable to compel an aged man to eat defiling foods, then in violent rage he commanded that others of the Hebrew captives be brought, and that any who ate defiling food would be freed after eating, but if any were to refuse, they would be tortured even more cruelly.

3 When the tyrant had given these orders, seven brothers—handsome, modest, noble, and accomplished in every way—were brought before him along with their aged mother. 4 When the tyrant saw them, grouped about their mother as though a chorus, he was pleased with them. And struck by their appearance and nobility, he smiled at them, and summoned them nearer and said, 5 "Young men, with favorable feelings I admire each and every one of you, and greatly respect the beauty and the number of such brothers. Not only do I advise you not to display the same madness as that of the old man who has just been tortured, but I also exhort you to yield to me and enjoy my friendship. 6 Just as I am able to punish those who disobey my orders, so I can be a benefactor to those who obey me. 7 Trust me, then, and you

a Other ancient authorities lack *divine* b Other ancient authorities lack *fiery* c Gk *the tautness of the body already loosed*

ἀρχὰς ἐπὶ τῶν ἐμῶν πραγμάτων ἡγεμονικὰς λήμψεσθε ἀρνησάμενοι τὸν πάτριον ὑμῶν τῆς πολιτείας θεσμόν· 8 καὶ μεταλαβόντες Ἑλληνικοῦ βίου καὶ μεταδιαιτηθέντες ἐντρυφήσατε ταῖς νεότησιν ὑμῶν· 9 ἐπεί, ἐὰν ὀργίλως με διάθησθε διὰ τῆς ἀπειθείας, ἀναγκάσετέ με ἐπὶ δειναῖς κολάσεσιν ἕνα ἕκαστον ὑμῶν διὰ τῶν βασάνων ἀπολέσαι. 10 κατελεήσατε οὖν ἑαυτούς, οὓς καὶ ὁ πολέμιος ἔγωγε καὶ τῆς ἡλικίας καὶ τῆς εὐμορφίας οἰκτίρομαι. 11 οὐ διαλογιεῖσθε τοῦτο, ὅτι οὐδὲν ὑμῖν ἀπειθήσασιν πλὴν τοῦ μετὰ στρεβλῶν ἀποθανεῖν ἀπόκειται;

12 Ταῦτα δὲ λέγων ἐκέλευσεν εἰς τὸ ἔμπροσθεν τιθέναι τὰ βασανιστήρια, ὅπως καὶ διὰ τοῦ φόβου πείσειεν αὐτοὺς μιαροφαγῆσαι. 13 ὡς δὲ τροχούς τε καὶ ἀρθρέμβολα, στρεβλωτήριά τε καὶ τροχαντῆρας καὶ καταπέλτας καὶ λέβητας, τήγανά τε καὶ δακτυλήθρας καὶ χεῖρας σιδηρᾶς καὶ σφῆνας καὶ τὰ ζώπυρα τοῦ πυρὸς οἱ δορυφόροι προέθεσαν, ὑπολαβὼν ὁ τύραννος ἔφη 14 Μειράκια, φοβήθητε, καὶ ἣν σέβεσθε δίκην, ἵλεως ὑμῖν ἔσται δι᾽ ἀνάγκην παρανομήσασιν.

15 Οἱ δὲ ἀκούσαντες ἐπαγωγὰ καὶ ὁρῶντες δεινὰ οὐ μόνον οὐκ ἐφοβήθησαν, ἀλλὰ καὶ ἀντεφιλοσόφησαν τῷ τυράννῳ καὶ διὰ τῆς εὐλογιστίας τὴν τυραννίδα αὐτοῦ κατέλυσαν. 16 καίτοι λογισώμεθα, εἰ δειλόψυχοί τινες ἦσαν ἐν αὐτοῖς καὶ ἄνανδροι, ποίοις ἂν ἐχρήσαντο λόγοις; οὐχὶ τούτοις; 17 Ὦ τάλανες ἡμεῖς καὶ λίαν ἀνόητοι· βασιλέως ἡμᾶς καλοῦντος καὶ ἐπὶ εὐεργεσίᾳ παρακαλοῦντος, εἰ πεισθείημεν αὐτῷ, 18 τί βουλήμασιν κενοῖς ἑαυτοὺς εὐφραίνομεν καὶ θανατηφόρον ἀπείθειαν τολμῶμεν; 19 οὐ φοβηθησόμεθα, ἄνδρες ἀδελφοί, τὰ βασανιστήρια καὶ λογιούμεθα τὰς τῶν βασάνων ἀπειλὰς καὶ φευξόμεθα τὴν κενοδοξίαν ταύτην καὶ ὀλεθροφόρον ἀλαζονείαν; 20 ἐλεήσωμεν τὰς ἑαυτῶν ἡλικίας καὶ κατοικτίρωμεν τὸ τῆς μητρὸς γῆρας 21 καὶ ἐνθυμηθῶμεν ὅτι ἀπειθοῦντες τεθνηξόμεθα. 22 συγγνώσεται δὲ ἡμῖν καὶ ἡ θεία δίκη δι᾽ ἀνάγκην τὸν βασιλέα φοβηθεῖσιν. 23 τί ἐξάγομεν ἑαυτοὺς τοῦ ἡδίστου βίου καὶ ἀποστεροῦμεν ἑαυτοὺς τοῦ γλυκέος κόσμου; 24 μὴ βιαζώμεθα τὴν ἀνάγκην μηδὲ κενοδοξήσωμεν ἐπὶ τῇ ἑαυτῶν στρέβλῃ. 25 οὐδ᾽ αὐτὸς ὁ νόμος ἑκουσίως ἡμᾶς θανατοῖ φοβηθέντας τὰ βασανιστήρια. 26 πόθεν ἡμῖν ἡ τοσαύτη ἐντέτηκε φιλονεικία καὶ ἡ θανατηφόρος ἀρέσκει καρτερία, παρὸν μετὰ ἀταραξίας ζῆν τῷ βασιλεῖ πεισθέντας; 27 ἀλλὰ τούτων οὐδὲν εἶπον οἱ νεανίαι βασανίζεσθαι μέλλοντες οὐδὲ ἐνεθυμήθησαν. 28 ἦσαν γὰρ περίφρονες τῶν παθῶν καὶ αὐτοκράτορες τῶν ἀλγηδόνων, 29 ὥστε ἅμα τῷ παύσασθαι τὸν τύραννον συμβουλεύοντα αὐτοῖς μιαροφαγῆσαι, πάντες διὰ μιᾶς φωνῆς ὁμοῦ ὥσπερ ἀπὸ τῆς αὐτῆς ψυχῆς εἶπον

9 Τί μέλλεις, ὦ τύραννε; ἕτοιμοι γάρ ἐσμεν ἀποθνήσκειν ἢ παραβαίνειν τὰς πατρίους ἡμῶν ἐντολάς. 2 αἰσχυνόμεθα γὰρ τοὺς προγόνους ἡμῶν εἰκότως, εἰ μὴ τῇ τοῦ νόμου εὐπειθείᾳ καὶ συμβούλῳ Μωυσεῖ χρησαίμεθα. 3 σύμβουλε τύραννε παρανομίας, μὴ ἡμᾶς μισῶν ὑπὲρ αὐτοὺς ἡμᾶς ἐλέα. 4 χαλεπώτερον γὰρ αὐτοῦ τοῦ θανάτου νομίζομεν εἶναί σου τὸν ἐπὶ τῇ παρανόμῳ σωτηρίᾳ ἡμῶν ἔλεον.

will have positions of authority in my government if you will renounce the ancestral tradition of your national life. 8 Enjoy your youth by adopting the Greek way of life and by changing your manner of living. 9 But if by disobedience you rouse my anger, you will compel me to destroy each and every one of you with dreadful punishments through tortures. 10 Therefore take pity on yourselves. Even I, your enemy, have compassion for your youth and handsome appearance. 11 Will you not consider this, that if you disobey, nothing remains for you but to die on the rack?"

12 When he had said these things, he ordered the instruments of torture to be brought forward so as to persuade them out of fear to eat the defiling food. 13 When the guards had placed before them wheels and joint-dislocators, rack and hooks[a] and catapults[b] and caldrons, braziers and thumbscrews and iron claws and wedges and bellows, the tyrant resumed speaking: 14 "Be afraid, young fellows; whatever justice you revere will be merciful to you when you transgress under compulsion."

15 But when they had heard the inducements and saw the dreadful devices, not only were they not afraid, but they also opposed the tyrant with their own philosophy, and by their right reasoning nullified his tyranny. 16 Let us consider, on the other hand, what arguments might have been used if some of them had been cowardly and unmanly. Would they not have been the following? 17 "O wretches that we are and so senseless! Since the king has summoned and exhorted us to accept kind treatment if we obey him, 18 why do we take pleasure in vain resolves and venture upon a disobedience that brings death? 19 O men and brothers, should we not fear the instruments of torture and consider the threats of torments, and give up this vain opinion and this arrogance that threatens to destroy us? 20 Let us take pity on our youth and have compassion on our mother's age; 21 and let us seriously consider that if we disobey we are dead! 22 Also, divine justice will excuse us for fearing the king when we are under compulsion. 23 Why do we banish ourselves from this most pleasant life and deprive ourselves of this delightful world? 24 Let us not struggle against compulsion[c] or take hollow pride in being put to the rack. 25 Not even the law itself would arbitrarily put us to death for fearing the instruments of torture. 26 Why does such contentiousness excite us and such a fatal stubbornness please us, when we can live in peace if we obey the king?"

27 But the youths, though about to be tortured, neither said any of these things nor even seriously considered them. 28 For they were contemptuous of the emotions and sovereign over agonies, 29 so that as soon as the tyrant had ceased counseling them to eat defiling food, all with one voice together, as from one mind, said:

9 "Why do you delay, O tyrant? For we are ready to die rather than transgress our ancestral commandments; 2 we are obviously putting our forebears to shame unless we should practice ready obedience to the law and to Moses[d] our counselor. 3 Tyrant and counselor of lawlessness, in your hatred for us do not pity us more than we pity ourselves.[a] 4 For we consider this pity of yours, which insures our safety through transgression of the law, to be more

a Meaning of Gk uncertain *b* Here and elsewhere in 4 Macc an instrument of torture *c* Or *fate* *d* Other ancient authorities read *knowledge*

GREEK OLD TESTAMENT

[5] ἐκφοβεῖς δὲ ἡμᾶς τὸν διὰ τῶν βασάνων θάνατον ἡμῖν ἀπειλῶν ὥσπερ οὐχὶ πρὸ βραχέως παρ᾽ Ελεαζαρου μαθών. [6] εἰ δ᾽
οἱ γέροντες τῶν Εβραίων διὰ τὴν εὐσέβειαν καὶ βασανι-
σμοὺς ὑπομείναντες εὐσέβησαν, ἀποθάνοιμεν ἂν δικαιό-
τερον ἡμεῖς οἱ νέοι τὰς βασάνους τῶν σῶν ἀναγκῶν ὑπεριδόντες, ἃς καὶ ὁ παιδευτὴς ἡμῶν γέρων ἐνίκησεν. [7] πεί-
ραζε τοιγαροῦν, τύραννε· καὶ τὰς ἡμῶν ψυχὰς εἰ θανατώ-
σεις διὰ τὴν εὐσέβειαν, μὴ νομίσῃς ἡμᾶς βλάπτειν βασανί-
ζων. [8] ἡμεῖς μὲν γὰρ διὰ τῆσδε τῆς κακοπαθείας καὶ
ὑπομονῆς τὰ τῆς ἀρετῆς ἆθλα ἕξομεν καὶ ἐσόμεθα παρὰ θεῷ,
δι᾽ ὃν καὶ πάσχομεν· [9] σὺ δὲ διὰ τὴν ἡμῶν μιαιφονίαν αὐτάρκη καρτερήσεις ὑπὸ τῆς θείας δίκης αἰώνιον βάσανον διὰ
πυρός.

[10] Ταῦτα αὐτῶν εἰπόντων οὐ μόνον ὡς κατὰ ἀπειθούντων
ἐχαλέπαινεν ὁ τύραννος, ἀλλὰ καὶ ὡς κατὰ ἀχαρίστων ὠργίσθη. [11] ὅθεν τὸν πρεσβύτατον αὐτῶν κελευσθέντες παρῆγον
οἱ ὑπασπισταὶ καὶ διαρρήξαντες τὸν χιτῶνα διέδησαν τὰς
χεῖρας αὐτοῦ καὶ τοὺς βραχίονας ἱμᾶσιν ἑκατέρωθεν. [12] ὡς
δὲ τύπτοντες ταῖς μάστιξιν ἐκοπίασαν μηδὲν ἀνύοντες,
ἀνέβαλον αὐτὸν ἐπὶ τὸν τροχόν· [13] περὶ ὃν κατατεινόμενος
ὁ εὐγενὴς νεανίας ἔξαρθρος ἐγίνετο. [14] καὶ κατὰ πᾶν μέλος
κλώμενος ἐκακηγόρει λέγων [15] Τύραννε μιαρώτατε καὶ τῆς
οὐρανίου δίκης ἐχθρὲ καὶ ὠμόφρων, οὐκ ἀνδροφονήσαντά με
τοῦτον καταικίζεις τὸν τρόπον οὐδὲ ἀσεβήσαντα ἀλλὰ θείου
νόμου προασπίζοντα. [16] καὶ τῶν δορυφόρων λεγόντων Ὁμο-
λόγησον φαγεῖν, ὅπως ἀπαλλαγῇς τῶν βασάνων, [17] ὁ δὲ
εἶπεν Οὐχ οὕτως ἰσχυρὸς ὑμῶν ἐστιν ὁ τροχός, ὦ μιαροὶ
διάκονοι, ὥστε μου τὸν λογισμὸν ἄγξαι· τέμνετέ μου τὰ
μέλη καὶ πυροῦτέ μου τὰς σάρκας καὶ στρεβλοῦτε τὰ ἄρθρα.
[18] διὰ πασῶν γὰρ ὑμᾶς πείσω τῶν βασάνων ὅτι μόνοι παῖδες
Εβραίων ὑπὲρ ἀρετῆς εἰσιν ἀνίκητοι. [19] ταῦτα λέγοντι ὑπέ-
στρωσαν πῦρ καὶ τὸ διερεθίζον τὸν τροχὸν προσεπικατέ-
τεινον· [20] ἐμολύνετο δὲ πάντοθεν αἵματι ὁ τροχός, καὶ ὁ
σωρὸς τῆς ἀνθρακιᾶς τοῖς τῶν ἰχώρων ἐσβέννυτο σταλαγ-
μοῖς, καὶ περὶ τοὺς ἄξονας τοῦ ὀργάνου περιέρρεον αἱ σάρ-
κες. [21] καὶ περιτετμημένον ἤδη ἔχων τὸ τῶν ὀστέων πῆγμα
ὁ μεγαλόφρων καὶ Αβραμιαῖος νεανίας οὐκ ἐστέναξεν,
[22] ἀλλ᾽ ὥσπερ ἐν πυρὶ μετασχηματιζόμενος εἰς ἀφθαρσίαν
ὑπέμεινεν εὐγενῶς τὰς στρέβλας [23] Μιμήσασθέ με, ἀδελφοί, λέγων, μή μου τὸν ἀγῶνα λειποτακτήσητε μηδὲ ἐξομό-
σησθέ μου τὴν τῆς εὐψυχίας ἀδελφότητα. [24] ἱερὰν καὶ εὐγενῆ στρατείαν στρατεύσασθε περὶ τῆς εὐσεβείας, δι᾽ ἧς
ἵλεως ἡ δικαία καὶ πάτριος ἡμῶν πρόνοια τῷ ἔθνει γενηθεῖσα τιμωρήσειεν τὸν ἀλάστορα τύραννον. [25] καὶ ταῦτα
εἰπὼν ὁ ἱεροπρεπὴς νεανίας ἀπέρρηξεν τὴν ψυχήν.

[26] Θαυμασάντων δὲ πάντων τὴν καρτεροψυχίαν αὐτοῦ
ἦγον οἱ δορυφόροι τὸν καθ᾽ ἡλικίαν τοῦ προτέρου δεύτερον
καὶ σιδηρᾶς ἐναρμοσάμενοι χεῖρας ὀξέσι τοῖς ὄνυξιν ὀργάνῳ
καὶ καταπέλτῃ προσέδησαν αὐτόν. [27] ὡς δ᾽ εἰ φαγεῖν βούλοιτο πρὶν βασανίζεσθαι πυνθανόμενοι τὴν εὐγενῆ γνώμην
ἤκουσαν, [28] ἀπὸ τῶν τενόντων ταῖς σιδηραῖς χερσὶν ἐπι-
σπασάμενοι μέχρι τῶν γενείων τὴν σάρκα πᾶσαν καὶ τὴν
τῆς κεφαλῆς δορὰν οἱ παρδάλειοι θῆρες ἀπέσυρον. ὁ δὲ ταύτην βαρέως τὴν ἀλγηδόνα καρτερῶν ἔλεγεν [29] Ὡς ἡδὺς πᾶς

NEW REVISED STANDARD VERSION

grievous than death itself. [5] You are trying to terrify us by
threatening us with death by torture, as though a short time
ago you learned nothing from Eleazar. [6] And if the aged men
of the Hebrews because of their religion lived piously[a] while
enduring torture, it would be even more fitting that we
young men should die despising your coercive tortures,
which our aged instructor also overcame. [7] Therefore, tyrant,
put us to the test; and if you take our lives because of our
religion, do not suppose that you can injure us by torturing
us. [8] For we, through this severe suffering and endurance,
shall have the prize of virtue and shall be with God, on
whose account we suffer; [9] but you, because of your blood-
thirstiness toward us, will deservedly undergo from the
divine justice eternal torment by fire."

[10] When they had said these things, the tyrant was not
only indignant, as at those who are disobedient, but also
infuriated, as at those who are ungrateful. [11] Then at his
command the guards brought forward the eldest, and having
torn off his tunic, they bound his hands and arms with
thongs on each side. [12] When they had worn themselves out
beating him with scourges, without accomplishing anything,
they placed him upon the wheel. [13] When the noble youth
was stretched out around this, his limbs were dislocated,
[14] and with every member disjointed he denounced the
tyrant, saying, [15] "Most abominable tyrant, enemy of heavenly justice, savage of mind, you are mangling me in this
manner, not because I am a murderer, or as one who acts
impiously, but because I protect the divine law." [16] And
when the guards said, "Agree to eat so that you may be
released from the tortures," [17] he replied, "You abominable
lackeys, your wheel is not so powerful as to strangle my reason. Cut my limbs, burn my flesh, and twist my joints;
[18] through all these tortures I will convince you that children
of the Hebrews alone are invincible where virtue is concerned." [19] While he was saying these things, they spread
fire under him, and while fanning the flames[b] they tightened
the wheel further. [20] The wheel was completely smeared with
blood, and the heap of coals was being quenched by the drip-
pings of gore, and pieces of flesh were falling off the axles of
the machine. [21] Although the ligaments joining his bones
were already severed, the courageous youth, worthy of Abraham, did not groan, [22] but as though transformed by fire
into immortality, he nobly endured the rackings. [23] "Imitate
me, brothers," he said. "Do not leave your post in my
struggle[c] or renounce our courageous family ties. [24] Fight
the sacred and noble battle for religion. Thereby the just
Providence of our ancestors may become merciful to our
nation and take vengeance on the accursed tyrant." [25] When
he had said this, the saintly youth broke the thread of life.

[26] While all were marveling at his courageous spirit, the
guards brought in the next eldest, and after fitting themselves with iron gauntlets having sharp hooks, they bound
him to the torture machine and catapult. [27] Before torturing
him, they inquired if he were willing to eat, and they heard
his noble decision.[d] [28] These leopard-like beasts tore out his
sinews with the iron hands, flayed all his flesh up to his
chin, and tore away his scalp. But he steadfastly endured
this agony and said, [29] "How sweet is any kind of death for

a Other ancient authorities read *died* *b* Meaning of Gk uncertain
c Other ancient authorities read *post forever* *d* Other ancient authorities
read *having heard his noble decision, they tore him to shreds*

GREEK OLD TESTAMENT

θανάτου τρόπος διὰ τὴν πάτριον ἡμῶν εὐσέβειαν. ἔφη τε
πρὸς τὸν τύραννον 30 Οὐ δοκεῖς, πάντων ὠμότατε τύραννε,
πλέον ἐμοῦ σε βασανίζεσθαι ὁρῶν σου νικώμενον τὸν τῆς
τυραννίδος ὑπερήφανον λογισμὸν ὑπὸ τῆς διὰ τὴν εὐσέβειαν
ἡμῶν ὑπομονῆς; 31 ἐγὼ μὲν γὰρ ταῖς διὰ τὴν ἀρετὴν
ἡδοναῖς τὸν πόνον ἐπικουφίζομαι, 32 σὺ δὲ ἐν ταῖς τῆς ἀσεβείας ἀπειλαῖς βασανίζῃ. οὐκ ἐκφεύξῃ δέ, μιαρώτατε τύραννε, τὰς τῆς θείας ὀργῆς δίκας.

10 Καὶ τούτου τὸν ἀοίδιμον θάνατον καρτερήσαντος ὁ
τρίτος ἤγετο παρακαλούμενος πολλὰ ὑπὸ πολλῶν
ὅπως ἀπογευσάμενος σῴζοιτο. 2 ὁ δὲ ἀναβοήσας ἔφη Ἀγνοεῖτε ὅτι αὐτός με τοῖς ἀποθανοῦσιν ἔσπειρεν πατήρ, καὶ ἡ
αὐτὴ μήτηρ ἐγέννησεν, καὶ ἐπὶ τοῖς αὐτοῖς ἀνετράφην δόγ-
μασιν; 3 οὐκ ἐξόμνυμαι τὴν εὐγενῆ τῆς ἀδελφότητος συγγένειαν. 5 οἱ δὲ πικρῶς ἐνέγκαντες τὴν παρρησίαν τοῦ ἀνδρὸς
ἀρθρεμβόλοις ὀργάνοις τὰς χεῖρας αὐτοῦ καὶ τοὺς πόδας
ἐξήρθρουν καὶ ἐξ ἁρμῶν ἀναμοχλεύοντες ἐξεμέλιζον, 6 τοὺς
δακτύλους καὶ τοὺς βραχίονας καὶ τὰ σκέλη καὶ τοὺς ἀγκῶ-
νας περιέκλων. 7 καὶ κατὰ μηδένα τρόπον ἰσχύοντες αὐτὸν
ἄγξαι περιλύσαντες τὰ ὄργανα σὺν ἄκραις ταῖς τῶν δακτύ-
λων κορυφαῖς ἀπεσκύθιζον. 8 καὶ εὐθέως ἦγον ἐπὶ τὸν τροχόν, περὶ ὃν ἐκ σπονδύλων ἐκμελιζόμενος ἑώρα τὰς ἑαυτοῦ
σάρκας περιλακιζομένας καὶ κατὰ σπλάγχνων σταγόνας
αἵματος ἀπορρεούσας. 9 μέλλων δὲ ἀποθνῄσκειν ἔφη
10 Ἡμεῖς μέν, ὦ μιαρώτατε τύραννε, διὰ παιδείαν καὶ
ἀρετὴν θεοῦ ταῦτα πάσχομεν· 11 σὺ δὲ διὰ τὴν ἀσέβειαν καὶ
μιαιφονίαν ἀκαταλύτους καρτερήσεις βασάνους.

12 Καὶ τούτου θανόντος ἀδελφοπρεπῶς τὸν τέταρτον ἐπε-
σπῶντο λέγοντες 13 Μὴ μανῇς καὶ σὺ τοῖς ἀδελφοῖς σου
τὴν αὐτὴν μανίαν, ἀλλὰ πεισθεὶς τῷ βασιλεῖ σῷζε σεαυτόν.
14 ὁ δὲ αὐτοῖς ἔφη Οὐχ οὕτως καυστικώτερον ἔχετε κατ'
ἐμοῦ τὸ πῦρ ὥστε με δειλανδρῆσαι. 15 μὰ τὸν μακάριον τῶν
ἀδελφῶν μου θάνατον καὶ τὸν αἰώνιον τοῦ τυράννου ὄλεθρον
καὶ τὸν ἀΐδιον τῶν εὐσεβῶν βίον, οὐκ ἀρνήσομαι τὴν εὐγενῆ
ἀδελφότητα. 16 ἐπινόει, τύραννε, βασάνους, ἵνα καὶ δι'
αὐτῶν μάθῃς ὅτι ἀδελφός εἰμι τῶν προβασανισθέντων.
17 ταῦτα ἀκούσας ὁ αἱμοβόρος καὶ φονώδης καὶ παμμιαρώ-
τατος Ἀντίοχος ἐκέλευσεν τὴν γλῶτταν αὐτοῦ ἐκτεμεῖν.
18 ὁ δὲ ἔφη Κἂν ἀφέλῃς τὸ τῆς φωνῆς ὄργανον, καὶ σιωπών-
των ἀκούει ὁ θεός. 19 ἰδοὺ προκεχάλασται ἡ γλῶσσα, τέμνε,
οὐ γὰρ παρὰ τοῦτο τὸν λογισμὸν ἡμῶν γλωττοτομήσεις.
20 ἡδέως ὑπὲρ τοῦ θεοῦ τὰ τοῦ σώματος μέλη ἀκρωτηριαζό-
μεθα. 21 σὲ δὲ ταχέως μετελεύσεται ὁ θεός, τὴν γὰρ τῶν
θείων ὕμνων μελῳδὸν γλῶτταν ἐκτέμνεις.

11 Ὡς δὲ καὶ οὗτος ταῖς βασάνοις καταικισθεὶς ἐναπέθανεν, ὁ πέμπτος παρεπήδησεν λέγων 2 Οὐ μέλλω,
τύραννε, πρὸς τὸν ὑπὲρ τῆς ἀρετῆς βασανισμὸν παραιτεῖσθαι, 3 αὐτὸς δ' ἀπ' ἐμαυτοῦ παρῆλθον, ὅπως κἀμὲ κατα-
κτείνας περὶ πλειόνων ἀδικημάτων ὀφειλήσῃς τῇ οὐρανίῳ
δίκῃ τιμωρίαν. 4 ὦ μισάρετε καὶ μισάνθρωπε, τί δράσαντας
ἡμᾶς τοῦτον πορθεῖς τὸν τρόπον; 5 ὅτι τὸν πάντων κτίστην
εὐσεβοῦμεν καὶ κατὰ τὸν ἐνάρετον αὐτοῦ ζῶμεν νόμον;

NEW REVISED STANDARD VERSION

the religion of our ancestors!" 30 To the tyrant he said, "Do
you not think, you most savage tyrant, that you are being
tortured more than I, as you see the arrogant design of your
tyranny being defeated by our endurance for the sake of religion? 31 I lighten my pain by the joys that come from virtue,
32 but you suffer torture by the threats that come from impiety. You will not escape, you most abominable tyrant, the
judgments of the divine wrath."

10 When he too had endured a glorious death, the third
was led in, and many repeatedly urged him to save
himself by tasting the meat. 2 But he shouted, "Do you not
know that the same father begot me as well as those who
died, and the same mother bore me, and that I was brought
up on the same teachings? 3 I do not renounce the noble kinship that binds me to my brothers."[a] 5 Enraged by the man's
boldness, they disjointed his hands and feet with their
instruments, dismembering him by prying his limbs from
their sockets, 6 and breaking his fingers and arms and legs
and elbows. 7 Since they were not able in any way to break
his spirit,[b] they abandoned the instruments[c] and scalped
him with their fingernails in a Scythian fashion. 8 They
immediately brought him to the wheel, and while his verte-
brae were being dislocated by this, he saw his own flesh torn
all around and drops of blood flowing from his entrails.
9 When he was about to die, he said, 10 "We, most abominable tyrant, are suffering because of our godly training and
virtue, 11 but you, because of your impiety and bloodthirsti-
ness, will undergo unceasing torments."

12 When he too had died in a manner worthy of his
brothers, they dragged in the fourth, saying, 13 "As for you,
do not give way to the same insanity as your brothers, but
obey the king and save yourself." 14 But he said to them,
"You do not have a fire hot enough to make me play the
coward. 15 No—by the blessed death of my brothers, by the
eternal destruction of the tyrant, and by the everlasting life
of the pious, I will not renounce our noble family ties.
16 Contrive tortures, tyrant, so that you may learn from them
that I am a brother to those who have just now been tortured." 17 When he heard this, the bloodthirsty, murderous,
and utterly abominable Antiochus gave orders to cut out his
tongue. 18 But he said, "Even if you remove my organ of
speech, God hears also those who are mute. 19 See, here is
my tongue; cut it off, for in spite of this you will not make
our reason speechless. 20 Gladly, for the sake of God, we let
our bodily members be mutilated. 21 God will visit you swiftly, for you are cutting out a tongue that has been melodious
with divine hymns."

11 When he too died, after being cruelly tortured, the
fifth leaped up, saying, 2 "I will not refuse, tyrant, to
be tortured for the sake of virtue. 3 I have come of my own
accord, so that by murdering me you will incur punishment
from the heavenly justice for even more crimes. 4 Hater of
virtue, hater of humankind, for what act of ours are you
destroying us in this way? 5 Is it because[d] we revere the
Creator of all things and live according to his virtuous law?

a Other ancient authorities add verse 4, *So if you have any instrument of torture, apply it to my body; for you cannot touch my soul, even if you wish."*
b Gk *to strangle him* *c* Other ancient authorities read *they tore off his skin* *d* Other ancient authorities read *Or does it seem evil to you that*

GREEK OLD TESTAMENT

[6]ἀλλὰ ταῦτα τιμῶν, οὐ βασάνων ἐστὶν ἄξια. [9]τοιαῦτα δὲ
λέγοντα οἱ δορυφόροι δήσαντες αὐτὸν εἷλκον ἐπὶ τὸν
καταπέλτην, [10]ἐφ' ὃν δήσαντες αὐτὸν ἐπὶ τὰ γόνατα καὶ
ταῦτα ποδάγραις σιδηραῖς ἐφαρμόσαντες τὴν ὀσφὺν αὐτοῦ
περὶ τροχιαῖον σφῆνα κατέκαμψαν, περὶ ὃν ὅλος περὶ τὸν
τροχὸν σκορπίου τρόπον ἀνακλώμενος ἐξεμελίζετο. [11]κατὰ
τοῦτον τὸν τρόπον καὶ τὸ πνεῦμα στενοχωρούμενος καὶ τὸ
σῶμα ἀγχόμενος [12]Καλάς, ἔλεγεν, ἄκων, ὦ τύραννε, χάριτας ἡμῖν χαρίζῃ διὰ γενναιοτέρων πόνων ἐπιδείξασθαι
παρέχων τὴν εἰς τὸν νόμον ἡμῶν καρτερίαν.

[13]Τελευτήσαντος δὲ καὶ τούτου ὁ ἕκτος ἤγετο μειρακί-
σκος, ὃς πυνθανομένου τοῦ τυράννου εἰ βούλοιτο φαγὼν
ἀπολύεσθαι, ὁ δὲ ἔφη [14]Ἐγὼ τῇ μὲν ἡλικίᾳ τῶν ἀδελφῶν
μού εἰμι νεώτερος, τῇ δὲ διανοίᾳ ἡλικιώτης. [15]εἰς ταὐτὰ
γὰρ γεννηθέντες καὶ ἀνατραφέντες ὑπὲρ τῶν αὐτῶν καὶ
ἀποθνήσκειν ὀφείλομεν ὁμοίως. [16]ὥστε εἴ σοι δοκεῖ βασανίζειν μὴ μιαροφαγοῦντα, βασάνιζε. [17]ταῦτα αὐτὸν εἰπόντα
παρῆγον ἐπὶ τὸν τροχόν, [18]ἐφ' οὗ κατατεινόμενος ἐπιμελῶς
καὶ ἐκσπονδυλιζόμενος ὑπεκαίετο. [19]καὶ ὀβελίσκους ὀξεῖς
πυρώσαντες τοῖς νώτοις προσέφερον καὶ τὰ πλευρὰ διαπεί-
ραντες αὐτοῦ τὰ σπλάγχνα διέκαιον. [20]ὁ δὲ βασανιζόμενος
Ὦ ἱεροπρεποῦς ἀγῶνος, ἔλεγεν, ἐφ' ὃν διὰ τὴν εὐσέβειαν
εἰς γυμνασίαν πόνων ἀδελφοὶ τοσοῦτοι κληθέντες οὐκ ἐνική-
θημεν. [21]ἀνίκητος γάρ ἐστιν, ὦ τύραννε, ἡ εὐσεβὴς ἐπιστήμη. [22]καλοκἀγαθίᾳ καθωπλισμένος τεθνήξομαι κἀγὼ
μετὰ τῶν ἀδελφῶν μου [23]μέγαν σοὶ καὶ αὐτὸς προσβάλλων
ἀλάστορα, καινουργὲ τῶν βασάνων καὶ πολέμιε τῶν ἀληθῶς
εὐσεβούντων. [24]ἓξ μειράκια καταλελύκαμέν σου τὴν τυραν-
νίδα· [25]τὸ γὰρ μὴ δυνηθῆναί σε μεταπεῖσαι τὸν λογισμὸν
ἡμῶν μήτε βιάσασθαι πρὸς τὴν μιαροφαγίαν οὐ κατάλυσίς
ἐστίν σου; [26]τὸ πῦρ σου ψυχρὸν ἡμῖν, καὶ ἄπονοι οἱ κατα-
πέλται, καὶ ἀδύνατος ἡ βία σου. [27]οὐ γὰρ τυράννου, ἀλλὰ
θείου νόμου προεστήκασιν ἡμῶν οἱ δορυφόροι· διὰ τοῦτο ἀνίκητον ἔχομεν τὸν λογισμόν.

12 Ὡς δὲ καὶ οὗτος μακαρίως ἀπέθανεν καταβληθεὶς
εἰς λέβητα, ὁ ἕβδομος παρεγίνετο πάντων νεώτερος.
[2]ὃν κατοικτίρας ὁ τύραννος, καίπερ δεινῶς ὑπὸ τῶν ἀδελφῶν αὐτοῦ κακισθείς, ὁρῶν ἤδη τὰ δεσμὰ περικείμενα
πλησιέστερον αὐτὸν μετεπέμψατο καὶ παρηγορεῖν ἐπειρᾶτο
λέγων [3]Τῆς μὲν τῶν ἀδελφῶν σου ἀπονοίας τὸ τέλος ὁρᾷς.
διὰ γὰρ ἀπείθειαν στρεβλωθέντες τεθνᾶσιν. [4]σὺ δὲ εἰ μὲν
μὴ πεισθείης, τάλας βασανισθεὶς καὶ αὐτὸς τεθνήξῃ πρὸ
ὥρας, [5]πεισθεὶς δὲ φίλος ἔσῃ καὶ τῶν ἐπὶ τῆς βασιλείας
ἀφηγήσῃ πραγμάτων. [6]καὶ ταῦτα παρακαλῶν τὴν μητέρα
τοῦ παιδὸς μετεπέμψατο, ὅπως αὐτὴν ἐλεήσας τοσούτων
υἱῶν στερηθεῖσαν παρορμήσειεν ἐπὶ τὴν σωτήριον εὐπεί-
θειαν τὸν περιλειπόμενον. [7]ὁ δὲ τῆς μητρὸς τῇ Εβραΐδι
φωνῇ προτρεψαμένης αὐτόν, ὡς ἐροῦμεν μετὰ μικρὸν ὕστερον, [8]Λύσατέ μέ φησιν, εἴπω τῷ βασιλεῖ καὶ τοῖς σὺν αὐτῷ
φίλοις πᾶσιν. [9]καὶ ἐπιχαρέντες μάλιστα ἐπὶ τῇ ἐπαγγελίᾳ
τοῦ παιδὸς ταχέως ἔλυσαν αὐτόν. [10]καὶ δραμὼν ἐπὶ πλησίον τῶν τηγάνων [11]Ἀνόσιέ, φησιν, καὶ πάντων πονηρῶν

NEW REVISED STANDARD VERSION

[6]But these deeds deserve honors, not tortures."[a] [9]While he
was saying these things, the guards bound him and dragged
him to the catapult; [10]they tied him to it on his knees, and
fitting iron clamps on them, they twisted his back[b] around
the wedge on the wheel,[c] so that he was completely curled
back like a scorpion, and all his members were disjointed.
[11]In this condition, gasping for breath and in anguish of
body, [12]he said, "Tyrant, they are splendid favors that you
grant us against your will, because through these noble sufferings you give us an opportunity to show our endurance
for the law."

13 When he too had died, the sixth, a mere boy, was led
in. When the tyrant inquired whether he was willing to eat
and be released, he said, [14]"I am younger in age than my
brothers, but I am their equal in mind. [15]Since to this end
we were born and bred, we ought likewise to die for the
same principles. [16]So if you intend to torture me for not eating defiling foods, go on torturing!" [17]When he had said
this, they led him to the wheel. [18]He was carefully stretched
tight upon it, his back was broken, and he was roasted[d]
from underneath. [19]To his back they applied sharp spits that
had been heated in the fire, and pierced his ribs so that his
entrails were burned through. [20]While being tortured he
said, "O contest befitting holiness, in which so many of us
brothers have been summoned to an arena of sufferings for
religion, and in which we have not been defeated! [21]For religious knowledge, O tyrant, is invincible. [22]I also, equipped
with nobility, will die with my brothers, [23]and I myself will
bring a great avenger upon you, you inventor of tortures and
enemy of those who are truly devout. [24]We six boys have
paralyzed your tyranny. [25]Since you have not been able to
persuade us to change our mind or to force us to eat defiling
foods, is not this your downfall? [26]Your fire is cold to us,
and the catapults painless, and your violence powerless.
[27]For it is not the guards of the tyrant but those of the divine
law that are set over us; therefore, unconquered, we hold
fast to reason."

12 When he too, thrown into the caldron, had died a
blessed death, the seventh and youngest of all came
forward. [2]Even though the tyrant had been vehemently
reproached by the brothers, he felt strong compassion for
this child when he saw that he was already in fetters. He
summoned him to come nearer and tried to persuade him,
saying, [3]"You see the result of your brothers' stupidity, for
they died in torments because of their disobedience. [4]You
too, if you do not obey, will be miserably tortured and die
before your time, [5]but if you yield to persuasion you will be
my friend and a leader in the government of the kingdom."
[6]When he had thus appealed to him, he sent for the boy's
mother to show compassion on her who had been bereaved
of so many sons and to influence her to persuade the surviv-
ing son to obey and save himself. [7]But when his mother
had exhorted him in the Hebrew language, as we shall tell a
little later, [8]he said, "Let me loose, let me speak to the king
and to all his friends that are with him." [9]Extremely pleased
by the boy's declaration, they freed him at once. [10]Running
to the nearest of the braziers, [11]he said, "You profane

a Other authorities add verses 7 and 8, [7]*If you but understood human feelings and had hope of salvation from God—* [8]*but, as it is, you are a stranger to God and persecute those who serve him."* *b* Gk *loins*
c Meaning of Gk uncertain *d* Other ancient authorities add *by fire*

ἀσεβέστατε τύραννε, οὐκ ᾐδέσθης παρὰ τοῦ θεοῦ λαβὼν τὰ ἀγαθὰ καὶ τὴν βασιλείαν τοὺς θεράποντας αὐτοῦ κατακτεῖναι καὶ τοὺς τῆς εὐσεβείας ἀσκητὰς στρεβλῶσαι; 12 ἀνθ' ὧν ταμιεύσεταί σε ἡ δίκη πυκνοτέρῳ καὶ αἰωνίῳ πυρὶ καὶ βασάνοις, αἳ εἰς ὅλον τὸν αἰῶνα οὐκ ἀνήσουσίν σε. 13 οὐκ ᾐδέσθης ἄνθρωπος ὤν, θηριωδέστατε, τοὺς ὁμοιοπαθεῖς καὶ ἐκ τῶν αὐτῶν γεγονότας στοιχείων γλωττοτομῆσαι καὶ τοῦτον καταικίσας τὸν τρόπον βασανίσαι. 14 ἀλλ' οἱ μὲν εὐγενῶς ἀποθανόντες ἐπλήρωσαν τὴν εἰς τὸν θεὸν εὐσέβειαν, σὺ δὲ κακῶς οἰμώξεις τοὺς τῆς ἀρετῆς ἀγωνιστὰς ἀναιτίως ἀποκτείνας. 15 ὅθεν καὶ αὐτὸς ἀποθνῄσκειν μέλλων ἔφη 16 Οὐκ ἀπαυτομολῶ τῆς τῶν ἀδελφῶν μου ἀριστείας. 17 ἐπικαλοῦμαι δὲ τὸν πατρῷον θεὸν ὅπως ἵλεως γένηται τῷ ἔθνει ἡμῶν. 18 σὲ δὲ καὶ ἐν τῷ νῦν βίῳ καὶ θανόντα τιμωρήσεται. 19 καὶ ταῦτα κατευξάμενος ἑαυτὸν ἔρριψε κατὰ τῶν τηγάνων, καὶ οὕτως ἀπέδωκεν.

13 Εἰ δὲ τοίνυν τῶν μέχρι θανάτου πόνων ὑπερεφρόνησαν οἱ ἑπτὰ ἀδελφοί, συνομολογεῖται πανταχόθεν ὅτι αὐτοδέσποτός ἐστιν τῶν παθῶν ὁ εὐσεβὴς λογισμός. 2 εἰ γὰρ τοῖς πάθεσι δουλωθέντες ἐμιαροφάγησαν, ἐλέγομεν ἂν τούτοις αὐτοὺς νενικῆσθαι· 3 νυνὶ δὲ οὐχ οὕτως, ἀλλὰ τῷ ἐπαινουμένῳ παρὰ θεῷ λογισμῷ περιεγένοντο τῶν παθῶν, 4 ὧν οὐκ ἔστιν παριδεῖν τὴν ἡγεμονίαν τῆς διανοίας, ἐπεκράτησαν γὰρ καὶ πάθους καὶ πόνων. 5 πῶς οὖν οὐκ ἔστιν τούτοις τὴν τῆς εὐλογιστίας παθοκράτειαν ὁμολογεῖν, οἳ τῶν μὲν διὰ πυρὸς ἀλγηδόνων οὐκ ἐπεστράφησαν; 6 καθάπερ γὰρ προβλῆτες λιμένων πύργοι τὰς τῶν κυμάτων ἀπειλὰς ἀνακόπτοντες γαληνὸν παρέχουσι τοῖς εἰσπλέουσι τὸν ὅρμον, 7 οὕτως ἡ ἑπτάπυργος τῶν νεανίσκων εὐλογιστία τὸν τῆς εὐσεβείας ὀχυρώσασα λιμένα τὴν τῶν παθῶν ἐνίκησεν ἀκολασίαν. 8 ἱερὸν γὰρ εὐσεβείας στήσαντες χορὸν παρεθάρσυνον ἀλλήλους λέγοντες 9 Ἀδελφικῶς ἀποθάνωμεν, ἀδελφοί, περὶ τοῦ νόμου· μιμησώμεθα τοὺς τρεῖς τοὺς ἐπὶ τῆς Ἀσσυρίας νεανίσκους, οἳ τῆς ἰσοπολίτιδος καμίνου κατεφρόνησαν. 10 μὴ δειλανδρήσωμεν πρὸς τὴν τῆς εὐσεβείας ἐπίδειξιν. 11 καὶ ὁ μέν Θάρρει, ἀδελφέ ἔλεγεν, ὁ δέ Εὐγενῶς καρτέρησον, 12 ὁ δὲ καταμνησθεὶς ἔλεγεν Μνήσθητε πόθεν ἐστέ, ἢ τίνος πατρὸς χειρὶ σφαγιασθῆναι διὰ τὴν εὐσέβειαν ὑπέμεινεν Ισαακ. 13 εἷς δὲ ἕκαστος ἀλλήλους ὁμοῦ πάντες ἐφορῶντες φαιδροὶ καὶ μάλα θαρραλέοι Ἑαυτούς, ἔλεγον, τῷ θεῷ ἀφιερώσωμεν ἐξ ὅλης τῆς καρδίας τῷ δόντι τὰς ψυχὰς καὶ χρήσωμεν τῇ περὶ τὸν νόμον φυλακῇ τὰ σώματα. 14 μὴ φοβηθῶμεν τὸν δοκοῦντα ἀποκτέννειν· 15 μέγας γὰρ ψυχῆς ἀγὼν καὶ κίνδυνος ἐν αἰωνίῳ βασάνῳ κείμενος τοῖς παραβᾶσι τὴν ἐντολὴν τοῦ θεοῦ. 16 καθοπλισώμεθα τοιγαροῦν τὴν τοῦ θείου λογισμοῦ παθοκρατείαν. 17 οὕτω γὰρ θανόντας ἡμᾶς Αβρααμ καὶ Ισαακ καὶ Ιακωβ ὑποδέξονται καὶ πάντες οἱ πατέρες ἐπαινέσουσιν. 18 καὶ ἑνὶ ἑκάστῳ τῶν ἀποσπωμένων αὐτῶν ἀδελφῶν ἔλεγον οἱ περιλειπόμενοι Μὴ καταισχύνῃς ἡμᾶς, ἀδελφέ, μηδὲ ψεύσῃ τοὺς προαποθανόντας ἡμῶν ἀδελφούς. 19 οὐκ ἀγνοεῖτε δὲ τὰ τῆς

tyrant, most impious of all the wicked, since you have received good things and also your kingdom from God, were you not ashamed to murder his servants and torture on the wheel those who practice religion? 12 Because of this, justice has laid up for you intense and eternal fire and tortures, and these throughout all time[a] will never let you go. 13 As a man, were you not ashamed, you most savage beast, to cut out the tongues of men who have feelings like yours and are made of the same elements as you, and to maltreat and torture them in this way? 14 Surely they by dying nobly fulfilled their service to God, but you will wail bitterly for having killed without cause the contestants for virtue." 15 Then because he too was about to die, he said, 16 "I do not desert the excellent example[b] of my brothers, 17 and I call on the God of our ancestors to be merciful to our nation;[c] 18 but on you he will take vengeance both in this present life and when you are dead." 19 After he had uttered these imprecations, he flung himself into the braziers and so ended his life.[d]

13 Since, then, the seven brothers despised sufferings even unto death, everyone must concede that devout reason is sovereign over the emotions. 2 For if they had been slaves to their emotions and had eaten defiling food, we would say that they had been conquered by these emotions. 3 But in fact it was not so. Instead, by reason, which is praised before God, they prevailed over their emotions. 4 The supremacy of the mind over these cannot be overlooked, for the brothers[e] mastered both emotions and pains. 5 How then can one fail to confess the sovereignty of right reason over emotion in those who were not turned back by fiery agonies? 6 For just as towers jutting out over harbors hold back the threatening waves and make it calm for those who sail into the inner basin, 7 so the seven-towered right reason of the youths, by fortifying the harbor of religion, conquered the tempest of the emotions. 8 For they constituted a holy chorus of religion and encouraged one another, saying, 9 "Brothers, let us die like brothers for the sake of the law; let us imitate the three youths in Assyria who despised the same ordeal of the furnace. 10 Let us not be cowardly in the demonstration of our piety." 11 While one said, "Courage, brother," another said, "Bear up nobly," 12 and another reminded them, "Remember whence you came, and the father by whose hand Isaac would have submitted to being slain for the sake of religion." 13 Each of them and all of them together looking at one another, cheerful and undaunted, said, "Let us with all our hearts consecrate ourselves to God, who gave us our lives,[f] and let us use our bodies as a bulwark for the law. 14 Let us not fear him who thinks he is killing us, 15 for great is the struggle of the soul and the danger of eternal torment lying before those who transgress the commandment of God. 16 Therefore let us put on the full armor of self-control, which is divine reason. 17 For if we so die,[g] Abraham and Isaac and Jacob will welcome us, and all the fathers will praise us." 18 Those who were left behind said to each of the brothers who were being dragged away, "Do not put us to shame, brother, or betray the brothers who have died before us."

19 You are not ignorant of the affection of family ties,

a Gk *throughout the whole age* *b* Other ancient authorities read *the witness* *c* Other ancient authorities read *my race* *d* Gk *and so gave up*; other ancient authorities read *gave up his spirit* or *his soul* *e* Gk *they* *f* Or *souls* *g* Other ancient authorities read *suffer*

GREEK OLD TESTAMENT

ἀδελφότητος φίλτρα, ἅπερ ἡ θεία καὶ πάνσοφος πρόνοια διὰ
πατέρων τοῖς γεννωμένοις ἐμέρισεν καὶ διὰ τῆς μητρῴας
φυτεύσασα γαστρός, 20 ἐν ᾗ τὸν ἴσον ἀδελφοὶ κατοική-
σαντες χρόνον καὶ ἐν τῷ αὐτῷ χρόνῳ πλασθέντες καὶ ἀπὸ
τοῦ αὐτοῦ αἵματος αὐξηθέντες καὶ διὰ τῆς αὐτῆς ψυχῆς
τελεσφορηθέντες 21 καὶ διὰ τῶν ἴσων ἀποτεχθέντες χρόνων
καὶ ἀπὸ τῶν αὐτῶν γαλακτοποτοῦντες πηγῶν, ἀφ' ὧν
συντρέφονται ἐναγκαλισμάτων φιλάδελφοι ψυχαί· 22 καὶ
αὔξονται σφοδρότερον διὰ συντροφίας καὶ τῆς καθ' ἡμέραν
συνηθείας καὶ τῆς ἄλλης παιδείας καὶ τῆς ἡμετέρας ἐν
νόμῳ θεοῦ ἀσκήσεως. 23 οὕτως δὴ τοίνυν καθεστηκυίης
συμπαθοῦς τῆς φιλαδελφίας οἱ ἑπτὰ ἀδελφοὶ συμπαθέστερον
ἔσχον πρὸς ἀλλήλους. 24 νόμῳ γὰρ τῷ αὐτῷ παιδευθέντες
καὶ τὰς αὐτὰς ἐξασκήσαντες ἀρετὰς καὶ τῷ δικαίῳ συν-
τραφέντες βίῳ μᾶλλον ἑαυτοὺς ἠγάπων. 25 ἡ γὰρ ὁμοζηλία
τῆς καλοκἀγαθίας ἐπέτεινεν αὐτῶν τὴν πρὸς ἀλλήλους
εὔνοιαν καὶ ὁμόνοιαν· 26 σὺν γὰρ τῇ εὐσεβείᾳ ποθεινοτέραν
αὐτοῖς κατεσκεύαζον τὴν φιλαδελφίαν. 27 ἀλλ' ὅμως καίπερ
τῆς φύσεως καὶ τῆς συνηθείας καὶ τῶν τῆς ἀρετῆς ἠθῶν τὰ
τῆς ἀδελφότητος αὐτοῖς φίλτρα συναυξόντων ἀνέσχοντο
διὰ τὴν εὐσέβειαν τοὺς ἀδελφοὺς οἱ ὑπολειπόμενοι, τοὺς
καταικιζομένους ὁρῶντες μέχρι θανάτου βασανιζομένους,

14 1 προσέτι καὶ ἐπὶ τὸν αἰκισμὸν ἐποτρύνοντες, ὡς μὴ
μόνον τῶν ἀλγηδόνων περιφρονῆσαι αὐτούς, ἀλλὰ καὶ
τῶν τῆς φιλαδελφίας παθῶν κρατῆσαι.

2 Ὦ βασιλέων λογισμοὶ βασιλικώτεροι καὶ ἐλευθέρων
ἐλευθερώτεροι. 3 ὦ ἱερᾶς καὶ εὐαρμόστου περὶ τῆς εὐσεβείας τῶν ἑπτὰ ἀδελφῶν συμφωνίας. 4 οὐδεὶς ἐκ τῶν ἑπτὰ
μειρακίων ἐδειλίασεν οὐδὲ πρὸς τὸν θάνατον ὤκνησεν,
5 ἀλλὰ πάντες ὥσπερ ἐπ' ἀθανασίας ὁδὸν τρέχοντες ἐπὶ τὸν
διὰ τῶν βασάνων θάνατον ἔσπευδον. 6 καθάπερ αἱ χεῖρες καὶ
οἱ πόδες συμφώνως τοῖς τῆς ψυχῆς ἀφηγήμασιν κινοῦνται,
οὕτως οἱ ἱεροὶ μείρακες ἐκεῖνοι ὡς ὑπὸ ψυχῆς ἀθανάτου τῆς
εὐσεβείας πρὸς τὸν ὑπὲρ αὐτῆς συνεφώνησαν θάνατον. 7 ὦ
πανάγιε συμφώνων ἀδελφῶν ἑβδομάς. καθάπερ γὰρ ἑπτὰ τῆς
κοσμοποιίας ἡμέραι περὶ τὴν εὐσέβειαν, 8 οὕτως περὶ τὴν
ἑβδομάδα χορεύοντες οἱ μείρακες ἐκύκλουν τὸν τῶν βασάνων
φόβον καταλύοντες. 9 νῦν ἡμεῖς ἀκούοντες τὴν θλῖψιν τῶν
νεανιῶν ἐκείνων φρίττομεν· οἱ δὲ οὐ μόνον ὁρῶντες, ἀλλ'
οὐδὲ μόνον ἀκούοντες τὸν παραχρῆμα ἀπειλῆς λόγον, ἀλλὰ
καὶ πάσχοντες ἐνεκαρτέρουν, καὶ τοῦτο ταῖς διὰ πυρὸς
ὀδύναις. 10 ὧν τί γένοιτο ἐπαλγέστερον; ὀξεῖα γὰρ καὶ σύν-
τομος οὖσα ἡ τοῦ πυρὸς δύναμις ταχέως διέλυεν τὰ σώματα.

11 Καὶ μὴ θαυμαστὸν ἡγεῖσθε εἰ ὁ λογισμὸς περιεκράτησε
τῶν ἀνδρῶν ἐκείνων ἐν ταῖς βασάνοις, ὅπου γε καὶ γυναικὸς
νοῦς πολυτροπωτέρων ὑπερεφρόνησεν ἀλγηδόνων· 12 ἡ
μήτηρ γὰρ τῶν ἑπτὰ νεανίσκων ὑπήνεγκεν τὰς ἐφ' ἑνὶ ἑκάστῳ τῶν τέκνων στρέβλας. 13 θεωρεῖτε δὲ πῶς πολύπλοκός
ἐστιν ἡ τῆς φιλοτεκνίας στοργὴ ἕλκουσα πάντα πρὸς τὴν
τῶν σπλάγχνων συμπάθειαν, 14 ὅπου γε καὶ τὰ ἄλογα ζῷα
ὁμοίαν τὴν εἰς τὰ ἐξ αὐτῶν γεννώμενα συμπάθειαν καὶ
στοργὴν ἔχει τοῖς ἀνθρώποις. 15 καὶ γὰρ τῶν πετεινῶν τὰ
μὲν ἥμερα κατὰ τὰς οἰκίας ὀροφοιτοῦντα προασπίζει τῶν
νεοττῶν, 16 τὰ δὲ κατὰ κορυφὰς ὀρέων καὶ φαράγγων ἀπορ-
ρῶγας καὶ δένδρων ὀπὰς καὶ τὰς τούτων ἄκρας ἐννοσσο-
ποιησάμενα ἀποτίκτει καὶ τὸν προσιόντα κωλύει· 17 εἰ δὲ

NEW REVISED STANDARD VERSION

which the divine and all-wise Providence has bequeathed
through the fathers to their descendants and which was
implanted in the mother's womb. 20 There each of the brothers spent the same length of time and was shaped during the
same period of time; and growing from the same blood and
through the same life, they were brought to the light of day.
21 When they were born after an equal time of gestation, they
drank milk from the same fountains. From such embraces
brotherly-loving souls are nourished; 22 and they grow
stronger from this common nurture and daily companionship, and from both general education and our discipline in
the law of God.

23 Therefore, when sympathy and brotherly affection had
been so established, the brothers were the more sympathetic
to one another. 24 Since they had been educated by the same
law and trained in the same virtues and brought up in right
living, they loved one another all the more. 25 A common
zeal for nobility strengthened their goodwill toward one
another, and their concord, 26 because they could make their
brotherly love more fervent with the aid of their religion.
27 But although nature and companionship and virtuous
habits had augmented the affection of family ties, those who
were left endured for the sake of religion, while watching
their brothers being maltreated and tortured to death.

14 Furthermore, they encouraged them to face the torture, so that they not only despised their agonies, but
also mastered the emotions of brotherly love.

2 O reason,[a] more royal than kings and freer than the
free! 3 O sacred and harmonious concord of the seven brothers on behalf of religion! 4 None of the seven youths proved
coward or shrank from death, 5 but all of them, as though
running the course toward immortality, hastened to death by
torture. 6 Just as the hands and feet are moved in harmony
with the guidance of the mind, so those holy youths, as
though moved by an immortal spirit of devotion, agreed to
go to death for its sake. 7 O most holy seven, brothers in harmony! For just as the seven days of creation move in choral
dance around religion, 8 so these youths, forming a chorus,
encircled the sevenfold fear of tortures and dissolved it.
9 Even now, we ourselves shudder as we hear of the suffering
of these young men; they not only saw what was happening,
not only heard the direct word of threat, but also bore the
sufferings patiently, and in agonies of fire at that. 10 What
could be more excruciatingly painful than this? For the
power of fire is intense and swift, and it consumed their bodies quickly.

11 Do not consider it amazing that reason had full command over these men in their tortures, since the mind of
woman despised even more diverse agonies, 12 for the mother of the seven young men bore up under the rackings of
each one of her children.

13 Observe how complex is a mother's love for her children, which draws everything toward an emotion felt in her
inmost parts. 14 Even unreasoning animals, as well as
human beings, have a sympathy and parental love for their
offspring. 15 For example, among birds, the ones that are
tame protect their young by building on the housetops,
16 and the others, by building in precipitous chasms and in
holes and tops of trees, hatch the nestlings and ward off the

a Or *O minds*

καὶ μὴ δύναιντο κωλύειν, περιιπτάμενα κυκλόθεν αὐτῶν ἀλ-
γοῦντα τῇ στοργῇ ἀνακαλούμενα τῇ ἰδίᾳ φωνῇ, καθ᾽ ὃ δύναται, βοηθεῖ τοῖς τέκνοις. 18 καὶ τί δεῖ τὴν διὰ τῶν ἀλόγων
ζῴων ἐπιδεικνύναι πρὸς τὰ τέκνα συμπάθειαν, 19 ὅπου γε
καὶ μέλισσαι περὶ τὸν τῆς κηρογονίας καιρὸν ἐπαμύνονται
τοὺς προσιόντας καὶ καθάπερ σιδήρῳ τῷ κέντρῳ πλήσσουσι
τοὺς προσιόντας τῇ νοσσιᾷ αὐτῶν καὶ ἀπαμύνουσιν ἕως
θανάτου; 20 ἀλλ᾽ οὐχὶ τὴν Αβρααμ ὁμόψυχον τῶν νεανίσκων
μητέρα μετεκίνησεν συμπάθεια τέκνων.

15 Ὦ λογισμὲ τέκνων παθῶν τύραννε καὶ εὐσέβεια μητρὶ τέκνων ποθεινοτέρα. 2 μήτηρ δυεῖν προκειμένων,
εὐσεβείας καὶ τῆς ἑπτὰ υἱῶν σωτηρίας προσκαίρου κατὰ τὴν
τοῦ τυράννου ὑπόσχεσιν, 3 τὴν εὐσέβειαν μᾶλλον ἠγάπησεν
τὴν σῴζουσαν εἰς αἰωνίαν ζωὴν κατὰ θεόν. 4 ὢ τίνα τρόπον
ἠθολογήσαιμι φιλότεκνα γονέων πάθη. ψυχῆς τε καὶ μορφῆς
ὁμοιότητα εἰς μικρὸν παιδὸς χαρακτῆρα θαυμάσιον ἐναπο-
σφραγίζομεν, μάλιστα διὰ τὸ τῶν παθῶν τοῖς γεννηθεῖσιν
τὰς μητέρας τῶν πατέρων καθεστάναι συμπαθεστέρας.
5 ὅσῳ γὰρ καὶ ἀσθενόψυχοι καὶ πολυγονώτεραι ὑπάρχουσιν
αἱ μητέρες, τοσούτῳ μᾶλλόν εἰσιν φιλοτεκνότεραι. 6 πασῶν
δὲ τῶν μητέρων ἐγένετο ἡ τῶν ἑπτὰ παίδων μήτηρ φιλοτε-
κνοτέρα, ἥτις ἑπτὰ κυοφορίαις τὴν πρὸς αὐτοὺς ἐπιφυ-
τευομένη φιλοστοργίαν 7 καὶ διὰ πολλὰς τὰς καθ᾽ ἕκαστον
αὐτῶν ὠδῖνας ἠναγκασμένη τὴν εἰς αὐτοὺς ἔχειν συμπάθειαν, 8 διὰ τὸν πρὸς τὸν θεὸν φόβον ὑπερεῖδεν τὴν τῶν
τέκνων πρόσκαιρον σωτηρίαν. 9 οὐ μὴν δὲ ἀλλὰ καὶ διὰ τὴν
καλοκἀγαθίαν τῶν υἱῶν καὶ τὴν πρὸς τὸν νόμον αὐτῶν εὐπεί-
θειαν μείζω τὴν ἐν αὐτοῖς ἔσχεν φιλοστοργίαν. 10 δίκαιοί
τε γὰρ ἦσαν καὶ σώφρονες καὶ ἀνδρεῖοι καὶ μεγαλόψυχοι καὶ
φιλάδελφοι καὶ φιλομήτορες οὕτως ὥστε καὶ μέχρι θανάτου
τὰ νόμιμα φυλάσσοντας πείθεσθαι αὐτῇ. 11 ἀλλ᾽ ὅμως καίπερ τοσούτων ὄντων τῶν περὶ τὴν φιλοτεκνίαν εἰς συμπάθειαν ἑλκόντων τὴν μητέρα, ἐπ᾽ οὐδενὸς αὐτῶν τὸν λογισμὸν
αὐτῆς αἱ παμποίκιλοι βάσανοι ἴσχυσαν μετατρέψαι, 12 ἀλλὰ
καὶ καθ᾽ ἕνα παῖδα καὶ ὁμοῦ πάντας ἡ μήτηρ ἐπὶ τὸν τῆς
εὐσεβείας προετρέπετο θάνατον. 13 ὢ φύσις ἱερὰ καὶ φίλτρα
γονέων καὶ γένεσι φιλόστοργε καὶ τροφεία καὶ μητέρων ἀδά-
μαστα πάθη. 14 καθένα στρεβλούμενον καὶ φλεγόμενον
ὁρῶσα μήτηρ οὐ μετεβάλλετο διὰ τὴν εὐσέβειαν. 15 τὰς σάρκας τῶν τέκνων ἑώρα περὶ τὸ πῦρ τηκομένας καὶ τοὺς τῶν
ποδῶν καὶ χειρῶν δακτύλους ἐπὶ γῆς σπαίροντας καὶ τὰς
τῶν κεφαλῶν μέχρι τῶν περὶ τὰ γένεια σάρκας ὥσπερ προσ-
ωπεῖα προκειμένας. 16 ὢ πικροτέρων νῦν πόνων πειρασθεῖσα
μήτηρ ἤπερ τῶν ἐπ᾽ αὐτοῖς ὠδίνων. 17 ὢ μόνη γύναι τὴν
εὐσέβειαν ὁλόκληρον ἀποκυήσασα. 18 οὐ μετέτρεψέν σε πρω-
τοτόκος ἀποπνέων οὐδὲ δεύτερος εἰς σὲ οἰκτρὸν βλέπων ἐν
βασάνοις, οὐ τρίτος ἀποψύχων, 19 οὐδὲ τοὺς ὀφθαλμοὺς ἑνὸς
ἑκάστου θεωροῦσα ταυρηδὸν ἐπὶ τῶν βασάνων ὁρῶντας τὸν
αὐτὸν αἰκισμὸν καὶ τοὺς μυκτῆρας προσημειουμένους τὸν
θάνατον αὐτῶν οὐκ ἔκλαυσας. 20 ἐπὶ σαρξὶν τέκνων ὁρῶσα
σάρκας τέκνων ἀποκαιομένας καὶ ἐπὶ χερσὶν χεῖρας

intruder. 17 If they are not able to keep the intruder[a] away,
they do what they can to help their young by flying in circles
around them in the anguish of love, warning them with their
own calls. 18 And why is it necessary to demonstrate sympathy for children by the example of unreasoning animals,
19 since even bees at the time for making honeycombs defend
themselves against intruders and, as though with an iron
dart, sting those who approach their hive and defend it even
to the death? 20 But sympathy for her children did not sway
the mother of the young men; she was of the same mind as
Abraham.

15 O reason of the children, tyrant over the emotions!
O religion, more desirable to the mother than her
children! 2 Two courses were open to this mother, that of
religion, and that of preserving her seven sons for a time, as
the tyrant had promised. 3 She loved religion more, the religion that preserves them for eternal life according to God's
promise.[b] 4 In what manner might I express the emotions of
parents who love their children? We impress upon the character of a small child a wondrous likeness both of mind and
of form. Especially is this true of mothers, who because of
their birth pangs have a deeper sympathy toward their offspring than do the fathers. 5 Considering that mothers are
the weaker sex and give birth to many, they are more devoted to their children.[c] 6 The mother of the seven boys, more
than any other mother, loved her children. In seven pregnancies she had implanted in herself tender love toward them,
7 and because of the many pains she suffered with each of
them she had sympathy for them; 8 yet because of the fear of
God she disdained the temporary safety of her children. 9 Not
only so, but also because of the nobility of her sons and their
ready obedience to the law, she felt a greater tenderness
toward them. 10 For they were righteous and self-controlled
and brave and magnanimous, and loved their brothers and
their mother, so that they obeyed her even to death in keeping the ordinances.

11 Nevertheless, though so many factors influenced the
mother to suffer with them out of love for her children, in the
case of none of them were the various tortures strong
enough to pervert her reason. 12 But each child separately
and all of them together the mother urged on to death for
religion's sake. 13 O sacred nature and affection of parental
love, yearning of parents toward offspring, nurture and
indomitable suffering by mothers! 14 This mother, who saw
them tortured and burned one by one, because of religion did
not change her attitude. 15 She watched the flesh of her children being consumed by fire, their toes and fingers
scattered[d] on the ground, and the flesh of the head to the
chin exposed like masks.

16 O mother, tried now by more bitter pains than even the
birth pangs you suffered for them! 17 O woman, who alone
gave birth to such complete devotion! 18 When the firstborn
breathed his last, it did not turn you aside, nor when the second in torments looked at you piteously nor when the third
expired; 19 nor did you weep when you looked at the eyes of
each one in his tortures gazing boldly at the same agonies,
and saw in their nostrils the signs of the approach of death.
20 When you saw the flesh of children burned upon the flesh

a Gk *it* b Gk *according to God* c Or *For to the degree that mothers are weaker and the more children they bear, the more they are devoted to their children.* d Or *quivering*

GREEK OLD TESTAMENT

ἀποτεμνομένας καὶ ἐπὶ κεφαλαῖς κεφαλὰς ἀποδειροτομ-
ουμένας καὶ ἐπὶ νεκροῖς νεκροὺς πίπτοντας καὶ πολυάνδριον
ὁρῶσα τῶν τέκνων τὸ χωρίον διὰ τῶν βασάνων οὐκ ἐδά-
κρυσας. 21 οὐχ οὕτως σειρήνιοι μελῳδίαι οὐδὲ κύκνειοι πρὸς
φιληκοΐαν φωναὶ τοὺς ἀκούοντας ἐφέλκονται ὡς τέκνων
φωναὶ μετὰ βασάνων μητέρα φωνούντων. 22 πηλίκαις καὶ πόσαις τότε ἡ μήτηρ τῶν υἱῶν βασανιζομένων τροχοῖς τε καὶ
καυτηρίοις ἐβασανίζετο βασάνοις. 23 ἀλλὰ τὰ σπλάγχνα
αὐτῆς ὁ εὐσεβὴς λογισμὸς ἐν αὐτοῖς τοῖς πάθεσιν ἀνδρει-
ώσας ἐπέτεινεν τὴν πρόσκαιρον φιλοτεκνίαν παριδεῖν.
24 καίπερ ἑπτὰ τέκνων ὁρῶσα ἀπώλειαν καὶ τὴν τῶν στρεβλῶν πολύπλοκον ποικιλίαν, ἁπάσας ἡ γενναία μήτηρ ἐξέ-
λυσεν διὰ τὴν πρὸς θεὸν πίστιν. 25 καθάπερ γὰρ ἐν βουλευ-
τηρίῳ τῇ ἑαυτῆς ψυχῇ δεινοὺς ὁρῶσα συμβούλους φύσιν καὶ
γένεσιν καὶ φιλοτεκνίαν καὶ τέκνων στρέβλας, 26 δύο ψή-
φους κρατοῦσα μήτηρ, θανατηφόρον τε καὶ σωτήριον, ὑπὲρ
τέκνων 27 οὐκ ἐπέγνω τὴν σῴζουσαν ἑπτὰ υἱοὺς πρὸς ὀλίγον
χρόνον σωτηρίαν, 28 ἀλλὰ τῆς θεοσεβοῦς Αβρααμ καρτερίας
ἡ θυγάτηρ ἐμνήσθη. 29 ὦ μήτηρ ἔθνους, ἔκδικε τοῦ νόμου καὶ
ὑπερασπίστρια τῆς εὐσεβείας καὶ τοῦ διὰ σπλάγχνων ἀγῶνος ἀθλοφόρε· 30 ὦ ἀρρένων πρὸς καρτερίαν γενναιοτέρα καὶ
ἀνδρῶν πρὸς ὑπομονὴν ἀνδρειοτέρα. 31 καθάπερ γὰρ ἡ Νωε
κιβωτὸς ἐν τῷ κοσμοπληθεῖ κατακλυσμῷ κοσμοφοροῦσα
καρτερῶς ὑπέμεινεν τοὺς κλύδωνας, 32 οὕτως σὺ ἡ νομοφύ-
λαξ πανταχόθεν ἐν τῷ τῶν παθῶν περιαντλουμένη κατακλυσμῷ καὶ καρτεροῖς ἀνέμοις, ταῖς τῶν υἱῶν βασάνοις,
συνεχομένη γενναίως ὑπέμεινας τοὺς ὑπὲρ τῆς εὐσεβείας
χειμῶνας.

16 Εἰ δὲ τοίνυν καὶ γυνὴ καὶ γεραιὰ καὶ ἑπτὰ παίδων
μήτηρ ὑπέμεινεν τὰς μέχρι θανάτου βασάνους τῶν
τέκνων ὁρῶσα, ὁμολογουμένως αὐτοκράτωρ ἐστὶν τῶν παθῶν
ὁ εὐσεβὴς λογισμός. 2 ἀπέδειξα οὖν ὅτι οὐ μόνον ἄνδρες
τῶν παθῶν ἐκράτησαν, ἀλλὰ καὶ γυνὴ τῶν μεγίστων βασάνων
ὑπερεφρόνησεν. 3 καὶ οὐχ οὕτως οἱ περὶ Δανιηλ λέοντες
ἦσαν ἄγριοι οὐδὲ ἡ Μισαηλ ἐκφλεγομένη κάμινος λαβροτάτῳ
πυρί, ὡς ἡ τῆς φιλοτεκνίας περιέκαιεν ἐκείνην φύσις ὁρῶ-
σαν αὐτῆς οὕτως ποικίλως βασανιζομένους τοὺς ἑπτὰ υἱούς.
4 ἀλλὰ τῷ λογισμῷ τῆς εὐσεβείας κατέσβεσεν τὰ τοσαῦτα
καὶ τηλικαῦτα πάθη ἡ μήτηρ.

5 Καὶ γὰρ τοῦτο ἐπιλογίσασθε, ὅτι δειλόψυχος εἰ ἦν ἡ
γυνὴ καίπερ μήτηρ οὖσα, ὠλοφύρετο ἂν ἐπ' αὐτοῖς καὶ ἴσως
ἂν ταῦτα εἶπεν 6 Ὢ μελέα ἔγωγε καὶ πολλάκις τρισαθλία,
ἥτις ἑπτὰ παῖδας τεκοῦσα οὐδενὸς μήτηρ γεγένημαι. 7 ὦ
μάταιοι ἑπτὰ κυοφορίαι καὶ ἀνόνητοι ἑπτὰ δεκάμηνοι καὶ
ἄκαρποι τιθηνίαι καὶ ταλαίπωροι γαλακτοτροφίαι. 8 μάτην
δὲ ἐφ' ὑμῖν, ὦ παῖδες, πολλὰς ὑπέμεινα ὠδῖνας καὶ χαλεπω-
τέρας φροντίδας ἀνατροφῆς. 9 ὦ τῶν ἐμῶν παίδων οἱ μὲν
ἄγαμοι, οἱ δὲ γήμαντες ἀνόνητοι· οὐκ ὄψομαι ὑμῶν τέκνα
οὐδὲ μάμμη κληθεῖσα μακαρισθήσομαι. 10 ὦ ἡ πολύπαις καὶ
καλλίπαις ἐγὼ γυνὴ χήρα καὶ μόνη πολύθρηνος. 11 οὐδ' ἂν
ἀποθάνω, θάπτοντα τῶν υἱῶν ἕξω τινά.

12 Ἀλλὰ τούτῳ τῷ θρήνῳ οὐδένα ὠλοφύρετο ἡ ἱερὰ
καὶ θεοσεβὴς μήτηρ οὐδ' ἵνα μὴ ἀποθάνωσιν ἀπέτρεπεν
αὐτῶν τινα οὐδ' ὡς ἀποθνῃσκόντων ἐλυπήθη, 13 ἀλλ' ὥσπερ

NEW REVISED STANDARD VERSION

of other children, severed hands upon hands, scalped heads
upon heads, and corpses fallen on other corpses, and when
you saw the place filled with many spectators of the tortur-
ings, you did not shed tears. 21 Neither the melodies of
sirens nor the songs of swans attract the attention of their
hearers as did the voices of the children in torture calling to
their mother. 22 How great and how many torments the
mother then suffered as her sons were tortured on the wheel
and with the hot irons! 23 But devout reason, giving her
heart a man's courage in the very midst of her emotions,
strengthened her to disregard, for the time, her parental love.

24 Although she witnessed the destruction of seven children and the ingenious and various rackings, this noble
mother disregarded all these[a] because of faith in God. 25 For
as in the council chamber of her own soul she saw mighty
advocates—nature, family, parental love, and the rackings of
her children— 26 this mother held two ballots, one bearing
death and the other deliverance for her children. 27 She did
not approve the deliverance that would preserve the seven
sons for a short time, 28 but as the daughter of God-fearing
Abraham she remembered his fortitude.

29 O mother of the nation, vindicator of the law and
champion of religion, who carried away the prize of the contest in your heart! 30 O more noble than males in steadfastness, and more courageous than men in endurance! 31 Just
as Noah's ark, carrying the world in the universal flood,
stoutly endured the waves, 32 so you, O guardian of the law,
overwhelmed from every side by the flood of your emotions
and the violent winds, the torture of your sons, endured
nobly and withstood the wintry storms that assail religion.

16 If, then, a woman, advanced in years and mother of
seven sons, endured seeing her children tortured to
death, it must be admitted that devout reason is sovereign
over the emotions. 2 Thus I have demonstrated not only that
men have ruled over the emotions, but also that a woman
has despised the fiercest tortures. 3 The lions surrounding
Daniel were not so savage, nor was the raging fiery furnace
of Mishael so intensely hot, as was her innate parental love,
inflamed as she saw her seven sons tortured in such varied
ways. 4 But the mother quenched so many and such great
emotions by devout reason.

5 Consider this also: If this woman, though a mother, had
been fainthearted, she would have mourned over them and
perhaps spoken as follows: 6 "O how wretched am I and
many times unhappy! After bearing seven children, I am now
the mother of none! 7 O seven childbirths all in vain, seven
profitless pregnancies, fruitless nurturings and wretched
nursings! 8 In vain, my sons, I endured many birth pangs for
you, and the more grievous anxieties of your upbringing.
9 Alas for my children, some unmarried, others married and
without offspring.[b] I shall not see your children or have the
happiness of being called grandmother. 10 Alas, I who had so
many and beautiful children am a widow and alone, with
many sorrows.[c] 11 And when I die, I shall have none of my
sons to bury me."

12 Yet that holy and God-fearing mother did not wail with
such a lament for any of them, nor did she dissuade any of
them from dying, nor did she grieve as they were dying.

a Other ancient authorities read *having bidden them farewell, surrendered them* *b* Gk *without benefit* *c* Or *much to be pitied*

GREEK OLD TESTAMENT

ἀδαμάντινον ἔχουσα τὸν νοῦν καὶ εἰς ἀθανασίαν ἀνατίκτουσα τὸν τῶν υἱῶν ἀριθμὸν μᾶλλον ὑπὲρ τῆς εὐσεβείας ἐπὶ τὸν θάνατον αὐτοὺς προετρέπετο ἱκετεύουσα. 14 ὦ μῆτερ δι᾽ εὐσέβειαν θεοῦ στρατιῶτι πρεσβῦτι καὶ γύναι, διὰ καρτερίαν καὶ τύραννον ἐνίκησας καὶ ἔργοις δυνατωτέρα καὶ λόγοις εὑρέθης ἀνδρός. 15 καὶ γὰρ ὅτε συνελήμφθης μετὰ τῶν παίδων, εἱστήκεις τὸν Ελεαζαρον ὁρῶσα βασανιζόμενον καὶ ἔλεγες τοῖς παισὶν ἐν τῇ Εβραΐδι φωνῇ 16 Ὦ παῖδες, γενναῖος ὁ ἀγών, ἐφ᾽ ὃν κληθέντες ὑπὲρ τῆς διαμαρτυρίας τοῦ ἔθνους ἐναγωνίσασθε προθύμως ὑπὲρ τοῦ πατρῴου νόμου· 17 καὶ γὰρ αἰσχρὸν τὸν μὲν γέροντα τοῦτον ὑπομένειν τὰς διὰ τὴν εὐσέβειαν ἀλγηδόνας, ὑμᾶς δὲ τοὺς νεανίσκους καταπλαγῆναι τὰς βασάνους. 18 ἀναμνήσθητε ὅτι διὰ τὸν θεὸν τοῦ κόσμου μετελάβετε καὶ τοῦ βίου ἀπελαύσατε, 19 καὶ διὰ τοῦτο ὀφείλετε πάντα πόνον ὑπομένειν διὰ τὸν θεόν, 20 δι᾽ ὃν καὶ ὁ πατὴρ ἡμῶν Αβρααμ ἔσπευδεν τὸν ἐθνοπάτορα υἱὸν σφαγιάσαι Ισαακ, καὶ τὴν πατρῴαν χεῖρα ξιφηφόρον καταφερομένην ἐπ᾽ αὐτὸν ὁρῶν οὐκ ἔπτηξεν. 21 καὶ Δανιηλ ὁ δίκαιος εἰς λέοντας ἐβλήθη, καὶ Ανανιας καὶ Αζαριας καὶ Μισαηλ εἰς κάμινον πυρὸς ἀπεσφενδονήθησαν καὶ ὑπέμειναν διὰ τὸν θεόν. 22 καὶ ὑμεῖς οὖν τὴν αὐτὴν πίστιν πρὸς τὸν θεὸν ἔχοντες μὴ χαλεπαίνετε. 23 ἀλόγιστον γὰρ εἰδότας εὐσέβειαν μὴ ἀνθίστασθαι τοῖς πόνοις.

24 Διὰ τούτων τῶν λόγων ἡ ἑπταμήτωρ ἕνα ἕκαστον τῶν υἱῶν παρακαλοῦσα ἀποθανεῖν ἔπεισεν μᾶλλον ἢ παραβῆναι τὴν ἐντολὴν τοῦ θεοῦ, 25 ἔτι δὲ καὶ ταῦτα εἰδότες ὅτι οἱ διὰ τὸν θεὸν ἀποθνῄσκοντες ζῶσιν τῷ θεῷ ὥσπερ Αβρααμ καὶ Ισαακ καὶ Ιακωβ καὶ πάντες οἱ πατριάρχαι.

17 Ἔλεγον δὲ καὶ τῶν δορυφόρων τινὲς ὅτι ὡς ἔμελλεν συλλαμβάνεσθαι καὶ αὐτὴ πρὸς θάνατον, ἵνα μὴ ψαύσειέν τις τοῦ σώματος αὐτῆς, ἑαυτὴν ἔρριψε κατὰ τῆς πυρᾶς.

2 Ὦ μήτηρ σὺν ἑπτὰ παισὶν καταλύσασα τὴν τοῦ τυράννου βίαν καὶ ἀκυρώσασα τὰς κακὰς ἐπινοίας αὐτοῦ καὶ δείξασα τὴν τῆς πίστεως γενναιότητα. 3 καθάπερ γὰρ σὺ στέγη ἐπὶ τοὺς στύλους τῶν παίδων γενναίως ἱδρυμένη ἀκλινὴς ὑπήνεγκας τὸν διὰ τῶν βασάνων σεισμόν. 4 θάρρει τοιγαροῦν, ὦ μήτηρ ἱερόψυχε, τὴν ἐλπίδα τῆς ὑπομονῆς βεβαίαν ἔχουσα πρὸς τὸν θεόν. 5 οὐχ οὕτως σελήνη κατ᾽ οὐρανὸν σὺν ἄστροις σεμνὴ καθέστηκεν, ὡς σὺ τοὺς ἰσαστέρους ἑπτὰ παῖδας φωταγωγήσασα πρὸς τὴν εὐσέβειαν ἔντιμος καθέστηκας θεῷ καὶ ἐστήρισαι σὺν αὐτοῖς ἐν οὐρανῷ· 6 ἦν γὰρ ἡ παιδοποιία σου ἀπὸ Αβρααμ τοῦ πατρός.

7 Εἰ δὲ ἐξὸν ἡμῖν ἦν ὥσπερ ἐπί τινος ζωγραφῆσαι τὴν τῆς εὐσεβείας σου ἱστορίαν, οὐκ ἂν ἔφριττον οἱ θεωροῦντες ὁρῶντες μητέρα ἑπτὰ τέκνων δι᾽ εὐσέβειαν ποικίλας βασάνους μέχρι θανάτου ὑπομείνασαν; 8 καὶ γὰρ ἄξιον ἦν καὶ ἐπ᾽ αὐτοῦ τοῦ ἐπιταφίου ἀναγράψαι καὶ ταῦτα τοῖς ἀπὸ τοῦ ἔθνους εἰς μνείαν λεγόμενα 9 Ἐνταῦθα γέρων ἱερεὺς καὶ γυνὴ γεραιὰ καὶ ἑπτὰ παῖδες ἐγκεκήδευνται διὰ τυράννου βίαν τὴν Εβραίων πολιτείαν καταλῦσαι θέλοντος, 10 οἳ καὶ ἐξεδίκησαν τὸ γένος εἰς θεὸν ἀφορῶντες καὶ μέχρι θανάτου τὰς βασάνους ὑπομείναντες.

11 Ἀληθῶς γὰρ ἦν ἀγὼν θεῖος ὁ δι᾽ αὐτῶν γεγενημένος. 12 ἠθλοθέτει γὰρ τότε ἀρετὴ δι᾽ ὑπομονῆς δοκιμάζουσα. τὸ

NEW REVISED STANDARD VERSION

13 On the contrary, as though having a mind like adamant and giving rebirth for immortality to the whole number of her sons, she implored them and urged them on to death for the sake of religion. 14 O mother, soldier of God in the cause of religion, elder and woman! By steadfastness you have conquered even a tyrant, and in word and deed you have proved more powerful than a man. 15 For when you and your sons were arrested together, you stood and watched Eleazar being tortured, and said to your sons in the Hebrew language, 16 "My sons, noble is the contest to which you are called to bear witness for the nation. Fight zealously for our ancestral law. 17 For it would be shameful if, while an aged man endures such agonies for the sake of religion, you young men were to be terrified by tortures. 18 Remember that it is through God that you have had a share in the world and have enjoyed life, 19 and therefore you ought to endure any suffering for the sake of God. 20 For his sake also our father Abraham was zealous to sacrifice his son Isaac, the ancestor of our nation; and when Isaac saw his father's hand wielding a knife[a] and descending upon him, he did not cower. 21 Daniel the righteous was thrown to the lions, and Hananiah, Azariah, and Mishael were hurled into the fiery furnace and endured it for the sake of God. 22 You too must have the same faith in God and not be grieved. 23 It is unreasonable for people who have religious knowledge not to withstand pain."

24 By these words the mother of the seven encouraged and persuaded each of her sons to die rather than violate God's commandment. 25 They knew also that those who die for the sake of God live to God, as do Abraham and Isaac and Jacob and all the patriarchs.

17 Some of the guards said that when she also was about to be seized and put to death she threw herself into the flames so that no one might touch her body.

2 O mother, who with your seven sons nullified the violence of the tyrant, frustrated his evil designs, and showed the courage of your faith! 3 Nobly set like a roof on the pillars of your sons, you held firm and unswerving against the earthquake of the tortures. 4 Take courage, therefore, O holy-minded mother, maintaining firm an enduring hope in God. 5 The moon in heaven, with the stars, does not stand so august as you, who, after lighting the way of your star-like seven sons to piety, stand in honor before God and are firmly set in heaven with them. 6 For your children were true descendants of father Abraham.[b]

7 If it were possible for us to paint the history of your religion as an artist might, would not those who first beheld it have shuddered as they saw the mother of the seven children enduring their varied tortures to death for the sake of religion? 8 Indeed it would be proper to inscribe on their tomb these words as a reminder to the people of our nation:[c]

9 "Here lie buried an aged priest and an aged woman and seven sons, because of the violence of the tyrant who wished to destroy the way of life of the Hebrews. 10 They vindicated their nation, looking to God and enduring torture even to death."

11 Truly the contest in which they were engaged was divine, 12 for on that day virtue gave the awards and tested

a Gk *sword* *b* Gk *For your childbearing was from Abraham the father*; other ancient authorities read *For . . . Abraham the servant* *c* Or *as a memorial to the heroes of our people*

νῖκος ἀφθαρσία ἐν ζωῇ πολυχρονίῳ. 13 Ελεαζαρ δὲ προηγωνί-
ζετο, ἡ δὲ μήτηρ τῶν ἑπτὰ παίδων ἐνήθλει, οἱ δὲ ἀδελφοὶ
ἠγωνίζοντο· 14 ὁ τύραννος ἀντηγωνίζετο· ὁ δὲ κόσμος καὶ ὁ
τῶν ἀνθρώπων βίος ἐθεώρει· 15 θεοσέβεια δὲ ἐνίκα τοὺς ἑαυτῆς ἀθλητὰς στεφανοῦσα. 16 τίνες οὐκ ἐθαύμασαν τοὺς τῆς
θείας νομοθεσίας ἀθλητάς; τίνες οὐκ ἐξεπλάγησαν;

17 Αὐτός γέ τοι ὁ τύραννος καὶ ὅλον τὸ συμβούλιον ἐθαύμασαν αὐτῶν τὴν ὑπομονήν, 18 δι᾽ ἣν καὶ τῷ θείῳ νῦν παρεστήκασιν θρόνῳ καὶ τὸν μακάριον βιοῦσιν αἰῶνα. 19 καὶ γάρ
φησιν ὁ Μωυσῆς Καὶ πάντες οἱ ἡγιασμένοι ὑπὸ τὰς χεῖράς
σου. 20 καὶ οὗτοι οὖν ἁγιασθέντες διὰ θεὸν τετίμηνται, οὐ
μόνον ταύτῃ τῇ τιμῇ, ἀλλὰ καὶ τῷ δι᾽ αὐτοὺς τὸ ἔθνος ἡμῶν
τοὺς πολεμίους μὴ ἐπικρατῆσαι 21 καὶ τὸν τύραννον
τιμωρηθῆναι καὶ τὴν πατρίδα καθαρισθῆναι, ὥσπερ ἀντίψυχον γεγονότας τῆς τοῦ ἔθνους ἁμαρτίας. 22 καὶ διὰ τοῦ
αἵματος τῶν εὐσεβῶν ἐκείνων καὶ τοῦ ἱλαστηρίου τοῦ θανάτου αὐτῶν ἡ θεία πρόνοια τὸν Ισραηλ προκακωθέντα διέ-
σωσεν.

23 Πρὸς γὰρ τὴν ἀνδρείαν αὐτῶν τῆς ἀρετῆς καὶ τὴν ἐπὶ
ταῖς βασάνοις αὐτῶν ὑπομονὴν ὁ τύραννος ἀπιδὼν ἀνε-
κήρυξεν ὁ Ἀντίοχος τοῖς στρατιώταις αὐτοῦ εἰς ὑπόδειγμα
τὴν ἐκείνων ὑπομονὴν 24 ἔσχεν τε αὐτοὺς γενναίους καὶ ἀν-
δρείους εἰς πεζομαχίαν καὶ πολιορκίαν καὶ ἐκπορθήσας ἐνίκησεν πάντας τοὺς πολεμίους.

18 Ὦ τῶν Αβραμιαίων σπερμάτων ἀπόγονοι παῖδες
Ισραηλῖται, πείθεσθε τῷ νόμῳ τούτῳ καὶ πάντα τρόπον εὐσεβεῖτε 2 γινώσκοντες ὅτι τῶν παθῶν ἐστιν δεσπότης
ὁ εὐσεβὴς λογισμὸς καὶ οὐ μόνον τῶν ἔνδοθεν, ἀλλὰ καὶ τῶν
ἔξωθεν πόνων.

3 Ἀνθ᾽ ὧν διὰ τὴν εὐσέβειαν προέμενοι τὰ σώματα τοῖς
πόνοις ἐκεῖνοι οὐ μόνον ὑπὸ τῶν ἀνθρώπων ἐθαυμάσθησαν,
ἀλλὰ καὶ θείας μερίδος κατηξιώθησαν.

4 Καὶ δι᾽ αὐτοὺς εἰρήνευσεν τὸ ἔθνος, καὶ τὴν εὐνομίαν
τὴν ἐπὶ τῆς πατρίδος ἀνανεωσάμενοι ἐκπεπόρθηκαν τοὺς
πολεμίους. 5 καὶ ὁ τύραννος Ἀντίοχος καὶ ἐπὶ γῆς τετιμώ-
ρηται καὶ ἀποθανὼν κολάζεται· ὡς γὰρ οὐδὲν οὐδαμῶς
ἴσχυσεν ἀναγκάσαι τοὺς Ιεροσολυμίτας ἀλλοφυλῆσαι καὶ
τῶν πατρίων ἐθῶν ἐκδιαιτηθῆναι, τότε ἀπάρας ἀπὸ τῶν
Ιεροσολύμων ἐστράτευσεν ἐπὶ Πέρσας.

6 Ἔλεγεν δὲ ἡ μήτηρ τῶν ἑπτὰ παίδων καὶ ταῦτα τὰ
δικαιώματα τοῖς τέκνοις 7 ὅτι Ἐγὼ ἐγενήθην παρθένος
ἁγνὴ οὐδὲ ὑπερέβην πατρικὸν οἶκον, ἐφύλασσον δὲ τὴν
ᾠκοδομημένην πλευράν. 8 οὐδὲ ἔφθειρέν με λυμεὼν ἐρημίας
φθορεὺς ἐν πεδίῳ, οὐδὲ ἐλυμήνατό μου τὰ ἁγνὰ τῆς παρθενίας λυμεὼν ἀπάτης ὄφις. 9 ἔμεινα δὲ χρόνον ἀκμῆς σὺν
ἀνδρί· τούτων δὲ ἐνηλίκων γενομένων ἐτελεύτησεν ὁ πατὴρ
αὐτῶν, μακάριος μὲν ἐκεῖνος, τὸν γὰρ τῆς εὐτεκνίας βίον
ἐπιζήσας τὸν τῆς ἀτεκνίας οὐκ ὠδυνήθη καιρόν. 10 ὃς ἐδί-
δασκεν ὑμᾶς ἔτι ὢν σὺν ὑμῖν τὸν νόμον καὶ τοὺς προφήτας.
11 τὸν ἀναιρεθέντα Αβελ ὑπὸ Καιν ἀνεγίνωσκέν τε ὑμῖν καὶ
τὸν ὁλοκαρπούμενον Ισαακ καὶ τὸν ἐν φυλακῇ Ιωσηφ.
12 ἔλεγεν δὲ ὑμῖν τὸν ζηλωτὴν Φινεες, ἐδίδασκέν τε ὑμᾶς
τοὺς ἐν πυρὶ Ανανιαν καὶ Αζαριαν καὶ Μισαηλ. 13 ἐδόξαζεν
δὲ καὶ τὸν ἐν λάκκῳ λεόντων Δανιηλ, ὃν ἐμακάριζεν. 14 ὑπε-
μίμνησκεν δὲ ὑμᾶς καὶ τὴν Ησαιου γραφὴν τὴν λέγουσαν

them for their endurance. The prize was immortality in endless life. 13 Eleazar was the first contestant, the mother of
the seven sons entered the competition, and the brothers
contended. 14 The tyrant was the antagonist, and the world
and the human race were the spectators. 15 Reverence for
God was victor and gave the crown to its own athletes.
16 Who did not admire the athletes of the divine[a] legislation?
Who were not amazed?

17 The tyrant himself and all his council marveled at
their[b] endurance, 18 because of which they now stand before
the divine throne and live the life of eternal blessedness.
19 For Moses says, "All who are consecrated are under your
hands." 20 These, then, who have been consecrated for the
sake of God,[c] are honored, not only with this honor, but also
by the fact that because of them our enemies did not rule
over our nation, 21 the tyrant was punished, and the homeland purified—they having become, as it were, a ransom for
the sin of our nation. 22 And through the blood of those
devout ones and their death as an atoning sacrifice, divine
Providence preserved Israel that previously had been mistreated.

23 For the tyrant Antiochus, when he saw the courage of
their virtue and their endurance under the tortures, proclaimed them to his soldiers as an example for their own
endurance, 24 and this made them brave and courageous for
infantry battle and siege, and he ravaged and conquered all
his enemies.

18 O Israelite children, offspring of the seed of
Abraham, obey this law and exercise piety in every
way, 2 knowing that devout reason is master of all emotions,
not only of sufferings from within, but also of those from
without.

3 Therefore those who gave over their bodies in suffering
for the sake of religion were not only admired by mortals,
but also were deemed worthy to share in a divine inheritance. 4 Because of them the nation gained peace, and by
reviving observance of the law in the homeland they ravaged
the enemy. 5 The tyrant Antiochus was both punished on
earth and is being chastised after his death. Since in no way
whatever was he able to compel the Israelites to become
pagans and to abandon their ancestral customs, he left
Jerusalem and marched against the Persians.

6 The mother of seven sons expressed also these principles to her children: 7 "I was a pure virgin and did not go
outside my father's house; but I guarded the rib from which
woman was made.[d] 8 No seducer corrupted me on a desert
plain, nor did the destroyer, the deceitful serpent, defile the
purity of my virginity. 9 In the time of my maturity I
remained with my husband, and when these sons had grown
up their father died. A happy man was he, who lived out his
life with good children, and did not have the grief of bereavement. 10 While he was still with you, he taught you the law
and the prophets. 11 He read to you about Abel slain by Cain,
and Isaac who was offered as a burnt offering, and about
Joseph in prison. 12 He told you of the zeal of Phinehas, and
he taught you about Hananiah, Azariah, and Mishael in the
fire. 13 He praised Daniel in the den of the lions and blessed
him. 14 He reminded you of the scripture of Isaiah, which

a Other ancient authorities read *true* *b* Other ancient authorities add *virtue and* *c* Other ancient authorities lack *for the sake of God*
d Gk *the rib that was built*

Κἂν διὰ πυρὸς διέλθῃς, φλὸξ οὐ κατακαύσει σε. 15 τὸν
ὑμνογράφον ἐμελῴδει ὑμῖν Δαυιδ λέγοντα Πολλαὶ αἱ θλίψεις
τῶν δικαίων. 16 τὸν Σαλωμῶντα ἐπαροιμίαζεν ὑμῖν λέγοντα
Ξύλον ζωῆς ἐστιν τοῖς ποιοῦσιν αὐτοῦ τὸ θέλημα. 17 τὸν
Ιεζεκιηλ ἐπιστοποίει τὸν λέγοντα Εἰ ζήσεται τὰ ὀστᾶ τὰ
ξηρὰ ταῦτα; 18 ᾠδὴν μὲν γάρ, ἣν ἐδίδαξεν Μωυσῆς, οὐκ
ἐπελάθετο διδάσκων τὴν λέγουσαν 19 Ἐγὼ ἀποκτενῶ καὶ ζῆν
ποιήσω· αὕτη ἡ ζωὴ ὑμῶν καὶ ἡ μακρότης τῶν ἡμερῶν.

20 Ὢ πικρᾶς τῆς τότε ἡμέρας καὶ οὐ πικρᾶς, ὅτε ὁ πικρὸς
Ἑλλήνων τύραννος πῦρ πυρὶ σβέσας λέβησιν ὠμοῖς καὶ ζέ-
ουσι θυμοῖς ἀγαγὼν ἐπὶ τὸν καταπέλτην καὶ πάλιν τὰς
βασάνους αὐτοῦ τοὺς ἑπτὰ παῖδας τῆς Αβρααμίτιδος 21 τὰς
τῶν ὀμμάτων κόρας ἐπήρωσεν καὶ γλώσσας ἐξέτεμεν καὶ
βασάνοις ποικίλαις ἀπέκτεινεν. 22 ὑπὲρ ὧν ἡ θεία δίκη
μετῆλθεν καὶ μετελεύσεται τὸν ἀλάστορα τύραννον. 23 οἱ δὲ
Αβραμιαῖοι παῖδες σὺν τῇ ἀθλοφόρῳ μητρὶ εἰς πατέρων
χορὸν συναγελάζονται ψυχὰς ἁγνὰς καὶ ἀθανάτους ἀπειλη-
φότες παρὰ τοῦ θεοῦ. 24 ᾧ ἡ δόξα εἰς τοὺς αἰῶνας τῶν αἰώ-
νων· αμην.

says, 'Even though you go through the fire, the flame shall
not consume you.' 15 He sang to you songs of the psalmist
David, who said, 'Many are the afflictions of the righteous.'
16 He recounted to you Solomon's proverb, 'There is a tree of
life for those who do his will.' 17 He confirmed the query of
Ezekiel, 'Shall these dry bones live?' 18 For he did not forget
to teach you the song that Moses taught, which says, 19 'I
kill and I make alive: this is your life and the length of your
days.' "

20 O bitter was that day—and yet not bitter—when that
bitter tyrant of the Greeks quenched fire with fire in his cruel
caldrons, and in his burning rage brought those seven sons
of the daughter of Abraham to the catapult and back again
to more[a] tortures, 21 pierced the pupils of their eyes and cut
out their tongues, and put them to death with various tortures. 22 For these crimes divine justice pursued and will pursue the accursed tyrant. 23 But the sons of Abraham with
their victorious mother are gathered together into the chorus
of the fathers, and have received pure and immortal[b] souls
from God, 24 to whom be glory forever and ever. Amen.

a Other ancient authorities read *to all his* *b* Other ancient authorities read *victorious*